American Statistics Index 1989

Covering Publications Issued
January 1–December 31, 1989

A comprehensive guide to the
statistical publications of the
U.S. Government

Index

 Congressional Information Service

ISSN 0091-1658
Key Title: American Statistics Index

The Library of Congress Cataloged the First Issue of This Title as Follows:

American Statistics Index, 1973-
 Washington. Congressional Information Service.
 annual.

 "A comprehensive guide and index to the statistical publications of the U.S. Government."

 1. United States-Statistics-Bibliography.
 2. United States-Statistics-Abstracts. I. Congressional Information Service.

Z7554.U5A46   016.3173   73-82599
ISSN 0091-1658   MARC-S

International Standard Book Number
For the Set: 0-88692-190-2
For Index Volume: 0-88692-191-0
For Abstract Volume: 0-88692-192-9

Published by Congressional Information Service
4520 East-West Highway
Bethesda, MD 20814 U.S.A.

 ™

The paper used in this publication meets the minimum requirements of American National Standard for Information Sciences-Permanence of Paper for Printed Library Materials, ANSI Z39.48-1984.

A privately organized reference service.
Printed and Bound in the United States of America.
Copyright © 1990 by Congressional Information Service All rights reserved.

CONTENTS

The American Statistics Index 1989 Annual
is published in two volumes, the contents
of which are summarized below.

Index

Abstracts

Detailed Table of Contents: Index Volume

USER GUIDE

INTRODUCTION TO THE AMERICAN STATISTICS INDEX

The U.S. Government is the world's most important and prolific publisher of statistics. Federal agencies produce a continual flow of facts and figures on virtually every aspect of life in America and on most matters of world-wide concern.

Until the initiation of the American Statistics Index (ASI) and related services in 1972, use of Government statistics was hampered by the absence of adequate tools to identify relevant publications and pinpoint the data within them, as well as by the difficulty of locating and acquiring the publications themselves.

Major statistical agencies, such as the Census Bureau, index their own publications and disseminate them widely; other agencies issue publications lists and partial indexes; many agencies do neither. Nowhere in the Government is this wealth of data indexed, or even listed, completely. Many of these publications are not available through the Government Printing Office nor listed in its *Monthly Catalog;* and many are unavailable at depository libraries.

ASI aims to be a master guide and index to all the statistical publications of the U.S. Government. It was created to meet the need expressed in 1971 by the President's Commission on Federal Statistics, for "a central catalog of data available in government agencies . . . a single source in which one could locate all data currently collected by the Federal Government on a particular subject."

Specifically, the purpose of ASI is to perform the following functions, promptly and comprehensively:

- **Identify** the statistical data published by all branches and agencies of the Federal Government.
- **Catalog** the publications in which these data appear, providing full bibliographic information about each publication.
- **Announce** new publications as they appear.
- **Describe** the contents of these publications fully.
- **Index** this information in full subject detail.
- **Micropublish** virtually all the publications covered by ASI, thereby providing, on a continuing basis, reliable access to the statistics themselves.

To assure comprehensiveness, ASI staff members monitor all published document listings and regularly visit or contact over 500 Federal offices. In 1989, ASI collected, abstracted, and micropublished approximately 5,000 titles, including 600 periodicals. To assure prompt coverage during the year, full abstracts and indexing for all publications, including statistical articles within individual issues of periodicals, are published in an ASI Monthly Supplement issued 5 to 6 weeks after the month in which publications are obtained. The source documents themselves are issued on ASI microfiche about two weeks later.

This ASI 1989 Annual cumulates and enhances ASI Monthly Supplement coverage of Federal statistical publications issued during 1989. It is meant to be used in coordination with other ASI publications and services that provide comprehensive coverage of Federal statistical publications issued since the 1960s.

The following User's Guide discusses how the ASI system is organized; what kinds of statistical publications and statistics are issued by the Federal Government and accessible through ASI; how these publications are cataloged for retrieval through ASI; how their contents are abstracted and indexed in ASI; and where one can obtain the publications in hardcopy or on ASI microfiche.

COVERAGE OF ASI ANNUAL AND MONTHLY EDITIONS

ASI full coverage of U.S. Government statistical publications dates from the 1960s. This coverage is achieved through a base ASI Retrospective Edition, covering publications issued from 1960-73; Annual editions, each covering publications issued during a single year of coverage, 1974-89; and Monthly Supplement editions, issued throughout each year.

Each ASI edition is issued in 2 sections: an Abstracts Section that contains full descriptions of the content and format of each publication, organized by ASI accession number; and an Index Section that contains comprehensive subject and name, category, title, and report number indexes, with references keyed to abstract accession numbers.

The separate ASI editions are more fully described below.

ASI 1989 Annual

The ASI 1989 Annual, covering publications issued Jan. 1-Dec. 31, 1989, cumulates coverage of all publications originally abstracted and indexed in the ASI 1989 Monthly Supplements. It replaces and fully supersedes those Monthly Supplements.

In addition, the 1989 Annual contains full abstracts and indexing for all periodicals actively being published in 1989. In this respect, it is also designed to serve as the base reference source for all periodicals currently publishing in 1990, and to be used in conjunction with the ASI 1990 Monthly Supplements for locating data contained in current periodicals. Abstracts of periodicals and other recurring publications in the 1989 Annual reflect the format and content of the latest issue received during the year, and include notations of any significant changes occurring during the year.

ASI 1990 Monthly Supplements

ASI 1990 Monthly Supplements provide current abstracts and indexing for all new publications issued during each month of 1990. These include wholly new publications, new items in series, and updates or new editions of annuals, semiannuals, or other publications covered in previous ASI editions.

Monthly Supplements may also include abstracts for some publications that were issued prior to 1990, but that only recently came to our attention. Such publications are covered, provided they are still current enough to be of general interest.

All statistical periodicals covered by ASI, whether quarterly, monthly, weekly, or daily, are reviewed by the ASI staff on a continuing basis, and the issues received

are listed in each Monthly Supplement in the "Periodicals Received and Reviewed" section. However, Monthly Supplements do not re-abstract or re-index periodicals that have remained substantially unchanged since this 1989 Annual.

Only those periodicals that show significant changes in content or format since the basic description in this 1989 Annual are re-abstracted and indexed in the detail necessary to describe the change.

Periodical articles that contain statistical data are abstracted and indexed individually each month.

Monthly Supplements are issued 5 to 6 weeks after the end of the month covered, generally by the 10th-12th of each month.

ASI Retrospective Coverage

This ASI 1989 Annual is the sixteenth annual cumulation issued since the publication of ASI's base 1974 Annual Retrospective Edition. The Retrospective Edition covers statistical publications in print as of Jan. 1, 1974, as well as significant publications issued since the early 1960s.

In the case of repetitive or continuing publications, such as annuals or periodicals, which present continuing series of statistics over long periods of time, the Retrospective Edition does not describe each issuance published since 1960. Rather, it describes in full the format and contents of the most recent edition received at the time, and, where possible, characterizes major changes in format that occurred prior to 1974.

Subsequent annual cumulations, taken together, provide comprehensive coverage of statistical publications issued since Jan. 1, 1974. These annuals are published as hardcover abstracts and index volumes in the spring following the year of coverage.

ASI Multi-year Cumulative Indexes

ASI has published three multiple-year cumulative indexes to date. The 1974–79 Cumulative Index, published in May 1990, which revises and supersedes the separate Annual Index volumes issued for 1974 through 1979, is designed to be used in conjunction with ASI First through Sixth Annual Supplements as originally published. A cumulation covering ASI 1980 through 1984 Index volumes was published in 1985, and a cumulation covering ASI 1985 through 1988 Index volumes was published in 1989. Subsequent cumulations will be issued every four years. For more information about these multiple-year indexes, consult the most recent CIS catalog.

STATISTICAL PUBLICATIONS COVERED BY ASI

Publications included in ASI cover a wide range of subjects, reflecting the many concerns of hundreds of central and regional Federal agencies. These issuing agencies are listed in the detailed table of contents in each Abstracts volume and in the list of "Issuing Agencies and ASI Accession Numbers" in the Index volume. ASI abstracts and indexes all Federal agency publications that contain social, economic, demographic, or natural resources data, and a selection of publications with scientific and technical data.

ASI includes all Federal publications that contain primary data of research value or secondary data collected on a special subject, and also special studies and analyses or other statistics-related materials. All types of publications are covered, whether published as periodicals, as special one-time reports, as items within a large continuing report series, or as annual or biennial reports.

For purposes of inclusion in ASI, the term "publication" is defined as all printed or duplicated materials that may be distributed by an agency to members of the public, whether on a broad or a limited basis. In a few cases, ASI has obtained single copies of materials that are not generally available for distribution, and has micropublished them for distribution. Press releases and other ephemera are included only if they contain basic data not readily available in another form.

The sections below describe selected examples of the approximately 5,000 titles covered every year by ASI.

Basic Social and Economic Statistical Data

Since its early organization, and as required by the U.S. Constitution, the Federal Government has been responsible for gathering basic national social and economic data. Today, six large Federal statistical agencies, each in a specialized field, have as their major function the regular collection, analysis, and publication of such data. Data published by these agencies are broadly characterized below:

- **Agricultural Statistics Board, Department of Agriculture** — Monthly to annual reports on every important U.S. crop, with data on production, yield, prices, prospective plantings, and indicated production for the season.

- **Bureau of the Census** — Decennial census of population and housing; quinquennial economic and agricultural censuses; Census of Governments; Current Housing Reports, Current Industrial Reports, monthly foreign trade data, and reports from the monthly Current Population Survey; and methodological studies, indexes, and guides.

- **Bureau of Labor Statistics** — Monthly reports on the Consumer Price Index and unemployment rate; and other periodic, serial, and annual reports on prices, wages and hours, benefits, collective bargaining, work stoppages, and productivity.

- **Energy Information Administration** — Weekly to annual reports on U.S. production, consumption, stocks, trade, and prices of all major energy resources; finances and operations of oil companies, electric utilities, and other energy industries; and projections of energy supply and demand.

- **National Center for Education Statistics** — Annual and other collections of data on elementary, secondary, and higher education schools, staff, students, finances, curricula, and graduates.

- **National Center for Health Statistics** — Monthly and annual collections of vital statistics; and periodic surveys of the health condition of the population, and of health care, personnel, and facilities.

Many additional departments and agencies regularly compile primary data, both from required reports in their areas of responsibility and from special surveys; for example: Bureau of Mines' *Mineral Industry Surveys,* Justice Department's *Uniform Crime Reports* and victimization surveys, Treasury Department income tax statistics, Federal Reserve data on finances and banking, Department of Transportation data on highways and air traffic, and National Science Foundation's *Surveys of Science Resources.*

Program Related Statistics

Almost all executive departments and administrative or regulatory agencies publish statistics on their own funding and programs.

These data cover agency financial statements, personnel, processing efficiency, workloads, accidents, persons served, and payments made. Some of these data have interest well beyond the functioning of the agency; for example, social security recipients and payments, food stamp recipients, aliens admitted, speed of handling court cases, nuclear power plant shutdowns and accidents, Federal civilian workforce, and military troop strengths.

ASI provides full coverage of these types of program statistics, but, where possible, selects agency-wide reports for inclusion, and excludes subagency reports that only repeat data in the reports of the larger unit.

For example, the basic financial publication for the entire Government, the *Budget of the U.S.,* is fully covered by ASI; but ASI does not also cover budget requests or justifications from individual agencies. ASI generally covers the annual report of each separate agency, but not those of sub-agencies unless they include unique data. Also, ASI covers data on grants, contracts, and procurements, as reported by a large agency as a whole (such as DOD *Prime Contract Awards*), but usually excludes reports by individual divisions.

Special Studies

Many agencies produce a steady stream of monographs, analyses, and studies on subjects within their areas of activity; these are covered by ASI whenever they include statistical data of probable research value. Some agencies also undertake large special studies from time to time; an example of this kind of study covered by ASI in 1989 is the Health Care Financing Administration's *Medicare/Medicaid Nursing Home Information* State report series, which presents detailed data on individual nursing homes.

In some cases, special commissions are created specifically for the purpose of studying a problem of current concern. Studies of this nature have been covered by ASI beginning with those from the early 1960s. For instance, this 1989 Annual covers *Death Before Life,* the report of the National Commission To Prevent Infant Mortality on the incidence, causes, and prevention of infant mortality.

Some original studies are included which, although not primarily quantitative in nature, present statistics unavailable anywhere else; a number of reports by the General Accounting Office fall into this category. Other publications in ASI are primarily non-statistical, but may contain significant statistical sections. Congressional committee hearings and prints are prime examples.

Non-Tabular Statistics-Related Materials

Publications selected for inclusion in ASI generally contain statistical data in tabular form. However, maps, charts, listings, and narrative materials have also been covered if they provide aid in locating statistical data or in understanding statistical programs. Thus, we cover narrative discussions of statistical methodology, classification guides, directories, and bibliographies that include references to a significant body of statistical materials.

In general, we have attempted to cover all such material issued by the major statistical agencies, but we have applied somewhat more rigid standards for inclusion of material from other agencies.

Exclusions and Selective Coverage

The following kinds of material are either excluded from ASI or covered only on a selective basis:

- **Scientific and technical data** — Highly technical studies, scientific and experimental observations, engineering data, clinical medical studies, and animal laboratory studies are generally excluded from ASI. These data are disseminated through such information services as NTIS, NASA, ERIC, and the National Library of Medicine; ASI makes no attempt to duplicate this coverage.

  We do provide selective coverage of technical data with broad social or economic implications or particular current interest, as well as the less technical publications of technically oriented agencies. For instance, we do cover epidemiological studies; a large number of reports on energy resources, use, and conservation; EPA publications presenting monitoring data and pollution abatement measures and technologies; NOAA weather observations and forecasting techniques; and selected NASA publications.

- **Contract studies** — ASI coverage of contract studies by private organizations is typically limited to those that have been issued by a Federal agency as its own publication, either directly through the agency, through GPO, or through NTIS. In special cases, additional contract studies are covered that we would normally exclude but that have been recommended by an agency as being of particular importance.

- **Classified and confidential data** — These data are not included.

- **Congressional publications** — Congressional publications that contain substantial statistical information are included in ASI. However, ASI does not include any appropriations hearings, which contain primarily Federal program data, and which are abstracted and indexed in detail in the comprehensive *CIS/Index to Publications of the U.S. Congress.*

  When ASI covers a congressional publication also covered by the CIS/Index, it is completely re-abstracted and indexed to highlight the statistical data.

ORGANIZATION OF ASI ABSTRACTS AND INDEXES

ASI provides access to statistical data through companion volumes of indexes and abstracts. In making a subject search, you should consult this 1989 Annual for descriptions of publications issued during 1989, and for basic descriptions of periodicals that continue publication in 1990. The 1990 Monthly Supplements will cover new publications issued during 1990, including new editions of annual reports, and will change and update information regarding 1990 issues of periodicals. To search for material issued prior to 1989, you should consult the ASI Retrospective Edition and the subsequent Annuals, and all multi-year ASI cumulative indexes.

ASI Indexes

Ordinarily, research in ASI will begin with the Index volume. The ASI indexes are designed to lead you to the

information you seek from a variety of starting points. The five basic ASI indexes are designed to answer the following types of questions:

- **Subject and Name Index** — "What publications provide statistical data on cost of living and related matters?" and "What publications were issued by the Office of Management and Budget?"
- **Category Index** — "What publications provide cost of living data broken down by city, or some other geographic category?"
- **Title Index** — "What statistical data are included in a periodical entitled *Monthly Labor Review*?"
- **Agency Report Number Index** — "Where in ASI will I find reports in the BLS Bulletin 3050 series?"
- **SuDoc Number Index** — "Does ASI cover the report with the Superintendent of Documents number E3.49:988?"

Each ASI index reference will lead you to an abstract. Descriptive abstracts are provided for every publication; they are designed to tell you enough about the information content of the publication to enable you to decide whether or not it is likely to contain the specific data for which you are looking.

This system depends upon a basic key — the ASI accession number — which identifies publications (or specific parts of publications) in both the index and the abstract volumes.

ASI Accession Numbers

Each ASI abstract carries a unique accession number, which identifies not only the individual publication, but also the issuing agency and the publication type (see Sample Abstracts on p. xxxiii-xxxv for an illustration of how accession numbers appear on abstracts). The accession number has four basic components, the form and functions of which are described below.

- **Issuing Agency** — In the accession number for any one publication's abstract, the first two to four digits (up to the digit before the hyphen) are keyed to an overall coding scheme and represent the agency that issued the publication. (Coding for large agencies may be broken down by subagency or subject matter area.)
- **Publication type** — The last digit before the

hyphen is keyed to the document's publication type, as follows:

- 2 = Current periodicals, daily through semi-annual
- 4 = annuals and biennials
- 6 = publications in series
- 8 = special and irregular publications
- 1, 3, 5, 7, 9 = special series and special groups of publications (such as census reports or crop reports) that do not fall into one of the four basic types or which are most clearly represented if kept together under a special heading.

- **Sequential ASI serial number** — The digits after the hyphen form a unique serial number, sequentially assigned, basically in order of ASI acquisition, so that every publication has its own unique number that can be easily found in the Abstracts volumes of ASI.
- **Analytic number** — In many cases, ASI describes publications by using a main abstract in coordination with subordinate abstracts called "analytics," which are printed after the main abstract and are identified and sequenced by decimal numbers (.1, .2, or .3, etc.) following the main abstract accession number.

Analytics are frequently used to describe and individually index distinct parts of a large publication. They are also used to abstract and separately index the individual publications comprising a series, or the statistical articles appearing in individual issues of periodicals.

To use the ASI indexes and abstracts effectively, you do not need to know the ASI agency-coding or publication-type coding schemes, which are incorporated into accession numbers, but familiarity with codes can speed interpretation of entries in the indexes.

Arrangement of Abstracts by Accession Number

All abstracts are arranged by accession number in ascending order. This system automatically catalogs all publications, first by issuing agency, then by publication type, and then by individual publication serial number. All index references are made to these accession numbers. For ease in referring from index to abstract, every page of

Sample: ASI Accession Numbers

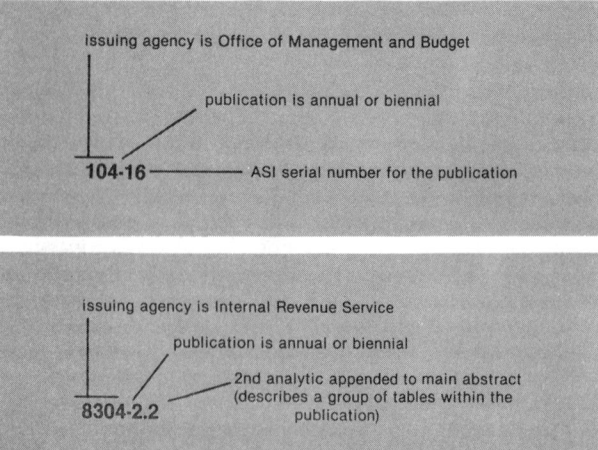

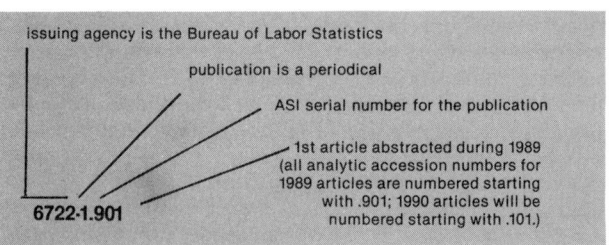

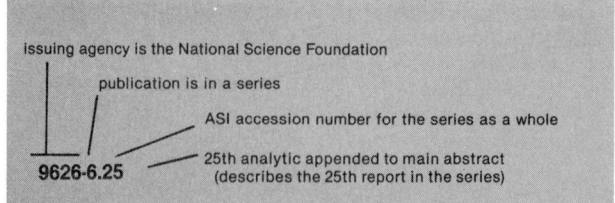

abstracts in the Abstracts volume carries a locator number in the upper right or left corner.

Continuity of Accession Numbers

Generally, once ASI has assigned an accession number to a publication, all successive issues or updates of that publication will receive the same accession number. If the number is changed, cross-references between the old and new numbers are included in the abstracts. The accession number will change if, for example, the periodicity of the publication changes from quarterly to annual, or if the issuing agency of the publication changes.

HOW ASI ABSTRACTS STATISTICAL PUBLICATIONS

All ASI abstracts are original and are based upon examination of the entire document. Abstracts differ substantially in degree of detail, depending on the type of publications and the kind of data being described. However, all abstracts are written to fulfill certain objectives.

These objectives are to describe a publication fully enough to allow you to determine if it is likely to contain the specific statistical data you seek; to provide the bibliographic data you need to identify and locate the publication if you wish to borrow or acquire it; and to tell you where in the publication you can find the data, often with specific page ranges.

Guidelines for Describing Statistical Contents

In describing the basic subject matter or statistical data of a publication, ASI does not attempt to summarize observations or conclusions. Rather, we attempt to state consistently what a publication is about; what specific data are presented, from what source, and at what level of detail; and what relationship the publication has to other statistical series. In describing a publication, ASI abstractors observe the following guidelines:
- State the subject matter and purpose of the publication as a whole.
- Identify sources of data presented, whether primary (based on original collection) or whether selected or reprinted from other published sources.
- Describe, if data are primary, the sample type and size, the survey methodology, or the information reporting requirement by which the data were gathered.
- Specify time span and geographic coverage of the data (special methods, discussed below, are used to describe time coverage and currency of data in periodicals).
- State periodicity of data collection and publication.
- Indicate breakdowns of the data and the level of detail they provide.
- Outline physical contents of the publication, such as number of charts and tables, and presence of narrative discussion, appendices, bibliographies, and index. Include page ranges to indicate the quantity and location of each type of material.

- List individual titles of all tables in publications that present continuing time series data or data from basic censuses (handling of table listings is further discussed below).
- Review continuity and length of time series data, providing references to ASI abstracts of earlier publications in the series (with the exception of semiannual or annual reports bearing the same accession number) and any breaks in publishing continuity since ASI coverage began.
- Indicate whether a serial publication has been temporarily suspended, discontinued, or transferred to another agency.
- Provide references to known related publications that present similar or identical source data in different analytical or publication formats.

In all cases, the aim is to specify as precisely as possible the actual data to be found in a publication. Particular pains are taken to distinguish among publications providing different data on similar subject matter.

Listing of Table Titles

For every publication, ASI attempts to identify, mention, and index the subjects and categories for which significant amounts of statistical data are presented. Often, the best way to describe in detail the data in a statistical publication is to list the titles of the tables it contains.

In general, ASI lists individual titles of tables that carry forward a continuing time series of data in biennial, annual or periodical publications. We also list table titles for publications presenting data from basic surveys and censuses. We usually list the titles exactly as they appear in the original publication. Where necessary for clarity or additional detail, these titles are augmented by material in brackets. Pagination for each table, or group of tables, is given.

Abstracts of special or irregular publications generally do not list tables, but describe the tables in varying degrees of detail, depending upon their number and complexity. If listing table titles is the clearest and briefest way to indicate the exact data present, it is done for any type of publication.

Special Aspects of Abstracts Describing Periodicals

This 1989 Annual contains full descriptions of all statistical periodicals that published any issues during 1989. Since most statistical periodicals retain constant format, features, and tables, it would be redundant to provide full abstracts for each issue. Therefore, abstracts of periodicals indicate the features common to all issues and list tables that appear in each issue or at regular intervals. Periodicals that were discontinued during 1989 are so annotated in this 1989 Annual; all others may be presumed to be continuing publication in 1990.

Statistical articles in periodicals are individually abstracted and indexed each month, and special tables that appear only in certain issues are listed. All such articles and special tables appearing in periodical issues during 1989 are included in this 1989 Annual.

In listing tables for periodicals, we do not give the time coverage of the data as a specific month or year, but describe it in a way that will apply to all issues. The abstracts do not include page ranges, which may change from issue to issue.

All abstracts of periodiclas in this annual include a notation of issues received, reviewed, and microfilmed during 1989. The cover dates of the issues are labeled (P) if they approximate the publication date: or (D) if they

represent the period covered by the data presented. The body of the abstract usually indicates the time lag between the data date and the publication date.

Periodical abstracts in the 1989 Annual serve as the base abstracts for continuing periodicals, to be used in conjunction with the 1990 Monthly Supplements. Issues of those periodicals received during 1990 will be listed in the Monthly Supplements "Periodicals Received and Reviewed" section as they are received, but will not be re-abstracted of re-indexed unless their contents change significantly.

Provision of Bibliographic Data

ASI abstracts for each publication provide, at a minimum, primary bibliographic information, such as title, date, collation, agency report number (if any), and periodicity. In addition, we include, whenever possible, the Superintendent of Documents classification number, the Library of Congress card number, the Government Printing Office (GPO) Monthly Catalog entry number, the GPO stock number, and the depository Item Number.

However, many Government publications covered in ASI have not been assigned all, or in some cases any, identification or classification numbers. Many of the publications we cover are not cataloged either in the GPO Monthly Catalog or in the issuing agency's own catalog or publication list, if one exists.

Each document abstract provides as much specific information on hardcopy availability as we are able to obtain at time of publication, and includes information on ASI microfiche availability and price. (For more information about the availability of documents or microfiche, see below "Acquiring the Documents.")

Usually, all bibliographic information for a publication is given at the head of the main abstract, following the title (see Sample Abstracts on p. xxiii-xxv for detailed labeling of bibliographic information provided). When analytic abstracts are being used to describe separate documents in a series, however (see sample abstract for publications in series), only bibliographic data common to the entire series are included in the main abstract, and information individual to each document is shown in its respective analytic abstract.

Frequently, a publication that is going to be cataloged by the GPO Monthly Catalog will not have been cataloged by the time ASI monthly abstracts are published. If such Monthly Catalog entries appear prior to the ASI Annual, information from them is included in the published Annual. Occasionally, items have not yet been covered in the Monthly Catalog, but are documents within continuing series for which established classification data exist; in such cases, we will publish classification data, based on precedent, in the absence of Monthly Catalog verification. In addition, ASI publishes bibliographic data revisions and additions in a special section at the end of each quarterly Monthly Supplement index volume. These revisions and additions are then cumulated annually and issued as separate pamphlets to supplement the bibliographic data in each past ASI Annual.

References to Publication Dates

When a date is included in the title of a publication, ASI prints it as part of the title; this date usually represents the period covered by the data or, sometimes, the year the report was prepared. When a date is given anywhere within a publication to indicate date of transmittal, final preparation, or printing, ASI lists this date in the bibliographic data. The user should remember, however, that schedules are often delayed and the publication may not actually have become available until later.

Some publications contain no date at all, and these, ASI lists in the bibliographic data the closest approximation it can determine of the year of actual release.

Uses of Main Abstracts and Analytic Abstracts

To handle the broad variety of materials it includes, ASI developed a flexible approach to document accessioning and abstracting. As described earlier in the section on the ASI accession number, we use a structured abstract system that provides for main abstracts and subordinate abstracts (analytics).

ASI uses analytics for the following purposes:

- To single out part of a publication for more detailed abstracting, or to divide the publication into parts, generally into groups of tables, which are then listed. Analytics may also be used for sections or chapters of a publication, each of which is then further described.

- To abstract individual publications in a series. The title and bibliographic data unique to the publication are given in the analytic; data common to the series as a whole are given in the main abstract.

- To abstract articles in periodicals. Article abstracts are identified by 3-digit analytics, beginning with .901 for the first article abstracted in 1989. Thus, article abstracts always follow table listings, which begin with .1.

ASI provides for each individual publication the descriptive information outlined in the above sections. For periodicals, annuals, or one-time publications, the basic information is usually given in the main abstract (see the Sample Abstracts on p. xxiii and xxiv).

For publications in series, information common to the series as a whole is given in the main abstract, and that peculiar to each individual publication in the series is given in its respective analytic (see Sample Abstract on p. xxv). This system allows complete descriptions of individual, related publications without extensive repetition of common characteristics.

The use of analytics also allows ASI to index to specific parts or even single tables in publications. Any index terms may be assigned to an analytic to indicate data specific only to that analytic, and the ASI accession number, with a decimal, will lead the user to it.

For example, the accession number 6224-2.2, under the index term "Counterfeiting and forgery," shows that the second analytic, not the publication as a whole, contains data on that topic. The main abstract, however, will contain the basic information on the subject, data type and source, and overall contents of the publication.

When index terms apply to the entire publication or to many of the analytics used, these terms are assigned to the main abstract only and are not repeated for the individual analytics to which they apply.

HOW ASI INDEXES STATISTICAL PUBLICATIONS

ASI indexes are designed to serve a wide range of needs and search approaches for locating statistical materials.

To accomplish this, the following five separate indexes have been provided:

- **Index by Subjects and Names,** which contains references to specific subject areas, places, and personal and corporate authors.
- **Index by Categories** (and accompanying Guide to Selected Standard Classifications), which contains references to tabular data breakdowns by twenty-one common geographic, demographic, and economic categories (e.g., by State, by sex, or by specific industry).
- **Index by Titles**
- **Index by Agency Report Numbers**
- **Index of Superintendent of Documents Numbers**

This section reviews basic ASI objectives and policies in building these five indexes; provides instructions and suggestions for using each of them; and gives specific hints on which indexes to use for answers to a number of different types of questions.

INDEX BY SUBJECTS AND NAMES

The Index by Subjects and Names provides access to:

- **Subjects** of publications and of specific data within publications.
- **Place names,** including names of cities, counties, States, and foreign countries to which data relate.
- **Government agency names,** including the Federal national or regional agencies, commissions, or congressional committees that issue publications or that are the subjects of data contained in publications.
- **Major Government programs or proposals** to which data relate (e.g., Work Incentive Program, Medicare).
- **Special classes of publications or data** (e.g., publications under the terms "Opinion and attitude surveys," "Statistical programs and activities," "Projections," "Directories," and "Bibliographies").
- **Individual personal names, companies, and institutions,** both as authors and as subjects of publications.
- **Major surveys** through which significant bodies of data have been collected (e.g., Current Population Survey).

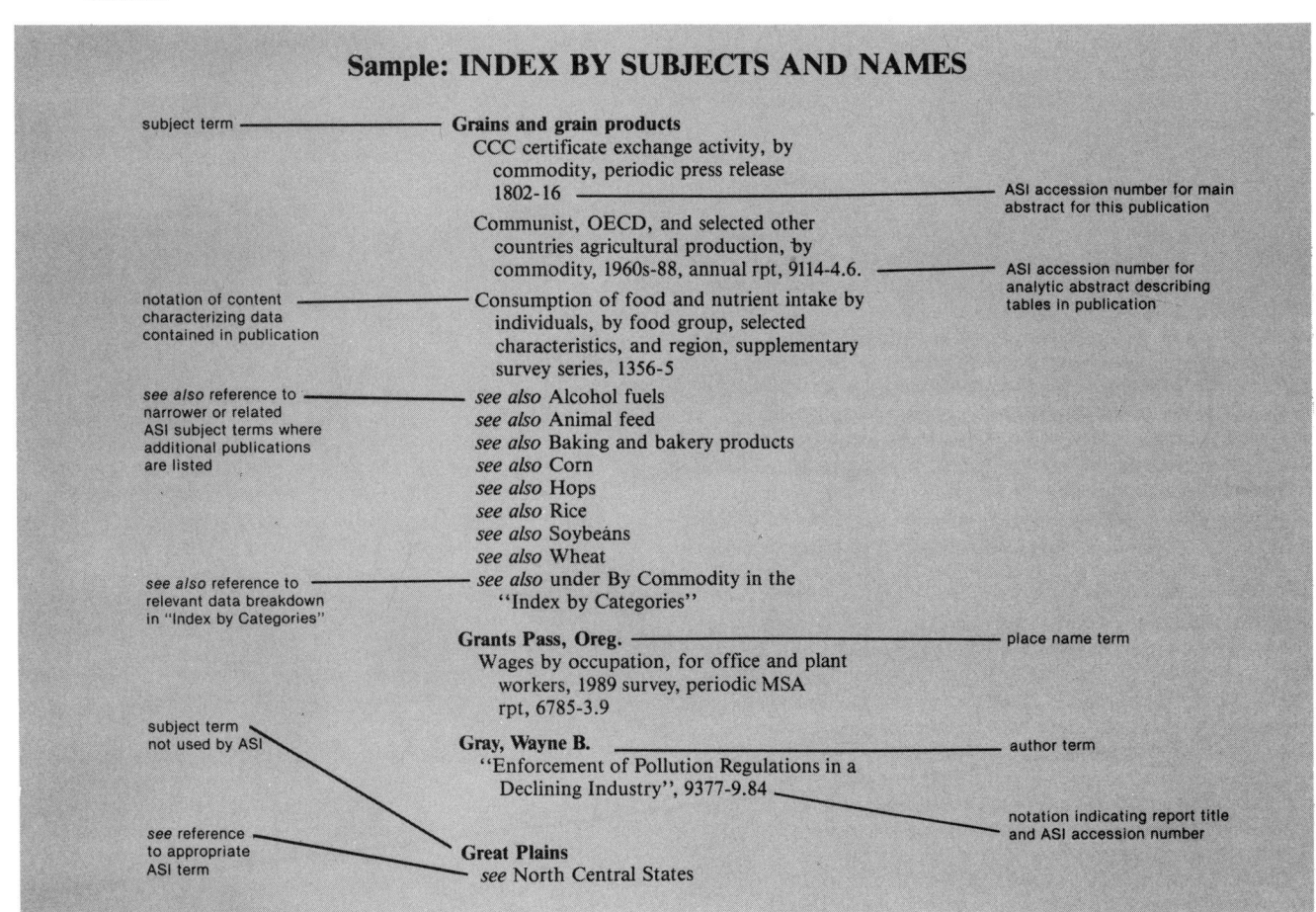

Sample: INDEX BY SUBJECTS AND NAMES

subject term — **Grains and grain products**
CCC certificate exchange activity, by commodity, periodic press release 1802-16 —— ASI accession number for main abstract for this publication

Communist, OECD, and selected other countries agricultural production, by commodity, 1960s-88, annual rpt, 9114-4.6. —— ASI accession number for analytic abstract describing tables in publication

notation of content characterizing data contained in publication —— Consumption of food and nutrient intake by individuals, by food group, selected characteristics, and region, supplementary survey series, 1356-5

see also reference to narrower or related ASI subject terms where additional publications are listed —— see also Alcohol fuels
see also Animal feed
see also Baking and bakery products
see also Corn
see also Hops
see also Rice
see also Soybeans
see also Wheat

see also reference to relevant data breakdown in "Index by Categories" —— see also under By Commodity in the "Index by Categories"

Grants Pass, Oreg. —— place name term
Wages by occupation, for office and plant workers, 1989 survey, periodic MSA rpt, 6785-3.9

subject term not used by ASI —— **Gray, Wayne B.** —— author term
"Enforcement of Pollution Regulations in a Declining Industry", 9377-9.84 —— notation indicating report title and ASI accession number

see reference to appropriate ASI term —— **Great Plains**
see North Central States

As illustrated in the above sample, this index consists of the following four basic structural elements:

- Subject and author terms (subject terms are based upon a controlled vocabulary).
- *See* and *see also* cross references directing the user to the appropriate index term or to terms under which additional related data may be found.
- Notations of content, which summarize the relevant data content and time coverage of each publication indexed to a particular term. Under an author's name the title is used as a notation of content.
- ASI accession numbers, which refer the user to the full ASI abstract for that publication.

ASI Subject Terms

Subject terms and cross references in the Index by Subjects and Names are based on a controlled vocabulary developed by ASI to meet the particular needs of ASI data coverage. This vocabulary is constantly reviewed and enlarged to respond to the ever expanding range of subjects receiving attention in Government publications.

Publications abstracted in ASI cover an extremely wide variety of subjects, and the data presented range from the very general to the very specific. In selecting subject index terms for the ASI controlled vocabulary, we have strived to maintain a middle level of specificity, which allows for adequate flexibility in indexing to specific subjects, but avoids too great a fragmentation and scattering of subject references. For example, in dealing with data on commodities, the ASI controlled vocabulary generally contains terms for commodity groups, such as the terms "Grains and grain products," "Animal feed," and "Baking and bakery products," found in the preceding sample. However, in the case of selected specific commodities, which are frequently dealt with in publications covered by ASI, we have established separate index terms (e.g., "Wheat," "Corn," "Rice," and "Soybeans" in the preceding sample).

ASI policy is to index to subject terms that reflect the principal subject matters and data contents of each publication abstracted. In addition, unusual items or items of special interest that occur in the body of a report or article, or in individual tables or groups of tables, will be indexed whether or not they relate to the primary focus of the publication at hand.

When indexing a publication to which a hierarchy of vocabulary terms might apply, we select the most specific applicable term or terms in the controlled vocabulary, and do not also index to broader or narrower terms that do not reflect so well its particular focus. But when the focus of the document is equally upon the more general and the more particular subject term, we place index entries under both terms.

For example, when indexing large compendia that present major data on commodities, we index both to the terms for commodity groups and also to those terms for specific commodities that have been established in the controlled vocabulary. Publications primarily focusing on a single commodity, such as wheat, corn, or rice, will be indexed only to the specific commodity terms and not to the more general term "Grains and grain products." Publications that focus on the general subject of grains, but contain a considerable amount of data on one or more of these specific commodities, will be indexed both to the specific commodity terms and to "Grains and grain products." Finally, publications that include some data on the specific commodities, but have a main focus that is on grains will be indexed only to "Grains and grain products."

Cross References

The *see also* references provided by ASI, such as those shown in the preceding sample, are designed to guide you to additional material to be found under the related or narrower terms cited, and to remind you of the need to check the Index by Categories where additional data may be available.

ASI also provides *see* references to aid in locating the specific form of phraseology of subject terms used by ASI. ("Great Plains," for example, is not a term used by ASI, but relevant entries will be found under the term "North Central States.")

Notations of Content

Each index entry under a subject or category term contains an ASI accession number and a "notation of content," a brief description of a report's subject matter or data content. These notations assist you in selecting relevant entries under any particular term and restricting the number of abstracts to which you need refer.

Notations of content are individually written for each publication indexed by ASI. They include, at a minimum, the main subject or subjects of the publication as they relate to the specific index term, and the data date. Additional information that may be noted, as relevant, includes geographic area of coverage, major data breakdowns, and periodicity of publication. Under an author term, the publication title is used as the notation of content.

In selecting the first words for notations of content, we have attempted to choose key words that will automatically group index entries according to their prime subject content. The key words perform some of the functions of a "second-level" index term (e.g., the word "Consumption" used in the preceding sample to group entries relating to food consumption). Although the informal type of grouping thus achieved can be helpful to you, these groups will not always bring together all related material. A complete search should include examination of all notations of content under a given term.

In general, only one notation of content for any one publication appears under a specific index term. This entry must reflect the full scope of the publication being indexed as it relates to that subject term. As a result, in many cases, the notation of content must be quite general, subsuming coverage of a great deal of specific data. In those cases, however, when the material relating to an index term is too diverse to be covered by a single notation of content, a second notation may be used under that term.

As stated above, usually only one notation of content for any one publication will appear under a specific index term. However, the wording of the notation of content for a single publication may be different for each of the index terms under which it appears. In such cases, the differences reflect an effort to relate the wording and initial key word of the notation of content to the specific index term under which it appears.

For example, the publication in the above index sample with the notation of content, "Communist, OECD, and selected other countries agricultural production, by commodity, 1960s-88, annual rpt," contains data on a wide variety of additional economic subjects relating to communist and other countries. Under the index term "Centrally planned economies," to reflect this broad scope, the notation of content reads "Economic conditions in Communist, OECD, and selected other countries, 1960s-88, annual rpt."

In all cases, it must be remembered that notations of content are brief and highly condensed guides, and cannot be used as substitutes for the abstracts. The full abstracts will further describe the extent and limitations of the data indicated in the index entry, and will often note the existence of related data that could not be indicated in the brief space occupied by the index entry.

Other Indexing Conventions

- **Alphabetization** — Following Library of Congress practice, ASI alphabetizes on a word-by-word basis. For example, "New Jersey" and "New York" precede "Newark," and "Fire departments" precedes

"Firearms." It is important to know if there is a word break in a term, since a compound word like "Airlines" will follow all terms beginning with the word "Air" (i.e., "Air pollution"). Hyphenated words are alphabetized as if they were two separate words.

- **Proper Names** — These have been entered in natural word order. Thus, you will find "Department of Labor" rather than "Labor Department," and "Bureau of Labor Statistics" rather than "Labor Statistics Bureau." However, names of individuals always have last name first, such as "Boyd, Gayle M."

- **References to the United States** — Because of the nature and scope of most U.S. Government statistical publications, "U.S." is an implied prefix for many of the subjects in the ASI Subject Index. Thus, you will find "Army" rather than "U.S. Army," and "Foreign relations" rather than "U.S. Government-foreign relations." In agency titles, the prefix "U.S." has been dropped whenever possible, except where necessary to conform to *U.S. Government Manual* usage (e.g., U.S. Postal Service). In notations of content, "U.S." is always implied unless "foreign," "world," or "by country" is specified.

Making a Subject Index Search

If you are seeking a specific piece of information in ASI, you will often find it quickly by referring to the obvious subject term or terms, locating the relevant group of notations of content, and selecting the one or ones most pertinent to your search. You should then consult the abstract for a full description of the publication and its availability.

If such a search does not yield the information required, or if you desire a more complete survey of possible data on the subject, additional steps should be taken. As previously noted, your first step should be to consult the more specific and related *see also* terms listed under the relevant subject terms in order to obtain additional leads.

Your next step should be to consult more general terms that encompass the subject matter sought. Despite our efforts to index to the most specific available term, some statistical publications are so wide-ranging or so detailed in their subject coverage that it is impractical to include references to all the specific topics they mention. It is wise, therefore, when checking the specific subject term in which you are interested, also to check the more general terms related to it.

Searching the subject terms, however, is only part of making a successful subject search in ASI. For instance, a publication that contains data on agriculture may break down these data by hundreds of different commodities, one of which is likely to be grains. The existence of these breakdowns by category adds a new dimension to statistical data retrieval. To help the researcher locate this kind of information quickly, ASI has provided an Index by Categories, which is discussed in detail below.

A limited amount of overlapping (or "double posting") occurs between the Index by Subjects and Names and the Index by Categories. Detailed data subject matter shown in tabular breakdowns (e.g., occupational breakdowns) are always indexed in the Index by Categories. In selected cases, where tabular breakdowns or cross-tabulations provide an extensive or particularly significant body of data on a given subject, references to these data have been included in both the Index of Subjects and Names (e.g., indexed to the subject terms "Clerical workers," "Nurses and nursing," "Blue-collar workers," etc.) and the Index by Categories (e.g., "By Occupation"). The existence of this limited overlap should not mislead the user with respect to the large amount of additional data available through the Index by Categories.

INDEX BY CATEGORIES

As mentioned above, to provide a ready access to the multiplicity of detailed statistical data in tabular breakdowns and cross-classifications, ASI has created a special type of supplementary index: the Index by Categories. This index includes references to all publications that contain comparative tabular data broken down in any or several of the following twenty-one standard categories:

- **Geographic Categories** — By census division; By city; By county; By foreign country; By outlying area (territories of the U.S.); By region; By SMSA or MSA; By State; and By urban-rural and metro-nonmetro.

- **Economic Categories** — By commodity; By Federal agency; By income; By individual company or institution; By industry; and By occupation.

- **Demographic Categories** — By age; By disease; By educational attainment; By marital status; By race and ethnic group; and By sex.

For easier use, index entries within each of the categories are grouped according to subject matter, under one of the following nineteen subheadings:

> Agriculture and Food
> Banking, Finance, and Insurance
> Communications and Transportation
> Education
> Energy Resources and Demand
> Geography and Climate
> Government and Defense
> Health and Vital Statistics
> Housing and Construction
> Industry and Commerce
> Labor and Employment
> Law Enforcement
> Natural Resources, Environment, and Pollution
> Population
> Prices and Cost of Living
> Public Welfare and Social Security
> Recreation and Leisure
> Science and Technology
> Veterans Affairs

In those instances where a reference might logically fit under two or more of the subheadings, we have tried to select the most obvious one and to place it there. A brief listing of the kinds of material referenced under each subheading is given at the beginning of the Index by Categories.

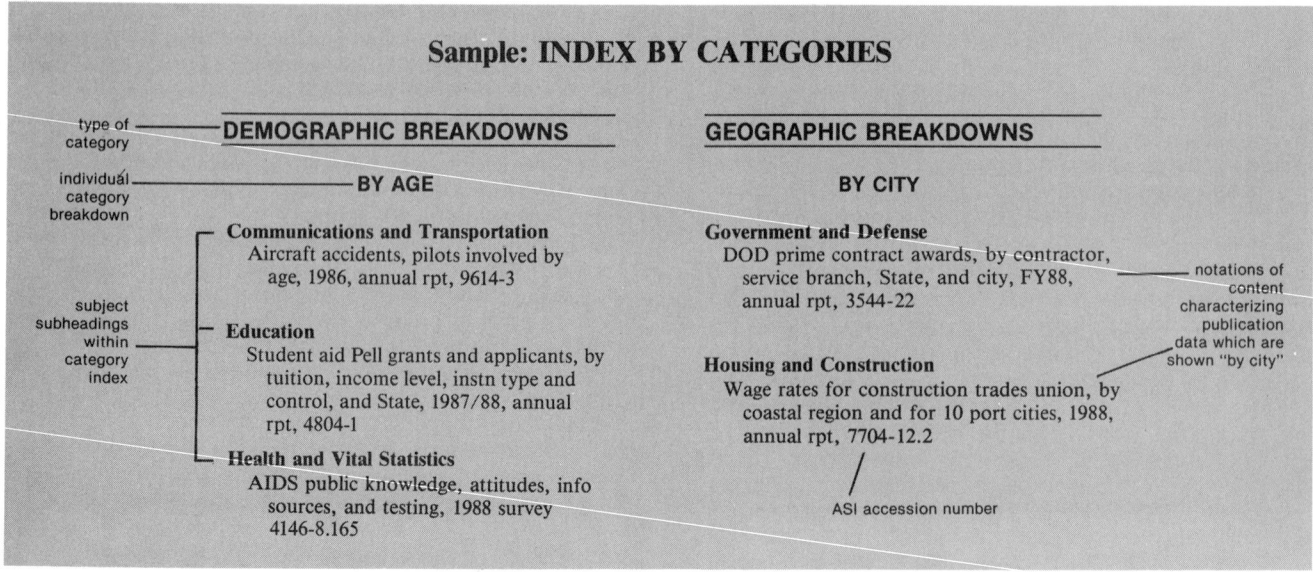

Sample: INDEX BY CATEGORIES

type of category → DEMOGRAPHIC BREAKDOWNS

individual category breakdown → BY AGE

subject subheadings within category index

Communications and Transportation
Aircraft accidents, pilots involved by age, 1986, annual rpt, 9614-3

Education
Student aid Pell grants and applicants, by tuition, income level, instn type and control, and State, 1987/88, annual rpt, 4804-1

Health and Vital Statistics
AIDS public knowledge, attitudes, info sources, and testing, 1988 survey 4146-8.165

GEOGRAPHIC BREAKDOWNS

BY CITY

Government and Defense
DOD prime contract awards, by contractor, service branch, State, and city, FY88, annual rpt, 3544-22 → notations of content characterizing publication data which are shown "by city"

Housing and Construction
Wage rates for construction trades union, by coastal region and for 10 port cities, 1988, annual rpt, 7704-12.2

← ASI accession number

As illustrated in the above sample, this index consists of the following four basic structural elements:

- Category terms, for the twenty-one categories listed above.

- Subject subheadings, to group entries within each category by subject matter. These are listed above.

- Notations of content, which are used just as in the Index by Subjects and Names to characterize further the data indexed to the category.

- ASI accession numbers, which refer the user to the full ASI abstract for that publication.

In the Index by Categories, data in the specified categories can be identified with greater detail and specificity than in the Index by Subjects and Names. This index also provides the best and most complete source for locating comparative data on a wide variety of subjects.

Breakdowns in individual tables, to which references are made in the Index by Categories, may vary considerably in the detail provided. Breakdowns "By sex" are, by definition, complete. Breakdowns "By State" are usually, but not always, for all 50 States. However, detail in breakdowns of such categories as "By city," "By SMSA," "By Federal agency," "By industry," "By commodity," and "By occupation," varies widely. In the abstracts of publications containing such breakdowns, we have, when possible, tried to include an indication of the degree of detail provided (i.e., "by detailed industries," "by major cause of death," "for 20 large cities," etc.).

In searching the Index by Categories for very detailed data, such as those on a small city, minor industry, or other specific entity, you are likely to find several entries referring to publications that could possibly contain the information you want. You will usually find it necessary to go back to the abstract to ascertain which publication has or is most likely to have that information. In some cases, where a high degree of specificity is desired, an examination of the Index by Categories and the abstracts will help to narrow the field of possibilities, but it may still be necessary actually to examine the text of two or three publications to be certain the exact information needed is there.

Examples and further instructions for making various types of Category Index searches follow.

Making a Search by Geographic Categories

Much data on Chicago can be located under the term "Chicago, Ill." in the Index by Subjects and Names. These entries represent instances where Chicago is the principal subject of a publication or where a significant body of information relating to Chicago can be found. There are considerable additional data, however, to be found in individual tables that have a breakdown by city, including Chicago. These data are located in the Index by Categories under the term "By city."

Similarly, you can find data on individual States, counties, SMSAs, MSAs, or foreign countries in the Index by Categories. The number of places included in reports indexed to these categories may vary considerably. Breakdowns by State or county are usually complete, unless the notation of content indicates that data are limited to a specific part of the country, or to "large counties" or "selected counties." In the case of cities or foreign countries, there may be wider variation; when practical, the notation of content indicates the degree of detail provided (e.g., "10 port cities" in the sample above).

Data on the regions of the U.S. can be found under the category "By region." Since, however, the different Federal agencies use a variety of regional delineations, such data may not be comparable from one report to another. To assist the user, ASI has provided lists of six major regional structures in the Guide to Selected Standard Classifications, further described below.

Making a Search by Economic Categories

The Index by Categories term "By Industry" will lead to reports and to individual tables which present a wealth of detailed data on both major and minor industries. These data can often be found only through the Index by Categories, since the Subject Index would become unwieldy if ASI attempted to index each column of every table.

In the same way as for cities, explained above, the notation of content will generally indicate the level of industry detail provided in each publication, and the abstract will specify further. In some cases, the degree of detail in the breakdowns may be based upon a standard classification system, such as the Standard Industrial Classification (SIC) which classifies all types of industries, businesses, and services for purposes of developing comparable statistical data. Whenever such a standard classification is used, this fact is noted in the abstract and frequently in the notation of content as well. Several of the most frequently used classifications, including the SIC, are listed in ASI's Guide to Standard Statistical Classifications, further described below.

The use of the SIC listing to find data on a specific industry is illustrated in the sample below. For example, if you want data on the typesetting industry, an industry for which there is no separate entry in the Subject Index, you can refer to the SIC listing to determine at what SIC level the typesetting service industry is specified. Since it is specified at the 4-digit level, you can then examine the entries under "By Industry" in the Category Index, and check the abstracts of likely references, to find reports and specific tables that present data broken down to the SIC 4-digit level.

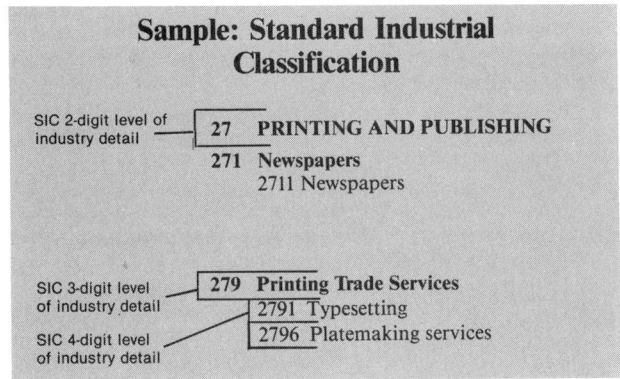

Sample: Standard Industrial Classification

SIC 2-digit level of industry detail — **27 PRINTING AND PUBLISHING**

271 Newspapers
2711 Newspapers

SIC 3-digit level of industry detail — **279 Printing Trade Services**
SIC 4-digit level of industry detail — 2791 Typesetting
2796 Platemaking services

Very detailed data on commodities can be found in the same way, using the category term "By Commodity." The industry and commodity categories only partially overlap, since many firms produce a wide range of commodities but are classified only in the industry of their major activity. ASI policy is to follow the classification— industry-based or commodity-based—used by the publication. To make a complete search for such economic data, you will probably want to examine both categories.

Data shown for individual entities of all kinds, including companies or their brand name products, universities, hospitals, foundations, and government projects may be found under "By Individual Company or Institution." Category indexing is also provided for data "By Federal Agency," "By Occupation," and "By Income," including both salary levels and total family income.

Making a Search by Demographic Categories

When you want data about specific groups of the population, the Category Index is a versatile tool to augment the Subject Index. For example, the following subjects can be thoroughly searched using this two-pronged approach:

- **Women** — Data may be found under the subject terms "Women," "Women's employment," or "Maternity." Quantities of additional data may be found under the category term "By Sex."
- **Age groups** — Look under subject terms "Children," "Youth," or "Aged and aging." Look also under the category term "By Age."

- **Blacks** — Look under such subject terms as "Black Americans," "Black students," or "Racial discrimination." More data can be found under the category term "By Race."
- **The poor** — The subject term "Poverty" will lead to reports dealing specifically with the poor. Additional data can be extracted from reports with breakdowns "By Income," found in the Category Index.
- **Divorced persons** — The subject term "Marriage and divorce" will lead to reports specifically on this subject. The category term "By Marital Status" will lead to additional data.

In a similar way you can find data on demographic groups under the categories "By Occupation," "By Industry," "By Educational Attainment," or "By Disease."

Making a Search for Comparative Data

A major advantage of the Index by Categories is the ease with which it enables you to locate comparative data on a subject. This index is the logical starting point for such search questions as: "Which cities have the highest unemployment rate?" "Which States have the lowest taxes?" "Which are the largest industries in the U.S. in specified States?" "Do people with more education really earn more money?" (These last two questions each combine two category terms: "By Industry" and "By State," and "By Income" and "By Educational Attainment.") Data pertinent to these questions will also be found under the subject terms "Employment and unemployment, general," "State and local taxes," etc. However, the most efficient search for such comparative data will begin with the Index by Categories.

ASI's Guide to Selected Standard Classifications

As stated above, Federal statistical data breakdowns are frequently presented in terms of several standard classification systems, and ASI abstracts generally make note of their use. To provide an easily accessible reference for the user, we have printed a number of major classification systems or lists in the "Guide to Selected Standard Classifications." The Guide, which appears at the end of the Index volume, includes the following listings:

- Census regions and divisions; outlying areas of the U.S.; Standard Federal Administrative Regions; farm production regions; Federal Reserve Districts; Federal Home Loan Bank Districts; and Bureau of Labor Statistics Regions.
- Metropolitan Statistical Areas (MSAs); Consolidated Metropolitan Statistical Areas; cities with population over 100,000 (based on the 1980 Census of Population and biennial updates); and Consumer Price Index cities.
- Standard Industrial Classification (SIC), providing 1- to 4-digit codes for industry divisions through individual industries.
- Standard Occupational Classification, providing 1- to 3-digit codes for major and minor occupational groups.
- Standard International Trade Classification (SITC), a system of 3-digit codes for commodities in world trade, developed by the United Nations, used for foreign trade data, and consistent with the 7-digit codes used for U.S. import-export data.

Even when data breakdowns do not correspond with one of these standard classification systems, these listings can still serve as useful guides to what may be included in breakdowns at varying levels of detail (i.e., "by major industry group" will approximate the 2-digit SIC level, and "by detailed industries" will approximate the 4-digit level).

Government publications that describe these and

other standard classification systems, survey methods, glossaries, and directories are abstracted and microfilmed by ASI, and can usually also be obtained in hard-copy by the user. Such publications are generally indexed to "Methodology" or "Classifications" as well as to their respective subjects.

INDEX BY TITLES

This index lists titles of all publications covered by ASI in the 1989 Annual. It also lists titles of periodical articles, conference papers, and reports within larger publications when these are separately abstracted.

This index lists all main titles and also analytic titles of individual monographs within a series, except when series reports are essentially identical, e.g., a series of State reports or country reports. In these cases, the name of each State or country can be found in the Index by Subjects and Names; the reports will also be listed, usually in alphabetical order, in the Abstracts volume under the ASI accession number for the series. Series reports on individual commodities or industries are listed in the Index by Titles under the name of the commodity, followed by the name of the series, e.g., "Footwear, Current Industrial Report."

Titles are listed alphabetically in natural word order, as they appear in the abstract. ASI routinely omits initial articles (a, an, the) in titles, both in the abstracts and in this index. Titles that begin with Arabic numbers (e.g., "1989 Economic Report of the President") appear at the end of the index.

To assist users in locating a publication, we provide in certain cases alternate word orders for titles, including all of those beginning with Arabic numerals. For example, census reports are generally listed under the overall title of the census and under the title of the individual report as well.

Sample: INDEX BY TITLES

publication title —— Canadian Travel to the U.S., 1988, 2904-7.

title of individual —— Capital Punishment, 1988, 6066-25.23
report in a series

article title —— CARD Linear Programming Model of U.S. Agriculture, 1502-3.902

Each title is followed by the ASI accession number, which directs the user to the abstract of the publication.

Anyone knowing the title of the publication desired can locate it most quickly in this index. Users should keep in mind that notations of content in the Index by Subjects and Names and in the Index by Categories bear no necessary relationship to a publication's title and should not be confused with it.

INDEX BY AGENCY REPORT NUMBERS

This index lists the report numbers assigned to publications by the issuing agency. It can be useful both for identifying one specific document and for locating an entire series of numbered publications.

We have grouped numbers in this index under the names of each issuing executive department, independent agency or commission, or congressional body, but generally have not attempted to group them by bureau, office, or committee within a department or independent agency. (Frequently, the alphabetical prefixes of the numbers themselves serve to identify agencies.)

Exceptions to this general rule are Census Bureau publication numbers, which are preceded with the word "Census" so that they group together and are not inter-

Sample: INDEX BY AGENCY REPORT NUMBERS

Federal department —— **DEPARTMENT OF EDUCATION**
or agency

              LP 89-705........................4874-1

Agency Report —— LP 89-720...................4874-1
Number   NCES 89-609..................4834-23

mixed with other Commerce Department reports. Also, the "DHHS" prefix in the Department of Health and Human Services report numbers has been omitted so that numbers will group more meaningfully.

INDEX OF SUPERINTENDENT OF DOCUMENTS NUMBERS

This index presents, in shelf list order, the Superintendent of Documents (SuDocs) Classification Numbers of publications abstracted by ASI during 1989, and provides references from the SuDocs numbers to ASI accession numbers.

The index enables a user who has obtained a SuDocs number from the Monthly Catalog or some other source to quickly locate the ASI abstract and then obtain the document.

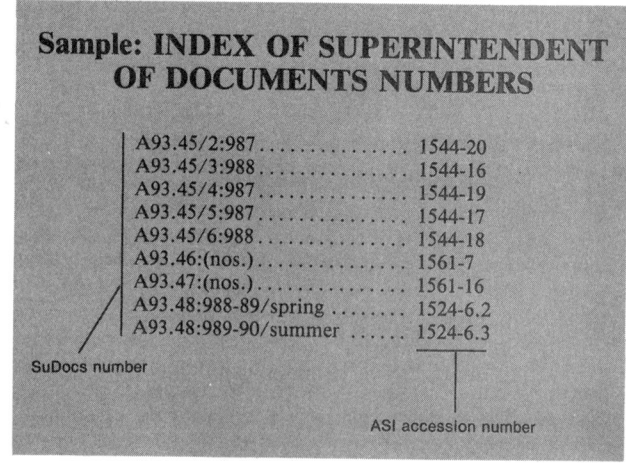

Sample: INDEX OF SUPERINTENDENT OF DOCUMENTS NUMBERS

    A93.45/2:987..............1544-20
    A93.45/3:988..............1544-16
    A93.45/4:987..............1544-19
    A93.45/5:987..............1544-17
    A93.45/6:988..............1544-18
    A93.46:(nos.)..............1561-7
    A93.47:(nos.)..............1561-16
    A93.48:988-89/spring........1524-6.2
    A93.48:989-90/summer......1524-6.3

SuDocs number

ASI accession number

Suggestions for Making Information Searches

The "best" information search technique to use with ASI abstracts and indexes depends upon the type of information needed and upon the amount and type of information with which the search begins. Listed below are some examples of the types of information you can obtain through ASI, together with suggested routes for searching.

IN ORDER TO ...	YOU SHOULD ...
Pinpoint specific statistical data on any subject treated in Federal Government publications.	Use the subject index.
Locate broad analyses of comprehensive studies.	Use the subject index; concentrate on the more general subject terms.
Determine whether data are available for specific parts of the U.S., such as States, cities, or counties; for specific industries or commodities; or for specific groups of people, such as races, men and women, or age, income, or occupational groups.	Use both the subject and category indexes.
Find comparative data for States, cities, foreign countries, Government agencies, commodities, industries, or groups of people.	Use the category index.
Find out what Federal Reserve district Florida is in.	Look in the Guide to Selected Standard Classifications.
Determine whether a large report, with a breakdown by industry, will include data on the dog food industry.	Look at the Standard Industrial Classification Codes listed in the Guide to Selected Standard Classifications to determine that the industry you are looking for has a 4-digit code. Look in the indexes for notations of content specifying detailed industry breakdowns. Look at the table listing in the abstract for tables specifying 4-digit detail.
Find data on Minneapolis.	Look in the subject index under "Minneapolis, Minn." Look also in the category index under "By city."
Be confident that you have found the latest data available.	Look at the dates in the notations of content that interest you in the ASI 1989 Annual. Check ASI 1990 Monthly Supplements under the same index terms to see if there are similar notations with later dates. ASI is current to 6-10 weeks after publication of the reports covered. If the notations of content indicate a periodical, locate the latest issue in the "Periodicals Received and Reviewed" section.
Find the latest issue of a periodical carrying forward a statistical time series.	Look in ASI 1989 Annual for description of the periodical. Look for the title in the "Periodicals Received and Reviewed" section of the latest ASI Monthly Supplements; the issues received each month will be listed.
Locate continuing monthly or quarterly reports on a particular subject.	Look in the subject index. The notations of content include the periodicity of the reports.
Determine the availability of comparable historical data.	Look in the Abstracts Section of each ASI edition, under the same accession number. The abstract will state whether the report is part of a continuing time series; e.g., "Twentieth annual report." Also, look in the abstract for references to earlier publications, changes in ASI accession numbers, or breaks in continuity.
Locate the report of a specific Board or Commission.	Look in the subject index under the name of the issuing agency.
Locate an agency publication list.	Look in the subject index under "Government publications lists."
Review the entire statistical output of any particular Federal Government agency or office.	Look in the detailed table of contents for the ASI accession number and page of the agency that interests you. Look in the Abstracts Section for all publications under this accession number.
Find out how many Federal Government agencies publish data on the same subject.	Look in the subject index, at the ASI accession numbers following the notations of content. The first two to four digits (minus the digit before the hyphen) indicate the issuing agency of the publication.
Locate a specific statistical article in a periodical.	Look in the title index or in the subject index under the author's name.
Determine the content of a specific publication when you know the title or agency report number.	Use the title index or the agency report number index to locate the pertinent abstract.
Locate all the reports in a specific series.	Look in the title index of each edition of ASI under the title of the series. If it is a numbered series, use the agency report number index.
Find a report you remember hearing about in the 1970s.	Start out by checking the ASI Retrospective Edition Index, followed by successive Annual Supplements.
Locate reports describing specific statistical methods; locate reports containing projected data.	Look in the subject index under "Methodology;" look in the subject index under "Projections."

ACQUIRING THE DOCUMENTS

Once you have identified a publication that appears to contain the data you seek, you may wish to borrow or acquire the publication itself, either in its original hardcopy form or in microform.

Acquiring Documents From a Library

Although there are no complete collections in existence, Government documents can be found in many libraries, particularly those that have been designated as U.S. Government depository libraries. There are usually at least two depositories in each congressional district, approximately 1,300 throughout the country.

The publication abstracts that contain a bullet (•) and an Item Number indicate publications that have been made available to depository libraries by the Government Printing Office. However, fewer than 50 depositories receive *all* the publications that are theoretically available to them, and even these libraries receive only about three-quarters of all the publications covered by ASI.

Libraries that subscribe to the ASI Microfiche Library will have complete collections of the materials abstracted and indexed in ASI.

Requesting or Purchasing Publications From the Government

Whether or not they are sent to depositories, many Government publications can be purchased while the supply lasts, either from the Government Printing Office, or, in certain cases, from the National Technical Information Service, or the issuing agency.

If a publication listed in ASI is available for sale, the price and source, when known, are listed in the abstract. It should be noted that the prices of Government publications are subject to frequent change. The price listed is that printed on the publication or in the GPO *Monthly Catalog*, or is based on firm information about a later price from another source.

When the publication abstract contains a single dagger (†), inquiries should be addressed directly to the issuing agency in order to determine whether copies are available for distribution. Principal agency addresses are listed in each Annual Abstracts volume in the section labeled "Where to Write for Statistical Publications."

Some publications intended for internal or official use only have been printed in small editions, and copies generally are not available for distribution. In some cases, the agency will honor a written request for a copy of one of these publications, but this will be decided by the agency on a case-by-case basis. Abstracts of publications in this category carry a double dagger (‡).

In some cases, we have been informed by the agency that there are absolutely no copies available for distribution outside the agency. Abstracts of publications in this category carry a diamond symbol (♦). In most of these cases, the agencies have cooperated with our attempt to make the data available to the public by permitting ASI to microfilm the publications for inclusion in the ASI Microfiche Library. The agency itself will not honor requests for publications that carry this symbol.

The ASI Microfiche Program

Because of the enormous difficulty of acquiring, cataloging, and maintaining a collection of all the publications covered by ASI, no complete hardcopy collection of these publications now exists in any library. For this reason, CIS has undertaken to make these publications available in American Standard microfiche on a continuing basis.

Our microfiche sheets measure 105 × 149 mm (approximately 4" × 6"), and contain up to 98 document pages. Each has an eye-readable "title header" that conclusively identifies the accession number, series title (if any), dates of periodical issues, and document title of each publication filmed. Documents are separated from each other, and they are plainly sequenced for file integrity and quick retrieval according to ASI accession number.

Researchers may view microfiche with the aid of a simple reader, such as those found in most libraries and offices. Individual pages from a microfiche can be reproduced in full size with the aid of a reader-printer; these machines are becoming increasingly available in libraries and offices.

With a few specific exclusions, all publications abstracted and indexed in ASI are available on ASI microfiche. The microfiche availability and unit count for a given publication are indicated by the notation "ASI/MF" in the publication's abstract. We have systematically excluded only publications that reprint other items in the ASI Microfiche Library, large or colored maps that are unsuitable for reproduction in standard microfiche, and large appendix volumes that are non-statistical (such as public hearing testimony) or highly technical.

Automatically updated collections of current publications, on silver-halide, archival-quality microfiche, are available on a subscription basis. Retrospective collections, shipped in their entirety and ready for use, may also be purchased. Collections may be ordered to contain the entire range of ASI publications, may be limited to "non-depository" publications (i.e., those not included in Government documents classes sent to depository libraries), or may be limited to publications of a single Government agency. For details, please write: CIS Library Services Manager.

ASI Documents on Demand

Since June 1, 1975, individual publications covered in ASI have been available on diazo microfiche or paper copy for purchase through our ASI DOCUMENTS ON DEMAND service. The price of any document is based on the "unit count" data indicated for the document, e.g. ASI/MF/3. (Note that a unit count of 3 is the minimum order for any document, regardless of size; each additional 100 pages or less equals 1 additional unit.) Please ask your librarian for additional ordering information; or write CIS Documents on Demand, P.O. Box 30056, Bethesda, MD 20814.

ADDITIONAL CIS SERVICES

Index to International Statistics and Statistical Reference Index

Beginning in January 1983, Congressional Information Service initiated publication of the Index to International Statistics (IIS), a comprehensive monthly index and abstracting service, covering the statistical publications

of international intergovernmental organizations, including UN, OECD, EC, OAS, and approximately 40 other important organizations.

Since 1980, Congressional Information Service has published the Statistical Reference Index (SRI), a monthly abstract and index publication with annual cumulations, covering statistical reports from a broad range of U.S. sources other than the Federal Government. These sources include trade, professional, and other nonprofit associations; business organizations; commercial publishers; independent research centers; State government agencies; and university research centers. SRI has selected from these sources a cross-section of documents presenting basic national and State data on business, industry, finance, economic and social conditions, the environment, and the population.

SRI and IIS complement ASI's coverage of statistical materials by providing access to data not collected by the Federal Government and to alternative sources and analyses of data. Because the abstracting and indexing styles of the two publications are quite similar, researchers can use ASI, SRI, and IIS without significantly changing their search methods.

Most of the documents covered in SRI and IIS are included in their respective Microfiche Libraries, available on a subscription basis. For more information about SRI, IIS, and their microfiche programs, contact the CIS Marketing Department.

Statistical Masterfile

In 1989, CIS introduced a new CD-ROM product, the Statistical Masterfile, which allows users to search simultaneously the abstracts and indexing from ASI, SRI, and IIS. The three component data bases may be purchased separately or in any combination. Both current year service and retrospective coverage are available for each data base. Current service subscribers receive quarterly CD-ROM disk updates.

For additional information, contact the CIS Marketing Department.

CIS On-Line Services

Through cooperative arrangements with on-line computer services, the CIS data base is made available to the public. This service makes possible direct on-line computer searching of the abstracts and indexing contained in all American Statistics Indexes and all CIS/Indexes, from our first publication to the present.

CIS/Indexes to Publications of the U.S. Congress

Since 1970, Congressional Information Service has published the CIS/Index, a monthly abstract and index publication with annual cumulations, which covers all publications of the U.S. Congress. Selected congressional publications containing statistical data are covered in ASI as well as CIS. Those covered by ASI are re-abstracted and re-indexed to focus on their statistical contents.

However, ASI does not repeat CIS/Index coverage of the wide range of congressional publications that contain no substantial statistical data. Nor does ASI abstract or index the publications of the Senate and House Appropriations Committees. Since CIS/Indexes provide detailed access to the extensive program statistics and background information contained in publications of these committees, we believe that reabstracting them for ASI would be a duplication of effort and service.

The CIS/Microfiche Library and CIS Documents on Demand services provide full-text availability of CIS/Index publications in a manner paralleling ASI microfiche services.

Other Services

In 1986, Congressional Information Service published a two-part *Guide to 1980 U.S. Decennial Census Publications*, covering all basic printed reports issued as part of the 1980 Census through May 1986. The abstracts and indexing in the Guide have been substantially reprinted from six ASI annual editions and have been combined in a single publication for the convenience of researchers. A companion microfiche collection of 1980 Census reports is also available.

The Census Guide and other CIS publications and microform collections are fully described in the CIS catalog, available on request.

Sample Abstract—Individual Publication

issuing agency —————

8304
INTERNAL REVENUE SERVICE
      Annuals and Biennials ————— publication type

ASI accession number for publication as a whole —————

8304–2   **STATISTICS OF INCOME,** ————— title and subtitle
          Individual Income Tax
          Returns, 1979 ————— collation

periodicity and date ————— Annual. 1982. viii+270 p. ————— agency report number
          IRS Pub. 79(3-82). —————

depository item number ————— ●Item 964. GPO $7.50. ————— hardcopy source and price
          ASI/MF/5 ————— ASI microfiche availability and unit count*

Superintendent of Documents classification number —————
          S/N 048-004-01845-4. ————— GPO stock number
          °T22.35/2:In2/979.
                    LC 61-37567. ————— Library of Congress number

description of publication as a whole —————

Final detailed annual tabulation of 1979 individual income tax returns, filed during 1980. Presents data on number of returns, sources of income, deductions and exemptions, tax computation and tax rates, age exemption, credit for the elderly, and high income returns; with breakdowns by State, marital status, and selected financial items, including size of adjusted gross income.

    Data are estimates based on a stratified sample of all individual tax returns filed for income year 1979. ————— data sources

Contains the following 9 sections:

    1-5. Current statistical sections, each with brief narrative, charts, and text tables; and 35 basic tables, listed below. (p. 1-143)

    6-7. Explanation of terms; and description of data sources and limitations and sampling methodology; with 5 methodological tables. (p. 145-185)

    8. High income returns. Brief narrative and 12 tables showing returns with 1979 taxable and nontaxable income of $200,000 or more, tabulated using 4 alternative definitions of income, by various income, deduction, credit, and tax status categories. (p.187-213) ————— organization of contents

    9. 1979 tax forms and filing instructions. (p. 215-270)

Report has been published annually since 1916.
    Data on high income returns have previously been published in a separate annual report. For description of report for 1975-76 tax years, see ASI 1978 Annual, 8004-11; reports for 1977-78 have not yet been published. ————— reference to previous reports in time series, and to related publications

detailed table listing —————

TABLES:
[All tables refer to 1979 and present data by adjusted gross income, unless otherwise noted.] ————— note on coverage of all tables

ASI accession number for group of related tables within publication —————

8304–2.1: Returns Filed and Sources of Income

    1.1. Selected income and tax items, by size and accumulated size of adjusted gross income. (p. 9) ————— titles and page locations of individual tables

    1.2. All returns: sources of income, deductions, and tax items, by marital status and sex of taxpayer [not by adjusted gross income]. (p. 12)

*for calculating ASI Documents on Demand fees; the number of physical fiche is generally two less than the ASI/MF unit count

Sample Abstract—Periodical Publication

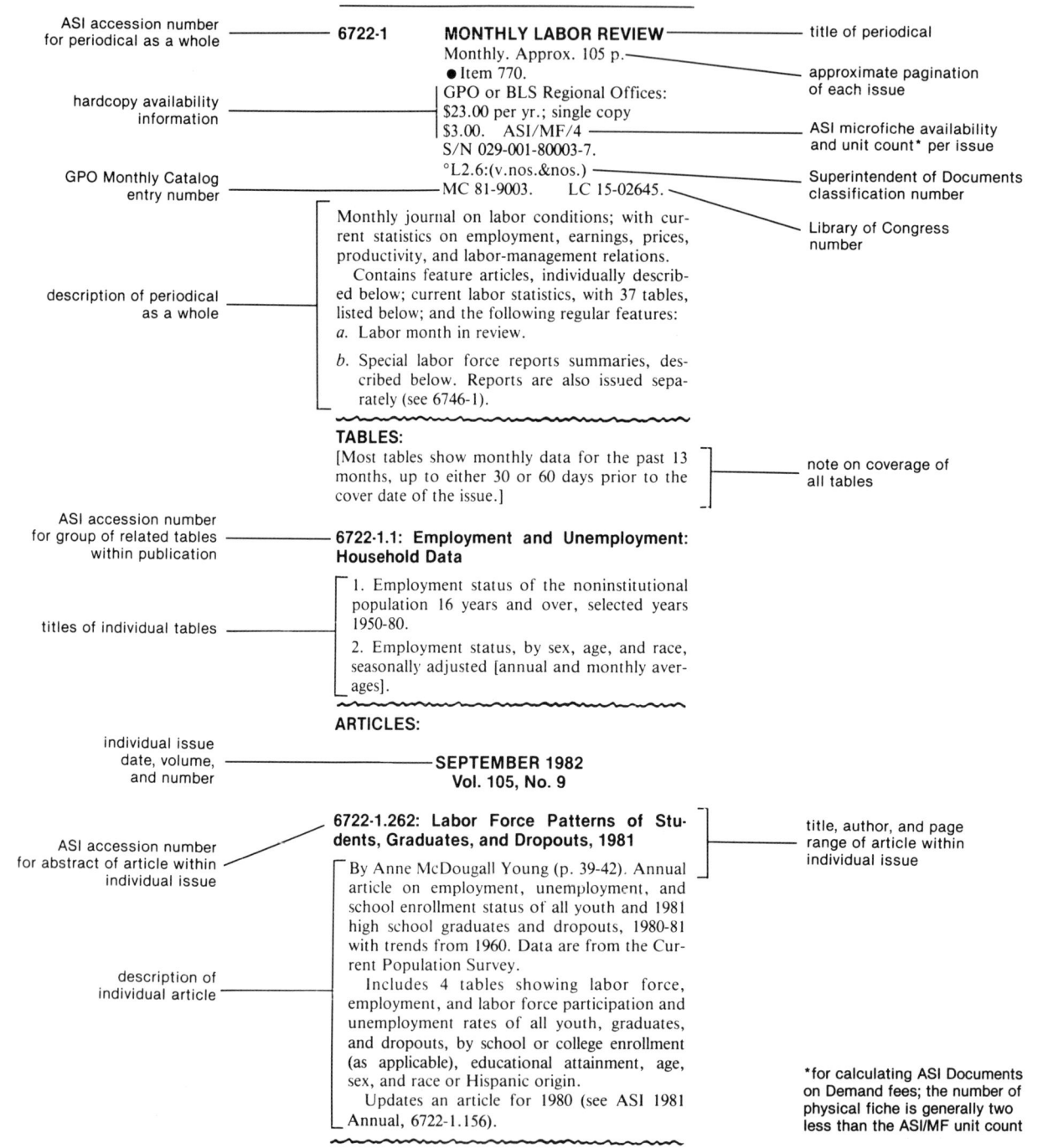

6722
BUREAU OF LABOR STATISTICS: GENERAL
Current Periodicals

ASI accession number for periodical as a whole

6722-1 **MONTHLY LABOR REVIEW** — title of periodical
Monthly. Approx. 105 p. — approximate pagination of each issue
● Item 770.

hardcopy availability information

GPO or BLS Regional Offices: $23.00 per yr.; single copy $3.00. ASI/MF/4 — ASI microfiche availability and unit count* per issue
S/N 029-001-80003-7.

GPO Monthly Catalog entry number

°L2.6:(v.nos.&nos.) — Superintendent of Documents classification number
MC 81-9003. LC 15-02645. — Library of Congress number

description of periodical as a whole

Monthly journal on labor conditions; with current statistics on employment, earnings, prices, productivity, and labor-management relations.

Contains feature articles, individually described below; current labor statistics, with 37 tables, listed below; and the following regular features:

a. Labor month in review.

b. Special labor force reports summaries, described below. Reports are also issued separately (see 6746-1).

TABLES:
[Most tables show monthly data for the past 13 months, up to either 30 or 60 days prior to the cover date of the issue.] — note on coverage of all tables

ASI accession number for group of related tables within publication

6722-1.1: Employment and Unemployment: Household Data

titles of individual tables

1. Employment status of the noninstitutional population 16 years and over, selected years 1950-80.

2. Employment status, by sex, age, and race, seasonally adjusted [annual and monthly averages].

ARTICLES:

individual issue date, volume, and number

SEPTEMBER 1982
Vol. 105, No. 9

ASI accession number for abstract of article within individual issue

6722-1.262: Labor Force Patterns of Students, Graduates, and Dropouts, 1981 — title, author, and page range of article within individual issue

description of individual article

By Anne McDougall Young (p. 39-42). Annual article on employment, unemployment, and school enrollment status of all youth and 1981 high school graduates and dropouts, 1980-81 with trends from 1960. Data are from the Current Population Survey.

Includes 4 tables showing labor force, employment, and labor force participation and unemployment rates of all youth, graduates, and dropouts, by school or college enrollment (as applicable), educational attainment, age, sex, and race or Hispanic origin.

Updates an article for 1980 (see ASI 1981 Annual, 6722-1.156).

*for calculating ASI Documents on Demand fees; the number of physical fiche is generally two less than the ASI/MF unit count

Sample Abstract—Publications in Series

2546
BUREAU OF CENSUS: POPULATION

Publications in Series

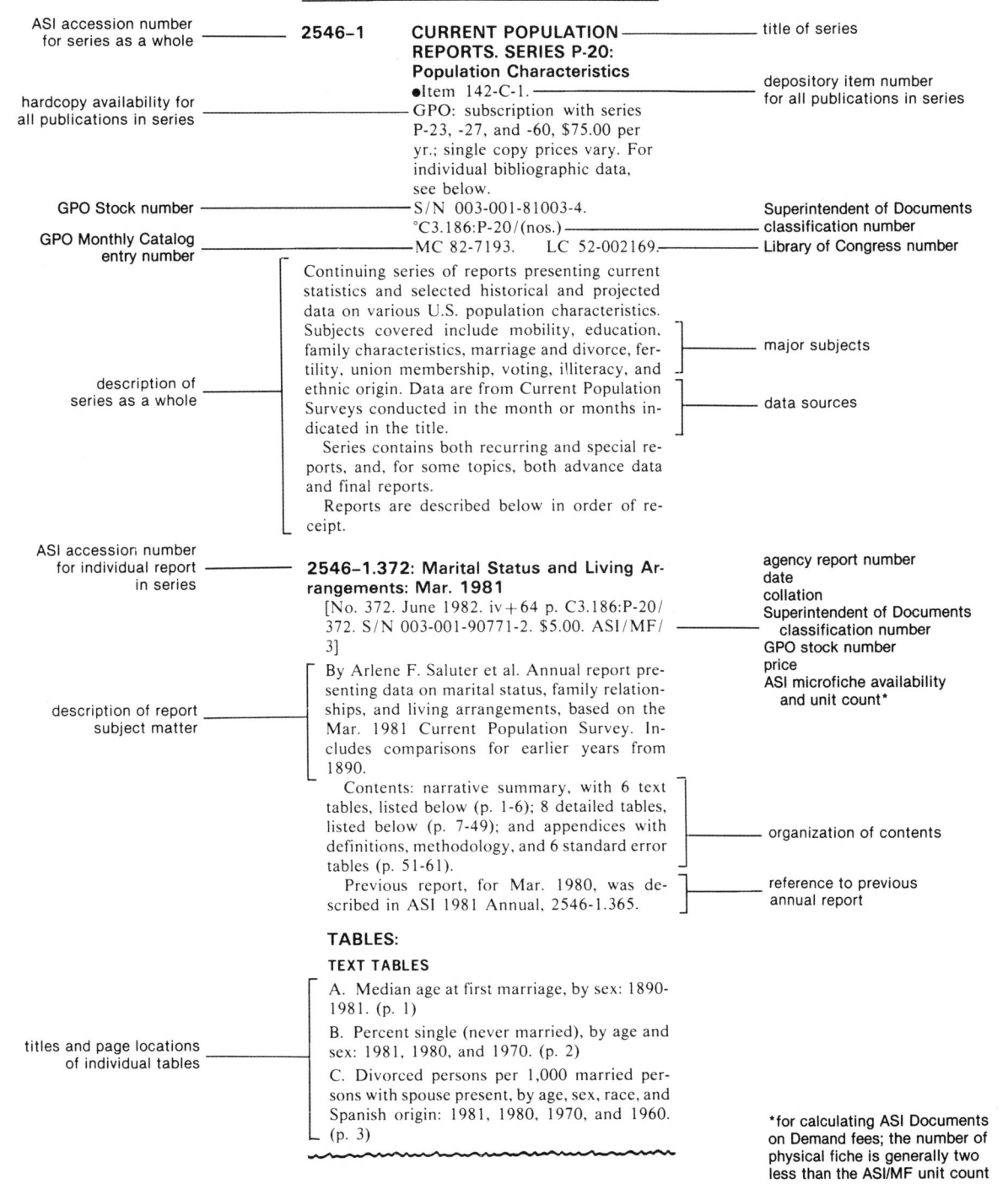

ASI accession number for series as a whole

2546-1 **CURRENT POPULATION REPORTS. SERIES P-20: Population Characteristics** — title of series

●Item 142-C-1. — depository item number for all publications in series

hardcopy availability for all publications in series — GPO: subscription with series P-23, -27, and -60, $75.00 per yr.; single copy prices vary. For individual bibliographic data, see below.

GPO Stock number — S/N 003-001-81003-4.

°C3.186:P-20/(nos.) — Superintendent of Documents classification number

GPO Monthly Catalog entry number — MC 82-7193.   LC 52-002169 — Library of Congress number

description of series as a whole — Continuing series of reports presenting current statistics and selected historical and projected data on various U.S. population characteristics. Subjects covered include mobility, education, family characteristics, marriage and divorce, fertility, union membership, voting, illiteracy, and ethnic origin. Data are from Current Population Surveys conducted in the month or months indicated in the title.

— major subjects

— data sources

Series contains both recurring and special reports, and, for some topics, both advance data and final reports.

Reports are described below in order of receipt.

ASI accession number for individual report in series — **2546-1.372: Marital Status and Living Arrangements: Mar. 1981**

[No. 372. June 1982. iv+64 p. C3.186:P-20/ 372. S/N 003-001-90771-2. $5.00. ASI/MF/ 3]

— agency report number
date
collation
Superintendent of Documents classification number
GPO stock number
price
ASI microfiche availability and unit count*

description of report subject matter — By Arlene F. Saluter et al. Annual report presenting data on marital status, family relationships, and living arrangements, based on the Mar. 1981 Current Population Survey. Includes comparisons for earlier years from 1890.

Contents: narrative summary, with 6 text tables, listed below (p. 1-6); 8 detailed tables, listed below (p. 7-49); and appendices with definitions, methodology, and 6 standard error tables (p. 51-61). — organization of contents

Previous report, for Mar. 1980, was described in ASI 1981 Annual, 2546-1.365. — reference to previous annual report

TABLES:

TEXT TABLES

titles and page locations of individual tables — A. Median age at first marriage, by sex: 1890-1981. (p. 1)

B. Percent single (never married), by age and sex: 1981, 1980, and 1970. (p. 2)

C. Divorced persons per 1,000 married persons with spouse present, by age, sex, race, and Spanish origin: 1981, 1980, 1970, and 1960. (p. 3)

*for calculating ASI Documents on Demand fees; the number of physical fiche is generally two less than the ASI/MF unit count

Sample
ASI Search

"How much did the chemicals industry invest in pollution control equipment in New Jersey?"

Step 1
Check the ASI Index Volume

Start with a "subject" approach where extensive cross-references will lead to to the proper index reference from almost any likely point of entry.

Index by Subjects and Names

Pollution
see Air pollution
see Electromagnetic radiation
see Environmental pollution and control
see Marine pollution
see Mercury pollution
see Noise
see Nuclear radiation
see Soil pollution
see Water pollution

Chemicals and chemical industry
Air pollution abatement equipment shipments by industry, exports, and new and backlog orders, by product, 1984, annual Current Industrial Rpt, 2506–12.5

Pollution abatement capital and operating costs, by SIC 2- to 4-digit industry, State, and SMSA, 1983, annual Current Industrial Rpt, 2506–3.6

Environmental pollution and control
Abatement capital and operating costs, by SIC 2- to 4-digit industry, State, and SMSA, 1982, annual Current Industrial Rpt, 2506–3.6
Abatement spending and govt regulation SIC 2- to 4-digit industry, State, and SMSA, 1983, annual Current Industrial Rpt, 2506–3.6

Index by Categories

An alternate approach is through the "Index by Categories." Since you are looking for information about a particular state, you can find it under "By State."

BY STATE

Natural Resources, Environment, and Pollution
Acid rain causes, air pollutant sources, health effects, and environmental and economic impacts of abatement proposals, 1900s-83 and projected to 2010, hearings, 21368–60

Pollution abatement capital and operating costs, by SIC 2- to 4-digit industry, State, and SMSA, 1983, annual Current Industrial Rpt, 2506–3.6

Step 2

Go from the index to the data description in the appropriate Abstracts volume

The ASI accession number in the index will lead to a publication entry that fully describes the document and pinpoints the tables containing the statistics you need.

**2506
BUREAU OF CENSUS:
MANUFACTURING**
**Publications
in series**

2506-3.6: Pollution Abatement Costs and Expenditures, 1983

[Annual. Apr. 1985. xv+79+App 4 p. MA200(83)-1. °C3.158:MA200(83)-1. LC 77-646295. $4.00. ASI/MF/3]

Annual report for 1983 on pollution abatement control capital expenditures and operating costs, for U.S. by SIC 4-digit industry, and for States by 2-digit industry. Data are from a survey of approximately 20,000 establishments selected as a subsample from the 57,000 1980 Annual Survey of Manufactures (ASM) establishments.

Contents: introduction, with 4 charts and 3 tables (p. v-xv); 10 tables, listed below (p. 1-79); and appendix, with facsimile survey form (4 p.).

TABLES:

[All data are for 1983, unless otherwise noted. Tables show data for establishments with 20 or more employees and are repeated for U.S. by SIC 2- to 4-digit industry (table A), and for States by SIC 2-digit industry (table B). Forms of abatement are water, air, and solid waste.]

CAPITAL EXPENDITURES AND OPERATING COSTS

1-2. Pollution abatement capital expenditures and operating costs, by form of abatement, major [SIC 2-digit] industry group, and State, 1979-83. (p. 1-7)

3A-3B. Pollution abatement capital expenditures [by air and water pollution abatement technique (end-of-line and production process change), by type of air pollutant, and for solid waste]. (p. 8-23)

Step 3

Retrieve the publication

The ASI abstract contains the bibliographic information you need to locate the publication in a library's hardcopy collection or to obtain it from the issuing source, if copies are available.

Alternatively, if you have access to an ASI Microfiche Library collecton, the ASI accession number will lead you directly to the correct microfiche. Or, individual publications abstracted in any ASI Monthly or Annual Supplement are available for purchase on microfiche directly from Congressional Information Service through our CIS & ASI Documents on Demand Service.

Order kits supplied to all ASI subscribers provide the necessary information about costs and how to place microfiche orders. (Details are also available by writing CIS, Documents on Demand, P.O. Box 30056, Bethesda, MD 20814.

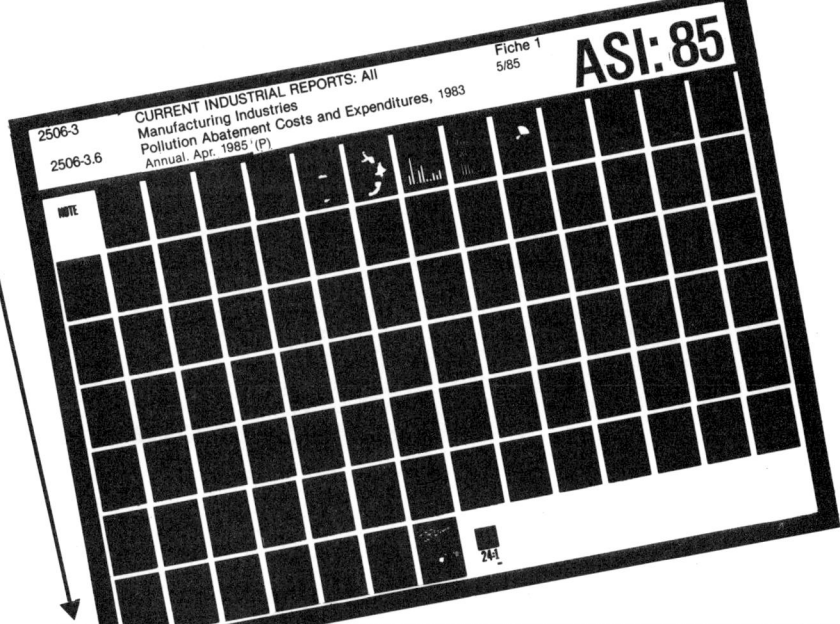

Table 3B. **Pollution Abatement Capital Expenditures, by State and Major Industry Group: 1983**

(Millions of dollars)

Where to Write for Statistical Publications

Publications abstracted in ASI are frequently available to the public from the Government Printing Office, the National Technical Information Service, or the issuing agency. In addition, a complete collection of abstracted publications is available in the ASI Microfiche Library.

Information about the source and availability of specific publications is given in each ASI abstract. (For illustrations, see the Sample Abstracts; for background information, see the section headed "Acquiring the Documents" on p. xx.)

The mailing addresses of GPO, NTIS, and principal issuing agency sources of publications are listed below.

When ordering publications from the issuing agency, requests should be directed to the specific subagency, Information Division, c/o the parent agency. Where the subagency has a separate mailing address, it is given.

There has been no attempt to list regional or field offices for every agency and subagency. Listings and addresses of these offices can be found in most agency catalogs, and in local telephone directories for the cities in which they are located.

Addresses have been provided for the sources of publications, periodicals, and/or specials and irregulars, which may be available only, or more conveniently, from offices in other locations than the central information office for an agency. Identification of other unusual sources will appear with the abstract of a publication.

GOVERNMENT PRINTING OFFICE (GPO)
Superintendent of Documents
Washington, DC 20402

NATIONAL TECHNICAL INFORMATION SERVICE (NTIS)
5285 Port Royal Rd
Springfield, VA 22161

EXECUTIVE OFFICE OF THE PRESIDENT
Publications Unit, Rm G236
New Executive Office Bldg
Washington, DC 20503

COUNCIL OF ECONOMIC ADVISERS
New Executive Office Bldg
Washington, DC 20506

COUNCIL ON ENVIRONMENTAL QUALITY
722 Jackson Pl., N.W.
Washington, DC 20006\

OFFICE OF MANAGEMENT & BUDGET
Publications Unit, Rm G236
New Executive Office Bldg
Washington, DC 20503

OFFICE OF SCIENCE AND TECHNOLOGY POLICY
New Executive Office Building
Washington, DC 20506

OFFICE OF THE U.S. TRADE REPRESENTATIVE
600 17th St., N.W.
Washington, DC 20506

DEPARTMENT OF AGRICULTURE
(Subagency Name)
Information Division
Washington, DC 20250

AGRICULTURAL MARKETING SERVICE
Information Staff   Rm 3068-S
Washington, DC 20250

Cotton Division
4841 Summer Ave.
Memphis, TN 38122

AGRICULTURAL STATISTICS
5820 S. Building
Washington, DC 20250

ECONOMIC RESEARCH SERVICE
ERS-NASS Publications
P.O. Box 1608
Rockville, MD 20850

FOREST SERVICE—Forest (and Range) Experiment Stations

Intermountain (INT)
324 25th St.
Ogden, UT 84401

North Central (NC)
1992 Folwell Ave.
St. Paul, MN 55108

Northeastern (NE)
370 Reed Rd
Broomall, PA 19008

Pacific Northwest (PNW)
P.O. Box 3890
Portland, OR 97208

Pacific Southwest (PSW)
1960 Addison St.
P.O. Box 245
Berkeley, CA 94701

Rocky Mountain (RM)
240 West Prospect St.
Fort Collins, CO 80526

Southeastern (SE)
200 Weaver Blvd.
Asheville, NC 28804

Southern (SO)
T-10210 Postal Services Bldg
701 Loyola Ave.
New Orleans, LA 70113

SOIL CONSERVATION SERVICE
(Western U.S.)
West Technical Service Center, Rm 510
511 N.W. Broadway
Portland, OR 97209

DEPARTMENT OF COMMERCE
(Subagency Name)
Office of Public Affairs
Washington, DC 20230

BUREAU OF ECONOMIC ANALYSIS
Information Services Division
1401 K St., N.W.
Washington, DC 20235

BUREAU OF THE CENSUS
Customer Services
Data User Services Division
Washington, DC 20233

NATIONAL INSTITUTE OF STANDARDS AND TECHNOLOGY
Office of Information Activities
Rm 640, Administration Bldg
Washington, DC 20234

NATIONAL OCEANIC AND ATMOSPHERIC ADMINISTRATION
Office of Public Affairs
WSC-5
Rockville, MD 20852

Environmental Satellite, Data, and Information Service
Library and Information Services Division
Rockville, MD 20852

Environmental Research Laboratories
Public Information Office
Boulder, CO 80302

National Climatic Data Center
EDIS
Federal Building
Asheville, NC 28801

National Marine Fisheries Service
Public Affairs
1825 Connecticut Ave., N.W.
Universal S. Building
Washington, DC 20235

National Ocean Service
Public Information Office
WSC-1
Rockville, MD 20852

National Weather Service
Rm 400, Gramax Bldg
8060 13th St.
Silver Spring, MD 20910

PATENT AND TRADEMARK OFFICE
Office of Public Affairs
2021 Jefferson Davis Highway
Arlington, VA 20231

DEPARTMENT OF COMMERCE DISTRICT OFFICES—INTERNATIONAL TRADE ADMINISTRATION

22 W. 7th Ave.
Anchorage, AK 99513

Suite 504, 1365 Peachtree St., N.E.
Atlanta, GA 30309

Rm 415, U.S. Customhouse
Baltimore, MD 21202

Berry Bldg., 2015 2nd Ave. N.,
Birmingham, AL 35203

Suite 307, World Trade Center
Commonwealth Pier Area
Boston, MA 02210

Rm 1312, 111 W. Huron St.
Buffalo, NY 14202

42 New Federal Building
500 Quarrier St.
Charleston, WV 26301

55 E. Monroe St.
Chicago, IL 60603

550 Main St.
Cincinnati, OH 45202

Rm 600, 666 Euclid Ave.
Cleveland, OH 44114

Suite 172, 1835 Assembly St.
Columbia, SC 29201

Rm 7A5, 1100 Commerce St.
Dallas, TX 75242

Suite 600, 1625 Broadway
Denver, CO 80202

Rm 817, 210 Walnut St.
Des Moines, IA 50309

1140 McNamara Bldg, 477 Michigan Ave.
Detroit, MI 48226

Rm 203, 324 W. Market St.
Greensboro, NC 27402

Rm 610-B, 450 Main St.
Hartford, CT 06103

P.O. Box 50026, 300 Ala Moana Blvd.
Honolulu, HI 96850

Rm 2625, 515 Rusk Ave.
Houston, TX 77002

Suite 520, One N. Capitol St.
Indianapolis, IN 46204

328 Jackson Mall Office Center
Jackson, MS 39213

Rm 635, 601 E. 12th St.
Kansas City, MO 64106

Suite 635, 320 W. Capitol Ave.
Little Rock, AR 72201

Rm 800, 11777 San Vincente Blvd
Los Angeles, CA 90049

Rm 636B, 601 W. Broadway
Louisville, KY 40202

Suite 224, 51 SW 1st Ave.
Miami, FL 33130

517 E. Wisconsin Ave.
Milwaukee, WI 53202

Rm 108, 110 S. 4th St.
Minneapolis, MN 55401

Suite 1114, Parkway Towers
Nashville, TN 27219

2 Canal St.
New Orleans, LA 70130

Rm 3718, Federal Office Bldg
New York, NY 10278

Suite 200, 5 Broadway Executive Park,
Oklahoma City, OK 73116

11133 O St.
Omaha, NE 68137

Suite 202, 475 Allendale Rd.
King of Prussia, PA 19406

Rm 3412, Federal Bldg and U.S. Courthouse
Phoenix, AZ 85025

Rm 2002, 1000 Liberty Ave.
Pittsburgh, PA 15222

Rm 618, 1220 S.W. 3rd Ave.
Portland, OR 97204

1755 E. Plumb La., No. 152
Reno, NV 89502

Rm 8010, 400 N. 8th St.
Richmond, VA 23240

Rm 340, 350 S. Main St.
Salt Lake City, UT 84101

6363 Greenwich Dr.
San Diego, CA 92122

Box 36013, 450 Golden Gate Ave.
San Francisco, CA 94102

Rm G-55, Federal Bldg, Chardon Ave.
San Juan, PR 00918

120 Barnard St., A-107
Savannah, GA 31402

Suite 290, 3131 Elliott Ave.
Seattle, WA 98121

Suite 610, 7911 Forsyth Blvd.
St. Louis, MO 63105

Suite 100, Bldg 6, 3131 Princeton Pike
Trenton, NJ 08648

DEPARTMENT OF DEFENSE

Office of the Assistant Secretary of Defense
(Public Affairs)
The Pentagon
Washington, DC 20301

Directorate for Information Operations
and Reports (DIOR)
Suite 1204, 1215 Jefferson Davis Hwy.
Arlington, VA 22202-4302

DEFENSE LOGISTICS AGENCY
Defense Fuel Supply Center
Public Affairs
Bldg 8, Cameron Station
Alexandria, VA 22314

U.S. AIR FORCE PUBLICATIONS
Office of the Secretary of the Air Force
Office of Information
Public Information Division
Headquarters, USAF
Washington, DC 20330

U.S. ARMY PUBLICATIONS
Public Information Office
Office of the Chief of Information
Headquarters, Department of the Army
Washington, DC 20310

U.S. ARMY CORPS OF ENGINEERS
Public Affairs Office
Forrestal Bldg
Washington, DC 20314

**U.S. ARMY CORPS OF ENGINEERS
REGIONAL OFFICES**
Alaska District
P.O. Box 7002
Anchorage, AK 99510

Detroit District
P.O. Box 1027
Detroit, MI 48281

Louisville District
P.O. Box 59
Louisville, KY 40201

Lower Mississippi Valley Division
P.O. Box 60
Vicksburg, MS 39180

Missouri River Division
Downtown Station, P.O. Box 103
Omaha, NE 68101

Mobile District
P.O. Box 2288
Mobile, AL 36828

Nashville District
P.O. Box 1070
Nashville, TN 37202

New England Division
424 Trapelo Rd
Waltham, MA 02154

New Orleans District
P.O. Box 60267
New Orleans, LA 70160

North Atlantic Division
90 Church St.
New York, NY 10007

North Central Division
536 S. Clark St.
Chicago, IL 60605

Ohio River Division
P.O. Box 1159
Cincinnati, OH 45201

South Atlantic Division
510 Title Bldg
30 Pryor St., S.W.
Atlanta, GA 30303

South Pacific Division
630 Sansome St.
San Francisco, CA 94111

Southwest Division
1114 Commerce St.
Dallas, TX 75242

U.S. NAVY PUBLICATIONS
Public Information Division
Office of Information
Department of the Navy
Washington, DC 20350

DEPARTMENT OF EDUCATION

(Specified Office)
400 Maryland Ave., S.W.
Washington, DC 20202

**NATIONAL CENTER FOR EDUCATION
STATISTICS**
OERI
555 New Jersey Ave., N.W.
Washington, DC 20208

**NATIONAL ASSESSMENT OF
EDUCATIONAL PROGRESS (NAEP)**
CN6710
Princeton, NJ 08541-6710

DEPARTMENT OF ENERGY

(Subagency Name)
Washington, DC 20585

BONNEVILLE POWER ADMINISTRATION
Public Involvement
P.O. Box 12999
Portland, OR 97212

ENERGY INFORMATION ADMINISTRATION
National Energy Information Center
EI-20, Mail Station 1F048
1000 Independence Ave., S.W.
Washington, DC 20585

**FEDERAL ENERGY REGULATORY
COMMISSION**
Public Information Office, Rm 1000
825 North Capitol St., N.E.
Washington, DC 20426

OAK RIDGE NATIONAL LABORATORY
Technical Information Center
P.O. Box 62
Oak Ridge, TN 37831

DEPARTMENT OF HEALTH
AND HUMAN SERVICES

Office of Public Affairs
Rm 647-D, HHH Bldg
200 Independence Ave., S.W.
Washington, DC 20201

CENTERS FOR DISEASE CONTROL
1600 Clifton Rd, N.E.
Atlanta, GA 30333

FOOD AND DRUG ADMINISTRATION
HFE 88
5600 Fishers La.
Rockville, MD 20857

HEALTH CARE FINANCING ADMINISTRATION
648 East High Rise Bldg
6401 Security Blvd
Baltimore, MD 21235

**HEALTH RESOURCES AND SERVICES
ADMINISTRATION**
(Subagency Name)
14-43 Parklawn Bldg
5600 Fishers La.
Rockville, MD 20857

NATIONAL CENTER FOR HEALTH STATISTICS
Rm 1-57, Federal Center Bldg #2
3700 East-West Hwy
Hyattsville, MD 20782

**NATIONAL CHILD SUPPORT
ENFORCEMENT CENTER**
Rm. 820, 6110 Executive Blvd.
Rockville, MD 20852

**NATIONAL CLEARINGHOUSE FOR
ALCOHOL INFORMATION**
P.O. Box 2345
Rockville, MD 20852

**NATIONAL CLEARINGHOUSE FOR
DRUG ABUSE INFORMATION**
10A-53 Parklawn Bldg
5600 Fishers La.
Rockville, MD 20857

NATIONAL INSTITUTES OF HEALTH
Office of Information
Rm 307, Bldg 1
9000 Rockville Pike
Bethesda, MD 20205

NATIONAL INSTITUTE OF MENTAL HEALTH
Public Inquiries
Rm 11A-21, 5600 Fishers La.
Rockville, MD 20857

**NATIONAL INSTITUTE FOR OCCUPATIONAL
SAFETY AND HEALTH**
Publications, DTS
4676 Columbia Parkway
Cincinnati, OH 45226

OFFICE OF HUMAN DEVELOPMENT SERVICES
Rm 329D, HHH Bldg
200 Independence Ave., S.W.
Washington, DC 20201

OFFICE ON SMOKING AND HEALTH
Rm 158, 5600 Fishers La.
Rockville, MD 20857

PUBLIC HEALTH SERVICE
Office of Public Affairs
Rm 740-G, HHH Bldg
200 Independence Ave., S.W.
Washington, DC 20201

OHIC/ODPHP
P.O. Box 1133
Washington, DC 20013-1133

SOCIAL SECURITY ADMINISTRATION
Printing and Records Management Branch
1121 Operations Bldg
6401 Security Blvd
Baltimore, MD 21235

DEPARTMENT OF HOUSING AND
URBAN DEVELOPMENT

Publication Service Center
Rm B-258
Washington, DC 20410

**OFFICE OF POLICY DEVELOPMENT
AND RESEARCH**
HUD USER
P.O. Box 280
Germantown, MD 20767

DEPARTMENT OF THE INTERIOR

(Subagency Name)
Office of Information
Washington, DC 20240

BUREAU OF MINES
Publication Distribution Section
4800 Forbes Ave.
Pittsburgh, PA 15213

FISH AND WILDLIFE SERVICE
Natl Coastal Ecosystems Team
NASA Slidell Computer Complex
1010 Gause Blvd.
Slidell, LA 709458

U.S. GEOLOGICAL SURVEY
USGS Books and Open-File Rpts. Section
Branch of Distribution
Box 25425, Federal Center
Denver, CO 80225

DEPARTMENT OF JUSTICE
Office of Public Information
10th and Constitution Ave., N.W.
Washington, DC 20530

BUREAU OF PRISONS
320 1st St., N.W.
Washington, DC 20534

DRUG ENFORCEMENT ADMINISTRATION
1405 I St., N.W.
Washington, DC 20537

FEDERAL BUREAU OF INVESTIGATION
9th and Pennsylvania Ave., N.W.
Washington, DC 20535

FOREIGN CLAIMS SETTLEMENT
COMMISSION OF THE U.S.
Vanguard Building
1111 20th St., N.W.
Washington, DC 20579

IMMIGRATION AND NATURALIZATION SERVICE
425 I St., N.W.
Attn: Tariff Rm 235
Washington, DC 20536

NATIONAL CRIMINAL JUSTICE
REFERENCE SERVICE (NCJRS)
Box 6000
Rockville, MD 20850

OFFICE OF JUSTICE PROGRAMS
633 Indiana Ave., N.W.
Washington, DC 20531

DEPARTMENT OF LABOR
Office of Information, Publications, and Reports
200 Constitution Ave., N.W.
Washington, DC 20210

BUREAU OF LABOR STATISTICS
Information Office
GAO Bldg
441 G St., N.W.
Washington, DC 20212

BUREAU OF LABOR STATISTICS
REGIONAL OFFICES
Region I
Rm 1603, JFK Federal Bldg
Government Center
Boston, MA 02203

Region II
1515 Broadway, Suite 3400
New York, NY 10036

Region III
3535 Market St.
P.O. Box 13309
Philadelphia, PA 19101

Region IV
1371 Peachtree St., N.E.
Atlanta, GA 30309

Region V
Federal Office Bldg
230 S. Dearborn St.
Chicago, IL 60604

Region VI
555 Griffin St., Rm 221
Dallas, TX 75202

Regions VII and VIII
911 Walnut St.
Kansas City, MO 64106

Regions IX and X
450 Golden Gate Ave.
Box 36017
San Francisco, CA 94102

EMPLOYMENT AND TRAINING ADMINISTRATION
Rm 10426, 601 D St., N.W.
Washington, DC 20213

MINE SAFETY AND HEALTH ADMINISTRATION
Office of Information
Ballston Tower #3, Rm 902
4015 Wilson Blvd
Arlington, VA 22203

DEPARTMENT OF STATE
(Subagency Name)
Bureau of Public Affairs
Washington, DC 20520

DEPARTMENT OF TRANSPORTATION
Office of Public & Consumer Affairs (S-81)
400 7th St., S.W.
Washington, DC 20590

Transporation Systems Center
Kendall Sq.
Cambridge, MA 02142

FEDERAL AVIATION ADMINISTRATION
Public Inquiry Center (APA-420)
800 Independence Ave., S.W.
Washington, DC 20590

FEDERAL HIGHWAY ADMINISTRATION
Office of Public Affairs (HPA-1)
400 7th St., S.W.
Washington, DC 20590

FEDERAL RAILROAD ADMINISTRATION
Office of Public Affairs (ROA-30)
400 7th St., S.W.
Washington, DC 20590

MARITIME ADMINISTRATION
Office of Public Affairs (MAR-240)
400 7th St., S.W.
Washington, DC 20590

NATIONAL HIGHWAY TRAFFIC SAFETY
ADMINISTRATION
400 7th St., S.W.
Washington, DC 20590

SAINT LAWRENCE SEAWAY
DEVELOPMENT CORPORATION
P.O. Box 44090
Washington, DC 20026-4090

URBAN MASS TRANSPORTATION ADMINISTRATION
Office of Public Affairs (UPA-1)
400 7th St., S.W.
Washington, DC 20590

U.S. COAST GUARD
Public Affairs Division (G-BPA)
2100 2nd St., S.W.
Washington, DC 20593

DEPARTMENT OF THE TREASURY
Public Affairs Office
15th and Pennsylvania Ave., N.W.
Washington, DC 20220

BUREAU OF ALCOHOL, TOBACCO
AND FIREARMS
Office of Public Affairs
1200 Pennsylvania Ave., N.W.
Washington, DC 20226

BUREAU OF ENGRAVING AND PRINTING
Public Affairs Section, Rm 602-11A
14th and C Sts., S.W.
Washington, DC 20228

BUREAU OF THE PUBLIC DEBT
Washington, DC 20226

COMPTROLLER OF THE CURRENCY
Communications Division
490 L'Enfant Plaza East, S.W.
Washington, DC 20219

FINANCIAL MANAGEMENT SERVICE
Pennsylvania Ave. and Madison Pl., N.W.
Washington, DC 20226

INTERNAL REVENUE SERVICE
Office of Public Affairs
1111 Constitution Ave., N.W.
Washington, DC 20224

OFFICE OF REVENUE SHARING
Office of Public Affairs
2401 E St., N.W.
Washington, DC 20226

OFFICE OF THRIFT SUPERVISION
1700 G St., N.W.
Washington, DC 20552

U.S. CUSTOMS SERVICE
Office of Public Affairs
1301 Constitution Ave., N.W.
Washington, DC 20229

U.S. MINT
Assistant to the Director for Public Affairs
501 13th St., N.W.
Washington, DC 20220

U.S. SAVINGS BOND DIVISION
Washington, DC 20226

U.S. SECRET SERVICE
Office of Public Affairs
1800 G St., N.W.
Washington, DC 20223

DEPARTMENT OF VETERANS AFFAIRS
Office of Public Affairs
810 Vermont Ave., N.W.
Washington, DC 20420

INDEPENDENT AGENCIES
ACTION
Office of Public Affairs
1100 Vermont Ave., N.W.
Washington, DC 20525

AMERICAN BATTLE MONUMENTS COMMISSION
20 Massachusetts Ave., N.W.
Washington, DC 20314

APPALACHIAN REGIONAL COMMISSION
Archivist
1666 Connecticut Ave., N.W.
Washington, DC 20235

CENTRAL INTELLIGENCE AGENCY
Photoduplication Service
Library of Congress
Washington, DC 20540

CONSUMER PRODUCT SAFETY COMMISSION
Bureau of Information and Education
Product Safety Information Division
5401 Westbard Ave.
Bethesda, MD 20207

ENVIRONMENTAL PROTECTION AGENCY
(Subagency Name)
401 M St., S.W.
Washington, DC 20460

Documents Distribution Division
1901 Ross Ave.
Cincinnati, OH 45212

Office of Air Quality Planning and Standards
Research Triangle Park, NC 27711

ENVIRONMENTAL PROTECTION AGENCY
REGIONAL OFFICES
Region I
Rm 2203, JFK Federal Bldg
Boston, MA 02203

Region II
Rm 1009, 26 Federal Plaza
New York, NY 10278

Region III
841 Chestnut St.
Philadelphia, PA 19107

Region IV
345 Courtland St., N.E.
Atlanta, GA 30308

Region V
230 South Dearborn St.
Chicago, IL 60604

Region VI
1201 Elm St.
Dallas, TX 75270

Region VII
726 Minnesota Ave.
Kansas City, KS 66101

Region VIII
999 18th St., Suite 500
Denver, CO 80202-2405

Region IX
215 Fremont St.
San Francisco, CA 94105

Region X
1200 6th Ave.
Seattle, WA 98101

EQUAL EMPLOYMENT OPPORTUNITY
COMMISSION
1801 L St., N.W.
Washington, DC 20507

EXPORT-IMPORT BANK OF THE
UNITED STATES
Public Affairs Office
811 Vermont Ave., N.W.
Washington, DC 20571

FARM CREDIT ADMINISTRATION
Information Division
1501 Farm Credit Dr.
McLean, VA 22102

FEDERAL COMMUNICATIONS COMMISSION
Public Information Office
1919 M St., N.W.
Washington, DC 20554

FEDERAL DEPOSIT INSURANCE
CORPORATION
Information Office
550 17th St., N.W.
Washington, DC 20429

FEDERAL ELECTION COMMISSION
999 E St., N.W.
Washington, DC 20463

FEDERAL EMERGENCY MANAGEMENT AGENCY
Office of Public Affairs
500 C St., S.W.
Washington, DC 20472

FEDERAL HOME LOAN BANKS

Federal Home Loan Bank of Atlanta
Peachtree Center Station
P.O. Box 56527
Atlanta, GA 30343

Federal Home Loan Bank of Boston
P.O. Box 2196
Boston, MA 02106

Federal Home Loan Bank of Chicago
111 E. Wacker Dr.
Chicago, IL 60601

Federal Home Loan Bank of Cincinnati
2500 DuBois Tower
P.O. Box 598
Cincinnati, OH 45201

Federal Home Loan Bank of Dallas
500 E. John Carpenter Freeway
P.O. Box 619026
Dallas/Ft. Worth, TX 75261

Federal Home Loan Bank of Des Moines
907 Walnut St.
Des Moines, IA 50309

Federal Home Loan Bank of Indianapolis
1350 Merchants Plaza, South Tower
115 W. Washington St.
P.O. Box 60
Indianapolis, IN 46206

Federal Home Loan Bank of New York
One World Trade Center
New York, NY 10048

Federal Home Loan Bank of Pittsburgh
11 Stanwix St.
Gateway Center
Pittsburgh, PA 15222

Federal Home Loan Bank of San Francisco
600 California St.
P.O. Box 7948
San Francisco, CA 94120

Federal Home Loan Bank of Seattle
600 Stewart St.
Seattle, WA 98101

Federal Home Loan Bank of Topeka
3 Townsite Plaza
P.O. Box 176   120 East 6th St.
Topeka, KS 66601

FEDERAL HOME LOAN MORTGAGE CORPORATION

1770 G St., N.W.
Washington, DC 20552

FEDERAL HOUSING FINANCE BOARD

1700 G St., N.W.
Washington, DC 20552

FEDERAL MARITIME COMMISSION

Public Information Office
1100 L St., N.W.
Washington, DC 20573

FEDERAL MEDIATION AND CONCILIATION SERVICE

2100 K St., N.W.
Washington, DC 20427

FEDERAL RESERVE SYSTEM

Board of Governors
Publications Section
Division of Administrative Services
Washington, DC 20551

Federal Reserve Bank of Atlanta
Research Department
P.O. Box 1731
Atlanta, GA 30301

Federal Reserve Bank of Boston
Bank & Public Information Center
600 Atlantic Ave.
Boston, MA 02106

Federal Reserve Bank of Chicago
Publications Division
P.O. Box 834
Chicago, IL 60690

Federal Reserve Bank of Cleveland
Research Department
P.O. Box 6387
Cleveland, OH 44101

Federal Reserve Bank of Dallas
Research Department
Station K
Dallas, TX 75222

Federal Reserve Bank of Kansas City
Research Department
925 Grand Ave.
Kansas City, MO 64198

Federal Reserve Bank of Minneapolis
Office of Public Information
Minneapolis, MN 55480

Federal Reserve Bank of New York
Public Information Department
33 Liberty St.
New York, NY 10045

Federal Reserve Bank of Philadelphia
Public Information Department
PO Box 66
Philadelphia, PA 19105

Federal Reserve Bank of Richmond
Bank and Public Relations Department
P.O. Box 27622
Richmond, VA 23261

Federal Reserve Bank of St. Louis
Research Department
Box 442
St. Louis, MO 63166

Federal Reserve Bank of San Francisco
Research Information Center
P.O. Box 7702
San Francisco, CA 94120

FEDERAL TRADE COMMISSION

Public Reference Room
Pennsylvania Ave. at 6th St., N.W.
Rm 130
Washington, DC 20580

GENERAL SERVICES ADMINISTRATION

Director of Information
Washington, DC 20405

INTERSTATE COMMERCE COMMISSION

Public Information Office
12th St. and Constitution Ave., N.W.
Washington, DC 20423

MERIT SYSTEMS PROTECTION BOARD

1120 Vermont Ave., N.W.
Washington, DC 20419

NATIONAL AERONAUTICS AND SPACE ADMINISTRATION

Headquarters, Information Center
Washington, DC 20546

NATIONAL ARCHIVES AND RECORDS ADMINISTRATION

Publications Services
Washington, DC 20408

NATIONAL CREDIT UNION ADMINISTRATION

Office of Public Information
1776 G St., N.W.
Washington, DC 20456

NATIONAL FOUNDATION ON THE ARTS AND HUMANITIES

1100 Pennsylvania, Ave., N.W.
Washington, DC 20506

NATIONAL LABOR RELATIONS BOARD

1717 Pennsylvania Ave., N.W.
Washington, DC 20570

NATIONAL MEDIATION BOARD

1425 K St., N.W.
Washington, DC 20572

NATIONAL SCIENCE FOUNDATION

Public Information Branch, Rm 531
1800 G St., N.W.
Washington, DC 20550

NATIONAL TRANSPORTATION SAFETY BOARD

Publications Unit
800 Independence Ave., S.W.
Washington, DC 20594

OFFICE OF PERSONNEL MANAGEMENT

Office of Public Affairs
1900 E St., N.W.
Washington, DC 20415

PANAMA CANAL COMMISSION

2000 L St., N.W.
Washington, DC 20036

PEACE CORPS

806 Connecticut Ave., N.W.
Washington, DC 20526

PENSION BENEFIT GUARANTY CORPORATION

2020 K St., N.W.
Washington, DC 20006

RAILROAD RETIREMENT BOARD

Division of Information Service
844 Rush St.
Chicago, IL 60611

RESOLUTION TRUST CORPORATION

Communications Unit
Washington, DC 20429

SECURITIES AND EXCHANGE COMMISSION

Office of Public Information
450 5th St., N.W.
Washington, DC 20549

SELECTIVE SERVICE SYSTEM

600 E St., N.W.
Washington, DC 20435

SMALL BUSINESS ADMINISTRATION

Office of Public Affairs
1441 L. St., N.W.
Washington, DC 20416

SMITHSONIAN INSTITUTION

Office of Public Affairs
Washington, DC 20560

TENNESSEE VALLEY AUTHORITY

Suite 300, 412 First St., S.E.
Washington, DC 20444

Public Affairs Office
400 W. Summit Hill Dr.
Knoxville, TN 37902-1499

Division of Energy Use and Distributor Relations
721 Power Building
Chattanooga, TN 37401

Division of Land and Forest Resources
Norris, TN 37828

National Fertilizer Development Center
Muscle Shoals, AL 35660

Technical Library
NFD 1A 100E
Muscle Shoals, AL 35660-1010

U.S. ARMS CONTROL AND DISARMAMENT AGENCY

Office of Public Affairs
320 21st St., N.W.
Washington, DC 20451

U.S. INFORMATION AGENCY

Office of Public Liaison
301 Fourth St., S.W.
Washington, DC 20547

U.S. INTERNATIONAL DEVELOPMENT COOPERATION AGENCY

Office of Public Affairs
Washington, DC 20523-0001

Agency for International Development
Director, Office of Public Affairs
Washington, DC 20523-0001

AID Document and Information Handling Facility
Suite 100, 7222 47th St.
Chevy Chase, MD 20815

Overseas Private Investment Corporation
1615 M St., N.W.
Washington, DC 20527

U.S. INTERNATIONAL TRADE COMMISSION

Office of the Secretary
500 E St., S.W.
Washington, DC 20436

U.S. POSTAL SERVICE

475 L'Enfant Plaza West, S.W.
Washington, DC 20260

SPECIAL BOARDS, COMMITTEES, AND COMMISSIONS

ADVISORY COMMISSION ON INTERGOVERNMENTAL RELATIONS

Suite 2000, Vanguard Bldg
111 20th St., N.W.
Washington, DC 20575

ADVISORY COMMITTEE ON FEDERAL PAY

Rm 205, 1730 K St., N.W.
Washington, DC 20006

ARCHITECTURAL AND TRANSPORTATION BARRIERS COMPLIANCE BOARD

Suite 501, 1111 18th St., N.W.
Washington, DC 20036

BOARD FOR INTERNATIONAL BROADCASTING

Suite 400, 1201 Connecticut Ave., N.W.
Washington, DC 20036

BOARD OF FOREIGN SCHOLARSHIPS

U.S. Information Agency
Rm 247, 301 4th St., S.W.
Washington, DC 20547

COMMISSION ON CIVIL RIGHTS

1121 Vermont Ave., N.W.
Washington, DC 20425

COMMODITY FUTURES TRADING COMMISSION
Office of Public Information
2033 K St., N.W.
Washington, DC 20581

Suite 4600, 233 S. Wacker Dr.
Chicago, IL 60606

Rm 400, 4901 Main St.
Kansas City, MO 64112

510 Grain Exchange Building
Minneapolis, MN 55415

Suite 4747, One World Trade Center
New York, NY 10048

**FEDERAL FINANCIAL INSTITUTIONS
EXAMINATION COUNCIL**
Suite 701, 1776 G St., N.W.
Washington, DC 20006

FEDERAL LABOR RELATIONS AUTHORITY
500 C St., S.W.
Washington, DC 20424

**HARRY S. TRUMAN SCHOLARSHIP
FOUNDATION**
712 Jackson Place, N.W.
Washington, DC 20006

INTER-AMERICAN FOUNDATION
1515 Wilson Blvd, 5th Fl.
Rosslyn, VA 22209

**INTERNATIONAL JOINT COMMISSION,
U.S. AND CANADA**
United States Section
2001 S St., N.W.
Washington, DC 20440

JAPAN-U.S. FRIENDSHIP COMMISSION
Rm 3416, 1200 Pennsylvania Ave., N.W.
Washington, DC 20004

MARINE MAMMAL COMMISSION
1625 I St., N.W.
Washington, DC 20006

**MIGRATORY BIRD CONSERVATION
COMMISSION**
18th & C Sts., N.W., 622 ARL.SQ
Washington, DC 20240

**NATIONAL ADVISORY COUNCIL ON
ADULT EDUCATION**
Rm 323, 425 13th St., N.W.
Washington, DC 20004

**NATIONAL ADVISORY COUNCIL ON
INDIAN EDUCATION**
330 C St., S.W., Room 4072
Switzer Bldg, Mail Stop 2419
Washington, DC 20202-7556

**NATIONAL ADVISORY COUNCIL ON
INTERNATIONAL MONETARY AND
FINANCIAL POLICIES**
Rm 5455
Department of the Treasury
Washington, DC 20220

**NATIONAL CAPITAL PLANNING
COMMISSION**
1325 G St., N.W.
Washington, DC 20576

**NATIONAL COMMISSION FOR
EMPLOYMENT POLICY**
1522 K St., N.W., Rm 300
Washington, DC 20005

**NATIONAL COMMISSION ON LIBRARIES
AND INFORMATION SCIENCE**
1111 18th St., N.W., Suite 310
Washington, DC 20036

**NAVAJO AND HOPI INDIAN
RELOCATION COMMISSION**
P.O. Box KK
Flagstaff, ZA 86002

**PRESIDENT'S COMMITTEE ON
EMPLOYMENT OF PEOPLE WITH
DISABILITIES**
1111 20th St., N.W., Suite 636
Washington, DC 20036

**PROSPECTIVE PAYMENT ASSESSMENT
COMMISSION**
300 7th St., S.W.
Washington, DC 20024

**U.S. ADVISORY COMMISSION
ON PUBLIC DIPLOMACY**
Rm 1008, 1750 Pennsylvania Ave., N.W.
Washington, DC 20547

JUDICIAL BRANCH
**ADMINISTRATIVE OFFICE OF
U.S. COURTS**
Washington, DC 20544

FEDERAL JUDICIAL CENTER
1520 H St., N.W.
Washington, DC 20005

SPECIAL COURTS
U.S. Court of International Trade
1 Federal Plaza
New York, NY 10007

U.S. Court of Claims
717 Madison Pl., N.W.
Washington, DC 20005

U.S. Tax Court
400 2nd St., N.W.
Washington, DC 20217

UNITED STATES CONGRESS
(House Committee Name)
U.S. House of Representatives
Washington, DC 20515

(Senate Committee Name)
U.S. Senate
Washington, DC 20510

(Joint Committee Name)
U.S. Congress
Washington, DC 20510

CONGRESSIONAL BUDGET OFFICE
Office of Intergovernmental Relations
2nd and D Sts., S.W.
Washington, DC 20515

LIBRARY OF CONGRESS
Publications Officer
Washington, DC 20540

OFFICE OF TECHNOLOGY ASSESSMENT
Office of Public Affairs
Washington, DC 20510

U.S. GENERAL ACCOUNTING OFFICE
Document Handling and Information
   Services Facility
P.O. Box 6015
Gaithersburg, MD 20877

QUASI-OFFICIAL AGENCIES
AMERICAN NATIONAL RED CROSS
Office of Public Affairs and
   Financial Development
17th and D Sts., N.W.
Washington, DC 20006

**NATIONAL RAILROAD PASSENGER
CORPORATION (AMTRAK)**
Vice President, Public Affairs
400 North Capitol St., N.W.
Washington, DC 20001

U.S. INSTITUTE OF PEACE
1550 M St., N.W.
Washington, DC 20005-1708

Document Availability Symbols

The following abbreviations and symbols are used to indicate the availability of documents abstracted by ASI. The symbols are provided in the bibliographic data section given at the head of each abstract.

GPO For sale by Government Printing Office, Washington, D.C., 20402.

The GPO stock number (S/N) is also given. The price is given if it has been announced at the time ASI goes to press; GPO prices change frequently, however.

NTIS For sale by National Technical Information Service, 5285 Port Royal Rd., Springfield, Va., 22161.

Order number and price are also given if available.

† or ‡ Inquire of the issuing agency.

† Copies are available at the time the document is issued, often free of charge, but supplies may be limited.

‡ Limited or restricted distribution has been specified by the agency. In some cases a request for a copy will be honored.

Addresses of major issuing agency offices are given in the Abstracts Volume, p. xxxvii; Index Volume, p. xxviii. If documents are available from another office, the name and address will be given in the bibliographic data section of the abstract.

◆ No distribution. Issuing agency has specified it should not be contacted.

ASI/MF Available on ASI microfiche. Microfiche collections are available in many libraries. The number following this notation indicates the unit count for ordering individual documents on microfiche through ASI "Documents on Demand." For information, see p. xxx.

● Item Depository item number, assigned to classes of documents issued to depository libraries.

ACRONYMS AND SELECTED ABBREVIATIONS

The following acronyms and abbreviations may be used without further identification:

ADAMHA	Alcohol, Drug Abuse and Mental Health Administration	FHLB	Federal Home Loan Bank	NSF	National Science Foundation
Admin	Administration	FHLBB	Federal Home Loan Bank Board	NTIS	National Technical Information Services
AFDC	Aid to Families with Dependent Children	FmHA	Farmers Home Administration	OAS	Organization of American States
AID	Agency for International Development	FSLIC	Federal Savings and Loan Insurance Corporation	OASDHI	Old-Age, Survivors, Disability, and Health Insurance Program
Amtrak	National Railroad Passenger Corporation	FTC	Federal Trade Commission	OCS	Outer continental shelf
Assn	Association	FY	Fiscal year	OECD	Organization for Economic Cooperation and Development
BEA	Bureau of Economic Analysis	GAO	General Accounting Office	OHDS	Office of Human Development Services
Bibl	Bibliography	GATT	General Agreement on Tariffs and Trade	OMB	Office of Management and Budget
BLS	Bureau of Labor Statistics	GDP	Gross Domestic Product	OPEC	Organization of Petroleum Exporting Countries
Bull	Bulletin	GNP	Gross National Product	OPM	Office of Personnel Management
Bur	Bureau	Govtl	Governmental	OSHA	Occupational Safety and Health Administration
CAB	Civil Aeronautics Board	GPO	Government Printing Office	PAD	Petroleum Administration for Defense (abolished in 1954 but acronym still in use)
CBO	Congressional Budget Office	GSA	General Services Administration		
CCC	Commodity Credit Corporation	GS	General Schedule		
CDC	Centers for Disease Control	HCFA	Health Care Financing Administration		
CES	Center for Educ Statistics	HHS	Department of Health and Human Services	PHS	Public Health Service
CETA	Comprehensive Employment and Training Act	HMO	Health maintenance organization	PPI	Producer Price Index
CIA	Central Intelligence Agency	HRSA	Health Resources and Services Administration	PRC	People's Republic of China
Conf	Conference	HUD	Department of Housing and Urban Development	Pub	Publication
CPI	Consumer Price Index			R&D	Research and Development
CRS	Congressional Research Service	Hwy	Highway	REA	Rural Electrification Administration
CY	Calendar year	ICC	Interstate Commerce Commission	Res	Research
DEA	Drug Enforcement Administration	IMF	International Monetary Fund	Rpt	Report
Dept	Department	Info	Information	S&L	Savings and Loan Association
Dev	Development	Inst	Institute	SALT	Strategic Arms Limitation Talks
Div	Division	Instn	Institution	SBA	Small Business Administration
DOD	Department of Defense	Intl	International	SEC	Securities and Exchange Commission
DOE	Department of Energy	IRA	Individual retirement arrangement		
DOT	Department of Transportation	IRS	Internal Revenue Service	SIC	Standard Industrial Classification
EC	European Community (formerly European Economic Community, EEC)	ITA	International Trade Administration	SITC	Standard International Trade Classification
		LC	Library of Congress		
EDA	Economic Development Administration	MarAd	Maritime Administration	SMSA	Standard Metropolitan Statistical Area (see MSA)
EIA	Energy Information Administration	Mgmt	Management		
EPA	Environmental Protection Agency	MSA	Metropolitan Statistical Area (formerly SMSA)	SRS	Statistical Reporting Service
ERS	Economic Research Service			SSA	Social Security Administration
ESEA	Elementary and Secondary Education Act	NASA	National Aeronautics and Space Administration	SSI	Supplemental Security Income
Eximbank	Export-Import Bank	NASS	National Agricultural Statistics Service	TSUSA	Tariff Schedules of the U.S., Annotated
FAA	Federal Aviation Administration	Natl	National		
FAO	Food and Agriculture Organization (UN)	NATO	North Atlantic Treaty Organization	TTPI	Trust Territory of the Pacific Islands
FAS	Foreign Agricultural Service	NCHS	National Center for Health Statistics	TVA	Tennessee Valley Authority
FBI	Federal Bureau of Investigation	NIH	National Institutes of Health	USDA	Department of Agriculture
FCC	Federal Communications Commission	NIMH	National Institute of Mental Health	USGS	U.S. Geological Survey
FDA	Food and Drug Administration	NLRB	National Labor Relations Board	USIA	U.S. Information Agency
FDIC	Federal Deposit Insurance Corporation	NOAA	National Oceanic and Atmospheric Administration	USITC	U.S. International Trade Commission
Fed	Federal			USPS	U.S. Postal Service
FERC	Federal Energy Regulatory Commission	NOW	Negotiable orders of withdrawal	VA	Veterans Administration
FHA	Federal Housing Administration	NRC	Nuclear Regulatory Commission		

Issuing Agencies and ASI Accession Numbers

Listed below are issuing agencies for all publications abstracted in this Annual. Agencies are arranged to reflect current departmental organizations.

EXECUTIVE OFFICE OF THE PRESIDENT

20	General
100	Office of Management and Budget
200	Council of Economic Advisers
230	Office of National Drug Control Policy
420	Office of Science and Technology Policy
430	Federal Coordinating Council for Science, Engineering and Technology
440	Office of the U.S. Trade Representative
480	Council on Environmental Quality

DEPARTMENT OF AGRICULTURE

1000	General
1120	Agricultural Cooperative Service
1180	Farmers Home Administration
1200	Forest Service
1240	Rural Electrification Administration
1260	Soil Conservation Service
1270	Office of Transportation
1290	Federal Grain Inspection Service
	Agricultural Marketing Service
1300	General
1309–
1319	Commodity Reports
1350	Human Nutrition Information Service
1360	Food and Nutrition Service
1370	Food Safety and Inspection Service
1380	Packers and Stockyards Administration
1390	Animal and Plant Health Inspection Service
	Economic Research Service
1500	General
1520	International
1540	National Economics
1560	National Economics, Commodities
1580	Natural Resources
1590	Economic Development
	National Agricultural Statistics Service
1610–
1631	Agricultural Statistics Board
1700	Agricultural Research Service
1740	Cooperative State Research Service
1760	Office of Grants and Program Systems
	Agricultural Stabilization and Conservation Service
1800	General
1820	Commodity Credit Corp.
1920	Foreign Agricultural Service
1950	Office of International Cooperation and Development

DEPARTMENT OF COMMERCE

2000	General
2040	International Trade Administration
2020	Bureau of Export Administration
2060	Economic Development Administration
2100	Minority Business Development Agency
	National Oceanic and Atmospheric Administration
2140	General
2150	National Environmental Satellite, Data, and Information Service
2160	National Marine Fisheries Service
2170	National Ocean Service
2180	National Weather Service
2210	National Institute of Standards and Technology
2220	National Technical Information Service
2240	Patent and Trademark Office
	Bureau of Census
2300	Bibliographies and Guides
2320	General
2330	1987 Census of Agriculture
2340	Agriculture
2370	1987 Census of Construction Industries
2380	Construction
2391	1987 Census of Service Industries
2397	1987 Census of Retail Trade
2405	1987 Census of Wholesale Trade
2410	Business
2420	Foreign Trade
2440	Geography
2450	1987 Census of Governments
2460	Governments
2480	Housing
2491	1987 Census of Manufactures
2500	Manufacturing
2511	1987 Census of Mineral Industries
2540	Population
2555	1980 Census of Population and Housing
2570	1987 Census of Transportation
2590	1987 Economic Censuses of Outlying Areas
2620	Methodology
2700	Bureau of Economic Analysis
2800	National Telecommunications and Information Administration
2900	U.S. Travel and Tourism Administration

DEPARTMENT OF ENERGY

3000	General
3020	Office of the Secretary of Energy
3080	Federal Energy Regulatory Commission
3100	Economic Regulatory Administration
3160	Energy Information Administration
3220	Bonneville Power Administration
3230	Southeastern Power Administration
3240	Southwestern Power Administration
3250	Western Area Power Administration
3300	Conservation and Renewable Energy
3320	Environment, Safety, and Health
3340	Defense Programs
3350	Nuclear Energy

3360 Civilian Radioactive Waste Management
3400 International Affairs and Energy Emergencies

DEPARTMENT OF DEFENSE

3500 General
3540 Office of the Secretary of Defense
3560 Joint Chiefs of Staff
3600 Department of Air Force
3700 Department of Army
3750 Army Corps of Engineers
3800 Department of Navy
3900 Defense Agencies

DEPARTMENT OF HEALTH AND HUMAN SERVICES

4000 General

Public Health Service

4040 General
4060 Food and Drug Administration
4080 Indian Health Service (transferred from HRSA)
Health Resources and Services Administration
  4100 General
  4110 Bureau of Health Professions
National Center for Health Statistics
  4120 Bibliographies and Guides
  4140 General
  4160 Methodology
4180 Agency for Health Care Policy and Research (formerly National Center for Health Services Research and Health Care Technology Assessment)
Centers for Disease Control
  4200 General
  4240 National Institute for Occupational Safety and Health
National Institutes of Health
  4430 General
  4460 National Library of Medicine
  4470 NIH Research Institutes
Alcohol, Drug Abuse and Mental Health Administration
  4480 National Institute on Alcohol Abuse and Alcoholism
  4490 National Institute on Drug Abuse
  4500 National Institute of Mental Health

4600 Office of Human Development Services
4650 Health Care Financing Administration
4690 Family Support Administration
Social Security Administration
  4700 General
  4740 Office of Policy

DEPARTMENT OF EDUCATION

4800 General
Office of Educational Research and Improvement
  4810 General
    National Center for Education Statistics
  4820 General
  4830 Elementary and Secondary Education
  4840 Postsecondary Education
  4860 Information Services
  4870 Library Programs
4890 National Assessment of Educational Progress
4940 Office of Special Education and Rehabilitative Services

DEPARTMENT OF HOUSING AND URBAN DEVELOPMENT

5000 General
5120 Community Planning and Development
5140 Housing (FHA)
5180 Policy Development and Research

DEPARTMENT OF INTERIOR

5300 General
5500 Fish and Wildlife Service
5540 National Park Service
Bureau of Mines
  5600 General
  5610 Mineral Industry Surveys
5640 Office of Surface Mining Reclamation and Enforcement
5660 Geological Survey
5700 Bureau of Indian Affairs
5720 Bureau of Land Management
5730 Minerals Management Service
5820 Bureau of Reclamation

DEPARTMENT OF JUSTICE

6000 General
6060 Office of Justice Programs
6220 Federal Bureau of Investigation
6240 Bureau of Prisons
6260 Immigration and Naturalization Service
6280 Drug Enforcement Administration
6290 U.S. Marshals Service

DEPARTMENT OF LABOR

6300 General
6360 Bureau of International Labor Affairs
6400 Employment and Training Administration
6500 Employment Standards Administration
6600 Occupational Safety and Health Administration
6660 Mine Safety and Health Administration
Bureau of Labor Statistics
  6720 General
  6740 Employment Analysis and Trends
  6760 Prices and Living Conditions
  6780 Wages and Industrial Relations
  6820 Productivity and Technology
  6840 Occupational Safety and Health
  6860 Foreign Labor Conditions
  6880 Methodology
  6920 Regional Office 2, New York
  6940 Regional Office 4, Atlanta
  6960 Regional Office 6, Dallas

DEPARTMENT OF STATE

7000 General
7140 Bureau of Intelligence and Research
7180 Bureau of Consular Affairs

DEPARTMENT OF TRANSPORTATION

7300 General
7400 Coast Guard
7500 Federal Aviation Administration

7550	Federal Highway Administration
7600	Federal Railroad Administration
7700	Maritime Administration
7740	Saint Lawrence Seaway Development Corp.
7760	National Highway Traffic Safety Administration
7880	Urban Mass Transportation Administration

DEPARTMENT OF TREASURY

8000	General
8060	Office of Revenue Sharing
8100	Financial Management Service
8140	U.S. Customs Service
8200	U.S. Mint
8240	Bureau of the Public Debt
8300	Internal Revenue Service
8400	Office of the Comptroller of Currency
8430	Office of Thrift Supervision (transferred from FHLBB)
8440	U.S. Savings Bonds Division
8460	U.S. Secret Service
8480	Bureau of Alcohol, Tobacco and Firearms

DEPARTMENT OF VETERANS AFFAIRS

8600	General
8650	Veterans Benefits Administration
8700	Veterans Health Services and Research Administration

INDEPENDENT AGENCIES

9020	ACTION
9080	Appalachian Regional Commission
9110	Central Intelligence Agency
9160	Consumer Product Safety Commission
	Environmental Protection Agency
9180	General
9190	Air and Radiation
9200	Water
9210	Solid Waste and Emergency Response
9230	Pesticides and Toxic Substances
9240	Equal Employment Opportunity Commission
9250	Export-Import Bank
9260	Farm Credit Administration
9270	Federal Election Commission

9280	Federal Communications Commission
9290	Federal Deposit Insurance Corp.
9300	Federal Home Loan Banks
9310	Federal Home Loan Bank Board
9330	Federal Maritime Commission
9340	Federal Mediation and Conciliation Service
9360	Federal Reserve Board of Governors
	Federal Reserve Banks
9371	Federal Reserve Bank of Atlanta
9373	Federal Reserve Bank of Boston
9375	Federal Reserve Bank of Chicago
9377	Federal Reserve Bank of Cleveland
9379	Federal Reserve Bank of Dallas
9381	Federal Reserve Bank of Kansas City
9383	Federal Reserve Bank of Minneapolis
9385	Federal Reserve Bank of New York
9387	Federal Reserve Bank of Philadelphia
9389	Federal Reserve Bank of Richmond
9391	Federal Reserve Bank of St. Louis
9393	Federal Reserve Bank of San Francisco
9400	Federal Trade Commission
9410	Federal Home Loan Mortgage Corp.
9450	General Services Administration
9480	Interstate Commerce Commission
9490	Merit Systems Protection Board
9500	National Aeronautics and Space Administration
9510	National Archives and Records Administration
9530	National Credit Union Administration
9560	National Foundation on the Arts and the Humanities
9580	National Labor Relations Board
9600	National Mediation Board
9610	National Transportation Safety Board
9620	National Science Foundation
9630	Nuclear Regulatory Commission
9650	Peace Corps
9660	Panama Canal Commission
9670	Pension Benefit Guaranty Corp.
9700	Railroad Retirement Board

9720	Resolution Trust Corp. (transferred from FHLBB)
9730	Securities and Exchange Commission
9740	Selective Service System
9760	Small Business Administration
9800	Tennessee Valley Authority
9820	U.S. Arms Control and Disarmament Agency
9840	Office of Personnel Management
9850	U.S. Information Agency
9860	U.S. Postal Service
9880	U.S. International Trade Commission
	U.S. International Development Cooperation Agency
9900	General
9910	Agency for International Development
9920	Veterans Administration (transferred to Dept of Veterans Affairs)

SPECIAL BOARDS, COMMITTEES, AND COMMISSIONS

10040	Advisory Commission on Intergovernmental Relations
10100	Advisory Committee on Federal Pay
10310	Board for International Broadcasting
10320	Board of Foreign Scholarships
11040	Commission on Civil Rights
11200	Commission on Merchant Marine and Defense
11710	Committee for Purchase from the Blind and Other Severely Handicapped
11920	Commodity Futures Trading Commission
12800	Federal Financing Bank
12900	Federal Council on the Aging
13000	Federal Financial Institutions Examination Council
13360	Federal Labor Relations Authority
14310	Harry S. Truman Scholarship Foundation
14350	Interagency Task Force on Acid Precipitation
14420	Inter-American Foundation
14640	International Joint Commission, U.S. and Canada
14690	Japan-U.S. Friendship Commission
14730	Marine Mammal Commission
14780	Migratory Bird Conservation Commission
14850	National Advisory Council on Child Nutrition
14870	National Advisory Council on

Index by
Subjects and
Names

Index by Subjects and Names

This index contains references to subjects, to corporate authors, and to individual authors.

References to individual items within a tabular breakdown (e.g. data about a particular State in a table that is broken down State-by-State) have been included only on a very selective basis. For complete references to information of this kind, please use the Index by Categories.

For information on how to make best use of both indexes, please consult the User Guide.

Abandoned property
see Vacant and abandoned property
Abernathy, Thomas J.
"Planned and Unplanned Home Births and Hospital Births in Calgary, Alberta, 1984-87", 4042–3.935
Abilene, Tex.
see also under By City and By SMSA or MSA in the "Index by Categories"
Abken, Peter A.
"Discrete Option Replication with Transactions Costs: An Analysis of Hedging Errors", 9371–10.37
"Survey and Analysis of Index-Linked Certificates of Deposit", 9371–10.38
Abnormalities
see Birth defects
Abortion
Deaths related to legal and illegal abortion, and hospitalization, for US and selected countries, 1950s-83, hearing, 21408–113
Deaths related to pregnancy, and rates, by detailed cause and demographic characteristics, 1986, US Vital Statistics annual rpt, 4144–2
Deaths related to pregnancy, rates, and risk, by pregnancy outcome, cause, and maternal characteristics, 1980-85, article, 4202–7.903
Deaths related to pregnancy, 1987, US Vital Statistics advance annual rpt, 4146–5.113
Health condition and health care resources, use, and spending, 1950s-87, annual data compilation, 4144–11
Human papillomavirus infection rates, by sexual and personal hygiene practices, and other patient characteristics, Brazil local area studies, 1989 article, 4472–1.908
Performance of abortions, by method, pregnancy history, and other characteristics of woman, 1985-86, US Vital Statistics annual rpt, 4146–5.108
Performance of abortions, by patient characteristics, and related deaths, 1972-85, article, 4202–7.906
Performance of abortions by patient characteristics, rates for all and 1st abortions, and related deaths in US and other countries, 1989 hearing, 21408–113
Public opinion on abortion, by sex, age, region, race, religion, educational attainment, political affiliation, and income, selected years 1972-89, annual rpt, 6064–6.2

Statistical Abstract of US, social, political, and economic data, 1790-2025, comprehensive annual compilation, 2324–1.1
Vital and Health Statistics series: reprints of monthly rpt supplements, 4147–24
Abraham, Sidney
"Comparison of Levels of Serum Cholesterol of Adults 18-74 Years of Age in the U.S. in 1960-62 and 1971-74", 4147–16.1
"Dietary Intake of Persons 1-74 Years of Age in the U.S.", 4147–16.1
"Height and Weight of Adults 18-74 Years of Age in the U.S.", 4147–16.1
"Total Serum Cholesterol Level of Adults 18-74 Years of Age, U.S., 1971-74", 4147–16.1
"Total Serum Cholesterol Levels of Children 4-17 Years of Age, U.S., 1971-74", 4147–16.1
"Weight by Height and Age of Adults 18-74 Years: U.S., 1971-74", 4147–16.2
Abrasive materials
Employment, earnings, and hours, by SIC 1- to 4-digit industry, monthly 1983-Feb 1989, annual rpt, 6744–4
Exports of US, detailed commodities by country, monthly rpt, 2422–3
Imports of US, detailed Schedule A commodities by country, monthly rpt, 2422–2
Manufacturing annual survey, 1986: financial and operating data, by SIC 2- to 4-digit industry, series, 2506–15
Manufacturing census, 1987: financial and operating data, for SIC 4-digit industries by product, preliminary rpt, 2491–1.50
Mineral Industry Surveys, commodity review of production, trade, stocks, and use, quarterly rpt, 5612–2.19
Mineral Industry Surveys, commodity reviews of production, trade, stocks, and use, monthly rpt series, 5612–1
Mineral Industry Surveys, commodity reviews of production, trade, use, and industry operations, advance annual rpt series, 5614–5
Mineral Industry Surveys, State reviews of production, 1988, preliminary annual rpt, 5614–6
Minerals Yearbook, 1987, Vol 1: commodity reviews of production, use, trade, prices, and mining operations, annual rpt, 5604–33
Minerals Yearbook, 1987, Vol 1 preprints: commodity review of production, reserves, supply, use, and trade, annual rpt, 5604–15.3
Minerals Yearbook, 1987, Vol 1 preprints: commodity reviews of production, reserves, supply, use, and trade, annual rpt series, 5604–15
Minerals Yearbook, 1987, Vol 2 preprints: State reviews of production and sales by commodity, and business activity, annual rpt series, 5604–16

Minerals Yearbook, 1987, Vol 2: State reviews of production, sales, and firms, by commodity, and business activity, annual rpt, 5604–34
Minerals Yearbook, 1987, Vol 3: foreign country reviews of production, trade, and policy, by commodity, annual rpt, 5604–35
Minerals Yearbook, 1987, Vol 3 preprints: foreign country reviews of production, trade, and policy, by commodity, annual rpt series, 5604–23
Minerals Yearbook, 1988, Vol 1: commodity reviews of production, reserves, supply, use, and trade, annual rpt series, 5604–20
Minerals Yearbook, 1988, Vol 2 rpts: State reviews of production and sales by commodity, and business activity, annual rpt series, 5604–22
Occupational injuries and incidence, employment, and hours in nonmetallic minerals mines and related operations, 1987, annual rpt, 6664–1
Occupational injury and illness rates, by SIC 2- to 4-digit industry, 1987, annual rpt, 6844–1
Price indexes (producer), by stage of processing and detailed commodity, monthly rpt, 6762–6
Price indexes (producer), by stage of processing and detailed commodity, monthly 1988, annual rpt, 6764–2
Production, prices, trade, use, employment, tariffs, and stockpiles, by mineral, with foreign comparisons, 1984-88, annual rpt, 5604–18
Stockpiling of strategic material, inventories and needs, by commodity, as of Sept 1988, annual rpt, 3544–37
Stockpiling of strategic material, inventories, costs, and goals by commodity, as of June 1989, semiannual rpt, 3902–3
Absenteeism
Cardiovascular diseases cases, health care services use and costs, and productivity losses, by selected characteristics, 1980, 4146–12.26
Census of Population and Housing, 1990: data item selection, questionnaire dev, and testing, 2626–11.1
Child care leave of absence for employees, policies, coverage, and attitudes, by employee characteristics, 1980-87, hearings, 25548–95
Child health condition indicators for low and normal birthweight children, by age, sex, mothers education, and race, 1981, article, 4042–3.904
Crime victimization rates, by victim and offender characteristics, circumstances, and offense, 1987 survey, annual rpt, 6066–3.41
Disability, acute and chronic health conditions, absenteeism, and health services use, by selected characteristics, 1988, annual rpt, 4147–10.170

Fed Govt civilian employee leave use and costs, by type of leave, 1987-88, annual article, 9842-1.906

High school dropout rates, and subsequent completion, by student and school characteristics, alternative estimates, 1988, annual rpt, 4834-23

High school students employment, academic and other characteristics, 1984-86, 4898-27

Labor force health condition and services use, by occupation and industry of longest job held, income, age, sex, and race, 1980, 4147-10.168

Labor force health condition, disability days, health services use, and disease prevalence, by occupation and sex, 1983-85, 4146-8.170

Labor force not at work, by reason, whether absence paid, and sex, 1957-83, 6728-38.1

Labor force not at work, unemployed, and working less than 35 hours, by reason, sex, race, region, and State, 1988, annual rpt, 6744-7.1; 6744-7.2

Longshore workers injuries resulting in lost time, FY76-87, annual rpt, 6504-10

Lumber mill occupational injury and illness rates and workdays lost, by selected State and SIC 4-digit industry, 1978-87, article, 6722-1.945

Meatpacking occupational injury and illness rates and workdays lost, 1977-86, article, 6722-1.901

Military personnel alcohol and drug abuse, prevalence and consequences, by selected characteristics, 1988, biennial rpt, 3504-19

Mine employees by selected occupational and other characteristics, injuries, and workdays lost, 1986, series, 5606-8

Mines (coal) and related operations occupational injuries and incidence, employment, and hours, 1987, annual rpt, 6664-4

Mines (metal) and related operations occupational injuries and incidence, employment, and hours, 1987, annual rpt, 6664-3

Mines (nonmetallic minerals) and related operations occupational injuries and incidence, employment, and hours, 1987, annual rpt, 6664-1

Mines (sand and gravel) and related operations occupational injuries and incidence, employment, and hours, 1987, annual rpt, 6664-2

Mines (stone) and related operations occupational injuries and incidence, employment, and hours, 1987, annual rpt, 6664-5

Mobile home industry occupational injury and illness rates and workdays lost, by selected State, 1978-87, article, 6722-1.932

Occupational injuries, by circumstances, body site, equipment type, and industry, with safety measures, series, 6846-1

Occupational injuries, illnesses, and workdays lost, by SIC 2-digit industry, 1987-88, annual press release, 6844-3

Occupational injury and illness rates, by SIC 2- to 4-digit industry, 1987, annual rpt, 6844-1

Pollutant ozone levels, urban areas failure to meet natl standards, emissions sources, exposure, and costs and benefits of reduction strategies, 1983-87 and projected to 2004, 26358-203

Postal Service employee disciplinary actions, by type of infraction and penalty, and region, 1985-88, GAO rpt, 26119-256

Railroad accidents, casualties, and damage, by cause, railroad, and State, 1988, annual rpt, 7604-1

Railroad accidents reported and not reported to Fed Railroad Admin, injuries, damage, and workdays lost, for 5 carriers, 1983-87, GAO rpt, 26113-410

Statistical Abstract of US, social, political, and economic data, 1790-2025, comprehensive annual compilation, 2324-1.1; 2324-1.3

Abt Associates, Inc.
"Administrative Costs of the Housing Voucher and Certificate Programs", 5186-14.2

"Agricultural Policy Analysis: A Manual for AID Agricultural and Rural Development Officers", 9916-3.55

"National Hospital Rate-Setting Study: Final Report", 4658-29

"Prosecution of Felony Arrests, 1986", 6064-27

Abu Dhabi
see United Arab Emirates

Accident insurance
see Automobile insurance

Accidental deaths
Aircraft accidents and circumstances, for US operations of domestic and foreign airlines and general aviation, periodic rpt, 9612-1

Aircraft accidents and deaths by carrier, 1978-88, annual rpt, 9614-1

Aircraft accidents, casualties, and damage, for commercial operations by detailed circumstances, 1986, annual rpt, 9614-2

Aircraft accidents, deaths, and circumstances, by carrier and carrier type, preliminary 1988, annual press release, 9614-9

Aircraft accidents in general aviation, by circumstances, characteristics of persons and aircraft involved, and type of flying, 1986, annual rpt, 9614-3

Aircraft hijackings, on-board explosions, and other crime, US and foreign incidents, 1983-87, annual rpt, 7504-31

Bombing incidents and casualties by target and circumstances, and explosives theft and recovery, by State, 1979-88, annual rpt, 8484-4

Bombing incidents, casualties, and damage, by target, circumstances, and State, 1988, annual rpt, 6224-5

Child death rates, by age, sex, race, and cause, for US and compared to 8 OECD countries, 1985 and trends from 1900, 4147-3.27

Consumer Product Safety Commission activities, recalls by brand, and casualties and societal costs, by product type, FY87, annual rpt, 9164-2

Deaths and rates, by cause, age, sex, marital status, race, and State, 1987, US Vital Statistics advance annual rpt, 4146-5.113

Deaths and rates, by cause and age, preliminary 1987-88, US Vital Statistics annual rpt, 4144-7

Deaths and rates, by detailed cause and demographic characteristics, 1986 and trends from 1900, US Vital Statistics annual rpt, 4144-2

Deaths and rates, by detailed location, cause, and demographic characteristics, 1987, US Vital Statistics annual rpt, 4144-3

Diving (underwater sport and occupational) deaths, by circumstances, diver characteristics, and location, 1970-87, annual rpt, 2144-5

Firearms-related deaths, and prevention recommendations, 1989 article, 4042-3.906

Firearms-related deaths of children, by motive, age, sex, and race, 1968-87, 4146-8.181

Fires in hotels and motels, casualties, and effectiveness of smoke detectors, sprinkler systems, and building and equipment design, 1989 hearing, 21708-127

Grain handling facility explosions and casualties, by firm, FY88, annual rpt, 1294-1

Hazardous material transport accidents, casualties, and damage, by mode of transport, with DOT control activities, 1988, annual rpt, 7304-4

Health care devices malfunction, injury, and death reports to FDA, and inspection findings and disposition, 1985-87, GAO rpt, 26131-57

Hurricanes and tropical storms in north Atlantic and Caribbean area, paths, surveillance, deaths, damage, and landfall probabilities by city, 1988, annual rpt, 2184-7

Hurricanes and tropical storms in north Atlantic Ocean, characteristics and deaths, 1988, annual article, 2152-8.902

Indian (Seneca Tribe) deaths and years of potential life lost, by selected cause and sex, various periods 1955-84, article, 4042-3.925

Indian Health Service facilities, funding, operations, and Indian health and other characteristics, 1950s-88, annual chartbook, 4084-1

Insurance (accidental death and dismemberment) coverage of employee plans, by plan provision and occupational group, 1988, article, 6722-1.944

Law enforcement officer assaults and deaths by circumstances, agency, victim and offender characteristics, and location, 1988, annual rpt, 6224-3

Military deaths by cause, age, race, and rank, and personnel captured and missing, by service branch, 2nd half FY88, semiannual rpt, 3542-21

Mine (coal) disabling injuries and deaths, 1937-87, biennial rpt, 3164-79

Mine safety and health enforcement, training, and funding, with casualties, by type of mine and State, FY87, annual rpt, 6664-6

Minerals industries injuries by circumstances, employment, and hours, by type of operation and State, quarterly rpt, 6662-1

Mines (coal) and related operations occupational injuries and incidence, employment, and hours, 1987, annual rpt, 6664-4

Fed Govt labor productivity, indexes of output and labor costs by function, FY67-87, annual rpt, 6824–1.6

Fed Govt mgmt cost control proposals, Reagan Admin initiatives, savings, and status, FY85-94, annual rpt, 104–23

Futures market trading abuses, Commodity Futures Trading Commission and exchanges enforcement activity, various periods 1984-FY90, GAO rpt, 26119–263

Futures market trading abuses, Commodity Futures Trading Commission, Chicago Board of Trade, and Chicago Mercantile Exchange enforcement activity, 1984-89, GAO rpt, 26119–247

GAO activities, operations, and resulting cost savings to Fed Govt, FY88, annual rpt, 26104–1

Hospital reimbursement by Medicare under prospective payment system, cost accounting alternatives, model description and results, FY84, article, 4652–1.948

Hospital reimbursement by Medicare under prospective payment system, impacts on cost accounting systems and marketing techniques, survey results, 1988 rpt, 17206–2.7

Insurance (health) plans of corporations for retirees, costs and liabilities under alternative accounting standards, 1983-88, technical paper, 9366–6.190

Insurance (property and casualty) industry solvency monitoring by States, activities, staff, and interstate info sharing, 1989 GAO rpt, 26119–273

Nursing home compliance with Medicare and Medicaid regulations, and patient characteristics, by facility, 1987/88, annual State rpt series, 4654–15

OASDHI future cost estimates, actuarial study series, 4706–1

OASDHI programs actuarial studies, series, 4706–2

Occupational injury and illness rates, by SIC 2- to 4-digit industry, 1987, annual rpt, 6844–1

Partnerships (master limited) finances, firms, partners, and tax reform impacts, by industry, 1986, technical paper, 8006–3.59

Pension plan financial status, impact of alternative accounting standards, 1978-87, technical paper, 9366–6.172

Railroad retirement system actuarial evaluation, 1989 and projected to 2013, annual rpt, 9704–1

Receipts for services, by SIC 2- to 4-digit kind of business, 1988, annual rpt, 2413–8

Science and engineering employment, by nonmanufacturing industry and field, 1987, triennial rpt, 9627–31

SEC staffing, pay, and turnover by occupation and city, with proposed fee revenues to improve work conditions, 1989 hearing, 21368–116

Service industries census, 1987: establishments, receipts, employment, and payroll, by SIC 2- to 4-digit kind of business, MSA, county, and city, State rpt series, 2391–1

Tax (income) returns of corporations, income and tax items by asset size and detailed industry, 1986, annual rpt, 8304–4; 8304–21

Tax (income) returns of partnerships, income statement items by industry group, 1986, annual article, 8302–2.903

Tax (income) returns of sole proprietorships, income statement items, by industry group, 1987, annual article, 8302–2.904; 8302–2.921

Tax (income) unpaid by reason, and compliance after audits and appeals, for individuals and corporations, 1970s-87 and projected to 1992, 8302–2.902; 8308–26

Tax assessments and collections resulting from IRS criminal investigations, by violation type, 1984, GAO rpt, 26119–244

Tax collection, enforcement, and litigation activity of IRS, with data by type of tax, region, and State, FY88, annual rpt, 8304–3

Tax preparation services use for individual income tax returns, 1986, annual article, 8302–2.901

Tax preparation services violations of income tax law, civil penalties assessed and abated, FY87-88, GAO rpt, 26119–265

see also Federal Inspectors General reports

see also Financial disclosure

Achievement tests

see Educational tests

Acid rain

Abatement spending, capital and operating costs by SIC 2- to 4-digit industry and State, 1986, annual Current Industrial Rpt, 2506–3.6

Coastal and estuarine pollutant discharges from agricultural, airborne, and other nonpoint sources, and regulatory issues, 1988 hearing, 21568–46

Distribution, pH levels, and composition of acid rain, monitoring results by site, 1987, annual rpt, 9194–20

Electric power plants coal and oil deliveries by sulfur content and location, and sulfur removal capacity use by plant, 1987-88, annual rpt, 3164–42

Electric power plants coal and oil receipts and average cost by sulfur content and State, quarterly rpt, 3162–39

Electric power plants sulfur dioxide emissions and control costs, alternative projections to 2000, 26306–3.108

Electric utilities serving aluminum smelters, effects of proposed sulfur dioxide abatement legislation on operating costs, 1985, 5608–155

Research on acid rain, activities, and funding by Federal agency, 1988, annual rpt, 14354–1

Soil, water, and environmental conservation and conditions, with data by State and region, 1989 quinquennial rpt, 1268–24

Sulfur dioxide and other air pollutants levels, and measurements exceeding natl standards, by site, 1987-88, annual rpt, 9194–5

Sulfur dioxide emissions and reductions of industrial and power plants, and acid rain control economic impacts, 1987 hearing, 21368–104

TVA financial and operating data by program and facility, FY88, annual rpt, 9804–32

Water supply and quality in streams and lakes, and groundwater levels in wells, by drainage basin, 1986, annual State rpt series, 5666–23

Water supply and quality in streams and lakes, and groundwater levels in wells, by drainage basin, 1987, annual State rpt series, 5666–10

Water supply and quality in streams and lakes, and groundwater levels in wells, by drainage basin, 1988, annual State rpt series, 5666–16

Ackerman, Karen Z.

"Review and Analysis of the EEP for Wheat", 1561–12.906

"Role of Government Programs in U.S. Rice Exports", 1561–8.903

Acquired immune deficiency syndrome

Army active duty personnel health condition, and use of Army medical services in US and abroad, monthly rpt, 3702–4.2

Black Americans AIDS knowledge, attitudes, info sources, and testing, 1988 survey, 4146–8.167

Budget of US, Bush Admin policy changes by program, FY90, 028–32

Budget of US, Reagan Admin policy changes by program, FY90, annual rpt, 104–21

Cases of AIDS and AIDS virus infection prevalence, by risk group and other patient characteristics, 1981-88 and projected to 1992, 4206–2.13

Cases of AIDS by risk group, race, sex, age, State, and SMSA, and deaths, monthly rpt, 4202–9

Cases of AIDS, projected by CDC and other forecasters, analysis of methodology, 1989 GAO rpt, 26131–55

CDC staffing and reallocations from other programs for AIDS and other new programs, FY81-88, GAO rpt, 26121–287

Child AIDS cases, by age, sex, and risk group, with related HHS funding, 1980s-88, 4438–15

Deaths and rates, by cause, age, sex, marital status, race, and State, 1987, US Vital Statistics advance annual rpt, 4146–5.113

Deaths and rates for AIDS virus infection, by age, race, and sex, preliminary 1988, annual rpt, 4144–7

Deaths from AIDS, by age, race, and sex, monthly rpt, annual table, 4142–1

Deaths from AIDS, by health and other characteristics, 1986, 4146–8.178

Developing countries economic and social conditions from 1960s, and Intl Dev Cooperation Agency and AID activities and funding, FY88-90, annual rpt, 9904–4

Drug abuse emergency room admissions and deaths, by drug type and source, sex, race, age, and major metro area, 1988, annual rpt, 4494–8

Drug abuse indicators for selected metro areas, research results, data collection, and policy issues, 1989 semiannual conf, 4492–5

Fed Govt financial and nonfinancial domestic aid, 1989 base edition with supplements, annual listing, 104–5

Health care and public safety workers AIDS and hepatitis B virus transmission, CDC prevention guidelines, 1989 rpt, 4206–2.15

Health care setting transmission of AIDS virus, facilities compliance with OSHA guidelines for worker protection, 1988 rpt, 26358-198

Health condition and health care resources, use, and spending, 1950s-87, annual data compilation, 4144-11

HHS financial aid, by program, recipient, State, and city, FY88, annual regional listings, 4004-3

Hispanic Americans AIDS knowledge, attitudes, info sources, and testing, 1988 survey, 4146-8.168

Homeless shelters services, operations, and client characteristics, 1988 survey, 5188-123

Homosexual men AIDS risk knowledge and high-risk activities, for cities with low and high AIDS rates, 1989 article, 4042-3.939

Labor laws enacted, by State, 1988, annual article, 6722-1.904

Medicaid claims and payments for AIDS patients, by type of care and whether AIDS-related, race, sex, and diagnosis, 1984-87, article, 4042-3.940

Medicaid enrollment of AIDS patients, services use, and charges, for California, 1981-84, article, 4652-1.907

Medicaid policies and State health insurance regulation for AIDS patients and persons with AIDS virus infection, with background data, 1987-88, article, 4652-1.953

Methadone patients participation in AIDS education and testing program, with characteristics and views, 1987 local area study, article, 4042-3.920

Military personnel knowledge of AIDS and changes in sexual practices, 1988, biennial rpt, 3504-19

Minority group sexually transmitted disease cases, by race, 1988, article, 4042-3.954

Morbidity and Mortality Weekly Report, infectious notifiable disease cases by age and State, and deaths, 1930s-88, annual rpt, 4204-1

Morbidity and Mortality Weekly Report, infectious notifiable disease cases by State, and public health issues, 4202-1

Natl Inst of Allergy and Infectious Diseases activities, grants by recipient and location, and disease incidence, FY81-88, annual rpt, 4474-30

NIH activities, funding by program and recipient type, staff, and clinic patients, by inst, FY87, annual rpt, 4434-3

Pneumonia (*pneumocystis carinii*) in AIDS patients, prevention and control, CDC guidelines, 1989 rpt, 4206-2.14

Prevention, prevalence, and treatment issues for AIDS, 1988 conf papers, 4042-3.905

Preventive disease and health improvement goals and recommended activities for 2000, with trends 1970s-80s, 4048-10

Prison cases of AIDS, test results, and prevention and control policies, by location, 1988 survey, annual rpt, 6064-22

Prisoners in Federal instns testing for AIDS, public opinion by respondent characteristics, 1987 survey, annual rpt, 6064-6.2

Public knowledge, attitudes, info sources, and testing for AIDS, 1988 survey, 4146-8.165; 4146-8.169; 4146-8.173

Public knowledge, attitudes, info sources, and testing for AIDS, 1989 survey, 4146-8.176; 4146-8.180

Public opinion on Surgeon General's AIDS info brochure, by age, sex, race, education, and income, 1988 survey, 4042-3.908

Research methods and design of health surveys, 1989 conf proceedings, 4188-60

Research on AIDS health care and epidemiology, methodological issues, 1988 conf, 4188-61

Research on AIDS health care, costs and effectiveness of alternative treatment methods, 1988, 4186-9.6

Research on AIDS health care services, status, needs, methods, and impacts on public health policy and funding, with data for selected cities, 1989 conf papers, 4188-59

Research on AIDS health care, social, and support services, data collection methods with background data, 1984-88, 4186-9.5

Research on AIDS, NIH grants and contracts by funding and approval status, and researcher age, experience, and sex, FY86, GAO rpt, 26121-267

Schools AIDS prevention programs, Fed Govt funding, FY88, annual rpt, 6064-11

Statistical Abstract of US, social, political, and economic data, 1790-2025, comprehensive annual compilation, 2324-1.1

Surgeons (orthopedic) views on treatment of patients with AIDS virus, and professional restriction of infected surgeons, 1986 survey, article, 4042-3.907

Testing for AIDS virus antibodies, demand, accuracy, and costs, data collection methods with background data, 1986-88, 4186-9.7

Testing for AIDS virus antibodies, Western blot interpretation and use guidelines, 1989 rpt, 4206-2.16

Treatment and social services availability for AIDS patients, for 5 cities, 1988, GAO rpt, 26121-307

Vermont AIDS public knowledge, by age and education, 1986-87 survey, article, 4042-3.938

Veterans health care centers AIDS cases, by facility and region, periodic tables, 8702-1; 9922-15

Acquisitions, business
see Business acquisitions and mergers

Acrylics
see Plastics and plastics industry

ACTION
Activities of ACTION, by program, FY88, annual rpt, 9024-2

Budget of US Appendix, obligations, appropriations, and personnel, by program and agency, FY90, annual rpt, 104-3

Budget of US, authoritative financial statements with appropriations, outlays, and receipts, by category and agency, FY88, annual rpt, 8104-2.2

Expenditures of Fed Govt in States, by type, program, agency, and State, FY88, annual rpt, 2464-2

Labor unions recognized in Fed Govt, agreements and membership by agency and facility, as of Jan 1989, biennial listing, 9844-14

see also Foster Grandparent Program
see also Retired Senior Volunteer Program
see also VISTA

Adami, Hans-Olov
"Increasing Survival Trend After Cancer Diagnosis in Sweden: 1960-84", 4472-1.929

Adams, Catherine F.
"Nutritive Value of American Foods in Common Units", 1358-3

Adams, E. Kathleen
"Utilization and Expenditures Under Medicaid for Supplemental Security Income Disabled", 4652-1.947

Adams, Jerry G.
"Collective Bargaining Calendar for the Southeast, 1989", 6946-1.73

Adams, Patricia F.
"Current Estimates from the National Health Interview Survey, 1988", 4147-10.170

Adams, Stephen D.
"Estimated Oil and Gas Reserves: Pacific Outer Continental Shelf (as of Dec. 31, 1988)", 5734-7

Aden
see Yemen, South

Adhesives
Hazardous substances health effects, environmental levels, and household products composition, with data by selected location, 1988 hearings, 21408-112

Manufacturing census, 1987: financial and operating data, for SIC 4-digit industries by product, preliminary rpt, 2491-1.40

Price indexes (producer), by stage of processing and detailed commodity, monthly rpt, 6762-6

Price indexes (producer), by stage of processing and detailed commodity, monthly 1988, annual rpt, 6764-2

Administration
see Administration of justice
see Administrative law and procedure
see Business management
see Executives and managers
see Health facilities administration
see Public administration
see School administration and staff

Administration for Children, Youth, and Families
see Office of Human Development Services

Administration for Native Americans
see Office of Human Development Services

Administration of justice
Budget of US, historical data, selected years FY34-88 and projected to FY94, annual rpt, 104-22

Data on crime, criminal justice admin and enforcement, and public opinion, data compilation, 1970s-88, annual rpt, 6064-6

Employment and payroll, by function and level of govt, 1987-88, annual rpt series, 2466-1

Employment, payroll, and spending for criminal justice, by level of govt, State, and selected city and county, FY71-85, annual rpt, 6064-9

Energy use in commercial buildings, costs and conservation, by building characteristics, survey rpt series, 3166-8

Finances of govts, by level of govt, State, and for large cities and counties, annual rpt series, 2466-2

Finances of govts, revenues by source and spending by function, natl income and product account, *Survey of Current Business*, monthly rpt, 2702–1.24

Foreign countries human rights conditions in 170 countries, 1988, annual rpt, 21384–3

Judicial Conf proceedings and findings, fall 1989, semiannual rpt, 18202–2

Justice Dept activities, FY81-87, annual rpt, 6004–1

State and local govt employment of minorities and women, by occupation, function, and pay level, 1986, annual rpt, 9244–6.4

see also Administrative law and procedure
see also Arrest
see also Civil procedure
see also Correctional institutions
see also Courts
see also Crime and criminals
see also Criminal procedure
see also Due process of law
see also Evidence
see also Extradition
see also Federal aid to law enforcement
see also Judges
see also Judicial reform
see also Juries
see also Law enforcement
see also Lawyers and legal services
see also Legal aid
see also Legal arbitration and mediation
see also Military law
see also Pardons
see also Parole and probation
see also Pretrial detention and release
see also Sentences, criminal procedure
see also Trials
see also Witnesses
see also under names of specific types of courts (listed under Courts)

Administration on Aging
see Office of Human Development Services

Administration on Developmental Disabilities
see Office of Human Development Services

Administrative agencies
see under Executive Office of the President
see under Federal boards, committees, and commissions
see under Federal executive departments
see under Federal independent agencies

Administrative Conference of the U.S.
Budget of US Appendix, obligations, appropriations, and personnel, by program and agency, FY90, annual rpt, 104–3

Budget of US, authoritative financial statements with appropriations, outlays, and receipts, by category and agency, FY88, annual rpt, 8104–2.2

Administrative law and procedure
Advisory committees of Fed Govt, and members, staff, meetings, and costs by agency, FY88, annual rpt, 9454–18

AFDC hearings dispositions, and fraud cases, referrals, and actions, by State, FY87, annual rpt, 4694–7.4; 4694–7.5

Airport security operations to prevent hijacking, screening results, enforcement actions, and hijacking attempts, 1st half 1988, semiannual rpt, 7502–5

Appeals filed involving Federal agency decisions, by circuit and agency, 1988, annual rpt, 18204–8.10

Census of Population and Housing, 1980: data collection issues and procedural and legal history, 2555–2.5

Coal leasing activity on Federal land, acreage, production, and reserves, by coal region and State, FY88, annual rpt, 5724–10

Criminal case processing in Federal district courts, and dispositions, by offense, district, and offender characteristics, 1984, annual rpt, 6064–29

Disability Insurance and SSI admin of Fed Govt and States, benefits, caseloads, and operations, 1980s, 4708–11

Disability Insurance and SSI benefit denials, appeals processing, caseloads, dispositions, and allowances by disability, 1986-88, GAO rpt, 26121–278

Disability Insurance and SSI eligibility reviews, and State administrators views of review standards, 1986-88, GAO rpt, 26121–258

Disability Insurance eligibility claims reviewed by SSA administrative law judges and Appeals Council, and dispositions, FY81-88, GAO rpt, 26121–290

Discrimination complaints of Federal employees, processing, and disposition, by complaint type and agency, FY87, annual rpt, 9244–11

Jail population by sex, race, and for 25 jurisdictions, and instn conditions, 1983-87, annual rpt, 6066–25.18

Jail population, capacity, and instns under court order to reduce population and improve conditions, 1983-86, annual rpt, 6064–26.1

Labor productivity of Federal employees, indexes of output and labor costs by function, FY67-87, annual rpt, 6824–1.6

Lands (public) acreage, grants, use, revenues, and allocations, by State, FY88, annual rpt, 5724–1.3

OMB regulatory review procedures, proposed and final rules by disposition and agency, 1981-89, GAO rpt, 26119–261

SSA activities, litigation, finances, and staff, FY88, annual rpt, 4704–6

Unemployment insurance programs of States, quality appraisal results, FY88, annual rpt, 6404–16

US attorneys case processing and collections, by case type and Federal district, FY88, annual rpt, 6004–2

VA benefit claims processing and efficiency at regional offices, and hearing officers salaries and travel costs, 1986-88, hearing, 21768–47

Veterans Appeals Board appeals and hearings, 1964-88, annual rpt, 8604–5.2

Veterans Appeals Board caseloads and dispositions, 1988 hearing, 25768–47

Veterans rehabilitation program admin, and participants earnings and tax liability before and after training, 1988 hearing, 25768–48

Workers compensation programs of States, admin, coverage, benefits, finances, processing, and staff, 1984-88, annual rpt, 6504–9

see also Antitrust law
see also Civil procedure
see also Commercial law
see also Consumer protection
see also Environmental impact statements

see also Federal Inspectors General reports
see also Freedom of information
see also Fuel allocation
see also Government and business
see also Government forms and paperwork
see also Labor law
see also Licenses and permits
see also Maritime law
see also Price regulation
see also Tax laws and courts
see also Tax protests and appeals
see also under names of individual regulatory commissions (listed under Federal independent agencies)

Administrative Office of the U.S. Courts
Budget of US Appendix, obligations, appropriations, and personnel, by program and agency, FY90, annual rpt, 104–3

Budget of US, authoritative financial statements with appropriations, outlays, and receipts, by category and agency, FY88, annual rpt, 8104–2.2

Caseloads (civil and criminal) for Federal district, appeals, and bankruptcy courts, by offense, circuit, and district, quarterly rpt, 18202–1

Caseloads (civil and criminal) for Federal district, appeals, and special courts, June 1989, annual rpt, 18204–2; 18204–8

Caseloads (criminal) in Federal district courts, by offense, disposition, and district, annual rpt, suspended, 18204–1

Caseloads, actions, procedure duration, judges, and jurors, by Federal district and appeals court, 1984-89, annual rpt, 18204–3

Judicial Conf proceedings and findings, fall 1989, semiannual rpt, 18202–2

Juror (grand and petit) use and costs, trials, and trial days, by Federal district court, 1981-88, annual rpt, 18204–4

Sentences for Federal offenses, offenders by length of imprisonment and probation, size of fine, and offense, annual rpt, suspended, 18204–13

Wiretaps authorized, costs, arrests, trials, and convictions, by offense and jurisdiction, 1988, annual rpt, 18204–7

Administrators
see Business management
see Executives and managers

Adolescents
see Youth

Adoption
Alien children adopted abroad and to be adopted, admissions to US by country of birth, FY82-88, annual rpt, 6264–2

Assistance programs under Ways and Means Committee jurisdiction, finances and operations, FY70s-88, annual rpt, 21784–11

Budget of US, Bush Admin policy changes by program, FY90, 028–32

Employee parental leave of absence, policies, coverage, and attitudes, by employee characteristics, 1980-87, hearings, 25548–95

HHS financial aid, by program, recipient, State, and city, FY88, annual regional listings, 4004–3

Household and family characteristics, by living arrangement, 1988 and trends from 1960, Current Population Rpt, 2546–2.148

Homeless population characteristics, needs, and impacts of govt aid programs and housing costs, 1988 conf papers, 10048-73

Homeowners Residential Community Assns, services provided, and relations with local govts, 1988 conf, 10048-75

Hwy admin and gasoline tax revenue proposed transfer from Fed Govt to States, issues, with motor fuel taxes by selected State, 1988 rpt, 10048-72

Intergovernmental Perspective, quarterly journal, 10042-1

Local govts in metro areas, finances, structure, and service delivery, local area rpt series, 10046-9

R&D funding by Fed Govt, by field, performer type, agency, and State, FY87-89, annual rpt, 9627-20

Tax revenue potential of State and local systems relative to natl average tax burden, by type of tax and State, 1986, annual rpt, 10044-7

Taxes, spending, and govt efficiency, public opinion by respondent characteristics, 1989 survey, annual rpt, 10044-2

Advisory Committee on Federal Pay

Budget of US Appendix, obligations, appropriations, and personnel, by program and agency, FY90, annual rpt, 104-3

Budget of US, authoritative financial statements with appropriations, outlays, and receipts, by category and agency, FY88, annual rpt, 8104-2.2

Pay comparability of Fed Govt with private industry, and recommended and actual pay adjustments, 1970s-89, annual rpt, 10104-1

Advisory Council on Historic Preservation

Budget of US Appendix, obligations, appropriations, and personnel, by program and agency, FY90, annual rpt, 104-3

Budget of US, authoritative financial statements with appropriations, outlays, and receipts, by category and agency, FY88, annual rpt, 8104-2.2

Aeronautical engineering

see Aviation sciences

Aeronautical navigation

Airport traffic, delays, capacity improvement projects and funding, runway length, and navigational operations, for hub and reliever airports, 1986-87 and forecast to 1996, 7508-67

Alaska airport dev plans and air systems operations, FY89-98, annual rpt, 7504-36

Charting and Geodetic Service of Natl Ocean Service activities and funding, by State, FY89-90, biennial rpt, 2174-10

FAA air traffic control and airway facilities improvement under Natl Airspace System Plan, 1981-85 and projected to 2000, annual rpt, 7504-12

FAA air traffic control facility traffic levels, by airport and State, FY88, annual rpt, 7504-27

FAA certifications for pilots and nonpilots by type, age, sex, region, and State, 1988, annual rpt, 7504-2

Flight service station workload of FAA, pilot briefs, contacts, and flight plans by facility, projected FY88-99 and trends from FY80, annual rpt, 7504-39

General aviation aircraft, flight hours, and equipment, by type, use, and model of aircraft, region, and State, 1988, annual rpt, 7504-29

Instrument flight rule aircraft handled, by user type, FAA traffic control center, and region, FY80-88 and projected to FY2000, annual rpt, 7504-15

Traffic, aircraft, pilots, airports, and fuel use, forecast FY89-2000 and trends from FY80, annual rpt, 7504-6

see also Radar

Aerospace industry

Business statistics, detailed data for major industries and economic indicators, *Survey of Current Business*, monthly rpt, 2702-1.20

County Business Patterns, 1987: employment, establishments, and payroll, by SIC 2- to 4-digit industry and county, annual State rpt series, 2326-8

Employment and Earnings, detailed data, monthly rpt, 6742-2.6

Employment and salaries in aerospace industry, by sex and race, 1979-87, GAO rpt, 26121-315

Employment Cost Index and alternative measure of compensation costs, by component, occupation, industry group, union status, and location, 1975-89, annual rpt, 6744-20

Employment Cost Index and percent change by occupational group, industry div, region, and metro-nonmetro area, quarterly press release, 6782-5

Employment Cost Index in aerospace manufacturing, by occupational group and industry, monthly rpt, 6782-1.1

Employment, earnings, and hours, by selected SIC 1- to 4-digit industry, State, and for 262 MSAs, 1972-87, 6748-81

Employment, earnings, and hours, by SIC 1- to 4-digit industry, monthly 1983-Feb 1989, annual rpt, 6744-4

Employment of minorities and women, by occupation, SIC 1- to 3-digit industry, State, and MSA, 1986, annual rpt, 9244-1

Exports and arms sales of US, foreign conditions on sales and impacts on US industry, 1973-87, annual rpt, 104-25

Finances and operations, by SIC 2- to 4-digit industry, forecast 1989 with trends from 1950s, annual rpt, 2044-28

Financial statements for manufacturing, mining, and trade corporations, by selected SIC 2- to 3-digit industry, quarterly rpt, 2502-1

Input-output structure of US economy, detailed interindustry transactions for 84 industries, and components of final demand, 1983, annual article, 2702-1.909

Labor hourly costs, by component, occupational group, union coverage, industry div, and region, 1989, annual rpt, 6744-21

Manufacturing annual survey, 1986: financial and operating data, by SIC 2- to 4-digit industry, series, 2506-15

Manufacturing census, 1987: financial and operating data, for SIC 4-digit industries by product, preliminary rpt, 2491-1.76

Minority employment in Los Angeles aerospace industry, by occupational group, 1980s-86, 21348-113

Occupational injury and illness rates, by SIC 2- to 4-digit industry, 1987, annual rpt, 6844-1

Price indexes (producer), by stage of processing and detailed commodity, monthly rpt, 6762-6

R&D funding, and scientists and engineers education and employment, for US and selected foreign countries, 1988, annual rpt, 9624-23.1

Sales, orders, backlog, and firms, by product for govt, military, and other customers, 1988, annual Current Industrial Rpt, 2506-12.22

Science, engineering, and technical employment in manufacturing, by field, occupation, and industry, 1986, triennial rpt, 9627-23

Shipments, trade, use, and firms, by type of craft and engine, monthly Current Industrial Rpt, 2506-12.24

Statistical Abstract of US, social, political, and economic data, 1790-2025, comprehensive annual compilation, 2324-1.3

Tax (income) returns of corporations, income and tax items by asset size and detailed industry, 1986, annual rpt, 8304-4; 8304-21

Wholesale trade census, 1987: employment, establishments, finances, and operations, by SIC 2- to 4-digit kind of business, MSA, county, and city, State rpt series, 2405-1

see also Aircraft

see also Missiles and rockets

see also Spacecraft

AFDC

see Aid to Families with Dependent Children

Afghanistan

Agricultural and food production and indexes, total and for selected commodities, by country, 1970s-88, annual rpt, 1524-12

Agricultural production, prices, and trade, by country, 1960s-89, annual world region rpt, 1524-4.2

Agricultural trade of US, by detailed commodity and country, 1988, semiannual rpt, 1522-4

AID activities and funding by project and function, FY90, and developing countries summary socioeconomic data from 1960s, annual rpt, 9904-4.6

AID economic aid to developing countries, obligations and disbursements by country, quarterly rpt, 9912-4

AID loans repayment status and terms by program and country, and status of predecessor agency loans, quarterly rpt, 9912-3

Economic and military aid and loans from US and intl agencies, by program and country, FY46-87, annual rpt, 9914-5

Economic, social, political, and geographic summary data, by country, 1989, annual factbook, 9114-2

Exports and imports of US with Communist countries, by detailed commodity and country, quarterly rpt with articles, 9882-2

Human rights conditions in 170 countries, 1988, annual rpt, 21384-3

Military aid of US, arms sales, and training programs costs and budget requests, by program, world region, and country, FY88-90, annual rpt, 7144-13

Military spending, arms trade, and force strengths, with govt spending and population, by country, 1977-87, annual rpt, 9824-1

Minerals production, reserves, and industry role in domestic economy and world supply, 1988 country rpt, 5606-1.17

Minerals Yearbook, 1987, Vol 3: foreign country reviews of production, trade, and policy, by commodity, annual rpt, 5604-35

Minerals Yearbook, 1987, Vol 3 preprints: foreign country review of production, trade, and policy, by commodity, annual rpt, 5604-23.86

Pakistan airspace violations by USSR and Afghanistan, and casualties, 1980-86, hearing, 21388-54

Population size, growth rates, and components of change, by country, projected 1989-2020 and trends from 1950, biennial rpt, 2324-9

Refugee resettlement programs and funding, arrivals by country of origin, and indicators of adjustment, by State, FY88, annual rpt, 4694-5

UN voting record and share of votes in agreement with US, by issue, country, and world area, 1988, annual rpt, 7004-18

see also under By Foreign Country in the "Index by Categories"

Africa

Agricultural and food aid to developing countries, and impacts on US exports, with background data, 1960s-89, 26308-85

Agricultural and food production and indexes, total and for selected commodities, by country, 1970s-88, annual rpt, 1524-12

Agricultural exports of Africa by commodity, and relation to economic conditions and other factors, by country, 1960s-87, 1528-280

Agricultural exports of US, for grains, oilseed products, hides, skins, and cotton, by country, weekly rpt, 1922-3

Agricultural production, prices, and trade, by country, 1960s-89, annual world region rpt, 1524-4.2

Agricultural trade of US, by commodity and country, bimonthly rpt with articles, 1522-1

Agricultural trade of US, by detailed commodity and country, 1988, semiannual rpt, 1522-4

Agricultural trade of US with Asia, Middle East, and North Africa, by commodity and country, 1962-86, 1528-277

AID activities and funding by project and function, FY90, and developing countries summary socioeconomic data from 1960s, annual rpt, 9904-4.5

AID contracts and grants for technical and support services, by instn, country, and State, FY88, annual listing, 9914-7

AID economic aid to developing countries, obligations and disbursements by country, quarterly rpt, 9912-4

AID housing and urban dev program financial statements, and loan guarantees by country, FY88, annual rpt, 9914-4

AID loans authorized, signed, and canceled, by country and world area, quarterly rpt, 9912-2

AID loans repayment status and terms by program and country, and status of predecessor agency loans, quarterly rpt, 9912-3

Businesses (foreign) activity in US, income tax returns, assets, and income statement items, by industry div, country, and world area, 1984-85, article, 8302-2.920

Construction contracts awarded US firms, and share of construction market by country of contractor, by world area, 1982-87, annual article, 2042-1.902

Economic and military aid and loans from US and intl agencies, by program and country, FY46-87, annual rpt, 9914-5

Energy producers finances and operations, by energy type for US firms domestic and foreign operations, 1987, annual rpt, 3164-44.2

Energy production by type, and oil prices, trade, and use, by country group and selected country, monthly rpt, 9112-2

Energy use by sector, and production, by fuel type, country, and country group, projected 1988-2000 and trends from 1970, annual rpt, 3164-84

English language program of USIA, enrollment and staff, by instn, world area, and country, FY88, annual rpt, 9854-2

Exchange and training programs of Federal agencies, participants by world area, and funding, by program, FY87, annual rpt, 9854-8

Exports and imports (waterborne) of US, by type of service, commodity, country, route, and US port, 1986-87, annual rpt, 7704-2

Exports and imports (waterborne) of US, by type of service, customs district, port, and world area, monthly rpt, 2422-7

Exports and imports of OECD, total and for 4 major countries, and US trade by country, by commodity, 1970-87, world area rpt, 9116-1.4

Exports and imports of US, by commodity group, world area, selected country, US coastal area and port, and mode of transport, monthly rpt, 2422-9

Exports and imports of US, by selected country, country group, and commodity group, 1988, annual rpt, 2044-37

Fertilizer components use, by world area, 1978-88 and projected to 2010, 5608-154

Food production and needs, and related economic outlook, by country, 1989/90, annual rpt, 1524-6

Food supply indicators for Sahel, by country, 1960s-2000, 1528-290

Immigrant and nonimmigrant visas of US issued and refused, by class, issuing office, and nationality, FY88, annual rpt, 7184-1

Immigrants admitted to US, by class of admission, country of birth, and State and MSA of destination, FY88, annual rpt, 6264-4

Immigrants admitted to US, by occupational group and country of birth, preliminary FY88, annual table, 6264-1

Immigration to US, alien workers, visitors, deportations, and naturalizations, by country, FY88 and trends from 1820, annual rpt, 6264-2

Investment (foreign direct) of US, by selected industry group and world area, 1986-88, annual article, 2702-1.930

Loans of US banks to foreigners at all US and foreign offices, by country group and country, quarterly rpt, 13002-1

Military aid of US, arms sales, and training, by country, FY50-88, annual rpt, 3904-3

Military aid programs and related activities of US, costs by country and intl agency, FY85-87 and cumulative from FY50, GAO rpt, 26123-30

Military spending and imports of developing countries, measures to determine eligibility for US economic aid, by country, 1985-86, annual rpt, 9914-1

Military spending, arms trade, and force strengths, with govt spending and population, by country, 1977-87, annual rpt, 9824-1

Minerals Yearbook, 1987, Vol 3: foreign country reviews of production, trade, and policy, by commodity, annual rpt, 5604-35

Multinatl firms US affiliates, finances, and operations, by industry, world area of parent firm, and State, 1987, annual rpt, 2704-4

Multinatl US firms and foreign affiliates finances and operations, by industry of parent firm and affiliate, world area, and country, preliminary 1987, annual rpt, 2704-5

Oil and gas reserves and discoveries, by country and country group, quarterly rpt, 3162-43

Peace Corps activities, funding by program, and volunteers, by country, FY90, annual rpt, 9654-1

Population size, growth rates, and components of change, by country, projected 1989-2020 and trends from 1950, biennial rpt, 2324-9

R&D funding by Fed Govt, by field, performer type, agency, and State, FY87-89, annual rpt, 9627-20

Refugee arrivals in US by world area and country of origin, and quotas, monthly rpt, 7002-4

Refugee arrivals in US by world area of origin and State of settlement, and Federal aid, FY88-90, annual rpt, 7004-16

Rhinoceros wild and captive population, poacher kills and enforcement action, and conservation issues, 1988 hearing, 21708-125

Science and engineering immigrants, by field, age, sex, country and world area of birth and last residence, and State, 1987 and trends from 1967, 9627-29

Terrorist (intl) incidents, casualties, and attacks on US targets, by attack type and country, 1980-88, 7008-56

Terrorist (intl) incidents, casualties, and attacks on US targets, by attack type and world area, 1968-88, annual rpt, 7004-13

Tide height and time daily at coastal points, forecast 1990, annual rpt, 2174-2.4; 2174-2.5

Travel to and from US, and travel receipts and payments, by world area, with data by country, 1984-88, annual rpt, 2904-10

Travel to and from US on US and foreign flag air carriers, by country, world area, and US port, monthly rpt, 7302-2

Travel to and from US on US and foreign flag airlines, by world area, 1980-88, annual rpt, 2904–13

Travel to US, by characteristics of visit and traveler, country, port city, and State of destination, quarterly rpt, 2902–1

Travel to US, spending by category, world area of residence, census div, and State, model results, 1985-86, 2908–28

UN voting record and share of votes in agreement with US, by issue, country, and world area, 1988, annual rpt, 7004–18

USIA library holdings, use, and staff, by country and city, FY88, annual rpt, 9854–4

Visas of US issued at Foreign Service posts, by category and world area, selected years FY84-88, annual rpt, 7184–4

Weather conditions and effect on agriculture, by US region, State, and city, and world area, weekly rpt, 2152–2

Weather events and anomalies, precipitation and temperature for US and foreign locations, weekly rpt, 2182–6

see also African Development Bank
see also African Development Fund
see also Algeria
see also Angola
see also Benin
see also Botswana
see also Burkina Faso
see also Burundi
see also Cameroon
see also Cape Verde
see also Central African Republic
see also Chad
see also Comoros
see also Congo
see also Djibouti
see also Egypt
see also Equatorial Guinea
see also Ethiopia
see also Gabon
see also Gambia
see also Ghana
see also Guinea
see also Guinea-Bissau
see also Ivory Coast
see also Kenya
see also Lesotho
see also Liberia
see also Libya
see also Madagascar
see also Malawi
see also Mali
see also Mauritania
see also Mauritius
see also Morocco
see also Mozambique
see also Namibia
see also Niger
see also Nigeria
see also Reunion
see also Rwanda
see also Sao Tome and Principe
see also Senegal
see also Seychelles
see also Sierra Leone
see also Somalia
see also South Africa
see also Sudan
see also Swaziland
see also Tanzania
see also Togo

see also Tunisia
see also Uganda
see also Western Sahara
see also Zaire
see also Zambia
see also Zimbabwe
see also under By Foreign Country in the "Index by Categories"

African Americans
see Black Americans

African Development Bank
AID loans repayment status and terms by program and country, and status of predecessor agency loans, quarterly rpt, 9912–3

Loans and grants for economic and military aid from US and intl agencies, by program and country, FY46-87, annual rpt, 9914–5

US contributions to multilateral dev banks, FY86-90, annual rpt, 9904–1.4

African Development Fund
US contributions to multilateral dev banks, FY86-90, annual rpt, 9904–1.4

Age
see Age discrimination
see Aged and aging
see Children
see Life expectancy
see Population characteristics
see Youth
see under By Age in the "Index by Categories"

Age discrimination
Education Dept Civil Rights Office, complaints, investigations, funding, and staff, various periods FY81-88, 21348–114

Fed Govt personnel action appeals, decisions of Merit Systems Protection Board by agency and region, FY88, annual rpt, 9494–2

Labor laws enacted, by State, 1988, annual article, 6722–1.904

Telecommunications industries minority employment and discrimination charges, with data by industry and selected firm, 1970s-88, hearings, 21368–113

Aged and aging
Arrest rates, by offense, sex, age, and race, 1987, annual rpt, 6224–7

Assets of older persons and relation to income, by selected characteristics, 1984, article, 4742–1.910

Assets of older persons and relation to income, 1984, technical paper, 4746–26.5

Board and care homes conditions, State licensing and enforcement activity, and client characteristics, 1970s-88, 21148–55

Board and care homes licensing and inspection by States, and client characteristics, 1989 GAO rpt, 26121–275

Cancer screening of aged by physicians and compliance with American Cancer Society schedules, by speciality, 1986 local area study, article, 4042–3.917

Consumer Expenditure Survey, household income by source, and itemized spending, by selected characteristics and region, 1984-87, annual rpt, 6764–5

Consumer Income, socioeconomic characteristics of persons, families, and households, detailed cross-tabulations, Current Population Rpt series, 2546–6

Deaths and rates, by detailed cause and demographic characteristics, 1986 and trends from 1900, US Vital Statistics annual rpt, 4144–2

Deaths and rates, by detailed location, cause, and demographic characteristics, 1987, US Vital Statistics annual rpt, 4144–3

Developing countries aged population and selected characteristics, 1980s and projected to 2020, country rpt series, 2326–19

Disability (functional) of aged, by activity type and selected characteristics, 1984, 4147–10.167

Disabled persons employment, labor force status, and other characteristics, 1988, Current Population Rpt, 2546–2.147

Drug and alcohol abuse treatment facilities, services, use, funding, and client characteristics, 1987, annual rpt, 4494–10

Employment and earnings covered under OASDHI, and social security contributions, by age, sex, race, State, and county, 1985, 4748–43

Employment and Training Admin activities, funding, and participant characteristics, by program, FY80-86, 6408–71

Employment in community services for aged, funding by recipient, 1989-90, press release, 6406–2.26

Employment of older persons, and earnings, reasons for working, and job training preferences, by selected characteristics, 1960-87, 6306–2.3

Energy use of aged, and compared to persons under 60 years old, by household end use, 1987 survey, 3166–7.30

Family members caring for aged, and potential caregivers, by relation and other characteristics, 1984, 4186–7.5

Family members caring for aged, stress levels and respite services, for King County, Wash, 1983-87, article, 4652–1.916

Family members caring for aged, tax subsidies in 2 States, 1981-84, article, 4652–1.915

Financial stress of aged, essential expenses cut and household economic characteristics, 1983, article, 1702–1.907

Foreign and US older persons institutionalized in medical and other care facilities, rates by selected country, 1980 and 1985, article, 4652–1.918

Health care (long-term) needs of aged with functional limitations, and costs by payment source, 1982-85, GAO rpt, 26121–266

Health care (preventive) program of California for aged, tests, results, referrals, and participant characteristics, 1985-86, article, 4042–3.918

Health care and condition research, survey design and research methods, 1989 conf proceedings, 4188–60

Health care services (preventive) for aged, effectiveness and costs of proposed Medicare coverage, series, 26356–7

Health care services and long term care for aged, series, 4186–7

Health care services use by aged, factors influencing level of care, literature review, 1988 article, 4652–1.905

Health care services use by aged, persons with high and low levels of care by selected health and other characteristics, 1971 and 1980 studies, 4186-2.22

Health care services use by aged related to marital status, living arrangements, and other characteristics, 1977, 4188-54

Health care spending of aged for instnl and community care, under alternative community care settings, 1979-84 study, article, 4652-1.932

Health condition and care access of older persons, data collection improvement needs, 1985 conf, 4147-4.26

Health condition and health care resources, use, and spending, 1950s-87, annual data compilation, 4144-11

Health condition improvement and disease prevention goals and recommended activities for 2000, with trends 1970s-80s, 4048-10

Health condition of aged, chronic and multiple illness prevalence by sex and age group, 1984, 4146-8.172

Health maintenance organizations case mgmt and home care services for frail aged, demonstration projects enrollment, 1986, article, 4652-1.913

Hispanic Americans socioeconomic characteristics, by detailed origin, 1988, Current Population Rpt, 2546-1.430; 2546-1.438

Homicide rates, and lifetime probability of victimization, by age, sex, and race, 1987, annual rpt, 6224-8

Hospice services awareness of aged, by age, sex, education, region, SMSA/non-SMSA residence, and cancer history, 1984 survey, article, 4042-3.915

Hospital service area population care need indicators, and travel distances, for rural and urban instns in New York State, 1983, 4188-53

Hospitalization of older persons, community care effect on hospital use, demonstration projects, 1989 article, 4652-1.911

Household and family characteristics, by living arrangement, 1988 and trends from 1960, Current Population Rpt, 2546-2.148

Household and family characteristics, by location, 1988, annual Current Population Rpt, 2546-1.437

Household composition, income, benefits, and labor force status, Survey of Income and Program Participation methodology, working paper series, 2626-10

Households and housing characteristics, MSA surveys, fact sheet series, 2485-11

Households and housing detailed characteristics, and unit and neighborhood quality, by location, 1985, biennial rpt, 2485-12

Households and housing detailed characteristics, and unit and neighborhood quality, MSA surveys, series, 2485-6

Households and housing unit summary characteristics, 1985 and trends, biennial chartbook, 2486-1.7

Housing aid of Fed Govt, with low income housing unit conditions and household characteristics, 1985-FY88 and alternative projections to 2008, 26306-6.134

Housing and community preferences of persons nearing retirement, by respondent characteristics, 1987 survey, article, 1702-1.905

Income (household) and poverty status under alternative income definitions, by recipient characteristics, 1986, Current Population Rpt, 2546-6.58

Income and poverty characteristics of aged, social security issues with data on Fed Govt spending and indicators of need, with bibl, 1988 compilation of papers, 25928-7

Income of aged, by source, 1962 and 1987, chartbook, 4748-42

Income of aged, ratios for couples to single persons, by age and sex, 1987, 26306-3.111

Indian housing condition and other characteristics, for aged, 1987 survey, 21148-53

Injuries from use of consumer products and related activities, by victim age and sex, 1988, annual rpt, 9164-7

Injuries from use of consumer products, by severity, victim age, and detailed product, 1988, annual rpt, 9164-6

Labor force participation of older persons, unemployment, displacement, and reemployment, by selected characteristics, 1969-88, 6306-2.2

Libraries (public) special programs, project descriptions and funding by level of govt, State, and city, 1984-87, annual rpt, 4874-4

Life expectancy of aged under independent and dependent living arrangements, by age, model results, 1989 article, 4042-3.919

Living arrangements of aged, by poverty status, 1988, annual rpt, 4744-3.1

Mississippi hospitals and community health centers, use, staff, and Medicare and other payments, 1988 hearing, 25548-97

Mortgage insurance programs of HUD, finances and lending activity by program, FY88, annual rpt, 5004-8

Nutritional status and related health condition and practices, by selected characteristics, 1970s-87, 4048-33

Pneumonia hospitalization and death rates for aged, and risk relation to health status indicators, aggregate 1982-84, article, 4042-3.934

Pollution (air) exposure of population and selected risk groups, by pollutant, MSA, and county, 1988, hearing, 21368-117

Population, health condition, and services needs of aged, issues and Federal policies, 1989 annual rpt, 25144-3

Population of aged, social and economic characteristics, 1900s-1986 and projected to 2050, biennial chartbook, 12904-1

Population size, by age, sex, and race, and components of change, alternative projections 1988-2080, Current Population Rpt, 2546-3.158

Poverty status of families and persons, by detailed characteristics, 1987, annual Current Population Rpt, 2546-6.60

Slowing of aging process, use of treatments and products not proven safe or effective, costs, and user characteristics, 1986 survey, 4008-86

Statistical Abstract of US, social, political, and economic data, with foreign comparisons, 1790-2025, comprehensive annual compilation, 2324-1

Surgical procedures performed in hospitals, by procedure type, age, sex, instn size, and payment source, 1983-87, 4146-8.171

Tax (income) returns of individuals, by filing status, tax item, and income level, 1987, annual article, 8302-2.901

Tax (income) returns of individuals, detailed data, 1986, annual rpt, 8304-2

Telephone service of households, by composition, income sources, and other characteristics, 1984-87, 9288-11

Traffic accidents, injuries, and deaths of older drivers, compared to other age groups, 1986, 7768-105

Unemployed displaced workers, by reason, industry, selected characteristics, and State, 1988, annual rpt, 6744-18

Vaccination activity, reactions, costs, and preventable disease cases and deaths, 1988 annual conf, 4204-15

Vermont older persons employment, income, and other characteristics, by sex and age, 1900-86, hearing, 21148-54

Voting and registration, by socioeconomic and demographic characteristics, 1988 presidential election, biennial Current Population Rpt, 2546-1.440

see also Adult day care
see also Age discrimination
see also Civil service pensions
see also Foster Grandparent Program
see also Geriatrics
see also Individual retirement arrangements
see also Medicare
see also Military benefits and pensions
see also Nursing homes
see also Old age assistance
see also Old-Age, Survivors, Disability, and Health Insurance
see also Pensions and pension funds
see also Retired Senior Volunteer Program
see also Retirement
see also Retirement communities
see also Social security
see also Supplemental Security Income
see also Veterans benefits and pensions
see also under By Age in the "Index by Categories"

Agency for International Development

Activities and funding of Intl Dev Cooperation Agency and AID, FY88-90, and developing countries economic and social conditions from 1960s, annual rpt, 9904-4

Budget of US, authoritative financial statements with appropriations, outlays, and receipts, by category and agency, FY88, annual rpt, 8104-2.2

Contract awards (noncompetitive) over $100,000, FY88, annual rpt, 9904-1.3

Contracts and grants of AID for technical and support services, by instn, country, and State, FY88, annual listing, 9914-7

Contracts and grants of AID to higher education instns, annual listing, discontinued, 9914-6

Contracts to disadvantaged and small businesses, awards and goals, FY88, annual rpt, 9904-1.2

Currency (foreign) accounts owned by US under AID admin and by foreign govts with joint AID control, status by program and country, quarterly rpt, 9912-1

Currency (foreign) trust funds of AID, mgmt and use by country, FY83-87, GAO rpt, 26123-221

Dev projects of AID, and socioeconomic impacts, evaluation rpt series, 9916-1

Dev projects of AID, special study series, 9916-3

Disaster preparedness and economic, population, and political data, country rpt series, 9916-2

Economic aid to developing countries, obligations and disbursements by country, quarterly rpt, 9912-4

Economic and military aid of US, by country and program, FY86-88, annual rpt, 9904-1.4

Exchange and training programs of Federal agencies, participants by world area, and funding, by program, FY87, annual rpt, 9854-8

Exports (agricultural) under federally financed programs, FY70-88, annual rpt, 1924-9

Housing and urban dev program of AID, financial statements, and loan guarantees by country, FY88, annual rpt, 9914-4

Labor unions recognized in Fed Govt, agreements and membership by agency and facility, as of Jan 1989, biennial listing, 9844-14

Liabilities (contingent) and claims paid by Fed Govt on federally insured and guaranteed contracts with foreign obligors, by country and program, periodic rpt, 8002-12

Loan repayment status and terms by program and country, AID and predecessor agencies, quarterly rpt, 9912-3

Loans and grants for economic and military aid from US and intl agencies, by program and country, FY46-87, annual rpt, 9914-5

Loans authorized, signed, and canceled, by country and world area, quarterly rpt, 9912-2

Military spending and imports of developing countries, measures to determine eligibility for US economic aid, by country, 1985-86, annual rpt, 9914-1

Nicaragua Contra forces humanitarian aid of AID, by type, 1988, GAO rpt, 26123-237

R&D and related funding of Fed Govt to higher education and nonprofit instns, by field, instn, agency, and State, FY87, annual rpt, 9627-17

R&D funding by Fed Govt, by field, performer type, agency, and State, FY87-89, annual rpt, 9627-20

Sri Lanka housing construction loans to rural low-income families, activities, and recipient characteristics, 1984-86, 9918-16

Agent Orange
see Dioxins

Aging Cell Culture Repository
Cell cultures for aging research, availability and cultures shipped, 1989 listing, 4478-187

Agricultural accidents and safety
Aircraft accidents in general aviation, by circumstances, characteristics of persons and aircraft involved, and type of flying, 1986, annual rpt, 9614-3

Deaths and rates, by cause, age, race, sex, and State, 1986, annual rpt, 4144-2.5

Grain handling facility explosions and casualties, by firm, FY88, annual rpt, 1294-1

Injuries from use of consumer products, by severity, victim age, and detailed product, 1988, annual rpt, 9164-6

Injuries, illnesses, and workdays lost, by SIC 2-digit industry, 1987-88, annual press release, 6844-3

Injury and illness rates by SIC 2- to 4-digit industry, and deaths by cause and industry div, 1987, annual rpt, 6844-1

Agricultural chemicals
see Fertilizers
see Pesticides

Agricultural commodities
Agricultural Statistics Board rpts, planned 1989, annual listing, 1614-1

Census of Agriculture, 1987: farms, farmland, production and costs, and operator characteristics, advance State and county rpt series, 2330-1

Data on agriculture, collection, methodology, and use for major time series of USDA, 1989 rpt, 1506-1.7

Economic Indicators of the Farm Sector, finances, income sources, expenses by type, assets, debts, and ratios, 1987, annual rpt, 1544-19

see also Agricultural exports and imports
see also Agricultural marketing
see also Agricultural prices
see also Agricultural production
see also Agricultural production costs
see also Agricultural production quotas and price supports
see also Agricultural stocks
see also Agricultural subsidies
see also Animal feed
see also Animals
see also Census of Agriculture
see also Citrus fruits
see also Cocoa and chocolate
see also Coffee
see also Corn
see also Cotton
see also Dairy industry and products
see also Flowers and nursery products
see also Food and food industry
see also Food consumption
see also Food prices
see also Food supply
see also Fruit and fruit products
see also Grains and grain products
see also Gum and wood chemicals
see also Hides and skins
see also Honey and beekeeping
see also Hops
see also Livestock and livestock industry
see also Lumber industry and products
see also Meat and meat products
see also Natural fibers
see also Nuts
see also Oils, oilseeds, and fats
see also Peanuts
see also Poultry industry and products
see also Rice
see also Seeds
see also Soybeans
see also Spices and herbs
see also Sugar industry and products
see also Tea

see also Tobacco industry and products
see also Vegetables and vegetable products
see also Wheat
see also Wool and wool trade
see also under By Commodity in the "Index by Categories"

Agricultural Cooperative Service
Budget of US Appendix, obligations, appropriations, and personnel, by program and agency, FY90, annual rpt, 104-3

Commercial members of agricultural cooperatives, characteristics and use of services, by region, 1980 and 1986, 1128-53

Cooperatives finances, aggregate for top 100 assns by commodity group, FY87, annual rpt, 1124-3

Cooperatives, finances, and membership, by type of service, commodity, and State, 1987, annual rpt, 1124-1

Cooperatives finances, operations, activities, and current issues, monthly journal, 1122-1

Cooperatives member characteristics, and use of services, by region, 1980 and 1986, 1128-54

Agricultural cooperatives
see Rural cooperatives

Agricultural credit
Agricultural Outlook, production, prices, marketing, and trade, by commodity, forecast and current situation, monthly rpt with articles, 1502-4

Agricultural Statistics, 1988, annual rpt, 1004-1.2

Assets and debts of private sector, balance sheets by segment, 1949-88, semiannual rpt, 9365-4.1

Assistance of Fed Govt to rural areas compared to urban areas, by program and degree of urbanization, FY85, periodic rpt, 1598-248

Banks (agricultural), by ratio of farm loans to capital, 1983-88, article, 9362-1.901

Banks (agricultural) financial impacts of drought, 1988, 1588-133

Banks (insured commercial and savings) finances, for foreign and domestic offices, by asset size, 1987, annual rpt, 9294-4.2

Banks (natl) domestic and intl operations, charters, mergers, and liquidations, by instn and State, quarterly rpt, 8402-3

Banks finances and operations, by metro-nonmetro location, 1986, annual rpt, 1544-29

Banks in rural areas, control by urban-based firms, and financial and market characteristics, 1960s-88, article, 1502-7.906

CCC certificate exchange activity, by commodity, weekly press release, 1802-16

CCC financial statements and operations, by program and commodity, FY88, annual rpt, 1824-4

CCC loan activities by commodity, and agency operating results, monthly press release, 1802-7

Census of Agriculture, 1987: farms, farmland, production and costs, and operator characteristics, advance State and county rpt series, 2330-1

Census of Agriculture, 1987: farms, farmland, production, finances, and operator characteristics, by county, final State rpt series, 2331-1

Mexico agricultural subsidies, and impacts of reductions on production, by commodity, 1982-87 and projected 1992, 1528–288

Rice market activities, prices, inspections, sales, trade, supply, and use, for US and selected foreign markets, weekly rpt, 1313–8

Saudi Arabia wheat production, use, prices, and subsidies, mid 1960s-89, article, 1522–3.903

Soil and water conservation funding by USDA, by program and State, FY86, annual rpt, 1264–12

Statistical Abstract of US, social, political, and economic data, 1790-2025, comprehensive annual compilation, 2324–1.3

Tax expenditures, Federal revenues forgone through income tax deductions and exclusions by type, FY90-94, annual rpt, 21784–10

Thailand rice production, consumption, exports, and subsidies, 1982-86, 1528–286

Thailand rice production, consumption, exports, and subsidies, 1982-87, article, 1522–3.915

Vegetables farms, acreage, and sales, by whether Federal farm program participant and State, 1987, article, 1561–11.907

Water Bank Program agreements, payments to farmers, and wetlands acreage, by State, FY72-89, annual rpt, 1804–21

Wheat export subsidy program costs to US and EC, 1980s-88, article, 9391–1.904

Wheat exports impacts of subsidies and exchange rates, by importing and exporting country, alternative model results, 1986/87, 1548–351

Wheat production and price impacts of proposed trade reforms affecting govt subsidies, 1989 article, 1561–12.905

see also Agricultural credit

see also Agricultural production quotas and price supports

Agricultural surpluses

Agricultural Stabilization and Conservation Service programs, annual commodity fact sheet series, 1806–4

CCC commodities for sale, and prices, monthly press release, 1802–4

CCC financial statements and operations, by program and commodity, FY88, annual rpt, 1824–4

CCC loan activities by commodity, and agency operating results, monthly press release, 1802–7

Cotton prices in 8 spot markets, futures prices at NYC exchange, farm prices, and CCC loan stocks, monthly rpt, 1309–1

Dairy products price support purchases, sales, donations, and inventories of CCC, monthly rpt, 1802–2

Grain stocks on and off farms, by crop, quarterly rpt, 1621–4

Grain support loan programs of USDA, activity and status by grain and State, monthly rpt, 1802–3

Irrigation subsidies of Reclamation Bur, costs to Fed Govt and surplus crop production, 1985-86, 21448–40

Production, trade, and price support activity and policy options, with foreign comparisons, 1950s-89, commodity rpt series, 1566–7

see also Agricultural production quotas and price supports

see also Agricultural stocks

see also Food assistance

see also Public Law 480

Agricultural Trade Development and Assistance Act

see Public Law 480

Agricultural transportation

see Agricultural marketing

Agricultural wages

Agricultural Outlook, production, prices, marketing, and trade, by commodity, forecast and current situation, monthly rpt with articles, 1502–4

Agricultural Statistics, 1988, annual rpt, 1004–1.2

Alien and US workers, evaluation of wage surveys to set minimum wage, with data by location, 1980s-87, GAO rpt, 26131–50

Alien workers (unauthorized) employer sanctions impacts on farm labor costs, by farm type, size, and region, 1986, 1598–250

Census of Agriculture, 1987: farms, farmland, production, finances, and operator characteristics, by county, final State rpt series, 2331–1

Earnings by industry div, and personal income per capita and by source, by State, MSA, and county, 1982-87, annual regional rpts, 2704–2

Earnings by major industry group, and personal income per capita and by source, by region and State, 1929-87, 2708–40

Earnings, employment, and days worked, for farm workers by selected characteristics and region, 1987, biennial rpt, 1594–2

Economic Indicators of the Farm Sector, balance sheets, and receipts by detailed commodity, by State, 1984-88, annual rpt, 1544–18

Economic Indicators of the Farm Sector, finances, income sources, expenses by type, assets, debts, and ratios, 1987, annual rpt, 1544–19

Economic Indicators of the Farm Sector, income, expenses, receipts by commodity, assets, and liabilities, 1988 and trends from 1945, annual rpt, 1544–16

Finances and operations of farms, by size, commodity, and region, 1986, annual rpt, 1544–27

Financial ratios of farms, benchmarks by type of operation and region, 1984-86, 1548–342

Income (household, family, and personal), by source, detailed characteristics, and region, 1987, annual Current Population Rpt, 2546–6.59

Labor costs for farms, for hired, contract, and family workers, by type of farm, 1986, article, 1561–16.901

Production itemized costs, by farm sales size and region, 1988, annual rpt, 1614–3

Production itemized costs, receipts, and returns, by crop and State, preliminary 1987, annual rpt, 1544–24

Production itemized costs, receipts, and returns, by selected commodity and region, 1975-87, 1548–345

Soviet Union personal income by source, disposable income, wage deductions by type, and savings, 1950s-87, 9118–7

Statistical Abstract of US, social, political, and economic data, 1790-2025, comprehensive annual compilation, 2324–1.3

Tobacco (burley) finances, operations, and labor, for Kentucky and Tennessee, 1984, 1568–277

Wages, employment, hours, and perquisites, for farm labor by State, quarterly rpt, 1631–1

Agriculture

Agricultural Statistics, 1988, annual rpt, 1004–1

Data coverage and availability of Census Bur rpts and data files, 1989 annual listing, 2304–2

Data on agriculture, collection, methodology, and use for major time series of USDA, series, 1506–1

Data on agriculture, compilation, 1987/88 and trends from 1920, annual rpt, 1004–14

Statistical Abstract of US, social, political, and economic data, 1790-2025, comprehensive annual compilation, 2324–1.3

TVA agriculture and fertilizer rpts, 1989 annual listing, 9804–28

see also Agricultural accidents and safety

see also Agricultural commodities

see also Agricultural credit

see also Agricultural education

see also Agricultural energy use

see also Agricultural exports and imports

see also Agricultural extension work

see also Agricultural finance

see also Agricultural insurance

see also Agricultural labor

see also Agricultural machinery and equipment

see also Agricultural marketing

see also Agricultural policy

see also Agricultural prices

see also Agricultural production

see also Agricultural production costs

see also Agricultural production quotas and price supports

see also Agricultural productivity

see also Agricultural sciences and research

see also Agricultural services

see also Agricultural stocks

see also Agricultural subsidies

see also Agricultural surpluses

see also Agricultural wages

see also Botany

see also Census of Agriculture

see also Drought

see also Farm income

see also Farm operators

see also Farms and farmland

see also Fertilizers

see also Food and food industry

see also Foreign agriculture

see also Forests and forestry

see also Irrigation

see also Pesticides

see also Pests and pest control

see also Rural areas

see also Soils and soil conservation

see also Wildlife and wildlife conservation

see also under By Industry in the "Index by Categories"

Air cargo

Exports and imports between US and outlying areas, by detailed commodity and mode of transport, monthly rpt, 2422-4

Exports and imports of US, by commodity group, world area, selected country, US coastal area and port, and mode of transport, monthly rpt, 2422-9

Finances, operations, vehicles, equipment, accidents, and energy use, by mode of transport, 1955-88, annual rpt, 7304-2

Financial data for airlines, by carrier, carrier group, and for total certificated system, quarterly rpt, 7302-7

Fruit and vegetable shipments, and arrivals in US and Canada cities, by mode of transport and State and country of origin, 1988, annual rpt series, 1311-4

Fruit and vegetable shipments by mode of transport, arrivals, and imports, by commodity and State and country of origin, weekly rpt, 1311-3

Hazardous material transport accidents, casualties, and damage, by mode of transport, with DOT control activities, 1988, annual rpt, 7304-4

Intercity freight, and carrier revenue, charges, and employment, by transport mode, 1986, annual rpt, 7704-7.1

Mail operating costs of USPS, itemized by class of mail, FY88, annual rpt, 9864-4

Mail revenue, costs, and volume, by class of mail, FY88, annual rpt, 9864-2

Tax (excise) collections of IRS, by source, quarterly rpt, 8302-1

Tax (excise) collections of IRS, by type of tax, region, and State, FY88, annual rpt, 8304-3.3

Traffic, aircraft, pilots, airports, and fuel use, forecast FY89-2000 and trends from FY80, annual rpt, 7504-6

Traffic, capacity, and performance, by carrier and type of operation, monthly rpt, 7302-6

Traffic, capacity, and performance for medium regional airlines, by carrier, quarterly rpt, 7302-8

see also Military airlift

Air conditioning

Air pollution indoor levels, effects of ventilation rates in commercial and public buildings, 1989 rpt, 3228-10

Apartment completions by region and metro-nonmetro location, and absorption rates, by size and rent class, preliminary 1988, annual Current Housing Rpt, 2484-3

Apartment market absorption rates and characteristics for nonsubsidized furnished and unfurnished units, 1987 and trends from 1970, annual Current Housing Rpt, 2484-2

Chlorofluorocarbon use, and costs and benefits of proposed reductions, projected to 2010, 3166-6.34

Energy use, costs, and conservation, and household and housing characteristics, survey rpt series, 3166-7

Energy use in commercial buildings, costs, and conservation, by building characteristics, survey rpt series, 3166-8

Energy use of households, and number with appliances, by type, selected years 1978-87, annual rpt, 3164-74.1

Equipment shipments, trade, use, and firms, by product, 1988, annual Current Industrial Rpt, 2506-12.7

Exports of US, detailed commodities by country, monthly rpt, 2422-3

Housing alteration and repair spending, by characteristics of property and region, 1984-88, annual rpt, 2384-4

Housing and households detailed characteristics, and unit and neighborhood quality, by location, 1985, biennial rpt, 2485-12

Housing and households detailed characteristics, and unit and neighborhood quality, MSA surveys, series, 2485-6

Housing energy conservation program of BPA, energy savings and indoor air quality under alternative methods, projected 1986-2006, 3228-9

Housing units completed, single and multifamily units by structural and financial characteristics, inside-outside MSAs, and region, 1984-88, annual rpt, 2384-1

Imports of US, detailed Schedule A commodities by country, monthly rpt, 2422-2

Injuries from use of consumer products and related activities, by victim age and sex, 1988, annual rpt, 9164-7

Injuries from use of consumer products, by severity, victim age, and detailed product, 1988, annual rpt, 9164-6

Manufacturing census, 1987: financial and operating data, for SIC 4-digit industries by product, preliminary rpt, 2491-1.67

Price indexes (producer), by stage of processing and detailed commodity, monthly rpt, 6762-6

Price indexes (producer), by stage of processing and detailed commodity, monthly 1988, annual rpt, 6764-2

Shipments and PPI for building materials, by type, bimonthly rpt, 2042-1.5; 2042-1.6

Solar collector and photovoltaic module shipments by end-use sector and State, R&D, and trade, 1988, annual rpt, 3164-62

TVA electric power purchases of municipal and cooperative distributors, and prices and use by distributor and consumer sector, monthly rpt, 9802-1

Wholesale trade census, 1987: employment, establishments, finances, and operations, by SIC 2- to 4-digit kind of business, MSA, county, and city, State rpt series, 2405-1

Air Force

Agent Orange exposure of Air Force personnel, deaths and rates by cause and selected characteristics, 1989 annual rpt, 3604-3

Birds collisions with military aircraft, and related costs, by service branch, 1975-88, GAO rpt, 26123-241

Bomber aircraft (B-1B) maintenance problems, and repair contracts, 1985-88 with costs projected to FY94, GAO rpt, 26123-218

Criminal case processing in military courts, and prisoners by facility, by service branch, 1960s-87, annual rpt, 6064-6.6

Criminal case processing in military courts, and prisoners by facility, by service branch, 1970s-88, annual rpt, 6064-6.5

Deaths by cause, age, race, and rank, and personnel captured and missing, by service branch, 2nd half FY88, semiannual rpt, 3542-21

Drug and alcohol abuse by military personnel, prevalence and consequences, by selected characteristics, 1988, biennial rpt, 3504-19

Health care facilities of DOD in US and abroad, beds, admissions, outpatient visits, and births, by service branch, quarterly rpt, 3542-15

Manpower active duty strength, civilian personnel, and dependents, by service branch and US and foreign location, quarterly rpt, 3542-20

Manpower active duty strength, recruits, and reenlistment, by race, sex, and service branch, quarterly press release, 3542-7

Manpower, contracts, and payroll of DOD, by service branch and location, with top 5 contractors and maps, by State and country, FY88, annual rpt, 3544-29

Manpower needs, costs, and force readiness, by service branch, FY90, annual rpt, 3504-1

Manpower of DOD, and organization, budget, weapons, and property, by service branch, State, and country, 1989 annual summary rpt, 3504-13

Manpower of DOD, by service branch, major installation, and State, as of Sept 1988, annual rpt, 3544-7

Manpower statistics for active duty, civilian, and reserve personnel, by service branch, FY88 and trends, annual rpt, 3544-1

Manpower statistics for active duty, civilian, and reserve personnel, by service branch, quarterly rpt, 3542-14

Manpower strengths in US and abroad, by service branch, world area, and country, quarterly press release, 3542-9

Manpower strengths, summary by service branch, monthly press release, 3542-2

NATO Europe members presence of US military and civilian personnel and dependents, by service branch, 1980-88, GAO rpt, 26123-252

NATO Europe members presence of US military and civilian personnel, and vacancies, by service branch, 1988, GAO rpt, 26123-251

Patents granted to Air Force personnel, FY81-88, annual rpt, 2244-1.2

Pilot needs, retention, incentive pay, and impacts of alternative bonus programs, FY89 and projected FY90-94, 26308-88

Reserve forces manpower strengths and characteristics, by component, quarterly rpt, 3542-4

Training and education programs of DOD, funding, staff, students, and facilities, by service branch, FY90, annual rpt, 3504-5

Women military personnel on active and reserve duty, by demographic and service characteristics and service branch, FY88, annual chartbook, 3544-26

see also Department of Air Force

Air Force Academy

see Service academies

Air freight

see Air cargo

Air National Guard

see National Guard

Air navigation

see Aeronautical navigation

Air piracy

Airport security operations to prevent hijacking, screening failures and proposed FAA penalties by carrier, 1989 press release, 7306-10.2; 7306-10.3

Airport security operations to prevent hijacking, screening results, enforcement actions, and hijacking attempts, 1st half 1988, semiannual rpt, 7502-5

Hijacking attempts on US and foreign aircraft, summary data 1974-84, annual rpt, 7304-1

Hijackings, on-board explosions, and other crime, US and foreign incidents, 1983-87, annual rpt, 7504-31

Hijackings, other crimes against aviation, and airport screening results, 1976-88, annual rpt, 6064-6.3

Sentences for Federal offenses, guidelines by offense and circumstances, 1989 rpt, 17668-1

Statistical Abstract of US, social, political, and economic data, 1790-2025, comprehensive annual compilation, 2324-1.3

Terrorist (intl) incidents, casualties, and attacks on US targets, by attack type and country, 1980-88, 7008-56

Terrorist (intl) incidents, casualties, and attacks on US targets, by attack type and world area, 1968-88, annual rpt, 7004-13

Air pollution

Abatement activity of EPA, compliance, and monitoring stations operating status, 1987, annual rpt, 9194-4

Abatement equipment shipments by industry, exports, and new and backlog orders, by product, 1988, annual Current Industrial Rpt, 2506-12.5

Abatement equipment spending of business, 1982-88, annual article, 2702-1.904

Abatement spending by govts, business, and consumers, 1983-87, annual article, 2702-1.919

Abatement spending, capital and operating costs by SIC 2- to 4-digit industry and State, 1986, annual Current Industrial Rpt, 2506-3.6

Assistance (financial and nonfinancial) of Fed Govt, 1989 base edition with supplements, annual listing, 104-5

Cancer (lung) risk relation to home heating and cooking facilities, air pollution exposure, and smoking, by sex, for Shenyang, PRC, 1985-87 study, article, 4472-1.931

Carbon dioxide and other pollutants in atmosphere, effects on climate, sea levels, and solar radiation, 1989 hearing, 25318-75

Carbon dioxide in atmosphere, measurement, methodology, and research results, series, 3006-11

Carbon monoxide emissions, by source, 1987 hearing, 21368-104

Chlorofluorocarbon use, and costs and benefits of proposed reductions, projected to 2010, 3166-6.34

Coastal areas environmental and socioeconomic conditions, and potential impact of oil and gas OCS leases, final statement series, 5736-1

Cost of living indexes for metro areas, relation of expenditure items and quality of life indicators, model results, 1973, working paper, 6886-6.9

Electric utilities privately owned, air pollution emissions and abatement equipment by fuel type and State,, 1987-88, annual rpt, 3164-11.5

Electric utilities privately owned, pollution abatement outlays by type of pollutant and equipment, and firm, 1987, annual rpt, 3164-23.1

Emissions levels for 5 pollutants, by detailed source and State, 1986, annual rpt, 9194-7

Emissions levels for 6 pollutants, and measurements exceeding natl standards, by site, 1987-88, annual rpt, 9194-5

Emissions levels for 6 pollutants, by source, region, and selected MSA, 1978-87, annual rpt, 9194-1

Emissions levels for 6 pollutants, by source, 1970-87 and trends from 1940, annual rpt, 9194-13

Environmental quality and protection programs, and intl issues, 1988 annual rpt, 484-1

EPA pollution control grant program activities, monthly rpt, 9182-8

Health care facilities medical waste disposal, hospital incinerator emissions, and regulation, 1988 rpt, 26358-198

Health condition and health care resources, use, and spending, 1950s-87, annual data compilation, 4144-11

Health effects of hazardous substances, concentrations in environment, and household products composition, with data by selected location, 1988 hearings, 21408-112

Health effects of selected pollutants, concentrations in food and environment, sources, and human intake, methodology and data needs, series, 9186-9

Health effects of selected pollutants, concentrations in food and environment, sources, human intake, and regulation, series, 9186-8

Indoor air pollution levels, impacts of BPA housing energy conservation program under alternative methods, projected 1986-2006, 3228-9

Industrial hazardous substances releases and reduction methods under EPA regulation, by chemical, source, industry, and location, 1987, annual rpt, 9234-6

Mine safety and health enforcement, training, and funding, with casualties, by type of mine and State, FY87, annual rpt, 6664-6

Ozone and carbon monoxide levels exceeding EPA standards, by MSA, 1988, annual press release, 9194-18

Ozone levels, urban areas failure to meet natl standards, emissions sources, exposure, and costs and benefits of reduction strategies, 1983-87 and projected to 2004, 26358-203

Ozone peak concentrations by selected city, 1983 and 1988, and health effects clinical test results, 1989 hearing, 21368-117

Pollution (air) indoor levels, effects of ventilation rates in commercial and public buildings, 1989 rpt, 3228-10

Polychlorinated biphenyls levels in Great Lakes environment, humans, and animals, and emissions sources, by site, 1970s-85, conf, 14648-19

Population and selected risk group exposure to air pollution, by pollutant, MSA, and county, 1988, hearing, 21368-117

Public opinion on taxes, spending, and govt efficiency, by respondent characteristics, 1989 survey, annual rpt, 10044-2

Soil, water, and environmental conservation and conditions, with data by State and region, 1989 quinquennial rpt, 1268-24

Statistical Abstract of US, social, political, and economic data, 1790-2025, comprehensive annual compilation, 2324-1.1

see also Acid rain
see also Motor vehicle exhaust
see also Radiation
see also Radon

Air safety

see Aviation accidents and safety

Air traffic control

Airport traffic, delays, capacity improvement projects and funding, runway length, and navigational operations, for hub and reliever airports, 1986-87 and forecast to 1996, 7508-67

Alaska airport dev plans and air systems operations, FY89-98, annual rpt, 7504-36

Certification of pilots and nonpilots, by certificate type, age, sex, region, and State, 1988, annual rpt, 7504-2

Collisions (mid-air) prevention measures of FAA, and near collisions by type of ATC facility and selected airport, 1986-88, GAO rpt, 26113-426

Delays of flights caused by ATC procedures and problems, and costs, with data by airport, 1976-86, 7508-68

Employment levels at ATC facilities, by selected characteristics of staff, FY88, annual rpt, 7504-41

Employment of DOT, by subagency, occupation, and selected personnel characteristics, FY88, annual rpt, 7304-18

Flight service station workload of FAA, pilot briefs, contacts, and flight plans by facility, projected FY88-99 and trends from FY80, annual rpt, 7504-39

Instrument flight rule aircraft handled, by user type, FAA traffic control center, and region, FY80-88 and projected to FY2000, annual rpt, 7504-15

Medical research and test results for aviation, technical rpt series, 7506-10

Operations and finances of FAA, and staff by region, FY87-88, annual rpt, 7504-10

Operations of FAA ATC facilities, improvement under Natl Airspace System Plan, 1981-85 and projected to 2000, annual rpt, 7504-12

Pension program of Fed Govt, benefits and coverage by age, type of beneficiary, and State, FY87, annual rpt, 9844-34

Safety of ATC system, working conditions, and traffic volume, various periods 1981-88, GAO rpt, 26113-220

Traffic, aircraft, pilots, airports, and fuel use, forecast FY89-2000 and trends from FY80, annual rpt, 7504-6

Traffic and other aviation activity forecasts of FAA, 1989 annual conf, 7504-28

Traffic and passenger enplanements, by airport, region, and State, projected FY89-2005 and trends from FY83, annual rpt, 7504-7

Traffic levels at FAA ATC facilities, by airport and State, FY88, annual rpt, 7504–27

see also Aviation accidents and safety

Air transportation

see Air cargo

see Air travel

see Airlines

see Airports and airways

see Military aviation

Air travel

Alaska airport dev plans and air systems operations, FY89-98, annual rpt, 7504–36

Canada travel to US by Province of residence, and characteristics of visit, by State, 1988, annual rpt, 2904–7

Communist and OECD countries air passenger-miles flown, 1960s-88, annual rpt, 9114–4.10

Consumer complaints against air carriers, agents, and cargo handlers, monthly rpt, 7302–11

Cuba economic conditions, agricultural and industrial production and distribution, trade, and intl economic relations, 1980-87 with trends from 1961, 9118–8

Energy use by mode of transport, fuel supply, and demographic and economic factors of vehicle use, 1970s-88, annual rpt, 3304–5

Fed Govt financial and nonfinancial domestic aid, 1989 base edition with supplements, annual listing, 104–5

Foreign travel from US, characteristics of visit and traveler, and world area of destination, 1988 in-flight survey, annual rpt, 2904–14

Foreign travel to and from US on US and foreign flag air carriers, by country, world area, and US port, monthly rpt, 7302–2

Foreign travel to and from US on US and foreign flag airlines, by world area, 1980-88, annual rpt, 2904–13

Foreign travel to US and Canada, market analyses with detailed trip and traveler characteristics, country rpt series, 2906–2

Foreign travel to US, by characteristics of visit and traveler, country, port city, and State of destination, monthly rpt, 2902–1

Foreign travel to US, characteristics of visit and traveler, world area of origin, and US destination, 1988 survey, annual rpt, 2904–12

Passenger enplanements and traffic, by airport, region, and State, projected FY89-2005 and trends from FY83, annual rpt, 7504–7

Passenger traffic, aircraft, pilots, airports, and fuel use, forecast FY89-2000 and trends from FY80, annual rpt, 7504–6

Passenger traffic, capacity, and performance, by carrier and type of operation, monthly rpt, 7302–6

Passenger traffic, capacity, and performance for medium regional airlines, by carrier, quarterly rpt, 7302–8

Price indexes for exports and imports of manufactured goods and services, quarterly press release, 6762–13

Reservation systems (computerized) finances, operations, and impacts on airline competitiveness, 1980s-86, 7308–193

Reservation systems (computerized) operating costs, fees, and market shares, by firm and location, 1984-87, hearing, 25528–108

Rural areas air service impacts of deregulation, and Federal subsidies, with data by location, 1978-87, 1278–17

Southeastern States, Fed Reserve 6th District, economic indicators by State and MSA, quarterly rpt, 9371–14

Statistical Abstract of US, social, political, and economic data, 1790-2025, comprehensive annual compilation, 2324–1.1; 2324–1.3

Tax (excise) collections of IRS, by source, quarterly rpt, 8302–1; 8302–2.1

Tax (excise) collections of IRS, by type of tax, region, and State, FY88, annual rpt, 8304–3.3

see also Aircraft

see also Airlines

see also Airports and airways

see also Aviation accidents and safety

see also Civil aviation

see also General aviation

see also Military aviation

see also Pilots

Aircraft

Alaska airport dev plans and air systems operations, FY89-98, annual rpt, 7504–36

Business statistics, detailed data for major industries and economic indicators, *Survey of Current Business*, monthly rpt, 2702–1.20

Communist, OECD, and selected other countries freight and carrier inventories, by mode of transport, 1960s-88, annual rpt, 9114–4.10

Costs of operating privately owned small planes by component, and Fed Govt mileage reimbursement rates, 1987, annual rpt, 9454–13

Customs Service activities, collections, entries processed by mode of transport, and seizures, FY84-88, annual rpt, 8144–1

Drug enforcement activities of State and local agencies, Federal aid by recipient, and background data, FY88, annual rpt, 6064–28

Drug smuggling aircraft interdiction activities of Fed Govt, funding, and radar system capabilities, by agency, FY82-89, GAO rpt, 26119–259

Exports of US, detailed commodities by country, monthly rpt, 2422–3

Flight and engine hours, and shutdown rates, by aircraft and engine model, and air carrier, monthly rpt, 7502–13

Foreign countries economic, social, political, and geographic summary data, by country, 1989, annual factbook, 9114–2

Freight (waterborne domestic and foreign) by commodity, traffic, and passengers, by port and waterway, 1987, annual rpt, 3754–3

General aviation aircraft, flight hours, and equipment, by type, use, and model of aircraft, region, and State, 1988, annual rpt, 7504–29

Herbicide use in natl forests, exposure and cancer risk by type and application mode, 1988 rpt, 1208–295

Imports of US, detailed Schedule A commodities by country, monthly rpt, 2422–2

Instrument flight rule aircraft handled, by user type, FAA traffic control center, and region, FY80-88 and projected to FY2000, annual rpt, 7504–15

Manufacturing annual survey, 1986: value of shipments, by SIC 4- to 5-digit product class, 2506–15.3

Manufacturing census, 1987: financial and operating data, for SIC 4-digit industries by product, preliminary rpt, 2491–1.76

OECD trade, total and for 4 major countries, and US trade by country, by commodity, 1970-87, world area rpt series, 9116–1

Police dept operations, staff, and expenses, for large cities by population size, 1987, 6066–19.51

Pollution (air) levels for 5 pollutants, by detailed source and State, 1986, annual rpt, 9194–7

Pollution (air) levels for 6 pollutants, by source, 1970-87 and trends from 1940, annual rpt, 9194–13

Price indexes (producer), by stage of processing and detailed commodity, monthly rpt, 6762–6

Price indexes (producer), by stage of processing and detailed commodity, monthly 1988, annual rpt, 6764–2

Registration of aircraft with FAA, by type and characteristics of aircraft, make, carrier, State, and county, 1988, annual rpt, 7504–3

Shipments, trade, use, and firms, by type of craft and engine, monthly Current Industrial Rpt, 2506–12.24

Statistical Abstract of US, social, political, and economic data, 1790-2025, comprehensive annual compilation, 2324–1.3

Traffic, aircraft, pilots, airports, and fuel use, forecast FY89-2000 and trends from FY80, annual rpt, 7504–6

Traffic and other aviation activity forecasts of FAA, 1989 annual conf, 7504–28

Whale (bowhead) population in Beaufort Sea, and aerial survey operations, Sept-Oct 1979-88, 5738–8

see also Aerospace industry

see also Aviation accidents and safety

see also Aviation fuels

see also Helicopters

see also Military aircraft

see also under By Commodity in the "Index by Categories"

Aircraft accidents

see Aviation accidents and safety

Aircraft carriers

see Naval vessels

Airlines

Air traffic control and airway facilities improvement activities under Natl Airspace System Plan, 1981-85 and projected to 2000, annual rpt, 7504–12

Aircraft registered with FAA, by type and characteristics of aircraft, make, carrier, State, and county, 1988, annual rpt, 7504–3

Business statistics, detailed data for major industries and economic indicators, *Survey of Current Business*, monthly rpt, 2702–1.8

Collective bargaining agreements expiring during year, and workers covered, by firm, union, industry group, and State, 1989, annual rpt, 6784–9

Commuter carrier and air taxi aircraft, hours flown, and equipment, by type and model of aircraft, region, and State, 1988, annual rpt, 7504–29

Competition and supply and demand factors impacts on fares, for flights to Cleveland, Ohio, 1987, article, 9377–1.903

Consumer complaints by reason, passengers denied boarding, and late flights, by reporting carrier and airport, monthly rpt, 7302–11

Consumer spending in metro and nonmetro areas, by item, 1987, article, 6722–1.962

County Business Patterns, 1987: employment, establishments, and payroll, by SIC 2- to 4-digit industry and county, annual State rpt series, 2326–8

CPI by component for US city average, and by region, population size, and for 27 metro areas, monthly rpt, 6762–2

Delays of flights caused by air traffic control procedures and problems, and costs, with data by airport, 1976-86, 7508–68

Developing countries disaster preparedness and economic, population, and political data, country rpt series, 9916–2

DOD shipments of military and personal property, passenger traffic, and costs, by service branch and mode of transport, quarterly rpt, 3702–1

Employee participation in decision-making and workplace reform, 1985-86 Western Airlines surveys, 6306–3.1; 6306–3.2

Employment, earnings, and hours, by selected SIC 1- to 4-digit industry, State, and for 262 MSAs, 1972-87, 6748–81

Employment, earnings, and hours, by SIC 1- to 4-digit industry, monthly 1983-Feb 1989, annual rpt, 6744–4

Employment of minorities and women, by occupation, SIC 1- to 3- digit industry, State, and MSA, 1986, annual rpt, 9244–1

Finances and operations, by SIC 2- to 4-digit industry, forecast 1989 with trends from 1950s, annual rpt, 2044–28

Finances, operations, vehicles, equipment, accidents, and energy use, by mode of transport, 1955-88, annual rpt, 7304–2

Financial data for airlines, by carrier, carrier group, and for total certificated system, quarterly rpt, 7302–7

Flight and engine hours, and shutdown rates, by aircraft and engine model, and air carrier, monthly rpt, 7502–13

Hijackings, on-board explosions, and other crime, US and foreign incidents, 1983-87, annual rpt, 7504–31

Labor disputes of airlines, Natl Mediation Board activities and caseloads, with data by carrier and union, FY85-86, annual rpt, 9604–1

Labor productivity, indexes of output, hours, and employment by SIC 2- to 4-digit industry, 1963-87, annual rpt, 6824–1.4

Merger of TWA and Ozark, impacts on fares and departures at St Louis, Mo, 1985-88, 7308–194

Reservation systems (computerized) for air travel, finances, operations, and impacts on airline competitiveness, 1980s-86, 7308–193

Rural areas air service impacts of deregulation, and Federal subsidies, with data by location, 1978-87, 1278–17

Science, engineering, and technical employment in transportation, utilities, and retail and wholesale trade, by field, occupation, and industry, 1985, triennial rpt, 9627–32

Statistical Abstract of US, social, political, and economic data, 1790-2025, comprehensive annual compilation, 2324–1.3

Tax (income) returns of corporations, income and tax items by asset size and detailed industry, 1986, annual rpt, 8304–4; 8304–21

Tax (income) returns of partnerships, income statement items by industry group, 1986, annual article, 8302–2.903

Tax (income) returns of sole proprietorships, income statement items, by industry group, 1987, annual article, 8302–2.904; 8302–2.921

Technological devs effect on labor force, composition, and productivity, by industry, 1960s-86 and projected to 2000, 6826–2.4

Traffic, aircraft, pilots, airports, and fuel use, forecast FY89-2000 and trends from FY80, annual rpt, 7504–6

Traffic and other aviation activity forecasts of FAA, 1989 annual conf, 7504–28

Traffic and passenger enplanements, by airport, region, and State, projected FY89-2005 and trends from FY83, annual rpt, 7504–7

Traffic, capacity, and performance, by carrier and type of operation, monthly rpt, 7302–6

Traffic, capacity, and performance for medium regional airlines, by carrier, quarterly rpt, 7302–8

Traffic levels at FAA air traffic control facilities, by airport and State, FY88, annual rpt, 7504–27

see also Aviation accidents and safety

see also By Industry in the "Index by Categories"

see also under By Individual Company or Institution in the "Index by Categories"

Airports and airways

Alaska airport dev plans and air systems operations, FY89-98, annual rpt, 7504–36

Alaska Arctic Natl Wildlife Refuge oil and gas production, reserves, exploration, and dev, 1981-89 and projected to 2003, 26358–200

Budget of US, special analysis of Federal capital spending by category, projected FY89-2005 and trends from FY81, annual rpt, 104–24

Charting and Geodetic Service of Natl Ocean Service activities and funding, by State, FY89-90, biennial rpt, 2174–10

Collisions (mid-air) prevention measures of FAA, and near collisions by type of air traffic control facility and selected airport, 1986-88, GAO rpt, 26113–426

Construction industries census, 1987: financial and operating data, preliminary industry rpt series, 2371–1

Crimes against civil aviation, and circumstances, US and worldwide, 1983-87, annual rpt, 7504–31

Developing countries disaster preparedness and economic, population, and political data, country rpt series, 9916–2

DOT planning and safety grants, by program, State, and for 38 SMSAs, FY88, annual rpt, 7304–7

FAA activities and finances, and staff by region, FY87-88, annual rpt, 7504–10

FAA air traffic control and airway facilities improvement under Natl Airspace System Plan, 1981-85 and projected to 2000, annual rpt, 7504–12

FAA airport improvement program grants and activities, by State and airport, FY88, annual rpt, 7504–38

FAA airport planning and dev project grants, by airport and location, quarterly press release, 7502–14

Fed Govt Airport and Airway Trust Fund finances and excise tax collections, FY71-88 and projected under alternative spending policies, FY89-94, 26308–84

Fed Govt Airport and Airway Trust Fund financial condition, monthly rpt, 8102–9.5

Fed Govt Airport and Airway Trust Fund funding and improvement spending, with data by airport and program, 1988 hearing, 21788–180

Fed Govt-owned real property inventory and costs, worldwide summary by purpose, agency, and location, 1987, annual rpt, 9454–5

Fed Govt spending in States, by type, program, agency, and State, FY88, annual rpt, 2464–2

Foreign countries economic, social, political, and geographic summary data, by country, 1989, annual factbook, 9114–2

Govt employment and payroll, by function, level of govt, and jurisdiction, 1987-88, annual rpt series, 2466–1

Govt finances, by level of govt, State, and for large cities and counties, annual rpt series, 2466–2

Immigration to US, alien workers, visitors, deportations, and naturalizations, by country, FY88 and trends from 1820, annual rpt, 6264–2

Passenger complaints, boarding denials, and late flights, by reporting carrier and airport, monthly rpt, 7302–11

Passenger travel to and from US on US and foreign flag air carriers, by country, world area, and US port, monthly rpt, 7302–2

Rural areas air service impacts of deregulation, and Federal subsidies, with data by location, 1978-87, 1278–17

Rural areas public transit services, operations and govt funding by region and State, 1986-87, 1278–11

Security operations of airports to prevent hijacking, screening failures and proposed FAA penalties by carrier, 1989 press release, 7306–10.2; 7306–10.3

Security operations of airports to prevent hijacking, screening results, enforcement actions, and hijacking attempts, 1st half 1988, semiannual rpt, 7502–5

Statistical Abstract of US, social, political, and economic data, 1790-2025, comprehensive annual compilation, 2324–1.3

Traffic, aircraft, pilots, airports, and fuel use, forecast FY89-2000 and trends from FY80, annual rpt, 7504–6

Traffic and other aviation activity forecasts of FAA, 1989 annual conf, 7504–28

Traffic and passenger enplanements, by airport, region, and State, projected FY89-2005 and trends from FY83, annual rpt, 7504–7

Traffic at top 50 airports, 1987, annual rpt, 7304–2.1

Traffic, delays, capacity improvement projects and funding, runway length, and navigational operations, for hub and reliever airports, 1986-87 and forecast to 1996, 7508–67

Traffic levels at FAA air traffic control facilities, by airport and State, FY88, annual rpt, 7504–27

Wilderness Natl Preservation System mgmt by Forest Service, regulation of commercial and recreational activities, and ranger views, 1985-88, GAO rpt, 26113–436

see also Air traffic control

see also Aviation accidents and safety

Aizcorbe, Ana M.

"Note on the Power of Nonparametric Tests", 6886–6.46

"Testing the Validity of Aggregates", 6886–6.32

Ajman

see United Arab Emirates

Akhtar, M. A.

"Adjustment of U.S. External Imbalances", 9385–2

"Developments in International Capital Mobility: A Perspective on the Underlying Forces and the Empirical Literature", 9385–9

"International Integration of Financial Markets and Domestic Monetary Policy: An Overview", 9385–9

"Monetary Policy Influence on the Economy: An Empirical Analysis", 9385–9

Akron, Ohio

CPI by component for US city average, and by region, population size, and for 15 metro areas, monthly rpt, 6762–1

CPI by component for US city average, and by region, population size, and for 27 metro areas, monthly rpt, 6762–2

see also under By City and By SMSA or MSA in the "Index by Categories"

Alabama

Agriculture census, 1987: farms, farmland, production and costs, and operator characteristics, advance State and county rpts, 2330–1.1

Agriculture census, 1987: farms, farmland, production, finances, and operator characteristics, by county, final State rpt, 2331–1.1

Appalachian Regional Commission funding, by project and State, planned FY89, annual rpt, 9084–3

Bank deposits in FDIC-insured commercial and savings banks, by instn, State, and county, as of June 1988, annual regional rpt, 9295–3.4

Births of low birthweight, by whether live, stillborn, and dying within 27 days, for Alabama, 1974-84, article, 4042–3.948

Coal production and mines by county, prices, productivity, miners, reserves, and stocks, by mining method and State, 1987-88, annual rpt, 3164–25

Collective bargaining calendar for southeastern States, 1989, annual rpt, 6946–1.73

County Business Patterns, 1987: employment, establishments, and payroll, by SIC 2- to 4-digit industry and county, annual State rpt, 2326–8.2

Deaths and rates, by detailed location, cause, and demographic characteristics, 1987, US Vital Statistics annual rpt, 4144–3.1

DOD prime contract awards, by contractor, service branch, State, and city, FY88, annual rpt, 3544–22

Economic indicators by State and MSA, Fed Reserve 6th District, quarterly rpt, 9371–14

Employment and housing market indicators by State, FHLB 4th District, quarterly rpt, 9302–36

Employment and unemployment, for 8 southeastern States, 1987-88, annual rpt, 6944–2

Employment by industry div, earnings, and hours, for 8 southeastern States, quarterly press release, 6942–7

Employment, earnings, and hours, by selected SIC 1- to 4-digit industry, State, and for 262 MSAs, 1972-87, 6748–81.1

Fed Govt spending in States and local areas, by type, State, county, and city, FY88, annual rpt, 2464–3

Fed Govt spending in States, by type, program, agency, and State, FY88, annual rpt, 2464–2

Fish and shellfish catch, wholesale receipts, prices, trade, and other market activities, weekly regional rpt, 2162–6.3

HHS financial aid, by program, recipient, State, and city, FY88, annual regional listing, 4004–3.4

Homeless children educational enrollment and needs, 1988, annual State rpt, 4804–35.2

Income (personal) per capita and by source, and earnings by industry div, by State, MSA, and county, 1982-87, annual regional rpt, 2704–2.4

Mineral Industry Surveys, State reviews of production, 1988, preliminary annual rpt, 5614–6

Minerals Yearbook, 1987, Vol 2 preprints: State review of production and sales by commodity, and business activity, annual rpt, 5604–16.2

Minerals Yearbook, 1987, Vol 2: State reviews of production, sales, and firms, by commodity, and business activity, annual rpt, 5604–34

Mobile home industry occupational injury and illness rates and workdays lost, by selected State, 1978-87, article, 6722–1.932

Retail trade census, 1987: employment, establishments, sales, and payroll, by SIC 2- to 4-digit kind of business, MSA, county, and city, State rpt, 2397–1.1

Savings instns, FHLB 4th District members finances and financial ratios, by State, quarterly rpt, 9302–3

Savings instns, FHLB 4th District members finances, by State, 1984-88, annual rpt, 9304–29.1

Service industries census, 1987: employment, establishments, receipts, and

payroll, by SIC 2- to 4-digit kind of business, MSA, county, and city, State rpt, 2391–1.1

Statistical Abstract of US, social, political, and economic data, with foreign comparisons, 1790-2025, comprehensive annual compilation, 2324–1

Textile mill employment, earnings, and hours, for 8 Southeastern States, quarterly press release, 6942–1

Water supply and quality in streams and lakes, and groundwater levels in wells, by drainage basin, 1987, annual State rpt, 5666–10.1

Water supply and quality in streams and lakes, and groundwater levels in wells, by drainage basin, 1988, annual State rpt, 5666–16.1

Wholesale trade census, 1987: employment, establishments, finances, and operations, by SIC 2- to 4-digit kind of business, MSA, county, and city, State rpt, 2405–1.1

Wildlife-related recreation, hunting, and fishing participation and spending, detailed data, 1985 survey, quinquennial State rpt, 5506–6.1

see also Birmingham, Ala.

see also Huntsville, Ala.

see also Jefferson County, Ala.

see also Mobile, Ala.

see also Montgomery, Ala.

see also Selma, Ala.

see also Walker County, Ala.

see also under By State in the "Index by Categories"

Alameda County, Calif.

Housing and households detailed characteristics, and unit and neighborhood quality, by location, 1985 survey, MSA rpt, 2485–6.10

Housing vacancy rates for single and multifamily units and mobile homes, by city and ZIP code, 1988, annual MSA rpt, 9304–20.13

Alamogordo, N.Mex.

Wages by occupation, for office and plant workers, 1989 survey, periodic MSA rpt, 6785–3.4

Alaska

Agricultural Statistics, 1988, annual rpt, 1004–1.2

Agriculture census, 1987: farms, farmland, production and costs, and operator characteristics, advance State and county rpts, 2330–1.2

Agriculture census, 1987: farms, farmland, production, finances, and operator characteristics, by county, final State rpt, 2331–1.2

Airport dev plans and air systems operations, for Alaska, FY89-98, annual rpt, 7504–36

Arctic Natl Wildlife Refuge oil and gas production and recovery, exploration and dev, and technologies, 1981-89 and projected to 2003, 26358–200

Arctic Natl Wildlife Refuge oil and gas resource assessment, with environmental impacts on North Slope and other locations, 1987 hearing, 21448–41

Arctic Natl Wildlife Refuge resources, native hunting activity, and energy exploration impact, 1985, last issue of annual rpt, 5504–26

Bank deposits in FDIC-insured commercial and savings banks, by instn, State, and county, as of June 1988, annual regional rpt, 9295-3.6

Birds (waterfowl) coastal population, breeding success, and diet, for murre and kittiwake at Cape Thompson, Alaska, 1960s-88, 5738-11

Coal production and mines by county, prices, productivity, miners, reserves, and stocks, by mining method and State, 1987-88, annual rpt, 3164-25

County Business Patterns, 1987: employment, establishments, and payroll, by SIC 2- to 4-digit industry and county, annual State rpt, 2326-8.3

Deaths and rates, by detailed location, cause, and demographic characteristics, 1987, US Vital Statistics annual rpt, 4144-3.1

DOD civilian and military personnel and dependents, by service branch and US and foreign location, quarterly rpt, 3542-20

DOD prime contract awards, by contractor, service branch, State, and city, FY88, annual rpt, 3544-22

Earthquakes in Alaska and Aleutian Islands, intensity, magnitude, time, and location, 1786-1981, 5668-87

Employment, earnings, and hours, by selected SIC 1- to 4-digit industry, State, and for 262 MSAs, 1972-87, 6748-81.1

Environmental conditions and oil dev impacts for Alaska OCS, compilation of papers, series, 2176-1

Fed Govt spending in States and local areas, by type, State, county, and city, FY88, annual rpt, 2464-3

Fed Govt spending in States, by type, program, agency, and State, FY88, annual rpt, 2464-2

Fish (Greenland turbot) catch, by Alaska coast fishery, 1960s-86, 2168-110

Fish and shellfish catch, wholesale receipts, prices, trade, and other market activities, weekly regional rpt, 2162-6.5

Freight (waterborne domestic and foreign) by commodity, traffic, and passengers, by port and waterway, 1987, annual rpt, 3754-3.4

HHS financial aid, by program, recipient, State, and city, FY88, annual regional listing, 4004-3.10

Homeless children educational enrollment and needs, 1988, annual State rpt, 4804-35.3

Ice conditions of Bering Sea and Alaska north coast, monthly rpt, 2182-5

Income (personal) per capita and by source, and earnings by industry div, by State, MSA, and county, 1982-87, annual regional rpt, 2704-2.5

Land area in Alaska by ownership, and availability for mineral exploration and dev, 1986, 5608-152

Marine mammal protection activities and funding, populations, and harvests, by species, 1987, annual rpt, 5504-12

Mineral Industry Surveys, State reviews of production, 1988, preliminary annual rpt, 5614-6

Minerals resources in sediment off north Alaska coast, 1985 study, 5668-95

Minerals resources of Alaska, production, oil and gas leases, and exploratory wells, with maps and bibl, 1987, annual rpt, 5664-11

Minerals Yearbook, 1987, Vol 2 preprints: State review of production and sales by commodity, and business activity, annual rpt, 5604-16.3

Minerals Yearbook, 1987, Vol 2: State reviews of production, sales, and firms, by commodity, and business activity, annual rpt, 5604-34

Nursing home compliance with Medicare and Medicaid regulations, and patient characteristics, by facility, 1987/88, annual State rpt, 4654-15.2

Oil and gas OCS reserves, and leasing and dev activity, 1988, annual regional rpt, 5736-3.1

Oil and gas OCS reserves of Fed Govt, leasing and exploration activity, production, revenue, and costs, by ocean area, FY88, annual rpt, 5734-4

Oil and gas supply, demand, and prices, alternative projections 1987-2000, annual rpt, 3164-89

Oil and lease condensate production on Alaska North Slope and other US areas, 1949-88, annual rpt, 3164-74.2

Oil crude, gas liquids, and refined products supply, demand, and movement, by PAD district and State, 1988 and trends from 1973, annual rpt, 3164-2

Radionuclide concentrations in air, water, humans, animals, and milk near Nevada and other nuclear test sites, 1988, annual rpt, 9194-17

Retail trade census, 1987: employment, establishments, sales, and payroll, by SIC 2- to 4-digit kind of business, MSA, county, and city, State rpt, 2397-1.2

Rural areas in Alaska, villages population characteristics and and subsistence activities, 1976-86, 5738-9

Savings instns, FHLB 12th District members deposits and lending, monthly press release, 9302-32.1

Service industries census, 1987: employment, establishments, receipts, and payroll, by SIC 2- to 4-digit kind of business, MSA, county, and city, State rpt, 2391-1.2

Statistical Abstract of US, social, political, and economic data, with foreign comparisons, 1790-2025, comprehensive annual compilation, 2324-1

Telecommunication domestic and overseas rates, by type of service and area served, various dates 1988, annual rpt, 9284-6.6

Tide height and time daily at coastal points, forecast 1990, annual rpt, 2174-2.1

Timber in northwestern US and British Columbia, production, prices, trade, and employment, quarterly rpt, 1202-3

Tsunamis intensity, time, location, and other characteristics, for US and territories, 1690-1988, 2158-52

Wages by occupation, for office and plant workers, 1989 survey, periodic labor market rpt, 6785-3.10

Water supply and quality in streams and lakes, and groundwater levels in wells, by drainage basin, 1987, annual State rpt, 5666-10.2

Water supply and quality in streams and lakes, and groundwater levels in wells, by drainage basin, 1988, annual State rpt, 5666-16.2

Water supply, and snow survey results, monthly State rpt, 1266-2.1

Water supply, and snow survey results, 1988, annual State rpt, 1264-14.2

Waterborne commerce (domestic) of US, freight by major commodity group, vessel type, and port, 1986, annual rpt, 7704-7

Wholesale trade census, 1987: employment, establishments, finances, and operations, by SIC 2- to 4-digit kind of business, MSA, county, and city, State rpt, 2405-1.2

Wildlife-related recreation, hunting, and fishing participation and spending, detailed data, 1985 survey, quinquennial State rpt, 5506-6.2

see also Alaska Natives
see also Aleutian Islands
see also Anchorage, Alaska
see also Fairbanks, Alaska
see also Gulf of Alaska
see also Nikishka, Alaska
see also Prudhoe Bay, Alaska
see also Seldovia, Alaska
see also Trans-Alaska Pipeline System
see also Valdez, Alaska
see also under By State in the "Index by Categories"

Alaska Natives

Alcohol use and abuse among minority groups, and related problems, by selected characteristics, 1985 conf papers, 4488-13

Arctic Natl Wildlife Refuge resources, native hunting activity, and energy exploration impact, 1985, last issue of annual rpt, 5504-26

Cancer cases and risk, for Alaska Natives by body site and ethnic group, 1969-83, article, 4042-3.963

Census of Population, 1980: selected socioeconomic data for Indians and Alaska Natives, by detailed origin, young readers pamphlet, 2326-1.6

Dental caries among Indian children from bottle feeding, prevention project effectiveness, 1985-89, article, 4042-3.961

Earnings of Indians and Alaska Natives, by urban-rural location and other characteristics, 1980, article, 1502-7.904

Education data compilation, students, staff, finances, and facilities, 1989 edition, annual rpt, 4824-2

Employment of minorities and women, by occupation, SIC 1- to 3-digit industry, State, and MSA, 1986, annual rpt, 9244-1

Health care spending, natl survey methodology, 1989 rpt, 4186-8.5

Health condition and other characteristics of Indians, and Indian Health Service facilities, funding, and operations, 1950s-88, annual chartbook, 4084-1

Hospitalization in Indian Health Service and contract facilities, by diagnosis, age, sex, and IHS service area, FY88, annual rpt, 4084-5; 4104-16

Housing and economic development program operations, by region, FY86-87, annual rpt, 5004-5

Land area in Alaska by ownership, and availability for mineral exploration and dev, 1986, 5608-152

Marine mammal protection activities and funding, populations, and harvests, by species, 1987, annual rpt, 5504–12

Rural areas in Alaska, villages population characteristics and and subsistence activities, 1976-86, 5738–9

Sexually transmitted disease cases among Indians, by State, 1988, article, 4042–3.955

Whale (bowhead) catch and quota for Eskimos, 1977-89, annual rpt, 14734–1

Alaska Power Administration

Finances and operations of Federal power admins, as of Sept 1987, annual rpt, 3164–23.4

Albania

Agricultural and food production and indexes, total and for selected commodities, by country, 1970s-88, annual rpt, 1524–12

Agricultural trade of US, by detailed commodity and country, 1988, semiannual rpt, 1522–4

Cuba economic conditions, agricultural and industrial production and distribution, trade, and intl economic relations, 1980-87 with trends from 1961, 9118–8

Economic and military aid and loans from US and intl agencies, by program and country, FY46-87, annual rpt, 9914–5

Economic, social, political, and geographic summary data, by country, 1989, annual factbook, 9114–2

Export licensing, monitoring, and enforcement activities, FY88, annual rpt, 2024–1

Exports and imports of US with Communist countries, by detailed commodity and country, quarterly rpt with articles, 9882–2

Human rights conditions in 170 countries, 1988, annual rpt, 21384–3

Military spending, arms trade, and force strengths, with govt spending and population, by country, 1977-87, annual rpt, 9824–1

Minerals Yearbook, 1987, Vol 3: foreign country reviews of production, trade, and policy, by commodity, annual rpt, 5604–35

Minerals Yearbook, 1987, Vol 3 preprints: foreign country review of production, trade, and policy, by commodity, annual rpt, 5604–23.2

Population size, growth rates, and components of change, by country, projected 1989-2020 and trends from 1950, biennial rpt, 2324–9

UN voting record and share of votes in agreement with US, by issue, country, and world area, 1988, annual rpt, 7004–18

see also under By Foreign Country in the "Index by Categories"

Albany, Ga.

see also under By SMSA or MSA in the "Index by Categories"

Albany, N.Y.

see also under By SMSA or MSA in the "Index by Categories"

Albritton, Robert B.

"Balanced Budgets and State Surpluses: The Politics of Budgeting in Illinois", 21528–72

Albuquerque, N.Mex.

Wages by occupation, for office and plant workers, 1989 survey, periodic MSA rpt, 6785–3.10

see also under By City and By SMSA or MSA in the "Index by Categories"

Alcohol abuse and treatment

Abuse of alcohol, related injury and illness, series, 4486–1

Abuse of drugs and alcohol, by type, age, sex, race, and region, 1988 survey, biennial rpt, 4494–5

Abuse of drugs in combination with alcohol, emergency room admissions and deaths by major metro area, July-Dec 1988, semiannual rpt, 4492–3

Abuse of drugs in combination with alcohol, emergency room admissions and deaths by sex, race, age, and major metro area, 1988, annual rpt, 4494–8

Abuse of drugs in combination with alcohol, indicators for selected metro areas, research results, data collection, and policy issues, 1989 semiannual conf, 4492–5

Arrests, by offense, offender characteristics, and location, 1988, annual rpt, 6224–2.2

Assistance (financial and nonfinancial) of Fed Govt, 1989 base edition with supplements, annual listing, 104–5

Crime, criminal justice admin and enforcement, and public opinion, data compilation, 1970s-88, annual rpt, 6064–6

Deaths and rates, by detailed cause and demographic characteristics, 1986 and trends from 1900, US Vital Statistics annual rpt, 4144–2

Genetic and other factors in drug abuse, 1986 conf papers, 4498–60

Genetic factors for alcoholism, for Asian and white populations, 1989 article, 4042–3.959

HHS financial aid, by program, recipient, State, and city, FY88, annual regional listings, 4004–3

High school seniors drug and alcohol use, by type and frequency, 1975-88, annual rpt, 4824–2.13

Homeless population characteristics, needs, and impacts of govt aid programs and housing costs, 1988 conf papers, 10048–73

Homeless shelters services, operations, and client characteristics, 1988 survey, 5188–123

Hospital mental health care units, length of stay related to patient, instn, and State Medicaid program characteristics, 1981, article, 4652–1.924

Hospitals alcohol abuse treatment, capacity, use, and patients by diagnosis, 1980 and 1985, 4186–9.3

Hospitals for mental health care of States and counties, patients and admissions by age, diagnosis, and State, FY87, annual rpt, 4504–2

Indian Health Service facilities, funding, operations, and Indian health and other characteristics, 1950s-88, annual chartbook, 4084–1

Indian youth suicide attempts, potential, and risk factors, longitudinal study, 1989 article, 4042–3.958

Insurance (health) coverage and provisions of employee benefit plans, by plan type and occupational group, 1988, annual rpt, 6784–19

Juvenile delinquency prevention funding, by program and Federal agency, FY88, annual rpt, 6064–11

Military deaths by cause, age, race, and rank, and personnel captured and missing, by service branch, 2nd half FY88, semiannual rpt, 3542–21

Military personnel alcohol and drug abuse, prevalence and consequences, by selected characteristics, 1988, biennial rpt, 3504–19

Minority group alcohol use and abuse, and related problems, by selected characteristics, 1985 conf papers, 4488–13

Navy drug and alcohol abuse education and treatment program activity, 2nd half FY88, semiannual tables, 3802–6

Parole and probation clients in program for drug- and alcohol-dependent Federal offenders, as of various dates 1984-89, annual rpt, 18204–2.5; 18204–8.4

Preventive disease and health improvement goals and recommended activities for 2000, with trends 1970s-80s, 4048–10

Prisoners in State instns, by offense, criminal history, and inmate, family, and victim characteristics, 1986, annual rpt, 6064–26.3

Public opinion on drinking and alcoholism, by respondent characteristics, 1985-87 surveys, annual rpt, 6064–6.3

Racial and ethnic groups alcohol use, abuse, treatment, and views, for US and native countries, by selected characteristics, 1988 compilation of papers, 4488–12

Research grants and awards of ADAMHA, by recipient, FY88, annual listing, 4044–13

Research on alcoholism, treatment programs, and patient characteristics, quarterly journal, 4482–1

Treatment facilities for alcohol abuse, and related services use, by program, facility type, and State, biennial rpt, discontinued, 4484–5

Treatment facilities for drug and alcohol abuse, services, use, funding, and client characteristics, 1987, annual rpt, 4494–10

Treatment facilities for drug and alcohol abuse, staff, and program characteristics, series, discontinued, 4496–8

Treatment facilities for drug and alcohol abuse, use, funding, and client and staff characteristics, series, discontinued, 4496–7

VA health care facilities mental health services, staff, research, and training programs, 1989 biennial listing, 8704–2

Youth drug, alcohol, and cigarette use and attitudes, by substance type and selected characteristics, 1975-88 surveys, annual rpt, 4494–4

see also Driving while intoxicated

see also Drug and alcohol testing

Alcohol, Drug Abuse, and Mental Health Administration

Budget of US Appendix, obligations, appropriations, and personnel, by program and agency, FY90, annual rpt, 104–3

Illegal aliens enforcement activity of Coast Guard, by nationality, 2nd half FY89, semiannual rpt, 7402–4

Illegal aliens welfare benefits, operations of Federal-State system to prevent payment, State official views, 1988, GAO rpt, 26121–276

Illegal entry and smuggling of aliens, Federal sentencing guidelines by offense and circumstances, 1989 rpt, 17668–1

Malaria cases in US, for military personnel and US and foreign civilians, and by country of infection, 1966-87, annual rpt, 4205–4

OASDI benefits for nonresident aliens, payments and withholdings, 1984-87 and alternative projections to 1997, actuarial rpt, 4706–1.103

Population not registered to vote, total and without US citizenship, by selected characteristics, 1988 presidential election, biennial Current Population Rpt, 2546–1.440

Science and engineering PhDs employment and other characteristics, by field and State, 1987, biennial rpt, 9627–18

Statistical Abstract of US, social, political, and economic data, 1790-2025, comprehensive annual compilation, 2324–1.1

Supplemental Security Income alien recipients, by legal status, for applications made 1974-87, annual rpt, 4744–3.8

Tuberculosis cases and deaths, by patient characteristics, State, and city, 1987 and trends from 1953, annual rpt, 4204–10

Visas of US issued and refused to immigrants and nonimmigrants, by class, issuing office, and nationality, FY88, annual rpt, 7184–1

Visas of US issued at Foreign Service posts, by category and world area, selected years FY84-88, annual rpt, 7184–4

see also Alien workers
see also Citizenship
see also Deportation
see also Foreign students
see also Immigration and emigration
see also Mexicans in the U.S.
see also Refugees

Alig, Ralph J.
"Economic Factors Influencing Land Use Changes in the South-Central U.S.", 1208–296

Alimony
see Child support and alimony

Allen-Hagen, Barbara
"Preliminary Estimates Developed on Stranger Abduction Homicides of Children", 6066–27.1

Allen, John W.
"Directions in Food Marketing: Responding to Consumers of Tommorrow", 1004–16.1

Allen, Linda
"Incentives To Engage in Bank Window-Dressing: Manager vs. Stockholder Conflicts", 9387–8.188

Allen, Richmond
"Effectiveness and Economic Development Impact of Policy-Based Cash Transfer Programs: The Case of Jamaica, 1981-87", 9916–3.56

Allentown, Pa.
see also under By City and By SMSA or MSA in the "Index by Categories"

Allergies
Cases of acute and chronic conditions, disability, absenteeism, and health services use, by selected characteristics, 1988, annual rpt, 4147–10.170

Deaths and rates, by detailed cause and demographic characteristics, 1986 and trends from 1900, US Vital Statistics annual rpt, 4144–2

Natl Inst of Allergy and Infectious Diseases activities, grants by recipient and location, and disease incidence, FY81-88, annual rpt, 4474–30

Allied health personnel
Educational and research grants and contracts of Health Professions Bur, by instn and program, FY88, annual listing, 4114–1

Emergency fire and medical services operations, staff, and finances, for DC and compared to other US and Canadian cities, 1986, hearing, 21308–25

Military health care personnel, and accessions by training source, by occupation, specialty, and service branch, FY87, annual rpt, 3544–24

Physicians assistants, by State, 1985-87, 25148–41

Rural areas health care facilities, staffing, services accessibility, and indicators of need, 1960s-88, 25148–41

Texas-Mexico border area health facilities and services, with background data, by Texas county, 1980s-88, GAO rpt, 26121–261

Training support grants of Bur of Health Professions, by program, region, and State, FY80-87, 4118–62

VA Medicine and Surgery Dept trainees, by detailed program and city, FY88, annual rpt, 8704–4

see also Clinical laboratory technicians
see also Dietitians and nutritionists
see also Midwives

Allred, Amy J.
"Sweetpotatoes vs. Yams: A Commodity Highlight", 1561–11.901

Alonso, Jose F.
"Cuba's Sugar Economy: Recent Performance and Challenges for the 1990's", 1561–14.903

Alpena, Mich.
Wages by occupation, for office and plant workers, 1989 survey, periodic MSA rpt, 6785–3.8

Alton, Ill.
see also under By SMSA or MSA in the "Index by Categories"

Alton, Miles S.
"Greenland Turbot, *Reinhardtius hippoglossoides,* of the Eastern Bering Sea and Aleutian Island Region", 2168–110

Altoona, Pa.
see also under By SMSA or MSA in the "Index by Categories"

Altus, Okla.
Wages by occupation, for office and plant workers, 1989 survey, periodic MSA rpt, 6785–3.4

Aluminum and aluminum industry
Building materials PPI, by type, bimonthly rpt, 2042–1.5

Business statistics, detailed data for major industries and economic indicators, *Survey of Current Business,* monthly rpt, 2702–1.14

Castings (nonferrous) shipments, by metal type, monthly Current Industrial Rpt, 2506–10.5

Communist, OECD, and selected other countries minerals production, by commodity, 1960s-88, annual rpt, 9114–4.7

County Business Patterns, 1987: employment, establishments, and payroll, by SIC 2- to 4-digit industry and county, annual State rpt series, 2326–8

Electric power use and prices, shipments, and trade, for 25 SIC 4-digit manufacturing industries, 1972-86, 2048–137

Electric utilities serving aluminum smelters, effects of proposed sulfur dioxide abatement legislation on operating costs, 1985, 5608–155

Employment, earnings, and hours, by SIC 1- to 4-digit industry, monthly 1983-Feb 1989, annual rpt, 6744–4

Energy use and prices for manufacturing industries, 1985 survey, series, 3166–13

Exports and imports of US shipped through Canada, by detailed commodity, customs district, and country, 1987, annual rpt, 7704–11

Exports of US, detailed commodities by country, monthly rpt, 2422–3

Finances and operations, by SIC 2- to 4-digit industry, forecast 1989 with trends from 1950s, annual rpt, 2044–28

Foreign and US aluminum plant ownership, capacity, energy and aluminum sources, and startup and closing dates, by plant and location, 1988, annual listing, 5604–49

Foreign countries mineral production, reserves, and industry role in domestic economy and world supply, world area and country rpt series, 5606–1

Freight (waterborne domestic and foreign) by commodity, traffic, and passengers, by port and waterway, 1987, annual rpt, 3754–3

Imports of US, detailed Schedule A commodities by country, monthly rpt, 2422–2

Imports of US given duty-free treatment for value of US material sent abroad, and impacts on US industry and employment, by commodity and country, 1987, annual rpt, 9884–14

Injuries from use of consumer products, by severity, victim age, and detailed product, 1988, annual rpt, 9164–6

Labor productivity, indexes of output, hours, and employment by SIC 2- to 4-digit industry, 1963-87, annual rpt, 6824–1.3

Manufacturing annual survey, 1986: financial and operating data, by SIC 2- to 4-digit industry, series, 2506–15

Manufacturing census, 1987: financial and operating data, for SIC 4-digit industries by product, preliminary rpt, 2491–1.52; 2491–1.53; 2491–1.54; 2491–1.55; 2491–1.57; 2491–1.58

Mineral Industry Surveys, commodity review of production, trade, stocks, and use, monthly rpt, 5612–1.1

Mineral Industry Surveys, commodity review of production, trade, stocks, and use, quarterly rpt, 5612–2.2

Minerals Yearbook, 1987, Vol 1: commodity reviews of production, use, trade, prices, and mining operations, annual rpt, 5604–33

Minerals Yearbook, 1987, Vol 1 preprints: commodity review of production, reserves, supply, use, and trade, annual rpt, 5604–15.4; 5604–15.8

Minerals Yearbook, 1987, Vol 2 preprints: State reviews of production and sales by commodity, and business activity, annual rpt series, 5604–16

Minerals Yearbook, 1987, Vol 2: State reviews of production, sales, and firms, by commodity, and business activity, annual rpt, 5604–34

Minerals Yearbook, 1987, Vol 3: foreign country reviews of production, trade, and policy, by commodity, annual rpt, 5604–35

Minerals Yearbook, 1987, Vol 3 preprints: foreign country reviews of production, trade, and policy, by commodity, annual rpt series, 5604–23

Minerals Yearbook, 1988, Vol 2 rpts: State reviews of production and sales by commodity, and business activity, annual rpt series, 5604–22

Occupational injuries and incidence, employment, and hours in metal mines and related operations, 1987, annual rpt, 6664–3

Occupational injury and illness rates, by SIC 2- to 4-digit industry, 1987, annual rpt, 6844–1

OECD trade, total and for 4 major countries, and US trade by country, by commodity, 1970-87, world area rpt series, 9116–1

Pacific Northwest aluminum industry electricity purchased from Bonneville Power Admin, by customer, FY88, annual rpt, 3224–1

Pacific Northwest aluminum industry electricity purchased from Bonneville Power Admin, by customer, 1988, semiannual rpt, 3222–1

Price indexes (producer), by stage of processing and detailed commodity, monthly rpt, 6762–6

Price indexes (producer), by stage of processing and detailed commodity, monthly 1988, annual rpt, 6764–2

Production, prices, trade, use, employment, tariffs, and stockpiles, by mineral, with foreign comparisons, 1984-88, annual rpt, 5604–18

Production, use, reserves, Federal lands availability for mining, and environmental impacts, for strategic minerals, 1950s-80s, 028–33

Science and engineering employment, by nonmanufacturing industry and field, 1987, triennial rpt, 9627–31

Shipments (defense and total), trade, use, and inventories of aluminum ingots and mill products, monthly Current Industrial Rpt, 2506–10.9

Statistical Abstract of US, social, political, and economic data, 1790-2025, comprehensive annual compilation, 2324–1.3

Stockpiling of strategic material by Fed Govt, activity, and inventory by commodity, as of Sept 1989, semiannual rpt, 3542–22; 3902–2

Stockpiling of strategic material, inventories and needs, by commodity, as of Sept 1988, annual rpt, 3544–37

Stockpiling of strategic material, inventories, costs, and goals by commodity, as of June 1989, semiannual rpt, 3902–3

Supply, demand, trade, and foreign and US industry devs by firm and country, for strategic minerals by commodity, bimonthly rpt with articles, 5602–4

Wire and cable (insulated) shipments, trade, use, and firms, by product, 1987-88, annual Current Industrial Rpt, 2506–10.8

see also under By Commodity in the "Index by Categories"

Aluminum Co. of America

Tennessee Valley river control activities, and hydroelectric power generation and capacity, 1984, annual rpt, 9804–7

Aluminum sulfate

see Chemicals and chemical industry

Alvic, Donald R.

"Potential Impact of Acid Rain Legislation on the Domestic Aluminum Smelting Industry", 5608–155

Amarillo, Tex.

see also under By City and By SMSA or MSA in the "Index by Categories"

Ambulatory aids

see Prosthetics and orthotics

Amel, Dean F.

"Do Firms Differ Much?", 9366–6.201

"Dynamics of Market Concentration", 9366–6.188

"Trends in Banking Structure Since the Mid-1970s", 9362–1.902

Amendola, G.

"Occurrence and Fate of PCDDs and PCDFs in Five Bleached Kraft Pulp and Paper Mills", 21368–112

American Battle Monuments Commission

Budget of US Appendix, obligations, appropriations, and personnel, by program and agency, FY90, annual rpt, 104–3

Budget of US, authoritative financial statements with appropriations, outlays, and receipts, by category and agency, FY88, annual rpt, 8104–2.2

American Federation of Teachers

Membership in AFT, 1955-87, article, 6722–1.931

American Forces Information Service

"Defense '89: Almanac", 3504–13

American Gas Association

"Peak-Quarter Conservation in the Residential Market: 1973-86", 21368–107

American Historical Association

Financial statements of AHA, and membership by State, 1988, annual rpt, 29574–2

American Housing Survey

Data coverage and availability of Census Bur rpts and data files, 1989 annual listing, 2304–2

Housing and households characteristics, MSA surveys, fact sheet series, 2485–11

Housing and households detailed characteristics, and unit and neighborhood quality, by location, 1985, biennial rpt, 2485–12

Housing and households detailed characteristics, and unit and neighborhood quality, MSA surveys, series, 2485–6

American Indians

see Indians

American Medical Association Council on Scientific Affairs

"Firearms Injuries and Deaths: A Critical Public Health Issue", 4042–3.906

American Motors Corp.

Safety of domestic and foreign autos, crash test results by model, model years 1984-88, 7768–111

American National Red Cross

Activities of Red Cross, finances, volunteers, and certificates issued, by program, FY88, annual rpt, 29254–1

Blood program activities of Red Cross, annual summary rpt, suspended, 29254–4

American Nurses' Association

Collective bargaining coverage and membership of ANA, 1956-88, article, 6722–1.946

American Samoa

Bank deposits in FDIC-insured commercial and savings banks, by instn, State, and county, as of June 1988, annual regional rpt, 9295–3.6

Census of Population and Housing, 1990: outlying areas preparations for count, hearings, 21628–74

Economic, social, political, and geographic summary data, by country, 1989, annual factbook, 9114–2

Exports and imports between US and outlying areas, by detailed commodity and mode of transport, monthly rpt, 2422–4

Fed Govt spending in States and local areas, by type, State, county, and city, FY88, annual rpt, 2464–3

Fed Govt spending in States, by type, program, agency, and State, FY88, annual rpt, 2464–2

Harbor traffic, facilities, dev, funding, and needs, for Pacific territories and Hawaii by port, as of 1987, 7308–195

HHS financial aid, by program, recipient, State, and city, FY88, annual regional listing, 4004–3.9

Minerals Yearbook, 1987, Vol 2: State reviews of production, sales, and firms, by commodity, and business activity, annual rpt, 5604–34

Population size and components of change, by outlying area, 1980-88, annual Current Population Rpt, 2546–3.162

Population size, growth rates, and components of change, by country, projected 1989-2020 and trends from 1950, biennial rpt, 2324–9

Water supply and quality in streams and lakes, and groundwater levels in wells, by drainage basin, 1987, annual State rpt, 5666–10.10

see also under By Outlying Area in the "Index by Categories"

American Schools and Hospitals Abroad

AID economic aid to developing countries, obligations and disbursements by country, quarterly rpt, 9912–4

Developing countries economic and social conditions from 1960s, and Intl Dev Cooperation Agency and AID activities and funding, FY88-90, annual rpt, 9904–4

American Stock Exchange
Capital gains tax rate changes effect on transactions by asset type, and stock exchange trading volume, late 1970s-88, article, 9373–1.901

Statistical Abstract of US, social, political, and economic data, 1790-2025, comprehensive annual compilation, 2324–1.3

Trading volume and new issue registrations, monthly rpt, 9732–1

Trading volume on New York and American Stock Exchanges, monthly rpt, 9362–1.1

Trading volume, securities listed by type, and finances, by exchange, selected years 1935-88, annual rpt, 9734–2.1; 9734–2.3

American Telephone and Telegraph Co.
Finances and operations, detail for telephone firms, 1987, annual rpt, 9284–6

Finances and operations of local and long distance firms, subscribership, and charges, 1970s-FY89, semiannual rpt, 9282–7

Finances, operations, and industry devs for telecommunications, with data by service type, firm, and country, 1950s-80s, 2808–27

Labor union (Intl Brotherhood of Electrical Workers) membership of AT&T workers, by local, 1981 and 1987, hearings, 21368–113

Rates for long distance intrastate calls, impact of State entry and price regulation, 1983-87, 9406–1.55

Ames Laboratory
see also Department of Energy National Laboratories

Amman, Gene D.
"Lodgepole Pine Vigor, Regeneration, and Infestation by Mountain Pine Beetle Following Partial Cutting on the Shoshone National Forest, Wyoming", 1208–297

Ammann, William C.
"National Urban Mass Transportation Statistics: 1986 Section 15 Annual Report", 7884–4

Ammonia
see Chemicals and chemical industry

Ammunition
County Business Patterns, 1987: employment, establishments, and payroll, by SIC 2- to 4-digit industry and county, annual State rpt series, 2326–8

Criminal cases by type and disposition, and collections, for US attorneys, by Federal district, FY88, annual rpt, 6004–2.1

DOD budget, procurement appropriations by item, service branch, and defense agency, FY88-91, annual rpt, 3544–32

DOD outlays and obligations, by function and service branch, quarterly rpt, 3542–3

DOD prime contract awards, by category, contract and contractor type, and service branch, FY79-88, semiannual rpt, 3542–1

DOD prime contract awards, by category, contractor type, and State, FY86-88, annual rpt, 3544–11

DOD prime contract awards, by detailed procurement category, FY85-88, annual rpt, 3544–18

DOD shipments of military and personal property, passenger traffic, and costs, by service branch and mode of transport, quarterly rpt, 3702–1

Employment, earnings, and hours, by SIC 1- to 4-digit industry, monthly 1983-Feb 1989, annual rpt, 6744–4

Exports of US, detailed commodities by country, monthly rpt, 2422–3

Freight (waterborne domestic and foreign) by commodity, traffic, and passengers, by port and waterway, 1987, annual rpt, 3754–3

Hunting, fishing, and other wildlife-related recreation participation and spending, detailed data by location, 1985 survey, quinquennial rpt, 5508–5

Hunting, fishing, and other wildlife-related recreation participation and spending, detailed data, 1985 survey, quinquennial State rpt series, 5506–6

Imports of US, detailed Schedule A commodities by country, monthly rpt, 2422–2

Imports of US given duty-free treatment for value of US material sent abroad, and impacts on US industry and employment, by commodity and country, 1987, annual rpt, 9884–14

Manufacturing annual survey, 1986: financial and operating data, by SIC 2- to 4-digit industry, series, 2506–15

Manufacturing census, 1987: financial and operating data, for SIC 4-digit industries by product, preliminary rpt, 2491–1.59

Occupational injury and illness rates, by SIC 2- to 4-digit industry, 1987, annual rpt, 6844–1

OECD trade, total and for 4 major countries, and US trade by country, by commodity, 1970-87, world area rpt series, 9116–1

Price indexes (producer), by stage of processing and detailed commodity, monthly rpt, 6762–6

Price indexes (producer), by stage of processing and detailed commodity, monthly 1988, annual rpt, 6764–2

Science, engineering, and technical employment in manufacturing, by field, occupation, and industry, 1986, triennial rpt, 9627–23

Tax (excise) collections of IRS, by source, quarterly rpt, 8302–1

Tax (excise) collections of IRS, by type of tax, region, and State, FY88, annual rpt, 8304–3.3

Tax (income) returns of corporations, income and tax items by asset size and detailed industry, 1986, annual rpt, 8304–4; 8304–21

Amnesties
see Pardons

Amtrak
see National Railroad Passenger Corp.

Anaheim, Calif.
CPI by component for US city average, and by region, population size, and for 15 metro areas, monthly rpt, 6762–1

CPI by component for US city average, and by region, population size, and for 27 metro areas, monthly rpt, 6762–2

Housing starts and completions authorized by building permits in 40 MSAs, quarterly rpt, 2382–9

Wages by occupation, and benefits for office and plant workers, 1988 survey, periodic MSA rpt, 6785–11.3

see also under By City and By SMSA or MSA in the "Index by Categories"

Anchorage, Alaska
CPI by component for US city average, and by region, population size, and for 27 metro areas, monthly rpt, 6762–2

Tide height and time daily at coastal points, forecast 1990, annual rpt, 2174–2.1

see also under By City and By SMSA or MSA in the "Index by Categories"

Anderson, Barbara A.
"Composition of Foods: Lamb, Veal, and Game Products", 1356–3.11

Anderson, Ind.
see also under By SMSA or MSA in the "Index by Categories"

Anderson, Margot
"Technology: Are We Running Out of Steam?", 1522–3.909

Anderson, S.C.
see also under By SMSA or MSA in the "Index by Categories"

Andorra
Economic, social, political, and geographic summary data, by country, 1989, annual factbook, 9114–2

Population size, growth rates, and components of change, by country, projected 1989-2020 and trends from 1950, biennial rpt, 2324–9

see also under By Foreign Country in the "Index by Categories"

Andrews, Roxanne M.
"Acquired Immunodeficiency Syndrome in California's Medicaid Program, 1981-84", 4652–1.907

Anemia
see Blood diseases and disorders
see Nutrition and malnutrition
see Sickle cell anemia

Anesthesiology
Educational and research grants and contracts of Health Professions Bur, by instn and program, FY88, annual listing, 4114–1

HHS financial aid, by program, recipient, State, and city, FY88, annual regional listings, 4004–3

Labor supply of certified RN anesthetists and anesthesiologists, by State, 1986, 25148–41

Malpractice claims and payments, by procedure and physician specialty, 1975-78, hearing, 21408–113

Medicare discharges, charges, and length of stay, by State and diagnosis, 1983 and 1985, article, 4652–1.925

Medicare enrollees physician and other services use, benefits, charges, and coinsurance and deductible obligations, 1982-86, article, 4652–1.901

Medicare physicians services use, charges, and reimbursement, by service type, setting, and specialty, 1986, article, 4652–1.936

Military health care personnel, and accessions by training source, by occupation, specialty, and service branch, FY87, annual rpt, 3544–24

Military reserve medical personnel, by specialty and reserve component, FY88, annual rpt, 3544–31.2

Training support grants of Bur of Health Professions, by program, region, and State, FY80-87, 4118–62

VA health care facilities physicians, dentists, and nurses, by selected employment characteristics and VA district, quarterly rpt, 8602–6

Angell, Wayne D.

"Economic Situation and Outlook", 1004–16.1

Angelo, Luigi

"Sugarbeet and Sugarcane Production and Processing Costs, 1987 Crop", 1561–14.906

Angola

Agricultural and food production and indexes, total and for selected commodities, by country, 1970s-88, annual rpt, 1524–12

Agricultural production, prices, and trade, by country, 1960s-89, annual world region rpt, 1524–4.2

Agricultural trade of US, by detailed commodity and country, 1988, semiannual rpt, 1522–4

Economic and military aid and loans from US and intl agencies, by program and country, FY46-87, annual rpt, 9914–5

Economic conditions, policy, and trade practices, by country, 1986-88, annual rpt, 21384–5

Economic, social, political, and geographic summary data, by country, 1989, annual factbook, 9114–2

Exports and imports of US, by commodity and country, 1970-87, world area rpt, 9116–1.4

Exports and imports of US, by selected country, country group, and commodity group, 1988, annual rpt, 2044–37

Human rights conditions in 170 countries, 1988, annual rpt, 21384–3

Military spending, arms trade, and force strengths, with govt spending and population, by country, 1977-87, annual rpt, 9824–1

Minerals Yearbook, 1987, Vol 3: foreign country reviews of production, trade, and policy, by commodity, annual rpt, 5604–35

Minerals Yearbook, 1987, Vol 3 preprints: foreign country review of production, trade, and policy, by commodity, annual rpt, 5604–23.4

Population size, growth rates, and components of change, by country, projected 1989-2020 and trends from 1950, biennial rpt, 2324–9

UN voting record and share of votes in agreement with US, by issue, country, and world area, 1988, annual rpt, 7004–18

see also under By Foreign Country in the "Index by Categories"

Anguilla

Economic, social, political, and geographic summary data, by country, 1989, annual factbook, 9114–2

Population size, growth rates, and components of change, by country, projected 1989-2020 and trends from 1950, biennial rpt, 2324–9

Animal and Plant Health Inspection Service

Animal protection, licensing, and inspection activities of USDA, and animals used in research, by State, FY88, annual rpt, 1394–10

Budget of US Appendix, obligations, appropriations, and personnel, by program and agency, FY90, annual rpt, 104–3

Cattle tuberculosis cases and cooperative Federal-State eradication activities, by State, FY88, annual rpt, 1394–13

Foreign and US animal disease outbreaks, quarterly rpt, 1392–3

Natl Veterinary Services Labs activities, biologic drug products evaluation and disease testing, FY88, annual rpt, 1394–17

Plant pests and diseases entering US, by type of pest and host, country, and State, FY87, annual rpt, 1394–16

Poultry Natl Improvement Plan coverage of hatcheries and birds, by species, disease program, and State, 1988, annual rpt, 1394–15

Animal diseases and zoonoses

Cattle tuberculosis cases and cooperative Federal-State eradication activities, by State, FY88, annual rpt, 1394–13

Deaths and rates, by detailed cause and demographic characteristics, 1986 and trends from 1900, US Vital Statistics annual rpt, 4144–2

Fish and shellfish aquaculture in US and Japan, mgmt, methods, and biological data for selected species, 1985 conf papers, annual rpt, 2164–15

Fish and Wildlife Service conservation and research project descriptions and results, FY87-88, biennial rpt, 5504–20

Fishery mgmt and R&D, Fed Govt grants by project and State, and rpts, 1987, annual listing, 2164–3

Fishery research of State fish and wildlife agencies, federally funded projects and costs by species and State, 1989, annual listing, 5504–23

Foreign and US animal disease outbreaks, quarterly rpt, 1392–3

Inspection of meat and poultry for domestic use and export, and rejections by cause, by type of animal and product, FY88, annual rpt, 1374–3

Morbidity and Mortality Weekly Report, infectious notifiable disease cases by age and State, and deaths, 1930s-88, annual rpt, 4204–1

Morbidity and Mortality Weekly Report, infectious notifiable disease cases by State, and public health issues, 4202–1

Natl Veterinary Services Labs activities, biologic drug products evaluation and disease testing, FY88, annual rpt, 1394–17

Poultry Natl Improvement Plan coverage of hatcheries and birds, by species, disease program, and State, 1988, annual rpt, 1394–15

Poultry slaughtered under Fed Govt inspection, pounds certified, and condemnations by cause, by State, monthly rpt, 1625–3

Research (agricultural) funding and staffing for USDA, State agencies, and other instns, by topic, FY88, annual rpt, 1744–2

Wildlife research of State fish and wildlife agencies, federally funded projects and costs by species and State, 1989, annual listing, 5504–24

see also Rabies

see also Veterinary medicine

Animal experimentation

Biotechnology legal, ethical, and economic issues, series, 26356–5

Cell cultures for aging research, availability and cultures shipped, 1989 listing, 4478–187

HHS financial aid, by program, recipient, State, and city, FY88, annual regional listings, 4004–3

Licensing and inspection of facilities, and other animal protection activities of USDA, with animals used in research, by State, FY88, annual rpt, 1394–10

NIH activities, funding by program and recipient type, staff, and clinic patients, by inst, FY87, annual rpt, 4434–3

Pollutants health effects, concentrations in food and environment, sources, and human intake methodology and data needs, series, 9186–9

Reproduction and population research, Fed Govt funding by project, FY87, annual listing, 4474–9

Animal feed

Acreage planted, by selected crop and State, 1980-88 and planned 1989, annual rpt, 1621–22

Agricultural data compilation, 1987/88 and trends from 1920, annual rpt, 1004–14

Agricultural Stabilization and Conservation Service producer payments, by program and State, 1988, annual rpt, 1804–12

Agricultural Stabilization and Conservation Service producer payments, by program, monthly rpt, 1802–10

Agricultural Statistics, 1988, annual rpt, 1004–1

Agriculture census, 1987: farms, farmland, production and costs, and operator characteristics, advance State and county rpt series, 2330–1

Agriculture census, 1987: farms, farmland, production, finances, and operator characteristics, by county, final State rpt series, 2331–1

Cattle and calves on feed, by State, as of July 1989, semiannual press release, 1623–1

Cattle and calves on feed, inventory and marketings by State, monthly release, 1623–2

China trade by SITC 1- to 5-digit commodity, 1970s-87, annual rpt, 9114–3

Cooperatives commercial member characteristics, and use of services, by region, 1980 and 1986, 1128–53

Costs of feeding livestock in selected locations, periodic situation rpt with articles, 1561–7

Cottonseed prices and quality, by State, seasonal weekly rpt, 1309–14

County Business Patterns, 1987: employment, establishments, and payroll, by SIC 2- to 4-digit industry and county, annual State rpt series, 2326–8

Dairy cattle, milk production, and grain and other concentrates fed, by State, monthly rpt, 1627–1

Dairy production by State, stocks, prices, and CCC price support activities, by product type, monthly rpt, 1627–3

Developing countries agricultural and food aid, and impacts on US exports, with background data, 1960s-89, 26308-85

Eastern Europe agricultural production, consumption, and trade, by country, 1970s-88, annual rpt, 1524-11

Eastern Europe and USSR agricultural production, acreage, and consumption, by commodity and country, 1965-85, 1528-284

EC imports of nongrain animal feed by type, 1966-86, 1528-276

Employment, earnings, and hours, by SIC 1- to 4-digit industry, monthly 1983-Feb 1989, annual rpt, 6744-4

Exports and imports (agricultural) commodity and country, prices, and world market devs, monthly rpt, 1922-12

Exports and imports (agricultural) of US, by commodity and country, bimonthly rpt with articles, 1522-1

Exports and imports (agricultural) of US, by commodity, monthly rpt, 1922-8

Exports and imports (agricultural) of US, by detailed commodity and country, 1988, semiannual rpt, 1522-4

Exports and imports of US shipped through Canada, by detailed commodity, customs district, and country, 1987, annual rpt, 7704-11

Exports of grains, oilseed products, hides, skins, and cotton, by country, weekly rpt, 1922-3

Exports of US, detailed commodities by country, monthly rpt, 2422-3

Farm finances and operations, by size, commodity, and region, 1986, annual rpt, 1544-27

Farm financial and marketing conditions, forecast 1988, conf papers, annual rpt, 1004-16

Farm income, expenses, receipts by commodity, assets, liabilities, and ratios, 1988 and trends from 1945, annual rpt, 1544-16

Farm production inputs, output, and productivity, by commodity and region, 1947-87, annual rpt, 1544-17

Farm production itemized costs, by farm sales size and region, 1988, annual rpt, 1614-3

Farm production itemized costs, receipts, and returns, by commodity and region, 1985-87, annual rpt, 1544-20

Farm receipts for 25 leading crops, by State, 1960-87, 1548-347

Farm sector balance sheet, and receipts by detailed commodity, by State, 1984-88, annual rpt, 1544-18

Farm sector finances, income sources, expenses by type, assets, debts, and ratios, 1987, annual rpt, 1544-19

FDA investigations and regulatory activities, quarterly rpt, 4062-3

Fish (processed) production by location, and trade, by species and product, 1987-88, annual rpts, 2166-6

Fish (trout) raised on farms, production, sales, prices, and losses, 1988-89, annual rpt, 1631-16

Fish and shellfish cold storage holdings, by product and species, preliminary data, monthly press release, 2162-2

Fish catch, trade, use, and fishery operations, with selected foreign data, by species, 1970s-88, annual rpt, 2164-1

Foreign and US agricultural production, trade, and weather devs, with US and Rotterdam prices and EC supports, weekly press release, 1922-4

Foreign and US agricultural supply and demand indicators, by selected crop, monthly rpt, 1522-5

Foreign and US grain production, prices, trade, stocks, and use, FAS periodic circular series, 1925-2

Foreign countries agricultural production, prices, and trade, by country, 1970s-89 and forecast 1990, annual world region rpt series, 1524-4

Freight (waterborne domestic and foreign) by commodity, traffic, and passengers, by port and waterway, 1987, annual rpt, 3754-3

Futures contracts risk hedging, for protein meals, model description and results, 1984-86, article, 1561-3.904

Hay (alfalfa and prairie) prices, for selected areas, weekly rpt, 1313-5

Hormones (growth) use impacts on livestock productivity, farm income, land use, and consumer prices, alternative estimates, 1985, 1548-346

Imports and quotas of dairy products, by commodity and country of origin, FAS monthly rpt, 1925-31

Imports of US, detailed Schedule A commodities by country, monthly rpt, 2422-2

Inspection of feed grain for export, current and proposed quality standards, 1989 article, 1561-4.904

Irrigation projects of Reclamation Bur in western US, crop production and acreage by commodity, State, and project, 1987, annual rpt, 5824-12.1

Labor productivity, indexes of output, hours, and employment by SIC 2- to 4-digit industry, 1963-87, annual rpt, 6824-1.3

Livestock, meat, and poultry production, consumption, and industry finances and operations, 1950s-86, 1568-280

Livestock, meat, poultry, and egg production, prices, trade, and stocks, monthly rpt, 1561-17

Manufacturing annual survey, 1986: financial and operating data, by SIC 2- to 4-digit industry, series, 2506-15

Manufacturing census, 1987: financial and operating data, for SIC 4-digit industries by product, preliminary rpt, 2491-1.4

Molasses (feed) production, wholesale prices by market area, and US imports and country, weekly rpt, 1311-16

Molasses supply, use, wholesale prices by market, and trade and production by country, 1983-88, annual rpt, 1311-19

Occupational injury and illness rates, by SIC 2- to 4-digit industry, 1987, annual rpt, 6844-1

OECD trade, total and for 4 major countries, and US trade by country, by commodity, 1970-87, world area rpt series, 9116-1

Oil and fat production, consumption by end use, and stocks, by type, monthly Current Industrial Rpt, 2506-4.4

Packers feeding and marketing of livestock, by animal type and State, 1987, annual rpt, 1384-1.2

PL 480 long-term credit sales allocations, by commodity and country, periodic press release, 1922-7

Potato production, prices, stocks, and use, by State, 1986-88, annual rpt, 1621-11

Poultry (chicken, egg, and turkey) production, prices, receipts, trade, and disposition, 1960-87, 1568-39

Price indexes (producer), by stage of processing and detailed commodity, monthly rpt, 6762-6

Price indexes (producer), by stage of processing and detailed commodity, monthly 1988, annual rpt, 6764-2

Price ratios between livestock and feed, for corn-fed hogs and beef steers, monthly 1970-87, 1568-285.3

Price support activity and policy options, with data on production, trade, use, and finances, and foreign comparisons, 1950s-89, commodity rpt series, 1566-7

Prices (producer and retail) of meat and fish, 1980-89, semiannual situation rpt, 1561-15.3

Prices and returns on grain, impacts of alternative farm inputs purchasing and marketing strategies, 1970s-86, article, 1561-4.901

Prices for nonfat milk and whey feeds in central States, and for dairy herd feed by selected State, 1988, annual rpt, 1317-1.4; 1317-1.6

Prices received and paid by farmers, by commodity and State, 1988, annual rpt, 1629-5

Prices received by farmers and production value, by detailed crop and State, 1986-88, annual rpt, 1621-2

Prices received by farmers for major products, and paid for farm inputs and living items, by State, monthly rpt, 1629-1

Production, acreage, stocks, use, trade, prices, and price supports, periodic situation rpt with articles, 1561-4

Production and operations of feed mills, detailed data by State, 1984, 1568-281

Production, farms, acreage, and related data, by selected crop and State, monthly rpt, 1621-1

Production, prices, trade, and marketing, by commodity, current situation and forecast, monthly rpt with articles, 1502-4

Production, prices, trade, and stocks, for feedstuffs and feed grains by type, weekly rpt, 1313-2

Production, receipts, and demand ratios, by commodity group and region, 1949-83, 1548-348

Rice market activities, prices, inspections, sales, trade, supply, and use, for US and selected foreign markets, weekly rpt, 1313-8

Seed exports, by type, world region, and country, FAS quarterly rpt, 1925-13

Wheat and rye foreign and US production, prices, trade, stocks, and use, quarterly situation rpt with articles, 1561-12

see also Pasture and rangeland

see also under By Commodity in the "Index by Categories"

Animal oils
see Oils, oilseeds, and fats

Animals

Accidents involving animals, deaths and rates by cause, age, race, sex, and State, 1986, US Vital Statistics annual rpt, 4144–2

China trade by SITC 1- to 5-digit commodity, 1970s-87, annual rpt, 9114–3

Exports of US, detailed commodities by country, monthly rpt, 2422–3

Imports of US, detailed Schedule A commodities by country, monthly rpt, 2422–2

Licensing and inspection of facilities, and other animal protection activities of USDA, with animals used in research, by State, FY88, annual rpt, 1394–10

see also Animal diseases and zoonoses

see also Animal experimentation

see also Animal feed

see also Birds and bird conservation

see also Endangered species

see also Fish and fishing industry

see also Fishing, sport

see also Hunting and trapping

see also Livestock and livestock industry

see also Marine mammals

see also Pasture and rangeland

see also Pets

see also Poultry industry and products

see also Rabies

see also Veterinary medicine

see also Wildlife and wildlife conservation

see also Wildlife refuges

see also Zoological parks

Ann Arbor, Mich.

CPI by component for US city average, and by region, population size, and for 15 metro areas, monthly rpt, 6762–1

CPI by component for US city average, and by region, population size, and for 27 metro areas, monthly rpt, 6762–2

see also under By City and By SMSA or MSA in the "Index by Categories"

Anniston, Ala.

see also under By SMSA or MSA in the "Index by Categories"

Annual Housing Survey

see American Housing Survey

Annual Survey of Manufactures

Data coverage and availability of Census Bur rpts and data files, 1989 annual listing, 2304–2

Financial and operating data, by SIC 2- to 4-digit industry, 1986 survey, series, 2506–15

Production indexes and exports by SIC 2-digit industry and State, 1986 and compared to 1985, model results, series, 2506–16

Antarctica

Environmental summary data, and intl claims and disputes, 1989 annual factbook, 9114–2

Marine Mammal Protection Act admin, and populations, strandings, and catch permits by species and location, 1987-88, annual rpt, 2164–11

NSF activities, finances, and funding by program, FY88, annual rpt, 9624–6

Weather (marine) forecast areas, and broadcast schedules and stations worldwide, as of Nov 1988, annual rpt, 2184–3

Anthropology

Employment and other characteristics of science and engineering PhDs, by field and State, 1987, biennial rpt, 9627–18

Employment characteristics of scientists and engineers, by field, 1988, biennial rpt, 9627–16

Enrollment in science and engineering grad programs, by field, source of funds, and characteristics of student and instn, 1975-87, annual rpt, 9627–7

Fed Govt aid to higher education and nonprofit instns for R&D and related activities, by field, instn, agency, and State, FY87, annual rpt, 9627–17

R&D funding by Fed Govt, by field, performer type, agency, and State, FY87-89, annual rpt, 9627–20

Anthropometry

see Body measurements

Anti-Drug Abuse Act

Fed Govt drug abuse and trafficking reduction aid to States, and grant processing time, FY87-88, GAO rpt, 26119–258

State and local govt drug enforcement activities, Federal aid by recipient, and background data, FY88, annual rpt, 6064–28

Antigua and Barbuda

AID loans repayment status and terms by program and country, and status of predecessor agency loans, quarterly rpt, 9912–3

Economic, social, political, and geographic summary data, by country, 1989, annual factbook, 9114–2

Human rights conditions in 170 countries, 1988, annual rpt, 21384–3

Investment (direct) incentives of Caribbean Basin Initiative, economic impacts, with finances and employment by country, 1984-88, 2048–141

Population size, growth rates, and components of change, by country, projected 1989-2020 and trends from 1950, biennial rpt, 2324–9

UN voting record and share of votes in agreement with US, by issue, country, and world area, 1988, annual rpt, 7004–18

see also under By Foreign Country in the "Index by Categories"

Antimony

see Metals and metal industries

Antiques

Exports of US, detailed commodities by country, monthly rpt, 2422–3

Imports of US, detailed Schedule A commodities by country, monthly rpt, 2422–2

Antitrust law

Banks (natl) domestic and intl operations, charters, mergers, and liquidations, by instn and State, quarterly rpt, 8402–3

Cases filed under antitrust law, by Fed Govt and private parties, 1975-87, annual rpt, 6064–6.5

Court caseloads for Federal district, appeals, and bankruptcy courts, by type of suit and offense, circuit, and district, quarterly rpt, 18202–1

Court civil and criminal caseloads for Federal district, appeals, and special courts, June 1989, annual rpt, 18204–2; 18204–8

Criminal case processing in Federal district courts, and dispositions, by offense, district, and offender characteristics, 1984, annual rpt, 6064–29

Sentences for Federal offenses, guidelines by offense and circumstances, 1989 rpt, 17668–1

Sham litigation countersuits disposition relation to market competition indicators, model results, 1972-85, 9406–1.59

US attorneys civil and criminal cases by type and disposition, and collections, by Federal district, FY88, annual rpt, 6004–2.1; 6004–2.7

Apartment houses

Alteration and repair spending for housing, by property type and region, 1984-88, annual rpt, 2384–4.1

American Housing Survey: unit and households detailed characteristics, and unit and neighborhood quality, MSA rpt series, 2485–6

American Housing Survey: unit and households detailed characteristics, and unit and neighborhood quality, 1985, biennial rpt, 2485–12

Arson incidents by whether structure occupied, property value, and arrest rate, by property type, 1988, annual rpt, 6224–2.1

Assets and debts of private sector, balance sheets by segment, 1949-88, semiannual rpt, 9365–4.1

Bond tax-exempt issues for private activity, by purpose, face value, major industry, and State, 1986, annual article, 8302–2.905

Chicago public housing projects structural and financial problems, and crime, 1979-88, GAO rpt, 26113–418

Construction industries census, 1987: establishments, employment, receipts, and expenditures, by SIC 4-digit industry and State, final industry rpt series, 2373–1

Construction industries census, 1987: financial and operating data, preliminary industry rpt series, 2371–1

Construction put in place, permits, housing sales, costs, material prices, and employment, bimonthly rpt with articles, 2042–1

Construction put in place, value of new public and private structures, by type, monthly rpt, 2382–4

Energy conservation (housing) program of BPA, energy savings and indoor air quality under alternative methods, projected 1986-2006, 3228–9

Energy-efficiency building codes effect on apartment building electricity use, for Tacoma, Wash, 1986-87, 3308–92

Energy use, costs, and conservation, and household and housing characteristics, survey rpt series, 3166–7

Fed Govt financial and nonfinancial domestic aid, 1989 base edition with supplements, annual listing, 104–5

Household and family characteristics, by location, 1988, annual Current Population Rpt, 2546–1.437

Housing and households summary characteristics, 1985 and trends, biennial chartbook, 2486–1.7

Market absorption rates and characteristics for nonsubsidized furnished and

unfurnished units, 1987 and trends from 1970, annual Current Housing Rpt, 2484–2

Market absorption rates for apartments and condominiums, and completions by rent class and sales price, quarterly rpt, 2482–2

Mortgage insurance programs of HUD, finances and lending activity by program, FY88, annual rpt, 5004–8

Mortgage loan activity, by type of lender, loan, and mortgaged property, monthly press release, 5142–18

Mortgage loan activity, by type of lender, loan, and mortgaged property, quarterly press release, 5142–30

Mortgage loan activity, by type of lender, loan, and mortgaged property, 1986-88, annual press release, 5144–22

Mortgage loan activity of FSLIC-insured savings instns, by purpose and State, various periods 1984-87, annual rpt, 9314–3

New apartment units completed by region and metro-nonmetro location, and absorption rates, by size and price class, preliminary 1988, annual Current Housing Rpt, 2484–3

New housing unit starts, by units per structure and metro-nonmetro location, and mobile home placements and prices, by region, monthly rpt, 2382–1

New housing units authorized, by region, State, selected MSA, and permit-issuing place, monthly rpt, 2382–5

New housing units authorized, by State, MSA, and permit-issuing place, 1988, annual rpt, 2384–2

New housing units completed and under construction, by units per structure, region, and inside-outside MSAs, monthly rpt, 2382–2

New single and multifamily units, by structural and financial characteristics, inside-outside MSAs, and region, 1984-88, annual rpt, 2384–1

North Central States, FHLB 7th District housing vacancy rates for single and multifamily units and mobile homes, by ZIP code, annual MSA rpt series, 9304–18

Rural and urban areas housing and households characteristics, 1930s-80, 1598–245

South Central States, FHLB 9th District housing vacancy rates for single and multifamily units and mobile homes by ZIP code, annual MSA rpt series, 9304–19

Southeastern States, Fed Reserve 6th District, economic indicators by State and MSA, quarterly rpt, 9371–14

Statistical Abstract of US, social, political, and economic data, 1790-2025, comprehensive annual compilation, 2324–1.3

Tax (property) revenue by level of govt, assessed values by locality, and exemptions, by property type and State, 1987 Census of Govts, 2453–1

Vacant housing characteristics and costs, and occupancy and vacancy rates, by region and metro-nonmetro location, quarterly rpt, 2482–1

Vacant housing characteristics, and occupancy and vacancy rates, by tenure, region, and metro-nonmetro location, selected years 1960-88, annual rpt, 2484–1

West Central States, FHLB 10th District housing vacancy rates for single and multifamily units and mobile homes, by ZIP code, annual MSA rpt series, 9304–22

Western States, FHLB 11th District housing vacancy rates for single and multifamily units and mobile homes, by ZIP code, annual MSA rpt series, 9304–20

Western States, FHLB 12th District housing vacancy rates for single and multifamily units and mobile homes, by ZIP code, annual MSA rpt series, 9304–21

Wiretaps authorized, costs, arrests, trials, and convictions, by offense and jurisdiction, 1988, annual rpt, 18204–7

see also Condominiums and cooperatives

see also Rooming and boarding houses

Appalachia

Agricultural Stabilization and Conservation Service producer payments, by program, monthly rpt, 1802–10

Apple production, marketing, and prices, for Appalachia and compared to other States, various periods 1986-89, annual rpt, 1311–13

Assistance dev project funding by Appalachian Regional Commission, by project and State, planned FY89, annual rpt, 9084–3

Coal production and mines by county, prices, productivity, miners, reserves, and stocks, by mining method and State, 1987-88, annual rpt, 3164–25

Dev projects in Appalachia, and funding by source, by program and State, FY88, annual rpt, 9084–1

Fed Govt spending in States, by type, program, agency, and State, FY88, annual rpt, 2464–2

HHS financial aid, by program, recipient, State, and city, FY88, annual regional listings, 4004–3

Hwy system and access roads funding and completion status, by State, quarterly tables, 9082–1

Peach production, marketing, and prices in 3 southeastern States and Appalachia, 1988, annual rpt, 1311–12

Population of Appalachia, by State and county, 1980 and 1987, annual rpt, 9084–1

Savings instns, FHLB 5th District members finances and lending by State, monthly rpt, 9302–8

see also under By Region in the "Index by Categories"

see also under names of individual States

Appalachian Regional Commission

Activities of ARC, local dev projects, and funding by source, by program and State, FY88, annual rpt, 9084–1

Budget of US Appendix, obligations, appropriations, and personnel, by program and agency, FY90, annual rpt, 104–3

Budget of US, authoritative financial statements with appropriations, outlays, and receipts, by category and agency, FY88, annual rpt, 8104–2.2

Expenditures by ARC, by project and State, planned FY89, annual rpt, 9084–3

Hwy system and access roads funding and completion status, by State, quarterly tables, 9082–1

R&D funding by Fed Govt, by field, performer type, agency, and State, FY87-89, annual rpt, 9627–20

Apparel

see Clothing and clothing industry

Appeals

see Court of Military Appeals

see Federal courts of appeals

see Supreme Court

see Tax protests and appeals

see U.S. Court of Appeals for the Federal Circuit

Applebee, Arthur N.

"Crossroads in American Education: A Summary of Findings", 4898–26

Apples

see Fruit and fruit products

Appleton, Wis.

see also under By SMSA or MSA in the "Index by Categories"

Appliances

see Household appliances and equipment

Apportionment

see Congressional apportionment

Apprenticeship

Employment and Training Admin activities, funding, and participant characteristics, by program, FY80-86, 6408–71

Europe and US apprentices, for selected countries, 1987, article, 6722–1.936

Participant characteristics, and sources of training, with data by employer size and major industry group, 1982-88, 6408–73

Public opinion on apprenticeship issues, 1988 rpt, 6408–72

Appropriations

see Budget of the U.S.

see Defense budgets and appropriations

Aptitude tests

see Educational tests

Aquaculture

Agriculture census, 1987: farms, farmland, production, finances, and operator characteristics, by county, final State rpt series, 2331–1

Bass (striped) stocks status on Atlantic coast, and sport and commercial catch by State, 1972-89, annual rpt, 5504–29

Catfish raised on farms, production, inventory, imports, and prices, by State, 1st half 1989, semiannual rpt, 1631–17

Catfish raised on farms, production, inventory, sales, prices, and imports, monthly release, 1631–14

Colorado River Storage Project finances and activities in western States, FY88, annual rpt, 5824–3

Farm financial and marketing conditions, forecast 1988, conf papers, annual rpt, 1004–16

Farm financial and marketing conditions, forecast 1989, annual chartbook, 1504–8

Farm income, expenses, receipts by commodity, assets, liabilities, and ratios, 1988 and trends from 1945, annual rpt, 1544–16

Great Lakes phosphorus loads and fish stocking effects on algal levels, 1966-85, conf, 14648–20

Hatcheries and research stations under Fish and Wildlife Service mgmt, acreage by site and State, as of Sept 1988, annual rpt, 5504–8

Japan and US aquaculture mgmt, methods, and biological data for selected species, 1985 conf papers, annual rpt, 2164–15

Natl Fish Hatchery System activities and deliveries, by species, hatchery, and jurisdiction of waters stocked, FY88, annual rpt, 5504–10

Oklahoma fish farming finances and operations, 1989, article, 1561–15.901

Production, costs, prices, sales, and hatcheries and farms, 1970s–89, semiannual situation rpt, 1561–15

R&D and mgmt of fisheries, Fed Govt grants by project and State, and rpts, 1987, annual listing, 2164–3

Research and education grants, USDA competitive awards by program and recipient, FY88, annual listing, 1764–1

Research of State fish and wildlife agencies, federally funded fishery projects and costs by species and State, 1989, annual listing, 5504–23

Shrimp raised on farms, yield and production by country, and US imports, 1980–89, article, 1522–3.924

Statistical Abstract of US, social, political, and economic data, 1790–2025, comprehensive annual compilation, 2324–1.3

Trout raised on farms, production, sales, and prices, 1988–89, annual rpt, 1631–16

Arab Republic of Egypt
see Egypt

Arabian Peninsula
see Oman
see Qatar
see Saudi Arabia
see United Arab Emirates
see Yemen, North
see Yemen, South

Arbitration
see Civil procedure
see Labor-management relations, general
see Labor-management relations in government
see Labor-management relations, local and regional
see Legal arbitration and mediation

Arboretums
see Botanical gardens

Architect of the Capitol
Activities of Capitol Architect, funding, costs, and contracts, FY86, annual rpt, 25944–1

Budget of US Appendix, obligations, appropriations, and personnel, by program and agency, FY90, annual rpt, 104–3

Expenditures for salaries, supplies, and services, itemized by payee and function, 1st half FY89, semiannual rpt, 25922–2

Architectural barriers to the handicapped
Building access for disabled to Federal and federally funded facilities, complaints by disposition and agency, FY88, annual rpt, 17614–1

Election polling places accessibility to aged and disabled, precincts by barrier type and State, 1988 natl elections, biennial rpt, 9274–6

Public and Indian housing stock and renovation needs, series, 5186–15

State govt and Federal compliance with disabled persons employment and architectural barrier removal laws, findings and recommendations, 1989 rpt, 10048–74

Architecture
Competitiveness (intl) of US construction and design industry, with selected foreign and US operating data, 1982–86, 2046–12.43

Degrees awarded in higher education, by level, field, race, and sex, 1989 edition, annual rpt, 4824–2.20

Fires in hotels and motels, casualties, and effectiveness of smoke detectors, sprinkler systems, and building and equipment design, 1989 hearing, 21708–127

Guam economic censuses, 1987: employment, firms, payroll, and receipts, by SIC 1- to 4-digit industry and election district, 2595–1

Historic and natural natl landmarks damaged and threatened, with owner, location, damage type, and recommended remedial action, 1988, annual listing, 5544–16

Industry finances and operations, by SIC 2- to 4-digit industry, forecast 1989 and trends from 1950s, annual rpt, 2044–28

Service industries census, 1987: establishments, receipts, employment, and payroll, by SIC 2- to 4-digit kind of business, MSA, county, and city, State rpt series, 2391–1

see also Architectural barriers to the handicapped

Arctic Ocean
Environmental conditions and oil dev impacts for Alaska OCS, compilation of papers, series, 2176–1

Environmental summary data, and intl claims and disputes, 1989 annual factbook, 9114–2

Marine Mammal Protection Act admin, and populations, strandings, and catch permits by species and location, 1987–88, annual rpt, 2164–11

see also Beaufort Sea
see also Chukchi Sea

Area studies
Arts Natl Endowment activities and grants, FY88, annual rpt, 9564–3

Exchange and training programs of Federal agencies, participants by world area, and funding, by program, FY87, annual rpt, 9854–8

Fed Govt aid to intl education programs, by program, FY86–88, annual rpt, 4804–28.5

Latin America dev grants of Inter-American Foundation by program area, and fellowships by field and instn, by country, FY71–88, annual rpt, 14424–2

Latin America dev grants of Inter-American Foundation by recipient, and fellowships, by country, FY88, annual rpt, 14424–1

Area wage surveys
Southeastern US wages of office and plant workers, for 36 MSAs, 1988, press release, 6946–3.14

Vacations, holidays, and relative pay levels, regional and metro area differences, 1983–86, article, 6722–1.909

Wages by occupation, and benefits for office and plant workers in selected MSAs, 1988, annual rpt, 6785–1

Wages by occupation, and benefits for office and plant workers, periodic MSA survey rpt series, 6785–3; 6785–11; 6785–12

Wages by occupation, for office and plant workers in metro areas, by industry div and region, Aug 1988, annual rpt, 6785–9

Wages by occupation, for office and plant workers in selected MSAs, 1989 survey, annual rpt, 6785–5

Wages by occupation, for office and plant workers in selected MSAs, 1989 survey, annual summary rpts, 6785–6

Wages for 3 occupational groups, relative pay levels in 92 labor market areas, 1988, annual rpt, 6785–13

Wages for 4 occupational groups, relative pay levels in 61 MSAs, 1988, annual rpt, 6785–8

see also Industry wage surveys

Arecibo, P.R.
see also under By SMSA or MSA in the "Index by Categories"

Argentina
Agricultural and food production and indexes, total and for selected commodities, by country, 1970s–88, annual rpt, 1524–12

Agricultural production, prices, and trade, by country, 1960s–89, annual world region rpt, 1524–4.2

Agricultural subsidies, consumer and producer equivalents by program, commodity, and major US trading partner, 1982–86, 1528–275

Agricultural trade of US, by detailed commodity and country, 1988, semiannual rpt, 1522–4

AID loans repayment status and terms by program and country, and status of predecessor agency loans, quarterly rpt, 9912–3

Background Notes, summary social, political, and economic data, 1988 rpt, 7006–2.3

Caribbean area sugar production and exports, and cruise ship tourist visits and spending, by country, 1981–88, hearing, 21788–179

Citrus production, trade, and use, 1970–89, and exports by country, 1988, by commodity, article, 1925–34.930

Economic and military aid and loans from US and intl agencies, by program and country, FY46–87, annual rpt, 9914–5

Economic conditions in Communist, OECD, and selected other countries, 1960s–88, annual rpt, 9114–4

Economic conditions, income, production, prices, employment, and trade, 1989 periodic country rpt, 2046–4.8; 2046–4.104

Economic conditions, policy, and trade practices, by country, 1986–88, annual rpt, 21384–5

Economic indicators of developing countries, problem debtors compared to other borrowers, by country, 1973–84, 1528–285

Economic, social, political, and geographic summary data, by country, 1989, annual factbook, 9114–2

Exports and imports of Latin America, and balance of trade with US, by country, 1988, annual rpt, 2044–34

Exports and imports of US, by commodity and country, 1970-87, world area rpt, 9116-1.5

Exports and imports of US, by selected country, country group, and commodity group, 1988, annual rpt, 2044-37

Fruit production, trade, use, and processing, by commodity for 5 countries, 1986-89, annual article, 1925-34.909

Grain production, use, exports, quality standards, storage, and prices, for 5 countries, 1960s-88, 26358-201.2

Human rights conditions in 170 countries, 1988, annual rpt, 21384-3

Imports of goods, services, and investment from US, trade barriers, impacts, and US actions, by country, 1988, annual rpt, 444-2

Military aid of US, arms sales, and training programs costs and budget requests, by program, world region, and country, FY88-90, annual rpt, 7144-13

Military spending, arms trade, and force strengths, with govt spending and population, by country, 1977-87, annual rpt, 9824-1

Minerals Yearbook, 1987, Vol 3: foreign country reviews of production, trade, and policy, by commodity, annual rpt, 5604-35

Minerals Yearbook, 1987, Vol 3 preprints: foreign country review of production, trade, and policy, by commodity, annual rpt, 5604-23.5

Multinatl US firms and foreign affiliates finances and operations, by industry of parent firm and affiliate, world area, and country, preliminary 1987, annual rpt, 2704-5

Nuclear power generation in US and 19 non-Communist countries, monthly rpt, 3162-24.10

Nuclear power plant capacity, generation, and operating status, by plant and foreign and US location, 1988 and projected to 2020, annual rpt, 3164-57

Pipes and tubes (light-walled steel) from Argentina at less than fair value, injury to US industry, investigation with background financial and operating data, 1989 rpt, 9886-14.262

Population size, growth rates, and components of change, by country, projected 1989-2020 and trends from 1950, biennial rpt, 2324-9

Soybean production itemized costs, by region, for US, Argentina, and Brazil, 1986-88, article, 1522-3.902

Tobacco acreage and production, and exports by country, for Argentina, 1985-89, article, 1925-16.906

UN voting record and share of votes in agreement with US, by issue, country, and world area, 1988, annual rpt, 7004-18

Wheat trade, elasticities of demand for US and 5 countries, alternative models description and results, 1950s-86, 1528-281

see also under By Foreign Country in the "Index by Categories"

Argon
see Gases

Argonne National Laboratory
"Energy Technologies and the Environment: Environmental Information Handbook", 3326-1.1

see also Department of Energy National Laboratories

Arid zones
Wyoming streamflow, annual peak by site, model description and results, 1985, 5668-84

Arizona
Agriculture census, 1987: farms, farmland, production and costs, and operator characteristics, advance State and county rpts, 2330-1.4

Agriculture census, 1987: farms, farmland, production, finances, and operator characteristics, by county, final State rpt, 2331-1.3

Bank deposits in FDIC-insured commercial and savings banks, by instn, State, and county, as of June 1988, annual regional rpt, 9295-3.6

Citrus production and use, by crop and State, 1981/82-1986/87, 1641-4

Coal production and mines by county, prices, productivity, miners, reserves, and stocks, by mining method and State, 1987-88, annual rpt, 3164-25

County Business Patterns, 1987: employment, establishments, and payroll, by SIC 2- to 4-digit industry and county, annual State rpt, 2326-8.4

Deaths and rates, by detailed location, cause, and demographic characteristics, 1987, US Vital Statistics annual rpt, 4144-3.1

DOD prime contract awards, by contractor, service branch, State, and city, FY88, annual rpt, 3544-22

Employment, earnings, and hours, by selected SIC 1- to 4-digit industry, State, and for 262 MSAs, 1972-87, 6748-81.1

Fed Govt spending in States and local areas, by type, State, county, and city, FY88, annual rpt, 2464-3

Fed Govt spending in States, by type, program, agency, and State, FY88, annual rpt, 2464-2

Health maintenance organizations providing alternative acute care, Arizona Medicaid demonstration project results, 1985 survey, article, 4652-1.951

HHS financial aid, by program, recipient, State, and city, FY88, annual regional listing, 4004-3.9

Homeless children educational enrollment and needs, 1988, annual State rpt, 4804-35.4

Income (personal) per capita and by source, and earnings by industry div, by State, MSA, and county, 1982-87, annual regional rpt, 2704-2.5

Indian (Navajo and Hopi) relocation program activities, caseloads, and finances, FY88, annual rpt, 16004-1

Mineral Industry Surveys, State reviews of production, 1988, preliminary annual rpt, 5614-6

Minerals Yearbook, 1987, Vol 2 preprints: State review of production and sales by commodity, and business activity, annual rpt, 5604-16.4

Minerals Yearbook, 1987, Vol 2: State reviews of production, sales, and firms, by commodity, and business activity, annual rpt, 5604-34

Mining shares of gross product, employment, earnings, and other economic impacts, 1977-86, article, 5602-4.902

Nursing home compliance with Medicare and Medicaid regulations, and patient characteristics, by facility, 1987/88, annual State rpt, 4654-15.3

Older persons care by family members, tax subsidies in 2 States, 1981-84, article, 4652-1.915

Retail trade census, 1987: employment, establishments, sales, and payroll, by SIC 2- to 4-digit kind of business, MSA, county, and city, State rpt, 2397-1.3

Savings instns, FHLB 11th District member offices, locations, savings balances, and accounts, quarterly listing, 9302-20

Service industries census, 1987: employment, establishments, receipts, and payroll, by SIC 2- to 4-digit kind of business, MSA, county, and city, State rpt, 2391-1.3

Statistical Abstract of US, social, political, and economic data, with foreign comparisons, 1790-2025, comprehensive annual compilation, 2324-1

Timber in Arizona, harvest, mill receipts, and residues, with methodology, 1984-85, 1208-294

Vegetables (broccoli, asparagus, cauliflower) industry intl competitiveness, investigation with background financial and operating data and foreign comparisons, 1988 rpt, 9886-4.133

Water supply and quality in streams and lakes, and groundwater levels in wells, by drainage basin, 1987, annual State rpt, 5666-10.3

Water supply, and snow survey results, monthly State rpt, 1266-2.2

Water supply, and snow survey results, 1988, annual State rpt, 1264-14.6

Wholesale trade census, 1987: employment, establishments, and operations, by SIC 2- to 4-digit kind of business, MSA, county, and city, State rpt, 2405-1.3

Wildlife-related recreation, hunting, and fishing participation and spending, detailed data, 1985 survey, quinquennial State rpt, 5506-6.3

Wood fuel harvest in Arizona, by species, ownership, and county, 1984, 1208-293

see also Douglas, Ariz.
see also Maricopa County, Ariz.
see also Mesa, Ariz.
see also Phoenix, Ariz.
see also Tucson, Ariz.
see also under By State in the "Index by Categories"

Arkansas
Agriculture census, 1987: farms, farmland, production and costs, and operator characteristics, advance State and county rpts, 2330-1.5

Agriculture census, 1987: farms, farmland, production, finances, and operator characteristics, by county, final State rpt, 2331-1.4

Bank deposits in FDIC-insured commercial and savings banks, by instn, State, and county, as of June 1988, annual regional rpt, 9295-3.4

Coal production and mines by county, prices, productivity, miners, reserves, and stocks, by mining method and State, 1987-88, annual rpt, 3164-25

Deaths and rates, by detailed location, cause, and demographic characteristics, 1987, US Vital Statistics annual rpt, 4144–3.1

Disaster relief program of Fed Emergency Mgmt Agency under State admin, impact of mgmt changes on benefits processing, 1986-88, GAO rpt, 26113–412

DOD prime contract awards, by contractor, service branch, State, and city, FY88, annual rpt, 3544–22

Economic and banking conditions, for Fed Reserve 8th District, quarterly rpt with articles, 9391–16

Employment by industry div, earnings, and hours, by southwestern State, monthly rpt, 6962–2

Employment, earnings, and hours, by selected SIC 1- to 4-digit industry, State, and for 262 MSAs, 1972-87, 6748–81.1

Fed Govt spending in States and local areas, by type, State, county, and city, FY88, annual rpt, 2464–3

Fed Govt spending in States, by type, program, agency, and State, FY88, annual rpt, 2464–2

HHS financial aid, by program, recipient, State, and city, FY88, annual regional listing, 4004–3.6

Homeless children educational enrollment and needs, 1988, annual State rpt, 4804–35.5

Income (personal) per capita and by source, and earnings by industry div, by State, MSA, and county, 1982-87, annual regional rpt, 2704–2.4

Mineral Industry Surveys, State reviews of production, 1988, preliminary annual rpt, 5614–6

Minerals Yearbook, 1987, Vol 2 preprints: State review of production and sales by commodity, and business activity, annual rpt, 5604–16.5

Minerals Yearbook, 1987, Vol 2: State reviews of production, sales, and firms, by commodity, and business activity, annual rpt, 5604–34

Nursing home compliance with Medicare and Medicaid regulations, and patient characteristics, by facility, 1987/88, annual State rpt, 4654–15.4

Retail trade census, 1987: employment, establishments, sales, and payroll, by SIC 2- to 4-digit kind of business, MSA, county, and city, State rpt, 2397–1.4

Rice market activities, prices, inspections, sales, trade, supply, and use, for US and selected foreign markets, weekly rpt, 1313–8

Savings instns, FHLB 9th District members finances and operations by State, monthly rpt, 9302–13

Savings instns, FHLB 9th District members finances and operations by State, quarterly rpt, 9302–31

Service industries census, 1987: employment, establishments, receipts, and payroll, by SIC 2- to 4-digit kind of business, MSA, county, and city, State rpt, 2391–1.4

Statistical Abstract of US, social, political, and economic data, with foreign comparisons, 1790-2025, comprehensive annual compilation, 2324–1

Water quality in Arkansas streams and rivers, by monitoring site, 1975-85, 5668–83

Water supply and quality in streams and lakes, and groundwater levels in wells, by drainage basin, 1987, annual State rpt, 5666–10.4

Water supply and quality in streams and lakes, and groundwater levels in wells, by drainage basin, 1988, annual State rpt, 5666–16.4

Wholesale trade census, 1987: employment, establishments, finances, and operations, by SIC 2- to 4-digit kind of business, MSA, county, and city, State rpt, 2405–1.4

Wildlife-related recreation, hunting, and fishing participation and spending, detailed data, 1985 survey, quinquennial State rpt, 5506–6.4

see also Fort Smith, Ark.

see also Little Rock, Ark.

see also North Little Rock, Ark.

see also under By State in the "Index by Categories"

Arkansas River

Freight (waterborne domestic and foreign) by commodity, traffic, and passengers, by port and waterway, 1987, annual rpt, 3754–3.2

Water supply and quality in streams and lakes, and groundwater levels in wells, by drainage basin, 1987, annual State rpt series, 5666–10

Water supply and quality in streams and lakes, and groundwater levels in wells, by drainage basin, 1988, annual State rpt series, 5666–16

Arlington, Tex.

Housing and households characteristics, 1985 survey, MSA fact sheet, 2485–11.11

Housing and households detailed characteristics, and unit and neighborhood quality, by location, 1985 survey, MSA rpt, 2485–6.7

see also under By City and By SMSA or MSA in the "Index by Categories"

Arlington, Va.

Fed Govt land acquisition and dev projects in DC metro area, characteristics and funding by agency and project, FY90-94, annual rpt, 15454–1

Police pay, benefits, and staffing, for US Park Police and compared to other Federal and local police units, FY85-88, GAO rpt, 26119–264

Armed services

see also Air Force

see also Armed services reserves

see also Army

see also Coast Guard

see also Department of Defense

see also Joint Chiefs of Staff

see also Marine Corps

see also Military personnel

see also Navy

see also Selective service

see also Voluntary military service

Armed services reserves

Army strategic capability, force strengths, budget, and mgmt, FY80-89, annual rpt, 3704–13

Base construction, renovation, and land acquisition, DOD budget requests by project, service branch, State, and country, FY90/91, annual rpt, 3544–15

Budget of DOD, procurement appropriations by item, service branch, and defense agency, FY88-91, annual rpt, 3544–32

Budget of DOD, R&D appropriations by item, service branch, and defense agency, FY88-91, annual rpt, 3544–33

Family social, economic, and other characteristics, and spouses attitudes, for reserve personnel, 1986 survey, 3508–30

Health care personnel and turnover, by specialty for reserves, FY87, annual rpt, 3544–24.8

Manpower active duty strength, recruits, and reenlistment, by race, sex, and service branch, quarterly press release, 3542–7

Manpower and equipment strengths, and readiness, by reserve component, FY88, annual rpt, 3544–31

Manpower and payroll for reserve units, by service branch, by State and country, FY88, annual rpt, 3544–29

Manpower, funding by category, procurement reductions, and needs, by reserve component, FY80-88, GAO rpt, 26123–220

Manpower needs, costs, and force readiness, by service branch, FY90, annual rpt, 3504–1

Manpower of DOD, and organization, budget, weapons, and property, by service branch, State, and country, 1989 annual summary rpt, 3504–13

Manpower social, economic, family, and service characteristics, and attitudes, by reserve component, 1986 survey, 3508–29

Manpower statistics for active duty and reserve recruits, aptitude test scores and retention rates, with data by sex, race, and service branch, various periods 1980-87, 26306–6.136

Manpower statistics for active duty, civilian, and reserve personnel, by service branch, quarterly rpt, 3542–14

Manpower strengths and characteristics, by reserve component, quarterly rpt, 3542–4

Manpower strengths for active duty, civilian, and reserve personnel, by service branch, selected years FY90-91, annual rpt, 3544–2

Manpower strengths for reserve components, by selected characteristics, FY88, annual rpt, 3544–1.5

NATO military forces compared to Warsaw Pact, and selected economic indicators, by country, 1900s-87, conf papers, 3908–6

Navy manpower strengths, accessions, and attrition, detailed statistics, quarterly rpt, 3802–4

Navy pilot proficiency program, aircraft hours flown and costs, FY83-87, GAO rpt, 26123–238

Statistical Abstract of US, social, political, and economic data, 1790-2025, comprehensive annual compilation, 2324–1.2

Training and education programs of DOD, funding, staff, students, and facilities, by service branch, FY90, annual rpt, 3504–5

Training of Army Reserve and Natl Guard personnel in combat and critical job task skills, resources, effectiveness, and officers views, FY87, GAO rpt, 26123–239

Women military personnel on active and reserve duty, by demographic and service characteristics and service branch, FY88, annual chartbook, 3544–26

Wiretaps authorized, costs, arrests, trials, and convictions, by offense and jurisdiction, 1988, annual rpt, 18204–7

Art

Copyrights Register activities, registrations by material type, and fees, FY87 and trends from 1790, annual rpt, 26404–2

Exports of US, detailed commodities by country, monthly rpt, 2422–3

Imports of US, detailed Schedule A commodities by country, monthly rpt, 2422–2

Library of Congress activities, acquisitions, services, and financial statements, FY88, annual rpt, 26404–1

Manufacturing census, 1987: financial and operating data, for SIC 4-digit industries by product, preliminary rpt, 2491–1.82

Natl Endowment for Arts activities and grants, FY88, annual rpt, 9564–3

OECD trade, total and for 4 major countries, and US trade by country, by commodity, 1970-87, world area rpt series, 9116–1

Service industries census, 1987: establishments, receipts, employment, and payroll, by SIC 2- to 4-digit kind of business, MSA, county, and city, State rpt series, 2391–1

Service industries receipts, by SIC 2- to 4-digit kind of business, 1988, annual rpt, 2413–8

Tariff Schedule of US, classifications and rates of duty by detailed imported commodity, 1990 base edition and supplements, 9886–13

Wholesale trade census, 1987: employment, establishments, finances, and operations, by SIC 2- to 4-digit kind of business, MSA, county, and city, State rpt series, 2405–1

Arterburn, Alfred B.

"Mutual to Stock Conversions as a Source of New Capital for Thrifts", 9302–33.902

"Proposed Minimum Capital Regulation for FSLIC-Insured Institutions", 9302–33.901

Arteriosclerosis

see Circulatory diseases

Arthritis

see Musculoskeletal diseases

Artificial fibers

see Synthetic fibers and fabrics

Artificial foods

see Synthetic food products

Artificial organs

see Medical transplants

Artificial satellites

see Communications satellites

see Meteorological satellites

see Satellites

Artificial sweeteners

see Syrups and sweeteners

Arts and the humanities

Degrees awarded in higher education, by level, field, race, and sex, 1989 edition, annual rpt, 4824–2.20

Japan-US Friendship Commission educational and cultural exchange activities, grants, and trust fund status, FY87-88, biennial report, 14694–1

Teachers bachelor degrees, by field and other characteristics, 1985-86, 4838–39

see also Antiques

see also Architecture

see also Art

see also Dance

see also Federal aid to arts and humanities

see also Foreign languages

see also Language arts

see also Motion pictures

see also Museums

see also Music

see also Performing arts

see also Photography and photographic equipment

see also Social sciences

see also Theater

Aruba

Background Notes, summary social, political, and economic data, 1989 rpt, 7006–2.10

Economic, social, political, and geographic summary data, by country, 1989, annual factbook, 9114–2

Investment (direct) incentives of Caribbean Basin Initiative, economic impacts, with finances and employment by country, 1984-88, 2048–141

Minerals Yearbook, 1987, Vol 3 preprints: foreign country review of production, trade, and policy, by commodity, annual rpt, 5604–23.83

Population size, growth rates, and components of change, by country, projected 1989-2020 and trends from 1950, biennial rpt, 2324–9

Ary, T. S.

"Health and Safety Research: Long-Range Plans of the Bureau of Mines", 5602–4.903

Asbestos

see Asbestos contamination

see Nonmetallic minerals and mines

Asbestos contamination

Abatement technical aid for asbestos, funding by State, 1985-88, hearing, 21248–119

Cancer incidence relation to exposure to asbestos in drinking water, by sex and cancer site, 1973-83, local area study, article, 4042–3.921

Carcinogens chemistry, sources, environment and health risks, and regulation, by substance and brand, 1989, annual rpt, 4044–15

Fed Govt asbestos trust fund financial condition, monthly rpt, 8102–9.13

Torts for product liability, asbestos-related personal injury caseload in Federal district courts, June 1989, annual rpt, 18204–2.12; 18204–8.11; 18204–8.14

Aschauer, David A.

"Public Investment and Productivity Growth in the Group of Seven", 9375–1.907

ASEAN

see Association of Southeast Asian Nations

Ash, Arlene

"Adjusting Medicare Capitation Payments Using Prior Hospitalization Data", 4652–1.939

Ash, Mark

"Oats: Background for 1990 Farm Legislation", 1566–7.5

"Recent Issues in Grain Quality", 1561–4.904

"U.S. Feed Manufacturing Industry, 1984", 1568–281

Asheville, N.C.

Wages by occupation, for office and plant workers, 1989 survey, periodic MSA rpt, 6785–3.4

see also under By SMSA or MSA in the "Index by Categories"

Ashland, Ky.

see also under By SMSA or MSA in the "Index by Categories"

Asia

Agricultural and food aid to developing countries, and impacts on US exports, with background data, 1960s-89, 26308–85

Agricultural and food production and indexes, total and for selected commodities, by country, 1970s-88, annual rpt, 1524–12

Agricultural exports of US, for grains, oilseed products, hides, skins, and cotton, by country, weekly rpt, 1922–3

Agricultural production, prices, and trade, by country, 1960s-89, annual world region rpt, 1524–4.2

Agricultural trade of US, by commodity and country, bimonthly rpt with articles, 1522–1

Agricultural trade of US, by detailed commodity and country, 1988, semiannual rpt, 1522–4

Agricultural trade of US with Asia, Middle East, and North Africa, by commodity and country, 1962-86, 1528–277

AID activities and funding by project and function, FY90, and developing countries summary socioeconomic data from 1960s, annual rpt, 9904–4.6

AID contracts and grants for technical and support services, by instn, country, and State, FY88, annual listing, 9914–7

AID economic aid to developing countries, obligations and disbursements by country, quarterly rpt, 9912–4

AID housing and urban dev program financial statements, and loan guarantees by country, FY88, annual rpt, 9914–4

AID loans authorized, signed, and canceled, by country and world area, quarterly rpt, 9912–2

AID loans repayment status and terms by program and country, and status of predecessor agency loans, quarterly rpt, 9912–3

Alcohol abuse hereditary factors, for Asian and white populations, 1989 article, 4042–3.959

Businesses (foreign) activity in US, income tax returns, assets, and income statement items, by industry div, country, and world area, 1984-85, article, 8302–2.920

Coal trade flows and reserves, by country, 1970s-87 and projected to 2000, annual rpt, 3164–77

Construction contracts awarded US firms, and share of construction market by country of contractor, by world area, 1982-87, annual article, 2042–1.902

Dollar exchange rate trade-weighted index of Fed Reserve Bank of Atlanta, by world area, monthly rpt, 9371–15

Dollar exchange rate trade-weighted index of Fed Reserve Bank of Dallas, by world area, monthly rpt, 9379–13

Economic and military aid and loans from US and intl agencies, by program and country, FY46-87, annual rpt, 9914–5

Economic conditions and trade devs and policy, for US and foreign countries, 1988 conf papers, 9373–3.32

English language program of USIA, enrollment and staff, by instn, world area, and country, FY88, annual rpt, 9854–2

Exchange and training programs of Federal agencies, participants by world area, and funding, by program, FY87, annual rpt, 9854–8

Export and import balances of US, and dollar exchange rates, with 4 Asian countries 1980s-89, semiannual rpt, 8002–14

Exports and imports (waterborne) of US, by type of service, commodity, country, route, and US port, 1986-87, annual rpt, 7704–2

Exports and imports (waterborne) of US, by type of service, customs district, port, and world area, monthly rpt, 2422–7

Exports and imports of OECD, total and for 4 major countries, and US trade by country, by commodity, 1970-87, world area rpt, 9116–1.2

Exports and imports of US, by commodity group, world area, selected country, US coastal area and port, and mode of transport, monthly rpt, 2422–9

Exports and imports of US, by selected country, country group, and commodity group, 1988, annual rpt, 2044–37

Fertilizer components use, by world area, 1978-88 and projected to 2010, 5608–154

Food production and needs, and related economic outlook, by country, 1989/90, annual rpt, 1524–6

Immigrant and nonimmigrant visas of US issued and refused, by class, issuing office, and nationality, FY88, annual rpt, 7184–1

Immigrants admitted to US, by class of admission, country of birth, and State and MSA of destination, FY88, annual rpt, 6264–4

Immigrants admitted to US, by occupational group and country of birth, preliminary FY88, annual table, 6264–1

Immigration to US, alien workers, visitors, deportations, and naturalizations, by country, FY88 and trends from 1820, annual rpt, 6264–2

Investment (foreign direct) of US, by selected industry group and world area, 1986-88, annual article, 2702–1.930

Loans of US banks to foreigners at all US and foreign offices, by country group and country, quarterly rpt, 13002–1

Manufacturing labor cost indexes, by selected country, 1980-89, article, 6722–1.926

Manufacturing labor costs and indexes, by selected country, 1975-88, annual rpt, 6824–3

Manufacturing labor costs and indexes, by selected country, 1975-88, semiannual rpt, 6822–3

Mexico industrial plants owned by US firms, employment impacts of US and Asia wages, 1975-87, technical paper, 9379–12.45

Military aid of US, arms sales, and training, by country, FY50-88, annual rpt, 3904–3

Military aid of US, arms sales, and training programs costs and budget requests, by program, world region, and country, FY88-90, annual rpt, 7144–13

Military aid programs and related activities of US, costs by country and intl agency, FY85-87 and cumulative from FY50, GAO rpt, 26123–30

Military, economic, technological, and trade conditions of Pacific Basin countries, 1970s-85, compilation of papers, 3908–4

Military spending and imports of developing countries, measures to determine eligibility for US economic aid, by country, 1985-86, annual rpt, 9914–1

Military spending, arms trade, and force strengths, with govt spending and population, by country, 1977-87, annual rpt, 9824–1

Minerals Yearbook, 1987, Vol 3: foreign country reviews of production, trade, and policy, by commodity, annual rpt, 5604–35

Multinatl firms US affiliates, finances, and operations, by industry, world area of parent firm, and State, 1987, annual rpt, 2704–4

Multinatl US firms and foreign affiliates finances and operations, by industry of parent firm and affiliate, world area, and country, preliminary 1987, annual rpt, 2704–5

Nuclear power plant capacity, generation, and operating status, by plant and foreign and US location, 1988 and projected to 2020, annual rpt, 3164–57

Nuclear power plant spent fuel and demand for uranium and enrichment service, for US and other country groups, projected 1989-2036, annual rpt, 3164–72

Oil and gas reserves and discoveries, by country and country group, quarterly rpt, 3162–43

Peace Corps activities, funding by program, and volunteers, by country, FY90, annual rpt, 9654–1

Population size, growth rates, and components of change, by country, projected 1989-2020 and trends from 1950, biennial rpt, 2324–9

R&D funding by Fed Govt, by field, performer type, agency, and State, FY87-89, annual rpt, 9627–20

Refugee arrivals in US by world area and country of origin, and quotas, monthly rpt, 7002–4

Refugee arrivals in US by world area of origin and State of settlement, and Federal aid, FY88-90, annual rpt, 7004–16

Science and engineering immigrants, by field, age, sex, country and world area of birth and last residence, and State, 1987 and trends from 1967, 9627–29

Terrorist (intl) incidents, casualties, and attacks on US targets, by attack type and country, 1980-88, 7008–56

Terrorist (intl) incidents, casualties, and attacks on US targets, by attack type and world area, 1968-88, annual rpt, 7004–13

Tidal currents, daily time and velocity by station for North America and Asia coasts, forecast 1990, annual rpt, 2174–1.1

Tide height and time daily at coastal points, forecast 1990, annual rpt, 2174–2.5

Travel to and from US, and travel receipts and payments, by world area, with data by country, 1984-88, annual rpt, 2904–10

Travel to and from US on US and foreign flag air carriers, by country, world area, and US port, monthly rpt, 7302–2

Travel to and from US on US and foreign flag airlines, by world area, 1980-88, annual rpt, 2904–13

Travel to US, by characteristics of visit and traveler, country, port city, and State of destination, quarterly rpt, 2902–1

Travel to US, spending by category, world area of residence, census div, and State, model results, 1985-86, 2908–28

UN voting record and share of votes in agreement with US, by issue, country, and world area, 1988, annual rpt, 7004–18

Unemployment rates in 7 Pacific basin countries, 1986-88, hearings, 23846–4.27

USIA library holdings, use, and staff, by country and city, FY88, annual rpt, 9854–4

Visas of US issued at Foreign Service posts, by category and world area, selected years FY84-88, annual rpt, 7184–4

Weather conditions and effect on agriculture, by US region, State, and city, and world area, weekly rpt, 2152–2

Weather events and anomalies, precipitation and temperature for US and foreign locations, weekly rpt, 2182–6

Weather forecasts for US and Northern Hemisphere, precipitation and temperature by location, semimonthly rpt, 2182–1

see also Afghanistan
see also Asian Development Bank
see also Bahrain
see also Bangladesh
see also Bhutan
see also Brunei
see also Burma
see also Cambodia
see also China, Peoples Republic
see also Hong Kong
see also India
see also Indonesia
see also Iran
see also Iraq
see also Israel
see also Japan
see also Jordan
see also Korea, North
see also Korea, South
see also Kuwait
see also Laos
see also Lebanon
see also Macao
see also Malaysia
see also Maldives
see also Middle East
see also Mongolia
see also Nepal
see also Oman
see also Pakistan
see also Philippines
see also Qatar
see also Saudi Arabia
see also Singapore
see also Southeast Asia
see also Sri Lanka
see also Syria

see also Taiwan
see also Thailand
see also Turkey
see also United Arab Emirates
see also Vietnam
see also Yemen, North
see also Yemen, South
see also under By Foreign Country in the
  "Index by Categories"

Asian Americans

Agriculture census, 1987: farms, farmland, production, finances, and operator characteristics, by county, final State rpt series, 2331–1

AIDS cases by risk group, race, sex, age, State, and MSA, and deaths, monthly rpt, 4202–9

Alcohol use, abuse, treatment, and views of racial and ethnic groups in US and native countries, by selected characteristics, 1988 compilation of papers, 4488–12

Alcohol use and abuse among minority groups, and related problems, by selected characteristics, 1985 conf papers, 4488–13

Arrests and prisoners, by offense, offender characteristics, and location, 1970s-87, annual rpt, 6064–6.4; 6064–6.6

Arrests, by offense, offender characteristics, and location, 1988, annual rpt, 6224–2.2

Births and rates, by characteristics of birth, infant, and parents, 1987 and trends from 1940, US Vital Statistics advance annual rpt, 4146–5.110

Business mgmt and financial aid from Minority Business Dev Centers, and characteristics of businesses, by region and State, FY88, annual rpt, 2104–6

Census of Population, 1980: selected socioeconomic data for Asian and Pacific Island Americans, by detailed origin, young readers pamphlet, 2326–1.5

Deaths and rates, by detailed cause and demographic characteristics, 1986 and trends from 1900, US Vital Statistics annual rpt, 4144–2

Disease (infectious notifiable) reporting to CDC, cases and rates by race, 1987, article, 4042–3.943

Earnings, and employment and other characteristics of Asian Americans, by detailed origin and whether foreign-born, 1980, 11046–7.2

Education data compilation, students, staff, finances, and facilities, 1989 edition, annual rpt, 4824–2

Employment of minorities and women, by occupation, SIC 1- to 3- digit industry, State, and MSA, 1986, annual rpt, 9244–1

Fed Equal Opportunity Recruitment Program activity, and employment by sex, race, pay grade, and selected occupation, FY88, annual rpt, 9844–33

Fed Govt employment of minorities, handicapped, and veterans, and years of service, by occupation, age, sex, and agency, as of Sept 1988, biennial rpt, 9844–27

FmHA loans, by type, borrower characteristics, and State, quarterly rpt, 1182–8

FmHA loans, by type, borrower race, and State, quarterly rpt, 1182–5

Indochina refugee population fertility indicators, by ethnic group, 1970s-84, article, 4042–3.910

Nutritional status and related health condition and practices, by selected characteristics, 1970s-87, 4048–33

Prisoners, movements, and characteristics, by State, 1986, annual rpt, 6064–26

Science and engineering grad enrollment, by field, source of funds, and characteristics of student and instn, 1975-87, annual rpt, 9627–7

Science and engineering labor supply, R&D funding, and other science indicators, with foreign comparisons, 1960s-89, annual chartbook, 9624–22

Science and engineering PhDs, by field, instn, employment prospects, sex, race, and other characteristics, 1960s-88, 9627–30

Science and engineering PhDs employment and other characteristics, by field and State, 1987, biennial rpt, 9627–18

Small business establishments, operations, owner characteristics, and job training, late 1950s-87, 9768–20

State and local govt employment of minorities and women, by occupation, function, pay level, and State, 1986, annual rpt, 9244–6

Statistical Abstract of US, social, political, and economic data, 1790-2025, comprehensive annual compilation, 2324–1.1

Telecommunications industries minority employment and discrimination charges, with data by industry and selected firm, 1970s-88, hearings, 21368–113

see also Pacific Islands Americans

see also under By Race and Ethnic Group in the "Index by Categories"

Asian Development Bank

Loans and grants for economic and military aid from US and intl agencies, by program and country, FY46-87, annual rpt, 9914–5

Technology transfer projects and spending of Bank, 1984, compilation of papers, 3908–4

US contributions to multilateral dev banks, FY86-90, annual rpt, 9904–1.4

Asphalt and tar

Bitumen-bearing tar sand deposits locations and characteristics, as of 1984, 5668–88

Building materials PPI, by type, bimonthly rpt, 2042–1.5

Carcinogens chemistry, sources, environment and health risks, and regulation, by substance and brand, 1989, annual rpt, 4044–15

Consumption of oil, switching to other fuels, capability by end-use sector, 1989, annual rpt, 3164–88

County Business Patterns, 1987: employment, establishments, and payroll, by SIC 2- to 4-digit industry and county, annual State rpt series, 2326–8

Exports and imports of US shipped through Canada, by detailed commodity, customs district, and country, 1987, annual rpt, 7704–11

Freight (waterborne domestic and foreign) by commodity, traffic, and passengers, by port and waterway, 1987, annual rpt, 3754–3

Hwy construction material use by type, and spending, by State, various periods 1944-88, annual rpt, 7554–29

Manufacturing census, 1987: financial and operating data, for SIC 4-digit industries by product, preliminary rpt, 2491–1.38; 2491–1.41

Occupational injury and illness rates, by SIC 2- to 4-digit industry, 1987, annual rpt, 6844–1

Ocean and beach plastic, tar, and other nondegradable debris, incidence and environmental impacts, 1970s-88, 14738–4

Price indexes (producer), by stage of processing and detailed commodity, monthly rpt, 6762–6

Price indexes (producer), by stage of processing and detailed commodity, monthly 1988, annual rpt, 6764–2

Prices and spending for fuel, by type, end-use sector, and State, 1987, annual rpt, 3164–64

Stone, sand, and gravel production, by end use, State, and district, 1985-86, 5608–157

Supply, demand, and movement of crude oil, gas liquids, and refined products, by PAD district and State, 1988 and trends from 1973, annual rpt, 3164–2

Aspirin

see Drugs

Assassination

Terrorist (intl) incidents, casualties, and attacks on US targets, by attack type and country, 1980-88, 7008–56

Terrorist (intl) incidents, casualties, and attacks on US targets, by attack type and world area, 1968-88, annual rpt, 7004–13

Terrorist incidents in US, related activity, and casualties, by attack type, target, group, and location, 1988, annual rpt, 6224–6

Assault

Arrest rates, by offense, sex, age, and race, 1987, annual rpt, 6224–7

Arrests by offender characteristics, prosecutions, convictions, and sentences by type, by felony offense, 1983-86, 6066–19.52

Board and care homes conditions, State licensing and enforcement activity, and client characteristics, 1970s-88, 21148–55

Court civil and criminal caseloads for Federal district, appeals, and special courts, June 1989, annual rpt, 18204–2; 18204–8

Crime, criminal justice admin and enforcement, and public opinion, data compilation, 1970s-88, annual rpt, 6064–6

Crime Index by population size and region, and offenses by large city, Jan-June 1989, semiannual rpt, 6222–1

Crimes, arrests by offender characteristics, and rates, by offense, and law enforcement employees, by population size and jurisdiction, 1988, annual rpt, 6224–2

Criminal case processing from arrest to sentencing, cases and duration by disposition, offense, and defendant characteristics, for selected cities, 1986, annual rpt, 6064–27

Criminal case processing in Federal district courts, and dispositions, by offense, district, and offender characteristics, 1984, annual rpt, 6064–29

Criminal case processing in Federal district courts, disposition by offense, 1980-87, 6066–19.50

Deaths and rates, by detailed cause and demographic characteristics, 1986 and trends from 1900, US Vital Statistics annual rpt, 4144–2

Diplomats and staff with immunity for foreign missions in US and US missions abroad, and foreign diplomats criminal cases, 1978-87, hearing, 25388–51

Drug test results at arrest, by drug type, offense, and sex, for selected urban areas, quarterly rpt, 6062–3

Juvenile court delinquency cases, by offense, referral source, disposition, age, sex, race, State, and county, 1985, annual rpt, 6064–12

Juvenile court referrals by offender characteristics, and dispositions, by offense, 1984, 6066–27.2

Juvenile delinquent and status offenses, by sex, race, age, income, and urban-rural location, 1976-86 surveys, annual rpt, 6064–6.3

Juvenile offenders recidivism rates, arrests, and court referrals, by offense, age, and sex, 1983 local area studies, 6068–227

Occupational deaths, by cause and industry div, 1987, annual rpt, 6844–1

Prison conditions, population, and problems, issues and bibl, 1989 compilation of papers, 25928–8

Prison time served ratio to offenses committed, by offense, 1958-86, 6068–229

Prisoners in State instns, by offense, criminal history, and inmate, family, and victim characteristics, 1986, annual rpt, 6064–26.3

Railroad accidents, casualties, and damage, by cause, railroad, and State, 1988, annual rpt, 7604–1

Recidivism rates of prisoners released in 1983, by offense and prisoner characteristics, 1983-86, 6066–19.48

Sentences by State courts for felony offenses, and sentence lengths and time served, by offense, 1986, 6066–25.19

Sentences for Federal crimes, guidelines use and results by offense and district, and Sentencing Commission activities, 1988, annual rpt, 17664–1

Sentences for Federal offenses, guidelines by offense and circumstances, 1989 rpt, 17668–1

Statistical Abstract of US, social, political, and economic data, 1790-2025, comprehensive annual compilation, 2324–1.1

Terrorist (intl) incidents, casualties, and attacks on US targets, by attack type and country, 1980-88, 7008–56

Terrorist (intl) incidents, casualties, and attacks on US targets, by attack type and world area, 1968-88, annual rpt, 7004–13

Victimization rates, by victim and offender characteristics, circumstances, and offense, survey rpt series, 6066–3

Victimizations and rates, by type of weapon, 1965-87, annual rpt, 6224–8

Victimizations, by offense, offender characteristics, and victim reactions and views, 1986-87, 6066–19.47

Victimizations of households, by offense, household characteristics, and location, 1975-88, annual rpt, 6066–25.22

Victimizations resulting in injury, by offense, type of injury and medical care received, and victim characteristics, 1979-86, 6066–19.49

see also Assaults on police
see also Domestic violence

Assaults on police

Assaults and deaths of law enforcement officers, by circumstances, agency, victim and offender characteristics, and location, 1988, annual rpt, 6224–3

Assaults and deaths of law enforcement officers, by circumstances, and offender characteristics, 1977-87, annual rpt, 6064–6.3

Assets and liabilities

see Business assets and liabilities, general
see Business assets and liabilities, specific industry
see Business inventories
see Government assets and liabilities
see Personal debt
see Wealth

Association of Southeast Asian Nations

Background Notes, ASEAN history, structure, and programs, 1989 rpt, 7006–2.17

Exports and imports of US with Asian countries by commodity, and free trade area proposal, 1985-88, 9886–4.135

UN voting record and share of votes in agreement with US, by issue, country, and world area, 1988, annual rpt, 7004–18

Association of State and Interstate Water Pollution Control Administrators

"America's Clean Water: The States' Nonpoint Source Assessment 1985", 21568–46

Associations

County Business Patterns, 1987: employment, establishments, and payroll, by SIC 2- to 4-digit industry and county, annual State rpt series, 2326–8

Earnings by major industry group, and personal income per capita and by source, by region and State, 1929-87, 2708–40

Employment, earnings, and hours, by selected SIC 1- to 4-digit industry, State, and for 262 MSAs, 1972-87, 6748–81

Employment, earnings, and hours, by SIC 1- to 4-digit industry, monthly 1983-Feb 1989, annual rpt, 6744–4

FmHA borrowers, by type of borrower and loan, and State, quarterly rpt, 1182–4

Lumber and wood products export market dev, assn listing, FAS quarterly circular, supplement, 1925–36

Occupational safety and health education grants, by recipient, 1989, press release, 6606–3.9

Schools (public) partnerships with community organizations, participation, activities, and contributions, by school characteristics and location, 1987/88, 4826–1.27

Science and engineering employment, by nonmanufacturing industry and field, 1987, triennial rpt, 9627–31

Service industries census, 1987: establishments, receipts, employment, and payroll, by SIC 2- to 4-digit kind of business, MSA, county, and city, State rpt series, 2391–1

Tax (income) returns of corporations, income and tax items by asset size and detailed industry, 1986, annual rpt, 8304–4; 8304–21

see also Consumer cooperatives
see also Cooperatives
see also Credit unions
see also Labor unions
see also Membership organizations
see also Nonprofit organizations and foundations
see also Political action committees
see also Rural cooperatives
see also Tax exempt organizations
see also By Industry in the "Index by Categories"

Asthma

see Respiratory diseases

Astronautics

see Astronauts
see Communications satellites
see Meteorological satellites
see Satellites
see Space program accidents and safety
see Space programs
see Space sciences

Astronauts

NASA project launch schedules and technical descriptions, press release series, 9506–2

Space launches and other activities of NASA and USSR, with flight data, 1957-88, annual rpt, 9504–6.1

Astronomy

Degrees (PhD) in science and engineering, by field, instn, employment prospects, sex, race, and other characteristics, 1960s-88, 9627–30

Employment and other characteristics of science and engineering PhDs, by field and State, 1987, biennial rpt, 9627–18

Employment characteristics of scientists and engineers, by field, 1988, biennial rpt, 9627–16

Employment of scientists, engineers, and technicians in manufacturing, by field, occupation, and industry, 1986, triennial rpt, 9627–23

Enrollment in science and engineering grad programs, by field, source of funds, and characteristics of student and instn, 1975-87, annual rpt, 9627–7

Fed Govt aid to higher education and nonprofit instns for R&D and related activities, by field, instn, agency, and State, FY87, annual rpt, 9627–17

NASA project launch schedules and technical descriptions, press release series, 9506–2

Observatories of higher education instns, purchases, 1982-83 and 1985-86, 9628–76

Planetary space probe findings, and NASA activities and finances, 1957-88, annual rpt, 9504–6.1

R&D funding by Fed Govt at large science facilities, by field, performer, and facility, FY86-88, hearings, 21708–128

R&D funding by Fed Govt, by field, performer type, agency, and State, FY87-89, annual rpt, 9627–20

R&D funding by higher education instns, by source and field, FY80-87, annual rpt, 9624–18.5

Star position tables, planet coordinates, time conversion factors, and listing of observatories worldwide, 1990, annual rpt, 3804–7

AT&T

see American Telephone and Telegraph Co.

Athens, Ga.

see also under By SMSA or MSA in the "Index by Categories"

Athletics

see Physical education and training

see Sporting goods

see Sports and athletics

Atlanta, Ga.

CPI by component for US city average, and by region, population size, and for 27 metro areas, monthly rpt, 6762–2

Drug abuse indicators for selected metro areas, research results, data collection, and policy issues, 1989 semiannual conf, 4492–5

Fruit and vegetable shipments, and arrivals in US and Canada cities, by mode of transport and State and country of origin, 1988, annual rpt, 1311–4.1

Housing starts and completions authorized by building permits in 40 MSAs, quarterly rpt, 2382–9

Wages by occupation, for office and plant workers, 1989 survey, periodic MSA rpt, 6785–12.5

see also under By City and By SMSA or MSA in the "Index by Categories"

Atlantic City, N.J.

Wages by occupation, for office and plant workers, 1989 survey, periodic MSA rpt, 6785–3.10

see also under By SMSA or MSA in the "Index by Categories"

Atlantic Ocean

Coastal areas environmental conditions and mgmt, map series, 2176–5

Coastal areas environmental conditions, fish, wildlife, use, and mgmt, 1989 rpt, 5506–9.35

Environmental summary data, and intl claims and disputes, 1989 annual factbook, 9114–2

Estuary environmental conditions and mgmt, for individual areas, conf series, 2146–6

Estuary environmental conditions, nitrogen and phosphorus levels, 1982, 2176–7.15

Estuary waters approved and prohibited for shellfish harvest, and pollution sources, 1985, 2176–7.11

Exports and imports (waterborne) of US, by type of service, commodity, country, route, and US port, 1986-87, annual rpt, 7704–2

Fish (striped bass) stocks status on Atlantic coast, and sport and commercial catch by State, 1979-87, annual rpt, 5504–29

Fish and shellfish catch, life cycles, and environmental needs, for selected coastal species and regions, series, 5506–8

Fish and shellfish distribution in Atlantic Ocean, bottom trawl survey evaluation with results by species and location, 1963-87, 2168–108

Fish and shellfish distribution in Atlantic Ocean, bottom trawl survey results by species and location, periodic rpt series, 2164–18

Fish catch, trade, use, and fishery operations, with selected foreign data, by species, 1970s-88, annual rpt, 2164–1

Fishing (ocean sport) catch and effort, and Natl Marine Fisheries Service tagging and research activity, by species and location, 1987, annual rpt, 2164–7

Florida straits coastal currents, temperatures, and salinity, series, 2146–7

Freight (waterborne domestic and foreign) by commodity, traffic, and passengers, by port and waterway, 1987, annual rpt, 3754–3.1

Hurricanes and tropical storms in north Atlantic and Caribbean area, paths, surveillance, deaths, damage, and landfall probabilities by city, 1988, annual rpt, 2184–7

Hurricanes and tropical storms in north Atlantic Ocean, characteristics and deaths, 1988, annual article, 2152–8.902

Marine Fisheries Review, US and foreign fisheries resources, dev, mgmt, and research, quarterly journal, 2162–1

Marine Mammal Protection Act admin, and populations, strandings, and catch permits by species and location, 1987-88, annual rpt, 2164–11

Mariners Weather Log, quarterly journal, 2152–8

Oil and gas OCS reserves of Fed Govt, leasing and exploration activity, production, revenue, and costs, by ocean area, FY88, annual rpt, 5734–4

Oil, gas, and minerals production, revenue, and leasing activity, for Federal OCS lands by ocean region and State, 1950s-87, annual rpt, 5734–3

Pollutant concentrations in coastal and estuarine sediments, by contaminant and selected site, 1984-87, 2176–3.7

Pollutant concentrations in coastal and estuarine shellfish, by pollutant and location, 1986-88, 2176–3.8

Pollution (water) incidents and discharges, by type, source, cause, and location, 1984-86, annual rpt, 7404–3

Research activities of Atlantic Oceanographic and Meteorological Lab, and bibl, FY88, annual rpt, 2144–19

Temperature of sea surface by ocean and for US coastal areas, and Bering Sea ice conditions, monthly rpt, 2182–5

Tidal currents, daily time and velocity by station for North America coasts, forecast 1990, annual rpt, 2174–1.2

Tide height and time daily at coastal points, forecast 1990, annual rpt, 2174–2.3; 2174–2.4

Weather (marine) forecast areas, and broadcast schedules and stations worldwide, as of Nov 1988, annual rpt, 2184–3

see also Caribbean area

see also New York Bight

Atmospheric sciences

Acid rain research activities and funding, by Federal agency, 1988 annual rpt, 14354–1

Atlantic Oceanographic and Meteorological Lab research activities and bibl, FY88, annual rpt, 2144–19

Carbon dioxide and other pollutants in atmosphere, effects on climate, sea levels, and solar radiation, 1989 hearing, 25318–75

Carbon dioxide in atmosphere, measurement, methodology, and research results, series, 3006–11

Degrees (PhD) in science and engineering, by field, instn, employment prospects, sex, race, and other characteristics, 1960s-88, 9627–30

Employment and earnings in science and engineering, by field and activity, and private and Federal R&D spending, by industry, 1975-88, 9626–6.29

Employment and other characteristics of science and engineering PhDs, by field and State, 1987, biennial rpt, 9627–18

Employment characteristics of scientists and engineers, by field, 1988, biennial rpt, 9627–16

Enrollment in science and engineering grad programs, by field, source of funds, and characteristics of student and instn, 1975-87, annual rpt, 9627–7

Fed Govt aid to higher education and nonprofit instns for R&D and related activities, by field, instn, agency, and State, FY87, annual rpt, 9627–17

Great Lakes Environmental Research Lab activities, 1987 annual rpt, 2144–26

Pacific Marine Environmental Lab research activities and bibl, FY88, annual rpt, 2144–21

R&D funding by Fed Govt at large science facilities, by field, performer, and facility, FY86-88, hearings, 21708–128

R&D funding by Fed Govt, by field, performer type, agency, and State, FY87-89, annual rpt, 9627–20

R&D funding by higher education instns, by source and field, FY80-87, annual rpt, 9624–18.5

Research activity of Fed Govt in atmospheric sciences, and funding by agency and program, FY84-87, biennial rpt, 434–1

Water chemistry, environmental impacts, analytic methods, and quality and mgmt issues, 1989 rpt, 5668–96

see also Meteorology

Atomic bombs

see Nuclear explosives and explosions

see Nuclear weapons

Atomic energy

see Nuclear power

Atomic explosives

see Nuclear explosives and explosions

Atomic weapons

see Nuclear weapons

Attitudes

see Opinion and attitude surveys

Attleboro, Mass.

see also under By SMSA or MSA in the "Index by Categories"

Attorneys-at-law

see Lawyers and legal services

Auburn, Maine

see also under By SMSA or MSA in the "Index by Categories"

Audiology

see Ear diseases and infections

see Hearing and hearing disorders

see Speech pathology and audiology

Audiovisual education

see Educational broadcasting

see Educational technology

Auditing
see Accounting and auditing

Auerbach, Barbara J.
"Work in American Prisons: The Private Sector Gets Involved", 6068–228

Auerbach, Mitchel I.
"Millwork Industry: Profile and Trends", 2042–1.911

Augusta, Ga.
Wages by occupation, and benefits for office and plant workers, 1989 survey, periodic MSA rpt, 6785–12.6
see also under By SMSA or MSA in the "Index by Categories"

Aurora, Colo.
see also under By City in the "Index by Categories"

Aurora, Ill.
Housing vacancy rates for single and multifamily units and mobile homes, by city and ZIP code, 1989, annual MSA rpt, 9304–18.2
see also under By SMSA or MSA in the "Index by Categories"

Auster, Peter J.
"Tautog and Cunner. Species Profiles: Life Histories and Environmental Requirements of Coastal Fishes and Invertebrates (North and Mid-Atlantic)", 5506–8.112

Austin, Tex.
Wages by occupation, and benefits for office and plant workers, 1988 survey, periodic MSA rpt, 6785–11.2
see also under By City and By SMSA or MSA in the "Index by Categories"

Australia
Agricultural and food production and indexes, total and for selected commodities, by country, 1970s-88, annual rpt, 1524–12
Agricultural subsidies, consumer and producer equivalents by program, commodity, and major US trading partner, 1982-86, 1528–275
Agricultural trade and market impacts of eliminating foreign and US protectionist policies, model description and results, 1986, 1528–282
Agricultural trade of US, by detailed commodity and country, 1988, semiannual rpt, 1522–4
Background Notes, summary social, political, and economic data, 1989 rpt, 7006–2.18
Bauxite proppants (calcined) from Australia at less than fair value, injury to US industry, investigation with background financial and operating data, 1989 rpt, 9886–14.257
Coal production and freight costs, and competitive position in selected markets, for Australia and US, 1987-89, 2048–143
Coal production, trade, and govt subsidies, by country and country group, 1973-87 and projected to 2000, 2048–144
Economic and military aid and loans from US and intl agencies, by program and country, FY46-87, annual rpt, 9914–5
Economic conditions in Communist and OECD countries, 1987, annual rpt, 7144–11
Economic conditions in Communist, OECD, and selected other countries, 1960s-88, annual rpt, 9114–4

Economic conditions, income, production, prices, employment, and trade, 1989 periodic country rpt, 2046–4.17; 2046–4.101
Economic conditions, investment and export opportunities, and trade practices, 1989 country market research rpt, 2046–6.10
Economic conditions, policy, and trade practices, by country, 1986-88, annual rpt, 21384–5
Economic, social, political, and geographic summary data, by country, 1989, annual factbook, 9114–2
Energy prices, by fuel type and end use, for 10 countries, 1980-88 annual rpt, 3164–50.6
Exports and imports (waterborne) of US, by type of service, commodity, country, route, and US port, 1986-87, annual rpt, 7704–2
Exports and imports (waterborne) of US, by type of service, customs district, port, and world area, monthly rpt, 2422–7
Exports and imports of US, by commodity group, world area, selected country, US coastal area and port, and mode of transport, monthly rpt, 2422–9
Exports and imports of US, by selected country, country group, and commodity group, 1988, annual rpt, 2044–37
Fish (groundfish) imports from Canada, New Zealand, and Australia to western US, by species, 1983-87, annual rpt, 2164–16.1
Fruit production, trade, use, and processing, by commodity for 5 countries, 1986-89, annual article, 1925–34.909
Grain production, use, exports, quality standards, storage, and prices, for 5 countries, 1960s-88, 26358–201.2
Human rights conditions in 170 countries, 1988, annual rpt, 21384–3
Imports of goods, services, and investment from US, trade barriers, impacts, and US actions, by country, 1988, annual rpt, 444–2
Labor conditions, union coverage, and work accidents, 1989 annual country rpt, 6366–4.31
Military aid of US, arms sales, and training programs costs and budget requests, by program, world region, and country, FY88-90, annual rpt, 7144–13
Military spending, arms trade, and force strengths, with govt spending and population, by country, 1977-87, annual rpt, 9824–1
Minerals Yearbook, 1987, Vol 3: foreign country reviews of production, trade, and policy, by commodity, annual rpt, 5604–35
Minerals Yearbook, 1987, Vol 3 preprints: foreign country review of production, trade, and policy, by commodity, annual rpt, 5604–23.6
Monetary aggregates forecasts, performance of alternative models, for Australia, late 1960s-87, technical paper, 9366–6.169
Multinatl firms US affiliates, finances, and operations, by industry, world area of parent firm, and State, 1987, annual rpt, 2704–4
Multinatl US firms and foreign affiliates finances and operations, by industry of parent firm and affiliate, world area, and country, preliminary 1987, annual rpt, 2704–5

Oil production, trade, use, and stocks, by selected country and country group, monthly rpt, 3162–42
Population size, growth rates, and components of change, by country, projected 1989-2020 and trends from 1950, biennial rpt, 2324–9
R&D funding by Fed Govt, by field, performer type, agency, and State, FY87-89, annual rpt, 9627–20
Raisin production, trade, use, and stocks for selected countries, 1985-89, article, 1925–34.924
Science and engineering immigrants, by field, age, sex, country and world area of birth and last residence, and State, 1987 and trends from 1967, 9627–29
Space satellites and other objects launched since 1957, quarterly listing, 9502–2
Steel export ceilings under voluntary restraint agreements, by country and product, with Western US steel industry impact, 1989 rpt, 9886–4.136
Steel imports of US under voluntary restraint agreement, by product, customs district, and country, with US industry operating data, monthly rpt, 9882–13
Travel to US and Canada, market analysis with detailed trip and traveler characteristics, 1988, country rpt, 2906–2.13
Travel to US, market research, major magazine ad costs and circulation, and trade show data, for selected countries, 1989-90, annual rpt, 2904–11
UN voting record and share of votes in agreement with US, by issue, country, and world area, 1988, annual rpt, 7004–18
Unemployment rates in 7 Pacific basin countries, 1986-88, hearings, 23846–4.27
Weather conditions and effect on agriculture, by US region, State, and city, and world area, weekly rpt, 2152–2
Wheat trade, elasticities of demand for US and 5 countries, alternative models description and results, 1950s-86, 1528–281
see also under By Foreign Country in the "Index by Categories"

Austria
Agricultural and food production and indexes, total and for selected commodities, by country, 1970s-88, annual rpt, 1524–12
Agricultural production, prices, and trade, by country, 1970s-88 and forecast 1990, annual world region rpt, 1524–4.1
Agricultural trade of US, by detailed commodity and country, 1988, semiannual rpt, 1522–4
AID loans repayment status and terms by program and country, and status of predecessor agency loans, quarterly rpt, 9912–3
Apprentices in US and 4 European countries, 1987, article, 6722–1.936
Auto imports from US, trade barriers by country, 1988, annual rpt, 444–2
Economic and military aid and loans from US and intl agencies, by program and country, FY46-87, annual rpt, 9914–5
Economic conditions, income, production, prices, employment, and trade, 1989 periodic country rpt, 2046–4.37

Economic conditions, policy, and trade practices, by country, 1986-88, annual rpt, 21384-5

Economic, social, political, and geographic summary data, by country, 1989, annual factbook, 9114-2

Exports and imports of US, by selected country, country group, and commodity group, 1988, annual rpt, 2044-37

Human rights conditions in 170 countries, 1988, annual rpt, 21384-3

Labor conditions, union coverage, and work accidents, 1989 annual country rpt, 6366-4.29; 6366-4.59

Military aid of US, arms sales, and training programs costs and budget requests, by program, world region, and country, FY88-90, annual rpt, 7144-13

Military spending, arms trade, and force strengths, with govt spending and population, by country, 1977-87, annual rpt, 9824-1

Minerals Yearbook, 1987, Vol 3: foreign country reviews of production, trade, and policy, by commodity, annual rpt, 5604-35

Minerals Yearbook, 1987, Vol 3 preprints: foreign country review of production, trade, and policy, by commodity, annual rpt, 5604-23.7

Multinatl US firms and foreign affiliates finances and operations, by industry of parent firm and affiliate, world area, and country, preliminary 1987, annual rpt, 2704-5

Oil production, trade, use, and stocks, by selected country and country group, monthly rpt, 3162-42

Population size, growth rates, and components of change, by country, projected 1989-2020 and trends from 1950, biennial rpt, 2324-9

Steel export ceilings under voluntary restraint agreements, by country and product, with Western US steel industry impact, 1989 rpt, 9886-4.136

Steel imports of US under voluntary restraint agreement, by product, customs district, and country, with US industry operating data, monthly rpt, 9882-13

UN voting record and share of votes in agreement with US, by issue, country, and world area, 1988, annual rpt, 7004-18

Unemployment insurance costs and beneficiaries, for US and 5 European countries, 1973-84, article, 6722-1.919

see also under By Foreign Country in the "Index by Categories"

Auten, Gerald E.
"Estimation and Interpretation of Capital Gains Realization Behavior: Evidence from Panel Data", 8006-3.63
"Private Activity Tax-Exempt Bonds, 1986", 8302-2.905

Authors
see Writers and writing

Automated tellers
see Electronic funds transfer

Automation
Air traffic control and airway facilities improvement activities under Natl Airspace System Plan, 1981-85 and projected to 2000, annual rpt, 7504-12
Air traffic control system safety, working conditions, and traffic volume, various periods 1981-88, GAO rpt series, 26113-220

Animal feed mill operations, detailed data by State, 1984, 1568-281

Banks in Fed Reserve System, expenses and operations itemized by service, office, and district, 1988, annual rpt, 9364-11

Customs Service imports inspection, automated selection system operations, FY88-1st qtr FY89, GAO rpt, 26125-35

Labor force, composition, and productivity effects of technological devs, by industry, 1960s-86 and projected to 2000, series, 6826-2

Manufacturing census, 1987: financial and operating data, for SIC 4-digit industries by product, preliminary rpt, 2491-1.65

Manufacturing high technology use and plans, with data by technology, selected industry, and firm and market characteristics, 1988 survey, 2508-1

Small business high technology sales, exports, siting, technology transfer, views on competitiveness, 1988 survey, hearing, 21728-69

Unemployed displaced workers, by reason, industry, selected characteristics, and State, 1988, annual rpt, 6744-18

Unemployment insurance systems of States, Labor Dept grants for automation, 1989, press release, 6406-2.24

see also Computer industry and products
see also Computer networks
see also Computer use
see also Electronic funds transfer
see also Industrial robots
see also Information storage and retrieval systems

Automobile exhaust
see Motor vehicle exhaust

Automobile industry
see Motor vehicle industry

Automobile insurance
Consumer Expenditure Survey, household income by source, and itemized spending, by selected characteristics and location, 1984-86, annual rpt, 6764-5.2

Costs of operating autos by component, and Fed Govt mileage reimbursement rates, 1988, annual rpt, 9454-13

Costs of owning and operating autos, by component, 1977-88, annual rpt, 7304-2.1

Coverage under auto insurance, premiums, and theft losses, with data by model and State, 1988 hearings, 21368-110

CPI by component for US city average, and by region, population size, and for 27 metro areas, monthly rpt, 6762-2

Profitability, income, and expenses, with premiums by company, 1977-87, 26119-267

Statistical Abstract of US, social, political, and economic data, 1790-2025, comprehensive annual compilation, 2324-1.3

Automobile parking
see Parking facilities

Automobile rental
see Motor vehicle rental

Automobile repair and maintenance
Collective bargaining agreements expiring during year, and workers covered, by firm, union, industry group, and State, 1989, annual rpt, 6784-9

Consumer Expenditure Survey, household income by source, and itemized spending, by selected characteristics and location, 1984-86, annual rpt, 6764-5.2

Costs of crash repair by State, and bodywork CPI, 1988 hearings, 21368-110

Costs of operating autos by component, and Fed Govt mileage reimbursement rates, 1988, annual rpt, 9454-13

Costs of owning and operating autos, by component, 1977-88, annual rpt, 7304-2.1

County Business Patterns, 1987: employment, establishments, and payroll, by SIC 2- to 4-digit industry and county, annual State rpt series, 2326-8

CPI by component for US city average, and by region, population size, and for 27 metro areas, monthly rpt, 6762-2

Earnings by major industry group, and personal income per capita and by source, by region and State, 1929-87, 2708-40

Employment, earnings, and hours, by selected SIC 1- to 4-digit industry, State, and for 262 MSAs, 1972-87, 6748-81

Employment, earnings, and hours, by SIC 1- to 4-digit industry, monthly 1983-Feb 1989, annual rpt, 6744-4

Employment in nonmanufacturing industries, by detailed occupation and SIC 2-digit industry, 1987, triennial rpt, 6748-60

Equipment for auto repair PPI, monthly 1988, annual rpt, 6764-2

Farm prices received and paid, by commodity and State, 1988, annual rpt, 1629-5

Fed Govt motor vehicle fleet costs and operating data, by agency, FY87, annual rpt, 9454-9

Guam economic censuses, 1987: employment, firms, payroll, and receipts, by SIC 1- to 4-digit industry and election district, 2595-1

Input-output structure of US economy, detailed interindustry transactions for 84 industries, and components of final demand, 1983, annual article, 2702-1.909

Labor productivity, indexes of output, hours, and employment by SIC 2- to 4-digit industry, 1963-87, annual rpt, 6824-1.4

Northern Mariana Islands economic census, 1987: employment, firms, payroll, and receipts, by SIC 1- to 4-digit industry, 2597-1

Occupational injury and illness rates, by SIC 2- to 4-digit industry, 1987, annual rpt, 6844-1

Retail of auto and home supplies, productivity trends and technological devs for stores, 1972-87, article, 6722-1.941

Science and engineering employment, by nonmanufacturing industry and field, 1987, triennial rpt, 9627-31

Service industries census, 1987: establishments, receipts, employment, and payroll, by SIC 2- to 4-digit kind of business, MSA, county, and city, State rpt series, 2391-1

Service industries receipts, by SIC 2- to 4-digit kind of business, 1988, annual rpt, 2413-8

Small business establishments, employment, and financial ratios, by SIC 1- to 2-digit industry and State, late 1960s-87, 9768-19

Tax (excise) collections of IRS, by type of tax, region, and State, FY88, annual rpt, 8304–3.3

Tax (excise) indexed to inflation, impacts on Federal revenue and family tax burden by commodity, projected under alternative proposals, 1989-93, GAO rpt, 26119–254

Tax (income) returns of sole proprietorships, income statement items, by industry group, 1987, annual article, 8302–2.904

Tax (property) revenue by level of govt, assessed values by locality, and exemptions, by property type and State, 1987 Census of Govts, 2453–1

Traffic volume in urban areas and detailed trip characteristics, by transport mode and city, 1950s-88, 7888–37

Transportation census, 1987: trucks, by detailed characteristics, miles traveled, and type of product carried, State rpt series, 2573–1

Transportation finances, operations, vehicles, equipment, accidents, and energy use, by mode of transport, 1955-88, annual rpt, 7304–2

Travel to US, spending by world area of residence, and economic impact, by spending category, census div, and State, model results, 1985-86, 2908–28

Wholesale trade census, 1987: employment, establishments, finances, and operations, by SIC 2- to 4-digit kind of business, MSA, county, and city, State rpt series, 2405–1

Wholesale trade sales and inventories, by SIC 2- to 3-digit kind of business, monthly rpt, 2413–7

see also Automobile insurance
see also Automobile repair and maintenance
see also Drivers licenses
see also Gasoline
see also Gasoline service stations
see also Motor vehicle exhaust
see also Motor vehicle exports and imports
see also Motor vehicle fleets
see also Motor vehicle industry
see also Motor vehicle registrations
see also Motor vehicle rental
see also Motor vehicle safety devices
see also Motor vehicle theft
see also Traffic accident fatalities
see also Traffic accidents and safety
see also under By Commodity in the "Index by Categories"

Autopsies

Aviation medicine research and test results, technical rpt series, 7506–10

Diving (underwater sport and occupational) deaths, by circumstances, diver characteristics, and location, 1970-87, annual rpt, 2144–5

Drug abuse emergency room admissions and deaths, by drug type and major metro area, July 1985-Dec 1988, semiannual rpt, 4492–3

Drug abuse emergency room admissions and deaths, by drug type and source, sex, race, age, and major metro area, 1988, annual rpt, 4494–8

Drug abuse indicators for selected metro areas, research results, data collection, and policy issues, 1989 semiannual conf, 4492–5

Performance of autopsies, by cause of death, age, race, and sex, 1986, US Vital Statistics annual rpt, 4144–2.1

Performance of autopsies, for 15 leading causes, 1987, US Vital Statistics advance annual rpt, 4146–5.113

Tuberculosis cases diagnosed at time of death, by State and city, 1987, annual rpt, 4204–10

Avery, David

"Southeastern Manufacturing: Recent Changes and Prospects", 9371–1.901

Avery, Robert B.

"Loan Commitments and Bank Risk Exposure", 9366–6.179

Avery, Roger

"Measuring Household Change at the Individual Level Using Data from SIPP", 2626–10.96

Aviation

see Aeronautical navigation
see Aerospace industry
see Air traffic control
see Air travel
see Aircraft
see Airlines
see Airports and airways
see Astronauts
see Aviation accidents and safety
see Aviation fuels
see Aviation medicine
see Aviation sciences
see Civil aviation
see General aviation
see Military aviation
see Space programs
see Space sciences
see Spacecraft

Aviation accidents and safety

Accident deaths and rates, by cause, age, race, sex, and State, 1986, US Vital Statistics annual rpt, 4144–2

Accidents and circumstances, for US operations of domestic and foreign airlines and general aviation, periodic rpt, 9612–1

Accidents and deaths, by mode of transport, 1955-88, annual rpt, 7304–2

Accidents, casualties, and damage for air carriers, by detailed circumstances, 1986, annual rpt, 9614–2

Accidents, deaths, and circumstances, for by carrier and carrier type, preliminary 1988, annual press release, 9614–9

Alaska airport dev plans and air systems operations, FY89-98, annual rpt, 7504–36

Bombing incidents and casualties, by target, circumstances, and State, 1979-88, annual rpt, 8484–4.1

Collisions (mid-air) prevention measures of FAA, and near collisions by type of air traffic control facility and selected airport, 1986-88, GAO rpt, 26113–426

DOT activities by subagency, budget, and summary accident data, FY85, annual rpt, 7304–1

General aviation accidents, by circumstances, characteristics of persons and aircraft involved, and type of flying, 1986, annual rpt, 9614–3

Hazardous material transport accidents, casualties, and damage, by mode of transport, with DOT control activities, 1988, annual rpt, 7304–4

Injury and illness rates by SIC 2- to 4-digit industry, and deaths by cause and industry div, 1987, annual rpt, 6844–1

Investigations and recommendations of Natl Transportation Safety Board, and aviation accidents and deaths by carrier, 1988, annual rpt, 9614–1

Medical research and test results for aviation, technical rpt series, 7506–10

Military aircraft bird collisions and related costs, by service branch, 1983-88, GAO rpt, 26123–241

Military deaths by cause, age, race, and rank, and personnel captured and missing, by service branch, 2nd half FY88, semiannual rpt, 3542–21

Natl Guard accident rates, by type, FY84-88, annual rpt, 3504–22.1

Public opinion on air travel safety and congestion, 1988 survey, hearing, 21788–180

Safety inspector training, FAA officals views on curriculum and adequacy, 1988 survey, GAO rpt, 26113–440

Weather services activities and funding, by Federal agency, planned FY89-90, annual rpt, 2144–2

see also Air piracy
see also Air traffic control
see also Space program accidents and safety

Aviation fuels

Business statistics, detailed data for major industries and economic indicators, *Survey of Current Business*, monthly rpt, 2702–1.15

Consumption, by detailed fuel type, end-use sector, and State, 1960-87, State Energy Data System annual rpt, 3164–39

Consumption of aviation fuels, forecast FY89-2000 and trends from FY80, annual rpt, 7504–6

Consumption of energy by mode of transport, fuel supply, and demographic and economic factors of vehicle use, 1970s-88, annual rpt, 3304–5

Consumption of energy by mode of transport, 1955-88, annual rpt, 7304–2

Consumption of fuel and jet load factors, projected 1985-2000, 3166–6.33

Consumption of fuel, total and per hour, by grade and aircraft type, 1988, annual rpt, 7504–29.3

Costs of operating privately owned small planes by component, and Fed Govt mileage reimbursement rates, 1987, annual rpt, 9454–13

Defense Fuel Supply Center procurement, prices, stocks, transport, and other activities and finances, FY88, annual rpt, 3904–8

Exports of US, detailed commodities by country, monthly rpt, 2422–3

Fed Govt energy use and efficiency, by agency and fuel type, FY88, annual rpt, 3304–22

Flight delays caused by air traffic control procedures and problems, and costs, with data by airport, 1976-86, 7508–68

Foreign and US oil production, trade, and stocks, by product and country, 1985-88, annual rpt, 3164–50.2

Freight (waterborne domestic and foreign) by commodity, traffic, and passengers, by port and waterway, 1987, annual rpt, 3754–3

Imports of US, detailed Schedule A commodities by country, monthly rpt, 2422–2

Manufacturing annual survey, 1986: financial and operating data, by SIC 2- to 4-digit industry, series, 2506–15

Manufacturing census, 1987: financial and operating data, for SIC 4-digit industries by product, preliminary rpt, 2491–1.41

Minerals Yearbook, 1987, Vol 3 preprints: foreign country reviews of production, trade, and policy, by commodity, annual rpt series, 5604–23

Price indexes (producer), by stage of processing and detailed commodity, monthly rpt, 6762–6

Price indexes (producer), by stage of processing and detailed commodity, monthly 1988, annual rpt, 6764–2

Prices and spending for fuel, by type, end-use sector, and State, 1987, annual rpt, 3164–64

Prices and volume of oil products sold and purchased by refiners, processors, and distributors, by product, end-use sector, PAD district, and State, monthly rpt with articles, 3162–11; 3164–85

Supply and demand of oil and refined products, refinery capacity and use, and prices, weekly rpt, 3162–32

Supply, demand, and movement of crude oil, gas liquids, and refined products, by PAD district and State, 1988 and trends from 1973, annual rpt, 3164–2

Supply, demand, and prices, by fuel type and end-use sector, projected under 3 oil price assumptions, 1988-2000, annual rpt, 3164–75

Supply, demand, and prices, by fuel type and end-use sector, with foreign comparisons, 1988 and trends from 1949, annual rpt, 3164–74.1; 3164–74.2

Supply, demand, and prices, by fuel type, end-use sector, and country, detailed data, monthly rpt, 3162–24

Supply, demand, and prices of energy, forecasts by resource type, quarterly rpt, 3162–34

Supply, demand, and prices of oil and gas, alternative projections 1987-2000, annual rpt, 3164–89

Supply, demand, trade, stocks, and refining of oil and gas liquids, by detailed product, State, and PAD district, monthly rpt with articles, 3162–6

Tax (excise) collections of IRS, by source, quarterly rpt, 8302–1

Tax (excise) collections of IRS, by type of tax, region, and State, FY88, annual rpt, 8304–3.3

Aviation industry
see Aerospace industry
see Aircraft
see Airlines
see Aviation accidents and safety

Aviation medicine
Military health care personnel, and accessions by training source, by occupation, specialty, and service branch, FY87, annual rpt, 3544–24

Research and test results for aviation medicine, technical rpt series, 7506–10

Aviation sciences
Aerial survey R&D rpts, and sources of natural resource and environmental data, quarterly listing, 9502–7

Degrees (bachelors) in aviation science, holders training performance compared to other FAA hires, 1988 technical rpt, 7506–10.54

Employment characteristics of scientists and engineers, by field, 1988, biennial rpt, 9627–16

Employment of scientists, engineers, and technicians in manufacturing, by field, occupation, and industry, 1986, triennial rpt, 9627–23

Employment of scientists, engineers, and technicians in transportation, utilities, and retail and wholesale trade, by field, occupation, and industry, 1985, triennial rpt, 9627–32

NASA R&D funding to higher education instns, by field, instn, and State, FY88, annual listing, 9504–7

R&D funding and staff of FAA, by program, FY87-88, GAO rpt, 26113–407

R&D funding by Fed Govt at large science facilities, by field, performer, and facility, FY86-88, hearings, 21708–128

R&D funding by Fed Govt, by field, performer type, agency, and State, FY87-89, annual rpt, 9627–20

R&D funding by higher education instns, by source and field, FY80-87, annual rpt, 9624–18.5

Wages of scientists and engineers in R&D, by field and educational, employment, and other characteristics, 1989, annual rpt, 3004–1

see also Space sciences

Awards, medals, and prizes
Educational partnerships of public schools with community organizations, participation, activities, and contributions, by school characteristics and location, 1987/88, 4826–1.27

Mint (US) activities, finances, coin and medals production and holdings, and gold and silver transactions, by facility, FY88, annual rpt, 8204–1

see also Employee bonuses and work incentives

see also Military awards, decorations, and medals

Ayres, Robert U.
"Historical Reconstruction of Major Pollutant Levels in the Hudson-Raritan Basin: 1880-1980", 2178–22

Babula, Ronald A.
"Contemporaneous Correlation and Modeling Canada's Imports of U.S. Crops", 1502–3.901

"Farmgate, Processor, and Consumer Price Transmissions in the Wheat Sector", 1502–3.903

Bachu, Amara
"Fertility of American Women: June 1988", 2546–1.436

Bacon, J. R.
"Regional Trends and Spatial Characteristics of U.S. Supply and Demand for Farm Output", 1548–348

Bags
see Packaging and containers

Bahamas
Agricultural and food production and indexes, total and for selected commodities, by country, 1970s-88, annual rpt, 1524–12

Agricultural trade of US, by detailed commodity and country, 1988, semiannual rpt, 1522–4

Economic and military aid and loans from US and intl agencies, by program and country, FY46-87, annual rpt, 9914–5

Economic conditions, income, production, prices, employment, and trade, 1989 periodic country rpt, 2046–4.72

Economic conditions, policy, and trade practices, by country, 1986-88, annual rpt, 21384–5

Economic, social, political, and geographic summary data, by country, 1989, annual factbook, 9114–2

Exports and imports of US, by commodity and country, 1970-87, world area rpt, 9116–1.1

Exports and imports of US, by selected country, country group, and commodity group, 1988, annual rpt, 2044–37

Human rights conditions in 170 countries, 1988, annual rpt, 21384–3

Investment (direct) incentives of Caribbean Basin Initiative, economic impacts, with finances and employment by country, 1984-88, 2048–141

Military aid of US, arms sales, and training programs costs and budget requests, by program, world region, and country, FY88-90, annual rpt, 7144–13

Minerals Yearbook, 1987, Vol 3: foreign country reviews of production, trade, and policy, by commodity, annual rpt, 5604–35

Minerals Yearbook, 1987, Vol 3 preprints: foreign country review of production, trade, and policy, by commodity, annual rpt, 5604–23.83

Multinatl US firms and foreign affiliates finances and operations, by industry of parent firm and affiliate, world area, and country, preliminary 1987, annual rpt, 2704–5

Oil exports to US by OPEC and non-OPEC countries, monthly rpt, 3162–24.3

Population size, growth rates, and components of change, by country, projected 1989-2020 and trends from 1950, biennial rpt, 2324–9

Ships in world merchant fleet, and tonnage, by country of registry, as of Jan 1988, annual rpt, 7704–3

UN voting record and share of votes in agreement with US, by issue, country, and world area, 1988, annual rpt, 7004–18

see also under By Foreign Country in the "Index by Categories"

Bahrain
Agricultural and food production and indexes, total and for selected commodities, by country, 1970s-88, annual rpt, 1524–12

Agricultural trade of US, by detailed commodity and country, 1988, semiannual rpt, 1522–4

AID economic aid to developing countries, obligations and disbursements by country, quarterly rpt, 9912–4

Economic and military aid and loans from US and intl agencies, by program and country, FY46-87, annual rpt, 9914–5

Economic conditions, income, production, prices, employment, and trade, 1989 periodic country rpt, 2046–4.51

Economic conditions, policy, and trade practices, by country, 1986-88, annual rpt, 21384–5

Economic, social, political, and geographic summary data, by country, 1989, annual factbook, 9114–2

Exports and imports of US, by commodity and country, 1970-87, world area rpt, 9116–1.3

Human rights conditions in 170 countries, 1988, annual rpt, 21384–3

Military aid of US, arms sales, and training programs costs and budget requests, by program, world region, and country, FY88-90, annual rpt, 7144–13

Military spending, arms trade, and force strengths, with govt spending and population, by country, 1977-87, annual rpt, 9824–1

Minerals Yearbook, 1987, Vol 3: foreign country reviews of production, trade, and policy, by commodity, annual rpt, 5604–35

Minerals Yearbook, 1987, Vol 3 preprints: foreign country review of production, trade, and policy, by commodity, annual rpt, 5604–23.86

Oil production, trade, use, and stocks, by selected country and country group, monthly rpt, 3162–42

Population size, growth rates, and components of change, by country, projected 1989-2020 and trends from 1950, biennial rpt, 2324–9

UN voting record and share of votes in agreement with US, by issue, country, and world area, 1988, annual rpt, 7004–18

see also under By Foreign Country in the "Index by Categories"

Bail

see Pretrial detention and release

Bailey, Kenneth W.

"Structural Econometric Model of the World Wheat Market", 1528–281

Bailey, Theodore M.

"Trichinosis Surveillance, U.S., 1986", 4202–7.901

Bailey, W. J.

"Fuel Performance Annual Report for 1987", 9634–8

Baker, D. A.

"Population Dose Commitments Due to Radioactive Releases from Nuclear Power Plant Sites in 1986", 9634–7

Baker, David B.

"Sediment, Nutrient and Pesticide Transport in Selected Lower Great Lakes Tributaries", 9208–129

Bakersfield, Calif.

Wages by occupation, for office and plant workers, 1989 survey, periodic MSA rpt, 6785–3.9

see also under By City and By SMSA or MSA in the "Index by Categories"

Baking and bakery products

Consumer Expenditure Survey, household income by source, and itemized spending, by selected characteristics and location, 1984-86, annual rpt, 6764–5.2

Consumption of food and nutrient intake by individuals, by food group, selected characteristics, and region, supplementary survey series, 1356–5

Consumption, supply, trade, prices, spending, and indexes, by food commodity, 1987, annual rpt, 1544–4

County Business Patterns, 1987: employment, establishments, and payroll, by SIC 2- to 4-digit industry and county, annual State rpt series, 2326–8

CPI by component for US city average, and by region, population size, and for 27 metro areas, monthly rpt, 6762–2

EC food supply and demand, market and support prices, and other economic indicators, by country and commodity, 1960-85, 1528–276

Employment, earnings, and hours, by selected SIC 1- to 4-digit industry, State, and for 262 MSAs, 1972-87, 6748–81

Employment, earnings, and hours, by SIC 1- to 4-digit industry, monthly 1983-Feb 1989, annual rpt, 6744–4

Employment of minorities and women, by occupation, SIC 1- to 3- digit industry, State, and MSA, 1986, annual rpt, 9244–1

Exports and imports (agricultural) of US, by detailed commodity and country, 1988, semiannual rpt, 1522–4

Exports of US, detailed commodities by country, monthly rpt, 2422–3

Fiber content in breakfast cereal and bread, health claim ads, and other factors affecting consumption, 1978-88, 9406–1.60

Finances and operations, by SIC 2- to 4-digit industry, forecast 1989 with trends from 1950s, annual rpt, 2044–28

Imports of US, detailed Schedule A commodities by country, monthly rpt, 2422–2

Labor productivity, indexes of output, hours, and employment by SIC 2- to 4-digit industry, 1963-87, annual rpt, 6824–1.3

Manufacturing annual survey, 1986: financial and operating data, by SIC 2- to 4-digit industry, series, 2506–15

Manufacturing census, 1987: financial and operating data, for SIC 4-digit industries by product, preliminary rpt, 2491–1.4; 2491–1.5

Nutrient and caloric composition of food, for raw, processed, and prepared food, 1988 rpt, 1358–3

Occupational injury and illness rates, by SIC 2- to 4-digit industry, 1987, annual rpt, 6844–1

Price indexes (producer), by stage of processing and detailed commodity, monthly rpt, 6762–6

Price indexes (producer), by stage of processing and detailed commodity, monthly 1988, annual rpt, 6764–2

Prices (farm-retail) for food, marketing cost components, and industry finances and productivity, 1950s-88, annual rpt, 1544–9

Retail trade census, 1987: employment, establishments, sales, and payroll, by SIC 2- to 4-digit kind of business, MSA, county, and city, State rpt series, 2397–1

Retail trade sales and inventories, by kind of business, region, and selected State, MSA, and city, monthly rpt, 2413–3

Retail trade sales, inventories, purchases, gross margin, and accounts receivable, by SIC 2- to 4-digit kind of business and form of ownership, 1987, annual rpt, 2413–5

Science, engineering, and technical employment in manufacturing, by field, occupation, and industry, 1986, triennial rpt, 9627–23

Science, engineering, and technical employment in transportation, utilities, and retail and wholesale trade, by field, occupation, and industry, 1985, triennial rpt, 9627–32

Tax (income) returns of corporations, income and tax items by asset size and detailed industry, 1986, annual rpt, 8304–4; 8304–21

Wheat flour bakery cost, quarterly situation rpt with articles, 1561–12

Wholesale trade census, 1987: employment, establishments, finances, and operations, by SIC 2- to 4-digit kind of business, MSA, county, and city, State rpt series, 2405–1

Balance of payments

Agricultural and food production and indexes, total and for selected commodities, by country, 1970s-88, annual rpt, 1524–12

Agricultural Outlook, production, prices, marketing, and trade, by commodity, forecast and current situation, monthly rpt with articles, 1502–2

Agricultural trade, outlook and current situation, quarterly rpt, 1542–4

Asia dollar exchange rate, and impacts of currency appreciation on current account and trade balances and economic indicators, for 3 countries, 1980s-90, GAO rpt, 26123–234

Banks (US) and nonbanking firms liabilities to and claims on foreigners, by country, 1986-87, annual rpt, 9364–5.10

Capital goods manufacturing productivity, labor cost indexes, and trade and trade balance impacts of economic conditions, with foreign comparisons, 1970s-88, article, 9385–1.909

Capital movements between US and foreign countries, *Treasury Bulletin*, quarterly rpt, 8002–4.11

China trade, by commodity, world area, and country, 1985-87, 9118–10

Communist and OECD countries economic conditions, 1987, annual rpt, 7144–11

Communist, OECD, and selected other countries economic conditions, 1960s-88, annual rpt, 9114–4

Communist, OECD, and selected other countries trade and balances, 1960s-88, annual rpt, 9114–4.9

Cuba economic conditions, agricultural and industrial production and distribution, trade, and intl economic relations, 1980-87 with trends from 1961, 9118–8

Current account balance and related economic indicators, for US and 4 countries, 1980s-87, article, 9389–1.908

Current account balance, by component, 1980-87 and projected under alternative growth and exchange rate assumptions, 1988-95, hearing, 23848–209

Current account balance of US, components and relation to foreign and US investment and economic conditions, 1970s-88 and projected to 1990s, article, 9385–1.905; 9385–1.906; 9385–1.907

Current account deficit, and impacts of alternative fiscal and monetary policies, 1980-88 and projected to 1999, 26306–6.135

Developing countries economic and social conditions from 1960s, and Intl Dev Cooperation Agency and AID activities and funding, FY88-90, annual rpt, 9904–4

Developing countries economic indicators, problem debtors compared to other borrowers, by country, 1973-84, 1528–285

Eastern Europe and USSR debt, trade, and balances with US and other western countries, with background data, 1980s-87, hearing, 21248–120

Economic indicators and components, current data and annual trends, monthly rpt, 23842–1.7

Economic Report of the President for 1989, economic effects of budget proposals, and trends and projections, 1929-99, annual hearings, 23844–4

Energy producers finances and operations, by energy type for US firms domestic and foreign operations, 1987, annual rpt, 3164–44

Exports and imports of US by country, and trade shifts by commodity, quarterly rpt, 9882–9

Exports and imports of US, by selected country, country group, and commodity group, 1988, annual rpt, 2044–37

Exports, imports, and balances of US by commodity group, world area, and country, and related employment, 1970s-88, annual rpt, 2044–26

Exports, imports, and balances of US with major trading partners, by product category, 1984-88, annual chartbook, 9884–21

Fed Govt financial operations, detailed data, *Treasury Bulletin*, quarterly rpt, 8002–4

Fed Reserve Board and Reserve banks finances, staff, and review of monetary policy and economic devs, 1988, annual rpt, 9364–1

Finance (intl) and trade studies, 1987 biennial compilation, 9375–14

Financial and business statistics, historic trends, 1988 annual chartbook, 9364–2.17

Flow-of-funds accounts, assets and liabilities by type and economic sector, outstanding at year-end 1965-88, annual rpt, 9364–3

Flow-of-funds and natl income and product accounts intl transactions, data reconciliation, 1989 technical paper, 9366–6.198

Flows of trade and investment, and economic indicators, for selected countries and country groups, selected years 1946-88, annual rpt, 204–1.9

Foreign and US economic conditions, and trade devs and balances, with data by selected country and country group, monthly rpt, 9882–14

Foreign and US economic conditions and trade devs and policy, 1988 conf papers, 9373–3.32

Foreign and US economic indicators, trade balances, and exchange rates, for selected OECD and Asian countries, 1980s-89, semiannual rpt, 8002–14

Foreign countries economic conditions and implications for US, periodic country rpt series, 2046–4

Intl transactions, *Business Conditions Digest*, monthly rpt, 2702–3.9

Intl transactions of US, and economic and monetary trends for US and 10 major trading partners, quarterly rpt, 9391–7

Intl transactions summary, monthly rpt, 9362–1.3

Intl transactions summary, 1980s-88, annual article, 9362–1.904

Intl transactions, *Survey of Current Business*, monthly rpt, quarterly tables, 2702–1.31

Investment (intl) position of US, by component, industry, world region, and country, 1987-88, annual article, 2702–1.922

Latin America trade, and balance of trade with US, by country, 1988, annual rpt, 2044–34

Lumber and wood products exports and export promotion of US by country, and trade balance, by commodity, FAS quarterly circular, 1925–36

Manufacturing capacity, output, and productivity growth, and trade balance by major industry group, 1973-87, article, 9391–1.903

Natl income and product accounts and components, *Survey of Current Business*, monthly rpt, 2702–1.21; 2702–1.25

OECD economic conditions for 6 countries and US, biweekly rpt, 9112–1

Overseas Business Reports: economic conditions, investment and export opportunities, and trade practices, country market research rpt series, 2046–6

Soviet Union economic conditions and military activity, 1960s-86, hearing, 23848–195

Soviet Union economic conditions under General Secretary Gorbachev, 1988 and trends from 1956, annual rpt, 9114–6

Statistical Abstract of US, social, political, and economic data, by outlying area and country, 1950s-87, comprehensive annual compilation, 2324–1.4

Taiwan and South Korea exports, imports, and trade balance with US, 1985-88, article, 9385–1.904

Taiwan and South Korea trade balance impacts of exchange rates and foreign and domestic economic indicators, 1974-87, article, 9393–8.905

Technology-intensive products trade balance of US, 1970-87, annual chartbook, 9624–22

Travel to and from US, and travel receipts and payments, by world area, with data by country, 1984-88, annual rpt, 2904–10

Unemployment rate relation to inflation, labor force, GNP, interest rate, and trade balance, various periods 1948-88, article, 9393–8.910

see also Foreign debts
see also Foreign exchange
see also Foreign investments
see also Foreign trade

Balance of trade
see Balance of payments

Balance sheets
see Business assets and liabilities, general
see Business assets and liabilities, specific industry
see Business income and expenses, general
see Business income and expenses, specific industry

see Government assets and liabilities

Balanced Budget and Emergency Deficit Control Act
Budget of US, CBO analysis of revenue and spending alternatives and projections of economic indicators, FY90-94, annual rpt, 26304–3

Budget of US, compact budgets by activity, function, and agency, FY90 and projected to FY94, annual rpt, 104–2

Budget of US, midsession review of FY90 budget, by function and agency, annual rpt, 104–7

Budget of US, overview, FY90, annual rpt, 104–6

Budget of US, Senate concurrent resolution, with spending and revenue targets, FY90, annual rpt, 25254–1

Budget of US, special analysis of baseline estimates required by Act, FY90, annual rpt, 104–1.1

Cancellation of budget authority under Act, by program, FY90, annual rpt, 104–27; 21924–1; 26304–6

Balke, Nathan
"Asymmetric Information and the Role of Fed Watching", 9379–12.35

Ballantyne, Harry C.
"Social Security Financing in North America", 4742–1.913

Ballenger, Louella
"Sole Proprietorship Returns, 1987", 8302–2.921

Ballenger, Nicole
"Agricultural Trade, Agreements, and Disputes in the Western Hemisphere", 1528–278

Ballistic missiles
see Missiles and rockets
see Nuclear weapons

Ballweg, John A.
"Comparison of Health Habits of Military Personnel with Civilian Populations", 4042–3.949

Baltimore, Md.
AIDS cases, and health and social services availability, for 5 cities, 1988, GAO rpt, 26121–307

CPI by component for US city average, and by region, population size, and for 15 metro areas, monthly rpt, 6762–1

CPI by component for US city average, and by region, population size, and for 27 metro areas, monthly rpt, 6762–2

Freight (waterborne domestic and foreign) by commodity, traffic, and passengers, by port and waterway, 1987, annual rpt, 3754–3.1

Fruit and vegetable shipments, and arrivals in US and Canada cities, by mode of transport and State and country of origin, 1988, annual rpt, 1311–4.1

Housing starts and completions authorized by building permits in 40 MSAs, quarterly rpt, 2382–9

Medicare enrollees health care alternatives, medical costs, training to select assigned-fee physicians, and physician attitudes, 1988 rpt, 4658–30

Wages by occupation, for office and plant workers, 1988 survey, periodic MSA rpt, 6785–11.2

see also under By City and By SMSA or MSA in the "Index by Categories"

Bangladesh

Agricultural and food production and indexes, total and for selected commodities, by country, 1970s-88, annual rpt, 1524–12

Agricultural production, prices, and trade, by country, 1960s-89, annual world region rpt, 1524–4.2

Agricultural trade of US, by detailed commodity and country, 1988, semiannual rpt, 1522–4

Agricultural trade of US with Asia, Middle East, and North Africa, by commodity and country, 1962-86, 1528–277

AID activities and funding by project and function, FY90, and developing countries summary socioeconomic data from 1960s, annual rpt, 9904–4.6

AID economic aid to developing countries, obligations and disbursements by country, quarterly rpt, 9912–4

AID loans repayment status and terms by program and country, and status of predecessor agency loans, quarterly rpt, 9912–3

Banks costs relation to loans, deposits, and input prices, for Bangladesh, 1983-84, working paper, 9371–10.39

Economic and military aid and loans from US and intl agencies, by program and country, FY46-87, annual rpt, 9914–5

Economic conditions, income, production, prices, employment, and trade, 1989 periodic country rpt, 2046–4.86

Economic conditions, policy, and trade practices, by country, 1986-88, annual rpt, 21384–5

Economic, social, political, and geographic summary data, by country, 1989, annual factbook, 9114–2

Exports and imports of US, by selected country, country group, and commodity group, 1988, annual rpt, 2044–37

Human rights conditions in 170 countries, 1988, annual rpt, 21384–3

Labor conditions, union coverage, and work accidents, 1989 annual country rpt, 6366–4.12; 6366–4.44

Military aid of US, arms sales, and training programs costs and budget requests, by program, world region, and country, FY88-90, annual rpt, 7144–13

Military spending, arms trade, and force strengths, with govt spending and population, by country, 1977-87, annual rpt, 9824–1

Minerals production, reserves, and industry role in domestic economy and world supply, 1988 country rpt, 5606–1.17

Minerals Yearbook, 1987, Vol 3: foreign country reviews of production, trade, and policy, by commodity, annual rpt, 5604–35

Minerals Yearbook, 1987, Vol 3 preprints: foreign country review of production, trade, and policy, by commodity, annual rpt, 5604–23.85

Population size, growth rates, and components of change, by country, projected 1989-2020 and trends from 1950, biennial rpt, 2324–9

UN voting record and share of votes in agreement with US, by issue, country, and world area, 1988, annual rpt, 7004–18

see also under By Foreign Country in the "Index by Categories"

Bangor, Maine

see also under By SMSA or MSA in the "Index by Categories"

Banister, Judith

"China: The Problem of Employing Surplus Rural Labor", 2326–18.48

Bank deposits

Appalachian States, FHLB 5th District savings instns finances and lending by State, monthly rpt, 9302–8

Assets and debts of private sector, balance sheets by segment, 1949-88, semiannual rpt, 9365–4.1

Brokered deposit holdings and financial indicators of banks, by size, region, and for failed instns, 1986-89, hearing, 21248–124

Business statistics, detailed data for major industries and economic indicators, *Survey of Current Business*, monthly rpt, 2702–1.6

Commercial and savings banks (insured) finances, by State, 1987, annual rpt, 9294–4

Commercial banks (insured) domestic and foreign office consolidated financial statements, monthly rpt, quarterly data, 9362–1.4

Commercial banks (insured) profitability, balance sheet items, and rates of return by asset size, 1984-88, annual article, 9362–1.907

Credit unions federally insured, finances by instn characteristics and State, as of June 1989, semiannual rpt, 9532–6

Credit unions federally insured, finances, 1987-88, annual rpt, 9534–1

Debits and turnover of demand and savings deposits, monthly rpt, 9362–1.1

Debits, deposits, and deposit turnover, for commercial banks by type of account, monthly rpt, 9365–2.5

Deposits in FDIC-insured commercial and savings banks, by instn, State, MSA, and county, as of June 1988, annual regional rpt series, 9295–3

Deposits in financial instns, by insurance status and instn type, 1980s-88, GAO rpt, 26119–241

Economic indicators and components, current data and annual trends, monthly rpt, 23842–1.5

Economic indicators compounded annual rates of change, 1969-88, annual rpt, 9391–9.1

Failures of banks and economic indicator variability, relation to bank branching and note issuance regulation, for US and Canada, various periods 1865-1987, article, 9383–6.904

Farm income, expenses, receipts by commodity, assets, liabilities, and ratios, 1988 and trends from 1945, annual rpt, 1544–16

Farm sector assets by type, 1988, annual rpt, 1544–16.2

Fed Reserve banks expenses and operations, itemized by service, office, and district, 1988, annual rpt, 9364–11

Fed Reserve banks finances and staff, 1988, annual rpt, 9364–1.1

Fed Reserve deposit reports, variability by district and financial instn type and size

groups, and recommendations for combining groups, various periods 1987-88, technical paper, 9366–6.186

Financial and business statistics, historic trends, 1988 annual chartbook, 9364–2.1; 9364–2.13

Financial and monetary conditions, selected US summary data, weekly rpt, 9391–4

Financial and operating conditions of banks, 1987, annual rpt, 9364–5

Financial, banking, and mortgage market activity, weekly rpt series, 9365–1

Financial condition and performance of insured commercial banks, by asset size and region, quarterly rpt, 9292–1

Financial instns financial and operating statements by deposit size, Fed Reserve functional cost analysis, 1988, annual rpt, 9364–6

Financial performance of banks, risk assessment, and regulation, 1988 annual conf papers, 9375–7

Florida banks and thrifts deposits and mortgages, building permits, population, and migration, with comparisons to other areas, 1980s-88, article, 9302–2.905

Flow-of-funds accounts, assets and liabilities by type and economic sector, outstanding at year-end 1965-88, annual rpt, 9364–3

Flow-of-funds accounts, savings, investments, and credit statements, quarterly rpt, 9365–3.3

Interest rates on bank deposits, relation to local bank market concentration and branching regulations, 1983-87, technical paper, 9366–6.166

Intl transactions, *Survey of Current Business*, monthly rpt, quarterly tables, 2702–1.31

Metro and nonmetro areas banks finances and operations, 1986, annual rpt, 1544–29

Middle Atlantic States, FHLB 2nd District member savings instns finances, quarterly rpt, 9302–14

Minority-owned banks, deposits from Fed Govt by agency, FY86-88, annual rpt, 2104–5

Monetary and Fed Govt budget trends, Fed Reserve Bank of St Louis monthly rpt, 9391–2

Money market deposit account interest rates relation to local bank market concentration, 1983-86, technical paper, 9366–6.173

New England States, banks, thrifts, and financial statements by type of instn and Fed deposit insurance, and State, 1987, annual rpt, 9304–3

New England States, FHLB 1st District thrift instns financial operations and housing industry indicators, monthly rpt, 9302–4

New England States financial instn assets and liabilities, Fed Reserve 1st District, monthly rpt, 9373–24

New England States financial instn assets and liabilities, Fed Reserve 1st District, quarterly rpt, 9373–2.5

Nonprofit charitable organizations finances, and assets and grants of top 10, 1985, article, 8302–2.923

North Central States business and economic conditions, Fed Reserve 9th District, quarterly journal, 9383–19

North Central States economic conditions, Fed Reserve 9th District, quarterly rpt, 9383–18

North Central States, FHLB 7th District insured thrifts, offices, and savings, by county, 1986-87, annual rpt, 9304–5

North Central States, FHLB 8th District S&Ls, locations, assets, and savings, 1989, annual listing, 9304–9

North Central States, FHLB 8th District savings instns financial operations by State and SMSA, monthly rpt, 9302–9

Panama govt assets in US blocked under economic sanctions, and conditions and procedures for release, 1989, press release, 8008–135

Savings and loan assns, FHLB 6th District insured members financial condition and operations by State, quarterly rpt, 9302–23

Savings instns (FSLIC-insured) assets, liabilities, and deposit and loan activity, and compared to all S&Ls, monthly rpt, 9312–4

Savings instns failure resolution activity of Resolution Trust Corp, with failed instn finances by instn, periodic press release, 9722–1

Savings instns failures, financial condition indicators, and liquidation and acquisition costs and tax benefits by instn and acquiring company, 1985-98, hearing, 21268–41

Savings instns finances and operations by district and State, mortgage lending activity and terms by MSA, and FHLB finances, 1987 with trends from 1900, annual rpt, 9314–3

Savings instns financial statements, FSLIC-insured instns by FHLB district and State, and FDIC-insured savings banks, 1988, annual rpt, 8434–1

Savings instns FSLIC-insured, offices, and deposits, by FHLB district, State, SMSA, and county, 1988, annual rpt, 9314–4

Savings instns insured by Savings Assn Insurance Fund, assets, liabilities, and deposit and loan activity, by conservatorship status, monthly rpt, 8432–1

Savings instns insured by Savings Assn Insurance Fund, finances by district, quarterly rpt, 8432–4

Savings instns regulatory issues, mgmt, and FHLB system and member finances and operations, monthly journal, 8432–2; 9312–1

South Central States, FHLB 9th District savings instns finances and operations by State, quarterly rpt, 9302–31

Southeastern States banks and thrifts industry structure impacts of market entry and branching regulation, by State, 1982-88, article, 9302–2.907

Southeastern States, Fed Reserve 5th District, economic indicators by State, quarterly rpt, 9389–16

Southeastern States, Fed Reserve 5th District insured commercial banks financial statements, by State, quarterly rpt, 9389–18

Southeastern States, Fed Reserve 8th District banking and economic conditions, quarterly rpt with articles, 9391–16

Southeastern States, FHLB 4th District thrifts finances, by State, 1984-88 annual rpt series, 9304–29

Statistical Abstract of US, social, political, and economic data, 1790-2025, comprehensive annual compilation, 2324–1.3

Supplemental Security Income beneficiaries, assets by type and eligibility class, FY87, article, 4742–1.922

Trust assets of banks, trust companies, and S&Ls, by type of asset and fund, selected firm, and State, 1988, annual rpt, 13004–1

West Central States, Fed Reserve 10th District banking industry structure, performance, and financial devs, 1988, annual rpt, 9381–14

West Central States, Fed Reserve 10th District depository instns deposits, loans, investments, and borrowings, monthly rpt, 9381–2

West Central States, Fed Reserve 10th District depository instns financial activity by State, and large commercial banks by city, monthly rpt, 9381–11

West Central States, FHLB 10th District savings instns finances and lending by State and MSA, monthly table, 9302–22

West Central States, FHLB 10th District savings instns financial condition, by State, quarterly rpt, 9302–34

Western States, FHLB 11th District S&Ls, offices, and financial condition, 1989 annual listing, 9304–23

Western States, FHLB 11th District thrift offices, locations, savings balances, and accounts, quarterly listing, 9302–20

Western States, FHLB 12th District savings instns deposits and lending by State, monthly press release series, 9302–32

see also Certificates of deposit
see also Checking accounts
see also Deposit insurance
see also Negotiable orders of withdrawal accounts
see also Savings

Bank for International Settlements
"International Banking Developments: Third Quarter 1987", 21248–120

Bank holding companies
Acquisitions of BHCs in southeastern States, as of Oct 1988, article, 9389–1.907

Assets, instns concentration ratios, and status changes of banks, by asset size, ownership, and location, and compared to other financial instns, 1976-87, article, 9362–1.902

Assets, offices, and deposits of BHCs, by State, 1987, annual rpt, 9364–5.11

Equity of BHCs, impact of credit and interest rate risk indicators and deposit insurance, 1986-87, technical paper, 9366–6.181; 9366–6.212

Fed Reserve Board and Reserve banks finances, staff, and review of monetary policy and economic devs, 1988, annual rpt, 9364–1

Financial and economic analysis, technical paper series, 9393–10

Financial performance of banks, risk assessment, and regulation, 1988 annual conf papers, 9375–7

Interstate banking offices by type of controlling organization and State, 1982-Feb 1989, article, 9371–1.909

Market concentration and State branching regulation impact on BHC risk, alternative regression results, various periods 1978-84, technical paper, 9366–6.182

Profit related to mgmt practices and market concentration and share, 1989 technical paper, 9366–6.201

Real estate lenders, commercial banks financial condition, 1989 technical paper, 9366–6.202

Savings instns regulatory issues, mgmt, and FHLB system and member finances and operations, monthly journal, 8432–2; 9312–1

Securities valuation by BHCs, impact of new issue announcements by issue type, 1982-86, working paper, 9371–10.34

Statistical Abstract of US, social, political, and economic data, 1790-2025, comprehensive annual compilation, 2324–1.3

Stock market returns of BHCs, relation to nonbanking activities and selected financial ratios, 1979-85, technical paper, 9375–11.20

Stock price effects of new issues and capital regulation, for BHCs, 1975-86, article, 9393–8.901

Stock prices relative to indexes by instn, and bond and supervisory ratings impact of BHC financial problems, 1970s-80s, article, 9373–1.911

Tax (income) returns of corporations, income and tax items by asset size and detailed industry, 1986, annual rpt, 8304–4; 8304–21

West Central States, Fed Reserve 10th District banking industry structure, performance, and financial devs, 1988, annual rpt, 9381–14.1

Bank reserve requirements
see Government and business

Bank reserves
see Banks and banking

Bankruptcy
Business bankruptcy filings with SEC participation, by firm, FY88, annual rpt, 9734–2.6

Employer bankruptcy probability, relationship to employees tenure-related earnings, 1979-83, technical paper, 9366–6.180

Farm finances, debts, assets, and receipts, and lenders financial condition, quarterly rpt with articles, 1541–1

Farms bankruptcy filings under Chapter 12 by State, and legal practitioners and creditors views on provisions, 1986-88, GAO rpt, 26113–415

FmHA loans and borrower supervision activities in farm and housing programs, by type and State, monthly rpt, 1182–1

Prisoners and movements, by offense, location, and selected other characteristics, data compilation, 1930s-89, annual rpt, 6064–6.6

Savings instns insolvency losses and uninsured certificate of deposit interest rates, impact of proposed depositor preference laws, model description and results, 1989 technical paper, 9316–1.154

Small business finances, operations, owner and employee characteristics, and Federal contracts, 1980s-88, annual rpt, 9764–6

Intl transactions, *Survey of Current Business*, monthly rpt, quarterly tables, 2702–1.31

Investments and loans of commercial banks, monthly rpt, 23842–1.5

Investments and loans of commercial banks, 1972-88, annual rpt, 204–1.5

Labor productivity, indexes of output, hours, and employment by SIC 2- to 4-digit industry, 1963-87, annual rpt, 6824–1.4

Land transfers, by source of credit financing and region, 1975-89, article, 1561–16.902

Market concentration of banks relation to money market deposit account interest rates, 1983-86, technical paper, 9366–6.173

Market concentration relation to excess profits and State branching regulation, various periods 1966-86, technical paper, 9366–6.188

Market entry probability relation to market characteristics and competition, for banks and S&Ls in rural areas, model description and results, 1980-84, working paper, 9377–9.76

Metro and nonmetro areas banks finances and operations, 1986, annual rpt, 1544–29

Natl banks domestic and intl operations, charters, and mergers, by instn and State, quarterly rpt, 8402–3

New England States, banks, thrifts, and financial statements by type of instn and Fed deposit insurance, and State, 1987, annual rpt, 9304–3

North Central States business and economic conditions, Fed Reserve 9th District, quarterly journal, 9383–19

North Central States economic conditions, Fed Reserve 9th District, quarterly rpt, 9383–18

Occupational injury and illness rates, by SIC 2- to 4-digit industry, 1987, annual rpt, 6844–1

Panics (banking) relation to production and business cycle, with data for NYC, 1857-1933, article, 9391–1.915

Profitability of banks relation to market concentration, impact of local market entry barriers, 1983, working paper, 9381–10.93

Profitability of insured commercial banks, balance sheet items, and rates of return by asset size, 1984-88, annual article, 9362–1.907

Puerto Rico and other US possessions corporations tax incentives, finances, and operations by industry, and impacts on local economy, 1970s-83, biennial rpt, 8004–12

Regulation of banks and related issues, quarterly journal, 9292–4

Regulation of market entry and deposit insurance by States, impacts on banks financial performance, model description and results, 1970-86, working paper, 9393–10.6

Regulatory costs of banks relation to corporate loans, alternative regression results, 1977-87, technical paper, 9366–6.177

Robberies and rates, by type of premises and weapon, 1973-87, annual rpt, 6224–8

Robberies, by type of premises, population size, and region, 1988, annual rpt, 6224–2.1

Robbery of banks and related crimes by State, casualties, and hostages, 1982-87, annual rpt, 6064–6.3

Robbery of banks, US attorneys cases by disposition, FY88, annual rpt, 6004–2.1; 6004–2.7

Rural and urban areas population and economic data, 1960s-88, annual chartbook, 1504–3

Rural areas banks, control by urban-based firms, and financial and market characteristics, 1960s-88, article, 1502–7.906

Science and engineering employment, by nonmanufacturing industry and field, 1987, triennial rpt, 9627–31

Securities (tax-exempt) holdings by investor type, and IRS enforcement of disallowance of interest deduction for financing holdings, mid 1970s-87, GAO rpt, 26119–239

Securities for subordinated debt issued by savings instns and banks, 1986-89, article, 9312–1.906

Services diversification of banks, impacts on costs, alternative indicators of cost impact by asset size, 1986, article, 9371–1.907

South Africa loans from US banks, and rescheduling issues, 1984-89, press release, 8008–136

South Central States bank performance indicators by asset size, Fed Reserve 8th District, 1985-88, annual article, 9391–1.912

South Central States farm yields by selected commodity, rainfall, and banks financial performance, with comparisons to US farm income trends, 1980s-88, annual article, 9391–1.911

Southeastern States banks and thrifts industry structure impacts of market entry and branching regulation, by State, 1982-88, article, 9302–2.907

Southeastern States, Fed Reserve 5th District banks financial performance, 1984-88, annual article, 9389–1.909

Southeastern States, Fed Reserve 8th District banking and economic conditions, quarterly rpt with articles, 9391–16

Southeastern US banks financial ratios, 1984-88, annual article, 9371–1.910

Statistical Abstract of US, social, political, and economic data, 1790-2025, comprehensive annual compilation, 2324–1.3

Stock prices and trading, impact of loan-loss reserve additions, with data by instn, 1987, working paper, 9387–8.186

Stock returns for banks involved in acquisitions, 1982-87, technical paper, 9366–6.178

Stock returns of banks, impacts of changes in State laws on interstate branching, 1988 working paper, 9387–8.174

Switzerland bank funds transfer system activity, by payment size and time of day, monthly 1987-88, article, 9389–1.903

Tax (income) returns of corporations, income and tax items by asset size and detailed industry, 1986, annual rpt, 8304–4; 8304–21

Tax (income) returns of partnerships, income statement items by industry group, 1986, annual article, 8302–2.903

Tax (income) returns of sole proprietorships, income statement items, by industry group, 1987, annual article, 8302–2.904; 8302–2.921

Technological devs adoption by banks relation to asset size, regression results, 1980s-86, working paper, 9371–10.33

Trust assets of banks, trust companies, and S&Ls, by type of asset and fund, selected firm, and State, 1988, annual rpt, 13004–1

West Central States, Fed Reserve 10th District banking industry structure, performance, and financial devs, 1988, annual rpt, 9381–14

see also Agricultural credit
see also Bank deposits
see also Bank holding companies
see also Checking accounts
see also Commercial credit
see also Consumer credit
see also Credit
see also Credit cards
see also Credit unions
see also Deposit insurance
see also Discrimination in credit
see also Electronic funds transfer
see also Eurocurrency
see also Export-Import Bank
see also Farm Credit System
see also Federal Financing Bank
see also Federal Home Loan Banks
see also Federal Reserve System
see also Flow-of-funds accounts
see also Foreign exchange
see also Interest rates
see also Loans
see also Money supply
see also Mortgages
see also Negotiable orders of withdrawal accounts
see also Savings
see also Savings institutions
see also By Industry in the "Index by Categories"

Banks for Cooperatives
see Farm Credit System

Banks, Vera
"Alternative Definitions of Farm People", 1598–249

Banta, Susan M.
"Consumer Expenditures in Different-Size Cities", 6722–1.962

Barbados
Agricultural and food production and indexes, total and for selected commodities, by country, 1970s-88, annual rpt, 1524–12

Agricultural trade of US, by detailed commodity and country, 1988, semiannual rpt, 1522–4

AID economic aid to developing countries, obligations and disbursements by country, quarterly rpt, 9912–4

Economic and military aid and loans from US and intl agencies, by program and country, FY46-87, annual rpt, 9914–5

Economic conditions, policy, and trade practices, by country, 1986-88, annual rpt, 21384–5

Economic, social, political, and geographic summary data, by country, 1989, annual factbook, 9114–2

Human rights conditions in 170 countries, 1988, annual rpt, 21384–3

Investment (direct) incentives of Caribbean Basin Initiative, economic impacts, with finances and employment by country, 1984-88, 2048-141

Military spending, arms trade, and force strengths, with govt spending and population, by country, 1977-87, annual rpt, 9824-1

Minerals Yearbook, 1987, Vol 3: foreign country reviews of production, trade, and policy, by commodity, annual rpt, 5604-35

Minerals Yearbook, 1987, Vol 3 preprints: foreign country review of production, trade, and policy, by commodity, annual rpt, 5604-23.83

Older persons population and selected characteristics, 1980s and projected to 2020, country rpt, 2326-19.1

Population size, growth rates, and components of change, by country, projected 1989-2020 and trends from 1950, biennial rpt, 2324-9

Rum imports (duty-free) of US under Caribbean Basin Initiative, by country, 1987-88, annual rpt, 9884-15

UN voting record and share of votes in agreement with US, by issue, country, and world area, 1988, annual rpt, 7004-18

see also under By Foreign Country in the "Index by Categories"

Barbash, Jack
"John R. Commons: Pioneer of Labor Economics", 6722-1.924

Barber and beauty shops
County Business Patterns, 1987: employment, establishments, and payroll, by SIC 2- to 4-digit industry and county, annual State rpt series, 2326-8

CPI by component for US city average, and by region, population size, and for 27 metro areas, monthly rpt, 6762-2

Employment, earnings, and hours, by SIC 1- to 4-digit industry, monthly 1983-Feb 1989, annual rpt, 6744-4

Guam economic censuses, 1987: employment, firms, payroll, and receipts, by SIC 1- to 4-digit industry and election district, 2595-1

Labor productivity, indexes of output, hours, and employment by SIC 2- to 4-digit industry, 1963-87, annual rpt, 6824-1.4

Northern Mariana Islands economic census, 1987: employment, firms, payroll, and receipts, by SIC 1- to 4-digit industry, 2597-1

Occupational injury and illness rates, by SIC 2- to 4-digit industry, 1987, annual rpt, 6844-1

Receipts for services, by SIC 2- to 4-digit kind of business, 1988, annual rpt, 2413-8

Senate receipts, itemized expenses by payee, and balances, 1st half FY89, semiannual listing, 25922-1

Service industries census, 1987: establishments, receipts, employment, and payroll, by SIC 2- to 4-digit kind of business, MSA, county, and city, State rpt series, 2391-1

Tax (income) returns of partnerships, income statement items by industry group, 1986, annual article, 8302-2.903

Tax (income) returns of sole proprietorships, income statement items, by industry group, 1987, annual article, 8302-2.904; 8302-2.921

Virgin Islands economic censuses, 1987: employment, firms, payroll, and receipts, by SIC 1- to 4-digit industry, island, and city, 2593-1

Wholesale trade census, 1987: employment, establishments, finances, and operations, by SIC 2- to 4-digit kind of business, MSA, county, and city, State rpt series, 2405-1

Barges
Construction and operating subsidies of MarAd by firm, and ship deliveries and fleet by country, by vessel type, FY88, annual rpt, 7704-14.1

Containers (intermodal) and equipment owned by shipping and leasing companies, inventory by type and size, 1989, annual rpt, 7704-10

Defense Fuel Supply Center procurement, prices, stocks, transport, and other activities and finances, FY88, annual rpt, 3904-8

Finances, operations, vehicles, equipment, accidents, and energy use, by mode of transport, 1955-88, annual rpt, 7304-2

Foreign and US merchant ships, and tonnage, by country of registry, as of Jan 1988, annual rpt, 7704-3

Freight (waterborne domestic), by major commodity group, vessel type, and port, 1986, annual rpt, 7704-7

Freight (waterborne domestic and foreign) by commodity, traffic, and passengers, by port and waterway, 1987, annual rpt, 3754-3

Grain shipments and rates for barge and rail loadings, periodic situation rpt with articles, 1561-4

Manufacturing census, 1987: financial and operating data, for SIC 4-digit industries by product, preliminary rpt, 2491-1.77

Ohio River basin waterway facilities, freight by commodity and port, and recreation, by waterway, 1986-87, annual rpt, 3754-6

Oil and refined products stocks, and interdistrict shipments by mode of transport, monthly rpt, 3162-6.3

Oil refinery crude received, by mode of transport and PAD district, 1988, annual rpt, 3164-2.1

Pollution (water) incidents and discharges, by type, source, cause, and location, 1984-86, annual rpt, 7404-3

St Lawrence Seaway ship, cargo, and passenger traffic, and toll revenue, 1988 and trends from 1959, annual rpt, 7744-2

Wartime capability of commercial ships, shipyards, and personnel, for merchant and reserve fleet, 1988-2000, 11208-1

Barite
see Nonmetallic minerals and mines

Barium
see Metals and metal industries

Barkema, Alan
"Agriculture and the GATT: A Time for Change", 9381-1.904

"U.S. Agriculture Shrugs off the Drought", 9381-1.902

Barkley, David L.
"Contributions of High-Tech Manufacturing to Rural Economies", 1502-7.912

Barley
see Animal feed
see Grains and grain products

Barlowe, Russell G.
"U.S. and World Cotton Outlook", 1004-16.1

Baron, Joan B.
"Collecting and Profiling School/Instructional Variables as Part of the State-NAEP Results Reporting: Some Technical and Political Issues", 4828-37.1

Barry, Lynn M.
"Commercial Real Estate Lending: A Growing Banking Risk", 9391-16.906

"Eighth District Banks: Back in the Black", 9391-1.912

"Eighth District Banks Rally in 1988", 9391-16.903

"U.S. Bank Failures Hit 200 in 1988", 9391-16.901

Barry, Peter J.,
"Publishing in Professional Journals", 1502-3.901

Barse, Joseph R.
"Economic Effects of Banning Soil Fumigants", 1588-136

Barth, James R.
"Alternative Federal Deposit Insurance Regimes", 9316-1.143

"Consolidation and Restructuring of the U.S. Thrift Industry Under the Financial Institutions Reform, Recovery, and Enforcement Act", 8436-1.1

"Cost of Liquidating Versus Selling Failed Thrift Institutions", 8436-1.2

"Determinants of Thrift Institution Resolution Costs", 8436-1.3

"Evolving Financial Services Sector, 1970-88", 8438-1

"Federal Deposit Insurance System: Origins and Omissions", 9316-1.144

"Moral Hazard and the Thrift Crisis: An Analysis of 1988 Resolutions", 9316-1.151

"Reforming Federal Deposit Insurance: What Can Be Learned from Private Insurance Practices?", 9316-1.152

Bartholomew, Ann M.
"Coal Mining: Characterization of the 1986 Mining Workforce", 5606-8.1

"Metal and Nonmetal Mining: Characterization of the 1986 Mining Workforce", 5606-8.2

"Metallic Mining: Characterization of the 1986 Mining Workforce", 5606-8.3

"Nonmetallic Mining: Characterization of the 1986 Mining Workforce", 5606-8.6

"Sand and Gravel Mining: Characterization of the 1986 Mining Workforce", 5606-8.5

"Stone Mining: Characterization of the 1986 Mining Workforce", 5606-8.4

Bartholomew, Philip F.
"As Canada's Thrifts Change, So Do Their Regulators", 9312-1.903

Basic Educational Opportunity Grant
see Student aid

Baskerville, Valerie G.
"Supplemental Security Income: State and County Data, December 1987", 4744-27

Basketball
Injuries from use of consumer products and related activities, by victim age and sex, 1988, annual rpt, 9164-7

Basketball
Injuries from use of consumer products, by
severity, victim age, and detailed product,
1988, annual rpt, 9164–6

Bass, Joel L.
"What School Children Need To Learn
About Injury Prevention", 4042–3.937

Bates, Jeffrey
"Individual Income Tax Returns,
Preliminary Data, 1987", 8302–2.917

Batkin, Ted
"Look into the Future for Fruits and
Vegetables", 1004–16.1

Baton Rouge, La.
Housing vacancy rates for single and
multifamily units and mobile homes, by
city and ZIP code, 1989, annual MSA rpt,
9304–19.2
Wages by occupation, and benefits for office
and plant workers, 1989 survey, periodic
MSA rpt, 6785–3.8
see also under By City and By SMSA or
MSA in the "Index by Categories"

Battelle Memorial Institute
see also Department of Energy National
Laboratories

Batteries
Business statistics, detailed data for major
industries and economic indicators, Survey
of Current Business, monthly rpt,
2702–1.14
County Business Patterns, 1987:
employment, establishments, and payroll,
by SIC 2- to 4-digit industry and county,
annual State rpt series, 2326–8
Employment, earnings, and hours, by SIC 1-
to 4-digit industry, monthly 1983-Feb
1989, annual rpt, 6744–4
Environmental impacts of energy
technologies, 1960s-80s, handbook series,
3326–1
Injuries from use of consumer products and
related activities, by victim age and sex,
1988, annual rpt, 9164–7
Manufacturing census, 1987: financial and
operating data, for SIC 4-digit industries
by product, preliminary rpt, 2491–1.74
Motorcycle batteries from Korea at less than
fair value, injury to US industry,
investigation with background financial
and operating data, 1989 rpt,
9886–14.265
Motorcycle batteries from Taiwan at less
than fair value, injury to US industry,
investigation with background financial
and operating data, 1989 rpt,
9886–14.268
Price indexes (producer), by stage of
processing and detailed commodity,
monthly rpt, 6762–6
Price indexes (producer), by stage of
processing and detailed commodity,
monthly 1988, annual rpt, 6764–2

Battle Creek, Mich.
Wages by occupation, for office and plant
workers, 1989 survey, periodic MSA rpt,
6785–3.9
see also under By SMSA or MSA in the
"Index by Categories"

Battleships
see Naval vessels

Bauer, Laura L.
"Tolerance-Width Groupings for Editing
Banking Deposits Data: An Analysis of
Variance of Variances", 9366–6.186

Bauer, Paul W.
"Decomposing TFP Growth in the Presence
of Cost Inefficiency, Nonconstant Returns
to Scale, and Technological Progress",
9377–9.69
"Determinants of Direct Air Fares to
Cleveland: How Competitive?",
9377–1.903

Bauxite
see Aluminum and aluminum industry

Baxter, Kenneth N.
"Commercial Bait Shrimp Fishery in
Galveston Bay, Texas, 1959-87",
2162–1.901

Bay City, Mich.
Wages by occupation, and benefits for office
and plant workers, 1989 survey, periodic
MSA rpt, 6785–3.10
see also under By SMSA or MSA in the
"Index by Categories"

BDM International, Inc.
"Gorbachev's Force Reductions and the
Restructuring of Soviet Forces",
21208–29

BEA
see Bureau of Economic Analysis

Beaches
see Lakes and lakeshores
see Seashores

Beall, Tommy
"Cattle Outlook", 1004–16.1

Beans
see Vegetables and vegetable products

Bearings
see Machines and machinery industry

Bears
see Wildlife and wildlife conservation

Beatty, Curt
"What Tomorrow's Foreign Customers Will
Want", 1004–16.1

Beaufort Sea
Environmental conditions and oil dev
impacts for Alaska OCS, compilation of
papers, series, 2176–1
Oil and gas resource assessment for Arctic
Natl Wildlife Refuge with environmental
impacts on North Slope and other
locations, 1987 hearing, 21448–41
Whale (bowhead) population in Beaufort
Sea, and aerial survey operations,
Sept-Oct 1979-88, 5738–8

Beaumont, Tex.
Ships in Natl Defense Reserve Fleet at
Beaumont harbor, as of Jan 1989,
semiannual listing, 7702–2
Wages by occupation, for office and plant
workers, 1989 survey, periodic MSA rpt,
6785–3.6
see also under By City and By SMSA or
MSA in the "Index by Categories"

Beautification of the landscape
see Urban beautification

Beauty aids
see Cosmetics and toiletries

Beauty parlors
see Barber and beauty shops

Beaver County, Pa.
see also under By SMSA or MSA in the
"Index by Categories"

Beazley, Doug
"Selected Trends in Collection Inventory
Revisited", 8304–8.1

Beck, Allen J.
"Recidivism of Prisoners Released in 1983",
6066–19.48

Beck, H.
"Occurrence of PCDD and PCDF in
Different Kinds of Paper", 21368–112

Becker, Paul R.
"Natural Oil Seeps in the Alaskan Marine
Environment", 2176–1.28

Becketti, Sean
"Prepayment Risk of Mortgage-Backed
Securities", 9381–1.905

Beckman, Barry A.
"Business Cycle Indicators: Revised
Composite Indexes", 2702–1.906;
2702–3

Beckman, Thomas J.
"Taxpayer Service Assistant Expert
System", 8304–8.1

Bednarzik, Robert W.
"Labor Market Changes and Adjustments:
How Do the U.S. and Japan Compare?",
6722–1.910

Beer and breweries
Agricultural exports of US, impacts of
foreign agricultural and trade policy, with
data by commodity and country, 1988,
annual rpt, 1924–8
Business statistics, detailed data for major
industries and economic indicators, Survey
of Current Business, monthly rpt,
2702–1.11
Consumption of alcohol, by beverage type,
region, and State, 1977-87, annual rpt,
4486–1.3; 4486–1.6; 4486–1.9
Consumption of food and nutrient intake by
individuals, by food group, selected
characteristics, and region, supplementary
survey series, 1356–5
Consumption, supply, trade, prices,
spending, and indexes, by food
commodity, 1987, annual rpt, 1544–4
County Business Patterns, 1987:
employment, establishments, and payroll,
by SIC 2- to 4-digit industry and county,
annual State rpt series, 2326–8
CPI by component for US city average, and
by region, population size, and for 27
metro areas, monthly rpt, 6762–2
Cuba economic conditions, agricultural and
industrial production and distribution,
trade, and intl economic relations,
1980-87 with trends from 1961, 9118–8
EC food supply and demand, market and
support prices, and other economic
indicators, by country and commodity,
1960-85, 1528–276
Employment, earnings, and hours, by SIC 1-
to 4-digit industry, monthly 1983-Feb
1989, annual rpt, 6744–4
Exports and imports (agricultural) of US, by
commodity and country, bimonthly rpt
with articles, 1522–1
Exports and imports (agricultural) of US, by
detailed commodity and country, 1988,
semiannual rpt, 1522–4
Exports of US, detailed commodities by
country, monthly rpt, 2422–3
Grain (feed) consumption, by end use,
periodic situation rpt with articles,
1561–4
Grain prices for brewers, rice and corn grits,
periodic situation rpt, 1561–8
Grain production, prices, trade, and export
inspections by US port and country of
destination, by grain type, weekly rpt,
1313–2

Hops production, stocks, use, and US trade by country, monthly rpt, 1313–7

Hops stocks held by growers, dealers, and brewers, 1987-89, semiannual press release, 1621–8

Imports of US, detailed Schedule A commodities by country, monthly rpt, 2422–2

Labor productivity, indexes of output, hours, and employment by SIC 2- to 4-digit industry, 1963-87, annual rpt, 6824–1.3

Manufacturing annual survey, 1986: financial and operating data, by SIC 2- to 4-digit industry, series, 2506–15

Manufacturing census, 1987: financial and operating data, for SIC 4-digit industries by product, preliminary rpt, 2491–1.8

Military personnel alcohol and drug abuse, prevalence and consequences, by selected characteristics, 1988, biennial rpt, 3504–19

Nutrient and caloric composition of food, for raw, processed, and prepared food, 1988 rpt, 1358–3

Occupational injury and illness rates, by SIC 2- to 4-digit industry, 1987, annual rpt, 6844–1

Price indexes (producer), by stage of processing and detailed commodity, monthly rpt, 6762–6

Price indexes (producer), by stage of processing and detailed commodity, monthly 1988, annual rpt, 6764–2

Production of beer, monthly rpt, 1313–7

Production, stocks, materials used, and tax-free and taxable removals by State, for beer, monthly rpt, 8486–1.1

Rice shipments, by end use, package size, and State of origin and destination, mid 1950s-87, biennial rpt, 1564–11

Tax (excise) collections of IRS, by source, quarterly rpt, 8302–1

Tax (excise) indexed to inflation, impacts on Federal revenue and family tax burden by commodity, projected under alternative proposals, 1989-93, GAO rpt, 26119–254

Tax (income) returns of corporations, income and tax items by asset size and detailed industry, 1986, annual rpt, 8304–4; 8304–21

Tax revenue potential of State and local systems relative to natl average tax burden, by type of tax and State, 1986, annual rpt, 10044–7

Wholesale trade census, 1987: employment, establishments, finances, and operations, by SIC 2- to 4-digit kind of business, MSA, county, and city, State rpt series, 2405–1

Bees and beeswax
see Honey and beekeeping

Behavior
see Intelligence levels
see Mental health and illness
see Sexual behavior
see Social sciences

Behavioral sciences
see Anthropology
see Psychology
see Social sciences
see Sociology

Beier, Ken
"Form W-4 Compliance: Evidence from Survey Data and Returns Processing", 8304–8.1

"Monitoring Tax Reform: A Comparison of 1987 and 1986 Returns", 8304–8.1

Beirne, Kenneth J.
"Hope for the Homeless: Local and State Response", 10048–73

Belgium
Agricultural and food production and indexes, total and for selected commodities, by country, 1970s-88, annual rpt, 1524–12

Agricultural production, prices, and trade, by country, 1970s-88 and forecast 1990, annual world region rpt, 1524–4.1

Agricultural trade of US, by detailed commodity and country, 1988, semiannual rpt, 1522–4

AID loans repayment status and terms by program and country, and status of predecessor agency loans, quarterly rpt, 9912–3

Auto imports from US, trade barriers by country, 1988, annual rpt, 444–2

Businesses (foreign) activity in US, income tax returns, assets, and income statement items, by industry div, country, and world area, 1984-85, article, 8302–2.920

Coal production, trade, and govt subsidies, by country and country group, 1973-87 and projected to 2000, 2048–144

Economic and military aid and loans from US and intl agencies, by program and country, FY46-87, annual rpt, 9914–5

Economic and monetary trends, compounded annual rates of change for US and 10 major trading partners, quarterly rpt, 9391–7

Economic conditions in Communist, OECD, and selected other countries, 1960s-88, annual rpt, 9114–4

Economic conditions, income, production, prices, employment, and trade, 1989 periodic country rpt, 2046–4.79

Economic conditions, policy, and trade practices, by country, 1986-88, annual rpt, 21384–5

Economic, social, political, and geographic summary data, by country, 1989, annual factbook, 9114–2

Exports and imports of US, by selected country, country group, and commodity group, 1988, annual rpt, 2044–37

Food supply and demand, market and support prices, and other economic indicators, by EC country and commodity, 1960-85, 1528–276

Human rights conditions in 170 countries, 1988, annual rpt, 21384–3

Intl transactions of US with 9 countries, 1986-88, *Survey of Current Business*, monthly rpt, annual table, 2702–1.31

Labor conditions, union coverage, and work accidents, 1989 annual country rpt, 6366–4.20

Manufacturing labor productivity and unit costs for 14 countries, 1950-88, annual press release, 6864–1

Military aid of US, arms sales, and training programs costs and budget requests, by program, world region, and country, FY88-90, annual rpt, 7144–13

Military spending, arms trade, and force strengths, with govt spending and population, by country, 1977-87, annual rpt, 9824–1

Minerals Yearbook, 1987, Vol 3: foreign country reviews of production, trade, and policy, by commodity, annual rpt, 5604–35

Minerals Yearbook, 1987, Vol 3 preprints: foreign country review of production, trade, and policy, by commodity, annual rpt, 5604–23.8

Multinatl US firms and foreign affiliates finances and operations, by industry of parent firm and affiliate, world area, and country, preliminary 1987, annual rpt, 2704–5

Nuclear power generation in US and 19 non-Communist countries, monthly rpt, 3162–24.10

Nuclear power plant capacity, generation, and operating status, by plant and foreign and US location, 1988 and projected to 2020, annual rpt, 3164–57

Oil production, trade, use, and stocks, by selected country and country group, monthly rpt, 3162–42

Population size, growth rates, and components of change, by country, projected 1989-2020 and trends from 1950, biennial rpt, 2324–9

UN voting record and share of votes in agreement with US, by issue, country, and world area, 1988, annual rpt, 7004–18

see also under By Foreign Country in the "Index by Categories"

Belinfante, Alexander
"Telephone Penetration and Family Characteristics", 9288–11

Belize
Agricultural and food production and indexes, total and for selected commodities, by country, 1970s-88, annual rpt, 1524–12

Agricultural trade of US, by detailed commodity and country, 1988, semiannual rpt, 1522–4

AID activities and funding by project and function, FY90, and developing countries summary socioeconomic data from 1960s, annual rpt, 9904–4.7

AID economic aid to developing countries, obligations and disbursements by country, quarterly rpt, 9912–4

AID loans repayment status and terms by program and country, and status of predecessor agency loans, quarterly rpt, 9912–3

Economic and military aid and loans from US and intl agencies, by program and country, FY46-87, annual rpt, 9914–5

Economic conditions, income, production, prices, employment, and trade, 1989 periodic country rpt, 2046–4.44

Economic conditions, policy, and trade practices, by country, 1986-88, annual rpt, 21384–5

Economic, social, political, and geographic summary data, by country, 1989, annual factbook, 9114–2

Human rights conditions in 170 countries, 1988, annual rpt, 21384–3

Investment (direct) incentives of Caribbean Basin Initiative, economic impacts, with finances and employment by country, 1984-88, 2048–141

Military aid of US, arms sales, and training programs costs and budget requests, by program, world region, and country, FY88-90, annual rpt, 7144–13

Minerals Yearbook, 1987, Vol 3: foreign country reviews of production, trade, and policy, by commodity, annual rpt, 5604–35

Minerals Yearbook, 1987, Vol 3 preprints: foreign country review of production, trade, and policy, by commodity, annual rpt, 5604–23.84

Population size, growth rates, and components of change, by country, projected 1989-2020 and trends from 1950, biennial rpt, 2324–9

UN voting record and share of votes in agreement with US, by issue, country, and world area, 1988, annual rpt, 7004–18

see also under By Foreign Country in the "Index by Categories"

Bell, Linda A.
"Incidence of Union Concessions in the 1980s: What, Where, and Why?", 9385–8.41
"Union Concessions in the 1980s", 9385–1.912

Bell Operating Companies
Finances and operations, detail for telephone firms, 1987, annual rpt, 9284–6
Finances and operations of local and long distance firms, subscribership, and charges, 1970s-FY89, semiannual rpt, 9282–7
Finances, operations, and industry devs for telecommunications, with data by service type, firm, and country, 1950s-80s, 2808–27
Local telephone rates and low-income subsidies, by region, company, and city, 1940-June 1989, semiannual rpt, 9282–8

Bellet, Adam Z.
"Employer-Sponsored Life Insurance: A New Look", 6722–1.951

Belleville, Ill.
see also under By SMSA or MSA in the "Index by Categories"

Bellingham, Wash.
see also under By SMSA or MSA in the "Index by Categories"

Beloit, Wis.
see also under By SMSA or MSA in the "Index by Categories"

Belongia, Michael T.
"Are Economic Forecasts by Government Agencies Biased? Accurate?", 9391–1.902
"Can a Central Bank Influence Its Currency's Real Value? The Swiss Case", 9391–1.907

Belous, Richard S.
"How Human Resource Systems Adjust to the Shift Toward Contingent Workers", 6722–1.913

Bengtsson, B.-E.
"Sublethal Effects of Tetrachloro-1,2-benzoquinone—A Component in Bleachery Effluents from Pulp Mills—On Vertebral Quality and Physiological Parameters in Fourhorn Sculpin", 21368–112

Benin
Agricultural and food production and indexes, total and for selected commodities, by country, 1970s-88, annual rpt, 1524–12
Agricultural trade of US, by detailed commodity and country, 1988, semiannual rpt, 1522–4

AID activities and funding by project and function, FY90, and developing countries summary socioeconomic data from 1960s, annual rpt, 9904–4.5

AID economic aid to developing countries, obligations and disbursements by country, quarterly rpt, 9912–4

AID loans repayment status and terms by program and country, and status of predecessor agency loans, quarterly rpt, 9912–3

Background Notes, summary social, political, and economic data, 1989 rpt, 7006–2.22

Economic and military aid and loans from US and intl agencies, by program and country, FY46-87, annual rpt, 9914–5

Economic conditions, income, production, prices, employment, and trade, 1989 periodic country rpt, 2046–4.61

Economic, social, political, and geographic summary data, by country, 1989, annual factbook, 9114–2

Exports and imports of US, by commodity and country, 1970-87, world area rpt, 9116–1.4

Human rights conditions in 170 countries, 1988, annual rpt, 21384–3

Military aid of US, arms sales, and training programs costs and budget requests, by program, world region, and country, FY88-90, annual rpt, 7144–13

Military spending, arms trade, and force strengths, with govt spending and population, by country, 1977-87, annual rpt, 9824–1

Minerals Yearbook, 1987, Vol 3: foreign country reviews of production, trade, and policy, by commodity, annual rpt, 5604–35

Minerals Yearbook, 1987, Vol 3 preprints: foreign country review of production, trade, and policy, by commodity, annual rpt, 5604–23.82

Population size, growth rates, and components of change, by country, projected 1989-2020 and trends from 1950, biennial rpt, 2324–9

UN voting record and share of votes in agreement with US, by issue, country, and world area, 1988, annual rpt, 7004–18

see also under By Foreign Country in the "Index by Categories"

Beningo, Steven
"Rural Air Service", 1278–17

Benites, Jose R.
"Low-Input Cropping for Acid Soils of the Humid Tropics", 21708–126

Bennefield, Robert L.
"Labor Force Status and Other Characteristics of Persons with a Work Disability: 1981-88", 2546–2.147

Benton Harbor, Mich.
see also under By SMSA or MSA in the "Index by Categories"

Berg, Gordon
"Frances Perkins and the Flowering of Economic and Social Policies", 6722–1.929

Bergen County, N.J.
Wages by occupation, for office and plant workers, 1988 survey, periodic MSA rpt, 6785–11.1
see also under By SMSA or MSA in the "Index by Categories"

Berger, Allen N.
"Collateral, Loan Quality, and Bank Risk", 9366–6.165
"Loan Commitments and Bank Risk Exposure", 9366–6.179
"Price Rigidity and Market Structure: Theory and Evidence from the Banking Industry", 9366–6.173
"Some Red Flags Concerning Market Value Accounting", 9366–6.199

Berger, Franklin D.
"Texas Industrial Production Index", 9379–1.908

Bergman, Bruce J.
"Area Wage Surveys, Selected Metropolitan Areas, 1988", 6785–1

Bergstrand, Jeffrey H.
"Selected Views of Exchange Rate Determination After a Decade of 'Floating'", 9375–14

Bering Sea
Environmental conditions and oil dev impacts for Alaska OCS, compilation of papers, series, 2176–1
Estuary environmental and fishery conditions, research results and methodology, 1988 rpt, 2176–7.8
Fish (Greenland turbot) catch, by Alaska coast fishery, 1960s-86, 2168–110
Ice conditions of Bering Sea and Alaska north coast, monthly rpt, 2182–5
Research activities of Pacific Marine Environmental Lab, and bibl, FY88, annual rpt, 2144–21

Berkeley, Calif.
see also under By City in the "Index by Categories"

Berlin, Martha
"Questionnaires and Data Collection Methods for the Household Survey and the Survey of American Indians and Alaska Natives. National Medical Expenditure Survey", 4186–8.5

Bermant, Gordon
"Alternative Dispute Resolution in a Bankruptcy Court: The Mediation Program in the Southern District of California", 18408–40

Bermuda
Agricultural trade of US, by detailed commodity and country, 1988, semiannual rpt, 1522–4
Businesses (foreign) activity in US, income tax returns, assets, and income statement items, by industry div, country, and world area, 1984-85, article, 8302–2.920
Economic and military aid and loans from US and intl agencies, by program and country, FY46-87, annual rpt, 9914–5
Economic, social, political, and geographic summary data, by country, 1989, annual factbook, 9114–2
Multinatl US firms and foreign affiliates finances and operations, by industry of parent firm and affiliate, world area, and country, preliminary 1987, annual rpt, 2704–5
Population size, growth rates, and components of change, by country, projected 1989-2020 and trends from 1950, biennial rpt, 2324–9

Bernanke, Ben S.
"Federal Funds Rate and the Channels of Monetary Transmission", 9387–8.189

Bernardo, Daniel J.
"Factor Demand in Irrigated Agriculture Under Conditions of Restricted Water Supplies", 1588–139

Bernauer, Kenneth
"Asian Dollar Market", 9375–14

Berries
see Fruit and fruit products

Berry, Janice T.
"1988 Fertilizer Summary Data", 9804–5

Bertelsen, Diane R.
"Financial and Production Management Benchmarks from Farm Operator Survey Data", 1548–342

Beryllium
see Metals and metal industries

Bessler, David A.
"Farmgate, Processor, and Consumer Price Transmissions in the Wheat Sector", 1502–3.903

Bethlehem, Pa.
see also under By SMSA or MSA in the "Index by Categories"

Betting
see Gambling
see Pari-mutuel wagering

Beverages
Apple juice production, use, stocks, and trade, and US imports, by country, 1983-89, article, 1925–34.908
China trade by SITC 1- to 5-digit commodity, 1970s-87, annual rpt, 9114–3
Consumer Expenditure Survey, household income by source, and itemized spending, by selected characteristics and location, 1984-86, annual rpt, 6764–5.2
Consumer research, food marketing, legislation, and regulation devs, and consumption and price trends, quarterly journal, 1541–7
Consumption of food and nutrient intake by individuals, by food group, selected characteristics, and region, supplementary survey series, 1356–5
Consumption, supply, trade, prices, spending, and indexes, by food commodity, 1987, annual rpt, 1544–4
County Business Patterns, 1987: employment, establishments, and payroll, by SIC 2- to 4-digit industry and county, annual State rpt series, 2326–8
CPI by component for US city average, and by region, population size, and for 27 metro areas, monthly rpt, 6762–2
Employment, earnings, and hours, by selected SIC 1- to 4-digit industry, State, and for 262 MSAs, 1972-87, 6748–81
Employment, earnings, and hours, by SIC 1- to 4-digit industry, monthly 1983-Feb 1989, annual rpt, 6744–4
Employment of minorities and women, by occupation, SIC 1- to 3- digit industry, State, and MSA, 1986, annual rpt, 9244–1
Exports and imports (agricultural) of US, by commodity and country, bimonthly rpt with articles, 1522–1
Exports and imports (agricultural) of US, by detailed commodity and country, 1988, semiannual rpt, 1522–4
Exports and imports (agricultural) of US with Asia, Middle East, and North Africa, by commodity and country, 1962-86, 1528–277

Exports and imports of US, by selected country, country group, and commodity group, 1988, annual rpt, 2044–37
Exports of US, detailed commodities by country, monthly rpt, 2422–3
Foreign and US fresh and processed fruit, vegetable, and nut production and trade, FAS monthly circular with articles, 1925–34
Fruit and vegetable processing industries finances and operations, consumption, farm production, and trade, by commodity, 1970s-88, 1568–275
Imports of US, detailed Schedule A commodities by country, monthly rpt, 2422–2
Manufacturing census, 1987: financial and operating data, for SIC 4-digit industries by product, preliminary rpt, 2491–1.8
Multinatl US firms and foreign affiliates finances and operations, by industry of parent firm and affiliate, world area, and country, preliminary 1987, annual rpt, 2704–5
Nutrient and caloric composition of food, for raw, processed, and prepared food, 1988 rpt, 1358–3
Occupational injury and illness rates, by SIC 2- to 4-digit industry, 1987, annual rpt, 6844–1
OECD trade, total and for 4 major countries, and US trade by country, by commodity, 1970-87, world area rpt series, 9116–1
Orange and grapefruit juice exports of US, by world area, 1985-87, tables, 1925–34.910
Orange juice (frozen) cold storage stocks, by census div, 1988, annual rpt, 1631–11
Orange juice (frozen) from Brazil, injury to US industry from import sales at less than fair value, investigation supplement, 1989 rpt, 9886–14.250
Pineapple (canned fruit and juice) production and exports, by country, 1986-89, annual article, 1925–34.920
Price indexes (producer), by stage of processing and detailed commodity, monthly rpt, 6762–6
Price indexes (producer), by stage of processing and detailed commodity, monthly 1988, annual rpt, 6764–2
Science, engineering, and technical employment in manufacturing, by field, occupation, and industry, 1986, triennial rpt, 9627–23
Statistical Abstract of US, social, political, and economic data, 1790-2025, comprehensive annual compilation, 2324–1.3
Tax (income) returns of corporations, income and tax items by asset size and detailed industry, 1986, annual rpt, 8304–4
Transportation census, 1987: trucks, by detailed characteristics, miles traveled, and type of product carried, State rpt series, 2573–1
see also Beer and breweries
see also Coffee
see also Liquor and liquor industry
see also Soft drink industry and products
see also Tea
see also Wine and winemaking

Bhutan
Agricultural and food production and indexes, total and for selected commodities, by country, 1970s-88, annual rpt, 1524–12
Economic and military aid and loans from US and intl agencies, by program and country, FY46-87, annual rpt, 9914–5
Economic, social, political, and geographic summary data, by country, 1989, annual factbook, 9114–2
Human rights conditions in 170 countries, 1988, annual rpt, 21384–3
Minerals production, reserves, and industry role in domestic economy and world supply, 1988 country rpt, 5606–1.17
Population size, growth rates, and components of change, by country, projected 1989-2020 and trends from 1950, biennial rpt, 2324–9
UN voting record and share of votes in agreement with US, by issue, country, and world area, 1988, annual rpt, 7004–18
see also under By Foreign Country in the "Index by Categories"

Bibliographies
Acid rain research activities and funding, by Federal agency, 1988 annual rpt, 14354–1
Agent Orange exposure health effects, literature review, 1987, annual rpt series, 8706–1
Agricultural policy impacts on economic dev, with background data for 6 developing countries, 1960s-86, 1528–283
Agricultural prices, income, and trade, and crop support levels by program, effect of Fed policies, 1989 semiannual rpt, 1542–6
Alaska Arctic Natl Wildlife Refuge resources, native hunting activity, and energy exploration impact, 1985, last issue of annual rpt, 5504–26
Alaska OCS environmental conditions and oil dev impacts, compilation of papers, series, 2176–1
Alcohol abuse research, treatment programs, and patient characteristics and health effects, quarterly journal, 4482–1
Atlantic Oceanographic and Meteorological Lab research activities and bibl, FY88, annual rpt, 2144–19
Autos powered by electricity, R&D activity and DOE funding shares, FY88, annual rpt, 3304–2
Coastal and estuarine pollutant concentrations in fish, shellfish, and environment, series, 2176–3
Coastal and riparian areas environmental conditions, fish, wildlife, use, and mgmt, for individual ecosystems, series, 5506–9
Crime, criminal justice admin and enforcement, and public opinion, data compilation, 1970s-88, annual rpt, 6064–6
Criminal justice issues, series, 6066–25
Employment and unemployment current statistics and articles, Monthly Labor Review, 6722–1
Energy rpts from DOE and other sources, monthly listing, 3002–2
Energy supply and demand summary data, DOE activities and finances, and bibl, 1987, annual rpt, 3024–2

Energy technologies environmental impacts, 1960s-80s, handbook series, 3326-1

Environmental and natural resource data sources, and aerial survey R&D rpts, quarterly listing, 9502-7

Estuary environmental conditions and mgmt, for individual areas, conf series, 2146-6

Fish and shellfish catch, life cycles, and environmental needs, for selected coastal species and regions, series, 5506-8

Fishery mgmt and R&D, Fed Govt grants by project and State, and rpts, 1987, annual listing, 2164-3

Foreign countries *Background Notes*, summary social, political, and economic data, series, 7006-2

Foreign countries economic and social conditions, working paper series, 2326-18

Foreign countries statistical abstracts and rpts, as of 1988, annual listing, 2324-1

Great Lakes Environmental Research Lab activities, 1987 annual rpt, 2144-26

Health care services delivery and costs, research rpts of NCHSR, 1985-July 1987, listing, 4188-57

Health condition and quality of life measurement, rpts and other info sources, quarterly listing, 4122-1

Household composition, income, benefits, and labor force status, Survey of Income and Program Participation methodology, working paper series, 2626-10

Marine Fisheries Review, US and foreign fisheries resources, dev, mgmt, and research, quarterly journal, 2162-1

Marine Mammal Protection Act admin, and populations, strandings, and catch permits by species and location, 1987-88, annual rpt, 2164-11

Marine mammal protection, Federal and intl regulatory and research activities, 1988, annual rpt, 14734-1

Medicare reimbursement of hospitals under prospective payment system, methodology, inputs, and data by diagnostic group, 1989 annual rpt, 17204-1

Medicine Natl Library activities, holdings, and grants, FY86-88, annual rpt, 4464-1

Minerals (strategic) supply and characteristics of individual deposits, by country, commodity rpt series, 5666-21

Minerals resources of Alaska, production, oil and gas leases, and exploratory wells, with maps and bibl, 1987, annual rpt, 5664-11

Minority group and women's income, economic status, and discrimination and govt policy impacts, series, 11046-7

Natl income and product accounts estimates, methodology and bibls, technical rpt series, 2706-6

NOAA Environmental Research Labs rpts, FY88, annual listing, 2144-25

Nutritional status and related health condition and practices, by selected characteristics, 1970s-87, 4048-33

Occupational safety and health research and demonstration grants by State, and project listing, FY87, annual rpt, 4244-2

Ocean and beach plastic, tar, and other nondegradable debris, incidence and environmental impacts, 1970s-88, 14738-4

Ocean pollution, estuary, and coastal waters monitoring and assessment, NOAA activities, funding, FY88, annual rpt, 2174-9

Oil and gas OCS reserves, and leasing and dev activity, periodic regional rpt series, 5736-3

Oil enhanced recovery research contracts of DOE, project summaries, funding, and bibl, quarterly rpt, 3002-14

Older persons social security issues, Fed Govt spending, and indicators of need, with bibl, 1988 compilation of papers, 25928-7

Pacific Marine Environmental Lab research activities and bibl, FY88, annual rpt, 2144-21

Paints used on ship hulls, impacts on environment and marine species, with bibl, 1960s-87, 2148-58

Pollutants health effects, concentrations in food and environment, sources, and human intake methodology and data needs, series, 9186-9

Pollutants health effects, concentrations in food and environment, sources, human intake, and regulation, series, 9186-8

Prison conditions, population, and problems, issues and bibl, 1989 compilation of papers, 25928-8

Science Resources Studies Div of NSF, project descriptions and rpts, 1988 annual listing, 9624-21

Smoking and health effects, with trends in smoking, related disease and death, and public attitudes, literature review, 1989 annual rpt, 4204-18

Smoking and health research rpts, 1988, last issue of annual listing, 4204-19

Smoking and health research summaries, bimonthly rpt, 4202-8

Soil, water, and environmental conservation and conditions, with data by State and region, 1989 quinquennial rpt, 1268-24

Solar photovoltaic R&D sponsored by DOE, projects, funding, and rpts, FY88, annual listing, 3304-20

State statistical abstracts and rpts, as of 1988, annual listing, 2324-1

Storms (severe) natl lab research activities and bibl, FY88, annual rpt, 2144-20

Tax (income) return processing, IRS workload forecasts, compliance, and enforcement, data compilation, 1989 annual rpt, 8304-8

Telecommunications and Info Natl Admin rpts, FY88, annual listing, 2804-3

Transit systems in rural areas, operations and govt funding by region and State, 1986-87, 1278-11

Transit systems research rpts, 1988, annual listing, 7884-11

Vaccination research rpts, 1988 annual listing, 4204-16

see also Computer data file guides

see also Government publications lists

Bicycles

Accident deaths and rates, by cause, age, race, sex, and State, 1986, US Vital Statistics annual rpt, 4144-2

Accident deaths involving alcohol, by driver and victim blood alcohol levels, and other characteristics, 1977-87, annual rpt, 4486-1.2; 4486-1.5; 4486-1.8

Accidents (fatal), circumstances, and characteristics of persons and vehicles involved, 1988, semiannual rpt, 7762-11

Accidents (fatal), deaths, and rates, by circumstances, characteristics of persons and vehicles involved, and location, 1987, annual rpt, 7764-10

Accidents and deaths, by mode of transport, 1977-88, annual rpt, 7304-2

Accidents involving consumer products and related activities, injuries by victim age and sex, 1988, annual rpt, 9164-7

Accidents involving consumer products, injuries by severity, victim age, and detailed product, 1988, annual rpt, 9164-6

Exports of US, detailed commodities by country, monthly rpt, 2422-3

Import restraint elimination, impact on domestic industry production and employment, by selected commodity, 1986-88, 9886-4.144

Imports of US, detailed Schedule A commodities by country, monthly rpt, 2422-2

Manufacturers finances and operations, by SIC 2- to 4-digit industry, forecast 1989 and trends from 1950s, annual rpt, 2044-28

Manufacturing annual survey, 1986: financial and operating data, by SIC 2- to 4-digit industry, series, 2506-15

Manufacturing census, 1987: financial and operating data, for SIC 4-digit industries by product, preliminary rpt, 2491-1.77

Price indexes (producer), by stage of processing and detailed commodity, monthly rpt, 6762-6

Price indexes (producer), by stage of processing and detailed commodity, monthly 1988, annual rpt, 6764-2

Suburban areas land use, commuting, employment, and housing characteristics, detailed data for traffic planning, 1986, 7888-75

Thefts, and value of property stolen and recovered, by property type, 1988, annual rpt, 6224-2.1

Thefts, by property type, 1973-87, annual rpt, 6224-8

Traffic volume in urban areas and detailed trip characteristics, by transport mode and city, 1950s-88, 7888-37

Biddle, Elyce A.

"Job Hazards Underscored in Woodworking Study", 6722-1.945

Bilingual education

see Compensatory education

Billings, Mont.

Housing vacancy rates for single and multifamily units and mobile homes, by city and ZIP code, 1989, annual MSA rpt, 9304-21.4

see also under By SMSA or MSA in the "Index by Categories"

Biloxi, Miss.

Wages by occupation, and benefits for office and plant workers, 1989 survey, periodic MSA rpt, 6785-3.10

see also under By SMSA or MSA in the "Index by Categories"

Binghamton, N.Y.

see also under By SMSA or MSA in the "Index by Categories"

Binnendijk, Annette

"AID's Experience with Rural Development: Project-Specific Factors Affecting Performance", 9916–3.54

Biologic drug products

County Business Patterns, 1987: employment, establishments, and payroll, by SIC 2- to 4-digit industry and county, annual State rpt series, 2326–8

Exports of US, detailed commodities by country, monthly rpt, 2422–3

FDA investigations and regulatory activities, quarterly rpt, 4062–3

Imports of US, detailed Schedule A commodities by country, monthly rpt, 2422–2

Manufacturers finances and operations, by SIC 2- to 4-digit industry, forecast 1989 and trends from 1950s, annual rpt, 2044–28

Manufacturing annual survey, 1986: value of shipments, by SIC 4- to 5-digit product class, 2506–15.3

Manufacturing census, 1987: financial and operating data, for SIC 4-digit industries by product, preliminary rpt, 2491–1.35

Occupational injury and illness rates, by SIC 2- to 4-digit industry, 1987, annual rpt, 6844–1

Prescriptions for new drugs, by category and brand, 1987, annual rpt, 4064–12.2

Price indexes (producer), by stage of processing and detailed commodity, monthly rpt, 6762–6

Price indexes (producer), by stage of processing and detailed commodity, monthly 1988, annual rpt, 6764–2

Veterinary Services Natl Labs activities, biologic drug products evaluation and disease testing, FY88, annual rpt, 1394–17

see also Vaccination and vaccines

Biological sciences

Alaska OCS environmental conditions and oil dev impacts, compilation of papers, series, 2176–1

Black colleges R&D funding by source, and characteristics of grad students and research staff, by field of science and instn, 1980s-87, 9628–78

Carbon dioxide in atmosphere, measurement, methodology, and research results, series, 3006–11

Degrees (bachelor and masters) awarded 1985/86, holders employment characteristics, 1987 survey, series, 4826–3

Degrees (PhD) in science and engineering, by field, instn, employment prospects, sex, race, and other characteristics, 1960s-88, 9627–30

Degrees awarded in higher education, by level, field, race, and sex, 1989 edition, annual rpt, 4824–2.20

Degrees in science and engineering, by field, level, and sex, 1950-86, 9628–77

DOE R&D projects and funding at natl labs, universities, and other instns, FY89, annual summary rpt, 3004–18.3

Education in science, elementary and secondary students proficiency, attitudes, factors affecting proficiency, and teacher background and views, natl assessment, 1977-86, 4898–25

Employment and earnings in science and engineering, by field and activity, and private and Federal R&D spending, by industry, 1975-88, 9626–6.29

Employment and other characteristics of science and engineering PhDs, by field and State, 1987, biennial rpt, 9627–18

Employment characteristics of scientists and engineers, by field, 1988, biennial rpt, 9627–16

Employment of scientists and engineers, and related topics, fact sheet series, 9626–2

Employment of scientists, engineers, and technicians, by nonmanufacturing industry and field, 1987, triennial rpt, 9627–31

Employment of scientists, engineers, and technicians in manufacturing, by field, occupation, and industry, 1986, triennial rpt, 9627–23

Employment of scientists, engineers, and technicians in transportation, utilities, and retail and wholesale trade, by field, occupation, and industry, 1985, triennial rpt, 9627–32

Enrollment in science and engineering, degrees, and student aid and sources, with data by field, race, sex, and instn, 1980s-87, 26358–202

Enrollment in science and engineering grad programs, by field, source of funds, and characteristics of student and instn, 1975-87, annual rpt, 9627–7

Estuary environmental conditions and mgmt, research projects and funding, FY87, annual listing, 2144–24

Fed Govt aid to higher education and nonprofit instns for R&D and related activities, by field, instn, agency, and State, FY87, annual rpt, 9627–17

Fed Govt science and engineering employment, by field, degree level, race, sex, agency, and State, 1987, annual rpt, 9627–5

NASA R&D funding to higher education instns, by field, instn, and State, FY88, annual listing, 9504–7

NIH grants for R&D, training, construction, and medical libraries, by location and recipient, FY88, annual listings, 4434–7

Oceanographic research and distribution activities of World Data Center A by country, and cruises by ship, 1987, annual rpt, 2144–15

R&D equipment of higher education instns, acquisition and service costs, condition, and financing, by field, 1982-83 and 1985-86, 9628–76

R&D funding by Fed Govt, by field, performer type, agency, and State, FY87-89, annual rpt, 9627–20

R&D funding by higher education instns, by source and field, FY80-87, annual rpt, 9624–18.5

R&D funding by source and performer, and related employment, by State, 1975-87, 9626–6.32

Research contracts and grants of Natl Inst of Child Health and Human Dev, by recipient and location, FY88, annual listing, 4474–36

Research on population and reproduction, Federal funding by project, FY87, annual listing, 4474–9

Research on population and reproduction, Natl Inst of Child Health and Human Dev funding and activities, 1988, annual rpt, 4474–33

Small business R&D grants of Fed Govt, by program area, agency, and State, FY88, annual rpt, 9764–7

Teachers bachelor degrees, by field and other characteristics, 1985-86, 4838–39

Wages of scientists and engineers in R&D, by field and educational, employment, and other characteristics, 1989, annual rpt, 3004–1

see also Biotechnology

see also Botany

see also Genetics

see also Physiology

see also Zoology

Biological warfare agents

see Chemical and biological warfare agents

Biomass energy

Consumption of wood, waste, and alcohol fuels, by region, 1980-84, annual rpt, 3164–74.7

Cuba economic conditions, agricultural and industrial production and distribution, trade, and intl economic relations, 1980-87 with trends from 1961, 9118–8

Environmental impacts of energy technologies, 1960s-80s, handbook series, 3326–1

see also Alcohol fuels

see also Gasohol

see also Wood fuel

Biotechnology

Agricultural research and education grants, USDA competitive awards by program and recipient, FY88, annual listing, 1764–1

Environmental quality and protection programs, and intl issues, 1988 annual rpt, 484–1

Fed Govt financial and nonfinancial domestic aid, 1989 base edition with supplements, annual listing, 104–5

Fish and shellfish aquaculture in US and Japan, mgmt, methods, and biological data for selected species, 1985 conf papers, annual rpt, 2164–15

Foreign and US agricultural research spending, public and private instns, and impacts on productivity, by world area, 1960s-87 and projected to 2000, article, 1522–3.909

HHS financial aid, by program, recipient, State, and city, FY88, annual regional listings, 4004–3

Japan biotechnology R&D spending, industry finances, and govt involvement, FY85-86, 2048–139

Legal, ethical, and economic issues involving biotechnology, series, 26356–5

Manufacturers finances and operations, by SIC 2- to 4-digit industry, forecast 1989 and trends from 1950s, annual rpt, 2044–28

NIH activities, funding by program and recipient type, staff, and clinic patients, by inst, FY87, annual rpt, 4434–3

Patents on biotechnology products, issues, and time lapse between application and issue, 1988, GAO rpt, 26113–406

Reproduction and population research, Fed Govt funding by project, FY87, annual listing, 4474–9

Small business high technology sales, exports, siting, technology transfer, views on competitiveness, 1988 survey, hearing, 21728–69

Refugee arrivals in US by world area of origin and State of settlement, and Federal aid, FY88-90, annual rpt, 7004–16

Science and engineering immigrants, by field, age, sex, country and world area of birth and last residence, and State, 1987 and trends from 1967, 9627–29

Statistical Abstract of US, social, political, and economic data, 1790-2025, comprehensive annual compilation, 2324–1.1

Births

Births and rates, by characteristics of birth, infant, and parents, 1987 and trends from 1940, US Vital Statistics advance annual rpt, 4146–5.110

Births and rates, by State, preliminary 1987-88, US Vital Statistics annual rpt, 4144–7

Births, fertility rates, and childless women, by selected characteristics, 1988, annual Current Population Rpt, 2546–1.436

Foreign countries population size, growth rates, and components of change, by country, projected 1989-2020 and trends from 1950, biennial rpt, 2324–9

Health condition and health care resources, use, and spending, 1950s-87, annual data compilation, 4144–11

Home births, by whether planned, outcome, and characteristics of mother and prenatal care, for Calgary, Canada, 1984-87, article, 4042–3.935

Indian Health Service facilities, funding, operations, and Indian health and other characteristics, 1950s-88, annual chartbook, 4084–1

Indian Health Service hospital admissions, length of stay, beds, births, and outpatient visits, by facility and IHS service area, FY70-88, annual rpt, 4084–4

Indian Health Service hospital capacity, use, births, and outpatient visits, by area and facility, quarterly rpt, 4082–1

Mexico population, labor force, and emigration, alternative projections 1990-2000, working paper, 2326–18.46

Military health care facilities of DOD in US and abroad, admissions, beds, outpatient visits, and births, by service branch, quarterly rpt, 3542–15

Minority group population, and components of change, by race, State, metro-nonmetro location, MSA, and county, 1980-85, Current Population Rpt, 2546–3.159

Older mothers over age 30, births and first births by age and race, 1970-86, 4147–21.47

Outlying areas population size and components of change, by area, 1980-88, annual Current Population Rpt, 2546–3.162

Pacific territories social, economic, health, and govtl data, FY88 and trends, annual rpt, 7004–6

Population size and characteristics, 1969-88, Current Population Rpt, annual rpt, 2546–2.146

Population size and components of change, alternative projections 1988-2080 and trends from 1900, annual actuarial rpt, 4706–1.104

Population size by age and sex, components of change, and households, by State, 1980-88, Current Population Rpt, 2546–3.161

Population size, by age, sex, and race, and components of change, alternative projections 1988-2080, Current Population Rpt, 2546–3.158

Population size, by MSA, county, metro-nonmetro location, and State, 1987, and for cities, 1986, with change from 1980 and trends from 1960, Current Population Rpt, 2546–3.160

Population size, July 1988 and compared to 1980 and 1987, and components of change, 1980-88, annual press release, 2324–10

Population size of counties, 1988, and components of change from 1980, annual Current Population Rpt, 2544–3

Statistical Abstract of US, social, political, and economic data, 1790-2025, comprehensive annual compilation, 2324–1.1

Vital and Health Statistics series: reprints of monthly rpt supplements, 4147–24

Vital statistics provisional data, monthly rpt, 4142–1

West Virginia poverty conditions, food aid participants, and birth outcomes, 1980-87, hearing, 21968–49

see also Abortion

see also Birth defects

see also Birthplace

see also Births out of wedlock

see also Birthweight

see also Fertility

see also Fetal deaths

see also Infant mortality

see also Maternity

see also Maternity benefits

see also Obstetrics and gynecology

see also Prenatal care

see also Teenage pregnancy

Births out of wedlock

Abortions, by method, pregnancy history, and other characteristics of woman, 1985-86, US Vital Statistics annual rpt, 4146–5.108

Births and rates, by characteristics of birth, infant, and parents, 1987 and trends from 1940, US Vital Statistics advance annual rpt, 4146–5.110

Births, fertility rates, and childless women, by selected characteristics, 1988, annual Current Population Rpt, 2546–1.436

Child support awards related to selected variables, 1970s-85, 4008–94

Fetal deaths and rates, by characteristics of mother and birth, 1986, US Vital Statistics annual rpt, 4144–2.3

Household and family characteristics, by living arrangement, 1988 and trends from 1960, Current Population Rpt, 2546–2.148

Households receipt of telephone service, by composition, income sources, and other characteristics, 1984-87, 9288–11

Income (household) and poverty status under alternative income definitions, by recipient characteristics, 1986, Current Population Rpt, 2546–6.58

Older mothers over age 30, births and first births by age and race, 1970-86, 4147–21.47

Population size and characteristics, 1969-88, Current Population Rpt, annual rpt, 2546–2.146

Public welfare programs beneficiaries, and benefits duration and share of income, by selected characteristics, 1983-86, 2546–20.8

Statistical Abstract of US, social, political, and economic data, 1790-2025, comprehensive annual compilation, 2324–1.1

Birthweight

Alabama low weight births, by outcome, 1974-84, article, 4042–3.948

Births and rates, by characteristics of birth, infant, and parents, 1987 and trends from 1940, US Vital Statistics advance annual rpt, 4146–5.110

Births of low birthweight, by race of child, and characteristics of mother, prenatal care, and birth, selected years 1975-87, 4147–21.48

Deaths and rates, by detailed cause and demographic characteristics, 1986 and trends from 1900, US Vital Statistics annual rpt, 4144–2

Deaths of infants, and prevention issues, for OECD, 1985 conf papers, 4148–28

Deaths of infants, causes, and prevention, recommendations and findings, 1988 rpt, 15838–1

Hazardous substances exposure of parents and relation to adverse birth outcomes, 1980, article, 4042–3.945

Health condition and health care resources, use, and spending, 1950s-87, annual data compilation, 4144–11

Health condition of low and normal birthweight children, indicators by age, sex, mothers education, and race, 1981, article, 4042–3.904

Indian Health Service facilities, funding, operations, and Indian health and other characteristics, 1950s-88, annual chartbook, 4084–1

Nutritional status and related health condition and practices, by selected characteristics, 1970s-87, 4048–33

Older mothers over age 30, births and first births by age and race, 1970-86, 4147–21.47

Statistical Abstract of US, social, political, and economic data, 1790-2025, comprehensive annual compilation, 2324–1.1

West Virginia poverty conditions, food aid participants, and birth outcomes, 1980-87, hearing, 21968–49

Bisenius, Donald

"Risk-Based Capital Still Fills the Bill", 9312–1.905

Bismarck, N.Dak.

see also under By SMSA or MSA in the "Index by Categories"

Bismuth

see Metals and metal industries

Bivens, Gordon E.

"Preliminary Examination of Uncommitted Funds of U.S. Consumer Units in 1985", 1004–16.1

Bixby, Ann K.

"Benefits and Beneficiaries Under Public Employee Retirement Systems, 1986", 4742–1.917

"Overview of Public Social Welfare Expenditures, FY87", 4742–1.929

"Public Social Welfare Expenditures, FY86", 4742–1.909

Black Americans

Abortions, by method, pregnancy history, and other characteristics of woman, 1985-86, US Vital Statistics annual rpt, 4146-5.108

Agriculture census, 1987: farms, farmland, production, finances, and operator characteristics, by county, final State rpt series, 2331-1

AIDS cases by risk group, race, sex, age, State, and MSA, and deaths, monthly rpt, 4202-9

AIDS public knowledge, attitudes, info sources, and testing, for blacks, 1988 survey, 4146-8.167

Alcohol use and abuse among minority groups, and related problems, by selected characteristics, 1985 conf papers, 4488-13

Army personnel, promotion, and training by race and for women, discrimination issues, and career attitudes, FY88, annual rpt, 3704-10

Births and rates, by characteristics of birth, infant, and parents, 1987 and trends from 1940, US Vital Statistics advance annual rpt, 4146-5.110

Cancer (breast and cervical) incidence, deaths, and survival rates, by race, average 1973-81, article, 4042-3.952

Cancer (cervical) screening and education program for black women, effectiveness and participant characteristics, 1988 local area study, article, 4042-3.953

Consumer Income, socioeconomic characteristics of persons, families, and households, detailed cross-tabulations, Current Population Rpt series, 2546-6

Crime, criminal justice admin and enforcement, and public opinion, data compilation, 1970s-88, annual rpt, 6064-6

Crimes, arrests, and rates, by offense, offender characteristics, population size, and jurisdiction, 1988, annual rpt, 6224-2.1; 6224-2.2

Deaths and rates, by detailed cause and demographic characteristics, 1986 and trends from 1900, US Vital Statistics annual rpt, 4144-2

Deaths and rates, by detailed location, cause, and demographic characteristics, 1987, US Vital Statistics annual rpt, 4144-3

Disabled persons employment, labor force status, and other characteristics, 1988, Current Population Rpt, 2546-2.147

Disease (infectious notifiable) reporting to CDC, cases and rates by race, 1987, article, 4042-3.943

Drug, alcohol, and cigarette use, by substance, age, sex, race, and region, 1988 survey, biennial rpt, 4494-5

Drug and alcohol abuse treatment facilities, services, use, funding, and client characteristics, 1987, annual rpt, 4494-10

Educational attainment, by sociodemographic characteristics and location, 1987 and trends from 1940, biennial Current Population Rpt, 2546-1.427; 2546-1.431

Employment of minorities and women, by occupation, SIC 1- to 3- digit industry, State, and MSA, 1986, annual rpt, 9244-1

Employment, unemployment, and labor force characteristics, by region, State, and selected metro area, 1988, annual rpt, 6744-7

Employment, unemployment, and labor force characteristics, Labor Statistics Handbook, 1940s-88 with trends from 1913, 6728-38.1; 6728-38.2

Farm population, by employment and socioeconomic characteristics, and region, 1988, annual Current Population Rpt, 2546-1.439

Fed Equal Opportunity Recruitment Program activity, and employment by sex, race, pay grade, and selected occupation, FY88, annual rpt, 9844-33

Fed Govt employment of minorities, handicapped, and veterans, and years of service, by occupation, age, sex, and agency, as of Sept 1988, biennial rpt, 9844-27

FmHA loans, by type, borrower characteristics, and State, quarterly rpt, 1182-8

FmHA loans, by type, borrower race, and State, quarterly rpt, 1182-5

Health condition and health care resources, use, and spending, 1950s-87, annual data compilation, 4144-11

Household and family characteristics, by location, 1988, annual Current Population Rpt, 2546-1.437

Household composition, income, benefits, and labor force status, Survey of Income and Program Participation methodology, working paper series, 2626-10

Households and housing detailed characteristics, and unit and neighborhood quality, by location, 1985, biennial rpt, 2485-12

Households and housing detailed characteristics, and unit and neighborhood quality, MSA surveys, series, 2485-6

Housing and households summary characteristics, 1985 and trends, biennial chartbook, 2486-1.7

Income (household), and expenses by type, for blacks by age and family composition, 1985, article, 1702-1.908

Income (household) and poverty status under alternative income definitions, by recipient characteristics, 1986, Current Population Rpt, 2546-6.58

Labor force participation, by race, detailed Hispanic origin, and sex, quarterly rpt, 6742-18

Labor force, wages, hours, and payroll costs, by major industry group and demographic characteristics, *Survey of Current Business*, monthly rpt, 2702-1.5

Living arrangements, family relationships, and marital status, by selected characteristics, 1988, annual Current Population Rpt, 2546-1.428; 2546-1.433

Marriages, divorces, and rates, by characteristics of spouses, State, and county, 1984 and trends from 1920, US Vital Statistics annual rpt, 4144-4

Mentally retarded persons facilities, beds, and residents, by ownership, resident age and race, and State, 1986, 4147-14.34

Military reserve personnel social, economic, family, and service characteristics, and attitudes, by reserve component, 1986 survey, 3508-29

Military reserve spouses attitudes, and family social, economic, and other characteristics, 1986 survey, 3508-30

Nursing home facility, staff, and resident detailed characteristics, 1985, 4147-13.97

Nursing homes, beds, and residents, by ownership, certification status, and State, 1986, 4147-14.33

Nutritional status and related health condition and practices, by selected characteristics, 1970s-87, 4048-33

Police dept operations, staff, and expenses, for large cities by population size, 1987, 6066-19.51

Population size, by age, sex, and race, and components of change, alternative projections 1988-2080, Current Population Rpt, 2546-3.158

Population size of minority groups, and components of change, by race, State, metro-nonmetro location, MSA, and county, 1980-85, Current Population Rpt, 2546-3.159

Prisoners, movements, and characteristics, by State, 1986, annual rpt, 6064-26

Science and engineering labor supply, R&D funding, and other science indicators, with foreign comparisons, 1960s-89, annual chartbook, 9624-22

Science and engineering PhDs, by field, instn, employment prospects, sex, race, and other characteristics, 1960s-88, 9627-30

Science and engineering PhDs employment and other characteristics, by field and State, 1987, biennial rpt, 9627-18

Sexually transmitted disease cases among minorities, by race, 1988, article, 4042-3.954

State and local govt employment of minorities and women, by occupation, function, pay level, and State, 1986, annual rpt, 9244-6

Statistical Abstract of US, social, political, and economic data, with foreign comparisons, 1790-2025, comprehensive annual compilation, 2324-1

Telecommunications industries minority employment and discrimination charges, with data by industry and selected firm, 1970s-88, hearings, 21368-113

Unemployed displaced workers, by reason, industry, selected characteristics, and State, 1988, annual rpt, 6744-18

Voting and registration, by socioeconomic and demographic characteristics, 1988 presidential election, biennial Current Population Rpt, 2546-1.440

see also Black colleges
see also Black students
see also Minority businesses
see also Racial discrimination
see also Sickle cell anemia
see also under By Race and Ethnic Group in the "Index by Categories"

Black colleges

Agricultural research funding and staffing for USDA, State agencies, and other instns, by topic, FY88, annual rpt, 1744-2

AID contracts to minority and women-owned businesses, awards and goals, FY88, annual rpt, 9904-1.2

Enrollment, degrees awarded, and finances of predominantly black instns, 1985-87, annual rpt, 4824–2.17

Fed Govt aid to higher education instns, by program and instn type and control, FY85-88, annual rpt, 4804–28.4; 4804–28.6

R&D and related funding of Fed Govt to higher education and nonprofit instns, by field, instn, agency, and State, FY87, annual rpt, 9627–17

R&D funding by source, and characteristics of grad students and research staff, for black colleges by field of science and instn, 1980s-87, 9628–78

Science and engineering grad enrollment, by field, source of funds, and characteristics of student and instn, 1975-87, annual rpt, 9627–7

Black, Harold A.
"Changes in Interstate Banking Laws: The Impact on Shareholder Wealth", 9387–8.174

Black lung disease
Assistance of Fed Govt, by type, program, agency, and State, FY88, annual rpt, 2464–2

Beneficiaries and benefits by recipient type, from 1970, and by State, 1987, annual rpt, 4744–3.7

Benefits and coverage under workers compensation, by type of program and insurer, and State, 1985-86, annual article, 4742–1.912

Benefits by county, FY88, annual regional listings, 4004–3

Benefits to miners, widows, and dependents, with data by State reported quarterly, monthly rpt, 4742–1.6; 4742–1.13

Coal production and freight costs, and competitive position in selected markets, for Australia and US, 1987-89, 2048–143

Compensation benefits and claims by State, trust fund receipts by source, and disbursements, 1987, annual rpt, 6504–3

Deaths and rates, by detailed cause and demographic characteristics, 1986 and trends from 1900, US Vital Statistics annual rpt, 4144–2

Statistical Abstract of US, social, political, and economic data, 1790-2025, comprehensive annual compilation, 2324–1.2

Tax (excise) collections of IRS, by source, quarterly rpt, 8302–2.1

Tax (excise) collections of IRS, by type of tax, region, and State, FY88, annual rpt, 8304–3.3

Tax (excise) collections of IRS for black lung benefits, quarterly rpt, 8302–1

Trust funds financial condition, for black lung, monthly rpt, 8102–9.10

Black market
see Underground economy

Black students
Condition of Education, detailed data on elementary, secondary, and higher education, 1920s-88 and projected to 1997, annual rpt, 4824–1

Digest of Education Statistics, detailed data on students, staff, finances, and facilities, 1989 edition, annual rpt, 4824–2

Enrollment, by grade, instn type and control, and student characteristics, 1986 and trends from 1947, annual Current Population Rpt, 2546–1.429; 2546–1.432

Enrollment by race, and other indicators of integration plans effectiveness, by school district and location, 1960s-85, 11048–189

High school class of 1972: education, employment, and family characteristics, activities, and attitudes, natl longitudinal study, series, 4836–1

Science and engineering grad enrollment, by field, source of funds, and characteristics of student and instn, 1975-87, annual rpt, 9627–7

Smoking prevention program for black high school students in urban areas, teacher and student views, 1989 local areas surveys, article, 4042–3.956

see also under By Race and Ethnic Group in the "Index by Categories"

Blackmore, William F., Jr.
"Introduction of Unleaded Midgrade Gasoline", 3162–11.902

Blalock, Joseph B.
"Who Are the Good Asset Managers?", 8432–2.901

Blalock, T. Carlton
"Tobacco Marketing Issues", 1004–16.1

Bleil, David F.
"Research Needs Concerning Organotin Compounds Used in Antifouling Paints in Coastal Environments", 2148–58

Blind
Children (handicapped) enrollment by age, and special education programs staff, funding, and needs, by type of handicap and State, 1987/88, annual rpt, 4944–4

Head Start handicapped enrollment, by handicap, State, and for Indian and migrant programs, 1985/86, annual rpt, 4604–1

Libraries for blind and handicapped, readership, circulation, staff, funding, and holdings, FY88, annual listing, 26404–3

Library of Congress activities, acquisitions, services, and financial statements, FY88, annual rpt, 26404–1

Statistical Abstract of US, social, political, and economic data, 1790-2025, comprehensive annual compilation, 2324–1.1

Tax (income) returns of individuals, detailed data, 1986, annual rpt, 8304–2

Vending facilities run by blind on Federal and non-Federal property, finances and operations by agency and State, FY88, annual rpt, 4944–9

see also Aid to blind
see also Supplemental Security Income

Blinder, Alan S.
"Federal Funds Rate and the Channels of Monetary Transmission", 9387–8.189

Blisard, W. Noel
"Quarterly Forecasting of Meat Retail Prices: A Vector Autoregression Approach", 1548–350

Blood
Exports of US, detailed commodities by country, monthly rpt, 2422–3

Red Cross activities, finances, volunteers, and certificates issued, by program, FY88, annual rpt, 29254–1

Red Cross blood program activities, annual summary rpt, suspended, 29254–4

Shipments of blood and blood products, 1986 Annual Survey of Manufactures, 2506–15.3

Transfusion recipients AIDS cases, by age group and race, 1981-88, 4206–2.13

Transfusion recipients AIDS cases, by age group, sex, race, and presence of other risk factors, monthly rpt, 4202–9

Transfusion recipients hepatitis cases, by strain, 1987 and trends from 1966, 4205–2

see also Blood diseases and disorders
see also Blood pressure
see also Septicemia

Blood diseases and disorders
Anemia and iron deficiency prevalence in selected population groups, 1970s-87, 4048–33

Cancer incidence, death, and survival rates, by sex, race, age, and body site, 1973-86, annual rpt, 4474–35

Cases of acute and chronic conditions, disability, absenteeism, and health services use, by selected characteristics, 1988, annual rpt, 4147–10.170

Deaths and rates, by cause, age, sex, marital status, race, and State, 1987, US Vital Statistics advance annual rpt, 4146–5.113

Deaths and rates, by detailed cause and demographic characteristics, 1986 and trends from 1900, US Vital Statistics annual rpt, 4144–2

Deaths and rates, by detailed location, cause, and demographic characteristics, 1987, US Vital Statistics annual rpt, 4144–3

Hemophiliac AIDS cases, by age group and race, 1981-88, 4206–2.13

Hemophiliac and coagulation disorder AIDS cases, by age group, sex, race, and presence of other risk factors, monthly rpt, 4202–9

HHS financial aid, by program, recipient, State, and city, FY88, annual regional listings, 4004–3

Hospital discharges and length of stay, by diagnosis, patient and instn characteristics, procedure performed, and payment source, 1987, annual rpt, 4147–13.99

Hospital discharges by detailed diagnostic and procedure category, primary diagnosis, and length of stay, by age, sex, and region, 1987, annual rpt, 4147–13.100

Indian Health Service and contract facilities hospitalization, by diagnosis, age, sex, and service area, FY88, annual rpt, 4084–5

Natl Heart, Lung, and Blood Inst activities and funding, FY87, annual narrative rpt, 4474–22

Natl Heart, Lung, and Blood Inst activities, and grants by recipient and location, FY88 with disease trends from 1940, annual rpt, 4474–15

Natl Heart, Lung, and Blood Inst grants, and Advisory Council recommendations, FY77-94, annual rpt, 4474–11

Nursing home facility, staff, and resident detailed characteristics, 1985, 4147–13.97

Pollutants health effects, concentrations in food and environment, sources, human intake, and regulation, series, 9186–8

see also Septicemia
see also Sickle cell anemia
see also under By Disease in the "Index by Categories"

Blood poisoning
see Septicemia
Blood pressure
Older persons preventive health care services use, and relation to selected characteristics, 1970s-80s, 26356-7.2
see also Hypertension
Bloom, Justin L.
"Survey of Supply/Demand Relationships for Japanese Technical Information in the U.S.: The Field of Advanced Ceramics Research and Development", 2008-28
Bloomington, Ill.
see also under By SMSA or MSA in the "Index by Categories"
Bloomington, Ind.
see also under By SMSA or MSA in the "Index by Categories"
Bloomquist, Leonard E.
"Too Few Jobs for Workfare To Put Many to Work", 1502-7.902
Blue collar workers
Cancer (stomach) incidence and risk relation to diet and refrigerator use, 1985-87 local area study, article, 4472-1.919
Earnings, annual average percent changes for selected occupational groups, selected MSAs, monthly rpt, 6782-1.1
Educational attainment, by sociodemographic characteristics and location, 1987 and trends from 1940, biennial Current Population Rpt, 2546-1.427; 2546-1.431
Employee flexible benefit plan coverage and provisions, by occupational group for private sector and govt workers, 1986-88, article, 6722-1.959
Employment and occupation of householder, by occupation of spouse, race, and family composition, 1988, annual Current Population Rpt, 2546-1.437
Employment Cost Index and alternative measure of compensation costs, by component, occupation, industry group, union status, and location, 1975-89, annual rpt, 6744-20
Employment, earnings, and hours, by SIC 1- to 4-digit industry, monthly 1983-Feb 1989, annual rpt, 6744-4
Employment, earnings, and hours, monthly press release, 6742-5
Employment in nonmanufacturing industries, by detailed occupation and SIC 2-digit industry, 1987, triennial rpt, 6748-60
Employment situation, earnings, hours, and other BLS economic indicators, transcripts of BLS Commissioner's monthly testimony, periodic rpt, 23846-4
Employment, unemployment, and labor force characteristics, by region, State, and selected metro area, 1988, annual rpt, 6744-7
Fed Govt civilian employee work-years, pay rates, and benefits use and costs, by agency, FY87, annual rpt, 9844-31
Fed Govt civilian employment and payroll, by occupation, pay grade, sex, agency, and location, 1987, biennial rpt, 9844-4
Fed Govt civilian employment by occupation, agency, and location, and language and math skill needs, 1966-87 and projected to 2000, 9848-37
Fed Govt pay comparability with private industry, and recommended and actual pay adjustments, 1970s-89, annual rpt, 10104-1

Fed Govt temporary employment, appointments and extensions, by occupational group, Jan-June 1983-85, GAO rpt, 26119-129
Govt services transfer to private contractors, impacts on govt workers, with data by worker characteristics, level of govt, and location, 1980s-87, 15496-1.5
Handbook of Labor Statistics, employment, unemployment, and labor force characteristics, 1940s-88 with trends from 1913, 6728-38
Health condition of labor force, and services use, by occupation and industry of longest job held, income, age, sex, and race. 1980, 4147-10.168
Immigrants admitted to US, by occupational group and country of birth, preliminary FY88, annual table, 6264-1
Immigration to US, alien workers, visitors, deportations, and naturalizations, by country, FY88 and trends from 1820, annual rpt, 6264-2
Income (household, family, and personal), by source, detailed characteristics, and region, 1987, annual Current Population Rpt, 2546-6.59
Industry finances and operations, by SIC 2- to 4-digit industry, forecast 1989 and trends from 1950s, annual rpt, 2044-28
Labor hourly costs, by component, occupational group, union coverage, industry div, and region, 1989, annual rpt, 6744-21
Manufacturing census, 1987: financial and operating data, for SIC 4-digit industries by product, preliminary industry rpt series, 2491-1
Minority group and women employment, by occupation, SIC 1- to 3- digit industry, State, and MSA, 1986, annual rpt, 9244-1
Occupational changes, by tenure and other worker characteristics, and labor mobility rates, 1965-86, article, 6722-1.943
State and local govt employment of minorities and women, by occupation, function, pay level, and State, 1986, annual rpt, 9244-6
Statistical Abstract of US, social, political, and economic data, 1790-2025, comprehensive annual compilation, 2324-1.3
Wages, hourly and weekly averages by industry div, monthly press release, 6742-3
see also Area wage surveys
see also Industry wage surveys
see also Production workers
see also Service workers
see also under By Occupation in the "Index by Categories"
see also under names of specific industries or industry groups
Blue Cross-Blue Shield
Employer-provided health insurance, coverage, employer and employee contributions, and plan operations, by carrier type, 1987, article, 4652-1.934
Hospice participation in Medicare, program provisions affecting participation, and claims processing time by carrier, 1987-89, GAO rpt, 26121-311
Hospital reimbursement by Medicare under prospective payment system, impacts on

instns, beneficiaries, and other care providers and payment sources, 1986, annual rpt, 4654-13
Ophthalmologist office visits, by characteristics of physician, practice, patient, and visit, with drug mentions by type and brand, 1985, 4146-8.166
Statistical Abstract of US, social, political, and economic data, 1790-2025, comprehensive annual compilation, 2324-1.1
Bluestone, Herman
"Growth Falters in Most Rural Counties: Manufacturing Both Hero and Goat", 1502-7.907
"Rural Development Data Book", 1598-244
Blum, Larry
"Issues in Timber Products Trade", 1004-16.1
Blyth, James E.
"Pulpwood Production in the North-Central Region by County, 1987", 1204-19
Board for International Broadcasting
Budget of US Appendix, obligations, appropriations, and personnel, by program and agency, FY90, annual rpt, 104-3
Budget of US, authoritative financial statements with appropriations, outlays, and receipts, by category and agency, FY88, annual rpt, 8104-2.2
Radio Free Europe and Radio Liberty broadcast and financial data, and compared to other intl broadcasters, FY88, annual rpt, 10314-1
Board of Foreign Scholarships
Fulbright-Hays academic exchanges, grants by purpose, and foreign govt share of costs, by country, FY88, annual rpt, 10324-1
Boarding houses
see Rooming and boarding houses
Boards of education
see School boards
Boats and boating
County Business Patterns, 1987: employment, establishments, and payroll, by SIC 2- to 4-digit industry and county, annual State rpt series, 2326-8
Drug and illegal alien enforcement activities of Coast Guard, 2nd half FY89, semiannual rpt, 7402-4
Drug enforcement activities of State and local agencies, Federal aid by recipient, and background data, FY88, annual rpt, 6064-28
Employment, earnings, and hours, by SIC 1- to 4-digit industry, monthly 1983-Feb 1989, annual rpt, 6744-4
Energy use by mode of transport, fuel supply, and demographic and economic factors of vehicle use, 1970s-88, annual rpt, 3304-5
Exports of US, detailed commodities by country, monthly rpt, 2422-3
Finances, operations, vehicles, equipment, accidents, and energy use, by mode of transport, 1955-88, annual rpt, 7304-2
Fishery employment, vessels, plants, and cooperatives, by State, 1988 and trends from 1970, annual rpt, 2164-1.10
Fishing (ocean sport) catch and effort, and Natl Marine Fisheries Service tagging and research activity, by species and location, 1987, annual rpt, 2164-7

Fishing (ocean sport) catch, by species, mode of fishing, and coastal region, 1988, annual rpt, 2164–1.2

Fishing, hunting, and other wildlife-related recreation participation and spending, detailed data by location, 1985 survey, quinquennial rpt, 5508–5

Fishing, hunting, and other wildlife-related recreation participation and spending, detailed data, 1985 survey, quinquennial State rpt series, 5506–6

Forests (natl) recreational use, by type of activity and State, 1988, annual rpt, 1204–17

Imports of US, detailed Schedule A commodities by country, monthly rpt, 2422–2

Manatees killed in Florida and other US waters, by cause, 1977-88, annual rpt, 14734–1

Manufacturing annual survey, 1986: financial and operating data, by SIC 2- to 4-digit industry, series, 2506–15

Manufacturing census, 1987: financial and operating data, for SIC 4-digit industries by product, preliminary rpt, 2491–1.77

New York Bight sport fishing catch and hours fished, by type of boat rental, 1971, article, 2162–1.901

Occupational injury and illness rates, by SIC 2- to 4-digit industry, 1987, annual rpt, 6844–1

Ohio River basin waterway facilities, freight by commodity and port, and recreation, by waterway, 1986-87, annual rpt, 3754–6

Pacific coast groundfish fleet size, characteristics, and revenues, by species and fishing method, 1981-87, annual rpt, 2164–16.1

Police dept operations, staff, and expenses, for large cities by population size, 1987, 6066–19.51

Price indexes (producer), by stage of processing and detailed commodity, monthly rpt, 6762–6

Price indexes (producer), by stage of processing and detailed commodity, monthly 1988, annual rpt, 6764–2

Public lands acreage, grants, use, revenues, and allocations, by State, FY88, annual rpt, 5724–1.2

Registrations of boats, and accidents, casualties, and damage by cause, by vessel characteristics and State, 1988, annual rpt, 7404–1

Retail trade census, 1987: employment, establishments, sales, and payroll, by SIC 2- to 4-digit kind of business, MSA, county, and city, State rpt series, 2397–1

see also Barges

see also Ferries

see also Inland water transportation

see also Marine accidents and safety

see also Ships and shipping

Bobbitt, Sharon A.

"Moonlighting Among Public School Teachers", 4838–36

"What Teachers Majored In: Bachelor's Degree Fields of Public and Private School Teachers", 4838–39

Boca Raton, Fla.

Housing starts and completions authorized by building permits in 40 MSAs, quarterly rpt, 2382–9

Wages by occupation, for office and plant workers, 1989 survey, periodic MSA rpt, 6785–3.10

see also under By SMSA or MSA in the "Index by Categories"

Body measurements

Cholesterol levels of youth related to physical characteristics, age, sex, and race, 1966-70 natl study, article, 4042–3.922

Hazardous substances exposure factors, and methodological guidelines, 1989 rpt, 9188–109

Hispanic Americans body measurements, obesity, and handedness, by detailed origin, age, and sex, 1982-84, 4147–11.207

Homeless persons nutritional status, 1987 local area study, article, 4042–3.942

Pneumonia hospitalization and death rates for aged, and risk relation to health status indicators, aggregate 1982-84, article, 4042–3.934

Statistical Abstract of US, social, political, and economic data, 1790-2025, comprehensive annual compilation, 2324–1.1

Traffic accidents, injuries, and deaths, by circumstances and characteristics of persons and vehicles involved, 1970s-87, series, 7766–14

Vital and Health Statistics series: health condition and body measurements, Natl Health and Nutrition Examination Survey results, 4147–11

see also Birthweight

see also Obesity

Boehly, William A.

"Papers on Car Size—Safety and Trends", 7766–14.4

Boemio, Thomas R.

"Asset Securitization: A Supervisory Perspective", 9362–1.909

Bogs

see Wetlands

Boise, Idaho

Wages by occupation, and benefits for office and plant workers, 1988 survey, periodic MSA rpt, 6785–11.3

see also under By City and By SMSA or MSA in the "Index by Categories"

Boland, Barbara

"Prosecution of Felony Arrests, 1986", 6064–27

Boleat, M. J.

"British Thrifts Thrive", 9312–1.901

Bolivia

Agricultural and food production and indexes, total and for selected commodities, by country, 1970s-88, annual rpt, 1524–12

Agricultural trade of US, by detailed commodity and country, 1988, semiannual rpt, 1522–4

AID activities and funding by project and function, FY90, and developing countries summary socioeconomic data from 1960s, annual rpt, 9904–4.7

AID economic aid to developing countries, obligations and disbursements by country, quarterly rpt, 9912–4

AID loans repayment status and terms by program and country, and status of predecessor agency loans, quarterly rpt, 9912–3

Auto imports from US, trade barriers by country, 1988, annual rpt, 444–2

Economic and military aid and loans from US and intl agencies, by program and country, FY46-87, annual rpt, 9914–5

Economic conditions, income, production, prices, employment, and trade, 1989 periodic country rpt, 2046–4.88

Economic conditions, investment and export opportunities, and trade practices, 1989 country market research rpt, 2046–6.4

Economic conditions, policy, and trade practices, by country, 1986-88, annual rpt, 21384–5

Economic, social, political, and geographic summary data, by country, 1989, annual factbook, 9114–2

Exports and imports of Latin America, and balance of trade with US, by country, 1988, annual rpt, 2044–34

Exports and imports of US, by commodity and country, 1970-87, world area rpt, 9116–1.5

Exports and imports of US, by selected country, country group, and commodity group, 1988, annual rpt, 2044–37

Human rights conditions in 170 countries, 1988, annual rpt, 21384–3

Military aid of US, arms sales, and training programs costs and budget requests, by program, world region, and country, FY88-90, annual rpt, 7144–13

Military spending, arms trade, and force strengths, with govt spending and population, by country, 1977-87, annual rpt, 9824–1

Minerals Yearbook, 1987, Vol 3: foreign country reviews of production, trade, and policy, by commodity, annual rpt, 5604–35

Minerals Yearbook, 1987, Vol 3 preprints: foreign country review of production, trade, and policy, by commodity, annual rpt, 5604–23.9

Population size, growth rates, and components of change, by country, projected 1989-2020 and trends from 1950, biennial rpt, 2324–9

UN voting record and share of votes in agreement with US, by issue, country, and world area, 1988, annual rpt, 7004–18

see also under By Foreign Country in the "Index by Categories"

Bolsinger, Charles L.

"Hardwoods of California's Timberlands, Woodlands, and Savannas", 1208–291

Bolts

see Hardware

Bombs

Aircraft hijackings, on-board explosions, and other crime, US and foreign incidents, 1983-87, annual rpt, 7504–31

Airport security operations to prevent hijacking, screening results, enforcement actions, and hijacking attempts, 1st half 1988, semiannual rpt, 7502–5

Homicides, by circumstance, victim and offender relationship, and type of weapon, 1988, annual rpt, 6224–2.1

Incidents of bombing, and casualties, by target and circumstances, with explosives theft and recovery, by State, 1979-88, annual rpt, 8484–4

Incidents of bombing, damage, and casualties, by target, circumstances, and State, 1988, annual rpt, 6224–5

Incidents of bombing, damage, and casualties, by target, 1973-87, annual rpt, 6064–6.3

Law enforcement officer assaults and deaths by circumstances, agency, victim and offender characteristics, and location, 1988, annual rpt, 6224–3

Military deaths by cause, age, race, and rank, and personnel captured and missing, by service branch, 2nd half FY88, semiannual rpt, 3542–21

Terrorist (intl) incidents, casualties, and attacks on US targets, by attack type and country, 1980-88, 7008–56

Terrorist (intl) incidents, casualties, and attacks on US targets, by attack type and world area, 1968-88, annual rpt, 7004–13

Terrorist incidents in US, related activity, and casualties, by attack type, target, group, and location, 1988, annual rpt, 6224–6

see also Military weapons
see also Nuclear explosives and explosions

Bonar, Scott A.
"Pink Salmon. Species Profiles: Life Histories and Environmental Requirements of Coastal Fishes and Invertebrates (Pacific Northwest)", 5506–8.95

Bondar, Joseph
"Effects of the Social Security Benefit Increase, December 1988", 4742–1.920

Bonds
see Government securities
see Municipal bonds
see Securities
see Surety bonds
see Tax exempt securities

Bonham, Gordon S.
"Expected Size of Completed Family Among Currently Married Women 15-44 Years of Age: U.S., 1973", 4147–16.1

Bonneville Power Administration
Activities of BPA, and Fed Columbia River Power System finances, operations, and sales by customer, FY88, annual rpt, 3224–1

Air pollution indoor levels, effects of ventilation rates in commercial and public buildings, 1989 rpt, 3228–10

Electric power capacity and use in Pacific Northwest, by end-use sector, projected under alternative fuel price cases, 1987-2010, annual rpt, 3224–4

Electric power capacity and use in Pacific Northwest, by energy source, projected under alternative load and demand cases, 1989-2008, annual rpt, 3224–3

Electric power use and prices in Pacific Northwest by end-use sector, and economic and demographic data, annual rpt, discontinued, 3224–2

Electric power wholesale purchases and costs for REA borrowers, by borrower, supplier, and State, 1940-87, annual rpt, 1244–5

Energy conservation (housing) program of BPA, energy savings and indoor air quality under alternative methods, projected 1986-2006, 3228–9

Energy conservation (housing) program of BPA in Hood River, Oreg, cost effectiveness and participation, 1983-86, series, 3226–2

Finances and operations of Federal power admins, as of Sept 1987, annual rpt, 3164–23.4

Finances and sales for Fed Columbia River Power System, summary data, quarterly rpt, 3222–2

Population, households, employment, income, and fuel prices, for Pacific Northwest, alternative projections 1990-2010 with trends from 1960, annual rpt, 3224–5

Sales, revenues, and rates of BPA, by customer and customer type, 1988, semiannual rpt, 3222–1

Bonuses
see Employee bonuses and work incentives

Books and bookselling
Consumer holdings of durable goods, by type, in current and constant dollars, 1985-88, annual article, 2702–1.931

County Business Patterns, 1987: employment, establishments, and payroll, by SIC 2- to 4-digit industry and county, annual State rpt series, 2326–8

Employment, earnings, and hours, by selected SIC 1- to 4-digit industry, State, and for 262 MSAs, 1972-87, 6748–81

Employment, earnings, and hours, by SIC 1- to 4-digit industry, monthly 1983-Feb 1989, annual rpt, 6744–4

Exports of US, detailed commodities by country, monthly rpt, 2422–3

GPO bookstores, 1989 annual listing, 2304–2

Imports of US, detailed Schedule A commodities by country, monthly rpt, 2422–2

Manufacturers finances and operations, by SIC 2- to 4-digit industry, forecast 1989 and trends from 1950s, annual rpt, 2044–28

Manufacturing annual survey, 1986: financial and operating data, by SIC 2- to 4-digit industry, series, 2506–15

Manufacturing census, 1987: financial and operating data, for SIC 4-digit industries by product, preliminary rpt, 2491–1.30; 2491–1.32

Occupational injury and illness rates, by SIC 2- to 4-digit industry, 1987, annual rpt, 6844–1

OECD trade, total and for 4 major countries, and US trade by country, by commodity, 1970-87, world area rpt series, 9116–1

Price indexes (producer), by stage of processing and detailed commodity, monthly rpt, 6762–6

Price indexes (producer), by stage of processing and detailed commodity, monthly 1988, annual rpt, 6764–2

Retail trade census, 1987: employment, establishments, sales, and payroll, by SIC 2- to 4-digit kind of business, MSA, county, and city, State rpt series, 2397–1

Retail trade sales and inventories, by kind of business, region, and selected State, MSA, and city, monthly rpt, 2413–3

Retail trade sales, inventories, purchases, gross margin, and accounts receivable, by SIC 2- to 4-digit kind of business and form of ownership, 1987, annual rpt, 2413–5

Science, engineering, and technical employment in manufacturing, by field, occupation, and industry, 1986, triennial rpt, 9627–23

Statistical Abstract of US, social, political, and economic data, 1790-2025, comprehensive annual compilation, 2324–1.1

Tax (income) returns of partnerships, income statement items by industry group, 1986, annual article, 8302–2.903

Tax (income) returns of sole proprietorships, income statement items, by industry group, 1987, annual article, 8302–2.904; 8302–2.921

see also Libraries

Boone, Jean F.
"Soviet Trade from Brezhnev's Stagnation to Gorbachev's Interdependence", 21248–120

Booze, Charles F., Jr.
"Prevalence of Disease Among Active Civil Airmen", 7506–10.55

Bordo, Michael D.
"Classical Gold Standard: Some Lessons for Today", 9375–14

Boron
see Gases

Bortner, James B.
"American Woodcock Harvest and Breeding Population Status, 1989", 5504–11

Boschen, John F.
"Real and Monetary Explanations of Permanent Movements in GNP", 9387–8.195

Bossert, Thomas
"Sustainability of U.S.-Supported Health, Population, and Nutrition Programs in Honduras: 1942-86", 9916–3.53

Bost, Kevin
"1989 Pork Outlook", 1004–16.1

Boston, Mass.
CPI by component for US city average, and by region, population size, and for 15 metro areas, monthly rpt, 6762–1

CPI by component for US city average, and by region, population size, and for 27 metro areas, monthly rpt, 6762–2

Drug abuse indicators for selected metro areas, research results, data collection, and policy issues, 1989 semiannual conf, 4492–5

Fish and shellfish catch, wholesale receipts, prices, trade, and other market activities, weekly regional rpt, 2162–6.1; 2162–6.2

Fruit and vegetable shipments, and arrivals in US and Canada cities, by mode of transport and State and country of origin, 1988, annual rpt, 1311–4.1

Housing and households characteristics, 1985 survey, MSA fact sheet, 2485–11.15

Housing and households detailed characteristics, and unit and neighborhood quality, by location, 1985 survey, MSA rpt, 2485–6.11

Housing costs appreciation impacts on income distribution in selected areas, 1978-88, article, 9373–1.907

Mortgages by lender type and related to neighborhood characteristics, for Boston, Mass, 1982-87, article, 9373–1.915

Wages by occupation, for office and plant workers, 1988 survey, periodic MSA rpt, 6785–11.2

Wages by occupation, for office and plant workers, 1989 survey, periodic MSA rpt, 6785–12.7

see also under By City and By SMSA or MSA in the "Index by Categories"

Botanical gardens

Inst of Museum Services grants, by recipient, FY89, annual press release series, 9564–6

Botany

Carbon dioxide in atmosphere, measurement, methodology, and research results, series, 3006–11

DOE R&D projects and funding at natl labs, universities, and other instns, FY89, annual summary rpt, 3004–18.3

Enrollment in science and engineering grad programs, by field, source of funds, and characteristics of student and instn, 1975-87, annual rpt, 9627–7

Research (agricultural) funding and staffing for USDA, State agencies, and other instns, by topic, FY88, annual rpt, 1744–2

Research and education grants, USDA competitive awards by program and recipient, FY88, annual listing, 1764–1

see also Botanical gardens
see also Flowers and nursery products
see also Forests and forestry
see also Fruit and fruit products
see also Plants and vegetation
see also Vegetables and vegetable products

Botswana

Agricultural and food production and indexes, total and for selected commodities, by country, 1970s-88, annual rpt, 1524–12

Agricultural trade of US, by detailed commodity and country, 1988, semiannual rpt, 1522–4

AID activities and funding by project and function, FY90, and developing countries summary socioeconomic data from 1960s, annual rpt, 9904–4.5

AID economic aid to developing countries, obligations and disbursements by country, quarterly rpt, 9912–4

AID loans repayment status and terms by program and country, and status of predecessor agency loans, quarterly rpt, 9912–3

Background Notes, summary social, political, and economic data, 1988 rpt, 7006–2.4

Economic and military aid and loans from US and intl agencies, by program and country, FY46-87, annual rpt, 9914–5

Economic conditions, policy, and trade practices, by country, 1986-88, annual rpt, 21384–5

Economic, social, political, and geographic summary data, by country, 1989, annual factbook, 9114–2

Human rights conditions in 170 countries, 1988, annual rpt, 21384–3

Military aid of US, arms sales, and training programs costs and budget requests, by program, world region, and country, FY88-90, annual rpt, 7144–13

Military spending, arms trade, and force strengths, with govt spending and population, by country, 1977-87, annual rpt, 9824–1

Minerals Yearbook, 1987, Vol 3: foreign country reviews of production, trade, and policy, by commodity, annual rpt, 5604–35

Minerals Yearbook, 1987, Vol 3 preprints: foreign country review of production, trade, and policy, by commodity, annual rpt, 5604–23.10

Population size, growth rates, and components of change, by country, projected 1989-2020 and trends from 1950, biennial rpt, 2324–9

UN voting record and share of votes in agreement with US, by issue, country, and world area, 1988, annual rpt, 7004–18

see also under By Foreign Country in the "Index by Categories"

Bottge, Robert G.

"Availability of Land for Mineral Exploration and Development in Western Alaska, 1986", 5608–152.3

Bottles

see Packaging and containers

Botulism

see Food and waterborne diseases

Botvin, Gilbert J.

"Psychosocial Approach to Smoking Prevention for Urban Black Youth", 4042–3.956

Boulder, Colo.

CPI by component for US city average, and by region, population size, and for 27 metro areas, monthly rpt, 6762–2

Housing starts and completions authorized by building permits in 40 MSAs, quarterly rpt, 2382–9

Housing vacancy rates for single and multifamily units and mobile homes, by city and ZIP code, 1988, annual MSA rpt, 9304–22.2

Wages by occupation, for office and plant workers, 1988 survey, periodic MSA rpt, 6785–11.3

see also under By SMSA or MSA in the "Index by Categories"

Bowman, Marjorie A.

"Family Physicians: Supply and Demand", 4042–3.926

Bowyer, Linda E.

"Who Does Rate Swaps?", 9312–1.902

Boxes

see Packaging and containers

Boxley, Robert F.

"Agricultural and Rural Data Paradigms", 1502–3.901

Boy Scouts of America

Statistical Abstract of US, social, political, and economic data, 1790-2025, comprehensive annual compilation, 2324–1.1

Boycotts

Exporters (US) antiboycott law violations and fines by firm, and invitations to boycott by country, FY88, annual rpt, 2024–1

Boyd, Gayle M.

"Smoking and Other Tobacco Use: U.S., 1987", 4147–10.169

Boyle, Maureen

"Spending Patterns and Income of Single and Married Parents", 6722–1.916

Bozeman, Earl L., Jr.

"Alewife and Blueback Herring. Species Profiles: Life Histories and Environmental Requirements of Coastal Fishes and Invertebrates (South Atlantic)", 5506–8.118

Bradbury, Katharine L.

"Geographic Patterns of Mortgage Lending in Boston, 1982-87", 9373–1.915

Bradenton, Fla.

Wages by occupation, for office and plant workers, 1989 survey, periodic MSA rpt, 6785–12.5

see also under By SMSA or MSA in the "Index by Categories"

Bragg, David

"Risk-Based Capital Still Fills the Bill", 9312–1.905

Brain diseases

see Cerebrovascular diseases
see Neurological disorders

Brancato, Carolyn K.

"Leveraged Buyouts and the Pot of Gold: 1989 Update", 21368–115

Branch, William

"Oklahoma Net-Pen Catfish Production: Estimated Attainable Production Levels and Their Associated Costs", 1561–15.901

Brand, Horst

"Productivity Trends in Agricultural Chemicals", 6722–1.915

Brand names

see Trademarks
see under By Individual Company or Institution in the "Index by Categories"

Brandt, Jeanette A.

"Housing and Community Preferences: Will They Change in Retirement?", 1004–16.1; 1702–1.905

Branson, William H.

"International Payments Imbalances in Japan, Germany, and the U.S.", 9373–3.32

Branstad, Terry E.

"State-Federal Cooperation", 1004–16.1

Brass

see Metals and metal industries

Brazell, David W.

"History of Federal Tax Depreciation Policy", 8006–3.60

Brazil

Agricultural and food production and indexes, total and for selected commodities, by country, 1970s-88, annual rpt, 1524–12

Agricultural production, prices, and trade, by country, 1960s-89, annual world region rpt, 1524–4.2

Agricultural subsidies, consumer and producer equivalents by program, commodity, and major US trading partner, 1982-86, 1528–275

Agricultural trade among western hemisphere countries, and US duty-free imports, with listing of trade disputes and outcomes, 1960s-85, 1528–278

Agricultural trade of US, by detailed commodity and country, 1988, semiannual rpt, 1522–4

AID economic aid to developing countries, obligations and disbursements by country, quarterly rpt, 9912–4

AID loans repayment status and terms by program and country, and status of predecessor agency loans, quarterly rpt, 9912–3

Debt (foreign) and debt burden and economic indicators for Brazil with comparisons to other developing countries, 1970s-88, hearings, 21248–122

Economic and military aid and loans from US and intl agencies, by program and country, FY46-87, annual rpt, 9914-5

Economic and monetary trends, compounded annual rates of change for US and 13 trading partners, quarterly rpt annual supplement, 9391-7

Economic conditions in Communist, OECD, and selected other countries, 1960s-88, annual rpt, 9114-4

Economic conditions, income, production, prices, employment, and trade, 1989 periodic country rpt, 2046-4.9; 2046-4.87

Economic conditions, investment and export opportunities, and trade practices, 1989 country market research rpt, 2046-6.11

Economic conditions, policy, and trade practices, by country, 1986-88, annual rpt, 21384-5

Economic indicators of developing countries, problem debtors compared to other borrowers, by country, 1973-84, 1528-285

Economic, social, political, and geographic summary data, by country, 1989, annual factbook, 9114-2

Exports and imports of Latin America, and balance of trade with US, by country, 1988, annual rpt, 2044-34

Exports and imports of US, by commodity and country, 1970-87, world area rpt, 9116-1.5

Exports and imports of US, by selected country, country group, and commodity group, 1988, annual rpt, 2044-37

Exports and imports, trade agreements and relations, and USITC investigations, 1988, annual rpt, 9884-5

Exports, imports, and balances of US by commodity group, world area, and country, and related employment, 1970s-88, annual rpt, 2044-26

Grain production, use, exports, quality standards, storage, and prices, for 5 countries, 1960s-88, 26358-201.2

Human papillomavirus infection rates, by sexual and personal hygiene practices, and other patient characteristics, Brazil local area studies, 1989 article, 4472-1.908

Human rights conditions in 170 countries, 1988, annual rpt, 21384-3

Imports of goods, services, and investment from US, trade barriers, impacts, and US actions, by country, 1988, annual rpt, 444-2

Imports of US given duty-free treatment for value of US material sent abroad, and impacts on US industry and employment, by commodity and country, 1987, annual rpt, 9884-14

Labor conditions, union coverage, and work accidents, 1989 annual country rpt, 6366-4.46

Military aid of US, arms sales, and training programs costs and budget requests, by program, world region, and country, FY88-90, annual rpt, 7144-13

Military spending, arms trade, and force strengths, with govt spending and population, by country, 1977-87, annual rpt, 9824-1

Minerals Yearbook, 1987, Vol 3: foreign country reviews of production, trade, and policy, by commodity, annual rpt, 5604-35

Minerals Yearbook, 1987, Vol 3 preprints: foreign country review of production, trade, and policy, by commodity, annual rpt, 5604-23.11

Multinatl US firms and foreign affiliates finances and operations, by industry of parent firm and affiliate, world area, and country, preliminary 1987, annual rpt, 2704-5

Nitrocellulose (industrial) from 7 countries at less than fair value, injury to US industry, investigation with background financial and operating data, 1989 rpt, 9886-14.270

Nuclear power generation in US and 19 non-Communist countries, monthly rpt, 3162-24.10

Nuclear power plant capacity, generation, and operating status, by plant and foreign and US location, 1988 and projected to 2020, annual rpt, 3164-57

Orange and frozen juice concentrate production, use, exports by country, and grower price, for Brazil, various periods 1966-90, article, 1925-34.922

Orange juice (frozen) from Brazil, injury to US industry from import sales at less than fair value, investigation supplement, 1989 rpt, 9886-14.250

Population size, growth rates, and components of change, by country, projected 1989-2020 and trends from 1950, biennial rpt, 2324-9

Ships in world merchant fleet, and tonnage, by country of registry, as of Jan 1988, annual rpt, 7704-3

Soybean production itemized costs, by region, for US, Argentina, and Brazil, 1986-88, article, 1522-3.902

Space satellites and other objects launched since 1957, quarterly listing, 9502-2

Steel disc wheels from Brazil at less than fair value, injury to US industry, investigation supplement, 1989 rpt, 9886-14.259

Steel export ceilings under voluntary restraint agreements, by country and product, with Western US steel industry impact, 1989 rpt, 9886-4.136

Steel imports of US under voluntary restraint agreement, by product, customs district, and country, with US industry operating data, monthly rpt, 9882-13

Steel wheels from Brazil, injury to US industry from foreign subsidized value imports, investigation with background financial and operating data, 1989 rpt, 9886-15.73

Stone (dimension) trade and price indexes by selected country, 1987, Mineral Industry Surveys, annual rpt, 5614-29

Tobacco acreage and production by province, and exports, 1980s-89, article, 1925-16.905

Travel to US and Canada, market analysis with detailed trip and traveler characteristics, 1988, country rpt, 2906-2.12

UN voting record and share of votes in agreement with US, by issue, country, and world area, 1988, annual rpt, 7004-18

see also under By Foreign Country in the "Index by Categories"

Brazoria, Tex.

CPI by component for US city average, and by region, population size, and for 15 metro areas, monthly rpt, 6762-1

CPI by component for US city average, and by region, population size, and for 27 metro areas, monthly rpt, 6762-2

Housing starts and completions authorized by building permits in 40 MSAs, quarterly rpt, 2382-9

see also under By SMSA or MSA in the "Index by Categories"

Bread

see Baking and bakery products

Breast-feeding

Nutritional status and related health condition and practices, by selected characteristics, 1970s-87, 4048-33

Bremerton, Wash.

see also under By SMSA or MSA in the "Index by Categories"

Breslin, John A.

"Health, Safety, and Economic Issues of Diesel Engines in Underground Mines", 5606-5.7

Brewer, Elijah, III

"Full-Blown Crisis, Half-Measure Cure", 9375-1.908

"Note on the Relationship Between Bank Holding Company Risk and Nonbank Activity", 9375-11.20

Bribery

see Corruption and bribery

Brick, J. Michael

"Comparison of Fall and Academic Year Student Aid Estimates", 4846-3.5

Bridgeport, Conn.

see also under By City and By SMSA or MSA in the "Index by Categories"

Bridges and tunnels

Army Corps of Engineers activities and projects, FY87 and trends from 1800s, annual rpt, 3754-1.2

Conditions, travel, and funding, by type of hwy, 1960s-87 and projected to 2005, biennial rpt, 7554-27

Construction industries census, 1987: financial and operating data, preliminary industry rpt series, 2371-1

Forest Service activities and finances, by region and State, FY88, annual rpt, 1204-1.1

Hwy Statistics, detailed data by State, 1988, annual rpt, 7554-1

Hwy Trust Fund obligations, by project and urban-rural location, 1982-86, 1278-12

Public lands acreage and use, and Land Mgmt Bur activities and finances, annual State rpt series, 5724-11

Reclamation Bur water storage and carriage facilities, capacity, and operating status, as of Sept 1988, biennial listing, 5824-7

Rural areas bridges conditions, needs, and funding, with data by State and compared to urban areas, 1988, 1278-16

Bridgeton, N.J.

see also under By SMSA or MSA in the "Index by Categories"

Bristol, Conn.

see also under By SMSA or MSA in the "Index by Categories"

Bristol, Ralph B., Jr.

"Tax Modelling and the Policy Environment of the 1990's", 8302-2.912

Bristol, Tenn.
see also under By SMSA or MSA in the "Index by Categories"

British Columbia Province, Canada
Tidal currents, daily time and velocity by station for North America and Asia coasts, forecast 1990, annual rpt, 2174–1.1
Timber in northwestern US and British Columbia, production, prices, trade, and employment, quarterly rpt, 1202–3

British Virgin Islands
Economic, social, political, and geographic summary data, by country, 1989, annual factbook, 9114–2
Population size, growth rates, and components of change, by country, projected 1989-2020 and trends from 1950, biennial rpt, 2324–9

Broadcasting
see Educational broadcasting
see Political broadcasting
see Public broadcasting
see Radio
see Television

Broaddus, Alfred
"Analysis of the Determinants of the Yields on Individual Municipal Securities", 9389–19.8

Brockman, Stanley R.
"Catalog of Intensities and Magnitudes for Earthquakes in Alaska and the Aleutian Islands—1786-1981", 5668–87

Brockton, Mass.
Housing and households detailed characteristics, and unit and neighborhood quality, by location, 1985 survey, MSA rpt, 2485–6.11
see also under By SMSA or MSA in the "Index by Categories"

Broderick, Eric
"Baby Bottle Tooth Decay in Native American Children in Head Start Centers", 4042–3.903

Brodsky, Melvin
"International Developments in Apprenticeship", 6722–1.936

Broehm, Karl A.
"Summary of Public Attitude Survey Findings", 8304–8.1

Brokers
see Futures trading
see Real estate business
see Stockbrokers

Bromine
see Nonmetallic minerals and mines

Brookhaven National Laboratory
see also Department of Energy National Laboratories

Brooks, Barbara G.
"Occupational Radiation Exposure at Commercial Nuclear Power Reactors and Other Facilities, 1986", 9634–3

Brooks, Douglas H.
"Metropolitan Growth and Agriculture: Farming in the City's Shadow", 1598–256
"Policy and Prosperity in Thailand's Rice Sector", 1561–8.904
"Reducing Support Using Aggregate Measures, Case Study: Thailand", 1528–286
"Thailand's Rice Sector in Transition", 1522–3.915

Brooks, Nora
"Effects of Population Growth and County Type on Farm Structure, 1970-80", 1598–253

Brooks, Sharon D.
"Apparent Per Capita Alcohol Consumption: National, State and Regional Trends, 1977-87", 4486–1.9

Broome, Carroll D.
"Default Experience of the FHA Graduated-Payment Mortgage", 9316–1.147

Brooms
see Household supplies and utensils

Brothers, Stephen L., Jr.
"Energy Management Annual Report, FY88", 9804–26

Broutman, Marlene A.
"Classified Shellfish Growing Waters by Estuary", 2176–7.3
"Quality of Shellfish Growing Waters in the Gulf of Mexico", 2176–7.5

Brown, Bob
"Hog Outlook for 1989", 1004–16.1

Brown, David L.
"Demographic Trends Relevant to Education in Nonmetropolitan America", 4818–6

Brown, Gretchen A.
"Prenatal, Delivery, and Infant Care Under Medicaid in Three States", 4652–1.938

Brown, Joseph V., Jr.
"Black Lung Benefits Act: Annual Report on Administration of the Act During 1987", 6504–3

Brown, Marilyn A.
"Energy-Related Inventions Program: An Assessment of Recent Commercial Progress", 3308–91

Brown, Mark J.
"Forest Statistics for North Georgia, 1989", 1206–26.11

Brown, Randall S.
"Biased Selection in the Medicare Competition Demonstrations", 4658–31

Brown, Stephen P.
"Econometric Analysis of U.S. Oil Demand", 9379–12.39
"Oil Demand and Prices in the 1990s", 9379–1.901
"Tax Policy and Texas Economic Development", 9379–12.28

Browne, Lynn E.
"Labor Force, Unemployment Rates, and Wage Pressures", 9373–1.902
"Shifting Regional Fortunes: The Wheel Turns", 9373–1.909

Brownsville, Tex.
see also under By City and By SMSA or MSA in the "Index by Categories"

Brucellosis
see Animal diseases and zoonoses

Brueggeman, John J.
"Aerial Surveys of Endangered Cetaceans and Other Marine Mammals in the Northwestern Gulf of Alaska and Southeastern Bering Sea", 2176–1.27
"Shipboard Surveys of Endangered Cetaceans in the Northwestern Gulf of Alaska", 2176–1.27

Bruerd, Bonnie
"Preventing Baby Bottle Tooth Decay in American Indian and Alaska Native Communities: A Model for Planning", 4042–3.961

Brunei
Agricultural and food production and indexes, total and for selected commodities, by country, 1970s-88, annual rpt, 1524–12
Agricultural trade of US, by detailed commodity and country, 1988, semiannual rpt, 1522–4
Economic and military aid and loans from US and intl agencies, by program and country, FY46-87, annual rpt, 9914–5
Economic, social, political, and geographic summary data, by country, 1989, annual factbook, 9114–2
Human rights conditions in 170 countries, 1988, annual rpt, 21384–3
Military aid of US, arms sales, and training programs costs and budget requests, by program, world region, and country, FY88-90, annual rpt, 7144–13
Minerals production, reserves, and industry role in domestic economy and world supply, 1988 country rpt, 5606–1.17
Minerals Yearbook, 1987, Vol 3: foreign country reviews of production, trade, and policy, by commodity, annual rpt, 5604–35
Minerals Yearbook, 1987, Vol 3 preprints: foreign country review of production, trade, and policy, by commodity, annual rpt, 5604–23.85
Population size, growth rates, and components of change, by country, projected 1989-2020 and trends from 1950, biennial rpt, 2324–9
UN voting record and share of votes in agreement with US, by issue, country, and world area, 1988, annual rpt, 7004–18
see also under By Foreign Country in the "Index by Categories"

Brunner, Karl
"Role of Money and Monetary Policy", 9391–1.921

Bruno, Rosalind R.
"Educational Attainment in the U.S.: March 1982 to 1985", 2546–1.427
"School Enrollment—Social and Economic Characteristics of Students: October 1985 and 1984", 2546–1.429
"School Enrollment—Social and Economic Characteristics of Students: October 1986", 2546–1.432

Brunswick, Ga.
Wages by occupation, and benefits for office and plant workers, 1989 survey, periodic MSA rpt, 6785–3.8

Bryan, Tex.
see also under By SMSA or MSA in the "Index by Categories"

Bryant, Kelly
"Productivity Trends in Agricultural Chemicals", 6722–1.915

Bucci, Gabriella A.
"Trends in the Voluntary Compliance of Taxpayers Who File Individual Income Tax Returns", 8304–8.1

Buchanan, Chester C.
"Marine Recreational Boat Fishery of the New York Bight Apex in 1971", 2162–1.901

Buchman, Michael F.
"Review and Summary of Trace Contaminant Data for Coastal and Estuarine Oregon", 2178–23

Buckley, Jack

"Rainbow Smelt. Species Profiles: Life Histories and Environmental Requirements of Coastal Fishes and Invertebrates (North Atlantic)", 5506–8.113

"Winter Flounder. Species Profiles: Life Histories and Environmental Requirements of Coastal Fishes and Invertebrates (North Atlantic)", 5506–8.94

Buckley, John E.

"Variations in Holidays, Vacations, and Area Pay Levels", 6722–1.909

Buckley, Katharine C.

"U.S. Fruit and Vegetable Processing Industries", 1568–275

Buczko, William

"Hospital Utilization and Expenditures in a Medicaid Population", 4652–1.949

Budget of the U.S.

Balanced budget proposed constitutional amendment, economic impacts, projected to FY94 and background data from 1940s, hearings, 21528–72

Budget of US Appendix, obligations, appropriations, and personnel, by program and agency, FY90, annual rpt, 104–3

Budget of US, authoritative financial statements with appropriations, outlays, and receipts, by agency, FY88, annual rpt, 8104–2

Budget of US, balances of budget authority obligated and unobligated, by function and agency, FY88-90, annual rpt, 104–8

Budget of US, Bush Admin policy changes by program, FY90, 028–32

Budget of US, CBO analysis and review of FY90 budget by function, annual rpt, 26304–2

Budget of US, CBO analysis of revenue and spending alternatives and projections of economic indicators, FY90-94, annual rpt, 26304–3

Budget of US, compact budgets by activity, function, and agency, FY90 and projected to FY94, annual rpt, 104–2

Budget of US, historical data, selected years FY34-88 and projected to FY94, annual rpt, 104–22

Budget of US, House concurrent resolution, with spending and revenue targets, FY90, annual rpt, 21264–2

Budget of US, midsession review of FY90 budget, by function and agency, annual rpt, 104–7

Budget of US, object class analysis of obligations, by agency, FY90, annual rpt, 104–9

Budget of US, overview, FY90, annual rpt, 104–6

Budget of US, Reagan Admin fiscal and economic projections made 1981 and actual trends, 1980s-87, article, 9391–1.905

Budget of US, Reagan Admin policy changes by program, FY90, annual rpt, 104–21

Budget of US, receipts and outlays on natl income and product basis, FY90, annual article, 2702–1.907

Budget of US, Senate concurrent resolution, with spending and revenue targets, FY90, annual rpt, 25254–1

Budget of US, special analyses by activity, function, and agency, FY90, annual rpt, 104–1

Budget of US, special analysis of Federal capital spending by category, projected FY89-2005 and trends from FY81, annual rpt, 104–24

Deficit impact of OASDI trust fund surpluses, projected FY89-2045, article, 9371–1.905

Deficit projections of CBO, FY86-1994, article, 9383–6.902

Deficit reduction recommendations, background data and testimony, 1989 rpt, 15888–2

Deficit reduction recommendations, 1989 rpt, 15888–1

Deficit reduction through increased excise and income taxes, and proposed value-added tax, projected FY89-94, article, 9381–1.906

Economic Report of the President for 1989, economic effects of budget proposals, and trends and projections, 1929-99, annual hearings, 23844–4

Economic Report of the President for 1989, Joint Economic Committee critique and policy recommendations, annual rpt, 23844–2

Economic Report of the President for 1989, with economic trends from 1929, annual rpt, 204–1

Fed Govt agency budget requests and program costs and characteristics, series, 26306–3

Fed Govt financial and business statistics, historic trends, 1988 annual chartbook, 9364–2.8

Gramm-Rudman Act budget deficit reduction, cancellation of budget authority by program, FY90, annual rpt, 104–27; 21924–1; 26304–6

OASDI trust funds finances, and impact on Federal budget, 1987-88 and projected to 2050, GAO rpt, 26121–269

OASDI trust funds surpluses impact on budget deficit, FY89-94, with surpluses projected to 2050, article, 9381–1.909

OASDI trust funds surpluses impact on budgets, 1960-86, article, 9373–1.905

Receipts and outlays, 1987, annual rpt, 9364–5.5

Receipts by source and outlays by agency, *Treasury Bulletin*, quarterly rpt, 8002–4.1

Receipts by source and outlays by function, monthly rpt, quarterly and annual data, 23842–1.6

Receipts by source, outlays by agency and program, and balances, monthly rpt, 8102–3

Receipts, outlays, and debt, Fed Reserve Bank of St Louis monthly rpt, 9391–2

Statistical Abstract of US, social, political, and economic data, 1790-2025, comprehensive annual compilation, 2324–1.2

Trust funds of Fed Govt, financial status by agency, and impacts on budget balance, FY47-93 and projected to FY93, GAO rpt, 26111–58

see also Defense budgets and appropriations

see also Executive impoundment of appropriated funds

see also Fiscal policy

see also Nonappropriated funds

see also Public debt

Budgets

see Budget of the U.S.

see Defense budgets and appropriations

see Family budgets

see Foreign budgets

Buehler, James W.

"Reporting of Race and Ethnicity in the National Notifiable Diseases Surveillance System", 4042–3.943

Buffalo, N.Y.

CPI by component for US city average, and by region, population size, and for 27 metro areas, monthly rpt, 6762–2

Freight (waterborne domestic and foreign) by commodity, traffic, and passengers, by port and waterway, 1987, annual rpt, 3754–3.3

Fruit and vegetable shipments, and arrivals in US and Canada cities, by mode of transport and State and country of origin, 1988, annual rpt, 1311–4.1

Wages by occupation, and benefits for office and plant workers, 1988 survey, periodic MSA rpt, 6785–11.3

see also under By City and By SMSA or MSA in the "Index by Categories"

Building abandonment

see Vacant and abandoned property

Building and loan association

see Savings institutions

Building codes

Energy-efficiency building codes effect on apartment building electricity use, for Tacoma, Wash, 1986-87, 3308–92

Fires in hotels and motels, casualties, and effectiveness of smoke detectors, sprinkler systems, and building and equipment design, 1989 hearing, 21708–127

Housing construction cost-saving methods, impacts of building codes and other factors, 1981, 9406–1.56

Building laws

see Building codes

see Building permits

Building materials

Acid rain research activities and funding, by Federal agency, 1988 annual rpt, 14354–1

Business statistics, detailed data for major industries and economic indicators, *Survey of Current Business*, monthly rpt, 2702–1.16; 2702–1.18

Canada construction products market trends and indicators, with imports by country, 1960s-86, article, 2042–1.905

China housing and commercial construction, and building materials production and trade by product group, 1984-85 and projected to 1990, article, 2042–1.910

Clay construction products production and shipments by region and State, trade, and use, by product, monthly Current Industrial Rpt, 2506–9.2

Construction industries census, 1987: establishments, employment, receipts, and expenditures, by SIC 4-digit industry and State, final industry rpt series, 2373–1

Construction industries census, 1987: financial and operating data, preliminary industry rpt series, 2371–1

County Business Patterns, 1987: employment, establishments, and payroll, by SIC 2- to 4-digit industry and county, annual State rpt series, 2326–8

Buildings

Buildings

see Apartment houses

see Architectural barriers to the handicapped

see Architecture

see Building codes

see Building materials

see Building permits

see Commercial buildings

see Condominiums and cooperatives

see Construction industry

see Elevators

see Housing condition and occupancy

see Housing construction

see Housing maintenance and repair

see Housing sales

see Housing supply and requirements

see Industrial plants and equipment

see Mobile homes

see Prefabricated buildings

see Public buildings

see Vacant and abandoned property

Bulgaria

Agricultural and food production and indexes, total and for selected commodities, by country, 1970s-88, annual rpt, 1524–12

Agricultural production, acreage, and consumption, by Eastern Europe country and commodity, 1965-85, 1528–284

Agricultural production, consumption, and trade, for Eastern Europe by country, 1970s-88, annual rpt, 1524–11

Agricultural trade of US, by detailed commodity and country, 1988, semiannual rpt, 1522–4

Cuba economic conditions, agricultural and industrial production and distribution, trade, and intl economic relations, 1980-87 with trends from 1961, 9118–8

Debt, trade, and balances of Eastern Europe and USSR with US and other western countries, with background data, 1980s-87, hearing, 21248–120

Economic conditions in Communist, OECD, and selected other countries, 1960s-88, annual rpt, 9114–4

Economic conditions, policy, and trade practices, by country, 1986-88, annual rpt, 21384–5

Economic, social, political, and geographic summary data, by country, 1989, annual factbook, 9114–2

Export licensing, monitoring, and enforcement activities, FY88, annual rpt, 2024–1

Exports and imports of US, by selected country, country group, and commodity group, 1988, annual rpt, 2044–37

Exports and imports of US with Communist countries, by detailed commodity and country, quarterly rpt with articles, 9882–2

Human rights conditions in 170 countries, 1988, annual rpt, 21384–3

Military spending, arms trade, and force strengths, with govt spending and population, by country, 1977-87, annual rpt, 9824–1

Military strength of USSR and Warsaw Pact, and proposed force reductions, with comparisons to NATO, 1980s-91, hearing, 21208–29

Minerals Yearbook, 1987, Vol 3: foreign country reviews of production, trade, and policy, by commodity, annual rpt, 5604–35

Minerals Yearbook, 1987, Vol 3 preprints: foreign country review of production, trade, and policy, by commodity, annual rpt, 5604–23.12

Nuclear power plant capacity and operating status, by plant and Communist country, as of Dec 1988, annual rpt, 3164–57.2

Population size, growth rates, and components of change, by country, projected 1989-2020 and trends from 1950, biennial rpt, 2324–9

UN voting record and share of votes in agreement with US, by issue, country, and world area, 1988, annual rpt, 7004–18

see also under By Foreign Country in the "Index by Categories"

Bull, Len

"Residue and Tillage Systems in 1987 Corn Production", 1561–16.901

Bunin, Greta R.

"Frequency of 13q Abnormalities Among 203 Patients with Retinoblastoma", 4472–1.909

Burack, Robert C.

"Detroit's Avoidable Mortality Project: Breast Cancer Control for Inner-City Women", 4042–3.951

Bureau for Refugee Programs, State Department

Arrivals in US by world area of origin and State of settlement, and Federal aid, FY88-90, annual rpt, 7004–16

Arrivals in US, by world area of origin, processing, and nationality, monthly rpt, 7002–4

Bureau of Alcohol, Tobacco and Firearms

Alcoholic beverages and tobacco production, removals, stocks, and material used, by State, monthly rpt series, 8486–1

Alcoholic beverages warning labels and other consumer protection methods, public views by selected characteristics, 1988 survey, 8488–5

Bombing incidents and casualties by target and circumstances, and explosives theft and recovery, by State, 1979-88, annual rpt, 8484–4

Budget of US Appendix, obligations, appropriations, and personnel, by program and agency, FY90, annual rpt, 104–3

Firearms violations enhanced and mandatory sentences, for cases under BATF investigation program, FY87-88, 8488–6

Bureau of Census

Activities, rpts, and user services of Census Bur, monthly rpt, 2302–3

American Housing Survey: unit and households characteristics, MSA fact sheet series, 2485–11

American Housing Survey: unit and households detailed characteristics, and unit and neighborhood quality, MSA rpt series, 2485–6

American Housing Survey: unit and households detailed characteristics, and unit and neighborhood quality, 1985, biennial rpt, 2485–12

Annual Survey of Manufacturers, 1986: production indexes and exports by SIC 2-digit industry and State, with comparisons to 1985, model results, series, 2506–16

Annual Survey of Manufactures, 1986: financial and operating data, by SIC 2- to 4-digit industry, series, 2506–15

Apartment and condominium completions and absorption rates, by size and price class, preliminary 1988, annual Current Housing Rpt, 2484–3

Apartment and condominium completions by rent class and sales price, and market absorption rates, quarterly rpt, 2482–2

Apartment market absorption rates and characteristics for nonsubsidized furnished and unfurnished units, 1987 and trends from 1970, annual Current Housing Rpt, 2484–2

Budget appropriations and staff for Commerce Dept, by subagency, FY88-90, annual rpt, 2004–6

Budget of US Appendix, obligations, appropriations, and personnel, by program and agency, FY90, annual rpt, 104–3

Buildings (commercial and public) alteration and repair spending, by type, size, age, and region, 1986, 2388–4

Census of Agriculture, 1987: data coverage and availability, for census and related statistics, 1989 guide, 2308–55

Census of Agriculture, 1987: farms, farmland, production and costs, and operator characteristics, advance State and county rpt series, 2330–1

Census of Agriculture, 1987: farms, farmland, production, finances, and operator characteristics, by county, final State rpt series, 2331–1

Census of Construction Industries, 1987: financial and operating data, by SIC 4-digit industry and State, final rpt series, 2373–1

Census of Construction Industries, 1987: financial and operating data, preliminary industry rpt series, 2371–1

Census of Govts, 1987: elected officials, by level of govt, race, sex, and State, preliminary rpt, 2450–2

Census of Govts, 1987: property tax revenue by level of govt, assessed values by locality, and exemptions, by property type and State, 2453–1

Census of Manufactures, 1987: financial and operating data, by SIC 4-digit industry and product, preliminary industry rpt series, 2491–1

Census of Mineral Industries, 1987: financial and operating data, preliminary industry rpt series, 2511–1

Census of Population and Housing, 1980: data collection procede, series, 2555–2

Census of Population and Housing, 1990: data collection procedure, and impacts on congressional apportionment by State, hearing, 25408–101

Census of Population and Housing, 1990: data collection procedure improvement and preparation for count, hearing, 21628–71

Census of Population and Housing, 1990: data coverage and availability for community and business dev projects, user guide, 2308–10

Census of Population and Housing, 1990: data coverage and products, 1989 guide, 2308–58

Census of Population and Housing, 1990: data item selection, questionnaire dev, and testing, series, 2626–11

Census of Population and Housing, 1990: outlying areas preparations for count, hearings, 21628–72; 21628–74

Manufacturing high technology use and plans, with data by technology, selected industry, and firm and market characteristics, 1988 survey, 2508-1

Manufacturing industries production, shipments, inventories, orders, and pollution control costs, periodic Current Industrial Rpt series, 2506-3

Maternity leave arrangements and work history of 1st-time mothers, by selected characteristics, 1960s-85, 2328-62

Metals (intermediate product) shipments, trade, and inventories, by product, periodic Current Industrial Rpt series, 2506-11

Metals (primary) production, shipments, trade, stocks, and material used, by product, periodic Current Industrial Rpt series, 2506-10

MSA population size, by area, 1988, annual press release, 2324-8

Population and housing data, and policy issues, fact sheet series, 2326-17

Population size, July 1988 and compared to 1980 and 1987, and components of change, 1980-88, annual press release, 2324-10

Retail trade sales and inventories, by kind of business, region, and selected State, MSA, and city, monthly rpt, 2413-3

Retail trade sales, by kind of business, advance monthly rpt, 2413-2

Retail trade sales, inventories, purchases, gross margin, and accounts receivable, by SIC 2- to 4-digit kind of business and form of ownership, 1987, annual rpt, 2413-5

Service industries receipts, by SIC 2- to 4-digit kind of business, 1988, annual rpt, 2413-8

Ships bunker fuel laden in US on vessels engaged in foreign trade, by fuel type and port, monthly rpt, 2422-5

Statistical Abstract of US, social, political, and economic data, with foreign comparisons, 1790-2025, comprehensive annual compilation, 2324-1

Survey of Income and Program Participation, data collection, methodology, and availability, 1987 users guide, 2628-24

Survey of Income and Program Participation, data collection, methodology, and comparisons to other data bases, working paper series, 2626-10

Survey of Income and Program Participation, data collection, methodology, and use, 1988 annual conf papers, 2624-1

Survey of Income and Program Participation, household income and socioeconomic characteristics, special study series, 2546-20

Tax revenues, by level of govt, type of tax, State, and selected large county, quarterly rpt, 2462-3

Textile mill production, trade, sales, stocks, and material used, by product, region, and State, periodic Current Industrial Rpt series, 2506-5

Truck and warehouse services finances and inventory, by SIC 2- to 4-digit industry, 1988 survey, annual rpt, 2413-14

Wholesale trade sales and inventories, by SIC 2- to 3-digit kind of business, monthly rpt, 2413-7

Wholesale trade sales, inventories, purchases, and gross margins, by SIC 2- to 3-digit kind of business and form of ownership, 1988, annual rpt, 2413-13

Bureau of Consular Affairs, State Department

Visas of US issued and refused to immigrants and nonimmigrants, by class, issuing office, and nationality, FY88, annual rpt, 7184-1

Visas of US issued at Foreign Service posts, by category and world area, selected years FY84-88, annual rpt, 7184-4

Bureau of Economic Analysis

Budget appropriations and staff for Commerce Dept, by subagency, FY88-90, annual rpt, 2004-6

Business Conditions Digest, economic, business, and financial devs and cyclical fluctuations, monthly rpt, 2702-3

Income (personal) per capita and by source, and earnings by industry div, by State, MSA, and county, 1982-87, annual regional rpts, 2704-2

Income (personal) per capita and by source, earnings by major industry group, and social insurance contributions, by region and State, 1929-87, 2708-40

Multinatl firms US affiliates, finances, and operations, by industry, world area of parent firm, and State, 1987, annual rpt, 2704-4

Multinatl US firms and foreign affiliates finances and operations, by industry of parent firm and affiliate, world area, and country, preliminary 1987, annual rpt, 2704-5

Natl income and product accounts estimates, methodology and bibls, technical rpt series, 2706-6

Survey of Current Business, detailed data for major industries and economic indicators, monthly rpt, 2702-1

Bureau of Engraving and Printing

Budget of US Appendix, obligations, appropriations, and personnel, by program and agency, FY90, annual rpt, 104-3

Bureau of Export Administration

Budget appropriations and staff for Commerce Dept, by subagency, FY88-90, annual rpt, 2004-6

Licensing of exports, monitoring, and enforcement activities, FY88, annual rpt, 2024-1

Military use potential of US exports, DOD and Commerce Dept licensing activities, staff, and costs, 1986-88, GAO rpt, 26123-250

Bureau of Health Professions

Data coverage and availability for health care resources geographic info system, 1989 rpt, 4118-61

Educational and research grants and contracts of BHPr, by instn and program, FY88, annual listing, 4114-1

Environmental and occupational health care personnel supply and needs, by field, 1987 conf, 4118-65

Grants of BHPr, by program, region, and State, FY80-87, 4118-62

Nurses recruitment and retention issues and indicators, 1988 conf papers, 4118-64

Teaching faculty dev programs for family medicine, Federal funding and trainees, by faculty status and region, 1978-87, 4118-63

Bureau of Health Services Research
see National Center for Health Services Research and Health Care Technology Assessment

Bureau of Indian Affairs

Cherokee Indian Agency activities in North Carolina, FY89, annual rpt, 5704-4

Crimes and enforcement activity in Montana Indian reservations, and Bur of Indian Affairs law enforcement officers training, 1985-87, GAO rpt, 26113-402

Education (special) enrollment by age, staff, funding, and needs, by type of handicap and State, 1987/88, annual rpt, 4944-4

Expenditures of Fed Govt in States, by type, program, agency, and State, FY88, annual rpt, 2464-2

Montana Indians social services funding of Federal, State, and tribal agencies, FY87, GAO rpt, 26121-257

Bureau of Intelligence and Research, State Department

Communist and OECD countries economic conditions, 1987, annual rpt, 7144-11

EC trade with US by country, and total agricultural trade, selected years 1958-88, annual rpt, 7144-7

Foreign countries *Geographic Notes*, boundaries, claims, nomenclature, and other devs, periodic rpt, 7142-3

Military aid of US, arms sales, and training programs costs and budget requests, by program, world region, and country, FY88-90, annual rpt, 7144-13

OECD members GNP and GNP growth, by country, 1978-88, annual rpt, 7144-8

Bureau of International Labor Affairs

Caribbean area duty-free exports to US, and imports from US, by country, and impact on US employment, by commodity, 1988, annual rpt, 6364-2

Foreign countries labor conditions, union coverage, and work accidents, annual country rpt series, 6366-4

Research contracts of Bur, FY83-89, annual listing, 6364-1

Bureau of Justice Assistance

Drug enforcement activities of State and local agencies, Federal aid by recipient, and background data, FY88, annual rpt, 6064-28

Bureau of Justice Statistics

Activities of BJS and States for criminal justice data collection, FY88, annual rpt, 6064-21

Crime and criminal justice data collection, methodology, and use, technical rpt series, 6066-23

Crime and criminal justice data collection programs and rpts, 1988, annual listing, 6064-25

Crime, criminal justice admin and enforcement, and public opinion, data compilation, 1970s-88, annual rpt, 6064-6

Crime victimization rates, by victim and offender characteristics, circumstances, and offense, survey rpt series, 6066-3

Criminal case processing from arrest to sentencing, cases and duration by disposition, offense, and defendant characteristics, for selected cities, 1986, annual rpt, 6064-27

Unemployment insurance coverage of establishments, employment, and wages, by SIC 4-digit industry and State, 1988, annual rpt, 6744–16

Wage and benefit changes from collective bargaining and mgmt decisions, by industry div, monthly rpt, 6782–1

Wages by occupation, and benefits for office and plant workers in selected MSAs, 1988, annual rpt, 6785–1

Wages by occupation, and benefits for office and plant workers, periodic MSA survey rpt series, 6785–3; 6785–11; 6785–12

Wages by occupation, for office and plant workers in metro areas, by industry div and region, Aug 1988, annual rpt, 6785–9

Wages by occupation, for office and plant workers in selected MSAs, 1989 survey, annual rpt, 6785–5

Wages by occupation, for office and plant workers in selected MSAs, 1989 survey, annual summary rpts, 6785–6

Wages for 3 occupational groups, relative pay levels in 92 labor market areas, 1988, annual rpt, 6785–13

Wages for 4 occupational groups, relative pay levels in 61 MSAs, 1988, annual rpt, 6785–8

Wages, hourly and weekly averages by industry div, monthly press release, 6742–3

Wages, hours, and employment by occupation, and benefits, for selected locations, industry survey rpt series, 6787–6

Wages of full- and part-time workers, by selected characteristics, quarterly press release, 6742–20

Wages of workers covered by unemployment insurance, by industry div, State, and MSA, 1987-88, annual press releases, 6784–17

Women's labor force participation, by age, race, and family status, quarterly rpt, 6742–17

Work stoppages, workers involved, and days idle, 1988 and trends from 1947, annual press release, 6784–12

Youth labor force participation by age, Apr and July 1989 and change from 1988, annual press release, 6744–13

Youth labor force status, by sex and race, summer 1985-89, annual press release, 6744–14

Bureau of Land Management

Activities and finances of BLM, and public land acreage and use, annual State rpt series, 5724–11

Activities of BLM and funding by State, and receipts by program, FY87, annual rpt, 5724–13

Coal leasing activity on Federal land, acreage, production, and reserves, by coal region and State, FY88, annual rpt, 5724–10

Expenditures of Fed Govt in States, by type, program, agency, and State, FY88, annual rpt, 2464–2

Finances and operations of BLM, 1936-87, 5728–30

Horse and burro wild herd areas in western States, population, adoption, and protection, and mgmt costs, as of FY87, biennial rpt, 5724–8

Mining claims on public lands, patents by type and State, and applications by disposition, 1978-87, GAO rpt, 26113–403

Oil and gas leasing activity on Federal land, production, revenue, and royalty rates, by whether competitively leased and western State, 1984-88, GAO rpt, 26113–413

Public lands acreage, grants, use, revenues, and allocations, by State, FY88 and trends, annual rpt, 5724–1

Public lands, Fed Govt payments to local govts in lieu of property taxes, by State and county, FY89, annual rpt, 5724–9

Recreation (outdoor) facilities of Fed Govt, fees and visitors by managing agency, 1988, annual rpt, 5544–14

Sedimentation control and research activity of Fed Govt, regional and project summaries, 1987, annual narrative rpt, 5664–9

Wilderness areas acreage by Federal agency and location, and sources of damage, with data for foreign countries, 1988 conf papers, 1208–301

Bureau of Mines

Alaska land area by ownership, and availability for mineral exploration and dev, 1986, 5608–152

Aluminum plant ownership, capacity, energy and aluminum sources, and startup and closing dates, by US and foreign plant and location, 1988, annual listing, 5604–49

Coal production and freight costs, and competitive position in selected markets, for Australia and US, 1987-89, 2048–143

Electric utilities serving aluminum smelters, effects of proposed sulfur dioxide abatement legislation on operating costs, 1985, 5608–155

Employees by selected occupational and other characteristics, injuries, and workdays lost, for mines, 1986, series, 5606–8

Explosives and blasting agents use, by type, industry, and State, 1988, Mineral Industry Surveys, annual rpt, 5614–22

Fertilizer components use, by world area, 1978-88 and projected to 2010, 5608–154

Foreign and US minerals industries operations, trends, and projections for selected countries, series, 5606–5

Foreign and US minerals supply under alternative market conditions, reserves, and background industry data, series, 5606–4

Foreign countries mineral production, reserves, and industry role in domestic economy and world supply, world area and country rpt series, 5606–1

Helium market demand and Bur production, sales, and financial statements, FY88, annual rpt, 5604–32

Helium resources in storage and natural gas reserves, by State, 1950-87 and projected to 2020, biennial rpt, 5604–44

Metals (primary) demand relation to consumption patterns and economic, trade, and technological factors, 1960s-82, 5608–159

Methane emissions control in coal mines, research results, techniques, and equipment, mid 1960s-79, 5608–156

Mineral Industry Surveys, commodity reviews of production, trade, stocks, and use, monthly rpt series, 5612–1

Mineral Industry Surveys, commodity reviews of production, trade, stocks, and use, quarterly rpt series, 5612–2

Mineral Industry Surveys, commodity reviews of production, trade, use, and industry operations, advance annual rpt series, 5614–5

Mineral Industry Surveys, State reviews of production, 1988, preliminary annual rpt, 5614–6

Mineral Industry Surveys, supply, demand, and foreign and US production, by commodity, annual rpt series, discontinued, 5614–28

Minerals of strategic and technological importance, supply, imports, and use, with foreign comparisons, commodity rpt series, 5606–9

Minerals production, prices, trade, use, employment, tariffs, and stockpiles, by mineral, with foreign comparisons, 1984-88, annual rpt, 5604–18

Minerals Yearbook, 1987, Vol 1: commodity reviews of production, use, trade, prices, and mining operations, annual rpt, 5604–33

Minerals Yearbook, 1987, Vol 1 preprints: commodity reviews of production, reserves, supply, use, and trade, annual rpt series, 5604–15

Minerals Yearbook, 1987, Vol 2 preprints: State reviews of production and sales by commodity, and business activity, annual rpt series, 5604–16

Minerals Yearbook, 1987, Vol 2: State reviews of production, sales, and firms, by commodity, and business activity, annual rpt, 5604–34

Minerals Yearbook, 1987, Vol 3: foreign country reviews of production, trade, and policy, by commodity, annual rpt, 5604–35

Minerals Yearbook, 1987, Vol 3 preprints: foreign country reviews of production, trade, and policy, by commodity, annual rpt series, 5604–23

Minerals Yearbook, 1988, Vol 1: commodity reviews of production, reserves, supply, use, and trade, annual rpt series, 5604–20

Minerals Yearbook, 1988, Vol 2 rpts: State reviews of production and sales by commodity, and business activity, annual rpt series, 5604–22

Natural gas composition and helium levels, analyses of individual wells and pipelines, by selected State and country, 1917-88, annual rpt, 5604–2

Phosphate rock production, sales, trade, and use, 1989, Mineral Industry Surveys, annual rpt, 5614–20

Potash production, prices, trade by country, use, and sales, 1988 crop year, Mineral Industry Surveys, annual rpt, 5614–19

Public lands minerals resources and availability, State rpt series, 5606–7

Publications and patents of Mines Bur, monthly listing, 5602–2

Publications of Bur of Mines, annual listing, suspended, 5604–40

Salt production capacity, and use in chlorine production, by firm and facility, 1988, annual listing, 5614–30

Soviet Union minerals production, trade, and use, by commodity, 1983-87, annual rpt, 5604-39

Stone (dimension) trade and price indexes by selected country, 1987, Mineral Industry Surveys, annual rpt, 5614-29

Stone, sand, and gravel production, by end use, State, and district, 1985-86, 5608-157

Strategic minerals supply, demand, trade, and foreign and US industry devs by firm and country, by commodity, bimonthly rpt with articles, 5602-4

Talc production, use, and trade, with foreign comparisons, selected years 1977-87, 5608-158

Water supply and use, and production, for minerals industries by commodity and State, 1950s-84 and projected to 2000, 5608-153

Bureau of Motor Carrier Safety
see Federal Highway Administration

Bureau of Prisons
Activities of Bur, and inmate and staff characteristics, FY88, annual rpt, 6244-2

Fed Prison Industries finances and operations, FY88, annual rpt, 6244-3

Prisoners in Federal instns, admissions, and releases, by offense, selected prisoner characteristics, instn, and location, annual rpt, suspended, 6244-1

Prisoners in Federal instns, by sex, prison, security level, contract facility type, and region, monthly rpt series, 6242-1

Bureau of Reclamation
Activities and finances of Bur, and project impacts in western US, annual rpts, 5824-12

Activities and finances of Bur, FY88, annual rpt, 5824-1

Colorado River Basin Project reservoir and power operations and revenues, 1987-88, annual rpt, 5824-6

Colorado River Storage Project finances and activities in western States, FY88, annual rpt, 5824-3

Fed Columbia River Power System projects, plant investment allocation schedule, FY88, annual rpt, 3224-1

Hydroelectric power plants capacity and other characteristics, for western US, FY88, annual rpt, 3254-1

Irrigation subsidies of Reclamation Bur, costs to Fed Govt and surplus crop production, 1985-86, 21448-40

Recreation (outdoor) facilities of Fed Govt, fees and visitors by managing agency, 1988, annual rpt, 5544-14

Sedimentation control and research activity of Fed Govt, regional and project summaries, 1987, annual narrative rpt, 5664-9

Water storage and carriage facilities of Bur, capacity, and operating status, as of Sept 1988, biennial listing, 5824-7

Bureau of Security and Consular Affairs
see Bureau of Consular Affairs, State Department

Bureau of the Mint
see U.S. Mint

Bureau of the Public Debt
Budget of US Appendix, obligations, appropriations, and personnel, by program and agency, FY90, annual rpt, 104-3

Public debt issued, redeemed, and outstanding, by series and source, and gifts to reduce debt, monthly rpt, 8242-2

Savings bonds issued, redeemed, and outstanding, by series, monthly table, 8242-1

Bureaucracy
see Civil service system
see Government efficiency
see Government employees
see International employees
see Political science
see Public administration

Burfisher, Mary E.
"Developing Countries' Performance in High-Value Agricultural Trade", 1522-3.921

"How the Dollar's Value Affects U.S. Agricultural Exports to Developing Countries", 1522-3.917

Burgdorf, Kenneth
"Academic Research Equipment in Selected Science/Engineering Fields: 1982-83 to 1985-86", 9628-76

Burglary
see Robbery and theft

Burial and burial laws
see Cemeteries and funerals
see Military cemeteries and funerals

Burkina Faso
Agricultural and food production and indexes, total and for selected commodities, by country, 1970s-88, annual rpt, 1524-12

Agricultural production, prices, and trade, by country, 1960s-89, annual world region rpt, 1524-4.2

Agricultural trade of US, by detailed commodity and country, 1988, semiannual rpt, 1522-4

AID activities and funding by project and function, FY90, and developing countries summary socioeconomic data from 1960s, annual rpt, 9904-4.5

AID economic aid to developing countries, obligations and disbursements by country, quarterly rpt, 9912-4

Economic and military aid and loans from US and intl agencies, by program and country, FY46-87, annual rpt, 9914-5

Economic conditions, income, production, prices, employment, and trade, 1988 periodic country rpt, 2046-4.1

Economic, social, political, and geographic summary data, by country, 1989, annual factbook, 9114-2

Food supply indicators for Sahel, by country, 1960s-2000, 1528-290

Human rights conditions in 170 countries, 1988, annual rpt, 21384-3

Military aid of US, arms sales, and training programs costs and budget requests, by program, world region, and country, FY88-90, annual rpt, 7144-13

Military spending, arms trade, and force strengths, with govt spending and population, by country, 1977-87, annual rpt, 9824-1

Minerals Yearbook, 1987, Vol 3: foreign country reviews of production, trade, and policy, by commodity, annual rpt, 5604-35

Minerals Yearbook, 1987, Vol 3 preprints: foreign country review of production, trade, and policy, by commodity, annual rpt, 5604-23.82

Population size, growth rates, and components of change, by country, projected 1989-2020 and trends from 1950, biennial rpt, 2324-9

UN voting record and share of votes in agreement with US, by issue, country, and world area, 1988, annual rpt, 7004-18

see also under By Foreign Country in the "Index by Categories"

Burlington, N.C.
Clothing (hosiery) production and related workers and wages by occupation and sex, and benefits, by location, 1987 survey, 6787-6.237

see also under By SMSA or MSA in the "Index by Categories"

Burlington, Vt.
see also under By SMSA or MSA in the "Index by Categories"

Burma
Agricultural and food production and indexes, total and for selected commodities, by country, 1970s-88, annual rpt, 1524-12

Agricultural production, prices, and trade, by country, 1960s-89, annual world region rpt, 1524-4.2

Agricultural trade of US, by detailed commodity and country, 1988, semiannual rpt, 1522-4

Agricultural trade of US with Asia, Middle East, and North Africa, by commodity and country, 1962-86, 1528-277

AID activities and funding by project and function, FY90, and developing countries summary socioeconomic data from 1960s, annual rpt, 9904-4.6

AID economic aid to developing countries, obligations and disbursements by country, quarterly rpt, 9912-4

AID loans repayment status and terms by program and country, and status of predecessor agency loans, quarterly rpt, 9912-3

Background Notes, summary social, political, and economic data, 1989 rpt, 7006-2.12

Economic and military aid and loans from US and intl agencies, by program and country, FY46-87, annual rpt, 9914-5

Economic conditions, policy, and trade practices, by country, 1986-88, annual rpt, 21384-5

Economic, social, political, and geographic summary data, by country, 1989, annual factbook, 9114-2

Human rights conditions in 170 countries, 1988, annual rpt, 21384-3

Military aid of US, arms sales, and training programs costs and budget requests, by program, world region, and country, FY88-90, annual rpt, 7144-13

Military spending, arms trade, and force strengths, with govt spending and population, by country, 1977-87, annual rpt, 9824-1

Minerals production, reserves, and industry role in domestic economy and world supply, 1988 country rpt, 5606-1.17

Minerals Yearbook, 1987, Vol 3: foreign country reviews of production, trade, and policy, by commodity, annual rpt, 5604-35

Minerals Yearbook, 1987, Vol 3 preprints: foreign country review of production, trade, and policy, by commodity, annual rpt, 5604-23.13

Population size, growth rates, and components of change, by country, projected 1989-2020 and trends from 1950, biennial rpt, 2324–9

UN voting record and share of votes in agreement with US, by issue, country, and world area, 1988, annual rpt, 7004–18

see also under By Foreign Country in the "Index by Categories"

Burns, Eugene M.

"Commercial Buildings Consumption and Expenditures, 1986. Nonresidential Buildings Energy Consumption Survey", 3166–8.8

Burr, Jeffrey A.

"Resource-Based Model of Living Arrangements Among the Unmarried Elderly", 2626–10.95

Burros, wild

see Wildlife and wildlife conservation

Burundi

Agricultural and food production and indexes, total and for selected commodities, by country, 1970s-88, annual rpt, 1524–12

Agricultural trade of US, by detailed commodity and country, 1988, semiannual rpt, 1522–4

AID activities and funding by project and function, FY90, and developing countries summary socioeconomic data from 1960s, annual rpt, 9904–4.5

AID economic aid to developing countries, obligations and disbursements by country, quarterly rpt, 9912–4

Economic and military aid and loans from US and intl agencies, by program and country, FY46-87, annual rpt, 9914–5

Economic, social, political, and geographic summary data, by country, 1989, annual factbook, 9114–2

Human rights conditions in 170 countries, 1988, annual rpt, 21384–3

Military aid of US, arms sales, and training programs costs and budget requests, by program, world region, and country, FY88-90, annual rpt, 7144–13

Military spending, arms trade, and force strengths, with govt spending and population, by country, 1977-87, annual rpt, 9824–1

Minerals Yearbook, 1987, Vol 3: foreign country reviews of production, trade, and policy, by commodity, annual rpt, 5604–35

Minerals Yearbook, 1987, Vol 3 preprints: foreign country review of production, trade, and policy, by commodity, annual rpt, 5604–23.81

Population size, growth rates, and components of change, by country, projected 1989-2020 and trends from 1950, biennial rpt, 2324–9

UN voting record and share of votes in agreement with US, by issue, country, and world area, 1988, annual rpt, 7004–18

see also under By Foreign Country in the "Index by Categories"

Busch, Lawrence

"Universities for Development: Report of the Joint Indo-U.S. Impact Evaluation of the Indian Agricultural Universities", 9916–1.67

Buses

Accidents (fatal), circumstances, and characteristics of persons and vehicles involved, 1988, semiannual rpt, 7762–11

Accidents (fatal), deaths, and rates, by circumstances, characteristics of persons and vehicles involved, and location, 1987, annual rpt, 7764–10

Accidents at hwy-railroad grade crossings, detailed data by State and railroad, 1988, annual rpt, 7604–2

Canada travel to US by Province of residence, and characteristics of visit, by State, 1988, annual rpt, 2904–7

County Business Patterns, 1987: employment, establishments, and payroll, by SIC 2- to 4-digit industry and county, annual State rpt series, 2326–8

Cuba economic conditions, agricultural and industrial production and distribution, trade, and intl economic relations, 1980-87 with trends from 1961, 9118–8

Customs Service activities, collections, entries processed by mode of transport, and seizures, FY84-88, annual rpt, 8144–1

DOD shipments of military and personal property, passenger traffic, and costs, by service branch and mode of transport, quarterly rpt, 3702–1

Drivers licenses issued and in force by age and sex, fees, and renewal, by license class and State, 1987, annual rpt, 7554–16

Drivers pay impacts of taxes dedicated to local bus systems funding and other factors, 1950s-85, working paper, 9377–9.73

Employment, earnings, and hours, by SIC 1- to 4-digit industry, monthly 1983-Feb 1989, annual rpt, 6744–4

Energy use and vehicle registrations, by vehicle type, 1960-88, annual rpt, 3164–74.1

Energy use by mode of transport, fuel supply, and demographic and economic factors of vehicle use, 1970s-88, annual rpt, 3304–5

Exhuast emissions reductions, truck and bus engine R&D and alternative fuels costs and economic impacts, 1988 hearing, 21708–124

Exports of US, detailed commodities by country, monthly rpt, 2422–3

Fed Govt motor vehicle fleet costs and operating data, by agency, FY87, annual rpt, 9454–9

Finances and operations of interstate carriers, by carrier, 1987, annual rpt, 9486–6.3

Finances and operations of transit systems, by mode of transport, size of fleet, and for 432 systems, 1986, annual rpt, 7884–4

Finances, costs, and needs of transit systems, by State and selected system, 1980-88, biennial rpt, 7884–8

Finances, operations, vehicles, equipment, accidents, and energy use, by mode of transport, 1955-88, annual rpt, 7304–2

Hwy Statistics, detailed data by State, 1988, annual rpt, 7554–1

Hwy Statistics, summary data by State, 1987-88, annual rpt, 7554–24

Imports of US, detailed Schedule A commodities by country, monthly rpt, 2422–2

Labor productivity, indexes of output, hours, and employment by SIC 2- to 4-digit industry, 1963-87, annual rpt, 6824–1.4

Maintenance of buses, relation to vehicle age and other system characteristics, for public and private systems, 1982-84, working paper, 9377–9.68

Manufacturing annual survey, 1986: financial and operating data, by SIC 2- to 4-digit industry, series, 2506–15

Manufacturing census, 1987: financial and operating data, for SIC 4-digit industries by product, preliminary rpt, 2491–1.75

Natl park system tour bus visits, by park, 1984-88, annual rpt, 5544–12

Nebraska intercity bus route, indicators of need, finances, and service and funding alternatives, 1980s, 7888–76

Occupational injury and illness rates, by SIC 2- to 4-digit industry, 1987, annual rpt, 6844–1

Park natl system visits and overnight stays, by park and State, monthly rpt, 5542–4

Price indexes (producer), by stage of processing and detailed commodity, monthly rpt, 6762–6

Price indexes (producer), by stage of processing and detailed commodity, monthly 1988, annual rpt, 6764–2

Ridership and selected revenue data, for individual large Class I bus carriers, quarterly rpt, 9482–13

Rural areas public transit services, operations and govt funding by region and State, 1986-87, 1278–11

Statistical Abstract of US, social, political, and economic data, 1790-2025, comprehensive annual compilation, 2324–1.3

Suburban areas land use, commuting, employment, and housing characteristics, detailed data for traffic planning, 1986, 7888–75

Traffic volume in urban areas and detailed trip characteristics, by transport mode and city, 1950s-88, 7888–37

Urban Mass Transportation Admin grants for transit systems, by city and State, FY88, annual rpt, 7884–10

Urban transit systems services and vehicles, 1988 annual listing, 7884–9

Used bus prices, and scrappage related to vehicle age and system characteristics, for public and private systems, 1982-85, working paper, 9377–9.67

Used bus prices by vehicle age, and bus maintenance rates, for public and private systems, 1980s, article, 9377–1.904

see also School busing

Business acquisitions and mergers

Airline merger of TWA and Ozark, impacts on fares and departures at St Louis, Mo, 1985-88, 7308–194

Announcements of acquisitions and mergers by type, 1976-86, article, 9373–2.901

Bank holding company acquisitions in southeastern States, as of Oct 1988, article, 9389–1.907

Banks (insured commercial and savings) finances, and changes in status, by State, 1987, annual rpt, 9294–4.1

Banks (natl) domestic and intl operations, charters, mergers, and liquidations, by instn and State, quarterly rpt, 8402–3

Banks acquired, financial characteristics related to purchase price, by region, 1981-86, article, 9371-1.911

Banks and bank branch formations, mergers, liquidations, and other changes in status, listing by instn, monthly rpt, 9365-2.23

Banks bought by small bank holding companies, financial performance by BHC debt/equity ratio, Fed Reserve 10th District, 1982-87, article, 9381-14.1

Banks financial performance, risk assessment, and regulation, 1988 annual conf papers, 9375-7

Banks financial position, accuracy of quarterly call rpts and relation to bank ownership and merger activity, 1978-86, working paper, 9387-8.188

Banks mergers and consolidations approved by Fed Reserve Board of Governors, 1988, annual rpt, 9364-1.2

Banks status changes, instns, assets, and concentration ratios by size, ownership, and location, and compared to other financial instns, 1976-87, article, 9362-1.902

Banks stock returns for instns involved in acquisitions, 1982-87, technical paper, 9366-6.178

Credit unions federally insured, finances, mergers, closings, and insurance fund losses and financial statements, FY88, annual rpt, 9534-7

Energy producers finances and operations, by energy type for US firms domestic and foreign operations, 1987, annual rpt, 3164-44

Energy resources of US, foreign direct investment by energy type and firm, US affiliates operations, and acquisitions, as of 1988, annual rpt, 3164-80

Food marketing sector finances, operations, and merger activity, for processors and distributors, as of 1988, annual rpt, 1544-22

Foreign direct investment in US by country, and finances, employment, and acreage owned, by industry group of business acquired or established, 1982-88, annual article, 2702-1.917

Foreign direct investment in US, major transactions by type, industry, country, and US location, 1987, annual rpt, 2044-20

Foreign firms hostile takeover of US firms, attempts by outcome, and transaction value, with data by firm, 1984-88, GAO rpt, 26123-222

Hostile takeover attempts by outcome, and other tender offers, 1978-87, article, 9375-1.901

Hostile takeover defense through repurchase of stock, stock price changes for selected firms, 1985-86, article, 9373-2.901

Leveraged buyout acquisitions, and stock price and economic impacts, 1960s-88, article, 9391-1.922

Leveraged buyout mergers and acquisitions, financing characteristics and policy issues, 1970s-88, 21368-115

Oil and gas companies mergers, impacts on domestic reserve purchases, exploration, and financial performance, 1982-86, 3168-112

Oil industry mergers and acquisitions impacts on market concentration, with background data, 1970-84, 9406-1.58

Oil refinery capacity, closings, and acquisitions by plant, and fuel used, by PAD district, 1973-88, annual rpt, 3164-2.1

Savings and loan assns failure resolution costs, and FSLIC finances and promissory notes issued, with data by instn, FY80s and projected to FY99, hearing, 25258-22

Savings and loan assns failures, assets, and FSLIC resolution costs and promissory notes, with data for acquired and acquiring instn in US and Texas, 1988 hearings, 21248-121

Savings and loan assns, FHLB 11th District members, offices, and financial condition, 1989 annual listing, 9304-23

Savings instns advances from FHLBs, assets, and liabilities, with data for failed and merged instns, by FHLB district, 1980s-88, GAO rpt, 26119-269

Savings instns assets and mortgage holdings, insured instns, and FSLIC failure resolution caseloads and costs, 1970s-88, 21788-177

Savings instns failure resolution activity of Resolution Trust Corp, with failed instn finances by instn, periodic press release, 9722-1

Savings instns failure resolution costs, financing problems, and FSLIC and acquiring instns tax benefits, 1988 and projected to FY99, hearings, 21788-181

Savings instns failure resolution costs to FSLIC for liquidation and sale, and financial characteristics of instn, 1988, technical paper, 8436-1.2

Savings instns failures, financial condition indicators, and liquidation and acquisition costs and tax benefits by instn and acquiring company, 1985-98, hearing, 21268-41

Savings instns regulatory issues, mgmt, and FHLB system and member finances and operations, monthly journal, 8432-2; 9312-1

Savings instns voluntary mergers, and failed instn FSLIC-assisted mergers by type, various periods 1934-88, technical paper, 8436-1.3

Savings instns voluntary, supervisory, and FSLIC-assisted mergers and FHLB membership changes, selected years 1970-87, annual rpt, 9314-3.1

Statistical Abstract of US, social, political, and economic data, 1790-2025, comprehensive annual compilation, 2324-1.3

Business and industry

Business America, foreign and domestic commerce, and US investment and trade opportunities, biweekly journal, 2042-24

Business Conditions Digest, economic, business, and financial devs and cyclical fluctuations, monthly rpt, 2702-3

Census of Population and Housing, 1990: data item selection, questionnaire dev, and testing, 2626-11.3

Classifications of occupations and industries used in 1970 and 1980 censuses, impact on labor force counts by industry, occupation, and sex, 1970, technical paper, 2626-2.59

Foreign countries economic and social conditions, working paper series, 2326-18

Health care R&D funding, by type of source and performer, 1978-87, annual rpt, 4434-3

R&D funding by source, and characteristics of grad students and research staff, for black colleges by field of science and instn, 1980s-87, 9628-78

R&D funding by source and performer, and related employment, by State, 1975-87, 9626-6.32

R&D funding, by source, performer, and for top 10 States, 1977-89, 9626-2.185

Science and engineering employment and earnings, by field and activity, and private and Federal R&D spending, by industry, 1975-88, 9626-6.29

Science and engineering employment in R&D, earnings by field and educational, employment, and other characteristics, 1989, annual rpt, 3004-1

Science and engineering labor supply by region and employment characteristics, and salaries by years of experience, 1987, 9626-2.184

Science and engineering PhDs, by field, instn, employment prospects, sex, race, and other characteristics, 1960s-88, 9627-30

Science and engineering PhDs employment and other characteristics, by field and State, 1987, biennial rpt, 9627-18

Survey of Current Business, detailed data for major industries and economic indicators, monthly rpt, 2702-1

Surveys of establishments by Fed Govt, analysis of errors, 1988 rpt, 106-4.9

see also Agriculture

see also Area wage surveys

see also Automation

see also Banks and banking

see also Business acquisitions and mergers

see also Business assets and liabilities, general

see also Business assets and liabilities, specific industry

see also Business cycles

see also Business education

see also Business ethics

see also Business failures and closings

see also Business firms and establishments, number

see also Business formations

see also Business income and expenses, general

see also Business income and expenses, specific industry

see also Business inventories

see also Business management

see also Business orders

see also Business outlook and attitude surveys

see also Capital investments, general

see also Capital investments, specific industry

see also Commercial buildings

see also Commercial credit

see also Commercial law

see also Communications industries

see also Competition

see also Construction industry

see also Consultants

see also Corporations

see also Credit

see also Defense industries

see also Depreciation
see also Divestiture
see also Earnings, general
see also Earnings, local and regional
see also Earnings, specific industry
see also Economic concentration and diversification
see also Electric power plants and equipment
see also Employee benefits
see also Employment and unemployment, general
see also Employment and unemployment, local and regional
see also Employment and unemployment, specific industry
see also Executives and managers
see also Financial institutions
see also Fish and fishing industry
see also Foreign corporations
see also Forests and forestry
see also Franchises
see also Government and business
see also Home-based offices and workers
see also Hours of labor
see also Industrial and commercial energy use
see also Industrial capacity and utilization
see also Industrial parks
see also Industrial plants and equipment
see also Industrial production
see also Industrial production indexes
see also Industrial purchasing
see also Industrial robots
see also Industrial siting
see also Industrial standards
see also Industry wage surveys
see also Input-output analysis
see also Insurance and insurance industry
see also Labor law
see also Labor-management relations, general
see also Labor-management relations, local and regional
see also Labor mobility
see also Labor productivity
see also Labor supply and demand
see also Labor turnover
see also Labor unions
see also Manufacturing
see also Marketing
see also Mines and mineral resources
see also Minority businesses
see also Multinational corporations
see also Occupational health and safety
see also Occupations
see also Ownership of enterprise
see also Partnerships
see also Payroll
see also Printing and publishing industry
see also Production costs
see also Productivity
see also Proprietorships
see also Public administration
see also Public utilities
see also Real estate business
see also Repair industries
see also Retail trade
see also Service industries
see also Small business
see also Standard Industrial Classification
see also Trade adjustment assistance
see also Trademarks
see also Transportation and transportation equipment

see also Value added tax
see also Wholesale trade
see also Women-owned businesses
see also under By Individual Company or Institution in the "Index by Categories"
see also under By Industry in the "Index by Categories"
see also under names of specific industries or industry groups

Business assets and liabilities, general

Acquisitions (hostile takeover) of US firms by foreign firms, attempts by outcome, and transaction value, with data by firm, 1984-88, GAO rpt, 26123-222

Assets and debts of private sector, balance sheets by segment, 1949-88, semiannual rpt, 9365-4.1

Business Conditions Digest, economic, business, and financial devs and cyclical fluctuations, monthly rpt, 2702-3

Capital stock growth, indexes, and variability, alternative BLS and BEA measures, various periods 1948-87, article, 9362-1.910

Caribbean Basin Initiative investment incentives, economic impacts, with finances and employment by country, 1984-88, 2048-141

Corporations finances, historic trends, 1988 annual chartbook, 9364-2.10

Corporations financial ratios, by industry div, and financing by source, 1900-88, article, 9373-1.912

Corporations financial statements for manufacturing, mining, and trade, by selected SIC 2- to 3-digit industry, quarterly rpt, 2502-1

Debt outstanding, by sector and type of debt and holder, monthly rpt, 9362-1.1

Economic indicators and components, current data and annual trends, monthly rpt, 23842-1.5

Flow-of-funds accounts, assets and liabilities by type and economic sector, outstanding at year-end 1965-88, annual rpt, 9364-3

Flow-of-funds accounts, savings, investments, and credit statements, quarterly rpt, 9365-3.3

Foreign corporate activity in US, income tax returns, assets, and income statement items, by industry div, country, and world area, 1984-85, article, 8302-2.920

Imports and tariff provisions effect on US industries and products, investigations with background financial and operating data, series, 9886-4

Insurance (health) for retirees, employer liabilities and costs by age group, 1988 and projected to 2043, GAO rpt, 26121-299

Intl capital markets outstanding debt, by borrower type, 1982-88, 21368-118

Labor collective bargaining agreement concessions relation to economic and industry financial conditions, with data by major industry and union, 1970s-88, technical paper, 9385-8.41

Mergers and acquisitions using leveraged buyout, financing characteristics and policy issues, 1970s-88, 21368-115

Multinatl firms US affiliates finances and operations, by industry div, country of parent firm, and State, 1986-87, annual article, 2702-1.925

Multinatl firms US affiliates, finances, and operations, by industry, world area of parent firm, and State, 1987, annual rpt, 2704-4

Multinatl US firms and foreign affiliates finances and operations, by industry of parent firm and affiliate, world area, and selected country, 1987, annual article, 2702-1.920; 2704-5

Partnership income tax returns, income statement items by industry group, 1986, annual article, 8302-2.903

Partnerships (master limited) finances, firms, partners, and tax reform impacts, by industry, 1986, technical paper, 8006-3.59

Pension plan financial status, impact of alternative accounting standards, 1978-87, technical paper, 9366-6.172

Puerto Rico and other US possessions corporations tax incentives, finances, and operations by industry, and impacts on local economy, 1970s-83, biennial rpt, 8004-12

Small business capital formation sources, 1988 annual conf, 9734-4

Small business finances, operations, owner and employee characteristics, and Federal contracts, 1980s-88, annual rpt, 9764-6

Statistical Abstract of US, social, political, and economic data, 1790-2025, comprehensive annual compilation, 2324-1.3

Tax (income) returns filed by type of filer, selected income items, quarterly rpt, 8302-2.1

Tax (income) returns of corporations, income and tax items by asset size and detailed industry, 1986, annual rpt, 8304-4; 8304-21

Tax (income) returns of corporations, summary data by asset size and industry div, 1986, annual article, 8302-2.922

see also Agricultural finance
see also Bankruptcy
see also Business assets and liabilities, specific industry
see also Business income and expenses, general
see also Business inventories
see also Capital investments, general
see also Depreciation
see also Divestiture
see also Foreign investments
see also Industrial plants and equipment
see also Investments
see also Mortgages
see also Operating ratios

Business assets and liabilities, specific industry

Agricultural cooperatives finances, aggregate for top 100 assns by commodity group, FY87, annual rpt, 1124-3

Agricultural cooperatives, finances, and membership, by type of service, commodity, and State, 1987, annual rpt, 1124-1

Agricultural cooperatives finances, operations, activities, and current issues, monthly journal, 1122-1

Airline financial data, by carrier, carrier group, and for total certificated system, quarterly rpt, 7302-7

American Historical Assn financial statements, and membership by State, 1988, annual rpt, 29574-2

Bank holding company risk, impact of market concentration and State branching regulation, alternative regression results, various periods 1978-84, technical paper, 9366-6.182

Bank holding company stock price effects of new issues and capital regulation, 1975-86, article, 9393-8.901

Banking and economic conditions, for Fed Reserve 8th District, quarterly rpt with articles, 9391-16

Banking and financial conditions, 1987, annual rpt, 9364-5

Banking industry structure, performance, and financial devs, for Fed Reserve 10th District, 1988, annual rpt, 9381-14.1

Banks (insured commercial) and offices, and summary assets and liabilities, 1987-88, annual rpt, 9364-1.2

Banks (insured commercial) assets, income, and financial ratios, by asset size and State, quarterly rpt, 13002-3

Banks (insured commercial) domestic and foreign office consolidated financial statements, monthly rpt, quarterly data, 9362-1.4

Banks (insured commercial), Fed Reserve 5th District members financial statements, by State, quarterly rpt, 9389-18

Banks (insured commercial) financial condition and performance, by asset size and region, quarterly rpt, 9292-1

Banks (insured commercial) profitability, balance sheet items, and rates of return by asset size, 1984-88, annual article, 9362-1.907

Banks (insured commercial and savings) finances, by State, 1987, annual rpt, 9294-4

Banks (intl) facilities of foreign and US banks in New York and total US, assets and liabilities, monthly rpt, 9365-2.22

Banks (natl) domestic and intl operations, charters, mergers, and liquidations, by instn and State, quarterly rpt, 8402-3

Banks (natl) financial performance, and Office of the Comptroller of Currency enforcement activities, 1978-88, 8408-18

Banks (US) foreign branches assets and liabilities, by world region and country, quarterly rpt, 9365-3.7

Banks (US) foreign branches, balance sheets, monthly rpt, 9362-1.3

Banks (US) loans to developing countries, and loan loss reserves, by money center bank, Sept 1988, hearings, 21248-122

Banks and thrifts finances by instn type, and Fed Financial Instns Exam Council financial statements, 1988, annual rpt, 13004-2

Banks and thrifts in New England, financial statements by type of instn and Fed deposit insurance, and State, 1987, annual rpt, 9304-3

Banks assets, income, and rates of return, by major instn for Fed Reserve 3rd District, quarterly rpt, annual table, 9387-10

Banks balance sheets, by Fed Reserve District, for major banks in NYC, and for US branches and agencies of foreign banks, weekly rpt, 9365-1.3

Banks brokered deposit holdings and financial indicators, by size, region, and for failed instns, 1986-89, hearing, 21248-124

Banks capital/asset ratios for Fed Reserve 5th District and other US banks, with intl capital adequacy standards, as of June 1988, article, 9389-1.904

Banks diversification impacts on costs, alternative indicators by asset size, 1986, article, 9371-1.907

Banks failed and assisted, FDIC mgmt and liquidation of acquired assets, 1980-88, GAO rpt, 26119-237

Banks failure forecasting accuracy, and failure relation to financial, regulatory, and other indicators, with data by instn, 1960s-89, working paper, 9377-9.77

Banks failures by bank type, asset size, region, and State, 1984-88, article, 9391-16.901

Banks finances and operations, by metro-nonmetro location, 1986, annual rpt, 1544-29

Banks finances and performance ratios, for North Central States, by State, quarterly journal, 9383-19

Banks financial performance, impact of loan commitments, various periods 1975-86, technical paper, 9366-6.179

Banks financial performance indicators by asset size, Fed Reserve 8th District, 1985-88, annual article, 9391-1.912

Banks financial performance, risk assessment, and regulation, 1988 annual conf papers, 9375-7

Banks financial position, accuracy of quarterly call rpts and relation to bank ownership and merger activity, 1978-86, working paper, 9387-8.188

Banks financial statistics, historic trends, 1988 annual chartbook, 9364-2.13

Banks in California owned by Japanese and other foreign banks, assets, portfolio composition, and cost of funds, 1987-88, article, 9393-8.906

Banks in Fed Reserve 1st District, assets and liabilities, monthly rpt, 9373-24

Banks in Fed Reserve 1st District, assets and liabilities, quarterly rpt, 9373-2.5

Banks in Fed Reserve 5th District, financial performance, 1984-88, annual article, 9389-1.909

Banks loan interest rates and default risk relation to loan collateral status, type, and other characteristics, 1977-87, technical paper, 9366-6.165

Banks market value accounting proposal, with assets and liabilities composition, loan ratios, and securities book and market value, 1984-88, working paper, 9389-19.12

Banks reserve requirements relation to interest rates, various periods 1882-1987, technical paper, 9379-12.43

Banks status changes, instns, assets, and concentration ratios by size, ownership, and location, and compared to other financial instns, 1976-87, article, 9362-1.902

Banks technological devs adoption relation to asset size, regression results, 1980s-86, working paper, 9371-10.33

Construction industries census, 1987: establishments, employment, receipts, and expenditures, by SIC 4-digit industry and State, final industry rpt series, 2373-1

Credit unions assets and location, 1989 annual listing, 9534-6

Credit unions federally insured, finances by instn characteristics and State, as of June 1989, semiannual rpt, 9532-6

Credit unions federally insured, finances, mergers, closings, and insurance fund losses and financial statements, FY88, annual rpt, 9534-7

Credit unions federally insured, finances, 1987-88, annual rpt, 9534-1

Electric power distribution loans from REA, and borrower operating and financial data, by firm and State, 1988, annual rpt, 1244-1

Electric power sales by customer, plants, and capacity of Southeastern Power Admin, FY88, annual rpt, 3234-1

Electric utilities finances and operations, detailed data for privately owned firms, and summary data for other utilities by type, 1987, annual rpt, 3164-23

Electric utilities finances and operations, detailed data for privately owned firms, 1986-88, annual rpt, 3164-11.4

Energy producers finances and operations, by energy type for US firms domestic and foreign operations, 1987, annual rpt, 3164-44

Energy resources of US, foreign direct investment by energy type and firm, and US affiliates operations, as of 1988, annual rpt, 3164-80

Finance companies assets and liabilities and business credit, 1987, annual rpt, 9364-5.7

Finance companies assets, liabilities, and credit and leasing activities, monthly rpt, 9365-2.7

Financial instns and Federal deposit insurance funds financial condition, 1980s-88, GAO rpt, 26119-241

Financial instns assets composition, growth, and distribution, by instn type, 1970s-88, 8438-1

Financial instns financial and operating statements by deposit size, Fed Reserve functional cost analysis, 1988, annual rpt, 9364-6

Financial instns holdings, for banks in and outside NYC, and for thrift instns, monthly rpt, 9362-1.1

Insurance (health) plans of corporations for retirees, costs and liabilities under alternative accounting standards, 1983-88, technical paper, 9366-6.190

Natural gas interstate pipeline company detailed financial and operating data, by firm, 1988, annual rpt, 3164-38

Nonprofit charitable organizations finances, and assets and grants of top 10, 1985, article, 8302-2.923

Oil company production and imports by type, and financial data, 1975-86, annual rpt, 3164-74.1

Oil industry mergers and acquisitions impacts on market concentration, with background data, 1970-84, 9406-1.58

Railroad (Class I) finances and operations, detailed data by firm, class of service, and district, 1987, annual rpt, 9486-6.1

Railroad (Class I) finances and operations, detailed data by firm, class of service, and district, 1988, annual rpt, 9486-5.1

Savings and loan assns assets and liabilities, by FHLB district and State, 1987 and trends from 1930, annual rpt, 9314-1

Savings and loan assns assets composition, and alternative estimates of net worth for insolvent instns allowed to remain open, 1982-88, article, 9375-1.908

Savings and loan assns failure resolution costs, and FSLIC finances and promissory notes issued, with data by instn, FY80s and projected to FY99, hearing, 25258-22

Savings and loan assns failures, assets, and FSLIC resolution costs and promissory notes, with data for acquired and acquiring instn in US and Texas, 1988 hearings, 21248-121

Savings and loan assns, FHLB 6th District insured members financial condition and operations by State, quarterly rpt, 9302-23

Savings and loan assns, FHLB 8th District members, locations, assets, and savings, 1989, annual listing, 9304-9

Savings and loan assns, FHLB 11th District members, offices, and financial condition, 1989 annual listing, 9304-23

Savings instns (FSLIC-insured) assets, liabilities, and deposit and loan activity, and compared to all S&Ls, monthly rpt, 9312-4

Savings instns advances from FHLBs, assets, and liabilities, with data for failed and merged instns, by FHLB district, 1980s-88, GAO rpt, 26119-269

Savings instns and assets, by solvency status under alternative risk-based capital requirements, Dec 1988, article, 9312-1.905

Savings instns and banks issues of subordinated debt, 1986-89, article, 9312-1.906

Savings instns assets and liabilities, by instn type, 1985-87, annual rpt, 9364-5.4

Savings instns assets and mortgage holdings, insured instns, and FSLIC failure resolution caseloads and costs, 1970s-88, 21788-177

Savings instns failure resolution activity of Resolution Trust Corp, with failed instn finances by instn, periodic press release, 9722-1

Savings instns failure resolution costs, financing problems, and FSLIC and acquiring instns tax benefits, 1988 and projected to FY99, hearings, 21788-181

Savings instns failure resolution costs to FSLIC by State, and instn financial characteristics, 1979-88, technical paper, 9316-1.151

Savings instns failure resolution costs to FSLIC for liquidation and sale, and financial characteristics of instn, 1988, technical paper, 8436-1.2

Savings instns failures, finances, and FSLIC and FDIC insurance premiums, coverage, losses, and reserves, 1930s-87, technical paper, 9316-1.143

Savings instns failures, financial condition indicators, and liquidation and acquisition costs and tax benefits by instn and acquiring company, 1985-98, hearing, 21268-41

Savings instns failures resolution costs to FSLIC relation to discount rate, instn financial characteristics, and State, alternative model results, 1980s-88, technical paper, 8436-1.3

Savings instns, FHLB 1st District members, financial condition, and locations, 1989, annual listing, 9304-26

Savings instns, FHLB 2nd District members capital and assets under capital requirements increase proposal, by State, 3rd qtr 1988, article, 9302-33.901

Savings instns, FHLB 2nd District members finances and operations, by State, quarterly rpt, 9302-14

Savings instns, FHLB 4th District members assets and financial ratios, by profitability and solvency status, various periods 1984-88, article, 9302-2.901

Savings instns, FHLB 4th District members finances and financial ratios, by State, quarterly rpt, 9302-3

Savings instns, FHLB 4th District members finances, by State, 1984-88, annual rpt series, 9304-29

Savings instns, FHLB 5th District members finances and lending by State, monthly rpt, 9302-8

Savings instns, FHLB 6th District members financial condition and operations by State, monthly rpt, 9302-11

Savings instns, FHLB 8th District members financial operations by State and SMSA, monthly rpt, 9302-9

Savings instns, FHLB 9th District members finances and operations by State, monthly rpt, 9302-13

Savings instns, FHLB 9th District members finances and operations by State, quarterly rpt, 9302-31

Savings instns, FHLB 10th District members financial condition, by State, quarterly rpt, 9302-34

Savings instns, FHLB 10th District members, locations, assets, and savings, 1989, annual listing, 9304-17

Savings instns finances and operations by district and State, mortgage lending activity and terms by MSA, and FHLB finances, 1987 with trends from 1900, annual rpt, 9314-3

Savings instns financial performance, for newly chartered instns by charter type, 1982-86, technical paper, 9316-1.146

Savings instns financial statements, FSLIC-insured instns by FHLB district and State, and FDIC-insured savings banks, 1988, annual rpt, 8434-1

Savings instns financial statistics, historic trends, 1988 annual chartbook, 9364-2.14

Savings instns financial status impact of Financial Instns Reform, Recovery, and Enforcement Act, June 1989, technical paper, 8436-1.1

Savings instns insured by Savings Assn Insurance Fund, assets, liabilities, and deposit and loan activity, by conservatorship status, monthly rpt, 8432-1

Savings instns insured by Savings Assn Insurance Fund, finances by district, quarterly rpt, 8432-4

Savings instns junk bond holdings, returns, defaults, and losses, 1985-88, GAO rpt, 26119-246

Savings instns members of Fed Home Loan Bank System, and assets, 1988, annual listing, 9314-5

Savings instns off-balance-sheet hedging activity, by type, asset size, and State, for FHLB 4th District, 1984-88, article, 9302-2.903

Savings instns regulatory issues, mgmt, and FHLB system and member finances and operations, monthly journal, 8432-2; 9312-1

Savings instns regulatory issues, 1988 annual conf, 9304-24

Securities industry finances, firms by type, and SEC applications and registrations, 1983-88, annual rpt, 9734-2.1; 9734-2.2

Shipping firms combined financial statements, Dec 1986-87, annual rpt, 7704-14.5

Small Business Investment Companies capital holdings, SBA obligation, and ownership, as of June 1989, semiannual listing, 9762-4

Small Business Investment Companies finances, funding, licensing, and loan activity, 1st half FY89, semiannual rpt, 9762-3

Steel (stainless and alloy tool) production, employment, finances, and US producers inventories and unfilled orders, 1987-88, annual rpt, 9884-22

Stockbrokers assets and liabilities, 1987, annual rpt, 9364-5.13

Stockbrokers issuing securities credit, balance sheet, as of June 1988, annual rpt, 9365-5.1

Telephone and electric loans for rural areas by State, and REA activities and finances, FY88 with trends from FY36, annual rpt, 1244-3

Telephone and telegraph firms detailed finances and operations, 1987, annual rpt, 9284-6

Telephone firms borrowing under Rural Telephone Program, and financial and operating data, 1988, annual rpt, 1244-2

Transit systems finances and operations, by mode of transport, size of fleet, and for 432 systems, 1986, annual rpt, 7884-4

Transportation finances, operations, vehicles, equipment, accidents, and energy use, by mode of transport, 1955-88, annual rpt, 7304-2

Truck interstate carriers finances and operations, by district, 1987, annual rpt, 9486-6.2

Trust assets of banks, trust companies, and S&Ls, by type of asset and fund, selected firm, and State, 1988, annual rpt, 13004-1

Uranium mining and milling industries finances and operations, with selected foreign comparisons, 1970s-87 and projected to 2000, annual rpt, 3164-82

see also Agricultural finance

see also Business income and expenses, specific industry

see also Business inventories

see also Capital investments, specific industry

see also Depreciation

see also Educational finance

see also under By Industry in the "Index by Categories"

Business assistance

see Government and business

see Subsidies

Farm finances, debts, assets, and receipts, and lenders financial condition, quarterly rpt with articles, 1541-1

Farm sector financial condition, debt by lender, and indicators of financial stress, 1988, annual GAO rpt, 26104-16

Financial instns and Federal deposit insurance funds financial condition, 1980s-88, GAO rpt, 26119-241

FmHA loans and borrower supervision activities in farm and housing programs, by type and State, monthly rpt, 1182-1

Hazardous waste treatment site liability insurance costs and availability, and reasons for site closure, 1982-87, GAO rpt, 26131-54

Hospital closures in 1987, operating characteristics, current use, and location, 1989 rpt, 4008-87

Hospital operations, ownership, staffing, and other characteristics, by urban-rural location, 1960s-88, 25148-41

Hospital reimbursement by Medicare under prospective payment system, and physician reimbursement, effect on services, finances, and beneficiary payments, 1970s-88, annual rpt, 17204-2

Hospital reimbursement by States under prospective payment programs, effects on operations, finances, and patient deaths, by State, 1970s-83, 4658-29

Hospitals in rural areas, risk of closure by characteristics of service area and hospital, aggregate 1980-87, article, 4042-3.930

Hydroelectric power plants retired, characteristics and location, as of 1989, annual listing, 3084-12

Insurance (property and casualty) industry solvency monitoring by States, activities, staff, and interstate info sharing, 1989 GAO rpt, 26119-273

Investment firm SEC applications, registrations, and terminations, FY41-88, annual rpt, 9734-2.2

Labor laws enacted, by State, 1988, annual article, 6722-1.904

North Central States business and economic conditions, Fed Reserve 9th District, quarterly journal, 9383-19

Nuclear power plant capacity, generation, and operating status, by plant and foreign and US location, 1988 and projected to 2020, annual rpt, 3164-57

Nuclear reactors for domestic use and export by function and operating status, with owner, operating characteristics, and location, 1988 annual listing, 3004-26

Oil refinery capacity, closings, and acquisitions by plant, and fuel used, by PAD district, 1973-88, annual rpt, 3164-2.1

Pension Benefit Guaranty Corp funding status, impact of pension plan terminations, alternative projections 1986-96, article, 9385-1.903

Savings and loan assns assets composition, and alternative estimates of net worth for insolvent instns allowed to remain open, 1982-88, article, 9375-1.908

Savings and loan assns failure resolution costs, and FSLIC finances and promissory notes issued, with data by instn, FY80s and projected to FY99, hearing, 25258-22

Savings and loan assns failures, assets, and FSLIC resolution costs and promissory notes, with data for acquired and acquiring instn in US and Texas, 1988 hearings, 21248-121

Savings and loan assns insolvency crisis, Bush Admin resolution proposals funding by source and use, projected FY89-99, press release, 8008-134

Savings instns advances from FHLBs, assets, and liabilities, with data for failed and merged instns, by FHLB district, 1980s-88, GAO rpt, 26119-269

Savings instns assets and mortgage holdings, insured instns, and FSLIC failure resolution caseloads and costs, 1970s-88, 21788-177

Savings instns crisis in Ohio, impact on certificates of deposit interest rates, 1983-85, technical paper, 9316-1.153

Savings instns failure resolution activity of Resolution Trust Corp, with failed instn finances by instn, periodic press release, 9722-1

Savings instns failure resolution costs, financing problems, and FSLIC and acquiring instns tax benefits, 1988 and projected to FY99, hearings, 21788-181

Savings instns failure resolution costs to FSLIC by State, and instn financial characteristics, 1979-88, technical paper, 9316-1.151

Savings instns failure resolution costs to FSLIC for liquidation and sale, and financial characteristics of instn, 1988, technical paper, 8436-1.2

Savings instns failures by State, with exam of mgmt weaknesses and regulatory activity, 1980s-87, GAO rpt, 26111-62

Savings instns failures, finances, and FSLIC and FDIC insurance premiums, coverage, losses, and reserves, 1930s-87, technical paper, 9316-1.143

Savings instns failures, financial condition indicators, and liquidation and acquisition costs and tax benefits by instn and acquiring company, 1985-98, hearing, 21268-41

Savings instns failures, real estate assets value, and disposition performance of FSLIC, Fed Asset Disposition Assn, and private contractors, 1988, article, 8432-2.901

Savings instns failures resolution costs to FSLIC relation to discount rate, instn financial characteristics, and State, alternative model results, 1980s-88, technical paper, 8436-1.3

Savings instns, FHLB 4th District members assets and financial ratios, by profitability and solvency status, various periods 1984-88, article, 9302-2.901

Savings instns insured by Savings Assn Insurance Fund, assets, liabilities, and deposit and loan activity, by conservatorship status, monthly rpt, 8432-1

Savings instns insured by Savings Assn Insurance Fund, finances by district, quarterly rpt, 8432-4

Schools of higher education closing, by instn type and control, 1960/61-1985/86, annual rpt, 4824-2.19

Small business establishments, employment, and financial ratios, by SIC 1- to 2-digit industry and State, late 1960s-87, 9768-19

Small business establishments, operations, owner characteristics, and job training, late 1950s-87, 9768-20

Small business finances, operations, owner and employee characteristics, and Federal contracts, 1980s-88, annual rpt, 9764-6

Statistical Abstract of US, social, political, and economic data, 1790-2025, comprehensive annual compilation, 2324-1.3

Steel plant closings relation to EPA pollution enforcement and compliance, model description and results, 1977-86, working paper, 9377-9.84

Survey of Current Business, detailed data for major industries and economic indicators, monthly rpt, 2702-1.1

Trucking industry deregulation in 1980, impacts on finances and safety, mid 1970s-88, hearing, 21648-55

Unemployed displaced older workers, and reemployment, by selected characteristics, 1969-88, 6306-2.2

Unemployed displaced workers, by reason, industry, selected characteristics, and State, 1988, annual rpt, 6744-18

Uranium mill capacity by plant, and production, by operating status, 1985-88, annual rpt, 3164-65.1

see also Bankruptcy

Business firms

see Bank holding companies

see Business acquisitions and mergers

see Business failures and closings

see Business firms and establishments, number

see Business formations

see Corporations

see Foreign corporations

see Franchises

see Government corporations and enterprises

see Holding companies

see Home-based offices and workers

see Industrial plants and equipment

see Industrial siting

see Minority businesses

see Multinational corporations

see Partnerships

see Proprietorships

see Public utilities

see Small business

see Small Business Investment Companies

see Women-owned businesses

see under By Individual Company or Institution in the "Index by Categories"

Business firms and establishments, number

Agricultural cooperatives, finances, and membership, by type of service, commodity, and State, 1987, annual rpt, 1124-1

Banking and financial conditions, 1987, annual rpt, 9364-5

Banking industry structure, performance, and financial devs, for Fed Reserve 10th District, 1988, annual rpt, 9381-14.1

Banks (commercial and savings) FDIC-insured, deposits by instn, State, MSA, and county, as of June 1988, annual regional rpt series, 9295-3

Banks (insured commercial) and offices, and summary assets and liabilities, 1987-88, annual rpt, 9364-1.2

Banks (insured commercial) assets, income, and financial ratios, by asset size and State, quarterly rpt, 13002-3

Banks (insured commercial and savings) finances, and changes in status, by State, 1987, annual rpt, 9294–4.1

Banks (natl) domestic and intl operations, charters, mergers, and liquidations, by instn and State, quarterly rpt, 8402–3

Banks and thrifts in New England, financial statements by type of instn and Fed deposit insurance, and State, 1987, annual rpt, 9304–3

Buildings (commercial) energy use, costs, and conservation, by building characteristics, survey rpt series, 3166–8

Chemicals (synthetic organic) production, sales, and manufacturer listing, by product, 1988, annual rpt, 9884–3

Chemicals and oil products shipments, firms, trade, and use, by product, periodic Current Industrial Rpt series, 2506–8

Coastal areas environmental impacts of economic dev and population growth, 1980s and projected to 2000, 2176–8.1

Construction industries census, 1987: establishments, employment, receipts, and expenditures, by SIC 4-digit industry and State, final industry rpt series, 2373–1

Construction industries census, 1987: financial and operating data, preliminary industry rpt series, 2371–1

Corporations income tax returns, income and tax items by asset size and detailed industry, 1986, annual rpt, 8304–4; 8304–21

Cotton gins by capacity, and utilization rates, by State, 1983-88, article, 1561–1.902

County Business Patterns, 1987: employment, establishments, and payroll, by SIC 2- to 4-digit industry and county, annual State rpt series, 2326–8

Credit unions federally insured, finances by instn characteristics and State, as of June 1989, semiannual rpt, 9532–6

Credit unions federally insured, finances, mergers, closings, and insurance fund losses and financial statements, FY88, annual rpt, 9534–7

Credit unions federally insured, finances, 1987-88, annual rpt, 9534–1

Drug testing of employees, coverage, policies, sponsors, treatment aid provided, and results, by industry div, 1988, 6728–37

Fertilizer (inorganic) shipments, trade, use, and firms, by product and State, with stocks, 1988, annual Current Industrial Rpt, 2506–8.13

Financial instns financial and operating statements by deposit size, Fed Reserve functional cost analysis, 1988, annual rpt, 9364–6

Fish (processed) production by location, and trade, by species and product, 1987-88, annual rpts, 2166–6

Fish processing plants on Pacific coast, and employment, by State, 1980-87, annual rpt, 2164–16.1

Fishery employment, vessels, plants, and cooperatives, by State, 1988 and trends from 1970, annual rpt, 2164–1.10

Food marketing sector finances, operations, and merger activity, for processors and distributors, as of 1988, annual rpt, 1544–22

Foreign corporate activity in US, income tax returns, assets, and income statement items, by industry div, country, and world area, 1984-85, article, 8302–2.920

Fruit and vegetable processing industries finances and operations, consumption, farm production, and trade, by commodity, 1970s-88, 1568–275

Glass (fibrous) production, shipments, and firms, by product, 1976-88, annual Current Industrial Rpt, 2506–9.5

Guam economic censuses, 1987: employment, firms, payroll, and receipts, by SIC 1- to 4-digit industry and election district, 2595–1

Hazardous substances industrial releases and reduction methods under EPA regulation, by chemical, source, industry, and location, 1987, annual rpt, 9234–6

Imports under Generalized System of Preferences, status, and US tariffs, trade by country, production, and use, for selected commodities, 1984-88, annual rpt, 9884–23

Industry (US) intl competitiveness, with selected foreign and US operating data by major firm and product, series, 2046–12

Livestock packers purchases and feeding, and livestock markets, dealers, and sales, by State, 1987, annual rpt, 1384–1

Machinery and equipment production, shipments, trade, stocks, orders, use, and firms, by product, periodic Current Industrial Rpt series, 2506–12

Manufacturing census, 1987: financial and operating data, for SIC 4-digit industries by product, preliminary industry rpt series, 2491–1

Metals (intermediate product) shipments, trade, and inventories, by product, periodic Current Industrial Rpt series, 2506–11

Mineral industries census, 1987: financial and operating data, preliminary industry rpt series, 2511–1

Minerals Yearbook, 1987, Vol 1: commodity reviews of production, use, trade, prices, and mining operations, annual rpt, 5604–33

Minerals Yearbook, 1987, Vol 2: State reviews of production, sales, and firms, by commodity, and business activity, annual rpt, 5604–34

Minority Business Dev Centers mgmt and financial aid, and characteristics of businesses, by region and State, FY88, annual rpt, 2104–6

Multinatl US firms and foreign affiliates finances and operations, by industry of parent firm and affiliate, world area, and country, preliminary 1987, annual rpt, 2704–5

Northern Mariana Islands economic census, 1987: employment, firms, payroll, and receipts, by SIC 1- to 4-digit industry, 2597–1

Partnership income tax returns, income statement items by industry group, 1986, annual article, 8302–2.903

Partnerships (master limited) finances, firms, partners, and tax reform impacts, by industry, 1986, technical paper, 8006–3.59

Potato chip plants and potatoes processed, by region, 1986-88, annual rpt, 1621–11

Puerto Rico and other US possessions corporations tax incentives, finances, and operations by industry, and impacts on local economy, 1970s-83, biennial rpt, 8004–12

Railroad (short-line) operations and regulation, for lines established 1834-1987, hearing, 21368–109

Railroad Retirement and Unemployment Insurance Acts coverage of employers, by class, Sept 1988, annual rpt, 9704–1

Retail trade census, 1987: employment, establishments, sales, and payroll, by SIC 2- to 4-digit kind of business, MSA, county, and city, State rpt series, 2397–1

Savings and loan assns assets and liabilities, by FHLB district and State, 1987 and trends from 1930, annual rpt, 9314–1

Savings instns (FSLIC-insured) assets, liabilities, and deposit and loan activity, and compared to all S&Ls, monthly rpt, 9312–4

Savings instns assets and mortgage holdings, insured instns, and FSLIC failure resolution caseloads and costs, 1970s-88, 21788–177

Savings instns, FHLB 1st District members by type and State, 1988, annual rpt, 9304–2

Savings instns finances and operations by district and State, mortgage lending activity and terms by MSA, and FHLB finances, 1987 with trends from 1900, annual rpt, 9314–3

Savings instns financial statements, FSLIC-insured instns by FHLB district and State, and FDIC-insured savings banks, 1988, annual rpt, 8434–1

Savings instns FSLIC-insured, offices, and deposits, by FHLB district, State, SMSA, and county, 1988, annual rpt, 9314–4

Savings instns insured by Savings Assn Insurance Fund, assets, liabilities, and deposit and loan activity, by conservatorship status, monthly rpt, 8432–1

Savings instns insured by Savings Assn Insurance Fund, finances by district, quarterly rpt, 8432–4

Savings instns regulatory issues, mgmt, and FHLB system and member finances and operations, monthly journal, 8432–2; 9312–1

Securities industry finances, firms by type, and SEC applications and registrations, 1983-88, annual rpt, 9734–2.1; 9734–2.2

Service industries census, 1987: establishments, receipts, employment, and payroll, by SIC 2- to 4-digit kind of business, MSA, county, and city, State rpt series, 2391–1

Small business establishments, employment, and financial ratios, by SIC 1- to 2-digit industry and State, late 1960s-87, 9768–19

Small business establishments, operations, owner characteristics, and job training, late 1950s-87, 9768–20

Small business finances, operations, owner and employee characteristics, and Federal contracts, 1980s-88, annual rpt, 9764–6

Small business loans, contracts, and financing by SBA program and firm, and SBA activities, FY88, annual rpt, 9764–1

Solar collector and photovoltaic module shipments by end-use sector and State, R&D, and trade, 1988, annual rpt, 3164-62

Sole proprietorship income tax returns, income statement items by industry group, 1987, annual article, 8302-2.904; 8302-2.921

Statistical Abstract of US, social, political, and economic data, 1790-2025, comprehensive annual compilation, 2324-1.3

Survey of Current Business, detailed data for major industries and economic indicators, monthly rpt, 2702-1.1

Telephone and telegraph firms detailed finances and operations, 1987, annual rpt, 9284-6

Telephone firms borrowing under Rural Telephone Program, and financial and operating data, 1988, annual rpt, 1244-2

Tobacco manufacturing firms, employment, and value added, by product, selected years 1977-82, 1568-276

Transit systems finances and operations, by mode of transport, size of fleet, and for 432 systems, 1986, annual rpt, 7884-4

Transportation finances, operations, vehicles, equipment, accidents, and energy use, by mode of transport, 1955-88, annual rpt, 7304-2

Truck and bus interstate carriers finances and operations, by district, 1987, annual rpt, 9486-6.3

Truck interstate carriers finances and operations, by district, 1987, annual rpt, 9486-6.2

Trust assets of banks, trust companies, and S&Ls, by type of asset and fund, selected firm, and State, 1988, annual rpt, 13004-1

TV and radio stations on the air, by class of operation, monthly press release, 9282-4

Unemployment insurance coverage of establishments, employment, and wages, by SIC 4-digit industry and State, 1988, annual rpt, 6744-16

Uranium mining and milling industries finances and operations, with selected foreign comparisons, 1970s-87 and projected to 2000, annual rpt, 3164-82

Uranium supply and industry operations, various periods 1947-88 and projected to 2000, annual rpt, 3164-65

Vending facilities run by blind on Federal and non-Federal property, finances and operations, by agency and State, FY88, annual rpt, 4944-2

Virgin Islands economic censuses, 1987: employment, firms, payroll, and receipts, by SIC 1- to 4-digit industry, island, and city, 2593-1

Wholesale trade census, 1987: employment, establishments, finances, and operations, by SIC 2- to 4-digit kind of business, MSA, county, and city, State rpt series, 2405-1

Wire and cable (insulated) shipments, trade, use, and firms, by product, 1987-88, annual Current Industrial Rpt, 2506-10.8

see also Business acquisitions and mergers
see also Business failures and closings
see also Business formations
see also Farms and farmland

see also Industrial plants and equipment
see also under By Industry in the "Index by Categories"

Business formations

Banks and bank branch formations, mergers, liquidations, and other changes in status, listing by instn, monthly rpt, 9365-2.23

Banks and thrifts industry structure impacts of market entry and branching regulation, by Southeastern State, 1982-88, article, 9302-2.907

Banks in New England, formations related to selected market indicators, 1970s-87, article, 9373-1.903

Banks status changes, instns, assets, and concentration ratios by size, ownership, and location, and compared to other financial instns, 1976-87, article, 9362-1.902

Credit unions federally insured, finances, mergers, closings, and insurance fund losses and financial statements, FY88, annual rpt, 9534-7

Credit unions federally insured, finances, 1987-88, annual rpt, 9534-1

Electric power plants summer capacity and fuel source, for new and retired units, 1988, annual rpt, 3164-11.1

Formation and failures of business, selected years 1945-88, annual rpt, 204-1.7

Hospital reimbursement by States under prospective payment programs, effects on operations, finances, and patient deaths, by State, 1970s-83, 4658-29

Incorporations of new businesses, by region and state, 1981-87, 9768-19

New England States economic indicators, Fed Reserve 1st District, quarterly rpt, 9373-2.3

North Central States business and economic conditions, Fed Reserve 9th District, quarterly journal, 9383-19

Railroad (short-line) operations and regulation, for lines established 1834-1987, hearing, 21368-109

Small business establishments, employment, and financial ratios, by SIC 1- to 2-digit industry and State, late 1960s-87, 9768-19

Small business establishments, operations, owner characteristics, and job training, late 1950s-87, 9768-20

Small business finances, operations, owner and employee characteristics, and Federal contracts, 1980s-88, annual rpt, 9764-6

Small business loans, contracts, and financing by SBA program and firm, and SBA activities, FY88, annual rpt, 9764-1

Statistical Abstract of US, social, political, and economic data, 1790-2025, comprehensive annual compilation, 2324-1.3

Survey of Current Business, detailed data for major industries and economic indicators, monthly rpt, 2702-1.1

Business income and expenses, general

Alien nonresidents income from US sources and tax withheld by country and US tax treaty status, 1986, annual article, 8302-2.915

Arms sales of US, foreign conditions on sales and impacts on US industry, with data by industry group and country, 1988 annual rpt, 104-25

Budget of US, CBO analysis of revenue and spending alternatives and projections of economic indicators, FY90-94, annual rpt, 26304-3

Business Conditions Digest, economic, business, and financial devs and cyclical fluctuations, monthly rpt, 2702-3

Caribbean Basin Initiative investment incentives, economic impacts, with finances and employment by country, 1984-88, 2048-141

Corporations finances, historic trends, 1988 annual chartbook, 9364-2.10

Corporations finances, monthly rpt, 9362-1.1

Corporations financial statements for manufacturing, mining, and trade, by selected SIC 2- to 3-digit industry, quarterly rpt, 2502-1

Economic indicators and components, current data and annual trends, monthly rpt, 23842-1.1; 23842-1.3; 23842-1.5

Economic indicators compounded annual rates of change, monthly rpt, 9391-3.2

Economic indicators compounded annual rates of change, 1969-88, annual rpt, 9391-9.2

Foreign corporate activity in US, income tax returns, assets, and income statement items, by industry div, country, and world area, 1984-85, article, 8302-2.920

Foreign direct investment in US by country, and finances, employment, and acreage owned, by industry group of business acquired or established, 1982-88, annual article, 2702-1.917

Foreign direct investment in US, by industry group and world area, 1987-88, annual article, 2702-1.929

Guam economic censuses, 1987: employment, firms, payroll, and receipts, by SIC 1- to 4-digit industry and election district, 2595-1

Health care spending of business, households, and govts, 1965-87, article, 4652-1.928

Imports and tariff provisions effect on US industries and products, investigations with background financial and operating data, series, 9886-4

Imports injury to US industries from foreign subsidized products and sales at less than fair value, investigations with background financial and operating data, series, 9886-19

Imports injury to US industries from foreign subsidized products, investigations with background financial and operating data, series, 9886-15

Imports injury to US industries from sales at less than fair value, investigations with background financial and operating data, series, 9886-14

Imports of US given duty-free treatment for value of US material sent abroad, and impacts on US industry and employment, by commodity and country, 1987, annual rpt, 9884-14

Income (personal) by source, and BEA and IRS adjusted gross income measures, 1986-87, annual article, 2702-1.927

Income (personal) per capita and by source, and earnings by industry div, by State, MSA, and county, 1982-87, annual regional rpts, 2704-2

Income (personal) per capita and by source, earnings by major industry group, and social insurance contributions, by region and State, 1929-82, 2708-40

Industry (US) intl competitiveness, with selected foreign and US operating data by major firm and product, series, 2046-12

Industry finances and operations, by SIC 2- to 4-digit industry, forecast 1989 and trends from 1950s, annual rpt, 2044-28

Labor collective bargaining agreement concessions relation to economic and industry financial conditions, with data by major industry and union, 1970s-88, technical paper, 9385-8.41

Manufacturing and trade inventories, sales, and inventory/sales ratios, quarterly article, 2702-1.33

Manufacturing census, 1987: financial and operating data, for SIC 4-digit industries by product, preliminary industry rpt series, 2491-1

Minority Business Dev Centers mgmt and financial aid, and characteristics of businesses, by region and State, FY88, annual rpt, 2104-6

Multinatl firms US affiliates finances and operations, by industry div, country of parent firm, and State, 1986-87, annual article, 2702-1.925

Multinatl firms US affiliates, finances, and operations, by industry, world area of parent firm, and State, 1987, annual rpt, 2704-4

Multinatl US firms and foreign affiliates finances and operations, by industry of parent firm and affiliate, world area, and selected country, 1987, annual article, 2702-1.920; 2704-5

Natl income and product accounts and components, *Survey of Current Business*, monthly rpt, 2702-1.21; 2702-1.27

Northern Mariana Islands economic census, 1987: employment, firms, payroll, and receipts, by SIC 1- to 4-digit industry, 2597-1

Partnership income tax returns, income statement items by industry group, 1986, annual article, 8302-2.903

Partnerships (master limited) finances, firms, partners, and tax reform impacts, by industry, 1986, technical paper, 8006-3.59

Political campaign financial activity reported to Fed Election Commission, by type of filer, 1988 natl elections, biennial rpt series, 9276-2

Pollution abatement capital and operating costs, by SIC 2-to 4-digit industry and State, 1986, annual Current Industrial Rpt, 2506-3.6

Pollution abatement spending by govts, business, and consumers, 1983-87, annual article, 2702-1.919

Productivity and costs of labor for private, nonfarm business, and manufacturing sectors, revised data, quarterly rpt, 6822-2

Puerto Rico and other US possessions corporations tax incentives, finances, and operations by industry, and impacts on local economy, 1970s-83, biennial rpt, 8004-12

Retail trade census, 1987: employment, establishments, sales, and payroll, by SIC 2- to 4-digit kind of business, MSA, county, and city, State rpt series, 2397-1

Retail trade sales and inventories, by kind of business, region, and selected State, MSA, and city, monthly rpt, 2413-3

Retail trade sales, by kind of business, advance monthly rpt, 2413-2

Retail trade sales, inventories, purchases, gross margin, and accounts receivable, by SIC 2- to 4-digit kind of business and form of ownership, 1987, annual rpt, 2413-5

Retail trade sales of consumer goods including autos, and manufacturers orders and shipments, 1950-88, annual chartbook, 9364-2.3

Retailer sales tax collection compliance costs, by industry group and for 7 States, 1981, hearings, 21528-73

Sales and ratio to inventories, by industry div, 1947-88, annual rpt, 204-1.1; 204-1.3; 204-1.7

Science and engineering employment and earnings, by field and activity, and private and Federal R&D spending, by industry, 1975-88, 9626-6.29

Securities offerings proceeds for common and preferred shares, by industry div, monthly rpt, 9732-1

Service industries census, 1987: establishments, receipts, employment, and payroll, by SIC 2- to 4-digit kind of business, MSA, county, and city, State rpt series, 2391-1

Service industries receipts, by SIC 2- to 4-digit kind of business, 1988, annual rpt, 2413-8

Small business establishments, employment, and financial ratios, by SIC 1- to 2-digit industry and State, late 1960s-87, 9768-19

Small business finances, operations, owner and employee characteristics, and Federal contracts, 1980s-88, annual rpt, 9764-6

Small business high technology sales, exports, siting, technology transfer, views on competitiveness, 1988 survey, hearing, 21728-69

Sole proprietorship income tax returns, income statement items by industry group, 1987, annual article, 8302-2.904; 8302-2.921

Statistical Abstract of US, social, political, and economic data, 1790-2025, comprehensive annual compilation, 2324-1.3

Survey of Current Business, detailed data for major industries and economic indicators, monthly rpt, 2702-1

Tax (income) returns filed by type of filer, selected income items, quarterly rpt, 8302-2.1

Tax (income) returns of corporations, income and tax items by asset size and detailed industry, 1986, annual rpt, 8304-4; 8304-21

Tax (income) returns of corporations, summary data by asset size and industry div, 1986, annual article, 8302-2.922

Tax (income) returns of individuals, by filing status, tax item, and income level, 1987, annual article, 8302-2.901

Tax (income) returns of individuals, detailed data, 1986, annual rpt, 8304-2

Tax (income) returns of individuals, selected income and tax items by income level, preliminary 1987, annual article, 8302-2.917

Virgin Islands economic censuses, 1987: employment, firms, payroll, and receipts, by SIC 1- to 4-digit industry, island, and city, 2593-1

Wholesale trade census, 1987: employment, establishments, finances, and operations, by SIC 2- to 4-digit kind of business, MSA, county, and city, State rpt series, 2405-1

Wholesale trade sales and inventories, by SIC 2- to 3-digit kind of business, monthly rpt, 2413-7

Wholesale trade sales, inventories, purchases, and gross margins, by SIC 2- to 3-digit kind of business and form of ownership, 1988, annual rpt, 2413-13

see also Agricultural finance

see also Agricultural marketing

see also Agricultural production costs

see also Business assets and liabilities, general

see also Business income and expenses, specific industry

see also Capital investments, general

see also Depreciation

see also Economic indicators

see also Employee benefits

see also Energy production costs

see also Farm income

see also Industrial and commercial energy use

see also Industrial purchasing

see also Labor costs and cost indexes

see also Operating ratios

see also Payroll

see also Production costs

see also Professionals' fees

see also Royalties

see also Value added tax

Business income and expenses, specific industry

Aerospace industry sales, orders, backlog, and firms, by product for govt, military, and other customers, 1988, annual Current Industrial Rpt, 2506-12.22

Agricultural cooperatives finances, aggregate for top 100 assns by commodity group, FY87, annual rpt, 1124-3

Agricultural cooperatives, finances, and membership, by type of service, commodity, and State, 1987, annual rpt, 1124-1

Agricultural cooperatives finances, operations, activities, and current issues, monthly journal, 1122-1

AID housing and urban dev program financial statements, and loan guarantees by country, FY88, annual rpt, 9914-4

Airline computer reservation systems finances, operations, and impacts on airline competitiveness, 1980s-86, 7308-193

Airline computer reservation systems operating costs, fees, and market shares, by firm and location, 1984-87, hearing, 25528-108

Airline financial data, by carrier, carrier group, and for total certificated system, quarterly rpt, 7302-7

American Historical Assn financial statements, and membership by State, 1988, annual rpt, 29574-2

Auto industry finances and operations, trade by country, and prices of selected US and foreign models, monthly rpt, 9882-8

Fed Reserve Bank of Dallas financial statements, 1987-88, annual rpt, 9379-2

Fed Reserve Bank of Kansas City financial statements, 1987-88, annual rpt, 9381-3

Fed Reserve Bank of Minneapolis financial statements, 1987-88, annual rpt, 9383-2

Fed Reserve Bank of New York financial statements, 1987-88, annual rpt, 9385-2

Fed Reserve Bank of Philadelphia financial statements, 1987-88, annual rpt, 9387-3

Fed Reserve Bank of Richmond financial statements, 1987-88, annual rpt, 9389-2

Fed Reserve Bank of San Francisco financial statements, 1987-88, annual rpt, 9393-2

Fed Reserve Board and Reserve banks finances, staff, and review of monetary policy and economic devs, 1988, annual rpt, 9364-1

Fed Reserve services provided depository instns, costs and revenue by service and district bank, 1987-88, article, 9362-1.908

Fed Reserve System, Board of Governors, and district banks financial statements, performance, and fiscal services, 1987-89, annual rpt, 9364-10

Financial instns financial and operating statements by deposit size, Fed Reserve functional cost analysis, 1988, annual rpt, 9364-6

Fish and shellfish catch, prices, and fisheries economic status, for Pacific coast, 1986-87, annual rpt series, 2164-16

Food marketing cost indexes, by expense category, monthly rpt with articles, 1502-4

Food marketing sector finances, operations, and merger activity, for processors and distributors, as of 1988, annual rpt, 1544-22

Food prices (farm-retail), marketing cost components, and industry finances and productivity, 1950s-88, annual rpt, 1544-9

Fruit and vegetable processing industries finances and operations, consumption, farm production, and trade, by commodity, 1970s-88, 1568-275

GPO activities, finances, and production, FY88, annual rpt, 26204-1

Health Care Financing Review, provider prices, price inputs and indexes, and labor, quarterly journal, 4652-1.1

Health care services (community and migrant) finances, operations, and staff, series, 4108-45

Helium market demand and Bur of Mines production, sales, and financial statements, FY88, annual rpt, 5604-32

Hospital burn injury units, case costs, Medicare reimbursement under prospective system, and instn losses under alternative payment plans, 1988 rpt, 17206-1.2

Hospital labor and total factor productivity, with background data, 1980-86, article, 4652-1.941

Hospital reimbursement by Medicare under prospective payment system, capital cost reimbursement adjustments financial impacts by instn characteristics, 1978-87, 17206-1.1

Hospital reimbursement by Medicare under prospective payment system, costs under alternative cost updating procedures, model results, 1976-84, article, 4652-1.921

Hospital reimbursement by Medicare under prospective payment system, impacts on costs, industry structure and operations, and quality of care, series, 17206-2

Hospital reimbursement by Medicare under prospective payment system, impacts on instns, beneficiaries, and other care providers and payment sources, 1986, annual rpt, 4654-13

Hospital reimbursement by Medicare under prospective payment system, impacts on profit margins, and instn characteristics, 1986/87, hearing, 21148-52

Hospital reimbursement by Medicare under prospective payment system, methodology, inputs, and data by diagnostic group, 1989 annual rpt, 17204-1

Hospital reimbursement by Medicare under prospective payment system, proposed inclusion of capital costs, with background data, FY84-88 and projected to 2008, 26308-83

Hospital reimbursement by States under prospective payment programs, effects on operations, finances, and patient deaths, by State, 1970s-83, 4658-29

Hospitals (children's) unreimbursed charges, expenses, and revenue, FY86, GAO rpt, 26121-291

Insurance (auto) industry profitability, income, and expenses, with premiums by company, 1977-87, 26119-267

Insurance (health) companies case mgmt for high-cost patients, savings, costs, and returns, 1984-86, article, 4652-1.914

Insurance (health) plans of corporations for retirees, costs and liabilities under alternative accounting standards, 1983-88, technical paper, 9366-6.190

Insurance (life) companies financial and tax impacts of Deficit Reduction Act and proposed reforms, for stock and mutual firms, 1984-88 and projected to FY94, 8008-138

Insurance (life) industry income, income taxes, and alternative methods of taxing dividends, for stock and mutual companies, 1980s-87, GAO rpt, 26119-274

Juvenile correctional and detention instns, inmates, and expenses, by instn and resident characteristics and State, 1975-85, biennial rpt, 6064-13

Meat, poultry, and livestock production, consumption, and industry finances and operations, 1950s-86, 1568-280

Mental health care hospitals, beds and caseload by State, patient characteristics, finances, and staff, for profit and nonprofit private instns, 1986, 4506-3.37

Metals (primary) production, shipments, trade, stocks, and material used, by product, periodic Current Industrial Rpt series, 2506-10

Military post exchange operations, and sales by commodity, by facility and location worldwide, FY87, annual rpt, 3504-10

Milk order market administrative expenses, by market area, 1988-89, article, 1317-4.903

Mineral industries census, 1987: financial and operating data, preliminary industry rpt series, 2511-1

Minerals (strategic) supply, demand, trade, and foreign and US industry devs by firm and country, by commodity, bimonthly rpt with articles, 5602-4

Minerals Yearbook, 1987, Vol 1: commodity reviews of production, use, trade, prices, and mining operations, annual rpt, 5604-33

Mint (US) activities, finances, coin and medals production and holdings, and gold and silver transactions, by facility, FY88, annual rpt, 8204-1

Natural and supplemental gas production, prices, trade, use, reserves, and pipeline company finances, by firm and State, monthly rpt with articles, 3162-4

Natural gas interstate pipeline company detailed financial and operating data, by firm, 1988, annual rpt, 3164-38

Nonprofit charitable organizations finances, and assets and grants of top 10, 1985, article, 8302-2.923

Nuclear power plant safety standards and research, design, licensing, construction, operation, and finances, with data by reactor, quarterly journal, 3352-4

Oil company production and imports by type, and financial data, 1975-86, annual rpt, 3164-74.1

Oil industry mergers and acquisitions impacts on market concentration, with background data, 1970-84, 9406-1.58

Overseas Private Investment Corp activities, and lists of grants and insured projects and firms, FY88, annual rpt, 9904-3

Overseas Private Investment Corp finances and activities, with list of insured projects and firms, FY88, annual rpt, 9904-2

Panama Canal Commission finances and activities, with Canal traffic and local govt operations, FY88, annual rpt, 9664-3

Pension Benefit Guaranty Corp activities and finances, FY88 and projected to FY98, annual rpt, 9674-1

Physicians malpractice insurance premium costs and growth rate, alternative estimates by risk class and State, 1975-85, 4658-27

Postal Service activities, financial statements, and employment, FY84-88, annual rpt, 9864-1

Postal Service finances, appropriations, and debt financing, selected years FY72-88, annual rpt, 9864-5.4

Postal Service inspection activities, expenses, and staff, FY88, annual rpt, 9864-8

Postal Service operating costs, itemized by class of mail, FY88, annual rpt, 9864-4

Postal Service revenue and mail volume by class, and special service transactions, quarterly rpt, 9862-1

Postal Service revenue, costs, and volume, by service type and class of mail, FY88, annual rpt, 9864-2

Poultry (broiler) production, slaughter, prices, and processing industry operations, 1950s-87, 1568-279

Prison Industries (Federal) finances and operations, FY88, annual rpt, 6244-3

Radio Free Europe and Radio Liberty broadcast and financial data, and compared to other intl broadcasters, FY88, annual rpt, 10314-1

Railroad (Amtrak) finances and operations, FY88, annual rpt, 29524-1

see also Depreciation

see also Educational finance

see also Energy production costs

see also Farm income

see also Operating ratios

see also Payroll

see also Production costs

see also under By Industry in the "Index by Categories"

Business inventories

Alcoholic beverages and tobacco production, removals, stocks, and material used, by State, monthly rpt series, 8486–1

Assets and debts of private sector, balance sheets by segment, 1949-88, semiannual rpt, 9365–4.1

Auto industry finances and operations, trade by country, and prices of selected US and foreign models, monthly rpt, 9882–8

Auto production, inventories, and inventory/sales ratio, model year 1988, annual article, 2702–1.901

Building materials production, shipments, and stocks, by type, bimonthly rpt, 2042–1.6

Business and financial statistics, historic trends, 1988 annual chartbook, 9364–2.3

Business Conditions Digest, economic, business, and financial devs and cyclical fluctuations, monthly rpt, 2702–3

Business statistics, detailed data for major industries and economic indicators, *Survey of Current Business*, monthly rpt, 2702–1

Chemicals and oil products shipments, firms, trade, and use, by product, periodic Current Industrial Rpt series, 2506–8

Clay and glass production, shipments, trade, and stocks, by product, periodic Current Industrial Rpt series, 2506–9

Construction industries census, 1987: establishments, employment, receipts, and expenditures, by SIC 4-digit industry and State, final industry rpt series, 2373–1

Cotton (long staple) production, prices, exports, stocks, and mill use, monthly rpt, 1309–12

Cotton linters production, stocks, use, and prices, monthly rpt, 1309–10

Cotton, wool, and synthetic fiber production, prices, trade, and use, periodic situation rpt with articles, 1561–1

Department store inventory price indexes, by class of item, monthly table, 6762–7

Economic indicators and components, and Fed Reserve 4th District business and financial conditions, monthly chartbook, 9377–10

Economic indicators and components, current data and annual trends, monthly rpt, 23842–1.1; 23842–1.3

Fertilizer (inorganic) shipments, trade, use, and firms, by product and State, with stocks, 1988, annual Current Industrial Rpt, 2506–8.13

Flow-of-funds accounts, savings, investments, and credit statements, quarterly rpt, 9365–3.3

Food (processed) production and stocks by State, shipments, exports, ingredients, and use, periodic Current Industrial Rpt series, 2506–4

Imports and tariff provisions effect on US industries and products, investigations with background financial and operating data, series, 9886–4

Imports injury to US industries from foreign subsidized products and sales at less than fair value, investigations with background financial and operating data, series, 9886–19

Imports injury to US industries from foreign subsidized products, investigations with background financial and operating data, series, 9886–15

Imports injury to US industries from sales at less than fair value, investigations with background financial and operating data, series, 9886–14

Input-output structure of US economy, detailed interindustry transactions for 84 industries, and components of final demand, 1983, annual article, 2702–1.909

Inventories and ratio to sales, by industry div, 1947-88, annual rpt, 204–1.1; 204–1.3

Lumber, paper, and related products shipments, trade, stocks, and use, periodic Current Industrial Rpt series, 2506–7

Machinery and equipment production, shipments, trade, stocks, orders, use, and firms, by product, periodic Current Industrial Rpt series, 2506–12

Manufacturers shipments, inventories, and orders, by SIC 2- to 3-digit industry, monthly Current Industrial Rpt, 2506–3.1

Manufacturing and trade inventories, sales, and inventory/sales ratios, quarterly article, 2702–1.33

Manufacturing census, 1987: financial and operating data, for SIC 4-digit industries by product, preliminary industry rpt series, 2491–1

Metals (intermediate product) shipments, trade, and inventories, by product, periodic Current Industrial Rpt series, 2506–11

Metals (primary) demand relation to consumption patterns and economic, trade, and technological factors, 1960s-82, 5608–159

Metals (primary) production, shipments, trade, stocks, and material used, by product, periodic Current Industrial Rpt series, 2506–10

Middle Atlantic States manufacturing business outlook, monthly survey rpt, 9387–11

Military commissaries in Europe, test sales of US beef and pork, and patron survey results, 1986, hearing, 21208–28

Mineral Industry Surveys, commodity reviews of production, trade, stocks, and use, monthly rpt series, 5612–1

Mineral Industry Surveys, commodity reviews of production, trade, stocks, and use, quarterly rpt series, 5612–2

Minerals (strategic) supply, demand, trade, and foreign and US industry devs by firm and country, by commodity, bimonthly rpt with articles, 5602–4

Minerals of strategic and technological importance, supply, imports, and use, with foreign comparisons, commodity rpt series, 5606–9

Mobile home placements and prices by State, and dealer inventories, by region, monthly rpt, 2382–1

Multinatl firms US affiliates, finances, and operations, by industry, world area of parent firm, and State, 1987, annual rpt, 2704–4

Multinatl US firms and foreign affiliates finances and operations, by industry of parent firm and affiliate, world area, and country, preliminary 1987, annual rpt, 2704–5

Natl income and product accounts and components, *Survey of Current Business*, monthly rpt, 2702–1.21; 2702–1.26

Nonprofit charitable organizations finances, and assets and grants of top 10, 1985, article, 8302–2.923

Phosphate rock production, sales, trade, and use, 1989, Mineral Industry Surveys, annual rpt, 5614–20

Rail shipments of grain, by commodity and port region, and car fleet requirements, 1949-88 with projections to 2001, 1278–14

Retail trade sales and inventories, by kind of business, region, and selected State, MSA, and city, monthly rpt, 2413–3

Retail trade sales, inventories, purchases, gross margin, and accounts receivable, by SIC 2- to 4-digit kind of business and form of ownership, 1987, annual rpt, 2413–5

Statistical Abstract of US, social, political, and economic data, 1790-2025, comprehensive annual compilation, 2324–1.3

Steel (stainless and alloy tool) production, employment, finances, and US producers inventories and unfilled orders, 1987-88, annual rpt, 9884–22

Steel export ceilings under voluntary restraint agreements, by country and product, with Western US steel industry impact, 1989 rpt, 9886–4.136

Steel industry finances and operations by product, and modernization efforts, as of June 1989, last issue of annual rpt, 9884–16

Tax (income) returns filed by type of filer, selected income items, quarterly rpt, 8302–2.1

Tax (income) returns of corporations, income and tax items by asset size and detailed industry, 1986, annual rpt, 8304–4; 8304–21

Tax (income) returns of partnerships, income statement items by industry group, 1986, annual article, 8302–2.903

Tax (income) returns of sole proprietorships, income statement items, by industry group, 1987, annual article, 8302–2.904

Textile mill production, trade, sales, stocks, and material used, by product, region, and State, periodic Current Industrial Rpt series, 2506–5

Truck and warehouse services finances and inventory, by SIC 2- to 4-digit industry, 1988 survey, annual rpt, 2413–14

Vaccine and toxoid shipments, by product type, July-Dec 1986, 4205–22

Wholesale trade census, 1987: employment, establishments, finances, and operations, by SIC 2- to 4-digit kind of business, MSA, county, and city, State rpt series, 2405–1

Wholesale trade sales and inventories, by SIC 2- to 3-digit kind of business, monthly rpt, 2413–7

Wholesale trade sales, inventories, purchases, and gross margins, by SIC 2- to 3-digit kind of business and form of ownership, 1988, annual rpt, 2413–13

see also Agricultural stocks

see also Business orders

see also Coal stocks

see also Energy stocks and inventories

see also Petroleum stocks

Business loans

see Commercial credit

Business machines and equipment

County Business Patterns, 1987: employment, establishments, and payroll, by SIC 2- to 4-digit industry and county, annual State rpt series, 2326–8

DOD prime contract awards, by detailed procurement category, FY85-88, annual rpt, 3544–18

Electric utilities privately owned, detailed finances and operations by firm, 1987, annual rpt, 3164–23.1

Employment, earnings, and hours, by selected SIC 1- to 4-digit industry, State, and for 262 MSAs, 1972-87, 6748–81

Employment, earnings, and hours, by SIC 1- to 4-digit industry, monthly 1983-Feb 1989, annual rpt, 6744–4

Employment of minorities and women, by occupation, SIC 1- to 3- digit industry, State, and MSA, 1986, annual rpt, 9244–1

Exports of US, detailed commodities by country, monthly rpt, 2422–3

Financial instns financial and operating statements by deposit size, Fed Reserve functional cost analysis, 1988, annual rpt, 9364–6

House of Representatives salaries, expenses, and contingent fund disbursement, detailed listings, quarterly rpt, 21942–1

Imports of US, detailed Schedule A commodities by country, monthly rpt, 2422–2

Imports of US given duty-free treatment for value of US material sent abroad, and impacts on US industry and employment, by commodity and country, 1987, annual rpt, 9884–14

Injuries from use of consumer products, by severity, victim age, and detailed product, 1988, annual rpt, 9164–6

Input-output structure of US economy, detailed interindustry transactions for 84 industries, and components of final demand, 1983, annual article, 2702–1.909

Manufacture of capital goods, productivity, labor cost indexes, and trade and trade balance impacts of economic conditions, with foreign comparisons, 1970s-88, article, 9385–1.909

Manufacturing annual survey, 1986: financial and operating data, by SIC 2- to 4-digit industry, series, 2506–15

Manufacturing census, 1987: financial and operating data, for SIC 4-digit industries by product, preliminary rpt, 2491–1.66

Multinatl US firms and foreign affiliates finances and operations, by industry of parent firm and affiliate, world area, and country, preliminary 1987, annual rpt, 2704–5

Natural gas interstate pipeline company detailed financial and operating data, by firm, 1988, annual rpt, 3164–38

Occupational injury and illness rates, by SIC 2- to 4-digit industry, 1987, annual rpt, 6844–1

OECD trade, total and for 4 major countries, and US trade by country, by commodity, 1970-87, world area rpt series, 9116–1

Pollution abatement capital and operating costs, by SIC 2-to 4-digit industry and State, 1986, annual Current Industrial Rpt, 2506–3.6

Price deflators and price indexes for computers and office equipment, 1983-88, article, 2702–1.902

Price indexes (producer), by stage of processing and detailed commodity, monthly rpt, 6762–6

Price indexes (producer), by stage of processing and detailed commodity, monthly 1988, annual rpt, 6764–2

Retail trade census, 1987: employment, establishments, sales, and payroll, by SIC 2- to 4-digit kind of business, MSA, county, and city, State rpt series, 2397–1

Science, engineering, and technical employment in manufacturing, by field, occupation, and industry, 1986, triennial rpt, 9627–23

Shipments, trade, use, and firms, for office machines by product, 1988, annual Current Industrial Rpt, 2506–12.2

Statistical Abstract of US, social, political, and economic data, 1790-2025, comprehensive annual compilation, 2324–1.3

Tax (income) returns of corporations, income and tax items by asset size and detailed industry, 1986, annual rpt, 8304–4; 8304–21

Thefts, and value of property stolen and recovered, by property type, 1988, annual rpt, 6224–2.1

Wholesale trade census, 1987: employment, establishments, finances, and operations, by SIC 2- to 4-digit kind of business, MSA, county, and city, State rpt series, 2405–1

see also Computer industry and products

see also Office supplies

see also under By Commodity in the "Index by Categories"

Business management

Banks failures, by type of charter and mgmt weakness, audit activity, asset size, age, and State, 1984-88, GAO rpt, 26111–61

Banks financial performance, risk assessment, and regulation, 1988 annual conf papers, 9375–7

County Business Patterns, 1987: employment, establishments, and payroll, by SIC 2- to 4-digit industry and county, annual State rpt series, 2326–8

Japan corporate investment spending relation to firm cash flow and bank and capital market borrowing, various periods 1977-86, technical paper, 9366–6.200

Japan corporate investment spending relation to firm cash flow, security holdings, and industry structure, 1977-82, technical paper, 9366–6.196

Minority Business Dev Centers mgmt and financial aid, and characteristics of businesses, by region and State, FY88, annual rpt, 2104–6

Multinatl US firms and foreign affiliates finances and operations, by industry of parent firm and affiliate, world area, and country, preliminary 1987, annual rpt, 2704–5

Natural gas interstate pipeline company detailed financial and operating data, by firm, 1988, annual rpt, 3164–38

Savings instns failures by State, with exam of mgmt weaknesses and regulatory activity, 1980s-87, GAO rpt, 26111–62

Savings instns regulatory issues, mgmt, and FHLB system and member finances and operations, monthly journal, 8432–2; 9312–1

Service industries census, 1987: establishments, receipts, employment, and payroll, by SIC 2- to 4-digit kind of business, MSA, county, and city, State rpt series, 2391–1

Statistical Abstract of US, social, political, and economic data, 1790-2025, comprehensive annual compilation, 2324–1.3

see also Business outlook and attitude surveys

see also Consultants

see also Executives and managers

see also Industrial purchasing

see also Industrial siting

see also Labor-management relations, general

see also Labor-management relations, local and regional

Business orders

Business and financial statistics, historic trends, 1988 annual chartbook, 9364–2.3

Business Conditions Digest, economic, business, and financial devs and cyclical fluctuations, monthly rpt, 2702–3

Business statistics, detailed data for major industries and economic indicators, Survey of Current Business, monthly rpt, 2702–1

Economic indicators and components, current data and annual trends, monthly rpt, 23842–1.3

Machinery and equipment production, shipments, trade, stocks, orders, use, and firms, by product, periodic Current Industrial Rpt series, 2506–12

Manufacturers shipments and new and unfilled orders, 1947-88, annual rpt, 204–1.3

Manufacturers shipments, inventories, and orders, by SIC 2- to 3-digit industry, monthly Current Industrial Rpt, 2506–3.1

Middle Atlantic States manufacturing business outlook, monthly survey rpt, 9387–11

Minerals (strategic) supply, demand, trade, and foreign and US industry devs by firm and country, by commodity, bimonthly rpt with articles, 5602–4

Minority Business Dev Centers mgmt and financial aid, and characteristics of businesses, by region and State, FY88, annual rpt, 2104–6

Natural gas interstate pipeline company capacity, use, sales, deliveries, and prices, by firm and Northeast State, 1980-88, 3166–6.35

Natural gas interstate pipeline company reserves and production, by firm, 1963-88 and deliverability projected to 2008, annual rpt, 3164–33

Shipbuilding costs, deliveries, and contracts, by coastal district and shipyard, various periods 1971-88, annual rpt, 7704–12.1

Ships under foreign flag owned by US firms and foreign affiliates, by type, owner, and country of registry and construction, as of July 1989, semiannual rpt, 7702–3

Statistical Abstract of US, social, political, and economic data, 1790-2025, comprehensive annual compilation, 2324–1.3

Steel (stainless and alloy tool) production, employment, finances, and US producers inventories and unfilled orders, 1987-88, annual rpt, 9884–22

Steel industry finances and operations by product, and modernization efforts, as of June 1989, last issue of annual rpt, 9884–16

Textile mill production, trade, sales, stocks, and material used, by product, region, and State, periodic Current Industrial Rpt series, 2506–5

Uranium marketing, contracts, prices, utility shipments, and trade, 1982-88 and projected to 2000, annual rpt, 3164–65.2

Uranium mining and milling industries finances and operations, with selected foreign comparisons, 1970s-87 and projected to 2000, annual rpt, 3164–82

Business outlook and attitude surveys

Alien workers (unauthorized) employer sanctions impacts on farm labor supply in Western US, with background data, 1986-89, GAO rpt, 26121–310

Assets (depreciable) class lives measurement, investment, and industry operations, asset class rpt series, 8006–5

Ceramics (advanced) technical info of Japan, US industry use and views on value, 1988 survey, 2008–28

Child care leave of absence for employees, policies, coverage, and attitudes, by employee characteristics, 1980-87, hearings, 25548–95

Farm credit conditions and real estate values, Fed Reserve 11th District, quarterly rpt, 9379–11

Farm credit conditions, earnings, and expenses, Fed Reserve 9th District, quarterly rpt, 9383–11

Hospice participation in Medicare, program provisions affecting participation, and claims processing time by carrier, 1987-89, GAO rpt, 26121–311

Middle Atlantic States manufacturing business outlook, monthly survey rpt, 9387–11

North Central States business and economic conditions, Fed Reserve 9th District, quarterly journal, 9383–19

North Central States farm credit conditions and economic devs, Fed Reserve 7th District, biweekly rpt, 9375–10

Physicians Medicare assigned-fee use, attitudes, and project to encourage patient use of assignment physician, 1988 rpt, 4658–30

Southeastern States farm credit conditions and real estate values, Fed Reserve 5th District, quarterly table, 9389–17

Technology-intensive manufacturing methods use and plans, with data by technology, selected industry, and firm and market characteristics, 1988 survey, 2508–1

Technology-intensive small businesses sales, exports, siting, technology transfer, views on competitiveness, 1988 survey, hearing, 21728–69

Western States farm real estate values, and nonreal estate farm loan trends, monthly rpt, quarterly data, 9381–2

Women-owned business mgmt issues, SBA loans, Federal contracts by agency, and owners views on Michigan business climate, FY79-88, hearings, 21728–68

see also National Survey of Small Business Finances

Business services

see Accounting and auditing

see Advertising

see Computer use

see Consultants

see Credit bureaus and agencies

see Direct marketing

see Employment services

see Janitorial and maintenance services

see Public relations

see Service industries

Busing

see School busing

Buss, Terry F.

"Entrepreneurs Find Niche Even in Rural Economies", 1502–7.913

Butani, Shail J.

"Coal Mining: Characterization of the 1986 Mining Workforce", 5606–8.1

"Metal and Nonmetal Mining: Characterization of the 1986 Mining Workforce", 5606–8.2

"Metallic Mining: Characterization of the 1986 Mining Workforce", 5606–8.3

"Nonmetallic Mining: Characterization of the 1986 Mining Workforce", 5606–8.6

"Sand and Gravel Mining: Characterization of the 1986 Mining Workforce", 5606–8.5

"Stone Mining: Characterization of the 1986 Mining Workforce", 5606–8.4

Butler, Gertrude S.

"Foreign Ownership of U.S. Agricultural Land Through Dec. 31, 1988: County-Level Data", 1584–3

Butler, Margaret A.

"Farm Entrepreneurial Population, 1987", 1598–252

Butter

see Dairy industry and products

Buxton, Boyd M.

"Economic Impact of Consumer Health Concerns About Alar on Apples", 1561–6.902

Buzzanell, Peter J.

"China's Sugar Industry: Performance and Prospects", 1561–14.901

"Cuba's Sugar Economy: Recent Performance and Challenges for the 1990's", 1561–14.903

Bye, Barry V.

"Eliminating the Medicare Waiting Period for Social Security Disabled-Worker Beneficiaries", 4742–1.915

"Statistical Methods for the Estimation of Costs in the Medicare Waiting Period for Social Security Disabled-Worker Beneficiaries", 4746–26.6

"Two Notes on Sampling Variance Estimates from the 1984 SIPP Public-Use Files", 2626–10.82

Byerly, Edwin

"State Population and Household Estimates, with Age, Sex, and Components of Change: 1981-88", 2546–3.161

Cable Communications Policy Act

Deregulation of CATV in 1986, impacts on prices, services, and finances, by system size, 1986-88, GAO rpt, 26113–431

Cable television

Copyright royalty fees from CATV, and funds available for distribution, 1986, annual rpt, 26404–2

CPI by component for US city average, and by region, population size, and for 27 metro areas, monthly rpt, 6762–2

Deregulation of CATV in 1986, impacts on prices, services, and finances, by system size, 1986-88, GAO rpt, 26113–431

Employment of minorities and discrimination charges in telecommunications industries, with data by industry and selected firm, 1970s-88, hearings, 21368–113

Finances, operations, and industry devs for telecommunications, with data by service type, firm, and country, 1950s-80s, 2808–27

Licensing activities of FCC, by class of operation, FY88, annual rpt, 9284–4

Price indexes (producer), by stage of processing and detailed commodity, monthly rpt, 6762–6

Price indexes (producer), by stage of processing and detailed commodity, monthly 1988, annual rpt, 6764–2

Statistical Abstract of US, social, political, and economic data, 1790-2025, comprehensive annual compilation, 2324–1.3

Cacy, J. A.

"U.S. Economy in 1989: An Uncertain Outlook", 9381–1.901

Cadmium

see Metals and metal industries

Cafferata, Gail L.

"Marital Status, Living Arrangements, and the Use of Health Services by Elderly Persons", 4188–54

Cage, Robert

"Spending Differences Across Occupational Fields", 6722–1.961

Caguas, P.R.

see also under By SMSA or MSA in the "Index by Categories"

Calabrese, Anthony

"Contaminants in Hudson-Raritan Estuary Water and Influence of Cold Storage upon Its Chemical Composition", 2168–109

Calcium

see Nonmetallic minerals and mines

see Vitamins and nutrients

California

Abortions by patient characteristics, rates for all and 1st abortions, and related deaths in US and other countries, 1989 hearing, 21408–113

Agriculture census, 1987: farms, farmland, production and costs, and operator characteristics, advance State and county rpts, 2330–1.6

Agriculture census, 1987: farms, farmland, production, finances, and operator characteristics, by county, final State rpt, 2331–1.5

AIDS patients Medicaid enrollment, services use, and charges, for California, 1981-84, article, 4652-1.907

Alien workers (unauthorized) employer sanctions, enforcement costs, compliance, and job discrimination, 1988 annual GAO rpt, 26104-19

Alien workers (unauthorized) employer sanctions impacts on farm labor supply in Western US, with background data, 1986-89, GAO rpt, 26121-310

Asian American earnings, and employment and other characteristics, by detailed origin and whether foreign-born, 1980, 11046-7.2

Bank deposits in FDIC-insured commercial and savings banks, by instn, State, and county, as of June 1988, annual regional rpt, 9295-3.6

Bankruptcy court mediation program caseloads and dispositions, for California southern district, 1986-88, 18408-40

Banks (foreign) US branches assets and liabilities, total and for 3 States, monthly rpt, quarterly data, 9362-1.4

Banks in California owned by Japanese and other foreign banks, assets, portfolio composition, and cost of funds, 1987-88, article, 9393-8.906

Bean (dried) prices by State, market activity, and foreign and US production, use, stocks, and trade, weekly rpt, 1311-17

Celery acreage planted and growing, by growing area, monthly rpt, 1621-14

Citrus production and use, by crop and State, 1981/82-1986/87, 1641-4

Coal production and mines by county, prices, productivity, miners, reserves, and stocks, by mining method and State, 1987-88, annual rpt, 3164-25

Coastal areas environmental conditions, fish, wildlife, use, and mgmt, 1989 rpt, 5506-9.36

County Business Patterns, 1987: employment, establishments, and payroll, by SIC 2- to 4-digit industry and county, annual State rpt, 2326-8.6

Dairy prices, by product and selected area, with related marketing data, 1988, annual rpt, 1317-1

Deaths and rates, by detailed location, cause, and demographic characteristics, 1987, US Vital Statistics annual rpt, 4144-3.1

Disabled SSI beneficiaries Medicaid services use and costs, by diagnosis and whether covered by Medicare, 1984, article, 4652-1.947

DOD prime contract awards, by contractor, service branch, State, and city, FY88, annual rpt, 3544-22

Employment, earnings, and hours, by selected SIC 1- to 4-digit industry, State, and for 262 MSAs, 1972-87, 6748-81.1

Fed Govt spending in States and local areas, by type, State, county, and city, FY88, annual rpt, 2464-3

Fed Govt spending in States, by type, program, agency, and State, FY88, annual rpt, 2464-2

Fish and shellfish catch, prices, and fisheries economic status, for Pacific coast, 1986-87, annual rpt series, 2164-16

HHS financial aid, by program, recipient, State, and city, FY88, annual regional listing, 4004-3.9

Homeless children educational enrollment and needs, 1988, annual State rpt, 4804-35.6

Hospital reimbursement by Medicare under prospective payment system, impacts on subacute care, 1988 rpt, 17206-2.8

Hospital use and costs of Medicaid enrollees related to selected characteristics, 1980, article, 4652-1.949

Housing costs appreciation impacts on income distribution in selected areas, 1978-88, article, 9373-1.907

Income (personal) per capita and by source, and earnings by industry div, by State, MSA, and county, 1982-87, annual regional rpt, 2704-2.5

Irrigation subsidies of Reclamation Bur, costs to Fed Govt and surplus crop production, 1985-86, 21448-40

Lettuce (iceberg) from California, price by marketing stage, 1980-88, article, 1561-11.904

Lumber mill occupational injury and illness rates and workdays lost, by selected State and SIC 4-digit industry, 1978-87, article, 6722-1.945

Medicaid enrollment, and service use and costs by service type, by eligibility type, for 5 States, 1980-84, article, 4652-1.919

Medicaid enrollment, services use, and costs, by eligibility type and length of enrollment, for 2 States, 1980-83, article, 4652-1.906

Mineral Industry Surveys, State reviews of production, 1988, preliminary annual rpt, 5614-6

Minerals Yearbook, 1987, Vol 2 preprints: State review of production and sales by commodity, and business activity, annual rpt, 5604-16.6

Minerals Yearbook, 1987, Vol 2: State reviews of production, sales, and firms, by commodity, and business activity, annual rpt, 5604-34

Mobile home industry occupational injury and illness rates and workdays lost, by selected State, 1978-87, article, 6722-1.932

Mortgage originations by type, with California fixed rate loans, rates, and secondary market placements, 1978-87, article, 9312-1.904

Nursing home admissions and discharges for Medicaid patients with prior hospitalization, for 3 States, 1981, article, 4652-1.942

Nursing home compliance with Medicare and Medicaid regulations, and patient characteristics, by facility, 1987/88, annual State rpt, 4654-15.5

Oil and gas extraction production workers and wages by occupation, and benefits, by location, 1988 survey, 6787-6.240

Older persons eligible for nursing home care, cost of home and community services, Medicaid waiver program in 2 States, 1981-84, article, 4652-1.943

Older persons in California preventive health care program, tests, results, referrals, and participant characteristics, 1985-86, article, 4042-3.918

Otter population off California coast, 1982-88, annual rpt, 14734-1

Peppers (dried chili and paprika) acreage and production in California and New Mexico, 1971-88, FAS annual circular, 1925-15.1

Pollution (air) ozone emissions from autos in southern California, under alternative reduction proposals, 1975-84, hearing, 21368-104

Pregnancy-related services use and costs, for Medicaid beneficiaries in 3 States, 1983-84, article, 4652-1.938

Retail trade census, 1987: employment, establishments, sales, and payroll, by SIC 2- to 4-digit kind of business, MSA, county, and city, State rpt, 2397-1.5

Rice market activities, prices, inspections, sales, trade, supply, and use, for US and selected foreign markets, weekly rpt, 1313-8

Rice stocks on and off farms and total in all positions, periodic rpt, 1621-7

River and stream environmental conditions, fish, wildlife, use, and mgmt, 1989 rpt, 5506-9.38; 5506-9.39

Savings and loan assns cost structure, for stock and mutual S&Ls in California, 1982, working paper, 9387-8.171

Savings and loan assns cost structure impacts on conversions from mutual to stock ownership, for California, 1982, working paper, 9387-8.172

Savings instns, FHLB 11th District member offices, locations, savings balances, and accounts, quarterly listing, 9302-20

Service industries census, 1987: employment, establishments, receipts, and payroll, by SIC 2- to 4-digit kind of business, MSA, county, and city, State rpt, 2391-1.5

Statistical Abstract of US, social, political, and economic data, with foreign comparisons, 1790-2025, comprehensive annual compilation, 2324-1

Timber in California, hardwood resources and mortality, by species, land class and ownership, and county, 1984-85, 1208-291

Timber in northwestern US and British Columbia, production, prices, trade, and employment, quarterly rpt, 1202-3

Trucking industry deregulation in 1980, impacts on finances and safety, mid 1970s-88, hearing, 21648-55

Vegetables (broccoli, asparagus, cauliflower) industry intl competitiveness, investigation with background financial and operating data and foreign comparisons, 1988 rpt, 9886-4.133

Vegetables production by leading county and crop, 1982, article, 1502-4.903

Vocational education for disadvantaged and handicapped funding of Fed Govt, by selected State and district, 1985-89 and projected to 2000, GAO rpt, 26121-286

Water quality in California, trace metal concentrations in San Joaquin river bed sediment, 1985, 5668-91

Water storage in San Joaquin Valley reservoirs, 1982, article, 1502-4.903

Water supply and quality in streams and lakes, and groundwater levels in wells, by drainage basin, 1987, annual State rpt, 5666-10.5

Water supply and quality in streams and lakes, and groundwater levels in wells, by drainage basin, 1988, annual State rpt, 5666-16.5

Waterborne commerce (domestic) of US, freight by major commodity group, vessel type, and port, 1986, annual rpt, 7704-7

Wholesale trade census, 1987: employment, establishments, finances, and operations, by SIC 2- to 4-digit kind of business, MSA, county, and city, State rpt, 2405–1.5

Wildlife-related recreation, hunting, and fishing participation and spending, detailed data, 1985 survey, quinquennial State rpt, 5506–6.5

Wind energy production, turbines, and air pollutant reductions, for California, 1988 and projected to 2000, hearing, 25318–75

see also Alameda County, Calif.

see also Anaheim, Calif.

see also Bakersfield, Calif.

see also Contra Costa County, Calif.

see also Fairfield, Calif.

see also Fresno, Calif.

see also Lompoc, Calif.

see also Long Beach, Calif.

see also Los Angeles, Calif.

see also Los Angeles County, Calif.

see also Marin County, Calif.

see also Monterey, Calif.

see also Napa, Calif.

see also Oakland, Calif.

see also Oxnard, Calif.

see also Petaluma, Calif.

see also Porterville, Calif.

see also Redding, Calif.

see also Riverside, Calif.

see also Sacramento, Calif.

see also Salinas, Calif.

see also San Bernardino, Calif.

see also San Diego, Calif.

see also San Francisco, Calif.

see also San Jose, Calif.

see also San Mateo County, Calif.

see also Santa Ana, Calif.

see also Santa Barbara, Calif.

see also Santa Cruz, Calif.

see also Santa Maria, Calif.

see also Santa Rosa, Calif.

see also Seaside, Calif.

see also Stockton, Calif.

see also Tulare County, Calif.

see also Vallejo, Calif.

see also Ventura, Calif.

see also Visalia, Calif.

see also Yuba City, Calif.

see also under By State in the "Index by Categories"

Calomiris, Charles W.

"Deposit Insurance: Lessons from the Record", 9375–1.904

Cambodia

Agricultural and food production and indexes, total and for selected commodities, by country, 1970s-88, annual rpt, 1524–12

Agricultural trade of US, by detailed commodity and country, 1988, semiannual rpt, 1522–4

AID activities and funding by project and function, FY90, and developing countries summary socioeconomic data from 1960s, annual rpt, 9904–4.6

AID economic aid to developing countries, obligations and disbursements by country, quarterly rpt, 9912–4

Economic and military aid and loans from US and intl agencies, by program and country, FY46-87, annual rpt, 9914–5

Economic, social, political, and geographic summary data, by country, 1989, annual factbook, 9114–2

Exports and imports of US with Communist countries, by detailed commodity and country, quarterly rpt with articles, 9882–2

Human rights conditions in 170 countries, 1988, annual rpt, 21384–3

Military aid of US, arms sales, and training programs costs and budget requests, by program, world region, and country, FY88-90, annual rpt, 7144–13

Military spending, arms trade, and force strengths, with govt spending and population, by country, 1977-87, annual rpt, 9824–1

Minerals production, reserves, and industry role in domestic economy and world supply, 1988 country rpt, 5606–1.17

Minerals Yearbook, 1987, Vol 3: foreign country reviews of production, trade, and policy, by commodity, annual rpt, 5604–35

Minerals Yearbook, 1987, Vol 3 preprints: foreign country review of production, trade, and policy, by commodity, annual rpt, 5604–23.85

Population size, growth rates, and components of change, by country, projected 1989-2020 and trends from 1950, biennial rpt, 2324–9

Refugee resettlement programs and funding, arrivals by country of origin, and indicators of adjustment, by State, FY88, annual rpt, 4694–5

Refugees from Indochina, arrivals, and departures, by country of origin and resettlement, camp, and ethnicity, monthly rpt, 7002–4

UN voting record and share of votes in agreement with US, by issue, country, and world area, 1988, annual rpt, 7004–18

see also under By Foreign Country in the "Index by Categories"

Cambridge, Mass.

Housing and households detailed characteristics, and unit and neighborhood quality, by location, 1985 survey, MSA rpt, 2485–6.11

Cameroon

Agricultural and food production and indexes, total and for selected commodities, by country, 1970s-88, annual rpt, 1524–12

Agricultural exports of Africa by commodity, and relation to economic conditions and other factors, by country, 1960s-87, 1528–280

Agricultural production, prices, and trade, by country, 1960s-89, annual world region rpt, 1524–4.2

Agricultural trade of US, by detailed commodity and country, 1988, semiannual rpt, 1522–4

AID activities and funding by project and function, FY90, and developing countries summary socioeconomic data from 1960s, annual rpt, 9904–4.5

AID economic aid to developing countries, obligations and disbursements by country, quarterly rpt, 9912–4

AID loans repayment status and terms by program and country, and status of predecessor agency loans, quarterly rpt, 9912–3

Economic and military aid and loans from US and intl agencies, by program and country, FY46-87, annual rpt, 9914–5

Economic, social, political, and geographic summary data, by country, 1989, annual factbook, 9114–2

Exports and imports of US, by commodity and country, 1970-87, world area rpt, 9116–1.4

Exports and imports of US, by selected country, country group, and commodity group, 1988, annual rpt, 2044–37

Human rights conditions in 170 countries, 1988, annual rpt, 21384–3

Military aid of US, arms sales, and training programs costs and budget requests, by program, world region, and country, FY88-90, annual rpt, 7144–13

Military spending, arms trade, and force strengths, with govt spending and population, by country, 1977-87, annual rpt, 9824–1

Minerals Yearbook, 1987, Vol 3: foreign country reviews of production, trade, and policy, by commodity, annual rpt, 5604–35

Minerals Yearbook, 1987, Vol 3 preprints: foreign country review of production, trade, and policy, by commodity, annual rpt, 5604–23.80

Population size, growth rates, and components of change, by country, projected 1989-2020 and trends from 1950, biennial rpt, 2324–9

UN voting record and share of votes in agreement with US, by issue, country, and world area, 1988, annual rpt, 7004–18

see also under By Foreign Country in the "Index by Categories"

Campaign funds

Fed Election Commission activities, and campaign finances, various periods 1975-88, annual rpt, 9274–1

Fed Election Commission activities, campaign finances, elections, and procedures, press release series, 9276–1

Financial activity reported to Fed Election Commission, by type of filer, 1988 natl elections, biennial rpt series, 9276–2

Presidential election campaign fund contributions from income tax return check-off, 1973-89, press release, 9276–1.70

Statistical Abstract of US, social, political, and economic data, 1790-2025, comprehensive annual compilation, 2324–1.2

Tax (income) returns of individuals, detailed data, 1986, annual rpt, 8304–2

see also Political action committees

Campbell, Bruce C.

"Using 1990 National MCH Objectives To Assess Health Status and Risk in an American Indian Community", 4042–3.960

Camping

Canada travel to US by Province of residence, and characteristics of visit, by State, 1988, annual rpt, 2904–7

County Business Patterns, 1987: employment, establishments, and payroll, by SIC 2- to 4-digit industry and county, annual State rpt series, 2326–8

Forest Service activities and finances, by region and State, FY88, annual rpt, 1204–1.1

Forests (natl) recreational use, by type of activity and State, 1988, annual rpt, 1204–17

Injuries from use of consumer products, by severity, victim age, and detailed product, 1988, annual rpt, 9164–6

Natl park system visits and overnight stays, by park and State, 1988 and trends from 1979, annual rpt, 5544–12

Park natl system visits and overnight stays, by park and State, monthly rpt, 5542–4

Public lands acreage, grants, use, revenues, and allocations, by State, FY88, annual rpt, 5724–1.2

Service industries census, 1987: establishments, receipts, employment, and payroll, by SIC 2- to 4-digit kind of business, MSA, county, and city, State rpt series, 2391–1

Tax (income) returns of partnerships, income statement items by industry group, 1986, annual article, 8302–2.903

Tax (income) returns of sole proprietorships, income statement items, by industry group, 1987, annual article, 8302–2.904; 8302–2.921

Wilderness Natl Preservation System mgmt by Forest Service, regulation of commercial and recreational activities, and ranger views, 1985-88, GAO rpt, 26113–436

Wildlife-related recreation, hunting, and fishing participation and spending, detailed data by location, 1985 survey, quinquennial rpt, 5508–5

Canada

Abortions in US, by place of woman's residence and selected State of occurrence, 1986, US Vital Statistics annual rpt, 4146–5.108

Agricultural and food production and indexes, total and for selected commodities, by country, 1970s-88, annual rpt, 1524–12

Agricultural imports demand of Canada for US cotton, rice, and soybeans, alternative model results, 1983-85, article, 1502–3.901

Agricultural subsidies, consumer and producer equivalents by program, commodity, and major US trading partner, 1982-86, 1528–275

Agricultural trade among western hemisphere countries, and US duty-free imports, with listing of trade disputes and outcomes, 1960s-85, 1528–278

Agricultural trade and market impacts of eliminating foreign and US protectionist policies, model description and results, 1986, 1528–282

Agricultural trade by commodity and country, prices, and world market devs, monthly rpt, 1922–12

Agricultural trade of US, by detailed commodity and country, 1988, semiannual rpt, 1522–4

AIDS cases in prisons, test results, and prevention and control policies, by location, 1988 survey, annual rpt, 6064–22

Arms sales of US, foreign conditions on sales and impacts on US industry, with data by industry group and country, 1988 annual rpt, 104–25

Auto industry finances and operations, trade by country, and prices of selected US and foreign models, monthly rpt, 9882–8

Auto trade of Canada and US, and production, sales, prices, and employment, selected years 1965-85, annual rpt, 2044–35

Background Notes, summary social, political, and economic data, 1989 rpt, 7006–2.34

Banks failures and economic indicator variability, relation to bank branching and note issuance regulation, for US and Canada, various periods 1865-1987, article, 9383–6.904

Birds (duck) breeding population, by species, State, and Canada Province, 1988-89 with trends from 1955, annual rpt, 5504–30

Birds (waterfowl) population, habitat conditions, and migratory flight forecasts, for Canada and US by region, 1989 and trends from 1955, annual rpt, 5504–27

Birds (woodcock) population in US and Canada from 1968, and hunter harvest, by State, 1989, annual rpt, 5504–11

Businesses (foreign) activity in US, income tax returns, assets, and income statement items, by industry div, country, and world area, 1984-85, article, 8302–2.920

Caribbean Basin exports to OECD members, and US imports under preferential treatment programs, by commodity, 1980s-87, 2048–138

China trade, by commodity, world area, and country, 1985-87, 9118–10

Coal exports of US to Canada by mode of transport, and overseas, by district of origin, quarterly rpt, 3162–8

Coal production, trade, and govt subsidies, by country and country group, 1973-87 and projected to 2000, 2048–144

Collective bargaining negotiated wages, relation to contract duration and inflation and unemployment rates, model description and results for Canada, 1970s-83, working paper, 9387–8.191

Construction products market trends and indicators for Canada, with imports by country, 1960s-86, article, 2042–1.905

Cooking appliance thermostatic plugs from 4 countries, injury to US industry from foreign subsidized and less than fair value imports, investigation with background financial and operating data, 1988 rpt, 9886–19.63

Current account balance and related economic indicators, for US and 4 countries, 1980s-87, article, 9389–1.908

Deaths in US, by State of occurrence and birthplace abroad, 1986, US Vital Statistics annual rpt, 4144–2.1

Developing countries debt burden and economic conditions, and trade with industrialized countries, by country, 1970s-87, hearings, 25248–108

Developing countries loans from banks and govts, debt exposure of 7 developed countries, various periods 1980-88, GAO rpt, 26123–255

Dollar exchange rate trade-weighted index of Fed Reserve Bank of Atlanta, by world area, monthly rpt, 9371–15

Dollar exchange rate trade-weighted index of Fed Reserve Bank of Dallas, by world area, monthly rpt, 9379–13

Drug (cephalexin) generic capsules from Canada at less than fair value, injury to US industry, investigation with background financial and operating data, 1989 rpt, 9886–14.267

Economic and military aid and loans from US and intl agencies, by program and country, FY46-87, annual rpt, 9914–5

Economic and monetary trends, compounded annual rates of change for US and 10 major trading partners, quarterly rpt, 9391–7

Economic conditions, and oil production, use, and imports, by country, biweekly rpt, 9112–1

Economic conditions, consumer and stock prices and production indexes, 6 OECD countries and US, *Business Conditions Digest*, monthly rpt, 2702–3.10

Economic conditions in Communist and OECD countries, 1987, annual rpt, 7144–11

Economic conditions in Communist, OECD, and selected other countries, 1960s-88, annual rpt, 9114–4

Economic conditions, income, production, prices, employment, and trade, 1989 periodic country rpt, 2046–4.21; 2046–4.62

Economic conditions, policy, and trade practices, by country, 1986-88, annual rpt, 21384–5

Economic indicators, and dollar exchange rates, for selected OECD countries, 1980s-89, semiannual rpt, 8002–14

Economic, social, political, and geographic summary data, by country, 1989, annual factbook, 9114–2

Electric power generation projects on Columbia River, returns to Canada, projected 1989-2008, annual rpt, 3224–3.2

Electric power trade of US with Canada and Mexico, 1966-85, annual rpt, 3404–6.3

Electric power trade of US with Canada, purchase agreements, and grid interconnection capacity, 1960s-88 and projected to 1992, GAO rpt, 26113–228

Emergency fire and medical services operations, staff, and finances, for DC and compared to other US and Canadian cities, 1986, hearing, 21308–25

Energy-intensive industry output and operations, and US investment barriers, for energy-rich countries, 1984-88, 9886–4.142

Energy prices, by fuel type and end use, for 10 countries, 1980-88 annual rpt, 3164–50.6

Energy producers finances and operations, by energy type for US firms domestic and foreign operations, 1987, annual rpt, 3164–44.2

Energy production by type, and oil prices, trade, and use, by country group and selected country, monthly rpt, 9112–2

Energy use by sector, and production, by fuel type, country, and country group, projected 1988-2000 and trends from 1970, annual rpt, 3164–84

Export credit activity of Eximbank and 6 OECD countries, 1988, annual rpt, 9254–3

Exports and imports (waterborne) of US, by type of service, customs district, port, and world area, monthly rpt, 2422–7

Exports and imports of New England States, impacts of Canada-US trade agreement, with data by industry, commodity, and State, 1987, article, 9373–2.902

Exports and imports of US, by commodity group, world area, selected country, US coastal area and port, and mode of transport, monthly rpt, 2422–9

Exports and imports of US, by selected country, country group, and commodity group, 1988, annual rpt, 2044–37

Exports and imports of US shipped through Canada, by detailed commodity, customs district, and country, 1987, annual rpt, 7704–11

Exports and imports, trade agreements and relations, and USITC investigations, 1988, annual rpt, 9884–5

Exports, imports, and balances of US by commodity group, world area, and country, and related employment, 1970s-88, annual rpt, 2044–26

Exports, imports, and balances of US with major trading partners, by product category, 1984-88, annual chartbook, 9884–21

Farmland (US) owned by foreigners, holdings, acreage, and value by land use, owner country, State, and county, 1988, annual rpt, 1584–3

Financial instns assets and liabilities by item and instn type, 1976 and 1986, article, 9312–1.903

Fish (groundfish) imports from Canada, New Zealand, and Australia to western US, by species, 1983-87, annual rpt, 2164–16.1

Freight (waterborne domestic and foreign) by commodity, traffic, and passengers, by port and waterway, 1987, annual rpt, 3754–3.3

Fruit and vegetable imports of Canada from US and worldwide, by commodity, 1986-88, annual article, 1925–34.932

Fruit and vegetable shipments, and arrivals in US and Canada cities, by mode of transport and State and country of origin, 1988, annual rpt series, 1311–4

GNP of Canada, Japan, and Germany, relation to foreign and domestic industry output, 1961-84, technical paper, 9366–6.189

Grain production, use, exports, quality standards, storage, and prices, for 5 countries, 1960s-88, 26358–201.2

Great Lakes ship pilotage activities, costs, and traffic for US and Canada, and US testing and certificates, 1960s-87, 7308–192

Great Lakes toxic spills and human error, with data by pollutant source and site, 1984-86, conf, 14648–21

Great Lakes trade between US and Canada, and other foreign trade, by type of vessel, 1986, annual rpt, 7704–7.3

Great Lakes water levels fluctuations, causes, and impacts of alternative mgmt strategies, 1900s-88, series, 14646–1

Human rights conditions in 170 countries, 1988, annual rpt, 21384–3

Immigrants admitted to US, by class of admission, country of birth, and State and MSA of destination, FY88, annual rpt, 6264–4

Immigration to US, alien workers, visitors, deportations, and naturalizations, by country, FY88 and trends from 1820, annual rpt, 6264–2

Imports from US, impacts on US employment by exporting sector and major importer, 1980s-87, 2048–103

Imports of goods, services, and investment from US, trade barriers, impacts, and US actions, by country, 1988, annual rpt, 444–2

Imports of US given duty-free treatment for value of US material sent abroad, and impacts on US industry and employment, by commodity and country, 1987, annual rpt, 9884–14

Interest rate differentials among countries, US and 4 industrialized countries, 1960s-88, article, 9385–1.902

Investment (foreign direct) in US, by industry group and world area, 1987-88, annual article, 2702–1.929

Investment (foreign direct) in US, major transactions by type, industry, country, and US location, 1987, annual rpt, 2044–20

Investment (foreign direct) of US, by selected industry group and world area, 1986-88, annual article, 2702–1.930

Labor conditions, union coverage, and work accidents, 1989 annual country rpt, 6366–4.56

Life expectancy, total and disability-free, for Canada, 1951 and 1978, conf paper, 4147–4.26

Limousines from Canada, injury to US industry from foreign subsidized and less than fair value imports, investigation with background financial and operating data, 1989 rpt, 9886–19.67

Lumber exports from northwestern US ports by selected country, and US imports from Canada, quarterly rpt, 1202–3

Manufacturing labor costs and indexes, by selected country, 1975-88, annual rpt, 6824–3

Manufacturing labor costs and indexes, by selected country, 1975-88, semiannual rpt, 6822–3

Manufacturing labor productivity and unit costs for 14 countries, 1950-88, annual press release, 6864–1

Military aid of US, arms sales, and training, by country, FY50-88, annual rpt, 3904–3

Military aid of US, arms sales, and training programs costs and budget requests, by program, world region, and country, FY88-90, annual rpt, 7144–13

Military spending, arms trade, and force strengths, with govt spending and population, by country, 1977-87, annual rpt, 9824–1

Minerals Yearbook, 1987, Vol 3: foreign country reviews of production, trade, and policy, by commodity, annual rpt, 5604–35

Minerals Yearbook, 1987, Vol 3 preprints: foreign country review of production, trade, and policy, by commodity, annual rpt, 5604–23.14

Multinatl firms US affiliates, finances, and operations, by industry, world area of parent firm, and State, 1987, annual rpt, 2704–4

Multinatl US firms and foreign affiliates finances and operations, by industry of parent firm and affiliate, world area, and country, preliminary 1987, annual rpt, 2704–5

Natural gas imports and contracted supply from Canada and Mexico, by US pipeline firm, 1987-88, annual rpt, 3164–33.6

Nuclear power generation in US and 19 non-Communist countries, monthly rpt, 3162–24.10

Nuclear power plant capacity, generation, and operating status, by plant and foreign and US location, 1988 and projected to 2020, annual rpt, 3164–57

Nuclear power plant spent fuel and demand for uranium and enrichment service, for US and other country groups, projected 1989-2036, annual rpt, 3164–72

Oil production, trade, use, and stocks, by selected country and country group, monthly rpt, 3162–42

Oil production, use, stocks, and exports and prices for US, by country, detailed data, monthly rpt, 3162–24

Population size, growth rates, and components of change, by country, projected 1989-2020 and trends from 1950, biennial rpt, 2324–9

Pork from Canada, injury to US industry from foreign subsidized imports, investigation with background financial and operating data, 1989 rpt, 9886–15.72; 9886–15.74

Potash production, prices, trade by country, use, and sales, 1988 crop year, Mineral Industry Surveys, annual rpt, 5614–19

R&D funding by Fed Govt, by field, performer type, agency, and State, FY87-89, annual rpt, 9627–20

Rabies cases in animals and humans, by location for US, Mexico, and Canada, 1988, annual rpt, 4202–7.904

Radiation and radionuclide concentrations in air, water, and milk, monitoring results by State and site, quarterly rpt, 9192–5

Rails (steel) from Canada, injury to US industry from foreign subsidized and less than fair value imports, investigation with background financial and operating data, 1989 rpt, 9886–19.68

Science and engineering immigrants, by field, age, sex, country and world area of birth and last residence, and State, 1987 and trends from 1967, 9627–29

Social security payroll tax rates, costs, and funding balance, for Canada and US earnings-related aged benefits, 1988 and projected to 2100, article, 4742–1.913

Social security trust funds surpluses impact on govt budgets, for 3 countries and US, 1960-86, article, 9373–1.905

Space satellites and other objects launched since 1957, quarterly listing, 9502–2

St Lawrence Seaway ship, cargo, and passenger traffic, and toll revenue, 1988 and trends from 1959, annual rpt, 7744–2

Statistical program dev in capital stock measurement and social policy simulation modeling, 1988 conf papers, 2702–1.918

Telecommunication domestic and overseas rates, by type of service and area served, various dates 1988, annual rpt, 9284–6.6

Carbon black
see Nonmetallic minerals and mines
Carbon dioxide
see Air pollution
Carbon monoxide
see Air pollution
Carcinogens
Chemistry, sources, environment and health risks, and regulation of carcinogens, by substance and brand, 1989, annual rpt, 4044–15
Cigarette smoke tar, nicotine, and carbon monoxide content, by brand, 1988, 9408–53
Great Lakes basin pollutant discharges, sources, and control program activities, 1987, biennial rpt, 14644–1
Health effects of hazardous substances, concentrations in environment, and household products composition, with data by selected location, 1988 hearings, 21408–112
Herbicide use in natl forests, exposure and cancer risk by type and application mode, 1988 rpt, 1208–295
Housing energy conservation program of BPA, energy savings and indoor air quality under alternative methods, projected 1986-2006, 3228–9
Lake Ontario eutrophication and pollutant levels, by contaminant type and site, 1967-85, 14648–22
Natl Cancer Inst contracts and grants, by recipient and location, FY88, annual listing, 4474–28
Pollutants health effects, concentrations in food and environment, sources, and human intake methodology and data needs, series, 9186–9
Pollutants health effects, concentrations in food and environment, sources, human intake, and regulation, series, 9186–8
Polychlorinated biphenyls levels in Great Lakes environment, humans, and animals, and emissions sources, by site, 1970s-85, conf, 14648–19
Research and testing activities under Natl Toxicology Program, FY87 and planned FY88, annual rpt, 4044–16
Smoking and health research rpts, 1988, last issue of annual listing, 4204–19
Smoking and health research summaries, bimonthly rpt, 4202–8
Tobacco (smokeless) use by youth and adults, user characteristics, and sales, 1970s-86, papers, 4478–188
Waste (hazardous) mgmt, effectiveness of alternative technologies, 1989 conf papers, biennial rpt, 9184–19
see also Asbestos contamination
see also Dioxins
see also Radiation
see also Radon
Cardiovascular diseases
Cases of acute and chronic conditions, disability, absenteeism, and health services use, by selected characteristics, 1988, annual rpt, 4147–10.170
Cases of cardiovascular diseases, health care services use and costs, and productivity losses, by selected characteristics, 1980, 4146–12.26
Deaths and rates, by cause, age, sex, marital status, race, and State, 1987, US Vital Statistics advance annual rpt, 4146–5.113

Deaths and rates, by cause and age, preliminary 1987-88, US Vital Statistics annual rpt, 4144–7
Deaths and rates, by detailed cause and demographic characteristics, 1986 and trends from 1900, US Vital Statistics annual rpt, 4144–2
Deaths and rates, by detailed location, cause, and demographic characteristics, 1987, US Vital Statistics annual rpt, 4144–3
Deaths from cardiovascular and cerebrovascular disease in New England, and prevention programs, by State, 1989 article, 4042–3.909
Deaths from heart disease, by health and other characteristics, 1986, 4146–8.177
Health condition and health care resources, use, and spending, 1950s-87, annual data compilation, 4144–11
HHS financial aid, by program, recipient, State, and city, FY88, annual regional listings, 4004–3
Hospital discharges and length of stay, by diagnosis, patient age and sex, surgical procedure performed, and region, 1965-86, 4147–13.101
Military deaths by cause, age, race, and rank, and personnel captured and missing, by service branch, 2nd half FY88, semiannual rpt, 3542–21
Mormons death risks from cancer and heart disease, by sex and health habits practiced, 1974 and 1979 studies, article, 4472–1.932
Natl Heart, Lung, and Blood Inst activities and funding, FY87, annual narrative rpt, 4474–22
Natl Heart, Lung, and Blood Inst activities, and grants by recipient and location, FY88 with disease trends from 1940, annual rpt, 4474–15
Natl Heart, Lung, and Blood Inst grants, and Advisory Council recommendations, FY77-94, annual rpt, 4474–11
Nursing home facility, staff, and resident detailed characteristics, 1985, 4147–13.97
Nutritional status and related health condition and practices, by selected characteristics, 1970s-87, 4048–33
Occupational deaths, by cause and industry div, 1987, annual rpt, 6844–1
Physicians (cardiologists) office visits, by characteristics of patient, physician, and visit, 1985, 4146–8.174
Pollutants health effects, concentrations in food and environment, sources, human intake, and regulation, series, 9186–8
Pollution (air) exposure of population and selected risk groups, by pollutant, MSA, and county, 1988, hearing, 21368–117
Smoking and health research rpts, 1988, last issue of annual listing, 4204–19
Smoking and health research summaries, bimonthly rpt, 4202–8
Smoking prevalence, related disease and deaths, and public attitudes, impact of Surgeon General rpts and antismoking campaigns, 1964-89, annual rpt, 4204–18
Statistical Abstract of US, social, political, and economic data, 1790-2025, comprehensive annual compilation, 2324–1.1

Surgery-related deaths and complications, by procedure and VA facility, and compared to non-VA instns, 1981-88, biennial rpt, 8704–1
Surgical procedures performed, costs, length of stay, and deaths, impacts of Medicare prospective payment system by procedure type, 1984-86, 17206–2.5
Surgical procedures performed in hospitals, by procedure type, age, sex, instn size, and payment source, 1983-87, 4146–8.171
West Virginia poverty conditions, food aid participants, and birth outcomes, 1980-87, hearing, 21968–49
see also Hypertension
see also under By Disease in the "Index by Categories"
Carey, Max L.
"Characteristics of Occupational Entrants", 6742–1.902
Cargill, Thomas F.
"Political Business Cycles in a Parliamentary Setting: The Case of Japan", 9393–10.7
Cargo
see Air cargo
see Freight
Carhill, Mike
"Critical Comparison of Alternative Thrift Management Strategies", 9302–2.901
"Fourth District Thrift Profitability in 1988", 9302–2.902
Caribbean area
Agricultural exports to US, by whether duty levied, commodity, and Caribbean country, 1983-88, annual article, 1925–34.923
Agricultural trade among western hemisphere countries, and US duty-free imports, with listing of trade disputes and outcomes, 1960s-85, 1528–278
Agricultural trade of US, by commodity and country, bimonthly rpt with articles, 1522–1
Agricultural trade of US, by detailed commodity and country, 1988, semiannual rpt, 1522–4
AID activities and funding by project and function, FY90, and developing countries summary socioeconomic data from 1960s, annual rpt, 9904–4.7
AID economic aid to developing countries, obligations and disbursements by country, quarterly rpt, 9912–4
AID loans repayment status and terms by program and country, and status of predecessor agency loans, quarterly rpt, 9912–3
Alcohol fuels (ethanol) from Caribbean basin, impacts of duty-free treatment on US industry, investigation with background financial and operating data, 1989 rpt, 9886–4.134
Businesses (foreign) activity in US, income tax returns, assets, and income statement items, by industry div, country, and world area, 1984-85, article, 8302–2.920
Drug abuse indicators, by world region and selected country, 1988 semiannual conf, 4492–5.1
Exports (duty-free) of Caribbean area to US, and imports from US, by country, and impact on US employment, by commodity, 1988, annual rpt, 6364–2

Exports (duty-free) of Caribbean area to US, and US exports and import duties on other goods, by commodity and country, 1984-88, annual rpt, 9884–20

Exports and imports (waterborne) of US, by type of service, commodity, country, route, and US port, 1986-87, annual rpt, 7704–2

Exports and imports (waterborne) of US, by type of service, customs district, port, and world area, monthly rpt, 2422–7

Exports and imports of Latin America, and balance of trade with US, by country, 1988, annual rpt, 2044–34

Exports and imports of OECD, total and for 4 major countries, and US trade by country, by commodity, 1970-87, world area rpt, 9116–1.1

Exports and imports of US, by selected country, country group, and commodity group, 1988, annual rpt, 2044–37

Exports of Caribbean area to OECD members, and US imports under preferential treatment programs, by commodity, 1980s-87, 2048–138

Fish distribution for coastal southeastern US and Caribbean, by season, species, and location, 1980-82, 2168–112

Fishing (ocean sport) catch and effort, and Natl Marine Fisheries Service tagging and research activity, by species and location, 1987, annual rpt, 2164–7

Food production and needs, and related economic outlook, by country, 1989/90, annual rpt, 1524–6

Hurricanes and tropical storms in north Atlantic and Caribbean area, paths, surveillance, deaths, damage, and landfall probabilities by city, 1988, annual rpt, 2184–7

Immigrants admitted to US, by class of admission, country of birth, and State and MSA of destination, FY88, annual rpt, 6264–4

Immigrants admitted to US, by occupational group and country of birth, preliminary FY88, annual table, 6264–1

Immigration to US, alien workers, visitors, deportations, and naturalizations, by country, FY88 and trends from 1820, annual rpt, 6264–2

Inter-American Foundation activities, grants by recipient, and fellowships, by country, FY88, annual rpt, 14424–1

Inter-American Foundation dev grants by program area, and fellowships by field and instn, by country, FY71-88, annual rpt, 14424–2

Investment (direct) incentives of Caribbean Basin Initiative, economic impacts, with finances and employment by country, 1984-88, 2048–141

Investment (foreign direct) in US, by industry group and world area, 1987-88, annual article, 2702–1.929

Loans of US banks to foreigners at all US and foreign offices, by country group and country, quarterly rpt, 13002–1

Military aid of US, arms sales, and training programs costs and budget requests, by program, world region, and country, FY88-90, annual rpt, 7144–13

Military aid programs and related activities of US, costs by country and intl agency, FY85-87 and cumulative from FY50, GAO rpt, 26123–30

Minerals Yearbook, 1987, Vol 3: foreign country reviews of production, trade, and policy, by commodity, annual rpt, 5604–35

Multinatl US firms and foreign affiliates finances and operations, by industry of parent firm and affiliate, world area, and country, preliminary 1987, annual rpt, 2704–5

Ocean currents, temperatures, and salinity, for Straits of Florida and Caribbean Sea, series, 2146–7

Oil exports to US by OPEC and non-OPEC countries, monthly rpt, 3162–24.3

Peace Corps activities, funding by program, and volunteers, by country, FY90, annual rpt, 9654–1

Plastic, tar, and other nondegradable ocean and beach debris, incidence and environmental impacts, 1970s-88, 14738–4

Refugee arrivals in US by world area and country of origin, and quotas, monthly rpt, 7002–4

Rum imports (duty-free) of US under Caribbean Basin Initiative, by country, 1987-88, annual rpt, 9884–15

Sugar production and exports, and cruise ship tourist visits and spending, by Caribbean area country, 1981-87, hearing, 21788–179

Textile imports under Multifiber Arrangement by product and country, and status of bilateral agreements, 1986-88, annual rpt, 9884–18

Travel to and from US on US and foreign flag airlines, by world area, 1980-88, annual rpt, 2904–13

Travel to US, by characteristics of visit and traveler, country, port city, and State of destination, quarterly rpt, 2902–1

Vegetables (winter fresh) from Florida, Mexico, and Caribbean area, shipments and costs by commodity, 1970s-87, article, 1561–11.902

see also Anguilla
see also Antigua and Barbuda
see also Aruba
see also Bahamas
see also Barbados
see also Bermuda
see also British Virgin Islands
see also Cayman Islands
see also Cuba
see also Dominica
see also Dominican Republic
see also Grenada
see also Haiti
see also Jamaica
see also Netherlands Antilles
see also Puerto Rico
see also St. Christopher and Nevis
see also St. Lucia
see also St. Vincent and The Grenadines
see also Trinidad and Tobago
see also U.S. Virgin Islands
see also under By Foreign Country in the "Index by Categories"

Caribbean Basin Initiative
see Trade agreements

Carlin, Thomas A.
"Farm Structure and Nearby Communities", 1502–7.909

Carlino, Gerald A.
"What Can Output Measures Tell Us About Deindustrialization in the Nation and Its Regions?", 9387–1.902

Carlisle, Pa.
see also under By SMSA or MSA in the "Index by Categories"

Carlson, Keith M.
"Federal Budget Trends and the 1981 Reagan Economic Plan", 9391–1.905

Carlstrom, Charles T.
"Money, Inflation, and Sectoral Shifts", 9377–9.70
"Two-Sector Implicit Contracting Model with Procyclical Quits and Involuntary Layoffs", 9377–9.75
"Why We Don't Know Whether Money Causes Output", 9377–1.906

Carman, Clifford M.
"Dairy Outlook: Industry Reaction", 1004–16.1

Carnevale, Anthony P.
"Learning Enterprise", 6408–73

Carpets and rugs
Building materials PPI, by type, bimonthly rpt, 2042–1.5

Business statistics, detailed data for major industries and economic indicators, *Survey of Current Business,* monthly rpt, 2702–1.19

County Business Patterns, 1987: employment, establishments, and payroll, by SIC 2- to 4-digit industry and county, annual State rpt series, 2326–8

Employment, earnings, and hours, by SIC 1- to 4-digit industry, monthly 1983-Feb 1989, annual rpt, 6744–4

Injuries from use of consumer products and related activities, by victim age and sex, 1988, annual rpt, 9164–7

Injuries from use of consumer products, by severity, victim age, and detailed product, 1988, annual rpt, 9164–6

Manufacturing census, 1987: financial and operating data, for SIC 4-digit industries by product, preliminary rpt, 2491–1.11

Price indexes (producer), by stage of processing and detailed commodity, monthly rpt, 6762–6

Price indexes (producer), by stage of processing and detailed commodity, monthly 1988, annual rpt, 6764–2

Retail trade census, 1987: employment, establishments, sales, and payroll, by SIC 2- to 4-digit kind of business, MSA, county, and city, State rpt series, 2397–1

Science, engineering, and technical employment in manufacturing, by field, occupation, and industry, 1986, triennial rpt, 9627–23

Shipments of carpets and rugs, trade, and use, by product, quarterly Current Industrial Rpt, 2506–5.9

Wholesale trade census, 1987: employment, establishments, finances, and operations, by SIC 2- to 4-digit kind of business, MSA, county, and city, State rpt series, 2405–1

Carpools
see Commuting

Carr, Gary
"Study of Mechanical and Driver-Related Systems of the Audi 5000 Capable of Producing Uncontrolled Sudden Acceleration Incidents. Examination of Sudden Acceleration, Appendix H", 7768–107.2

OECD trade, total and for 4 major countries, and US trade by country, by commodity, 1970-87, world area rpt series, 9116-1

Pollution (air) abatement equipment shipments by industry, exports, and new and backlog orders, by product, 1988, annual Current Industrial Rpt, 2506-12.5

Price indexes (producer), by stage of processing and detailed commodity, monthly rpt, 6762-6

Price indexes (producer), by stage of processing and detailed commodity, monthly 1988, annual rpt, 6764-2

Production and PPI for building materials, and cement shipments to census divs, Puerto Rico, and foreign countries, bimonthly rpt, 2042-1.5; 2042-1.6

Production, prices, trade, use, employment, tariffs, and stockpiles, by mineral, with foreign comparisons, 1984-88, annual rpt, 5604-18

Science, engineering, and technical employment in manufacturing, by field, occupation, and industry, 1986, triennial rpt, 9627-23

Statistical Abstract of US, social, political, and economic data, 1790-2025, comprehensive annual compilation, 2324-1.3

Stone, sand, and gravel production, by end use, State, and district, 1985-86, 5608-157

Tax (income) returns of corporations, income and tax items by asset size and detailed industry, 1986, annual rpt, 8304-4; 8304-21

Transportation census, 1987: trucks, by detailed characteristics, miles traveled, and type of product carried, State rpt series, 2573-1

Cemeteries and funerals

Casket manufacturers financial and operating data, by product, 1987 Census of Manufactures, preliminary rpt, 2491-1.83

Casket manufacturers financial and operating data, 1986 Annual Survey of Manufactures, series, 2506-15

Casket manufacturers occupational injury and illness rates, 1987, annual rpt, 6844-1

Casket manufacturers price indexes, monthly rpt, 6762-6

Casket manufacturers price indexes, monthly 1988, annual rpt, 6764-2

County Business Patterns, 1987: employment, establishments, and payroll, by SIC 2- to 4-digit industry and county, annual State rpt series, 2326-8

CPI by component for US city average, and by region, population size, and for 27 metro areas, monthly rpt, 6762-2

Employee paid leave days for funerals, by occupational group, 1988, annual rpt, 6784-19

Employment, earnings, and hours, by SIC 1- to 4-digit industry, monthly 1983-Feb 1989, annual rpt, 6744-4

Expenditures, arrangements, and preplanning for funerals, and knowledge of burial laws, 1986-87 survey, article, 1702-1.909

Guam economic censuses, 1987: employment, firms, payroll, and receipts, by SIC 1- to 4-digit industry and election district, 2595-1

Service industries census, 1987: establishments, receipts, employment, and payroll, by SIC 2- to 4-digit kind of business, MSA, county, and city, State rpt series, 2391-1

Service industries receipts, by SIC 2- to 4-digit kind of business, 1988, annual rpt, 2413-8

Tax (income) returns of partnerships, income statement items by industry group, 1986, annual article, 8302-2.903

Tax (income) returns of sole proprietorships, income statement items, by industry group, 1987, annual article, 8302-2.904; 8302-2.921

Workers compensation laws of States and Fed Govt, 1989 semiannual rpt, 6502-1

see also Military cemeteries and funerals

Censorship

Foreign countries human rights conditions in 170 countries, 1988, annual rpt, 21384-3

see also Freedom of the press

Census Bureau

see Bureau of Census

Census divisions

see under By Census Division in the "Index by Categories"

Census of Agriculture

Data coverage and availability for 1987 census and related statistics, 1989 guide, 2308-55

Data coverage and availability of Census Bur rpts and data files, 1989 annual listing, 2304-2

Data coverage, use, and availability, 1989 pamphlet, 2326-7.68

Farms, farmland, production and costs, and operator characteristics, 1987 census, advance State and county rpt series, 2330-1

Farms, farmland, production, finances, and operator characteristics, by county, 1987 census, final State rpt series, 2331-1

Census of Construction Industries

Data coverage and availability for 1987 economic censuses and related statistics, 1989 preliminary guide, 2308-5

Financial and operating data, by SIC 4-digit industry and State, 1987 census, final rpt series, 2373-1

Financial and operating data, 1987 census, preliminary industry rpt series, 2371-1

Census of Governments

Data coverage and availability for 1987 Census of Agriculture and related statistics, 1989 guide, 2308-55

Data coverage and availability of Census Bur rpts and data files, 1989 annual listing, 2304-2

Officials (elected), by level of govt, race, sex, and State, 1987 census, preliminary rpt, 2450-2

Property tax revenue by level of govt, assessed values by locality, and exemptions, by property type and State, 1987 census, 2453-1

Census of Housing

Data coverage and availability of Census Bur rpts and data files, 1989 annual listing, 2304-2

see also Census of Population and Housing

Census of Manufactures

Classification codes for SIC industries and SIC-based products, 1987 census, listing, 2628-10

Data coverage and availability for 1987 economic censuses and related statistics, 1989 preliminary guide, 2308-5

Employment, establishments, and other financial and operating data, by SIC 4-digit industry and product, 1987 census, preliminary industry rpt series, 2491-1

Census of Mineral Industries

Classification codes for SIC industries and SIC-based products, 1987 census, listing, 2628-10

Data coverage and availability for 1987 economic censuses and related statistics, 1989 preliminary guide, 2308-5

Establishments, employment, payroll, and other financial and operating data, 1987 census, preliminary industry rpt series, 2511-1

Census of Minority-Owned Business Enterprises

see Survey of Minority-Owned Business Enterprises

Census of Outlying Areas

Data coverage and availability for 1987 economic censuses and related statistics, 1989 preliminary guide, 2308-5

Guam economic censuses, 1987: employment, firms, payroll, and receipts, by SIC 1- to 4-digit industry and election district, 2595-1

Northern Mariana Islands economic census, 1987: employment, firms, payroll, and receipts, by SIC 1- to 4-digit industry, 2597-1

Virgin Islands economic censuses, 1987: employment, firms, payroll, and receipts, by SIC 1- to 4-digit industry, island, and city, 2593-1

Census of Population

Aliens (illegal) and immigration impact on congressional apportionment, alternative estimates by State, 1950s-80 with projections to 2010, hearing, 21628-70

Data coverage and availability of Census Bur rpts and data files, 1989 annual listing, 2304-2

Labor force counts under occupation and industry classifications used in 1970 and 1980 censuses, by industry, occupation, and sex, 1970, technical paper, 2626-2.59

Population socioeconomic characteristics, selected data, 1980 census, young readers pamphlet series, 2326-1

see also Census of Population and Housing

Census of Population and Housing

Data collection procedure, and impacts on congressional apportionment by State, 1990 census, hearing, 25408-101

Data collection procedure improvement and preparation for count, 1990 census, hearing, 21628-71

Data collection procedure, 1980 census, series, 2555-2

Data coverage and availability for community and business dev projects, 1990 census, user guide, 2308-10

Data coverage and availability for 1987 Census of Agriculture and related statistics, 1989 guide, 2308-55

Data coverage and availability of Census Bur rpts and data files, 1989 annual listing, 2304-2

Data coverage and products of 1990 census, 1989 guide, 2308-58

Data item selection, questionnaire dev, and testing, 1990 census, series, 2626–11

Mental health care facilities needs assessment and program evaluation for communities, methodology, use of census data, analysis, and sample data, series, 4506–8

Outlying areas preparations for count, 1990 census, hearings, 21628–72; 21628–74

see also Census of Housing

see also Census of Population

Census of Retail Trade

Data coverage and availability for 1987 economic censuses and related statistics, 1989 preliminary guide, 2308–5

Employment, establishments, sales, and payroll, by SIC 2- to 4-digit kind of business, MSA, county, and city, 1987 census, State rpt series, 2397–1

Census of Service Industries

Data coverage and availability for 1987 economic censuses and related statistics, 1989 preliminary guide, 2308–5

Establishments, receipts, employment, and payroll, by SIC 2- to 4-digit kind of business, MSA, city, and county, 1987 census, State rpt series, 2391–1

Census of Transportation

Data coverage and availability for 1987 economic censuses and related statistics, 1989 preliminary guide, 2308–5

Trucks, by detailed characteristics, miles traveled, and type of product carried, 1987 census, State rpt series, 2573–1

Census of Wholesale Trade

Data coverage and availability for 1987 economic censuses and related statistics, 1989 preliminary guide, 2308–5

Employment, establishments, and operations, by SIC 2- to 4-digit kind of business, MSA, county, and city, 1987 census, State rpt series, 2405–1

Census of Women-Owned Businesses

see Survey of Women-Owned Businesses

Center for Immigration Studies

"Impact of Immigration on Congressional Representation", 21628–70

Center for Research for Mothers and Children

Activities and funding of CRMC, FY88, annual rpt, 4474–31

Centers for Disease Control

AIDS and other new programs of CDC, staffing and reallocations from other programs, FY81-88, GAO rpt, 26121–287

AIDS cases by risk group, race, sex, age, State, and MSA, and deaths, monthly rpt, 4202–9

AIDS cases forecasts, analysis of CDC and other methodology, 1989 GAO rpt, 26131–55

Budget of US Appendix, obligations, appropriations, and personnel, by program and agency, FY90, annual rpt, 104–3

Expenditures of Fed Govt in States, by type, program, agency, and State, FY88, annual rpt, 2464–2

Financial aid of HHS, by program, recipient, State, and city, FY88, annual regional listings, 4004–3

Hepatitis cases by infection source, age, sex, race, and State, and deaths, by strain, 1987 and trends from 1966, 4205–2

Infectious notifiable diseases reporting to CDC, cases and rates by race, 1987, article, 4042–3.943

Malaria cases in US, for military personnel and US and foreign civilians, and by country of infection, 1966-87, annual rpt, 4205–4

Morbidity and Mortality Weekly Report, infectious notifiable disease cases and deaths, and other public health issues, periodic journal, 4202–7

Morbidity and Mortality Weekly Report, infectious notifiable disease cases by age and State, and deaths, 1930s-88, annual rpt, 4204–1

Morbidity and Mortality Weekly Report, infectious notifiable disease cases by State, and public health issues, 4202–1

Morbidity and Mortality Weekly Report, special supplements, series, 4206–2

Prospective payment system research activities and funding of PHS, by project and subagency, FY88, annual rpt, 4184–3

Research and evaluation programs of HHS, 1970-FY87, annual listing, 4004–30

Tuberculosis cases and deaths, by patient characteristics, State, and city, 1987 and trends from 1953, annual rpt, 4204–10

Vaccination activity, reactions, costs, and preventable disease cases and deaths, 1988 annual conf, 4204–15

Vaccination needs for intl travel by country, and disease prevention recommendations, 1989 annual rpt, 4204–11

Vaccination research rpts, 1988 annual listing, 4204–16

Vaccine and toxoid shipments, by product type, July-Dec 1986, 4205–22

see also National Institute for Occupational Safety and Health

see also Office on Smoking and Health

CENTO

see Central Treaty Organization

Central African Republic

Agricultural and food production and indexes, total and for selected commodities, by country, 1970s-88, annual rpt, 1524–12

Agricultural trade of US, by detailed commodity and country, 1988, semiannual rpt, 1522–4

AID activities and funding by project and function, FY90, and developing countries summary socioeconomic data from 1960s, annual rpt, 9904–4.5

AID economic aid to developing countries, obligations and disbursements by country, quarterly rpt, 9912–4

Economic and military aid and loans from US and intl agencies, by program and country, FY46-87, annual rpt, 9914–5

Economic conditions, income, production, prices, employment, and trade, 1989 periodic country rpt, 2046–4.19

Economic, social, political, and geographic summary data, by country, 1989, annual factbook, 9114–2

Human rights conditions in 170 countries, 1988, annual rpt, 21384–3

Military aid of US, arms sales, and training programs costs and budget requests, by program, world region, and country, FY88-90, annual rpt, 7144–13

Military spending, arms trade, and force strengths, with govt spending and population, by country, 1977-87, annual rpt, 9824–1

Minerals Yearbook, 1987, Vol 3: foreign country reviews of production, trade, and policy, by commodity, annual rpt, 5604–35

Minerals Yearbook, 1987, Vol 3 preprints: foreign country review of production, trade, and policy, by commodity, annual rpt, 5604–23.80

Population size, growth rates, and components of change, by country, projected 1989-2020 and trends from 1950, biennial rpt, 2324–9

UN voting record and share of votes in agreement with US, by issue, country, and world area, 1988, annual rpt, 7004–18

see also under By Foreign Country in the "Index by Categories"

Central America

Agricultural exports of US, for grains, oilseed products, hides, skins, and cotton, by country, weekly rpt, 1922–3

Agricultural trade among western hemisphere countries, and US duty-free imports, with listing of trade disputes and outcomes, 1960s-85, 1528–278

Agricultural trade of US, by detailed commodity and country, 1988, semiannual rpt, 1522–4

AID activities and funding by project and function, FY90, and developing countries summary socioeconomic data from 1960s, annual rpt, 9904–4.7

Businesses (foreign) activity in US, income tax returns, assets, and income statement items, by industry div, country, and world area, 1984-85, article, 8302–2.920

Economic and military aid and loans from US and intl agencies, by program and country, FY46-87, annual rpt, 9914–5

Exports (duty-free) of Caribbean area to US, and imports from US, by country, and impact on US employment, by commodity, 1988, annual rpt, 6364–2

Exports (duty-free) of Caribbean area to US, and US exports and import duties on other goods, by commodity and country, 1984-88, annual rpt, 9884–20

Exports and imports (waterborne) of US, by type of service, commodity, country, route, and US port, 1986-87, annual rpt, 7704–2

Exports and imports (waterborne) of US, by type of service, customs district, port, and world area, monthly rpt, 2422–7

Exports and imports of OECD, total and for 4 major countries, and US trade by country, by commodity, 1970-87, world area rpt, 9116–1.6

Exports and imports of US, by commodity group, world area, selected country, US coastal area and port, and mode of transport, monthly rpt, 2422–9

Exports of Caribbean area to OECD members, and US imports under preferential treatment programs, by commodity, 1980s-87, 2048–138

Food production and needs, and related economic outlook, by country, 1989/90, annual rpt, 1524–6

Immigrants admitted to US, by class of admission, country of birth, and State and MSA of destination, FY88, annual rpt, 6264–4

Immigrants admitted to US, by occupational group and country of birth, preliminary FY88, annual table, 6264-1

Immigration to US, alien workers, visitors, deportations, and naturalizations, by country, FY88 and trends from 1820, annual rpt, 6264-2

Inter-American Foundation activities, grants by recipient, and fellowships, by country, FY88, annual rpt, 14424-1

Inter-American Foundation dev grants by program area, and fellowships by field and instn, by country, FY71-88, annual rpt, 14424-2

Investment (direct) incentives of Caribbean Basin Initiative, economic impacts, with finances and employment by country, 1984-88, 2048-141

Investment (foreign direct) of US, by selected industry group and world area, 1986-88, annual article, 2702-1.930

Military aid of US, arms sales, and training programs costs and budget requests, by program, world region, and country, FY88-90, annual rpt, 7144-13

Military aid programs and related activities of US, costs by country and intl agency, FY85-87 and cumulative from FY50, GAO rpt, 26123-30

Minerals Yearbook, 1987, Vol 3: foreign country reviews of production, trade, and policy, by commodity, annual rpt, 5604-35

Multinatl US firms and foreign affiliates finances and operations, by industry of parent firm and affiliate, world area, and country, preliminary 1987, annual rpt, 2704-5

Peace Corps activities, funding by program, and volunteers, by country, FY90, annual rpt, 9654-1

R&D funding by Fed Govt, by field, performer type, agency, and State, FY87-89, annual rpt, 9627-20

Refugees from Nicaragua, El Salvador, and Guatemala receiving UN aid, resettlement in other Central American countries, and repatriations, 1984-88, GAO rpt, 26123-232

Terrorist (intl) incidents, casualties, and attacks on US targets, by attack type and country, 1980-88, 7008-56

Travel to and from US on US and foreign flag airlines, by world area, 1980-88, annual rpt, 2904-13

Travel to US, by characteristics of visit and traveler, country, port city, and State of destination, quarterly rpt, 2902-1

Weather events and anomalies, precipitation and temperature for US and foreign locations, weekly rpt, 2182-6

see also Belize
see also Caribbean area
see also Central American Common Market
see also Costa Rica
see also El Salvador
see also Guatemala
see also Honduras
see also Inter-American Development Bank
see also Latin American Integration Association
see also Nicaragua
see also Panama
see also under By Foreign Country in the "Index by Categories"

Central American Common Market
Exports and imports of US, by commodity group, world area, selected country, US coastal area and port, and mode of transport, monthly rpt, 2422-9

Central business districts
Traffic volume in urban areas and detailed trip characteristics, by transport mode and city, 1950s-88, 7888-37

Vacancy rates for office buildings in 16 cities, 1960s-87, article, 9387-1.903

Central cities
Births, fertility rates, and childless women, by selected characteristics, 1988, annual Current Population Rpt, 2546-1.436

Consumer Income, socioeconomic characteristics of persons, families, and households, detailed cross-tabulations, Current Population Rpt series, 2546-6

Definitions of MSAs and central cities, and revisions, periodic listings, series, 108-35

Educational enrollment, by grade, instn type and control, and student characteristics, 1986 and trends from 1947, annual Current Population Rpt, 2546-1.429; 2546-1.432

Employment and unemployment in metro and nonmetro areas, monthly rpt, quarterly data, 6742-2.9

Employment, unemployment, and labor force characteristics, Labor Statistics Handbook, 1940s-88 with trends from 1913, 6728-38.1

Expenditures of local govts, impacts of competition among govtl units, migration, and other factors, 1976-77, working paper, 9377-9.82

Food consumption and nutrient intake by individuals, by food group, selected characteristics, and region, supplementary survey series, 1356-5

Household and family characteristics, by location, 1988, annual Current Population Rpt, 2546-1.437

Housing and households detailed characteristics, and unit and neighborhood quality, by location, 1985, biennial rpt, 2485-12

Housing and households detailed characteristics, and unit and neighborhood quality, MSA surveys, series, 2485-6

Housing energy use, costs, and conservation, and household and housing characteristics, survey rpt series, 3166-7

Housing vacancy and occupancy rates, and vacant unit characteristics and costs, by region and metro-nonmetro location, quarterly rpt, 2482-1

Income (household) and poverty status under alternative income definitions, by recipient characteristics, 1986, Current Population Rpt, 2546-6.58

Medicare enrollment, and use by type of service, by age, sex, race, region, State, and MSA, 1986-87, annual rpt, 4657-5

Migration since 1986, mover characteristics by same or different area, and compared to nonmovers, 1987, annual Current Population Rpt, 2546-1.435

Population size, by MSA, county, metro-nonmetro location, and State, 1987, and for cities, 1986, with change from 1980 and trends from 1960, Current Population Rpt, 2546-3.160

Voting and registration, by socioeconomic and demographic characteristics, 1988 presidential election, biennial Current Population Rpt, 2546-1.440
see also Central business districts
see also Urban renewal

Central Intelligence Agency
Budget of US Appendix, obligations, appropriations, and personnel, by program and agency, FY90, annual rpt, 104-3

Budget of US, authoritative financial statements with appropriations, outlays, and receipts, by category and agency, FY88, annual rpt, 8104-2.2

Chiefs of State and Cabinet members, by country, bimonthly listing, 9112-4

China economic conditions and trade, annual rpt, discontinued, 9114-5

China trade, by commodity, world area, and country, 1985-87, 9118-10

China trade by SITC 1- to 5-digit commodity, 1970s-87, annual rpt, 9114-3

China trade with US by commodity, and foreign investment by source country, 1988, 9118-9

Communist, OECD, and selected other countries economic conditions, 1960s-88, annual rpt, 9114-4

Cuba economic conditions, agricultural and industrial production and distribution, trade, and intl economic relations, 1980-87 with trends from 1961, 9118-8

Economic conditions, and oil production, use, and imports, by OECD country, and OPEC prices, biweekly rpt, 9112-1

Economic, social, political, and geographic summary data, by country, 1989, annual factbook, 9114-2

Energy production by type, and oil prices, trade, and use, by country group and selected country, monthly rpt, 9112-2

OECD trade, total and for 4 major countries, and US trade by country, by commodity, 1970-87, world area rpt series, 9116-1

Soviet Union budget deficits and financing, revenues, and spending, with retail prices, 1970-88, 9118-6

Soviet Union economic conditions under General Secretary Gorbachev, Soviet and CIA measurement methods with background data, 1987 conf papers, 9118-4

Soviet Union economic conditions under General Secretary Gorbachev, Soviet and CIA measures, 1950s-87, 9118-5

Soviet Union economic conditions under General Secretary Gorbachev, 1988 and trends from 1956, annual rpt, 9114-6

Soviet Union officials public appearances in and outside USSR, 1988, annual rpt, 9114-1

Soviet Union personal income by source, disposable income, wage deductions by type, and savings, 1950s-87, 9118-7

Central Treaty Organization
Economic and military aid and loans from US and intl agencies, by program and country, FY46-87, annual rpt, 9914-5

Centrally planned economies
Agricultural and food production and indexes, total and for selected commodities, by country, 1970s-88, annual rpt, 1524-12

Economic and military aid and loans from US and intl agencies, by program and country, FY46-87, annual rpt, 9914–5

Economic conditions, income, production, prices, employment, and trade, 1989 periodic country rpt, 2046–4.102

Economic, social, political, and geographic summary data, by country, 1989, annual factbook, 9114–2

Food supply indicators for Sahel, by country, 1960s-2000, 1528–290

Human rights conditions in 170 countries, 1988, annual rpt, 21384–3

Military aid of US, arms sales, and training programs costs and budget requests, by program, world region, and country, FY88-90, annual rpt, 7144–13

Military spending, arms trade, and force strengths, with govt spending and population, by country, 1977-87, annual rpt, 9824–1

Minerals Yearbook, 1987, Vol 3: foreign country reviews of production, trade, and policy, by commodity, annual rpt, 5604–35

Minerals Yearbook, 1987, Vol 3 preprints: foreign country review of production, trade, and policy, by commodity, annual rpt, 5604–23.80

Population size, growth rates, and components of change, by country, projected 1989-2020 and trends from 1950, biennial rpt, 2324–9

UN voting record and share of votes in agreement with US, by issue, country, and world area, 1988, annual rpt, 7004–18

see also under By Foreign Country in the "Index by Categories"

Chakrabarty, Rameswar P.
"Composite Estimation for SIPP Annual Estimates", 2626–10.90
"Multivariate Analysis by Users of SIPP Micro-Data Files", 2626–10.94

Chalupa, Karel V.
"Foreign Currency Futures: Reducing Foreign Exchange Risk", 9375–14

Chamberlain, P. G.
"Technological Improvements Needed by the U.S. Mineral Industry by the Year 2000", 5606–5.7

Champ, Michael A.
"Research Needs Concerning Organotin Compounds Used in Antifouling Paints in Coastal Environments", 2148–58

Champaign, Ill.
Wages by occupation, and benefits for office and plant workers, 1988 survey, periodic MSA rpt, 6785–11.3
see also under By SMSA or MSA in the "Index by Categories"

CHAMPUS
see Civilian Health and Medical Program of the Uniformed Services

Chandrakantha, M. S.
"On the Use of Variance Ratios in the Analysis of Nonstationary Time Series", 9366–6.211

Chaney, Bradford
"Academic Research Equipment in Selected Science/Engineering Fields: 1982-83 to 1985-86", 9628–76

Charity
see Gifts and private contributions
see Nonprofit organizations and foundations

Charles River Associates
"Characteristics of Urban Transportation Demand, An Update", 7888–37

Charleston, S.C.
Freight (waterborne domestic and foreign) by commodity, traffic, and passengers, by port and waterway, 1987, annual rpt, 3754–3.1
Wages by occupation, and benefits for office and plant workers, 1988 survey, periodic MSA rpt, 6785–11.1
see also under By SMSA or MSA in the "Index by Categories"

Charleston, W.Va.
see also under By SMSA or MSA in the "Index by Categories"

Charlotte Amalie, V.I.
Economic Censuses of Outlying Areas, 1987: Virgin Islands employment, firms, payroll, and receipts, by SIC 1- to 4-digit industry, island, and city, 2593–1

Charlotte, N.C.
Housing starts and completions authorized by building permits in 40 MSAs, quarterly rpt, 2382–9
Wages by occupation, for office and plant workers, 1988 survey, periodic MSA rpt, 6785–11.2
see also under By City and By SMSA or MSA in the "Index by Categories"

Charlottesville, Va.
see also under By SMSA or MSA in the "Index by Categories"

Chartbooks
Agricultural production, marketing, trade, food consumption, and nutrition programs, 1960s-88, annual chartbook, 1504–3
Economic indicators and components, and Fed Reserve 4th District business and financial conditions, monthly chartbook, 9377–10
Exports, imports, and balances of US with major trading partners, by product category, 1984-88, annual chartbook, 9884–21
Farm financial and marketing conditions, forecast 1989, annual chartbook, 1504–8
Financial and business statistics, historic trends, 1988 annual chartbook, 9364–2
Financial data for US and selected foreign countries, including exchange rates, interest rates, gold prices, and security yields, weekly chartbook, 9365–1.5
Household and family composition, and factors affecting change, 1960s-88, chartbook, 2546–2.149
Housing and households summary characteristics, 1985 and trends, biennial chartbook, 2486–1.7
Indian Health Service facilities, funding, operations, and Indian health and other characteristics, 1950s-88, annual chartbook, 4084–1
Military health care benefits and costs under Civilian Health and Medical Program of Uniformed Services, FY83-FY89, 3508–31
Military women personnel on active and reserve duty, by demographic and service characteristics and service branch, FY88, annual chartbook, 3544–26
Older persons socioeconomic characteristics, 1900s-86 and projected to 2050, biennial chartbook, 12904–1

Public welfare programs benefits, beneficiaries, and summary program data, selected years 1937-89, chartbook, 4748–42
R&D funding, labor supply, and other science indicators, with foreign comparisons, 1960s-89, annual chartbook, 9624–22
Travel to and from US, by world area, forecast 1989-90, annual rpt, 2904–9
see also Maps

Chattanooga, Tenn.
Wages by occupation, for office and plant workers, 1989 survey, periodic MSA rpt, 6785–3.10
see also under By City and By SMSA or MSA in the "Index by Categories"

Chavez, Ernest L.
"Mexican American and White American School Dropouts' Drug Use, Health Status, and Involvement in Violence", 4042–3.957

Checking accounts
Assets and debts of private sector, balance sheets by segment, 1949-88, semiannual rpt, 9365–4.1
Budget of US, authoritative financial statements with appropriations, outlays, and receipts, by category and agency, FY88, annual rpt, 8104–2.2
Commercial banks finances, for foreign and domestic offices, by asset size, 1987, annual rpt, 9294–4.2
Commercial banks holdings of demand deposits of individuals, partnerships, and corporations, monthly rpt, 9362–1.1
Deposits, debits, and deposit turnover at financial instns, 1987, annual rpt, 9364–5.1
Deposits in FDIC-insured commercial and savings banks, by instn, State, MSA, and county, as of June 1988, annual regional rpt series, 9295–3
Economic indicators and components, current data and annual trends, monthly rpt, 23842–1.5
Economic indicators compounded annual rates of change, 1969-88, annual rpt, 9391–9.1
Farm sector assets by type, 1988, annual rpt, 1544–16.2
Fed Reserve and private check collection systems competition issues, finances, and operations, 1984-87, GAO rpt, 26119–255
Fed Reserve banks expenses and operations, itemized by service, office, and district, 1988, annual rpt, 9364–11
Fed Reserve services provided depository instns, costs and revenue by service and district bank, 1987-88, article, 9362–1.908
Financial and monetary conditions, selected US summary data, weekly rpt, 9391–4
Financial instns financial and operating statements by deposit size, Fed Reserve functional cost analysis, 1988, annual rpt, 9364–6
Flow-of-funds accounts, assets and liabilities by type and economic sector, outstanding at year-end 1965-88, annual rpt, 9364–3
Flow-of-funds accounts, savings, investments, and credit statements, quarterly rpt, 9365–3.3

Manufacturing census, 1987: financial and operating data, for SIC 4-digit industries by product, preliminary industry rpt series, 2491-1

Manufacturing industries production, shipments, inventories, orders, and pollution control costs, periodic Current Industrial Rpt series, 2506-3

Mineral industries census, 1987: financial and operating data, preliminary industry rpt, 2511-1.11

Multinatl firms US affiliates, finances, and operations, by industry, world area of parent firm, and State, 1987, annual rpt, 2704-4

Multinatl US firms and foreign affiliates finances and operations, by industry of parent firm and affiliate, world area, and country, preliminary 1987, annual rpt, 2704-5

Nitrocellulose (industrial) from 7 countries at less than fair value, injury to US industry, investigation with background financial and operating data, 1989 rpt, 9886-14.270

Occupational injury and illness rates, by SIC 2- to 4-digit industry, 1987, annual rpt, 6844-1

OECD trade, total and for 4 major countries, and US trade by country, by commodity, 1970-87, world area rpt series, 9116-1

Ohio River basin waterway facilities, freight by commodity and port, and recreation, by waterway, 1986-87, annual rpt, 3754-6

Pacific Northwest population, households, employment, income, and fuel prices, alternative projections 1990-2010 with trends from 1960, annual rpt, 3224-5

Pollution (air) abatement equipment shipments by industry, exports, and new and backlog orders, by product, 1988, annual Current Industrial Rpt, 2506-12.5

Pollution (air) levels for 5 pollutants, by detailed source and State, 1986, annual rpt, 9194-7

Pollution abatement capital and operating costs, by SIC 2-to 4-digit industry and State, 1986, annual Current Industrial Rpt, 2506-3.6

Price indexes (producer), by stage of processing and detailed commodity, monthly rpt, 6762-6

Price indexes (producer), by stage of processing and detailed commodity, monthly 1988, annual rpt, 6764-2

Production and sales of synthetic organic chemicals, and manufacturer listing, by product, 1988, annual rpt, 9884-3

Production, shipments, firms, trade, and use, by product, periodic Current Industrial Rpt series, 2506-8

R&D funding, and scientists and engineers education and employment, for US and selected foreign countries, 1988, annual rpt, 9624-23.1

Rail shipments of grain and other commodities by car type, 1986, and rail car fleet size, 1978-88, 1278-15

Science, engineering, and technical employment in manufacturing, by field, occupation, and industry, 1986, triennial rpt, 9627-23

Science, engineering, and technical employment in transportation, utilities, and retail and wholesale trade, by field, occupation, and industry, 1985, triennial rpt, 9627-32

Small business establishments, employment, and financial ratios, by SIC 1- to 2-digit industry and State, late 1960s-87, 9768-19

Statistical Abstract of US, social, political, and economic data, 1790-2025, comprehensive annual compilation, 2324-1.3

Synthetic organic chemical production, by detailed product, quarterly rpt, 9882-1

Tariff Schedule of US, classifications and rates of duty by detailed imported commodity, 1990 base edition and supplements, 9886-13

Tax (excise) collections of IRS, by source, quarterly rpt, 8302-1

Tax (income) returns of corporations, income and tax items by asset size and detailed industry, 1986, annual rpt, 8304-4; 8304-21

Tax (income) returns of partnerships, income statement items by industry group, 1986, annual article, 8302-2.903

Tax (income) returns of sole proprietorships, income statement items, by industry group, 1987, annual article, 8302-2.904; 8302-2.921

Transportation census, 1987: trucks, by detailed characteristics, miles traveled, and type of product carried, State rpt series, 2573-1

Wholesale trade census, 1987: employment, establishments, finances, and operations, by SIC 2- to 4-digit kind of business, MSA, county, and city, State rpt series, 2405-1

Wholesale trade sales and inventories, by SIC 2- to 3-digit kind of business, monthly rpt, 2413-7

Wholesale trade sales, inventories, purchases, and gross margins, by SIC 2- to 3-digit kind of business and form of ownership, 1988, annual rpt, 2413-13

see also Adhesives

see also Chemical and biological warfare agents

see also Dioxins

see also Drugs

see also Explosives

see also Fertilizers

see also Food ingredients and additives

see also Gases

see also Gum and wood chemicals

see also Hazardous substances

see also Hazardous waste and disposal

see also Paints and varnishes

see also Pesticides

see also Petrochemicals

see also Pharmaceutical industry

see also Plastics and plastics industry

see also Soap and detergent industry

see also Synthetic fibers and fabrics

see also By Industry in the "Index by Categories"

see also under By Commodity in the "Index by Categories"

Chemistry

Degrees (PhD) in science and engineering, by field, instn, employment prospects, sex, race, and other characteristics, 1960s-88, 9627-30

Degrees awarded in higher education, by level, field, race, and sex, 1989 edition, annual rpt, 4824-2.20

Degrees in science and engineering, by field, level, and sex, 1950-86 9628-77

Employment and earnings in science and engineering, by field and activity, and private and Federal R&D spending, by industry, 1975-88, 9626-6.29

Employment and other characteristics of science and engineering PhDs, by field and State, 1987, biennial rpt, 9627-18

Employment characteristics of scientists and engineers, by field, 1988, biennial rpt, 9627-16

Employment of scientists, engineers, and technicians, by nonmanufacturing industry and field, 1987, triennial rpt, 9627-31

Employment of scientists, engineers, and technicians in manufacturing, by field, occupation, and industry, 1986, triennial rpt, 9627-23

Enrollment in science and engineering grad programs, by field, source of funds, and characteristics of student and instn, 1975-87, annual rpt, 9627-7

Fed Govt aid to higher education and nonprofit instns for R&D and related activities, by field, instn, agency, and State, FY87, annual rpt, 9627-17

Hazardous waste mgmt, effectiveness of alternative technologies, 1989 conf papers, biennial rpt, 9184-19

Labor force, Federal and university research funding, and educational data, 1989 rpt, 9626-6.28

R&D funding by Fed Govt, by field, performer type, agency, and State, FY87-89, annual rpt, 9627-20

R&D funding by higher education instns, by source and field, FY80-87, annual rpt, 9624-18.5

Wages of scientists and engineers in R&D, by field and educational, employment, and other characteristics, 1989, annual rpt, 3004-1

Water chemistry, environmental impacts, analytic methods, and quality and mgmt issues, 1989 rpt, 5668-96

see also Chemicals and chemical industry

Chemotherapy

Cancer (breast) survival rates, for patients receiving chemotherapy after surgery, for diagnoses made 1975-85, GAO rpt, 26131-58

Cancer (osteosarcoma) progress and deaths, by disease and treatment characteristics, 1977-85 study, article, 4472-1.901

Cheng, Fred F.

"Fish Toxicity Screening Data", 9238-69

Cherries

see Fruit and fruit products

Chesapeake Bay

Army Corps of Engineers water resources dev projects, characteristics, and costs, 1950s-89, biennial State rpt series, 3756-1

Pollutant concentrations in coastal and estuarine sediments, by contaminant and selected site, 1984-87, 2176-3.7

Pollutant concentrations in coastal and estuarine shellfish, by pollutant and location, 1986-88, 2176-3.8

Pollutant discharges in coastal areas and estuaries from agricultural, airborne, and other nonpoint sources, and regulatory issues, 1988 hearing, 21568-46

Tidal currents, daily time and velocity by station for North America coasts, forecast 1990, annual rpt, 2174-1.2

Water supply and quality in streams and lakes, and groundwater levels in wells, by drainage basin, 1986, annual State rpt series, 5666-23

Water supply and quality in streams and lakes, and groundwater levels in wells, by drainage basin, 1987, annual State rpt series, 5666-10

Water supply and quality in streams and lakes, and groundwater levels in wells, by drainage basin, 1988, annual State rpt series, 5666-16

Chesapeake, Va.
see also under By City in the "Index by Categories"

Chessie System
Railroad accidents, casualties, and damage, with data by carrier, for Pennsylvania and US, 1984-87, GAO rpt, 26113-390

Chew, Siew T.
"Agroforestry Projects for Small Farmers: A Project Manager's Reference", 9916-3.52

Cheyenne, Wyo.
see also under By SMSA or MSA in the "Index by Categories"

Chicago, Ill.
Airport and Airway Trust Fund funding and improvement spending, with data by airport and program, 1988 hearing, 21788-180

CPI by component for US city average, and by region, population size, and for 15 metro areas, monthly rpt, 6762-1

CPI by component for US city average, and by region, population size, and for 27 metro areas, monthly rpt, 6762-2

Drug abuse indicators for selected metro areas, research results, data collection, and policy issues, 1989 semiannual conf, 4492-5

Drug test results at arrest, by drug type, offense, and sex, for selected urban areas, quarterly rpt, 6062-3

Freight (waterborne domestic and foreign) by commodity, traffic, and passengers, by port and waterway, 1987, annual rpt, 3754-3.3

Fruit and vegetable shipments, and arrivals in US and Canada cities, by mode of transport and State and country of origin, 1988, annual rpt, 1311-4.2

Fruit and vegetable wholesale prices in NYC, Chicago, and selected shipping points, by crop, 1988, annual rpt, 1311-8

Hazardous substances industrial releases and reduction methods under EPA regulation, by chemical, source, industry, and location, 1987, annual rpt, 9234-6

Hispanic Americans employment discrimination cases filed in Chicago, 1987-88, annual GAO rpt, 26104-19

Homeless persons aid programs, and shelter capacity and voucher programs, for 5 major cities, 1988, 5188-122

Household and family characteristics, by location, 1988, annual Current Population Rpt, 2546-1.437

Housing (public) projects in Chicago structural and financial problems, and crime, 1979-88, GAO rpt, 26113-418

Housing starts and completions authorized by building permits in 40 MSAs, quarterly rpt, 2382-9

Housing vacancy rates for single and multifamily units and mobile homes, by city and ZIP code, 1989, annual MSA rpt, 9304-18.7

Manufacturing employment in Chicago compared to Illinois and other Great Lakes States, various periods 1969-88, working paper, 9375-13.14

see also under By City and By SMSA or MSA in the "Index by Categories"

Chicanos
see Hispanic Americans
see Mexicans in the U.S.

Chickens
see Poultry industry and products

Chico, Calif.
see also under By SMSA or MSA in the "Index by Categories"

Child abuse and neglect
Abduction and murder of children by strangers, and rates, by victim sex, age, and race, 1976-84, 6066-27.1

Cases of abuse and neglect reported, and victim characteristics, 1982-86, annual rpt, 6064-6.3

Court delinquency and neglect case dispositions, by State and county, 1985, annual rpt, 6064-12

Deaths and rates, by cause, age, sex, marital status, race, and State, 1987, US Vital Statistics advance annual rpt, 4146-5.113

Deaths and rates, by detailed cause and demographic characteristics, 1986 and trends from 1900, US Vital Statistics annual rpt, 4144-2

Facilities for juvenile correction and detention, inmates, and expenses, by instn and resident characteristics and State, 1975-85, biennial rpt, 6064-13

Fed Govt funding for juvenile delinquency prevention, by program and agency, FY88, annual rpt, 6064-11

HHS financial aid, by program, recipient, State, and city, FY88, annual regional listings, 4004-3

Homeless and runaway youth programs, funding, activities, and participant characteristics, FY86, annual rpt, 4604-3

Labor laws enacted, by State, 1988, annual article, 6722-1.904

Pornography involving children, USPS investigations, arrests, and convictions, 1987, annual rpt, 9864-8

Sentences for Federal offenses, guidelines by offense and circumstances, 1989 rpt, 17668-1

State allocation of Federal educational funds, by program, recipient type, and State, 1987/88, annual rpt, 4804-8

Statistical Abstract of US, social, political, and economic data, 1790-2025, comprehensive annual compilation, 2324-1.1

US attorneys civil and criminal cases by type and disposition, and collections, by Federal district, FY88, annual rpt, 6004-2.1

Child day care
AFDC job training and related aid, participants, costs, and budget impact, projected FY89-93, 26306-3.102

AFDC recipients demographic and financial characteristics, by State, FY87, annual rpt, 4694-1

Arrangements for child care, and costs, by income and other characteristics of family, 1984-86, press release, 2328-61

Budget of US, Bush Admin policy changes by program, FY90, 028-32

Employee parental leave of absence, policies, coverage, and attitudes, by employee characteristics, 1980-87, hearings, 25548-95

Expenditures by category, and income, effects of wives' employment by household characteristics, 1984-86, article, 6722-1.908

Food aid programs of USDA, costs and participation by program, region, and State, monthly rpt, 1362-14

Handicapped children home health care and support services availability and need, 1988, GAO report, 26121-300

Hepatitis cases by infection source, age, sex, race, and State, and deaths, by strain, 1987 and trends from 1966, 4205-2

Homeless shelters services, operations, and client characteristics, 1988 survey, 5188-123

Household and family composition, and factors affecting change, 1960s-88, chartbook, 2546-2.149

Labor force participation of mothers related to child care costs, 1984, Survey of Income and Program Participation, working paper, 2626-10.97

Labor laws enacted, by State, 1988, annual article, 6722-1.904

Military bases child day care services use, capacity, and waiting list backlog, by service branch, as of Feb 1988, GAO rpt, 26121-279

Military installation child care availability for civilian employees, and need, 1988 survey, GAO rpt, 26121-262

Military reserve spouses attitudes, and family social, economic, and other characteristics, 1986 survey, 3508-30

Occupational injury and illness rates, by SIC 2- to 4-digit industry, 1987, annual rpt, 6844-1

Receipts for services, by SIC 2- to 4-digit kind of business, 1988, annual rpt, 2413-8

Science and engineering employment, by nonmanufacturing industry and field, 1987, triennial rpt, 9627-31

Service industries census, 1987: establishments, receipts, employment, and payroll, by SIC 2- to 4-digit kind of business, MSA, county, and city, State rpt series, 2391-1

Statistical Abstract of US, social, political, and economic data, 1790-2025, comprehensive annual compilation, 2324-1.2

Tax (income) returns filed by type of filer, selected income items, quarterly rpt, 8302-2.1

Tax (income) returns of individuals, detailed data, 1986, annual rpt, 8304-2

Tax expenditures, Federal revenues forgone through income tax deductions and exclusions by type, FY90-94, annual rpt, 21784–10

Child labor

Labor laws enacted, by State, 1988, annual article, 6722–1.904

Child mortality

Abduction and murder of children by strangers, and rates, by victim sex, age, and race, 1976-84, 6066–27.1

AIDS cases among children, by age, sex, and risk group, with related HHS funding, 1980s-88, 4438–15

AIDS cases by risk group, race, sex, age, State, and MSA, and deaths, monthly rpt, 4202–9

Death rates of children, by age, sex, race, and cause, for US and compared to 8 OECD countries, 1985 and trends from 1900, 4147–3.27

Deaths and rates, by cause, age, sex, marital status, race, and State, 1987, US Vital Statistics advance annual rpt, 4146–5.113

Deaths and rates, by cause, age, sex, race, and State, preliminary 1987-88 and trends from 1960, US Vital Statistics annual rpt, 4144–7

Deaths and rates, by detailed cause and demographic characteristics, 1986 and trends from 1900, US Vital Statistics annual rpt, 4144–2

Deaths and rates, by detailed location, cause, and demographic characteristics, 1987, US Vital Statistics annual rpt, 4144–3

Developing countries economic and social conditions from 1960s, and Intl Dev Cooperation Agency and AID activities and funding, FY88-90, annual rpt, 9904–4

Firearms-related deaths of children, by motive, age, sex, and race, 1968-87, 4146–8.181

Health condition and health care resources, use, and spending, 1950s-87, annual data compilation, 4144–11

Homicide rates, and lifetime probability of victimization, by age, sex, and race, 1987, annual rpt, 6224–8

Traffic accident child deaths and survivors, by restraint type and use, age, and seat position, 1982-87, 7768–104

Traffic accident child deaths, effects of State laws mandating safety restraint use, 1978-88, 7768–108

see also Infant mortality

Child support and alimony

AFDC application denials, by reason and State, FY87, annual rpt, 4694–7.3

Assistance programs under Ways and Means Committee jurisdiction, finances and operations, FY70s-88, annual rpt, 21784–11

Awards and payment status of child support and alimony, by selected characteristics of woman, 1985, biennial Current Population Rpt, 2546–2.145

Awards for child support related to selected variables, 1970s-85, 4008–94

Collection of child support, State automated enforcement systems operational status by State and whether federally funded, 1985-88, GAO rpt, 26121–272

Collection of child support, State programs operations, costs, and Federal incentive payments, by State, FY86-1987, 4698–3

HHS financial aid, by program, recipient, State, and city, FY88, annual regional listings, 4004–3

Household and family composition, and factors affecting change, 1960s-88, chartbook, 2546–2.149

Income (household, family, and personal), by source, detailed characteristics, and region, 1987, annual Current Population Rpt, 2546–6.59

Interstate collection of child support, processing, officials views on mgmt, and Child Support Enforcement Office demonstration projects, 1987-88, GAO rpt, 26121–271

Statistical Abstract of US, social, political, and economic data, 1790-2025, comprehensive annual compilation, 2324–1.2

Tax (income) returns of individuals, by filing status, tax item, and income level, 1987, annual article, 8302–2.901

Tax (income) returns of individuals, detailed data, 1986, annual rpt, 8304–2

Tax (income) returns of individuals, selected income and tax items by income level, preliminary 1987, annual article, 8302–2.917

Telephone service of households, by composition, income sources, and other characteristics, 1984-87, 9288–11

Child Support Enforcement Program

State child support enforcement automated systems, operational status by State and whether federally funded, 1985-88, GAO rpt, 26121–272

Child welfare

Appalachia local dev projects, and funding by source, by program and State, FY88, annual rpt, 9084–1

Assistance (financial and nonfinancial) of Fed Govt, 1989 base edition with supplements, annual listing, 104–5

Assistance programs under Ways and Means Committee jurisdiction, finances and operations, FY70s-88, annual rpt, 21784–11

Benefits, beneficiary characteristics, and trust funds of OASDHI, Medicaid, SSI, and related programs, selected years 1937-87, annual rpt, 4744–3

Budget of US, House concurrent resolution, with spending and revenue targets, FY90, annual rpt, 21264–2

Civil service retirement system actuarial valuation, and benefits and coverage by age, type of beneficiary, and State, FY87, annual rpt, 9844–34

Employee parental leave of absence, policies, coverage, and attitudes, by employee characteristics, 1980-87, hearings, 25548–95

Expenditures, coverage, and benefits for social welfare programs, late 1930s-87, annual rpt, 4744–3.1

Expenditures for public welfare by program, and private health care spending, FY50s-86, annual article, 4742–1.909

Food aid program of USDA for women, infants, and children, participants and costs by State and Indian agency, FY87, annual rpt, 1364–12

Food aid program of USDA for women, infants, and children, participants, clinics, and costs by State and Indian agency, monthly tables, 1362–16

Food aid programs of USDA, costs and participation by program, region, and State, monthly rpt, 1362–14

Food aid programs of USDA for children, evaluation, 1988, biennial narrative rpt, 14854–1

Food stamp eligibility and payment errors, by type, recipient characteristics, and State, FY87, annual rpt, 1364–15

HHS financial aid, by program, recipient, State, and city, FY88, annual regional listings, 4004–3

Homeless and runaway youth programs, funding, activities, and participant characteristics, FY86, annual rpt, 4604–3

Indochina Amerasian children arriving in US and refugee camps under Orderly Departure Program, monthly rpt, 7002–4

Local govt health and welfare programs for high-risk infants and children, for Los Angeles and San Francisco, 1988 hearing, 21968–48

Medicaid coverage, participation, payments, admin, and legislative history, with data by State, 1980s-88, 21368–105

Medicaid eligibility extension to pregnant women and children with incomes over AFDC levels, with data by State, 1986-89, GAO rpt, 26121–303

OASDI benefit payments, trust fund finances, and economic and demographic assumptions, 1970-87 and alternative projections to 1997, actuarial rpt, 4706–1.103

PL 480 exports by commodity, and recipients, by program, sponsor, and country, FY87 and cumulative from FY55, annual rpt, 1924–7

Railroad employee retirement, survivors, unemployment, and health insurance programs, monthly rpt, 9702–2

Refugee resettlement programs and funding, arrivals by country of origin, and indicators of adjustment, by State, FY88, annual rpt, 4694–5

Supplemental Security Income and Medicaid eligibility and payment provisions, and beneficiaries living arrangements, by State, 1989, annual rpt, 4704–13

Veterans compensation and pension recipients, for each US war, 1775-1988, annual rpt, 8604–2

Veterans disability and death compensation and pension cases, by type of entitlement and period of service, monthly rpt, 8602–5; 9922–10

Veterans disability and death compensation cases of VA, by entitlement type, period of service, and sex, as of Mar 1989, semiannual rpt, 8602–8

Veterans disability and death compensation cases of VA, by entitlement type, period of service, sex, age, and State, FY88, annual rpt, 8604–7

Workers compensation laws of States and Fed Govt, 1989 semiannual rpt, 6502–1

see also Adoption

see also Aid to Families with Dependent Children

see also Child abuse and neglect

see also Child day care
see also Child support and alimony
see also Foster home care
see also Head Start Project
see also School lunch and breakfast
programs

Childbirth
see Births
see Birthweight
see Infant mortality
see Maternity
see Midwives
see Obstetrics and gynecology

Childers, Thomas
"Public Library Effectiveness Study: Final
Report", 4878-3

Children
AIDS cases among children, by age, sex,
and risk group, with related HHS funding,
1980s-88, 4438-15
AIDS cases and AIDS virus infection
prevalence, by risk group and other
patient characteristics, 1981-88 and
projected to 1992, 4206-2.13
AIDS cases, and health and social services
availability, for 5 cities, 1988, GAO rpt,
26121-307
AIDS cases by risk group, race, sex, age,
State, and MSA, and deaths, monthly rpt,
4202-9
Clothing expenditures, by family member
and selected family characteristics,
1984-85, working paper, 6886-6.61
Clothing expenses, by family member and
selected family characteristics, 1984-85,
working paper, 6886-6.44
Consumer Expenditure Survey, household
income by source, and itemized spending,
by selected characteristics and region,
1984-87, annual rpt, 6764-5
Consumer Income, socioeconomic
characteristics of persons, families, and
households, detailed cross-tabulations,
Current Population Rpt series, 2546-6
Costs of rearing children, by age, region,
and urban-rural location, quarterly rpt,
1702-1
Divorces and children involved, by
characteristics of spouses and whether 1st
marriage, 1950s-84, 4147-21.46
Divorces and children involved, by marriage
duration, race and age of spouses, and
State, 1984 and trends from 1950, US
Vital Statistics annual rpt, 4144-4.2
Divorces by age of spouses and duration of
marriage, and children involved, by State,
1986 with trends from 1940, US Vital
Statistics advance annual rpt, 4146-5.109
Family characteristics of children, and
family income, 1974-88, article,
6722-1.963
Farm population, by employment and
socioeconomic characteristics, and region,
1988, annual Current Population Rpt,
2546-1.439
Fiber content in breakfast cereal and bread,
health claim ads, and other factors
affecting consumption, 1978-88,
9406-1.60
Food consumption and nutrient intake by
individuals, by food group, selected
characteristics, and region, 1986
supplementary survey, 1356-5.1
Health condition and care of mothers and
children, research activities and funding,
FY88, annual rpt, 4474-31

Health condition and health care resources,
use, and spending, 1950s-87, annual data
compilation, 4144-11
Health education programs for child
nutrition and smoking deterrence,
effectiveness, 1979-85 local area study,
article, 4472-1.916
Hispanic Americans socioeconomic
characteristics, by detailed origin, 1988,
Current Population Rpt, 2546-1.430;
2546-1.438
Homeless children, by type of
accommodation, urban-rural location, and
State, alternative estimates, 1988, GAO
rpt, 26131-61
Homeless children educational enrollment
and needs, 1988, annual State rpt series,
4804-35
Hospitals (children's) unreimbursed charges,
expenses, and revenue, FY86, GAO rpt,
26121-291
Household and family characteristics, by
living arrangement, 1988 and trends from
1960, Current Population Rpt,
2546-2.148
Household and family characteristics, by
location, 1988, annual Current Population
Rpt, 2546-1.437
Household and family composition, and
factors affecting change, 1960s-88,
chartbook, 2546-2.149
Household composition, income, benefits,
and labor force status, Survey of Income
and Program Participation methodology,
working paper series, 2626-10
Households and housing detailed
characteristics, and unit and neighborhood
quality, by location, 1985, biennial rpt,
2485-12
Households and housing detailed
characteristics, and unit and neighborhood
quality, MSA surveys, series, 2485-6
Households and housing unit summary
characteristics, 1985 and trends, biennial
chartbook, 2486-1.7
Housing aid of Fed Govt, with low income
housing unit conditions and household
characteristics, 1985-FY88 and alternative
projections to 2008, 26306-6.134
Immigrant and nonimmigrant visas of US
issued and refused, by class, issuing office,
and nationality, FY88, annual rpt,
7184-1
Immigration to US, alien workers, visitors,
deportations, and naturalizations, by
country, FY88 and trends from 1820,
annual rpt, 6264-2
Income (household) and poverty status
under alternative income definitions, by
recipient characteristics, 1986, Current
Population Rpt, 2546-6.58
Indian children tooth decay from bottle
feeding, prevention project effectiveness,
1985-89, article, 4042-3.961
Indian children tooth decay from overnight
bottle feeding with sugar solution, 1985
local areas study, article, 4042-3.903
Injuries from use of consumer products and
related activities, by victim age and sex,
1988, annual rpt, 9164-7
Injuries from use of consumer products, by
severity, victim age, and detailed product,
1988, annual rpt, 9164-6
Lead poisoning among children, and
children at risk in Massachusetts, by city,
1985-87, hearing, 21248-119

Lead poisoning among children, and impacts
of lead removal from housing, gasoline,
and water, 1987 conf, 4108-46
Living arrangements, family relationships,
and marital status, by selected
characteristics, 1988, annual Current
Population Rpt, 2546-1.428;
2546-1.433
Mental health treatment of children in
short-stay hospitals, by age, race, and
facility and physician characteristics,
1977, 4188-55
Migration since 1986, mover characteristics
by same or different area, and compared
to nonmovers, 1987, annual Current
Population Rpt, 2546-1.435
Military reserve spouses attitudes, and
family social, economic, and other
characteristics, 1986 survey, 3508-30
Nutritional status and related health
condition and practices, by selected
characteristics, 1970s-87, 4048-33
Pollution (air) exposure of population and
selected risk groups, by pollutant, MSA,
and county, 1988, hearing, 21368-117
Population of children from age 10 and from
birth, by county, 1985, annual rpt,
6064-12
Population size, by age, sex, and race, and
components of change, alternative
projections 1988-2080, Current Population
Rpt, 2546-3.158
Poverty status of families and persons, by
detailed characteristics, 1987, annual
Current Population Rpt, 2546-6.60
Radiation exposure of population near
commercial reactors, by body site, age
group, and selected plant, 1986, annual
rpt, 9634-7
Research contracts and grants of Natl Inst
of Child Health and Human Dev, by
recipient and location, FY88, annual
listing, 4474-36
Safety-related behavior of children, 1988
local area survey, article, 4042-3.937
Statistical Abstract of US, social, political,
and economic data, with foreign
comparisons, 1790-2025, comprehensive
annual compilation, 2324-1
Surgical procedures performed in hospitals,
by procedure type, age, sex, instn size,
and payment source, 1983-87,
4146-8.171
Tax (income) returns of individuals, by filing
status, tax item, and income level, 1987,
annual article, 8302-2.901
Tax (income) returns of individuals, detailed
data, 1986, annual rpt, 8304-2
Telephone service of households, by
composition, income sources, and other
characteristics, 1984-87, 9288-11
Traffic accident child deaths and survivors,
by restraint type and use, age, and seat
position, 1982-87, 7768-104
Vaccination activity, reactions, costs, and
preventable disease cases and deaths,
1988 annual conf, 4204-15
Vitamin and mineral supplements use by
adults and children, by type and user
characteristics, 1986, 4146-8.175
Wildlife-related recreation, hunting, and
fishing participation and spending,
detailed data by location, 1985 survey,
quinquennial rpt, 5508-5

Wildlife-related recreation, hunting, and fishing participation and spending, detailed data, 1985 survey, quinquennial State rpt series, 5506-6

see also Adoption

see also Aid to Families with Dependent Children

see also Birth defects

see also Births

see also Births out of wedlock

see also Breast-feeding

see also Child abuse and neglect

see also Child day care

see also Child labor

see also Child mortality

see also Child support and alimony

see also Child welfare

see also Compensatory education

see also Educational enrollment

see also Elementary and secondary education

see also Foster home care

see also Handicapped children

see also Head Start Project

see also Infant mortality

see also Juvenile courts and cases

see also Juvenile delinquency

see also Juvenile detention and correctional institutions

see also Old-Age, Survivors, Disability, and Health Insurance

see also Parents

see also Pediatrics

see also Preschool education

see also Remedial education

see also School lunch and breakfast programs

see also Special education

see also Students

see also Youth

see also Youth employment

see also under By Age in the "Index by Categories"

Childress, Carolyn J.

"Water-Quality Data-Collection Activities in Colorado and Ohio: Phase II—Evaluation of 1984 Field and Laboratory Quality-Assurance Practices", 5668-94

Childs, Nathan W.

"Changing Role of the U.S. in the World Rice Market", 1561-8.902

"U.S. Rice Distribution Patterns: An Overview of Crop Year 1986/87", 1561-8.901

"U.S. Rice Distribution Patterns, 1986/87", 1564-11

Chile

Agricultural and food production and indexes, total and for selected commodities, by country, 1970s-88, annual rpt, 1524-12

Agricultural production, prices, and trade, by country, 1960s-89, annual world region rpt, 1524-4.2

Agricultural trade of US, by detailed commodity and country, 1988, semiannual rpt, 1522-4

AID economic aid to developing countries, obligations and disbursements by country, quarterly rpt, 9912-4

AID loans repayment status and terms by program and country, and status of predecessor agency loans, quarterly rpt, 9912-3

Economic and military aid and loans from US and intl agencies, by program and country, FY46-87, annual rpt, 9914-5

Economic conditions, income, production, prices, employment, and trade, 1989 periodic country rpt, 2046-4.16

Economic conditions, policy, and trade practices, by country, 1986-88, annual rpt, 21384-5

Economic indicators of developing countries, problem debtors compared to other borrowers, by country, 1973-84, 1528-285

Economic, social, political, and geographic summary data, by country, 1989, annual factbook, 9114-2

Exports and imports of Latin America, and balance of trade with US, by country, 1988, annual rpt, 2044-34

Exports and imports of US, by commodity and country, 1970-87, world area rpt, 9116-1.5

Exports and imports of US, by selected country, country group, and commodity group, 1988, annual rpt, 2044-37

Fruit production, trade, and use, and fruit and vegetable exports to US, for Chile, by commodity, 1978-89, article, 1925-34.911

Fruit production, trade, use, and processing, by commodity for 5 countries, 1986-89, annual article, 1925-34.909

Human rights conditions in 170 countries, 1988, annual rpt, 21384-3

Imports of goods, services, and investment from US, trade barriers, impacts, and US actions, by country, 1988, annual rpt, 444-2

Labor conditions, union coverage, and work accidents, 1989 annual country rpt, 6366-4.53

Military aid of US, arms sales, and training programs costs and budget requests, by program, world region, and country, FY88-90, annual rpt, 7144-13

Military spending, arms trade, and force strengths, with govt spending and population, by country, 1977-87, annual rpt, 9824-1

Minerals Yearbook, 1987, Vol 3: foreign country reviews of production, trade, and policy, by commodity, annual rpt, 5604-35

Minerals Yearbook, 1987, Vol 3 preprints: foreign country review of production, trade, and policy, by commodity, annual rpt, 5604-23.15

Multinatl US firms and foreign affiliates finances and operations, by industry of parent firm and affiliate, world area, and country, preliminary 1987, annual rpt, 2704-5

Population size, growth rates, and components of change, by country, projected 1989-2020 and trends from 1950, biennial rpt, 2324-9

UN voting record and share of votes in agreement with US, by issue, country, and world area, 1988, annual rpt, 7004-18

see also under By Foreign Country in the "Index by Categories"

Chillicothe, Ohio

Wages by occupation, for office and plant workers, 1989 survey, periodic MSA rpt, 6785-3.4

Chin, E.

"Emerging Mineral Industry of China", 5606-5.7

China, Nationalist

see Taiwan

China, Peoples Republic

Agricultural and food production and indexes, total and for selected commodities, by country, 1970s-88, annual rpt, 1524-12

Agricultural exports of US, for grains, oilseed products, hides, skins, and cotton, by country, weekly rpt, 1922-3

Agricultural production, prices, and trade, by country, 1960s-89, annual world region rpt, 1524-4.2

Agricultural production, prices, and trade, for PRC, 1988 and forecast 1989, annual rpt, 1524-4.3

Agricultural subsidies, consumer and producer equivalents by program, commodity, and major US trading partner, 1982-86, 1528-275

Agricultural trade by commodity and country, prices, and world market devs, monthly rpt, 1922-12

Agricultural trade of US, by detailed commodity and country, 1988, semiannual rpt, 1522-4

Building materials production and trade by product group, and housing and commercial construction, for PRC, 1984-85 and projected to 1990, article, 2042-1.910

Cancer (lung) risk relation to home heating and cooking facilities, air pollution exposure, and smoking, by sex, for Shenyang, PRC, 1985-87 study, article, 4472-1.931

Cancer (stomach) by intake of allium vegetables, for China, 1984-86, article, 4472-1.903

Coal production, trade, and govt subsidies, by country and country group, 1973-87 and projected to 2000, 2048-144

Cotton acreage, production, consumption, stocks, and trade of PRC, 1975-88, article, 1561-1.901

Cotton production, trade, and use, for selected countries, FAS monthly circular, 1925-4.2

Cuba economic conditions, agricultural and industrial production and distribution, trade, and intl economic relations, 1980-87 with trends from 1961, 9118-8

Economic and military aid and loans from US and intl agencies, by program and country, FY46-87, annual rpt, 9914-5

Economic conditions and trade, for PRC, annual rpt, discontinued, 9114-5

Economic conditions in Communist and OECD countries, 1987, annual rpt, 7144-11

Economic conditions in Communist, OECD, and selected other countries, 1960s-88, annual rpt, 9114-4

Economic conditions in PRC before reform movement crackdown in 1989, with US trade by commodity, and foreign investment by source country, 1988, 9118-9

Economic conditions, income, production, prices, employment, and trade, 1989 periodic country rpt, 2046-4.108

Economic conditions, investment and export opportunities, and trade practices, 1988 country market research rpt, 2046–6.1

Economic conditions, policy, and trade practices, by country, 1986-88, annual rpt, 21384–5

Economic, social, political, and geographic summary data, by country, 1989, annual factbook, 9114–2

Employment by sector, urban-rural location, and Province, with surplus rural labor and urban jobs assigned, for PRC, 1950s-87 and projected to 2000, working paper, 2326–18.48

Energy-intensive industry output and operations, and US investment barriers, for energy-rich countries, 1984-88, 9886–4.142

Export license applications for high-technology trade with PRC, by disposition, 1973-84, compilation of papers, 3908–4

Export licensing, monitoring, and enforcement activities, FY88, annual rpt, 2024–1

Exports and imports of PRC, by commodity, world area, and country, 1985-87, 9118–10

Exports and imports of PRC, by SITC 1- to 5-digit commodity, 1970s-87, annual rpt, 9114–3

Exports and imports of US, by commodity and country, 1970-87, world area rpt, 9116–1.2

Exports and imports of US, by selected country, country group, and commodity group, 1988, annual rpt, 2044–37

Exports and imports of US with Communist countries, by detailed commodity and country, quarterly rpt with articles, 9882–2

Exports and imports of US with PRC, by selected commodity, 1980-86, hearing, 23848–195

Exports, imports, and balances of US by commodity group, world area, and country, and related employment, 1970s-88, annual rpt, 2044–26

Exports of footwear, games, and toys, to US from PRC and other countries, 1983-88, article, 9882–2.901

Grain exports to USSR and PRC under long-term bilateral agreements, 1976-88, 26123–227

Grain production, consumption, and trade of PRC, impact of re-centralization policies, 1989 article, 1522–3.914

Hats and caps (cloth) from PRC at less than fair value, injury to US industry, investigation with background financial and operating data, 1988 rpt, 9886–14.261

Human rights conditions in 170 countries, 1988, annual rpt, 21384–3

Imports of goods, services, and investment from US, trade barriers, impacts, and US actions, by country, 1988, annual rpt, 444–2

Labor conditions and work accidents, 1989 annual country rpt, 6366–4.22

Military aid of US, arms sales, and training programs costs and budget requests, by program, world region, and country, FY88-90, annual rpt, 7144–13

Military spending, arms trade, and force strengths, with govt spending and population, by country, 1977-87, annual rpt, 9824–1

Minerals production and trade of PRC, by commodity, estimated 1986-87, compilation of papers, 5606–5.7

Minerals production, reserves, and industry role in domestic economy and world supply, 1988 country rpt, 5606–1.17

Minerals Yearbook, 1987, Vol 3: foreign country reviews of production, trade, and policy, by commodity, annual rpt, 5604–35

Minerals Yearbook, 1987, Vol 3 preprints: foreign country review of production, trade, and policy, by commodity, annual rpt, 5604–23.16

Nitrocellulose (industrial) from 7 countries at less than fair value, injury to US industry, investigation with background financial and operating data, 1989 rpt, 9886–14.270

Nuclear power plant capacity and operating status, by plant and Communist country, as of Dec 1988, annual rpt, 3164–57.2

Oil production, and exports by country, for PRC, monthly rpt, 9112–2

Oil production by major exporting countries, monthly rpt, 3162–24.10

Oil production, trade, use, and stocks, by selected country and country group, monthly rpt, 3162–42

Population size, growth rates, and components of change, by country, projected 1989-2020 and trends from 1950, biennial rpt, 2324–9

Port facilities, operations, and impacts on US agricultural exports, for major Far East Asia ports, 1970s-87, 1278–13

Ships in world merchant fleet, and tonnage, by country of registry, as of Jan 1988, annual rpt, 7704–3

Space satellites and other objects launched since 1957, quarterly listing, 9502–2

Steel export ceilings under voluntary restraint agreements, by country and product, with Western US steel industry impact, 1989 rpt, 9886–4.136

Steel imports of US under voluntary restraint agreement, by product, customs district, and country, with US industry operating data, monthly rpt, 9882–13

Sugar production, consumption, and trade of PRC, selected years 1960-89, article, 1561–14.901

Tidal currents, daily time and velocity by station for North America and Asia coasts, forecast 1990, annual rpt, 2174–1.1

Timber in northwestern US and British Columbia, production, prices, trade, and employment, quarterly rpt, 1202–3

UN voting record and share of votes in agreement with US, by issue, country, and world area, 1988, annual rpt, 7004–18

Wheat yield of PRC compared to 11 other countries, 1978 and 1987, article, 1561–12.907

see also under By Foreign Country in the "Index by Categories"

Chinese Americans
see Asian Americans

Chiropractic and naturopathy
County Business Patterns, 1987: employment, establishments, and payroll, by SIC 2- to 4-digit industry and county, annual State rpt series, 2326–8

Health condition and health care resources, use, and spending, 1950s-87, annual data compilation, 4144–11

Medicare physicians services use, charges, and reimbursement, by service type, setting, and specialty, 1986, article, 4652–1.936

Safety and effectiveness of health care, use of unproven treatments and products, costs, and user characteristics, 1986 survey, 4008–86

Service industries census, 1987: establishments, receipts, employment, and payroll, by SIC 2- to 4-digit kind of business, MSA, county, and city, State rpt series, 2391–1

Service industries receipts, by SIC 2- to 4-digit kind of business, 1988, annual rpt, 2413–8

Tax (income) returns of partnerships, income statement items by industry group, 1986, annual article, 8302–2.903

Tax (income) returns of sole proprietorships, income statement items, by industry group, 1987, annual article, 8302–2.904; 8302–2.921

Chlorine
see Gases

Chlorofluorocarbons
see Chemicals and chemical industry

Chmura, Christine
"Changes in Manufacturing Employment in North Carolina Counties, 1980-85", 9389–1.915

Chocolate
see Cocoa and chocolate

Choi, Jai W.
"Exercise and Participation in Sports Among Persons 20 Years of Age and Over: U.S., 1975", 4147–16.2

Cholesterol
see Vitamins and nutrients

Chovonec, Mike
"Taxpayer Perceptions About the Quality of Taxpayer Service", 8304–8.1

Christensen, Lee A.
"Future Directions and Challenges in Egg Marketing", 1561–7.902

Christensen, Sandra
"Medicare Catastrophic Coverage Act of 1988", 26306–3.105

Christiansted, V.I.
Economic Censuses of Outlying Areas, 1987: Virgin Islands employment, firms, payroll, and receipts, by SIC 1- to 4-digit industry, island, and city, 2593–1

Christmas Island
Economic, social, political, and geographic summary data, by country, 1989, annual factbook, 9114–2

Minerals Yearbook, 1987, Vol 3 preprints: foreign country review of production, trade, and policy, by commodity, annual rpt, 5604–23.85

Chromium
see Metals and metal industries

Chronic health conditions
see Diseases and disorders
see Health condition

Chronologies

Agricultural trade among western hemisphere countries, and US duty-free imports, with listing of trade disputes and outcomes, 1960s-85, 1528–278

Aircraft accidents, casualties, and damage, for commercial operations by detailed circumstances, 1986, annual rpt, 9614–2

Aircraft accidents, deaths, and circumstances, by carrier and carrier type, preliminary 1988, annual press release, 9614–9

Aircraft hijackings and attempts, persons involved, and location, for US and foreign carriers, 1st half 1988, semiannual rpt, 7502–5

Aircraft hijackings, on-board explosions, and other crime, US and foreign incidents, 1983-87, annual rpt, 7504–31

Arms control treaties status, and Arms Control and Disarmament Agency activities, 1988, annual rpt, 9824–2

Bank deposit insurance systems of States, banks, and bank failure rates, for selected States, various periods 1829-1930, article, 9375–1.904

Banks and thrifts deposit insurance of FDIC and FSLIC, legislative history, 1933-87, technical paper, 9316–1.143

Capitol Architect outlays for salaries, supplies, and services, itemized by payee and function, 1st half FY89, semiannual rpt, 25922–2

Consumer Product Safety Commission activities, recalls by brand, and casualties and societal costs, by product type, FY87, annual rpt, 9164–2

Disasters by State, Natl Guard emergency response and strengths, FY88, annual rpt, 3504–22.1

Earthquakes and other ground motion, intensity by station, and info sources, 1986, annual rpt, 5664–14

Earthquakes in Alaska and Aleutian Islands, intensity, magnitude, time, and location, 1786-1981, 5668–87

Economic Report of the President for 1989, listing of deregulation initiatives, 1971-88, annual rpt, 204–1

Electric power shortages and disturbances of service, listing of occurrences, quarterly rpt, 3162–39.4

Export and import agreements, negotiations, anticompetitive investigations, and related legislation, FY86-88, annual rpt, 444–1

Exporters (US) antiboycott law violations and fines by firm, and invitations to boycott by country, FY88, annual rpt, 2024–1

Fed Govt civilian pay legislation, 1945-88, annual rpt, 9844–6.7

Fed Govt civilian pay rates, by pay schedule and grade, 1989 and trends from 1789, annual rpt, 21624–4

Fed Govt debt subject to statutory limits, and legislative history, FY40-88 and projected to FY94, annual rpt, 104–22

Fed Govt financial and nonfinancial domestic aid programs and changes since 1965, by agency, 1989 base edition with supplements, annual listing, 104–5

Foreign countries *Geographic Notes*, nations gaining sovereignty since 1943, and other devs, periodic rpt, 7142–3

Futures and options trading volume, by commodity and exchange, FY88, annual rpt, 11924–2

Gold deposits location, discovery, and geologic indicators, 1799-1982, compilation of papers, 5668–90

House of Representatives salaries, expenses, and contingent fund disbursement, detailed listings, quarterly rpt, 21942–1

Hurricanes and tropical storms in north Atlantic and Caribbean area, paths, surveillance, deaths, damage, and landfall probabilities by city, 1988, annual rpt, 2184–7

Hurricanes and tropical storms in northeastern Pacific Ocean, paths and surveillance, 1988, annual rpt, 2184–8

Income tax law changes, 1916-50, article, 8302–2.913

Labor-mgmt collective bargaining agreements expiring during year, and workers covered, by firm, union, industry group, and State, 1989, annual rpt, 6784–9

Oil and gas OCS operations accidents, spills, casualties, and circumstances, 1956-86, listing, 5738–7

Patent and Trademark Office activities, patent applications and grants, and trademark registrations and renewals, 1790-1988, 2248–2

Radioactive waste from DOE military activities, disposal plans and funding, FY87-93, last issue of annual rpt, 3344–1

Railroad accidents, circumstances, severity, and railroad involved, periodic rpt, 9612–3

Senate receipts, itemized expenses by payee, and balances, 1st half FY89, semiannual listing, 25922–1

Smithsonian Instn activities, rpts, and funding by donor, FY88, annual rpt, 29574–1.2

Smoking prevalence, related disease and deaths, and public attitudes, impact of Surgeon General rpts and antismoking campaigns, 1964-89, annual rpt, 4204–18

Soviet Union grain imports from US, 1970s-88 and commitments through 1990, FAS press release, 1928–10

Soviet Union officials public appearances in and outside USSR, 1988, annual rpt, 9114–1

Soviet Union space program activities, plans, and characteristics of flights and vehicles, 1981-87, 25268–76.2

Space launches and other activities of NASA and USSR, with flight data, 1957-88, annual rpt, 9504–6.1

Star position tables, planet coordinates, time conversion factors, and listing of observatories worldwide, 1990, annual rpt, 3804–7

Terrorist (intl) incidents, casualties, and attacks on US targets, by attack type and country, 1980-88, 7008–56

Terrorist (intl) incidents, casualties, and attacks on US targets, by attack type and world area, 1968-88, annual rpt, 7004–13

Terrorist incidents in US, related activity, and casualties, by attack type, target, group, and location, 1988, annual rpt, 6224–6

Transportation accident investigations and recommendations by Natl Transportation Safety Board, 1988, annual rpt, 9614–1

Tsunamis intensity, time, location, and other characteristics, for US and territories, 1690-1988, 2158–52

Weather data by census div and State, historical trends, indexes, major events, and maps, series, 2156–17

Chrysler Corp.
Energy economy, sales, and market shares, by size and model for domestic and foreign makes, 1989 model year, semiannual rpt, 3302–4

Energy economy test results, 1990 model year, annual rpt, 3304–11

Safety of domestic and foreign autos, crash test results by model, model years 1984-88, 7768–111

Safety of domestic and foreign autos, crash test results by model, press release series, 7766–7

Chrystal, K. Alec
"Guide to Foreign Exchange Markets", 9375–14

Chukchi Sea
Birds (waterfowl) coastal population, breeding success, and diet, for murre and kittiwake at Cape Thompson, Alaska, 1960s-88, 5738–11

Environmental conditions and oil dev impacts for Alaska OCS, compilation of papers, series, 2176–1

Minerals resources in sediment off north Alaska coast, 1985 study, 5668–95

Chula Vista, Calif.
see also under By City in the "Index by Categories"

Chung, Edward
"Private Activity Tax-Exempt Bonds, 1986", 8302–2.905

Church and state
see also Religious liberty

Churches
see Religious organizations

CIA
see Central Intelligence Agency

Cigarettes and cigars
see Smoking
see Tobacco industry and products

Cincinnati, Ohio
CPI by component for US city average, and by region, population size, and for 27 metro areas, monthly rpt, 6762–2

Driving while intoxicated enforcement and publicity strategies, NHSTA deterrence project results, 1984-85, 7768–109

Fruit and vegetable shipments, and arrivals in US and Canada cities, by mode of transport and State and country of origin, 1988, annual rpt, 1311–4.1

Wages by occupation, and benefits for office and plant workers, 1989 survey, periodic MSA rpt, 6785–12.7

see also under By City and By SMSA or MSA in the "Index by Categories"

Cinema
see Motion pictures

Circulatory diseases
Cases of acute and chronic conditions, disability, absenteeism, and health services use, by selected characteristics, 1988, annual rpt, 4147–10.170

Cholesterol levels among aged, screening and treatment effectiveness, and costs under proposed Medicare coverage, 1978-89, 26356–7.3

Deaths and rates, by cause, age, sex, marital status, race, and State, 1987, US Vital Statistics advance annual rpt, 4146–5.113

Deaths and rates, by cause and age, preliminary 1987-88, US Vital Statistics annual rpt, 4144–7

Deaths and rates, by detailed cause and demographic characteristics, 1986 and trends from 1900, US Vital Statistics annual rpt, 4144–2

Deaths and rates, by detailed location, cause, and demographic characteristics, 1987, US Vital Statistics annual rpt, 4144–3

Hospital discharges and length of stay, by diagnosis, patient and instn characteristics, procedure performed, and payment source, 1987, annual rpt, 4147–13.99

Hospital discharges by detailed diagnostic and procedure category, primary diagnosis, and length of stay, by age, sex, and region, 1987, annual rpt, 4147–13.100

Indian (Seneca Tribe) deaths and years of potential life lost, by selected cause and sex, various periods 1955-84, article, 4042–3.925

Indian Health Service and contract facilities hospitalization, by diagnosis, age, sex, and service area, FY87, annual rpt, 4104–16

Indian Health Service and contract facilities hospitalization, by diagnosis, age, sex, and service area, FY88, annual rpt, 4084–5

Nursing home facility, staff, and resident detailed characteristics, 1985, 4147–13.97

Surgical procedures performed, costs, length of stay, and deaths, impacts of Medicare prospective payment system by procedure type, 1984-86, 17206–2.5

see also Cardiovascular diseases
see also Cerebrovascular diseases
see also Hypertension
see also under By Disease in the "Index by Categories"

Cirrhosis of liver
see Digestive diseases

Cities
AIDS risk knowledge and high-risk activities of homosexual men in cities with low and high AIDS rates, 1989 article, 4042–3.939

Crimes, arrests by offender characteristics, and rates, by offense, and law enforcement employees, by population size and jurisdiction, 1988, annual rpt, 6224–2

Criminal justice spending, employment, and payroll, by level of govt, State, and selected city and county, FY71-85, annual rpt, 6064–9

Fed Govt spending in States and local areas, by type, State, county, and city, FY88, annual rpt, 2464–3.2

Govt (local) in metro areas, finances, structure, and service delivery, local area rpt series, 10046–9

Govt census, 1987: elected officials, by level of govt, race, sex, and State, preliminary rpt, 2450–2

Govt census, 1987: property tax revenue by level of govt, assessed values by locality, and exemptions, by property type and State, 2453–1

Govt employment and payroll, by function, for 295 largest cities, 1988, annual rpt, 2466–1.3; 2466–1.6

Govt finances, by level of govt, State, and for large cities and counties, annual rpt series, 2466–2

Govt finances, tax systems and revenue, and fiscal structure, by level of govt and State, selected years 1929-91, annual rpt, 10044–1

Govt services transfer to private contractors, impacts on govt workers, with data by worker characteristics, level of govt, and location, 1980s-87, 15496–1.5

Labor surplus areas eligible for preferential Fed Govt contracts, monthly listing, 6402–1

Population size, by MSA, county, metro-nonmetro location, and State, 1987, and for cities, 1986, with change from 1980 and trends from 1960, Current Population Rpt, 2546–3.160

Population size of cities with population over 100,000, as of July 1988, biennial press release, 2324–7

Statistical Abstract of US, social, political, and economic data, with foreign comparisons, 1790-2025, comprehensive annual compilation, 2324–1

Urban Dev Action Grants, funding sources, project descriptions, and economic impacts, by city, periodic press releases, 5002–7

see also Central business districts
see also Central cities
see also City and town planning
see also Harbors and ports
see also Metropolitan Statistical Areas
see also Neighborhoods
see also Suburbs
see also Urban areas
see also ZIP codes
see also under By City and By SMSA or MSA in the "Index by Categories"
see also under names of individual cities

Citizen-government relations
see Government-citizen relations

Citizen lawsuits
see Government-citizen lawsuits

Citizenship
Criminal cases by type and disposition, and collections, for US attorneys, by Federal district, FY88, annual rpt, 6004–2.1

Criminal sentences for Federal offenses, guidelines by offense and circumstances, 1989 rpt, 17668–1

DOD civilian employment, by service branch and defense agency, with summary military employment data, quarterly rpt, 3542–16

DOD civilian employment, by US citizenship, service branch, and country, quarterly rpt, 3542–20

Fed Govt civilian employment, by citizenship status and location, bimonthly rpt, 9842–1

Foreign countries human rights conditions in 170 countries, 1988, annual rpt, 21384–3

Military reserve spouses attitudes and family social, economic, and other characteristics, 1986 survey, 3508–30

Naturalization petitions filed and granted, by Federal district court, June 1988 and trends from 1970s, annual rpt, 18204–8.11; 18204–8.24

Naturalizations, by selected characteristics and country, FY88 and trends from 1907, annual rpt, 6264–2

Refugee arrivals and resettlement in US, by age, sex, sponsoring agency, State, and country, monthly rpt, 4692–2

Statistical Abstract of US, social, political, and economic data, 1790-2025, comprehensive annual compilation, 2324–1.1

see also Alien workers
see also Aliens
see also Foreign medical graduates
see also Foreign students

Citrus fruits
Agricultural Statistics, 1988, annual rpt, 1004–1

Agriculture census, 1987: farms, farmland, production and costs, and operator characteristics, advance State and county rpt series, 2330–1

Agriculture census, 1987: farms, farmland, production, finances, and operator characteristics, by county, final State rpt series, 2331–1

Consumption of food and nutrient intake by individuals, by food group, selected characteristics, and region, supplementary survey series, 1356–5

Consumption, supply, trade, prices, spending, and indexes, by food commodity, 1987, annual rpt, 1544–4

CPI by component for US city average, and by region, population size, and for 27 metro areas, monthly rpt, 6762–2

Cuba economic conditions, agricultural and industrial production and distribution, trade, and intl economic relations, 1980-87 with trends from 1961, 9118–8

Exports and imports (agricultural) of US, by commodity and country, bimonthly rpt with articles, 1522–1

Exports and imports (agricultural) of US, by detailed commodity and country, 1988, semiannual rpt, 1522–4

Exports of US, detailed commodities by country, monthly rpt, 2422–3

Farm income, expenses, receipts by commodity, assets, liabilities, and ratios, 1988 and trends from 1945, annual rpt, 1544–16

Farm receipts for 25 leading crops, by State, 1960-87, 1548–347

Farm sector balance sheet, and receipts by detailed commodity, by State, 1984-88, annual rpt, 1544–18

Foreign and US fresh and processed fruit, vegetable, and nut production and trade, FAS monthly circular with articles, 1925–34

Foreign countries agricultural production, prices, and trade, by country, 1970s-89 and forecast 1990, annual world region rpt series, 1524–4

Futures and options trading volume, by commodity and exchange, FY88, annual rpt, 11924–2

Futures contracts on commodities, financial instruments, and indexes, options trading in NYC, Chicago, and other markets, monthly rpt, 11922–6

Futures trading in selected commodities and financial instruments and indexes, NYC, Chicago, and other markets activity, monthly rpt, 11922–5

Imports of US, detailed Schedule A
commodities by country, monthly rpt,
2422–2

Nutrient and caloric composition of food,
for raw, processed, and prepared food,
1988 rpt, 1358–3

Orange and grapefruit juice exports of US,
by world area, 1985-87, tables,
1925–34.910

Orange exports of US, by world area,
1985-87, table, 1925–34.906

Orange juice (frozen) cold storage stocks, by
census div, 1988, annual rpt, 1631–11

Orange juice (frozen) from Brazil, injury to
US industry from import sales at less than
fair value, investigation supplement, 1989
rpt, 9886–14.250

Pesticide (soil fumigant) use, impacts of
bans of selected fumigants on production,
farm income, and retail prices, by crop
and region, 1988 rpt, 1588–136

Price indexes (producer), by stage of
processing and detailed commodity,
monthly rpt, 6762–6

Price indexes (producer), by stage of
processing and detailed commodity,
monthly 1988, annual rpt, 6764–2

Prices (farm-retail) for food, marketing cost
components, and industry finances and
productivity, 1950s-88, annual rpt,
1544–9

Prices (wholesale) for fresh fruit and
vegetables in NYC, Chicago, and selected
shipping points, by crop, 1988, annual rpt,
1311–8

Prices received and paid by farmers, by
commodity and State, 1988, annual rpt,
1629–5

Prices received by farmers and production
value, by detailed crop and State,
1986-88, annual rpt, 1621–2

Prices received by farmers for major
products, and paid for farm inputs and
living items, by State, monthly rpt,
1629–1

Production and use of citrus fruit, by crop
and producer State, 1981/82-1986/87,
1641–4

Production, farms, acreage, and related data,
by selected crop and State, monthly rpt,
1621–1

Production of fruit and vegetables for
processing, industries finances and
operations, consumption, and trade, by
commodity, 1970s-88, 1568–275

Production, prices, and use of fruit and nuts,
1986-89, annual rpt series, 1621–18

Production, prices, trade, stocks, and use, by
selected crop, periodic situation rpt with
articles, 1561–6

Shipments by mode of transport, arrivals,
and imports, for fruit and vegetables by
commodity and State and country of
origin, weekly rpt, 1311–3

Shipments of fruit and vegetables, and
arrivals in US and Canada cities, by mode
of transport and State and country of
origin, 1988, annual rpt series, 1311–4

see also under By Commodity in the "Index
by Categories"

City and town planning

Economic Dev Admin activities, and
funding by program, recipient, State, and
county, FY87 and cumulative from FY66,
annual rpt, 2064–2

Historic and natural natl landmarks
damaged and threatened, with owner,
location, damage type, and recommended
remedial action, 1988, annual listing,
5544–16

City taxation

see State and local taxes

Civil aviation

Communist, OECD, and selected other
countries freight and carrier inventories,
by mode of transport, 1960s-88, annual
rpt, 9114–4.10

Pilots and nonpilots certified by FAA, by
certificate type, age, sex, region, and
State, 1988, annual rpt, 7504–2

Statistical Abstract of US, social, political,
and economic data, 1790-2025,
comprehensive annual compilation,
2324–1.3

see also Aerospace industry
see also Air cargo
see also Air piracy
see also Air traffic control
see also Aircraft
see also Airlines
see also Airports and airways
see also Aviation accidents and safety
see also General aviation
see also Pilots

Civil defense

Assistance (financial and nonfinancial) of
Fed Govt, 1989 base edition with
supplements, annual listing, 104–5

Expenditures of Fed Govt in States, by type,
program, agency, and State, FY88, annual
rpt, 2464–2

see also National Guard

Civil engineering

see Bridges and tunnels
see Canals
see Dams
see Harbors and ports
see Highways, streets, and roads
see Irrigation
see Public works
see Reclamation of land
see Rivers and waterways
see Traffic engineering

Civil liberties

see Civil rights
see Due process of law
see Electronic surveillance
see Habeas corpus
see Right of privacy
see Searches and seizures

Civil-military relations

see also Defense contracts and procurement
see also Defense industries
see also Impacted areas

Civil procedure

Aliens exclusion and deportation cases,
appeals, bond postings, and investigations,
for NYC and Los Angeles, 1987, GAO
rpt, 26119–271

Diplomats and staff with immunity for
foreign missions in US and US missions
abroad, and foreign diplomats criminal
cases, 1978-87, hearing, 25388–51

Federal district and appeals court caseloads,
actions, procedure duration, judges, and
jurors, by court, 1984-89, annual rpt,
18204–3

Federal district, appeals, and bankruptcy
courts, civil cases terminated by circuit
and district, quarterly rpt, 18202–1

Federal district, appeals, and special courts
civil and criminal caseloads, 1989, annual
rpt, 18204–2; 18204–8

Judicial Conf proceedings and findings, fall
1989, semiannual rpt, 18202–2

Patent and trademark litigation, by court,
FY88, annual rpt, 2244–1.5

SSA activities, litigation, finances, and staff,
FY88, annual rpt, 4704–6

US attorneys case processing and
collections, by case type and Federal
district, FY88, annual rpt, 6004–2

see also Administrative law and procedure
see also Adoption
see also Bankruptcy
see also Child support and alimony
see also Claims
see also Contempt of court
see also Contracts
see also Divestiture
see also Evidence
see also Extradition
see also Government-citizen lawsuits
see also Guardianship
see also Habeas corpus
see also Judgments, civil procedure
see also Juries
see also Legal arbitration and mediation
see also Marriage and divorce
see also Tax protests and appeals
see also Torts
see also Trials

Civil rights

Court caseloads for Federal district, appeals,
and bankruptcy courts, by type of suit and
offense, circuit, and district, quarterly rpt,
18202–1

Court civil and criminal caseloads for
Federal district, appeals, and special
courts, June 1989, annual rpt, 18204–2;
18204–8

Criminal sentences for Federal offenses,
guidelines by offense and circumstances,
1989 rpt, 17668–1

Foreign countries human rights conditions in
170 countries, 1988, annual rpt, 21384–3

Helsinki Final Act implementation by
NATO and Warsaw Pact, Oct 1988-Mar
1989, semiannual rpt, 7002–1

UN voting record and share of votes in
agreement with US, by issue, country, and
world area, 1988, annual rpt, 7004–18

US attorneys case processing and
collections, by case type and Federal
district, FY88, annual rpt, 6004–2

see also Age discrimination
see also Discrimination against the
handicapped
see also Discrimination in credit
see also Discrimination in education
see also Discrimination in employment
see also Discrimination in housing
see also Due process of law
see also Freedom of information
see also Racial discrimination
see also Religious liberty
see also Right of assembly
see also Right of privacy
see also Sex discrimination

Civil Rights Commission

see Commission on Civil Rights

Civil service pensions

Assets composition, growth, and distribution
for financial instns, by instn type,
1970s-88, 8438–1

Beneficiaries and taxes collected for social insurance programs since 1940, monthly rpt, 4742-1.1

Benefits and beneficiaries of govt pension plans, by type of plan and eligibility, and level of govt, selected years 1954-85, article, 4742-1.917

Budget of US Appendix, obligations, appropriations, and personnel, by program and agency, FY90, annual rpt, 104-3

Budget of US, CBO analysis of revenue and spending alternatives and projections of economic indicators, FY90-94, annual rpt, 26304-3

Budget of US, compact budgets by activity, function, and agency, FY90 and projected to FY94, annual rpt, 104-2

Budget of US, historical data, selected years FY34-88 and projected to FY94, annual rpt, 104-22

Budget of US, midsession review of FY90 budget, by function and agency, annual rpt, 104-7

Budget of US, object class analysis of obligations, by agency, FY90, annual rpt, 104-9

Budget of US, receipts by source, outlays by agency and program, and balances, monthly rpt, 8102-3

DOD civilian employee voluntary early retirement program, costs and savings, FY88, GAO rpt, 26119-253

Expenditures, coverage, and benefits for social welfare programs, late 1930s-87, annual rpt, 4744-3.1; 4744-3.3; 4744-3.7

Expenditures for public welfare by program, and private health care spending, FY50s-86, annual article, 4742-1.909

Expenditures of Fed Govt in States, by type, program, agency, and State, FY88, annual rpt, 2464-2

Fed Govt civil service retirement annuity adjustments, 1948-89, annual rpt, 21624-4

Fed Govt civil service retirement system actuarial valuation, and benefits and coverage by age, type of beneficiary, and State, FY87, annual rpt, 9844-34

Fed Govt civilian employee work-years, pay rates, and benefits use and costs, by agency, FY87, annual rpt, 9844-31

Fed Govt civilian employees demographic and employment characteristics, as of Sept 1988, article, 9842-1.901

Finances of govts, by level of govt, State, and for large cities and counties, annual rpt series, 2466-2

Flow-of-funds accounts, assets and liabilities by type and economic sector, outstanding at year-end 1965-88, annual rpt, 9364-3

Flow-of-funds accounts, savings, investments, and credit statements, quarterly rpt, 9365-3.3

Income (household, family, and personal), by source, detailed characteristics, and region, 1987, annual Current Population Rpt, 2546-6.59

Income (personal) by source including transfer payments, and social insurance contributions, by region, 1948 and 1987, 2708-40

Income from transfer payments, natl income and product account, *Survey of Current Business*, monthly rpt, 2702-1.23

Insurance (health) for Federal employees and annuitants, enrollment, costs, and Medicare coverage, with data for selected plans, 1980-89, 21628-73

Judicial Survivors Annuity Fund financial condition and annuitants, June 1982-89, annual rpt, 18204-2.8; 18204-8.8

Mortgage loan activity, by type of lender, loan, and mortgaged property, monthly press release, 5142-18

Mortgage loan activity, by type of lender, loan, and mortgaged property, quarterly press release, 5142-30

Mortgage loan activity, by type of lender, loan, and mortgaged property, 1986-88, annual press release, 5144-22

Police pay, benefits, and staffing, for US Park Police and compared to other Federal and local police units, FY85-88, GAO rpt, 26119-264

Securities (tax-exempt) holdings by investor type, and IRS enforcement of disallowance of interest deduction for financing holdings, mid 1970s-87, GAO rpt, 26119-239

Senior Executive Service membership characteristics, entries, exits, and awards, FY80-1987, annual rpt, 9844-36

State and local govt retirement systems, cash and security holdings and finances, quarterly rpt, 2462-2

Statistical Abstract of US, social, political, and economic data, 1790-2025, comprehensive annual compilation, 2324-1.2

Tax expenditures from employee benefits, for income and payroll tax by benefit type, 1950-87 and projected to 2065, article, 9373-1.913

Telephone service of households, by composition, income sources, and other characteristics, 1984-87, 9288-11

Transit systems finances and operations, by mode of transport, size of fleet, and for 432 systems, 1986, annual rpt, 7884-4

TVA managers salaries, incentive payments by program, and supplemental pensions, 1979-88, GAO rpt, 26113-420

Women (older) pension coverage, sources, payments, and effect on income and poverty status, 1982, article, 4742-1.901

Civil service system

Equal Opportunity Recruitment Program activity, and Fed Govt employment by sex, race, pay grade, and selected occupation, FY88, annual rpt, 9844-33

Fed Govt noncareer employees conversions to career appointments, by agency, quarterly rpt, 26102-5

Fed Govt noncareer employees conversions to career appointments not reported, by agency, 1987-88, GAO rpt, 26119-250

Merit system oversight and enforcement activities of OPM, series, 9496-2

Merit Systems Protection Board decisions on appeals of Fed Govt personnel actions, by agency and region, FY88, annual rpt, 9494-2

OMB mgmt of Federal employees, budget, and info systems, indicators of effectiveness, FY81-90, GAO rpt, 26119-251

Senior Executive Service membership characteristics, entries, exits, and awards, FY80-1987, annual rpt, 9844-36

Violations and prohibited political activity reported by Federal employees, cases by type, FY88, annual rpt, 9494-3

see also Civil service pensions

see also Federal employees

see also State and local employees

Civil works

see Public works

Civilian Health and Medical Program of the Uniformed Services

Benefits and costs under CHAMPUS, FY83-89, 3508-31

Commercial activities of DOD performed in-house, and work-years, by service branch, installation, and State, FY88, annual rpt, 3544-25

Costs for military hospitals and CHAMPUS, and reduction in military hospital admissions, with background data, FY85-87, GAO rpt, 26121-288

Claims

AID economic aid to developing countries, obligations and disbursements by country, quarterly rpt, 9912-4

Banks (US) and nonbanking firms claims on foreigners, by type and country, *Treasury Bulletin*, quarterly rpt, 8002-4.11

Banks (US) and nonbanking firms liabilities to and claims on foreigners, by country, 1986-87, annual rpt, 9364-5.10

Fed Govt contingent liabilities and claims paid on insured and guaranteed contracts with foreign obligors, by country and program, periodic rpt, 8002-12

Foreign govt claims of US natls, by claim type and country, 1988, annual rpt, 6004-16

Medical malpractice claims against military hospitals by disposition, and costs, 1982-87, hearing, 21208-27

Mining claims on public lands, cumulative FY76-88, annual rpt, 5724-1.2

Mining claims on public lands, patents by type and State, and applications by disposition, 1978-87, GAO rpt, 26113-403

Public lands acreage and use, and Land Mgmt Bur activities and finances, annual State rpt series, 5724-11

Radiation exposure of Navy personnel on nuclear-powered vessels and at support facilities, and injury claims, 1950s-88, annual rpt, 3804-10

Railroad safety violation claims settled, by carrier, FY88, annual rpt, 7604-10

Truck transport of household goods, performance and disposition of damage claims, for selected carriers, 1988, annual rpt, 9484-11

US attorneys civil cases, by type and disposition, FY88, annual rpt, 6004-2.5

see also Insurance and insurance industry

see also under specific types of insurance (listed under Insurance and insurance industry)

Clair, Robert T.

"Clearing House Interbank Payments System: A Description of Its Operation and Risk Management", 9379-12.42

"Daylight Overdrafts: Who Really Bears the Risk?", 9379-12.40

Clark, Gilbert B.

"Annual Data and Verification Tabulation, Atlantic Tropical Cyclones, 1988", 2184-7

"Annual Data and Verification Tabulation, Eastern Pacific Tropical Cyclones, 1988", 2184–8

Clark, Jeffrey A.
"Entry Barriers, Market Concentration and Bank Profitability: A Switching Regression Approach", 9381–10.93

Clark, Wallace H., Jr.
"Model Predicting Survival in Stage I Melanoma Based on Tumor Progression", 4472–1.935

Clarksville, Tenn.
Wages by occupation, for office and plant workers, 1989 survey, periodic MSA rpt, 6785–3.4
see also under By SMSA or MSA in the "Index by Categories"

Clary, Warren P.
"Test of RPA Production Coefficients and Local Assumptions for the Pinyon-Juniper Ecosystem in Central Utah", 1208–307

Class actions
see Government-citizen lawsuits

Classifications
AIDS health care services research status, needs, methods, and impacts on public health policy and funding, with data for selected cities, 1989 conf papers, 4188–59

Computer systems purchase and use, and data recording, processing, and transfer, Fed Govt standards, series, 2216–2

Export statistics classification codes of Census Bur for countries, commodities, and customs districts, 1990 base edition, 2428–5

Labor force counts under occupation and industry classifications used in 1970 and 1980 censuses, by industry, occupation, and sex, 1970, technical paper, 2626–2.59

Library of Congress rpts and products, 1989, annual listing, 26404–6

Manufacturing and mineral industries censuses, 1987: SIC industry and SIC-based product codes, listing, 2628–10

Medicare reimbursement of hospitals under prospective payment system, regulatory adjustments review and diagnostic group weight calibration, FY90, annual rpt, 17204–3

MSA and central city definitions and revisions, periodic listings, series, 108–35

Oil and gas field codes and locations, 1988, annual listing, 3164–70

Rural areas aid from Fed Govt, by agency and program, with county classifications by population density, FY85 and FY87, GAO rpt, 26113–401

Tariff Schedule of US, classifications and rates of duty by detailed imported commodity, 1990 base edition and supplements, 9886–13

Textile Agreement Category System import classification codes, correlation with TSUSA, 1989 annual rpt, 2044–31

Urban areas farms, acreage, finances, and operators, under alternative MSA definitions, 1960s-82, 1598–256
see also Standard Industrial Classification
see also "Guide to Selected Standard Classifications" section in ASI Annual

Classified information
see Internal security

Clauson, Annette L.
"Characteristics of Burley Tobacco Farms", 1568–277
"Costs of Producing and Selling Flue-Cured Tobacco: 1987, 1988, and Preliminary 1989", 1561–10.902
"Flue-Cured Tobacco Labor Use and Availability", 1561–10.901
"1988 Cost of Production Estimates for Sugarbeet and Sugarcane Operations", 1561–14.907

Clay industry and products
Business statistics, detailed data for major industries and economic indicators, *Survey of Current Business*, monthly rpt, 2702–1.18

Ceramics (advanced) technical info of Japan, US industry use and views on value, 1988 survey, 2008–28

Construction industries census, 1987: financial and operating data, preliminary industry rpt, 2371–1.15

County Business Patterns, 1987: employment, establishments, and payroll, by SIC 2- to 4-digit industry and county, annual State rpt series, 2326–8

Earnings by major industry group, and personal income per capita and by source, by region and State, 1929-87, 2708–40

Employment, earnings, and hours, by selected SIC 1- to 4-digit industry, State, and for 262 MSAs, 1972-87, 6748–81

Employment, earnings, and hours, by SIC 1- to 4-digit industry, monthly 1983-Feb 1989, annual rpt, 6744–4

Exports of US, detailed commodities by country, monthly rpt, 2422–3

Finances and operations, by SIC 2- to 4-digit industry, forecast 1989 with trends from 1950s, annual rpt, 2044–28

Freight (waterborne domestic and foreign) by commodity, traffic, and passengers, by port and waterway, 1987, annual rpt, 3754–3

Hwy construction material use by type, and spending, by State, various periods 1944-88, annual rpt, 7554–29

Import restraint elimination, impact on domestic industry production and employment, by selected commodity, 1986-88, 9886–4.144

Imports, exports, and employment impacts, by SIC 2- to 4-digit industry and commodity, quarterly rpt, 2322–2

Imports of US, detailed Schedule A commodities by country, monthly rpt, 2422–2

Labor productivity, indexes of output, hours, and employment by SIC 2- to 4-digit industry, 1963-87, annual rpt, 6824–1.3

Manufacturing annual survey, 1986: financial and operating data, by SIC 2- to 4-digit industry, series, 2506–15

Manufacturing census, 1987: financial and operating data, for SIC 4-digit industries by product, preliminary rpt, 2491–1.47; 2491–1.48

Mineral industries census, 1987: financial and operating data, preliminary industry rpt, 2511–1.10

Mineral Industry Surveys, State reviews of production, 1988, preliminary annual rpt, 5614–6

Minerals Yearbook, 1987, Vol 1: commodity reviews of production, use, trade, prices, and mining operations, annual rpt, 5604–33

Minerals Yearbook, 1987, Vol 1 preprints: commodity review of production, reserves, supply, use, and trade, annual rpt, 5604–15.17

Minerals Yearbook, 1987, Vol 2 preprints: State reviews of production and sales by commodity, and business activity, annual rpt series, 5604–16

Minerals Yearbook, 1987, Vol 2: State reviews of production, sales, and firms, by commodity, and business activity, annual rpt, 5604–34

Minerals Yearbook, 1987, Vol 3: foreign country reviews of production, trade, and policy, by commodity, annual rpt, 5604–35

Minerals Yearbook, 1987, Vol 3 preprints: foreign country reviews of production, trade, and policy, by commodity, annual rpt series, 5604–23

Minerals Yearbook, 1988, Vol 2 rpts: State reviews of production and sales by commodity, and business activity, annual rpt series, 5604–22

Occupational injuries and incidence, employment, and hours in nonmetallic minerals mines and related operations, 1987, annual rpt, 6664–1

Occupational injury and illness rates, by SIC 2- to 4-digit industry, 1987, annual rpt, 6844–1

Pollution abatement capital and operating costs, by SIC 2-to 4-digit industry and State, 1986, annual Current Industrial Rpt, 2506–3.6

Price indexes (producer), by stage of processing and detailed commodity, monthly rpt, 6762–6

Price indexes (producer), by stage of processing and detailed commodity, monthly 1988, annual rpt, 6764–2

Production, prices, trade, use, employment, tariffs, and stockpiles, by mineral, with foreign comparisons, 1984-88, annual rpt, 5604–18

Production, shipments, and PPI for building materials, by type, bimonthly rpt, 2042–1.5; 2042–1.6

Production, shipments, trade, and stocks, by clay product, periodic Current Industrial Rpt series, 2506–9

Science and engineering employment, by nonmanufacturing industry and field, 1987, triennial rpt, 9627–31

Science, engineering, and technical employment in manufacturing, by field, occupation, and industry, 1986, triennial rpt, 9627–23
see also Pottery and porcelain products
see also By Industry in the "Index by Categories"
see also under By Commodity in the "Index by Categories"

Clean Water Act
Wastewater facilities of Fed Govt, compliance with pollution control regulations, FY86-87, GAO rpt, 26113–388

Cleaning services
see Domestic workers and services
see Janitorial and maintenance services
see Laundry and cleaning services

Clearwater, Fla.
Housing starts and completions authorized by building permits in 40 MSAs, quarterly rpt, 2382-9
Wages by occupation, for office and plant workers, 1988 survey, periodic MSA rpt, 6785-11.2
Wages by occupation, for office and plant workers, 1989 survey, periodic MSA rpt, 6785-12.6
see also under By SMSA or MSA in the "Index by Categories"

Clemency
Criminal case processing in Federal courts, by offense, disposition, and jurisdiction, 1950s-88, annual rpt, 6064-6.5
Execution, commutation of sentence, and other removals of inmates from death row, 1987, annual rpt, 6064-6.6
Prisoners released from sentences and death row, by reason and State, 1986, annual rpt, 6064-26.4; 6064-26.6
Prisoners removed from death row, by reason, 1973-88, annual rpt, 6066-25.23
see also Pardons

Clement Associates, Inc.
"Review of Literature on Herbicides, Including Phenoxy Herbicides and Associated Dioxins. Volume XI: Analysis of Recent Literature on Health Effects Published in 1987; Volume XII: Annotated Bibliography of Recent Literature on Health Effects", 8706-1.1

Clergy
Army chaplains and accession goals, by race and sex, 1985-88, annual rpt, 3704-10.1
Health care facilities of VA, Medicine and Surgery Dept chaplaincy trainees by city, FY88, annual rpt, 8704-4
Immigrants admitted to US, by class and country, FY82-88, annual rpt, 6264-2

Clerical workers
Air traffic control and airway facilities staff, by selected employment and demographic characteristics, FY88, annual rpt, 7504-41
Cancer (bladder) risk for men in selected occupations, by employment characteristics, 1977-78, article, 4472-1.925
DOT employment, by subagency, occupation, and selected personnel characteristics, FY88, annual rpt, 7304-18
Earnings, annual average percent changes for selected occupational groups, selected MSAs, monthly rpt, 6782-1.1
Employment and occupation of householder, by occupation of spouse, race, and family composition, 1988, annual Current Population Rpt, 2546-1.437
Employment Cost Index and alternative measure of compensation costs, by component, occupation, industry group, union status, and location, 1975-89, annual rpt, 6744-20
Employment, earnings, and hours, monthly press release, 6742-5
Employment in nonmanufacturing industries, by detailed occupation and SIC 2-digit industry, 1987, triennial rpt, 6748-60

Employment situation, earnings, hours, and other BLS economic indicators, transcripts of BLS Commissioner's monthly testimony, periodic rpt, 23846-4
Employment, unemployment, and labor force characteristics, by region, State, and selected metro area, 1988, annual rpt, 6744-7
Fed Govt civilian employment by occupation, agency, and location, and language and math skill needs, 1966-87 and projected to 2000, 9848-37
Fed Govt pay comparability with private industry, and recommended pay rate adjustments, 1989, annual rpt, 104-16
Handbook of Labor Statistics, employment, unemployment, and labor force characteristics, 1940s-88 with trends from 1913, 6728-38
Health condition of labor force, and services use, by occupation and industry of longest job held, income, age, sex, and race. 1980, 4147-10.168
Immigrants admitted to US, by occupational group and country of birth, preliminary FY88, annual table, 6264-1
Immigration to US, alien workers, visitors, deportations, and naturalizations, by country, FY88 and trends from 1820, annual rpt, 6264-2
Income (household, family, and personal), by source, detailed characteristics, and region, 1987, annual Current Population Rpt, 2546-6.59
Minority group and women employment, by occupation, SIC 1- to 3- digit industry, State, and MSA, 1986, annual rpt, 9244-1
Occupational changes, by tenure and other worker characteristics, and labor mobility rates, 1965-86, article, 6722-1.943
SEC staffing, pay, and turnover by occupation and city, with proposed fee revenues to improve work conditions, 1989 hearing, 21368-116
Service industries census, 1987: establishments, receipts, employment, and payroll, by SIC 2- to 4-digit kind of business, MSA, county, and city, State rpt series, 2391-1
State and local govt employment of minorities and women, by occupation, function, pay level, and State, 1986, annual rpt, 9244-6
Statistical Abstract of US, social, political, and economic data, 1790-2025, comprehensive annual compilation, 2324-1.3
Training and remedial education program for clerical workers, effectiveness, local area program, 1973-88, article, 9373-1.918
see also Area wage surveys
see also Industry wage surveys
see also Wage surveys
see also under By Occupation in the "Index by Categories"

Cleveland County, Okla.
Housing and households detailed characteristics, and unit and neighborhood quality, by location, 1984 survey, MSA rpt, 2485-6.3

Cleveland, Ohio
Airline fares relation to competition and supply and demand factors, for flights to Cleveland, Ohio, 1987, article, 9377-1.903
CPI by component for US city average, and by region, population size, and for 15 metro areas, monthly rpt, 6762-1
CPI by component for US city average, and by region, population size, and for 27 metro areas, monthly rpt, 6762-2
Drug test results at arrest, by drug type, offense, and sex, for selected urban areas, quarterly rpt, 6062-3
Wages by occupation, for office and plant workers, 1988 survey, periodic MSA rpt, 6785-11.2
Wages by occupation, for office and plant workers, 1989 survey, periodic MSA rpt, 6785-12.7
see also under By City and By SMSA or MSA in the "Index by Categories"

Cleveland, Robert W.
"Earnings of Married-Couple Families: 1987", 2546-6.61

Clifton, Daphne G.
"Trace Elements in Bed Sediments of the San Joaquin River and Its Tributary Streams, California, 1985", 5668-91

Climate
see Meteorology
see Weather

Clinical laboratory technicians
Indian Health Service outpatient visits, by type of provider, selected hospital, and IHS service area, FY87-88, annual rpt, 4084-3
Military health care personnel, and accessions by training source, by occupation, specialty, and service branch, FY87, annual rpt, 3544-24
VA Medicine and Surgery Dept trainees, by detailed program and city, FY88, annual rpt, 8704-4

Clinics
Army personnel health condition, and use of Army medical services in US and abroad by personnel, retirees, and dependents, monthly rpt, 3702-4.1
County Business Patterns, 1987: employment, establishments, and payroll, by SIC 2- to 4-digit industry and county, annual State rpt series, 2326-8
Drug and alcohol abuse treatment facilities, services, use, funding, and client characteristics, 1987, annual rpt, 4494-10
Employment, earnings, and hours, by SIC 1- to 4-digit industry, monthly 1983-Feb 1989, annual rpt, 6744-4
Food aid program of USDA for women, infants, and children, participants and costs by State and Indian agency, FY87, annual rpt, 1364-12
Food aid program of USDA for women, infants, and children, participants, clinics, and costs by State and Indian agency, monthly tables, 1362-16
Food aid program of USDA for women, infants, and children, prenatal enrollees by trimester of enrollment and other characteristics, 1984, article, 4042-3.929
Indian health clinic services use and staff, and effectiveness of prenatal care program, 1970s-86 local area study, article, 4042-3.960

Indian Health Service facilities, funding, operations, and Indian health and other characteristics, 1950s-88, annual chartbook, 4084-1

Medicaid beneficiaries and payments, by service type, FY72-87, annual rpt, 4744-3.6

Medicaid coverage, participation, payments, admin, and legislative history, with data by State, 1980s-88, 21368-105

Medicare and Medicaid beneficiaries and program operations, 1988, annual fact book, 4654-18

Medicare and Medicaid eligibility, participation, coverage, and program finances, various periods 1966-89, biennial rpt, 4654-1

Medicare physicians services use, charges, and reimbursement, by service type, setting, and specialty, 1986, article, 4652-1.936

Medicare reimbursement of hospitals under prospective payment system, impacts on industry structure, 1975-86, 17206-2.2

Mental health care facilities, staff, and patient characteristics, *Statistical Notes* series, 4506-3

Military health care facilities of DOD in US and abroad, admissions, beds, outpatient visits, and births, by service branch, quarterly rpt, 3542-15

NIH activities, funding by program and recipient type, staff, and clinic patients, by inst, FY87, annual rpt, 4434-3

Occupational injury and illness rates, by SIC 2- to 4-digit industry, 1987, annual rpt, 6844-1

Pacific territories social, economic, health, and govtl data, FY88 and trends, annual rpt, 7004-6

Receipts for services, by SIC 2- to 4-digit kind of business, 1988, annual rpt, 2413-8

Rural areas health care facilities, staffing, services accessibility, and indicators of need, 1960s-88, 25148-41

Service industries census, 1987: establishments, receipts, employment, and payroll, by SIC 2- to 4-digit kind of business, MSA, county, and city, State rpt series, 2391-1

Texas-Mexico border area health facilities and services, with background data, by Texas county, 1980s-88, GAO rpt, 26121-261

VA health care facilities mental health services, staff, research, and training programs, 1989 biennial listing, 8704-2

Veterans health care, patients, visits, costs, and operating beds, by VA and contract facility, and region, quarterly rpt, 8602-4

Veterans in VA and non-VA health facilities, by type, FY64-88, annual rpt, 8604-5.3

see also Clinical laboratory technicians

see also Hospitals

see also Medical examinations and tests

Clocks

see Watches and clocks

Cloe, William W.

"Selected Occupational Fatalities Related to Logging as Found in Reports of OSHA Fatality/Catastrophe Investigations", 6606-2.15

Clothing and clothing industry

Alien workers (unauthorized) employer sanctions, enforcement costs, compliance, and job discrimination, 1988 annual GAO rpt, 26104-19

Business statistics, detailed data for major industries and economic indicators, *Survey of Current Business*, monthly rpt, 2702-1.19

Caribbean Basin Initiative investment incentives, economic impacts, with finances and employment by country, 1984-88, 2048-141

China trade by SITC 1- to 5-digit commodity, 1970s-87, annual rpt, 9114-3

Collective bargaining agreements expiring during year, and workers covered, by firm, union, industry group, and State, 1989, annual rpt, 6784-9

Consumer Expenditure Survey, household income by source, and itemized spending, by selected characteristics and region, 1984-87, annual rpt, 6764-5

Consumer Expenditure Survey, spending by category, and income, by selected household characteristics and location, 1987, press release, 6726-1.23

Consumer Expenditure Survey, spending by category, selected household characteristics, and region, quarterly rpt, 6762-14

Consumer spending and income effects of wives' employment, by expenditure category and household characteristics, 1984-86, article, 6722-1.908

Consumer spending for clothing, by family member and selected family characteristics, 1984-85, technical paper, 6886-6.44; 6886-6.61

Consumer spending in metro and nonmetro areas, by item, 1987, article, 6722-1.962

Consumer spending, natl income and product account, *Survey of Current Business*, monthly rpt, 2702-1.23

Consumer spending, price changes, imports by fiber and country, and cotton market share, for clothing, mid 1970s-88, article, 1702-1.902

Consumer spending related to occupational group, 1986-87, article, 6722-1.961

Cost of living indexes for metro areas, relation of expenditure items and quality of life indicators, model results, 1973, working paper, 6886-6.9

County Business Patterns, 1987: employment, establishments, and payroll, by SIC 2- to 4-digit industry and county, annual State rpt series, 2326-8

CPI by component for US city average, and by region, population size, and for 27 metro areas, monthly rpt, 6762-2

CPI by major component and selected metro area, 1940s-88 with trends from 1913, 6728-38.8

CPI components relative importance, by selected SMSA, region, population size, and for US city average, 1988, annual rpt, 6884-1

Earnings by major industry group, and personal income per capita and by source, by region and State, 1929-87, 2708-40

Employment and wages in clothing industry, impact of prohibition against hiring undocumented aliens, with data by State, 1975-85, article, 9393-8.904

Employment, earnings, and hours, by selected SIC 1- to 4-digit industry, State, and for 262 MSAs, 1972-87, 6748-81

Employment, earnings, and hours, by SIC 1- to 4-digit industry, monthly 1983-Feb 1989, annual rpt, 6744-4

Employment of minorities and women, by occupation, SIC 1- to 3- digit industry, State, and MSA, 1986, annual rpt, 9244-1

Employment, unemployment, and labor force characteristics, by region and census div, 1988, annual rpt, 6744-7.1

Energy use and prices for manufacturing industries, 1985 survey, series, 3166-13

Exports and imports of US, by commodity group, world area, selected country, US coastal area and port, and mode of transport, monthly rpt, 2422-9

Exports of US, detailed commodities by country, monthly rpt, 2422-3

Finances and operations, by SIC 2- to 4-digit industry, forecast 1989 with trends from 1950s, annual rpt, 2044-28

Freight (waterborne domestic and foreign) by commodity, traffic, and passengers, by port and waterway, 1987, annual rpt, 3754-3

Hats and caps (cloth) from PRC at less than fair value, injury to US industry, investigation with background financial and operating data, 1988 rpt, 9886-14.261

Hazardous substances industrial releases and reduction methods under EPA regulation, by chemical, source, industry, and location, 1987, annual rpt, 9234-6

Hosiery production and related workers and wages by occupation and sex, and benefits, by location, 1987 survey, 6787-6.237

Hunting, fishing, and other wildlife-related recreation participation and spending, detailed data by location, 1985 survey, quinquennial rpt, 5508-5

Import quotas filled for cotton textiles, by product and country of origin, 1987-88, article, 1561-1.905

Import restraint elimination, impact on domestic industry production and employment, by selected commodity, 1986-88, 9886-4.144

Imports, exports, and employment impacts, by SIC 2- to 4-digit industry and commodity, quarterly rpt, 2322-2

Imports of textiles, by country of origin, monthly rpt, 2042-27

Imports of textiles, by product and country of origin, periodic rpt series, 2046-8; 2046-9

Imports of textiles, production, and imports share of use, by Multifiber Arrangement product, quarterly rpt, 2042-32

Imports of textiles under Multifiber Arrangement by product and country, and status of bilateral agreements, 1986-88, annual rpt, 9884-18

Imports of US, detailed Schedule A commodities by country, monthly rpt, 2422-2

Imports of US given duty-free treatment for value of US material sent abroad, and impacts on US industry and employment, by commodity and country, 1987, annual rpt, 9884-14

Injuries from use of consumer products and related activities, by victim age and sex, 1988, annual rpt, 9164-7

Injuries from use of consumer products, by severity, victim age, and detailed product, 1988, annual rpt, 9164-6

Input-output structure of US economy, detailed interindustry transactions for 84 industries, and components of final demand, 1983, annual article, 2702-1.909

Labor productivity, indexes of output, hours, and employment by SIC 2- to 4-digit industry, 1963-87, annual rpt, 6824-1.3

Manufacturing annual survey, 1986: financial and operating data, by SIC 2- to 4-digit industry, series, 2506-15

Manufacturing census, 1987: financial and operating data, for SIC 4-digit industries by product, preliminary industry rpt series, 2491-1

Manufacturing census, 1987: financial and operating data, for SIC 4-digit industries by product, preliminary rpt, 2491-1.42

Manufacturing industries production, shipments, inventories, orders, and pollution control costs, periodic Current Industrial Rpt series, 2506-3

Natl income and product accounts and components, *Survey of Current Business*, monthly rpt, 2702-1.21

New York and northeastern New Jersey employment by industry div, unemployment, and consumer price changes by selected commodity, 1978-June 1989, press release, 6926-2.40

Northern Mariana Islands economic census, 1987: employment, firms, payroll, and receipts, by SIC 1- to 4-digit industry, 2597-1

Occupational injury and illness rates, by SIC 2- to 4-digit industry, 1987, annual rpt, 6844-1

OECD trade, total and for 4 major countries, and US trade by country, by commodity, 1970-87, world area rpt series, 9116-1

Price indexes (producer), by stage of processing and detailed commodity, monthly rpt, 6762-6

Price indexes (producer), by stage of processing and detailed commodity, monthly 1988, annual rpt, 6764-2

Production, shipments, trade, and use of clothes, by product, periodic Current Industrial Rpt series, 2506-6

Retail trade census, 1987: employment, establishments, sales, and payroll, by SIC 2- to 4-digit kind of business, MSA, county, and city, State rpt series, 2397-1

Retail trade sales and inventories, by kind of business, region, and selected State, MSA, and city, monthly rpt, 2413-3

Retail trade sales, by kind of business, advance monthly rpt, 2413-2

Retail trade sales, inventories, purchases, gross margin, and accounts receivable, by SIC 2- to 4-digit kind of business and form of ownership, 1987, annual rpt, 2413-5

Science, engineering, and technical employment in manufacturing, by field, occupation, and industry, 1986, triennial rpt, 9627-23

Science, engineering, and technical employment in transportation, utilities, and retail and wholesale trade, by field, occupation, and industry, 1985, triennial rpt, 9627-32

Service industries census, 1987: establishments, receipts, employment, and payroll, by SIC 2- to 4-digit kind of business, MSA, county, and city, State rpt series, 2391-1

Small business establishments, employment, and financial ratios, by SIC 1- to 2-digit industry and State, late 1960s-87, 9768-19

Statistical Abstract of US, social, political, and economic data, 1790-2025, comprehensive annual compilation, 2324-1.3

Sweaters from 3 countries at less than fair value, injury to US industry, investigation with background financial and operating data, 1989 rpt, 9886-14.272

Tax (income) returns of corporations, income and tax items by asset size and detailed industry, 1986, annual rpt, 8304-4; 8304-21

Tax (income) returns of partnerships, income statement items by industry group, 1986, annual article, 8302-2.903

Tax (income) returns of sole proprietorships, income statement items, by industry group, 1987, annual article, 8302-2.904; 8302-2.921

Thefts, and value of property stolen and recovered, by property type, 1988, annual rpt, 6224-2.1

Tuxedo rental industry depreciable assets class lives measurement, investment, and industry operations, 1989 asset class rpt, 8006-5.1

Uniforms (martial arts) from Taiwan at less than fair value, injury to US industry, investigation with background financial and operating data, 1989 rpt, 9886-14.247; 9886-14.269

Wholesale trade census, 1987: employment, establishments, finances, and operations, by SIC 2- to 4-digit kind of business, MSA, county, and city, State rpt series, 2405-1

see also Shoes and shoe industry

see also By Industry in the "Index by Categories"

see also under By Commodity in the "Index by Categories"

Clough, Debora L.
"Airway Science Curriculum Demonstration Project: Summary of Initial Evaluation Findings", 7506-10.54

Clover
see Animal feed
see Pasture and rangeland

CMEA
see Council for Mutual Economic Assistance

Coal and coal mining
Abandoned coal mines emergency complaint processing by Office of Surface Mining Reclamation and Enforcement, efficiency, 1983-87, GAO rpt, 26113-398

Acid rain control economic impacts, and sulfur dioxide emissions and reductions of industrial and power plants, 1987 hearing, 21368-104

Alaska minerals resources, production, oil and gas leases, and exploratory wells, with maps and bibl, 1987, annual rpt, 5664-11

Ash from coal burning, contaminant levels, removal, EPA toxicity standards, and State disposal laws, 1988 rpt, 2048-140

Australia and US coal production and freight costs, and competitive position in selected markets, 1987, 2048-143

Business statistics, detailed data for major industries and economic indicators, *Survey of Current Business*, monthly rpt, 2702-1.15

Collective bargaining agreements expiring during year, and workers covered, by firm, union, industry group, and State, 1989, annual rpt, 6784-9

Communist, OECD, and selected other countries energy reserves, production, and use, and oil trade and revenue, 1960s-88, annual rpt, 9114-4.5

Consumption, by detailed fuel type, end-use sector, and State, 1960-87, State Energy Data System annual rpt, 3164-39

Consumption of energy, by air pollutant source, fuel type, and State, 1986, annual rpt, 9194-14

County Business Patterns, 1987: employment, establishments, and payroll, by SIC 2- to 4-digit industry and county, annual State rpt series, 2326-8

Defense Fuel Supply Center procurement, prices, stocks, transport, and other activities and finances, FY88, annual rpt, 3904-8

Earnings by major industry group, and personal income per capita and by source, by region and State, 1929-87, 2708-40

Electric power and industrial plants prohibited from oil and gas primary use, and gas use by State, 1988, annual rpt, 3104-8

Electric power plants (steam) fuel receipts, costs, and quality, by fuel, plant, utility, and State, 1988, annual rpt, 3164-42

Electric power plants and capacity, by fuel used, owner, location, and operating status, 1988 and for units planned 1989-98, annual listing, 3164-36

Electric power plants production and capital costs, operations, and fuel use, by fuel type, plant, utility, and location, 1987, annual rpt, 3164-9

Electric power plants production, capacity, sales, and fuel stocks, use, and costs, by State, 1984-88, annual rpt, 3164-11

Electric power plants production, fuel use, stocks, and costs by fuel type, and sales, by State, monthly rpt, 3162-35

Electric power plants sulfur dioxide emissions and control costs, alternative projections to 2000, 26306-3.108

Electric utilities fuel cost, quality, use, receipts, and stocks, and power plant production, by energy source, State and utility, quarterly rpt, 3162-39

Employment by selected occupational and other characteristics, injuries, and workdays lost, for mines, 1986, 5606-8.1

Employment, earnings, and hours, by selected SIC 1- to 4-digit industry, State, and for 262 MSAs, 1972-87, 6748-81

Employment, earnings, and hours, by SIC 1- to 4-digit industry, monthly 1983-Feb 1989, annual rpt, 6744-4

Employment in nonmanufacturing industries, by detailed occupation and SIC 2-digit industry, 1987, triennial rpt, 6748-60

Environmental impacts of energy technologies, 1960s-80s, handbook series, 3326–1

Explosives and blasting agents use, by type, industry, and State, 1988, Mineral Industry Surveys, annual rpt, 5614–22

Fed Govt and Indian land oil, gas, and minerals production and revenue, by State, 1988 and trends from 1920, annual rpt, 5734–2

Fed Govt coal leasing activity, acreage, production, and reserves, by coal region and State, FY88, annual rpt, 5724–10

Fed Govt coal leasing competitive effects, annual narrative rpt, discontinued, 6004–12

Fed Govt coal purchases, chemical analyses by mine and location, FY85, annual rpt, 3004–15

Fed Govt energy use and efficiency, by agency and fuel type, FY88, annual rpt, 3304–22

Finances and operations, by SIC 2- to 4-digit industry, forecast 1989 with trends from 1950s, annual rpt, 2044–28

Finances and operations of energy producers, by energy type for US firms domestic and foreign operations, 1987, annual rpt, 3164–44

Financial statements for manufacturing, mining, and trade corporations, by selected SIC 2- to 3-digit industry, quarterly rpt, 2502–1

Foreign and US coal production, trade, and govt subsidies, by country and country group, 1973-87 and projected to 2000, 2048–144

Foreign and US coal trade flows and reserves, by country, 1970s-87 and projected to 2000, annual rpt, 3164–77

Foreign and US energy production, trade, use, and reserves, and oil and refined products supply and prices, by country, 1980-88, annual rpt, 3164–50

Foreign and US energy use by sector, and production, by fuel type, country, and country group, projected 1988-2000 and trends from 1970, annual rpt, 3164–84

Foreign countries mineral production, reserves, and industry role in domestic economy and world supply, world area and country rpt series, 5606–1

Foreign direct investment in US energy sources by type and firm, and US affiliates operations, as of 1988, annual rpt, 3164–80

Freight (waterborne domestic and foreign) by commodity, traffic, and passengers, by port and waterway, 1987, annual rpt, 3754–3

Housing and households detailed characteristics, and unit and neighborhood quality, by location, 1985, biennial rpt, 2485–12

Housing and households detailed characteristics, and unit and neighborhood quality, MSA surveys, series, 2485–6

Housing energy use, costs, and conservation, and household and housing characteristics, survey rpt series, 3166–7

Hudson-Raritan River basin pollutant levels and sources, model description and results, 1880s-1982, 2178–22

Injuries by circumstances, employment, and hours, for mineral industries by type of operation and State, quarterly rpt, 6662–1

Input-output structure of US economy, detailed interindustry transactions for 84 industries, and components of final demand, 1983, annual article, 2702–1.909

Labor productivity, indexes of output, hours, and employment by SIC 2- to 4-digit industry, 1963-87, annual rpt, 6824–1.2

Manufacturing energy use and prices, 1985 survey, series, 3166–13

Methane emissions control in coal mines, research results, techniques, and equipment, mid 1960s-79, 5608–156

Mineral industries census, 1987: financial and operating data, preliminary industry rpt, 2511–1.4

Minerals Yearbook, 1987, Vol 3: foreign country reviews of production, trade, and policy, by commodity, annual rpt, 5604–35

Minerals Yearbook, 1987, Vol 3 preprints: foreign country reviews of production, trade, and policy, by commodity, annual rpt series, 5604–23

Occupational injuries and incidence, employment, and hours in coal mines and related operations, 1987, annual rpt, 6664–4

Occupational injuries and incidence, employment, and hours in metal mines and related operations, 1987, annual rpt, 6664–3

Occupational injury and illness rates, by SIC 2- to 4-digit industry, 1987, annual rpt, 6844–1

Occupational safety and health enforcement, training, and funding, with casualties, by type of mine and State, FY87, annual rpt, 6664–6

Ohio River basin waterway facilities, freight by commodity and port, and recreation, by waterway, 1986-87, annual rpt, 3754–6

Pollution (air) abatement equipment shipments by industry, exports, and new and backlog orders, by product, 1988, annual Current Industrial Rpt, 2506–12.5

Pollution (air) carbon dioxide emissions by fuel type and consuming sector, projected under alternative conservation methods, 1990s-2010, 3006–11.11

Pollution (air) levels for 5 pollutants, by detailed source and State, 1986, annual rpt, 9194–7

Pollution (air) levels for 6 pollutants, by source, 1970-87 and trends from 1940, annual rpt, 9194–13

Pollution abatement capital and operating costs, by SIC 2-to 4-digit industry and State, 1986, annual Current Industrial Rpt, 2506–3.6

Production and mines by county, prices, productivity, miners, reserves, and stocks, by mining method and State, 1987-88, annual rpt, 3164–25

Production and sales of synthetic organic chemicals, and manufacturer listing, by product, 1988, annual rpt, 9884–3

Production and stocks of coal by district, and shipments by district of origin, State of destination, end-use sector, and mode of transport, quarterly rpt, 3162–8

Production by State and region, trade, use, and stocks, weekly rpt, 3162–1

Production, dev, and distribution firms revenues and income, quarterly rpt, 3162–38

Production of coal by region, exports, and use by sector, projected 1988-2000 and trends from 1975, annual rpt, 3164–68

Production of coal, reserves, use, and prices by State, exports by country, and employment, 1900s-87, biennial rpt, 3164–79

Public lands acreage, grants, use, revenues, and allocations, by State, FY88, annual rpt, 5724–1.2

Reclamation of coal mining land, Office of Surface Mining Reclamation and Enforcement activities and funding, by State and Indian tribe, FY87, annual rpt, 5644–1

Science and engineering employment, by nonmanufacturing industry and field, 1987, triennial rpt, 9627–31

Ships bunker fuel laden in US on vessels engaged in foreign trade, by fuel type and port, monthly rpt, 2422–5

Small business establishments, employment, and financial ratios, by SIC 1- to 2-digit industry and State, late 1960s-87, 9768–19

Statistical Abstract of US, social, political, and economic data, 1790-2025, comprehensive annual compilation, 2324–1.3

Supply, demand, and distribution of energy, and impacts of legislation, series, 3166–6

Supply, demand, and prices, by fuel type and end-use sector, projected under 3 oil price assumptions, 1988-2000, annual rpt, 3164–75

Supply, demand, and prices, by fuel type and end-use sector, with foreign comparisons, 1988 and trends from 1949, annual rpt, 3164–74

Supply, demand, and prices, by fuel type and end use, with foreign comparisons, 1976-88, annual summary rpt, 3164–76

Supply, demand, and prices, by fuel type, end-use sector, and country, detailed data, monthly rpt, 3162–24

Supply, demand, and prices of energy, forecasts by resource type, quarterly rpt, 3162–34

Supply, demand, prices, trade, and stocks of coal, coke, and breeze, by end-use sector and State, quarterly rpt, 3162–37

Surface mining-related civil actions, attorneys fees and expenses awarded by case, 1989, GAO rpt, 26113–421

Tax (excise) on coal and other black lung trust fund receipts, fund disbursements, and claims and benefits by State, 1987, annual rpt, 6504–3

Tax (income) returns of corporations, income and tax items by asset size and detailed industry, 1986, annual rpt, 8304–4; 8304–21

Tax (income) returns of partnerships, income statement items by industry group, 1986, annual article, 8302–2.903

Tax (income) returns of sole proprietorships, income statement items, by industry group, 1987, annual article, 8302–2.904; 8302–2.921

Transportation finances, operations, vehicles, equipment, accidents, and energy use, by mode of transport, 1955-88, annual rpt, 7304–2

Water quality effects of coal mining operations, sediment discharges effects of alternative mining and mgmt methods and reclamation, for Pennsylvania, 1980-83, 5668–93

Wholesale trade census, 1987: employment, establishments, finances, and operations, by SIC 2- to 4-digit kind of business, MSA, county, and city, State rpt series, 2405–1

see also Black lung disease
see also Coal exports and imports
see also Coal prices
see also Coal reserves
see also Coal stocks
see also By Industry in the "Index by Categories"
see also under By Commodity in the "Index by Categories"

Coal exports and imports

Australia and US coal production and freight costs, and competitive position in selected markets, 1987, 2048–143

Business statistics, detailed data for major industries and economic indicators, *Survey of Current Business*, monthly rpt, 2702–1.15

China trade by SITC 1- to 5-digit commodity, 1970s-87, annual rpt, 9114–3

Cuba economic conditions, agricultural and industrial production and distribution, trade, and intl economic relations, 1980-87 with trends from 1961, 9118–8

Electric utilities coal imports, by utility and country of origin, 1984-88, annual rpt, 3164–42

Exports and imports of coal, by country of origin and destination, 1987, annual rpt, 3164–50.4

Exports, imports, and average price, by country of destination and origin, weekly rpt, monthly data, 3162–1.2

Exports of coal, by country of destination, selected years 1900-87, biennial rpt, 3164–79

Exports of coal from US and other countries, by world area of destination, projected 1988-2000 and trends from 1975, annual rpt, 3164–68

Exports of coal to Canada by mode of transport, and overseas, by district of origin, quarterly rpt, 3162–8

Exports of US, detailed commodities by country, monthly rpt, 2422–3

Foreign and US coal production, trade, and govt subsidies, by country and country group, 1973-87 and projected to 2000, 2048–144

Foreign and US coal trade flows and reserves, by country, 1970s-87 and projected to 2000, annual rpt, 3164–77

Foreign countries mineral production, reserves, and industry role in domestic economy and world supply, world area and country rpt series, 5606–1

Imports, exports, and employment impacts, by SIC 2- to 4-digit industry and commodity, quarterly rpt, 2322–2

Imports of US, detailed Schedule A commodities by country, monthly rpt, 2422–2

Minerals Yearbook, 1987, Vol 3 preprints: foreign country reviews of production, trade, and policy, by commodity, annual rpt series, 5604–23

OECD trade, total and for 4 major countries, and US trade by country, by commodity, 1970-87, world area rpt series, 9116–1

Shipborne commerce (domestic and foreign) of US, freight by commodity, traffic, and passengers, by port and waterway, 1987, annual rpt, 3754–3

Statistical Abstract of US, social, political, and economic data, 1790-2025, comprehensive annual compilation, 2324–1.3

Supply, demand, and prices, by fuel type and end-use sector, projected under 3 oil price assumptions, 1988-2000, annual rpt, 3164–75

Supply, demand, and prices, by fuel type and end-use sector, with foreign comparisons, 1988 and trends from 1949, annual rpt, 3164–74

Supply, demand, and prices, by fuel type and end use, with foreign comparisons, 1976-88, annual summary rpt, 3164–76

Supply, demand, and prices, by fuel type, end-use sector, and country, detailed data, monthly rpt, 3162–24

Supply, demand, and prices of energy, forecasts by resource type, quarterly rpt, 3162–34

Supply, demand, prices, trade, and stocks of coal, coke, and breeze, by end-use sector and State, quarterly rpt, 3162–37

Coal prices

Business statistics, detailed data for major industries and economic indicators, *Survey of Current Business*, monthly rpt, 2702–1.15

Electric power plants (steam) fuel receipts, costs, and quality, by fuel, plant, utility, and State, 1988, annual rpt, 3164–42

Electric power plants production, capacity, sales, and fuel stocks, use, and costs, by State, 1984-88, annual rpt, 3164–11

Electric power plants production, fuel use, stocks, and costs by fuel type, and sales, by State, monthly rpt, 3162–35

Electric utilities coal receipts, use, stocks, and delivered price, by State, and import and export prices, weekly rpt, monthly data, 3162–1.2

Electric utilities fuel cost, quality, use, receipts, and stocks, and power plant production, by energy source, State and utility, quarterly rpt, 3162–39

OECD energy prices, by fuel type and end use, for 10 countries, 1980-88 annual rpt, 3164–50.6

Pacific Northwest population, households, employment, income, and fuel prices, alternative projections 1990-2010 with trends from 1960, annual rpt, 3224–5

Prices and spending for fuel, by type, end-use sector, and State, 1987, annual rpt, 3164–64

Prices of coal, production, reserves, and use by State, exports by country, and employment, 1900s-87, biennial rpt, 3164–79

Prices, productivity, miners, reserves, stocks, and production and mines by county, by mining method and State, 1987-88, annual rpt, 3164–25

Prices, supply, and demand, by fuel type and end-use sector, projected under 3 oil price assumptions, 1988-2000, annual rpt, 3164–75

Prices, supply, and demand, by fuel type and end-use sector, with foreign comparisons, 1988 and trends from 1949, annual rpt, 3164–74

Prices, supply, and demand, by fuel type and end use, with foreign comparisons, 1976-88, annual summary rpt, 3164–76

Prices, supply, and demand of energy, forecasts by resource type, quarterly rpt, 3162–34

Prices, supply, demand, trade, and stocks of coal, coke, and breeze, by end-use sector and State, quarterly rpt, 3162–37

Producer price indexes, by stage of processing and detailed commodity, monthly rpt, 6762–6

Producer price indexes, by stage of processing and detailed commodity, monthly 1988, annual rpt, 6764–2

Statistical Abstract of US, social, political, and economic data, 1790-2025, comprehensive annual compilation, 2324–1.3

Coal reserves

Communist, OECD, and selected other countries energy reserves, production, and use, and oil trade and revenue, 1960s-88, annual rpt, 9114–4.5

Fed Govt coal leasing activity, acreage, production, and reserves, by coal region and State, FY88, annual rpt, 5724–10

Foreign and US coal trade flows and reserves, by country, 1970s-87 and projected to 2000, annual rpt, 3164–77

Foreign and US energy reserves, by type of fuel and country, as of Jan 1989, annual rpt, 3164–50.7

Foreign countries mineral production, reserves, and industry role in domestic economy and world supply, world area and country rpt series, 5606–1

Minerals Yearbook, 1987, Vol 3 preprints: foreign country reviews of production, trade, and policy, by commodity, annual rpt series, 5604–23

Producers finances and operations, by energy type for US firms domestic and foreign operations, 1987, annual rpt, 3164–44.4

Public lands minerals resources and availability, State rpt series, 5606–7

Reserves of coal, by heat and sulfur content, mining method, and State, 1987, 3168–114

Reserves of coal, production, use, and prices by State, exports by country, and employment, 1900s-87, biennial rpt, 3164–79

Reserves, stocks, prices, productivity, miners, and production and mines by county, by mining method and State, 1987-88, annual rpt, 3164–25

Supply, demand, and prices, by fuel type and end-use sector, with foreign comparisons, 1988 and trends from 1949, annual rpt, 3164–74

Coal stocks

Business statistics, detailed data for major industries and economic indicators, *Survey of Current Business*, monthly rpt, 2702–1.15

Electric power plants production, capacity, sales, and fuel stocks, use, and costs, by State, 1984-88, annual rpt, 3164–11

Electric power plants production, fuel use, stocks, and costs by fuel type, and sales, by State, monthly rpt, 3162–35

Electric utilities coal receipts, use, stocks, and delivered price, by State, weekly rpt, monthly data, 3162–1.2

Electric utilities, coke plants, and other industry stocks of coal, monthly rpt, 3162–24.6

Electric utilities, coke plants, other industrial, producer, and distributor coal stocks, and total coke and breeze stocks, quarterly rpt, 3162–37

Electric utilities fuel cost, quality, use, receipts, and stocks, and power plant production, by energy source, State and utility, quarterly rpt, 3162–39

Stocks of coal, by district, quarterly rpt, 3162–8

Stocks, prices, productivity, miners, reserves, and production and mines by county, by mining method and State, 1987-88, annual rpt, 3164–25

Supply, demand, and prices, by fuel type and end-use sector, with foreign comparisons, 1988 and trends from 1949, annual rpt, 3164–74.4

Supply, demand, and prices, by fuel type, end-use sector, and country, detailed data, monthly rpt, 3162–24

Supply, demand, and prices of energy, forecasts by resource type, quarterly rpt, 3162–34

Coast Guard

Boat registrations, and accidents, casualties, and damage by cause, by vessel characteristics and State, 1988, annual rpt, 7404–1

Budget of US Appendix, obligations, appropriations, and personnel, by program and agency, FY90, annual rpt, 104–3

Courts (military) cases and actions, FY88, annual rpt, 3504–3

Criminal case processing in military courts, and prisoners by facility, by service branch, 1960s-88, annual rpt, 6064–6.5

Drug and illegal alien enforcement activities of USCG, 2nd half FY89, semiannual rpt, 7402–4

Drug enforcement training of US for foreign govts, enrollment in US and host countries by program, FY88, annual rpt, 7004–17

Drug smuggling aircraft interdiction activities of Fed Govt, funding, and radar system capabilities, by agency, FY82-89, GAO rpt, 26119–259

Employment of DOT, by subagency, occupation, and selected personnel characteristics, FY88, annual rpt, 7304–18

Expenditures of Fed Govt in States, by type, program, agency, and State, FY88, annual rpt, 2464–2

Financial statements and activities of USCG, FY85, annual rpt, 7304–1

Pollution (water) incidents and discharges, by type, source, cause, and location, 1984-86, annual rpt, 7404–3

Statistical Abstract of US, social, political, and economic data, 1790-2025, comprehensive annual compilation, 2324–1.2

Women military personnel on active and reserve duty, by demographic and service characteristics and service branch, FY88, annual chartbook, 3544–26

see also Coast Guard Reserve

Coast Guard Academy

see Service academies

Coast Guard Reserve

Family social, economic, and other characteristics, and spouses attitudes, for reserve personnel, 1986 survey, 3508–30

Manpower and equipment strengths, and readiness, by reserve component, FY88, annual rpt, 3544–31

Manpower, funding by category, procurement reductions, and needs, by reserve component, FY80-88, GAO rpt, 26123–220

Manpower social, economic, family, and service characteristics, and attitudes, by reserve component, 1986 survey, 3508–29

Manpower strengths and characteristics, by reserve component, quarterly rpt, 3542–4

Manpower strengths for reserve components, by selected characteristics, FY88, annual rpt, 3544–1.5

Coastal areas

Alaska Arctic Natl Wildlife Refuge resources, native hunting activity, and energy exploration impact, 1985, last issue of annual rpt, 5504–26

Army Corps of Engineers activities and projects, FY87 and trends from 1800s, annual rpt, 3754–1.2

Birds (waterfowl) coastal breeding population and colonies, by species and location for Washington, 1978-82, atlas, 5508–101

Birds (waterfowl) coastal breeding population and colonies, by species and location, 1976-82 surveys, 5508–100

Birds (waterfowl) coastal population, breeding success, and diet, for murre and kittiwake at Cape Thompson, Alaska, 1960s-88, 5738–11

Cargo (containerized) carried over principal trade routes, by flag of vessel, port, and US coastal district, 1984, annual rpt, 7704–8

Coast Guard drug and illegal alien enforcement activities, 2nd half FY89, semiannual rpt, 7402–4

Environmental and socioeconomic conditions, and potential impact of oil and gas OCS leases, final statement series, 5736–1

Environmental conditions and mgmt of coastal areas, map series, 2176–5

Environmental conditions, fish, wildlife, use, and mgmt, for individual coastal and riparian ecosystems, series, 5506–9

Environmental conditions of coastal areas and estuaries, research results and methodology, series, 2176–7

Environmental impacts of coastal areas economic dev and population growth, 1980s and projected to 2000, series, 2176–8

Environmental quality and protection programs, and intl issues, 1988 annual rpt, 484–1

Fish and shellfish catch, life cycles, and environmental needs, for selected coastal species and regions, series, 5506–8

Fish catch, trade, use, and fishery operations, with selected foreign data, by species, 1970s-88, annual rpt, 2164–1

Fish distribution for coastal southeastern US and Caribbean, by season, species, and location, 1980-82, 2168–112

Marine Fisheries Review, US and foreign fisheries resources, dev, mgmt, and research, quarterly journal, 2162–1

Marine Mammal Protection Act admin, and populations, strandings, and catch permits by species and location, 1987-88, annual rpt, 2164–11

NOAA activities and funding for ocean pollution, estuary, and coastal waters monitoring and assessment, FY88, annual rpt, 2174–9

Ocean surface temperature by ocean and for US coastal areas, and Bering Sea ice conditions, monthly rpt, 2182–5

Pollutant (PCB and pesticide) concentrations in coastal and estuarine fish and shellfish, by species and location, 1965-84, 2178–21

Pollutant concentrations in coastal and estuarine fish, shellfish, and environment, series, 2176–3

Pollutant discharges in coastal areas and estuaries, by source, pollutant type, and location, series, 2176–4

Pollutant discharges in coastal areas and estuaries from agricultural, airborne, and other nonpoint sources, and regulatory issues, 1988 hearing, 21568–46

Pollution (water) incidents and discharges, by type, source, cause, and location, 1984-86, annual rpt, 7404–3

Sewage pipelines and dump sites authorized in coastal areas, status and EPA enforcement activities by State, 1982-87, hearings, 21568–45

Statistical Abstract of US, social, political, and economic data, 1790-2025, comprehensive annual compilation, 2324–1.1

Tidal currents, daily time and velocity by station for North America and Asia coasts, forecast 1990, annual rpts, 2174–1

Tide height and time daily at coastal points worldwide, forecast 1990, annual rpt series, 2174–2

see also Chesapeake Bay

see also Continental shelf

see also Estuaries

see also Harbors and ports

see also New York Bight

see also Offshore mineral resources

see also Offshore oil and gas

see also Puget Sound

see also San Francisco Bay

see also Seashores

see also Territorial waters

see also Wetlands

Cobalt

see Metals and metal industries

Cobb, Steven A.

"Interarea Cost of Living Measurement with Nonmarket Goods: A Demand Systems Approach", 6886–6.9

Cocaine

Abuse of drugs and alcohol, by type, age, sex, race, and region, 1988 survey, biennial rpt, 4494–5

Abuse of drugs, emergency room admissions and deaths by drug type and major metro area, July-Dec 1988, semiannual rpt, 4492–3

Abuse of drugs, emergency room admissions and deaths by drug type and source, sex, race, age, and major metro area, 1988, annual rpt, 4494-8

Abuse of drugs, indicators for selected metro areas, research results, data collection, and policy issues, 1989 semiannual conf, 4492-5

Arrests for drug- and nondrug-related offenses, urine test results by drug type, offense, and sex, for selected urban areas, quarterly rpt, 6062-3

Coast Guard drug and illegal alien enforcement activities, 2nd half FY89, semiannual rpt, 7402-4

Customs Service activities, collections, entries processed by mode of transport, and seizures, FY84-88, annual rpt, 8144-1

DC metro area drug abuse, deaths, arrests, convictions, and seizures by drug type, 1980-87, hearing, 21308-24

Deaths and rates, by detailed cause and demographic characteristics, 1986 and trends from 1900, US Vital Statistics annual rpt, 4144-2

Fed Govt interdiction of drug smuggling by aircraft, activities, funding, and radar system capabilities, by agency, FY82-89, GAO rpt, 26119-259

Foreign countries drug production, eradication, and seizures, by illegal substance, with US aid, by country, 1985-89, annual rpt, 7004-17

Health condition and health care resources, use, and spending, 1950s-87, annual data compilation, 4144-11

High school seniors drug and alcohol use, by type and frequency, 1975-88, annual rpt, 4824-2.13

Immigration and Naturalization Service illegal alien and narcotics activities, FY81-88, annual rpt, 6264-2

Military personnel alcohol and drug abuse, prevalence and consequences, by selected characteristics, 1988, biennial rpt, 3504-19

Organized Crime Drug Enforcement Task Forces regional investigation activities by agency and region, and background data, FY83-88, annual rpt, 6004-17

Public opinion on crime and crime-related issues, by respondent characteristics, 1970s-89, annual rpt, 6064-6.2

Research on drug abuse and treatment, summaries of findings, resource materials, and grant listings, periodic rpt, 4492-4

Sentences for Federal offenses, guidelines by offense and circumstances, 1989 rpt, 17668-1

State and local govt drug enforcement activities, Federal aid by recipient, and background data, FY88, annual rpt, 6064-28

Statistical Abstract of US, social, political, and economic data, 1790-2025, comprehensive annual compilation, 2324-1.1

Supply of drugs in US by country of origin, abuse, deaths, prices, and seizures, by substance, 1988, annual rpt, 6284-2

Treatment facilities for drug and alcohol abuse, services, use, funding, and client characteristics, 1987, annual rpt, 4494-10

Youth drug, alcohol, and cigarette use and attitudes, by substance type and selected characteristics, 1975-88 surveys, annual rpt, 4494-4

Cochrane, Nancy J.
"Agricultural Performance in Eastern Europe, 1988", 1524-11
"Agricultural Statistics of Eastern Europe and the Soviet Union, 1965-85", 1528-284

Cocoa and chocolate
Africa agricultural exports by commodity, and relation to economic conditions and other factors, by country, 1960s-87, 1528-280

Agricultural Statistics, 1988, annual rpt, 1004-1

Business statistics, detailed data for major industries and economic indicators, *Survey of Current Business*, monthly rpt, 2702-1.11

Consumption, supply, trade, prices, spending, and indexes, by food commodity, 1987, annual rpt, 1544-4

County Business Patterns, 1987: employment, establishments, and payroll, by SIC 2- to 4-digit industry and county, annual State rpt series, 2326-8

Developing countries export revenue effects of trade policy changes in developing and developed countries, model results, 1989 article, 1522-3.922

Exports and imports (agricultural) of US, by commodity and country, bimonthly rpt with articles, 1522-1

Exports and imports (agricultural) of US, by commodity, monthly rpt, 1922-8

Exports and imports (agricultural) of US, by detailed commodity and country, 1988, semiannual rpt, 1522-4

Exports of US, detailed commodities by country, monthly rpt, 2422-3

Foreign and US agricultural production, trade, and weather devs, weekly press release, 1922-4

Foreign and US cocoa and cocoa products production, prices, and trade, 1988-90, FAS semiannual circular, 1925-9

Foreign countries agricultural production, prices, and trade, by country, 1970s-89 and forecast 1990, annual world region rpt series, 1524-4

Freight (waterborne domestic and foreign) by commodity, traffic, and passengers, by port and waterway, 1987, annual rpt, 3754-3

Futures and options trading volume, by commodity and exchange, FY88, annual rpt, 11924-2

Futures contracts on commodities, financial instruments, and indexes, options trading in NYC, Chicago, and other markets, monthly rpt, 11922-6

Futures trading in selected commodities and financial instruments and indexes, NYC, Chicago, and other markets activity, monthly rpt, 11922-5

Imports and quotas of dairy products, by commodity and country of origin, FAS monthly rpt, 1925-31

Imports of chocolate, and milk content, FY80-89, GAO rpt, 26113-427

Imports of US, detailed Schedule A commodities by country, monthly rpt, 2422-2

Manufacturing annual survey, 1986: financial and operating data, by SIC 2- to 4-digit industry, series, 2506-15

Manufacturing census, 1987: financial and operating data, for SIC 4-digit industries by product, preliminary rpt, 2491-1.6

Nutrient and caloric composition of food, for raw, processed, and prepared food, 1988 rpt, 1358-3

Occupational injury and illness rates, by SIC 2- to 4-digit industry, 1987, annual rpt, 6844-1

OECD trade, total and for 4 major countries, and US trade by country, by commodity, 1970-87, world area rpt series, 9116-1

Price indexes (producer), by stage of processing and detailed commodity, monthly rpt, 6762-6

Price indexes (producer), by stage of processing and detailed commodity, monthly 1988, annual rpt, 6764-2

Coconut oil
see Oils, oilseeds, and fats

Coder, John
"Longitudinal vs. Retrospective Measures of Work Experience", 2626-10.83
"Look at Welfare Dependency Using the 1984 SIPP Panel File", 2626-10.78

Cody, Brian J.
"Evaluating Commodity Prices as a Gauge for Monetary Policy", 9387-8.184
"Optimal Exchange Market Intervention: Evidence from France and West Germany During the Post-Bretton Woods Era", 9387-8.181

Coffee
Africa agricultural exports by commodity, and relation to economic conditions and other factors, by country, 1960s-87, 1528-280

Agricultural Statistics, 1988, annual rpt, 1004-1

Business statistics, detailed data for major industries and economic indicators, *Survey of Current Business*, monthly rpt, 2702-1.11

Communist, OECD, and selected other countries agricultural production, by commodity, 1960s-88, annual rpt, 9114-4.6

Consumption of food and nutrient intake by individuals, by food group, selected characteristics, and region, supplementary survey series, 1356-5

Consumption, supply, trade, prices, spending, and indexes, by food commodity, 1987, annual rpt, 1544-4

County Business Patterns, 1987: employment, establishments, and payroll, by SIC 2- to 4-digit industry and county, annual State rpt series, 2326-8

CPI by component for US city average, and by region, population size, and for 27 metro areas, monthly rpt, 6762-2

Cuba economic conditions, agricultural and industrial production and distribution, trade, and intl economic relations, 1980-87 with trends from 1961, 9118-8

Developing countries export revenue effects of trade policy changes in developing and developed countries, model results, 1989 article, 1522-3.922

Exports and imports (agricultural) of US, by commodity and country, bimonthly rpt with articles, 1522-1

Exports and imports (agricultural) of US, by commodity, monthly rpt, 1922-8

Exports and imports (agricultural) of US, by detailed commodity and country, 1988, semiannual rpt, 1522-4

Exports and imports (agricultural) of US with Asia, Middle East, and North Africa, by commodity and country, 1962-86, 1528-277

Exports of US, detailed commodities by country, monthly rpt, 2422-3

Farm income, expenses, receipts by commodity, assets, liabilities, and ratios, 1988 and trends from 1945, annual rpt, 1544-16

Foreign and US agricultural production, trade, and weather devs, weekly press release, 1922-4

Foreign countries agricultural production, prices, and trade, by country, 1970s-89 and forecast 1990, annual world region rpt series, 1524-4

Freight (waterborne domestic and foreign) by commodity, traffic, and passengers, by port and waterway, 1987, annual rpt, 3754-3

Futures and options trading volume, by commodity and exchange, FY88, annual rpt, 11924-2

Futures contracts on commodities, financial instruments, and indexes, options trading in NYC, Chicago, and other markets, monthly rpt, 11922-6

Futures trading in selected commodities and financial instruments and indexes, NYC, Chicago, and other markets activity, monthly rpt, 11922-5

Imports of US, detailed Schedule A commodities by country, monthly rpt, 2422-2

Manufacturing annual survey, 1986: financial and operating data, by SIC 2- to 4-digit industry, series, 2506-15

Manufacturing census, 1987: financial and operating data, for SIC 4-digit industries by product, preliminary rpt, 2491-1.9

Mormons death risks from cancer and heart disease, by sex and health habits practiced, 1974 and 1979 studies, article, 4472-1.932

Nutrient and caloric composition of food, for raw, processed, and prepared food, 1988 rpt, 1358-3

Occupational injury and illness rates, by SIC 2- to 4-digit industry, 1987, annual rpt, 6844-1

OECD trade, total and for 4 major countries, and US trade by country, by commodity, 1970-87, world area rpt series, 9116-1

Price indexes (producer), by stage of processing and detailed commodity, monthly rpt, 6762-6

Price indexes (producer), by stage of processing and detailed commodity, monthly 1988, annual rpt, 6764-2

Prices received by farmers and production value, by detailed crop and State, 1986-88, annual rpt, 1621-2

Production, farms, acreage, and related data, by selected crop and State, monthly rpt, 1621-1

Production, trade and quotas, and use, by country, with US and intl prices, FAS periodic circular, 1925-5

Puerto Rico farms, farmland, production, finances, and operator characteristics, by municipio, 1987 Census of Agriculture, final State rpt, 2331-1.52

Coffey, Osa
"Employee Drug-Testing Policies in Prison Systems", 6066-26.1

Coffman, Joseph S.
"Barite Availability: Market Economy Countries. A Minerals Availability Appraisal", 5606-4.26

Cogeneration of heat and electricity
see Electric power and heat cogeneration

Coggon, David
"Stomach Cancer and Food Storage", 4472-1.919

Cohen, Marc A.
"Life Care: New Options for Financing and Delivering Long-Term Care", 4652-1.917

Coins and coinage
Banks in Fed Reserve System, expenses and operations itemized by service, office, and district, 1988, annual rpt, 9364-11

China trade by SITC 1- to 5-digit commodity, 1970s-87, annual rpt, 9114-3

Currency and coin outstanding and in circulation, by type and denomination, *Treasury Bulletin*, quarterly rpt, 8002-4.16

Exports of US, detailed commodities by country, monthly rpt, 2422-3

Fed Reserve banks finances and staff, 1988, annual rpt, 9364-1.1

Fed Reserve costs of new currency, by item, 1987-89, annual rpt, 9364-10

Imports of US, detailed Schedule A commodities by country, monthly rpt, 2422-2

Injuries from use of consumer products and related activities, by victim age and sex, 1988, annual rpt, 9164-7

Injuries from use of consumer products, by severity, victim age, and detailed product, 1988, annual rpt, 9164-6

Production of coins, and use and holdings of monetary metals, by metal type and US Mint facility, FY88, annual rpt, 8204-1

Production of coins by US Mint, for US by denomination and mint, and for foreign countries, monthly table, 8202-1

Seigniorage in Fed Govt consolidated financial statements, FY87-88, annual rpt, 8104-5

Seigniorage in Fed Govt authoritative financial statements, FY88, annual rpt, 8104-2.2

Thefts, and value of property stolen and recovered, by property type, 1988, annual rpt, 6224-2.1

see also Counterfeiting and forgery
see also Money supply

Coke
see Coal and coal mining

Colangelo, Eugene J.
"Injuries to Seat Occupants of Light Airplanes", 7506-10.57

Cold storage and refrigeration
Agricultural Statistics, 1988, annual rpt, 1004-1

Business statistics, detailed data for major industries and economic indicators, *Survey of Current Business*, monthly rpt, 2702-1.11

Cancer (stomach) incidence and risk relation to diet and refrigerator use, 1985-87 local area study, article, 4472-1.919

Chlorofluorocarbon use, and costs and benefits of proposed reductions, projected to 2010, 3166-6.34

Containers (intermodal) and equipment owned by shipping and leasing companies, inventory by type and size, 1989, annual rpt, 7704-10

County Business Patterns, 1987: employment, establishments, and payroll, by SIC 2- to 4-digit industry and county, annual State rpt series, 2326-8

Dairy storage holdings, total and for USDA by product, 1988, annual rpt, 1317-1.1

DOD prime contract awards, by detailed procurement category, FY85-88, annual rpt, 3544-18

Employment, earnings, and hours, by selected SIC 1- to 4-digit industry, State, and for 262 MSAs, 1972-87, 6748-81

Employment, earnings, and hours, by SIC 1- to 4-digit industry, monthly 1983-Feb 1989, annual rpt, 6744-4

Energy use in commercial buildings, costs, and conservation, by building characteristics, survey rpt series, 3166-8

Energy use of households, and number with appliances, by type, selected years 1978-87, annual rpt, 3164-74.1

Equipment shipments, trade, use, and firms, by product, 1988, annual Current Industrial Rpt, 2506-12.7

Exports of US, detailed commodities by country, monthly rpt, 2422-3

Fish (processed) production by location, and trade, by species and product, 1987-88, annual rpts, 2166-6

Fish and shellfish catch, wholesale receipts, prices, trade, and other market activities, weekly regional rpts, 2162-6

Fish and shellfish cold storage holdings, by product and species, preliminary data, monthly press release, 2162-2

Fish catch, prices, trade by country, cold storage holdings, and market devs, for Japan, semimonthly press release, 2162-7

Fish catch, trade, use, and fishery operations, with selected foreign data, by species, 1970s-88, annual rpt, 2164-1

Food (frozen) composition, nutrients and calories for raw, processed, and prepared food, 1988 rpt, 1358-3

Food stocks in cold storage by commodity and census div, and warehouse space use, by State, monthly rpt, 1631-1

Food stocks in cold storage, by commodity and region, 1988, annual rpt, 1631-11

Fruit and nut production, prices, and use, 1986-89, annual rpt series, 1621-18

Imports of US, detailed Schedule A commodities by country, monthly rpt, 2422-2

Manufacturing annual survey, 1986: financial and operating data, by SIC 2- to 4-digit industry, series, 2506-15

Manufacturing census, 1987: financial and operating data, for SIC 4-digit industries by product, preliminary rpt, 2491-1.67; 2491-1.70

Meat, poultry, and egg production, prices, trade, and stocks, monthly rpt, 1561-17

Meat stocks in cold storage, 1970-87, 1568-285.4

Military Sealift Command shipping operations, finances, and personnel, FY88, annual rpt, 3804–14

Nut cold storage holdings, by type and region, weekly rpt, periodic data, 1311–1

Pollutant effects of refrigeration, for water samples by pollutant, 1988 rpt, 2168–109

Poultry (broiler) production, slaughter, prices, and processing industry operations, 1950s-87, 1568–279

Poultry (chicken, egg, and turkey) production, prices, receipts, trade, and disposition, 1960-87, 1568–39

Poultry and egg prices and marketing, by selected region, State, and city, monthly and weekly 1988, annual rpt, 1317–2

Price indexes (producer), by stage of processing and detailed commodity, monthly rpt, 6762–6

Price indexes (producer), by stage of processing and detailed commodity, monthly 1988, annual rpt, 6764–2

Science, engineering, and technical employment in manufacturing, by field, occupation, and industry, 1986, triennial rpt, 9627–23

Ships under foreign flag owned by US firms and foreign affiliates, by type, owner, and country of registry and construction, as of July 1989, semiannual rpt, 7702–3

Transportation census, 1987: trucks, by detailed characteristics, miles traveled, and type of product carried, State rpt series, 2573–1

Vegetables production, prices, trade, stocks, and use, for selected fresh and processing crops, periodic situation rpt with articles, 1561–11

Warehouse services finances, by SIC 3- to 4-digit industry, 1988 survey, annual rpt, 2413–14

Wholesale trade census, 1987: employment, establishments, finances, and operations, by SIC 2- to 4-digit kind of business, MSA, county, and city, State rpt series, 2405–1

see also Ice, manufactured

Coleman, Michael J.
"Statistics of Income Studies of Individual Income and Taxes", 8302–2.909

Coliform bacteria
see Food and waterborne diseases

Collective bargaining
see Labor-management relations, general
see Labor-management relations, local and regional
see Labor unions

College Station, Tex.
see also under By SMSA or MSA in the "Index by Categories"

Colleges and universities
see Black colleges
see Federal aid to higher education
see Federal aid to medical education
see Higher education
see Junior colleges
see State funding for higher education
see under By Individual Company or Institution in the "Index by Categories"

Collin County, Tex.
Housing and households detailed characteristics, and unit and neighborhood quality, by location, 1985 survey, MSA rpt, 2485–6.12

Collins, Dorothy
"Statistics of Income Studies of Business Income and Taxes", 8302–2.910

Collins, John G.
"Health Characteristics of Workers by Occupation and Sex: U.S., 1983-85", 4146–8.170

Collins, William E.
"Relationships of Anxiety Scores to Academy and Field Training Performance of Air Traffic Control Specialists", 7506–10.60

Colombia
Agricultural and food production and indexes, total and for selected commodities, by country, 1970s-88, annual rpt, 1524–12

Agricultural production, prices, and trade, by country, 1960s-89, annual world region rpt, 1524–4.2

Agricultural trade of US, by detailed commodity and country, 1988, semiannual rpt, 1522–4

AID economic aid to developing countries, obligations and disbursements by country, quarterly rpt, 9912–4

AID loans repayment status and terms by program and country, and status of predecessor agency loans, quarterly rpt, 9912–3

Coal production, trade, and govt subsidies, by country and country group, 1973-87 and projected to 2000, 2048–144

Economic and military aid and loans from US and intl agencies, by program and country, FY46-87, annual rpt, 9914–5

Economic conditions, income, production, prices, employment, and trade, 1988 periodic country rpt, 2046–4.6

Economic conditions, policy, and trade practices, by country, 1986-88, annual rpt, 21384–5

Economic, social, political, and geographic summary data, by country, 1989, annual factbook, 9114–2

Exports and imports of Latin America, and balance of trade with US, by country, 1988, annual rpt, 2044–34

Exports and imports of US, by commodity and country, 1970-87, world area rpt, 9116–1.5

Exports and imports of US, by selected country, country group, and commodity group, 1988, annual rpt, 2044–37

Flowers (cut roses) US industry intl competitiveness, investigation with background financial and operating data and foreign comparisons, 1989 rpt, 9886–4.137

Food demand price elasticities, by commodity for Colombia, 1989 article, 1522–3.911

Human rights conditions in 170 countries, 1988, annual rpt, 21384–3

Imports of goods, services, and investment from US, trade barriers, impacts, and US actions, by country, 1988, annual rpt, 444–2

Labor conditions, union coverage, and work accidents, 1989 annual country rpt, 6366–4.8; 6366–4.57

Military aid of US, arms sales, and training programs costs and budget requests, by program, world region, and country, FY88-90, annual rpt, 7144–13

Military spending, arms trade, and force strengths, with govt spending and population, by country, 1977-87, annual rpt, 9824–1

Minerals Yearbook, 1987, Vol 3: foreign country reviews of production, trade, and policy, by commodity, annual rpt, 5604–35

Minerals Yearbook, 1987, Vol 3 preprints: foreign country review of production, trade, and policy, by commodity, annual rpt, 5604–23.17

Multinatl US firms and foreign affiliates finances and operations, by industry of parent firm and affiliate, world area, and country, preliminary 1987, annual rpt, 2704–5

Population size, growth rates, and components of change, by country, projected 1989-2020 and trends from 1950, biennial rpt, 2324–9

UN voting record and share of votes in agreement with US, by issue, country, and world area, 1988, annual rpt, 7004–18

see also under By Foreign Country in the "Index by Categories"

Colombo, P.
"Waste Package Performance Criteria for Deepsea Disposal of Low-Level Radioactive Waste", 9198–119

Colorado
Agriculture census, 1987: farms, farmland, production and costs, and operator characteristics, advance State and county rpts, 2330–1.8

Agriculture census, 1987: farms, farmland, production, finances, and operator characteristics, by county, final State rpt, 2331–1.6

Bank deposits in FDIC-insured commercial and savings banks, by instn, State, and county, as of June 1988, annual regional rpt, 9295–3.6

Coal production and mines by county, prices, productivity, miners, reserves, and stocks, by mining method and State, 1987-88, annual rpt, 3164–25

County Business Patterns, 1987: employment, establishments, and payroll, by SIC 2- to 4-digit industry and county, annual State rpt, 2326–8.7

Deaths and rates, by detailed location, cause, and demographic characteristics, 1987, US Vital Statistics annual rpt, 4144–3.1

DOD prime contract awards, by contractor, service branch, State, and city, FY88, annual rpt, 3544–22

Drug abuse indicators for selected metro areas, research results, data collection, and policy issues, 1989 semiannual conf, 4492–5

Employment, earnings, and hours, by selected SIC 1- to 4-digit industry, State, and for 262 MSAs, 1972-87, 6748–81.1

Fed Govt spending in States and local areas, by type, State, county, and city, FY88, annual rpt, 2464–3

Fed Govt spending in States, by type, program, agency, and State, FY88, annual rpt, 2464–2

Forests (aspen) bird and rodent population relation to aspen and conifer mix, for Colorado, 1988 rpt, 1208–299

HHS financial aid, by program, recipient, State, and city, FY88, annual regional listing, 4004–3.8

Homeless children educational enrollment and needs, 1988, annual State rpt, 4804–35.7

Income (personal) per capita and by source, and earnings by industry div, by State, MSA, and county, 1982-87, annual regional rpt, 2704–2.5

Mineral Industry Surveys, State reviews of production, 1988, preliminary annual rpt, 5614–6

Minerals Yearbook, 1987, Vol 2 preprints: State review of production and sales by commodity, and business activity, annual rpt, 5604–16.7

Minerals Yearbook, 1987, Vol 2: State reviews of production, sales, and firms, by commodity, and business activity, annual rpt, 5604–34

Nuclear power plant (helium-cooled) at Fort St Vrain, occupational radiation exposure, 1974-86, annual rpt, 9634–3

Nursing home compliance with Medicare and Medicaid regulations, and patient characteristics, by facility, 1987/88, annual State rpt, 4654–15.6

Oil and gas leasing activity on Federal land, production, revenue, and royalty rates, by whether competitively leased and western State, 1984-88, GAO rpt, 26113–413

Retail trade census, 1987: employment, establishments, sales, and payroll, by SIC 2- to 4-digit kind of business, MSA, county, and city, State rpt, 2397–1.6

Savings instns, FHLB 10th District members finances and lending by State and MSA, monthly table, 9302–22

Savings instns, FHLB 10th District members financial condition, by State, quarterly rpt, 9302–34

Service industries census, 1987: employment, establishments, receipts, and payroll, by SIC 2- to 4-digit kind of business, MSA, county, and city, State rpt, 2391–1.6

Statistical Abstract of US, social, political, and economic data, with foreign comparisons, 1790-2025, comprehensive annual compilation, 2324–1

Water quality data collection activities and quality, for 2 States, 1984, 5668–94

Water supply and quality in streams and lakes, and groundwater levels in wells, by drainage basin, 1987, annual State rpt, 5666–10.6

Water supply and quality in streams and lakes, and groundwater levels in wells, by drainage basin, 1988, annual State rpt, 5666–16.6

Water supply, and snow survey results, monthly State rpt, 1266–2.3

Water supply, and snow survey results, 1988, annual State rpt, 1264–14.4

Wholesale trade census, 1987: employment, establishments, and operations, by SIC 2- to 4-digit kind of business, MSA, county, and city, State rpt, 2405–1.6

Wildlife-related recreation, hunting, and fishing participation and spending, detailed data, 1985 survey, quinquennial State rpt, 5506–6.6

see also Boulder, Colo.

see also Colorado Springs, Colo.
see also Denver, Colo.
see also Fort Collins, Colo.
see also Loveland, Colo.
see also Pueblo, Colo.
see also under By State in the "Index by Categories"

Colorado River

Agricultural Stabilization and Conservation Service producer payments, by program, monthly rpt, 1802–10

Reservoir and power operations and revenues, for Colorado River Basin Project, 1987-88, annual rpt, 5824–6

Soil salinity impacts on yields and off-farm water quality, and costs and benefits of extending erosion control program to saline cropland, 1989 rpt, 1588–144

Water storage project for Colorado River, finances and activities in western States, FY88, annual rpt, 5824–3

Water supply and quality in streams and lakes, and groundwater levels in wells, by drainage basin, 1986, annual State rpt series, 5666–23

Water supply and quality in streams and lakes, and groundwater levels in wells, by drainage basin, 1987, annual State rpt series, 5666–10

Water supply and quality in streams and lakes, and groundwater levels in wells, by drainage basin, 1988, annual State rpt series, 5666–16

Colorado Springs, Colo.

Housing starts and completions authorized by building permits in 40 MSAs, quarterly rpt, 2382–9

Housing vacancy rates for single and multifamily units and mobile homes, by city and ZIP code, 1988, annual MSA rpt, 9304–22.1

Wages by occupation, and benefits for office and plant workers, 1988 survey, periodic MSA rpt, 6785–3.2

see also under By City and By SMSA or MSA in the "Index by Categories"

Coltrane, Robert

"Farm Labor Inputs", 1561–16.901

Columbia, Mo.

see also under By SMSA or MSA in the "Index by Categories"

Columbia River

Bonneville Power Admin mgmt of Fed Columbia River Power System, finances, operations, and sales by customer, FY88, annual rpt, 3224–1

Electric power capacity and use in Pacific Northwest, by energy source, projected under alternative load and demand cases, 1989-2008, annual rpt, 3224–3

Estuary environmental conditions, research results and methodology, 1988 local area rpt, 2176–7.10

Fish and shellfish catch, wholesale receipts, prices, trade, and other market activities, weekly regional rpt, 2162–6.5

Freight (waterborne domestic and foreign) by commodity, traffic, and passengers, by port and waterway, 1987, annual rpt, 3754–3.4

Pollution levels for Oregon coastal and estuarine waters, by pollutant and location, 1960s-87, 2178–23

Water supply and quality in streams and lakes, and groundwater levels in wells, by drainage basin, 1986, annual State rpt series, 5666–23

Water supply and quality in streams and lakes, and groundwater levels in wells, by drainage basin, 1987, annual State rpt series, 5666–10

Water supply and quality in streams and lakes, and groundwater levels in wells, by drainage basin, 1988, annual State rpt series, 5666–16

Water supply in US and southern Canada, streamflow, surface and groundwater conditions, and reservoir levels, by location, monthly rpt, 5662–3

Columbia, S.C.

Fruit and vegetable shipments, and arrivals in US and Canada cities, by mode of transport and State and country of origin, 1988, annual rpt, 1311–4.1

see also under By SMSA or MSA in the "Index by Categories"

Columbus, Ga.

Wages by occupation, for office and plant workers, 1989 survey, periodic MSA rpt, 6785–3.5

see also under By City and By SMSA or MSA in the "Index by Categories"

Columbus, Miss.

Wages by occupation, for office and plant workers, 1989 survey, periodic MSA rpt, 6785–3.8

Columbus, Ohio

see also under By City and By SMSA or MSA in the "Index by Categories"

Commemorations and memorials
see Monuments and memorials

Commerce
see Foreign trade
see Interstate commerce

Commerce Department
see Department of Commerce

Commercial banking
see Banks and banking

Commercial buildings

Alteration and repair spending for commercial and public buildings, by type, size, age, and region, 1986, 2388–4

Alteration and repair spending for commercial and public buildings, by type, 1986, article, 2042–1.906

Assets and debts of private sector, balance sheets by segment, 1949-88, semiannual rpt, 9365–4.1

Bombing incidents and casualties, by target, circumstances, and State, 1979-88, annual rpt, 8484–4.1

Bombing incidents, casualties, and damage, by target, circumstances, and State, 1988, annual rpt, 6224–5

China housing and commercial construction, and building materials production and trade by product group, 1984-85 and projected to 1990, article, 2042–1.910

Construction industries census, 1987: establishments, employment, receipts, and expenditures, by SIC 4-digit industry and State, final industry rpt series, 2373–1

Construction industries census, 1987: financial and operating data, preliminary industry rpt series, 2371–1

Construction put in place, permits, housing sales, costs, material prices, and employment, bimonthly rpt with articles, 2042–1

Construction put in place, value of new public and private structures, by type, monthly rpt, 2382–4

Crime victimization rates, by victim and offender characteristics, circumstances, and offense, 1987 survey, annual rpt, 6066–3.41

Energy use in commercial buildings, costs, and conservation, by building characteristics, survey rpt series, 3166–8

Fed Govt-owned real property inventory and costs, worldwide summary by purpose, agency, and location, 1987, annual rpt, 9454–5

Flow-of-funds accounts, savings, investments, and credit statements, quarterly rpt, 9365–3.3

Harbor traffic, facilities, dev, funding, and needs, for Pacific territories and Hawaii by port, as of 1987, 7308–195

Historic and natural natl landmarks damaged and threatened, with owner, location, damage type, and recommended remedial action, 1988, annual listing, 5544–16

Historic buildings rehabilitation tax incentives, projects, costs, ownership, use, and tax reform impacts, FY77-88, annual rpt, 5544–17

Mortgage loan activity, by type of lender, loan, and mortgaged property, monthly press release, 5142–18

Multinatl firms US affiliates finances and operations, by industry div, country of parent firm, and State, 1986-87, annual article, 2702–1.925

Multinatl firms US affiliates, finances, and operations, by industry, world area of parent firm, and State, 1987, annual rpt, 2704–4

Neighborhood and housing quality, indicators and attitudes, by householder type and location, 1985, biennial rpt, 2485–12

Pollution (air) indoor levels, effects of ventilation rates in commercial and public buildings, 1989 rpt, 3228–10

Pollution (air) levels for 5 pollutants, by detailed source and State, 1986, annual rpt, 9194–7

Puerto Rico and other US possessions corporations tax incentives, finances, and operations by industry, and impacts on local economy, 1970s-83, biennial rpt, 8004–12

Robberies and rates, by type of premises and weapon, 1973-87, annual rpt, 6224–8

Robberies, by type of premises, population size, and region, 1988, annual rpt, 6224–2.1

Statistical Abstract of US, social, political, and economic data, 1790-2025, comprehensive annual compilation, 2324–1.3

Suburban areas land use, commuting, employment, and housing characteristics, detailed data for traffic planning, 1986, 7888–75

Tax (property) revenue by level of govt, assessed values by locality, and exemptions, by property type and State, 1987 Census of Govts, 2453–1

Terrorist incidents in US, related activity, and casualties, by attack type, target, group, and location, 1988, annual rpt, 6224–6

Vacancy rates for office buildings in 16 cities, 1960s-87, article, 9387–1.903

Wiretaps authorized, costs, arrests, trials, and convictions, by offense and jurisdiction, 1988, annual rpt, 18204–7

Commercial credit

Agricultural cooperatives debt financing, by source, for top 100 cooperatives, 1987-88, article, 1122–1.911

Agricultural cooperatives finances, aggregate for top 100 assns by commodity group, FY87, annual rpt, 1124–3

Assets and debts of private sector, balance sheets by segment, 1949-88, semiannual rpt, 9365–4.1

Banks (commercial) business loans, and commercial paper of nonfinancial companies, weekly rpt, 9391–4

Banks regulatory costs relation to corporate loans, alternative regression results, 1977-87, technical paper, 9366–6.177

Financial and business detailed statistics, *Fed Reserve Bulletin*, monthly rpt with articles, 9362–1

Flow-of-funds accounts, assets and liabilities by type and economic sector, outstanding at year-end 1965-88, annual rpt, 9364–3

Flow-of-funds accounts, savings, investments, and credit statements, quarterly rpt, 9365–3.3

Mergers and acquisitions using leveraged buyout, financing characteristics and policy issues, 1970s-88, 21368–115

Minority Business Dev Centers mgmt and financial aid, and characteristics of businesses, by region and State, FY88, annual rpt, 2104–6

North Central States business and economic conditions, Fed Reserve 9th District, quarterly journal, 9383–19

Overseas Business Reports: economic conditions, investment and export opportunities, and trade practices, country market research rpt series, 2046–6

Savings instns insured by Savings Assn Insurance Fund, assets, liabilities, and deposit and loan activity, by conservatorship status, monthly rpt, 8432–1

Savings instns regulatory issues, mgmt, and FHLB system and member finances and operations, monthly journal, 8432–2; 9312–1

Small business financing sources, and business financial data by size, type, and industry, various periods 1980-88, annual rpt, 9764–6.2

Southeastern States, Fed Reserve 5th District insured commercial banks financial statements, by State, quarterly rpt, 9389–18

Southeastern States, FHLB 4th District thrifts finances, by State, 1984-88 annual rpt series, 9304–29

Survey of Current Business, detailed data for major industries and economic indicators, monthly rpt, 2702–1.6

Tax (income) returns of corporations, income and tax items by asset size and detailed industry, 1986, annual rpt, 8304–21

West Central States, FHLB 10th District savings instns finances and lending by State and MSA, monthly table, 9302–22

Commercial education
  see Business education

Commercial finance companies
  see Finance companies

Commercial law

Bank deposits interest rates relation to local bank market concentration and branching regulations, 1983-87, technical paper, 9366–6.166

Banking (interstate) laws of States, impacts of changes on bank stock returns, 1988 working paper, 9387–8.174

Court civil and criminal caseloads for Federal district, appeals, and special courts, June 1989, annual rpt, 18204–2

Industry structure, conduct, and govt regulation, effects on competition, series, 9406–1

Savings instns insolvency losses and uninsured certificate of deposit interest rates, impact of proposed depositor preference laws, model description and results, 1989 technical paper, 9316–1.154

  see also Antitrust law
  see also Bankruptcy
  see also Interstate commerce
  see also Licenses and permits
  see also Maritime law
  see also Patents
  see also Price regulation
  see also Trademarks

Commercial treaties
  see Trade agreements

Commissaries
  see Military post exchanges and commissaries

Commission of Fine Arts

Budget of US, authoritative financial statements with appropriations, outlays, and receipts, by category and agency, FY88, annual rpt, 8104–2.2

Commission on Civil Rights

Budget of US Appendix, obligations, appropriations, and personnel, by program and agency, FY90, annual rpt, 104–3

Budget of US, authoritative financial statements with appropriations, outlays, and receipts, by category and agency, FY88, annual rpt, 8104–2.2

Income and economic status of minority groups and women, and discrimination and govt policy impacts, series, 11046–7

Labor unions recognized in Fed Govt, agreements and membership by agency and facility, as of Jan 1989, biennial listing, 9844–14

School desegregation, indicators of integration plans effectiveness by school district and location, 1960s-85, 11048–189

Commission on Merchant Marine and Defense

Ships, shipyards, and personnel wartime capability, for merchant and reserve fleet, revised estimates, 1985-2000, 11208–3

Ships, shipyards, and personnel wartime capability, for merchant and reserve fleet, 1988-2000, 11208–1

Commissions of the Federal Government
  see Federal boards, committees, and commissions
  see Federal independent agencies

Committee for Purchase from the Blind and Other Severely Handicapped

Budget of US Appendix, obligations, appropriations, and personnel, by program and agency, FY90, annual rpt, 104-3

Budget of US, authoritative financial statements with appropriations, outlays, and receipts, by category and agency, FY88, annual rpt, 8104-2.2

Workshops for blind and handicapped, finances, operations, and Federal procurement, FY80-88, annual rpt, 11714-1

Committees of Congress

see Congressional committees

see Congressional joint committees

Commodities

see Agricultural commodities

see Foreign trade

see Futures trading

see Manufacturing

see Mines and mineral resources

see Natural resources

see Stockpiling

see Strategic materials

see under By Commodity in the "Index by Categories"

see under names of specific commodities or commodity groups

Commodity Credit Corp.

Activities and finances of CCC, by program, FY87, last issue of annual rpt, 1824-1

Agricultural Stabilization and Conservation Service programs, annual commodity fact sheet series, 1806-4

Agricultural Statistics, 1988, annual rpt, 1004-1

Agriculture census, 1987: farms, farmland, production, finances, and operator characteristics, by county, final State rpt series, 2331-1

Budget of US Appendix, obligations, appropriations, and personnel, by program and agency, FY90, annual rpt, 104-3

Certificate (generic commodity) program of CCC, issues and exchanges by commodity, and wheat auction sales, 1987-89, article, 1502-4.904

Certificate exchange activity of CCC, by commodity, weekly press release, 1802-16

Cotton loan activity of CCC, monthly press release, 1802-17

Cotton loan rates, and micronaire differentials of CCC, monthly rpt, annual tables, 1309-12

Cotton prices at selected spot markets, NYC futures prices, and CCC loan rates, 1988/89 and trends from 1940, annual rpt, 1309-2

Cotton prices in 8 spot markets, futures prices at NYC exchange, farm prices, and CCC loan stocks, monthly rpt, 1309-1

Cotton production, trade, and use, for selected countries, FAS monthly circular, 1925-4.2

Dairy production by State, stocks, prices, and CCC price support activities, by product type, monthly rpt, 1627-3

Dairy products price support purchases, sales, donations, and inventories of CCC, monthly rpt, 1802-2

Dairy products uncommitted stocks, periodic situation rpt with articles, 1561-2

Developing countries economic and military aid from US, by country and program, FY86, annual rpt, 9904-1.4

Economic Indicators of the Farm Sector, balance sheets, and receipts by detailed commodity, by State, 1984-88, annual rpt, 1544-18

Economic Indicators of the Farm Sector, finances, income sources, expenses by type, assets, debts, and ratios, 1987, annual rpt, 1544-19

Exports (agricultural) competitiveness, and subsidy and credit program costs, with data by commodity, 1980s-89, GAO rpt, 26113-404

Exports (agricultural) under federally financed programs, FY70-88, annual rpt, 1924-9

Exports under federally financed programs, by commodity and country, bimonthly rpt, periodic data, 1522-1.4

Finances of govts, revenues by source and spending by function, natl income and product account, *Survey of Current Business*, monthly rpt, 2702-1.24

Financial statements and operations of CCC, by program and commodity, annual rpt, discontinued, 1824-3

Financial statements and operations of CCC, by program and commodity, FY88, annual rpt, 1824-4

Grain and feed trade, and export and support prices, for US and major producer countries, FAS monthly circular, 1925-2.4

Grain futures contracts, stocks in deliverable position by type, weekly tables, 11922-4

Grain production, prices, trade, and export inspections by US port and country of destination, by grain type, weekly rpt, 1313-2

Grain storage facility and equipment loans to farmers under CCC program, by State, FY68-89, annual table, 1804-14

Honey production, prices, trade, stocks, marketing, and CCC honey loan and distribution activities, monthly rpt, 1311-2

Liabilities (contingent) and claims paid by Fed Govt on federally insured and guaranteed contracts with foreign obligors, by country and program, periodic rpt, 8002-12

Loan and support programs payment activity of CCC, with data by commodity, 1986-88 and projected to 1994, 26308-86

Loans (farm) outstanding, and lenders financial condition, quarterly rpt with articles, 1541-1

Loans, and other finances and operations of farms, by size, commodity, and region, 1986, annual rpt, 1544-27

Loans of CCC, activities and operating results, monthly release, 1802-7

Loans of CCC, and liquidations, by commodity, monthly 1983-88, annual rpt, 1544-16

Lumber and wood products exports and export promotion of US by country, and trade balance, by commodity, FAS quarterly circular, 1925-36

Oils, oilseeds, and fats foreign and US production and trade, FAS periodic circular series, 1925-1

PL 480 exports by commodity, and recipients, by program, sponsor, and country, FY87 and cumulative from FY55, annual rpt, 1924-7

Price support activity and policy options, with data on production, trade, use, and finances, and foreign comparisons, 1950s-89, commodity rpt series, 1566-7

Rice foreign and US production, prices, trade, stocks, and use, periodic situation rpt, 1561-8

Rice market activities, prices, inspections, sales, trade, supply, and use, for US and selected foreign markets, weekly rpt, 1313-8

Sale offerings of CCC commodities, and prices, monthly press release, 1802-4

Seed exports, by type, world region, and country, FAS quarterly rpt, 1925-13

Statistical Abstract of US, social, political, and economic data, 1790-2025, comprehensive annual compilation, 2324-1.3

Storage facility and equipment loans to farmers under CCC grain program, by State, monthly table, 1802-9

Wheat pledged under CCC nonrecourse loans, and relation to price and loan rate, 1965-88, article, 1561-12.902

Commodity Exchange Authority

see Commodity Futures Trading Commission

Commodity futures

see Futures trading

Commodity Futures Trading Commission

Activities, funding, and staff of CFTC, and futures and options trading volume by commodity and exchange, FY88, annual rpt, 11924-2

Budget of US Appendix, obligations, appropriations, and personnel, by program and agency, FY90, annual rpt, 104-3

Budget of US, authoritative financial statements with appropriations, outlays, and receipts, by category and agency, FY88, annual rpt, 8104-2.2

Cotton futures unfixed call sales and purchases and open contracts on NYC exchange, weekly rpt, 11922-3

Enforcement activities of CFTC, Chicago Board of Trade, and Chicago Mercantile Exchange, 1984-89, GAO rpt, 26119-247

Enforcement activity of CFTC and exchanges, various periods 1984-FY90, GAO rpt, 26119-263

Futures trading in selected commodities and financial instruments and indexes, NYC, Chicago, and other markets activity, monthly rpt, 11922-5

Grain futures contracts, stocks in deliverable position by type, weekly tables, 11922-4

Labor unions recognized in Fed Govt, agreements and membership by agency and facility, as of Jan 1989, biennial listing, 9844-14

Options on commodity, financial instrument, and index futures contracts, trading in NYC, Chicago, and other markets, monthly rpt, 11922-6

Common carriers

see Airlines

see Buses

see Passenger ships

see Public utilities

see Railroads
see Ships and shipping
see Taxicabs
see Trucks and trucking industry

Common markets and free trade areas
Asia countries trade with US by commodity, and free trade area proposal, 1985-88, 9886-4.135
Export and import agreements, negotiations, anticompetitive investigations, and related legislation, FY86-88, annual rpt, 444-1
Exports and imports, trade agreements and relations, and USITC investigations, 1988, annual rpt, 9884-5
Loans of US banks to foreigners at all US and foreign offices, by country group and country, quarterly rpt, 13002-1
US foreign trade zone operations and movement of goods, by zone and commodity, FY86, annual rpt, 2044-30
US foreign trade zones, applications, and shipments, with data for auto assembly, FY70s-87, GAO rpt, 26123-223
see also Central American Common Market
see also Council for Mutual Economic Assistance
see also European Community
see also Latin American Integration Association

Communicable diseases
see Acquired immune deficiency syndrome
see Animal diseases and zoonoses
see Infective and parasitic diseases
see Pneumonia and influenza
see Rabies
see Sexually transmitted diseases
see Tuberculosis

Communications industries
Collective bargaining agreements expiring during year, and workers covered, by firm, union, industry group, and State, 1989, annual rpt, 6784-9
County Business Patterns, 1987: employment, establishments, and payroll, by SIC 2- to 4-digit industry and county, annual State rpt series, 2326-8
Criminal cases by type and disposition, and collections, for US attorneys, by Federal district, FY88, annual rpt, 6004-2.1
DOD budget, manpower needs, costs, and force readiness by service branch, FY90, annual rpt, 3504-1
DOD budget, R&D appropriations by item, service branch, and defense agency, FY88-91, annual rpt, 3544-33
DOD prime contract awards, by detailed procurement category, FY85-88, annual rpt, 3544-18
Earnings by major industry group, and personal income per capita and by source, by region and State, 1929-87, 2708-40
Employment, earnings, and hours, by selected SIC 1- to 4-digit industry, State, and for 262 MSAs, 1972-87, 6748-81
Employment, earnings, and hours, by SIC 1- to 4-digit industry, monthly 1983-Feb 1989, annual rpt, 6744-4
Employment of minorities and women, by occupation, SIC 1- to 3- digit industry, State, and MSA, 1986, annual rpt, 9244-1
Foreign direct investment in US, major transactions by type, industry, country, and US location, 1987, annual rpt, 2044-20

Input-output structure of US economy, detailed interindustry transactions for 84 industries, and components of final demand, 1983, annual article, 2702-1.909
Licensing activities of FCC, by class of operation, FY88, annual rpt, 9284-4
Manufacturing census, 1987: financial and operating data, for SIC 4-digit industries by product, preliminary rpt, 2491-1.72
Natl income and product accounts and components, *Survey of Current Business*, monthly rpt, 2702-1.27
Occupational injury and illness rates, by SIC 2- to 4-digit industry, 1987, annual rpt, 6844-1
SEC registration, firms required to file annual rpts, as of Sept 1988, annual listing, 9734-5
Senate receipts, itemized expenses by payee, and balances, 1st half FY89, semiannual listing, 25922-1
Tax (income) returns of corporations, income and tax items by asset size and detailed industry, 1986, annual rpt, 8304-4; 8304-21
Tax (income) returns of partnerships, income statement items by industry group, 1986, annual article, 8302-2.903
Tax (income) returns of sole proprietorships, income statement items, by industry group, 1987, annual article, 8302-2.904; 8302-2.921
see also Books and bookselling
see also Cable television
see also Communications satellites
see also Educational broadcasting
see also Home video and audio equipment
see also Information services
see also Motion pictures
see also Newspapers
see also Periodicals
see also Political broadcasting
see also Printing and publishing industry
see also Public broadcasting
see also Radio
see also Recording industry
see also Telecommunication
see also Telegraph
see also Telephones and telephone industry
see also Television
see also under By Industry in the "Index by Categories"

Communications Satellite Corp.
Finances and operations of COMSAT, 1986-87, annual rpt, 9284-6.7

Communications satellites
DOD procurement cost estimates for weapons and communications systems, by service branch, quarterly summary rpt, 3502-1
Foreign countries economic, social, political, and geographic summary data, by country, 1989, annual factbook, 9114-2
Launches and other activities of NASA and Soviet Union, with flight data, 1957-88, annual rpt, 9504-6.1
Manufacturers finances and operations, by SIC 2- to 4-digit industry, forecast 1989 and trends from 1950s, annual rpt, 2044-28
Price indexes (producer), by stage of processing and detailed commodity, monthly rpt, 6762-6

Price indexes (producer), by stage of processing and detailed commodity, monthly 1988, annual rpt, 6764-2
Telephone and telegraph firms detailed finances and operations, 1987, annual rpt, 9284-6
TV satellite dish and decoder sales, ownership, subscribers, and program ratings compared to local stations, 1980s-88, hearings, 21528-74

Communism
see Centrally planned economies
see Communist parties
see Socialism

Communist countries
see Centrally planned economies
see East-West trade

Communist parties
Foreign countries economic, social, political, and geographic summary data, by country, 1989, annual factbook, 9114-2
Soviet Union officials public appearances in and outside USSR, 1988, annual rpt, 9114-1
Soviet Union personal income by source, disposable income, wage deductions by type, and savings, 1950s-87, 9118-7

Community-based correctional programs
Federal correctional instn inmates, by sex, prison, security level, contract facility type, and region, monthly rpt series, 6242-1
Juvenile correctional and detention instns, inmates, and expenses, by instn and resident characteristics and State, 1975-85, biennial rpt, 6064-13
Sentences for Federal offenses, guidelines by offense and circumstances, 1989 rpt, 17668-1
Sex offenders treatment programs for adults and juveniles, by program type and State, 1986-88, annual rpt, 6064-6.1
Statistical Abstract of US, social, political, and economic data, 1790-2025, comprehensive annual compilation, 2324-1.1

Community colleges
see Junior colleges

Community development
Appalachia local dev projects, and funding by source, by program and State, FY88, annual rpt, 9084-1
Assistance (financial and nonfinancial) of Fed Govt, 1989 base edition with supplements, annual listing, 104-5
Budget of US Appendix, obligations, appropriations, and personnel, by program and agency, FY90, annual rpt, 104-3
Budget of US, CBO analysis of revenue and spending alternatives and projections of economic indicators, FY90-94, annual rpt, 26304-3
Budget of US, compact budgets by activity, function, and agency, FY90 and projected to FY94, annual rpt, 104-2
Budget of US, historical data, selected years FY34-88 and projected to FY94, annual rpt, 104-22
Budget of US, House concurrent resolution, with spending and revenue targets, FY90, annual rpt, 21264-2
Budget of US, Senate concurrent resolution, with spending and revenue targets, FY90, annual rpt, 25254-1

Budget of US, special analysis of Federal capital spending by category, projected FY89-2005 and trends from FY81, annual rpt, 104–24

Census of Population and Housing, 1990: data coverage and availability for community and business dev projects, user guide, 2308–10

Economic Dev Admin activities, and funding by program, recipient, State, and county, FY87 and cumulative from FY66, annual rpt, 2064–2

Education in community dev, HUD work-study grants and students by sponsor instn, 1988-89, press release, 5006–3.64

Enterprise zone program of Maryland, participants characteristics and views on incentives, and proposed Federal program tax expenditures, 1983-88, GAO rpt, 26131–53

Expenditures of Fed Govt in States, by type, program, agency, and State, FY88, annual rpt, 2464–2

FmHA activities, and loans and grants by program and State, FY88 and trends from FY69, annual rpt, 1184–17

Govt employment and payroll, by function, level of govt, and jurisdiction, 1987-88, annual rpt series, 2466–1

HHS financial aid, by program, recipient, State, and city, FY88, annual regional listings, 4004–3

HUD community dev programs funding and activities, by program and State, FY88, annual rpt, 5124–5

HUD grants for moderate-income homeownership loans, by recipient, 1989, press release, 5006–3.70

Indian (Navajo and Hopi) relocation program activities and caseloads, monthly rpt, 16002–1

Public opinion on taxes, spending, and govt efficiency, by respondent characteristics, 1989 survey, annual rpt, 10044–2

R&D funding by Fed Govt, by detailed function, program, and agency, FY88-90, annual rpt, 9627–9

State and local govt employment of minorities and women, by occupation, function, and pay level, 1986, annual rpt, 9244–6.4

TVA financial and operating data by program and facility, FY88, annual rpt, 9804–32

see also City and town planning
see also Community Development Block Grants
see also Urban beautification
see also Urban Development Action Grants
see also Urban renewal

Community Development Block Grants

Assistance (block and categorical grants) programs for State and local govts, FY89, biennial listing, 10044–8

Expenditures and activities for HUD community dev programs, by program and State, FY88, annual rpt, 5124–5

Expenditures of Fed Govt in States, by type, program, agency, and State, FY88, annual rpt, 2464–2

Homeless persons aid programs, and shelter capacity and voucher programs, for 5 major cities, 1988, 5188–122

Indian and Alaska Native housing and economic development program operations, by region, FY86-87, annual rpt, 5004–5

Revenue sharing reduction impacts on rural local govts budgets, and other funding sources, with data for Ohio, 1980s-86, 1598–254

Rural areas aid from Fed Govt compared to urban areas, by program and degree of urbanization, FY85, periodic rpt, 1598–248

Southeastern States community dev grants from HUD, by purpose and location, quarterly rpt, 9389–16

Community health services

Children (handicapped) home health care and support services availability and need, 1988, GAO report, 26121–300

Drug and alcohol abuse treatment facilities, services, use, funding, and client characteristics, 1987, annual rpt, 4494–10

Finances, operations, and staff of community and migrant health services, series, 4108–45

HHS financial aid, by program, recipient, State, and city, FY88, annual regional listings, 4004–3

Homeless persons in rural areas, health condition, services use, and other characteristics, local area studies, 1989 rpt, 4186–9.1

Indian Health Service facilities, funding, operations, and Indian health and other characteristics, 1950s-88, annual chartbook, 4084–1

Indian youth health center use, by type of visit, for demonstration projects in New Mexico, 1987-88, article, 4042–3.924

Medicaid coverage, participation, payments, admin, and legislative history, with data by State, 1980s-88, 21368–105

Mental health care facilities needs assessment and program evaluation for communities, methodology, use of census data, analysis, and sample data, series, 4506–8

Mental health care facilities, staff, and patient characteristics, *Statistical Notes* series, 4506–3

Mental health care in general hospitals, length of stay related to patient, instn, and State Medicaid program characteristics, 1981, article, 4652–1.924

Mississippi hospitals and community health centers, use, staff, and Medicare and other payments, 1988 hearing, 25548–97

Older frail persons community and home-based care under prepaid care plan, enrollees health condition and services use, for San Francisco, 1987, article, 4652–1.912

Older persons at risk for chronic hospitalization, community care effect on hospital use, demonstration projects, 1989 article, 4652–1.911

Older persons eligible for nursing home care, cost of home and community services, Medicaid waiver program in 2 States, 1981-84, article, 4652–1.943

Older persons health care spending for instnl and community care, under alternative community settings, 1979-84 study, article, 4652–1.932

Rural areas health care facilities, staffing, services accessibility, and indicators of need, 1960s-88, 25148–41

Service industries census, 1987: establishments, receipts, employment, and payroll, by SIC 2- to 4-digit kind of business, MSA, county, and city, State rpt series, 2391–1

see also Group homes for the handicapped
see also Home health services
see also Respite care

Community mental health centers
see Community health services
see Mental health facilities and services

Community Planning and Development, HUD

Expenditures and activities for HUD community dev programs, by program and State, FY88, annual rpt, 5124–5

Urban areas economic and social conditions, biennial rpt, issuing agency change, 5124–4

Community Relations Service

Activities of CRS, investigation and mediation of minority discrimination disputes, FY87, annual rpt, 6004–9

Cuba refugees entering US during 1980 boatlift, Federal funding for youth mental health services, and participation, 1981-88, GAO rpt, 26121–270

Community treatment centers
see Community-based correctional programs
see Community health services
see Group homes for the handicapped

Commuter air carriers
see Airlines

Commuting

Census of Population and Housing, 1990: data item selection, questionnaire dev, and testing, 2626–11.4

Cost of living indexes for metro areas, relation of expenditure items and quality of life indicators, model results, 1973, working paper, 6886–6.9

Energy use by mode of transport, fuel supply, and demographic and economic factors of vehicle use, 1970s-88, annual rpt, 3304–5

Hwy Statistics, summary data by State, 1987-88, annual rpt, 7554–24

Rural areas population and net migration, by region and commuting population share, various periods 1960-87, Current Population Rpt, 2546–3.160

Statistical Abstract of US, social, political, and economic data, 1790-2025, comprehensive annual compilation, 2324–1.3

Suburban areas land use, commuting, employment, and housing characteristics, detailed data for traffic planning, 1986, 7888–75

Urban areas traffic volume and detailed trip characteristics, by transport mode and city, 1950s-88, 7888–37

see also Buses
see also Pedestrians
see also Subways
see also Urban transportation

Comoros

Agricultural and food production and indexes, total and for selected commodities, by country, 1970s-88, annual rpt, 1524–12

Agricultural trade of US, by detailed commodity and country, 1988, semiannual rpt, 1522–4

AID activities and funding by project and function, FY90, and developing countries summary socioeconomic data from 1960s, annual rpt, 9904–4.5

AID economic aid to developing countries, obligations and disbursements by country, quarterly rpt, 9912–4

Economic and military aid and loans from US and intl agencies, by program and country, FY46-87, annual rpt, 9914–5

Economic, social, political, and geographic summary data, by country, 1989, annual factbook, 9114–2

Human rights conditions in 170 countries, 1988, annual rpt, 21384–3

Military aid of US, arms sales, and training programs costs and budget requests, by program, world region, and country, FY88-90, annual rpt, 7144–13

Minerals Yearbook, 1987, Vol 3: foreign country reviews of production, trade, and policy, by commodity, annual rpt, 5604–35

Minerals Yearbook, 1987, Vol 3 preprints: foreign country review of production, trade, and policy, by commodity, annual rpt, 5604–23.81

Population size, growth rates, and components of change, by country, projected 1989-2020 and trends from 1950, biennial rpt, 2324–9

UN voting record and share of votes in agreement with US, by issue, country, and world area, 1988, annual rpt, 7004–18

see also under By Foreign Country in the "Index by Categories"

Companies
see Business acquisitions and mergers
see Business failures and closings
see Business firms and establishments, number
see Business formations
see Corporations
see Ownership of enterprise
see Partnerships
see Proprietorships
see under By Individual Company or Institution in the "Index by Categories"

Compensation
see Claims
see Earnings, general
see Earnings, local and regional
see Earnings, specific industry
see Employee benefits
see Federal pay
see Military pay
see Payroll
see State and local employees pay
see Torts

Compensatory education
Bilingual education program activities, Federal and State aid, and enrollment, FY86-87, biennial rpt, 4804–14

Education Dept programs funding, operations, and effectiveness, FY88, annual rpt, 4804–5

Expenditures of Fed Govt in States, by type, program, agency, and State, FY88, annual rpt, 2464–2

Private schools students federally funded compensatory education programs, and costs, for selected school districts, 1984-89, GAO rpt, 26121–308

State allocation of Federal educational funds, by program, recipient type, and State, 1987/88, annual rpt, 4804–8

see also Head Start Project
see also Remedial education
see also Special education

Competition
Agricultural research and education grants, USDA competitive awards by program and recipient, FY88, annual listing, 1764–1

Airline fares relation to competition and supply and demand factors, for flights to Cleveland, Ohio, 1987, article, 9377–1.903

Airline merger of TWA and Ozark, impacts on fares and departures at St Louis, Mo, 1985-88, 7308–194

Banks and thrifts market entry probability relation to market characteristics and competition, for rural areas, model description and results, 1980-84, working paper, 9377–9.76

Banks financial performance, impacts of State entry regulation and deposit insurance, model description and results, 1970-86, working paper, 9393–10.6

Check collection systems of Fed Reserve and private services, competition issues, finances, and operations, 1984-87, GAO rpt, 26119–255

DOD competitive and formally advertised awards, by contractor type and service branch, various periods FY79-88, semiannual rpt, 3542–1.2

DOD prime contract awards, by size and type of contract, service branch, competitive status, category, and labor standard, FY88, annual rpt, 3544–19

Fed Govt procurement contract awards, by procurement and contractor type, agency, State, and for top 100 contractors, quarterly rpt, 102–6

Industry structure, conduct, and govt regulation, effects on competition, series, 9406–1

NASA procurement contract awards, by type, contractor, State, and country, FY89, semiannual rpt, 9502–6

Navy procurement, by contractor and location, FY88, annual rpt, 3804–13

NIH activities, funding by program and recipient type, staff, and clinic patients, by inst, FY87, annual rpt, 4434–3

TV satellite dish and decoder sales, ownership, subscribers, and program ratings compared to local stations, 1980s-88, hearings, 21528–74

see also Antitrust law
see also Dumping
see also Economic concentration and diversification
see also Foreign competition

Comprehensive Anti-Apartheid Act
South Africa loans from US banks, and rescheduling issues, 1984-89, press release, 8008–136

Comptroller General of the U.S.
see General Accounting Office

Compulsory military service
see Draft evasion and protest
see Selective service

Computer data file guides
BEA rpts, data coverage, and availability, 1989 article, 2702–1.912

Census Bur activities, rpts, and user services, monthly rpt, 2302–3

Census Bur data coverage and availability for 1982 economic censuses and related statistics, 1989 preliminary guide, 2308–5

Census Bur rpts and data files, coverage and availability, 1989 annual listing, 2304–2

Census Bur rpts and data files, coverage, availability, and use, series, 2326–7

Census Bur rpts and data files, monthly listing, 2302–6

Census of Agriculture, 1987: data coverage and availability, for census and related statistics, 1989 guide, 2308–55

Census of Population and Housing, 1980: data processing, coverage, and availability, 2555–2.4

Census of Population and Housing, 1990: data coverage and products, 1989 guide, 2308–58

Energy Info Admin activities, 1988, annual rpt, 3164–29

Energy use, costs, and conservation, and household and housing characteristics, survey rpt series, 3166–7

Fed Govt standards for data recording, processing, and transfer, and for purchase and use of computer systems, series, 2216–2

Health care resources geographic info system, data coverage and availability, 1989 rpt, 4118–61

HHS data projects and systems, by subagency, FY88, 4008–92

NTIS computer data files, 1989 annual listing, 2224–3; 2224–5

Ocean pollution research projects, rpts and data files, FY78-83, listing, 2158–51

Social security beneficiary microdata sample file, description and use, 1989 article, 4742–1.919

Survey of Income and Program Participation, data collection, methodology, and availability, 1987 users guide, 2628–24

Telecommunications and Info Natl Admin rpts, FY88, annual listing, 2804–3

Computer industry and products
Banks in Fed Reserve System, expenses and operations itemized by service, office, and district, 1988, annual rpt, 9364–11

County Business Patterns, 1987: employment, establishments, and payroll, by SIC 2- to 4-digit industry and county, annual State rpt series, 2326–8

DOD prime contract awards, by detailed procurement category, FY85-88, annual rpt, 3544–18

Employment, earnings, and hours, by SIC 1- to 4-digit industry, monthly 1983-Feb 1989, annual rpt, 6744–4

Exports of US, detailed commodities by country, monthly rpt, 2422–3

Fed Govt computer systems and equipment, by type, make, and agency, 1st half FY89, semiannual listing, 9452–9

Fed Govt standards for data recording, processing, and transfer, and for purchase and use of computer systems, series, 2216–2

Finances and operations, by SIC 2- to 4-digit industry, forecast 1989 with trends from 1950s, annual rpt, 2044–28

Finances, operations, and industry devs for telecommunications, with data by service type, firm, and country, 1950s-80s, 2808–27

Fed Govt computer systems with sensitive info, and plans submitted to oversight agencies, by agency, 1989, GAO rpt, 26125–34

Computer software
see Computer industry and products

Computer use
Air Force fiscal mgmt system operations and techniques, quarterly rpt, 3602–1

Air traffic control and airway facilities staff, by selected employment and demographic characteristics, FY88, annual rpt, 7504–41

Banks in Fed Reserve System, expenses and operations itemized by service, office, and district, 1988, annual rpt, 9364–11

County Business Patterns, 1987: employment, establishments, and payroll, by SIC 2- to 4-digit industry and county, annual State rpt series, 2326–8

DOD Ada computer programming language implementation and use, costs and technical issues, FY82-89, GAO rpt, 26125–32

DOD in-house commercial activities work-years, by service branch, State, and installation, FY88, annual rpt, 3544–25

Earnings, annual average percent changes for selected occupational groups, selected MSAs, monthly rpt, 6782–1.1

Education in science, methods, materials, and factors affecting elementary and secondary student proficiency, views of students, teachers, and administrators, 1983-85 surveys, 4828–37.1

Education statistics, detailed data on elementary and secondary education, 1920s-88 and projected to 1997, annual rpt, 4824–1.1

Employment and occupation of householder, by occupation of spouse, race, and family composition, 1988, annual Current Population Rpt, 2546–1.437

Employment, earnings, and hours, by SIC 1- to 4-digit industry, monthly 1983-Feb 1989, annual rpt, 6744–4

Employment in nonmanufacturing industries, by detailed occupation and SIC 2-digit industry, 1987, triennial rpt, 6748–60

Employment, unemployment, and labor force characteristics, by region and census div, 1988, annual rpt, 6744–7.1

Fed Govt computer systems security training activities, by agency, 1988, GAO rpt, 26125–31

Fed Govt standards for data recording, processing, and transfer, and for purchase and use of computer systems, series, 2216–2

Fed Reserve System, Board of Governors, and district banks financial statements, performance, and fiscal services, 1987-89, annual rpt, 9364–10

Financial instns financial and operating statements by deposit size, Fed Reserve functional cost analysis, 1988, annual rpt, 9364–6

Industry finances and operations, by SIC 2- to 4-digit industry, forecast 1989 and trends from 1950s, annual rpt, 2044–28

Manufacturing high technology use and plans, with data by technology, selected industry, and firm and market characteristics, 1988 survey, 2508–1

Multinatl US firms and foreign affiliates finances and operations, by industry of parent firm and affiliate, world area, and country, preliminary 1987, annual rpt, 2704–5

Occupational injury and illness rates, by SIC 2- to 4-digit industry, 1987, annual rpt, 6844–1

Police agencies employment, spending, and operations, FY87, 6066–25.20

Police dept operations, staff, and expenses, for large cities by population size, 1987, 6066–19.51

Schools (elementary and secondary) computer use, by grade level, 1989 edition, annual rpt, 4824–2.30

Science and engineering employment, by nonmanufacturing industry and field, 1987, triennial rpt, 9627–31

SEC staffing, pay, and turnover by occupation and city, with proposed fee revenues to improve work conditions, 1989 hearing, 21368–116

Service industries census, 1987: establishments, receipts, employment, and payroll, by SIC 2- to 4-digit kind of business, MSA, county, and city, State rpt series, 2391–1

Service industries receipts, by SIC 2- to 4-digit kind of business, 1988, annual rpt, 2413–8

Statistical Abstract of US, social, political, and economic data, 1790-2025, comprehensive annual compilation, 2324–1.1

Stock market crash of 1987, market performance, foreign futures market activity, and computer-aided trading impacts on price variability, 1980s-88, hearings, 25168–70

Tax (income) return processing, IRS workload forecasts, compliance, and enforcement, data compilation, 1989 annual rpt, 8304–8

Tax (income) returns of partnerships, income statement items by industry group, 1986, annual article, 8302–2.903

Tax (income) returns of sole proprietorships, income statement items, by industry group, 1987, annual article, 8302–2.904; 8302–2.921

Tax (income) withholding and related documents filed, by type and IRS service center, 1988 and projected 1989-96, annual rpt, 8304–22

Wages and workers in computer and data processing services by occupation and sex, and benefits, by selected MSA, 1987 survey, 6787–6.236

Wages for 4 occupational groups, relative pay levels in 61 MSAs, 1988, annual rpt, 6785–8

Young adults computer use, by selected characteristics, 1984, annual rpt, 4824–2.30

see also Automation
see also Computer networks
see also Computer sciences
see also Economic and econometric models

COMSAT
see Communications Satellite Corp.

Concentration, business
see Economic concentration and diversification

Concord, Calif.
see also under By City in the "Index by Categories"

Concrete
see Cement and concrete

Condemnation of property
see Property condemnation

Condominiums and cooperatives
American Housing Survey: unit and households detailed characteristics, and unit and neighborhood quality, MSA rpt series, 2485–6

American Housing Survey: unit and households detailed characteristics, and unit and neighborhood quality, 1985, biennial rpt, 2485–12

Housing and households summary characteristics, 1985 and trends, biennial chartbook, 2486–1.7

Market absorption rate and characteristics, 1987 and trends from 1970, annual Current Housing Rpt, 2484–2

Market absorption rates for condominiums, and completions by sales price, quarterly rpt, 2482–2

Mortgage insurance programs of HUD, finances and lending activity by program, FY88, annual rpt, 5004–8

Mortgages by lender type and related to neighborhood characteristics, for Boston, Mass, 1982-87, article, 9373–1.915

Mortgages FHA-insured for 1-family units, by loan type and mortgage characteristics, quarterly rpt, 5142–45

New condominium units completed and absorption rates, by size and price class, preliminary 1988, annual Current Housing Rpt, 2484–3

New condominium units completed, by size, price, and location, 1984-88, annual rpt, 2384–1.7

New condominiums, by intended use, units per structure, tenure, and region, monthly rpt, annual tables, 2382–1

Services provided by Residential Community Assns, and RCAs relations with local govts, 1988 conf, 10048–75

Tax (income) returns of corporations, income and tax items by asset size and detailed industry, 1986, annual rpt, 8304–4; 8304–21

Confectionery products
see Candy and confectionery products

Conference Board
"Marketer's Guide to Discretionary Income", 2308–54

Conferences
AIDS health care and epidemiological research, methodological issues, 1988 conf, 4188–61

AIDS health care services research status, needs, methods, and impacts on public health policy and funding, with data for selected cities, 1989 conf papers, 4188–59

AIDS prevention, prevalence, and treatment, 1988 conf papers, 4042–3.905

Air traffic and other aviation activity forecasts of FAA, 1989 annual conf, 7504–28

Alcohol use and abuse among minority groups, and related problems, by selected characteristics, 1985 conf papers, 4488–13

Banks financial performance, risk assessment, and regulation, 1988 annual conf papers, 9375-7

Capital stock measurement and social policy simulation model dev, for Canada, 1988 conf papers, 2702-1.918

Drug abuse genetic and other factors, 1986 conf papers, 4498-60

Drug abuse indicators for selected metro areas, research results, data collection, and policy issues, 1989 semiannual conf, 4492-5

Drunk driving testing methods and analysis, technical data, 1986 conf, 6228-2

Economic data collection by Fed Govt, methods of improving existing surveys, 1988 conf papers, 2702-1.905; 2702-1.911

Estuary environmental conditions and mgmt, for individual areas, conf series, 2146-6

Farm financial and marketing conditions, forecast 1988, conf papers, annual rpt, 1004-16

Financial and monetary studies, Fed Reserve Bank of Boston conf series, 9373-3

Financial and monetary studies, Fed Reserve Bank of Kansas City conf series, 9381-13

Fish and shellfish aquaculture in US and Japan, mgmt, methods, and biological data for selected species, 1985 conf papers, annual rpt, 2164-15

Great Lakes phosphorus loads and fish stocking effects on algal levels, 1966-85, conf, 14648-20

Great Lakes polychlorinated biphenyls levels in environment, humans, and animals, and emissions sources, by site, 1970s-85, conf, 14648-19

Great Lakes toxic spills and human error, with data by pollutant source and site, 1984-86, conf, 14648-21

Great Plains rangeland acreage, soil erosion, and other impacts of Conservation Reserve program, 1987 conf papers, 1208-290

Hazardous waste mgmt, effectiveness of alternative technologies, 1989 conf papers, biennial rpt, 9184-19

Health care and condition research, survey design and research methods, 1989 conf proceedings, 4188-60

Health care personnel supply and needs, for environmental and occupational health fields, 1987 conf, 4118-65

Health condition and quality of life measurement, rpts and other info sources, quarterly listing, 4122-1

Hereditary disease and genetic screening, counseling, and treatment services use, costs, and payment sources, 1987 conf, 4108-47

Homeless population characteristics, needs, and impacts of govt aid programs and housing costs, 1988 conf papers, 10048-73

Homeowners Residential Community Assns, services provided, and relations with local govts, 1988 conf, 10048-75

Infant deaths and prevention issues, for OECD, 1985 conf papers, 4148-28

Judicial Conf proceedings and findings, fall 1989, semiannual rpt, 18202-2

Lead poisoning among children, and impacts of lead removal from housing, gasoline, and water, 1987 conf, 4108-46

Maine coastal marine resources and ocean floor ecology, 1983-87, conf papers, 2148-55

Mental health services use, spending, facility ownership, and Medicaid reimbursement, with data for 9 multifacility firms, 1987 conf papers, 4508-9

NATO military forces compared to Warsaw Pact, and selected economic indicators, by country, 1900s-87, conf papers, 3908-6

NIH intl program activities and funding, by inst and country, FY88, annual rpt, 4474-6

Nurses recruitment and retention issues and indicators, 1988 conf papers, 4118-64

Older persons health condition and care access, data collection improvement needs, 1985 conf papers, 4147-4.26

Pacific basin countries military, economic, technological, and trade conditions, 1970s-85, compilation of papers, 3908-4

Savings instns regulatory issues, 1988 annual conf, 9304-24

Small business training confs of SBA, cosponsors by type, and compliance with SBA regulations, by region, 1988, GAO rpt, 26113-425

Soviet Union economic conditions under General Secretary Gorbachev, Soviet and CIA measurement methods with background data, 1987 conf papers, 9118-4

Soviet Union education issues, 1988 conf, 4814-1

Survey of Income and Program Participation, data collection, methodology, and use, 1988 annual conf papers, 2624-1

Sweden multinatl firms domestic and foreign production, exports, employment, and sales, with data by commodity and firm, 1960s-86, conf, 23848-208

Telecommunications and Info Natl Admin rpts, FY88, annual listing, 2804-3

Timber in southeastern US, resources mgmt and research, 1988 biennial conf papers, 1204-35

Timber mountain pine beetle infestation in Western US and Canada, characteristics and control measures, 1988 conf papers, 1208-306

Vaccination activity, reactions, costs, and preventable disease cases and deaths, 1988 annual conf, 4204-15

Vital and Health Statistics Natl Committee activities, FY88, annual narrative rpt, 4164-1

Weights, measures, and performance standards dev, proposals, and policies, 1988 annual conf, 2214-7

Wilderness areas acreage by Federal agency and location, and sources of damage, with data for foreign countries, 1988 conf papers, 1208-301

Wildlife damage to crops, livestock, and property in Great Plains, and effectiveness of mgmt methods, 1988 conf, 1208-304

Wildlife habitat mgmt issues, for amphibians, reptiles, and small mammals, 1988 conf papers, 1208-302

Conflict of interests

Fed Govt and private sector executive exchange program, host and participant views on experimental payment provisions, 1988-89 survey, GAO rpt, 26119-249

Sentences for Federal offenses, guidelines by offense and circumstances, 1989 rpt, 17668-1

US attorneys civil and criminal cases by type and disposition, and collections, by Federal district, FY88, annual rpt, 6004-2.1

Congenital malformations

see Birth defects

Conglomerates

see Business acquisitions and mergers

see Economic concentration and diversification

Congo

Agricultural and food production and indexes, total and for selected commodities, by country, 1970s-88, annual rpt, 1524-12

Agricultural trade of US, by detailed commodity and country, 1988, semiannual rpt, 1522-4

AID activities and funding by project and function, FY90, and developing countries summary socioeconomic data from 1960s, annual rpt, 9904-4.5

AID economic aid to developing countries, obligations and disbursements by country, quarterly rpt, 9912-4

Economic and military aid and loans from US and intl agencies, by program and country, FY46-87, annual rpt, 9914-5

Economic conditions, income, production, prices, employment, and trade, 1989 periodic country rpt, 2046-4.94

Economic, social, political, and geographic summary data, by country, 1989, annual factbook, 9114-2

Exports and imports of US, by commodity and country, 1970-87, world area rpt, 9116-1.4

Exports and imports of US, by selected country, country group, and commodity group, 1988, annual rpt, 2044-37

Human rights conditions in 170 countries, 1988, annual rpt, 21384-3

Military aid of US, arms sales, and training programs costs and budget requests, by program, world region, and country, FY88-90, annual rpt, 7144-13

Military spending, arms trade, and force strengths, with govt spending and population, by country, 1977-87, annual rpt, 9824-1

Minerals Yearbook, 1987, Vol 3: foreign country reviews of production, trade, and policy, by commodity, annual rpt, 5604-35

Minerals Yearbook, 1987, Vol 3 preprints: foreign country review of production, trade, and policy, by commodity, annual rpt, 5604-23.80

Population size, growth rates, and components of change, by country, projected 1989-2020 and trends from 1950, biennial rpt, 2324-9

UN voting record and share of votes in agreement with US, by issue, country, and world area, 1988, annual rpt, 7004-18

Water supply and quality in streams and lakes, and groundwater levels in wells, by drainage basin, 1988, annual State rpt, 5666–16.7

Water supply in northeastern US, precipitation and stream runoff by station, monthly rpt, 2182–3

Wholesale trade census, 1987: employment, establishments, finances, and operations, by SIC 2- to 4-digit kind of business, MSA, county, and city, State rpt, 2405–1.7

Wildlife-related recreation, hunting, and fishing participation and spending, detailed data, 1985 survey, quinquennial State rpt, 5506–6.7

see also Danbury, Conn.

see also New Haven, Conn.

see also under By State in the "Index by Categories"

Connelly, Rachel

"Effect of Child Care Costs on Married Women's Labor Force Participation", 2626–10.97

Conrail

see Consolidated Rail Corp.

Conscription

see Draft evasion and protest

see Selective service

Conservation of natural resources

Agricultural Conservation Program participation and payments, by practice and State, FY87, annual rpt, 1804–7

Agricultural Stabilization and Conservation Service producer payments, by program and State, 1988, annual rpt, 1804–12

Agricultural Stabilization and Conservation Service producer payments, by program, monthly rpt, 1802–10

Agricultural Statistics, 1988, annual rpt, 1004–1.2

Appalachia local dev projects, and funding by source, by program and State, FY88, annual rpt, 9084–1

Assistance (block and categorical grants) programs for State and local govts, FY89, biennial listing, 10044–8

Assistance (financial and nonfinancial) of Fed Govt, 1989 base edition with supplements, annual listing, 104–5

Budget deficit reduction under Gramm-Rudman Act, cancellation of budget authority by program, FY90, annual rpt, 104–27; 26304–6

Budget of US Appendix, obligations, appropriations, and personnel, by program and agency, FY90, annual rpt, 104–3

Budget of US, balances of budget authority obligated and unobligated, by function and agency, FY88-90, annual rpt, 104–8

Budget of US, Bush Admin policy changes by program, FY90, 028–32

Budget of US, compact budgets by activity, function, and agency, FY90 and projected to FY94, annual rpt, 104–2

Budget of US, historical data, selected years FY34-88 and projected to FY94, annual rpt, 104–22

Budget of US, House concurrent resolution, with spending and revenue targets, FY90, annual rpt, 21264–2

Budget of US, midsession review of FY90 budget, by function and agency, annual rpt, 104–7

Budget of US, Reagan Admin policy changes by program, FY90, annual rpt, 104–21

Budget of US, receipts by source, outlays by agency and program, and balances, monthly rpt, 8102–3

Budget of US, Senate concurrent resolution, with spending and revenue targets, FY90, annual rpt, 25254–1

Conservation and conditions of soil, water, and environment, with data by State and region, 1989 quinquennial rpt, 1268–24

Construction industries census, 1987: financial and operating data, preliminary industry rpt series, 2371–1

Construction put in place, permits, housing sales, costs, material prices, and employment, bimonthly rpt with articles, 2042–1

Construction put in place, value of new public and private structures, by type, monthly rpt, 2382–4

Construction spending by Fed Govt, by program and type of structure, FY82-90, annual article, 2042–1.901

Criminal cases by type and disposition, and collections, for US attorneys, by Federal district, FY88, annual rpt, 6004–2.1

DOD prime contract awards, by detailed procurement category, FY85-88, annual rpt, 3544–18

Environmental quality and protection programs, and intl issues, 1988 annual rpt, 484–1

Expenditures of Fed Govt in States, by type, program, agency, and State, FY88, annual rpt, 2464–2

Fed Govt construction spending, by program and type of structure, FY82-90, annual article, 2042–1.907

Fed Govt labor productivity, indexes of output and labor costs by function, FY67-87, annual rpt, 6824–1.6

Fish and Wildlife Service restoration programs finances by State, and excise tax collections, FY88, annual rpt, 5504–13

Fish and Wildlife Service restoration programs funding, land purchases, and project listing, by State, FY87, annual rpt, 5504–1

Forest Service activities and finances, by region and State, FY88, annual rpt, 1204–1

Govt employment and payroll, by function, level of govt, and jurisdiction, 1987-88, annual rpt series, 2466–1

Govt finances, by level of govt, State, and for large cities and counties, annual rpt series, 2466–2

Govt revenues by source and spending by function, natl income and product account, *Survey of Current Business*, monthly rpt, 2702–1.24

Interior Dept programs fraud and abuse, audits and investigations, 2nd half FY89, semiannual rpt, 5302–2

Land Mgmt Bur activities and finances, and public land acreage and use, annual State rpt series, 5724–11

Land Mgmt Bur finances and operations, 1936-87, 5728–30

Landmarks (natl historic and natural) damaged and threatened, with owner, location, damage type, and recommended remedial action, 1988, annual listing, 5544–16

R&D funding by Fed Govt, by detailed function, program, and agency, FY88-90, annual rpt, 9627–9

Rural areas aid from Fed Govt compared to urban areas, by program and degree of urbanization, FY85, periodic rpt, 1598–248

State and local govt employment of minorities and women, by occupation, function, and pay level, 1986, annual rpt, 9244–6.4

Tax expenditures, Federal revenues forgone through income tax deductions and exclusions by type, FY90-94, annual rpt, 21784–10

TVA financial and operating data by program and facility, FY88, annual rpt, 9804–32

Wetlands preservation under Water Bank Program, acreage, agreements, and payments, by State, monthly rpt, 1802–5

see also Birds and bird conservation

see also Endangered species

see also Energy conservation

see also Environmental pollution and control

see also Flood control

see also Forests and forestry

see also International cooperation in conservation

see also Land use

see also Marine resources conservation

see also National forests

see also National parks

see also Plants and vegetation

see also Reclamation of land

see also Recycling of waste materials

see also Severance taxes

see also Soils and soil conservation

see also State forests

see also Water resources development

see also Wilderness areas

see also Wildlife and wildlife conservation

see also Wildlife refuges

Consiglieri, Lewis D.

"Seasonal Distribution and Relative Abundance of Marine Mammals in the Gulf of Alaska", 2176–1.27

Consolidated Metropolitan Statistical Areas

see Metropolitan Statistical Areas

see under By SMSA or MSA in the "Index by Categories"

Consolidated Rail Corp.

Finances and operations of Class I railroads, detailed data by firm, class of service, and district, 1987, annual rpt, 9486–6.1

Finances and operations of Class I railroads, detailed data by firm, class of service, and district, 1988, annual rpt, 9486–5.1

Railroad accidents, casualties, and damage, with data by carrier, for Pennsylvania and US, 1984-87, GAO rpt, 26113–390

Constitutional law

Budget of US, balanced budget proposed constitutional amendment, economic impacts, projected to FY94 and background data from 1940s, hearings, 21528–72

Court civil and criminal caseloads for Federal district, appeals, and special courts, June 1989, annual rpt, 18204–2; 18204–8

US attorneys civil and criminal cases by type and disposition, and collections, by Federal district, FY88, annual rpt, 6004–2.1

Libraries (public) services for Indians and Hawaii Natives, project listing and funding by tribe and State, FY88 rpt, 4874–5

Libraries (public) special programs, project descriptions and funding by level of govt, State, and city, 1984-87, annual rpt, 4874–4

Loan activity for mortgages, by type of lender, loan, and mortgaged property, monthly press release, 5142–18

Loan activity for mortgages, by type of lender, loan, and mortgaged property, quarterly press release, 5142–30

Loan activity for mortgages, by type of lender, loan, and mortgaged property, 1986-88, annual press release, 5144–22

Loans for construction and industrial dev, bank interest rates and terms by type of loan, 1987, annual rpt, 9364–5.3

Machinery for construction, shipments and other data, by SIC 4-digit manufacturing industry and product, 1987 census, preliminary rpt, 2491–1.62

Machinery for construction, shipments, exports, and firms by product, quarterly Current Industrial Rpt, 2506–12.3

Middle Atlantic States economic conditions, Fed Reserve 3rd District, quarterly rpt, 9387–10

Military aid of US, arms sales, and training, by country, FY50-88, annual rpt, 3904–3

Multinatl US firms and foreign affiliates finances and operations, by industry of parent firm and affiliate, world area, and country, preliminary 1987, annual rpt, 2704–5

Natl Guard (Army and Air) outlays, by function and State, FY88, annual rpt, 3504–22.1

Natl income and product accounts and components, *Survey of Current Business*, monthly rpt, 2702–1.27

Natural gas interstate pipeline company detailed financial and operating data, by firm, 1988, annual rpt, 3164–38

New construction (public and private) activity, and new housing starts, 1929-88, annual rpt, 204–1.3

New construction (public and private) put in place, value by type, monthly rpt, 2382–4

New England States economic indicators, Fed Reserve 1st District, monthly rpt, 9373–24

New England States economic indicators, Fed Reserve 1st District, quarterly rpt, 9373–2.4

New England States employment, BLS benchmark revisions by industry div and State, 1987-88, article, 9373–2.903

NIH activities, funding by program and recipient type, staff, and clinic patients, by inst, FY87, annual rpt, 4434–3

NIH grants and awards, quarterly listing, 4432–1

Northern Mariana Islands economic census, 1987: employment, firms, payroll, and receipts, by SIC 1- to 4-digit industry, 2597–1

Nuclear power plant capacity, generation, and operating status, by plant and foreign and US location, 1988 and projected to 2020, annual rpt, 3164–57

Nuclear power plant construction costs and status, and capacity, by plant, as of Dec 1988, annual rpt, 3164–69

Occupational injuries, illnesses, and workdays lost, by SIC 2-digit industry, 1987-88, annual press release, 6844–3

Occupational injury and illness rates, by SIC 2- to 4-digit industry, 1987, annual rpt, 6844–1

Price indexes (producer), by stage of processing and detailed commodity, monthly 1988, annual rpt, 6764–2

Price indexes (producer) for material inputs, by construction industry, monthly rpt, 6762–6

Science and engineering employment and education, and R&D spending, for US and selected foreign countries, 1988, annual rpt, 9624–23.2

Science and engineering employment, by nonmanufacturing industry and field, 1987, triennial rpt, 9627–31

SEC registration, firms required to file annual rpts, as of Sept 1988, annual listing, 9734–5

Small business establishments, employment, and financial ratios, by SIC 1- to 2-digit industry and State, late 1960s-87, 9768–19

Small business finances, operations, owner and employee characteristics, and Federal contracts, 1980s-88, annual rpt, 9764–6

Statistical Abstract of US, social, political, and economic data, 1790-2025, comprehensive annual compilation, 2324–1.3

Steel imports from EC and other countries, impact of voluntary restraint agreements on US user industries exports, sales, and prices, 1989 rpt, 9886–4.138

Tax (income) returns filed by type of filer, selected income items, quarterly rpt, 8302–2.1

Tax (income) returns for foreign corporate activity in US, assets, and income statement items, by industry div, country, and world area, 1984-85, article, 8302–2.920

Tax (income) returns of corporations, income and tax items by asset size and detailed industry, 1986, annual rpt, 8304–4; 8304–21

Tax (income) returns of partnerships, income statement items by industry group, 1986, annual article, 8302–2.903

Tax (income) returns of sole proprietorships, income statement items, by industry group, 1987, annual article, 8302–2.904; 8302–2.921

Technological devs effect on labor force, composition, and productivity, by industry, 1960s-86 and projected to 2000, 6826–2.4

Transportation census, 1987: trucks, by detailed characteristics, miles traveled, and type of product carried, State rpt series, 2573–1

Unemployment insurance coverage, impact of changes in labor market and UI policy, and trust fund finances of 11 States, 1971-86, 6406–6.24

Uranium tailings at inactive mills, remedial action proposals, costs, site characteristics, and environmental, socioeconomic, and health impacts, series, 3356–4

Urban Dev Action Grants, funding sources, project descriptions, and economic impacts, by city, periodic press releases, 5002–7

VA health care, nursing home, and other facilities construction projects, costs and completion status by site, FY88, annual rpt, 8604–3.5

Virgin Islands economic censuses, 1987: employment, firms, payroll, and receipts, by SIC 1- to 4-digit industry, island, and city, 2593–1

Wage and benefit changes from collective bargaining and mgmt decisions, by industry div, monthly rpt, 6782–1

Wage rates for construction trades union, by coastal region and for 10 port cities, 1988, annual rpt, 7704–12.2

see also Building codes
see also Building materials
see also Building permits
see also Cement and concrete
see also Census of Construction Industries
see also Housing construction
see also Housing maintenance and repair
see also Plumbing and heating
see also Shipbuilding and repairing
see also Wrecking and demolition
see also under By Industry in the "Index by Categories"

Consultants

Credit unions federally insured, finances by instn characteristics and State, as of June 1989, semiannual rpt, 9532–6

DOD prime contract awards, by detailed procurement category, FY85-88, annual rpt, 3544–18

Employment, earnings, and hours, by SIC 1- to 4-digit industry, monthly 1983-Feb 1989, annual rpt, 6744–4

Finances and operations, by SIC 2- to 4-digit industry, forecast 1989 with trends from 1950s, annual rpt, 2044–28

Guam economic censuses, 1987: employment, firms, payroll, and receipts, by SIC 1- to 4-digit industry and election district, 2595–1

Investment advisors for trust, employee benefit, and other accounts, assets involved for all and top 15 firms, 1988, annual rpt, 13004–1

Mental health services, staffing, research, and training programs in VA facilities, 1989 biennial listing, 8704–2

Minority Business Dev Centers mgmt and financial aid, and characteristics of businesses, by region and State, FY88, annual rpt, 2104–6

Northern Mariana Islands economic census, 1987: employment, firms, payroll, and receipts, by SIC 1- to 4-digit industry, 2597–1

Nuclear Regulatory Commission budget, staff, and activities, by program, FY88-91, annual rpt, 9634–9

Physicians consulting and attending at VA facilities, by specialty, quarterly rpt, 8602–6

Receipts for services, by SIC 2- to 4-digit kind of business, 1988, annual rpt, 2413–8

Science and engineering employment characteristics, by field, 1988, biennial rpt, 9627–16

Science and engineering labor force, Federal and university research funding, and educational data, series, 9626-6

Science and engineering labor supply by region and employment characteristics, and salaries by years of experience, 1987, 9626-2.184

Science and engineering PhDs employment and other characteristics, by field and State, 1987, biennial rpt, 9627-18

Senate receipts, itemized expenses by payee, and balances, 1st half FY89, semiannual listing, 25922-1

Service industries census, 1987: establishments, receipts, employment, and payroll, by SIC 2- to 4-digit kind of business, MSA, county, and city, State rpt series, 2391-1

Tax (income) returns of partnerships, income statement items by industry group, 1986, annual article, 8302-2.903

Tax (income) returns of sole proprietorships, income statement items, by industry group, 1987, annual article, 8302-2.904; 8302-2.921

Virgin Islands economic censuses, 1987: employment, firms, payroll, and receipts, by SIC 1- to 4-digit industry, island, and city, 2593-1

Consumer complaints
see Consumer protection

Consumer cooperatives
Food consumer research, marketing, legislation, and regulation devs, and consumption and price trends, quarterly journal, 1541-7
see also Rural cooperatives

Consumer credit
Airline consumer complaints to DOT about service by US and foreign carrier, and for travel and cargo service, by reason, monthly rpt, 7302-11

Assets and debts of private sector, balance sheets by segment, 1949-88, semiannual rpt, 9365-4.1

Auto, mobile home, and other consumer installment credit loans, monthly rpt, 23842-1.5

Banks (insured commercial and savings) finances, for foreign and domestic offices, by asset size, 1987, annual rpt, 9294-4.2

Banks (natl) domestic and intl operations, charters, mergers, and liquidations, by instn and State, quarterly rpt, 8402-3

Business Conditions Digest, cyclical indicators, by economic process, monthly rpt, 2702-3.3

Business statistics, detailed data for major industries and economic indicators, *Survey of Current Business*, monthly rpt, 2702-1.6

Debt outstanding for installment and noninstallment credit, monthly rpt series, 9365-2

Electric and gas utilities standard for service disconnection, status and coverage of consumers and sales, 1988, annual rpt, 3104-7

Financial and business detailed statistics, *Fed Reserve Bulletin*, monthly rpt with articles, 9362-1

Financial and business statistics, historic trends, 1988 annual chartbook, 9364-2.11

Flow-of-funds accounts, assets and liabilities by type and economic sector, outstanding at year-end 1965-88, annual rpt, 9364-3

Flow-of-funds accounts, savings, investments, and credit statements, quarterly rpt, 9365-3.3

Household debt and interest-earning assets, interest paid and received, and consumption expenditures, by selected characteristics, 1960s-88, article, 9385-1.913

Installment credit outstanding, by lender type, 1983-88, annual rpt, 9534-1.2

Installment credit outstanding, extensions, and liquidations, monthly rpt, 9362-1.1

Installment credit outstanding, extensions, liquidations, and terms, 1985-87, annual rpt, 9364-5.7; 9364-5.13

New England States financial instn assets and liabilities, Fed Reserve 1st District, quarterly rpt, 9373-2.5

North Central States business and economic conditions, Fed Reserve 9th District, quarterly journal, 9383-19

North Central States, FHLB 6th District insured savings instns financial condition and operations by State, monthly rpt, 9302-11

North Central States, FHLB 8th District savings instns financial operations by State and SMSA, monthly rpt, 9302-9

Outstanding installment credit by type, and noninstallment credit, 1950-88, annual rpt, 204-1.5

Retail trade sales, inventories, purchases, gross margin, and accounts receivable, by SIC 2- to 4-digit kind of business and form of ownership, 1987, annual rpt, 2413-5

Savings instns (FSLIC-insured) assets, liabilities, and deposit and loan activity, and compared to all S&Ls, monthly rpt, 9312-4

Savings instns financial statements, FSLIC-insured instns by FHLB district and State, and FDIC-insured savings banks, 1988, annual rpt, 8434-1

Savings instns insured by Savings Assn Insurance Fund, assets, liabilities, and deposit and loan activity, by conservatorship status, monthly rpt, 8432-1

South Central States, FHLB 9th District savings instns finances and operations by State, quarterly rpt, 9302-31

Southeastern States, Fed Reserve 5th District, economic indicators by State, quarterly rpt, 9389-16

Southeastern States, Fed Reserve 5th District insured commercial banks financial statements, by State, quarterly rpt, 9389-18

Southeastern States, Fed Reserve 8th District banking and economic conditions, quarterly rpt with articles, 9391-16

Southeastern States, FHLB 4th District thrifts finances, by State, 1984-88 annual rpt series, 9304-29

Statistical Abstract of US, social, political, and economic data, 1790-2025, comprehensive annual compilation, 2324-1.3

West Central States, Fed Reserve 10th District depository instns financial activity by State, and large commercial banks by city, monthly rpt, 9381-11

West Central States, FHLB 10th District savings instns finances and lending by State and MSA, monthly table, 9302-22
see also Credit bureaus and agencies
see also Credit cards
see also Credit unions
see also Discrimination in credit
see also Finance companies
see also Personal debt

Consumer Expenditure Survey
Economic indicators, prices, labor costs, and productivity, BLS econometric analyses and methodology, working paper series, 6886-6

Expenditures by category and age of household head, Consumer Expenditure Survey, 1987, semiannual pamphlet, 2322-3

Expenditures by category, and income, by selected household characteristics and location, 1987 survey, press release, 6726-1.23

Expenditures by category, selected household characteristics, and region, quarterly rpt, 6762-14

Expenditures by commodity, and household income by source, by selected characteristics and region, 1984-87 surveys, annual rpt, 6764-5

Expenditures in metro and nonmetro areas, by item, 1987 survey, article, 6722-1.962

Expenditures related to occupational group, 1986-87, article, 6722-1.961

Married couple families with both spouses working, effects on consumer spending by category, and income, by household characteristics, 1984-86, article, 6722-1.908

Single-parent household income sources and spending by category, by sex, age, race, and household size, 1984-85, article, 1702-1.901

Consumer expenditures
see Personal consumption

Consumer income
see Personal and household income

Consumer Price Index
Agricultural Outlook, production, prices, marketing, and trade, by commodity, forecast and current situation, monthly rpt with articles, 1502-4

Budget of US, CBO analysis of revenue and spending alternatives and projections of economic indicators, FY90-94, annual rpt, 26304-3

Business statistics, detailed data for major industries and economic indicators, *Survey of Current Business*, monthly rpt, 2702-1.2

Communist, OECD, and selected other countries economic conditions, 1960s-88, annual rpt, 9114-4.2

CPI by component for US city average, and by region, population size, and for 15 metro areas, monthly rpt, 6762-1

CPI by component for US city average, and by region, population size, and for 27 metro areas, monthly rpt, 6762-2

CPI by major component and selected metro area, 1940s-88 with trends from 1913, 6728-38.8

CPI components relative importance, by selected SMSA, region, population size, and for US city average, 1988, annual rpt, 6884-1

US attorneys civil and criminal cases by type and disposition, and collections, by Federal district, FY88, annual rpt, 6004-2.1

Continental shelf
Alaska OCS environmental conditions and oil dev impacts, compilation of papers, series, 2176-1
Environmental conditions, fish, wildlife, use, and mgmt, for individual coastal and riparian ecosystems, series, 5506-9
Workers compensation programs under Federal admin, finances and operations, FY87, annual rpt, 6504-10
see also Coastal areas
see also Offshore mineral resources
see also Offshore oil and gas
see also Territorial waters

Continuing education
see Adult education

Continuing Survey of Food Intakes by Individuals
Food consumption and nutrient intake by individuals, by food group, selected characteristics, and region, supplementary survey series, 1356-5
Nutritional status and related health condition and practices, by selected characteristics, 1970s-87, 4048-33

Contra Costa County, Calif.
Housing vacancy rates for single and multifamily units and mobile homes, by city and ZIP code, 1988, annual MSA rpt, 9304-20.13

Contraband
Customs Service activities, collections, entries processed by mode of transport, and seizures, FY84-88, annual rpt, 8144-1
Endangered animals and plants US trade and permits, by species, purpose, disposition, and country, 1987, annual rpt, 5504-19
see also Drug and narcotics offenses

Contraception
see Contraceptives
see Family planning
see Sexual sterilization

Contraceptives
Abortions by patient characteristics, rates for all and 1st abortions, and related deaths in US and other countries, 1989 hearing, 21408-113
AIDS public knowledge, attitudes, info sources, and testing, for blacks, 1988 survey, 4146-8.167
AIDS public knowledge, attitudes, info sources, and testing, for Hispanics, 1988 survey, 4146-8.168
AIDS public knowledge, attitudes, info sources, and testing, 1988 survey, 4146-8.165; 4146-8.169; 4146-8.173
AIDS public knowledge, attitudes, info sources, and testing, 1989 survey, 4146-8.176; 4146-8.180
Cancer (breast) risk, by oral contraceptives use and menopausal status, 1976-86 study, article, 4472-1.923
Cancer (breast) risk relation to oral contraceptives use, by age at first use and duration, Sweden study, 1979-85, article, 4472-1.917
Deaths related to pregnancy, abortion, and contraception, by age, 1975 and 1982, hearing, 21408-113

Exports of US, detailed commodities by country, monthly rpt, 2422-3
Foreign countries contraception use by women, by age and country, 1989 biennial rpt, 2324-9
Health condition and health care resources, use, and spending, 1950s-87, annual data compilation, 4144-11
Human papillomavirus infection rates, by sexual and personal hygiene practices, and other patient characteristics, Brazil local area studies, 1989 article, 4472-1.908
Injuries from use of consumer products, by severity, victim age, and detailed product, 1988, annual rpt, 9164-6
Oral contraceptive prescriptions, 1987, annual rpt, 4064-12
Research contracts and grants of Natl Inst of Child Health and Human Dev, by recipient and location, FY88, annual listing, 4474-36
Research on population and reproduction, Federal funding by project, FY87, annual listing, 4474-9
Research on population and reproduction, Natl Inst of Child Health and Human Dev funding and activities, 1988, annual rpt, 4474-33
Statistical Abstract of US, social, political, and economic data, 1790-2025, comprehensive annual compilation, 2324-1.1

Contract labor
see Temporary and seasonal employment

Contracts
Arms sales of US, foreign conditions on sales and impacts on US industry, with data by industry group and country, 1988 annual rpt, 104-25
Construction (industrial and commercial) contracts, *Business Conditions Digest*, cyclical indicators, monthly rpt, 2702-3.3
Construction industries census, 1987: establishments, employment, receipts, and expenditures, by SIC 4-digit industry and State, final industry rpt series, 2373-1
Construction industries census, 1987: financial and operating data, preliminary industry rpt series, 2371-1
Court caseloads for Federal district, appeals, and bankruptcy courts, by type of suit and offense, circuit, and district, quarterly rpt, 18202-1
Court civil and criminal caseloads for Federal district, appeals, and special courts, June 1989, annual rpt, 18204-2; 18204-8
CPI use in escalator clauses of collective bargaining agreements and other contracts, with conversion factors for index rebasing, 1989 guide, 6888-34
Electric power trade of US with Canada, purchase agreements, and grid interconnection capacity, 1960s-88 and projected to 1992, GAO rpt, 26113-228
Housing alteration and repair spending, by type of job and for work under contract, quarterly rpt, 2382-7
Housing alteration and repair spending, by type of job and for work under contract, 1984-88, annual rpt, 2384-4.2
Labor laws enacted, by State, 1988, annual article, 6722-1.904
Mental health care hospitals, beds and caseload by State, patient characteristics, finances, and staff, for profit and nonprofit private instns, 1986, 4506-3.37

Natural gas interstate pipeline company sales, contract deliveries, and prices, with data by firm and location, 1982-87, 3168-113
Uranium marketing, contracts, prices, utility shipments, and trade, 1982-88 and projected to 2000, annual rpt, 3164-65.2
Western Area Power Admin activities by plant, financial statements, and sales by customer, FY88, annual rpt, 3254-1
see also Agricultural production quotas and price supports
see also Business orders
see also Defense contracts and procurement
see also Defense industries
see also Escalator clauses
see also Futures trading
see also Government contracts and procurement
see also Labor-management relations, general
see also Labor-management relations in government
see also Labor-management relations, local and regional

Contributions
see Campaign funds
see Gifts and private contributions

Controlled substances
see Alcoholic beverages control laws
see Cocaine
see Drug abuse and treatment
see Drug and narcotics offenses
see Marijuana

Convalescent homes
see Nursing homes

Convenience stores
see Food stores

Conventions
see Political conventions
see Treaties and conventions

Convictions, criminal
see Sentences, criminal procedure

Cook Islands
Economic, social, political, and geographic summary data, by country, 1989, annual factbook, 9114-2

Cook, John S.
"Review of Valdez Oil Spill Market Impacts", 3162-11.901; 3162-24.902

Cook, Leah
"Distributional Effects of Housing Price Booms: Winners and Losers in Boston, 1980-88", 9373-1.907

Cook, Timothy
"Analysis of the Determinants of the Yields on Individual Municipal Securities", 9389-19.8
"Determinants of the Federal Funds Rate: 1979-82", 9389-1.905; 9389-19.7

Cooke, Patrick W.
"Update of U.S. Participation in International Standards Activities", 2218-80

Cooking equipment
see Household appliances and equipment

Cooking utensils
see Household supplies and utensils

Cooper, Sharon P.
"Health Characteristics by Occupation and Industry of Longest Employment", 4147-10.168

Cooperative State Research Service

Budget of US Appendix, obligations, appropriations, and personnel, by program and agency, FY90, annual rpt, 104–3

Expenditures and staffing for agricultural research by USDA, State agencies, and other instns, by topic, FY88, annual rpt, 1744–2

Expenditures of Fed Govt in States, by type, program, agency, and State, FY88, annual rpt, 2464–2

Cooperatives

Political action committees, by type, 1974-89, semiannual press release, 9276–1.61; 9276–1.67

Political action committees contributions by office and party, and finances by PAC, 1988 natl elections, press release, 9276–1.65

Political campaign financial activity reported to Fed Election Commission, by type of filer, 1988 natl elections, biennial rpt series, 9276–2

Soviet Union personal income by source, disposable income, wage deductions by type, and savings, 1950s-87, 9118–7

Statistical Abstract of US, social, political, and economic data, 1790-2025, comprehensive annual compilation, 2324–1.3

Tax (income) withholding and related documents filed, by type and IRS service center, 1988 and projected 1989-96, annual rpt, 8304–22

Wholesale trade census, 1987: employment, establishments, finances, and operations, by SIC 2- to 4-digit kind of business, MSA, county, and city, State rpt series, 2405–1

see also Condominiums and cooperatives
see also Consumer cooperatives
see also Credit unions
see also Rural cooperatives

Cooperman, Elizabeth S.

"Effect of the 1985 Ohio Thrift Crisis on the Interest Cost of Retail CDs", 9316–1.153

Copiers, office

see Business machines and equipment

Copper and copper industry

Africa agricultural exports by commodity, and relation to economic conditions and other factors, by country, 1960s-87, 1528–280

Building materials PPI, by type, bimonthly rpt, 2042–1.5

Business statistics, detailed data for major industries and economic indicators, *Survey of Current Business*, monthly rpt, 2702–1.14

Castings (nonferrous) shipments, by metal type, monthly Current Industrial Rpt, 2506–10.5

Coin production and monetary metals use and holdings of US Mint, by metal type, FY88, annual rpt, 8204–1

Communist, OECD, and selected other countries minerals production, by commodity, 1960s-88, annual rpt, 9114–4.7

County Business Patterns, 1987: employment, establishments, and payroll, by SIC 2- to 4-digit industry and county, annual State rpt series, 2326–8

Cuba economic conditions, agricultural and industrial production and distribution, trade, and intl economic relations, 1980-87 with trends from 1961, 9118–8

Employment, earnings, and hours, by selected SIC 1- to 4-digit industry, State, and for 262 MSAs, 1972-87, 6748–81

Employment, earnings, and hours, by SIC 1- to 4-digit industry, monthly 1983-Feb 1989, annual rpt, 6744–4

Exports of US, detailed commodities by country, monthly rpt, 2422–3

Finances and operations, by SIC 2- to 4-digit industry, forecast 1989 with trends from 1950s, annual rpt, 2044–28

Foreign countries mineral production, reserves, and industry role in domestic economy and world supply, world area and country rpt series, 5606–1

Freight (waterborne domestic and foreign) by commodity, traffic, and passengers, by port and waterway, 1987, annual rpt, 3754–3

Futures contracts on commodities, financial instruments, and indexes, options trading in NYC, Chicago, and other markets, monthly rpt, 11922–6

Futures trading in selected commodities and financial instruments and indexes, NYC, Chicago, and other markets activity, monthly rpt, 11922–5

Imports of US, detailed Schedule A commodities by country, monthly rpt, 2422–2

Labor productivity, indexes of output, hours, and employment by SIC 2- to 4-digit industry, 1963-87, annual rpt, 6824–1.2; 6824–1.3

Manufacturing annual survey, 1986: financial and operating data, by SIC 2- to 4-digit industry, series, 2506–15

Manufacturing census, 1987: financial and operating data, for SIC 4-digit industries by product, preliminary rpt, 2491–1.52; 2491–1.53; 2491–1.54; 2491–1.58

Mineral industries census, 1987: financial and operating data, preliminary industry rpt, 2511–1.2

Mineral Industry Surveys, commodity review of production, trade, stocks, and use, monthly rpt, 5612–1.6

Mineral Industry Surveys, State reviews of production, 1988, preliminary annual rpt, 5614–6

Minerals Yearbook, 1987, Vol 1: commodity reviews of production, use, trade, prices, and mining operations, annual rpt, 5604–33

Minerals Yearbook, 1987, Vol 1 preprints: commodity review of production, reserves, supply, use, and trade, annual rpt, 5604–15.20

Minerals Yearbook, 1987, Vol 2 preprints: State reviews of production and sales by commodity, and business activity, annual rpt series, 5604–16

Minerals Yearbook, 1987, Vol 2: State reviews of production, sales, and firms, by commodity, and business activity, annual rpt, 5604–34

Minerals Yearbook, 1987, Vol 3: foreign country reviews of production, trade, and policy, by commodity, annual rpt, 5604–35

Minerals Yearbook, 1987, Vol 3 preprints: foreign country reviews of production, trade, and policy, by commodity, annual rpt series, 5604–23

Minerals Yearbook, 1988, Vol 2 rpts: State reviews of production and sales by commodity, and business activity, annual rpt series, 5604–22

Occupational injuries and incidence, employment, and hours in metal mines and related operations, 1987, annual rpt, 6664–3

Occupational injury and illness rates, by SIC 2- to 4-digit industry, 1987, annual rpt, 6844–1

OECD trade, total and for 4 major countries, and US trade by country, by commodity, 1970-87, world area rpt series, 9116–1

Price indexes (producer), by stage of processing and detailed commodity, monthly rpt, 6762–6

Price indexes (producer), by stage of processing and detailed commodity, monthly 1988, annual rpt, 6764–2

Production cost impacts of occupational safety and environmental regulation, factors affecting US mineral industry competitiveness, 1989 compilation of papers, 5606–5.7

Production, prices, trade, use, employment, tariffs, and stockpiles, by mineral, with foreign comparisons, 1984-88, annual rpt, 5604–18

Production, use, reserves, Federal lands availability for mining, and environmental impacts, for strategic minerals, 1950s-80s, 028–33

Science and engineering employment, by nonmanufacturing industry and field, 1987, triennial rpt, 9627–31

Statistical Abstract of US, social, political, and economic data, 1790-2025, comprehensive annual compilation, 2324–1.3

Stockpiling of strategic material by Fed Govt, activity, and inventory by commodity, as of Sept 1989, semiannual rpt, 3542–22; 3902–2

Stockpiling of strategic material, inventories and needs, by commodity, as of Sept 1988, annual rpt, 3544–37

Stockpiling of strategic material, inventories, costs, and goals by commodity, as of June 1989, semiannual rpt, 3902–3

Supply, demand, trade, and foreign and US industry devs by firm and country, for strategic minerals by commodity, bimonthly rpt with articles, 5602–4

Wire and cable (insulated) shipments, trade, use, and firms, by product, 1987-88, annual Current Industrial Rpt, 2506–10.8

see also under By Commodity in the "Index by Categories"

Copyright

Court civil and criminal caseloads for Federal district, appeals, and special courts, June 1989, annual rpt, 18204–2; 18204–8

Criminal and civil immunity for diplomatic missions in US and US missions abroad, and foreign diplomats criminal cases, 1978-87, hearing, 25388–51

Criminal cases by type and disposition, and collections, for US attorneys, by Federal district, FY88, annual rpt, 6004–2.1

Criminal sentences for Federal offenses, guidelines by offense and circumstances, 1989 rpt, 17668-1

Exports of goods, services, and investment, trade barriers, impacts, and US actions, by country, 1988, annual rpt, 444-2

Foreign countries economic conditions, policy, and trade practices, by country, 1986-88, annual rpt, 21384-5

Intl agreements of US establishing copyright relations, by country, as of Jan 1989, annual listing, 7004-1

Register of Copyrights activities, registrations by material type, and fees, FY87 and trends from 1790, annual rpt, 26404-2

Registrations and claims and fees collected by type of material, claims and fees, and fee transfers, for Library of Congress Copyright Office, FY88, annual rpt, 26404-1

Statistical Abstract of US, social, political, and economic data, 1790-2025, comprehensive annual compilation, 2324-1.3

see also Patents

see also Trademarks

Copyright Royalty Tribunal

Royalty fees from cable TV and jukeboxes available for distribution by Tribunal, 1986-87, annual rpt, 26404-2

Coral reefs and islands

Alaska OCS environmental conditions and oil dev impacts, compilation of papers, series, 2176-1

Birds (waterfowl) coastal breeding population and colonies, by species and location for Washington, 1978-82, atlas, 5508-101

Corley, Audrey E.

"Comparisons of Independent Statistics on Petroleum Supply", 3162-6.903

Corn

Acreage planted, by selected crop and State, 1980-88 and planned 1989, annual rpt, 1621-22

Acreage under Agricultural Stabilization and Conservation Service programs, rankings by commodity and congressional district, 1987, biennial rpt, 1804-17

Agricultural data compilation, 1987/88 and trends from 1920, annual rpt, 1004-14

Agricultural Statistics, 1988, annual rpt, 1004-1

Agriculture census, 1987: farms, farmland, production and costs, and operator characteristics, advance State and county rpt series, 2330-1

Agriculture census, 1987: farms, farmland, production, finances, and operator characteristics, by county, final State rpt series, 2331-1

Alcohol fuels (ethanol) production costs and Federal loan guarantees, 1987-88, 1588-132

Alcoholic beverages production, stocks, materials used, and taxable and tax-free removals, for beer and distilled spirits by State, monthly rpt, 8486-1.1; 8486-1.3

Business statistics, detailed data for major industries and economic indicators, *Survey of Current Business*, monthly rpt, 2702-1.11

CCC certificate exchange activity, by commodity, weekly press release, 1802-16

CCC loan and support programs payment activity, with data by commodity, 1986-88 and projected to 1994, 26308-86

Consumption, supply, trade, prices, spending, and indexes, by food commodity, 1987, annual rpt, 1544-4

County Business Patterns, 1987: employment, establishments, and payroll, by SIC 2- to 4-digit industry and county, annual State rpt series, 2326-8

Drought of 1988, impacts on farm production and income, and compared to other droughts from 1928, 1588-129

Eastern Europe agricultural production, consumption, and trade, by country, 1970s-88, annual rpt, 1524-11

Eastern Europe and USSR agricultural production, acreage, and consumption, by commodity and country, 1965-85, 1528-284

EC food supply and demand, market and support prices, and other economic indicators, by country and commodity, 1960-85, 1528-276

Exports and imports (agricultural) commodity and country, prices, and world market devs, monthly rpt, 1922-12

Exports and imports (agricultural) of US, by commodity and country, bimonthly rpt with articles, 1522-1

Exports and imports (agricultural) of US, by commodity, monthly rpt, 1922-8

Exports and imports (agricultural) of US, by detailed commodity and country, 1988, semiannual rpt, 1522-4

Exports and prices, by type of grain, weekly rpt, 1272-2

Exports of grain, competitiveness and quality issues, with background data and comparisons to other countries, 1960s-88, 26358-201

Exports of grains, oilseed products, hides, skins, and cotton, by country, weekly rpt, 1922-3

Exports of US, detailed commodities by country, monthly rpt, 2422-3

Farm income, expenses, receipts by commodity, assets, liabilities, and ratios, 1988 and trends from 1945, annual rpt, 1544-16

Farm receipts for 25 leading crops, by State, 1960-87, 1548-347

Farm sales of corn, and price support payments by program, 1971-88, article, 1561-4.905

Farm sector balance sheet, and receipts by detailed commodity, by State, 1984-88, annual rpt, 1544-18

Farm sector finances, income sources, expenses by type, assets, debts, and ratios, 1987, annual rpt, 1544-19

Fertilizer use by crop and State, and prices, by fertilizer type, 1960s-88, 1588-113

Foreign and US agricultural supply and demand indicators, by selected crop, monthly rpt, 1522-5

Foreign and US grain production, prices, trade, stocks, and use, FAS periodic circular series, 1925-2

Foreign and US oils, oilseeds, and fats production and trade, FAS periodic circular series, 1925-1

Foreign countries agricultural production, prices, and trade, by country, 1970s-89 and forecast 1990, annual world region rpt series, 1524-4

Freight (waterborne domestic and foreign) by commodity, traffic, and passengers, by port and waterway, 1987, annual rpt, 3754-3

Futures and options trading volume, by commodity and exchange, FY88, annual rpt, 11924-2

Futures contracts on commodities, financial instruments, and indexes, options trading in NYC, Chicago, and other markets, monthly rpt, 11922-6

Futures contracts, stocks in deliverable position by type, weekly table, 11922-4.3

Futures contracts yield and price risk hedging, for corn and soybeans, by selected county and State, model results, 1961-83, 1548-352

Futures trading in selected commodities and financial instruments and indexes, NYC, Chicago, and other markets activity, monthly rpt, 11922-5

Imports of US, detailed Schedule A commodities by country, monthly rpt, 2422-2

Inspection of corn, test results by State, 1988, annual rpt, 1294-3.3

Inspection of grain for domestic use and export, and foreign buyers complaints, FY88, annual rpt, 1294-1

Inspection of grain for export, test results by commodity and port region, 1988, annual rpt series, 1294-2

Irrigation projects of Reclamation Bur in western US, crop production and acreage by commodity, State, and project, 1987, annual rpt, 5824-12.1

Labor productivity, indexes of output, hours, and employment by SIC 2- to 4-digit industry, 1963-87, annual rpt, 6824-1.3

Loan support programs of USDA for grains, activity and status by grain and State, monthly rpt, 1802-3

Manufacturing annual survey, 1986: financial and operating data, by SIC 2- to 4-digit industry, series, 2506-15

Manufacturing census, 1987: financial and operating data, for SIC 4-digit industries by product, preliminary rpt, 2491-1.4; 2491-1.9

Mexico agricultural subsidies, and impacts of reductions on production, by commodity, 1982-87 and projected 1992, 1528-288

Mill production workers and wages, by occupation and sex, and benefits, by region, 1987 survey, 6787-6.239

Nutrient and caloric composition of food, for raw, processed, and prepared food, 1988 rpt, 1358-3

OECD trade, total and for 4 major countries, and US trade by country, by commodity, 1970-87, world area rpt series, 9116-1

Price indexes (producer), by stage of processing and detailed commodity, monthly rpt, 6762-6

Price indexes (producer), by stage of processing and detailed commodity, monthly 1988, annual rpt, 6764-2

Price support activity and policy options, with data on production, trade, use, and finances, and foreign comparisons, 1950s-89, commodity rpt, 1566-7.4

Prices on US farms and for imports at Rotterdam, and EC price supports, by type of grain, weekly press release, 1922-4

Stock performance of individual firms relative to market index, relation to firm characteristics by firm, alternative models results, 1963-81, technical paper, 9366-6.183

Stockbrokers finances, firms by type of organization and State, and SEC applications and registrations, 1983-88, annual rpt, 9734-2.1

Survey of Current Business, detailed data for major industries and economic indicators, monthly rpt, 2702-1

Tax (income) and other govt finances, by level of govt and State, selected years 1929-91, annual rpt, 10044-1

Tax (income) collection, enforcement, and litigation activity of IRS, with data by type of tax, region, and State, FY88, annual rpt, 8304-3

Tax (income) return processing, IRS workload forecasts, compliance, and enforcement, data compilation, 1989 annual rpt, 8304-8

Tax (income) returns and supplemental documents filed, by type, FY88 and projected to FY97, semiannual rpt, 8302-4

Tax (income) returns filed by type of filer, selected income items, quarterly rpt, 8302-2.1

Tax (income) returns filed, by type of return and IRS region and service center, projected 1988-95 and trends from 1977, annual rpt, 8304-9

Tax (income) returns of corporations, income and tax items by asset size and detailed industry, 1986, annual rpt, 8304-4; 8304-21

Tax (income) returns of corporations, summary data by asset size and industry div, 1986, annual article, 8302-2.922

Tax (income) unpaid by reason, and compliance after audits and appeals, for individuals and corporations, 1970s-87 and projected to 1992, 8302-2.902; 8308-26

Tax collections of State govts by detailed type of tax, and tax rates, by State, FY88, annual rpt, 2466-2.3

Tax expenditures, Federal revenues forgone through income tax deductions and exclusions by type, FY90-94, annual rpt, 21784-10

Tax returns and supplemental documents filed, by type, FY88 and projected to FY97, semiannual rpt, 8302-2.916

Tax revenue potential of State and local systems relative to natl average tax burden, by type of tax and State, 1986, annual rpt, 10044-7

Tax revenues, by level of govt, type of tax, State, and selected large county, quarterly rpt, 2462-3

Terrorist (intl) incidents, casualties, and attacks on US targets, by attack type and country, 1980-88, 7008-56

Terrorist (intl) incidents, casualties, and attacks on US targets, by attack type and world area, 1968-88, annual rpt, 7004-13

Truck and warehouse services finances and inventory, by SIC 2- to 4-digit industry, 1988 survey, annual rpt, 2413-14

Virgin Islands economic censuses, 1987: employment, firms, payroll, and receipts, by SIC 1- to 4-digit industry, island, and city, 2593-1

Wholesale trade sales, inventories, purchases, and gross margins, by SIC 2- to 3-digit kind of business and form of ownership, 1988, annual rpt, 2413-13

see also Bank holding companies
see also Business acquisitions and mergers
see also Economic concentration and diversification
see also Foreign corporations
see also Government corporations and enterprises
see also Holding companies
see also Multinational corporations
see also Public utilities
see also under By Individual Company or Institution in the "Index by Categories"

Corps of Engineers
see Army Corps of Engineers

Corpus Christi, Tex.
see also under By City and By SMSA or MSA in the "Index by Categories"

Correctional institutions
AIDS cases in prisons, test results, and prevention and control policies, by location, 1988 survey, annual rpt, 6064-22

Conditions, population, and problems of prisons, issues and bibl, 1989 compilation of papers, 25928-8

Data on crime, criminal justice admin and enforcement, and public opinion, data compilation, 1970s-88, annual rpt, 6064-6

Drug testing of prison employees, and training and treatment referrals provided, 1988 rpt, 6066-26.1

Employment, earnings, facilities, and inmates of State correctional instns, by facility characteristics and State, 1980s-87 with trends from 1976, annual rpt, 6064-6.1; 6064-6.6

Employment, payroll, and spending for criminal justice, by level of govt, State, and selected city and county, FY71-85, annual rpt, 6064-9

Fed Bur of Prisons activities, and inmate and staff characteristics, FY88, annual rpt, 6244-2

Fed Govt spending in States, by type, program, agency, and State, FY88, annual rpt, 2464-2

Federal and State correctional instns population by sex, admissions, and instn capacity and overcrowding, by State, 1980s-88, annual rpt, 6066-25.21

Foreign countries human rights conditions in 170 countries, 1988, annual rpt, 21384-3

Govt employment and payroll, by function, level of govt, and jurisdiction, 1987-88, annual rpt series, 2466-1

Govt revenues by source and spending by function, natl income and product account, *Survey of Current Business*, monthly rpt, 2702-1.24

Jail population by sex, race, and for 25 jurisdictions, and instn conditions, 1983-87, annual rpt, 6066-25.18

Jail population, capacity, and instns under court order to reduce population and improve conditions, 1983-86, annual rpt, 6064-26.1

Pacific territories social, economic, health, and govtl data, FY88 and trends, annual rpt, 7004-6

see also Community-based correctional programs
see also Juvenile detention and correctional institutions
see also Military prisons
see also Parole and probation
see also Prison work programs
see also Prisoners
see also Rehabilitation of criminals

Correspondence courses
Service industries census, 1987: establishments, receipts, employment, and payroll, by SIC 2- to 4-digit kind of business, MSA, county, and city, State rpt series, 2391-1

Corruption and bribery
Court civil and criminal caseloads for Federal district, appeals, and special courts, June 1989, annual rpt, 18204-2; 18204-8

Criminal case processing in Federal district courts, and dispositions, by offense, district, and offender characteristics, 1984, annual rpt, 6064-29

Drug enforcement regional task forces investigation of organized crime, activities by agency and region, and background data, FY83-88, annual rpt, 6004-17

Govt officials prosecuted and convicted for corruption, by judicial district and level of govt, 1978-88, annual rpt, 6004-13

Govt officials prosecuted and convicted for corruption, by level of govt, 1970-87, annual rpt, 6064-6.5

Sentences for Federal crimes, guidelines use and results by offense and district, and Sentencing Commission activities, 1988, annual rpt, 17664-1

Sentences for Federal offenses, guidelines by offense and circumstances, 1989 rpt, 17668-1

Statistical Abstract of US, social, political, and economic data, 1790-2025, comprehensive annual compilation, 2324-1.1

US attorneys civil and criminal cases by type and disposition, and collections, by Federal district, FY88, annual rpt, 6004-2.1; 6004-2.7

Wiretaps authorized, costs, arrests, trials, and convictions, by offense and jurisdiction, 1988, annual rpt, 18204-7

see also Federal Inspectors General reports

Corson, Walter
"Examination of Declining UI Claims During the 1980s", 6406-6.24
"New Jersey Unemployment Insurance Reemployment Demonstration Project", 6406-6.27

Corundum
see Abrasive materials

Cosmetics and toiletries
Carcinogens chemistry, sources, environment and health risks, and regulation, by substance and brand, 1989, annual rpt, 4044-15

China trade by SITC 1- to 5-digit commodity, 1970s-87, annual rpt, 9114-3

Consumer Expenditure Survey, spending by category, and income, by selected household characteristics and location, 1987, press release, 6726-1.23

County Business Patterns, 1987: employment, establishments, and payroll, by SIC 2- to 4-digit industry and county, annual State rpt series, 2326-8

Prices of cotton at selected spot markets, NYC futures prices, and CCC loan rates, 1988/89 and trends from 1940, annual rpt, 1309-2

Prices received and paid by farmers, by commodity and State, 1988, annual rpt, 1629-5

Prices received by farmers and production value, by detailed crop and State, 1986-88, annual rpt, 1621-2

Prices received by farmers for major products, and paid for farm inputs and living items, by State, monthly rpt, 1629-1

Production, farms, acreage, and related data, by selected crop and State, monthly rpt, 1621-1

Production inputs, output, and productivity for farms, by commodity and region, 1947-87, annual rpt, 1544-17

Production itemized costs, receipts, and returns, by commodity and region, 1985-87, annual rpt, 1544-20

Production itemized costs, receipts, and returns, by crop and State, preliminary 1987, annual rpt, 1544-24

Production itemized costs, receipts, and returns, by selected commodity and region, 1975-87, 1548-345

Production, prices, exports, stocks, and mill use of long staple cotton, monthly rpt, 1309-12

Production, prices, trade, and marketing, by commodity, current situation and forecast, monthly rpt with articles, 1502-4

Production, prices, trade, and use of cotton, wool, and synthetic fibers, periodic situation rpt with articles, 1561-1

Production, trade, sales, stocks, and material used, by product, region, and State, periodic Current Industrial Rpt series, 2506-5

Science, engineering, and technical employment in manufacturing, by field, occupation, and industry, 1986, triennial rpt, 9627-23

Statistical Abstract of US, social, political, and economic data, 1790-2025, comprehensive annual compilation, 2324-1.3

Wholesale trade census, 1987: employment, establishments, finances, and operations, by SIC 2- to 4-digit kind of business, MSA, county, and city, State rpt series, 2405-1

see also under By Commodity in the "Index by Categories"

Cottonseed
see Oils, oilseeds, and fats

Coughlin, Cletus C.
"Dubious Success of Export Subsidies for Wheat", 9391-1.904

"Have Federal Spending and Taxation Contributed to the Divergence of State Per Capita Incomes in the 1980s?", 9391-1.918

"Introduction to Non-Tariff Barriers to Trade", 9391-1.906

Council for Mutual Economic Assistance
Debt, trade, and balances of Eastern Europe and USSR with US and other western countries, with background data, 1980s-87, hearing, 21248-120

Economic conditions in Communist and OECD countries, 1987, annual rpt, 7144-11

Council of Economic Advisers
Budget of US Appendix, obligations, appropriations, and personnel, by program and agency, FY90, annual rpt, 104-3

Budget of US, authoritative financial statements with appropriations, outlays, and receipts, by category and agency, FY88, annual rpt, 8104-2.2

Economic indicators and components, current data and annual trends, monthly rpt, 23842-1

Economic Report of the President for 1989, with economic trends from 1929, annual rpt, 204-1

Council on Environmental Quality
Budget of US Appendix, obligations, appropriations, and personnel, by program and agency, FY90, annual rpt, 104-3

Budget of US, authoritative financial statements with appropriations, outlays, and receipts, by category and agency, FY88, annual rpt, 8104-2.2

Environmental quality and protection programs, and intl issues, 1988 annual rpt, 484-1

Councils of government
see Regional planning

Counselors and counseling
AIDS virus antibody testing services demand, accuracy, and costs, data collection methods with background data, 1986-88, 4186-9.7

Community organizations partnerships with public schools, participation, activities, and contributions, by school characteristics and location, 1987/88, 4826-1.27

Crime victim aid programs of law enforcement agencies, funding levels, staff, and needs, 1986, 6066-26.3

Drug and alcohol abuse treatment facilities, services, use, funding, and client characteristics, 1987, annual rpt, 4494-10

Education (special) enrollment by age, staff, funding, and needs, by type of handicap and State, 1987/88, annual rpt, 4944-4

Health condition improvement and disease prevention goals and recommended activities for 2000, with trends 1970s-80s, 4048-10

Hereditary disease and genetic screening, counseling, and treatment services use, costs, and payment sources, 1987 conf, 4108-47

Homeless and runaway youth programs, funding, activities, and participant characteristics, FY86, annual rpt, 4604-3

Homeless shelters services, operations, and client characteristics, 1988 survey, 5188-123

Physicians (cardiologists) office visits, by characteristics of patient, physician, and visit, 1985, 4146-8.174

Prenatal care risk assessment and health promotion services, findings and recommendations, 1989 narrative rpt, 4048-32

Special education enrollment by disability, transfers to public schools from State instns, services provided, and Federal funding, with data by State, 1987-88, GAO rpt, 26121-294

VA health care facilities mental health services, staff, research, and training programs, 1989 biennial listing, 8704-2

VA Medicine and Surgery Dept trainees, by detailed program and city, FY88, annual rpt, 8704-4

Veterans rehabilitative and educational counseling provided, 1964-88, annual rpt, 8604-5.2

see also Clergy
see also Psychiatry
see also Social work
see also Vocational guidance

Counterfeiting and forgery
Arrest rates, by offense, sex, age, and race, 1987, annual rpt, 6224-7

Arrests, by offense, offender characteristics, and location, 1988, annual rpt, 6224-2.2

Court civil and criminal caseloads for Federal district, appeals, and special courts, June 1989, annual rpt, 18204-2; 18204-8

Crime, criminal justice admin and enforcement, and public opinion, data compilation, 1970s-88, annual rpt, 6064-6

Criminal case processing in Federal district courts, and dispositions, by offense, district, and offender characteristics, 1984, annual rpt, 6064-29

Criminal case processing in Federal district courts, disposition by offense, 1980-87, 6066-19.50

Diplomats and staff with immunity for foreign missions in US and US missions abroad, and foreign diplomats criminal cases, 1978-87, hearing, 25388-51

Postal Service inspection activities, expenses, and staff, FY88, annual rpt, 9864-8

Secret Service counterfeiting and other investigations and arrests by type, and disposition, by field office, FY88 and trends from FY79, annual rpt, 8464-1

Sentences for Federal crimes, guidelines use and results by offense and district, and Sentencing Commission activities, 1988, annual rpt, 17664-1

Sentences for Federal offenses, guidelines by offense and circumstances, 1989 rpt, 17668-1

US attorneys civil and criminal cases by type and disposition, and collections, by Federal district, FY88, annual rpt, 6004-2.1

Value of counterfeit money seized and in circulation, and operations suppressed by Secret Service, FY72-87, annual rpt, 6064-6.4

Counties
Agricultural Conservation Program, counties served by State, FY87, annual rpt, 1804-7

Agriculture census, 1987: farms, farmland, production and costs, and operator characteristics, advance State and county rpt series, 2330-1

Crimes, arrests by offender characteristics, and rates, by offense, and law enforcement employees, by population size and jurisdiction, 1988, annual rpt, 6224-2

Criminal justice spending, employment, and payroll, by level of govt, State, and selected city and county, FY71-85, annual rpt, 6064-9

Farmland damaged by natural disaster, Emergency Conservation Program aid and participation by State, FY87, annual rpt, 1804-22

Govt (local) in metro areas, finances, structure, and service delivery, local area rpt series, 10046-9

Govt census, 1987: elected officials, by level of govt, race, sex, and State, preliminary rpt, 2450-2

Govt census, 1987: property tax revenue by level of govt, assessed values by locality, and exemptions, by property type and State, 2453-1

Govt employment and payroll, by function and population size, for 398 largest counties, 1987, annual rpt, 2466-1.4

Govt employment and payroll, by function, for 410 large counties, annual rpt, discontinued, 2466-1.2

Govt finances, by level of govt, State, and for large cities and counties, annual rpt series, 2466-2

Govt finances, tax systems and revenue, and fiscal structure, by level of govt and State, selected years 1929-91, annual rpt, 10044-1

Govt services transfer to private contractors, impacts on govt workers, with data by worker characteristics, level of govt, and location, 1980s-87, 15496-1.5

Health care resources geographic info system, data coverage and availability, 1989 rpt, 4118-61

Income (personal) per capita and by source, and earnings by industry div, by State, MSA, and county, 1982-87, annual regional rpts, 2704-2

Labor surplus areas eligible for preferential Fed Govt contracts, monthly listing, 6402-1

Migration since 1986, mover characteristics by same or different area, and compared to nonmovers, 1987, annual Current Population Rpt, 2546-1.435

Nonmetro counties employment by industry sector and degree of urbanization, and compared to metro counties, various periods 1969-86, 1598-244

Population size, by MSA, county, metro-nonmetro location, and State, 1987, and for cities, 1986, with change from 1980 and trends from 1960, Current Population Rpt, 2546-3.160

Population size of counties, 1988, and components of change from 1980, annual Current Population Rpt, 2544-3

Rural areas aid from Fed Govt, by agency and program, with county classifications by population density, FY85 and FY87, GAO rpt, 26113-401

Rural areas economic and social conditions, dev, and problems, periodic journal, 1502-7

Rural counties with employment growth and decline, by leading industry div, various periods 1969-84, article, 1502-7.907

Soil surveys and maps for counties, 1899-1987, annual listing, 1264-11

Statistical Abstract of US, social, political, and economic data, with foreign comparisons, 1790-2025, comprehensive annual compilation, 2324-1

Unemployment insurance extended benefits provision in substate areas, model results and cost estimates, 1980-86, 6406-6.28

see also County Business Patterns

see also under By County in the "Index by Categories"

County Business Patterns

Employment, establishments, and payroll, by SIC 2- to 4-digit industry and county, 1987, annual State rpt series, 2326-8

Court of International Trade

Budget of US Appendix, obligations, appropriations, and personnel, by program and agency, FY90, annual rpt, 104-3

Budget of US, authoritative financial statements with appropriations, outlays, and receipts, by category and agency, FY88, annual rpt, 8104-2.2

Caseloads of Court of Intl Trade, decisions, and appeals, FY88-89, annual rpt, 18224-2

Cases filed and terminated, 1987-88, annual rpt, 18204-8.17

Pay rates of Fed Govt civilian employees, by pay schedule and grade, 1989 and trends from 1789, annual rpt, 21624-4

Court of Military Appeals

Cases and actions of military courts, FY88, annual rpt, 3504-3

Courtless, Joan C.

"Recent Trends in Clothing and Textiles", 1702-1.902

Courts

Bankruptcy courts of US, caseloads by type of estate, Code chapter, circuit, and district, quarterly rpt, 18202-1

Budget deficit reduction under Gramm-Rudman Act, cancellation of budget authority by program, FY90, annual rpt, 104-27; 21924-1; 26304-6

Budget of US Appendix, obligations, appropriations, and personnel, by program and agency, FY90, annual rpt, 104-3

Budget of US, authoritative financial statements with appropriations, outlays, and receipts, by agency, FY88, annual rpt, 8104-2

Budget of US, compact budgets by activity, function, and agency, FY90 and projected to FY94, annual rpt, 104-2

Budget of US, historical data, selected years FY34-88 and projected to FY94, annual rpt, 104-22

Budget of US, object class analysis of obligations, by agency, FY90, annual rpt, 104-9

Budget of US, receipts by source, outlays by agency and program, and balances, monthly rpt, 8102-3

Caseloads (civil and criminal) for Federal district, appeals, and special courts, June 1989, annual rpt, 18204-2; 18204-8

Congressional Directory, members of 101st Congress, other officials, elections, and districts, 1989-90, biennial rpt, 23874-1

Employment, earnings, and hours, by SIC 1- to 4-digit industry, monthly 1983-Feb 1989, annual rpt, 6744-4

Employment, payroll, and spending for criminal justice, by level of govt, State, and selected city and county, FY71-85, annual rpt, 6064-9

Fed Govt consolidated financial statements based on business accounting methods, FY87-88, annual rpt, 8104-5

Judicial Conf proceedings and findings, fall 1989, semiannual rpt, 18202-2

Labor productivity of Federal employees, indexes of output and labor costs by function, FY67-87, annual rpt, 6824-1.6

Statistical Abstract of US, social, political, and economic data, 1790-2025, comprehensive annual compilation, 2324-1.1; 2324-1.2

see also Administrative Office of the U.S. Courts

see also Civil procedure

see also Contempt of court

see also Court of International Trade

see also Court of Military Appeals

see also Courts-martial and courts of inquiry

see also Criminal procedure

see also D.C. courts

see also Federal bankruptcy courts

see also Federal courts of appeals

see also Federal district courts

see also Federal Judicial Center

see also Judges

see also Judicial Conference of the U.S.

see also Judicial powers

see also Judicial reform

see also Juries

see also Juvenile courts and cases

see also Parole and probation

see also Sentences, criminal procedure

see also State courts

see also Supreme Court

see also Tax Court of the U.S.

see also Tax laws and courts

see also Traffic laws and courts

see also Trials

see also U.S. Claims Court

see also U.S. Court of Appeals for the Federal Circuit

see also Witnesses

Courts martial and courts of inquiry

Army criminal offenders, by sex and race, FY87-88, annual rpt, 3704-10.5

Cases and actions of military courts, FY88, annual rpt, 3504-3

Criminal case processing in military courts, and prisoners by facility, by service branch, 1960s-88, annual rpt, 6064-6.5; 6064-6.6

Drug and alcohol abuse by military personnel, prevalence and consequences, by selected characteristics, 1988, biennial rpt, 3504-19

Cows

see Dairy industry and products

see Livestock and livestock industry

Cox, Brenda G.

"National Survey of Small Business Finances: Description and Preliminary Evaluation", 9366-6.207

Cox, E. Jane

"Agricultural Work Force of 1987: A Statistical Profile", 1594-2

Cox, W. Michael

"Money and Inflation in a Deregulated Financial Environment: An Overview", 9379-1.905

CPI

see Consumer Price Index

Crabbe, Leland

"International Gold Standard and U.S. Monetary Policy from World War I to the New Deal", 9362-1.906

Crabs

see Shellfish

Craig, Peter C.

"Evaluation of Environmental Information for the Unimak Pass Area, Alaska", 2176-1.24

"Fish Resources of the Chukchi Sea: Status of Existing Information and Field Program Design", 2176–1.29

Cranberries

see Fruit and fruit products

Cranston, R.I.

Housing and households detailed characteristics, and unit and neighborhood quality, by location, 1984 survey, MSA rpt, 2485–6.2

Crawford, Terry

"Livestock Costs and Returns, 1988-89", 1561–7.903

Credit

Assets and debts of private sector, balance sheets by segment, 1949-88, semiannual rpt, 9365–4.1

Budget of US, Bush Admin policy changes by program, FY90, 028–32

Budget of US, CBO analysis of revenue and spending alternatives and projections of economic indicators, FY90-94, annual rpt, 26304–3

Budget of US, historical data, selected years FY34-88 and projected to FY94, annual rpt, 104–22

Budget of US, House concurrent resolution, with spending and revenue targets, FY90, annual rpt, 21264–2

Budget of US, overview, FY90, annual rpt, 104–6

Budget of US, Reagan Admin policy changes by program, FY90, annual rpt, 104–21

Budget of US, Senate concurrent resolution, with spending and revenue targets, FY90, annual rpt, 25254–1

Budget of US, special analysis of credit programs, FY90, annual rpt, 104–1.6

Demand for credit, activity indicators, 1979-88, annual rpt, 204–1.5

Economic indicator performance, and Fed Reserve monetary policy objectives, as of July 1989, semiannual rpt, 9362–4

Economic indicators and components, current data and annual trends, monthly rpt, 23842–1.5

Economic indicators targets and performance, 1960s-88 and projected to 1994, annual article, 9381–1.901

Fed Govt mgmt cost control proposals, Reagan Admin initiatives, savings, and status, FY85-94, annual rpt, 104–23

Financial and business detailed statistics, *Fed Reserve Bulletin*, monthly rpt with articles, 9362–1

Flow-of-funds accounts, assets and liabilities by type and economic sector, outstanding at year-end 1965-88, annual rpt, 9364–3

GNP, interest rates, and inflation related to private and Federal credit, model description and results, 1960s-87, working paper, 9381–10.94

Home equity loans by lender type, and homeowner participation and characteristics, 1988, article, 9362–1.905

see also Agricultural credit

see also Business assets and liabilities, general

see also Business assets and liabilities, specific industry

see also Commercial credit

see also Commodity Credit Corp.

see also Consumer credit

see also Credit bureaus and agencies

see also Credit cards

see also Credit unions

see also Discrimination in credit

see also Finance companies

see also Foreign debts

see also Government assets and liabilities

see also Interest payments

see also International finance

see also Loan delinquency and default

see also Loans

see also Mortgages

see also Public debt

Credit bureaus and agencies

County Business Patterns, 1987: employment, establishments, and payroll, by SIC 2- to 4-digit industry and county, annual State rpt series, 2326–8

Employment, earnings, and hours, by SIC 1- to 4-digit industry, monthly 1983-Feb 1989, annual rpt, 6744–4

Employment in nonmanufacturing industries, by detailed occupation and SIC 2-digit industry, 1987, triennial rpt, 6748–60

Flow-of-funds accounts, assets and liabilities by type and economic sector, outstanding at year-end 1965-88, annual rpt, 9364–3

Mortgage loan activity, by type of lender, loan, and mortgaged property, monthly press release, 5142–18

Mortgage loan activity, by type of lender, loan, and mortgaged property, quarterly press release, 5142–30

Mortgage loan activity, by type of lender, loan, and mortgaged property, 1986-88, annual press release, 5144–22

Occupational injury and illness rates, by SIC 2- to 4-digit industry, 1987, annual rpt, 6844–1

Science and engineering employment, by nonmanufacturing industry and field, 1987, triennial rpt, 9627–31

Service industries census, 1987: establishments, receipts, employment, and payroll, by SIC 2- to 4-digit kind of business, MSA, county, and city, State rpt series, 2391–1

Service industries receipts, by SIC 2- to 4-digit kind of business, 1988, annual rpt, 2413–8

Tax (income) returns of corporations, income and tax items by asset size and detailed industry, 1986, annual rpt, 8304–4; 8304–21

Tax (income) returns of partnerships, income statement items by industry group, 1986, annual article, 8302–2.903

Tax (income) returns of sole proprietorships, income statement items, by industry group, 1987, annual article, 8302–2.904; 8302–2.921

Credit cards

Banks (natl) domestic and intl operations, charters, mergers, and liquidations, by instn and State, quarterly rpt, 8402–3

Financial instns financial and operating statements by deposit size, Fed Reserve functional cost analysis, 1988, annual rpt, 9364–6

Statistical Abstract of US, social, political, and economic data, 1790-2025, comprehensive annual compilation, 2324–1.3

Tax (income) returns of individuals, detailed data, 1986, annual rpt, 8304–2

Credit unions

Assets and liabilities of depository instns, monthly rpt, 9362–1.1

Assets and liabilities of financial instns, by instn type, 1985-87, annual rpt, 9364–5.4

Assets and location of credit unions, 1989 annual listing, 9534–6

Assets composition, growth, and distribution for financial instns, by instn type, 1970s-88, 8438–1

County Business Patterns, 1987: employment, establishments, and payroll, by SIC 2- to 4-digit industry and county, annual State rpt series, 2326–8

Finances, mergers, and closings of federally insured credit unions, and insurance fund losses and financial statements, FY88, annual rpt, 9534–7

Finances of banks and thrifts, by instn type, 1988, annual rpt, 13004–2

Finances of federally insured credit unions, by instn characteristics and State, as of June 1989, semiannual rpt, 9532–6

Finances of federally insured credit unions, 1987-88, annual rpt, 9534–1

Financial condition of Federal deposit insurance funds, and of financial instns by type, 1980s-88, GAO rpt, 26119–241

Flow-of-funds accounts, assets and liabilities by type and economic sector, outstanding at year-end 1965-88, annual rpt, 9364–3

Flow-of-funds accounts, savings, investments, and credit statements, quarterly rpt, 9365–3.3

Installment credit outstanding, and terms, by lender and credit type, monthly rpt, 9365–2.6

Installment credit outstanding, by type of holder, *Survey of Current Business*, monthly rpt, 2702–1.6

North Central States economic conditions, Fed Reserve 9th District, quarterly rpt, 9383–18

Rural Credit Unions cooperatives, memberships, and loans, by State, 1987, annual rpt, 1124–1

Science and engineering employment, by nonmanufacturing industry and field, 1987, triennial rpt, 9627–31

Statistical Abstract of US, social, political, and economic data, 1790-2025, comprehensive annual compilation, 2324–1.3

Tax (income) returns of corporations, income and tax items by asset size and detailed industry, 1986, annual rpt, 8304–4

Crime and criminals

Aliens excluded and deported from US by cause and country, 1892-1988, annual rpt, 6264–2

Chicago public housing projects structural and financial problems, and crime, 1979-88, GAO rpt, 26113–418

Cost of living indexes for metro areas, relation of expenditure items and quality of life indicators, model results, 1973, working paper, 6886–6.9

Crimes, arrests by offender characteristics, and rates, by offense, and law enforcement employees, by population size and jurisdiction, 1988, annual rpt, 6224–2

Data on crime and criminal justice, activities of Bur of Justice Statistics and States, FY88, annual rpt, 6064–21

Data on crime and criminal justice, collection, methodology, and use, technical rpt series, 6066–23

Data on crime and criminal justice, programs and rpts, 1988, annual listing, 6064–25

Data on crime and criminal justice, research results, series, 6066–20; 6066–26

Data on crime, criminal justice admin and enforcement, and public opinion, data compilation, 1970s-88, annual rpt, 6064–6

Data on criminal justice issues, series, 6066–19; 6066–25

Diplomats and staff with immunity for foreign missions in US and US missions abroad, and foreign diplomats criminal cases, 1978-87, hearing, 25388–51

Index of crime by population size and region, and offenses by large city, Jan-June 1989, semiannual rpt, 6222–1

Index of crime, victimizations and arrest by offense, circumstances, and location, 1970s-87, annual rpt, 6064–6.3; 6064–6.4

Indian reservation crimes and enforcement activity in Montana, and Bur of Indian Affairs law enforcement officers training, 1985-87, GAO rpt, 26113–402

Mental health services for criminals, use, availability, staff, and funding, by facility type, 1985, 4506–3.36

Neighborhood and housing quality, indicators and attitudes, by householder type and location, 1985, biennial rpt, 2485–12

Neighborhood and housing quality, indicators and attitudes, MSA surveys, series, 2485–6

Older persons crime victimization rates, by offense and victim age, 1970s-85, annual rpt, 25144–3.2

Pacific territories social, economic, health, and govtl data, FY88 and trends, annual rpt, 7004–6

Statistical Abstract of US, social, political, and economic data, 1790-2025, comprehensive annual compilation, 2324–1.1

Victim aid programs of law enforcement agencies, funding levels, staff, and needs, 1986, 6066–26.3

Victimization rates, by victim and offender characteristics, circumstances, and offense, survey rpt series, 6066–3

Wiretaps authorized, costs, arrests, trials, and convictions, by offense and jurisdiction, 1988, annual rpt, 18204–7

see also Air piracy
see also Arrest
see also Arson
see also Assassination
see also Assault
see also Assaults on police
see also Bombs
see also Child abuse and neglect
see also Contraband
see also Correctional institutions
see also Corruption and bribery
see also Counterfeiting and forgery
see also Courts

see also Criminal investigations
see also Criminal procedure
see also Detective and protective services
see also Domestic violence
see also Driving while intoxicated
see also Drug and narcotics offenses
see also Fraud
see also Gambling
see also Homicide
see also Hostages
see also Juvenile delinquency
see also Kidnapping
see also Law enforcement
see also Motor vehicle theft
see also Organized crime
see also Parole and probation
see also Pretrial detention and release
see also Prisoners
see also Prostitution
see also Rape
see also Recidivism
see also Rehabilitation of criminals
see also Robbery and theft
see also Sentences, criminal procedure
see also Sex crimes
see also Smuggling
see also Terrorism
see also Trials
see also Vandalism
see also Violence

Criminal investigations

Banks and other financial instns fraud and insider misconduct cases, Federal regulatory and enforcement activities, and losses, 1981-87, hearing, 21408–111

Data on crime, criminal justice admin and enforcement, and public opinion, data compilation, 1970s-88, annual rpt, 6064–6

DOD criminal investigation activities, funding, and case dispositions, by service branch, FY84-88, GAO rpt, 26123–242

Drug enforcement regional task forces investigation of organized crime, activities by agency and region, and background data, FY83-88, annual rpt, 6004–17

Federal district court criminal case processing, disposition by offense, 1980-87, 6066–19.50

Firearms violations enhanced and mandatory sentences, for cases under Bur of Alcohol, Tobacco, and Firearms investigation program, FY87-88, 8488–6

Indian reservation crimes and enforcement activity in Montana, and Bur of Indian Affairs law enforcement officers training, 1985-87, GAO rpt, 26113–402

Marijuana crop eradication activities of DEA and local agencies by State, and drug potency, 1982-88, annual rpt, 6284–4

Postal Service inspection activities, expenses, and staff, FY88, annual rpt, 9864–8

Postal Service inspection activities, FY88, annual rpt, 9864–9

Secret Service counterfeiting and other investigations and arrests by type, and disposition, by field office, FY88 and trends from FY79, annual rpt, 8464–1

Securities law enforcement activities of SEC, FY88, annual rpt, 9734–2.5

Small Business Admin programs fraud and abuse, Inspector General indictments and convictions, FY84-88, annual rpt, 9764–1

Tax assessments and collections resulting from IRS criminal investigations, by violation type, 1984, GAO rpt, 26119–244

Tax litigation and enforcement activity of IRS, FY88, annual rpt, 8304–3.1

Terrorist incidents in US, related activity, and casualties, by attack type, target, group, and location, 1988, annual rpt, 6224–6

Wiretaps authorized, costs, arrests, trials, and convictions, by offense and jurisdiction, 1988, annual rpt, 18204–7

see also Police
see also Searches and seizures

Criminal Justice Associates

"Work in American Prisons: The Private Sector Gets Involved", 6068–228

Criminal procedure

Aliens exclusion and deportation cases, appeals, bond postings, and investigations, for NYC and Los Angeles, 1987, GAO rpt, 26119–271

Case processing from arrest to sentencing, cases and duration by disposition, offense, and defendant characteristics, for selected cities, 1986, annual rpt, 6064–27

Court caseloads for Federal district, appeals, and bankruptcy courts, by type of suit and offense, circuit, and district, quarterly rpt, 18202–1

Data on crime and criminal justice, activities of Bur of Justice Statistics and States, FY88, annual rpt, 6064–21

Data on crime and criminal justice, collection, methodology, and use, technical rpt series, 6066–23

Data on crime and criminal justice, programs and rpts, 1988, annual listing, 6064–25

Data on crime and criminal justice, research results, series, 6066–20; 6066–26

Data on crime, criminal justice admin and enforcement, and public opinion, data compilation, 1970s-88, annual rpt, 6064–6

Data on criminal justice issues, series, 6066–19; 6066–25

Diplomats and staff with immunity for foreign missions in US and US missions abroad, and foreign diplomats criminal cases, 1978-87, hearing, 25388–51

Drug enforcement regional task forces investigation of organized crime, activities by agency and region, and background data, FY83-88, annual rpt, 6004–17

Federal district and appeals court caseloads, actions, procedure duration, judges, and jurors, by court, 1984-89, annual rpt, 18204–3

Federal district, appeals, and special courts civil and criminal caseloads, 1989, annual rpt, 18204–2; 18204–8

Felony arrests by offender characteristics, prosecutions, convictions, and sentences by type, by offense, 1983-86, 6066–19.52

Immigration and nationality violations, prosecutions, fines, imprisonment, and convictions, and deportation and exclusion cases, FY82-88, annual rpt, 6264–2

Indian reservation crimes and enforcement activity in Montana, and Bur of Indian Affairs law enforcement officers training, 1985-87, GAO rpt, 26113–402

Judicial Conf proceedings and findings, fall 1989, semiannual rpt, 18202–2

Juvenile arrests, by disposition and population size, 1988, annual rpt, 6224–2.2

Secret Service counterfeiting and other investigations and arrests by type, and disposition, by field office, FY88 and trends from FY79, annual rpt, 8464–1

US attorneys case processing and collections, by case type and Federal district, FY88, annual rpt, 6004–2

see also Arrest

see also Capital punishment

see also Evidence

see also Extradition

see also Habeas corpus

see also Juries

see also Pardons

see also Parole and probation

see also Pretrial detention and release

see also Searches and seizures

see also Sentences, criminal procedure

see also Trials

Crom, Richard J.
"Economics of the U.S. Meat Industry", 1568–280

Cromarty, William A.
"Sweetener Outlook, Industry Reaction", 1004–16.1

Cromer, Shauna
"U.S. Egg and Poultry Statistical Series, 1960-87", 1568–39

Cromwell, Brian A.
"Capital Subsidies and the Infrastructure Crisis: Evidence from the Local Mass-Transit Industry", 9377–1.904
"Dedicated Taxes and Rent Capture by Public Employees", 9377–9.73
"Federal Grant Policies and Public Sector Scrappage Decisions", 9377–9.67
"Impact of Capital Grants on Maintenance in the Local Public Sector", 9377–9.68

Cromwell, Jerry
"Does One National Prospective Payment System Market Basket Make Sense?", 4652–1.921
"Estimates of Hospital Industry Total Factor Productivity for the Period 1980-86", 17206–2.1
"Trends in Hospital Labor and Total Factor Productivity, 1981-86", 4652–1.941

Crone, Theodore M.
"Office Vacancy Rates: How Should We Interpret Them?", 9387–1.903

Cronkhite, Fred R.
"BLS Establishment Estimates Revised to March 1988 Benchmarks", 6742–2.903
"New Seasonal Adjustment Factors for the Establishment Data Series", 6742–2.905

Crook, Frederick W.
"China's Wheat Economy", 1524–4.3
"Long Term Prospects for China's Wheat Imports", 1561–12.907

Crop insurance
see Agricultural insurance

Crops
see Agricultural commodities

Crouch, Glenn L.
"Summer Birds and Mammals of Aspen-Conifer Forests in West-Central Colorado", 1208–299

Croushore, Dean D.
"Transactions Costs and Optimal Inflation", 9387–8.199

Crowder, Bradley M.
"Cotton Acreage in Major Producing Areas", 1561–1.903
"Soybeans: Background for 1990 Farm Legislation", 1566–7.1

Crutchfield, Stephen R.
"U.S. Agriculture and Water Quality: Scope and Extent of the Problem", 1561–16.904

Crysdale, Bonnie L.
"Bitumen-Bearing Deposits of the U.S.", 5668–88

Crystal, Stephen
"Economic Resources of the Elderly: A Comprehensive Income Approach", 2626–10.93

Cuba
Agricultural and food production and indexes, total and for selected commodities, by country, 1970s-88, annual rpt, 1524–12

Agricultural trade of US, by detailed commodity and country, 1988, semiannual rpt, 1522–4

Aircraft hijackings, on-board explosions, and other crime, US and foreign incidents, 1983-87, annual rpt, 7504–31

Deaths in US, by State of occurrence and birthplace abroad, 1986, US Vital Statistics annual rpt, 4144–2.1

Economic and military aid and loans from US and intl agencies, by program and country, FY46-87, annual rpt, 9914–5

Economic conditions in Cuba, agricultural and industrial production and distribution, trade, and intl economic relations, 1980-87 with trends from 1961, 9118–8

Economic, social, political, and geographic summary data, by country, 1989, annual factbook, 9114–2

Exports and imports of US with Communist countries, by detailed commodity and country, quarterly rpt with articles, 9882–2

Exports, imports, and USSR economic aid, for Cuba, 1960s-87, annual rpt, 9114–4.9

Human rights conditions in 170 countries, 1988, annual rpt, 21384–3

Immigration to US, alien workers, visitors, deportations, and naturalizations, by country, FY88 and trends from 1820, annual rpt, 6264–2

Military spending, arms trade, and force strengths, with govt spending and population, by country, 1977-87, annual rpt, 9824–1

Minerals Yearbook, 1987, Vol 3: foreign country reviews of production, trade, and policy, by commodity, annual rpt, 5604–35

Minerals Yearbook, 1987, Vol 3 preprints: foreign country review of production, trade, and policy, by commodity, annual rpt, 5604–23.83

Multinatl US firms foreign affiliates trade with Cuba, by country, FY82-87, press release, 8008–137

Nuclear power plant capacity and operating status, by plant and Communist country, as of Dec 1988, annual rpt, 3164–57.2

Population size, growth rates, and components of change, by country, projected 1989-2020 and trends from 1950, biennial rpt, 2324–9

Refugee resettlement programs and funding, arrivals by country of origin, and indicators of adjustment, by State, FY88, annual rpt, 4694–5

Refugees from Cuba entering US during 1980 boatlift, Federal funding for youth mental health services, and participation, 1981-88, GAO rpt, 26121–270

Sugar production, millings, consumption, and exports, for Cuba, 1950s-89, article, 1561–14.903

UN voting record and share of votes in agreement with US, by issue, country, and world area, 1988, annual rpt, 7004–18

see also under By Foreign Country in the "Index by Categories"

Cuban Americans
see Hispanic Americans

Cullison, William E.
"Changing Labor Force: Some Provocative Findings", 9389–1.914
"On Recognizing Inflation", 9389–19.6
"U.S. Productivity Slowdown: What the Experts Say", 9389–1.911

Cultural activities
see also Anthropology
see also Area studies
see also Art
see also Arts and the humanities
see also Dance
see also Educational exchanges
see also Exchange of persons programs
see also Federal aid to arts and humanities
see also International cooperation in cultural activities
see also Language arts
see also Motion pictures
see also Museums
see also Music
see also Performing arts
see also Theater

Cumberland, Md.
see also under By SMSA or MSA in the "Index by Categories"

Cumella, Edward J.
"Capitation Payment: Using Predictors of Medical Utilization To Adjust Rates", 4652–1.905

Cummings, K. Michael
"Adoption of Smoking Policies by Automobile Dealerships", 4042–3.950

Cummins, David
"Co-op Share of Supply Sales Up: Marketings Slip During 1980s", 1122–1.901

Cunningham, Rosemary T.
"What's the 'Surprise' in Money Supply Announcements?", 9371–10.32

Cunningham, Thomas J.
"Federal Budget Deficit and the Social Security Surplus", 9371–1.905
"What's the 'Surprise' in Money Supply Announcements?", 9371–10.32

Curran, Thomas C.
"National Air Quality and Emissions Trends Report, 1987", 9194–1

Currency
see Coins and coinage
see Flow-of-funds accounts
see Foreign exchange
see Money supply
see Special foreign currency programs

Current Employment Survey

Employment and Earnings, detailed data, monthly rpt, 6742–2

Employment change by industry div, alternative estimates, 1982-1989, article, 6722–1.938

Current Population Reports

see Current Population Survey

see Survey of Income and Program Participation

Current Population Survey

Consumer Income, socioeconomic characteristics of persons, families, and households, detailed cross-tabulations, series, 2546–6

Data collection, methodology, and comparisons to other data bases, Survey of Income and Program Participation, working paper series, 2626–10

Data coverage and availability of Census Bur rpts and data files, 1989 annual listing, 2304–2

Employment and Earnings, detailed data, monthly rpt, 6742–2

Employment change by industry div, alternative estimates, 1982-1989, article, 6722–1.938

Employment, unemployment, and labor force characteristics, by region, State, and selected metro area, 1988, annual rpt, 6744–7

Farm population, by employment and socioeconomic characteristics, and region, 1988, annual rpt, 2546–1.439

Labor force characteristics, press release series, 6726–1

Population and housing data, and policy issues, fact sheet series, 2326–17

Population demographic, social, and economic characteristics, series, 2546–1

Population demographic subjects, special study series, 2546–2

Population estimates and projections, by region and State, series, 2546–3

Population estimates for civilian, resident, and total population, monthly rpt, 2542–1

Population size of counties, 1988, and components of change from 1980, annual rpt, 2544–3

Smoking rates, by sex, age, race, occupation, region, and State, 1985 CPS, article, 4472–1.910

Unemployment, by State and metro area, monthly press release, 6742–12

Curricula

Condition of Education, detailed data on elementary, secondary, and higher education, 1920s-88 and projected to 1997, annual rpt, 4824–1

Digest of Education Statistics, detailed data on students, staff, finances, and facilities, 1989 edition, annual rpt, 4824–2

High school class of 1972: education, employment, and family characteristics, activities, and attitudes, natl longitudinal study, series, 4836–1

High school classes of 1980 and 1982: education, employment, and family characteristics, activities, and attitudes, natl longitudinal study, series, 4826–2

Statistical Abstract of US, social, political, and economic data, 1790-2025, comprehensive annual compilation, 2324–1.1

see also Agricultural education
see also Area studies
see also Arts and the humanities
see also Astronomy
see also Biological sciences
see also Business education
see also Chemistry
see also Earth sciences
see also Economics
see also Educational reform
see also Environmental sciences
see also Foreign languages
see also Geography
see also Health education
see also History
see also Home economics
see also Information sciences
see also Journalism
see also Language arts
see also Legal education
see also Mathematics
see also Medical education
see also Military education
see also Physical education and training
see also Physical sciences
see also Physics
see also Political science
see also Psychology
see also Scientific education
see also Sex education
see also Social sciences
see also Social work
see also Sociology
see also Teacher education

Curry, Timothy J.

"Who Are the Good Asset Managers?", 8432–2.901

Customs administration

Court of Intl Trade caseloads, decisions, and appeals, FY88-89, annual rpt, 18224–2

Criminal cases by type and disposition, and collections, for US attorneys, by Federal district, FY88, annual rpt, 6004–2.1

Customs Service activities, collections, entries processed by mode of transport, and seizures, FY84-88, annual rpt, 8144–1

Customs Service imports inspection, automated selection system operations, FY88-1st qtr FY89, GAO rpt, 26125–35

Duties on US imports under antidumping and countervailing orders, and duty assessment and reporting errors, 1987-88, GAO rpt, 26119–270

FDA detention of imports, by reason, product, shipper, brand, and country, monthly listing, 4062–2

FDA investigations and regulatory activities, quarterly rpt, 4062–3

Feed grain inspected for export, current and proposed quality standards, 1989 article, 1561–4.904

Grain inspected for domestic use and export, foreign buyers complaints, and handling facilities explosions, FY88, annual rpt, 1294–1

Grain inspected for export, test results by commodity and port region, 1988, annual rpt, 1294–2

Grain shipments, rail loadings, export sales and inspections, prices, and ocean freight rates, weekly rpt, 1272–2

Housewares (ceramic) lead and cadmium levels, FDA import inspection activity by country, and food safety funding and staff, 1983-88, hearing, 21368–108

Meat and poultry inspection activities and staff of Federal, State, and foreign govts, FY88, annual rpt, 1374–1

Meat and poultry inspection for domestic use and export, and rejections by cause, by type of animal and product, FY88, annual rpt, 1374–3

Meat plants inspected and certified for exporting to US, by country, 1988, annual listing, 1374–2

Plant pests and diseases entering US, by type of pest and host, country, and State, FY87, annual rpt, 1394–16

Soybeans inspected for export, current and proposed quality standards, 1989 article, 1561–3.903

Tea imports inspected by FDA, by type and country, 1983-88, FAS annual circular, 1925–15.3

Tobacco leaf stocks, production, sales, and import inspections by country, by product, quarterly rpt, 1319–3

see also Smuggling

Customs duties

see Tariffs and foreign trade controls

Customs Service

see U.S. Customs Service

Cutcher-Gershenfeld, Joel

"Institutionalizing and Diffusing Innovations in Industrial Relations", 6306–3.1

Cutlery

see Household supplies and utensils

Cyclones

see Storms

Cypress, Beulah K.

"National Ambulatory Medical Care Survey of Visits to General and Family Practitioners, January-December 1975", 4147–16.2

"Office Visits to Internists: National Ambulatory Medical Care Survey, U.S., 1975", 4147–16.2

Cyprus

Agricultural and food production and indexes, total and for selected commodities, by country, 1970s-88, annual rpt, 1524–12

Agricultural trade of US, by detailed commodity and country, 1988, semiannual rpt, 1522–4

AID activities and funding by project and function, FY90, and developing countries summary socioeconomic data from 1960s, annual rpt, 9904–4.6

AID loans repayment status and terms by program and country, and status of predecessor agency loans, quarterly rpt, 9912–3

Economic and military aid and loans from US and intl agencies, by program and country, FY46-87, annual rpt, 9914–5

Economic conditions, income, production, prices, employment, and trade, 1989 periodic country rpt, 2046–4.113

Economic conditions, policy, and trade practices, by country, 1986-88, annual rpt, 21384–5

Economic, social, political, and geographic summary data, by country, 1989, annual factbook, 9114–2

Human rights conditions in 170 countries, 1988, annual rpt, 21384–3

Military aid of US, arms sales, and training programs costs and budget requests, by program, world region, and country, FY88-90, annual rpt, 7144–13

Military spending, arms trade, and force strengths, with govt spending and population, by country, 1977-87, annual rpt, 9824–1

Minerals Yearbook, 1987, Vol 3: foreign country reviews of production, trade, and policy, by commodity, annual rpt, 5604–35

Minerals Yearbook, 1987, Vol 3 preprints: foreign country review of production, trade, and policy, by commodity, annual rpt, 5604–23.18

Population size, growth rates, and components of change, by country, projected 1989-2020 and trends from 1950, biennial rpt, 2324–9

Ships in world merchant fleet, and tonnage, by country of registry, as of Jan 1988, annual rpt, 7704–3

UN voting record and share of votes in agreement with US, by issue, country, and world area, 1988, annual rpt, 7004–18

see also under By Foreign Country in the "Index by Categories"

Czajka, John L.
"Evaluation of the Feasibility of a Substate Area Extended Benefit Program: Final Report", 6406–6.28

Czechoslovakia

Agricultural and food production and indexes, total and for selected commodities, by country, 1970s-88, annual rpt, 1524–12

Agricultural production, acreage, and consumption, by Eastern Europe country and commodity, 1965-85, 1528–284

Agricultural production, consumption, and trade, for Eastern Europe by country, 1970s-88, annual rpt, 1524–11

Agricultural trade of US, by detailed commodity and country, 1988, semiannual rpt, 1522–4

Cuba economic conditions, agricultural and industrial production and distribution, trade, and intl economic relations, 1980-87 with trends from 1961, 9118–8

Debt, trade, and balances of Eastern Europe and USSR with US and other western countries, with background data, 1980s-87, hearing, 21248–120

Economic and military aid and loans from US and intl agencies, by program and country, FY46-87, annual rpt, 9914–5

Economic conditions in Communist, OECD, and selected other countries, 1960s-88, annual rpt, 9114–4

Economic conditions, income, production, prices, employment, and trade, 1989 periodic country rpt, 2046–4.41

Economic conditions, policy, and trade practices, by country, 1986-88, annual rpt, 21384–5

Economic, social, political, and geographic summary data, by country, 1989, annual factbook, 9114–2

Export licensing, monitoring, and enforcement activities, FY88, annual rpt, 2024–1

Exports and imports of US, by selected country, country group, and commodity group, 1988, annual rpt, 2044–37

Exports and imports of US with Communist countries, by detailed commodity and country, quarterly rpt with articles, 9882–2

Human rights conditions in 170 countries, 1988, annual rpt, 21384–3

Military spending, arms trade, and force strengths, with govt spending and population, by country, 1977-87, annual rpt, 9824–1

Military strength of USSR and Warsaw Pact, and proposed force reductions, with comparisons to NATO, 1980s-91, hearing, 21208–29

Minerals Yearbook, 1987, Vol 3: foreign country reviews of production, trade, and policy, by commodity, annual rpt, 5604–35

Minerals Yearbook, 1987, Vol 3 preprints: foreign country review of production, trade, and policy, by commodity, annual rpt, 5604–23.19

Nuclear power plant capacity and operating status, by plant and Communist country, as of Dec 1988, annual rpt, 3164–57.2

Population size, growth rates, and components of change, by country, projected 1989-2020 and trends from 1950, biennial rpt, 2324–9

Refugee resettlement programs and funding, arrivals by country of origin, and indicators of adjustment, by State, FY88, annual rpt, 4694–5

Space satellites and other objects launched since 1957, quarterly listing, 9502–2

Steel export ceilings under voluntary restraint agreements, by country and product, with Western US steel industry impact, 1989 rpt, 9886–4.136

Steel imports of US under voluntary restraint agreement, by product, customs district, and country, with US industry operating data, monthly rpt, 9882–13

UN voting record and share of votes in agreement with US, by issue, country, and world area, 1988, annual rpt, 7004–18

see also under By Foreign Country in the "Index by Categories"

Daberkow, Stan G.
"Common Crop Rotations Among Major Field Crops", 1561–16.903
"Outlook for Farm Inputs", 1004–16.1

Daft, Lynn M.
"Farm Policy Challenges Facing the Next Administration", 1004–16.1

Dahl, Carol
"Dynamic Comparison of an Oil Tariff, a Producer Subsidy, and a Gasoline Tax", 9379–12.44

Dahomey
see Benin

Dairy industry and products
Acreage under Agricultural Stabilization and Conservation Service programs, rankings by commodity and congressional district, 1987, biennial rpt, 1804–17

Agricultural data compilation, 1987/88 and trends from 1920, annual rpt, 1004–14

Agricultural exports of US, impacts of foreign agricultural and trade policy, with data by commodity and country, 1988, annual rpt, 1924–8

Agricultural Stabilization and Conservation Service dairy programs, 1949-1988/89, annual fact sheet, 1806–4.1

Agricultural Stabilization and Conservation Service producer payments, by program and State, 1988, annual rpt, 1804–12

Agricultural Stabilization and Conservation Service producer payments, by program, monthly rpt, 1802–10

Agricultural Statistics, 1988, annual rpt, 1004–1

Agriculture census, 1987: farms, farmland, production, finances, and operator characteristics, by county, final State rpt series, 2331–1

Business statistics, detailed data for major industries and economic indicators, *Survey of Current Business*, monthly rpt, 2702–1.11

Cattle and calves for beef and milk, by State, as of July 1989, semiannual press release, 1623–1

Cattle, milk production, and grain and other concentrates fed, by State, monthly rpt, 1627–1

CCC dairy price support purchases, sales, donations, and inventories, monthly rpt, 1802–2

China trade by SITC 1- to 5-digit commodity, 1970s-87, annual rpt, 9114–3

Chocolate imports and milk content, FY80-89, GAO rpt, 26113–427

Cold storage food stocks by commodity and census div, and warehouse space use, by State, monthly rpt, 1631–5

Cold storage food stocks, by commodity and census div, 1988, annual rpt, 1631–11

Communist countries agricultural, mineral, and consumer and producer goods production, by commodity, 1960s-88, annual rpt, 9114–4.4

Consumer Expenditure Survey, household income by source, and itemized spending, by selected characteristics and location, 1984-86, annual rpt, 6764–5.2

Consumption of food and nutrient intake by individuals, by food group, selected characteristics, and region, supplementary survey series, 1356–5

Consumption, supply, trade, prices, spending, and indexes, by food commodity, 1987, annual rpt, 1544–4

Cooperatives commercial member characteristics, and use of services, by region, 1980 and 1986, 1128–53

Cooperatives member characteristics, and use of services, by region, 1980 and 1986, 1128–54

County Business Patterns, 1987: employment, establishments, and payroll, by SIC 2- to 4-digit industry and county, annual State rpt series, 2326–8

CPI by component for US city average, and by region, population size, and for 27 metro areas, monthly rpt, 6762–2

Cuba economic conditions, agricultural and industrial production and distribution, trade, and intl economic relations, 1980-87 with trends from 1961, 9118–8

Developing countries food production and needs, and related economic outlook, by country, 1989/90, annual rpt, 1524–6

Eastern Europe agricultural production, consumption, and trade, by country, 1970s-88, annual rpt, 1524–11

Eastern Europe and USSR agricultural production, acreage, and consumption, by commodity and country, 1965-85, 1528–284

Wholesale trade census, 1987: employment, establishments, finances, and operations, by SIC 2- to 4-digit kind of business, MSA, county, and city, State rpt series, 2405-1

see also under By Commodity in the "Index by Categories"

Daley, Judy R.
"Profiles in Safety and Health: Work Hazards of Mobile Homes", 6722-1.932

Dallas County, Tex.
Housing and households detailed characteristics, and unit and neighborhood quality, by location, 1985 survey, MSA rpt, 2485-6.12

Dallas, Tex.
CPI by component for US city average, and by region, population size, and for 15 metro areas, monthly rpt, 6762-1

CPI by component for US city average, and by region, population size, and for 27 metro areas, monthly rpt, 6762-2

CPI by major component for 2 Texas MSAs, monthly rpt, 6962-2

Drug test results at arrest, by drug type, offense, and sex, for selected urban areas, quarterly rpt, 6062-3

Employment, earnings, hours, and CPI changes, for Dallas-Fort Worth metro area, 1970s-88, annual rpt, 6964-2

Fruit and vegetable shipments, and arrivals in US and Canada cities, by mode of transport and State and country of origin, 1988, annual rpt, 1311-4.2

Housing and households characteristics, 1985 survey, MSA fact sheet, 2485-11.14

Housing and households detailed characteristics, and unit and neighborhood quality, by location, 1985 survey, MSA rpt, 2485-6.12

Housing starts and completions authorized by building permits in 40 MSAs, quarterly rpt, 2382-9

Wages by occupation, for office and plant workers, 1988 survey, periodic MSA rpt, 6785-11.3

see also under By City and By SMSA or MSA in the "Index by Categories"

Dams
Army Corps of Engineers activities and projects, FY87 and trends from 1800s, annual rpt, 3754-1.2

Army Corps of Engineers water resources dev projects, characteristics, and costs, 1950s-87, biennial State rpt series, 3756-2

Army Corps of Engineers water resources dev projects, characteristics, and costs, 1950s-89, biennial State rpt series, 3756-1

Hydroelectric power plants capacity, dev status, and ownership, by State and river basin, as of Jan 1988, quadrennial rpt, 3088-14

Indiana water supply, annual high and low levels by lake, 1940s-85, 5668-89

Ohio River basin waterway facilities, freight by commodity and port, and recreation, by waterway, 1986-87, annual rpt, 3754-6

Reclamation Bur water storage and carriage facilities, capacity, and operating status, as of Sept 1988, biennial listing, 5824-7

Tennessee Valley river control activities, and hydroelectric power generation and capacity, 1984, annual rpt, 9804-7

TVA financial and operating data by program and facility, FY88, annual rpt, 9804-32

see also Reservoirs

Danbury, Conn.
Wages by occupation, for office and plant workers, 1989 survey, periodic MSA rpt, 6785-12.6

see also under By SMSA or MSA in the "Index by Categories"

Dance
County Business Patterns, 1987: employment, establishments, and payroll, by SIC 2- to 4-digit industry and county, annual State rpt series, 2326-8

Injuries from use of consumer products and related activities, by victim age and sex, 1988, annual rpt, 9164-7

Injuries from use of consumer products, by severity, victim age, and detailed product, 1988, annual rpt, 9164-6

Natl Endowment for Arts activities and grants, FY88, annual rpt, 9564-3

Service industries census, 1987: establishments, receipts, employment, and payroll, by SIC 2- to 4-digit kind of business, MSA, county, and city, State rpt series, 2391-1

Danville, Va.
see also under By SMSA or MSA in the "Index by Categories"

Data processing
see Computer industry and products
see Computer networks
see Computer sciences
see Computer use
see Information storage and retrieval systems

Data Resources, Inc.
"Simulation of the Macroeconomic Effects of the Balanced Budget Amendment", 21528-72

Dates
see Chronologies

Daugherty, Arthur B.
"U.S. Grazing Lands: 1950-82", 1588-130

Davenport, Edgar L.
"Pulpwood Prices in the Southeast, 1987", 1204-22

Davenport, Iowa
Wages by occupation, and benefits for office and plant workers, 1989 survey, periodic MSA rpt, 6785-12.3

see also under By SMSA or MSA in the "Index by Categories"

David, Martin H.
"Database Design for Large-Scale, Complex Data", 2626-10.103

Davidson, Donald R.
"Top 100 Cooperatives, 1987 Financial Profile", 1124-3

Davies, Katherine
"Concentrations and Dietary Intake of Selected Organochlorides, Including PCBs, PCDDs and PCDFs in Fresh Food Composites Grown in Ontario, Canada", 21368-112

Davila, Natalie A.
"Unemployment Insurance: A State Economic Development Perspective", 9375-13.9

"Unemployment Insurance and Regional Economic Development", 9375-1.902

Davis, Lester A.
"Contribution of Exports to U.S. Employment, 1980-87", 2048-103

Davis, Sally M.
"Improving the Health of Indian Teenagers: A Demonstration Program in Rural New Mexico", 4042-3.924

Davis, Stacy C.
"Transportation Energy Data Book: Edition 10", 3304-5

Davis, William M.
"Collective Bargaining in 1989: Negotiators Will Face Diverse Issues", 6722-1.902

"Major Collective Bargaining Settlements in Private Industry in 1988", 6722-1.923

Davison, Cecil W.
"Box-Cox Estimation of U.S. Soybean Exports", 1502-3.903

"Changes in Food Demand", 1522-3.911

"Soybeans: Background for 1990 Farm Legislation", 1566-7.1

DAWN
see Drug Abuse Warning Network

Dawson, Deborah A.
"AIDS Knowledge and Attitudes of Black Americans. Provisional Data from the 1988 National Health Interview Survey", 4146-8.167

"AIDS Knowledge and Attitudes of Hispanic Americans. Provisional Data from the 1988 National Health Interview Survey", 4146-8.168

"AIDS Knowledge and Attitudes. Provisional Data from the National Health Interview Survey", 4146-8.169; 4146-8.173; 4146-8.176

Day, Anne L.
"New Dynamics of Produce Marketing", 1004-16.1

Day care programs
see Adult day care
see Child day care

Day, John C.
"Soil and Water Management in West Africa: An Economic Analysis", 1528-289

Daylight hours
see Time of day

Dayton, Mark R.
"Status of the Airport and Airway Trust Fund", 26308-84

Dayton, Ohio
Wages by occupation, for office and plant workers, 1988 survey, periodic MSA rpt, 6785-3.1

see also under By City and By SMSA or MSA in the "Index by Categories"

Daytona Beach, Fla.
Wages by occupation, for office and plant workers, 1989 survey, periodic MSA rpt, 6785-3.10

see also under By SMSA or MSA in the "Index by Categories"

D.C.
Bank deposits in FDIC-insured commercial and savings banks, by instn, State, and county, as of June 1988, annual regional rpt, 9295-3.2

Banks (insured commercial), Fed Reserve 5th District members financial statements, by State, quarterly rpt, 9389-18

Budget of US Appendix, obligations, appropriations, and personnel, by program and agency, FY90, annual rpt, 104-3

Budget of US, authoritative financial statements with appropriations, outlays, and receipts, by category and agency, FY88, annual rpt, 8104–2.2

Congressional Directory, members of 101st Congress, other officials, elections, and districts, 1989-90, biennial rpt, 23874–1

County Business Patterns, 1987: employment, establishments, and payroll, by SIC 2- to 4-digit industry and county, annual State rpt, 2326–8.10

CPI by component for US city average, and by region, population size, and for 15 metro areas, monthly rpt, 6762–1

CPI by component for US city average, and by region, population size, and for 27 metro areas, monthly rpt, 6762–2

Deaths and rates, by detailed location, cause, and demographic characteristics, 1987, US Vital Statistics annual rpt, 4144–3.1

Diplomats and staff with immunity for foreign missions in US and US missions abroad, and foreign diplomats criminal cases, 1978-87, hearing, 25388–51

DOD civilian and military employment in DC metro area, FY88, and in Pentagon from 1945, annual rpt, 3544–1.1

DOD prime contract awards, by contractor, service branch, State, and city, FY88, annual rpt, 3544–22

Drug abuse, deaths, arrests, convictions, and seizures by drug type, for DC metro area, 1980-87, hearing, 21308–24

Drug abuse indicators for selected metro areas, research results, data collection, and policy issues, 1989 semiannual conf, 4492–5

Drug test results at arrest, by drug type, offense, and sex, for selected urban areas, quarterly rpt, 6062–3

Economic indicators by State, Fed Reserve 5th District, quarterly rpt, 9389–16

Education funding by Federal agency, program, and recipient type, and instn spending, FY80-88, 4828–21

Emergency fire and medical services operations, staff, and finances, for DC and compared to other US and Canadian cities, 1986, hearing, 21308–25

Employment and housing market indicators by State, FHLB 4th District, quarterly rpt, 9302–36

Employment, earnings, and hours, by selected SIC 1- to 4-digit industry, State, and for 262 MSAs, 1972-87, 6748–81.1

Fed Govt civilian employment and payroll, by agency in DC metro area, total US, and abroad, bimonthly rpt, 9842–1

Fed Govt civilian employment and payroll, by occupation, pay grade, sex, agency, and location, 1987, biennial rpt, 9844–4

Fed Govt civilian employment and payroll, by pay system, agency, and location, 1988, annual rpt, 9844–6

Fed Govt civilian employment by occupation, agency, and location, and language and math skill needs, 1966-87 and projected to 2000, 9848–37

Fed Govt land acquisition and dev projects in DC metro area, characteristics and funding by agency and project, FY90-94, annual rpt, 15454–1

Fed Govt spending in States and local areas, by type, State, county, and city, FY88, annual rpt, 2464–3

Fed Govt spending in States, by type, program, agency, and State, FY88, annual rpt, 2464–2

Fruit and vegetable shipments, and arrivals in US and Canada cities, by mode of transport and State and country of origin, 1988, annual rpt, 1311–4.1

HHS financial aid, by program, recipient, State, and city, FY88, annual regional listing, 4004–3.3

Homeless children educational enrollment and needs, 1988, annual State rpt, 4804–35.10

Housing and households characteristics, 1985 survey, MSA fact sheet, 2485–11.6

Housing and households detailed characteristics, and unit and neighborhood quality, by location, 1985 survey, MSA rpt, 2485–6.4

Housing starts and completions authorized by building permits in 40 MSAs, quarterly rpt, 2382–9

Income (personal) per capita and by source, and earnings by industry div, by State, MSA, and county, 1982-87, annual regional rpt, 2704–2.2

Labor unions recognized in Fed Govt, agreements and membership for DC govt employees, Jan 1989, biennial listing, 9844–14

Police pay, benefits, and staffing, for US Park Police and compared to other Federal and local police units, FY85-88, GAO rpt, 26119–264

Retail trade census, 1987: employment, establishments, sales, and payroll, by SIC 2- to 4-digit kind of business, MSA, county, and city, State rpt, 2397–1.9

Savings instns, FHLB 4th District members finances and financial ratios, by State, quarterly rpt, 9302–3

Savings instns, FHLB 4th District members finances, by State, 1984-88, annual rpt, 9304–29.2

Service industries census, 1987: employment, establishments, receipts, and payroll, by SIC 2- to 4-digit kind of business, MSA, county, and city, State rpt, 2391–1.9

Statistical Abstract of US, social, political, and economic data, with foreign comparisons, 1790-2025, comprehensive annual compilation, 2324–1

Wages by occupation, for office and plant workers, 1989 survey, periodic MSA rpt, 6785–12.2

Wholesale trade census, 1987: employment, establishments, finances, and operations, by SIC 2- to 4-digit kind of business, MSA, county, and city, State rpt, 2405–1.9

Workers compensation programs under Federal admin, finances and operations, FY87, annual rpt, 6504–10

see also D.C. courts

see also under By City, By SMSA or MSA, and By State in the "Index by Categories"

D.C. courts

Caseloads (civil and criminal) for Federal district, appeals, and bankruptcy courts, by offense, circuit, and district, quarterly rpt, 18202–1

Caseloads (civil and criminal) for Federal district, appeals, and special courts, June 1989, annual rpt, 18204–2; 18204–8

de Janvry, Alain

"Foreign Aid's Effect on U.S. Farm Exports: Benefits or Penalties?", 1528–291

de Leeuw, Frank

"Leading Indicators and the 'Prime Mover' View", 2702–1.926

Deaf

Children (handicapped) enrollment by age, and special education programs staff, funding, and needs, by type of handicap and State, 1987/88, annual rpt, 4944–4

Educational enrollment of disabled in postsecondary instns, by disability, educational, and other characteristics, fall 1986, 4846–3.6

Head Start handicapped enrollment, by handicap, State, and for Indian and migrant programs, 1985/86, annual rpt, 4604–1

Dean, Edwin

"Alternative Measures of Capital Inputs in Japanese Manufacturing", 6886–6.58

DeAre, Diana

"Rural and Rural Farm Population: 1988", 2546–1.439

Death penalty

see Capital punishment

Deaths

AFDC recipients demographic and financial characteristics, by State, FY87, annual rpt, 4694–1

Agent Orange exposure of Air Force personnel, deaths and rates by cause and selected characteristics, 1989 annual rpt, 3604–3

AIDS deaths and rates, by age group, monthly rpt, 4202–9

AIDS deaths, by health and other characteristics, 1986, 4146–8.178

Alcohol use and abuse among minority groups, and related problems, by selected characteristics, 1985 conf papers, 4488–13

Army active duty personnel health condition, and use of Army medical services in US and abroad, monthly rpt, 3702–4.2

Cancer (breast and cervical) incidence, deaths, and survival rates, by race, average 1973-81, article, 4042–3.952

Cancer (lung) incidence and death rates, by age, sex, and race, various periods 1950-86, article, 4472–1.926

Cancer dev and death risk, and death risk from other causes, relation to cholesterol levels, by sex, 1963-84 study, article, 4472–1.936

Cancer incidence, death, and survival rates, by sex, race, age, and body site, 1973-86, annual rpt, 4474–35

Cirrhosis of liver deaths, by age, sex, race, and whether alcohol involved, 1986 and trends from 1910, 4486–1.4; 4486–1.7

Deaths and rates, by cause, age, sex, marital status, race, and State, 1987, US Vital Statistics advance annual rpt, 4146–5.113

Deaths and rates, by cause, age, sex, race, and State, preliminary 1987-88 and trends from 1960, US Vital Statistics annual rpt, 4144–7

Deaths and rates, by detailed cause and demographic characteristics, 1986 and trends from 1900, US Vital Statistics annual rpt, 4144–2

Veterans disability and death compensation cases of VA, by entitlement type, period of service, and sex, as of Mar 1989, semiannual rpt, 8602–8

Veterans disability and death compensation cases of VA, by entitlement type, period of service, sex, age, and State, FY88, annual rpt, 8604–7

Veterans disability by type, and deaths, by period of service, and VA activities, FY88, annual rpt, 8604–3.6

Vital and Health Statistics series: reprints of monthly rpt supplements, 4147–24

Vital statistics provisional data, monthly rpt, 4142–1

see also Accidental deaths
see also Autopsies
see also Capital punishment
see also Cemeteries and funerals
see also Child mortality
see also Drowning
see also Fetal deaths
see also Homicide
see also Infant mortality
see also Poisoning and drug reaction
see also Suicide
see also Traffic accident fatalities
see also War casualties

DeBraal, J. Peter
"Foreign Investment in U.S. Cropland: Some Evidence on the Role of Exchange Rates, Interest Rates, and Returns on Cropland", 1528–287
"Foreign Ownership of U.S. Agricultural Land Through Dec. 31, 1988", 1584–2
"Foreign Ownership of U.S. Agricultural Land Through Dec. 31, 1988: County-Level Data", 1584–3

Debt
see Agricultural credit
see Business assets and liabilities, general
see Business assets and liabilities, specific industry
see Commercial credit
see Consumer credit
see Credit
see Credit bureaus and agencies
see Foreign debts
see Government assets and liabilities
see Government securities
see Loans
see Mortgages
see Municipal bonds
see Personal debt
see Public debt
see U.S. savings bonds

DeByle, Norbert V.
"Forage Quality in Burned and Unburned Aspen Communities", 1208–309

Decatur, Ala.
see also under By SMSA or MSA in the "Index by Categories"

Decatur, Ill.
see also under By SMSA or MSA in the "Index by Categories"

Decontrol of prices
see Price regulation

DeCosse, Jerome J.
"Effect of Wheat Fiber and Vitamins C and E on Rectal Polyps in Patients with Familial Adenomatous Polyposis", 4472–1.921

Default
see Bankruptcy
see Loan delinquency and default

Defective products
Aircraft accidents, casualties, and damage, for commercial operations by detailed circumstances, 1986, annual rpt, 9614–2

Aircraft accidents in general aviation, by circumstances, characteristics of persons and aircraft involved, and type of flying, 1986, annual rpt, 9614–3

Auto and auto equipment recalls for safety-related defects, by make, quarterly listing, 7762–2

Auto sudden acceleration incidents involving Audi 5000 and selected other models, investigation results, 1986-88, 7768–107

Consumer Product Safety Commission activities, recalls by brand, and casualties and societal costs, by product type, FY87, annual rpt, 9164–2

Health care devices malfunction, injury, and death reports to FDA, and inspection findings and disposition, 1985-87, GAO rpt, 26131–57

Imports detained by FDA, by reason, product, shipper, brand, and country, monthly listing, 4062–2

Defense
see Civil defense
see Department of Defense
see National defense

Defense agencies
Base construction, renovation, and land acquisition, DOD budget requests by project, service branch, State, and country, FY90/91, annual rpt, 3544–15

Budget of DOD, manpower needs, costs, and force readiness by service branch, FY90, annual rpt, 3504–1

Budget of DOD, procurement appropriations by item, service branch, and defense agency, FY88-91, annual rpt, 3544–32

Budget of DOD, R&D appropriations by item, service branch, and defense agency, FY88-91, annual rpt, 3544–33

Commercial activities of DOD performed in-house, and work-years, by service branch, installation, and State, FY88, annual rpt, 3544–25

Employment (civilian and military) of DOD, by service branch and defense agency, quarterly rpt, 3542–14.1

Expenditures and obligations of DOD, by function and service branch, quarterly rpt, 3542–3

NATO Europe members presence of US military and civilian personnel and dependents, by service branch, 1980-88, GAO rpt, 26123–252

Property, supply, and equipment inventory of DOD, by service branch, 1988, annual rpt, 3544–6

see also Defense Communications Agency
see also Defense Contract Audit Agency
see also Defense Fuel Supply Center
see also Defense Intelligence Agency
see also Defense Investigative Service
see also Defense Logistics Agency
see also Defense Mapping Agency
see also Defense Nuclear Agency
see also Defense Security Assistance Agency
see also National Defense University

Defense budgets and appropriations
Air Force fiscal mgmt system operations and techniques, quarterly rpt, 3602–1

Air Force supply inventory stock fund balances, refunds to customers, and procurement cost effects of reducing balances, FY84-88, GAO rpt, 26111–60

Army Dept activities, manpower, logistics, R&D, and budget, FY86, annual rpt, 3704–11

Army strategic capability, force strengths, budget, and mgmt, FY80-89, annual rpt, 3704–13

Base construction, renovation, and land acquisition, DOD budget requests by project, service branch, State, and country, FY90/91, annual rpt, 3544–15

Budget deficit reduction under Gramm-Rudman Act, cancellation of budget authority by program, FY90, annual rpt, 104–27; 26304–6

Budget of DOD, justification, programs, and policies, FY90-91, annual rpt, 3544–2

Budget of DOD, manpower and spending under alternative spending growth rates, FY89-94, 26306–3.107

Budget of DOD, organization, personnel, weapons, and property, by service branch, State, and country, 1989 annual summary rpt, 3504–13

Budget of DOD, summary justification, plans, and funding requests, FY90-91, annual rpt, 3544–30

Budget of US Appendix, obligations, appropriations, and personnel, by program and agency, FY90, annual rpt, 104–3

Budget of US, authoritative financial statements with appropriations, outlays, and receipts, by category and agency, FY88, annual rpt, 8104–2.2

Budget of US, balances of budget authority obligated and unobligated, by function and agency, FY88-90, annual rpt, 104–8

Budget of US, Bush Admin policy changes by program, FY90, 028–32

Budget of US, CBO analysis and review of FY90 budget by function, annual rpt, 26304–2

Budget of US, CBO analysis of revenue and spending alternatives and projections of economic indicators, FY90-94, annual rpt, 26304–3

Budget of US, compact budgets by activity, function, and agency, FY90 and projected to FY94, annual rpt, 104–2

Budget of US, historical data, selected years FY34-88 and projected to FY94, annual rpt, 104–22

Budget of US, House concurrent resolution, with spending and revenue targets, FY90, annual rpt, 21264–2

Budget of US, midsession review of FY90 budget, by function and agency, annual rpt, 104–7

Budget of US, object class analysis of obligations, by agency, FY90, annual rpt, 104–9

Budget of US, overview, FY90, annual rpt, 104–6

Budget of US, Reagan Admin policy changes by program, FY90, annual rpt, 104–21

Budget of US, receipts by source, outlays by agency and program, and balances, monthly rpt, 8102–3

Budget of US, Senate concurrent resolution, with spending and revenue targets, FY90, annual rpt, 25254-1

Civilian Health and Medical Program of Uniformed Services benefits and costs, FY83-89, 3508-31

Employment (civilian) of DOD, voluntary early retirement program costs and savings, FY88, GAO rpt, 26119-253

Foreign countries military aid of US, arms sales, and training programs costs and budget requests, by program, world region, and country, FY88-90, annual rpt, 7144-13

Foreign countries military aid proposed budget, by program, FY89, 26123-30

Manpower needs, costs, and force readiness, by service branch, FY90, annual rpt, 3504-1

Natl Guard (Army and Air) activities, manpower, and facilities, FY88, annual rpt, 3504-22

Navy budget, manpower, procurement, and equipment, planned FY89-91, annual fact sheet, 3804-16

Procurement appropriations, by item, service branch, and defense agency, FY88-91, annual rpt, 3544-32

R&D funding by item, service branch, and defense agency, FY88-91, annual rpt, 3544-33

Reserve forces manpower and equipment strengths, and readiness, by reserve component, FY88, annual rpt, 3544-31

Reserve forces manpower, funding by category, procurement reductions, and needs, by component, FY80-88, GAO rpt, 26123-220

Statistical Abstract of US, social, political, and economic data, 1790-2025, comprehensive annual compilation, 2324-1.2

Strategic Defense Initiative R&D costs, and benefits, under alternative system capabilities, projected FY90-94, 26308-87

Training and education programs of DOD, funding, staff, students, and facilities, by service branch, FY90, annual rpt, 3504-5

Transport of personnel and property, Military Traffic Mgmt Command finances and operations, FY88, annual rpt, 3704-14

Weapons acquisition costs by system and service branch, DOD budget, FY89-91, annual rpt, 3504-2

see also Defense expenditures

Defense Communications Agency

Commercial activities of DOD performed in-house, and work-years, by service branch, installation, and State, FY88, annual rpt, 3544-25

Employment (civilian and military) of DOD, by service branch and defense agency, quarterly rpt, 3542-14.1

Labor unions recognized in Fed Govt, agreements and membership by agency and facility, as of Jan 1989, biennial listing, 9844-14

Defense Contract Audit Agency

Employment (civilian and military) of DOD, by service branch and defense agency, quarterly rpt, 3542-14.1

Labor unions recognized in Fed Govt, agreements and membership by agency and facility, as of Jan 1989, biennial listing, 9844-14

Defense contracts and procurement

Advertising spending of Fed Govt, and subcontracts to small and disadvantaged firms, by agency and medium, FY86, GAO rpt, 26113-428

Aerospace industry sales, orders, backlog, and firms, by product for govt, military, and other customers, 1988, annual Current Industrial Rpt, 2506-12.22

Agricultural Statistics, 1988, annual rpt, 1004-1.2

Air Force B-1B aircraft maintenance problems, and repair contracts, 1985-88 with costs projected to FY94, GAO rpt, 26123-218

Air Force property mgmt, validation of unfilled orders for aircraft spare parts, 1985-87, GAO rpt, 26123-245

Army spare parts procurement in advance of reorder dates, excess costs by item, FY87-88, GAO rpt, 26123-254

Budget of DOD, justification, programs, and policies, FY90-91, annual rpt, 3544-2

Budget of DOD, organization, personnel, weapons, and property, by service branch, State, and country, 1989 annual summary rpt, 3504-13

Budget of DOD, procurement appropriations by item, service branch, and defense agency, FY88-91, annual rpt, 3544-32

Budget of US, authoritative financial statements with appropriations, outlays, and receipts, by category and agency, FY88, annual rpt, 8104-2.2

Budget of US, object class analysis of obligations, by agency, FY90, annual rpt, 104-9

Business Conditions Digest, defense activity indicators, monthly rpt, 2702-3.8

Computer mainframe and related equipment procurement, compatibility, and operating system contracts, for Navy, FY86-89, GAO rpt, 26125-37

Defense Fuel Supply Center procurement, prices, stocks, transport, and other activities and finances, FY88, annual rpt, 3904-8

Expenditures and obligations of DOD, by function and service branch, quarterly rpt, 3542-3

Expenditures of Fed Govt in States and local areas, by type, State, county, and city, FY88, annual rpt, 2464-3

Expenditures of Fed Govt in States, by type, program, agency, and State, FY88, annual rpt, 2464-2

Fraud and abuse in DOD programs, audits and investigations, 1st half FY89, semiannual rpt, 3542-18

Input-output structure of US economy, detailed interindustry transactions for 84 industries, and components of final demand, 1983, annual article, 2702-1.909

Manufacturing high technology use and plans, with data by technology, selected industry, and firm and market characteristics, 1988 survey, 2508-1

Marine Corps amphibious ships, procurement, and costs, projected under alternative proposals, FY90-2000, 26308-90

Minority business funding, by program and Federal agency, FY86-88, annual rpt, 2104-5

Natl Guard (Army and Air) outlays, by function and State, FY88, annual rpt, 3504-22.1

Natl income and product accounts and components, *Survey of Current Business*, monthly rpt, 2702-1.21

Natl income and product accounts govt transactions component estimates, methodology and bibl, 1988 technical rpt, 2706-6.5

Navy budget, manpower, procurement, and equipment, planned FY89-91, annual fact sheet, 3804-16

Navy procurement, by contractor and location, FY88, annual rpt, 3804-13

Navy small and disadvantaged business procurement offices and location, 1988 annual listing, 3804-5

Post exchange operations, and sales by commodity, by facility and location worldwide, FY87, annual rpt, 3504-10

Prime contract awards by category, contractor type, and State, FY86-88, annual rpt, 3544-11

Prime contract awards of DOD, by category, contract and contractor type, and service branch, FY79-88, semiannual rpt, 3542-1

Prime contract awards of DOD, by contractor, service branch, State, and city, FY88, annual rpt, 3544-22

Prime contract awards of DOD, by detailed procurement category, FY85-88, annual rpt, 3544-18

Prime contract awards of DOD, by service branch and State, FY88, semiannual rpt, 3542-5

Prime contract awards of DOD, by size and type of contract, service branch, competitive status, category, and labor standard, FY88, annual rpt, 3544-19

Prime contract awards of DOD, for top 100 contractors, FY88, annual listing, 3544-5

Prime contract awards of DOD in labor surplus areas, by service branch, State, and area, FY88, semiannual rpt, 3542-19

Prime contracts, payroll, and personnel of DOD, by service branch and location, with top 5 contractors and maps, by State and country, FY88, annual rpt, 3544-29

Procurement contract awards of Fed Govt, by State, agency, procurement and contractor type, and for top 100 contractors, quarterly rpt, 102-6

R&D prime contract awards of DOD, for top 500 contractors, FY88, annual listing, 3544-4

R&D prime contract awards of DOD to US and foreign nonprofit instns and govt agencies, by instn and location, FY88, annual listing, 3544-17

Reserve forces manpower and equipment strengths, and readiness, by reserve component, FY88, annual rpt, 3544-31

Reserve forces manpower, funding by category, procurement reductions, and needs, by component, FY80-88, GAO rpt, 26123-220

Rural areas aid from Fed Govt compared to urban areas, by program and degree of urbanization, FY85, periodic rpt, 1598-248

Service contracts of Fed Govt compared with work performed in-house, savings and employment effects by agency, 1978-87, GAO rpt, 26119-238

Small business finances, operations, owner and employee characteristics, and Federal contracts, 1980s-88, annual rpt, 9764-6

Statistical Abstract of US, social, political, and economic data, 1790-2025, comprehensive annual compilation, 2324-1.2

Strategic Defense Initiative R&D costs, and benefits, under alternative system capabilities, projected FY90-94, 26308-87

Subcontract awards by DOD contractors to small and disadvantaged business, by firm and service branch, quarterly rpt, 3542-17

Weapons acquisition costs by system and service branch, DOD budget, FY89-91, annual rpt, 3504-2

Weapons and communications systems cost estimates, by service branch, quarterly summary rpt, 3502-1

Workers compensation programs under Federal admin, finances and operations, FY87, annual rpt, 6504-10

Defense Department
see Department of Defense

Defense expenditures
Air Force fiscal mgmt system operations and techniques, quarterly rpt, 3602-1

Assistance (block and categorical grants) programs for State and local govts, FY89, biennial listing, 10044-8

Base closings, costs and savings, 1970s, 26306-3.104

Budget of US, special analysis of Federal capital spending by category, projected FY89-2005 and trends from FY81, annual rpt, 104-24

Business Conditions Digest, defense activity indicators, monthly rpt, 2702-3.8

Communist and OECD countries economic conditions, 1987, annual rpt, 7144-11

Communist, OECD, and selected other countries economic conditions, 1960s-88, annual rpt, 9114-4.2

Computer programming language (Ada) implementation and use by DOD, costs and technical issues, FY82-89, GAO rpt, 26125-32

Construction spending by Fed Govt, by program and type of structure, FY82-90, annual article, 2042-1.901

Developing countries economic and social conditions from 1960s, and Intl Dev Cooperation Agency and AID activities and funding, FY88-90, annual rpt, 9904-4

Developing countries receiving US economic aid, military spending and imports measures to determine aid eligibility, by country, 1985-86, annual rpt, 9914-1

Economic indicators compounded annual rates of change, 1969-88, annual rpt, 9391-9.2

Energy use and efficiency of Fed Govt, by agency and fuel type, FY88, annual rpt, 3304-22

Expenditures and obligations of DOD, by function and service branch, quarterly rpt, 3542-3

Expenditures of DOD for contracts and payroll, and personnel, by service branch and location, with top 5 contractors and maps, by State and country, FY88, annual rpt, 3544-29

Expenditures of Fed Govt by type, and other finances, selected years 1954-87, annual rpt, 10044-1

Expenditures of Fed Govt in States and local areas, by type, State, county, and city, FY88, annual rpt, 2464-3

Expenditures of Fed Govt in States, by type, program, agency, and State, FY88, annual rpt, 2464-2

Finances of govts, revenues by source and spending by function, natl income and product account, *Survey of Current Business*, monthly rpt, 2702-1.24

Financial consolidated statements of Fed Govt based on business accounting methods, FY87-88, annual rpt, 8104-5

Foreign countries economic, social, political, and geographic summary data, by country, 1989, annual factbook, 9114-2

Foreign countries military spending, arms trade, and force strengths, with govt spending and population, by country, 1977-87, annual rpt, 9824-1

Hazardous waste site remedial action at military installations, activities and funding by site and State, FY88, annual rpt, 3544-36

Income (personal) per capita impacts of Federal and defense spending and taxation, by State, 1950s-87, article, 9391-1.918

Loans and loan guarantees of of Fed Govt, outstanding amounts by agency and program, *Treasury Bulletin*, quarterly rpt, 8002-4.9

Metals (primary) demand relation to consumption patterns and economic, trade, and technological factors, 1960s-82, 5608-159

Metro area employment and manufacturing output growth, relation to labor costs and area economic conditions, 1976-85, working paper, 9375-13.8

Natl Guard (Army and Air) activities, manpower, and facilities, FY88, annual rpt, 3504-22

Natl income and product accounts and components, *Survey of Current Business*, monthly rpt, 2702-1.21

NATO and Japan military spending and indicators of ability to support common defense, by country, 1960s-87, annual rpt, 3544-28

Pacific basin countries military, economic, technological, and trade conditions, 1970s-85, compilation of papers, 3908-4

Pakistan military strengths, spending, weapons systems, and arms imports, with comparisons to India, 1980s-87, hearing, 21388-54

Sealift Military Command shipping operations, finances, and personnel, FY88, annual rpt, 3804-14

Soviet Union economic conditions and military activity, 1960s-86, hearing, 23848-195

Space program funding by NASA and DOD, by category, FY81-89, GAO rpt, 26123-152

Statistical Abstract of US, social, political, and economic data, 1790-2025, comprehensive annual compilation, 2324-1.2

Training and education programs of DOD, funding, staff, students, and facilities, by service branch, FY90, annual rpt, 3504-5

see also Budget of the U.S.
see also Defense budgets and appropriations
see also Defense contracts and procurement
see also Defense research
see also Military pay

Defense Fuel Supply Center
Procurement, prices, stocks, transport, and other activities and finances of DFSC, FY88, annual rpt, 3904-8

Defense industries
Aluminum ingot and mill product defense and total shipments, trade, use, and inventories, monthly Current Industrial Rpt, 2506-10.9

Arms sales of US, foreign conditions on sales and impacts on US industry, with data by industry group and country, 1988 annual rpt, 104-25

Business Conditions Digest, defense activity indicators, monthly rpt, 2702-3.8

Commercial activities of DOD performed in-house, and work-years, by service branch, installation, and State, FY88, annual rpt, 3544-25

Statistical Abstract of US, social, political, and economic data, 1790-2025, comprehensive annual compilation, 2324-1.2

see also Arms trade
see also Defense contracts and procurement

Defense Intelligence Agency
Soviet Union economic conditions under General Secretary Gorbachev, 1988 and trends from 1956, annual rpt, 9114-6

Defense Investigative Service
Employment (civilian and military) of DOD, by service branch and defense agency, quarterly rpt, 3542-14.1

Defense Logistics Agency
Commercial activities of DOD performed in-house, and work-years, by service branch, installation, and State, FY88, annual rpt, 3544-25

Employment (civilian and military) of DOD, by service branch and defense agency, quarterly rpt, 3542-14.1

Fishery products purchases of DLA, by base of destination, weekly regional rpt, 2162-6.5

Labor unions recognized in Fed Govt, agreements and membership by agency and facility, as of Jan 1989, biennial listing, 9844-14

Procurement, DOD prime contract awards by category, contract and contractor type, and service branch, FY79-88, semiannual rpt, 3542-1

Procurement, DOD prime contract awards by contractor, service branch, State, and city, FY88, annual rpt, 3544-22

Procurement, DOD prime contract awards by service branch and State, FY88, semiannual rpt, 3542-5

Procurement, DOD prime contract awards by size and type of contract, service branch, competitive status, category, and labor standard, FY88, annual rpt, 3544-19

Procurement, DOD prime contract awards in labor surplus areas, by service branch, State, and area, FY88, semiannual rpt, 3542-19

Procurement, subcontract awards by DOD contractors to small and disadvantaged business, by firm and service branch, quarterly rpt, 3542-17

Property, supply, and equipment inventory of DOD, by service branch, 1988, annual rpt, 3544–6

Shipments by DOD of military and personal property, passenger traffic, and costs, by service branch and mode of transport, quarterly rpt, 3702–1

Stockpiling of strategic material by Fed Govt, activity, and inventory by commodity, as of Sept 1989, semiannual rpt, 3902–2

Stockpiling of strategic material, inventories, costs, and goals by commodity, as of June 1989, semiannual rpt, 3902–3

see also Defense Fuel Supply Center

Defense Mapping Agency

Commercial activities of DOD performed in-house, and work-years, by service branch, installation, and State, FY88, annual rpt, 3544–25

Employment (civilian and military) of DOD, by service branch and defense agency, quarterly rpt, 3542–14.1

Labor unions recognized in Fed Govt, agreements and membership by agency and facility, as of Jan 1989, biennial listing, 9844–14

Defense Nuclear Agency

Commercial activities of DOD performed in-house, and work-years, by service branch, installation, and State, FY88, annual rpt, 3544–25

Employment (civilian and military) of DOD, by service branch and defense agency, quarterly rpt, 3542–14.1

Labor unions recognized in Fed Govt, agreements and membership by agency and facility, as of Jan 1989, biennial listing, 9844–14

Defense research

Budget of DOD, justification, programs, and policies, FY90-91, annual rpt, 3544–2

Budget of DOD, manpower and spending under alternative spending growth rates, FY89-94, 26306–3.107

Budget of DOD, manpower needs, costs, and force readiness by service branch, FY90, annual rpt, 3504–1

Budget of DOD, organization, personnel, weapons, and property, by service branch, State, and country, 1989 annual summary rpt, 3504–13

Budget of DOD, R&D appropriations by item, service branch, and defense agency, FY88-91, annual rpt, 3544–33

Budget of DOD, weapons acquisition costs by system and service branch, FY89-91, annual rpt, 3504–2

Budget of US, historical data, selected years FY34-88 and projected to FY94, annual rpt, 104–22

Commercial activities of DOD performed in-house, and work-years, by service branch, installation, and State, FY88, annual rpt, 3544–25

Expenditures and obligations of DOD, by function and service branch, quarterly rpt, 3542–3

Expenditures for R&D, and scientists and engineers education and employment, for US and selected foreign countries, 1988, annual rpt, 9624–23

Expenditures for R&D by Fed Govt, by detailed function, program, and agency, FY88-90, annual rpt, 9627–9

Expenditures for R&D by Fed Govt, by field, performer type, agency, and State, FY87-89, annual rpt, 9627–20

Expenditures for R&D by source and field, selected years 1953-89, annual rpt, 9624–18

Foreign countries military aid programs and related activities of US, costs by country and intl agency, FY85-87 and cumulative from FY50, GAO rpt, 26123–30

Manufacturing census, 1987: financial and operating data, for SIC 4-digit industries by product, preliminary rpt, 2491–1.76

Nuclear reactors for domestic use and export by function and operating status, with owner, operating characteristics, and location, 1988 annual listing, 3004–26

Prime contract awards by category, contractor type, and State, FY86-88, annual rpt, 3544–11

Prime contract awards of DOD, by category, contract and contractor type, and service branch, FY79-88, semiannual rpt, 3542–1

Prime contract awards of DOD, by detailed procurement category, FY85-88, annual rpt, 3544–18

Prime contract awards of DOD for R&D, for top 500 contractors, FY88, annual listing, 3544–4

Prime contract awards of DOD for R&D to US and foreign nonprofit instns and govt agencies, by instn and location, FY88, annual listing, 3544–17

Prime contracts, payroll, and personnel of DOD, by service branch and location, with top 5 contractors and maps, by State and country, FY88, annual rpt, 3544–29

Procurement contract awards of Fed Govt, by State, agency, procurement and contractor type, and for top 100 contractors, quarterly rpt, 102–6

Radioactive waste and spent fuel generation, inventory, and disposal, 1960s-88 and projected to 2020, annual rpt, 3364–2

Small business R&D grants of Fed Govt, by program area, agency, and State, FY88, annual rpt, 9764–7

Soviet Union and Warsaw Pact military weapons systems, aid, presence, and force strengths, and compared to US and NATO, 1989 annual rpt, 3504–20

Space program funding by NASA and DOD, by category, FY81-89, GAO rpt, 26123–152

Statistical Abstract of US, social, political, and economic data, 1790-2025, comprehensive annual compilation, 2324–1.2

Superconductivity (high temperature) R&D spending by Federal agency, and US and Japan industry funding and employment, by application, 1981-89, hearing, 25408–100

Weather services activities and funding, by Federal agency, planned FY89-90, annual rpt, 2144–2

see also Military science

see also Strategic Defense Initiative

Defense Security Assistance Agency

Fed Financing Bank loans outstanding, and loan prepayment activity and costs, 1985-88, GAO rpt, 26111–63

Foreign countries military aid of US, arms sales, and training, by country, FY50-88, annual rpt, 3904–3

Foreign Military Sales program loans outstanding, prepayments, delinquency, and refinancing, by country, 1988-89, GAO rpt, 26123–253

Liabilities (contingent) and claims paid by Fed Govt on federally insured and guaranteed contracts with foreign obligors, by country and program, periodic rpt, 8002–12

Deficit Reduction Act

Insurance (life) companies financial and tax impacts of Deficit Reduction Act and proposed reforms, for stock and mutual firms, 1984-88 and projected to FY94, 8008–138

DeFina, Robert H.

"Optimal Response of Monetary Policy to Oil Price Shocks", 9387–8.193

Degrees, educational

see Degrees, higher education

see Educational attainment

see under By Educational Attainment in the "Index by Categories"

Degrees, higher education

AIDS research grants and contracts of NIH, by funding and approval status, and researcher age, experience, and sex, FY86, GAO rpt, 26121–267

Aviation science bachelor degree holders training performance compared to other FAA hires, 1988 technical rpt, 7506–10.54

Condition of Education, detailed data on higher education, 1960s-88, annual rpt, 4824–1.2

Data on education, enrollment, degrees, teachers, and spending, 1974/75-1988/89 and alternative projections to 1999/2000, annual rpt, 4824–4

Degrees awarded, by sex, degree level, and instn level and control, 1986/87-1987/88, annual rpt, 4844–14

Degrees awarded in higher education, by level, 1980s-90, annual press release, 4804–19

Degrees awarded in higher education, by level, 1986/87 and projected 1992/93, annual rpt, 4826–8.2

Digest of Education Statistics, detailed data on students, staff, finances, and facilities, 1989 edition, annual rpt, 4824–2

Earnings relation to completion of college, model description and results, 1989 working paper, 6886–6.65

Employment characteristics of holders of bachelor and masters degrees awarded 1985/86, 1987 survey, series, 4826–3

Engineering PhD awards to US and foreign students, and minority bachelors and masters degree recipients, 1977-87, 9626–2.182

Epidemiologists in State health depts, ratios to population and professional characteristics, 1983, article, 4042–3.914

Fed Govt civilian employees demographic and employment characteristics, as of Sept 1988, article, 9842–1.901

High school class of 1972: education, employment, and family characteristics, activities, and attitudes, natl longitudinal study, series, 4836–1

High school class of 1980: postsecondary enrollment, transfers, part-time attendance, degrees, and dropouts, by selected characteristics, 1980-86, natl longitudinal study, 4826–2.50

High school classes of 1972 and 1980: enrollment in 2-year colleges, credits earned and dropout rate, by student characteristics, as of 1984, 4848-38

High school classes of 1972, 1980, and 1982: educational attainment by selected characteristics, 1976-87, 4848-36

High school classes of 1972, 1980, and 1982: postsecondary enrollment and degrees, by sex, race, and income level, natl longitudinal surveys, 4848-35

Indian education funding of Fed Govt, enrollment, and degrees, late 1960s-FY88, annual rpt, 14874-1

Nuclear engineering enrollment and degrees by instn and State, and women grads plans and employment, 1972-88, 3006-8.8

Nurses (RN) in nursing homes, degrees held by employment status and instn characteristics, 1985, 4147-13.97

Radiation protection and health physics enrollment and degrees granted by instn and State, and women grads plans and employment, 1972-88, 3006-8.9

Science and engineering degrees, by field, level, and sex, 1950-86, 9628-77

Science and engineering education enrollment, degrees, and student aid and sources, with data by field, race, sex, and instn, 1980s-87, 26358-202

Science and engineering employment and earnings, by field and activity, and private and Federal R&D spending, by industry, 1975-88, 9626-6.29

Science and engineering employment and education, and R&D spending, for US and selected foreign countries, 1988, annual rpt, 9624-23.2

Science and engineering employment in Fed Govt, by field, degree level, race, sex, agency, and State, 1987, annual rpt, 9627-5

Science and engineering employment in R&D, earnings at DOE labs and non-DOE facilities, 1989, annual rpt, 3004-9

Science and engineering employment in R&D, earnings by field and educational, employment, and other characteristics, 1989, annual rpt, 3004-1

Science and engineering labor force, Federal and university research funding, and educational data, series, 9626-6

Science and engineering labor supply, R&D funding, and other science indicators, with foreign comparisons, 1960s-89, annual chartbook, 9624-22

Science and engineering PhDs, by field, instn, employment prospects, sex, race, and other characteristics, 1960s-88, 9627-30

Science and engineering PhDs employment and other characteristics, by field and State, 1987, biennial rpt, 9627-18

Science PhD recipients by whether foreign, race, and sex, and instnl support, 1978 and 1987-88, 9626-2.187

Statistical Abstract of US, social, political, and economic data, 1790-2025, comprehensive annual compilation, 2324-1.1

Teachers bachelor degrees, by field and other characteristics, 1985-86, 4838-39

Vocational and academic AA degree and certificate recipients and credits, by field, and student and instn characteristics, 1984, 4848-37

Vocational education aid recipients and sources, and characteristics of programs and students, 1970s-89, series, 4806-3

see also under By Educational Attainment in the "Index by Categories"

Deily, Mary E.

"Enforcement of Pollution Regulations in a Declining Industry", 9377-9.84

"Factor-Adjustment Costs at the Industry Level", 9377-9.83

Delaware

Agriculture census, 1987: farms, farmland, production, finances, and operator characteristics, by county, final State rpt, 2331-1.8

Bank deposits in FDIC-insured commercial and savings banks, by instn, State, and county, as of June 1988, annual regional rpt, 9295-3.2

County Business Patterns, 1987: employment, establishments, and payroll, by SIC 2- to 4-digit industry and county, annual State rpt, 2326-8.9

Deaths and rates, by detailed location, cause, and demographic characteristics, 1987, US Vital Statistics annual rpt, 4144-3.1

DOD prime contract awards, by contractor, service branch, State, and city, FY88, annual rpt, 3544-22

Employment, earnings, and hours, by selected SIC 1- to 4-digit industry, State, and for 262 MSAs, 1972-87, 6748-81.1

Employment growth and unemployment rates, Fed Reserve 3rd District, quarterly rpt, 9387-10

Fed Govt spending in States and local areas, by type, State, county, and city, FY88, annual rpt, 2464-3

Fed Govt spending in States, by type, program, agency, and State, FY88, annual rpt, 2464-2

HHS financial aid, by program, recipient, State, and city, FY88, annual regional listing, 4004-3.3

Homeless children educational enrollment and needs, 1988, annual State rpt, 4804-35.9

Income (personal) per capita and by source, and earnings by industry div, by State, MSA, and county, 1982-87, annual regional rpt, 2704-2.2

Mineral Industry Surveys, State reviews of production, 1988, preliminary annual rpt, 5614-6

Minerals Yearbook, 1987, Vol 2 preprints: State review of production and sales by commodity, and business activity, annual rpt, 5604-16.9

Minerals Yearbook, 1987, Vol 2: State reviews of production, sales, and firms, by commodity, and business activity, annual rpt, 5604-34

Nursing home compliance with Medicare and Medicaid regulations, and patient characteristics, by facility, 1987/88, annual State rpt, 4654-15.8

Retail trade census, 1987: employment, establishments, sales, and payroll, by SIC 2- to 4-digit kind of business, MSA, county, and city, State rpt, 2397-1.8

Service industries census, 1987: employment, establishments, receipts, and payroll, by SIC 2- to 4-digit kind of business, MSA, county, and city, State rpt, 2391-1.8

Statistical Abstract of US, social, political, and economic data, with foreign comparisons, 1790-2025, comprehensive annual compilation, 2324-1

Wages by occupation, and benefits for office and plant workers, 1989 survey, periodic labor market rpt, 6785-3.9

Water supply and quality in streams and lakes, and groundwater levels in wells, by drainage basin, 1987, annual State rpt, 5666-10.19

Wholesale trade census, 1987: employment, establishments, finances, and operations, by SIC 2- to 4-digit kind of business, MSA, county, and city, State rpt, 2405-1.8

Wildlife-related recreation, hunting, and fishing participation and spending, detailed data, 1985 survey, quinquennial State rpt, 5506-6.8

see also Wilmington, Del.

see also under By State in the "Index by Categories"

Delaware County, Pa.

Housing and households detailed characteristics, and unit and neighborhood quality, by location, 1985 survey, MSA rpt, 2485-6.8

Delaware River

Army Corps of Engineers water resources dev projects, characteristics, and costs, 1950s-87, biennial State rpt series, 3756-2

Army Corps of Engineers water resources dev projects, characteristics, and costs, 1950s-89, biennial State rpt series, 3756-1

Freight (waterborne domestic and foreign) by commodity, traffic, and passengers, by port and waterway, 1987, annual rpt, 3754-3.1

Tidal currents, daily time and velocity by station for North America coasts, forecast 1990, annual rpt, 2174-1.2

Water supply and quality in streams and lakes, and groundwater levels in wells, by drainage basin, 1986, annual State rpt series, 5666-23

Water supply and quality in streams and lakes, and groundwater levels in wells, by drainage basin, 1987, annual State rpt series, 5666-10

Water supply and quality in streams and lakes, and groundwater levels in wells, by drainage basin, 1988, annual State rpt series, 5666-16

Water supply in northeastern US, precipitation and stream runoff by station, monthly rpt, 2182-3

Water supply in US and southern Canada, streamflow, surface and groundwater conditions, and reservoir levels, by location, monthly rpt, 5662-3

Delaware River Basin Commission

Budget of US, authoritative financial statements with appropriations, outlays, and receipts, by category and agency, FY88, annual rpt, 8104-2.2

DeLozier, J.
"Ambulatory Care: France, Federal Republic of Germany, and U.S.", 4147–5.5

Delray Beach, Fla.
Wages by occupation, for office and plant workers, 1989 survey, periodic MSA rpt, 6785–3.10
see also under By SMSA or MSA in the "Index by Categories"

Demand deposits
see Checking accounts
see Negotiable orders of withdrawal accounts

Demers, Raymond Y.
"Mortality Among Pulp and Paper Workers", 21368–112

Demirguc-Kunt, Asli
"Modeling Large Commercial-Bank Failures: A Simultaneous-Equation Analysis", 9377–9.77

Democratic Party
Campaign finances, elections, procedures, and Fed Election Commission activities, press release series, 9276–1
Campaign financial activity reported to Fed Election Commission, by type of filer, 1988 natl elections, biennial rpt series, 9276–2
Congressional Directory, members of 101st Congress, other officials, elections, and districts, 1989-90, biennial rpt, 23874–1
Election results impacts of inflation, for Democratic share of presidential vote, 1916-88, hearing, 25248–109
Statistical Abstract of US, social, political, and economic data, 1790-2025, comprehensive annual compilation, 2324–1.2
Votes cast by party, candidate, and State, 1988 natl elections, biennial rpt, 9274–5; 21944–3

Democratic Peoples Republic of Korea
see Korea, North

Demography
see Population characteristics
see Population size
see Vital statistics
see under Demographic Breakdowns in the "Index by Categories"

Demolition
see Wrecking and demolition

Demonstration and pilot projects
AIDS health care research on costs and effectiveness of alternative treatment methods, 1988, 4186–9.6
Assistance (financial and nonfinancial) of Fed Govt, 1989 base edition with supplements, annual listing, 104–5
Aviation science bachelor degree holders training performance compared to other FAA hires, 1988 technical rpt, 7506–10.54
Child support interstate collection processing, officials views on mgmt, and Child Support Enforcement Office demonstration projects, 1987-88, GAO rpt, 26121–271
Developing countries sociodemographic data, and AID dev projects, special study series, 9916–3
Driving while intoxicated enforcement and publicity strategies, NHSTA deterrence project results, 1984-85, 7768–109
Economic Dev Admin research grants, by project, FY87, annual listing, 2064–2.3

Education (early childhood) for handicapped children, project descriptions, 1988/89, annual listing, 4944–10
Energy conservation (housing) program of BPA in Hood River, Oreg, cost effectiveness and participation, 1983-86, series, 3226–2
Head Start demonstration program grants, by recipient, 1985, 4608–25
Health care and condition research, survey design and research methods, 1989 conf proceedings, 4188–60
Health Care Financing Admin research activities and grants, by program, as of Mar 1989, annual listing, 4654–10
Health Care Financing Review, quarterly journal, 4652–1
Health care services quality and effectiveness, Patient Outcome Assessment Research Program project listing, FY87-89, 4186–9.4
Health maintenance organization Medicare enrollees, reimbursement and other characteristics by plan, and compared to fee-for-service, mid-1980s, 4658–31
Heart, Lung, and Blood Natl Inst activities, and grants by recipient and location, FY88 with disease trends from 1940, annual rpt, 4474–15
HHS research and evaluation programs, 1970-FY87, annual listing, 4004–30
Housing finance, construction, and improvement aid programs of HUD, press release series, 5006–3
Kidney end-stage disease research of CDC and HCFA, project listing, 1988 annual rpt, 4654–16
Libraries (research) funding of Education Dept, by project, instn, and State, FY88, annual listing, 4874–2
Medicaid coverage, participation, payments, admin, and legislative history, with data by State, 1980s-88, 21368–105
Medicare enrollees health care alternatives, medical costs, training to select assigned-fee physicians, and physician attitudes, 1988 rpt, 4658–30
Occupational Safety and Health Admin activities and grants, press release series, 6606–3
Occupational safety and health research and demonstration grants by State, and project listing, FY87, annual rpt, 4244–2
Older and handicapped persons cash aid in place of food stamps, pilot project results by area, 1988, semiannual rpt, 1362–6
Public Health Reports, bimonthly journal, 4042–3
Railroad-hwy grade-crossing warning devices, costs and effectiveness of alternative devices, local area study, 1985-86, 7558–108
Unemployed displaced workers, labor-mgmt committee aid recipients by selected characteristics, for 4 State programs, 1988, GAO rpt, 26121–316
Unemployment insurance reemployment and training services, and bonus for early reemployment, New Jersey demonstration project results, 1987-88, 6406–6.27

DeNavas, Carmen
"Hispanic Population in the U.S.: March 1986 and 1987", 2546–1.430
"Hispanic Population in the U.S.: March 1988", 2546–1.438

Dendy, Dallas L., Jr.
"Statistics of the Presidential and Congressional Election of Nov. 8, 1988", 21944–3

Denison, Tex.
Wages by occupation, for office and plant workers, 1989 survey, periodic MSA rpt, 6785–3.9
see also under By SMSA or MSA in the "Index by Categories"

Denmark
Agricultural and food production and indexes, total and for selected commodities, by country, 1970s-88, annual rpt, 1524–12
Agricultural production, prices, and trade, by country, 1970s-88 and forecast 1990, annual world region rpt, 1524–4.1
Agricultural trade of US, by detailed commodity and country, 1988, semiannual rpt, 1522–4
AID loans repayment status and terms by program and country, and status of predecessor agency loans, quarterly rpt, 9912–3
Auto imports from US, trade barriers by country, 1988, annual rpt, 444–2
Background Notes, summary social, political, and economic data, 1988 rpt, 7006–2.5
Economic and military aid and loans from US and intl agencies, by program and country, FY46-87, annual rpt, 9914–5
Economic conditions, income, production, prices, employment, and trade, 1989 periodic country rpt, 2046–4.30
Economic conditions, investment and export opportunities, and trade practices, 1989 country market research rpt, 2046–6.6
Economic conditions, policy, and trade practices, by country, 1986-88, annual rpt, 21384–5
Economic, social, political, and geographic summary data, by country, 1989, annual factbook, 9114–2
Exports and imports of US, by selected country, country group, and commodity group, 1988, annual rpt, 2044–37
Food supply and demand, market and support prices, and other economic indicators, by EC country and commodity, 1960-85, 1528–276
Human rights conditions in 170 countries, 1988, annual rpt, 21384–3
Manufacturing labor productivity and unit costs for 14 countries, 1950-88, annual press release, 6864–1
Military aid of US, arms sales, and training programs costs and budget requests, by program, world region, and country, FY88-90, annual rpt, 7144–13
Military spending, arms trade, and force strengths, with govt spending and population, by country, 1977-87, annual rpt, 9824–1
Minerals Yearbook, 1987, Vol 3: foreign country reviews of production, trade, and policy, by commodity, annual rpt, 5604–35
Minerals Yearbook, 1987, Vol 3 preprints: foreign country review of production, trade, and policy, by commodity, annual rpt, 5604–23.20
Multinatl US firms and foreign affiliates finances and operations, by industry of parent firm and affiliate, world area, and country, preliminary 1987, annual rpt, 2704–5

Oil production, trade, use, and stocks, by selected country and country group, monthly rpt, 3162–42

Population size, growth rates, and components of change, by country, projected 1989-2020 and trends from 1950, biennial rpt, 2324–9

UN voting record and share of votes in agreement with US, by issue, country, and world area, 1988, annual rpt, 7004–18

see also under By Foreign Country in the "Index by Categories"

Dennehy, Kevin F.
"Water Movement in the Unsaturated Zone at a Low-Level Radioactive-Waste Burial Site Near Barnwell, S.C.", 5668–98

Dennison, Norma Jean
"Ambulatory Medical Care Rendered in Physicians' Offices: U.S., 1975", 4147–16.2

Dental condition
Acute and chronic health conditions, disability, absenteeism, and health services use, by selected characteristics, 1988, annual rpt, 4147–10.170

Deaths and rates, by detailed cause and demographic characteristics, 1986 and trends from 1900, US Vital Statistics annual rpt, 4144–2

HHS financial aid, by program, recipient, State, and city, FY88, annual regional listings, 4004–3

Indian children tooth decay from bottle feeding, prevention project effectiveness, 1985-89, article, 4042–3.961

Indian children tooth decay from overnight bottle feeding with sugar solution, 1985 local areas study, article, 4042–3.903

Preventive disease and health improvement goals and recommended activities for 2000, with trends 1970s-80s, 4048–10

Research and training grants of Natl Inst of Dental Research, by recipient instn, FY88, annual listing, 4474–19

Dentists and dentistry
Community and migrant health services finances, operations, and staff, 1988 rpt, 4108–45.1

County Business Patterns, 1987: employment, establishments, and payroll, by SIC 2- to 4-digit industry and county, annual State rpt series, 2326–8

CPI by component for US city average, and by region, population size, and for 27 metro areas, monthly rpt, 6762–2

Degrees awarded in higher education, by level, field, race, and sex, 1989 edition, annual rpt, 4824–2.20

Educational and research grants and contracts of Health Professions Bur, by instn and program, FY88, annual listing, 4114–1

Employment, earnings, and hours, by SIC 1- to 4-digit industry, monthly 1983-Feb 1989, annual rpt, 6744–4

Enrollment in science and engineering grad programs, by field, source of funds, and characteristics of student and instn, 1975-87, annual rpt, 9627–7

Expenditures for health care, by service type, payment source, and sector, 1960s-87, annual article, 4652–1.926

Fed Govt financial and nonfinancial domestic aid, 1989 base edition with supplements, annual listing, 104–5

Head Start program operations, enrollment by handicap, and family characteristics, for North Central States, 1987/88, annual rpt, 4604–12

Health Care Financing Review, provider prices, price inputs and indexes, and labor, quarterly journal, 4652–1.1

Health condition and health care resources, use, and spending, 1950s-87, annual data compilation, 4144–11

Hepatitis cases by infection source, age, sex, race, and State, and deaths, by strain, 1987 and trends from 1966, 4205–2

HHS financial aid, by program, recipient, State, and city, FY88, annual regional listings, 4004–3

Indian Health Service facilities, funding, operations, and Indian health and other characteristics, 1950s-88, annual chartbook, 4084–1

Insurance (health) coverage and provisions of employee benefit plans, by plan type and occupational group, 1988, annual rpt, 6784–19

Insurance (health) coverage of employees, out-of-pocket expenses, benefits, and premiums, 1970s-86 and projected to 2000, 4188–56

Labor force health condition and services use, by occupation and industry of longest job held, income, age, sex, and race, 1980, 4147–10.168

Manufacturing census, 1987: financial and operating data, for SIC 4-digit industries by product, preliminary rpt, 2491–1.79

Medicaid beneficiaries and payments, by service type, FY72-87, annual rpt, 4744–3.6

Medicaid coverage, participation, payments, admin, and legislative history, with data by State, 1980s-88, 21368–105

Medicare and Medicaid beneficiaries and program operations, 1988, annual fact book, 4654–18

Medicare and Medicaid eligibility, participation, coverage, and program finances, various periods 1966-89, biennial rpt, 4654–1

Military health care personnel, and accessions by training source, by occupation, specialty, and service branch, FY87, annual rpt, 3544–24

Mississippi hospitals and community health centers, use, staff, and Medicare and other payments, 1988 hearing, 25548–97

Navy manpower strengths, accessions, and attrition, detailed statistics, quarterly rpt, 3802–4

Pregnancy-related services use and costs, for Medicaid beneficiaries in 3 States, 1983-84, article, 4652–1.938

Receipts for services, by SIC 2- to 4-digit kind of business, 1988, annual rpt, 2413–8

Research and training grants of Natl Inst of Dental Research, by recipient instn, FY88, annual listing, 4474–19

Rural areas health care facilities, staffing, services accessibility, and indicators of need, 1960s-88, 25148–41

Service industries census, 1987: establishments, receipts, employment, and payroll, by SIC 2- to 4-digit kind of business, MSA, county, and city, State rpt series, 2391–1

Statistical Abstract of US, social, political, and economic data, 1790-2025, comprehensive annual compilation, 2324–1.1

Tax (income) returns of corporations, income and tax items by asset size and detailed industry, 1986, annual rpt, 8304–4; 8304–21

Tax (income) returns of partnerships, income statement items by industry group, 1986, annual article, 8302–2.903

Tax (income) returns of sole proprietorships, income statement items, by industry group, 1987, annual article, 8302–2.904; 8302–2.921

Texas-Mexico border area health facilities and services, with background data, by Texas county, 1980s-88, GAO rpt, 26121–261

Training support grants of Bur of Health Professions, by program, region, and State, FY80-87, 4118–62

VA health care facilities employment, FY64-88, annual rpt, 8604–5.1

VA health care facilities physicians, dentists, and nurses, by selected employment characteristics and VA district, quarterly rpt, 8602–6

VA health care professionals employment, by district and facility, quarterly rpt, 8602–4

VA Medicine and Surgery Dept trainees, by detailed program and city, FY88, annual rpt, 8704–4

see also Dental condition

Denver, Colo.
CPI by component for US city average, and by region, population size, and for 27 metro areas, monthly rpt, 6762–2

Drug abuse indicators for selected metro areas, research results, data collection, and policy issues, 1989 semiannual conf, 4492–5

Fruit and vegetable shipments, and arrivals in US and Canada cities, by mode of transport and State and country of origin, 1988, annual rpt, 1311–4.2

Housing starts and completions authorized by building permits in 40 MSAs, quarterly rpt, 2382–9

Housing vacancy rates for single and multifamily units and mobile homes, by city and ZIP code, 1988, annual MSA rpt, 9304–22.2

Wages by occupation, for office and plant workers, 1988 survey, periodic MSA rpt, 6785–11.3

see also under By City and By SMSA or MSA in the "Index by Categories"

Department of Agriculture
Activities and programs of USDA, by subagency, FY88, annual rpt, 1004–3

Agricultural data compilation, 1987/88 and trends from 1920, annual rpt, 1004–14

Agricultural Statistics, 1988, annual rpt, 1004–1

Atmospheric sciences research activity of Fed Govt, and funding by agency and program, FY84-87, biennial rpt, 434–1

Budget deficit reduction under Gramm-Rudman Act, cancellation of budget authority by program, FY90, annual rpt, 104–27; 21924–1; 26304–6

Budget of US Appendix, obligations, appropriations, and personnel, by program and agency, FY90, annual rpt, 104–3

Budget of US, authoritative financial statements with appropriations, outlays, and receipts, by category and agency, FY88, annual rpt, 8104–2.2

Drought of 1988, impacts on agriculture and other sectors, and Federal aid, 1008–53

Education funding by Federal agency, program, and recipient type, and instn spending, FY80-88, 4828–21

Employee productivity improvement program of Fed Govt, coverage and impacts by function for selected agencies, FY86-87 and projected to 1992, 26306–3.103

Employment discrimination complaints, and awards by funding source, for 3 Federal agencies, FY87-88, GAO rpt, 26121–313

Expenditures of Fed Govt in States, by type, program, agency, and State, FY88, annual rpt, 2464–2

Farm financial and marketing conditions, forecast 1988, conf papers, annual rpt, 1004–16

Fraud and abuse in USDA programs, audits and investigations, 2nd half FY89, semiannual rpt, 1002–4

Labor unions recognized in Fed Govt, agreements and membership by agency and facility, as of Jan 1989, biennial listing, 9844–14

Mgmt of farms, finances, operations, environmental issues, and info sources, *1989 Yearbook of Agriculture*, annual rpt, 1004–18

Nutritional status and related health condition and practices, by selected characteristics, 1970s-87, 4048–33

R&D and related funding of Fed Govt to higher education and nonprofit instns, by field, instn, agency, and State, FY87, annual rpt, 9627–17

R&D funding by Fed Govt, by field, performer type, agency, and State, FY87-89, annual rpt, 9627–20

Rural areas dev aid by Fed Govt, Reagan Admin programs and initiatives, FY88, annual rpt, 1004–17

Science and engineering employment in Fed Govt, by field, degree level, race, sex, agency, and State, 1987, annual rpt, 9627–5

Science and engineering grad enrollment, by field, source of funds, and characteristics of student and instn, 1975-87, annual rpt, 9627–7

Soil and water conservation programs of USDA, activities, 1988-97, 1008–41

Wilderness Preservation Natl System acreage, by site and State, 1987, annual rpt, 1004–15

see also Agricultural Cooperative Service
see also Agricultural Marketing Service
see also Agricultural Research Service
see also Agricultural Stabilization and Conservation Service
see also Agricultural Statistics Board
see also Animal and Plant Health Inspection Service
see also Commodity Credit Corp.
see also Cooperative State Research Service
see also Economic Research Service
see also Farmers Home Administration
see also Federal Crop Insurance Corp.
see also Federal Grain Inspection Service

see also Food and Nutrition Service
see also Food Safety and Inspection Service
see also Foreign Agricultural Service
see also Forest Service
see also Human Nutrition Information Service
see also National Agricultural Statistics Service
see also Office of Grants and Program Systems, USDA
see also Office of International Cooperation and Development, USDA
see also Office of Transportation, USDA
see also Packers and Stockyards Administration
see also Rural Electrification Administration
see also Soil Conservation Service
see also under By Federal Agency in the "Index by Categories"

Department of Air Force

Agent Orange exposure of Air Force personnel, deaths and rates by cause and selected characteristics, 1989 annual rpt, 3604–3

Base construction, renovation, and land acquisition, DOD budget requests by project, service branch, State, and country, FY90/91, annual rpt, 3544–15

Budget of DOD, justification, programs, and policies, FY90-91, annual rpt, 3544–2

Budget of DOD, procurement appropriations by item, service branch, and defense agency, FY88-91, annual rpt, 3544–32

Budget of DOD, R&D appropriations by item, service branch, and defense agency, FY88-91, annual rpt, 3544–33

Budget of DOD, weapons acquisition costs by system and service branch, FY89-91, annual rpt, 3504–2

Commercial activities of DOD performed in-house, and work-years, by service branch, installation, and State, FY88, annual rpt, 3544–25

Courts (military) cases and actions, FY88, annual rpt, 3504–3

Criminal investigation activities of DOD, funding and case dispositions, by service branch, FY84-88, GAO rpt, 26123–242

Employment (civilian) of DOD, by service branch and defense agency, with summary military employment data, quarterly rpt, 3542–16

Employment (civilian and military) of DOD, by service branch, major installation, and State, as of Sept 1988, annual rpt, 3544–7

Expenditures and obligations of DOD, by function and service branch, quarterly rpt, 3542–3

Fiscal mgmt system operations and techniques of Air Force, quarterly rpt, 3602–1

Health care personnel, and accessions by training source, by occupation, specialty, and service branch, FY87, annual rpt, 3544–24

Labor unions recognized in Fed Govt, agreements and membership by agency and facility, as of Jan 1989, biennial listing, 9844–14

Medical malpractice claims against military hospitals by disposition, and costs, 1982-87, hearing, 21208–27

Pacific basin airlift of aircraft parts, traffic, shipments, and impacts on force readiness, for Air Force, 1986-88, GAO rpt, 26123–230

Procurement, DOD prime contract awards by category, contract and contractor type, and service branch, FY79-88, semiannual rpt, 3542–1

Procurement, DOD prime contract awards by contractor, service branch, State, and city, FY88, annual rpt, 3544–22

Procurement, DOD prime contract awards by service branch and State, FY88, semiannual rpt, 3542–5

Procurement, DOD prime contract awards by size and type of contract, service branch, competitive status, category, and labor standard, FY88, annual rpt, 3544–19

Procurement, DOD prime contract awards in labor surplus areas, by service branch, State, and area, FY88, semiannual rpt, 3542–19

Procurement, subcontract awards by DOD contractors to small and disadvantaged business, by firm and service branch, quarterly rpt, 3542–17

Property mgmt of Air Force, validation of unfilled orders for aircraft spare parts, 1985-87, GAO rpt, 26123–245

Property, supply, and equipment inventory of DOD, by service branch, 1988, annual rpt, 3544–6

Science and engineering employment in Fed Govt, by field, degree level, race, sex, agency, and State, 1987, annual rpt, 9627–5

Shipments by DOD of military and personal property, passenger traffic, and costs, by service branch and mode of transport, quarterly rpt, 3702–1

Supply inventory stock fund balances, refunds to customers, and procurement cost effects of reducing balances, FY84-88, GAO rpt, 26111–60

Weapons and communications systems cost estimates, by service branch, quarterly summary rpt, 3502–1

see also Air Force
see also terms beginning with Defense and with Military

Department of Army

Activities, personnel, logistics, R&D, and budget, FY86 summary data, annual rpt, 3704–11

Base construction, renovation, and land acquisition, DOD budget requests by project, service branch, State, and country, FY90/91, annual rpt, 3544–15

Budget of DOD, justification, programs, and policies, FY90-91, annual rpt, 3544–2

Budget of DOD, procurement appropriations by item, service branch, and defense agency, FY88-91, annual rpt, 3544–32

Budget of DOD, R&D appropriations by item, service branch, and defense agency, FY88-91, annual rpt, 3544–33

Budget of DOD, weapons acquisition costs by system and service branch, FY89-91, annual rpt, 3504–2

Budget of US Appendix, obligations, appropriations, and personnel, by program and agency, FY90, annual rpt, 104–3

Commercial activities of DOD performed in-house, and work-years, by service branch, installation, and State, FY88, annual rpt, 3544–25

Courts (military) cases and actions, FY88, annual rpt, 3504–3

Drug smuggling aircraft interdiction activities of Fed Govt, funding, and radar system capabilities, by agency, FY82-89, GAO rpt, 26119-259

Education funding by Federal agency, program, and recipient type, and instn spending, FY80-88, 4828-21

Employment (civilian) of DOD, by service branch and defense agency, with summary military employment data, quarterly rpt, 3542-16

Employment (civilian) of DOD, voluntary early retirement program costs and savings, FY88, GAO rpt, 26119-253

Employment (civilian) of Fed Govt, by work schedule, selected agency, State, and MSA, as of Dec 1988, article, 9842-1.904

Employment (civilian and military) of DOD, by service branch, major installation, and State, as of Sept 1988, annual rpt, 3544-7

Employment, earnings, and hours, by SIC 1- to 4-digit industry, monthly 1983-Feb 1989, annual rpt, 6744-4

Expenditures of Fed Govt in States, by type, program, agency, and State, FY88, annual rpt, 2464-2

Export licensing of goods with potential military uses, DOD and Commerce Dept activities, staff, and costs, 1986-88, GAO rpt, 26123-250

Foreign countries military aid of US, arms sales, and training programs costs and budget requests, by program, world region, and country, FY88-90, annual rpt, 7144-13

Foreign countries military aid of US, DOD notifications to Congress of changes from Admin budget request, and funds affected by country, FY86-87, GAO rpt, 26123-219

Fraud and abuse in DOD programs, audits and investigations, 1st half FY89, semiannual rpt, 3542-18

Headquarters personnel reduction proposals for joint and service commands, by service branch, FY90-91, GAO rpt, 26123-236

Intl exchange and training programs of Federal agencies, participants by world area, and funding, by program, FY87, annual rpt, 9854-8

Labor unions recognized in Fed Govt, agreements and membership by agency and facility, as of Jan 1989, biennial listing, 9844-14

Manpower statistics for active duty, civilian, and reserve personnel, by service branch, FY88 and trends, annual rpt, 3544-1

Manpower statistics for active duty, civilian, and reserve personnel, by service branch, quarterly rpt, 3542-14

Natl Guard (Army and Air) activities, manpower, and facilities, FY88, annual rpt, 3504-22

NATO Europe members presence of US military and civilian personnel and dependents, by service branch, 1980-88, GAO rpt, 26123-252

NATO Europe members presence of US military and civilian personnel, and vacancies, by service branch, 1988, GAO rpt, 26123-251

Officers assigned to multiservice organizations, quality and promotion indicators by service branch, 1985-88, GAO rpt, 26123-231

Post exchange operations, and sales by commodity, by facility and location worldwide, FY87, annual rpt, 3504-10

Procurement, DOD prime contract awards by category, contract and contractor type, and service branch, FY79-88, semiannual rpt, 3542-1

Procurement, DOD prime contract awards by contractor, service branch, State, and city, FY88, annual rpt, 3544-22

Procurement, DOD prime contract awards by service branch and State, FY88, semiannual rpt, 3542-5

Procurement, DOD prime contract awards in labor surplus areas, by service branch, State, and area, FY88, semiannual rpt, 3542-19

Property (real) of Fed Govt, inventory and costs, worldwide summary by location, agency, and use, 1987, annual rpt, 9454-5

Property (real) of Fed Govt, leased inventory and rental costs, worldwide summary by location and agency, 1987, annual rpt, 9454-10

Property, supply, and equipment inventory of DOD, by service branch, 1988, annual rpt, 3544-6

R&D and related funding of Fed Govt to higher education and nonprofit instns, by field, instn, agency, and State, FY87, annual rpt, 9627-17

R&D funding by Fed Govt, by field, performer type, agency, and State, FY87-89, annual rpt, 9627-20

Reserve personnel social, economic, family, and service characteristics, and attitudes, by reserve component, 1986 survey, 3508-29

Reserve personnel spouses attitudes, and family social, economic, and other characteristics, 1986 survey, 3508-30

Science and engineering employment in Fed Govt, by field, degree level, race, sex, agency, and State, 1987, annual rpt, 9627-5

Science and engineering grad enrollment, by field, source of funds, and characteristics of student and instn, 1975-87, annual rpt, 9627-7

Soviet Union and Warsaw Pact military weapons systems, aid, presence, and force strengths, and compared to US and NATO, 1989 annual rpt, 3504-20

Space launches and other activities of NASA and USSR, with flight data, 1957-88, annual rpt, 9504-6.1

Space program funding by NASA and DOD, by category, FY81-89, GAO rpt, 26123-152

Stars and Stripes coverage of sensitive topics, FY88-89, GAO rpt, 26123-226

Training and education programs of DOD, funding, staff, students, and facilities, by service branch, FY90, annual rpt, 3504-5

Weapons and communications systems cost estimates, by service branch, quarterly summary rpt, 3502-1

see also Army Corps of Engineers
see also Court of Military Appeals

see also Defense agencies
see also Defense Communications Agency
see also Defense Contract Audit Agency
see also Defense Fuel Supply Center
see also Defense Intelligence Agency
see also Defense Investigative Service
see also Defense Logistics Agency
see also Defense Mapping Agency
see also Defense Nuclear Agency
see also Defense Security Assistance Agency
see also Department of Air Force
see also Department of Army
see also Department of Navy
see also Joint Chiefs of Staff
see also Marine Corps
see also National Defense University
see also Office of the Secretary of Defense
see also terms beginning with Defense and with Military
see also under By Federal Agency in the "Index by Categories"

Department of Education

Athlete grad rates for NCAA Div I college programs, and reporting of academic performance to Education Dept, 1987-89, GAO rpt, 26121-305

Bilingual education program activities, Federal and State aid, and enrollment, FY86-87, biennial rpt, 4804-14

Budget deficit reduction under Gramm-Rudman Act, cancellation of budget authority by program, FY90, annual rpt, 104-27; 21924-1; 26304-6

Budget of US Appendix, obligations, appropriations, and personnel, by program and agency, FY90, annual rpt, 104-3

Budget of US, authoritative financial statements with appropriations, outlays, and receipts, by category and agency, FY88, annual rpt, 8104-2.2

Civil Rights Office of Education Dept, complaints, investigations, funding, and staff, various periods FY81-88, 21348-114

Contract admin at 4 agencies, and contract deficiencies by type, 1980s, GAO rpt, 26119-268

Education data, selected performance and financial indicators by State, 1982-88, annual table with supplements, 4804-32

Enrollment, staff, and spending, by instn level and control, and teacher salaries, 1980s-90, annual press release, 4804-19

Expenditures for education by Federal agency, program, and recipient type, and instn spending, FY80-88, 4828-21

Expenditures of Fed Govt in States, by type, program, agency, and State, FY88, annual rpt, 2464-2

Expenditures, operations, and effectiveness of Education Dept programs, FY88, annual rpt, 4804-5

Financial aid programs of Education Dept, 1989 annual listing, 4804-3

Fraud and abuse in Education Dept programs, audits and investigations, 2nd half FY89, semiannual rpt, 4802-1

Fulbright-Hays academic exchanges, grants by purpose, and foreign govt share of costs, by country, FY88, annual rpt, 10324-1

Handicapped children early education project descriptions, 1988/89, annual listing, 4944-10

Homeless children educational enrollment and needs, 1988, annual State rpt series, 4804-35

Intl exchange and training programs of Federal agencies, participants by world area, and funding, by program, FY87, annual rpt, 9854-8

Labor unions recognized in Fed Govt, agreements and membership by agency and facility, as of Jan 1989, biennial listing, 9844-14

Pell grants and applicants, by tuition, family and student income, instn type and control, and State, 1987/88, annual rpt, 4804-1

R&D and related funding of Fed Govt to higher education and nonprofit instns, by field, instn, agency, and State, FY87, annual rpt, 9627-17

R&D funding by Fed Govt, by field, performer type, agency, and State, FY87-89, annual rpt, 9627-20

State allocation of Federal educational funds, by program, recipient type, and State, 1987/88, annual rpt, 4804-8

Student aid funding and participation, by Federal program, instn type and control, and State, various periods 1959-88, annual rpt, 4804-28

Student aid supplemental grants, loans, and work-study awards, Federal share by instn and State, 1989/90, annual listing, 4804-17

Student guaranteed loan default rate, and borrowers in repayment status, by instn, State and outlying area, FY87, annual rpt, 4804-34

Student loans of Fed Govt in default, losses, and rates, by instn and State, as of June 1988, annual rpt, 4804-18

Vocational education aid recipients and sources, and characteristics of programs and students, 1970s-89, series, 4806-3

see also National Assessment of Educational Progress

see also Office of Educational Research and Improvement

see also Office of Special Education and Rehabilitative Services

see also under By Federal Agency in the "Index by Categories"

Department of Energy

Activities and finances of DOE, summary energy supply and demand data, and bibl, 1987, annual rpt, 3024-2

Alcohol fuels (methanol) prices, distribution, and gasoline displacement, with background data, 1985-86 and projected to 2000, 3008-122

Atmospheric sciences research activity of Fed Govt, and funding by agency and program, FY84-87, biennial rpt, 434-1

Auto and light truck fuel economy, sales, and market shares, annual rpt, issuing agency change, 3304-27

Budget deficit reduction under Gramm-Rudman Act, cancellation of budget authority by program, FY90, annual rpt, 104-27; 21924-1; 26304-6

Budget of DOE, authority by program and subagency, annual rpt, discontinued, 3004-14

Budget of US Appendix, obligations, appropriations, and personnel, by program and agency, FY90, annual rpt, 104-3

Budget of US, authoritative financial statements with appropriations, outlays, and receipts, by category and agency, FY88, annual rpt, 8104-2.2

Carbon dioxide in atmosphere, measurement, methodology, and research results, series, 3006-11

Coal purchases by Fed Govt, chemical analyses by mine and location, FY84, annual rpt, 3004-15

Contract admin at 4 agencies, and contract deficiencies by type, 1980s, GAO rpt, 26119-268

Contracts and grants of DOE, by category, State, and for top contractors, FY88, annual rpt, 3004-21

Data collection forms of DOE and related rpts, 1988, annual listing, 3164-86

Education funding by Federal agency, program, and recipient type, and instn spending, FY80-88, 4828-21

Employee security clearances and investigations of DOE, 1986-88, GAO rpt, 26113-387

Employment in energy-related fields, manpower studies and devs, series, 3006-8

Energy conservation aid of DOE, State officials views on administrative appeal procedures, 1989, GAO rpt, 26113-414

Energy use, costs, and conservation, for DOE, by end use, fuel type, and field office, FY88, annual rpt, 3004-27

Expenditures of Fed Govt in States, by type, program, agency, and State, FY88, annual rpt, 2464-2

Fraud and abuse in DOE programs, audits and investigations, 2nd half FY89, semiannual rpt, 3002-12

Inventions recommended by Natl Inst of Standards and Technology for DOE support, awards, and evaluation status, 1988, annual listing, 2214-5

Labor unions recognized in Fed Govt, agreements and membership by agency and facility, as of Jan 1989, biennial listing, 9844-14

Naval Petroleum and Oil Shale Reserves production and revenue by fuel type, sales by purchaser, and wells, by reserve, FY88, annual rpt, 3004-22

Nuclear material inventory discrepancies at DOE and contractor facilities, 2nd half FY87, semiannual rpt, 3002-4

Nuclear reactors for domestic use and export by function and operating status, with owner, operating characteristics, and location, 1988 annual listing, 3004-26

Oil enhanced recovery research contracts of DOE, project summaries, funding, and bibl, quarterly rpt, 3002-14

Property (real) of DOE owned and leased, by type, subagency, contractor, and site, FY87, annual rpt, 3004-28

Publications on energy from DOE and other sources, monthly listing, 3002-2

R&D and related funding of Fed Govt to higher education and nonprofit instns, by field, instn, agency, and State, FY87, annual rpt, 9627-17

R&D funding by Fed Govt, by field, performer type, agency, and State, FY87-89, annual rpt, 9627-20

R&D projects and funding of DOE at natl labs, universities, and other instns, periodic summary rpt series, 3004-18

Radioactive waste (military) disposal at New Mexico Waste Isolation Pilot Plant, environmental impacts, 1989 supplemental statement, 3008-33

Science and engineering employment in Fed Govt, by field, degree level, race, sex, agency, and State, 1987, annual rpt, 9627-5

Science and engineering employment in R&D, earnings at DOE labs and non-DOE facilities, 1989, annual rpt, 3004-9

Science and engineering employment in R&D, earnings by field and educational, employment, and other characteristics, 1989, annual rpt, 3004-1

Strategic Petroleum Reserve capacity, inventory, fill rate, and finances, quarterly rpt, 3002-13

Strategic Petroleum Reserve funding and activities, by site, as of Sept 1988, semiannual GAO rpt, 26102-3

Toxicology Natl Program research and testing activities, FY87 and planned FY88, annual rpt, 4044-16

see also Alaska Power Administration

see also Bonneville Power Administration

see also Department of Energy: Civilian Radioactive Waste Management

see also Department of Energy: Conservation and Renewable Energy

see also Department of Energy: Defense Programs

see also Department of Energy: Environment, Safety, and Health

see also Department of Energy: International Affairs and Energy Emergencies

see also Department of Energy National Laboratories

see also Department of Energy: Nuclear Energy

see also Economic Regulatory Administration

see also Energy Information Administration

see also Federal Energy Regulatory Commission

see also Office of the Secretary of Energy

see also Southeastern Power Administration

see also Southwestern Power Administration

see also Western Area Power Administration

see also under By Federal Agency in the "Index by Categories"

Department of Energy: Civilian Radioactive Waste Management

Nuclear Waste Fund finances and CRWM activities, quarterly GAO rpt, 26102-4

Nuclear Waste Fund finances, and CRWM project budgets alternative projections, quarterly rpt, 3362-1

Spent fuel and radioactive waste generation, inventory, and disposal, 1960s-88 and projected to 2020, annual rpt, 3364-2

Department of Energy: Conservation and Renewable Energy

Auto and light truck fuel economy, sales, and market shares, by size and model for US and foreign makes, 1989 model year, semiannual rpt, 3302-4

Auto engine and power train R&D projects, DOE contracts and funding by recipient, FY88, annual rpt, 3304-17

Auto fuel economy test results for US and foreign makes, 1990 model year, annual rpt, 3304-11

Education funding by Federal agency, program, and recipient type, and instn spending, FY80-88, 4828-21

Employee productivity improvement program of Fed Govt, coverage and impacts by function for selected agencies, FY86-87 and projected to 1992, 26306-3.103

Expenditures of Fed Govt in States, by type, program, agency, and State, FY88, annual rpt, 2464-2

Labor unions recognized in Fed Govt, agreements and membership by agency and facility, as of Jan 1989, biennial listing, 9844-14

R&D funding by Fed Govt, by field, performer type, agency, and State, FY87-89, annual rpt, 9627-20

US attorneys case processing and collections, by case type and Federal district, FY88, annual rpt, 6004-2

see also Bureau of Justice Assistance

see also Bureau of Justice Statistics

see also Bureau of Prisons

see also Community Relations Service

see also Drug Enforcement Administration

see also Federal Bureau of Investigation

see also Foreign Claims Settlement Commission

see also Immigration and Naturalization Service

see also National Institute of Justice

see also Office of Justice Programs

see also Office of Juvenile Justice and Delinquency Prevention

see also U.S. Marshals Service

see also U.S. Parole Commission

see also under By Federal Agency in the "Index by Categories"

Department of Labor

Activities and funding of DOL, by program and State, FY88, annual rpt, 6304-1

Budget deficit reduction under Gramm-Rudman Act, cancellation of budget authority by program, FY90, annual rpt, 104-27; 21924-1; 26304-6

Budget of US Appendix, obligations, appropriations, and personnel, by program and agency, FY90, annual rpt, 104-3

Budget of US, authoritative financial statements with appropriations, outlays, and receipts, by category and agency, FY88, annual rpt, 8104-2.2

Collective bargaining agreements, innovations and issues, series, 6306-3

Education funding by Federal agency, program, and recipient type, and instn spending, FY80-88, 4828-21

Employment discrimination complaints, and awards by funding source, for 3 Federal agencies, FY87-88, GAO rpt, 26121-313

Expenditures of Fed Govt in States, by type, program, agency, and State, FY88, annual rpt, 2464-2

Farm labor wage surveys to set minimum wage for US and alien workers, evaluation with data by location, 1980s-87, GAO rpt, 26131-50

Fraud and abuse in DOL programs, audits and investigations, 2nd half FY89, semiannual rpt, 6302-2

Job Training Partnership Act State and local admin, funding, effectiveness, and participants, GAO rpt series, 26106-8

Labor force issues and trends, 1980s, series, 6306-2

Labor unions recognized in Fed Govt, agreements and membership by agency and facility, as of Jan 1989, biennial listing, 9844-14

Pension laws admin and enforcement under Employee Retirement Income Security Act (ERISA), 1987, annual rpt, 6304-4

Pension plan regulation enforcement of DOL and IRS, violations, and penalties, FY85-88, GAO rpt, 26121-259

R&D and related funding of Fed Govt to higher education and nonprofit instns, by field, instn, agency, and State, FY87, annual rpt, 9627-17

R&D funding by Fed Govt, by field, performer type, agency, and State, FY87-89, annual rpt, 9627-20

see also Bureau of International Labor Affairs

see also Bureau of Labor Statistics

see also Employment and Training Administration

see also Employment Standards Administration

see also Mine Safety and Health Administration

see also Occupational Safety and Health Administration

see also under By Federal Agency in the "Index by Categories"

Department of Navy

Base construction, renovation, and land acquisition, DOD budget requests by project, service branch, State, and country, FY90/91, annual rpt, 3544-15

Budget of DOD, justification, programs, and policies, FY90-91, annual rpt, 3544-2

Budget of DOD, procurement appropriations by item, service branch, and defense agency, FY88-91, annual rpt, 3544-32

Budget of DOD, R&D appropriations by item, service branch, and defense agency, FY88-91, annual rpt, 3544-33

Budget of DOD, weapons acquisition costs by system and service branch, FY89-91, annual rpt, 3504-2

Budget of Navy, manpower, procurement, and equipment, planned FY89-91, annual fact sheet, 3804-16

Commercial activities of DOD performed in-house, and work-years, by service branch, installation, and State, FY88, annual rpt, 3544-25

Computer mainframe and related equipment procurement, compatibility, and operating system contracts, for Navy, FY86-89, GAO rpt, 26125-37

Courts (military) cases and actions, FY88, annual rpt, 3504-3

Criminal investigation activities of DOD, funding and case dispositions, by service branch, FY84-88, GAO rpt, 26123-242

Drug and alcohol abuse education and treatment programs activity of Navy, 2nd half FY88, semiannual tables, 3802-6

Employment (civilian) of DOD, by service branch and defense agency, with summary military employment data, quarterly rpt, 3542-16

Employment (civilian and military) of DOD, by service branch, major installation, and State, as of Sept 1988, annual rpt, 3544-7

Expenditures and obligations of DOD, by function and service branch, quarterly rpt, 3542-3

Health care personnel, and accessions by training source, by occupation, specialty, and service branch, FY87, annual rpt, 3544-24

Labor unions recognized in Fed Govt, agreements and membership by agency and facility, as of Jan 1989, biennial listing, 9844-14

Manpower strengths, accessions, and attrition, detailed statistics for Navy and Naval Reserve, quarterly rpt, 3802-4

Military Sealift Command shipping operations, finances, and personnel, FY88, annual rpt, 3804-14

Procurement, DOD prime contract awards by category, contract and contractor type, and service branch, FY79-88, semiannual rpt, 3542-1

Procurement, DOD prime contract awards by contractor, service branch, State, and city, FY88, annual rpt, 3544-22

Procurement, DOD prime contract awards by service branch and State, FY88, semiannual rpt, 3542-5

Procurement, DOD prime contract awards by size and type of contract, service branch, competitive status, category, and labor standard, FY88, annual rpt, 3544-19

Procurement, DOD prime contract awards in labor surplus areas, by service branch, State, and area, FY88, semiannual rpt, 3542-19

Procurement of Navy, by contractor and location, FY88, annual rpt, 3804-13

Procurement, subcontract awards by DOD contractors to small and disadvantaged business, by firm and service branch, quarterly rpt, 3542-17

Property, supply, and equipment inventory of DOD, by service branch, 1988, annual rpt, 3544-6

Radiation exposure of Navy personnel on nuclear-powered vessels and at support facilities, and injury claims, 1950s-88, annual rpt, 3804-10

Radioactive waste from Navy nuclear-powered vessels and support facilities, releases in harbors, and public exposure, 1970s-88, annual rpt, 3804-11

Science and engineering employment in Fed Govt, by field, degree level, race, sex, agency, and State, 1987, annual rpt, 9627-5

Shipments by DOD of military and personal property, passenger traffic, and costs, by service branch and mode of transport, quarterly rpt, 3702-1

Small business procurement offices of Navy, and location, 1988 annual listing, 3804-5

Weapons and communications systems cost estimates, by service branch, quarterly summary rpt, 3502-1

see also Marine Corps

see also Marine Reserve

see also Naval Oceanography Command

see also Navy

see also U.S. Naval Observatory

see also terms beginning with Defense and with Military

Department of State

Budget deficit reduction under Gramm-Rudman Act, cancellation of budget authority by program, FY90, annual rpt, 104-27; 21924-1; 26304-6

Budget of US Appendix, obligations, appropriations, and personnel, by program and agency, FY90, annual rpt, 104-3

Budget of US, authoritative financial statements with appropriations, outlays, and receipts, by category and agency, FY88, annual rpt, 8104-2.2

Drugs (illegal) production, eradication, and seizures, by substance, with US aid, by country, 1985-89, annual rpt, 7004-17

Education funding by Federal agency, program, and recipient type, and instn spending, FY80-88, 4828-21

Foreign countries Background Notes, summary social, political, and economic data, series, 7006-2

Foreign Service Inst enrollment and training hours, by course, 1983-87, GAO rpt, 26123-248

Fraud and abuse in State Dept programs, audits and investigations, 2nd half FY89, semiannual rpt, 7002-6

Freedom of info requests and security reviews of State Dept, processing, 1985-88, GAO rpt, 26119-243

Helsinki Final Act implementation by NATO and Warsaw Pact, Oct 1988-Mar 1989, semiannual rpt, 7002-1

Labor unions recognized in Fed Govt, agreements and membership by agency and facility, as of Jan 1989, biennial listing, 9844-14

Loan repayment status and terms by program and country, AID and predecessor agencies, quarterly rpt, 9912-3

Maritime claims and boundary agreements of coastal countries, series, 7006-8

Minority group and women employment and hires of State Dept, and Foreign Service exam results and officer appointments, annual rpt, discontinued, 7004-11

Minority group and women employment and hires of State Dept, and Foreign Service officer appointments, annual rpt, discontinued, 7004-20

Minority group and women employment, hires, and promotions in Foreign Service, 1981-87, GAO rpt, 26123-247

Minority group and women employment in State Dept and Foreign Service, FY88, annual rpt, 7004-21

Pacific territories social, economic, health, and govtl data, FY88 and trends, annual rpt, 7004-6

Passport and visa applicant screening, State Dept info system records by reason for exclusion, 1989, GAO rpt, 26125-36

R&D funding by Fed Govt, by field, performer type, agency, and State, FY87-89, annual rpt, 9627-20

Terrorist (intl) incidents, casualties, and attacks on US targets, by attack type and country, 1980-88, 7008-56

Terrorist (intl) incidents, casualties, and attacks on US targets, by attack type and world area, 1968-88, annual rpt, 7004-13

Treaties and other bilateral and multilateral agreements of US in force, by country, as of Jan 1989, annual listing, 7004-1

UN participation of US, and member and nonmember shares of UN budget by country, FY86-88, annual rpt, 7004-5

UN voting record and share of votes in agreement with US, by issue, country, and world area, 1988, annual rpt, 7004-18

see also Bureau for Refugee Programs, State Department

see also Bureau of Consular Affairs, State Department

see also Bureau of Intelligence and Research, State Department

see also under By Federal Agency in the "Index by Categories"

Department of Transportation

Activities of DOT by subagency, budget, and summary accident data, FY85, annual rpt, 7304-1

Air travel to and from US on US and foreign flag carriers, by country, world area, and US port, monthly rpt, 7302-2

Airline computer reservation systems finances, operations, and impacts on airline competitiveness, 1980s-86, 7308-193

Airline consumer complaints by reason, passengers denied boarding, and late flights, by reporting carrier and airport, monthly rpt, 7302-11

Airline financial data, by carrier, carrier group, and for total certificated system, quarterly rpt, 7302-7

Airline merger of TWA and Ozark, impacts on fares and departures at St Louis, Mo, 1985-88, 7308-194

Airline traffic, capacity, and performance, by carrier and type of operation, monthly rpt, 7302-6

Airline traffic, capacity, and performance for medium regionals, by carrier, quarterly rpt, 7302-8

Atmospheric sciences research activity of Fed Govt, and funding by agency and program, FY84-87, biennial rpt, 434-1

Budget deficit reduction under Gramm-Rudman Act, cancellation of budget authority by program, FY90, annual rpt, 104-27; 21924-1; 26304-6

Budget of US Appendix, obligations, appropriations, and personnel, by program and agency, FY90, annual rpt, 104-3

Budget of US, authoritative financial statements with appropriations, outlays, and receipts, by category and agency, FY88, annual rpt, 8104-2.2

Education funding by Federal agency, program, and recipient type, and instn spending, FY80-88, 4828-21

Employee productivity improvement program of Fed Govt, coverage and impacts by function for selected agencies, FY86-87 and projected to 1992, 26306-3.103

Employment of DOT, by subagency, occupation, and selected personnel characteristics, FY88, annual rpt, 7304-18

Expenditures of Fed Govt in States, by type, program, agency, and State, FY88, annual rpt, 2464-2

Finances and staff of DOT, by subagency, FY88-90, annual rpt, 7304-10

Fraud and abuse in DOT programs, audits and investigations, 2nd half FY89, semiannual rpt, 7302-4

Grants and contracts of DOT to higher education instns, by instn, subagency, and State, annual listing, discontinued, 7304-13

Grants of DOT for planning and safety, by program, State, and for 38 SMSAs, FY88, annual rpt, 7304-7

Great Lakes ship pilotage activities, costs, and traffic for US and Canada, and US testing and certificates, 1960s-87, 7308-192

Harbor traffic, facilities, dev, funding, and needs, for Pacific territories and Hawaii by port, as of 1987, 7308-195

Hazardous material transport accidents, casualties, and damage, by mode of transport, with DOT control activities, 1988, annual rpt, 7304-4

Labor unions recognized in Fed Govt, agreements and membership by agency and facility, as of Jan 1989, biennial listing, 9844-14

Pipeline accidents, casualties, safety enforcement activity, and Federal funding, by State, 1987, annual rpt, 7304-5

R&D and related funding of Fed Govt to higher education and nonprofit instns, by field, instn, agency, and State, FY87, annual rpt, 9627-17

R&D funding by Fed Govt, by field, performer type, agency, and State, FY87-89, annual rpt, 9627-20

Safety monitoring activities of DOT, press release series, 7306-10

Science and engineering employment in Fed Govt, by field, degree level, race, sex, agency, and State, 1987, annual rpt, 9627-5

Transportation finances, operations, vehicles, equipment, accidents, and energy use, by mode of transport, 1955-88, annual rpt, 7304-2

see also Coast Guard

see also Coast Guard Reserve

see also Federal Aviation Administration

see also Federal Highway Administration

see also Federal Railroad Administration

see also Maritime Administration

see also National Highway Traffic Safety Administration

see also St. Lawrence Seaway Development Corp.

see also Urban Mass Transportation Administration

see also under By Federal Agency in the "Index by Categories"

Department of Treasury

Assets (depreciable) class lives measurement, investment, and industry operations, asset class rpt series, 8006-5

Bill offerings, auction results by Fed Reserve District, and terms, periodic press release series, 8002-7

Budget deficit reduction under Gramm-Rudman Act, cancellation of budget authority by program, FY90, annual rpt, 104-27; 21924-1; 26304-6

Budget of US Appendix, obligations, appropriations, and personnel, by program and agency, FY90, annual rpt, 104-3

Budget of US, authoritative financial statements with appropriations, outlays, and receipts, by category and agency, FY88, annual rpt, 8104-2.2

Cuba trade with multinatl US firms foreign affiliates, by country, FY82-87, press release, 8008-137

Developing countries economic aid from US, bilateral and through intl dev banks, by world region and country, 1970s-FY88, annual rpt, 9904-1

Education funding by Federal agency, program, and recipient type, and instn spending, FY80-88, 4828-21

Employee productivity improvement program of Fed Govt, coverage and impacts by function for selected agencies, FY86-87 and projected to 1992, 26306-3.103

Expenditures of Fed Govt in States, by type, program, agency, and State, FY88, annual rpt, 2464-2

Fed Govt contingent liabilities and claims paid on insured and guaranteed contracts with foreign obligors, by country and program, periodic rpt, 8002-12

Fed Govt financial operations, detailed data, *Treasury Bulletin*, quarterly rpt, 8002-4

Foreign and US economic indicators, trade balances, and exchange rates, for selected OECD and Asian countries, 1980s-89, semiannual rpt, 8002-14

Foreign govt and private obligors debt to US, by country and program, periodic rpt, 8002-6

Insurance (life) companies financial and tax impacts of Deficit Reduction Act and proposed reforms, for stock and mutual firms, 1984-88 and projected to FY94, 8008-138

Labor unions recognized in Fed Govt, agreements and membership by agency and facility, as of Jan 1989, biennial listing, 9844-14

Panama govt assets in US blocked under economic sanctions, and conditions and procedures for release, 1989, press release, 8008-135

Puerto Rico and other US possessions corporations tax incentives, finances, and operations by industry, and impacts on local economy, 1970s-83, biennial rpt, 8004-12

R&D funding by Fed Govt, by field, performer type, agency, and State, FY87-89, annual rpt, 9627-20

Savings and loan assns insolvency crisis, Bush Admin resolution proposals funding by source and use, projected FY89-99, press release, 8008-134

South Africa loans from US banks, and rescheduling issues, 1984-89, press release, 8008-136

Tax-related economic and fiscal topics, technical paper series, 8006-3

see also Bureau of Alcohol, Tobacco and Firearms

see also Bureau of Engraving and Printing

see also Bureau of the Public Debt

see also Federal Open Market Committee

see also Financial Management Service

see also Internal Revenue Service

see also Office of the Comptroller of Currency

see also Office of Thrift Supervision

see also U.S. Customs Service

see also U.S. Mint

see also U.S. Savings Bonds Division

see also U.S. Secret Service

see also under By Federal Agency in the "Index by Categories"

Department of Veterans Affairs

Activities and programs of VA, and veterans characteristics, FY88, annual rpt, 8604-3

Activities and programs of VA, monthly rpt, 8602-3

Board of Veterans Appeals caseloads and dispositions, 1988 hearing, 25768-47

Budget deficit reduction under Gramm-Rudman Act, cancellation of budget authority by program, FY90, annual rpt, 104-27; 21924-1; 26304-6

Budget of US Appendix, obligations, appropriations, and personnel, by program and agency, FY90, annual rpt, 104-3

Compensation and pension cases of VA, by type of entitlement and period of service, monthly rpt, 8602-5

Disability and death compensation cases of VA, by entitlement type, period of service, and sex, as of Mar 1989, semiannual rpt, 8602-8

Disability and death compensation cases of VA, by entitlement type, period of service, sex, age, and State, FY88, annual rpt, 8604-7

Disability compensation and pensions, VA claims processing and disposition, FY87, GAO rpt, 26121-293

Disability compensation cases of VA, effects of eliminating non-service connected disabilities, with background data, 1986, GAO rpt, 26121-295

Employee productivity improvement program of Fed Govt, coverage and impacts by function for selected agencies, FY86-87 and projected to 1992, 26306-3.103

Expenditures and beneficiaries of VA compensation, health, and rehabilitation programs, FY64-88, annual rpt, 8604-5

Expenditures for VA programs, by State, county, and congressional district, FY88, annual rpt, 8604-6

Fraud and abuse in VA programs, audits and investigations, 2nd half FY89, semiannual rpt, 8602-2

Health care clinics outpatient care applications, denials, appointments, and waiting periods, for 4 Florida VA clinics, FY88, GAO rpt, 26121-283

Health care facilities physicians staffing, and rehabilitation programs admin and effectiveness, for VA, 1988 hearing, 25768-48

Health care for veterans, patients, visits, costs, and operating beds, by VA and contract facility, and region, quarterly rpt, 8602-4

Health care professionals of VA, by selected employment characteristics and VA district, quarterly rpt, 8602-6

Insurance (life) for veterans and servicepersons, actuarial analysis of VA programs, 1988, annual rpt, 8604-1

Insurance (life) for veterans and servicepersons, finances and coverage by program and State, 1988, annual rpt, 8604-4

Labor unions recognized in Fed Govt, agreements and membership by agency and facility, as of Jan 1989, biennial listing, 9844-14

Loan guarantee operations of VA, quarterly rpt, 8602-2

Pay comparability of Fed Govt with private industry, and recommended pay rate adjustments, 1989, annual rpt, 104-16

Population of veterans, and benefits programs awareness and use, by age, sex, income, race, and period of service, 1987 survey, 8608-1

Population of veterans, by period of service, age, and State, as of Mar 1989, semiannual rpt, 8602-7

R&D funding by Fed Govt, by field, performer type, agency, and State, FY87-89, annual rpt, 9627-20

War participants, deaths, veterans living, and compensation and pension recipients, for each US war, 1775-1988, annual rpt, 8604-2

see also Veterans Administration

see also Veterans Benefits Administration

see also Veterans Health Services and Research Administration

see also under By Federal Agency in the "Index by Categories"

Department stores

Census of Retail Trade, 1987: employment, establishments, sales, and payroll, by SIC 2- to 4-digit kind of business, MSA, county, and city, State rpt series, 2397-1

Collective bargaining agreements expiring during year, and workers covered, by firm, union, industry group, and State, 1989, annual rpt, 6784-9

Construction authorized by building permits, by type of construction, region, State, and MSA, bimonthly rpt, 2042-1.3

County Business Patterns, 1987: employment, establishments, and payroll, by SIC 2- to 4-digit industry and county, annual State rpt series, 2326-8

Employment, earnings, and hours, by selected SIC 1- to 4-digit industry, State, and for 262 MSAs, 1972-87, 6748-81

Employment, earnings, and hours, by SIC 1- to 4-digit industry, monthly 1983-Feb 1989, annual rpt, 6744-4

Employment of minorities and women, by occupation, SIC 1- to 3- digit industry, State, and MSA, 1986, annual rpt, 9244-1

Finances and operations, by SIC 2- to 4-digit industry, forecast 1989 with trends from 1950s, annual rpt, 2044-28

Financial statements for manufacturing, mining, and trade corporations, by selected SIC 2- to 3-digit industry, quarterly rpt, 2502-1

Guam economic censuses, 1987: employment, firms, payroll, and receipts, by SIC 1- to 4-digit industry and election district, 2595-1

Inventory price indexes for department stores, by class of item, monthly table, 6762-7

Labor productivity, indexes of output, hours, and employment by SIC 2- to 4-digit industry, 1963-87, annual rpt, 6824-1.4

Military post exchange operations, and sales by commodity, by facility and location worldwide, FY87, annual rpt, 3504-10

Northern Mariana Islands economic census, 1987: employment, firms, payroll, and receipts, by SIC 1- to 4-digit industry, 2597-1

Fed Govt consolidated financial statements based on business accounting methods, FY87-88, annual rpt, 8104–5

Housing (rental) depreciation, age as an indicator of unit quality, and other factors, model description and results, 1988 working paper, 6886–6.29; 6886–6.35

Mental health care hospitals, beds and caseload by State, patient characteristics, finances, and staff, for profit and nonprofit private instns, 1986, 4506–3.37

Mergers and acquisitions using leveraged buyout, financing characteristics and policy issues, 1970s-88, 21368–115

Multinatl firms US affiliates, finances, and operations, by industry, world area of parent firm, and State, 1987, annual rpt, 2704–4

Multinatl US firms and foreign affiliates finances and operations, by industry of parent firm and affiliate, world area, and country, preliminary 1987, annual rpt, 2704–5

Natl income and product accounts and components, *Survey of Current Business*, monthly rpt, 2702–1.21; 2702–1.27

Natural gas interstate pipeline company detailed financial and operating data, by firm, 1988, annual rpt, 3164–38

Nonprofit charitable organizations finances, and assets and grants of top 10, 1985, article, 8302–2.923

Pollution abatement capital and operating costs, by SIC 2-to 4-digit industry and State, 1986, annual Current Industrial Rpt, 2506–3.6

Railroad (Class I) finances and operations, detailed data by firm, class of service, and district, 1987, annual rpt, 9486–6.1

Railroad (Class I) finances and operations, detailed data by firm, class of service, and district, 1988, annual rpt, 9486–5.1

Tax (income) depreciation accounting, with mean retention period of selected assets by type, 1989 technical paper, 8006–3.60

Tax (income) returns filed by type of filer, selected income items, quarterly rpt, 8302–2.1

Tax (income) returns of corporations, income and tax items by asset size and detailed industry, 1986, annual rpt, 8304–4; 8304–21

Tax (income) returns of corporations, summary data by asset size and industry div, 1986, annual article, 8302–2.922

Tax (income) returns of individuals, by filing status, tax item, and income level, 1987, annual article, 8302–2.901

Tax (income) returns of partnerships, income statement items by industry group, 1986, annual article, 8302–2.903

Tax (income) returns of sole proprietorships, income statement items, by industry group, 1987, annual article, 8302–2.904; 8302–2.921

Tax expenditures, Federal revenues forgone through income tax deductions and exclusions by type, FY90-94, annual rpt, 21784–10

Telephone and telegraph firms detailed finances and operations, 1987, annual rpt, 9284–6

Telephone firms borrowing under Rural Telephone Program, and financial and operating data, 1988, annual rpt, 1244–2

Truck and warehouse services finances and inventory, by SIC 2- to 4-digit industry, 1988 survey, annual rpt, 2413–14

Truck interstate carriers finances and operations, by district, 1987, annual rpt, 9486–6.2

Truck itemized costs per mile, finances, and operations, for agricultural carriers, 1988, annual rpt, 1311–15

Truck transport of fruit and vegetables, itemized costs per mile by item for fleets and owner-operator trucks, monthly table, 1272–1

TVA financial and operating data by program and facility, FY88, annual rpt, 9804–32

Depressions
see Business cycles

Deregulation
see Government and business
see Price regulation

Des Moines, Iowa
Wages by occupation, for office and plant workers, 1989 survey, periodic MSA rpt, 6785–3.8
see also under By City and By SMSA or MSA in the "Index by Categories"

Desegregation of schools
see Discrimination in education

Deserts
see Arid zones

Destroyers
see Naval vessels

Detective and protective services
Banks in Fed Reserve System, expenses and operations itemized by service, office, and district, 1988, annual rpt, 9364–11

County Business Patterns, 1987: employment, establishments, and payroll, by SIC 2- to 4-digit industry and county, annual State rpt series, 2326–8

Employment and occupation of householder, by occupation of spouse, race, and family composition, 1988, annual Current Population Rpt, 2546–1.437

Employment, earnings, and hours, by SIC 1- to 4-digit industry, monthly 1983-Feb 1989, annual rpt, 6744–4

Employment, unemployment, and labor force characteristics, by region and census div, 1988, annual rpt, 6744–7.1

Equipment for communications and security, FCC authorizations by type, FY88, annual rpt, 9284–4

Fed Reserve services provided depository instns, costs and revenue by service and district bank, 1987-88, article, 9362–1.908

Handbook of Labor Statistics, employment, unemployment, and labor force characteristics, 1940s-88 with trends from 1913, 6728–38

Higher education instn law enforcement personnel, by instn, 1988, annual rpt, 6224–2.3

Marshals Service activities, FY88, annual rpt, 6294–1

Receipts for services, by SIC 2- to 4-digit kind of business, 1988, annual rpt, 2413–8

Service industries census, 1987: establishments, receipts, employment, and payroll, by SIC 2- to 4-digit kind of business, MSA, county, and city, State rpt series, 2391–1

State and local govt employment of minorities and women, by occupation, function, pay level, and State, 1986, annual rpt, 9244–6

Detention
see Arrest
see Correctional institutions
see Habeas corpus
see Juvenile detention and correctional institutions
see Pretrial detention and release
see Prisoners

Detergent industry
see Soap and detergent industry

Detroit, Mich.
CPI by component for US city average, and by region, population size, and for 15 metro areas, monthly rpt, 6762–1

CPI by component for US city average, and by region, population size, and for 27 metro areas, monthly rpt, 6762–2

Drug abuse indicators for selected metro areas, research results, data collection, and policy issues, 1989 semiannual conf, 4492–5

Drug test results at arrest, by drug type, offense, and sex, for selected urban areas, quarterly rpt, 6062–3

Freight (waterborne domestic and foreign) by commodity, traffic, and passengers, by port and waterway, 1987, annual rpt, 3754–3.3

Fruit and vegetable shipments, and arrivals in US and Canada cities, by mode of transport and State and country of origin, 1988, annual rpt, 1311–4.1

Housing and households characteristics, 1985 survey, MSA fact sheet, 2485–11.13

Housing and households detailed characteristics, and unit and neighborhood quality, by location, 1985 survey, MSA rpt, 2485–6.9

Mammography referral services for low-income women, use and client characteristics, 1987-88 local area study, article, 4042–3.951

see also under By City and By SMSA or MSA in the "Index by Categories"

Developing countries
Agricultural and food aid to developing countries, and impacts on US exports, with background data, 1960s-89, 26308–85

Agricultural and food production and indexes, total and for selected commodities, by country, 1970s-88, annual rpt, 1524–12

Agricultural exports, for tropical and temperate commodities, 1986, article, 1522–3.919

Agricultural exports of high-value commodities from developing countries to OECD members, 1970s-87, article, 1522–3.921

Agricultural imports from US by world area, and grain trade impacts on production, for developing countries, 1960s-87, article, 1541–7.903

Agricultural policy impacts on economic dev, with background data for 6 developing countries, 1960s-86, 1528–283

Agricultural production, prices, and trade, by country, 1960s-89, annual world region rpt, 1524–4.2

Agricultural trade and market impacts of eliminating foreign and US protectionist policies, model description and results, 1986, 1528–282

Agricultural trade of US, by commodity and country, bimonthly rpt with articles, 1522–1

Agricultural trade of US, by detailed commodity and country, 1988, semiannual rpt, 1522–4

Agricultural trade share of production and total trade, by commodity and country group, 1960s-87, article, 1522–3.912

AID dev projects and socioeconomic impacts, evaluation rpt series, 9916–1

AID dev projects, special study series, 9916–3

AID economic aid to developing countries, obligations and disbursements by country, quarterly rpt, 9912–4

AID loans authorized, signed, and canceled, by country and world area, quarterly rpt, 9912–2

AID loans repayment status and terms by program and country, and status of predecessor agency loans, quarterly rpt, 9912–3

China trade, by commodity, world area, and country, 1985-87, 9118–10

Debt (foreign) and debt burden indicators, for Brazil and other developing countries, and aggregate loans from 9 US money center banks by bank, 1970s-88, hearings, 21248–122

Debt burden and economic conditions, and trade with industrialized countries, by developing country, 1970s-87, hearings, 25248–108

Debt reduction proposals for developing countries, and Eximbank export financing programs, with background data, 1986-89, 2048–142

Disaster preparedness and economic, population, and political data, country rpt series, 9916–2

Economic aid of US, bilateral and through intl dev banks, by world region and country, 1970s-FY87, annual rpt, 9904–1

Economic and military aid and loans from US and intl agencies, by program and country, FY46-87, annual rpt, 9914–5

Economic and social conditions of developing countries from 1960s, and Intl Dev Cooperation Agency and AID activities and funding, FY88-90, annual rpt, 9904–4

Economic conditions and food spending, for developing countries, 1987, article, 1522–3.911

Economic conditions and trade devs and policy, for US and foreign countries, 1988 conf papers, 9373–3.32

Economic conditions in Communist, OECD, and selected other countries, 1960s-88, annual rpt, 9114–4

Economic indicators of developing countries, problem debtors compared to other borrowers, by country, 1973-84, 1528–285

Exchange rate of dollar, indexes for 22 developing countries, 1972-86, article, 1522–3.917

Export revenues of developing countries, effects of trade policy changes in developing and developed countries, model results, 1989 article, 1522–3.922

Exports and imports of US, by commodity group, world area, selected country, US coastal area and port, and mode of transport, monthly rpt, 2422–9

Exports and imports of US, by selected country, country group, and commodity group, 1988, annual rpt, 2044–37

Exports, imports, and balances of US by commodity group, world area, and country, and related employment, 1970s-88, annual rpt, 2044–26

Exports, imports, and balances of US with major trading partners, by product category, 1984-88, annual chartbook, 9884–21

Fertilizer (nitrogen) production, and energy and other capital investments, for developing countries, various periods 1955-89, article, 1522–3.905

Finance (intl) and trade studies, 1987 biennial compilation, 9375–14

Fish catch and consumption, for Eastern Europe and other countries, 1970s-86, article, 2162–1.901

Food aid impacts on developing countries economic conditions and demand for US grain exports, model description and results, 1960s-84, 1528–291

Food production and needs, and related economic outlook, by country, 1989/90, annual rpt, 1524–6

Imports of US given duty-free treatment for value of US material sent abroad, and impacts on US industry and employment, by commodity and country, 1987, annual rpt, 9884–14

Investment (foreign direct) of US, by selected industry group and world area, 1986-88, annual article, 2702–1.930

Loans of banks and govts to developing countries, debt exposure of 7 developed countries, various periods 1980-88, GAO rpt, 26123–255

Loans of US banks to developing countries, ratios and reserves as share of loans, for leading instns, 1988, working paper, 9389–19.12

Loans of US banks to foreigners at all US and foreign offices, by country group and country, quarterly rpt, 13002–1

Military spending and imports of developing countries, measures to determine eligibility for US economic aid, by country, 1985-86, annual rpt, 9914–1

Military spending, arms trade, and force strengths, with govt spending and population, by country, 1977-87, annual rpt, 9824–1

Multinatl US firms and foreign affiliates finances and operations, by industry of parent firm and affiliate, world area, and selected country, 1987, annual article, 2702–1.920; 2704–5

Older persons in developing countries, population and selected characteristics, 1980s and projected to 2020, country rpt series, 2326–19

Overseas Private Investment Corp activities, and lists of grants and insured projects and firms, FY88, annual rpt, 9904–3

Overseas Private Investment Corp finances and activities, with list of insured projects and firms, FY88, annual rpt, 9904–2

Peace Corps activities, funding by program, and volunteers, by country, FY90, annual rpt, 9654–1

Population size, growth rates, and components of change, by country, projected 1989-2020 and trends from 1950, biennial rpt, 2324–9

Soviet Union and Warsaw Pact military weapons systems, aid, presence, and force strengths, and compared to US and NATO, 1989 annual rpt, 3504–20

Soviet Union arms sales to developing countries and Nicaragua, 1981-86, hearing, 23848–195

Statistical Abstract of US, social, political, and economic data, by outlying area and country, 1950s-87, comprehensive annual compilation, 2324–1.4

see also under By Foreign Country in the "Index by Categories"

see also under names of individual countries

Devesa, Susan S.

"Declining Lung Cancer Rates Among Young Men and Women in the U.S.: A Cohort Analysis", 4472–1.926

Devine, Patricia R.

"Effects of Economic Growth, Technology Change, Consumption Pattern Change, and Foreign Trade on Domestic Demand for Primary Metals, 1963-82", 5608–159

Dewald, William G.

"Effects of Disinflationary Policies on Monetary Velocity", 9377–9.74

DeWire, Elinor

"Sentinels on Watch", 2152–8.903

"Sentinels on Watch—2", 2152–8.904

Diabetes

Cases of acute and chronic conditions, disability, absenteeism, and health services use, by selected characteristics, 1988, annual rpt, 4147–10.170

Deaths and rates, by cause, age, sex, marital status, race, and State, 1987, US Vital Statistics advance annual rpt, 4146–5.113

Deaths and rates, by cause and age, preliminary 1987-88, US Vital Statistics annual rpt, 4144–7

Deaths and rates, by detailed cause and demographic characteristics, 1986 and trends from 1900, US Vital Statistics annual rpt, 4144–2

Deaths and rates, by detailed location, cause, and demographic characteristics, 1987, US Vital Statistics annual rpt, 4144–3

Hospital discharges and length of stay, by diagnosis, patient age and sex, surgical procedure performed, and region, 1965-86, 4147–13.101

Indian diabetes cases, by tribe, for New Mexico, 1985, article, 4042–3.964

Indian Health Service facilities, funding, operations, and Indian health and other characteristics, 1950s-88, annual chartbook, 4084–1

Indians with non-insulin-dependent diabetes trated at rural and urban clinics, glucose control levels and other health indicators, 1984-86 study, article, 4042–3.946

Kidney end-stage disease program of Medicare, enrollment and survival of dialysis and transplant patients by age, sex, race, and primary diagnosis, 1980-85, annual rpt, 4654–16.1; 4654–16.3

Nursing home facility, staff, and resident detailed characteristics, 1985, 4147–13.97

Fed Govt employment of minorities, handicapped, and veterans, and years of service, by occupation, age, sex, and agency, as of Sept 1988, biennial rpt, 9844-27

Fed Govt personnel action appeals, decisions of Merit Systems Protection Board by agency and region, FY88, annual rpt, 9494-2

Fed Govt spending in States, by type, program, agency, and State, FY88, annual rpt, 2464-2

Fed Govt violations of personnel practices, cases by type, FY88, annual rpt, 9494-3

Foreign Service minority and women employment, hires, and promotions, 1981-87, GAO rpt, 26123-247

Income and economic status of minority groups and women, and discrimination and govt policy impacts, series, 11046-7

Labor laws enacted, by State, 1988, annual article, 6722-1.904

Minority group and women employment, by occupation, SIC 1- to 3- digit industry, State, and MSA, 1986, annual rpt, 9244-1

State and local govt employment of minorities and women, by occupation, function, pay level, and State, 1986, annual rpt, 9244-6

State Dept and Foreign Service minority and women employment, FY88, annual rpt, 7004-21

State govt and Federal compliance with disabled persons employment and architectural barrier removal laws, findings and recommendations, 1989 rpt, 10048-74

Telecommunications industries minority employment and discrimination charges, with data by industry and selected firm, 1970s-88, hearings, 21368-113

Veterans (disabled) employment and promotion in Fed Govt by agency, and recruitment coordinator activities, FY81-87, GAO rpt, 26119-245

Discrimination in housing

Assistance (financial and nonfinancial) of Fed Govt, 1989 base edition with supplements, annual listing, 104-5

Fed Govt spending in States, by type, program, agency, and State, FY88, annual rpt, 2464-2

Diseases and disorders

Agent Orange exposure health effects, literature review, 1987, annual rpt series, 8706-1

Agent Orange exposure of Air Force personnel, deaths and rates by cause and selected characteristics, 1989 annual rpt, 3604-3

Aircraft pilots disease rates, by disease and age, 1988 technical rpt, 7506-10.55

Army active duty personnel health condition, and use of Army medical services in US and abroad, monthly rpt, 3702-4.2

Cases of acute and chronic conditions, disability, absenteeism, and health services use, by selected characteristics, 1988, annual rpt, 4147-10.170

Deaths and rates, by detailed cause and demographic characteristics, 1986 and trends from 1900, US Vital Statistics annual rpt, 4144-2

Developing countries disaster preparedness and economic, population, and political data, country rpt series, 9916-2

HHS financial aid, by program, recipient, State, and city, FY88, annual regional listings, 4004-3

Hospital discharges by detailed diagnostic and procedure category, primary diagnosis, and length of stay, by age, sex, and region, 1987, annual rpt, 4147-13.100

Indian Health Service facilities, funding, operations, and Indian health and other characteristics, 1950s-88, annual chartbook, 4084-1

Indian Health Service outpatient visits, by reason for visit and age, FY87-88, annual rpt, 4084-2

Military deaths by cause, age, race, and rank, and personnel captured and missing, by service branch, 2nd half FY88, semiannual rpt, 3542-21

Morbidity and Mortality Weekly Report, infectious notifiable disease cases by State, and public health issues, 4202-1

NIH rpts, 1989 annual listing, 4434-2

Nursing home use rates, charges, and resident length of stay, care needs, and other characteristics, 1985, 4147-13.102

Older persons health condition, chronic and multiple illness prevalence by sex and age group, 1984, 4146-8.172

Older persons social security issues, Fed Govt spending, and indicators of need, with bibl, 1988 compilation of papers, 25928-7

Older persons socioeconomic characteristics, 1900s-86 and projected to 2050, biennial chartbook, 12904-1

Pacific territories social, economic, health, and govtl data, FY88 and trends, annual rpt, 7004-6

Pollutants health effects, concentrations in food and environment, sources, and human intake methodology and data needs, series, 9186-9

Pollutants health effects, concentrations in food and environment, sources, human intake, and regulation, series, 9186-8

Statistical Abstract of US, social, political, and economic data, 1790-2025, comprehensive annual compilation, 2324-1.1

Texas-Mexico border area health facilities and services, with background data, by Texas county, 1980s-88, GAO rpt, 26121-261

Treatments and health products not proven safe or effective, use, costs, and user characteristics, 1986 survey, 4008-86

see also Accidents and accident prevention

see also Acquired immune deficiency syndrome

see also Alcohol abuse and treatment

see also Allergies

see also Animal diseases and zoonoses

see also Birth defects

see also Black lung disease

see also Blood diseases and disorders

see also Cardiovascular diseases

see also Cerebrovascular diseases

see also Circulatory diseases

see also Diabetes

see also Digestive diseases

see also Drug abuse and treatment

see also Ear diseases and infections

see also Epidemiology and epidemiologists

see also Eye diseases and defects

see also Food and waterborne diseases

see also Health condition

see also Hearing and hearing disorders

see also Hereditary diseases

see also Hypertension

see also Immunity disorders

see also Infective and parasitic diseases

see also Mental health and illness

see also Mental retardation

see also Metabolic and endocrine diseases

see also Mobility limitations

see also Musculoskeletal diseases

see also Neoplasms

see also Neurological disorders

see also Nose and throat disorders

see also Nutrition and malnutrition

see also Obesity

see also Occupational health and safety

see also Pathology

see also Pneumonia and influenza

see also Poisoning and drug reaction

see also Rabies

see also Respiratory diseases

see also Septicemia

see also Sexually transmitted diseases

see also Sickle cell anemia

see also Skin diseases

see also Spinal cord injuries

see also Tuberculosis

see also Urogenital diseases

see also Vaccination and vaccines

see also under By Disease in the "Index by Categories"

Displaced workers

see Labor turnover

Disposable income

see Personal and household income

Distillate fuels

see Diesel fuel

see Fuel oil

see Kerosene

Distribution of income

see Business income and expenses, general

see Earnings, general

see National income and product accounts

see Personal and household income

see Poverty

see Wealth

District courts

see Federal district courts

District of Columbia

see D.C.

Districts

see Central business districts

see Common markets and free trade areas

see Congressional districts

see School districts

see Special districts

Diversification of business

see Economic concentration and diversification

Divestiture

Energy producers finances and operations, by energy type for US firms domestic and foreign operations, 1987, annual rpt, 3164-44

Food marketing sector finances, operations, and merger activity, for processors and distributors, as of 1988, annual rpt, 1544-22

UK and France govt-owned corporations stock issues, value, new shareholders, and revenue effects, 1960s-88, article, 9385–1.911

Diving
  see Swimming

Division of Health Maintenance Organizations
  see Office of Health Maintenance Organizations

Division of Research Resources, NIH
  Activities and funding of DRR, by program, FY87, annual rpt, 4434–12
  Activities of NIH, funding, and advisory council recommendations, by inst, FY87-88, biennial rpt, 4434–16

Divorce
  see Marriage and divorce

Dixit, Praveen M.
  "Economic Implications of Agricultural Policy Reforms in Industrial Market Economies", 1528–282

Djibouti
  Agricultural and food production and indexes, total and for selected commodities, by country, 1970s-88, annual rpt, 1524–12
  Agricultural trade of US, by detailed commodity and country, 1988, semiannual rpt, 1522–4
  AID activities and funding by project and function, FY90, and developing countries summary socioeconomic data from 1960s, annual rpt, 9904–4.5
  AID economic aid to developing countries, obligations and disbursements by country, quarterly rpt, 9912–4
  Economic and military aid and loans from US and intl agencies, by program and country, FY46-87, annual rpt, 9914–5
  Economic, social, political, and geographic summary data, by country, 1989, annual factbook, 9114–2
  Human rights conditions in 170 countries, 1988, annual rpt, 21384–3
  Military aid of US, arms sales, and training programs costs and budget requests, by program, world region, and country, FY88-90, annual rpt, 7144–13
  Minerals Yearbook, 1987, Vol 3: foreign country reviews of production, trade, and policy, by commodity, annual rpt, 5604–35
  Minerals Yearbook, 1987, Vol 3 preprints: foreign country review of production, trade, and policy, by commodity, annual rpt, 5604–23.81
  Population size, growth rates, and components of change, by country, projected 1989-2020 and trends from 1950, biennial rpt, 2324–9
  UN voting record and share of votes in agreement with US, by issue, country, and world area, 1988, annual rpt, 7004–18
  see also under By Foreign Country in the "Index by Categories"

Doctors
  see Physicians

Documents
  see Bibliographies
  see Environmental impact statements
  see Government documents
  see Government forms and paperwork
  see Government publications lists

DOD
  see Department of Defense

DOE
  see Department of Energy

Dolbeare, Cushing N.
  "Low-Income Housing Crisis and Its Impact on Homelessness", 10048–73

Dolton, David D.
  "Mourning Dove Breeding Population Status, 1989", 5504–15

Dombey, Bonita J.
  "Strategic Defenses: Alternative Missions and Their Costs", 26308–87

Domestic International Sales Corporations
  Tax (income) returns filed by type of filer, selected income items, quarterly rpt, 8302–2.1
  Tax (income) returns of corporations, income and tax items by asset size and detailed industry, 1986, annual rpt, 8304–4; 8304–21
  Tax collection activity of IRS, by type of tax, FY88, annual rpt, 8304–3.3

Domestic relations
  see Child abuse and neglect
  see Domestic violence
  see Families and households
  see Marriage and divorce

Domestic violence
  Arrests, by offense, offender characteristics, and location, 1988, annual rpt, 6224–2.2
  Crimes, arrests, and rates, by offense, offender characteristics, population size, and jurisdiction, 1988, annual rpt, 6224–2.1; 6224–2.2
  Fed Govt financial and nonfinancial domestic aid, 1989 base edition with supplements, annual listing, 104–5
  Homeless shelters services, operations, and client characteristics, 1988 survey, 5188–123
  Homicides, by circumstance, victim and offender relationship, and type of weapon, 1988, annual rpt, 6224–2.1
  Police response to disturbances, officers assaulted and killed, by circumstances, 1988, annual rpt, 6224–3
  Shelters and support services for victims of domestic violence, HUD grants by recipient, 1989, press release, 5006–3.66
  Victimization rates, by victim and offender characteristics, circumstances, and offense, 1987 survey, annual rpt, 6066–3.41
  Victimizations and arrest, by offense, circumstances, and location, 1970s-87, annual rpt, 6064–6.3; 6064–6.4
  Victimizations, by offense, offender characteristics, and victim reactions and views, 1986-87, 6066–19.47
  see also Child abuse and neglect

Domestic workers and services
  Consumer spending, natl income and product account, *Survey of Current Business*, monthly rpt, 2702–1.23
  CPI by component for US city average, and by region, population size, and for 27 metro areas, monthly rpt, 6762–2
  Earnings by major industry group, and personal income per capita and by source, by region and State, 1929-87, 2708–40
  Educational attainment, by sociodemographic characteristics and location, 1987 and trends from 1940, biennial Current Population Rpt, 2546–1.427; 2546–1.431

Employment and Earnings, detailed data, monthly rpt, 6742–2
  Employment and occupation of householder, by occupation of spouse, race, and family composition, 1988, annual Current Population Rpt, 2546–1.437
  Employment, earnings, and hours, monthly press release, 6742–5
  Employment, unemployment, and labor force characteristics, by region and census div, 1988, annual rpt, 6744–7.1
  Handbook of Labor Statistics, employment, unemployment, and labor force characteristics, 1940s-88 with trends from 1913, 6728–38
  Health condition of labor force, and services use, by occupation and industry of longest job held, income, age, sex, and race. 1980, 4147–10.168
  Income (household, family, and personal), by source, detailed characteristics, and region, 1987, annual Current Population Rpt, 2546–6.59
  Workers compensation laws of States and Fed Govt, 1989 semiannual rpt, 6502–1
  Youth labor force status, by sex and race, summer 1985-89, annual press release, 6744–14
  see also Homemaker services

Domiciliary care
  see Group homes for the handicapped
  see Home health services
  see Homemaker services
  see Nursing homes
  see Respite care
  see Veterans health facilities and services

Dominica
  Economic conditions, income, production, prices, employment, and trade, 1989 periodic country rpt, 2046–4.18
  Economic, social, political, and geographic summary data, by country, 1989, annual factbook, 9114–2
  Human rights conditions in 170 countries, 1988, annual rpt, 21384–3
  Investment (direct) incentives of Caribbean Basin Initiative, economic impacts, with finances and employment by country, 1984-88, 2048–141
  Population size, growth rates, and components of change, by country, projected 1989-2020 and trends from 1950, biennial rpt, 2324–9
  UN voting record and share of votes in agreement with US, by issue, country, and world area, 1988, annual rpt, 7004–18
  see also under By Foreign Country in the "Index by Categories"

Dominican Republic
  Agricultural and food production and indexes, total and for selected commodities, by country, 1970s-88, annual rpt, 1524–12
  Agricultural production, prices, and trade, by country, 1960s-89, annual world region rpt, 1524–4.2
  Agricultural trade of US, by detailed commodity and country, 1988, semiannual rpt, 1522–4
  AID activities and funding by project and function, FY90, and developing countries summary socioeconomic data from 1960s, annual rpt, 9904–4.7
  AID economic aid to developing countries, obligations and disbursements by country, quarterly rpt, 9912–4

AID loans repayment status and terms by program and country, and status of predecessor agency loans, quarterly rpt, 9912-3

Economic and military aid and loans from US and intl agencies, by program and country, FY46-87, annual rpt, 9914-5

Economic conditions, income, production, prices, employment, and trade, 1989 periodic country rpt, 2046-4.70

Economic conditions, policy, and trade practices, by country, 1986-88, annual rpt, 21384-5

Economic, social, political, and geographic summary data, by country, 1989, annual factbook, 9114-2

Exports and imports of US, by commodity and country, 1970-87, world area rpt, 9116-1.1

Exports and imports of US, by selected country, country group, and commodity group, 1988, annual rpt, 2044-37

Exports of Caribbean area to OECD members, and US imports under preferential treatment programs, by commodity, 1980s-87, 2048-138

Human rights conditions in 170 countries, 1988, annual rpt, 21384-3

Investment (direct) incentives of Caribbean Basin Initiative, economic impacts, with finances and employment by country, 1984-88, 2048-141

Labor conditions, union coverage, and work accidents, 1989 annual country rpt, 6366-4.36

Military aid of US, arms sales, and training programs costs and budget requests, by program, world region, and country, FY88-90, annual rpt, 7144-13

Military spending, arms trade, and force strengths, with govt spending and population, by country, 1977-87, annual rpt, 9824-1

Minerals Yearbook, 1987, Vol 3: foreign country reviews of production, trade, and policy, by commodity, annual rpt, 5604-35

Minerals Yearbook, 1987, Vol 3 preprints: foreign country review of production, trade, and policy, by commodity, annual rpt, 5604-23.83

Population size, growth rates, and components of change, by country, projected 1989-2020 and trends from 1950, biennial rpt, 2324-9

Rum imports (duty-free) of US under Caribbean Basin Initiative, by country, 1987-88, annual rpt, 9884-15

Sugar production and exports, and cruise ship tourist visits and spending, by Caribbean area country, 1981-87, hearing, 21788-179

UN voting record and share of votes in agreement with US, by issue, country, and world area, 1988, annual rpt, 7004-18

see also under By Foreign Country in the "Index by Categories"

Dommen, Arthur J.
"World Situation in Perspective", 1522-3.906

Donald, James R.
"World and U.S. Agricultural Outlook", 1004-16.1

Donovan, Michael L.
"Land Use and the Nation's Estuaries", 2176-7.4

Dormitories
see Group quarters

Dornbusch, Rudiger
"Adjustment Mechanism: Theory and Problems", 9373-3.32

Dorwart, Robert A.
"Privatization of Mental Health Care and Directions for Mental Health Services Research", 4508-9

DOT
see Department of Transportation

Dothan, Ala.
see also under By SMSA or MSA in the "Index by Categories"

Dotsey, Michael
"Examination of International Trade Data in the 1980s", 9389-1.908

Doty, Pamela
"Long-Term Care in International Perspective", 4652-1.918

Douglas, Ariz.
Wages by occupation, and benefits for office and plant workers, 1989 survey, periodic MSA rpt, 6785-3.10

Douglas, Dean
"U.S. Petroleum Trade Trends: 1988", 3162-6.902

Dover, N.H.
see also under By SMSA or MSA in the "Index by Categories"

Drabenstott, Mark
"Agriculture and the GATT: The Link to U.S. Farm Policy", 9381-1.908
"U.S. Agriculture Shrugs off the Drought", 9381-1.902

Draft
see Draft evasion and protest
see Selective service

Draft evasion and protest
Prisoners and movements, by offense, location, and selected other characteristics, data compilation, 1930s-89, annual rpt, 6064-6.6
Sentences for Federal offenses, guidelines by offense and circumstances, 1989 rpt, 17668-1
US attorneys civil and criminal cases by type and disposition, and collections, by Federal district, FY88, annual rpt, 6004-2.1

Drain, Mary C.
"Heavy Rail Transit Safety, 1987 Annual Report", 7884-5

Drake, Dennis L.
"Composition of Foods: Cereal Grains and Pasta", 1356-3.12

Dran, Ellen M.
"Balanced Budgets and State Surpluses: The Politics of Budgeting in Illinois", 21528-72

Dredging
Army Corps of Engineers activities and projects, FY87 and trends from 1800s, annual rpt, 3754-1.2
Army Corps of Engineers water resources dev projects, characteristics, and costs, 1950s-87, biennial State rpt series, 3756-2
Army Corps of Engineers water resources dev projects, characteristics, and costs, 1950s-89, biennial State rpt series, 3756-1

Coastal areas environmental and socioeconomic conditions, and potential impact of oil and gas OCS leases, final statement series, 5736-1

Estuary shorelines, channels, area, and dredged material disposal area, by estuary, 1985, 2176-7.6

Great Lakes water levels fluctuations, causes, and impacts of alternative mgmt strategies, 1900s-88, series, 14646-1

Pacific territories and Hawaii harbor traffic, facilities, dev, funding, and needs, by port, as of 1987, 7308-195

Panama Canal dredging operations, FY88, annual rpt, 9664-3.2

Sedimentation control and research activity of Fed Govt, regional and project summaries, 1987, annual narrative rpt, 5664-9

Wetlands acreage conserved and disturbed in southeastern US, by disturbance type and State, 1987, article, 2162-1.902

Drinking places
see Restaurants and drinking places

Drinking water
see Water fluoridation
see Water supply and use

Drivers licenses
Accidents (fatal), deaths, and rates, by circumstances, characteristics of persons and vehicles involved, and location, 1987, annual rpt, 7764-10
Hwy Statistics, detailed data by State, 1988, annual rpt, 7554-1
Hwy Statistics, summary data by State, 1987-88, annual rpt, 7554-24
Licenses issued and in force by age and sex, fees, and renewal, by license class and State, 1987, annual rpt, 7554-16
Revenue potential of State and local tax systems relative to natl average tax burden, by type of tax and State, 1986, annual rpt, 10044-7
Revenues, by level of govt, type of tax, State, and selected large county, quarterly rpt, 2462-3
Revenues of State govts by detailed source, and tax rates, by State, FY88, annual rpt, 2466-2.3
Statistical Abstract of US, social, political, and economic data, 1790-2025, comprehensive annual compilation, 2324-1.3
Truck driver multi-State license prohibition, FHwA enforcement activities by region, 1987-88, GAO rpt, 26113-396

Driving while intoxicated
Accident deaths impacts of drinking age laws, by State, 1975-87, 7768-103
Accident deaths involving alcohol, by driver and victim blood alcohol levels, and other characteristics, 1977-87, annual rpt, 4486-1.2; 4486-1.5; 4486-1.8
Accident impacts of speed limits, with accident circumstances and speed averages, for States with 55 and 65 mph limit, 1986-87, annual rpt, 7764-15
Accidents (fatal), alcohol levels of drivers and others involved, by circumstances and characteristics of persons and vehicles, 1988, annual rpt, 7764-16
Accidents (fatal), alcohol levels of drivers and others involved, 1982-88, fact sheet, 7766-15.3

Health condition and health care resources, use, and spending, 1950s-87, annual data compilation, 4144-11

Hepatitis cases by infection source, age, sex, race, and State, and deaths, by strain, 1987 and trends from 1966, 4205-2

HHS financial aid, by program, recipient, State, and city, FY88, annual regional listings, 4004-3

High school seniors drug and alcohol use, by type and frequency, 1975-88, annual rpt, 4824-2.13

Homeless population characteristics by city, and Federal funding by program, 1980s-89, hearings, 21248-123

Homeless population characteristics, needs, and impacts of govt aid programs and housing costs, 1988 conf papers, 10048-73

Homeless shelters services, operations, and client characteristics, 1988 survey, 5188-123

Hospital mental health care units, length of stay related to patient, instn, and State Medicaid program characteristics, 1981, article, 4652-1.924

Hospitals for mental health care, beds and caseload by State, patient characteristics, finances, and staff, for profit and nonprofit private instns, 1986, 4506-3.37

Hospitals for mental health care of States and counties, patients and admissions by age, diagnosis, and State, FY87, annual rpt, 4504-2

Indian Health Service facilities, funding, operations, and Indian health and other characteristics, 1950s-88, annual chartbook, 4084-1

Insurance (health) coverage and provisions of employee benefit plans, by plan type and occupational group, 1988, annual rpt, 6784-19

Juvenile delinquency prevention funding, by program and Federal agency, FY88, annual rpt, 6064-11

Juvenile delinquent and status offenses, by sex, race, age, income, and urban-rural location, 1976-86 surveys, annual rpt, 6064-6.3

Labor laws enacted, by State, 1988, annual article, 6722-1.904

Methamphetamine abuse, emergency room admissions and deaths by selected city, and lab seizures, 1980s-87, 4498-61

Mexican American high school dropouts health condition, substance abuse, and involvement with violence, 1988-89 survey, article, 4042-3.957

Military deaths by cause, age, race, and rank, and personnel captured and missing, by service branch, 2nd half FY88, semiannual rpt, 3542-21

Military personnel alcohol and drug abuse, prevalence and consequences, by selected characteristics, 1988, biennial rpt, 3504-19

Navy drug and alcohol abuse education and treatment program activity, 2nd half FY88, semiannual tables, 3802-6

Nursing home use rates, charges, and resident length of stay, care needs, and other characteristics, 1985, 4147-13.102

Paraphernalia for drug abuse, mail order imports of US, proposed tariff schedule revisions, 1989 rpt, 9886-4.145

Parole and probation clients in program for drug- and alcohol-dependent Federal offenders, as of various dates 1984-89, annual rpt, 18204-2.5; 18204-8.4

PCP (phencyclidine) treatment admissions and deaths in selected areas, and emergency visits by patient sex, race, and age, 1987, article, 4042-3.931

Preventive disease and health improvement goals and recommended activities for 2000, with trends 1970s-80s, 4048-10

Prison conditions, population, and problems, issues and bibl, 1989 compilation of papers, 25928-8

Prisoners in State instns, by offense, criminal history, and inmate, family, and victim characteristics, 1986, annual rpt, 6064-26.3

Public opinion on taxes, spending, and govt efficiency, by respondent characteristics, 1989 survey, annual rpt, 10044-2

Research grants and awards of ADAMHA, by recipient, FY88, annual listing, 4044-13

Research on drug abuse and treatment, summaries of findings, resource materials, and grant listings, periodic rpt, 4492-4

Statistical Abstract of US, social, political, and economic data, 1790-2025, comprehensive annual compilation, 2324-1.1

Tobacco (smokeless) use by youth and adults, user characteristics, and sales, 1970s-86, papers, 4478-188

Treatment facilities for drug and alcohol abuse, services, use, funding, and client characteristics, 1987, annual rpt, 4494-10

Treatment facilities for drug and alcohol abuse, staff, and program characteristics, series, discontinued, 4496-8

Treatment facilities for drug and alcohol abuse, use, funding, and client and staff characteristics, series, discontinued, 4496-7

VA health care facilities mental health services, staff, research, and training programs, 1989 biennial listing, 8704-2

VA health care facilities physicians, dentists, and nurses, by selected employment characteristics and VA district, quarterly rpt, 8602-6

Youth drug, alcohol, and cigarette use and attitudes, by substance type and selected characteristics, 1975-88 surveys, annual rpt, 4494-4

see also Alcohol abuse and treatment
see also Cocaine
see also Drug and alcohol testing
see also Drug and narcotics offenses
see also Marijuana

Drug Abuse Warning Network

Emergency room admissions and deaths, by drug type and major metro area, July-Dec 1988, semiannual rpt, 4492-3

Emergency room admissions and deaths, by drug type and source, sex, race, age, and major metro area, 1988, annual rpt, 4494-8

Emergency room admissions, for selected metro areas, 1989 semiannual conf, 4492-5

Drug and alcohol testing

Arrests for drug- and nondrug-related offenses, urine test results by drug type, offense, and sex, for selected urban areas, quarterly rpt, 6062-3

Driving while intoxicated enforcement and publicity strategies, NHSTA deterrence project results, 1984-85, 7768-109

Driving while intoxicated, testing methods and analysis, technical data, 1986 conf, 6228-2

Employee drug testing, coverage, policies, sponsors, treatment aid provided, and results, by industry div, 1988, 6728-37

Navy drug and alcohol abuse education and treatment program activity, 2nd half FY88, semiannual tables, 3802-6

Prison employees drug testing, and training and treatment referrals provided, 1988 rpt, 6066-26.1

Public opinion on drug testing of selected groups, 1985-86 survey, annual rpt, 6064-6.2

Railroad accidents, circumstances, severity, and railroad involved, periodic rpt, 9612-3

State and local govt drug enforcement activities, Federal aid by recipient, and background data, FY88, annual rpt, 6064-28

Traffic accident deaths involving alcohol, by driver and victim blood alcohol levels and other characteristics, 1977-87, annual rpt, 4486-1.2; 4486-1.5; 4486-1.8

Traffic accidents and deaths, by alcohol level of driver, 1982-86, annual rpt, 6064-6.3

Traffic fatal accidents, alcohol levels of drivers and others, by circumstances and characteristics of persons and vehicles, 1988, annual rpt, 7764-16

Drug and narcotics offenses

Abuse of drugs, indicators for selected metro areas, research results, data collection, and policy issues, 1989 semiannual conf, 4492-5

Aliens excluded and deported from US by cause, and Immigration and Naturalization Service narcotics control, FY81-88, annual rpt, 6264-2

Arrest rates, by offense, sex, age, and race, 1987, annual rpt, 6224-7

Arrests by offender characteristics, prosecutions, convictions, and sentences by type, by felony offense, 1983-86, 6066-19.52

Arrests, by offense, offender characteristics, and location, 1970s-87, annual rpt, 6064-6.4

Arrests, by offense, offender characteristics, and location, 1988, annual rpt, 6224-2.2

Arrests for drug- and nondrug-related offenses, urine test results by drug type, offense, and sex, for selected urban areas, quarterly rpt, 6062-3

Budget of US, Bush Admin policy changes by program, FY90, 028-32

Budget of US, Reagan Admin policy changes by program, FY90, annual rpt, 104-21

Coast Guard drug and illegal alien enforcement activities, 2nd half FY89, semiannual rpt, 7402-4

Court civil and criminal caseloads for Federal district, appeals, and special courts, June 1989, annual rpt, 18204-2; 18204-8

Crime, criminal justice admin and enforcement, and public opinion, data compilation, 1970s-88, annual rpt, 6064-6

Crimes, arrests, and rates, by offense, offender characteristics, population size, and jurisdiction, 1988, annual rpt, 6224-2.1; 6224-2.2

Criminal case processing from arrest to sentencing, cases and duration by disposition, offense, and defendant characteristics, for selected cities, 1986, annual rpt, 6064-27

Criminal case processing in Federal district courts, and dispositions, by offense, district, and offender characteristics, 1984, annual rpt, 6064-29

Criminal case processing in Federal district courts, disposition by offense, 1980-87, 6066-19.50

Customs Service activities, collections, entries processed by mode of transport, and seizures, FY84-88, annual rpt, 8144-1

DC metro area drug abuse, deaths, arrests, convictions, and seizures by drug type, 1980-87, hearing, 21308-24

Diplomats and staff with immunity for foreign missions in US and US missions abroad, and foreign diplomats criminal cases, 1978-87, hearing, 25388-51

Fed Govt drug abuse and trafficking reduction programs by agency, and Bush Admin budget request, by program area, FY87-90, 238-1

Fed Govt financial and nonfinancial domestic aid, 1989 base edition with supplements, annual listing, 104-5

Fed Govt interdiction of drug smuggling by aircraft, activities, funding, and radar system capabilities, by agency, FY82-89, GAO rpt, 26119-259

Firearms violations enhanced and mandatory sentences, for cases under Bur of Alcohol, Tobacco, and Firearms investigation program, FY87-88, 8488-6

Foreign countries drug production, eradication, and seizures, by illegal substance, with US aid, by country, 1985-89, annual rpt, 7004-17

Foreign countries economic and military aid loans and grants from US and intl agencies, by program and country, FY46-87, annual rpt, 9914-5

Homicides, by circumstance, victim and offender relationship, and type of weapon, 1988, annual rpt, 6224-2.1

Juvenile court delinquency cases, by offense, referral source, disposition, age, sex, race, State, and county, 1985, annual rpt, 6064-12

Juvenile court referrals by offender characteristics, and dispositions, by offense, 1984, 6066-27.2

Juvenile delinquent and status offenses, by sex, race, age, income, and urban-rural location, 1976-86 surveys, annual rpt, 6064-6.3

Juvenile offenders recidivism rates, arrests, and court referrals, by offense, age, and sex, 1983 local area studies, 6068-227

Marijuana crop eradication activities of DEA and local agencies by State, and drug potency, 1982-88, annual rpt, 6284-4

Methamphetamine abuse, emergency room admissions and deaths by selected city, and lab seizures, 1980s-87, 4498-61

Organized Crime Drug Enforcement Task Forces regional investigation activities by agency and region, and background data, FY83-88, annual rpt, 6004-17

Postal Service inspection activities, expenses, and staff, FY88, annual rpt, 9864-8

Postal Service inspection activities, FY88, annual rpt, 9864-9

Postal Service inspection and law enforcement activities, by type, FY88, annual rpt, 9864-5.3

Prisoners in Federal and State instns by sex, admissions, and instn capacity and overcrowding, by State, 1980s-87, annual rpt, 6066-25.21

Prisoners in State instns, by offense, criminal history, and inmate, family, and victim characteristics, 1986, annual rpt, 6064-26.3

Recidivism rates of prisoners released in 1983, by offense and prisoner characteristics, 1983-86, 6066-19.48

Sentences by State courts for felony offenses, and sentence lengths and time served, by offense, 1986, 6066-25.19

Sentences for Federal crimes, guidelines use and results by offense and district, and Sentencing Commission activities, 1988, annual rpt, 17664-1

Sentences for Federal offenses, guidelines by offense and circumstances, 1989 rpt, 17668-1

State and local govt drug enforcement activities, Federal aid by recipient, and background data, FY88, annual rpt, 6064-28

Statistical Abstract of US, social, political, and economic data, 1790-2025, comprehensive annual compilation, 2324-1.1

Supply of drugs in US by country of origin, abuse, deaths, prices, and seizures, by substance, 1988, annual rpt, 6284-2

Tax litigation and enforcement activity of IRS, FY88, annual rpt, 8304-3.1

US attorneys civil and criminal cases by type and disposition, and collections, by Federal district, FY88, annual rpt, 6004-2.1; 6004-2.7

Wiretaps authorized, costs, arrests, trials, and convictions, by offense and jurisdiction, 1988, annual rpt, 18204-7

Drug Enforcement Administration

Budget of US Appendix, obligations, appropriations, and personnel, by program and agency, FY90, annual rpt, 104-3

DC metro area drug arrests, convictions, and seizures by drug type, and DEA staff by occupational group, 1980-87, hearing, 21308-24

Foreign countries drug enforcement personnel training of US, enrollment in US and host countries by program, FY88, annual rpt, 7004-17

Marijuana crop eradication activities of DEA and local agencies by State, and drug potency, 1982-88, annual rpt, 6284-4

Supply of drugs in US by country of origin, abuse, deaths, prices, and seizures, by substance, 1988, annual rpt, 6284-2

Drug industry
see Pharmaceutical industry

Drug Use Forecasting System

Drug test results at arrest, by drug type, offense, and sex, for selected urban areas, quarterly rpt, 6062-3

Drugs

AIDS patients and persons with AIDS virus infection, Medicaid policies and State health insurance regulation, with background data, 1987-88, article, 4652-1.953

AIDS patients Medicaid claims and payments, by type of care and whether AIDS-related, race, sex, and diagnosis, 1984-87, article, 4042-3.940

AIDS patients Medicaid enrollment, services use, and charges, for California, 1981-84, article, 4652-1.907

Allergy and Infectious Diseases Natl Inst activities, grants by recipient and location, and disease incidence, FY81-88, annual rpt, 4474-30

Biotechnology in Japan, R&D spending, industry finances, and govt involvement, FY85-86, 2048-139

Carcinogens chemistry, sources, environment and health risks, and regulation, by substance and brand, 1989, annual rpt, 4044-15

Cardiologist office visits, by characteristics of patient, physician, and visit, 1985, 4146-8.174

Cardiovascular diseases cases, health care services use and costs, and productivity losses, by selected characteristics, 1980, 4146-12.26

Cephalexin capsules (generic) from Canada at less than fair value, injury to US industry, investigation with background financial and operating data, 1989 rpt, 9886-14.267

China trade by SITC 1- to 5-digit commodity, 1970s-87, annual rpt, 9114-3

Consumer Expenditure Survey, household income by source, and itemized spending, by selected characteristics and location, 1984-86, annual rpt, 6764-5.2

Consumer spending in metro and nonmetro areas, by item, 1987, article, 6722-1.962

Controlled drugs provided during physician office visits, by drug, patient, and provider characteristics, 1985, 4146-8.179

CPI by component for US city average, and by region, population size, and for 27 metro areas, monthly rpt, 6762-2

Disabled college student alcohol and drug abuse, and prescription drug use, local area study, 1989 article, 4482-1.904

Epilepsy patients cancer risk relation to anticonvulsant drug treatment and radioactive thorium dioxide exposure, 1989 article, 4472-1.914

Expenditures for health care, by service type, payment source, and sector, 1960s-87, annual article, 4652-1.926

Exports and imports (agricultural) of US, by commodity and country, bimonthly rpt with articles, 1522-1

Exports and imports (agricultural) of US, by detailed commodity and country, 1988, semiannual rpt, 1522-4

Exports of US, detailed commodities by country, monthly rpt, 2422-3

Freight (waterborne domestic and foreign) by commodity, traffic, and passengers, by port and waterway, 1987, annual rpt, 3754–3

Health Care Financing Review, provider prices, price inputs and indexes, and labor, quarterly journal, 4652–1.1

Heart transplants performed by hospital, charges, payment sources, nonpaying patients, and waiting periods, 1986-88, GAO rpt, 26121–281

Imports detained by FDA, by reason, product, shipper, brand, and country, monthly listing, 4062–2

Imports of US, detailed Schedule A commodities by country, monthly rpt, 2422–2

Input-output structure of US economy, detailed interindustry transactions for 84 industries, and components of final demand, 1983, annual article, 2702–1.909

Insurance (health) coverage and provisions of employee benefit plans, by plan type and occupational group, 1988, annual rpt, 6784–19

Manufacturing annual survey, 1986: value of shipments, by SIC 4- to 5-digit product class, 2506–15.3

Manufacturing census, 1987: financial and operating data, for SIC 4-digit industries by product, preliminary rpt, 2491–1.35

Medicaid beneficiaries and payments, by service type, FY72-87, annual rpt, 4744–3.6

Medicaid coverage, participation, payments, admin, and legislative history, with data by State, 1980s-88, 21368–105

Medicaid enrollment, and service use and costs by service type, by eligibility type, for 5 States, 1980-84, article, 4652–1.919

Medicaid enrollment, services use, and costs, by eligibility type and length of enrollment, for 2 States, 1980-83, article, 4652–1.906

Medicaid reimbursement for prescription drugs under alternative methods of determining pharmacy costs, for Wisconsin, 1986, article, 4652–1.933

Medicare and Medicaid beneficiaries and program operations, 1988, annual fact book, 4654–18

Medicare and Medicaid eligibility, participation, coverage, and program finances, various periods 1966-89, biennial rpt, 4654–1

Medicare and other insurance programs catastrophic illness coverage, benefits, premiums, costs, and program finances, projected 1988-93, 26306–3.105

Medicare beneficiaries prescription drug use and spending, and costs of catastrophic coverage, 1987 and projected to 1993, 26308–89

Medicare beneficiaries prescription drug use and spending, by selected characteristics, 1987, 4186–8.3

Medicare discharges, charges, and length of stay, by State and diagnosis, 1983 and 1985, article, 4652–1.925

Medicare reimbursement of hospitals under prospective payment system, and of physicians, effect on services, finances, and beneficiary payments, 1970s-88, annual rpt, 17204–2

Nursing home compliance with Medicare and Medicaid regulations, and patient characteristics, by facility, 1987/88, annual State rpt series, 4654–15

Nursing home facility, staff, and resident detailed characteristics, 1985, 4147–13.97

OECD trade, total and for 4 major countries, and US trade by country, by commodity, 1970-87, world area rpt series, 9116–1

Older persons health care services use, persons with high and low levels of care by selected health and other characteristics, 1971 and 1980 studies, 4186–2.22

Ophthalmologist office visits, by characteristics of physician, practice, patient, and visit, with drug mentions by type and brand, 1985, 4146–8.166

Orphan drug tax credit, corporate income tax returns by asset size and detailed industry, 1986, annual rpt, 8304–4; 8304–21

Orphan drug tax credit, corporate income tax returns, quarterly rpt, 8302–2.1

Pregnancy-related services use and costs, for Medicaid beneficiaries in 3 States, 1983-84, article, 4652–1.938

Prescription drug abuse, emergency room admissions by drug type and major metro area, 1988, annual rpt, 4494–1

Prescriptions for drugs, by drug type and brand, and for new drugs, 1987, annual rpt, 4064–12

Price indexes (producer), by stage of processing and detailed commodity, monthly rpt, 6762–6

Price indexes (producer), by stage of processing and detailed commodity, monthly 1988, annual rpt, 6764–2

Production and sales of synthetic organic chemicals, and manufacturer listing, by product, 1988, annual rpt, 9884–3

Production of synthetic organic chemicals, by detailed product, quarterly rpt, 9882–1

Regulatory and investigation activities of FDA, quarterly rpt, 4062–3

Reproduction and population research, Fed Govt funding by project, FY87, annual listing, 4474–9

Safety and effectiveness of health care, use of unproven treatments and products, costs, and user characteristics, 1986 survey, 4008–86

Sexually transmitted disease treatment and diagnosis guidelines, 1989 rpt, 4206–2.17

Statistical Abstract of US, social, political, and economic data, 1790-2025, comprehensive annual compilation, 2324–1.1

Stockpiling of strategic material by Fed Govt, activity, and inventory by commodity, as of Sept 1989, semiannual rpt, 3542–22; 3902–2

Stockpiling of strategic material, inventories and needs, by commodity, as of Sept 1988, annual rpt, 3544–37

Stockpiling of strategic material, inventories, costs, and goals by commodity, as of June 1989, semiannual rpt, 3902–3

Wholesale trade census, 1987: employment, establishments, finances, and operations, by SIC 2- to 4-digit kind of business, MSA, county, and city, State rpt series, 2405–1

see also Biologic drug products
see also Chemotherapy
see also Cocaine
see also Drug abuse and treatment
see also Drug and alcohol testing
see also Drug and narcotics offenses
see also Drugstores
see also Hormones
see also Marijuana
see also Pharmaceutical industry
see also Poisoning and drug reaction
see also Vaccination and vaccines
see also under By Commodity in the "Index by Categories"

Drugstores

Census of Retail Trade, 1987: employment, establishments, sales, and payroll, by SIC 2- to 4-digit kind of business, MSA, county, and city, State rpt series, 2397–1

County Business Patterns, 1987: employment, establishments, and payroll, by SIC 2- to 4-digit industry and county, annual State rpt series, 2326–8

Employment, earnings, and hours, by SIC 1- to 4-digit industry, monthly 1983-Feb 1989, annual rpt, 6744–4

Employment of minorities and women, by occupation, SIC 1- to 3- digit industry, State and MSA, 1986, annual rpt, 9244–1

Finances and operations, by SIC 2- to 4-digit industry, forecast 1989 with trends from 1950s, annual rpt, 2044–28

Guam economic censuses, 1987: employment, firms, payroll, and receipts, by SIC 1- to 4-digit industry and election district, 2595–1

Labor productivity, indexes of output, hours, and employment by SIC 2- to 4-digit industry, 1963-87, annual rpt, 6824–1.4

Occupational injury and illness rates, by SIC 2- to 4-digit industry, 1987, annual rpt, 6844–1

Sales and inventories, by kind of retail business, region, and selected State, MSA, and city, monthly rpt, 2413–3

Sales, inventories, purchases, gross margin, and accounts receivable, by SIC 2- to 4-digit kind of business and form of ownership, 1987, annual rpt, 2413–5

Sales of retailers, by kind of business, advance monthly rpt, 2413–2

Science, engineering, and technical employment in transportation, utilities, and retail and wholesale trade, by field, occupation, and industry, 1985, triennial rpt, 9627–32

Tax (income) returns of corporations, income and tax items by asset size and detailed industry, 1986, annual rpt, 8304–4; 8304–21

Tax (income) returns of partnerships, income statement items by industry group, 1986, annual article, 8302–2.903

Tax (income) returns of sole proprietorships, income statement items, by industry group, 1987, annual article, 8302–2.904; 8302–2.921

Virgin Islands economic censuses, 1987: employment, firms, payroll, and receipts, by SIC 1- to 4-digit industry, island, and city, 2593–1

Drunk drivers
see Driving while intoxicated

Drunkenness
see Alcohol abuse and treatment

Drury, Thomas F.
"Access to Ambulatory Health Care: U.S., 1974", 4147–16.2

Dubai
see United Arab Emirates

Dubin, Elliott J.
"Do Federal Funds Help Spur Rural Development?", 1502–7.901
"Geographic Distribution of Federal Funds in 1985", 1598–248

Dubuque, Iowa
see also under By SMSA or MSA in the "Index by Categories"

Due process of law
Court caseloads, actions, procedure duration, judges, and jurors, by Federal district and appeals court, 1984-89, annual rpt, 18204–3
Court civil and criminal caseloads for Federal district, appeals, and special courts, June 1989, annual rpt, 18204–2; 18204–8
Criminal case processing from arrest to sentencing, cases and duration by disposition, offense, and defendant characteristics, for selected cities, 1986, annual rpt, 6064–27
Foreign countries human rights conditions in 170 countries, 1988, annual rpt, 21384–3
Torts for product liability, dispositions, awards, case processing time, and plaintiff injury severity and other characteristics, 1983-85, GAO rpt, 26121–317
US attorneys civil and criminal cases by type and disposition, and collections, by Federal district, FY88, annual rpt, 6004–2.1; 6004–2.7
see also Civil procedure
see also Criminal procedure

Duewer, Lawrence A.
"Effects of Meat Imports on the Puerto Rican Livestock-Meat Industry", 1568–282

Duffield, James A.
"Farm Labor Inputs", 1561–16.901
"Labor Expenditures Help Determine Farms Affected by Immigration Reform", 1598–250

Duffy-Deno, Kevin T.
"Public Infrastructure and Regional Economic Development: A Simultaneous Equations Approach", 9377–9.81

Dufour, Mary C.
"Alcohol-Related Morbidity Among the Disabled: The Medicare Experience 1985", 4482–1.905

Duke, John
"Multifactor Productivity Slips in the Nonrubber Footwear Industry", 6722–1.920

Duke, Richard
"Local Building Codes and the Use of Cost-Saving Methods", 9406–1.56

Duleep, Harriet O.
"Economic Status of Americans of Asian Descent: An Exploratory Investigation", 11046–7.2

Duluth, Minn.
see also under By SMSA or MSA in the "Index by Categories"

Dumper, Thomas A.
"Magnitude and Extent of Water Quality Problems in the U.S.", 1004–16.1

Dumping
Communist countries imports of US, status of dumping investigations by product, quarterly rpt with articles, 9882–2
Duties on US imports under antidumping and countervailing orders, and duty assessment and reporting errors, 1987-88, GAO rpt, 26119–270
Export and import agreements, negotiations, anticompetitive investigations, and related legislation, FY86-88, annual rpt, 444–1
Imports injury to US industries from foreign subsidized products and sales at less than fair value, investigations with background financial and operating data, series, 9886–19
Imports injury to US industries from foreign subsidized products, investigations with background financial and operating data, series, 9886–15
Imports injury to US industries from sales at less than fair value, investigations with background financial and operating data, series, 9886–14
USITC activities, investigations, and rpts, FY88, annual rpt, 9884–1
see also Trade adjustment assistance

Dumps
see Hazardous waste and disposal
see Landfills
see Radioactive waste and disposal
see Refuse and refuse disposal

Duncan, Douglas
"1988 Drought Did Not Dry Up Credit", 1502–7.916

Duncan, Marvin R.
"Revitalizing the Farm Credit System", 1004–16.1

Dunham, Constance R.
"New Banks in New England", 9373–1.903

Dunham, Denis
"Food Cost Review, 1988", 1544–9

Dunkirk, N.Y.
see also under By SMSA or MSA in the "Index by Categories"

Dupre, William R.
"Yukon Delta Coastal Processes Study", 2176–1.24

Durant, Sharon L.
"Testing Telephone Interviewing in the Survey of Income and Program Participation and Some Early Results", 2626–10.74

Durham, N.C.
Wages by occupation, and benefits for office and plant workers, 1989 survey, periodic MSA rpt, 6785–3.7
see also under By City and By SMSA or MSA in the "Index by Categories"

Durst, Ron L.
"Recent Developments in Federal Income Taxation for Farmers", 1541–1.905

Dursthoff, Clay
"Significant Features of Fiscal Federalism, 1989 Edition. Volume I", 10044–1.1
"Significant Features of Fiscal Federalism, 1989 Edition. Volume II", 10044–1.2

Duties
see Tariffs and foreign trade controls

Dwyer, Gerald P., Jr.
"Are National Stock Markets Linked?", 9391–1.901
"Bank Runs and Private Remedies", 9391–1.915
"Interest Rates and Economic Announcements", 9391–1.909

Dyes
see Paints and varnishes

Dykacz, Janice M.
"Postrecovery Experience of Disabled-Worker Beneficiaries", 4742–1.924
"Projected Outcomes and Length of Time in the Disability Insurance Program", 4742–1.923

Eagle, Eva
"Postsecondary Enrollment, Persistence, and Attainment for 1972, 1980, and 1982 High School Graduates", 4848–35

Ear diseases and infections
Cases of acute and chronic conditions, disability, absenteeism, and health services use, by selected characteristics, 1988, annual rpt, 4147–10.170
Deaths and rates, by detailed cause and demographic characteristics, 1986 and trends from 1900, US Vital Statistics annual rpt, 4144–2
Hospital discharges and length of stay, by diagnosis, patient age and sex, surgical procedure performed, and region, 1965-86, 4147–13.101
see also under By Disease in the "Index by Categories"

Earley, Thomas C.
"Relative Price Support Levels for Sugar and Other Crops", 1004–16.1

Earnings, general
AFDC recipients demographic and financial characteristics, by State, FY87, annual rpt, 4694–1
Alien workers (unauthorized) employer sanctions impacts on wages and output under alternative levels of enforcement, 1988 technical paper, 9379–12.33
Asian American earnings, and employment and other characteristics, by detailed origin and whether foreign-born, 1980, 11046–7.2
Budget of US, CBO analysis of revenue and spending alternatives and projections of economic indicators, FY90-94, annual rpt, 26304–3
Business and financial statistics, historic trends, 1988 annual chartbook, 9364–2.4
Business Conditions Digest, earnings and compensation indexes, monthly rpt, 2702–3.6
Child support awards related to selected variables, 1970s-85, 4008–94
Collective bargaining contract expirations, wage increases, and coverage, by major industry and selected firm and union, 1989, annual article, 6722–1.902
Collective bargaining wage and benefit changes and coverage, by industry sector and whether contract includes escalator clause and lump sum payment, 1968-88, annual article, 6722–1.923
Collective bargaining wage and benefit changes, by industry div, monthly rpt, 6782–1

Collective bargaining wage and benefit changes, by sector, 1954-88, 6728-38.7

Collective bargaining wage and benefit changes, quarterly press release, 6782-2

Collective bargaining wage and benefit concessions and workers affected, by type of concession and major industry group, 1975-88, article, 9385-1.912

Consumer spending relation to income and earnings, alternative models description and results, various periods 1929-87, technical paper, 9366-6.171

Degrees (bachelor) awarded 1985/86, holders annual salary by field and occupation, 1987, biennial rpt, 4826-3.1

Disabled persons employment, labor force status, and other characteristics, 1988, Current Population Rpt, 2546-2.147

Disabled persons rehabilitation, Federal and State activities and funding, FY88, annual rpt, 4944-1

Distribution of earnings, alternative measures by race, sex, industry sector, and region, 1960-80, article, 6722-1.917

Earnings and hours of production or nonsupervisory workers on nonagricultural payrolls, monthly rpt, 6742-2.6

Earnings by industry div, and personal income per capita and by source, by State, MSA, and county, 1982-87, annual regional rpts, 2704-2

Earnings by industry group, region, and State, 1986-88, annual article, 2702-1.928

Earnings by major industry group, and personal income per capita and by source, by region and State, 1929-87, 2708-40

Earnings, employment, hours, and productivity, by industry div, selected years 1929-88, annual rpt, 204-1.2

Earnings, income, population, and employment growth rates, by area population size and region, 1969-79 and 1979-87, article, 2702-1.915

Earnings per hour in private economy, natl compounded annual rates of change, monthly rpt, 9391-3.2

Economic indicators and components, and Fed Reserve 4th District business and financial conditions, monthly chartbook, 9377-10

Economic indicators and components, current data and annual trends, monthly rpt, 23842-1.2

Economic indicators compounded annual rates of change, 1969-88, annual rpt, 9391-9.2

Economic indicators, prices, labor costs, and productivity, BLS econometric analyses and methodology, working paper series, 6886-6

Education statistics, detailed data on higher education, 1960s-88, annual rpt, 4824-1.2

Employment conditions, alternative BLS projections to 2000 and trends 1970s-88, biennial article, 6722-1.955

Employment, earnings, and hours, by selected SIC 1- to 4-digit industry, State, and for 262 MSAs, 1972-87, 6748-81

Employment, earnings, and hours, by SIC 1- to 4-digit industry, monthly 1983-Feb 1989, annual rpt, 6744-4

Employment, earnings, and hours, monthly press release, 6742-5

Employment services participation, placement rates, wages relative to community rates, and Federal funding, 1980-87, GAO rpt, 26121-296

Employment shifts among industries, factors and impacts on wage growth, with data by industry group, 1948-87, 23848-207

Employment situation, earnings, hours, and other BLS economic indicators, transcripts of BLS Commissioner's monthly testimony, periodic rpt, 23846-4

Family members employment status and earnings, by family composition and race, quarterly press release, 6742-21

Food stamp eligibility and payment errors, by type, recipient characteristics, and State, FY87, annual rpt, 1364-15

Handbook of Labor Statistics, employment, unemployment, and labor force characteristics, 1940s-88 with trends from 1913, 6728-38

Higher education grads and advanced degree recipients, average salaries by field, 1989 edition, annual rpt, 4824-2.28

Hispanic Americans socioeconomic characteristics, by detailed origin, 1988, Current Population Rpt, 2546-1.430; 2546-1.438

Household composition, income, benefits, and labor force status, Survey of Income and Program Participation methodology, working paper series, 2626-10

Imports and tariff provisions effect on US industries and products, investigations with background financial and operating data, series, 9886-4

Imports injury to US industries from foreign subsidized products and sales at less than fair value, investigations with background financial and operating data, series, 9886-19

Imports injury to US industries from foreign subsidized products, investigations with background financial and operating data, series, 9886-15

Imports injury to US industries from sales at less than fair value, investigations with background financial and operating data, series, 9886-14

Income (household) by source, and itemized spending, by selected characteristics and region, 1984-87 Consumer Expenditure Surveys, annual rpt, 6764-5

Income (household, family, and personal), by source, detailed characteristics, and region, 1987, annual Current Population Rpt, 2546-6.59

Income (personal) by source, and BEA and IRS adjusted gross income measures, 1984-86 with trends from 1947, article, 8302-2.914

Income (personal) by source, and BEA and IRS adjusted gross income measures, 1986-87, annual article, 2702-1.927

Indian and Alaska Native earnings, by urban-rural location and other characteristics, 1980, article, 1502-7.904

Industry finances and operations, by SIC 2- to 4-digit industry, forecast 1989 and trends from 1950s, annual rpt, 2044-28

Insurance (health) coverage of total and working population, by selected characteristics, 1987, 4186-8.1

Job Training Partnership Act occupational training and other services provision, and outcomes, by participant characteristics, 1982-86, GAO rpt, 26106-8.8

Job Training Partnership Act participant occupational training and placements by occupation and skill level, and placement wages, by sex, 1982-86, GAO rpt, 26106-8.9

Labor force composition, and wages relation to inflation and unemployment, late 1930s-88, article, 9373-1.902

Labor force, wages, hours, and payroll costs, by major industry group and demographic characteristics, *Survey of Current Business*, monthly rpt, 2702-1.5

Labor laws enacted, by State, 1988, annual article, 6722-1.904

Law enforcement spending and employment, by activity and level of govt, 1970s-88, annual rpt, 6064-6.1

Manufacturing census, 1987: financial and operating data, for SIC 4-digit industries by product, preliminary industry rpt series, 2491-1

Married couple earnings, by employment status, occupation, age, and education of spouses, and age of children, 1987, Current Population Rpt, 2546-6.61

Monthly Labor Review, current statistics and articles, 6722-1

Natl income and product accounts and components, *Survey of Current Business*, monthly rpt, 2702-1.21; 2702-1.22; 2702-1.27

OASDHI admin, and SSA activities, 1930s-89 and projected to 2063, data compilation, annual rpt, 4704-12

OASDHI coverage of employment and earnings, and social security contributions, by age, sex, race, State, and county, 1985, 4748-43

OASDHI coverage of employment and earnings, late 1930s-87, annual rpt, 4744-3.1; 4744-3.2; 4744-3.3

OASDI coverage of wages, 1970-87 and alternative projections to 1997, actuarial rpt, 4706-1.103

OASI beneficiaries affected by earnings limits by selected characteristics, and Federal outlays, under alternative limits, 1986, 26306-3.110

Occupational Outlook Quarterly, journal, 6742-1

Older persons employment, earnings, reasons for working, and job training preferences, by selected characteristics, 1960-87, 6306-2.3

Older persons labor force participation, unemployment, displacement, and reemployment, by selected characteristics, 1969-88, 6306-2.2

Older persons socioeconomic characteristics, 1900s-86 and projected to 2050, biennial chartbook, 12904-1

Pay comparability of Fed Govt with private industry, and recommended pay rate adjustments, 1989, annual rpt, 104-16

Population size and characteristics, 1969-88, Current Population Rpt, annual rpt, 2546-2.146

Poverty level labor force employment, earnings, and other characteristics, 1987, article, 6722-1.948

Poverty status of families and persons, by detailed characteristics, 1987, annual Current Population Rpt, 2546-6.60

Refugee resettlement programs and funding, arrivals by country of origin, and indicators of adjustment, by State, FY88, annual rpt, 4694-5

Regional income and earnings per capita relative to US average, analysis of differential by census div, various periods 1969-87, article, 9373-1.909

Rural areas economic and social conditions, dev, and problems, periodic journal, 1502-7

Rural areas employment, economic conditions, and population characteristics, 1970s-85, compilation of papers, 1598-243

Science and engineering employment in R&D, earnings at DOE labs and non-DOE facilities, 1989, annual rpt, 3004-9

Science and engineering employment in R&D, earnings by field and educational, employment, and other characteristics, 1989, annual rpt, 3004-1

Science and engineering labor force, Federal and university research funding, and educational data, series, 9626-6

Science and engineering PhDs employment and other characteristics, by field and State, 1987, biennial rpt, 9627-18

Small business establishments, employment, and financial ratios, by SIC 1- to 2-digit industry and State, late 1960s-87, 9768-19

Soviet Union personal income by source, disposable income, wage deductions by type, and savings, 1950s-87, 9118-7

Statistical Abstract of US, social, political, and economic data, 1790-2025, comprehensive annual compilation, 2324-1.3

Student aid Pell grants and applicants, by tuition, income level, instn type and control, and State, 1987/88, annual rpt, 4804-1

Survey of Current Business, detailed financial and business data, and economic indicators, monthly rpt, 2702-1.1

Tax (income) returns filed by type of filer, selected income items, quarterly rpt, 8302-2.1

Tax (income) returns of individuals, by filing status, tax item, and income level, 1987, annual article, 8302-2.901

Tax (income) returns of individuals, detailed data, 1986, annual rpt, 8304-2

Tax (income) returns of individuals, selected income and tax items by income level, preliminary 1987, annual article, 8302-2.917

Tax (income) returns of individuals with foreign earned income, returns, exclusions, credits, and US revenue losses, with data by country, 1983, quadrennial rpt, 8308-34

Telephone service of households, by composition, income sources, and other characteristics, 1984-87, 9288-11

Tenure-related earnings, relationship to probability of employer bankruptcy, 1979-83, technical paper, 9366-6.180

Unemployed displaced workers earnings losses and unemployment duration, relation to educational attainment, by selected characteristics, 1984-86, article, 6722-1.942

Unemployed displaced workers, labor-mgmt committee aid recipients by selected characteristics, for 4 State programs, 1988, GAO rpt, 26121-316

Unemployment insurance coverage of establishments, employment, and wages, by SIC 4-digit industry and State, 1988, annual rpt, 6744-16

Unemployment insurance coverage, wages by industry div, State, and MSA, 1987-88, annual press releases, 6784-17

Unemployment insurance long-term claimants employment services use, work experience, and reemployment, by selected characteristics and county, 1987-88, 6406-6.25; 6406-6.26

Unemployment insurance programs of States and Fed Govt, benefits adequacy, and work disincentives, series, 6406-6

Unemployment insurance programs of States, benefits, coverage, exhaustions, and finances by State, 1987, annual tables, 6404-10

Unemployment spells duration, frequency, insurance coverage, and outcome, by age, sex, and race, 1984, Current Population Rpt, 2546-20.9

Unemployment, underemployment, and related earnings losses, by worker characteristics and location, 1986, 1598-251

Veterans rehabilitation program admin, and participants earnings and tax liability before and after training, 1988 hearing, 25768-48

Wage differentials among census divs related to worker and job characteristics, 1973-87, article, 9377-1.905

Wage differentials among employers, relation to occupation, sex, establishment size, and industry, 1975-82, working paper, 9377-9.78

Wage differentials between service and manufacturing sectors related to worker characteristics, 1987, article, 9377-1.901

Wages, hourly and weekly averages by industry div, monthly press release, 6742-3

Wages of full- and part-time workers, by selected characteristics, quarterly press release, 6742-20

Women awarded child support and alimony, award amount, and payment status, by selected characteristics of woman, 1985, biennial Current Population Rpt, 2546-2.145

Women's earnings losses and other costs of maternity, and effect of employee leave benefit coverage, 1979-84, hearings, 25548-95

see also Agricultural wages
see also Area wage surveys
see also Earnings, local and regional
see also Earnings, specific industry
see also Educational employees pay
see also Employee benefits
see also Employee bonuses and work incentives
see also Escalator clauses
see also Farm income
see also Federal pay
see also Foreign labor conditions
see also Industry wage surveys
see also Labor costs and cost indexes
see also Military pay
see also Minimum wage
see also Payroll
see also Professionals' fees

see also State and local employees pay
see also Tips and tipping
see also Wage deductions
see also Wage surveys

Earnings, local and regional

Dallas-Fort Worth metro area employment, earnings, hours, and CPI changes, 1970s-88, annual rpt, 6964-2

Houston metro area employment, earnings, hours, and CPI changes, 1970s-88, annual rpt, 6964-1

New England States economic indicators, Fed Reserve 1st District, monthly rpt, 9373-24

New England States economic indicators, Fed Reserve 1st District, quarterly rpt, 9373-2.1

North Central States business and economic conditions, Fed Reserve 9th District, quarterly journal, 9383-19

North Central States economic conditions, Fed Reserve 9th District, quarterly rpt, 9383-18

Puerto Rico economic conditions, 1986 hearings, 21448-39

Southeastern States collective bargaining calendar, deferred wage increases, 1989, annual rpt, 6946-1.73

Southeastern States manufacturing employment and earnings, by industry group, State, and urban-rural location, 1970s-85, article, 9371-1.901

Southeastern US manufacturing hours and earnings, for 8 States, quarterly press release, 6942-7

Southwestern States employment by industry div, earnings, and hours, by State, monthly rpt, 6962-2

Tennessee Valley industrial dev, employment, and electricity demand, by SIC 2-digit industry, firm, and location, 1988, annual rpt, 9804-3

see also Area wage surveys
see also under By Census Division, By City, By County, By Region, By SMSA or MSA, and By State in the "Index by Categories"

Earnings, specific industry

Aerospace industry employment and salaries, by sex and race, 1979-87, GAO rpt, 26121-315

Construction employment, earnings, and hours, by selected SIC 2- to 3-digit industry, bimonthly rpt, 2042-1.7

Food marketing sector hourly and weekly earnings, selected years 1962-87, annual rpt, 1544-22.3

Food prices (farm-retail), marketing cost components, and industry finances and productivity, 1950s-88, annual rpt, 1544-9.2

Health Care Financing Review, provider prices, price inputs and indexes, and labor, quarterly journal, 4652-1.1

Health care services (community and migrant) finances, operations, and staff, series, 4108-45

Hospital workers wages relation to supervisory levels and other factors, 1985, working paper, 9377-9.79

Housing (manufactured) production, shipments, production workers, and finances, 1970s-89, annual article, 2042-1.902

Marketing and sales industries employment and earnings, by occupation, 1986-87 and projected 2000, article, 6742-1.901

Meat, poultry, and livestock production, consumption, and industry finances and operations, 1950s-86, 1568-280

Mineral industries census, 1987: financial and operating data, preliminary industry rpt series, 2511-1

Nuclear power plant mgmt salaries by position, and plant capacity, for TVA compared to private utilities, 1985-87, hearing, 21648-57

Nursing labor supply and shortage indicators, and earnings, by State, 1970s-80s, 25148-41

Prison industries involvement of private sector, operations by prison and firm, and State provisions, as of 1987, 6068-228

Railroad (Amtrak) officers salaries compared to industry average, 1986, hearing, 21368-103

Railroad employment and compensation, by age, sex, occupation, and years of service, 1984, annual rpt, 9704-2.4

Railroad employment, earnings, and hours, by occupation for Class I railroads, 1988, annual table, 9484-5

Shipyard employment and wage rates, by coastal district, 1986-88, annual rpt, 7704-12.2

Temporary help supply services industry employment and earnings for permanent and temporary workers, by occupation, Sept 1987, article, 6722-1.912

Textile mill employment, earnings, and hours, for 8 Southeastern States, quarterly press release, 6942-1

Transportation employment, wages, and average annual earnings, by mode of transport, 1977-87, annual rpt, 7304-2.2

Vending facilities run by blind on Federal and non-Federal property, finances and operations by agency and State, FY88, annual rpt, 4944-2

see also Agricultural wages
see also Educational employees pay
see also Farm income
see also Federal pay
see also Industry wage surveys
see also Military pay
see also Payroll
see also State and local employees pay
see also under By Industry in the "Index by Categories"

Earth sciences

Degrees (PhD) in science and engineering, by field, instn, employment prospects, sex, race, and other characteristics, 1960s-88, 9627-30

Degrees in science and engineering, by field, level, and sex, 1950-86, 9628-77

DOD budget, manpower needs, costs, and force readiness by service branch, FY90, annual rpt, 3504-1

DOE R&D projects and funding at natl labs, universities, and other instns, FY88, annual summary rpt, 3004-18.1

Employment and earnings in science and engineering, by field and activity, and private and Federal R&D spending, by industry, 1975-88, 9626-6.29

Employment and other characteristics of science and engineering PhDs, by field and State, 1987, biennial rpt, 9627-18

Employment characteristics of scientists and engineers, by field, 1988, biennial rpt, 9627-16

Enrollment in science and engineering grad programs, by field, source of funds, and characteristics of student and instn, 1975-87, annual rpt, 9627-7

Fed Govt aid to higher education and nonprofit instns for R&D and related activities, by field, instn, agency, and State, FY87, annual rpt, 9627-17

NASA project launch schedules and technical descriptions, press release series, 9506-2

R&D funding by higher education instns, by source and field, FY80-87, annual rpt, 9624-18.5

see also Geography
see also Geology
see also Hydrology
see also Oceanography

Earthquakes

Alaska and Aleutian Islands earthquakes, intensity, magnitude, time, and location, 1786-1981, 5668-87

Alaska OCS environmental conditions and oil dev impacts, compilation of papers, series, 2176-1

Developing countries disaster preparedness and economic, population, and political data, country rpt series, 9916-2

Intensity of ground motion by station, and info sources, 1986, annual rpt, 5664-14

Mexico City earthquake, injuries by type, Sept 1985, article, 4042-3.947

East Pakistan

see Bangladesh

East-West trade

Agricultural trade and market impacts of eliminating foreign and US protectionist policies, model description and results, 1986, 1528-282

Agricultural trade of US, by detailed commodity and country, 1988, semiannual rpt, 1522-4

China trade, by commodity, world area, and country, 1985-87, 9118-10

China trade with US by commodity, and foreign investment by source country, 1988, 9118-9

China trade with US, by selected commodity, 1980-86, hearing, 23848-195

Cuba economic conditions, agricultural and industrial production and distribution, trade, and intl economic relations, 1980-87 with trends from 1961, 9118-8

Eastern Europe agricultural production, consumption, and trade, by country, 1970s-88, annual rpt, 1524-11

Eastern Europe and USSR debt, trade, and balances with US and other western countries, with background data, 1980s-87, hearing, 21248-120

Export licensing, monitoring, and enforcement activities, FY88, annual rpt, 2024-1

Export licensing of goods with potential military uses, DOD and Commerce Dept activities, staff, and costs, 1986-88, GAO rpt, 26123-250

Exports and imports of US, by commodity group, world area, selected country, US coastal area and port, and mode of transport, monthly rpt, 2422-9

Exports and imports of US, by selected country, country group, and commodity group, 1988, annual rpt, 2044-37

Exports and imports of US with Communist countries, by detailed commodity and country, quarterly rpt with articles, 9882-2

Exports, imports, and balances of US by commodity group, world area, and country, and related employment, 1970s-88, annual rpt, 2044-26

Oil exports to centrally planned economies from market economy countries, monthly rpt, 3162-42.2

Soviet Union economic conditions under General Secretary Gorbachev, 1988 and trends from 1956, annual rpt, 9114-6

Soviet Union hard currency trade by commodity, and balance of payments, 1960s-88, annual rpt, 9114-4.3

Eastern Europe

Agricultural and food production and indexes, total and for selected commodities, by country, 1970s-88, annual rpt, 1524-12

Agricultural exports of US, for grains, oilseed products, hides, skins, and cotton, by country, weekly rpt, 1922-3

Agricultural production, acreage, and consumption, by Eastern Europe country and commodity, 1965-85, 1528-284

Agricultural production, consumption, and trade, for Eastern Europe by country, 1970s-88, 1524-11

Agricultural trade of US, by commodity and country, bimonthly rpt with articles, 1522-1

Agricultural trade of US, by detailed commodity and country, 1988, semiannual rpt, 1522-4

Coal trade flows and reserves, by country, 1970s-87 and projected to 2000, annual rpt, 3164-77

Debt, trade, and balances of Eastern Europe and USSR with US and other western countries, with background data, 1980s-87, hearing, 21248-120

Economic and military aid and loans from US and intl agencies, by program and country, FY46-87, annual rpt, 9914-5

Economic conditions in Communist and OECD countries, 1987, annual rpt, 7144-11

Economic conditions in Communist, OECD, and selected other countries, 1960s-88, annual rpt, 9114-4

Energy production, by fuel type, country, and country group, projected 1988-2000 and trends from 1970, annual rpt, 3164-84

Export licensing, monitoring, and enforcement activities, FY88, annual rpt, 2024-1

Exports and imports (waterborne) of US, by type of service, customs district, port, and world area, monthly rpt, 2422-7

Exports and imports of US, by commodity group, world area, selected country, US coastal area and port, and mode of transport, monthly rpt, 2422-9

Exports and imports of US, by selected country, country group, and commodity group, 1988, annual rpt, 2044-37

Exports and imports of US with Communist countries, by detailed commodity and country, quarterly rpt with articles, 9882-2

Exports, imports, and balances of US by commodity group, world area, and country, and related employment, 1970s-88, annual rpt, 2044–26

Fertilizer components use, by world area, 1978-88 and projected to 2010, 5608–154

Fish catch and consumption, for Eastern Europe and other countries, 1970s-86, article, 2162–1.901

Labor reform prospects in Eastern Europe, 1989 narrative rpt, 6366–4.43

Loans of US banks to foreigners at all US and foreign offices, by country group and country, quarterly rpt, 13002–1

Military strength of USSR and Warsaw Pact, and proposed force reductions, with comparisons to NATO, 1980s-91, hearing, 21208–29

Oil and gas production, use, and trade by country, for Communist countries, monthly rpt, 9112–2

Radio Free Europe and Radio Liberty broadcast and financial data, and compared to other intl broadcasters, FY88, annual rpt, 10314–1

Refugee arrivals in US by world area and country of origin, and quotas, monthly rpt, 7002–4

Refugee arrivals in US by world area of origin and State of settlement, and Federal aid, FY88-90, annual rpt, 7004–16

Refugee resettlement programs and funding, arrivals by country of origin, and indicators of adjustment, by State, FY88, annual rpt, 4694–5

Science and engineering immigrants, by field, age, sex, country and world area of birth and last residence, and State, 1987 and trends from 1967, 9627–29

Terrorist (intl) incidents, casualties, and attacks on US targets, by attack type and world area, 1968-88, annual rpt, 7004–13

Travel to US, by characteristics of visit and traveler, country, port city, and State of destination, quarterly rpt, 2902–1

UN voting record and share of votes in agreement with US, by issue, country, and world area, 1988, annual rpt, 7004–18

USIA library holdings, use, and staff, by country and city, FY88, annual rpt, 9854–4

see also Albania
see also Bulgaria
see also Council for Mutual Economic Assistance
see also Czechoslovakia
see also Germany, East
see also Hungary
see also Poland
see also Romania
see also Soviet Union
see also Warsaw Pact
see also Yugoslavia
see also under By Foreign Country in the "Index by Categories"

Eau Claire, Wis.
see also under By SMSA or MSA in the "Index by Categories"

Eavesdropping
see Electronic surveillance

Eberts, Randall W.
"Accounting for the Recent Divergence in Regional Wage Differentials", 9377–1.905
"Do the Earnings of Manufacturing and Service Workers Grow at the Same Rate over Their Careers?", 9377–1.901
"Public Infrastructure and Regional Economic Development: A Simultaneous Equations Approach", 9377–9.81
"Structure, Conduct, and Performance in the Local Public Sector", 9377–9.82

Ecology
see Conservation of natural resources
see Environmental pollution and control
see Environmental sciences
see Marine pollution
see Marine resources conservation
see Wildlife and wildlife conservation

Economic and econometric models
Agricultural Economics Research, quarterly journal, 1502–3

Agricultural production cost efficiency of USSR, by Republic, model description and results, 1960s-85, 1528–292

Agricultural trade and market impacts of eliminating foreign and US protectionist policies, model description and results, 1986, 1528–282

Banks financial performance, risk assessment, and regulation, 1988 annual conf papers, 9375–7

BLS econometric analyses and methodology, for economic indicators, prices, labor costs, and productivity, working paper series, 6886–6

Budget of US, balanced budget proposed constitutional amendment, economic impacts, projected to FY94 and background data from 1940s, hearings, 21528–72

Capital flows (intl) impacts on monetary policy instruments, and financial and economic indicators, 1987 compilation of papers, 9385–9

Capital investment spending relation to financial and economic indicators, model description and results, 1953-86, working paper, 9393–10.9

Capital stock measurement and social policy simulation model dev, for Canada, 1988 conf papers, 2702–1.918

Corn and soybean futures contract yield and price risk hedging strategies, by selected county and State, model results, 1961-83, 1548–352

Developing countries economic indicators, problem debtors compared to other borrowers, by country, 1973-84, 1528–285

Economic indicator forecasts, assessment of bias and accuracy of Fed Govt and private sector models, 1976-87, article, 9391–1.902

Electric power demand related to economic dev and weather, by census div, model results, quarterly 1977-85, 3028–2

Energy supply, demand, and prices, by fuel type and end-use sector, projected under 3 oil price assumptions, 1988-2000, annual rpt, 3164–75

Energy supply, demand, distribution, and impacts of legislation, series, 3166–6

Farm financial ratios, model description and results, 1986, 1548–341

Financial and banking devs in southeastern States, working paper series, 9371–10

Financial and economic analysis and forecasting methodology, technical paper series, 9366–6; 9377–9

Financial and economic analysis and methodology, technical paper series, 9375–11

Financial and economic analysis of banking and nonbanking sectors, working paper series, 9381–10

Financial and economic analysis, technical paper series, 9379–12; 9385–8; 9389–19; 9393–10

Financial and economic devs, Fed Reserve Bank of Richmond bimonthly journal, 9389–1

Financial and monetary research and econometric analyses, working paper series, 9387–8

Food aid impacts on developing countries economic conditions and demand for US grain exports, model description and results, 1960s-84, 1528–291

Foreign countries economic and social conditions, working paper series, 2326–18

GNP and inflation forecasts, analysis of errors among alternative models, 1989 article, 9373–1.904

GNP relation to economic indicators, model description and results, various periods 1958-88, working paper, 9393–10.4

GNP relation to inflation variability, model description and results, 1959-88, article, 9391–1.919

Housing finance studies, technical paper series, 8436–1; 9306–1; 9316–1

Import quotas on steel, autos, and textiles, employment and income impacts by industry, model description and results, 1984, 9406–1.57

Interest rate impacts of Fed Govt deficit reduction, alternative model results, 1989 rpt, 26306–3.100; 26306–3.101

Manufacturing output forecasts, performance of alternative regional indexes by SIC 2-digit industry, 1970s-85, article, 9375–1.905

Meat price quarterly forecasts, by product, alternative model results, 1989 rpt, 1548–350

Nut (tree) prices related to production, use, and other nut prices, for 5 commodities, model description and results, 1970-88, article, 1561–6.904

Survey of Income and Program Participation, household composition, income, benefits, and labor force status, methodology, working paper series, 2626–10

Tax-related economic and fiscal topics, technical paper series, 8006–3

Travel to US, spending by world area of residence, and economic impact, by spending category, census div, and State, model results, 1985-86, 2908–28

Wheat exports impacts of subsidies and exchange rates, by importing and exporting country, alternative model results, 1986/87, 1548–351

Wheat trade, elasticities of demand for US and 5 countries, alternative models description and results, 1950s-86, 1528–281

see also Input-output analysis
see also Mathematic models and modeling
Economic assistance
  see Economic policy
  see International assistance
  see Military assistance
Economic censuses
  Data coverage and availability for 1987 Census of Agriculture and related statistics, 1989 guide, 2308–55
  Data coverage and availability for 1987 economic censuses and related statistics, 1989 preliminary guide, 2308–5
  Data coverage and availability of Census Bur rpts and data files, 1989 annual listing, 2304–2
  see also Census of Construction Industries
  see also Census of Manufactures
  see also Census of Mineral Industries
  see also Census of Outlying Areas
  see also Census of Retail Trade
  see also Census of Service Industries
  see also Census of Transportation
  see also Census of Wholesale Trade
  see also Enterprise Statistics Program
  see also Survey of Minority-Owned Business Enterprises
  see also Survey of Women-Owned Businesses
Economic concentration and diversification
  Agricultural cooperatives shares of food and tobacco industry sales and exports, 1985-86, article, 1122–1.906
  Agriculture census, 1987: farms, farmland, production, finances, and operator characteristics, by county, final State rpt series, 2331–1
  Airline computer reservation systems finances, operations, and impacts on airline competitiveness, 1980s-86, 7308–193
  Airline computer reservation systems operating costs, fees, and market shares, by firm and location, 1984-87, hearing, 25528–108
  Auto and light truck fuel economy, sales, and market shares, by size and model for US and foreign makes, 1989 model year, semiannual rpt, 3302–4
  Bank deposits interest rates relation to local bank market concentration and branching regulations, 1983-87, technical paper, 9366–6.166
  Bank holding company profit related to mgmt practices and market concentration and share, 1989 technical paper, 9366–6.201
  Bank holding company risk, impact of market concentration and State branching regulation, alternative regression results, various periods 1978-84, technical paper, 9366–6.182
  Banking industry structure, performance, and financial devs, for Fed Reserve 10th District, 1988, annual rpt, 9381–14.1
  Banks (commercial) and trust companies, assets and liabilities of 10 largest organizations by State, 1987, annual rpt, 9364–5.11
  Banks (natl) domestic and intl operations, charters, mergers, and liquidations, by instn and State, quarterly rpt, 8402–3
  Banks diversification impacts on costs, alternative indicators by asset size, 1986, article, 9371–1.907

Banks financial performance, risk assessment, and regulation, 1988 annual conf papers, 9375–7
Banks market concentration ratios, impact of automated teller machines adoption by large and small banks, 1971-79, technical paper, 9366–6.187
Banks market concentration relation to excess profits and State branching regulation, various periods 1966-86, technical paper, 9366–6.188
Banks market concentration relation to money market deposit account interest rates, 1983-86, technical paper, 9366–6.173
Banks profitability relation to market concentration, impact of local market entry barriers, 1983, working paper, 9381–10.93
Banks status changes, instns, assets, and concentration ratios by size, ownership, and location, and compared to other financial instns, 1976-87, article, 9362–1.902
Cigarette ad and promotion costs by media, and market shares, by cigarette type, with sales and use, 1963-87, annual rpt, 9404–4
Construction industries census, 1987: establishments, employment, receipts, and expenditures, by SIC 4-digit industry and State, final industry rpt series, 2373–1
Food marketing sector finances, operations, and merger activity, for processors and distributors, as of 1988, annual rpt, 1544–22
Fruit and vegetable processing industries finances and operations, consumption, farm production, and trade, by commodity, 1970s-88, 1568–275
Hospital reimbursement by Medicare under prospective payment system, impacts on costs, industry structure and operations, and quality of care, series, 17206–2
Imports from Communist countries, market share by selected commodity, quarterly rpt, 9882–2
Imports injury to US industries from sales at less than fair value, investigations with background financial and operating data, series, 9886–14
Manufacturing index of diversification, for establishments and firms by SIC 2- and 4-digit industry, census years 1963-82, technical paper, 2626–2.58
Meat, poultry, and livestock production, consumption, and industry finances and operations, 1950s-86, 1568–280
Oil industry mergers and acquisitions impacts on market concentration, with background data, 1970-84, 9406–1.58
Poultry (broiler) production, slaughter, prices, and processing industry operations, 1950s-87, 1568–279
Southeastern States banks and thrifts deposit concentration index, by selected MSA, 1984 and 1988, article, 9302–2.905
Telecommunications industry devs, finances, and operations, with data by service type, firm, and country, 1950s-80s, 2808–27
West Central States, Fed Reserve 10th District depository instns financial activity by State, and large commercial banks by city, monthly rpt, 9381–11

see also Antitrust law
see also Business acquisitions and mergers
see also Competition
see also Holding companies
see also Ownership of enterprise
Economic crises and depressions
  see Business cycles
Economic development
  Assistance (block and categorical grants) programs for State and local govts, FY89, biennial listing, 10044–8
  Bond tax-exempt issues for private activity, by purpose, face value, major industry, and State, 1986, annual article, 8302–2.905
  Budget deficit reduction under Gramm-Rudman Act, cancellation of budget authority by program, FY90, annual rpt, 104–27; 26304–6
  Budget of US Appendix, obligations, appropriations, and personnel, by program and agency, FY90, annual rpt, 104–3
  Budget of US, compact budgets by activity, function, and agency, FY90 and projected to FY94, annual rpt, 104–2
  Budget of US, historical data, selected years FY34-88 and projected to FY94, annual rpt, 104–22
  Budget of US, House concurrent resolution, with spending and revenue targets, FY90, annual rpt, 21264–2
  Budget of US, Reagan Admin policy changes by program, FY90, annual rpt, 104–21
  Coastal areas environmental and socioeconomic conditions, and potential impact of oil and gas OCS leases, final statement series, 5736–1
  Coastal areas environmental impacts of economic dev and population growth, 1980s and projected to 2000, series, 2176–8
  Economic Dev Admin activities, and funding by program, recipient, State, and county, FY87 and cumulative from FY66, annual rpt, 2064–2
  Economic Dev Admin funding, and loans forgiven, with data by project and location, FY84-88, hearing, 21648–56
  Electric power demand related to economic dev and weather, by census div, model results, quarterly 1977-85, 3028–2
  Expenditures of Fed Govt in States, by type, program, agency, and State, FY88, annual rpt, 2464–2
  Fed Govt financial and nonfinancial domestic aid, 1989 base edition with supplements, annual listing, 104–5
  FmHA borrowers, by type of borrower and loan, and State, quarterly rpt, 1182–4
  Forest Service mgmt of public lands and resources dev, environmental, economic, and social impacts of alternative programs, projected to 2030, 1208–24
  Govt revenues by source and spending by function, natl income and product account, *Survey of Current Business*, monthly rpt, 2702–1.24
  Indian and Alaska Native housing and economic development program operations, by region, FY86-87, annual rpt, 5004–5
  Labor laws enacted, by State, 1988, annual article, 6722–1.904

Metals (primary) demand relation to consumption patterns and economic, trade, and technological factors, 1960s-82, 5608-159

R&D funding by Fed Govt, by detailed function, program, and agency, FY88-90, annual rpt, 9627-9

Rural areas aid from Fed Govt, by agency and program, with county classifications by population density, FY85 and FY87, GAO rpt, 26113-401

Rural areas aid from Fed Govt compared to urban areas, by program and degree of urbanization, FY85, periodic rpt, 1598-248

Rural areas dev aid by Fed Govt, Reagan Admin programs and initiatives, FY88, annual rpt, 1004-17

Rural areas economic and social conditions, dev, and problems, periodic journal, 1502-7

Tax expenditures, Federal revenues forgone through income tax deductions and exclusions by type, FY90-94, annual rpt, 21784-10

Tennessee Valley industrial dev, employment, and electricity demand, by SIC 2-digit industry, firm, and location, 1988, annual rpt, 9804-3

TVA financial and operating data by program and facility, FY88, annual rpt, 9804-32

see also Business cycles
see also Community development
see also Community Development Block Grants
see also Developing countries
see also Economic indicators
see also Job creation
see also Regional planning
see also State funding for economic development
see also Urban Development Action Grants
see also Urban renewal

Economic Development Administration

Activities of EDA, and funding by program, recipient, State, and county, FY87 and cumulative from FY66, annual rpt, 2064-2

Budget appropriations and staff for Commerce Dept, by subagency, FY88-90, annual rpt, 2004-6

Budget of US Appendix, obligations, appropriations, and personnel, by program and agency, FY90, annual rpt, 104-3

Expenditures of EDA, and loans forgiven, with data by project and location, FY84-88, hearing, 21648-56

Expenditures of Fed Govt in States, by type, program, agency, and State, FY88, annual rpt, 2464-2

Economic indicators

Africa agricultural exports by commodity, and relation to economic conditions and other factors, by country, 1960s-87, 1528-280

Agricultural Outlook, production, prices, marketing, and trade, by commodity, forecast and current situation, monthly rpt with articles, 1502-4

Asia dollar exchange rate, and impacts of currency appreciation on current account and trade balances and economic indicators, for 3 countries, 1980s-90, GAO rpt, 26123-234

Banking and financial conditions, 1987, annual rpt, 9364-5

Banks failures and economic indicator variability, relation to bank branching and note issuance regulation, for US and Canada, various periods 1865-1987, article, 9383-6.904

Brazil foreign debt, debt burden, and other economic indicators, with comparisons to other developing countries, 1970s-88, hearings, 21248-122

Budget deficit reduction recommendations, background data and testimony, 1989 rpt, 15888-2

Budget of US, CBO analysis and review of FY90 budget by function, annual rpt, 26304-2

Budget of US, CBO analysis of revenue and spending alternatives and projections of economic indicators, FY90-94, annual rpt, 26304-3

Budget of US, compact budgets by activity, function, and agency, FY90 and projected to FY94, annual rpt, 104-2

Budget of US, economic assumptions, FY89-94, midsession review of FY90 budget, annual rpt, 104-7

Budget of US, House concurrent resolution, with spending and revenue targets, FY90, annual rpt, 21264-2

Budget of US, overview, FY90, annual rpt, 104-6

Budget of US, Reagan Admin fiscal and economic projections made 1981 and actual trends, 1980s-87, article, 9391-1.905

Budget of US, special analyses by activity, function, and agency, FY90, annual rpt, 104-1

Business America, foreign and domestic commerce, and US investment and trade opportunities, biweekly journal, 2042-24

Business Conditions Digest, economic, business, and financial devs and cyclical fluctuations, monthly rpt, 2702-3

Capital flows (intl) impacts on monetary policy instruments, and financial and economic indicators, 1987 compilation of papers, 9385-9

Caribbean Basin Initiative investment incentives, economic impacts, with finances and employment by country, 1984-88, 2048-141

Communist and OECD countries economic conditions, 1987, annual rpt, 7144-11

Communist, OECD, and selected other countries economic conditions, 1960s-88, annual rpt, 9114-4

Consumer spending related to cash holdings, interest rates, and other economic indicators, 1950s-86, technical paper, 9379-12.38

Current account balance of US, components and relation to foreign and US investment and economic conditions, 1970s-88 and projected to 1990s, article, 9385-1.905; 9385-1.906

Current account deficit, and impacts of alternative fiscal and monetary policies, 1980-88 and projected to 1999, 26306-6.135

Data series and collections of Fed Govt, adequacy to address economic devs and policy issues, 1989 rpt, 26358-207

Data series revisions and methodological issues, 1989 article, 9371-1.906

Developing countries agricultural and food aid, and impacts on US exports, with background data, 1960s-89, 26308-85

Developing countries agricultural policy impacts on economic dev, with background data for 6 countries, 1960s-86, 1528-283

Developing countries debt burden and economic conditions, and trade with industrialized countries, by country, 1970s-87, hearings, 25248-108

Developing countries disaster preparedness and economic, population, and political data, country rpt series, 9916-2

Developing countries economic and social conditions from 1960s, and Intl Dev Cooperation Agency and AID activities and funding, FY88-90, annual rpt, 9904-4

Developing countries economic indicators, problem debtors compared to other borrowers, by country, 1973-84, 1528-285

Developing countries food spending and economic conditions, 1987, article, 1522-3.911

Developing countries sociodemographic data, and AID dev projects, special study series, 9916-3

Eastern Europe and USSR debt, trade, and balances with US and other western countries, with background data, 1980s-87, hearing, 21248-120

EC economic integration impact on EC employment, GDP, and other economic indicators, projected 1992, article, 9373-1.908

Economic and employment conditions, alternative BLS projections to 2000 and trends 1970s-88, biennial article, 6722-1.953

Economic indicator performance, and Fed Reserve monetary policy objectives, as of July 1989, semiannual rpt, 9362-4

Economic indicator performance from 1961, and Commerce Dept rpts, biweekly listing, 2002-1

Economic indicators and components, and Fed Reserve 4th District business and financial conditions, monthly chartbook, 9377-10

Economic indicators and components, current data and annual trends, monthly rpt, 23842-1

Economic indicators compounded annual rates of change, monthly rpt, 9391-3

Economic indicators compounded annual rates of change, 1969-88, annual rpt, 9391-9

Economic indicators, monthly table, 9302-26

Economic indicators summary, monthly rpt, 2302-3

Economic indicators targets and performance, 1960s-88 and projected to 1994, annual article, 9381-1.901

Economic Report of the President for 1989, economic effects of budget proposals, and trends and projections, 1929-99, annual hearings, 23844-4

Economic Report of the President for 1989, Joint Economic Committee critique and policy recommendations, annual rpt, 23844-2

see also Business assets and liabilities, general
see also Business cycles
see also Business income and expenses, general
see also Business inventories
see also Capital investments, general
see also Consumer Price Index
see also Credit
see also Earnings, general
see also Economic and econometric models
see also Employment and unemployment, general
see also Flow-of-funds accounts
see also Gross National Product
see also Housing costs and financing
see also Housing sales
see also Industrial capacity and utilization
see also Industrial production
see also Industrial production indexes
see also Inflation
see also Job creation
see also Job vacancy
see also Labor productivity
see also Labor turnover
see also Money supply
see also National income and product accounts
see also Personal and household income
see also Personal consumption
see also Prices
see also Producer Price Index

Economic policy

Banks in Fed Reserve System, expenses and operations itemized by service, office, and district, 1988, annual rpt, 9364–11

Budget of US, CBO analysis of revenue and spending alternatives and projections of economic indicators, FY90-94, annual rpt, 26304–3

Budget of US, economic assumptions, FY89-94, midsession review of FY90 budget, annual rpt, 104–7

Costa Rica cash transfer payments of AID linked to economic and policy reforms, effectiveness, 1960-87, 9916–3.51

Data series and collections of Fed Govt, adequacy to address economic devs and policy issues, 1989 rpt, 26358–207

Economic Report of the President for 1989, economic effects of budget proposals, and trends and projections, 1929-99, annual hearings, 23844–4

Economic Report of the President for 1989, Joint Economic Committee critique and policy recommendations, annual rpt, 23844–2

Economic Report of the President for 1989, with economic trends from 1929, annual rpt, 204–1

Financial and economic analysis, technical paper series, 9379–12; 9389–19

Financial and economic devs, Fed Reserve Bank of Atlanta bimonthly rpt with articles, 9371–1

Financial and economic devs, Fed Reserve Bank of Chicago bimonthly journal, 9375–1

Financial and economic devs, Fed Reserve Bank of Dallas bimonthly journal, 9379–1

Financial and economic devs, Fed Reserve Bank of Kansas City monthly journal, 9381–1

Financial and economic devs, Fed Reserve Bank of Minneapolis quarterly journal, 9383–6

Financial and economic devs, Fed Reserve Bank of New York quarterly journal, 9385–1

Financial and economic devs, Fed Reserve Bank of Philadelphia bimonthly journal, 9387–1

Financial and economic devs, Fed Reserve Bank of Richmond bimonthly journal, 9389–1

Financial and economic devs, Fed Reserve Bank of San Francisco quarterly journal, 9393–8

Financial and economic devs, Fed Reserve Bank of St Louis bimonthly journal, 9391–1

Foreign and US economic conditions and trade devs and policy, 1988 conf papers, 9373–3.32

Foreign countries economic conditions and implications for US, periodic country rpt series, 2046–4

Foreign countries economic conditions, policy, and trade practices, by country, 1986-88, annual rpt, 21384–5

Jamaica cash transfers from AID linked to economic and policy reforms, effectiveness, 1981-87, 9916–3.56

Overseas Business Reports: economic conditions, investment and export opportunities, and trade practices, country market research rpt series, 2046–6

Soviet Union economic conditions under General Secretary Gorbachev, Soviet and CIA measurement methods with background data, 1987 conf papers, 9118–4

Soviet Union economic conditions under General Secretary Gorbachev, Soviet and CIA measures, 1950s-87, 9118–5

Soviet Union economic conditions under General Secretary Gorbachev, 1988 and trends from 1956, annual rpt, 9114–6

Soviet Union planning for science and technology, and relation to economic plans, 1989 working paper, 2326–18.45

see also Business cycles
see also Defense expenditures
see also Economic development
see also Employment and unemployment, general
see also Fiscal policy
see also Foreign economic relations
see also Foreign trade
see also Foreign trade promotion
see also Government spending
see also Inflation
see also Interest rates
see also International assistance
see also International sanctions
see also Military assistance
see also Monetary policy
see also Price regulation
see also Prices
see also Subsidies
see also Tariffs and foreign trade controls
see also terms beginning with Federal aid

Economic Regulatory Administration

Electric and gas utility ratemaking and regulatory standards, status and coverage of consumers and sales, 1988, annual rpt, 3104–7

Electric power and industrial plants prohibited from oil and gas primary use, and gas use by State, 1988, annual rpt, 3104–8

Electric power trade of US with Canada and Mexico, by utility and US region, annual rpt, discontinued, 3104–10

Economic relations

see Foreign economic relations

Economic Research Service

Activities, funding, and staff of ERS, by branch, planned FY89, annual rpt, 1504–6

Africa (Sahel) food supply indicators, by country, 1960s-2000, 1528–290

Africa agricultural exports by commodity, and relation to economic conditions and other factors, by country, 1960s-87, 1528–280

Africa food imports and aid needs under alternative weather assumptions, for 17 African countries, projected to 1995, 1528–279

Agricultural Economics Research, quarterly journal, 1502–3

Agricultural Outlook, production, prices, marketing, and trade, by commodity, forecast and current situation, monthly rpt with articles, 1502–4

Agricultural situation and farm-related topics, monthly rpt, 1502–6

Alcohol fuels (ethanol) production costs and Federal loan guarantees, 1987-88, 1588–132

Alien workers (unauthorized) employer sanctions impacts on farm labor costs, by farm type, size, and region, 1986, 1598–250

Animal feed mill operations, detailed data by State, 1984, 1568–281

Banks finances and operations, by metro-nonmetro location, 1986, annual rpt, 1544–29

Budget of US Appendix, obligations, appropriations, and personnel, by program and agency, FY90, annual rpt, 104–3

Corn and soybean futures contract yield and price risk hedging strategies, by selected county and State, model results, 1961-83, 1548–352

Cotton ginning activity and charges, by State, 1988/89, annual rpt, 1564–3

Cotton, wool, and synthetic fiber production, prices, trade, and use, periodic situation rpt with articles, 1561–1

Counties (nonmetro) employment by industry sector and degree of urbanization, and compared to metro counties, various periods 1969-86, 1598–244

Dairy production, prices, trade, and use, periodic situation rpt with articles, 1561–2

Data on agriculture, collection, methodology, and use for major time series of USDA, series, 1506–1

Developing countries agricultural policy impacts on economic dev, with background data for 6 countries, 1960s-86, 1528–283

Developing countries food production and needs, and related economic outlook, by country, 1989/90, annual rpt, 1524–6

Drought of 1988, impacts on farm production and income, and compared to other droughts from 1928, 1588–129

Livestock, meat, poultry, and egg production, prices, trade, and stocks, monthly rpt, 1561-17

Livestock, meat, poultry, and egg production, prices, trade, stocks, and use, periodic situation rpt with articles, 1561-7

Mali farm income and production impacts of alternative soil and water mgmt strategies, model results, 1989 rpt, 1528-289

Meat price quarterly forecasts, by product, alternative model results, 1989 rpt, 1548-350

Mexico agricultural subsidies, and impacts of reductions on production, by commodity, 1982-87 and projected 1992, 1528-288

Milk order market policy alternatives impact on producer costs and income, prices, and supply, by region, 1985, 1568-274

Mortgage (farm) debt by lender, impact of establishment of secondary market, 1987 and trends from 1950, 1548-343

Oils, oilseeds, and fats production, prices, trade, and use, periodic situation rpt with articles, 1561-3

Pesticide (soil fumigant) use, impacts of bans of selected fumigants on production, farm income, and retail prices, by crop and region, 1988 rpt, 1588-136

Pesticide use, costs, toxicity, and application rates, and losses from pests, for cotton by pest type and State, 1981-84, 1568-278

Pollution (water) from agricultural sources, USDA abatement program benefits and costs, projected 1990, 1588-141

Population of farm operators and farming-dependent households, by selected characteristics, under alternative definitions, 1987, 1598-252

Population on farms, by employment and socioeconomic characteristics, and region, 1988, annual Current Population Rpt, 2546-1.439

Population on farms under alternative definitions, by selected characteristics, 1983, 1598-249

Poultry (broiler) production, slaughter, prices, and processing industry operations, 1950s-87, 1568-279

Poultry (chicken, egg, and turkey) production, prices, receipts, trade, and disposition, 1960-87, 1568-39

Price support activity and policy options, with data on production, trade, use, and finances, and foreign comparisons, 1950s-89, commodity rpt series, 1566-7

Production costs and prices, impacts of alternative crop, marketing, and futures contract purchase strategies, model results, 1971-86, 1548-353

Production inputs, finances, mgmt, and land value and transfers, periodic situation rpt with articles, 1561-16

Production itemized costs, receipts, and returns, by crop and State, preliminary 1987, annual rpt, 1544-24

Production itemized costs, receipts, and returns, by selected commodity and region, 1975-87, 1548-345

Production mandatory control programs impacts on farm income, acreage, govt payments, and consumers, projected under alternative program provisions, 1986-90, 1548-354

Production, receipts, and demand ratios, by commodity group and region, 1949-83, 1548-348

Puerto Rico meat production, prices, consumption, imports, and impact of import restrictions, 1950s-85, 1568-282

Railroad deregulation impacts on grain shipping rates and revenues, 1981-85, 1548-349

Revenue sharing reduction impacts on rural local govts budgets, and other funding sources, with data for Ohio, 1980s-86, 1598-254

Rice foreign and US production, prices, trade, stocks, and use, periodic situation rpt, 1561-8

Rice shipments, by end use, package size, and State of origin and destination, mid 1950s-87, biennial rpt, 1564-11

Rural areas aid from Fed Govt compared to urban areas, by program and degree of urbanization, FY85, periodic rpt, 1598-248

Rural areas economic and social conditions, dev, and problems, periodic journal, 1502-7

Rural areas employment, economic conditions, and population characteristics, 1970s-85, compilation of papers, 1598-243

Saline soil impacts on yields and off-farm water quality, and costs and benefits of extending erosion control program to saline cropland, 1989 rpt, 1588-144

Soil conservation and other land improvement capital investment, impacts of govt programs and economic factors, 1983-86, 1588-137

Soviet Union agricultural production cost efficiency, by Republic, model description and results, 1960s-85, 1528-292

Sugar and sweeteners production, prices, trade, supply, and use, quarterly situation rpt with articles, 1561-14

Thailand rice production, consumption, exports, and subsidies, 1982-86, 1528-286

Tobacco (burley) finances, operations, and labor, for Kentucky and Tennessee, 1984, 1568-277

Tobacco industry review, quarterly situation rpt articles, 1561-10

Tobacco production, use, prices, and trade, by variety and product, 1950s-87, 1568-276

Unemployment, underemployment, and related earnings losses, by worker characteristics and location, 1986, 1598-251

Urban areas farms, acreage, finances, and operators, under alternative MSA definitions, 1960s-82, 1598-256

Vegetables production, prices, trade, stocks, and use, for selected fresh and processing crops, periodic situation rpt with articles, 1561-11

Water supply in rural areas, public system financial and operating characteristics, by region, 1980, 1598-247

Weather data for farmland, average precipitation and temperature by State, monthly 1950-88, biennial rpt, 1544-28

Wheat and rye foreign and US production, prices, trade, stocks, and use, quarterly situation rpt with articles, 1561-12

Wheat exports impacts of subsidies and exchange rates, by importing and exporting country, alternative model results, 1986/87, 1548-351

Wheat production, acreage, and sales, for winter, durum, and other wheat, by State, 1949-88, 1568-284

Wheat trade, elasticities of demand for US and 5 countries, alternative models description and results, 1950s-86, 1528-281

Economics
Agricultural Economics Research, quarterly journal, 1502-3

Agricultural research funding and staffing for USDA, State agencies, and other instns, by topic, FY88, annual rpt, 1744-2

Degrees awarded in higher education, by level, field, race, and sex, 1989 edition, annual rpt, 4824-2.20

Degrees in science and engineering, by field, level, and sex, 1950-86, 9628-77

Employment and earnings in science and engineering, by field and activity, and private and Federal R&D spending, by industry, 1975-88, 9626-6.29

Employment and other characteristics of science and engineering PhDs, by field and State, 1987, biennial rpt, 9627-18

Employment characteristics of scientists and engineers, by field, 1988, biennial rpt, 9627-16

Enrollment in science and engineering grad programs, by field, source of funds, and characteristics of student and instn, 1975-87, annual rpt, 9627-7

Fed Govt aid to higher education and nonprofit instns for R&D and related activities, by field, instn, agency, and State, FY87, annual rpt, 9627-17

Labor force, Federal and university research funding, and educational data, 1988 rpt, 9626-6.30

R&D funding by Fed Govt, by field, performer type, agency, and State, FY87-89, annual rpt, 9627-20

R&D funding by higher education instns, by source and field, FY80-87, annual rpt, 9624-18.5

see also Economic and econometric models
see also Economic policy

Ectopic pregnancy
see Maternity

Ecuador
Agricultural and food production and indexes, total and for selected commodities, by country, 1970s-88, annual rpt, 1524-12

Agricultural policy impacts on economic dev, with background data for 6 developing countries, 1960s-86, 1528-283

Agricultural production, prices, and trade, by country, 1960s-89, annual world region rpt, 1524-4.2

Agricultural trade of US, by detailed commodity and country, 1988, semiannual rpt, 1522-4

AID activities and funding by project and function, FY90, and developing countries summary socioeconomic data from 1960s, annual rpt, 9904-4.7

AID economic aid to developing countries, obligations and disbursements by country, quarterly rpt, 9912–4

AID loans repayment status and terms by program and country, and status of predecessor agency loans, quarterly rpt, 9912–3

Auto imports from US, trade barriers by country, 1988, annual rpt, 444–2

Economic and military aid and loans from US and intl agencies, by program and country, FY46-87, annual rpt, 9914–5

Economic conditions, income, production, prices, employment, and trade, 1989 periodic country rpt, 2046–4.59

Economic conditions, investment and export opportunities, and trade practices, 1989 country market research rpt, 2046–6.16

Economic conditions, policy, and trade practices, by country, 1986-88, annual rpt, 21384–5

Economic, social, political, and geographic summary data, by country, 1989, annual factbook, 9114–2

Exports and imports of Latin America, and balance of trade with US, by country, 1988, annual rpt, 2044–34

Exports and imports of US, by commodity and country, 1970-87, world area rpt, 9116–1.5

Exports and imports of US, by selected country, country group, and commodity group, 1988, annual rpt, 2044–37

Human rights conditions in 170 countries, 1988, annual rpt, 21384–3

Military aid of US, arms sales, and training programs costs and budget requests, by program, world region, and country, FY88-90, annual rpt, 7144–13

Military spending, arms trade, and force strengths, with govt spending and population, by country, 1977-87, annual rpt, 9824–1

Minerals Yearbook, 1987, Vol 3: foreign country reviews of production, trade, and policy, by commodity, annual rpt, 5604–35

Minerals Yearbook, 1987, Vol 3 preprints: foreign country review of production, trade, and policy, by commodity, annual rpt, 5604–23.87

Multinatl US firms and foreign affiliates finances and operations, by industry of parent firm and affiliate, world area, and country, preliminary 1987, annual rpt, 2704–5

Oil production, trade, use, and stocks, by selected country and country group, monthly rpt, 3162–42

Population size, growth rates, and components of change, by country, projected 1989-2020 and trends from 1950, biennial rpt, 2324–9

UN voting record and share of votes in agreement with US, by issue, country, and world area, 1988, annual rpt, 7004–18

see also under By Foreign Country in the "Index by Categories"

Edinburg, Tex.
see also under By SMSA or MSA in the "Index by Categories"

Editorial occupations
see Journalism
see Writers and writing

Edmonds, J. A.
"Preliminary Analysis of U.S. CO2 Emissions Reduction Potential from Energy Conservation and the Substitution of Natural Gas for Coal in the Period to 2010", 3006–11.11

Education
Condition of Education, detailed data on elementary, secondary, and higher education, 1920s-88 and projected to 1997, annual rpt, 4824–1

Data on education, projections, annual rpt series, 4826–8

Developing countries disaster preparedness and economic, population, and political data, country rpt series, 9916–2

Digest of Education Statistics, detailed data on students, staff, finances, and facilities, 1989 edition, annual rpt, 4824–2

Statistical Abstract of US, social, political, and economic data, 1790-2025, comprehensive annual compilation, 2324–1.1

see also Adult education
see also Agricultural education
see also American Schools and Hospitals Abroad
see also Area studies
see also Black colleges
see also Black students
see also Business education
see also Compensatory education
see also Correspondence courses
see also Curricula
see also Degrees, higher education
see also Discrimination in education
see also Educational attainment
see also Educational broadcasting
see also Educational employees pay
see also Educational enrollment
see also Educational exchanges
see also Educational facilities
see also Educational finance
see also Educational materials
see also Educational reform
see also Educational research
see also Educational retention rates
see also Educational technology
see also Educational tests
see also Elementary and secondary education
see also Federal aid to education
see also Federal aid to higher education
see also Federal aid to medical education
see also Federal aid to vocational education
see also Head Start Project
see also Health education
see also Higher education
see also Legal education
see also Libraries
see also Medical education
see also Military education
see also National Assessment of Educational Progress
see also Physical education and training
see also Preschool education
see also Private schools
see also Remedial education
see also School administration and staff
see also School boards
see also School busing
see also School districts
see also School dropouts
see also School lunch and breakfast programs

see also Scientific education
see also Sex education
see also Special education
see also Student aid
see also Student discipline
see also Students
see also Teacher education
see also Teachers
see also Tuition and fees
see also Veterans education
see also Vocational education and training
see also Work-study programs
see also By Industry in the "Index by Categories"

Education Commission of the States
see National Assessment of Educational Progress

Education of handicapped children
see Special education

Educational attainment
Asian American earnings, and employment and other characteristics, by detailed origin and whether foreign-born, 1980, 11046–7.2

Athlete grad rates for NCAA Div I college programs, and reporting of academic performance to Education Dept, 1987-89, GAO rpt, 26121–305

Athlete grad rates for NCAA Div I college programs, by region, aggregate 1982-87, GAO rpt, 26121–285

Births, fertility rates, and childless women, by selected characteristics, 1988, annual Current Population Rpt, 2546–1.436

Condition of Education, detailed data on elementary, secondary, and higher education, 1920s-88 and projected to 1997, annual rpt, 4824–1

Consumer Income, socioeconomic characteristics of persons, families, and households, detailed cross-tabulations, Current Population Rpt series, 2546–6

Digest of Education Statistics, detailed data on students, staff, finances, and facilities, 1989 edition, annual rpt, 4824–2

Educational attainment, by sociodemographic characteristics and location, 1987 and trends from 1940, biennial Current Population Rpt, 2546–1.427; 2546–1.431

Employment, unemployment, and labor force characteristics, Labor Statistics Handbook, 1940s-88 with trends from 1913, 6728–38.2

Farm operators leaving farming, employment prospects, indicators by region, various periods 1969-86, article, 1502–7.911

High school class of 1972: education, employment, and family characteristics, activities, and attitudes, natl longitudinal study, series, 4836–1

High school classes of 1972, 1980, and 1982: educational attainment by selected characteristics, 1976-87, 4848–36

High school grads, by instn control, 1980s-90, annual press release, 4804–19

High school grads from public schools, 1986/87-1987/88 and projected to 1992/93, annual rpt, 4826–8.1

High school students employment, academic and other characteristics, 1984-86, 4898–27

Hispanic Americans socioeconomic characteristics, by detailed origin, 1988, Current Population Rpt, 2546–1.430; 2546–1.438

Household and family characteristics, by location, 1988, annual Current Population Rpt, 2546-1.437

Income (household) and poverty status under alternative income definitions, by recipient characteristics, 1986, Current Population Rpt, 2546-6.58

Military recruits, percent high school grads by sex and service branch, quarterly press release, 3542-7

Older persons health care services use related to marital status, living arrangements, and other characteristics, 1977, 4188-54

Older persons socioeconomic characteristics, 1900s-86 and projected to 2050, biennial chartbook, 12904-1

Police agencies employment, spending, and operations, FY87, 6066-25.20

Population size and characteristics, 1969-88, Current Population Rpt, annual rpt, 2546-2.146

Reading ability and literacy of young adults, relation to educational attainment and race, natl assessment, 1985, 4828-36

Rural areas employment, economic conditions, and population characteristics, 1970s-85, compilation of papers, 1598-243

Statistical Abstract of US, social, political, and economic data, 1790-2025, comprehensive annual compilation, 2324-1.1

Texas-Mexico border area health facilities and services, with background data, by Texas county, 1980s-88, GAO rpt, 26121-261

Unemployed displaced workers earnings losses and unemployment duration, relation to educational attainment, by selected characteristics, 1984-86, article, 6722-1.942

see also Degrees, higher education

see also Educational retention rates

see also National Assessment of Educational Progress

see also School dropouts

see also under By Educational Attainment in the "Index by Categories"

Educational broadcasting

Humanities Natl Endowment activities and grants, FY88, annual rpt, 9564-2

TV and radio stations on the air, by class of operation, monthly press release, 9282-4

Educational development

see Educational reform

Educational employees pay

Collective bargaining agreements expiring during year, and workers covered, by firm, union, industry group, and State, 1989, annual rpt, 6784-9

Condition of Education, detailed data on elementary, secondary, and higher education, 1920s-88 and projected to 1997, annual rpt, 4824-1

County Business Patterns, 1987: employment, establishments, and payroll, by SIC 2- to 4-digit industry and county, annual State rpt series, 2326-8

Digest of Education Statistics, detailed data on students, staff, finances, and facilities, 1989 edition, annual rpt, 4824-2

Early childhood education centers, services, costs, and teacher salaries, FY88, GAO rpt, 26121-297

Earnings by major industry group, and personal income per capita and by source, by region and State, 1929-87, 2708-40

Elementary and secondary public education agency revenues by source, and outlays, by State, FY86-87, annual rpt, 4834-6

Employee flexible benefit plan coverage and provisions, by occupational group for private sector and govt workers, 1986-88, article, 6722-1.959

Employment, earnings, and hours, by selected SIC 1- to 4-digit industry, State, and for 262 MSAs, 1972-87, 6748-81

Employment, earnings, and hours, by SIC 1- to 4-digit industry, monthly 1983-Feb 1989, annual rpt, 6744-4

Insurance (short term disability) coverage and provisions, by occupational group, 1986-87, article, 6722-1.925

Payroll and employment, by function and level of govt, 1987-88, annual rpt series, 2466-4

Payroll and employment of State and local govts, monthly rpt, 6742-4

Public schools teachers salaries, 1974/75-1988/89 and alternative projections to 1999/2000, annual rpt, 4824-4

Science and engineering employment and earnings, by field and activity, and private and Federal R&D spending, by industry, 1975-88, 9626-6.29

Science and engineering employment in R&D, earnings by field and educational, employment, and other characteristics, 1989, annual rpt, 3004-1

Science and engineering PhDs employment and other characteristics, by field and State, 1987, biennial rpt, 9627-18

Service industries census, 1987: establishments, receipts, employment, and payroll, by SIC 2- to 4-digit kind of business, MSA, county, and city, State rpt series, 2391-1

Teachers in public and private schools, salaries by selected characteristics, 1984/85-1985/86, 4838-37

Teachers moonlighting, by selected employment and other characteristics, 1985, 4838-36

Teachers salaries, by State, 1982-88, annual table with supplements, 4804-32

Teachers salaries in elementary and secondary education, 1986/87 and projected to 1992/93, annual rpt, 4826-8.3

Teachers salaries, 1980s-90, annual press release, 4804-19

Educational enrollment

Abortions by patient characteristics, rates for all and 1st abortions, and related deaths in US and other countries, 1989 hearing, 21408-113

Alaska rural villages population characteristics and subsistence activities, 1976-86, 5738-9

Bilingual education program activities, Federal and State aid, and enrollment, FY86-87, biennial rpt, 4804-14

Black colleges R&D funding by source, and characteristics of grad students and research staff, by field of science and instn, 1980s-87, 9628-78

Community organizations partnerships with public schools, participation, activities,

and contributions, by school characteristics and location, 1987/88, 4826-1.27

Compensatory education programs federally funded, private school students served, and costs, for selected districts, 1984-89, GAO rpt, 26121-308

Condition of Education, detailed data on elementary, secondary, and higher education, 1920s-88 and projected to 1997, annual rpt, 4824-1

Data on education, enrollment, degrees, teachers, and spending, 1974/75-1988/89 and alternative projections to 1999/2000, annual rpt, 4824-4

Desegregation of schools, indicators of integration plans effectiveness by school district and location, 1960s-85, 11048-189

Digest of Education Statistics, detailed data on students, staff, finances, and facilities, 1989 edition, annual rpt, 4824-2

Elementary and secondary education enrollment, teachers, high school grads, and spending, by State, 1988/89, annual rpt, 4834-19

Elementary and secondary public school enrollment, 1987 and projected to 1993, annual rpt, 4826-8.5

Elementary and secondary public schools, enrollment and other characteristics, for top 55 districts, 1987-88, annual rpt, 4834-22

Elementary and secondary public schools, enrollment, and teachers, by level and State, 1987/88, annual rpt, 4834-17

Employment, unemployment, and labor force characteristics, Labor Statistics Handbook, 1940s-88 with trends from 1913, 6728-38.2

Enrollment, by grade, instn type and control, and student characteristics, 1986 and trends from 1947, annual Current Population Rpt, 2546-1.429; 2546-1.432

Enrollment, staff, and spending, by instn level and control, and teacher salaries, 1980s-90, annual press release, 4804-19

Head Start enrollment, funding, and staff, FY88, annual rpt, 4604-8

Head Start handicapped enrollment, by handicap, State, and for Indian and migrant programs, 1985/86, annual rpt, 4604-1

Head Start program operations, enrollment by handicap, and family characteristics, for North Central States, 1987/88, annual rpt, 4604-12

High school class of 1972: education, employment, and family characteristics, activities, and attitudes, natl longitudinal study, series, 4836-1

High school class of 1988: college enrollment, and labor force participation of grads and dropouts, by race and sex, press release, 6726-1.22

High school classes of 1972, 1980, and 1982: postsecondary enrollment and degrees, by sex, race, and income level, natl longitudinal surveys, 4848-35

Higher education enrollment and degrees awarded by sex, and instn finances, by instn level and control, 1987-88, annual rpt, 4844-14

Literacy programs of libraries, activities, and relation to community and instn characteristics, 1986, 4878–2

Mail revenue and appropriation for revenue forgone, by class of mail, FY88, annual rpt, 9864–5.4

Mail revenue and subsidy for revenue forgone, by class of mail, FY88, and volume from FY84, annual rpt, 9864–1

Mail revenue, costs, and volume, by class of mail, FY88, annual rpt, 9864–2

Manufacturing census, 1987: financial and operating data, for SIC 4-digit industries by product, preliminary rpt, 2491–1.30

Price indexes (producer), by stage of processing and detailed commodity, monthly rpt, 6762–6

Science education methods, materials, and factors affecting student proficiency, views of students, teachers, and administrators, 1983-85 surveys, 4828–37.1

Science proficiency, attitudes, factors affecting proficiency, and teacher background and views, natl assessment of elementary and high school students, 1977-86, 4898–25

Educational reform

Community organizations partnerships with public schools, participation, activities, and contributions, by school characteristics and location, 1987/88, 4826–1.27

Effective schools programs for improving academic achievement, characteristics of schools, districts, and students, 1987/88, GAO rpt, 26121–304

Elementary and secondary educational curricula standards, minimum compentency testing, and other academic reform, 1989 edition, annual rpt, 4824–2.14

High school academic requirement reform, impacts on test scores by subject and race, 1982-88, GAO rpt, 26131–62

Educational research

Assistance (financial and nonfinancial) of Fed Govt, 1989 base edition with supplements, annual listing, 104–5

Bilingual education program activities, Federal and State aid, and enrollment, FY86-87, biennial rpt, 4804–14

Education Dept programs funding, operations, and effectiveness, FY88, annual rpt, 4804–5

Fast Response Survey System, estimates for education data, series, 4826–1

Fed Govt funding for R&D, by detailed function, program, and agency, FY88-90, annual rpt, 9627–9

Fed Govt procurement contract awards, by procurement and contractor type, agency, State, and for top 100 contractors, quarterly rpt, 102–6

Handicapped children early education project descriptions, 1988/89, annual listing, 4944–10

Office of Educational Research and Improvement activities, FY88, annual narrative rpt, 4814–1

Office of Educational Research and Improvement rpts, 1988-89, listing, 4868–9

Reading ability test scores for natl assessment, comparison to scores on other tests, findings, 1989 rpt, 4828–37

Tax (income) returns of corporations, income and tax items by asset size and detailed industry, 1986, annual rpt, 8304–4

see also National Assessment of Educational Progress

Educational retention rates

Condition of Education, detailed data on elementary and secondary education, 1920s-88 and projected to 1997, annual rpt, 4824–1.1

Data on education, enrollment, degrees, teachers, and spending, 1974/75-1988/89 and alternative projections to 1999/2000, annual rpt, 4824–4

Data on education, selected performance and financial indicators by State, 1982-88, annual table with supplements, 4804–32

Digest of Education Statistics, detailed data on students, staff, finances, and facilities, 1989 edition, annual rpt, 4824–2

Elementary and secondary education enrollment, teachers, high school grads, and spending, by State, 1988/89, annual rpt, 4834–19

High school class of 1972: postsecondary enrollment, transfers, and completions, by selected characteristics, 1972-84, natl longitudinal study, 4836–1.12

High school class of 1980: postsecondary enrollment, transfers, part-time attendance, degrees, and dropouts, by selected characteristics, 1980-86, natl longitudinal study, 4826–2.50

High school classes of 1972 and 1980: enrollment in 2-year colleges, credits earned and dropout rate, by student characteristics, as of 1984, 4848–38

High school classes of 1972, 1980, and 1982: educational attainment by selected characteristics, 1976-87, 4848–36

High school completion rates, by age group and race, 1976-86, article, 6722–1.956

High school dropout rates, and subsequent completion, by student and school characteristics, alternative estimates, 1988, annual rpt, 4834–23

Private elementary and secondary schools, enrollment, teachers, and high school grads, by instn religious orientation, 1988/89, annual rpt, 4834–21

Special education programs, enrollment by age, staff, funding, and needs, by type of handicap and State, 1987/88, annual rpt, 4944–4

Statistical Abstract of US, social, political, and economic data, 1790-2025, comprehensive annual compilation, 2324–1.1

Vocational education aid recipients and sources, and characteristics of programs and students, 1970s-89, series, 4806–3

see also School dropouts

Educational technology

Computer use in elementary and secondary schools, by grade level, 1989 edition, annual rpt, 4824–2.30

Manufacturing census, 1987: financial and operating data, for SIC 4-digit industries by product, preliminary rpt, 2491–1.74

see also Educational broadcasting

Educational television

see Educational broadcasting

Educational Testing Service

"Crossroads in American Education, A Summary of Findings", 4898–26

Educational tests

Condition of Education, detailed data on elementary and secondary education, 1920s-88 and projected to 1997, annual rpt, 4824–1.1

Data on education, selected performance and financial indicators by State, 1982-88, annual table with supplements, 4804–32

Digest of Education Statistics, detailed data on students, staff, finances, and facilities, 1989 edition, annual rpt, 4824–2

DOD Dependents Schools basic skills and college entrance test scores, 1988/89, annual rpt, 3504–16

DOD Dependents Schools students college admission test scores, annual rpt, discontinued, 3504–17

Effective schools programs for improving academic achievement, characteristics of schools, districts, and students, 1987/88, GAO rpt, 26121–304

High school academic requirement reform, impacts on test scores by subject and race, 1982-88, GAO rpt, 26131–62

High school classes of 1980 and 1982: education, employment, and family characteristics, activities, and attitudes, natl longitudinal study, series, 4826–2

Reading ability test scores for natl assessment, comparison to scores on other tests, findings, 1989 rpt, 4828–37

Science and engineering education in elementary and secondary schools, and student persistence in postsecondary education, 1977-88, 26358–199

St Louis metro area local govt finances, structure, and service delivery, mid-1980s, 10046–9.1

Statistical Abstract of US, social, political, and economic data, 1790-2025, comprehensive annual compilation, 2324–1.1

see also National Assessment of Educational Progress

Edwards, Brad

"Questionnaires and Data Collection Methods for the Institutional Population Component. National Medical Expenditure Survey", 4186–8.4

Edwards, Franklin R.

"Policies To Curb Stock Market Volatility", 9381–13.1

Edwards, Gerald A., Jr.

"Asset Securitization: A Supervisory Perspective", 9362–1.909

Edwards, W. Sherman

"Questionnaires and Data Collection Methods for the Household Survey and the Survey of American Indians and Alaska Natives. National Medical Expenditure Survey", 4186–8.5

"Questionnaires and Data Collection Methods for the Institutional Population Component. National Medical Expenditure Survey", 4186–8.4

Edwards, Winston O.

"Physician Charges and Utilization Trends", 4652–1.955

EG&G Idaho, Inc.

"Environmental Monitoring for EG&G Idaho Facilities at the Idaho National Engineering Laboratory, Annual Report, 1988", 3354–10

Eggert, Gerald M.
"Need for Special Interventions for Multiple Hospital Admission Patients", 4652–1.911

Eggs
see Poultry industry and products

Egypt
Agricultural and food production and indexes, total and for selected commodities, by country, 1970s-88, annual rpt, 1524–12

Agricultural exports of Africa by commodity, and relation to economic conditions and other factors, by country, 1960s-87, 1528–280

Agricultural exports of Egypt, for high-value and other commodities, 1982-89, article, 1522–3.925

Agricultural production, prices, and trade, by country, 1960s-89, annual world region rpt, 1524–4.2

Agricultural subsidies of Egypt, transfers to consumers and govt and from producers, and impacts on farm revenue and returns, by crop, semiannual rpt, 1542–6

Agricultural trade by commodity and country, prices, and world market devs, monthly rpt, 1922–12

Agricultural trade of US, by detailed commodity and country, 1988, semiannual rpt, 1522–4

Agricultural trade of US with Asia, Middle East, and North Africa, by commodity and country, 1962-86, 1528–277

AID activities and funding by project and function, FY90, and developing countries summary socioeconomic data from 1960s, annual rpt, 9904–4.6

AID economic aid to developing countries, obligations and disbursements by country, quarterly rpt, 9912–4

AID loans repayment status and terms by program and country, and status of predecessor agency loans, quarterly rpt, 9912–3

AID local currency trust funds mgmt and use, by country, FY83-87, GAO rpt, 26123–221

Cotton subsidies in Egypt, impacts on production and trade, 1981-88, article, 1522–3.904

Economic and military aid and loans from US and intl agencies, by program and country, FY46-87, annual rpt, 9914–5

Economic conditions in Communist, OECD, and selected other countries, 1960s-88, annual rpt, 9114–4

Economic conditions, income, production, prices, employment, and trade, 1989 periodic country rpt, 2046–4.54

Economic conditions, policy, and trade practices, by country, 1986-88, annual rpt, 21384–5

Economic indicators of developing countries, problem debtors compared to other borrowers, by country, 1973-84, 1528–285

Economic, social, political, and geographic summary data, by country, 1989, annual factbook, 9114–2

Exports and imports of US, by commodity and country, 1970-87, world area rpt, 9116–1.3

Exports and imports of US, by selected country, country group, and commodity group, 1988, annual rpt, 2044–37

Human rights conditions in 170 countries, 1988, annual rpt, 21384–3

Imports of goods, services, and investment from US, trade barriers, impacts, and US actions, by country, 1988, annual rpt, 444–2

Labor conditions, union coverage, and work accidents, 1989 annual country rpt, 6366–4.34

Military aid of US, arms sales, and training programs costs and budget requests, by program, world region, and country, FY88-90, annual rpt, 7144–13

Military spending, arms trade, and force strengths, with govt spending and population, by country, 1977-87, annual rpt, 9824–1

Minerals Yearbook, 1987, Vol 3: foreign country reviews of production, trade, and policy, by commodity, annual rpt, 5604–35

Minerals Yearbook, 1987, Vol 3 preprints: foreign country review of production, trade, and policy, by commodity, annual rpt, 5604–23.21

Multinatl US firms and foreign affiliates finances and operations, by industry of parent firm and affiliate, world area, and country, preliminary 1987, annual rpt, 2704–5

Nuclear power plant capacity, generation, and operating status, by plant and foreign and US location, 1988 and projected to 2020, annual rpt, 3164–57

Population size, growth rates, and components of change, by country, projected 1989-2020 and trends from 1950, biennial rpt, 2324–9

UN voting record and share of votes in agreement with US, by issue, country, and world area, 1988, annual rpt, 7004–18

see also under By Foreign Country in the "Index by Categories"

Eisenbeis, Robert A.
"Are Real Estate Specializing Depositories Viable? The Evidence from Commercial Banks", 9366–6.202

El Paso, Tex.
Wages by occupation, for office and plant workers, 1989 survey, periodic MSA rpt, 6785–3.4

see also under By City and By SMSA or MSA in the "Index by Categories"

El Salvador
Agricultural and food production and indexes, total and for selected commodities, by country, 1970s-88, annual rpt, 1524–12

Agricultural trade of US, by detailed commodity and country, 1988, semiannual rpt, 1522–4

AID activities and funding by project and function, FY90, and developing countries summary socioeconomic data from 1960s, annual rpt, 9904–4.7

AID economic aid to developing countries, obligations and disbursements by country, quarterly rpt, 9912–4

AID loans repayment status and terms by program and country, and status of predecessor agency loans, quarterly rpt, 9912–3

Economic and military aid and loans from US and intl agencies, by program and country, FY46-87, annual rpt, 9914–5

Economic conditions, income, production, prices, employment, and trade, 1989 periodic country rpt, 2046–4.31

Economic conditions, policy, and trade practices, by country, 1986-88, annual rpt, 21384–5

Economic, social, political, and geographic summary data, by country, 1989, annual factbook, 9114–2

Exports and imports of US, by commodity and country, 1970-87, world area rpt, 9116–1.6

Exports and imports of US, by selected country, country group, and commodity group, 1988, annual rpt, 2044–37

Human rights conditions in 170 countries, 1988, annual rpt, 21384–3

Investment (direct) incentives of Caribbean Basin Initiative, economic impacts, with finances and employment by country, 1984-88, 2048–141

Military aid of US, arms sales, and training programs costs and budget requests, by program, world region, and country, FY88-90, annual rpt, 7144–13

Military spending, arms trade, and force strengths, with govt spending and population, by country, 1977-87, annual rpt, 9824–1

Minerals Yearbook, 1987, Vol 3: foreign country reviews of production, trade, and policy, by commodity, annual rpt, 5604–35

Minerals Yearbook, 1987, Vol 3 preprints: foreign country review of production, trade, and policy, by commodity, annual rpt, 5604–23.84

Population size, growth rates, and components of change, by country, projected 1989-2020 and trends from 1950, biennial rpt, 2324–9

Refugees from Nicaragua, El Salvador, and Guatemala receiving UN aid, resettlement in other Central American countries, and repatriations, 1984-88, GAO rpt, 26123–232

UN voting record and share of votes in agreement with US, by issue, country, and world area, 1988, annual rpt, 7004–18

see also under By Foreign Country in the "Index by Categories"

Elderly
see Aged and aging

Eldridge, Peter J.
"Southeast Area Monitoring and Assessment Program (SEAMAP): A State-Federal-University Program for Collection, Management, and Dissemination of Fishery-Independent Data and Information in the Southeastern U.S.", 2162–1.901

Elections
Congressional Directory, members of 101st Congress, other officials, elections, and districts, 1989-90, biennial rpt, 23874–1

Criminal cases by type and disposition, and collections, for US attorneys, by Federal district, FY88, annual rpt, 6004–2.1

Criminal sentences for Federal offenses, guidelines by offense and circumstances, 1989 rpt, 17668–1

Developing countries disaster preparedness and economic, population, and political data, country rpt series, 9916–2

Colorado River Storage Project finances and activities in western States, FY88, annual rpt, 5824–3

Communist countries agricultural, mineral, and consumer and producer goods production, by commodity, 1960s-88, annual rpt, 9114–4.4

Connecticut energy use by consuming sector, and prices, by energy type, 1960s-86, hearing, 21448–38

Construction industries census, 1987: establishments, employment, receipts, and expenditures, by SIC 4-digit industry and State, final industry rpt series, 2373–1

Construction industries census, 1987: financial and operating data, preliminary industry rpt series, 2371–1

Construction put in place, permits, housing sales, costs, material prices, and employment, bimonthly rpt with articles, 2042–1

Construction put in place, private and public, by type and region, monthly rpt, annual tables, 2382–4

Construction put in place, value of new public and private structures, by type, monthly rpt, 2382–4

County Business Patterns, 1987: employment, establishments, and payroll, by SIC 2- to 4-digit industry and county, annual State rpt series, 2326–8

Employment, earnings, and hours, by SIC 1- to 4-digit industry, monthly 1983-Feb 1989, annual rpt, 6744–4

Employment of minorities and women, by occupation, SIC 1- to 3- digit industry, State, and MSA, 1986, annual rpt, 9244–1

Energy prices and spending, by fuel type, end-use sector, and State, 1987, annual rpt, 3164–64

Energy supply, demand, and prices, by fuel type and end-use sector, projected under 3 oil price assumptions, 1988-2000, annual rpt, 3164–75

Energy supply, demand, and prices, by fuel type, end-use sector, and country, detailed data, monthly rpt, 3162–24

Energy supply, demand, and prices, forecasts by resource type, quarterly rpt, 3162–34

Energy use, by detailed fuel type, end-use sector, and State, 1960-87, State Energy Data System annual rpt, 3164–39

Energy use, by fuel pollutant source, fuel type, and State, 1986, annual rpt, 9194–14

Energy use, cost, quality, receipts, and stocks, and power plant production, by energy source, State and utility, quarterly rpt, 3162–39

Energy use, generation, capacity, and prices, 1988 and trends from 1949, annual rpt, 3164–74.5

Energy use in transportation and other sectors, by fuel type, 1970s-88, annual rpt, 3304–5

Energy use, production, stocks, and costs by fuel type, and sales, by State, monthly rpt, 3162–35

Environmental impacts of energy technologies, 1960s-80s, handbook series, 3326–1

Eximbank loans for energy-related products and services, by country and firm, 1988, annual rpt, 9254–3

Exports of US, detailed commodities by country, monthly rpt, 2422–3

Fed Govt-owned real property inventory and costs, worldwide summary by purpose, agency, and location, 1987, annual rpt, 9454–5

FERC activities, licensing, and rate regulation, FY88, annual rpt, 3084–9

Foreign and US energy use by sector, and production, by fuel type, country, and country group, projected 1988-2000 and trends from 1970, annual rpt, 3164–84

Hydroelectric power generation and capacity, for TVA projects, 1984, annual rpt, 9804–7

Hydroelectric power plants capacity, dev status, and ownership, by State and river basin, as of Jan 1988, quadrennial rpt, 3088–14

Hydroelectric power plants retired, characteristics and location, as of 1989, annual listing, 3084–12

Imports of US, detailed Schedule A commodities by country, monthly rpt, 2422–2

Imports of US given duty-free treatment for value of US material sent abroad, and impacts on US industry and employment, by commodity and country, 1987, annual rpt, 9884–14

Labor productivity, indexes of output, hours, and employment by SIC 2- to 4-digit industry, 1963-87, annual rpt, 6824–1.3

Manufacturers finances and operations, by SIC 2- to 4-digit industry, forecast 1989 and trends from 1950s, annual rpt, 2044–28

Manufacturing annual survey, 1986: financial and operating data, by SIC 2- to 4-digit industry, series, 2506–15

Manufacturing census, 1987: financial and operating data, for SIC 4-digit industries by product, preliminary rpt, 2491–1.61

Natl forests revenue, by source, forest, and State, FY88, annual rpt, 1204–34

Natural and supplemental gas production, prices, trade, use, reserves, and pipeline company finances, by firm and State, monthly rpt with articles, 3162–4

Natural gas interstate pipeline company sales, contract deliveries, and prices, with data by firm and location, 1982-87, 3168–113

Natural gas supply, demand, distribution, and prices, by State, 1984-88 annual rpt, 3164–4

Natural gas use by electric power plants, and fuel and electricity prices, with data by region, 1987-88 and alternative projections to 2000, 3166–6.31

Nuclear power plant capacity and uranium needs, projected 1987-2000, annual rpt, 3164–82

Nuclear power plant capacity, generation, and operating status, by plant and foreign and US location, 1988 and projected to 2020, annual rpt, 3164–57

Nuclear power plant capital and operating costs per kilowatt, by plant, semiannual rpt, discontinued, 9802–5

Nuclear power plant construction costs and status, and capacity, by plant, as of Dec 1988, annual rpt, 3164–69

Nuclear power plant fuel assembly performance and failures, by fuel vendor and reactor, 1987, annual rpt, 9634–8

Nuclear power plant mgmt salaries by position, and plant capacity, for TVA compared to private utilities, 1985-87, hearing, 21648–57

Nuclear power plant radioactive waste, releases and waste composition by plant, 1986, annual rpt, 9634–1

Nuclear power plant safety standards and research, design, licensing, construction, operation, and finances, with data by reactor, quarterly journal, 3352–4

Nuclear power plant spent fuel and demand for uranium and enrichment service, for US and other country groups, projected 1989-2036, annual rpt, 3164–72

Nuclear power plant spent fuel and waste generation, inventory, and disposal, 1960s-88 and projected to 2020, annual rpt, 3364–2

Nuclear power plant spent fuel discharges and additional storage capacity needed, by reactor, 1987 and projected 1988-2007, annual rpt, 3354–2

Nuclear reactors for domestic use and export by function and operating status, with owner, operating characteristics, and location, 1988 annual listing, 3004–26

Nuclear reactors inspections and operations, by commercial facility, monthly rpt, 9632–1

Nuclear Regulatory Commission activities, finances, and staff, with data for individual power plants, FY88, annual rpt, 9634–2

Occupational injury and illness rates, by SIC 2- to 4-digit industry, 1987, annual rpt, 6844–1

OECD trade, total and for 4 major countries, and US trade by country, by commodity, 1970-87, world area rpt series, 9116–1

Oil and gas primary use prohibited for power and industrial plants, and gas use by State, 1988, annual rpt, 3104–8

Oil and gas supply, demand, and prices, alternative projections 1987-2000, annual rpt, 3164–89

Oil fuel switching to other fuels, capability by end-use sector, 1989, annual rpt, 3164–88

Oil products sales, and purchases of refiners, processors, and distributors, by product, end-use sector, PAD district, and State, 1988, annual rpt, 3164–85

Pacific Northwest electric power capacity and use, by energy source, projected under alternative load and demand cases, 1989-2008, annual rpt, 3224–3

Pollution (air) abatement equipment shipments by industry, exports, and new and backlog orders, by product, 1988, annual Current Industrial Rpt, 2506–12.5

Pollution (air) emissions and abatement equipment, for privately owned electric utilities by fuel type and State, 1987-88, annual rpt, 3164–11.5

Pollution (air) levels for 5 pollutants, by detailed source and State, 1986, annual rpt, 9194–7

Pollution (air) levels for 6 pollutants, by source, 1970-87 and trends from 1940, annual rpt, 9194–13

Pollution (air) sulfur dioxide emissions of electric power plants, and control costs, alternative projections to 2000, 26306–3.108

Price indexes (producer), by stage of processing and detailed commodity, monthly rpt, 6762–6

Reclamation Bur activities, finances, and project impacts in western US, annual rpts, 5824–12

Rural Electrification Admin financed electric power plants, with location, capacity, and owner, as of Jan 1989, annual listing, 1244–6

Rural Electrification Admin loans, and borrower operating and financial data, by distribution firm and State, 1988, annual rpt, 1244–1

Science, engineering, and technical employment in manufacturing, by field, occupation, and industry, 1986, triennial rpt, 9627–23

Science, engineering, and technical employment in transportation, utilities, and retail and wholesale trade, by field, occupation, and industry, 1985, triennial rpt, 9627–32

Solar collector and photovoltaic module shipments by end-use sector and State, R&D, and trade, 1988, annual rpt, 3164–62

Southeastern Power Admin sales by customer, plants, capacity, and Southeastern Fed Power Program financial statements, FY88, annual rpt, 3234–1

Southwestern Fed Power System financial statements, sales by customer, and operations and costs by project, FY88, annual rpt, 3244–1

Steam-driven power plants fuel receipts, costs, and quality, by fuel, plant, utility, and State, 1988, annual rpt, 3164–42

TVA financial and operating data by program and facility, FY88, annual rpt, 9804–32

Utilities finances and operations, detailed data for privately owned firms, and summary data for other utilities by type, 1987, annual rpt, 3164–23

Utilities finances and operations, detailed data for privately owned firms, 1986-88, annual rpt, 3164–11.4

Western Area Power Admin activities by plant, financial statements, and sales by customer, FY88, annual rpt, 3254–1

see also Electric power and heat cogeneration

see also Nuclear accidents and safety

Electric power prices

Bonneville Power Admin sales, revenues, and rates, by customer and customer type, 1988, semiannual rpt, 3222–1

CPI by component for US city average, and by region, population size, and for 27 metro areas, monthly rpt, 6762–2

Farm electric power use and average monthly bill, monthly rpt, annual table, 1629–1

Food marketing cost indexes, by expense category, monthly rpt with articles, 1502–4

Housing average electric power bills, and rankings, by State, as of Jan 1988, annual rpt, 1244–1.6

Import price indexes for electric power, quarterly press release, 6762–13

Manufacturing electric power use and prices, shipments, and trade, for 25 SIC 4-digit industries, 1972-86, 2048–137

Natural gas use by electric power plants, and fuel and electricity prices, with data by region, 1987-88 and alternative projections to 2000, 3166–6.31

OECD energy prices, by fuel type and end use, for 10 countries, 1980-88 annual rpt, 3164–50.6

Pacific Northwest electric power capacity and use, by end-use sector, projected under alternative fuel price cases, 1987-2010, annual rpt, 3224–4

Prices and spending for fuel, by type, end-use sector, and State, 1987, annual rpt, 3164–64

Prices, supply, and demand, by fuel type and end-use sector, projected under 3 oil price assumptions, 1988-2000, annual rpt, 3164–75

Prices, supply, and demand, by fuel type and end-use sector, with foreign comparisons, 1988 and trends from 1949, annual rpt, 3164–74

Prices, supply, and demand, by fuel type and end use, with foreign comparisons, 1976-88, annual summary rpt, 3164–76

Prices, supply, and demand of energy, forecasts by resource type, quarterly rpt, 3162–34

Producer price indexes, by stage of processing and detailed commodity, monthly rpt, 6762–6

Producer price indexes, by stage of processing and detailed commodity, monthly 1988, annual rpt, 6764–2

Puerto Rico economic conditions, 1986 hearings, 21448–39

Rate schedules by user type, utility, and city, as of Jan 1988, annual rpt, 3164–40

Regulation, licensing, and other activities of FERC, FY88, annual rpt, 3084–9

Regulatory and ratemaking standards of utilities, status and coverage of consumers and sales by standard, 1988, annual rpt, 3104–7

Retail electric power prices, by end-use sector, monthly rpt, 3162–24.9; 3162–35

Retail electric power sales, prices, and revenue, by end-use sector, 1984-88, annual rpt, 3164–11.3

Rural Electrification Admin borrowers wholesale purchases and costs, by borrower, supplier, and State, 1940-87, annual rpt, 1244–5

Statistical Abstract of US, social, political, and economic data, 1790-2025, comprehensive annual compilation, 2324–1.3

TVA electric power purchases and resales, with electricity use, average bills, and rates by customer class, by distributor, 1988, annual tables, 9804–11

TVA electric power purchases of municipal and cooperative distributors, and prices and use by distributor and consumer sector, monthly rpt, 9802–1

Electric utilities

see Electric power

see Electric power plants and equipment

see Electric power prices

see Rural electrification

Electrical machinery and equipment

Building materials PPI, by type, bimonthly rpt, 2042–1.5

Business statistics, detailed data for major industries and economic indicators, *Survey of Current Business*, monthly rpt, 2702–1.14

China trade by SITC 1- to 5-digit commodity, 1970s-87, annual rpt, 9114–3

Collective bargaining agreements expiring during year, and workers covered, by firm, union, industry group, and State, 1989, annual rpt, 6784–9

Construction industries census, 1987: financial and operating data, by SIC 4-digit industry and State, final rpt, 2373–1.12

County Business Patterns, 1987: employment, establishments, and payroll, by SIC 2- to 4-digit industry and county, annual State rpt series, 2326–8

DOD prime contract awards, by detailed procurement category, FY85-88, annual rpt, 3544–18

DOD shipments of military and personal property, passenger traffic, and costs, by service branch and mode of transport, quarterly rpt, 3702–1

Earnings by major industry group, and personal income per capita and by source, by region and State, 1929-87, 2708–40

Employment, earnings, and hours, by selected SIC 1- to 4-digit industry, State, and for 262 MSAs, 1972-87, 6748–81

Employment, earnings, and hours, by SIC 1- to 4-digit industry, monthly 1983-Feb 1989, annual rpt, 6744–4

Employment of minorities and women, by occupation, SIC 1- to 3- digit industry, State, and MSA, 1986, annual rpt, 9244–1

Employment, unemployment, and labor force characteristics, by region and census div, 1988, annual rpt, 6744–7.1

Energy use and prices for manufacturing industries, 1985 survey, series, 3166–13

Exports of US, detailed commodities by country, monthly rpt, 2422–3

Financial statements for manufacturing, mining, and trade corporations, by selected SIC 2- to 3-digit industry, quarterly rpt, 2502–1

Foreign direct investment of US, by selected industry group and world area, 1986-88, annual article, 2702–1.930

Freight (waterborne domestic and foreign) by commodity, traffic, and passengers, by port and waterway, 1987, annual rpt, 3754–3

Hazardous substances industrial releases and reduction methods under EPA regulation, by chemical, source, industry, and location, 1987, annual rpt, 9234–6

Imports, exports, and employment impacts, by SIC 2- to 4-digit industry and commodity, quarterly rpt, 2322–2

Imports of US, detailed Schedule A commodities by country, monthly rpt, 2422–2

Imports of US given duty-free treatment for value of US material sent abroad, and impacts on US industry and employment, by commodity and country, 1987, annual rpt, 9884–14

Injuries from use of consumer products, by severity, victim age, and detailed product, 1988, annual rpt, 9164–6

Input-output structure of US economy, detailed interindustry transactions for 84 industries, and components of final demand, 1983, annual article, 2702–1.909

Labor productivity, indexes of output, hours, and employment by SIC 2- to 4-digit industry, 1963-87, annual rpt, 6824–1.3

Light (fluorescent) ballast shipments, trade, and firms, by ballast type, quarterly Current Industrial Rpt, 2506–12.14

Light bulb production, shipments, stocks, trade, and firms, by type, monthly and quarterly Current Industrial Rpts, 2506–12.13; 2506–12.33

Lighting equipment use in commercial buildings, and conservation, by building characteristics, survey rpt series, 3166–8

Lighting fixture shipments, trade, firms, and use, by product, 1988, annual Current Industrial Rpt, 2506–12.19

Manufacturers finances and operations, by SIC 2- to 4-digit industry, forecast 1989 and trends from 1950s, annual rpt, 2044–28

Manufacturing annual survey, 1986: financial and operating data, by SIC 2- to 4-digit industry, series, 2506–15

Manufacturing annual survey, 1986: production indexes and exports by SIC 2-digit industry and State, with comparisons to 1985, model results, series, 2506–16

Manufacturing census, 1987: financial and operating data, for SIC 4-digit industries by product, preliminary industry rpt series, 2491–1

Manufacturing industries production, shipments, inventories, orders, and pollution control costs, periodic Current Industrial Rpt series, 2506–3

Multinatl firms US affiliates, finances, and operations, by industry, world area of parent firm, and State, 1987, annual rpt, 2704–4

Multinatl US firms and foreign affiliates finances and operations, by industry of parent firm and affiliate, world area, and country, preliminary 1987, annual rpt, 2704–5

Occupational injury and illness rates, by SIC 2- to 4-digit industry, 1987, annual rpt, 6844–1

OECD trade, total and for 4 major countries, and US trade by country, by commodity, 1970-87, world area rpt series, 9116–1

Pollution abatement capital and operating costs, by SIC 2-to 4-digit industry and State, 1986, annual Current Industrial Rpt, 2506–3.6

Price indexes (producer), by stage of processing and detailed commodity, monthly rpt, 6762–6

Price indexes (producer), by stage of processing and detailed commodity, monthly 1988, annual rpt, 6764–2

Science, engineering, and technical employment in manufacturing, by field, occupation, and industry, 1986, triennial rpt, 9627–23

Science, engineering, and technical employment in transportation, utilities, and retail and wholesale trade, by field, occupation, and industry, 1985, triennial rpt, 9627–32

Service industries census, 1987: establishments, receipts, employment, and payroll, by SIC 2- to 4-digit kind of business, MSA, county, and city, State rpt series, 2391–1

Small business establishments, employment, and financial ratios, by SIC 1- to 2-digit industry and State, late 1960s-87, 9768–19

Statistical Abstract of US, social, political, and economic data, 1790-2025, comprehensive annual compilation, 2324–1.3

Switchgear, switchboard apparatus, relays, and other equipment shipments, trade, use, and firms, by product, 1988, annual Current Industrial Rpt, 2506–12.11

Tax (income) returns of corporations, income and tax items by asset size and detailed industry, 1986, annual rpt, 8304–4; 8304–21

Tax (income) returns of partnerships, income statement items by industry group, 1986, annual article, 8302–2.903

Tax (income) returns of sole proprietorships, income statement items, by industry group, 1987, annual article, 8302–2.904; 8302–2.921

Technology-intensive manufacturing methods use and plans, with data by technology, selected industry, and firm and market characteristics, 1988 survey, 2508–1

Wholesale trade census, 1987: employment, establishments, finances, and operations, by SIC 2- to 4-digit kind of business, MSA, county, and city, State rpt series, 2405–1

Wholesale trade sales and inventories, by SIC 2- to 3-digit kind of business, monthly rpt, 2413–7

Wholesale trade sales, inventories, purchases, and gross margins, by SIC 2- to 3-digit kind of business and form of ownership, 1988, annual rpt, 2413–13

Wire and cable (insulated) shipments, trade, use, and firms, by product, 1987-88, annual Current Industrial Rpt, 2506–10.8

see also Batteries
see also Electric power plants and equipment
see also Electronics industry and products
see also Engines and motors
see also Household appliances and equipment
see also By Industry in the "Index by Categories"
see also under By Commodity in the "Index by Categories"

Electromagnetic radiation
see Nuclear medicine and radiology
see Radiation
see X-rays

Electronic data processing
see Computer industry and products
see Computer sciences
see Computer use
see Electronic funds transfer
see Information storage and retrieval systems

Electronic funds transfer
Banks account debits, deposits, and deposit turnover, for commercial banks by type of account, monthly rpt, 9365–2.5
Banks in Fed Reserve System, expenses and operations itemized by service, office, and district, 1988, annual rpt, 9364–11

Banks market concentration ratios, impact of automated teller machines adoption by large and small banks, 1971-79, technical paper, 9366–6.187

Budget of US, authoritative financial statements with appropriations, outlays, and receipts, by category and agency, FY88, annual rpt, 8104–2.2

Check collection systems of Fed Reserve and private services, competition issues, finances, and operations, 1984-87, GAO rpt, 26119–255

Fed Govt finances, cash and debt transactions, daily tables, 8102–4

Fed Reserve services provided depository instns, costs and revenue by service and district bank, 1987-88, article, 9362–1.908

Fed Reserve System, Board of Governors, and district banks financial statements, performance, and fiscal services, 1987-89, annual rpt, 9364–10

OASDI beneficiaries using direct deposit, and benefits, by beneficiary type, race, and sex, 1986, annual rpt, 4744–3.3

Overdrafts (daylight) on Clearing House Interbank Payments System, and transactions and average payments, various periods 1970-88, technical paper, 9379–12.42

Overdrafts (daylight) on Fed Reserve and private EFT systems, and impact of overdraft limits, 1985-88, technical paper, 9379–12.40

Overdrafts (daylight) on Fed Reserve and private systems, and potential impact of overdraft charges, 1985-88, article, 9389–1.910

Statistical Abstract of US, social, political, and economic data, 1790-2025, comprehensive annual compilation, 2324–1.3

Switzerland bank funds transfer system activity, by payment size and time of day, monthly 1987-88, article, 9389–1.903

Telegraph firms money order operations and revenue, 1987, annual rpt, 9284–6.5

Electronic mail
see Computer networks
see Postal service

Electronic surveillance
Criminal sentences for Federal offenses, guidelines by offense and circumstances, 1989 rpt, 17668–1

Statistical Abstract of US, social, political, and economic data, 1790-2025, comprehensive annual compilation, 2324–1.1

Wiretaps and results by offense and location, and public opinion, 1970s-88, annual rpt, 6064–6.2; 6064–6.5

Wiretaps authorized, costs, arrests, trials, and convictions, by offense and jurisdiction, 1988, annual rpt, 18204–7

see also Radar

Electronics industry and products
Communications and security equipment authorizations of FCC, by type, FY88, annual rpt, 9284–4

County Business Patterns, 1987: employment, establishments, and payroll, by SIC 2- to 4-digit industry and county, annual State rpt series, 2326–8

DOD prime contract awards, by category, contract and contractor type, and service branch, FY79-88, semiannual rpt, 3542–1

DOD prime contract awards, by category, contractor type, and State, FY86-88, annual rpt, 3544–11

DOD prime contract awards, by detailed procurement category, FY85-88, annual rpt, 3544–18

DOD prime contract awards, by size and type of contract, service branch, competitive status, category, and labor standard, FY88, annual rpt, 3544–19

Earnings by major industry group, and personal income per capita and by source, by region and State, 1929-87, 2708–40

Employment, earnings, and hours, by selected SIC 1- to 4-digit industry, State, and for 262 MSAs, 1972-87, 6748–81

Employment, earnings, and hours, by SIC 1- to 4-digit industry, monthly 1983-Feb 1989, annual rpt, 6744–4

Employment of minorities and women, by occupation, SIC 1- to 3- digit industry, State, and MSA, 1986, annual rpt, 9244–1

Exports of US, detailed commodities by country, monthly rpt, 2422–3

Finances and operations, by SIC 2- to 4-digit industry, forecast 1989 with trends from 1950s, annual rpt, 2044–28

Financial statements for manufacturing, mining, and trade corporations, by selected SIC 2- to 3-digit industry, quarterly rpt, 2502–1

Foreign and US technology dev and competition issues, fundings and recommendations, 1980s-87, 21708–123

Foreign direct investment of US, by selected industry group and world area, 1986-88, annual article, 2702–1.930

Health care electronic equipment shipments, trade, use, and firms, by product, 1988, annual Current Industrial Rpt, 2506–12.34

Import restraint elimination, impact on domestic industry production and employment, by selected commodity, 1986-88, 9886–4.144

Imports detained by FDA, by reason, product, shipper, brand, and country, monthly listing, 4062–2

Imports of US, detailed Schedule A commodities by country, monthly rpt, 2422–2

Imports of US given duty-free treatment for value of US material sent abroad, and impacts on US industry and employment, by commodity and country, 1987, annual rpt, 9884–14

Input-output structure of US economy, detailed interindustry transactions for 84 industries, and components of final demand, 1983, annual article, 2702–1.909

Labor productivity, indexes of output, hours, and employment by SIC 2- to 4-digit industry, 1963-87, annual rpt, 6824–1.3

Manufacturing annual survey, 1986: financial and operating data, by SIC 2- to 4-digit industry, series, 2506–15

Manufacturing census, 1987: financial and operating data, for SIC 4-digit industries by product, preliminary industry rpt series, 2491–1

Multinatl US firms and foreign affiliates finances and operations, by industry of parent firm and affiliate, world area, and country, preliminary 1987, annual rpt, 2704–5

Occupational injury and illness rates, by SIC 2- to 4-digit industry, 1987, annual rpt, 6844–1

OECD trade, total and for 4 major countries, and US trade by country, by commodity, 1970-87, world area rpt series, 9116–1

Price indexes (producer), by stage of processing and detailed commodity, monthly rpt, 6762–6

Price indexes (producer), by stage of processing and detailed commodity, monthly 1988, annual rpt, 6764–2

Radiation from electronic devices, incidents by type of device, and FDA control activities, 1988, annual rpt, 4064–13

Retail trade census, 1987: employment, establishments, sales, and payroll, by SIC 2- to 4-digit kind of business, MSA, county, and city, State rpt series, 2397–1

Science, engineering, and technical employment in manufacturing, by field, occupation, and industry, 1986, triennial rpt, 9627–23

Small business R&D grants of Fed Govt, by program area, agency, and State, FY88, annual rpt, 9764–7

Statistical Abstract of US, social, political, and economic data, 1790-2025, comprehensive annual compilation, 2324–1.3

Switchgear, switchboard apparatus, relays, and other equipment shipments, trade, use, and firms, by product, 1988, annual Current Industrial Rpt, 2506–12.11

Tariff Schedule of US, classifications and rates of duty by detailed imported commodity, 1990 base edition and supplements, 9886–13

Tax (income) returns of corporations, income and tax items by asset size and detailed industry, 1986, annual rpt, 8304–4; 8304–21

Wholesale trade census, 1987: employment, establishments, finances, and operations, by SIC 2- to 4-digit kind of business, MSA, county, and city, State rpt series, 2405–1

see also Computer industry and products
see also Electronic funds transfer
see also Electronic surveillance
see also Home video and audio equipment
see also Lasers
see also Radio
see also Television
see also Video recordings and equipment
see also By Industry in the "Index by Categories"
see also under By Commodity in the "Index by Categories"

Elementary and secondary education

Assistance (financial and nonfinancial) of Fed Govt, 1989 base edition with supplements, annual listing, 104–5

Community organizations partnerships with public schools, participation, activities, and contributions, by school characteristics and location, 1987/88, 4826–1.27

Condition of Education, detailed data on elementary and secondary education, 1920s-88 and projected to 1997, annual rpt, 4824–1.1

Data on education, estimates from Fast Response Survey System, series, 4826–1

Data on education, projections, annual rpt series, 4826–8

Data on education, selected performance and financial indicators by State, 1982-88, annual table with supplements, 4804–32

Data on elementary and secondary public schools, enrollment and other characteristics, for top 55 districts, 1987-88, annual rpt, 4834–22

Digest of Education Statistics, detailed data on students, staff, finances, and facilities, 1989 edition, annual rpt, 4824–2

High school classes of 1980 and 1982: education, employment, and family characteristics, activities, and attitudes, natl longitudinal study, series, 4826–2

Minority group education, schools participating in natl surveys, 1969-88, listing, 4828–38

Public opinion on taxes, spending, and govt efficiency, by respondent characteristics, 1989 survey, annual rpt, 10044–2

Science and engineering education in elementary and secondary schools, and student persistence in postsecondary education, 1977-88, 26358–199

Science and engineering PhDs employment and other characteristics, by field and State, 1987, biennial rpt, 9627–18

Statistical Abstract of US, social, political, and economic data, 1790-2025, comprehensive annual compilation, 2324–1.1

see also Compensatory education
see also Curricula
see also Discrimination in education
see also Educational attainment
see also Educational broadcasting
see also Educational enrollment
see also Educational exchanges
see also Educational facilities
see also Educational finance
see also Educational materials
see also Educational reform
see also Educational research
see also Educational technology
see also Educational tests
see also Federal aid to education
see also Head Start Project
see also National Assessment of Educational Progress
see also Preschool education
see also Private schools
see also Remedial education
see also School administration and staff
see also School districts
see also School lunch and breakfast programs
see also Special education
see also State funding for education
see also Students
see also Teacher education
see also Teachers
see also Vocational education and training

Elevators

County Business Patterns, 1987: employment, establishments, and payroll, by SIC 2- to 4-digit industry and county, annual State rpt series, 2326–8

Housing and households detailed characteristics, and unit and neighborhood quality, by location, 1985, biennial rpt, 2485–12

Housing and households detailed characteristics, and unit and neighborhood quality, MSA surveys, series, 2485–6

Coverage and provisions of employee benefit plans, by plan type and occupational group, 1988, annual rpt, 6784–19

Criminal sentences for Federal offenses, guidelines by offense and circumstances, 1989 rpt, 17668–1

Disabled persons employment, labor force status, and other characteristics, 1988, Current Population Rpt, 2546–2.147

Educational finance, elementary and secondary public education agency revenues by source, and outlays, by State, FY86-87, annual rpt, 4834–6

Electric utilities privately owned, detailed finances and operations by firm, 1987, annual rpt, 3164–23.1

Expenditures (private) for social welfare, by category, 1970s-87, annual article, 4742–1.928

Farm finances and operations, by size, commodity, and region, 1986, annual rpt, 1544–27

Farm income, expenses, receipts by commodity, assets, liabilities, and ratios, 1988 and trends from 1945, annual rpt, 1544–16

Farm labor, wages, hours, and perquisites, by State, quarterly rpt, 1631–1

Farm production itemized costs, by farm sales size and region, 1988, annual rpt, 1614–3

Fed Govt civilian employee leave use and costs, by type of leave, 1987-88, annual article, 9842–1.906

Fed Govt civilian employee work-years, pay rates, and benefits use and costs, by agency, FY87, annual rpt, 9844–31

Fed Govt civilian regular work-years by schedule, overtime, holidays, and personnel cost components, FY87-88, annual article, 9842–1.905

Fed Govt consolidated financial statements based on business accounting methods, FY87-88, annual rpt, 8104–5

Fed Govt obligations object class analysis, by agency, Budget of US, FY90, annual rpt, 104–9

Fed Govt spending in States, by type, program, agency, and State, FY88, annual rpt, 2464–2

Flexible benefit plan coverage and provisions, by occupational group for private sector and govt workers, 1986-88, article, 6722–1.959

Foreign countries labor conditions, output, earnings, and price indexes, by selected country, 1950-88, 6728–38.11

Govt finances, by level of govt, State, and for large cities and counties, annual rpt series, 2466–2

Govt services transfer to private contractors, impacts on govt workers, with data by worker characteristics, level of govt, and location, 1980s-87, 15496–1.5

Handbook of Labor Statistics, employment, unemployment, and labor force characteristics, 1940s-88 with trends from 1913, 6728–38.12

Health Care Financing Review, provider prices, price inputs and indexes, and labor, quarterly journal, 4652–1.1

Income from US sources and tax withheld for foreign natls not residing in US, by country and tax treaty status, 1986, annual article, 8302–2.915

Investment funds (collective) assets, instns involved, and accounts, by type of fund and holding, 1988, annual rpt, 13004–1.3

Labor laws enacted, by State, 1988, annual article, 6722–1.904

Multinatl firms US affiliates, finances, and operations, by industry, world area of parent firm, and State, 1987, annual rpt, 2704–4

Natl income and product accounts and components, *Survey of Current Business*, monthly rpt, 2702–1.27; 2702–1.29

Natural gas interstate pipeline company detailed financial and operating data, by firm, 1988, annual rpt, 3164–38

Nonprofit charitable organizations finances, and assets and grants of top 10, 1985, article, 8302–2.923

Postal Service finances, appropriations, and debt financing, selected years FY72-88, annual rpt, 9864–5.4

Railroad employee benefits and beneficiaries by type, and railroad employment and payroll, FY85, annual rpt, 9704–2

Railroad employee retirement, survivors, unemployment, and health insurance programs, monthly rpt, 9702–2

Railroad employment, and benefits program finances and beneficiaries, FY88, annual rpt, 9704–1

Railroad employment, earnings, and hours, by occupation for Class I railroads, 1988, annual table, 9484–5

Science and engineering employment in R&D, earnings at DOE labs and non-DOE facilities, 1989, annual rpt, 3004–9

Science and engineering employment in R&D, earnings by field and educational, employment, and other characteristics, 1989, annual rpt, 3004–1

Senate receipts, itemized expenses by payee, and balances, 1st half FY89, semiannual listing, 25922–1

Statistical Abstract of US, social, political, and economic data, 1790-2025, comprehensive annual compilation, 2324–1.2; 2324–1.3

Tax (excise) collections of IRS, by source, quarterly rpt, 8302–1

Tax (excise) collections of IRS, by type of tax, region, and State, FY88, annual rpt, 8304–3

Tax (income) returns filed by type of filer, selected income items, quarterly rpt, 8302–2.1

Tax (income) returns of corporations, income and tax items by asset size and detailed industry, 1986, annual rpt, 8304–4; 8304–21

Tax (income) returns of partnerships, income statement items by industry group, 1986, annual article, 8302–2.903

Tax (income) returns of sole proprietorships, income statement items, by industry group, 1987, annual article, 8302–2.904

Tax expenditures, Federal revenues forgone through income tax deductions and exclusions by type, FY90-94, annual rpt, 21784–10

Tax expenditures from employee benefits, for income and payroll tax by benefit type, 1950-87 and projected to 2065, article, 9373–1.913

Tax returns and supplemental documents filed, by type, FY88 and projected to FY97, semiannual rpt, 8302–2.916; 8302–4

Tax returns filed, by type of tax and IRS region and service center, projected 1988-95 and trends from 1977, annual rpt, 8304–9

Telephone and telegraph firms detailed finances and operations, 1987, annual rpt, 9284–6.4; 9284–6.5

Transit systems finances and operations, by mode of transport, size of fleet, and for 432 systems, 1986, annual rpt, 7884–4

Truck and warehouse services finances and inventory, by SIC 2- to 4-digit industry, 1988 survey, annual rpt, 2413–14

Truck interstate carriers finances and operations, by district, 1987, annual rpt, 9486–6.2

Trust assets of banks, trust companies, and S&Ls, by type of asset and fund, selected firm, and State, 1988, annual rpt, 13004–1

Value of employee benefits, alternative measurement methodologies, 1989 article, 6722–1.960

Wage and benefit changes from collective bargaining and mgmt decisions, by industry div, monthly rpt, 6782–1

see also Area wage surveys
see also Civil service pensions
see also Disability benefits and insurance
see also Employee bonuses and work incentives
see also Health insurance
see also Industry wage surveys
see also Labor costs and cost indexes
see also Life insurance
see also Military benefits and pensions
see also Pensions and pension funds
see also Vacations and holidays
see also Wage deductions
see also Wage surveys

Employee bonuses and work incentives

Air Force pilot needs, retention, incentive pay, and impacts of alternative bonus programs, FY89 and projected FY90-94, 26308–88

Costs (hourly) of labor, by component, occupational group, union coverage, industry div, and region, 1989, annual rpt, 6744–21

Fed Govt civilian regular work-years by schedule, overtime, holidays, and personnel cost components, FY87-88, annual article, 9842–1.905

Fed Govt employee incentive awards, costs, and benefits, by award type and agency, FY88, annual rpt, 9844–20

Fed Govt R&D labs technology transfer cooperative agreements, royalties, and incentive payments to employees, by agency, FY87-88, GAO rpt, 26113–422

Fed Govt Senior Executive Service former members reasons for leaving, and views on SES statutory compliance, 1988 survey, 9498–3

Fed Govt Senior Executive Service membership characteristics, entries, exits, and awards, FY80-1987, annual rpt, 9844–36

NASA staff characteristics and personnel actions, FY88, annual rpt, 9504–1

Teachers incentive programs of public schools, and participation, by instn and teacher characteristics, with effectiveness ratings, 1985, 4838–38

TVA managers salaries, incentive payments by program, and supplemental pensions, 1979-88, GAO rpt, 26113–420

UK and France govt-owned corporations stock issues, value, new shareholders, and revenue effects, 1960s-88, article, 9385–1.911

Employee development

Air Force fiscal mgmt system operations and techniques, quarterly rpt, 3602–1

Air traffic control system safety, working conditions, and traffic volume, various periods 1981-88, GAO rpt series, 26113–220

Air travel safety inspector training, FAA officals views on curriculum and adequacy, 1988 survey, GAO rpt, 26113–440

Aviation science bachelor degree holders training performance compared to other FAA hires, 1988 technical rpt, 7506–10.54

Banks in Fed Reserve System, expenses and operations itemized by service, office, and district, 1988, annual rpt, 9364–11

Clerical workers remedial education and training programs, effectiveness, local area program, 1973-88, article, 9373–1.918

DOD training and education programs funding, staff, students, and facilities, by service branch, FY90, annual rpt, 3504–5

Earnings relation to job training, by source of training and employee characteristics, model results, 1983, working paper, 6886–6.34

Fed Govt computer systems security training activities, by agency, 1988, GAO rpt, 26125–31

Fed Govt Senior Executive Service membership characteristics, entries, exits, and awards, FY80-1987, annual rpt, 9844–36

Fed Govt Senior Executive Service training and dev program activities, participant views, 1987 survey, GAO rpt, 26119–272

Foreign countries industrial trainees admitted to US, by country, FY78-88, annual rpt, 6264–2

Foreign Service Inst enrollment and training hours, by course, 1983-87, GAO rpt, 26123–248

Marshals Service activities, FY88, annual rpt, 6294–1

Mine employees by selected occupational and other characteristics, injuries, and workdays lost, 1986, series, 5606–8

Mine safety and health enforcement, training, and funding, with casualties, by type of mine and State, FY87, annual rpt, 6664–6

NASA staff characteristics and personnel actions, FY88, annual rpt, 9504–1

Participant characteristics, and sources of training, with data by employer size and major industry group, 1982-88, 6408–73

Police agencies employment, spending, and operations, FY87, 6066–25.20

Police dept operations, staff, and expenses, for large cities by population size, 1987, 6066–19.51

Small business establishments, operations, owner characteristics, and job training, late 1950s-87, 9768–20

SSA employees with poor performance, mgmt activities, outcomes, and supervisors views, 1985-87, GAO rpt, 26119–240

Teachers incentive programs of public schools, and participation, by instn and teacher characteristics, with effectiveness ratings, 1985, 4838–38

Employee-management relations

see Labor-management relations, general

see Labor-management relations in government

see Labor-management relations, local and regional

Employment and Training Administration

Activities of ETA, funding, and participant characteristics, by program, FY80-86, 6408–71

Apprenticeship issues and public opinion, 1988 rpt, 6408–72

Budget of US Appendix, obligations, appropriations, and personnel, by program and agency, FY90, annual rpt, 104–3

Employment programs, training, and unemployment compensation, current devs and grants to States, press release series, 6406–2

Employment services participation, placement rates, wages relative to community rates, and Federal funding, 1980-87, GAO rpt, 26121–296

Expenditures of Fed Govt in States, by type, program, agency, and State, FY88, annual rpt, 2464–2

Labor surplus areas eligible for preferential Fed Govt contracts, monthly listing, 6402–1

Participant characteristics, and sources of training, with data by employer size and major industry group, 1982-88, 6408–73

Trade adjustment aid for workers, petitions by disposition, selected industry, union, and State, monthly rpt, 6402–13

Unemployment insurance claims, by program, weekly press release, 6402–14

Unemployment insurance laws of States, comparison of provisions, as of Jan 1989, semiannual revisions to base edition, 6402–2

Unemployment insurance programs of States and Fed Govt, benefits adequacy, and work disincentives, series, 6406–6

Unemployment insurance programs of States, benefits, coverage, and tax provisions, as of July 1989, semiannual listing, 6402–7

Unemployment insurance programs of States, benefits, coverage, exhaustions, and finances by State, 1987, annual tables, 6404–10

Unemployment insurance programs of States, quality appraisal results, FY88, annual rpt, 6404–16

Employment and unemployment, general

Abortions by patient characteristics, rates for all and 1st abortions, and related deaths in US and other countries, 1989 hearing, 21408–113

AFDC recipients demographic and financial characteristics, by State, FY87, annual rpt, 4694–1

AFDC unemployed parent cases and payments, by State, quarterly FY87, annual rpt, 4694–7.1; 4694–7.2

Agriculture-related sectors employment and value added, selected years 1975-87, annual rpt, 1544–19

Alcohol use and abuse among minority groups, and related problems, by selected characteristics, 1985 conf papers, 4488–13

Arms sales of US, foreign conditions on sales and impacts on US industry, with data by industry group and country, 1988 annual rpt, 104–25

Asian American earnings, and employment and other characteristics, by detailed origin and whether foreign-born, 1980, 11046–7.2

Budget of US, CBO analysis of revenue and spending alternatives and projections of economic indicators, FY90-94, annual rpt, 26304–3

Business activity indicators, 1987, annual rpt, 9364–5.9

Business and financial statistics, historic trends, 1988 annual chartbook, 9364–2.4

Business Conditions Digest, economic, business, and financial devs and cyclical fluctuations, monthly rpt, 2702–3

Census of Population and Housing, 1990: data item selection, questionnaire dev, and testing, 2626–11.1; 2626–11.3

Coastal areas environmental and socioeconomic conditions, and potential impact of oil and gas OCS leases, final statement series, 5736–1

Coastal areas environmental impacts of economic dev and population growth, 1980s and projected to 2000, 2176–8.1

Consumer Income, socioeconomic characteristics of persons, families, and households, detailed cross-tabulations, Current Population Rpt series, 2546–6

Consumer spending relation to income, unemployment rate, and interest rate, various periods 1949-88, article, 9393–8.911

Counties (nonmetro) employment by industry sector and degree of urbanization, and compared to metro counties, various periods 1969-86, 1598–244

County Business Patterns, 1987: employment, establishments, and payroll, by SIC 2- to 4-digit industry and county, annual State rpt series, 2326–8

Crime victimizations resulting in injury, by offense, type of injury and medical care received, and victim characteristics, 1979-86, 6066–19.49

Criminal case processing in Federal district courts, and dispositions, by offense, district, and offender characteristics, 1984, annual rpt, 6064–29

Degrees (bachelor and masters) awarded 1985/86, holders employment characteristics, 1987 survey, series, 4826–3

Disability Insurance and SSI admin of Fed Govt and States, benefits, caseloads, and operations, 1980s, 4708–11

Disability Insurance beneficiaries health insurance coverage, by type and selected beneficiary characteristics, fall 1982, article, 4742–1.927

Disabled persons employment, labor force status, and other characteristics, 1988, Current Population Rpt, 2546–2.147

Disabled persons rehabilitation, Federal and State activities and funding, FY88, annual rpt, 4944–1

DOD prime contract awards in labor surplus areas, by service branch, State, and area, FY88, semiannual rpt, 3542–19

Drugs (prescription) use and spending by Medicare beneficiaries, by selected characteristics, 1987, 4186–8.3

Economic and monetary trends, compounded annual rates of change for US and 10 major trading partners, quarterly rpt, 9391–7

Economic conditions, and oil production, use, and imports, by country, biweekly rpt, 9112–1

Economic indicator performance, and Fed Reserve monetary policy objectives, as of July 1989, semiannual rpt, 9362–4

Economic indicators and components, and Fed Reserve 4th District business and financial conditions, monthly chartbook, 9377–10

Economic indicators and components, current data and annual trends, monthly rpt, 23842–1.2

Economic indicators compounded annual rates of change, monthly rpt, 9391–3.1

Economic indicators compounded annual rates of change, 1969–88, annual rpt, 9391–9.2

Economic indicators, monthly rpt, 9362–1.2

Economic indicators, monthly table, 9302–26

Economic Report of the President for 1989, Joint Economic Committee critique and policy recommendations, annual rpt, 23844–2

Education statistics, detailed data on elementary, secondary, and higher education, 1920s–88 and projected to 1997, annual rpt, 4824–1

Educational enrollment, by grade, instn type and control, and student characteristics, 1986 and trends from 1947, annual Current Population Rpt, 2546–1.429; 2546–1.432

Employment and Earnings, detailed data, monthly rpt, 6742–2

Employment change by industry div, alternative estimates, 1982-1989, article, 6722–1.938

Employment, earnings, and hours, by selected SIC 1- to 4-digit industry, State, and for 262 MSAs, 1972-87, 6748–81

Employment, earnings, and hours, by SIC 1- to 4-digit industry, monthly 1983-Feb 1989, annual rpt, 6744–4

Employment, earnings, and hours, monthly press release, 6742–5

Employment, earnings, income, and population growth rates, by area population size and region, 1969-79 and 1979-87, article, 2702–1.915

Employment in manufacturing and nonagricultural industries, by MSA, 1987-88, annual press release, 6946–3.12

Employment in nonmanufacturing industries, by detailed occupation and SIC 2-digit industry, 1987, triennial rpt, 6748–60

Employment situation, earnings, hours, and other BLS economic indicators, transcripts of BLS Commissioner's monthly testimony, periodic rpt, 23846–4

Employment, unemployment, and labor force characteristics, by region, State, and selected metro area, 1988, annual rpt, 6744–7

Export-related employment, by industry div, 1980s-87, 2048–103

Exports, imports, and balances of US by commodity group, world area, and country, and related employment, 1970s-88, annual rpt, 2044–26

Family members employment status and earnings, by family composition and race, quarterly press release, 6742–21

Farm operators leaving farming, employment prospects, indicators by region, various periods 1969-86, article, 1502–7.911

Farm population, by employment and socioeconomic characteristics, and region, 1988, annual Current Population Rpt, 2546–1.439

Food stamp eligibility and payment errors, by type, recipient characteristics, and State, FY87, annual rpt, 1364–15

Forecasts of economic and employment conditions, alternative BLS projections to 2000 and trends 1970s-88, biennial article, 6722–1.953

Forecasts of employment conditions, alternative BLS projections to 2000 and trends 1970s-88, biennial article, 6722–1.952

Forecasts of inflation and unemployment, performance of commodity price indexes, with regression results and forecast errors, 1965-88, article, 9393–8.902

Foreign direct investment in US by country, and finances, employment, and acreage owned, by industry group of business acquired or established, 1982-88, annual article, 2702–1.917

Foreign travelers spending in US by world area of residence, and economic impact, by spending category, census div, and State, model results, 1985-86, 2908–28

GNP forecasts for current quarter, performance of monthly employment, production, and retail sales, 1978-88, article, 9393–8.903

Handbook of Labor Statistics, employment, unemployment, and labor force characteristics, 1940s-88 with trends from 1913, 6728–38

Health condition of labor force, disability days, health services use, and disease prevalence, by occupation and sex, 1983-85, 4146–8.170

High school and college grads and dropouts employment status and income, 1989 edition, annual rpt, 4824–2.28

High school class of 1972: education, employment, and family characteristics, activities, and attitudes, natl longitudinal study, series, 4836–1

High school class of 1988: college enrollment, and labor force participation of grads and dropouts, by race and sex, press release, 6726–1.22

Hispanic Americans socioeconomic characteristics, by detailed origin, 1988, Current Population Rpt, 2546–1.430; 2546–1.438

Homeless population characteristics by city, and Federal funding by program, 1980s-89, hearings, 21248–123

Household and family characteristics, by living arrangement, 1988 and trends from 1960, Current Population Rpt, 2546–2.148

Household and family characteristics, by location, 1988, annual Current Population Rpt, 2546–1.437

Household and family composition, and factors affecting change, 1960s-88, chartbook, 2546–2.149

Household composition, income, benefits, and labor force status, Survey of Income and Program Participation methodology, working paper series, 2626–10

Import quotas on steel, autos, and textiles, employment and income impacts by industry, model description and results, 1984, 9406–1.57

Imports (duty-free) from Caribbean area, impact on US employment by industry, 1988, annual rpt, 6364–2

Imports and tariff provisions effect on US industries and products, investigations with background financial and operating data, series, 9886–4

Imports, exports, and employment impacts, by SIC 2- to 4-digit industry and commodity, quarterly rpt, 2322–2

Imports injury to US industries from foreign subsidized products and sales at less than fair value, investigations with background financial and operating data, series, 9886–19

Imports under Generalized System of Preferences, status, and US tariffs, trade by country, production, and use, for selected commodities, 1984-88, annual rpt, 9884–23

Income (household) and poverty status under alternative income definitions, by recipient characteristics, 1986, Current Population Rpt, 2546–6.58

Income (household) before and after taxes, and discretionary, by sociodemographic characteristics, 1986, 2308–54

Income (personal) and poverty status, change by selected socioeconomic characteristics, 1984-85, Current Population Rpt, 2546–20.10

Industrial employment shifts, factors and impacts on wage growth, with data by industry group, 1948-87, 23848–207

Industry (US) intl competitiveness, with selected foreign and US operating data by major firm and product, series, 2046–12

Industry finances and operations, by SIC 2- to 4-digit industry, forecast 1989 and trends from 1950s, annual rpt, 2044–28

Inflation relation to employment variability, 1951-80, working paper, 9377–9.70

Insurance (health) coverage of total and working population, by selected characteristics, 1987, 4186–8.1

Insurance (health) coverage, uninsured persons employment and income characteristics, hospital charges, and care expenses, 1977-85, GAO rpt, 26121–274

Labor force characteristics, press release series, 6726–1

Labor force composition, and wages relation to inflation and unemployment, late 1930s-88, article, 9373–1.902

Labor force counts under occupation and industry classifications used in 1970 and 1980 censuses, by industry, occupation, and sex, 1970, technical paper, 2626–2.59

Labor force issues and trends, 1980s, series, 6306-2

Labor force status by race and sex, employment by industry div, and unemployment duration and reason, selected years 1929-88, annual rpt, 204-1.2

Labor force, wages, hours, and payroll costs, by major industry group and demographic characteristics, *Survey of Current Business*, monthly rpt, 2702-1.5

Living arrangements, family relationships, and marital status, by selected characteristics, 1988, annual Current Population Rpt, 2546-1.428; 2546-1.433

Local areas with labor surplus and eligible for preferential Fed Govt contracts, monthly listing, 6402-1

Manufacturing annual survey, 1986: exports and export-related employment, by SIC 2-digit industry and State, and compared to 1985, model results, annual rpt, 2506-16.1

Manufacturing census, 1987: financial and operating data, for SIC 4-digit industries by product, preliminary industry rpt series, 2491-1

Manufacturing employment, and export and import shares, by SIC 2-digit industry, 1950s-88, article, 9373-1.906

Manufacturing employment change during periods of exchange rate volatility, by industry trade orientation and and census div, 1973-87, article, 9373-1.917

Manufacturing share of output by State, and employment and output shares by industry div for US and Fed Reserve 3rd District, 1967-86, article, 9387-1.902

Married couple earnings, by employment status, occupation, age, and education of spouses, and age of children, 1987, Current Population Rpt, 2546-6.61

Metro area employment and manufacturing output growth, relation to labor costs and area economic conditions, 1976-85, working paper, 9375-13.8

Migration since 1986, mover characteristics by same or different area, and compared to nonmovers, 1987, annual Current Population Rpt, 2546-1.435

Military reserve service impacts on civilian job, and employer support, reservists views, 1986 survey, 3508-29

Military reserve spouses attitudes, and family social, economic, and other characteristics, 1986 survey, 3508-30

Minority Business Dev Centers mgmt and financial aid, and characteristics of businesses, by region and State, FY88, annual rpt, 2104-6

Minority group and women employment, by occupation, SIC 1- to 3- digit industry, State, and MSA, 1986, annual rpt, 9244-1

Minority group labor force participation, by race, detailed Hispanic origin, and sex, quarterly rpt, 6742-18

Monthly Labor Review, current statistics and articles, 6722-1

Multinatl firms US affiliates finances and operations, by industry div, country of parent firm, and State, 1986-87, annual article, 2702-1.925

Multinatl firms US affiliates, finances, and operations, by industry, world area of parent firm, and State, 1987, annual rpt, 2704-4

Multinatl US firms and foreign affiliates finances and operations, by industry of parent firm and affiliate, world area, and selected country, 1987, annual article, 2702-1.920; 2704-5

Natl Commission for Employment Policy activities and rpts, 1989 annual rpt, 15494-1

Natl income and product accounts and components, *Survey of Current Business*, monthly rpt, 2702-1.27

NATO and Japan military spending and indicators of ability to support common defense, by country, 1960s-87, annual rpt, 3544-28

OASDHI admin, and SSA activities, 1930s-89 and projected to 2063, data compilation, annual rpt, 4704-12

OASDHI coverage of employment and earnings, and social security contributions, by age, sex, race, State, and county, 1985, 4748-43

OASDHI coverage of employment and earnings, late 1930s-87, annual rpt, 4744-3.1; 4744-3.2

OASDI benefit payments, trust fund finances, and economic and demographic assumptions, 1970-87 and alternative projections to 1997, actuarial rpt, 4706-1.103

OASI beneficiaries retiring before age 62, employment, income, and benefits, by selected characteristics, 1982, article, 4742-1.911

Occupational Outlook Quarterly, journal, 6742-1

Older persons employment, earnings, reasons for working, and job training preferences, by selected characteristics, 1960-87, 6306-2.3

Older persons labor force participation, unemployment, displacement, and reemployment, by selected characteristics, 1969-88, 6306-2.2

Older persons socioeconomic characteristics, 1900s-86 and projected to 2050, biennial chartbook, 12904-1

Poor householders employment status and reasons for not working, by sex, 1959-86, article, 6722-1.939

Population size and characteristics, 1969-88, Current Population Rpt, annual rpt, 2546-2.146

Poverty level labor force employment, earnings, and other characteristics, 1987, article, 6722-1.948

Poverty status of families and persons, by detailed characteristics, 1987, annual Current Population Rpt, 2546-6.60

Prisoners in State instns, by offense, criminal history, and inmate, family, and victim characteristics, 1986, annual rpt, 6064-26.3

Public welfare programs beneficiaries, and benefits duration and share of income, by selected characteristics, 1983-86, 2546-20.8

Refugee resettlement programs and funding, arrivals by country of origin, and indicators of adjustment, by State, FY88, annual rpt, 4694-5

Retail trade census, 1987: employment, establishments, sales, and payroll, by SIC 2- to 4-digit kind of business, MSA, county, and city, State rpt series, 2397-1

Rural and urban areas population and economic data, 1960s-88, annual chartbook, 1504-3

Rural areas aid from Fed Govt compared to urban areas, by program and degree of urbanization, FY85, periodic rpt, 1598-248

Rural areas economic and social conditions, dev, and problems, periodic journal, 1502-7

Rural areas employment, economic conditions, and population characteristics, 1970s-85, compilation of papers, 1598-243

Rural areas high-technology employment, by industry div and size of firm, and compared to urban areas, selected years 1972-86, hearing, 25728-41

Rural areas high-technology manufacturing employment in western States, by occupational group, 1986 survey results, article, 1502-7.912

Rural counties with employment growth and decline, by leading industry div, various periods 1969-84, article, 1502-7.907

Service industries census, 1987: establishments, receipts, employment, and payroll, by SIC 2- to 4-digit kind of business, MSA, county, and city, State rpt series, 2391-1

Single-parent household income and spending, and selected characteristics, with comparison to households with married parents, 1984-86, article, 6722-1.916

Small business establishments, employment, and financial ratios, by SIC 1- to 2-digit industry and State, late 1960s-87, 9768-19

Small business establishments, operations, owner characteristics, and job training, late 1950s-87, 9768-20

Small business finances, operations, owner and employee characteristics, and Federal contracts, 1980s-88, annual rpt, 9764-6

Smoking prevalence, related disease and deaths, and public attitudes, impact of Surgeon General rpts and antismoking campaigns, 1964-89, annual rpt, 4204-18

Special Labor Force Reports, series, discontinued, 6746-1

Statistical Abstract of US, social, political, and economic data, 1790-2025, comprehensive annual compilation, 2324-1.3

Suburban areas land use, commuting, employment, and housing characteristics, detailed data for traffic planning, 1986, 7888-75

Tax policy of Reagan Admin and business cycle indicators, impacts on labor force participation rate by sex and age, 1976-88, article, 9389-1.914

Taxes, spending, and govt efficiency, public opinion by respondent characteristics, 1989 survey, annual rpt, 10044-2

Technological devs effect on labor force, composition, and productivity, by industry, 1960s-86 and projected to 2000, series, 6826-2

Southeastern States manufacturing employment and earnings, by industry group, State, and urban-rural location, 1970s-85, article, 9371-1.901

Southeastern US economic and employment conditions, for 4 largest MSAs, 1977-87, article, 9391-16.902

Southeastern US employment by industry div, earnings, and hours, for 8 States, quarterly press release, 6942-7

Southeastern US employment by industry div, unemployment, and CPI, for 8 States, 1987-88, annual rpt, 6944-2

Southeastern US employment conditions, with comparisons to other regions, press release series, 6946-3

Southeastern US employment of multinatl firms US affiliates, by industry, State, and country, 1977 and 1987, article, 9371-1.913

Southeastern US textile mill employment, earnings, and hours, for 8 States, quarterly press release, 6942-1

Southern US lumber and paper industries productivity, impact on economy, and employment compared to other industries, 1970s-80, State rpt series, 1206-36

Southern US textile mill employment, 1951-88, annual rpt, 6944-1

Southwestern States employment by industry div, earnings, and hours, by State, monthly rpt, 6962-2

Tennessee Valley industrial dev, employment, and electricity demand, by SIC 2-digit industry, firm, and location, 1988, annual rpt, 9804-3

Texas employment by major industry group, and relation to oil prices and employment in other States, mid 1970s-88, article, 9379-1.902

Texas employment variability, employment shares, and potential impact of diversification, by major industry group, 1970s-88, article, 9379-1.907

Vermont older persons employment, income, and other characteristics, by sex and age, 1900-86, hearing, 21148-54

Virgin Islands economic censuses, 1987: employment, firms, payroll, and receipts, by SIC 1- to 4-digit industry, island, and city, 2593-1

see also Area wage surveys

see also Earnings, local and regional

see also Labor-management relations, local and regional

see also under By Census Division, By City, By County, By Region, By SMSA or MSA, and By State in the "Index by Categories"

Employment and unemployment, specific industry

Aerospace industry employment and salaries, by sex and race, 1979-87, GAO rpt, 26121-315

Aerospace industry minority employment in Los Angeles area, by occupational group, 1980s-86, 21348-113

Animal feed mill operations, detailed data by State, 1984, 1568-281

Auto and home supply stores productivity trends and technological devs, 1972-87, article, 6722-1.941

Auto industry finances and operations, trade by country, and prices of selected US and foreign models, monthly rpt, 9882-8

Auto trade of Canada and US, and production, sales, prices, and employment, selected years 1965-85, annual rpt, 2044-35

Banks (Fed Reserve) and branch officers, staff, and salary, 1988, annual rpt, 9364-1.1

Banks (insured commercial) employment, by asset size and State, 1987, annual rpt, 9294-4.3

Banks (insured commercial), Fed Reserve 5th District members financial statements, by State, quarterly rpt, 9389-18

Banks (insured commercial) financial condition and performance, by asset size and region, quarterly rpt, 9292-1

Banks employment relation to labor costs, output, and technological change, US and 5 OECD countries, 1980-86, working paper, 9371-10.42

Banks in Fed Reserve System, expenses and operations itemized by service, office, and district, 1988, annual rpt, 9364-11

Clothing industry employment and wages impact of prohibition against hiring undocumented aliens, with data by State, 1975-85, article, 9393-8.904

Coal miners working daily, mines, and labor productivity, quarterly rpt, 3162-37.4

Coal production and freight costs, and competitive position in selected markets, for Australia and US, 1987-89, 2048-143

Coal production and mines by county, prices, productivity, miners, reserves, and stocks, by mining method and State, 1987-88, annual rpt, 3164-25

Coal production, reserves, use, and prices by State, exports by country, and employment, 1900s-87, biennial rpt, 3164-79

Construction employment, earnings, and hours, by selected SIC 2- to 3-digit industry, bimonthly rpt, 2042-1.7

Construction industries census, 1987: establishments, employment, receipts, and expenditures, by SIC 4-digit industry and State, final industry rpt series, 2373-1

Construction industries census, 1987: financial and operating data, preliminary industry rpt series, 2371-1

Credit unions federally insured, finances by instn characteristics and State, as of June 1989, semiannual rpt, 9532-6

Electric power distribution loans from REA, and borrower operating and financial data, by firm and State, 1988, annual rpt, 1244-1

Electric power plants production and capital costs, operations, and fuel use, by fuel type, plant, utility, and location, 1987, annual rpt, 3164-9

Electric utilities privately owned, detailed finances and operations by firm, 1987, annual rpt, 3164-23.1

Energy-related fields manpower studies and devs, series, 3006-8

Engine carburetors, pistons, and valves, industry productivity and technological devs, for 1972-86, article, 6722-1.911

Fed Reserve System, Board of Governors, and district banks financial statements, performance, and fiscal services, 1987-89, annual rpt, 9364-10

Financial instns assets composition, growth, and distribution, by instn type, 1970s-88, 8438-1

Financial instns financial and operating statements by deposit size, Fed Reserve functional cost analysis, 1988, annual rpt, 9364-6

Fish processing plants on Pacific coast, and employment, by State, 1980-87, annual rpt, 2164-16.1

Fishery employment, vessels, plants, and cooperatives, by State, 1988 and trends from 1970, annual rpt, 2164-1.10

Food consumer research, marketing, legislation, and regulation devs, and consumption and price trends, quarterly journal, 1541-7

Food marketing sector finances, operations, and merger activity, for processors and distributors, as of 1988, annual rpt, 1544-22

Footwear production, employment, use, prices, and US trade by country, quarterly rpt, 9882-6

Fruit and vegetable processing industries finances and operations, consumption, farm production, and trade, by commodity, 1970s-88, 1568-275

Health care facilities excluded from Medicare prospective payment system, labor and capital productivity indicators by instn type, 1976-86, 17206-2.1

Health Care Financing Review, provider prices, price inputs and indexes, and labor, quarterly journal, 4652-1.1

Health care services (community and migrant) finances, operations, and staff, series, 4108-45

Hospital reimbursement by States under prospective payment programs, effects on operations, finances, and patient deaths, by State, 1970s-83, 4658-29

Hotel industry of the Caribbean area, rooms and employment, by country, 1987, hearing, 21788-179

Housing (manufactured) production, shipments, production workers, and finances, 1970s-89, annual article, 2042-1.902

Lumber (hardwood) production, prices, employment, and trade, quarterly rpt, 1202-4

Lumber and paper industries productivity, impact on southern US economy, and employment compared to other industries, 1970s-80, State rpt series, 1206-36

Marketing and sales industries employment and earnings, by occupation, 1986-87 and projected 2000, article, 6742-1.901

Meat, poultry, and livestock production, consumption, and industry finances and operations, 1950s-86, 1568-280

Mine employees by selected occupational and other characteristics, injuries, and workdays lost, 1986, series, 5606-8

Mineral industries census, 1987: financial and operating data, preliminary industry rpt series, 2511-1

Mineral Industry Surveys, commodity reviews of production, trade, use, and industry operations, advance annual rpt series, 5614-5

Minerals (strategic) supply, demand, trade, and foreign and US industry devs by firm and country, by commodity, bimonthly rpt with articles, 5602-4

Minerals industries injuries by circumstances, employment, and hours, by type of operation and State, quarterly rpt, 6662-1

Minerals production, prices, trade, use, employment, tariffs, and stockpiles, by mineral, with foreign comparisons, 1984-88, annual rpt, 5604–18

Mines (coal) and related operations occupational injuries and incidence, employment, and hours, 1987, annual rpt, 6664–4

Mines (metal) and related operations occupational injuries and incidence, employment, and hours, 1987, annual rpt, 6664–3

Mines (nonmetallic minerals) and related operations occupational injuries and incidence, employment, and hours, 1987, annual rpt, 6664–1

Mines (sand and gravel) and related operations occupational injuries and incidence, employment, and hours, 1987, annual rpt, 6664–2

Mines (stone) and related operations occupational injuries and incidence, employment, and hours, 1987, annual rpt, 6664–5

Natural gas interstate pipeline company detailed financial and operating data, by firm, 1988, annual rpt, 3164–38

Oil and gas exploratory rigs in operation, wells and footage drilled, and seismic exploration crews, monthly rpt, 3162–24.5

Prison industries involvement of private sector, operations by prison and firm, and State provisions, as of 1987, 6068–228

Railroad (short-line) operations and regulation, for lines established 1834-1987, hearing, 21368–109

Railroad employment, and benefits program finances and beneficiaries, FY88, annual rpt, 9704–1

Railroad employment and compensation, by age, sex, occupation, and years of service, 1984, annual rpt, 9704–2.4

Railroad employment by occupation from 1957, and Railroad Retirement Account finances, alternative projections 1987-2010, GAO rpt, 26121–280

Railroad employment by occupational group, for Class I line-haul railroads, monthly rpt, 9482–3

Railroad employment, earnings, and hours, by occupation for Class I railroads, 1988, annual table, 9484–5

Ship-related employment, FY87-88, annual rpt, 7704–14.3

Shipbuilding and repair facilities, capacity, and employment, by shipyard, 1988, annual rpt, 7704–9

Ships in US merchant fleet, operating subsidies, and ship-related employment, monthly rpt, 7702–1

Ships, shipyards, and personnel wartime capability, for merchant and reserve fleet, 1988-2000, 11208–1

Shipyard employment and wage rates, by coastal district, 1986-88, annual rpt, 7704–12.2

Steel (stainless and alloy tool) production, employment, finances, and US producers inventories and unfilled orders, 1987-88, annual rpt, 9884–22

Steel export ceilings under voluntary . restraint agreements, by country and product, with Western US steel industry impact, 1989 rpt, 9886–4.136

Steel imports of US under voluntary restraint agreement, by product, customs district, and country, with US industry operating data, monthly rpt, 9882–13

Steel imports of US under voluntary restraint agreements, with industry finances, operations, and foreign comparisons, various periods 1979-89, 21788–182

Steel industry finances and operations by product, and modernization efforts, as of June 1989, last issue of annual rpt, 9884–16

Telecommunications industries minority employment and discrimination charges, with data by industry and selected firm, 1970s-88, hearings, 21368–113

Telephone and telegraph firms detailed finances and operations, 1987, annual rpt, 9284–6

Telephone firms borrowing under Rural Telephone Program, and financial and operating data, 1988, annual rpt, 1244–2

Temporary help supply services industry employment and earnings for permanent and temporary workers, by occupation, Sept 1987, article, 6722–1.912

Textile mill employment, earnings, and hours, for 8 Southeastern States, quarterly press release, 6942–1

Textile mill employment in southern US, 1951-88, annual rpt, 6944–1

Timber in northwestern US and British Columbia, production, prices, trade, and employment, quarterly rpt, 1202–3

Timber sales of Forest Service, expenses, and operations, by region, State, and natl forest, FY88, annual rpts, 1204–36

Tobacco manufacturing firms, employment, and value added, by product, selected years 1977-82, 1568–276

Transport of intercity freight, and carrier revenue, charges, and employment, by transport mode, 1986, annual rpt, 7704–7.1

Transportation employment, wages, and average annual earnings, by mode of transport, 1977-87, annual rpt, 7304–2.2

Truck and bus interstate carriers finances and operations, by district, 1987, annual rpt, 9486–6.3

Truck interstate carriers finances and operations, by district, 1987, annual rpt, 9486–6.2

Trucking industry deregulation in 1980, impacts on finances and safety, mid 1970s-88, hearing, 21648–55

Uranium mining and milling industries finances and operations, with selected foreign comparisons, 1970s-87 and projected to 2000, annual rpt, 3164–82

Uranium reserves and industry operations, by region and State, various periods 1966-88, annual rpt, 3164–65.1

Uranium tailings at inactive mills, remedial action proposals, costs, site characteristics, and environmental, socioeconomic, and health impacts, series, 3356–4

see also Agricultural labor
see also Earnings, specific industry
see also Federal employees
see also Government employees
see also Health occupations
see also Industry wage surveys

see also Military personnel
see also State and local employees
see also Teachers
see also under By Industry in the "Index by Categories"
see also under By Occupation in the "Index by Categories"

Employment Cost Index
see Labor costs and cost indexes

Employment services
Assistance (block and categorical grants) programs for State and local govts, FY89, biennial listing, 10044–8

Assistance (financial and nonfinancial) of Fed Govt, 1989 base edition with supplements, annual listing, 104–5

County Business Patterns, 1987: employment, establishments, and payroll, by SIC 2- to 4-digit industry and county, annual State rpt series, 2326–8

Employment and Training Admin activities, funding, and participant characteristics, by program, FY80-86, 6408–71

Employment, earnings, and hours, by SIC 1- to 4-digit industry, monthly 1983-Feb 1989, annual rpt, 6744–4

Employment programs, training, and unemployment compensation, current devs and grants to States, press release series, 6406–2

Homeless shelters services, operations, and client characteristics, 1988 survey, 5188–123

Labor Dept activities and funding, by program and State, FY88, annual rpt, 6304–1

Labor laws enacted, by State, 1988, annual article, 6722–1.904

Northern Mariana Islands economic census, 1987: employment, firms, payroll, and receipts, by SIC 1- to 4-digit industry, 2597–1

Occupational injury and illness rates, by SIC 2- to 4-digit industry, 1987, annual rpt, 6844–1

Railroad employment, and benefits program finances and beneficiaries, FY88, annual rpt, 9704–1

Receipts for services, by SIC 2- to 4-digit kind of business, 1988, annual rpt, 2413–8

Service industries census, 1987: establishments, receipts, employment, and payroll, by SIC 2- to 4-digit kind of business, MSA, county, and city, State rpt series, 2391–1

State and local govt employment of minorities and women, by occupation, function, and pay level, 1986, annual rpt, 9244–6.4

Statistical Abstract of US, social, political, and economic data, 1790-2025, comprehensive annual compilation, 2324–1.3

Unemployed displaced workers, labor-mgmt committee aid recipients by selected characteristics, for 4 State programs, 1988, GAO rpt, 26121–316

Unemployment insurance employment service program job placements and wage ratios by State, and Federal administrative funding, 1980-87, GAO rpt, 26121–296

Unemployment insurance long-term claimants employment services use, work experience, and reemployment, by selected characteristics and county, 1987-88, 6406–6.25; 6406–6.26

Unemployment insurance reemployment and training services, and bonus for early reemployment, New Jersey demonstration project results, 1987-88, 6406-6.27

Employment Standards Administration

Black lung benefits and claims by State, trust fund receipts by source, and disbursements, 1987, annual rpt, 6504-3

Budget of US Appendix, obligations, appropriations, and personnel, by program and agency, FY90, annual rpt, 104-3

Workers compensation laws of States and Fed Govt, 1989 semiannual rpt, 6502-1

Workers compensation programs of States, admin, coverage, benefits, finances, processing, and staff, 1984-88, annual rpt, 6504-9

Workers compensation programs under Federal admin, finances and operations, FY87, annual rpt, 6504-10

Encephalitis

see Infective and parasitic diseases

Endangered species

Coastal and riparian areas environmental conditions, fish, wildlife, use, and mgmt, for individual ecosystems, series, 5506-9

Coastal areas environmental and socioeconomic conditions, and potential impact of oil and gas OCS leases, final statement series, 5736-1

Environmental quality and protection programs, and intl issues, 1988 annual rpt, 484-1

Exports, imports, and permits for endangered animals and plants, by species, purpose, disposition, and country, 1987, annual rpt, 5504-19

Fish and Wildlife Service conservation and research project descriptions and results, FY87-88, biennial rpt, 5504-20

Fish Hatchery Natl System activities and deliveries, by species, hatchery, and jurisdiction of waters stocked, FY88, annual rpt, 5504-10

Marine Mammal Protection Act admin, and populations, strandings, and catch permits by species and location, 1987-88, annual rpt, 2164-11

Marine mammal protection activities and funding, populations, and harvests, by species, 1987, annual rpt, 5504-12

Marine mammal protection, Federal and intl regulatory and research activities, 1988, annual rpt, 14734-1

Public lands acreage, grants, use, revenues, and allocations, by State, FY88, annual rpt, 5724-1.2

Recovery plans for endangered species, and funding by Federal agencies and others, by species, FY72-87, GAO rpt, 26113-391

Research of State fish and wildlife agencies, federally funded fishery projects and costs by species and State, 1989, annual listing, 5504-23

Research of State fish and wildlife agencies, federally funded wildlife projects and costs by species and State, 1989, annual listing, 5504-24

Rhinoceros wild and captive population, poacher kills and enforcement action, and conservation issues, 1988 hearing, 21708-125

Statistical Abstract of US, social, political, and economic data, 1790-2025, comprehensive annual compilation, 2324-1.1

Turtles (sea) catch, population monitoring, shrimping kills, and effects of drilling rig removal, 1970s-80s, article, 2162-1.902

Whale (bowhead) population in Beaufort Sea, and aerial survey operations, Sept-Oct 1979-88, 5738-8

Woodpecker (red-cockaded) habitat preservation, costs and timber revenue losses, 1989 article, 1502-3.902

Endocrine diseases

see Metabolic and endocrine diseases

Energy conservation

Auto engine and power train R&D projects, DOE contracts and funding by recipient, FY88, annual rpt, 3304-17

Auto fuel economy test results for US and foreign makes, 1990 model year, annual rpt, 3304-11

Bonneville Power Admin housing energy conservation program, energy savings and indoor air quality under alternative methods, projected 1986-2006, 3228-9

Bonneville Power Admin housing energy conservation program in Hood River, Oreg, cost effectiveness and participation, 1983-86, series, 3226-2

Building codes for energy efficiency, effect on apartment building electricity use, for Tacoma, Wash, 1986-87, 3308-92

Commercial buildings energy use, costs, and conservation, by building characteristics, survey rpt series, 3166-8

DOE activities and finances, summary energy supply and demand data, and bibl, 1987, annual rpt, 3024-2

DOE energy conservation aid activities, funding, and grants by State, by program, FY88, annual rpt, 3304-21

DOE energy conservation aid, State officials views on administrative appeals procedures, 1989, GAO, 26113-414

DOE energy use, costs, and conservation, by end use, fuel type, and field office, FY88, annual rpt, 3004-27

Environmental impacts of energy technologies, 1960s-80s, handbook series, 3326-1

Expenditures of Fed Govt in States, by type, program, agency, and State, FY88, annual rpt, 2464-2

Fed Govt building energy use and efficiency, by agency, FY85-88, annual rpt, 3304-25

Fed Govt energy use and efficiency, by agency and fuel type, FY88, annual rpt, 3304-22

Fed Govt financial and nonfinancial domestic aid, 1989 base edition with supplements, annual listing, 104-5

Housing (public and Indian) stock and renovation needs, series, 5186-15

Housing energy use, costs, and conservation, and household and housing characteristics, survey rpt series, 3166-7

Oil and gas primary use prohibited for power and industrial plants, and gas use by State, 1988, annual rpt, 3104-8

Oil fuel switching to other fuels, capability by end-use sector, 1989, annual rpt, 3164-88

Oil stocks and conservation measures of Intl Energy Program countries, 1987-88 and projected to 1990, GAO rpt, 26123-225

Pacific Northwest electric power capacity and use, by end-use sector, projected under alternative fuel price cases, 1987-2010, annual rpt, 3224-4

Pollution (air) carbon dioxide emissions by fuel type and consuming sector, projected under alternative conservation methods, 1990s-2010, 3006-11.11

Public and nonprofit private instns conservation grants of Fed Govt, by building type and State, 1988, annual rpt, 3304-15

R&D spending of DOE and private sector for conservation R&D, 1984-85, hearings, 21368-107

Research on energy, rpts from DOE and other sources, monthly listing, 3002-2

Supply and demand summary data, DOE activities and finances, and bibl, 1987, annual rpt, 3024-2

Supply, demand, and distribution of energy, and impacts of legislation, series, 3166-6

Tax (income) returns of individuals, by filing status, tax item, and income level, 1987, annual article, 8302-2.901

Tax expenditures, Federal revenues forgone through income tax deductions and exclusions by type, FY90-94, annual rpt, 21784-10

Transportation census, 1987: trucks, by detailed characteristics, miles traveled, and type of product carried, State rpt series, 2573-1

Transportation energy use by mode, fuel supply, and demographic and economic factors of vehicle use, 1970s-88, annual rpt, 3304-5

Transportation finances, operations, vehicles, equipment, accidents, and energy use, by mode of transport, 1955-88, annual rpt, 7304-2

TVA energy use by fuel type, and conservation costs and savings, FY88, annual rpt, 9804-26

see also Alcohol fuels
see also Biomass energy
see also Electric power and heat cogeneration
see also Fuel allocation
see also Insulation
see also Solar energy
see also Synthetic fuels
see also Wind energy

Energy consumption

see Agricultural energy use
see Energy conservation
see Energy resources and consumption
see Government energy use
see Housing energy use
see Industrial and commercial energy use
see Transportation energy use
see under names of specific types of energy (listed under Energy resources and consumption)

Energy exploration and drilling

Aerial survey R&D rpts, and sources of natural resource and environmental data, quarterly listing, 9502-7

Alaska Arctic Natl Wildlife Refuge oil and gas production, reserves, exploration, and dev, 1981-89 and projected to 2003, 26358-200

Alaska Arctic Natl Wildlife Refuge oil and gas resource assessment, with environmental impacts on North Slope and other locations, 1987 hearing, 21448-41

Alaska Arctic Natl Wildlife Refuge resources, native hunting activity, and energy exploration impact, 1985, last issue of annual rpt, 5504-26

Energy exports and imports

Imports of US, detailed Schedule A commodities by country, monthly rpt, 2422–2

Latin America trade, and balance of trade with US, by country, 1988, annual rpt, 2044–34

Manufacturing annual survey, 1986: exports and export-related employment, by SIC 2-digit industry and State, and compared to 1985, model results, annual rpt, 2506–16.1

Minerals Yearbook, 1987, Vol 3 preprints: foreign country reviews of production, trade, and policy, by commodity, annual rpt series, 5604–23

OECD trade, total and for 4 major countries, and US trade by country, by commodity, 1970-87, world area rpt series, 9116–1

Pacific Northwest electric power capacity and use, by energy source, projected under alternative load and demand cases, 1989-2008, annual rpt, 3224–3

Solar collector and photovoltaic module shipments by end-use sector and State, R&D, and trade, 1988, annual rpt, 3164–62

Statistical Abstract of US, social, political, and economic data, 1790-2025, comprehensive annual compilation, 2324–1.3

Supply and demand summary data, DOE activities and finances, and bibl, 1987, annual rpt, 3024–2

Supply, demand, and prices, by fuel type and end-use sector, projected under 3 oil price assumptions, 1988-2000, annual rpt, 3164–75

Supply, demand, and prices, by fuel type and end-use sector, with foreign comparisons, 1988 and trends from 1949, annual rpt, 3164–74

Supply, demand, and prices, by fuel type and end use, with foreign comparisons, 1976-88, annual summary rpt, 3164–76

Supply, demand, and prices of energy, forecasts by resource type, quarterly rpt, 3162–34

Uranium marketing, contracts, prices, utility shipments, and trade, 1982-88 and projected to 2000, annual rpt, 3164–65.2

Uranium mining and milling industries finances and operations, with selected foreign comparisons, 1970s-87 and projected to 2000, annual rpt, 3164–82

see also Coal exports and imports
see also Natural gas exports and imports
see also Petroleum exports and imports

Energy Information Administration

Activities of EIA, 1988, annual rpt, 3164–29

Buildings (commercial) energy use, costs, and conservation, by building characteristics, survey rpt series, 3166–8

Coal, coke, and breeze supply, demand, prices, trade, and stocks, by end-use sector and State, quarterly rpt with articles, 3162–37

Coal production and mines by county, prices, productivity, miners, reserves, and stocks, by mining method and State, 1987-88, annual rpt, 3164–25

Coal production and stocks by district, and shipments by district of origin, State of destination, end-use sector, and mode of transport, quarterly rpt, 3162–8

Coal production by region, exports, and use by sector, projected 1988-2000 and trends from 1975, annual rpt, 3164–68

Coal production by State and region, trade, use, and stocks, weekly rpt, 3162–1

Coal production, reserves, use, and prices by State, exports by country, and employment, 1900s-87, biennial rpt, 3164–79

Coal reserves, by heat and sulfur content, mining method, and State, 1987, 3168–114

Coal trade flows and reserves, by country, 1970s-87 and projected to 2000, annual rpt, 3164–77

Data collection forms of DOE and related rpts, 1988, annual listing, 3164–86

Distillate fuel production, imports, stocks, and prices, by selected PAD district and northern State, seasonal monthly rpt, 3162–40

Electric power plants (steam) fuel receipts, costs, and quality, by fuel, plant, utility, and State, 1988, annual rpt, 3164–42

Electric power plants and capacity, by fuel used, owner, location, and operating status, 1988 and for units planned 1989-98, annual listing, 3164–36

Electric power plants production and capital costs, operations, and fuel use, by fuel type, plant, utility, and location, 1987, annual rpt, 3164–9

Electric power plants production, capacity, sales, and fuel stocks, use, and costs, by State, 1984-88, annual rpt, 3164–11

Electric power plants production, fuel use, stocks, and costs by fuel type, and sales, by State, monthly rpt, 3162–35

Electric power rate schedules, by user type, utility, and city, as of Jan 1988, annual rpt, 3164–40

Electric utilities finances and operations, detailed data for privately owned firms, and summary data for other utilities by type, 1987, annual rpt, 3164–23

Electric utilities fuel cost, quality, use, receipts, and stocks, and power plant production, by energy source, State and utility, quarterly rpt, 3162–39

Energy Info Admin and alternative estimates of energy supply, demand, prices, and trade, with methodology, series, 3166–12

Energy producers finances and operations, by energy type for US firms domestic and foreign operations, 1987, annual rpt, 3164–44

Energy production, dev, and distribution firms revenues and income, quarterly rpt, 3162–38

Energy supply, demand, and prices, by fuel type and end-use sector, projected under 3 oil price assumptions, 1988-2000, annual rpt, 3164–75

Energy supply, demand, and prices, by fuel type and end-use sector, with foreign comparisons, 1988 and trends from 1949, annual rpt, 3164–74

Energy supply, demand, and prices, by fuel type and end use, with foreign comparisons, 1976-88, annual summary rpt, 3164–76

Energy supply, demand, and prices, by fuel type, end-use sector, and country, detailed data, monthly rpt, 3162–24

Energy supply, demand, and prices, forecasts by resource type, quarterly rpt, 3162–34

Energy supply, demand, distribution, and impacts of legislation, series, 3166–6

Energy use, by detailed fuel type, end-use sector, and State, 1960-87, State Energy Data System annual rpt, 3164–39

Foreign and US energy production, trade, use, and reserves, and oil and refined products supply and prices, by country, 1980-88, annual rpt, 3164–50

Foreign and US energy use by sector, and production, by fuel type, country, and country group, projected 1988-2000 and trends from 1970, annual rpt, 3164–84

Foreign countries oil and gas reserves and discoveries, by country and country group, quarterly rpt, 3162–43

Foreign direct investment in US energy sources by type and firm, and US affiliates operations, as of 1988, annual rpt, 3164–80

Housing energy use, costs, and conservation, and household and housing characteristics, survey rpt series, 3166–7

Manufacturing energy use and prices, 1985 survey, series, 3166–13

Natural and supplemental gas production, prices, trade, use, reserves, and pipeline company finances, by firm and State, monthly rpt with articles, 3162–4

Natural gas interstate pipeline company detailed financial and operating data, by firm, 1988, annual rpt, 3164–38

Natural gas interstate pipeline company reserves and production, by firm, 1963-88 and deliverability projected to 2008, annual rpt, 3164–33

Natural gas interstate pipeline company sales, contract deliveries, and prices, with data by firm and location, 1982-87, 3168–113

Natural gas production, wells drilled, and contract prices, by Natural Gas Policy Act section, producer, State, and field, late 1970s-86, 3168–90

Natural gas supply, demand, distribution, and prices, by State, 1984-88 annual rpt, 3164–4

Nuclear power plant capacity, generation, and operating status, by plant and foreign and US location, 1988 and projected to 2020, annual rpt, 3164–57

Nuclear power plant construction costs and status, and capacity, by plant, as of Dec 1988, annual rpt, 3164–69

Nuclear power plant spent fuel and demand for uranium and enrichment service, for US and other country groups, projected 1989-2036, annual rpt, 3164–72

Oil and gas companies mergers, impacts on domestic reserve purchases, exploration, and financial performance, 1982-86, 3168–112

Oil and gas field codes and locations, 1988, annual listing, 3164–70

Oil and gas supply, demand, and prices, alternative projections 1987-2000, annual rpt, 3164–89

Oil and refined products supply and demand, refinery capacity and use, and prices, weekly rpt, 3162–32

Oil crude, gas liquids, and refined products supply, demand, and movement, by PAD district and State, 1988 and trends from 1973, annual rpt, 3164–2

Coal production, trade, and govt subsidies, by country and country group, 1973-87 and projected to 2000, 2048-144

Coal trade flows and reserves, by country, 1970s-87 and projected to 2000, annual rpt, 3164-77

Electric power capacity and use in Pacific Northwest, by energy source, projected under alternative load and demand cases, 1989-2008, annual rpt, 3224-3

Electric power plants capacity additions of utilities and nonutilities, projected under 3 oil price assumptions, 1989-2000, article, 3162-35.901

Electric power plants capacity additions, projected 1989-98, annual rpt, 3164-11.8

Electric power seasonal peak demand and generating capacity, by region, 1987 and projected 1988-97, annual rpt, 3404-6

Foreign and US energy use by sector, and production, by fuel type, country, and country group, projected 1988-2000 and trends from 1970, annual rpt, 3164-84

Natural gas interstate pipeline company reserves and production, by firm, 1963-88 and deliverability projected to 2008, annual rpt, 3164-33

Natural gas reserves, by State, 1950-87 and projected to 2020, biennial rpt, 5604-44

Nuclear power plant capacity, generation, and operating status, by plant and foreign and US location, 1988 and projected to 2020, annual rpt, 3164-57

Nuclear power plant spent fuel and demand for uranium and enrichment service, for US and other country groups, projected 1989-2036, annual rpt, 3164-72

Nuclear power plant spent fuel discharges and additional storage capacity needed, by reactor, 1987 and projected 1988-2007, annual rpt, 3354-2

Oil and gas supply, demand, and prices, alternative projections 1987-2000, annual rpt, 3164-89

Oil demand related to GNP and oil prices, 1972-88 and alternative projections to 2000, article, 9379-1.901

Oil prices and US and OPEC industry impacts of alternative US protective policies, projected 2037, technical paper, 9379-12.44

Pacific Northwest electric power capacity and use, by end-use sector, projected under alternative fuel price cases, 1987-2010, annual rpt, 3224-4

Pacific Northwest electric power use and prices by end-use sector, and economic and demographic data, annual rpt, discontinued, 3224-2

Pacific Northwest population, households, employment, income, and fuel prices, alternative projections 1990-2010 with trends from 1960, annual rpt, 3224-5

Strategic Petroleum Reserve capacity, inventory, fill rate, and finances, quarterly rpt, 3002-13

Supply, demand, and distribution of energy, and impacts of legislation, series, 3166-6

Supply, demand, and prices, by fuel type and end-use sector, projected under 3 oil price assumptions, 1988-2000, annual rpt, 3164-75

Supply, demand, and prices of energy, forecasts by resource type, quarterly rpt, 3162-34

Uranium marketing, contracts, prices, utility shipments, and trade, 1982-88 and projected to 2000, annual rpt, 3164-65.2

Uranium mining and milling industries finances and operations, with selected foreign comparisons, 1970s-87 and projected to 2000, annual rpt, 3164-82

Energy research and development

Autos powered by electricity, R&D activity and DOE funding shares, FY88, annual rpt, 3304-2

Carbon dioxide in atmosphere, measurement, methodology, and research results, series, 3006-11

Conservation R&D spending of DOE and private sector, and housing natural gas use indicators, hearings, 21368-107

DOE real property owned and leased, by type, subagency, contractor, and site, FY87, annual rpt, 3004-28

Electric utilities privately owned, detailed finances and operations by firm, 1987, annual rpt, 3164-23.1

Environmental impacts of energy technologies, 1960s-80s, handbook series, 3326-1

Foreign and US funding for R&D, and scientists and engineering employment and education, 1988, annual rpt, 9624-23.1

Inventions recommended by Natl Inst of Standards and Technology for DOE support, awards, and evaluation status, 1988, annual listing, 2214-5

Inventions supported by DOE, sales, jobs created, and inventor characteristics, 1980-86, 3308-91

Minerals Yearbook, 1987, Vol 3 preprints: foreign country reviews of production, trade, and policy, by commodity, annual rpt series, 5604-23

Natural gas interstate pipeline company detailed financial and operating data, by firm, 1988, annual rpt, 3164-38

Nuclear power plant safety standards and research, design, licensing, construction, operation, and finances, with data by reactor, quarterly journal, 3352-4

Nuclear reactors for domestic use and export by function and operating status, with owner, operating characteristics, and location, 1988 annual listing, 3004-26

Nuclear reactors for research and experimental purposes, by location, monthly rpt, 9632-1.4

Producers finances and operations, by energy type for US firms domestic and foreign operations, 1987, annual rpt, 3164-44.5

Publications on energy from DOE and other sources, monthly listing, 3002-2

Radioactive waste and spent fuel generation, inventory, and disposal, 1960s-88 and projected to 2020, annual rpt, 3364-2

Science and engineering employment in R&D, earnings at DOE labs and non-DOE facilities, 1989, annual rpt, 3004-9

Science and engineering employment related to energy, for PhDs by field and work activity, various periods 1975-87, 3006-8.10

Solar collector and photovoltaic module shipments by end-use sector and State, R&D, and trade, 1988, annual rpt, 3164-62

Superconductivity (high temperature) R&D spending by Federal agency, and US and Japan industry funding and employment, by application, 1981-89, hearing, 25408-100

Tax (income) returns of corporations, income and tax items by asset size and detailed industry, 1986, annual rpt, 8304-4; 8304-21

see also Department of Energy National Laboratories

see also Energy exploration and drilling

see also Federal funding for energy programs

Energy reserves

Foreign and US land, water, and energy resources, by world area, 1960s-80s and projected to 2050, article, 1522-3.908

Foreign countries mineral production, reserves, and industry role in domestic economy and world supply, world area and country rpt series, 5606-1

Minerals Yearbook, 1987, Vol 3 preprints: foreign country reviews of production, trade, and policy, by commodity, annual rpt series, 5604-23

Uranium mining and milling industries finances and operations, with selected foreign comparisons, 1970s-87 and projected to 2000, annual rpt, 3164-82

Uranium reserves and industry operations, by region and State, various periods 1966-88, annual rpt, 3164-65.1

see also Coal reserves

see also Natural gas reserves

see also Petroleum reserves

Energy resources and consumption

Capacity use for selected industries, monthly rpt, 9365-2.19

Coastal areas environmental impacts of economic dev and population growth, 1980s and projected to 2000, 2176-8.1

Communist, OECD, and selected other countries energy reserves, production, and use, and oil trade and revenue, 1960s-88, annual rpt, 9114-4.5

Consumption, by detailed fuel type, end-use sector, and State, 1960-87, State Energy Data System annual rpt, 3164-39

Developing countries economic and social conditions from 1960s, and Intl Dev Cooperation Agency and AID activities and funding, FY88-90, annual rpt, 9904-4

Electric power plants production, fuel use, stocks, and costs by fuel type, and sales, by State, monthly rpt, 3162-35

Employment in energy-related fields, manpower studies and devs, series, 3006-8

Foreign and US energy production, trade, use, and reserves, and oil and refined products supply and prices, by country, 1980-88, annual rpt, 3164-50

Foreign and US energy use by sector, and production, by fuel type, country, and country group, projected 1988-2000 and trends from 1970, annual rpt, 3164-84

Foreign and US land, water, and energy resources, by world area, 1960s-80s and projected to 2050, article, 1522-3.908

Gross product growth rates relation to natural resources sector share of State output, 1963-86, article, 9393-8.909

Input-output structure of US economy, detailed interindustry transactions for 84

industries, and components of final demand, 1983, annual article, 2702–1.909

Natl income and product accounts and components, *Survey of Current Business*, monthly rpt, 2702–1.21

Research on energy, rpts from DOE and other sources, monthly listing, 3002–2

Soviet Union minerals production, trade, and use, by commodity, 1983-87, annual rpt, 5604–39

Statistical Abstract of US, social, political, and economic data, 1790-2025, comprehensive annual compilation, 2324–1.3

Supply and demand summary data, DOE activities and finances, and bibl, 1987, annual rpt, 3024–2

Supply, demand, and prices, by fuel type and end-use sector, projected under 3 oil price assumptions, 1988-2000, annual rpt, 3164–75

Supply, demand, and prices, by fuel type and end-use sector, with foreign comparisons, 1988 and trends from 1949, annual rpt, 3164–74

Supply, demand, and prices, by fuel type and end use, with foreign comparisons, 1976-88, annual summary rpt, 3164–76

Supply, demand, and prices of energy, forecasts by resource type, quarterly rpt, 3162–34

Supply, demand, prices, and trade, EIA and alternative estimates, with methodology, series, 3166–12

see also Agricultural energy use
see also Alcohol fuels
see also Aviation fuels
see also Biomass energy
see also Coal and coal mining
see also Coal exports and imports
see also Coal prices
see also Coal reserves
see also Coal stocks
see also Department of Energy National Laboratories
see also Diesel fuel
see also Electric power
see also Electric power and heat cogeneration
see also Electric power plants and equipment
see also Electric power prices
see also Energy conservation
see also Energy exploration and drilling
see also Energy exports and imports
see also Energy prices
see also Energy production costs
see also Energy projections
see also Energy research and development
see also Energy reserves
see also Energy stocks and inventories
see also Federal funding for energy programs
see also Fuel allocation
see also Fuel oil
see also Gasohol
see also Gasoline
see also Geothermal resources
see also Government energy use
see also Housing energy use
see also Hydroelectric power
see also Industrial and commercial energy use
see also Kerosene
see also Liquefied petroleum gas

see also Motor fuels
see also Natural gas and gas industry
see also Natural gas exports and imports
see also Natural gas liquids
see also Natural gas prices
see also Natural gas reserves
see also Nuclear power
see also Offshore oil and gas
see also Oil shale
see also Oil spills
see also Petrochemicals
see also Petroleum and petroleum industry
see also Petroleum exports and imports
see also Petroleum prices
see also Petroleum reserves
see also Petroleum stocks
see also Solar energy
see also Synthetic fuels
see also Tar sands
see also Transportation energy use
see also Uranium
see also Water power
see also Wind energy
see also Wood fuel

Energy stocks and inventories

Defense Fuel Supply Center procurement, prices, stocks, transport, and other activities and finances, FY88, annual rpt, 3904–8

Electric utilities fuel use and end of month stocks, by prime mover and energy resource, monthly rpt, 3162–24.7

Natural and supplemental gas production, prices, trade, use, reserves, and pipeline company finances, by firm and State, monthly rpt with articles, 3162–4

Natural gas in underground storage, weekly rpt, 3162–32.2

Natural gas interstate pipeline company detailed financial and operating data, by firm, 1988, annual rpt, 3164–38

Natural gas liquids supply, demand, and movement, by PAD district and State, 1988 and trends from 1973, annual rpt, 3164–2

Natural gas liquids supply, demand, trade, stocks, and refining, by detailed product and PAD district, monthly rpt with articles, 3162–6

Natural gas supply, demand, distribution, and prices, by State, 1984-88 annual rpt, 3164–4

Nuclear fuel inventory discrepancy, by facility, 1st half 1988, semiannual rpt, 9632–3

Supply, demand, and prices, by fuel type and end-use sector, with foreign comparisons, 1988 and trends from 1949, annual rpt, 3164–74

Supply, demand, and prices, by fuel type and end use, with foreign comparisons, 1976-88, annual summary rpt, 3164–76

Supply, demand, and prices of energy, forecasts by resource type, quarterly rpt, 3162–34

Tax (income) returns of corporations, income and tax items by asset size and detailed industry, 1986, annual rpt, 8304–4

Uranium enrichment facilities of DOE, financial statements, operations, and stocks, FY87-88, annual rpt, 3354–7

Uranium marketing, contracts, prices, utility shipments, and trade, 1982-88 and projected to 2000, annual rpt, 3164–65.2

Uranium mining and milling industries finances and operations, with selected foreign comparisons, 1970s-87 and projected to 2000, annual rpt, 3164–82

see also Coal stocks
see also Naval Petroleum Reserves
see also Petroleum stocks
see also Strategic Petroleum Reserve

Energy use

see Agricultural energy use
see Energy conservation
see Energy resources and consumption
see Government energy use
see Housing energy use
see Industrial and commercial energy use
see Transportation energy use
see under names of specific types of energy (listed under Energy resources and consumption)

Eng, Catherine

"Case Management in Capitated Long-Term Care", 4652–1.912

Eng, Thomas R.

"Rabies Surveillance, U.S., 1988", 4202–7.904

Engineering & Economics Research, Inc.

"Statistical Abstract of the Unsewered U.S. Population", 9208–128

Engineers and engineering

Air traffic control and airway facilities staff, by selected employment and demographic characteristics, FY88, annual rpt, 7504–41

Army Corps of Engineers activities, FY87, annual rpt, 3754–1

Black colleges R&D funding by source, and characteristics of grad students and research staff, by field of science and instn, 1980s-87, 9628–78

Ceramics (advanced) technical info of Japan, US industry use and views on value, 1988 survey, 2008–28

Competitiveness (intl) of US construction and design industry, with selected foreign and US operating data, 1982-86, 2046–12.43

County Business Patterns, 1987: employment, establishments, and payroll, by SIC 2- to 4-digit industry and county, annual State rpt series, 2326–8

Degrees (bachelor and masters) awarded 1985/86, holders employment characteristics, 1987 survey, series, 4826–3

Degrees (PhD) in science and engineering, by field, instn, employment prospects, sex, race, and other characteristics, 1960s-88, 9627–30

Degrees awarded in higher education, by level, field, race, and sex, 1989 edition, annual rpt, 4824–2.20

Degrees in science and engineering, by field, level, and sex, 1950-86, 9628–77

DOD budget, R&D appropriations by item, service branch, and defense agency, FY88-91, annual rpt, 3544–33

DOE R&D projects and funding at natl labs, universities, and other instns, FY88, annual summary rpt, 3004–18.2

DOT employment, by subagency, occupation, and selected personnel characteristics, FY88, annual rpt, 7304–18

Earnings of scientists and engineers in R&D at DOE labs and non-DOE facilities, 1989, annual rpt, 3004–9

Education in science and engineering in elementary and secondary schools, and student persistence in postsecondary education, 1977-88, 26358–199

Employment and education of scientists and engineers, and R&D spending, for US and selected foreign countries, 1988, annual rpt, 9624–23.2

Employment and occupation of householder, by occupation of spouse, race, and family composition, 1988, annual Current Population Rpt, 2546–1.437

Employment and other characteristics of science and engineering PhDs, by field and State, 1987, biennial rpt, 9627–18

Employment characteristics of scientists and engineers, by field, 1988, biennial rpt, 9627–16

Employment, earnings, and hours, by SIC 1- to 4-digit industry, monthly 1983-Feb 1989, annual rpt, 6744–4

Employment in nonmanufacturing industries, by detailed occupation and SIC 2-digit industry, 1987, triennial rpt, 6748–60

Employment of scientists and engineers, and related topics, fact sheet series, 9626–2

Employment of scientists, engineers, and technicians, by nonmanufacturing industry and field, 1987, triennial rpt, 9627–31

Employment of scientists, engineers, and technicians in manufacturing, by field, occupation, and industry, 1986, triennial rpt, 9627–23

Employment of scientists, engineers, and technicians in transportation, utilities, and retail and wholesale trade, by field, occupation, and industry, 1985, 9627–32

Employment, unemployment, and labor force characteristics, by region and census div, 1988, annual rpt, 6744–7.1

Energy-related employment of scientists and engineers with PhDs, by field and work activity, various periods 1975-87, 3006–8.10

Enrollment in science and engineering, degrees, and student aid and sources, with data by field, race, sex, and instn, 1980s-87, 26358–202

Enrollment in science and engineering grad programs, by field, source of funds, and characteristics of student and instn, 1975-87, annual rpt, 9627–7

Fed Govt aid to higher education and nonprofit instns for R&D and related activities, by field, instn, agency, and State, FY87, annual rpt, 9627–17

Fed Govt science and engineering employment, by field, degree level, race, sex, agency, and State, 1987, annual rpt, 9627–5

Flight engineers certified by FAA, by age, sex, region, and State, 1988, annual rpt, 7504–2

Guam economic censuses, 1987: employment, firms, payroll, and receipts, by SIC 1- to 4-digit industry and election district, 2595–1

Handbook of Labor Statistics, employment, unemployment, and labor force characteristics, 1940s-88 with trends from 1913, 6728–38

Immigrant scientists and engineers, by field, age, sex, country and world area of origin, and State, 1987 and trends from 1967, 9627–29

Industry finances and operations, by SIC 2- to 4-digit industry, forecast 1989 and trends from 1950s, annual rpt, 2044–28

Labor force, Federal and university research funding, and educational data, for science and engineering, series, 9626–6

Labor supply, R&D funding, and other science indicators, with foreign comparisons, 1960s-89, annual chartbook, 9624–22

Manufacturing high technology use and plans, with data by technology, selected industry, and firm and market characteristics, 1988 survey, 2508–1

Multinatl US firms and foreign affiliates finances and operations, by industry of parent firm and affiliate, world area, and country, preliminary 1987, annual rpt, 2704–5

NASA R&D funding to higher education instns, by field, instn, and State, FY88, annual listing, 9504–7

Navy manpower strengths, accessions, and attrition, detailed statistics, quarterly rpt, 3802–4

Northern Mariana Islands economic census, 1987: employment, firms, payroll, and receipts, by SIC 1- to 4-digit industry, 2597–1

NSF activities, finances, and funding by program, FY88, annual rpt, 9624–6

NSF Science Resources Studies Div project descriptions and rpts, 1988 annual listing, 9624–21

Nuclear engineering enrollment and degrees by instn and State, and women grads plans and employment, 1972-88, 3006–8.8

Occupational injury and illness rates, by SIC 2- to 4-digit industry, 1987, annual rpt, 6844–1

R&D equipment of higher education instns, acquisition and service costs, condition, and financing, by field, 1982-83 and 1985-86, 9628–76

R&D funding by Fed Govt at large science facilities, by field, performer, and facility, FY86-88, hearings, 21708–128

R&D funding by Fed Govt, by field, performer type, agency, and State, FY87-89, annual rpt, 9627–20

R&D funding by source and field, selected years 1953-89, annual rpt, 9624–18

Receipts for services, by SIC 2- to 4-digit kind of business, 1988, annual rpt, 2413–8

Research and education engineering grants of NSF, FY88, annual listing, 9624–24

Service industries census, 1987: establishments, receipts, employment, and payroll, by SIC 2- to 4-digit kind of business, MSA, county, and city, State rpt series, 2391–1

Statistical Abstract of US, social, political, and economic data, 1790-2025, comprehensive annual compilation, 2324–1.3

Superconductivity (high temperature) R&D spending by Federal agency, and US and Japan industry funding and employment, by application, 1981-89, hearing, 25408–100

Tax (income) returns of corporations, income and tax items by asset size and detailed industry, 1986, annual rpt, 8304–4; 8304–21

Tax (income) returns of partnerships, income statement items by industry group, 1986, annual article, 8302–2.903

Tax (income) returns of sole proprietorships, income statement items, by industry group, 1987, annual article, 8302–2.904; 8302–2.921

Telecommunications and Info Natl Admin rpts, FY88, annual listing, 2804–3

TVA nuclear power plant mgmt salaries by position, and plant capacity, compared to private utilities, 1985-87, hearing, 21648–57

Uranium tailings at inactive mills, remedial action proposals, costs, site characteristics, and environmental, socioeconomic, and health impacts, series, 3356–4

Virgin Islands economic censuses, 1987: employment, firms, payroll, and receipts, by SIC 1- to 4-digit industry, island, and city, 2593–1

Wages of scientists and engineers in R&D, by field and educational, employment, and other characteristics, 1989, annual rpt, 3004–1

see also Architecture
see also Biotechnology
see also Technological innovations
see also Traffic engineering

Engines and motors

Aircraft engine shipments, trade, use, and firms, by type, monthly Current Industrial Rpt, 2506–12.24

Auto and light truck fuel economy, sales, and market shares, by size and model for US and foreign makes, 1989 model year, semiannual rpt, 3302–4

Auto engine and power train R&D projects, DOE contracts and funding by recipient, FY88, annual rpt, 3304–17

County Business Patterns, 1987: employment, establishments, and payroll, by SIC 2- to 4-digit industry and county, annual State rpt series, 2326–8

Employment, earnings, and hours, by SIC 1- to 4-digit industry, monthly 1983-Feb 1989, annual rpt, 6744–4

Exports and imports of US shipped through Canada, by detailed commodity, customs district, and country, 1987, annual rpt, 7704–11

Price indexes (producer), by stage of processing and detailed commodity, monthly rpt, 6762–6

Price indexes (producer), by stage of processing and detailed commodity, monthly 1988, annual rpt, 6764–2

Recalls of motor vehicles and equipment with safety-related defects, by make, quarterly listing, 7762–2

Science, engineering, and technical employment in manufacturing, by field, occupation, and industry, 1986, triennial rpt, 9627–23

Shipments of motors and generators, trade, use, and firms, by product, 1988, annual Current Industrial Rpt, 2506–12.17

Shipments, trade, use, and firms, for internal combustion engines by product, 1988, annual Current Industrial Rpt, 2506–12.6

see also Electric power plants and equipment

England
see United Kingdom

English language
see Language arts
see Language use and ability

Enid, Okla.
see also under By SMSA or MSA in the "Index by Categories"

Enlistment
see Voluntary military service

Enrollment
see Educational enrollment

Enstrom, James E.
"Health Practices and Cancer Mortality Among Active California Mormons", 4472–1.932

Enterovirus infections
see Infective and parasitic diseases

Enterprise Statistics Program
Data coverage and availability for 1987 economic censuses and related statistics, 1989 preliminary guide, 2308–5

Entertainment
see Performing arts
see Recreation

Environmental assessments
see Environmental impact statements

Environmental Data and Information Service
see National Environmental Satellite, Data, and Information Service

Environmental impact statements
Alaska Arctic Natl Wildlife Refuge oil and gas resource assessment, with environmental impacts on North Slope and other locations, 1987 hearing, 21448–41
Alaska Arctic Natl Wildlife Refuge resources, native hunting activity, and energy exploration impact, 1985, last issue of annual rpt, 5504–26
Alaska OCS environmental conditions and oil dev impacts, compilation of papers, series, 2176–1
Coal Surface Mining Reclamation and Enforcement Office activities and funding, by State and Indian tribe, FY87, annual rpt, 5644–1
Energy conservation (housing) program of BPA, energy savings and indoor air quality under alternative methods, projected 1986-2006, 3228–9
Environmental quality and protection programs, and intl issues, 1988 annual rpt, 484–1
Forest Service mgmt of public lands and resources dev, environmental, economic, and social impacts of alternative programs, projected to 2030, 1208–24
New Mexico Waste Isolation Pilot Plant disposal of military radioactive waste, environmental impacts, 1989 supplemental statement, 3008–33
Nuclear weapons test areas in Nevada and other sites, radionuclide concentrations in air, water, humans, animals, and milk, 1988, annual rpt, 9194–17
Oil and gas OCS leases environmental and socioeconomic impact and coastal area description, final statement series, 5736–1
Oil and gas OCS production water discharges, and impacts on Gulf of Mexico coastal habitats, 1983-88, 5738–10

Public lands acreage and use, and Land Mgmt Bur activities and finances, annual State rpt series, 5724–11
Uranium tailings at inactive mills, remedial action proposals, costs, site characteristics, and environmental, socioeconomic, and health impacts, series, 3356–4

Environmental pollution and control
Abatement equipment spending of business, 1982-88, annual article, 2702–1.904
Abatement spending by govts, business, and consumers, 1983-87, annual article, 2702–1.919
Abatement spending, capital and operating costs by SIC 2- to 4-digit industry and State, 1986, annual Current Industrial Rpt, 2506–3.6
Abatement spending impact on labor productivity, 1960s-80s, article, 9389–1.911
Agricultural Conservation Program participation and payments, by practice and State, FY87, annual rpt, 1804–7
Alaska OCS environmental conditions and oil dev impacts, compilation of papers, series, 2176–1
Assistance (block and categorical grants) programs for State and local govts, FY89, biennial listing, 10044–8
Assistance (financial and nonfinancial) of Fed Govt, 1989 base edition with supplements, annual listing, 104–5
Bond tax-exempt issues for private activity, by purpose, face value, major industry, and State, 1986, annual article, 8302–2.905
Budget of US Appendix, obligations, appropriations, and personnel, by program and agency, FY90, annual rpt, 104–3
Budget of US, historical data, selected years FY34-88 and projected to FY94, annual rpt, 104–22
Carcinogens chemistry, sources, environment and health risks, and regulation, by substance and brand, 1989, annual rpt, 4044–15
Court civil and criminal caseloads for Federal district, appeals, and special courts, June 1989, annual rpt, 18204–2; 18204–8
Criminal sentences for Federal offenses, guidelines by offense and circumstances, 1989 rpt, 17668–1
Electric utilities privately owned, pollution abatement outlays by type of pollutant and equipment, and firm, 1987, annual rpt, 3164–23.1
Energy rpts from DOE and other sources, monthly listing, 3002–2
Energy technologies environmental impacts, 1960s-80s, handbook series, 3326–1
Environmental quality and protection programs, and intl issues, 1988 annual rpt, 484–1
EPA pollution control grant program activities, monthly rpt, 9182–8
EPA programs fraud and abuse, audits and investigations, 2nd half FY89, semiannual rpt, 9182–10
EPA regulatory and protection programs operations and mgmt goals, progress and activities, by office, quarterly rpt, 9182–11
EPA rpts in NTIS collection, quarterly listing, 9182–5

Farm mgmt, finances, operations, environmental issues, and info sources, *1989 Yearbook of Agriculture*, annual rpt, 1004–18
Fed Govt spending in States, by type, program, agency, and State, FY88, annual rpt, 2464–2
Fish and Wildlife Service conservation and research project descriptions and results, FY87-88, biennial rpt, 5504–20
Forest Service mgmt of public lands and resources dev, environmental, economic, and social impacts of alternative programs, projected to 2030, 1208–24
Health care personnel supply and needs, for environmental and occupational health fields, 1987 conf, 4118–65
Health condition and health care resources, use, and spending, 1950s-87, annual data compilation, 4144–11
Health condition improvement and disease prevention goals and recommended activities for 2000, with trends 1970s-80s, 4048–10
Health effects of selected pollutants, concentrations in food and environment, sources, and human intake, methodology and data needs, series, 9186–9
Health effects of selected pollutants, concentrations in food and environment, sources, human intake, and regulation, series, 9186–8
HHS financial aid, by program, recipient, State, and city, FY88, annual regional listings, 4004–3
Historic and natural natl landmarks damaged and threatened, with owner, location, damage type, and recommended remedial action, 1988, annual listing, 5544–16
Insurance (liability) for pollution releases, coverage and costs, 1982-87, GAO rpt, 26131–54
Minerals (strategic) production, use, reserves, Federal lands availability for mining, and environmental impacts, 1950s-80s, 028–33
Minerals industry production cost impacts of occupational safety and environmental regulation, factors affecting US competitiveness, 1989 compilation of papers, 5606–5.7
Regulatory costs by agency, reform proposals, and environmental regulation costs to govts and businesses, 1988 hearings, 25408–99
Small Business Admin pollution control loan guarantees, FY83-88, annual rpt, 9764–1
Statistical Abstract of US, social, political, and economic data, 1790-2025, comprehensive annual compilation, 2324–1.1
Steel plant closings relation to EPA pollution enforcement and compliance, model description and results, 1977-86, working paper, 9377–9.84
Tax (excise) collections of IRS, by source, quarterly rpt, 8302–1
Tax (excise) collections of IRS, by type of tax, region, and State, FY88, annual rpt, 8304–3.3
Timber in southeastern US, resources mgmt and research, 1988 biennial conf papers, 1204–35

TVA financial and operating data by program and facility, FY88, annual rpt, 9804-32

see also Acid rain
see also Air pollution
see also Dioxins
see also Environmental impact statements
see also Hazardous waste and disposal
see also International cooperation in environmental sciences
see also Landfills
see also Lead poisoning and pollution
see also Marine pollution
see also Mercury pollution
see also Motor vehicle exhaust
see also Noise
see also Oil spills
see also Pesticides
see also Radiation
see also Radioactive waste and disposal
see also Radon
see also Reclamation of land
see also Recycling of waste materials
see also Refuse and refuse disposal
see also Soil pollution
see also Trace metals
see also Water pollution

Environmental Protection Agency

Acid rain distribution, pH levels, and composition, monitoring results by site, 1987, annual rpt, 9194-20

Activities and progress for EPA regulatory and protection programs operations and mgmt goals, by office, quarterly rpt, 9182-11

Air pollution abatement activity of EPA, compliance, and monitoring stations operating status, 1987, annual rpt, 9194-4

Air pollution levels for 5 pollutants, by detailed source and State, 1986, annual rpt, 9194-7

Air pollution levels for 6 pollutants, and measurements exceeding natl standards, by site, 1987-88, annual rpt, 9194-5

Air pollution levels for 6 pollutants, by source, region, and selected MSA, 1978-87, annual rpt, 9194-1

Air pollution levels for 6 pollutants, by source, 1970-87 and trends from 1940, annual rpt, 9194-13

Asbestos abatement and technical aid, funding by State, 1985-88, hearing, 21248-119

Atmospheric sciences research activity of Fed Govt, and funding by agency and program, FY84-87, biennial rpt, 434-1

Auto emissions control device tampering and fuel-switching incidence in 15 urban areas, 1988, annual rpt, 9194-15

Auto fuel economy test results for US and foreign makes, 1990 model year, annual rpt, 3304-11

Budget deficit reduction under Gramm-Rudman Act, cancellation of budget authority by program, FY90, annual rpt, 104-27; 21924-1; 26304-6

Budget of US Appendix, obligations, appropriations, and personnel, by program and agency, FY90, annual rpt, 104-3

Budget of US, authoritative financial statements with appropriations, outlays, and receipts, by category and agency, FY88, annual rpt, 8104-2.2

Coastal and estuarine pollutant discharges from agricultural, airborne, and other nonpoint sources, and regulatory issues, 1988 hearing, 21568-46

Energy use, by fuel pollutant source, fuel type, and State, 1986, annual rpt, 9194-14

Environmental quality and protection programs, and intl issues, 1988 annual rpt, 484-1

Estuary environmental conditions and mgmt, for individual areas, conf series, 2146-6

Expenditures of Fed Govt in States, by type, program, agency, and State, FY88, annual rpt, 2464-2

Fish hazardous substances toxicity levels, by detailed compound, 1989 rpt, 9238-68; 9238-69

Fraud and abuse in EPA programs, audits and investigations, 2nd half FY89, semiannual rpt, 9182-10

Grants for pollution control, EPA program activities, monthly rpt, 9182-8

Great Lakes pollution loadings from nonpoint sources, for Lake Erie and Lake Ontario tributaries, 1982-85, 9208-129

Great Lakes water quality indicators, by water basin and lake, 1970s-85, annual rpt, 9204-14

Hazardous substances exposure factors, and methodological guidelines, 1989 rpt, 9188-109

Hazardous substances industrial releases and reduction methods under EPA regulation, by chemical, source, industry, and location, 1987, annual rpt, 9234-6

Hazardous waste mgmt, effectiveness of alternative technologies, 1989 conf papers, biennial rpt, 9184-19

Health effects of selected pollutants, concentrations in food and environment, sources, and human intake, methodology and data needs, series, 9186-9

Health effects of selected pollutants, concentrations in food and environment, sources, human intake, and regulation, series, 9186-8

Labor unions recognized in Fed Govt, agreements and membership by agency and facility, as of Jan 1989, biennial listing, 9844-14

Ozone and carbon monoxide levels exceeding EPA standards, by MSA, 1988, annual press release, 9194-18

Publications of EPA in NTIS collection, quarterly listing, 9182-5

R&D and related funding of Fed Govt to higher education and nonprofit instns, by field, instn, agency, and State, FY87, annual rpt, 9627-17

R&D funding by Fed Govt, by field, performer type, agency, and State, FY87-89, annual rpt, 9627-20

Radiation and radionuclide concentrations in air, water, and milk, monitoring results by State and site, quarterly rpt, 9192-5

Radioactive waste containers for ocean disposal, performance criteria, with waste production and inventory, 1984-85 and projected to 2020, 9198-119

Radionuclide concentrations in air, water, humans, animals, and milk near Nevada and other nuclear test sites, 1988, annual rpt, 9194-17

Radon indoor air pollution levels, by county and State, 1989, annual rpt, 9194-19

Regulatory costs by agency, reform proposals, and environmental regulation costs to govts and businesses, 1988 hearings, 25408-99

Science and engineering employment in Fed Govt, by field, degree level, race, sex, agency, and State, 1987, annual rpt, 9627-5

Septic tanks, cesspools, and other nonpublic sewer systems, housing and household characteristics, 1970 and 1980, 9208-128

Sewage pipelines and dump sites authorized in coastal areas, status and EPA enforcement activities by State, 1982-87, hearings, 21568-45

Superfund hazardous waste site remedial action, current and proposed sites descriptions and status, periodic listings, series, 9216-3

Superfund hazardous waste site remedial action, current and proposed sites priority ranking and status by location, as of July 1989, listing, 9218-64

Superfund hazardous waste site remedial action, deadlines and compliance of govts and businesses, as of Mar 1989, GAO rpt, 26113-394

Superfund hazardous waste site remedial action, enforcement, spending, and cost recovery, 1986-88, GAO rpt, 26113-386

Timber resources surveys of Forest Service, coverage and methodology, 1932-89, 9188-110

Toxicology Natl Program research and testing activities, FY87 and planned FY88, annual rpt, 4044-16

Wastewater facilities of Fed Govt, compliance with pollution control regulations, FY86-87, GAO rpt, 26113-388

Wastewater treatment and collection facility construction funding needs and Fed Govt grants, by State, 1988 and projected to 2008, biennial rpt, 9204-7

Wastewater treatment facility construction grants of EPA to State and local govts, by project, monthly listing, 9202-3

Water (groundwater) protection standards, States use of EPA and alternative standards by type of water use, and contaminant test results, 1976-88, GAO rpt, 26131-56

Environmental sciences

Acid rain research activities and funding, by Federal agency, 1988 annual rpt, 14354-1

Alaska OCS environmental conditions and oil dev impacts, compilation of papers, series, 2176-1

Black colleges R&D funding by source, and characteristics of grad students and research staff, by field of science and instn, 1980s-87, 9628-78

Carbon dioxide in atmosphere, measurement, methodology, and research results, series, 3006-11

Degrees (PhD) in science and engineering, by field, instn, employment prospects, sex, race, and other characteristics, 1960s-88, 9627-30

Employment and earnings in science and engineering, by field and activity, and private and Federal R&D spending, by industry, 1975-88, 9626-6.29

Employment and other characteristics of science and engineering PhDs, by field and State, 1987, biennial rpt, 9627–18

Employment characteristics of scientists and engineers, by field, 1988, biennial rpt, 9627–16

Enrollment in science and engineering grad programs, by field, source of funds, and characteristics of student and instn, 1975-87, annual rpt, 9627–7

Environmental quality and protection programs, and intl issues, 1988 annual rpt, 484–1

Fed Govt aid to higher education and nonprofit instns for R&D and related activities, by field, instn, agency, and State, FY87, annual rpt, 9627–17

Fish and Wildlife Service conservation and research project descriptions and results, FY87-88, biennial rpt, 5504–20

Foreign and US funding for R&D, and scientists and engineering employment and education, 1988, annual rpt, 9624–23.1

NASA R&D funding to higher education instns, by field, instn, and State, FY88, annual listing, 9504–7

NOAA Environmental Research Labs rpts, FY88, annual listing, 2144–25

NSF activities, finances, and funding by program, FY88, annual rpt, 9624–6

R&D equipment of higher education instns, acquisition and service costs, condition, and financing, by field, 1982-83 and 1985-86, 9628–76

R&D funding by Fed Govt, by field, performer type, agency, and State, FY87-89, annual rpt, 9627–20

R&D funding by higher education instns, by source and field, FY77-87, annual rpt, 9626–2.188

R&D funding by higher education instns, by source and field, FY80-87, annual rpt, 9624–18.5

R&D funding by source and performer, and related employment, by State, 1975-87, 9626–6.32

Small business R&D grants of Fed Govt, by program area, agency, and State, FY88, annual rpt, 9764–7

see also Astronomy

see also Atmospheric sciences

see also Earth sciences

see also Energy research and development

see also International cooperation in environmental sciences

see also Meteorology

see also Oceanography

Epidemiology and epidemiologists

AIDS health care and epidemiological research, methodological issues, 1988 conf, 4188–61

Animal disease outbreaks in US and foreign countries, quarterly rpt, 1392–3

Environmental and occupational health care personnel supply and needs, by field, 1987 conf, 4118–65

Health condition improvement and disease prevention goals and recommended activities for 2000, with trends 1970s-80s, 4048–10

HHS financial aid, by program, recipient, State, and city, FY88, annual regional listings, 4004–3

Morbidity and Mortality Weekly Report, infectious notifiable disease cases by State, and public health issues, 4202–1

Morbidity and Mortality Weekly Report, special supplements, series, 4206–2

Public Health Reports, bimonthly journal, 4042–3

State health dept epidemiologists, ratios to population and professional characteristics, 1983, article, 4042–3.914

see also Diseases and disorders

see also Public health

Epilepsy

see Neurological disorders

Epstein, Arnold M.

"Capitation Payment: Using Predictors of Medical Utilization To Adjust Rates", 4652–1.905

Equal employment opportunity

see Discrimination in employment

Equal Employment Opportunity Commission

Budget of US Appendix, obligations, appropriations, and personnel, by program and agency, FY90, annual rpt, 104–3

Budget of US, authoritative financial statements with appropriations, outlays, and receipts, by category and agency, FY88, annual rpt, 8104–2.2

Expenditures of Fed Govt in States, by type, program, agency, and State, FY88, annual rpt, 2464–2

Fed Govt employment discrimination complaints, processing, and disposition, by complaint type and agency, FY87, annual rpt, 9244–11

Fed Govt employment of minorities and women by occupation, and handicapped employment, by agency, FY87, annual rpt, 9244–10

Labor unions recognized in Fed Govt, agreements and membership by agency and facility, as of Jan 1989, biennial listing, 9844–14

Minority group and women employment, by occupation, SIC 1- to 3- digit industry, State, and MSA, 1986, annual rpt, 9244–1

State and local govt employment of minorities and women, by occupation, function, pay level, and State, 1986, annual rpt, 9244–6

Equatorial Guinea

Agricultural and food production and indexes, total and for selected commodities, by country, 1970s-88, annual rpt, 1524–12

Agricultural trade of US, by detailed commodity and country, 1988, semiannual rpt, 1522–4

AID activities and funding by project and function, FY90, and developing countries summary socioeconomic data from 1960s, annual rpt, 9904–4.5

AID economic aid to developing countries, obligations and disbursements by country, quarterly rpt, 9912–4

Background Notes, summary social, political, and economic data, 1989 rpt, 7006–2.13

Economic and military aid and loans from US and intl agencies, by program and country, FY46-87, annual rpt, 9914–5

Economic, social, political, and geographic summary data, by country, 1989, annual factbook, 9114–2

Human rights conditions in 170 countries, 1988, annual rpt, 21384–3

Military aid of US, arms sales, and training programs costs and budget requests, by program, world region, and country, FY88-90, annual rpt, 7144–13

Military spending, arms trade, and force strengths, with govt spending and population, by country, 1977-87, annual rpt, 9824–1

Minerals Yearbook, 1987, Vol 3: foreign country reviews of production, trade, and policy, by commodity, annual rpt, 5604–35

Minerals Yearbook, 1987, Vol 3 preprints: foreign country review of production, trade, and policy, by commodity, annual rpt, 5604–23.80

Population size, growth rates, and components of change, by country, projected 1989-2020 and trends from 1950, biennial rpt, 2324–9

UN voting record and share of votes in agreement with US, by issue, country, and world area, 1988, annual rpt, 7004–18

see also under By Foreign Country in the "Index by Categories"

Erickson, Kenneth

"Major Statistical Series of the U.S. Department of Agriculture, Volume 11: Balance Sheet", 1506–1.8

Erie, Pa.

see also under By City and By SMSA or MSA in the "Index by Categories"

Ernsberger, C. Nicole

"Public Pension Surpluses and National Saving: Foreign Experience", 9373–1.905

Ernst, Lawrence

"Excluding Sample That Misses Some Interviews from SIPP Longitudinal Estimates", 2626–10.75

Erosion

see Soils and soil conservation

Escalator clauses

Collective bargaining agreement concessions relation to economic and industry financial conditions, with data by major industry and union, 1970s-88, technical paper, 9385–8.41

Collective bargaining contract expirations, wage increases, and coverage, by major industry and selected firm and union, 1989, annual article, 6722–1.902

Collective bargaining wage and benefit changes and coverage, by industry sector and whether contract includes escalator clause and lump sum payment, 1968-88, annual article, 6722–1.923

Collective bargaining wage and benefit changes, quarterly press release, 6782–2

CPI use in escalator clauses of collective bargaining agreements and other contracts, with conversion factors for index rebasing, 1989 guide, 6888–34

Fed Govt civilian pay rates, by pay schedule and grade, 1989 and trends from 1789, annual rpt, 21624–4

State and local govt collective bargaining, wage and benefit changes and coverage, 1st half 1989, semiannual press release, 6782–6

Supplemental Security Income and Medicaid eligibility and payment provisions, and beneficiaries living arrangements, by State, 1989, annual rpt, 4704–13

Wage adjustments in collective bargaining, Monthly Labor Review, 6722–1.3

Wage and benefit changes from collective bargaining and mgmt decisions, by industry div, monthly rpt, 6782–1

Escowitz, Edward C.
"Grain-Size, Heavy-Mineral, and Geochemical Analyses of Sediments from the Chukchi Sea, Alaska", 5668–95

Eskimos
see Alaska Natives

Espionage
Sentences for Federal offenses, guidelines by offense and circumstances, 1989 rpt, 17668–1

Essential oils
see Spices and herbs

Estate tax
Budget of US, authoritative financial statements with appropriations, outlays, and receipts, by category and agency, FY88, annual rpt, 8104–2.2

Budget of US, CBO analysis of revenue and spending alternatives and projections of economic indicators, FY90-94, annual rpt, 26304–3

Budget of US, historical data, selected years FY34-88 and projected to FY94, annual rpt, 104–22

Budget of US, receipts by source, outlays by agency and program, and balances, monthly rpt, 8102–3

Fed Govt consolidated financial statements based on business accounting methods, FY87-88, annual rpt, 8104–5

Fed Govt finances, cash and debt transactions, daily tables, 8102–4

Fed Govt internal revenue and refunds, by type of tax, quarterly rpt, 8302–2.1

Fed Govt receipts by source and outlays by agency, *Treasury Bulletin*, quarterly rpt, 8002–4.1

Finances of govts, revenues by source and spending by function, natl income and product account, *Survey of Current Business*, monthly rpt, 2702–1.24

Govt finances, tax systems and revenue, and fiscal structure, by level of govt and State, selected years 1929-91, annual rpt, 10044–1

IRS collections, enforcement, and litigation activity, with data by type of tax, region, and State, FY88, annual rpt, 8304–3

Returns and supplemental documents filed, by type, FY88 and projected to FY97, semiannual rpt, 8302–2.916; 8302–4

Returns filed, by type of tax, region, and IRS service center, projected 1988-95 and trends from 1977, annual rpt, 8304–9

State and local revenue potential relative to natl average tax burden, by type of tax and State, 1986, annual rpt, 10044–7

State govt tax collections by detailed type of tax, and tax rates, by State, FY88, annual rpt, 2466–2.3
see also Gift tax

Estrella, Arturo
"Estimating the Funding Gap of the Pension Benefit Guaranty Corporation", 9385–1.903

Estuaries
Army Corps of Engineers activities and projects, FY87 and trends from 1800s, annual rpt, 3754–1.2

Environmental conditions and mgmt, for individual estuaries, conf series, 2146–6

Environmental conditions and mgmt of coastal areas, map series, 2176–5

Environmental conditions, fish, wildlife, use, and mgmt, for individual coastal and riparian ecosystems, series, 5506–9

Environmental conditions of coastal areas and estuaries, research results and methodology, series, 2176–7

Fishery research of State fish and wildlife agencies, federally funded projects and costs by species and State, 1989, annual listing, 5504–23

Hudson-Raritan River basin pollutant levels and sources, model description and results, 1880s-1982, 2178–22

NOAA activities and funding for ocean pollution, estuary, and coastal waters monitoring and assessment, FY88, annual rpt, 2174–9

Oregon coastal and estuarine pollutant levels, by pollutant and location, 1960s-87, 2178–23

Pollutant (PCB and pesticide) concentrations in coastal and estuarine fish and shellfish, by species and location, 1965-84, 2178–21

Pollutant concentrations in coastal and estuarine fish, shellfish, and environment, series, 2176–3

Pollutant discharges in coastal areas and estuaries, by source, pollutant type, and location, series, 2176–4

Pollutant discharges in coastal areas and estuaries from agricultural, airborne, and other nonpoint sources, and regulatory issues, 1988 hearing, 21568–46

Research on estuary environmental conditions and mgmt, projects and funding, FY87, annual listing, 2144–24
see also Wetlands

Ethanol
see Alcohol fuels

Ethics
High school classes of 1972 and 1982: ratings of selected life values, 1972-86 surveys, annual rpt, 4824–2.28
see also Business ethics
see also Conflict of interests
see also Financial disclosure
see also Judicial ethics
see also Legal ethics
see also Medical ethics
see also Political ethics
see also Scientific ethics

Ethiopia
Agricultural and food production and indexes, total and for selected commodities, by country, 1970s-88, annual rpt, 1524–12

Agricultural exports of Africa by commodity, and relation to economic conditions and other factors, by country, 1960s-87, 1528–280

Agricultural imports and food aid needs under alternative weather assumptions, for 17 African countries, projected to 1995, 1528–279

Agricultural production, prices, and trade, by country, 1960s-89, annual world region rpt, 1524–4.2

Agricultural trade of US, by detailed commodity and country, 1988, semiannual rpt, 1522–4

Agricultural university in Ethiopia, impacts of AID-Ethiopia govt joint project, 1950s-88, 9916–1.69

AID economic aid to developing countries, obligations and disbursements by country, quarterly rpt, 9912–4

AID loans repayment status and terms by program and country, and status of predecessor agency loans, quarterly rpt, 9912–3

Economic and military aid and loans from US and intl agencies, by program and country, FY46-87, annual rpt, 9914–5

Economic conditions, income, production, prices, employment, and trade, 1989 periodic country rpt, 2046–4.78

Economic conditions, policy, and trade practices, by country, 1986-88, annual rpt, 21384–5

Economic, social, political, and geographic summary data, by country, 1989, annual factbook, 9114–2

Exports and imports of US, by commodity and country, 1970-87, world area rpt, 9116–1.4

Human rights conditions in 170 countries, 1988, annual rpt, 21384–3

Military spending, arms trade, and force strengths, with govt spending and population, by country, 1977-87, annual rpt, 9824–1

Minerals Yearbook, 1987, Vol 3: foreign country reviews of production, trade, and policy, by commodity, annual rpt, 5604–35

Minerals Yearbook, 1987, Vol 3 preprints: foreign country review of production, trade, and policy, by commodity, annual rpt, 5604–23.81

Population size, growth rates, and components of change, by country, projected 1989-2020 and trends from 1950, biennial rpt, 2324–9

Refugee resettlement programs and funding, arrivals by country of origin, and indicators of adjustment, by State, FY88, annual rpt, 4694–5

UN voting record and share of votes in agreement with US, by issue, country, and world area, 1988, annual rpt, 7004–18
see also under By Foreign Country in the "Index by Categories"

Ethnic groups
see Hispanic Americans
see Minority groups
see under By Race and Ethnic Group in the "Index by Categories"

Etzel, Phil
"Affirmative Employment Statistics for Executive Branch (Non-Postal) Agencies, as of Sept. 30, 1988", 9842–1.902

Eugene, Oreg.
Housing vacancy rates for single and multifamily units and mobile homes, by city and ZIP code, 1989, annual MSA rpt, 9304–21.5

Wages by occupation, and benefits for office and plant workers, 1989 survey, periodic MSA rpt, 6785–3.9
see also under By City and By SMSA or MSA in the "Index by Categories"

Eurocurrency
Eastern Europe and USSR debt, trade, and balances with US and other western countries, with background data, 1980s-87, hearing, 21248–120

Eurodollar and total market liabilities, US bank foreign branches market share, and Eurodollar deposit rates, quarterly rpt, 9391–7.1

Eurodollar deposit rates, weekly chartbook, 9365–1.5

Futures and options trading volume, by commodity and exchange, FY88, annual rpt, 11924–2

Futures contracts on commodities, financial instruments, and indexes, options trading in NYC, Chicago, and other markets, monthly rpt, 11922–6

Futures trading in selected commodities and financial instruments and indexes, NYC, Chicago, and other markets activity, monthly rpt, 11922–5

Intl finance and trade studies, 1987 biennial compilation, 9375–14

Europe

Agricultural and food production and indexes, total and for selected commodities, by country, 1970s–88, annual rpt, 1524–12

Agricultural exports of US, for grains, oilseed products, hides, skins, and cotton, by country, weekly rpt, 1922–3

Agricultural production, prices, and trade, by country, 1970s–88 and forecast 1990, annual world region rpt, 1524–4.1

Agricultural trade of US, by commodity and country, bimonthly rpt with articles, 1522–1

Agricultural trade of US, by detailed commodity and country, 1988, semiannual rpt, 1522–4

AID contracts and grants for technical and support services, by instn, country, and State, FY88, annual listing, 9914–7

AID economic aid to developing countries, obligations and disbursements by country, quarterly rpt, 9912–4

Banks (central) gold and foreign exchange reserves, for Europe and France, 1924–32, article, 9362–1.906

Businesses (foreign) activity in US, income tax returns, assets, and income statement items, by industry div, country, and world area, 1984–85, article, 8302–2.920

Coal production and freight costs, and competitive position in selected markets, for Australia and US, 1987–89, 2048–143

Coal trade flows and reserves, by country, 1970s–87 and projected to 2000, annual rpt, 3164–77

Construction contracts awarded US firms, and share of construction market by country of contractor, by world area, 1982–87, annual article, 2042–1.902

Current account balance of US, components and relation to foreign and US investment and economic conditions, 1970s–88 and projected to 1990s, article, 9385–1.907

Dollar exchange rate trade-weighted index of Fed Reserve Bank of Atlanta, by world area, monthly rpt, 9371–15

Dollar exchange rate trade-weighted index of Fed Reserve Bank of Dallas, by world area, monthly rpt, 9379–13

Economic and military aid and loans from US and intl agencies, by program and country, FY46–87, annual rpt, 9914–5

Energy producers finances and operations, by energy type for US firms domestic and foreign operations, 1987, annual rpt, 3164–44.2

Energy production by type, and oil prices, trade, and use, by country group and selected country, monthly rpt, 9112–2

Energy use by sector, and production, by fuel type, country, and country group, projected 1988–2000 and trends from 1970, annual rpt, 3164–84

English language program of USIA, enrollment and staff, by instn, world area, and country, FY88, annual rpt, 9854–2

Exchange and training programs of Federal agencies, participants by world area, and funding, by program, FY87, annual rpt, 9854–8

Exports and imports (waterborne) of US, by type of service, commodity, country, route, and US port, 1986–87, annual rpt, 7704–2

Exports and imports (waterborne) of US, by type of service, customs district, port, and world area, monthly rpt, 2422–7

Exports and imports of US, by commodity group, world area, selected country, US coastal area and port, and mode of transport, monthly rpt, 2422–9

Exports and imports of US, by selected country, country group, and commodity group, 1988, annual rpt, 2044–37

Fertilizer components use, by world area, 1978–88 and projected to 2010, 5608–154

Immigrant and nonimmigrant visas of US issued and refused, by class, issuing office, and nationality, FY88, annual rpt, 7184–1

Immigrants admitted to US, by class of admission, country of birth, and State and MSA of destination, FY88, annual rpt, 6264–4

Immigrants admitted to US, by occupational group and country of birth, preliminary FY88, annual table, 6264–1

Immigration to US, alien workers, visitors, deportations, and naturalizations, by country, FY88 and trends from 1820, annual rpt, 6264–2

Investment (foreign direct) in US, by industry group and world area, 1987–88, annual article, 2702–1.929

Investment (foreign direct) of US, by selected industry group and world area, 1986–88, annual article, 2702–1.930

Loans of US banks to foreigners at all US and foreign offices, by country group and country, quarterly rpt, 13002–1

Manufacturing labor cost indexes, by selected country, 1980–89, article, 6722–1.926

Manufacturing labor costs and indexes, by selected country, 1975–88, annual rpt, 6824–3

Manufacturing labor costs and indexes, by selected country, 1975–88, semiannual rpt, 6822–3

Military aid of US, arms sales, and training, by country, FY50–88, annual rpt, 3904–3

Military aid of US, arms sales, and training programs costs and budget requests, by program, world region, and country, FY88–90, annual rpt, 7144–13

Military aid programs and related activities of US, costs by country and intl agency, FY85–87 and cumulative from FY50, GAO rpt, 26123–30

Military spending, arms trade, and force strengths, with govt spending and population, by country, 1977–87, annual rpt, 9824–1

Multinatl firms US affiliates, finances, and operations, by industry, world area of parent firm, and State, 1987, annual rpt, 2704–4

Multinatl US firms and foreign affiliates finances and operations, by industry of parent firm and affiliate, world area, and country, preliminary 1987, annual rpt, 2704–5

Nuclear power plant capacity, generation, and operating status, by plant and foreign and US location, 1988 and projected to 2020, annual rpt, 3164–57

Nuclear power plant spent fuel and demand for uranium and enrichment service, for US and other country groups, projected 1989–2036, annual rpt, 3164–72

Oil and gas reserves and discoveries, by country and country group, quarterly rpt, 3162–43

Population size, growth rates, and components of change, by country, projected 1989–2020 and trends from 1950, biennial rpt, 2324–9

R&D funding by Fed Govt, by field, performer type, agency, and State, FY87–89, annual rpt, 9627–20

Science and engineering immigrants, by field, age, sex, country and world area of birth and last residence, and State, 1987 and trends from 1967, 9627–29

Terrorist (intl) incidents, casualties, and attacks on US targets, by attack type and country, 1980–88, 7008–56

Terrorist (intl) incidents, casualties, and attacks on US targets, by attack type and world area, 1968–88, annual rpt, 7004–13

Tide height and time daily at coastal points, forecast 1990, annual rpt, 2174–2.4

Travel to and from US, and travel receipts and payments, by world area, with data by country, 1984–88, annual rpt, 2904–10

Travel to and from US, by world area, forecast 1989–90, annual rpt, 2904–9

Travel to and from US on US and foreign flag air carriers, by country, world area, and US port, monthly rpt, 7302–2

Travel to and from US on US and foreign flag airlines, by world area, 1980–88, annual rpt, 2904–13

Travel to US, by characteristics of visit and traveler, country, port city, and State of destination, quarterly rpt, 2902–1

Travel to US, spending by category, world area of residence, census div, and State, model results, 1985–86, 2908–28

UN voting record and share of votes in agreement with US, by issue, country, and world area, 1988, annual rpt, 7004–18

US military commissaries in Europe, test sales of US beef and pork, and patron survey results, 1986, hearing, 21208–28

USIA library holdings, use, and staff, by country and city, FY88, annual rpt, 9854–4

Visas of US issued at Foreign Service posts, by category and world area, selected years FY84–88, annual rpt, 7184–4

Weather conditions and effect on agriculture, by US region, State, and city, and world area, weekly rpt, 2152–2

Weather events and anomalies, precipitation and temperature for US and foreign locations, weekly rpt, 2182-6

Weather forecasts for US and Northern Hemisphere, precipitation and temperature by location, semimonthly rpt, 2182-1

see also Albania
see also Andorra
see also Austria
see also Belgium
see also Bulgaria
see also Central Treaty Organization
see also Cyprus
see also Czechoslovakia
see also Denmark
see also Eastern Europe
see also Eurocurrency
see also European Community
see also European Space Agency
see also Finland
see also France
see also Germany, East
see also Germany, West
see also Gibraltar
see also Greece
see also Hungary
see also Iceland
see also Ireland
see also Italy
see also Liechtenstein
see also Luxembourg
see also Malta
see also Monaco
see also Netherlands
see also North Atlantic Treaty Organization
see also Norway
see also Organization for Economic Cooperation and Development
see also Poland
see also Portugal
see also Romania
see also San Marino
see also Soviet Union
see also Spain
see also Sweden
see also Switzerland
see also United Kingdom
see also Yugoslavia
see also under By Foreign Country in the "Index by Categories"

European Community

Agricultural export subsidies of EC by commodity and destination, FAS monthly circular, 1925-32

Agricultural exports and market shares of US and EC, for 4 high-value processed commodities, 1970s-87, article, 1522-3.920

Agricultural exports of US, for grains, oilseed products, hides, skins, and cotton, by country, weekly rpt, 1922-3

Agricultural exports of US, impacts of foreign agricultural and trade policy, with data by commodity and country, 1988, annual rpt, 1924-8

Agricultural imports from US and other countries, and food spending and consumption, for EC, 1980s, article, 1541-7.903

Agricultural price support thresholds and planned threshold reductions, for selected fruit of Spain and EC, 1987-1992, tables, 1925-34.905

Agricultural production, acreage, and yield for selected crops, forecasts by selected world region and country, FAS monthly circular, 1925-28

Agricultural production, prices, and trade, by country, 1970s-88 and forecast 1990, annual world region rpt, 1524-4.1

Agricultural subsidies, consumer and producer equivalents by program, commodity, and major US trading partner, 1982-86, 1528-275

Agricultural trade and market impacts of eliminating foreign and US protectionist policies, model description and results, 1986, 1528-282

Agricultural trade by commodity and country, prices, and world market devs, monthly rpt, 1922-12

Agricultural trade of US, by commodity and country, bimonthly rpt with articles, 1522-1

Agricultural trade of US, by detailed commodity and country, 1988, semiannual rpt, 1522-4

AID loans repayment status and terms by program and country, and status of predecessor agency loans, quarterly rpt, 9912-3

Apple exports of US to EC and 4 north European countries, 1984-89, article, 1925-34.939

Businesses (foreign) activity in US, income tax returns, assets, and income statement items, by industry div, country, and world area, 1984-85, article, 8302-2.920

Caribbean Basin exports to OECD members, and US imports under preferential treatment programs, by commodity, 1980s-87, 2048-138

Dairy imports under quota by commodity, and meat imports under Meat Import Act, by country of origin, FAS monthly rpt, 1925-31

Developing countries debt burden and economic conditions, and trade with industrialized countries, by country, 1970s-87, hearings, 25248-108

Economic conditions in Communist and OECD countries, 1987, annual rpt, 7144-11

Economic conditions in Communist, OECD, and selected other countries, 1960s-88, annual rpt, 9114-4

Economic conditions, policy, and trade practices, by country, 1986-88, annual rpt, 21384-5

Economic integration of EC impacts on domestic economic conditions and US trade, with trade by commodity and country, 1984-87, 9886-4.140

Exports and imports of high-value agricultural commodities between US and EC, 1985-87, article, 1502-4.905

Exports and imports of US, by commodity group, world area, selected country, US coastal area and port, and mode of transport, monthly rpt, 2422-9

Exports and imports of US, by selected country, country group, and commodity group, 1988, annual rpt, 2044-37

Exports and imports of US with EC by country, and total agricultural trade, selected years 1958-88, annual rpt, 7144-7

Exports and imports, trade agreements and relations, and USITC investigations, 1988, annual rpt, 9884-5

Exports, imports, and balances of US by commodity group, world area, and country, and related employment, 1970s-88, annual rpt, 2044-26

Exports, imports, and balances of US with major trading partners, by product category, 1984-88, annual chartbook, 9884-21

Flowers (cut roses) US industry intl competitiveness, investigation with background financial and operating data and foreign comparisons, 1989 rpt, 9886-4.137

Food supply and demand, market and support prices, and other economic indicators, by EC country and commodity, 1960-85, 1528-276

GNP and GNP growth of OECD members, by country, 1978-88, annual rpt, 7144-8

GNP, employment, and other economic indicators of EC, impact of economic integration by source, projected 1992, article, 9373-1.908

Grain and soybean import prices at Rotterdam, and EC import levies and supports, by type of grain, weekly press release, 1922-4

Grain production, supply, trade, and use, by country and world region, forecasts and trends, FAS monthly circular, 1925-2.1

Imports from US, impacts on US employment by exporting sector and major importer, 1980s-87, 2048-103

Imports of goods, services, and investment from US, trade barriers, impacts, and US actions, by country, 1988, annual rpt, 444-2

Imports of OECD countries covered by non-tariff trade barriers, by barrier type and commodity group, 1981-86, article, 9391-1.906

Investment (foreign direct) in US, by industry group and world area, 1987-88, annual article, 2702-1.929

Investment (foreign direct) of US, by selected industry group and world area, 1986-88, annual article, 2702-1.930

Loans and grants for economic and military aid from US and intl agencies, by program and country, FY46-87, annual rpt, 9914-5

Meat trade of EC and US, FY84-88, article, 1502-4.902

Multinatl firms US affiliates, finances, and operations, by industry, world area of parent firm, and State, 1987, annual rpt, 2704-4

Multinatl US firms and foreign affiliates finances and operations, by industry of parent firm and affiliate, world area, and country, preliminary 1987, annual rpt, 2704-5

Raisin production, trade, use, and stocks for selected countries, and EC subsidies, various periods 1981-90, annual article, 1925-34.944

Seed exports, by type, world region, and country, FAS quarterly rpt, 1925-13

Steel export ceilings under voluntary restraint agreements, by country and product, with Western US steel industry impact, 1989 rpt, 9886-4.136

Steel imports from EC and other countries, impact of voluntary restraint agreements on US user industries exports, sales, and prices, 1989 rpt, 9886-4.138

Steel imports of US under voluntary restraint agreement, by product, customs district, and country, with US industry operating data, monthly rpt, 9882-13

Textile imports under Multifiber Arrangement by product and country, and status of bilateral agreements, 1986-88, annual rpt, 9884–18

Tomato, peach, and pear grower price, subsidy, and processor cost, by EC member, various periods 1979-90, annual tables, 1925–34.934

Tomato production quotas, by processed product and EC country, 1989/90, article, 1925–34.927

Wheat export subsidies of EC and US, impacts on exports and prices, mid 1970s-86, 1528–293

Wheat export subsidy program costs to US and EC, 1980s-88, article, 9391–1.904

Wheat trade, elasticities of demand for US and 5 countries, alternative models description and results, 1950s-86, 1528–281

European Space Agency
Launchings of satellites and other space objects since 1957, quarterly listing, 9502–2

Eutrophication
Coastal and estuarine environmental conditions, research results and methodology, series, 2176–7

Coastal and estuarine pollutant discharges, by source, pollutant type, and location, series, 2176–4

Estuary environmental conditions and mgmt, for individual areas, conf series, 2146–6

Great Lakes phosphorus loads and fish stocking effects on algal levels, 1966-85, conf, 14648–20

Great Lakes pollution loadings from nonpoint sources, for Lake Erie and Lake Ontario tributaries, 1982-85, 9208–129

Great Lakes water quality indicators, by water basin and lake, 1970s-85, annual rpt, 9204–14

Lake Ontario eutrophication and pollutant levels, by contaminant type and site, 1967-85, 14648–22

Evans, Conrad
"Ethiopia: Alemaya University of Agriculture", 9916–1.69

Evans, Sam
"Effects of the Triple Base Proposal on Soybeans and Sunflowers", 1561–3.905

Evansville, Ind.
see also under By City and By SMSA or MSA in the "Index by Categories"

Everett, Rebecca J.
"Population Genetic Structure of Arctic Char (Salvelinus alpinus) from Rivers of the North Slope of Alaska", 2176–1.29

Evidence
Criminal case processing from arrest to sentencing, cases and duration by disposition, offense, and defendant characteristics, for selected cities, 1986, annual rpt, 6064–27

Drunk driving testing methods and analysis, technical data, 1986 conf, 6228–2

Wiretaps authorized, costs, arrests, trials, and convictions, by offense and jurisdiction, 1988, annual rpt, 18204–7

Exceptional children
see Handicapped children
see Special education

Exchange of persons programs
Admissions to US, by country, FY88, annual rpt, 6264–2

Admissions to US of aliens, by class of admission, port, country, and State of destination, quarterly rpt, 6262–2

Executive exchange program of Fed Govt and private sector, host and participant views on experimental payment provisions, 1988-89 survey, GAO rpt, 26119–249

Fed Govt and other organization exchange of employees, program activities and costs, with data by agency, FY84-88, GAO rpt, 26119–260

Japan-US Friendship Commission educational and cultural exchange activities, grants, and trust fund status, FY87-88, biennial report, 14694–1

NIH intl program activities and funding, by inst and country, FY88, annual rpt, 4474–6

Participation in intl exchange and training programs, by world region, and funding, by Federal agency, FY87, annual rpt, 9854–8

see also Educational exchanges

Exchange rates
see Foreign exchange

Excise tax
Airport and Airway Trust Fund finances and excise tax collections, FY71-88 and projected under alternative spending policies, FY89-94, 26308–84

Alcoholic beverages and tobacco production, removals, stocks, and material used, by State, monthly rpt series, 8486–1

Auto equipment excise taxes of Fed Govt and States, 1988, annual rpt, 7554–1

Budget deficit reduction through increased excise and income taxes, and proposed value-added tax, projected FY89-94, article, 9381–1.906

Budget of US, authoritative financial statements with appropriations, outlays, and receipts, by category and agency, FY88, annual rpt, 8104–2.2

Budget of US, CBO analysis of revenue and spending alternatives and projections of economic indicators, FY90-94, annual rpt, 26304–3

Budget of US, historical data, selected years FY34-88 and projected to FY94, annual rpt, 104–22

Budget of US, midsession review of FY90 budget, by function and agency, annual rpt, 104–7

Budget of US, receipts by source, outlays by agency and program, and balances, monthly rpt, 8102–3

Cigarette excise tax rates, and impacts on smoking by age, annual rpt, 4204–18

Coal excise tax and other black lung trust fund receipts, fund disbursements, and claims and benefits by State, 1987, annual rpt, 6504–3

Coal Surface Mining Reclamation and Enforcement Office activities and funding, by State and Indian tribe, FY87, annual rpt, 5644–1

Energy producers finances and operations, by energy type for US firms domestic and foreign operations, 1987, annual rpt, 3164–44.1

Fed Govt consolidated financial statements based on business accounting methods, FY87-88, annual rpt, 8104–5

Fed Govt finances, cash and debt transactions, daily tables, 8102–4

Fed Govt internal revenue and refunds, by type of tax, quarterly rpt, 8302–2.1

Fed Govt receipts by source and outlays by agency, *Treasury Bulletin*, quarterly rpt, 8002–4.1

Fish and Wildlife Service restoration programs finances by State, and excise tax collections, FY88, annual rpt, 5504–13

Govt finances, by level of govt, State, and for large cities and counties, annual rpt series, 2466–2

Govt finances, tax systems and revenue, and fiscal structure, by level of govt and State, selected years 1929-91, annual rpt, 10044–1

Govt revenues by source and expenditures by function, natl income and product account, *Survey of Current Business*, monthly rpt, 2702–1.24

Income tax returns of individuals, by filing status, tax item, and income level, 1987, annual article, 8302–2.901

Inflation-indexed excise taxes impacts on Federal revenue and family tax burden by commodity, projected under alternative proposals, 1989-93, GAO rpt, 26119–254

IRS collections, by excise tax source, quarterly rpt, 8302–1

IRS collections, enforcement, and litigation activity, with data by type of tax, region, and State, FY88, annual rpt, 8304–3

Motorcycle operating costs by component, for 4 makes, and Fed Govt mileage reimbursement rates, 1987, annual rpt, 9454–13

Natl income and product accounts and components, *Survey of Current Business*, monthly rpt, 2702–1.21

New England States economic indicators, Fed Reserve 1st District, quarterly rpt, 9373–2.3

Nonprofit charitable organizations finances, and assets and grants of top 10, 1985, article, 8302–2.923

Pension plan excise tax collections of IRS, and returns examined, 1976-88, article, 8304–8.1

Pension plan regulation enforcement by Labor Dept and IRS, violations, and penalties, FY85-88, GAO rpt, 26121–259

Returns and supplemental documents filed, by type, FY88 and projected to FY97, semiannual rpt, 8302–2.916; 8302–4

Returns filed, by type of tax, region, and IRS service center, projected 1988-95 and trends from 1977, annual rpt, 8304–9

State and local revenue potential relative to natl average tax burden, by type of tax and State, 1986, annual rpt, 10044–7

Telephone and telegraph firms detailed finances and operations, 1987, annual rpt, 9284–6.4; 9284–6.5

Tobacco tax rates and receipts of Fed Govt and States, FY83-88, annual rpt, 1319–1.4

Tobacco tax revenues, by level of govt, 1950-86, 1568–276

Transit systems finances and operations, by mode of transport, size of fleet, and for 432 systems, 1986, annual rpt, 7884–4

Transportation finances, operations, vehicles, equipment, accidents, and energy use, by mode of transport, 1955-88, annual rpt, 7304-2
see also Fuel tax
see also Sales tax
see also Tolls
see also Windfall profit tax

Executive agreements
Bilateral and multilateral treaties and other agreements in force, by country, as of Jan 1989, annual listing, 7004-1

Executive clemency
see Pardons

Executive-congressional relations
see Congressional-executive relations

Executive departments
see Federal executive departments

Executive impoundment of appropriated funds
Budget of US Appendix, obligations, appropriations, and personnel, by program and agency, FY90, annual rpt, 104-3
Rescissions and deferrals of budget authority, monthly rpt, 102-2

Executive Office of the President
Budget deficit reduction under Gramm-Rudman Act, cancellation of budget authority by program, FY90, annual rpt, 104-27; 21924-1; 26304-6
Budget of US Appendix, obligations, appropriations, and personnel, by program and agency, FY90, annual rpt, 104-3
Budget of US, authoritative financial statements with appropriations, outlays, and receipts, by category and agency, FY88, annual rpt, 8104-2.2
Budget of US, Bush Admin policy changes by program, FY90, 028-32
Budget of US, receipts by source, outlays by agency and program, and balances, monthly rpt, 8102-3
Minerals (strategic) production, use, reserves, Federal lands availability for mining, and environmental impacts, 1950s-80s, 028-33
Services of Fed Govt, demand and mgmt, outlook for 2000, 028-30
see also Council of Economic Advisers
see also Council on Environmental Quality
see also Federal Coordinating Council for Science, Engineering and Technology
see also National Security Council
see also Office of Management and Budget
see also Office of National Drug Control Policy
see also Office of Policy Development
see also Office of Science and Technology Policy
see also Office of the U.S. Trade Representative
see also Office of the Vice President
see also under names of individual Presidential commissions (starting with Presidential or President's)

Executives and managers
Aerospace industry employment and salaries, by sex and race, 1979-87, GAO rpt, 26121-315
Aircraft (general aviation), flight hours, and equipment, by type, use, and model of aircraft, region, and State, 1988, annual rpt, 7504-29
Banks (Fed Reserve) and branch officers, staff, and salary, 1988, annual rpt, 9364-1.1

Educational attainment, by sociodemographic characteristics and location, 1987 and trends from 1940, biennial Current Population Rpt, 2546-1.427; 2546-1.431
Employment and occupation of householder, by occupation of spouse, race, and family composition, 1988, annual Current Population Rpt, 2546-1.437
Employment Cost Index and alternative measure of compensation costs, by component, occupation, industry group, union status, and location, 1975-89, annual rpt, 6744-20
Employment in nonmanufacturing industries, by detailed occupation and SIC 2-digit industry, 1987, triennial rpt, 6748-60
Employment training participant characteristics, and sources of training, with data by employer size and major industry group, 1982-88, 6408-73
Employment, unemployment, and labor force characteristics, by region, State, and selected metro area, 1988, annual rpt, 6744-7
Fed Govt and private sector executive exchange program, host and participant views on experimental payment provisions, 1988-89 survey, GAO rpt, 26119-249
Fed Govt civilian employment and payroll, by pay system, agency, and location, 1988, annual rpt, 9844-6
Fed Govt civilian pay rates, by pay schedule and grade, 1989 and trends from 1789, annual rpt, 21624-4
Fed Govt executive and excepted service employees, and political appointments, by category, branch, and selected agency, Sept 1988, article, 9842-1.903
Fed Govt Senior Executive Service career position longterm vacancies, by reason and agency, 1989, GAO rpt, 26119-252
Fed Govt Senior Executive Service former members reasons for leaving, and views on SES statutory compliance, 1988 survey, 9498-3
Fed Govt Senior Executive Service membership characteristics, entries, exits, and awards, FY80-1987, annual rpt, 9844-36
Fed Govt Senior Executive Service training and dev program activities, participant views, 1987 survey, GAO rpt, 26119-272
Handbook of Labor Statistics, employment, unemployment, and labor force characteristics, 1940s-88 with trends from 1913, 6728-38
Health condition of labor force, and services use, by occupation and industry of longest job held, income, age, sex, and race. 1980, 4147-10.168
Immigrants admitted to US, by occupational group and country of birth, preliminary FY88, annual table, 6264-1
Immigration to US, alien workers, visitors, deportations, and naturalizations, by country, FY88 and trends from 1820, annual rpt, 6264-2
Minority group and women employment, by occupation, SIC 1- to 3- digit industry, State, and MSA, 1986, annual rpt, 9244-1

Occupational changes, by tenure and other worker characteristics, and labor mobility rates, 1965-86, article, 6722-1.943
Science and engineering employment characteristics, by field, 1988, biennial rpt, 9627-16
Science and engineering employment in R&D, earnings by field and educational, employment, and other characteristics, 1989, annual rpt, 3004-1
Science and engineering labor force, Federal and university research funding, and educational data, series, 9626-6
Science and engineering labor supply by region and employment characteristics, and salaries by years of experience, 1987, 9626-2.184
Science and engineering PhDs employment and other characteristics, by field and State, 1987, biennial rpt, 9627-18
State Dept and Foreign Service minority and women employment, FY88, annual rpt, 7004-21
Suburban areas land use, commuting, employment, and housing characteristics, detailed data for traffic planning, 1986, 7888-75
Telecommunications industries minority employment and discrimination charges, with data by industry and selected firm, 1970s-88, hearings, 21368-113
TVA managers salaries, incentive payments by program, and supplemental pensions, 1979-88, GAO rpt, 26113-420
TVA nuclear power plant mgmt salaries by position, and plant capacity, compared to private utilities, 1985-87, hearing, 21648-57
see also Business management
see also Officials

Exercise
see Physical exercise
see Sports and athletics

Exhibitions and trade fairs
Business America, foreign and domestic commerce, and US investment and trade opportunities, biweekly journal, 2042-24
Construction industry intl trade fairs and other events, FY89/90 listing, article, 2042-1.904; 2042-1.908
Travel to US, market research, major magazine ad costs and circulation, and trade show data, for selected countries, 1989-90, annual rpt, 2904-11

Eximbank
see Export-Import Bank

Exploration, natural resources
see Energy exploration and drilling
see Mines and mineral resources

Explosives
Accident deaths and rates, by cause, age, race, sex, and State, 1986, US Vital Statistics annual rpt, 4144-2
Accidents (occupational) injury and illness rates by SIC 2- to 4-digit industry, and deaths by cause and industry div, 1987, annual rpt, 6844-1
Accidents involving consumer products and related activities, injuries by victim age and sex, 1988, annual rpt, 9164-7
Accidents involving consumer products, injuries by severity, victim age, and detailed product, 1988, annual rpt, 9164-6

China trade by SITC 1- to 5-digit commodity, 1970s-87, annual rpt, 9114-3

Consumption of explosives and blasting agents, by type, industry, and State, 1988, Mineral Industry Surveys, annual rpt, 5614-22

County Business Patterns, 1987: employment, establishments, and payroll, by SIC 2- to 4-digit industry and county, annual State rpt series, 2326-8

Criminal sentences for Federal offenses, guidelines by offense and circumstances, 1989 rpt, 17668-1

Exports of US, detailed commodities by country, monthly rpt, 2422-3

Hwy construction material use by type, and spending, by State, various periods 1944-88, annual rpt, 7554-29

Imports of US, detailed Schedule A commodities by country, monthly rpt, 2422-2

Manufacturing annual survey, 1986: financial and operating data, by SIC 2- to 4-digit industry, series, 2506-15

Manufacturing census, 1987: financial and operating data, for SIC 4-digit industries by product, preliminary rpt, 2491-1.40

Mineral industries census, 1987: financial and operating data, preliminary industry rpt series, 2511-1

Minerals Yearbook, 1987, Vol 1: commodity reviews of production, use, trade, prices, and mining operations, annual rpt, 5604-33

OECD trade, total and for 4 major countries, and US trade by country, by commodity, 1970-87, world area rpt series, 9116-1

Postal Service inspection activities, FY88, annual rpt, 9864-9

Price indexes (producer), by stage of processing and detailed commodity, monthly rpt, 6762-6

Price indexes (producer), by stage of processing and detailed commodity, monthly 1988, annual rpt, 6764-2

Theft and recovery of explosives by State, and accidental detonations by place of occurrence, 1979-88, annual rpt, 8484-4

Transport of hazardous material, accidents, casualties, and damage, by mode of transport, with DOT control activities, 1988, annual rpt, 7304-4

Transportation census, 1987: trucks, by detailed characteristics, miles traveled, and type of product carried, State rpt series, 2573-1

see also Ammunition

see also Bombs

see also Nuclear explosives and explosions

Export controls

see Tariffs and foreign trade controls

Export-Import Bank

Budget of US Appendix, obligations, appropriations, and personnel, by program and agency, FY90, annual rpt, 104-3

Budget of US, authoritative financial statements with appropriations, outlays, and receipts, by category and agency, FY88, annual rpt, 8104-2.2

Credit programs for exports, activities of Eximbank and 6 OECD countries, 1988, annual rpt, 9254-3

Debt to US of foreign govts and private obligors, by country and program, periodic rpt, 8002-6

Developing countries debt reduction proposals, and Eximbank export financing programs, with background data, 1986-89, 2048-142

Developing countries economic and military aid from US, by country and program, FY86, annual rpt, 9904-1.4

Financial condition, credit and insurance authorizations, and loan activity and delinquencies, by country, FY88, annual rpt, 9254-1

Labor unions recognized in Fed Govt, agreements and membership by agency and facility, as of Jan 1989, biennial listing, 9844-14

Liabilities (contingent) and claims paid by Fed Govt on federally insured and guaranteed contracts with foreign obligors, by country and program, periodic rpt, 8002-12

Loans and grants for economic and military aid from US and intl agencies, by program and country, FY46-87, annual rpt, 9914-5

Small business loans of Eximbank, by firm, 1984-88, hearing, 21728-70

Export promotion

see Foreign trade promotion

Exports and imports

see Agricultural exports and imports

see Balance of payments

see Coal exports and imports

see East-West trade

see Energy exports and imports

see Foreign trade

see Motor vehicle exports and imports

see Natural gas exports and imports

see Petroleum exports and imports

see under names of specific commodities or commodity groups

Expositions

see Exhibitions and trade fairs

Expropriation of alien property

Claims against foreign govts by US natls, by claim type and country, 1988, annual rpt, 6004-16

Extension work

see Agricultural extension work

Exterminator services

see Pests and pest control

Extradition

Criminal cases by type and disposition, and collections, for US attorneys, by Federal district, FY88, annual rpt, 6004-2.1

Drug enforcement regional task forces investigation of organized crime, activities by agency and region, and background data, FY83-88, annual rpt, 6004-17

Exxon Corp.

Alaska oil spill from tanker Exxon Valdez, impacts on gasoline and crude oil supply and prices, 1988-89, article, 3162-11.901; 3162-24.902

Alaska oil spills, for Exxon North Slope and Beaufort Sea operations, 1977-87, listing, 21448-41

Eye diseases and defects

Cancer (retinoblastoma) relation to chromosome 13 abnormality, 1982-85 study, article, 4472-1.909

Cancer incidence, death, and survival rates, by sex, race, age, and body site, 1973-86, annual rpt, 4474-35

Cases of acute and chronic conditions, disability, absenteeism, and health services use, by selected characteristics, 1988, annual rpt, 4147-10.170

Deaths and rates, by detailed cause and demographic characteristics, 1986 and trends from 1900, US Vital Statistics annual rpt, 4144-2

Educational enrollment of disabled in postsecondary instns, by disability, educational, and other characteristics, fall 1986, 4846-3.6

Glaucoma incidence, screening and treatment effectiveness, and costs under proposed Medicare coverage, 1988, 26356-7.1

Head Start handicapped enrollment, by handicap, State, and for Indian and migrant programs, 1985/86, annual rpt, 4604-1

HHS financial aid, by program, recipient, State, and city, FY88, annual regional listings, 4004-3

Nursing home facility, staff, and resident detailed characteristics, 1985, 4147-13.97

see also Blind

see also Optometry

see also under By Disease in the "Index by Categories"

Ezzati, Trena

"Ambulatory Medical Care Rendered in Pediatricians' Offices During 1975", 4147-16.2

"Office Visits to Obstetrician-Gynecologists: National Ambulatory Medical Care Survey, U.S., 1975", 4147-16.2

FAA

see Federal Aviation Administration

Faber, Phyllis M.

"Ecology of Riparian Habitats of the Southern California Coastal Region: A Community Profile", 5506-9.36

Fabrics

see Synthetic fibers and fabrics

see Textile industry and fabrics

Fackler, James S.

"Federal Credit, Private Credit, and Economic Activity", 9381-10.94

Factories

see Industrial plants and equipment

Factory closings

see Business failures and closings

Factory workers

see Production workers

Faculty

see Educational employees pay

see School administration and staff

see Teachers

Fadell, Alicia

"Trends in the Refund Offset Program", 8304-8.1

Fadely, Brian S.

"Populations, Productivity, and Feeding Habits of Seabirds at Cape Thompson, Alaska", 5738-11

Fair employment practices

see Discrimination in employment

Fair housing

see Discrimination in housing

Hunting, fishing, and other wildlife-related recreation participation and spending, detailed data by location, 1985 survey, quinquennial rpt, 5508-5

Immigrant and nonimmigrant visas of US issued and refused, by class, issuing office, and nationality, FY88, annual rpt, 7184-1

Immigrants admitted to US, by class of admission, country of birth, and State and MSA of destination, FY88, annual rpt, 6264-4

Immigration to US, alien workers, visitors, deportations, and naturalizations, by country, FY88 and trends from 1820, annual rpt, 6264-2

Immigration to US by category and for relatives of US natls, FY49-88 and alternative projections to FY99, GAO rpt, 26131-59

Indian (Navajo and Hopi) relocation program activities, caseloads, and finances, by location, annual rpt, discontinued, 16004-4

Indian (Navajo and Hopi) relocation program activities, caseloads, and finances, FY88, annual rpt, 16004-1

Indian reservation water supply projects in South Dakota, costs and indicators of need, with health and housing data for other reservations, 1980s-87, hearing, 21448-37

Indian youth suicide attempts, potential, and risk factors, longitudinal study, 1989 article, 4042-3.958

Insurance (health) coverage of adolescents by selected characteristics, and impacts of mandated employer and expanded Medicaid coverage, 1979-87, 26358-205

Migration since 1986, mover characteristics by same or different area, and compared to nonmovers, 1987, annual Current Population Rpt, 2546-1.435

Natl income and product accounts and components, *Survey of Current Business*, monthly rpt, 2702-1.22

OASDI beneficiary households income, assets, and economic status changes, by beneficiary type, 1983-84, article, 4742-1.904

Older persons assets and relation to income, 1984, technical paper, 4746-26.5

Older persons care by family members, caregivers and potential caregivers by relation and other characteristics, 1984, 4186-7.5

Older persons care by family members, caregivers stress and respite services, for King County, Wash, 1983-87, article, 4652-1.916

Older persons care by family members, tax subsidies in 2 States, 1981-84, article, 4652-1.915

Older persons socioeconomic characteristics, 1900s-86 and projected to 2050, biennial chartbook, 12904-1

Pacific Northwest population, households, employment, income, and fuel prices, alternative projections 1990-2010 with trends from 1960, annual rpt, 3224-5

Population size and characteristics, 1969-88, Current Population Rpt, annual rpt, 2546-2.146

Poverty level labor force employment, earnings, and other characteristics, 1987, article, 6722-1.948

Poverty status by age group and living arrangements, and family poverty threshold, late 1930s-87, annual rpt, 4744-3.1

Poverty status of families and persons, by detailed characteristics, 1987, annual Current Population Rpt, 2546-6.60

Prisoners in State instns, by offense, criminal history, and inmate, family, and victim characteristics, 1986, annual rpt, 6064-26.3

Research on population and reproduction, Federal funding by project, FY87, annual listing, 4474-9

Rural and urban areas housing and households characteristics, 1930s-80, 1598-245

Rural and urban areas population and economic data, 1960s-88, annual chartbook, 1504-3

Southern US poverty rates, by household composition, race, and urban-rural location, 1986, article, 9371-1.903

Statistical Abstract of US, social, political, and economic data, 1790-2025, comprehensive annual compilation, 2324-1.1

Supplemental Security Income aged and disabled beneficiary characteristics, payments, and eligibility, for awards made 1981, 1985, article, 4742-1.907

Supplemental Security Income and Medicaid eligibility and payment provisions, and beneficiaries living arrangements, by State, 1989, annual rpt, 4704-13

Survey of Income and Program Participation, data collection, methodology, and availability, 1987 users guide, 2628-24

Survey of Income and Program Participation, data collection, methodology, and use, 1988 annual conf papers, 2624-1

Survey of Income and Program Participation, household composition, income, benefits, and labor force status, methodology, working paper series, 2626-10

Survey of Income and Program Participation, household income and socioeconomic characteristics, special study series, 2546-20

Telephone service of households, by composition, income sources, and other characteristics, 1984-87, 9288-11

Telephone service subscribership, charges, and local and long distance firm finances and operations, 1970s-FY89, semiannual rpt, 9282-7

Traffic volume in urban areas and detailed trip characteristics, by transport mode and city, 1950s-88, 7888-37

Transportation census, 1987: trucks, by detailed characteristics, miles traveled, and type of product carried, State rpt series, 2573-1

Visas of US issued at Foreign Service posts, by category and world area, selected years FY84-88, annual rpt, 7184-4

Warsaw Pact and US citizens divided family cases pending as of Sept 1988, semiannual rpt, 7002-1

Women's labor force participation, by age, race, and family status, quarterly rpt, 6742-17

see also Adoption
see also Aid to Families with Dependent Children
see also Child abuse and neglect
see also Child support and alimony
see also Child welfare
see also Children
see also Domestic violence
see also Family budgets
see also Family planning
see also Group quarters
see also Housing energy use
see also Living arrangements
see also Marriage and divorce
see also Maternity benefits
see also Military dependents
see also Parents
see also Personal and household income
see also Unpaid family workers
see also Widows and widowers

Family budgets

Alaska rural villages population characteristics and and subsistence activities, 1976-86, 5738-9

Assets and debts of private sector, balance sheets by segment, 1949-88, semiannual rpt, 9365-4.1

Assets and liabilities in flow-of-funds accounts, by type and economic sector, outstanding at year-end 1965-88, annual rpt, 9364-3

Child care arrangements and costs, by income and other characteristics of family, 1984-86, press release, 2328-61

Consumer Expenditure Survey, household income by source, and itemized spending, by selected characteristics and region, 1984-87, annual rpt, 6764-5

Economic indicators, prices, labor costs, and productivity, BLS econometric analyses and methodology, working paper series, 6886-6

Family Economics Review, consumer goods prices and supply, and home economics, quarterly rpt with articles, 1702-1

Health care costs to families for care of handicapped and chronically ill children at home, literature review, 1978-85, article, 4042-3.912

Higher education instn student aid and other sources of support, with student expenses and characteristics, by instn type and control, 1987 triennial study, series, 4846-3

Married couple families with both spouses working, effects on consumer spending by category, and income, by household characteristics, 1984-86, article, 6722-1.908

Older persons assets and relation to income, by selected characteristics, 1984, article, 4742-1.910

Securities (tax-exempt) holdings by investor type, and IRS enforcement of disallowance of interest deduction for financing holdings, mid 1970s-87, GAO rpt, 26119-239

Single-parent household income sources and spending by category, by sex, age, race, and household size, 1984-85, article, 1702-1.901

Supplemental Security Income beneficiaries, assets by type and eligibility class, FY87, article, 4742-1.922

Taxes, spending, and govt efficiency, public opinion by respondent characteristics, 1989 survey, annual rpt, 10044–2

Telephone local service charges and low-income subsidies, by region, company, and city, 1940-June 1989, semiannual rpt, 9282–8

Telephone service subscribership, charges, and local and long distance firm finances and operations, 1970s-FY89, semiannual rpt, 9282–7

see also Personal consumption

Family income

see Personal and household income

see under By Income in the "Index by Categories"

Family planning

Developing countries economic and social conditions from 1960s, and Intl Dev Cooperation Agency and AID activities and funding, FY88-90, annual rpt, 9904–4

Foreign countries contraception use by women, by age and country, 1989 biennial rpt, 2324–9

Health condition and health care resources, use, and spending, 1950s-87, annual data compilation, 4144–11

HHS financial aid, by program, recipient, State, and city, FY88, annual regional listings, 4004–3

Honduras health care projects of AID, design and mgmt effects on sustainability, 1942-86, 9916–3.53

Indian Health Service outpatient visits, by type of provider, selected hospital, and IHS service area, FY87-88, annual rpt, 4084–3

Medicaid beneficiaries and payments, by service type, FY72-87, annual rpt, 4744–3.6

Medicaid coverage, participation, payments, admin, and legislative history, with data by State, 1980s-88, 21368–105

Medicare and Medicaid beneficiaries and program operations, 1988, annual fact book, 4654–18

Medicare and Medicaid eligibility, participation, coverage, and program finances, various periods 1966-89, biennial rpt, 4654–1

Research on population and reproduction, Federal funding by project, FY87, annual listing, 4474–9

Research on population and reproduction, Natl Inst of Child Health and Human Dev funding and activities, 1988, annual rpt, 4474–33

Statistical Abstract of US, social, political, and economic data, 1790-2025, comprehensive annual compilation, 2324–1.1

see also Abortion

see also Contraceptives

see also Sex education

see also Sexual sterilization

Family Support Act

Job training and related aid, AFDC participants, costs, and budget impact, projected FY89-93, 26306–3.102

Family Support Administration

AFDC beneficiaries by county, payments, application processing and disposition, hearings, and fraud cases, by State, FY87, annual rpt, 4694–7

AFDC eligibility and payment errors, by type and State, semiannual rpt, discontinued, 4692–1

AFDC provisions, by State, FY88, annual rpt, 4694–4

AFDC recipients demographic and financial characteristics, by State, FY87, annual rpt, 4694–1

AFDC State admin agencies performance measures, caseloads, payments, and costs, by State, annual rpt, discontinued, 4694–2

Budget of US Appendix, obligations, appropriations, and personnel, by program and agency, FY90, annual rpt, 104–3

Child support collection programs of States, operations, costs, and Federal incentive payments, by State, FY86-1987, 4698–3

Child support enforcement automated systems of States, operational status by State and whether federally funded, 1985-88, GAO rpt, 26121–272

Child Support Enforcement Office demonstration projects for interstate collection, as of Aug 1988, GAO rpt, 26121–271

Data projects and systems of HHS, by subagency, FY88, 4008–92

Expenditures of Fed Govt in States, by type, program, agency, and State, FY88, annual rpt, 2464–3

Refugee arrivals and resettlement in US, by age, sex, sponsoring agency, State, and country, monthly rpt, 4692–2

Refugee resettlement programs and funding, arrivals by country of origin, and indicators of adjustment, by State, FY88, annual rpt, 4694–5

Research and evaluation programs of HHS, 1970-FY87, annual listing, 4004–30

Famine

see Food supply

Famulari, Melissa

"Empirical Test of the Labor Market Discrimination Hypothesis for People with Epilepsy", 6886–6.59

"Employer-Provided Benefits: Employer Cost Versus Employee Value", 6722–1.960

Fantel, R. J.

"Phosphate Availability and Supply. A Minerals Availability Appraisal", 5606–4.27

Farber, Kit D.

"Pollution Abatement and Control Expenditures, 1984-87", 2702–1.919

Fargo, N.Dak.

see also under By SMSA or MSA in the "Index by Categories"

Farley, Reynolds

"Analyzing the Characteristics of Blacks: A Comparison of Data from SIPP and CPS", 2626–10.84

Farm costs

see Agricultural finance

see Agricultural production costs

Farm Costs and Returns Survey

Alien workers (unauthorized) employer sanctions impacts on farm labor costs, by farm type, size, and region, 1986, 1598–250

Economic Indicators of the Farm Sector, itemized production costs, receipts, and returns, by commodity and region, 1985-87, annual rpt, 1544–20

Finances and operations of farms, by size, commodity, and region, 1986, annual rpt, 1544–27

Financial condition of farms, estimates under alternative measures of sales size, 1985, 1548–344

Production itemized costs, receipts, and returns, by crop and State, preliminary 1987, annual rpt, 1544–24

Tobacco (burley) finances, operations, and labor, for Kentucky and Tennessee, 1984, 1568–277

Farm Credit Administration

Budget of US Appendix, obligations, appropriations, and personnel, by program and agency, FY90, annual rpt, 104–3

Budget of US, authoritative financial statements with appropriations, outlays, and receipts, by category and agency, FY88, annual rpt, 8104–2.2

Credit and financial conditions of farms, forecast 1989, annual rpt, 9264–10

Farm Credit System financial statements and loan activity by lender type and district, and borrower characteristics, 1988, annual rpt, 9264–2

Financial condition of Farm Credit System, quarterly rpt, 9262–2

Financial statements of Farm Credit System banks, 1988, annual rpt, 9264–5

Farm Credit Banks

see Farm Credit System

Farm Credit System

Agricultural Statistics, 1988, annual rpt, 1004–1.2

Budget of US Appendix, financial statements of federally sponsored enterprises, FY90, annual rpt, 104–3.4

Business statistics, detailed data for major industries and economic indicators, *Survey of Current Business*, monthly rpt, 2702–1.6

Cooperatives loans, assets, net worth, and assns, for FCS by district, 1987, annual rpt, 1124–1

Credit and financial conditions of farms, forecast 1989, annual rpt, 9264–10

Economic Indicators of the Farm Sector, balance sheets, and receipts by detailed commodity, by State, 1984-88, annual rpt, 1544–18

Financial condition of FCS, quarterly rpt, 9262–2

Financial statements and loan activity by district and type of lender, and borrower characteristics, 1988, annual rpt, 9264–2

Financial statements of FCS banks, 1988, annual rpt, 9264–5

Flow-of-funds accounts, savings, investments, and credit statements, quarterly rpt, 9365–3.3

Foreclosure of farm property, by lender, quarterly 1984-88, article, 1541–1.903

Land transfers, by source of credit financing and region, 1975-89, article, 1561–16.902

Loans (farm) by purpose and source, quarterly rpt, 9365–3.10

Loans (farm) outstanding, and lenders financial condition, quarterly rpt with articles, 1541–1

Loans (farm) outstanding, by lender type, with indicators of financial stress, 1988, annual GAO rpt, 26104–16

Loans (farm) outstanding, by lender type, 1988, annual rpt, 1544–16.2

Foreign investment in US farm and commercial real estate, by owner country, 1977-89, GAO rpt, 26123–244

Foreign investment in US farmland related to exchange rate, interest rate, and cropland returns, by leading country, 1981-88, 1528–287

Foreign ownership of US farmland, holdings, acquisitions, and disposals by land use, owner type and country, and State, 1988, annual rpt, 1584–2

Foreign ownership of US farmland, holdings, acreage, and value by land use, owner country, State, and county, 1988, annual rpt, 1584–3

Fruit and vegetable processing industries finances and operations, consumption, farm production, and trade, by commodity, 1970s-88, 1568–275

Hogs and pigs production, inventory, and farms, by State, 1983-87, 1641–10

Hogs inventory, value, farrowings, and farms, by State, quarterly release, 1623–3

Livestock productivity, farm income, land use, and consumer prices impacts of growth hormones use, alternative estimates, 1985, 1548–346

Metro and nonmetro areas farms, sales, size, and operator tenure, impacts of population growth, with data by State, 1969-82, 1598–253

Mink and pelt production, prices, and farms, selected years 1969-89, annual rpt, 1631–7

North Central States agricultural credit conditions and farmland market values, Fed Reserve 9th District, quarterly rpt, 9383–11

Oregon (western) non-Federal land, by use and county, 1971-74 and 1982, 1206–19.9

Pollutant discharges in coastal areas and estuaries from agricultural, airborne, and other nonpoint sources, and regulatory issues, 1988 hearing, 21568–46

Pollution (water) from agricultural sources, USDA abatement program benefits and costs, projected 1990, 1588–141

Property tax revenue by level of govt, assessed values by locality, and exemptions, by property type and State, 1987 Census of Govts, 2453–1

Research (agricultural) funding and staffing for USDA, State agencies, and other instns, by topic, FY88, annual rpt, 1744–2

Rural areas aid from Fed Govt compared to urban areas, by program and degree of urbanization, FY85, periodic rpt, 1598–248

Sheep, lamb, and goat inventory, by State, 1987-89, annual press release, 1623–4

Small business establishments, employment, and financial ratios, by SIC 1- to 2-digit industry and State, late 1960s-87, 9768–19

Southeastern States farm credit conditions and real estate values, Fed Reserve 5th District, quarterly table, 9389–17

Southwestern States farm credit conditions and real estate values, Fed Reserve 11th District, quarterly rpt, 9379–11

Soviet Union agricultural production cost efficiency, by Republic, model description and results, 1960s-85, 1528–292

Statistical Abstract of US, social, political, and economic data, 1790-2025, comprehensive annual compilation, 2324–1.3

Storage facility and equipment loans to farmers under CCC grain program, by State, FY68-89, annual table, 1804–14

Storage facility and equipment loans to farmers under CCC grain program, by State, monthly table, 1802–9

Supplemental Security Income beneficiaries, assets by type and eligibility class, FY87, article, 4742–1.922

Tobacco production, use, prices, and trade, by variety and product, 1950s-87, 1568–276

Urban areas farms, acreage, finances, and operators, under alternative MSA definitions, 1960s-82, 1598–256

Value and transfers of farmland, production inputs, finances, and mgmt, periodic situation rpt with articles, 1561–16

Value of farmland, and other finances and operations of farms, by size, commodity, and region, 1986, annual rpt, 1544–27

Vegetables farms, acreage, and sales, by whether Federal farm program participant and State, 1987, article, 1561–11.907

Weather data for farmland, average precipitation and temperature by State, monthly 1950-88, biennial rpt, 1544–28

Western States farm real estate values, and nonreal estate farm loan trends, monthly rpt, quarterly data, 9381–2

Wildlife damage to crops, livestock, and property in Great Plains, and effectiveness of mgmt methods, 1988 conf, 1208–304

Wisconsin timber resources and removals, by species, forest type, ownership, and county, series, 1206–34

see also Agricultural accidents and safety

see also Agricultural commodities

see also Agricultural credit

see also Agricultural education

see also Agricultural energy use

see also Agricultural exports and imports

see also Agricultural extension work

see also Agricultural finance

see also Agricultural insurance

see also Agricultural labor

see also Agricultural machinery and equipment

see also Agricultural marketing

see also Agricultural policy

see also Agricultural prices

see also Agricultural production

see also Agricultural production costs

see also Agricultural production quotas and price supports

see also Agricultural productivity

see also Agricultural sciences and research

see also Agricultural stocks

see also Agricultural subsidies

see also Agricultural surpluses

see also Agricultural wages

see also Farm income

see also Farm operators

see also Farm population

see also Farmers Home Administration

see also Irrigation

see also Pasture and rangeland

see also Soil pollution

see also Soils and soil conservation

see also By Industry in the "Index by Categories"

Fats and oils
see Oils, oilseeds, and fats

Fayette County, Ky.
Wages by occupation, and benefits for office and plant workers, 1988 survey, periodic MSA rpt, 6785–3.1
see also under By SMSA or MSA in the "Index by Categories"

Fayetteville, Ark.
see also under By SMSA or MSA in the "Index by Categories"

Fayetteville, N.C.
Wages by occupation, for office and plant workers, 1989 survey, periodic MSA rpt, 6785–3.2
see also under By SMSA or MSA in the "Index by Categories"

Fazzari, Steven
"Price Flexibility and Macroeconomic Stability: An Empirical Simulation Analysis", 9381–10.96

FBI
see Federal Bureau of Investigation

FCC
see Federal Communications Commission

FDA
see Food and Drug Administration

Federal advisory bodies
see Federal boards, committees, and commissions

Federal agencies
see Federal boards, committees, and commissions
see Federal executive departments
see Federal independent agencies
see under By Federal Agency in the "Index by Categories"

Federal agencies fraud, waste, and abuse investigations
see Federal Inspectors General reports

Federal aid programs
Assistance (financial and nonfinancial) of Fed Govt, 1989 base edition with supplements, annual listing, 104–5

Budget deficit reduction under Gramm-Rudman Act, cancellation of budget authority by program, FY90, annual rpt, 104–27; 26304–6

Budget of US Appendix, obligations, appropriations, and personnel, by program and agency, FY90, annual rpt, 104–3

Budget of US, authoritative financial statements with appropriations, outlays, and receipts, by category and agency, FY88, annual rpt, 8104–2.2

Budget of US, balances of budget authority obligated and unobligated, by function and agency, FY88-90, annual rpt, 104–8

Budget of US, Bush Admin policy changes by program, FY90, 028–32

Budget of US, CBO analysis and review of FY90 budget by function, annual rpt, 26304–2

Budget of US, CBO analysis of revenue and spending alternatives and projections of economic indicators, FY90-94, annual rpt, 26304–3

Budget of US, compact budgets by activity, function, and agency, FY90 and projected to FY94, annual rpt, 104–2

Budget of US, historical data, selected years FY34-88 and projected to FY94, annual rpt, 104–22

Budget of US, House concurrent resolution, with spending and revenue targets, FY90, annual rpt, 21264–2

Budget of US, midsession review of FY90 budget, by function and agency, annual rpt, 104–7

Budget of US, object class analysis of obligations, by agency, FY90, annual rpt, 104–9

Budget of US, overview, FY90, annual rpt, 104–6

Budget of US, Reagan Admin policy changes by program, FY90, annual rpt, 104–21

Budget of US, receipts by source, outlays by agency and program, and balances, monthly rpt, 8102–3

Budget of US, Senate concurrent resolution, with spending and revenue targets, FY90, annual rpt, 25254–1

Budget of US, special analyses by activity, function, and agency, FY90, annual rpt, 104–1

Cost control proposals for Fed Govt mgmt, Reagan Admin initiatives, savings, and status, FY85-94, annual rpt, 104–23

Criminal cases by type and disposition, and collections, for US attorneys, by Federal district, FY88, annual rpt, 6004–2.1

Expenditures of Fed Govt in States and local areas, by type, State, county, and city, FY88, annual rpt, 2464–3

Expenditures of Fed Govt in States, by type, program, agency, and State, FY88, annual rpt, 2464–2

Finances of Fed Govt, cash and debt transactions, daily tables, 8102–4

Finances of govts, revenues by source and spending by function, natl income and product account, *Survey of Current Business*, monthly rpt, 2702–1.24

Financial consolidated statements of Fed Govt based on business accounting methods, FY87-88, annual rpt, 8104–5

Labor productivity of Federal employees, indexes of output and labor costs by function, FY67-87, annual rpt, 6824–1.6

Loan and physical asset sales of Fed Govt, and budget impacts, by program, FY90, annual rpt, 104–7

Loans and loan guarantees of of Fed Govt, outstanding amounts by agency and program, *Treasury Bulletin*, quarterly rpt, 8002–4.9

Loans, loan guarantees, and insurance programs of Fed Govt, outstanding amounts by agency and program, FY65-88, GAO rpt, 26111–65

Natl income and product accounts govt transactions component estimates, methodology and bibl, 1988 technical rpt, 2706–6.5

Puerto Rico economic conditions and govt finances, 1975-89, GAO rpt, 26121–298

Statistical Abstract of US, social, political, and economic data, 1790-2025, comprehensive annual compilation, 2324–1.2

see also Agricultural credit

see also Agricultural production quotas and price supports

see also Agricultural subsidies

see also Agricultural surpluses

see also Aid to Families with Dependent Children

see also Child welfare

see also Community Development Block Grants

see also Federal aid to arts and humanities

see also Federal aid to education

see also Federal aid to higher education

see also Federal aid to highways

see also Federal aid to housing

see also Federal aid to law enforcement

see also Federal aid to libraries

see also Federal aid to local areas

see also Federal aid to medical education

see also Federal aid to medicine

see also Federal aid to railroads

see also Federal aid to rural areas

see also Federal aid to States

see also Federal aid to transportation

see also Federal aid to vocational education

see also Federal funding for energy programs

see also Federal funding for research and development

see also Federally Funded R&D Centers

see also Food assistance

see also Food stamp programs

see also Government and business

see also Head Start Project

see also Income maintenance

see also Legal aid

see also Manpower training programs

see also Medicaid

see also Medical assistance

see also Medicare

see also Old-Age, Survivors, Disability, and Health Insurance

see also Public housing

see also Public service employment

see also Public welfare programs

see also Rent supplements

see also Revenue sharing

see also School lunch and breakfast programs

see also Shipbuilding and operating subsidies

see also Social security

see also Student aid

see also Subsidies

see also Supplemental Security Income

see also Tax expenditures

see also Unemployment insurance

see also Urban Development Action Grants

see also Veterans benefits and pensions

see also Veterans health facilities and services

see also Veterans housing

Federal aid to agriculture

see Agricultural credit

see Agricultural production quotas and price supports

see Agricultural subsidies

see Agricultural surpluses

see Federal aid to rural areas

Federal aid to arts and humanities

Assistance (financial and nonfinancial) of Fed Govt, 1989 base edition with supplements, annual listing, 104–5

Education Dept programs funding, operations, and effectiveness, FY88, annual rpt, 4804–5

Expenditures of Fed Govt in States, by type, program, agency, and State, FY88, annual rpt, 2464–2

Museum Services Inst activities and finances, and grants by recipient, FY88, annual rpt, 9564–7

Museum Services Inst grants, by recipient, FY89, annual press release series, 9564–6

Natl Endowment for Arts activities and grants, FY88, annual rpt, 9564–3

Natl Endowment for Arts matching grants, by instn, annual rpt, discontinued, 9564–5

Natl Endowment for Humanities activities and grants, FY88, annual rpt, 9564–2

Smithsonian Instn activities and finances, FY88, annual rpt, 29574–1

Statistical Abstract of US, social, political, and economic data, 1790-2025, comprehensive annual compilation, 2324–1.1

Federal aid to business

see Government and business

see Subsidies

Federal aid to cities

see Federal aid to local areas

Federal aid to education

Appalachia local dev projects, and funding by source, by program and State, FY88, annual rpt, 9084–1

Arts Natl Endowment activities and grants, FY88, annual rpt, 9564–3

Assistance (block and categorical grants) programs for State and local govts, FY89, biennial listing, 10044–8

Assistance (financial and nonfinancial) of Fed Govt, 1989 base edition with supplements, annual listing, 104–5

Bilingual education program activities, Federal and State aid, and enrollment, FY86-87, biennial rpt, 4804–14

Budget of US Appendix, obligations, appropriations, and personnel, by program and agency, FY90, annual rpt, 104–3

Budget of US, balances of budget authority obligated and unobligated, by function and agency, FY88-90, annual rpt, 104–8

Budget of US, Bush Admin policy changes by program, FY90, 028–32

Budget of US, CBO analysis of revenue and spending alternatives and projections of economic indicators, FY90-94, annual rpt, 26304–3

Budget of US, compact budgets by activity, function, and agency, FY90 and projected to FY94, annual rpt, 104–2

Budget of US, historical data, selected years FY34-88 and projected to FY94, annual rpt, 104–22

Budget of US, House concurrent resolution, with spending and revenue targets, FY90, annual rpt, 21264–2

Budget of US, Reagan Admin policy changes by program, FY90, annual rpt, 104–21

Budget of US, receipts by source, outlays by agency and program, and balances, monthly rpt, 8102–3

Compensatory education programs federally funded, private school students served, and costs, for selected districts, 1984-89, GAO rpt, 26121–308

Condition of Education, detailed data on elementary, secondary, and higher education, 1920s-88 and projected to 1997, annual rpt, 4824–1

Construction put in place, by type of construction, bimonthly rpt, 2042–1.1

Data on education, selected performance and financial indicators by State, 1982-88, annual table with supplements, 4804–32

Digest of Education Statistics, detailed data on students, staff, finances, and facilities, 1989 edition, annual rpt, 4824–2

Indian (Navajo and Hopi) relocation program activities and caseloads, monthly rpt, 16002–1

Indian (Navajo and Hopi) relocation program activities, caseloads, and finances, by location, annual rpt, discontinued, 16004–4

Indian (Navajo and Hopi) relocation program activities, caseloads, and finances, FY88, annual rpt, 16004–1

Indian and Alaska Native housing and economic development program operations, by region, FY86-87, annual rpt, 5004–5

Loans and loan guarantees of of Fed Govt, outstanding amounts by agency and program, *Treasury Bulletin*, quarterly rpt, 8002–4.9

Low income housing stock effects of alternative Federal actions and spending levels, projected 1988-2002, hearing, 21248–116

Older and handicapped persons housing projects, HUD construction and rehabilitation loans, annual listing, suspended, 5004–6

Rural areas aid from Fed Govt compared to urban areas, by program and degree of urbanization, FY85, periodic rpt, 1598–248

Statistical Abstract of US, social, political, and economic data, 1790-2025, comprehensive annual compilation, 2324–1.2

Tax (income) returns of individuals, detailed data, 1986, annual rpt, 8304–2

Tax expenditures, Federal revenues forgone through income tax deductions and exclusions by type, FY90-94, annual rpt, 21784–10

Urban Dev Action Grants, funding sources, project descriptions, and economic impacts, by city, periodic press releases, 5002–7

see also Farmers Home Administration
see also Housing (FHA), HUD
see also Mortgages
see also Public housing
see also Rent supplements
see also Veterans housing

Federal aid to law enforcement

Assistance (block and categorical grants) programs for State and local govts, FY89, biennial listing, 10044–8

Assistance (financial and nonfinancial) of Fed Govt, 1989 base edition with supplements, annual listing, 104–5

Budget deficit reduction under Gramm-Rudman Act, cancellation of budget authority by program, FY90, annual rpt, 104–27; 26304–6

Budget of US Appendix, obligations, appropriations, and personnel, by program and agency, FY90, annual rpt, 104–3

Budget of US, Bush Admin policy changes by program, FY90, 028–32

Budget of US, CBO analysis of revenue and spending alternatives and projections of economic indicators, FY90-94, annual rpt, 26304–3

Budget of US, compact budgets by activity, function, and agency, FY90 and projected to FY94, annual rpt, 104–2

Budget of US, historical data, selected years FY34-88 and projected to FY94, annual rpt, 104–22

Budget of US, House concurrent resolution, with spending and revenue targets, FY90, annual rpt, 21264–2

Budget of US, midsession review of FY90 budget, by function and agency, annual rpt, 104–7

Budget of US, Reagan Admin policy changes by program, FY90, annual rpt, 104–21

Budget of US, receipts by source, outlays by agency and program, and balances, monthly rpt, 8102–3

Budget of US, Senate concurrent resolution, with spending and revenue targets, FY90, annual rpt, 25254–1

Drug abuse and trafficking reduction aid to States, and grant processing time, FY87-88, GAO rpt, 26119–258

Drug abuse and trafficking reduction programs funding by Federal agency, and Bush Admin budget request, by program area, FY87-90, 238–1

Drug enforcement activities of State and local agencies, Federal aid by recipient, and background data, FY88, annual rpt, 6064–28

Drug enforcement regional task forces investigation of organized crime, activities by agency and region, and background data, FY83-88, annual rpt, 6004–17

Drug smuggling aircraft interdiction activities of Fed Govt, funding, and radar system capabilities, by agency, FY82-89, GAO rpt, 26119–259

Employment, payroll, and spending for criminal justice, by level of govt, State, and selected city and county, FY71-85, annual rpt, 6064–9

Expenditures and employment for law enforcement, by activity and level of govt, FY84-88, annual rpt, 6064–6.1

Expenditures of Fed Govt in States, by type, program, agency, and State, FY88, annual rpt, 2464–2

Finances of govts, revenues by source and spending by function, natl income and product account, *Survey of Current Business*, monthly rpt, 2702–1.24

Juvenile delinquency prevention funding, by program and Federal agency, FY88, annual rpt, 6064–11

Marijuana crop eradication activities of DEA and local agencies by State, and drug potency, 1982-88, annual rpt, 6284–4

Marine mammal protection activities and funding, populations, and harvests, by species, 1987, annual rpt, 5504–12

Marshals Service activities, FY88, annual rpt, 6294–1

Office of Justice Programs activities, FY88, annual narrative rpt, 6064–18

Prison conditions, population, and problems, issues and bibl, 1989 compilation of papers, 25928–8

Public defender grants, by State, FY90-91, Judicial Conf proceedings, semiannual rpt, 18202–2

R&D funding by Fed Govt, by detailed function, program, and agency, FY88-90, annual rpt, 9627–9

Rural areas aid from Fed Govt compared to urban areas, by program and degree of urbanization, FY85, periodic rpt, 1598–248

Statistical Abstract of US, social, political, and economic data, 1790-2025, comprehensive annual compilation, 2324–1.1

Federal aid to libraries

Assistance (financial and nonfinancial) of Fed Govt, 1989 base edition with supplements, annual listing, 104–5

Blind and handicapped libraries, readership, circulation, staff, funding, and holdings, FY88, annual listing, 26404–3

Education Dept programs funding, operations, and effectiveness, FY88, annual rpt, 4804–5

Expenditures for education by Federal agency, program, and recipient type, and instn spending, FY80-88, 4828–21

HHS financial aid, by program, recipient, State, and city, FY88, annual regional listings, 4004–3

Humanities Natl Endowment activities and grants, FY88, annual rpt, 9564–2

Indian and Hawaii Native public libraries services, project listing and funding by tribe and State, FY88, annual rpt, 4874–5

Literacy programs of public libraries, descriptions and funding, FY87, annual listing, 4874–3

Mail operating costs of USPS, itemized by class of mail, FY88, annual rpt, 9864–4

Mail revenue and appropriation for revenue forgone, by class of mail, FY88, annual rpt, 9864–5

Mail revenue, costs, and volume, by class of mail, FY88, annual rpt, 9864–2

Medicine Natl Library activities, holdings, and grants, FY86-88, annual rpt, 4464–1

Natl Archives and Records Admin activities, finances, holdings, and staff, FY88, annual rpt, 9514–2

Natl Commission on Libraries and Info Science activities, FY88, annual rpt, 15634–1

NIH grants and awards, quarterly listing, 4432–1

NIH grants for R&D, training, construction, and medical libraries, by location and recipient, FY88, annual listings, 4434–7

Public libraries special programs, project descriptions and funding by level of govt, State, and city, 1984-87, annual rpt, 4874–4

Research library funding of Education Dept, by project, instn, and State, FY88, annual listing, 4874–2

State allocation of Federal educational funds, by program, recipient type, and State, 1987/88, annual rpt, 4804–8

Technological aid to libraries, project descriptions and funding, FY88, annual listing, 4874–6

Training in library science, grants for disadvantaged students, by instn and State, FY89, annual listing, 4874–1

Federal aid to local areas

Alaska rural villages population characteristics and and subsistence activities, 1976-86, 5738–9

Appalachian Regional Commission funding, by project and State, planned FY89, annual rpt, 9084–3

Arts Natl Endowment activities and grants, FY88, annual rpt, 9564–3

Federal aid to medical education

Federal aid to medicine

Budget of US, Reagan Admin policy changes by program, FY90, annual rpt, 104-21

Budget of US, receipts by source, outlays by agency and program, and balances, monthly rpt, 8102-3

Budget of US, special analysis of Federal capital spending by category, projected FY89-2005 and trends from FY81, annual rpt, 104-24

Cancer Natl Inst contracts and grants, by recipient and location, FY88, annual listing, 4474-28

Child and maternal health research activities and funding, FY88, annual rpt, 4474-31

Child Health and Human Dev Natl Inst contracts and grants, by recipient and location, FY88, annual listing, 4474-36

Children (handicapped) health care services block grants of Fed Govt, State and other funding, and children served, by State, FY87, GAO rpt, 26121-301

Construction and rehabilitation mortgages for hospitals insured by HUD, principal, and defaults, 1988, GAO rpt, 26121-263

Construction put in place, by type of construction, bimonthly rpt, 2042-1.1

Construction spending by Fed Govt, by program and type of structure, FY82-90, annual article, 2042-1.901; 2042-1.907

Data projects and systems of HHS, by subagency, FY88, 4008-92

Dental Research Natl Inst research and training grants, by recipient, FY88, annual listing, 4474-19

Diabetes research and care services programs and funding, by Federal agency and NIH inst, FY88, annual rpt, 4474-34

Disabled persons rehabilitation, Federal and State activities and funding, FY88, annual rpt, 4944-1

Drug abuse and treatment research summaries, and resource materials and grant listings, periodic rpt, 4492-4

Drug and alcohol abuse treatment facilities, services, use, funding, and client characteristics, 1987, annual rpt, 4494-10

Expenditures for health care, by service type, payment source, and sector, 1960s-87, annual article, 4652-1.926

Expenditures for health care of business, households, and govts, 1965-87, article, 4652-1.928

Expenditures for public welfare by program, and private health care spending, FY50s-86, annual article, 4742-1.909

Expenditures of Fed Govt in States, by type, program, agency, and State, FY88, annual rpt, 2464-2

Finances of govts, by level of govt, State, and for large cities and counties, annual rpt series, 2466-2

Finances of govts, revenues by source and spending by function, natl income and product account, *Survey of Current Business*, monthly rpt, 2702-1.24

Fraud and abuse in HHS programs, audits and investigations, 2nd half FY89, semiannual rpt, 4002-6

Health Care Financing Admin research activities and grants, by program, as of Mar 1989, annual listing, 4654-10

Health condition and health care resources, use, and spending, 1950s-87, annual data compilation, 4144-11

Heart, Lung, and Blood Natl Inst activities and funding, FY87, annual narrative rpt, 4474-22

Heart, Lung, and Blood Natl Inst activities, and grants by recipient and location, FY88 with disease trends from 1940, annual rpt, 4474-15

Heart, Lung, and Blood Natl Inst grants and Advisory Council recommendations, FY77-94, annual rpt, 4474-11

HHS financial aid, by program, recipient, State, and city, FY88, annual regional listings, 4004-3

Home health care funding by Fed Govt, long-term care costs, and ability to pay, 1988 survey, hearing, 21148-51

Homeless population characteristics, needs, and impacts of govt aid programs and housing costs, 1988 conf papers, 10048-73

Infant deaths, causes, and prevention, recommendations and findings, 1988 rpt, 15838-1

Kidney end-stage disease research of CDC and HCFA, project listing, 1988 annual rpt, 4654-16

Library of Medicine of NIH, activities, holdings, and grants, FY86-88, annual rpt, 4464-1

Loans and loan guarantees of Fed Govt, outstanding amounts by agency and program, *Treasury Bulletin*, quarterly rpt, 8002-4.9

Mental health care hospitals, beds and caseload by State, patient characteristics, finances, and staff, for profit and nonprofit private instns, 1986, 4506-3.37

Mental stress-related disorder prevention and research grants of NIMH, by subject, FY87, GAO rpt, 26121-302

NASA R&D funding to higher education instns, by field, instn, and State, FY88, annual listing, 9504-7

NIH activities, funding, and advisory council recommendations, by inst, FY87-88, biennial rpt, 4434-16

NIH activities, funding by program and recipient type, staff, and clinic patients, by inst, FY87, annual rpt, 4434-3

NIH grants and awards, quarterly listing, 4432-1

NIH grants and contracts, by inst and type of recipient, FY79-88, annual rpt, 4434-9

NIH grants for R&D, training, construction, and medical libraries, by location and recipient, FY88, annual listings, 4434-7

NIH intl program activities and funding, by inst and country, FY88, annual rpt, 4474-6

NIH research contract awards to higher education instns, and research staff, related charges, and time allocated to projects, 1984-88, 4008-89

NIH Research Resources Div activities and funding, by program, FY87, annual rpt, 4434-12

Nutrition biomedical and behavioral research and training, NIH activities and funding by inst, FY87, annual rpt, 4434-15

Older persons aid and policies of Fed Govt, program funding, and grants awarded, FY80-89, annual rpt, 25144-3.2

Prospective payment system research activities and funding of PHS, by project and subagency, FY88, annual rpt, 4184-3

R&D and related funding of Fed Govt to higher education and nonprofit instns, by field, instn, agency, and State, FY87, annual rpt, 9627-17

R&D funding by Fed Govt, by detailed function, program, and agency, FY88-90, annual rpt, 9627-9

R&D funding by Fed Govt, by field, performer type, agency, and State, FY87-89, annual rpt, 9627-20

R&D price index for medicine, NIH index by component, and compared to other indexes, FY79-86, article, 4042-3.901

Reproduction and population research, Fed Govt funding by project, FY87, annual listing, 4474-9

Reproduction and population research, Natl Inst of Child Health and Human Dev funding and activities, 1988, annual rpt, 4474-33

Rural areas aid from Fed Govt compared to urban areas, by program and degree of urbanization, FY85, periodic rpt, 1598-248

Rural areas health care facilities, staffing, services accessibility, and indicators of need, 1960s-88, 25148-41

Smoking and health, HHS spending, by agency, FY79-86, annual rpt, 4204-18

Statistical Abstract of US, social, political, and economic data, 1790-2025, comprehensive annual compilation, 2324-1.1; 2324-1.2

Tax expenditures, Federal revenues forgone through income tax deductions and exclusions by type, FY90-94, annual rpt, 21784-10

Toxicology Natl Program research and testing activities, FY87 and planned FY88, annual rpt, 4044-16

see also Civilian Health and Medical Program of the Uniformed Services

see also Federal aid to medical education

see also Medicaid

see also Medicare

see also Military health facilities and services

see also Supplemental Security Income

see also Veterans health facilities and services

Federal aid to railroads

Amtrak finances and operations, FY88, annual rpt, 29524-1

Assistance (financial and nonfinancial) of Fed Govt, 1989 base edition with supplements, annual listing, 104-5

Budget of US, special analysis of Federal capital spending by category, projected FY89-2005 and trends from FY81, annual rpt, 104-24

DOT planning and safety grants, by program, State, and for 38 SMSAs, FY88, annual rpt, 7304-7

Expenditures of Fed Govt in States, by type, program, agency, and State, FY88, annual rpt, 2464-2

Lands (public) acreage and grants, by State, FY88 and trends, annual rpt, 5724-1.1

Transit systems finances, costs, and needs, by State and selected system, 1980-88, biennial rpt, 7884–8

Urban Mass Transportation Admin grants for transit systems, by city and State, FY88, annual rpt, 7884–10

Urban Mass Transportation Admin research and training grants to higher education instns, by project, FY88, annual listing, 7884–7

see also Federal aid to highways

see also Federal aid to railroads

see also Shipbuilding and operating subsidies

Federal aid to vocational education

Assistance (block and categorical grants) programs for State and local govts, FY89, biennial listing, 10044–8

Assistance (financial and nonfinancial) of Fed Govt, 1989 base edition with supplements, annual listing, 104–5

Assistance for vocational education by type of recipient and source, and characteristics of programs and students, 1970s-89, series, 4806–3

Budget of US Appendix, obligations, appropriations, and personnel, by program and agency, FY90, annual rpt, 104–3

Budget of US, compact budgets by activity, function, and agency, FY90 and projected to FY94, annual rpt, 104–2

Disadvantaged and handicapped vocational education funding of Fed Govt, by selected State and district, 1985-89 and projected to 2000, GAO rpt, 26121–286

Education Dept programs funding, operations, and effectiveness, FY88, annual rpt, 4804–5

Expenditures and participation in employment training and vocational education programs, for 6 Federal agencies, FY89-90, GAO rpt, 26121–277

Expenditures for education, by Federal agency, program, and State, FY80-89, annual rpt, 4824–2.27

Expenditures of Fed Govt in States, by type, program, agency, and State, FY88, annual rpt, 2464–2

HHS financial aid, by program, recipient, State, and city, FY88, annual regional listings, 4004–3

State allocation of Federal educational funds, by program, recipient type, and State, 1987/88, annual rpt, 4804–8

Student aid funding and participation, by Federal program, instn type and control, and State, various periods 1959-88, annual rpt, 4804–28

Federal Asset Disposition Association

Savings instns failures, real estate assets value, and disposition performance of FSLIC, Fed Asset Disposition Assn, and private contractors, 1988, article, 8432–2.901

Federal Aviation Administration

Activities and finances of FAA, and staff by region, FY87-88, annual rpt, 7504–10

Air traffic control and airway facilities improvement activities under Natl Airspace System Plan, 1981-85 and projected to 2000, annual rpt, 7504–12

Air traffic control and airway facilities staff, by selected employment and demographic characteristics, FY88, annual rpt, 7504–41

Air traffic control system safety, working conditions, and traffic volume, various periods 1981-88, GAO rpt series, 26113–220

Air traffic, pilots, airports, and fuel use, forecast FY89-2000 and trends from FY80, annual rpt, 7504–6

Aircraft (general aviation), flight hours, and equipment, by type, use, and model of aircraft, region, and State, 1988, annual rpt, 7504–29

Aircraft registered with FAA, by type and characteristics of aircraft, make, carrier, State, and county, 1988, annual rpt, 7504–3

Airport and Airway Trust Fund finances and excise tax collections, FY71-88 and projected under alternative spending policies, FY89-94, 26308–84

Airport and Airway Trust Fund funding and improvement spending, with data by airport and program, 1988 hearing, 21788–180

Airport improvement program of FAA, grants and activities by State and airport, FY88, annual rpt, 7504–38

Airport planning and dev project grants of FAA, by airport and location, quarterly press release, 7502–14

Airport security operations to prevent hijacking, screening failures and proposed FAA penalties by carrier, 1989 press release, 7306–10.2; 7306–10.3

Airport security operations to prevent hijacking, screening results, enforcement actions, and hijacking attempts, 1st half 1988, semiannual rpt, 7502–5

Airport traffic, delays, capacity improvement projects and funding, runway length, and navigational operations, for hub and reliever airports, 1986-87 and forecast to 1996, 7508–67

Alaska airport dev plans and air systems operations, FY89-98, annual rpt, 7504–36

Budget of US Appendix, obligations, appropriations, and personnel, by program and agency, FY90, annual rpt, 104–3

Delays of flights caused by air traffic control procedures and problems, and costs, with data by airport, 1976-86, 7508–68

Employment of DOT, by subagency, occupation, and selected personnel characteristics, FY88, annual rpt, 7304–18

Expenditures of Fed Govt in States, by type, program, agency, and State, FY88, annual rpt, 2464–2

Flight and engine hours, and shutdown rates, by aircraft and engine model, and air carrier, monthly rpt, 7502–13

Flight service station workload of FAA, pilot briefs, contacts, and flight plans by facility, projected FY88-99 and trends from FY80, annual rpt, 7504–39

Hijackings, on-board explosions, and other crime, US and foreign incidents, 1983-87, annual rpt, 7504–31

Instrument flight rule aircraft handled, by user type, FAA traffic control center, and region, FY80-88 and projected to FY2000, annual rpt, 7504–15

Medical research and test results for aviation, technical rpt series, 7506–10

Pilots and nonpilots certified by FAA, by certificate type, age, sex, region, and State, 1988, annual rpt, 7504–2

R&D funding and staff of FAA, by program, FY87-88, GAO rpt, 26113–407

Safety inspector training, FAA officals views on curriculum and adequacy, 1988 survey, GAO rpt, 26113–440

Traffic and other aviation activity forecasts of FAA, 1989 annual conf, 7504–28

Traffic and passenger enplanements, by airport, region, and State, projected FY89-2005 and trends from FY83, annual rpt, 7504–7

Traffic levels at FAA air traffic control facilities, by airport and State, FY88, annual rpt, 7504–27

Federal bankruptcy courts

Caseloads (civil and criminal) for Federal district, appeals, and bankruptcy courts, by offense, circuit, and district, quarterly rpt, 18202–1

Caseloads (civil and criminal) for Federal district, appeals, and special courts, June 1989, annual rpt, 18204–2; 18204–8

Farms bankruptcy filings under Chapter 12 by State, and legal practitioners and creditors views on provisions, 1986-88, GAO rpt, 26113–415

Judicial Conf proceedings and findings, fall 1989, semiannual rpt, 18202–2

Mediation program caseloads and dispositions, for California southern district bankruptcy court, 1986-88, 18408–40

Pay rates of Fed Govt civilian employees, by pay schedule and grade, 1989 and trends from 1789, annual rpt, 21624–4

US attorneys work hours, by type of court and Federal district, FY88, annual rpt, 6004–2.6

Federal boards, committees, and commissions

Advisory committees of Fed Govt, and members, staff, meetings, and costs by agency, FY88, annual rpt, 9454–18

Budget deficit reduction under Gramm-Rudman Act, cancellation of budget authority by program, FY90, annual rpt, 104–27; 21924–1; 26304–6

Budget of US Appendix, obligations, appropriations, and personnel, by program and agency, FY90, annual rpt, 104–3

Budget of US, authoritative financial statements with appropriations, outlays, and receipts, by category and agency, FY88, annual rpt, 8104–2.2

Budget of US, compact budgets by activity, function, and agency, FY90 and projected to FY94, annual rpt, 104–2

Budget of US, receipts by source, outlays by agency and program, and balances, monthly rpt, 8102–3

Budget of US, special analyses by activity, function, and agency, FY90, annual rpt, 104–1

Education funding by Federal agency, program, and recipient type, and instn spending, FY80-88, 4828–21

Employment and payroll (civilian) of Fed Govt, by agency in DC metro area, total US, and abroad, bimonthly rpt, 9842–1

Financial operations of Fed Govt, detailed data, *Treasury Bulletin*, quarterly rpt, 8002–4

Labor unions recognized in Fed Govt, agreements and membership by agency and facility, as of Jan 1989, biennial listing, 9844–14

see also Advisory Commission on Intergovernmental Relations
see also Advisory Committee on Federal Pay
see also Board for International Broadcasting
see also Board of Foreign Scholarships
see also Commission on Civil Rights
see also Commission on Merchant Marine and Defense
see also Committee for Purchase from the Blind and Other Severely Handicapped
see also Commodity Futures Trading Commission
see also Delaware River Basin Commission
see also Federal Committee on Statistical Methodology
see also Federal Council on the Aging
see also Federal Election Commission
see also Federal Financial Institutions Examination Council
see also Federal Financing Bank
see also Federal independent agencies
see also Federal Labor Relations Authority
see also Federal Mine Safety and Health Review Commission
see also Interagency Council on the Homeless
see also Interagency Drought Policy Committee
see also Interagency Task Force on Acid Precipitation
see also Interdepartment Radio Advisory Committee
see also International Boundary and Water Commission, U.S. and Mexico
see also International Joint Commission, U.S. and Canada
see also Interstate Commission on the Potomac River Basin
see also Japan-U.S. Friendship Commission
see also Marine Mammal Commission
see also Migratory Bird Conservation Commission
see also National Advisory Council on Child Nutrition
see also National Advisory Council on Educational Research and Improvement
see also National Advisory Council on Indian Education
see also National Capital Planning Commission
see also National Commission for Employment Policy
see also National Commission on Libraries and Information Science
see also National Commission to Prevent Infant Mortality
see also National Committee on Vital and Health Statistics
see also National Economic Commission
see also National Narcotics Intelligence Consumers Committee
see also Navajo and Hopi Indian Relocation Commission
see also Organized Crime Drug Enforcement Task Forces
see also Prospective Payment Assessment Commission
see also Susquehanna River Basin Commission

see also Truman, Harry S., Scholarship Foundation
see also U.S. Advisory Commission on Public Diplomacy
see also U.S. Architectural and Transportation Barriers Compliance Board
see also U.S. Holocaust Memorial Council
see also U.S. Sentencing Commission
see also Water Resources Council
see also under By Federal Agency in the "Index by Categories"
see also under names of individual Presidential commissions (starting with Presidential or President's)

Federal budget
see Budget of the U.S.

Federal buildings
see Public buildings

Federal Bureau of Investigation
Arrest rates, by offense, sex, age, and race, 1987, annual rpt, 6224–7
Assaults and deaths of law enforcement officers, by circumstances, agency, victim and offender characteristics, and location, 1988, annual rpt, 6224–3
Bombing incidents, casualties, and damage, by target, circumstances, and State, 1988, annual rpt, 6224–5
Budget of US Appendix, obligations, appropriations, and personnel, by program and agency, FY90, annual rpt, 104–3
Crime Index by population size and region, and offenses by large city, Jan-June 1989, semiannual rpt, 6222–1
Crime victimization rates, by circumstances and offense, 1965-87, annual rpt, 6224–8
Crimes, arrests by offender characteristics, and rates, by offense, and law enforcement employees, by population size and jurisdiction, 1988, annual rpt, 6224–2
Drunk driving testing methods and analysis, technical data, 1986 conf, 6228–2
Indian reservation crimes and enforcement activity in Montana, and Bur of Indian Affairs law enforcement officers training, 1985-87, GAO rpt, 26113–402
Terrorist incidents in US, related activity, and casualties, by attack type, target, group, and location, 1988, annual rpt, 6224–6

Federal Bureau of Prisons
see Bureau of Prisons

Federal Committee on Statistical Methodology
Fed Govt policies relating to statistical programs technical operation, methodology, and use of data, working paper series, 106–4

Federal Communications Commission
Budget of US Appendix, obligations, appropriations, and personnel, by program and agency, FY90, annual rpt, 104–3
Budget of US, authoritative financial statements with appropriations, outlays, and receipts, by category and agency, FY88, annual rpt, 8104–2.2
Labor unions recognized in Fed Govt, agreements and membership by agency and facility, as of Jan 1989, biennial listing, 9844–14
Licensing activities of FCC, by class of operation, FY88, annual rpt, 9284–4
R&D funding by Fed Govt, by field, performer type, agency, and State, FY87-89, annual rpt, 9627–20

Telephone and telegraph firms detailed finances and operations, 1987, annual rpt, 9284–6
Telephone local service charges and low-income subsidies, by region, company, and city, 1940-June 1989, semiannual rpt, 9282–8
Telephone service of households, by composition, income sources, and other characteristics, 1984-87, 9288–11
Telephone service subscribership, charges, and local and long distance firm finances and operations, 1970s-FY89, semiannual rpt, 9282–7
TV and radio stations on the air, by class of operation, monthly press release, 9282–4
TV channel allocation and license status, for commercial and noncommercial UHF and VHF TV by market, as of June 1989, semiannual rpt, 9282–6

Federal contracts
see Government contracts and procurement

Federal Coordinating Council for Science, Engineering and Technology
Atmospheric sciences research activity of Fed Govt, and funding by agency and program, FY84-87, biennial rpt, 434–1

Federal corporations
see Government corporations and enterprises

Federal Council on the Aging
Older persons socioeconomic characteristics, 1900s-86 and projected to 2050, biennial chartbook, 12904–1

Federal courts
see Administrative Office of the U.S. Courts
see Court of International Trade
see Court of Military Appeals
see Courts
see Federal bankruptcy courts
see Federal courts of appeals
see Federal district courts
see Supreme Court
see Tax Court of the U.S.
see U.S. Claims Court
see U.S. Court of Appeals for the Federal Circuit

Federal courts of appeals
Budget of US Appendix, obligations, appropriations, and personnel, by program and agency, FY90, annual rpt, 104–3
Budget of US, authoritative financial statements with appropriations, outlays, and receipts, by category and agency, FY88, annual rpt, 8104–2.2
Caseloads (civil and criminal) for Federal district, appeals, and bankruptcy courts, by offense, circuit, and district, quarterly rpt, 18202–1
Caseloads (civil and criminal) for Federal district, appeals, and special courts, June 1989, annual rpt, 18204–2
Caseloads (civil and criminal), June 1989, annual rpt, 18204–8
Caseloads, actions, procedure duration, judges, and jurors, by Federal district and appeals court, 1984-89, annual rpt, 18204–3
Criminal case processing in Federal courts, by offense, disposition, and jurisdiction, 1950s-88, annual rpt, 6064–6.5
Judicial Conf proceedings and findings, fall 1989, semiannual rpt, 18202–2
Labor Relations Natl Board activities, cases, elections conducted, and litigation, FY85, annual rpt, 9584–1

Pay rates of Fed Govt civilian employees, by pay schedule and grade, 1989 and trends from 1789, annual rpt, 21624–4

Statistical Abstract of US, social, political, and economic data, 1790-2025, comprehensive annual compilation, 2324–1.1

Tax Court of US caseloads and appeals by disposition, procedure duration, and recoveries, FY88, annual rpt, 18224–5

Tax litigation, prosecutions, and interpretive law decisions, FY88, annual rpt, 8304–3.2

US attorneys work hours, by type of court and Federal district, FY88, annual rpt, 6004–2.6

see also U.S. Court of Appeals for the Federal Circuit

Federal Crop Insurance Corp.

Budget of US Appendix, obligations, appropriations, and personnel, by program and agency, FY90, annual rpt, 104–3

Disaster relief programs of USDA, costs by program, and crop insurance participation and funding sources, FY80-88, GAO rpt, 26113–437

Federal Deposit Insurance Corp.

Banks (insured commercial) financial condition and performance, by asset size and region, quarterly rpt, 9292–1

Banks (insured commercial and savings) finances, by State, 1987, annual rpt, 9294–4

Banks failed and assisted, FDIC mgmt and liquidation of acquired assets, 1980-88, GAO rpt, 26119–237

Budget of US Appendix, obligations, appropriations, and personnel, by program and agency, FY90, annual rpt, 104–3

Budget of US, authoritative financial statements with appropriations, outlays, and receipts, by category and agency, FY88, annual rpt, 8104–2.2

Deposits in FDIC-insured commercial and savings banks, by instn, State, MSA, and county, as of June 1988, annual regional rpt series, 9295–3

Failures of banks, by type, asset size, region, and State, 1984-88, article, 9391–16.901

Finances and operations of FDIC, insured deposits, and finances of banks needing FDIC aid, 1988 and trends from 1934, annual rpt, 9294–1

Financial condition of Federal deposit insurance funds, and of financial instns by type, 1980s-88, GAO rpt, 26119–241

Fraud and insider misconduct at financial instns, cases, Federal regulatory and enforcement activities, and losses, 1981-87, hearing, 21408–111

Labor unions recognized in Fed Govt, agreements and membership by agency and facility, as of Jan 1989, biennial listing, 9844–14

Regulation of banks and related issues, quarterly journal, 9292–4

Savings banks federally chartered and FDIC-insured, financial statements, 1988, annual rpt, 8434–1

Savings instns failures, finances, and FSLIC and FDIC insurance premiums, coverage, losses, and reserves, 1930s-87, technical paper, 9316–1.143

Federal district courts

Budget of US Appendix, obligations, appropriations, and personnel, by program and agency, FY90, annual rpt, 104–3

Caseloads (civil and criminal) for Federal district, appeals, and bankruptcy courts, by offense, circuit, and district, quarterly rpt, 18202–1

Caseloads (civil and criminal) for Federal district, appeals, and special courts, June 1989, annual rpt, 18204–2

Caseloads (civil and criminal), June 1989, annual rpt, 18204–8

Caseloads (criminal) in Federal district courts, by offense, disposition, and district, annual rpt, suspended, 18204–1

Caseloads, actions, procedure duration, judges, and jurors, by Federal district and appeals court, 1984-89, annual rpt, 18204–3

Corrupt govt officials prosecuted and convicted, by judicial district and level of govt, 1978-88, annual rpt, 6004–13

Criminal case processing in Federal district courts, and dispositions, by offense, district, and offender characteristics, 1984, annual rpt, 6064–29

Criminal case processing in Federal district courts, disposition by offense, 1980-87, 6066–19.50

Criminal caseload of Federal district courts, by district, 1970-87, annual rpt, 6064–6.1; 6064–6.5

Judicial Conf proceedings and findings, fall 1989, semiannual rpt, 18202–2

Juror (grand and petit) use and costs, trials, and trial days, by Federal district court, 1981-88, annual rpt, 18204–4

Pay rates of Fed Govt civilian employees, by pay schedule and grade, 1989 and trends from 1789, annual rpt, 21624–4

Statistical Abstract of US, social, political, and economic data, 1790-2025, comprehensive annual compilation, 2324–1.1

Tax litigation, prosecutions, and interpretive law decisions, FY88, annual rpt, 8304–3.2

Torts for product liability, dispositions, awards, case processing time, and plaintiff injury severity and other characteristics, 1983-85, GAO rpt, 26121–317

US attorneys case processing and collections, by case type and Federal district, FY88, annual rpt, 6004–2

Wiretaps authorized, costs, arrests, trials, and convictions, by offense and jurisdiction, 1988, annual rpt, 18204–7

see also Federal bankruptcy courts

Federal Election Commission

Activities of FEC, and election campaign finances, various periods 1975-88, annual rpt, 9274–1

Activities of FEC, elections, procedures, and campaign finances, press release series, 9276–1

Budget of US Appendix, obligations, appropriations, and personnel, by program and agency, FY90, annual rpt, 104–3

Budget of US, authoritative financial statements with appropriations, outlays, and receipts, by category and agency, FY88, annual rpt, 8104–2.2

Campaign financial activity reported to FEC, by type of filer, 1988 natl elections, biennial rpt series, 9276–2

Labor unions recognized in Fed Govt, agreements and membership by agency and facility, as of Jan 1989, biennial listing, 9844–14

Polling places accessibility to aged and handicapped, precincts by barrier type and State, 1988 natl elections, biennial rpt, 9274–6

Voter participation in 1984 and 1988 presidential elections, and returns by candidate and State, article, 9278–7

Votes cast by party, candidate, and State, 1988 natl elections, biennial rpt, 9274–5

Federal Emergency Management Agency

Budget of US Appendix, obligations, appropriations, and personnel, by program and agency, FY90, annual rpt, 104–3

Budget of US, authoritative financial statements with appropriations, outlays, and receipts, by category and agency, FY88, annual rpt, 8104–2.2

Disaster relief program of FEMA under State admin, impact of mgmt changes on benefits processing, 1986-88, GAO rpt, 26113–412

Expenditures of Fed Govt in States, by type, program, agency, and State, FY88, annual rpt, 2464–2

Homeless persons housing and food aid under HUD and FEMA programs, funding and operations, FY87-88, GAO rpt, 26113–411

Labor unions recognized in Fed Govt, agreements and membership by agency and facility, as of Jan 1989, biennial listing, 9844–14

Federal employees

Advisory committees of Fed Govt, and members, staff, meetings, and costs by agency, FY88, annual rpt, 9454–18

Air traffic control and airway facilities improvement activities under Natl Airspace System Plan, 1981-85 and projected to 2000, annual rpt, 7504–12

Air traffic control and airway facilities staff, by selected employment and demographic characteristics, FY88, annual rpt, 7504–41

Air traffic control system safety, working conditions, and traffic volume, various periods 1981-88, GAO rpt series, 26113–220

Assaults and deaths of law enforcement officers, by circumstances, agency, victim and offender characteristics, and location, 1988, annual rpt, 6224–3

Budget of US Appendix, obligations, appropriations, and personnel, by program and agency, FY90, annual rpt, 104–3

Budget of US, CBO analysis of revenue and spending alternatives and projections of economic indicators, FY90-94, annual rpt, 26304–3

Budget of US, compact budgets by activity, function, and agency, FY90 and projected to FY94, annual rpt, 104–2

Budget of US, overview, FY90, annual rpt, 104–6

Budget of US, Reagan Admin policy changes by program, FY90, annual rpt, 104–21

Budget of US, special analysis of Federal employment and compensation, FY90, annual rpt, 104–1.9

Corrupt govt officials prosecuted and convicted, by judicial district and level of govt, 1978-88, annual rpt, 6004–13

Cost control proposals for Fed Govt mgmt, Reagan Admin initiatives, savings, and status, FY85-94, annual rpt, 104–23

Criminal justice spending, employment, and payroll, by level of govt, State, and selected city and county, FY71-85, annual rpt, 6064–9

Disabled persons employment and architectural barrier removal laws, Federal and State govt compliance, findings and recommendations, 1989 rpt, 10048–74

Discrimination in employment, complaints, and awards by funding source, for 3 Federal agencies, FY87-88, GAO rpt, 26121–313

DOD military and civilian personnel, and vacancies, for NATO Europe countries, by service branch, 1988, GAO rpt, 26123–251

Employment (civilian) of Fed Govt by occupation, agency, and location, and language and math skill needs, 1966-87 and projected to 2000, 9848–37

Employment (civilian) of Fed Govt, work-years, pay rates, and benefits use and costs, by agency, FY87, annual rpt, 9844–31

Employment and payroll (civilian) of Fed Govt, by agency in DC metro area, total US, and abroad, bimonthly rpt, 9842–1

Employment and payroll (civilian) of Fed Govt, by occupation, pay grade, sex, agency, and location, 1987, biennial rpt, 9844–4

Employment and payroll (civilian) of Fed Govt, by pay system, agency, and location, 1988, annual rpt, 9844–6

Employment and payroll, by function, level of govt, and State, 1988, annual rpt, 2466–1.1; 2466–1.5

Employment, earnings, and hours, by selected SIC 1- to 4-digit industry, State, and for 262 MSAs, 1972-87, 6748–81

Employment, earnings, and hours, by SIC 1- to 4-digit industry, monthly 1983-Feb 1989, annual rpt, 6744–4

Employment situation, earnings, hours, and other BLS economic indicators, transcripts of BLS Commissioner's monthly testimony, periodic rpt, 23846–4

Exchange of employees between Fed Govt and other organizations, program activities and costs, with data by agency, FY84-88, GAO rpt, 26119–260

Health Care Financing Review, provider prices, price inputs and indexes, and labor, quarterly journal, 4652–1.1

Immigrants admitted to US, by class and country, FY82-88, annual rpt, 6264–2

Insurance (health) for Federal employees and annuitants, enrollment, costs, and Medicare coverage, with data for selected plans, 1980-89, 21628–73

Judicial personnel, by position, June 1988-89, annual rpt, 18204–2.7; 18204–8.7

Labor productivity of Federal employees, indexes of output and labor costs by function, FY67-87, annual rpt, 6824–1.6

Law enforcement personnel and hiring of Fed Govt, by agency, 1982-FY87, GAO rpt, 26119–242

Law enforcement spending and employment, by activity and level of govt, 1970s-88, annual rpt, 6064–6.1

Military reserve spouses attitudes, and family social, economic, and other characteristics, 1986 survey, 3508–30

Minority group and women employment of Fed Govt by occupation, and handicapped employment, by agency, FY87, annual rpt, 9244–10

Minority group, handicapped, and veteran employment in Fed Govt, and years of service, by occupation, age, sex, and agency, as of Sept 1988, biennial rpt, 9844–27

Productivity improvement program of Fed Govt, coverage and impacts by function for selected agencies, FY86-87 and projected to 1992, 26306–3.103

Radiation exposure of Federal employees, by age, occupation, and selected agency, 1986-87, biennial rpt, 4064–15

Royalties and incentive payments to Fed Govt R&D lab employees, by agency, FY87-88, GAO rpt, 26113–422

Science and engineering employment characteristics, by field, 1988, biennial rpt, 9627–16

Science and engineering employment in Fed Govt, by field, degree level, race, sex, agency, and State, 1987, annual rpt, 9627–5

Science and engineering labor force, Federal and university research funding, and educational data, series, 9626–6

Science and engineering labor supply by region and employment characteristics, and salaries by years of experience, 1987, 9626–2.184

Science and engineering PhDs employment and other characteristics, by field and State, 1987, biennial rpt, 9627–18

Security clearance of Fed Govt and contractor employees, polygraph use, prepublication reviews, and unauthorized disclosures and investigations, 1986-88, GAO rpt, 26123–66

Senior Executive Service career position longterm vacancies, by reason and agency, 1989, GAO rpt, 26119–252

Senior Executive Service former members reasons for leaving, and views on SES statutory compliance, 1988 survey, 9498–3

Senior Executive Service membership characteristics, entries, exits, and awards, FY80-1987, annual rpt, 9844–36

Senior Executive Service training and dev program activities, participant views, 1987 survey, GAO rpt, 26119–272

Service contracts of Fed Govt compared with work performed in-house, savings and employment effects by agency, 1978-87, GAO rpt, 26119–238

Services transfer from govts to private contractors, impacts on govt workers, with data by worker characteristics, level of govt, and location, 1980s-87, 15496–1.5

Southwestern States employment by industry div, earnings, and hours, by State, monthly rpt, 6962–2

Statistical Abstract of US, social, political, and economic data, 1790-2025, comprehensive annual compilation, 2324–1.2

Temporary employment in Fed Govt, appointments and extensions, by occupational group, 1983-87, GAO rpt, 26119–129

Travel expenses of Fed Govt employees, operating costs for private autos and reimbursement rates for business use, 1988, annual rpt, 9454–13

Unemployment insurance claims, by program, weekly press release, 6402–14

Unemployment insurance coverage of establishments, employment, and wages, by SIC 4-digit industry and State, 1988, annual rpt, 6744–16

Veterans (disabled) employment and promotion in Fed Govt by agency, and recruitment coordinator activities, FY81-87, GAO rpt, 26119–245

Vietnam Orderly Departure Program, former Fed Govt employees arrivals in US and refugee camps, monthly rpt, 7002–4

Weather services activities and funding, by Federal agency, planned FY89-90, annual rpt, 2144–2

Workers compensation coverage and benefits, by type of program and insurer, and State, 1985-86, annual article, 4742–1.912

Workers compensation laws of States and Fed Govt, 1989 semiannual rpt, 6502–1

see also Civil service pensions
see also Civil service system
see also Congressional employees
see also Diplomatic and consular service
see also Federal pay
see also Labor-management relations in government
see also Military personnel
see also Postal employees
see also Presidential appointments
see also under names of individual Federal departments and agencies

Federal Energy Administration
see Department of Energy

Federal Energy Regulatory Commission
Activities of FERC, licensing, and rate regulation, FY88, annual rpt, 3084–9

Electric power plants certification applications filed with FERC, for small production and cogeneration facilities, FY80-88, annual listing, 3084–13

Hydroelectric power plants capacity, dev status, and ownership, by State and river basin, as of Jan 1988, quadrennial rpt, 3088–14

Hydroelectric power plants retired, characteristics and location, as of 1989, annual listing, 3084–12

Labor unions recognized in Fed Govt, agreements and membership by agency and facility, as of Jan 1989, biennial listing, 9844–14

Federal executive departments
Budget of US Appendix, obligations, appropriations, and personnel, by program and agency, FY90, annual rpt, 104–3

Budget of US, compact budgets by activity, function, and agency, FY90 and projected to FY94, annual rpt, 104–2

Budget of US, object class analysis of obligations, by agency, FY90, annual rpt, 104–9

Budget of US, receipts by source, outlays by agency and program, and balances, monthly rpt, 8102–3

Budget of US, special analyses by activity, function, and agency, FY90, annual rpt, 104–1

Congressional Directory, members of 101st Congress, other officials, elections, and districts, 1989-90, biennial rpt, 23874–1

Employment (civilian) of Fed Govt, work-years, pay rates, and benefits use and costs, by agency, FY87, annual rpt, 9844–31

Employment and payroll (civilian) of Fed Govt, by agency in DC metro area, total US, and abroad, bimonthly rpt, 9842–1

Financial consolidated statements of Fed Govt based on business accounting methods, FY87-88, annual rpt, 8104–5

Financial operations of Fed Govt, detailed data, *Treasury Bulletin*, quarterly rpt, 8002–4

Labor unions recognized in Fed Govt, agreements and membership by agency and facility, as of Jan 1989, biennial listing, 9844–14

see also Federal boards, committees, and commissions

see also Federal independent agencies

see also under By Federal Agency in the "Index by Categories"

see also under names of individual Federal departments and agencies

Federal expenditures

see Budget of the U.S.

see Defense expenditures

see Government contracts and procurement

see Government spending

see terms beginning with Federal aid and Federal funding

Federal Financial Institutions Examination Council

Banks (insured commercial) assets, income, and financial ratios, by asset size and State, quarterly rpt, 13002–3

Financial statements of FFIEC, and bank and thrift finances by instn type, 1988, annual rpt, 13004–2

Loans of US banks to foreigners at all US and foreign offices, by country group and country, quarterly rpt, 13002–1

Trust assets of banks, trust companies, and S&Ls, by type of asset and fund, selected firm, and State, 1988, annual rpt, 13004–1

Federal Financing Bank

Budget of US Appendix, obligations, appropriations, and personnel, by program and agency, FY90, annual rpt, 104–3

Finances and operations of programs under Ways and Means Committee jurisdiction, FY70s-88, annual rpt, 21784–11

Holdings and transactions of Fed Financing Bank, by borrower, monthly press release, 12802–1

Liabilities (contingent) and claims paid by Fed Govt on federally insured and guaranteed contracts with foreign obligors, by country and program, periodic rpt, 8002–12

Loans of Bank outstanding, and loan prepayment activity and costs, 1985-88, GAO rpt, 26111–63

Federal funding for energy programs

Agricultural research and education grants, USDA competitive awards by program and recipient, FY88, annual listing, 1764–1

Alcohol fuels (ethanol) production costs and Federal loan guarantees, 1987-88, 1588–132

Assistance (block and categorical grants) programs for State and local govts, FY89, biennial listing, 10044–8

Assistance (financial and nonfinancial) of Fed Govt, 1989 base edition with supplements, annual listing, 104–5

Auto engine and power train R&D projects, DOE contracts and funding by recipient, FY88, annual rpt, 3304–17

Autos powered by electricity, R&D activity and DOE funding shares, FY88, annual rpt, 3304–2

Budget deficit reduction under Gramm-Rudman Act, cancellation of budget authority by program, FY90, annual rpt, 104–27; 26304–6

Budget of US Appendix, obligations, appropriations, and personnel, by program and agency, FY90, annual rpt, 104–3

Budget of US, balances of budget authority obligated and unobligated, by function and agency, FY88-90, annual rpt, 104–8

Budget of US, CBO analysis of revenue and spending alternatives and projections of economic indicators, FY90-94, annual rpt, 26304–3

Budget of US, compact budgets by activity, function, and agency, FY90 and projected to FY94, annual rpt, 104–2

Budget of US, historical data, selected years FY34-88 and projected to FY94, annual rpt, 104–22

Budget of US, House concurrent resolution, with spending and revenue targets, FY90, annual rpt, 21264–2

Budget of US, midsession review of FY90 budget, by function and agency, annual rpt, 104–7

Budget of US, Reagan Admin policy changes by program, FY90, annual rpt, 104–21

Budget of US, receipts by source, outlays by agency and program, and balances, monthly rpt, 8102–3

Budget of US, Senate concurrent resolution, with spending and revenue targets, FY90, annual rpt, 25254–1

Budget of US, special analysis of Federal capital spending by category, projected FY89-2005 and trends from FY81, annual rpt, 104–24

Conservation aid of DOE, activities, funding, and grants by State, by program, FY88 annual rpt, 3304–21

Conservation grants of Fed Govt to public and nonprofit private instns, by building type and State, 1988, annual rpt, 3304–15

Conservation R&D spending of DOE and private sector, and housing natural gas use indicators, hearings, 21368–107

Contracts and grants of DOE, by category, State, and for top contractors, FY88, annual rpt, 3004–21

DOE activities and finances, summary energy supply and demand data, and bibl, 1987, annual rpt, 3024–2

DOE budget authority, by program and subagency, annual rpt, discontinued, 3004–14

Expenditures for R&D by Fed Govt, by detailed function, program, and agency, FY88-90, annual rpt, 9627–9

Expenditures for R&D by Fed Govt, by field, performer type, agency, and State, FY87-89, annual rpt, 9627–20

Expenditures of Fed Govt in States, by type, program, agency, and State, FY88, annual rpt, 2464–2

Finances of Fed Govt, cash and debt transactions, daily tables, 8102–4

Finances of govts, revenues by source and spending by function, natl income and product account, *Survey of Current Business*, monthly rpt, 2702–1.24

Fraud and abuse in DOE programs, audits and investigations, 2nd half FY89, semiannual rpt, 3002–12

HHS financial aid, by program, recipient, State, and city, FY88, annual regional listings, 4004–3

Housing (low income) energy aid, by type of aid and State, 1982-87, annual rpt, 4744–3.8

Housing energy aid, beneficiary households by aid type, FY88, article, 4742–1.921

Hydrogen energy R&D activity and funding of DOE, and project listing, FY88, annual rpt, 3304–18

Inventions recommended by Natl Inst of Standards and Technology for DOE support, awards, and evaluation status, 1988, annual listing, 2214–5

Inventions supported by DOE, sales, jobs created, and inventor characteristics, 1980-86, 3308–91

Loans and loan guarantees of of Fed Govt, outstanding amounts by agency and program, *Treasury Bulletin*, quarterly rpt, 8002–4.9

Nuclear power plant safety standards and research, design, licensing, construction, operation, and finances, with data by reactor, quarterly journal, 3352–4

Nuclear Regulatory Commission budget, staff, and activities, by program, FY88-91, annual rpt, 9634–9

Nuclear Waste Fund finances, and DOE Civilian Radioactive Waste Mgmt Office activities, quarterly GAO rpt, 26102–4

Nuclear Waste Fund finances, and DOE Civilian Radioactive Waste Mgmt Office project budgets alternative projections, quarterly rpt, 3362–1

Oil enhanced recovery research contracts of DOE, project summaries, funding, and bibl, quarterly rpt, 3002–14

Procurement contract awards of Fed Govt, by State, agency, procurement and contractor type, and for top 100 contractors, quarterly rpt, 102–6

R&D funding by Fed Govt at large science facilities, by field, performer, and facility, FY86-88, hearings, 21708–128

R&D projects and funding of DOE at natl labs, universities, and other instns, periodic summary rpt series, 3004–18

Radioactive waste from DOE military activities, disposal plans and funding, FY87-93, last issue of annual rpt, 3344–1

Rural Electrification Admin loans, and borrower operating and financial data, by distribution firm and State, 1988, annual rpt, 1244–1

Small business R&D grants of Fed Govt, by program area, agency, and State, FY88, annual rpt, 9764–7

Ocean pollution research, monitoring, and resources dev activities of Fed Govt, funding and project descriptions, FY87, annual rpt, 2144-23

Ocean pollution research, monitoring, and resources dev activities of Fed Govt, 5-year plan and funding by agency, FY84-89, triennial rpt, 2148-56

Population and reproduction research, Fed Govt funding by project, FY87, annual listing, 4474-9

Procurement contract awards of Fed Govt, by State, agency, procurement and contractor type, and for top 100 contractors, quarterly rpt, 102-6

Property (real) of Fed Govt, inventory and costs, worldwide summary by location, agency, and use, 1987, annual rpt, 9454-5

Science and engineering grad enrollment, by field, source of funds, and characteristics of student and instn, 1975-87, annual rpt, 9627-7

Science and engineering PhDs employment and other characteristics, by field and State, 1987, biennial rpt, 9627-18

Small business R&D grants of Fed Govt, administrators views on effectiveness, FY86-87, GAO rpt, 26113-393

Small business R&D grants of Fed Govt, by program area, agency, and State, FY88, annual rpt, 9764-7

Smithsonian Instn activities and finances, FY88, annual rpt, 29574-1

Space program funding by NASA and DOD, by category, FY81-89, GAO rpt, 26123-152

Statistical Abstract of US, social, political, and economic data, 1790-2025, comprehensive annual compilation, 2324-1.3

Superconductivity (high temperature) R&D spending by Federal agency, and US and Japan industry funding and employment, by application, 1981-89, hearing, 25408-100

Tax expenditures, Federal revenues forgone through income tax deductions and exclusions by type, FY90-94, annual rpt, 21784-10

Technology Assessment Office activities and rpts, FY88, annual rpt, 26354-3

Technology transfer by Fed Govt R&D labs, cooperative agreements, royalties, and incentive payments to employees, by agency, FY87-88, GAO rpt, 26113-422

Telecommunications and Info Natl Admin rpts, FY88, annual listing, 2804-3

Transportation R&D spending, by Federal agency and transport mode, selected years 1970-88, annual rpt, 7304-2.2

Urban Mass Transportation Admin R&D projects and funding, FY88, annual listing, 7884-1

Urban Mass Transportation Admin research and training grants to higher education instns, by project, FY88, annual listing, 7884-7

Weather research, monitoring, and impact assessment activities of Fed Govt, and funding by agency, FY87, annual rpt, 2144-17

Weather services activities and funding, by Federal agency, planned FY89-90, annual rpt, 2144-2

Wildlife research of State fish and wildlife agencies, federally funded projects and costs by species and State, 1989, annual listing, 5504-24

see also Defense research

see also Department of Energy National Laboratories

see also Federal aid to medicine

see also Federal funding for energy programs

see also Federally Funded R&D Centers

Federal Grain Inspection Service

Activities and finances of FGIS, domestic and export inspections, foreign buyers complaints, and handling facilities explosions, FY88, annual rpt, 1294-1

Budget of US Appendix, obligations, appropriations, and personnel, by program and agency, FY90, annual rpt, 104-3

Export of grains, inspection results by commodity and port region, 1988, annual rpt, 1294-2

Feed grain inspected for export, current and proposed quality standards, 1989 article, 1561-4.904

Inspection of grain, test results by commodity and State, 1988, annual rpt series, 1294-3

Soybeans inspected for export, current and proposed quality standards, 1989 article, 1561-3.903

Federal grants

see terms beginning with Federal aid and Federal funding

Federal Highway Administration

Activities of FHwA, funding, and inspections, FY85, annual rpt, 7304-1

Budget of US Appendix, obligations, appropriations, and personnel, by program and agency, FY90, annual rpt, 104-3

Construction bids and contracts for Federal-aid hwys, by State, 1st half 1989, semiannual rpt, 7552-12

Construction material prices and indexes for Federal-aid hwy system, by type of material and urban-rural location, quarterly rpt, 7552-7

Construction material prices and indexes for Federal-aid hwy system, by type of material, quarterly press release, 7552-16

Construction material use by type, and spending for hwys, by State, various periods 1944-88, annual rpt, 7554-29

Drivers licenses issued and in force by age and sex, fees, and renewal, by license class and State, 1987, annual rpt, 7554-16

Employment of DOT, by subagency, occupation, and selected personnel characteristics, FY88, annual rpt, 7304-18

Expenditures, costs, and completion status of Federal-aid hwy system, by State, as of June 1989, semiannual rpt, 7552-5

Expenditures of Fed Govt in States, by type, program, agency, and State, FY88, annual rpt, 2464-2

Gasoline and fuel oil retail prices and sales, EIA and alternative estimates 1984-88, article, 3162-11.903

Gasoline and other motor fuel tax rates, by State, 1978-87, annual table, 7554-32

Gasoline and other motor fuel use and tax rates, by State, monthly rpt, 7552-1

Hwy and bridge conditions, travel, and funding, by type of hwy, 1960s-87 and projected to 2005, biennial rpt, 7554-27

Hwy Statistics, detailed data by State, 1988, annual rpt, 7554-1

Hwy Statistics, summary data by State, 1987-88, annual rpt, 7554-24

Minority- and women-owned businesses awards for Federal-aid hwy construction, FHwA and State reviews, FY83-87, GAO rpt, 26113-389

R&D for hwy design and construction, quarterly journal, 7552-3

Railroad-hwy grade-crossing warning devices, costs and effectiveness of alternative devices, local area study, 1985-86, 7558-108

Safety program funding, and accident and death reductions, by State, FY88, annual rpt, 7554-26

Safety program funding by Fed Govt, by programs and State, quarterly rpt, discontinued, 7552-9

Speed averages and vehicles exceeding 55 mph, by State, quarterly rpt, 7552-14

Traffic volume on rural roads and city streets, monthly rpt, 7552-8

Federal Home Loan Bank Board

Budget of US Appendix, obligations, appropriations, and personnel, by program and agency, FY90, annual rpt, 104-3

Budget of US, authoritative financial statements with appropriations, outlays, and receipts, by category and agency, FY88, annual rpt, 8104-2.2

Finances and operations of FHLB system and members, and savings instns regulatory issues and mgmt, monthly journal, 9312-1

Financial and operating performance of FHLBB, FSLIC, Financing Corp, and district banks, annual rpt, issuing agency change, 9314-7

Financial condition of FHLBs, bonds issued and outstanding, bond rates, and members, monthly press release, discontinued, 9312-8

Financial statements of FHLBB, FSLIC, Financing Corp, and FHLBs, 1988, annual rpt, 8434-2

Fraud and insider misconduct at financial instns, cases, Federal regulatory and enforcement activities, and losses, 1981-87, hearing, 21408-111

Housing finance studies, technical paper series, 9316-1

Labor unions recognized in Fed Govt, agreements and membership by agency and facility, as of Jan 1989, biennial listing, 9844-14

Members of Fed Home Loan Bank System, and assets, 1988, annual listing, 9314-5

Mortgage terms on conventional loans closed, and commitment rates, by type of loan and lender and for 32 SMSAs, monthly rpt, 9312-2

New England States, thrift instn FHLB advances, by type of instn and Fed deposit insurance, and State, 1987, annual rpt, 9304-3

R&D funding by Fed Govt, by field, performer type, agency, and State, FY87-89, annual rpt, 9627-20

Savings and loan assns assets and liabilities, by FHLB district and State, 1987 and trends from 1930, annual rpt, 9314-1

Savings instns (FSLIC-insured) assets, liabilities, and deposit and loan activity, and compared to all S&Ls, monthly rpt, 9312-4

Federal Home Loan Mortgage Corp.

Budget of US Appendix, financial statements of federally sponsored enterprises, FY90, annual rpt, 104–3.4

Financial statements and activities of FHLMC, 1988, annual rpt, 9414–1

Mortgage debt outstanding by purpose and holder type, 1977-87, annual rpt, 9314–3.3

Mortgage terms and yields, secondary market activity, and debt outstanding, 1984-87, annual rpt, 9364–5.7

Securities backed by mortgages, corporate and union pension funds and life insurance firms investments, by issuer, quarterly rpt, 5002–10

Securities backed by mortgages issued through private and govt issuers, 1984-88, article, 9362–1.909

Federal Housing Administration

see Housing (FHA), HUD

Federal Housing Finance Board

Financial statements of FHLBs, monthly rpt, 9442–1

Federal independent agencies

Budget deficit reduction under Gramm-Rudman Act, cancellation of budget authority by program, FY90, annual rpt, 104–27; 21924–1; 26304–6

Budget of US Appendix, obligations, appropriations, and personnel, by program and agency, FY90, annual rpt, 104–3

Budget of US, authoritative financial statements with appropriations, outlays, and receipts, by category and agency, FY88, annual rpt, 8104–2.2

Budget of US, compact budgets by activity, function, and agency, FY90 and projected to FY94, annual rpt, 104–2

Budget of US, object class analysis of obligations, by agency, FY90, annual rpt, 104–9

Budget of US, receipts by source, outlays by agency and program, and balances, monthly rpt, 8102–3

Budget of US, special analyses by activity, function, and agency, FY90, annual rpt, 104–1

Congressional Directory, members of 101st Congress, other officials, elections, and districts, 1989-90, biennial rpt, 23874–1

Education funding by Federal agency, program, and recipient type, and instn spending, FY80-88, 4828–21

Employment (civilian) of Fed Govt, work-years, pay rates, and benefits use and costs, by agency, FY87, annual rpt, 9844–31

Employment and payroll (civilian) of Fed Govt, by agency in DC metro area, total US, and abroad, bimonthly rpt, 9842–1

Financial consolidated statements of Fed Govt based on business accounting methods, FY87-88, annual rpt, 8104–5

Financial operations of Fed Govt, detailed data, *Treasury Bulletin*, quarterly rpt, 8002–4

Flow-of-funds accounts, savings, investments, and credit statements, quarterly rpt, 9365–3.3

Labor unions recognized in Fed Govt, agreements and membership by agency and facility, as of Jan 1989, biennial listing, 9844–14

see also ACTION
see also Administrative Conference of the U.S.
see also Advisory Council on Historic Preservation
see also American Battle Monuments Commission
see also Appalachian Regional Commission
see also Central Intelligence Agency
see also Commission of Fine Arts
see also Consumer Product Safety Commission
see also Environmental Protection Agency
see also Equal Employment Opportunity Commission
see also Export-Import Bank
see also Farm Credit Administration
see also Federal boards, committees, and commissions
see also Federal Communications Commission
see also Federal Deposit Insurance Corp.
see also Federal Emergency Management Agency
see also Federal Home Loan Bank Board
see also Federal Housing Finance Board
see also Federal Maritime Commission
see also Federal Mediation and Conciliation Service
see also Federal Reserve System
see also Federal Trade Commission
see also General Services Administration
see also Government corporations and enterprises
see also Interstate Commerce Commission
see also Merit Systems Protection Board
see also National Aeronautics and Space Administration
see also National Archives and Records Administration
see also National Credit Union Administration
see also National Foundation on the Arts and the Humanities
see also National Labor Relations Board
see also National Mediation Board
see also National Railroad Adjustment Board
see also National Science Foundation
see also National Transportation Safety Board
see also Neighborhood Reinvestment Corp.
see also Nuclear Regulatory Commission
see also Occupational Safety and Health Review Commission
see also Office of Personnel Management
see also Panama Canal Commission
see also Peace Corps
see also Railroad Retirement Board
see also Resolution Trust Corp.
see also Securities and Exchange Commission
see also Selective Service System
see also Small Business Administration
see also Tennessee Valley Authority
see also U.S. Arms Control and Disarmament Agency
see also U.S. Information Agency
see also U.S. International Development Cooperation Agency
see also U.S. International Trade Commission
see also U.S. Postal Service
see also Veterans Administration

see also under By Federal Agency in the "Index by Categories"

Federal Inspectors General reports

Activities of Inspectors General, and fraud and abuse audits and investigations by agency, FY88, annual rpt, 104–29

Activities of Inspectors General, and fraud and abuse audits and investigations by agency, 2nd half FY87, semiannual rpt, 102–5

Commerce Dept programs fraud and abuse, audits and investigations, 2nd half FY89, semiannual rpt, 2002–5

DOD programs fraud and abuse, audits and investigations, 1st half FY89, semiannual rpt, 3542–18

DOE programs fraud and abuse, audits and investigations, 2nd half FY89, semiannual rpt, 3002–12

DOT programs fraud and abuse, audits and investigations, 2nd half FY89, semiannual rpt, 7302–4

Education Dept programs fraud and abuse, audits and investigations, 2nd half FY89, semiannual rpt, 4802–1

EPA programs fraud and abuse, audits and investigations, 2nd half FY89, semiannual rpt, 9182–10

GSA programs fraud and abuse, audits and investigations, 2nd half FY89, semiannual rpt, 9452–8

Health care professionals licensing and disciplinary actions of State medical boards, 1950s-87, series, 4006–8

HHS programs fraud and abuse, audits and investigations, 2nd half FY89, semiannual rpt, 4002–6

Hospital closures in 1987, operating characteristics, current use, and location, 1989 rpt, 4008–87

HUD programs fraud and abuse, audits and investigations, 2nd half FY89, semiannual rpt, 5002–8; 5002–11

Interior Dept programs fraud and abuse, audits and investigations, 2nd half FY89, semiannual rpt, 5302–2

Labor Dept programs fraud and abuse, audits and investigations, 2nd half FY89, semiannual rpt, 6302–2

NASA programs fraud and abuse, audits and investigations, 1st half FY89, semiannual rpt, 9502–9

NIH research contract awards to higher education instns, and research staff, related charges, and time allocated to projects, 1984-88, 4008–89

Nursing chief officers in hospitals, activities, responsibilities, and role in nurse hiring and retention, 1988 survey, 4008–91

Physicians ownership of labs and medical equipment services, referrals to own businesses, and excess Medicare costs from referrals, 1987, 4008–90

Small Business Admin programs fraud and abuse, audits and investigations, 1st half FY89, semiannual rpt, 9762–5

State Dept programs fraud and abuse, audits and investigations, 2nd half FY89, semiannual rpt, 7002–6

Surgeries performed in rural hospitals by itinerant surgeons, quality of care issues and Medicare overpayments, 1985-86, 4008–93

USDA programs fraud and abuse, audits and investigations, 2nd half FY89, semiannual rpt, 1002–4

VA programs fraud and abuse, audits and investigations, 2nd half FY89, semiannual rpt, 8602–1

Veterans rehabilitation program admin, and participants earnings and tax liability before and after training, 1988 hearing, 25768–48

Virgin Islands govt fiscal condition, annual rpt, discontinued, 5304–10

Federal Intermediate Credit Banks
see Farm Credit System

Federal Judicial Center
Bankruptcy court mediation program caseloads and dispositions, for California southern district, 1986-88, 18408–40

Budget of US Appendix, obligations, appropriations, and personnel, by program and agency, FY90, annual rpt, 104–3

Budget of US, authoritative financial statements with appropriations, outlays, and receipts, by category and agency, FY88, annual rpt, 8104–2.2

Federal Labor Relations Authority
Activities of FLRA and Fed Service Impasses Panel, and cases by union, agency, and State, FY79-87, annual rpt, 13364–1

Budget of US Appendix, obligations, appropriations, and personnel, by program and agency, FY90, annual rpt, 104–3

Budget of US, authoritative financial statements with appropriations, outlays, and receipts, by category and agency, FY88, annual rpt, 8104–2.2

Federal land banks
see Farm Credit System

Federal lands
see Government supplies and property
see Military bases, posts, and reservations
see Public lands

Federal-local relations
Army Corps of Engineers activities and projects, FY87 and trends from 1800s, annual rpt, 3754–1.2

Army Corps of Engineers water resources dev projects, characteristics, and costs, 1950s-87, biennial State rpt series, 3756–2

Army Corps of Engineers water resources dev projects, characteristics, and costs, 1950s-89, biennial State rpt series, 3756–1

Hazardous waste site remedial action under Superfund, deadlines and compliance of govts and businesses, as of Mar 1989, GAO rpt, 26113–394

Historic and natural natl landmarks damaged and threatened, with owner, location, damage type, and recommended remedial action, 1988, annual listing, 5544–16

see also Federal aid to local areas
see also Revenue sharing

Federal Maritime Commission
Activities of FMC, case filings by type and disposition, and civil penalties by shipper, FY88, annual rpt, 9334–1

Budget of US Appendix, obligations, appropriations, and personnel, by program and agency, FY90, annual rpt, 104–3

Budget of US, authoritative financial statements with appropriations, outlays, and receipts, by category and agency, FY88, annual rpt, 8104–2.2

Federal Mediation and Conciliation Service
Activities of FMCS, and cases by issue, region, and State, FY82-87, annual rpt, 9344–1

Budget of US Appendix, obligations, appropriations, and personnel, by program and agency, FY90, annual rpt, 104–3

Budget of US, authoritative financial statements with appropriations, outlays, and receipts, by category and agency, FY88, annual rpt, 8104–2.2

Labor unions recognized in Fed Govt, agreements and membership by agency and facility, as of Jan 1989, biennial listing, 9844–14

Federal Mine Safety and Health Act
Enforcement of mine safety and health, training, and funding, with casualties, by type of mine and State, FY87, annual rpt, 6664–6

Federal Mine Safety and Health Review Commission
Budget of US Appendix, obligations, appropriations, and personnel, by program and agency, FY90, annual rpt, 104–3

Budget of US, authoritative financial statements with appropriations, outlays, and receipts, by category and agency, FY88, annual rpt, 8104–2.2

Federal National Mortgage Association
Budget of US Appendix, financial statements of federally sponsored enterprises, FY90, annual rpt, 104–3.4

Mortgage debt outstanding by purpose and holder type, 1977-87, annual rpt, 9314–3.3

Mortgage terms and yields, secondary market activity, and debt outstanding, 1984-87, annual rpt, 9364–5.7

Securities backed by mortgages, corporate and union pension funds and life insurance firms investments, by issuer, quarterly rpt, 5002–10

Securities backed by mortgages, Fed Natl Mortgage Assn pools prepayment rates, Jan 1987-June 1988, article, 9381–1.905

Securities backed by mortgages issued through private and govt issuers, 1984-88, article, 9362–1.909

Federal officials
see Officials

Federal Open Market Committee
Fed Reserve Board and Reserve banks finances, staff, and review of monetary policy and economic devs, 1988, annual rpt, 9364–1

Monetary aggregates growth and related devs, and Fed Open Market Committee activity, annual article, 9385–1

Monetary aggregates targeted and actual growth, and Fed funds rate, 1987-89, annual article, 9391–1.908

Policies and transactions, *Fed Reserve Bulletin*, monthly rpt with articles, 9362–1

Federal pay
Advisory committees of Fed Govt, and members, staff, meetings, and costs by agency, FY88, annual rpt, 9454–18

Budget of US Appendix, obligations, appropriations, and personnel, by program and agency, FY90, annual rpt, 104–3

Budget of US, authoritative financial statements with appropriations, outlays, and receipts, by category and agency, FY88, annual rpt, 8104–2.2

Budget of US, historical data, selected years FY34-88 and projected to FY94, annual rpt, 104–22

Budget of US, object class analysis of obligations, by agency, FY90, annual rpt, 104–9

Budget of US, special analysis of Federal employment and compensation, FY90, annual rpt, 104–1.9

Criminal justice spending, employment, and payroll, by level of govt, State, and selected city and county, FY71-85, annual rpt, 6064–9

Earnings by industry div, and personal income per capita and by source, by State, MSA, and county, 1982-87, annual regional rpts, 2704–2

Earnings by major industry group, and personal income per capita and by source, by region and State, 1929-87, 2708–40

Executive exchange program of Fed Govt and private sector, host and participant views on experimental payment provisions, 1988-89 survey, GAO rpt, 26119–249

Finances of Fed Govt, cash and debt transactions, daily tables, 8102–4

Financial consolidated statements of Fed Govt based on business accounting methods, FY87-88, annual rpt, 8104–5

House of Representatives salaries, expenses, and contingent fund disbursement, detailed listings, quarterly rpt, 21942–1

Incentive awards to Federal employees, costs, and benefits, by award type and agency, FY88, annual rpt, 9844–20

Income (household, family, and personal), by source, detailed characteristics, and region, 1987, annual Current Population Rpt, 2546–6.59

Insurance (health) for Federal employees, State taxes on plan underwriters, 1987, GAO rpt, 26119–262

Law enforcement spending and employment, by activity and level of govt, 1970s-88, annual rpt, 6064–6.1

Merit system oversight and enforcement activities of OPM, series, 9496–2

Minority group and women employment of Fed Govt, by pay grade, 1976-86, 9848–37

Natl income and product accounts and components, *Survey of Current Business*, monthly rpt, 2702–1.21

Natl income and product accounts govt transactions component estimates, methodology and bibl, 1988 technical rpt, 2706–6.5

Pay comparability of Fed Govt with private industry, and recommended and actual pay adjustments, 1970s-89, annual rpt, 10104–1

Pay comparability of Fed Govt with private industry, and recommended pay rate adjustments, 1989, annual rpt, 104–16

Pay rates, employment, work-years, and benefits use and costs, by agency, FY87, annual rpt, 9844–31

Pay rates of Fed Govt civilian employees, by pay schedule and grade, 1989 and trends from 1789, annual rpt, 21624–4

Payroll and employment (civilian) of Fed Govt, by agency in DC metro area, total US, and abroad, bimonthly rpt, 9842–1

Financial and economic analysis of banking and nonbanking sectors, working paper series, 9381–10

Financial and economic devs, monthly journal, 9381–1

Financial and monetary studies, conf series, 9381–13

Financial statements of Bank, 1987-88, annual rpt, 9381–3

Federal Reserve Bank of Minneapolis

Business and economic conditions, Fed Reserve 9th District, quarterly journal, 9383–19

Economic conditions, Fed Reserve 9th District, quarterly rpt, 9383–18

Farm credit conditions, earnings, and expenses, Fed Reserve 9th District, quarterly rpt, 9383–11

Financial and economic devs, quarterly journal, 9383–6

Financial statements of Bank, 1987-88, annual rpt, 9383–2

Federal Reserve Bank of New York

Capital flows (intl) impacts on monetary policy instruments, and financial and economic indicators, 1987 compilation of papers, 9385–9

Financial and economic analysis, technical paper series, 9385–8

Financial and economic devs, quarterly journal, 9385–1

Financial statements of Bank, 1987-88, annual rpt, 9385–2

Federal Reserve Bank of Philadelphia

Economic conditions, Fed Reserve 3rd District, quarterly rpt, 9387–10

Financial and economic devs, bimonthly journal, 9387–1

Financial and monetary research and econometric analyses, working paper series, 9387–8

Financial statements of Bank, 1987-88, annual rpt, 9387–3

Manufacturing business outlook, for Fed Reserve 3rd District, monthly survey rpt, 9387–11

Middle Atlantic States manufacturing output index, monthly rpt, 9387–12

Federal Reserve Bank of Richmond

Banks (insured commercial), Fed Reserve 5th District members financial statements, by State, quarterly rpt, 9389–18

Economic indicators by State, Fed Reserve 5th District, quarterly rpt, 9389–16

Farm credit conditions and real estate values, Fed Reserve 5th District, quarterly rpt, 9389–17

Financial and economic analysis, technical paper series, 9389–19

Financial and economic devs, bimonthly journal, 9389–1

Financial statements of Bank, 1987-88, annual rpt, 9389–2

Federal Reserve Bank of San Francisco

Financial and economic analysis, technical paper series, 9393–10

Financial and economic devs, quarterly journal, 9393–8

Financial statements of Bank, 1987-88, annual rpt, 9393–2

Federal Reserve Bank of St. Louis

Economic and banking conditions, for Fed Reserve 8th District, quarterly rpt with articles, 9391–16

Economic indicators compounded annual rates of change, monthly rpt, 9391–3

Economic indicators compounded annual rates of change, 1969-88, annual rpt, 9391–9

Financial and economic devs, bimonthly journal, 9391–1

Financial and monetary conditions, selected US summary data, weekly rpt, 9391–4

Intl transactions of US, and economic and monetary trends for US and 10 major trading partners, quarterly rpt, 9391–7

Monetary and Fed Govt budget trends, monthly rpt, 9391–2

Federal Reserve Board of Governors

Assets and debts of private sector, balance sheets by segment, 1949-88, semiannual rpt series, 9365–4

Banking and financial conditions, 1987, annual rpt, 9364–5

Budget of US Appendix, financial statements of federally sponsored enterprises, FY90, annual rpt, 104–3.4

Credit, interest rates, banking activity, bank status changes, and industrial production, monthly rpt series, 9365–2

Data concordance for *Federal Reserve Bulletin* and *Annual Statistical Digest*, 1988 annual rpt, 9364–8

Expenses and operations of Fed Reserve banks, itemized by service, office, and district, 1988, annual rpt, 9364–11

Finances and staff of Fed Reserve Board and Reserve banks, and review of monetary policy and economic devs, 1988, annual rpt, 9364–1

Financial and business detailed statistics, *Fed Reserve Bulletin*, monthly rpt with articles, 9362–1

Financial and business statistics, historic trends, 1988 annual chartbook, 9364–2

Financial and economic analysis and forecasting methodology, technical paper series, 9366–6

Financial, banking, and mortgage market activity, weekly rpt series, 9365–1

Financial instns financial and operating statements by deposit size, Fed Reserve functional cost analysis, 1988, annual rpt, 9364–6

Financial statements, performance, and fiscal services, for Fed Reserve System, Board of Governors, and district banks, 1987-89, annual rpt, 9364–10

Flow-of-funds accounts, assets and liabilities by type and economic sector, outstanding at year-end 1965-88, annual rpt, 9364–3

Flow-of-funds accounts, US banks foreign branches assets and liabilities, and agricultural credit, quarterly rpt series, 9365–3

Fraud and insider misconduct at financial instns, cases, Federal regulatory and enforcement activities, and losses, 1981-87, hearing, 21408–111

Monetary aggregates and velocities, monthly rpt, 9362–6

Monetary policy objectives of Fed Reserve, and performance of major economic indicators, as of July 1989, semiannual rpt, 9362–4

Securities credit issues of stockbrokers and other nonbank lenders, as of June 1987, annual rpt series, 9365–5

Federal Reserve System

Banking and financial conditions, 1987, annual rpt, 9364–5

Budget of US, historical data, selected years FY34-88 and projected to FY94, annual rpt, 104–22

Business statistics, detailed data for major industries and economic indicators, *Survey of Current Business*, monthly rpt, 2702–1.6

Check collection systems of Fed Reserve and private services, competition issues, finances, and operations, 1984-87, GAO rpt, 26119–255

County Business Patterns, 1987: employment, establishments, and payroll, by SIC 2- to 4-digit industry and county, annual State rpt series, 2326–8

Credit and reserves of depository instns, 1959-88, annual rpt, 204–1.5

Expenses and operations of Fed Reserve banks, itemized by service, office, and district, 1988, annual rpt, 9364–11

Finances and staff of Fed Reserve Board and Reserve banks, and review of monetary policy and economic devs, 1988, annual rpt, 9364–1

Financial and business statistics, historic trends, 1988 annual chartbook, 9364–2

Financial and operating statements of financial instns by deposit size, Fed Reserve functional cost analysis, 1988, annual rpt, 9364–6

Financial, banking, and mortgage market activity, weekly rpt series, 9365–1

Financial operations of Fed Govt, detailed data, *Treasury Bulletin*, quarterly rpt, 8002–4

Financial statements for Fed Reserve services, by service and district bank, 1987-88, article, 9362–1.908

Financial statements for Fed Reserve services, monthly rpt, periodic data, 9362–1.4

Financial statements, performance, and fiscal services, for Fed Reserve System, Board of Governors, and district banks, 1987-89, annual rpt, 9364–10

Flow-of-funds accounts, assets and liabilities by type and economic sector, outstanding at year-end 1965-88, annual rpt, 9364–3

Monetary policy objectives of Fed Reserve, and performance of major economic indicators, as of July 1989, semiannual rpt, 9362–4

Reserves and borrowings of all member banks, monthly rpt, 23842–1.5

Reserves of depository instns, reserve and margin requirements, and borrowings from Fed Reserve, monthly rpt, 9362–1.1

Statistical Abstract of US, social, political, and economic data, 1790-2025, comprehensive annual compilation, 2324–1.3

Transactions of US Treasury with Fed Reserve Banks, daily tables, 8102–4

see also Federal Open Market Committee

see also Federal Reserve Bank of Atlanta

see also Federal Reserve Bank of Boston

see also Federal Reserve Bank of Chicago

see also Federal Reserve Bank of Cleveland

see also Federal Reserve Bank of Dallas

see also Federal Reserve Bank of Kansas City

see also Federal Reserve Bank of
Minneapolis
see also Federal Reserve Bank of New York
see also Federal Reserve Bank of
Philadelphia
see also Federal Reserve Bank of Richmond
see also Federal Reserve Bank of San
Francisco
see also Federal Reserve Bank of St. Louis
see also Federal Reserve Board of Governors

Federal Savings and Loan Insurance Corp.
Assets and liabilities of S&Ls insured by
FSLIC, by FHLB district and State, 1987
and trends from 1930, annual rpt,
9314-1
Budget deficit reduction under
Gramm-Rudman Act, cancellation of
budget authority by program, FY90,
annual rpt, 104-27
Budget of US, compact budgets by activity,
function, and agency, FY90 and projected
to FY94, annual rpt, 104-2
Budget of US, Reagan Admin policy
changes by program, FY90, annual rpt,
104-21
Deposits in FSLIC-insured thrifts, and
offices, by FHLB district, State, SMSA,
and county, 1988, annual rpt, 9314-4
Failures of S&Ls, assets, and FSLIC
resolution costs and promissory notes,
with data for acquired and acquiring instn
in US and Texas, 1988 hearings,
21248-121
Failures of S&Ls, Bush Admin proposals for
resolving insolvency crisis, funding by
source and use, projected FY89-99, press
release, 8008-134
Failures of savings instns, resolution costs,
financing problems, and FSLIC and
acquiring instns tax benefits, 1988 and
projected to FY99, hearings, 21788-181
Finances of FSLIC, alternative projections
to FY94, with thrift instn failure
resolution caseloads and costs, 1970s-88,
21788-177
Finances of FSLIC and promissory notes
issued, and S&L failure resolution costs,
with data by instn, FY80s and projected
to FY99, hearing, 25258-22
Financial condition of Federal deposit
insurance funds, and of financial instns by
type, 1980s-88, GAO rpt, 26119-241
Financial statements of FHLBB, FSLIC,
Financing Corp, and FHLBs, 1988, annual
rpt, 8434-2
Financial statements of FSLIC-insured
instns, by FHLB district and State, 1988,
annual rpt, 8434-1
Insurance premiums, coverage, losses, and
reserves, for FDIC and FSLIC, 1930s-87,
technical paper, 9316-1.143
Savings instns failure resolution costs to
FSLIC by State, and instn financial
characteristics, 1979-88, technical paper,
9316-1.151
Savings instns failure resolution costs to
FSLIC for liquidation and sale, and
financial characteristics of instn, 1988,
technical paper, 8436-1.2
Savings instns failures, real estate assets
value, and disposition performance of
FSLIC, Fed Asset Disposition Assn, and
private contractors, 1988, article,
8432-2.901

Savings instns failures resolution costs to
FSLIC relation to discount rate, instn
financial characteristics, and State,
alternative model results, 1980s-88,
technical paper, 8436-1.3
Savings instns regulatory issues, mgmt, and
FHLB system and member finances and
operations, monthly journal, 8432-2;
9312-1

Federal Service Impasses Panel
see Federal Labor Relations Authority

Federal-State relations
Air pollution abatement activity of EPA,
compliance, and monitoring stations
operating status, 1987, annual rpt,
9194-4
Aliens (illegal) welfare benefits, operations
of Federal-State system to prevent
payment, State official views, 1988, GAO
rpt, 26121-276
Cattle tuberculosis cases and cooperative
Federal-State eradication activities, by
State, FY88, annual rpt, 1394-13
Coal Surface Mining Reclamation and
Enforcement Office activities and funding,
by State and Indian tribe, FY87, annual
rpt, 5644-1
Disaster relief program of Fed Emergency
Mgmt Agency under State admin, impact
of mgmt changes on benefits processing,
1986-88, GAO rpt, 26113-412
EPA regulatory and protection programs
operations and mgmt goals, progress and
activities, by office, quarterly rpt,
9182-11
Geological Survey activities and funding,
FY88, annual rpt, 5664-8
Hazardous waste site remedial action under
Superfund, deadlines and compliance of
govts and businesses, as of Mar 1989,
GAO rpt, 26113-394
Historic and natural natl landmarks
damaged and threatened, with owner,
location, damage type, and recommended
remedial action, 1988, annual listing,
5544-16
Hwy admin and gasoline tax revenue
proposed transfer from Fed Govt to
States, issues, with motor fuel taxes by
selected State, 1988 rpt, 10048-72
Meat and poultry inspection activities and
staff of Federal, State, and foreign govts,
FY88, annual rpt, 1374-1
Truck driver multi-State license prohibition,
FHwA enforcement activities by region,
1987-88, GAO rpt, 26113-396
Unemployment insurance programs of States
and Fed Govt, benefits adequacy, and
work disincentives, series, 6406-6
Unemployment insurance programs of States
and Fed Govt, benefits, coverage,
exhaustions, and finances, by State, and
beneficiary characteristics, 1940s-FY89,
21788-175
Unemployment insurance programs of
States, benefits, coverage, exhaustions,
and finances by State, 1987, annual tables,
6404-10
see also Federal aid to States

Federal stockpiles
see Stockpiling

Federal Technology Transfer Act
Labs of Fed Govt, technology transfer
cooperative agreements, royalties, and
incentive payments to employees, by
agency, FY87-88, GAO rpt, 26113-422

Federal Trade Commission
Activities of FTC, FY86, annual narrative
rpt, 9404-1
Budget of US Appendix, obligations,
appropriations, and personnel, by program
and agency, FY90, annual rpt, 104-3
Budget of US, authoritative financial
statements with appropriations, outlays,
and receipts, by category and agency,
FY88, annual rpt, 8104-2.2
Cigarette ad and promotion costs by media,
and market shares, by cigarette type, with
sales and use, 1963-87, annual rpt,
9404-4
Cigarette smoke tar, nicotine, and carbon
monoxide content, by brand, 1988,
9408-53
Industry structure, conduct, and govt
regulation, effects on competition, series,
9406-1
Labor unions recognized in Fed Govt,
agreements and membership by agency
and facility, as of Jan 1989, biennial
listing, 9844-14
R&D funding by Fed Govt, by field,
performer type, agency, and State,
FY87-89, annual rpt, 9627-20

Federally Funded R&D Centers
Expenditures for R&D and related activities
of higher education and nonprofit instns
by Fed Govt, by field, instn, agency, and
State, FY87, annual rpt, 9627-17.1
Expenditures for R&D by Fed Govt, by
field, performer type, agency, and State,
FY87-89, annual rpt, 9627-20
Expenditures for R&D by source and field,
selected years 1953-89, annual rpt,
9624-18
Expenditures for R&D by source and
performer, and related employment, by
State, 1975-87, 9626-6.32
Expenditures for R&D, by source,
performer, and for top 10 States, 1977-89,
9626-2.185
NASA procurement contract awards, by
type, contractor, State, and country,
FY89, semiannual rpt, 9502-6
Science and engineering employment in
R&D, earnings at DOE labs and
non-DOE facilities, 1989, annual rpt,
3004-9
Wages of scientists and engineers in R&D,
by field and educational, employment, and
other characteristics, 1989, annual rpt,
3004-1
see also Department of Energy National
Laboratories

Federally impacted areas
see Impacted areas

Federated States of Micronesia
see Micronesia Federated States

**Federation of American Societies for
Experimental Biology**
"Nutrition Monitoring in the U.S. An
Update Report on Nutrition Monitoring",
4048-33

Feeds
see Animal feed

Feedstocks, petrochemical
see Petrochemicals

Feinstein, Steven P.
"Forecasting Stock-Market Volatility Using
Options on Index Futures", 9371-1.908
"Source of Unbiased Implied Volatility
Forecasts", 9371-10.36

Feldman, Robert A.
"Dollar Appreciation, Foreign Trade, and the U.S. Economy", 9375–14

Feldman, Roger
"Employer-Based Health Insurance", 4186–2.23

Fellowships
see Student aid

Felmy, John C.
"Simulation of the Macroeconomic Effects of the Balanced Budget Amendment", 21528–72

Ferguson, Roy A.
"Maximum Primary Insurance Amounts in 1988", 4706–2.131

Ferguson, Walter L.
"Economic Effects of Banning a Widely Used and Relatively Cheap Pesticide: The Case of Parathion and Vegetables", 1561–11.906

Ferries
Customs Service activities, collections, entries processed by mode of transport, and seizures, FY84-88, annual rpt, 8144–1

Finances and operations of transit systems, by mode of transport, size of fleet, and for 432 systems, 1986, annual rpt, 7884–4

Finances, operations, vehicles, equipment, accidents, and energy use, by mode of transport, 1955-88, annual rpt, 7304–2

Manufacturing census, 1987: financial and operating data, for SIC 4-digit industries by product, preliminary rpt, 2491–1.77

Urban Mass Transportation Admin grants for transit systems, by city and State, FY88, annual rpt, 7884–10

Urban transit systems services and vehicles, 1988 annual listing, 7884–9

Ferris, John W.
"Productivity in the Carburetors, Pistons, and Valves Industry", 6722–1.911

Ferroalloys
see Iron and steel industry

Fertility
Births and rates, by characteristics of birth, infant, and parents, 1987 and trends from 1940, US Vital Statistics advance annual rpt, 4146–5.110

Births, fertility rates, and childless women, by selected characteristics, 1988, annual Current Population Rpt, 2546–1.436

Developing countries economic and social conditions from 1960s, and Intl Dev Cooperation Agency and AID activities and funding, FY88-90, annual rpt, 9904–4

Farm population, by employment and socioeconomic characteristics, and region, 1988, annual Current Population Rpt, 2546–1.439

Foreign countries population size, growth rates, and components of change, by country, projected 1987-2050 and trends from 1950, biennial rpt, 2324–9

Health condition and health care resources, use, and spending, 1950s-87, annual data compilation, 4144–11

Hispanic Americans socioeconomic characteristics, by detailed origin, 1988, Current Population Rpt, 2546–1.430; 2546–1.438

Household and family composition, and factors affecting change, 1960s-88, chartbook, 2546–2.149

Indochina refugee population fertility indicators, by ethnic group, 1970s-84, article, 4042–3.910

Mexico population, labor force, and emigration, alternative projections 1990-2000, working paper, 2326–18.46

OASDI benefit payments, trust fund finances, and economic and demographic assumptions, 1970-87 and alternative projections to 1997, actuarial rpt, 4706–1.103

Population size and characteristics, 1969-88, Current Population Rpt, annual rpt, 2546–2.146

Population size and components of change, alternative projections 1988-2080 and trends from 1900, annual actuarial rpt, 4706–1.104

Population size, by age, sex, and race, and components of change, alternative projections 1988-2080, Current Population Rpt, 2546–3.158

Research contracts and grants of Natl Inst of Child Health and Human Dev, by recipient and location, FY88, annual listing, 4474–36

Research on population and reproduction, Federal funding by project, FY87, annual listing, 4474–9

Research on population and reproduction, Natl Inst of Child Health and Human Dev funding and activities, 1988, annual rpt, 4474–33

Statistical Abstract of US, social, political, and economic data, 1790-2025, comprehensive annual compilation, 2324–1.1

see also Abortion
see also Births
see also Family planning
see also Population size

Fertilizers
Agricultural Outlook, production, prices, marketing, and trade, by commodity, forecast and current situation, monthly rpt with articles, 1502–4

Agricultural Statistics, 1988, annual rpt, 1004–1.2

Agriculture census, 1987: farms, farmland, production, finances, and operator characteristics, by county, final State rpt series, 2331–1

Business statistics, detailed data for major industries and economic indicators, *Survey of Current Business*, monthly rpt, 2702–1.9

China trade by SITC 1- to 5-digit commodity, 1970s-87, annual rpt, 9114–3

Coastal and estuarine pollutant discharges, by source, pollutant type, and location, series, 2176–4

Communist countries fertilizer production, 1960s-88, annual rpt, 9114–4.4

Communist, OECD, and selected other countries consumer and producer goods production, 1960s-88, annual rpt, 9114–4.8

Consumption and costs for fertilizer by type, and harvested acreage, by State, 1988 and trends from 1965, biennial rpt, 9804–5

Consumption of fertilizer and pesticide, under alternative crop mgmt methods, model results, 1986, hearing, 25168–69

Consumption of fertilizer by crop and State, and prices, by fertilizer type, 1960s-88, 1588–113

Consumption of fertilizer, by fertilizer type and State, as of June 1987-88, annual rpt, 9804–30

Consumption of fertilizer, by type and region, 1947-87, annual rpt, 1544–17.2

Cooperatives commercial member characteristics, and use of services, by region, 1980 and 1986, 1128–53

Costs of production, receipts, and returns, itemized by selected commodity and region, 1975-87, 1548–345

County Business Patterns, 1987: employment, establishments, and payroll, by SIC 2- to 4-digit industry and county, annual State rpt series, 2326–8

Cuba economic conditions, agricultural and industrial production and distribution, trade, and intl economic relations, 1980-87 with trends from 1961, 9118–8

Developing countries nitrogen fertilizer production, and energy and other capital investments, various periods 1955-89, article, 1522–3.905

Eastern Europe and USSR agricultural production, acreage, and consumption, by commodity and country, 1965-85, 1528–284

EC food supply and demand, market and support prices, and other economic indicators, by country and commodity, 1960-85, 1528–276

Electric power use and prices, shipments, and trade, for 25 SIC 4-digit manufacturing industries, 1972-86, 2048–137

Employment, earnings, and hours, by SIC 1- to 4-digit industry, monthly 1983-Feb 1989, annual rpt, 6744–4

Energy use and prices for manufacturing industries, 1985 survey, series, 3166–13

Environmental quality and protection programs, and intl issues, 1988 annual rpt, 484–1

Exports and imports (agricultural) of US, by commodity and country, bimonthly rpt with articles, 1522–1

Exports and imports (agricultural) of US, by detailed commodity and country, 1988, semiannual rpt, 1522–4

Exports and imports of fertilizer, by type and country, FY70-88, 1588–142

Exports of US, detailed commodities by country, monthly rpt, 2422–3

Farm finances and operations, by size, commodity, and region, 1986, annual rpt, 1544–27

Farm income, expenses, receipts by commodity, assets, liabilities, and ratios, 1988 and trends from 1945, annual rpt, 1544–16

Farm prices received for major products and paid for farm inputs and living items, by commodity and State, monthly rpt, 1629–1

Farm production inputs supply, demand, and prices, 1970s-88 and projected to 1993, articles, 1561–16.901

Farm production itemized costs, by farm sales size and region, 1988, annual rpt, 1614–3

Farm production itemized costs, receipts, and returns, by commodity and region, 1985-87, annual rpt, 1544–20

Farm production itemized costs, receipts, and returns, by crop and State, preliminary 1987, annual rpt, 1544–24

Farm sector balance sheet, and marketing receipts by detailed commodity, by State, 1984-88, annual rpt, 1544–18

Farm sector finances, income sources, expenses by type, assets, debts, and ratios, 1983-87, annual rpt, 1544–19

Foreign countries agricultural production, prices, and trade, by country, 1970s-89 and forecast 1990, annual world region rpt series, 1524–4

Foreign countries energy-intensive industry output and operations, and US investment barriers, for energy-rich countries, 1984-88, 9886-4.142

Foreign countries use of fertilizer components, by world area, 1978-88 and projected to 2010, 5608–154

Freight (waterborne domestic and foreign) by commodity, traffic, and passengers, by port and waterway, 1987, annual rpt, 3754–3

Great Lakes basin pollutant discharges, sources, and control program activities, 1987, biennial rpt, 14644–1

Great Lakes pollution loadings from nonpoint sources, for Lake Erie and Lake Ontario tributaries, 1982-85, 9208–129

Hudson-Raritan River basin pollutant levels and sources, model description and results, 1880s-1982, 2178–22

Imports of US, detailed Schedule A commodities by country, monthly rpt, 2422–2

Injuries from use of consumer products, by severity, victim age, and detailed product, 1988, annual rpt, 9164–6

Irrigation water supply restriction and compensatory use of other production inputs, 1984-85, 1588–139

Labor productivity, indexes of output, hours, and employment by SIC 2- to 4-digit industry, 1963-87, annual rpt, 6824–1.3

Lake Ontario eutrophication and pollutant levels, by contaminant type and site, 1967-85, 14648–22

Manufacturers finances and operations, by SIC 2- to 4-digit industry, forecast 1989 and trends from 1950s, annual rpt, 2044–28

Manufacturing annual survey, 1986: financial and operating data, by SIC 2- to 4-digit industry, series, 2506–15

Manufacturing census, 1987: financial and operating data, for SIC 4-digit industries by product, preliminary rpt, 2491–1.39

Mineral industries census, 1987: financial and operating data, preliminary industry rpt, 2511–1.11

Minerals Yearbook, 1987, Vol 1: commodity reviews of production, use, trade, prices, and mining operations, annual rpt, 5604–33

Minerals Yearbook, 1987, Vol 2 preprints: State reviews of production and sales by commodity, and business activity, annual rpt series, 5604–16

Minerals Yearbook, 1987, Vol 3 preprints: foreign country reviews of production, trade, and policy, by commodity, annual rpt series, 5604–23

Minerals Yearbook, 1988, Vol 2 rpts: State reviews of production and sales by commodity, and business activity, annual rpt series, 5604–22

Occupational injury and illness rates, by SIC 2- to 4-digit industry, 1987, annual rpt, 6844–1

OECD trade, total and for 4 major countries, and US trade by country, by commodity, 1970-87, world area rpt series, 9116–1

Price indexes (producer), by stage of processing and detailed commodity, monthly rpt, 6762–6

Price indexes (producer), by stage of processing and detailed commodity, monthly 1988, annual rpt, 6764–2

Prices received and paid by farmers, by commodity and State, 1988, annual rpt, 1629–5

Production of inorganic fertilizer by State, stocks, trade, and use, by product, monthly Current Industrial Rpt, 2506–8.2

Productivity of labor, indexes and annual rates of change, for fertilizer and pesticide industry, 1972-86, article, 6722–1.915

Rail shipments of grain and other commodities by car type, 1986, and rail car fleet size, 1978-88, 1278–15

Shipments, trade, use, and firms, by product and State, with stocks, for inorganic fertilizers, 1988, annual Current Industrial Rpt, 2506–8.13

Soil, water, and environmental conservation and conditions, with data by State and region, 1989 quinquennial rpt, 1268–24

Soviet Union agricultural production cost efficiency, by Republic, model description and results, 1960s-85, 1528–292

Statistical Abstract of US, social, political, and economic data, 1790-2025, comprehensive annual compilation, 2324–1.3

Tobacco (burley) finances, operations, and labor, for Kentucky and Tennessee, 1984, 1568–277

TVA agriculture and fertilizer rpts, 1989 annual listing, 9804–28

TVA financial and operating data by program and facility, FY88, annual rpt, 9804–32

Fescue
see Pasture and rangeland

Fetal deaths

Alabama low weight births, by outcome, 1974-84, article, 4042–3.948

Deaths and rates, by detailed cause and demographic characteristics, 1986 and trends from 1900, US Vital Statistics annual rpt, 4144–1

Deaths and rates, by detailed location, cause, and demographic characteristics, 1987, US Vital Statistics annual rpt, 4144–3

Hazardous substances exposure of parents and relation to adverse birth outcomes, 1980, article, 4042–3.945

Health condition and health care resources, use, and spending, 1950s-87, annual data compilation, 4144–11

Maternal deaths, rates, and risk, by pregnancy outcome, cause, and maternal characteristics, 1980-85, article, 4202–7.903

Maternal deaths related to spontaneous abortion, 1972-85, article, 4202–7.906

Perinatal deaths and rates, by race, sex, State, census div, and metro-nonmetro location, 1950s-85, 4146–5.107

Statistical Abstract of US, social, political, and economic data, 1790-2025, comprehensive annual compilation, 2324–1.1

West Virginia poverty conditions, food aid participants, and birth outcomes, 1980-87, hearing, 21968–49

see also Abortion
see also Infant mortality

FHA
see Housing (FHA), HUD

FHwA
see Federal Highway Administration

Fiber, dietary
see Vitamins and nutrients

Fiber optics

DOD prime contract awards, by detailed procurement category, FY85-88, annual rpt, 3544–18

Manufacturers finances and operations, by SIC 2- to 4-digit industry, forecast 1989 and trends from 1950s, annual rpt, 2044–28

Production and shipments of fibrous glass, and firms, by product, 1976-88, annual Current Industrial Rpt, 2506–9.5

Small business high technology sales, exports, siting, technology transfer, views on competitiveness, 1988 survey, hearing, 21728–69

Telephone fiber optics line mileage, by firm, 1987, 2808–27

Wire and cable (insulated) shipments, trade, use, and firms, by product, 1987-88, annual Current Industrial Rpt, 2506–10.8

Fibers
see Cotton
see Natural fibers
see Silk
see Synthetic fibers and fabrics
see Wool and wool trade

FICA
see Social security tax

Field seeds
see Seeds

Fieleke, Norman S.
"Budget Deficit: Are the International Consequences Unfavorable?", 9375–14
"Europe in 1992", 9373–1.908
"International Payments Imbalances in Heavily Indebted Developing Countries", 9373–3.32

Fiji

Agricultural and food production and indexes, total and for selected commodities, by country, 1970s-88, annual rpt, 1524–12

AID activities and funding by project and function, FY90, and developing countries summary socioeconomic data from 1960s, annual rpt, 9904–4.6

AID economic aid to developing countries, obligations and disbursements by country, quarterly rpt, 9912–4

Economic, social, political, and geographic summary data, by country, 1989, annual factbook, 9114–2

Human rights conditions in 170 countries, 1988, annual rpt, 21384–3

Military aid of US, arms sales, and training programs costs and budget requests, by program, world region, and country, FY88-90, annual rpt, 7144–13

Military spending, arms trade, and force strengths, with govt spending and population, by country, 1977-87, annual rpt, 9824–1

Minerals Yearbook, 1987, Vol 3: foreign country reviews of production, trade, and policy, by commodity, annual rpt, 5604–35

Minerals Yearbook, 1987, Vol 3 preprints: foreign country review of production, trade, and policy, by commodity, annual rpt, 5604–23.88

Population size, growth rates, and components of change, by country, projected 1989-2020 and trends from 1950, biennial rpt, 2324–9

UN voting record and share of votes in agreement with US, by issue, country, and world area, 1988, annual rpt, 7004–18

see also under By Foreign Country in the "Index by Categories"

Filipino Americans
see Pacific Islands Americans

Films
see Motion pictures

Finance
Fed Govt financial operations, detailed data, *Treasury Bulletin*, quarterly rpt, 8002–4

Federal Reserve Bulletin, detailed financial statistics, monthly rpt with articles, 9362–1

Financial and banking devs in southeastern States, working paper series, 9371–10

Financial and business statistics, historic trends, 1988 annual chartbook, 9364–2

Financial and economic analysis and forecasting methodology, technical paper series, 9377–9

Financial and economic analysis of banking and nonbanking sectors, working paper series, 9381–10

Financial and economic analysis, technical paper series, 9379–12; 9385–8; 9389–19; 9393–10

Financial and economic devs, Fed Reserve Bank of Atlanta bimonthly journal, 9371–1

Financial and economic devs, Fed Reserve Bank of Chicago bimonthly journal, 9375–1

Financial and economic devs, Fed Reserve Bank of Cleveland quarterly journal, 9377–1

Financial and economic devs, Fed Reserve Bank of Dallas bimonthly journal, 9379–1

Financial and economic devs, Fed Reserve Bank of Kansas City monthly journal, 9381–1

Financial and economic devs, Fed Reserve Bank of Minneapolis quarterly journal, 9383–6

Financial and economic devs, Fed Reserve Bank of New York quarterly journal, 9385–1

Financial and economic devs, Fed Reserve Bank of Philadelphia bimonthly journal, 9387–1

Financial and economic devs, Fed Reserve Bank of Richmond bimonthly journal, 9389–1

Financial and economic devs, Fed Reserve Bank of San Francisco quarterly journal, 9393–8

Financial and economic devs, Fed Reserve Bank of St Louis bimonthly journal, 9391–1

Financial and monetary research and econometric analyses, working paper series, 9387–8

Financial and monetary studies, Fed Reserve Bank of Boston conf series, 9373–3

Financial and monetary studies, Fed Reserve Bank of Kansas City conf series, 9381–13

Statistical Abstract of US, social, political, and economic data, 1790-2025, comprehensive annual compilation, 2324–1.3

see also Agricultural credit
see also Agricultural finance
see also Bankruptcy
see also Banks and banking
see also Certificates of deposit
see also Commercial credit
see also Consumer credit
see also Credit
see also Educational finance
see also Financial institutions
see also Fiscal policy
see also Flow-of-funds accounts
see also Foreign exchange
see also Futures trading
see also Government securities
see also Gross National Product
see also Housing costs and financing
see also Individual retirement arrangements
see also Inflation
see also Input-output analysis
see also Insurance and insurance industry
see also Interest rates
see also International finance
see also Investments
see also Loans
see also Monetary policy
see also Money supply
see also Municipal bonds
see also National income and product accounts
see also New York Stock Exchange
see also Prices
see also Securities
see also Stock exchanges

Finance companies
Assets, liabilities, and business credit, 1987, annual rpt, 9364–5.7

Assets, liabilities, and business loans of finance companies, monthly rpt, 9362–1.1

Assets, liabilities, and credit activities, monthly rpt series, 9365–2

Employment, earnings, and hours, by SIC 1- to 4-digit industry, monthly 1983-Feb 1989, annual rpt, 6744–4

Financial and business statistics, historic trends, 1988 annual chartbook, 9364–2.14

Flow-of-funds accounts, assets and liabilities by type and economic sector, outstanding at year-end 1965-88, annual rpt, 9364–3

Flow-of-funds accounts, savings, investments, and credit statements, quarterly rpt, 9365–3.3

Mortgage loan activity, by type of lender, loan, and mortgaged property, monthly press release, 5142–18

Mortgage loan activity, by type of lender, loan, and mortgaged property, quarterly press release, 5142–30

Mortgage loan activity, by type of lender, loan, and mortgaged property, 1986-88, annual press release, 5144–22

Mortgage terms on conventional loans closed, and commitment rates, by type of loan and lender and for 32 SMSAs, monthly rpt, 8432–3; 9312–2

Occupational injury and illness rates, by SIC 2- to 4-digit industry, 1987, annual rpt, 6844–1

Small business financing sources, and business financial data by size, type, and industry, various periods 1980-88, annual rpt, 9764–6.2

Statistical Abstract of US, social, political, and economic data, 1790-2025, comprehensive annual compilation, 2324–1.3

Tax (income) returns of corporations, income and tax items by asset size and detailed industry, 1986, annual rpt, 8304–4

Texas finance companies loan terms relation to borrower socioeconomic characteristics, 1973, technical paper, 9366–6.174

Financial crises and depressions
see Business cycles

Financial disclosure
Banks financial position, accuracy of quarterly call rpts and relation to bank ownership and merger activity, 1978-86, working paper, 9387–8.188

Election campaign finances and FEC activities, various periods 1975-88, annual rpt, 9274–1

Election campaign financial activity reported to FEC, by type of filer, 1988 natl elections, biennial rpt series, 9276–2

Elections, procedures, campaign finances, and Fed Election Commission activities, press release series, 9276–1

Fed Reserve deposit rpts, variability by district and financial instn type and size groups, and recommendations for combining groups, various periods 1987-88, technical paper, 9366–6.186

Pension plan regulation enforcement by Labor Dept and IRS, violations, and penalties, FY85-88, GAO rpt, 26121–259

SEC registration, firms required to file annual rpts, as of Sept 1988, annual listing, 9734–5

Financial institutions
AID loans repayment status and terms by program and country, and status of predecessor agency loans, quarterly rpt, 9912–3

Assets and debts of private sector, balance sheets by segment, 1949-88, semiannual rpt, 9365–4.1

Assets and liabilities in flow-of-funds accounts, by type and economic sector, outstanding at year-end 1965-88, annual rpt, 9364–3

Assets composition, growth, and distribution for financial instns, by instn type, 1970s-88, 8438–1

Assets, instns, concentration ratios, and status changes of banks, by asset size, ownership, and location, and compared to other financial instns, 1976-87, article, 9362–1.902

Bombing incidents, casualties, and damage, by target, circumstances, and State, 1988, annual rpt, 6224–5

Business statistics, detailed data for major industries and economic indicators, *Survey of Current Business*, monthly rpt, 2702–1.6

Canada financial instns assets and liabilities, by item and instn type, 1976 and 1986, article, 9312–1.903

Budget of US, receipts by source, outlays by agency and program, and balances, monthly rpt, 8102-3

Currency (foreign) holdings of US, transactions and balances by program and country, 1st half FY89, semiannual rpt, 8102-7

Currency (foreign) purchases of US with dollars, by country, 1st half FY89, semiannual rpt, 8102-5

Finances of Fed Govt, cash and debt transactions, daily tables, 8102-4

Financial consolidated statements of Fed Govt based on business accounting methods, FY87-88, annual rpt, 8104-5

Foreign exchange rates offered by US disbursing offices, by country, quarterly rpt, 8102-6

Surety companies authorized to post bonds with Fed Govt, location and bonding limits, as of July 1989, annual listing, 8104-4

Trust funds of Fed Govt, financial condition, periodic rpt series, 8102-9

Financial ratios
see Operating ratios

Financial statements
see Business assets and liabilities, general
see Business assets and liabilities, specific industry
see Business income and expenses, general
see Business income and expenses, specific industry
see Government assets and liabilities
see Operating ratios

Financing Corp.
Financial statements of FHLBB, FSLIC, Financing Corp, and FHLBs, 1988, annual rpt, 8434-2

Savings and loan assns failure resolution costs, and FSLIC finances and promissory notes issued, with data by instn, FY80s and projected to FY99, hearing, 25258-22

Savings and loan assns failures, assets, and FSLIC resolution costs and promissory notes, with data for acquired and acquiring instn in US and Texas, 1988 hearings, 21248-121

Fine arts
see Art
see Arts and the humanities

Fines
see Administrative law and procedure
see Judgments, civil procedure
see Sentences, criminal procedure

Fingerhut, Lois A.
"Firearm Mortality Among Children and Youth", 4146-8.181

"Trends and Current Status in Childhood Mortality: U.S., 1900-85. Vital and Health Statistics Series 3", 4147-3.27

Finland
Agricultural and food production and indexes, total and for selected commodities, by country, 1970s-88, annual rpt, 1524-12

Agricultural production, prices, and trade, by country, 1970s-88 and forecast 1990, annual world region rpt, 1524-4.1

Agricultural trade of US, by detailed commodity and country, 1988, semiannual rpt, 1522-4

AID loans repayment status and terms by program and country, and status of predecessor agency loans, quarterly rpt, 9912-3

Apple exports of US to EC and 4 north European countries, 1984-89, article, 1925-34.939

Economic and military aid and loans from US and intl agencies, by program and country, FY46-87, annual rpt, 9914-5

Economic conditions, income, production, prices, employment, and trade, 1989 periodic country rpt, 2046-4.60

Economic conditions, investment and export opportunities, and trade practices, 1989 country market research rpt, 2046-6.7

Economic conditions, policy, and trade practices, by country, 1986-88, annual rpt, 21384-5

Economic, social, political, and geographic summary data, by country, 1989, annual factbook, 9114-2

Exports and imports of US, by selected country, country group, and commodity group, 1988, annual rpt, 2044-37

Human rights conditions in 170 countries, 1988, annual rpt, 21384-3

Imports of goods, services, and investment from US, trade barriers, impacts, and US actions, by country, 1988, annual rpt, 444-2

Labor conditions, union coverage, and work accidents, 1989 annual country rpt, 6366-4.66

Military aid of US, arms sales, and training programs costs and budget requests, by program, world region, and country, FY88-90, annual rpt, 7144-13

Military spending, arms trade, and force strengths, with govt spending and population, by country, 1977-87, annual rpt, 9824-1

Minerals Yearbook, 1987, Vol 3: foreign country reviews of production, trade, and policy, by commodity, annual rpt, 5604-35

Minerals Yearbook, 1987, Vol 3 preprints: foreign country review of production, trade, and policy, by commodity, annual rpt, 5604-23.22

Multinatl US firms and foreign affiliates finances and operations, by industry of parent firm and affiliate, world area, and country, preliminary 1987, annual rpt, 2704-5

Nuclear power generation in US and 19 non-Communist countries, monthly rpt, 3162-24.10

Nuclear power plant capacity, generation, and operating status, by plant and foreign and US location, 1988 and projected to 2020, annual rpt, 3164-57

Oil production, trade, use, and stocks, by selected country and country group, monthly rpt, 3162-42

Paper mill products and effluents levels of dioxins and other hazardous substances, and environmental and health effects, 1988 hearing, 21368-112

Population size, growth rates, and components of change, by country, projected 1989-2020 and trends from 1950, biennial rpt, 2324-9

Steel export ceilings under voluntary restraint agreements, by country and product, with Western US steel industry impact, 1989 rpt, 9886-4.136

Steel imports of US under voluntary restraint agreement, by product, customs district, and country, with US industry operating data, monthly rpt, 9882-13

Stone (dimension) trade and price indexes by selected country, 1987, Mineral Industry Surveys, annual rpt, 5614-29

UN voting record and share of votes in agreement with US, by issue, country, and world area, 1988, annual rpt, 7004-18

see also under By Foreign Country in the "Index by Categories"

Fire departments
DC emergency fire and medical services operations, staff, and finances, with comparisons to other US and Canadian cities, 1986, hearing, 21308-25

Employment and payroll, by function and level of govt, 1987-88, annual rpt series, 2466-1

Finances of govts, by level of govt, State, and for large cities and counties, annual rpt series, 2466-2

Finances of govts, revenues by source and spending by function, natl income and product account, *Survey of Current Business*, monthly rpt, 2702-1.24

St Louis metro area local govt finances, structure, and service delivery, mid-1980s, 10046-9.1

State and local govt employment of minorities and women, by occupation, function, and pay level, 1986, annual rpt, 9244-6.4

Firearms
Aircraft hijackings, on-board explosions, and other crime, US and foreign incidents, 1983-87, annual rpt, 7504-31

Airport security operations to prevent hijacking, screening results, enforcement actions, and hijacking attempts, 1st half 1988, semiannual rpt, 7502-5

Arrests, by offense, offender characteristics, and location, 1988, annual rpt, 6224-2.2

Assaults and rates, by type of weapon, 1965-87, annual rpt, 6224-8

Child deaths from firearms, by motive, age, sex, and race, 1968-87 1987 with trends from 1968, 4146-8.181

County Business Patterns, 1987: employment, establishments, and payroll, by SIC 2- to 4-digit industry and county, annual State rpt series, 2326-8

Court civil and criminal caseloads for Federal district, appeals, and special courts, June 1989, annual rpt, 18204-2; 18204-8

Crime, criminal justice admin and enforcement, and public opinion, data compilation, 1970s-88, annual rpt, 6064-6

Crime victimization rates, by victim and offender characteristics, circumstances, and offense, 1987 survey, annual rpt, 6066-3.41

Crimes, arrests, and rates, by offense, offender characteristics, population size, and jurisdiction, 1988, annual rpt, 6224-2.1; 6224-2.2

Criminal cases by type and disposition, and collections, for US attorneys, by Federal district, FY88, annual rpt, 6004-2.1

Criminal sentences for Federal offenses, guidelines by offense and circumstances, 1989 rpt, 17668-1

Deaths and rates, by detailed cause and demographic characteristics, 1986 and trends from 1900, US Vital Statistics annual rpt, 4144-2

Financial and economic analysis, technical paper series, 9379–12

Foreign and US economic conditions and trade devs and policy, 1988 conf papers, 9373–3.32

Govt finances, by level of govt, State, and for large cities and counties, annual rpt series, 2466–2

Income distribution relation to fiscal and monetary policy, alternative regression results, 1947-86, technical paper, 9379–12.41

Interest rate impacts of Fed Govt deficit reduction, alternative model results, 1989 rpt, 26306–3.100; 26306–3.101

Local govts in metro areas, finances, structure, and service delivery, local area rpt series, 10046–9

Production impacts of dollar exchange rate and fiscal policy, by industry div, 1970-87, working paper, 9393–10.5

Research on tax-related economic and fiscal topics, technical paper series, 8006–3

State admin of hwys and gasoline tax revenue, proposed transfer from Fed Govt to States, issues, with motor fuel taxes by selected State, 1988 rpt, 10048–72

State govt fiscal policy, budgets, and tax and spending provisions, as of 1988, annual rpt, 10044–1.1

see also Budget of the U.S.
see also Economic policy
see also Government assets and liabilities
see also Government spending
see also Income taxes
see also Monetary policy
see also Public debt
see also Subsidies
see also Tax expenditures
see also Tax incentives and shelters
see also Tax laws and courts
see also Tax reform
see also Taxation
see also terms beginning with Federal aid

Fish and fishing industry

Agricultural Statistics, 1988, annual rpt, 1004–1.2

Alaska Arctic Natl Wildlife Refuge resources, native hunting activity, and energy exploration impact, 1985, last issue of annual rpt, 5504–26

Alaska OCS environmental conditions and oil dev impacts, compilation of papers, series, 2176–1

Alaska rural villages population characteristics and and subsistence activities, 1976-86, 5738–9

Atlantic Ocean fish and shellfish distribution, bottom trawl survey evaluation with results by species and location, 1963-87, 2168–108

Atlantic Ocean fish and shellfish distribution, bottom trawl survey results by species and location, periodic rpt series, 2164–18

Bass (striped) stocks status on Atlantic coast, and sport and commercial catch by State, 1972-89, annual rpt, 5504–29

Business statistics, detailed data for major industries and economic indicators, *Survey of Current Business*, monthly rpt, 2702–1.11

China trade by SITC 1- to 5-digit commodity, 1970s-87, annual rpt, 9114–3

Coastal and estuarine environmental conditions, research results and methodology, series, 2176–7

Coastal and riparian areas environmental conditions, fish, wildlife, use, and mgmt, for individual ecosystems, series, 5506–9

Coastal areas environmental and socioeconomic conditions, and potential impact of oil and gas OCS leases, final statement series, 5736–1

Coastal areas environmental conditions and mgmt, 1988 map, 2176–5.7

Coastal areas fish and shellfish catch, life cycles, and environmental needs, for selected species and regions, series, 5506–8

Cold storage holdings of fish and shellfish, by product and species, preliminary data, monthly press release, 2162–2

Communist, OECD, and selected other countries fishing fleets, and Communist countries fish catch, 1960s-88, annual rpt, 9114–4.4; 9114–4.10

Conservation and research projects of FWS, descriptions and results by program, FY87-88, biennial rpt, 5504–20

Consumer Expenditure Survey, household income by source, and itemized spending, by selected characteristics and location, 1984-86, annual rpt, 6764–5.2

Consumption of food and nutrient intake by individuals, by food group, selected characteristics, and region, supplementary survey series, 1356–5

Consumption, supply, trade, prices, spending, and indexes, by food commodity, 1987, annual rpt, 1544–4

County Business Patterns, 1987: employment, establishments, and payroll, by SIC 2- to 4-digit industry and county, annual State rpt series, 2326–8

CPI by component for US city average, and by region, population size, and for 27 metro areas, monthly rpt, 6762–2

Cuba economic conditions, agricultural and industrial production and distribution, trade, and intl economic relations, 1980-87 with trends from 1961, 9118–8

Employment, earnings, and hours, by selected SIC 1- to 4-digit industry, State, and for 262 MSAs, 1972-87, 6748–81

Endangered species recovery plans, and funding by Federal agencies and others, by species, FY72-87, GAO rpt, 26113–391

Environmental quality and protection programs, and intl issues, 1988 annual rpt, 484–1

Estuary environmental conditions and mgmt, for individual areas, conf series, 2146–6

Estuary environmental conditions and mgmt, research projects and funding, FY87, annual listing, 2144–24

Exports and imports (agricultural) of US, by commodity and country, bimonthly rpt with articles, 1522–1

Exports and imports (agricultural) of US, by detailed commodity and country, 1988, semiannual rpt, 1522–4

Exports and imports (agricultural) of US with Asia, Middle East, and North Africa, by commodity and country, 1962-86, 1528–277

Exports of US, detailed commodities by country, monthly rpt, 2422–3

Fed Govt financial and nonfinancial domestic aid, 1989 base edition with supplements, annual listing, 104–5

Finances and operations, by SIC 2- to 4-digit industry, forecast 1989 with trends from 1950s, annual rpt, 2044–28

Foreign and US oils, oilseeds, and fats production and trade, FAS periodic circular series, 1925–1

Foreign countries economic, social, political, and geographic summary data, by country, 1989, annual factbook, 9114–2

Foreign countries maritime claims and boundary agreements, series, 7006–8

Freight (waterborne domestic and foreign) by commodity, traffic, and passengers, by port and waterway, 1987, annual rpt, 3754–3

Great Lakes basin pollutant discharges, sources, and control program activities, 1987, biennial rpt, 14644–1

Hatcheries and research stations under Fish and Wildlife Service mgmt, acreage by site and State, as of Sept 1988, annual rpt, 5504–8

Hazardous substances toxicity levels for fish, by detailed compound, 1989 rpt, 9238–68; 9238–69

Import restraint elimination, impact on domestic industry production and employment, by selected commodity, 1986-88, 9886–4.144

Imports of US, detailed Schedule A commodities by country, monthly rpt, 2422–2

Japan fish catch, prices, trade by country, cold storage holdings, import quotas, and market devs, semimonthly press release, 2162–7

Lake Ontario eutrophication and pollutant levels, by contaminant type and site, 1967-85, 14648–22

Landings and trade of commercial fisheries, by species, 1980-88, semiannual rpt, 1561–15.1

Landings, trade, use, and fishery operations, with selected foreign data, by species, 1970s-88, annual rpt, 2164–1

Landings, wholesale receipts, prices, trade, and other market activities, by region, weekly rpts, 2162–6

Maine coastal marine resources and ocean floor ecology, 1983-87, conf papers, 2148–55

Manufacturing annual survey, 1986: financial and operating data, by SIC 2- to 4-digit industry, series, 2506–15

Manufacturing census, 1987: financial and operating data, for SIC 4-digit industries by product, preliminary rpt, 2491–1.7; 2491–1.9

Marine Fisheries Review, US and foreign fisheries resources, dev, mgmt, and research, quarterly journal, 2162–1

Nuclear radiation exposure of population near commercial reactors, by body site, age group, and selected plant, 1986, annual rpt, 9634–7

Nutrient and caloric composition of food, for raw, processed, and prepared food, 1988 rpt, 1358–3

Nutrient and fatty acid composition of fish, by northeastern US species, 1985-87, 2168–111

Fisher, Charles R.
"Physician Charges and Utilization Trends",
4652–1.955
"Trends in Medicare Enrollee Use of
Physician and Supplier Services,
1983-86", 4652–1.901
Fisher, Jacob
"Postwar Changes in the Income Position of
the Aged", 4742–1.903
Fisheries
see Fish and fishing industry
Fishing, sport
Agricultural Statistics, 1988, annual rpt,
1004–1.2
Bass (striped) stocks status on Atlantic
coast, and sport and commercial catch by
State, 1972-89, annual rpt, 5504–29
Coastal areas fish and shellfish catch, life
cycles, and environmental needs, for
selected species and regions, series,
5506–8
Estuary environmental conditions and
mgmt, for individual areas, conf series,
2146–6
Forest Service activities and finances, by
region and State, FY88, annual rpt,
1204–1.1
Forest Service mgmt of public lands and
resources dev, environmental, economic,
and social impacts of alternative
programs, projected to 2030, 1208–24
Forests (natl) recreational use, by type of
activity and State, 1988, annual rpt,
1204–17
Hatcheries and research stations under Fish
and Wildlife Service mgmt, acreage by
site and State, as of Sept 1988, annual rpt,
5504–8
Hatchery Natl System activities and
deliveries, by species, hatchery, and
jurisdiction of waters stocked, FY88,
annual rpt, 5504–10
Hazardous substances exposure factors, and
methodological guidelines, 1989 rpt,
9188–109
Injuries from use of consumer products and
related activities, by victim age and sex,
1988, annual rpt, 9164–7
Injuries from use of consumer products, by
severity, victim age, and detailed product,
1988, annual rpt, 9164–6
Licenses for fishing and hunting issued, and
costs, by State, FY88, annual press
release, 5504–16
New York Bight sport fishing catch and
hours fished, by type of boat rental, 1971,
article, 2162–1.901
Ocean sport fishing catch and effort, and
Natl Marine Fisheries Service tagging and
research activity, by species and location,
1987, annual rpt, 2164–7
Ocean sport fishing catch, by species, mode
of fishing, and coastal region, 1988,
annual rpt, 2164–1.2
Participation and spending for hunting,
fishing, and other wildlife-related
recreation, detailed data by location, 1985
survey, quinquennial rpt, 5508–5
Participation and spending for hunting,
fishing, and other wildlife-related
recreation, detailed data, 1985 survey,
quinquennial State rpt series, 5506–6
Public lands acreage and use, and Land
Mgmt Bur activities and finances, annual
State rpt series, 5724–11

Public lands acreage, grants, use, revenues,
and allocations, by State, FY88, annual
rpt, 5724–1.2
Research of State fish and wildlife agencies,
federally funded fishery projects and costs
by species and State, 1989, annual listing,
5504–23
Restoration programs of Fish and Wildlife
Service, finances by State, and excise tax
collections, FY88, annual rpt, 5504–13
Restoration programs of Fish and Wildlife
Service, funding, land purchases, and
project listing, by State, FY87, annual rpt,
5504–1
Tax collections of State govts by detailed
type of tax, and tax rates, by State, FY88,
annual rpt, 2466–2.3
TVA financial and operating data by
program and facility, FY88, annual rpt,
9804–32
Fissionable materials
see Radioactive materials
see Uranium
Fitchburg, Mass.
see also under By SMSA or MSA in the
"Index by Categories"
Fitti, Joseph E.
"AIDS Knowledge and Attitudes.
Provisional Data from the National
Health Interview Survey", 4146–8.165
Fixed investment
see Capital investments, general
see Capital investments, specific industry
Fixler, Dennis J.
"Commercial Bank Output Price Index",
6886–6.48
"Measuring the Nominal Value of Financial
Services in the National Income
Accounts", 6886–6.62
Flaim, Paul O.
"How Many New Jobs Since 1982? Data
from Two Surveys Differ", 6722–1.938
Flammable materials
see Inflammable materials
Flax
see Natural fibers
Flaxseed
see Oils, oilseeds, and fats
Fletcher, John C.
"International Survey of Attitudes of
Medical Geneticists Toward Mass
Screening and Access to Results",
4042–3.902
Flint, Mich.
see also under By City and By SMSA or
MSA in the "Index by Categories"
Flood control
Agricultural Statistics, 1988, annual rpt,
1004–1.2
Army Corps of Engineers activities and
projects, FY87 and trends from 1800s,
annual rpt, 3754–1.2
Army Corps of Engineers water resources
dev projects, characteristics, and costs,
1950s-87, biennial State rpt series,
3756–2
Army Corps of Engineers water resources
dev projects, characteristics, and costs,
1950s-89, biennial State rpt series,
3756–1
Assistance (financial and nonfinancial) of
Fed Govt, 1989 base edition with
supplements, annual listing, 104–5
Colorado River Storage Project finances and
activities in western States, FY88, annual
rpt, 5824–3

Conservation and conditions of soil, water,
and environment, with data by State and
region, 1989 quinquennial rpt, 1268–24
Developing countries disaster preparedness
and economic, population, and political
data, country rpt series, 9916–2
Expenditures of Fed Govt in States, by type,
program, agency, and State, FY88, annual
rpt, 2464–2
Fed Govt-owned real property inventory
and costs, worldwide summary by
purpose, agency, and location, 1987,
annual rpt, 9454–5
FmHA activities, and loans and grants by
program and State, FY88 and trends from
FY69, annual rpt, 1184–17
Forest Service activities and finances, by
region and State, FY88, annual rpt,
1204–1
Great Lakes flood prevention activities of
Army Corps of Engineers and Intl Joint
Commission, monthly rpt and
supplements, 3752–1
Reclamation Bur activities in western US,
land and population served, and recreation
areas, by location, 1987, annual rpt,
5824–12.1
Reclamation Bur water storage and carriage
facilities, capacity, and operating status, as
of Sept 1988, biennial listing, 5824–7
Tennessee Valley river control activities, and
hydroelectric power generation and
capacity, 1984, annual rpt, 9804–7
TVA financial and operating data by
program and facility, FY88, annual rpt,
9804–32
Water supply and quality in streams and
lakes, and groundwater levels in wells, by
drainage basin, 1986, annual State rpt
series, 5666–23
Water supply and quality in streams and
lakes, and groundwater levels in wells, by
drainage basin, 1987, annual State rpt
series, 5666–10
Water supply and quality in streams and
lakes, and groundwater levels in wells, by
drainage basin, 1988, annual State rpt
series, 5666–16
see also Dams
see also Dredging
see also Reservoirs
see also Watershed projects
Floods
Agricultural water supply, crop moisture,
and drought indexes, weekly rpt, seasonal
data, 2152–2
Army Corps of Engineers activities and
projects, FY87 and trends from 1800s,
annual rpt, 3754–1.2
Army Corps of Engineers water resources
dev projects, characteristics, and costs,
1950s-87, biennial State rpt series,
3756–2
Army Corps of Engineers water resources
dev projects, characteristics, and costs,
1950s-89, biennial State rpt series,
3756–1
Developing countries disaster preparedness
and economic, population, and political
data, country rpt series, 9916–2
Environmental quality and protection
programs, and intl issues, 1988 annual rpt,
484–1
Farmland damaged by natural disaster,
Emergency Conservation Program aid and
participation by State, FY87, annual rpt,
1804–22

Water supply in US and southern Canada, streamflow, surface and groundwater conditions, and reservoir levels, by location, monthly rpt, 5662–3

Weather events and anomalies, precipitation and temperature for US and foreign locations, weekly rpt, 2182–6

see also Flood control

see also Tsunamis

Floor coverings

see Carpets and rugs

Florence, Ala.

see also under By SMSA or MSA in the "Index by Categories"

Florence, S.C.

see also under By SMSA or MSA in the "Index by Categories"

Florida

Agriculture census, 1987: farms, farmland, production and costs, and operator characteristics, advance State and county rpts, 2330–1.12

Agriculture census, 1987: farms, farmland, production, finances, and operator characteristics, by county, final State rpt, 2331–1.9

Alien workers (unauthorized) employer sanctions, enforcement costs, compliance, and job discrimination, 1988 annual GAO rpt, 26104–19

Bank deposits in FDIC-insured commercial and savings banks, by instn, State, and county, as of June 1988, annual regional rpt, 9295–3.2

Banks and thrifts deposits and mortgages, building permits, population, and migration, for Florida with comparisons to other areas, 1980s-88, article, 9302–2.905

Banks and thrifts industry structure impacts of market entry and branching regulation, by Southeastern State, 1982-88, article, 9302–2.907

Celery acreage planted and growing, by growing area, monthly rpt, 1621–14

Citrus production and use, by crop and State, 1981/82-1986/87, 1641–4

Coastal areas environmental conditions, fish, wildlife, use, and mgmt, 1989 rpt, 5506–9.40

Coastal areas environmental conditions, fish, wildlife, use, and use, and mgmt, 1989 rpt, 5506–9.37

Coastal currents, temperatures, and salinity, for Straits of Florida, series, 2146–7

Collective bargaining calendar for southeastern States, 1989, annual rpt, 6946–1.73

County Business Patterns, 1987: employment, establishments, and payroll, by SIC 2- to 4-digit industry and county, annual State rpt, 2326–8.11

Deaths and rates, by detailed location, cause, and demographic characteristics, 1987, US Vital Statistics annual rpt, 4144–3.1

DOD prime contract awards, by contractor, service branch, State, and city, FY88, annual rpt, 3544–22

Economic indicators by State and MSA, Fed Reserve 6th District, quarterly rpt, 9371–14

Employment and housing market indicators by State, FHLB 4th District, quarterly rpt, 9302–36

Employment and unemployment, for 8 southeastern States, 1987-88, annual rpt, 6944–2

Employment by industry div, earnings, and hours, for 8 southeastern States, quarterly press release, 6942–7

Employment, earnings, and hours, by selected SIC 1- to 4-digit industry, State, and for 262 MSAs, 1972-87, 6748–81.1

Estuary environmental conditions and mgmt, 1987 conf, 2146–6.9

Fed Govt spending in States and local areas, by type, State, county, and city, FY88, annual rpt, 2464–3

Fed Govt spending in States, by type, program, agency, and State, FY88, annual rpt, 2464–2

Fish and shellfish catch, wholesale receipts, prices, trade, and other market activities, weekly regional rpt, 2162–6.3

HHS financial aid, by program, recipient, State, and city, FY88, annual regional listing, 4004–3.4

Homeless children educational enrollment and needs, 1988, annual State rpt, 4804–35.11

Housing starts and population growth rates, for Florida by MSA, 1988, article, 9302–2.906

Hwy admin and gasoline tax revenue proposed transfer from Fed Govt to States, issues, with motor fuel taxes by selected State, 1988 rpt, 10048–72

Income (personal) per capita and by source, and earnings by industry div, by State, MSA, and county, 1982-87, annual regional rpt, 2704–2.4

Lumber and paper industries productivity, impact on economy, and employment compared to other industries, 1970s-80, State rpt, 1206–36.12

Manatees killed in Florida and other US waters, by cause, 1977-88, annual rpt, 14734–1

Mineral Industry Surveys, State reviews of production, 1988, preliminary annual rpt, 5614–6

Minerals Yearbook, 1987, Vol 2 preprints: State review of production and sales by commodity, and business activity, annual rpt, 5604–16.10

Minerals Yearbook, 1987, Vol 2: State reviews of production, sales, and firms, by commodity, and business activity, annual rpt, 5604–34

Mobile home industry occupational injury and illness rates and workdays lost, by selected State, 1978-87, article, 6722–1.932

Nursing home compliance with Medicare and Medicaid regulations, and patient characteristics, by facility, 1987/88, annual State rpt, 4654–15.10

Peach production, marketing, and prices in 3 southeastern States and Appalachia, 1988, annual rpt, 1311–12

Retail trade census, 1987: employment, establishments, sales, and payroll, by SIC 2- to 4-digit kind of business, MSA, county, and city, State rpt, 2397–1.10

Savings instns, FHLB 4th District members finances and financial ratios, by State, quarterly rpt, 9302–3

Savings instns, FHLB 4th District members finances, by State, 1984-88, annual rpt, 9304–29.3

Service industries census, 1987: employment, establishments, receipts, and payroll, by SIC 2- to 4-digit kind of business, MSA, county, and city, State rpt, 2391–1.10

Statistical Abstract of US, social, political, and economic data, with foreign comparisons, 1790-2025, comprehensive annual compilation, 2324–1

Textile mill employment, earnings, and hours, for 8 Southeastern States, quarterly press release, 6942–1

Unemployment insurance extended benefits provision in substate areas, model results and cost estimates, 1980-86, 6406–6.28

VA health care clinics outpatient care applications, denials, appointments, and waiting periods, for 4 Florida clinics, FY88, GAO rpt, 26121–283

Vegetables (winter fresh) from Florida, Mexico, and Caribbean area, shipments and costs by commodity, 1970s-87, article, 1561–11.902

Wages by occupation, for office and plant workers, 1989 survey, periodic labor market rpt, 6785–3.10

Water supply and quality in streams and lakes, and groundwater levels in wells, by drainage basin, 1987, annual State rpt, 5666–10.8

Water supply and quality in streams and lakes, and groundwater levels in wells, by drainage basin, 1988, annual State rpt, 5666–16.8

Wholesale trade census, 1987: employment, establishments, finances, and operations, by SIC 2- to 4-digit kind of business, MSA, county, and city, State rpt, 2405–1.10

Wildlife-related recreation, hunting, and fishing participation and spending, detailed data, 1985 survey, quinquennial State rpt, 5506–6.9

see also Boca Raton, Fla.

see also Bradenton, Fla.

see also Clearwater, Fla.

see also Daytona Beach, Fla.

see also Delray Beach, Fla.

see also Fort Lauderdale, Fla.

see also Hialeah, Fla.

see also Hollywood, Fla.

see also Jacksonville, Fla.

see also Melbourne, Fla.

see also Miami, Fla.

see also Orlando, Fla.

see also Palm Bay, Fla.

see also Pinellas County, Fla.

see also Pompano Beach, Fla.

see also St. Petersburg, Fla.

see also Tampa, Fla.

see also Titusville, Fla.

see also West Palm Beach, Fla.

see also under By State in the "Index by Categories"

Florists

see Flowers and nursery products

Flour

see Baking and bakery products

see Grains and grain products

Flow-of-funds accounts

Assets and debts of private sector, balance sheets by segment, 1949-88, semiannual rpt, 9365–4.1

Assets and liabilities in flow-of-funds accounts, by type and economic sector, outstanding at year-end 1965-88, annual rpt, 9364–3

Business Conditions Digest, cyclical indicators, by economic process, monthly rpt, 2702–3.3

Credit market debt outstanding, and statements of assets and liabilities, by sector, 1976-87, annual rpt, 9364–5.8

Credit markets, direct and indirect sources of funds, monthly rpt, 9362–1.1

Fed Govt cash flow items, by agency, *Treasury Bulletin*, quarterly rpt, annual data, 8002–4.9

Flow-of-funds accounts, savings, investments, and credit statements, quarterly rpt, 9365–3.3

Foreign countries economic indicators, and trade and investment flows, for selected countries and country groups, selected years 1946-88, annual rpt, 204–1.9

Foreign direct investment of US, by selected industry group and world area, 1986-88, annual article, 2702–1.930

Intl investment position of US, by component, industry, world region, and country, 1987-88, annual article, 2702–1.922

Intl transactions in flow-of-funds and natl income and product accounts, data reconciliation, 1989 technical paper, 9366–6.198

Statistical Abstract of US, social, political, and economic data, 1790-2025, comprehensive annual compilation, 2324–1.3

Flowers and nursery products

Agricultural Statistics, 1988, annual rpt, 1004–1

Agriculture census, 1987: farms, farmland, production and costs, and operator characteristics, advance State and county rpt series, 2330–1

Agriculture census, 1987: farms, farmland, production, finances, and operator characteristics, by county, final State rpt series, 2331–1

Competitiveness (intl) of US fresh cut rose industry, investigation with background financial and operating data and foreign comparisons, 1989 rpt, 9886–4.137

Endangered animals and plants US trade and permits, by species, purpose, disposition, and country, 1987, annual rpt, 5504–19

Exports and imports (agricultural) of US, by commodity and country, bimonthly rpt with articles, 1522–1

Exports and imports (agricultural) of US, by commodity, monthly rpt, 1922–8

Exports and imports (agricultural) of US, by detailed commodity and country, 1988, semiannual rpt, 1522–4

Exports of US, detailed commodities by country, monthly rpt, 2422–3

Farm finances and operations, by size, commodity, and region, 1986, annual rpt, 1544–27

Farm income, expenses, receipts by commodity, assets, liabilities, and ratios, 1988 and trends from 1945, annual rpt, 1544–16

Farm labor costs impacts of illegal aliens employer sanctions, by farm type, size, and region, 1986, 1598–250

Farm receipts for 25 leading crops, by State, 1960-87, 1548–347

Farm sector balance sheet, and receipts by detailed commodity, by State, 1984-88, annual rpt, 1544–18

Farm sector finances, income sources, expenses by type, assets, debts, and ratios, 1987, annual rpt, 1544–16

Imports of cut flowers, by type and country, FAS monthly circular with articles, 1925–34

Imports of US, detailed Schedule A commodities by country, monthly rpt, 2422–2

Injuries from use of consumer products, by severity, victim age, and detailed product, 1988, annual rpt, 9164–6

Production, sales, prices, and growers, by flower and foliage crop and State, 1987-88 and planting planned 1989, annual rpt, 1631–8

Retail trade census, 1987: employment, establishments, sales, and payroll, by SIC 2- to 4-digit kind of business, MSA, county, and city, State rpt series, 2397–1

Shipments of domestic and imported cut flowers and decorative greens, by State and country of origin, weekly rpt, 1311–3

Statistical Abstract of US, social, political, and economic data, 1790-2025, comprehensive annual compilation, 2324–1.1

Tree seedlings produced for forest and windbarrier planting, by nursery ownership and State, FY88, annual rpt, 1204–7.2

Wholesale trade census, 1987: employment, establishments, finances, and operations, by SIC 2- to 4-digit kind of business, MSA, county, and city, State rpt series, 2405–1

see also Seeds

see also under By Commodity in the "Index by Categories"

Flu

see Pneumonia and influenza

Fluoridation

see Water fluoridation

Fluorine

see Gases

Fluorocarbons

see Chemicals and chemical industry

Fluorspar

see Nonmetallic minerals and mines

FNMA

see Federal National Mortgage Association

Fogarty International Center for Advanced Study in the Health Sciences

Activities of NIH, funding, and advisory council recommendations, by inst, FY87-88, biennial rpt, 4434–16

Intl programs of NIH, activities and funding by inst and country, FY88, annual rpt, 4474–6

Fomby, Thomas B.

"Texas in Transition: Dependence on Oil and the National Economy", 9379–1.902

Fontana, C. A.

"Off-Site Environmental Monitoring Report: Radiation Monitoring Around U.S. Nuclear Test Areas, 1988", 9194–17

Food and Drug Administration

Activities of FDA, quarterly rpt, 4062–3

Budget of US Appendix, obligations, appropriations, and personnel, by program and agency, FY90, annual rpt, 104–3

Drug prescriptions, by drug type and brand, and for new drugs, 1987, annual rpt, 4064–12

Employment and turnover, facilities, and equipment, for FDA, FY80-89, GAO rpt, 26121–309

Financial aid of HHS, by program, recipient, State, and city, FY88, annual regional listings, 4004–3

Health care devices malfunction, injury, and death reports to FDA, and inspection findings and disposition, 1985-87, GAO rpt, 26131–57

Housewares (ceramic) lead and cadmium levels, FDA import inspection activity by country, and food safety funding and staff, 1983-88, hearing, 21368–108

Imports detained by FDA, by reason, product, shipper, brand, and country, monthly listing, 4062–2

Radiation exposure of Federal employees, by age, occupation, and selected agency, 1986-87, biennial rpt, 4064–15

Radiation from electronic devices, incidents by type of device, and FDA control activities, 1988, annual rpt, 4064–13

Research and evaluation programs of HHS, 1970-FY87, annual listing, 4004–30

Toxicology Natl Program research and testing activities, FY87 and planned FY88, annual rpt, 4044–16

Food and food industry

Agricultural Statistics, 1988, annual rpt, 1004–1

Alien workers (unauthorized) employer sanctions, enforcement costs, compliance, and job discrimination, 1988 annual GAO rpt, 26104–19

Business statistics, detailed data for major industries and economic indicators, *Survey of Current Business*, monthly rpt, 2702–1.11

China trade by SITC 1- to 5-digit commodity, 1970s-87, annual rpt, 9114–3

Collective bargaining agreements expiring during year, and workers covered, by firm, union, industry group, and State, 1989, annual rpt, 6784–9

Cooperatives share of food and tobacco industry sales and exports, 1985-86, article, 1122–1.906

County Business Patterns, 1987: employment, establishments, and payroll, by SIC 2- to 4-digit industry and county, annual State rpt series, 2326–8

Cuba economic conditions, agricultural and industrial production and distribution, trade, and intl economic relations, 1980-87 with trends from 1961, 9118–8

Drought of 1988, impacts on farm, rural areas, and food industry financial conditions, with trends from 1970, 1588–133

Earnings by major industry group, and personal income per capita and by source, by region and State, 1929-87, 2708–40

Employment and value added in food and fiber sectors, selected years 1975-87, annual rpt, 1544–19

Employment, earnings, and hours, by selected SIC 1- to 4-digit industry, State, and for 262 MSAs, 1972-87, 6748–81

Employment, earnings, and hours, by SIC 1- to 4-digit industry, monthly 1983-Feb 1989, annual rpt, 6744–4

Purchases by food aid programs, by commodity, firm, and shipping point or destination, weekly rpt, 1302–3

Rice exports under Federal programs, periodic situation rpt, 1561–8

Statistical Abstract of US, social, political, and economic data, 1790-2025, comprehensive annual compilation, 2324–1.2

USDA child nutrition programs funding, by program and State, FY86-88, annual rpt, 4824–2.27

USDA food aid programs costs and participation, by program, 1960s-88, annual chartbook, 1504–3

USDA food aid programs participants and costs, by program, region, and State, monthly rpt, 1362–14

West Virginia poverty conditions, food aid participants, and birth outcomes, 1980-87, hearing, 21968–49

Women, infants, and children food aid program of USDA, participants and costs by State and Indian agency, FY87, annual rpt, 1364–12

Women, infants, and children food aid program of USDA, participants, clinics, and costs by State and Indian agency, monthly tables, 1362–16

Women, infants, and children food aid program of USDA, prenatal enrollees by trimester of enrollment and other characteristics, 1984, article, 4042–3.929

see also Food stamp programs

see also Public Law 480

see also School lunch and breakfast programs

Food consumption

Agricultural Outlook, production, prices, marketing, and trade, by commodity, forecast and current situation, monthly rpt with articles, 1502–4

Agricultural Statistics, 1988, annual rpt, 1004–1

Alaska rural villages population characteristics and and subsistence activities, 1976-86, 5738–9

Bean (dried) prices by State, market activity, and foreign and US production, use, stocks, and trade, weekly rpt, 1311–17

Cancer (breast) risk relation to diet and nutrient intake, for northwestern Italy, 1983-85 study, article, 4472–1.906

Cancer (stomach) by intake of allium vegetables, for China, 1984-86, article, 4472–1.903

Cancer (stomach) incidence and risk relation to diet and refrigerator use, 1985-87 local area study, article, 4472–1.919

Cancer cases, and prevention and risk activities and attitudes, 1987 survey, annual rpt, 4474–35

Consumption of food and nutrient intake by individuals, by food group, selected characteristics, and region, supplementary survey series, 1356–5

Consumption of nutrients, nutritional status, and related health condition and practices, by selected characteristics, 1970s-86, 4048–33

Consumption per capita of selected food items and groups, selected years 1967-87, annual rpt, 1544–19

Consumption, production, trade, use, farm finances, and price support activity and policy options, with foreign comparisons, 1950s-89, commodity rpt series, 1566–7

Consumption, supply, trade, prices, spending, and indexes, by food commodity, 1987, annual rpt, 1544–4

Dairy production, prices, trade, and use, periodic situation rpt with articles, 1561–2

Dairy products foreign and US production, trade, use, and prices, forecast 1990 and trends from 1983, FAS semiannual circular, 1925–10

Data on agriculture, collection, methodology, and use for major time series of USDA, 1989 rpt, 1506–1.11

Demand for food, impacts of price and quality, model description and results, 1987 working paper, 6886–6.37

Developing countries agricultural and food aid, and impacts on US exports, with background data, 1960s-89, 26308–85

Developing countries disaster preparedness and economic, population, and political data, country rpt series, 9916–2

Developing countries food production and needs, and related economic outlook, by country, 1989/90, annual rpt, 1524–6

Dioxin levels in paper products and pulp mill effluents, and environmental and health effects, 1988 hearing, 21368–112

Eastern Europe agricultural production, consumption, and trade, by country, 1970s-88, annual rpt, 1524–11

Eastern Europe and USSR agricultural production, acreage, and consumption, by commodity and country, 1965-85, 1528–284

Expenditures by category, and income, by selected household characteristics and location, Consumer Expenditure Survey, 1987, press release, 6726–1.23

Expenditures by category, selected household characteristics, and region, Consumer Expenditure Survey, quarterly rpt, 6762–14

Expenditures by detailed category, and household income by source, by selected characteristics and region, Consumer Expenditure Survey, 1984-87, annual rpt, 6764–5

Expenditures for food, consumption, and other consumer finances, 1960s-88, annual chartbook, 1504–3

Expenditures for food, 1975-88, annual rpt, 1544–9

Expenditures in metro and nonmetro areas, by item, 1987 survey, article, 6722–1.962

Expenditures of consumers, natl income and product account, *Survey of Current Business*, monthly rpt, 2702–1.23

Expenditures related to occupational group, 1986-87, article, 6722–1.961

Farm finances and operations, by size, commodity, and region, 1986, annual rpt, 1544–27

Farm financial and marketing conditions, forecast 1989, annual chartbook, 1504–8

Farm home use of meat raised on premises, by species and State, 1987-88, annual rpt, 1623–4

Farm households consumption of crops and livestock, 1945-88, annual rpt, 1544–16

Farm sector financial condition, debt by lender, and indicators of financial stress, 1988, annual GAO rpt, 26104–16

Fiber content in breakfast cereal and bread, health claim ads, and other factors affecting consumption, 1978-88, 9406–1.60

Fish and fish products per capita use for US, 1909-88, and by country, average 1982-84, annual rpt, 2164–1.8

Foreign and US agricultural and food production and indexes, total and for selected commodities, by country, 1970s-88, annual rpt, 1524–12

Foreign and US agricultural production, prices, trade, and use, periodic rpt with articles, 1522–3

Foreign and US agricultural supply and demand indicators, by selected crop, monthly rpt, 1522–5

Foreign countries agricultural production, prices, and trade, by country, 1970s-89 and forecast 1990, annual world region rpt series, 1524–4

Fruit and nut production, prices, trade, stocks, and use, by selected crop, periodic situation rpt with articles, 1561–6

Fruit and vegetable processing industries finances and operations, consumption, farm production, and trade, by commodity, 1970s-88, 1568–275

Hazardous substances exposure factors, and methodological guidelines, 1989 rpt, 9188–109

Health-related behavior of runners, for 7 habits, by sex, age, education, income, and average miles run per week, 1985 survey, article, 4042–3.933

Homeless persons nutritional status, 1987 local area study, article, 4042–3.942

Meat and poultry foreign and US production, trade, and use, by selected country, forecast 1990, FAS annual circular, 1925–33

Meat and poultry production, trade, and consumption, quarterly 1960-87, 1568–285.2

Meat, poultry, and egg consumption per capita, periodic situation rpt with articles, 1561–7

Meat, poultry, and livestock production, consumption, and industry finances and operations, 1950s-86, 1568–280

Metro area cost of living indexes, relation of expenditure items and quality of life indicators, model results, 1973, working paper, 6886–6.9

Military personnel health-related behavior, for 7 habits, by age, education, race, and health status, 1985 survey, article, 4042–3.949

Milk order market policy alternatives impact on producer costs and income, prices, and supply, by region, 1985, 1568–274

Natl income and product accounts and components, *Survey of Current Business*, monthly rpt, 2702–1.21

Oils, oilseeds, and fats foreign and US production and trade, FAS periodic circular series, 1925–1

Oils, oilseeds, and fats production, prices, trade, and use, periodic situation rpt with articles, 1561–3

Polychlorinated biphenyls levels in Great Lakes environment, humans, and animals, and emissions sources, by site, 1970s-85, conf, 14648–19

Poultry (broiler) production, slaughter, prices, and processing industry operations, 1950s-87, 1568–279

Poultry (chicken, egg, and turkey) production, prices, receipts, trade, and disposition, 1960-87, 1568–39

Food shortage
see Food supply
see Nutrition and malnutrition

Food stamp programs

Assistance (financial and nonfinancial) of Fed Govt, 1989 base edition with supplements, annual listing, 104–5

Assistance programs under Ways and Means Committee jurisdiction, finances and operations, FY70s-88, annual rpt, 21784–11

Banks in Fed Reserve System, expenses and operations itemized by service, office, and district, 1988, annual rpt, 9364–11

Beneficiaries of public welfare programs, and benefits duration and share of income, by selected characteristics, 1983-86, 2546–20.8

Benefits cash value, alternative measures by household type, 1980, technical paper, 6886–6.42

Benefits payment and eligibility errors, by type, recipient characteristics, and State, FY87, annual rpt, 1364–15

Benefits temporary termination, by reason and duration, for 2 States, FY87, GAO rpt, 26113–423

Budget of US, CBO analysis of revenue and spending alternatives and projections of economic indicators, FY90-94, annual rpt, 26304–3

Budget of US, midsession review of FY90 budget, by function and agency, annual rpt, 104–7

Consumer research, food marketing, legislation, and regulation devs, and consumption and price trends, quarterly journal, 1541–7

Disabled persons employment, labor force status, and other characteristics, 1988, Current Population Rpt, 2546–2.147

Expenditures, coverage, and benefits for social welfare programs, late 1930s-87, annual rpt, 4744–3.1; 4744–3.3; 4744–3.8

Expenditures of Fed Govt in States, by type, program, agency, and State, FY88, annual rpt, 2464–2

Fed Govt policy issues and effects on agricultural production, prices, income, and trade, and crop support levels by program, 1989 semiannual rpt, 1542–6

Fed Reserve banks finances and staff, 1988, annual rpt, 9364–1.1

Finances of Fed Govt, cash and debt transactions, daily tables, 8102–4

Household composition, income, benefits, and labor force status, Survey of Income and Program Participation methodology, working paper series, 2626–10

Housing and households detailed characteristics, and unit and neighborhood quality, by location, 1985, biennial rpt, 2485–12

Housing and households detailed characteristics, and unit and neighborhood quality, MSA surveys, series, 2485–6

Income (household) and poverty status under alternative income definitions, by recipient characteristics, 1986, Current Population Rpt, 2546–6.58

Income (personal) by source including transfer payments, and social insurance contributions, by region, 1984, 2708–40

Indian food aid programs participation and eligibility, for 4 reservations, 1988, GAO rpt, 26113–439

Job training and related aid, AFDC participants, costs, and budget impact, projected FY89-93, 26306–3.102

Participation and costs of USDA food aid programs, by program, region, and State, monthly rpt, 1362–14

Participation and coupons issued, by State and county, as of July 1988, semiannual rpt, 1362–6

Participation in program and reasons for nonparticipation by eligible households, 1979 and 1986, GAO rpt, 26131–52

Statistical Abstract of US, social, political, and economic data, 1790-2025, comprehensive annual compilation, 2324–1.2

West Virginia poverty conditions, food aid participants, and birth outcomes, 1980-87, hearing, 21968–49

Women and children participating in food stamp program, food consumption and nutrient intake by food group, selected characteristics, and region, 1986 supplementary survey, 1356–5.1

Food stocks
see Agricultural stocks
see Food supply

Food stores

Census of Retail Trade, 1987: employment, establishments, sales, and payroll, by SIC 2- to 4-digit kind of business, MSA, county, and city, State rpt series, 2397–1

Collective bargaining agreements expiring during year, and workers covered, by firm, union, industry group, and State, 1989, annual rpt, 6784–9

County Business Patterns, 1987: employment, establishments, and payroll, by SIC 2- to 4-digit industry and county, annual State rpt series, 2326–8

Employment, earnings, and hours, by selected SIC 1- to 4-digit industry, State, and for 262 MSAs, 1972-87, 6748–31

Employment, earnings, and hours, by SIC 1- to 4-digit industry, monthly 1983-Feb 1989, annual rpt, 6744–4

Employment of minorities and women, by occupation, SIC 1- to 3- digit industry, State, and MSA, 1986, annual rpt, 9244–1

Energy use in commercial buildings, costs, and conservation, by building characteristics, survey rpt series, 3166–8

Expenditures for food and alcoholic beverages, by place of purchase, 1966-87, annual rpt, 1544–4.6

Finances and operations, by SIC 2- to 4-digit industry, forecast 1989 with trends from 1950s, annual rpt, 2044–28

Finances, operations, and merger activity, for food processors and distributors, as of 1988, annual rpt, 1544–22

Financial statements for manufacturing, mining, and trade corporations, by selected SIC 2- to 3-digit industry, quarterly rpt, 2502–1

Guam economic censuses, 1987: employment, firms, payroll, and receipts, by SIC 1- to 4-digit industry and election district, 2595–1

Labor productivity, indexes of output, hours, and employment by SIC 2- to 4-digit industry, 1963-87, annual rpt, 6824–1.4

Meat, poultry, and livestock production, consumption, and industry finances and operations, 1950s-86, 1568–280

Milk home delivery, and sales by wholesale outlet type, by region, 1987 survey, article, 1317–4.901

Milk order market sales, by container size and type, outlet type, and market area, 1987, biennial rpt, 1317–6

Northern Mariana Islands economic census, 1987: employment, firms, payroll, and receipts, by SIC 1- to 4-digit industry, 2597–1

Occupational injury and illness rates, by SIC 2- to 4-digit industry, 1987, annual rpt, 6844–1

Prices (farm-retail) for food, marketing cost components, and industry finances and productivity, 1950s-88, annual rpt, 1544–9

Robberies and rates, by type of premises and weapon, 1973-87, annual rpt, 6224–8

Robberies, by type of premises, population size, and region, 1988, annual rpt, 6224–2.1

Sales and inventories, by kind of retail business, region, and selected State, MSA, and city, monthly rpt, 2413–3

Sales, inventories, purchases, gross margin, and accounts receivable, by SIC 2- to 4-digit kind of business and form of ownership, 1987, annual rpt, 2413–5

Sales of retailers, by kind of business, advance monthly rpt, 2413–2

Science, engineering, and technical employment in transportation, utilities, and retail and wholesale trade, by field, occupation, and industry, 1985, triennial rpt, 9627–32

Small business establishments, employment, and financial ratios, by SIC 1- to 2-digit industry and State, late 1960s-87, 9768–19

Statistical Abstract of US, social, political, and economic data, 1790-2025, comprehensive annual compilation, 2324–1.3

Tax (income) returns of corporations, income and tax items by asset size and detailed industry, 1986, annual rpt, 8304–4; 8304–21

Tax (income) returns of partnerships, income statement items by industry group, 1986, annual article, 8302–2.903

Tax (income) returns of sole proprietorships, income statement items, by industry group, 1987, annual article, 8302–2.904; 8302–2.921

Virgin Islands economic censuses, 1987: employment, firms, payroll, and receipts, by SIC 1- to 4-digit industry, island, and city, 2593–1

see also By Industry in the "Index by Categories"

Food supply

Africa (Sahel) food supply indicators, by country, 1960s-2000, 1528–290

Africa food imports and aid needs under alternative weather assumptions, for 17 African countries, projected to 1995, 1528–279

Agricultural Outlook, production, prices, marketing, and trade, by commodity, forecast and current situation, monthly rpt with articles, 1502–4

Developing countries receiving US economic aid, military spending and imports measures to determine aid eligibility, by country, 1985-86, annual rpt, 9914-1

Economic conditions in foreign countries and implications for US, periodic country rpt series, 2046-4

Economic, social, political, and geographic summary data, by country, 1989, annual factbook, 9114-2

Military spending, arms trade, and force strengths, with govt spending and population, by country, 1977-87, annual rpt, 9824-1

OECD and Arab countries dev aid, total, per capita, and share of GNP and budget, by country, 1987, annual rpt, 9904-1.4

Overseas Business Reports: economic conditions, investment and export opportunities, and trade practices, country market research rpt series, 2046-6

Pacific basin countries military, economic, technological, and trade conditions, 1970s-85, compilation of papers, 3908-4

Portugal and Turkey economic indicators and govt finances, 1982-86, hearing, 21388-53

Social security trust funds surpluses impact on govt budgets, for 3 countries and US, 1960-86, article, 9373-1.905

Soviet Union budget deficits and financing, revenues, and spending, with retail prices, 1970-88, 9118-6

Statistical Abstract of US, social, political, and economic data, by outlying area and country, 1950s-87, comprehensive annual compilation, 2324-1.4

UN participation of US, and member and nonmember shares of UN budget by country, FY86-88, annual rpt, 7004-5

UN voting record and share of votes in agreement with US, by issue, country, and world area, 1988, annual rpt, 7004-18

Foreign Claims Settlement Commission

Claims against foreign govts by US natls, by claim type and country, 1988, annual rpt, 6004-16

Foreign competition

Agricultural exports competitiveness, and subsidy and credit program costs, with data by commodity, 1980s-89, GAO rpt, 26113-404

Agricultural imports of US, competitive and noncompetitive, by commodity and country, bimonthly rpt, 1522-1.2

Agricultural trade and market impacts of eliminating foreign and US protectionist policies, model description and results, 1986, 1528-282

Caribbean area duty-free exports to US, and imports from US, by country, and impact on US employment, by commodity, 1988, annual rpt, 6364-2

Coal production and freight costs, and competitive position in selected markets, for Australia and US, 1987-89, 2048-143

Credit programs for exports, activities of Eximbank and 6 OECD countries, 1988, annual rpt, 9254-3

EC economic integration impact on EC employment, GDP, and other economic indicators, projected 1992, article, 9373-1.908

Export and import agreements, negotiations, anticompetitive investigations, and related legislation, FY86-88, annual rpt, 444-1

Export competitiveness of US, findings and recommendations, 1988 rpt, 028-31

Grain exports competitiveness and quality issues, with background data and comparisons to other countries, 1960s-88, 26358-201

Imports and tariff provisions effect on US industries and products, investigations with background financial and operating data, series, 9886-4

Imports injury to US industries from foreign subsidized products and sales at less than fair value, investigations with background financial and operating data, series, 9886-19

Imports injury to US industries from foreign subsidized products, investigations with background financial and operating data, series, 9886-15

Imports injury to US industries from sales at less than fair value, investigations with background financial and operating data, series, 9886-14

Imports under Generalized System of Preferences, status, and US tariffs, trade by country, production, and use, for selected commodities, 1984-88, annual rpt, 9884-23

Industry (US) intl competitiveness, with selected foreign and US operating data by major firm and product, series, 2046-12

Minerals industry production cost impacts of occupational safety and environmental regulation, factors affecting US competitiveness, 1989 compilation of papers, 5606-5.7

Ship foreign and US flag competition in US Exclusive Economic Zone, impacts of extending cabotage laws, with background data, 1970s-80s, 26358-206   •

Small business high technology sales, exports, siting, technology transfer, views on competitiveness, 1988 survey, hearing, 21728-69

Steel imports of US under voluntary restraint agreement, by product, customs district, and country, with US industry operating data, monthly rpt, 9882-13

Sweden multinatl firms domestic and foreign production, exports, employment, and sales, with data by commodity and firm, 1960s-86, conf, 23848-208

Technology dev and foreign competition issues for US, fundings and recommendations, 1980s-87, 21708-123

Unemployed displaced workers, by reason, industry, selected characteristics, and State, 1988, annual rpt, 6744-18

see also Dumping

see also Foreign trade

Foreign corporations

Airport security operations to prevent hijacking, screening results, enforcement actions, and hijacking attempts, 1st half 1988, semiannual rpt, 7502-5

Aluminum plant ownership, capacity, energy and aluminum sources, and startup and closing dates, by US and foreign plant and location, 1988, annual listing, 5604-49

Auto and light truck fuel economy, sales, and market shares, by size and model for US and foreign makes, 1989 model year, semiannual rpt, 3302-4

Background Notes, foreign countries summary social, political, and economic data, series, 7006-2

Banks branches and agencies of foreign banks, assets and liabilities, monthly rpt, 9362-1.1

Banks branches and agencies of foreign banks, assets and liabilities, monthly rpt, quarterly data, 9362-1.4

Banks interstate offices, by type of controlling organization and State, 1982-Feb 1989, article, 9371-1.909

Biotechnology in Japan, R&D spending, industry finances, and govt involvement, FY85-86, 2048-139

Business America, foreign and domestic commerce, and US investment and trade opportunities, biweekly journal, 2042-24

Capital cost indicators for US, Japan, West Germany, and UK, various periods 1977-88, article, 9385-1.910

Competitiveness (intl) of US industries, with selected foreign and US operating data by major firm and product, series, 2046-12

DOD prime contract awards, by category, contract and contractor type, and service branch, FY79-88, semiannual rpt, 3542-1

DOD prime contract awards for R&D, for top 500 contractors, FY88, annual listing, 3544-4

Farmland (US) investment of foreigners related to exchange rate, interest rate, and cropland returns, by leading country, 1981-88, 1528-287

Farmland (US) owned by foreigners, holdings, acquisitions, and disposals by land use, owner type and country, and State, 1988, annual rpt, 1584-2

Imports and tariff provisions effect on US industries and products, investigations with background financial and operating data, series, 9886-4

Imports injury to US industries from foreign subsidized products and sales at less than fair value, investigations with background financial and operating data, series, 9886-19

Income from US sources and tax withheld for foreign natls not residing in US, by country and tax treaty status, 1986, annual article, 8302-2.915

Minerals (strategic) supply, demand, trade, and foreign and US industry devs by firm and country, by commodity, bimonthly rpt with articles, 5602-4

Minerals foreign and US supply under alternative market conditions, reserves, and background industry data, series, 5606-4

Minerals production, reserves, and industry role in domestic economy and world supply, world area and country rpt, series, 5606-1

Navy procurement, by contractor and location, FY88, annual rpt, 3804-13

Nuclear power plant capacity, generation, and operating status, by plant and foreign and US location, 1988 and projected to 2020, annual rpt, 3164-57

Overseas Business Reports: economic conditions, investment and export opportunities, and trade practices, country market research rpt series, 2046-6

Patents (US) granted to US and foreign applicants, by applicant and country, 1960s-88, annual rpt, 2244-3

Tax (income) returns of corporations, income and tax items by asset size and detailed industry, 1986, annual rpt, 8304-4; 8304-21

Tax expenditures, Federal revenues forgone through income tax deductions and exclusions by type, FY90-94, annual rpt, 21784-10

UK and France govt-owned corporations stock issues, value, new shareholders, and revenue effects, 1960s-88, article, 9385-1.911

see also Multinational corporations

Foreign countries

Abortion-related deaths and hospitalization, for selected countries restricting abortions, 1950s-83, hearing, 21408-113

Aircraft hijackings, on-board explosions, and other crime, US and foreign incidents, 1983-87, annual rpt, 7504-31

Background Notes, foreign countries summary social, political, and economic data, series, 7006-2

Cement (portland) shipments to foreign countries, bimonthly rpt, 2042-1.6

Census Bur rpts and data files, coverage and availability, 1989 annual listing, 2304-2

Chiefs of State and Cabinet members, by country, bimonthly listing, 9112-4

Classification codes for countries and ports under Tariff Schedule of US, 1990 base edition and supplements, 9886-13

Classification codes for countries, commodities, and customs districts for Census Bur export statistics, 1990 base edition, 2428-5

Economic and monetary trends, compounded annual rates of change for US and 10 major trading partners, quarterly rpt, 9391-7

Economic and social conditions of foreign countries, working paper series, 2326-18

Economic conditions in Communist, OECD, and selected other countries, 1960s-88, annual rpt, 9114-4

Economic, social, political, and geographic summary data, by country, 1989, annual factbook, 9114-2

Education data for foreign countries, and students enrolled in US higher education instns, 1989 edition, annual rpt, 4824-2.29

Education statistics, detailed data on elementary and secondary education, 1920s-88 and projected to 1997, annual rpt, 4824-1.1

Geographic Notes, foreign countries boundaries, claims, nomenclature, and other devs, periodic rpt, 7142-3

Health condition and health care resources, use, and spending, 1950s-87, annual data compilation, 4144-11

Health, welfare, and research aid from HHS, by program, recipient, and country, FY88, annual listing, 4004-3.10

Living costs abroad, State Dept indexes, housing allowances, and hardship differentials by country and major city, quarterly rpt, 6862-1

Mail (US) revenue, FY88, and volume from FY84, annual rpt, 9864-1

Mail (US) to foreign countries, USPS itemized operating costs, FY88, annual rpt, 9864-4

Mail (US) to foreign countries, USPS revenue, and costs and miles by class of mail, FY88, annual rpt, 9864-2

Mail (US) to foreign countries, USPS revenue and volume, quarterly rpt, 9862-1

Mail (US) to foreign countries, USPS revenue, FY88, annual rpt, 9864-5

Medicare enrollment, by region and abroad, 1966-87, article, 4652-1.937

Minerals foreign and US supply under alternative market conditions, reserves, and background industry data, series, 5606-4

Minerals industry operations, trends, and projections for selected countries, series, 5606-5

Minerals of strategic and technological importance, supply, imports, and use, with foreign comparisons, commodity rpt series, 5606-9

Minerals production, prices, trade, use, employment, tariffs, and stockpiles, by mineral, with foreign comparisons, 1984-88, annual rpt, 5604-18

Minerals production, reserves, and industry role in domestic economy and world supply, world area and country rpt, series, 5606-1

Minerals Yearbook, 1987, Vol 1 preprints: commodity reviews of production, reserves, supply, use, and trade, annual rpt series, 5604-15

Minerals Yearbook, 1987, Vol 3: foreign country reviews of production, trade, and policy, by commodity, annual rpt, 5604-35

Minerals Yearbook, 1987, Vol 3 preprints: foreign country reviews of production, trade, and policy, by commodity, annual rpt series, 5604-23

Minerals Yearbook, 1988, Vol 1: commodity reviews of production, reserves, supply, use, and trade, annual rpt series, 5604-20

Older persons institutionalization in medical and other care facilities, rates by selected country, 1980 and 1985, article, 4652-1.918

Patents (US) granted to US and foreign applicants, by applicant and country, 1960s-88, annual rpt, 2244-3

Population size, growth rates, and components of change, by country, projected 1989-2020 and trends from 1950, biennial rpt, 2324-9

Science and engineering labor supply, R&D funding, and other science indicators, with foreign comparisons, 1960s-89, annual chartbook, 9624-22

Social security programs and spending by type, with background data, for selected OECD countries, 1940s-80s and projected to 2040, 4742-1.908

Social security programs coverage, funding, eligibility, and benefits, by country, 1987, biennial rpt, 4746-4.60

Statistical Abstract of US, social, political, and economic data, with foreign comparisons, 1790-2025, comprehensive annual compilation, 2324-1

Travel from US, characteristics of visit and traveler, and world area of destination, 1988 in-flight survey, annual rpt, 2904-14

Travel to and from US, and travel receipts and payments, by world area, with data by country, 1984-88, annual rpt, 2904-10

Travel to and from US on US and foreign flag air carriers, by country, world area, and US port, monthly rpt, 7302-2

Travel to US and Canada, market analysis with detailed trip and traveler characteristics, country rpt series, 2906-2

Travel to US, characteristics of visit and traveler, world area of origin, and US destination, 1988 survey, annual rpt, 2904-12

Travel to US, spending by world area of residence, and economic impact, by spending category, census div, and State, model results, 1985-86, 2908-28

Travel to US, tour promotion by region of destination and country of traveler, 1987, 2908-31

US govt civil service pension beneficiaries and benefits overseas, FY87, annual rpt, 9844-34

US govt civilian employment and payroll abroad, by agency, bimonthly rpt, 9842-1

US govt civilian employment and payroll, by occupation, pay grade, sex, agency, and location, 1987, biennial rpt, 9844-4

US govt civilian employment and payroll, by pay system and location, 1988, annual rpt, 9844-6.1

US govt-leased real property inventory and rental costs, worldwide summary by location and agency, 1987, annual rpt, 9454-10

US govt-owned real property inventory and costs, worldwide summary by location, agency, and use, 1987, annual rpt, 9454-5

US Medicare recipients living abroad, 1986-87, annual rpt, 4657-5

US military and civilian personnel and dependents, by service branch, world area, and country, quarterly rpt, 3542-20

US military draft registrants residing abroad, 2nd half FY88, semiannual rpt, 9742-1

US military hospitals abroad, admissions, beds, outpatient visits, and births, by service branch, quarterly rpt, 3542-15

US military personnel abroad, by service branch, world area, and country, quarterly news release, 3542-9

US military prime contract awards for R&D to US and foreign nonprofit instns and govt agencies, by instn and location, FY88, annual listing, 3544-17

US personal transfer payments to foreigners, *Survey of Current Business*, monthly rpt, 2702-1.1; 2702-1.21

US veterans living abroad, VA expenses by type and location, FY88, annual rpt, 8604-3.9

Vaccination needs for intl travel by country, and disease prevention recommendations, 1989 annual rpt, 4204-11

Vital and Health Statistics series: foreign and US comparative data, 4147-5

Weather data for surface and upper air, averages by foreign and US station, monthly rpt, 2152-4

Weather events and anomalies, precipitation and temperature for US and foreign locations, weekly rpt, 2182-6

Wilderness areas acreage by Federal agency and location, and sources of damage, with data for foreign countries, 1988 conf papers, 1208-301

Wildlife-related recreation, hunting, and fishing participation by US residents in other countries, 1985 survey, quinquennial rpt, 5508-5

see also Africa
see also Agricultural exports and imports
see also Alien workers
see also Aliens
see also Asia
see also Balance of payments
see also Caribbean area
see also Central America
see also Centrally planned economies
see also Citizenship
see also Deportation
see also Developing countries
see also Diplomatic and consular service
see also East-West trade
see also Eastern Europe
see also Educational exchanges
see also Europe
see also Foreign agriculture
see also Foreign budgets
see also Foreign competition
see also Foreign corporations
see also Foreign debts
see also Foreign economic relations
see also Foreign exchange
see also Foreign investments
see also Foreign labor conditions
see also Foreign languages
see also Foreign medical graduates
see also Foreign opinion of U.S.
see also Foreign relations
see also Foreign students
see also Foreign trade
see also Foreign trade promotion
see also Immigration and emigration
see also International assistance
see also International cooperation in conservation
see also International cooperation in cultural activities
see also International cooperation in environmental sciences
see also International cooperation in law enforcement
see also International cooperation in science and technology
see also International finance
see also International military forces
see also International sanctions
see also Latin America
see also Middle East
see also Military assistance
see also North America
see also Oceania
see also Refugees
see also South America
see also Southeast Asia
see also Tariffs and foreign trade controls
see also Trade agreements
see also Treaties and conventions
see also under By Foreign Country in the "Index by Categories"
see also under names of individual countries

Foreign currency programs
see Special foreign currency programs

Foreign debts
AID loans authorized, signed, and canceled, by country and world area, quarterly rpt, 9912-2
AID loans repayment status and terms by program and country, and status of predecessor agency loans, quarterly rpt, 9912-3
Assets and debts of private sector, balance sheets by segment, 1949-88, semiannual rpt, 9365-4.1

Assistance (financial and nonfinancial) of Fed Govt, 1989 base edition with supplements, annual listing, 104-5
Banks (US) and nonbanking firms liabilities to and claims on foreigners, by country, 1986-87, annual rpt, 9364-5.10
Banks (US) domestic and intl operations, charters, mergers, and liquidations, by instn and State, quarterly rpt, 8402-3
Banks (US) foreign lending at all US and foreign offices, by country group and country, quarterly rpt, 13002-1
Banks and nonbank liabilities to and claims on foreigners, by type and world area, monthly rpt, 9362-1.3
Budget of US, special analysis of outstanding debt and interest costs, FY90, annual rpt, 104-1.5
Cuba economic conditions, agricultural and industrial production and distribution, trade, and intl economic relations, 1980-87 with trends from 1961, 9118-8
Currency (foreign) positions of US firms and foreign branches or affiliates, *Treasury Bulletin*, quarterly rpt, 8002-4.12
Current account balance of US, components and relation to foreign and US investment and economic conditions, 1970s-88 and projected to 1990s, article, 9385-1.907
Developing countries debt burden and economic conditions, and trade with industrialized countries, by country, 1970s-87, hearings, 25248-108
Developing countries debt reduction proposals, and Eximbank export financing programs, with background data, 1986-89, 2048-142
Developing countries economic aid from US, bilateral and through intl dev banks, by world region and country, 1970s-FY88, annual rpt, 9904-1
Developing countries economic and social conditions from 1960s, and Intl Dev Cooperation Agency and AID activities and funding, FY88-90, annual rpt, 9904-4
Developing countries economic indicators, problem debtors compared to other borrowers, by country, 1973-84, 1528-285
Developing countries food production and needs, and related economic outlook, by country, 1989/90, annual rpt, 1524-6
Developing countries loans from banks and govts, debt exposure of 7 developed countries, various periods 1980-88, GAO rpt, 26123-255
Developing countries loans from US banks, ratios and reserves as share of loans, for leading instns, 1988, working paper, 9389-19.12
Developing countries loans of 9 US money center banks, and debt indicators by selected country, 1970s-88, hearings, 21248-122
Eastern Europe and USSR debt, trade, and balances with US and other western countries, with background data, 1980s-87, hearing, 21248-120
Eastern Europe debt by source, and developing country debt, 1970s-88, annual rpt, 9114-4.2
Economic and military aid and loans from US and intl agencies, by program and country, FY46-87, annual rpt, 9914-5

Economic conditions and trade devs and policy, for US and foreign countries, 1988 conf papers, 9373-3.32
Eximbank financial condition, credit and insurance authorizations, and loan activity and delinquencies, by country, FY88, annual rpt, 9254-1
Fed Govt finances, cash and debt transactions, daily tables, 8102-4
Flow-of-funds accounts, assets and liabilities by type and economic sector, outstanding at year-end 1965-88, annual rpt, 9364-3
Intl finance and trade studies, 1987 biennial compilation, 9375-14
Investment (foreign direct) in US, and US investment abroad, by type, selected years 1975-87, article, 9391-1.910
Investment (intl) position of US, by component, industry, world region, and country, 1987-88, annual article, 2702-1.922
Outstanding debt to US of foreign govts and private obligors, by country and program, periodic rpt, 8002-6
Pacific basin countries military, economic, technological, and trade conditions, 1970s-85, compilation of papers, 3908-4
Portugal and Turkey economic indicators and govt finances, 1982-86, hearing, 21388-53
South Africa loans from US banks, and rescheduling issues, 1984-89, press release, 8008-136
Soviet Union economic conditions under General Secretary Gorbachev, 1988 and trends from 1956, annual rpt, 9114-6
Soviet Union hard currency debt to western countries, and balance of payments 1960s-88, annual rpt, 9114-4.3
Statistical Abstract of US, social, political, and economic data, by outlying area and country, 1950s-87, comprehensive annual compilation, 2324-1.4
Survey of Current Business, monthly rpt, quarterly tables, 2702-1.31
UN voting record and share of votes in agreement with US, by issue, country, and world area, 1988, annual rpt, 7004-18
US foreign debt economic impact, 1970s-80s and projected to 2000, article, 9387-1.905
US govt contingent liabilities and claims paid on federally insured and guaranteed contracts with foreign obligors, by country and program, periodic rpt, 8002-12
US govt liabilities to foreigners and foreign official instns, *Treasury Bulletin*, quarterly rpt, 8002-4.10
US natls claims against foreign govts, by claim type and country, 1988, annual rpt, 6004-16
see also Balance of payments
see also Public debt

Foreign economic relations
Asia dollar exchange rate, and impacts of currency appreciation on current account and trade balances and economic indicators, for 3 countries, 1980s-90, GAO rpt, 26123-234
Assistance (financial and nonfinancial) of Fed Govt, 1989 base edition with supplements, annual listing, 104-5
Background Notes, foreign countries summary social, political, and economic data, series, 7006-2

Farmland (US) investment of foreigners related to exchange rate, interest rate, and cropland returns, by leading country, 1981-88, 1528–287

Fed Reserve Board and Reserve banks finances, staff, and review of monetary policy and economic devs, 1988, annual rpt, 9364–1

Financial and business statistics, historic trends, 1988 annual chartbook, 9364–2.17

Flow-of-funds accounts, assets and liabilities by type and economic sector, outstanding at year-end 1965-88, annual rpt, 9364–3

Flow-of-funds accounts, savings, investments, and credit statements, quarterly rpt, 9365–3.3

Futures and options trading volume, by commodity and exchange, FY88, annual rpt, 11924–2

Futures contracts on commodities, financial instruments, and indexes, options trading in NYC, Chicago, and other markets, monthly rpt, 11922–6

Futures trading in selected commodities and financial instruments and indexes, NYC, Chicago, and other markets activity, monthly rpt, 11922–5

Germany (West) and France exchange rate variability impact of monetary policy, model description and results, 1973-88, working paper, 9387–8.181

Germany (West) money supply impact of central bank foreign exchange intervention, various periods 1978-88, article, 9391–1.924

Interest rate differentials among countries, US and 4 industrialized countries, 1960s-88, article, 9385–1.902

Interest rates relation to intl rates, exchange rates, and US money supply, for 7 OECD countries, 1979-88, article, 9391–1.920

Intl finance and trade studies, 1987 biennial compilation, 9375–14

Intl transactions summary, 1980s-88, annual article, 9362–1.904

Investment (intl) position of US, by component, industry, world region, and country, 1987-88, annual article, 2702–1.922

Manufacturing employment change during periods of exchange rate volatility, by industry trade orientation and and census div, 1973-87, article, 9373–1.917

Money supply changes, financial markets response, regression results, late 1970s-84, working paper, 9371–10.32

North Carolina counties manufacturing employment, by industry group and whether urban, with exchange rate impacts, 1980-85, article, 9389–1.915

OECD and US exchange rate indexes, for 7 countries, 1981-88, annual rpt, 9254–3

OECD current account balance and related economic indicators, for US and 4 countries, 1980s-87, article, 9389–1.908

Production impacts of dollar exchange rate and fiscal policy, by industry div, 1970-87, working paper, 9393–10.5

Statistical Abstract of US, social, political, and economic data, by outlying area and country, 1950s-87, comprehensive annual compilation, 2324–1.4

Switzerland franc exchange rate against dollar and German mark, impact of monetary policy, 1973-86, article, 9391–1.907

Taiwan and South Korea trade balance impacts of exchange rates and foreign and domestic economic indicators, 1974-87, article, 9393–8.905

Treasury and Fed Reserve foreign exchange operations, *Fed Reserve Bulletin*, monthly rpt, quarterly article, 9362–1

Treasury and Fed Reserve foreign exchange operations, quarterly journal, 9385–1

Unemployment rate impact of exchange rate variability, model description and results, 1963-85, technical paper, 9366–6.206

Wheat exports impacts of subsidies and exchange rates, by importing and exporting country, alternative model results, 1986/87, 1548–351

see also Balance of payments

see also Eurocurrency

Foreign investments

Acquisitions (hostile takeover) of US firms by foreign firms, attempts by outcome, and transaction value, with data by firm, 1984-88, GAO rpt, 26123–222

Arms sales of US, foreign conditions on sales and impacts on US industry, with data by industry group and country, 1988 annual rpt, 104–25

Assets and debts of private sector, balance sheets by segment, 1949-88, semiannual rpt, 9365–4.1

Banks (insured commercial and savings) finances, for foreign and domestic offices, by asset size, 1987, annual rpt, 9294–4.2

Banks (US) and nonbanking firms liabilities to and claims on foreigners, by country, 1986-87, annual rpt, 9364–5.10

Banks in California owned by Japanese and other foreign banks, assets, portfolio composition, and cost of funds, 1987-88, article, 9393–8.906

Bond (low-grade) issues by industry div, holdings by owner type, yields, and defaults, 1977-88, 21248–118

Business America, foreign and domestic commerce, and US investment and trade opportunities, biweekly journal, 2042–24

Business and financial statistics, historic trends, 1988 annual chartbook, 9364–2.17

Capital flows (intl) impacts on monetary policy instruments, and financial and economic indicators, 1987 compilation of papers, 9385–9

Caribbean area foreign investment of US, by industry div, 1988, annual rpt, 9884–20.2

Caribbean Basin Initiative investment incentives, economic impacts, with finances and employment by country, 1984-88, 2048–141

China trade with US by commodity, and foreign investment by source country, 1988, 9118–9

Corporations and govt securities of US, foreign transactions, monthly rpt, 9362–1.3

Currency (foreign) positions of US firms and foreign branches or affiliates, *Treasury Bulletin*, quarterly rpt, 8002–4.12

Current account balance and net capital flows, 1988-89, semiannual rpt, 8002–14

Current account balance of US, components and relation to foreign and US investment and economic conditions, 1970s-88 and projected to 1990s, article, 9385–1.906; 9385–1.907

Developing countries economic aid from US, bilateral and through intl dev banks, by world region and country, 1970s-FY88, annual rpt, 9904–1

Direct foreign investment and trade of US, barriers, impacts, and US actions, by country, 1988, annual rpt, 444–2

Direct foreign investment in and by US, and net position, 1970-88, annual rpt, 2044–26

Direct foreign investment in North Central States and other US regions by country and major industry group, and for auto industry, 1978-88, working paper, 9375–13.12

Direct foreign investment in US, and US investment abroad, by type, selected years 1975-87, article, 9391–1.910

Direct foreign investment in US by country, and finances, employment, and acreage owned, by industry group of business acquired or established, 1982-88, annual article, 2702–1.917

Direct foreign investment in US, by industry group and world area, 1987-88, annual article, 2702–1.929

Direct foreign investment in US, major transactions by type, industry, country, and US location, 1987, annual rpt, 2044–20

Direct foreign investment of US, by selected industry group and world area, 1986-88, annual article, 2702–1.930

Economic conditions and trade devs and policy, for US and foreign countries, 1988 conf papers, 9373–3.32

Economic conditions, policy, and trade practices, by country, 1986-88, annual rpt, 21384–5

Energy-intensive industry output and operations, and US investment barriers, for energy-rich countries, 1984-88, 9886–4.142

Energy producers finances and operations, by energy type for US firms domestic and foreign operations, 1987, annual rpt, 3164–44

Energy resources of US, foreign direct investment by energy type and firm, US affiliates operations, and acquisitions, as of 1988, annual rpt, 3164–80

Farmland (US) investment of foreigners related to exchange rate, interest rate, and cropland returns, by leading country, 1981-88, 1528–287

Farmland (US) owned by foreigners, by owner country and State, as of Dec 1988, article, 1561–16.902

Farmland (US) owned by foreigners, holdings, acquisitions, and disposals by land use, owner type and country, and State, 1988, annual rpt, 1584–2

Farmland (US) owned by foreigners, holdings, acreage, and value by land use, owner country, State, and county, 1988, annual rpt, 1584–3

Flow-of-funds accounts, assets and liabilities by type and economic sector, outstanding at year-end 1965-88, annual rpt, 9364–3

Flow-of-funds accounts, savings, investments, and credit statements, quarterly rpt, 9365–3.3

Flows of trade and investment, and economic indicators, for selected countries and country groups, selected years 1946-88, annual rpt, 204–1.1; 204–1.9

Mexico industrial plants owned by US firms, employment impacts of US and Asia wages, 1975-87, technical paper, 9379-12.45

Mexico labor supply and conditions, with data by major city, selected years 1969-88, working paper, 2326-18.49

Mexico population, labor force, and emigration, alternative projections 1990-2000, working paper, 2326-18.46

Minerals (strategic) supply, demand, trade, and foreign and US industry devs by firm and country, by commodity, bimonthly rpt with articles, 5602-4

Minerals production, reserves, and industry role in domestic economy and world supply, world area and country rpt, series, 5606-1

Multinatl US firms and foreign affiliates finances and operations, by industry of parent firm and affiliate, world area, and selected country, 1987, annual article, 2702-1.920; 2704-5

OECD economic conditions for 6 countries and US, biweekly rpt, 9112-1

Overseas Business Reports: economic conditions, investment and export opportunities, and trade practices, country market research rpt series, 2046-6

Pacific basin countries unemployment rates, for 7 countries, 1986-88, hearings, 23846-4.27

Paper and wood products production and trade, and industry operations by firm, by country, world region rpt series, 2046-14

R&D funding and science and technology employment for selected countries, selected years 1961-87, annual rpt, 9624-18.2

Research contracts of Bur of Intl Labor Affairs, FY83-89, annual listing, 6364-1

Science and engineering labor supply, R&D funding, and other science indicators, with foreign comparisons, 1960s-89, annual chartbook, 9624-22

Social security programs and spending by type, with background data, for selected OECD countries, 1940s-80s and projected to 2040, 4742-1.908

Soviet Union personal income by source, disposable income, wage deductions by type, and savings, 1950s-87, 9118-7

Statistical Abstract of US, social, political, and economic data, by outlying area and country, 1950s-87, comprehensive annual compilation, 2324-1.4

Steel imports of US under voluntary restraint agreements, with industry finances, operations, and foreign comparisons, various periods 1979-89, 21788-182

Sweden multinatl firms domestic and foreign production, exports, employment, and sales, with data by commodity and firm, 1960s-86, conf, 23848-208

Foreign languages

Background Notes, foreign countries summary social, political, and economic data, series, 7006-2

Court interpreter use in Federal district and bankruptcy courts, by language, June 1989, annual rpt, 18204-2.8; 18204-8.8

Degrees awarded in higher education, by level, field, race, and sex, 1989 edition, annual rpt, 4824-2.20

Developing countries disaster preparedness and economic, population, and political data, country rpt series, 9916-2

Fed Govt aid to intl education programs, by program, FY86-88, annual rpt, 4804-28.5

Foreign countries economic, social, political, and geographic summary data, by country, 1989, annual factbook, 9114-2

High school enrollment in foreign language classes, by language, 1948-85, annual rpt, 4824-2.8

Japan-US Friendship Commission educational and cultural exchange activities, grants, and trust fund status, FY87-88, biennial report, 14694-1

Military reserve spouses attitudes, and family social, economic, and other characteristics, 1986 survey, 3508-30

Radio Free Europe and Radio Liberty broadcast and financial data, and compared to other intl broadcasters, FY88, annual rpt, 10314-1

Refugee resettlement programs and funding, arrivals by country of origin, and indicators of adjustment, by State, FY88, annual rpt, 4694-5

SSA employment of Hispanics by regional office, and Spanish-speaking employees in California, 1987, GAO rpt, 26121-268

Teachers bachelor degrees, by field and other characteristics, 1985-86, 4838-39

see also Language use and ability

Foreign loans

see Export-Import Bank
see Foreign debts
see International assistance
see Military assistance

Foreign medical graduates

Admissions to US of immigrants, alien workers, and visitors, deportations, and naturalizations, by country, FY88 and trends from 1820, annual rpt, 6264-2

Developing countries population/physician ratios, by country, 1960s-83, annual rpt, 9904-4

Enrollment in science and engineering grad programs, by field, source of funds, and characteristics of student and instn, 1975-87, annual rpt, 9627-7

Health condition and health care resources, use, and spending, 1950s-87, annual data compilation, 4144-11

Military health care personnel, and accessions by training source, by occupation, specialty, and service branch, FY87, annual rpt, 3544-24

Nurses with alien resident status and temporary work visas, by State and source country, 1985-90, GAO rpt, 26121-314

Physicians (family practice) by age, ratios to population, and residents, and percent women and foreign medical grads, 1960s-88 and projected to 2010, article, 4042-3.926

VA health care personnel born abroad, and English proficiency, as of Mar 1988, GAO rpt, 26121-273

Foreign military sales

see Arms trade
see Military assistance

Foreign opinion of U.S.

Travel to US and Canada, market analysis with detailed trip and traveler characteristics, country rpt series, 2906-2

Foreign relations

Background Notes, foreign countries summary social, political, and economic data, series, 7006-2

Budget deficit reduction under Gramm-Rudman Act, cancellation of budget authority by program, FY90, annual rpt, 104-27; 26304-6

Budget of US Appendix, obligations, appropriations, and personnel, by program and agency, FY90, annual rpt, 104-3

Budget of US, CBO analysis of revenue and spending alternatives and projections of economic indicators, FY90-94, annual rpt, 26304-3

Budget of US, compact budgets by activity, function, and agency, FY90 and projected to FY94, annual rpt, 104-2

Budget of US, historical data, selected years FY34-88 and projected to FY94, annual rpt, 104-22

Budget of US, midsession review of FY90 budget, by function and agency, annual rpt, 104-7

Budget of US, Reagan Admin policy changes by program, FY90, annual rpt, 104-21

Criminal cases by type and disposition, and collections, for US attorneys, by Federal district, FY88, annual rpt, 6004-2.1

Helsinki Final Act implementation by NATO and Warsaw Pact, Oct 1988-Mar 1989, semiannual rpt, 7002-1

Loans and loan guarantees of Fed Govt, outstanding amounts by agency and program, *Treasury Bulletin*, quarterly rpt, 8002-4.9

State Dept programs fraud and abuse, audits and investigations, 2nd half FY89, semiannual rpt, 7002-6

UN voting record and share of votes in agreement with US, by issue, country, and world area, 1988, annual rpt, 7004-18

USIA activities, finances, and info services, FY89, annual rpt, 17594-1

see also Arms trade
see also Diplomatic and consular service
see also East-West trade
see also Educational exchanges
see also Exchange of persons programs
see also Executive agreements
see also Foreign countries
see also Foreign debts
see also Foreign economic relations
see also Foreign opinion of U.S.
see also Foreign students
see also Foreign trade
see also Foreign trade promotion
see also International assistance
see also International cooperation in conservation
see also International cooperation in cultural activities
see also International cooperation in environmental sciences
see also International cooperation in law enforcement
see also International cooperation in science and technology
see also International sanctions
see also Military assistance
see also Treaties and conventions
see also War

Foreign Sales Corporations
see Domestic International Sales
Corporations

Foreign Service
see Diplomatic and consular service

Foreign Service Act
Employee dev, Foreign Service Inst
enrollment and training hours by course,
1983-87, GAO rpt, 26123-248

Foreign students
Admissions to US of immigrants, alien
workers, and visitors, deportations, and
naturalizations, by country, FY88 and
trends from 1820, annual rpt, 6264-2

Black colleges R&D funding by source, and
characteristics of grad students and
research staff, by field of science and
instn, 1980s-87, 9628-78

Condition of Education, detailed data on
higher education, 1960s-88, annual rpt,
4824-1.2

Degrees awarded in higher education, by
level, field, race, and sex, 1989 edition,
annual rpt, 4824-2.20

Digest of Education Statistics, detailed data
on students, staff, finances, and facilities,
1989 edition, annual rpt, 4824-2

Drug enforcement training of US for foreign
govts, enrollment in US and host
countries by program, FY88, annual rpt,
7004-17

Engineering PhD awards to US and foreign
students, and minority bachelors and
masters degree recipients, 1977-87,
9626-2.182

Expenditures of foreign visitors to US, by
trip purpose and world area of residence,
model results, 1985-86, 2908-28

Latin America dev grants of Inter-American
Foundation by program area, and
fellowships by field and instn, by country,
FY71-88, annual rpt, 14424-2

Latin America dev grants of Inter-American
Foundation by recipient, and fellowships,
by country, FY88, annual rpt, 14424-1

Science and engineering education
enrollment, degrees, and student aid and
sources, with data by field, race, sex, and
instn, 1980s-87, 26358-202

Science and engineering employment and
education, and R&D spending, for US and
selected foreign countries, 1988, annual
rpt, 9624-23.2

Science and engineering grad enrollment, by
field, source of funds, and characteristics
of student and instn, 1975-87, annual rpt,
9627-7

Science and engineering labor force, Federal
and university research funding, and
educational data, series, 9626-6

Science and engineering labor supply, R&D
funding, and other science indicators, with
foreign comparisons, 1960s-89, annual
chartbook, 9624-22

Science and engineering PhDs, by field,
instn, employment prospects, sex, race,
and other characteristics, 1960s-88,
9627-30

Science PhD recipients by whether foreign,
race, and sex, and instnl support, 1978
and 1987-88, 9626-2.187

Statistical Abstract of US, social, political,
and economic data, 1790-2025,
comprehensive annual compilation,
2324-1.1

Travel to US, by characteristics of visit and
traveler, country, port city, and State of
destination, quarterly rpt, 2902-1
see also Educational exchanges
see also Foreign medical graduates

Foreign trade
Air cargo trade of US, by world area and
US customs district and city, monthly rpt,
suspended, 2422-8

Asia countries trade with US by commodity,
and free trade area proposal, 1985-88,
9886-4.135

Background Notes, foreign countries
summary social, political, and economic
data, series, 7006-2

Budget of US, balanced budget proposed
constitutional amendment, economic
impacts, projected to FY94 and
background data from 1940s, hearings,
21528-72

Business America, foreign and domestic
commerce, and US investment and trade
opportunities, biweekly journal, 2042-24

Business statistics, detailed data for major
industries and economic indicators, Survey
of Current Business, monthly rpt, 2702-1

Canada-US trade agreement impacts on
New England States trade, with data by
industry, commodity, and State, 1987,
article, 9373-2.902

Capital goods manufacturing productivity,
labor cost indexes, and trade and trade
balance impacts of economic conditions,
with foreign comparisons, 1970s-88,
article, 9385-1.909

Caribbean area duty-free exports to US, and
imports from US, by country, and impact
on US employment, by commodity, 1988,
annual rpt, 6364-2

Caribbean area duty-free exports to US, and
US exports and import duties on other
goods, by commodity and country,
1984-88, annual rpt, 9884-20

Caribbean Basin exports to OECD members,
and US imports under preferential
treatment programs, by commodity,
1980s-87, 2048-138

Caribbean Basin Initiative investment
incentives, economic impacts, with
finances and employment by country,
1984-88, 2048-141

Census Bur rpts and data files, coverage and
availability, 1989 annual listing, 2304-2

China housing and commercial construction,
and building materials production and
trade by product group, 1984-85 and
projected to 1990, article, 2042-1.910

China trade, by commodity, world area, and
country, 1985-87, 9118-10

China trade by SITC 1- to 5-digit
commodity, 1970s-87, annual rpt,
9114-3

Classification codes for countries,
commodities, and customs districts for
Census Bur export statistics, 1990 base
edition, 2428-5

Communist and OECD countries economic
conditions, 1987, annual rpt, 7144-11

Communist, OECD, and selected other
countries trade and balances, 1960s-88,
annual rpt, 9114-4.9

Containerized cargo carried over principal
trade routes, by flag of vessel, port, and
US coastal district, 1984, annual rpt,
7704-8

Cuba economic conditions, agricultural and
industrial production and distribution,
trade, and intl economic relations,
1980-87 with trends from 1961, 9118-8

Developing countries debt burden and
economic conditions, and trade with
industrialized countries, by country,
1970s-87, hearings, 25248-108

Developing countries disaster preparedness
and economic, population, and political
data, country rpt series, 9916-2

Developing countries economic and social
conditions from 1960s, and Intl Dev
Cooperation Agency and AID activities
and funding, FY88-90, annual rpt,
9904-4

Developing countries economic indicators,
problem debtors compared to other
borrowers, by country, 1973-84,
1528-285

Developing countries food production and
needs, and related economic outlook, by
country, 1989/90, annual rpt, 1524-6

Developing countries receiving US economic
aid, military spending and imports
measures to determine aid eligibility, by
country, 1985-86, annual rpt, 9914-1

Dollar exchange rate trade-weighted index
of Fed Reserve Bank of Atlanta, by world
area, monthly rpt, 9371-15

Dollar exchange rate trade-weighted index
of Fed Reserve Bank of Dallas, by world
area, monthly rpt, 9379-13

EC economic integration impact on EC
employment, GDP, and other economic
indicators, projected 1992, article,
9373-1.908

EC economic integration impacts on
domestic economic conditions and US
trade, with trade by commodity and
country, 1984-87, 9886-4.140

EC trade with US by country, and total
agricultural trade, selected years 1958-88,
annual rpt, 7144-7

Economic and employment conditions,
alternative BLS projections to 2000 and
trends 1970s-88, biennial article,
6722-1.953

Economic conditions, and trade devs and
balances, with data by selected country
and country group, monthly rpt, 9882-14

Economic conditions and trade devs and
policy, for US and foreign countries, 1988
conf papers, 9373-3.32

Economic conditions in foreign countries
and implications for US, periodic country
rpt series, 2046-4

Economic conditions, policy, and trade
practices, by country, 1986-88, annual rpt,
21384-5

Economic indicators and components, and
Fed Reserve 4th District business and
financial conditions, monthly chartbook,
9377-10

Economic indicators and components,
current data and annual trends, monthly
rpt, 23842-1.7

Economic Report of the President for 1989,
Joint Economic Committee critique and
policy recommendations, annual rpt,
23844-2

Economic Report of the President for 1989,
with economic trends from 1929, annual
rpt, 204-1

Economic, social, political, and geographic summary data, by country, 1989, annual factbook, 9114-2

Employment related to exports, by industry div, 1980s-87, 2048-103

Export and import balance, by component, 1987-89, semiannual rpt, 8002-14

Export competitiveness of US, findings and recommendations, 1988 rpt, 028-31

Exports and imports, *Business Conditions Digest*, monthly rpt, 2702-3.5; 2702-3.9

Exports and imports of US, and trade balance, by major commodity group, selected country, world area, and State, monthly rpt, suspended, 2422-6

Exports and imports of US, by commodity group, world area, selected country, US coastal area and port, and mode of transport, monthly rpt, 2422-9

Exports and imports of US by country, and trade shifts by commodity, quarterly rpt, 9882-9

Exports and imports of US, by selected country, country group, and commodity group, 1988, annual rpt, 2044-37

Exports and imports of US shipped through Canada, by detailed commodity, customs district, and country, 1987, annual rpt, 7704-11

Exports and imports, trade agreements and relations, and USITC investigations, 1988, annual rpt, 9884-5

Exports, imports, and balances, monthly rpt, 9362-1.3

Exports, imports, and balances of US by commodity group, world area, and country, and related employment, 1970s-88, annual rpt, 2044-26

Exports, imports, and balances of US with major trading partners, by product category, 1984-88, annual chartbook, 9884-21

Exports of US, detailed commodities by country, monthly rpt, 2422-3

Financial and business statistics, historic trends, 1988 annual chartbook, 9364-2.17

Flows of trade and investment, and economic indicators, for selected countries and country groups, selected years 1946-88, annual rpt, 204-1.1; 204-1.9

Flows of trade relation to country commodity demand patterns, 1975, technical paper, 9379-12.31

Generalized System of Preferences status, and US tariffs, trade by country, production, and use, for selected commodities, 1984-88, annual rpt, 9884-23

Great Lakes trade between US and Canada, and other foreign trade, by type of vessel, 1986, annual rpt, 7704-7.3

Imports and tariff provisions effect on US industries and products, investigations with background financial and operating data, series, 9886-4

Imports, exports, and employment impacts, by SIC 2- to 4-digit industry and commodity, quarterly rpt, 2322-2

Imports injury to US industries from foreign subsidized products, investigations with background financial and operating data, series, 9886-15

Imports injury to US industries from sales at less than fair value, investigations with background financial and operating data, series, 9886-14

Imports of US, detailed Schedule A commodities by country, monthly rpt, 2422-2

Imports of US given duty-free treatment for value of US material sent abroad, and impacts on US industry and employment, by commodity and country, 1987, annual rpt, 9884-14

Indexes of trade indicators, alternative measures, quarterly 1978-84, working paper, 6886-6.14

Industry finances and operations, by SIC 2- to 4-digit industry, forecast 1989 and trends from 1950s, annual rpt, 2044-28

Input-output structure of US economy, detailed interindustry transactions for 84 industries, and components of final demand, 1983, annual article, 2702-1.909

Intl transactions summary, 1980s-88, annual article, 9362-1.904

Latin America trade, and balance of trade with US, by country, 1988, annual rpt, 2044-34

Manufacturing annual survey, 1986: exports and export-related employment, by SIC 2-digit industry and State, and compared to 1985, model results, annual rpt, 2506-16.1

Manufacturing electric power use and prices, shipments, and trade, for 25 SIC 4-digit industries, 1972-86, 2048-137

Manufacturing employment, and export and import shares, by SIC 2-digit industry, 1950s-88, article, 9373-1.906

Manufacturing employment change during periods of exchange rate volatility, by industry trade orientation and and census div, 1973-87, article, 9373-1.917

Manufacturing export shares by industry group, region, and country of destination, 1987, article, 9381-1.903

Metro area employment and manufacturing output growth, relation to labor costs and area economic conditions, 1976-85, working paper, 9375-13.8

Multinatl firms US affiliates finances and operations, by industry div, country of parent firm, and State, 1986-87, annual article, 2702-1.925

Multinatl firms US affiliates, finances, and operations, by industry, world area of parent firm, and State, 1987, annual rpt, 2704-4

Multinatl US firms and foreign affiliates finances and operations, by industry of parent firm and affiliate, world area, and selected country, 1987, annual article, 2702-1.920; 2704-5

Natl income and product accounts and components, *Survey of Current Business*, monthly rpt, 2702-1.21; 2702-1.25

OECD economic conditions for 6 countries and US, biweekly rpt, 9112-1

OECD trade, total and for 4 major countries, and US trade by country, by commodity, 1970-87, world area rpt series, 9116-1

Outlying areas trade with US, by detailed commodity and mode of transport, monthly rpt, 2422-4

Overseas Business Reports: economic conditions, investment and export opportunities, and trade practices, country market research rpt series, 2046-6

Overseas Private Investment Corp projects, and exports and export-related employment generated, FY88, annual rpt, 9904-2; 9904-3

Pacific basin countries military, economic, technological, and trade conditions, 1970s-85, compilation of papers, 3908-4

Pacific territories social, economic, health, and govtl data, FY88 and trends, annual rpt, 7004-6

Portugal and Turkey economic indicators and govt finances, 1982-86, hearing, 21388-53

Price indexes for exports and imports, and share of 1985 trade value, by selected commodity group, various periods 1986-88, annual article, 6722-1.922

Price indexes for exports and imports, by commodity, 1980-88, 6728-38.8

Price indexes for exports and imports, by selected end-use category, monthly press release, 6762-15

Price indexes for exports and imports of goods and services, and dollar exchange rate indexes, quarterly press release, 6762-13

Price indexes for exports and imports of US, by SITC commodity, end-use, and SIC industry, Monthly Labor Review, 6722-1.4

Small business high technology sales, exports, siting, technology transfer, views on competitiveness, 1988 survey, hearing, 21728-69

Soviet Union budget deficits and financing, revenues, and spending, with retail prices, 1970-88, 9118-6

Soviet Union economic conditions and military activity, 1960s-86, hearing, 23848-195

Soviet Union economic conditions under General Secretary Gorbachev, 1988 and trends from 1956, annual rpt, 9114-6

Statistical Abstract of US, social, political, and economic data, with foreign comparisons, 1790-2025, comprehensive annual compilation, 2324-1.3; 2324-1.4

Sweden multinatl firms domestic and foreign production, exports, employment, and sales, with data by commodity and firm, 1960s-86, conf, 23848-208

Taiwan and South Korea exports, imports, and trade balance with US, 1985-88, article, 9385-1.904

Technology dev and foreign competition issues for US, fundings and recommendations, 1980s-87, 21708-123

USITC activities, investigations, and rpts, FY88, annual rpt, 9884-1

USITC rpts, 1982-88, annual listing, 9884-12

Wholesale trade census, 1987: employment, establishments, finances, and operations, by SIC 2- to 4-digit kind of business, MSA, county, and city, State rpt series, 2405-1

see also Agricultural exports and imports
see also Arms trade
see also Balance of payments
see also Coal exports and imports
see also Common markets and free trade areas
see also Contraband
see also Customs administration

Forest Service timber resources inventories coverage and methodology, 1932-89, 9188-110

Georgia timber resources and removals, by species, ownership class, and county, 1988-89, series, 1206-26

Grazing land acreage, erosion, value, and livestock fed, by region and State, 1950-82, 1588-130

Gross product growth rates relation to natural resources sector share of State output, 1963-86, article, 9393-8.909

Illinois timber resources, removals, and products, by species, forest characteristics, ownership, and county, 1960s-85 and projected to 2015, 1208-292

Improvement program for private timberland, Fed Govt cost-sharing funds by region and State, monthly table, 1802-11

Improvement program for private timberland, participation and payments by State, as of FY87, annual rpt, 1804-20

Indian (Cherokee) Agency activities in North Carolina, FY89, annual rpt, 5704-4

Insect (mountain pine beetle) infestation in Western US and Canada, characteristics and control measures, 1988 conf papers, 1208-306

Insect and disease incidence and damage in forests, annual regional rpt series, 1206-11

Insect and disease incidence and damage in forests, by State, 1988, annual rpt, 1204-8

Mgmt of public lands and resources dev, environmental, economic, and social impacts of alternative Forest Service programs, projected to 2030, 1208-24

New Mexico timber acreage and resources, by species, ownership class, and county, 1986-87, series, 1206-23

New Mexico timber resources and harvest, 1987, 1208-310

Northeastern US timber resources and removals, by species, ownership, and county, State rpt series, 1206-12

Northwestern US and British Columbia forest industry production, prices, trade, and employment, quarterly rpt, 1202-3

Northwestern US timber resources and removals, projected under 5 mgmt alternatives, 1988 rpt, 1208-300

Occupational injury and illness rates, by SIC 2- to 4-digit industry, 1987, annual rpt, 6844-1

Oregon (western) non-Federal land, by use and county, 1971-74 and 1982, 1206-19.9

Oregon timber resources, by species, ownership, and county, 1983-86, series, 1206-19

Pesticide (soil fumigant) use, impacts of bans of selected fumigants on production, farm income, and retail prices, by crop and region, 1988 rpt, 1588-136

Pine (lodgepole) losses from beetle infestation, and effects of thinning stands, 1985 study, 1208-297

Planting and dev of forests and windbarriers, by State, FY88, annual rpt, 1204-7

Public lands acreage, grants, use, revenues, and allocations, by State, FY88, annual rpt, 5724-1.2

R&D funding, and scientists and engineers education and employment, for US and selected foreign countries, 1988, annual rpt, 9624-23.1

Research (agricultural) funding and staffing for USDA, State agencies, and other instns, by topic, FY88, annual rpt, 1744-2

Research and education grants, USDA competitive awards by program and recipient, FY88, annual listing, 1764-1

Research and mgmt of timber resources, for southeast US, 1988 biennial conf papers, 1204-35

Rocky Mountain States timber and mill residue production, by species, ownership, and county, series, 1206-17

Rural areas employment, economic conditions, and population characteristics, 1970s-85, compilation of papers, 1598-243

Southeastern US pine resources and removals, 1950s-85, hearing, 21368-104

Statistical Abstract of US, social, political, and economic data, 1790-2025, comprehensive annual compilation, 2324-1.1; 2324-1.3

Tax (income) returns of partnerships, income statement items by industry group, 1986, annual article, 8302-2.903

Tax (income) returns of sole proprietorships, income statement items, by industry group, 1987, annual article, 8302-2.904; 8302-2.921

Tennessee timber acreage and resources, by species, ownership class, and county, 1989, series, 1206-27

Transportation census, 1987: trucks, by detailed characteristics, miles traveled, and type of product carried, State rpt series, 2573-1

Tropical deforestation, land degradation, and salinization of irrigated cropland, by world area, late 1970s-84, article, 1522-3.910

TVA financial and operating data by program and facility, FY88, annual rpt, 9804-32

Wisconsin timber resources and removals, by species, forest type, ownership, and county, series, 1206-34

see also Forest fires
see also Gum and wood chemicals
see also Lumber industry and products
see also National forests
see also National parks
see also State forests
see also Wood fuel
see also By Industry in the "Index by Categories"

Forgery
see Counterfeiting and forgery

Forgione, Pascal D., Jr.
"Collecting and Profiling School/Instructional Variables as Part of the State-NAEP Results Reporting: Some Technical and Political Issues", 4828-37.1

Forrest, Jacqueline D.
"Unintended Pregnancy Among American Women", 21408-113

Forstall, Richard L.
"Patterns of Metropolitan Area and County Population Growth: 1980-87", 2546-3.160

Forsyth County, N.C.
Cancer (cervical) screening and education program for black women, effectiveness and participant characteristics, 1988 local area study, article, 4042-3.953

Fort Collins, Colo.
Housing vacancy rates for single and multifamily units and mobile homes, by city and ZIP code, 1989, annual MSA rpt, 9304-22.5
see also under By SMSA or MSA in the "Index by Categories"

Fort Lauderdale, Fla.
CPI by component for US city average, and by region, population size, and for 15 metro areas, monthly rpt, 6762-1
CPI by component for US city average, and by region, population size, and for 27 metro areas, monthly rpt, 6762-2
Drug test results at arrest, by drug type, offense, and sex, for selected urban areas, quarterly rpt, 6062-3
Housing starts and completions authorized by building permits in 40 MSAs, quarterly rpt, 2382-9
Wages by occupation, for office and plant workers, 1989 survey, periodic MSA rpt, 6785-3.10
see also under By City and By SMSA or MSA in the "Index by Categories"

Fort Myers, Fla.
see also under By SMSA or MSA in the "Index by Categories"

Fort Pierce, Fla.
see also under By SMSA or MSA in the "Index by Categories"

Fort Smith, Ark.
Wages by occupation, for office and plant workers, 1988 survey, periodic MSA rpt, 6785-3.1
see also under By SMSA or MSA in the "Index by Categories"

Fort Walton Beach, Fla.
see also under By SMSA or MSA in the "Index by Categories"

Fort Wayne, Ind.
Wages by occupation, for office and plant workers, 1989 survey, periodic MSA rpt, 6785-3.7
see also under By City and By SMSA or MSA in the "Index by Categories"

Fort Worth, Tex.
CPI by component for US city average, and by region, population size, and for 15 metro areas, monthly rpt, 6762-1
CPI by component for US city average, and by region, population size, and for 27 metro areas, monthly rpt, 6762-2
CPI by major component for 2 Texas MSAs, monthly rpt, 6962-2
Employment, earnings, hours, and CPI changes, for Dallas-Fort Worth metro area, 1970s-88, annual rpt, 6964-2
Housing and households characteristics, 1985 survey, MSA fact sheet, 2485-11.11
Housing and households detailed characteristics, and unit and neighborhood quality, by location, 1985 survey, MSA rpt, 2485-6.7
Housing starts and completions authorized by building permits in 40 MSAs, quarterly rpt, 2382-9
Wages by occupation, for office and plant workers, 1988 survey, periodic MSA rpt, 6785-11.3

see also under By City and By SMSA or
MSA in the "Index by Categories"

Fortier, Diana L.
"Hostile Takeovers and the Market for
Corporate Control", 9375–1.901

Foscarinis, Maria
"Homelessness: Federal and State
Legislative Solutions", 10048–73

Foster, Christian J.
"Outlook for Soviet Wheat Imports in the
1990's", 1561–12.908

Foster Grandparent Program
Activities of ACTION, by program, FY88,
annual rpt, 9024–2

Foster home care
Assistance programs under Ways and Means
Committee jurisdiction, finances and
operations, FY70s-88, annual rpt,
21784–11

HHS financial aid, by program, recipient,
State, and city, FY88, annual regional
listings, 4004–3

Local govt health and welfare programs for
high-risk infants and children, for Los
Angeles and San Francisco, 1988 hearing,
21968–48

Supplemental Security Income and Medicaid
eligibility and payment provisions, and
beneficiaries living arrangements, by State,
1989, annual rpt, 4704–13

Foundations
see Nonprofit organizations and foundations

Foundries
Aluminum plant ownership, capacity, energy
and aluminum sources, and startup and
closing dates, by US and foreign plant and
location, 1988, annual listing, 5604–49

Electric power use and prices, shipments,
and trade, for 25 SIC 4-digit
manufacturing industries, 1972-86,
2048–137

Energy use and prices for manufacturing
industries, 1985 survey, series, 3166–13

Hazardous substances industrial releases and
reduction methods under EPA regulation,
by chemical, source, industry, and
location, 1987, annual rpt, 9234–6

Manufacturing annual survey, 1986:
financial and operating data, by SIC 2- to
4-digit industry, series, 2506–15

Manufacturing annual survey, 1986:
production indexes and exports by SIC
2-digit industry and State, with
comparisons to 1985, model results, series,
2506–16

Manufacturing census, 1987: financial and
operating data, for SIC 4-digit industries
by product, preliminary industry rpt
series, 2491–1

Manufacturing industries production,
shipments, inventories, orders, and
pollution control costs, periodic Current
Industrial Rpt series, 2506–3

Metal-forming presses (automatic) from
Japan at less than fair market value, injury
to US industry, investigation with
background financial and operating data,
1989 rpt, 9886–14.253

Minerals (strategic) supply, demand, trade,
and foreign and US industry devs by firm
and country, by commodity, bimonthly
rpt with articles, 5602–4

Occupational injury and illness rates, by SIC
2- to 4-digit industry, 1987, annual rpt,
6844–1

Pollution (air) abatement equipment
shipments by industry, exports, and new
and backlog orders, by product, 1988,
annual Current Industrial Rpt, 2506–12.5

Pollution (air) levels for 5 pollutants, by
detailed source and State, 1986, annual
rpt, 9194–7

Pollution abatement capital and operating
costs, by SIC 2-to 4-digit industry and
State, 1986, annual Current Industrial
Rpt, 2506–3.6

Steel industry finances and operations by
product, and modernization efforts, as of
June 1989, last issue of annual rpt,
9884–16

Technology-intensive manufacturing
methods use and plans, with data by
technology, selected industry, and firm
and market characteristics, 1988 survey,
2508–1

Fowler, Kathleen K.
"Annual Maximum and Minimum Lake
Levels for Indiana, Water Years 1942-85",
5668–89

Frain, Lewis F.
"Monthly OASDI One-Percent Sample
File", 4742–1.919

France
Agricultural and food production and
indexes, total and for selected
commodities, by country, 1970s-88,
annual rpt, 1524–12

Agricultural production, prices, and trade,
by country, 1970s-88 and forecast 1990,
annual world region rpt, 1524–4.1

Agricultural trade of US, by detailed
commodity and country, 1988, semiannual
rpt, 1522–4

AID loans repayment status and terms by
program and country, and status of
predecessor agency loans, quarterly rpt,
9912–3

Apprentices in US and 4 European
countries, 1987, article, 6722–1.936

Background Notes, summary social, political,
and economic data, 1989 rpt, 7006–2.35

Banks (central) gold and foreign exchange
reserves, for Europe and France, 1924-32,
article, 9362–1.906

Bearings (antifriction) from 9 countries,
injury to US industry from foreign
subsidized and less than fair value
imports, investigation with background
financial and operating data, 1989 rpt,
9886–19.65

Businesses (foreign) activity in US, income
tax returns, assets, and income statement
items, by industry div, country, and world
area, 1984-85, article, 8302–2.920

Coal production, trade, and govt subsidies,
by country and country group, 1973-87
and projected to 2000, 2048–144

Developing countries loans from banks and
govts, debt exposure of 7 developed
countries, various periods 1980-88, GAO
rpt, 26123–255

Economic and military aid and loans from
US and intl agencies, by program and
country, FY46-87, annual rpt, 9914–5

Economic and monetary trends,
compounded annual rates of change for
US and 10 major trading partners,
quarterly rpt, 9391–7

Economic conditions, and oil production,
use, and imports, by country, biweekly
rpt, 9112–1

Economic conditions, consumer and stock
prices and production indexes, 6 OECD
countries and US, *Business Conditions
Digest*, monthly rpt, 2702–3.10

Economic conditions in Communist, OECD,
and selected other countries, 1960s-88,
annual rpt, 9114–4

Economic conditions, income, production,
prices, employment, and trade, 1989
periodic country rpt, 2046–4.26;
2046–4.81

Economic conditions, investment and export
opportunities, and trade practices, 1989
country market research rpt, 2046–6.15

Economic conditions, policy, and trade
practices, by country, 1986-88, annual rpt,
21384–5

Economic indicators, and dollar exchange
rates, for selected OECD countries,
1980s-89, semiannual rpt, 8002–14

Economic, social, political, and geographic
summary data, by country, 1989, annual
factbook, 9114–2

Energy prices, by fuel type and end use, for
10 countries, 1980-88 annual rpt,
3164–50.6

Energy production by type, and oil prices,
trade, and use, by country group and
selected country, monthly rpt, 9112–2

Exchange rate variability impact of
monetary policy, for West Germany and
France, model description and results,
1973-88, working paper, 9387–8.181

Export credit activity of Eximbank and 6
OECD countries, 1988, annual rpt,
9254–3

Exports and imports of OECD, total and for
4 major countries, and US trade by
country, by commodity, 1970-87, world
area rpt series, 9116–1

Exports and imports of US, by selected
country, country group, and commodity
group, 1988, annual rpt, 2044–37

Farmland (US) owned by foreigners,
holdings, acreage, and value by land use,
owner country, State, and county, 1988,
annual rpt, 1584–3

Food supply and demand, market and
support prices, and other economic
indicators, by EC country and
commodity, 1960-85, 1528–276

Govt-owned corporations stock issues, value,
new shareholders, and revenue effects, for
UK and France, 1960s-88, article,
9385–1.911

Grain production, use, exports, quality
standards, storage, and prices, for 5
countries, 1960s-88, 26358–201.2

Hospital beds, and use by diagnosis and
patient characteristics, by instn ownership,
with deaths by cause, for France and US,
1981, 4147–5.4

Human rights conditions in 170 countries,
1988, annual rpt, 21384–3

Imports of goods, services, and investment
from US, trade barriers, impacts, and US
actions, by country, 1988, annual rpt,
444–2

Imports of US given duty-free treatment for
value of US material sent abroad, and
impacts on US industry and employment,
by commodity and country, 1987, annual
rpt, 9884–14

Intl transactions of US with 9 countries,
1986-88, *Survey of Current Business*,
monthly rpt, annual table, 2702–1.31

Investment (foreign direct) in US, major transactions by type, industry, country, and US location, 1987, annual rpt, 2044–20

Labor conditions, union coverage, and work accidents, 1989 annual country rpt, 6366–4.50

Manufacturing labor productivity and unit costs for 14 countries, 1950-88, annual press release, 6864–1

Military aid of US, arms sales, and training programs costs and budget requests, by program, world region, and country, FY88-90, annual rpt, 7144–13

Military spending, arms trade, and force strengths, with govt spending and population, by country, 1977-87, annual rpt, 9824–1

Minerals Yearbook, 1987, Vol 3: foreign country reviews of production, trade, and policy, by commodity, annual rpt, 5604–35

Minerals Yearbook, 1987, Vol 3 preprints: foreign country review of production, trade, and policy, by commodity, annual rpt, 5604–23.23

Multinatl firms US affiliates, finances, and operations, by industry, world area of parent firm, and State, 1987, annual rpt, 2704–4

Multinatl US firms and foreign affiliates finances and operations, by industry of parent firm and affiliate, world area, and country, preliminary 1987, annual rpt, 2704–5

Nuclear power generation in US and 19 non-Communist countries, monthly rpt, 3162–24.10

Nuclear power plant capacity, generation, and operating status, by plant and foreign and US location, 1988 and projected to 2020, annual rpt, 3164–57

Oil production, trade, use, and stocks, by selected country and country group, monthly rpt, 3162–42

Oil use and stocks for selected OECD countries, monthly rpt, 3162–24.10

Physicians, and visits by reason and patient age and sex, by specialty, for France, Germany, and US, 1981-83, 4147–5.5

Polychloroprene from 2 countries at less than fair value, injury to US industry, investigation with background financial and operating data, 1989 rpt, 9886–14.271

Population size, growth rates, and components of change, by country, projected 1989-2020 and trends from 1950, biennial rpt, 2324–9

R&D funding and science and technology employment for selected countries, selected years 1961-87, annual rpt, 9624–18.2

Science and engineering employment and education, and R&D spending, for US and selected foreign countries, 1988, annual rpt, 9624–23

Space satellites and other objects launched since 1957, quarterly listing, 9502–2

Transportation energy use, fuel prices, and vehicle registrations, by selected country, 1970s-88, annual rpt, 3304–5.1

Travel to US, market research, major magazine ad costs and circulation, and trade show data, for selected countries, 1989-90, annual rpt, 2904–11

UN voting record and share of votes in agreement with US, by issue, country, and world area, 1988, annual rpt, 7004–18

Unemployment insurance costs and beneficiaries, for US and 5 European countries, 1973-84, article, 6722–1.919

see also French Guiana

see also Monaco

see also New Caledonia

see also under By Foreign Country in the "Index by Categories"

Franchises

Business opportunities for franchises by firm and kind of business, and sources of aid and info, annual listing, suspended, 2044–27

Establishments (franchise) by State, sales, and operations, by kind of business, annual rpt, suspended, 2044–2

Food marketing sector finances, operations, and merger activity, for processors and distributors, as of 1988, annual rpt, 1544–22

Statistical Abstract of US, social, political, and economic data, 1790-2025, comprehensive annual compilation, 2324–1.3

Franco, Eduardo L.

"Epidemiologic Correlates of Cervical Neoplasia and Risk of Human Papillomavirus Infection in Asymptomatic Women in Brazil", 4472–1.908

Frank, Richard G.

"Factors Affecting Medicaid Patients' Length of Stay in Psychiatric Units", 4652–1.924

Frankel, Allen B.

"International Banking Part I: U.S. Banks Abroad", 9375–14

Frankel, Jeffrey A.

"International Capital Mobility and Exchange Rate Volatility", 9373–3.32

Franklin, C. G.

"Trends in Returns with Itemized Versus Non-Itemized Deductions", 8304–8.1

Franks, Adele L.

"Isoniazid Hepatitis Among Pregnant and Postpartum Hispanic Patients", 4042–3.911

Frase, Mary J.

"Dropout Rates in the U.S.: 1988", 4834–23

Fratanduono, Richard J.

"Trends in the Voluntary Compliance of Taxpayers Who File Individual Income Tax Returns", 8304–8.1

Fraud

AFDC fraud cases, referrals, and disposition, by State, FY87, annual rpt, 4694–7.5

Arrest rates, by offense, sex, age, and race, 1987, annual rpt, 6224–7

Arrests, by offense, offender characteristics, and location, 1988, annual rpt, 6224–2.2

Banks and other financial instns fraud and insider misconduct cases, Federal regulatory and enforcement activities, and losses, 1981-87, hearing, 21408–111

Court civil and criminal caseloads for Federal district, appeals, and special courts, June 1989, annual rpt, 18204–2; 18204–8

Crime, criminal justice admin and enforcement, and public opinion, data compilation, 1970s-88, annual rpt, 6064–6

Criminal case processing from arrest to sentencing, cases and duration by disposition, offense, and defendant characteristics, for selected cities, 1986, annual rpt, 6064–27

Criminal case processing in Federal district courts, and dispositions, by offense, district, and offender characteristics, 1984, annual rpt, 6064–29

Criminal case processing in Federal district courts, disposition by offense, 1980-87, 6066–19.50

Diplomats and staff with immunity for foreign missions in US and US missions abroad, and foreign diplomats criminal cases, 1978-87, hearing, 25388–51

DOD Civilian Health and Medical Program of Uniformed Services fraud and abuse cases and referrals, FY87-88, 3508–31.4

DOD criminal investigation activities, funding, and case dispositions, by service branch, FY84-88, GAO rpt, 26123–242

Gasoline octane labeling, State testing programs, violations, and penalties, as of Feb 1988, GAO rpt, 26113–409

Immigration and Naturalization Service illegal alien and narcotics activities, FY81-88, annual rpt, 6264–2

Juvenile delinquent and status offenses, by sex, race, age, income, and urban-rural location, 1979-86 surveys, annual rpt, 6064–6.3

Juvenile offenders recidivism rates, arrests, and court referrals, by offense, age, and sex, 1983 local area studies, 6068–227

Postal Service inspection activities, expenses, and staff, FY88, annual rpt, 9864–8

Postal Service inspection activities, FY88, annual rpt, 9864–9

Postal Service inspection and law enforcement activities, by type, FY88, annual rpt, 9864–5.3

Prisoners in State instns, by offense, criminal history, and inmate, family, and victim characteristics, 1986, annual rpt, 6064–26.3

Recidivism rates of prisoners released in 1983, by offense and prisoner characteristics, 1983-86, 6066–19.48

Secret Service counterfeiting and other investigations and arrests by type, and disposition, by field office, FY88 and trends from FY79, annual rpt, 8464–1

Securities law enforcement activities of SEC, FY88, annual rpt, 9734–2.5

Sentences for Federal crimes, guidelines use and results by offense and district, and Sentencing Commission activities, 1988, annual rpt, 17664–1

Sentences for Federal offenses, guidelines by offense and circumstances, 1989 rpt, 17668–1

Sentences for felonies, by sentence type and offense, 1983-86, 6066–19.52

Surety bonds use to guarantee Federal small business construction contracts, and fraud cases, by agency, 1985-89, GAO rpt, 26113–438

Unemployment insurance programs of States, quality appraisal results, FY88, annual rpt, 6404–16

US attorneys case processing and collections, by case type and Federal district, FY88, annual rpt, 6004–2

Wiretaps authorized, costs, arrests, trials, and convictions, by offense and jurisdiction, 1988, annual rpt, 18204–7
see also Counterfeiting and forgery
see also Federal Inspectors General reports

Fravel, Frederic D.
"Comprehensive Study of Intercity Bus Service in Nebraska", 7888–76

Frazis, Harley
"Is There a College Diploma Effect?", 6886–6.65

Frederick, Martha
"Rural Development Data Book", 1598–244

Frederiksted, V.I.
Economic Censuses of Outlying Areas, 1987: Virgin Islands employment, firms, payroll, and receipts, by SIC 1- to 4-digit industry, island, and city, 2593–1

Freeborn, Donald K.
"Consistently High and Low Elderly Users of Medical Care: Final Report", 4186–2.22

Freedom of information
Court civil and criminal caseloads for Federal district, appeals, and special courts, June 1989, annual rpt, 18204–2; 18204–8
Fed Govt info security measures and classification actions monitored by Info Security Oversight Office, FY88, annual rpt, 9454–21
HHS Freedom of Info Act requests, disposition, costs, and fees, 1988, annual rpt, 4004–21
State Dept freedom of info requests and security reviews, processing, 1985-88, GAO rpt, 26119–243
USDA programs fraud and abuse, audits and investigations, 2nd half FY89, semiannual rpt, 1002–4
see also Censorship
see also Freedom of the press

Freedom of the press
Foreign countries human rights conditions in 170 countries, 1988, annual rpt, 21384–3
Military newspaper *Stars and Stripes* coverage of sensitive topics, FY88-89, GAO rpt, 26123–226

Freeman, Jean L.
"Potential for Inpatient-Outpatient Substitution with Diagnosis-Related Groups", 4652–1.940

Freeways
see Highways, streets, and roads

Freight
Agricultural production, marketing, trade, food consumption, and nutrition programs, 1960s-88, annual chartbook, 1504–3
Agricultural Statistics, 1988, annual rpt, 1004–1
Alcohol fuels (methanol) prices, distribution, and gasoline displacement, with background data, 1985-86 and projected to 2000, 3008–122
Animal feed mill operations, detailed data by State, 1984, 1568–281
Animal protection, licensing, and inspection activities of USDA, and animals used in research, by State, FY88, annual rpt, 1394–10
Apple (red delicious) prices by marketing stage, and trucking rates, 1980-89, article, 1561–6.903

Apple production, marketing, and prices, for Appalachia and compared to other States, various periods 1986-89, annual rpt, 1311–13
Bus (intercity) route in Nebraska, indicators of need, finances, and service and funding alternatives, 1980s, 7888–76
Business statistics, detailed data for major industries and economic indicators, *Survey of Current Business*, monthly rpt, 2702–1.8
Carriage of freight for trucks, rail, and water, by industry group, 1985, 3166–6.33
Coal production and freight costs, and competitive position in selected markets, for Australia and US, 1987-89, 2048–143
Coal production and stocks by district, and shipments by district of origin, State of destination, end-use sector, and mode of transport, quarterly rpt, 3162–8
Communist, OECD, and selected other countries freight and carrier inventories, by mode of transport, 1960s-88, annual rpt, 9114–4.10
County Business Patterns, 1987: employment, establishments, and payroll, by SIC 2- to 4-digit industry and county, annual State rpt series, 2326–8
Cuba economic conditions, agricultural and industrial production and distribution, trade, and intl economic relations, 1980-87 with trends from 1961, 9118–8
Defense Fuel Supply Center procurement, prices, stocks, transport, and other activities and finances, FY88, annual rpt, 3904–8
DOD shipments of military and personal property, passenger traffic, and costs, by service branch and mode of transport, quarterly rpt, 3702–1
Employment, earnings, and hours, by SIC 1- to 4-digit industry, monthly 1983-Feb 1989, annual rpt, 6744–4
Energy use by mode of transport, fuel supply, and demographic and economic factors of vehicle use, 1970s-88, annual rpt, 3304–5
Farm, food, grain, and all products rail freight index, and selected shipments by mode, monthly rpt with articles, 1502–4
Farm production itemized costs, by farm sales size and region, 1988, annual rpt, 1614–3
Food marketing cost indexes, by expense category, monthly rpt with articles, 1502–4
Food prices (farm-retail), marketing cost components, and industry finances and productivity, 1950s-88, annual rpt, 1544–9
Foreign trade zones (US) operations and movement of goods, by zone and commodity, FY86, annual rpt, 2044–30
Fruit and vegetable shipments, and arrivals in US and Canada cities, by mode of transport and State and country of origin, 1988, annual rpt series, 1311–4
Fruit and vegetable shipments by mode of transport, arrivals, and imports, by commodity and State and country of origin, weekly rpt, 1311–3
Fruit and vegetable shipments by truck, monthly by State and country of origin, and rates weekly by growing area and market, 1988, annual rpt, 1311–15

Grain and other commodities shipments by rail by car type, 1986, and rail car fleet size, 1978-88, 1278–15
Grain shipments and rates for barge and rail loadings, periodic sitiuation rpt with articles, 1561–4
Grain shipments by rail, and car fleets and shortages, with data by firm, 1970s-88 and forecast to 1995, hearing, 21368–114
Grain shipments by rail, by commodity and port region, and car fleet requirements, 1949-88 with projections to 2001, 1278–14
Grain shipments, rail loadings, export sales and inspections, prices, and ocean freight rates, weekly rpt, 1272–2
Grain shipping rates and revenues, impacts of rail deregulation, 1981-85, 1548–349
Great Lakes ship pilotage activities, costs, and traffic for US and Canada, and US testing and certificates, 1960s-87, 7308–192
Household goods carriers financial and operating data by firm, quarterly rpt, 9482–14
Intercity freight, and carrier revenue, charges, and employment, by transport mode, 1986, annual rpt, 7704–7.1
Military Sealift Command shipping operations, finances, and personnel, FY88, annual rpt, 3804–14
Occupational injury and illness rates, by SIC 2- to 4-digit industry, 1987, annual rpt, 6844–1
Ohio River basin waterway facilities, freight by commodity and port, and recreation, by waterway, 1986-87, annual rpt, 3754–6
Pacific territories and Hawaii harbor traffic, facilities, dev, funding, and needs, by port, as of 1987, 7308–195
Poultry (broiler) production, slaughter, prices, and processing industry operations, 1950s-87, 1568–279
Price indexes (producer), by stage of processing and detailed commodity, monthly 1988, annual rpt, 6764–2
Pulpwood and residue prices, spending, and transport shares by mode, for southeast US, 1986-87, annual rpt, 1204–22
Railroad (Class I) finances and operations, detailed data by firm, class of service, and district, 1987, annual rpt, 9486–6.1
Railroad (Class I) finances and operations, detailed data by firm, class of service, and district, 1988, annual rpt, 9486–5.1
Railroad freight volume and revenue, by commodity and region of origin and destination, 1987, annual rpt, 7604–6
Railroad revenue, income, freight, and rate of return, by Class I freight railroad and district, quarterly rpt, 9482–2
Science, engineering, and technical employment in transportation, utilities, and retail and wholesale trade, by field, occupation, and industry, 1985, triennial rpt, 9627–32
Shipborne commerce (domestic and foreign) of US, freight by commodity, traffic, and passengers, by port and waterway, 1987, annual rpt, 3754–3
Shipborne trade of US, by type of service, commodity, country, route, and US port, 1986-87, annual rpt, 7704–2

Ships, shipyards, and personnel wartime
capability, for merchant and reserve fleet,
1988-2000, 11208–1
St Lawrence Seaway ship, cargo, and
passenger traffic, and toll revenue, 1988
and trends from 1959, annual rpt,
7744–2
Statistical Abstract of US, social, political,
and economic data, 1790-2025,
comprehensive annual compilation,
2324–1.3
Tax (income) returns of partnerships,
income statement items by industry group,
1986, annual article, 8302–2.903
Tax (income) returns of sole proprietorships,
income statement items, by industry
group, 1987, annual article, 8302–2.904;
8302–2.921
Transportation census, 1987: trucks, by
detailed characteristics, miles traveled,
and type of product carried, State rpt
series, 2573–1
Transportation finances, operations, vehicles,
equipment, accidents, and energy use, by
mode of transport, 1955-88, annual rpt,
7304–2
Truck and bus interstate carriers finances
and operations, by district, 1987, annual
rpt, 9486–6.3
Truck and warehouse services finances and
inventory, by SIC 2- to 4-digit industry,
1988 survey, annual rpt, 2413–14
Truck interstate carriers finances and
operations, by district, 1987, annual rpt,
9486–6.2
Truck transport of property, financial and
operating data by region and firm,
quarterly rpt, 9482–5
Vegetables truck rates, by crop, growing
area, and market, periodic situation rpt
with articles, 1561–11
Waterborne commerce (domestic) of US,
freight by major commodity group, vessel
type, and port, 1986, annual rpt, 7704–7
Waterborne commerce (domestic) of US,
freight by major commodity group,
1981-86, annual rpt, 3754–1.1
Waterborne trade of US, and Fed Govt
sponsored cargo by agency, total and
US-flag share by vessel type, selected
years 1978-87, annual rpt, 7704–14.2;
7704–14.3
see also Air cargo
see also Containerization
see also Hazardous substances transport
Fremont, Calif.
see also under By City in the "Index by
Categories"
French Guiana
Agricultural trade of US, by detailed
commodity and country, 1988, semiannual
rpt, 1522–4
Background Notes, summary social, political,
and economic data, 1989 rpt, 7006–2.7
Economic, social, political, and geographic
summary data, by country, 1989, annual
factbook, 9114–2
Minerals Yearbook, 1987, Vol 3: foreign
country reviews of production, trade, and
policy, by commodity, annual rpt,
5604–35
Minerals Yearbook, 1987, Vol 3 preprints:
foreign country review of production,
trade, and policy, by commodity, annual
rpt, 5604–23.87

Population size, growth rates, and
components of change, by country,
projected 1989-2020 and trends from
1950, biennial rpt, 2324–9
French West Indies
see Caribbean area
Frenkel, Jacob A.
"Exchange Rate Volatility and
Misalignment: Evaluating Some Proposals
for Reform", 9381–13.1
Fresno, Calif.
Housing vacancy rates for single and
multifamily units and mobile homes, by
city and ZIP code, 1988, annual MSA rpt,
9304–20.12
see also under By City and By SMSA or
MSA in the "Index by Categories"
Freund, James L.
"Evolving Financial Services Sector,
1970-88", 8438–1
Fribush, Lillian A.
"Earnings and Employment Data for Wage
and Salary Workers Covered Under Social
Security by State and County, 1985",
4748–43
Friedenberg, Howard L.
"Per Capita Personal Income: Continued
Widening of Regional Differences in
1988", 2702–1.914
Friedman, Benjamin M.
"Substitutability of U.S. and Foreign
Assets", 9385–9
Friedman, Bernard
"Changing Structure of the Health Care
Industry and the Influence of Medicare
Prospective Payments", 17206–2.2
Friedman, Bruce
"Need for Special Interventions for Multiple
Hospital Admission Patients",
4652–1.911
Friel, E. A.
"Low-Flow Characteristics of Streams in
West Virginia", 5668–92
Fringe benefits
see Employee benefits
Frisch, Daniel J.
"Recent Issues in Transfer Pricing",
8006–3.57
Fritz, Richard G.
"Florida's Housing Market: Prospects for
the 1990s", 9302–2.906
Fritzsche, Ronald A.
"Pile Perch, Striped Seaperch, and Rubberlip
Seaperch. Species Profiles: Life Histories
and Environmental Requirements of
Coastal Fishes and Invertebrates (Pacific
Southwest)", 5506–8.110
Froeb, Luke
"Do Firms Differ Much?", 9366–6.201
Frost, Kathryn J.
"Ringed Seal Monitoring: Relationships of
Distribution and Abundance to Habitat
Attributes and Industrial Activities",
2176–1.27
Fruit and fruit products
Agricultural exports of US, impacts of
foreign agricultural and trade policy, with
data by commodity and country, 1988,
annual rpt, 1924–8
Agricultural Statistics, 1988, annual rpt,
1004–1
Agriculture census, 1987: farms, farmland,
production and costs, and operator
characteristics, advance State and county
rpt series, 2330–1

Agriculture census, 1987: farms, farmland,
production, finances, and operator
characteristics, by county, final State rpt
series, 2331–1
Apple (red delicious) prices by marketing
stage, and trucking rates, 1980-89, article,
1561–6.903
Apple and pear trade, by world region and
country, 1986-88, article, 1925–34.937
Apple exports of US to EC and 4 north
European countries, 1984-89, article,
1925–34.939
Apple juice production, use, stocks, and
trade, and US imports, by country,
1983-89, article, 1925–34.908
Apple price impacts of consumer awareness
of use of chemical growth regulator Alar,
monthly 1986-June 1989, article,
1561–6.902
Apple production, and exports by country of
destination, for US and 3 other countries,
mid 1970s-87, article, 1561–6.901
Apple production, marketing, and prices, for
Appalachia and compared to other States,
various periods 1986-89, annual rpt,
1311–13
Cancer (lung) risk, by intake of selected
nutrients, fruits, and vegetables, by
smoking history and sex, 1983-85 local
area study, article, 4472–1.918
Cherry production, by State, 1989, annual
rpt, 1621–18.3
China trade by SITC 1- to 5-digit
commodity, 1970s-87, annual rpt,
9114–3
Cold storage food stocks by commodity and
census div, and warehouse space use, by
State, monthly rpt, 1631–5
Cold storage food stocks, by commodity and
census div, 1988, annual rpt, 1631–11
Consumer Expenditure Survey, household
income by source, and itemized spending,
by selected characteristics and location,
1984-86, annual rpt, 6764–5.2
Consumption of food and nutrient intake by
individuals, by food group, selected
characteristics, and region, supplementary
survey series, 1356–5
Consumption, supply, trade, prices,
spending, and indexes, by food
commodity, 1987, annual rpt, 1544–4
County Business Patterns, 1987:
employment, establishments, and payroll,
by SIC 2- to 4-digit industry and county,
annual State rpt series, 2326–8
CPI by component for US city average, and
by region, population size, and for 27
metro areas, monthly rpt, 6762–2
Cranberry production, prices, use, and
acreage, for selected States, 1987-88 and
forecast 1989, annual rpt, 1621–18.4
Cuba economic conditions, agricultural and
industrial production and distribution,
trade, and intl economic relations,
1980-87 with trends from 1961, 9118–8
Eastern Europe and USSR agricultural
production, acreage, and consumption, by
commodity and country, 1965-85,
1528–284
Employment, earnings, and hours, by
selected SIC 1- to 4-digit industry, State,
and for 262 MSAs, 1972-87, 6748–81
Employment, earnings, and hours, by SIC 1-
to 4-digit industry, monthly 1983-Feb
1989, annual rpt, 6744–4

Exports and imports (agricultural) of US, by commodity and country, bimonthly rpt with articles, 1522–1

Exports and imports (agricultural) of US, by commodity, monthly rpt, 1922–8

Exports and imports (agricultural) of US, by detailed commodity and country, 1988, semiannual rpt, 1522–4

Exports and imports (agricultural) of US with Asia, Middle East, and North Africa, by commodity and country, 1962-86, 1528–277

Exports of US, detailed commodities by country, monthly rpt, 2422–3

Farm financial and marketing conditions, forecast 1988, conf papers, annual rpt, 1004–16

Farm financial and marketing conditions, forecast 1989, annual chartbook, 1504–8

Farm income, expenses, receipts by commodity, assets, liabilities, and ratios, 1988 and trends from 1945, annual rpt, 1544–16

Farm labor costs impacts of illegal aliens employer sanctions, by farm type, size, and region, 1986, 1598–250

Farm receipts for 25 leading crops, by State, 1960-87, 1548–347

Farm sector balance sheet, and receipts by detailed commodity, by State, 1984-88, annual rpt, 1544–18

Farm sector finances, income sources, expenses by type, assets, debts, and ratios, 1987, annual rpt, 1544–19

Foreign and US agricultural production, trade, and weather devs, weekly press release, 1922–4

Foreign and US fresh and processed fruit, vegetable, and nut production and trade, FAS monthly circular with articles, 1925–34

Foreign countries agricultural production, prices, and trade, by country, 1970s-89 and forecast 1990, annual world region rpt series, 1524–4

Freight (waterborne domestic and foreign) by commodity, traffic, and passengers, by port and waterway, 1987, annual rpt, 3754–3

Imports of US, detailed Schedule A commodities by country, monthly rpt, 2422–2

Irrigation projects of Reclamation Bur in western US, crop production and acreage by commodity, State, and project, 1987, annual rpt, 5824–12.1

Labor productivity, indexes of output, hours, and employment by SIC 2- to 4-digit industry, 1963-87, annual rpt, 6824–1.3

Liquor production, stocks, materials used, and taxable and tax-free removals, by State, monthly rpt, 8486–1.3

Manufacturers finances and operations, by SIC 2- to 4-digit industry, forecast 1989 and trends from 1950s, annual rpt, 2044–28

Manufacturing annual survey, 1986: financial and operating data, by SIC 2- to 4-digit industry, series, 2506–15

Manufacturing census, 1987: financial and operating data, for SIC 4-digit industries by product, preliminary rpt, 2491–1.3

Nutrient and caloric composition of food, for raw, processed, and prepared food, 1988 rpt, 1358–3

Occupational injury and illness rates, by SIC 2- to 4-digit industry, 1987, annual rpt, 6844–1

OECD trade, total and for 4 major countries, and US trade by country, by commodity, 1970-87, world area rpt series, 9116–1

Peach (canned) production, costs, subsidy, trade, consumption, and stocks, 1982-89, article, 1925–34.945

Peach production, marketing, and prices in 3 southeastern States and Appalachia, 1988, annual rpt, 1311–12

Pineapple (canned fruit and juice) production and exports, by country, 1986-89, annual article, 1925–34.920

Price indexes (producer), by stage of processing and detailed commodity, monthly rpt, 6762–6

Price indexes (producer), by stage of processing and detailed commodity, monthly 1988, annual rpt, 6764–2

Prices (farm-retail) for food, marketing cost components, and industry finances and productivity, 1950s-88, annual rpt, 1544–9

Prices (wholesale) for fresh fruit and vegetables in NYC, Chicago, and selected shipping points, by crop, 1988, annual rpt, 1311–8

Prices received and paid by farmers, by commodity and State, 1988, annual rpt, 1629–5

Prices received by farmers and production value, by detailed crop and State, 1986-88, annual rpt, 1621–2

Prices received by farmers for major products, and paid for farm inputs and living items, by State, monthly rpt, 1629–1

Production, acreage, and yield, current and forecast for melons and strawberries by State, periodic rpt, 1621–12

Production, farms, acreage, and related data, by selected crop and State, monthly rpt, 1621–1

Production inputs, output, and productivity for farms, by commodity and region, 1947-87, annual rpt, 1544–17

Production of fruit and vegetables for processing, industries finances and operations, consumption, and trade, by commodity, 1970s-88, 1568–275

Production, prices, and acreage, for melons and strawberries, by State, 1986-88, annual rpts, 1621–25

Production, prices, and use of fruit and nuts, 1986-89, annual rpt series, 1621–18

Production, prices, trade, and marketing, by commodity, current situation and forecast, monthly rpt with articles, 1502–4

Production, prices, trade, stocks, and use, by selected crop, periodic situation rpt with articles, 1561–6

Production, receipts, and demand ratios, by commodity group and region, 1949-83, 1548–348

Prune production, trade, use, and stocks for selected countries, 1985-89, table, 1925–34.925

Raisin production, trade, use, and stocks for selected countries, and EC subsidies, various periods 1981-90, annual article, 1925–34.944

Raisin production, trade, use, and stocks for selected countries, 1985-89, article, 1925–34.924

Retail trade census, 1987: employment, establishments, sales, and payroll, by SIC 2- to 4-digit kind of business, MSA, county, and city, State rpt series, 2397–1

Science, engineering, and technical employment in manufacturing, by field, occupation, and industry, 1986, triennial rpt, 9627–23

Shipments by mode of transport, arrivals, and imports, for fruit and vegetables by commodity and State and country of origin, weekly rpt, 1311–3

Shipments of fruit and vegetables, and arrivals in US and Canada cities, by mode of transport and State and country of origin, 1988, annual rpt series, 1311–4

Statistical Abstract of US, social, political, and economic data, 1790-2025, comprehensive annual compilation, 2324–1.3

Tax (income) returns of corporations, income and tax items by asset size and detailed industry, 1986, annual rpt, 8304–21

Tax (income) returns of partnerships, income statement items by industry group, 1986, annual article, 8302–2.903

Truck rates for fruit and vegetables weekly by growing area and market, and shipments monthly by State and country of origin, 1988, annual rpt, 1311–15

Truck transport of fruit and vegetables, itemized costs per mile by item for fleets and owner-operator trucks, monthly table, 1272–1

Wholesale trade census, 1987: employment, establishments, finances, and operations, by SIC 2- to 4-digit kind of business, MSA, county, and city, State rpt series, 2405–1

see also Citrus fruits
see also Nuts
see also Vegetables and vegetable products
see also under By Commodity in the "Index by Categories"

Fryar, Edward O., Jr.
"Hedging and Cross-Hedging Selected Protein Meals", 1561–3.904

FTC
see Federal Trade Commission

FTC Communications
Finances and operations, detail for telegraph firms, 1987, annual rpt, 9284–6.5

Fuel
see Fuel tax
see Kerosene
see Motor fuels
see Natural gas liquids
see terms listed under Energy resources and consumption

Fuel allocation
Intl Energy Program countries oil stocks and conservation measures, 1987-88 and projected to 1990, GAO rpt, 26123–225

Fuel oil
Buildings (commercial) energy use, costs, and conservation, by building characteristics, survey rpt series, 3166–8

Business statistics, detailed data for major industries and economic indicators, *Survey of Current Business*, monthly rpt, 2702–1.15

Consumer Expenditure Survey, household income by source, and itemized spending, by selected characteristics and location, 1984-86, annual rpt, 6764-5.2

Consumption, by detailed fuel type, end-use sector, and State, 1960-87, State Energy Data System annual rpt, 3164-39

Consumption of oil, switching to other fuels, capability by end-use sector, 1989, annual rpt, 3164-88

CPI by component for US city average, and by region, population size, and for 27 metro areas, monthly rpt, 6762-2

Fed Govt energy use and efficiency, by agency and fuel type, FY88, annual rpt, 3304-22

Foreign and US oil prices, by refined product and country, 1980-88, annual rpt, 3164-50.6

Freight (waterborne domestic and foreign) by commodity, traffic, and passengers, by port and waterway, 1987, annual rpt, 3754-3

Futures and options trading volume, by commodity and exchange, FY88, annual rpt, 11924-2

Futures contracts on commodities, financial instruments, and indexes, options trading in NYC, Chicago, and other markets, monthly rpt, 11922-6

Futures trading in selected commodities and financial instruments and indexes, NYC, Chicago, and other markets activity, monthly rpt, 11922-5

Household utilities spending, by household size, income, householder age and race, and region, 1983, article, 1702-1.904

Housing and households detailed characteristics, and unit and neighborhood quality, by location, 1985, biennial rpt, 2485-12

Housing and households detailed characteristics, and unit and neighborhood quality, MSA surveys, series, 2485-6

Housing energy use, costs, and conservation, and household and housing characteristics, survey rpt series, 3166-7

Housing heating and air conditioning equipment shipments by type of fuel used, monthly rpt, 2042-1.6

Housing units completed, single and multifamily units by structural and financial characteristics, inside-outside MSAs, and region, 1984-88, annual rpt, 2384-1

Imports of US, detailed Schedule A commodities by country, monthly rpt, 2422-2

Manufacturing census, 1987: financial and operating data, for SIC 4-digit industries by product, preliminary rpt, 2491-1.41

Minerals Yearbook, 1987, Vol 3 preprints: foreign country reviews of production, trade, and policy, by commodity, annual rpt series, 5604-23

Pacific Northwest population, households, employment, income, and fuel prices, alternative projections 1990-2010 with trends from 1960, annual rpt, 3224-5

Pollution (air) levels for 6 pollutants, by source, 1970-87 and trends from 1940, annual rpt, 9194-13

Price indexes (producer), by stage of processing and detailed commodity, monthly 1988, annual rpt, 6764-2

Prices and sales of gasoline and fuel oil, EIA and alternative estimates 1984-88, article, 3162-11.903

Prices and spending for fuel, by type, end-use sector, and State, 1987, annual rpt, 3164-64

Prices and stocks of heating oil, for 14 northern States, seasonal monthly rpt, 3162-40

Prices and volume of oil products sold and purchased by refiners, processors, and distributors, by product, end-use sector, PAD district, and State, monthly rpt with articles, 3162-11; 3164-85

Retail trade census, 1987: employment, establishments, sales, and payroll, by SIC 2- to 4-digit kind of business, MSA, county, and city, State rpt series, 2397-1

Ships bunker fuel laden in US on vessels engaged in foreign trade, by fuel type and port, monthly rpt, 2422-5

Statistical Abstract of US, social, political, and economic data, 1790-2025, comprehensive annual compilation, 2324-1.3

Supply and demand of oil and refined products, refinery capacity and use, and prices, weekly rpt, 3162-32

Supply, demand, and movement of crude oil, gas liquids, and refined products, by PAD district and State, 1988 and trends from 1973, annual rpt, 3164-2

Supply, demand, and prices, by fuel type and end-use sector, projected under 3 oil price assumptions, 1988-2000, annual rpt, 3164-75

Supply, demand, and prices, by fuel type and end-use sector, with foreign comparisons, 1988 and trends from 1949, annual rpt, 3164-74.2

Supply, demand, and prices, by fuel type, end-use sector, and country, detailed data, monthly rpt, 3162-24

Supply, demand, and prices of energy, forecasts by resource type, quarterly rpt, 3162-34

Supply, demand, and prices of oil and gas, alternative projections 1987-2000, annual rpt, 3164-89

Supply, demand, trade, stocks, and refining of oil and gas liquids, by detailed product, State, and PAD district, monthly rpt with articles, 3162-6

Supply of oil products, EIA and alternative estimates, 1979-88, annual article, 3162-6.903

Transportation energy use by mode, fuel supply, and demographic and economic factors of vehicle use, 1970s-88, annual rpt, 3304-5

Fuel tax

Budget of US, authoritative financial statements with appropriations, outlays, and receipts, by category and agency, FY88, annual rpt, 8104-2.2

Budget of US, CBO analysis of revenue and spending alternatives and projections of economic indicators, FY90-94, annual rpt, 26304-3

Collections of excise tax, by source, quarterly rpt, 8302-2.1

Collections of excise taxes by IRS, by type of tax, FY88, annual rpt, 8304-3.3

Collections of taxes, by level of govt, type of tax, State, and selected counties, quarterly rpt, 2462-3

Finances of govts, revenues by source and spending by function, natl income and product account, *Survey of Current Business*, monthly rpt, 2702-1.24

Foreign and US retail gasoline and diesel prices and tax rates, for US and 4 countries, monthly rpt, 9112-2

Gasohol use, and tax rates on all motor fuels, by State, 1987-88, annual rpt, 3304-9

Gasoline and diesel fuel Federal and State tax rates, by State, monthly rpt, 3162-11

gasoline and diesel fuel Federal and State tax rates, by State, 1988, annual rpt, 3164-85

Gasoline and fuel oil retail prices and sales, EIA and alternative estimates 1984-88, article, 3162-11.903

Gasoline and other motor fuel tax rates, by selected State, as of Oct 1987, 10048-72

Gasoline tax rates and provisions, by State, as of various dates 1978-88, 10044-1

Hwy Statistics, summary data by State, 1987-88, annual rpt, 7554-24

Income tax returns of individuals, detailed data, 1986, annual rpt, 8304-2

IRS collections, by excise tax source, quarterly rpt, 8302-1

Middle Atlantic State hwy construction costs, funding, mileage, and traffic, by project, 1989 article, 9387-1.904

Oil prices and US and OPEC industry impacts of alternative US protective policies, projected 2037, technical paper, 9379-12.44

State and local revenue potential relative to natl average tax burden, by type of tax and State, 1986, annual rpt, 10044-7

State govt tax collections by detailed type of tax, and tax rates, by State, FY88, annual rpt, 2466-2.3

State tax rates on motor fuel, by fuel type and State, monthly rpt, 7552-1

State tax rates on motor fuel, by State, 1978-87, annual table, 7554-32

State tax rates on motor fuel, by State, 1988, annual rpt, 7554-1

see also Severance taxes

Fuhrer, Jeff
"Monetary Policy Rules and the Indicator Properties of Asset Prices", 9366-6.203
"Stability of Wicksell's Monetary Policy Rule", 9366-6.208

Fuhrmann, M.
"Waste Package Performance Criteria for Deepsea Disposal of Low-Level Radioactive Waste", 9198-119

Fujairah
see United Arab Emirates

Fujimura, Robert K.
"Biotechnology in Japan", 2048-139

Fuller, Len C.
"Effect of Lifestyle on Energy Use Estimations and Predicted Savings", 3226-2.11

Fullerton, Calif.
see also under By City in the "Index by Categories"

Fullerton, Howard N., Jr.
"New Labor Force Projections, Spanning 1988 to 2000", 6722-1.952

Fulton, John P.
"Physical Functioning of the Aged, U.S., 1984", 4147-10.167

Functional limitations
  see Mobility limitations
Funerals
  see Cemeteries and funerals
  see Military cemeteries and funerals
Fungicides
  see Pesticides
Furlong, Frederick T.
  "Commodity Prices as a Guide for
    Monetary Policy", 9393–8.902
Furniture and furnishings
  China trade by SITC 1- to 5-digit
    commodity, 1970s-87, annual rpt,
    9114–3
  Consumer Expenditure Survey, household
    income by source, and itemized spending,
    by selected characteristics and region,
    1984-87, annual rpt, 6764–5
  Consumer Expenditure Survey, spending by
    category, and income, by selected
    household characteristics and location,
    1987, press release, 6726–1.23
  Consumer Expenditure Survey, spending by
    category, selected household
    characteristics, and region, quarterly rpt,
    6762–14
  Consumer holdings of durable goods, by
    type, in current and constant dollars,
    1985-88, annual article, 2702–1.931
  Consumer spending in metro and nonmetro
    areas, by item, 1987, article, 6722–1.962
  Consumer spending, natl income and
    product account, *Survey of Current
    Business*, monthly rpt, 2702–1.23
  Cost of living indexes for metro areas,
    relation of expenditure items and quality
    of life indicators, model results, 1973,
    working paper, 6886–6.9
  County Business Patterns, 1987:
    employment, establishments, and payroll,
    by SIC 2- to 4-digit industry and county,
    annual State rpt series, 2326–8
  CPI by component for US city average, and
    by region, population size, and for 27
    metro areas, monthly rpt, 6762–2
  CPI components relative importance, by
    selected SMSA, region, population size,
    and for US city average, 1988, annual rpt,
    6884–1
  DOD prime contract awards, by detailed
    procurement category, FY85-88, annual
    rpt, 3544–18
  DOD shipments of military and personal
    property, passenger traffic, and costs, by
    service branch and mode of transport,
    quarterly rpt, 3702–1
  Earnings by major industry group, and
    personal income per capita and by source,
    by region and State, 1929-87, 2708–40
  Employment, earnings, and hours, by
    selected SIC 1- to 4-digit industry, State,
    and for 262 MSAs, 1972-87, 6748–81
  Employment, earnings, and hours, by SIC 1-
    to 4-digit industry, monthly 1983-Feb
    1989, annual rpt, 6744–4
  Employment of minorities and women, by
    occupation, SIC 1- to 3- digit industry,
    State, and MSA, 1986, annual rpt,
    9244–1
  Employment, unemployment, and labor
    force characteristics, by region and census
    div, 1988, annual rpt, 6744–7.1
  Energy use and prices for manufacturing
    industries, 1985 survey, series, 3166–13

  Exports and imports between US and
    outlying areas, by detailed commodity and
    mode of transport, monthly rpt, 2422–4
  Exports and imports of US, by commodity
    group, world area, selected country, US
    coastal area and port, and mode of
    transport, monthly rpt, 2422–9
  Exports of US, detailed commodities by
    country, monthly rpt, 2422–3
  Farm sector assets by type, 1988, annual
    rpt, 1544–16.2
  Farm sector balance sheet, and marketing
    receipts by detailed commodity, by State,
    1984-88, annual rpt, 1544–18
  Fires in hotels and motels, casualties, and
    effectiveness of smoke detectors, sprinkler
    systems, and building and equipment
    design, 1989 hearing, 21708–127
  Freight (waterborne domestic and foreign)
    by commodity, traffic, and passengers, by
    port and waterway, 1987, annual rpt,
    3754–3
  Hazardous substances industrial releases and
    reduction methods under EPA regulation,
    by chemical, source, industry, and
    location, 1987, annual rpt, 9234–6
  Imports, exports, and employment impacts,
    by SIC 2- to 4-digit industry and
    commodity, quarterly rpt, 2322–2
  Imports of textiles under Multifiber
    Arrangement by product and country, and
    status of bilateral agreements, 1986-88,
    annual rpt, 9884–18
  Imports of US, detailed Schedule A
    commodities by country, monthly rpt,
    2422–2
  Imports of US given duty-free treatment for
    value of US material sent abroad, and
    impacts on US industry and employment,
    by commodity and country, 1987, annual
    rpt, 9884–14
  Injuries from use of consumer products and
    related activities, by victim age and sex,
    1988, annual rpt, 9164–7
  Injuries from use of consumer products, by
    severity, victim age, and detailed product,
    1988, annual rpt, 9164–6
  Injuries from use of consumer products,
    related deaths and costs, and recalls by
    brand, by product type, FY87, annual rpt,
    9164–2
  Input-output structure of US economy,
    detailed interindustry transactions for 84
    industries, and components of final
    demand, 1983, annual article,
    2702–1.909
  Japan lumber use by industry, and
    construction activity and indicators of
    demand, 1970-88, article, 2042–1.909
  Labor productivity, indexes of output, hours,
    and employment by SIC 2- to 4-digit
    industry, 1963-87, annual rpt, 6824–1.3
  Manufacturers finances and operations, by
    SIC 2- to 4-digit industry, forecast 1989
    and trends from 1950s, annual rpt,
    2044–28
  Manufacturing annual survey, 1986:
    financial and operating data, by SIC 2- to
    4-digit industry, series, 2506–15
  Manufacturing annual survey, 1986:
    production indexes and exports by SIC
    2-digit industry and State, with
    comparisons to 1985, model results, series,
    2506–16

  Manufacturing census, 1987: financial and
    operating data, for SIC 4-digit industries
    by product, preliminary industry rpt
    series, 2491–1
  Manufacturing census, 1987: financial and
    operating data, for SIC 4-digit industries
    by product, preliminary rpt, 2491–1.22;
    2491–1.25
  Manufacturing industries production,
    shipments, inventories, orders, and
    pollution control costs, periodic Current
    Industrial Rpt series, 2506–3
  Military Sealift Command shipping
    operations, finances, and personnel, FY88,
    annual rpt, 3804–14
  Natl income and product accounts and
    components, *Survey of Current Business*,
    monthly rpt, 2702–1.21
  Occupational injury and illness rates, by SIC
    2- to 4-digit industry, 1987, annual rpt,
    6844–1
  OECD trade, total and for 4 major
    countries, and US trade by country, by
    commodity, 1970-87, world area rpt
    series, 9116–1
  Pollution abatement capital and operating
    costs, by SIC 2-to 4-digit industry and
    State, 1986, annual Current Industrial
    Rpt, 2506–3.6
  Price indexes (producer), by stage of
    processing and detailed commodity,
    monthly rpt, 6762–6
  Price indexes (producer), by stage of
    processing and detailed commodity,
    monthly 1988, annual rpt, 6764–2
  Price indexes for department store
    inventories, by class of item, monthly
    table, 6762–7
  Production, prices, employment, and trade,
    for hardwood lumber and products,
    quarterly rpt, 1202–4
  Retail trade census, 1987: employment,
    establishments, sales, and payroll, by SIC
    2- to 4-digit kind of business, MSA,
    county, and city, State rpt series, 2397–1
  Retail trade sales and inventories, by kind of
    business, region, and selected State, MSA,
    and city, monthly rpt, 2413–3
  Retail trade sales, by kind of business,
    advance monthly rpt, 2413–2
  Retail trade sales, inventories, purchases,
    gross margin, and accounts receivable, by
    SIC 2- to 4-digit kind of business and
    form of ownership, 1987, annual rpt,
    2413–5
  Science, engineering, and technical
    employment in manufacturing, by field,
    occupation, and industry, 1986, triennial
    rpt, 9627–23
  Science, engineering, and technical
    employment in transportation, utilities,
    and retail and wholesale trade, by field,
    occupation, and industry, 1985, triennial
    rpt, 9627–32
  Small business establishments, employment,
    and financial ratios, by SIC 1- to 2-digit
    industry and State, late 1960s-87,
    9768–19
  Southern US lumber and paper industries
    productivity, impact on economy, and
    employment compared to other industries,
    1970s-80, State rpt series, 1206–36
  Tax (income) returns of corporations,
    income and tax items by asset size and
    detailed industry, 1986, annual rpt,
    8304–4; 8304–21

Tax (income) returns of partnerships, income statement items by industry group, 1986, annual article, 8302–2.903

Tax (income) returns of sole proprietorships, income statement items, by industry group, 1987, annual article, 8302–2.904; 8302–2.921

Transportation census, 1987: trucks, by detailed characteristics, miles traveled, and type of product carried, State rpt series, 2573–1

Truck transport of household goods, financial and operating data by firm, quarterly rpt, 9482–14

Truck transport of household goods, performance and disposition of damage claims, for selected carriers, 1988, annual rpt, 9484–11

Warehouse services finances, by SIC 3- to 4-digit industry, 1988 survey, annual rpt, 2413–14

Wholesale trade census, 1987: employment, establishments, finances, and operations, by SIC 2- to 4-digit kind of business, MSA, county, and city, State rpt series, 2405–1

Wholesale trade sales and inventories, by SIC 2- to 3-digit kind of business, monthly rpt, 2413–7

Wholesale trade sales, inventories, purchases, and gross margins, by SIC 2- to 3-digit kind of business and form of ownership, 1988, annual rpt, 2413–13

see also Antiques

see also Carpets and rugs

see also Household appliances and equipment

see also Household supplies and utensils

see also By Industry in the "Index by Categories"

see also under By Commodity in the "Index by Categories"

Furs and fur industry

Agricultural Statistics, 1988, annual rpt, 1004–1

Agriculture census, 1987: farms, farmland, production, finances, and operator characteristics, by county, final State rpt series, 2331–1

County Business Patterns, 1987: employment, establishments, and payroll, by SIC 2- to 4-digit industry and county, annual State rpt series, 2326–8

Endangered animals and plants US trade and permits, by species, purpose, disposition, and country, 1987, annual rpt, 5504–19

Exports and imports (agricultural) of US, by commodity and country, bimonthly rpt with articles, 1522–1

Exports and imports (agricultural) of US, by detailed commodity and country, 1988, semiannual rpt, 1522–4

Exports and imports of dairy, livestock, and poultry products, by commodity and country, FAS monthly circular, 1925–32

Exports of US, detailed commodities by country, monthly rpt, 2422–3

Imports of US, detailed Schedule A commodities by country, monthly rpt, 2422–2

Manufacturing annual survey, 1986: financial and operating data, by SIC 2- to 4-digit industry, series, 2506–15

Manufacturing census, 1987: financial and operating data, for SIC 4-digit industries by product, preliminary rpt, 2491–1.19; 2491–1.83

Mink and pelt production, prices, and farms, selected years 1969-89, annual rpt, 1631–7

Price indexes (producer), by stage of processing and detailed commodity, monthly rpt, 6762–6

Price indexes (producer), by stage of processing and detailed commodity, monthly 1988, annual rpt, 6764–2

Retail trade census, 1987: employment, establishments, sales, and payroll, by SIC 2- to 4-digit kind of business, MSA, county, and city, State rpt series, 2397–1

see also Hides and skins

Furst, P.

"Interaction Between Sample and Packaging Material—A Potential Source of Contamination with PCDDs and PCDFs", 21368–112

Future

see Projections and forecasts

Futures trading

Banks (insured commercial and savings) finances, for foreign and domestic offices, by asset size, 1987, annual rpt, 9294–4.2

Cocoa bean futures prices at NYC exchange, 1988-90, FAS semiannual circular, 1925–9

Corn and soybean futures contract yield and price risk hedging strategies, by selected county and State, model results, 1961-83, 1548–352

Cotton futures unfixed call sales and purchases and open contracts on NYC exchange, weekly rpt, 11922–3

Cotton prices at selected spot markets, NYC futures prices, and CCC loan rates, 1988/89 and trends from 1940, annual rpt, 1309–2

Cotton prices in 8 spot markets, futures prices at NYC exchange, farm prices, and CCC loan stocks, monthly rpt, 1309–1

Dairy prices, by product and selected area, with related marketing data, 1988, annual rpt, 1317–1

Exchange activity by commodity and exchange, and Commodity Futures Trading Commission oversight, FY88, annual rpt, 11924–2

Exchange activity in selected commodities and financial instruments and indexes, NYC, Chicago, and other markets, monthly rpt, 11922–5

Farm production costs and prices, impacts of alternative crop, marketing, and futures contract purchase strategies, model results, 1971-86, 1548–353

Gold and silver futures trading, Mineral Industry Surveys, monthly rpt, 5612–1.10

Grain futures contracts, stocks in deliverable position by type, weekly tables, 11922–4

Grain futures settlement prices, by commodity and exchange, weekly rpt, 1313–2

Grains farm inputs purchases and marketing, impacts of alternative strategies on prices and returns, 1970s-86, article, 1561–4.901

Market crash of 1987, market performance, foreign futures market activity, and computer-aided trading impacts on price variability, 1980s-88, hearings, 25168–70

Rice market activities, prices, inspections, sales, trade, supply, and use, for US and selected foreign markets, weekly rpt, 1313–8

Savings instns off-balance-sheet hedging activity, by type, asset size, and State, for FHLB 4th District, 1984-88, article, 9302–2.903

Soybean and other protein meal futures contracts risk hedging, model description and results, 1984-86, article, 1561–3.904

Statistical Abstract of US, social, political, and economic data, 1790-2025, comprehensive annual compilation, 2324–1.3

Stock price volatility forecasting performance of options on stock index futures, alternative model results, various periods 1983-88, article, 9371–1.908

Trading abuses in futures market, Commodity Futures Trading Commission and exchanges enforcement activity, various periods 1984-FY90, GAO rpt, 26119–263

Trading abuses in futures markets, Commodity Futures Trading Commission, Chicago Board of Trade, and Chicago Mercantile Exchange enforcement activity, 1984-89, GAO rpt, 26119–247

Treasury bill interest rate forecasts, performance of futures rates and survey forecasts, 1977-87, article, 9391–1.914

see also Options trading

Gabel, Jon

"Conventional Health Insurance: A Decade Later", 4652–1.934

Gabon

Agricultural and food production and indexes, total and for selected commodities, by country, 1970s-88, annual rpt, 1524–12

Agricultural trade of US, by detailed commodity and country, 1988, semiannual rpt, 1522–4

AID economic aid to developing countries, obligations and disbursements by country, quarterly rpt, 9912–4

Economic and military aid and loans from US and intl agencies, by program and country, FY46-87, annual rpt, 9914–5

Economic conditions, income, production, prices, employment, and trade, 1989 periodic country rpt, 2046–4.34

Economic, social, political, and geographic summary data, by country, 1989, annual factbook, 9114–2

Exports and imports of US, by commodity and country, 1970-87, world area rpt, 9116–1.4

Exports and imports of US, by selected country, country group, and commodity group, 1988, annual rpt, 2044–37

Human rights conditions in 170 countries, 1988, annual rpt, 21384–3

Military aid of US, arms sales, and training programs costs and budget requests, by program, world region, and country, FY88-90, annual rpt, 7144–13

Military spending, arms trade, and force strengths, with govt spending and population, by country, 1977-87, annual rpt, 9824–1

Minerals Yearbook, 1987, Vol 3: foreign country reviews of production, trade, and policy, by commodity, annual rpt, 5604–35

Minerals Yearbook, 1987, Vol 3 preprints: foreign country review of production, trade, and policy, by commodity, annual rpt, 5604–23.24

Oil production, trade, use, and stocks, by selected country and country group, monthly rpt, 3162–42

Population size, growth rates, and components of change, by country, projected 1989-2020 and trends from 1950, biennial rpt, 2324–9

UN voting record and share of votes in agreement with US, by issue, country, and world area, 1988, annual rpt, 7004–18

see also under By Foreign Country in the "Index by Categories"

Gadsden, Ala.
see also under By SMSA or MSA in the "Index by Categories"

Gady, Richard
"World Wheat Outlook: Policy Implications", 1004–16.1

Gail, Mitchell H.
"Projecting Individualized Probabilities of Developing Breast Cancer for White Females Who Are Being Examined Annually", 4472–1.934

Gainer, Leila J.
"Learning Enterprise", 6408–73

Gainesville, Fla.
see also under By SMSA or MSA in the "Index by Categories"

Gajewski, Gregory R.
"1988 Drought Did Not Dry Up Credit", 1502–7.916

Galanter, Marc
"Alcohol and Drug Abuse as a Subspecialty: Credentialing and Specialization", 4482–1.901

Gallicchio, Salvatore J.
"Two Notes on Sampling Variance Estimates from the 1984 SIPP Public-Use Files", 2626–10.82

Gallipolis, Ohio
Wages by occupation, for office and plant workers, 1989 survey, periodic MSA rpt, 6785–3.4

Gallium
see Metals and metal industries

Gallo, Frank
"Can Employee Associations Negotiate New Growth?", 6722–1.931
"Collective Bargaining and Private Sector Professionals", 6722–1.946

Galveston, Tex.
CPI by component for US city average, and by region, population size, and for 15 metro areas, monthly rpt, 6762–1
CPI by component for US city average, and by region, population size, and for 27 metro areas, monthly rpt, 6762–2
Freight (waterborne domestic and foreign) by commodity, traffic, and passengers, by port and waterway, 1987, annual rpt, 3754–3.2
Housing starts and completions authorized by building permits in 40 MSAs, quarterly rpt, 2382–9
Oil drilling rig removal using explosives, impacts on sea turtles and dolphins off Galveston, 1988 article, 2162–1.902

Shrimp (bait) catch in Galveston Bay, 1959-87, article, 2162–1.901
see also under By SMSA or MSA in the "Index by Categories"

Gamber, Edward N.
"Money, Inflation, and Sectoral Shifts", 9377–9.70
"Why We Don't Know Whether Money Causes Output", 9377–1.906

Gambia
Agricultural and food production and indexes, total and for selected commodities, by country, 1970s-88, annual rpt, 1524–12
Agricultural imports and food aid needs under alternative weather assumptions, for 17 African countries, projected to 1995, 1528–279
Agricultural trade of US, by detailed commodity and country, 1988, semiannual rpt, 1522–4
AID activities and funding by project and function, FY90, and developing countries summary socioeconomic data from 1960s, annual rpt, 9904–4.5
AID economic aid to developing countries, obligations and disbursements by country, quarterly rpt, 9912–4
Economic and military aid and loans from US and intl agencies, by program and country, FY46-87, annual rpt, 9914–5
Economic, social, political, and geographic summary data, by country, 1989, annual factbook, 9114–2
Food supply indicators for Sahel, by country, 1960s-2000, 1528–290
Human rights conditions in 170 countries, 1988, annual rpt, 21384–3
Military aid of US, arms sales, and training programs costs and budget requests, by program, world region, and country, FY88-90, annual rpt, 7144–13
Military spending, arms trade, and force strengths, with govt spending and population, by country, 1977-87, annual rpt, 9824–1
Minerals Yearbook, 1987, Vol 3: foreign country reviews of production, trade, and policy, by commodity, annual rpt, 5604–35
Minerals Yearbook, 1987, Vol 3 preprints: foreign country review of production, trade, and policy, by commodity, annual rpt, 5604–23.82
Population size, growth rates, and components of change, by country, projected 1989-2020 and trends from 1950, biennial rpt, 2324–9
UN voting record and share of votes in agreement with US, by issue, country, and world area, 1988, annual rpt, 7004–18
see also under By Foreign Country in the "Index by Categories"

Gambling
Arrest rates, by offense, sex, age, and race, 1987, annual rpt, 6224–7
Arrests, by offense, offender characteristics, and location, 1970s-87, annual rpt, 6064–6.4
Arrests, by offense, offender characteristics, and location, 1988, annual rpt, 6224–2.2
Court civil and criminal caseloads for Federal district, appeals, and special courts, June 1989, annual rpt, 18204–2; 18204–8

Criminal case processing in Federal district courts, and dispositions, by offense, district, and offender characteristics, 1984, annual rpt, 6064–29
Sentences for Federal crimes, guidelines use and results by offense and district, and Sentencing Commission activities, 1988, annual rpt, 17664–1
Sentences for Federal offenses, guidelines by offense and circumstances, 1989 rpt, 17668–1
Statistical Abstract of US, social, political, and economic data, 1790-2025, comprehensive annual compilation, 2324–1.2
Tax (excise) collections of IRS, by source, quarterly rpt, 8302–1
Tax (excise) collections of IRS, by type of tax, region, and State, FY88, annual rpt, 8304–3.3
Tax (excise) indexed to inflation, impacts on Federal revenue and family tax burden by commodity, projected under alternative proposals, 1989-93, GAO rpt, 26119–254
Tax (income) withholding and related documents filed, by type and IRS service center, 1988 and projected 1989-96, annual rpt, 8304–22
Tax revenue potential of State and local systems relative to natl average tax burden, by type of tax and State, 1986, annual rpt, 10044–7
US attorneys civil and criminal cases by type and disposition, and collections, by Federal district, FY88, annual rpt, 6004–2.1
Wiretaps authorized, costs, arrests, trials, and convictions, by offense and jurisdiction, 1988, annual rpt, 18204–7
see also Horse racing
see also Lotteries
see also Pari-mutuel wagering

Game
see Birds and bird conservation
see Hunting and trapping
see Wildlife and wildlife conservation

Games
see Toys and games

Gangs, criminal
see Organized crime

GAO
see General Accounting Office

Garbage
see Landfills
see Refuse and refuse disposal

Garber, Alan M.
"Costs and Effectiveness of Cholesterol Screening in the Elderly", 26356–7.3

Garden Grove, Calif.
see also under By City in the "Index by Categories"

Gardening
see Flowers and nursery products
see Lawn and garden equipment

Gardiner, Walter H.
"EC Cereals Incorporation Scheme: A Cure for Grain Surpluses?", 1524–4.1

Gardner, George R.
"Implications of Changes in Egypt's Cotton Policy", 1522–3.904

Garfinkel, Michelle R.
"Causes and Consequences of Leveraged Buyouts", 9391–1.922
"FOMC in 1988: Uncertainty's Effects on Monetary Policy", 9391–1.908

"Link Between M1 and the Monetary Base in the 1980s", 9391–1.923

"What Is an 'Acceptable' Rate of Inflation?—A Review of the Issues", 9391–1.916

Garland, Tex.
see also under By City in the "Index by Categories"

Garment industry
see Clothing and clothing industry

Garner, C. Alan
"Commodity Prices: Policy Target or Information Variable?", 9381–10.91
"Social Security Surplus: A Solution to the Federal Budget Deficit?", 9381–1.909

Garner, Thesia I.
"Consumer Expenditures and Inequality: An Analysis Using the Gini Coefficient", 6886–6.66
"Gift-Giving Behavior: An Economic Perspective", 6886–6.49

Garnick, Daniel H.
"Growth in Metropolitan and Nonmetropolitan Areas: An Update", 2702–1.915

Garnishment of wages
see Wage deductions

Garrison, Louis
"Impact of Medicare Prospective Payment on the Use of Expensive Devices, 1984-86", 17206–2.3

Gary, Ind.
CPI by component for US city average, and by region, population size, and for 15 metro areas, monthly rpt, 6762–1
CPI by component for US city average, and by region, population size, and for 27 metro areas, monthly rpt, 6762–2
Housing starts and completions authorized by building permits in 40 MSAs, quarterly rpt, 2382–9
see also under By City and By SMSA or MSA in the "Index by Categories"

Gas appliances
see Household appliances and equipment

Gas utilities
see Natural gas and gas industry

Gas wells
see Energy exploration and drilling

Gases
Accident deaths and rates, by cause, age, race, sex, and State, 1986, US Vital Statistics annual rpt, 4144–2
Accidents (occupational) injury and illness rates by SIC 2- to 4-digit industry, and deaths by cause and industry div, 1987, annual rpt, 6844–1
Business statistics, detailed data for major industries and economic indicators, *Survey of Current Business*, monthly rpt, 2702–1.9
County Business Patterns, 1987: employment, establishments, and payroll, by SIC 2- to 4-digit industry and county, annual State rpt series, 2326–8
Electric power use and prices, shipments, and trade, for 25 SIC 4-digit manufacturing industries, 1972-86, 2048–137
Exports of US, detailed commodities by country, monthly rpt, 2422–3
Foreign countries mineral production, reserves, and industry role in domestic economy and world supply, world area and country rpt series, 5606–1

Helium and other components of natural gas, analyses of individual wells and pipelines, 1917-88, annual rpt, 5604–2
Helium market demand and Bur of Mines production, sales, and financial statements, FY88, annual rpt, 5604–32
Helium resources in storage and natural gas reserves, by State, 1950-87 and projected to 2020, biennial rpt, 5604–44
Hydrogen energy R&D activity and funding of DOE, and project listing, FY88, annual rpt, 3304–18
Manufacturing annual survey, 1986: financial and operating data, by SIC 2- to 4-digit industry, series, 2506–15
Manufacturing census, 1987: financial and operating data, for SIC 4-digit industries by product, preliminary rpt, 2491–1.33; 2491–1.38
Methane emissions control in coal mines, research results, techniques, and equipment, mid 1960s-79, 5608–156
Minerals Yearbook, 1987, Vol 1: commodity reviews of production, use, trade, prices, and mining operations, annual rpt, 5604–33
Minerals Yearbook, 1987, Vol 1 preprints: commodity reviews of production, reserves, supply, use, and trade, annual rpt series, 5604–15
Minerals Yearbook, 1987, Vol 2 preprints: State reviews of production and sales by commodity, and business activity, annual rpt series, 5604–16
Minerals Yearbook, 1987, Vol 2: State reviews of production, sales, and firms, by commodity, and business activity, annual rpt, 5604–34
Minerals Yearbook, 1987, Vol 3: foreign country reviews of production, trade, and policy, by commodity, annual rpt, 5604–35
Minerals Yearbook, 1987, Vol 3 preprints: foreign country reviews of production, trade, and policy, by commodity, annual rpt series, 5604–23
Minerals Yearbook, 1988, Vol 1: commodity reviews of production, reserves, supply, use, and trade, annual rpt series, 5604–20
Minerals Yearbook, 1988, Vol 2 rpts: State reviews of production and sales by commodity, and business activity, annual rpt series, 5604–22
Price indexes (producer), by stage of processing and detailed commodity, monthly rpt, 6762–6
Price indexes (producer), by stage of processing and detailed commodity, monthly 1988, annual rpt, 6764–2
Production of industrial gases, by product, monthly Current Industrial Rpt, 2506–8.3
Production, prices, trade, use, employment, tariffs, and stockpiles, by mineral, with foreign comparisons, 1984-88, annual rpt, 5604–18
Supply, imports, and use of strategic and technologically important minerals, with foreign comparisons, commodity rpt series, 5606–9
Transportation census, 1987: trucks, by detailed characteristics, miles traveled, and type of product carried, State rpt series, 2573–1

Wholesale trade census, 1987: employment, establishments, finances, and operations, by SIC 2- to 4-digit kind of business, MSA, county, and city, State rpt series, 2405–1
see also Air pollution
see also Liquefied petroleum gas
see also Natural gas and gas industry
see also Natural gas liquids
see also Radon
see also under By Commodity in the "Index by Categories"

Gasohol
Consumption and tax rates for motor fuel, by fuel type and State, monthly rpt, 7552–1
Consumption of gasohol, and tax rates, by State, 1987-88, annual rpt, 3304–9
Consumption of gasohol, by State, 1980-87, annual rpt, 3304–5.2
Consumption of gasohol, by State, 1988, annual rpt, 7554–1.1
Defense Fuel Supply Center procurement, prices, stocks, transport, and other activities and finances, FY88, annual rpt, 3904–8
Energy use by mode of transport, fuel supply, and demographic and economic factors of vehicle use, 1970s-88, annual rpt, 3304–5
Tax (excise) on gasoline and other motor fuels, rates by selected State, as of Oct 1987, 10048–72
Tax (excise) rates for motor fuels, by State, 1978-87, annual table, 7554–32

Gasoline
Agriculture census, 1987: farms, farmland, production, finances, and operator characteristics, by county, final State rpt series, 2331–1
Alcohol fuels (methanol) prices, distribution, and gasoline displacement, with background data, 1985-86 and projected to 2000, 3008–122
Auto fuel economy test results for US and foreign makes, 1990 model year, annual rpt, 3304–11
Auto operating costs by component, and Fed Govt mileage reimbursement rates, 1988, annual rpt, 9454–13
Business statistics, detailed data for major industries and economic indicators, *Survey of Current Business*, monthly rpt, 2702–1.15
Consumption and tax rates for motor fuel, by fuel type and State, monthly rpt, 7552–1
Consumption, by detailed fuel type, end-use sector, and State, 1960-87, State Energy Data System annual rpt, 3164–39
Consumption of energy, by air pollutant source, fuel type, and State, 1986, annual rpt, 9194–14
Consumption of gasoline, and taxes, by State, 1987-88, annual rpt, 7554–24
Consumption of motor fuel, by consuming sector and State, 1988, annual rpt, 7554–1.1
Costs of owning and operating autos, by component, 1977-88, annual rpt, 7304–2.1
CPI by component for US city average, and by region, population size, and for 27 metro areas, monthly rpt, 6762–2

Tax (income) returns of corporations, income and tax items by asset size and detailed industry, 1986, annual rpt, 8304–4; 8304–21

Tax (income) returns of partnerships, income statement items by industry group, 1986, annual article, 8302–2.903

Tax (income) returns of sole proprietorships, income statement items, by industry group, 1987, annual article, 8302–2.904; 8302–2.921

Virgin Islands economic censuses, 1987: employment, firms, payroll, and receipts, by SIC 1- to 4-digit industry, island, and city, 2593–1

see also Automobile repair and maintenance

Gasoline tax
see Fuel tax

Gastonia, N.C.
Housing starts and completions authorized by building permits in 40 MSAs, quarterly rpt, 2382–9

Wages by occupation, for office and plant workers, 1988 survey, periodic MSA rpt, 6785–11.2

see also under By SMSA or MSA in the "Index by Categories"

Gastrointestinal diseases
see Digestive diseases

Gates, Gerald W.
"Census Bureau Microdata: Providing Useful Research Data While Protecting the Anonymity of Respondents", 2626–10.79

GATT
see Trade agreements

Gavin, William T.
"Effects of Disinflationary Policies on Monetary Velocity", 9377–9.74

Gbur, Philip M.
"Testing Telephone Interviewing in the Survey of Income and Program Participation and Some Early Results", 2626–10.74

Gedney, Donald R.
"Changes in Land Use in Western Oregon Between 1971-74 and 1982", 1206–19.9

Geier-Hayes, Kathleen
"Vegetation Response to Helicopter Logging and Broadcast Burning in Douglas-fir Habitat Types at Silver Creek, Central Idaho", 1208–305

Geiman, Rusty
"Selected Trends in Collection Inventory Revisited", 8304–8.1

Geisinger, Kenneth
"Airline Delay: 1976-86, Based upon the Standardized Delay Reporting System", 7508–68

Gelfand, Matthew D.
"Simple Microanalytics of Payments System Risk", 9366–6.175

Gemstones
Exports of US, detailed commodities by country, monthly rpt, 2422–3

Imports of US, detailed Schedule A commodities by country, monthly rpt, 2422–2

Manufacturing census, 1987: financial and operating data, for SIC 4-digit industries by product, preliminary rpt, 2491–1.80

Mineral Industry Surveys, State reviews of production, 1988, preliminary annual rpt, 5614–6

Minerals Yearbook, 1987, Vol 1: commodity reviews of production, use, trade, prices, and mining operations, annual rpt, 5604–33

Minerals Yearbook, 1987, Vol 2 preprints: State reviews of production and sales by commodity, and business activity, annual rpt series, 5604–16

Minerals Yearbook, 1987, Vol 2: State reviews of production, sales, and firms, by commodity, and business activity, annual rpt, 5604–34

Minerals Yearbook, 1987, Vol 3: foreign country reviews of production, trade, and policy, by commodity, annual rpt, 5604–35

Minerals Yearbook, 1987, Vol 3 preprints: foreign country reviews of production, trade, and policy, by commodity, annual rpt series, 5604–23

Minerals Yearbook, 1988, Vol 2 rpts: State reviews of production and sales by commodity, and business activity, annual rpt series, 5604–22

Occupational injuries and incidence, employment, and hours in nonmetallic minerals mines and related operations, 1987, annual rpt, 6664–1

Production, prices, trade, use, employment, tariffs, and stockpiles, by mineral, with foreign comparisons, 1984-88, annual rpt, 5604–18

Stockpiling of strategic material by Fed Govt, activity, and inventory by commodity, as of Sept 1989, semiannual rpt, 3542–22; 3902–2

Stockpiling of strategic material, inventories and needs, by commodity, as of Sept 1988, annual rpt, 3544–37

Stockpiling of strategic material, inventories, costs, and goals by commodity, as of June 1989, semiannual rpt, 3902–3

see also Jewelry

see also under By Commodity in the "Index by Categories"

General Accounting Office
Activities and operations of GAO, and resulting cost savings to Fed Govt, FY88, annual rpt, 26104–1

Advertising spending of Fed Govt, and subcontracts to small and disadvantaged firms, by agency and medium, FY86, GAO rpt, 26113–428

Aerospace industry employment and salaries, by sex and race, 1979-87, GAO rpt, 26121–315

Agricultural exports competitiveness, and subsidy and credit program costs, with data by commodity, 1980s-89, GAO rpt, 26113–404

AID local currency trust funds mgmt and use, by country, FY83-87, GAO rpt, 26123–221

AIDS and other new programs of CDC, staffing and reallocations from other programs, FY81-88, GAO rpt, 26121–287

AIDS cases, and health and social services availability, for 5 cities, 1988, GAO rpt, 26121–307

AIDS cases forecasts, analysis of CDC and other methodology, 1989 GAO rpt, 26131–55

AIDS research grants and contracts of NIH, by funding and approval status, and researcher age, experience, and sex, FY86, GAO rpt, 26121–267

Air Force B-1B aircraft maintenance problems, and repair contracts, 1985-88 with costs projected to FY94, GAO rpt, 26123–218

Air Force Pacific basin airlift of aircraft parts, traffic, shipments, and impacts on force readiness, 1986-88, GAO rpt, 26123–230

Air Force property mgmt, validation of unfilled orders for aircraft spare parts, 1985-87, GAO rpt, 26123–245

Air Force supply inventory stock fund balances, refunds to customers, and procurement cost effects of reducing balances, FY84-88, GAO rpt, 26111–60

Air traffic control system safety, working conditions, and traffic volume, various periods 1981-88, GAO rpt series, 26113–220

Air travel safety inspector training, FAA officals views on curriculum and adequacy, 1988 survey, GAO rpt, 26113–440

Aircraft mid-air collision prevention measures of FAA, and near collisions by type of ATC facility and selected airport, 1986-88, GAO rpt, 26113–426

Alien workers (unauthorized) employer sanctions, enforcement costs, compliance, and job discrimination, 1988 annual GAO rpt, 26104–19

Alien workers (unauthorized) employer sanctions impacts on farm labor supply in Western US, with background data, 1986-89, GAO rpt, 26121–310

Aliens (illegal) welfare benefits, operations of Federal-State system to prevent payment, State official views, 1988, GAO rpt, 26121–276

Aliens exclusion and deportation cases, appeals, bond postings, and investigations, for NYC and Los Angeles, 1987, GAO rpt, 26119–271

Army Reserve and Natl Guard combat and critical job task training, resources, effectiveness, and officers views, FY87, GAO rpt, 26123–239

Army spare parts procurement in advance of reorder dates, excess costs by item, FY87-88, GAO rpt, 26123–254

Asia dollar exchange rate, and impacts of currency appreciation on current account and trade balances and economic indicators, for 3 countries, 1980s-90, GAO rpt, 26123–234

Athlete grad rates for NCAA Div I college programs, and reporting of academic performance to Education Dept, 1987-89, GAO rpt, 26121–305

Athlete grad rates for NCAA Div I college programs, by region, aggregate 1982-87, GAO rpt, 26121–285

Aviation R&D funding and staff of FAA, by program, FY87-88, GAO rpt, 26113–407

Banks failures, by type of charter and mgmt weakness, audit activity, asset size, age, and State, 1984-88, GAO rpt, 26111–61

Biotechnology patent issues, and time lapse between application and issue, 1988, GAO rpt, 26113–406

Board and care homes licensing and inspection by States, and client characteristics, 1989 GAO rpt, 26121–275

Bond (low-grade) holdings of thrift instns, returns, defaults, and losses, 1985-88, GAO rpt, 26119–246

Budget of US Appendix, obligations, appropriations, and personnel, by program and agency, FY90, annual rpt, 104–3

Military bases child day care services use, capacity, and waiting list backlog, by service branch, as of Feb 1988, GAO rpt, 26121-279

Military headquarters personnel reduction proposals for joint and service commands, by service branch, FY90-91, GAO rpt, 26123-236

Military health care facilities quality of care, patient views, 1988-89 survey, GAO rpt, 26121-318

Military hospitals and CHAMPUS costs, and reduction in military hospital admissions, with background data, FY85-87, GAO rpt, 26121-288

Military installation child care availability for civilian employees, and need, 1988 survey, GAO rpt, 26121-262

Military newspaper *Stars and Stripes* coverage of sensitive topics, FY88-89, GAO rpt, 26123-226

Military officers assigned to multiservice organizations, quality and promotion indicators by service branch, 1985-88, GAO rpt, 26123-231

Military sales program loans outstanding, prepayments, delinquency, and refinancing, by country, 1988-89, GAO rpt, 26123-253

Minerals (strategic) production, by country and for South Africa companies controlled by multinatl firms, 1987, GAO rpt, 26123-233

Mining claims on public lands, patents by type and State, and applications by disposition, 1978-87, GAO rpt, 26113-403

Mortgage servicing transfers among lenders, and consumer complaints, 1984-89, GAO rpt, 26113-441

NATO Europe members presence of US military and civilian personnel and dependents, by service branch, 1980-88, GAO rpt, 26123-252

NATO Europe members presence of US military and civilian personnel, and vacancies, by service branch, 1988, GAO rpt, 26123-251

Navy computer mainframe and related equipment procurement, compatibility, and operating system contracts, FY86-89, GAO rpt, 26125-37

Navy pilot proficiency program, aircraft hours flown and costs, FY83-87, GAO rpt, 26123-238

Nicaragua Contra forces humanitarian aid of AID, by type, 1988, GAO rpt, 26123-237

Nuclear power plant performance ratings, violations, penalties, and unplanned outages, by plant, 1970s-87, GAO rpt, 26113-416

Nuclear Waste Fund finances, and DOE Civilian Radioactive Waste Mgmt Office activities, quarterly GAO rpt, 26102-4

Nurses with alien resident status and temporary work visas, by State and source country, 1985-90, GAO rpt, 26121-314

OASDI trust funds finances, and impact on Federal budget, 1987-88 and projected to 2050, GAO rpt, 26121-269

Oil and gas leasing activity on Federal land, production, revenue, and royalty rates, by whether competitively leased and western State, 1984-88, GAO rpt, 26113-413

Oil company overcharge settlements, and use for State legal expenses, by State, firm, and case, as of 1988, GAO rpt, 26113-408

Oil stocks and conservation measures of Intl Energy Program countries, 1987-88 and projected to 1990, GAO rpt, 26123-225

Older persons with functional limitations, long-term health care needs, and costs by payment source, 1982-85, GAO rpt, 26121-266

OMB mgmt of Federal employees, budget, and info systems, indicators of effectiveness, FY81-90, GAO rpt, 26119-251

OPM activities and funding, and Federal personnel officers and OPM employees views on leadership and support in labor mgmt issues, 1984-88, GAO rpt, 26119-236

Passport and visa applicant screening, State Dept info system records by reason for exclusion, 1989, GAO rpt, 26125-36

Peace Corps activities, funding, and volunteers characteristics, FY62-88, GAO rpt, 26123-243

Pension plan regulation enforcement by Labor Dept and IRS, violations, and penalties, FY85-88, GAO rpt, 26121-259

Pension plan vesting and other provisions by plan size, and compliance with Federal rules, 1984-85, GAO rpt, 26121-306

Police pay, benefits, and staffing, for US Park Police and compared to other Federal and local police units, FY85-88, GAO rpt, 26119-264

Postal Service employee disciplinary actions, by type of infraction and penalty, and region, 1985-88, GAO rpt, 26119-256

Postal Service land purchases and needs, FY87, GAO rpt, 26119-266

Presidential directives released through Natl Security Council, by purpose and admin, 1961-88, GAO rpt, 26123-224

Publications of GAO, FY88, annual listing, 26104-17

Puerto Rico economic conditions and govt finances, 1975-89, GAO rpt, 26121-298

Railroad accidents, casualties, and damage, with data by carrier, for Pennsylvania and US, 1984-87, GAO rpt, 26113-390

Railroad accidents reported and not reported to Fed Railroad Admin, injuries, damage, and workdays lost, for 5 carriers, 1983-87, GAO rpt, 26113-410

Railroad employment by occupation from 1957, and Railroad Retirement Account finances, alternative projections 1987-2010, GAO rpt, 26121-280

Refugees from Nicaragua, El Salvador, and Guatemala receiving UN aid, resettlement in other Central American countries, and repatriations, 1984-88, GAO rpt, 26123-232

Regulatory review procedures of OMB, proposed and final rules by disposition and agency, 1981-89, GAO rpt, 26119-261

Reserve forces manpower, funding by category, procurement reductions, and needs, by component, FY80-88, GAO rpt, 26123-220

Rural areas aid from Fed Govt, by agency and program, with county classifications by population density, FY85 and FY87, GAO rpt, 26113-401

Savings instns advances from FHLBs, assets, and liabilities, with data for failed and merged instns, by FHLB district, 1980s-88, GAO rpt, 26119-269

Savings instns failures by State, with exam of mgmt weaknesses and regulatory activity, 1980s-87, GAO rpt, 26111-62

Securities (tax-exempt) holdings by investor type, and IRS enforcement of disallowance of interest deduction for financing holdings, mid 1970s-87, GAO rpt, 26119-239

Securities intl transaction activity, by country, 1982-88, GAO rpt, 26123-235

Senior Executive Service career position longterm vacancies, by reason and agency, 1989, GAO rpt, 26119-252

Senior Executive Service training and dev program activities, participant views, 1987 survey, GAO rpt, 26119-272

Service contracts of Fed Govt compared with work performed in-house, savings and employment effects by agency, 1978-87, GAO rpt, 26119-238

Shipboard employment of women in merchant marine, Natl Marine Fisheries Service, and fishing, with rpts of sexual assault, 1980s-88, GAO rpt, 26113-397

Small Business Investment Companies disbursements, by State, 1983-87, GAO rpt, 26113-417

Small business R&D grants of Fed Govt, administrators views on effectiveness, FY86-87, GAO rpt, 26113-393

Small business training confs of SBA, cosponsors by type, and compliance with SBA regulations, by region, 1988, GAO rpt, 26113-425

Space program funding by NASA and DOD, by category, FY81-89, GAO rpt, 26123-152

SSA employees with poor performance, mgmt activities, outcomes, and supervisors views, 1985-87, GAO rpt, 26119-240

SSA employment of Hispanics by regional office, and Spanish-speaking employees in California, 1987, GAO rpt, 26121-268

State Dept freedom of info requests and security reviews, processing, 1985-88, GAO rpt, 26119-243

Steel import voluntary restraint agreements, ITA review of requests for restraint waivers because of supply shortages, 1985-88, GAO rpt, 26123-240

Strategic Petroleum Reserve funding and activities, by site, as of Sept 1988, semiannual GAO rpt, 26102-3

Student guaranteed loan default rates, and claims paid by guaranty agencies, by State, and borrower characteristics, FY87, GAO rpt, 26121-292

Student guaranteed loan defaults, losses, and rates, by instn, 1983-Sept 1987, GAO rpt, 26121-289

Surety bonds use to guarantee Federal small business construction contracts, and fraud cases, by agency, 1985-89, GAO rpt, 26113-438

Tax (excise) indexed to inflation, impacts on Federal revenue and family tax burden by commodity, projected under alternative proposals, 1989-93, GAO rpt, 26119-254

Tax (income) aid telephone system of IRS, accessibility and accuracy, 1988 survey, GAO rpt, 26119-190

Tax (income) law violations civil penalties assessed and abated, FY87-88, GAO rpt, 26119-265

Tax assessments and collections resulting from IRS criminal investigations, by violation type, 1984, GAO rpt, 26119-244

Temporary employment in Fed Govt, appointments and extensions, by occupational group, 1983-87, GAO rpt, 26119-129

Torts for product liability, dispositions, awards, case processing time, and plaintiff injury severity and other characteristics, 1983-85, GAO rpt, 26121-317

Truck driver multi-State license prohibition, FHwA enforcement activities by region, 1987-88, GAO rpt, 26113-396

Truck drivers training in private and public programs, requirements, cost, and staffing, 1989, GAO rpt, 26113-432

Trust funds of Fed Govt, financial status by agency, and impacts on budget balance, FY47-93 and projected to FY93, GAO rpt, 26111-58

TVA managers salaries, incentive payments by program, and supplemental pensions, 1979-88, GAO rpt, 26113-420

UN Environment Program activities, and funding by source, program, and country, 1986-89, GAO rpt, 26123-246

Unemployed displaced workers, labor-mgmt committee aid recipients by selected characteristics, for 4 State programs, 1988, GAO rpt, 26121-316

Unemployment insurance administrative funding by Fed Govt, impacts of reductions on State program operations, FY80-88, GAO rpt, 26121-284

Urban Dev Action Grant eligibility rating system of HUD, and project costs and economic impacts, as of Nov 1988, GAO rpt, 26113-424

Urban Dev Action Grant projects and funding, impacts of changes in selection criteria, by city and State, 1988, GAO rpt, 26113-395

VA disability ratings system, evaluation of methods, 1987 survey, GAO rpt, 26121-264

VA health care clinics outpatient care applications, denials, appointments, and waiting periods, for 4 Florida clinics, FY88, GAO rpt, 26121-283

VA health care personnel born abroad, and English proficiency, as of Mar 1988, GAO rpt, 26121-273

Veterans (disabled) employment and promotion in Fed Govt by agency, and recruitment coordinator activities, FY81-87, GAO rpt, 26119-245

Veterans disability compensation and pensions, VA claims processing and disposition, FY87, GAO rpt, 26121-293

Veterans disability compensation, effects of eliminating non-service connected disabilities, with background data, 1986, GAO rpt, 26121-295

Vocational education for disadvantaged and handicapped funding of Fed Govt, by selected State and district, 1985-89 and projected to 2000, GAO rpt, 26121-286

Wastewater facilities of Fed Govt, compliance with pollution control regulations, FY86-87, GAO rpt, 26113-388

Water (groundwater) pollution from soil injection of oil and gas refining wastes, by State, 1987, GAO rpt, 26113-429

Water (groundwater) protection standards, States use of EPA and alternative standards by type of water use, and contaminant test results, 1976-88, GAO rpt, 26131-56

Wilderness Natl Preservation System mgmt by Forest Service, regulation of commercial and recreational activities, and ranger views, 1985-88, GAO rpt, 26113-436

Wildlife (endangered species) recovery plans, and funding by Federal agencies and others, by species, FY72-87, GAO rpt, 26113-391

Wildlife refuge impacts of recreational, commercial, and military use, by type of activity, 1988-89, GAO rpt, 26113-434

General Agreement on Tariffs and Trade
see Trade agreements

General aviation

Accidents and circumstances, for US operations of domestic and foreign airlines and general aviation, periodic rpt, 9612-1

Accidents, deaths, and circumstances, for by carrier and carrier type, preliminary 1988, annual press release, 9614-9

Accidents in general aviation, by circumstances, characteristics of persons and aircraft involved, and type of flying, 1986, annual rpt, 9614-3

Air traffic control and airway facilities improvement activities under Natl Airspace System Plan, 1981-85 and projected to 2000, annual rpt, 7504-12

Aircraft (general aviation), flight hours, and equipment, by type, use, and model of aircraft, region, and State, 1988, annual rpt, 7504-29

Aircraft registered with FAA, by type and characteristics of aircraft, make, carrier, State, and county, 1988, annual rpt, 7504-3

Finances, operations, vehicles, equipment, accidents, and energy use, by mode of transport, 1955-88, annual rpt, 7304-2

Hijacking attempts and airport security operations, screening results, and enforcement actions, 1st half 1988, semiannual rpt, 7502-5

Hijackings, on-board explosions, and other crime, US and foreign incidents, 1983-87, annual rpt, 7504-31

Instrument flight rule aircraft handled, by user type, FAA traffic control center, and region, FY80-88 and projected to FY2000, annual rpt, 7504-15

Pilots and nonpilots certified by FAA, by certificate type, age, sex, region, and State, 1988, annual rpt, 7504-2

Traffic, aircraft, pilots, airports, and fuel use, forecast FY89-2000 and trends from FY80, annual rpt, 7504-6

Traffic and other aviation activity forecasts of FAA, 1989 annual conf, 7504-28

Traffic and passenger enplanements, by airport, region, and State, projected FY89-2005 and trends from FY83, annual rpt, 7504-7

Traffic levels at FAA air traffic control facilities, by airport and State, FY88, annual rpt, 7504-27

General Motors Corp.

Energy economy, sales, and market shares, by size and model for domestic and foreign makes, 1989 model year, semiannual rpt, 3302-4

Energy economy test results, 1990 model year, annual rpt, 3304-11

Hazardous substances industrial releases and reduction methods under EPA regulation, by chemical, source, industry, and location, 1987, annual rpt, 9234-6

Safety of domestic and foreign autos, crash test results by model, model years 1984-88, 7768-111

Safety of domestic and foreign autos, crash test results by model, press release series, 7766-7

General Services Administration

Activities and finances of GSA, FY88, annual rpt, 9454-1

Advisory committees of Fed Govt, and members, staff, meetings, and costs by agency, FY88, annual rpt, 9454-18

Assistance (financial and nonfinancial) of Fed Govt, 1989 base edition with supplements, annual listing, 104-5

Auto fleet of Fed Govt, costs and operating data by agency, FY87, annual rpt, 9454-9

Auto operating costs by component, and Fed Govt mileage reimbursement rates, 1988, annual rpt, 9454-13

Budget deficit reduction under Gramm-Rudman Act, cancellation of budget authority by program, FY90, annual rpt, 104-27; 21924-1; 26304-6

Budget of US Appendix, obligations, appropriations, and personnel, by program and agency, FY90, annual rpt, 104-3

Budget of US, authoritative financial statements with appropriations, outlays, and receipts, by category and agency, FY88, annual rpt, 8104-2.2

Computer systems and equipment of Fed Govt, by type, make, and agency, 1st half FY89, semiannual listing, 9452-9

Fraud and abuse in GSA programs, audits and investigations, 2nd half FY89, semiannual rpt, 9452-8

Info Security Oversight Office monitoring of Federal security measures and classification actions, FY88, annual rpt, 9454-21

Labor unions recognized in Fed Govt, agreements and membership by agency and facility, as of Jan 1989, biennial listing, 9844-14

Procurement contract awards of Fed Govt, by State, agency, procurement and contractor type, and for top 100 contractors, quarterly rpt, 102-6

Property (real) of Fed Govt, inventory and costs, worldwide summary by location, agency, and use, 1987, annual rpt, 9454-5

Property (real) of Fed Govt, leased inventory and rental costs, worldwide summary by location and agency, 1987, annual rpt, 9454-10

R&D funding by Fed Govt, by field, performer type, agency, and State, FY87-89, annual rpt, 9627-20

Small business construction contracts of Fed Govt, surety bonds use and fraud cases, by agency, 1985-89, GAO rpt, 26113-438

Bank deposits in FDIC-insured commercial and savings banks, by instn, State, and county, as of June 1988, annual regional rpt, 9295-3.2

Collective bargaining calendar for southeastern States, 1989, annual rpt, 6946-1.73

County Business Patterns, 1987: employment, establishments, and payroll, by SIC 2- to 4-digit industry and county, annual State rpt, 2326-8.12

Deaths and rates, by detailed location, cause, and demographic characteristics, 1987, US Vital Statistics annual rpt, 4144-3.1

Disabled SSI beneficiaries Medicaid services use and costs, by diagnosis and whether covered by Medicare, 1984, article, 4652-1.947

DOD prime contract awards, by contractor, service branch, State, and city, FY88, annual rpt, 3544-22

Economic indicators by State and MSA, Fed Reserve 6th District, quarterly rpt, 9371-14

Employment and housing market indicators by State, FHLB 4th District, quarterly rpt, 9302-36

Employment and unemployment, for 8 southeastern States, 1987-88, annual rpt, 6944-2

Employment and unemployment in Georgia, by sex and race, 1988, press release, 6946-3.13

Employment by industry div, earnings, and hours, for 8 southeastern States, quarterly press release, 6942-7

Employment, earnings, and hours, by selected SIC 1- to 4-digit industry, State, and for 262 MSAs, 1972-87, 6748-81.1

Estuary environmental conditions and mgmt, 1989 conf, 2146-6.13

Farm operators displaced worker programs under Job Training Partnership Act, funding, participation, and results by selected State, 1982-87, 15496-1.2

Fed Govt spending in States and local areas, by type, State, county, and city, FY88, annual rpt, 2464-3

Fed Govt spending in States, by type, program, agency, and State, FY88, annual rpt, 2464-2

Food stamp program temporary termination of benefits, by reason and duration, for 2 States, FY87, GAO rpt, 26113-423

HHS financial aid, by program, recipient, State, and city, FY88, annual regional listing, 4004-3.4

Homeless children educational enrollment and needs, 1988, annual State rpt, 4804-35.12

Income (personal) per capita and by source, and earnings by industry div, by State, MSA, and county, 1982-87, annual regional rpt, 2704-2.4

Medicaid enrollment, and service use and costs by service type, by eligibility type, for 5 States, 1980-84, article, 4652-1.919

Medicaid enrollment, services use, and costs, by eligibility type and length of enrollment, for 2 States, 1980-83, article, 4652-1.906

Mineral Industry Surveys, State reviews of production, 1988, preliminary annual rpt, 5614-6

Minerals Yearbook, 1987, Vol 2 preprints: State review of production and sales by commodity, and business activity, annual rpt, 5604-16.11

Minerals Yearbook, 1987, Vol 2: State reviews of production, sales, and firms, by commodity, and business activity, annual rpt, 5604-34

Nursing home compliance with Medicare and Medicaid regulations, and patient characteristics, by facility, 1987/88, annual State rpt, 4654-15.11

Older persons eligible for nursing home care, cost of home and community services, Medicaid waiver program in 2 States, 1981-84, article, 4652-1.943

Peach production, marketing, and prices in 3 southeastern States and Appalachia, 1988, annual rpt, 1311-12

Pregnancy-related services use and costs, for Medicaid beneficiaries in 3 States, 1983-84, article, 4652-1.938

Retail trade census, 1987: employment, establishments, sales, and payroll, by SIC 2- to 4-digit kind of business, MSA, county, and city, State rpt, 2397-1.11

Savings instns, FHLB 4th District members finances and financial ratios, by State, quarterly rpt, 9302-3

Savings instns, FHLB 4th District members finances, by State, 1984-88, annual rpt, 9304-29.4

Service industries census, 1987: employment, establishments, receipts, and payroll, by SIC 2- to 4-digit kind of business, MSA, county, and city, State rpt, 2391-1.11

Statistical Abstract of US, social, political, and economic data, with foreign comparisons, 1790-2025, comprehensive annual compilation, 2324-1

Textile mill employment, earnings, and hours, for 8 Southeastern States, quarterly press release, 6942-1

Timber in Georgia, resources and removals by species, ownership class, and county, 1988-89, series, 1206-26

Water supply and quality in streams and lakes, and groundwater levels in wells, by drainage basin, 1987, annual State rpt, 5666-10.9

Water supply and quality in streams and lakes, and groundwater levels in wells, by drainage basin, 1988, annual State rpt, 5666-16.9

Wholesale trade census, 1987: employment, establishments, finances, and operations, by SIC 2- to 4-digit kind of business, MSA, county, and city, State rpt, 2405-1.11

Wildlife-related recreation, hunting, and fishing participation and spending, detailed data, 1985 survey, quinquennial State rpt, 5506-6.10

see also Atlanta, Ga.

see also Augusta, Ga.

see also Brunswick, Ga.

see also Columbus, Ga.

see also Macon, Ga.

see also Savannah, Ga.

see also Warner Robins, Ga.

see also under By State in the "Index by Categories"

Geothermal resources

Consumption, by detailed fuel type, end-use sector, and State, 1960-87, State Energy Data System annual rpt, 3164-39

Electric power plants and capacity, by fuel used, owner, location, and operating status, 1988 and for units planned 1989-98, annual listing, 3164-36

Environmental impacts of energy technologies, 1960s-80s, handbook series, 3326-1

Foreign and US energy production and use, by energy type and country, 1980-88, annual rpt, 3164-50.5

Pacific Northwest electric power capacity and use, by energy source, projected under alternative load and demand cases, 1989-2008, annual rpt, 3224-3

Public lands acreage and use, and Land Mgmt Bur activities and finances, annual State rpt series, 5724-11

Public lands acreage, grants, use, revenues, and allocations, by State, FY88, annual rpt, 5724-1.2

Public lands minerals resources and availability, State rpt series, 5606-7

Supply, demand, and prices, by fuel type and end-use sector, with foreign comparisons, 1988 and trends from 1949, annual rpt, 3164-74

Gerald, Debra E.

"Projections of Education Statistics to 2000", 4824-4

Gerbert, Barbara

"Public Acceptance of the Surgeon General's Brochure on AIDS", 4042-3.908

Geriatrics

Cell cultures for aging research, availability and cultures shipped, 1989 listing, 4478-187

Educational and research grants and contracts of Health Professions Bur, by instn and program, FY88, annual listing, 4114-1

Health care services and long term care for aged, series, 4186-7

HHS financial aid, by program, recipient, State, and city, FY88, annual regional listings, 4004-3

Long-term health care for aged, funding by Fed Govt, public views, 1987 survey, hearings, 21368-106

Long-term health care needs of aged with functional limitations, and costs by payment source, 1982-85, GAO rpt, 26121-266

VA health care facilities mental health services, staff, research, and training programs, 1989 biennial listing, 8704-2

VA health care facilities physicians, dentists, and nurses, by selected employment characteristics and VA district, quarterly rpt, 8602-6

VA Medicine and Surgery Dept trainees, by detailed program and city, FY88, annual rpt, 8704-4

German Democratic Republic

see Germany, East

Germanium

see Metals and metal industries

Germany, East

Agricultural and food production and indexes, total and for selected commodities, by country, 1970s-88, annual rpt, 1524-12

Agricultural production, acreage, and consumption, by Eastern Europe country and commodity, 1965-85, 1528–284

Agricultural production, consumption, and trade, for Eastern Europe by country, 1970s-88, annual rpt, 1524–11

Agricultural trade of US, by detailed commodity and country, 1988, semiannual rpt, 1522–4

Cuba economic conditions, agricultural and industrial production and distribution, trade, and intl economic relations, 1980-87 with trends from 1961, 9118–8

Debt, trade, and balances of Eastern Europe and USSR with US and other western countries, with background data, 1980s-87, hearing, 21248–120

Economic and military aid and loans from US and intl agencies, by program and country, FY46-87, annual rpt, 9914–5

Economic conditions in Communist, OECD, and selected other countries, 1960s-88, annual rpt, 9114–4

Economic conditions, income, production, prices, employment, and trade, 1989 periodic country rpt, 2046–4.49

Economic conditions, policy, and trade practices, by country, 1986-88, annual rpt, 21384–5

Economic, social, political, and geographic summary data, by country, 1989, annual factbook, 9114–2

Export licensing, monitoring, and enforcement activities, FY88, annual rpt, 2024–1

Exports and imports of US, by selected country, country group, and commodity group, 1988, annual rpt, 2044–37

Exports and imports of US with Communist countries, by detailed commodity and country, quarterly rpt with articles, 9882–2

Human rights conditions in 170 countries, 1988, annual rpt, 21384–3

Military spending, arms trade, and force strengths, with govt spending and population, by country, 1977-87, annual rpt, 9824–1

Military strength of USSR and Warsaw Pact, and proposed force reductions, with comparisons to NATO, 1980s-91, hearing, 21208–29

Minerals Yearbook, 1987, Vol 3: foreign country reviews of production, trade, and policy, by commodity, annual rpt, 5604–35

Minerals Yearbook, 1987, Vol 3 preprints: foreign country review of production, trade, and policy, by commodity, annual rpt, 5604–23.25

Nuclear power plant capacity and operating status, by plant and Communist country, as of Dec 1988, annual rpt, 3164–57.2

Population size, growth rates, and components of change, by country, projected 1989-2020 and trends from 1950, biennial rpt, 2324–9

Steel export ceilings under voluntary restraint agreements, by country and product, with Western US steel industry impact, 1989 rpt, 9886–4.136

Steel imports of US under voluntary restraint agreement, by product, customs district, and country, with US industry operating data, monthly rpt, 9882–13

UN voting record and share of votes in agreement with US, by issue, country, and world area, 1988, annual rpt, 7004–18

see also under By Foreign Country in the "Index by Categories"

Germany, West

Agricultural and food production and indexes, total and for selected commodities, by country, 1970s-88, annual rpt, 1524–12

Agricultural production, prices, and trade, by country, 1970s-88 and forecast 1990, annual world region rpt, 1524–4.1

Agricultural trade of US, by detailed commodity and country, 1988, semiannual rpt, 1522–4

AID loans repayment status and terms by program and country, and status of predecessor agency loans, quarterly rpt, 9912–3

Apprentices in US and 4 European countries, 1987, article, 6722–1.936

Background Notes, summary social, political, and economic data, 1989 rpt, 7006–2.29

Bearings (antifriction) from 9 countries, injury to US industry from foreign subsidized and less than fair value imports, investigation with background financial and operating data, 1989 rpt, 9886–19.65

Businesses (foreign) activity in US, income tax returns, assets, and income statement items, by industry div, country, and world area, 1984-85, article, 8302–2.920

Capital cost indicators for US, Japan, West Germany, and UK, various periods 1977-88, article, 9385–1.910

China trade, by commodity, world area, and country, 1985-87, 9118–10

Coal production, trade, and govt subsidies, by country and country group, 1973-87 and projected to 2000, 2048–144

Current account balance and related economic indicators, for US and 4 countries, 1980s-87, article, 9389–1.908

Current account balance of US, components and relation to foreign and US investment and economic conditions, 1970s-88 and projected to 1990s, article, 9385–1.907

Developing countries loans from banks and govts, debt exposure of 7 developed countries, various periods 1980-88, GAO rpt, 26123–255

Drug abuse indicators, for selected countries, 1989 semiannual conf, 4492–5.2

Economic and military aid and loans from US and intl agencies, by program and country, FY46-87, annual rpt, 9914–5

Economic and monetary trends, compounded annual rates of change for US and 10 major trading partners, quarterly rpt, 9391–7

Economic conditions, and oil production, use, and imports, by country, biweekly rpt, 9112–1

Economic conditions and trade devs and policy, for US and foreign countries, 1988 conf papers, 9373–3.32

Economic conditions, consumer and stock prices and production indexes, 6 OECD countries and US, *Business Conditions Digest,* monthly rpt, 2702–3.10

Economic conditions in Communist, OECD, and selected other countries, 1960s-88, annual rpt, 9114–4

Economic conditions, policy, and trade practices, by country, 1986-88, annual rpt, 21384–5

Economic indicators, and dollar exchange rates, for selected OECD countries, 1980s-89, semiannual rpt, 8002–14

Economic, social, political, and geographic summary data, by country, 1989, annual factbook, 9114–2

Energy prices, by fuel type and end use, for 10 countries, 1980-88 annual rpt, 3164–50.6

Energy production by type, and oil prices, trade, and use, by country group and selected country, monthly rpt, 9112–2

Exchange rate variability impact of monetary policy, for West Germany and France, model description and results, 1973-88, working paper, 9387–8.181

Export credit activity of Eximbank and 6 OECD countries, 1988, annual rpt, 9254–3

Exports and imports of OECD, total and for 4 major countries, and US trade by country, by commodity, 1970-87, world area rpt series, 9116–1

Exports and imports of US, by commodity group, world area, selected country, US coastal area and port, and mode of transport, monthly rpt, 2422–9

Exports and imports of US, by selected country, country group, and commodity group, 1988, annual rpt, 2044–37

Farmland (US) owned by foreigners, holdings, acreage, and value by land use, owner country, State, and county, 1988, annual rpt, 1584–3

Food supply and demand, market and support prices, and other economic indicators, by EC country and commodity, 1960-85, 1528–276

GNP of Canada, Japan, and Germany, relation to foreign and domestic industry output, 1961-84, technical paper, 9366–6.189

Human rights conditions in 170 countries, 1988, annual rpt, 21384–3

Imports of goods, services, and investment from US, trade barriers, impacts, and US actions, by country, 1988, annual rpt, 444–2

Imports of US given duty-free treatment for value of US material sent abroad, and impacts on US industry and employment, by commodity and country, 1987, annual rpt, 9884–14

Interest rate differentials among countries, US and 4 industrialized countries, 1960s-88, article, 9385–1.902

Intl transactions of US with 9 countries, 1986-88, *Survey of Current Business,* monthly rpt, annual table, 2702–1.31

Investment (foreign direct) in US, major transactions by type, industry, country, and US location, 1987, annual rpt, 2044–20

Labor conditions, union coverage, and work accidents, 1989 annual country rpt, 6366–4.13; 6366–4.62

Machinery belts from 8 countries, injury to US industry from foreign subsidized and less than fair value imports, investigation with background financial and operating data, 1989 rpt, 9886–19.66

Manufacturing labor productivity and unit costs for 14 countries, 1950-88, annual press release, 6864–1

Military aid of US, arms sales, and training programs costs and budget requests, by program, world region, and country, FY88-90, annual rpt, 7144–13

Military spending, arms trade, and force strengths, with govt spending and population, by country, 1977-87, annual rpt, 9824–1

Minerals Yearbook, 1987, Vol 3: foreign country reviews of production, trade, and policy, by commodity, annual rpt, 5604–35

Minerals Yearbook, 1987, Vol 3 preprints: foreign country review of production, trade, and policy, by commodity, annual rpt, 5604–23.26

Money supply impact of central bank foreign exchange intervention, various periods 1978-88, article, 9391–1.924

Money supply target and actual growth in West Germany, 1975-89, article, 9381–1.907

Multinatl firms US affiliates, finances, and operations, by industry, world area of parent firm, and State, 1987, annual rpt, 2704–4

Multinatl US firms and foreign affiliates finances and operations, by industry of parent firm and affiliate, world area, and country, preliminary 1987, annual rpt, 2704–5

Nitrocellulose (industrial) from 7 countries at less than fair value, injury to US industry, investigation with background financial and operating data, 1989 rpt, 9886–14.270

Nuclear power generation in US and 19 non-Communist countries, monthly rpt, 3162–24.10

Nuclear power plant capacity, generation, and operating status, by plant and foreign and US location, 1988 and projected to 2020, annual rpt, 3164–57

Oil production, trade, use, and stocks, by selected country and country group, monthly rpt, 3162–42

Oil use and stocks for selected OECD countries, monthly rpt, 3162–24.10

Physicians, and visits by reason and patient age and sex, by specialty, for France, Germany, and US, 1981-83, 4147–5.5

Polychloroprene from 2 countries at less than fair value, injury to US industry, investigation with background financial and operating data, 1989 rpt, 9886–14.271

Population size, growth rates, and components of change, by country, projected 1989-2020 and trends from 1950, biennial rpt, 2324–9

R&D funding and science and technology employment for selected countries, selected years 1961-87, annual rpt, 9624–18.2

Science and engineering employment and education, and R&D spending, for US and selected foreign countries, 1988, annual rpt, 9624–23

Space satellites and other objects launched since 1957, quarterly listing, 9502–2

Stock price index correlations among US and 3 countries, various periods 1957-88, article, 9391–1.901

Switzerland franc exchange rate against dollar and German mark, impact of monetary policy, 1973-86, article, 9391–1.907

Transportation energy use, fuel prices, and vehicle registrations, by selected country, 1970s-88, annual rpt, 3304–5.1

Travel to US, market research, major magazine ad costs and circulation, and trade show data, for selected countries, 1989-90, annual rpt, 2904–11

UN voting record and share of votes in agreement with US, by issue, country, and world area, 1988, annual rpt, 7004–18

Unemployment insurance costs and beneficiaries, for US and 5 European countries, 1973-84, article, 6722–1.919

see also under By Foreign Country in the "Index by Categories"

Gerrish, Harold P.

"Eastern North Pacific Hurricanes—1988", 2152–8.903

Gertler, Mark

"Financial Factors in Business Fluctuations", 9381–13.1

Getzen, Thomas E.

"Longlife Insurance: A Prototype for Funding Long-Term Care", 4652–1.923

Ghana

Agricultural and food production and indexes, total and for selected commodities, by country, 1970s-88, annual rpt, 1524–12

Agricultural production, prices, and trade, by country, 1960s-89, annual world region rpt, 1524–4.2

Agricultural trade of US, by detailed commodity and country, 1988, semiannual rpt, 1522–4

AID activities and funding by project and function, FY90, and developing countries summary socioeconomic data from 1960s, annual rpt, 9904–4.5

AID economic aid to developing countries, obligations and disbursements by country, quarterly rpt, 9912–4

AID loans repayment status and terms by program and country, and status of predecessor agency loans, quarterly rpt, 9912–3

Auto imports from US, trade barriers by country, 1988, annual rpt, 444–2

Economic and military aid and loans from US and intl agencies, by program and country, FY46-87, annual rpt, 9914–5

Economic conditions, policy, and trade practices, by country, 1986-88, annual rpt, 21384–5

Economic, social, political, and geographic summary data, by country, 1989, annual factbook, 9114–2

Exports and imports of US, by commodity and country, 1970-87, world area rpt, 9116–1.4

Human rights conditions in 170 countries, 1988, annual rpt, 21384–3

Labor conditions, union coverage, and work accidents, 1989 annual country rpt, 6366–4.33

Military aid of US, arms sales, and training programs costs and budget requests, by program, world region, and country, FY88-90, annual rpt, 7144–13

Military spending, arms trade, and force strengths, with govt spending and population, by country, 1977-87, annual rpt, 9824–1

Minerals Yearbook, 1987, Vol 3: foreign country reviews of production, trade, and policy, by commodity, annual rpt, 5604–35

Minerals Yearbook, 1987, Vol 3 preprints: foreign country review of production, trade, and policy, by commodity, annual rpt, 5604–23.27

Population size, growth rates, and components of change, by country, projected 1989-2020 and trends from 1950, biennial rpt, 2324–9

UN voting record and share of votes in agreement with US, by issue, country, and world area, 1988, annual rpt, 7004–18

see also under By Foreign Country in the "Index by Categories"

Ghelfi, Linda M.

"About That Lower Cost of Living in Nonmetro Areas", 1502–7.905

GI Bill

see Veterans education

Gibraltar

Agricultural trade of US, by detailed commodity and country, 1988, semiannual rpt, 1522–4

Economic, social, political, and geographic summary data, by country, 1989, annual factbook, 9114–2

Population size, growth rates, and components of change, by country, projected 1989-2020 and trends from 1950, biennial rpt, 2324–9

Giese, Alenka S.

"New Approach to Regional Capital Stock Estimation: Measurement and Performance", 9375–13.13

"Opening of Midwest Manufacturing to Foreign Companies: The Influx of Foreign Direct Investment", 9375–13.12

"Regional Specialization and Technology in Manufacturing", 9375–13.15

"Window of Opportunity Opens for Regional Economic Analysis: BEA Releases Gross State Product Data", 9375–13.10

Gift tax

Budget of US, CBO analysis of revenue and spending alternatives and projections of economic indicators, FY90-94, annual rpt, 26304–3

Budget of US, midsession review of FY90 budget, by function and agency, annual rpt, 104–7

Budget of US, receipts by source, outlays by agency and program, and balances, monthly rpt, 8102–3

Fed Govt internal revenue and refunds, by type of tax, quarterly rpt, 8302–2.1

Fed Govt receipts by source and outlays by agency, *Treasury Bulletin*, quarterly rpt, 8002–4.1

Fed Govt tax revenues, by type of tax, quarterly rpt, 2462–3

Govt finances, tax systems and revenue, and fiscal structure, by level of govt and State, selected years 1929-91, annual rpt, 10044–1

IRS collections, enforcement, and litigation activity, with data by type of tax, region, and State, FY88, annual rpt, 8304–3

Returns and supplemental documents filed, by type, FY88 and projected to FY97, semiannual rpt, 8302–2.916; 8302–4

OECD trade, total and for 4 major countries, and US trade by country, by commodity, 1970-87, world area rpt series, 9116-1

Pollution abatement capital and operating costs, by SIC 2-to 4-digit industry and State, 1986, annual Current Industrial Rpt, 2506-3.6

Price indexes (producer), by stage of processing and detailed commodity, monthly rpt, 6762-6

Price indexes (producer), by stage of processing and detailed commodity, monthly 1988, annual rpt, 6764-2

Production, shipments, trade, and stocks, by glass product, periodic Current Industrial Rpt series, 2506-9

Science, engineering, and technical employment in manufacturing, by field, occupation, and industry, 1986, triennial rpt, 9627-23

Tax (income) returns of corporations, income and tax items by asset size and detailed industry, 1986, annual rpt, 8304-4; 8304-21

Transportation census, 1987: trucks, by detailed characteristics, miles traveled, and type of product carried, State rpt series, 2573-1

Wholesale trade census, 1987: employment, establishments, finances, and operations, by SIC 2- to 4-digit kind of business, MSA, county, and city, State rpt series, 2405-1

see also under By Commodity in the "Index by Categories"

Glauber, Joseph W.
"Federal Crop Insurance for Wheat: An Assessment of Program Options", 1561-12.903
"Net Returns Analysis of the Flexible Plantings Provision for Soybeans and Sunflowers", 1561-3.902

Glaucoma
see Eye diseases and defects

Glaz, B.
"Evaluation of New Canal Point Sugarcane Clones, 1988-89 Harvest Season", 1704-2

Glaze, Dargan
"Distribution of Costs of Production for Wheat Farms", 1541-1.902

Glendale, Ariz.
see also under By City in the "Index by Categories"

Glendale, Calif.
see also under By City in the "Index by Categories"

Glens Falls, N.Y.
see also under By SMSA or MSA in the "Index by Categories"

Glick, Reuven
"Does Exchange Rate Appreciation 'Deindustrialize' the Open Economy? A Critique of U.S. Evidence", 9393-10.5

Glossaries
Agricultural data compilation, 1987/88 and trends from 1920, annual rpt, 1004-14
Astronomical tables, time conversion factors, and listing of observatories worldwide, 1990, annual rpt, 3804-7
Computer systems purchase and use, and data recording, processing, and transfer, Fed Govt standards, series, 2216-2

Consumption, by detailed fuel type, end-use sector, and State, 1960-87, State Energy Data System annual rpt, 3164-39

Electric power plants production and capital costs, operations, and fuel use, by fuel type, plant, utility, and location, 1987, annual rpt, 3164-9

Electric power plants production, fuel use, stocks, and costs by fuel type, and sales, by State, monthly rpt, 3162-35

Electric utilities finances and operations, detailed data for privately owned firms, and summary data for other utilities by type, 1987, annual rpt, 3164-23

Energy technologies environmental impacts, 1960s-80s, handbook series, 3326-1

Energy use, costs, and conservation, and household and housing characteristics, survey rpt series, 3166-7

Futures and options trading volume, by commodity and exchange, FY88, annual rpt, 11924-2

Natural and supplemental gas production, prices, trade, use, reserves, and pipeline company finances, by firm and State, monthly rpt with articles, 3162-4

Oil and gas OCS reserves, and leasing and dev activity, periodic regional rpt series, 5736-3

Oil and gas supply, demand, and prices, alternative projections 1987-2000, annual rpt, 3164-89

Radioactive waste (military) disposal at New Mexico Waste Isolation Pilot Plant, environmental impacts, 1989 supplemental statement, 3008-33

Radioactive waste and spent fuel generation, inventory, and disposal, 1960s-88 and projected to 2020, annual rpt, 3364-2

Superconductivity (high temperature) R&D spending by Federal agency, and US and Japan industry funding and employment, by application, 1981-89, hearing, 25408-100

Supply, demand, trade, stocks, and refining of oil and gas liquids, by detailed product, State, and PAD district, monthly rpt with articles, 3162-6

Tidal currents, daily time and velocity by station for North America and Asia coasts, forecast 1990, annual rpts, 2174-1

Transit systems finances and operations, by mode of transport, size of fleet, and for 432 systems, 1986, annual rpt, 7884-4

Gloucester, Mass.
Fish and shellfish catch, wholesale receipts, prices, trade, and other market activities, weekly regional rpt, 2162-6.1; 2162-6.2
see also under By SMSA or MSA in the "Index by Categories"

Gloves and mittens
see Clothing and clothing industry

Gluck, Michael E.
"Use of Preventive Services by the Elderly", 26356-7.2

GNMA
see Government National Mortgage Association

GNP
see Gross National Product

Goats
see Livestock and livestock industry

Goddard, Katherine J.
"Comments on Revised New England Employment Data", 9373-2.903

Godin, Gaston
"Factors Influencing Intentions of Pregnant Women To Exercise After Giving Birth", 4042-3.916

Gold
Budget of US, authoritative financial statements with appropriations, outlays, and receipts, by category and agency, FY88, annual rpt, 8104-2.2

Business statistics, detailed data for major industries and economic indicators, *Survey of Current Business*, monthly rpt, 2702-1.6

Coin production and monetary metals use and holdings of US Mint, by metal type, FY88, annual rpt, 8204-1

Communist, OECD, and selected other countries minerals production, by commodity, 1960s-88, annual rpt, 9114-4.7

County Business Patterns, 1987: employment, establishments, and payroll, by SIC 2- to 4-digit industry and county, annual State rpt series, 2326-8

Deposits of gold, location, discovery, and geologic indicators, 1799-1982, compilation of papers, 5668-90

Europe central banks gold and foreign exchange reserves, 1924-32, article, 9362-1.906

Exports of US, detailed commodities by country, monthly rpt, 2422-3

Fed Reserve banks finances and staff, 1988, annual rpt, 9364-1.1

Financial and business statistics, historic trends, 1988 annual chartbook, 9364-2.17

Flow-of-funds accounts, savings, investments, and credit statements, quarterly rpt, 9365-3.3

Foreign countries economic conditions and implications for US, periodic country rpt series, 2046-4

Foreign countries mineral production, reserves, and industry role in domestic economy and world supply, world area and country rpt series, 5606-1

Foreign countries production of strategic minerals, by country and for South Africa companies controlled by multinatl firms, 1987, GAO rpt, 26123-233

Foreign direct investment in US and US investment abroad, by type, selected years 1975-87, article, 9391-1.910

Futures and options trading volume, by commodity and exchange, FY88, annual rpt, 11924-2

Futures contracts on commodities, financial instruments, and indexes, options trading in NYC, Chicago, and other markets, monthly rpt, 11922-6

Futures trading in selected commodities and financial instruments and indexes, NYC, Chicago, and other markets activity, monthly rpt, 11922-5

Imports of US, detailed Schedule A commodities by country, monthly rpt, 2422-2

Intl finance and trade studies, 1987 biennial compilation, 9375-14

Investment (intl) position of US, by component, industry, world region, and country, 1987-88, annual article, 2702-1.922

Budget of US Appendix, obligations, appropriations, and personnel, by program and agency, FY90, annual rpt, 104–3

Budget of US, Bush Admin policy changes by program, FY90, 028–32

Budget of US, compact budgets by activity, function, and agency, FY90 and projected to FY94, annual rpt, 104–2

Budget of US, House concurrent resolution, with spending and revenue targets, FY90, annual rpt, 21264–2

Budget of US, midsession review of FY90 budget, by function and agency, annual rpt, 104–7

Budget of US, Reagan Admin policy changes by program, FY90, annual rpt, 104–21

Budget of US, receipts by source, outlays by agency and program, and balances, monthly rpt, 8102–3

Budget of US, Senate concurrent resolution, with spending and revenue targets, FY90, annual rpt, 25254–1

Budget of US, special analysis of credit programs, FY90, annual rpt, 104–1.6

Computer systems purchase and use, and data recording, processing, and transfer, Fed Govt standards, series, 2216–2

Construction spending by Fed Govt, by program and type of structure, FY82-90, annual article, 2042–1.901; 2042–1.907

Corporations anti-takeover laws of States, with merger announcements by type and stock price changes for firms paying greenmail by firm, 1970s-86, article, 9373–2.901

Cost control proposals for Fed Govt mgmt, Reagan Admin initiatives, savings, and status, FY85-94, annual rpt, 104–23

Economic Dev Admin activities, and funding by program, recipient, State, and county, FY87 and cumulative from FY66, annual rpt, 2064–2

Economic Report of the President for 1989, with economic trends from 1929, annual rpt, 204–1

Electric and gas utility ratemaking and regulatory standards, status and coverage of consumers and sales, 1988, annual rpt, 3104–7

Electronic payments daylight overdrafts on Fed Reserve and private systems, and impact of overdraft limits, 1985-88, technical paper, 9379–12.40

Electronic payments daylight overdrafts on Fed Reserve and private systems, and impact of proposed overdraft charges, 1985-88, article, 9389–1.910

Energy technologies environmental impacts, 1960s-80s, handbook series, 3326–1

Executive exchange program of Fed Govt and private sector, host and participant views on experimental payment provisions, 1988-89 survey, GAO rpt, 26119–249

Export and import product standards under GATT, Natl Inst of Standards and Technology info activities, and proposed standards by agency and country, 1988, annual rpt, 2214–6

Export credit activity of Eximbank and 6 OECD countries, 1988, annual rpt, 9254–3

Fed Reserve Board and Reserve banks finances, staff, and review of monetary policy and economic devs, 1988, annual rpt, 9364–1

Fed Reserve System, Board of Governors, and district banks financial statements, performance, and fiscal services, 1987-89, annual rpt, 9364–10

Finances of govts, revenues by source and spending by function, natl income and product account, *Survey of Current Business*, monthly rpt, 2702–1.24

Financial instns deregulation impact on monetary policy targets, 1960s-88, article, 9379–1.905

Financial system crises of banks and nonfinancial corporations, relation to financial ratios and deregulation, alternative regression results, 1946-87, technical paper, 9366–6.192

FmHA activities, and loans and grants by program and State, FY88 and trends from FY69, annual rpt, 1184–17

Food consumer research, marketing, legislation, and regulation devs, and consumption and price trends, quarterly journal, 1541–7

Hazardous waste site remedial action under Superfund, deadlines and compliance of govts and businesses, as of Mar 1989, GAO rpt, 26113–394

Industry structure, conduct, and govt regulation, effects on competition, series, 9406–1

Insurance (health) for long term care, State regulation and enforcement actions, 1986-88, GAO rpt, 26121–282

Insurance (property and casualty) industry solvency monitoring by States, activities, staff, and interstate info sharing, 1989 GAO rpt, 26119–273

Japan capital market deregulation, impact on firm investment spending relation to cash flow and bank and capital market borrowing, various periods 1977-86, technical paper, 9366–6.200

Lands (public) acreage and grants, by State, FY88 and trends, annual rpt, 5724–1.1

Loans and loan guarantees of of Fed Govt, outstanding amounts by agency and program, *Treasury Bulletin*, quarterly rpt, 8002–4.9

Market regulation impacts on industry wages and turnover, model description and results, 1987 working paper, 6886–6.21; 6886–6.33

Minority Business Dev Centers mgmt and financial aid, and characteristics of businesses, by region and State, FY88, annual rpt, 2104–6

Minority business funding, by program and Federal agency, FY86-88, annual rpt, 2104–5

Nuclear Regulatory Commission budget, staff, and activities, by program, FY88-91, annual rpt, 9634–9

Oil and gas primary use prohibited for power and industrial plants, and gas use by State, 1988, annual rpt, 3104–8

Overseas Business Reports: economic conditions, investment and export opportunities, and trade practices, country market research rpt series, 2046–6

Pesticide (soil fumigant) use, impacts of bans of selected fumigants on production, farm income, and retail prices, by crop and region, 1988 rpt, 1588–136

Pollution abatement spending by govts, business, and consumers, 1983-87, annual article, 2702–1.919

Prison industries involvement of private sector, operations by prison and firm, and State provisions, as of 1987, 6068–228

Railroad deregulation impacts on grain shipping rates and revenues, 1981-85, 1548–349

Regulatory costs by agency, reform proposals, and environmental regulation costs to govts and businesses, 1988 hearings, 25408–99

Rural areas aid from Fed Govt compared to urban areas, by program and degree of urbanization, FY85, periodic rpt, 1598–248

Rural Electrification Program lending, by State, as of FY88, annual rpt, 1244–7

Savings instns and assets, by solvency status under alternative risk-based capital requirements, Dec 1988, article, 9312–1.905

Savings instns, FHLB 2nd District members capital and assets under capital requirements increase proposal, by State, 3rd qtr 1988, article, 9302–33.901

Savings instns financial performance, for newly chartered instns by charter type, 1982-86, technical paper, 9316–1.146

Savings instns financial status impact of Financial Instns Reform, Recovery, and Enforcement Act, June 1989, technical paper, 8436–1.1

Savings instns insolvency losses and uninsured certificate of deposit interest rates, impact of proposed depositor preference laws, model description and results, 1989 technical paper, 9316–1.154

Savings instns regulatory issues, mgmt, and FHLB system and member finances and operations, monthly journal, 8432–2; 9312–1

Savings instns regulatory issues, 1988 annual conf, 9304–24

Securities backed by assets, risk weights under regulatory capital guidelines, by security type, 1989 article, 9362–1.909

Small Business Admin loan and contract activity by program and firm, and financial condition, FY88, annual rpt, 9764–1

Small business capital formation sources, 1988 annual conf, 9734–4

Small business financial and technical aid of States, 1988 listing, 9768–15

Small business loans of Eximbank, by firm, 1984-88, hearing, 21728–70

Small business training confs of SBA, cosponsors by type, and compliance with SBA regulations, by region, 1988, GAO rpt, 26113–425

Southeastern States banks and thrifts industry structure impacts of market entry and branching regulation, by State, 1982-88, article, 9302–2.907

Space launches and other activities of NASA and USSR, with flight data, 1957-88, annual rpt, 9504–6.1

Steel plant closings relation to EPA pollution enforcement and compliance, model description and results, 1977-86, working paper, 9377–9.84

Telephone firms borrowing under Rural Telephone Program, loan activity by State, FY88, annual tables, 1244–8

Telephone intrastate long distance call rates, impact of State entry and price regulation, 1983-87, 9406–1.55

State and local govt retirement systems, cash and security holdings and finances, quarterly rpt, 2462-2

TVA finances and electric power sales, FY88, annual rpt, 9804-1

TVA financial and operating data by program and facility, FY88, annual rpt, 9804-32

Uranium enrichment facilities of DOE, financial statements, operations, and stocks, FY87-88, annual rpt, 3354-7

Water supply in rural areas, public system financial and operating characteristics, by region, 1980, 1598-247

Western Area Power Admin activities by plant, financial statements, and sales by customer, FY88, annual rpt, 3254-1

Workers compensation programs under Federal admin, finances and operations, FY87, annual rpt, 6504-10

see also Defense budgets and appropriations

see also Foreign budgets

see also Foreign debts

see also Government revenues

see also Government securities

see also Government spending

see also Government supplies and property

see also Government trust funds

see also Military supplies and property

see also Municipal bonds

see also Public debt

see also State government spending

see also U.S. savings bonds

Government bonds

see Government securities

see Municipal bonds

see Tax exempt securities

see U.S. savings bonds

Government buildings

see Public buildings

Government census

see Census of Governments

Government-citizen lawsuits

Claims Court caseload by type of suit, and judgments, FY89, annual rpt, 18224-1

Coal surface mining-related civil actions, attorneys fees and expenses awarded by case, 1989, GAO rpt, 26113-421

Court civil and criminal caseloads for Federal district, appeals, and special courts, June 1989, annual rpt, 18204-2; 18204-8

US attorneys case processing and collections, by case type and Federal district, FY88, annual rpt, 6004-2

Government-citizen relations

FDA investigations and regulatory activities, quarterly rpt, 4062-3

Fed Govt services demand and mgmt, outlook for 2000, 028-30

Forest Service mgmt plans and timber sales appeals processing, for selected States, 1985-88, GAO rpt, 26113-400

Historic and natural natl landmarks damaged and threatened, with owner, location, damage type, and recommended remedial action, 1988, annual listing, 5544-16

Homeowners Residential Community Assns, services provided, and relations with local govts, 1988 conf, 10048-75

IRS collections, enforcement, and litigation activity, with data by type of tax, region, and State, FY88, annual rpt, 8304-3

IRS telephone system for income tax aid, accessibility and accuracy, and other IRS workload indicators, 1988 hearing, 21788-178

IRS telephone system for income tax aid, accessibility and accuracy, 1988 survey, GAO rpt, 26119-190

Public opinion on taxes, spending, and govt efficiency, by respondent characteristics, 1989 survey, annual rpt, 10044-2

see also Civil rights

see also Elections

see also Government and business

see also Government-citizen lawsuits

see also Impacted areas

see also Lobbying and lobbying groups

see also Taxation

Government contracts and procurement

Admin of contracts at 4 agencies, and contract deficiencies by type, 1980s, GAO rpt, 26119-268

Advertising spending of Fed Govt, and subcontracts to small and disadvantaged firms, by agency and medium, FY86, GAO rpt, 26113-428

Aerospace industry minority employment in Los Angeles area, by occupational group, 1980s-86, 21348-113

Aerospace industry sales, orders, backlog, and firms, by product for govt, military, and other customers, 1988, annual Current Industrial Rpt, 2506-12.22

Agricultural Statistics, 1988, annual rpt, 1004-1.2

AID contracts and grants for technical and support services, by instn, country, and State, FY88, annual listing, 9914-7

AID contracts to minority and women-owned businesses, awards and goals, FY88, annual rpt, 9904-1.2

AID housing and urban dev program financial statements, and loan guarantees by country, FY88, annual rpt, 9914-4

AID noncompetitive contract awards over $100,000, FY88, annual rpt, 9904-1.3

AIDS research grants and contracts of NIH, by funding and approval status, and researcher age, experience, and sex, FY86, GAO rpt, 26121-267

Audiovisual activities and spending of Fed Govt, by whether performed in-house and agency, FY87, annual rpt, 9514-1

Auto fleet of Fed Govt, costs and operating data by agency, FY87, annual rpt, 9454-9

Budget of US, authoritative financial statements with appropriations, outlays, and receipts, by category and agency, FY88, annual rpt, 8104-2.2

Budget of US, object class analysis of obligations, by agency, FY90, annual rpt, 104-9

Budget of US, special analyses by activity, function, and agency, FY90, annual rpt, 104-1

Cancer Natl Inst contracts and grants, by recipient and location, FY88, annual listing, 4474-28

Capitol Architect activities, funding, costs, and contracts, FY86, annual rpt, 25944-1

Capitol Architect outlays for salaries, supplies, and services, itemized by payee and function, 1st half FY89, semiannual rpt, 25922-2

Coal purchases by Fed Govt, chemical analyses by mine and location, FY84, annual rpt, 3004-15

Commerce Dept programs fraud and abuse, audits and investigations, 2nd half FY89, semiannual rpt, 2002-3

Cost control proposals for Fed Govt mgmt, Reagan Admin initiatives, savings, and status, FY85-94, annual rpt, 104-23

DC metro area land acquisition and dev projects of Fed Govt, characteristics and funding by agency and project, FY90-94, annual rpt, 15454-1

Disabled persons workshops finances, operations, and Federal procurement, FY80-88, annual rpt, 11714-1

DOE real property owned and leased, by type, subagency, contractor, and site, FY87, annual rpt, 3004-28

DOT programs fraud and abuse, audits and investigations, 2nd half FY89, semiannual rpt, 7302-4

Economic indicators compounded annual rates of change, monthly rpt, 9391-3.2

Electric power capacity and use in Pacific Northwest, by energy source, projected under alternative load and demand cases, 1989-2008, annual rpt, 3224-3

EPA programs fraud and abuse, audits and investigations, 2nd half FY89, semiannual rpt, 9182-10

Expenditures of Fed Govt in States and local areas, by type, State, county, and city, FY88, annual rpt, 2464-3

Expenditures of Fed Govt in States, by type, program, agency, and State, FY88, annual rpt, 2464-2

Export licensing of goods with potential military uses, DOD and Commerce Dept activities, staff, and costs, 1986-88, GAO rpt, 26123-250

Fed Govt consolidated financial statements based on business accounting methods, FY87-88, annual rpt, 8104-5

Fed Govt obligations by function and agency, *Treasury Bulletin*, quarterly rpt, 8002-4.2

Finances of govts, revenues by source and spending by function, natl income and product account, *Survey of Current Business*, monthly rpt, 2702-1.24

Finances of govts, tax systems and revenue, and fiscal structure, by level of govt and State, selected years 1929-91, annual rpt, 10044-1

Food aid programs purchases, by commodity, firm, and shipping point or destination, weekly rpt, 1302-3

Fraud and abuse in Fed Govt, audits and investigations by agency, FY88, annual rpt, 104-29

Fraud and abuse in Fed Govt, audits and investigations by agency, 2nd half FY87, semiannual rpt, 102-5

GPO activities, finances, and production, FY88, annual rpt, 26204-1

GSA programs fraud and abuse, audits and investigations, 2nd half FY89, semiannual rpt, 9452-8

HHS financial aid, by program, recipient, State, and city, FY88, annual regional listings, 4004-3

HHS programs fraud and abuse, audits and investigations, 2nd half FY89, semiannual rpt, 4002-6

HUD programs fraud and abuse, audits and investigations, 2nd half FY89, semiannual rpt, 5002–8; 5002–11

Hwy construction bids and contracts for Federal-aid hwys, by State, 1st half 1989, semiannual rpt, 7552–12

Hwy construction contracts for Federal-aid system, awards to minority- and women-owned businesses, FHwA and State reviews, FY83-87, GAO rpt, 26113–389

Indian Health Service and contract facilities hospitalization, by diagnosis, age, sex, and service area, FY87, annual rpt, 4104–16

Indian Health Service and contract facilities hospitalization, by diagnosis, age, sex, and service area, FY88, annual rpt, 4084–5

Info security compliance of Federal agencies, computer systems with sensitive info, and plans submitted to oversight agencies, by agency, 1989, GAO rpt, 26125–34

Input-output structure of US economy, detailed interindustry transactions for 84 industries, and components of final demand, 1983, annual article, 2702–1.909

Interior Dept programs fraud and abuse, audits and investigations, 2nd half FY89, semiannual rpt, 5302–2

Labor laws enacted, by State, 1988, annual article, 6722–1.904

Labor productivity of Federal employees, indexes of output and labor costs by function, FY67-87, annual rpt, 6824–1.6

Labor surplus areas eligible for preferential Fed Govt contracts, monthly listing, 6402–1

Land Mgmt Bur activities and funding by State, and receipts by program, FY87, annual rpt, 5724–13

Manufacturing high technology use and plans, with data by technology, selected industry, and firm and market characteristics, 1988 survey, 2508–1

Medicare hospital claims processing under contract, HCFA controls adequacy and payment errors, 1985-88, GAO rpt, 26121–260

Medicare peer review organizations review of hospital claims, activities, and membership, 1984-88, GAO rpt, 26131–51

Medicare physicians assigned fee participation related to selected physician, practice, and community characteristics, 1984, article, 4652–1.902

Microfiche shipment to depository libraries, GPO contract awards, and supply and quality problems, 1988, GAO rpt, 26119–248

Minority Business Dev Centers mgmt and financial aid, and characteristics of businesses, by region and State, FY88, annual rpt, 2104–6

Minority business funding, by program and Federal agency, FY86-88, annual rpt, 2104–5

NASA funding by program and type of performer, and contract awards by State, FY88, annual rpt, 9504–6.2

NASA procurement economic benefits by industry group, jobs created, and sales, by State, FY90, 9508–35

NASA programs fraud and abuse, audits and investigations, 1st half FY89, semiannual rpt, 9502–9

Natl income and product accounts and components, *Survey of Current Business*, monthly rpt, 2702–1.21

Natl income and product accounts govt transactions component estimates, methodology and bibl, 1988 technical rpt, 2706–6.5

New England States economic indicators, Fed Reserve 1st District, quarterly rpt, 9373–2.3

NIH grants and contracts, by inst and type of recipient, FY79-88, annual rpt, 4434–9

NIH grants for R&D, training, construction, and medical libraries, by location and recipient, FY88, annual listings, 4434–7

North Central States business and economic conditions, Fed Reserve 9th District, quarterly journal, 9383–19

Prison Industries (Federal) finances and operations, FY88, annual rpt, 6244–3

Procurement contract awards of Fed Govt, by State, agency, procurement and contractor type, and for top 100 contractors, quarterly rpt, 102–6

Procurement of goods and services by level of govt, *Business Conditions Digest*, monthly rpt, 2702–3.5

Rural areas aid from Fed Govt compared to urban areas, by program and degree of urbanization, FY85, periodic rpt, 1598–248

Savings instns failures, real estate assets value, and disposition performance of FSLIC, Fed Asset Disposition Assn, and private contractors, 1988, article, 8432–2.901

Security clearance of Fed Govt and contractor employees, polygraph use, prepublication reviews, and unauthorized disclosures and investigations, 1986-88, GAO rpt, 26123–66

Service contracts of Fed Govt compared with work performed in-house, savings and employment effects by agency, 1978-87, GAO rpt, 26119–238

Services transfer from govts to private contractors, impacts on govt workers, with data by worker characteristics, level of govt, and location, 1980s-87, 15496–1.5

Shipbuilding costs, deliveries, and contracts, by coastal district and shipyard, various periods 1971-88, annual rpt, 7704–12.1

Small Business Admin loan and contract activity by program and firm, and financial condition, FY88, annual rpt, 9764–1

Small Business Admin programs fraud and abuse, audits and investigations, 1st half FY89, semiannual rpt, 9762–5

Small business contracts and obligations of Fed Govt, by program and recipient type, for North Carolina and total US, FY77-87, hearings, 21728–67

Small business establishments, operations, owner characteristics, and job training, late 1950s-87, 9768–20

Small business finances, operations, owner and employee characteristics, and Federal contracts, 1980s-88, annual rpt, 9764–6

Small business financial and technical aid of States, 1988 listing, 9768–15

Space program procurement contract awards of NASA, by type, contractor, State, and country, FY89, semiannual rpt, 9502–6

State Dept programs fraud and abuse, audits and investigations, 2nd half FY89, semiannual rpt, 7002–6

State govt procedures for prompt payment of contractors and private vendors, 1988-89, GAO rpt, 26111–64

State law provisions and terms for prompt payment of contractors and private vendors, by State, 1988, GAO rpt, 26111–59

Statistical programs of Fed Govt, funding by agency, FY87-89, annual rpt, 104–10

Surety bonds use to guarantee Federal small business construction contracts, and fraud cases, by agency, 1985-89, GAO rpt, 26113–438

TVA financial and operating data by program and facility, FY88, annual rpt, 9804–32

US attorneys civil and criminal cases by type and disposition, and collections, by Federal district, FY88, annual rpt, 6004–2.1; 6004–2.5

USDA programs fraud and abuse, audits and investigations, 2nd half FY89, semiannual rpt, 1002–4

VA and non-VA facilities health services sharing contracts, by service type and region, FY88, annual rpt, 8704–5

VA programs fraud and abuse, audits and investigations, 2nd half FY89, semiannual rpt, 8602–1

Wastewater facilities of Fed Govt, compliance with pollution control regulations, FY86-87, GAO rpt, 26113–388

Women-owned business mgmt issues, SBA loans, Federal contracts by agency, and owners views on Michigan business climate, FY79-88, hearings, 21728–68

see also Defense contracts and procurement
see also Federal funding for energy programs
see also Federal funding for research and development

Government corporations and enterprises

Budget deficit reduction under Gramm-Rudman Act, cancellation of budget authority by program, FY90, annual rpt, 104–27; 26304–6

Budget of US Appendix, obligations, appropriations, and personnel, by program and agency, FY90, annual rpt, 104–3

Budget of US, compact budgets by activity, function, and agency, FY90 and projected to FY94, annual rpt, 104–2

Budget of US, object class analysis of obligations, by agency, FY90, annual rpt, 104–9

Budget of US, Reagan Admin policy changes by program, FY90, annual rpt, 104–21

Budget of US, receipts by source, outlays by agency and program, and balances, monthly rpt, 8102–3

Budget of US, special analyses by activity, function, and agency, FY90, annual rpt, 104–1

Construction spending by Fed Govt, by program and type of structure, FY82-90, annual article, 2042–1.901

Cost control proposals for Fed Govt mgmt, Reagan Admin initiatives, savings, and status, FY85-94, annual rpt, 104–23

Financial consolidated statements of Fed Govt based on business accounting methods, FY87-88, annual rpt, 8104-5

Financial operations of Fed Govt, detailed data, *Treasury Bulletin*, quarterly rpt, 8002-4

Input-output structure of US economy, detailed interindustry transactions for 84 industries, and components of final demand, 1983, annual article, 2702-1.909

Loans, loan guarantees, and insurance programs of Fed Govt, outstanding amounts by agency and program, FY65-88, GAO rpt, 26111-65

Mortgage loan activity, by type of lender, loan, and mortgaged property, monthly press release, 5142-18

Mortgage loan activity, by type of lender, loan, and mortgaged property, quarterly press release, 5142-30

Natl income and product accounts and components, *Survey of Current Business*, monthly rpt, 2702-1.22; 2702-1.27

UK and France govt-owned corporations stock issues, value, new shareholders, and revenue effects, 1960s-88, article, 9385-1.911

see also Commodity Credit Corp.

see also Communications Satellite Corp.

see also Corporation for Public Broadcasting

see also Export-Import Bank

see also Federal Crop Insurance Corp.

see also Federal Deposit Insurance Corp.

see also Federal Home Loan Mortgage Corp.

see also Federal National Mortgage Association

see also Federal Prison Industries

see also Federal Savings and Loan Insurance Corp.

see also Financing Corp.

see also Government National Mortgage Association

see also Inter-American Foundation

see also Legal Services Corp.

see also National Railroad Passenger Corp.

see also Neighborhood Reinvestment Corp.

see also Overseas Private Investment Corp.

see also Pennsylvania Avenue Development Corp.

see also Pension Benefit Guaranty Corp.

see also Rural Telephone Bank

see also St. Lawrence Seaway Development Corp.

see also Student Loan Marketing Association

see also Tennessee Valley Authority

see also U.S. Postal Service

see also U.S. Synthetic Fuels Corp.

Government debt

see Public debt

Government documents

GPO activities, finances, and production, FY88, annual rpt, 26204-1

Labor productivity of Federal employees, indexes of output and labor costs by function, FY67-87, annual rpt, 6824-1.6

Microfiche shipment to depository libraries, GPO contract awards, and supply and quality problems, 1988, GAO rpt, 26119-248

Natl Archives and Records Admin activities, finances, holdings, and staff, FY88, annual rpt, 9514-2

see also Environmental impact statements

see also Federal Inspectors General reports

see also Government forms and paperwork

see also Government publications lists

Government efficiency

AFDC application processing duration, and time from hearing requests to decision, by State, FY87, annual rpt, 4694-7.3; 4694-7.4

Air Force fiscal mgmt system operations and techniques, quarterly rpt, 3602-1

Banks in Fed Reserve System, expenses and operations itemized by service, office, and district, 1988, annual rpt, 9364-11

Budget of US, Reagan Admin policy changes by program, FY90, annual rpt, 104-21

Cost control proposals for Fed Govt mgmt, Reagan Admin initiatives, savings, and status, FY85-94, annual rpt, 104-23

Court caseloads, actions, procedure duration, judges, and jurors, by Federal district and appeals court, 1984-89, annual rpt, 18204-3

Court civil and criminal case dispositions and trials, and time to trial and case disposition, June 1989, annual rpt, 18204-2

Disability Insurance and SSI eligibility determinations for mental impairment, caseload and review activities by impairment type and State, 1984-86, hearing, 21788-176

Economic data series and collections of Fed Govt, adequacy to address devs and policy issues, 1989 rpt, 26358-207

Employee productivity improvement program of Fed Govt, coverage and impacts by function for selected agencies, FY86-87 and projected to 1992, 26306-3.103

Employment discrimination complaints, processing, and disposition, by complaint type and Federal agency, FY87, annual rpt, 9244-11

Energy use and efficiency of Fed Govt, by agency and fuel type, FY88, annual rpt, 3304-22

EPA regulatory and protection programs operations and mgmt goals, progress and activities, by office, quarterly rpt, 9182-11

Federal district and appeals court civil and criminal trials, and time to trial and case disposition, June 1989, annual rpt, 18204-8.11; 18204-8.14

FmHA activities, and loans and grants by program and State, FY88 and trends from FY69, annual rpt, 1184-17

Food stamp eligibility and payment errors, by type, recipient characteristics, and State, FY87, annual rpt, 1364-15

GAO activities, operations, and resulting cost savings to Fed Govt, FY88, annual rpt, 26104-1

Incentive awards to Federal employees, costs, and benefits, by award type and agency, FY88, annual rpt, 9844-20

Info collection of Fed Govt under Paperwork Reduction Act, effects on requirements and respondent burden by agency, FY87-89, annual rpt, 104-19

Info collection of Fed Govt under Paperwork Reduction Act, respondent burden by paperwork and respondent type, 1985-87, GAO rpt, 26131-60

Info collection of Fed Govt under Paperwork Reduction Act, respondent burden, OMB reviews, and violations, 1981-88, annual rpt, 104-26

IRS operating costs, collections, and ratios, FY88, annual rpt, 8304-3.3

IRS telephone system for income tax aid, accessibility and accuracy, and other IRS workload indicators, 1988 hearing, 21788-178

Labor productivity and productivity for other inputs, indexes and changes for 2- to 4-digit industry and govt functions, 1982-87, annual article, 6722-1.914

Labor productivity for govt employees, indexes of output and labor costs by function, FY67-87, annual rpt, 6824-1.6

Labor productivity indexes for Fed Govt, by function, 1972-87, 6728-38.6

Merit system oversight and enforcement activities of OPM, series, 9496-2

Merit Systems Protection Board decisions on appeals of Fed Govt personnel actions, by agency and region, FY88, annual rpt, 9494-2

OMB mgmt of Federal employees, budget, and info systems, indicators of effectiveness, FY81-90, GAO rpt, 26119-251

Postal Service activities, financial statements, and employment, FY84-88, annual rpt, 9864-1

Postal Service stamped and metered mail delivery performance, FY87-88, annual rpt, 9864-5.2

Public opinion on taxes, spending, and govt efficiency, by respondent characteristics, 1989 survey, annual rpt, 10044-2

Savings instns failures, real estate assets value, and disposition performance of FSLIC, Fed Asset Disposition Assn, and private contractors, 1988, article, 8432-2.901

Senior Executive Service former members reasons for leaving, and views on SES statutory compliance, 1988 survey, 9498-3

Service contracts of Fed Govt compared with work performed in-house, savings and employment effects by agency, 1978-87, GAO rpt, 26119-238

SSA activities, and OASDHI admin, 1930s-89 and projected to 2063, data compilation, annual rpt, 4704-12

SSA activities, litigation, finances, and staff, FY88, annual rpt, 4704-6

Tax (income) return processing, IRS workload forecasts, compliance, and enforcement, data compilation, 1989 annual rpt, 8304-8

Unemployment insurance programs of States, quality appraisal results, FY88, annual rpt, 6404-16

VA benefit claims processing and efficiency at regional offices, and hearing officers salaries and travel costs, 1986-88, hearing, 21768-47

see also Federal Inspectors General reports

see also General Accounting Office

Government employees

Census of Population and Housing, 1990: data item selection, questionnaire dev, and testing, 2626-11.3

Counties (nonmetro) employment by industry sector and degree of

Tax (income) returns filed by type of filer, selected income items, quarterly rpt, 8302–2.1

Tax (income) returns of individuals, by filing status, tax item, and income level, 1987, annual article, 8302–2.901

Tax (income) withholding and related documents filed, by type and IRS service center, 1988 and projected 1989-96, annual rpt, 8304–22

Tax returns and supplemental documents filed, by type, FY88 and projected to FY97, semiannual rpt, 8302–2.916

Tax returns filed, by type of tax and IRS region and service center, projected 1988-95 and trends from 1977, annual rpt, 8304–9

see also Licenses and permits

Government grants

see Community Development Block Grants

see Federal aid programs

see Federal funding for research and development

see Revenue sharing

see Urban Development Action Grants

see terms beginning with Federal aid

Government housing

see Public housing

Government information

Advisory committees of Fed Govt, and members, staff, meetings, and costs by agency, FY88, annual rpt, 9454–18

Assistance (financial and nonfinancial) of Fed Govt, 1989 base edition with supplements, annual listing, 104–5

Coastal and estuarine pollutant discharges, Natl Ocean Service data provided by source of request, 1984-88, 2176–4.10

Export and import product standards under GATT, Natl Inst of Standards and Technology info activities, and proposed standards by agency and country, 1988, annual rpt, 2214–6

Fed Reserve data concordance for *Federal Reserve Bulletin* and *Annual Statistical Digest*, 1988 annual rpt, 9364–8

Fishery info and rpts of Natl Marine Fisheries Service, 1988, annual rpt, 2164–1

Geological Survey activities and funding, FY88, annual rpt, 5664–8

HHS data projects and systems, by subagency, FY88, 4008–92

Labor productivity of Federal employees, indexes of output and labor costs by function, FY67-87, annual rpt, 6824–1.6

Land Mgmt Bur activities and finances, and public land acreage and use, annual State rpt series, 5724–11

Ocean coastal currents, temperatures, and salinity, for Straits of Florida, series, 2146–7

Ocean subsurface temperature data collection activities, for Pacific Ocean, 1985-87, annual rpt, 2154–12

Pension laws admin and enforcement under Employee Retirement Income Security Act (ERISA), 1987, annual rpt, 6304–4

Security clearance of Fed Govt and contractor employees, polygraph use, prepublication reviews, and unauthorized disclosures and investigations, 1986-88, GAO rpt, 26123–66

Security compliance of Federal agencies, computer systems with sensitive info, and plans submitted to oversight agencies, by agency, 1989, GAO rpt, 26125–34

Security measures and classification actions of Fed Govt monitored by Info Security Oversight Office, FY88, annual rpt, 9454–21

Security measures of Fed Govt, computer security training activities, by agency, 1988, GAO rpt, 26125–31

USIA activities, finances, and info services, FY89, annual rpt, 17594–1

Weather services activities and funding, by Federal agency, planned FY89-90, annual rpt, 2144–2

see also Computer data file guides

see also Freedom of information

see also Government and the press

see also Government documents

see also Government forms and paperwork

see also Government publications lists

see also Statistical programs and activities

Government inspections

Animal protection, licensing, and inspection activities of USDA, and animals used in research, by State, FY88, annual rpt, 1394–10

Assistance (financial and nonfinancial) of Fed Govt, 1989 base edition with supplements, annual listing, 104–5

Auto emissions control device tampering and fuel-switching incidence in 15 urban areas, 1988, annual rpt, 9194–15

Auto safety, crash test results by domestic and foreign model, model years 1984-88, 7768–111

Auto safety, crash test results by domestic and foreign model, press release series, 7766–7

Banks failure forecasting accuracy, and failure relation to financial, regulatory, and other indicators, with data by instn, 1960s-89, working paper, 9377–9.77

Banks in Fed Reserve System, expenses and operations itemized by service, office, and district, 1988, annual rpt, 9364–11

Board and care homes licensing and inspection by States, and client characteristics, 1989 GAO rpt, 26121–275

Coal Surface Mining Reclamation and Enforcement Office activities and funding, by State and Indian tribe, FY87, annual rpt, 5644–1

Customs Service activities, collections, entries processed by mode of transport, and seizures, FY84-88, annual rpt, 8144–1

Customs Service imports inspection, automated selection system operations, FY88-1st qtr FY89, GAO rpt, 26125–35

DOT employment, by subagency, occupation, and selected personnel characteristics, FY88, annual rpt, 7304–18

FDA investigations and regulatory activities, quarterly rpt, 4062–3

Fed Reserve deposit reports, variability by district and financial instn type and size groups, and recommendations for combining groups, various periods 1987-88, technical paper, 9366–6.186

Gasoline octane labeling, State testing programs, violations, and penalties, as of Feb 1988, GAO rpt, 26113–409

Hazardous material transport accidents, casualties, and damage, by mode of transport, with DOT control activities, 1988, annual rpt, 7304–4

Health care devices malfunction, injury, and death reports to FDA, and inspection findings and disposition, 1985-87, GAO rpt, 26131–57

Hearing aid performance test results, by make and model, 1989 annual rpt, 8704–3

Housewares (ceramic) lead and cadmium levels, FDA import inspection activity by country, and food safety funding and staff, 1983-88, hearing, 21368–108

Hwy funding and inspection activity of FHwA, FY85, annual rpt, 7304–1

Imports detained by FDA, by reason, product, shipper, brand, and country, monthly listing, 4062–2

Labor productivity of Federal employees, indexes of output and labor costs by function, FY67-87, annual rpt, 6824–1.6

Labs (clinical) under HCFA regulation, and labs with violations by Medicare termination and license status, 1983-87, hearings, 25408–98

Mine safety and health enforcement, training, and funding, with casualties, by type of mine and State, FY87, annual rpt, 6664–6

Nuclear reactors inspections and operations, by commercial facility, monthly rpt, 9632–1

Nuclear Regulatory Commission activities, finances, and staff, with data for individual power plants, FY88, annual rpt, 9634–2

Nuclear Regulatory Commission budget, staff, and activities, by program, FY88-91, annual rpt, 9634–9

Nursing home compliance with Medicare and Medicaid regulations, and patient characteristics, by facility, 1987/88, annual State rpt series, 4654–15

Occupational safety inspections at firms with high injury rates, impacts on injury rates, 1979-85, working paper, 6886–6.63

Occupational safety inspections at firms with high injury rates, impacts on injury reporting, 1979-85, working paper, 6886–6.41

Pipeline accidents, casualties, safety enforcement activity, and Federal funding, by State, 1987, annual rpt, 7304–5

Postal Service inspection activities, expenses, and staff, FY88, annual rpt, 9864–8

Postal Service inspection activities, FY88, annual rpt, 9864–9

Railroad accidents, casualties, and damage, Fed Railroad Admin activities, and safety inspectors by State, 1987, annual rpt, 7604–12

Railroad accidents, casualties, and Federal safety activities, late 1970s-87, hearing, 21368–103

Savings instns failures by State, with exam of mgmt weaknesses and regulatory activity, 1980s-87, GAO rpt, 26111–62

Security measures and classification actions of Fed Govt monitored by Info Security Oversight Office, FY88, annual rpt, 9454–21

Wastewater facilities of Fed Govt, compliance with pollution control regulations, FY86-87, GAO rpt, 26113–388

see also Federal Inspectors General reports

see also Food inspection
see also Government investigations
Government investigations

Airport security operations to prevent hijacking, screening failures and proposed FAA penalties by carrier, 1989 press release, 7306-10.2; 7306-10.3

Airport security operations to prevent hijacking, screening results, enforcement actions, and hijacking attempts, 1st half 1988, semiannual rpt, 7502-5

Assistance (financial and nonfinancial) of Fed Govt, 1989 base edition with supplements, annual listing, 104-5

Auto sudden acceleration incidents involving Audi 5000 and selected other models, investigation results, 1986-88, 7768-107

Banks and other financial instns fraud and insider misconduct cases, Federal regulatory and enforcement activities, and losses, 1981-87, hearing, 21408-111

Communist countries trade with US, by detailed commodity and country, quarterly rpt with articles, 9882-2

Community Relations Service investigation and mediation of minority discrimination disputes, FY87, annual rpt, 6004-9

Education Dept Civil Rights Office, complaints, investigations, funding, and staff, various periods FY81-88, 21348-114

Election campaign finances and FEC activities, various periods 1975-88, annual rpt, 9274-1

Export and import agreements, negotiations, anticompetitive investigations, and related legislation, FY86-88, annual rpt, 444-1

Exports and imports, trade agreements and relations, and USITC investigations, 1988, annual rpt, 9884-5

Futures market trading abuses, Commodity Futures Trading Commission and exchanges enforcement activity, various periods 1984-FY90, GAO rpt, 26119-263

Futures market trading abuses, Commodity Futures Trading Commission, Chicago Board of Trade, and Chicago Mercantile Exchange enforcement activity, 1984-89, GAO rpt, 26119-247

HHS research and evaluation programs, 1970-FY87, annual listing, 4004-30

Imports and tariff provisions effect on US industries and products, investigations with background financial and operating data, series, 9886-4

Imports injury to US industries from foreign subsidized products and sales at less than fair value, investigations with background financial and operating data, series, 9886-19

Imports injury to US industries from foreign subsidized products, investigations with background financial and operating data, series, 9886-15

Imports injury to US industries from sales at less than fair value, investigations with background financial and operating data, series, 9886-14

Imports injury to US industry, USITC activities, investigations, and rpts, FY88, annual rpt, 9884-1

Imports injury to US industry, USITC rpts, 1982-88, annual listing, 9884-12

Imports under Generalized System of Preferences, status, and US tariffs, trade by country, production, and use, for selected commodities, 1984-88, annual rpt, 9884-23

Maritime Commission activities, case filings by type and disposition, and civil penalties by shipper, FY88, annual rpt, 9334-1

Mine safety and health enforcement, training, and funding, with casualties, by type of mine and State, FY87, annual rpt, 6664-6

Nuclear material inventory discrepancies at DOE and contractor facilities, 2nd half FY87, semiannual rpt, 3002-4

Occupational deaths, by equipment type, circumstances, and OSHA standards violated, series, 6606-2

Pension laws admin and enforcement under Employee Retirement Income Security Act (ERISA), 1987, annual rpt, 6304-4

Pension plan regulation enforcement by Labor Dept and IRS, violations, and penalties, FY85-88, GAO rpt, 26121-259

Railroad accidents, casualties, and damage, Fed Railroad Admin investigations in Pennsylvania, 1984-87, GAO rpt, 26113-390

Railroad accidents, casualties, damage, and circumstances, by incident, 1986, annual rpt, 7604-3

Railroad accidents, circumstances, severity, and railroad involved, periodic rpt, 9612-3

Securities law enforcement activities of SEC, FY88, annual rpt, 9734-2.5

Security clearance of Fed Govt and contractor employees, polygraph use, prepublication reviews, and unauthorized disclosures and investigations, 1986-88, GAO rpt, 26123-66

Toxicology Natl Program research and testing activities, FY87 and planned FY88, annual rpt, 4044-16

Transportation accident investigations and recommendations by Natl Transportation Safety Board, 1988, annual rpt, 9614-1

see also Congressional investigations
see also Criminal investigations
see also Environmental impact statements
see also Federal Inspectors General reports
see also General Accounting Office
see also Government inspections

Government lands
see Public lands

Government loans and grants
see Federal aid programs
see Federal funding for research and development
see terms beginning with Federal aid

Government National Mortgage Association

Budget of US Appendix, obligations, appropriations, and personnel, by program and agency, FY90, annual rpt, 104-3

Securities backed by mortgages, corporate and union pension funds and life insurance firms investments, by issuer, quarterly rpt, 5002-10

Securities backed by mortgages, GNMA prepayment rates relation to interest rates and security age, 1983-85, technical paper, 9316-1.141

Securities backed by mortgages issued through private and govt issuers, 1984-88, article, 9362-1.909

Servicing of mortgages, transfers among lenders and consumer complaints, 1984-89, GAO rpt, 26113-441

Government ownership

Electric power wholesale purchases and costs for REA borrowers, by borrower, supplier, and State, 1940-87, annual rpt, 1244-5

Electric utilities publicly owned, finances and operations, 1987, annual rpt, 3164-23.2

France and US hospital and long-term care beds, by facility type and ownership, 1981, 4147-5.4

Hospital reimbursement by Medicare under prospective payment system, impacts on instns, beneficiaries, and other care providers and payment sources, 1986, annual rpt, 4654-13

Mental health care facilities, staff, and patient characteristics, *Statistical Notes* series, 4506-3

Mental health services use, spending, facility ownership, and Medicaid reimbursement, with data for 9 multifacility firms, 1987 conf papers, 4508-9

Mentally retarded persons facilities, beds, and residents, by ownership, resident age and race, and State, 1986, 4147-14.34

Nursing home compliance with Medicare and Medicaid regulations, and patient characteristics, by facility, 1987/88, annual State rpt series, 4654-15

Nursing home facility, staff, and resident detailed characteristics, 1985, 4147-13.97

Nursing homes, beds, and residents, by ownership, certification status, and State, 1986, 4147-14.33

Statistical Abstract of US, social, political, and economic data, 1790-2025, comprehensive annual compilation, 2324-1.2

Uranium supply and industry operations, various periods 1947-88 and projected to 2000, annual rpt, 3164-65

Water supply in rural areas, public system financial and operating characteristics, by region, 1980, 1598-247

see also Expropriation of alien property
see also Government corporations and enterprises
see also Government supplies and property
see also Military bases, posts, and reservations
see also Military health facilities and services
see also Military supplies and property
see also Public buildings
see also Public lands
see also Socialism
see also Surplus government property
see also Veterans health facilities and services

Government pay
see also Civil service pensions
see also Educational employees pay
see also Federal pay
see also Military benefits and pensions
see also Military pay
see also State and local employees pay

Government price control
see Price regulation

Government Printing Office

Activities, finances, and production of GPO, FY88, annual rpt, 26204–1

Budget of US Appendix, obligations, appropriations, and personnel, by program and agency, FY90, annual rpt, 104–3

Budget of US, authoritative financial statements with appropriations, outlays, and receipts, by category and agency, FY88, annual rpt, 8104–2.2

Labor unions recognized in Fed Govt, agreements and membership by agency and facility, as of Jan 1989, biennial listing, 9844–14

Libraries (depository), and users by selected characteristics, for academic and public instns, 1988 survey, 26208–1

Microfiche shipment to depository libraries, GPO contract awards, and supply and quality problems, 1988, GAO rpt, 26119–248

Government publications

see Government documents

see Government publications lists

Government publications lists

Acid rain research activities and funding, by Federal agency, 1988 annual rpt, 14354–1

Agricultural data collection, methodology, and use, for major time series of USDA, series, 1506–1

Agricultural data compilation, 1987/88 and trends from 1920, annual rpt, 1004–14

Agricultural Statistics Board rpts, planned 1989, annual listing, 1614–1

BEA rpts, data coverage, and availability, 1989 article, 2702–1.912

Census Bur activities, rpts, and user services, monthly rpt, 2302–3

Census Bur rpts and data files, coverage and availability, 1989 annual listing, 2304–2

Census Bur rpts and data files, coverage, availability, and use, series, 2326–7

Census Bur rpts and data files, monthly listing, 2302–6

Census of Agriculture, 1987: data coverage and availability, for census and related statistics, 1989 guide, 2308–55

Census of Population and Housing, 1980: data processing, coverage, and availability, 2555–2.4

Census of Population and Housing, 1990: data coverage and products, 1989 guide, 2308–58

Commerce Dept rpts, biweekly listing, 2002–1

Crime and criminal justice data collection activities of Bur of Justice Statistics and States, FY88, annual rpt, 6064–21

Crime and criminal justice data collection programs and rpts, 1988, annual listing, 6064–25

Criminal justice issues and research, rpts and videotapes, 1984-88, listing, 6066–26.2

DOE data collection forms and related rpts, 1988, annual listing, 3164–86

DOE rpts, monthly listing, 3002–2

Drug abuse and treatment research summaries, resource materials and grant listings, periodic rpt, 4492–4

Educational Research and Improvement Office rpts, 1988-89, listing, 4868–9

Employment Policy Natl Commission activities and rpts, 1989 annual rpt, 15494–1

Energy Info Admin activities, 1988, annual rpt, 3164–29

Energy use, costs, and conservation, and household and housing characteristics, survey rpt series, 3166–7

EPA rpts in NTIS collection, quarterly listing, 9182–5

Fed Info Processing Standards rpts, 1968-89, listing, 2216–2.184

Fishery info and rpts of Natl Marine Fisheries Service, 1988, annual rpt, 2164–1

Foreign countries *Background Notes*, summary social, political, and economic data, 1989 listing, 7006–2.1; 7006–2.16; 7006–2.23; 7006–2.44; 7006–2.50

FTC activities, FY86, annual narrative rpt, 9404–1

GAO rpts, FY88, annual listing, 26104–17

Geological Survey rpts and research journal articles, monthly listing, 5662–1

Geological Survey rpts, 1988, annual listing, 5664–4

Health care resources geographic info system, data coverage and availability, 1989 rpt, 4118–61

Health care services delivery and costs, research rpts of NCHSR, 1985-July 1987, listing, 4188–57

Health Statistics Natl Center rpts, quarterly listing, 4122–2

HHS research and evaluation programs, 1970-FY87, annual listing, 4004–30

Hwy construction and design R&D, quarterly journal, 7552–3

Intergovernmental Perspective, quarterly journal, 10042–1

Intl Trade Admin rpts, biweekly rpt, annual listing, 2042–24

Libraries and Info Science Natl Commission activities, FY88, annual rpt, 15634–1

Library of Congress rpts and products, 1989, annual listing, 26404–6

Library of Congress rpts and recordings, 1989, biennial listing, 26404–5

MarAd activities, finances, subsidies, and world merchant fleet operations, FY88, annual rpt, 7704–14

Medicine Natl Library activities, holdings, and grants, FY86-88, annual rpt, 4464–1

Minerals resources of Alaska, production, oil and gas leases, and exploratory wells, with maps and bibl, 1987, annual rpt, 5664–11

Mines Bur rpts and patents, monthly listing, 5602–2

Mines Bur rpts, annual listing, suspended, 5604–40

Natl Archives and Records Admin activities, finances, holdings, and staff, FY88, annual rpt, 9514–2

NCES rpts, periodic listing, 4822–1

NIH rpts, 1989 annual listing, 4434–2

NOAA Environmental Research Labs rpts, FY88, annual listing, 2144–25

NSF rpts, 1985-88, annual chartbook, 9624–22

NSF rpts, 1989 annual listing, 9624–16

NSF Science Resources Studies Div rpts, 1978-88, listing, 9627–22

Ocean pollution research projects, rpts and data files, FY78-83, listing, 2158–51

Oil enhanced recovery research contracts of DOE, project summaries, funding, and bibl, quarterly rpt, 3002–14

Older persons aid and policies of Fed Govt, and issues of aging, 1989 annual rpt, 25144–3.1

Older persons social security issues, Fed Govt spending, and indicators of need, with bibl, 1988 compilation of papers, 25928–7

Prison conditions, population, and problems, issues and bibl, 1989 compilation of papers, 25928–8

Science Resources Studies Div of NSF, project descriptions and rpts, 1988 annual listing, 9624–21

Smithsonian Instn activities, rpts, and funding by donor, FY88, annual rpt, 29574–1.2

Social Security Bulletin, indexes, 1980-88, 4748–32

Soil surveys and maps for counties, 1899-1987, annual listing, 1264–11

SSA activities, litigation, finances, and staff, FY88, annual rpt, 4704–6

Standards and Technology Natl Inst rpts, 1988, annual listing, 2214–1

Statistical Abstract of US, guide to sources, 1989 annual rpt, 2324–1

Survey of Income and Program Participation, data collection, methodology, and availability, 1987 users guide, 2628–24

Technology Assessment Office activities and rpts, FY88, annual rpt, 26354–3

Telecommunications and Info Natl Admin rpts, FY88, annual listing, 2804–3

Toxicology Natl Program research and testing activities, FY87 and planned FY88, annual rpt, 4044–16

TVA agriculture and fertilizer rpts, 1989 annual listing, 9804–28

USITC activities, investigations, and rpts, FY88, annual rpt, 9884–1

USITC rpts, 1982-88, annual listing, 9884–12

Vital and Health Statistics series and other NCHS rpts, 1980-88, annual listing, 4124–1

Government regulation

see Administrative law and procedure

see Antitrust law

see Government and business

see Government forms and paperwork

see Government inspections

see Interstate commerce

see Licenses and permits

see Price regulation

Government reorganization

Budget of US, Reagan Admin policy changes by program, FY90, annual rpt, 104–21

Cost control proposals for Fed Govt mgmt, Reagan Admin initiatives, savings, and status, FY85-94, annual rpt, 104–23

Unemployment insurance administrative funding by Fed Govt, impacts of reductions on State program operations, FY80-88, GAO rpt, 26121–284

Government revenues

Budget of US, Reagan Admin fiscal and economic projections made 1981 and actual trends, 1980s-87, article, 9391–1.905

Cost control proposals for Fed Govt mgmt, Reagan Admin initiatives, savings, and status, FY85-94, annual rpt, 104–23

see also Military bases, posts, and
reservations
see also Military supplies and property
see also Public buildings
see also Public lands
see also Surplus government property

Government trust funds

Abandoned Mine Reclamation Fund
financial status, FY87, annual rpt,
5644–1

AID local currency trust funds mgmt and
use, by country, FY83-87, GAO rpt,
26123–221

Airport and Airway Trust Fund finances
and excise tax collections, FY71-88 and
projected under alternative spending
policies, FY89-94, 26308–84

Alaska rural villages population
characteristics and and subsistence
activities, 1976-86, 5738–9

Birds (waterfowl) refuge and breeding area
acreage acquired by Fed Govt, and costs,
by site and State, FY89, annual rpt,
14784–1

Black lung benefits and claims by State,
trust fund receipts by source, and
disbursements, 1987, annual rpt, 6504–3

Budget deficit reduction recommendations,
background data and testimony, 1989 rpt,
15888–2

Budget deficit reduction under
Gramm-Rudman Act, cancellation of
budget authority by program, FY90,
annual rpt, 104–27; 26304–6

Budget of US Appendix, obligations,
appropriations, and personnel, by program
and agency, FY90, annual rpt, 104–3

Budget of US, authoritative financial
statements with appropriations, outlays,
and receipts, by agency, FY88, annual rpt,
8104–2

Budget of US, balances of budget authority
obligated and unobligated, by function and
agency, FY88-90, annual rpt, 104–8

Budget of US, CBO analysis of revenue and
spending alternatives and projections of
economic indicators, FY90-94, annual rpt,
26304–3

Budget of US, compact budgets by activity,
function, and agency, FY90 and projected
to FY94, annual rpt, 104–2

Budget of US, historical data, selected years
FY34-88 and projected to FY94, annual
rpt, 104–22

Budget of US, object class analysis of
obligations, by agency, FY90, annual rpt,
104–9

Budget of US, receipts by source, outlays by
agency and program, and balances,
monthly rpt, 8102–3

Budget of US, special analysis of trust fund
receipts and outlays by fund, FY90,
annual rpt, 104–1.3

Civil service retirement system actuarial
valuation, and benefits and coverage by
age, type of beneficiary, and State, FY87,
annual rpt, 9844–34

Credit unions federally insured, finances,
mergers, closings, and insurance fund
losses and financial statements, FY88,
annual rpt, 9534–7

Currency (foreign) accounts owned by US
under AID admin and by foreign govts
with joint AID control, status by program
and country, quarterly rpt, 9912–1

Currency (foreign) holdings of US,
transactions and balances by program and
country, 1st half FY89, semiannual rpt,
8102–7

DOD outlays and obligations, by function
and service branch, quarterly rpt, 3542–3

Expenditures of Fed Govt in States, by type,
program, agency, and State, FY88, annual
rpt, 2464–2

Fed Govt trust funds financial condition, by
fund, periodic rpt series, 8102–9

Finances and operations of programs under
Ways and Means Committee jurisdiction,
FY70s-88, annual rpt, 21784–11

Finances of govts, by level of govt, State,
and for large cities and counties, annual
rpt series, 2466–2

Financial status of Federal trust funds, by
agency, and impacts on budget balance,
FY47-93 and projected to FY93, GAO
rpt, 26111–58

Fish and Wildlife Service restoration
programs finances by State, and excise tax
collections, FY88, annual rpt, 5504–13

Helium market demand and Bur of Mines
production, sales, and financial statements,
FY88, annual rpt, 5604–32

Historic Preservation Fund grants, by State,
FY90, annual table, 5544–9

Hwy Trust Fund obligations, by project and
urban-rural location, 1982-86, 1278–12

Hwy Trust Fund receipts by source, and
apportionments, by State, 1988, annual
rpt, 7554–1.3

Hwy Trust Fund status and net revenues,
FY57-88, annual rpt, 7554–24

Japan-US Friendship Commission
educational and cultural exchange
activities, grants, and trust fund status,
FY87-88, biennial report, 14694–1

Judicial Survivors Annuity Fund financial
condition and annuitants, June 1982-89,
annual rpt, 18204–2.8; 18204–8.8

Labor Dept activities and funding, by
program and State, FY88, annual rpt,
6304–1

Lands (public) acreage, grants, use,
revenues, and allocations, by State, FY88,
annual rpt, 5724–1.3

Library of Congress activities, acquisitions,
services, and financial statements, FY88,
annual rpt, 26404–1

Medicare and Medicaid beneficiaries and
program operations, 1988, annual fact
book, 4654–18

Medicare and Medicaid eligibility,
participation, coverage, and program
finances, various periods 1966-89, biennial
rpt, 4654–1

Medicare and other insurance programs
catastrophic illness coverage, benefits,
premiums, costs, and program finances,
projected 1988-93, 26306–3.105

Medicare beneficiaries prescription drug use
and spending, and costs of catastrophic
coverage, 1987 and projected to 1993,
26308–89

Medicare catastrophic illness coverage and
premium collection, effects of revisions on
Federal budget and enrollees, projected
1989-93, 25368–161

Medicare trust funds finances, various
periods 1966-88 and projected to 1992,
annual rpt, 4654–12

Medicare trust funds finances, 1966-88 and
alternative projections to 1991, annual rpt,
4654–11

Medicare trust funds finances, 1987 and
projected to 2062, annual rpt, 4654–8

Natl Archives and Records Admin
activities, finances, holdings, and staff,
FY88, annual rpt, 9514–2

NTIS activities, finances, and modernization
plans, FY88, annual rpt, 2224–6

Nuclear Waste Fund finances, and DOE
Civilian Radioactive Waste Mgmt Office
activities, quarterly GAO rpt, 26102–4

Nuclear Waste Fund finances, and DOE
Civilian Radioactive Waste Mgmt Office
project budgets alternative projections,
quarterly rpt, 3362–1

OASDHI admin, and SSA activities,
1930s-89 and projected to 2063, data
compilation, annual rpt, 4704–12

OASDHI, Medicaid, SSI, and related
programs benefits, beneficiary
characteristics, and trust funds, selected
years 1937-87, annual rpt, 4744–3

OASDHI trust funds receipts, outlays, and
assets since 1940, monthly rpt, 4742–1.2

OASDI benefit payments, trust fund
finances, and economic and demographic
assumptions, 1970-87 and alternative
projections to 1997, actuarial rpt,
4706–1.103

OASDI trust funds finances, and impact on
Federal budget, 1987-88 and projected to
2050, GAO rpt, 26121–269

OASDI trust funds finances, FY88 and
projected to 2060s, annual article,
4742–1.918

OASDI trust funds income and outlays,
FY88, annual rpt, 4704–6

OASDI trust funds surpluses impact on
budget deficit, FY89-94, with surpluses
projected to 2050, article, 9381–1.909

Pension Benefit Guaranty Corp activities
and finances, FY88 and projected to
FY98, annual rpt, 9674–1

Pension fund assets, for public and private
funds, 1976-87, annual rpt, 9364–5.12

Public debt issued, redeemed, and
outstanding, by series and source, and
gifts to reduce debt, monthly rpt, 8242–2

Railroad employment, and benefits program
finances and beneficiaries, FY88, annual
rpt, 9704–1

Railroad employment by occupation from
1957, and Railroad Retirement Account
finances, alternative projections
1987-2010, GAO rpt, 26121–280

Railroad retirement and unemployment
insurance accounts status, and interchange
with OASDHI fund, FY85, annual rpt,
9704–2.1

Receipts, outlays, debt, and assets, by fund,
Treasury Bulletin, quarterly rpt,
8002–4.1; 8002–4.4; 8002–4.15

Red Cross financial statements, FY87-88,
annual rpt, 29254–1.2

Rural areas electric and telephone loans by
State, and REA activities and finances,
FY88 with trends from FY36, annual rpt,
1244–3

Small Business Admin loan and contract
activity by program and firm, and
financial condition, FY88, annual rpt,
9764–1

see also Hops
see also Oils, oilseeds, and fats
see also Rice
see also Soybeans
see also Wheat
see also under By Commodity in the "Index by Categories"

Gramm-Rudman Act
see Balanced Budget and Emergency Deficit Control Act

Grammatikos, Theoharry
"Additions to Bank Loan-Loss Reserves Good News or Bad News?", 9387-8.186

Grand Forks, N.Dak.
see also under By SMSA or MSA in the "Index by Categories"

Grand Island, Nebr.
Wages by occupation, for office and plant workers, 1989 survey, periodic MSA rpt, 6785-3.10

Grand Rapids, Mich.
see also under By City and By SMSA or MSA in the "Index by Categories"

Grant, Bridget F.
"Liver Cirrhosis Mortality in the U.S., 1971-85", 4486-1.4
"Liver Cirrhosis Mortality in the U.S., 1972-86", 4486-1.7

Grant, Dwight
"Optimal Futures Positions for Corn and Soybean Growers Facing Price and Yield Risk", 1548-352

Grants and grants-in-aid
see State funding for economic development
see State funding for education
see State funding for health and hospitals
see State funding for higher education
see State funding for local areas
see State funding for public safety
see State funding for social welfare
see State government spending
see terms beginning with Federal aid

Grants Pass, Oreg.
Wages by occupation, and benefits for office and plant workers, 1989 survey, periodic MSA rpt, 6785-3.9

Grapefruit
see Citrus fruits

Graphics
see Advertising
see Art
see Chartbooks
see Photography and photographic equipment
see Printing and publishing industry

Graphite
see Nonmetallic minerals and mines

Grasses
see Animal feed
see National grasslands
see Pasture and rangeland
see Plants and vegetation

Gravel
see Stone products and quarries

Graves, Edmund J.
"Detailed Diagnoses and Procedures, National Hospital Discharge Survey, 1987", 4147-13.100
"National Hospital Discharge Survey: Annual Summary, 1987", 4147-13.99

Gray, Arthur W.
"Availability of Federal Land for Mineral Exploration and Development in Western States: New Mexico, 1987", 5606-7.5

Gray, Fred
"U.S. Imports of Sugar in Sugar-Containing Products, 1977-88", 1561-14.905

Gray, Wayne B.
"Enforcement of Pollution Regulations in a Declining Industry", 9377-9.84

Grazing
see Pasture and rangeland

Grease
see Oils, oilseeds, and fats
see Petroleum and petroleum industry

Great Britain
see United Kingdom

Great Falls, Mont.
see also under By SMSA or MSA in the "Index by Categories"

Great Lakes
Algal levels in Great Lakes, effects of phosphorus loads, and fish stocking, 1966-85, conf, 14648-20
Army Corps of Engineers water resources dev projects, characteristics, and costs, 1950s-87, biennial State rpt, 3756-2.15
Army Corps of Engineers water resources dev projects, characteristics, and costs, 1950s-87, biennial State rpt series, 3756-2
Army Corps of Engineers water resources dev projects, characteristics, and costs, 1950s-89, biennial State rpt series, 3756-1
Coal production and stocks by district, and shipments by district of origin, State of destination, end-use sector, and mode of transport, quarterly rpt, 3162-8
Conservation and research projects of Fish and Wildlife Service, descriptions and results by program, FY87-88, biennial rpt, 5504-20
Environmental quality and protection programs, and intl issues, 1988 annual rpt, 484-1
Environmental research lab for Great Lakes, activities, annual conf, discontinued, 2144-22
Environmental research lab for Great Lakes, activities, 1987 annual rpt, 2144-26
Estuary environmental conditions and mgmt, for individual areas, conf series, 2146-6
Exports and imports (waterborne) of US, by type of service, commodity, country, route, and US port, 1986-87, annual rpt, 7704-2
Fish catch, trade, use, and fishery operations, with selected foreign data, by species, 1970s-88, annual rpt, 2164-1
Fish Hatchery Natl System activities and deliveries, by species, hatchery, and jurisdiction of waters stocked, FY88, annual rpt, 5504-10
Fishing, hunting, and other wildlife-related recreation participation and spending, detailed data by location, 1985 survey, quinquennial rpt, 5508-5
Fishing, hunting, and other wildlife-related recreation participation and spending, detailed data, 1985 survey, quinquennial State rpt series, 5506-7
Freight (waterborne domestic), by major commodity group, vessel type, and port, 1986, annual rpt, 7704-7
Freight (waterborne domestic and foreign) by commodity, traffic, and passengers, by port and waterway, 1987, annual rpt, 3754-3.3

Lake Ontario eutrophication and pollutant levels, by contaminant type and site, 1967-85, 14648-22
Pollutant discharges, sources, and control program activities for Great Lakes basin, 1987, biennial rpt, 14644-1
Pollutant polychlorinated biphenyls levels in Great Lakes environment, humans, and animals, and emissions sources, by site, 1970s-85, conf, 14648-19
Pollution (toxic) spills in Great Lakes, and human error, with data by pollutant source and site, 1984-86, conf, 14648-21
Pollution (water) incidents and discharges, by type, source, cause, and location, 1984-86, annual rpt, 7404-3
Pollution loadings from nonpoint sources, for Lake Erie and Lake Ontario tributaries, 1982-85, 9208-129
Ship pilotage activities, costs, and traffic for US and Canada, and US testing and certificates, for Great Lakes, 1960s-87, 7308-192
Shipbuilding costs, deliveries, contracts, employment, and wage rates, by coastal district and shipyard, 1988, annual rpt, 7704-12
Ships in Great Lakes fleet, and tonnage, by activity status and vessel type, FY88, annual rpt, 7704-14.2
Ships in US merchant fleet, operating subsidies, and ship-related employment, monthly rpt, 7702-1
Ships in world bulk carrier fleet, characteristics by country of registry, as of Jan 1989, annual listing, 7704-13
Transportation finances, operations, vehicles, equipment, accidents, and energy use, by mode of transport, 1955-88, annual rpt, 7304-2
Water levels in Great Lakes, fluctuations, causes, and impacts of alternative mgmt strategies, 1900s-88, series, 14646-1
Water levels in Great Lakes, impacts of water supply mgmt and weather phenomena, model description, 1900-85, 2148-59
Water levels of Great Lakes and connecting channels, and forecasts, semimonthly rpt, 3752-2
Water levels of Great Lakes, and forecasts, monthly rpt and supplements, 3752-1
Water quality indicators for Great Lakes by water basin and lake, 1970s-85, annual rpt, 9204-14
Water supply and quality in streams and lakes, and groundwater levels in wells, by drainage basin, 1986, annual State rpt series, 5666-23
Water supply and quality in streams and lakes, and groundwater levels in wells, by drainage basin, 1987, annual State rpt series, 5666-10
Water supply and quality in streams and lakes, and groundwater levels in wells, by drainage basin, 1988, annual State rpt series, 5666-16
Water supply in northeastern US, precipitation and stream runoff by station, monthly rpt, 2182-3
Weather (marine) forecast areas, and broadcast schedules and stations worldwide, as of Nov 1988, annual rpt, 2184-3

Grise, Verner N.

"Costs of Producing and Selling Flue-Cured Tobacco: 1987, 1988, and Preliminary 1989", 1561–10.902

"Tobacco: Background for 1990 Farm Legislation", 1566–7.6

"U.S. Tobacco Industry", 1568–276

"1989 Outlook for Tobacco", 1004–16.1

Grocery stores

see Food stores

Gronberg, Timothy J.

"Structure, Conduct, and Performance in the Local Public Sector", 9377–9.82

Groshen, Erica L.

"Do the Earnings of Manufacturing and Service Workers Grow at the Same Rate over Their Careers?", 9377–1.901

"Do Wage Differences Among Employers Last?", 9377–9.78

"Structure of Supervision and Pay in Hospitals", 9377–9.79

Gross, James M.

"North Atlantic Tropical Cyclones, 1988", 2152–8.902

Gross National Product

Budget of US, CBO analysis of revenue and spending alternatives and projections of economic indicators, FY90-94, annual rpt, 26304–3

Budget of US, historical data, selected years FY34-88 and projected to FY94, annual rpt, 104–22

Business and financial statistics, historic trends, 1988 annual chartbook, 9364–2.2

Business Conditions Digest, economic, business, and financial devs and cyclical fluctuations, monthly rpt, 2702–3

Business statistics, detailed data for major industries and economic indicators, Survey of Current Business, monthly rpt, 2702–1

Communist and OECD countries economic conditions, 1987, annual rpt, 7144–11

Communist, OECD, and selected other countries economic conditions, 1960s-88, annual rpt, 9114–4

Credit (private and Federal) related to GNP, interest rates, and inflation, model description and results, 1960s-87, working paper, 9381–10.94

Cuba economic conditions, agricultural and industrial production and distribution, trade, and intl economic relations, 1980-87 with trends from 1961, 9118–8

Current account balance, by component, 1980-87 and projected under alternative growth and exchange rate assumptions, 1988-95, hearing, 23848–209

Current account balance of US, components and relation to foreign and US investment and economic conditions, 1970s-88 and projected to 1990s, article, 9385–1.906

Developing countries disaster preparedness and economic, population, and political data, country rpt series, 9916–2

Developing countries economic and social conditions from 1960s, and Intl Dev Cooperation Agency and AID activities and funding, FY88-90, annual rpt, 9904–4

Developing countries economic indicators, problem debtors compared to other borrowers, by country, 1973-84, 1528–285

Developing countries receiving US economic aid, military spending and imports measures to determine aid eligibility, by country, 1985-86, annual rpt, 9914–1

EC economic integration impact on EC employment, GDP, and other economic indicators, projected 1992, article, 9373–1.908

EC food supply and demand, market and support prices, and other economic indicators, by country and commodity, 1960-85, 1528–276

Economic and employment conditions, alternative BLS projections to 2000 and trends 1970s-88, biennial article, 6722–1.953; 6722–1.954

Economic indicator performance, and Fed Reserve monetary policy objectives, as of July 1989, semiannual rpt, 9362–4

Economic indicators and components, and Fed Reserve 4th District business and financial conditions, monthly chartbook, 9377–10

Economic indicators and components, current data and annual trends, monthly rpt, 23842–1.1

Economic indicators and relation to govt finances by level of govt, selected years 1929-87, annual rpt, 10044–1

Economic indicators compounded annual rates of change, monthly rpt, 9391–3.2

Economic indicators compounded annual rates of change, 1969-88, annual rpt, 9391–9.2

Economic indicators, monthly rpt, 9362–1.2

Economic indicators, monthly table, 9302–26

Economic indicators relation to GNP, model description and results, various periods 1958-88, working paper, 9393–10.4

Economic indicators targets and performance, 1960s-88 and projected to 1994, annual article, 9381–1.901

Economic Report of the President for 1989, with economic trends from 1929, annual rpt, 204–1

Financial and economic analysis and forecasting methodology, technical paper series, 9366–6

Financial and economic indicators relation to GNP, model description and results, 1948-86, working paper, 9387–8.195

Forecasts of GNP and inflation, analysis of errors among alternative models, 1989 article, 9373–1.904

Forecasts of GNP for current quarter, performance of monthly employment, production, and retail sales, 1978-88, article, 9393–8.903

Foreign and domestic industry output relation to GNP, for Canada, Japan, and Germany, 1961-84, technical paper, 9366–6.189

Foreign and US economic indicators, trade balances, and exchange rates, for selected OECD and Asian countries, 1980s-89, semiannual rpt, 8002–14

Foreign countries Background Notes, summary social, political, and economic data, series, 7006–2

Foreign countries economic and monetary trends, compounded annual rates of change for US and 10 major trading partners, quarterly rpt, 9391–7

Foreign countries economic conditions and implications for US, periodic country rpt series, 2046–4

Foreign countries economic conditions, policy, and trade practices, by country, 1986-88, annual rpt, 21384–5

Foreign countries economic indicators, and trade and investment flows, for selected countries and country groups, selected years 1946-88, annual rpt, 204–1.9

Foreign countries economic, social, political, and geographic summary data, by country, 1989, annual factbook, 9114–2

Foreign countries military spending, arms trade, and force strengths, with govt spending and population, by country, 1977-87, annual rpt, 9824–1

GNP by component in 1982 and 1987 dollars, 1982-88, and methodological issues, article, 2702–1.913

Health care spending share of GNP, by component, 1960s-87, article, 4652–1.927

Inflation relation to labor costs and GNP, 1959-88, working paper, 9389–19.9

Inflation relation to M2, GNP, and interest rates, various periods 1952-88, working paper, 9389–19.10

Inflation variability impact on GNP, model description and results, 1959-88, article, 9391–1.919

Monetary base alternative measures, performance in forecasting GNP, 1959-87, technical paper, 9379–12.32

Monetary reserves relation to GNP, alternative measures, model description and results, 1959-89, technical paper, 9379–12.46

Money supply growth rates relation to GNP and Fed funds and other interest rates, various periods 1964-88, article, 9362–1.903

Natl income and product accounts and components, Survey of Current Business, monthly rpt, 2702–1.21; 2702–1.22

NATO and Japan military spending and indicators of ability to support common defense, by country, 1960s-87, annual rpt, 3544–28

NATO military forces compared to Warsaw Pact, and selected economic indicators, by country, 1900s-87, conf papers, 3908–6

OASDI benefit payments, trust fund finances, and economic and demographic assumptions, 1970-87 and alternative projections to 1997, actuarial rpt, 4706–1.103

OECD and Arab countries dev aid, total, per capita, and share of GNP, by country, 1987, annual rpt, 9904–1.4

OECD current account balance and related economic indicators, for US and 4 countries, 1980s-87, article, 9389–1.908

OECD economic conditions for 6 countries and US, biweekly rpt, 9112–1

OECD members GNP and GNP growth, by country, 1978-88, annual rpt, 7144–8

Oil demand related to GNP and oil prices, 1972-88 and alternative projections to 2000, article, 9379–1.901

Oil use relation to crude oil prices, GNP, and industrial production, 1972-88, technical paper, 9379–12.39

Overseas Business Reports: economic conditions, investment and export opportunities, and trade practices, country market research rpt series, 2046–6

Pacific basin countries military, economic, technological, and trade conditions, 1970s-85, compilation of papers, 3908-4

Pacific territories social, economic, health, and govtl data, FY88 and trends, annual rpt, 7004-6

Portugal and Turkey economic indicators and govt finances, 1982-86, hearing, 21388-53

Puerto Rico economic conditions and govt finances, 1975-89, GAO rpt, 26121-298

Southeastern States gross product, by major industry group and State, 1982-86, article, 9389-16

Southeastern US industrial output, by major industry group, 1986 with growth since 1963, article, 9391-16.905

Southeastern US mining industry output relative to gross State product, by type of mining and State, 1986, article, 9391-16.904

Soviet Union economic conditions and military activity, 1960s-86, hearing, 23848-195

Soviet Union economic conditions under General Secretary Gorbachev, Soviet and CIA measurement methods with background data, 1987 conf papers, 9118-4

Soviet Union economic conditions under General Secretary Gorbachev, Soviet and CIA measures, 1950s-87, 9118-5

Soviet Union economic conditions under General Secretary Gorbachev, 1988 and trends from 1956, annual rpt, 9114-6

State gross product growth rates relation to natural resources sector share of State output, 1963-86, article, 9393-8.909

Statistical Abstract of US, social, political, and economic data, 1790-2025, comprehensive annual compilation, 2324-1.3

Taiwan and South Korea trade balance impacts of exchange rates and foreign and domestic economic indicators, 1974-87, article, 9393-8.905

Transportation energy use by mode, fuel supply, and demographic and economic factors of vehicle use, 1970s-88, annual rpt, 3304-5.2

Unemployment rate relation to inflation, labor force, GNP, interest rate, and trade balance, various periods 1948-88, article, 9393-8.910

Gross, Thomas P.
"Outbreak of Acute Infectious Nonbacterial Gastroenteritis in a High School in Maryland", 4042-3.913

Grosse, Daniel J.
"Amphipods. Species Profiles: Life Histories and Environmental Requirements of Coastal Fishes and Invertebrates", 5506-8.99

Grossman, Sanford J.
"Report on Program Trading: An Analysis of Interday Relationships", 25168-70

Groundwater
see Hydrology
see Rivers and waterways
see Water supply and use

Group health
see Blue Cross-Blue Shield
see Health insurance
see Health maintenance organizations

Group homes for the handicapped
Drug and alcohol abuse treatment facilities, services, use, funding, and client characteristics, 1987, annual rpt, 4494-10

Homeless persons transitional housing, HUD grants by recipient, 1989, press release, 5006-3.66

Homeless persons with handicaps, HUD group housing grants by recipient, 1989, press release, 5006-3.67

HUD loans for disabled persons housing, by recipient, 1989, press release, 5006-3.72

Licensing and enforcement activity by States, conditions of board and care homes, and client characteristics, 1970s-88, 21148-55

Licensing and inspection of board and care homes by States, and client characteristics, 1989 GAO rpt, 26121-275

Mentally retarded persons facilities, beds, and residents, by ownership, resident age and race, and State, 1986, 4147-14.34

Supplemental Security Income and Medicaid eligibility and payment provisions, and beneficiaries living arrangements, by State, 1989, annual rpt, 4704-13

Group quarters
Accident deaths and rates, by cause, age, race, sex, and State, 1986, annual rpt, 4144-2.5

County Business Patterns, 1987: employment, establishments, and payroll, by SIC 2- to 4-digit industry and county, annual State rpt series, 2326-8

Foreign and US older persons institutionalized in medical and other care facilities, rates by selected country, 1980 and 1985, article, 4652-1.918

Higher education instn student aid and other sources of support, with student expenses and characteristics, by instn type and control, 1987 triennial study, series, 4846-3

Living arrangements, family relationships, and marital status, by selected characteristics, 1988, annual Current Population Rpt, 2546-1.428; 2546-1.433

Poverty status of families and persons, by detailed characteristics, 1987, annual Current Population Rpt, 2546-6.60

Service industries census, 1987: establishments, receipts, employment, and payroll, by SIC 2- to 4-digit kind of business, MSA, county, and city, State rpt series, 2391-1

Service industries receipts, by SIC 2- to 4-digit kind of business, 1988, annual rpt, 2413-8

Statistical Abstract of US, social, political, and economic data, 1790-2025, comprehensive annual compilation, 2324-1.1

see also Group homes for the handicapped
see also Transient housing

Grubb, W. Norton
"Sources of Increasing Inequality in Wages and Salaries, 1960-80", 6722-1.917

Gruben, William C.
"Diversifying Texas: Recent History and Prospects", 9379-1.907
"Do Maquiladoras Take American Jobs? Some Tentative Econometric Results", 9379-12.45

"Unionization and Unemployment Rates: Re-Examination of Olson's Labor Cartelization Hypothesis", 9379-12.29

GSA
see General Services Administration

Guam
Agriculture census, 1987: farms, farmland, production, finances, and operator characteristics, by election district, final outlying area rpt, 2331-1.53

Bank deposits in FDIC-insured commercial and savings banks, by instn, State, and county, as of June 1988, annual regional rpt, 9295-3.6

Census of Population and Housing, 1990: outlying areas preparations for count, hearings, 21628-74

Deaths and rates, by detailed location, cause, and demographic characteristics, 1987, US Vital Statistics annual rpt, 4144-3.2

Economic Censuses of Outlying Areas, 1987: Guam employment, firms, payroll, and receipts, by SIC 1- to 4-digit industry and election district, 2595-1

Economic, social, political, and geographic summary data, by country, 1989, annual factbook, 9114-2

Exports and imports between US and outlying areas, by detailed commodity and mode of transport, monthly rpt, 2422-4

Fed Govt spending in States and local areas, by type, State, county, and city, FY88, annual rpt, 2464-3

Fed Govt spending in States, by type, program, agency, and State, FY88, annual rpt, 2464-2

Harbor traffic, facilities, dev, funding, and needs, for Pacific territories and Hawaii by port, as of 1987, 7308-195

HHS financial aid, by program, recipient, State, and city, FY88, annual regional listing, 4004-3.9

Minerals Yearbook, 1987, Vol 2: State reviews of production, sales, and firms, by commodity, and business activity, annual rpt, 5604-34

Population size and components of change, by outlying area, 1980-88, annual Current Population Rpt, 2546-3.162

Population size, growth rates, and components of change, by country, projected 1989-2020 and trends from 1950, biennial rpt, 2324-9

Water supply and quality in streams and lakes, and groundwater levels in wells, by drainage basin, 1987, annual State rpt, 5666-10.10

see also under By Outlying Area in the "Index by Categories"

Guaranteed income
see Income maintenance

Guaranteed Student Loan Program
see Student aid

Guarantees and warranties
see also Surety bonds

Guardianship
OASDI and SSI recipients with representative payee, by beneficiary type, 1986-87, annual rpt, 4744-3.8

Veterans benefits under guardianship, for incompetent and minor recipients, 1964-88, annual rpt, 8604-5.2

Guatemala

Agricultural and food production and indexes, total and for selected commodities, by country, 1970s-88, annual rpt, 1524-12

Agricultural policy impacts on economic dev, with background data for 6 developing countries, 1960s-86, 1528-283

Agricultural production, prices, and trade, by country, 1960s-89, annual world region rpt, 1524-4.2

Agricultural trade of US, by detailed commodity and country, 1988, semiannual rpt, 1522-4

AID activities and funding by project and function, FY90, and developing countries summary socioeconomic data from 1960s, annual rpt, 9904-4.7

AID economic aid to developing countries, obligations and disbursements by country, quarterly rpt, 9912-4

AID loans repayment status and terms by program and country, and status of predecessor agency loans, quarterly rpt, 9912-3

Economic and military aid and loans from US and intl agencies, by program and country, FY46-87, annual rpt, 9914-5

Economic conditions, policy, and trade practices, by country, 1986-88, annual rpt, 21384-5

Economic, social, political, and geographic summary data, by country, 1989, annual factbook, 9114-2

Exports and imports of US, by commodity and country, 1970-87, world area rpt, 9116-1.6

Exports and imports of US, by selected country, country group, and commodity group, 1988, annual rpt, 2044-37

Human rights conditions in 170 countries, 1988, annual rpt, 21384-3

Investment (direct) incentives of Caribbean Basin Initiative, economic impacts, with finances and employment by country, 1984-88, 2048-141

Military aid of US, arms sales, and training programs costs and budget requests, by program, world region, and country, FY88-90, annual rpt, 7144-13

Military spending, arms trade, and force strengths, with govt spending and population, by country, 1977-87, annual rpt, 9824-1

Minerals Yearbook, 1987, Vol 3: foreign country reviews of production, trade, and policy, by commodity, annual rpt, 5604-35

Minerals Yearbook, 1987, Vol 3 preprints: foreign country review of production, trade, and policy, by commodity, annual rpt, 5604-23.84

Population size, growth rates, and components of change, by country, projected 1989-2020 and trends from 1950, biennial rpt, 2324-9

Refugees from Nicaragua, El Salvador, and Guatemala receiving UN aid, resettlement in other Central American countries, and repatriations, 1984-88, GAO rpt, 26123-232

UN voting record and share of votes in agreement with US, by issue, country, and world area, 1988, annual rpt, 7004-18

see also under By Foreign Country in the "Index by Categories"

Guinea

Agricultural and food production and indexes, total and for selected commodities, by country, 1970s-88, annual rpt, 1524-12

Agricultural trade of US, by detailed commodity and country, 1988, semiannual rpt, 1522-4

AID activities and funding by project and function, FY90, and developing countries summary socioeconomic data from 1960s, annual rpt, 9904-4.5

AID economic aid to developing countries, obligations and disbursements by country, quarterly rpt, 9912-4

AID loans repayment status and terms by program and country, and status of predecessor agency loans, quarterly rpt, 9912-3

Background Notes, summary social, political, and economic data, 1989 rpt, 7006-2.45

Economic and military aid and loans from US and intl agencies, by program and country, FY46-87, annual rpt, 9914-5

Economic conditions, income, production, prices, employment, and trade, 1989 periodic country rpt, 2046-4.64

Economic, social, political, and geographic summary data, by country, 1989, annual factbook, 9114-2

Human rights conditions in 170 countries, 1988, annual rpt, 21384-3

Military aid of US, arms sales, and training programs costs and budget requests, by program, world region, and country, FY88-90, annual rpt, 7144-13

Military spending, arms trade, and force strengths, with govt spending and population, by country, 1977-87, annual rpt, 9824-1

Minerals Yearbook, 1987, Vol 3: foreign country reviews of production, trade, and policy, by commodity, annual rpt, 5604-35

Minerals Yearbook, 1987, Vol 3 preprints: foreign country review of production, trade, and policy, by commodity, annual rpt, 5604-23.29

Population size, growth rates, and components of change, by country, projected 1989-2020 and trends from 1950, biennial rpt, 2324-9

UN voting record and share of votes in agreement with US, by issue, country, and world area, 1988, annual rpt, 7004-18

see also under By Foreign Country in the "Index by Categories"

Guinea-Bissau

Agricultural and food production and indexes, total and for selected commodities, by country, 1970s-88, annual rpt, 1524-12

AID activities and funding by project and function, FY90, and developing countries summary socioeconomic data from 1960s, annual rpt, 9904-4.5

AID economic aid to developing countries, obligations and disbursements by country, quarterly rpt, 9912-4

Background Notes, summary social, political, and economic data, 1989 rpt, 7006-2.8

Economic and military aid and loans from US and intl agencies, by program and country, FY46-87, annual rpt, 9914-5

Economic, social, political, and geographic summary data, by country, 1989, annual factbook, 9114-2

Human rights conditions in 170 countries, 1988, annual rpt, 21384-3

Military aid of US, arms sales, and training programs costs and budget requests, by program, world region, and country, FY88-90, annual rpt, 7144-13

Military spending, arms trade, and force strengths, with govt spending and population, by country, 1977-87, annual rpt, 9824-1

Minerals Yearbook, 1987, Vol 3 preprints: foreign country review of production, trade, and policy, by commodity, annual rpt, 5604-23.82

Population size, growth rates, and components of change, by country, projected 1989-2020 and trends from 1950, biennial rpt, 2324-9

UN voting record and share of votes in agreement with US, by issue, country, and world area, 1988, annual rpt, 7004-18

see also under By Foreign Country in the "Index by Categories"

Gulf of Alaska

Army Corps of Engineers water resources dev projects, characteristics, and costs, 1950s-87, biennial State rpt series, 3756-2

Army Corps of Engineers water resources dev projects, characteristics, and costs, 1950s-89, biennial State rpt series, 3756-1

Coastal areas environmental conditions and mgmt, map series, 2176-5

Environmental conditions and oil dev impacts for Alaska OCS, compilation of papers, series, 2176-1

Fish catch, trade, use, and fishery operations, with selected foreign data, by species, 1970s-88, annual rpt, 2164-1

Gulf of Mexico

Coastal areas environmental conditions and mgmt, map series, 2176-5

Coastal areas environmental conditions, fish, wildlife, use, and mgmt, 1989 rpt, 5506-9.35; 5506-9.40

Estuary drainage basin area and daily flows, by monitoring site for Gulf coast, 1988, 2176-4.11

Estuary environmental and fishery conditions, research results and methodology, 1988 rpt, 2176-7.9

Estuary environmental and fishery conditions, research results and methodology, 1989 rpt, 2176-7.16

Estuary environmental conditions and mgmt, for individual areas, conf series, 2146-6

Estuary environmental conditions, nitrogen and phosphorus levels, 1982, 2176-7.14

Estuary waters approved and prohibited for shellfish harvest, and pollution sources, 1985, 2176-7.5

Fish and shellfish catch, life cycles, and environmental needs, for selected coastal species and regions, series, 5506-8

Fish and shellfish catch, wholesale receipts, prices, trade, and other market activities, weekly regional rpt, 2162-6.3

Fish catch, trade, use, and fishery operations, with selected foreign data, by species, 1970s-88, annual rpt, 2164-1

Fishing (ocean sport) catch and effort, and Natl Marine Fisheries Service tagging and research activity, by species and location, 1987, annual rpt, 2164–7

Freight (waterborne domestic), by major commodity group, vessel type, and port, 1986, annual rpt, 7704–7

Freight (waterborne domestic and foreign) by commodity, traffic, and passengers, by port and waterway, 1987, annual rpt, 3754–3.2

Grain vessels in port, loaded, and due in Gulf coast, weekly rpt, 1272–2

Hurricanes and tropical storms in north Atlantic and Caribbean area, paths, surveillance, deaths, damage, and landfall probabilities by city, 1988, annual rpt, 2184–7

Marine Fisheries Review, US and foreign fisheries resources, dev, mgmt, and research, quarterly journal, 2162–1

Mineral industries census, 1987: financial and operating data, preliminary summary rpt, 2511–1.13

Oil and gas OCS lease sales in Gulf of Mexico, by company and tract, 1988, annual rpt, 5734–8

Oil and gas OCS leases environmental and socioeconomic impact and coastal area description, final statement series, 5736–1

Oil and gas OCS operations accidents, spills, casualties, and circumstances, 1956-86, listing, 5738–7

Oil and gas OCS production water discharges, and impacts on Gulf of Mexico coastal habitats, 1983-88, 5738–10

Oil and gas OCS reserves of Fed Govt, leasing and exploration activity, production, revenue, and costs, by ocean area, FY88, annual rpt, 5734–4

Oil and gas OCS reserves, production, and leasing status, for Gulf of Mexico by location, 1987, annual rpt, 5734–6

Oil, gas, and minerals production, revenue, and leasing activity, for Federal OCS lands by ocean region and State, 1950s-87, annual rpt, 5734–3

Pollutant concentrations in coastal and estuarine sediments, by contaminant and selected site, 1984-87, 2176–3.7

Pollutant concentrations in coastal and estuarine shellfish, by pollutant and location, 1986-88, 2176–3.8

Pollution (water) incidents and discharges, by type, source, cause, and location, 1984-86, annual rpt, 7404–3

Temperature of sea surface by ocean and for US coastal areas, and Bering Sea ice conditions, monthly rpt, 2182–5

Tidal currents, daily time and velocity by station for North America coasts, forecast 1990, annual rpt, 2174–1.2

Tide height and time daily at coastal points, forecast 1990, annual rpt, 2174–2.3

Turtles (sea) catch, population monitoring, shrimping kills, and effects of drilling rig removal, 1970s-80s, article, 2162–1.902

Water runoff for streams draining eastern Mississippi coastal plain, 1939-85, 5668–85

Water supply and quality in streams and lakes, and groundwater levels in wells, by drainage basin, 1987, annual State rpt series, 5666–10

Water supply and quality in streams and lakes, and groundwater levels in wells, by drainage basin, 1988, annual State rpt series, 5666–16

Weather (marine) forecast areas, and broadcast schedules and stations worldwide, as of Nov 1988, annual rpt, 2184–3

Gulfport, Miss.

Wages by occupation, and benefits for office and plant workers, 1989 survey, periodic MSA rpt, 6785–3.10

see also under By SMSA or MSA in the "Index by Categories"

Gum and wood chemicals

County Business Patterns, 1987: employment, establishments, and payroll, by SIC 2- to 4-digit industry and county, annual State rpt series, 2326–8

Employment, earnings, and hours, by SIC 1- to 4-digit industry, monthly 1983-Feb 1989, annual rpt, 6744–4

Exports of US, detailed commodities by country, monthly rpt, 2422–3

Freight (waterborne domestic and foreign) by commodity, traffic, and passengers, by port and waterway, 1987, annual rpt, 3754–3

Health effects of hazardous substances, concentrations in environment, and household products composition, with data by selected location, 1988 hearings, 21408–112

Imports of US, detailed Schedule A commodities by country, monthly rpt, 2422–2

Manufacturers finances and operations, by SIC 2- to 4-digit industry, forecast 1989 and trends from 1950s, annual rpt, 2044–28

Manufacturing annual survey, 1986: financial and operating data, by SIC 2- to 4-digit industry, series, 2506–15

Manufacturing census, 1987: financial and operating data, for SIC 4-digit industries by product, preliminary rpt, 2491–1.38

Occupational injury and illness rates, by SIC 2- to 4-digit industry, 1987, annual rpt, 6844–1

Price indexes (producer), by stage of processing and detailed commodity, monthly rpt, 6762–6

Price indexes (producer), by stage of processing and detailed commodity, monthly 1988, annual rpt, 6764–2

Gunn, Robert A.

"State Epidemiology Programs and State Epidemiologists: Results of a National Study", 4042–3.914

Guns

see Firearms

see Military weapons

Gup, Benton E.

"Performance of De Novo Thrift Institutions: Risk, Return, and Charter Type", 9316–1.146

Guralnik, Jack M.

"Aging in the Eighties: The Prevalence of Comorbidity and Its Association with Disability", 4146–8.172

Guyana

Agricultural and food production and indexes, total and for selected commodities, by country, 1970s-88, annual rpt, 1524–12

Agricultural trade of US, by detailed commodity and country, 1988, semiannual rpt, 1522–4

AID activities and funding by project and function, FY90, and developing countries summary socioeconomic data from 1960s, annual rpt, 9904–4.7

AID economic aid to developing countries, obligations and disbursements by country, quarterly rpt, 9912–4

AID loans repayment status and terms by program and country, and status of predecessor agency loans, quarterly rpt, 9912–3

Background Notes, summary social, political, and economic data, 1989 rpt, 7006–2.30

Economic and military aid and loans from US and intl agencies, by program and country, FY46-87, annual rpt, 9914–5

Economic, social, political, and geographic summary data, by country, 1989, annual factbook, 9114–2

Human rights conditions in 170 countries, 1988, annual rpt, 21384–3

Labor conditions, union coverage, and work accidents, 1989 annual country rpt, 6366–4.39

Military aid of US, arms sales, and training programs costs and budget requests, by program, world region, and country, FY88-90, annual rpt, 7144–3

Military spending, arms trade, and force strengths, with govt spending and population, by country, 1977-87, annual rpt, 9824–1

Minerals Yearbook, 1987, Vol 3: foreign country reviews of production, trade, and policy, by commodity, annual rpt, 5604–35

Minerals Yearbook, 1987, Vol 3 preprints: foreign country review of production, trade, and policy, by commodity, annual rpt, 5604–23.87

Population size, growth rates, and components of change, by country, projected 1989-2020 and trends from 1950, biennial rpt, 2324–9

UN voting record and share of votes in agreement with US, by issue, country, and world area, 1988, annual rpt, 7004–18

see also under By Foreign Country in the "Index by Categories"

Guynes, Randall

"Difficult Clients, Large Caseloads Plague Probation, Parole Agencies", 6066–26.4

"Employee Drug-Testing Policies in Prison Systems", 6066–26.1

Gypsum

see Nonmetallic minerals and mines

Haanes-Olsen, Leif

"Worldwide Trends and Developments in Social Security, 1985-87", 4742–1.908

Habeas corpus

Court civil and criminal caseloads for Federal district, appeals, and special courts, June 1989, annual rpt, 18204–2; 18204–8

Deportation and exclusion cases, writs of habeas corpus, judicial review, and declaratory judgments, FY82-88, annual rpt, 6264–2

Executions by whether writ of habeas corpus used to appeal, race, and State, with military death row inmates, 1977-87, hearing, 21408–110

Prisoner petitions filed in Federal courts of appeals and district courts, by type of petition, circuit, and district, quarterly rpt, 18202–1

US attorneys case processing and collections, by case type and Federal district, FY88, annual rpt, 6004–2

Haber, Sheldon E.
"Training, Wage Growth, Firm Size", 2626–10.71

Hafer, R. W.
"Are National Stock Markets Linked?", 9391–1.901
"Comparing Futures and Survey Forecasts of Near-Term Treasury Bill Rates", 9391–1.914
"Does Dollar Depreciation Cause Inflation?", 9391–1.917
"Interest Rates and Economic Announcements", 9391–1.909

Hafnium
see Metals and metal industries

Hagemeyer, D.
"Occupational Radiation Exposure at Commercial Nuclear Power Reactors and Other Facilities, 1986", 9634–3

Hagerstown, Md.
see also under By SMSA or MSA in the "Index by Categories"

Hahn, Jerold T.
"Wisconsin's Forest Statistics, 1987: An Inventory Update", 1206–34.8

Hahn, Robert A.
"Chronic Disease Reports in the Morbidity and Mortality Weekly Report (MMWR)", 4206–2.10
"Ohio River Basin Navigation System 1988 Report", 3754–6

Hahn, William F.
"Estimating Forage Values for Grazing National Forest Lands", 1588–145

Haines, Pamela S.
"Eating Out: Who and Where", 1004–16.1

Hainly, Robert A.
"Suspended-Sediment Yields from an Unmined Area and from Mined Areas Before and After Reclamation in Pennsylvania, June 1978-September 1983", 5668–93

Haiti
Agricultural and food production and indexes, total and for selected commodities, by country, 1970s-88, annual rpt, 1524–12
Agricultural trade of US, by detailed commodity and country, 1988, semiannual rpt, 1522–4
AID activities and funding by project and function, FY90, and developing countries summary socioeconomic data from 1960s, annual rpt, 9904–4.7
AID economic aid to developing countries, obligations and disbursements by country, quarterly rpt, 9912–4
AID loans repayment status and terms by program and country, and status of predecessor agency loans, quarterly rpt, 9912–3
Aliens (illegal) enforcement activity of Coast Guard, by nationality, 2nd half FY89, semiannual rpt, 7402–4
Economic and military aid and loans from US and intl agencies, by program and country, FY46-87, annual rpt, 9914–5

Economic conditions, income, production, prices, employment, and trade, 1989 periodic country rpt, 2046–4.52
Economic conditions, policy, and trade practices, by country, 1986-88, annual rpt, 21384–5
Economic, social, political, and geographic summary data, by country, 1989, annual factbook, 9114–2
Exports and imports of US, by commodity and country, 1970-87, world area rpt, 9116–1.1
Exports and imports of US, by selected country, country group, and commodity group, 1988, annual rpt, 2044–37
Human rights conditions in 170 countries, 1988, annual rpt, 21384–3
Investment (direct) incentives of Caribbean Basin Initiative, economic impacts, with finances and employment by country, 1984-88, 2048–141
Military aid of US, arms sales, and training programs costs and budget requests, by program, world region, and country, FY88-90, annual rpt, 7144–13
Military spending, arms trade, and force strengths, with govt spending and population, by country, 1977-87, annual rpt, 9824–1
Minerals Yearbook, 1987, Vol 3: foreign country reviews of production, trade, and policy, by commodity, annual rpt, 5604–35
Minerals Yearbook, 1987, Vol 3 preprints: foreign country review of production, trade, and policy, by commodity, annual rpt, 5604–23.83
Population size, growth rates, and components of change, by country, projected 1989-2020 and trends from 1950, biennial rpt, 2324–9
Rum imports (duty-free) of US under Caribbean Basin Initiative, by country, 1987-88, annual rpt, 9884–15
UN voting record and share of votes in agreement with US, by issue, country, and world area, 1988, annual rpt, 7004–18
see also under By Foreign Country in the "Index by Categories"

Hakkio, Craig S.
"Exchange Rates in the 1980s", 9381–10.98

Hales, L. S.
"Spot. Species Profiles: Life Histories and Environmental Requirements of Coastal Fishes and Invertebrates (South Atlantic)", 5506–8.98

Haley, Stephen L.
"Evaluation of Export Enhancement, Dollar Depreciation, and Loan Rate Reduction for Wheat", 1548–351

Halfway houses
see Community-based correctional programs
see Group homes for the handicapped
see Sheltered workshops

Hall, Margaret J.
"Trends in Medicare Use of Post-Hospital Care", 4652–1.909

Hall, Mark W.
"Mali: A Country Profile", 9916–2.70

Haltmaier, Jane
"Use of Survey Data in Forecasting Business Fixed Investment", 9366–6.170

Hamak, J. E.
"Analyses of Natural Gases, 1988", 5604–2

Hamer, Thomas P.
"New Regional Economic Indicator: The Mid-Atlantic Manufacturing Index", 9387–1.901

Hamilton, Frederick, and Schneiders
"Survey of Americans' Attitudes Toward Air Travel", 21788–180

Hamilton, Milo C.
"Rice and Commodity Trading", 1004–16.1

Hamilton, Ohio
CPI by component for US city average, and by region, population size, and for 27 metro areas, monthly rpt, 6762–2
see also under By SMSA or MSA in the "Index by Categories"

Hamm, Shannon R.
"1989 Outlook for Vegetables", 1004–16.1

Hammett, Theodore M.
"1988 Update: AIDS in Correctional Facilities", 6064–22

Hammond, Ind.
see also under By SMSA or MSA in the "Index by Categories"

Hampton, Va.
see also under By City in the "Index by Categories"

Hanchar, John J.
"Irrigated Agriculture in the U.S.: State-Level Data", 1588–131

Hand tools
see Tools

Handbags
see Leather industry and products

Handedness
see Physical characteristics

Handicapped
see Architectural barriers to the handicapped
see Blind
see Deaf
see Disabled and handicapped persons
see Discrimination against the handicapped
see Group homes for the handicapped
see Handicapped children
see Mental retardation
see Mobility limitations
see Rehabilitation of the disabled

Handicapped children
Education data compilation, students, staff, finances, and facilities, 1989 edition, annual rpt, 4824–2
Education data, selected performance and financial indicators by State, 1982-88, annual table with supplements, 4804–32
Head Start handicapped enrollment, by handicap, State, and for Indian and migrant programs, 1985/86, annual rpt, 4604–1
Head Start program operations, enrollment by handicap, and family characteristics, for North Central States, 1987/88, annual rpt, 4604–12
Health care services for handicapped children, Fed Govt block grants, State and other funding, and children served, by State, FY87, GAO rpt, 26121–301
HHS financial aid, by program, recipient, State, and city, FY88, annual regional listings, 4004–3
Hispanic children with chronic illness, family characteristics and impact by English fluency, 1977 local area survey, article, 4042–3.936

Home health care and support services availability and need, for chronically ill children, 1988, GAO rpt, 26121–300

Home health care costs to families for care of handicapped and chronically ill children, literature review, 1978-85, article, 4042–3.912

Medicaid coverage of home care for chronically ill children, applications disposition under income waiver program, for Minnesota, 1985-87, article, 4042–3.944

Mental health care facilities, staff, and patient characteristics, *Statistical Notes* series, 4506–3

Mental health care hospitals of States and counties, patients and admissions by age, diagnosis, and State, FY87, annual rpt, 4504–2

Military reserve spouses attitudes, and family social, economic, and other characteristics, 1986 survey, 3508–30

Research contracts and grants of Natl Inst of Child Health and Human Dev, by recipient and location, FY88, annual listing, 4474–36

see also Birth defects

see also Old-Age, Survivors, Disability, and Health Insurance

see also Special education

see also Supplemental Security Income

Hanford Engineering Development Laboratory

see also Department of Energy National Laboratories

Hannan, Timothy H.

"Foundations of the Structure-Conduct-Performance Paradigm", 9366–6.197

"Impact of Bank Regulatory Requirements on Large Corporate Lending", 9366–6.177

"Impact of Technology Adoption on Market Structure", 9366–6.187

"Price Rigidity and Market Structure: Theory and Evidence from the Banking Industry", 9366–6.173

"Returns to Bidders and Targets in the Acquisition Process: Evidence from the Banking Industry", 9366–6.178

Hansen, Kristin A.

"Geographical Mobility: March 1986-March 1987", 2546–1.435

Hanson, Gregory D.

"Alternative Measures of Farm Output To Classify Farms by Size", 1548–344

"Farm Finance Outlook", 1004–16.1

Harbors and ports

Aliens admitted to US, by class of admission, port, country, and State of destination, quarterly rpt, 6262–2

Army Corps of Engineers activities and projects, FY87 and trends from 1800s, annual rpt, 3754–1.2

Army Corps of Engineers water resources dev projects, characteristics, and costs, 1950s-87, biennial State rpt series, 3756–2

Army Corps of Engineers water resources dev projects, characteristics, and costs, 1950s-89, biennial State rpt series, 3756–1

Asia port facilities, operations, and impacts on US agricultural exports, for major Far East ports, 1970s-87, 1278–13

Bunker fuel laden in US on vessels engaged in foreign trade, by fuel type and port, monthly rpt, 2422–5

Classification codes for countries and ports under Tariff Schedule of US, 1990 base edition and supplements, 9886–13

Coal production and freight costs, and competitive position in selected markets, for Australia and US, 1987-89, 2048–143

Coal production and stocks by district, and shipments by district of origin, State of destination, end-use sector, and mode of transport, quarterly rpt, 3162–8

Construction industries census, 1987: financial and operating data, preliminary industry rpt series, 2371–1

Containerized cargo carried over principal trade routes, by flag of vessel, port, and US coastal district, 1984, annual rpt, 7704–8

Customs collections, for top 15 ports, quarterly rpt, 8142–1

Developing countries disaster preparedness and economic, population, and political data, country rpt series, 9916–2

DOD shipments of military and personal property, passenger traffic, and costs, by service branch and mode of transport, quarterly rpt, 3702–1

Estuary environmental conditions and mgmt, for individual areas, conf series, 2146–6

Export statistics classification codes of Census Bur for countries, commodities, and customs districts, 1990 base edition, 2428–5

Exports and imports (agricultural) of US, by commodity, country, and US port, 1950s-89, annual rpt, 1924–9

Exports and imports (waterborne) of US, by type of service, commodity, country, route, and US port, 1986-87, annual rpt, 7704–2

Exports and imports (waterborne) of US, by type of service, customs district, port, and world area, monthly rpt, 2422–7

Exports and imports of US, by commodity group, world area, selected country, US coastal area and port, and mode of transport, monthly rpt, 2422–9

Fed Govt Harbor Maintenance Trust Fund financial condition, monthly rpt, 8102–9.12

Fed Govt-owned real property inventory and costs, worldwide summary by purpose, agency, and location, 1987, annual rpt, 9454–5

Fish and shellfish catch, wholesale receipts, prices, trade, and other market activities, weekly regional rpts, 2162–6

Fish catch, by species, use, region, State, and major port, 1970s-88, annual rpt, 2164–1.1

Foreign countries economic, social, political, and geographic summary data, by country, 1989, annual factbook, 9114–2

Foreign countries ports accessible to tankers of 200,000 tons and larger, by country, Jan 1989, annual rpt, 9114–4.10

Freight (waterborne domestic), by major commodity group, vessel type, and port, 1986, annual rpt, 7704–7

Freight (waterborne domestic and foreign) by commodity, traffic, and passengers, by port and waterway, 1987, annual rpt, 3754–3

Govt employment and payroll, by function, level of govt, and jurisdiction, 1987-88, annual rpt series, 2466–1

Grain shipments by rail, by commodity and port region, and car fleet requirements, 1949-88 with projections to 2001, 1278–14

Immigration to US, alien workers, visitors, deportations, and naturalizations, by country, FY88 and trends from 1820, annual rpt, 6264–2

Navy nuclear-powered vessels and support facilities radioactive waste, releases in harbors, and public exposure, 1970s-88, annual rpt, 3804–11

Ohio River basin waterway facilities, freight by commodity and port, and recreation, by waterway, 1986-87, annual rpt, 3754–6

Pacific territories and Hawaii harbor traffic, facilities, dev, funding, and needs, by port, as of 1987, 7308–195

Pollutant concentrations in coastal and estuarine sediments, by contaminant and selected site, 1984-87, 2176–3.7

Pollutant concentrations in coastal and estuarine shellfish, by pollutant and location, 1986-88, 2176–3.8

Pollution (water) incidents and discharges, by type, source, cause, and location, 1984-86, annual rpt, 7404–3

St Lawrence Seaway ship, cargo, and passenger traffic, and toll revenue, 1988 and trends from 1959, annual rpt, 7744–2

Tidal currents, daily time and velocity by station for North America and Asia coasts, forecast 1990, annual rpts, 2174–1

Tide height and time daily at coastal points worldwide, forecast 1990, annual rpt series, 2174–2

Workers compensation programs under Federal admin, finances and operations, FY87, annual rpt, 6504–10

see also Dredging

Hardig, Jan

"Long-Term Effects of Bleached Kraft Mill Effluents on Red and White Blood Cell Status, Ion Balance, and Vertebral Structure in Fish", 21368–112

Hardt, John P.

"Soviet Trade from Brezhnev's Stagnation to Gorbachev's Interdependence", 21248–120

Hardware

County Business Patterns, 1987: employment, establishments, and payroll, by SIC 2- to 4-digit industry and county, annual State rpt series, 2326–8

CPI by component for US city average, and by region, population size, and for 27 metro areas, monthly rpt, 6762–2

DOD prime contract awards, by detailed procurement category, FY85-88, annual rpt, 3544–18

Employment, earnings, and hours, by selected SIC 1- to 4-digit industry, State, and for 262 MSAs, 1972-87, 6748–81

Employment, earnings, and hours, by SIC 1- to 4-digit industry, monthly 1983-Feb 1989, annual rpt, 6744–4

Exports of US, detailed commodities by country, monthly rpt, 2422–3

Imports of US, detailed Schedule A commodities by country, monthly rpt, 2422–2

Injuries from use of consumer products and related activities, by victim age and sex, 1988, annual rpt, 9164–7

Injuries from use of consumer products, by severity, victim age, and detailed product, 1988, annual rpt, 9164–6

Locks (residential door) from Taiwan at less than fair value, injury to US industry, investigation with background financial and operating data, 1989 rpt, 9886–14.264

Manufacturing annual survey, 1986: financial and operating data, by SIC 2- to 4-digit industry, series, 2506–15

Manufacturing census, 1987: financial and operating data, for SIC 4-digit industries by product, preliminary rpt, 2491–1.55; 2491–1.58; 2491–1.60

Occupational injury and illness rates, by SIC 2- to 4-digit industry, 1987, annual rpt, 6844–1

Price indexes (producer), by stage of processing and detailed commodity, monthly rpt, 6762–6

Price indexes (producer), by stage of processing and detailed commodity, monthly 1988, annual rpt, 6764–2

Retail trade census, 1987: employment, establishments, sales, and payroll, by SIC 2- to 4-digit kind of business, MSA, county, and city, State rpt series, 2397–1

Retail trade sales and inventories, by kind of business, region, and selected State, MSA, and city, monthly rpt, 2413–3

Retail trade sales, by kind of business, advance monthly rpt, 2413–2

Retail trade sales, inventories, purchases, gross margin, and accounts receivable, by SIC 2- to 4-digit kind of business and form of ownership, 1987, annual rpt, 2413–5

Science, engineering, and technical employment in manufacturing, by field, occupation, and industry, 1986, triennial rpt, 9627–23

Science, engineering, and technical employment in transportation, utilities, and retail and wholesale trade, by field, occupation, and industry, 1985, triennial rpt, 9627–32

Shipments and PPI for building materials, by type, bimonthly rpt, 2042–1.5; 2042–1.6

Tax (income) returns of corporations, income and tax items by asset size and detailed industry, 1986, annual rpt, 8304–4

Transportation census, 1987: trucks, by detailed characteristics, miles traveled, and type of product carried, State rpt series, 2573–1

Wholesale trade census, 1987: employment, establishments, finances, and operations, by SIC 2- to 4-digit kind of business, MSA, county, and city, State rpt series, 2405–1

Wholesale trade sales and inventories, by SIC 2- to 3-digit kind of business, monthly rpt, 2413–7

Wholesale trade sales, inventories, purchases, and gross margins, by SIC 2- to 3-digit kind of business and form of ownership, 1988, annual rpt, 2413–13

see also Tools
see also under By Commodity in the "Index by Categories"

Hardy, Ann M.
"AIDS Knowledge and Attitudes of Black Americans. Provisional Data from the 1988 National Health Interview Survey", 4146–8.167
"AIDS Knowledge and Attitudes of Hispanic Americans. Provisional Data from the 1988 National Health Interview Survey", 4146–8.168
"AIDS Knowledge and Attitudes. Provisional Data from the National Health Interview Survey", 4146–8.169; 4146–8.173; 4146–8.180
"Current Estimates from the National Health Interview Survey, 1988", 4147–10.170

Hargett, Norman L.
"1988 Fertilizer Summary Data", 9804–5

Hargroves, Jeannette S.
"Basic Skills Crisis: One Bank Looks at Its Training Investment", 9373–1.918

Harlan, William R.
"Health Care Utilization and Costs of Adult Cardiovascular Conditions U.S., 1980", 4146–12.26

Harlingen, Tex.
see also under By SMSA or MSA in the "Index by Categories"

Harlow, Caroline W.
"Injuries from Crime", 6066–19.49

Harper, Michael J.
"Rates of Return and Capital Aggregation Using Alternative Rental Prices", 6886–6.39

Harper, Robert G., III
"Comparisons of Independent Statistics on Petroleum Supply", 3162–6.903

Harris, Ethan S.
"Monetary Policy Influence on the Economy: An Empirical Analysis", 9385–9

Harris, Louis, and Associates, Inc.
"Health, Information and the Use of Questionable Treatments: A Study of the American Public", 4008–86

Harris, Walter M.
"Federal Offshore Statistics: 1987, Leasing, Exploration, Production, and Revenues", 5734–3

Harrisburg, Pa.
see also under By SMSA or MSA in the "Index by Categories"

Harry S. Truman Scholarship Foundation
see Truman, Harry S., Scholarship Foundation

Hartford, Conn.
see also under By City and By SMSA or MSA in the "Index by Categories"

Hartmann, Heidi
"Employment of Mothers and the Prevention of Poverty", 2626–10.76

Hartmann, Holly C.
"Potential Variation of Great Lakes Water Levels: A Hydrologic Response Analysis", 2148–59

Hartwell, Steven
"Alternative Dispute Resolution in a Bankruptcy Court: The Mediation Program in the Southern District of California", 18408–40

Harvey, James
"Highly Leveraged Bank Holding Companies and Subsidiary Bank Performance", 9381–14.1

Harwood, Joy L.
"Federal Crop Insurance for Wheat: An Assessment of Program Options", 1561–12.903
"Trade Liberalization in the World Wheat Market", 1561–12.905
"Wheat: Background for 1990 Farm Legislation", 1566–7.7

Hasan, Iftekhar
"More Branching Is Increasing Competition for the Florida Thrift Industry", 9302–2.907

Haslag, Joseph H.
"Asymmetric Information and the Role of Fed Watching", 9379–12.35
"Evidence on the Two Monetary Base Measures and Economic Activity", 9379–12.32
"Federal Reserve System Reserve Requirements: 1959–88, A Note", 9379–12.36
"Macroeconomic Policy and Income Inequality: An Error-Correction Representation", 9379–12.41
"Nominal GNP Growth and Adjusted Reserve Growth: Nonnested Tests of the St. Louis and Board Measures", 9379–12.46
"Reserve Requirements, the Monetary Base, and Economic Activity", 9379–1.903

Hassler, Thomas J.
"Brown Rockfish, Copper Rockfish, and Black Rockfish. Species Profiles: Life Histories and Environmental Requirements of Coastal Fishes and Invertebrates (Pacific Southwest)", 5506–8.120
"Pile Perch, Striped Seaperch, and Rubberlip Seaperch. Species Profiles: Life Histories and Environmental Requirements of Coastal Fishes and Invertebrates (Pacific Southwest)", 5506–8.110
"Pismo Clam. Species Profiles: Life Histories and Environmental Requirements of Coastal Fishes and Invertebrates", 5506–8.102

Hastings, Nebr.
Wages by occupation, for office and plant workers, 1989 survey, periodic MSA rpt, 6785–3.10

Haugen, Steven E.
"Employment Gains Slow in the First Half of 1989", 6722–1.937

Havas, Stephen
"Report of the New England Task Force on Reducing Heart Disease and Stroke Risk", 4042–3.909

Haverhill, Mass.
see also under By SMSA or MSA in the "Index by Categories"

Hawaii
Agriculture census, 1987: farms, farmland, production and costs, and operator characteristics, advance State and county rpts, 2330–1.15
Agriculture census, 1987: farms, farmland, production, finances, and operator characteristics, by county, final State rpt, 2331–1.11
Asian American earnings, and employment and other characteristics, by detailed origin and whether foreign-born, 1980, 11046–7.2

Bank deposits in FDIC-insured commercial and savings banks, by instn, State, and county, as of June 1988, annual regional rpt, 9295–3.6

Census of Population and Housing, 1990: outlying areas preparations for count, hearings, 21628–74

County Business Patterns, 1987: employment, establishments, and payroll, by SIC 2- to 4-digit industry and county, annual State rpt, 2326–8.13

Deaths and rates, by detailed location, cause, and demographic characteristics, 1987, US Vital Statistics annual rpt, 4144–3.1

DOD civilian and military personnel and dependents, by service branch and US and foreign location, quarterly rpt, 3542–20

DOD prime contract awards, by contractor, service branch, State, and city, FY88, annual rpt, 3544–22

Employment, earnings, and hours, by selected SIC 1- to 4-digit industry, State, and for 262 MSAs, 1972-87, 6748–81.1

Fed Govt spending in States and local areas, by type, State, county, and city, FY88, annual rpt, 2464–3

Fed Govt spending in States, by type, program, agency, and State, FY88, annual rpt, 2464–2

Freight (waterborne domestic and foreign) by commodity, traffic, and passengers, by port and waterway, 1987, annual rpt, 3754–3.4

Ginger acreage and production in Hawaii, 1977-88, FAS annual circular, 1925–15.1

Harbor traffic, facilities, dev, funding, and needs, for Pacific territories and Hawaii by port, as of 1987, 7308–195

HHS financial aid, by program, recipient, State, and city, FY88, annual regional listing, 4004–3.9

Income (personal) per capita and by source, and earnings by industry div, by State, MSA, and county, 1982-87, annual regional rpt, 2704–2.5

Libraries (public) services for Indians and Hawaii Natives, project listing and funding by tribe and State, FY88 rpt, 4874–5

Mineral Industry Surveys, State reviews of production, 1988, preliminary annual rpt, 5614–6

Minerals Yearbook, 1987, Vol 2 preprints: State review of production and sales by commodity, and business activity, annual rpt, 5604–16.12

Minerals Yearbook, 1987, Vol 2: State reviews of production, sales, and firms, by commodity, and business activity, annual rpt, 5604–34

Nursing home compliance with Medicare and Medicaid regulations, and patient characteristics, by facility, 1987/88, annual State rpt, 4654–15.12

Retail trade census, 1987: employment, establishments, sales, and payroll, by SIC 2- to 4-digit kind of business, MSA, county, and city, State rpt, 2397–1.12

Savings instns, FHLB 12th District members deposits and lending, monthly press release, 9302–32.3

Service industries census, 1987: employment, establishments, receipts, and payroll, by SIC 2- to 4-digit kind of business, MSA, county, and city, State rpt, 2391–1.12

Statistical Abstract of US, social, political, and economic data, with foreign comparisons, 1790-2025, comprehensive annual compilation, 2324–1

Telecommunication domestic and overseas rates, by type of service and area served, various dates 1988, annual rpt, 9284–6.6

Tide height and time daily at coastal points, forecast 1990, annual rpt, 2174–2.2

Tsunamis intensity, time, location, and other characteristics, for US and territories, 1690-1988, 2158–52

Water supply and quality in streams and lakes, and groundwater levels in wells, by drainage basin, 1987, annual State rpt, 5666–10.10

Waterborne commerce (domestic) of US, freight by major commodity group, vessel type, and port, 1986, annual rpt, 7704–7

Wholesale trade census, 1987: employment, establishments, and operations, by SIC 2- to 4-digit kind of business, MSA, county, and city, State rpt, 2405–1.12

Wildlife-related recreation, hunting, and fishing participation and spending, detailed data, 1985 survey, quinquennial State rpt, 5506–6.11

see also Honolulu, Hawaii

see also under By State in the "Index by Categories"

Hay

see Animal feed

see Pasture and rangeland

Hay Group

"Comparison of Compensation of Research and Development Scientists and Engineers, DOE Laboratories Compared to National Survey, Jan. 15, 1989 Data", 3004–9

"1989 National Compensation Survey of Research and Development Scientists and Engineers, Final Report", 3004–1

Hayghe, Howard V.

"Children in 2-Worker Families and Real Family Income", 6722–1.963

Hayward, Becky J.

"Handicapped and Disadvantaged Students: Access to Quality Vocational Education. National Assessment of Vocational Education", 4806–3.6

Hayward, Calif.

see also under By City in the "Index by Categories"

Hazard, John W.

"Forest Survey Methods Used in the USDA Forest Service", 9188–110

Hazardous substances

Burns (chemical) occupational injury, by body site, circumstances, and characteristics of persons and equipment involved, 1985 survey, 6846–1.19

Criminal cases by type and disposition, and collections, for US attorneys, by Federal district, FY88, annual rpt, 6004–2.1

Criminal sentences for Federal offenses, guidelines by offense and circumstances, 1989 rpt, 17668–1

Exposure limits for hazardous substances, Occupational Safety and Health Admin regulations, 1989, press release, 6606–3.8

Fed Govt spending in States, by type, program, agency, and State, FY88, annual rpt, 2464–2

Fish hazardous substances toxicity levels, by detailed compound, 1989 rpt, 9238–68; 9238–69

Health effects of hazardous substances, concentrations in environment, and household products composition, with data by selected location, 1988 hearings, 21408–112

Health effects of selected pollutants, concentrations in food and environment, sources, and human intake, methodology and data needs, series, 9186–9

Health effects of selected pollutants, concentrations in food and environment, sources, human intake, and regulation, series, 9186–8

HHS financial aid, by program, recipient, State, and city, FY88, annual regional listings, 4004–3

Industrial hazardous substances releases and reduction methods under EPA regulation, by chemical, source, industry, and location, 1987, annual rpt, 9234–6

Injuries from use of consumer products and related activities, by victim age and sex, 1988, annual rpt, 9164–7

Nicotine and other chemicals in tobacco and cigarette smoke, literature review, 1988 annual rpt, 4204–18

Nicotine, tar, and carbon monoxide content of cigarettes, by brand, 1988, 9408–53

Occupational exposure to hazardous substances and conditions, and prevention and control measures, 1981-83 survey, 4248–86

Occupational illness rates, by cause and SIC 2- to 3-digit industry, 1987, annual rpt, 6844–1

Research and testing activities under Natl Toxicology Program, FY87 and planned FY88, annual rpt, 4044–16

Tax (excise) collections of IRS, by source, quarterly rpt, 8302–1

see also Air pollution

see also Asbestos contamination

see also Carcinogens

see also Dioxins

see also Hazardous substances transport

see also Hazardous waste and disposal

see also Inflammable materials

see also Lead poisoning and pollution

see also Marine pollution

see also Mercury pollution

see also Motor vehicle exhaust

see also Pesticides

see also Poisoning and drug reaction

see also Product safety

see also Radiation

see also Radioactive materials

see also Radioactive waste and disposal

see also Radon

see also Soil pollution

see also Trace metals

see also Water pollution

Hazardous substances transport

Accidents, casualties, and property damage involving hazardous substances, by mode of transport, with DOT control activities, 1988, annual rpt, 7304–4

Airport security inspections of hazardous cargo, enforcement actions, 1st half 1988, semiannual rpt, 7502–5

DOT activities by subagency, budget, and summary accident data, FY85, annual rpt, 7304–1

Great Lakes toxic spills and human error, with data by pollutant source and site, 1984-86, conf, 14648–21

Industrial hazardous substances releases and reduction methods under EPA regulation, by chemical, source, industry, and location, 1987, annual rpt, 9234-6

Pipeline accidents, casualties, safety enforcement activity, and Federal funding, by State, 1987, annual rpt, 7304-5

Radioactive waste (military) disposal at New Mexico Waste Isolation Pilot Plant, environmental impacts, 1989 supplemental statement, 3008-33

Radioactive waste and spent fuel generation, inventory, and disposal, 1960s-88 and projected to 2020, annual rpt, 3364-2

Radioactive waste from nuclear power plants, releases and waste composition by plant, 1986, annual rpt, 9634-1

Railroad accidents and cars releasing hazardous materials, and persons evacuated, for Pennsylvania and US, 1984-87, GAO rpt, 26113-390

Railroad accidents, casualties, and damage, Fed Railroad Admin activities, and safety inspectors by State, 1987, annual rpt, 7604-12

Railroad accidents, casualties, and Federal safety activities, late 1970s-87, hearing, 21368-103

Railroad accidents, circumstances, severity, and railroad involved, periodic rpt, 9612-3

Railroad accidents involving hazardous materials, damage, and persons evacuated, by cause, railroad, and State, 1988, annual rpt, 7604-1

Railroad freight volume and revenue, by commodity and region of origin and destination, 1987, annual rpt, 7604-6

Railroad safety violation claims settled, by carrier, FY88, annual rpt, 7604-10

Shipborne commerce (domestic and foreign) of US, freight by commodity, traffic, and passengers, by port and waterway, 1987, annual rpt, 3754-3

Traffic accident impacts of speed limits, with accident circumstances and speed averages, for States with 55 and 65 mph limit, 1986-87, annual rpt, 7764-15

Transportation census, 1987: trucks, by detailed characteristics, miles traveled, and type of product carried, State rpt series, 2573-1

Water pollution incidents and discharges, by type, source, cause, and location, 1984-86, annual rpt, 7404-3

Hazardous waste and disposal

Budget of US, Reagan Admin policy changes by program, FY90, annual rpt, 104-21

Coal ash contaminant levels, removal, EPA toxicity standards, and State disposal laws, 1988 rpt, 2048-140

Coastal areas environmental impacts of economic dev and population growth, 1980s and projected to 2000, 2176-8.1

Environmental quality and protection programs, and intl issues, 1988 annual rpt, 484-1

EPA pollution control grant program activities, monthly rpt, 9182-8

Fed Govt financial and nonfinancial domestic aid, 1989 base edition with supplements, annual listing, 104-5

Health care facilities medical waste disposal, hospital incinerator emissions, and regulation, 1988 rpt, 26358-198

HHS financial aid, by program, recipient, State, and city, FY88, annual regional listings, 4004-3

Industrial hazardous substances releases and reduction methods under EPA regulation, by chemical, source, industry, and location, 1987, annual rpt, 9234-6

Insurance (liability) for hazardous waste treatment sites, costs and availability, and reasons for site closure, 1982-87, GAO rpt, 26131-54

Mgmt of hazardous waste, effectiveness of alternative technologies, 1989 conf papers, biennial rpt, 9184-19

Military installations hazardous waste site remedial action, activities and funding by site and State, FY88, annual rpt, 3544-36

Pollutant ozone levels, urban areas failure to meet natl standards, emissions sources, exposure, and costs and benefits of reduction strategies, 1983-87 and projected to 2004, 26358-203

Superfund financial condition, monthly rpt, 8102-9.6

Superfund hazardous waste site remedial action, current and proposed sites descriptions and status, periodic listings, series, 9216-3

Superfund hazardous waste site remedial action, current and proposed sites priority ranking and status by location, as of July 1989, listing, 9218-64

Superfund hazardous waste site remedial action, deadlines and compliance of govts and businesses, as of Mar 1989, GAO rpt, 26113-394

Superfund hazardous waste site remedial action, enforcement, spending, and cost recovery, 1986-88, GAO rpt, 26113-386

Tax (excise) collections of IRS, by source, quarterly rpt, 8302-2.1

Water (groundwater) pollution from soil injection of oil and gas refining wastes, by State, 1987, GAO rpt, 26113-429

see also Radioactive waste and disposal

Head Start Project

Demonstration program grants under Head Start Project, by recipient, 1985, 4608-25

Dental caries among Indian children from bottle feeding, prevention project effectiveness, 1985-89, article, 4042-3.961

Enrollment, funding, and staff for Head Start, FY88, annual rpt, 4604-8

Expenditures for program, by recipient agency and location, FY88, annual regional listings, 4004-3

Handicapped children enrollment in Head Start, by handicap, State, and for Indian and migrant programs, 1985/86, annual rpt, 4604-1

North Central States Head Start program operations, enrollment by handicap, and family characteristics, by State, 1987/88, annual rpt, 4604-12

Health care costs

see Medical costs

Health Care Financing Administration

Budget of US Appendix, obligations, appropriations, and personnel, by program and agency, FY90, annual rpt, 104-3

Data projects and systems of HHS, by subagency, FY88, 4008-92

Financial aid of HHS, by program, recipient, State, and city, FY88, annual regional listings, 4004-3

Health Care Financing Review, quarterly journal, 4652-1

Health care use and costs, methodology and findings of natl survey and Medicare and Medicaid records, 1980, series, 4146-12

Health maintenance organization Medicare enrollees, reimbursement and other characteristics by plan, and compared to fee-for-service, mid-1980s, 4658-31

Hospital reimbursement by States under prospective payment programs, effects on operations, finances, and patient deaths, by State, 1970s-83, 4658-29

Kidney end-stage disease treatment facilities approved by Medicare, dialysis and transplant services and ownership, 1989 annual listing, 4654-17

Kidney end-stage disease treatment facilities, Medicare enrollment and reimbursement, survival, and patient characteristics, 1980-86, annual rpt, 4654-16

Labs (clinical) under HCFA regulation, and labs with violations by Medicare termination and license status, 1983-87, hearings, 25408-98

Malpractice insurance premium costs and growth rate for physicians, alternative estimates by risk class and State, 1975-85, 4658-27

Medicare admin, finances, and activities of end-stage renal disease and accreditation programs, annual rpt, discontinued, 4654-5

Medicare and Medicaid beneficiaries and program operations, 1988, annual fact book, 4654-18

Medicare and Medicaid eligibility, participation, coverage, and program finances, various periods 1966-89, biennial rpt, 4654-1

Medicare enrollees health care alternatives, medical costs, training to select assigned-fee physicians, and physician attitudes, 1988 rpt, 4658-30

Medicare enrollment, and use by type of service, by age, sex, race, region, State, and MSA, 1986-87, annual rpt, 4657-5

Medicare hospital claims processing under contract, HCFA controls adequacy and payment errors, 1985-88, GAO rpt, 26121-260

Medicare peer review organizations review of hospital claims, activities, and membership, 1984-88, GAO rpt, 26131-51

Medicare reimbursement of hospitals under prospective payment system, impacts on instns, beneficiaries, and other care providers and payment sources, 1986, annual rpt, 4654-13

Medicare trust funds finances, various periods 1966-88 and projected to 1992, annual rpt, 4654-12

Medicare trust funds finances, 1966-88 and alternative projections to 1991, annual rpt, 4654-11

Medicare trust funds finances, 1987 and projected to 2062, annual rpt, 4654-8

Nursing home and home care case mix, quality of care, and outcomes, impacts of Medicare prospective payment system, 1980s-86, 4658-28

Nursing home compliance with Medicare and Medicaid regulations, and patient characteristics, by facility, 1987/88, annual State rpt series, 4654-15

Older persons aid and policies of Fed Govt, program funding, and grants awarded, FY80-89, annual rpt, 25144-3.2

Research activities and grants of HCFA, by program, as of Mar 1989, annual listing, 4654-10

Research and evaluation programs of HHS, 1970-FY87, annual listing, 4004-30

Health condition

Army personnel health condition, and use of Army medical services in US and abroad by personnel, retirees, and dependents, monthly rpt, 3702-4

Aviation medicine research and test results, technical rpt series, 7506-10

Birthweight relation to child health condition, indicators for low and normal weight by age, sex, mothers education, and race, 1981, article, 4042-3.904

Data coverage and availability for health care resources geographic info system, 1989 rpt, 4118-61

Data on health condition and health care resources, use, and spending, 1950s-86, annual data compilation, 4144-11

Data on health condition and quality of life measures, rpts and other info sources, quarterly listing, 4122-1

Developing countries aged population and selected characteristics, 1980s and projected to 2020, country rpt series, 2326-19

Drugs (prescription) use and spending by Medicare beneficiaries, by selected characteristics, 1987, 4186-8.3

Expenditures for health care, effects of health condition and prior services use, 1974-82 study, article, 4652-1.931

Hazardous substances health effects, environmental levels, and household products composition, with data by selected location, 1988 hearings, 21408-112

Health care services needs, delivery, and costs, series, 4186-9

Health care use and costs, methodology and findings of natl survey and Medicare and Medicaid records, 1980, series, 4146-12

Health condition improvement and disease prevention goals and recommended activities for 2000, with trends 1970s-80s, 4048-10

Health maintenance organization enrollment of Medicare enrollees, services use, charges, and survival, compared to fee-for-service, 1980-82 study, article, 4652-1.904

Health maintenance organization Medicare enrollees, reimbursement and other characteristics by plan, and compared to fee-for-service, mid-1980s, 4658-31

Homeless population characteristics, needs, and impacts of govt aid programs and housing costs, 1988 conf papers, 10048-73

Indian Health Service facilities, funding, operations, and Indian health and other characteristics, 1950s-88, annual chartbook, 4084-1

Indian housing condition and other characteristics, for aged, 1987 survey, 21148-53

Indian reservation water supply projects in South Dakota, costs and indicators of need, with health and housing data for other reservations, 1980s-87, hearing, 21448-37

Labor force health condition, disability days, health services use, and disease prevalence, by occupation and sex, 1983-85, 4146-8.170

Lead poisoning among children, and impacts of lead removal from housing, gasoline, and water, 1987 conf, 4108-46

Medicare enrollees health care alternatives, medical costs, training to select assigned-fee physicians, and physician attitudes, 1988 rpt, 4658-30

Medicare enrollees hospital readmissions related to selected characteristics, for Michigan, 1982-83, article, 4652-1.903

Medicare reimbursement of hospitals under prospective payment system, and of physicians, effect on services, finances, and beneficiary payments, 1970s-88, annual rpt, 17204-2

Mexican American high school dropouts health condition, substance abuse, and involvement with violence, 1988-89 survey, article, 4042-3.957

Military personnel alcohol and drug abuse, prevalence and consequences, by selected characteristics, 1988, biennial rpt, 3504-19

Military personnel health-related behavior, for 7 habits, by age, education, race, and health status, 1985 survey, article, 4042-3.949

Mormons death risks from cancer and heart disease, by sex and health habits practiced, 1974 and 1979 studies, article, 4472-1.932

Nursing home and home care case mix, quality of care, and outcomes, impacts of Medicare prospective payment system, 1980s-86, 4658-28

Nursing home facility, staff, and resident detailed characteristics, 1985, 4147-13.97

Nursing home rehabilitation services use, by service type and patient characteristics, 1st qtr 1983, 4188-58

Older persons health care services use, persons with high and low levels of care by selected health and other characteristics, 1971 and 1980 studies, 4186-2.22

Older persons health care services use related to marital status, living arrangements, and other characteristics, 1977, 4188-54

Older persons socioeconomic characteristics, 1900s-86 and projected to 2050, biennial chartbook, 12904-1

Pneumonia hospitalization and death rates for aged, and risk relation to health status indicators, aggregate 1982-84, article, 4042-3.934

Public Health Reports, bimonthly journal, 4042-3

Research methods and design of health surveys, 1989 conf proceedings, 4188-60

Statistical Abstract of US, social, political, and economic data, 1790-2025, comprehensive annual compilation, 2324-1.1

Treatments and health products not proven safe or effective, use, costs, and user characteristics, 1986 survey, 4008-86

Uranium tailings at inactive mills, remedial action proposals, costs, site characteristics, and environmental, socioeconomic, and health impacts, series, 3356-4

Veterans population, and benefits programs awareness and use, by age, sex, income, race, and period of service, 1987 survey, 8608-1

Vital and Health Statistics series: advance data rpts, 4146-8

Vital and Health Statistics series and other NCHS rpts, 1980-88, annual listing, 4124-1

Vital and Health Statistics series: foreign and US comparative data, 4147-5

Vital and Health Statistics series: health condition and body measurements, Natl Health and Nutrition Examination Survey results, 4147-11

Vital and Health Statistics series: health condition, medical costs, and use of facilities and services, 4147-10

Vital and Health Statistics series: reprints of advance data rpts, 4147-16

see also Absenteeism

see also Dental condition

see also Disabled and handicapped persons

see also Diseases and disorders

see also Handicapped children

see also Hospitalization

see also Medical examinations and tests

see also Mental health and illness

see also Mobility limitations

see also Nutrition and malnutrition

see also Obesity

see also Occupational health and safety

see also Vital statistics

Health Economics Research, Inc.

"Estimates of Hospital Industry Total Factor Productivity for the Period 1980-86", 17206-2.1

Health education

AIDS cases in prisons, test results, and prevention and control policies, by location, 1988 survey, annual rpt, 6064-22

AIDS info brochure of Surgeon General, public views by age, sex, race, education, and income, 1988 survey, 4042-3.908

AIDS prevention education in schools, Fed Govt funding, FY88, annual rpt, 6064-11

AIDS public knowledge, attitudes, info sources, and testing, for blacks, 1988 survey, 4146-8.167

AIDS public knowledge, attitudes, info sources, and testing, for Hispanics, 1988 survey, 4146-8.168

AIDS public knowledge, attitudes, info sources, and testing, 1988 survey, 4146-8.165; 4146-8.169; 4146-8.173

AIDS public knowledge, attitudes, info sources, and testing, 1989 survey, 4146-8.176; 4146-8.180

Assistance (financial and nonfinancial) of Fed Govt, 1989 base edition with supplements, annual listing, 104-5

Cancer (cervical) screening and education program for black women, effectiveness and participant characteristics, 1988 local area study, article, 4042-3.953

by selected health and other characteristics, 1971 and 1980 studies, 4186–2.22

Ophthalmologist office visits, by characteristics of physician, practice, patient, and visit, with drug mentions by type and brand, 1985, 4146–8.166

Statistical Abstract of US, social, political, and economic data, 1790-2025, comprehensive annual compilation, 2324–1.1

Health occupations

AIDS and hepatitis B transmission to health care and public safety workers, CDC prevention guidelines, 1989 rpt, 4206–2.15

Army health care personnel and accession goals, by race and sex, 1985-88, annual rpt, 3704–10.1

Community and migrant health services finances, operations, and staff, series, 4108–45

Data coverage and availability for health care resources geographic info system, 1989 rpt, 4118–61

Data on health condition and health care resources, use, and spending, 1950s-87, annual data compilation, 4144–11

DOD budget, manpower needs, costs, and force readiness by service branch, FY90, annual rpt, 3504–1

Drug and alcohol abuse treatment facilities, services, use, funding, and client characteristics, 1987, annual rpt, 4494–10

Educational and research grants and contracts of Health Professions Bur, by instn and program, FY88, annual listing, 4114–1

Employment and occupation of householder, by occupation of spouse, race, and family composition, 1988, annual Current Population Rpt, 2546–1.437

Employment Cost Index and alternative measure of compensation costs, by component, occupation, industry group, union status, and location, 1975-89, annual rpt, 6744–20

Employment in nonmanufacturing industries, by detailed occupation and SIC 2-digit industry, 1987, triennial rpt, 6748–60

Employment, unemployment, and labor force characteristics, by region and census div, 1988, annual rpt, 6744–7.1

Environmental and occupational health care personnel supply and needs, by field, 1987 conf, 4118–65

Handbook of Labor Statistics, employment, unemployment, and labor force characteristics, 1940s-88 with trends from 1913, 6728–38

Hepatitis cases by infection source, age, sex, race, and State, and deaths, by strain, 1987 and trends from 1966, 4205–2

HHS financial aid, by program, recipient, State, and city, FY88, annual regional listings, 4004–3

Hospital labor and total factor productivity, with background data, 1980-86, article, 4652–1.941

Licensing and discipline of health professionals by State medical boards, 1950s-87, series, 4006–8

Military health care personnel, and accessions by training source, by occupation, specialty, and service branch, FY87, annual rpt, 3544–24

Nursing home facility, staff, and resident detailed characteristics, 1985, 4147–13.97

Pacific territories social, economic, health, and govtl data, FY88 and trends, annual rpt, 7004–6

Radiation exposure of Federal employees, by age, occupation, and selected agency, 1986-87, biennial rpt, 4064–15

Statistical Abstract of US, social, political, and economic data, 1790-2025, comprehensive annual compilation, 2324–1.1

VA health care employment and average salary, by pay system and occupational group, 1988, annual rpt, 9844–6

VA health care employment, work-years, pay rates, and benefits use and costs, by agency, FY87, annual rpt, 9844–31

VA health care personnel born abroad, and English proficiency, as of Mar 1988, GAO rpt, 26121–273

VA health care personnel pay rates, by pay schedule and grade, 1989, annual rpt, 21624–4

VA Medicine and Surgery Dept trainees, by detailed program and city, FY88, annual rpt, 8704–4

VA pay comparability with private industry, and recommended pay rate adjustments, 1989, annual rpt, 104–16

Vital and Health Statistics series: health care facilities manpower and resources, 4147–14

Vital and Health Statistics series: health care facilities use and labor force, 4147–13

Wages of hospital workers relation to supervisory levels and other factors, 1985, working paper, 9377–9.79

see also Allied health personnel

see also Anesthesiology

see also Chiropractic and naturopathy

see also Clinical laboratory technicians

see also Dentists and dentistry

see also Dietitians and nutritionists

see also Epidemiology and epidemiologists

see also Foreign medical graduates

see also Geriatrics

see also Health facilities administration

see also Medical education

see also Midwives

see also Nuclear medicine and radiology

see also Nurses and nursing

see also Obstetrics and gynecology

see also Occupational therapy

see also Optometry

see also Orthopedics

see also Osteopathy

see also Pathology

see also Pediatrics

see also Pharmacists and pharmacy

see also Physical therapy

see also Physicians

see also Podiatry

see also Psychiatry

see also Respiratory therapy

see also Social work

see also Speech pathology and audiology

see also Surgeons and surgery

see also Veterinary medicine

see also under Medicine and terms beginning with Medical

Health of workers

see Absenteeism

see Occupational health and safety

Health planning and evaluation

AIDS cases in prisons, test results, and prevention and control policies, by location, 1988 survey, annual rpt, 6064–22

Assistance (financial and nonfinancial) of Fed Govt, 1989 base edition with supplements, annual listing, 104–5

Data coverage and availability for health care resources geographic info system, 1989 rpt, 4118–61

Data on health condition and health care resources, use, and spending, 1950s-87, annual data compilation, 4144–11

Data projects and systems of HHS, by subagency, FY88, 4008–92

Delivery of health services and related topics, series, 4186–2

Demand for health services, needs, delivery, and costs, series, 4186–9

Environmental and occupational health care personnel supply and needs, by field, 1987 conf, 4118–65

HHS financial aid, by program, recipient, State, and city, FY88, annual regional listings, 4004–3

HHS research and evaluation programs, 1970-FY87, annual listing, 4004–30

Mental health care facilities data collection needs, implementation, uses, and costs, series, 4506–2

Mental health care facilities needs assessment and program evaluation for communities, methodology, use of census data, analysis, and sample data, series, 4506–8

Preventive disease and health improvement goals and recommended activities for 2000, with trends 1970s-80s, 4048–10

Prospective payment system research activities and funding of PHS, by project and subagency, FY88, annual rpt, 4184–3

Public Health Reports, bimonthly journal, 4042–3

Research activities and grants of HCFA, by program, as of Mar 1989, annual listing, 4654–10

Research methods and design of health surveys, 1989 conf proceedings, 4188–60

Research on health care services delivery and costs, NCHSR rpts, 1985-July 1987, listing, 4188–57

VA Medicine and Surgery Dept trainees, by detailed program and city, FY88, annual rpt, 8704–4

see also Regional medical programs

Health Resources and Services Administration

Budget of US Appendix, obligations, appropriations, and personnel, by program and agency, FY90, annual rpt, 104–3

Community and migrant health services finances, operations, and staff, series, 4108–45

Expenditures of Fed Govt in States, by type, program, agency, and State, FY88, annual rpt, 2464–2

Financial aid of HHS, by program, recipient, State, and city, FY88, annual regional listings, 4004–3

Hereditary disease and genetic screening, counseling, and treatment services use, costs, and payment sources, 1987 conf, 4108–47

Lead poisoning among children, and impacts of lead removal from housing, gasoline, and water, 1987 conf, 4108–46

Prospective payment system research activities and funding of PHS, by project and subagency, FY88, annual rpt, 4184–3

Research and evaluation programs of HHS, 1970–FY87, annual listing, 4004–30
see also Bureau of Health Professions
see also Office of Health Maintenance Organizations

Health surveys
see under names of individual surveys (listed under Surveys)

Hearing aids
see Medical supplies and equipment

Hearing and hearing disorders
Educational enrollment of disabled in postsecondary instns, by disability, educational, and other characteristics, fall 1986, 4846–3.6

Fed Govt employment of minorities, handicapped, and veterans, and years of service, by occupation, age, sex, and agency, as of Sept 1988, biennial rpt, 9844–27

Head Start handicapped enrollment, by handicap, State, and for Indian and migrant programs, 1985/86, annual rpt, 4604–1

Hearing aid performance test results, by make and model, 1989 annual rpt, 8704–3

Nursing home facility, staff, and resident detailed characteristics, 1985, 4147–13.97

Statistical Abstract of US, social, political, and economic data, 1790-2025, comprehensive annual compilation, 2324–1.1

Workers compensation laws of States and Fed Govt, 1989 semiannual rpt, 6502–1
see also Deaf
see also Ear diseases and infections
see also Speech pathology and audiology

Heart diseases
see Cardiovascular diseases

Heart transplants
see Medical transplants

Heathington, K. W.
"Field Evaluation of Innovative Active Warning Devices for Use at Railroad-Highway Grade Crossings", 7558–108

Heating
see Plumbing and heating

Heating oil
see Fuel oil

Hedging
see Futures trading

Height
see Body measurements

Heimlich, Ralph E.
"Metropolitan Growth and Agriculture: Farming in the City's Shadow", 1598–256
"Productivity and Erodibility of U.S. Cropland", 1588–135
"Productivity of Highly Erodible Cropland", 1502–3.903

Hein, Scott E.
"Comparing Futures and Survey Forecasts of Near-Term Treasury Bill Rates", 9391–1.914
"Evidence on the Two Monetary Base Measures and Economic Activity", 9379–12.32
"Federal Reserve System Reserve Requirements: 1959-88, A Note", 9379–12.36
"Nominal GNP Growth and Adjusted Reserve Growth: Nonnested Tests of the St. Louis and Board Measures", 9379–12.46
"Reserve Requirements, the Monetary Base, and Economic Activity", 9379–1.903

Heinemann, M. Edith
"Nurse Educators Look at Alcohol Education for the Profession", 4482–1.902

Heinemeier, Meredith M.
"USSR: The Belorussian Railroad Experiment", 2326–18.47

Helbing, Charles
"Medicare: Short-Stay Hospital Services, by Leading Diagnosis-Related Groups, 1983 and 1985", 4652–1.925
"Use and Cost of Home Health Agency Services Under Medicare", 4652–1.908
"Use and Cost of Physician and Supplier Services Under Medicare, 1986", 4652–1.936
"Use and Cost of Short-Stay Hospital Inpatient Services Under Medicare, 1986", 4652–1.945

Helicopters
Accidents and circumstances, for US operations of domestic and foreign airlines and general aviation, periodic rpt, 9612–1
Accidents in general aviation, by circumstances, characteristics of persons and aircraft involved, and type of flying, 1986, annual rpt, 9614–3
Air traffic control and airway facilities improvement activities under Natl Airspace System Plan, 1981-85 and projected to 2000, annual rpt, 7504–12
Airport traffic, delays, capacity improvement projects and funding, runway length, and navigational operations, for hub and reliever airports, 1986-87 and forecast to 1996, 7508–67
DOD budget, weapons acquisition costs by system and service branch, FY89-91, annual rpt, 3504–2
DOD procurement cost estimates for weapons and communications systems, by service branch, quarterly summary rpt, 3502–1
Flight and engine hours, and shutdown rates, by aircraft and engine model, and air carrier, monthly rpt, 7502–13
Foreign countries military spending, arms trade, and force strengths, with govt spending and population, by country, 1977-87, annual rpt, 9824–1
General aviation aircraft, flight hours, and equipment, by type, use, and model of aircraft, region, and State, 1988, annual rpt, 7504–29
Hijackings, on-board explosions, and other crime, US and foreign incidents, 1983-87, annual rpt, 7504–31

Pilots and nonpilots certified by FAA, by certificate type, age, sex, region, and State, 1988, annual rpt, 7504–2
Police dept operations, staff, and expenses, for large cities by population size, 1987, 6066–19.51
Price indexes (producer), by stage of processing and detailed commodity, monthly rpt, 6762–6
Price indexes (producer), by stage of processing and detailed commodity, monthly 1988, annual rpt, 6764–2
Registration of aircraft with FAA, by type and characteristics of aircraft, make, carrier, State, and county, 1988, annual rpt, 7504–3
Shipments, trade, use, and firms, by type of craft and engine, monthly Current Industrial Rpt, 2506–12.24
Soviet Union and Warsaw Pact military weapons systems, aid, presence, and force strengths, and compared to US and NATO, 1989 annual rpt, 3504–20
Traffic, aircraft, pilots, airports, and fuel use, forecast FY89-2000 and trends from FY80, annual rpt, 7504–6

Helium
see Gases

Helwege, Jean
"Capital Structure, Bankruptcy Costs, and Firm-Specific Human Capital", 9366–6.180

Hem, John D.
"Study and Interpretation of the Chemical Characteristics of Natural Water", 5668–96

Hemophilia
see Blood diseases and disorders

Hemp
see Natural fibers

Hendershot, Gerry E.
"Pregnant Workers in the U.S.", 4147–16.2

Hendershott, Patric H.
"Do Home Mortgage Portfolio Lenders Have a Future?", 9312–1.904

Henderson, David
"Community Ties to the Farm", 1502–7.914

Henderson, Faye I.
"Philippines: A Country Profile", 9916–2.71

Henderson, Mary G.
"Private Sector Initiatives in Case Management", 4652–1.914

Henderson, Yolanda K.
"Capital Gains Rates and Revenues", 9373–1.901
"Emergence of the Venture Capital Industry", 9373–1.914

Hendrickson, Michael C.
"State Tax Incentives for Persons Giving Informal Care to the Elderly", 4652–1.915

Heneman, Burr
"Persistent Marine Debris in the North Sea, Northwest Atlantic Ocean, Wider Caribbean Area, and the West Coast of Baja California", 14738–4

Hennepin County, Minn.
Housing and households detailed characteristics, and unit and neighborhood quality, by location, 1985 survey, MSA rpt, 2485–6.5

Hennessey, John C.
"Postrecovery Experience of Disabled-Worker Beneficiaries", 4742–1.924
"Projected Outcomes and Length of Time in the Disability Insurance Program", 4742–1.923

Henshaw, Stanley K.
"Characteristics and Prior Contraceptive Use of U.S. Abortion Patients", 21408–113

Henson, Mary F.
"Earnings of Married-Couple Families: 1987", 2546–6.61

Hepatitis
see Infective and parasitic diseases

Herbicides
see Pesticides

Herbold, Bruce
"Ecology of the Sacramento-San Joaquin Delta: A Community Profile", 5506–9.38

Herbs
see Spices and herbs

Hereditary diseases
Deaths and rates, by detailed cause and demographic characteristics, 1986 and trends from 1900, US Vital Statistics annual rpt, 4144–2
HHS financial aid, by program, recipient, State, and city, FY88, annual regional listings, 4004–3
Screening, counseling, and treatment services for hereditary disease and genetic problems, use, costs, and payment sources, 1987 conf, 4108–47
Screening for hereditary disease, mass testing, and access to results by employer, insurer, and others, foreign and US geneticists views, 1987 survey, article, 4042–3.902
see also Birth defects

Herlihy, Michael T.
"Agricultural Statistics of the European Community, 1960-85", 1528–276
"EC Cereals Incorporation Scheme: A Cure for Grain Surpluses?", 1524–4.1

Herman, Arthur S.
"Productivity Continued To Rise in Many Industries During 1987", 6722–1.914

Hermann, Werner
"Can a Central Bank Influence Its Currency's Real Value? The Swiss Case", 9391–1.907

Hernandez, Donald J.
"Components of Longitudinal Household Change for 1984-85: An Evaluation of National Estimates from the SIPP", 2626–10.102

Hernon, Peter
"Users of Academic and Public GPO Depository Libraries", 26208–1

Heroin
see Drug abuse and treatment
see Drug and narcotics offenses

Herr, Ellen M.
"U.S. Business Enterprises Acquired or Established by Foreign Direct Investors in 1988", 2702–1.917

Herrero, Rolando
"Invasive Cervical Cancer and Smoking in Latin America", 4472–1.905

Herriot, Roger
"Enhanced Demographic-Economic Data Sets", 2626–10.85

Hertel, Thomas W.
"CARD Linear Programming Model of U.S. Agriculture", 1502–3.902

Hertz, Milton
"Conservation Reserve Program: Progress and Prospects", 1004–16.1

Hertzberg, Marie P.
"Business Cycle Indicators: Revised Composite Indexes", 2702–1.906; 2702–3

Hertzler, Glenn, Jr.
"Restructuring Farmers Home Administration Loans", 1004–16.1

Hervey, Jack L.
"Bankers' Acceptances Revisited", 9375–14
"New Dollar Indexes Are No Different from the Old Ones", 9375–14

Herz, Diane E.
"Institutional Barriers to Employment of Older Workers", 6722–1.918
"Labor Market Problems of Older Workers", 6306–2.2

Herzenberg, Stephen
"Labor-Management Conflict and Cooperation: The Role of Shop Floor Leaders", 6306–3.3

Hester, Thomas
"Federal Criminal Cases, 1980-87", 6066–19.50
"Probation and Parole, 1987", 6066–25.17

Hetzel, Robert L.
"M2 and Monetary Policy", 9389–1.913

HEW
see Department of Education
see Department of Health and Human Services

Hialeah, Fla.
Housing starts and completions authorized by building permits in 40 MSAs, quarterly rpt, 2382–9
Wages by occupation, for office and plant workers, 1988 survey, periodic MSA rpt, 6785–11.1
see also under By City and By SMSA or MSA in the "Index by Categories"

Hickok, Susan
"Consumer Cost of U.S. Trade Restraints", 9375–14
"U.S. Trade with Taiwan and South Korea", 9385–1.904

Hickory, N.C.
Clothing (hosiery) production and related workers and wages by occupation and sex, and benefits, by location, 1987 survey, 6787–6.237
see also under By SMSA or MSA in the "Index by Categories"

Hides and skins
Africa agricultural exports by commodity, and relation to economic conditions and other factors, by country, 1960s-87, 1528–280
Agricultural Statistics, 1988, annual rpt, 1004–1
Agriculture census, 1987: farms, farmland, production, finances, and operator characteristics, by county, final State rpt series, 2331–1
China trade by SITC 1- to 5-digit commodity, 1970s-87, annual rpt, 9114–3
Eastern Europe agricultural production, consumption, and trade, by country, 1970s-88, annual rpt, 1524–11

Endangered animals and plants US trade and permits, by species, purpose, disposition, and country, 1987, annual rpt, 5504–19
Export licensing, monitoring, and enforcement activities, FY88, annual rpt, 2024–1
Exports and imports (agricultural) of US, by commodity and country, bimonthly rpt with articles, 1522–1
Exports and imports (agricultural) of US, by detailed commodity and country, 1988, semiannual rpt, 1522–4
Exports and imports of dairy, livestock, and poultry products, by commodity and country, FAS monthly circular, 1925–32
Exports of grains, oilseed products, hides, skins, and cotton, by country, weekly rpt, 1922–3
Exports of US, detailed commodities by country, monthly rpt, 2422–3
Farm sector balance sheet, and receipts by detailed commodity, by State, 1984-88, annual rpt, 1544–18
Foreign and US production, trade, and use, by selected country, forecast 1990, FAS annual circular, 1925–33
Foreign countries agricultural production, prices, and trade, by country, 1970s-89 and forecast 1990, annual world region rpt series, 1524–4
Imports of US, detailed Schedule A commodities by country, monthly rpt, 2422–2
Manufacturing annual survey, 1986: financial and operating data, by SIC 2- to 4-digit industry, series, 2506–15
Manufacturing census, 1987: financial and operating data, for SIC 4-digit industries by product, preliminary rpt, 2491–1.1; 2491–1.44
Marketing data for livestock, meat, and wool, by species and market, weekly rpt, 1315–1
OECD trade, total and for 4 major countries, and US trade by country, by commodity, 1970-87, world area rpt series, 9116–1
Price indexes (producer), by stage of processing and detailed commodity, monthly rpt, 6762–6
Price indexes (producer), by stage of processing and detailed commodity, monthly 1988, annual rpt, 6764–2
Wholesale trade census, 1987: employment, establishments, finances, and operations, by SIC 2- to 4-digit kind of business, MSA, county, and city, State rpt series, 2405–1
see also Furs and fur industry
see also Leather industry and products

Hiemstra, Stephen W.
"Farmer Mac Secondary Market: Prospects for 1989", 1541–1.904
"Prospects for a Secondary Market for Farm Mortgages", 1548–343

Higgins, E. Arnold
"'Operation Workload': A Study of Passenger Energy Expenditure During an Emergency Evacuation", 7506–10.58
"Performance Evaluation of the Puritan-Bennett Crewmember Portable Protective Breathing Device as Prescribed by Portions of FAA Action Notice A-8150.2", 7506–10.61

High Point, N.C.

Clothing (hosiery) production and related workers and wages by occupation and sex, and benefits, by location, 1987 survey, 6787-6.237

see also under By SMSA or MSA in the "Index by Categories"

High School and Beyond Survey

Educational attainment of high school classes of 1972, 1980, and 1982, by selected characteristics, 1976-87, 4848-36

Higher education enrollment and degrees by sex, race, and income level, for high school classes of 1972, 1980, and 1982, natl longitudinal surveys, 4848-35

Student education, employment, and family characteristics, activities, and attitudes, classes of 1980 and 1982, natl longitudinal study, series, 4826-2

High schools

see Elementary and secondary education

Higher education

Condition of Education, detailed data on higher education, 1960s-88, annual rpt, 4824-1.2

Digest of Education Statistics, detailed data on students, staff, finances, and facilities, 1989 edition, annual rpt, 4824-2

Elementary and secondary public schools partnerships with community organizations, participation, activities, and contributions, by school characteristics and location, 1987/88, 4826-1.27

High school class of 1972: education, employment, and family characteristics, activities, and attitudes, natl longitudinal study, series, 4836-1

Libraries (depository), and users by selected characteristics, for academic and public instns, 1988 survey, 26208-1

Minority group education, schools participating in natl surveys, 1969-88, listing, 4828-38

Patents (US) granted to US and foreign applicants, by applicant and country, 1960s-88, annual rpt, 2244-3

R&D equipment of higher education instns, acquisition and service costs, condition, and financing, by field, 1982-83 and 1985-86, 9628-76

R&D facilities of higher education instns, equipment spending by funding source, and retirement and acquisition rates, by field, 1982/83-1985/86, 9626-2.180

R&D funding by source and performer, and related employment, by State, 1975-87, 9626-6.32

R&D funding, by source, performer, and for top 10 States, 1977-89, 9626-2.185

Statistical Abstract of US, social, political, and economic data, 1790-2025, comprehensive annual compilation, 2324-1.1

see also Adult education
see also Agricultural education
see also Area studies
see also Black colleges
see also Business education
see also Curricula
see also Degrees, higher education
see also Educational attainment
see also Educational broadcasting
see also Educational enrollment

see also Educational exchanges
see also Educational facilities
see also Educational finance
see also Educational materials
see also Educational research
see also Educational technology
see also Educational tests
see also Federal aid to higher education
see also Federal aid to medical education
see also Junior colleges
see also Legal education
see also Medical education
see also Reserve Officers Training Corps
see also School administration and staff
see also Scientific education
see also Service academies
see also State funding for higher education
see also Student aid
see also Students
see also Teacher education
see also Teachers
see also Veterans education
see also Vocational education and training
see also Work-study programs
see also under By Individual Company or Institution in the "Index by Categories"

Highway speed limit

see Traffic laws and courts

Highways, streets, and roads

Accident deaths and rates, by cause, age, race, sex, and State, 1986, annual rpt, 4144-2.5

Alaska Arctic Natl Wildlife Refuge oil and gas production, reserves, exploration, and dev, 1981-89 and projected to 2003, 26358-200

Appalachia hwy system and access roads funding and completion status, by State, quarterly tables, 9082-1

Appalachia local dev projects, and funding by source, by program and State, FY88, annual rpt, 9084-1

Coastal areas environmental impacts of economic dev and population growth, 1980s and projected to 2000, 2176-8.1

Conditions, travel, and funding, by type of hwy, 1960s-87 and projected to 2005, biennial rpt, 7554-27

Construction contracts for hwys, State awards to minority- and women-owned firms, FY85-88, GAO, 26113-399

Construction industries census, 1987: establishments, employment, receipts, and expenditures, by SIC 4-digit industry and State, final industry rpt series, 2373-1

Construction industries census, 1987: financial and operating data, preliminary industry rpt series, 2371-1

Construction material PPI, by construction industry, monthly rpt, 6762-6

Construction material prices and indexes for Federal-aid hwy system, by type of material and urban-rural location, quarterly rpt, 7552-7

Construction material prices and indexes for Federal-aid hwy system, by type of material, quarterly press release, 7552-16

Construction material use by type, and spending for hwys, by State, various periods 1944-88, annual rpt, 7554-29

Construction put in place and cost indexes, by type of construction, bimonthly rpt, 2042-1.1; 2042-1.5

Construction put in place, value of new public and private structures, by type, monthly rpt, 2382-4

County Business Patterns, 1987: employment, establishments, and payroll, by SIC 2- to 4-digit industry and county, annual State rpt series, 2326-8

Crime victimization rates, by victim and offender characteristics, circumstances, and offense, 1987 survey, annual rpt, 6066-3.41

Developing countries disaster preparedness and economic, population, and political data, country rpt series, 9916-2

Energy use by mode of transport, fuel supply, and demographic and economic factors of vehicle use, 1970s-88, annual rpt, 3304-5

Finances, operations, vehicles, equipment, accidents, and energy use, by mode of transport, 1955-88, annual rpt, 7304-2

Foreign countries economic, social, political, and geographic summary data, by country, 1989, annual factbook, 9114-2

Forest Service mgmt of public lands and resources dev, environmental, economic, and social impacts of alternative programs, projected to 2030, 1208-24

Govt employment and payroll, by function, level of govt, and jurisdiction, 1987-88, annual rpt series, 2466-1

Govt finances, by level of govt, State, and for large cities and counties, annual rpt series, 2466-2

Hwy Statistics, detailed data by State, 1988, annual rpt, 7554-1

Hwy Statistics, summary data by State, 1987-88, annual rpt, 7554-24

Middle Atlantic State hwy construction costs, funding, mileage, and traffic, by project, 1989 article, 9387-1.904

Neighborhood and housing quality, indicators and attitudes, by householder type and location, 1985, biennial rpt, 2485-12

Neighborhood and housing quality, indicators and attitudes, MSA surveys, series, 2485-6

Pacific territories social, economic, health, and govtl data, FY88 and trends, annual rpt, 7004-6

Pollution (water) incidents and discharges, by type, source, cause, and location, 1984-86, annual rpt, 7404-3

Public lands acreage and use, and Land Mgmt Bur activities and finances, annual State rpt series, 5724-11

R&D for hwy design and construction, quarterly journal, 7552-3

Robberies and rates, by type of premises and weapon, 1973-87, annual rpt, 6224-8

Robberies, by type of premises, population size, and region, 1988, annual rpt, 6224-2.1

St Louis metro area local govt finances, structure, and service delivery, mid-1980s, 10046-9.1

State admin of hwys and gasoline tax revenue, proposed transfer from Fed Govt to States, issues, with motor fuel taxes by selected State, 1988 rpt, 10048-72

State and local govt employment of minorities and women, by occupation, function, and pay level, 1986, annual rpt, 9244-6.4

Statistical Abstract of US, social, political, and economic data, 1790-2025, comprehensive annual compilation, 2324-1.1; 2324-1.3

Suburban areas land use, commuting, employment, and housing characteristics, detailed data for traffic planning, 1986, 7888-75

Traffic volume on rural roads and city streets, monthly rpt, 7552-8

Urban areas traffic volume and detailed trip characteristics, by transport mode and city, 1950s-88, 7888-37

see also Bridges and tunnels

see also Federal aid to highways

see also Traffic accident fatalities

see also Traffic accidents and safety

see also Traffic engineering

see also Traffic laws and courts

Hijacking of aircraft

see Air piracy

Hildreth, R. J.

"Critique of the World Agricultural Economics Research Establishment", 1502-3.902

Hill, Daniel H.

"Poisson Model of Response and Procedural Error Analysis of SIPP Reinterview Data", 2626-10.92

Hill, Jennifer

"Blue Crab. Species Profiles: Life Histories and Environmental Requirements of Coastal Fishes and Invertebrates (Mid-Atlantic)", 5506-8.105

Hill, John K.

"Incidence of Sanctions Against U.S. Employers of Illegal Aliens", 9379-12.33

"Money, Wages, and Factor Scarcity as Predictors of Inflation", 9379-1.906

Hill, Martha

"Employment of Mothers and the Prevention of Poverty", 2626-10.76

Hilton, R. Spence

"Capacity Constraints and the Prospects for External Adjustment and Economic Growth: 1989-90", 9385-1.908

"Interest Rate and Exchange Rate Effects in Selected Manufacturing Industries", 9385-9

Hing, Esther

"Effects of the Prospective Payment System on Nursing Homes", 4147-13.98

"National Nursing Home Survey: 1985 Summary for the U.S.", 4147-13.97

"Nursing Home Utilization by Current Residents: U.S., 1985. Vital and Health Statistics Series 13", 4147-13.102

Hinton, David

"U.S. Petroleum Developments: 1988", 3162-6.901

Hires

see Labor turnover

Hirschberg, Joseph G.

"Texas in Transition: Dependence on Oil and the National Economy", 9379-1.902

Hirschhorn, Eric

"Policies To Change the Priority of Claimants: The Case of Depositor Preference Laws", 9316-1.154

Hirtle, Beverly

"Estimating the Funding Gap of the Pension Benefit Guaranty Corporation", 9385-1.903

Hiserote, Bruce A.

"Changes in Land Use in Western Oregon Between 1971-74 and 1982", 1206-19.9

Hispanic Americans

Agriculture census, 1987: farms, farmland, production, finances, and operator characteristics, by county, final State rpt series, 2331-1

AIDS cases by risk group, race, sex, age, State, and MSA, and deaths, monthly rpt, 4202-9

AIDS public knowledge, attitudes, info sources, and testing, for Hispanics, 1988 survey, 4146-8.168

Alcohol use, abuse, treatment, and views of racial and ethnic groups in US and native countries, by selected characteristics, 1988 compilation of papers, 4488-12

Alcohol use and abuse among minority groups, and related problems, by selected characteristics, 1985 conf papers, 4488-13

Army personnel, promotion, and training by race and for women, discrimination issues, and career attitudes, FY88, annual rpt, 3704-10

Births and rates, by characteristics of birth, infant, and parents, 1987 and trends from 1940, US Vital Statistics advance annual rpt, 4146-5.110

Business mgmt and financial aid from Minority Business Dev Centers, and characteristics of businesses, by region and State, FY88, annual rpt, 2104-6

Children (handicapped) family characteristics and impact, for Hispanic families by English fluency, 1977 local area survey, article, 4042-3.936

Consumer Income, socioeconomic characteristics of persons, families, and households, detailed cross-tabulations, Current Population Rpt series, 2546-6

Crime, criminal justice admin and enforcement, and public opinion, data compilation, 1970s-88, annual rpt, 6064-6

Crimes, arrests, and rates, by offense, offender characteristics, population size, and jurisdiction, 1988, annual rpt, 6224-2.1; 6224-2.2

Deaths and rates, by detailed cause and demographic characteristics, 1986 and trends from 1900, US Vital Statistics annual rpt, 4144-2

Disabled persons employment, labor force status, and other characteristics, 1988, Current Population Rpt, 2546-2.147

Drug, alcohol, and cigarette use, by substance, age, sex, race, and region, 1988 survey, biennial rpt, 4494-5

Drug and alcohol abuse treatment facilities, services, use, funding, and client characteristics, 1987, annual rpt, 4494-10

Education data compilation, students, staff, finances, and facilities, 1989 edition, annual rpt, 4824-2

Education statistics, detailed data on elementary, secondary, and higher education, 1920s-88 and projected to 1997, annual rpt, 4824-1

Educational attainment, by sociodemographic characteristics and location, 1987 and trends from 1940, biennial Current Population Rpt, 2546-1.427; 2546-1.431

Educational enrollment, by grade, instn type and control, and student characteristics,

1986 and trends from 1947, annual Current Population Rpt, 2546-1.429; 2546-1.432

Employment and unemployment current statistics and articles, Monthly Labor Review, 6722-1

Employment, earnings, and hours, monthly press release, 6742-5

Employment of minorities and women, by occupation, SIC 1- to 3- digit industry, State, and MSA, 1986, annual rpt, 9244-1

Employment, unemployment, and labor force characteristics, by region, State, and selected metro area, 1988, annual rpt, 6744-7

Employment, unemployment, and labor force characteristics, Labor Statistics Handbook, 1940s-88 with trends from 1913, 6728-38.1; 6728-38.2

Enrollment by race, and other indicators of integration plans effectiveness, by school district and location, 1960s-85, 11048-189

Farm population, by employment and socioeconomic characteristics, and region, 1988, annual Current Population Rpt, 2546-1.439

Fed Equal Opportunity Recruitment Program activity, and employment by sex, race, pay grade, and selected occupation, FY88, annual rpt, 9844-33

Fed Govt employment of minorities, handicapped, and veterans, and years of service, by occupation, age, sex, and agency, as of Sept 1988, biennial rpt, 9844-27

FmHA loans, by type, borrower characteristics, and State, quarterly rpt, 1182-8

FmHA loans, by type, borrower race, and State, quarterly rpt, 1182-5

High school class of 1972: education, employment, and family characteristics, activities, and attitudes, natl longitudinal study, series, 4836-1

High school classes of 1980 and 1982: education, employment, and family characteristics, activities, and attitudes, natl longitudinal study, series, 4826-2

High school dropouts health condition, substance abuse, and involvement with violence, for Mexican Americans, 1988-89 survey, article, 4042-3.957

Household and family characteristics, by location, 1988, annual Current Population Rpt, 2546-1.437

Household composition, income, benefits, and labor force status, Survey of Income and Program Participation methodology, working paper series, 2626-10

Households and housing detailed characteristics, and unit and neighborhood quality, by location, 1985, biennial rpt, 2485-12

Households and housing detailed characteristics, and unit and neighborhood quality, MSA surveys, series, 2485-6

Housing and households summary characteristics, 1985 and trends, biennial chartbook, 2486-1.7

Hwy construction contracts awards of States to minority- and women-owned firms, FY85-88, GAO rpt, 26113-399

Income (household) and poverty status under alternative income definitions, by recipient characteristics, 1986, Current Population Rpt, 2546–6.58

Labor force participation, by race, detailed Hispanic origin, and sex, quarterly rpt, 6742–18

Labor force, wages, hours, and payroll costs, by major industry group and demographic characteristics, *Survey of Current Business*, monthly rpt, 2702–1.5

Living arrangements, family relationships, and marital status, by selected characteristics, 1988, annual Current Population Rpt, 2546–1.428; 2546–1.433

Mentally retarded persons facilities, beds, and residents, by ownership, resident age and race, and State, 1986, 4147–14.34

Military reserve personnel social, economic, family, and service characteristics, and attitudes, by reserve component, 1986 survey, 3508–29

Military reserve spouses attitudes, and family social, economic, and other characteristics, 1986 survey, 3508–30

Nursing home facility, staff, and resident detailed characteristics, 1985, 4147–13.97

Nursing homes, beds, and residents, by ownership, certification status, and State, 1986, 4147–14.33

Nutritional status and related health condition and practices, by selected characteristics, 1970s-87, 4048–33

Police dept operations, staff, and expenses, for large cities by population size, 1987, 6066–19.51

Population size of minority groups, and components of change, by race, State, metro-nonmetro location, MSA, and county, 1980-85, Current Population Rpt, 2546–3.159

Population socioeconomic characteristics, for Hispanics by detailed origin, 1988, Current Population Rpt, 2546–1.430; 2546–1.438

Prisoners, movements, and characteristics, by State, 1986, annual rpt, 6064–26

Science and engineering grad enrollment, by field, source of funds, and characteristics of student and instn, 1975-87, annual rpt, 9627–7

Science and engineering PhDs, by field, instn, employment prospects, sex, race, and other characteristics, 1960s-88, 9627–30

Science and engineering PhDs employment and other characteristics, by field and State, 1987, biennial rpt, 9627–18

Sexually transmitted disease cases among minorities, by race, 1988, article, 4042–3.954

Small business establishments, operations, owner characteristics, and job training, late 1950s-87, 9768–20

Smoking rates, by sex, age, race, occupation, region, and State, 1985 Current Population Survey, article, 4472–1.910

SSA employment of Hispanics by regional office, and Spanish-speaking employees in California, 1987, GAO rpt, 26121–268

State and local govt employment of minorities and women, by occupation, function, pay level, and State, 1986, annual rpt, 9244–6

Statistical Abstract of US, social, political, and economic data, with foreign comparisons, 1790-2025, comprehensive annual compilation, 2324–1

Telecommunications industries minority employment and discrimination charges, with data by industry and selected firm, 1970s-88, hearings, 21368–113

Telephone service of households, by composition, income sources, and other characteristics, 1984-87, 9288–11

Texas-Mexico border area health facilities and services, with background data, by Texas county, 1980s-88, GAO rpt, 26121–261

Unemployed displaced workers, by reason, industry, selected characteristics, and State, 1988, annual rpt, 6744–18

Voting and registration, by socioeconomic and demographic characteristics, 1988 presidential election, biennial Current Population Rpt, 2546–1.440

Weight, height, other body measurements, obesity, and handedness, by detailed Hispanic origin, age, and sex, 1982-84, 4147–11.207

see also under By Race and Ethnic Group in the "Index by Categories"

Hispanic Health and Nutrition Examination Survey

Alcohol use and abuse among minority groups, and related problems, by selected characteristics, 1985 conf papers, 4488–13

Data coverage and availability, 1989 rpt, 4147–1.24

Nutritional status and related health condition and practices, by selected characteristics, 1970s-87, 4048–33

Historic events
see Chronologies

Historic sites

Acreage of land under Natl Park Service mgmt, by site, ownership, and region, 1989 semiannual rpt, 5542–1

Coastal areas environmental and socioeconomic conditions, and potential impact of oil and gas OCS leases, final statement series, 5736–1

Criminal cases by type and disposition, and collections, for US attorneys, by Federal district, FY88, annual rpt, 6004–2.1

Damaged and threatened natl historic and natural landmarks, with owner, location, damage type, and recommended remedial action, 1988, annual listing, 5544–16

Fed Govt financial and nonfinancial domestic aid, 1989 base edition with supplements, annual listing, 104–5

Fed Govt spending in States, by type, program, agency, and State, FY88, annual rpt, 2464–2

Lighthouses historic preservation grants, by State, FY89, press release, 5306–4.1

Preservation Fund grants, by State, FY90, annual table, 5544–9

Preservation of historic buildings, tax incentives, projects, costs, ownership, use, and tax reform impacts, FY77-88, annual rpt, 5544–17

Tax expenditures, Federal revenues forgone through income tax deductions and exclusions by type, FY90-94, annual rpt, 21784–10

Visits in natl park system, by park and State, monthly rpt, 5542–4

Visits in natl park system, by park and State, 1988 and trends from 1979, annual rpt, 5544–12

see also Monuments and memorials

History

American Historical Assn financial statements, and membership by State, 1988, annual rpt, 29574–2

Degrees awarded in higher education, by level, field, race, and sex, 1989 edition, annual rpt, 4824–2.20

Education statistics, detailed data on elementary and secondary education, 1920s-88 and projected to 1997, annual rpt, 4824–1.1

Fed Govt aid to higher education and nonprofit instns for R&D and related activities, by field, instn, agency, and State, FY87, annual rpt, 9627–17

Fed Govt classified info access and denials to historians and former presidential appointees, 1986-87, GAO rpt, 26123–66

Hitchner, Roger E.
"Outlook for Farm Commodity Program Spending, FY89-94", 26308–86

HIV virus group
see Acquired immune deficiency syndrome

Hjort, Kim
"Wheat Substitution in Developing Country Markets", 1522–3.916

Hobbs, Frank B.
"Mexico's Total, Employed, and Excess Labor Force: Future Prospects, 1985 to 2000", 2326–18.46

Hobbs, James R.
"Foreign Investment and Activity in the U.S. Through Corporations, 1984-85", 8302–2.920
"Statistics of Income Studies of International Income and Taxes", 8302–2.907

Hoekzema, Robert
"Mineral Future of Alaska", 5606–5.7

Hoff, Frederic L.
"Honey: Background for 1990 Farm Legislation", 1566–7.3
"U.S. Honey Price Support Policy", 1561–14.902

Hoffman, Agnes L.
"Nurse Educators Look at Alcohol Education for the Profession", 4482–1.902

Hoffman, Charlene M.
"Federal Support for Education, FY80-88", 4828–21

Hoffman, Daniel A.
"Breast Cancer in Women with Scoliosis Exposed to Multiple Diagnostic X-Rays", 4472–1.922

Hoffman, Gene D.
"Marketing Strategies for Agribusiness Firms", 1004–16.1

Hoffman, Linwood A.
"Oats: Background for 1990 Farm Legislation", 1566–7.5
"Sorghum: Background for 1990 Farm Legislation", 1566–7.9

Hog cholera
see Animal diseases and zoonoses

Hogan, Christopher
"Patterns of Travel for Rural Individuals Hospitalized in New York State: Relationships Between Distance, Destination, and Casemix", 4188–53

Hogarth, Jeanne M.
"Saving and Dissaving in Retirement", 1004–16.1; 1702–1.906

Hogs
see Livestock and livestock industry

Holahan, John
"Assessing Medicare Reimbursement Options for Skilled Nursing Facility Care", 4652–1.929

Holding companies
County Business Patterns, 1987: employment, establishments, and payroll, by SIC 2- to 4-digit industry and county, annual State rpt series, 2326–8

Employment, earnings, and hours, by SIC 1- to 4-digit industry, monthly 1983-Feb 1989, annual rpt, 6744–4

Employment in nonmanufacturing industries, by detailed occupation and SIC 2-digit industry, 1987, triennial rpt, 6748–60

Multinatl US firms and foreign affiliates finances and operations, by industry of parent firm and affiliate, world area, and country, preliminary 1987, annual rpt, 2704–5

Occupational injury and illness rates, by SIC 2- to 4-digit industry, 1987, annual rpt, 6844–1

Partnerships (master limited) finances, firms, partners, and tax reform impacts, by industry, 1986, technical paper, 8006–3.59

Science and engineering employment, by nonmanufacturing industry and field, 1987, triennial rpt, 9627–31

Tax (income) returns of corporations, income and tax items by asset size and detailed industry, 1986, annual rpt, 8304–4; 8304–21

Tax (income) returns of partnerships, income statement items by industry group, 1986, annual article, 8302–2.903

Telephone and telegraph corporate control and holding company finances and operations, 1987, annual rpt, 9284–6.1

Trust assets of banks, trust companies, and S&Ls, by type of asset and fund, selected firm, and State, 1988, annual rpt, 13004–1
see also Bank holding companies

Holidays
see Vacations and holidays

Holik, Daniel
"Individual Income Tax Rates, 1986", 8302–2.918

Holland
see Netherlands

Hollingsworth, Jane A.
"Chicago Seiches", 2152–8.902

Holloway, James J.
"Clinical and Sociodemographic Risk Factors for Readmission of Medicare Beneficiaries", 4652–1.903

Holloway, Thomas M.
"Price Index for Biomedical Research and Development", 4042–3.901

Holly, Elizabeth A.
"Anal Cancer Incidence: Genital Warts, Anal Fissure or Fistula, Hemorrhoids, and Smoking", 4472–1.930

Hollywood, Fla.
Housing starts and completions authorized by building permits in 40 MSAs, quarterly rpt, 2382–9

Wages by occupation, for office and plant workers, 1989 survey, periodic MSA rpt, 6785–3.10
see also under By City and By SMSA or MSA in the "Index by Categories"

Holm, Lars-Erik
"Cancer Risk in Population Examined with Diagnostic Doses of Iodine-131", 4472–1.907
"Dietary Habits and Prognostic Factors in Breast Cancer", 4472–1.920

Holtz-Eakin, Douglas
"Intertemporal Analysis of State and Local Government Spending: Theory and Tests", 9387–8.183

Holy See
see Vatican City

Home-based offices and workers
American Housing Survey: unit and households detailed characteristics, and unit and neighborhood quality, 1985, biennial rpt, 2485–12

Urban areas traffic volume and detailed trip characteristics, by transport mode and city, 1950s-88, 7888–37

Home economics
Education Dept programs funding, operations, and effectiveness, FY88, annual rpt, 4804–5

Farm financial and marketing conditions, forecast 1988, conf papers, annual rpt, 1004–16

State allocation of Federal educational funds, by program, recipient type, and State, 1987/88, annual rpt, 4804–8
see also Family budgets

Home equity loans
see Credit

Home health services
AIDS deaths, by health and other characteristics, 1986, 4146–8.178

AIDS patients and persons with AIDS virus infection, Medicaid policies and State health insurance regulation, with background data, 1987-88, article, 4652–1.953

AIDS patients Medicaid claims and payments, by type of care and whether AIDS-related, race, sex, and diagnosis, 1984-87, article, 4042–3.940

Children (handicapped) home health care and support services availability and need, 1988, GAO report, 26121–300

Children (handicapped) requiring home care, Medicaid applications disposition under income waiver program, for Minnesota, 1985-87, article, 4042–3.944

Costs for home health visits, relation to agency caseload and patient and operating characteristics, 1987, article, 4042–3.932

Fed Govt aid for home care, long-term care costs, and ability to pay, 1988 survey, hearing, 21148–51

Health Care Financing Review, provider prices, price inputs and indexes, and labor, quarterly journal, 4652–1.1

Heart disease deaths, by health and other characteristics, 1986, 4146–8.177

HHS financial aid, by program, recipient, State, and city, FY88, annual regional listings, 4004–3

Insurance (health) coverage and provisions

of employee benefit plans, by plan type and occupational group, 1988, annual rpt, 6784–19

Kidney end-stage disease treatment facilities, Medicare enrollment and reimbursement, survival, and patient characteristics, 1980-86, annual rpt, 4654–16

Long-term health care case mix, quality of care, and outcomes, impacts of Medicare prospective payment system, 1980s-86, 4658–28

Medicaid coverage, participation, payments, admin, and legislative history, with data by State, 1980s-88, 21368–105

Medicare and Medicaid beneficiaries and program operations, 1988, annual fact book, 4654–18

Medicare and Medicaid eligibility, participation, coverage, and program finances, various periods 1966-89, biennial rpt, 4654–1

Medicare and Medicaid enrollees, benefits, reimbursements, and services use, mid-1960s-87, annual rpt, 4744–3.5; 4744–3.6

Medicare and other insurance programs catastrophic illness coverage, benefits, premiums, costs, and program finances, projected 1988-93, 26306–3.105

Medicare claims approved, charges, and reimbursements by type of service, from 1974, monthly rpt, quarterly data, 4742–1.11

Medicare disabled and aged enrollees home health care services use and costs, by age, sex, service type, and diagnosis, mid 1970s-86, article, 4652–1.908

Medicare payments for post-hospitalization care by diagnosis, for nursing home, home care, and rehabilitation, 1980s-87, article, 4652–1.909

Medicare reimbursement of hospitals under prospective payment system, and of physicians, effect on services, finances, and beneficiary payments, 1970s-88, annual rpt, 17204–2

Medicare reimbursement of hospitals under prospective payment system, impacts on industry structure, 1975-86, 17206–2.2

Medicare reimbursement of hospitals under prospective payment system, impacts on instns, beneficiaries, and other care providers and payment sources, 1986, annual rpt, 4654–13

Medicare reimbursement of hospitals under prospective payment system, impacts on subacute care, 1988 rpt, 17206–2.8

Older frail persons community and home-based care under prepaid care plan, enrollees health condition and services use, for San Francisco, 1987, article, 4652–1.912

Older persons aid and policies of Fed Govt, and issues of aging, 1989 annual rpt, 25144–3

Older persons eligible for nursing home care, cost of home and community services, Medicaid waiver program in 2 States, 1981-84, article, 4652–1.943

Older persons health care (long-term) funding by Fed Govt, public views, 1987 survey, hearings, 21368–106

Older persons poverty risk from long-term care costs, by duration of care, income, and marital status, model results, 1987 rpt, 25928–7

Older persons with functional limitations, long-term health care needs, and costs by payment source, 1982-85, GAO rpt, 26121–266

Physicians Medicare services use, charges, and reimbursement, by service type, setting, and specialty, 1986, article, 4652–1.936

Service industries census, 1987: establishments, receipts, employment, and payroll, by SIC 2- to 4-digit kind of business, MSA, county, and city, State rpt series, 2391–1

Veterans disability and death compensation cases of VA, by entitlement type, period of service, and sex, as of Mar 1989, semiannual rpt, 8602–8

Veterans disability and death compensation cases of VA, by entitlement type, period of service, sex, age, and State, FY88, annual rpt, 8604–7

see also Respite care

Home ownership
see Housing sales
see Housing tenure

Home video and audio equipment
Consumer Expenditure Survey, household income by source, and itemized spending, by selected characteristics and region, 1984-87, annual rpt, 6764–5

Consumer spending in metro and nonmetro areas, by item, 1987, article, 6722–1.962

County Business Patterns, 1987: employment, establishments, and payroll, by SIC 2- to 4-digit industry and county, annual State rpt series, 2326–8

CPI by component for US city average, and by region, population size, and for 27 metro areas, monthly rpt, 6762–2

Exports of US, detailed commodities by country, monthly rpt, 2422–3

Imports of US, detailed Schedule A commodities by country, monthly rpt, 2422–2

Imports of US given duty-free treatment for value of US material sent abroad, and impacts on US industry and employment, by commodity and country, 1987, annual rpt, 9884–14

Injuries from use of consumer products and related activities, by victim age and sex, 1988, annual rpt, 9164–7

Injuries from use of consumer products, by severity, victim age, and detailed product, 1988, annual rpt, 9164–6

Manufacturing annual survey, 1986: value of shipments, by SIC 4- to 5-digit product class, 2506–15.3

Manufacturing census, 1987: financial and operating data, for SIC 4-digit industries by product, preliminary rpt, 2491–1.72

OECD trade, total and for 4 major countries, and US trade by country, by commodity, 1970-87, world area rpt series, 9116–1

Price indexes (producer), by stage of processing and detailed commodity, monthly rpt, 6762–6

Price indexes (producer), by stage of processing and detailed commodity, monthly 1988, annual rpt, 6764–2

Retail trade sales, inventories, purchases, gross margin, and accounts receivable, by SIC 2- to 4-digit kind of business and form of ownership, 1987, annual rpt, 2413–5

Service industries census, 1987: establishments, receipts, employment, and payroll, by SIC 2- to 4-digit kind of business, MSA, county, and city, State rpt series, 2391–1

Statistical Abstract of US, social, political, and economic data, 1790-2025, comprehensive annual compilation, 2324–1.1

see also Radio
see also Television
see also Video recordings and equipment

Homeless population
Assistance (financial and nonfinancial) of Fed Govt, 1989 base edition with supplements, annual listing, 104–5

Assistance of Fed Govt to homeless and hungry, public opinion by respondent characteristics, 1988 survey, hearings, 25248–107

Assistance of Fed Govt to homeless by program and Federal agency, and indicators of need, 1988, annual rpt, 14364–1

Assistance programs for homeless, and shelter capacity and voucher programs, for 5 major cities, 1988, 5188–122

Assistance to homeless persons, HUD and Fed Emergency Mgmt Agency housing and food programs funding and operations, FY87-88, GAO rpt, 26113–411

Budget of US, Bush Admin policy changes by program, FY90, 028–32

Children (homeless) by type of accommodation, urban-rural location, and State, alternative estimates, 1988, GAO rpt, 26131–61

Community dev programs of HUD, funding and activities by program and State, FY88, annual rpt, 5124–5

Developing countries disaster preparedness and economic, population, and political data, country rpt series, 9916–2

Disabled homeless persons group housing, HUD grants by recipient, 1989, press release, 5006–3.67

Educational enrollment and needs of homeless children, 1988, annual State rpt, 4804–35

HHS financial aid, by program, recipient, State, and city, FY88, annual regional listings, 4004–3

Housing (transitional) for homeless persons, HUD grants by recipient, 1989, press release, 5006–3.66

Housing aid of HUD for homeless, project listing, 1988 rpt, 5188–121

Housing for homeless persons in rehabilitated single occupancy units, HUD grants by recipient, 1989, press release, 5006–3.68

Nutritional status of homeless population, 1987 local area study, article, 4042–3.942

Older persons aid and policies of Fed Govt, with program funding, 1980s-89, annual rpt, 25144–3.1

Population characteristics and needs of homeless, and impacts of govt aid programs and housing costs, 1988 conf papers, 10048–73

Population characteristics of homeless by city, and Federal funding by program, 1980s-89, hearings, 21248–123

Public opinion on taxes, spending, and govt efficiency, by respondent characteristics, 1989 survey, annual rpt, 10044–2

Rural areas homeless persons health condition, services use, and other characteristics, local area studies, 1989 rpt, 4186–9.1

Shelters for homeless, services, operations, and client characteristics, 1988 survey, 5188–123

Youth (homeless and runaway) programs, funding, activities, and participant characteristics, FY86, annual rpt, 4604–3

Homemaker services
Children (handicapped) home health care and support services availability and need, 1988, GAO report, 26121–300

Employment, earnings, and hours, by SIC 1- to 4-digit industry, monthly 1983-Feb 1989, annual rpt, 6744–4

Older persons health care spending for instnl and community care, under alternative community settings, 1979-84 study, article, 4652–1.932

Homeowner's insurance
see Property and casualty insurance

Homesteads
Public lands acreage and grants, by State, FY88 and trends, annual rpt, 5724–1.1

Tax (property) revenue by level of govt, assessed values by locality, and exemptions, by property type and State, 1987 Census of Govts, 2453–1

Urban Homesteading Program properties, units, and rehabilitation costs by financing source, FY88, annual rpt, 5124–5

Homicide
Alcohol blood levels of homicide victims, by race, Hispanic origin, and other characteristics, for Los Angeles, 1970-79, conf papers, 4488–13

Arrest rates, by offense, sex, age, and race, 1987, annual rpt, 6224–7

Bombing incidents and casualties, by target, circumstances, and State, 1979-88, annual rpt, 8484–4.1

Child death rates, by age, sex, race, and cause, for US and compared to 8 OECD countries, 1985 and trends from 1900, 4147–3.27

Children abducted and murdered by strangers, and rates, by victim sex, age, and race, 1976-84, 6066–27.1

Court civil and criminal caseloads for Federal district, appeals, and special courts, June 1989, annual rpt, 18204–2; 18204–8

Crime, criminal justice admin and enforcement, and public opinion, data compilation, 1970s-88, annual rpt, 6064–6

Crime Index by population size and region, and offenses by large city, Jan-June 1989, semiannual rpt, 6222–1

Crimes, arrests by offender characteristics, and rates, by offense, and law enforcement employees, by population size and jurisdiction, 1988, annual rpt, 6224–2

Criminal case processing from arrest to sentencing, cases and duration by disposition, offense, and defendant characteristics, for selected cities, 1986, annual rpt, 6064–27

Criminal case processing in Federal district courts, and dispositions, by offense, district, and offender characteristics, 1984, annual rpt, 6064–29

Criminal case processing in Federal district courts, disposition by offense, 1980-87, 6066–19.50

Deaths and rates, by cause, age, sex, marital status, race, and State, 1987, US Vital Statistics advance annual rpt, 4146–5.113

Deaths and rates, by cause and age, preliminary 1987-88, US Vital Statistics annual rpt, 4144–7

Deaths and rates, by detailed cause and demographic characteristics, 1986 and trends from 1900, US Vital Statistics annual rpt, 4144–2

Deaths and rates, by detailed location, cause, and demographic characteristics, 1987, US Vital Statistics annual rpt, 4144–3

Deaths by cause, age, race, and sex, 1950s-86, annual rpt, 4144–11

Drug test results at arrest, by drug type, offense, and sex, for selected urban areas, quarterly rpt, 6062–3

Executions of prisoners, by offense and race, 1930-86, annual rpt, 6064–26.6

Executions since 1930, and prisoners under death sentence by prison control and prisoner characteristics, by State, 1973-88, annual rpt, 6066–25.23

Firearms-related deaths of children, by motive, age, sex, and race, 1968-87, 4146–8.181

Indian Health Service facilities, funding, operations, and Indian health and other characteristics, 1950s-88, annual chartbook, 4084–1

Juvenile court delinquency cases, by offense, referral source, disposition, age, sex, race, State, and county, 1985, annual rpt, 6064–12

Juvenile court referrals by offender characteristics, and dispositions, by offense, 1984, 6066–27.2

Juvenile offenders recidivism rates, arrests, and court referrals, by offense, age, and sex, 1983 local area studies, 6068–227

Military deaths by cause, age, race, and rank, and personnel captured and missing, by service branch, 2nd half FY88, semiannual rpt, 3542–21

Prison time served ratio to offenses committed, by offense, 1958-86, 6068–229

Prisoners in Federal and State instns, deaths by cause, sex, and State, 1986, annual rpt, 6064–26.4

Prisoners in State instns, by offense, criminal history, and inmate, family, and victim characteristics, 1986, annual rpt, 6064–26.3

Recidivism rates of prisoners released in 1983, by offense and prisoner characteristics, 1983-86, 6066–19.48

Sentences by State courts for felony offenses, and sentence lengths and time served, by offense, 1986, 6066–25.19

Sentences for Federal crimes, guidelines use and results by offense and district, and Sentencing Commission activities, 1988, annual rpt, 17664–1

Sentences for Federal offenses, guidelines by offense and circumstances, 1989 rpt, 17668–1

Sentences for felonies, by sentence type and offense, 1983-86, 6066–19.52

Statistical Abstract of US, social, political, and economic data, 1790-2025, comprehensive annual compilation, 2324–1.1

Terrorist (intl) incidents, casualties, and attacks on US targets, by attack type and country, 1980-88, 7008–56

Terrorist (intl) incidents, casualties, and attacks on US targets, by attack type and world area, 1968-88, annual rpt, 7004–13

Victimization rates, and lifetime probability of murder, by age, sex, and race, 1987, annual rpt, 6224–8

Wiretaps authorized, costs, arrests, trials, and convictions, by offense and jurisdiction, 1988, annual rpt, 18204–7

see also Assaults on police

Homosexuality

AIDS cases and AIDS virus infection prevalence, by risk group and other patient characteristics, 1981-88 and projected to 1992, 4206–2.13

AIDS cases and deaths, by whether intravenous drug user and sexual orientation, for selected metro areas, 1989 semiannual conf, 4492–5

AIDS cases, and health and social services availability, for 5 cities, 1988, GAO rpt, 26121–307

AIDS cases by risk group, race, sex, age, State, and MSA, and deaths, monthly rpt, 4202–9

AIDS risk knowledge and high-risk activities of homosexual men in cities with low and high AIDS rates, 1989 article, 4042–3.939

Aliens excluded and deported from US by cause and country, 1892-1988, annual rpt, 6264–2

Cancer (anal) risk, by sex and history of urogenital disorders, homosexual activity, and smoking, 1989 article, 4472–1.930

Hepatitis cases by infection source, age, sex, race, and State, and deaths, by strain, 1987 and trends from 1966, 4205–2

Honduras

Agricultural and food production and indexes, total and for selected commodities, by country, 1970s-88, annual rpt, 1524–12

Agricultural trade of US, by detailed commodity and country, 1988, semiannual rpt, 1522–4

AID activities and funding by project and function, FY90, and developing countries summary socioeconomic data from 1960s, annual rpt, 9904–4.7

AID economic aid to developing countries, obligations and disbursements by country, quarterly rpt, 9912–4

AID loans repayment status and terms by program and country, and status of predecessor agency loans, quarterly rpt, 9912–3

AID local currency trust funds mgmt and use, by country, FY83-87, GAO rpt, 26123–221

Economic and military aid and loans from US and intl agencies, by program and country, FY46-87, annual rpt, 9914–5

Economic conditions, income, production, prices, employment, and trade, 1989 periodic country rpt, 2046–4.73

Economic conditions, policy, and trade practices, by country, 1986-88, annual rpt, 21384–5

Economic, social, political, and geographic summary data, by country, 1989, annual factbook, 9114–2

Exports and imports of US, by commodity and country, 1970-87, world area rpt, 9116–1.6

Exports and imports of US, by selected country, country group, and commodity group, 1988, annual rpt, 2044–37

Health care projects of AID, design and implementation effects on sustainability, 1940s-86, 9916–3.53

Human rights conditions in 170 countries, 1988, annual rpt, 21384–3

Investment (direct) incentives of Caribbean Basin Initiative, economic impacts, with finances and employment by country, 1984-88, 2048–141

Labor conditions, union coverage, and work accidents, 1989 annual country rpt, 6366–4.35

Military aid of US, arms sales, and training programs costs and budget requests, by program, world region, and country, FY88-90, annual rpt, 7144–13

Military spending, arms trade, and force strengths, with govt spending and population, by country, 1977-87, annual rpt, 9824–1

Minerals Yearbook, 1987, Vol 3: foreign country reviews of production, trade, and policy, by commodity, annual rpt, 5604–35

Minerals Yearbook, 1987, Vol 3 preprints: foreign country review of production, trade, and policy, by commodity, annual rpt, 5604–23.84

Population size, growth rates, and components of change, by country, projected 1989-2020 and trends from 1950, biennial rpt, 2324–9

Refugees from Nicaragua, El Salvador, and Guatemala receiving UN aid, resettlement in other Central American countries, and repatriations, 1984-88, GAO rpt, 26123–232

UN voting record and share of votes in agreement with US, by issue, country, and world area, 1988, annual rpt, 7004–18

see also under By Foreign Country in the "Index by Categories"

Honey and beekeeping

Acreage under Agricultural Stabilization and Conservation Service programs, rankings by commodity and congressional district, 1987, biennial rpt, 1804–17

Agricultural Stabilization and Conservation Service honey programs, 1960-88, annual fact sheet, 1806–4.7

Agricultural Statistics, 1988, annual rpt, 1004–1

Agriculture census, 1987: farms, farmland, production, finances, and operator characteristics, by county, final State rpt series, 2331–1

CCC certificate exchange activity, by commodity, weekly press release, 1802–16

Exports of US, detailed commodities by country, monthly rpt, 2422–3

Farm sector balance sheet, and receipts by detailed commodity, by State, 1984-88, annual rpt, 1544–18

Foreign and US production, prices, trade, and use, FAS periodic circular series, 1925–14

Imports of honey, quarterly situation rpt, 1561–14.2

Imports of US, detailed Schedule A commodities by country, monthly rpt, 2422–2

Manufacturing census, 1987: financial and operating data, for SIC 4-digit industries by product, preliminary rpt, 2491–1.9

Nutrient and caloric composition of food, for raw, processed, and prepared food, 1988 rpt, 1358–3

Price support activity and policy options, with data on production, trade, use, and finances, and foreign comparisons, 1950s–89, commodity rpt, 1566–7.3

Production, prices, and stocks of honey, and bee colonies, by State, 1987-88, annual rpt, 1631–6

Production, prices, trade, stocks, and marketing of honey, and CCC loan and distribution activities, monthly rpt, 1311–2

Honeycutt, T. Crawford
"Higher Prices Yield Improved Energy Industry Financial Results in the First Half of 1989", 3162–24.903

"Increased Refining Income Led U.S. Energy Industry Financial Recovery in 1988", 3162–24.901

Hong Kong
Agricultural and food production and indexes, total and for selected commodities, by country, 1970s-88, annual rpt, 1524–12

Agricultural trade of US, by detailed commodity and country, 1988, semiannual rpt, 1522–4

Background Notes, summary social, political, and economic data, 1988 rpt, 7006–2.6

Businesses (foreign) activity in US, income tax returns, assets, and income statement items, by industry div, country, and world area, 1984-85, article, 8302–2.920

China trade, by commodity, world area, and country, 1985-87, 9118–10

Dollar exchange rates, and impacts of currency appreciation on current account and trade balances and economic indicators, for 3 Asian countries, 1980s-90, GAO rpt, 26123–234

Economic and military aid and loans from US and intl agencies, by program and country, FY46-87, annual rpt, 9914–5

Economic conditions, policy, and trade practices, by country, 1986-88, annual rpt, 21384–5

Economic, social, political, and geographic summary data, by country, 1989, annual factbook, 9114–2

Export and import balances of US, and dollar exchange rates, with 4 Asian countries 1980s-89, semiannual rpt, 8002–14

Exports and imports of US, by commodity and country, 1970-87, world area rpt, 9116–1.2

Exports and imports of US, by selected country, country group, and commodity group, 1988, annual rpt, 2044–37

Labor conditions and work accidents, 1989 annual country rpt, 6366–4.65

Minerals production, reserves, and industry role in domestic economy and world supply, 1988 country rpt, 5606–1.17

Minerals Yearbook, 1987, Vol 3: foreign country reviews of production, trade, and policy, by commodity, annual rpt, 5604–35

Minerals Yearbook, 1987, Vol 3 preprints: foreign country review of production, trade, and policy, by commodity, annual rpt, 5604–23.85

Multinatl US firms and foreign affiliates finances and operations, by industry of parent firm and affiliate, world area, and country, preliminary 1987, annual rpt, 2704–5

Population size, growth rates, and components of change, by country, projected 1989-2020 and trends from 1950, biennial rpt, 2324–9

Sweaters from 3 countries at less than fair value, injury to US industry, investigation with background financial and operating data, 1989 rpt, 9886–14.272

Honolulu, Hawaii
CPI by component for US city average, and by region, population size, and for 27 metro areas, monthly rpt, 6762–2

Housing vacancy rates for single and multifamily units and mobile homes, by city and ZIP code, 1989, annual MSA rpt, 9304–21.6

see also under By City and By SMSA or MSA in the "Index by Categories"

Hooker, Sarah A.
"Reconciliation of Flow of Funds and Commerce Department Statistics on U.S. International Transactions and Foreign Investment Position", 9366–6.198

Hooper, Peter
"U.S. International Transactions in 1988", 9362–1.904

Hopkinsville, Ky.
Wages by occupation, for office and plant workers, 1989 survey, periodic MSA rpt, 6785–3.4

see also under By SMSA or MSA in the "Index by Categories"

Hoppe, Robert A.
"Defining and Measuring Nonmetro Poverty: Results from the Survey of Income and Program Participation", 2626–10.72

"Short-Term Poor Need Help, Too", 1502–7.915

Hops
Agricultural Statistics, 1988, annual rpt, 1004–1

Agriculture census, 1987: farms, farmland, production, finances, and operator characteristics, by county, final State rpt series, 2331–1

Beer production, stocks, material used, tax-free removals, and taxable removals by State, monthly rpt, 8486–1.1

Exports and imports (agricultural) of US, by commodity and country, bimonthly rpt with articles, 1522–1

Exports and imports (agricultural) of US, by detailed commodity and country, 1988, semiannual rpt, 1522–4

Farm income, expenses, receipts by commodity, assets, liabilities, and ratios, 1988 and trends from 1945, annual rpt, 1544–16

Farm sector balance sheet, and receipts by detailed commodity, by State, 1984-88, annual rpt, 1544–18

Foreign and US fresh and processed fruit, vegetable, and nut production and trade, FAS monthly circular with articles, 1925–34

Prices received by farmers and production value, by detailed crop and State, 1986-88, annual rpt, 1621–2

Production, farms, acreage, and related data, by selected crop and State, monthly rpt, 1621–1

Production, stocks, and use of hops, and US trade by country, monthly rpt, 1313–7

Stocks held by growers, dealers, and brewers, 1987-89, semiannual press release, 1621–8

Hormones
Cancer (breast) risk for women by smoking history, and menopausal and estrogen receptor status, 1976-86 study, article, 4472–1.928

Carcinogens chemistry, sources, environment and health risks, and regulation, by substance and brand, 1989, annual rpt, 4044–15

Exports of US, detailed commodities by country, monthly rpt, 2422–3

Imports of US, detailed Schedule A commodities by country, monthly rpt, 2422–2

Livestock productivity, farm income, land use, and consumer prices impacts of growth hormones use, alternative estimates, 1985, 1548–346

Prescriptions for drugs, by drug type and brand, and for new drugs, 1987, annual rpt, 4064–12

Production and sales of synthetic organic chemicals, and manufacturer listing, by product, 1988, annual rpt, 9884–3

Research on population and reproduction, Federal funding by project, FY87, annual listing, 4474–9

see also Metabolic and endocrine diseases

Hornig, Susanna
"Ghost Shrimp and Blue Mud Shrimp. Species Profiles: Life Histories and Environmental Requirements of Coastal Fishes and Invertebrates", 5506–8.100

Horse racing
County Business Patterns, 1987: employment, establishments, and payroll, by SIC 2- to 4-digit industry and county, annual State rpt series, 2326–8

Service industries census, 1987: establishments, receipts, employment, and payroll, by SIC 2- to 4-digit kind of business, MSA, county, and city, State rpt series, 2391–1

Horses
see Horse racing
see Livestock and livestock industry

Horticulture
see also Flowers and nursery products

Hoshi, Takeo
"Bank Monitoring and Investment: Evidence from the Changing Structure of Japanese Corporate Banking Relations", 9366–6.200

"Corporate Structure, Liquidity, and Investment: Evidence from Japanese Industrial Groups", 9366–6.196

Medicaid enrollees hospital use and costs related to selected characteristics, 1980, article, 4652–1.949

Medicaid enrollment, and service use and costs by service type, by eligibility type, for 5 States, 1980-84, article, 4652–1.919

Medicaid enrollment, services use, and costs, by eligibility type and length of enrollment, for 2 States, 1980-83, article, 4652–1.906

Medicare and Medicaid beneficiaries and program operations, 1988, annual fact book, 4654–18

Medicare and Medicaid eligibility, participation, coverage, and program finances, various periods 1966-89, biennial rpt, 4654–1

Medicare and Medicaid enrollees, benefits, reimbursements, and services use, mid-1960s-87, annual rpt, 4744–3.5; 4744–3.6

Medicare claims approved, charges, and reimbursements by type of service, from 1974, monthly rpt, quarterly data, 4742–1.11

Medicare discharges, charges, and length of stay, by State and diagnosis, 1983 and 1985, article, 4652–1.925

Medicare discharges, charges, and length of stay, for facilities excluded from prospective payment system, FY84-88, article, 4652–1.935

Medicare enrollees health care alternatives, medical costs, training to select assigned-fee physicians, and physician attitudes, 1988 rpt, 4658–30

Medicare enrollees hospital readmissions related to selected characteristics, for Michigan, 1982-83, article, 4652–1.903

Medicare enrollees physician and other services use, benefits, charges, and coinsurance and deductible obligations, 1982-86, article, 4652–1.901

Medicare hospital claims processing under contract, HCFA controls adequacy and payment errors, 1985-88, GAO rpt, 26121–260

Medicare payments for post-hospitalization care by diagnosis, for nursing home, home care, and rehabilitation, 1980s-87, article, 4652–1.909

Medicare peer review organizations review of hospital claims, activities, and membership, 1984-88, GAO rpt, 26131–51

Medicare reimbursement of hospitals under prospective payment system, and of physicians, effect on services, finances, and beneficiary payments, 1970s-88, annual rpt, 17204–2

Medicare reimbursement of hospitals under prospective payment system, impacts on costs, industry structure and operations, and quality of care, series, 17206–2

Medicare reimbursement of hospitals under prospective payment system, impacts on instns, beneficiaries, and other care providers and payment sources, 1986, annual rpt, 4654–13

Mental health care facilities, staff, and patient characteristics, *Statistical Notes* series, 4506–3

Mental health care hospitals of States and counties, patients and admissions by age, diagnosis, and State, FY87, annual rpt, 4504–2

Mental health care in general hospitals, length of stay related to patient, instn, and State Medicaid program characteristics, 1981, article, 4652–1.924

Military health care benefits and costs under Civilian Health and Medical Program of Uniformed Services, FY83-FY89, 3508–31

Military health care facilities of DOD in US and abroad, admissions, beds, outpatient visits, and births, by service branch, quarterly rpt, 3542–15

Mississippi hospitals and community health centers, use, staff, and Medicare and other payments, 1988 hearing, 25548–97

NIH activities, funding by program and recipient type, staff, and clinic patients, by inst, FY87, annual rpt, 4434–3

Nursing facility service use and costs for Medicare enrollees, by selected characteristics and State, 1970s-87, article, 4652–1.954

Nursing home admissions and discharges for Medicaid patients with prior hospitalization, for 3 States, 1981, article, 4652–1.942

Nursing home and home care case mix, quality of care, and outcomes, impacts of Medicare prospective payment system, 1980s-86, 4658–28

Nursing home facility, staff, and resident detailed characteristics, 1985, 4147–13.97

Nursing home reimbursement by Medicare under prospective payment system, and admissions by prior hospitalization status and duration, and patient characteristics, mid 1970s-85, 4147–13.98

Nursing home use rates, charges, and resident length of stay, care needs, and other characteristics, 1985, 4147–13.102

Occupational injuries, by circumstances, body site, equipment type, and industry, with safety measures, series, 6846–1

Older persons at risk for chronic hospitalization, community care effect on hospital use, demonstration projects, 1989 article, 4652–1.911

Older persons health care services use, persons with high and low levels of care by selected health and other characteristics, 1971 and 1980 studies, 4186–2.22

Older persons health care services use related to marital status, living arrangements, and other characteristics, 1977, 4188–54

Older persons socioeconomic characteristics, 1900s-86 and projected to 2050, biennial chartbook, 12904–1

Pacific territories social, economic, health, and govtl data, FY88 and trends, annual rpt, 7004–6

Pneumonia hospitalization and death rates for aged, and risk relation to health status indicators, aggregate 1982-84, article, 4042–3.934

Pregnancy-related services use and costs, for Medicaid beneficiaries in 3 States, 1983-84, article, 4652–1.938

Rural areas health care facilities, staffing, services accessibility, and indicators of need, 1960s-88, 25148–41

Rural areas hospitals, use, staff, and funding sources, by instn characteristics, 1980s-86, hearing, 25148–42

State govt reimbursement of hospitals under prospective payment programs, effects on operations, finances, and patient deaths, by State, 1970s-83, 4658–29

Statistical Abstract of US, social, political, and economic data, 1790-2025, comprehensive annual compilation, 2324–1.1

Supplemental Security Income beneficiaries Medicaid services use and costs, by diagnosis and whether covered by Medicare, 1984, article, 4652–1.947

Surgical admissions and costs for inpatients and outpatients, by diagnostic group, for Manitoba, Canada, 1982-84, article, 4652–1.940

Surgical procedures performed in hospitals, by procedure type, age, sex, instn size, and payment source, 1983-87, 4146–8.171

Teaching hospitals Medicare payments, and cost factors, compared to non-teaching instns, FY80-85 and projected to FY96, GAO rpt, 26121–265

Traffic accidents, injuries, and deaths, by circumstances and characteristics of persons and vehicles involved, 1970s-87, series, 7766–14

VA activities and programs, and veterans characteristics, FY88, annual rpt, 8604–3

Veterans health care, patients, visits, costs, and operating beds, by VA and contract facility, and region, quarterly rpt, 8602–4

Veterans in VA and non-VA health facilities, by type, FY64-88, annual rpt, 8604–5.3

Veterans population, and benefits programs awareness and use, by age, sex, income, race, and period of service, 1987 survey, 8608–1

Vital and Health Statistics series: health care facilities use and labor force, 4147–13

Hospitalization insurance
see Health insurance

Hospitals

Alcohol abuse treatment in hospitals, capacity, use, and patients by diagnosis, 1980 and 1985, 4186–9.3

Alcohol, Drug Abuse and Mental Health Admin research grants and awards, by recipient, FY88, annual listing, 4044–13

Allergy and Infectious Diseases Natl Inst activities, grants by recipient and location, and disease incidence, FY81-88, annual rpt, 4474–30

Children's hospitals unreimbursed charges, expenses, and revenue, FY86, GAO rpt, 26121–291

Closings of hospitals in 1987, operating characteristics, current use, and location, 1989 rpt, 4008–87

Construction and rehabilitation mortgages for hospitals insured by HUD, principal, and defaults, 1988, GAO rpt, 26121–263

Construction put in place, permits, housing sales, costs, material prices, and employment, bimonthly rpt with articles, 2042–1

Construction put in place, value of new public and private structures, by type, monthly rpt, 2382–4

County Business Patterns, 1987: employment, establishments, and payroll, by SIC 2- to 4-digit industry and county, annual State rpt series, 2326–8

Tax (income) returns of sole proprietorships, income statement items, by industry group, 1987, annual article, 8302–2.904; 8302–2.921

Texas-Mexico border area health facilities and services, with background data, by Texas county, 1980s-88, GAO rpt, 26121–261

Wages of hospital workers relation to supervisory levels and other factors, 1985, working paper, 9377–9.79

Workers compensation regulation of physician fees and hospital rates, provisions by State, 1989 semiannual rpt, 6502–1

see also American Schools and Hospitals Abroad

see also Clinics

see also Emergency medical service

see also Health facilities administration

see also Health maintenance organizations

see also Hospitalization

see also Mental health facilities and services

see also Military health facilities and services

see also Nursing homes

see also Veterans health facilities and services

Hostages

Aircraft hijackings, on-board explosions, and other crime, US and foreign incidents, 1983-87, annual rpt, 7504–31

Bank roberries and related crimes by State, casualties, and hostages, 1982-87, annual rpt, 6064–6.3

Terrorist (intl) incidents, casualties, and attacks on US targets, by attack type and country, 1980-88, 7008–56

Terrorist (intl) incidents, casualties, and attacks on US targets, by attack type and world area, 1968-88, annual rpt, 7004–13

Hostetter, Susan

"Individual Income Tax Returns, Preliminary Data, 1987", 8302–2.917

Hotels and motels

Alteration and repair spending for commercial and public buildings, by type, size, age, and region, 1986, 2388–4

Business statistics, detailed data for major industries and economic indicators, *Survey of Current Business*, monthly rpt, 2702–1.8

Canada travel to US by Province of residence, and characteristics of visit, by State, 1988, annual rpt, 2904–7

Caribbean area hotel rooms and employment, by country, 1987, hearing, 21788–179

Construction industries census, 1987: establishments, employment, receipts, and expenditures, by SIC 4-digit industry and State, final industry rpt series, 2373–1

Construction industries census, 1987: financial and operating data, preliminary industry rpt series, 2371–1

Construction put in place, and authorized by region, by type, bimonthly rpt, 2042–1.1; 2042–1.3

Construction put in place, value of new public and private structures, by type, monthly rpt, 2382–4

County Business Patterns, 1987: employment, establishments, and payroll, by SIC 2- to 4-digit industry and county, annual State rpt series, 2326–8

CPI by component for US city average, and by region, population size, and for 27 metro areas, monthly rpt, 6762–2

Earnings by major industry group, and personal income per capita and by source, by region and State, 1929-87, 2708–40

Employment, earnings, and hours, by selected SIC 1- to 4-digit industry, State, and for 262 MSAs, 1972-87, 6748–81

Employment, earnings, and hours, by SIC 1- to 4-digit industry, monthly 1983-Feb 1989, annual rpt, 6744–4

Employment in nonmanufacturing industries, by detailed occupation and SIC 2-digit industry, 1987, triennial rpt, 6748–60

Employment of minorities and women, by occupation, SIC 1- to 3- digit industry, State, and MSA, 1986, annual rpt, 9244–1

Energy use in commercial buildings, costs, and conservation, by building characteristics, survey rpt series, 3166–8

Finances and operations, by SIC 2- to 4-digit industry, forecast 1989 with trends from 1950s, annual rpt, 2044–28

Fires in hotels and motels, casualties, and effectiveness of smoke detectors, sprinkler systems, and building and equipment design, 1989 hearing, 21708–127

Food and alcoholic beverage spending, by place of purchase, 1966-87, annual rpt, 1544–4.6

Foreign travel to US and Canada, market analyses with detailed trip and traveler characteristics, country rpt series, 2906–2

Foreign travelers spending in US by world area of residence, and economic impact, by spending category, census div, and State, model results, 1985-86, 2908–28

Guam economic censuses, 1987: employment, firms, payroll, and receipts, by SIC 1- to 4-digit industry and election district, 2595–1

Homeless persons housing in rehabilitated single occupancy units, HUD grants by recipient, 1989, press release, 5006–3.68

Labor productivity, indexes of output, hours, and employment by SIC 2- to 4-digit industry, 1963-87, annual rpt, 6824–1.4

Multinatl US firms and foreign affiliates finances and operations, by industry of parent firm and affiliate, world area, and country, preliminary 1987, annual rpt, 2704–5

Northern Mariana Islands economic census, 1987: employment, firms, payroll, and receipts, by SIC 1- to 4-digit industry, 2597–1

Occupational injury and illness rates, by SIC 2- to 4-digit industry, 1987, annual rpt, 6844–1

Pacific territories social, economic, health, and govtl data, FY88 and trends, annual rpt, 7004–6

Park natl system visits and overnight stays, by park and State, monthly rpt, 5542–4

Park natl system visits and overnight stays, by park and State, 1988 and trends from 1979, annual rpt, 5544–12

Receipts for services, by SIC 2- to 4-digit kind of business, 1988, annual rpt, 2413–8

Science and engineering employment, by nonmanufacturing industry and field, 1987, triennial rpt, 9627–31

Service industries census, 1987: establishments, receipts, employment, and payroll, by SIC 2- to 4-digit kind of business, MSA, county, and city, State rpt series, 2391–1

Small business establishments, employment, and financial ratios, by SIC 1- to 2-digit industry and State, late 1960s-87, 9768–19

Statistical Abstract of US, social, political, and economic data, 1790-2025, comprehensive annual compilation, 2324–1.3

Tax (income) returns of corporations, income and tax items by asset size and detailed industry, 1986, annual rpt, 8304–4; 8304–21

Tax (income) returns of partnerships, income statement items by industry group, 1986, annual article, 8302–2.903

Tax (income) returns of sole proprietorships, income statement items, by industry group, 1987, annual article, 8302–2.904; 8302–2.921

Virgin Islands economic censuses, 1987: employment, firms, payroll, and receipts, by SIC 1- to 4-digit industry, island, and city, 2593–1

Wages and employment by occupation and sex, and benefits, for hotel and motel service workers in 18 MSAs, 1988 survey, 6787–6.242

Wildlife-related recreation, hunting, and fishing participation and spending, detailed data by location, 1985 survey, quinquennial rpt, 5508–5

Wildlife-related recreation, hunting, and fishing participation and spending, detailed data, 1985 survey, quinquennial State rpt series, 5506–6

Houchens, Robert L.

"Developing a Measure of Complexity of Illness Within DRGs", 17206–2.6

Houff, James N.

"Analyzing Short-Term Disability Benefits", 6722–1.925

Houlihan, William A.

"Issue Subordinated Debt for Good Reason", 9312–1.906

Houma, La.

see also under By SMSA or MSA in the "Index by Categories"

Hours of labor

Agricultural Statistics, 1988, annual rpt, 1004–1.2

Agriculture census, 1987: farms, farmland, production, finances, and operator characteristics, by county, final State rpt series, 2331–1

Asian American earnings, and employment and other characteristics, by detailed origin and whether foreign-born, 1980, 11046–7.2

Auto and home supply stores productivity trends and technological devs, 1972-87, article, 6722–1.941

Banks in Fed Reserve System, expenses and operations itemized by service, office, and district, 1988, annual rpt, 9364–11

Business and financial statistics, historic trends, 1988 annual chartbook, 9364–2.2

Business Conditions Digest, cyclical indicators, by economic process, monthly rpt, 2702–3.3

Work stoppages, workers involved, and days
idle, 1988 and trends from 1947, annual
press release, 6784-12

see also Absenteeism

see also Area wage surveys

see also Earnings, general

see also Earnings, local and regional

see also Industry wage surveys

see also Labor productivity

see also Moonlighting

see also Overtime

see also Part-time employment

see also Temporary and seasonal
employment

see also Underemployment

House Aging Committee, Select

Board and care homes conditions, State
licensing and enforcement activity, and
client characteristics, 1970s-88,
21148-55

Health care (long-term) needs, ability to
pay, and views on Federal aid for home
care, 1988 survey, hearing, 21148-51

Hospital reimbursement by Medicare under
prospective payment system, impacts on
profit margins, and instn characteristics,
1986/87, hearing, 21148-52

Indian housing condition and other
characteristics, for aged, 1987 survey,
21148-53

Vermont older persons employment, income,
and other characteristics, by sex and age,
1900-86, hearing, 21148-54

House Agriculture Committee

Production itemized costs, by selected
commodity, projected 1986-97, hearing,
21168-40

House Armed Services Committee

Medical malpractice claims against military
hospitals by disposition, and costs,
1982-87, hearing, 21208-27

Military commissaries in Europe, test sales
of US beef and pork, and patron survey
results, 1986, hearing, 21208-28

Warsaw Pact and USSR military strength,
and proposed force reductions, with
comparisons to NATO, 1980s-91, hearing,
21208-29

House Banking Committee

Bond (low-grade) issues by industry div,
holdings by owner type, yields, and
defaults, 1977-88, 21248-118

**House Banking, Finance, and Urban Affairs
Committee**

Banks (US) loans to developing countries,
and loan loss reserves, by money center
bank, Sept 1988, hearings, 21248-122

Banks brokered deposit holdings and
financial indicators, by size, region, and
for failed instns, 1986-89, hearing,
21248-124

Eastern Europe and USSR debt, trade, and
balances with US and other western
countries, with background data,
1980s-87, hearing, 21248-120

Homeless population characteristics by city,
and Federal funding by program,
1980s-89, hearings, 21248-123

Lead poisoning among children, and
children at risk in Massachusetts, by city,
1985-87, hearing, 21248-119

Low income housing stock effects of
alternative Federal actions and spending
levels, projected 1988-2002, hearing,
21248-116

Rural areas rental housing units, vacancy,
and rent exceeding 30% of renter income,
by type of rental aid and State, FY88,
hearing, 21248-117

Savings and loan assns failures, assets, and
FSLIC resolution costs and promissory
notes, with data for acquired and
acquiring instn in US and Texas, 1988
hearings, 21248-121

House Budget Committee

Budget of US, House concurrent resolution,
with spending and revenue targets, FY90,
annual rpt, 21264-2

Savings instns failures, financial condition
indicators, and liquidation and acquisition
costs and tax benefits by instn and
acquiring company, 1985-98, hearing,
21268-41

**House Children, Youth, and Families
Committee, Select**

Child health and welfare programs of local
agencies for high-risk infants and children,
for Los Angeles and San Francisco, 1988
hearing, 21968-48

House District of Columbia Committee

Drug abuse, deaths, arrests, convictions, and
seizures by drug type, for DC metro area,
1980-87, hearing, 21308-24

Emergency fire and medical services
operations, staff, and finances, for DC and
compared to other US and Canadian
cities, 1986, hearing, 21308-25

House Documents

Budget deficit reduction under
Gramm-Rudman Act, cancellation of
budget authority by program, FY90,
annual rpt, 21924-1

House, Donald

"Comparison of Physician Malpractice
Insurance Indices", 4658-27

House Education and Labor Committee

Aerospace industry minority employment in
Los Angeles area, by occupational group,
1980s-86, 21348-113

Education Dept Civil Rights Office,
complaints, investigations, funding, and
staff, various periods FY81-88,
21348-114

House Energy and Commerce Committee

Acid rain control economic impacts, and
sulfur dioxide emissions and reductions of
industrial and power plants, 1987 hearing,
21368-104

Auto insurance coverage, premiums, and
theft losses, with data by model and State,
1988 hearings, 21368-110

Conservation R&D spending of DOE and
private sector, and housing natural gas use
indicators, hearings, 21368-107

Dioxin levels in paper products and pulp
mill effluents, and environmental and
health effects, 1988 hearing, 21368-112

Health care (long-term) for aged, funding by
Fed Govt, public views, 1987 survey,
hearings, 21368-106

Housewares (ceramic) lead and cadmium
levels, FDA import inspection activity by
country, and food safety funding and staff,
1983-88, hearing, 21368-108

Medicaid coverage, participation, payments,
admin, and legislative history, with data
by State, 1980s-88, 21368-105

Mergers and acquisitions using leveraged
buyout, financing characteristics and
policy issues, 1970s-88, 21368-115

Pollution (air) exposure of population and
selected risk groups, by pollutant, MSA,
and county, 1988, hearing, 21368-117

Rail shipments of grain, and car fleets and
shortages, with data by firm, 1970s-88 and
forecast to 1995, hearing, 21368-114

Railroad (short-line) operations and
regulation, for lines established
1834-1987, hearing, 21368-109

Railroad accidents, casualties, and Federal
safety activities, late 1970s-87, hearing,
21368-103

SEC staffing, pay, and turnover by
occupation and city, with proposed fee
revenues to improve work conditions,
1989 hearing, 21368-116

Securities issues, placements, and intl and
US transactions by type, 1982-88,
21368-118

Stock market crash of 1987, consumer
complaints by reason, security type, and
State, Nov-Dec 1987, hearings,
21368-111

Telecommunications industries minority
employment and discrimination charges,
with data by industry and selected firm,
1970s-88, hearings, 21368-113

House Foreign Affairs Committee

Economic conditions, policy, and trade
practices, by country, 1986-88, annual rpt,
21384-5

Human rights conditions in 170 countries,
1988, annual rpt, 21384-3

Pakistan military strengths, spending,
weapons systems, and arms imports, with
comparisons to India, 1980s-87, hearing,
21388-54

Portugal and Turkey economic indicators
and govt finances, 1982-86, hearing,
21388-53

House Government Operations Committee

Abortions by patient characteristics, rates
for all and 1st abortions, and related
deaths in US and other countries, 1989
hearing, 21408-113

Banks and other financial instns fraud and
insider misconduct cases, Federal
regulatory and enforcement activities, and
losses, 1981-87, hearing, 21408-111

Executions by whether writ of habeas corpus
used to appeal, race, and State, with
military death row inmates, 1977-87,
hearing, 21408-110

Hazardous substances health effects,
environmental levels, and household
products composition, with data by
selected location, 1988 hearings,
21408-112

House Hunger Committee, Select

West Virginia poverty conditions, food aid
participants, and birth outcomes, 1980-87,
hearing, 21968-49

House Interior and Insular Affairs Committee

Alaska Arctic Natl Wildlife Refuge oil and
gas resource assessment, with
environmental impacts on North Slope
and other locations, 1987 hearing,
21448-41

Connecticut energy use by consuming
sector, and prices, by energy type,
1960s-86, hearing, 21448-38

Indian reservation water supply projects in
South Dakota, costs and indicators of
need, with health and housing data for
other reservations, 1980s-87, hearing,
21448-37

Irrigation subsidies of Reclamation Bur, costs to Fed Govt and surplus crop production, 1985-86, 21448-40

Puerto Rico economic conditions, 1986 hearings, 21448-39

House Judiciary Committee

Budget of US, balanced budget proposed constitutional amendment, economic impacts, projected to FY94 and background data from 1940s, hearings, 21528-72

Mail order sales from out of State, tax revenues and rates under proposed collection system, by State, 1988 hearings, 21528-73

TV satellite dish and decoder sales, ownership, subscribers, and program ratings compared to local stations, 1980s-88, hearings, 21528-74

House Merchant Marine and Fisheries Committee

Pollutant discharges in coastal areas and estuaries from agricultural, airborne, and other nonpoint sources, and regulatory issues, 1988 hearing, 21568-46

Sewage pipelines and dump sites authorized in coastal areas, status and EPA enforcement activities by State, 1982-87, hearings, 21568-45

Tuna fishery porpoise kill, purse seine vessels in Pacific Ocean, and porpoise population, 1960s-90, hearing, 21568-47

House Narcotics Abuse and Control Committee, Select

Drug abuse, deaths, arrests, convictions, and seizures by drug type, for DC metro area, 1980-87, hearing, 21308-24

House of Representatives

Budget of US Appendix, obligations, appropriations, and personnel, by program and agency, FY90, annual rpt, 104-3

Budget of US, authoritative financial statements with appropriations, outlays, and receipts, by category and agency, FY88, annual rpt, 8104-2.2

Buildings and grounds under Capitol Architect supervision, itemized outlays by payee and function, 1st half FY89, semiannual rpt, 25922-2

Congressional Directory, members of 101st Congress, other officials, elections, and districts, 1989-90, biennial rpt, 23874-1

Election campaign finances and FEC activities, various periods 1975-88, annual rpt, 9274-1

Election campaign financial activity reported to FEC, by type of filer, 1988 natl elections, biennial rpt series, 9276-2

Election campaign funds raised and spent by party committees, by candidate, 1988, press release, 9276-1.64

Election campaign receipts and spending of congressional candidates, by candidate, 1987-88, press release, 9276-1.62; 9276-1.63

Salaries, expenses, and contingent fund disbursement, detailed listings, quarterly rpt, 21942-1

Seats in House by State, Census of Population use in apportionment, 1972-90, article, 9278-7

Statistical Abstract of US, social, political, and economic data, 1790-2025, comprehensive annual compilation, 2324-1.2

Votes cast by party, candidate, and State, 1988 natl elections, biennial rpt, 9274-5; 21944-3

see also House Documents

see also House Special Publications

see also under names of individual committees (starting with House or Joint)

see also under names of individual subcommittees (starting with Subcommittee)

House Post Office and Civil Service Committee

Aliens (illegal) and immigration impact on congressional apportionment, alternative estimates by State, 1950s-80 with projections to 2010, hearing, 21628-70

Census of Population and Housing, 1990: data collection procedure improvement and preparation for count, hearing, 21628-71

Census of Population and Housing, 1990: outlying areas preparations for count, hearings, 21628-72; 21628-74

Insurance (health) for Federal employees and annuitants, enrollment, costs, and Medicare coverage, with data for selected plans, 1980-89, 21628-73

Pay rates of Fed Govt civilian employees, by pay schedule and grade, 1989 and trends from 1789, annual rpt, 21624-4

House Public Works and Transportation Committee

Economic Dev Admin funding, and loans forgiven, with data by project and location, FY84-88, hearing, 21648-56

Hwy (interstate) system expenditures, costs, and mileage, by State, as of 1988 and forecast FY91-92, 21648-58

Hwy conditions, travel, and funding, by type of hwy, biennial rpt, issuing agency change, 21644-2

Trucking industry deregulation in 1980, impacts on finances and safety, mid 1970s-88, hearing, 21648-55

TVA nuclear power plant mgmt salaries by position, and plant capacity, compared to private utilities, 1985-87, hearing, 21648-57

House Science, Space, and Technology Committee

Fires in hotels and motels, casualties, and effectiveness of smoke detectors, sprinkler systems, and building and equipment design, 1989 hearing, 21708-127

Foreign and US technology dev and competition issues, fundings and recommendations, 1980s-87, 21708-123

Foreign countries food and agricultural conditions, and relationship to population growth, with background data, 1950s-88 and projections to 2050, hearing, 21708-126

R&D funding by Fed Govt at large science facilities, by field, performer, and facility, FY86-88, hearings, 21708-128

Rhinoceros wild and captive population, poacher kills and enforcement action, and conservation issues, 1988 hearing, 21708-125

Truck and bus engine R&D and alternative fuels to reduce exhaust emissions costs and economic impacts, 1988 hearing, 21708-124

House Small Business Committee

Fed Govt contracts and obligations for small business, by program and recipient type, for North Carolina and total US, FY77-87, hearings, 21728-67

Small business high technology sales, exports, siting, technology transfer, views on competitiveness, 1988 survey, hearing, 21728-69

Small business loans of Eximbank, by firm, 1984-88, hearing, 21728-70

Women-owned business mgmt issues, SBA loans, Federal contracts by agency, and owners views on Michigan business climate, FY79-88, hearings, 21728-68

House Special Publications

House of Representatives salaries, expenses, and contingent fund disbursement, detailed listings, quarterly rpt, 21942-1

Votes cast by party, candidate, and State, 1988 natl elections, biennial rpt, 21944-3

House trailers

see Mobile homes

House Veterans Affairs Committee

Benefits claims processing and efficiency at regional VA offices, and hearing officers salaries and travel costs, 1986-88, hearing, 21768-47

Health care centers canteen services discontinuing tobacco sales, impacts on finances, FY83-FY88, hearing, 21768-49

Health care facilities of VA, beds closed because of nurse shortages, and malpractice claim rates, FY85-88, hearing, 21768-48

House Ways and Means Committee

Airport and Airway Trust Fund funding and improvement spending, with data by airport and program, 1988 hearing, 21788-180

Caribbean area sugar production and exports, and cruise ship tourist visits and spending, by country, 1981-88, hearing, 21788-179

Disability Insurance and SSI eligibility determinations for mental impairment, caseload and review activities by impairment type and State, 1984-86, hearing, 21788-176

Fed Govt programs under Committee jurisdiction, finances and operations, FY70s-88, annual rpt, 21784-11

Foreign countries economic conditions, policy, and trade practices, by country, 1986-88, annual rpt, 21384-5

Savings instns assets and mortgage holdings, insured instns, and FSLIC failure resolution caseloads and costs, 1970s-88, 21788-177

Savings instns failure resolution costs, financing problems, and FSLIC and acquiring instns tax benefits, 1988 and projected to FY99, hearings, 21788-181

Steel imports of US under voluntary restraint agreements, with industry finances, operations, and foreign comparisons, various periods 1979-89, 21788-182

Tax (income) aid telephone system of IRS, accessibility and accuracy, and other IRS workload indicators, 1988 hearing, 21788-178

Tax expenditures, Federal revenues forgone through income tax deductions and exclusions by type, FY90-94, annual rpt, 21784-10

Energy conservation (housing) program of BPA, energy savings and indoor air quality under alternative methods, projected 1986-2006, 3228–9

Farmland value, rent, taxes, foreign ownership, and transfers by probable use and lender type, with data by region and State, 1975-89, article, 1561–16.902

Fed Govt financial and nonfinancial domestic aid, 1989 base edition with supplements, annual listing, 104–5

Finances and operations, by SIC 2- to 4-digit industry, forecast 1989 with trends from 1950s, annual rpt, 2044–28

Financial and business statistics, historic trends, 1988 annual chartbook, 9364–2.12

Flow-of-funds accounts, savings, investments, and credit statements, quarterly rpt, 9365–3.3

Housing and households summary characteristics, 1985 and trends, biennial chartbook, 2486–1.7

Indian (Navajo and Hopi) relocation program activities and caseloads, monthly rpt, 16002–1

Indian and Alaska Native housing and economic development program operations, by region, FY86-87, annual rpt, 5004–5

Japan lumber use by industry, and construction activity and indicators of demand, 1970-88, article, 2042–1.909

Japan wood products, selected economic and housing demand indicators, 1989 rpt, 2046–14.2

Loan rates for FHA and conventional construction loans by region, and builders with declining, stable, and advancing trends in new plans and unsold units, monthly press release, 5142–20

Middle Atlantic States, FHLB 2nd District economic and housing indicators, by State, quarterly rpt with articles, 9302–33

Mortgage applications to FHA for new and existing units, refinancings, and housing starts, monthly rpt, 5142–44

Mortgage loan activity, by type of lender, loan, and mortgaged property, monthly press release, 5142–18

Mortgage loan activity, by type of lender, loan, and mortgaged property, quarterly press release, 5142–30

Mortgage loan activity, by type of lender, loan, and mortgaged property, 1986-88, annual press release, 5144–22

Mortgage loan activity of FSLIC-insured savings instns, by purpose and State, various periods 1984-87, annual rpt, 9314–3

Mortgages by lender type and related to neighborhood characteristics, for Boston, Mass, 1982-87, article, 9373–1.915

Natl income and product accounts and components, *Survey of Current Business*, monthly rpt, 2702–1.22

New construction (public and private) put in place, value by type, monthly rpt, 2382–4

New England States economic indicators, Fed Reserve 1st District, monthly rpt, 9373–24

New England States economic indicators, Fed Reserve 1st District, quarterly rpt, 9373–2.4

New England States, FHLB 1st District thrift instns financial operations and housing industry indicators, monthly rpt, 9302–4

New housing construction and sales by region, permits by State and MSA, costs, and material prices, bimonthly rpt with articles, 2042–1

New housing starts and authorizations, 1959-88 with trends from 1929, annual rpt, 204–1.3

New housing starts and completions authorized by building permits in 40 MSAs, quarterly rpt, 2382–9

New housing unit starts, by units per structure and metro-nonmetro location, and mobile home placements and prices, by region, monthly rpt, 2382–1

New housing units authorized, by region, State, selected MSA, and permit-issuing place, monthly rpt, 2382–5

New housing units authorized, by State, MSA, and permit-issuing place, 1988, annual rpt, 2384–2

New housing units completed and under construction, by units per structure, region, and inside-outside MSAs, monthly rpt, 2382–2

New single and multifamily units, by structural and financial characteristics, inside-outside MSAs, and region, 1984-88, annual rpt, 2384–1

New single-family houses sold and for sale, by price, stage of construction, months on market, and region, monthly rpt, 2382–3

North Central States, FHLB 7th District housing vacancy rates for single and multifamily units and mobile homes, by ZIP code, annual MSA rpt series, 9304–18

Occupational injury and illness rates, by SIC 2- to 4-digit industry, 1987, annual rpt, 6844–1

Older persons low-income rental housing construction and rehabilitation loans, by recipient, 1989, press release HUD loans for older persons low-income rental housing construction and rehabilitation, by recipient, 1989, press release, 5006–3.71

Pacific Northwest population, households, employment, income, and fuel prices, alternative projections 1990-2010 with trends from 1960, annual rpt, 3224–5

Puerto Rico and other US possessions corporations tax incentives, finances, and operations by industry, and impacts on local economy, 1970s-83, biennial rpt, 8004–12

Rural and urban areas housing and households characteristics, 1930s-80, 1598–245

Science and engineering employment, by nonmanufacturing industry and field, 1987, triennial rpt, 9627–31

South Central States, FHLB 9th District housing vacancy rates for single and multifamily units and mobile homes by ZIP code, annual MSA rpt series, 9304–19

Southeastern States, Fed Reserve 6th District, economic indicators by State and MSA, quarterly rpt, 9371–14

Sri Lanka housing construction loans to rural low-income families, activities, and recipient characteristics, 1984-86, 9918–16

Statistical Abstract of US, social, political, and economic data, 1790-2025, comprehensive annual compilation, 2324–1.3

Urban Dev Action Grant eligibility rating system of HUD, and project costs and economic impacts, as of Nov 1988, GAO rpt, 26113–424

West Central States, FHLB 10th District housing vacancy rates for single and multifamily units and mobile homes, by ZIP code, annual MSA rpt series, 9304–22

Western States, FHLB 11th District housing vacancy rates for single and multifamily units and mobile homes, by ZIP code, annual MSA rpt series, 9304–20

Western States, FHLB 12th District housing vacancy rates for single and multifamily units and mobile homes, by ZIP code, annual MSA rpt series, 9304–21

see also Building materials
see also Federal aid to housing
see also Housing condition and occupancy
see also Housing costs and financing
see also Housing maintenance and repair
see also Insulation
see also Prefabricated buildings
see also Property value
see also Public housing
see also Wrecking and demolition

Housing costs and financing
Alteration and repair spending for housing, by characteristics of property and region, 1984-88, annual rpt, 2384–4

American Housing Survey: unit and households characteristics, MSA fact sheet series, 2485–11

American Housing Survey: unit and households detailed characteristics, and unit and neighborhood quality, MSA rpt series, 2485–6

American Housing Survey: unit and households detailed characteristics, and unit and neighborhood quality, 1985, biennial rpt, 2485–12

Bond tax-exempt issues for private activity, by purpose, face value, major industry, and State, 1986, annual article, 8302–2.905

Community dev programs of HUD, funding and activities by program and State, FY88, annual rpt, 5124–5

Condominium completions and absorption rates, by size and price class, preliminary 1988, annual Current Housing Rpt, 2484–3

Condominium completions by rent class and sales price, and market absorption rates, quarterly rpt, 2482–2

Consumer Expenditure Survey, household income by source, and itemized spending, by selected characteristics and region, 1984-87, annual rpt, 6764–5

Consumer Expenditure Survey, spending by category, and income, by selected household characteristics and location, 1987, press release, 6726–1.23

Consumer Expenditure Survey, spending by category, selected household characteristics, and region, quarterly rpt, 6762–14

Consumer spending and income effects of wives' employment, by expenditure category and household characteristics, 1984-86, article, 6722–1.908

Indian Health Service facilities, funding, operations, and Indian health and other characteristics, 1950s-88, annual chartbook, 4084-1

Japan lumber use by industry, and construction activity and indicators of demand, 1970-88, article, 2042-1.909

Loan activity of FSLIC-insured savings instns by FHLB district and State, and for FDIC-insured savings banks, 1988, annual rpt, 8434-1

Low income housing stock effects of alternative Federal actions and spending levels, projected 1988-2002, hearing, 21248-116

Mortgage insurance programs of HUD, finances and lending activity by program, FY88, annual rpt, 5004-8

Mortgages FHA-insured for 1-family units, by loan type and mortgage characteristics, quarterly rpt, 5142-45

Older persons low-income rental housing construction and rehabilitation loans, by recipient, 1989, press release HUD loans for older persons low-income rental housing construction and rehabilitation, by recipient, 1989, press release, 5006-3.71

Price indexes (producer) for material inputs, by construction industry, monthly rpt, 6762-6

Price indexes for department store inventories, by class of item, monthly table, 6762-7

Public and Indian housing stock and renovation needs, series, 5186-15

Rental housing rehabilitation loans under HUD Section 312, program operations, FY86-88, annual rpt, 5124-5

Statistical Abstract of US, social, political, and economic data, 1790-2025, comprehensive annual compilation, 2324-1.3

Urban Homesteading Program properties, units, and rehabilitation costs by financing source, FY88, annual rpt, 5124-5

Value of private residential additions and alterations, monthly rpt, 2382-4

see also Insulation

Housing rehabilitation

see Housing maintenance and repair

see Urban renewal

Housing sales

Business activity indicators, 1987, annual rpt, 9364-5.9

Condominium absorption rates, by sales class and size, 1987 and trends from 1970, annual Current Housing Rpt, 2484-2

Condominium completions and absorption rates, by size and price class, preliminary 1988, annual Current Housing Rpt, 2484-3

FmHA property acquired through foreclosure, 1-family homes, value, sales, and leases, by State, monthly rpt, 1182-7

Indian (Navajo and Hopi) relocation program activities and caseloads, monthly rpt, 16002-1

Indian (Navajo and Hopi) relocation program activities, caseloads, and finances, FY88, annual rpt, 16004-1

Inventory of unsold new units, share of builders reporting declining, stable, and advancing trends, monthly press release, 5142-20

Mortgages by lender type and related to neighborhood characteristics, for Boston, Mass, 1982-87, article, 9373-1.915

Mortgages FHA-insured, characteristics of first time and other buyers, 1988, 5148-8

New and existing housing units sold, and average price, by region, bimonthly rpt, 2042-1.2

New England States, FHLB 1st District thrift instns financial operations and housing industry indicators, monthly rpt, 9302-4

New single and multifamily units, by structural and financial characteristics, inside-outside MSAs, and region, 1984-88, annual rpt, 2384-1

New single-family houses sold and for sale, by price, stage of construction, months on market, and region, monthly rpt, 2382-3

New single-family houses sold, prices and price index by region, quarterly rpt, 2382-8

Southeastern States, FHLB 4th District, employment and housing market indicators by State, quarterly rpt, 9302-36

Statistical Abstract of US, social, political, and economic data, 1790-2025, comprehensive annual compilation, 2324-1.3

Tax (income) returns of individuals, by filing status, tax item, and income level, 1987, annual article, 8302-2.901

Housing starts

see Housing construction

Housing supply and requirements

Alaska rural villages population characteristics and and subsistence activities, 1976-86, 5738-9

Apartment and condominium completions by rent class and sales price, and market absorption rates, quarterly rpt, 2482-2

Apartment market absorption rates and characteristics for nonsubsidized furnished and unfurnished units, 1987 and trends from 1970, annual Current Housing Rpt, 2484-2

Census Bur rpts and data files, coverage and availability, 1989 annual listing, 2304-2

Coastal areas environmental impacts of economic dev and population growth, 1980s and projected to 2000, 2176-8.1

Housing units completed, single and multifamily units by structural and financial characteristics, inside-outside MSAs, and region, 1984-88, annual rpt, 2384-1

Low income housing stock effects of alternative Federal actions and spending levels, projected 1988-2002, hearing, 21248-116

Low income housing stock, units eligible for subsidized mortgage prepayment, and index of affordable housing needs, by State, 1982-2006, article, 1702-1.903

New single-family houses sold and for sale, by price, stage of construction, months on market, and region, monthly rpt, 2382-3

North Central States, FHLB 7th District housing vacancy rates for single and multifamily units and mobile homes, by ZIP code, annual MSA rpt series, 9304-18

Pacific Northwest population, households, employment, income, and fuel prices, alternative projections 1990-2010 with trends from 1960, annual rpt, 3224-5

Public and Indian housing stock and renovation needs, series, 5186-15

Rural areas rental housing units, vacancy, and rent exceeding 30% of renter income, by type of rental aid and State, FY88, hearing, 21248-117

South Central States, FHLB 9th District housing vacancy rates for single and multifamily units and mobile homes by ZIP code, annual MSA rpt series, 9304-19

Vacant housing characteristics and costs, and occupancy and vacancy rates, by region and metro-nonmetro location, quarterly rpt, 2482-1

West Central States, FHLB 10th District housing vacancy rates for single and multifamily units and mobile homes, by ZIP code, annual MSA rpt series, 9304-22

Western States, FHLB 11th District housing vacancy rates for single and multifamily units and mobile homes, by ZIP code, annual MSA rpt series, 9304-20

Western States, FHLB 12th District housing vacancy rates for single and multifamily units and mobile homes, by ZIP code, annual MSA rpt series, 9304-21

see also Building permits

see also Housing condition and occupancy

see also Housing construction

see also Housing costs and financing

see also Housing sales

see also Urban renewal

see also Wrecking and demolition

Housing tenure

Alteration and repair spending for housing, by characteristics of property and region, 1984-88, annual rpt, 2384-4

Alteration and repair spending for housing, by tenure, quarterly rpt, 2382-7

American Housing Survey: unit and households characteristics, MSA fact sheet series, 2485-11

American Housing Survey: unit and households detailed characteristics, and unit and neighborhood quality, MSA rpt series, 2485-6

American Housing Survey: unit and households detailed characteristics, and unit and neighborhood quality, 1985, biennial rpt, 2485-12

Capital (fixed), govt and private nonresidential structures and equipment, residential capital, and consumer-owned durable goods, 1985-88, annual article, 2702-1.931; 2702-1.937

Child support and alimony awards, and payment status, by selected characteristics of woman, 1985, biennial Current Population Rpt, 2546-2.145

Consumer Expenditure Survey, household income by source, and itemized spending, by selected characteristics and region, 1984-87, annual rpt, 6764-5

Consumer Expenditure Survey, spending by category, and income, by selected household characteristics and location, 1987, press release, 6726-1.23

Consumer Income, socioeconomic characteristics of persons, families, and households, detailed cross-tabulations, Current Population Rpt series, 2546-6

Consumer spending and income effects of wives' employment, by expenditure category and household characteristics, 1984-86, article, 6722-1.908

Cost of living indexes for metro areas, relation of expenditure items and quality of life indicators, model results, 1973, working paper, 6886–6.9

Crime victimization rates, by victim and offender characteristics, circumstances, and offense, 1987 survey, annual rpt, 6066–3.41

Farm population under alternative definitions, by selected characteristics, 1983, 1598–249

Household and family characteristics, by location, 1988, annual Current Population Rpt, 2546–1.437

Housing and households summary characteristics, 1985 and trends, biennial chartbook, 2486–1.7

Housing energy use, costs, and conservation, and household and housing characteristics, survey rpt series, 3166–7

Income (household) before and after taxes, and discretionary, by sociodemographic characteristics, 1986, 2308–54

Indian housing condition and other characteristics, for aged, 1987 survey, 21148–53

Living arrangements, family relationships, and marital status, by selected characteristics, 1988, annual Current Population Rpt, 2546–1.428; 2546–1.433

Low income housing aid of Fed Govt, unit conditions, and household characteristics, 1985-FY88 and alternative projections to 2008, 26306–6.134

Military reserve spouses attitudes, and family social, economic, and other characteristics, 1986 survey, 3508–30

Older persons socioeconomic characteristics, 1900s-86 and projected to 2050, biennial chartbook, 12904–1

Ownership of homes, rates by location, quarterly rpt, 2482–1

Ownership rate, by age of household head, 1974-87, article, 1702–1.903

Ownership rates and unit costs, by income, age, family composition, and region, 1967-87, hearings, 25248–107

Retirees housing and community preferences, by respondent characteristics, 1987 survey, article, 1702–1.905

Rural and urban areas housing and households characteristics, 1930s-80, 1598–245

Single-parent household income and spending, and selected characteristics, with comparison to households with married parents, 1984-86, article, 6722–1.916

Statistical Abstract of US, social, political, and economic data, 1790-2025, comprehensive annual compilation, 2324–1.1; 2324–1.3

Suburban areas land use, commuting, employment, and housing characteristics, detailed data for traffic planning, 1986, 7888–75

Supplemental Security Income beneficiaries, assets by type and eligibility class, FY87, article, 4742–1.922

Taxes, spending, and govt efficiency, public opinion by respondent characteristics, 1989 survey, annual rpt, 10044–2

Vacant housing characteristics and costs, and occupancy and vacancy rates, by region and metro-nonmetro location, quarterly rpt, 2482–1

Vacant housing characteristics, and occupancy and vacancy rates, by tenure, region, and metro-nonmetro location, selected years 1960-88, annual rpt, 2484–1
see also Apartment houses
see also Condominiums and cooperatives
see also Housing sales
see also Rent

Housing voucher programs
see Rent supplements

Houston, Tex.
CPI by component for US city average, and by region, population size, and for 15 metro areas, monthly rpt, 6762–1
CPI by component for US city average, and by region, population size, and for 27 metro areas, monthly rpt, 6762–2
CPI by major component for 2 Texas MSAs, monthly rpt, 6962–2
Drug test results at arrest, by drug type, offense, and sex, for selected urban areas, quarterly rpt, 6062–3
Employment, earnings, hours, and CPI changes, for Houston metro area, 1970s-88, annual rpt, 6964–1
Homeless persons aid programs, and shelter capacity and voucher programs, for 5 major cities, 1988, 5188–122
Housing starts and completions authorized by building permits in 40 MSAs, quarterly rpt, 2382–9
Wages by occupation, for office and plant workers, 1989 survey, periodic MSA rpt, 6785–12.3
see also under By City and By SMSA or MSA in the "Index by Categories"

Howe, Holly L.
"Cancer Incidence Following Exposure to Drinking Water with Asbestos Leachate", 4042–3.921

Howe, Wayne J.
"Labor Market Completes Sixth Year of Expansion in 1988", 6722–1.907

Howell, Craig
"Price Highlights of 1988: Rising Pressures on Consumer Prices", 6722–1.921

Howell, Embry M.
"Longitudinal Patterns of Enrollment and Expenditures for a Medicaid Cohort", 4652–1.906
"Patterns of Medicaid Utilization and Expenditures in Selected States: 1980-84", 4652–1.919
"Prenatal, Delivery, and Infant Care Under Medicaid in Three States", 4652–1.938

Howenstine, Ned G.
"U.S. Affiliates of Foreign Companies: 1987 Benchmark Survey Results", 2702–1.925

Howland, Marie
"Urban-Oriented Program Helped Rural Communities", 1502–7.903

Hu, Patricia S.
"Light-Duty Vehicle Summary: Model Year 1976 to the First Half of Model Year 1989", 3302–4

Huang, Ben W.
"1989 Outlook for Fruit and Tree Nuts", 1004–16.1

Hubbard, R. Glenn
"Financial Factors in Business Fluctuations", 9381–13.1

Huckabee, David C.
"Proposed Exclusion of Illegal Aliens from the Population Used To Apportion the House of Representatives: A Methodological and Policy Analysis", 21628–70

HUD
see Department of Housing and Urban Development

Hudson Institute
"Civil Service 2000", 9848–37

Hudson River
Freight (waterborne domestic and foreign) by commodity, traffic, and passengers, by port and waterway, 1987, annual rpt, 3754–3.1
Pollutant levels and sources for Hudson-Raritan River basin, model description and results, 1880s-1982, 2178–22
Pollution levels in Hudson-Raritan estuary, and effects of refrigeration on pollutant samples, 1983-84, 2168–109
Pollution of oceans, estuaries, and coastal waters monitoring and assessment, NOAA activities and funding, FY88, annual rpt, 2174–9
Water supply and quality in streams and lakes, and groundwater levels in wells, by drainage basin, 1986, annual State rpt series, 5666–23
Water supply and quality in streams and lakes, and groundwater levels in wells, by drainage basin, 1987, annual State rpt series, 5666–10
Water supply and quality in streams and lakes, and groundwater levels in wells, by drainage basin, 1988, annual State rpt series, 5666–16
Water supply in northeastern US, precipitation and stream runoff by station, monthly rpt, 2182–3
Water supply in US and southern Canada, streamflow, surface and groundwater conditions, and reservoir levels, by location, monthly rpt, 5662–3

Huffman, Gregory W.
"Tax Analysis in a Dynamic Stochastic Model: On Measuring Harberger Triangles and Okun Gaps", 9381–10.95

Hughes, Vergie
"Producer Milk Marketed Under Federal Milk Orders by State of Origin", 1317–4.904

Hull, David B.
"Feed Grain Situation and Outlook", 1004–16.1

Hull, Everson
"Who Suffers Most from Downturns?", 8432–2.902

Hulten, Charles R.
"Energy, Obsolescence, and the Productivity Slowdown", 6886–6.45

Human experimentation
Allergy and Infectious Diseases Natl Inst activities, grants by recipient and location, and disease incidence, FY81-88, annual rpt, 4474–30
Biotechnology legal, ethical, and economic issues, series, 26356–5
Cell cultures for aging research, availability and cultures shipped, 1989 listing, 4478–187
NIH activities, funding by program and recipient type, staff, and clinic patients, by inst, FY87, annual rpt, 4434–3

Ozone peak concentrations by selected city, 1983 and 1988, and health effects clinical test results, 1989 hearing, 21368–117

Human immunodeficiency virus
see Acquired immune deficiency syndrome

Human Nutrition Information Service
Budget of US Appendix, obligations, appropriations, and personnel, by program and agency, FY90, annual rpt, 104–3

Food composition, detailed data on nutrients, calories, and waste, for raw, processed, and prepared foods, series, 1356–3

Food consumption and nutrient intake by individuals, by food group, selected characteristics, and region, supplementary survey series, 1356–5

Nutrient and caloric composition of food, for raw, processed, and prepared food, 1988 rpt, 1358–3

Human rights
see Civil rights

Humanities
see Arts and the humanities

Humphrey, David B.
"Market Responses to Pricing Fedwire Daylight Overdrafts", 9389–1.910

Hung, Juann
"Financial Implications of the U.S. External Deficit", 9385–1.907

Hungary
Agricultural and food production and indexes, total and for selected commodities, by country, 1970s-88, annual rpt, 1524–12

Agricultural production, acreage, and consumption, by Eastern Europe country and commodity, 1965-85, 1528–284

Agricultural production, consumption, and trade, for Eastern Europe by country, 1970s-88, annual rpt, 1524–1

Agricultural trade of US, by detailed commodity and country, 1988, semiannual rpt, 1522–4

Background Notes, summary social, political, and economic data, 1989 rpt, 7006–2.31

Cuba economic conditions, agricultural and industrial production and distribution, trade, and intl economic relations, 1980-87 with trends from 1961, 9118–8

Debt, trade, and balances of Eastern Europe and USSR with US and other western countries, with background data, 1980s-87, hearing, 21248–120

Economic and military aid and loans from US and intl agencies, by program and country, FY46-87, annual rpt, 9914–5

Economic conditions in Communist, OECD, and selected other countries, 1960s-88, annual rpt, 9114–4

Economic conditions, income, production, prices, employment, and trade, 1989 periodic country rpt, 2046–4.27

Economic conditions, policy, and trade practices, by country, 1986-88, annual rpt, 21384–5

Economic, social, political, and geographic summary data, by country, 1989, annual factbook, 9114–2

Export licensing, monitoring, and enforcement activities, FY88, annual rpt, 2024–1

Exports and imports of US, by selected country, country group, and commodity group, 1988, annual rpt, 2044–37

Exports and imports of US with Communist countries, by detailed commodity and country, quarterly rpt with articles, 9882–2

Human rights conditions in 170 countries, 1988, annual rpt, 21384–3

Military spending, arms trade, and force strengths, with govt spending and population, by country, 1977-87, annual rpt, 9824–1

Military strength of USSR and Warsaw Pact, and proposed force reductions, with comparisons to NATO, 1980s-91, hearing, 21208–29

Minerals Yearbook, 1987, Vol 3: foreign country reviews of production, trade, and policy, by commodity, annual rpt, 5604–35

Minerals Yearbook, 1987, Vol 3 preprints: foreign country review of production, trade, and policy, by commodity, annual rpt, 5604–23.30

Nuclear power plant capacity and operating status, by plant and Communist country, as of Dec 1988, annual rpt, 3164–57.2

Population size, growth rates, and components of change, by country, projected 1989-2020 and trends from 1950, biennial rpt, 2324–9

Refugee resettlement programs and funding, arrivals by country of origin, and indicators of adjustment, by State, FY88, annual rpt, 4694–5

Steel export ceilings under voluntary restraint agreements, by country and product, with Western US steel industry impact, 1989 rpt, 9886–4.136

Steel imports of US under voluntary restraint agreement, by product, customs district, and country, with US industry operating data, monthly rpt, 9882–13

UN voting record and share of votes in agreement with US, by issue, country, and world area, 1988, annual rpt, 7004–18

see also under By Foreign Country in the "Index by Categories"

Hunger
see Food assistance
see Food supply
see Nutrition and malnutrition

Hunter, Linda
"Contribution of Nonhomothetic Preferences to Trade", 9379–12.31

Hunter, William C.
"Bank Merger Motivations: A Review of the Evidence and an Examination of Key Target Bank Characteristics", 9371–1.911

"Demand for Labor at the World's Largest Banking Organizations", 9371–10.42

"Does Multiproduct Production in Large Banks Reduce Costs?", 9371–1.907

"Examination of Cost Subadditivity and Multiproduct Production in Large U.S. Banks", 9371–10.40

"Technological Change in Large U.S. Commercial Banks", 9371–10.33

Hunterdon County, N.J.
see also under By SMSA or MSA in the "Index by Categories"

Hunting and trapping
Agricultural Statistics, 1988, annual rpt, 1004–1.2

Alaska Arctic Natl Wildlife Refuge resources, native hunting activity, and energy exploration impact, 1985, last issue of annual rpt, 5504–26

Alaska rural villages population characteristics and and subsistence activities, 1976-86, 5738–9

Bears (grizzly) in Yellowstone Natl Park area, monitoring results, 1988, annual rpt, 5544–4

Birds (mourning dove) population, by hunting and nonhunting State, 1966-89, annual rpt, 5504–15

Birds (sandhill crane) hunting activity and permits, by State and county, 1987/88-1988/89, annual rpt, 5504–31

Birds (waterfowl) hunter harvest, age and sex ratios by species, State, and flyway, 1984-88, annual rpt, 5504–32

Birds (waterfowl) hunter harvest and unretrieved kills, and duck stamps sold, by species, State, and flyway, 1987-88, annual rpt, 5504–28

Birds (woodcock) population in US and Canada from 1968, and hunter harvest, by State, 1989, annual rpt, 5504–11

County Business Patterns, 1987: employment, establishments, and payroll, by SIC 2- to 4-digit industry and county, annual State rpt series, 2326–8

Duck hunting stamps philatelic and sales info, 1934/35-1988/89, annual rpt, 5504–25

Earnings by major industry group, and personal income per capita and by source, by region and State, 1929-87, 2708–40

Fish and Wildlife Service restoration programs finances by State, and excise tax collections, FY88, annual rpt, 5504–13

Fish and Wildlife Service restoration programs funding, land purchases, and project listing, by State, FY87, annual rpt, 5504–1

Forest Service activities and finances, by region and State, FY88, annual rpt, 1204–1.1

Forests (natl) recreational use, by type of activity and State, 1988, annual rpt, 1204–17

Licenses for fishing and hunting issued, and costs, by State, FY88, annual press release, 5504–16

Marine mammal protection activities and funding, populations, and harvests, by species, 1987, annual rpt, 5504–12

Occupational injury and illness rates, by SIC 2- to 4-digit industry, 1987, annual rpt, 6844–1

Participation and spending for hunting, fishing, and other wildlife-related recreation, detailed data by location, 1985 survey, quinquennial rpt, 5508–5

Participation and spending for hunting, fishing, and other wildlife-related recreation, detailed data, 1985 survey, quinquennial State rpt series, 5506–6

Public lands acreage, grants, use, revenues, and allocations, by State, FY88, annual rpt, 5724–1.2

Research of State fish and wildlife agencies, federally funded wildlife projects and costs by species and State, 1989, annual listing, 5504–24

Rhinoceros wild and captive population, poacher kills and enforcement action, and conservation issues, 1988 hearing, 21708–125

Statistical Abstract of US, social, political, and economic data, 1790-2025, comprehensive annual compilation, 2324–1.1

Tax collections of State govts by detailed type of tax, and tax rates, by State, FY88, annual rpt, 2466–2.3
see also Fish and fishing industry
see also Fishing, sport

Huntington Beach, Calif.
see also under By City in the "Index by Categories"

Huntington, W.Va.
Freight (waterborne domestic and foreign) by commodity, traffic, and passengers, by port and waterway, 1987, annual rpt, 3754–3.2
see also under By SMSA or MSA in the "Index by Categories"

Huntsville, Ala.
Wages by occupation, and benefits for office and plant workers, 1989 survey, periodic MSA rpt, 6785–12.4
see also under By City and By SMSA or MSA in the "Index by Categories"

Huntzinger, Thomas L.
"Experiment in Representative Ground-Water Sampling for Water-Quality Analysis", 5668–97

Hurd, Michael
"Joint Retirement Decision of Husbands and Wives", 4742–1.906

Hurricanes
see Storms

Hutchins, Cecil C., Jr.
"Southern Pulpwood Production, 1987", 1204–23

Hutchinson, T. Q.
"Grain Transportation: A Forecast", 1561–4.903

Hutchison, Michael M.
"Central Bank Secrecy and Money Surprises: International Evidence", 9393–10.8
"Does Exchange Rate Appreciation 'Deindustrialize' the Open Economy? A Critique of U.S. Evidence", 9393–10.5
"Political Business Cycles in a Parliamentary Setting: The Case of Japan", 9393–10.7

Hyde, Pamela S.
"Ohio's Coordinated Response to the Problems of Homelessness", 10048–73

Hyde, William F.
"Marginal Costs of Managing Endangered Species: The Case of the Red-Cockaded Woodpecker", 1502–3.902

Hydrocarbons
see Petrochemicals

Hydroelectric power
Army Corps of Engineers activities and projects, FY87 and trends from 1800s, annual rpt, 3754–1.2
Army Corps of Engineers water resources dev projects, characteristics, and costs, 1950s-87, biennial State rpt series, 3756–2
Army Corps of Engineers water resources dev projects, characteristics, and costs, 1950s-89, biennial State rpt series, 3756–1
Bond tax-exempt issues for private activity, by purpose, face value, major industry, and State, 1986, annual article, 8302–2.905
Bonneville Power Admin mgmt of Fed Columbia River Power System, finances, operations, and sales by customer, FY88, annual rpt, 3224–1

Business statistics, detailed data for major industries and economic indicators, Survey of Current Business, monthly rpt, 2702–1.10
Colorado River Basin Project reservoir and power operations and revenues, 1987-88, annual rpt, 5824–6
Colorado River Storage Project finances and activities in western States, FY88, annual rpt, 5824–3
Consumption, by detailed fuel type, end-use sector, and State, 1960-87, State Energy Data System annual rpt, 3164–39
Cuba economic conditions, agricultural and industrial production and distribution, trade, and intl economic relations, 1980-87 with trends from 1961, 9118–8
Environmental impacts of energy technologies, 1960s-80s, handbook series, 3326–1
FERC activities, licensing, and rate regulation, FY88, annual rpt, 3084–9
Foreign and US energy production and use, by energy type and country, 1980-88, annual rpt, 3164–50.1; 3164–50.5; 3164–50.8
Foreign and US energy use by sector, and production, by fuel type, country, and country group, projected 1988-2000 and trends from 1970, annual rpt, 3164–84
Pacific Northwest electric power capacity and use, by energy source, projected under alternative load and demand cases, 1989-2008, annual rpt, 3224–3
Power plants (hydroelectric) retired, characteristics and location, as of 1989, annual listing, 3084–12
Power plants and capacity, by fuel used, owner, location, and operating status, 1988, and for units planned 1989-98, annual listing, 3164–36
Power plants capacity, dev status, and ownership, for hydroelectric plants by State and river basin, as of Jan 1988, quadrennial rpt, 3088–14
Power plants capital and production costs, operations, and fuel use, by fuel type, plant, utility, and location, 1987, annual rpt, 3164–9
Power plants production, fuel use, stocks, and costs by fuel type, and sales, by State, monthly rpt, 3162–35
Production of electric power and fuel use, receipts, cost, quality, and stocks, by energy source, State, and utility, quarterly rpt with articles, 3162–39
Production, plant capacity, and fuel use, by fuel type, census div, and State, 1984-88, annual rpt, 3164–11.1
Reclamation Bur activities, finances, and project impacts in western US, annual rpts, 5824–12
Rural Electrification Admin financed electric power plants, with location, capacity, and owner, as of Jan 1989, annual listing, 1244–6
Southwestern Fed Power System financial statements, sales by customer, and operations and costs by project, FY88, annual rpt, 3244–1
Statistical Abstract of US, social, political, and economic data, 1790-2025, comprehensive annual compilation, 2324–1.3

Supply, demand, and prices, by fuel type and end-use sector, projected under 3 oil price assumptions, 1988-2000, annual rpt, 3164–75
Supply, demand, and prices, by fuel type and end-use sector, with foreign comparisons, 1988 and trends from 1949, annual rpt, 3164–74
Supply, demand, and prices, by fuel type, end-use sector, and country, detailed data, monthly rpt, 3162–24
Supply, demand, and prices of energy, forecasts by resource type, quarterly rpt, 3162–34
Tennessee Valley river control activities, and hydroelectric power generation and capacity, 1984, annual rpt, 9804–7
TVA financial and operating data by program and facility, FY88, annual rpt, 9804–32
Utilities finances and operations, detailed data for privately owned firms, and summary data for other utilities by type, 1987, annual rpt, 3164–23
Western Area Power Admin activities by plant, financial statements, and sales by customer, FY88, annual rpt, 3254–1

Hydrogen
see Gases

Hydrology
Arkansas water quality in streams and rivers, by monitoring site, 1975-85, 5668–83
Chemistry of surface and groundwater, environmental impacts, analytic methods, and quality and mgmt issues, 1989 rpt, 5668–96
Coastal and estuarine environmental conditions, research results and methodology, series, 2176–7
Coastal and riparian areas environmental conditions, fish, wildlife, use, and mgmt, for individual ecosystems, series, 5506–9
DOE R&D projects and funding at natl labs, universities, and other instns, FY88, annual summary rpt, 3004–18.1
Estuary environmental conditions and mgmt, for individual areas, conf series, 2146–6
Estuary environmental conditions and mgmt, research projects and funding, FY87, annual listing, 2144–24
Geological Survey activities and funding, FY88, annual rpt, 5664–8
Great Lakes Environmental Research Lab activities, 1987 annual rpt, 2144–26
Great Lakes water levels fluctuations, causes, and impacts of alternative mgmt strategies, 1900s-88, series, 14446–1
Great Lakes water levels impacts of water supply mgmt and weather, model description, 1900s-85, 2148–59
New Mexico water resources data collection and analysis activities of USGS, with project descriptions, FY88, 5668–86
Radioactive waste repository sites, water movement through soil near sites in humid areas, 1989 rpt, 5668–98
Water quality data collection, aquifer hydrologic and chemical properties impacts on representative groundwater sampling, local area study, 1988 rpt, 5668–97
Water supply in US and southern Canada, streamflow, surface and groundwater conditions, and reservoir levels, by location, monthly rpt, 5662–3

see also Oceanography
see also Water area
see also Water pollution
see also Water power
see also Water resources development
see also Water supply and use
see also Watershed projects
Hydrothermal power
see Geothermal resources
Hypertension
Cancer (breast) risk, relation to hypertension diagnosis before and after pregnancy, 1989 article, 4472–1.927
Cases of acute and chronic conditions, disability, absenteeism, and health services use, by selected characteristics, 1988, annual rpt, 4147–10.170
Cases of cardiovascular diseases, health care services use and costs, and productivity losses, by selected characteristics, 1980, 4146–12.26
Deaths and rates, by cause, age, sex, marital status, race, and State, 1987, US Vital Statistics advance annual rpt, 4146–5.113
Deaths and rates, by cause and age, preliminary 1987-88, US Vital Statistics annual rpt, 4144–7
Deaths and rates, by detailed cause and demographic characteristics, 1986 and trends from 1900, US Vital Statistics annual rpt, 4144–2
Deaths and rates, by detailed location, cause, and demographic characteristics, 1987, US Vital Statistics annual rpt, 4144–3
Developing countries aged population and selected characteristics, 1980s and projected to 2020, country rpt series, 2326–19
Health condition and health care resources, use, and spending, 1950s-87, annual data compilation, 4144–11
Kidney end-stage disease program of Medicare, enrollment and survival of dialysis and transplant patients by age, sex, race, and primary diagnosis, 1980-85, annual rpt, 4654–16.1; 4654–16.3
Military personnel alcohol and drug abuse, prevalence and consequences, by selected characteristics, 1988, biennial rpt, 3504–19
Natl Heart, Lung, and Blood Inst activities, and grants by recipient and location, FY88 with disease trends from 1940, annual rpt, 4474–15
Nutritional status and related health condition and practices, by selected characteristics, 1970s-87, 4048–33
Preventive disease and health improvement goals and recommended activities for 2000, with trends 1970s-80s, 4048–10
see also under By Disease in the "Index by Categories"
Hysterectomy
see Sexual sterilization

IBRD
see International Bank for Reconstruction and Development
ICC
see Interstate Commerce Commission

Ice conditions
Alaska OCS environmental conditions and oil dev impacts, compilation of papers, series, 2176–1
Bering Sea and Alaska north coast ice conditions, monthly rpt, 2182–5
Whale (bowhead) population in Beaufort Sea, and aerial survey operations, Sept-Oct 1979-88, 5738–8
Ice, manufactured
County Business Patterns, 1987: employment, establishments, and payroll, by SIC 2- to 4-digit industry and county, annual State rpt series, 2326–8
Fishing, hunting, and other wildlife-related recreation participation and spending, detailed data by location, 1985 survey, quinquennial rpt, 5508–5
Fishing, hunting, and other wildlife-related recreation participation and spending, detailed data, 1985 survey, quinquennial State rpt series, 5506–6
Freight (waterborne domestic and foreign) by commodity, traffic, and passengers, by port and waterway, 1987, annual rpt, 3754–3
Manufacturing annual survey, 1986: financial and operating data, by SIC 2- to 4-digit industry, series, 2506–15
Manufacturing census, 1987: financial and operating data, for SIC 4-digit industries by product, preliminary rpt, 2491–1.9
Occupational injury and illness rates, by SIC 2- to 4-digit industry, 1987, annual rpt, 6844–1
Price indexes (producer), by stage of processing and detailed commodity, monthly rpt, 6762–6
Price indexes (producer), by stage of processing and detailed commodity, monthly 1988, annual rpt, 6764–2
Iceland
Agricultural and food production and indexes, total and for selected commodities, by country, 1970s-88, annual rpt, 1524–12
Agricultural trade of US, by detailed commodity and country, 1988, semiannual rpt, 1522–4
AID loans repayment status and terms by program and country, and status of predecessor agency loans, quarterly rpt, 9912–3
Apple exports of US to EC and 4 north European countries, 1984-89, article, 1925–34.939
Economic and military aid and loans from US and intl agencies, by program and country, FY46-87, annual rpt, 9914–5
Economic conditions, income, production, prices, employment, and trade, 1989 periodic country rpt, 2046–4.28
Economic conditions, policy, and trade practices, by country, 1986-88, annual rpt, 21384–5
Economic, social, political, and geographic summary data, by country, 1989, annual factbook, 9114–2
Human rights conditions in 170 countries, 1988, annual rpt, 21384–3
Labor conditions, union coverage, and work accidents, 1989 annual country rpt, 6366–4.21
Military aid of US, arms sales, and training programs costs and budget requests, by program, world region, and country, FY88-90, annual rpt, 7144–13

Military spending, arms trade, and force strengths, with govt spending and population, by country, 1977-87, annual rpt, 9824–1
Minerals Yearbook, 1987, Vol 3: foreign country reviews of production, trade, and policy, by commodity, annual rpt, 5604–35
Minerals Yearbook, 1987, Vol 3 preprints: foreign country review of production, trade, and policy, by commodity, annual rpt, 5604–23.31
Oil production, trade, use, and stocks, by selected country and country group, monthly rpt, 3162–42
Population size, growth rates, and components of change, by country, projected 1989-2020 and trends from 1950, biennial rpt, 2324–9
UN voting record and share of votes in agreement with US, by issue, country, and world area, 1988, annual rpt, 7004–18
see also under By Foreign Country in the "Index by Categories"
ICF, Inc.
"Future Accrual of Capital Repair and Replacement Needs of Public Housing: Final Report", 5186–15.2
Idaho
Agriculture census, 1987: farms, farmland, production and costs, and operator characteristics, advance State and county rpts, 2330–1.16
Agriculture census, 1987: farms, farmland, production, finances, and operator characteristics, by county, final State rpt, 2331–1.12
Bank deposits in FDIC-insured commercial and savings banks, by instn, State, and county, as of June 1988, annual regional rpt, 9295–3.6
Bears (grizzly) in Yellowstone Natl Park area, monitoring results, 1988, annual rpt, 5544–4
County Business Patterns, 1987: employment, establishments, and payroll, by SIC 2- to 4-digit industry and county, annual State rpt, 2326–8.14
Deaths and rates, by detailed location, cause, and demographic characteristics, 1987, US Vital Statistics annual rpt, 4144–3.1
DOD prime contract awards, by contractor, service branch, State, and city, FY88, annual rpt, 3544–22
Employment, earnings, and hours, by selected SIC 1- to 4-digit industry, State, and for 262 MSAs, 1972-87, 6748–81.1
Fed Govt spending in States and local areas, by type, State, county, and city, FY88, annual rpt, 2464–3
Fed Govt spending in States, by type, program, agency, and State, FY88, annual rpt, 2464–2
Fires effects on forage nutrient concentration, for Idaho aspen forests, by species, 1982-83, 1208–309
Gold deposits location, discovery, and geologic indicators, 1799-1982, compilation of papers, 5668–90
HHS financial aid, by program, recipient, State, and city, FY88, annual regional listing, 4004–3.10
Homeless children educational enrollment and needs, 1988, annual State rpt, 4804–35.13

Income (personal) per capita and by source, and earnings by industry div, by State, MSA, and county, 1982-87, annual regional rpt, 2704–2.5

Irrigation system sediment control costs and benefits, by technique, for Idaho project, 1981-86 and projected to 2030, 1588–138

Land Mgmt Bur activities and finances, and public land acreage and use, FY87, annual State rpt, 5724–11.1

Mineral Industry Surveys, State reviews of production, 1988, preliminary annual rpt, 5614–6

Minerals Yearbook, 1987, Vol 2 preprints: State review of production and sales by commodity, and business activity, annual rpt, 5604–16.13

Minerals Yearbook, 1987, Vol 2: State reviews of production, sales, and firms, by commodity, and business activity, annual rpt, 5604–34

Nursing home compliance with Medicare and Medicaid regulations, and patient characteristics, by facility, 1987/88, annual State rpt, 4654–15.13

Older persons care by family members, tax subsidies in 2 States, 1981-84, article, 4652–1.915

Population, households, employment, income, and fuel prices, for Pacific Northwest, alternative projections 1990-2010 with trends from 1960, annual rpt, 3224–5

Radiation monitoring results of Idaho Natl Engineering Lab, for facilities and nearby areas, 1988, annual rpt, 3354–10

Retail trade census, 1987: employment, establishments, sales, and payroll, by SIC 2- to 4-digit kind of business, MSA, county, and city, State rpt, 2397–1.13

River and stream environmental conditions, fish, wildlife, use, and mgmt, 1989 rpt, 5506–9.39

Savings instns, FHLB 12th District members deposits and lending, monthly press release, 9302–32.2

Service industries census, 1987: employment, establishments, receipts, and payroll, by SIC 2- to 4-digit kind of business, MSA, county, and city, State rpt, 2391–1.13

Statistical Abstract of US, social, political, and economic data, with foreign comparisons, 1790-2025, comprehensive annual compilation, 2324–1

Timber (Douglas fir) controlled burning, plant succession by species, 1976-86, 1208–305

Timber in northwestern US and British Columbia, production, prices, trade, and employment, quarterly rpt, 1202–3

Transportation census, 1987: trucks, by detailed characteristics, miles traveled, and type of product carried, State rpt, 2573–1.13

Unemployed displaced workers, labor-mgmt committee aid recipients by selected characteristics, for 4 State programs, 1988, GAO rpt, 26121–316

Water supply and quality in streams and lakes, and groundwater levels in wells, by drainage basin, 1987, annual State rpt, 5666–10.11

Water supply and quality in streams and lakes, and groundwater levels in wells, by drainage basin, 1988, annual State rpt, 5666–16.11

Water supply, and snow survey results, monthly State rpt, 1266–2.4

Water supply, and snow survey results, 1988, annual State rpt, 1264–14.7

Wholesale trade census, 1987: employment, establishments, and operations, by SIC 2- to 4-digit kind of business, MSA, county, and city, State rpt, 2405–1.13

Wildlife-related recreation, hunting, and fishing participation and spending, detailed data, 1985 survey, quinquennial State rpt, 5506–6.12

see also Boise, Idaho

see also under By State in the "Index by Categories"

Idaho National Engineering Laboratory

see also Department of Energy National Laboratories

Iden, George

"Deficits and Interest Rates: Theoretical Issues and Empirical Evidence", 26306–3.101

Identification papers

see Government forms and paperwork

IEC

see International Electrotechnical Commission

Ihrig, Jane

"Changes in Manufacturing Employment in North Carolina Counties, 1980-85", 9389–1.915

Illegitimacy

see Births out of wedlock

Illinois

Agriculture census, 1987: farms, farmland, production and costs, and operator characteristics, advance State and county rpts, 2330–1.17

Agriculture census, 1987: farms, farmland, production, finances, and operator characteristics, by county, final State rpt, 2331–1.13

Alien workers (unauthorized) employer sanctions, enforcement costs, compliance, and job discrimination, 1988 annual GAO rpt, 26104–19

Asian American earnings, and employment and other characteristics, by detailed origin and whether foreign-born, 1980, 11046–7.2

Bank deposits in FDIC-insured commercial and savings banks, by instn, State, and county, as of June 1988, annual regional rpt, 9295–3.3

Banks (foreign) US branches assets and liabilities, total and for 3 States, monthly rpt, quarterly data, 9362–1.4

Coal production and mines by county, prices, productivity, miners, reserves, and stocks, by mining method and State, 1987-88, annual rpt, 3164–25

Deaths and rates, by detailed location, cause, and demographic characteristics, 1987, US Vital Statistics annual rpt, 4144–3.1

Disaster relief program of Fed Emergency Mgmt Agency under State admin, impact of mgmt changes on benefits processing, 1986-88, GAO rpt, 26113–412

DOD prime contract awards, by contractor, service branch, State, and city, FY88, annual rpt, 3544–22

Employment, earnings, and hours, by selected SIC 1- to 4-digit industry, State, and for 262 MSAs, 1972-87, 6748–81.2

Fed Govt spending in States and local areas, by type, State, county, and city, FY88, annual rpt, 2464–3

Fed Govt spending in States, by type, program, agency, and State, FY88, annual rpt, 2464–2

Govt budget for Illinois, balances and spending, FY55-84, hearings, 21528–72

Head Start program operations, enrollment by handicap, and family characteristics, for North Central States, 1987/88, annual rpt, 4604–12

HHS financial aid, by program, recipient, State, and city, FY88, annual regional listing, 4004–3.5

Homeless children educational enrollment and needs, 1988, annual State rpt, 4804–35.14

Housing vacancy rates for single and multifamily units and mobile homes in FHLB 7th District, by ZIP code, annual MSA rpt series, 9304–15

Hwy admin and gasoline tax revenue proposed transfer from Fed Govt to States, issues, with motor fuel taxes by selected State, 1988 rpt, 10048–72

Income (personal) per capita and by source, and earnings by industry div, by State, MSA, and county, 1982-87, annual regional rpt, 2704–2.2

Manufacturing employment in Illinois compared to other Great Lakes States, by industry group, various periods 1960-88, working paper, 9375–13.14

Mineral Industry Surveys, State reviews of production, 1988, preliminary annual rpt, 5614–6

Minerals Yearbook, 1987, Vol 2 preprints: State review of production and sales by commodity, and business activity, annual rpt, 5604–16.14

Minerals Yearbook, 1987, Vol 2: State reviews of production, sales, and firms, by commodity, and business activity, annual rpt, 5604–34

Mortgage interest fixed and adjustable rates and fees offered by Illinois S&Ls, monthly rpt, 9302–6

Nursing home compliance with Medicare and Medicaid regulations, and patient characteristics, by facility, 1987/88, annual State rpt, 4654–15.14

Retail trade census, 1987: employment, establishments, sales, and payroll, by SIC 2- to 4-digit kind of business, MSA, county, and city, State rpt, 2397–1.14

Savings instns, FHLB 7th District and natl cost of funds indexes, and mortgage rates, monthly rpt, 9302–30

Savings instns, FHLB 7th District insured members, offices, and savings, by county, 1985-86, annual rpt, 9304–5

Service industries census, 1987: employment, establishments, receipts, and payroll, by SIC 2- to 4-digit kind of business, MSA, county, and city, State rpt, 2391–1.14

Statistical Abstract of US, social, political, and economic data, with foreign comparisons, 1790-2025, comprehensive annual compilation, 2324–1

Timber in Illinois, resources, removals, and products by species, forest characteristics, ownership, and county, 1960s-85 and projected to 2015, 1208-292

Water supply and quality in streams and lakes, and groundwater levels in wells, by drainage basin, 1987, annual State rpt, 5666-10.12

Water supply and quality in streams and lakes, and groundwater levels in wells, by drainage basin, 1988, annual State rpt, 5666-16.12

Wholesale trade census, 1987: employment, establishments, finances, and operations, by SIC 2- to 4-digit kind of business, MSA, county, and city, State rpt, 2405-1.14

Wildlife-related recreation, hunting, and fishing participation and spending, detailed data, 1985 survey, quinquennial State rpt, 5506-6.13

see also Aurora, Ill.

see also Champaign, Ill.

see also Chicago, Ill.

see also Elgin, Ill.

see also Joliet, Ill.

see also Kankakee, Ill.

see also Lake County, Ill.

see also Moline, Ill.

see also Peoria, Ill.

see also Rantoul, Ill.

see also Rock Island, Ill.

see also Rockford, Ill.

see also Urbana, Ill.

see also under By State in the "Index by Categories"

Illinois River

Freight (waterborne domestic and foreign) by commodity, traffic, and passengers, by port and waterway, 1987, annual rpt, 3754-3.2; 3754-3.3

Water supply and quality in streams and lakes, and groundwater levels in wells, by drainage basin, 1986, annual State rpt series, 5666-23

Water supply and quality in streams and lakes, and groundwater levels in wells, by drainage basin, 1987, annual State rpt series, 5666-10

Water supply and quality in streams and lakes, and groundwater levels in wells, by drainage basin, 1988, annual State rpt series, 5666-16

Illiteracy

see Literacy and illiteracy

Illness

see Disabled and handicapped persons

see Diseases and disorders

see Hospitalization

Imamura, Carolyn K.

"Ocean Transportation Needs of the American Pacific Islands: Report to Congress", 7308-195

Imitation food products

see Synthetic food products

Immigration Act

Admissions to US, visas, and waiting periods, effects of immigration reform affecting persons with needed labor skills and persons otherwise excluded, 1990-99, GAO rpt, 26131-64

Immigration and emigration

Admissions to US of immigrants, alien workers, and visitors, deportations, and naturalizations, by country, FY88 and trends from 1820, annual rpt, 6264-2

Admissions to US of immigrants, by class of admission, country of birth, and State and MSA of destination, FY88, annual rpt, 6264-4

Admissions to US of immigrants, by occupational group and country of birth, preliminary FY88, annual table, 6264-1

Admissions to US of relatives of US natls and other immigrants, FY49-88 and alternative projections to FY99, GAO rpt, 26131-59

Admissions to US, visas, and waiting periods, effects of immigration reform affecting persons with needed labor skills and persons otherwise excluded, 1990-99, GAO rpt, 26131-64

Asian American earnings, and employment and other characteristics, by detailed origin and whether foreign-born, 1980, 11046-7.2

Congressional apportionment impact of immigration and illegal aliens, alternative estimates by State, 1950s-80 with projections to 2010, hearing, 21628-70

Court civil and criminal caseloads for Federal district, appeals, and special courts, June 1989, annual rpt, 18204-2; 18204-8

Crime, criminal justice admin and enforcement, and public opinion, data compilation, 1970s-88, annual rpt, 6064-6

Criminal case processing in Federal district courts, and dispositions, by offense, district, and offender characteristics, 1984, annual rpt, 6064-29

Criminal case processing in Federal district courts, disposition by offense, 1980-87, 6066-19.50

Criminal cases by type and disposition, and collections, for US attorneys, by Federal district, FY88, annual rpt, 6004-2.1; 6004-2.7

Criminal sentences for Federal offenses, guidelines use and results by offense and district, and Sentencing Commission activities, 1988, annual rpt, 17664-1

Education Dept programs funding, operations, and effectiveness, FY88, annual rpt, 4804-5

Education funding of Fed Govt, State allocation by program, recipient type, and State, 1987/88, annual rpt, 4804-8

Foreign countries human rights conditions in 170 countries, 1988, annual rpt, 21384-3

Illegal entry and smuggling of aliens, Federal sentencing guidelines by offense and circumstances, 1989 rpt, 17668-1

Mexico population, labor force, and emigration, alternative projections 1990-2000, working paper, 2326-18.46

Migration since 1986, mover characteristics by same or different area, and compared to nonmovers, 1987, annual Current Population Rpt, 2546-1.435

Minority group population, and components of change, by race, State, metro-nonmetro location, MSA, and county, 1980-85, Current Population Rpt, 2546-3.159

Population size and characteristics, 1969-88, Current Population Rpt, annual rpt, 2546-2.146

Population size and components of change, alternative projections 1988-2080 and trends from 1900, annual actuarial rpt, 4706-1.104

Population size, by age, sex, and race, and components of change, alternative projections 1988-2080, Current Population Rpt, 2546-3.158

Science and engineering employment and education, and R&D spending, for US and selected foreign countries, 1988, annual rpt, 9624-23.2

Science and engineering immigrants, by field, age, sex, country and world area of birth and last residence, and State, 1987 and trends from 1967, 9627-29

Statistical Abstract of US, social, political, and economic data, 1790-2025, comprehensive annual compilation, 2324-1.1

Visas of US issued and refused to immigrants and nonimmigrants, by class, issuing office, and nationality, FY88, annual rpt, 7184-1

Visas of US issued at Foreign Service posts, by category and world area, selected years FY84-88, annual rpt, 7184-4

see also Alien workers

see also Aliens

see also Deportation

see also Foreign medical graduates

see also Foreign students

see also Mexicans in the U.S.

see also Passports and visas

see also Refugees

Immigration and Naturalization Service

Admissions to US of aliens, by class of admission, port, country, and State of destination, quarterly rpt, 6262-2

Admissions to US of immigrants, alien workers, and visitors, deportations, and naturalizations, by country, FY88 and trends from 1820, annual rpt, 6264-2

Admissions to US of immigrants, by class of admission, country of birth, and State and MSA of destination, FY88, annual rpt, 6264-4

Admissions to US of immigrants, by occupational group and country of birth, preliminary FY88, annual table, 6264-1

Budget of US Appendix, obligations, appropriations, and personnel, by program and agency, FY90, annual rpt, 104-3

Deportation and exclusion cases, appeals, bond postings, and investigations, for NYC and Los Angeles, 1987, GAO rpt, 26119-271

Illegal alien workers employer sanctions, enforcement costs, compliance, and job discrimination, 1988 annual GAO rpt, 26104-19

Illegal aliens welfare benefits, operations of Federal-State system to prevent payment, State official views, 1988, GAO rpt, 26121-276

Immigration Reform and Control Act

Employer sanctions for hiring illegal aliens, effect on wages and output under alternative levels of enforcement, 1988 technical paper, 9379-12.33

Employer sanctions for hiring illegal aliens, enforcement costs, compliance, and job discrimination, 1988 annual GAO rpt, 26104-19

Farm labor costs impacts of illegal aliens employer sanctions, by farm type, size, and region, 1986, 1598-250

Farm labor supply impacts of employer sanctions for illegal alien workers, for Western US, with background data, 1986-89, GAO rpt, 26121-310

Telephone service of households, by composition, income sources, and other characteristics, 1984-87, 9288-11

Women awarded child support and alimony, award amount, and payment status, by selected characteristics of woman, 1985, biennial Current Population Rpt, 2546-2.145

see also Aid to Families with Dependent Children

see also Disability benefits and insurance

see also Food stamp programs

see also Maternity benefits

see also Medicaid

see also Medicare

see also Old-Age, Survivors, Disability, and Health Insurance

see also Public welfare programs

see also Rent supplements

see also Social security

see also State funding for social welfare

see also Supplemental Security Income

see also Unemployment insurance

see also Workers compensation

Income taxes

Assets and debts of private sector, balance sheets by segment, 1949-88, semiannual rpt, 9365-4.1

Banks and thrifts in New England, financial statements by type of instn and Fed deposit insurance, and State, 1987, annual rpt, 9304-3

Budget deficit reduction through increased excise and income taxes, and proposed value-added tax, projected FY89-94, article, 9381-1.906

Budget of US, authoritative financial statements with appropriations, outlays, and receipts, by category and agency, FY88, annual rpt, 8104-2.2

Budget of US, CBO analysis of revenue and spending alternatives and projections of economic indicators, FY90-94, annual rpt, 26304-3

Budget of US, historical data, selected years FY34-88 and projected to FY94, annual rpt, 104-22

Budget of US, midsession review of FY90 budget, by function and agency, annual rpt, 104-7

Budget of US, receipts by source, outlays by agency and program, and balances, monthly rpt, 8102-3

Budget of US, special analysis of tax expenditures, FY90, annual rpt, 104-1.7

Capital gains tax rate changes effect on transactions by asset type, and stock exchange trading volume, late 1970s-88, article, 9373-1.901

Capital gains tax rate changes effects on revenue, alternative model results, 1988, 26306-3.106

Capital gains tax rate changes relation to realized gains and tax revenue, alternative estimates, various periods 1948-87, technical paper, 8006-3.61; 8006-3.62; 8006-3.63

Coal production and freight costs, and competitive position in selected markets, for Australia and US, 1987-89, 2048-143

Collections, enforcement, and litigation activity of IRS, with data by type of tax, region, and State, FY88, annual rpt, 8304-3

Collections of taxes, by level of govt, type of tax, State, and selected counties, quarterly rpt, 2462-3

Consumer Expenditure Survey, household income by source, and itemized spending, by selected characteristics and location, 1984-86, annual rpt, 6764-5.2

Corporations and individual income taxes, monthly rpt, quarterly and annual data, 23842-1.6

Corporations income tax returns, income and tax items by asset size and detailed industry, 1986, annual rpt, 8304-4; 8304-21

Corporations income tax returns, summary data by asset size and industry div, 1986, annual article, 8302-2.922

CPI tax liability components, by tax type, 1967-85, working paper, 6886-6.18

Depreciation accounting under income tax, with mean retention period of selected assets by type, 1989 technical paper, 8006-3.60

Electric utilities privately owned, detailed finances and operations by firm, 1987, annual rpt, 3164-23.1

Employee benefits impact on income and payroll tax revenue, by benefit type, 1950-87 and projected to 2065, article, 9373-1.913

Energy producers finances and operations, by energy type for US firms domestic and foreign operations, 1987, annual rpt, 3164-44

Farm sector balance sheet, and marketing receipts by detailed commodity, by State, 1984-88, annual rpt, 1544-18

Fed Govt consolidated financial statements based on business accounting methods, FY87-88, annual rpt, 8104-5

Fed Govt finances, cash and debt transactions, daily tables, 8102-4

Fed Govt financial and business statistics, historic trends, 1988 annual chartbook, 9364-2.8

Fed Govt internal revenue and refunds, by type of tax, quarterly rpt, 8302-2.1

Fed Govt mgmt cost control proposals, Reagan Admin initiatives, savings, and status, FY85-94, annual rpt, 104-23

Fed Govt receipts by source and outlays by agency, Treasury Bulletin, quarterly rpt, 8002-4.1

Finances of govts, revenues by source and spending by function, natl income and product account, Survey of Current Business, monthly rpt, 2702-1.24

Flow-of-funds accounts, savings, investments, and credit statements, quarterly rpt, 9365-3.3

Foreign corporate activity in US, income tax returns, assets, and income statement items, by industry div, country, and world area, 1984-85, article, 8302-2.920

Foreign earned income on US individual returns, exclusions, credits, and US revenue losses, with data by country, 1983, quadrennial rpt, 8308-34

Govt finances, by level of govt, State, and for large cities and counties, annual rpt series, 2466-2

Govt finances, tax systems and revenue, and fiscal structure, by level of govt and State, selected years 1929-91, annual rpt, 10044-1

Household income and poverty status under alternative income definitions, by recipient characteristics, 1986, Current Population Rpt, 2546-6.58

Household income before and after taxes, and discretionary, by sociodemographic characteristics, 1986, 2308-54

Income (personal) per capita impacts of Federal and defense spending and taxation, by State, 1950s-87, article, 9391-1.918

Individual income tax liability and payments, and total and taxable personal income, quarterly 1983-87, annual article, 2702-1.932

Individual income tax returns, data compilation, semiannual rpt, suspended, 8302-5

Individual income tax returns, detailed data, 1986, annual rpt, 8304-2

Individual income tax returns, income and tax shares, and tax rates, by income level, 1916-50, article, 8302-2.913

Individual income tax returns, income and tax shares, and tax rates, by income level, 1951-86, article, 8302-2.919

Individual income tax returns, selected income and tax items by income level, preliminary 1987, annual article, 8302-2.917

Individual income tax returns, taxable income, and tax generated, by tax rate and income level, 1986, annual article, 8302-2.918

Indochina refugee indicators of social and economic adjustment, FY88, annual rpt, 4694-5

Insurance (life) companies financial and tax impacts of Deficit Reduction Act and proposed reforms, for stock and mutual firms, 1984-88 and projected to FY94, 8008-138

Insurance (life) industry income, income taxes, and alternative methods of taxing dividends, for stock and mutual companies, 1980s-87, GAO rpt, 26119-274

Medicare catastrophic illness coverage and premium collection, effects of revisions on Federal budget and enrollees, projected 1989-93, 25368-161

Multinatl firms US affiliates, finances, and operations, by industry, world area of parent firm, and State, 1987, annual rpt, 2704-4

Multinatl US firms and foreign affiliates finances and operations, by industry of parent firm and affiliate, world area, and country, preliminary 1987, annual rpt, 2704-5

Natl income and product accounts and components, Survey of Current Business, monthly rpt, 2702-1.21; 2702-1.27

Natl income and product accounts govt transactions component estimates, methodology and bibl, 1988 technical rpt, 2706-6.5

Natural gas interstate pipeline company detailed financial and operating data, by firm, 1988, annual rpt, 3164-38

New England States economic indicators, Fed Reserve 1st District, quarterly rpt, 9373-2.3

Nonprofit charitable organizations finances, and assets and grants of top 10, 1985, article, 8302-2.923

North Central States, FHLB 6th District insured S&Ls financial condition and operations by State, quarterly rpt, 9302–23

OASDI benefit payments, trust fund finances, and economic and demographic assumptions, 1970-87 and alternative projections to 1997, actuarial rpt, 4706–1.103

Partnership income tax returns, income statement items by industry group, 1986, annual article, 8302–2.903

Partnerships (master limited) finances, firms, partners, and tax reform impacts, by industry, 1986, technical paper, 8006–3.59

Presidential election campaign fund contributions from income tax return check-off, 1973-89, press release, 9276–1.70

Public opinion on taxes, spending, and govt efficiency, by respondent characteristics, 1989 survey, annual rpt, 10044–2

Puerto Rico and other US possessions corporations tax incentives, finances, and operations by industry, and impacts on local economy, 1970s-83, biennial rpt, 8004–12

Puerto Rico economic conditions and govt finances, 1975-89, GAO rpt, 26121–298

Returns and supplemental documents filed, by type, FY88 and projected to FY97, semiannual rpt, 8302–4

Returns filed, by type of filer, detailed preliminary and supplementary data, quarterly rpt with articles, 8302–2

Returns filed, by type of tax, region, and IRS service center, projected 1988-95 and trends from 1977, annual rpt, 8304–9

Returns processing, IRS workload forecasts, compliance, and enforcement, data compilation, 1989 annual rpt, 8304–8

Savings instns, FHLB 4th District members finances, by State, 1984-88, annual rpt series, 9304–29

Savings instns, FHLB 9th District members finances and operations by State, quarterly rpt, 9302–31

Savings instns financial statements, FSLIC-insured instns by FHLB district and State, and FDIC-insured savings banks, 1988, annual rpt, 8434–1

Savings instns insured by Savings Assn Insurance Fund, finances by district, quarterly rpt, 8432–4

Savings instns regulatory issues, mgmt, and FHLB system and member finances and operations, monthly journal, 8432–2; 9312–1

Securities (tax-exempt) holdings by investor type, and IRS enforcement of disallowance of interest deduction for financing holdings, mid 1970s-87, GAO rpt, 26119–239

Sole proprietorship income tax returns, income statement items by industry group, 1987, annual article, 8302–2.904; 8302–2.921

Southeastern States, Fed Reserve 5th District insured commercial banks financial statements, by State, quarterly rpt, 9389–18

Soviet Union personal income by source, disposable income, wage deductions by type, and savings, 1950s-87, 9118–7

State and local revenue potential relative to natl average tax burden, by type of tax and State, 1986, annual rpt, 10044–7

State and local tax deduction from income taxes, subsidy rates by State, 1985, article, 9373–1.910

Statistical Abstract of US, social, political, and economic data, 1790-2025, comprehensive annual compilation, 2324–1.2

Tax and Price Index by household characteristics, 1978-88, working paper, 6886–6.68

Tax expenditures, Federal revenues forgone through income tax deductions and exclusions by type, FY90-94, annual rpt, 21784–10

Telephone and telegraph firms detailed finances and operations, 1987, annual rpt, 9284–6

Telephone firms borrowing under Rural Telephone Program, and financial and operating data, 1988, annual rpt, 1244–2

Telephone system of IRS for income tax questions, accessibility and accuracy, and other IRS workload indicators, 1988 hearing, 21788–178

Telephone system of IRS for income tax questions, accessibility and accuracy, 1988 survey, GAO rpt, 26119–190

Timber sales of Forest Service, expenses, and operations, by region, State, and natl forest, FY88, annual rpts, 1204–36

Transit systems finances and operations, by mode of transport, size of fleet, and for 432 systems, 1986, annual rpt, 7884–4

Truck and bus interstate carriers finances and operations, by district, 1987, annual rpt, 9486–6.3

Veterans rehabilitation program admin, and participants earnings and tax liability before and after training, 1988 hearing, 25768–48

Violations of income tax law, civil penalties assessed and abated, FY87-88, GAO rpt, 26119–265

see also Tax incentives and shelters
see also Tax protests and appeals
see also Windfall profit tax
see also Withholding tax

Incontinence
see Digestive diseases
see Urogenital diseases

Independence, Mo.
see also under By City in the "Index by Categories"

Independent agencies
see Federal independent agencies

Indexes
see Bibliographies
see Computer data file guides
see Consumer Price Index
see Cost of living
see Directories
see Government publications lists
see Industrial production indexes
see Labor costs and cost indexes
see Producer Price Index

India
Agricultural and food production and indexes, total and for selected commodities, by country, 1970s-88, annual rpt, 1524–12

Agricultural exports of US, for grains, oilseed products, hides, skins, and cotton, by country, weekly rpt, 1922–3

Agricultural production, prices, and trade, by country, 1960s-89, annual world region rpt, 1524–4.2

Agricultural subsidies, consumer and producer equivalents by program, commodity, and major US trading partner, 1982-86, 1528–275

Agricultural trade of US, by detailed commodity and country, 1988, semiannual rpt, 1522–4

Agricultural trade of US with Asia, Middle East, and North Africa, by commodity and country, 1962-86, 1528–277

Agricultural universities in India, impacts of AID-India govt joint project, FY60s-78, 9916–1.67

AID activities and funding by project and function, FY90, and developing countries summary socioeconomic data from 1960s, annual rpt, 9904–4.6

AID economic aid to developing countries, obligations and disbursements by country, quarterly rpt, 9912–4

AID loans repayment status and terms by program and country, and status of predecessor agency loans, quarterly rpt, 9912–3

Background Notes, summary social, political, and economic data, 1989 rpt, 7006–2.20

Coal production, trade, and govt subsidies, by country and country group, 1973-87 and projected to 2000, 2048–144

Economic and military aid and loans from US and intl agencies, by program and country, FY46-87, annual rpt, 9914–5

Economic conditions in Communist, OECD, and selected other countries, 1960s-88, annual rpt, 9114–4

Economic conditions, income, production, prices, employment, and trade, 1989 periodic country rpt, 2046–4.29; 2046–4.85

Economic conditions, policy, and trade practices, by country, 1986-88, annual rpt, 21384–5

Economic indicators of developing countries, problem debtors compared to other borrowers, by country, 1973-84, 1528–285

Economic, social, political, and geographic summary data, by country, 1989, annual factbook, 9114–2

Exports and imports of US, by commodity and country, 1970-87, world area rpt, 9116–1.2

Exports and imports of US, by selected country, country group, and commodity group, 1988, annual rpt, 2044–37

Human rights conditions in 170 countries, 1988, annual rpt, 21384–3

Imports of goods, services, and investment from US, trade barriers, impacts, and US actions, by country, 1988, annual rpt, 444–2

Military aid of US, arms sales, and training programs costs and budget requests, by program, world region, and country, FY88-90, annual rpt, 7144–13

Military spending, arms trade, and force strengths, with govt spending and population, by country, 1977-87, annual rpt, 9824–1

Military strengths, spending, weapons systems, and arms imports, for Pakistan and India, 1980s-87, hearing, 21388–54

Minerals production, reserves, and industry role in domestic economy and world supply, 1988 country rpt, 5606–1.17

Minerals Yearbook, 1987, Vol 3: foreign country reviews of production, trade, and policy, by commodity, annual rpt, 5604–35

Minerals Yearbook, 1987, Vol 3 preprints: foreign country review of production, trade, and policy, by commodity, annual rpt, 5604–23.32

Multinatl US firms and foreign affiliates finances and operations, by industry of parent firm and affiliate, world area, and country, preliminary 1987, annual rpt, 2704–5

Nuclear power generation in US and 19 non-Communist countries, monthly rpt, 3162–24.10

Nuclear power plant capacity, generation, and operating status, by plant and foreign and US location, 1988 and projected to 2020, annual rpt, 3164–57

Population size, growth rates, and components of change, by country, projected 1989-2020 and trends from 1950, biennial rpt, 2324–9

Space satellites and other objects launched since 1957, quarterly listing, 9502–2

UN voting record and share of votes in agreement with US, by issue, country, and world area, 1988, annual rpt, 7004–18

see also under By Foreign Country in the "Index by Categories"

Indian Health Service

Budget of US Appendix, obligations, appropriations, and personnel, by program and agency, FY90, annual rpt, 104–3

Facilities, funding, and operations of IHS, and Indian health and other characteristics, annual chartbook, issuing agency transfer, 4104–13

Facilities, funding, and operations of IHS, and Indian health and other characteristics, 1950s-88, annual chartbook, 4084–1

Financial aid of HHS, by program, recipient, State, and city, FY88, annual regional listings, 4004–3

Hospital admissions, length of stay, beds, births, and outpatient visits, by facility and IHS service area, annual rpt, issuing agency transfer, 4104–12

Hospital admissions, length of stay, beds, births, and outpatient visits, by facility and IHS service area, FY70-88, annual rpt, 4084–4

Hospital capacity, use, births, and outpatient visits, by area and IHS facility, quarterly rpt, 4082–1

Hospital capacity, use, births, and outpatient visits, by area and IHS facility, quarterly rpt, issuing agency transfer, 4102–3

Hospitalization in IHS and contract facilities, by diagnosis, age, sex, and service area, FY87, annual rpt, 4104–16

Hospitalization in IHS and contract facilities, by diagnosis, age, sex, and service area, FY88, annual rpt, 4084–5

Montana Indians social services funding of Federal, State, and tribal agencies, FY87, GAO rpt, 26121–257

Outpatient visits, by type of provider, selected hospital, and IHS service area, annual rpt, issuing agency transfer, 4104–14

Outpatient visits, by type of provider, selected hospital, and IHS service area, FY87-88, annual rpt, 4084–3

Outpatient visits to IHS facilities, by reason for visit and age, annual rpt, issuing agency transfer, 4104–10

Outpatient visits to IHS facilities, by reason for visit and age, FY87-88, annual rpt, 4084–2

Research and evaluation programs of HHS, 1970-FY87, annual listing, 4004–30

Indian Ocean

Environmental summary data, and intl claims and disputes, 1989 annual factbook, 9114–2

Hurricanes and tropical storms in north Indian Ocean, characteristics, 1987, article, 2152–8.901

Hurricanes and tropical storms in Pacific and Indian Oceans, paths and surveillance, 1988, annual rpt, 3804–8

Mariners Weather Log, quarterly journal, 2152–8

Temperature of sea surface by ocean and for US coastal areas, and Bering Sea ice conditions, monthly rpt, 2182–5

Tide height and time daily at coastal points, forecast 1990, annual rpt, 2174–2.5

Weather (marine) forecast areas, and broadcast schedules and stations worldwide, as of Nov 1988, annual rpt, 2184–3

Indiana

Agriculture census, 1987: farms, farmland, production and costs, and operator characteristics, advance State and county rpts, 2330–1.18

Agriculture census, 1987: farms, farmland, production, finances, and operator characteristics, by county, final State rpt, 2331–1.14

Bank deposits in FDIC-insured commercial and savings banks, by instn, State, and county, as of June 1988, annual regional rpt, 9295–3.3

Coal production and mines by county, prices, productivity, miners, reserves, and stocks, by mining method and State, 1987-88, annual rpt, 3164–25

Deaths and rates, by detailed location, cause, and demographic characteristics, 1987, US Vital Statistics annual rpt, 4144–3.1

DOD prime contract awards, by contractor, service branch, State, and city, FY88, annual rpt, 3544–22

Employment, earnings, and hours, by selected SIC 1- to 4-digit industry, State, and for 262 MSAs, 1972-87, 6748–81.2

Fed Govt spending in States and local areas, by type, State, county, and city, FY88, annual rpt, 2464–3

Fed Govt spending in States, by type, program, agency, and State, FY88, annual rpt, 2464–2

Head Start program operations, enrollment by handicap, and family characteristics, for North Central States, 1987/88, annual rpt, 4604–12

HHS financial aid, by program, recipient, State, and city, FY88, annual regional listing, 4004–3.5

Homeless children educational enrollment and needs, 1988, annual State rpt, 4804–35.15

Income (personal) per capita and by source, and earnings by industry div, by State, MSA, and county, 1982-87, annual regional rpt, 2704–2.2

Mineral Industry Surveys, State reviews of production, 1988, preliminary annual rpt, 5614–6

Minerals Yearbook, 1987, Vol 2 preprints: State review of production and sales by commodity, and business activity, annual rpt, 5604–16.15

Minerals Yearbook, 1987, Vol 2: State reviews of production, sales, and firms, by commodity, and business activity, annual rpt, 5604–34

Mobile home industry occupational injury and illness rates and workdays lost, by selected State, 1978-87, article, 6722–1.932

Nursing home compliance with Medicare and Medicaid regulations, and patient characteristics, by facility, 1987/88, annual State rpt, 4654–15.15

Retail trade census, 1987: employment, establishments, sales, and payroll, by SIC 2- to 4-digit kind of business, MSA, county, and city, State rpt, 2397–1.15

Savings and loan assns, FHLB 6th District insured members financial condition and operations by State, quarterly rpt, 9302–23

Savings instns, FHLB 6th District members financial condition and operations by State, monthly rpt, 9302–11

Service industries census, 1987: employment, establishments, receipts, and payroll, by SIC 2- to 4-digit kind of business, MSA, county, and city, State rpt, 2391–1.15

Statistical Abstract of US, social, political, and economic data, with foreign comparisons, 1790-2025, comprehensive annual compilation, 2324–1

Water resources dev projects of Army Corps of Engineers, characteristics, and costs, 1950s-87, biennial State rpt, 3756–2.15

Water supply and quality in streams and lakes, and groundwater levels in wells, by drainage basin, 1987, annual State rpt, 5666–10.13

Water supply and quality in streams and lakes, and groundwater levels in wells, by drainage basin, 1988, annual State rpt, 5666–16.13

Water supply in Indiana, annual high and low levels by lake, 1940s-85, 5668–89

Wholesale trade census, 1987: employment, establishments, finances, and operations, by SIC 2- to 4-digit kind of business, MSA, county, and city, State rpt, 2405–1.15

Wildlife-related recreation, hunting, and fishing participation and spending, detailed data, 1985 survey, quinquennial State rpt, 5506–6.14

see also Fort Wayne, Ind.

see also Gary, Ind.

see also Indianapolis, Ind.

see also Lake County, Ind.

see also under By State in the "Index by Categories"

Indianapolis, Ind.

Driving while intoxicated enforcement and publicity strategies, NHSTA deterrence project results, 1984-85, 7768–109

Drug test results at arrest, by drug type, offense, and sex, for selected urban areas, quarterly rpt, 6062-3

Housing and households characteristics, 1984 survey, MSA fact sheet, 2485-11.2

Wages by occupation, and benefits for office and plant workers, 1988 survey, periodic MSA rpt, 6785-11.1

see also under By City and By SMSA or MSA in the "Index by Categories"

Indians

Agriculture census, 1987: farms, farmland, production, finances, and operator characteristics, by county, final State rpt series, 2331-1

AIDS cases by risk group, race, sex, age, State, and MSA, and deaths, monthly rpt, 4202-9

Alcohol use and abuse among minority groups, and related problems, by selected characteristics, 1985 conf papers, 4488-13

Arrests and prisoners, by offense, offender characteristics, and location, 1970s-87, annual rpt, 6064-6.4; 6064-6.6

Arrests, by offense, offender characteristics, and location, 1988, annual rpt, 6224-2.2

Assistance (financial and nonfinancial) of Fed Govt, 1989 base edition with supplements, annual listing, 104-5

Births and rates, by characteristics of birth, infant, and parents, 1987 and trends from 1940, US Vital Statistics advance annual rpt, 4146-5.110

Budget of US, historical data, selected years FY34-88 and projected to FY94, annual rpt, 104-22

Business mgmt and financial aid from Minority Business Dev Centers, and characteristics of businesses, by region and State, FY88, annual rpt, 2104-6

Census of Population, 1980: selected socioeconomic data for Indians and Alaska Natives, by detailed origin, young readers pamphlet, 2326-1.6

Cherokee Indian Agency activities in North Carolina, FY89, annual rpt, 5704-4

Coal leasing activity on Federal and Indian lands, acreage, production, and revenues, by State, 1981-87, biennial rpt, 3164-79

Coal leasing activity, reserves, and acreage on Federal, State, and Indian lands, by State, FY88, annual rpt, 5724-10

Coal Surface Mining Reclamation and Enforcement Office activities and funding, by State and Indian tribe, FY87, annual rpt, 5644-1

Crimes and enforcement activity in Montana Indian reservations, and Bur of Indian Affairs law enforcement officers training, 1985-87, GAO rpt, 26113-402

Criminal cases by type and disposition, and collections, for US attorneys, by Federal district, FY88, annual rpt, 6004-2.1; 6004-2.7

Deaths among Seneca Indians and years of potential life lost, by selected cause and sex, various periods 1955-84, article, 4042-3.925

Deaths and rates, by detailed cause and demographic characteristics, 1986 and trends from 1900, US Vital Statistics annual rpt, 4144-2

Dental caries among Indian children from bottle feeding, prevention project effectiveness, 1985-89, article, 4042-3.961

Dental caries among Indian children from overnight bottle feeding with sugar solution, 1985 local areas study, article, 4042-3.903

Diabetes cases among Indians, by tribe, for New Mexico, 1985, article, 4042-3.964

Diabetes control levels, and other health indicators, for non-insulin-dependent Indians treated at rural and urban clinics, 1984-86 study, article, 4042-3.946

Disease (infectious notifiable) reporting to CDC, cases and rates by race, 1987, article, 4042-3.943

Drug and alcohol abuse treatment facilities, services, use, funding, and client characteristics, 1987, annual rpt, 4494-10

Earnings of Indians and Alaska Natives, by urban-rural location and other characteristics, 1980, article, 1502-7.904

Education data compilation, students, staff, finances, and facilities, 1989 edition, annual rpt, 4824-2

Education Dept programs funding, operations, and effectiveness, FY88, annual rpt, 4804-5

Education funding of Fed Govt, enrollment, and degrees, for Indians, late 1960s-FY88, annual rpt, 14874-1

Employment of minorities and women, by occupation, SIC 1- to 3- digit industry, State, and MSA, 1986, annual rpt, 9244-1

EPA pollution control grant program activities, monthly rpt, 9182-8

Fed Equal Opportunity Recruitment Program activity, and employment by sex, race, pay grade, and selected occupation, FY88, annual rpt, 9844-33

Fed Govt and other organization exchange of employees, program activities and costs, with data by agency, FY84-88, GAO rpt, 26119-260

Fed Govt employment of minorities, handicapped, and veterans, and years of service, by occupation, age, sex, and agency, as of Sept 1988, biennial rpt, 9844-27

Fed Govt spending in States, by type, program, agency, and State, FY88, annual rpt, 2464-2

Fish Hatchery Natl System activities and deliveries, by species, hatchery, and jurisdiction of waters stocked, FY88, annual rpt, 5504-10

FmHA activities, and loans and grants by program and State, FY88 and trends from FY69, annual rpt, 1184-17

FmHA borrowers, by type of borrower and loan, and State, quarterly rpt, 1182-4

FmHA loans, by type, borrower characteristics, and State, quarterly rpt, 1182-8

FmHA loans, by type, borrower race, and State, quarterly rpt, 1182-5

Food aid program of USDA for women, infants, and children, participants and costs by State and Indian agency, FY87, annual rpt, 1364-12

Food aid program of USDA for women, infants, and children, participants, clinics, and costs by State and Indian agency, monthly tables, 1362-16

Food aid programs of USDA, costs and participation by program, region, and State, monthly rpt, 1362-14

Food aid programs participation and eligibility, for 4 reservations, 1988, GAO rpt, 26113-439

Head Start enrollment, funding, and staff, FY88, annual rpt, 4604-8

Head Start handicapped enrollment, by handicap, State, and for Indian and migrant programs, 1985/86, annual rpt, 4604-1

Health care centers for Indian youth, use by type of visit, for demonstration projects in New Mexico, 1987-88, article, 4042-3.924

Health care clinic services use and staff, and effectiveness of prenatal care program, 1970s-86 local area study, article, 4042-3.960

Health care facilities of Indian Health Service, outpatient visits by reason for visit and age, FY87-88, annual rpt, 4084-2

Health care facilities of Indian Health Service, outpatient visits by type of provider, selected hospital, and IHS service area, FY87-88, annual rpt, 4084-3

Health care spending, natl survey methodology, 1989 rpt, 4186-8.5

Health condition and other characteristics of Indians, and Indian Health Service facilities, funding, and operations, 1950s-88, annual chartbook, 4084-1

HHS financial aid, by program, recipient, State, and city, FY88, annual regional listings, 4004-3

Higher education instn support from Fed Govt, by program and instn type and control, FY85-88, annual rpt, 4804-28.6

Hospital admissions, length of stay, beds, births, and outpatient visits, by Indian Health Service facility and service area, FY70-88, annual rpt, 4084-4

Hospital capacity, use, births, and outpatient visits, by area and Indian Health Service facility, quarterly rpt, 4082-1

Hospitalization in Indian Health Service and contract facilities, by diagnosis, age, sex, and IHS service area, FY88, annual rpt, 4084-5; 4104-16

Housing (public and Indian) stock and renovation needs, series, 5186-15

Housing and economic development program operations, by region, FY86-87, annual rpt, 5004-5

Housing condition and other characteristics, for aged Indians, 1987 survey, 21148-53

Hwy construction contracts awards of States to minority- and women-owned firms, FY85-88, GAO rpt, 26113-399

Lands (public) acreage, grants, use, revenues, and allocations, by State, FY88, annual rpt, 5724-1.3

Libraries (public) services for Indians and Hawaii Natives, project listing and funding by tribe and State, FY88 rpt, 4874-5

Minerals resources and availability on public lands, State rpt series, 5606-7

Nutritional status and related health condition and practices, by selected characteristics, 1970s-87, 4048-33

Oil, gas, and minerals production and revenue on Federal and Indian land, by State, 1988 and trends from 1920, annual rpt, 5734-2

Older persons aid and policies of Fed Govt, program funding, and grants awarded, FY80-89, annual rpt, 25144–3.2

Prisoners, movements, and characteristics, by State, 1986, annual rpt, 6064–26

Radon indoor air pollution levels, by county and State, 1989, annual rpt, 9194–19

Relocation program for Navajo and Hopi, activities and caseloads, monthly rpt, 16002–1

Relocation program for Navajo and Hopi, activities, caseloads, and finances, FY88, annual rpt, 16004–1

Relocation program for Navajo and Hopi, caseloads, activities, and finances, by location, annual rpt, discontinued, 16004–4

Rural areas aid from Fed Govt compared to urban areas, by program and degree of urbanization, FY85, periodic rpt, 1598–248

Science and engineering grad enrollment, by field, source of funds, and characteristics of student and instn, 1975-87, annual rpt, 9627–7

Science and engineering PhDs, by field, instn, employment prospects, sex, race, and other characteristics, 1960s-88, 9627–30

Science and engineering PhDs employment and other characteristics, by field and State, 1987, biennial rpt, 9627–18

Sexually transmitted disease cases among Indians, by State, 1988, article, 4042–3.955

Social services for Indians, Federal, State, and tribal agencies funding, with reservation land property tax, for Montana, FY87, GAO rpt, 26121–257

Special education programs, enrollment by age, staff, funding, and needs, by type of handicap and State, 1987/88, annual rpt, 4944–4

State and local govt employment of minorities and women, by occupation, function, pay level, and State, 1986, annual rpt, 9244–6

Statistical Abstract of US, social, political, and economic data, 1790-2025, comprehensive annual compilation, 2324–1.1

Suicide attempts, potential, and risk factors for Indian youth, longitudinal study, 1989 article, 4042–3.958

Telecommunications industries minority employment and discrimination charges, with data by industry and selected firm, 1970s-88, hearings, 21368–113

Tobacco (smokeless) use by youth and adults, user characteristics, and sales, 1970s-86, papers, 4478–188

Uranium reserves and industry operations, by region and State, various periods 1966-88, annual rpt, 3164–65.1

Water supply projects for South Dakota Indian reservation, costs and indicators of need, with health and housing data for other reservations, 1980s-87, hearing, 21448–37

Wisconsin timber resources and removals, by species, forest type, ownership, and county, series, 1206–34

see also under By Race and Ethnic Group in the "Index by Categories"

Indigent defense
see Legal aid

Individual retirement arrangements

Assets of collective investment funds, instns involved, and accounts, by type of fund and holding, 1988, annual rpt, 13004–1.3

Banks (insured commercial) domestic and foreign office consolidated financial statements, monthly rpt, quarterly data, 9362–1.4

Banks (insured commercial and savings) finances, for foreign and domestic offices, by asset size, 1987, annual rpt, 9294–4.2

Credit unions federally insured, finances by instn characteristics and State, as of June 1989, semiannual rpt, 9532–6

Credit unions federally insured, finances, 1987-88, annual rpt, 9534–1

Employee pension coverage, by whether contributed to IRA, plan type, and other characteristics, 1970s-88, article, 4742–1.925; 4746–26.7

Financial instns financial and operating statements by deposit size, Fed Reserve functional cost analysis, 1988, annual rpt, 9364–6

North Central States, FHLB 8th District savings instns financial operations by State and SMSA, monthly rpt, 9302–9

Savings instns regulatory issues, mgmt, and FHLB system and member finances and operations, monthly journal, 8432–2; 9312–1

South Central States, FHLB 9th District savings instns finances and operations by State, quarterly rpt, 9302–31

Southeastern States, Fed Reserve 5th District insured commercial banks financial statements, by State, quarterly rpt, 9389–18

Southeastern States, FHLB 4th District thrifts finances, by State, 1984-88 annual rpt series, 9304–29

Statistical Abstract of US, social, political, and economic data, 1790-2025, comprehensive annual compilation, 2324–1.2

Tax (excise) collections of IRS, and returns examined, for employee plans, 1976-88, article, 8304–8.1

Tax (income) returns filed by type of filer, selected income items, quarterly rpt, 8302–2.1

Tax (income) returns of individuals, by filing status, tax item, and income level, 1987, annual article, 8302–2.901

Tax (income) returns of individuals, detailed data, 1986, annual rpt, 8304–2

Tax (income) returns of individuals, selected income and tax items by income level, preliminary 1987, annual article, 8302–2.917

Tax (income) withholding and related documents filed, by type and IRS service center, 1988 and projected 1989-96, annual rpt, 8304–22

Tax expenditures, Federal revenues forgone through income tax deductions and exclusions by type, FY90-94, annual rpt, 21784–10

Indochina
see Cambodia
see Laos
see Southeast Asia

see Vietnam

Indonesia

Agricultural and food production and indexes, total and for selected commodities, by country, 1970s-88, annual rpt, 1524–12

Agricultural production, prices, and trade, by country, 1960s-89, annual world region rpt, 1524–4.2

Agricultural subsidies, consumer and producer equivalents by program, commodity, and major US trading partner, 1982-86, 1528–275

Agricultural trade of US, by detailed commodity and country, 1988, semiannual rpt, 1522–4

Agricultural trade of US with Asia, Middle East, and North Africa, by commodity and country, 1962-86, 1528–277

Agricultural universities in Indonesia, impacts of AID-Indonesia govt joint project, 1957-86, 9916–1.68

AID activities and funding by project and function, FY90, and developing countries summary socioeconomic data from 1960s, annual rpt, 9904–4.6

AID economic aid to developing countries, obligations and disbursements by country, quarterly rpt, 9912–4

AID loans repayment status and terms by program and country, and status of predecessor agency loans, quarterly rpt, 9912–3

Background Notes, summary social, political, and economic data, 1989 rpt, 7006–2.26

Coal production, trade, and govt subsidies, by country and country group, 1973-87 and projected to 2000, 2048–144

Economic and military aid and loans from US and intl agencies, by program and country, FY46-87, annual rpt, 9914–5

Economic conditions in Communist, OECD, and selected other countries, 1960s-88, annual rpt, 9114–4

Economic conditions, income, production, prices, employment, and trade, 1989 periodic country rpt, 2046–4.32; 2046–4.71

Economic conditions, policy, and trade practices, by country, 1986-88, annual rpt, 21384–5

Economic indicators of developing countries, problem debtors compared to other borrowers, by country, 1973-84, 1528–285

Economic, social, political, and geographic summary data, by country, 1989, annual factbook, 9114–2

Energy-intensive industry output and operations, and US investment barriers, for energy-rich countries, 1984-88, 9886–4.142

Exports and imports of US, by commodity and country, 1970-87, world area rpt, 9116–1.2

Exports and imports of US, by selected country, country group, and commodity group, 1988, annual rpt, 2044–37

Food consumption and spending, by item for Indonesia, 1978-84, 26308–85

Human rights conditions in 170 countries, 1988, annual rpt, 21384–3

Imports of goods, services, and investment from US, trade barriers, impacts, and US actions, by country, 1988, annual rpt, 444–2

Military aid of US, arms sales, and training programs costs and budget requests, by program, world region, and country, FY88-90, annual rpt, 7144–13

Military spending, arms trade, and force strengths, with govt spending and population, by country, 1977-87, annual rpt, 9824–1

Minerals production, reserves, and industry role in domestic economy and world supply, 1988 country rpt, 5606–1.17

Minerals Yearbook, 1987, Vol 3: foreign country reviews of production, trade, and policy, by commodity, annual rpt, 5604–35

Minerals Yearbook, 1987, Vol 3 preprints: foreign country review of production, trade, and policy, by commodity, annual rpt, 5604–23.33

Multinatl US firms and foreign affiliates finances and operations, by industry of parent firm and affiliate, world area, and country, preliminary 1987, annual rpt, 2704–5

Oil production, and exports and prices for US, by major exporting country, detailed data, monthly rpt, 3162–24

Oil production, trade, use, and stocks, by selected country and country group, monthly rpt, 3162–42

Population size, growth rates, and components of change, by country, projected 1989-2020 and trends from 1950, biennial rpt, 2324–9

Space satellites and other objects launched since 1957, quarterly listing, 9502–2

UN voting record and share of votes in agreement with US, by issue, country, and world area, 1988, annual rpt, 7004–18

see also under By Foreign Country in the "Index by Categories"

Industrial accidents and safety
see Hazardous substances
see Mine accidents and safety
see Occupational health and safety
see Railroad accidents and safety
see Transportation accidents and safety

Industrial and commercial energy use
Aluminum plant ownership, capacity, energy and aluminum sources, and startup and closing dates, by US and foreign plant and location, 1988, annual listing, 5604–49

Bonneville Power Admin mgmt of Fed Columbia River Power System, finances and sales, summary data, quarterly rpt, 3222–2

Bonneville Power Admin mgmt of Fed Columbia River Power System, finances, operations, and sales by customer, FY88, annual rpt, 3224–1

Bonneville Power Admin sales, revenues, and rates, by customer and customer type, 1988, semiannual rpt, 3222–1

Buildings (commercial) energy use, costs, and conservation, by building characteristics, survey rpt series, 3166–8

Business statistics, detailed data for major industries and economic indicators, *Survey of Current Business*, monthly rpt, 2702–1.10; 2702–1.15

Coal, coke, and breeze supply, demand, prices, trade, and stocks, by end-use sector and State, quarterly rpt with articles, 3162–37

Coal production and mines by county, prices, productivity, miners, reserves, and stocks, by mining method and State, 1987-88, annual rpt, 3164–25

Coal production and stocks by district, and shipments by district of origin, State of destination, end-use sector, and mode of transport, quarterly rpt, 3162–8

Coal production by region, exports, and use by sector, projected 1988-2000 and trends from 1975, annual rpt, 3164–68

Coal receipts, use, stocks, and delivered price to electric utilities, by State, weekly rpt, monthly data, 3162–1.2

Connecticut energy use by consuming sector, and prices, by energy type, 1960s-86, hearing, 21448–38

Construction industries census, 1987: establishments, employment, receipts, and expenditures, by SIC 4-digit industry and State, final industry rpt series, 2373–1

Construction industries census, 1987: financial and operating data, preliminary industry rpt series, 2371–1

Electric and gas utility ratemaking and regulatory standards, status and coverage of consumers and sales, 1988, annual rpt, 3104–7

Electric power plants production and capital costs, operations, and fuel use, by fuel type, plant, utility, and location, 1987, annual rpt, 3164–9

Electric power plants production, capacity, sales, and fuel stocks, use, and costs, by State, 1984-88, annual rpt, 3164–11

Electric power plants production, fuel use, stocks, and costs by fuel type, and sales, by State, monthly rpt, 3162–35

Electric power rate schedules, by user type, utility, and city, as of Jan 1988, annual rpt, 3164–40

Electric power sales, by end-use sector, census div, and State, and fuel use and costs, EIA and alternative estimates, with methodology, 1982-87, 3166–12.5

Electric power use and prices, shipments, and trade, for 25 SIC 4-digit manufacturing industries, 1972-86, 2048–137

Electric power use indexes, by SIC 2- to 4-digit industry, monthly rpt, 9365–2.10

Electric utilities finances and operations, detailed data for privately owned firms, and summary data for other utilities by type, 1987, annual rpt, 3164–23

Electric utilities fuel cost, quality, use, receipts, and stocks, and power plant production, by energy source, State and utility, quarterly rpt, 3162–39

Energy demand indicators, and use by fuel type and region, 1983, 3166–6.33

Energy supply, demand, and prices, by fuel type and end-use sector, projected under 3 oil price assumptions, 1988-2000, annual rpt, 3164–75

Energy supply, demand, and prices, by fuel type and end-use sector, with foreign comparisons, 1988 and trends from 1949, annual rpt, 3164–74

Energy supply, demand, and prices, by fuel type and end use, with foreign comparisons, 1976-88, annual summary rpt, 3164–76

Energy supply, demand, and prices, by fuel type, end-use sector, and country, detailed data, monthly rpt, 3162–24

Energy supply, demand, and prices, forecasts by resource type, quarterly rpt, 3162–34

Energy use, by detailed fuel type, end-use sector, and State, 1960-87, State Energy Data System annual rpt, 3164–39

Energy use, by fuel pollutant source, fuel type, and State, 1986, annual rpt, 9194–14

Energy use in transportation and other sectors, by fuel type, 1970s-88, annual rpt, 3304–5

Environmental impacts of energy technologies, 1960s-80s, handbook series, 3326–1

Foreign and US energy use by sector, and production, by fuel type, country, and country group, projected 1988-2000 and trends from 1970, annual rpt, 3164–84

Foreign countries energy-intensive industry output and operations, and US investment barriers, for energy-rich countries, 1984-88, 9886–4.142

Gasoline and other motor fuel use, by consuming sector and State, 1988, annual rpt, 7554–1.1

Health Care Financing Review, provider prices, price inputs and indexes, and labor, quarterly journal, 4652–1.1

Manufacturing energy use and prices, 1985 survey, series, 3166–13

Mineral industries census, 1987: financial and operating data, preliminary industry rpt series, 2511–1

Natural and supplemental gas production, prices, trade, use, reserves, and pipeline company finances, by firm and State, monthly rpt with articles, 3162–4

Natural gas interstate pipeline company detailed financial and operating data, by firm, 1988, annual rpt, 3164–38

Natural gas interstate pipeline company sales, by customer, SIC 2-digit industry group, and State, monthly rpt, annual tables, 3162–4.6

Natural gas interstate pipeline company sales, contract deliveries, and prices, with data by firm and location, 1982-87, 3168–113

Natural gas supply, demand, distribution, and prices, by State, 1984-88 annual rpt, 3164–4

New England States electric power sales, Fed Reserve 1st District, monthly rpt, 9373–24

New England States electric power sales, Fed Reserve 1st District, quarterly rpt, 9373–2.6

Oil and gas primary use prohibited for power and industrial plants, and gas use by State, 1988, annual rpt, 3104–8

Oil and gas supply, demand, and prices, alternative projections 1987-2000, annual rpt, 3164–89

Oil fuel switching to other fuels, capability by end-use sector, 1989, annual rpt, 3164–88

Oil products sales and purchases of refiners, processors, and distributors, by product, end-use sector, PAD district, and State, monthly rpt with articles, 3162–11; 3164–85

Oil refinery capacity, closings, and acquisitions by plant, and fuel used, by PAD district, 1973-88, annual rpt, 3164–2.1

Science, engineering, and technical employment in manufacturing, by field, occupation, and industry, 1986, triennial rpt, 9627-23

Shipbuilding and repair facilities, capacity, and employment, by shipyard, 1988, annual rpt, 7704-9

Solar collector and photovoltaic module shipments by end-use sector and State, R&D, and trade, 1988, annual rpt, 3164-62

Statistical Abstract of US, social, political, and economic data, 1790-2025, comprehensive annual compilation, 2324-1.3

Tax (income) returns of corporations, income and tax items by asset size and detailed industry, 1986, annual rpt, 8304-4; 8304-21

Tax (property) revenue by level of govt, assessed values by locality, and exemptions, by property type and State, 1987 Census of Govts, 2453-1

Technology-intensive manufacturing methods use and plans, with data by technology, selected industry, and firm and market characteristics, 1988 survey, 2508-1

Telephone and telegraph firms detailed finances and operations, 1987, annual rpt, 9284-6

Tennessee Valley industrial dev, employment, and electricity demand, by SIC 2-digit industry, firm, and location, 1988, annual rpt, 9804-3

Uranium tailings at inactive mills, remedial action proposals, costs, site characteristics, and environmental, socioeconomic, and health impacts, series, 3356-4

Wholesale trade census, 1987: employment, establishments, finances, and operations, by SIC 2- to 4-digit kind of business, MSA, county, and city, State rpt series, 2405-1

see also Business firms and establishments, number

see also Business machines and equipment

see also Capital investments, general

see also Capital investments, specific industry

see also Depreciation

see also Electric power plants and equipment

see also Foundries

see also Industrial capacity and utilization

see also Industrial robots

see also Industrial siting

see also Railroad equipment and vehicles

see also Warehouses

Industrial pollution

see Air pollution

see Environmental pollution and control

see Hazardous waste and disposal

see Lead poisoning and pollution

see Marine pollution

see Noise

see Water pollution

Industrial production

Alien workers (unauthorized) employer sanctions impacts on wages and output under alternative levels of enforcement, 1988 technical paper, 9379-12.33

Banking panics relation to production and business cycle, with data for NYC, 1857-1933, article, 9391-1.915

Business and financial statistics, historic trends, 1988 annual chartbook, 9364-2.2; 9364-2.5

Business Conditions Digest, economic, business, and financial devs and cyclical fluctuations, monthly rpt, 2702-3

Capital flows (intl) impacts on monetary policy instruments, and financial and economic indicators, 1987 compilation of papers, 9385-9

Communist and OECD countries economic conditions, 1987, annual rpt, 7144-11

Communist, OECD, and selected other countries economic conditions, 1960s-88, annual rpt, 9114-4

Competitiveness (intl) of US industries, with selected foreign and US operating data by major firm and product, series, 2046-12

Cuba economic conditions, agricultural and industrial production and distribution, trade, and intl economic relations, 1980-87 with trends from 1961, 9118-8

Dollar exchange rate and fiscal policy impacts on production, by industry div, 1970-87, working paper, 9393-10.5

Economic and employment conditions, alternative BLS projections to 2000 and trends 1970s-88, biennial article, 6722-1.954

Economic indicators and components, and Fed Reserve 4th District business and financial conditions, monthly chartbook, 9377-10

Economic indicators and components, current data and annual trends, monthly rpt, 23842-1.3

Economic indicators compounded annual rates of change, 1969-88, annual rpt, 9391-9.2

Economic indicators, monthly rpt, 9362-1.2

Exchange rate impact on inflation and output, 1960s-87, working paper, 9381-10.99

Forecasts of industrial production based on preliminary and revised composite leading index of economic indicators, accuracy assessment, 1969-88, technical paper, 9366-6.204

Foreign and domestic industry output relation to GNP, for Canada, Japan, and Germany, 1961-84, technical paper, 9366-6.189

Foreign and US economic conditions, and trade devs and balances, with data by selected country and country group, monthly rpt, 9882-14

Foreign countries economic and monetary trends, compounded annual rates of change for US and 10 major trading partners, quarterly rpt, 9391-7

Foreign countries economic conditions and implications for US, periodic country rpt series, 2046-4

Foreign countries economic indicators, and trade and investment flows, for selected countries and country groups, selected years 1946-88, annual rpt, 204-1.9

GNP forecasts for current quarter, performance of monthly employment, production, and retail sales, 1978-88, article, 9393-8.903

Imports and tariff provisions effect on US industries and products, investigations with background financial and operating data, series, 9886-4

Imports injury to US industries from foreign subsidized products, investigations with background financial and operating data, series, 9886-15

Imports injury to US industries from sales at less than fair value, investigations with background financial and operating data, series, 9886-14

Industry finances and operations, by SIC 2- to 4-digit industry, forecast 1989 and trends from 1950s, annual rpt, 2044-28

Input-output structure of US economy, detailed interindustry transactions for 84 industries, and components of final demand, 1983, annual article, 2702-1.909

Interest and inflation rates impact of unanticipated changes in money supply, industrial production, and inflation, 1959-86, technical paper, 9379-12.34

Manufacturers shipments and new and unfilled orders, 1947-88, annual rpt, 204-1.3

Manufacturers shipments, inventories, and orders, by SIC 2- to 3-digit industry, monthly Current Industrial Rpt, 2506-3.1

Manufacturing annual survey, 1986: production indexes and exports by SIC 2-digit industry and State, with comparisons to 1985, model results, series, 2506-16

Manufacturing annual survey, 1986: value of shipments, by SIC 4- to 5-digit product class, 2506-15.3

Manufacturing capacity, output, and productivity growth, and trade balance by major industry group, 1973-87, article, 9391-1.903

Manufacturing census, 1987: financial and operating data, for SIC 4-digit industries by product, preliminary industry rpt series, 2491-1

Manufacturing electric power use and prices, shipments, and trade, for 25 SIC 4-digit industries, 1972-86, 2048-137

Manufacturing share of output by State, and employment and output shares by industry div for US and Fed Reserve 3rd District, 1967-86, article, 9387-1.902

Middle Atlantic States manufacturing business outlook, monthly survey rpt, 9387-11

Monetary policy target forecasting performance, impact of commodity prices, model description and results, 1959-87, working paper, 9387-8.184

Oil use relation to crude oil prices, GNP, and industrial production, 1972-88, technical paper, 9379-12.39

Overseas Business Reports: economic conditions, investment and export opportunities, and trade practices, country market research rpt series, 2046-6

Regional manufacturing output measures of BEA, assessment of methods, 1989 working paper, 9375-13.11

Small business establishments, operations, owner characteristics, and job training, late 1950s-87, 9768-20

Southeastern US industrial output, by major industry group, 1986 with growth since 1963, article, 9391-16.905

Soviet Union economic conditions under General Secretary Gorbachev, Soviet and

see also Acquired immune deficiency
syndrome
see also Animal diseases and zoonoses
see also Food and waterborne diseases
see also Pneumonia and influenza
see also Rabies
see also Septicemia
see also Sexually transmitted diseases
see also Tuberculosis
see also Vaccination and vaccines
see also under By Disease in the "Index by
Categories"

Inflammable materials
Hotel and motel fires, casualties, and
effectiveness of smoke detectors, sprinkler
systems, and building and equipment
design, 1989 hearing, 21708–127
Injuries from use of consumer products, by
severity, victim age, and detailed product,
1988, annual rpt, 9164–6
Transport of hazardous material, accidents,
casualties, and damage, by mode of
transport, with DOT control activities,
1988, annual rpt, 7304–4
Transportation census, 1987: trucks, by
detailed characteristics, miles traveled,
and type of product carried, State rpt
series, 2573–1

Inflation
Africa (Sahel) food supply indicators, by
country, 1960s-2000, 1528–290
Budget of US, CBO analysis of revenue and
spending alternatives and projections of
economic indicators, FY90-94, annual rpt,
26304–3
Budget of US, historical data, selected years
FY34-88 and projected to FY94, annual
rpt, 104–22
Business statistics, detailed data for major
industries and economic indicators, Survey
of Current Business, monthly rpt,
2702–1.2
Capacity utilization rate impact on inflation,
for all manufacturing and for chemical
industry, 1971-88, article, 9375–1.903
Child support awards related to selected
variables, 1970s-85, 4008–94
Collective bargaining negotiated wages,
relation to contract duration and inflation
and unemployment rates, model
description and results for Canada,
1970s-83, working paper, 9387–8.191
CPI and Personal Consumption Expenditure
Index inflation measures under alternative
weighting systems, monthly rpt, quarterly
article, 6762–2
Credit (private and Federal) related to
GNP, interest rates, and inflation, model
description and results, 1960s-87, working
paper, 9381–10.94
Developing countries economic and social
conditions from 1960s, and Intl Dev
Cooperation Agency and AID activities
and funding, FY88-90, annual rpt,
9904–4
Dollar exchange rate impact on inflation,
1973-88, article, 9391–1.917
Economic indicator performance, and Fed
Reserve monetary policy objectives, as of
July 1989, semiannual rpt, 9362–4
Economic indicators and relation to govt
finances by level of govt, selected years
1929-87, annual rpt, 10044–1
Economic indicators compounded annual
rates of change, 1969-88, annual rpt,
9391–9.2

Economic indicators targets and
performance, 1960s-88 and projected to
1994, annual article, 9381–1.901
Economic Report of the President for 1989,
with economic trends from 1929, annual
rpt, 204–1
Election results impacts of inflation, for
Democratic share of presidential vote,
1916-88, hearing, 25248–109
Employment variability relation to inflation,
1951-80, working paper, 9377–9.70
Exchange rate impact on inflation and
output, 1960s-87, working paper,
9381–10.99
Forecasts of GNP and inflation, analysis of
errors among alternative models, 1989
article, 9373–1.904
Forecasts of GNP deflator and selected
economic indicators relation to actual
inflation, 1968-86, article, 9383–6.903
Forecasts of inflation, alternative model
results and forecast errors, 1960s-87,
article, 9389–1.901
Forecasts of inflation and unemployment,
performance of commodity price indexes,
with regression results and forecast errors,
1965-88, article, 9393–8.902
Forecasts of inflation, performance impacts
of forecast announcements, 1981-83,
working paper, 9387–8.185
Forecasts of inflation, performance of
alternative forecasts, 1970s-82, working
paper, 9389–19.6
Forecasts of inflation, performance of
commodity price indexes, alternative
regression results, 1954-88, article,
9389–1.902
Forecasts of inflation, performance of
financial and nonfinancial indicators,
model description and results, 1970s-88,
article, 9373–1.916
Forecasts of inflation, performance of money
supply and other economic indicators,
with inflation rates in 15 countries,
1960s-1988 and forecast to 1990, article,
9379–1.906
Forecasts of monetary policy targets and
inflation, performance of commodity price
indexes, with regression results, 1950s-87,
working paper, 9381–10.91
Foreign and US economic indicators, trade
balances, and exchange rates, for selected
OECD and Asian countries, 1980s-89,
semiannual rpt, 8002–14
Foreign countries economic and monetary
trends, compounded annual rates of
change for US and 10 major trading
partners, quarterly rpt, 9391–7
Foreign debt of US, economic impact,
1970s-80s and projected to 2000, article,
9387–1.905
GNP implicit price deflators, monthly rpt,
quarterly data, 23842–1.1
GNP implicit price deflators, natl
compounded annual rates of change,
monthly rpt, 9391–3.2
GNP implicit price deflators, total and
major components, quarterly data with
benchmark revisions, Survey of Current
Business, monthly rpt, 2702–1.28
GNP implicit price deflators, total and
major components, Survey of Current
Business, monthly rpt, 2702–1.21
GNP relation to inflation variability, model
description and results, 1959-88, article,
9391–1.919

Inflation and unemployment rates, 1979-88,
article, 9391–1.916
Interest rates relation to inflation and
money supply, 1954-87, working paper,
9387–8.187
Labor costs relation to inflation and GNP,
1959-88, working paper, 9389–19.9
Labor force composition, and wages relation
to inflation and unemployment, late
1930s-88, article, 9373–1.902
Monetary aggregates velocity relation to
inflation, for US and 39 countries, various
periods 1908-87, working paper,
9377–9.74
Monetary policy target forecasting
performance, impact of commodity prices,
model description and results, 1959-87,
working paper, 9387–8.184
Money supply, GNP, and interest rates,
relation to inflation, various periods
1952-88, working paper, 9389–19.10
Money supply, industrial production, and
inflation, impact of unanticipated changes
on interest and inflation rates, 1959-86,
technical paper, 9379–12.34
Money supply, monetary base, and
commodity price index inflation
forecasting performance, 1960s-87,
working paper, 9371–10.35
Natl income and product accounts govt
transactions component estimates,
methodology and bibl, 1988 technical rpt,
2706–6.5
OECD current account balance and related
economic indicators, for US and 4
countries, 1980s-87, article, 9389–1.908
Statistical Abstract of US, social, political,
and economic data, 1790-2025,
comprehensive annual compilation,
2324–1.3
Stock prices correlation with inflation rates
in US and 6 other countries, 1950s-86,
article, 9379–1.904
Stock yields relation to inflation and
monetary policy, 1969-87, technical paper,
9379–12.37
Survey of Current Business, detailed
financial and business data, and economic
indicators, monthly rpt, 2702–1.1
Tax (excise) indexed to inflation, impacts on
Federal revenue and family tax burden by
commodity, projected under alternative
proposals, 1989-93, GAO rpt, 26119–254
Unemployment rate relation to inflation,
labor force, GNP, interest rate, and trade
balance, various periods 1948-88, article,
9393–8.910
see also Consumer Price Index
see also Cost of living
see also Food prices
see also Interest rates
see also Monetary policy
see also Money supply
see also Price regulation
see also Prices
see also Producer Price Index

Influenza
see Pneumonia and influenza

Information access
see Freedom of information
see Government information
see Information sciences
see Information services
see Information storage and retrieval systems

Information sciences

Degrees awarded in higher education, by level, field, race, and sex, 1989 edition, annual rpt, 4824-2.20

Degrees in science and engineering, by field, level, and sex, 1950-86, 9628-77

Natl Commission on Libraries and Info Science activities, FY88, annual rpt, 15634-1

Training in library science, grants for disadvantaged students, by instn and State, FY89, annual listing, 4874-1

see also Computer sciences

Information services

County Business Patterns, 1987: employment, establishments, and payroll, by SIC 2- to 4-digit industry and county, annual State rpt series, 2326-8

Farm mgmt, finances, operations, environmental issues, and info sources, *1989 Yearbook of Agriculture*, annual rpt, 1004-18

Finances and operations, by SIC 2- to 4-digit industry, forecast 1989 with trends from 1950s, annual rpt, 2044-28

Finances, operations, and industry devs for telecommunications, with data by service type, firm, and country, 1950s-80s, 2808-27

Telecommunications info services for home and business, availability, use, and market indicators, for Us and other OECD countries, 1980s and projected to 1992, 2808-28

Weather services activities and funding, by Federal agency, planned FY89-90, annual rpt, 2144-2

see also Government information
see also Information storage and retrieval systems
see also Libraries
see also Mass media
see also Research

Information storage and retrieval systems

Air Force fiscal mgmt system operations and techniques, quarterly rpt, 3602-1

Airline computer reservation systems finances, operations, and impacts on airline competitiveness, 1980s-86, 7308-193

Airline computer reservation systems operating costs, fees, and market shares, by firm and location, 1984-87, hearing, 25528-108

Aliens (illegal) welfare benefits, operations of Federal-State system to prevent payment, State official views, 1988, GAO rpt, 26121-276

Census of Population and Housing, 1980: data processing, coverage, and availability, 2555-2.4

Child support enforcement automated systems of States, operational status by State and whether federally funded, 1985-88, GAO rpt, 26121-272

DOD procurement cost estimates for weapons and communications systems, by service branch, quarterly summary rpt, 3502-1

Environmental and natural resource data sources, and aerial survey R&D rpts, quarterly listing, 9502-7

Fed Govt computer systems and equipment, by type, make, and agency, 1st half FY89, semiannual listing, 9452-9

Fed Govt computer systems mgmt deficiencies, and corrective actions and delays, by agency, 1983-87, GAO rpt, 26125-33

Fed Govt computer systems security training activities, by agency, 1988, GAO rpt, 26125-31

Fed Govt computer systems with sensitive info, and plans submitted to oversight agencies, by agency, 1989, GAO rpt, 26125-34

Fed Govt mgmt cost control proposals, Reagan Admin initiatives, savings, and status, FY85-94, annual rpt, 104-23

Fed Govt standards for data recording, processing, and transfer, and for purchase and use of computer systems, series, 2216-2

HHS data projects and systems, by subagency, FY88, 4008-92

Industry finances and operations, by SIC 2- to 4-digit industry, forecast 1989 and trends from 1950s, annual rpt, 2044-28

Library of Congress activities, acquisitions, services, and financial statements, FY88, annual rpt, 26404-1

Medicine Natl Library activities, holdings, and grants, FY86-88, annual rpt, 4464-1

NIH Natl Library of Medicine MEDLINE on-line data base user info needs and other characteristics, 1987 survey, 4468-3

OMB mgmt of Federal employees, budget, and info systems, indicators of effectiveness, FY81-90, GAO rpt, 26119-251

Passport and visa applicant screening, State Dept info system records by reason for exclusion, 1989, GAO rpt, 26125-36

Police dept operations, staff, and expenses, for large cities by population size, 1987, 6066-19.51

Service industries census, 1987: establishments, receipts, employment, and payroll, by SIC 2- to 4-digit kind of business, MSA, county, and city, State rpt series, 2391-1

Survey of Income and Program Participation, data collection, methodology, and availability, 1987 users guide, 2628-24

Survey of Income and Program Participation, data collection, methodology, and comparisons to other data bases, working paper series, 2626-10

Survey of Income and Program Participation, data collection, methodology, and use, 1988 annual conf papers, 2624-1

see also Computer data file guides
see also Computer industry and products
see also Computer networks
see also Microforms
see also Statistical programs and activities

Infrastructure

see Public works

Inglewood, Calif.

see also under By City in the "Index by Categories"

Inhalation therapy

see Respiratory therapy

Inheritance tax

see Estate tax

Injuries

see Accidental deaths
see Accidents and accident prevention
see Agricultural accidents and safety
see Aviation accidents and safety
see Drowning
see Marine accidents and safety
see Mine accidents and safety
see Occupational health and safety
see Railroad accidents and safety
see Spinal cord injuries
see Traffic accidents and safety
see Transportation accidents and safety

Inland water transportation

Army Corps of Engineers activities and projects, FY87 and trends from 1800s, annual rpt, 3754-1.2

Army Corps of Engineers water resources dev projects, characteristics, and costs, 1950s-87, biennial State rpt series, 3756-2

Army Corps of Engineers water resources dev projects, characteristics, and costs, 1950s-89, biennial State rpt series, 3756-1

Coal production and stocks by district, and shipments by district of origin, State of destination, end-use sector, and mode of transport, quarterly rpt, 3162-8

Communist, OECD, and selected other countries freight and carrier inventories, by mode of transport, 1960s-88, annual rpt, 9114-4.10

County Business Patterns, 1987: employment, establishments, and payroll, by SIC 2- to 4-digit industry and county, annual State rpt series, 2326-8

Developing countries disaster preparedness and economic, population, and political data, country rpt series, 9916-2

DOD shipments of military and personal property, passenger traffic, and costs, by service branch and mode of transport, quarterly rpt, 3702-1

Employment, earnings, and hours, by SIC 1- to 4-digit industry, monthly 1983-Feb 1989, annual rpt, 6744-4

Energy use by mode of transport, fuel supply, and demographic and economic factors of vehicle use, 1970s-88, annual rpt, 3304-5

Exports and imports (waterborne) of US, by type of service, customs district, port, and world area, monthly rpt, 2422-7

Fed Govt Inland Waterways Trust Fund financial condition, monthly rpt, 8102-9.8

Finances, operations, vehicles, equipment, accidents, and energy use, by mode of transport, 1955-88, annual rpt, 7304-2

Foreign countries economic, social, political, and geographic summary data, by country, 1989, annual factbook, 9114-2

Freight (waterborne domestic), by major commodity group, vessel type, and port, 1986, annual rpt, 7704-7

Freight (waterborne domestic), by major commodity group, 1981-86, annual rpt, 3754-1.1

Freight (waterborne domestic and foreign) by commodity, traffic, and passengers, by port and waterway, 1987, annual rpt, 3754-3

Govt employment and payroll, by function, level of govt, and jurisdiction, 1987-88, annual rpt series, 2466–1

Govt finances, by level of govt, State, and for large cities and counties, annual rpt series, 2466–2

Grain shipments and rates for barge and rail loadings, periodic sitiuation rpt with articles, 1561–4

Grain shipments for exports, effects of rail car availability and major river water levels, 1979-87, article, 1561–4.903

Occupational injury and illness rates, by SIC 2- to 4-digit industry, 1987, annual rpt, 6844–1

Ohio River basin waterway facilities, freight by commodity and port, and recreation, by waterway, 1986-87, annual rpt, 3754–6

Pollution (water) incidents and discharges, by type, source, cause, and location, 1984-86, annual rpt, 7404–3

Science, engineering, and technical employment in transportation, utilities, and retail and wholesale trade, by field, occupation, and industry, 1985, triennial rpt, 9627–32

St Lawrence Seaway ship, cargo, and passenger traffic, and toll revenue, 1988 and trends from 1959, annual rpt, 7744–2

Statistical Abstract of US, social, political, and economic data, 1790-2025, comprehensive annual compilation, 2324–1.3

TVA financial and operating data by program and facility, FY88, annual rpt, 9804–32

see also Barges

see also Dredging

Inner cities
see Central cities

Inoculation
see Vaccination and vaccines

Inorganic chemicals
see Chemicals and chemical industry

Input-output analysis
Input-output structure of US economy, detailed interindustry transactions for 84 industries, and components of final demand, 1983, annual article, 2702–1.909

Insecticides
see Pesticides

Insects
see Animal diseases and zoonoses
see Honey and beekeeping
see Infective and parasitic diseases
see Pests and pest control

Inspection of industrial products
see Quality control and testing

Inspectors General reports
see Federal Inspectors General reports

Installment credit
see Consumer credit

Institute of Museum Services
see National Foundation on the Arts and the Humanities

Institute of Peace
see U.S. Institute of Peace

Instructional materials
see Educational materials

Instruments and measuring devices
Aerial survey R&D rpts, and sources of natural resource and environmental data, quarterly listing, 9502–7

Air traffic levels at FAA-operated control facilities, including instrument operations, by airport and State, FY88, annual rpt, 7504–27

Aircraft (general aviation), flight hours, and equipment, by type, use, and model of aircraft, region, and State, 1988, annual rpt, 7504–29

Aircraft flight service station workload of FAA, pilot briefs, contacts, and flight plans by facility, projected FY88-99 and trends from FY80, annual rpt, 7504–39

Aircraft handled by instrument flight rule, by user type, FAA traffic control center, and region, FY80-88 and projected to FY2000, annual rpt, 7504–15

Aircraft pilots instrument ratings, by certificate type and region, 1988, annual rpt, 7504–2

China trade by SITC 1- to 5-digit commodity, 1970s-87, annual rpt, 9114–3

Collective bargaining agreements expiring during year, and workers covered, by firm, union, industry group, and State, 1989, annual rpt, 6784–9

County Business Patterns, 1987: employment, establishments, and payroll, by SIC 2- to 4-digit industry and county, annual State rpt series, 2326–8

Digital readout systems and components from Japan at less than fair value, injury to US industry, investigation with background financial and operating data, 1989 rpt, 9886–14.249

DOD prime contract awards, by detailed procurement category, FY85-88, annual rpt, 3544–18

Drafting machines from Japan at less than fair value, injury to US industry, investigation with background financial and operating data, 1989 rpt, 9886–14.263

Earnings by major industry group, and personal income per capita and by source, by region and State, 1929-87, 2708–40

Electric and gas utility ratemaking and regulatory standards, status and coverage of consumers and sales, 1988, annual rpt, 3104–7

Employment, earnings, and hours, by selected SIC 1- to 4-digit industry, State, and for 262 MSAs, 1972-87, 6748–81

Employment, earnings, and hours, by SIC 1- to 4-digit industry, monthly 1983-Feb 1989, annual rpt, 6744–4

Employment of minorities and women, by occupation, SIC 1- to 3- digit industry, State, and MSA, 1986, annual rpt, 9244–1

Employment, unemployment, and labor force characteristics, by region and census div, 1988, annual rpt, 6744–7.1

Energy use and prices for manufacturing industries, 1985 survey, series, 3166–13

Exports and imports of US, by commodity group, world area, selected country, US coastal area and port, and mode of transport, monthly rpt, 2422–9

Exports of US, detailed commodities by country, monthly rpt, 2422–3

Financial statements for manufacturing, mining, and trade corporations, by selected SIC 2- to 3-digit industry, quarterly rpt, 2502–1

Fires in hotels and motels, casualties, and effectiveness of smoke detectors, sprinkler systems, and building and equipment design, 1989 hearing, 21708–127

Freight (waterborne domestic and foreign) by commodity, traffic, and passengers, by port and waterway, 1987, annual rpt, 3754–3

Hazardous substances industrial releases and reduction methods under EPA regulation, by chemical, source, industry, and location, 1987, annual rpt, 9234–6

Imports, exports, and employment impacts, by SIC 2- to 4-digit industry and commodity, quarterly rpt, 2322–2

Imports of US, detailed Schedule A commodities by country, monthly rpt, 2422–2

Imports of US given duty-free treatment for value of US material sent abroad, and impacts on US industry and employment, by commodity and country, 1987, annual rpt, 9884–14

Industrial control equipment shipments, trade, use, and firms, by product, 1988, annual Current Industrial Rpt, 2506–12.11

Injuries from use of consumer products, by severity, victim age, and detailed product, 1988, annual rpt, 9164–6

Input-output structure of US economy, detailed interindustry transactions for 84 industries, and components of final demand, 1983, annual article, 2702–1.909

Labor productivity, indexes of output, hours, and employment by SIC 2- to 4-digit industry, 1963-87, annual rpt, 6824–1.3

Manufacturers finances and operations, by SIC 2- to 4-digit industry, forecast 1989 and trends from 1950s, annual rpt, 2044–28

Manufacturing annual survey, 1986: financial and operating data, by SIC 2- to 4-digit industry, series, 2506–15

Manufacturing annual survey, 1986: production indexes and exports by SIC 2-digit industry and State, with comparisons to 1985, model results, series, 2506–16

Manufacturing census, 1987: financial and operating data, for SIC 4-digit industries by product, preliminary industry rpt series, 2491–1

Manufacturing industries production, shipments, inventories, orders, and pollution control costs, periodic Current Industrial Rpt series, 2506–3

Multinatl US firms and foreign affiliates finances and operations, by industry of parent firm and affiliate, world area, and country, preliminary 1987, annual rpt, 2704–5

Natural gas interstate pipeline company detailed financial and operating data, by firm, 1988, annual rpt, 3164–38

Occupational injury and illness rates, by SIC 2- to 4-digit industry, 1987, annual rpt, 6844–1

OECD trade, total and for 4 major countries, and US trade by country, by commodity, 1970-87, world area rpt series, 9116–1

Science and engineering employment, by nonmanufacturing industry and field, 1987, triennial rpt, 9627–31

SEC registration, firms required to file annual rpts, as of Sept 1988, annual listing, 9734–5

Securities (tax-exempt) holdings by investor type, and IRS enforcement of disallowance of interest deduction for financing holdings, mid 1970s-87, GAO rpt, 26119–239

Small business establishments, employment, and financial ratios, by SIC 1- to 2-digit industry and State, late 1960s-87, 9768–19

Small business finances, operations, owner and employee characteristics, and Federal contracts, 1980s-88, annual rpt, 9764–6

Soviet Union personal income by source, disposable income, wage deductions by type, and savings, 1950s-87, 9118–7

Statistical Abstract of US, social, political, and economic data, 1790-2025, comprehensive annual compilation, 2324–1.3

Student guaranteed loan default rates, and claims paid by guaranty agencies, by State, and borrower characteristics, FY87, GAO rpt, 26121–292

Tax (excise) collections of IRS, by source, quarterly rpt, 8302–1

Tax (income) returns filed by type of filer, selected income items, quarterly rpt, 8302–2.1

Tax (income) returns of corporations, income and tax items by asset size and detailed industry, 1986, annual rpt, 8304–4; 8304–21

Tax (income) returns of partnerships, income statement items by industry group, 1986, annual article, 8302–2.903

Tax (income) returns of sole proprietorships, income statement items, by industry group, 1987, annual article, 8302–2.904; 8302–2.921

Tax collections of State govts by detailed type of tax, and tax rates, by State, FY88, annual rpt, 2466–2.3

Tax expenditures, Federal revenues forgone through income tax deductions and exclusions by type, FY90-94, annual rpt, 21784–10

Tax revenue potential of State and local systems relative to natl average tax burden, by type of tax and State, 1986, annual rpt, 10044–7

see also Agricultural insurance
see also Automobile insurance
see also Deposit insurance
see also Disability benefits and insurance
see also Employee benefits
see also Federal Deposit Insurance Corp.
see also Federal Savings and Loan Insurance Corp.
see also Health insurance
see also Life insurance
see also Medicare
see also Old-Age, Survivors, Disability, and Health Insurance
see also Property and casualty insurance
see also Servicepersons life insurance programs
see also Surety bonds
see also Unemployment insurance

see also Workers compensation
see also under By Industry in the "Index by Categories"

Insurgency
Nicaragua Contra forces humanitarian aid of AID, by type, 1988, GAO rpt, 26123–237

Intelligence levels
Improvement of intelligence and memory, use of treatments and products not proven safe or effective, costs, and user characteristics, 1986 survey, 4008–86
Military reserve forces manpower strengths and characteristics, by component, quarterly rpt, 3542–4
see also Educational tests
see also Literacy and illiteracy
see also Mental health and illness
see also Mental retardation

Intelligence services
see also Bureau of Intelligence and Research, State Department
see also Central Intelligence Agency
see also Defense Intelligence Agency
see also Defense Security Assistance Agency
see also Detective and protective services
see also Espionage
see also Military intelligence

Intelligence tests
see Intelligence levels

INTELSAT
see International Telecommunications Satellite Organization

Inter-American Development Bank
Loans and grants for economic and military aid from US and intl agencies, by program and country, FY46-87, annual rpt, 9914–5
US contributions to multilateral dev banks, FY86-90, annual rpt, 9904–1.4

Inter-American Foundation
Activities, grants by recipient, and fellowships of IAF, by country, FY88, annual rpt, 14424–1
Budget of US, authoritative financial statements with appropriations, outlays, and receipts, by category and agency, FY88, annual rpt, 8104–2.2
Grants by program area, and fellowships by field and instn, by country, with IAF finances and staff, FY71-88, annual rpt, 14424–2

Interagency Council on the Homeless
Assistance of Fed Govt to homeless by program and Federal agency, and indicators of need, 1988, annual rpt, 14364–1

Interagency Drought Policy Committee
Drought of 1988, impacts on agriculture and other sectors, and Federal aid, 1008–53

Interagency Task Force on Acid Precipitation
Research on acid rain, activities, and funding by Federal agency, 1988, annual rpt, 14354–1

Interdepartment Radio Advisory Committee
Radio frequency assignments for Federal use, by agency, 2nd half 1988, semiannual rpt, 2802–1

Interest groups
see Lobbying and lobbying groups
see Nonprofit organizations and foundations
see Political action committees

Interest payments
Agricultural Statistics, 1988, annual rpt, 1004–1.2
Agriculture census, 1987: farms, farmland, production, finances, and operator characteristics, by county, final State rpt series, 2331–1
AID loans repayment status and terms by program and country, and status of predecessor agency loans, quarterly rpt, 9912–5
Auto operating costs, by component, 1977-88, annual rpt, 7304–2.1
Banks (insured commercial) financial condition and performance, by asset size and region, quarterly rpt, 9292–1
Banks (insured commercial and savings) finances, for foreign and domestic offices, by asset size, 1987, annual rpt, 9294–4.2
Banks and thrifts in New England, financial statements by type of instn and Fed deposit insurance, and State, 1987, annual rpt, 9304–3
Budget deficit reduction under Gramm-Rudman Act, cancellation of budget authority by program, FY90, annual rpt, 104–27
Budget of US Appendix, obligations, appropriations, and personnel, by program and agency, FY90, annual rpt, 104–3
Budget of US, authoritative financial statements with appropriations, outlays, and receipts, by category and agency, FY88, annual rpt, 8104–2.2
Budget of US, CBO analysis and review of FY90 budget by function, annual rpt, 26304–2
Budget of US, CBO analysis of revenue and spending alternatives and projections of economic indicators, FY90-94, annual rpt, 26304–3
Budget of US, compact budgets by activity, function, and agency, FY90 and projected to FY94, annual rpt, 104–2
Budget of US, historical data, selected years FY34-88 and projected to FY94, annual rpt, 104–22
Budget of US, House concurrent resolution, with spending and revenue targets, FY90, annual rpt, 21264–2
Budget of US, midsession review of FY90 budget, by function and agency, annual rpt, 104–7
Budget of US, overview, FY90, annual rpt, 104–6
Budget of US, receipts by source, outlays by agency and program, and balances, monthly rpt, 8102–3
Budget of US, Senate concurrent resolution, with spending and revenue targets, FY90, annual rpt, 25254–1
Budget of US, special analysis of outstanding debt and interest costs, FY90, annual rpt, 104–1.5
CCC loan and support programs payment activity, with data by commodity, 1986-88 and projected to 1994, 26308–86
Census of Agriculture, 1987: farms, farmland, production and costs, and operator characteristics, advance State and county rpt series, 2330–1
Consumer interest paid to business, and interest received as personal income, 1929-88, annual rpt, 204–1.1

Wisconsin S&Ls, mortgage interest fixed and adjustable rates and fees offered, monthly rpt, 9302–7

Intergovernmental relations

Assistance (financial and nonfinancial) of Fed Govt, 1989 base edition with supplements, annual listing, 104–5

Budget of US Appendix, obligations, appropriations, and personnel, by program and agency, FY90, annual rpt, 104–3

Intergovernmental Perspective, quarterly journal, 10042–1

Policy, intergovtl relations, and finances of Federal, State, and local govts, series, 10046–8

see also Federal-local relations

see also Federal-State relations

see also Foreign relations

see also International cooperation in law enforcement

see also Interstate relations

see also Regional planning

see also State-local relations

Interindustry transactions

see Input-output analysis

Interior Department

see Department of Interior

Internal combustion engines

see Engines and motors

Internal Revenue Service

Activities of IRS, collection, enforcement, and litigation, with data by type of tax, region, and State, FY88, annual rpt, 8304–3

Budget of US Appendix, obligations, appropriations, and personnel, by program and agency, FY90, annual rpt, 104–3

Corporations income tax returns, income and tax items by asset size and detailed industry, 1986, annual rpt, 8304–4; 8304–21

Criminal investigations of IRS resulting in tax assessment and collection, by violation type, 1984, GAO rpt, 26119–244

Employee benefit plan applications to IRS, and coverage, by disposition and plan type, July 1987-FY88, annual rpt, 8304–23

Excise tax collections of IRS, by source, quarterly rpt, 8302–1

Foreign earned income on US individual returns, exclusions, credits, and US revenue losses, with data by country, 1983, quadrennial rpt, 8308–34

Income tax unpaid by reason, and compliance after audits and appeals, for individuals and corporations, 1970s-87 and projected to 1992, 8308–26

Individual income tax returns, data compilation, semiannual rpt, suspended, 8302–5

Individual income tax returns, detailed data, 1986, annual rpt, 8304–2

Partnership income tax returns, income statement items by industry group, annual rpt, suspended, 8304–18

Pension plan regulation enforcement by Labor Dept and IRS, violations, and penalties, FY85-88, GAO rpt, 26121–259

Returns and supplemental documents filed, by type, FY88 and projected to FY97, semiannual rpt, 8302–4

Returns filed, by type of filer, detailed preliminary and supplementary data, quarterly rpt with articles, 8302–2

Returns filed, by type of tax, region, and IRS service center, projected 1988-95 and trends from 1977, annual rpt, 8304–9

Returns processing, IRS workload forecasts, compliance, and enforcement, data compilation, 1989 annual rpt, 8304–8

Securities (tax-exempt) holdings by investor type, and IRS enforcement of disallowance of interest deduction for financing holdings, mid 1970s-87, GAO rpt, 26119–239

Telephone system of IRS for income tax questions, accessibility and accuracy, and other IRS workload indicators, 1988 hearing, 21788–178

Telephone system of IRS for income tax questions, accessibility and accuracy, 1988 survey, GAO rpt, 26119–190

Violations of income tax law, civil penalties assessed and abated, FY87-88, GAO rpt, 26119–265

Withholding and related documents filed, by type and IRS service center, 1988 and projected 1989-96, annual rpt, 8304–22

Internal security

DOE security clearances and investigations, 1986-88, GAO rpt, 26113–387

Info security clearance of Fed Govt and contractor employees, polygraph use, prepublication reviews, and unauthorized disclosures and investigations, 1986-88, GAO rpt, 26123–66

Info security compliance of Federal agencies, computer systems security training activities, by agency, 1988, GAO rpt, 26125–31

Info security compliance of Federal agencies, computer systems with sensitive info, and plans submitted to oversight agencies, by agency, 1989, GAO rpt, 26125–34

Info Security Oversight Office monitoring of Federal security measures and classification actions, FY88, annual rpt, 9454–21

Labor laws enacted, by State, 1988, annual article, 6722–1.904

Labor productivity of Federal employees, indexes of output and labor costs by function, FY67-87, annual rpt, 6824–1.6

Natl Archives and Records Admin activities, finances, holdings, and staff, FY88, annual rpt, 9514–2

US attorneys civil and criminal cases by type and disposition, and collections, by Federal district, FY88, annual rpt, 6004–2.7

International agreements

see Executive agreements

see Trade agreements

see Treaties and conventions

International assistance

Agricultural and food aid to developing countries, and impacts on US exports, with background data, 1960s-89, 26308–85

Agricultural research grants of USDA, by program, subagency, and country, FY88, annual listing, 1954–3

Agricultural technical aid of USDA, personnel and agreements by project, world area, and country, FY87, annual rpt, 1954–2

AID contracts and grants for technical and support services, by instn, country, and State, FY88, annual listing, 9914–7

AID dev projects and socioeconomic impacts, evaluation rpt series, 9916–1

AID dev projects, special study series, 9916–3

AID economic aid to developing countries, obligations and disbursements by country, quarterly rpt, 9912–4

AID loans authorized, signed, and canceled, by country and world area, quarterly rpt, 9912–2

AID loans repayment status and terms by program and country, and status of predecessor agency loans, quarterly rpt, 9912–3

Background Notes, foreign countries summary social, political, and economic data, series, 7006–2

Budget of US Appendix, obligations, appropriations, and personnel, by program and agency, FY90, annual rpt, 104–3

Budget of US, balances of budget authority obligated and unobligated, by function and agency, FY88-90, annual rpt, 104–8

Budget of US, compact budgets by activity, function, and agency, FY90 and projected to FY94, annual rpt, 104–2

Budget of US, historical data, selected years FY34-88 and projected to FY94, annual rpt, 104–22

Budget of US, House concurrent resolution, with spending and revenue targets, FY90, annual rpt, 21264–2

Budget of US, receipts by source, outlays by agency and program, and balances, monthly rpt, 8102–3

Budget of US, Senate concurrent resolution, with spending and revenue targets, FY90, annual rpt, 25254–1

Cuba economic conditions, agricultural and industrial production and distribution, trade, and intl economic relations, 1980-87 with trends from 1961, 9118–8

Currency (foreign) accounts owned by US under AID admin and by foreign govts with joint AID control, status by program and country, quarterly rpt, 9912–1

Currency (foreign) holdings of US, transactions and balances by program and country, 1st half FY89, semiannual rpt, 8102–7

Debt to US of foreign govts and private obligors, by country and program, periodic rpt, 8002–6

Developing countries economic aid from US, bilateral and through intl dev banks, by world region and country, 1970s-FY88, annual rpt, 9904–1

Developing countries economic and military aid from US, Communist, and selected other countries, 1946-88, annual rpt, 9114–4.9

Developing countries economic and social conditions from 1960s, and Intl Dev Cooperation Agency and AID activities and funding, FY88-90, annual rpt, 9904–4

Developing countries receiving US economic aid, military spending and imports measures to determine aid eligibility, by country, 1985-86, annual rpt, 9914–1

Disaster preparedness and economic, population, and political data, country rpt series, 9916–2

Economic conditions, policy, and trade practices, by country, 1986-88, annual rpt, 21384–5

Economic, social, political, and geographic summary data, by country, 1989, annual factbook, 9114–2

Fed Govt contingent liabilities and claims paid on insured and guaranteed contracts with foreign obligors, by country and program, periodic rpt, 8002–12

Finances of govts, revenues by source and spending by function, natl income and product account, *Survey of Current Business*, monthly rpt, 2702–1.24

Food aid impacts on developing countries economic conditions and demand for US grain exports, model description and results, 1960s-84, 1528–291

Food and agricultural conditions of foreign countries, and relationship to population growth, with background data, 1950s-88 and projections to 2050, hearing, 21708–126

Housing and urban dev program of AID, financial statements, and loan guarantees by country, FY88, annual rpt, 9914–4

Inter-American Foundation activities, grants by recipient, and fellowships, by country, FY88, annual rpt, 14424–1

Inter-American Foundation dev grants by program area, and fellowships by field and instn, by country, FY71-88, annual rpt, 14424–2

Loans and grants for economic and military aid from US and intl agencies, by program and country, FY46-87, annual rpt, 9914–5

Loans and loan guarantees of Fed Govt, outstanding amounts by agency and program, *Treasury Bulletin*, quarterly rpt, 8002–4.9

NATO members economic aid to developing countries, for 11 members, 1982-87, annual rpt, 3544–28

Nicaragua Contra forces humanitarian aid of AID, by type, 1988, GAO rpt, 26123–237

Peace Corps activities, funding by program, and volunteers, by country, FY90, annual rpt, 9654–1

R&D funding by Fed Govt, by detailed function, program, and agency, FY88-90, annual rpt, 9627–9

Red Cross domestic and intl services, volunteers, and certificates issued, by program, FY88, annual rpt, 29254–1.1

Refugee arrivals in US by world area of origin and State of settlement, and Federal aid, FY88-90, annual rpt, 7004–16

Rice exports under Federal programs, periodic situation rpt, 1561–8

Statistical Abstract of US, social, political, and economic data, by outlying area and country, 1950s-87, comprehensive annual compilation, 2324–1.4

USIA English language program enrollment and staff, by instn, world area, and country, FY88, annual rpt, 9854–2

see also Export-Import Bank

see also Military assistance

see also Public Law 480

see also Refugees

see also War relief

International Bank for Reconstruction and Development

Loans and grants for economic and military aid from US and intl agencies, by program and country, FY46-87, annual rpt, 9914–5

US contributions to multilateral dev banks, FY86-90, annual rpt, 9904–1.4

see also International Development Association

see also International Finance Corp.

International Boundary and Water Commission, U.S. and Mexico

Hydroelectric power plants capacity and other characteristics, for western US, FY88, annual rpt, 3254–1

Labor unions recognized in Fed Govt, agreements and membership by agency and facility, as of Jan 1989, biennial listing, 9844–14

International Brotherhood of Electrical Workers

AT&T workers membership in IBEW, by local, 1981 and 1987, hearings, 21368–113

International cooperation in conservation

Endangered animals and plants US trade and permits, by species, purpose, disposition, and country, 1987, annual rpt, 5504–19

EPA pollution control grant program activities, monthly rpt, 9182–8

Fish Hatchery Natl System activities and deliveries, by species, hatchery, and jurisdiction of waters stocked, FY88, annual rpt, 5504–10

Marine Mammal Protection Act admin, and populations, strandings, and catch permits by species and location, 1987-88, annual rpt, 2164–11

Marine mammal protection, Federal and intl regulatory and research activities, 1988, annual rpt, 14734–1

Oil stocks and conservation measures of Intl Energy Program countries, 1987-88 and projected to 1990, GAO rpt, 26123–225

Rhinoceros wild and captive population, poacher kills and enforcement action, and conservation issues, 1988 hearing, 21708–125

Treaties and other bilateral and multilateral agreements of US in force, by country, as of Jan 1989, annual listing, 7004–1

see also International cooperation in environmental sciences

International cooperation in cultural activities

Arts Natl Endowment activities and grants, FY88, annual rpt, 9564–3

English language program of USIA, enrollment and staff, by instn, world area, and country, FY88, annual rpt, 9854–2

Japan-US Friendship Commission educational and cultural exchange activities, grants, and trust fund status, FY87-88, biennial report, 14694–1

Smithsonian Instn activities and finances, FY88, annual rpt, 29574–1

Treaties and other bilateral and multilateral agreements of US in force, by country, as of Jan 1989, annual listing, 7004–1

USIA library holdings, use, and staff, by country and city, FY88, annual rpt, 9854–4

see also Educational exchanges

see also Exchange of persons programs

International cooperation in environmental sciences

Exchange and training programs of Federal agencies, participants by world area, and funding, by program, FY87, annual rpt, 9854–8

Geological Survey activities and funding, FY88, annual rpt, 5664–8

Oceanographic research and distribution activities of World Data Center A by country, and cruises by ship, 1987, annual rpt, 2144–15

Radiation and radionuclide concentrations, monitoring results of intl and foreign agencies, quarterly rpt, 9192–5

Treaties and other bilateral and multilateral agreements of US in force, by country, as of Jan 1989, annual listing, 7004–1

UN Environment Program activities, and funding by source, program, and country, 1986-89, GAO rpt, 26123–246

Weather services activities and funding, by Federal agency, planned FY89-90, annual rpt, 2144–2

see also International cooperation in conservation

International cooperation in law enforcement

Drug abuse indicators for selected metro areas, research results, data collection, and policy issues, 1989 semiannual conf, 4492–5

Drugs (illegal) production, eradication, and seizures, by substance, with US aid, by country, 1985-89, annual rpt, 7004–17

Terrorist incidents in US, related activity, and casualties, by attack type, target, group, and location, 1988, annual rpt, 6224–6

Treaties and other bilateral and multilateral agreements of US in force, by country, as of Jan 1989, annual listing, 7004–1

International cooperation in science and technology

Allergy and Infectious Diseases Natl Inst activities, grants by recipient and location, and disease incidence, FY81-88, annual rpt, 4474–30

Assistance (financial and nonfinancial) of Fed Govt, 1989 base edition with supplements, annual listing, 104–5

Dental Research Natl Inst research and training grants, by recipient, FY88, annual listing, 4474–19

Economic and military aid of US, by country and program, FY86-88, annual rpt, 9904–1.4

Exchange and training programs of Federal agencies, participants by world area, and funding, by program, FY87, annual rpt, 9854–8

Heart, Lung, and Blood Natl Inst activities, and grants by recipient and location, FY88 with disease trends from 1940, annual rpt, 4474–15

HHS financial aid, by program, recipient, State, and city, FY88, annual regional listings, 4004–3

Industry (US) intl competitiveness, with selected foreign and US operating data by major firm and product, series, 2046–12

NASA R&D funding to higher education instns, by field, instn, and State, FY88, annual listing, 9504–7

NIH activities, funding by program and recipient type, staff, and clinic patients, by inst, FY87, annual rpt, 4434–3

NIH grants for R&D, training, construction, and medical libraries, by location and recipient, FY88, annual listings, 4434–7

NIH intl program activities and funding, by inst and country, FY88, annual rpt, 4474–6

NSF grants and contracts, by field, inst, State, and country, FY88, annual rpt, 9624–26

NSF Science Resources Studies Div project descriptions and rpts, 1988 annual listing, 9624–21

R&D Fed Govt policies and programs, 1985-88, biennial rpt, 424–2

R&D funding by Fed Govt, by field, performer type, agency, and State, FY87-89, annual rpt, 9627–20

Space launches and other activities of NASA and USSR, with flight data, 1957-88, annual rpt, 9504–6.1

Standards (intl) assns participation by US and other countries, 1989, 2218–80

Treaties and other bilateral and multilateral agreements of US in force, by country, as of Jan 1989, annual listing, 7004–1

see also European Space Agency

see also International cooperation in environmental sciences

see also Technology transfer

International corporations

see Foreign corporations

see Multinational corporations

International crime

see also Air piracy

see also International cooperation in law enforcement

see also Smuggling

see also Terrorism

International debts

see Foreign debts

International Development Association

Loans and grants for economic and military aid from US and intl agencies, by program and country, FY46-87, annual rpt, 9914–5

US contributions to multilateral dev banks, FY86-90, annual rpt, 9904–1.4

International Development Cooperation Agency

see U.S. International Development Cooperation Agency

International economic relations

see Balance of payments

see Foreign competition

see Foreign debts

see Foreign economic relations

see Foreign investments

see Foreign trade

see International finance

see Multinational corporations

International Electrotechnical Commission

US and other countries participation in intl standards assns, 1989, 2218–80

International employees

Admissions to US, by class of admission, port, country, and State of destination, quarterly rpt, 6262–2

Admissions to US, by country, FY88, annual rpt, 6264–2

Congressional Directory, members of 101st Congress, other officials, elections, and districts, 1989-90, biennial rpt, 23874–1

Criminal and civil immunity for diplomatic missions in US and US missions abroad, and foreign diplomats criminal cases, 1978-87, hearing, 25388–51

UN employment, and US natls share of staff, by agency, 1988, annual rpt, 7004–5

International Energy Agency

Oil stocks and conservation measures of Intl Energy Program countries, 1987-88 and projected to 1990, GAO rpt, 26123–225

International finance

Banks (intl) facilities of foreign and US banks in New York and total US, assets and liabilities, monthly rpt, 9365–2.22

Banks (US) foreign lending at all US and foreign offices, by country group and country, quarterly rpt, 13002–1

Banks balance sheets, by Fed Reserve District, for major banks in NYC, and for US branches and agencies of foreign banks, weekly rpt, 9365–1.3

Banks capital/asset ratios for Fed Reserve 5th District and other US banks, with intl capital adequacy standards, as of June 1988, article, 9389–1.904

Capital flows (intl) impacts on monetary policy instruments, and financial and economic indicators, 1987 compilation of papers, 9385–9

Capital movements between US and foreign countries, *Treasury Bulletin*, quarterly rpt, 8002–4.11

Financial and business statistics, historic trends, 1988 annual chartbook, 9364–2.17

Financial and economic analysis, technical paper series, 9385–8

Foreign and US intl transactions, debt, security holdings, interest and exchange rates, and US reserve assets, monthly rpt, 9362–1.3

Intl finance and trade studies, 1987 biennial compilation, 9375–14

Statistical Abstract of US, social, political, and economic data, 1790-2025, comprehensive annual compilation, 2324–1.3

see also African Development Bank

see also African Development Fund

see also Asian Development Bank

see also Balance of payments

see also Eurocurrency

see also Export-Import Bank

see also Foreign debts

see also Foreign economic relations

see also Foreign exchange

see also Foreign investments

see also Inter-American Development Bank

see also Inter-American Foundation

see also International Bank for Reconstruction and Development

see also International Development Association

see also International Monetary Fund

see also Multinational corporations

see also Organization for Economic Cooperation and Development

see also Overseas Private Investment Corp.

see also Special Drawing Rights

International Finance Corp.

Loans and grants for economic and military aid from US and intl agencies, by program and country, FY46-87, annual rpt, 9914–5

US contributions to multilateral dev banks, FY86-90, annual rpt, 9904–1.4

International Joint Commission, U.S. and Canada

Great Lakes basin pollutant discharges, sources, and control program activities, 1987, biennial rpt, 14644–1

Great Lakes flood prevention activities of Army Corps of Engineers and Intl Joint Commission, monthly rpt and supplements, 3752–1

Great Lakes phosphorus loads and fish stocking effects on algal levels, 1966-85, conf, 14648–20

Great Lakes polychlorinated biphenyls levels in environment, humans, and animals, and emissions sources, by site, 1970s-85, conf, 14648–19

Great Lakes toxic spills and human error, with data by pollutant source and site, 1984-86, conf, 14648–21

Great Lakes water levels fluctuations, causes, and impacts of alternative mgmt strategies, 1900s-88, series, 14646–1

Lake Ontario eutrophication and pollutant levels, by contaminant type and site, 1967-85, 14648–22

International labor

see Foreign labor conditions

International law

see also Citizenship

see also Diplomatic and consular service

see also Executive agreements

see also Expropriation of alien property

see also International cooperation in law enforcement

see also International military forces

see also International sanctions

see also Maritime law

see also Passports and visas

see also Territorial waters

see also Treaties and conventions

International military forces

Military aid programs and related activities of US, costs by country and intl agency, FY85-87 and cumulative from FY50, GAO rpt, 26123–30

UN voting record and share of votes in agreement with US, by issue, country, and world area, 1988, annual rpt, 7004–18

US military aid, arms sales, and training programs costs and budget requests, by program, world region, and country, FY88-90, annual rpt, 7144–13

International Monetary Fund

Budget of US, authoritative financial statements with appropriations, outlays, and receipts, by category and agency, FY88, annual rpt, 8104–2.2

Fed Govt receipts by source and outlays by agency, *Treasury Bulletin*, quarterly rpt, 8002–4.1

Investment (intl) position of US, by component, industry, world region, and country, 1987-88, annual article, 2702–1.922

Reserve assets of US by type, *Treasury Bulletin*, quarterly rpt, 8002–4.10

International Organization for Standardization

see International Standardization Organization

International organizations

AID economic aid to developing countries, obligations and disbursements by country, quarterly rpt, 9912–4

AID loans repayment status and terms by program and country, and status of predecessor agency loans, quarterly rpt, 9912–3

Budget of US Appendix, obligations, appropriations, and personnel, by program and agency, FY90, annual rpt, 104–3

Congressional Directory, members of 101st Congress, other officials, elections, and districts, 1989-90, biennial rpt, 23874-1

Disaster preparedness and economic, population, and political data, country rpt series, 9916-2

Economic and military aid of US, by country and program, FY86-88, annual rpt, 9904-1.4

Economic, social, political, and geographic summary data, by country, 1989, annual factbook, 9114-2

Loans and grants for economic and military aid from US and intl agencies, by program and country, FY46-87, annual rpt, 9914-5

Loans of US banks to foreigners at all US and foreign offices, by country group and country, quarterly rpt, 13002-1

Military aid of US, arms sales, and training, by country, FY50-88, annual rpt, 3904-3

Military aid programs and related activities of US, costs by country and intl agency, FY85-87 and cumulative from FY50, GAO rpt, 26123-30

PL 480 exports by commodity, and recipients, by program, sponsor, and country, FY87 and cumulative from FY55, annual rpt, 1924-7

R&D funding by Fed Govt, by field, performer type, agency, and State, FY87-89, annual rpt, 9627-20

Treaties and other bilateral and multilateral agreements of US in force, by country, as of Jan 1989, annual listing, 7004-1

see also African Development Bank

see also African Development Fund

see also Asian Development Bank

see also Association of Southeast Asian Nations

see also Bank for International Settlements

see also Central Treaty Organization

see also Common markets and free trade areas

see also European Space Agency

see also Inter-American Development Bank

see also International Bank for Reconstruction and Development

see also International Development Association

see also International Electrotechnical Commission

see also International employees

see also International Energy Agency

see also International Finance Corp.

see also International Monetary Fund

see also International Standardization Organization

see also International Telecommunications Satellite Organization

see also North Atlantic Treaty Organization

see also Organization for Economic Cooperation and Development

see also Red Cross

see also United Nations

see also Warsaw Pact

International relations

see Diplomatic and consular service

see Foreign economic relations

see Foreign relations

see International military forces

see International sanctions

see United Nations

International sanctions

Cuba trade with multinatl US firms foreign affiliates, by country, FY82-87, press release, 8008-137

Panama govt assets in US blocked under economic sanctions, and conditions and procedures for release, 1989, press release, 8008-135

South Africa loans from US banks, and rescheduling issues, 1984-89, press release, 8008-136

UN voting record and share of votes in agreement with US, by issue, country, and world area, 1988, annual rpt, 7004-18

see also Boycotts

International Standardization Organization

US and other countries participation in intl standards assns, 1989, 2218-80

International Telecommunications Satellite Organization

Launchings of satellites and other space objects since 1957, quarterly listing, 9502-2

International trade

see Balance of payments

see Foreign competition

see Foreign exchange

see Foreign investments

see Foreign trade

see Foreign trade promotion

see Maritime law

see Multinational corporations

see Ships and shipping

see Tariffs and foreign trade controls

see Trade agreements

International Trade Administration

Auto trade of Canada and US, and production, sales, prices, and employment, selected years 1965-85, annual rpt, 2044-35

Biotechnology in Japan, R&D spending, industry finances, and govt involvement, FY85-86, 2048-139

Budget appropriations and staff for Commerce Dept, by subagency, FY88-90, annual rpt, 2004-6

Budget of US Appendix, obligations, appropriations, and personnel, by program and agency, FY90, annual rpt, 104-3

Business America, foreign and domestic commerce, and US investment and trade opportunities, biweekly journal, 2042-24

Caribbean Basin exports to OECD members, and US imports under preferential treatment programs, by commodity, 1980s-87, 2048-138

Caribbean Basin Initiative investment incentives, economic impacts, with finances and employment by country, 1984-88, 2048-141

Coal ash contaminant levels, removal, EPA toxicity standards, and State disposal laws, 1988 rpt, 2048-140

Coal production and freight costs, and competitive position in selected markets, for Australia and US, 1987-89, 2048-143

Coal production, trade, and govt subsidies, by country and country group, 1973-87 and projected to 2000, 2048-144

Competitiveness (intl) of US industries, with selected foreign and US operating data by major firm and product, series, 2046-12

Construction put in place, permits, housing sales, costs, material prices, and employment, bimonthly rpt with articles, 2042-1

Developing countries debt reduction proposals, and Eximbank export financing programs, with background data, 1986-89, 2048-142

Employment related to exports, by industry div, 1980s-87, 2048-103

Exports and imports of US, by selected country, country group, and commodity group, 1988, annual rpt, 2044-37

Exports, imports, and balances of US by commodity group, world area, and country, and related employment, 1970s-88, annual rpt, 2044-26

Foreign countries economic conditions and implications for US, periodic country rpt series, 2046-4

Franchise business opportunities by firm and kind of business, and sources of aid and info, annual listing, suspended, 2044-27

Franchise establishments by State, sales, and operations, by kind of business, annual rpt, suspended, 2044-2

Industry finances and operations, by SIC 2- to 4-digit industry, forecast 1989 and trends from 1950s, annual rpt, 2044-28

Investment (foreign direct) in US, major transactions by type, industry, country, and US location, 1987, annual rpt, 2044-20

Latin America trade, and balance of trade with US, by country, 1988, 2044-34

Manufacturing electric power use and prices, shipments, and trade, for 25 SIC 4-digit industries, 1972-86, 2048-137

Overseas Business Reports: economic conditions, investment and export opportunities, and trade practices, country market research rpt series, 2046-6

Paper and wood products production and trade, and industry operations by firm, by country, world region rpt series, 2046-14

Steel import voluntary restraint agreements, ITA review of requests for restraint waivers because of supply shortages, 1985-88, GAO rpt, 26123-240

Textile Agreement Category System import classification codes, correlation with TSUSA, 1989 annual rpt, 2044-31

Textile imports, by country of origin, monthly rpt, 2042-27

Textile imports, by product and country of origin, periodic rpt series, 2046-8; 2046-9

Textile imports of US, production, and imports share of use, by Multifiber Arrangement product, quarterly rpt, 2042-32

see also Foreign Trade Zones Board

International Trade Commission

see U.S. International Trade Commission

International transactions

see Balance of payments

Interstate commerce

Banking (interstate) laws of States, impacts of changes on bank stock returns, 1988 working paper, 9387-8.174

Banks interstate offices, by type of controlling organization and State, 1982-Feb 1989, article, 9371-1.909

Criminal cases by type and disposition, and collections, for US attorneys, by Federal district, FY88, annual rpt, 6004-2.1

Criminal sentences for Federal offenses, guidelines by offense and circumstances, 1989 rpt, 17668-1

Mail order sales from out of State, tax revenues and rates under proposed collection system, by State, 1988 hearings, 21528-73

Telecommunication domestic and overseas rates, by type of service and area served, various dates 1988, annual rpt, 9284-6.6

see also Antitrust law

see also Buses

see also Contraband

see also Freight

see also Inland water transportation

see also Pipelines

see also Railroads

see also Ships and shipping

see also Transportation and transportation equipment

see also Trucks and trucking industry

Interstate Commerce Commission

Budget of US Appendix, obligations, appropriations, and personnel, by program and agency, FY90, annual rpt, 104-3

Budget of US, authoritative financial statements with appropriations, outlays, and receipts, by category and agency, FY88, annual rpt, 8104-2.2

Bus (Class I) passengers and selected revenue data, for individual large carriers, quarterly rpt, 9482-13

Labor unions recognized in Fed Govt, agreements and membership by agency and facility, as of Jan 1989, biennial listing, 9844-14

Railroad employment by occupational group, for Class I line-haul railroads, monthly rpt, 9482-3

Railroad employment, earnings, and hours, by occupation for Class I railroads, 1988, annual table, 9484-5

Railroad revenue, income, freight, and rate of return, by Class I freight railroad and district, quarterly rpt, 9482-2

Truck, bus, and rail carriers finances and operations, detailed data, 1987, annual rpt series, 9486-6

Truck, bus, and rail carriers finances and operations, detailed data, 1988, annual rpt series, 9486-5

Truck transport of household goods, financial and operating data by firm, quarterly rpt, 9482-14

Truck transport of household goods, performance and disposition of damage claims, for selected carriers, 1988, annual rpt, 9484-11

Truck transport of property, financial and operating data by region and firm, quarterly rpt, 9482-5

Interstate Commission on the Potomac River Basin

Budget of US, authoritative financial statements with appropriations, outlays, and receipts, by category and agency, FY88, annual rpt, 8104-2.2

Interstate highways

see Highways, streets, and roads

Interstate relations

Child support interstate collection processing, officials views on mgmt, and Child Support Enforcement Office demonstration projects, 1987-88, GAO rpt, 26121-271

Insurance (property and casualty) industry solvency monitoring by States, activities, staff, and interstate info sharing, 1989 GAO rpt, 26119-273

see also Regional planning

Inventions

Energy-related inventions recommended by Natl Inst of Standards and Technology for DOE support, awards, and evaluation status, 1988, annual listing, 2214-5

Energy-related inventions supported by DOE, sales, jobs created, and inventor characteristics, 1980-86, 3308-91

Fed Govt employee incentive awards, costs, and benefits, by award type and agency, FY88, annual rpt, 9844-20

see also Patents

see also Technological innovations

see also Technology transfer

Inventories

see Agricultural stocks

see Agricultural surpluses

see Business inventories

see Energy stocks and inventories

see Stockpiling

Inventory of Long-Term Care Places

Mentally retarded persons facilities, beds, and residents, by ownership, resident age and race, and State, 1986, 4147-14.34

Nursing homes, beds, and residents, by ownership, certification status, and State, 1986, 4147-14.33

Investigations

see Congressional investigations

see Criminal investigations

see Government investigations

Investments

AFDC recipients demographic and financial characteristics, by State, FY87, annual rpt, 4694-1

Airline financial data, by carrier, carrier group, and for total certificated system, quarterly rpt, 7302-7

Assets and debts of private sector, balance sheets by segment, 1949-88, semiannual rpt, 9365-4.1

Banking and financial conditions, 1987, annual rpt, 9364-5

Banks (commercial) loans and investments, 1972-88, annual rpt, 204-1.5

Banks (natl) domestic and intl operations, charters, mergers, and liquidations, by instn and State, quarterly rpt, 8402-3

Business Conditions Digest, economic, business, and financial devs and cyclical fluctuations, monthly rpt, 2702-3

Capital gains counted as income, and other income definitions effects on household income and poverty status, by recipient characteristics, 1986, Current Population Rpt, 2546-6.58

Capital gains tax rate changes effect on transactions by asset type, and stock exchange trading volume, late 1970s-88, article, 9373-1.901

Capital gains tax rate changes effects on revenue, alternative model results, 1988, 26306-3.106

Capital gains tax rate changes relation to realized gains and tax revenue, alternative estimates, various periods 1948-87, technical paper, 8006-3.61; 8006-3.62; 8006-3.63

County Business Patterns, 1987: employment, establishments, and payroll, by SIC 2- to 4-digit industry and county, annual State rpt series, 2326-8

Credit unions federally insured, finances by instn characteristics and State, as of June 1989, semiannual rpt, 9532-6

Credit unions federally insured, finances, 1987-88, annual rpt, 9534-1

Current account balance of US, components and relation to foreign and US investment and economic conditions, 1970s-88 and projected to 1990s, article, 9385-1.905; 9385-1.906

Economic indicators and components, and Fed Reserve 4th District business and financial conditions, monthly chartbook, 9377-10

Economic indicators and components, current data and annual trends, monthly rpt, 23842-1.5

Economic indicators compounded annual rates of change, monthly rpt, 9391-3.2

Economic indicators compounded annual rates of change, 1969-88, annual rpt, 9391-9.2

Economic Report of the President for 1989, with economic trends from 1929, annual rpt, 204-1.1

Electric utilities finances and operations, detailed data for privately owned firms, and summary data for other utilities by type, 1987, annual rpt, 3164-23

Electric utilities finances and operations, detailed data for privately owned firms, 1986-88, annual rpt, 3164-11.4

Energy producers finances and operations, by energy type for US firms domestic and foreign operations, 1987, annual rpt, 3164-44

Financial and business statistics, historic trends, 1988 annual chartbook, 9364-2.13

Flow-of-funds accounts, assets and liabilities by type and economic sector, outstanding at year-end 1965-88, annual rpt, 9364-3

Flow-of-funds accounts, savings, investments, and credit statements, quarterly rpt, 9365-3.3

Household debt and interest-earning assets, interest paid and received, and consumption expenditures, by selected characteristics, 1960s-88, article, 9385-1.913

Households receipt of telephone service, by composition, income sources, and other characteristics, 1984-87, 9288-11

Income (household, family, and personal), by source, detailed characteristics, and region, 1987, annual Current Population Rpt, 2546-6.59

Income (personal) by source, and BEA and IRS adjusted gross income measures, 1984-86 with trends from 1947, article, 8302-2.914

Income (personal) by source, and BEA and IRS adjusted gross income measures, 1986-87, annual article, 2702-1.927

Income (personal) per capita and by source, and earnings by industry div, by State, MSA, and county, 1982-87, annual regional rpts, 2704-2

Income (personal) per capita and by source, earnings by major industry group, and social insurance contributions, by region and State, 1929-87, 2708-40

Input-output structure of US economy, detailed interindustry transactions for 84 industries, and components of final demand, 1983, annual article, 2702-1.909

Insurance (life) companies financial and tax impacts of Deficit Reduction Act and proposed reforms, for stock and mutual firms, 1984-88 and projected to FY94, 8008–138

Monetary and Fed Govt budget trends, Fed Reserve Bank of St Louis monthly rpt, 9391–2

Multinatl firms US affiliates, finances, and operations, by industry, world area of parent firm, and State, 1987, annual rpt, 2704–4

Multinatl US firms and foreign affiliates finances and operations, by industry of parent firm and affiliate, world area, and country, preliminary 1987, annual rpt, 2704–5

Natl income and product accounts and components, *Survey of Current Business*, monthly rpt, 2702–1.21

Natural gas interstate pipeline company detailed financial and operating data, by firm, 1988, annual rpt, 3164–38

Nonprofit charitable organizations finances, and assets and grants of top 10, 1985, article, 8302–2.923

North Central States business and economic conditions, Fed Reserve 9th District, quarterly journal, 9383–19

North Central States economic conditions, Fed Reserve 9th District, quarterly rpt, 9383–18

North Central States, FHLB 6th District insured S&Ls financial condition and operations by State, quarterly rpt, 9302–23

Older persons socioeconomic characteristics, 1900s-86 and projected to 2050, biennial chartbook, 12904–1

Poverty status of families and persons, by detailed characteristics, 1987, annual Current Population Rpt, 2546–6.60

Puerto Rico and other US possessions corporations tax incentives, finances, and operations by industry, and impacts on local economy, 1970s-83, biennial rpt, 8004–12

Railroad (Class I) finances and operations, detailed data by firm, class of service, and district, 1987, annual rpt, 9486–6.1

Railroad (Class I) finances and operations, detailed data by firm, class of service, and district, 1988, annual rpt, 9486–5.1

Retirees savings maintenance and liquidation, by selected financial and other characteristics, 1971-79, article, 1702–1.906

Savings instns, FHLB 9th District members finances and operations by State, quarterly rpt, 9302–31

Savings instns financial statements, FSLIC-insured instns by FHLB district and State, and FDIC-insured savings banks, 1988, annual rpt, 8434–1

Savings instns regulatory issues, mgmt, and FHLB system and member finances and operations, monthly journal, 8432–2; 9312–1

Southeastern States, Fed Reserve 5th District insured commercial banks financial statements, by State, quarterly rpt, 9389–18

Survey of Current Business, detailed financial and business data, and economic indicators, monthly rpt, 2702–1.1

Tax (income) returns filed by type of filer, selected income items, quarterly rpt, 8302–2.1

Tax (income) returns for foreign corporate activity in US, assets, and income statement items, by industry div, country, and world area, 1984-85, article, 8302–2.920

Tax (income) returns of corporations, income and tax items by asset size and detailed industry, 1986, annual rpt, 8304–4; 8304–21

Tax (income) returns of individuals, by filing status, tax item, and income level, 1987, annual article, 8302–2.901

Tax (income) returns of individuals, detailed data, 1986, annual rpt, 8304–2

Tax (income) returns of individuals, selected income and tax items by income level, preliminary 1987, annual article, 8302–2.917

Tax (income) returns of partnerships, income statement items by industry group, 1986, annual article, 8302–2.903

Tax (income) withholding and related documents filed, by type and IRS service center, 1988 and projected 1989-96, annual rpt, 8304–22

Telephone and telegraph firms detailed finances and operations, 1987, annual rpt, 9284–6

Telephone firms borrowing under Rural Telephone Program, and financial and operating data, 1988, annual rpt, 1244–2

Trust assets of banks, trust companies, and S&Ls, by type of asset and fund, selected firm, and State, 1988, annual rpt, 13004–1

Urban Dev Action Grants, funding, and jobs and taxes generated, by city, FY88, annual rpt, 5124–5

Urban Dev Action Grants, funding sources, project descriptions, and economic impacts, by city, periodic press releases, 5002–7

West Central States, Fed Reserve 10th District depository instns financial activity by State, and large commercial banks by city, monthly rpt, 9381–11

Western States, FHLB 11th District S&Ls, offices, and financial condition, 1989 annual listing, 9304–23

see also Capital investments, general

see also Capital investments, specific industry

see also Divestiture

see also Foreign investments

see also Futures trading

see also Government securities

see also Individual retirement arrangements

see also Joint ventures

see also Loans

see also Mortgages

see also Mutual funds

see also New York Stock Exchange

see also Options trading

see also Securities

see also Stock exchanges

see also Venture capital

Iocozzia, James T.

"Trends in Taxpayer Paperwork Burden", 8304–8.1

Iowa

Agriculture census, 1987: farms, farmland, production and costs, and operator characteristics, advance State and county rpts, 2330–1.19

Agriculture census, 1987: farms, farmland, production, finances, and operator characteristics, by county, final State rpt, 2331–1.15

Bank deposits in FDIC-insured commercial and savings banks, by instn, State, and county, as of June 1988, annual regional rpt, 9295–3.5

Coal production and mines by county, prices, productivity, miners, reserves, and stocks, by mining method and State, 1987-88, annual rpt, 3164–25

Corn and soybean futures contract yield and price risk hedging strategies, by selected county and State, model results, 1961-83, 1548–352

County Business Patterns, 1987: employment, establishments, and payroll, by SIC 2- to 4-digit industry and county, annual State rpt, 2326–8.17

Dairy prices for cows, milk, and feed, by selected State, and cows slaughtered by region, 1988, annual rpt, 1317–1.6

Deaths and rates, by detailed location, cause, and demographic characteristics, 1987, US Vital Statistics annual rpt, 4144–3.1

DOD prime contract awards, by contractor, service branch, State, and city, FY88, annual rpt, 3544–22

Employment, earnings, and hours, by selected SIC 1- to 4-digit industry, State, and for 262 MSAs, 1972-87, 6748–81.2

Farm operators displaced worker programs under Job Training Partnership Act, funding, participation, and results by selected State, 1982-87, 15496–1.2

Fed Govt spending in States and local areas, by type, State, county, and city, FY88, annual rpt, 2464–3

Fed Govt spending in States, by type, program, agency, and State, FY88, annual rpt, 2464–2

HHS financial aid, by program, recipient, State, and city, FY88, annual regional listing, 4004–3.7

Homeless children educational enrollment and needs, 1988, annual State rpt, 4804–35.16

Income (personal) per capita and by source, and earnings by industry div, by State, MSA, and county, 1982-87, annual regional rpt, 2704–2.3

Mineral Industry Surveys, State reviews of production, 1988, preliminary annual rpt, 5614–6

Minerals Yearbook, 1987, Vol 2 preprints: State review of production and sales by commodity, and business activity, annual rpt, 5604–16.16

Minerals Yearbook, 1987, Vol 2: State reviews of production, sales, and firms, by commodity, and business activity, annual rpt, 5604–34

Nursing home compliance with Medicare and Medicaid regulations, and patient characteristics, by facility, 1987/88, annual State rpt, 4654–15.16

Retail trade census, 1987: employment, establishments, sales, and payroll, by SIC 2- to 4-digit kind of business, MSA, county, and city, State rpt, 2397–1.16

Savings instns, FHLB 8th District members financial operations by State and SMSA, monthly rpt, 9302–9

Service industries census, 1987: employment, establishments, receipts, and payroll, by SIC 2- to 4-digit kind of business, MSA, county, and city, State rpt, 2391–1.16

Statistical Abstract of US, social, political, and economic data, with foreign comparisons, 1790-2025, comprehensive annual compilation, 2324–1

Water resources dev projects of Army Corps of Engineers, characteristics, and costs, 1950s-89, biennial State rpt, 3756–1.16

Water supply and quality in streams and lakes, and groundwater levels in wells, by drainage basin, 1987, annual State rpt, 5666–10.14

Wholesale trade census, 1987: employment, establishments, finances, and operations, by SIC 2- to 4-digit kind of business, MSA, county, and city, State rpt, 2405–1.16

Wildlife-related recreation, hunting, and fishing participation and spending, detailed data, 1985 survey, quinquennial State rpt, 5506–6.15

see also Davenport, Iowa

see also Des Moines, Iowa

see also under By State in the "Index by Categories"

Iowa City, Iowa

see also under By SMSA or MSA in the "Index by Categories"

Ippolito, Pauline M.

"Health Claims in Advertising and Labeling", 9406–1.60

Iran

Agricultural and food production and indexes, total and for selected commodities, by country, 1970s-88, annual rpt, 1524–12

Agricultural production, prices, and trade, by country, 1960s-89, annual world region rpt, 1524–4.2

Agricultural trade of US, by detailed commodity and country, 1988, semiannual rpt, 1522–4

AID loans repayment status and terms by program and country, and status of predecessor agency loans, quarterly rpt, 9912–3

Economic and military aid and loans from US and intl agencies, by program and country, FY46-87, annual rpt, 9914–5

Economic conditions, policy, and trade practices, by country, 1986-88, annual rpt, 21384–5

Economic, social, political, and geographic summary data, by country, 1989, annual factbook, 9114–2

Exports and imports of US, by commodity and country, 1970-87, world area rpt, 9116–1.3

Exports and imports of US, by selected country, country group, and commodity group, 1988, annual rpt, 2044–37

Human rights conditions in 170 countries, 1988, annual rpt, 21384–3

Military spending, arms trade, and force strengths, with govt spending and population, by country, 1977-87, annual rpt, 9824–1

Minerals Yearbook, 1987, Vol 3: foreign country reviews of production, trade, and policy, by commodity, annual rpt, 5604–35

Minerals Yearbook, 1987, Vol 3 preprints: foreign country review of production, trade, and policy, by commodity, annual rpt, 5604–23.34

Oil production, and exports and prices for US, by major exporting country, detailed data, monthly rpt, 3162–24

Oil production, trade, use, and stocks, by selected country and country group, monthly rpt, 3162–42

Population size, growth rates, and components of change, by country, projected 1989-2020 and trends from 1950, biennial rpt, 2324–9

Refugee resettlement programs and funding, arrivals by country of origin, and indicators of adjustment, by State, FY88, annual rpt, 4694–5

UN voting record and share of votes in agreement with US, by issue, country, and world area, 1988, annual rpt, 7004–18

see also under By Foreign Country in the "Index by Categories"

Iraq

Agricultural and food production and indexes, total and for selected commodities, by country, 1970s-88, annual rpt, 1524–12

Agricultural production, prices, and trade, by country, 1960s-89, annual world region rpt, 1524–4.2

Agricultural trade by commodity and country, prices, and world market devs, monthly rpt, 1922–12

Agricultural trade of US, by detailed commodity and country, 1988, semiannual rpt, 1522–4

Economic and military aid and loans from US and intl agencies, by program and country, FY46-87, annual rpt, 9914–5

Economic conditions, income, production, prices, employment, and trade, 1989 periodic country rpt, 2046–4.13; 2046–4.105

Economic conditions, policy, and trade practices, by country, 1986-88, annual rpt, 21384–5

Economic, social, political, and geographic summary data, by country, 1989, annual factbook, 9114–2

Exports and imports of US, by commodity and country, 1970-87, world area rpt, 9116–1.3

Exports and imports of US, by selected country, country group, and commodity group, 1988, annual rpt, 2044–37

Human rights conditions in 170 countries, 1988, annual rpt, 21384–3

Military spending, arms trade, and force strengths, with govt spending and population, by country, 1977-87, annual rpt, 9824–1

Minerals Yearbook, 1987, Vol 3: foreign country reviews of production, trade, and policy, by commodity, annual rpt, 5604–35

Minerals Yearbook, 1987, Vol 3 preprints: foreign country review of production, trade, and policy, by commodity, annual rpt, 5604–23.35

Oil production by major exporting countries, monthly rpt, 3162–24.10

Oil production, trade, use, and stocks, by selected country and country group, monthly rpt, 3162–42

Population size, growth rates, and components of change, by country, projected 1989-2020 and trends from 1950, biennial rpt, 2324–9

UN voting record and share of votes in agreement with US, by issue, country, and world area, 1988, annual rpt, 7004–18

see also under By Foreign Country in the "Index by Categories"

Ireland

Agricultural and food production and indexes, total and for selected commodities, by country, 1970s-88, annual rpt, 1524–12

Agricultural production, prices, and trade, by country, 1970s-88 and forecast 1990, annual world region rpt, 1524–4.1

Agricultural trade of US, by detailed commodity and country, 1988, semiannual rpt, 1522–4

AID activities and funding by project and function, FY90, and developing countries summary socioeconomic data from 1960s, annual rpt, 9904–4.6

AID loans repayment status and terms by program and country, and status of predecessor agency loans, quarterly rpt, 9912–3

Economic and military aid and loans from US and intl agencies, by program and country, FY46-87, annual rpt, 9914–5

Economic conditions, income, production, prices, employment, and trade, 1989 periodic country rpt, 2046–4.89

Economic conditions, policy, and trade practices, by country, 1986-88, annual rpt, 21384–5

Economic, social, political, and geographic summary data, by country, 1989, annual factbook, 9114–2

Exports and imports of US, by selected country, country group, and commodity group, 1988, annual rpt, 2044–37

Food supply and demand, market and support prices, and other economic indicators, by EC country and commodity, 1960-85, 1528–276

Human rights conditions in 170 countries, 1988, annual rpt, 21384–3

Labor conditions, union coverage, and work accidents, 1989 annual country rpt, 6366–4.58

Military aid of US, arms sales, and training programs costs and budget requests, by program, world region, and country, FY88-90, annual rpt, 7144–13

Military spending, arms trade, and force strengths, with govt spending and population, by country, 1977-87, annual rpt, 9824–1

Minerals Yearbook, 1987, Vol 3: foreign country reviews of production, trade, and policy, by commodity, annual rpt, 5604–35

Minerals Yearbook, 1987, Vol 3 preprints: foreign country review of production, trade, and policy, by commodity, annual rpt, 5604–23.36

Multinatl US firms and foreign affiliates finances and operations, by industry of

parent firm and affiliate, world area, and country, preliminary 1987, annual rpt, 2704–5

Oil production, trade, use, and stocks, by selected country and country group, monthly rpt, 3162–42

Population size, growth rates, and components of change, by country, projected 1989-2020 and trends from 1950, biennial rpt, 2324–9

UN voting record and share of votes in agreement with US, by issue, country, and world area, 1988, annual rpt, 7004–18

see also under By Foreign Country in the "Index by Categories"

Iron and steel industry

Building materials shipments and PPI, by type, bimonthly rpt, 2042–1.5; 2042–1.6

Business statistics, detailed data for major industries and economic indicators, *Survey of Current Business*, monthly rpt, 2702–1.14

China trade by SITC 1- to 5-digit commodity, 1970s-87, annual rpt, 9114–3

Communist, OECD, and selected other countries minerals production, by commodity, 1960s-88, annual rpt, 9114–4.7

Construction industries census, 1987: financial and operating data, preliminary industry rpt, 2371–1.21

County Business Patterns, 1987: employment, establishments, and payroll, by SIC 2- to 4-digit industry and county, annual State rpt series, 2326–8

Cuba economic conditions, agricultural and industrial production and distribution, trade, and intl economic relations, 1980-87 with trends from 1961, 9118–8

Demand for primary metals, relation to consumption patterns and economic, trade, and technological factors, 1960s-82, 5608–159

DOD shipments of military and personal property, passenger traffic, and costs, by service branch and mode of transport, quarterly rpt, 3702–1

Drums and pails (steel shipping) shipments, trade, use, and firms, quarterly Current Industrial Rpt, 2506–11.5

Employment, earnings, and hours, by selected SIC 1- to 4-digit industry, State, and for 262 MSAs, 1972-87, 6748–81

Employment, earnings, and hours, by SIC 1- to 4-digit industry, monthly 1983-Feb 1989, annual rpt, 6744–4

Employment of minorities and women, by occupation, SIC 1- to 3- digit industry, State, and MSA, 1986, annual rpt, 9244–1

Energy use and prices for manufacturing industries, 1985 survey, series, 3166–13

Export ceilings on steel under voluntary restraint agreements, by country and product, with Western US steel industry impact, 1989 rpt, 9886–4.136

Exports and imports of US shipped through Canada, by detailed commodity, customs district, and country, 1987, annual rpt, 7704–11

Exports of US, detailed commodities by country, monthly rpt, 2422–3

Finances and operations by product, and modernization efforts of steel industry, as of June 1989, last issue of annual rpt, 9884–16

Finances and operations, by SIC 2- to 4-digit industry, forecast 1989 with trends from 1950s, annual rpt, 2044–28

Financial statements for manufacturing, mining, and trade corporations, by selected SIC 2- to 3-digit industry, quarterly rpt, 2502–1

Foreign and US hourly compensation costs, for iron and steel industry by country, 1975-88, 6826–3.2; 6826–3.5

Foreign countries economic, social, political, and geographic summary data, by country, 1989, annual factbook, 9114–2

Foreign countries energy-intensive industry output and operations, and US investment barriers, for energy-rich countries, 1984-88, 9886–4.142

Foreign countries mineral production, reserves, and industry role in domestic economy and world supply, world area and country rpt series, 5606–1

Freight (waterborne domestic and foreign) by commodity, traffic, and passengers, by port and waterway, 1987, annual rpt, 3754–3

Hwy construction material prices and indexes for Federal-aid system, by type of material and urban-rural location, quarterly rpt, 7552–7

Hwy construction material prices and indexes for Federal-aid system, by type of material, quarterly press release, 7552–16

Hwy construction material use by type, and spending, by State, various periods 1944-88, annual rpt, 7554–29

Import of steel voluntary restraint agreements, ITA review of requests for restraint waivers because of supply shortages, 1985-88, GAO rpt, 26123–240

Import quotas on steel, autos, and textiles, employment and income impacts by industry, model description and results, 1984, 9406–1.57

Import restraint elimination, impact on domestic industry production and employment, by selected commodity, 1986-88, 9886–4.144

Imports injury to US industries from foreign subsidized products and sales at less than fair value, investigations with background financial and operating data, series, 9886–19

Imports injury to US industries from foreign subsidized products, investigations with background financial and operating data, series, 9886–15

Imports injury to US industries from sales at less than fair value, investigations with background financial and operating data, series, 9886–14

Imports of steel from EC and other countries, impact of voluntary restraint agreements on US user industries exports, sales, and prices, 1989 rpt, 9886–4.138

Imports of steel under voluntary restraint agreement, by product, customs district, and country, with US industry operating data, monthly rpt, 9882–13

Imports of steel under voluntary restraint agreements, with industry finances, operations, and foreign comparisons, various periods 1979-89, 21788–182

Imports of US, detailed Schedule A commodities by country, monthly rpt, 2422–2

Imports of US given duty-free treatment for value of US material sent abroad, and impacts on US industry and employment, by commodity and country, 1987, annual rpt, 9884–14

Input-output structure of US economy, detailed interindustry transactions for 84 industries, and components of final demand, 1983, annual article, 2702–1.909

Manufacturing annual survey, 1986: financial and operating data, by SIC 2- to 4-digit industry, series, 2506–15

Manufacturing census, 1987: financial and operating data, for SIC 4-digit industries by product, preliminary rpt, 2491–1.51; 2491–1.52; 2491–1.55; 2491–1.57; 2491–1.58

Mineral industries census, 1987: financial and operating data, preliminary industry rpt, 2511–1.1; 2511–1.3

Mineral Industry Surveys, commodity review of production, trade, stocks, and use, monthly rpt, 5612–1.11; 5612–1.12

Minerals Yearbook, 1987, Vol 1: commodity reviews of production, use, trade, prices, and mining operations, annual rpt, 5604–33

Minerals Yearbook, 1987, Vol 1 preprints: commodity review of production, reserves, supply, use, and trade, annual rpt, 5604–15.32

Minerals Yearbook, 1987, Vol 1 preprints: commodity reviews of production, reserves, supply, use, and trade, annual rpt series, 5604–15

Minerals Yearbook, 1987, Vol 2 preprints: State reviews of production and sales by commodity, and business activity, annual rpt series, 5604–16

Minerals Yearbook, 1987, Vol 2: State reviews of production, sales, and firms, by commodity, and business activity, annual rpt, 5604–34

Minerals Yearbook, 1987, Vol 3: foreign country reviews of production, trade, and policy, by commodity, annual rpt, 5604–35

Minerals Yearbook, 1987, Vol 3 preprints: foreign country reviews of production, trade, and policy, by commodity, annual rpt series, 5604–23

Minerals Yearbook, 1988, Vol 1: commodity reviews of production, reserves, supply, use, and trade, annual rpt series, 5604–20

Minerals Yearbook, 1988, Vol 2 rpts: State reviews of production and sales by commodity, and business activity, annual rpt series, 5604–22

Multinatl US firms and foreign affiliates finances and operations, by industry of parent firm and affiliate, world area, and country, preliminary 1987, annual rpt, 2704–5

North Central States business and economic conditions, Fed Reserve 9th District, quarterly journal, 9383–19

Occupational injuries and incidence, employment, and hours in metal mines and related operations, 1987, annual rpt, 6664–3

Occupational injury and illness rates, by SIC 2- to 4-digit industry, 1987, annual rpt, 6844–1

OECD trade, total and for 4 major countries, and US trade by country, by commodity, 1970-87, world area rpt series, 9116-1

Ohio River basin waterway facilities, freight by commodity and port, and recreation, by waterway, 1986-87, annual rpt, 3754-6

Pension plan financial status, impact of alternative accounting standards, 1978-87, technical paper, 9366-6.172

Pollution (air) abatement equipment shipments by industry, exports, and new and backlog orders, by product, 1988, annual Current Industrial Rpt, 2506-12.5

Pollution control enforcement of EPA and industry compliance, relation to steel plant closings, mcodel description and results, 1977-86, working paper, 9377-9.84

Price indexes (producer), by stage of processing and detailed commodity, monthly rpt, 6762-6

Price indexes (producer), by stage of processing and detailed commodity, monthly 1988, annual rpt, 6764-2

Production costs relation to labor and other input changes in steel industry, model description and results, 1954-85, working paper, 9377-9.83

Production, prices, trade, use, employment, tariffs, and stockpiles, by mineral, with foreign comparisons, 1984-88, annual rpt, 5604-18

Production, shipments, trade, stocks, and material used, for primary metals by product, periodic Current Industrial Rpt series, 2506-10

Productivity of labor and capital, and indexes of output, hours, and employment, 1963-87, annual rpt, 6824-1.2; 6824-1.3; 6824-1.5

Science and engineering employment, by nonmanufacturing industry and field, 1987, triennial rpt, 9627-31

Science, engineering, and technical employment in manufacturing, by field, occupation, and industry, 1986, triennial rpt, 9627-23

Stainless steel and alloy tool production, employment, finances, and US producers inventories and unfilled orders, 1987-88, annual rpt, 9884-22

Statistical Abstract of US, social, political, and economic data, 1790-2025, comprehensive annual compilation, 2324-1.3

Supply, demand, trade, and foreign and US industry devs by firm and country, for strategic minerals by commodity, bimonthly rpt with articles, 5602-4

Tax (income) returns of corporations, income and tax items by asset size and detailed industry, 1986, annual rpt, 8304-4; 8304-21

Wholesale trade census, 1987: employment, establishments, finances, and operations, by SIC 2- to 4-digit kind of business, MSA, county, and city, State rpt series, 2405-1

see also under By Commodity in the "Index by Categories"

Irrigation

Africa (Sahel) food supply indicators, by country, 1960s-2000, 1528-290

Agricultural Conservation Program participation and payments, by practice and State, FY87, annual rpt, 1804-7

Agricultural data compilation, 1987/88 and trends from 1920, annual rpt, 1004-14

Agricultural Statistics, 1988, annual rpt, 1004-1.2

Army Corps of Engineers activities and projects, FY87 and trends from 1800s, annual rpt, 3754-1.2

Army Corps of Engineers water resources dev projects, characteristics, and costs, 1950s-87, biennial State rpt series, 3756-2

Army Corps of Engineers water resources dev projects, characteristics, and costs, 1950s-89, biennial State rpt series, 3756-1

Census of Agriculture, 1987: farms, farmland, production and costs, and operator characteristics, advance State and county rpt series, 2330-1

Census of Agriculture, 1987: farms, farmland, production, finances, and operator characteristics, by county, final State rpt series, 2331-1

Colorado River Storage Project finances and activities in western States, FY88, annual rpt, 5824-3

Conservation Reserve Program coverage of irrigated acreage, and acreage idled, by western State, as of 1987 and projected 1990, 1588-143

Costs of production (itemized), receipts, and returns, by crop and State, preliminary 1987, annual rpt, 1544-24

Costs of production, itemized by farm sales size and region, 1988, annual rpt, 1614-3

County Business Patterns, 1987: employment, establishments, and payroll, by SIC 2- to 4-digit industry and county, annual State rpt series, 2326-8

Farm production inputs, finances, mgmt, and land value and transfers, periodic situation rpt with articles, 1561-16

Farm production itemized costs, receipts, and returns, by commodity and region, 1985-87, annual rpt, 1544-20

Farm production itemized costs, receipts, and returns, by selected commodity and region, 1975-87, 1548-345

Farms irrigated, by selected characteristics of farm and operator, and State, 1982, 1588-131

Fed Columbia River Power System projects, plant investment allocation schedule, FY88, annual rpt, 3224-1

FmHA activities, and loans and grants by program and State, FY88 and trends from FY69, annual rpt, 1184-17

Groundwater protection standards, States use of EPA and alternative standards by type of water use, and contaminant test results, 1976-88, GAO rpt, 26131-56

Occupational injury and illness rates, by SIC 2- to 4-digit industry, 1987, annual rpt, 6844-1

Pacific Northwest electric power capacity and use, by end-use sector, projected under alternative fuel price cases, 1987-2010, annual rpt, 3224-4

Science, engineering, and technical employment in transportation, utilities, and retail and wholesale trade, by field, occupation, and industry, 1985, triennial rpt, 9627-32

Sediment control techniques for irrigation systems, costs and benefits by technique, for Idaho project, 1981-86 and projected to 2030, 1588-138

Soil salinity impacts on yields and off-farm water quality, and costs and benefits of extending erosion control program to saline cropland, 1989 rpt, 1588-144

Soil, water, and environmental conservation and conditions, with data by State and region, 1989 quinquennial rpt, 1268-24

Statistical Abstract of US, social, political, and economic data, 1790-2025, comprehensive annual compilation, 2324-1.3

Water chemistry, environmental impacts, analytic methods, and quality and mgmt issues, 1989 rpt, 5668-96

Water supply restriction and compensatory use of other production inputs, 1984-85, 1588-139

Western Area Power Admin activities by plant, financial statements, and sales by customer, FY88, annual rpt, 3254-1

Western US irrigation projects of Reclamation Bur, crop production and acreage by commodity, State, and project, 1987, annual rpt, 5824-12.1

Western US irrigation subsidies of Reclamation Bur, costs to Fed Govt and surplus crop production, 1985-86, 21448-40

see also Watershed projects

IRS

see Internal Revenue Service

Irvine, Calif.

see also under By City in the "Index by Categories"

Irving, Tex.

see also under By City in the "Index by Categories"

Isherwood, R. J.

"Regulation in the Domestic Mineral Industry: A Case Study of Lead", 5606-5.7

Islands

see Coral reefs and islands

ISO

see International Standardization Organization

Israel

Agricultural and food production and indexes, total and for selected commodities, by country, 1970s-88, annual rpt, 1524-12

Agricultural trade of US, by detailed commodity and country, 1988, semiannual rpt, 1522-4

Agricultural trade of US with Asia, Middle East, and North Africa, by commodity and country, 1962-86, 1528-277

AID activities and funding by project and function, FY90, and developing countries summary socioeconomic data from 1960s, annual rpt, 9904-4.6

AID economic aid to developing countries, obligations and disbursements by country, quarterly rpt, 9912-4

AID loans repayment status and terms by program and country, and status of predecessor agency loans, quarterly rpt, 9912-3

Auto imports from US, trade barriers by country, 1988, annual rpt, 444–2

Economic and military aid and loans from US and intl agencies, by program and country, FY46-87, annual rpt, 9914–5

Economic conditions, income, production, prices, employment, and trade, 1989 periodic country rpt, 2046–4.99

Economic conditions, policy, and trade practices, by country, 1986-88, annual rpt, 21384–5

Economic, social, political, and geographic summary data, by country, 1989, annual factbook, 9114–2

Exports and imports of US, by selected country, country group, and commodity group, 1988, annual rpt, 2044–37

Flowers (cut roses) US industry intl competitiveness, investigation with background financial and operating data and foreign comparisons, 1989 rpt, 9886–4.137

Human rights conditions in 170 countries, 1988, annual rpt, 21384–3

Labor conditions, union coverage, and work accidents, 1989 annual country rpt, 6366–4.14

Machinery belts from 8 countries, injury to US industry from foreign subsidized and less than fair value imports, investigation with background financial and operating data, 1989 rpt, 9886–19.66

Military aid of US, arms sales, and training programs costs and budget requests, by program, world region, and country, FY88-90, annual rpt, 7144–13

Military spending, arms trade, and force strengths, with govt spending and population, by country, 1977-87, annual rpt, 9824–1

Minerals Yearbook, 1987, Vol 3: foreign country reviews of production, trade, and policy, by commodity, annual rpt, 5604–35

Minerals Yearbook, 1987, Vol 3 preprints: foreign country review of production, trade, and policy, by commodity, annual rpt, 5604–23.37

Multinatl US firms and foreign affiliates finances and operations, by industry of parent firm and affiliate, world area, and country, preliminary 1987, annual rpt, 2704–5

Nuclear power plant capacity, generation, and operating status, by plant and foreign and US location, 1988 and projected to 2020, annual rpt, 3164–57

Population size, growth rates, and components of change, by country, projected 1989-2020 and trends from 1950, biennial rpt, 2324–9

Space satellites and other objects launched since 1957, quarterly listing, 9502–2

UN voting record and share of votes in agreement with US, by issue, country, and world area, 1988, annual rpt, 7004–18

see also under By Foreign Country in the "Index by Categories"

Israilevich, Philip R.
"Determining Manufacturing Output for States and Regions", 9375–13.11
"Geography of Value Added", 9375–1.906
"Reconsidering the Regional Manufacturing Indexes", 9375–1.905

Italy

Agricultural and food production and indexes, total and for selected commodities, by country, 1970s-88, annual rpt, 1524–12

Agricultural production, prices, and trade, by country, 1970s-88 and forecast 1990, annual world region rpt, 1524–4.1

Agricultural trade of US, by detailed commodity and country, 1988, semiannual rpt, 1522–4

AID economic aid to developing countries, obligations and disbursements by country, quarterly rpt, 9912–4

AID loans repayment status and terms by program and country, and status of predecessor agency loans, quarterly rpt, 9912–3

Background Notes, summary social, political, and economic data, 1989 rpt, 7006–2.32

Bearings (antifriction) from 9 countries, injury to US industry from foreign subsidized and less than fair value imports, investigation with background financial and operating data, 1989 rpt, 9886–19.65

Cancer (breast) risk relation to diet and nutrient intake, for northwestern Italy, 1983-85 study, article, 4472–1.906

Developing countries loans from banks and govts, debt exposure of 7 developed countries, various periods 1980-88, GAO rpt, 26123–255

Drug abuse indicators, by world region and selected country, 1988 semiannual conf, 4492–5.1

Drug abuse indicators, for selected countries, 1989 semiannual conf, 4492–5.2

Economic and military aid and loans from US and intl agencies, by program and country, FY46-87, annual rpt, 9914–5

Economic and monetary trends, compounded annual rates of change for US and 10 major trading partners, quarterly rpt, 9391–7

Economic conditions, and oil production, use, and imports, by country, biweekly rpt, 9112–1

Economic conditions, consumer and stock prices and production indexes, 6 OECD countries and US, *Business Conditions Digest*, monthly rpt, 2702–3.10

Economic conditions in Communist, OECD, and selected other countries, 1960s-88, annual rpt, 9114–4

Economic conditions, income, production, prices, employment, and trade, 1989 periodic country rpt, 2046–4.83

Economic conditions, policy, and trade practices, by country, 1986-88, annual rpt, 21384–5

Economic indicators, and dollar exchange rates, for selected OECD countries, 1980s-89, semiannual rpt, 8002–14

Economic, social, political, and geographic summary data, by country, 1989, annual factbook, 9114–2

Energy prices, by fuel type and end use, for 10 countries, 1980-88 annual rpt, 3164–50.6

Energy production by type, and oil prices, trade, and use, by country group and selected country, monthly rpt, 9112–2

Export credit activity of Eximbank and 6 OECD countries, 1988, annual rpt, 9254–3

Exports and imports of US, by selected country, country group, and commodity group, 1988, annual rpt, 2044–37

Food supply and demand, market and support prices, and other economic indicators, by EC country and commodity, 1960-85, 1528–276

Human rights conditions in 170 countries, 1988, annual rpt, 21384–3

Imports of goods, services, and investment from US, trade barriers, impacts, and US actions, by country, 1988, annual rpt, 444–2

Imports of US given duty-free treatment for value of US material sent abroad, and impacts on US industry and employment, by commodity and country, 1987, annual rpt, 9884–14

Intl transactions of US with 9 countries, 1986-88, *Survey of Current Business*, monthly rpt, annual table, 2702–1.31

Labor conditions, union coverage, and work accidents, 1988 annual country rpt, 6366–4.1

Machinery belts from 8 countries, injury to US industry from foreign subsidized and less than fair value imports, investigation with background financial and operating data, 1989 rpt, 9886–19.66

Manufacturing labor productivity and unit costs for 14 countries, 1950-88, annual press release, 6864–1

Military aid of US, arms sales, and training programs costs and budget requests, by program, world region, and country, FY88-90, annual rpt, 7144–13

Military spending, arms trade, and force strengths, with govt spending and population, by country, 1977-87, annual rpt, 9824–1

Minerals Yearbook, 1987, Vol 3: foreign country reviews of production, trade, and policy, by commodity, annual rpt, 5604–35

Minerals Yearbook, 1987, Vol 3 preprints: foreign country review of production, trade, and policy, by commodity, annual rpt, 5604–23.38

Multinatl US firms and foreign affiliates finances and operations, by industry of parent firm and affiliate, world area, and country, preliminary 1987, annual rpt, 2704–5

Nuclear power generation in US and 19 non-Communist countries, monthly rpt, 3162–24.10

Nuclear power plant capacity, generation, and operating status, by plant and foreign and US location, 1988 and projected to 2020, annual rpt, 3164–57

Oil production, trade, use, and stocks, by selected country and country group, monthly rpt, 3162–42

Oil use and stocks for selected OECD countries, monthly rpt, 3162–24.10

Population size, growth rates, and components of change, by country, projected 1989-2020 and trends from 1950, biennial rpt, 2324–9

Ships in world merchant fleet, and tonnage, by country of registry, as of Jan 1988, annual rpt, 7704–3

Space satellites and other objects launched since 1957, quarterly listing, 9502–2

Stone (dimension) trade and price indexes by selected country, 1987, Mineral Industry Surveys, annual rpt, 5614–29

Transportation energy use, fuel prices, and vehicle registrations, by selected country, 1970s-88, annual rpt, 3304–5.1

Travel to US and Canada, market analysis with detailed trip and traveler characteristics, 1988, country rpt, 2906–2.14

Travel to US, market research, major magazine ad costs and circulation, and trade show data, for selected countries, 1989-90, annual rpt, 2904–11

UN voting record and share of votes in agreement with US, by issue, country, and world area, 1988, annual rpt, 7004–18

see also San Marino

see also Vatican City

see also under By Foreign Country in the "Index by Categories"

Iversen, Edwin S.

"Black, Red, and Nassau Groupers. Species Profiles: Life Histories and Environmental Requirements of Coastal Fishes and Invertebrates (South Florida)", 5506–8.117

Ivory Coast

Agricultural and food production and indexes, total and for selected commodities, by country, 1970s-88, annual rpt, 1524–12

Agricultural exports of Africa by commodity, and relation to economic conditions and other factors, by country, 1960s-87, 1528–280

Agricultural production, prices, and trade, by country, 1960s-89, annual world region rpt, 1524–4.2

Agricultural trade of US, by detailed commodity and country, 1988, semiannual rpt, 1522–4

AID activities and funding by project and function, FY90, and developing countries summary socioeconomic data from 1960s, annual rpt, 9904–4.5

AID economic aid to developing countries, obligations and disbursements by country, quarterly rpt, 9912–4

AID loans repayment status and terms by program and country, and status of predecessor agency loans, quarterly rpt, 9912–3

Economic and military aid and loans from US and intl agencies, by program and country, FY46-87, annual rpt, 9914–5

Economic conditions, income, production, prices, employment, and trade, 1989 periodic country rpt, 2046–4.107

Economic conditions, policy, and trade practices, by country, 1986-88, annual rpt, 21384–5

Economic, social, political, and geographic summary data, by country, 1989, annual factbook, 9114–2

Exports and imports of US, by commodity and country, 1970-87, world area rpt, 9116–1.4

Exports and imports of US, by selected country, country group, and commodity group, 1988, annual rpt, 2044–37

Human rights conditions in 170 countries, 1988, annual rpt, 21384–3

Military aid of US, arms sales, and training programs costs and budget requests, by program, world region, and country, FY88-90, annual rpt, 7144–13

Military spending, arms trade, and force strengths, with govt spending and population, by country, 1977-87, annual rpt, 9824–1

Minerals Yearbook, 1987, Vol 3 preprints: foreign country review of production, trade, and policy, by commodity, annual rpt, 5604–23.82

Population size, growth rates, and components of change, by country, projected 1989-2020 and trends from 1950, biennial rpt, 2324–9

UN voting record and share of votes in agreement with US, by issue, country, and world area, 1988, annual rpt, 7004–18

see also under By Foreign Country in the "Index by Categories"

Jackson, Mich.

see also under By SMSA or MSA in the "Index by Categories"

Jackson, Miss.

Wages by occupation, and benefits for office and plant workers, 1989 survey, periodic MSA rpt, 6785–12.1

see also under By City and By SMSA or MSA in the "Index by Categories"

Jackson, Tenn.

see also under By SMSA or MSA in the "Index by Categories"

Jacksonville, Fla.

Freight (waterborne domestic and foreign) by commodity, traffic, and passengers, by port and waterway, 1987, annual rpt, 3754–3.1; 3754–3.2

Housing starts and completions authorized by building permits in 40 MSAs, quarterly rpt, 2382–9

Wages by occupation, and benefits for office and plant workers, 1988 survey, periodic MSA rpt, 6785–3.1

see also under By City and By SMSA or MSA in the "Index by Categories"

Jacksonville, N.C.

Wages by occupation, and benefits for office and plant workers, 1989 survey, periodic MSA rpt, 6785–3.2

see also under By SMSA or MSA in the "Index by Categories"

Jacobs, Eva

"Families of Working Wives Spending More on Services and Nondurables", 6722–1.908

Jacobs, Fred

"Highlighting Recent Advances in IRS Volunteer Programs—Understanding Taxes", 8304–8.1

"Tax Supplement—New Approaches to Media Placement Problems", 8304–8.1

Jacobs, Philip

"Family Caregiver Costs of Chronically Ill and Handicapped Children: Method and Literature Review", 4042–3.912

Jacobson, Kristina

"Lessons from West German Monetary Policy", 9381–1.907

Jacowski, Michael J.

"Trends in Banking Structure Since the Mid-1970s", 9362–1.902

Jagger, Craig

"Effects of the CRP: Focus on Wheat Production", 1561–12.904

Jails

see Correctional institutions

Jain, Raj K.

"Infinite Polynomial Distributed Lag Model and Its Estimation", 6886–6.54

"Seasonal Adjustment Procedures for the Consumer Prices Indexes: Some Empirical Results", 6886–6.53

Jamaica

Agricultural and food production and indexes, total and for selected commodities, by country, 1970s-88, annual rpt, 1524–12

Agricultural trade of US, by detailed commodity and country, 1988, semiannual rpt, 1522–4

AID activities and funding by project and function, FY90, and developing countries summary socioeconomic data from 1960s, annual rpt, 9904–4.7

AID cash transfers to Jamaica linked to economic and policy reforms, effectiveness, 1981-87, 9916–3.56

AID economic aid to developing countries, obligations and disbursements by country, quarterly rpt, 9912–4

AID loans repayment status and terms by program and country, and status of predecessor agency loans, quarterly rpt, 9912–3

Economic and military aid and loans from US and intl agencies, by program and country, FY46-87, annual rpt, 9914–5

Economic conditions, income, production, prices, employment, and trade, 1989 periodic country rpt, 2046–4.46

Economic conditions, policy, and trade practices, by country, 1986-88, annual rpt, 21384–5

Economic, social, political, and geographic summary data, by country, 1989, annual factbook, 9114–2

Exports and imports of US, by commodity and country, 1970-87, world area rpt, 9116–1.1

Exports and imports of US, by selected country, country group, and commodity group, 1988, annual rpt, 2044–37

Exports of Caribbean area to OECD members, and US imports under preferential treatment programs, by commodity, 1980s-87, 2048–138

Human rights conditions in 170 countries, 1988, annual rpt, 21384–3

Investment (direct) incentives of Caribbean Basin Initiative, economic impacts, with finances and employment by country, 1984-88, 2048–141

Labor conditions, union coverage, and work accidents, 1989 annual country rpt, 6366–4.15

Military aid of US, arms sales, and training programs costs and budget requests, by program, world region, and country, FY88-90, annual rpt, 7144–13

Military spending, arms trade, and force strengths, with govt spending and population, by country, 1977-87, annual rpt, 9824–1

Minerals Yearbook, 1987, Vol 3: foreign country reviews of production, trade, and policy, by commodity, annual rpt, 5604–35

Economic indicators variability and correlation with GNP, for US, Japan, and UK, alternative estimates, for business cycles 1954-86, article, 9377-1.902

Economic, social, political, and geographic summary data, by country, 1989, annual factbook, 9114-2

Educational and cultural exchange activities of Japan-US Friendship Commission, grants, and trust fund status, FY87-88, biennial rpt, 14694-1

Election results and timing in Japan, relation to economic indicators, 1946-86, working paper, 9393-10.7

Energy prices, by fuel type and end use, for 10 countries, 1980-88 annual rpt, 3164-50.6

Energy production by type, and oil prices, trade, and use, by country group and selected country, monthly rpt, 9112-2

Energy use by sector, and production, by fuel type, country, and country group, projected 1988-2000 and trends from 1970, annual rpt, 3164-84

Export credit activity of Eximbank and 6 OECD countries, 1988, annual rpt, 9254-3

Exports and imports of OECD, total and for 4 major countries, and US trade by country, by commodity, 1970-87, world area rpt series, 9116-1

Exports and imports of US, by commodity group, world area, selected country, US coastal area and port, and mode of transport, monthly rpt, 2422-9

Exports and imports of US, by selected country, country group, and commodity group, 1988, annual rpt, 2044-37

Exports and imports, trade agreements and relations, and USITC investigations, 1988, annual rpt, 9884-5

Exports, imports, and balances of US by commodity group, world area, and country, and related employment, 1970s-88, annual rpt, 2044-26

Exports, imports, and balances of US with major trading partners, by product category, 1984-88, annual chartbook, 9884-21

Fish (Greenland turbot) catch, by Alaska coast fishery, 1960s-86, 2168-110

Fish and shellfish aquaculture in US and Japan, mgmt, methods, and biological data for selected species, 1985 conf papers, annual rpt, 2164-15

Fish catch, prices, trade by country, cold storage holdings, and market devs, for Japan, semimonthly press release, 2162-7

Fishery mgmt agency budget for Japan, FY87-88, article, 2162-1.902

Flowers (cut roses) US industry intl competitiveness, investigation with background financial and operating data and foreign comparisons, 1989 rpt, 9886-4.137

GNP of Canada, Japan, and Germany, relation to foreign and domestic industry output, 1961-84, technical paper, 9366-6.189

Grain imports, and change in per capita consumption, by commodity for Japan, 1955-87, article, 1522-3.913

Human rights conditions in 170 countries, 1988, annual rpt, 21384-3

Import restraint elimination by US, impact on domestic industry production and employment, by selected commodity, 1987, 9886-4.144

Imports from US, impacts on US employment by exporting sector and major importer, 1980s-87, 2048-103

Imports of goods, services, and investment from US, trade barriers, impacts, and US actions, by country, 1988, annual rpt, 444-2

Imports of US given duty-free treatment for value of US material sent abroad, and impacts on US industry and employment, by commodity and country, 1987, annual rpt, 9884-14

Interest rate differentials among countries, US and 4 industrialized countries, 1960s-88, article, 9385-1.902

Investment (foreign direct) in US, by industry group and world area, 1987-88, annual article, 2702-1.929

Investment (foreign direct) in US, major transactions by type, industry, country, and US location, 1987, annual rpt, 2044-20

Labor conditions, union coverage, and work accidents, 1989 annual country rpt, 6366-4.2; 6366-4.64

Labor force participation by selected characteristics, productivity, and unit labor costs, for Japan and US, 1960s-87, article, 6722-1.910

Lumber products of Japan, selected economic and housing demand indicators, 1989 rpt, 2046-14.2

Lumber use by industry, and construction activity and indicators of demand, for Japan, 1970-88, article, 2042-1.909

Machinery belts from 8 countries, injury to US industry from foreign subsidized and less than fair value imports, investigation with background financial and operating data, 1989 rpt, 9886-19.66

Manganese dioxide (electrolytic) from 2 countries at less than fair value, injury to US industry, investigation with background financial and operating data, 1989 rpt, 9886-14.260

Manufacturing capital stock relation to productivity, alternative measures, for Japan, model results, 1955-81, working paper, 6886-6.58

Manufacturing labor costs and indexes, by selected country, 1975-88, annual rpt, 6824-3

Manufacturing labor costs and indexes, by selected country, 1975-88, semiannual rpt, 6822-3

Manufacturing labor productivity and unit costs for 14 countries, 1950-88, annual press release, 6864-1

Metal-forming presses (automatic) from Japan at less than fair market value, injury to US industry, investigation with background financial and operating data, 1989 rpt, 9886-14.253

Military aid of US, arms sales, and training programs costs and budget requests, by program, world region, and country, FY88-90, annual rpt, 7144-13

Military bases of US, maintenance costs contributed, FY81-90, GAO rpt, 26123-249

Military, economic, technological, and trade conditions of Pacific Basin countries, 1970s-85, compilation of papers, 3908-4

Military spending and indicators of ability to support common defense, for NATO members and Japan, 1971-87, annual rpt, 3544-28

Military spending, arms trade, and force strengths, with govt spending and population, by country, 1977-87, annual rpt, 9824-1

Minerals production, reserves, and industry role in domestic economy and world supply, 1988 country rpt, 5606-1.17

Minerals Yearbook, 1987, Vol 3: foreign country reviews of production, trade, and policy, by commodity, annual rpt, 5604-35

Minerals Yearbook, 1987, Vol 3 preprints: foreign country review of production, trade, and policy, by commodity, annual rpt, 5604-23.39

Money supply forecast accuracy impact of monetary target announcements, for US and Japan, 1978-88, working paper, 9393-10.8

Multinatl firms US affiliates, finances, and operations, by industry, world area of parent firm, and State, 1987, annual rpt, 2704-4

Multinatl US firms and foreign affiliates finances and operations, by industry of parent firm and affiliate, world area, and country, preliminary 1987, annual rpt, 2704-5

Nitrocellulose (industrial) from 7 countries at less than fair value, injury to US industry, investigation with background financial and operating data, 1989 rpt, 9886-14.270

Nuclear power generation in US and 19 non-Communist countries, monthly rpt, 3162-24.10

Nuclear power plant capacity, generation, and operating status, by plant and foreign and US location, 1988 and projected to 2020, annual rpt, 3164-57

Oil production, trade, use, and stocks, by selected country and country group, monthly rpt, 3162-42

Oil use and stocks for selected OECD countries, monthly rpt, 3162-24.10

Population size, growth rates, and components of change, by country, projected 1989-2020 and trends from 1950, biennial rpt, 2324-9

Port facilities, operations, and impacts on US agricultural exports, for major Far East Asia ports, 1970s-87, 1278-13

R&D funding and science and technology employment for selected countries, selected years 1961-87, annual rpt, 9624-18.2

Recreational all-terrain vehicles from Japan at less than fair value, injury to US industry, investigation with background financial and operating data, 1989 rpt, 9886-14.254

Science and engineering employment and education, and R&D spending, for US and selected foreign countries, 1988, annual rpt, 9624-23

Securities intl transactions, for US govt and other securities, and for Japan purchases by country, late 1970s-87, hearing, 23848-209

Ships in world merchant fleet, and tonnage, by country of registry, as of Jan 1988, annual rpt, 7704–3

Social security trust funds surpluses impact on govt budgets, for 3 countries and US, 1960-86, article, 9373–1.905

Space satellites and other objects launched since 1957, quarterly listing, 9502–2

Steel export ceilings under voluntary restraint agreements, by country and product, with Western US steel industry impact, 1989 rpt, 9886–4.136

Steel imports of US under voluntary restraint agreement, by product, customs district, and country, with US industry operating data, monthly rpt, 9882–13

Stock market crash of 1987, US stock prices relation to prices on Tokyo and London exchanges, 1987-88, technical paper, 9366–6.164

Stock price index correlations among US and 3 countries, various periods 1957-88, article, 9391–1.901

Stone (dimension) trade and price indexes by selected country, 1987, Mineral Industry Surveys, annual rpt, 5614–29

Superconductivity (high temperature) R&D spending by Federal agency, and US and Japan industry funding and employment, by application, 1981-89, hearing, 25408–100

Telephones (cellular mobile) from Japan at less than fair value, injury to US industry, investigation with background financial and operating data, investigation supplement, 1989 rpt, 9886–14.252

Telephones and equipment from 3 countries at less than fair value, injury to US industry, investigation with background financial and operating data, 1989 rpt, 9886–14.251; 9886–14.274

Tidal currents, daily time and velocity by station for North America and Asia coasts, forecast 1990, annual rpt, 2174–1.1

Timber in northwestern US and British Columbia, production, prices, trade, and employment, quarterly rpt, 1202–3

Tobacco trade of US with 3 Asian countries, 1984-88, article, 1925–16.908

Transmissions for riding mowers from Japan at less than fair value, injury to US industry, investigation with background financial and operating data, 1989 rpt, 9886–14.248

Transportation energy use, fuel prices, and vehicle registrations, by selected country, 1970s-88, annual rpt, 3304–5.1

Travel to US, market research, major magazine ad costs and circulation, and trade show data, for selected countries, 1989-90, annual rpt, 2904–11

UN voting record and share of votes in agreement with US, by issue, country, and world area, 1988, annual rpt, 7004–18

Unemployment rates and labor force participation in Japan by sex, alternative estimates, 1984-88, article, 6722–1.930

US Air Force Pacific basin airlift of aircraft parts, traffic, shipments, and impacts on force readiness, 1986-88, GAO rpt, 26123–230

Wheat trade, elasticities of demand for US and 5 countries, alternative models description and results, 1950s-86, 1528–281

Wine (grape) production, imports by country, and duty, for Japan, selected years 1978-89, article, 1925–34.928

see also under By Foreign Country in the "Index by Categories"

Japan-U.S. Friendship Commission

Budget of US Appendix, obligations, appropriations, and personnel, by program and agency, FY90, annual rpt, 104–3

Budget of US, authoritative financial statements with appropriations, outlays, and receipts, by category and agency, FY88, annual rpt, 8104–2.2

Educational and cultural exchange activities, grants, and trust fund status, FY87-88, biennial rpt, 14694–1

Japanese Americans

see Asian Americans

Jappinen, Paavo

"Cancer Incidence of Workers in the Finnish Pulp and Paper Industry", 21368–112

Jarrell, Jerry D.

"Avoid the Typhoon", 2152–8.901

Jayne, Thomas S.

"Technology and Agricultural Productivity in the Sahel", 1528–290

Jefferson County, Ala.

Housing and households detailed characteristics, and unit and neighborhood quality, by location, 1984 survey, MSA rpt, 2485–6.1

Jenkins, Lynn B.

"Science Report Card, Elements of Risk and Recovery: Trends and Achievement Based on the 1986 National Assessment", 4898–25

Jennings, Jerry T.

"Voting and Registration in the Election of November 1988", 2546–1.440

Jersey City, N.J.

see also under By City and By SMSA or MSA in the "Index by Categories"

Jessop, Dorothy J.

"Measuring Health Variables Among Hispanic and Non-Hispanic Children with Chronic Conditions", 4042–3.936

Jet fuel

see Aviation fuels

Jewelry

Consumer holdings of durable goods, by type, in current and constant dollars, 1985-88, annual article, 2702–1.931

County Business Patterns, 1987: employment, establishments, and payroll, by SIC 2- to 4-digit industry and county, annual State rpt series, 2326–8

CPI by component for US city average, and by region, population size, and for 27 metro areas, monthly rpt, 6762–2

Employment, earnings, and hours, by selected SIC 1- to 4-digit industry, State, and for 262 MSAs, 1972-87, 6748–81

Employment, earnings, and hours, by SIC 1- to 4-digit industry, monthly 1983-Feb 1989, annual rpt, 6744–4

Endangered animals and plants US trade and permits, by species, purpose, disposition, and country, 1987, annual rpt, 5504–19

Exports of US, detailed commodities by country, monthly rpt, 2422–3

Import restraint elimination, impact on domestic industry production and employment, by selected commodity, 1986-88, 9886–4.144

Imports of US, detailed Schedule A commodities by country, monthly rpt, 2422–2

Imports of US given duty-free treatment for value of US material sent abroad, and impacts on US industry and employment, by commodity and country, 1987, annual rpt, 9884–14

Injuries from use of consumer products and related activities, by victim age and sex, 1988, annual rpt, 9164–7

Injuries from use of consumer products, by severity, victim age, and detailed product, 1988, annual rpt, 9164–6

Manufacturers finances and operations, by SIC 2- to 4-digit industry, forecast 1989 and trends from 1950s, annual rpt, 2044–28

Manufacturing annual survey, 1986: financial and operating data, by SIC 2- to 4-digit industry, series, 2506–15

Manufacturing census, 1987: financial and operating data, for SIC 4-digit industries by product, preliminary rpt, 2491–1.80; 2491–1.82

Occupational injury and illness rates, by SIC 2- to 4-digit industry, 1987, annual rpt, 6844–1

OECD trade, total and for 4 major countries, and US trade by country, by commodity, 1970-87, world area rpt series, 9116–1

Price indexes (producer), by stage of processing and detailed commodity, monthly rpt, 6762–6

Price indexes (producer), by stage of processing and detailed commodity, monthly 1988, annual rpt, 6764–2

Price indexes for department store inventories, by class of item, monthly table, 6762–7

Retail trade census, 1987: employment, establishments, sales, and payroll, by SIC 2- to 4-digit kind of business, MSA, county, and city, State rpt series, 2397–1

Retail trade sales and inventories, by kind of business, region, and selected State, MSA, and city, monthly rpt, 2413–3

Retail trade sales, inventories, purchases, gross margin, and accounts receivable, by SIC 2- to 4-digit kind of business and form of ownership, 1987, annual rpt, 2413–5

Science, engineering, and technical employment in manufacturing, by field, occupation, and industry, 1986, triennial rpt, 9627–23

Thefts, and value of property stolen and recovered, by property type, 1988, annual rpt, 6224–2.1

Wholesale trade census, 1987: employment, establishments, finances, and operations, by SIC 2- to 4-digit kind of business, MSA, county, and city, State rpt series, 2405–1

see also Gemstones

Job Corps

Forest Service activities and finances, by region and State, FY88, annual rpt, 1204–1.4

Participant characteristics, activities, and funding, for Employment and Training Admin programs, FY80-86, 6408–71

Reclamation Bur activities and finances, FY88, annual rpt, 5824–1

Job creation

Employment conditions, alternative BLS projections to 2000 and trends 1970s-88, biennial article, 6722-1.954; 6722-1.955

Energy-related inventions supported by DOE, sales, jobs created, and inventor characteristics, 1980-86, 3308-91

Export-related employment generated by Overseas Private Investment Corp projects, FY88, annual rpt, 9904-3

Exports and export-related employment generated by Overseas Private Investment Corp projects, FY88, annual rpt, 9904-2

NASA procurement economic benefits by industry group, jobs created, and sales, by State, FY90, 9508-35

Rural and urban areas jobs created under AFDC workfare program, 1986 and estimated 1988, article, 1502-7.902

Rural areas investment and employment impacts of Urban Dev Action Grant funding, 1978-87, article, 1502-7.903

Ship foreign and US flag competition in US Exclusive Economic Zone, impacts of extending cabotage laws, with background data, 1970s-80s, 26358-206

Small business establishments, employment, and financial ratios, by SIC 1- to 2-digit industry and State, late 1960s-87, 9768-19

Small business establishments, operations, owner characteristics, and job training, late 1950s-87, 9768-20

Small business finances, operations, owner and employee characteristics, and Federal contracts, 1980s-88, annual rpt, 9764-6

Tax (income) returns filed by type of filer, selected income items, quarterly rpt, 8302-2.1

Tax (income) returns of individuals, by filing status, tax item, and income level, 1987, annual article, 8302-2.901

Tax (income) returns of individuals, detailed data, 1986, annual rpt, 8304-2

Tax (income) returns of partnerships, income statement items by industry group, 1986, annual article, 8302-2.903

Tax (income) returns of sole proprietorships, income statement items, by industry group, 1987, annual article, 8302-2.904

Tax expenditures, Federal revenues forgone through income tax deductions and exclusions by type, FY90-94, annual rpt, 21784-10

Tennessee Valley industrial dev, employment, and electricity demand, by SIC 2-digit industry, firm, and location, 1988, annual rpt, 9804-3

Urban Dev Action Grant eligibility rating system of HUD, and project costs and economic impacts, as of Nov 1988, GAO rpt, 26113-424

Urban Dev Action Grants, funding, and jobs and taxes generated, by city, FY88, annual rpt, 5124-5

Urban Dev Action Grants, funding sources, project descriptions, and economic impacts, by city, periodic press releases, 5002-7

Job discrimination

see Discrimination in employment

Job placement

see Employment services

Job tenure

Cancer (bladder) risk for men in selected occupations, by employment characteristics, 1977-78, article, 4472-1.924; 4472-1.925

Clerical workers remedial education and training programs, effectiveness, local area program, 1973-88, article, 9373-1.918

Displaced workers, labor-mgmt committee aid recipients by selected characteristics, for 4 State programs, 1988, GAO rpt, 26121-316

Earnings related to tenure, relationship to probability of employer bankruptcy, 1979-83, technical paper, 9366-6.180

Education data compilation, students, staff, finances, and facilities, 1989 edition, annual rpt, 4824-2

Fed Govt employment of minorities, handicapped, and veterans, and years of service, by occupation, age, sex, and agency, as of Sept 1988, biennial rpt, 9844-27

Health condition of labor force, and services use, by occupation and industry of longest job held, income, age, sex, and race. 1980, 4147-10.168

Labor force supply and mobility, by age, and educational level needs, 1960-86 and projected to 2000, 6306-2.4

Military reserve personnel social, economic, family, and service characteristics, and attitudes, by reserve component, 1986 survey, 3508-29

Military reserve spouses attitudes, and family social, economic, and other characteristics, 1986 survey, 3508-30

Military women personnel on active and reserve duty, by demographic and service characteristics and service branch, FY88, annual chartbook, 3544-26

NASA staff characteristics and personnel actions, FY88, annual rpt, 9504-1

Nurses (RN) in nursing homes, years of service by employment status and instn characteristics, 1985, 4147-13.97

Occupational changes, by tenure and other worker characteristics, and labor mobility rates, 1965-86, article, 6722-1.943

Pension coverage, by plan type and worker characteristics, 1970s-88, article, 4742-1.925; 4746-26.7

Science and engineering labor supply by region and employment characteristics, and salaries by years of experience, 1987, 9626-2.184

SEC staffing, pay, and turnover by occupation and city, with proposed fee revenues to improve work conditions, 1989 hearing, 21368-116

Teachers bachelor degrees, by field and other characteristics, 1985-86, 4838-39

Teachers in public and private schools, salaries by selected characteristics, 1984/85-1985/86, 4838-37

Teachers incentive programs of public schools, and participation, by instn and teacher characteristics, with effectiveness ratings, 1985, 4838-38

see also Labor mobility

see also Labor turnover

Job training

see Apprenticeship

see Employee development

see Manpower training programs

see Vocational education and training

see Vocational rehabilitation

Job Training Partnership Act

Displaced workers program grants under JTPA, 1989, press release, 6406-2.25

Expenditures of Fed Govt in States, by type, program, agency, and State, FY88, annual rpt, 2464-2

Participant characteristics, activities, and funding, for Employment and Training Admin programs, FY80-86, 6408-71

Participation in JTPA, by selected characteristics, FY88, annual rpt, 6304-1

State and local govt JTPA admin, funding, effectiveness, and participants, GAO rpt series, 26106-8

Unemployed displaced workers and other hard to serve groups, factors contributing to unemployment, and training programs operations, series, 15496-1

Unemployment, employment, and labor force of States and local areas eligible for JTPA funding, monthly rpt, supplement, 6742-22

Unemployment insurance reemployment and training services, and bonus for early reemployment, New Jersey demonstration project results, 1987-88, 6406-6.27

Job vacancy

Business Conditions Digest, cyclical indicators, by economic process, monthly rpt, 2702-3.3

Fed Govt Senior Executive Service career position longterm vacancies, by reason and agency, 1989, GAO rpt, 26119-252

Health care personnel supply and needs, for environmental and occupational health fields, 1987 conf, 4118-65

Help-wanted ads index and ratio to unemployment, *Business Conditions Digest*, cyclical indicators, monthly rpt, 2702-3.3

Judgeships vacant, by Federal district and appeals court, 1984-89, annual rpt, 18204-3

Labor force, wages, hours, and payroll costs, by major industry group and demographic characteristics, *Survey of Current Business*, monthly rpt, 2702-1.5

New England States economic indicators, Fed Reserve 1st District, quarterly rpt, 9373-2.1

New England States, FHLB 1st District thrift instns financial operations and housing industry indicators, monthly rpt, 9302-4

North Central States business and economic conditions, Fed Reserve 9th District, quarterly journal, 9383-19

Nurses (RN) employment, shortages, recruitment, and retention, findings and recommendations, 1988 rpt, 4008-88

Nursing chief officers in hospitals, activities, responsibilities, and role in nurse hiring and retention, 1988 survey, 4008-91

Nursing labor supply and shortage indicators, and earnings, by State, 1970s-80s, 25148-41

Police pay, benefits, and staffing, for US Park Police and compared to other Federal and local police units, FY85-88, GAO rpt, 26119-264

Statistical Abstract of US, social, political, and economic data, 1790-2025, comprehensive annual compilation, 2324-1.3

VA health care facilities physicians staffing, vacancies, and positions filled, by speciality, 1982-87, hearing, 25768-48

see also Labor turnover

Jobs

see Employment and unemployment, general

see Employment and unemployment, local and regional

see Employment and unemployment, specific industry

see Job creation

see Job vacancy

see Labor turnover

see Occupations

see Part-time employment

see Temporary and seasonal employment

see Veterans employment

see Women's employment

see Youth employment

see under By Occupation in the "Index by Categories"

Johnson City, Tenn.

see also under By SMSA or MSA in the "Index by Categories"

Johnson, David W.

"Forest Pest Conditions in the Rocky Mountain Region, 1988", 1206-11.2

Johnson, Dwight L.

"We, the Asian and Pacific Islander Americans", 2326-1.5

"We, the First Americans", 2326-1.6

Johnson, Mae D.

"Cotton Ginning Charges, Harvesting Practices, and Selected Marketing Costs, 1988/89 Season", 1564-3

Johnson, Marie-Louise T.

"Prevalence of Dermatological Disease Among Persons 1-74 Years of Age: U.S.", 4147-16.1

Johnson, Martha

"Residential Energy Consumption Survey: Housing Characteristics, 1987", 3166-7.29

Johnson, Tony G.

"Forest Statistics for North Central Georgia, 1989", 1206-26.12

Johnsrud, Myron D.

"Global Dimensions: Revitalization of Rural America", 1004-16.1

Johnston, Lloyd D.

"Drug Use, Drinking and Smoking: National Survey Results from High School, College, and Young Adult Populations, 1975-88", 4494-4

Johnston, William B.

"Civil Service 2000", 9848-37

Johnstown, Pa.

see also under By SMSA or MSA in the "Index by Categories"

Joint Chiefs of Staff

NATO and US weapons and troop strength compared to Warsaw Pact and USSR, annual rpt, discontinued, 3564-1

Joint committees

see Congressional joint committees

Joint Economic Committee

Current account balance, by component, 1980-87 and projected under alternative growth and exchange rate assumptions, 1988-95, hearing, 23848-209

Economic indicators and components, current data and annual trends, monthly rpt, 23842-1

Economic Report of the President for 1989, economic effects of budget proposals, and trends and projections, 1929-99, annual hearings, 23844-4

Economic Report of the President for 1989, Joint Economic Committee critique and policy recommendations, annual rpt, 23844-2

Employment shifts among industries, factors and impacts on wage growth, with data by industry group, 1948-87, 23848-207

Employment situation, earnings, hours, and other BLS economic indicators, transcripts of BLS Commissioner's monthly testimony, periodic rpt, 23846-4

Soviet Union economic conditions and military activity, 1960s-86, hearing, 23848-195

Sweden multinatl firms domestic and foreign production, exports, employment, and sales, with data by commodity and firm, 1960s-86, conf, 23848-208

Joint Printing Committee

Congressional Directory, members of 101st Congress, other officials, elections, and districts, 1989-90, biennial rpt, 23874-1

Joint Taxation Committee

Medicare catastrophic illness coverage and premium collection, effects of revisions on Federal budget and enrollees, projected 1989-93, 25368-161

Tax expenditures, Federal revenues forgone through income tax deductions and exclusions by type, FY90-94, annual rpt, 21784-10

Joint ventures

AID dev projects and socioeconomic impacts, evaluation rpt series, 9916-1

Energy resources of US, foreign direct investment by energy type and firm, and US affiliates operations, as of 1988, annual rpt, 3164-80

Foreign direct investment in US, major transactions by type, industry, country, and US location, 1987, annual rpt, 2044-20

Joliet, Ill.

Housing vacancy rates for single and multifamily units and mobile homes, by city and ZIP code, 1989, annual MSA rpt, 9304-18.1

Wages by occupation, and benefits for office and plant workers, 1988 survey, periodic MSA rpt, 6785-11.3

see also under By SMSA or MSA in the "Index by Categories"

Jones, Jonathan D.

"Analysis of Aggregate Time Series Capital Gains Equations", 8006-3.61

Joplin, Mo.

see also under By SMSA or MSA in the "Index by Categories"

Jordan

Agricultural and food production and indexes, total and for selected commodities, by country, 1970s-88, annual rpt, 1524-12

Agricultural trade of US, by detailed commodity and country, 1988, semiannual rpt, 1522-4

Agricultural trade of US with Asia, Middle East, and North Africa, by commodity and country, 1962-86, 1528-277

AID activities and funding by project and function, FY90, and developing countries summary socioeconomic data from 1960s, annual rpt, 9904-4.6

AID economic aid to developing countries, obligations and disbursements by country, quarterly rpt, 9912-4

AID loans repayment status and terms by program and country, and status of predecessor agency loans, quarterly rpt, 9912-3

Economic and military aid and loans from US and intl agencies, by program and country, FY46-87, annual rpt, 9914-5

Economic conditions, policy, and trade practices, by country, 1986-88, annual rpt, 21384-5

Economic, social, political, and geographic summary data, by country, 1989, annual factbook, 9114-2

Exports and imports of US, by commodity and country, 1970-87, world area rpt, 9116-1.3

Human rights conditions in 170 countries, 1988, annual rpt, 21384-3

Military aid of US, arms sales, and training programs costs and budget requests, by program, world region, and country, FY88-90, annual rpt, 7144-13

Military spending, arms trade, and force strengths, with govt spending and population, by country, 1977-87, annual rpt, 9824-1

Minerals Yearbook, 1987, Vol 3: foreign country reviews of production, trade, and policy, by commodity, annual rpt, 5604-35

Minerals Yearbook, 1987, Vol 3 preprints: foreign country review of production, trade, and policy, by commodity, annual rpt, 5604-23.40

Population size, growth rates, and components of change, by country, projected 1989-2020 and trends from 1950, biennial rpt, 2324-9

UN voting record and share of votes in agreement with US, by issue, country, and world area, 1988, annual rpt, 7004-18

see also under By Foreign Country in the "Index by Categories"

Jory, Darryl E.

"Black, Red, and Nassau Groupers. Species Profiles: Life Histories and Environmental Requirements of Coastal Fishes and Invertebrates (South Florida)", 5506-8.117

Journalism

County Business Patterns, 1987: employment, establishments, and payroll, by SIC 2- to 4-digit industry and county, annual State rpt series, 2326-8

Foreign countries media representatives admitted to US, by country, FY78-88, annual rpt, 6264-2

Foreign countries media representatives admitted to US, quarterly rpt, 6262-2

Hwy speed limit increase coverage by newspapers and TV, 1987, 7768-110

Science and engineering employment, by nonmanufacturing industry and field, 1987, triennial rpt, 9627-31

Service industries census, 1987: establishments, receipts, employment, and payroll, by SIC 2- to 4-digit kind of business, MSA, county, and city, State rpt series, 2391-1

see also Freedom of the press

see also Government and the press

see also Newspapers

see also Periodicals

Judd, John P.
"Central Bank Secrecy and Money
Surprises: International Evidence",
9393–10.8
"Unemployment-Rate Dynamics:
Aggregate-Demand and -Supply
Interactions", 9393–8.910

Judges
Army judges and accession goals, by race
and sex, 1985-88, annual rpt, 3704–10.1 .
Assaults and deaths of law enforcement
officers, by circumstances, agency, victim
and offender characteristics, and location,
1988, annual rpt, 6224–3
Criminal caseload, positions authorized,
misconduct, terms, salaries, and selected
other characteristics of judges, 1970s-88,
annual rpt, 6064–6.1; 6064–6.5
Fed Govt civilian pay rates, by pay schedule
and grade, 1989 and trends from 1789,
annual rpt, 21624–4
Federal district and appeals court caseloads,
actions, procedure duration, judges, and
jurors, by court, 1984-89, annual rpt,
18204–3
Federal district and appeals court judgeships
and visiting judge services, June 1989,
annual rpt, 18204–8.7; 18204–8.25
Federal district and appeals court
judgeships, June 1989, annual rpt,
18204–2.7
Judicial Conf proceedings and findings, fall
1989, semiannual rpt, 18202–2
Wiretaps authorized, costs, arrests, trials,
and convictions, by offense and
jurisdiction, 1988, annual rpt, 18204–7
Workers compensation contested claims,
contested caseload, and commissioners
and hearing officers, by State, 1988,
annual rpt, 6504–9
see also Judicial ethics
see also Judicial powers
see also Judicial reform

Judgments, civil procedure
Airport security operations to prevent
hijacking, screening failures and proposed
FAA penalties by carrier, 1989 press
release, 7306–10.2; 7306–10.3
Airport security operations to prevent
hijacking, screening results, enforcement
actions, and hijacking attempts, 1st half
1988, semiannual rpt, 7502–5
Alien workers (unauthorized) employer
sanctions, enforcement costs, compliance,
and job discrimination, 1988 annual GAO
rpt, 26104–19
Bankruptcy court mediation program
caseloads and dispositions, for California
southern district, 1986-88, 18408–40
Budget of US, authoritative financial
statements with appropriations, outlays,
and receipts, by category and agency,
FY88, annual rpt, 8104–2.2
Claims Court caseload by type of suit, and
judgments, FY89, annual rpt, 18224–1
Coal Surface Mining Reclamation and
Enforcement Office activities and funding,
by State and Indian tribe, FY87, annual
rpt, 5644–1
Coal surface mining-related civil actions,
attorneys fees and expenses awarded by
case, 1989, GAO rpt, 26113–421
Customs Service activities, collections,
entries processed by mode of transport,
and seizures, FY84-88, annual rpt,
8144–1

Exporters (US) antiboycott law violations
and fines by firm, and invitations to
boycott by country, FY88, annual rpt,
2024–1
Fed Govt benefit programs overpayment
recovery and judgment enforcement cases
filed in Federal district courts, June 1989,
annual rpt, 18204–2.12; 18204–8.11
Fed Govt employment discrimination
complaints, and awards by funding source,
for 3 agencies, FY87-88, GAO rpt,
26121–313
Federal district, appeals, and bankruptcy
courts, civil cases terminated by circuit
and district, quarterly rpt, 18202–1
Futures market trading abuses, Commodity
Futures Trading Commission and
exchanges enforcement activity, various
periods 1984-FY90, GAO rpt,
26119–263
Futures market trading abuses, Commodity
Futures Trading Commission, Chicago
Board of Trade, and Chicago Mercantile
Exchange enforcement activity, 1984-89,
GAO rpt, 26119–247
HHS programs fraud and abuse, audits and
investigations, 2nd half FY89, semiannual
rpt, 4002–6
Maritime Commission activities, case filings
by type and disposition, and civil penalties
by shipper, FY88, annual rpt, 9334–1
Medical malpractice claims against military
hospitals by disposition, and costs,
1982-87, hearing, 21208–27
Mine safety and health enforcement,
training, and funding, with casualties, by
type of mine and State, FY87, annual rpt,
6664–6
Nuclear power plant performance ratings,
violations, penalties, and unplanned
outages, by plant, 1970s-87, GAO rpt,
26113–416
Nuclear Regulatory Commission activities,
finances, and staff, with data for
individual power plants, FY88, annual rpt,
9634–2
Oil company overcharge settlements, and
use for State legal expenses, by State,
firm, and case, as of 1988, GAO rpt,
26113–408
Pension laws admin and enforcement under
Employee Retirement Income Security
Act (ERISA), 1987, annual rpt, 6304–4
Pension plan regulation enforcement by
Labor Dept and IRS, violations, and
penalties, FY85-88, GAO rpt, 26121–259
Pipeline accidents, casualties, safety
enforcement activity, and Federal funding,
by State, 1987, annual rpt, 7304–5
Railroad accidents, casualties, and Federal
safety activities, late 1970s-87, hearing,
21368–103
Railroad safety violation claims settled, by
carrier, FY88, annual rpt, 7604–10
Tax (income) law violations civil penalties
assessed and abated, FY87-88, GAO rpt,
26119–265
Tax collection, enforcement, and litigation
activity of IRS, with data by type of tax,
region, and State, FY88, annual rpt,
8304–3
Tax Court of US caseloads and appeals by
disposition, procedure duration, and
recoveries, FY88, annual rpt, 18224–5

Tax Court of US caseloads and tax due, by
disposition, FY89, annual tables,
18224–3
Torts for product liability, dispositions,
awards, case processing time, and plaintiff
injury severity and other characteristics,
1983-85, GAO rpt, 26121–317
US attorneys case processing and
collections, by case type and Federal
district, FY88, annual rpt, 6004–2
see also Child support and alimony

Judicial Branch
see Administrative Office of the U.S. Courts
see Court of International Trade
see Court of Military Appeals
see Federal bankruptcy courts
see Federal courts of appeals
see Federal district courts
see Federal Judicial Center
see Supreme Court
see U.S. Court of Appeals for the Federal
Circuit

Judicial Conference of the U.S.
Proceedings and findings of conf, fall 1989,
semiannual rpt, 18202–2
Proceedings and findings of semiannual
confs, 1988, annual rpt, 18204–8

Judicial ethics
Judges misconduct cases by disposition, and
judicial conduct commissions staff and
budgets, by State, 1986, annual rpt,
6064–6.5
Judicial Conf proceedings and findings, fall
1989, semiannual rpt, 18202–2
Public opinion on crime and crime-related
issues, by respondent characteristics,
1970s-89, annual rpt, 6064–6.2

Judicial powers
Judicial Conf proceedings and findings, fall
1989, semiannual rpt, 18202–2

Judicial reform
Habeas corpus used to appeal capital
convictions, and executions by race, by
State, with military death row inmates,
1977-87, hearing, 21408–110
Judicial Conf proceedings and findings, fall
1989, semiannual rpt, 18202–2
Prison conditions, population, and problems,
issues and bibl, 1989 compilation of
papers, 25928–8
Sentences for Federal crimes, guidelines use
and results by offense and district, and
Sentencing Commission activities, 1988,
annual rpt, 17664–1
Sentences for Federal offenses, guidelines by
offense and circumstances, 1989 rpt,
17668–1
Sentencing guidelines use and results, for
Minnesota, 1978-84, 6066–20.20

Junior colleges
Condition of Education, detailed data on
higher education, 1960s-88, annual rpt,
4824–1.2
Digest of Education Statistics, detailed data
on students, staff, finances, and facilities,
1989 edition, annual rpt, 4824–2
Enrollment and degrees awarded by sex, and
instn finances, by instn level and control,
1987-88, annual rpt, 4844–14
Enrollment, by grade, instn type and
control, and student characteristics, 1986
and trends from 1947, annual Current
Population Rpt, 2546–1.429;
2546–1.432

Enrollment, degrees, teachers, and spending, 1974/75-1988/89 and alternative projections to 1999/2000, annual rpt, 4824-4

Pell grants and applicants, by tuition, family and student income, instn type and control, and State, 1987/88, annual rpt, 4804-1

R&D and related funding of Fed Govt to higher education and nonprofit instns, by field, instn, agency, and State, FY87, annual rpt, 9627-17

Statistical Abstract of US, social, political, and economic data, 1790-2025, comprehensive annual compilation, 2324-1.1

Student aid and other sources of support, with student expenses and characteristics, by instn type and control, 1987 triennial study, series, 4846-3

Student aid funding and participation, by Federal program, instn type and control, and State, various periods 1959-88, annual rpt, 4804-28

Vocational education aid recipients and sources, and characteristics of programs and students, 1970s-89, series, 4806-3

Juries

Employee paid leave days for jury duty, by occupational group, 1988, annual rpt, 6784-19

Federal district and appeals court caseloads, actions, procedure duration, judges, and jurors, by court, 1984-89, annual rpt, 18204-3

Federal district court grand and petit juror use and costs, trials, and trial days, by court, 1981-88, annual rpt, 18204-4

Federal district court grand and petit juror use, June 1982-89, annual rpt, 18204-2; 18204-8

Federal district courts grand and petit juror use, by circuit and district, quarterly rpt, annual tables, 18202-1

Fees paid, size and vote required for decision, and jury use, by State and for Federal system, various periods 1976-88, annual rpt, 6064-6.1

US attorneys case processing and collections, by case type and Federal district, FY88, annual rpt, 6004-2

Jurisdiction

see Administration of justice

see Administrative law and procedure

see Courts

see Law

Justice Department

see Department of Justice

Jute

see Natural fibers

Juvenile courts and cases

Caseloads of Federal district courts, June 1989, annual rpt, 18204-2.12; 18204-8.14

Cases (delinquency), by offense, referral source, disposition, age, sex, race, State, and county, 1985, annual rpt, 6064-12

Data on juvenile justice issues, young offenders and victims, series, 6066-27

Recidivism rates of juvenile offenders, arrests, and court referrals, by offense, age, and sex, 1983 local area studies, 6068-227

Statistical Abstract of US, social, political, and economic data, 1790-2025, comprehensive annual compilation, 2324-1.1

US attorneys civil and criminal cases by type and disposition, and collections, by Federal district, FY88, annual rpt, 6004-2.1

Juvenile delinquency

Arrests, by offense, offender characteristics, and location, 1988, annual rpt, 6224-2.2

Data on crime, criminal justice admin and enforcement, and public opinion, data compilation, 1970s-88, annual rpt, 6064-6

Data on juvenile justice issues, young offenders and victims, series, 6066-27

Fed Govt funding for juvenile delinquency prevention, by program and agency, FY88, annual rpt, 6064-11

Jail population by sex, race, and for 25 jurisdictions, and instn conditions, 1983-87, annual rpt, 6066-25.18

Recidivism rates of juvenile offenders, arrests, and court referrals, by offense, age, and sex, 1983 local area studies, 6068-227

Sentences for Federal offenses, guidelines by offense and circumstances, 1989 rpt, 17668-1

State allocation of Federal educational funds, by program, recipient type, and State, 1987/88, annual rpt, 4804-8

Statistical Abstract of US, social, political, and economic data, 1790-2025, comprehensive annual compilation, 2324-1.1

see also Juvenile courts and cases

see also Juvenile detention and correctional institutions

see also Missing persons and runaways

Juvenile detention and correctional institutions

Court cases of juvenile delinquency, by offense, referral source, disposition, age, sex, race, State, and county, 1985, annual rpt, 6064-12

Court referrals by juvenile offender characteristics, and dispositions, by offense, 1984, 6066-27.2

Education (special) enrollment by age, staff, funding, and needs, by type of handicap and State, 1987/88, annual rpt, 4944-4

Facilities for juvenile correction and detention, inmates, and expenses, by instn and resident characteristics and State, 1975-85, biennial rpt, 6064-13

Jail population, for juveniles by sex, 1983-86, annual rpt, 6064-26.1

Prisoners and movements, by offense, location, and selected other characteristics, data compilation, 1930s-89, annual rpt, 6064-6.6

Prisoners in Federal instns, by sex, prison, security level, contract facility type, and region, monthly rpt series, 6242-1

Statistical Abstract of US, social, political, and economic data, 1790-2025, comprehensive annual compilation, 2324-1.1

Kahley, William J.

"Interregional Migration: Boon or Bane for the South?", 9371-1.902

"U.S. and Foreign Direct Investment Patterns", 9371-1.913

Kahn, George A.

"Lessons from West German Monetary Policy", 9381-1.907

"Output and Inflation Effects of Dollar Depreciation", 9381-10.99

Kaiser Foundation Research Institute

"Consistently High and Low Elderly Users of Medical Care: Final Report", 4186-2.22

Kalamazoo, Mich.

see also under By SMSA or MSA in the "Index by Categories"

Kalbacher, Judith Z.

"Rural and Rural Farm Population: 1988", 2546-1.439

Kampe, Ronald E.

"Rural and Urban Housing, 1930-80", 1598-245

Kampuchea

see Cambodia

Kan, William

"Long and Short of Industrial Strength Pricing", 9366-6.213

Kane, Michael D.

"Improved Ag Economy, Management Help Top 100 Co-ops Improve Returns to Members", 1122-1.910

"Nation's Largest Farmer Cooperatives Continued Economic Recovery in 1988", 1122-1.909

"Top 100 Ag Cooperatives Built '88 Cash Reserves", 1122-1.911

Kane, Sally M.

"Economics of Ethanol Production in the U.S.", 1588-132

Kankakee, Ill.

Housing vacancy rates for single and multifamily units and mobile homes, by city and ZIP code, 1989, annual MSA rpt, 9304-18.3

see also under By SMSA or MSA in the "Index by Categories"

Kansas

Agriculture census, 1987: farms, farmland, production and costs, and operator characteristics, advance State and county rpts, 2330-1.20

Agriculture census, 1987: farms, farmland, production, finances, and operator characteristics, by county, final State rpt, 2331-1.16

Bank deposits in FDIC-insured commercial and savings banks, by instn, State, and county, as of June 1988, annual regional rpt, 9295-3.5

Coal production and mines by county, prices, productivity, miners, reserves, and stocks, by mining method and State, 1987-88, annual rpt, 3164-25

County Business Patterns, 1987: employment, establishments, and payroll, by SIC 2- to 4-digit industry and county, annual State rpt, 2326-8.18

Deaths and rates, by detailed location, cause, and demographic characteristics, 1987, US Vital Statistics annual rpt, 4144-3.1

DOD prime contract awards, by contractor, service branch, State, and city, FY88, annual rpt, 3544-22

Employment, earnings, and hours, by selected SIC 1- to 4-digit industry, State, and for 262 MSAs, 1972-87, 6748-81.2

Fed Govt spending in States and local areas, by type, State, county, and city, FY88, annual rpt, 2464-3

Fed Govt spending in States, by type, program, agency, and State, FY88, annual rpt, 2464–2

HHS financial aid, by program, recipient, State, and city, FY88, annual regional listing, 4004–3.7

Homeless children educational enrollment and needs, 1988, annual State rpt, 4804–35.17

Hwy admin and gasoline tax revenue proposed transfer from Fed Govt to States, issues, with motor fuel taxes by selected State, 1988 rpt, 10048–72

Income (personal) per capita and by source, and earnings by industry div, by State, MSA, and county, 1982-87, annual regional rpt, 2704–2.3

Mineral Industry Surveys, State reviews of production, 1988, preliminary annual rpt, 5614–6

Minerals Yearbook, 1987, Vol 2 preprints: State review of production and sales by commodity, and business activity, annual rpt, 5604–16.17

Minerals Yearbook, 1987, Vol 2: State reviews of production, sales, and firms, by commodity, and business activity, annual rpt, 5604–34

Nursing home compliance with Medicare and Medicaid regulations, and patient characteristics, by facility, 1987/88, annual State rpt, 4654–15.17

Retail trade census, 1987: employment, establishments, sales, and payroll, by SIC 2- to 4-digit kind of business, MSA, county, and city, State rpt, 2397–1.17

Savings instns, FHLB 10th District members finances and lending by State and MSA, monthly table, 9302–22

Savings instns, FHLB 10th District members financial condition, by State, quarterly rpt, 9302–34

Service industries census, 1987: employment, establishments, receipts, and payroll, by SIC 2- to 4-digit kind of business, MSA, county, and city, State rpt, 2391–1.17

Statistical Abstract of US, social, political, and economic data, with foreign comparisons, 1790-2025, comprehensive annual compilation, 2324–1

Water supply and quality in streams and lakes, and groundwater levels in wells, by drainage basin, 1987, annual State rpt, 5666–10.15

Wholesale trade census, 1987: employment, establishments, finances, and operations, by SIC 2- to 4-digit kind of business, MSA, county, and city, State rpt, 2405–1.17

Wildlife-related recreation, hunting, and fishing participation and spending, detailed data, 1985 survey, quinquennial State rpt, 5506–6.16

see also Kansas City, Kans.

see also Topeka, Kans.

see also Wichita, Kans.

see also under By State in the "Index by Categories"

Kansas City, Kans.

CPI by component for US city average, and by region, population size, and for 27 metro areas, monthly rpt, 6762–2

Drug test results at arrest, by drug type, offense, and sex, for selected urban areas, quarterly rpt, 6062–3

Housing starts and completions authorized by building permits in 40 MSAs, quarterly rpt, 2382–9

Wages by occupation, and benefits for office and plant workers, 1988 survey, periodic MSA rpt, 6785–11.3

Wages by occupation, for office and plant workers, 1989 survey, periodic MSA rpt, 6785–12.7

see also under By City and By SMSA or MSA in the "Index by Categories"

Kansas City, Mo.

CPI by component for US city average, and by region, population size, and for 27 metro areas, monthly rpt, 6762–2

Drug test results at arrest, by drug type, offense, and sex, for selected urban areas, quarterly rpt, 6062–3

Housing starts and completions authorized by building permits in 40 MSAs, quarterly rpt, 2382–9

Wages by occupation, and benefits for office and plant workers, 1988 survey, periodic MSA rpt, 6785–11.3

Wages by occupation, for office and plant workers, 1989 survey, periodic MSA rpt, 6785–12.7

see also under By City and By SMSA or MSA in the "Index by Categories"

Kapantais, Gloria

"Characteristics of Persons Dying from AIDS. Preliminary Data from the 1986 National Mortality Followback Survey", 4146–8.178

"Characteristics of Persons Dying of Diseases of Heart. Preliminary Data from the 1986 National Mortality Followback Survey", 4146–8.177

Kaplan, Carol G.

"Federal Criminal Cases, 1980-87", 6066–19.50

Kappel, Steven

"AIDS Knowledge and Attitudes Among Adults in Vermont", 4042–3.938

Karber, Phillip A.

"Gorbachev's Force Reductions and the Restructuring of Soviet Forces", 21208–29

Karrenbrock, Jeffrey D.

"Changing Role of Mining in the Eighth District", 9391–16.904

"1988 Drought: Its Impact on District Agriculture", 9391–1.911

Kasman, Bruce

"Examination of Interest Rate Divergences Among the Major Industrial Countries", 9385–9

"External Adjustment and U.S. Macroeconomic Performance", 9385–1.906

"Interest Rate Divergences Among the Major Industrial Nations", 9385–1.902

"U.S. Interest Rates and Exchange Rates: Analysis and Interpretation", 9385–9

Kasper, Judith D.

"Beneficiary Selection, Use, and Charges in Two Medicare Capitation Demonstrations", 4652–1.904

Kasprzyk, Daniel

"Survey of Income and Program Participation: An Overview and Discussion of Research Issues", 2626–10.80

Kasten, Rick

"Medicare Catastrophic Coverage Act of 1988", 26306–3.105

Keane, Michael P.

"Are Economic Forecasts Rational?", 9383–6.903

Keeley, Michael C.

"Deposit Insurance, Risk, and Market Power in Banking", 9393–10.6

"Stock Price Effects of Bank Holding Company Securities Issuance", 9393–8.901

Keene, Roger E.

"Use and Cost of Physician and Supplier Services Under Medicare, 1986", 4652–1.936

"Use and Cost of Short-Stay Hospital Inpatient Services Under Medicare, 1986", 4652–1.945

"Use and Cost of Skilled Nursing Facility Services Under Medicare, 1987", 4652–1.954

Kelch, David R.

"Europe 1992: Implications for Agriculture", 1524–4.1

Kelley, James

"National Transportation Statistics: Annual Report, 1989", 7304–2

Kelly, Brendan P.

"Ringed Seal Winter Ecology and Effects of Noise Disturbance", 2176–1.27

Kelly, S. T.

"Trends in Duck Breeding Populations, 1955-89", 5504–30

Kelly, William F.

"Comparison of Selected EIA-782 Data with Other Data Sources", 3162–11.903

Kelso, Wash.

Housing vacancy rates for single and multifamily units and mobile homes, by city and ZIP code, 1988, annual MSA rpt, 9304–21.2

Kemp, Donald S.

"Balance-of-Payments Concepts—What Do They Really Mean?", 9375–14

Kemper, Peter

"Spouses and Children of Disabled Elders: Potential and Active Caregivers", 4186–7.5

Kenadjian, Berdj

"Gross Tax Gap Trends According to New IRS Estimates, Income Years 1973-92", 8302–2.902

Kendell, James M.

"Future of Electric Generating Capacity", 3162–35.901

Kennedy, James E.

"Effect of Bayesian Priors on the Moving-Average Representation of Vector Autoregressions", 9366–6.193

Kennedy, Stephen D.

"Administrative Costs of the Housing Voucher and Certificate Programs", 5186–14.2

Kennewick, Wash.

see also under By SMSA or MSA in the "Index by Categories"

Kenosha, Wis.

see also under By SMSA or MSA in the "Index by Categories"

Kentucky

Agriculture census, 1987: farms, farmland, production and costs, and operator characteristics, advance State and county rpts, 2330–1.21

Agriculture census, 1987: farms, farmland, production, finances, and operator characteristics, by county, final State rpt, 2331–1.17

Appalachian Regional Commission funding, by project and State, planned FY89, annual rpt, 9084–3

Bank deposits in FDIC-insured commercial and savings banks, by instn, State, and county, as of June 1988, annual regional rpt, 9295–3.3

Coal production and mines by county, prices, productivity, miners, reserves, and stocks, by mining method and State, 1987-88, annual rpt, 3164–25

Collective bargaining calendar for southeastern States, 1989, annual rpt, 6946–1.73

County Business Patterns, 1987: employment, establishments, and payroll, by SIC 2- to 4-digit industry and county, annual State rpt, 2326–8.19

Deaths and rates, by detailed location, cause, and demographic characteristics, 1987, US Vital Statistics annual rpt, 4144–3.1

DOD prime contract awards, by contractor, service branch, State, and city, FY88, annual rpt, 3544–22

Economic and banking conditions, for Fed Reserve 8th District, quarterly rpt with articles, 9391–16

Employment and unemployment, for 8 southeastern States, 1987-88, annual rpt, 6944–2

Employment by industry div, earnings, and hours, for 8 southeastern States, quarterly press release, 6942–7

Employment, earnings, and hours, by selected SIC 1- to 4-digit industry, State, and for 262 MSAs, 1972-87, 6748–81.2

Employment stability in rural areas, impacts of industrial growth and other factors, 1979, 1598–255

Fed Govt spending in States and local areas, by type, State, county, and city, FY88, annual rpt, 2464–3

Fed Govt spending in States, by type, program, agency, and State, FY88, annual rpt, 2464–2

HHS financial aid, by program, recipient, State, and city, FY88, annual regional listing, 4004–3.4

Homeless children educational enrollment and needs, 1988, annual State rpt, 4804–35.18

Income (personal) per capita and by source, and earnings by industry div, by State, MSA, and county, 1982-87, annual regional rpt, 2704–2.4

Mineral Industry Surveys, State reviews of production, 1988, preliminary annual rpt, 5614–6

Minerals Yearbook, 1987, Vol 2 preprints: State review of production and sales by commodity, and business activity, annual rpt, 5604–16.18

Minerals Yearbook, 1987, Vol 2: State reviews of production, sales, and firms, by commodity, and business activity, annual rpt, 5604–34

Nursing home compliance with Medicare and Medicaid regulations, and patient characteristics, by facility, 1987/88, annual State rpt, 4654–15.18

Retail trade census, 1987: employment, establishments, sales, and payroll, by SIC 2- to 4-digit kind of business, MSA, county, and city, State rpt, 2397–1.18

Savings instns, FHLB 5th District members finances and lending by State, monthly rpt, 9302–8

Service industries census, 1987: employment, establishments, receipts, and payroll, by SIC 2- to 4-digit kind of business, MSA, county, and city, State rpt, 2391–1.18

Statistical Abstract of US, social, political, and economic data, with foreign comparisons, 1790-2025, comprehensive annual compilation, 2324–1

Textile mill employment, earnings, and hours, for 8 Southeastern States, quarterly press release, 6942–1

Tobacco (burley) finances, operations, and labor, for Kentucky and Tennessee, 1984, 1568–277

Water resources dev projects of Army Corps of Engineers, characteristics, and costs, 1950s-87, biennial State rpt, 3756–2.18

Water supply and quality in streams and lakes, and groundwater levels in wells, by drainage basin, 1987, annual State rpt, 5666–10.16

Wholesale trade census, 1987: employment, establishments, finances, and operations, by SIC 2- to 4-digit kind of business, MSA, county, and city, State rpt, 2405–1.18

Wildlife-related recreation, hunting, and fishing participation and spending, detailed data, 1985 survey, quinquennial State rpt, 5506–6.17

see also Fayette County, Ky.

see also Hopkinsville, Ky.

see also Lexington, Ky.

see also Louisville, Ky.

see also under By State in the "Index by Categories"

Kenya

Agricultural and food production and indexes, total and for selected commodities, by country, 1970s-88, annual rpt, 1524–12

Agricultural exports of Africa by commodity, and relation to economic conditions and other factors, by country, 1960s-87, 1528–280

Agricultural imports and food aid needs under alternative weather assumptions, for 17 African countries, projected to 1995, 1528–279

Agricultural policy impacts on economic dev, with background data for 6 developing countries, 1960s-86, 1528–283

Agricultural production, prices, and trade, by country, 1960s-89, annual world region rpt, 1524–4.2

Agricultural trade of US, by detailed commodity and country, 1988, semiannual rpt, 1522–4

AID activities and funding by project and function, FY90, and developing countries summary socioeconomic data from 1960s, annual rpt, 9904–4.5

AID economic aid to developing countries, obligations and disbursements by country, quarterly rpt, 9912–4

AID loans repayment status and terms by program and country, and status of predecessor agency loans, quarterly rpt, 9912–3

Auto imports from US, trade barriers by country, 1988, annual rpt, 444–2

Economic and military aid and loans from US and intl agencies, by program and country, FY46-87, annual rpt, 9914–5

Economic conditions, policy, and trade practices, by country, 1986-88, annual rpt, 21384–5

Economic, social, political, and geographic summary data, by country, 1989, annual factbook, 9114–2

Exports and imports of US, by commodity and country, 1970-87, world area rpt, 9116–1.4

Human rights conditions in 170 countries, 1988, annual rpt, 21384–3

Labor conditions, union coverage, and work accidents, 1989 annual country rpt, 6366–4.10

Military aid of US, arms sales, and training programs costs and budget requests, by program, world region, and country, FY88-90, annual rpt, 7144–13

Military spending, arms trade, and force strengths, with govt spending and population, by country, 1977-87, annual rpt, 9824–1

Minerals Yearbook, 1987, Vol 3: foreign country reviews of production, trade, and policy, by commodity, annual rpt, 5604–35

Minerals Yearbook, 1987, Vol 3 preprints: foreign country review of production, trade, and policy, by commodity, annual rpt, 5604–23.81

Older persons population and selected characteristics, 1980s and projected to 2020, country rpt, 2326–19.2

Population size, growth rates, and components of change, by country, projected 1989-2020 and trends from 1950, biennial rpt, 2324–9

UN voting record and share of votes in agreement with US, by issue, country, and world area, 1988, annual rpt, 7004–18

see also under By Foreign Country in the "Index by Categories"

Keogh plans

see Individual retirement arrangements

Kerns, Wilmer L.

"Private Social Welfare Expenditures, 1972-87", 4742–1.928

Kerosene

Freight (waterborne domestic and foreign) by commodity, traffic, and passengers, by port and waterway, 1987, annual rpt, 3754–3

Housing and households detailed characteristics, and unit and neighborhood quality, MSA surveys, series, 2485–6

Housing energy use, costs, and conservation, and household and housing characteristics, survey rpt series, 3166–7

Manufacturing census, 1987: financial and operating data, for SIC 4-digit industries by product, preliminary rpt, 2491–1.41

Minerals Yearbook, 1987, Vol 3 preprints: foreign country reviews of production, trade, and policy, by commodity, annual rpt series, 5604–23

Price indexes (producer), by stage of processing and detailed commodity, monthly rpt, 6762–6

Price indexes (producer), by stage of processing and detailed commodity, monthly 1988, annual rpt, 6764–2

Prices and spending for fuel, by type, end-use sector, and State, 1987, annual rpt, 3164–64

Prices and volume of oil products sold and purchased by refiners, processors, and distributors, by product, end-use sector, PAD district, and State, monthly rpt with articles, 3162–11; 3164–85

Supply, demand, and movement of crude oil, gas liquids, and refined products, by PAD district and State, 1988 and trends from 1973, annual rpt, 3164–2

Supply, demand, and prices, by fuel type and end-use sector, with foreign comparisons, 1988 and trends from 1949, annual rpt, 3164–74.1

Key, Sydney J.
"Activities of International Banking Facilities: The Early Experience", 9375–14

Kickbacks
see Corruption and bribery

Kidnapping
Aircraft hijackings, on-board explosions, and other crime, US and foreign incidents, 1983-87, annual rpt, 7504–31

Children abducted and murdered by strangers, and rates, by victim sex, age, and race, 1976-84, 6066–27.1

Court civil and criminal caseloads for Federal district, appeals, and special courts, June 1989, annual rpt, 18204–2; 18204–8

Criminal case processing in Federal courts by disposition, and prisoners, by offense and jurisdiction, 1985-87, annual rpt, 6064–6.5; 6064–6.6

Criminal case processing in Federal district courts, and dispositions, by offense, district, and offender characteristics, 1984, annual rpt, 6064–29

Criminal case processing in Federal district courts, disposition by offense, 1980-87, 6066–19.50

Prisoners in State instns, by offense, criminal history, and inmate, family, and victim characteristics, 1986, annual rpt, 6064–26.3

Recidivism rates of prisoners released in 1983, by offense and prisoner characteristics, 1983-86, 6066–19.48

Sentences for Federal crimes, guidelines use and results by offense and district, and Sentencing Commission activities, 1988, annual rpt, 17664–1

Sentences for Federal offenses, guidelines by offense and circumstances, 1989 rpt, 17668–1

Sentences for felonies, by sentence type and offense, 1983-86, 6066–19.52

Terrorist (intl) incidents, casualties, and attacks on US targets, by attack type and country, 1980-88, 7008–56

Terrorist (intl) incidents, casualties, and attacks on US targets, by attack type and world area, 1968-88, annual rpt, 7004–13

US attorneys civil and criminal cases by type and disposition, and collections, by Federal district, FY88, annual rpt, 6004–2.1

Wiretaps authorized, costs, arrests, trials, and convictions, by offense and jurisdiction, 1988, annual rpt, 18204–7
see also Hostages

Kidney diseases
see Urogenital diseases

Kilgore, Catherine C.
"Barite Availability: Market Economy Countries. A Minerals Availability Appraisal", 5606–4.26

Killeen, Tex.
see also under By SMSA or MSA in the "Index by Categories"

Kincaid, D. Lawrence
"Getting the Message: The Communication for Young People Project", 9916–3.50

Kindergarten
see Preschool education

King, B. Frank
"Interstate Banking Developments in the 1980s", 9371–1.909

King County, Wash.
Older persons care by family members, caregivers stress and respite services, for King County, Wash, 1983-87, article, 4652–1.916

Pedestrian deaths, by circumstances and characteristics of victim, injury, and vehicle, 1985-86 local area study, article, 4042–3.927

Kingsport, Tenn.
see also under By SMSA or MSA in the "Index by Categories"

Kinoshita, Richard K.
"Economic Status of the Washington, Oregon, and California Groundfish Fishery in 1987", 2164–16.1

Kiribati
Economic, social, political, and geographic summary data, by country, 1989, annual factbook, 9114–2

Human rights conditions in 170 countries, 1988, annual rpt, 21384–3

Population size, growth rates, and components of change, by country, projected 1989-2020 and trends from 1950, biennial rpt, 2324–9
see also under By Foreign Country in the "Index by Categories"

Kirstein, Bruce E.
"Ocean-Ice Oil-Weathering Computer Program User's Manual", 2176–1.25

Kitchen, John
"Foreign Investment in U.S. Cropland: Some Evidence on the Role of Exchange Rates, Interest Rates, and Returns on Cropland", 1528–287

"Interest Rates and Commodity Prices", 1502–3.902

Kitchen utensils and appliances
see Household appliances and equipment
see Household supplies and utensils

Klamath Falls, Oreg.
Wages by occupation, and benefits for office and plant workers, 1989 survey, periodic MSA rpt, 6785–3.9

Klarquist, Virginia L.
"Productivity in the Carburetors, Pistons, and Valves Industry", 6722–1.911

Kleckner, Dean R.
"Farmer's View", 1004–16.1

Klein, Bruce W.
"Profile of the Working Poor", 6722–1.948

Klein, C. John, III
"Characterization of Salinity and Temperature for Mobile Bay", 2176–7.12

Klein, Christopher C.
"Economics of Sham Litigation: Theory, Cases, and Policy", 9406–1.59

Klein, Deborah P.
"Developing Statistics To Meet Society's Needs", 6722–1.949

Kleingartner, Larry
"Sunflower Markets: A Function of Government Production Policy and Oil Export Program", 1004–16.1

Kleinman, Joel C.
"Firearm Mortality Among Children and Youth", 4146–8.181

"Trends and Current Status in Childhood Mortality: U.S., 1900-85. Vital and Health Statistics Series 3", 4147–3.27

Klima, Edward F.
"Impacts of Explosive Removal of Offshore Petroleum Platforms on Sea Turtles and Dolphins", 2162–1.902

Klindworth, Keith A.
"Railcar Shortages for Grain Shippers, A Current Overview", 1278–15

"Railcars for Grain: Future Need and Availability", 1278–14

Kline, Susan
"Jail Inmates, 1987", 6066–25.18

Klitgaard, Thomas
"Exploring the Effects of Capital Movements on M1 and the Economy", 9385–9

"U.S. Trade with Taiwan and South Korea", 9385–1.904

Knepper, Paula R.
"Student Progress in College: NLS-72 Postsecondary Education Transcript Study, 1984", 4836–1.12

Knickman, James R.
"Comparing the Cost Effectiveness of Alternative Models for Organizing Services for Persons with AIDS", 4186–9.6

Knight, Richard R.
"Yellowstone Grizzly Bear Investigations, Annual Report of the Interagency Study Team, 1988", 5544–4

Knit fabrics
see Clothing and clothing industry
see Textile industry and fabrics

Knoxville, Tenn.
Railroad-hwy grade-crossing warning devices, costs and effectiveness of alternative devices, local area study, 1985-86, 7558–108
see also under By City and By SMSA or MSA in the "Index by Categories"

Knudson, Mary
"Technology: Are We Running Out of Steam?", 1522–3.909

Knutilla, R. L.
"Water Resources Activities of the USGS in New Mexico, FY88", 5668–86

Koch, Hugo K.
"Ambulatory Medical Care Rendered in Physicians' Offices: U.S., 1975", 4147–16.2

"Practice Patterns of the Office-Based Ophthalmologist, National Ambulatory Medical Care Survey, 1985", 4146–8.166

"Utilization of Controlled Drugs in Office-Based Ambulatory Care: National Ambulatory Medical Care Survey, 1985", 4146–8.179

Koch, Peter
"Proposed Wood Products Plant To Utilize Sub-Sawlog Size and Dead Lodgepole Pine in Northwestern Montana: A Technical and Economic Feasibility Analysis", 1208–308

Kochan, Thomas A.
"Institutionalizing and Diffusing Innovations in Industrial Relations", 6306–3.1

Kochanek, Kenneth D.
"Induced Terminations of Pregnancy: Reporting States, 1985 and 1986", 4146–5.108

Koenig, Evan F.
"Are the Permanent-Income Model of Consumption and the Accelerator Model of Investment Compatible?", 9379–12.47
"Investment and the Nominal Interest Rate, the Variable Velocity Case", 9379–12.27
"Real Money Balances and the Timing of Consumption: An Empirical Investigation", 9379–12.38

Kokomo, Ind.
see also under By SMSA or MSA in the "Index by Categories"

Kokoski, Mary F.
"Autocovariance of Expenditure Shares from Consumer Expenditure Survey Data", 6886–6.60
"Changes in Taxes, Prices, and the Cost-of-Living: An Analysis of Tax Reform", 6886–6.68
"Consumer Price Indices by Demographic Group", 6886–6.36
"Cost-of-Living Measures and Substitution Bias by Demographic Group", 6886–6.27
"Empirical Analysis of Intertemporal and Demographic Variations in Consumer Preferences", 6886–6.13
"Empirical Performance of Aggregate, Fixed Weight Cost-of-Living Indices", 6886–6.17
"Experimental Cost-of-Living Indexes: A Summary of Current Research", 6722–1.935
"Indices of Household Welfare and the Value of Leisure Time", 6886–6.28

Kominski, Robert
"Educational Attainment in the U.S.: March 1987 and 1986", 2546–1.431

Koonin, Lisa M.
"Maternal Mortality Surveillance, U.S., 1980-85", 4202–7.903

Koopman, Robert B.
"Efficiency and Growth in Agriculture: A Comparative Study of the Soviet Union, U.S., Canada, and Finland", 1528–292

Kopcke, Richard W.
"Roles of Debt and Equity in Financing Corporate Investments", 9373–1.912

Korb, Roslyn
"Student Financing of Graduate and Professional Education", 4846–3.2

Korea, North
Agricultural and food production and indexes, total and for selected commodities, by country, 1970s-88, annual rpt, 1524–12
Agricultural trade of US, by detailed commodity and country, 1988, semiannual rpt, 1522–4
Background Notes, summary social, political, and economic data, 1989 rpt, 7006–2.46
Cuba economic conditions, agricultural and industrial production and distribution, trade, and intl economic relations, 1980-87 with trends from 1961, 9118–8

Economic, social, political, and geographic summary data, by country, 1989, annual factbook, 9114–2
Exports and imports of US with Communist countries, by detailed commodity and country, quarterly rpt with articles, 9882–2
Human rights conditions in 170 countries, 1988, annual rpt, 21384–3
Military, economic, technological, and trade conditions of Pacific Basin countries, 1970s-85, compilation of papers, 3908–4
Military spending, arms trade, and force strengths, with govt spending and population, by country, 1977-87, annual rpt, 9824–1
Minerals production, reserves, and industry role in domestic economy and world supply, 1988 country rpt, 5606–1.17
Minerals Yearbook, 1987, Vol 3: foreign country reviews of production, trade, and policy, by commodity, annual rpt, 5604–35
Minerals Yearbook, 1987, Vol 3 preprints: foreign country review of production, trade, and policy, by commodity, annual rpt, 5604–23.85
Population size, growth rates, and components of change, by country, projected 1989-2020 and trends from 1950, biennial rpt, 2324–9
see also under By Foreign Country in the "Index by Categories"

Korea, South
Agricultural and food production and indexes, total and for selected commodities, by country, 1970s-88, annual rpt, 1524–12
Agricultural subsidies, consumer and producer equivalents by program, commodity, and major US trading partner, 1982-86, 1528–275
Agricultural trade by commodity and country, prices, and world market devs, monthly rpt, 1922–12
Agricultural trade of US, by detailed commodity and country, 1988, semiannual rpt, 1522–4
Agricultural trade of US with Asia, Middle East, and North Africa, by commodity and country, 1962-86, 1528–277
AID loans repayment status and terms by program and country, and status of predecessor agency loans, quarterly rpt, 9912–3
Alcohol use, abuse, treatment, and views of racial and ethnic groups in US and native countries, by selected characteristics, 1988 compilation of papers, 4488–12
Batteries for motorcycles from Korea at less than fair value, injury to US industry, investigation with background financial and operating data, 1989 rpt, 9886–14.265
Businesses (foreign) activity in US, income tax returns, assets, and income statement items, by industry div, country, and world area, 1984-85, article, 8302–2.920
Coal production, trade, and govt subsidies, by country and country group, 1973-87 and projected to 2000, 2048–144
Dollar exchange rates, and impacts of currency appreciation on current account and trade balances and economic indicators, for 3 Asian countries, 1980s-90, GAO rpt, 26123–234

Economic and military aid and loans from US and intl agencies, by program and country, FY46-87, annual rpt, 9914–5
Economic conditions in Communist, OECD, and selected other countries, 1960s-88, annual rpt, 9114–4
Economic conditions, income, production, prices, employment, and trade, 1989 periodic country rpt, 2046–4.74
Economic conditions, policy, and trade practices, by country, 1986-88, annual rpt, 21384–5
Economic indicators of developing countries, problem debtors compared to other borrowers, by country, 1973-84, 1528–285
Economic, social, political, and geographic summary data, by country, 1989, annual factbook, 9114–2
Export and import balance impacts of exchange rates and foreign and domestic economic indicators, for Taiwan and South Korea, 1974-87, article, 9393–8.905
Export and import balances of US, and dollar exchange rates, with 4 Asian countries 1980s-89, semiannual rpt, 8002–14
Exports and imports of US, by commodity and country, 1970-87, world area rpt, 9116–1.2
Exports and imports of US, by selected country, country group, and commodity group, 1988, annual rpt, 2044–37
Exports and imports of US with Asian countries by commodity, and free trade area proposal, 1985-88, 9886–4.135
Exports and imports, trade agreements and relations, and USITC investigations, 1988, annual rpt, 9884–5
Exports, imports, and trade balance of South Korea and Taiwan with US, 1985-88, article, 9385–1.904
Fruit production, consumption, trade, and tariffs, for South Korea, by commodity, 1977-88, article, 1925–34.907
Human rights conditions in 170 countries, 1988, annual rpt, 21384–3
Imports of goods, services, and investment from US, trade barriers, impacts, and US actions, by country, 1988, annual rpt, 444–2
Imports of US given duty-free treatment for value of US material sent abroad, and impacts on US industry and employment, by commodity and country, 1987, annual rpt, 9884–14
Labor conditions, union coverage, and work accidents, 1989 annual country rpt, 6366–4.24; 6366–4.61
Machinery belts from 8 countries, injury to US industry from foreign subsidized and less than fair value imports, investigation with background financial and operating data, 1989 rpt, 9886–19.66
Manufacturing labor productivity and unit costs for 14 countries, 1950-88, annual press release, 6864–1
Military aid of US, arms sales, and training programs costs and budget requests, by program, world region, and country, FY88-90, annual rpt, 7144–13
Military, economic, technological, and trade conditions of Pacific Basin countries, 1970s-85, compilation of papers, 3908–4

Military spending, arms trade, and force strengths, with govt spending and population, by country, 1977-87, annual rpt, 9824-1

Minerals production, reserves, and industry role in domestic economy and world supply, 1988 country rpt, 5606-1.17

Minerals Yearbook, 1987, Vol 3: foreign country reviews of production, trade, and policy, by commodity, annual rpt, 5604-35

Minerals Yearbook, 1987, Vol 3 preprints: foreign country review of production, trade, and policy, by commodity, annual rpt, 5604-23.41

Multinatl US firms and foreign affiliates finances and operations, by industry of parent firm and affiliate, world area, and country, preliminary 1987, annual rpt, 2704-5

Mushroom (canned) trade by selected country, supply and use for 2 Asia countries, and US production and imports, various periods 1979-89, annual article, 1925-34.935

Nitrocellulose (industrial) from 7 countries at less than fair value, injury to US industry, investigation with background financial and operating data, 1989 rpt, 9886-14.270

Nuclear power generation in US and 19 non-Communist countries, monthly rpt, 3162-24.10

Nuclear power plant capacity, generation, and operating status, by plant and foreign and US location, 1988 and projected to 2020, annual rpt, 3164-57

Population size, growth rates, and components of change, by country, projected 1989-2020 and trends from 1950, biennial rpt, 2324-9

Port facilities, operations, and impacts on US agricultural exports, for major Far East Asia ports, 1970s-87, 1278-13

Ships in world merchant fleet, and tonnage, by country of registry, as of Jan 1988, annual rpt, 7704-3

Steel export ceilings under voluntary restraint agreements, by country and product, with Western US steel industry impact, 1989 rpt, 9886-4.136

Steel imports of US under voluntary restraint agreement, by product, customs district, and country, with US industry operating data, monthly rpt, 9882-13

Sweaters from 3 countries at less than fair value, injury to US industry, investigation with background financial and operating data, 1989 rpt, 9886-14.272

Telephones and equipment from 3 countries at less than fair value, injury to US industry, investigation with background financial and operating data, 1989 rpt, 9886-14.251

Tobacco and cigarette production, trade, and use, for South Korea, 1980-88, article, 1925-16.902

Tobacco trade of US with 3 Asian countries, 1984-88, article, 1925-16.908

US Air Force Pacific basin airlift of aircraft parts, traffic, shipments, and impacts on force readiness, 1986-88, GAO rpt, 26123-230

see also under By Foreign Country in the "Index by Categories"

Korean War
see Veterans benefits and pensions
see War

Korson, Charles S.
"Economic Status of the California Dungeness Crab Fishery in 1986-87", 2164-16.3
"Economic Status of the Washington, Oregon, and California Groundfish Fishery in 1987", 2164-16.1
"Economic Status of the Washington, Oregon and California Pink Shrimp Fishery in 1987", 2164-16.2

Kosrae
see Micronesia Federated States

Kovar, Mary G.
"Data Systems of the National Center for Health Statistics: Vital and Health Series 1", 4147-1.24

Kowalczyk, George I.
"Using Marginal Analysis To Evaluate Health Spending Trends", 4652-1.927

Kowalewski, K. J.
"Bankruptcy in the Life-Cycle Consumption Model", 9377-9.72

Kozak, Lola J.
"Hospital Inpatient Surgery: U.S., 1983-87", 4146-8.171
"Hospital Use in France and the U.S.", 4147-5.4

Kozielec, John A.
"Statistics of Income Domestic Special Studies", 8302-2.908

Kraenzle, Charles A.
"California Replaces Iowa as Leading State in Cooperative Business Volume", 1122-1.908
"Dairy Farmers Make Greatest Use of Co-ops for Marketing, Supplies", 1122-1.903
"Farmer Cooperatives: Commercial Farmers Members and Use", 1128-53
"Farmer Cooperatives: Members and Use", 1128-54
"Majority of Farmers Using Co-ops Do Most of Business with Them", 1122-1.904

Krajewski, R.
"Soybean Costs of Production in Argentina, Brazil, and the U.S.: A Regional Farm Budget Analysis", 1522-3.902

Kramer, Deborah A.
"Gallium and Gallium Arsenide: Supply, Technology, and Uses", 5606-9.1

Krause, Kenneth R.
"Farmer Buying/Selling Strategies and Growth of Crop Farms", 1548-353
"Market Exchange Economies and Other Factors in the Growth of Crop Farms", 1561-4.901

Krauss, Ulrich H.
"International Strategic Minerals Inventory Summary Reports: Natural Graphite", 5666-21.8

Kreicher, Lawrence L.
"Eurodollar Arbitrage", 9375-14

Kreling, David H.
"Assessing Potential Prescription Reimbursement Changes: Estimated Acquisition Costs in Wisconsin", 4652-1.933

Krieger, Reva
"Real Exchange Rates, Sectoral Shifts, and Aggregate Unemployment", 9366-6.206

"Sectoral and Aggregate Shocks to Industrial Output in Germany, Japan and Canada", 9366-6.189

Krissoff, Barry
"When Does Trade Liberalization in Tropical Beverages Improve Export Revenues?", 1522-3.922

Kronick, Richard
"Adolescent Health Insurance Status", 26358-205.

Krueger, Alan B.
"Structure of Supervision and Pay in Hospitals", 9377-9.79

Krzynowek, Judith
"Proximate Composition and Fatty Acid and Cholesterol Content of 22 Species of Northwest Atlantic Finfish", 2168-111

Ku, Leighton
"Factors Influencing Early Prenatal Enrollment in the WIC Program", 4042-3.929

Kuchler, Fred
"Issues Raised by New Agricultural Technologies: Livestock Growth Hormones", 1548-346

Kuczmarski, Robert J.
"Anthropometric Data and Prevalence of Overweight for Hispanics: 1982-84", 4147-11.207

Kuester, Kathleen A.
"Bank Equity Values, Bank Risk, and the Implied Market Value of Banks' Assets, Liabilities, and Deposit Insurance", 9366-6.212
"Bank Equity Values, Bank Risk, and the Implied Market Values of Banks' Assets and Liabilities", 9366-6.181

Kuo, Chin S.
"Emerging Mineral Industry of China", 5606-5.7

Kupiec, Paul H.
"Animal Spirits, Margin Requirements, and Stock Price Volatility", 9366-6.205
"Futures Margins and Stock Price Volatility: Is There Any Link?", 9366-6.209
"Initial Margin Requirements and Stock Returns Volatility: Another Look", 9366-6.167
"Microeconomic Sources of Beta Risk Instability", 9366-6.183
"Survey of Exchange-Traded Basket Instruments", 9366-6.176

Kushnirsky, Fyodor
"New Challenges to Soviet Official Statistics: A Methodological Survey", 9118-4

Kutscher, Ronald E.
"Projections Summary and Emerging Issues", 6722-1.956

Kuwait
Agricultural and food production and indexes, total and for selected commodities, by country, 1970s-88, annual rpt, 1524-12

Agricultural trade of US, by detailed commodity and country, 1988, semiannual rpt, 1522-4

Auto imports from US, trade barriers by country, 1988, annual rpt, 444-2

Economic and military aid and loans from US and intl agencies, by program and country, FY46-87, annual rpt, 9914-5

Economic conditions, income, production, prices, employment, and trade, 1989 periodic country rpt, 2046-4.12; 2046-4.109

Economic conditions, policy, and trade practices, by country, 1986-88, annual rpt, 21384–5

Economic, social, political, and geographic summary data, by country, 1989, annual factbook, 9114–2

Exports and imports of US, by commodity and country, 1970-87, world area rpt, 9116–1.3

Exports and imports of US, by selected country, country group, and commodity group, 1988, annual rpt, 2044–37

Human rights conditions in 170 countries, 1988, annual rpt, 21384–3

Labor conditions, union coverage, and work accidents, 1989 annual country rpt, 6366–4.23

Military aid of US, arms sales, and training programs costs and budget requests, by program, world region, and country, FY88-90, annual rpt, 7144–13

Military spending, arms trade, and force strengths, with govt spending and population, by country, 1977-87, annual rpt, 9824–1

Minerals Yearbook, 1987, Vol 3: foreign country reviews of production, trade, and policy, by commodity, annual rpt, 5604–35

Minerals Yearbook, 1987, Vol 3 preprints: foreign country review of production, trade, and policy, by commodity, annual rpt, 5604–23.42

Oil production by major exporting countries, monthly rpt, 3162–24.10

Oil production, trade, use, and stocks, by selected country and country group, monthly rpt, 3162–42

Population size, growth rates, and components of change, by country, projected 1989-2020 and trends from 1950, biennial rpt, 2324–9

UN voting record and share of votes in agreement with US, by issue, country, and world area, 1988, annual rpt, 7004–18

see also under By Foreign Country in the "Index by Categories"

Kvasnicka, Joseph G.
"Central Banks Move To Halt the Dollar's Rise", 9375–14
"Collapse and Restructuring of the International Monetary System", 9375–14
"Dealing with the Developing Countries' 'Debt Crisis'", 9375–14
'Eurodollar Futures', 9375–14
"Eurodollars—An Important Source of Funds for American Banks", 9375–14
"European Monetary System", 9375–14
"International Banking Part II: Foreign Banks in the U.S.", 9375–14
"International Monetary Fund", 9375–14
"Net U.S. International Wealth", 9375–14
"Options on German Mark Futures Contracts", 9375–14
"Primer on Devaluation", 9375–14
"Special Drawing Rights", 9375–14
"Transactions in the U.S. Foreign Exchange Markets", 9375–14
"U.S. Balance-of-Payments Statistics: What They Are and What Do They Tell Us", 9375–14
"Why the U.S. Is Trying To Reduce the Dollar's Value", 9375–14

Kwast, Myron L.
"Are Real Estate Specializing Depositories Viable? The Evidence from Commercial Banks", 9366–6.202

Kyanite
see Nonmetallic minerals and mines

La Crosse, Wis.
Wages by occupation, for office and plant workers, 1989 survey, periodic MSA rpt, 6785–3.9
see also under By SMSA or MSA in the "Index by Categories"

Labat-Anderson, Inc.
"Mali: A Country Profile", 9916–2.70
"Philippines: A Country Profile", 9916–2.71

Labate, John
"Individual Income Tax Rates, 1986", 8302–2.918

Labeling
Alcoholic beverages warning labels and other consumer protection methods, public views by selected characteristics, 1988 survey, 8488–5
Exports of goods, services, and investment, trade barriers, impacts, and US actions, by country, 1988, annual rpt, 444–2
Fiber content in breakfast cereal and bread, health claim ads, and other factors affecting consumption, 1978-88, 9406–1.60
Gasoline octane labeling, State testing programs, violations, and penalties, as of Feb 1988, GAO rpt, 26113–409
Imports detained by FDA, by reason, product, shipper, brand, and country, monthly listing, 4062–2
Meat and poultry inspection activities and staff of Federal, State, and foreign govts, FY88, annual rpt, 1374–1
see also Trademarks

Labor
see terms listed under Employment and unemployment, general, Labor supply and demand, and Occupations

Labor Agreement Information Retrieval System
Collective bargaining multi-unit agreements of Fed Govt, by agency and labor union, as of Aug 1988, annual listing, 9847–4

Labor costs and cost indexes
Banks employment relation to labor costs, output, and technological change, US and 5 OECD countries, 1980-86, working paper, 9371–10.42
Business Conditions Digest, cyclical indicators, by economic process, monthly rpt, 2702–3.3; 2702–3.6
Capital goods manufacturing productivity, labor cost indexes, and trade and trade balance impacts of economic conditions, with foreign comparisons, 1970s-88, article, 9385–1.909
Costs and productivity of labor for private, nonfarm business, and manufacturing sectors, revised data, quarterly rpt, 6822–2
Costs and productivity of labor, indexes by sector and selected industry, 1947-88, 6728–38.6
Costs and productivity of labor, indexes, preliminary data, quarterly rpt, 6822–1

Economic indicators, prices, labor costs, and productivity, BLS econometric analyses and methodology, working paper series, 6886–6
Economic indicators targets and performance, 1960s-88 and projected to 1994, annual article, 9381–1.901
Employment and Earnings, detailed data, monthly rpt, 6742–2.7
Employment Cost Index and alternative measure of compensation costs, by component, occupation, industry group, union status, and location, 1975-89, annual rpt, 6744–20
Employment Cost Index and percent change by occupational group, industry div, region, and metro-nonmetro area, quarterly press release, 6782–5
Employment Cost Index by occupational group, industry div, union coverage, region, and metro-nonmetro area, 1975-88, 6728–38.7
Employment Cost Index, by region, selected quarters 1988-89, press release, 6946–3.15
Employment Cost Index changes for nonfarm workers, by occupation, industry div, region, and bargaining status, monthly rpt, 6782–1
Employment Cost Index, current data and annual trends, monthly rpt, 23842–1.2
Employment, earnings, and hours, by SIC 1- to 4-digit industry, monthly 1983-Feb 1989, annual rpt, 6744–4
Employment, earnings, and hours, monthly press release, 6742–5
Food marketing cost indexes, by expense category, monthly rpt with articles, 1502–4
Foreign and US manufacturing hourly compensation costs, by industry and country, series, 6826–3
Foreign and US manufacturing labor costs and indexes, by selected country, 1975-88, annual rpt, 6824–3
Foreign and US manufacturing labor costs and indexes, by selected country, 1975-88, semiannual rpt, 6822–3
Foreign and US manufacturing labor productivity and unit costs, for 14 countries, 1950-88, annual press release, 6864–1
Foreign and US output, compensation, unit labor costs, and indexes, Monthly Labor Review, 6722–1.6
Foreign countries labor conditions, output, earnings, and price indexes, by selected country, 1950-88, 6728–38.11
Foreign countries labor cost indexes, by selected country, 1980-89, article, 6722–1.926
Health Care Financing Review, provider prices, price inputs and indexes, and labor, quarterly journal, 4652–1.1
Hospital operations, ownership, staffing, and other characteristics, by urban-rural location, 1960s-88, 25148–41
Hospital reimbursement by Medicare under prospective payment system, and physician reimbursement, effect on services, finances, and beneficiary payments, 1970s-88, annual rpt, 17204–2
Hospital reimbursement by Medicare under prospective payment system, costs related to hospital characteristics, and alternative case mix indexes, 1984, article, 4652–1.922

Hospital reimbursement by Medicare under prospective payment system, methodology, inputs, and data by diagnostic group, 1989 annual rpt, 17204-1

Hourly costs, by component, occupational group, union coverage, industry div, and region, 1989, annual rpt, 6744-21

Inflation relation to labor costs and GNP, 1959-88, working paper, 9389-19.9

Japan and US labor force participation by selected characteristics, productivity, and unit labor costs, 1960s-87, article, 6722-1.910

Labor force, wages, hours, and payroll costs, by major industry group and demographic characteristics, *Survey of Current Business*, monthly rpt, 2702-1.5

Metro area employment and manufacturing output growth, relation to labor costs and area economic conditions, 1976-85, working paper, 9375-13.8

Middle Atlantic States economic conditions, Fed Reserve 3rd District, quarterly rpt, 9387-10

Monthly Labor Review, output, compensation, unit labor costs, and indexes, 6722-1.1; 6722-1.3; 6722-1.5

Statistical Abstract of US, social, political, and economic data, 1790-2025, comprehensive annual compilation, 2324-1.3

see also Employee benefits
see also Payroll
see also Social security tax
see also Unemployment insurance tax
see also Workers compensation

Labor Department
see Department of Labor

Labor force
see Employment and unemployment, general
see Employment and unemployment, local and regional
see Employment and unemployment, specific industry
see Foreign labor conditions
see Labor supply and demand

Labor law
Alien workers (unauthorized) employer sanctions, enforcement costs, compliance, and job discrimination, 1988 annual GAO rpt, 26104-19

Alien workers (unauthorized) employer sanctions impacts on farm labor supply in Western US, with background data, 1986-89, GAO rpt, 26121-310

Alien workers (unauthorized) employer sanctions impacts on wages and output under alternative levels of enforcement, 1988 technical paper, 9379-12.33

Black lung benefits and claims by State, trust fund receipts by source, and disbursements, 1987, annual rpt, 6504-3

Collective bargaining devs, 1988, annual narrative article, 6722-1.903

Court caseloads for Federal district, appeals, and bankruptcy courts, by type of suit and offense, circuit, and district, quarterly rpt, 18202-1

Court civil and criminal caseloads for Federal district, appeals, and special courts, June 1989, annual rpt, 18204-2; 18204-8

Criminal case processing in Federal district courts, and dispositions, by offense, district, and offender characteristics, 1984, annual rpt, 6064-29

DOD prime contract awards, by size and type of contract, service branch, competitive status, category, and labor standard, FY88, annual rpt, 3544-19

Farm labor costs impacts of illegal aliens employer sanctions, by farm type, size, and region, 1986, 1598-250

Fed Labor Relations Authority and Fed Service Impasses Panel activities, and cases by union, agency, and State, FY79-87, annual rpt, 13364-1

Industrial relations devs and collective bargaining agreements expiring during month, Monthly Labor Review, 6722-1

Mine safety and health enforcement, training, and funding, with casualties, by type of mine and State, FY87, annual rpt, 6664-6

Natl Labor Relations Board activities, cases, elections conducted, and litigation, FY85, annual rpt, 9584-1

Pension laws admin and enforcement under Employee Retirement Income Security Act (ERISA), 1987, annual rpt, 6304-4

State labor laws enacted, by State, 1988 annual article, 6722-1.904

Unemployment insurance laws of States, changes in coverage, benefits, tax rates, and penalties, by State, 1988, annual article, 6722-1.905

Unemployment insurance laws of States, comparison of provisions, as of Jan 1989, semiannual revisions to base edition, 6402-2

US attorneys civil and criminal cases by type and disposition, and collections, by Federal district, FY88, annual rpt, 6004-2.1; 6004-2.7

Workers compensation laws of States and Fed Govt, 1989 semiannual rpt, 6502-1

Workers compensation laws of States, changes in coverage, benefits, and premium rates, by State, 1988, annual article, 6722-1.906

see also Minimum wage

Labor-management relations, general
Assistance (financial and nonfinancial) of Fed Govt, 1989 base edition with supplements, annual listing, 104-5

Bombing incidents and casualties, by target, circumstances, and State, 1979-88, annual rpt, 8484-4.1

Collective bargaining agreement concessions relation to economic and industry financial conditions, with data by major industry and union, 1970s-88, technical paper, 9385-8.41

Collective bargaining agreement coverage of plant and office workers, by industry div and MSA, aggregate 1985-88, annual rpt, 6784-1.3

Collective bargaining agreements expiring during year, and workers covered, by firm, union, industry group, and State, 1989, annual rpt, 6784-9

Collective bargaining agreements, innovations and issues, series, 6306-3

Collective bargaining contract expirations, and industrial relations devs, current statistics and articles, Monthly Labor Review, 6722-1

Collective bargaining contract expirations, wage increases, and coverage, by major industry and selected firm and union, 1989, annual article, 6722-1.902

Collective bargaining devs, 1988, annual narrative article, 6722-1.903

Collective bargaining negotiated wages, relation to contract duration and inflation and unemployment rates, model description and results for Canada, 1970s-83, working paper, 9387-8.191

Collective bargaining wage and benefit changes and coverage, by industry sector and whether contract includes escalator clause and lump sum payment, 1968-88, annual article, 6722-1.923

Collective bargaining wage and benefit changes, by sector, 1954-88, 6728-38.7

Collective bargaining wage and benefit changes, quarterly press release, 6782-2

Collective bargaining wage and benefit concessions and workers affected, by type of concession and major industry group, 1975-88, article, 9385-1.912

Drug testing of employees, coverage, policies, sponsors, treatment aid provided, and results, by industry div, 1988, 6728-37

Employee participation in decision-making and workplace reform, 1985-86 Western Airlines surveys, 6306-3.1; 6306-3.2

Foreign countries labor conditions, union coverage, and work accidents, annual country rpt series, 6366-4

Labor laws enacted, by State, 1988, annual article, 6722-1.904

Mediation and arbitration activities of Fed Mediation and Conciliation Service, and cases by issue, region, and State, FY82-87, annual rpt, 9344-1

Military reserve service impacts on civilian job, and employer support, reservists spouses views, 1986 survey, 3508-30

Military reserve service impacts on civilian job, and employer support, reservists views, 1986 survey, 3508-29

Natl Labor Relations Board activities, cases, elections conducted, and litigation, FY85, annual rpt, 9584-1

Nurses recruitment and retention issues and indicators, 1988 conf papers, 4118-64

Nursing chief officers in hospitals, activities, responsibilities, and role in nurse hiring and retention, 1988 survey, 4008-91

Railroad and airline labor disputes, and Federal mediation activities and caseloads, with data by carrier and union, FY85-86, annual rpt, 9604-1

Representation elections conducted by NLRB, results, monthly rpt, 9582-2

Statistical Abstract of US, social, political, and economic data, 1790-2025, comprehensive annual compilation, 2324-1.3

Unemployed displaced workers, by reason, industry, selected characteristics, and State, 1988, annual rpt, 6744-18

Unemployed displaced workers, labor-mgmt committee aid recipients by selected characteristics, for 4 State programs, 1988, GAO rpt, 26121-316

Wage and benefit changes from collective bargaining and mgmt decisions, by industry div, monthly rpt, 6782-1

Wage-benefit negotiated decisions, annual rates of change, *Business Conditions Digest*, monthly rpt, 2702-3.6

see also Absenteeism

see also Discrimination in employment
see also Employee benefits
see also Escalator clauses
see also Labor-management relations in
government
see also Labor-management relations, local
and regional
see also Labor unions
see also Pensions and pension funds
see also Work conditions
see also Work stoppages

Labor-management relations in government

Air traffic control system safety, working
conditions, and traffic volume, various
periods 1981-88, GAO rpt series,
26113–220

Collective bargaining agreements expiring
during year, and workers covered, by
firm, union, industry group, and State,
1989, annual rpt, 6784–9

Collective bargaining contract expirations,
wage increases, and coverage, by major
industry and selected firm and union,
1989, annual article, 6722–1.902

Collective bargaining multi-unit agreements
of Fed Govt, by agency and labor union,
as of Aug 1988, annual listing, 9847–4

Discrimination complaints of Federal
employees, processing, and disposition, by
complaint type and agency, FY87, annual
rpt, 9244–11

Fed Govt civilian employees demographic
and employment characteristics, as of Sept
1988, article, 9842–1.901

Fed Govt labor unions recognized,
agreements and membership by agency
and facility, as of Jan 1989, biennial
listing, 9844–14

Fed Labor Relations Authority and Fed
Service Impasses Panel activities, and
cases by union, agency, and State,
FY79-87, annual rpt, 13364–1

Mediation and arbitration activities of Fed
Mediation and Conciliation Service, and
cases by issue, region, and State,
FY82-87, annual rpt, 9344–1

Merit system oversight and enforcement
activities of OPM, series, 9496–2

Merit Systems Protection Board decisions
on appeals of Fed Govt personnel actions,
by agency and region, FY88, annual rpt,
9494–2

NASA staff characteristics and personnel
actions, FY88, annual rpt, 9504–1

OPM activities and funding, and Federal
personnel officers and OPM employees
views on leadership and support in labor
mgmt issues, 1984-88, GAO rpt,
26119–236

Postal Service employee disciplinary actions,
by type of infraction and penalty, and
region, 1985-88, GAO rpt, 26119–256

SSA employees with poor performance,
mgmt activities, outcomes, and supervisors
views, 1985-87, GAO rpt, 26119–240

State and local govt collective bargaining,
wage and benefit changes and coverage,
1st half 1989, semiannual press release,
6782–6

Statistical Abstract of US, social, political,
and economic data, 1790-2025,
comprehensive annual compilation,
2324–1.2

Wage and benefit changes from collective
bargaining and mgmt decisions, by
industry div, monthly rpt, 6782–1

**Labor-management relations, local and
regional**

Southeastern States collective bargaining
calendar, 1989, annual rpt, 6946–1.73

Labor mobility

Displaced workers, labor-mgmt committee
aid recipients by selected characteristics,
for 4 State programs, 1988, GAO rpt,
26121–316

Fed Govt Senior Executive Service
membership characteristics, entries, exits,
and awards, FY80-1987, annual rpt,
9844–36

Housing characteristics of recent movers for
new and previous unit, and household
characteristics, by location, 1985, biennial
rpt, 2485–12

Housing characteristics of recent movers for
new and previous unit, and household
characteristics, MSA surveys, series,
2485–6

Labor force supply and mobility, by age, and
educational level needs, 1960-86 and
projected to 2000, 6306–2.4

Migration since 1986, mover characteristics
by same or different area, and compared
to nonmovers, 1987, annual Current
Population Rpt, 2546–1.435

Occupational changes, by tenure and other
worker characteristics, and labor mobility
rates, 1965-86, article, 6722–1.943

Older persons labor force participation,
unemployment, displacement, and
reemployment, by selected characteristics,
1969-88, 6306–2.2

see also Job tenure
see also Labor turnover
see also Migrant workers
see also Migration

Labor productivity

Auto and home supply stores productivity
trends and technological devs, 1972-87,
article, 6722–1.941

Banks employment relation to labor costs,
output, and technological change, US and
5 OECD countries, 1980-86, working
paper, 9371–10.42

Business and financial statistics, historic
trends, 1988 annual chartbook, 9364–2.2;
9364–2.4

Business Conditions Digest, economic,
business, and financial devs and cyclical
fluctuations, monthly rpt, 2702–3

Capital goods manufacturing productivity,
labor cost indexes, and trade and trade
balance impacts of economic conditions,
with foreign comparisons, 1970s-88,
article, 9385–1.909

Cardiovascular diseases cases, health care
services use and costs, and productivity
losses, by selected characteristics, 1980,
4146–12.26

Child care leave of absence for employees,
policies, coverage, and attitudes, by
employee characteristics, 1980-87,
hearings, 25548–95

Coal miners working daily, mines, and labor
productivity, quarterly rpt, 3162–37.4

Coal mining productivity, by mine type,
1949-87, annual rpt, 3164–68.2

Coal production and mines by county,
prices, productivity, miners, reserves, and
stocks, by mining method and State,
1987-88, annual rpt, 3164–25

Coal production per workhour, 1987 and
trends from 1949, annual rpt, 3164–74.4

Coal production, reserves, use, and prices by
State, exports by country, and
employment, 1900s-87, biennial rpt,
3164–79

Competitiveness (intl) of US industries, with
selected foreign and US operating data by
major firm and product, series, 2046–12

Economic indicators and components,
current data and annual trends, monthly
rpt, 23842–1.2

Economic indicators compounded annual
rates of change, monthly rpt, 9391–3.2

Economic indicators compounded annual
rates of change, 1969-88, annual rpt,
9391–9.2

Economic Report of the President for 1989,
Joint Economic Committee critique and
policy recommendations, annual rpt,
23844–2

Employment and unemployment current
statistics, Monthly Labor Review,
6722–1.1

Employment shifts among industries, factors
and impacts on wage growth, with data by
industry group, 1948-87, 23848–207

Engine carburetors, pistons, and valves,
industry productivity and technological
devs, for 1972-86, article, 6722–1.911

Farm production inputs, output, and
productivity, by commodity and region,
1947-87, annual rpt, 1544–17

Fertilizer and pesticide industry productivity
of labor, indexes and annual rates of
change, 1972-86, article, 6722–1.915

Food marketing sector finances, operations,
and merger activity, for processors and
distributors, as of 1988, annual rpt,
1544–22

Food prices (farm-retail), marketing cost
components, and industry finances and
productivity, 1950s-88, annual rpt,
1544–9.2

Foreign and US manufacturing labor
productivity and unit costs, for 14
countries, 1950-88, annual press release,
6864–1

Foreign and US output, compensation, unit
labor costs, and indexes, Monthly Labor
Review, 6722–1.6

Foreign countries labor conditions, output,
earnings, and price indexes, by selected
country, 1950-88, 6728–38.11

Foreign countries labor conditions, union
coverage, and work accidents, annual
country rpt series, 6366–4

Govt spending related to labor productivity,
for 7 OECD countries, 1966-85, article,
9375–1.907

Health care facilities excluded from
Medicare prospective payment system,
labor and capital productivity indicators
by instn type, 1976-86, 17206–2.1

Hospital labor and total factor productivity,
with background data, 1980-86, article,
4652–1.941

Hospital reimbursement by Medicare under
prospective payment system, and
physician reimbursement, effect on
services, finances, and beneficiary
payments, 1970s-88, annual rpt, 17204–2

Hospital reimbursement by Medicare under
prospective payment system,
methodology, inputs, and data by
diagnostic group, 1989 annual rpt,
17204–1

Hospital reimbursement by States under prospective payment programs, effects on operations, finances, and patient deaths, by State, 1970s-83, 4658–29

Imports injury to US industries from foreign subsidized products and sales at less than fair value, investigations with background financial and operating data, series, 9886–19

Japan and US labor force participation by selected characteristics, productivity, and unit labor costs, 1960s-87, article, 6722–1.910

Military personnel alcohol and drug abuse, prevalence and consequences, by selected characteristics, 1988, biennial rpt, 3504–19

Mines (coal) and related operations occupational injuries and incidence, employment, and hours, 1987, annual rpt, 6664–4

Output, compensation, labor and nonlabor unit costs, and indexes, Monthly Labor Review, 6722–1.5

Output per hour, and compensation and unit labor costs, percent change, monthly rpt, 6742–2.7

Output per hour, and compensation and unit labor costs, 1947-88, annual rpt, 204–1.1; 204–1.2

Pacific Northwest population, households, employment, income, and fuel prices, alternative projections 1990-2010 with trends from 1960, annual rpt, 3224–5

Productivity and costs of labor for private, nonfarm business, and manufacturing sectors, revised data, quarterly rpt, 6822–2

Productivity and costs of labor, indexes by sector and selected industry, 1947-88, 6728–38.6

Productivity and costs of labor, indexes, preliminary data, quarterly rpt, 6822–1

Productivity growth indicators, and impacts of pollution abatement spending and other factors, for US and selected OECD countries, various periods 1948-86, article, 9389–1.911

Productivity of labor and for other inputs, indexes and changes for 2- to 4-digit industry and govt functions, 1982-87, annual article, 6722–1.914

Productivity of labor, indexes of output, hours, and employment by SIC 2- to 4-digit industry, 1963-87, annual rpt, 6824–1

Puerto Rico economic conditions, 1986 hearings, 21448–39

Shoe (nonrubber) industry productivity measures, 1958-86, article, 6722–1.920

Small business finances, operations, owner and employee characteristics, and Federal contracts, 1980s-88, annual rpt, 9764–6

Smoking restrictions in workplace, and personnel directors views on morale, productivity, and smoking impacts, 1987 local area survey, article, 4472–1.904

Statistical Abstract of US, social, political, and economic data, 1790-2025, comprehensive annual compilation, 2324–1.3

Steel industry finances and operations by product, and modernization efforts, as of June 1989, last issue of annual rpt, 9884–16

Technological devs effect on labor force, composition, and productivity, by industry, 1960s-86 and projected to 2000, series, 6826–2

Tire and inner tube industry productivity measures, 1958-86, article, 6722–1.928

see also Government efficiency

see also Industrial production indexes

see also Labor costs and cost indexes

see also Production costs

Labor supply and demand

Economic indicators and components, current data and annual trends, monthly rpt, 23842–1.2

Forecasts of employment conditions, alternative BLS projections to 2000 and trends 1970s-88, biennial article, 6722–1.952

Labor force supply and mobility, by age, and educational level needs, 1960-86 and projected to 2000, 6306–2.4

Labor force, wages, hours, and payroll costs, by major industry group and demographic characteristics, *Survey of Current Business*, monthly rpt, 2702–1.5

Monthly Labor Review, current statistics and articles, 6722–1

New England States economic indicators, Fed Reserve 1st District, quarterly rpt, 9373–2.1

Rural and urban areas jobs created under AFDC workfare program, 1986 and estimated 1988, article, 1502–7.902

see also Absenteeism

see also Agricultural labor

see also Alien workers

see also Blue collar workers

see also Child labor

see also Clerical workers

see also Employee benefits

see also Employee development

see also Employment and unemployment, general

see also Employment and unemployment, local and regional

see also Employment and unemployment, specific industry

see also Federal employees

see also Forced labor

see also Foreign labor conditions

see also Health occupations

see also Hours of labor

see also Job tenure

see also Job vacancy

see also Labor law

see also Labor-management relations, general

see also Labor-management relations, local and regional

see also Labor mobility

see also Labor productivity

see also Labor turnover

see also Labor unions

see also Manpower training programs

see also Merchant seamen

see also Migrant workers

see also Military personnel

see also Occupational health and safety

see also Occupational testing and certification

see also Occupations

see also Old-Age, Survivors, Disability, and Health Insurance

see also Part-time employment

see also Pensions and pension funds

see also Production workers

see also Professional and technical workers

see also Retirement

see also Sales workers

see also State and local employees

see also Temporary and seasonal employment

see also Underemployment

see also Unemployment insurance

see also Unpaid family workers

see also Vacations and holidays

see also Veterans employment

see also Women's employment

see also Youth employment

see also under names of specific occupations

Labor turnover

Displaced workers and other hard to serve groups, factors contributing to unemployment, and training programs operations, series, 15496–1

Displaced workers, by reason, industry, selected characteristics, and State, 1988, annual rpt, 6744–18

Displaced workers changing occupations for new job, by previous job tenure, occupational group, and industry div, 1986, article, 6722–1.943

Displaced workers earnings losses and unemployment duration, relation to educational attainment, by selected characteristics, 1984-86, article, 6722–1.942

Displaced workers, labor-mgmt committee aid recipients by selected characteristics, for 4 State programs, 1988, GAO rpt, 26121–316

Displaced workers program grants under Job Training Partnership Act, 1989, press release, 6406–2.25

Employee benefit plan coverage and provisions, by plan type and occupational group, 1988, annual rpt, 6784–19

Employment of DOT, by subagency, occupation, and selected personnel characteristics, FY88, annual rpt, 7304–18

Fed Govt civilian employee accessions and separations, by citizenship status and agency for DC metro area and elsewhere, bimonthly rpt, 9842–1.3

Fed Govt employment of minorities and women by occupation, and handicapped employment, by agency, FY87, annual rpt, 9244–10

Fed Govt personnel action appeals, decisions of Merit Systems Protection Board by agency and region, FY88, annual rpt, 9494–2

Fed Govt Senior Executive Service former members reasons for leaving, and views on SES statutory compliance, 1988 survey, 9498–3

Fed Govt Senior Executive Service membership characteristics, entries, exits, and awards, FY80-1987, annual rpt, 9844–36

Fed Govt service contracts compared with work performed in-house, savings and employment effects by agency, 1978-87, GAO rpt, 26119–238

Govt services transfer to private contractors, impacts on govt workers, with data by worker characteristics, level of govt, and location, 1980s-87, 15496–1.5

Handbook of Labor Statistics, employment, unemployment, and labor force characteristics, 1940s-88 with trends from 1913, 6728-38

Household composition, income, benefits, and labor force status, Survey of Income and Program Participation methodology, working paper series, 2626-10

Imports, exports, and employment impacts, by SIC 2- to 4-digit industry and commodity, quarterly rpt, 2322-2

Labor force entrants, by age, sex, race, part-time status, and detailed occupation, Jan 1987, article, 6742-1.902

Labor force not at work, unemployed, and working less than 35 hours, by reason, sex, race, region, and State, 1988, annual rpt, 6744-7.1; 6744-7.2

Labor laws enacted, by State, 1988, annual article, 6722-1.904

Market regulation impacts on industry wages and turnover, model description and results, 1987 working paper, 6886-6.21

Military enlistments and reenlistment rates, by service branch, FY79-88, annual rpt, 3544-1.2

Military personnel on active duty, recruits, and reenlistment, by race, sex, and service branch, quarterly press release, 3542-7

Military recruits and reenlistment rates, by service branch, quarterly rpt, 3542-14.4

Military women personnel on active and reserve duty, by demographic and service characteristics and service branch, FY88, annual chartbook, 3544-26

Minerals (strategic) supply, demand, trade, and foreign and US industry devs by firm and country, by commodity, bimonthly rpt with articles, 5602-4

NASA staff characteristics and personnel actions, FY88, annual rpt, 9504-1

Nuclear power plant occupational radiation exposure, by site, 1968-86, annual rpt, 9634-3

Nurses (RN) employment, shortages, recruitment, and retention, findings and recommendations, 1988 rpt, 4008-88

Nurses (RN) in nursing homes, factors related to recruitment and retention, 1985 survey, 4147-13.97

Occupational changes, by tenure and other worker characteristics, and labor mobility rates, 1965-86, article, 6722-1.943

Older persons labor force participation, unemployment, displacement, and reemployment, by selected characteristics, 1969-88, 6306-2.2

Police pay, benefits, and staffing, for US Park Police and compared to other Federal and local police units, FY85-88, GAO rpt, 26119-264

Rural areas employment stability impacts of industrial growth and other factors, 1979, 1598-255

Science personnel quit and turnover rates for Fed Govt and FDA, by field, FY85-88, GAO rpt, 26121-309

SEC staffing, pay, and turnover by occupation and city, with proposed fee revenues to improve work conditions, 1989 hearing, 21368-116

Small business establishments, employment, and financial ratios, by SIC 1- to 2-digit industry and State, late 1960s-87, 9768-19

Small business finances, operations, owner and employee characteristics, and Federal contracts, 1980s-88, annual rpt, 9764-6

Statistical Abstract of US, social, political, and economic data, 1790-2025, comprehensive annual compilation, 2324-1.3

Unemployment by reason, detailed data, monthly rpt, 6742-2

Unemployment by reason, monthly press release, 6742-5

Unemployment by reason, transcripts of BLS Commissioner's monthly testimony, periodic rpt, 23846-4

Unemployment, by reason, 1947-88, annual rpt, 204-1.2

Unemployment insurance long-term claimants employment services use, work experience, and reemployment, by selected characteristics and county, 1987-88, 6406-6.25; 6406-6.26

Unemployment spells duration, frequency, insurance coverage, and outcome, by age, sex, and race, 1984, Current Population Rpt, 2546-20.9

see also Job tenure

see also Job vacancy

Labor unions

AT&T workers membership in Intl Brotherhood of Electrical Workers, by local, 1981 and 1987, hearings, 21368-113

Bus drivers pay impacts of taxes dedicated to local systems funding and other factors, 1950s-85, working paper, 9377-9.73

Collective bargaining agreement concessions relation to economic and industry financial conditions, with data by major industry and union, 1970s-88, technical paper, 9385-8.41

Collective bargaining agreements expiring during year, and workers covered, by firm, union, industry group, and State, 1989, annual rpt, 6784-9

Collective bargaining agreements, innovations and issues, series, 6306-3

County Business Patterns, 1987: employment, establishments, and payroll, by SIC 2- to 4-digit industry and county, annual State rpt series, 2326-8

Coverage by unions of workers and earnings, by age, sex, race, occupational group, and industry div, annual article, 6782-1.2

Criminal sentences for Federal offenses, guidelines by offense and circumstances, 1989 rpt, 17668-1

Drug testing of employees, coverage, policies, sponsors, treatment aid provided, and results, by industry div, 1988, 6728-37

Elections for representation conducted by NLRB, results, monthly rpt, 9582-2

Employment Cost Index and alternative measure of compensation costs, by component, occupation, industry group, union status, and location, 1975-89, annual rpt, 6744-20

Employment Cost Index and percent change by occupational group, industry div, region, and metro-nonmetro area, quarterly press release, 6782-5

Employment Cost Index, by industry sector and union status, monthly rpt, 6782-1.1

Employment, earnings, and hours, by SIC 1- to 4-digit industry, monthly 1983-Feb 1989, annual rpt, 6744-4

Employment training participant characteristics, and sources of training, with data by employer size and major industry group, 1982-88, 6408-73

Fed Govt collective bargaining multi-unit agreements, by agency and labor union, as of Aug 1988, annual listing, 9847-4

Fed Govt labor unions recognized, agreements and membership by agency and facility, as of Jan 1989, biennial listing, 9844-14

Fed Labor Relations Authority and Fed Service Impasses Panel activities, and cases by union, agency, and State, FY79-87, annual rpt, 13364-1

Foreign countries economic, social, political, and geographic summary data, by country, 1989, annual factbook, 9114-2

Foreign countries labor conditions, union coverage, and work accidents, annual country rpt series, 6366-4

Govt services transfer to private contractors, impacts on govt workers, with data by worker characteristics, level of govt, and location, 1980s-87, 15496-1.5

Health care (long-term) needs, ability to pay, and views on Federal aid for home care, 1988 survey, hearing, 21148-51

Insurance (health) coverage of total and working population, by selected characteristics, 1987, 4186-8.1

Labor hourly costs, by component, occupational group, union coverage, industry div, and region, 1989, annual rpt, 6744-21

Membership of selected unions, and percent of workers accepting concessionary contracts, 1975-88, article, 6385-1.912

Multinatl firms US affiliates, finances, and operations, by industry, world area of parent firm, and State, 1987, annual rpt, 2704-4

Natl Labor Relations Board activities, cases, elections conducted, and litigation, FY85, annual rpt, 9584-1

Nurses American Assn membership and collective bargaining coverage, 1956-88, article, 6722-1.946

Occupational safety and health education grants, by recipient, 1989, press release, 6606-3.9

Pension coverage, by plan type and worker characteristics, 1970s-88, article, 4742-1.925; 4746-26.7

Pension funds investment in mortgage-backed securities, by issuer, quarterly rpt, 5002-10

Police agencies employment, spending, and operations, FY87, 6066-25.20

Political action committees, by type, 1974-89, semiannual press release, 9276-1.61; 9276-1.67

Political action committees contributions by office and party, and finances by PAC, 1988 natl elections, press release, 9276-1.65

Political campaign financial activity reported to Fed Election Commission, by type of filer, 1988 natl elections, biennial rpt series, 9276-2

Railroad and airline labor disputes, and Federal mediation activities and caseloads, with data by carrier and union, FY85-86, annual rpt, 9604-1

Army Corps of Engineers water resources dev projects, characteristics, and costs, 1950s-87, biennial State rpt series, 3756-2

Army Corps of Engineers water resources dev projects, characteristics, and costs, 1950s-89, biennial State rpt series, 3756-1

Developing countries disaster preparedness and economic, population, and political data, country rpt series, 9916-2

Environmental conditions, fish, wildlife, use, and mgmt, for individual coastal and riparian ecosystems, series, 5506-9

Fish and Wildlife Service restoration programs funding, land purchases, and project listing, by State, FY87, annual rpt, 5504-1

Fish Hatchery Natl System activities and deliveries, by species, hatchery, and jurisdiction of waters stocked, FY88, annual rpt, 5504-10

Fishery research of State fish and wildlife agencies, federally funded projects and costs by species and State, 1989, annual listing, 5504-23

Fishing, hunting, and other wildlife-related recreation participation and spending, detailed data, 1985 survey, quinquennial State rpt series, 5506-6

Freight (waterborne domestic and foreign) by commodity, traffic, and passengers, by port and waterway, 1987, annual rpt, 3754-3

Indiana water supply, annual high and low levels by lake, 1940s-85, 5668-89

Natl park system and other land under Natl Park Service mgmt, acreage by site, ownership, and region, 1989 semiannual rpt, 5542-1

Natl park system visits and overnight stays, by park and State, monthly rpt, 5542-4

Pollution (water) incidents and discharges, by type, source, cause, and location, 1984-86, annual rpt, 7404-3

Public lands acreage, grants, use, revenues, and allocations, by State, FY88, annual rpt, 5724-1.2

Water supply and quality in streams and lakes, and groundwater levels in wells, by drainage basin, 1986, annual State rpt series, 5666-23

Water supply and quality in streams and lakes, and groundwater levels in wells, by drainage basin, 1987, annual State rpt series, 5666-10

Water supply and quality in streams and lakes, and groundwater levels in wells, by drainage basin, 1988, annual State rpt series, 5666-16

Western US activities of Reclamation Bur, land and population served, and recreation areas, by location, 1987, annual rpt, 5824-12.1

Wildlife-related recreation, hunting, and fishing participation and spending, detailed data by location, 1985 survey, quinquennial rpt, 5508-5

see also Dredging
see also Great Lakes
see also National parks
see also Reservoirs
see also Wetlands

Lakewood, Colo.
see also under By City in the "Index by Categories"

Lamas, Enrique
"Training, Wage Growth, Firm Size", 2626-10.71

Lambert, Miles J.
"Agricultural Performance in Eastern Europe, 1988", 1524-11

Lamfalussy, Alexandre
"Globalization of Financial Markets: International Supervisory and Regulatory Issues", 9381-13.1

Lamps, electric
see Electrical machinery and equipment
see Household appliances and equipment

Lancaster, Pa.
see also under By SMSA or MSA in the "Index by Categories"

Land
see Arid zones
see Farms and farmland
see Forests and forestry
see Geography
see Homesteads
see Land area
see Land ownership and rights
see Land use
see Pasture and rangeland
see Property condemnation
see Public lands
see Real estate business
see Reclamation of land
see Soil pollution
see Soils and soil conservation
see Topography

Land area
Coal leasing activity on Federal land, acreage, production, and reserves, by coal region and State, FY88, annual rpt, 5724-10

Coastal areas environmental impacts of economic dev and population growth, 1980s and projected to 2000, 2176-8.1

Conservation and conditions of soil, water, and environment, with data by State and region, 1989 quinquennial rpt, 1268-24

Developing countries disaster preparedness and economic, population, and political data, country rpt series, 9916-2

DOE real property owned and leased, by type, subagency, contractor, and site, FY87, annual rpt, 3004-28

Fed Govt-leased real property inventory and rental costs, worldwide summary by location and agency, 1987, annual rpt, 9454-10

Fed Govt-owned real property inventory and costs, worldwide summary by purpose, agency, and location, 1987, annual rpt, 9454-5

Fish and Wildlife Service restoration programs funding, land purchases, and project listing, by State, FY87, annual rpt, 5504-1

Foreign countries economic, social, political, and geographic summary data, by country, 1989, annual factbook, 9114-2

Foreign countries *Geographic Notes*, boundaries, claims, nomenclature, and other devs, periodic rpt, 7142-3

Foreign countries population size, growth rate, and area, for 94 largest cities, 1989 biennial rpt, 2324-9

Forest Service revenue, share paid to States and natl forest acreage by forest, region, county, and congressional district, FY88, annual rpt, 1204-33

Forests (natl) and other lands under Forest Service mgmt, acreage by forest and location, 1988, annual rpt, 1204-2

Illinois timber resources, removals, and products, by species, forest characteristics, ownership, and county, 1960s-85 and projected to 2015, 1208-292

New Mexico timber acreage and resources, by species, ownership class, and county, 1986-87, series, 1206-23

New Mexico water resources data collection and analysis activities of USGS, with project descriptions, FY88, 5668-86

Northeastern US timber resources and removals, by species, ownership, and county, State rpt series, 1206-12

Park natl system and other land under Natl Park Service mgmt, acreage by site, ownership, and region, 1989, semiannual rpt, 5542-1

Park natl system visits and overnight stays, by park and State, 1988 and trends from 1979, annual rpt, 5544-12

Public lands acreage, grants, use, revenues, and allocations, by State, FY88 and trends, annual rpt, 5724-1

Public lands minerals resources and availability, State rpt series, 5606-7

Puerto Rico land area and topography, 1986 hearings, 21448-39

St Louis metro area local govt finances, structure, and service delivery, mid-1980s, 10046-9.1

Statistical Abstract of US, social, political, and economic data, with foreign comparisons, 1790-2025, comprehensive annual compilation, 2324-1

Statistical Abstract of US, social, political, and economic data, 1790-2025, comprehensive annual compilation, 2324-1.1

Tennessee timber acreage and resources, by species, ownership class, and county, 1989, series, 1206-27

Timber and windbarrier planting and dev, by State, FY88, annual rpt, 1204-7

Timber improvement program for private land, participation and payments by State, as of FY87, annual rpt, 1804-20

Timber insect and disease incidence and damage, annual regional rpt series, 1206-11

Timber insect and disease incidence and damage, by State, 1988, annual rpt, 1204-8

Western US activities of Reclamation Bur, land and population served, and recreation areas, by location, 1987, annual rpt, 5824-12.1

Wetlands acreage acquired by Fed Govt, and costs, by site and State, FY89, annual rpt, 14784-1

Wetlands acreage, and agreements and payments to farmers under Water Bank Program, by State, FY72-89, annual rpt, 1804-21

Wetlands preservation under Water Bank Program, acreage, agreements, and payments, by State, monthly rpt, 1802-5

Wilderness Preservation Natl System acreage, by site and State, 1987, annual rpt, 1004-15

Wildlife refuges and other land under Fish and Wildlife Service mgmt, acreage by site and State, as of Sept 1988, annual rpt, 5504–8

Wisconsin timber resources and removals, by species, forest type, ownership, and county, series, 1206–34

see also Farms and farmland

see also Land use

Land ownership and rights

Agricultural Statistics, 1988, annual rpt, 1004–1.2

Agriculture census, 1987: farms, farmland, production, finances, and operator characteristics, by county, final State rpt series, 2331–1

Alaska land area by ownership, and availability for mineral exploration and dev, 1986, 5608–152

Arizona wood fuel harvest, by tree species, ownership, and county, 1984, 1208–293

Assets and debts of private sector, balance sheets by segment, 1949-88, semiannual rpt, 9365–4.1

California timber resources and mortality, by hardwood species, land class and ownership, and county, 1984-85, 1208–291

Cotton farm operators by selected characteristics, and farms by size, by State, 1982 and 1987, article, 1561–1.907

Farm finances and operations, by size, commodity, and region, 1986, annual rpt, 1544–27

Farm production inputs, finances, mgmt, and land value and transfers, periodic situation rpt with articles, 1561–16

Farmland (US) investment of foreigners related to exchange rate, interest rate, and cropland returns, by leading country, 1981-88, 1528–287

Farmland (US) owned by foreigners, holdings, acquisitions, and disposals by land use, owner type and country, and State, 1988, annual rpt, 1584–2

Farmland (US) owned by foreigners, holdings, acreage, and value by land use, owner country, State, and county, 1988, annual rpt, 1584–3

Farms in urban areas, acreage, finances, and operators, under alternative MSA definitions, 1960s-82, 1598–256

Financial ratios of farms, model description and results, 1986, 1548–341

Foreign direct investment in US by country, and finances, employment, and acreage owned, by industry group of business acquired or established, 1982-88, annual article, 2702–1.917

Foreign direct investment in US, major transactions by type, industry, country, and US location, 1987, annual rpt, 2044–20

Foreign investment in US farm and commercial real estate, by owner country, 1977-89, GAO rpt, 26123–244

Georgia timber resources and removals, by species, ownership class, and county, 1988-89, series, 1206–26

Historic and natural natl landmarks damaged and threatened, with owner, location, damage type, and recommended remedial action, 1988, annual listing, 5544–16

Historic buildings rehabilitation tax incentives, projects, costs, ownership, use, and tax reform impacts, FY77-88, annual rpt, 5544–17

Illinois timber resources, removals, and products, by species, forest characteristics, ownership, and county, 1960s-85 and projected to 2015, 1208–292

Loan activity for mortgages, by type of lender, loan, and mortgaged property, monthly press release, 5142–18

Loan activity for mortgages, by type of lender, loan, and mortgaged property, quarterly press release, 5142–30

Loan activity for mortgages, by type of lender, loan, and mortgaged property, 1986-88, annual press release, 5144–22

Minerals foreign and US supply under alternative market conditions, reserves, and background industry data, series, 5606–4

Multinatl firms US affiliates finances and operations, by industry div, country of parent firm, and State, 1986-87, annual article, 2702–1.925

Multinatl firms US affiliates, finances, and operations, by industry, world area of parent firm, and State, 1987, annual rpt, 2704–4

New Mexico fuelwood harvest, by species, ownership, and county, 1986, 1208–303

New Mexico timber acreage and resources, by species, ownership class, and county, 1986-87, series, 1206–23

Northeastern US timber resources and removals, by species, ownership, and county, State rpt series, 1206–12

Oregon timber resources, by species, ownership, and county, 1983-86, series, 1206–19

Park natl system and other land under Natl Park Service mgmt, acreage by site, ownership, and region, 1989, semiannual rpt, 5542–1

Rocky Mountain States timber and mill residue production, by species, ownership, and county, series, 1206–17

Southeastern US land and mineral rights ownership by foreigners, by State, 1987, article, 9371–1.913

Statistical Abstract of US, social, political, and economic data, 1790-2025, comprehensive annual compilation, 2324–1.1

Tax (income) returns filed by type of filer, selected income items, quarterly rpt, 8302–2.1

Tennessee timber acreage and resources, by species, ownership class, and county, 1989, series, 1206–27

Timber insect and disease incidence and damage, annual regional rpt series, 1206–11

Timber insect and disease incidence and damage, by State, 1988, annual rpt, 1204–8

Tobacco (burley) finances, operations, and labor, for Kentucky and Tennessee, 1984, 1568–277

Uranium reserves and industry operations, by region and State, various periods 1966-88, annual rpt, 3164–65.1

Wildlife-related recreation, hunting, and fishing participation and spending, detailed data by location, 1985 survey, quinquennial rpt, 5508–5

Wildlife-related recreation, hunting, and fishing participation and spending, detailed data, 1985 survey, quinquennial State rpt series, 5506–6

Wisconsin timber resources and removals, by species, forest type, ownership, and county, series, 1206–34

see also Government supplies and property

see also Homesteads

see also Public lands

see also Real estate business

see also Vacant and abandoned property

Land reclamation

see Reclamation of land

Land surveying

see Land area

Land tax

see Property tax

Land use

Aerial survey R&D rpts, and sources of natural resource and environmental data, quarterly listing, 9502–7

Coastal areas environmental and socioeconomic conditions, and potential impact of oil and gas OCS leases, final statement series, 5736–1

Coastal areas environmental impacts of economic dev and population growth, 1980s and projected to 2000, series, 2176–8

Conservation and conditions of soil, water, and environment, with data by State and region, 1989 quinquennial rpt, 1268–24

Developing countries disaster preparedness and economic, population, and political data, country rpt series, 9916–2

Environmental quality and protection programs, and intl issues, 1988 annual rpt, 484–1

Estuary drainage areas land use, research results and methodology, 1987 rpt, 2176–7.4

Estuary environmental conditions and mgmt, for individual areas, conf series, 2146–6

Foreign and US land, water, and energy resources, by world area, 1960s-80s and projected to 2050, article, 1522–3.908

Foreign countries economic, social, political, and geographic summary data, by country, 1989, annual factbook, 9114–2

Foreign ownership of US farmland, holdings, acquisitions, and disposals by land use, owner type and country, and State, 1988, annual rpt, 1584–2

Foreign ownership of US farmland, holdings, acreage, and value by land use, owner country, State, and county, 1988, annual rpt, 1584–3

Forest Service mgmt of public lands and resources dev, environmental, economic, and social impacts of alternative programs, projected to 2030, 1208–24

Great Lakes water area, depth, and shoreline acreage by land use, 1989 rpt, 14646–1.1

Hudson-Raritan River basin pollutant levels and sources, model description and results, 1880s-1982, 2178–22

Research (agricultural) funding and staffing for USDA, State agencies, and other instns, by topic, FY88, annual rpt, 1744–2

Southeastern States land use factors, regression results, 1988 rpt, 1208–296

Statistical Abstract of US, social, political, and economic data, 1790-2025, comprehensive annual compilation, 2324-1.1

Suburban areas land use, commuting, employment, and housing characteristics, detailed data for traffic planning, 1986, 7888-75

Tax (property) revenue by level of govt, assessed values by locality, and exemptions, by property type and State, 1987 Census of Govts, 2453-1

Uranium tailings at inactive mills, remedial action proposals, costs, site characteristics, and environmental, socioeconomic, and health impacts, series, 3356-4

Western US activities of Reclamation Bur, land and population served, and recreation areas, by location, 1987, annual rpt, 5824-12.1

see also City and town planning
see also Farms and farmland
see also Forests and forestry
see also Industrial siting
see also Land ownership and rights
see also Mines and mineral resources
see also Pasture and rangeland
see also Property condemnation
see also Public lands
see also Reclamation of land
see also Regional planning

Lande, James L.
"Telephone Rates Update", 9282-8

Lander, James F.
"U.S. Tsunamis (Including U.S. Possessions), 1690-1988", 2158-52

Landfills
Cleanup of landfills, sites requiring action under Federal and State programs, by operating status, disposition of site expansion applications, and State, 1986-88, GAO rpt, 26113-430

Landscape protection
see Environmental pollution and control
see Land use

Lang, William W.
"Examination of Wage Behavior in Macroeconomic Models with Long Term Contracts", 9387-8.191
"Information Losses in a Dynamic Model of Credit", 9387-8.173
"Learning in the Marketplace: Free Entry Is Free Riding", 9387-8.192

Langan, Patrick A.
"Felony Sentences in State Courts, 1986", 6066-25.19

Langenbrunner, John C.
"Developing Payment Refinements and Reforms Under Medicare for Excluded Hospitals", 4652-1.935
"Physician Incomes and Work Patterns Across Specialties: 1975 and 1983-84", 4652-1.920

Langley, Jim
"Quantity of Wheat Placed Under Nonrecourse Loan", 1561-12.902
"State-Level Wheat Statistics, 1949-88", 1568-284

Langley, Suchada
"State-Level Wheat Statistics, 1949-88", 1568-284

Language arts
Degrees awarded in higher education, by level, field, race, and sex, 1989 edition, annual rpt, 4824-2.20

DOD Dependents Schools basic skills and college entrance test scores, 1988/89, annual rpt, 3504-16

Education statistics, detailed data on elementary and secondary education, 1920s-88 and projected to 1997, annual rpt, 4824-1.1

Educational progress by subject and selected student characteristics, standard test results and credits, 1989 edition, annual rpt, 4824-2.12

Elementary and secondary students performance in selected subjects, and factors affecting proficiency, natl assessments, 1969-86, 4898-26

Enrollment in science and engineering grad programs, by field, source of funds, and characteristics of student and instn, 1975-87, annual rpt, 9627-7

Fed Govt aid to higher education and nonprofit instns for R&D and related activities, by field, instn, agency, and State, FY87, annual rpt, 9627-17

Natl Endowment for Arts activities and grants, FY88, annual rpt, 9564-3

Teachers bachelor degrees, by field and other characteristics, 1985-86, 4838-39

USIA English language program enrollment and staff, by instn, world area, and country, FY88, annual rpt, 9854-2

see also Area studies
see also Writers and writing

Language use and ability
Asian American earnings, and employment and other characteristics, by detailed origin and whether foreign-born, 1980, 11046-7.2

Children with limited English proficiency, fall 1985-86, annual rpt, 4804-14

Condition of Education, detailed data on elementary and secondary education, 1920s-88 and projected to 1997, annual rpt, 4824-1.1

DOD Dependents Schools basic skills and college entrance test scores, 1988/89, annual rpt, 3504-16

Educational progress by subject and selected student characteristics, standard test results and credits, 1989 edition, annual rpt, 4824-2.12

Fed Govt civilian employment by occupation, agency, and location, and language and math skill needs, 1966-87 and projected to 2000, 9848-37

Health care personnel of VA born abroad, and English proficiency, as of Mar 1988, GAO rpt, 26121-273

High school dropout rates, and subsequent completion, by student and school characteristics, alternative estimates, 1988, annual rpt, 4834-23

Hispanic children with chronic illness, family characteristics and impact by English fluency, 1977 local area survey, article, 4042-3.936

Job Training Partnership Act participants, by selected characteristics, FY88, annual rpt, 6304-1

Refugee resettlement programs and funding, arrivals by country of origin, and indicators of adjustment, by State, FY88, annual rpt, 4694-5

Special education programs, enrollment by age, staff, funding, and needs, by type of handicap and State, 1987/88, annual rpt, 4944-4

see also Compensatory education
see also Foreign languages
see also Language arts
see also Literacy and illiteracy
see also Reading ability and habits
see also Speech pathology and audiology
see also Writers and writing

Lanier, Anne P.
"Cancer in Alaskan Indians, Eskimos, and Aleuts, 1969-83: Implications for Etiology and Control", 4042-3.963

Lansing, Mich.
see also under By City and By SMSA or MSA in the "Index by Categories"

Laos
Agricultural and food production and indexes, total and for selected commodities, by country, 1970s-88, annual rpt, 1524-12

Agricultural trade of US, by detailed commodity and country, 1988, semiannual rpt, 1522-4

AID loans repayment status and terms by program and country, and status of predecessor agency loans, quarterly rpt, 9912-3

Economic and military aid and loans from US and intl agencies, by program and country, FY46-87, annual rpt, 9914-5

Economic, social, political, and geographic summary data, by country, 1989, annual factbook, 9114-2

Exports and imports of US with Communist countries, by detailed commodity and country, quarterly rpt with articles, 9882-2

Human rights conditions in 170 countries, 1988, annual rpt, 21384-3

Military spending, arms trade, and force strengths, with govt spending and population, by country, 1977-87, annual rpt, 9824-1

Minerals production, reserves, and industry role in domestic economy and world supply, 1988 country rpt, 5606-1.17

Minerals Yearbook, 1987, Vol 3: foreign country reviews of production, trade, and policy, by commodity, annual rpt, 5604-35

Minerals Yearbook, 1987, Vol 3 preprints: foreign country review of production, trade, and policy, by commodity, annual rpt, 5604-23.85

Population size, growth rates, and components of change, by country, projected 1989-2020 and trends from 1950, biennial rpt, 2324-9

Refugee resettlement programs and funding, arrivals by country of origin, and indicators of adjustment, by State, FY88, annual rpt, 4694-5

Refugees from Indochina, arrivals, and departures, by country of origin and resettlement, camp, and ethnicity, monthly rpt, 7002-4

UN voting record and share of votes in agreement with US, by issue, country, and world area, 1988, annual rpt, 7004-18

see also under By Foreign Country in the "Index by Categories"

Larceny
see Robbery and theft

Lard
see Oils, oilseeds, and fats

Laredo, Tex.
see also under By City and By SMSA or MSA in the "Index by Categories"

Larson, Bruce A.
"Dynamic Factor Demands Using Intertemporal Duality", 1502–3.901

Larson, Donald K.
"Employment Stability Among Workers: A Case Study from Nine Nonmetro Kentucky Counties, 1979", 1598–255

Larson, Scott C.
"Brown Shrimp. Species Profiles: Life Histories and Environmental Requirements of Coastal Fishes and Invertebrates (South Atlantic)", 5506–8.97

Las Cruces, N.Mex.
Wages by occupation, for office and plant workers, 1989 survey, periodic MSA rpt, 6785–3.4
see also under By SMSA or MSA in the "Index by Categories"

Las Vegas, Nev.
Housing starts and completions authorized by building permits in 40 MSAs, quarterly rpt, 2382–9
Wages by occupation, for office and plant workers, 1988 survey, periodic MSA rpt, 6785–3.1
see also under By City and By SMSA or MSA in the "Index by Categories"

Lasers
Manufacturing census, 1987: financial and operating data, for SIC 4-digit industries by product, preliminary rpt, 2491–1.74
Manufacturing high technology use and plans, with data by technology, selected industry, and firm and market characteristics, 1988 survey, 2508–1
Price indexes (producer), by stage of processing and detailed commodity, monthly rpt, 6762–6
Price indexes (producer), by stage of processing and detailed commodity, monthly 1988, annual rpt, 6764–2

Lasley, Floyd A.
"U.S. Broiler Industry", 1568–279

Lassuy, Dennis R.
"English Sole. Species Profiles: Life Histories and Environmental Requirements of Coastal Fishes and Invertebrates (Pacific Northwest)", 5506–8.109
"Pacific Razor Clam. Species Profiles: Life Histories and Environmental Requirements of Coastal Fishes and Invertebrates (Pacific Northwest)", 5506–8.96

Latin America
Abortion-related deaths and hospitalization, for selected countries restricting abortions, 1950s-83, hearing, 21408–113
Agricultural production, prices, and trade, by country, 1960s-89, annual world region rpt, 1524–4.2
Agricultural trade among western hemisphere countries, and US duty-free imports, with listing of trade disputes and outcomes, 1960s-85, 1528–278
AID activities and funding by project and function, FY90, and developing countries summary socioeconomic data from 1960s, annual rpt, 9904–4.7

AID loans authorized, signed, and canceled, by country and world area, quarterly rpt, 9912–2
Businesses (foreign) activity in US, income tax returns, assets, and income statement items, by industry div, country, and world area, 1984-85, article, 8302–2.920
Cancer (cervical) cases and risk relation to smoking and other characteristics, for 4 Latin American countries, 1986-87 study, article, 4472–1.905
Coal trade flows and reserves, by country, 1970s-87 and projected to 2000, annual rpt, 3164–77
Construction contracts awarded US firms, and share of construction market by country of contractor, by world area, 1982-87, annual article, 2042–1.902
Drug abuse indicators, by world region and selected country, 1988 semiannual conf, 4492–5.1
Energy production by type, and oil prices, trade, and use, by country group and selected country, monthly rpt, 9112–2
Energy use by sector, and production, by fuel type, country, and country group, projected 1988-2000 and trends from 1970, annual rpt, 3164–84
English language program of USIA, enrollment and staff, by instn, world area, and country, FY88, annual rpt, 9854–2
Exchange and training programs of Federal agencies, participants by world area, and funding, by program, FY87, annual rpt, 9854–8
Exports and imports (waterborne) of US, by type of service, commodity, country, route, and US port, 1986-87, annual rpt, 7704–2
Exports and imports (waterborne) of US, by type of service, customs district, port, and world area, monthly rpt, 2422–7
Exports and imports of Latin America, and balance of trade with US, by country, 1988, annual rpt, 2044–34
Exports and imports of US, by commodity group, world area, selected country, US coastal area and port, and mode of transport, monthly rpt, 2422–9
Exports and imports of US, by selected country, country group, and commodity group, 1988, annual rpt, 2044–37
Exports, imports, and balances of US by commodity group, world area, and country, and related employment, 1970s-88, annual rpt, 2044–26
Fertilizer components use, by world area, 1978-88 and projected to 2010, 5608–154
Fishery exports of Latin America, by country, 1980-87, article, 2162–1.902
Immigrant and nonimmigrant visas of US issued and refused, by class, issuing office, and nationality, FY88, annual rpt, 7184–1
Immigrants admitted to US, by class of admission, country of birth, and State and MSA of destination, FY88, annual rpt, 6264–4
Immigrants admitted to US, by occupational group and country of birth, preliminary FY88, annual table, 6264–1
Immigration to US, alien workers, visitors, deportations, and naturalizations, by country, FY88 and trends from 1820, annual rpt, 6264–2

Inter-American Foundation activities, grants by recipient, and fellowships, by country, FY88, annual rpt, 14424–1
Inter-American Foundation dev grants by program area, and fellowships by field and instn, by country, FY71-88, annual rpt, 14424–2
Investment (foreign direct) in US, by industry group and world area, 1987-88, annual article, 2702–1.929
Investment (foreign direct) of US, by selected industry group and world area, 1986-88, annual article, 2702–1.930
Loans of US banks to foreigners at all US and foreign offices, by country group and country, quarterly rpt, 13002–1
Military aid of US, arms sales, and training programs costs and budget requests, by program, world region, and country, FY88-90, annual rpt, 7144–13
Military aid programs and related activities of US, costs by country and intl agency, FY85-87 and cumulative from FY50, GAO rpt, 26123–30
Military spending and imports of developing countries, measures to determine eligibility for US economic aid, by country, 1985-86, annual rpt, 9914–1
Military spending, arms trade, and force strengths, with govt spending and population, by country, 1977-87, annual rpt, 9824–1
Minerals Yearbook, 1987, Vol 3: foreign country reviews of production, trade, and policy, by commodity, annual rpt, 5604–35
Multinatl firms US affiliates, finances, and operations, by industry, world area of parent firm, and State, 1987, annual rpt, 2704–4
Multinatl US firms and foreign affiliates finances and operations, by industry of parent firm and affiliate, world area, and country, preliminary 1987, annual rpt, 2704–5
Peace Corps activities, funding by program, and volunteers, by country, FY90, annual rpt, 9654–1
Refugee arrivals in US by world area and country of origin, and quotas, monthly rpt, 7002–4
Refugee arrivals in US by world area of origin and State of settlement, and Federal aid, FY88-90, annual rpt, 7004–16
Science and engineering immigrants, by field, age, sex, country and world area of birth and last residence, and State, 1987 and trends from 1967, 9627–29
Terrorist (intl) incidents, casualties, and attacks on US targets, by attack type and world area, 1968-88, annual rpt, 7004–13
Tide height and time daily at coastal points, forecast 1990, annual rpt, 2174–2.2; 2174–2.3
Travel to and from US, and travel receipts and payments, by world area, with data by country, 1984-88, annual rpt, 2904–10
Travel to and from US on US and foreign flag air carriers, by country, world area, and US port, monthly rpt, 7302–2
UN voting record and share of votes in agreement with US, by issue, country, and world area, 1988, annual rpt, 7004–18

USIA library holdings, use, and staff, by
country and city, FY88, annual rpt,
9854–4

Visas of US issued at Foreign Service posts,
by category and world area, selected years
FY84-88, annual rpt, 7184–4

Weather conditions and effect on
agriculture, by US region, State, and city,
and world area, weekly rpt, 2152–2

Weather events and anomalies, precipitation
and temperature for US and foreign
locations, weekly rpt, 2182–6

Youth sexual behavior, impact of popular
music promoting responsibility, for Latin
America, 1986, 9916–3.50

see also Anguilla
see also Antigua and Barbuda
see also Argentina
see also Aruba
see also Bahamas
see also Belize
see also Bermuda
see also Bolivia
see also Brazil
see also British Virgin Islands
see also Caribbean area
see also Cayman Islands
see also Central America
see also Central American Common Market
see also Chile
see also Colombia
see also Costa Rica
see also Cuba
see also Dominica
see also Dominican Republic
see also Ecuador
see also El Salvador
see also French Guiana
see also Grenada
see also Guatemala
see also Guyana
see also Haiti
see also Honduras
see also Inter-American Development Bank
see also Jamaica
see also Latin American Integration
Association
see also Mexico
see also Netherlands Antilles
see also Nicaragua
see also Panama
see also Paraguay
see also Peru
see also Puerto Rico
see also South America
see also St. Christopher and Nevis
see also St. Lucia
see also St. Vincent and The Grenadines
see also Suriname
see also Trinidad and Tobago
see also Uruguay
see also U.S. Virgin Islands
see also Venezuela
see also under By Foreign Country in the
"Index by Categories"

Latin American Free Trade Association
see Latin American Integration Association

Latin American Integration Association
Exports and imports of US, by commodity
group, world area, selected country, US
coastal area and port, and mode of
transport, monthly rpt, 2422–9

Latinos
see Hispanic Americans
see Mexicans in the U.S.

Latta, Viola B.
"Medicare: Short-Stay Hospital Services, by
Leading Diagnosis-Related Groups, 1983
and 1985", 4652–1.925
"Use and Cost of Skilled Nursing Facility
Services Under Medicare, 1987",
4652–1.954

Laundry and cleaning services
Cancer (bladder) risk for men in selected
occupations, by employment
characteristics, 1977-78, article,
4472–1.925
County Business Patterns, 1987:
employment, establishments, and payroll,
by SIC 2- to 4-digit industry and county,
annual State rpt series, 2326–8
CPI by component for US city average, and
by region, population size, and for 27
metro areas, monthly rpt, 6762–2
Employment, earnings, and hours, by SIC 1-
to 4-digit industry, monthly 1983-Feb
1989, annual rpt, 6744–4
Employment of minorities and women, by
occupation, SIC 1- to 3- digit industry,
State, and MSA, 1986, annual rpt,
9244–1
Guam economic censuses, 1987:
employment, firms, payroll, and receipts,
by SIC 1- to 4-digit industry and election
district, 2595–1
Labor productivity, indexes of output, hours,
and employment by SIC 2- to 4-digit
industry, 1963-87, annual rpt, 6824–1.4
Northern Mariana Islands economic census,
1987: employment, firms, payroll, and
receipts, by SIC 1- to 4-digit industry,
2597–1
Occupational injury and illness rates, by SIC
2- to 4-digit industry, 1987, annual rpt,
6844–1
Pollutant ozone levels, urban areas failure to
meet natl standards, emissions sources,
exposure, and costs and benefits of
reduction strategies, 1983-87 and
projected to 2004, 26358–203
Receipts for services, by SIC 2- to 4-digit
kind of business, 1988, annual rpt,
2413–8
Science and engineering employment, by
nonmanufacturing industry and field,
1987, triennial rpt, 9627–31
Service industries census, 1987:
establishments, receipts, employment, and
payroll, by SIC 2- to 4-digit kind of
business, MSA, county, and city, State rpt
series, 2391–1
Tax (income) returns of partnerships,
income statement items by industry group,
1986, annual article, 8302–2.903
Tax (income) returns of sole proprietorships,
income statement items, by industry
group, 1987, annual article, 8302–2.904;
8302–2.921
Virgin Islands economic censuses, 1987:
employment, firms, payroll, and receipts,
by SIC 1- to 4-digit industry, island, and
city, 2593–1
Wholesale trade census, 1987: employment,
establishments, finances, and operations,
by SIC 2- to 4-digit kind of business,
MSA, county, and city, State rpt series,
2405–1

see also Janitorial and maintenance services

Lave, Judith R.
"Factors Affecting Medicaid Patients'
Length of Stay in Psychiatric Units",
4652–1.924

Law
Foreign countries economic, social, political,
and geographic summary data, by country,
1989, annual factbook, 9114–2
Smoking and health research rpts, 1988, last
issue of annual listing, 4204–19
see also Administration of justice
see also Administrative law and procedure
see also Alcoholic beverages control laws
see also Antitrust law
see also Building codes
see also Civil procedure
see also Commercial law
see also Constitutional law
see also Courts
see also Criminal procedure
see also Due process of law
see also Government-citizen lawsuits
see also International cooperation in law
enforcement
see also Labor law
see also Law enforcement
see also Lawyers and legal services
see also Legal aid
see also Legal education
see also Maritime law
see also Military law
see also State laws
see also Tax laws and courts
see also Traffic laws and courts
see also U.S. statutes

Law, Beverly E.
"Forest Survey Methods Used in the USDA
Forest Service", 9188–110

Law enforcement
Data on crime and criminal justice, activities
of Bur of Justice Statistics and States,
FY88, annual rpt, 6064–21
Data on crime, criminal justice admin and
enforcement, and public opinion, data
compilation, 1970s-88, annual rpt,
6064–6
Employment, payroll, and spending for
criminal justice, by level of govt, State,
and selected city and county, FY71-85,
annual rpt, 6064–9
Federal law enforcement personnel and
hiring, by agency, 1982-FY87, GAO rpt,
26119–242
Pacific territories social, economic, health,
and govtl data, FY88 and trends, annual
rpt, 7004–6
Statistical Abstract of US, social, political,
and economic data, 1790-2025,
comprehensive annual compilation,
2324–1.1
Victim aid programs of law enforcement
agencies, funding levels, staff, and needs,
1986, 6066–26.3
see also Administration of justice
see also Administrative law and procedure
see also Arrest
see also Correctional institutions
see also Courts
see also Crime and criminals
see also Criminal investigations
see also Criminal procedure
see also Electronic surveillance
see also Federal aid to law enforcement

see also Forensic sciences
see also International cooperation in law enforcement
see also Juvenile detention and correctional institutions
see also Organized crime
see also Police
see also Pretrial detention and release
see also Searches and seizures
see also State funding for public safety
see also Traffic laws and courts

Law of the sea
see Maritime law

Law schools
see Legal education

Lawler, John V.
"Raw Fiber Equivalent of U.S. Textile Trade, by Country and Fiber, 1988", 1561–1.904

Lawn and garden equipment
County Business Patterns, 1987: employment, establishments, and payroll, by SIC 2- to 4-digit industry and county, annual State rpt series, 2326–8
CPI by component for US city average, and by region, population size, and for 27 metro areas, monthly rpt, 6762–2
Exports of US, detailed commodities by country, monthly rpt, 2422–3
Imports of US, detailed Schedule A commodities by country, monthly rpt, 2422–2
Injuries from use of consumer products and related activities, by victim age and sex, 1988, annual rpt, 9164–7
Injuries from use of consumer products, by severity, victim age, and detailed product, 1988, annual rpt, 9164–6
Injuries from use of consumer products, related deaths and costs, and recalls by brand, by product type, FY87, annual rpt, 9164–2
Labor productivity, indexes of output, hours, and employment by SIC 2- to 4-digit industry, 1963-87, annual rpt, 6824–1.3
Manufacturers finances and operations, by SIC 2- to 4-digit industry, forecast 1989 and trends from 1950s, annual rpt, 2044–28
Manufacturing annual survey, 1986: financial and operating data, by SIC 2- to 4-digit industry, series, 2506–15
Manufacturing census, 1987: financial and operating data, for SIC 4-digit industries by product, preliminary rpt, 2491–1.61
Occupational injury and illness rates, by SIC 2- to 4-digit industry, 1987, annual rpt, 6844–1
Price indexes (producer), by stage of processing and detailed commodity, monthly rpt, 6762–6
Price indexes (producer), by stage of processing and detailed commodity, monthly 1988, annual rpt, 6764–2
Riding mower transmissions from Japan at less than fair value, injury to US industry, investigation with background financial and operating data, 1989 rpt, 9886–14.248
Service industries census, 1987: establishments, receipts, employment, and payroll, by SIC 2- to 4-digit kind of business, MSA, county, and city, State rpt series, 2391–1

Wholesale trade census, 1987: employment, establishments, finances, and operations, by SIC 2- to 4-digit kind of business, MSA, county, and city, State rpt series, 2405–1

Lawnmowers
see Lawn and garden equipment

Lawrence Berkeley Laboratory
see also Department of Energy National Laboratories

Lawrence, Edward C.
"Discrimination in Consumer Lending", 9366–6.174

Lawrence, Kans.
see under By SMSA or MSA in the "Index by Categories"

Lawrence Livermore National Laboratory
see also Department of Energy National Laboratories

Lawrence, Mass.
CPI by component for US city average, and by region, population size, and for 15 metro areas, monthly rpt, 6762–1
CPI by component for US city average, and by region, population size, and for 27 metro areas, monthly rpt, 6762–2
see also under By SMSA or MSA in the "Index by Categories"

Lawrence, Miles B.
"North Atlantic Tropical Cyclones, 1988", 2152–8.902

Lawson, Herschel W.
"Abortion Surveillance, U.S., 1984-85", 4202–7.906
"Ectopic Pregnancy Surveillance, U.S., 1970-85", 4202–7.902
"Ectopic Pregnancy Surveillance, U.S., 1970-86", 4202–7.905

Lawton, Okla.
Housing vacancy rates for single and multifamily units and mobile homes, by city and ZIP code, 1989, annual MSA rpt, 9304–22.4
Wages by occupation, for office and plant workers, 1989 survey, periodic MSA rpt, 6785–3.4
see also under By SMSA or MSA in the "Index by Categories"

Lawyers and legal services
AFDC hearings dispositions, by type of claimant representation, FY87, annual rpt, 4694–7.4
Coal surface mining-related civil actions, attorneys fees and expenses awarded by case, 1989, GAO rpt, 26113–421
County Business Patterns, 1987: employment, establishments, and payroll, by SIC 2- to 4-digit industry and county, annual State rpt series, 2326–8
CPI by component for US city average, and by region, population size, and for 27 metro areas, monthly rpt, 6762–2
Earnings by major industry group, and personal income per capita and by source, by region and State, 1929-87, 2708–40
Employment and spending for law enforcement, by activity and level of govt, FY84-86, annual rpt, 6064–6.1
Employment, earnings, and hours, by selected SIC 1- to 4-digit industry, State, and for 262 MSAs, 1972-87, 6748–81
Employment, earnings, and hours, by SIC 1- to 4-digit industry, monthly 1983-Feb 1989, annual rpt, 6744–4

Employment in nonmanufacturing industries, by detailed occupation and SIC 2-digit industry, 1987, triennial rpt, 6748–60
Employment, payroll, and spending for criminal justice, by level of govt, State, and selected city and county, FY71-85, annual rpt, 6064–9
Federal judicial personnel, by position, June 1988-89, annual rpt, 18204–2.7; 18204–8.7
Guam economic censuses, 1987: employment, firms, payroll, and receipts, by SIC 1- to 4-digit industry and election district, 2595–1
Northern Mariana Islands economic census, 1987: employment, firms, payroll, and receipts, by SIC 1- to 4-digit industry, 2597–1
Occupational injury and illness rates, by SIC 2- to 4-digit industry, 1987, annual rpt, 6844–1
Oil company overcharge settlements, and use for State legal expenses, by State, firm, and case, as of 1988, GAO rpt, 26113–408
Receipts for services, by SIC 2- to 4-digit kind of business, 1988, annual rpt, 2413–8
Science and engineering employment, by nonmanufacturing industry and field, 1987, triennial rpt, 9627–31
SEC staffing, pay, and turnover by occupation and city, with proposed fee revenues to improve work conditions, 1989 hearing, 21368–116
Senate receipts, itemized expenses by payee, and balances, 1st half FY89, semiannual listing, 25922–1
Service industries census, 1987: establishments, receipts, employment, and payroll, by SIC 2- to 4-digit kind of business, MSA, county, and city, State rpt series, 2391–1
Small business establishments, employment, and financial ratios, by SIC 1- to 2-digit industry and State, late 1960s-87, 9768–19
Statistical Abstract of US, social, political, and economic data, 1790-2025, comprehensive annual compilation, 2324–1.1
Tax (income) returns of corporations, income and tax items by asset size and detailed industry, 1986, annual rpt, 8304–4; 8304–21
Tax (income) returns of partnerships, income statement items by industry group, 1986, annual article, 8302–2.903
Tax (income) returns of sole proprietorships, income statement items, by industry group, 1987, annual article, 8302–2.904; 8302–2.921
Tax Court of US caseloads and appeals by disposition, procedure duration, and recoveries, FY88, annual rpt, 18224–5
Virgin Islands economic censuses, 1987: employment, firms, payroll, and receipts, by SIC 1- to 4-digit industry, island, and city, 2593–1
Workers compensation contested claims cases represented by attorneys, by State, 1988, annual rpt, 6504–9
Workers compensation laws of States and Fed Govt, 1989 semiannual rpt, 6502–1

see also Judges
see also Legal aid
see also Legal arbitration and mediation
see also Legal education
see also Legal ethics
see also U.S. attorneys
see also By Industry in the "Index by Categories"

Lay, Rick
"Highly Leveraged Bank Holding Companies and Subsidiary Bank Performance", 9381-14.1

Layoffs
see Labor turnover

Le Marchand, Loic
"Vegetable Consumption and Lung Cancer Risk: A Population-Based Case-Control Study in Hawaii", 4472-1.918

Lead and lead industry
Business statistics, detailed data for major industries and economic indicators, *Survey of Current Business*, monthly rpt, 2702-1.14
Castings (nonferrous) shipments, by metal type, monthly Current Industrial Rpt, 2506-10.5
Communist countries agricultural, mineral, and consumer and producer goods production, by commodity, 1960s-88, annual rpt, 9114-4.4
County Business Patterns, 1987: employment, establishments, and payroll, by SIC 2- to 4-digit industry and county, annual State rpt series, 2326-8
Exports of US, detailed commodities by country, monthly rpt, 2422-3
Finances and operations, by SIC 2- to 4-digit industry, forecast 1989 with trends from 1950s, annual rpt, 2044-28
Imports of US, detailed Schedule A commodities by country, monthly rpt, 2422-2
Manufacturing annual survey, 1986: financial and operating data, by SIC 2- to 4-digit industry, series, 2506-15
Manufacturing census, 1987: financial and operating data, for SIC 4-digit industries by product, preliminary rpt, 2491-1.53; 2491-1.54
Mineral industries census, 1987: financial and operating data, preliminary industry rpt, 2511-1.2
Mineral Industry Surveys, commodity review of production, trade, stocks, and use, monthly rpt, 5612-1.13
Mineral Industry Surveys, State reviews of production, 1988, preliminary annual rpt, 5614-6
Minerals Yearbook, 1987, Vol 1: commodity reviews of production, use, trade, prices, and mining operations, annual rpt, 5604-33
Minerals Yearbook, 1987, Vol 1 preprints: commodity review of production, reserves, supply, use, and trade, annual rpt, 5604-15.38
Minerals Yearbook, 1987, Vol 2 preprints: State reviews of production and sales by commodity, and business activity, annual rpt series, 5604-16
Minerals Yearbook, 1987, Vol 2: State reviews of production, sales, and firms, by commodity, and business activity, annual rpt, 5604-34

Minerals Yearbook, 1987, Vol 3: foreign country reviews of production, trade, and policy, by commodity, annual rpt, 5604-35
Minerals Yearbook, 1987, Vol 3 preprints: foreign country reviews of production, trade, and policy, by commodity, annual rpt series, 5604-23
Minerals Yearbook, 1988, Vol 2 rpts: State reviews of production and sales by commodity, and business activity, annual rpt series, 5604-22
Occupational injuries and incidence, employment, and hours in metal mines and related operations, 1987, annual rpt, 6664-3
Occupational injury and illness rates, by SIC 2- to 4-digit industry, 1987, annual rpt, 6844-1
Price indexes (producer), by stage of processing and detailed commodity, monthly rpt, 6762-6
Price indexes (producer), by stage of processing and detailed commodity, monthly 1988, annual rpt, 6764-2
Production cost impacts of occupational safety and environmental regulation, factors affecting US mineral industry competitiveness, 1989 compilation of papers, 5606-5.7
Production, prices, trade, use, employment, tariffs, and stockpiles, by mineral, with foreign comparisons, 1984-88, annual rpt, 5604-18
Statistical Abstract of US, social, political, and economic data, 1790-2025, comprehensive annual compilation, 2324-1.3
Stockpiling of strategic material by Fed Govt, activity, and inventory by commodity, as of Sept 1989, semiannual rpt, 3542-22; 3902-2
Stockpiling of strategic material, inventories and needs, by commodity, as of Sept 1988, annual rpt, 3544-37
Stockpiling of strategic material, inventories, costs, and goals by commodity, as of June 1989, semiannual rpt, 3902-3
Supply, demand, trade, and foreign and US industry devs by firm and country, for strategic minerals by commodity, bimonthly rpt with articles, 5602-4
see also Lead poisoning and pollution
see also under By Commodity in the "Index by Categories"

Lead poisoning and pollution
Abatement spending, capital and operating costs by SIC 2- to 4-digit industry and State, 1986, annual Current Industrial Rpt, 2506-3.6
Air pollution abatement activity of EPA, compliance, and monitoring stations operating status, 1987, annual rpt, 9194-4
Air pollution levels for 6 pollutants, and measurements exceeding natl standards, by site, 1987-88, annual rpt, 9194-5
Air pollution levels for 6 pollutants, by source, region, and selected MSA, 1978-87, annual rpt, 9194-1
Air pollution levels for 6 pollutants, by source, 1970-87 and trends from 1940, annual rpt, 9194-13
Arkansas water quality in streams and rivers, by monitoring site, 1975-85, 5668-83

California water quality, trace metal concentrations in San Joaquin river bed sediment, 1985, 5668-91
Carcinogens chemistry, sources, environment and health risks, and regulation, by substance and brand, 1989, annual rpt, 4044-15
Child lead poisoning, and children at risk, for Massachusetts, by city, 1985-87, hearing, 21248-119
Child lead poisoning, and impacts of lead removal from housing, gasoline, and water, 1987 conf, 4108-46
Coastal and estuarine pollutant concentrations in fish, shellfish, and environment, series, 2176-3
Coastal and estuarine pollutant discharges, by source, pollutant type, and location, series, 2176-4
Health condition and health care resources, use, and spending, 1950s-87, annual data compilation, 4144-11
Housewares (ceramic) lead and cadmium levels, FDA import inspection activity by country, and food safety funding and staff, 1983-88, hearing, 21368-108
Housing (public and Indian) stock and renovation needs, series, 5186-15
Hudson-Raritan River basin pollutant levels and sources, model description and results, 1880s-1982, 2178-22
Imports detained by FDA, by reason, product, shipper, brand, and country, monthly listing, 4062-2
Industrial hazardous substances releases and reduction methods under EPA regulation, by chemical, source, industry, and location, 1987, annual rpt, 9234-6
Lake Ontario eutrophication and pollutant levels, by contaminant type and site, 1967-85, 14648-22
Water supply and quality in streams and lakes, and groundwater levels in wells, by drainage basin, 1986, annual State rpt series, 5666-23
Water supply and quality in streams and lakes, and groundwater levels in wells, by drainage basin, 1987, annual State rpt series, 5666-10
Water supply and quality in streams and lakes, and groundwater levels in wells, by drainage basin, 1988, annual State rpt series, 5666-16

Leading indicators
see Economic indicators

Leasing
see Mineral leases
see Motor vehicle rental
see Oil and gas leases
see Rental industries

Leather industry and products
Business statistics, detailed data for major industries and economic indicators, *Survey of Current Business*, monthly rpt, 2702-1.12
China trade by SITC 1- to 5-digit commodity, 1970s-87, annual rpt, 9114-3
Collective bargaining agreements expiring during year, and workers covered, by firm, union, industry group, and State, 1989, annual rpt, 6784-9
County Business Patterns, 1987: employment, establishments, and payroll, by SIC 2- to 4-digit industry and county, annual State rpt series, 2326-8

Earnings by major industry group, and personal income per capita and by source, by region and State, 1929-87, 2708-40

Employment, earnings, and hours, by selected SIC 1- to 4-digit industry, State, and for 262 MSAs, 1972-87, 6748-81

Employment, earnings, and hours, by SIC 1- to 4-digit industry, monthly 1983-Feb 1989, annual rpt, 6744-4

Endangered animals and plants US trade and permits, by species, purpose, disposition, and country, 1987, annual rpt, 5504-19

Energy use and prices for manufacturing industries, 1985 survey, series, 3166-13

Exports and imports of dairy, livestock, and poultry products, by commodity and country, FAS monthly circular, 1925-32

Exports and imports of US, by commodity group, world area, selected country, US coastal area and port, and mode of transport, monthly rpt, 2422-9

Exports of US, detailed commodities by country, monthly rpt, 2422-3

Finances and operations, by SIC 2- to 4-digit industry, forecast 1989 with trends from 1950s, annual rpt, 2044-28

Freight (waterborne domestic and foreign) by commodity, traffic, and passengers, by port and waterway, 1987, annual rpt, 3754-3

Hazardous substances industrial releases and reduction methods under EPA regulation, by chemical, source, industry, and location, 1987, annual rpt, 9234-6

Import restraint elimination, impact on domestic industry production and employment, by selected commodity, 1986-88, 9886-4.144

Imports, exports, and employment impacts, by SIC 2- to 4-digit industry and commodity, quarterly rpt, 2322-2

Imports of US, detailed Schedule A commodities by country, monthly rpt, 2422-2

Input-output structure of US economy, detailed interindustry transactions for 84 industries, and components of final demand, 1983, annual article, 2702-1.909

Manufacturing annual survey, 1986: financial and operating data, by SIC 2- to 4-digit industry, series, 2506-15

Manufacturing annual survey, 1986: production indexes and exports by SIC 2-digit industry and State, with comparisons to 1985, model results, series, 2506-16

Manufacturing census, 1987: financial and operating data, for SIC 4-digit industries by product, preliminary rpt, 2491-1.19; 2491-1.44; 2491-1.45

Manufacturing industries production, shipments, inventories, orders, and pollution control costs, periodic Current Industrial Rpt series, 2506-3

Occupational injury and illness rates, by SIC 2- to 4-digit industry, 1987, annual rpt, 6844-1

OECD trade, total and for 4 major countries, and US trade by country, by commodity, 1970-87, world area rpt series, 9116-1

Pollution abatement capital and operating costs, by SIC 2-to 4-digit industry and State, 1986, annual Current Industrial Rpt, 2506-3.6

Price indexes (producer), by stage of processing and detailed commodity, monthly rpt, 6762-6

Price indexes (producer), by stage of processing and detailed commodity, monthly 1988, annual rpt, 6764-2

Retail trade census, 1987: employment, establishments, sales, and payroll, by SIC 2- to 4-digit kind of business, MSA, county, and city, State rpt series, 2397-1

Science, engineering, and technical employment in manufacturing, by field, occupation, and industry, 1986, triennial rpt, 9627-23

Small business establishments, employment, and financial ratios, by SIC 1- to 2-digit industry and State, late 1960s-87, 9768-19

Tariff Schedule of US, classifications and rates of duty by detailed imported commodity, 1990 base edition and supplements, 9886-13

Tax (income) returns of corporations, income and tax items by asset size and detailed industry, 1986, annual rpt, 8304-4; 8304-21

Tax (income) returns of partnerships, income statement items by industry group, 1986, annual article, 8302-2.903

Tax (income) returns of sole proprietorships, income statement items, by industry group, 1987, annual article, 8302-2.904; 8302-2.921

see also Hides and skins

see also Shoes and shoe industry

see also By Industry in the "Index by Categories"

see also under By Commodity in the "Index by Categories"

Leatherberry, Earl C.

"Illinois' Forest Resource", 1208-292

Lebanon

Agricultural and food production and indexes, total and for selected commodities, by country, 1970s-88, annual rpt, 1524-12

Agricultural trade of US, by detailed commodity and country, 1988, semiannual rpt, 1522-4

AID activities and funding by project and function, FY90, and developing countries summary socioeconomic data from 1960s, annual rpt, 9904-4.6

AID economic aid to developing countries, obligations and disbursements by country, quarterly rpt, 9912-4

AID loans repayment status and terms by program and country, and status of predecessor agency loans, quarterly rpt, 9912-3

Economic and military aid and loans from US and intl agencies, by program and country, FY46-87, annual rpt, 9914-5

Economic conditions, policy, and trade practices, by country, 1986-88, annual rpt, 21384-5

Economic, social, political, and geographic summary data, by country, 1989, annual factbook, 9114-2

Hostages held and kidnappings in Lebanon, 1988, 7008-56

Human rights conditions in 170 countries, 1988, annual rpt, 21384-3

Military aid of US, arms sales, and training programs costs and budget requests, by program, world region, and country, FY88-90, annual rpt, 7144-13

Military spending, arms trade, and force strengths, with govt spending and population, by country, 1977-87, annual rpt, 9824-1

Minerals Yearbook, 1987, Vol 3: foreign country reviews of production, trade, and policy, by commodity, annual rpt, 5604-35

Minerals Yearbook, 1987, Vol 3 preprints: foreign country review of production, trade, and policy, by commodity, annual rpt, 5604-23.86

Population size, growth rates, and components of change, by country, projected 1989-2020 and trends from 1950, biennial rpt, 2324-9

UN voting record and share of votes in agreement with US, by issue, country, and world area, 1988, annual rpt, 7004-18

see also under By Foreign Country in the "Index by Categories"

Lebanon, Pa.

see also under By SMSA or MSA in the "Index by Categories"

Lee, Hyunok

"Transactor Characteristics and Rural Land Prices", 1561-16.902

Lee, Linda K.

"Estimating the Offsite Household Damages from Wind Erosion in the Western U.S.", 1588-140

Leesville, La.

Wages by occupation, for office and plant workers, 1989 survey, periodic MSA rpt, 6785-3.5

Leeward and Windward Islands

see Caribbean area

Lefebvre, R. Craig

"Performance Characteristics of a Blood Cholesterol Measuring Instrument Used in Screening Programs", 4042-3.923

Legal aid

Assistance (financial and nonfinancial) of Fed Govt, 1989 base edition with supplements, annual listing, 104-5

Employment and spending for law enforcement, by activity and level of govt, 1982-86, annual rpt, 6064-6.1

Employment, payroll, and spending for criminal justice, by level of govt, State, and selected city and county, FY71-85, annual rpt, 6064-9

Fed Govt spending in States, by type, program, agency, and State, FY88, annual rpt, 2464-2

Homeless shelters services, operations, and client characteristics, 1988 survey, 5188-123

Public defender caseloads in Federal district courts, by district, quarterly rpt, annual tables, 18202-1

Public defender grants, by State, FY90-91, Judicial Conf proceedings, semiannual rpt, 18202-2

Public defender workloads in Federal district courts, and Equal Access to Justice Act petitions and decisions, 1989, annual rpt, 18204-2.9; 18204-2.17; 18204-8

Service industries census, 1987: establishments, receipts, employment, and payroll, by SIC 2- to 4-digit kind of business, MSA, county, and city, State rpt series, 2391-1

Legal arbitration and mediation

Community Relations Service investigation and mediation of minority discrimination disputes, FY87, annual rpt, 6004–9

Labor disputes of airlines and railroads, Natl Mediation Board activities and caseloads, with data by carrier, union, and occupation, FY85-86, annual rpt, 9604–1

Labor-mgmt mediation and arbitration activities of Fed Mediation and Conciliation Service, and cases by issue, region, and State, FY82-87, annual rpt, 9344–1

Legal education

Education Dept programs funding, operations, and effectiveness, FY88, annual rpt, 4804–5

Fed Govt aid to higher education instns, by program and instn type and control, FY85-88, annual rpt, 4804–28.4

Legal ethics

Public opinion on crime and crime-related issues, by respondent characteristics, 1970s-89, annual rpt, 6064–6.2

see also Judicial ethics

Legal services

see Lawyers and legal services

see Legal aid

Legal Services Corp.

Budget of US, authoritative financial statements with appropriations, outlays, and receipts, by category and agency, FY88, annual rpt, 8104–2.2

Expenditures of Fed Govt in States, by type, program, agency, and State, FY88, annual rpt, 2464–2

Leger, Mireille L.

"Administrative Costs of the Housing Voucher and Certificate Programs", 5186–14.2

Leginski, Walter A.

"Data Standards for Mental Health Decision Support Systems", 4506–2.7

Legislative bodies

see Congress

see House of Representatives

see Senate

see State legislatures

Legumes

see Vegetables and vegetable products

Leisure activities

see Recreation

Lemons

see Citrus fruits

Lennon, Robert E.

"Toxicity of 1,085 Chemicals to Fish", 9238–68

Lentils

see Vegetables and vegetable products

Lentjes, Donna M.

"Planned and Unplanned Home Births and Hospital Births in Calgary, Alberta, 1984-87", 4042–3.935

Leominster, Mass.

see also under By SMSA or MSA in the "Index by Categories"

Leonard, Barbara J.

"Providing Access to Home Care for Disabled Children: Minnesota's Medicaid Model Waiver Program", 4042–3.944

Leonard, Dorothy L.

"Classified Shellfish Growing Waters by Estuary", 2176–7.3

"Quality of Shellfish Growing Waters in the Gulf of Mexico", 2176–7.5

"Quality of Shellfish Growing Waters on the East Coast of the U.S.", 2176–7.11

Leptospirosis

see Animal diseases and zoonoses

Lerman, Donald L.

"Rural Poverty: Do Assets Matter?", 1502–7.908

Lerner, Philip R.

"OASDI Beneficiaries by State and County, December 1987", 4744–28

Lesotho

Agricultural and food production and indexes, total and for selected commodities, by country, 1970s-88, annual rpt, 1524–12

Agricultural imports and food aid needs under alternative weather assumptions, for 17 African countries, projected to 1995, 1528–279

Agricultural trade of US, by detailed commodity and country, 1988, semiannual rpt, 1522–4

AID activities and funding by project and function, FY90, and developing countries summary socioeconomic data from 1960s, annual rpt, 9904–4.5

AID economic aid to developing countries, obligations and disbursements by country, quarterly rpt, 9912–4

Economic and military aid and loans from US and intl agencies, by program and country, FY46-87, annual rpt, 9914–5

Economic conditions, income, production, prices, employment, and trade, 1989 periodic country rpt, 2046–4.82

Economic conditions, policy, and trade practices, by country, 1986-88, annual rpt, 21384–5

Economic, social, political, and geographic summary data, by country, 1989, annual factbook, 9114–2

Human rights conditions in 170 countries, 1988, annual rpt, 21384–3

Military aid of US, arms sales, and training programs costs and budget requests, by program, world region, and country, FY88-90, annual rpt, 7144–13

Military spending, arms trade, and force strengths, with govt spending and population, by country, 1977-87, annual rpt, 9824–1

Minerals Yearbook, 1987, Vol 3: foreign country reviews of production, trade, and policy, by commodity, annual rpt, 5604–35

Minerals Yearbook, 1987, Vol 3 preprints: foreign country review of production, trade, and policy, by commodity, annual rpt, 5604–23.81

Population size, growth rates, and components of change, by country, projected 1989-2020 and trends from 1950, biennial rpt, 2324–9

UN voting record and share of votes in agreement with US, by issue, country, and world area, 1988, annual rpt, 7004–18

see also under By Foreign Country in the "Index by Categories"

Lessler, Judith T.

"Questionnaire Design in the Cognitive Research Laboratory. Vital and Health Statistics Series 6", 4147–6.1

Letsch, Suzanne W.

"National Health Expenditures, 1987", 4652–1.926

Letter carriers

see Postal employees

Lettuce

see Vegetables and vegetable products

Leukemia

see Blood diseases and disorders

Levin, David J.

"Alternative Measure of the State and Local Government Fiscal Position: Revised and Updated Estimates", 2702–1.903

Levine, Richard M.

"Mineral Industries of the USSR", 5604–39

Levit, Katharine R.

"Health Spending and Ability To Pay: Business, Individuals, and Government", 4652–1.928

Levitan, Sar A.

"Can Employee Associations Negotiate New Growth?", 6722–1.931

"Collective Bargaining and Private Sector Professionals", 6722–1.946

Lewin/ICF

"Subacute Care in Hospitals, Synthesis of Findings from the 1987 Survey of Hospitals and Care Studies in Five States", 17206–2.8

Lewis, Jeannine T.

"U.S. Public Health Service Personnel Monitoring Program, 1986-87", 4064–15

Lewis, Margaret P.

"Foreign Recipients of U.S. Income, and Tax Withheld, 1986", 8302–2.915

Lewiston, Maine

see also under By SMSA or MSA in the "Index by Categories"

Lexington, Ky.

Wages by occupation, and benefits for office and plant workers, 1988 survey, periodic MSA rpt, 6785–3.1

see also under By City and By SMSA or MSA in the "Index by Categories"

Li, Li

"Comparison of Health Habits of Military Personnel with Civilian Populations", 4042–3.949

Liability insurance

see Property and casualty insurance

Liang, J. Nellie

"Dynamics of Market Concentration", 9366–6.188

"Systematic Risk, Market Structure and Entry Barriers", 9366–6.182

Liapis, Peter S.

"Estimation and Evaluation of Economic Community Wheat Export Subsidies", 1528–293

Libel and slander

Court caseloads for Federal district courts, June 1989, annual rpt, 18204–2.12; 18204–8.14

Liberia

Agricultural and food production and indexes, total and for selected commodities, by country, 1970s-88, annual rpt, 1524–12

Agricultural imports and food aid needs under alternative weather assumptions, for 17 African countries, projected to 1995, 1528–279

Agricultural trade of US, by detailed commodity and country, 1988, semiannual rpt, 1522–4

AID activities and funding by project and function, FY90, and developing countries summary socioeconomic data from 1960s, annual rpt, 9904-4.5

AID economic aid to developing countries, obligations and disbursements by country, quarterly rpt, 9912-4

AID loans repayment status and terms by program and country, and status of predecessor agency loans, quarterly rpt, 9912-3

Economic and military aid and loans from US and intl agencies, by program and country, FY46-87, annual rpt, 9914-5

Economic conditions, income, production, prices, employment, and trade, 1989 periodic country rpt, 2046-4.22

Economic conditions, policy, and trade practices, by country, 1986-88, annual rpt, 21384-5

Economic, social, political, and geographic summary data, by country, 1989, annual factbook, 9114-2

Human rights conditions in 170 countries, 1988, annual rpt, 21384-3

Labor conditions, union coverage, and work accidents, 1989 annual country rpt, 6366-4.18; 6366-4.47

Military aid of US, arms sales, and training programs costs and budget requests, by program, world region, and country, FY88-90, annual rpt, 7144-13

Military spending, arms trade, and force strengths, with govt spending and population, by country, 1977-87, annual rpt, 9824-1

Minerals Yearbook, 1987, Vol 3: foreign country reviews of production, trade, and policy, by commodity, annual rpt, 5604-35

Minerals Yearbook, 1987, Vol 3 preprints: foreign country review of production, trade, and policy, by commodity, annual rpt, 5604-23.43

Multinatl US firms and foreign affiliates finances and operations, by industry of parent firm and affiliate, world area, and country, preliminary 1987, annual rpt, 2704-5

Population size, growth rates, and components of change, by country, projected 1989-2020 and trends from 1950, biennial rpt, 2324-9

Ships in world merchant fleet, and tonnage, by country of registry, as of Jan 1988, annual rpt, 7704-3

UN voting record and share of votes in agreement with US, by issue, country, and world area, 1988, annual rpt, 7004-18

see also under By Foreign Country in the "Index by Categories"

Librarians

Blind and handicapped libraries, readership, circulation, staff, funding, and holdings, FY88, annual listing, 26404-3

Education Dept programs funding, operations, and effectiveness, FY88, annual rpt, 4804-5

Employment and payroll, by function and level of govt, 1987-88, annual rpt series, 2466-1

Fed Govt labor productivity, indexes of output and labor costs by function, FY67-87, annual rpt, 6824-1.6

Indian and Hawaii Native public libraries services, project listing and funding by tribe and State, FY88, annual rpt, 4874-5

Public libraries, outlets, and staff, by hours open, service population size, and selected State, 1987, annual rpt, 4824-6

Public libraries services effectiveness, public opinion survey methodology and results, 1989 rpt, 4878-3

Training in library science, grants for disadvantaged students, by instn and State, FY89, annual listing, 4874-1

USIA library holdings, use, and staff, by country and city, FY88, annual rpt, 9854-4

VA Medicine and Surgery Dept trainees, by detailed program and city, FY88, annual rpt, 8704-4

Libraries

Audiovisual activities and spending of Fed Govt, by whether performed in-house and agency, FY87, annual rpt, 9514-1

Banks in Fed Reserve System, expenses and operations itemized by service, office, and district, 1988, annual rpt, 9364-11

Blind and handicapped libraries, readership, circulation, staff, funding, and holdings, FY88, annual listing, 26404-3

County Business Patterns, 1987: employment, establishments, and payroll, by SIC 2- to 4-digit industry and county, annual State rpt series, 2326-8

Depository libraries, and users by selected characteristics, for academic and public instns, 1988 survey, 26208-1

Depository libraries for Federal publications, 1989 annual listing, 2214-1; 2304-2

Depository libraries microfiche shipments from GPO, contract awards, and supply and quality problems, 1988, GAO rpt, 26119-248

Govt finances, by level of govt, State, and for large cities and counties, annual rpt series, 2466-2

Govt revenues by source and spending by function, natl income and product account, *Survey of Current Business*, monthly rpt, 2702-1.24

Japan-US Friendship Commission educational and cultural exchange activities, grants, and trust fund status, FY87-88, biennial report, 14694-1

Library of Congress activities, acquisitions, services, and financial statements, FY88, annual rpt, 26404-1

Literacy programs of libraries, activities, and relation to community and instn characteristics, 1986, 4878-2

Literacy programs of public libraries, descriptions and funding, FY87, annual listing, 4874-3

Mail revenue and subsidy for revenue forgone, by class of mail, FY88, and volume from FY84, annual rpt, 9864-1

Natl Archives and Records Admin activities, finances, holdings, and staff, FY88, annual rpt, 9514-2

Presidential libraries holdings, use, and costs, by instn, FY88, annual rpt, 9514-2

Public libraries, outlets, and staff, by hours open, service population size, and selected State, 1987, annual rpt, 4824-6

Public libraries services effectiveness, public opinion survey methodology and results, 1989 rpt, 4878-3

Public libraries special programs, project descriptions and funding by level of govt, State, and city, 1984-87, annual rpt, 4874-4

School and public libraries, selected data, 1989 edition, annual rpt, 4824-2.30

Service industries census, 1987: establishments, receipts, employment, and payroll, by SIC 2- to 4-digit kind of business, MSA, county, and city, State rpt series, 2391-1

Statistical Abstract of US, social, political, and economic data, 1790-2025, comprehensive annual compilation, 2324-1.1

USIA library holdings, use, and staff, by country and city, FY88, annual rpt, 9854-4

see also Federal aid to libraries
see also Librarians
see also Medical libraries

Library of Congress

Activities, acquisitions, services, and financial statements of LC, FY88, annual rpt, 26404-1

Blind and handicapped libraries, readership, circulation, staff, funding, and holdings, FY88, annual listing, 26404-3

Budget of US Appendix, obligations, appropriations, and personnel, by program and agency, FY90, annual rpt, 104-3

Budget of US, authoritative financial statements with appropriations, outlays, and receipts, by category and agency, FY88, annual rpt, 8104-2.2

Buildings and grounds under Capitol Architect supervision, itemized outlays by payee and function, 1st half FY89, semiannual rpt, 25922-2

Copyrights Register activities, registrations by material type, and fees, FY87 and trends from 1790, annual rpt, 26404-2

Education funding by Federal agency, program, and recipient type, and instn spending, FY80-88, 4828-21

Labor unions recognized in Fed Govt, agreements and membership by agency and facility, as of Jan 1989, biennial listing, 9844-14

Police pay, benefits, and staffing, for US Park Police and compared to other Federal and local police units, FY85-88, GAO rpt, 26119-264

Publications and products of LC, 1989, annual listing, 26404-6

Publications and recordings of LC, 1989, biennial listing, 26404-5

R&D funding by Fed Govt, by field, performer type, agency, and State, FY87-89, annual rpt, 9627-20

see also Congressional Research Service
see also Copyright Royalty Tribunal

Library sciences

see Information sciences

Libya

Agricultural and food production and indexes, total and for selected commodities, by country, 1970s-88, annual rpt, 1524-12

Agricultural trade of US, by detailed commodity and country, 1988, semiannual rpt, 1522-4

AID loans repayment status and terms by program and country, and status of predecessor agency loans, quarterly rpt, 9912-3

Radio (mobile) licenses, by service type, 1983-87, 2808-27

SEC activities, securities industry finances, and exchange activity, selected years 1935-88, annual rpt, 9734-2

Sewage pipelines and dump sites authorized in coastal areas, status and EPA enforcement activities by State, 1982-87, hearings, 21568-45

Small Business Admin loan and contract activity by program and firm, and financial condition, FY88, annual rpt, 9764-1

Small Business Investment Companies capital holdings, SBA obligation, and ownership, as of June 1989, semiannual listing, 9762-4

Small Business Investment Companies finances, funding, licensing, and loan activity, 1st half FY89, semiannual rpt, 9762-3

Truck itemized costs per mile, finances, and operations, for agricultural carriers, 1988, annual rpt, 1311-15

Truck transport of fruit and vegetables, itemized costs per mile by item for fleets and owner-operator trucks, monthly table, 1272-4

TV channel allocation and license status, for commercial and noncommercial UHF and VHF TV by market, as of June 1989, semiannual rpt, 9282-6

see also Building permits

see also Drivers licenses

see also Motor vehicle registrations

see also Occupational testing and certification

see also Royalties

see also Water permits

Liebrand, Carolyn B.

"Milk Costs of Production, 1985-87", 1561-2.901

"Milk Production Costs and Returns, 1986, 1987, Preliminary 1988, and Forecast 1989", 1561-2.903

Liechtenstein

Background Notes, summary social, political, and economic data, 1989 rpt, 7006-2.9

Economic, social, political, and geographic summary data, by country, 1989, annual factbook, 9114-2

Population size, growth rates, and components of change, by country, projected 1989-2020 and trends from 1950, biennial rpt, 2324-9

see also under By Foreign Country in the "Index by Categories"

Life expectancy

AIDS health care services research status, needs, methods, and impacts on public health policy and funding, with data for selected cities, 1989 conf papers, 4188-59

AIDS health care, social, and support services research, data collection methods with background data, 1984-88, 4186-9.5

Cancer (breast and cervical) incidence, deaths, and survival rates, by race, average 1973-81, article, 4042-3.952

Cancer (melanoma) survival rates, by sex, for Sweden, for diagnoses made 1960-82, article, 4472-1.912

Cancer (melanoma) 8-year survival rates, model description and results, 1989 article, 4472-1.935

Cancer survival rates 2- to 10-years following diagnosis, by sex, for Sweden and US, 1960s-84, article, 4472-1.929

Communist, OECD, and selected other countries living standards and commodity production, 1960s-88, annual rpt, 9114-4.1

Deaths and years of potential life lost from selected chronic diseases, weekly rpt, monthly table, 4202-1

Developing countries aged population and selected characteristics, 1980s and projected to 2020, country rpt series, 2326-19

Developing countries disaster preparedness and economic, population, and political data, country rpt series, 9916-2

Developing countries economic and social conditions from 1960s, and Intl Dev Cooperation Agency and AID activities and funding, FY88-90, annual rpt, 9904-4

Foreign countries economic, social, political, and geographic summary data, by country, 1989, annual factbook, 9114-2

Foreign countries population size, growth rates, and components of change, by country, projected 1987-2050 and trends from 1950, biennial rpt, 2324-9

France and US life expectancy, by sex, 1981, 4147-5.4

Hazardous substances exposure factors, and methodological guidelines, 1989 rpt, 9188-109

Health condition and health care resources, use, and spending, 1950s-87, annual data compilation, 4144-11

Homicide rates, and lifetime probability of victimization, by age, sex, and race, 1987, annual rpt, 6224-8

Indian Health Service facilities, funding, operations, and Indian health and other characteristics, 1950s-88, annual chartbook, 4084-1

Life tables, abridged, 1987, US Vital Statistics advance annual rpt, 4146-5.113

Life tables, 1986 and trends from 1900, US Vital Statistics annual rpt, 4144-2.6

Life tables, 1988, and life expectancy by race and sex, from 1950, US Vital Statistics annual rpt, 4144-7

Mexico population, labor force, and emigration, alternative projections 1990-2000, working paper, 2326-18.46

OASDI benefit payments, trust fund finances, and economic and demographic assumptions, 1970-87 and alternative projections to 1997, actuarial rpt, 4706-1.103

Older persons health condition and care access, data collection improvement needs, 1985 conf papers, 4147-4.26

Older persons life expectancy under independent and dependent living arrangements, by age, model results, 1989 article, 4042-3.919

Older persons socioeconomic characteristics, 1900s-86 and projected to 2050, biennial chartbook, 12904-1

Population size and characteristics, 1969-88, Current Population Rpt, annual rpt, 2546-2.146

Population size and components of change, alternative projections 1988-2080 and trends from 1900, annual actuarial rpt, 4706-1.104

Population size, by age, sex, and race, and components of change, alternative projections 1988-2080, Current Population Rpt, 2546-3.158

Statistical Abstract of US, social, political, and economic data, 1790-2025, comprehensive annual compilation, 2324-1.1

Life insurance

Assets and debts of private sector, balance sheets by segment, 1949-88, semiannual rpt, 9365-4.1

Assets and liabilities of financial instns, by instn type, 1985-87, annual rpt, 9364-5.4

Assets and liabilities of life insurance companies, monthly rpt, 9362-1.1

Assets composition, growth, and distribution for financial instns, by instn type, 1970s-88, 8438-1

Consumer Expenditure Survey, household income by source, and itemized spending, by selected characteristics and location, 1984-86, annual rpt, 6764-5.2

Employee benefit plan coverage and provisions, by plan type and occupational group, 1988, annual rpt, 6784-19

Employer-provided accidental death and dismemberment plans, coverage by plan provision and occupational group, 1988, article, 6722-1.944

Employer-provided life insurance plans, coverage and benefits by length of service and other employee characteristics, 1988, article, 6722-1.951

Employment, earnings, and hours, by SIC 1- to 4-digit industry, monthly 1983-Feb 1989, annual rpt, 6744-4

Expenditures, coverage, and benefits for social welfare programs, late 1930s-87, annual rpt, 4744-3.1

Fed Govt civilian employee work-years, pay rates, and benefits use and costs, by agency, FY87, annual rpt, 9844-31

Fed Govt civilian employees demographic and employment characteristics, as of Sept 1988, article, 9842-1.901

Fed Home Loan Bank System members and assets, 1988, annual listing, 9314-5

Financial and business statistics, historic trends, 1988 annual chartbook, 9364-2.14

Financial and tax impacts of Deficit Reduction Act and proposed reforms, for stock and mutual life insurance firms, 1984-86 and projected to FY94, 8008-138

Flow-of-funds accounts, assets and liabilities by type and economic sector, outstanding at year-end 1965-88, annual rpt, 9364-3

Income, income taxes, and alternative methods of taxing dividends, for stock and mutual life insurance companies, 1980s-87, GAO rpt, 26119-274

Mortgage-backed securities investment by corporate and union pension funds and life insurance firms, by issuer, quarterly rpt, 5002-10

Mortgage commitments of life insurance companies, 1985-87, annual rpt, 9364-5.13

Occupational injury and illness rates, by SIC 2- to 4-digit industry, 1987, annual rpt, 6844-1

Police pay, benefits, and staffing, for US Park Police and compared to other Federal and local police units, FY85-88, GAO rpt, 26119-264

Smoker-nonsmoker differentials in life insurance premiums, 1986-87, annual rpt, 4204–18

Statistical Abstract of US, social, political, and economic data, 1790-2025, comprehensive annual compilation, 2324–1.3

Supplemental Security Income beneficiaries, assets by type and eligibility class, FY87, article, 4742–1.922

Tax expenditures from employee benefits, for income and payroll tax by benefit type, 1950-87 and projected to 2065, article, 9373–1.913

Veterans and servicepersons life insurance, actuarial analysis of VA programs, 1988, annual rpt, 8604–1

Veterans and servicepersons life insurance of VA, finances and coverage by program and State, 1988, annual rpt, 8604–4

see also Area wage surveys

see also Old-Age, Survivors, Disability, and Health Insurance

see also Servicepersons life insurance programs

Light
see also Fiber optics
see also Lasers

Light, Audrey
"New Evidence on School Desegregation", 11048–189

Light bulbs
see Household supplies and utensils

Lighthouses and lightships
Historic preservation grants for lighthouses, by State, FY89, press release, 5306–4.1
Mariners Weather Log, quarterly journal, 2152–8

Lighting equipment
see Electrical machinery and equipment

Lima, Ohio
Wages by occupation, for office and plant workers, 1989 survey, periodic MSA rpt, 6785–3.10
see also under By SMSA or MSA in the "Index by Categories"

Lime
see Fertilizers
see Nonmetallic minerals and mines

Lin, William
"Proposed Changes in the Cu-Sum Plan: What Will Be the Impact on the U.S. Soybean Industry?", 1561–3.903
"Sorghum: Background for 1990 Farm Legislation", 1566–7.9

Lincoln, Nebr.
see also under By City and By SMSA or MSA in the "Index by Categories"

Lindsey, David E.
"Simple Microanalytics of Payments System Risk", 9366–6.175

Lindsey, Phoebe A.
"Medicaid Utilization Control Programs: Results of a 1987 Study", 4652–1.944

Linens
see Household supplies and utensils

Lino, Mark
"Consumer Decisions, Expenditures, and Knowledge Regarding Funerals", 1702–1.909
"Financial Status of Single-Parent Households", 1702–1.901

Linseed
see Oils, oilseeds, and fats

Lipovsky, William A.
"Rum: Annual Report (Covering 1987 and 1988) on Selected Economic Indicators", 9884–15

Liquefied natural gas
see Natural gas liquids

Liquefied petroleum gas
Agriculture census, 1987: farms, farmland, production, finances, and operator characteristics, by county, final State rpt series, 2331–1

Business statistics, detailed data for major industries and economic indicators, *Survey of Current Business*, monthly rpt, 2702–1.15

Consumption, by detailed fuel type, end-use sector, and State, 1960-87, State Energy Data System annual rpt, 3164–39

Consumption of oil, switching to other fuels, capability by end-use sector, 1989, annual rpt, 3164–88

Farm prices received and paid, by commodity and State, 1988, annual rpt, 1629–5

Farm prices received for major products and paid for farm inputs and living items, by commodity and State, monthly rpt, 1629–1

Farm production inputs supply, demand, and prices, 1970s-89, article, 1561–16.903

Farm production itemized costs, by farm sales size and region, 1988, annual rpt, 1614–3

Foreign and US oil prices, by refined product and country, 1980-88, annual rpt, 3164–50.6

Freight (waterborne domestic and foreign) by commodity, traffic, and passengers, by port and waterway, 1987, annual rpt, 3754–3

Futures trading in selected commodities and financial instruments and indexes, NYC, Chicago, and other markets activity, monthly rpt, 11922–5

Housing and households detailed characteristics, and unit and neighborhood quality, by location, 1985, biennial rpt, 2485–12

Housing and households detailed characteristics, and unit and neighborhood quality, MSA surveys, series, 2485–6

Housing energy use, costs, and conservation, and household and housing characteristics, survey rpt series, 3166–7

Manufacturing census, 1987: financial and operating data, for SIC 4-digit industries by product, preliminary rpt, 2491–1.41

Manufacturing energy use and prices, 1985 survey, series, 3166–13

Minerals Yearbook, 1987, Vol 3 preprints: foreign country reviews of production, trade, and policy, by commodity, annual rpt series, 5604–23

Naval Petroleum and Oil Shale Reserves production and revenue by fuel type, sales by purchaser, and wells, by reserve, FY88, annual rpt, 3004–22

Pollution (air) levels for 5 pollutants, by detailed source and State, 1986, annual rpt, 9194–7

Price indexes (producer), by stage of processing and detailed commodity, monthly rpt, 6762–6

Prices and spending for fuel, by type, end-use sector, and State, 1987, annual rpt, 3164–64

Retail trade census, 1987: employment, establishments, sales, and payroll, by SIC 2- to 4-digit kind of business, MSA, county, and city, State rpt series, 2397–1

Supply, demand, and movement of crude oil, gas liquids, and refined products, by PAD district and State, 1988 and trends from 1973, annual rpt, 3164–2

Supply, demand, and prices, by fuel type and end-use sector, projected under 3 oil price assumptions, 1988-2000, annual rpt, 3164–75

Supply, demand, and prices, by fuel type and end-use sector, with foreign comparisons, 1988 and trends from 1949, annual rpt, 3164–74.1; 3164–74.2

Supply, demand, and prices, by fuel type, end-use sector, and country, detailed data, monthly rpt, 3162–24

Supply, demand, trade, stocks, and refining of oil and gas liquids, by detailed product, State, and PAD district, monthly rpt with articles, 3162–6

Tax (excise) on gasoline and other motor fuels, rates by selected State, as of Oct 1987, 10048–72

Tax rates for motor fuel, by fuel type and State, monthly rpt, 7552–1

Transportation census, 1987: trucks, by detailed characteristics, miles traveled, and type of product carried, State rpt series, 2573–1

Transportation energy use by mode, fuel supply, and demographic and economic factors of vehicle use, 1970s-88, annual rpt, 3304–5

Wholesale trade census, 1987: employment, establishments, finances, and operations, by SIC 2- to 4-digit kind of business, MSA, county, and city, State rpt series, 2405–1

Liquor and liquor industry
Business statistics, detailed data for major industries and economic indicators, *Survey of Current Business*, monthly rpt, 2702–1.11

Consumption of alcohol, by beverage type, region, and State, 1977-87, annual rpt, 4486–1.3; 4486–1.6; 4486–1.9

Consumption, supply, trade, prices, spending, and indexes, by food commodity, 1987, annual rpt, 1544–4

County Business Patterns, 1987: employment, establishments, and payroll, by SIC 2- to 4-digit industry and county, annual State rpt series, 2326–8

CPI by component for US city average, and by region, population size, and for 27 metro areas, monthly rpt, 6762–2

Employment, earnings, and hours, by SIC 1- to 4-digit industry, monthly 1983-Feb 1989, annual rpt, 6744–4

Exports and imports (agricultural) of US, by commodity, monthly rpt, 1922–8

Exports of US, detailed commodities by country, monthly rpt, 2422–3

Finances and operations, by SIC 2- to 4-digit industry, forecast 1989 with trends from 1950s, annual rpt, 2044–28

Food marketing sector finances, operations, and merger activity, for processors and distributors, as of 1988, annual rpt, 1544–22

Freight (waterborne domestic and foreign) by commodity, traffic, and passengers, by port and waterway, 1987, annual rpt, 3754–3

Govt finances, by level of govt, State, and for large cities and counties, annual rpt series, 2466–2

Grain (feed) consumption, by end use, periodic situation rpt with articles, 1561–4

Grain production, prices, trade, and export inspections by US port and country of destination, by grain type, weekly rpt, 1313–2

Imports of US, detailed Schedule A commodities by country, monthly rpt, 2422–2

Manufacturing annual survey, 1986: financial and operating data, by SIC 2- to 4-digit industry, series, 2506–15

Manufacturing census, 1987: financial and operating data, for SIC 4-digit industries by product, preliminary rpt, 2491–1.8

Molasses supply, use, wholesale prices by market, and trade and production by country, 1983-88, annual rpt, 1311–19

Nutrient and caloric composition of food, for raw, processed, and prepared food, 1988 rpt, 1358–3

Occupational injury and illness rates, by SIC 2- to 4-digit industry, 1987, annual rpt, 6844–1

Price indexes (producer), by stage of processing and detailed commodity, monthly rpt, 6762–6

Price indexes (producer), by stage of processing and detailed commodity, monthly 1988, annual rpt, 6764–2

Production of distilled spirits, stocks, materials used, and taxable and tax-free removals, by State, monthly rpt, 8486–1.3

Retail trade census, 1987: employment, establishments, sales, and payroll, by SIC 2- to 4-digit kind of business, MSA, county, and city, State rpt series, 2397–1

Retail trade sales and inventories, by kind of business, region, and selected State, MSA, and city, monthly rpt, 2413–3

Retail trade sales, by kind of business, advance monthly rpt, 2413–2

Retail trade sales, inventories, purchases, gross margin, and accounts receivable, by SIC 2- to 4-digit kind of business and form of ownership, 1987, annual rpt, 2413–5

Rum production, trade by country, and use, 1987-88, annual rpt, 9884–15

Science, engineering, and technical employment in transportation, utilities, and retail and wholesale trade, by field, occupation, and industry, 1985, triennial rpt, 9627–32

State liquor store employment and payroll, by State, 1988, annual rpt series, 2466–1.1; 2466–1.5

State liquor store labor productivity and indexes of output, FY67-87, annual rpt, 6824–1.6

Statistical Abstract of US, social, political, and economic data, 1790-2025, comprehensive annual compilation, 2324–1.2; 2324–1.3

Tax (excise) collections of IRS, by source, quarterly rpt, 8302–1; 8302–2.1

Tax (excise) collections of IRS, by type of tax, region, and State, FY88, annual rpt, 8304–3

Tax (excise) indexed to inflation, impacts on Federal revenue and family tax burden by commodity, projected under alternative proposals, 1989-93, GAO rpt, 26119–254

Tax (income) returns of corporations, income and tax items by asset size and detailed industry, 1986, annual rpt, 8304–4; 8304–21

Tax rates and revenue of State and local govts, by source and State, 1989 annual rpt, 10044–1

Tax revenue potential of State and local systems relative to natl average tax burden, by type of tax and State, 1986, annual rpt, 10044–7

Tax revenues, by level of govt, type of tax, State, and selected large county, quarterly rpt, 2462–3

Wholesale trade census, 1987: employment, establishments, finances, and operations, by SIC 2- to 4-digit kind of business, MSA, county, and city, State rpt series, 2405–1

Wholesale trade sales and inventories, by SIC 2- to 3-digit kind of business, monthly rpt, 2413–7

Wholesale trade sales, inventories, purchases, and gross margins, by SIC 2- to 3-digit kind of business and form of ownership, 1988, annual rpt, 2413–13

see also Alcohol abuse and treatment
see also Alcohol use
see also Alcoholic beverages control laws
see also Beer and breweries
see also Wine and winemaking

Liquor laws
see Alcoholic beverages control laws

Listerosis
see Animal diseases and zoonoses

Literacy and illiteracy
Aliens excluded and deported from US by cause and country, 1892-1988, annual rpt, 6264–2

Asian American earnings, and employment and other characteristics, by detailed origin and whether foreign-born, 1980, 11046–7.2

Communist, OECD, and selected other countries living standards and commodity production, 1960s-88, annual rpt, 9114–4.1

Developing countries aged population and selected characteristics, 1980s and projected to 2020, country rpt series, 2326–19

Developing countries disaster preparedness and economic, population, and political data, country rpt series, 9916–2

Developing countries economic and social conditions from 1960s, and Intl Dev Cooperation Agency and AID activities and funding, FY88-90, annual rpt, 9904–4

Foreign countries economic, social, political, and geographic summary data, by country, 1989, annual factbook, 9114–2

Health care personnel of VA born abroad, and English proficiency, as of Mar 1988, GAO rpt, 26121–273

Libraries (public) literacy project descriptions and funding, FY88, annual listing, 4874–3

Libraries literacy program activities, and relation to community and instn characteristics, 1986, 4878–2

Young adults literacy and reading scores, by race and education, 1985, annual rpt, 4824–2.28

Young adults literacy skills, relation to educational attainment and race, natl assessment, 1985, 4828–36

see also Reading ability and habits

Literature
see Language arts

Lithium
see Metals and metal industries

Litter
see Refuse and refuse disposal

Little, Jane S.
"Economic Effects of the U.S.-Canada Free Trade Agreement on New England", 9373–2.902
"Exchange Rates and Structural Change in U.S. Manufacturing Employment", 9373–1.906

Little Rock, Ariz.
see also under By City and By SMSA or MSA in the "Index by Categories"

Little Rock, Ark.
Economic and banking conditions, for Fed Reserve 8th District, quarterly rpt with articles, 9391–16

Freight (waterborne domestic and foreign) by commodity, traffic, and passengers, by port and waterway, 1987, annual rpt, 3754–3.2

Housing vacancy rates for single and multifamily units and mobile homes, by city and ZIP code, 1989, annual MSA rpt, 9304–19.3

Wages by occupation, and benefits for office and plant workers, 1989 survey, periodic MSA rpt, 6785–12.7

Littman, Mark S.
"Poverty in the U.S., 1987", 2546–6.60
"Poverty in the 1980's: Are the Poor Getting Poorer?", 6722–1.927
"Reasons for Not Working: Poor and Nonpoor Householders", 6722–1.939
"Transitions in Income and Poverty Status: 1984-85", 2546–20.10

Litz, Diane
"Multifactor Productivity Advances in the Tires and Inner Tubes Industry", 6722–1.928

Liver diseases
see Digestive diseases

Livestock and livestock industry
Agricultural data compilation, 1987/88 and trends from 1920, annual rpt, 1004–14

Agricultural exports of US, impacts of foreign agricultural and trade policy, with data by commodity and country, 1988, annual rpt, 1924–8

Agricultural Stabilization and Conservation Service producer payments, by program and State, 1988, annual rpt, 1804–12

Agricultural Statistics, 1988, annual rpt, 1004–1

Agriculture census, 1987: farms, farmland, production and costs, and operator characteristics, advance State and county rpt series, 2330–1

Agriculture census, 1987: farms, farmland, production, finances, and operator characteristics, by county, final State rpt series, 2331–1

Transportation census, 1987: trucks, by detailed characteristics, miles traveled, and type of product carried, State rpt series, 2573–1

Water (groundwater) protection standards, States use of EPA and alternative standards by type of water use, and contaminant test results, 1976-88, GAO rpt, 26131–56

Wholesale trade census, 1987: employment, establishments, finances, and operations, by SIC 2- to 4-digit kind of business, MSA, county, and city, State rpt series, 2405–1

Wildlife damage to crops, livestock, and property in Great Plains, and effectiveness of mgmt methods, 1988 conf, 1208–304

see also Animal diseases and zoonoses

see also Dairy industry and products

see also Hides and skins

see also Meat and meat products

see also Pasture and rangeland

see also Poultry industry and products

see also Veterinary medicine

see also By Industry in the "Index by Categories"

see also under By Commodity in the "Index by Categories"

Livezey, Janet

"Setting for the 1990 Farm Bill", 1561–8.905

Living arrangements

Abortions by patient characteristics, rates for all and 1st abortions, and related deaths in US and other countries, 1989 hearing, 21408–113

AIDS deaths, by health and other characteristics, 1986, 4146–8.178

Alaska rural villages population characteristics and and subsistence activities, 1976-86, 5738–9

Children (handicapped) enrollment by age, and special education programs staff, funding, and needs, by type of handicap and State, 1987/88, annual rpt, 4944–4

Consumer Income, socioeconomic characteristics of persons, families, and households, detailed cross-tabulations, Current Population Rpt series, 2546–6

Disabled persons employment, labor force status, and other characteristics, 1988, Current Population Rpt, 2546–2.147

Heart disease deaths, by health and other characteristics, 1986, 4146–8.177

Homeless children, by type of accommodation, urban-rural location, and State, alternative estimates, 1988, GAO rpt, 26131–61

Household and family characteristics, by living arrangement, 1988 and trends from 1960, Current Population Rpt, 2546–2.148

Household and family composition, and factors affecting change, 1960s-88, chartbook, 2546–2.149

Household composition, income, benefits, and labor force status, Survey of Income and Program Participation methodology, working paper series, 2626–10

Income (household) and poverty status under alternative income definitions, by recipient characteristics, 1986, Current Population Rpt, 2546–6.58

Insurance (health) coverage of adolescents by selected characteristics, and impacts of mandated employer and expanded Medicaid coverage, 1979-87, 26358–205

Living arrangements and household composition, 1988, advance annual Current Population Rpt, 2546–1.441

Living arrangements, family relationships, and marital status, by selected characteristics, 1988, annual Current Population Rpt, 2546–1.428; 2546–1.433

Nursing home facility, staff, and resident detailed characteristics, 1985, 4147–13.97

Nursing home residents, by living arrangement prior to admission and other characteristics, 1985, 4147–13.102

Older persons functional limitations, by activity type and selected characteristics, 1984, 4147–10.167

Older persons health care services use related to marital status, living arrangements, and other characteristics, 1977, 4188–54

Older persons health care spending for instnl and community care, under alternative community settings, 1979-84 study, article, 4652–1.932

Older persons life expectancy under independent and dependent living arrangements, by age, model results, 1989 article, 4042–3.919

Older persons living arrangements, by poverty status, 1988, annual rpt, 4744–3.1

Older persons socioeconomic characteristics, 1900s-86 and projected to 2050, biennial chartbook, 12904–1

Statistical Abstract of US, social, political, and economic data, 1790-2025, comprehensive annual compilation, 2324–1.1

Supplemental Security Income aged and disabled beneficiary characteristics, payments, and eligibility, for awards made 1981, 1985, article, 4742–1.907

Supplemental Security Income and Medicaid eligibility and payment provisions, and beneficiaries living arrangements, by State, 1989, annual rpt, 4704–13

Supplemental Security Income beneficiaries, by race and sex, monthly rpt, 4742–1.12

Supplemental Security Income recipients, by eligibility type and living arrangement, 1987, annual rpt, 4744–3.8

Vermont older persons employment, income, and other characteristics, by sex and age, 1900-86, hearing, 21148–54

see also Families and households

see also Foster home care

see also Group quarters

see also Homeless population

see also Housing condition and occupancy

see also Retirement communities

see also Rooming and boarding houses

see also Transient housing

Living standard

see Cost of living

see Family budgets

see Personal and household income

see Quality of life

Livingston, Lori A.

"U.S. Import and Export Prices Continued To Register Sizeable Gains in 1988", 6722–1.922

Livonia, Mich.

see also under By City in the "Index by Categories"

Loan delinquency and default

Agricultural banks financial performance, impacts of drought by region, 1988, article, 1502–7.916

AID housing and urban dev program financial statements, and loan guarantees by country, FY88, annual rpt, 9914–4

AID loans repayment status and terms by program and country, and status of predecessor agency loans, quarterly rpt, 9912–3

Banks (insured commercial) assets, income, and financial ratios, by asset size and State, quarterly rpt, 13002–3

Banks (insured commercial) financial condition and performance, by asset size and region, quarterly rpt, 9292–1

Banks (insured commercial) profitability, balance sheet items, and rates of return by asset size, 1984-88, annual article, 9362–1.907

Banks (insured commercial and savings) finances, for foreign and domestic offices, by asset size, 1987, annual rpt, 9294–4.2

Banks (natl) domestic and intl operations, charters, mergers, and liquidations, by instn and State, quarterly rpt, 8402–3

Banks (natl) financial performance, and Office of the Comptroller of Currency enforcement activities, 1978-88, 8408–18

Banks (US) loans to developing countries, and loan loss reserves, by money center bank, Sept 1988, hearings, 21248–122

Banks failed and assisted, FDIC mgmt and liquidation of acquired assets, 1980-88, GAO rpt, 26119–237

Banks financial performance, impact of loan commitments, various periods 1975-86, technical paper, 9366–6.179

Banks financial performance indicators by asset size, Fed Reserve 8th District, 1985-88, annual article, 9391–1.912

Banks financial performance, risk assessment, and regulation, 1988 annual conf papers, 9375–7

Banks in Fed Reserve 5th District, financial performance, 1984-88, annual article, 9389–1.909

Banks loan interest rates and default risk relation to loan collateral status, type, and other characteristics, 1977-87, technical paper, 9366–6.165

Banks stock price and trading impact of loan-loss reserve additions, with data by instn, 1987, working paper, 9387–8.186

Bond (low-grade) holdings of thrift instns, returns, defaults, and losses, 1985-88, GAO rpt, 26119–246

Bond (low-grade) issues by industry div, holdings by owner type, yields, and defaults, 1977-88, 21248–118

Budget of US, compact budgets by activity, function, and agency, FY90 and projected to FY94, annual rpt, 104–2

Budget of US, special analysis of credit programs, FY90, annual rpt, 104–1.6

Business Conditions Digest, economic, business, and financial devs and cyclical fluctuations, monthly rpt, 2702–3

CCC financial statements and operations, by program and commodity, FY88, annual rpt, 1824–4

West Central States, FHLB 10th District savings instns finances and lending by State and MSA, monthly table, 9302–22

Western States, FHLB 11th District S&Ls, offices, and financial condition, 1989 annual listing, 9304–23

Western States, FHLB 12th District savings instns deposits and lending by State, monthly press release series, 9302–32

see also Agricultural credit
see also Commercial credit
see also Consumer credit
see also Credit
see also Credit unions
see also Discrimination in credit
see also Export-Import Bank
see also Farm Credit System
see also Federal aid programs
see also Federal aid to arts and humanities
see also Federal aid to education
see also Federal aid to higher education
see also Federal aid to highways
see also Federal aid to housing
see also Federal aid to law enforcement
see also Federal aid to libraries
see also Federal aid to local areas
see also Federal aid to medical education
see also Federal aid to medicine
see also Federal aid to railroads
see also Federal aid to rural areas
see also Federal aid to States
see also Federal aid to transportation
see also Federal aid to vocational education
see also Federal funding for energy programs
see also Federal funding for research and development
see also Finance companies
see also Foreign debts
see also Government and business
see also Government assets and liabilities
see also Interest payments
see also Interest rates
see also International assistance
see also Loan delinquency and default
see also Military assistance
see also Mortgages
see also Public debt
see also Student aid
see also Veterans benefits and pensions
see also Veterans housing

Lobbying and lobbying groups
Tax (excise) collections of IRS, by source, quarterly rpt, 8302–1
Tax (excise) collections of IRS, by type of tax, region, and State, FY88, annual rpt, 8304–3.3
see also Political action committees

Lobsters
see Shellfish

Local-Federal relations
see Federal-local relations

Local government
Construction put in place, value of new public and private structures, by type, monthly rpt, 2382–4
Criminal justice spending, employment, and payroll, by level of govt, State, and selected city and county, FY71-85, annual rpt, 6064–9
Drug enforcement activities of State and local agencies, Federal aid by recipient, and background data, FY88, annual rpt, 6064–28
Environmental protection budgets and aid of EPA and State, and regulation impacts on local govts credit availability and farm income, 1988 hearings, 25408–99

Expenditures of local govts, impacts of competition among govtl units, migration, and other factors, 1976-77, working paper, 9377–9.82

Finances of govts, by level of govt, State, and for large cities and counties, annual rpt series, 2466–2

Finances of govts, revenues by source and spending by function, natl income and product account, *Survey of Current Business*, monthly rpt, 2702–1.24

Finances of govts, tax systems and revenue, and fiscal structure, by level of govt and State, selected years 1929-91, annual rpt, 10044–1

Finances of State and local govts, revenues by source and outlays by type, 1985-88, annual article, 2702–1.908; 2702–1.935

Finances, policy, and intergovtl relations of Federal, State, and local govts, series, 10046–8

Finances, structure, and service delivery of local govts in metro areas, local area rpt series, 10046–9

Financial and business statistics, historic trends, 1988 annual chartbook, 9364–2.9

Flow-of-funds accounts, savings, investments, and credit statements, quarterly rpt, 9365–3.3

Hwy funding by function, and revenue, by level of govt and type of hwy, 1960-87, biennial rpt, 7554–27.2

Hwy Statistics, detailed data by State, 1988, annual rpt, 7554–1

Job Training Partnership Act State and local admin, funding, effectiveness, and participants, GAO rpt series, 26106–8

Law enforcement spending and employment, by activity and level of govt, 1970s-88, annual rpt, 6064–6.1

Procurement of goods and services by level of govt, *Business Conditions Digest*, monthly rpt, 2702–3.5

Public opinion on taxes, spending, and govt efficiency, by respondent characteristics, 1989 survey, annual rpt, 10044–2

Retirement systems of State and local govts, cash and security holdings and finances, quarterly rpt, 2462–2

Statistical Abstract of US, social, political, and economic data, 1790-2025, comprehensive annual compilation, 2324–1.2
see also Census of Governments
see also City and town planning
see also Federal aid to local areas
see also Federal-local relations
see also Fire departments
see also Municipal bonds
see also Police
see also School districts
see also Special districts
see also State and local employees
see also State and local employees pay
see also State and local taxes
see also State funding for local areas
see also State-local relations

Location of industries
see Industrial siting

Lockouts
see Labor-management relations, general

Lockridge, Patricia A.
"U.S. Tsunamis (Including U.S. Possessions), 1690-1988", 2158–52

Locks
see Hardware

Locomotives
see Railroad equipment and vehicles

Lodging
see Hotels and motels

Logistics
DOD budget, manpower needs, costs, and force readiness by service branch, FY90, annual rpt, 3504–1
DOD budget, R&D appropriations by item, service branch, and defense agency, FY88-91, annual rpt, 3544–33
DOD shipments of military and personal property, passenger traffic, and costs, by service branch and mode of transport, quarterly rpt, 3702–1
Fed Govt labor productivity, indexes of output and labor costs by function, FY67-87, annual rpt, 6824–1.6
Military Traffic Mgmt Command finances and operations, FY88, annual rpt, 3704–14
Soviet Union and Warsaw Pact military weapons systems, aid, presence, and force strengths, and compared to US and NATO, 1989 annual rpt, 3504–20
see also Military supplies and property

Lompoc, Calif.
Wages by occupation, and benefits for office and plant workers, 1989 survey, periodic MSA rpt, 6785–3.9
see also under By SMSA or MSA in the "Index by Categories"

London, Kathryn A.
"Children of Divorce. Vital and Health Statistics Series 21", 4147–21.46

London, Stephanie J.
"Prospective Study of Smoking and the Risk of Breast Cancer", 4472–1.928

Long Beach, Calif.
Household and family characteristics, by location, 1988, annual Current Population Rpt, 2546–1.437
Housing and households characteristics, 1985 survey, MSA fact sheet, 2485–11.12
Housing and households detailed characteristics, and unit and neighborhood quality, by location, 1985 survey, MSA rpt, 2485–6.13
Housing starts and completions authorized by building permits in 40 MSAs, quarterly rpt, 2382–9
Older frail persons HMO case mgmt and home care services, demonstration projects enrollment, 1986, article, 4652–1.913
Wages by occupation, for office and plant workers, 1988 survey, periodic MSA rpt, 6785–11.2
see also under By City and By SMSA or MSA in the "Index by Categories"

Long, Celeste A.
"Growth Falters in Most Rural Counties: Manufacturing Both Hero and Goat", 1502–7.907

Long Island, N.Y.
CPI by component for US city average, and by region, population size, and for 15 metro areas, monthly rpt, 6762–1
CPI by component for US city average, and by region, population size, and for 27 metro areas, monthly rpt, 6762–2

Housing starts and completions authorized
by building permits in 40 MSAs, quarterly
rpt, 2382–9

Long, Stephen H.
"Updated Estimates of Medicare's
Catastrophic Drug Insurance Program",
26308–89

Long, William T., III
"Texas Industrial Production Index",
9379–1.908

Longmont, Colo.
see also under By SMSA or MSA in the
"Index by Categories"

Longshoremen
Collective bargaining agreements expiring
during year, and workers covered, by
firm, union, industry group, and State,
1989, annual rpt, 6784–9
Employment shipboard, shipyard, and
longshore, FY87-88, annual rpt,
7704–14.3
Labor supply in 4 coastal regions, monthly
rpt, 7702–1
Occupational injuries of longshoremen, by
body site, circumstances, and
characteristics of persons and equipment
involved, 1985-86 survey, 6846–1.18
Workers compensation laws of States and
Fed Govt, 1989 semiannual rpt, 6502–1
Workers compensation programs under
Federal admin, finances and operations,
FY87, annual rpt, 6504–10

Longview, Tex.
Wages by occupation, for office and plant
workers, 1989 survey, periodic MSA rpt,
6785–12.6
see also under By SMSA or MSA in the
"Index by Categories"

Longview, Wash.
Housing vacancy rates for single and
multifamily units and mobile homes, by
city and ZIP code, 1988, annual MSA rpt,
9304–21.2

Lorain, Ohio
CPI by component for US city average, and
by region, population size, and for 15
metro areas, monthly rpt, 6762–1
CPI by component for US city average, and
by region, population size, and for 27
metro areas, monthly rpt, 6762–2
see also under By SMSA or MSA in the
"Index by Categories"

Lord, Ronald C.
"U.S. Imports of Sugar in Sugar-Containing
Products, 1977-88", 1561–14.905
"World Sugar and HFCS Production Costs,
1979/80-1986/87", 1561–14.904

Los Alamos Scientific Laboratory
see also Department of Energy National
Laboratories

Los Angeles, Calif.
Aerospace industry employment and
salaries, by sex and race, 1979-87, GAO
rpt, 26121–315
Aerospace industry minority employment in
Los Angeles area, by occupational group,
1980s-86, 21348–113
Alcohol fuels (methanol) prices, distribution,
and gasoline displacement, with
background data, 1985-86 and projected
to 2000, 3008–122
Aliens exclusion and deportation cases,
appeals, bond postings, and investigations,
for NYC and Los Angeles, 1987, GAO
rpt, 26119–271

Child health and welfare programs of local
agencies for high-risk infants and children,
for Los Angeles and San Francisco, 1988
hearing, 21968–48
CPI by component for US city average, and
by region, population size, and for 15
metro areas, monthly rpt, 6762–1
CPI by component for US city average, and
by region, population size, and for 27
metro areas, monthly rpt, 6762–2
Drug abuse emergency room admissions and
deaths, by drug type and source, sex, race,
age, and major metro area, 1988, annual
rpt, 4494–8
Drug abuse indicators for selected metro
areas, research results, data collection, and
policy issues, 1989 semiannual conf,
4492–5
Drug test results at arrest, by drug type,
offense, and sex, for selected urban areas,
quarterly rpt, 6062–3
Freight (waterborne domestic and foreign)
by commodity, traffic, and passengers, by
port and waterway, 1987, annual rpt,
3754–3.4
Fruit and vegetable shipments, and arrivals
in US and Canada cities, by mode of
transport and State and country of origin,
1988, annual rpt, 1311–4.2
Homeless persons aid programs, and shelter
capacity and voucher programs, for 5
major cities, 1988, 5188–122
Homicide victims alcohol blood levels, by
race, Hispanic origin, and other
characteristics, for Los Angeles, 1970-79,
conf papers, 4488–13
Household and family characteristics, by
location, 1988, annual Current Population
Rpt, 2546–1.437
Housing and households characteristics,
1985 survey, MSA fact sheet,
2485–11.12
Housing and households detailed
characteristics, and unit and neighborhood
quality, by location, 1985 survey, MSA
rpt, 2485–6.13
Housing starts and completions authorized
by building permits in 40 MSAs, quarterly
rpt, 2382–9
Wages by occupation, for office and plant
workers, 1988 survey, periodic MSA rpt,
6785–11.2
see also under By City and By SMSA or
MSA in the "Index by Categories"

Los Angeles County, Calif.
Govt services transfer to private contractors,
impacts on govt workers, with data by
worker characteristics, level of govt, and
location, 1980s-87, 15496–1.5
Housing and households detailed
characteristics, and unit and neighborhood
quality, by location, 1985 survey, MSA
rpt, 2485–6.13

Lotteries
Govt finances, tax systems and revenue, and
fiscal structure, by level of govt and State,
selected years 1929-91, annual rpt,
10044–1.2
Statistical Abstract of US, social, political,
and economic data, 1790-2025,
comprehensive annual compilation,
2324–1.2
Virgin Islands economic censuses, 1987:
employment, firms, payroll, and receipts,
by SIC 1- to 4-digit industry, island, and
city, 2593–1

Loudoun County, Va.
Fed Govt land acquisition and dev projects
in DC metro area, characteristics and
funding by agency and project, FY90-94,
annual rpt, 15454–1

Louisiana
Agriculture census, 1987: farms, farmland,
production and costs, and operator
characteristics, advance State and county
rpts, 2330–1.22
Agriculture census, 1987: farms, farmland,
production, finances, and operator
characteristics, by county, final State rpt,
2331–1.18
Bank deposits in FDIC-insured commercial
and savings banks, by instn, State, and
county, as of June 1988, annual regional
rpt, 9295–3.4
Coal production and mines by county,
prices, productivity, miners, reserves, and
stocks, by mining method and State,
1987-88, annual rpt, 3164–25
Deaths and rates, by detailed location,
cause, and demographic characteristics,
1987, US Vital Statistics annual rpt,
4144–3.1
Disaster relief program of Fed Emergency
Mgmt Agency under State admin, impact
of mgmt changes on benefits processing,
1986-88, GAO rpt, 26113–412
DOD prime contract awards, by contractor,
service branch, State, and city, FY88,
annual rpt, 3544–22
Economic indicators by State and MSA,
Fed Reserve 6th District, quarterly rpt,
9371–14
Employment by industry div, earnings, and
hours, by southwestern State, monthly rpt,
6962–2
Employment, earnings, and hours, by
selected SIC 1- to 4-digit industry, State,
and for 262 MSAs, 1972-87, 6748–81.2
Estuary environmental conditions, research
results and methodology, 1989 local area
rpt, 2176–7.13
Fed Govt spending in States and local areas,
by type, State, county, and city, FY88,
annual rpt, 2464–3
Fed Govt spending in States, by type,
program, agency, and State, FY88, annual
rpt, 2464–2
Fish and shellfish catch, wholesale receipts,
prices, trade, and other market activities,
weekly regional rpt, 2162–6.3
HHS financial aid, by program, recipient,
State, and city, FY88, annual regional
listing, 4004–3.6
Homeless children educational enrollment
and needs, 1988, annual State rpt,
4804–35.19
Hospital reimbursement by Medicare under
prospective payment system, impacts on
subacute care, 1988 rpt, 17206–2.8
Income (personal) per capita and by source,
and earnings by industry div, by State,
MSA, and county, 1982-87, annual
regional rpt, 2704–2.4
Mineral Industry Surveys, State reviews of
production, 1988, preliminary annual rpt,
5614–6
Minerals Yearbook, 1987, Vol 2 preprints:
State review of production and sales by
commodity, and business activity, annual
rpt, 5604–16.19

Minerals Yearbook, 1987, Vol 2: State reviews of production, sales, and firms, by commodity, and business activity, annual rpt, 5604-34

Nursing home compliance with Medicare and Medicaid regulations, and patient characteristics, by facility, 1987/88, annual State rpt, 4654-15.19

Oil and gas extraction production workers and wages by occupation, and benefits, by location, 1988 survey, 6787-6.240

Oil and gas OCS production water discharges, and impacts on Gulf of Mexico coastal habitats, 1983-88, 5738-10

Retail trade census, 1987: employment, establishments, sales, and payroll, by SIC 2- to 4-digit kind of business, MSA, county, and city, State rpt, 2397-1.19

Rice market activities, prices, inspections, sales, trade, supply, and use, for US and selected foreign markets, weekly rpt, 1313-8

Savings instns, FHLB 9th District members finances and operations by State, monthly rpt, 9302-13

Savings instns, FHLB 9th District members finances and operations by State, quarterly rpt, 9302-31

Service industries census, 1987: employment, establishments, receipts, and payroll, by SIC 2- to 4-digit kind of business, MSA, county, and city, State rpt, 2391-1.19

Statistical Abstract of US, social, political, and economic data, with foreign comparisons, 1790-2025, comprehensive annual compilation, 2324-1

Water supply and quality in streams and lakes, and groundwater levels in wells, by drainage basin, 1987, annual State rpt, 5666-10.17

Wholesale trade census, 1987: employment, establishments, finances, and operations, by SIC 2- to 4-digit kind of business, MSA, county, and city, State rpt, 2405-1.19

Wildlife-related recreation, hunting, and fishing participation and spending, detailed data, 1985 survey, quinquennial State rpt, 5506-6.18

see also Alexandria, La.

see also Baton Rouge, La.

see also Lake Charles, La.

see also Leesville, La.

see also New Orleans, La.

see also Shreveport, La.

see also under By State in the "Index by Categories"

Louisville, Ky.

Economic and banking conditions, for Fed Reserve 8th District, quarterly rpt with articles, 9391-16

Freight (waterborne domestic and foreign) by commodity, traffic, and passengers, by port and waterway, 1987, annual rpt, 3754-3.2

see also under By City and By SMSA or MSA in the "Index by Categories"

Love, Douglas O.

"Using a Consumer Price Index Database To Measure Intercity Differences in Living Costs", 6886-6.55

Loveland, Colo.

Housing vacancy rates for single and multifamily units and mobile homes, by city and ZIP code, 1989, annual MSA rpt, 9304-22.5

see also under By SMSA or MSA in the "Index by Categories"

Low-income housing

American Housing Survey: unit and households detailed characteristics, and unit and neighborhood quality, MSA rpt series, 2485-6

American Housing Survey: unit and households detailed characteristics, and unit and neighborhood quality, 1985, biennial rpt, 2485-12

Assistance of Fed Govt to low-income housing, unit conditions, and household characteristics, 1985-FY88 and alternative projections to 2008, 26306-6.134

Community dev programs of HUD, funding and activities by program and State, FY88, annual rpt, 5124-5

Energy aid for low income households, by type of aid and State, 1982-87, annual rpt, 4744-3.8

Fed Govt financial and nonfinancial domestic aid, 1989 base edition with supplements, annual listing, 104-5

Fed Govt spending in States, by type, program, agency, and State, FY88, annual rpt, 2464-2

FmHA activities, and loans and grants by program and State, FY88 and trends from FY69, annual rpt, 1184-17

FmHA borrowers, by type of borrower and loan, and State, quarterly rpt, 1182-4

FmHA loans and borrower supervision activities in farm and housing programs, by type and State, monthly rpt, 1182-1

Homeless population characteristics, needs, and impacts of govt aid programs and housing costs, 1988 conf papers, 10048-73

Income (household) and poverty status under alternative income definitions, by recipient characteristics, 1986, Current Population Rpt, 2546-6.58

Indian and Alaska Native housing and economic development program operations, by region, FY86-87, annual rpt, 5004-5

Mortgages FHA-insured for 1-family units, by loan type and mortgage characteristics, quarterly rpt, 5142-45

Older persons low-income rental housing construction and rehabilitation loans, by recipient, 1989, press release HUD loans for older persons low-income rental housing construction and rehabilitation, by recipient, 1989, press release, 5006-3.71

Supply of low income housing, effects of alternative Federal actions and spending levels, projected 1988-2002, hearing, 21248-116

Supply of low income housing, units eligible for subsidized mortgage prepayment, and index of affordable housing needs, by State, 1982-2006, article, 1702-1.903

see also Public housing

see also Rent supplements

Lowell, Mass.

see also under By SMSA or MSA in the "Index by Categories"

Lowham, H. W.

"Streamflows in Wyoming", 5668-84

Lown, Cara S.

"Are Reserve Requirement Changes Really Exogenous? An Example of Regulatory Accommodation of Industry Goals", 9379-12.43

Lowry, Lloyd F.

"Ringed Seal Monitoring: Relationships of Distribution and Abundance to Habitat Attributes and Industrial Activities", 2176-1.27

Loyacono, Laura L.

"State Budget Implications: Child Support Enforcement", 4698-3

LPG

see Liquefied petroleum gas

Lubbock, Tex.

see also under By City and By SMSA or MSA in the "Index by Categories"

Luby, Patrick J.

"What's Ahead in Livestock and Meat Marketing", 1004-16.1

Lucier, Gary

"Characteristics of U.S. Vegetable Farms by Participation in Farm Programs", 1561-11.907

"1989 Outlook for Vegetables", 1004-16.1

Luder, Elisabeth

"Assessment of the Nutritional Status of Urban Homeless Adults", 4042-3.942

Luepke, Gretchen

"Grain-Size, Heavy-Mineral, and Geochemical Analyses of Sediments from the Chukchi Sea, Alaska", 5668-95

Luggage

see Leather industry and products

Lukasiewicz, John

"Projections of Occupational Employment, 1988-2000", 6722-1.955

Lumber industry and products

Agricultural exports of US, impacts of foreign agricultural and trade policy, with data by commodity and country, 1988, annual rpt, 1924-8

Agricultural Statistics, 1988, annual rpt, 1004-1.2

Agriculture census, 1987: farms, farmland, production, finances, and operator characteristics, by county, final State rpt series, 2331-1

Arizona timber harvest, mill receipts, and residues, with methodology, 1984-85, 1208-294

Business statistics, detailed data for major industries and economic indicators, *Survey of Current Business*, monthly rpt, 2702-1.13

California timber resources and mortality, by hardwood species, land class and ownership, and county, 1984-85, 1208-291

China trade by SITC 1- to 5-digit commodity, 1970s-87, annual rpt, 9114-3

Collective bargaining agreements expiring during year, and workers covered, by firm, union, industry group, and State, 1989, annual rpt, 6784-9

Communist countries agricultural, mineral, and consumer and producer goods production, by commodity, 1960s-88, annual rpt, 9114-4.4

County Business Patterns, 1987: employment, establishments, and payroll, by SIC 2- to 4-digit industry and county, annual State rpt series, 2326-8

Prices (stumpage) for sawtimber sold from natl forests, by species and region, quarterly rpt, 1202–1

Production of wood products from damaged and dead timber, feasibility of proposed Montana plant, 1989 rpt, 1208–308

Production, prices, employment, and trade, for hardwood lumber and products, quarterly rpt, 1202–4

Production, shipments, PPI, stocks, and trade of lumber products, by type, bimonthly rpt, 2042–1.5; 2042–1.6

Production, shipments, trade, stocks, and use of wood, paper, and related products, periodic Current Industrial Rpt series, 2506–7

Public lands acreage and use, and Land Mgmt Bur activities and finances, annual State rpt series, 5724–11

Public lands acreage, grants, use, revenues, and allocations, by State, FY88, annual rpt, 5724–1.2

Rocky Mountain States timber and mill residue production, by species, ownership, and county, series, 1206–17

Science, engineering, and technical employment in manufacturing, by field, occupation, and industry, 1986, triennial rpt, 9627–23

Small business establishments, employment, and financial ratios, by SIC 1- to 2-digit industry and State, late 1960s-87, 9768–19

Southeastern US pulpwood and residue prices, spending, and transport shares by mode, 1986-87, annual rpt, 1204–22

Southern US lumber and paper industries productivity, impact on economy, and employment compared to other industries, 1970s-80, State rpt series, 1206–36

Southern US pulpwood production by county, and mill capacity by firm, by State, 1987, annual rpt, 1204–23

Statistical Abstract of US, social, political, and economic data, 1790-2025, comprehensive annual compilation, 2324–1.3

Tariff Schedule of US, classifications and rates of duty by detailed imported commodity, 1990 base edition and supplements, 9886–13

Tax (income) returns of corporations, income and tax items by asset size and detailed industry, 1986, annual rpt, 8304–4; 8304–21

Tax (income) returns of partnerships, income statement items by industry group, 1986, annual article, 8302–2.903

Tax (income) returns of sole proprietorships, income statement items, by industry group, 1987, annual article, 8302–2.904; 8302–2.921

Transportation census, 1987: trucks, by detailed characteristics, miles traveled, and type of product carried, State rpt series, 2573–1

Wholesale trade census, 1987: employment, establishments, finances, and operations, by SIC 2- to 4-digit kind of business, MSA, county, and city, State rpt series, 2405–1

Wholesale trade sales and inventories, by SIC 2- to 3-digit kind of business, monthly rpt, 2413–7

Wisconsin timber resources and removals, by species, forest type, ownership, and county, series, 1206–34

see also Forests and forestry
see also Furniture and furnishings
see also Gum and wood chemicals
see also Paper and paper products
see also Wood fuel
see also By Industry in the "Index by Categories"
see also under By Commodity in the "Index by Categories"

Lung diseases
see Black lung disease
see Pneumonia and influenza
see Respiratory diseases
see Tuberculosis

Lussier, Frances M.
"Effects of a Constrained Budget on U.S. Military Forces", 26306–3.107

Luxembourg
Agricultural and food production and indexes, total and for selected commodities, by country, 1970s-88, annual rpt, 1524–12

Agricultural production, prices, and trade, by country, 1970s-88 and forecast 1990, annual world region rpt, 1524–4.1

Agricultural trade of US, by detailed commodity and country, 1988, semiannual rpt, 1522–4

AID loans repayment status and terms by program and country, and status of predecessor agency loans, quarterly rpt, 9912–3

Economic and military aid and loans from US and intl agencies, by program and country, FY46-87, annual rpt, 9914–5

Economic conditions, policy, and trade practices, by country, 1986-88, annual rpt, 21384–5

Economic, social, political, and geographic summary data, by country, 1989, annual factbook, 9114–2

Exports and imports of US, by selected country, country group, and commodity group, 1988, annual rpt, 2044–37

Food supply and demand, market and support prices, and other economic indicators, by EC country and commodity, 1960-85, 1528–276

Human rights conditions in 170 countries, 1988, annual rpt, 21384–3

Intl transactions of US with 9 countries, 1986-88, *Survey of Current Business*, monthly rpt, annual table, 2702–1.31

Military aid of US, arms sales, and training programs costs and budget requests, by program, world region, and country, FY88-90, annual rpt, 7144–13

Military spending, arms trade, and force strengths, with govt spending and population, by country, 1977-87, annual rpt, 9824–1

Minerals Yearbook, 1987, Vol 3: foreign country reviews of production, trade, and policy, by commodity, annual rpt, 5604–35

Minerals Yearbook, 1987, Vol 3 preprints: foreign country review of production, trade, and policy, by commodity, annual rpt, 5604–23.8

Multinatl US firms and foreign affiliates finances and operations, by industry of parent firm and affiliate, world area, and country, preliminary 1987, annual rpt, 2704–5

Oil production, trade, use, and stocks, by selected country and country group, monthly rpt, 3162–42

Population size, growth rates, and components of change, by country, projected 1989-2020 and trends from 1950, biennial rpt, 2324–9

UN voting record and share of votes in agreement with US, by issue, country, and world area, 1988, annual rpt, 7004–18

see also under By Foreign Country in the "Index by Categories"

Luytjes, Jan E.
"Determining the Appropriate Measure of Interest-Rate Risk from a Regulatory Perspective", 9316–1.145

Lynchburg, Va.
see also under By SMSA or MSA in the "Index by Categories"

Maas, Kenneth M.
"Availability of Land for Mineral Exploration and Development in Southwestern Alaska, 1986", 5608–152.4

Mabbs-Zeno, Carl
"Importance of Tropical Products in the GATT", 1522–3.919
"When Does Trade Liberalization in Tropical Beverages Improve Export Revenues?", 1522–3.922

Macao
Agricultural and food production and indexes, total and for selected commodities, by country, 1970s-88, annual rpt, 1524–12

Agricultural trade of US, by detailed commodity and country, 1988, semiannual rpt, 1522–4

Economic, social, political, and geographic summary data, by country, 1989, annual factbook, 9114–2

Minerals production, reserves, and industry role in domestic economy and world supply, 1988 country rpt, 5606–1.17

Population size, growth rates, and components of change, by country, projected 1989-2020 and trends from 1950, biennial rpt, 2324–9

MacAuley, Patrick H.
"Federal Construction-Related Expenditures, 1981-89", 2042–1.901
"Federal Construction-Related Expenditures, 1982-90", 2042–1.907

MacDonald, James M.
"Effects of Railroad Deregulation on Grain Transportation", 1548–349

MacDonald, Stephen A.
"Defining Bulk and High-Value Products", 1522–3.918

Macera, C. A.
"Runners' Health Habits, 1985: 'The Alameda 7' Revisited", 4042–3.933

Machine-readable data file guides
see Computer data file guides

Machine tools
see Machines and machinery industry

Machines and machinery industry
Accident deaths and rates, by cause, age, race, sex, and State, 1986, US Vital Statistics annual rpt, 4144–4

Bearings (antifriction) from 9 countries, injury to US industry from foreign subsidized and less than fair value imports, investigation with background financial and operating data, 1989 rpt, 9886–19.65

Belts for machinery from 8 countries, injury to US industry from foreign subsidized and less than fair value imports, investigation with background financial and operating data, 1989 rpt, 9886–19.66

Business statistics, detailed data for major industries and economic indicators, *Survey of Current Business*, monthly rpt, 2702–1.14

China trade by SITC 1- to 5-digit commodity, 1970s-87, annual rpt, 9114–3

Collective bargaining agreements expiring during year, and workers covered, by firm, union, industry group, and State, 1989, annual rpt, 6784–9

Communist countries agricultural, mineral, and consumer and producer goods production, by commodity, 1960s-88, annual rpt, 9114–4.4

Communist countries trade with US, by detailed commodity and country, quarterly rpt with articles, 9882–2

Competitiveness (intl) of US paper-making machinery industry, with selected foreign and US operating data, selected years 1958-87, 2046–12.44

Construction industries census, 1987: establishments, employment, receipts, and expenditures, by SIC 4-digit industry and State, final industry rpt series, 2373–1

Construction industries census, 1987: financial and operating data, preliminary industry rpt series, 2371–1

Construction machinery PPI, bimonthly rpt, 2042–1.5

County Business Patterns, 1987: employment, establishments, and payroll, by SIC 2- to 4-digit industry and county, annual State rpt series, 2326–8

DOD prime contract awards, by detailed procurement category, FY85-88, annual rpt, 3544–18

DOD shipments of military and personal property, passenger traffic, and costs, by service branch and mode of transport, quarterly rpt, 3702–1

Earnings by major industry group, and personal income per capita and by source, by region and State, 1929-87, 2708–40

Employment, earnings, and hours, by selected SIC 1- to 4-digit industry, State, and for 262 MSAs, 1972-87, 6748–81

Employment, earnings, and hours, by SIC 1- to 4-digit industry, monthly 1983-Feb 1989, annual rpt, 6744–4

Employment of minorities and women, by occupation, SIC 1- to 3- digit industry, State, and MSA, 1986, annual rpt, 9244–1

Employment, unemployment, and labor force characteristics, by region and census div, 1988, annual rpt, 6744–7.1

Energy use and prices for manufacturing industries, 1985 survey, series, 3166–13

Exports and imports between US and outlying areas, by detailed commodity and mode of transport, monthly rpt, 2422–4

Exports and imports of US, by commodity group, world area, selected country, US coastal area and port, and mode of transport, monthly rpt, 2422–9

Exports and imports of US by country, and trade shifts by commodity, quarterly rpt, 9882–9

Exports and imports of US, by selected country, country group, and commodity group, 1988, annual rpt, 2044–37

Exports of agricultural products and nonelectrical machinery, *Business Conditions Digest*, monthly rpt, 2702–3.9

Exports of US, detailed commodities by country, monthly rpt, 2422–3

Finances and operations, by SIC 2- to 4-digit industry, forecast 1989 with trends from 1950s, annual rpt, 2044–28

Financial statements for manufacturing, mining, and trade corporations, by selected SIC 2- to 3-digit industry, quarterly rpt, 2502–1

Foreign direct investment in US, by industry group and world area, 1987-88, annual article, 2702–1.929

Foreign direct investment of US, by selected industry group and world area, 1986-88, annual article, 2702–1.930

Freight (waterborne domestic and foreign) by commodity, traffic, and passengers, by port and waterway, 1987, annual rpt, 3754–3

Hazardous substances industrial releases and reduction methods under EPA regulation, by chemical, source, industry, and location, 1987, annual rpt, 9234–6

Import restraint elimination, impact on domestic industry production and employment, by selected commodity, 1986-88, 9886–4.144

Imports, exports, and employment impacts, by SIC 2- to 4-digit industry and commodity, quarterly rpt, 2322–2

Imports of US, detailed Schedule A commodities by country, monthly rpt, 2422–2

Imports of US given duty-free treatment for value of US material sent abroad, and impacts on US industry and employment, by commodity and country, 1987, annual rpt, 9884–14

Injuries from use of consumer products, by severity, victim age, and detailed product, 1988, annual rpt, 9164–6

Input-output structure of US economy, detailed interindustry transactions for 84 industries, and components of final demand, 1983, annual article, 2702–1.909

Labor productivity and technological devs for carburetors, pistons, and valves industry, 1972-86, article, 6722–1.911

Labor productivity, indexes of output, hours, and employment by SIC 2- to 4-digit industry, 1963-87, annual rpt, 6824–1.3

Latin America trade, and balance of trade with US, by country, 1988, annual rpt, 2044–34

Manufacturing annual survey, 1986: financial and operating data, by SIC 2- to 4-digit industry, series, 2506–15

Manufacturing annual survey, 1986: production indexes and exports by SIC 2-digit industry and State, with comparisons to 1985, model results, series, 2506–16

Manufacturing census, 1987: financial and operating data, for SIC 4-digit industries by product, preliminary industry rpt series, 2491–1

Manufacturing industries production, shipments, inventories, orders, and pollution control costs, periodic Current Industrial Rpt series, 2506–3

Mineral industries census, 1987: financial and operating data, preliminary industry rpt series, 2511–1

Multinatl firms US affiliates, finances, and operations, by industry, world area of parent firm, and State, 1987, annual rpt, 2704–4

Multinatl US firms and foreign affiliates finances and operations, by industry of parent firm and affiliate, world area, and country, preliminary 1987, annual rpt, 2704–5

Occupational deaths, by equipment type, circumstances, and OSHA standards violated, series, 6606–2

Occupational injury and illness rates, by SIC 2- to 4-digit industry, 1987, annual rpt, 6844–1

OECD trade, total and for 4 major countries, and US trade by country, by commodity, 1970-87, world area rpt series, 9116–1

Pollution abatement capital and operating costs, by SIC 2-to 4-digit industry and State, 1986, annual Current Industrial Rpt, 2506–3.6

Price indexes (producer), by stage of processing and detailed commodity, monthly rpt, 6762–6

Price indexes (producer), by stage of processing and detailed commodity, monthly 1988, annual rpt, 6764–2

Production, shipments, trade, stocks, orders, use, and firms, by product, periodic Current Industrial Rpt series, 2506–12

R&D funding, and scientists and engineers education and employment, for US and selected foreign countries, 1988, annual rpt, 9624–23.1

Rubber mechanical goods shipments, by product, 1988, annual Current Industrial Rpt, 2506–8.17

Science, engineering, and technical employment in manufacturing, by field, occupation, and industry, 1986, triennial rpt, 9627–23

Science, engineering, and technical employment in transportation, utilities, and retail and wholesale trade, by field, occupation, and industry, 1985, triennial rpt, 9627–32

Service industries census, 1987: establishments, receipts, employment, and payroll, by SIC 2- to 4-digit kind of business, MSA, county, and city, State rpt series, 2391–1

Small business establishments, employment, and financial ratios, by SIC 1- to 2-digit industry and State, late 1960s-87, 9768–19

Statistical Abstract of US, social, political, and economic data, 1790-2025, comprehensive annual compilation, 2324–1.3

Steel imports from EC and other countries, impact of voluntary restraint agreements on US user industries exports, sales, and prices, 1989 rpt, 9886–4.138

Tariff Schedule of US, classifications and rates of duty by detailed imported commodity, 1990 base edition and supplements, 9886–13

Tax (income) returns of corporations, income and tax items by asset size and detailed industry, 1986, annual rpt, 8304–4; 8304–21

Tax (income) returns of partnerships, income statement items by industry group, 1986, annual article, 8302–2.903

Tax (income) returns of sole proprietorships, income statement items, by industry group, 1987, annual article, 8302–2.904; 8302–2.921

Technology-intensive manufacturing methods use and plans, with data by technology, selected industry, and firm and market characteristics, 1988 survey, 2508–1

Transportation census, 1987: trucks, by detailed characteristics, miles traveled, and type of product carried, State rpt series, 2573–1

Wholesale trade census, 1987: employment, establishments, finances, and operations, by SIC 2- to 4-digit kind of business, MSA, county, and city, State rpt series, 2405–1

Wholesale trade sales and inventories, by SIC 2- to 3-digit kind of business, monthly rpt, 2413–7

Wholesale trade sales, inventories, purchases, and gross margins, by SIC 2- to 3-digit kind of business and form of ownership, 1988, annual rpt, 2413–13

see also Agricultural machinery and equipment

see also Electric power plants and equipment

see also Electrical machinery and equipment

see also Engines and motors

see also Hardware

see also Industrial plants and equipment

see also Industrial robots

see also Lawn and garden equipment

see also Tools

see also Transportation and transportation equipment

see also Vending machines and stands

see also By Industry in the "Index by Categories"

see also under By Commodity in the "Index by Categories"

Mackie, Philip L.
"Oilseeds and Products Outlook", 1004–16.1

MacKnight, Peggy J.
"U.S. Imports of Textiles and Apparel Under the Multifiber Arrangement: Statistical Report Through 1988", 9884–18

Macon, Ga.
Wages by occupation, and benefits for office and plant workers, 1988 survey, periodic MSA rpt, 6785–3.1

see also under By City and By SMSA or MSA in the "Index by Categories"

MacPhee, Craig
"Fish Toxicity Screening Data", 9238–69

Macro Systems, Inc.
"Referral of Long-Term Unemployment Insurance (UI) Claimants to Reemployment Services", 6406–6.25; 6406–6.26

Madagascar
Agricultural and food production and indexes, total and for selected commodities, by country, 1970s-88, annual rpt, 1524–12

Agricultural exports of Africa by commodity, and relation to economic conditions and other factors, by country, 1960s-87, 1528–280

Agricultural imports and food aid needs under alternative weather assumptions, for 17 African countries, projected to 1995, 1528–279

Agricultural production, prices, and trade, by country, 1960s-89, annual world region rpt, 1524–4.2

Agricultural trade of US, by detailed commodity and country, 1988, semiannual rpt, 1522–4

AID activities and funding by project and function, FY90, and developing countries summary socioeconomic data from 1960s, annual rpt, 9904–4.5

AID economic aid to developing countries, obligations and disbursements by country, quarterly rpt, 9912–4

AID loans repayment status and terms by program and country, and status of predecessor agency loans, quarterly rpt, 9912–3

Economic and military aid and loans from US and intl agencies, by program and country, FY46-87, annual rpt, 9914–5

Economic conditions, investment and export opportunities, and trade practices, 1988 country market research rpt, 2046–6.3

Economic, social, political, and geographic summary data, by country, 1989, annual factbook, 9114–2

Human rights conditions in 170 countries, 1988, annual rpt, 21384–3

Military aid of US, arms sales, and training programs costs and budget requests, by program, world region, and country, FY88-90, annual rpt, 7144–13

Military spending, arms trade, and force strengths, with govt spending and population, by country, 1977-87, annual rpt, 9824–1

Minerals Yearbook, 1987, Vol 3: foreign country reviews of production, trade, and policy, by commodity, annual rpt, 5604–35

Minerals Yearbook, 1987, Vol 3 preprints: foreign country review of production, trade, and policy, by commodity, annual rpt, 5604–23.45

Population size, growth rates, and components of change, by country, projected 1989-2020 and trends from 1950, biennial rpt, 2324–9

UN voting record and share of votes in agreement with US, by issue, country, and world area, 1988, annual rpt, 7004–18

see also under By Foreign Country in the "Index by Categories"

Madison, Wis.
Wages by occupation, for office and plant workers, 1989 survey, periodic MSA rpt, 6785–3.10

see also under By City and By SMSA or MSA in the "Index by Categories"

Maffei, Helen M.
"Annual Southwestern Region Pest Conditions Report, 1988", 1206–11.1

Magazines
see Periodicals

Mager, Andreas, Jr.
"National Marine Fisheries Service Habitat Conservation Efforts in the Coastal Southeastern U.S. for 1987", 2162–1.902

Magistrates
see Judges

Magleby, Richard
"Economics of Controlling Sediment from Irrigation: An Idaho Example", 1588–138

Magnesium
see Metals and metal industries

Maguire, Bryan
"Public Acceptance of the Surgeon General's Brochure on AIDS", 4042–3.908

Magura, Stephen
"Correlates of Participation in AIDS Education and HIV Antibody Testing by Methadone Patients", 4042–3.920

Mahoney, Martin C.
"Years of Potential Life Lost Among a Native American Population", 4042–3.925

Mail
see Postal service

Mail order business
see Direct marketing

Maine
Agriculture census, 1987: farms, farmland, production and costs, and operator characteristics, advance State and county rpts, 2330–1.23

Agriculture census, 1987: farms, farmland, production, finances, and operator characteristics, by county, final State rpt, 2331–1.19

Bank deposits in FDIC-insured commercial and savings banks, by instn, State, and county, as of June 1988, annual regional rpt, 9295–3.1

Banks and thrifts in New England, financial statements by type of instn and Fed deposit insurance, and State, 1987, annual rpt, 9304–3

County Business Patterns, 1987: employment, establishments, and payroll, by SIC 2- to 4-digit industry and county, annual State rpt, 2326–8.21

Deaths and rates, by detailed location, cause, and demographic characteristics, 1987, US Vital Statistics annual rpt, 4144–3.1

DOD prime contract awards, by contractor, service branch, State, and city, FY88, annual rpt, 3544–22

Economic indicators for New England States, Fed Reserve 1st District, monthly rpt, 9373–24

Economic indicators for New England States, Fed Reserve 1st District, quarterly rpt with articles, 9373–2

Employment, earnings, and hours, by selected SIC 1- to 4-digit industry, State, and for 262 MSAs, 1972-87, 6748–81.2

Fed Govt spending in States and local areas, by type, State, county, and city, FY88, annual rpt, 2464–3

Fed Govt spending in States, by type, program, agency, and State, FY88, annual rpt, 2464–2

Fish and shellfish catch, wholesale receipts, prices, trade, and other market activities, weekly regional rpt, 2162–6.2

HHS financial aid, by program, recipient, State, and city, FY88, annual regional listing, 4004–3.1

Homeless children educational enrollment and needs, 1988, annual State rpt, 4804–35.20

Income (personal) per capita and by source, and earnings by industry div, by State, MSA, and county, 1982-87, annual regional rpt, 2704-2.2

Marine resources of coastal Maine, and ocean floor ecology, 1983-87, conf papers, 2148-55

Mineral Industry Surveys, State reviews of production, 1988, preliminary annual rpt, 5614-6

Minerals Yearbook, 1987, Vol 2 preprints: State review of production and sales by commodity, and business activity, annual rpt, 5604-16.20

Minerals Yearbook, 1987, Vol 2: State reviews of production, sales, and firms, by commodity, and business activity, annual rpt, 5604-34

Nursing home compliance with Medicare and Medicaid regulations, and patient characteristics, by facility, 1987/88, annual State rpt, 4654-15.20

Retail trade census, 1987: employment, establishments, sales, and payroll, by SIC 2- to 4-digit kind of business, MSA, county, and city, State rpt, 2397-1.20

Savings instns, FHLB 1st District members financial operations and related economic and housing indicators, monthly rpt, 9302-4

Service industries census, 1987: employment, establishments, receipts, and payroll, by SIC 2- to 4-digit kind of business, MSA, county, and city, State rpt, 2391-1.20

Statistical Abstract of US, social, political, and economic data, with foreign comparisons, 1790-2025, comprehensive annual compilation, 2324-1

Transportation census, 1987: trucks, by detailed characteristics, miles traveled, and type of product carried, State rpt, 2573-1.20

Wages by occupation, and benefits for office and plant workers, 1988 survey, periodic labor market rpt, 6785-3.2

Water supply and quality in streams and lakes, and groundwater levels in wells, by drainage basin, 1987, annual State rpt, 5666-10.18

Water supply in northeastern US, precipitation and stream runoff by station, monthly rpt, 2182-3

Wholesale trade census, 1987: employment, establishments, finances, and operations, by SIC 2- to 4-digit kind of business, MSA, county, and city, State rpt, 2405-1.20

Wildlife-related recreation, hunting, and fishing participation and spending, detailed data, 1985 survey, quinquennial State rpt, 5506-6.19

see also Portland, Maine

see also under By State in the "Index by Categories"

Mak, Marion W.
"Projections of Returns To Be Filed in FY89-96", 8302-2.916
"Trends in the Filing of Withholding and Information Documents", 8304-8.1

Maki, Wilbur R.
"Florida's Forest Products Industry: Performance and Contribution to the State's Economy, 1970-80", 1206-36.12

Malagasy Republic
see Madagascar

Malaria
see Infective and parasitic diseases

Malawi
Agricultural and food production and indexes, total and for selected commodities, by country, 1970s-88, annual rpt, 1524-12

Agricultural policy impacts on economic dev, with background data for 6 developing countries, 1960s-86, 1528-283

Agricultural production, prices, and trade, by country, 1960s-89, annual world region rpt, 1524-4.2

Agricultural trade of US, by detailed commodity and country, 1988, semiannual rpt, 1522-4

AID activities and funding by project and function, FY90, and developing countries summary socioeconomic data from 1960s, annual rpt, 9904-4.5

AID economic aid to developing countries, obligations and disbursements by country, quarterly rpt, 9912-4

AID loans repayment status and terms by program and country, and status of predecessor agency loans, quarterly rpt, 9912-3

Background Notes, summary social, political, and economic data, 1989 rpt, 7006-2.14

Economic and military aid and loans from US and intl agencies, by program and country, FY46-87, annual rpt, 9914-5

Economic conditions, income, production, prices, employment, and trade, 1989 periodic country rpt, 2046-4.77

Economic, social, political, and geographic summary data, by country, 1989, annual factbook, 9114-2

Human rights conditions in 170 countries, 1988, annual rpt, 21384-3

Military aid of US, arms sales, and training programs costs and budget requests, by program, world region, and country, FY88-90, annual rpt, 7144-13

Military spending, arms trade, and force strengths, with govt spending and population, by country, 1977-87, annual rpt, 9824-1

Minerals Yearbook, 1987, Vol 3: foreign country reviews of production, trade, and policy, by commodity, annual rpt, 5604-35

Minerals Yearbook, 1987, Vol 3 preprints: foreign country review of production, trade, and policy, by commodity, annual rpt, 5604-23.81

Population size, growth rates, and components of change, by country, projected 1989-2020 and trends from 1950, biennial rpt, 2324-9

UN voting record and share of votes in agreement with US, by issue, country, and world area, 1988, annual rpt, 7004-18

see also under By Foreign Country in the "Index by Categories"

Malaysia
Agricultural and food production and indexes, total and for selected commodities, by country, 1970s-88, annual rpt, 1524-12

Agricultural policy impacts on economic dev, with background data for 6 developing countries, 1960s-86, 1528-283

Agricultural production, prices, and trade, by country, 1960s-89, annual world region rpt, 1524-4.2

Agricultural trade of US, by detailed commodity and country, 1988, semiannual rpt, 1522-4

AID loans repayment status and terms by program and country, and status of predecessor agency loans, quarterly rpt, 9912-3

Coal production, trade, and govt subsidies, by country and country group, 1973-87 and projected to 2000, 2048-144

Cooking appliance thermostatic plugs from 4 countries, injury to US industry from foreign subsidized and less than fair value imports, investigation with background financial and operating data, 1988 rpt, 9886-19.63

Economic and military aid and loans from US and intl agencies, by program and country, FY46-87, annual rpt, 9914-5

Economic conditions, income, production, prices, employment, and trade, 1989 periodic country rpt, 2046-4.15; 2046-4.65

Economic conditions, policy, and trade practices, by country, 1986-88, annual rpt, 21384-5

Economic indicators of developing countries, problem debtors compared to other borrowers, by country, 1973-84, 1528-285

Economic, social, political, and geographic summary data, by country, 1989, annual factbook, 9114-2

Exports and imports of US, by commodity and country, 1970-87, world area rpt, 9116-1.2

Exports and imports of US, by selected country, country group, and commodity group, 1988, annual rpt, 2044-37

Human rights conditions in 170 countries, 1988, annual rpt, 21384-3

Imports of goods, services, and investment from US, trade barriers, impacts, and US actions, by country, 1988, annual rpt, 444-2

Imports of US given duty-free treatment for value of US material sent abroad, and impacts on US industry and employment, by commodity and country, 1987, annual rpt, 9884-14

Labor conditions, union coverage, and work accidents, 1989 annual country rpt, 6366-4.16

Military aid of US, arms sales, and training programs costs and budget requests, by program, world region, and country, FY88-90, annual rpt, 7144-13

Military spending, arms trade, and force strengths, with govt spending and population, by country, 1977-87, annual rpt, 9824-1

Minerals production, reserves, and industry role in domestic economy and world supply, 1988 country rpt, 5606-1.17

Minerals Yearbook, 1987, Vol 3: foreign country reviews of production, trade, and policy, by commodity, annual rpt, 5604-35

Minerals Yearbook, 1987, Vol 3 preprints: foreign country review of production, trade, and policy, by commodity, annual rpt, 5604-23.47

Multinatl US firms and foreign affiliates
finances and operations, by industry of
parent firm and affiliate, world area, and
country, preliminary 1987, annual rpt,
2704–5

Population size, growth rates, and
components of change, by country,
projected 1989-2020 and trends from
1950, biennial rpt, 2324–9

UN voting record and share of votes in
agreement with US, by issue, country, and
world area, 1988, annual rpt, 7004–18

see also under By Foreign Country in the
"Index by Categories"

Maldives

Agricultural and food production and
indexes, total and for selected
commodities, by country, 1970s-88,
annual rpt, 1524–12

Economic, social, political, and geographic
summary data, by country, 1989, annual
factbook, 9114–2

Human rights conditions in 170 countries,
1988, annual rpt, 21384–3

Military aid of US, arms sales, and training
programs costs and budget requests, by
program, world region, and country,
FY88-90, annual rpt, 7144–13

Population size, growth rates, and
components of change, by country,
projected 1989-2020 and trends from
1950, biennial rpt, 2324–9

UN voting record and share of votes in
agreement with US, by issue, country, and
world area, 1988, annual rpt, 7004–18

see also under By Foreign Country in the
"Index by Categories"

Mali

Agricultural and food production and
indexes, total and for selected
commodities, by country, 1970s-88,
annual rpt, 1524–12

Agricultural exports of Africa by
commodity, and relation to economic
conditions and other factors, by country,
1960s-87, 1528–280

Agricultural imports and food aid needs
under alternative weather assumptions, for
17 African countries, projected to 1995,
1528–279

Agricultural production, prices, and trade,
by country, 1960s-89, annual world region
rpt, 1524–4.2

Agricultural trade of US, by detailed
commodity and country, 1988, semiannual
rpt, 1522–4

AID activities and funding by project and
function, FY90, and developing countries
summary socioeconomic data from 1960s,
annual rpt, 9904–4.5

AID economic aid to developing countries,
obligations and disbursements by country,
quarterly rpt, 9912–4

AID loans repayment status and terms by
program and country, and status of
predecessor agency loans, quarterly rpt,
9912–3

Disaster preparedness and economic,
population, and political data, 1988
country rpt, 9916–2.70

Economic and military aid and loans from
US and intl agencies, by program and
country, FY46-87, annual rpt, 9914–5

Economic, social, political, and geographic
summary data, by country, 1989, annual
factbook, 9114–2

Farm income and production impacts of
alternative soil and water mgmt strategies,
for Mali, model results, 1989 rpt,
1528–289

Food supply indicators for Sahel, by
country, 1960s-2000, 1528–290

Human rights conditions in 170 countries,
1988, annual rpt, 21384–3

Military aid of US, arms sales, and training
programs costs and budget requests, by
program, world region, and country,
FY88-90, annual rpt, 7144–13

Military spending, arms trade, and force
strengths, with govt spending and
population, by country, 1977-87, annual
rpt, 9824–1

Minerals Yearbook, 1987, Vol 3 preprints:
foreign country review of production,
trade, and policy, by commodity, annual
rpt, 5604–23.82

Population size, growth rates, and
components of change, by country,
projected 1989-2020 and trends from
1950, biennial rpt, 2324–9

UN voting record and share of votes in
agreement with US, by issue, country, and
world area, 1988, annual rpt, 7004–18

see also under By Foreign Country in the
"Index by Categories"

Malnutrition

see Nutrition and malnutrition

Malpractice

see Medical malpractice

see Property and casualty insurance

Malt

see Beer and breweries

see Grains and grain products

Malta

Agricultural and food production and
indexes, total and for selected
commodities, by country, 1970s-88,
annual rpt, 1524–12

Agricultural trade of US, by detailed
commodity and country, 1988, semiannual
rpt, 1522–4

AID loans repayment status and terms by
program and country, and status of
predecessor agency loans, quarterly rpt,
9912–3

Economic and military aid and loans from
US and intl agencies, by program and
country, FY46-87, annual rpt, 9914–5

Economic, social, political, and geographic
summary data, by country, 1989, annual
factbook, 9114–2

Human rights conditions in 170 countries,
1988, annual rpt, 21384–3

Military aid of US, arms sales, and training
programs costs and budget requests, by
program, world region, and country,
FY88-90, annual rpt, 7144–13

Military spending, arms trade, and force
strengths, with govt spending and
population, by country, 1977-87, annual
rpt, 9824–1

Minerals Yearbook, 1987, Vol 3: foreign
country reviews of production, trade, and
policy, by commodity, annual rpt,
5604–35

Minerals Yearbook, 1987, Vol 3 preprints:
foreign country review of production,
trade, and policy, by commodity, annual
rpt, 5604–23.46

Population size, growth rates, and
components of change, by country,
projected 1989-2020 and trends from
1950, biennial rpt, 2324–9

UN voting record and share of votes in
agreement with US, by issue, country, and
world area, 1988, annual rpt, 7004–18

see also under By Foreign Country in the
"Index by Categories"

Management

see Business management

see Consultants

see Executives and managers

see Government efficiency

see Health facilities administration

see Labor-management relations, general

see Labor-management relations in
government

see Labor-management relations, local and
regional

see School administration and staff

Management Information Services, Inc.

"Private Sector Economic and Employment
Benefits to the Nation and to Each State
of Proposed FY90 NASA Procurement
Expenditures", 9508–35

Manchester, N.H.

see also under By SMSA or MSA in the
"Index by Categories"

Mandelbaum, Thomas B.

"Eighth District Business Economy in 1988:
Still Expanding, but More Slowly",
9391–1.913

"Have Federal Spending and Taxation
Contributed to the Divergence of State
Per Capita Incomes in the 1980s?",
9391–1.918

"In Search of a Regional Economic
Identity", 9391–16.905

"Relative Performance of the District's
Major Metropolitan Areas", 9391–16.902

Manen, Carol-Ann

"Natural Oil Seeps in the Alaskan Marine
Environment", 2176–1.28

Manganese

see Metals and metal industries

Manganese dioxide

see Chemicals and chemical industry

Mangeno, J. J.

"Environmental Monitoring and Disposal of
Radioactive Wastes from U.S. Naval
Nuclear-Powered Ships and Their Support
Facilities, 1988", 3804–11

"Occupational Radiation Exposure from
U.S. Naval Nuclear Propulsion Plants and
Their Support Facilities, 1988", 3804–10

Manitoba Province, Canada

Surgical admissions and costs for inpatients
and outpatients, by diagnostic group, for
Manitoba, Canada, 1982-84, article,
4652–1.940

Manned space flight

see Astronauts

Manning, Carol A.

"Prediction of Success in FAA Air Traffic
Control Field Training as a Function of
Selection and Screening Test
Performance", 7506–10.59

Manpower

see Labor supply and demand

see under names of specific occupations

Manpower training programs

Assistance (block and categorical grants)
programs for State and local govts, FY89,
biennial listing, 10044–8

Assistance (financial and nonfinancial) of
Fed Govt, 1989 base edition with
supplements, annual listing, 104–5

Budget of US Appendix, obligations, appropriations, and personnel, by program and agency, FY90, annual rpt, 104–3

Budget of US, compact budgets by activity, function, and agency, FY90 and projected to FY94, annual rpt, 104–2

Budget of US, historical data, selected years FY34-88 and projected to FY94, annual rpt, 104–22

Employment and Training Admin activities, funding, and participant characteristics, by program, FY80-86, 6408–71

Employment, earnings, and hours, by SIC 1- to 4-digit industry, monthly 1983-Feb 1989, annual rpt, 6744–4

Employment programs, training, and unemployment compensation, current devs and grants to States, press release series, 6406–2

Expenditures and participation in employment training and vocational education programs, for 6 Federal agencies, FY89-90, GAO rpt, 26121–277

Expenditures of Fed Govt in States, by type, program, agency, and State, FY88, annual rpt, 2464–2

Fed Govt procurement contract awards, by procurement and contractor type, agency, State, and for top 100 contractors, quarterly rpt, 102–6

Govt revenues by source and spending by function, natl income and product account, *Survey of Current Business*, monthly rpt, 2702–1.24

Homeless persons aid by program and Federal agency, and indicators of need, 1988, annual rpt, 14364–1

Homeless population characteristics, needs, and impacts of govt aid programs and housing costs, 1988 conf papers, 10048–73

Job Training Partnership Act participants, by selected characteristics, FY88, annual rpt, 6304–1

Job Training Partnership Act State and local admin, funding, effectiveness, and participants, GAO rpt series, 26106–8

Labor laws enacted, by State, 1988, annual article, 6722–1.904

Natl Commission for Employment Policy activities and rpts, 1989 annual rpt, 15494–1

Rural areas aid from Fed Govt compared to urban areas, by program and degree of urbanization, FY85, periodic rpt, 1598–248

Unemployed displaced workers and other hard to serve groups, factors contributing to unemployment, and training programs operations, series, 15496–1

Unemployment insurance reemployment and training services, and bonus for early reemployment, New Jersey demonstration project results, 1987-88, 6406–6.27

see also Apprenticeship

see also Employee development

see also Military training

see also Vocational education and training

see also Vocational rehabilitation

see also Work incentive programs

see also Youth Conservation Corps

Manser, Marilyn E.

"Analysis of Substitution Bias in Measuring Inflation, 1959-82", 6886–6.11

"Cash-Equivalent Values from In-Kind Benefits: Estimates from a Complete Demand System Using Household Data", 6886–6.42

"Employer-Provided Benefits: Employer Cost Versus Employee Value", 6722–1.960

"Real Wages Over the Business Cycle: Estimates Using a Fixed-Weight Wage Index", 6886–6.56

Mansfield, Ohio

see also under By SMSA or MSA in the "Index by Categories"

Manson, Spero M.

"Risk Factors for Suicide Among Indian Adolescents at a Boarding School", 4042–3.958

Manton, Kenneth G.

"Measurements of Health and Disease, a Transitional Perspective", 4147–4.26

Manufactured gas

see Synthetic fuels

Manufactured housing

see Mobile homes

Manufacturing

Business and financial statistics, historic trends, 1988 annual chartbook, 9364–2.3

Business Conditions Digest, economic, business, and financial devs and cyclical fluctuations, monthly rpt, 2702–3

Business statistics, detailed data for major industries and economic indicators, *Survey of Current Business*, monthly rpt, 2702–1

Capital expenditures for plant and equipment, by industry div, monthly rpt, quarterly data, 23842–1.1

Capital investment, capacity, and output relation to domestic demand and trade, 1970s-88, article, 9385–1.908

Census Bur rpts and data files, coverage and availability, 1989 annual listing, 2304–2

China trade by SITC 1- to 5-digit commodity, 1970s-87, annual rpt, 9114–3

Coal receipts and prices at manufacturing plants, by SIC 2-digit industry, quarterly rpt, 3162–37.2

Collective bargaining agreements expiring during year, and workers covered, by firm, union, industry group, and State, 1989, annual rpt, 6784–9

Collective bargaining wage and benefit changes and coverage, by industry sector and whether contract includes escalator clause and lump sum payment, 1968-88, annual article, 6722–1.923

Collective bargaining wage and benefit changes, by sector, 1954-88, 6728–38.7

Collective bargaining wage and benefit changes, quarterly press release, 6782–2

Collective bargaining wage and benefit concessions and workers affected, by type of concession and major industry group, 1975-88, article, 9385–1.912

Communist countries trade with US, by detailed commodity and country, quarterly rpt with articles, 9882–2

Counties (nonmetro) employment by industry sector and degree of urbanization, and compared to metro counties, various periods 1969-86, 1598–244

County Business Patterns, 1987: employment, establishments, and payroll, by SIC 2- to 4-digit industry and county, annual State rpt series, 2326–8

Diversification index for establishments and firms by SIC 2- and 4-digit manufacturing industry, census years 1963-82, technical paper, 2626–2.58

Earnings and hours of work, weekly averages, monthly rpt, 23842–1.2

Earnings by industry div, and personal income per capita and by source, by State, MSA, and county, 1982-87, annual regional rpts, 2704–2

Earnings by major industry group, and personal income per capita and by source, by region and State, 1929-87, 2708–40

Electric power use and prices, shipments, and trade, for 25 SIC 4-digit manufacturing industries, 1972-86, 2048–137

Employment and Earnings, detailed data, monthly rpt, 6742–2.5; 6742–2.6

Employment, and export and import shares in manufacturing, by SIC 2-digit industry, 1950s-88, article, 9373–1.906

Employment change during periods of exchange rate volatility, by industry trade orientation and census div, 1973-87, article, 9373–1.917

Employment Cost Index and alternative measure of compensation costs, by component, occupation, industry group, union status, and location, 1975-89, annual rpt, 6744–20

Employment Cost Index and percent change by occupational group, industry div, region, and metro-nonmetro area, quarterly press release, 6782–5

Employment, earnings, and hours, by industry div and major manufacturing group, Monthly Labor Review, 6722–1.2

Employment, earnings, and hours, by selected SIC 1- to 4-digit industry, State, and for 262 MSAs, 1972-87, 6748–81

Employment, earnings, and hours, by SIC 1- to 4-digit industry, monthly 1983-Feb 1989, annual rpt, 6744–4

Employment, earnings, and hours, monthly press release, 6742–5

Employment in manufacturing and nonagricultural industries, by MSA, 1987-88, annual press release, 6946–3.12

Employment of minorities and women, by occupation, SIC 1- to 3- digit industry, State, and MSA, 1986, annual rpt, 9244–1

Employment shifts among industries, factors and impacts on wage growth, with data by industry group, 1948-87, 23848–207

Employment situation, earnings, hours, and other BLS economic indicators, transcripts of BLS Commissioner's monthly testimony, periodic rpt, 23846–4

Employment, unemployment, and labor force characteristics, by region, State, and selected metro area, 1988, annual rpt, 6744–7

Employment, unemployment, and labor force characteristics, Labor Statistics Handbook, 1940s-88 with trends from 1913, 6728–38

Energy use and prices for manufacturing industries, 1985 survey, series, 3166–13

Energy use in commercial buildings, costs, and conservation, by building characteristics, survey rpt series, 3166–8

Export and import price indexes, by selected end-use category, monthly press release, 6762–15

Science and engineering employment and education, and R&D spending, for US and selected foreign countries, 1988, annual rpt, 9624–23.2

Science and engineering employment, by field and industry div, 1977, 1986, and alternative projections to 2000, 9626–2.181

Science and engineering employment concentration, by industry group and census div, 1989 working paper, 9375–13.15

Science, engineering, and technical employment in manufacturing, by field, occupation, and industry, 1986, triennial rpt, 9627–23

SEC registration, firms required to file annual rpts, as of Sept 1988, annual listing, 9734–5

Shipments, inventories, orders, capacity use, and pollution control costs of manufacturers, periodic Current Industrial Rpt series, 2506–3

Small business establishments, employment, and financial ratios, by SIC 1- to 2-digit industry and State, late 1960s-87, 9768–19

Small business establishments, operations, owner characteristics, and job training, late 1950s-87, 9768–20

Small business finances, operations, owner and employee characteristics, and Federal contracts, 1980s-88, annual rpt, 9764–6

Small business high technology sales, exports, siting, technology transfer, views on competitiveness, 1988 survey, hearing, 21728–69

Southeastern States, Fed Reserve 5th District, economic indicators by State, quarterly rpt, 9389–16

Southeastern States manufacturing employment and earnings, by industry group, State, and urban-rural location, 1970s-85, article, 9371–1.901

Southeastern US industrial output, by major industry group, 1986 with growth since 1963, article, 9391–16.905

Statistical Abstract of US, social, political, and economic data, 1790-2025, comprehensive annual compilation, 2324–1.3

Sweden multinatl firms domestic and foreign production, exports, employment, and sales, with data by commodity and firm, 1960s-86, conf, 23848–208

Tariff Schedule of US, classifications and rates of duty by detailed imported commodity, 1990 base edition and supplements, 9886–13

Tax (income) returns filed by type of filer, selected income items, quarterly rpt, 8302–2.1

Tax (income) returns for foreign corporate activity in US, assets, and income statement items, by industry div, country, and world area, 1984-85, article, 8302–2.920

Tax (income) returns of corporations, income and tax items by asset size and detailed industry, 1986, annual rpt, 8304–4; 8304–21

Tax (income) returns of partnerships, income statement items by industry group, 1986, annual article, 8302–2.903

Tax (income) returns of sole proprietorships, income statement items, by industry group, 1987, annual article, 8302–2.904; 8302–2.921

Technology-intensive manufacturing methods use and plans, with data by technology, selected industry, and firm and market characteristics, 1988 survey, 2508–1

Trade zones (US) operations and movement of goods, by zone and commodity, FY86, annual rpt, 2044–30

Transportation census, 1987: trucks, by detailed characteristics, miles traveled, and type of product carried, State rpt series, 2573–1

Unemployment insurance coverage, impact of changes in labor market and UI policy, and trust fund finances of 11 States, 1971-86, 6406–6.24

Value added in manufacturing, allocation to States and SMSAs, assessment of Census Bur methodology, 1989 article, 9375–1.906

Virgin Islands economic censuses, 1987: employment, firms, payroll, and receipts, by SIC 1- to 4-digit industry, island, and city, 2593–1

Wage and benefit changes from collective bargaining and mgmt decisions, by industry div, monthly rpt, 6782–1

Wage differentials between service and manufacturing sectors related to worker characteristics, 1987, article, 9377–1.901

Wages by occupation, and benefits for office and plant workers in selected MSAs, 1988, annual rpt, 6785–1

Wages by occupation, and benefits for office and plant workers, periodic MSA survey rpt series, 6785–11; 6785–12

Wages for 4 occupational groups, relative pay levels in 61 MSAs, 1988, annual rpt, 6785–8

see also Aerospace industry
see also Aircraft
see also Aluminum and aluminum industry
see also Annual Survey of Manufactures
see also Business machines and equipment
see also Cement and concrete
see also Census of Manufactures
see also Chemicals and chemical industry
see also Clay industry and products
see also Clothing and clothing industry
see also Copper and copper industry
see also Electrical machinery and equipment
see also Electronics industry and products
see also Food and food industry
see also Furniture and furnishings
see also Furs and fur industry
see also Glass and glass industry
see also Gum and wood chemicals
see also Household appliances and equipment
see also Ice, manufactured
see also Industrial capacity and utilization
see also Industrial plants and equipment
see also Industrial production
see also Instruments and measuring devices
see also Iron and steel industry
see also Leather industry and products
see also Lumber industry and products
see also Machines and machinery industry
see also Metals and metal industries
see also Motor vehicle industry

see also Musical instruments
see also Paints and varnishes
see also Paper and paper products
see also Petroleum and petroleum industry
see also Pharmaceutical industry
see also Plastics and plastics industry
see also Printing and publishing industry
see also Production workers
see also Rubber and rubber industry
see also Shipbuilding and repairing
see also Sporting goods
see also Stone products and quarries
see also Textile industry and fabrics
see also Tires and tire industry
see also Tobacco industry and products
see also Toys and games
see also Transportation and transportation equipment
see also Zinc and zinc industry
see also under By Commodity in the "Index by Categories"
see also under By Industry in the "Index by Categories"

Manzella, Sharon

"Kemp's Ridley, *Lepidochelys kempi*, Sea Turtle Head Start Tag Recoveries: Distribution, Habitat, and Method of Recovery", 2162–1.902

Maps

Air traffic control and airway facilities improvement activities under Natl Airspace System Plan, 1981-85 and projected to 2000, annual rpt, 7504–12

Alaska Arctic Natl Wildlife Refuge resources, native hunting activity, and energy exploration impact, 1985, last issue of annual rpt, 5504–26

Alaska land area by ownership, and availability for mineral exploration and dev, 1986, 5608–152

Alaska minerals resources, production, oil and gas leases, and exploratory wells, with maps and bibl, 1987, annual rpt, 5664–11

Alaska OCS environmental conditions and oil dev impacts, compilation of papers, series, 2176–1

Birds (mourning dove) population, by hunting and nonhunting State, 1966-89, annual rpt, 5504–15

Birds (waterfowl) coastal breeding population and colonies, by species and location for Washington, 1978-82, atlas, 5508–101

Birds (waterfowl) coastal breeding population and colonies, by species and location, 1976-82 surveys, 5508–100

Birds (waterfowl) population, habitat conditions, and migratory flight forecasts, for Canada and US by region, 1989 and trends from 1955, annual rpt, 5504–27

Birds (waterfowl) refuge and breeding area acreage acquired by Fed Govt, and costs, by site and State, FY89, annual rpt, 14784–1

Census Bur rpts and data files, coverage and availability, 1989 annual listing, 2304–2

Census Bur rpts and data files, coverage, availability, and use, series, 2326–7

Census of Population and Housing, 1980: data processing, coverage, and availability, 2555–2.4

Census of Population and Housing, 1990: data coverage and products, 1989 guide, 2308–58

Fed Govt interdiction of drug smuggling by aircraft, activities, funding, and radar system capabilities, by agency, FY82-89, GAO rpt, 26119-259

Foreign countries drug production, eradication, and seizures, by illegal substance, with US aid, by country, 1985-89, annual rpt, 7004-17

Health condition and health care resources, use, and spending, 1950s-87, annual data compilation, 4144-11

High school seniors drug and alcohol use, by type and frequency, 1975-88, annual rpt, 4824-2.13

Immigration and Naturalization Service illegal alien and narcotics activities, FY81-88, annual rpt, 6264-2

Military personnel alcohol and drug abuse, prevalence and consequences, by selected characteristics, 1988, biennial rpt, 3504-19

Organized Crime Drug Enforcement Task Forces regional investigation activities by agency and region, and background data, FY83-88, annual rpt, 6004-17

Public opinion on crime and crime-related issues, by respondent characteristics, 1970s-89, annual rpt, 6064-6.2

Research on drug abuse and treatment, summaries of findings, resource materials, and grant listings, periodic rpt, 4492-4

Sentences for Federal offenses, guidelines by offense and circumstances, 1989 rpt, 17668-1

State and local govt drug enforcement activities, Federal aid by recipient, and background data, FY88, annual rpt, 6064-28

Statistical Abstract of US, social, political, and economic data, 1790-2025, comprehensive annual compilation, 2324-1.1

Supply of drugs in US by country of origin, abuse, deaths, prices, and seizures, by substance, 1988, annual rpt, 6284-2

Youth drug, alcohol, and cigarette use and attitudes, by substance type and selected characteristics, 1975-88 surveys, annual rpt, 4494-4

Marin County, Calif.

Housing vacancy rates for single and multifamily units and mobile homes, by city and ZIP code, 1988, annual MSA rpt, 9304-20.8

Marine accidents and safety

Accident deaths and rates, by cause, age, race, sex, and State, 1986, US Vital Statistics annual rpt, 4144-4

Accidents and deaths, by mode of transport, 1955-88, annual rpt, 7304-2

Boat registrations, and accidents, casualties, and damage by cause, by vessel characteristics and State, 1988, annual rpt, 7404-1

Diving (underwater sport and occupational) deaths, by circumstances, diver characteristics, and location, 1970-87, annual rpt, 2144-5

DOT planning and safety grants, by program, State, and for 38 SMSAs, FY88, annual rpt, 7304-7

Fed Govt spending in States, by type, program, agency, and State, FY88, annual rpt, 2464-2

Hazardous material transport accidents, casualties, and damage, by mode of transport, with DOT control activities, 1988, annual rpt, 7304-4

Injury and illness rates and causes, by SIC 2- to 4-digit industry, 1987, annual rpt, 6844-1

Military deaths by cause, age, race, and rank, and personnel captured and missing, by service branch, 2nd half FY88, semiannual rpt, 3542-21

Pollution (water) incidents and discharges, by type, source, cause, and location, 1984-86, annual rpt, 7404-3

Statistical Abstract of US, social, political, and economic data, 1790-2025, comprehensive annual compilation, 2324-1.3

Weather services activities and funding, by Federal agency, planned FY89-90, annual rpt, 2144-2

see also Drowning

see also Oil spills

Marine Corps

Budget of DOD, procurement appropriations by item, service branch, and defense agency, FY88-91, annual rpt, 3544-32

Budget of DOD, weapons acquisition costs by system and service branch, FY89-91, annual rpt, 3504-2

Commercial activities of DOD performed in-house, and work-years, by service branch, installation, and State, FY88, annual rpt, 3544-25

Computer mainframe and related equipment procurement, compatibility, and operating system contracts, for Navy, FY86-89, GAO rpt, 26125-37

Criminal case processing in military courts, and prisoners by facility, by service branch, 1960s-87, annual rpt, 6064-6.6

Deaths by cause, age, race, and rank, and personnel captured and missing, by service branch, 2nd half FY88, semiannual rpt, 3542-21

Drug and alcohol abuse by military personnel, prevalence and consequences, by selected characteristics, 1988, biennial rpt, 3504-19

Health care facilities of DOD in US and abroad, beds, admissions, outpatient visits, and births, by service branch, quarterly rpt, 3542-15

Manpower active duty strength, civilian personnel, and dependents, by service branch and US and foreign location, quarterly rpt, 3542-20

Manpower active duty strength, recruits, and reenlistment, by race, sex, and service branch, quarterly press release, 3542-7

Manpower needs, costs, and force readiness, by service branch, FY90, annual rpt, 3504-1

Manpower of DOD, and organization, budget, weapons, and property, by service branch, State, and country, 1989 annual summary rpt, 3504-13

Manpower, procurement, equipment, and budget of Navy, planned FY89-91, annual fact sheet, 3804-16

Manpower statistics for active duty, civilian, and reserve personnel, by service branch, FY88 and trends, annual rpt, 3544-1

Manpower statistics for active duty, civilian, and reserve personnel, by service branch, quarterly rpt, 3542-14

Manpower strengths in US and abroad, by service branch, world area, and country, quarterly press release, 3542-9

Manpower strengths, summary by service branch, monthly press release, 3542-2

NATO Europe members presence of US military and civilian personnel and dependents, by service branch, 1980-88, GAO rpt, 26123-252

NATO Europe members presence of US military and civilian personnel, and vacancies, by service branch, 1988, GAO rpt, 26123-251

Procurement of Navy, by contractor and location, FY88, annual rpt, 3804-13

Shipments by DOD of military and personal property, passenger traffic, and costs, by service branch and mode of transport, quarterly rpt, 3702-1

Ships (amphibious), procurement, and costs, for Marine Corps, projected under alternative proposals, FY90-2000, 26308-90

Statistical Abstract of US, social, political, and economic data, 1790-2025, comprehensive annual compilation, 2324-1.2

Training and education programs of DOD, funding, staff, students, and facilities, by service branch, FY90, annual rpt, 3504-5

Women military personnel on active and reserve duty, by demographic and service characteristics and service branch, FY88, annual chartbook, 3544-26

see also Marine Reserve

Marine Mammal Commission

Budget of US Appendix, obligations, appropriations, and personnel, by program and agency, FY90, annual rpt, 104-3

Budget of US, authoritative financial statements with appropriations, outlays, and receipts, by category and agency, FY88, annual rpt, 8104-2.2

Plastic, tar, and other nondegradable ocean and beach debris, incidence and environmental impacts, 1970s-88, 14738-4

Protection of marine mammals, Federal and intl regulatory and research activities, with bibl, 1988, annual rpt, 14734-1

Marine Mammal Protection Act

Admin of Act, and marine mammal population, strandings, and catch permits by species and location, 1987-88, annual rpt, 2164-11

Marine mammals

Alaska OCS environmental conditions and oil dev impacts, compilation of papers, series, 2176-1

Alaska rural villages population characteristics and and subsistence activities, 1976-86, 5738-9

Coastal and riparian areas environmental conditions, fish, wildlife, use, and mgmt, for individual ecosystems, series, 5506-9

Coastal areas environmental and socioeconomic conditions, and potential impact of oil and gas OCS leases, final statement series, 5736-1

Environmental quality and protection programs, and intl issues, 1988 annual rpt, 484-1

Plastic, tar, and other nondegradable ocean and beach debris, incidence and environmental impacts, 1970s-88, 14738-4

Population of marine mammals, strandings, and catch permits by species and location, 1987-88, annual rpt, 2164–11

Porpoise population, and tuna fishery kills, 1960s-90, hearing, 21568–47

Protection of marine mammals, activities, funding, populations, and harvests, by species, 1987, annual rpt, 5504–12

Protection of marine mammals, Federal and intl regulatory and research activities, with bibl, 1988, annual rpt, 14734–1

Recreation related to wildlife, hunting, and fishing participation and spending, detailed data by location, 1985 survey, quinquennial rpt, 5508–5

Whale (bowhead) population in Beaufort Sea, and aerial survey operations, Sept-Oct 1979-88, 5738–8

Marine pollution

Alaska OCS environmental conditions and oil dev impacts, compilation of papers, series, 2176–1

Coastal and estuarine environmental conditions, research results and methodology, series, 2176–7

Coastal and estuarine PCB and pesticide concentrations in fish and shellfish, by species and location, 1965-84, 2178–21

Coastal and estuarine pollutant concentrations in fish, shellfish, and environment, series, 2176–3

Coastal and estuarine pollutant discharges, by source, pollutant type, and location, series, 2176–4

Coastal and riparian areas environmental conditions, fish, wildlife, use, and mgmt, for individual ecosystems, series, 5506–9

Coastal areas environmental and socioeconomic conditions, and potential impact of oil and gas OCS leases, final statement series, 5736–1

Environmental quality and protection programs, and intl issues, 1988 annual rpt, 484–1

Estuary environmental conditions and mgmt, for individual areas, conf series, 2146–6

Estuary environmental conditions and mgmt, research projects and funding, FY87, annual listing, 2144–24

Fish (striped bass) stocks status on Atlantic coast, and sport and commercial catch by State, 1979-87, annual rpt, 5504–29

Fish and shellfish catch, life cycles, and environmental needs, for selected coastal species and regions, series, 5506–8

Incidents and discharges, by type, source, cause, and location, 1984-86, annual rpt, 7404–3

NOAA activities and funding for ocean pollution, estuary, and coastal waters monitoring and assessment, FY88, annual rpt, 2174–9

Oil and gas OCS production water discharges, and impacts on Gulf of Mexico coastal habitats, 1983-88, 5738–10

Oil and gas OCS production water discharges, for Pacific lands under Federal lease by drilling platform, 1960s-88, annual rpt, 5734–9

Oregon coastal and estuarine pollutant levels, by pollutant and location, 1960s-87, 2178–23

Paints used on ship hulls, impacts on environment and marine species, with bibl, 1960s-87, 2148–58

Plastic, tar, and other nondegradable ocean and beach debris, incidence and environmental impacts, 1970s-88, 14738–4

Radioactive waste and spent fuel generation, inventory, and disposal, 1960s-88 and projected to 2020, annual rpt, 3364–2

Radioactive waste containers for ocean disposal, performance criteria, with waste production and inventory, 1984-85 and projected to 2020, 9198–119

Radioactive waste from Navy nuclear-powered vessels and support facilities, releases in harbors, and public exposure, 1970s-88, annual rpt, 3804–11

Research and distribution of oceanographic data, World Data Center A activities by country, and cruises by ship, 1987, annual rpt, 2144–15

Research on ocean pollution, monitoring, and resources dev activities of Fed Govt, funding and project descriptions, FY87, annual listing, 2144–23

Research on ocean pollution, monitoring, and resources dev activities of Fed Govt, 5-year plan and funding by agency, FY84-89, triennial rpt, 2148–56

Research on ocean pollution, project rpts and data files, FY78-83, listing, 2158–51

Researchers rankings of seriousness of marine pollution events, by event type, 1987 survey, 2148–57

Sewage pipelines and dump sites authorized in coastal areas, status and EPA enforcement activities by State, 1982-87, hearings, 21568–45

see also Oil spills

Marine Reserve

Family social, economic, and other characteristics, and spouses attitudes, for reserve personnel, 1986 survey, 3508–30

Manpower and equipment strengths, and readiness, by reserve component, FY88, annual rpt, 3544–31

Manpower, funding by category, procurement reductions, and needs, by reserve component, FY80-88, GAO rpt, 26123–220

Manpower social, economic, family, and service characteristics, and attitudes, by reserve component, 1986 survey, 3508–29

Manpower strengths and characteristics, by reserve component, quarterly rpt, 3542–4

Manpower strengths for reserve components, by selected characteristics, FY88, annual rpt, 3544–1.5

Women military personnel on active and reserve duty, by demographic and service characteristics and service branch, FY88, annual chartbook, 3544–26

Marine resources

Aerial survey R&D rpts, and sources of natural resource and environmental data, quarterly listing, 9502–7

Coastal areas environmental and socioeconomic conditions, and potential impact of oil and gas OCS leases, final statement series, 5736–1

see also Coastal areas

see also Continental shelf

see also Coral reefs and islands

see also Fish and fishing industry

see also Marine mammals

see also Marine pollution

see also Marine resources conservation

see also Offshore mineral resources

see also Offshore oil and gas

see also Oil spills

see also Shellfish

see also Water resources development

Marine resources conservation

Coastal and estuarine environmental conditions, research results and methodology, series, 2176–7

Coastal and riparian areas environmental conditions, fish, wildlife, use, and mgmt, for individual ecosystems, series, 5506–9

Coastal areas environmental conditions and mgmt, map series, 2176–5

Environmental quality and protection programs, and intl issues, 1988 annual rpt, 484–1

Estuary environmental conditions and mgmt, for individual areas, conf series, 2146–6

Estuary environmental conditions and mgmt, research projects and funding, FY87, annual listing, 2144–24

Fish and shellfish catch, life cycles, and environmental needs, for selected coastal species and regions, series, 5506–8

Fish and Wildlife Service conservation and research project descriptions and results, FY87-88, biennial rpt, 5504–20

Fishery mgmt and R&D, Fed Govt grants by project and State, and rpts, 1987, annual listing, 2164–3

Maine coastal marine resources and ocean floor ecology, 1983-87, conf papers, 2148–55

Marine Fisheries Review, US and foreign fisheries resources, dev, mgmt, and research, quarterly journal, 2162–1

Research on ocean pollution, monitoring, and resources dev activities of Fed Govt, funding and project descriptions, FY87, annual listing, 2144–23

Research on ocean pollution, monitoring, and resources dev activities of Fed Govt, 5-year plan and funding by agency, FY84-89, triennial rpt, 2148–56

see also Marine mammals

see also Marine pollution

Marine safety

see Marine accidents and safety

Marital status

see Marriage and divorce

see Widows and widowers

see under By Marital Status in the "Index by Categories"

Maritime academies

see Service academies

Maritime Administration

Activities, finances, and subsidies of MarAd, and world merchant fleet operations, FY88, annual rpt, 7704–14

Budget of US Appendix, obligations, appropriations, and personnel, by program and agency, FY90, annual rpt, 104–3

Bulk carrier ships in world fleet, characteristics by country of registry, and for Great Lakes fleet by owner, as of Jan 1989, annual listing, 7704–13

Containerized cargo carried over principal trade routes, by flag of vessel, port, and US coastal district, 1984, annual rpt, 7704–8

Containers (intermodal) and equipment owned by shipping and leasing companies, inventory by type and size, 1989, annual rpt, 7704–10

Employment of DOT, by subagency, occupation, and selected personnel characteristics, FY88, annual rpt, 7304–18

Exports and imports (waterborne) of US, by type of service, commodity, country, route, and US port, 1986-87, annual rpt, 7704–2

Exports and imports of US shipped through Canada, by detailed commodity, customs district, and country, 1987, annual rpt, 7704–11

Foreign and US merchant ships, and tonnage, by country of registry, as of Jan 1988, annual rpt, 7704–3

Foreign-flag ships owned by US firms and foreign affiliates, by type, owner, and country of registry and construction, as of July 1989, semiannual rpt, 7702–3

Merchant ships in US fleet and Natl Defense Reserve Fleet, vessels, tonnage, and owner, as of Jan 1989, semiannual listing, 7702–2

Shipbuilding and deliveries, by vessel type and country of construction and registry, 1988, annual rpt, 7704–4

Shipbuilding and repair facilities, capacity, and employment, by shipyard, 1988, annual rpt, 7704–9

Shipbuilding costs, deliveries, contracts, employment, and wage rates, by coastal district and shipyard, 1988, annual rpt, 7704–12

Ships in US merchant fleet, operating subsidies, and ship-related employment, monthly rpt, 7702–1

Tanker ships in world fleet, characteristics by country of registry, as of Jan 1989, annual listing, 7704–17

Waterborne commerce (domestic) of US, freight by major commodity group, vessel type, and port, 1986, annual rpt, 7704–7

Maritime industry
see Inland water transportation
see Longshoremen
see Marine accidents and safety
see Merchant seamen
see Shipbuilding and operating subsidies
see Shipbuilding and repairing
see Ships and shipping

Maritime law
Court civil and criminal caseloads for Federal district, appeals, and special courts, June 1989, annual rpt, 18204–2; 18204–8

Marine Mammal Protection Act admin, and populations, strandings, and catch permits by species and location, 1987-88, annual rpt, 2164–11

Maritime Commission activities, case filings by type and disposition, and civil penalties by shipper, FY88, annual rpt, 9334–1

Treaties and other bilateral and multilateral agreements of US in force, by country, as of Jan 1989, annual listing, 7004–1

US attorneys civil and criminal cases by type and disposition, and collections, by Federal district, FY88, annual rpt, 6004–2.5

Market Facts of Canada Ltd.
"Pleasure Travel Markets to North America", 2906–2

Market research
Agricultural exports of US, impacts of foreign agricultural and trade policy, with data by commodity and country, 1988, annual rpt, 1924–8

Agricultural production, consumption, and policies for selected countries, and US export dev and promotion, monthly journal, 1922–2

Agricultural trade by commodity and country, prices, and world market devs, monthly rpt, 1922–12

Agricultural trade, outlook and current situation, quarterly rpt, 1542–4

Business America, foreign and domestic commerce, and US investment and trade opportunities, biweekly journal, 2042–24

Census of Population and Housing, 1990: data coverage and availability for community and business dev projects, user guide, 2308–10

Overseas Business Reports: economic conditions, investment and export opportunities, and trade practices, country market research rpt series, 2046–6

Paper and wood products production and trade, and industry operations by firm, by country, world region rpt series, 2046–14

Travel to US and Canada, market analysis with detailed trip and traveler characteristics, country rpt series, 2906–2

Travel to US, market research, major magazine ad costs and circulation, and trade show data, for selected countries, 1989-90, annual rpt, 2904–11

see also Consumer surveys

Market shares
see Economic concentration and diversification

Marketing
Employment and earnings in marketing and sales industries, by occupation, 1986-87 and projected 2000, article, 6742–1.901

Hospital reimbursement by Medicare under prospective payment system, impacts on cost accounting systems and marketing techniques, survey results, 1988 rpt, 17206–2.7

Savings instns financial statements, FSLIC-insured instns by FHLB district and State, and FDIC-insured savings banks, 1988, annual rpt, 8434–1

see also Advertising
see also Agricultural marketing
see also Competition
see also Consumer credit
see also Consumer protection
see also Consumer surveys
see also Credit
see also Direct marketing
see also Economic concentration and diversification
see also Foreign trade promotion
see also Labeling
see also Market research
see also Packaging and containers
see also Price regulation
see also Prices
see also Retail trade
see also Sales promotion
see also Sales workers

see also Shopping centers
see also Wholesale trade
see also under names of specific commodities or commodity groups

Marketing quotas
see Agricultural production quotas and price supports

Markey, James P.
"Occupational Change: Pursuing a Different Kind of Work", 6722–1.943

Marquis, Kent H.
"Using Administrative Record Data To Describe SIPP Response Errors", 2626–10.77

Marriage and divorce
AFDC recipients demographic and financial characteristics, by State, FY87, annual rpt, 4694–1

Asian American earnings, and employment and other characteristics, by detailed origin and whether foreign-born, 1980, 11046–7.2

Consumer Income, socioeconomic characteristics of persons, families, and households, detailed cross-tabulations, Current Population Rpt series, 2546–6

Deaths and rates, by cause, marital status, age, race, and sex, 1986, annual rpt, 4144–2.1

Divorce property settlement, by type, whether child support and alimony received, and selected characteristics of woman, 1985, biennial Current Population Rpt, 2546–2.145

Divorces and children involved, by characteristics of spouses and whether 1st marriage, 1950s-84, 4147–21.46

Divorces by age of spouses and duration of marriage, and children involved, by State, 1986 with trends from 1940, US Vital Statistics advance annual rpt, 4146–5.109

Earnings of married couples, by employment status, occupation, age, and education of spouses, and age of children, 1987, Current Population Rpt, 2546–6.61

Educational attainment, by sociodemographic characteristics and location, 1987 and trends from 1940, biennial Current Population Rpt, 2546–1.427; 2546–1.431

Employment, unemployment, and labor force characteristics, Labor Statistics Handbook, 1940s-88 with trends from 1913, 6728–38.2

Farm population, by employment and socioeconomic characteristics, and region, 1988, annual Current Population Rpt, 2546–1.439

Hispanic Americans socioeconomic characteristics, by detailed origin, 1988, Current Population Rpt, 2546–1.430; 2546–1.438

Household and family characteristics, by living arrangement, 1988 and trends from 1960, Current Population Rpt, 2546–2.148

Household and family characteristics, by location, 1988, annual Current Population Rpt, 2546–1.437

Household and family composition, and factors affecting change, 1960s-88, chartbook, 2546–2.149

Household composition, income, benefits, and labor force status, Survey of Income and Program Participation methodology, working paper series, 2626–10

Housing characteristics of recent movers for new and previous unit, and household characteristics, by location, 1985, biennial rpt, 2485-12

Immigrant and nonimmigrant visas of US issued and refused, by class, issuing office, and nationality, FY88, annual rpt, 7184-1

Immigration to US, alien workers, visitors, deportations, and naturalizations, by country, FY88 and trends from 1820, annual rpt, 6264-2

Income (household) and poverty status under alternative income definitions, by recipient characteristics, 1986, Current Population Rpt, 2546-6.58

Living arrangements, family relationships, and marital status, by selected characteristics, 1988, annual Current Population Rpt, 2546-1.428; 2546-1.433

Marriages and rates, by age, race, education, previous marital status of spouses, and State, 1986, US Vital Statistics advance annual rpt, 4146-5.111; 4146-5.112

Marriages, by prior marital status, interval between marriages, other characteristics of spouses, type of ceremony, and State, with divorces, 1970s-83, 4147-21.45

Marriages, divorces, and rates, by characteristics of spouses, State, and county, 1984 and trends from 1920, US Vital Statistics annual rpt, 4144-4

Marriages, divorces, and rates, by State, preliminary 1987-88, US Vital Statistics annual rpt, 4144-7

Military reserve personnel social, economic, family, and service characteristics, and attitudes, by reserve component, 1986 survey, 3508-29

Military reserve spouses attitudes, and family social, economic, and other characteristics, 1986 survey, 3508-30

OASDI benefit payments, trust fund finances, and economic and demographic assumptions, 1970-87 and alternative projections to 1997, actuarial rpt, 4706-1.103

Older persons care by family members, caregivers and potential caregivers by relation and other characteristics, 1984, 4186-7.5

Older persons health care services use related to marital status, living arrangements, and other characteristics, 1977, 4188-54

Older persons socioeconomic characteristics, 1900s-86 and projected to 2050, biennial chartbook, 12904-1

Population size and characteristics, 1969-88, Current Population Rpt, annual rpt, 2546-2.146

Population size and components of change, alternative projections 1988-2080 and trends from 1900, annual actuarial rpt, 4706-1.104

Railroad employee benefits and beneficiaries, by type, FY85, annual rpt, 9704-2.2

Railroad employee retirement benefits for divorced spouses, monthly rpt, 9702-2

Research on population and reproduction, Federal funding by project, FY87, annual listing, 4474-9

Retirement timing of married couples, differences in age and retirement age of spouses, 1982, article, 4742-1.906

Statistical Abstract of US, social, political, and economic data, 1790-2025, comprehensive annual compilation, 2324-1.1

Tax (income) returns of individuals, by filing status, tax item, and income level, 1987, annual article, 8302-2.901

Telephone service of households, by composition, income sources, and other characteristics, 1984-87, 9288-11

Vital and Health Statistics series: reprints of monthly rpt supplements, 4147-24

Vital statistics provisional data, monthly rpt, 4142-1

Wages of full- and part-time workers, by selected characteristics, quarterly press release, 6742-20

Warsaw Pact and US citizens binatl marriage cases pending as of Sept 1988, semiannual rpt, 7002-1

see also Births out of wedlock

see also Child support and alimony

see also Families and households

see also Widows and widowers

see also under By Marital Status in the "Index by Categories"

Marshall Islands

Bank deposits in FDIC-insured commercial and savings banks, by instn, State, and county, as of June 1988, annual regional rpt, 9295-3.6

Economic, social, political, and geographic summary data, by country, 1989, annual factbook, 9114-2

Human rights conditions in 170 countries, 1988, annual rpt, 21384-3

Population size, growth rates, and components of change, by country, projected 1989-2020 and trends from 1950, biennial rpt, 2324-9

Population social, economic, health, and govtl data, by TTPI govt, FY88 and selected trends, detailed annual rpt, 7004-6

see also under By Foreign Country in the "Index by Categories"

Marshall, Tex.

Wages by occupation, for office and plant workers, 1989 survey, periodic MSA rpt, 6785-12.6

see also under By SMSA or MSA in the "Index by Categories"

Marshals Service

see U.S. Marshals Service

Marshes

see Wetlands

Martens, Joann

"Master Limited Partnerships: A View from Their 1986 Tax Returns", 8006-3.59

Martin, Douglas J.

"Distribution and Seasonal Abundance of Juvenile Salmon and Other Fishes in the Yukon Delta", 2176-1.29

Martin, Philip L.

"Dislocated Farmers: Number, Distribution, and Impacts", 15496-1.1

Maryland

Agriculture census, 1987: farms, farmland, production, finances, and operator characteristics, by county, final State rpt, 2331-1.20

Appalachian Regional Commission funding, by project and State, planned FY89, annual rpt, 9084-3

Apple production, marketing, and prices, for Appalachia and compared to other States, various periods 1986-89, annual rpt, 1311-13

Bank deposits in FDIC-insured commercial and savings banks, by instn, State, and county, as of June 1988, annual regional rpt, 9295-3.2

Banks (insured commercial), Fed Reserve 5th District members financial statements, by State, quarterly rpt, 9389-18

Coal production and mines by county, prices, productivity, miners, reserves, and stocks, by mining method and State, 1987-88, annual rpt, 3164-25

County Business Patterns, 1987: employment, establishments, and payroll, by SIC 2- to 4-digit industry and county, annual State rpt, 2326-8.22

Deaths and rates, by detailed location, cause, and demographic characteristics, 1987, US Vital Statistics annual rpt, 4144-3.1

DOD prime contract awards, by contractor, service branch, State, and city, FY88, annual rpt, 3544-22

Economic indicators by State, Fed Reserve 5th District, quarterly rpt, 9389-16

Employment and housing market indicators by State, FHLB 4th District, quarterly rpt, 9302-36

Employment, earnings, and hours, by selected SIC 1- to 4-digit industry, State, and for 262 MSAs, 1972-87, 6748-81.2

Enterprise zone program of Maryland, participants characteristics and views on incentives, and proposed Federal program tax expenditures, 1983-88, GAO rpt, 26131-53

Fed Govt spending in States and local areas, by type, State, county, and city, FY88, annual rpt, 2464-3

Fed Govt spending in States, by type, program, agency, and State, FY88, annual rpt, 2464-2

HHS financial aid, by program, recipient, State, and city, FY88, annual regional listing, 4004-3.3

Homeless children educational enrollment and needs, 1988, annual State rpt, 4804-35.21

Housing and households characteristics, 1985 survey, MSA fact sheet, 2485-11.6

Hwy admin and gasoline tax revenue proposed transfer from Fed Govt to States, issues, with motor fuel taxes by selected State, 1988 rpt, 10048-72

Income (personal) per capita and by source, and earnings by industry div, by State, MSA, and county, 1982-87, annual regional rpt, 2704-2.2

Mineral Industry Surveys, State reviews of production, 1988, preliminary annual rpt, 5614-6

Minerals Yearbook, 1987, Vol 2 preprints: State review of production and sales by commodity, and business activity, annual rpt, 5604-16.21

Minerals Yearbook, 1987, Vol 2: State reviews of production, sales, and firms, by commodity, and business activity, annual rpt, 5604-34

Retail trade census, 1987: employment, establishments, sales, and payroll, by SIC 2- to 4-digit kind of business, MSA, county, and city, State rpt, 2397–1.21

Savings instns, FHLB 4th District members finances and financial ratios, by State, quarterly rpt, 9302–3

Savings instns, FHLB 4th District members finances, by State, 1984-88, annual rpt, 9304–29.5

Service industries census, 1987: employment, establishments, receipts, and payroll, by SIC 2- to 4-digit kind of business, MSA, county, and city, State rpt, 2391–1.21

Statistical Abstract of US, social, political, and economic data, with foreign comparisons, 1790-2025, comprehensive annual compilation, 2324–1

Suicide incidence rates related to age, sex, race, marital status, and month, for Maryland, 1970-80, article, 4042–3.928

Suicides in Maryland prisons, by selected characteristics, 1979-87, 4186–9.2

Wages by occupation, and benefits for office and plant workers, 1989 survey, periodic labor market rpt, 6785–3.9

Water supply and quality in streams and lakes, and groundwater levels in wells, by drainage basin, 1987, annual State rpt, 5666–10.19

Wholesale trade census, 1987: employment, establishments, finances, and operations, by SIC 2- to 4-digit kind of business, MSA, county, and city, State rpt, 2405–1.21

Wildlife-related recreation, hunting, and fishing participation and spending, detailed data, 1985 survey, quinquennial State rpt, 5506–6.20

see also Baltimore, Md.

see also Montgomery County, Md.

see also Prince George's County, Md.

see also under By State in the "Index by Categories"

Mass media

AIDS public knowledge, attitudes, info sources, and testing, for blacks, 1988 survey, 4146–8.167

AIDS public knowledge, attitudes, info sources, and testing, for Hispanics, 1988 survey, 4146–8.168

AIDS public knowledge, attitudes, info sources, and testing, 1988 survey, 4146–8.165; 4146–8.169; 4146–8.173

AIDS public knowledge, attitudes, info sources, and testing, 1989 survey, 4146–8.176; 4146–8.180

Fed Govt audiovisual activities and spending, by whether performed in-house and agency, FY87, annual rpt, 9514–1

Statistical Abstract of US, social, political, and economic data, 1790-2025, comprehensive annual compilation, 2324–1.3

see also Advertising

see also Motion pictures

see also Newspapers

see also Periodicals

see also Public broadcasting

see also Radio

see also Television

Mass transit

see Airlines

see Buses

see National Railroad Passenger Corp.

see Railroads

see Subways

see Urban transportation

Massachusetts

Agriculture census, 1987: farms, farmland, production and costs, and operator characteristics, advance State and county rpts, 2330–1.25

Agriculture census, 1987: farms, farmland, production, finances, and operator characteristics, by county, final State rpt, 2331–1.21

Bank deposits in FDIC-insured commercial and savings banks, by instn, State, and county, as of June 1988, annual regional rpt, 9295–3.1

Banks and thrifts in New England, financial statements by type of instn and Fed deposit insurance, and State, 1987, annual rpt, 9304–3.1

County Business Patterns, 1987: employment, establishments, and payroll, by SIC 2- to 4-digit industry and county, annual State rpt, 2326–8.23

Cranberry production, prices, use, and acreage, for selected States, 1987-88 and forecast 1989, annual rpt, 1621–18.4

Deaths and rates, by detailed location, cause, and demographic characteristics, 1987, US Vital Statistics annual rpt, 4144–3.1

DOD prime contract awards, by contractor, service branch, State, and city, FY88, annual rpt, 3544–22

Economic indicators for New England States, Fed Reserve 1st District, monthly rpt, 9373–24

Economic indicators for New England States, Fed Reserve 1st District, quarterly rpt with articles, 9373–2

Employment, earnings, and hours, by selected SIC 1- to 4-digit industry, State, and for 262 MSAs, 1972-87, 6748–81.2

Fed Govt spending in States and local areas, by type, State, county, and city, FY88, annual rpt, 2464–3

Fed Govt spending in States, by type, program, agency, and State, FY88, annual rpt, 2464–2

Fish and shellfish catch, wholesale receipts, prices, trade, and other market activities, weekly regional rpt, 2162–6.2

HHS financial aid, by program, recipient, State, and city, FY88, annual regional listing, 4004–3.1

Homeless children educational enrollment and needs, 1988, annual State rpt, 4804–35.22

Income (personal) per capita and by source, and earnings by industry div, by State, MSA, and county, 1982-87, annual regional rpt, 2704–2.2

Lead poisoning among children, and children at risk in Massachusetts, by city, 1985-87, hearing, 21248–119

Medicare physicians assigned-fee laws of 4 States, impacts on care cost and availability, 1985-89, GAO rpt, 26121–312

Mineral Industry Surveys, State reviews of production, 1988, preliminary annual rpt, 5614–6

Minerals Yearbook, 1987, Vol 2 preprints: State review of production and sales by commodity, and business activity, annual rpt, 5604–16.22

Minerals Yearbook, 1987, Vol 2: State reviews of production, sales, and firms, by commodity, and business activity, annual rpt, 5604–34

Nursing home compliance with Medicare and Medicaid regulations, and patient characteristics, by facility, 1987/88, annual State rpt, 4654–15.22

Retail trade census, 1987: employment, establishments, sales, and payroll, by SIC 2- to 4-digit kind of business, MSA, county, and city, State rpt, 2397–1.22

Savings instns, FHLB 1st District members financial operations and related economic and housing indicators, monthly rpt, 9302–4

Service industries census, 1987: employment, establishments, receipts, and payroll, by SIC 2- to 4-digit kind of business, MSA, county, and city, State rpt, 2391–1.22

Statistical Abstract of US, social, political, and economic data, with foreign comparisons, 1790-2025, comprehensive annual compilation, 2324–1

Timber resources and removals, by species, ownership class, and county, 1972 and 1985, State rpt, 1206–12.12

Wages by occupation, and benefits for office and plant workers in southeastern Massachusetts, 1989 survey, periodic labor market rpt, 6785–3.2

Water supply and quality in streams and lakes, and groundwater levels in wells, by drainage basin, 1986, annual State rpt, 5666–23.20

Water supply and quality in streams and lakes, and groundwater levels in wells, by drainage basin, 1987, annual State rpt, 5666–10.20

Wholesale trade census, 1987: employment, establishments, finances, and operations, by SIC 2- to 4-digit kind of business, MSA, county, and city, State rpt, 2405–1.22

Wildlife-related recreation, hunting, and fishing participation and spending, detailed data, 1985 survey, quinquennial State rpt, 5506–6.21

see also Boston, Mass.

see also Brockton, Mass.

see also Cambridge, Mass.

see also Gloucester, Mass.

see also Lawrence, Mass.

see also New Bedford, Mass.

see also Salem, Mass.

see also Woburn, Mass.

see also under By State in the "Index by Categories"

Massey, James T.

"Design and Estimation for the National Health Interview Survey, 1985-94. Vital and Health Statistics Series 2", 4147–2.110

Mataloni, Raymond J., Jr.

"Capital Expenditures by Majority-Owned Foreign Affiliates of U.S. Companies, 1990", 2702–1.933

Maternity

Abortions, by method, pregnancy history, and other characteristics of woman, 1985-86, US Vital Statistics annual rpt, 4146-5.108

AIDS cases and AIDS virus infection prevalence, by risk group and other patient characteristics, 1981-88 and projected to 1992, 4206-2.13

Births, fertility rates, and childless women, by selected characteristics, 1988, annual Current Population Rpt, 2546-1.436

Cancer (breast) risk, relation to hypertension diagnosis before and after pregnancy, 1989 article, 4472-1.927

Deaths and rates, by cause and age, preliminary 1987-88, US Vital Statistics annual rpt, 4144-7

Deaths and rates, by detailed location, cause, and demographic characteristics, 1987, US Vital Statistics annual rpt, 4144-3

Deaths related to pregnancy, abortion, and contraception, by age, 1975 and 1982, hearing, 21408-113

Deaths related to pregnancy, and rates, by detailed cause and demographic characteristics, 1986, US Vital Statistics annual rpt, 4144-2

Deaths related to pregnancy, rates, and risk, by pregnancy outcome, cause, and maternal characteristics, 1980-85, article, 4202-7.903

Deaths related to pregnancy, 1987, US Vital Statistics advance annual rpt, 4146-5.113

Disability related to pregnancy, absenteeism, and health services use, by selected characteristics, 1988, annual rpt, 4147-10.170

Ectopic pregnancies and related deaths, by race, age, and region, 1970-86, article, 4202-7.902; 4202-7.905

Employment history and maternity leave arrangements of 1st-time mothers, by selected characteristics, 1960s-85, 2328-62

Exercise following delivery, intention relationship to age, education, and exercise attitudes and habits, local area study, 1989 article, 4042-3.916

Health condition and care of mothers and children, research activities and funding, FY88, annual rpt, 4474-31

Health condition and health care resources, use, and spending, 1950s-87, annual data compilation, 4144-11

Health condition improvement and disease prevention goals and recommended activities for 2000, with trends 1970s-80s, 4048-10

Hepatitis risk for pregnant and postpartum women related to isoniazid treatment for tuberculosis, by age group, 1981-82 study, article, 4042-3.911

Hospital discharges and length of stay, by diagnosis, patient and instn characteristics, procedure performed, and payment source, 1987, annual rpt, 4147-13.99

Hospital discharges by detailed diagnostic and procedure category, primary diagnosis, and length of stay, by age, sex, and region, 1987, annual rpt, 4147-13.100

Indian Health Service facilities, funding, operations, and Indian health and other characteristics, 1950s-88, annual chartbook, 4084-1

Nutritional status and related health condition and practices, by selected characteristics, 1970s-87, 4048-33

Pollution (air) exposure of population and selected risk groups, by pollutant, MSA, and county, 1988, hearing, 21368-117

Research contracts and grants of Natl Inst of Child Health and Human Dev, by recipient and location, FY88, annual listing, 4474-36

Smoking and health research rpts, 1988, last issue of annual listing, 4204-19

Smoking and health research summaries, bimonthly rpt, 4202-8

Statistical Abstract of US, social, political, and economic data, 1790-2025, comprehensive annual compilation, 2324-1.1

see also Birth defects
see also Births
see also Births out of wedlock
see also Birthweight
see also Breast-feeding
see also Family planning
see also Fertility
see also Fetal deaths
see also Infant mortality
see also Maternity benefits
see also Midwives
see also Obstetrics and gynecology
see also Prenatal care
see also Teenage pregnancy

Maternity benefits

Assistance (financial and nonfinancial) of Fed Govt, 1989 base edition with supplements, annual listing, 104-5

Coverage and provisions of parental leave policies, by occupational group, 1988, article, 6722-1.950

Employee benefit plan coverage and provisions, by plan type and occupational group, 1988, annual rpt, 6784-19

Employee maternity leave arrangements and work history of 1st-time mothers, by selected characteristics, 1960s-85, 2328-62

Employee parental leave of absence, policies, coverage, and attitudes, by employee characteristics, 1980-87, hearings, 25548-95

Food aid program of USDA for women, infants, and children, participants, clinics, and costs by State and Indian agency, monthly tables, 1362-16

Food aid program of USDA for women, infants, and children, prenatal enrollees by trimester of enrollment and other characteristics, 1984, article, 4042-3.929

Food aid programs of USDA, costs and participation by program, region, and State, monthly rpt, 1362-14

Foreign countries social security programs coverage, funding, eligibility, and benefits, by country, 1987, biennial rpt, 4746-4.60

Labor laws enacted, by State, 1988, annual article, 6722-1.904

Medicaid beneficiaries maternity services use and costs, in 3 States, 1983-84, article, 4652-1.938

Medicaid eligibility extension to pregnant women and children with incomes over AFDC levels, with data by State, 1986-89, GAO rpt, 26121-303

Mathematic models and modeling

Africa food imports and aid needs under alternative weather assumptions, for 17 African countries, projected to 1995, 1528-279

AIDS health care and epidemiological research, methodological issues, 1988 conf, 4188-61

AIDS health care services research status, needs, methods, and impacts on public health policy and funding, with data for selected cities, 1989 conf papers, 4188-59

Cancer (breast) long-term risk among women with selected risk factors, model description and results, 1989 article, 4472-1.934

Cancer (melanoma) 8-year survival rates, model description and results, 1989 article, 4472-1.935

Energy supply, demand, distribution, and impacts of legislation, series, 3166-6

Futures contracts risk hedging, for soybean and other protein meals, model description and results, 1984-86, article, 1561-3.904

Great Lakes water levels impacts of water supply mgmt and weather, model description, 1900s-85, 2148-59

Health care costs related to cost of prior hospitalization, model description and results, 1974-80, article, 4652-1.939

Hudson-Raritan River basin pollutant levels and sources, model description and results, 1880s-1982, 2178-22

Nuclear radiation exposure of population near commercial reactors, by body site, age group, and selected plant, 1986, annual rpt, 9634-7

OASDI disabled worker beneficiaries, duration, and exits by reason, by selected characteristics, model description and results, 1972-80, article, 4742-1.923

Unemployment insurance extended benefits provision in substate areas, model results and cost estimates, 1980-86, 6406-6.28

Unemployment insurance programs of States and Fed Govt, benefits adequacy, and work disincentives, series, 6406-6

Water supply in West Virginia, low streamflow frequency by site, model description and results, 1980-83, 5668-92

Water supply in Wyoming, annual peak streamflow by site, model description and results, 1985, 5668-84

see also Economic and econometric models

Mathematica Policy Research, Inc.

"Biased Selection in the Medicare Competition Demonstrations", 4658-31

"Evaluation of the Feasibility of a Substate Area Extended Benefit Program: Final Report", 6406-6.28

"Examination of Declining UI Claims During the 1980s", 6406-6.24

"New Jersey Unemployment Insurance Reemployment Demonstration Project", 6406-6.27

Mathematics

Black colleges R&D funding by source, and characteristics of grad students and research staff, by field of science and instn, 1980s-87, 9628-78

Degrees (PhD) in science and engineering, by field, instn, employment prospects, sex, race, and other characteristics, 1960s-88, 9627-30

Degrees awarded in higher education, by level, field, race, and sex, 1989 edition, annual rpt, 4824-2.20

Degrees in science and engineering, by field, level, and sex, 1950-86, 9628-77

DOD Dependents Schools basic skills and college entrance test scores, 1988/89, annual rpt, 3504-16

Education in science and engineering in elementary and secondary schools, and student persistence in postsecondary education, 1977-88, 26358-199

Education statistics, detailed data on elementary, secondary, and higher education, 1920s-88 and projected to 1997, annual rpt, 4824-1

Educational progress by subject and selected student characteristics, standard test results and credits, 1989 edition, annual rpt, 4824-2.12

Elementary and secondary students performance in selected subjects, and factors affecting proficiency, natl assessments, 1969-86, 4898-26

Employment and earnings in science and engineering, by field and activity, and private and Federal R&D spending, by industry, 1975-88, 9626-6.29

Employment and other characteristics of science and engineering PhDs, by field and State, 1987, biennial rpt, 9627-18

Employment characteristics of scientists and engineers, by field, 1988, biennial rpt, 9627-16

Employment of scientists and engineers, and related topics, fact sheet series, 9626-2

Employment of scientists, engineers, and technicians, by nonmanufacturing industry and field, 1987, triennial rpt, 9627-31

Employment of scientists, engineers, and technicians in manufacturing, by field, occupation, and industry, 1986, triennial rpt, 9627-23

Employment of scientists, engineers, and technicians in transportation, utilities, and retail and wholesale trade, by field, occupation, and industry, 1985, triennial rpt, 9627-32

Employment, unemployment, and labor force characteristics, by region and census div, 1988, annual rpt, 6744-7.1

Enrollment in science and engineering grad programs, by field, source of funds, and characteristics of student and instn, 1975-87, annual rpt, 9627-7

Fed Govt aid to higher education and nonprofit instns for R&D and related activities, by field, instn, agency, and State, FY87, annual rpt, 9627-17

Fed Govt civilian employment by occupation, agency, and location, and language and math skill needs, 1966-87 and projected to 2000, 9848-37

Fed Govt science and engineering employment, by field, degree level, race, sex, agency, and State, 1987, annual rpt, 9627-5

Foreign and US funding for R&D, and scientists and engineering employment and education, 1988, annual rpt, 9624-23.1

Foreign and US technology dev and competition issues, fundings and recommendations, 1980s-87, 21708-123

High school academic requirement reform, impacts on test scores by subject and race, 1982-88, GAO rpt, 26131-62

High school students employment, academic and other characteristics, 1984-86, 4898-27

Immigrant scientists and engineers, by field, age, sex, country and world area of origin, and State, 1987 and trends from 1967, 9627-29

NASA R&D funding to higher education instns, by field, instn, and State, FY88, annual listing, 9504-7

NSF activities, finances, and funding by program, FY88, annual rpt, 9624-6

R&D funding by Fed Govt, by field, performer type, agency, and State, FY87-89, annual rpt, 9627-20

R&D funding by higher education instns, by source and field, FY80-87, annual rpt, 9624-18.5

R&D funding by source and performer, and related employment, by State, 1975-87, 9626-6.32

State allocation of Federal educational funds, by program, recipient type, and State, 1987/88, annual rpt, 4804-8

Teachers bachelor degrees, by field and other characteristics, 1985-86, 4838-39

Wages of scientists and engineers in R&D, by field and educational, employment, and other characteristics, 1989, annual rpt, 3004-1

see also Computer sciences

see also Mathematic models and modeling

see also Statisticians

Mathios, Alan D.
"Health Claims in Advertising and Labeling", 9406-1.60
"Impact of State Price and Entry Regulation on Intrastate Long Distance Telephone Rates", 9406-1.55

Mathiowetz, Nancy A.
"Prescribed Medicines: A Summary of Use and Expenditures by Medicare Beneficiaries. National Medical Expenditure Survey", 4186-8.3

Mattresses
see Furniture and furnishings

Mauldin, Patrick D.
"Critical Comparison of Alternative Thrift Management Strategies", 9302-2.901
"Use of Mortgage Derivative Products by Southeast Thrifts", 9302-2.904

Maurer, Kurt
"Blood Pressure of Persons 6-74 Years of Age in the U.S.", 4147-16.1

Mauritania
Agricultural and food production and indexes, total and for selected commodities, by country, 1970s-88, annual rpt, 1524-12

Agricultural trade of US, by detailed commodity and country, 1988, semiannual rpt, 1522-4

AID activities and funding by project and function, FY90, and developing countries summary socioeconomic data from 1960s, annual rpt, 9904-4.5

AID economic aid to developing countries, obligations and disbursements by country, quarterly rpt, 9912-4

Economic and military aid and loans from US and intl agencies, by program and country, FY46-87, annual rpt, 9914-5

Economic conditions, income, production, prices, employment, and trade, 1989 periodic country rpt, 2046-4.69

Economic, social, political, and geographic summary data, by country, 1989, annual factbook, 9114-2

Food supply indicators for Sahel, by country, 1960s-2000, 1528-290

Human rights conditions in 170 countries, 1988, annual rpt, 21384-3

Military aid of US, arms sales, and training programs costs and budget requests, by program, world region, and country, FY88-90, annual rpt, 7144-13

Military spending, arms trade, and force strengths, with govt spending and population, by country, 1977-87, annual rpt, 9824-1

Minerals Yearbook, 1987, Vol 3: foreign country reviews of production, trade, and policy, by commodity, annual rpt, 5604-35

Minerals Yearbook, 1987, Vol 3 preprints: foreign country review of production, trade, and policy, by commodity, annual rpt, 5604-23.48

Population size, growth rates, and components of change, by country, projected 1989-2020 and trends from 1950, biennial rpt, 2324-9

UN voting record and share of votes in agreement with US, by issue, country, and world area, 1988, annual rpt, 7004-18

see also under By Foreign Country in the "Index by Categories"

Mauritius
Agricultural and food production and indexes, total and for selected commodities, by country, 1970s-88, annual rpt, 1524-12

Agricultural trade of US, by detailed commodity and country, 1988, semiannual rpt, 1522-4

AID activities and funding by project and function, FY90, and developing countries summary socioeconomic data from 1960s, annual rpt, 9904-4.5

AID economic aid to developing countries, obligations and disbursements by country, quarterly rpt, 9912-4

Economic and military aid and loans from US and intl agencies, by program and country, FY46-87, annual rpt, 9914-5

Economic conditions, income, production, prices, employment, and trade, 1989 periodic country rpt, 2046-4.53

Economic, social, political, and geographic summary data, by country, 1989, annual factbook, 9114-2

Human rights conditions in 170 countries, 1988, annual rpt, 21384-3

Military aid of US, arms sales, and training programs costs and budget requests, by program, world region, and country, FY88-90, annual rpt, 7144-13

Military spending, arms trade, and force strengths, with govt spending and population, by country, 1977-87, annual rpt, 9824-1

Minerals Yearbook, 1987, Vol 3: foreign country reviews of production, trade, and policy, by commodity, annual rpt, 5604-35

Minerals Yearbook, 1987, Vol 3 preprints: foreign country review of production, trade, and policy, by commodity, annual rpt, 5604-23.81

Population size, growth rates, and components of change, by country, projected 1989-2020 and trends from 1950, biennial rpt, 2324-9

UN voting record and share of votes in agreement with US, by issue, country, and world area, 1988, annual rpt, 7004-18

see also under By Foreign Country in the "Index by Categories"

May, Dennis M.
"Forest Statistics for East Tennessee Counties", 1206-27.6

Mayaguez, P.R.
see also under By SMSA or MSA in the "Index by Categories"

Mayes, Fred, Jr.
"Annual Prospects for World Coal Trade, 1989", 3164-77

Mayfield, Max
"Eastern North Pacific Hurricanes—1988", 2152-8.903

McAfee, Carol L.
"Forest Statistics for Massachusetts, 1972 and 1985", 1206-12.12

McAllen, Tex.
see also under By SMSA or MSA in the "Index by Categories"

McAndrews, James J.
"Entry-Deterring Debt", 9387-8.194
"Strategic Role Complementarity", 9387-8.182

McAniff, John J.
"U.S. Underwater Diving Fatality Statistics, 1986-87, With a Preliminary Assessment of 1988 Fatalities", 2144-5

McArthur, Timmie
"Trends in the Refund Offset Program", 8304-8.1

McCall, Nelda
"Access and Satisfaction in the Arizona Health Care Cost Containment System", 4652-1.951

McCarthy, Mary A.
"Federal Civilian Leave Usage in the Executive Branch for Leave Year 1988", 9842-1.906
"Federal Civilian Work Years and Personnel Costs in the Executive Branch for FY88", 9842-1.905
"Salary and Wage Statistics, Full-Time Employment in Non-Postal Agencies, Mar. 31, 1989", 9842-1.907

McCauley, Robert N.
"Explaining International Differences in the Cost of Capital", 9385-1.910

McClelland, John
"Issues Raised by New Agricultural Technologies: Livestock Growth Hormones", 1548-346

McClure, Charles R.
"Users of Academic and Public GPO Depository Libraries", 26208-1

McCoy, John L.
"Disabled-Worker Beneficiaries and Disabled SSI Recipients: A Profile of Demographic and Program Characteristics", 4742-1.916

McCracken, Roger
"Analysis of Acid Precipitation Samples Collected by State Agencies: January-December 1987", 9194-20

McCracken, Vicki A.
"U.S. Demand for Vegetables", 1561-11.903

McCray, Jacquelyn W.
"Housing Affordability: Concept and Reality", 1004-16.1; 1702-1.903

McCubbin, Janet
"Individual Income Tax Shares and Average Tax Rates, Tax Years 1916-50", 8302-2.913
"Individual Income Tax Shares and Average Tax Rates, Tax Years 1951-86", 8302-2.919

McDermott, Suzanne
"Family Caregiver Costs of Chronically Ill and Handicapped Children: Method and Literature Review", 4042-3.912

McDevitt, Roland D.
"Assessing the Adequacy of the Medicare Cost Report Data", 17206-2.4

McDonald, Richard J.
"Analysis of Substitution Bias in Measuring Inflation, 1959-82", 6886-6.11

McDowell, John M.
"Impact of Technology Adoption on Market Structure", 9366-6.187

McElroy, Robert G.
"Costs of Production for Major U.S. Crops, 1975-87", 1548-345
"Developing and Using Cost-of-Production Data", 1541-1.901
"State-Level Costs of Production, 1987", 1544-24

McGovern, R. Gordon
"Commodity Marketing Opportunities and Challenges", 1004-16.1

McGuire, Thomas G.
"Financing and Reimbursement for Mental Health Services", 4508-9

McGurk, Michael D.
"Early Life History of Pacific Herring in Auke Bay, Alaska: Relationships of Growth and Survival to Environmental Conditions", 2176-1.29

McHenry, Rose Ann
"Changes in the Availability of Economic Data Under Gorbachev", 9118-4

McIntire, Robert J.
"New Seasonal Adjustment Factors for Household Data Series", 6742-2.904
"Revision of Seasonally Adjusted Labor Force Series", 6742-2.901

McKay, Steven F.
"Short-Range Actuarial Projections of the Old-Age, Survivors, and Disability Insurance Program, 1988", 4706-1.103

McKinney Homeless Assistance Act
Assistance of Fed Govt to homeless by program and Federal agency, and indicators of need, 1988, annual rpt, 14364-1
Homeless persons housing and food aid under HUD and Fed Emergency Mgmt Agency programs, funding and operations, FY87-88, GAO rpt, 26113-411
Homeless population characteristics by city, and Federal funding by program, 1980s-89, hearings, 21248-123

McLain, William H.
"Arizona's 1984 Fuelwood Harvest", 1208-293
"Logging Utilization: Arizona, 1985", 1208-294
"Logging Utilization: New Mexico, 1987", 1208-310

"New Mexico's Timber Production and Mill Residue, 1986", 1206-17.11
"New Mexico's 1986 Fuelwood Harvest", 1208-303

McLaughlin, Mary M.
"Recent Developments in the Profitability and Lending Practices of Commercial Banks", 9362-1.907

McMahon, Peter B.
"Water Movement in the Unsaturated Zone at a Low-Level Radioactive-Waste Burial Site Near Barnwell, S.C.", 5668-98

McNees, Stephen K.
"How Well Do Financial Markets Predict the Inflation Rate?", 9373-1.916
"Why Do Forecasts Differ?", 9373-1.904

McNeil, John M.
"Characteristics of Persons Receiving Benefits from Major Assistance Programs", 2546-20.8
"Labor Force Status and Other Characteristics of Persons with a Work Disability: 1981-88", 2546-2.147
"Measuring the Effect of Benefits and Taxes on Income and Poverty: 1986", 2546-6.58

Meade, Ellen E.
"U.S. International Transactions in 1988", 9362-1.904

Means, Barbara
"Autobiographical Memory for Health-Related Events. Vital and Health Statistics Series 6", 4147-6.2

Mearns, Alan J.
"PCB and Chlorinated Pesticide Contamination in U.S. Fish and Shellfish: A Historical Assessment Report", 2178-21

Measles
see Infective and parasitic diseases

Measures
see Industrial standards
see Instruments and measuring devices
see Weights and measures

Meat and meat products
Agricultural Statistics, 1988, annual rpt, 1004-1

Agriculture census, 1987: farms, farmland, production, finances, and operator characteristics, by county, final State rpt series, 2331-1

Business statistics, detailed data for major industries and economic indicators, *Survey of Current Business*, monthly rpt, 2702-1.11

China trade by SITC 1- to 5-digit commodity, 1970s-87, annual rpt, 9114-3

Cold storage food stocks by commodity and census div, and warehouse space use, by State, monthly rpt, 1631-5

Cold storage food stocks, by commodity and census div, 1988, annual rpt, 1631-11

Communist countries agricultural, mineral, and consumer and producer goods production, by commodity, 1960s-88, annual rpt, 9114-4.4

Consumer Expenditure Survey, household income by source, and itemized spending, by selected characteristics and location, 1984-86, annual rpt, 6764-5.2

Consumption of food and nutrient intake by individuals, by food group, selected characteristics, and region, supplementary survey series, 1356-5

Consumption, supply, trade, prices, spending, and indexes, by food commodity, 1987, annual rpt, 1544-4

County Business Patterns, 1987: employment, establishments, and payroll, by SIC 2- to 4-digit industry and county, annual State rpt series, 2326-8

CPI by component for US city average, and by region, population size, and for 27 metro areas, monthly rpt, 6762-2

Cuba economic conditions, agricultural and industrial production and distribution, trade, and intl economic relations, 1980-87 with trends from 1961, 9118-8

Eastern Europe agricultural production, consumption, and trade, by country, 1970s-88, annual rpt, 1524-11

Eastern Europe and USSR agricultural production, acreage, and consumption, by commodity and country, 1965-85, 1528-284

EC and US meat trade, FY84-88, article, 1502-4.902

EC food supply and demand, market and support prices, and other economic indicators, by country and commodity, 1960-85, 1528-276

Electric power use and prices, shipments, and trade, for 25 SIC 4-digit manufacturing industries, 1972-86, 2048-137

Employment, earnings, and hours, by selected SIC 1- to 4-digit industry, State, and for 262 MSAs, 1972-87, 6748-81

Employment, earnings, and hours, by SIC 1- to 4-digit industry, monthly 1983-Feb 1989, annual rpt, 6744-4

Employment of minorities and women, by occupation, SIC 1- to 3- digit industry, State, and MSA, 1986, annual rpt, 9244-1

Exports and imports (agricultural) commodity and country, prices, and world market devs, monthly rpt, 1922-12

Exports and imports (agricultural) of US, by commodity and country, bimonthly rpt with articles, 1522-1

Exports and imports (agricultural) of US, by commodity, monthly rpt, 1922-8

Exports and imports (agricultural) of US, by detailed commodity and country, 1988, semiannual rpt, 1522-4

Exports and imports of dairy, livestock, and poultry products, by commodity and country, FAS monthly circular, 1925-32

Exports of US, detailed commodities by country, monthly rpt, 2422-3

Farm sector finances, income sources, expenses by type, assets, debts, and ratios, 1987, annual rpt, 1544-19

Foreign and US agricultural production, prices, trade, and use, periodic rpt with articles, 1522-3

Foreign and US agricultural production, trade, and weather devs, weekly press release, 1922-4

Foreign and US agricultural trade and market impacts of eliminating protectionist policies, model description and results, 1986, 1528-282

Foreign and US production, trade, and use, by selected country, forecast 1990, FAS annual circular, 1925-33

Foreign countries agricultural production, prices, and trade, by country, 1970s-89 and forecast 1990, annual world region rpt series, 1524-4

Freight (waterborne domestic and foreign) by commodity, traffic, and passengers, by port and waterway, 1987, annual rpt, 3754-3

Futures and options trading volume, by commodity and exchange, FY88, annual rpt, 11924-2

Futures contracts on commodities, financial instruments, and indexes, options trading in NYC, Chicago, and other markets, monthly rpt, 11922-6

Futures trading in selected commodities and financial instruments and indexes, NYC, Chicago, and other markets activity, monthly rpt, 11922-5

Hormones (growth) use impacts on livestock productivity, farm income, land use, and consumer prices, alternative estimates, 1985, 1548-346

Imports of meat under Meat Import Act, by country of origin, FAS monthly rpt, 1925-31

Imports of US, detailed Schedule A commodities by country, monthly rpt, 2422-2

Inspection and certification of meat plants for export to US, by country, 1988, annual listing, 1374-2

Inspection of meat and poultry, Federal, State, and foreign govts activities and staff, FY88, annual rpt, 1374-1

Inspection of meat and poultry for domestic use and export, and rejections by cause, by type of animal and product, FY88, annual rpt, 1374-3

Labor productivity, indexes of output, hours, and employment by SIC 2- to 4-digit industry, 1963-87, annual rpt, 6824-1.3

Manufacturers finances and operations, by SIC 2- to 4-digit industry, forecast 1989 and trends from 1950s, annual rpt, 2044-28

Manufacturing annual survey, 1986: financial and operating data, by SIC 2- to 4-digit industry, series, 2506-15

Manufacturing census, 1987: financial and operating data, for SIC 4-digit industries by product, preliminary rpt, 2491-1.1; 2491-1.7

Marketing data for livestock, meat, and wool, by species and market, weekly rpt, 1315-1

Military commissaries in Europe, test sales of US beef and pork, and patron survey results, 1986, hearing, 21208-28

Nutrient and caloric composition of food, for raw, processed, and prepared food, 1988 rpt, 1358-3

Nutrient, caloric, and waste composition, detailed data for raw, processed, and prepared lamb, veal, and game meats, 1989 rpt, 1356-3.11

Occupational injury and illness rates and workdays lost in meatpacking, 1977-86, article, 6722-1.901

Occupational injury and illness rates, by SIC 2- to 4-digit industry, 1987, annual rpt, 6844-1

OECD trade, total and for 4 major countries, and US trade by country, by commodity, 1970-87, world area rpt series, 9116-1

Pork from Canada, injury to US industry from foreign subsidized imports, investigation with background financial and operating data, 1989 rpt, 9886-15.72; 9886-15.74

Pork production and trade, 1975-88 and forecast 1989, article, 1561-7.904

Price indexes (producer), by stage of processing and detailed commodity, monthly rpt, 6762-6

Price indexes (producer), by stage of processing and detailed commodity, monthly 1988, annual rpt, 6764-2

Prices (farm-retail) for food, marketing cost components, and industry finances and productivity, 1950s-88, annual rpt, 1544-9

Prices (producer and retail) of meat and fish, 1980-89, semiannual situation rpt, 1561-15.3

Prices for meat, quarterly forecasts by product, alternative model results, 1989 rpt, 1548-350

Production, consumption, and industry finances and operations, for livestock, meat, and poultry, 1950s-86, 1568-280

Production of meat and livestock slaughter, by livestock type and State, monthly rpt, 1623-9

Production of meat, by species and State, 1988, annual rpt, 1623-10

Production, prices, and trade of livestock and meat, annual rpt, discontinued, 1564-6

Production, prices, and trade of livestock and meat, 1970-88, 1568-285

Production, prices, receipts, and disposition for meat animals, by species and State, 1987-88, annual rpt, 1623-8

Production, prices, trade, and marketing, by commodity, current situation and forecast, monthly rpt with articles, 1502-4

Production, prices, trade, and stocks, monthly rpt, 1561-17

Production, prices, trade, stocks, and use, periodic situation rpt with articles, 1561-7

Production, receipts, and demand ratios, by commodity group and region, 1949-83, 1548-348

Puerto Rico meat production, prices, consumption, imports, and impact of import restrictions, 1950s-85, 1568-282

Retail trade census, 1987: employment, establishments, sales, and payroll, by SIC 2- to 4-digit kind of business, MSA, county, and city, State rpt series, 2397-1

Retail trade sales and inventories, by kind of business, region, and selected State, MSA, and city, monthly rpt, 2413-3

Retail trade sales, inventories, purchases, gross margin, and accounts receivable, by SIC 2- to 4-digit kind of business and form of ownership, 1987, annual rpt, 2413-5

Science, engineering, and technical employment in manufacturing, by field, occupation, and industry, 1986, triennial rpt, 9627-23

Statistical Abstract of US, social, political, and economic data, 1790-2025, comprehensive annual compilation, 2324-1.3

Supply and demand indicators for livestock and dairy products, and for selected foreign and US crops, monthly rpt, 1522-5

Tax (income) returns of corporations, income and tax items by asset size and detailed industry, 1986, annual rpt, 8304-4; 8304-21

Hearing aid performance test results, by make and model, 1989 annual rpt, 8704-3

Import restraint elimination, impact on domestic industry production and employment, by selected commodity, 1986-88, 9886-4.144

Imports detained by FDA, by reason, product, shipper, brand, and country, monthly listing, 4062-2

Imports of US, detailed Schedule A commodities by country, monthly rpt, 2422-2

Imports of US given duty-free treatment for value of US material sent abroad, and impacts on US industry and employment, by commodity and country, 1987, annual rpt, 9884-14

Injuries from use of consumer products, by severity, victim age, and detailed product, 1988, annual rpt, 9164-6

Manufacturers finances and operations, by SIC 2- to 4-digit industry, forecast 1989 and trends from 1950s, annual rpt, 2044-28

Manufacturing annual survey, 1986: financial and operating data, by SIC 2- to 4-digit industry, series, 2506-15

Manufacturing census, 1987: financial and operating data, for SIC 4-digit industries by product, preliminary rpt, 2491-1.26; 2491-1.79

Medicare discharges, charges, and length of stay, by State and diagnosis, 1983 and 1985, article, 4652-1.925

Nicaragua Contra forces humanitarian aid of AID, by type, 1988, GAO rpt, 26123-237

Nursing home compliance with Medicare and Medicaid regulations, and patient characteristics, by facility, 1987/88, annual State rpt series, 4654-15

Nursing home facility, staff, and resident detailed characteristics, 1985, 4147-13.97

Occupational injury and illness rates, by SIC 2- to 4-digit industry, 1987, annual rpt, 6844-1

OECD trade, total and for 4 major countries, and US trade by country, by commodity, 1970-87, world area rpt series, 9116-1

Optical goods employment, establishments, sales, and payroll, by MSA, county, and city, 1987 Census of Retail Trade, State rpt series, 2397-1

Physicians ownership of labs and medical equipment services, referrals to own businesses, and excess Medicare costs from referrals, 1987, 4008-90

Price indexes (producer), by stage of processing and detailed commodity, monthly rpt, 6762-6

Price indexes (producer), by stage of processing and detailed commodity, monthly 1988, annual rpt, 6764-2

Radiation from electronic devices, incidents by type of device, and FDA control activities, 1988, annual rpt, 4064-13

Science, engineering, and technical employment in manufacturing, by field, occupation, and industry, 1986, triennial rpt, 9627-23

Service industries census, 1987: establishments, receipts, employment, and

payroll, by SIC 2- to 4-digit kind of business, MSA, county, and city, State rpt series, 2391-1

Shipments, trade, use, and firms, for electronic medical equipment, by product, 1988, annual Current Industrial Rpt, 2506-12.34

Statistical Abstract of US, social, political, and economic data, 1790-2025, comprehensive annual compilation, 2324-1.1

Tax (income) returns of corporations, income and tax items by asset size and detailed industry, 1986, annual rpt, 8304-4; 8304-21

Wholesale trade census, 1987: employment, establishments, finances, and operations, by SIC 2- to 4-digit kind of business, MSA, county, and city, State rpt series, 2405-1

see also Biologic drug products
see also Drugs
see also Prosthetics and orthotics
see also Vaccination and vaccines
see also X-rays

Medical technicians
see Allied health personnel
see Clinical laboratory technicians
see Health occupations

Medical transplants
Heart transplants performed by hospital, charges, payment sources, nonpaying patients, and waiting periods, 1986-88, GAO rpt, 26121-281

Kidney end-stage disease treatment facilities approved by Medicare, dialysis and transplant services and ownership, 1989 annual listing, 4654-17

Kidney end-stage disease treatment facilities, Medicare enrollment and reimbursement, survival, and patient characteristics, 1980-86, annual rpt, 4654-16

Medicaid coverage, participation, payments, admin, and legislative history, with data by State, 1980s-88, 21368-105

Statistical Abstract of US, social, political, and economic data, 1790-2025, comprehensive annual compilation, 2324-1.1

VA health care facilities surgery-related deaths and complications, by procedure and instn, and compared to to non-VA instns, 1981-88, biennial rpt, 8704-1

Medicare
Actuarial studies, Medicare and OASDI future cost estimates and past experience analyses, series, 4706-1

Admin of Medicare, finances, and activities of end-stage renal disease and accreditation programs, annual rpt, discontinued, 4654-5

AIDS deaths, by health and other characteristics, 1986, 4146-8.178

AIDS health care services research status, needs, methods, and impacts on public health policy and funding, with data for selected cities, 1989 conf papers, 4188-59

Alcohol-related illness hospital discharges for disabled Medicare beneficiaries, by diagnosis, 1985, article, 4482-1.905

Assistance (financial and nonfinancial) of Fed Govt, 1989 base edition with supplements, annual listing, 104-5

Assistance of Fed Govt, by type, program, agency, and State, FY88, annual rpt, 2464-2

Beneficiaries and program operations, for Medicare and Medicaid, 1989, annual fact book, 4654-18

Beneficiaries, eligibility, coverage, and program finances, for Medicare and Medicaid, various periods 1966-89, biennial rpt, 4654-1

Benefits, beneficiaries, and summary program data for selected public welfare programs, selected years 1937-89, chartbook, 4748-42

Benefits by county, FY88, annual regional listings, 4004-3

Benefits overpayment recovery and judgment enforcement cases filed in Federal district courts, June 1988, annual rpt, 18204-8.11

Budget deficit reduction under Gramm-Rudman Act, cancellation of budget authority by program, FY90, annual rpt, 104-27; 26304-6

Budget of US Appendix, obligations, appropriations, and personnel, by program and agency, FY90, annual rpt, 104-3

Budget of US, CBO analysis of revenue and spending alternatives and projections of economic indicators, FY90-94, annual rpt, 26304-3

Budget of US, compact budgets by activity, function, and agency, FY90 and projected to FY94, annual rpt, 104-2

Budget of US, historical data, selected years FY34-88 and projected to FY94, annual rpt, 104-22

Budget of US, House concurrent resolution, with spending and revenue targets, FY90, annual rpt, 21264-2

Budget of US, midsession review of FY90 budget, by function and agency, annual rpt, 104-7

Budget of US, Reagan Admin policy changes by program, FY90, annual rpt, 104-21

Budget of US, receipts by source, outlays by agency and program, and balances, monthly rpt, 8102-3

Budget of US, Senate concurrent resolution, with spending and revenue targets, FY90, annual rpt, 25254-1

Burn injury units of hospitals, case costs, Medicare reimbursement under prospective system, and instn losses under alternative payment plans, 1988 rpt, 17206-1.2

Cardiovascular diseases cases, health care services use and costs, and productivity losses, by selected characteristics, 1980, 4146-12.26

Catastrophic illness coverage under Medicare and other insurance programs, benefits, premiums, costs, and program finances, projected 1988-93, 26306-3.105

Catastrophic illness coverage under Medicare, and premium collection, effects of revisions on Federal budget and enrollees, projected 1989-93, 25368-161

Claims approved, charges, and reimbursements by type of service, from 1974, monthly rpt, quarterly data, 4742-1.11

Claims processing under contract for Medicare hospital payments, HCFA controls adequacy and errors, 1985-88, GAO rpt, 26121-260

Older persons care by family members, caregivers stress and respite services, for King County, Wash, 1983-87, article, 4652-1.916

Older persons health care (long-term) funding by Fed Govt, public views, 1987 survey, hearings, 21368-106

Older persons health care services use related to marital status, living arrangements, and other characteristics, 1977, 4188-54

Older persons preventive health care services, effectiveness and costs of proposed Medicare coverage, series, 26356-7

Older persons with functional limitations, long-term health care needs, and costs by payment source, 1982-85, GAO rpt, 26121-266

Ophthalmologist office visits, by characteristics of physician, practice, patient, and visit, with drug mentions by type and brand, 1985, 4146-8.166

Peer review organizations review of Medicare hospital claims, activities, and membership, 1984-88, GAO rpt, 26131-51

Physicians and other services use under Medicare, benefits, charges, and coinsurance and deductible obligations, 1982-86, article, 4652-1.901

Physicians and other supplementary providers under Medicare, program payments, copayment obligations, and balances billed, 1975-87, article, 4652-1.955

Physicians Medicare assigned-fee laws of 4 States, impacts on care cost and availability, 1985-89, GAO rpt, 26121-312

Physicians Medicare assigned-fee participation related to selected physician, practice, and community characteristics, 1984, article, 4652-1.902

Physicians Medicare assigned-fee use, attitudes, and project to encourage patient use of assignment physician, 1988 rpt, 4658-30

Physicians Medicare services use, charges, and reimbursement, by service type, setting, and specialty, 1986, article, 4652-1.936

Physicians ownership of labs and medical equipment services, referrals to own businesses, and excess Medicare costs from referrals, 1987, 4008-90

Prospective payment system research activities and funding of PHS, by project and subagency, FY88, annual rpt, 4184-3

Research activities and grants of HCFA, by program, as of Mar 1989, annual listing, 4654-10

Retirees health insurance coverage, by source, and former industry and occupation, 1987, 4186-8.2

Rural areas health care facilities, staffing, services accessibility, and indicators of need, 1960s-88, 25148-41

Rural areas hospitals, use, staff, and funding sources, by instn characteristics, 1980s-86, hearing, 25148-42

Statistical Abstract of US, social, political, and economic data, 1790-2025, comprehensive annual compilation, 2324-1.1; 2324-1.2

Supplemental Security Income beneficiaries Medicaid services use and costs, by diagnosis and whether covered by Medicare, 1984, article, 4652-1.947

Surgeries performed in rural hospitals by itinerant surgeons, quality of care issues and Medicare overpayments, 1985-86, 4008-93

Tax expenditures, Federal revenues forgone through income tax deductions and exclusions by type, FY90-94, annual rpt, 21784-10

Teaching hospitals Medicare payments, and cost factors, compared to non-teaching instns, FY80-85 and projected to FY96, GAO rpt, 26121-265

Trust funds finances of Medicare, receipts, outlays, and assets since 1966, monthly rpt, 4742-1.2

Trust funds finances of Medicare, various periods 1966-88 and projected to 1992, annual rpt, 4654-12

Trust funds finances of Medicare, 1966-88 and alternative projections to 1991, annual rpt, 4654-11

Trust funds finances of Medicare, 1987 and projected to 2062, annual rpt, 4654-8

Trust funds financial condition, for Hospital Insurance, monthly rpt, 8102-9.15

Trust funds financial condition, for Medicare, monthly rpt, 8102-9.3

see also Old-Age, Survivors, Disability, and Health Insurance

Medicine

Statistical Abstract of US, social, political, and economic data, 1790-2025, comprehensive annual compilation, 2324-1.1

see also Anesthesiology

see also Aviation medicine

see also Biologic drug products

see also Chemotherapy

see also Chiropractic and naturopathy

see also Dentists and dentistry

see also Diseases and disorders

see also Drugs

see also Epidemiology and epidemiologists

see also Federal aid to medical education

see also Federal aid to medicine

see also Geriatrics

see also Health condition

see also Health education

see also Health facilities administration

see also Health facilities and services

see also Health insurance

see also Health maintenance organizations

see also Health occupations

see also Hospitals

see also Medicaid

see also Medical assistance

see also Medical costs

see also Medical education

see also Medical ethics

see also Medical examinations and tests

see also Medical libraries

see also Medical malpractice

see also Medical research

see also Medical supplies and equipment

see also Medical transplants

see also Medicare

see also Nurses and nursing

see also Nursing homes

see also Obstetrics and gynecology

see also Optometry

see also Orthopedics

see also Osteopathy

see also Pathology

see also Pediatrics

see also Pharmaceutical industry

see also Pharmacists and pharmacy

see also Physicians

see also Physiology

see also Podiatry

see also Prenatal care

see also Preventive medicine

see also Psychiatry

see also Public health

see also Regional medical programs

see also State funding for health and hospitals

see also Surgeons and surgery

see also Vaccination and vaccines

see also Veterinary medicine

Mediterranean Sea

Exports and imports (waterborne) of US, by type of service, commodity, country, route, and US port, 1986-87, annual rpt, 7704-2

Tide height and time daily at coastal points, forecast 1990, annual rpt, 2174-2.4

Weather (marine) forecast areas, and broadcast schedules and stations worldwide, as of Nov 1988, annual rpt, 2184-3

Mehra, Yash P.

"Cointegration and a Test of the Quantity Theory of Money", 9389-19.10

"Forecast Performance of Alternative Models of Inflation", 9389-1.901

"Some Further Results on the Source of Shift in M1 Demand in the 1980s", 9389-1.912

"Wage Growth and the Inflation Process: An Empirical Note", 9389-19.9

Meisenheimer, Joseph R., II

"Employer Provisions for Parental Leave", 6722-1.950

"Flexible Benefits Plans: Employees Who Have a Choice", 6722-1.959

Melancon, J. Michael

"Estimated Oil and Gas Reserves, Gulf of Mexico, Dec. 31, 1987", 5734-6

Melanoma

see Skin diseases

Melbourne, Fla.

Wages by occupation, for office and plant workers, 1989 survey, periodic MSA rpt, 6785-3.4

see also under By SMSA or MSA in the "Index by Categories"

Mellman and Lazarus

"Survey of Attitudes Toward Hunger and Homelessness in America, Jan. 8-19, 1988", 25248-107

Melnick, Glenn A.

"Prospective Payments to Hospitals: Should Emergency Admissions Have Higher Rates?", 4652-1.930

Melons

see Fruit and fruit products

Membership organizations

American Historical Assn financial statements, and membership by State, 1988, annual rpt, 29574-2

County Business Patterns, 1987: employment, establishments, and payroll, by SIC 2- to 4-digit industry and county, annual State rpt series, 2326-8

CPI by component for US city average, and by region, population size, and for 27 metro areas, monthly rpt, 6762–2

Earnings by major industry group, and personal income per capita and by source, by region and State, 1929-87, 2708–40

Employment, earnings, and hours, by SIC 1- to 4-digit industry, monthly 1983-Feb 1989, annual rpt, 6744–4

Employment in nonmanufacturing industries, by detailed occupation and SIC 2-digit industry, 1987, triennial rpt, 6748–60

Homeowners Residential Community Assns, services provided, and relations with local govts, 1988 conf, 10048–75

Service industries census, 1987: establishments, receipts, employment, and payroll, by SIC 2- to 4-digit kind of business, MSA, county, and city, State rpt series, 2391–1

Service industries receipts, by SIC 2- to 4-digit kind of business, 1988, annual rpt, 2413–8

Teachers assn membership, by instn level, 1955-87, article, 6722–1.931

Wildlife-related recreation, hunting, and fishing participation and spending, detailed data, 1985 survey, quinquennial State rpt series, 5506–6

see also Associations
see also Consumer cooperatives
see also Cooperatives
see also Credit unions
see also Labor unions
see also Rural cooperatives

Memorials
see Monuments and memorials

Memphis, Tenn.
Economic and banking conditions, for Fed Reserve 8th District, quarterly rpt with articles, 9391–16

Freight (waterborne domestic and foreign) by commodity, traffic, and passengers, by port and waterway, 1987, annual rpt, 3754–3.2

Hazardous substances industrial releases and reduction methods under EPA regulation, by chemical, source, industry, and location, 1987, annual rpt, 9234–6

Housing and households characteristics, 1984 survey, MSA fact sheet, 2485–11.1

Housing vacancy rates for single and multifamily units and mobile homes, by city and ZIP code, 1988, annual MSA rpt, 9304–19.1

see also under By City and By SMSA or MSA in the "Index by Categories"

Men
AIDS cases by risk group, race, sex, age, State, and MSA, and deaths, monthly rpt, 4202–9

AIDS risk knowledge and high-risk activities of homosexual men in cities with low and high AIDS rates, 1989 article, 4042–3.939

Arrest rates, by offense, sex, age, and race, 1987, annual rpt, 6224–7

Asian American earnings, and employment and other characteristics, by detailed origin and whether foreign-born, 1980, 11046–7.2

Cancer (bladder) risk for men in selected occupations, by employment characteristics, 1977-78, article, 4472–1.924; 4472–1.925

Crimes, arrests, and rates, by offense, offender characteristics, population size, and jurisdiction, 1988, annual rpt, 6224–2.1; 6224–2.2

Deaths and rates, by detailed cause and demographic characteristics, 1986 and trends from 1900, US Vital Statistics annual rpt, 4144–2

Deaths and rates, by detailed location, cause, and demographic characteristics, 1987, US Vital Statistics annual rpt, 4144–3

Divorces by age of spouses and duration of marriage, and children involved, by State, 1986 with trends from 1940, US Vital Statistics advance annual rpt, 4146–5.109

Drug, alcohol, and cigarette use, by substance, age, sex, race, and region, 1988 survey, biennial rpt, 4494–5

Health condition and health care resources, use, and spending, 1950s-87, annual data compilation, 4144–11

Homeless shelters services, operations, and client characteristics, 1988 survey, 5188–123

Homicide rates, and lifetime probability of victimization, by age, sex, and race, 1987, annual rpt, 6224–8

Household composition, income, benefits, and labor force status, Survey of Income and Program Participation methodology, working paper series, 2626–10

Marriages and rates, by age, race, education, previous marital status of spouses, and State, 1986, US Vital Statistics advance annual rpt, 4146–5.111; 4146–5.112

Marriages, by prior marital status, interval between marriages, other characteristics of spouses, type of ceremony, and State, with divorces, 1970s-83, 4147–21.45

Marriages, divorces, and rates, by characteristics of spouses, State, and county, 1984 and trends from 1920, US Vital Statistics annual rpt, 4144–4

Military draft registrants by State, 2nd half FY88, semiannual rpt, 9742–1

Nurses employed by VA, men licensed practical nurses and nursing assistants, by grade, quarterly rpt, 8602–6

Nutritional status and related health condition and practices, by selected characteristics, 1970s-87, 4048–33

OASDHI, Medicaid, SSI, and related programs benefits, beneficiary characteristics, and trust funds, selected years 1937-87, annual rpt, 4744–3

Population size, by age, sex, and race, and components of change, alternative projections 1988-2080, Current Population Rpt, 2546–3.158

Prisoners, movements, and characteristics, by State, 1986, annual rpt, 6064–26

Statistical Abstract of US, social, political, and economic data, with foreign comparisons, 1790-2025, comprehensive annual compilation, 2324–1

Voting and registration, by socioeconomic and demographic characteristics, 1988 presidential election, biennial Current Population Rpt, 2546–1.440

see also Families and households
see also Parents
see also under By Sex in the "Index by Categories"

Menefee, John A.
"Economic Data and the Analysis of Health-Related Issues of the Elderly", 4147–4.26

Mengle, David L.
"Banking Under Changing Rules: The Fifth District Since 1970", 9389–1.907; 9389–2

"Feasibility of Market Value Accounting for Commercial Banks", 9389–19.12

"SIC: Switzerland's New Electronic Interbank Payment System", 9389–1.903

Meningitis
see Infective and parasitic diseases

Mental health and illness
AIDS deaths, by health and other characteristics, 1986, 4146–8.178

Alcohol-related disorder hospital discharges, by sex, 1979-84, annual rpt, 4486–1.1

Alcohol use and abuse among minority groups, and related problems, by selected characteristics, 1985 conf papers, 4488–13

Assistance (financial and nonfinancial) of Fed Govt, 1989 base edition with supplements, annual listing, 104–5

Board and care homes conditions, State licensing and enforcement activity, and client characteristics, 1970s-88, 21148–55

Board and care homes licensing and inspection by States, and client characteristics, 1989 GAO rpt, 26121–275

Children (handicapped) enrollment by age, and special education programs staff, funding, and needs, by type of handicap and State, 1987/88, annual rpt, 4944–4

Court insanity caseloads for Federal district courts, June 1989, annual rpt, 18204–2.12; 18204–8.11; 18204–8.14

Deaths and rates, by detailed cause and demographic characteristics, 1986 and trends from 1900, US Vital Statistics annual rpt, 4144–2

Disability Insurance and SSI eligibility determinations for mental impairment, caseload and review activities by impairment type and State, 1984-86, hearing, 21788–176

Drug (antidepressant) prescriptions, by brand, 1987, annual rpt, 4064–12

Head Start handicapped enrollment, by handicap, State, and for Indian and migrant programs, 1985/86, annual rpt, 4604–1

Health condition and health care resources, use, and spending, 1950s-87, annual data compilation, 4144–11

Health condition improvement and disease prevention goals and recommended activities for 2000, with trends 1970s-80s, 4048–10

HHS financial aid, by program, recipient, State, and city, FY88, annual regional listings, 4004–3

Homeless persons in rural areas, health condition, services use, and other characteristics, local area studies, 1989 rpt, 4186–9.1

Homeless population characteristics by city, and Federal funding by program, 1980s-89, hearings, 21248–123

Homeless population characteristics, needs, and impacts of govt aid programs and housing costs, 1988 conf papers, 10048–73

Homeless shelters services, operations, and client characteristics, 1988 survey, 5188-123

Hospital discharges and length of stay, by diagnosis, patient age and sex, surgical procedure performed, and region, 1965-86, 4147-13.101

Hospital discharges and length of stay, by diagnosis, patient and instn characteristics, procedure performed, and payment source, 1987, annual rpt, 4147-13.99

Hospital discharges by detailed diagnostic and procedure category, primary diagnosis, and length of stay, by age, sex, and region, 1987, annual rpt, 4147-13.100

Indian Health Service and contract facilities hospitalization, by diagnosis, age, sex, and service area, FY87, annual rpt, 4104-16

Indian Health Service and contract facilities hospitalization, by diagnosis, age, sex, and service area, FY88, annual rpt, 4084-5

Indian youth suicide attempts, potential, and risk factors, longitudinal study, 1989 article, 4042-3.958

Nursing home compliance with Medicare and Medicaid regulations, and patient characteristics, by facility, 1987/88, annual State rpt series, 4654-15

Nursing home facility, staff, and resident detailed characteristics, 1985, 4147-13.97

Nursing home use rates, charges, and resident length of stay, care needs, and other characteristics, 1985, 4147-13.102

Older persons health care services use, persons with high and low levels of care by selected health and other characteristics, 1971 and 1980 studies, 4186-2.22

Palau mental illness diagnoses, by type, selected years 1980-87, annual rpt, 7004-6

Prison conditions, population, and problems, issues and bibl, 1989 compilation of papers, 25928-8

Research grants and awards of ADAMHA, by recipient, FY88, annual listing, 4044-13

Stress reduction, use of treatments and products not proven safe or effective, costs, and user characteristics, 1986 survey, 4008-86

Stress-related disorder prevention and research grants of NIMH, by subject, FY87, GAO rpt, 26121-302

Veterans (Vietnam) post-traumatic stress cases, claims, and VA disposition, 1985-88, hearing, 25768-46

see also Intelligence levels
see also Mental health facilities and services
see also Mental retardation
see also Neurological disorders
see also Psychiatry
see also Psychology
see also Suicide

Mental health facilities and services

AIDS deaths, by health and other characteristics, 1986, 4146-8.178

Alcohol, Drug Abuse and Mental Health Admin research grants and awards, by recipient, FY88, annual listing, 4044-13

Assistance (financial and nonfinancial) of Fed Govt, 1989 base edition with supplements, annual listing, 104-5

Child mental health treatment in short-stay hospitals, by age, race, and facility and physician characteristics, 1977, 4188-55

Community mental health care facilities needs assessment and program evaluation, methodology, use of census data, analysis, and sample data, series, 4506-8

Criminal mental health services use, availability, staff, and funding, by facility type, 1985, 4506-3.36

Criminal sentences for Federal offenses, guidelines by offense and circumstances, 1987 rpt, 17668-1

Cuba refugees entering US during 1980 boatlift, Federal funding for youth mental health services, and participation, 1981-88, GAO rpt, 26121-270

Data collection needs, implementation, uses, and costs, for mental health facilities, series, 4506-2

Employment, earnings, and hours, by SIC 1- to 4-digit industry, monthly 1983-Feb 1989, annual rpt, 6744-4

Facilities ownership, use, spending, and Medicaid reimbursement for mental health services, with data for 9 multifacility firms, 1987 conf papers, 4508-9

Facilities, patients, services, and staff characteristics, *Statistical Notes* series, 4506-3

France and US hospital and long-term care beds, by facility type and ownership, 1981, 4147-5.4

Health condition and health care resources, use, and spending, 1950s-87, annual data compilation, 4144-11

HHS financial aid, by program, recipient, State, and city, FY88, annual regional listings, 4004-3

Homeless persons in rural areas, health condition, services use, and other characteristics, local area studies, 1989 rpt, 4186-9.1

Homeless persons transitional housing, HUD grants by recipient, 1989, press release, 5006-3.66

Hospital mental health care units, length of stay related to patient, instn, and State Medicaid program characteristics, 1981, article, 4652-1.924

Insurance (health) coverage and provisions of employee benefit plans, by plan type and occupational group, 1988, annual rpt, 6784-19

Juvenile correctional and detention instns, inmates, and expenses, by instn and resident characteristics and State, 1975-85, biennial rpt, 6064-13

Medicaid beneficiaries and payments, by service type, FY72-87, annual rpt, 4744-3.6

Medicaid coverage, participation, payments, admin, and legislative history, with data by State, 1980s-88, 21368-105

Medicare and Medicaid beneficiaries and program operations, 1988, annual fact book, 4654-18

Medicare and Medicaid eligibility, participation, coverage, and program finances, various periods 1966-89, biennial rpt, 4654-1

Medicare discharges, charges, and length of stay, for facilities excluded from prospective payment system, FY84-88, article, 4652-1.935

Medicare reimbursement of hospitals under prospective payment system, and of physicians, effect on services, finances, and beneficiary payments, 1970s-88, annual rpt, 17204-2

Mentally retarded persons facilities, beds, and residents, by ownership, resident age and race, and State, 1986, 4147-14.34

Military health care benefits and costs under Civilian Health and Medical Program of Uniformed Services, FY83-FY89, 3508-31

NIH grants for R&D, training, construction, and medical libraries, by location and recipient, FY88, annual listings, 4434-7

Nursing home facility, staff, and resident detailed characteristics, 1985, 4147-13.97

Older persons health care services use, persons with high and low levels of care by selected health and other characteristics, 1971 and 1980 studies, 4186-2.22

Patients and admissions of State and county mental hospitals, by age, diagnosis, and State, FY87, annual rpt, 4504-2

Productivity of labor and capital, indicators for health facilities excluded from Medicare prospective payment system by instn type, 1976-86, 17206-2.1

Safety and effectiveness of health care, use of unproven treatments and products, costs, and user characteristics, 1986 survey, 4008-86

Service industries census, 1987: establishments, receipts, employment, and payroll, by SIC 2- to 4-digit kind of business, MSA, county, and city, State rpt series, 2391-1

State mental hospitals and costs per patient, by State, selected years 1969-87, 21148-55

Statistical Abstract of US, social, political, and economic data, 1790-2025, comprehensive annual compilation, 2324-1.1

VA health care facilities mental health services, staff, research, and training programs, 1989 biennial listing, 8704-2

VA hospitals admissions and discharges by diagnosis, facilities operating costs, and other VA activities, FY88, annual rpt, 8604-3.3

Veterans health care, patients, visits, costs, and operating beds, by VA and contract facility, and region, quarterly rpt, 8602-4

see also Psychiatry

Mental retardation

Board and care homes licensing and inspection by States, and client characteristics, 1989 GAO rpt, 26121-275

Children (handicapped) enrollment by age, and special education programs staff, funding, and needs, by type of handicap and State, 1987/88, annual rpt, 4944-4

Deaths and rates, by detailed cause and demographic characteristics, 1986 and trends from 1900, US Vital Statistics annual rpt, 4144-2

Disability Insurance and SSI eligibility determinations for mental impairment, caseload and review activities by impairment type and State, 1984-86, hearing, 21788-176

Facilities for mentally retarded, beds, and residents, by ownership, resident age and race, and State, 1986, 4147-14.34

Head Start handicapped enrollment, by handicap, State, and for Indian and migrant programs, 1985/86, annual rpt, 4604-1

Hospital mental health care units, length of stay related to patient, instn, and State Medicaid program characteristics, 1981, article, 4652-1.924

Hospitals for mental health care, beds and caseload by State, patient characteristics, finances, and staff, for profit and nonprofit private instns, 1986, 4506-3.37

Medicaid coverage, participation, payments, admin, and legislative history, with data by State, 1980s-88, 21368-105

Medicare and Medicaid eligibility, participation, coverage, and program finances, various periods 1966-89, biennial rpt, 4654-1

Nursing home use rates, charges, and resident length of stay, care needs, and other characteristics, 1985, 4147-13.102

Patients and admissions of State and county mental hospitals, by age, diagnosis, and State, FY87, annual rpt, 4504-2

Statistical Abstract of US, social, political, and economic data, 1790-2025, comprehensive annual compilation, 2324-1.1

Menzie, Keith

"History of Farm Income for U.S. Corn Producers", 1561-4.905

Merced, Calif.

see also under By SMSA or MSA in the "Index by Categories"

Mercer, Linda P.

"Black Sea Bass. Species Profiles: Life Histories and Environmental Requirements of Coastal Fishes and Invertebrates (South Atlantic)", 5506-8.107

"Weakfish. Species Profiles: Life Histories and Environmental Requirements of Coastal Fishes and Invertebrates (Mid-Atlantic)", 5506-8.116

Merchant marine

see Merchant seamen

see Ships and shipping

Merchant Marine Academy

see Service academies

Merchant seamen

Collective bargaining agreements expiring during year, and workers covered, by firm, union, industry group, and State, 1989, annual rpt, 6784-9

Competition in Exclusive Economic Zone between foreign and US flag ships, impacts of extending cabotage laws, with background data, 1970s-80s, 26358-206

Employment, by type and ownership of vessel and license status of sailor, monthly rpt, 7702-1

Employment shipboard, shipyard, and longshore, FY87-88, annual rpt, 7704-14.3

Fed Govt civilian employee work-years, pay rates, and benefits use and costs, by agency, FY87, annual rpt, 9844-31

Immigration to US, alien workers, visitors, deportations, and naturalizations, by country, FY88 and trends from 1820, annual rpt, 6264-2

Wartime capability of commercial ships, shipyards, and personnel, for merchant and reserve fleet, 1988-2000, 11208-1

Women's employment in merchant marine, Natl Marine Fisheries Service, and fishing, with rpts of sexual assault, 1980s-88, GAO rpt, 26113-397

Mercier, Stephanie

"Corn: Background for 1990 Farm Legislation", 1566-7.4

"Costs of Combining Dockage and Foreign Material in the Grading Standards for Wheat Exports", 1561-12.901

"History of Farm Income for U.S. Corn Producers", 1561-4.905

"Recent Issues in Grain Quality", 1561-4.904

Mercury

see Mercury pollution

see Metals and metal industries

Mercury pollution

California water quality, trace metal concentrations in San Joaquin river bed sediment, 1985, 5668-91

Coastal and estuarine pollutant concentrations in fish, shellfish, and environment, series, 2176-3

Coastal and estuarine pollutant discharges, by source, pollutant type, and location, series, 2176-4

Hudson-Raritan River basin pollutant levels and sources, model description and results, 1880s-1982, 2178-22

Lake Ontario eutrophication and pollutant levels, by contaminant type and site, 1967-85, 14648-22

Water supply and quality in streams and lakes, and groundwater levels in wells, by drainage basin, 1986, annual State rpt series, 5666-23

Water supply and quality in streams and lakes, and groundwater levels in wells, by drainage basin, 1987, annual State rpt series, 5666-10

Water supply and quality in streams and lakes, and groundwater levels in wells, by drainage basin, 1988, annual State rpt series, 5666-16

Mergers

see Business acquisitions and mergers

Meriden, Conn.

see also under By SMSA or MSA in the "Index by Categories"

Meridian, Miss.

Wages by occupation, and benefits for office and plant workers, 1989 survey, periodic MSA rpt, 6785-3.10

Merit Systems Protection Board

Appeals decisions on Fed Govt personnel actions, by agency and region, FY88, annual rpt, 9494-2

Budget of US Appendix, obligations, appropriations, and personnel, by program and agency, FY90, annual rpt, 104-3

Budget of US, authoritative financial statements with appropriations, outlays, and receipts, by category and agency, FY88, annual rpt, 8104-2.2

Labor unions recognized in Fed Govt, agreements and membership by agency and facility, as of Jan 1989, biennial listing, 9844-14

Personnel Mgmt Office merit system oversight and enforcement activities, series, 9496-2

Senior Executive Service former members reasons for leaving, and views on SES statutory compliance, 1988 survey, 9498-3

Senior Executive Service of Fed Govt former members reasons for leaving, and views on SES statutory compliance, periodicity change, 9494-4

Violations and prohibited political activity reported by Federal employees, cases by type, FY88, annual rpt, 9494-3

Merriam, Ida C.

"Commentary: Economic Status of the Aged", 4742-1.902

Merrifield, Susan G.

"Ladyfish and Tarpon. Species Profiles: Life Histories and Environmental Requirements of Coastal Fishes and Invertebrates (South Florida)", 5506-8.111

Mesa, Ariz.

Housing and households detailed characteristics, and unit and neighborhood quality, by location, 1985 survey, MSA rpt, 2485-6.14

see also under By City in the "Index by Categories"

Mester, Loretta J.

"Are Production Economies a Motive for Mutual to Stock Conversions in the Savings and Loan Industry?", 9387-8.172

"Credit Card Rate Stickiness in a Screening Model of Consumer Credit", 9387-8.178

"Testing Strategy for Expense Preference Behavior", 9387-8.171

"Viability in Multiproduct Industries", 9387-8.179

Metabolic and endocrine diseases

Cancer incidence, death, and survival rates, by sex, race, age, and body site, 1973-86, annual rpt, 4474-35

Deaths and rates, by detailed cause and demographic characteristics, 1986 and trends from 1900, US Vital Statistics annual rpt, 4144-2

Health condition and health care resources, use, and spending, 1950s-87, annual data compilation, 4144-11

HHS financial aid, by program, recipient, State, and city, FY88, annual regional listings, 4004-3

Hospital discharges and length of stay, by diagnosis, patient and instn characteristics, procedure performed, and payment source, 1987, annual rpt, 4147-13.99

Hospital discharges by detailed diagnostic and procedure category, primary diagnosis, and length of stay, by age, sex, and region, 1987, annual rpt, 4147-13.100

Indian (Seneca Tribe) deaths and years of potential life lost, by selected cause and sex, various periods 1955-84, article, 4042-3.925

Indian Health Service and contract facilities hospitalization, by diagnosis, age, sex, and service area, FY87, annual rpt, 4104-16

Indian Health Service and contract facilities hospitalization, by diagnosis, age, sex, and service area, FY88, annual rpt, 4084-5

Nursing home facility, staff, and resident detailed characteristics, 1985, 4147-13.97

Pollutants health effects, concentrations in food and environment, sources, human intake, and regulation, series, 9186-8

see also Allergies

see also Diabetes

see also Immunity disorders

see also Nutrition and malnutrition

see also under By Disease in the "Index by Categories"

Metals and metal industries

Alaska minerals resources, production, oil and gas leases, and exploratory wells, with maps and bibl, 1987, annual rpt, 5664-11

Building materials production and PPI, by type, bimonthly rpt, 2042-1.5; 2042-1.6

Business statistics, detailed data for major industries and economic indicators, *Survey of Current Business*, monthly rpt, 2702-1.14

China trade by SITC 1- to 5-digit commodity, 1970s-87, annual rpt, 9114-3

Coin production and monetary metals use and holdings of US Mint, by metal type, FY88, annual rpt, 8204-1

Collective bargaining agreements expiring during year, and workers covered, by firm, union, industry group, and State, 1989, annual rpt, 6784-9

Communist, OECD, and selected other countries minerals production, by commodity, 1960s-88, annual rpt, 9114-4.7

County Business Patterns, 1987: employment, establishments, and payroll, by SIC 2- to 4-digit industry and county, annual State rpt series, 2326-8

Cuba economic conditions, agricultural and industrial production and distribution, trade, and intl economic relations, 1980-87 with trends from 1961, 9118-8

Demand for primary metals, relation to consumption patterns and economic, trade, and technological factors, 1960s-82, 5608-159

DOD prime contract awards, by detailed procurement category, FY85-88, annual rpt, 3544-18

Earnings by major industry group, and personal income per capita and by source, by region and State, 1929-87, 2708-40

Electric power use and prices, shipments, and trade, for 25 SIC 4-digit manufacturing industries, 1972-86, 2048-137

Employment, earnings, and hours, by selected SIC 1- to 4-digit industry, State, and for 262 MSAs, 1972-87, 6748-81

Employment, earnings, and hours, by SIC 1- to 4-digit industry, monthly 1983-Feb 1989, annual rpt, 6744-4

Employment in nonmanufacturing industries, by detailed occupation and SIC 2-digit industry, 1987, triennial rpt, 6748-60

Employment of minorities and women, by occupation, SIC 1- to 3- digit industry, State, and MSA, 1986, annual rpt, 9244-1

Employment, unemployment, and labor force characteristics, by region and census div, 1988, annual rpt, 6744-7.1

Explosives and blasting agents use, by type, industry, and State, 1988, Mineral Industry Surveys, annual rpt, 5614-22

Exports and imports of US, by commodity group, world area, selected country, US coastal area and port, and mode of transport, monthly rpt, 2422-9

Exports and imports of US, by selected country, country group, and commodity group, 1988, annual rpt, 2044-37

Exports of US, detailed commodities by country, monthly rpt, 2422-3

Finances and operations, by SIC 2- to 4-digit industry, forecast 1989 with trends from 1950s, annual rpt, 2044-28

Financial statements for manufacturing, mining, and trade corporations, by selected SIC 2- to 3-digit industry, quarterly rpt, 2502-1

Foreign and US minerals industries operations, trends, and projections for selected countries, series, 5606-5

Foreign and US minerals supply under alternative market conditions, reserves, and background industry data, series, 5606-4

Foreign countries mineral production, reserves, and industry role in domestic economy and world supply, world area and country rpt series, 5606-1

Foreign direct investment in US, by industry group and world area, 1987-88, annual article, 2702-1.929

Foreign direct investment of US, by selected industry group and world area, 1986-88, annual article, 2702-1.930

Freight (waterborne domestic and foreign) by commodity, traffic, and passengers, by port and waterway, 1987, annual rpt, 3754-3

Futures and options trading volume, by commodity and exchange, FY88, annual rpt, 11924-2

Futures trading in selected commodities and financial instruments and indexes, NYC, Chicago, and other markets activity, monthly rpt, 11922-5

Hazardous substances industrial releases and reduction methods under EPA regulation, by chemical, source, industry, and location, 1987, annual rpt, 9234-6

Hudson-Raritan River basin pollutant levels and sources, model description and results, 1880s-1982, 2178-22

Idaho gold, silver, and other metals production, by location, late 1800s-1982, 5668-90

Imports, exports, and employment impacts, by SIC 2- to 4-digit industry and commodity, quarterly rpt, 2322-2

Imports of US, detailed Schedule A commodities by country, monthly rpt, 2422-2

Imports of US given duty-free treatment for value of US material sent abroad, and impacts on US industry and employment, by commodity and country, 1987, annual rpt, 9884-14

Input-output structure of US economy, detailed interindustry transactions for 84 industries, and components of final demand, 1983, annual article, 2702-1.909

Labor productivity, indexes of output, hours, and employment by SIC 2- to 4-digit industry, 1963-87, annual rpt, 6824-1.3

Machinery for metalworking, shipments, unfilled orders, trade, and use, quarterly Current Industrial Rpt, 2506-12.12

Manufacturing annual survey, 1986: financial and operating data, by SIC 2- to 4-digit industry, series, 2506-15

Manufacturing annual survey, 1986: production indexes and exports by SIC 2-digit industry and State, with comparisons to 1985, model results, series, 2506-16

Manufacturing census, 1987: financial and operating data, for SIC 4-digit industries by product, preliminary industry rpt series, 2491-1

Manufacturing industries production, shipments, inventories, orders, and pollution control costs, periodic Current Industrial Rpt series, 2506-3

Mine employment by selected occupational and other characteristics, injuries, and workdays lost, for mines, 1986, 5606-8.2; 5606-8.3

Mineral industries census, 1987: financial and operating data, preliminary industry rpt, 2511-1.3

Mineral Industry Surveys, commodity reviews of production, trade, stocks, and use, monthly rpt series, 5612-1

Mineral Industry Surveys, commodity reviews of production, trade, stocks, and use, quarterly rpt series, 5612-2

Mineral Industry Surveys, commodity reviews of production, trade, use, and industry operations, advance annual rpt series, 5614-5

Mineral Industry Surveys, State reviews of production, 1988, preliminary annual rpt, 5614-6

Minerals Yearbook, 1987, Vol 1: commodity reviews of production, use, trade, prices, and mining operations, annual rpt, 5604-33

Minerals Yearbook, 1987, Vol 1 preprints: commodity reviews of production, reserves, supply, use, and trade, annual rpt series, 5604-15

Minerals Yearbook, 1987, Vol 2 preprints: State reviews of production and sales by commodity, and business activity, annual rpt series, 5604-16

Minerals Yearbook, 1987, Vol 2: State reviews of production, sales, and firms, by commodity, and business activity, annual rpt, 5604-34

Minerals Yearbook, 1987, Vol 3: foreign country reviews of production, trade, and policy, by commodity, annual rpt, 5604-35

Minerals Yearbook, 1987, Vol 3 preprints: foreign country reviews of production, trade, and policy, by commodity, annual rpt series, 5604-23

Minerals Yearbook, 1988, Vol 1: commodity reviews of production, reserves, supply, use, and trade, annual rpt series, 5604-20

Minerals Yearbook, 1988, Vol 2 rpts: State reviews of production and sales by commodity, and business activity, annual rpt series, 5604-22

Multinatl firms US affiliates, finances, and operations, by industry, world area of parent firm, and State, 1987, annual rpt, 2704-4

Multinatl US firms and foreign affiliates finances and operations, by industry of parent firm and affiliate, world area, and country, preliminary 1987, annual rpt, 2704-5

Occupational injuries and incidence, employment, and hours in metal mines and related operations, 1987, annual rpt, 6664–3

Occupational injuries by circumstances, employment, and hours, for mining industries by type of operation and State, quarterly rpt, 6662–1

Occupational injury and illness rates, by SIC 2- to 4-digit industry, 1987, annual rpt, 6844–1

OECD trade, total and for 4 major countries, and US trade by country, by commodity, 1970-87, world area rpt series, 9116–1

Price indexes (producer), by stage of processing and detailed commodity, monthly rpt, 6762–6

Price indexes (producer), by stage of processing and detailed commodity, monthly 1988, annual rpt, 6764–2

Production, prices, trade, use, employment, tariffs, and stockpiles, by mineral, with foreign comparisons, 1984-88, annual rpt, 5604–18

Production, shipments, trade, stocks, and material used, for primary metals by product, periodic Current Industrial Rpt series, 2506–10

Public lands minerals resources and availability, State rpt series, 5606–7

Rail shipments of grain and other commodities by car type, 1986, and rail car fleet size, 1978-88, 1278–15

Science and engineering employment, by nonmanufacturing industry and field, 1987, triennial rpt, 9627–31

Science, engineering, and technical employment in manufacturing, by field, occupation, and industry, 1986, triennial rpt, 9627–23

Science, engineering, and technical employment in transportation, utilities, and retail and wholesale trade, by field, occupation, and industry, 1985, triennial rpt, 9627–32

Shipments, trade, and inventories of intermediate metal products, periodic Current Industrial Rpt series, 2506–11

Small business establishments, employment, and financial ratios, by SIC 1- to 2-digit industry and State, late 1960s-87, 9768–19

Soviet Union minerals production, trade, and use, by commodity, 1983-87, annual rpt, 5604–39

Statistical Abstract of US, social, political, and economic data, 1790-2025, comprehensive annual compilation, 2324–1.3

Stockpiling of strategic material, inventories and needs, by commodity, as of Sept 1988, annual rpt, 3544–37

Supply, imports, and use of strategic and technologically important minerals, with foreign comparisons, commodity rpt series, 5606–9

Tariff Schedule of US, classifications and rates of duty by detailed imported commodity, 1990 base edition and supplements, 9886–13

Tax (income) returns of corporations, income and tax items by asset size and detailed industry, 1986, annual rpt, 8304–4; 8304–21

Tax (income) returns of partnerships, income statement items by industry group, 1986, annual article, 8302–2.903

Tax (income) returns of sole proprietorships, income statement items, by industry group, 1987, annual article, 8302–2.904; 8302–2.921

Transportation census, 1987: trucks, by detailed characteristics, miles traveled, and type of product carried, State rpt series, 2573–1

Wholesale trade census, 1987: employment, establishments, finances, and operations, by SIC 2- to 4-digit kind of business, MSA, county, and city, State rpt series, 2405–1

see also Abrasive materials

see also Aluminum and aluminum industry

see also Copper and copper industry

see also Foundries

see also Gold

see also Hardware

see also Iron and steel industry

see also Lead and lead industry

see also Lead poisoning and pollution

see also Mercury pollution

see also Offshore mineral resources

see also Scrap metals

see also Silver

see also Stockpiling

see also Strategic materials

see also Tin and tin industry

see also Trace metals

see also Uranium

see also Zinc and zinc industry

see also By Industry in the "Index by Categories"

see also under By Commodity in the "Index by Categories"

Meteorological satellites

Fed Govt weather services activities and funding, by agency, planned FY89-90, annual rpt, 2144–2

Hurricanes and tropical storms in north Atlantic and Caribbean area, paths, surveillance, deaths, damage, and landfall probabilities by city, 1988, annual rpt, 2184–7

Hurricanes and tropical storms in northeastern Pacific Ocean, paths and surveillance, 1988, annual rpt, 2184–8

Hurricanes and tropical storms in Pacific and Indian Oceans, paths and surveillance, 1988, annual rpt, 3804–8

Launches and other activities of NASA and Soviet Union, with flight data, 1957-88, annual rpt, 9504–6.1

Meteorology

Agricultural research funding and staffing for USDA, State agencies, and other instns, by topic, FY88, annual rpt, 1744–2

Atlantic Oceanographic and Meteorological Lab research activities and bibl, FY88, annual rpt, 2144–19

Fed Govt weather services activities and funding, by agency, planned FY89-90, annual rpt, 2144–2

Great Lakes Environmental Research Lab activities, 1987 annual rpt, 2144–26

Oceanographic research and distribution activities of World Data Center A by country, and cruises by ship, 1987, annual rpt, 2144–15

Pacific Marine Environmental Lab research activities and bibl, FY88, annual rpt, 2144–21

Research activity of Fed Govt in atmospheric sciences, and funding by agency and program, FY84-87, biennial rpt, 434–1

Research on weather, monitoring, and impact assessment activities of Fed Govt, and funding by agency, FY87, annual rpt, 2144–17

Storms (severe) natl lab research activities and bibl, FY88, annual rpt, 2144–20

see also Meteorological satellites

see also Weather

Methadone treatment

see Drug abuse and treatment

Methane

see Gases

Methanol

see Alcohol fuels

Methodology

Agricultural Economics Research, quarterly journal, 1502–3

Agricultural research funding and staffing for USDA, State agencies, and other instns, by topic, FY88, annual rpt, 1744–2

AIDS cases forecasts, analysis of CDC and other methodology, 1989 GAO rpt, 26131–55

AIDS health care and epidemiological research, methodological issues, 1988 conf, 4188–61

Air traffic and other aviation activity forecasts of FAA, 1989 annual conf, 7504–28

Alaska OCS environmental conditions and oil dev impacts, compilation of papers, series, 2176–1

Astronomical tables, time conversion factors, and listing of observatories worldwide, 1990, annual rpt, 3804–7

Atlantic Ocean fish and shellfish distribution, bottom trawl survey evaluation with results by species and location, 1963-87, 2168–108

Aviation medicine research and test results, technical rpt series, 7506–10

Business cycle composite indexes of performance, BEA methodological revisions, 1989 article, 2702–1.906

Carbon dioxide in atmosphere, measurement, methodology, and research results, series, 3006–11

Coastal and estuarine environmental conditions, research results and methodology, series, 2176–7

CPI under alternative weighting systems, and experimental price indexes, 1967-85, article, 6722–1.935

CPI use in escalator clauses of collective bargaining agreements and other contracts, with conversion factors for index rebasing, 1989 guide, 6888–34

Economic data series revisions and methodological issues, 1989 article, 9371–1.906

Employee benefits value, alternative measurement methodologies, 1989 article, 6722–1.960

Employment, earnings, and hours benchmarks by SIC 2- to 4-digit industry, 1981-88, and revised seasonal adjustment factors by major industry group, 1989, semiannual article, 6742–2.903

Employment, earnings, and hours seasonal adjustment factors by major industry group, Oct 1989-Mar 1990, semiannual article, 6742-2.905

Energy conservation (housing) program of Bonneville Power Admin in Hood River, Oreg, cost effectiveness and participation, 1983-86, series, 3226-2

Energy use, costs, and conservation, and household and housing characteristics, survey rpt series, 3166-7

Farm financial condition, estimates under alternative measures of sales size, 1985, 1548-344

Farm labor wage surveys to set minimum wage for US and alien workers, evaluation with data by location, 1980s-87, GAO rpt, 26131-50

Farm operators and farming-dependent households, population by selected characteristics, under alternative definitions, 1987, 1598-252

Farm population under alternative definitions, by selected characteristics, 1983, 1598-249

Financial and economic analysis and forecasting methodology, technical paper series, 9366-6; 9377-9

Financial and economic analysis of banking and nonbanking sectors, working paper series, 9381-10

Foreign countries economic and social conditions, working paper series, 2326-18

GNP by component in 1982 and 1987 dollars, 1982-88, and methodological issues, article, 2702-1.913

Hazardous substances exposure factors, and methodological guidelines, 1989 rpt, 9188-109

Health care and condition research, survey design and research methods, 1989 conf proceedings, 4188-60

Health condition and quality of life measurement, rpts and other info sources, quarterly listing, 4122-1

High school dropout rates, and subsequent completion, by student and school characteristics, alternative estimates, 1988, annual rpt, 4834-23

Hospital reimbursement by Medicare under prospective payment system, impacts on costs, industry structure and operations, and quality of care, series, 17206-2

Inflation measured by CPI and Personal Consumption Expenditure Index, under alternative weighting systems, monthly rpt, quarterly article, 6762-2

Labor Intl Affairs Bur research contracts, FY83-89, annual listing, 6364-1

Libraries (public) services effectiveness, public opinion survey methodology and results, 1989 rpt, 4878-3

Manufacturing output regional measures of BEA, assessment of methods, 1989 working paper, 9375-13.11

Manufacturing value added, allocation to States and SMSAs, assessment of Census Bur methodology, 1989 article, 9375-1.906

Medicaid reimbursement of nursing homes, case mix classification methodology, for New York State, 1987, article, 4652-1.910

Medical R&D price index of NIH by component, and compared to other indexes, FY79-86, article, 4042-3.901

Medicare reimbursement of hospitals under prospective payment system, methodology, inputs, and data by diagnostic group, 1989 annual rpt, 17204-1

Mental health care facilities needs assessment and program evaluation for communities, methodology, use of census data, analysis, and sample data, series, 4506-8

Middle Atlantic States manufacturing output index, methodology, 1989 article, 9387-1.901

Natl income and product accounts estimates, methodology and bibls, technical rpt series, 2706-6

Natl income and product accounts revisions, methodology, and data sources, various periods 1986-89, annual article, 2702-1.923

Pollutants health effects, concentrations in food and environment, sources, and human intake methodology and data needs, series, 9186-9

Social security programs and related issues, technical paper series, 4746-26

Statistical Abstract of US, social, political, and economic data, with foreign comparisons, 1790-2025, comprehensive annual compilation, 2324-1

Tax (income) return processing, IRS workload forecasts, compliance, and enforcement, data compilation, 1989 annual rpt, 8304-8

Timber in Arizona, harvest, mill receipts, and residues, with methodology, 1984-85, 1208-294

Unemployment insurance programs of States and Fed Govt, benefits adequacy, and work disincentives, series, 6406-6

Uranium tailings at inactive mills, remedial action proposals, costs, site characteristics, and environmental, socioeconomic, and health impacts, series, 3356-4

Water chemistry, environmental impacts, analytic methods, and quality and mgmt issues, 1989 rpt, 5668-96

Water quality data collection activities and quality, for 2 States, 1984, 5668-94

Water quality data collection, aquifer hydrologic and chemical properties impacts on representative groundwater sampling, local area study, 1988 rpt, 5668-97

see also Classifications
see also Demonstration and pilot projects
see also Economic and econometric models
see also Mathematic models and modeling
see also Seasonal adjustment factors
see also Statistical programs and activities
see also under names of individual surveys (listed under Surveys)

Metrica, Inc.
"Comparison of Physician Malpractice Insurance Indices", 4658-27

Metrication
see Weights and measures

Metroliner
see National Railroad Passenger Corp.

Metropolitan areas
see Central cities
see Metropolitan Statistical Areas
see Suburbs
see Urban areas
see under By City, By SMSA or MSA, and By Urban-Rural and Metro-Nonmetro in the "Index by Categories"

Metropolitan Statistical Areas
Consumer Income, socioeconomic characteristics of persons, families, and households, detailed cross-tabulations, Current Population Rpt series, 2546-6

Crimes, arrests by offender characteristics, and rates, by offense, and law enforcement employees, by population size and jurisdiction, 1988, annual rpt, 6224-2

Definitions of MSAs and central cities, and revisions, periodic listings, series, 108-35

Employment and manufacturing output growth, relation to labor costs and metro area economic conditions, 1976-85, working paper, 9375-13.8

Farms in urban areas, acreage, finances, and operators, under alternative MSA definitions, 1960s-82, 1598-256

Govt (local) in metro areas, finances, structure, and service delivery, local area rpt series, 10046-9

Health care resources geographic info system, data coverage and availability, 1989 rpt, 4118-61

Housing starts and completions authorized by building permits in 40 MSAs, quarterly rpt, 2382-9

Income (personal) per capita and by source, and earnings by industry div, by State, MSA, and county, 1982-87, annual regional rpts, 2704-2

Migration since 1986, mover characteristics by same or different area, and compared to nonmovers, 1987, annual Current Population Rpt, 2546-1.435

Population size, by MSA, county, metro-nonmetro location, and State, 1987, and for cities, 1986, with change from 1980 and trends from 1960, Current Population Rpt, 2546-3.160

Population size, by MSA, 1988, annual press release, 2324-8

Southeastern US economic and employment conditions, for 4 largest MSAs, 1977-87, article, 9391-16.902

Statistical Abstract of US, social, political, and economic data, with foreign comparisons, 1790-2025, comprehensive annual compilation, 2324-1

Unemployment insurance extended benefits provision in substate areas, model results and cost estimates, 1980-86, 6406-6.28

see also Area wage surveys
see also Central business districts
see also Central cities
see also under By SMSA or MSA in the "Index by Categories"

Mexican Americans
see Hispanic Americans
see Mexicans in the U.S.

Mexicans in the U.S.
Admissions to US of aliens, by class of admission, port, country, and State of destination, quarterly rpt, 6262-2

Admissions to US of immigrants, alien workers, and visitors, deportations, and naturalizations, by country, FY88 and trends from 1820, annual rpt, 6264-2

Travel to US, market research, major magazine ad costs and circulation, and trade show data, for selected countries, 1989-90, annual rpt, 2904–11

Travel to US, spending by category, world area of residence, census div, and State, model results, 1985-86, 2908–28

Turtles (sea) catch, population monitoring, shrimping kills, and effects of drilling rig removal, 1970s-80s, article, 2162–1.902

UN voting record and share of votes in agreement with US, by issue, country, and world area, 1988, annual rpt, 7004–18

Vegetables (broccoli, asparagus, cauliflower) industry intl competitiveness, investigation with background financial and operating data and foreign comparisons, 1988 rpt, 9886–4.133

Vegetables (winter fresh) from Florida, Mexico, and Caribbean area, shipments and costs by commodity, 1970s-87, article, 1561–11.902

Vegetables, melon, and strawberry exports to US from Mexico, 1979-88, article, 1925–34.918

Water use from Colorado River Basin Project, by State and for Mexico, 1981-85, annual rpt, 5824–6

Youth sexual behavior, impact of popular music promoting responsibility, for Latin America, 1986, 9916–3.50

see also Gulf of Mexico

see also Mexicans in the U.S.

see also Mexico City, Mexico

see also under By Foreign Country in the "Index by Categories"

Mexico City, Mexico

Earthquake-related injuries, by type, for Mexico City, Sept 1985, article, 4042–3.947

Meyer, Leslie A.

"Portrait of Cotton Farm Operators and Their Farms: 1987 Census of Agriculture", 1561–1.907

"Recent Trends in Quota Shipments for Cotton Textiles", 1561–1.905

Meyer, Stephen A.

"U.S. as a Debtor Country: Causes, Prospects, and Policy Implications", 9387–1.905

Miami, Fla.

CPI by component for US city average, and by region, population size, and for 15 metro areas, monthly rpt, 6762–1

CPI by component for US city average, and by region, population size, and for 27 metro areas, monthly rpt, 6762–2

Drug abuse indicators for selected metro areas, research results, data collection, and policy issues, 1989 semiannual conf, 4492–5

Drug test results at arrest, by drug type, offense, and sex, for selected urban areas, quarterly rpt, 6062–3

Fruit and vegetable shipments, and arrivals in US and Canada cities, by mode of transport and State and country of origin, 1988, annual rpt, 1311–4.1

Housing starts and completions authorized by building permits in 40 MSAs, quarterly rpt, 2382–9

Wages by occupation, for office and plant workers, 1988 survey, periodic MSA rpt, 6785–11.1

see also under By City and By SMSA or MSA in the "Index by Categories"

Mica

see Nonmetallic minerals and mines

Michielutte, Robert

"Development of a Community Cancer Education Program: The Forsyth County, N.C., Cervical Cancer Prevention Project", 4042–3.953

Michigan

Agriculture census, 1987: farms, farmland, production and costs, and operator characteristics, advance State and county rpts, 2330–1.26

Agriculture census, 1987: farms, farmland, production, finances, and operator characteristics, by county, final State rpt, 2331–1.22

AIDS patients Medicaid claims and payments, by type of care and whether AIDS-related, race, sex, and diagnosis, 1984-87, article, 4042–3.940

Bank deposits in FDIC-insured commercial and savings banks, by instn, State, and county, as of June 1988, annual regional rpt, 9295–3.3

Business and economic conditions, Fed Reserve 9th District, quarterly journal, 9383–19

Celery acreage planted and growing, by growing area, monthly rpt, 1621–14

Dairy prices, by product and selected area, with related marketing data, 1988, annual rpt, 1317–1

Deaths and rates, by detailed location, cause, and demographic characteristics, 1987, US Vital Statistics annual rpt, 4144–3.1

Disabled SSI beneficiaries Medicaid services use and costs, by diagnosis and whether covered by Medicare, 1984, article, 4652–1.947

DOD prime contract awards, by contractor, service branch, State, and city, FY88, annual rpt, 3544–22

Economic conditions, Fed Reserve 9th District, quarterly rpt, 9383–18

Employment, earnings, and hours, by selected SIC 1- to 4-digit industry, State, and for 262 MSAs, 1972-87, 6748–81.2

Farm operators displaced worker programs under Job Training Partnership Act, funding, participation, and results by selected State, 1982-87, 15496–1.2

Fed Govt spending in States and local areas, by type, State, county, and city, FY88, annual rpt, 2464–3

Fed Govt spending in States, by type, program, agency, and State, FY88, annual rpt, 2464–2

Head Start program operations, enrollment by handicap, and family characteristics, for North Central States, 1987/88, annual rpt, 4604–12

HHS financial aid, by program, recipient, State, and city, FY88, annual regional listing, 4004–3.5

Hospital use and costs of Medicaid enrollees related to selected characteristics, 1980, article, 4652–1.949

Income (personal) per capita and by source, and earnings by industry div, by State, MSA, and county, 1982-87, annual regional rpt, 2704–2.2

Medicaid enrollment, and service use and costs by service type, by eligibility type, for 5 States, 1980-84, article, 4652–1.919

Medicare enrollees hospital readmissions related to selected characteristics, for Michigan, 1982-83, article, 4652–1.903

Mineral Industry Surveys, State reviews of production, 1988, preliminary annual rpt, 5614–6

Minerals Yearbook, 1987, Vol 2 preprints: State review of production and sales by commodity, and business activity, annual rpt, 5604–16.23

Minerals Yearbook, 1987, Vol 2: State reviews of production, sales, and firms, by commodity, and business activity, annual rpt, 5604–34

Nursing home admissions and discharges for Medicaid patients with prior hospitalization, for 3 States, 1981, article, 4652–1.942

Nursing home compliance with Medicare and Medicaid regulations, and patient characteristics, by facility, 1987/88, annual State rpt, 4654–15.23

Pregnancy-related services use and costs, for Medicaid beneficiaries in 3 States, 1983-84, article, 4652–1.938

Retail trade census, 1987: employment, establishments, sales, and payroll, by SIC 2- to 4-digit kind of business, MSA, county, and city, State rpt, 2397–1.23

Savings and loan assns, FHLB 6th District insured members financial condition and operations by State, quarterly rpt, 9302–23

Savings instns, FHLB 6th District members financial condition and operations by State, monthly rpt, 9302–11

Service industries census, 1987: employment, establishments, receipts, and payroll, by SIC 2- to 4-digit kind of business, MSA, county, and city, State rpt, 2391–1.23

Statistical Abstract of US, social, political, and economic data, with foreign comparisons, 1790-2025, comprehensive annual compilation, 2324–1

Unemployed displaced workers, labor-mgmt committee aid recipients by selected characteristics, for 4 State programs, 1988, GAO rpt, 26121–316

Water supply and quality in streams and lakes, and groundwater levels in wells, by drainage basin, 1987, annual State rpt, 5666–10.21

Wholesale trade census, 1987: employment, establishments, finances, and operations, by SIC 2- to 4-digit kind of business, MSA, county, and city, State rpt, 2405–1.23

Wildlife-related recreation, hunting, and fishing participation and spending, detailed data, 1985 survey, quinquennial State rpt, 5506–6.22

Women-owned business mgmt issues, SBA loans, Federal contracts by agency, and owners views on Michigan business climate, FY79-88, hearings, 21728–68

see also Alpena, Mich.

see also Ann Arbor, Mich.

see also Battle Creek, Mich.

see also Bay City, Mich.

see also Detroit, Mich.

see also Oakland County, Mich.
see also Saginaw, Mich.
see also Standish, Mich.
see also Tawas City, Mich.
see also Wayne County, Mich.
see also under By State in the "Index by Categories"

Microforms

Census Bur activities, rpts, and user services, monthly rpt, 2302–3

Census Bur data coverage and availability for 1987 economic censuses and related statistics, 1989 preliminary guide, 2308–5

Census Bur rpts and data files, coverage and availability, 1989 annual listing, 2304–2

Census Bur rpts and data files, coverage, availability, and use, series, 2326–7

Census Bur rpts and data files, monthly listing, 2302–6

Census of Agriculture, 1987: data coverage and availability, for census and related statistics, 1989 guide, 2308–55

Census of Population and Housing, 1980: data processing, coverage, and availability, 2555–2.4

Census of Population and Housing, 1990: data coverage and products, 1989 guide, 2308–58

Fed Govt standards for data recording, processing, and transfer, and for purchase and use of computer systems, series, 2216–2

Geological Survey rpts and research journal articles, monthly listing, 5662–1

GPO microfiche shipment to depository libraries, contract awards, and supply and quality problems, 1988, GAO rpt, 26119–248

Library of Congress activities, acquisitions, services, and financial statements, FY88, annual rpt, 26404–1

Library of Congress rpts and products, 1989, annual listing, 26404–6

Natl Archives and Records Admin activities, finances, holdings, and staff, FY88, annual rpt, 9514–2

Price indexes (producer), by stage of processing and detailed commodity, monthly rpt, 6762–6

Micronesia Federated States

Bank deposits in FDIC-insured commercial and savings banks, by instn, State, and county, as of June 1988, annual regional rpt, 9295–3.6

Economic, social, political, and geographic summary data, by country, 1989, annual factbook, 9114–2

Human rights conditions in 170 countries, 1988, annual rpt, 21384–3

Population size, growth rates, and components of change, by country, projected 1989-2020 and trends from 1950, biennial rpt, 2324–9

Population social, economic, health, and govtl data, by TTPI govt, FY88 and selected trends, detailed annual rpt, 7004–6

Water supply and quality in streams and lakes, and groundwater levels in wells, by drainage basin, 1987, annual State rpt, 5666–10.10

see also under By Foreign Country in the "Index by Categories"

Microscopes

see Scientific equipment and apparatus

Middle Atlantic States

Clothing (hosiery) production and related workers and wages by occupation and sex, and benefits, by location, 1987 survey, 6787–6.237

Economic and housing indicators for FHLB 2nd District, by State, quarterly rpt with articles, 9302–33

Economic conditions, Fed Reserve 3rd District, quarterly rpt, 9387–10

Employment, earnings, and consumer prices in BLS Middle Atlantic region, press release series, 6926–2

Financial and economic devs, Fed Reserve Bank of Philadelphia bimonthly journal, 9387–1

Financial and economic devs, Fed Reserve Bank of Richmond bimonthly journal, 9389–1

Fish and shellfish catch, life cycles, and environmental needs, for selected coastal species and regions, series, 5506–8

Freight (waterborne domestic and foreign) by commodity, traffic, and passengers, by port and waterway, 1987, annual rpt, 3754–3.1

HHS financial aid, by program, recipient, State, and city, FY88, annual regional listing, 4004–3.2; 4004–3.3

Hwy construction costs, funding, mileage, and traffic, for Middle Atlantic States by project, 1989 article, 9387–1.904

Income (personal) per capita and by source, and earnings by industry div, by State, MSA, and county, 1982-87, annual regional rpt, 2704–2.2

Income (personal) per capita and by source, earnings by major industry group, and social insurance contributions, by region and State, 1929-87, 2708–40

Lumber (pulpwood) production by species and county, and shipments, by northeastern State, 1987, annual rpt, 1204–18

Manufacturing business outlook, for Fed Reserve 3rd District, monthly survey rpt, 9387–11

Manufacturing output index for Middle Atlantic States, monthly rpt, 9387–12

Manufacturing share of output by State, and employment and output shares by industry div for US and Fed Reserve 3rd District, 1967-86, article, 9387–1.902

Natural gas interstate pipeline company capacity, use, sales, deliveries, and prices, by firm and Northeast State, 1980-88, 3166–6.35

Savings instns, FHLB 2nd District members finances and operations, by State, quarterly rpt, 9302–14

Shipbuilding costs, deliveries, contracts, employment, and wage rates, by coastal district and shipyard, 1988, annual rpt, 7704–12

Statistical Abstract of US, social, political, and economic data, with foreign comparisons, 1790-2025, comprehensive annual compilation, 2324–1

Tide height and time daily at coastal points, forecast 1990, annual rpt, 2174–2.3

see also Appalachia

see also under By Census Division in the "Index by Categories"

see also under names of individual States

Middle East

Agricultural and food aid to developing countries, and impacts on US exports, with background data, 1960s-89, 26308–85

Agricultural and food production and indexes, total and for selected commodities, by country, 1970s-88, annual rpt, 1524–12

Agricultural production, prices, and trade, by country, 1960s-89, annual world region rpt, 1524–4.2

Agricultural trade of US, by commodity and country, bimonthly rpt with articles, 1522–1

Agricultural trade of US, by detailed commodity and country, 1988, semiannual rpt, 1522–4

Agricultural trade of US with Asia, Middle East, and North Africa, by commodity and country, 1962-86, 1528–277

AID activities and funding by project and function, FY90, and developing countries summary socioeconomic data from 1960s, annual rpt, 9904–4.6

AID contracts and grants for technical and support services, by instn, country, and State, FY88, annual listing, 9914–7

AID economic aid to developing countries, obligations and disbursements by country, quarterly rpt, 9912–4

AID housing and urban dev program financial statements, and loan guarantees by country, FY88, annual rpt, 9914–4

AID loans authorized, signed, and canceled, by country and world area, quarterly rpt, 9912–2

AID loans repayment status and terms by program and country, and status of predecessor agency loans, quarterly rpt, 9912–3

Construction contracts awarded US firms, and share of construction market by country of contractor, by world area, 1982-87, annual article, 2042–1.902

Dev aid of OECD and Arab countries, total, per capita, and share of GNP, by country, 1987, annual rpt, 9904–1.4

Economic and military aid and loans from US and intl agencies, by program and country, FY46-87, annual rpt, 9914–5

Energy producers finances and operations, by energy type for US firms domestic and foreign operations, 1987, annual rpt, 3164–44.2

Energy production by type, and oil prices, trade, and use, by country group and selected country, monthly rpt, 9112–2

Energy use by sector, and production, by fuel type, country, and country group, projected 1988-2000 and trends from 1970, annual rpt, 3164–28

English language program of USIA, enrollment and staff, by instn, world area, and country, FY88, annual rpt, 9854–2

Exchange and training programs of Federal agencies, participants by world area, and funding, by program, FY87, annual rpt, 9854–8

Exports and imports (waterborne) of US, by type of service, commodity, country, route, and US port, 1986-87, annual rpt, 7704–2

Exports and imports of OECD, total and for 4 major countries, and US trade by country, by commodity, 1970-87, world area rpt, 9116–1.3

Exports and imports of US, by selected country, country group, and commodity group, 1988, annual rpt, 2044–37

Food production and needs, and related economic outlook, by country, 1989/90, annual rpt, 1524–6

Immigration to US, alien workers, visitors, deportations, and naturalizations, by country, FY88 and trends from 1820, annual rpt, 6264–2

Imports of goods, services, and investment from US, trade barriers, impacts, and US actions, by country, 1988, annual rpt, 444–2

Investment (foreign direct) in US, by industry group and world area, 1987-88, annual article, 2702–1.929

Investment (foreign direct) of US, by selected industry group and world area, 1986-88, annual article, 2702–1.930

Military aid of US, arms sales, and training, by country, FY50-88, annual rpt, 3904–3

Military aid of US, arms sales, and training programs costs and budget requests, by program, world region, and country, FY88-90, annual rpt, 7144–13

Military aid programs and related activities of US, costs by country and intl agency, FY85-87 and cumulative from FY50, GAO rpt, 26123–30

Military spending and imports of developing countries, measures to determine eligibility for US economic aid, by country, 1985-86, annual rpt, 9914–1

Military spending, arms trade, and force strengths, with govt spending and population, by country, 1977-87, annual rpt, 9824–1

Minerals Yearbook, 1987, Vol 3: foreign country reviews of production, trade, and policy, by commodity, annual rpt, 5604–35

Multinatl firms US affiliates, finances, and operations, by industry, world area of parent firm, and State, 1987, annual rpt, 2704–4

Multinatl US firms and foreign affiliates finances and operations, by industry of parent firm and affiliate, world area, and country, preliminary 1987, annual rpt, 2704–5

Oil and gas reserves and discoveries, by country and country group, quarterly rpt, 3162–43

Population size, growth rates, and components of change, by country, projected 1989-2020 and trends from 1950, biennial rpt, 2324–9

R&D funding by Fed Govt, by field, performer type, agency, and State, FY87-89, annual rpt, 9627–20

Refugee arrivals in US by world area and country of origin, and quotas, monthly rpt, 7002–4

Refugee arrivals in US by world area of origin and State of settlement, and Federal aid, FY88-90, annual rpt, 7004–16

River water annual discharge, for 4 Middle East rivers, 1989 hearing, 21708–126

Science and engineering immigrants, by field, age, sex, country and world area of birth and last residence, and State, 1987 and trends from 1967, 9627–29

Terrorist (intl) incidents, casualties, and attacks on US targets, by attack type and country, 1980-88, 7008–56

Terrorist (intl) incidents, casualties, and attacks on US targets, by attack type and world area, 1968-88, annual rpt, 7004–13

Tide height and time daily at coastal points, forecast 1990, annual rpt, 2174–2.5

Travel to and from US, and travel receipts and payments, by world area, with data by country, 1984-88, annual rpt, 2904–10

Travel to US, by characteristics of visit and traveler, country, port city, and State of destination, quarterly rpt, 2902–1

Travel to US, spending by category, world area of residence, census div, and State, model results, 1985-86, 2908–28

UN voting record and share of votes in agreement with US, by issue, country, and world area, 1988, annual rpt, 7004–18

USIA library holdings, use, and staff, by country and city, FY88, annual rpt, 9854–4

Weather forecasts for US and Northern Hemisphere, precipitation and temperature by location, semimonthly rpt, 2182–1

see also Bahrain
see also Central Treaty Organization
see also Cyprus
see also Egypt
see also Iran
see also Iraq
see also Israel
see also Jordan
see also Kuwait
see also Lebanon
see also Mediterranean Sea
see also Oman
see also Organization of Petroleum Exporting Countries
see also Qatar
see also Saudi Arabia
see also Syria
see also Turkey
see also United Arab Emirates
see also Yemen, North
see also Yemen, South
see also under By Foreign Country in the "Index by Categories"

Middlesex County, N.J.
see also under By SMSA or MSA in the "Index by Categories"

Middletown, Conn.
see also under By SMSA or MSA in the "Index by Categories"

Midland, Mich.
Wages by occupation, and benefits for office and plant workers, 1989 survey, periodic MSA rpt, 6785–3.10
see also under By SMSA or MSA in the "Index by Categories"

Midland, Tex.
see also under By SMSA or MSA in the "Index by Categories"

Midway Islands
Economic, social, political, and geographic summary data, by country, 1989, annual factbook, 9114–2

Midwestern States
see North Central States
see under By Region in the "Index by Categories"

Midwives
Births and rates, by characteristics of birth, infant, and parents, 1987 and trends from 1940, US Vital Statistics advance annual rpt, 4146–5.110

Indian Health Service outpatient visits, by type of provider, selected hospital, and IHS service area, FY87-88, annual rpt, 4084–3

Military health care personnel, and accessions by training source, by occupation, specialty, and service branch, FY87, annual rpt, 3544–24

Mielke, Myles J.
"Government Intervention in the Mexican Crop Sector", 1528–288

Miethe, Terance D.
"Sentencing Guidelines: Their Effect in Minnesota", 6066–20.20

Migrant workers
Agricultural Statistics, 1988, annual rpt, 1004–1.2

Assistance (financial and nonfinancial) of Fed Govt, 1989 base edition with supplements, annual listing, 104–5

Education Dept programs funding, operations, and effectiveness, FY88, annual rpt, 4804–5

Education funding of Fed Govt, State allocation by program, recipient type, and State, 1987/88, annual rpt, 4804–8

Farm hired workers employment, days worked, and migrant and alien workers, 1945-87, 1598–246

Farm worker migrant labor force and housing supply, for Western US, 1989 GAO rpt, 26121–310

Head Start enrollment, funding, and staff, FY88, annual rpt, 4604–8

Head Start handicapped enrollment, by handicap, State, and for Indian and migrant programs, 1985/86, annual rpt, 4604–1

Health care services (community and migrant) finances, operations, and staff, series, 4108–45

HHS financial aid, by program, recipient, State, and city, FY88, annual regional listings, 4004–3

Migration
Consumer Income, socioeconomic characteristics of persons, families, and households, detailed cross-tabulations, Current Population Rpt series, 2546–6

Deaths in US, by State of occurrence and birth, and birthplace abroad, 1986, US Vital Statistics annual rpt, 4144–2.1

Fetal deaths and rates, by characteristics of mother and birth, 1986, US Vital Statistics annual rpt, 4144–2.3

Florida banks and thrifts deposits and mortgages, building permits, population, and migration, with comparisons to other areas, 1980s-88, article, 9302–2.905

Govt (local) spending, impacts of competition among govtl units, migration, and other factors, 1976-77, working paper, 9377–9.82

Hazardous substances exposure factors, and methodological guidelines, 1989 rpt, 9188–109

Higher education enrollment of State and out-of-State residents, by State, fall 1986, annual rpt, 4824–2.17

Household and family characteristics, by location, 1988, annual Current Population Rpt, 2546–1.437

Household composition, income, benefits, and labor force status, Survey of Income and Program Participation methodology, working paper series, 2626–10 .

Housing and households characteristics, MSA surveys, fact sheet series, 2485–11

Housing characteristics of recent movers for new and previous unit, and household characteristics, by location, 1985, biennial rpt, 2485–12

Housing characteristics of recent movers for new and previous unit, and household characteristics, MSA surveys, series, 2485–6

Migration since 1986, mover characteristics by same or different area, and compared to nonmovers, 1987, annual Current Population Rpt, 2546–1.435

Minority group population, and components of change, by race, State, metro-nonmetro location, MSA, and county, 1980-85, Current Population Rpt, 2546–3.159

Older persons socioeconomic characteristics, 1900s-86 and projected to 2050, biennial chartbook, 12904–1

Outlying areas population size and components of change, by area, 1980-88, annual Current Population Rpt, 2546–3.162

Population size by age and sex, components of change, and households, by State, 1980-88, Current Population Rpt, 2546–3.161

Population size, by MSA, county, metro-nonmetro location, and State, 1987, and for cities, 1986, with change from 1980 and trends from 1960, Current Population Rpt, 2546–3.160

Population size, July 1988 and compared to 1980 and 1987, and components of change, 1980-88, annual press release, 2324–10

Population size of counties, 1988, and components of change from 1980, annual Current Population Rpt, 2544–3

Research on population and reproduction, Federal funding by project, FY87, annual listing, 4474–9

Rural areas employment, economic conditions, and population characteristics, 1970s-85, compilation of papers, 1598–243

Science and engineering PhDs, by field, instn, employment prospects, sex, race, and other characteristics, 1960s-88, 9627–30

Southern US in- and out-migration, by migrant characteristics and location, 1970s-87 and alternative projections to 2000, article, 9371–1.902

Statistical Abstract of US, social, political, and economic data, 1790-2025, comprehensive annual compilation, 2324–1.1

see also Alien workers
see also Immigration and emigration
see also Labor mobility
see also Mexicans in the U.S.

see also Migrant workers
see also Refugees
see also Relocation

Migratory Bird Conservation Commission
Refuges and breeding areas for migratory waterfowl, acreage acquired by Fed Govt, and costs, by site and State, FY89, annual rpt, 14784–1

Mikesell, James J.
"Nonmetro, Metro, and U.S. Bank Operating Statistics, 1986", 1544–29
"Rural Poverty: Do Assets Matter?", 1502–7.908

Milford, Conn.
see also under By SMSA or MSA in the "Index by Categories"

Milham, Samuel, Jr.
"Mortality Among Pulp and Paper Workers", 21368–112

Military aircraft
Birds collisions with military aircraft, and related costs, by service branch, 1975-88, GAO rpt, 26123–241

Bomber aircraft (B-1B) maintenance problems, and repair contracts, 1985-88 with costs projected to FY94, GAO rpt, 26123–218

Budget of DOD, justification, programs, and policies, FY90-91, annual rpt, 3544–2

Budget of DOD, organization, personnel, weapons, and property, by service branch, State, and country, 1989 annual summary rpt, 3504–13

Budget of DOD, procurement appropriations by item, service branch, and defense agency, FY88-91, annual rpt, 3544–32

Budget of DOD, weapons acquisition costs by system and service branch, FY89-91, annual rpt, 3504–2

Coast Guard drug and illegal alien enforcement activities, 2nd half FY89, semiannual rpt, 7402–4

Customs Service activities, collections, entries processed by mode of transport, and seizures, FY84-88, annual rpt, 8144–1

Expenditures and obligations of DOD, by function and service branch, quarterly rpt, 3542–3

Exports of US, detailed commodities by country, monthly rpt, 2422–3

Foreign countries military aid and arms sales of US, by weapon type, as of Sept 1988, annual rpt, 3904–3

Foreign countries military spending, arms trade, and force strengths, with govt spending and population, by country, 1977-87, annual rpt, 9824–1

Manufacturing annual survey, 1986: value of shipments, by SIC 4- to 5-digit product class, 2506–15.3

Manufacturing census, 1987: financial and operating data, for SIC 4-digit industries by product, preliminary rpt, 2491–1.76

Natl Guard aircraft, FY88, annual rpt, 3504–22.1

NATO and Japan military spending and indicators of ability to support common defense, by country, 1960s-87, annual rpt, 3544–28

Navy budget, manpower, procurement, and equipment, planned FY89-91, annual fact sheet, 3804–6

Pacific basin airlift of aircraft parts, traffic, shipments, and impacts on force readiness, for Air Force, 1986-88, GAO rpt, 26123–230

Pollution (air) levels for 5 pollutants, by detailed source and State, 1986, annual rpt, 9194–7

Price indexes (producer), by stage of processing and detailed commodity, monthly rpt, 6762–6

Price indexes (producer), by stage of processing and detailed commodity, monthly 1988, annual rpt, 6764–2

Procurement cost estimates for weapons and communications systems, by service branch, quarterly summary rpt, 3502–1

Procurement, DOD prime contract awards by category, contract and contractor type, and service branch, FY79-88, semiannual rpt, 3542–1

Procurement, DOD prime contract awards by category, contractor type, and State, FY86-88, annual rpt, 3544–11

Procurement, DOD prime contract awards by detailed procurement category, FY85-88, annual rpt, 3544–18

Procurement, DOD prime contract awards by size and type of contract, service branch, competitive status, category, and labor standard, FY88, annual rpt, 3544–19

Reserve forces manpower and equipment strengths, and readiness, by reserve component, FY88, annual rpt, 3544–31

Soviet Union and Warsaw Pact military weapons systems, aid, presence, and force strengths, and compared to US and NATO, 1989 annual rpt, 3504–20

Spare parts unfilled orders validation of Air Force, 1985-87, GAO rpt, 26123–245

Warsaw Pact and USSR military strength, and proposed force reductions, with comparisons to NATO, 1980s-91, hearing, 21208–29

Military airlift
Pacific basin airlift of aircraft parts, traffic, shipments, and impacts on force readiness, for Air Force, 1986-88, GAO rpt, 26123–230

Shipments by DOD of military and personal property, passenger traffic, and costs, by service branch and mode of transport, quarterly rpt, 3702–1

Military appropriations
see Defense budgets and appropriations

Military assistance
Budget of DOD, justification, programs, and policies, FY90-91, annual rpt, 3544–2

Budget of DOD, organization, personnel, weapons, and property, by service branch, State, and country, 1989 annual summary rpt, 3504–13

Budget of DOD, R&D appropriations by item, service branch, and defense agency, FY88-91, annual rpt, 3544–33

Budget of US Appendix, obligations, appropriations, and personnel, by program and agency, FY90, annual rpt, 104–3

Business Conditions Digest, defense activity indicators, monthly rpt, 2702–3.8

Currency (foreign) holdings of US, transactions and balances by program and country, 1st half FY89, semiannual rpt, 8102–7

Debt to US of foreign govts and private obligors, by country and program, periodic rpt, 8002–6

Developing countries economic and military aid from US, Communist, and selected other countries, 1946-88, annual rpt, 9114–4.9

Military intelligence

Budget of DOD, justification, programs, and policies, FY90-91, annual rpt, 3544-2

Budget of DOD, manpower needs, costs, and force readiness by service branch, FY90, annual rpt, 3504-1

Budget of DOD, R&D appropriations by item, service branch, and defense agency, FY88-91, annual rpt, 3544-33

see also Defense Intelligence Agency

see also Defense Security Assistance Agency

Military law

Navy manpower strengths, accessions, and attrition, detailed statistics, quarterly rpt, 3802-4

US attorneys civil and criminal cases by type and disposition, and collections, by Federal district, FY88, annual rpt, 6004-2.1

see also Court of Military Appeals

see also Courts-martial and courts of inquiry

Military pay

Air Force pilot needs, retention, incentive pay, and impacts of alternative bonus programs, FY89 and projected FY90-94, 26308-88

Budget of DOD, justification, programs, and policies, FY90-91, annual rpt, 3544-2

Budget of US, historical data, selected years FY34-88 and projected to FY94, annual rpt, 104-22

Budget of US, object class analysis of obligations, by agency, FY90, annual rpt, 104-9

Earnings by industry div, and personal income per capita and by source, by State, MSA, and county, 1982-87, annual regional rpts, 2704-2

Earnings by major industry group, and personal income per capita and by source, by region and State, 1929-87, 2708-40

Expenditures and obligations of DOD, by function and service branch, quarterly rpt, 3542-3

Income (household, family, and personal), by source, detailed characteristics, and region, 1987, annual Current Population Rpt, 2546-6.59

Manpower of DOD, and organization, budget, weapons, and property, by service branch, State, and country, 1989 annual summary rpt, 3504-13

Natl Guard (Army and Air) outlays, by function and State, FY88, annual rpt, 3504-22.1

Natl income and product accounts and components, Survey of Current Business, monthly rpt, 2702-1.21

Natl income and product accounts govt transactions component estimates, methodology and bibl, 1988 technical rpt, 2706-6.5

Navy budget, manpower, procurement, and equipment, planned FY89-91, annual fact sheet, 3804-16

Pay comparability of Fed Govt with private industry, and recommended and actual pay adjustments, 1970s-89, annual rpt, 10104-1

Payroll and employment, by function, level of govt, and State, 1988, annual rpt, 2466-1.1; 2466-1.5

Payroll of Fed Govt, by State and county, FY88, annual rpt, 2464-3.1

Payroll of Fed Govt, spending for civilian, military, and postal workers by State, FY88, annual rpt, 2464-2

Payroll, personnel, and contracts of DOD, by service branch and location, with top 5 contractors and maps, by State and country, FY88, annual rpt, 3544-29

Reserve forces manpower, funding by category, procurement reductions, and needs, by component, FY80-88, GAO rpt, 26123-220

Reserve forces manpower strengths and characteristics, by component, quarterly rpt, 3542-4

Reserve personnel social, economic, family, and service characteristics, and attitudes, by reserve component, 1986 survey, 3508-29

Reserve personnel spouses attitudes, and family social, economic, and other characteristics, 1986 survey, 3508-30

Rural areas aid from Fed Govt compared to urban areas, by program and degree of urbanization, FY85, periodic rpt, 1598-248

Science and engineering PhDs employment and other characteristics, by field and State, 1987, biennial rpt, 9627-18

Sealift Military Command shipping operations, finances, and personnel, FY88, annual rpt, 3804-14

Soviet Union personal income by source, disposable income, wage deductions by type, and savings, 1950s-87, 9118-7

Statistical Abstract of US, social, political, and economic data, 1790-2025, comprehensive annual compilation, 2324-1.2

see also Military benefits and pensions

Military personnel

Agent Orange exposure health effects, literature review, 1987, annual rpt series, 8706-1

Agent Orange exposure of Air Force personnel, deaths and rates by cause and selected characteristics, 1989 annual rpt, 3604-3

Aliens serving in US armed forces, citizenship petitions granted by country, 1907-88, annual rpt, 6264-2

Army Dept activities, manpower, logistics, R&D, and budget, FY86, annual rpt, 3704-11

Army personnel health condition, and use of Army medical services in US and abroad by personnel, retirees, and dependents, monthly rpt, 3702-4

Army strategic capability, force strengths, budget, and mgmt, FY80-89, annual rpt, 3704-13

Budget of DOD, justification, programs, and policies, FY90-91, annual rpt, 3544-2

Budget of DOD, manpower and spending under alternative spending growth rates, FY89-94, 26306-3.107

Budget of DOD, manpower needs, costs, and force readiness by service branch, FY90, annual rpt, 3504-1

Budget of US Appendix, obligations, appropriations, and personnel, by program and agency, FY90, annual rpt, 104-3

Budget of US, CBO analysis and review of FY90 budget by function, annual rpt, 26304-2

Budget of US, compact budgets by activity, function, and agency, FY90 and projected to FY94, annual rpt, 104-2

Business Conditions Digest, defense activity indicators, monthly rpt, 2702-3.8

Criminal case processing in military courts, and prisoners by facility, by service branch, 1960s-88, annual rpt, 6064-6.5; 6064-6.6

Deaths by cause, age, race, and rank, and personnel captured and missing, by service branch, 2nd half FY88, semiannual rpt, 3542-21

Deaths of military personnel by service branch and age group, and veterans death rates, 1966-88, annual rpt, 8654-1

Defense Fuel Supply Center procurement, prices, stocks, transport, and other activities and finances, FY88, annual rpt, 3904-8

Discrimination issues in Army, personnel, promotion, and training by race and sex, and career attitudes, FY88, annual rpt, 3704-10

Drug and alcohol abuse by military personnel, prevalence and consequences, by selected characteristics, 1988, biennial rpt, 3504-19

Economic indicators and components, current data and annual trends, monthly rpt, 23842-1.2

Employee paid leave days for military duty, by occupational group, 1988, annual rpt, 6784-19

Employment (civilian) of DOD, by service branch and defense agency, with summary military employment data, quarterly rpt, 3542-16

Employment and Earnings, detailed data, monthly rpt, 6742-2.4

Employment and occupation of householder, by occupation of spouse, race, and family composition, 1988, annual Current Population Rpt, 2546-1.437

Employment and payroll, by function, level of govt, and State, 1988, annual rpt, 2466-1.1; 2466-1.5

Employment, earnings, and hours, monthly press release, 6742-5

Employment situation, earnings, hours, and other BLS economic indicators, transcripts of BLS Commissioner's monthly testimony, periodic rpt, 23846-4

Employment, unemployment, and labor force characteristics, Labor Statistics Handbook, 1940s-88 with trends from 1913, 6728-38.1

Foreign countries economic, social, political, and geographic summary data, by country, 1989, annual factbook, 9114-2

Foreign countries military aid of US, arms sales, and training programs costs and budget requests, by program, world region, and country, FY88-90, annual rpt, 7144-13

Foreign countries military spending, arms trade, and force strengths, with govt spending and population, by country, 1977-87, annual rpt, 9824-1

Headquarters personnel reduction proposals for joint and service commands, by service branch, FY90-91, GAO rpt, 26123-236

Health care costs for military hospitals and CHAMPUS, and reduction in military hospital admissions, with background data, FY85-87, GAO rpt, 26121-288

Poultry (chicken, egg, and turkey)
production, prices, receipts, trade, and
disposition, 1960-87, 1568-39

Sales by commodity, and operations, by post
exchange and location worldwide, FY87,
annual rpt, 3504-10

Military prisons

Executions by whether writ of habeas corpus
used to appeal, race, and State, with
military death row inmates, 1977-87,
hearing, 21408-110

Prisoners in Federal instns, by sex, prison,
security level, contract facility type, and
region, monthly rpt series, 6242-1

Prisoners in military prisons, and capacity,
by service branch and facility, 1970s-87,
annual rpt, 6064-6.6

Military research

see Defense research

Military reserves

see Armed services reserves

Military science

Budget of DOD, R&D appropriations by
item, service branch, and defense agency,
FY88-91, annual rpt, 3544-33

Soviet Union and Warsaw Pact military
weapons systems, aid, presence, and force
strengths, and compared to US and
NATO, 1989 annual rpt, 3504-20

see also Arms control and disarmament

see also Civil defense

see also Defense research

see also Logistics

see also Military strategy

Military service

see Selective service

see Voluntary military service

Military service academies

see Service academies

Military strategy

Army strategic capability, force strengths,
budget, and mgmt, FY80-89, annual rpt,
3704-13

Budget of DOD, justification, programs, and
policies, FY90-91, annual rpt, 3544-2

Budget of DOD, manpower needs, costs,
and force readiness by service branch,
FY90, annual rpt, 3504-1

Budget of DOD, R&D appropriations by
item, service branch, and defense agency,
FY88-91, annual rpt, 3544-33

Foreign countries military aid of US, arms
sales, and training programs costs and
budget requests, by program, world
region, and country, FY88-90, annual rpt,
7144-13

NATO military forces compared to Warsaw
Pact, and selected economic indicators, by
country, 1900s-87, conf papers, 3908-6

Reserve forces manpower and equipment
strengths, and readiness, by reserve
component, FY88, annual rpt, 3544-31

Ships, shipyards, and personnel wartime
capability, for merchant and reserve fleet,
revised estimates, 1985-2000, 11208-3

Ships, shipyards, and personnel wartime
capability, for merchant and reserve fleet,
1988-2000, 11208-1

Soviet Union and Warsaw Pact military
weapons systems, aid, presence, and force
strengths, and compared to US and
NATO, 1989 annual rpt, 3504-20

Military supplies and property

Air Force property mgmt, validation of
unfilled orders for aircraft spare parts,
1985-87, GAO rpt, 26123-245

Air Force supply inventory stock fund
balances, refunds to customers, and
procurement cost effects of reducing
balances, FY84-88, GAO rpt, 26111-60

Bombing incidents and casualties by target
and circumstances, and explosives theft
and recovery, by State, 1979-88, annual
rpt, 8484-4

Budget of DOD, justification, programs, and
policies, FY90-91, annual rpt, 3544-2

Budget of DOD, R&D appropriations by
item, service branch, and defense agency,
FY88-91, annual rpt, 3544-33

Budget of DOD, weapons acquisition costs
by system and service branch, FY89-91,
annual rpt, 3504-2

Capital (fixed), govt and private
nonresidential structures and equipment,
residential capital, and consumer-owned
durable goods, 1985-88, annual article,
2702-1.931

Commercial activities of DOD performed
in-house, and work-years, by service
branch, installation, and State, FY88,
annual rpt, 3544-25

Computer systems and equipment of Fed
Govt, by type, make, and agency, 1st half
FY89, semiannual listing, 9452-9

Defense Fuel Supply Center procurement,
prices, stocks, transport, and other
activities and finances, FY88, annual rpt,
3904-8

Expenditures and obligations of DOD, by
function and service branch, quarterly rpt,
3542-3

Exports of US, detailed commodities by
country, monthly rpt, 2422-3

Foreign countries military aid and arms
sales of US, by weapon type, as of Sept
1988, annual rpt, 3904-3

Foreign countries military aid of US, arms
sales, and training programs costs and
budget requests, by program, world
region, and country, FY88-90, annual rpt,
7144-13

Freight (waterborne domestic and foreign)
by commodity, traffic, and passengers, by
port and waterway, 1987, annual rpt,
3754-3

Imports of US, detailed Schedule A
commodities by country, monthly rpt,
2422-2

Inventory of DOD property, supplies, and
equipment, by service branch, 1988,
annual rpt, 3544-6

Navy budget, manpower, procurement, and
equipment, planned FY89-91, annual fact
sheet, 3804-16

Pacific basin countries military, economic,
technological, and trade conditions,
1970s-85, compilation of papers, 3908-4

Reserve forces manpower and equipment
strengths, and readiness, by reserve
component, FY88, annual rpt, 3544-31

Reserve forces manpower, funding by
category, procurement reductions, and
needs, by component, FY80-88, GAO rpt,
26123-220

Reserve personnel social, economic, family,
and service characteristics, and attitudes,
by reserve component, 1986 survey,
3508-29

Sealift Military Command shipping
operations, finances, and personnel, FY88,
annual rpt, 3804-14

Shipments by DOD of military and personal
property, passenger traffic, and costs, by
service branch and mode of transport,
quarterly rpt, 3702-1

Soviet Union and Warsaw Pact military
weapons systems, aid, presence, and force
strengths, and compared to US and
NATO, 1989 annual rpt, 3504-20

see also Ammunition

see also Arms trade

see also Defense contracts and procurement

see also Logistics

see also Military assistance

see also Military bases, posts, and
reservations

see also Military vehicles

see also Military weapons

Military training

Air Force B-1B aircraft maintenance
problems, and repair contracts, 1985-88
with costs projected to FY94, GAO rpt,
26123-218

Army personnel, promotion, and training by
race and for women, discrimination issues,
and career attitudes, FY88, annual rpt,
3704-10

Army Reserve and Natl Guard combat and
critical job task training, resources,
effectiveness, and officers views, FY87,
GAO rpt, 26123-239

Budget of DOD, justification, programs, and
policies, FY90-91, annual rpt, 3544-2

Budget of DOD, manpower needs, costs,
and force readiness by service branch,
FY90, annual rpt, 3504-1

Budget of DOD, R&D appropriations by
item, service branch, and defense agency,
FY88-91, annual rpt, 3544-33

Commercial activities of DOD performed
in-house, and work-years, by service
branch, installation, and State, FY88,
annual rpt, 3544-25

Developing countries military, academic,
and technical training aid from
Communist countries, 1970s-88, annual
rpt, 9114-4.9

Exchange and training programs of Federal
agencies, participants by world area, and
funding, by program, FY87, annual rpt,
9854-8

Expenditures, staff, students, and facilities
for DOD training and education
programs, by service branch, FY90,
annual rpt, 3504-5

Foreign countries economic and military aid
loans and grants from US and intl
agencies, by program and country,
FY46-87, annual rpt, 9914-5

Foreign countries military aid of US, arms
sales, and training, by country, FY50-88,
annual rpt, 3904-3

Foreign countries military aid of US, arms
sales, and training programs costs and
budget requests, by program, world
region, and country, FY88-90, annual rpt,
7144-13

Foreign countries military aid programs and
related activities of US, costs by country
and intl agency, FY85-87 and cumulative
from FY50, GAO rpt, 26123-30

Health care personnel, and accessions by
training source, by occupation, specialty,
and service branch, FY87, annual rpt,
3544-24

Manpower of DOD, and organization, budget, weapons, and property, by service branch, State, and country, 1989 annual summary rpt, 3504–13

Natl Guard (Army and Air) activities, manpower, and facilities, FY88, annual rpt, 3504–22

Navy manpower strengths, accessions, and attrition, detailed statistics, quarterly rpt, 3802–4

Navy pilot proficiency program, aircraft hours flown and costs, FY83-87, GAO rpt, 26123–238

Participant characteristics, and sources of training, with data by employer size and major industry group, 1982-88, 6408–73

Procurement, DOD prime contract awards by detailed procurement category, FY85-88, annual rpt, 3544–18

Reserve forces manpower and equipment strengths, and readiness, by reserve component, FY88, annual rpt, 3544–31

Reserve forces manpower, funding by category, procurement reductions, and needs, by component, FY80-88, GAO rpt, 26123–220

Reserve personnel social, economic, family, and service characteristics, and attitudes, by reserve component, 1986 survey, 3508–29

Wildlife refuge impacts of recreational, commercial, and military use, by type of activity, 1988-89, GAO rpt, 26113–434

see also Military education

see also Reserve Officers Training Corps

see also Service academies

Military tribunals

see Courts-martial and courts of inquiry

Military vehicles

Budget of DOD, justification, programs, and policies, FY90-91, annual rpt, 3544–2

Budget of DOD, procurement appropriations by item, service branch, and defense agency, FY88-91, annual rpt, 3544–32

Budget of DOD, weapons acquisition costs by system and service branch, FY89-91, annual rpt, 3504–2

Budget of US, object class analysis of obligations, by agency, FY90, annual rpt, 104–9

Energy use by mode of transport, fuel supply, and demographic and economic factors of vehicle use, 1970s-88, annual rpt, 3304–5

Exports of US, detailed commodities by country, monthly rpt, 2422–3

Foreign countries military aid and arms sales of US, by weapon type, as of Sept 1988, annual rpt, 3904–3

Foreign countries military spending, arms trade, and force strengths, with govt spending and population, by country, 1977-87, annual rpt, 9824–1

Imports of US, detailed Schedule A commodities by country, monthly rpt, 2422–2

Manufacturing annual survey, 1986: financial and operating data, by SIC 2- to 4-digit industry, series, 2506–15

Manufacturing census, 1987: financial and operating data, for SIC 4-digit industries by product, preliminary rpt, 2491–1.75; 2491–1.77

Occupational injury and illness rates, by SIC 2- to 4-digit industry, 1987, annual rpt, 6844–1

Oil products sales, and purchases of refiners, processors, and distributors, by product, end-use sector, PAD district, and State, 1988, annual rpt, 3164–85

Procurement cost estimates for weapons and communications systems, by service branch, quarterly summary rpt, 3502–1

Procurement, DOD prime contract awards by category, contract and contractor type, and service branch, FY79-88, semiannual rpt, 3542–1

Procurement, DOD prime contract awards by category, contractor type, and State, FY86-88, annual rpt, 3544–11

Procurement, DOD prime contract awards by detailed procurement category, FY85-88, annual rpt, 3544–18

Shipments by DOD of military and personal property, passenger traffic, and costs, by service branch and mode of transport, quarterly rpt, 3702–1

Soviet Union and Warsaw Pact military weapons systems, aid, presence, and force strengths, and compared to US and NATO, 1989 annual rpt, 3504–20

Warsaw Pact and USSR military strength, and proposed force reductions, with comparisons to NATO, 1980s-91, hearing, 21208–29

Military weapons

Army strategic capability, force strengths, budget, and mgmt, FY80-89, annual rpt, 3704–13

Budget of DOD, justification, programs, and policies, FY90-91, annual rpt, 3544–2

Budget of DOD, organization, personnel, weapons, and property, by service branch, State, and country, 1989 annual summary rpt, 3504–13

Budget of DOD, R&D appropriations by item, service branch, and defense agency, FY88-91, annual rpt, 3544–33

Exports of US, detailed commodities by country, monthly rpt, 2422–3

Foreign countries military aid of US, arms sales, and training programs costs and budget requests, by program, world region, and country, FY88-90, annual rpt, 7144–13

Foreign countries military spending, arms trade, and force strengths, with govt spending and population, by country, 1977-87, annual rpt, 9824–1

Japan weapons equipment levels, by system, planned 1986-90, annual rpt, 3544–28

Manufacturing census, 1987: financial and operating data, for SIC 4-digit industries by product, preliminary rpt, 2491–1.59

Military deaths by cause, age, race, and rank, and personnel captured and missing, by service branch, 2nd half FY88, semiannual rpt, 3542–21

NATO and US weapons and troop strength compared to Warsaw Pact and USSR, annual rpt, discontinued, 3564–1

NATO military forces compared to Warsaw Pact, and selected economic indicators, by country, 1900s-87, conf papers, 3908–6

Pakistan military strengths, spending, weapons systems, and arms imports, with comparisons to India, 1980s-87, hearing, 21388–54

Price indexes (producer), by stage of processing and detailed commodity, monthly 1988, annual rpt, 6764–2

Sealift Military Command shipping operations, finances, and personnel, FY88, annual rpt, 3804–14

Shipments by DOD of military and personal property, passenger traffic, and costs, by service branch and mode of transport, quarterly rpt, 3702–1

Soviet Union and Warsaw Pact military weapons systems, aid, presence, and force strengths, and compared to US and NATO, 1989 annual rpt, 3504–20

Soviet Union economic conditions and military activity, 1960s-86, hearing, 23848–195

Statistical Abstract of US, social, political, and economic data, 1790-2025, comprehensive annual compilation, 2324–1.2

Warsaw Pact and USSR military strength, and proposed force reductions, with comparisons to NATO, 1980s-91, hearing, 21208–29

see also Ammunition

see also Arms trade

see also Chemical and biological warfare agents

see also Defense contracts and procurement

see also Defense expenditures

see also Military aircraft

see also Military assistance

see also Military vehicles

see also Missiles and rockets

see also Naval vessels

see also Nuclear weapons

see also Torpedoes

Militia

see National Guard

Milk and milk products

see Dairy industry and products

Milkove, Daniel L.

"Should Rural Communities Fear Bank Deregulation?", 1502–7.906

Miller, Glenn H.

"Federal Excise Taxes: Approaching Deficit Reduction from the Revenue Side", 9381–1.906

Miller, James J.

"Outlook for Dairy", 1004–16.1

Miller, Joan N.

"U.S. Public Health Service Personnel Monitoring Program, 1986-87", 4064–15

Miller, Louisa F.

"Married-Couple Families with Children", 2546–2.148

Miller, Preston J.

"Gramm-Rudman-Hollings' Hold on Budget Policy: Losing Its Grip?", 9383–6.902

"How Little We Know About Budget Policy Effects", 9371–10.41

"U.S. Economy in 1989 and 1990: Walking a Fine Line", 9383–6.901

Miller, Richard D.

"Helium Resources of the U.S., 1987", 5604–44

Miller, Ted

"Urban-Oriented Program Helped Rural Communities", 1502–7.903

Millionaires

see Wealth

Mills, Leonard O.

"Evaluating Commodity Prices as a Gauge for Monetary Policy", 9387–8.184

"Real and Monetary Explanations of Permanent Movements in GNP", 9387–8.195

Millville, N.J.
see also under By SMSA or MSA in the "Index by Categories"

Milonas, Nikolaos T.
"Examination of GNMA Prepayments", 9316-1.141

Milwaukee, Wis.
CPI by component for US city average, and by region, population size, and for 27 metro areas, monthly rpt, 6762-2

Homeless population characteristics, needs, and impacts of govt aid programs and housing costs, 1988 conf papers, 10048-73

Wages by occupation, for office and plant workers, 1989 survey, periodic MSA rpt, 6785-12.4

see also under By City and By SMSA or MSA in the "Index by Categories"

Mine accidents and safety
Coal mining accidents occuring underground, costs of deaths and work-time lost, 1987, article, 5602-4.903

Coal mining and related operations occupational injuries and incidence, employment, and hours, 1987, annual rpt, 6664-4

Coal mining disabling injuries and deaths, 1937-87, biennial rpt, 3164-79

Coal mining methane emissions control, research results, techniques, and equipment, mid 1960s-79, 5608-156

Coal production and freight costs, and competitive position in selected markets, for Australia and US, 1987-89, 2048-143

Deaths and rates, by cause, age, race, sex, and State, 1986, annual rpt, 4144-2.5

Fed Govt spending in States, by type, program, agency, and State, FY88, annual rpt, 2464-2

Injuries by circumstances, employment, and hours, for mineral industries by type of operation and State, quarterly rpt, 6662-1

Injuries, illnesses, and workdays lost, by SIC 2-digit industry, 1987-88, annual press release, 6844-3

Injuries, workdays lost, and employee characteristics, for mines, 1986, series, 5606-8

Injury and illness rates by SIC 2- to 4-digit industry, and deaths by cause and industry div, 1987, annual rpt, 6844-1

Metal mines and related operations occupational injuries and incidence, employment, and hours, 1987, annual rpt, 6664-3

Nonmetallic minerals mines and related operations occupational injuries and incidence, employment, and hours, 1987, annual rpt, 6664-1

Safety and health enforcement, training, and funding, with casualties, by type of mine and State, FY87, annual rpt, 6664-6

Sand and gravel mines and related operations occupational injuries and incidence, employment, and hours, 1987, annual rpt, 6664-2

Statistical Abstract of US, social, political, and economic data, 1790-2025, comprehensive annual compilation, 2324-1.3

Stone mines and related operations occupational injuries and incidence, employment, and hours, 1987, annual rpt, 6664-5

see also Black lung disease

Mine Safety and Health Administration
Budget of US Appendix, obligations, appropriations, and personnel, by program and agency, FY90, annual rpt, 104-3

Coal mining and related operations occupational injuries and incidence, employment, and hours, 1987, annual rpt, 6664-4

Enforcement activities of MSHA, training, and funding, with casualties, by type of mine and State, FY87, annual rpt, 6664-6

Expenditures of Fed Govt in States, by type, program, agency, and State, FY88, annual rpt, 2464-2

Injuries by circumstances, employment, and hours, for mineral industries by type of operation and State, quarterly rpt, 6662-1

Metal mines and related operations occupational injuries and incidence, employment, and hours, 1987, annual rpt, 6664-3

Nonmetallic minerals mines and related operations occupational injuries and incidence, employment, and hours, 1987, annual rpt, 6664-1

Sand and gravel mines and related operations occupational injuries and incidence, employment, and hours, 1987, annual rpt, 6664-2

Stone mines and related operations occupational injuries and incidence, employment, and hours, 1987, annual rpt, 6664-5

Mineral Industry Surveys
Explosives and blasting agents use, by type, industry, and State, 1988, annual rpt, 5614-22

Phosphate rock production, sales, trade, and use, 1989, annual rpt, 5614-20

Potash production, prices, trade by country, use, and sales, 1988 crop year, annual rpt, 5614-19

Production of minerals, 1988, annual preliminary rpt, 5614-6

Production, trade, stocks, and use of minerals, monthly commodity rpt series, 5612-1

Production, trade, stocks, and use of minerals, quarterly commodity rpt series, 5612-2

Production, trade, use, and industry operations, advance annual commodity rpt series, 5614-5

Stone (dimension) trade and price indexes by selected country, 1987, annual rpt, 5614-29

Supply, demand, and foreign and US production, by commodity, annual rpt series, discontinued, 5614-28

Mineral leases
Alaska land area by ownership, and availability for mineral exploration and dev, 1986, 5608-152

Coal and other fossil fuel production on Federal land, 1988 and trends from 1949, annual rpt, 3164-74.1

Coal leasing activity on Federal and Indian lands, acreage, production, and revenues, by State, 1981-87, biennial rpt, 3164-79

Coal leasing activity on Federal land, acreage, production, and reserves, by coal region and State, FY88, annual rpt, 5724-10

Expenditures of Fed Govt in States, by type, program, agency, and State, FY88, annual rpt, 2464-2

Fed Govt receipts by source and outlays by agency, *Treasury Bulletin*, quarterly rpt, 8002-4.1

Flow-of-funds accounts, savings, investments, and credit statements, quarterly rpt, 9365-3.3

Forest Service activities and finances, by region and State, FY88, annual rpt, 1204-1.1

Forests (natl) revenue, by source, forest, and State, FY88, annual rpt, 1204-34

Land Mgmt Bur activities and funding by State, and receipts by program, FY87, annual rpt, 5724-13

Multinatl firms US affiliates finances and operations, by industry div, country of parent firm, and State, 1986-87, annual article, 2702-1.925

Multinatl firms US affiliates, finances, and operations, by industry, world area of parent firm, and State, 1987, annual rpt, 2704-4

Offshore oil, gas, and minerals production, revenue, and leasing activity, for Federal OCS lands by ocean area and State, 1950s-87, annual rpt, 5734-3

Production and revenue from oil, gas, and minerals on Federal and Indian lands, by State, 1988 and trends from 1920, annual rpt, 5734-2

Public lands acreage and use, and Land Mgmt Bur activities and finances, annual State rpt series, 5724-11

Public lands acreage, grants, use, revenues, and allocations, by State, FY88 and trends, annual rpt, 5724-1

Public lands minerals resources and availability, State rpt series, 5606-7

Southeastern US land and mineral rights ownership by foreigners, by State, 1987, article, 9371-1.913

State and local revenue potential relative to natl average tax burden, by type of tax and State, 1986, annual rpt, 10044-7

Statistical Abstract of US, social, political, and economic data, 1790-2025, comprehensive annual compilation, 2324-1.2

see also Oil and gas leases

Minerals Management Service
Activities of MMS, press release series, 5736-4

Alaska rural villages population characteristics and and subsistence activities, 1976-86, 5738-9

Birds (waterfowl) coastal breeding population and colonies, by species and location for Washington, 1978-82, atlas, 5508-101

Birds (waterfowl) coastal breeding population and colonies, by species and location, 1976-82 surveys, 5508-100

Birds (waterfowl) coastal population, breeding success, and diet, for murre and kittiwake at Cape Thompson, Alaska, 1960s-88, 5738-11

Expenditures of Fed Govt in States, by type, program, agency, and State, FY88, annual rpt, 2464-2

Gulf of Mexico oil and gas leases, by company and tract, 1988, annual rpt, 5734-8

Mineral Industry Surveys, commodity reviews of production, trade, stocks, and use, quarterly rpt series, 5612-2

Mineral Industry Surveys, commodity reviews of production, trade, use, and industry operations, advance annual rpt series, 5614-5

Mineral Industry Surveys, State reviews of production, 1988, preliminary annual rpt, 5614-6

Mineral Industry Surveys, supply, demand, and foreign and US production, by commodity, annual rpt series, discontinued, 5614-28

Minerals Yearbook, 1987, Vol 1: commodity reviews of production, use, trade, prices, and mining operations, annual rpt, 5604-33

Minerals Yearbook, 1987, Vol 1 preprints: commodity reviews of production, reserves, supply, use, and trade, annual rpt series, 5604-15

Minerals Yearbook, 1987, Vol 2 preprints: State reviews of production and sales by commodity, and business activity, annual rpt series, 5604-16

Minerals Yearbook, 1987, Vol 2: State reviews of production, sales, and firms, by commodity, and business activity, annual rpt, 5604-34

Minerals Yearbook, 1987, Vol 3: foreign country reviews of production, trade, and policy, by commodity, annual rpt, 5604-35

Minerals Yearbook, 1987, Vol 3 preprints: foreign country reviews of production, trade, and policy, by commodity, annual rpt series, 5604-23

Minerals Yearbook, 1988, Vol 1: commodity reviews of production, reserves, supply, use, and trade, annual rpt series, 5604-20

Minerals Yearbook, 1988, Vol 2 rpts: State reviews of production and sales by commodity, and business activity, annual rpt series, 5604-22

Multinatl firms US affiliates, finances, and operations, by industry, world area of parent firm, and State, 1987, annual rpt, 2704-4

Multinatl US firms and foreign affiliates finances and operations, by industry of parent firm and affiliate, world area, and country, preliminary 1987, annual rpt, 2704-5

Natl income and product accounts and components, *Survey of Current Business*, monthly rpt, 2702-1.27

OECD trade, total and for 4 major countries, and US trade by country, by commodity, 1970-87, world area rpt series, 9116-1

Ohio River basin waterway facilities, freight by commodity and port, and recreation, by waterway, 1986-87, annual rpt, 3754-6

Pollution (air) levels for 5 pollutants, by detailed source and State, 1986, annual rpt, 9194-7

Price indexes (producer), by stage of processing and detailed commodity, monthly rpt, 6762-6

Price indexes (producer), by stage of processing and detailed commodity, monthly 1988, annual rpt, 6764-2

Producer Price Index, by major commodity group and subgroup, and processing stage, monthly press release, 6762-5

Production indexes, by SIC 2- to 4-digit industry, monthly rpt, 9365-2.10

Production, prices, trade, use, employment, tariffs, and stockpiles, by mineral, with foreign comparisons, 1984-88, annual rpt, 5604-18

Public lands acreage and use, and Land Mgmt Bur activities and finances, annual State rpt series, 5724-11

Public lands minerals resources and availability, State rpt series, 5606-7

Public lands mining claims, patents by type and State, and applications by disposition, 1978-87, GAO rpt, 26113-403

Publications and patents of Mines Bur, monthly listing, 5602-2

Rural areas aid from Fed Govt compared to urban areas, by program and degree of urbanization, FY85, periodic rpt, 1598-248

Rural areas employment, economic conditions, and population characteristics, 1970s-85, compilation of papers, 1598-243

Science and engineering employment and education, and R&D spending, for US and selected foreign countries, 1988, annual rpt, 9624-23.2

Science and engineering employment, by field and industry div, 1977, 1986, and alternative projections to 2000, 9626-2.181

Science and engineering employment, by nonmanufacturing industry and field, 1987, triennial rpt, 9627-31

SEC registration, firms required to file annual rpts, as of Sept 1988, annual listing, 9734-5

Small business establishments, employment, and financial ratios, by SIC 1- to 2-digit industry and State, late 1960s-87, 9768-19

Small business finances, operations, owner and employee characteristics, and Federal contracts, 1980s-88, annual rpt, 9764-6

Southeastern US mining industry output relative to gross State product, by type of mining and State, 1986, article, 9391-16.904

Soviet Union minerals production, trade, and use, by commodity, 1983-87, annual rpt, 5604-39

Statistical Abstract of US, social, political, and economic data, 1790-2025, comprehensive annual compilation, 2324-1.3

Supply, imports, and use of strategic and technologically important minerals, with foreign comparisons, commodity rpt series, 5606-9

Tariff Schedule of US, classifications and rates of duty by detailed imported commodity, 1990 base edition and supplements, 9886-13

Tax (income) returns filed by type of filer, selected income items, quarterly rpt, 8302-2.1

Tax (income) returns for foreign corporate activity in US, assets, and income statement items, by industry div, country, and world area, 1984-85, article, 8302-2.920

Tax (income) returns of corporations, income and tax items by asset size and detailed industry, 1986, annual rpt, 8304-4; 8304-21

Tax (income) returns of partnerships, income statement items by industry group, 1986, annual article, 8302-2.903

Tax (income) returns of sole proprietorships, income statement items, by industry group, 1987, annual article, 8302-2.904; 8302-2.921

Tax expenditures, Federal revenues forgone through income tax deductions and exclusions by type, FY90-94, annual rpt, 21784-10

Transportation census, 1987: trucks, by detailed characteristics, miles traveled, and type of product carried, State rpt series, 2573-1

Wage and benefit changes from collective bargaining and mgmt decisions, by industry div, monthly rpt, 6782-1

Water supply and use, and production, for minerals industries by commodity and State, 1950s-84 and projected to 2000, 5608-153

Wholesale trade census, 1987: employment, establishments, finances, and operations, by SIC 2- to 4-digit kind of business, MSA, county, and city, State rpt series, 2405-1

Wholesale trade sales and inventories, by SIC 2- to 3-digit kind of business, monthly rpt, 2413-7

Wholesale trade sales, inventories, purchases, and gross margins, by SIC 2- to 3-digit kind of business and form of ownership, 1988, annual rpt, 2413-13

Wilderness Natl Preservation System mgmt by Forest Service, regulation of commercial and recreational activities, and ranger views, 1985-88, GAO rpt, 26113-436

see also Aluminum and aluminum industry
see also Cement and concrete
see also Census of Mineral Industries
see also Clay industry and products
see also Coal and coal mining
see also Copper and copper industry
see also Gases
see also Gemstones
see also Gold
see also Iron and steel industry
see also Lead and lead industry
see also Metals and metal industries
see also Mine accidents and safety
see also Mineral leases
see also Natural gas and gas industry
see also Nonmetallic minerals and mines
see also Offshore mineral resources
see also Offshore oil and gas
see also Oil shale
see also Petroleum and petroleum industry
see also Phosphate
see also Potash
see also Radioactive materials
see also Severance taxes
see also Silver
see also Stockpiling
see also Stone products and quarries
see also Strategic materials
see also Tar sands
see also Tin and tin industry
see also Uranium

see also Zinc and zinc industry

see also under By Commodity in the "Index by Categories"

see also under By Industry in the "Index by Categories"

Minimum income

see Income maintenance

Minimum wage

Fair Labor Standards Act minimum wage rates, 1938-87, annual rpt, 4744-3.1

Farm labor wage surveys to set minimum wage for US and alien workers, evaluation with data by location, 1980s-87, GAO rpt, 26131-50

Foreign countries labor conditions, union coverage, and work accidents, annual country rpt series, 6366-4

Labor laws enacted, by State, 1988, annual article, 6722-1.904

Poverty level labor force earnings characteristics, and adjusted minimum wage values, 1967-87, article, 6722-1.948

Statistical Abstract of US, social, political, and economic data, 1790-2025, comprehensive annual compilation, 2324-1.3

Mining

see Mine accidents and safety

see Mines and mineral resources

Minneapolis, Minn.

CPI by component for US city average, and by region, population size, and for 27 metro areas, monthly rpt, 6762-2

Drug abuse indicators for selected metro areas, research results, data collection, and policy issues, 1989 semiannual conf, 4492-5

Housing and households characteristics, 1985 survey, MSA fact sheet, 2485-11.8

Housing and households detailed characteristics, and unit and neighborhood quality, by location, 1985 survey, MSA rpt, 2485-6.5

Housing starts and completions authorized by building permits in 40 MSAs, quarterly rpt, 2382-9

Older frail persons HMO case mgmt and home care services, demonstration projects enrollment, 1986, article, 4652-1.913

Wages by occupation, for office and plant workers, 1989 survey, periodic MSA rpt, 6785-12.4

see also under By City and By SMSA or MSA in the "Index by Categories"

Minnesota

Agriculture census, 1987: farms, farmland, production and costs, and operator characteristics, advance State and county rpts, 2330-1.27

Agriculture census, 1987: farms, farmland, production, finances, and operator characteristics, by county, final State rpt, 2331-1.23

Bank deposits in FDIC-insured commercial and savings banks, by instn, State, and county, as of June 1988, annual regional rpt, 9295-3.5

Business and economic conditions, Fed Reserve 9th District, quarterly journal, 9383-19

Children (handicapped) requiring home care, Medicaid applications disposition under income waiver program, for Minnesota, 1985-87, article, 4042-3.944

County Business Patterns, 1987: employment, establishments, and payroll, by SIC 2- to 4-digit industry and county, annual State rpt, 2326-8.25

Criminal sentencing guidelines use and results, for Minnesota, 1978-84, 6066-20.20

Dairy prices, by product and selected area, with related marketing data, 1988, annual rpt, 1317-1

Deaths and rates, by detailed location, cause, and demographic characteristics, 1987, US Vital Statistics annual rpt, 4144-3.1

DOD prime contract awards, by contractor, service branch, State, and city, FY88, annual rpt, 3544-22

Economic conditions, Fed Reserve 9th District, quarterly rpt, 9383-18

Employment, earnings, and hours, by selected SIC 1- to 4-digit industry, State, and for 262 MSAs, 1972-87, 6748-81.3

Fed Govt spending in States and local areas, by type, State, county, and city, FY88, annual rpt, 2464-3

Fed Govt spending in States, by type, program, agency, and State, FY88, annual rpt, 2464-2

Head Start program operations, enrollment by handicap, and family characteristics, for North Central States, 1987/88, annual rpt, 4604-12

HHS financial aid, by program, recipient, State, and city, FY88, annual regional listing, 4004-3.5

Homeless children educational enrollment and needs, 1988, annual State rpt, 4804-35.23

Income (personal) per capita and by source, and earnings by industry div, by State, MSA, and county, 1982-87, annual regional rpt, 2704-2.3

Mineral Industry Surveys, State reviews of production, 1988, preliminary annual rpt, 5614-6

Minerals Yearbook, 1987, Vol 2 preprints: State review of production and sales by commodity, and business activity, annual rpt, 5604-16.24

Minerals Yearbook, 1987, Vol 2: State reviews of production, sales, and firms, by commodity, and business activity, annual rpt, 5604-34

Nursing home compliance with Medicare and Medicaid regulations, and patient characteristics, by facility, 1987/88, annual State rpt, 4654-15.24

Retail trade census, 1987: employment, establishments, sales, and payroll, by SIC 2- to 4-digit kind of business, MSA, county, and city, State rpt, 2397-1.24

Savings instns, FHLB 8th District members financial operations by State and SMSA, monthly rpt, 9302-9

Service industries census, 1987: employment, establishments, receipts, and payroll, by SIC 2- to 4-digit kind of business, MSA, county, and city, State rpt, 2391-1.24

Statistical Abstract of US, social, political, and economic data, with foreign comparisons, 1790-2025, comprehensive annual compilation, 2324-1

Water supply and quality in streams and lakes, and groundwater levels in wells, by drainage basin, 1986, annual State rpt, 5666-23.22

Wholesale trade census, 1987: employment, establishments, finances, and operations, by SIC 2- to 4-digit kind of business, MSA, county, and city, State rpt, 2405-1.24

Wildlife-related recreation, hunting, and fishing participation and spending, detailed data, 1985 survey, quinquennial State rpt, 5506-6.23

see also Hennepin County, Minn.

see also Minneapolis, Minn.

see also St. Cloud, Minn.

see also St. Paul, Minn.

see also under By State in the "Index by Categories"

Minority Business Development Agency

Budget appropriations and staff for Commerce Dept, by subagency, FY88-90, annual rpt, 2004-6

Budget of US Appendix, obligations, appropriations, and personnel, by program and agency, FY90, annual rpt, 104-3

Fed Govt funding of minority businesses, by program and agency, FY86-88, annual rpt, 2104-5

Franchise business opportunities by firm and kind of business, and sources of aid and info, annual listing, suspended, 2044-27

Mgmt and financial aid from Minority Business Dev Centers, and characteristics of businesses, by region and State, FY88, annual rpt, 2104-6

Minority businesses

Advertising spending of Fed Govt, and subcontracts to small and disadvantaged firms, by agency and medium, FY86, GAO rpt, 26113-428

Agriculture census, 1987: farms, farmland, production, finances, and operator characteristics, by county, final State rpt series, 2331-1

AID contracts to minority and women-owned businesses, awards and goals, FY88, annual rpt, 9904-1.2

Banks minority-owned, selected assets and liabilities, 1987, annual rpt, 9364-5.11

Defense Fuel Supply Center procurement, prices, stocks, transport, and other activities and finances, FY88, annual rpt, 3904-8

DOD contractor subcontract awards to small and disadvantaged business, by firm and service branch, quarterly rpt, 3542-17

DOE contracts and grants, by category, State, and for top contractors, FY88, annual rpt, 3004-21

Fed Govt contracts and obligations for small business, by program and recipient type, for North Carolina and total US, FY77-87, hearings, 21728-67

Fed Govt financial and nonfinancial domestic aid, 1989 base edition with supplements, annual listing, 104-5

Fed Govt funding of minority businesses, by program and agency, FY86-88, annual rpt, 2104-5

Fed Govt procurement contract awards, by procurement and contractor type, agency, State, and for top 100 contractors, quarterly rpt, 102-6

Fed Govt small business construction contracts, surety bonds use and fraud cases, by agency, 1985-89, GAO rpt, 26113-438

Hwy construction contracts awards of States to minority- and women-owned firms, FY85-88, GAO rpt, 26113-399

Hwy construction contracts for Federal-aid system, awards to minority- and women-owned businesses, FHwA and State reviews, FY83-87, GAO rpt, 26113-389

Mgmt and financial aid from Minority Business Dev Centers, and characteristics of businesses, by region and State, FY88, annual rpt, 2104-6

NASA procurement contract awards, by type, contractor, State, and country, FY89, semiannual rpt, 9502-6

Navy procurement awards to disadvantaged and women-owned businesses, FY88, annual rpt, 3804-13.3

Navy small and disadvantaged business procurement offices and location, 1988 annual listing, 3804-5

NIH activities, funding by program and recipient type, staff, and clinic patients, by inst, FY87, annual rpt, 4434-3

R&D funding by Fed Govt to small business, by program area, agency, and State, FY88, annual rpt, 9764-7

R&D grants of Fed Govt to small business, administrators views on effectiveness, FY86-87, GAO rpt, 26113-393

Small Business Admin loan and contract activity by program and firm, and financial condition, FY88, annual rpt, 9764-1

Small business establishments, operations, owner characteristics, and job training, late 1950s-87, 9768-20

Small business finances, operations, owner and employee characteristics, and Federal contracts, 1980s-88, annual rpt, 9764-6

Small business financial and technical aid of States, 1988 listing, 9768-15

Small Business Investment Companies capital holdings, SBA obligation, and ownership, as of June 1989, semiannual listing, 9762-4

Small Business Investment Companies disbursements, by State, 1983-87, GAO rpt, 26113-417

Small Business Investment Companies finances, funding, licensing, and loan activity, 1st half FY89, semiannual rpt, 9762-3

Statistical Abstract of US, social, political, and economic data, 1790-2025, comprehensive annual compilation, 2324-1.3

Telecommunications industries purchases from minority- and women-owned businesses, 1986-87, hearings, 21368-113

see also Survey of Minority-Owned Business Enterprises

Minority Enterprise Small Business Investment Companies

see Small Business Investment Companies

Minority groups

Aerospace industry minority employment in Los Angeles area, by occupational group, 1980s-86, 21348-113

AFDC recipients demographic and financial characteristics, by State, FY87, annual rpt, 4694-1

Alcohol use, abuse, treatment, and views of racial and ethnic groups in US and native countries, by selected characteristics, 1988 compilation of papers, 4488-12

Alcohol use and abuse among minority groups, and related problems, by selected characteristics, 1985 conf papers, 4488-13

Arrest rates, by offense, sex, age, and race, 1987, annual rpt, 6224-7

Arts Natl Endowment activities and grants, FY88, annual rpt, 9564-3

Cancer (bladder) risk for men in selected occupations, by employment characteristics, 1977-78, article, 4472-1.925

Child health and welfare programs of local agencies for high-risk infants and children, for Los Angeles and San Francisco, 1988 hearing, 21968-48

Community dev programs of HUD, funding and activities by program and State, FY88, annual rpt, 5124-5

Community dev work-study program of HUD, students and awards by sponsor instn, 1988-89, press release, 5006-3.64

Defense Fuel Supply Center procurement, prices, stocks, transport, and other activities and finances, FY88, annual rpt, 3904-8

Developing countries disaster preparedness and economic, population, and political data, country rpt series, 9916-2

DOT activities by subagency, budget, and summary accident data, FY85, annual rpt, 7304-1

Education data compilation, students, staff, finances, and facilities, 1989 edition, annual rpt, 4824-2

Education data, selected performance and financial indicators by State, 1982-88, annual table with supplements, 4804-32

Education Dept programs funding, operations, and effectiveness, FY88, annual rpt, 4804-5

Education of minorities, schools participating in natl surveys, 1969-88, listing, 4828-38

Employment of minorities and women, by occupation, SIC 1- to 3- digit industry, State, and MSA, 1986, annual rpt, 9244-1

Engineering PhD awards to US and foreign students, and minority bachelors and masters degree recipients, 1977-87, 9626-2.182

Fed Govt civilian employment of minorities and women, by pay grade, 1976-86, 9848-37

Fed Govt employment of minorities and women by occupation, and handicapped employment, by agency, FY87, annual rpt, 9244-10

Fed Govt employment of minorities, handicapped, and veterans, and years of service, by occupation, age, sex, and agency, as of Sept 1988, biennial rpt, 9844-27

Foreign countries economic, social, political, and geographic summary data, by country, 1989, annual factbook, 9114-2

Foreign Service minority and women employment, hires, and promotions, 1981-87, GAO rpt, 26123-247

Health Professions Bur training and research grants and contracts, by instn and program, FY88, annual listing, 4114-1

Health Professions Bur training support grants, by program, region, and State, FY80-87, 4118-62

Heart, Lung, and Blood Natl Inst activities, and grants by recipient and location, FY88 with disease trends from 1940, annual rpt, 4474-15

Household composition, income, benefits, and labor force status, Survey of Income and Program Participation methodology, working paper series, 2626-10

Income and economic status of minority groups and women, and discrimination and govt policy impacts, series, 11046-7

Infant deaths, causes, and prevention, recommendations and findings, 1988 rpt, 15838-1

NASA staff characteristics and personnel actions, FY88, annual rpt, 9504-1

Older persons health care services use related to marital status, living arrangements, and other characteristics, 1977, 4188-54

Population size of minority groups, and components of change, by race, State, metro-nonmetro location, MSA, and county, 1980-85, Current Population Rpt, 2546-3.159

Science and engineering grad enrollment, by field, source of funds, and characteristics of student and instn, 1975-87, annual rpt, 9627-7

Science and engineering PhDs employment and other characteristics, by field and State, 1987, biennial rpt, 9627-18

Sexually transmitted disease cases among minorities, by race, 1988, article, 4042-3.954

SSA activities, and OASDHI admin, 1930s-89 and projected to 2063, data compilation, annual rpt, 4704-12

SSA minority, handicapped, and women employees, by pay grade, FY88, annual rpt, 4704-6

St Louis metro area local govt finances, structure, and service delivery, mid-1980s, 10046-9.1

State Dept and Foreign Service minority and women employment, FY88, annual rpt, 7004-21

Statistical Abstract of US, social, political, and economic data, with foreign comparisons, 1790-2025, comprehensive annual compilation, 2324-1

Telecommunications industries minority employment and discrimination charges, with data by industry and selected firm, 1970s-88, hearings, 21368-113

Tuberculosis cases among minorities, by age and race, 1987, article, 4042-3.962

see also Alaska Natives

see also Asian Americans

see also Black Americans

see also Black students

see also Civil rights

see also Hispanic Americans

see also Indians

see also Minority businesses

see also Pacific Islands Americans

see also Racial discrimination

see also Survey of Minority-Owned Business Enterprises

see also under By Race and Ethnic Group in the "Index by Categories"

Minority-Owned Business Enterprise Survey

see Survey of Minority-Owned Business Enterprises

Minshall, G. Wayne
"Ecology of Stream and Riparian Habitats
of the Great Basin Region: A Community
Profile", 5506–9.39
Mint
see Spices and herbs
Mint Bureau
see U.S. Mint
Miscarriage
see Fetal deaths
Mishawaka, Ind.
see also under By SMSA or MSA in the
"Index by Categories"
Missiles and rockets
County Business Patterns, 1987:
employment, establishments, and payroll,
by SIC 2- to 4-digit industry and county,
annual State rpt series, 2326–8
DOD budget justification, programs, and
policies, FY88-91, annual rpt, 3544–2
DOD budget, organization, personnel,
weapons, and property, by service branch,
State, and country, 1989 annual summary
rpt, 3504–13
DOD budget, procurement appropriations
by item, service branch, and defense
agency, FY88-91, annual rpt, 3544–32
DOD budget, weapons acquisition costs by
system and service branch, FY89-91,
annual rpt, 3504–2
DOD outlays and obligations, by function
and service branch, quarterly rpt, 3542–3
DOD prime contract awards, by category,
contract and contractor type, and service
branch, FY79-88, semiannual rpt, 3542–1
DOD prime contract awards, by category,
contractor type, and State, FY86-88,
annual rpt, 3544–11
DOD prime contract awards, by detailed
procurement category, FY85-88, annual
rpt, 3544–18
DOD prime contract awards, by size and
type of contract, service branch,
competitive status, category, and labor
standard, FY88, annual rpt, 3544–19
DOD procurement cost estimates for
weapons and communications systems, by
service branch, quarterly summary rpt,
3502–1
Employment, earnings, and hours, by SIC 1-
to 4-digit industry, monthly 1983-Feb
1989, annual rpt, 6744–4
Foreign countries military aid and arms
sales of US, by weapon type, as of Sept
1988, annual rpt, 3904–3
Foreign countries military spending, arms
trade, and force strengths, with govt
spending and population, by country,
1977-87, annual rpt, 9824–1
Manufacturers finances and operations, by
SIC 2- to 4-digit industry, forecast 1989
and trends from 1950s, annual rpt,
2044–28
Manufacturing annual survey, 1986: value of
shipments, by SIC 4- to 5-digit product
class, 2506–15.3
Manufacturing census, 1987: financial and
operating data, for SIC 4-digit industries
by product, preliminary rpt, 2491–1.76
NATO and Japan military spending and
indicators of ability to support common
defense, by country, 1960s-87, annual rpt,
3544–28
Soviet Union and Warsaw Pact military
weapons systems, aid, presence, and force
strengths, and compared to US and
NATO, 1989 annual rpt, 3504–20

Soviet Union space program activities, plans,
and characteristics of flights and vehicles,
1981-87, 25268–76
Missing persons and runaways
Arrests, by offense, offender characteristics,
and location, 1970s-87, annual rpt,
6064–6.4
Arrests, by offense, offender characteristics,
and location, 1988, annual rpt, 6224–2.2
Children abducted and murdered by
strangers, and rates, by victim sex, age,
and race, 1976-84, 6066–27.1
Detention and correctional instns for
juveniles, inmates, and expenses, by instn
and resident characteristics and State,
1975-85, biennial rpt, 6064–13
Fed Govt funding for juvenile delinquency
prevention, by program and agency,
FY88, annual rpt, 6064–11
HHS financial aid, by program, recipient,
State, and city, FY88, annual regional
listings, 4004–3
Juvenile court delinquency cases, by offense,
referral source, disposition, age, sex, race,
State, and county, 1985, annual rpt,
6064–12
Juvenile delinquent and status offenses, by
sex, race, age, income, and urban-rural
location, 1976-80 surveys, annual rpt,
6064–6.3
Juvenile offenders recidivism rates, arrests,
and court referrals, by offense, age, and
sex, 1983 local area studies, 6068–227
Military deaths by cause, age, race, and
rank, and personnel captured and missing,
by service branch, 2nd half FY88,
semiannual rpt, 3542–21
Youth (homeless and runaway) programs,
funding, activities, and participant
characteristics, FY86, annual rpt, 4604–3
Mission, Tex.
see also under By SMSA or MSA in the
"Index by Categories"
Mississippi
Agriculture census, 1987: farms, farmland,
production and costs, and operator
characteristics, advance State and county
rpts, 2330–1.28
Agriculture census, 1987: farms, farmland,
production, finances, and operator
characteristics, by county, final State rpt,
2331–1.24
Appalachian Regional Commission funding,
by project and State, planned FY89,
annual rpt, 9084–3
Bank deposits in FDIC-insured commercial
and savings banks, by instn, State, and
county, as of June 1988, annual regional
rpt, 9295–3.4
Collective bargaining calendar for
southeastern States, 1989, annual rpt,
6946–1.73
County Business Patterns, 1987:
employment, establishments, and payroll,
by SIC 2- to 4-digit industry and county,
annual State rpt, 2326–8.26
Deaths and rates, by detailed location,
cause, and demographic characteristics,
1987, US Vital Statistics annual rpt,
4144–3.1
DOD prime contract awards, by contractor,
service branch, State, and city, FY88;
annual rpt, 3544–22
Economic indicators by State and MSA,
Fed Reserve 6th District, quarterly rpt,
9371–14

Employment and unemployment, for 8
southeastern States, 1987-88, annual rpt,
6944–2
Employment by industry div, earnings, and
hours, for 8 southeastern States, quarterly
press release, 6942–7
Employment, earnings, and hours, by
selected SIC 1- to 4-digit industry, State,
and for 262 MSAs, 1972-87, 6748–81.3
Fed Govt spending in States and local areas,
by type, State, county, and city, FY88,
annual rpt, 2464–3
Fed Govt spending in States, by type,
program, agency, and State, FY88, annual
rpt, 2464–2
Fish and shellfish catch, wholesale receipts,
prices, trade, and other market activities,
weekly regional rpt, 2162–6.3
HHS financial aid, by program, recipient,
State, and city, FY88, annual regional
listing, 4004–3.4
Homeless children educational enrollment
and needs, 1988, annual State rpt,
4804–35.24
Hospitals and community health centers in
Mississippi, and use, staff, and Medicare
and other payments, 1988 hearing,
25548–97
Income (personal) per capita and by source,
and earnings by industry div, by State,
MSA, and county, 1982-87, annual
regional rpt, 2704–2.4
Lumber and paper industries productivity,
impact on economy, and employment
compared to other industries, 1970s-80,
State rpt, 1206–36.13
Mineral Industry Surveys, State reviews of
production, 1988, preliminary annual rpt,
5614–6
Minerals Yearbook, 1987, Vol 2 preprints:
State review of production and sales by
commodity, and business activity, annual
rpt, 5604–16.25
Minerals Yearbook, 1987, Vol 2: State
reviews of production, sales, and firms, by
commodity, and business activity, annual
rpt, 5604–34
Nursing home compliance with Medicare
and Medicaid regulations, and patient
characteristics, by facility, 1987/88,
annual State rpt, 4654–15.25
Radionuclide concentrations in air, water,
humans, animals, and milk near Nevada
and other nuclear test sites, 1988, annual
rpt, 9194–17
Retail trade census, 1987: employment,
establishments, sales, and payroll, by SIC
2- to 4-digit kind of business, MSA,
county, and city, State rpt, 2397–1.25
Savings instns, FHLB 9th District members
finances and operations by State, monthly
rpt, 9302–13
Savings instns, FHLB 9th District members
finances and operations by State, quarterly
rpt, 9302–31
Service industries census, 1987:
employment, establishments, receipts, and
payroll, by SIC 2- to 4-digit kind of
business, MSA, county, and city, State
rpt, 2391–1.25
Statistical Abstract of US, social, political,
and economic data, with foreign
comparisons, 1790-2025, comprehensive
annual compilation, 2324–1

Textile mill employment, earnings, and hours, for 8 Southeastern States, quarterly press release, 6942–1

Water runoff for streams draining eastern Mississippi coastal plain, 1939-85, 5668–85

Water supply and quality in streams and lakes, and groundwater levels in wells, by drainage basin, 1987, annual State rpt, 5666–10.23

Water supply and quality in streams and lakes, and groundwater levels in wells, by drainage basin, 1988, annual State rpt, 5666–16.23

Wholesale trade census, 1987: employment, establishments, finances, and operations, by SIC 2- to 4-digit kind of business, MSA, county, and city, State rpt, 2405–1.25

Wildlife-related recreation, hunting, and fishing participation and spending, detailed data, 1985 survey, quinquennial State rpt, 5506–6.24

see also Biloxi, Miss.

see also Columbus, Miss.

see also Gulfport, Miss.

see also Jackson, Miss.

see also Meridian, Miss.

see also Pascagoula, Miss.

see also Vicksburg, Miss.

see also under By State in the "Index by Categories"

Mississippi River

Army Corps of Engineers water resources dev projects, characteristics, and costs, 1950s-87, biennial State rpt, 3756–2.15; 3756–2.18; 3756–2.43

Army Corps of Engineers water resources dev projects, characteristics, and costs, 1950s-87, biennial State rpt series, 3756–2

Army Corps of Engineers water resources dev projects, characteristics, and costs, 1950s-89, biennial State rpt series, 3756–1

Estuary environmental conditions, research results and methodology, 1989 local area rpt, 2176–7.13

Freight (waterborne domestic), by major commodity group, vessel type, and port, 1986, annual rpt, 7704–7

Freight (waterborne domestic), by major commodity group, 1981-86, annual rpt, 3754–1.1

Freight (waterborne domestic and foreign) by commodity, traffic, and passengers, by port and waterway, 1987, annual rpt, 3754–3.2

Water supply and quality in streams and lakes, and groundwater levels in wells, by drainage basin, 1986, annual State rpt series, 5666–23

Water supply and quality in streams and lakes, and groundwater levels in wells, by drainage basin, 1987, annual State rpt series, 5666–10

Water supply and quality in streams and lakes, and groundwater levels in wells, by drainage basin, 1988, annual State rpt series, 5666–16

Water supply in US and southern Canada, streamflow, surface and groundwater conditions, and reservoir levels, by location, monthly rpt, 5662–3

Missouri

Agriculture census, 1987: farms, farmland, production and costs, and operator characteristics, advance State and county rpts, 2330–1.29

Agriculture census, 1987: farms, farmland, production, finances, and operator characteristics, by county, final State rpt, 2331–1.25

Bank deposits in FDIC-insured commercial and savings banks, by instn, State, and county, as of June 1988, annual regional rpt, 9295–3.5

Coal production and mines by county, prices, productivity, miners, reserves, and stocks, by mining method and State, 1987-88, annual rpt, 3164–25

County Business Patterns, 1987: employment, establishments, and payroll, by SIC 2- to 4-digit industry and county, annual State rpt, 2326–8.27

Deaths and rates, by detailed location, cause, and demographic characteristics, 1987, US Vital Statistics annual rpt, 4144–3.1

DOD prime contract awards, by contractor, service branch, State, and city, FY88, annual rpt, 3544–22

Economic and banking conditions, for Fed Reserve 8th District, quarterly rpt with articles, 9391–16

Employment, earnings, and hours, by selected SIC 1- to 4-digit industry, State, and for 262 MSAs, 1972-87, 6748–81.3

Fed Govt spending in States and local areas, by type, State, county, and city, FY88, annual rpt, 2464–3

Fed Govt spending in States, by type, program, agency, and State, FY88, annual rpt, 2464–2

HHS financial aid, by program, recipient, State, and city, FY88, annual regional listing, 4004–3.7

Homeless children educational enrollment and needs, 1988, annual State rpt, 4804–35.25

Income (personal) per capita and by source, and earnings by industry div, by State, MSA, and county, 1982-87, annual regional rpt, 2704–2.3

Mineral Industry Surveys, State reviews of production, 1988, preliminary annual rpt, 5614–6

Minerals Yearbook, 1987, Vol 2 preprints: State review of production and sales by commodity, and business activity, annual rpt, 5604–16.26

Minerals Yearbook, 1987, Vol 2: State reviews of production, sales, and firms, by commodity, and business activity, annual rpt, 5604–34

Nursing home compliance with Medicare and Medicaid regulations, and patient characteristics, by facility, 1987/88, annual State rpt, 4654–15.26

Retail trade census, 1987: employment, establishments, sales, and payroll, by SIC 2- to 4-digit kind of business, MSA, county, and city, State rpt, 2397–1.26

Savings instns, FHLB 8th District members financial operations by State and SMSA, monthly rpt, 9302–9

Service industries census, 1987: employment, establishments, receipts, and payroll, by SIC 2- to 4-digit kind of business, MSA, county, and city, State rpt, 2391–1.26

Statistical Abstract of US, social, political, and economic data, with foreign comparisons, 1790-2025, comprehensive annual compilation, 2324–1

Water supply and quality in streams and lakes, and groundwater levels in wells, by drainage basin, 1987, annual State rpt, 5666–10.24

Wholesale trade census, 1987: employment, establishments, finances, and operations, by SIC 2- to 4-digit kind of business, MSA, county, and city, State rpt, 2405–1.26

Wildlife-related recreation, hunting, and fishing participation and spending, detailed data, 1985 survey, quinquennial State rpt, 5506–6.25

see also Kansas City, Mo.

see also St. Louis, Mo.

see also under By State in the "Index by Categories"

Missouri River

Army Corps of Engineers water resources dev projects, characteristics, and costs, 1950s-87, biennial State rpt series, 3756–2

Army Corps of Engineers water resources dev projects, characteristics, and costs, 1950s-89, biennial State rpt series, 3756–1

Freight (waterborne domestic and foreign) by commodity, traffic, and passengers, by port and waterway, 1987, annual rpt, 3754–3.2

Water supply and quality in streams and lakes, and groundwater levels in wells, by drainage basin, 1986, annual State rpt series, 5666–23

Water supply and quality in streams and lakes, and groundwater levels in wells, by drainage basin, 1987, annual State rpt series, 5666–10

Water supply and quality in streams and lakes, and groundwater levels in wells, by drainage basin, 1988, annual State rpt series, 5666–16

Water supply in US and southern Canada, streamflow, surface and groundwater conditions, and reservoir levels, by location, monthly rpt, 5662–3

Mitchell, Janet B.

"To Sign or Not To Sign: Physician Participation in Medicare, 1984", 4652–1.902

Mobile, Ala.

Estuary environmental conditions, research results and methodology, 1989 local area rpt, 2176–7.12

Freight (waterborne domestic and foreign) by commodity, traffic, and passengers, by port and waterway, 1987, annual rpt, 3754–3.2

see also under By City and By SMSA or MSA in the "Index by Categories"

Mobile homes

American Housing Survey: unit and households detailed characteristics, and unit and neighborhood quality, MSA rpt series, 2485–6

American Housing Survey: unit and households detailed characteristics, and unit and neighborhood quality, 1985, biennial rpt, 2485–12

County Business Patterns, 1987: employment, establishments, and payroll, by SIC 2- to 4-digit industry and county, annual State rpt series, 2326–8

Employment, earnings, and hours, by SIC 1- to 4-digit industry, monthly 1983-Feb 1989, annual rpt, 6744–4

Energy conservation (housing) program of BPA, energy savings and indoor air quality under alternative methods, projected 1986-2006, 3228–9

Energy use, costs, and conservation, and household and housing characteristics, survey rpt series, 3166–7

Exports of US, detailed commodities by country, monthly rpt, 2422–3

Finance companies assets, liabilities, and credit and leasing activities, monthly rpt, 9365–2.7

Flow-of-funds accounts, savings, investments, and credit statements, quarterly rpt, 9365–3.3

Housing and households summary characteristics, 1985 and trends, biennial chartbook, 2486–1.7

Injuries from use of consumer products, by severity, victim age, and detailed product, 1988, annual rpt, 9164–6

Loan activity of FSLIC-insured savings instns by FHLB district and State, and for FDIC-insured savings banks, 1988, annual rpt, 8434–1

Loans for mobile homes, monthly rpt, 23842–1.5

Loans for mobile homes outstanding, *Survey of Current Business*, monthly rpt, 2702–1.6

Loans outstanding, and terms, by lender and credit type, monthly rpt, 9365–2.6

Manufacturing annual survey, 1986: financial and operating data, by SIC 2- to 4-digit industry, series, 2506–15

Manufacturing census, 1987: financial and operating data, for SIC 4-digit industries by product, preliminary rpt, 2491–1.24; 2491–1.75

Mortgage insurance programs of HUD, finances and lending activity by program, FY88, annual rpt, 5004–8

New single and multifamily units, by structural and financial characteristics, inside-outside MSAs, and region, 1984-88, annual rpt, 2384–1

North Central States, FHLB 7th District housing vacancy rates for single and multifamily units and mobile homes, by ZIP code, annual MSA rpt series, 9304–18

Occupational injury and illness rates and workdays lost in mobile home industry, by selected State, 1978-87, article, 6722–1.932

Occupational injury and illness rates, by SIC 2- to 4-digit industry, 1987, annual rpt, 6844–1

Pacific Northwest population, households, employment, income, and fuel prices, alternative projections 1990-2010 with trends from 1960, annual rpt, 3224–5

Price indexes (producer), by stage of processing and detailed commodity, monthly rpt, 6762–6

Price indexes (producer), by stage of processing and detailed commodity, monthly 1988, annual rpt, 6764–2

Retail trade census, 1987: employment, establishments, sales, and payroll, by SIC 2- to 4-digit kind of business, MSA, county, and city, State rpt series, 2397–1

Safety standards for mobile homes, biennial rpt, suspended, 5004–4

Science, engineering, and technical employment in transportation, utilities, and retail and wholesale trade, by field, occupation, and industry, 1985, triennial rpt, 9627–32

Shipments and PPI for mobile homes, bimonthly rpt, 2042–1.2; 2042–1.5

Shipments of mobile homes, by State, monthly rpt, quarterly table, 2382–5

Shipments of mobile homes, by State, 1986-88, annual rpt, 2384–2

Shipments of mobile homes, dealer inventories, and home characteristics, by region, and placements and prices by State, monthly rpt, 2382–1

Shipments of mobile homes, production, production workers, and finances, 1970s-89, annual article, 2042–1.902

Shipments of mobile homes, *Survey of Current Business*, monthly rpt, 2702–1.3

South Central States, FHLB 9th District housing vacancy rates for single and multifamily units and mobile homes by ZIP code, annual MSA rpt series, 9304–19

Statistical Abstract of US, social, political, and economic data, 1790-2025, comprehensive annual compilation, 2324–1.3

Supplemental Security Income beneficiaries, assets by type and eligibility class, FY87, article, 4742–1.922

VA activities and programs, monthly rpt, 8602–3; 9922–2

VA loan guarantee operations, quarterly rpt, 8602–2

West Central States, FHLB 10th District housing vacancy rates for single and multifamily units and mobile homes, by ZIP code, annual MSA rpt series, 9304–22

Western States, FHLB 11th District housing vacancy rates for single and multifamily units and mobile homes, by ZIP code, annual MSA rpt series, 9304–20

Western States, FHLB 12th District housing vacancy rates for single and multifamily units and mobile homes, by ZIP code, annual MSA rpt series, 9304–21

see also Recreational vehicles

Mobile radio

Cellular telephones from Japan at less than fair value, injury to US industry, investigation with background financial and operating data, investigation supplement, 1989 rpt, 9886–14.252

Finances, operations, and industry devs for telecommunications, with data by service type, firm, and country, 1950s-80s, 2808–27

Licensing activities of FCC, by class of operation, FY88, annual rpt, 9284–4

Manufacturers finances and operations, by SIC 2- to 4-digit industry, forecast 1989 and trends from 1950s, annual rpt, 2044–28

Price indexes (producer), by stage of processing and detailed commodity, monthly rpt, 6762–6

Price indexes (producer), by stage of processing and detailed commodity, monthly 1988, annual rpt, 6764–2

Telephone firms borrowing under Rural Telephone Program, and financial and operating data, 1988, annual rpt, 1244–2

Telephone firms mobile operations and revenue, 1987, annual rpt, 9284–6.3; 9284–6.4

Weather (marine) forecast areas, and broadcast schedules and stations worldwide, as of Nov 1988, annual rpt, 2184–3

Mobile telephones
see Mobile radio

Mobility
see Labor mobility
see Migration
see Mobility limitations

Mobility limitations

AIDS deaths, by health and other characteristics, 1986, 4146–8.178

Birthweight relation to child health condition, indicators for low and normal weight by age, sex, mothers education, and race, 1981, article, 4042–3.904

Board and care homes licensing and inspection by States, and client characteristics, 1989 GAO rpt, 26121–275

Bus (intercity) route in Nebraska, indicators of need, finances, and service and funding alternatives, 1980s, 7888–76

Cardiovascular diseases cases, health care services use and costs, and productivity losses, by selected characteristics, 1980, 4146–12.26

Cases of acute and chronic conditions, disability, absenteeism, and health services use, by selected characteristics, 1988, annual rpt, 4147–10.170

Children (handicapped) enrollment by age, and special education programs staff, funding, and needs, by type of handicap and State, 1987/88, annual rpt, 4944–4

Educational enrollment of disabled in postsecondary instns, by disability, educational, and other characteristics, fall 1986, 4846–3.6

Head Start handicapped enrollment, by handicap, State, and for Indian and migrant programs, 1985/86, annual rpt, 4604–1

Health condition and health care resources, use, and spending, 1950s-87, annual data compilation, 4144–11

Labor force health condition and services use, by occupation and industry of longest job held, income, age, sex, and race, 1980, 4147–10.168

Labor force health condition, disability days, health services use, and disease prevalence, by occupation and sex, 1983-85, 4146–8.170

Nursing home and home care case mix, quality of care, and outcomes, impacts of Medicare prospective payment system, 1980s-86, 4658–28

Nursing home compliance with Medicare and Medicaid regulations, and patient characteristics, by facility, 1987/88, annual State rpt series, 4654–15

Nursing home facility, staff, and resident detailed characteristics, 1985, 4147–13.97

Nursing home rehabilitation services use, by service type and patient characteristics, 1st qtr 1983, 4188–58

Nursing home reimbursement by Medicare under prospective payment system, and admissions by prior hospitalization status and duration, and patient characteristics, mid 1970s-85, 4147–13.98

Nursing home use rates, charges, and resident length of stay, care needs, and other characteristics, 1985, 4147–13.102

Older persons functional limitations, by activity type and selected characteristics, 1984, 4147–10.167

Older persons health care services use related to marital status, living arrangements, and other characteristics, 1977, 4188–54

Older persons health condition, chronic and multiple illness prevalence by sex and age group, 1984, 4146–8.172

Older persons socioeconomic characteristics, 1900s-86 and projected to 2050, biennial chartbook, 12904–1

Older persons transportation requirements, by urban-rural location and mobility limitation status, projected 2000, annual rpt, 25144–3.1

Older persons with functional limitations, long-term health care needs, and costs by payment source, 1982-85, GAO rpt, 26121–266

Statistical Abstract of US, social, political, and economic data, 1790-2025, comprehensive annual compilation, 2324–1.1

see also Architectural barriers to the handicapped

Mobs
see Riots and disorders

Models
see Demonstration and pilot projects
see Economic and econometric models
see Mathematic models and modeling

Modems
see Telecommunication

Modesto, Calif.
see also under By City and By SMSA or MSA in the "Index by Categories"

Modigliani, Andre
"Growth of the Federal Deficit and the Role of Public Attitudes", 21528–72

Modigliani, Franco
"Growth of the Federal Deficit and the Role of Public Attitudes", 21528–72

Moeller, John F.
"Prescribed Medicines: A Summary of Use and Expenditures by Medicare Beneficiaries. National Medical Expenditure Survey", 4186–8.3

Moen, Jon R.
"Poverty in the South", 9371–1.903

Moffatt, Ronald E.
"Oceanographic Data Exchange, 1987", 2144–15

Mohair
see Wool and wool trade

Molasses
see Sugar industry and products
see Syrups and sweeteners

Moline, Ill.
Wages by occupation, and benefits for office and plant workers, 1989 survey, periodic MSA rpt, 6785–12.3
see also under By SMSA or MSA in the "Index by Categories"

Molybdenum
see Metals and metal industries

Monaco
Economic, social, political, and geographic summary data, by country, 1989, annual factbook, 9114–2

Population size, growth rates, and components of change, by country, projected 1989-2020 and trends from 1950, biennial rpt, 2324–9
see also under By Foreign Country in the "Index by Categories"

Monaco, Mark E.
"Distribution and Abundance of Fishes and Invertebrates in Texas Estuaries", 2176–7.16

"Estuarine Living Marine Resources Project, Washington State Component", 2176–7.7

"Living Marine Resources Component, Preliminary West Coast Study", 2176–7.1

Monahan, James L.
"From Homogeneity to Heterogeneity: An Index of Diversification", 2626–2.58

Monetary Control Act
Money supply relation to monetary base, impact of financial instn reserve and operating requirements under Act, 1973-88, article, 9391–1.923

Monetary policy
Banks in Fed Reserve System, expenses and operations itemized by service, office, and district, 1988, annual rpt, 9364–11

Banks reserve requirements relation to interest rates, various periods 1882-1987, technical paper, 9379–12.43

Capital flows (intl) impacts on monetary policy instruments, and financial and economic indicators, 1987 compilation of papers, 9385–9

Current account balance of US, components and relation to foreign and US investment and economic conditions, 1970s-88 and projected to 1990s, article, 9385–1.906

Current account deficit, and impacts of alternative fiscal and monetary policies, 1980-88 and projected to 1999, 26306–6.135

Dollar exchange rate and other economic indicators, impact of fiscal policy under alternative money policy and exchange rate assumptions, 1981-88, article, 9393–8.908

Economic Report of the President for 1989, economic effects of budget proposals, and trends and projections, 1929-99, annual hearings, 23844–4

Economic Report of the President for 1989, Joint Economic Committee critique and policy recommendations, annual rpt, 23844–2

Economic Report of the President for 1989, with economic trends from 1929, annual rpt, 204–1

Exchange rate variability impact of monetary policy, for West Germany and France, model description and results, 1973-88, working paper, 9387–8.181

Fed funds rate relation to monetary policy, bank loans, and other economic indicators, 1959-88, working paper, 9387–8.189

Fed funds rates, impact of discretionary monetary policy, various periods 1979-82, article, 9389–1.905; 9389–19.7

Fed Reserve Board and Reserve banks finances, staff, and review of monetary policy and economic devs, 1988, annual rpt, 9364–1

Fed Reserve monetary policy objectives, and performance of major economic indicators, as of July 1989, semiannual rpt, 9362–4

Fed Reserve monetary policy objectives and US and foreign economic indicators, 1988 hearing, 25248–109

Fed Reserve System, Board of Governors, and district banks financial statements, performance, and fiscal services, 1987-89, annual rpt, 9364–10

Financial and economic analysis of banking and nonbanking sectors, working paper series, 9381–10

Financial and economic analysis, technical paper series, 9379–12; 9389–19; 9393–10

Financial and economic devs, Fed Reserve Bank of Dallas bimonthly journal, 9379–1

Financial and economic devs, Fed Reserve Bank of Minneapolis quarterly journal, 9383–6

Financial and economic devs, Fed Reserve Bank of New York quarterly journal, 9385–1

Financial and economic devs, Fed Reserve Bank of Philadelphia bimonthly journal, 9387–1

Financial and economic devs, Fed Reserve Bank of St Louis bimonthly journal, 9391–1

Forecasts of monetary policy targets and inflation, performance of commodity price indexes, with regression results, 1950s-87, working paper, 9381–10.91

Foreign and US economic conditions and trade devs and policy, 1988 conf papers, 9373–3.32

Foreign countries economic and monetary trends, compounded annual rates of change and monetary targets for US and 10 major trading partners, quarterly rpt, 9391–7

Germany (West) money supply impact of central bank foreign exchange intervention, various periods 1978-88, article, 9391–1.924

Germany (West) money supply target and actual growth rates, 1975-89, article, 9381–1.907

Income distribution relation to fiscal and monetary policy, alternative regression results, 1947-86, technical paper, 9379–12.41

Inflation and other monetary policy target forecasting performance, impact of commodity prices, model description and results, 1959-87, working paper, 9387–8.184

Inflation forecasting performance of commodity price indexes, alternative regression results, 1954-88, article, 9389–1.902

Inflation forecasting performance of M1, monetary base, and commodity price index, 1960s-87, working paper, 9371–10.35

Interest rate impact of foreign financial conditions, 1979-87, article, 9385–1.901

Monetary aggregate (M2) relation to income, interest rates, and other economic indicators, various periods 1946-89, article, 9389-1.913

Monetary policy targets, performance of source base and adjustments for reserve requirements as measures of monetary base, various dates 1979-89, article, 9379-1.903

Oil price changes, impact on monetary policy relation to economic indicators, model description and results, 1956-87, working paper, 9387-8.193

Stock yields relation to inflation and monetary policy, 1969-87, technical paper, 9379-12.37

Switzerland franc exchange rate against dollar and German mark, impact of monetary policy, 1973-86, article, 9391-1.907

see also Credit
see also Fiscal policy
see also Foreign exchange
see also Inflation
see also Money supply

Money market funds
see Mutual funds

Money supply

Australia monetary aggregates forecasts, performance of alternative models, late 1960s-87, technical paper, 9366-6.169

Banking panics relation to production and business cycle, with data for NYC, 1857-1933, article, 9391-1.915

Budget of US, CBO analysis of revenue and spending alternatives and projections of economic indicators, FY90-94, annual rpt, 26304-3

Business Conditions Digest, cyclical indicators, by economic process, monthly rpt, 2702-3.3

Business statistics, detailed data for major industries and economic indicators, Survey of Current Business, monthly rpt, 2702-1.6

Consumer spending related to cash holdings, interest rates, and other economic indicators, 1950s-86, technical paper, 9379-12.38

Currency and coin outstanding and in circulation, by type and denomination, Treasury Bulletin, quarterly rpt, 8002-4.16

Current account deficit, and impacts of alternative fiscal and monetary policies, 1980-88 and projected to 1999, 26306-6.135

Economic indicators and components, and Fed Reserve 4th District business and financial conditions, monthly chartbook, 9377-10

Economic indicators and components, current data and annual trends, monthly rpt, 23842-1.5

Economic indicators compounded annual rates of change, 1969-88, annual rpt, 9391-9.1

Economic indicators, monthly table, 9302-26

Economic indicators targets and performance, 1960s-88 and projected to 1994, annual article, 9381-1.901

Fed funds rates, impact of discretionary monetary policy, various periods 1979-82, article, 9389-1.905; 9389-19.7

Fed Reserve costs of new currency, by item, 1987-89, annual rpt, 9364-10

Fed Reserve monetary policy objectives, and performance of major economic indicators, as of July 1989, semiannual rpt, 9362-4

Financial and business statistics, historic trends, 1988 annual chartbook, 9364-2.1

Financial and economic analysis and forecasting methodology, technical paper series, 9366-6

Financial and economic analysis, technical paper series, 9385-8; 9393-10

Financial and economic devs, Fed Reserve Bank of St Louis bimonthly journal, 9391-1

Financial and monetary conditions, selected US summary data, weekly rpt, 9391-4

Financial instns deregulation impact on monetary policy targets, 1960s-88, article, 9379-1.905

Financial markets response to money supply changes, regression results, late 1970s-84, working paper, 9371-10.32

Forecasts of inflation and unemployment, performance of commodity price indexes, with regression results and forecast errors, 1965-88, article, 9393-8.902

Forecasts of monetary policy targets and inflation, performance of commodity price indexes, with regression results, 1950s-87, working paper, 9381-10.91

Forecasts of money supply, impacts of monetary target announcements on accuracy, for US and Japan, 1978-88, working paper, 9393-10.8

Foreign countries economic and monetary trends, compounded annual rates of change for US and 10 major trading partners, quarterly rpt, 9391-7

Foreign countries economic conditions and implications for US, periodic country rpt series, 2046-4

Germany (West) money supply impact of central bank foreign exchange intervention, various periods 1978-88, article, 9391-1.924

GNP correlation with monetary base and other economic indicators, 1959-88, article, 9377-1.906

GNP forecasting performance of alternative monetary base measures, 1959-87, technical paper, 9379-12.32

GNP, interest rate, and introduction of interest on checking accounts and other financial change indicators, impact on M1 and M2, 1952-88, article, 9389-1.912

GNP relation to alternative measures of monetary reserves, model description and results, 1959-89, technical paper, 9379-12.46

Inflation forecasting performance of financial and nonfinancial indicators, model description and results, 1970s-88, article, 9373-1.916

Inflation forecasting performance of money supply and other economic indicators, with inflation rates in 15 countries, 1960s-1988 and forecast to 1990, article, 9379-1.906

Inflation forecasting performance of M1, monetary base, and commodity price index, 1960s-87, working paper, 9371-10.35

Inflation relation to monetary aggregates velocity, for US and 39 countries, various periods 1908-87, working paper, 9377-9.74

Inflation relation to M2, GNP, and interest rates, various periods 1952-88, working paper, 9389-19.10

Interest and inflation rates impact of unanticipated changes in money supply, industrial production, and inflation, 1959-86, technical paper, 9379-12.34

Interest rate expectations impact of money supply growth, model description and results, 1950s-87, working paper, 9387-8.177

Interest rates, Fed funds rate, and GNP relation to money supply growth rates, various periods 1964-88, article, 9362-1.903

Interest rates relation to inflation and money supply, 1954-87, working paper, 9387-8.187

Interest rates relation to intl rates, exchange rates, and US money supply, for 7 OECD countries, 1979-88, article, 9391-1.920

Monetary aggregate (M2) relation to income, interest rates, and other economic indicators, various periods 1946-89, article, 9389-1.913

Monetary aggregates and money stock, 1984-87, annual rpt, 9364-5.1

Monetary aggregates and velocities, monthly rpt, 9362-6

Monetary aggregates components, with estimation data sources and availability of time series, as of 1988, article, 9389-1.906

Monetary aggregates, money stock measures and components, monthly rpt, 9362-1.1

Monetary aggregates targeted and actual growth, and Fed funds rate, 1987-89, annual article, 9391-1.908

Monetary and Fed Govt budget trends, Fed Reserve Bank of St Louis monthly rpt, 9391-2

Money stock components, 1959-88, annual rpt, 204-1.5

OECD current account balance and related economic indicators, for US and 4 countries, 1980s-87, article, 9389-1.908

OECD economic conditions for 6 countries and US, biweekly rpt, 9112-1

Statistical Abstract of US, social, political, and economic data, 1790-2025, comprehensive annual compilation, 2324-1.3

see also Coins and coinage
see also Counterfeiting and forgery
see also Credit
see also Eurocurrency
see also Flow-of-funds accounts
see also Foreign exchange
see also Monetary policy
see also Special foreign currency programs

Mongolia

Agricultural and food production and indexes, total and for selected commodities, by country, 1970s-88, annual rpt, 1524-12

Agricultural trade of US, by detailed commodity and country, 1988, semiannual rpt, 1522-4

Cuba economic conditions, agricultural and industrial production and distribution, trade, and intl economic relations, 1980-87 with trends from 1961, 9118-8

Economic, social, political, and geographic summary data, by country, 1989, annual factbook, 9114–2

Exports and imports of US with Communist countries, by detailed commodity and country, quarterly rpt with articles, 9882–2

Human rights conditions in 170 countries, 1988, annual rpt, 21384–3

Military spending, arms trade, and force strengths, with govt spending and population, by country, 1977-87, annual rpt, 9824–1

Minerals production, reserves, and industry role in domestic economy and world supply, 1988 country rpt, 5606–1.17

Minerals Yearbook, 1987, Vol 3: foreign country reviews of production, trade, and policy, by commodity, annual rpt, 5604–35

Minerals Yearbook, 1987, Vol 3 preprints: foreign country review of production, trade, and policy, by commodity, annual rpt, 5604–23.85

Population size, growth rates, and components of change, by country, projected 1989-2020 and trends from 1950, biennial rpt, 2324–9

UN voting record and share of votes in agreement with US, by issue, country, and world area, 1988, annual rpt, 7004–18

see also under By Foreign Country in the "Index by Categories"

Monheit, Alan C.
"Health Insurance Coverage of Retired Persons. National Medical Expenditure Survey", 4186–8.2

Monmouth County, N.J.
Wages by occupation, for office and plant workers, 1989 survey, periodic MSA rpt, 6785–12.4

see also under By SMSA or MSA in the "Index by Categories"

Monopolies and cartels
see also Antitrust law
see also Organization of Petroleum Exporting Countries

Monroe County, N.Y.
Medicare enrollees health care alternatives, medical costs, training to select assigned-fee physicians, and physician attitudes, 1988 rpt, 4658–30

Monroe, La.
see also under By SMSA or MSA in the "Index by Categories"

Montana
Agriculture census, 1987: farms, farmland, production and costs, and operator characteristics, advance State and county rpts, 2330–1.30

Agriculture census, 1987: farms, farmland, production, finances, and operator characteristics, by county, final State rpt, 2331–1.26

Bank deposits in FDIC-insured commercial and savings banks, by instn, State, and county, as of June 1988, annual regional rpt, 9295–3.6

Bears (grizzly) in Yellowstone Natl Park area, monitoring results, 1988, annual rpt, 5544–4

Business and economic conditions, Fed Reserve 9th District, quarterly journal, 9383–19

Coal production and mines by county, prices, productivity, miners, reserves, and stocks, by mining method and State, 1987-88, annual rpt, 3164–25

County Business Patterns, 1987: employment, establishments, and payroll, by SIC 2- to 4-digit industry and county, annual State rpt, 2326–8.28

Deaths and rates, by detailed location, cause, and demographic characteristics, 1987, US Vital Statistics annual rpt, 4144–3.1

DOD prime contract awards, by contractor, service branch, State, and city, FY88, annual rpt, 3544–22

Economic conditions, Fed Reserve 9th District, quarterly rpt, 9383–18

Employment, earnings, and hours, by selected SIC 1- to 4-digit industry, State, and for 262 MSAs, 1972-87, 6748–81.3

Farm operators displaced worker programs under Job Training Partnership Act, funding, participation, and results by selected State, 1982-87, 15496–1.2

Fed Govt spending in States and local areas, by type, State, county, and city, FY88, annual rpt, 2464–3

Fed Govt spending in States, by type, program, agency, and State, FY88, annual rpt, 2464–2

HHS financial aid, by program, recipient, State, and city, FY88, annual regional listing, 4004–3.8

Homeless children educational enrollment and needs, 1988, annual State rpt, 4804–35.26

Income (personal) per capita and by source, and earnings by industry div, by State, MSA, and county, 1982-87, annual regional rpt, 2704–2.5

Indian reservation crimes and enforcement activity in Montana, and Bur of Indian Affairs law enforcement officers training, 1985-87, GAO rpt, 26113–402

Indian social services funding by Federal, State, and tribal agencies, with reservation land property tax, for Montana, FY87, GAO rpt, 26121–257

Lumber production from damaged and dead timber, feasibility of proposed Montana plant, 1989 rpt, 1208–308

Mineral Industry Surveys, State reviews of production, 1988, preliminary annual rpt, 5614–6

Minerals Yearbook, 1987, Vol 2 preprints: State review of production and sales by commodity, and business activity, annual rpt, 5604–16.27

Minerals Yearbook, 1987, Vol 2: State reviews of production, sales, and firms, by commodity, and business activity, annual rpt, 5604–34

Nursing home compliance with Medicare and Medicaid regulations, and patient characteristics, by facility, 1987/88, annual State rpt, 4654–15.27

Oil and gas leasing activity on Federal land, production, revenue, and royalty rates, by whether competitively leased and western State, 1984-88, GAO rpt, 26113–413

Population, households, employment, income, and fuel prices, for Pacific Northwest, alternative projections 1990-2010 with trends from 1960, annual rpt, 3224–5

Retail trade census, 1987: employment, establishments, sales, and payroll, by SIC 2- to 4-digit kind of business, MSA, county, and city, State rpt, 2397–1.27

Savings instns, FHLB 12th District members deposits and lending, monthly press release, 9302–32.4

Service industries census, 1987: employment, establishments, receipts, and payroll, by SIC 2- to 4-digit kind of business, MSA, county, and city, State rpt, 2391–1.27

Statistical Abstract of US, social, political, and economic data, with foreign comparisons, 1790-2025, comprehensive annual compilation, 2324–1

Timber in northwestern US and British Columbia, production, prices, trade, and employment, quarterly rpt, 1202–3

Water supply and quality in streams and lakes, and groundwater levels in wells, by drainage basin, 1987, annual State rpt, 5666–10.25

Water supply, and snow survey results, monthly State rpt, 1266–2.5

Water supply, and snow survey results, 1988, annual State rpt, 1264–14.8

Water supply in Montana, precipitation, snow cover, and reservoir storage, by river basin, annual rpt, discontinued, 1264–7

Wholesale trade census, 1987: employment, establishments, finances, and operations, by SIC 2- to 4-digit kind of business, MSA, county, and city, State rpt, 2405–1.27

Wildlife-related recreation, hunting, and fishing participation and spending, detailed data, 1985 survey, quinquennial State rpt, 5506–6.26

see also Billings, Mont.

see also under By State in the "Index by Categories"

Monterey, Calif.
Housing vacancy rates for single and multifamily units and mobile homes, by city and ZIP code, 1988, annual MSA rpt, 9304–20.4

see also under By SMSA or MSA in the "Index by Categories"

Montgomery, Ala.
Wages by occupation, for office and plant workers, 1989 survey, periodic MSA rpt, 6785–3.4

see also under By City and By SMSA or MSA in the "Index by Categories"

Montgomery County, Md.
Fed Govt land acquisition and dev projects in DC metro area, characteristics and funding by agency and project, FY90-94, annual rpt, 15454–1

Police pay, benefits, and staffing, for US Park Police and compared to other Federal and local police units, FY85-88, GAO rpt, 26119–264

Montgomery County, Pa.
Housing and households detailed characteristics, and unit and neighborhood quality, by location, 1985 survey, MSA rpt, 2485–6.8

Montgomery, John M., Jr.
"Price Competitiveness Issues", 1004–16.1

Montgomery, Rhonda J.
"Respite Care: Lessons from a Controlled Design Study", 4652–1.916

Montreal, Canada

Fruit and vegetable shipments, and arrivals in US and Canada cities, by mode of transport and State and country of origin, 1988, annual rpt, 1311–4.1

Monuments and memorials

Acreage of land under Forest Service mgmt, by forest and location, 1988, annual rpt, 1204–2

Acreage of land under Natl Park Service mgmt, by site, ownership, and region, 1989 semiannual rpt, 5542–1

Damaged and threatened natl historic and natural landmarks, with owner, location, damage type, and recommended remedial action, 1988, annual listing, 5544–16

Inventory and costs of real property owned by Fed Govt, worldwide summary by location, agency, and use, 1987, annual rpt, 9454–5

Visits and overnight stays in natl park system, by park and State, monthly rpt, 5542–4

Visits and overnight stays in natl park system, by park and State, 1988 and trends from 1979, annual rpt, 5544–12

Moolgavkar, Suresh H.

"Cigarette Smoking and Lung Cancer: Reanalysis of the British Doctors' Data", 4472–1.911

Mooney, Michael J.

"Malstrom—The Legend and the Reality", 2152–8.901

Moonlighting

Hours per week and reasons for moonlighting, and worker and primary and other secondary job characteristics, 1989, press release, 6726–1.24

Statistical Abstract of US, social, political, and economic data, 1790-2025, comprehensive annual compilation, 2324–1.3

Teachers moonlighting, by selected employment and other characteristics, 1985, 4838–36

Moore, Charles A.

"Sentencing Guidelines: Their Effect in Minnesota", 6066–20.20

Moore, Dennis

"Alcohol and Other Drug Use Among Orthopedically Impaired College Students", 4482–1.904

Moore, George

"Monetary Policy Rules and the Indicator Properties of Asset Prices", 9366–6.203

"Stability of Wicksell's Monetary Policy Rule", 9366–6.208

Moore, Jeffrey C.

"Using Administrative Record Data To Describe SIPP Response Errors", 2626–10.77

Moore, Linda

"Multifactor Productivity Advances in the Tires and Inner Tubes Industry", 6722–1.928

Moorhead, Minn.

see also under By SMSA or MSA in the "Index by Categories"

Moorman, Jeanne E.

"Married-Couple Families with Children", 2546–2.148

Mor, Vincent

"Awareness of Hospice Services: Results of a National Survey", 4042–3.915

Moran, John S.

"Impact of Sexually Transmitted Diseases on Minority Populations", 4042–3.954

Moran, Larry R.

"Motor Vehicles, Model Year 1988", 2702–1.901

Morbidity

see Diseases and disorders

Morehart, Mitchell J.

"Development and Use of Financial Ratios for the Evaluation of Farm Businesses", 1548–341

"Farm Operating and Financial Characteristics, 1986", 1544–27

"Financial Characteristics of Dairy Farms", 1561–2.902

Morehouse, David

"Summary of 'An Examination of Domestic Natural Gas Resource Estimates'", 3162–4.902

Moreno, Ramon

"Exchange Rates and Trade Adjustment in Taiwan and Korea", 9393–8.905

Morgan, Donald

"Bank Credit Commitments and Credit Rationing", 9381–10.100

Morgan, James J.

"Economic Status of the California Dungeness Crab Fishery in 1986-87", 2164–16.3

Morocco

Agricultural and food production and indexes, total and for selected commodities, by country, 1970s-88, annual rpt, 1524–12

Agricultural exports of Africa by commodity, and relation to economic conditions and other factors, by country, 1960s-87, 1528–280

Agricultural imports and food aid needs under alternative weather assumptions, for 17 African countries, projected to 1995, 1528–279

Agricultural production, prices, and trade, by country, 1960s-89, annual world region rpt, 1524–4.2

Agricultural trade of US, by detailed commodity and country, 1988, semiannual rpt, 1522–4

Agricultural trade of US with Asia, Middle East, and North Africa, by commodity and country, 1962-86, 1528–277

AID activities and funding by project and function, FY90, and developing countries summary socioeconomic data from 1960s, annual rpt, 9904–4.6

AID economic aid to developing countries, obligations and disbursements by country, quarterly rpt, 9912–4

AID loans repayment status and terms by program and country, and status of predecessor agency loans, quarterly rpt, 9912–3

Auto imports from US, trade barriers by country, 1988, annual rpt, 444–2

Background Notes, summary social, political, and economic data, 1989 rpt, 7006–2.48

Economic and military aid and loans from US and intl agencies, by program and country, FY46-87, annual rpt, 9914–5

Economic conditions, income, production, prices, employment, and trade, 1989 periodic country rpt, 2046–4.14

Economic conditions, policy, and trade practices, by country, 1986-88, annual rpt, 21384–5

Economic indicators of developing countries, problem debtors compared to other borrowers, by country, 1973-84, 1528–285

Economic, social, political, and geographic summary data, by country, 1989, annual factbook, 9114–2

Exports and imports of US, by commodity and country, 1970-87, world area rpt, 9116–1.3

Exports and imports of US, by selected country, country group, and commodity group, 1988, annual rpt, 2044–37

Human rights conditions in 170 countries, 1988, annual rpt, 21384–3

Labor conditions, union coverage, and work accidents, 1989 annual country rpt, 6366–4.49

Military aid of US, arms sales, and training programs costs and budget requests, by program, world region, and country, FY88-90, annual rpt, 7144–13

Military spending, arms trade, and force strengths, with govt spending and population, by country, 1977-87, annual rpt, 9824–1

Minerals Yearbook, 1987, Vol 3: foreign country reviews of production, trade, and policy, by commodity, annual rpt, 5604–35

Minerals Yearbook, 1987, Vol 3 preprints: foreign country review of production, trade, and policy, by commodity, annual rpt, 5604–23.50

Phosphate rock exports of Morocco by country of destination, Mineral Industry Surveys, monthly rpt, periodic table, 5612–1.30

Population size, growth rates, and components of change, by country, projected 1989-2020 and trends from 1950, biennial rpt, 2324–9

UN voting record and share of votes in agreement with US, by issue, country, and world area, 1988, annual rpt, 7004–18

see also under By Foreign Country in the "Index by Categories"

Morris, J. Glenn, Jr.

"Foodborne Disease: A Look at a Continuing Problem", 1004–16.1

Mortality

see Accidental deaths

see Child mortality

see Deaths

see Fetal deaths

see Homicide

see Infant mortality

see Life expectancy

see Suicide

see Traffic accident fatalities

see Vital statistics

Mortgages

American Housing Survey: unit and households detailed characteristics, and unit and neighborhood quality, MSA rpt series, 2485–6

American Housing Survey: unit and households detailed characteristics, and unit and neighborhood quality, 1985, biennial rpt, 2485–12

Appalachian States, FHLB 5th District savings instns finances and lending by State, monthly rpt, 9302–8

Assets and debts of private sector, balance sheets by segment, 1949-88, semiannual rpt, 9365–4.1

Savings instns finances and operations by district and State, mortgage lending activity and terms by MSA, and FHLB finances, 1987 with trends from 1900, annual rpt, 9314–3

Savings instns financial statements, FSLIC-insured instns by FHLB district and State, and FDIC-insured savings banks, 1988, annual rpt, 8434–1

Savings instns insured by Savings Assn Insurance Fund, assets, liabilities, and deposit and loan activity, by conservatorship status, monthly rpt, 8432–1

Savings instns regulatory issues, mgmt, and FHLB system and member finances and operations, monthly journal, 8432–2; 9312–1

Securities backed by mortgages and Treasury securities yield spreads, relation to interest rate variability, 1970s-87, technical paper, 9316–1.148

Securities backed by mortgages, corporate and union pension funds and life insurance firms investments, by issuer, quarterly rpt, 5002–10

Securities backed by mortgages, Fed Natl Mortgage Assn pools prepayment rates, Jan 1987-June 1988, article, 9381–1.905

Securities backed by mortgages, Govt Natl Mortgage Assn prepayment rates relation to interest rates and security age, 1983-85, technical paper, 9316–1.141

Servicing of mortgages, transfers among lenders and consumer complaints, 1984-89, GAO rpt, 26113–441

Small business financing sources, and business financial data by size, type, and industry, various periods 1980-88, annual rpt, 9764–6.2

South Central States, FHLB 9th District savings instns finances and operations by State, monthly rpt, 9302–13

South Central States, FHLB 9th District savings instns finances and operations by State, quarterly rpt, 9302–31

Southeastern States, Fed Reserve 5th District, economic indicators by State, quarterly rpt, 9389–16

Southeastern States, Fed Reserve 5th District insured commercial banks financial statements, by State, quarterly rpt, 9389–18

Southeastern States, Fed Reserve 8th District banking and economic conditions, quarterly rpt with articles, 9391–16

Southeastern States, FHLB 4th District savings instns finances, financial ratios, and mortgage loans, by State, quarterly rpt, 9302–3

Southeastern States, FHLB 4th District thrifts finances, by State, 1984-88 annual rpt series, 9304–29

State and local govt retirement systems, cash and security holdings and finances, quarterly rpt, 2462–2

Statistical Abstract of US, social, political, and economic data, 1790-2025, comprehensive annual compilation, 2324–1.3

Tax (income) returns filed by type of filer, selected income items, quarterly rpt, 8302–2.1

Tax (income) returns of corporations, income and tax items by asset size and detailed industry, 1986, annual rpt, 8304–4; 8304–21

Tax (income) returns of individuals, detailed data, 1986, annual rpt, 8304–2

Tax (income) returns of sole proprietorships, income statement items, by industry group, 1987, annual article, 8302–2.904

Tax (income) withholding and related documents filed, by type and IRS service center, 1988 and projected 1989-96, annual rpt, 8304–22

Tax expenditures, Federal revenues forgone through income tax deductions and exclusions by type, FY90-94, annual rpt, 21784–10

Terms on conventional mortgages closed, and commitment rates, by type of loan and lender and for 32 SMSAs, monthly rpt, 8432–3; 9312–2

Terms, yields, secondary market activity, and debt outstanding, monthly rpt, 9362–1.1

Terms, yields, secondary market activity, and debt outstanding, 1984-87, annual rpt, 9364–5.7

Trust assets of banks, trust companies, and S&Ls, by type of asset and fund, selected firm, and State, 1988, annual rpt, 13004–1

UK mortgages, by type of holder, as of Dec 1987, article, 9312–1.901

West Central States, FHLB 10th District savings instns finances and lending by State and MSA, monthly table, 9302–22

West Central States, FHLB 10th District savings instns financial condition, by State, quarterly rpt, 9302–34

Western States, FHLB 11th District S&Ls, offices, and financial condition, 1989 annual listing, 9304–23

Western States, FHLB 12th District savings instns deposits and lending by State, monthly press release series, 9302–32

Wisconsin S&Ls, mortgage interest fixed and adjustable rates and fees offered, monthly rpt, 9302–7

see also Agricultural credit
see also Farm Credit System
see also Veterans housing

Morticians
see Cemeteries and funerals

Morton, Timothy
"Bay Anchovy. Species Profiles: Life Histories and Environmental Requirements of Coastal Fishes and Invertebrates", 5506–8.103

Moskowitz, Warren E.
"Global Asset and Liability Management at Commercial Banks", 9375–14

Moss, Abigail J.
"Hypertension: U.S., 1974", 4147–16.1
"Use of Vitamin and Mineral Supplements in the U.S.: Current Users, Types of Products, and Nutrients", 4146–8.175

Motels
see Hotels and motels

Mothers
see Births
see Breast-feeding
see Families and households
see Fertility
see Maternity
see Maternity benefits
see Parents
see Teenage pregnancy
see Women

Motion pictures
Box office ticket prices, 1963-87, 2808–27

Collective bargaining agreements expiring during year, and workers covered, by firm, union, industry group, and State, 1989, annual rpt, 6784–9

Copyrights Register activities, registrations by material type, and fees, FY87 and trends from 1790, annual rpt, 26404–2

County Business Patterns, 1987: employment, establishments, and payroll, by SIC 2- to 4-digit industry and county, annual State rpt series, 2326–8

Earnings by major industry group, and personal income per capita and by source, by region and State, 1929-87, 2708–40

Employment, earnings, and hours, by selected SIC 1- to 4-digit industry, State, and for 262 MSAs, 1972-87, 6748–81

Employment, earnings, and hours, by SIC 1- to 4-digit industry, monthly 1983-Feb 1989, annual rpt, 6744–4

Employment in nonmanufacturing industries, by detailed occupation and SIC 2-digit industry, 1987, triennial rpt, 6748–60

Exports of US, detailed commodities by country, monthly rpt, 2422–3

Fed Govt audiovisual activities and spending, by whether performed in-house and agency, FY87, annual rpt, 9514–1

Finances and operations, by SIC 2- to 4-digit industry, forecast 1989 with trends from 1950s, annual rpt, 2044–28

Imports of US, detailed Schedule A commodities by country, monthly rpt, 2422–2

Library of Congress activities, acquisitions, services, and financial statements, FY88, annual rpt, 26404–1

Military post exchange operations, and sales by commodity, by facility and location worldwide, FY87, annual rpt, 3504–10

Multinatl US firms and foreign affiliates finances and operations, by industry of parent firm and affiliate, world area, and country, preliminary 1987, annual rpt, 2704–5

Natl Archives and Records Admin activities, finances, holdings, and staff, FY88, annual rpt, 9514–2

Natl Endowment for Arts activities and grants, FY88, annual rpt, 9564–3

Occupational injury and illness rates, by SIC 2- to 4-digit industry, 1987, annual rpt, 6844–1

Price indexes (producer), by stage of processing and detailed commodity, monthly rpt, 6762–6

Receipts for services, by SIC 2- to 4-digit kind of business, 1988, annual rpt, 2413–8

Science and engineering employment, by nonmanufacturing industry and field, 1987, triennial rpt, 9627–31

Service industries census, 1987: establishments, receipts, employment, and payroll, by SIC 2- to 4-digit kind of business, MSA, county, and city, State rpt series, 2391–1

Small business establishments, employment, and financial ratios, by SIC 1- to 2-digit industry and State, late 1960s-87, 9768–19

Motor vehicle industry

Business statistics, detailed data for major industries and economic indicators, *Survey of Current Business*, monthly rpt, 2702–1.20

Cancer (bladder) risk for men in selected occupations, by employment characteristics, 1977-78, article, 4472–1.925

Communist, OECD, and selected other countries consumer and producer goods production, 1960s-88, annual rpt, 9114–4.8

County Business Patterns, 1987: employment, establishments, and payroll, by SIC 2- to 4-digit industry and county, annual State rpt series, 2326–8

Earnings by major industry group, and personal income per capita and by source, by region and State, 1929-87, 2708–40

Economic indicators and components, and Fed Reserve 4th District business and financial conditions, monthly chartbook, 9377–10

Electric power use and prices, shipments, and trade, for 25 SIC 4-digit manufacturing industries, 1972-86, 2048–137

Electric-powered autos, R&D activity and DOE funding shares, FY88, annual rpt, 3304–2

Employment, earnings, and hours, by selected SIC 1- to 4-digit industry, State, and for 262 MSAs, 1972-87, 6748–81

Employment, earnings, and hours, by SIC 1- to 4-digit industry, monthly 1983-Feb 1989, annual rpt, 6744–4

Employment of minorities and women, by occupation, SIC 1- to 3- digit industry, State, and MSA, 1986, annual rpt, 9244–1

Employment, unemployment, and labor force characteristics, by region and census div, 1988, annual rpt, 6744–7.1

Finances and operations, by SIC 2- to 4-digit industry, forecast 1989 with trends from 1950s, annual rpt, 2044–28

Finances and operations of US auto industry, trade by country, and prices of selected US and foreign models, monthly rpt, 9882–8

Financial statements for manufacturing, mining, and trade corporations, by selected SIC 2- to 3-digit industry, quarterly rpt, 2502–1

Foreign and US hourly compensation costs, for motor vehicle and equipment industry by country, 1975-88, 6826–3.3; 6826–3.5

Foreign and US technology dev and competition issues, fundings and recommendations, 1980s-87, 21708–123

Foreign direct investment in North Central States and other US regions by country and major industry group, and for auto industry, 1978-88, working paper, 9375–13.12

Foreign trade zones, applications, and shipments, with data for auto assembly, FY70s-87, GAO rpt, 26123–223

Input-output structure of US economy, detailed interindustry transactions for 84 industries, and components of final demand, 1983, annual article, 2702–1.909

Manufacturing annual survey, 1986: financial and operating data, by SIC 2- to 4-digit industry, series, 2506–15

Manufacturing census, 1987: financial and operating data, for SIC 4-digit industries by product, preliminary rpt, 2491–1.20; 2491–1.58; 2491–1.71; 2491–1.75

Market shares, sales, and fuel economy, by size and model for domestic and foreign makes, 1989 model year, semiannual rpt, 3302–4

Multinatl US firms and foreign affiliates finances and operations, by industry of parent firm and affiliate, world area, and country, preliminary 1987, annual rpt, 2704–5

Natl income and product accounts and components, *Survey of Current Business*, monthly rpt, 2702–1.22

Occupational injury and illness rates, by SIC 2- to 4-digit industry, 1987, annual rpt, 6844–1

Price indexes (producer), by stage of processing and detailed commodity, monthly rpt, 6762–6

Price indexes (producer), by stage of processing and detailed commodity, monthly 1988, annual rpt, 6764–2

Production indexes, by SIC 2- to 4-digit industry, monthly rpt, 9365–2.10

Productivity of labor and capital, and indexes of output, hours, and employment, 1963-87, annual rpt, 6824–1.3; 6824–1.5

R&D funding, and scientists and engineers education and employment, for US and selected foreign countries, 1988, annual rpt, 9624–23.1

Recalls of motor vehicles and equipment with safety-related defects, by make, quarterly listing, 7762–2

Retail trade census, 1987: employment, establishments, sales, and payroll, by SIC 2- to 4-digit kind of business, MSA, county, and city, State rpt series, 2397–1

Science, engineering, and technical employment in manufacturing, by field, occupation, and industry, 1986, triennial rpt, 9627–23

Science, engineering, and technical employment in transportation, utilities, and retail and wholesale trade, by field, occupation, and industry, 1985, triennial rpt, 9627–32

Statistical Abstract of US, social, political, and economic data, 1790-2025, comprehensive annual compilation, 2324–1.3

Steel imports from EC and other countries, impact of voluntary restraint agreements on US user industries exports, sales, and prices, 1989 rpt, 9886–4.138

Tax (income) returns of corporations, income and tax items by asset size and detailed industry, 1986, annual rpt, 8304–4; 8304–21

Wholesale trade census, 1987: employment, establishments, finances, and operations, by SIC 2- to 4-digit kind of business, MSA, county, and city, State rpt series, 2405–1

Wholesale trade sales, inventories, purchases, and gross margins, by SIC 2- to 3-digit kind of business and form of ownership, 1988, annual rpt, 2413–13

see also Automobile repair and maintenance
see also Automobiles
see also Buses
see also Chrysler Corp.
see also Ford Motor Co.
see also General Motors Corp.
see also Motor vehicle exhaust
see also Motor vehicle exports and imports
see also Motor vehicle fleets
see also Motor vehicle registrations
see also Motor vehicle rental
see also Motor vehicle safety devices
see also Motorcycles
see also Recreational vehicles
see also Tires and tire industry
see also Trucks and trucking industry

Motor vehicle registrations

Business statistics, detailed data for major industries and economic indicators, *Survey of Current Business*, monthly rpt, 2702–1.20

Communist, OECD, and selected other countries living standards and commodity production, 1960s-88, annual rpt, 9114–4.1

Costs of operating autos by component, and Fed Govt mileage reimbursement rates, 1988, annual rpt, 9454–13

Costs of owning and operating autos, by component, 1977-88, annual rpt, 7304–2.1

CPI by component for US city average, and by region, population size, and for 27 metro areas, monthly rpt, 6762–2

Energy use by mode of transport, fuel supply, and demographic and economic factors of vehicle use, 1970s-88, annual rpt, 3304–5

Foreign countries transportation energy use, fuel prices, and vehicle registrations, by selected country, 1970s-88, annual rpt, 3304–5.1

Hwy receipts by source, and spending by function, by level of govt and State, 1988, annual rpt, 7554–1.3

Hwy Statistics, summary data by State, 1987-88, annual rpt, 7554–24

Pacific territories social, economic, health, and govtl data, FY88 and trends, annual rpt, 7004–6

Registrations and fuel use, by vehicle type, 1960-88, annual rpt, 3164–74.1

Registrations by public and private ownership and vehicle type, and revenues, by State, 1988, annual rpt, 7554–1.2

Revenue potential of State and local tax systems relative to natl average tax burden, by type of tax and State, 1986, annual rpt, 10044–7

Revenues, by level of govt, type of tax, State, and selected large county, quarterly rpt, 2462–3

Revenues of State govts by detailed source, and tax rates, by State, FY88, annual rpt, 2466–2.3

Sentences for Federal offenses, guidelines by offense and circumstances, 1989 rpt, 17668–1

Statistical Abstract of US, social, political, and economic data, 1790-2025, comprehensive annual compilation, 2324–1.3

Truck interstate carriers finances and operations, by district, 1987, annual rpt, 9486–6.2

Price indexes (producer), by stage of processing and detailed commodity, monthly 1988, annual rpt, 6764–2

Recalls of motor vehicles and equipment with safety-related defects, by make, quarterly listing, 7762–2

Retail trade census, 1987: employment, establishments, sales, and payroll, by SIC 2- to 4-digit kind of business, MSA, county, and city, State rpt series, 2397–1

Statistical Abstract of US, social, political, and economic data, 1790-2025, comprehensive annual compilation, 2324–1.3

Traffic volume in urban areas and detailed trip characteristics, by transport mode and city, 1950s-88, 7888–37

Transportation finances, operations, vehicles, equipment, accidents, and energy use, by mode of transport, 1955-88, annual rpt, 7304–2

Motors

see Engines and motors

Moulton, Brent R.

"Alternative Tests of the Error Components Model", 6886–6.38

"Diagnostics for Group Effects in Regression Analysis", 6886–6.25

"Illustration of a Pitfall in Estimating the Effects of Aggregate Variables on Micro Units", 6886–6.50

"Latent Family Influences on Individual Expenditures for Clothing", 6886–6.61

"Random Group Effects and the Precision of Regression Estimates", 6886–6.26

Mountain-Plains States

see Western States

see under By Region in the "Index by Categories"

Movie industry

see Motion pictures

see Video recordings and equipment

Moyle, Peter B.

"Ecology of the Sacramento-San Joaquin Delta: A Community Profile", 5506–9.38

Mozambique

Agricultural and food production and indexes, total and for selected commodities, by country, 1970s-88, annual rpt, 1524–12

Agricultural production, prices, and trade, by country, 1960s-89, annual world region rpt, 1524–4.2

Agricultural trade of US, by detailed commodity and country, 1988, semiannual rpt, 1522–4

AID activities and funding by project and function, FY90, and developing countries summary socioeconomic data from 1960s, annual rpt, 9904–4.5

AID economic aid to developing countries, obligations and disbursements by country, quarterly rpt, 9912–4

Background Notes, summary social, political, and economic data, 1989 rpt, 7006–2.36

Economic and military aid and loans from US and intl agencies, by program and country, FY46-87, annual rpt, 9914–5

Economic conditions, income, production, prices, employment, and trade, 1989 periodic country rpt, 2046–4.58

Economic conditions, policy, and trade practices, by country, 1986-88, annual rpt, 21384–5

Economic, social, political, and geographic summary data, by country, 1989, annual factbook, 9114–2

Human rights conditions in 170 countries, 1988, annual rpt, 21384–3

Military spending, arms trade, and force strengths, with govt spending and population, by country, 1977-87, annual rpt, 9824–1

Minerals Yearbook, 1987, Vol 3: foreign country reviews of production, trade, and policy, by commodity, annual rpt, 5604–35

Minerals Yearbook, 1987, Vol 3 preprints: foreign country review of production, trade, and policy, by commodity, annual rpt, 5604–23.81

Population size, growth rates, and components of change, by country, projected 1989-2020 and trends from 1950, biennial rpt, 2324–9

UN voting record and share of votes in agreement with US, by issue, country, and world area, 1988, annual rpt, 7004–18

see also under By Foreign Country in the "Index by Categories"

MSA

see Metropolitan Statistical Areas

see under By SMSA or MSA in the "Index by Categories"

Muhn, James

"Opportunity and Challenge: The Story of BLM", 5728–30

Mullally, Joseph C., II

"China Sea Rescue", 2152–8.904

Muller, L. Scott

"Health Insurance Coverage Among Recently Entitled Disability Insurance Beneficiaries: Findings from the New Beneficiary Survey", 4742–1.927

Mullis, Ina V.

"Science Report Card, Elements of Risk and Recovery: Trends and Achievement Based on the 1986 National Assessment", 4898–25

Mullner, Ross M.

"Rural Community Hospitals and Factors Correlated with Their Risk of Closing", 4042–3.930

Multilateral development banks

see African Development Bank

see Asian Development Bank

see Inter-American Development Bank

see International Bank for Reconstruction and Development

Multinational corporations

Banks (insured commercial and savings) finances, for foreign and domestic offices, by asset size, 1987, annual rpt, 9294–4.2

Banks (intl) facilities of foreign and US banks in New York and total US, assets and liabilities, monthly rpt, 9365–2.22

Banks (natl) domestic and intl operations, charters, mergers, and liquidations, by instn and State, quarterly rpt, 8402–3

Banks (US) foreign branches assets and liabilities, by world region and country, quarterly rpt, 9365–3.7

Banks (US) foreign lending at all US and foreign offices, by country group and country, quarterly rpt, 13002–1

Banks balance sheets, by Fed Reserve District, for major banks in NYC, and for US branches and agencies of foreign banks, weekly rpt, 9365–1.3

Capital expenditures of multinatl US firms foreign affiliates, by major industry group, world area, and country, 1984-89, semiannual article, 2702–1.910; 2702–1.933

Cuba trade with multinatl US firms foreign affiliates, by country, FY82-87, press release, 8008–137

Currency (foreign) positions of US firms and foreign branches or affiliates, *Treasury Bulletin*, quarterly rpt, 8002–4.12

Employees of intl corporations transferred to US, by country, FY78-88, annual rpt, 6264–2

Employees of intl corporations transferred to US, quarterly rpt, 6262–2

Energy producers finances and operations, by energy type for US firms domestic and foreign operations, 1987, annual rpt, 3164–44

Energy resources of US, foreign direct investment by energy type and firm, and US affiliates operations, as of 1988, annual rpt, 3164–80

Finances and operations of foreign firms US affiliates, by industry div, country of parent firm, and State, 1986-87, annual article, 2702–1.925

Finances and operations of foreign firms US affiliates, by industry, world area of parent firm, and State, 1987, annual rpt, 2704–4

Finances and operations of multinatl US firms and foreign affiliates, by industry of parent firm and affiliate, world area, and selected country, 1987, annual article, 2702–1.920; 2704–5

Foreign direct investment in US, by industry group and world area, 1987-88, annual article, 2702–1.929

Foreign direct investment in US, major transactions by type, industry, country, and US location, 1987, annual rpt, 2044–20

Foreign direct investment of US, by selected industry group and world area, 1986-88, annual article, 2702–1.930

Imports of US given duty-free treatment for value of US material sent abroad, and impacts on US industry and employment, by commodity and country, 1987, annual rpt, 9884–14

Mexico industrial plants owned by US firms, employment impacts of US and Asia wages, 1975-87, technical paper, 9379–12.45

Ships under foreign flag owned by US firms and foreign affiliates, by type, owner, and country of registry and construction, as of July 1989, semiannual rpt, 7702–3

Southeastern US employment of multinatl firms US affiliates, by industry, State, and country, 1977 and 1987, article, 9371–1.913

Statistical Abstract of US, social, political, and economic data, by outlying area and country, 1950s-87, comprehensive annual compilation, 2324–1.4

Statistical Abstract of US, social, political, and economic data, 1790-2025, comprehensive annual compilation, 2324–1.3

Sweden multinatl firms domestic and foreign production, exports, employment, and sales, with data by commodity and firm, 1960s-86, conf, 23848–208

Tax (income) returns for foreign corporate activity in US, assets, and income statement items, by industry div, country, and world area, 1984-85, article, 8302-2.920

Mulvey, Janemarie J.
"Simulation of the Macroeconomic Effects of the Balanced Budget Amendment", 21528-72

Muncie, Ind.
see also under By SMSA or MSA in the "Index by Categories"

Municipal bonds
Finances of govts, by level of govt, State, and for large cities and counties, annual rpt series, 2466-2
Financial and business statistics, historic trends, 1988 annual chartbook, 9364-2.9
Futures and options trading volume, by commodity and exchange, FY88, annual rpt, 11924-2
Futures trading in selected commodities and financial instruments and indexes, NYC, Chicago, and other markets activity, monthly rpt, 11922-5
Hwy receipts by source, and spending by function, by level of govt and State, 1988, annual rpt, 7554-1.3
Interest rates for commercial paper, govt securities, other financial instruments, and home mortgages, monthly rpt, 9365-2.14
Issues by local govts, 1987, annual rpt, 9364-5.5
Securities industry finances, firms by type, and SEC applications and registrations, 1983-88, annual rpt, 9734-2.1
State and local govt retirement systems, cash and security holdings and finances, quarterly rpt, 2462-2
Trust assets of banks, trust companies, and S&Ls, by type of asset and fund, selected firm, and State, 1988, annual rpt, 13004-1
Yields and interest rates, *Business Conditions Digest*, cyclical indicators, monthly rpt, 2702-3.3
Yields of Treasury, corporate, and municipal long-term bonds, *Treasury Bulletin*, quarterly rpt, 8002-4.8
Yields relation to natl and regional financial indicators and issue and underwriter characteristics, by maturity and bond type, 1977-78, working paper, 9389-19.8

Municipal government
see Census of Governments
see Local government

Municipal taxation
see State and local taxes

Municipal transportation
see Urban transportation

Munnell, Alicia H.
"It's Time To Tax Employee Benefits", 9373-1.913
"Public Pension Surpluses and National Saving: Foreign Experience", 9373-1.905

Munson, Martha L.
"Wanted and Unwanted Births Reported by Mothers 15-44 Years of Age: U.S., 1973", 4147-16.1

Murder
see Homicide

Murphy, J. Austin
"Effect of Interest Rate Volatility on Mortgage Instrument Values", 9316-1.149

"Hedging Fixed-Rate Mortgage Investments Against Interest-Rate Risk", 9316-1.150

Murtaugh, Christopher M.
"Nursing Home Reimbursement and the Allocation of Rehabilitation Therapy Resources", 4188-58

Musculoskeletal diseases
Arthritis patients use of treatments and health products not proven safe or effective, costs, and user characteristics, 1986 survey, 4008-86
Cancer (breast) risk of scoliosis patients x-rayed during childhood, by diagnosis and other characteristics, 1922-86, local area study, article, 4472-1.922
Cancer (osteosarcoma) progress and deaths, by disease and treatment characteristics, 1977-85 study, article, 4472-1.901
Cancer incidence, death, and survival rates, by sex, race, age, and body site, 1973-86, annual rpt, 4474-35
Children (handicapped) enrollment by age, and special education programs staff, funding, and needs, by type of handicap and State, 1987/88, annual rpt, 4944-4
Deaths and rates, by cause, age, sex, marital status, race, and State, 1987, US Vital Statistics advance annual rpt, 4146-5.113
Deaths and rates, by detailed cause and demographic characteristics, 1986 and trends from 1900, US Vital Statistics annual rpt, 4144-2
Dental Research Natl Inst research and training grants, by recipient, FY88, annual listing, 4474-19
Drug and alcohol abuse, and prescription drug use, for disabled college students, local area study, 1989 article, 4482-1.904
Health condition and health care resources, use, and spending, 1950s-87, annual data compilation, 4144-11
HHS financial aid, by program, recipient, State, and city, FY88, annual regional listings, 4004-3
Hospital discharges and length of stay, by diagnosis, patient age and sex, surgical procedure performed, and region, 1965-86, 4147-13.101
Hospital discharges and length of stay, by diagnosis, patient and instn characteristics, procedure performed, and payment source, 1987, annual rpt, 4147-13.99
Hospital discharges by detailed diagnostic and procedure category, primary diagnosis, and length of stay, by age, sex, and region, 1987, annual rpt, 4147-13.100
Indian Health Service and contract facilities hospitalization, by diagnosis, age, sex, and service area, FY87, annual rpt, 4104-16
Indian Health Service and contract facilities hospitalization, by diagnosis, age, sex, and service area, FY88, annual rpt, 4084-5
Nursing home facility, staff, and resident detailed characteristics, 1985, 4147-13.97
Surgical procedures performed, costs, length of stay, and deaths, impacts of Medicare prospective payment system by procedure type, 1984-86, 17206-2.5
see also under By Disease in the "Index by Categories"

Musell, R. Mark
"Productivity Improvement Under the Government's Productivity Improvement Initiative", 26306-3.103

Museums
County Business Patterns, 1987: employment, establishments, and payroll, by SIC 2- to 4-digit industry and county, annual State rpt series, 2326-8
Earnings by major industry group, and personal income per capita and by source, by region and State, 1929-87, 2708-40
Education Dept funding of research libraries, by project, instn, and State, FY88, annual listing, 4874-2
Employment, earnings, and hours, by SIC 1- to 4-digit industry, monthly 1983-Feb 1989, annual rpt, 6744-4
Employment in nonmanufacturing industries, by detailed occupation and SIC 2-digit industry, 1987, triennial rpt, 6748-60
Endangered animals and plants US trade and permits, by species, purpose, disposition, and country, 1987, annual rpt, 5504-19
Fed Govt spending in States, by type, program, agency, and State, FY88, annual rpt, 2464-2
Inst of Museum Services activities and finances, and grants by recipient, FY88, annual rpt, 9564-7
Inst of Museum Services grants, by recipient, FY89, annual press release series, 9564-6
Natl Archives and Records Admin activities, finances, holdings, and staff, FY88, annual rpt, 9514-2
Natl Endowment for Arts activities and grants, FY88, annual rpt, 9564-3
Natl Endowment for Humanities activities and grants, FY88, annual rpt, 9564-2
Occupational injury and illness rates, by SIC 2- to 4-digit industry, 1987, annual rpt, 6844-1
Science and engineering employment, by nonmanufacturing industry and field, 1987, triennial rpt, 9627-31
Service industries census, 1987: establishments, receipts, employment, and payroll, by SIC 2- to 4-digit kind of business, MSA, county, and city, State rpt series, 2391-1
Smithsonian Instn activities and finances, FY88, annual rpt, 29574-1
Statistical Abstract of US, social, political, and economic data, 1790-2025, comprehensive annual compilation, 2324-1.1
see also Botanical gardens
see also Zoological parks

Musgrave, John C.
"Fixed Reproducible Tangible Wealth in the U.S., 1985-88", 2702-1.931

Mushrooms
see Vegetables and vegetable products

Music
Exports of music books and sheet music, by country, monthly rpt, 2422-3
Imports of music books and sheet music, by country, monthly rpt, 2422-2
Industry finances and operations, by SIC 2- to 4-digit industry, forecast 1989 and trends from 1950s, annual rpt, 2044-28

Library of Congress activities, acquisitions, services, and financial statements, FY88, annual rpt, 26404-1

Natl Endowment for Arts activities and grants, FY88, annual rpt, 9564-3

Service industries census, 1987: establishments, receipts, employment, and payroll, by SIC 2- to 4-digit kind of business, MSA, county, and city, State rpt series, 2391-1

Sheet music manufacturers financial and operating data, 1987 Census of Manufactures, preliminary rpt, 2491-1.30

Youth sexual behavior, impact of popular music promoting responsibility, for Latin America, 1986, 9916-3.50

Musical instruments

County Business Patterns, 1987: employment, establishments, and payroll, by SIC 2- to 4-digit industry and county, annual State rpt series, 2326-8

Employment, earnings, and hours, by SIC 1- to 4-digit industry, monthly 1983-Feb 1989, annual rpt, 6744-4

Exports of US, detailed commodities by country, monthly rpt, 2422-3

Imports of US, detailed Schedule A commodities by country, monthly rpt, 2422-2

Injuries from use of consumer products, by severity, victim age, and detailed product, 1988, annual rpt, 9164-6

Manufacturers finances and operations, by SIC 2- to 4-digit industry, forecast 1989 and trends from 1950s, annual rpt, 2044-28

Manufacturing annual survey, 1986: financial and operating data, by SIC 2- to 4-digit industry, series, 2506-15

Manufacturing census, 1987: financial and operating data, for SIC 4-digit industries by product, preliminary rpt, 2491-1.81

Occupational injury and illness rates, by SIC 2- to 4-digit industry, 1987, annual rpt, 6844-1

OECD trade, total and for 4 major countries, and US trade by country, by commodity, 1970-87, world area rpt series, 9116-1

Price indexes (producer), by stage of processing and detailed commodity, monthly rpt, 6762-6

Price indexes (producer), by stage of processing and detailed commodity, monthly 1988, annual rpt, 6764-2

Retail trade census, 1987: employment, establishments, sales, and payroll, by SIC 2- to 4-digit kind of business, MSA, county, and city, State rpt series, 2397-1

Science, engineering, and technical employment in manufacturing, by field, occupation, and industry, 1986, triennial rpt, 9627-23

Wholesale trade census, 1987: employment, establishments, finances, and operations, by SIC 2- to 4-digit kind of business, MSA, county, and city, State rpt series, 2405-1

Muskegon, Mich.

see also under By SMSA or MSA in the "Index by Categories"

Musselman, Bryan L.

"Filing Characteristics of U.S. Passport Applicants Resident Abroad", 8304-8.1

Mutchler, Jan E.

"Resource-Based Model of Living Arrangements Among the Unmarried Elderly", 2626-10.95

Mutual funds

Assets and debts of private sector, balance sheets by segment, 1949-88, semiannual rpt, 9365-4.1

Assets composition, growth, and distribution for financial instns, by instn type, 1970s-88, 8438-1

Assets of trusts under mgmt of banks, trust companies, and S&Ls, by type of asset and fund, selected firm, and State, 1988, annual rpt, 13004-1

Credit unions federally insured, finances by instn characteristics and State, as of June 1989, semiannual rpt, 9532-6

Finances, firms, and SEC registrations and terminations, by type of investment firm, 1983-88, annual rpt, 9734-2.2

Finances of open-end investment companies, monthly 1986-87, annual rpt, 9364-5.6

Flow-of-funds accounts, assets and liabilities by type and economic sector, outstanding at year-end 1965-88, annual rpt, 9364-3

Flow-of-funds accounts, savings, investments, and credit statements, quarterly rpt, 9365-3.3

Industry finances and operations, by SIC 2- to 4-digit industry, forecast 1989 and trends from 1950s, annual rpt, 2044-28

OECD economic conditions for 6 countries and US, biweekly rpt, 9112-1

Securities (tax-exempt) holdings by investor type, and IRS enforcement of disallowance of interest deduction for financing holdings, mid 1970s-87, GAO rpt, 26119-239

Statistical Abstract of US, social, political, and economic data, 1790-2025, comprehensive annual compilation, 2324-1.3

Transactions and new issue registrations, monthly rpt, 9732-1

Myanmar

see Burma

Mycoses

see Infective and parasitic diseases

Mye, L. Randolph

"Caribbean and Central American Export Performance, 1980-87", 2048-138

Myers, Forest

"Bank Earnings Analysis: U.S., Tenth District, and Tenth District States", 9381-14.1

Najjar, Matthew F.

"Anthropometric Data and Prevalence of Overweight for Hispanics: 1982-84", 4147-11.207

Nakamura, Leonard I.

"Entry-Deterring Debt", 9387-8.194

"Information Losses in a Dynamic Model of Credit", 9387-8.173

"Learning in the Marketplace: Free Entry Is Free Riding", 9387-8.192

"Loan Workouts and Commercial Bank Information: Why Banks Are Special", 9387-8.190

Namibia

Agricultural and food production and indexes, total and for selected commodities, by country, 1970s-88, annual rpt, 1524-12

Agricultural trade of US, by detailed commodity and country, 1988, semiannual rpt, 1522-4

Economic, social, political, and geographic summary data, by country, 1989, annual factbook, 9114-2

Human rights conditions in 170 countries, 1988, annual rpt, 21384-3

Minerals Yearbook, 1987, Vol 3: foreign country reviews of production, trade, and policy, by commodity, annual rpt, 5604-35

Minerals Yearbook, 1987, Vol 3 preprints: foreign country review of production, trade, and policy, by commodity, annual rpt, 5604-23.51

Population size, growth rates, and components of change, by country, projected 1989-2020 and trends from 1950, biennial rpt, 2324-9

Napa, Calif.

Housing vacancy rates for single and multifamily units and mobile homes, by city and ZIP code, 1988, annual MSA rpt, 9304-20.1

Wages by occupation, for office and plant workers, 1989 survey, periodic MSA rpt, 6785-3.9

see also under By SMSA or MSA in the "Index by Categories"

Naples, Fla.

see also under By SMSA or MSA in the "Index by Categories"

Narcotics

see Drug abuse and treatment

see Drug and narcotics offenses

see Drugs

Nardone, Thomas

"On the Definition of 'Contingent Work' ", 6722-1.958

NASA

see National Aeronautics and Space Administration

Nashua, N.H.

see also under By SMSA or MSA in the "Index by Categories"

Nashville, Tenn.

Freight (waterborne domestic and foreign) by commodity, traffic, and passengers, by port and waterway, 1987, annual rpt, 3754-3.2

Wages by occupation, and benefits for office and plant workers, 1989 survey, periodic MSA rpt, 6785-12.7

see also under By City and By SMSA or MSA in the "Index by Categories"

Nason, James M.

"Nonparametric Exchange Rate Prediction?", 9366-6.195

Nassau County, N.Y.

Wages by occupation, for office and plant workers, 1988 survey, periodic MSA rpt, 6785-11.2

Wages by occupation, for office and plant workers, 1989 survey, periodic MSA rpt, 6785-12.7

see also under By SMSA or MSA in the "Index by Categories"

Nathan, Robert R., Associates, Inc.

"Effectiveness and Economic Development Impact of Policy-Based Cash Transfer Programs: The Case of Jamaica, 1981-87", 9916-3.56

"Effectiveness and Economic Development Impact of Policy-Based Cash Transfer Programs: The Case of Costa Rica", 9916-3.51

National accounts
see National income and product accounts
National Advisory Council on Child Nutrition
USDA child nutrition programs evaluation, 1988, biennial narrative rpt, 14854-1
National Advisory Council on Educational Research and Improvement
Office of Educational Research and Improvement activities, FY88, annual narrative rpt, 4814-1
National Advisory Council on Indian Education
Activities of NACIE, with Indian education funding of Fed Govt, enrollment, and degrees, late 1960s-FY88, annual rpt, 14874-1
National Aeronautics and Space Administration
Activities and finances of NASA, and data on US and USSR space launches, 1957-88, annual rpt, 9504-6
Aerial survey R&D rpts, and sources of natural resource and environmental data, quarterly listing, 9502-7
Atmospheric sciences research activity of Fed Govt, and funding by agency and program, FY84-87, biennial rpt, 434-1
Budget deficit reduction under Gramm-Rudman Act, cancellation of budget authority by program, FY90, annual rpt, 104-27; 21924-1; 26304-6
Budget of US Appendix, obligations, appropriations, and personnel, by program and agency, FY90, annual rpt, 104-3
Budget of US, authoritative financial statements with appropriations, outlays, and receipts, by category and agency, FY88, annual rpt, 8104-2.2
Debris from spacecraft in orbit, hazards, and tracking, with data for individual fragmented craft, 1961-88, 9508-34
Employee characteristics and personnel actions, FY88, annual rpt, 9504-1
Expenditures of Fed Govt in States, by type, program, agency, and State, FY88, annual rpt, 2464-2
Expenditures of NASA and DOD for space programs, by category, FY81-89, GAO rpt, 26123-152
Fraud and abuse in NASA programs, audits and investigations, 1st half FY89, semiannual rpt, 9502-9
Labor unions recognized in Fed Govt, agreements and membership by agency and facility, as of Jan 1989, biennial listing, 9844-14
Launch schedules and technical descriptions of NASA projects, press release series, 9506-2
Launchings of satellites and other space objects since 1957, quarterly listing, 9502-2
Procurement by NASA, economic benefits by industry group, jobs created, and sales, by State, FY90, 9508-35
Procurement contract awards of NASA, by type, contractor, State, and country, FY89, semiannual rpt, 9502-6
R&D and related funding of Fed Govt to higher education and nonprofit instns, by field, instn, agency, and State, FY87, annual rpt, 9627-17
R&D funding by Fed Govt, by field, performer type, agency, and State, FY87-89, annual rpt, 9627-20

R&D funding by NASA to higher education instns, by field, instn, and State, FY88, annual listing, 9504-7
Science and engineering employment in Fed Govt, by field, degree level, race, sex, agency, and State, 1987, annual rpt, 9627-5
National Agricultural Statistics Service
Budget of US Appendix, obligations, appropriations, and personnel, by program and agency, FY90, annual rpt, 104-3
see also Agricultural Statistics Board
National Ambulatory Medical Care Survey
Cardiologist office visits, by characteristics of patient, physician, and visit, 1985, 4146-8.174
Data coverage and availability, 1989 rpt, 4147-1.24
Drugs (controlled) provided during physician office visits, by drug, patient, and provider characteristics, 1985, 4146-8.179
National Archives and Records Administration
Activities, finances, holdings, and staff of NARA, FY88, annual rpt, 9514-2
Audiovisual activities and spending of Fed Govt, by whether performed in-house and agency, FY87, annual rpt, 9514-1
Budget of US Appendix, obligations, appropriations, and personnel, by program and agency, FY90, annual rpt, 104-3
Budget of US, authoritative financial statements with appropriations, outlays, and receipts, by category and agency, FY88, annual rpt, 8104-2.2
Labor unions recognized in Fed Govt, agreements and membership by agency and facility, as of Jan 1989, biennial listing, 9844-14
R&D funding by Fed Govt, by field, performer type, agency, and State, FY87-89, annual rpt, 9627-20
National Assessment of Educational Progress
Educational progress by subject and selected student characteristics, standard test results and credits, 1989 edition, annual rpt, 4824-2.12
Elementary and secondary students performance in selected subjects, and factors affecting proficiency, natl assessments, 1969-86, 4898-26
Employment of high school students, academic and other characteristics, 1984-86, 4898-27
Reading ability and literacy of young adults, relation to educational attainment and race, natl assessment, 1985, 4828-36
Reading ability test scores for natl assessment, comparison to scores on other tests, findings, 1989 rpt, 4828-37
Science proficiency, attitudes, factors affecting proficiency, and teacher background and views, natl assessment of elementary and high school students, 1977-86, 4898-25
National Association of Blue Shield Plans
see Blue Cross-Blue Shield
National Association of Social Workers
"Report of the Geographic Distribution of Mental Health Providers", 25148-42
National Bureau of Standards
see National Institute of Standards and Technology

National Cancer Institute
Activities of NIH, funding, and advisory council recommendations, by inst, FY87-88, biennial rpt, 4434-16
Cases of cancer, death, and survival rates, by age, sex, race, and body site, 1973-86, annual rpt, 4474-35
Contracts and grants of NCI, by recipient and location, FY88, annual listing, 4474-28
Research on cancer epidemiology and biochemistry, semimonthly journal, 4472-1
Tobacco (smokeless) use by youth and adults, user characteristics, and sales, 1970s-86, papers, 4478-188
National Capital Planning Commission
Budget of US Appendix, obligations, appropriations, and personnel, by program and agency, FY90, annual rpt, 104-3
Budget of US, authoritative financial statements with appropriations, outlays, and receipts, by category and agency, FY88, annual rpt, 8104-2.2
Land acquisition and dev projects of Fed Govt in DC metro area, characteristics and funding by agency and project, FY90-94, annual rpt, 15454-1
National Center for Education Statistics
see Office of Educational Research and Improvement
National Center for Health Services Research and Health Care Technology Assessment
AIDS health care and epidemiological research, methodological issues, 1988 conf, 4188-61
AIDS health care services research status, needs, methods, and impacts on public health policy and funding, with data for selected cities, 1989 conf papers, 4188-59
Child mental health treatment in short-stay hospitals, by age, race, and facility and physician characteristics, 1977, 4188-55
Health care and condition research, survey design and research methods, conf proceedings, periodicity change, 4184-1
Health care and condition research, survey design and research methods, 1989 conf proceedings, 4188-60
Health care services delivery and related topics, series, 4186-2
Health care services needs, delivery, and costs, series, 4186-9
Health care use and costs, methodology and findings of natl survey, series, 4186-8
Hospital service area population care need indicators, and travel distances, for rural and urban instns in New York State, 1983, 4188-53
Insurance (health) coverage of employees, out-of-pocket expenses, benefits, and premiums, 1970s-86 and projected to 2000, 4188-56
Nursing home rehabilitation services use, by service type and patient characteristics, 1st qtr 1983, 4188-58
Older persons health care services and long term care, series, 4186-7
Older persons health care services use related to marital status, living arrangements, and other characteristics, 1977, 4188-54
Prospective payment system research activities and funding of PHS, by project and subagency, FY88, annual rpt, 4184-3

Prospective payment system research activities and funding of PHS, periodic rpt, periodicity change, 4182–1

Publications of NCHSR on health care services delivery and costs, 1985-July 1987, listing, 4188–57

National Center for Health Statistics

Deaths and rates, by detailed cause and demographic characteristics, 1986 and trends from 1900, US Vital Statistics annual rpt, 4144–2

Deaths and rates, by detailed location, cause, and demographic characteristics, 1987, US Vital Statistics annual rpt, 4144–3

Health care use and costs, methodology and findings of natl survey and Medicare and Medicaid records, 1980, series, 4146–12

Health condition and health care resources, use, and spending, 1950s-87, annual data compilation, 4144–11

Health condition and quality of life measurement, rpts and other info sources, quarterly listing, 4122–1

Infant deaths and prevention issues, for OECD, 1985 conf papers, 4148–28

Marriages, divorces, and rates, by characteristics of spouses, State, and county, 1984 and trends from 1920, US Vital Statistics annual rpt, 4144–4

Prospective payment system research activities and funding of PHS, by project and subagency, FY88, annual rpt, 4184–3

Publications of NCHS, quarterly listing, 4122–2

Publications of NCHS, 1980-88, annual listing, 4124–1

Vital and Health Statistics Natl Committee activities, FY88, annual narrative rpt, 4164–1

Vital and Health Statistics series: advance data rpts, 4146–8

Vital and Health Statistics series: analytical and epidemiological studies, 4147–3

Vital and Health Statistics series: conf rpts, 4147–4

Vital and Health Statistics series: foreign and US comparative data, 4147–5

Vital and Health Statistics series: health care facilities manpower and resources, 4147–14

Vital and Health Statistics series: health care facilities use and labor force, 4147–13

Vital and Health Statistics series: health condition and body measurements, Natl Health and Nutrition Examination Survey results, 4147–11

Vital and Health Statistics series: health condition, medical costs, and use of facilities and services, 4147–10

Vital and Health Statistics series: methodology, survey design, and data evaluation, 4147–2

Vital and Health Statistics series: natality, marriage, and divorce trends, 4147–21

Vital and Health Statistics series: program and data collection procedures, 4147–1

Vital and Health Statistics series: reprints of advance data rpts, 4147–16

Vital and Health Statistics series: reprints of monthly rpt supplements, 4147–24

Vital and Health Statistics series: survey questionnaire dev and testing, 4147–6

Vital statistics, preliminary 1987-88 and trends from 1950, annual rpt, 4144–7

Vital statistics provisional data, monthly rpt, 4142–1

Vital statistics provisional data, supplements to monthly rpts, series, 4146–5

National Center for Nursing Research

Activities of NIH, funding, and advisory council recommendations, by inst, FY87-88, biennial rpt, 4434–16

National Clearinghouse for Smoking and Health

see Office on Smoking and Health

National Coal Association

"Reduction in Sulfur Dioxide Emissions at Coal-Fired Electric Utilities: The Trend Continues", 21368–104

National Commission for Employment Policy

Activities and rpts of NCEP, 1989 annual rpt, 15494–1

Unemployed displaced workers and other hard to serve groups, factors contributing to unemployment, and training programs operations, series, 15496–1

National Commission on Libraries and Information Science

Activities of NCLIS, FY88, annual rpt, 15634–1

Budget of US Appendix, obligations, appropriations, and personnel, by program and agency, FY90, annual rpt, 104–3

Budget of US, authoritative financial statements with appropriations, outlays, and receipts, by category and agency, FY88, annual rpt, 8104–2.2

National Commission To Prevent Infant Mortality

Prevention and causes of infant deaths, recommendations and findings, 1988 rpt, 15838–1

National commissions

see Federal boards, committees, and commissions

see Federal independent agencies

National Committee on Vital and Health Statistics

Vital and health statistics series: conf rpts, 4147–4

National Conference of State Legislatures

"State Budget Implications: Child Support Enforcement", 4698–3

National Council of the Paper Industry for Air and Stream Improvement, Inc.

"Summary and Interpretation of USDA Forest Service Report on 'Pine Growth Reductions in the Southeast'", 21368–104

National Credit Union Administration

Assets and location of credit unions, 1989 annual listing, 9534–6

Budget of US Appendix, obligations, appropriations, and personnel, by program and agency, FY90, annual rpt, 104–3

Budget of US, authoritative financial statements with appropriations, outlays, and receipts, by category and agency, FY88, annual rpt, 8104–2.2

Finances of federally insured credit unions, by instn characteristics and State, as of June 1989, semiannual rpt, 9532–6

Financial condition of Federal deposit insurance funds, and of financial instns by type, 1980s-88, GAO rpt, 26119–241

Financial statements of Central Liquidity Facility, FY88, annual rpt, 9534–5

Financial statements of NCUA and credit unions, 1987-88, annual rpt, 9534–1

Fraud and insider misconduct at financial instns, cases, Federal regulatory and enforcement activities, and losses, 1981-87, hearing, 21408–111

Insurance fund of NCUA, losses and financial statements, with federally insured credit union finances, mergers, and closings, FY88, annual rpt, 9534–7

National Crime Survey

Data collection, methodology, and use, technical rpt series, 6066–23

Victimization rates, by victim and offender characteristics, circumstances, and offense, survey rpt series, 6066–3

National debt

see Foreign debts

see Government assets and liabilities

see Public debt

National defense

Foreign countries economic, social, political, and geographic summary data, by country, 1989, annual factbook, 9114–2

Pacific basin countries military, economic, technological, and trade conditions, 1970s-85, compilation of papers, 3908–4

Pakistan military strengths, spending, weapons systems, and arms imports, with comparisons to India, 1980s-87, hearing, 21388–54

Soviet Union and Warsaw Pact military weapons systems, aid, presence, and force strengths, and compared to US and NATO, 1989 annual rpt, 3504–20

Soviet Union economic conditions and military activity, 1960s-86, hearing, 23848–195

Statistical Abstract of US, social, political, and economic data, 1790-2025, comprehensive annual compilation, 2324–1.2

see also Armed services reserves

see also Arms control and disarmament

see also Arms trade

see also Chemical and biological warfare agents

see also Civil defense

see also Defense agencies

see also Defense budgets and appropriations

see also Defense contracts and procurement

see also Defense expenditures

see also Defense industries

see also Defense research

see also Department of Defense

see also Espionage

see also Internal security

see also Logistics

see also Military aircraft

see also Military airlift

see also Military assistance

see also Military aviation

see also Military awards, decorations, and medals

see also Military bases, posts, and reservations

see also Military benefits and pensions

see also Military education

see also Military health facilities and services

see also Military housing

see also Military intelligence

see also Military law

see also Military pay

see also Military personnel
see also Military post exchanges and
commissaries
see also Military prisons
see also Military science
see also Military strategy
see also Military supplies and property
see also Military training
see also Military vehicles
see also Military weapons
see also National Guard
see also Naval vessels
see also Nuclear weapons
see also Service academies
see also Strategic Defense Initiative
see also Strategic materials
see also War

National Defense University
NATO military forces compared to Warsaw
Pact, and selected economic indicators, by
country, 1900s-87, conf papers, 3908-6
Pacific basin countries military, economic,
technological, and trade conditions,
1970s-85, compilation of papers, 3908-4

**National Drug and Alcoholism Treatment
Utilization Survey**
Treatment facilities for drug and alcohol
abuse, services, use, funding, and client
characteristics, 1987, annual rpt,
4494-10

National Economic Commission
Deficit reduction recommendations,
background data and testimony, 1989 rpt,
15888-2
Deficit reduction recommendations, 1989
rpt, 15888-1

National Education Association
Membership in NEA, 1955-87, article,
6722-1.931

National Endowment for the Arts
see National Foundation on the Arts and the
Humanities

National Endowment for the Humanities
see National Foundation on the Arts and the
Humanities

National Environmental Policy Act
Environmental quality and protection
programs, and intl issues, 1988 annual rpt,
484-1

**National Environmental Satellite, Data, and
Information Service**
Heating and cooling degree days weighted
by population, by census div and State,
with area-weighted temperature and
precipitation, monthly rpt, 2152-13
Mariners Weather Log, quarterly journal,
2152-8
Ocean pollution research projects, rpts and
data files, FY78-83, listing, 2158-51
Pacific Ocean subsurface temperature data
collection activities, 1985-87, annual rpt,
2154-12
Storms and unusual weather phenomena
characteristics, casualties, and property
damage, by State, monthly listing,
2152-3
Tsunamis intensity, time, location, and other
characteristics, for US and territories,
1690-1988, 2158-52
Weather conditions and effect on
agriculture, by US region, State, and city,
and world area, weekly rpt, 2152-2
Weather data by census div and State,
historical trends, indexes, major events,
and maps, series, 2156-17

Weather data for stations in continental US
and outlying areas, 1988 and historic
trends, annual rpt, 2154-8
Weather data for surface and upper air,
averages by foreign and US station,
monthly rpt, 2152-4

National Eye Institute
Activities of NIH, funding, and advisory
council recommendations, by inst,
FY87-88, biennial rpt, 4434-16

National Fetal Mortality Survey
Data coverage and availability, 1989 rpt,
4147-1.24
Hazardous substances exposure of parents
and relation to adverse birth outcomes,
1980, article, 4042-3.945

National forests
Acreage, grants, use, revenues, and
allocations, for public lands by State,
FY88 and trends, annual rpt, 5724-1
Acreage of land under Forest Service mgmt,
by forest and location, 1988, annual rpt,
1204-2
Acreage of natl forests, and share of Forest
Service revenue paid to States, by forest,
region, county, and congressional district,
FY88, annual rpt, 1204-33
Agricultural Statistics, 1988, annual rpt,
1004-1.2
Arizona wood fuel harvest, by tree species,
ownership, and county, 1984, 1208-293
California timber resources and mortality, by
hardwood species, land class and
ownership, and county, 1984-85,
1208-291
Expenditures of Fed Govt in States, by type,
program, agency, and State, FY88, annual
rpt, 2464-2
Forest Service activities and finances, by
region and State, FY88, annual rpt,
1204-1
Georgia timber resources and removals, by
species, ownership class, and county,
1988-89, series, 1206-26
Grazing of livestock on natl forest land,
acreage, use, fees, and rancher costs and
returns, by region under alternative fee
levels, 1980s-86, 1588-145
Grazing of livestock on natl forest lands, by
region and State, FY88, annual rpt,
1204-5
Herbicide use in natl forests, exposure and
cancer risk by type and application mode,
1988 rpt, 1208-295
Horse and burro wild herd areas in western
States, population, adoption, and
protection, and mgmt costs, as of FY87,
biennial rpt, 5724-8
Illinois timber resources, removals, and
products, by species, forest characteristics,
ownership, and county, 1960s-85 and
projected to 2015, 1208-292
Insect and disease incidence and damage in
forests, annual regional rpt series,
1206-11
Insect and disease incidence and damage in
forests, by State, 1988, annual rpt,
1204-8
Inventory and costs of real property owned
by Fed Govt, worldwide summary by
location, agency, and use, 1987, annual
rpt, 9454-5
Land Mgmt Bur activities and funding by
State, and receipts by program, FY87,
annual rpt, 5724-13

Lumber production from damaged and dead
timber, feasibility of proposed Montana
plant, 1989 rpt, 1208-308
Mgmt of public lands and resources dev,
environmental, economic, and social
impacts of alternative Forest Service
programs, projected to 2030, 1208-24
Mgmt plans and timber sales of Forest
Service, appeals processing, for selected
States, 1985-88, GAO, 26113-400
Minerals resources and availability on public
lands, State rpt series, 5606-7
New Mexico fuelwood harvest, by species,
ownership, and county, 1986, 1208-303
Northeastern US timber resources and
removals, by species, ownership, and
county, State rpt series, 1206-12
Northwestern US and British Columbia
forest industry production, prices, trade,
and employment, quarterly rpt, 1202-3
Planting and dev of forests and windbarriers,
by State, FY88, annual rpt, 1204-7
Recreational use of natl forests, by type of
activity and State, 1988, annual rpt,
1204-17
Revenue of natl forest land, by source,
forest, and State, FY88, annual rpt,
1204-34
Rocky Mountain States timber and mill
residue production, by species, ownership,
and county, series, 1206-17
Statistical Abstract of US, social, political,
and economic data, 1790-2025,
comprehensive annual compilation,
2324-1.1; 2324-1.3
Timber resources surveys of Forest Service,
coverage and methodology, 1932-89,
9188-110
Timber sales in natl forests, logging and
road construction costs, model results,
1989 rpt, 1208-298
Timber sales of Forest Service, expenses,
and operations, by region, State, and natl
forest, FY88, annual rpts, 1204-36
Timber stumpage prices, for sawtimber sold
from natl forests by species and region,
quarterly rpt, 1202-1
Trail maintenance and construction needs,
by region, and Forest Service budget,
FY80-89 and projected to 1993, GAO rpt,
26113-435
Visits and fees for Federal outdoor
recreation facilities, by managing agency,
1988, annual rpt, 5544-14
Wisconsin timber resources and removals,
by species, forest type, ownership, and
county, series, 1206-34
see also Wilderness areas

**National Foundation on the Arts and the
Humanities**
Arts Natl Endowment activities and grants,
FY88, annual rpt, 9564-3
Budget of US Appendix, obligations,
appropriations, and personnel, by program
and agency, FY90, annual rpt, 104-3
Budget of US, authoritative financial
statements with appropriations, outlays,
and receipts, by category and agency,
FY88, annual rpt, 8104-2.2
Expenditures of Fed Govt in States, by type,
program, agency, and State, FY88, annual
rpt, 2464-2
Grants (matching) of Natl Endowment for
Arts, by instn, annual rpt, discontinued,
9564-5

Humanities Natl Endowment activities and grants, FY88, annual rpt, 9564–2

Museum Services Inst activities and finances, and grants by recipient, FY88, annual rpt, 9564–7

Museum Services Inst grants, by recipient, FY89, annual press release series, 9564–6

National grasslands

Acreage and use of public lands, and Land Mgmt Bur activities and finances, annual State rpt series, 5724–11

Acreage, grants, use, revenues, and allocations, for public lands by State, FY88 and trends, annual rpt, 5724–1

Acreage of land under Forest Service mgmt, by forest and location, 1988, annual rpt, 1204–2

Agricultural Statistics, 1988, annual rpt, 1004–1.2

Expenditures of Fed Govt in States, by type, program, agency, and State, FY88, annual rpt, 2464–2

Grazing of livestock on natl forest land, acreage, use, fees, and rancher costs and returns, by region under alternative fee levels, 1980s-86, 1588–145

Grazing of livestock on natl forest lands, by region and State, FY88, annual rpt, 1204–5

Great Plains rangeland acreage, soil erosion, and other impacts of Conservation Reserve program, 1987 conf papers, 1208–290

Inventory and costs of real property owned by Fed Govt, worldwide summary by location, agency, and use, 1987, annual rpt, 9454–5

Land Mgmt Bur activities and funding by State, and receipts by program, FY87, annual rpt, 5724–13

Statistical Abstract of US, social, political, and economic data, 1790-2025, comprehensive annual compilation, 2324–1.2

National Guard

Activities, manpower, and facilities of Army and Air Natl Guard, FY88, annual rpt, 3504–22

Activities, personnel, logistics, R&D, and budget, FY86 summary data, annual rpt, 3704–11

Expenditures of Fed Govt in States, by type, program, agency, and State, FY88, annual rpt, 2464–2

Family social, economic, and other characteristics, and spouses attitudes, for reserve personnel, 1986 survey, 3508–30

Labor unions recognized in Fed Govt, agreements and membership by agency and facility, as of Jan 1989, biennial listing, 9844–14

Manpower active duty strength, recruits, and reenlistment, by race, sex, and service branch, quarterly press release, 3542–7

Manpower and equipment strengths, and readiness, by reserve component, FY88, annual rpt, 3544–31

Manpower, funding by category, procurement reductions, and needs, by reserve component, FY80-88, GAO rpt, 26123–220

Manpower social, economic, family, and service characteristics, and attitudes, by reserve component, 1986 survey, 3508–29

Manpower strengths and characteristics, by reserve component, quarterly rpt, 3542–4

Manpower strengths for reserve components, by selected characteristics, FY88, annual rpt, 3544–1.5

Statistical Abstract of US, social, political, and economic data, 1790-2025, comprehensive annual compilation, 2324–1.2

Training and education programs of DOD, funding, staff, students, and facilities, by service branch, FY90, annual rpt, 3504–5

Training of Army Reserve and Natl Guard personnel in combat and critical job task skills, resources, effectiveness, and officers views, FY87, GAO rpt, 26123–239

Women military personnel on active and reserve duty, by demographic and service characteristics and service branch, FY88, annual chartbook, 3544–26

National Health and Nutrition Examination Survey

Alcohol use and abuse among minority groups, and related problems, by selected characteristics, 1985 conf papers, 4488–13

Data coverage and availability, 1989 rpt, 4147–1.24

Health condition and body measurements, Vital and Health Statistics series, 4147–11

Nutritional status and related health condition and practices, by selected characteristics, 1970s-87, 4048–33

National Health Examination Survey

see National Health and Nutrition Examination Survey

National Health Interview Survey

Alcohol use and abuse among minority groups, and related problems, by selected characteristics, 1985 conf papers, 4488–13

Data coverage and availability, 1989 rpt, 4147–1.24

Health condition, medical costs, and use of health facilities and services, Vital and Health Statistics series, 4147–10

Hospice services awareness of aged, by age, sex, education, region, SMSA/non-SMSA residence, and cancer history, 1984 survey, article, 4042–3.915

Methodology, sample design, and estimation procedures for 1985-94 NHIS, 1989 rpt, 4147–2.110

Vital and Health Statistics series: advance data rpts, 4146–8

Vital and Health Statistics series: reprints of advance data rpts, 4147–16

National Health Interview Survey of Health Promotion and Disease Prevention

Military personnel health-related behavior, for 7 habits, by age, education, race, and health status, 1985 survey, article, 4042–3.949

National Health Survey

see Hispanic Health and Nutrition Examination Survey

see National Ambulatory Medical Care Survey

see National Fetal Mortality Survey

see National Health and Nutrition Examination Survey

see National Health Interview Survey

see National Health Interview Survey of Health Promotion and Disease Prevention

see National Hospital Discharge Survey

see National Master Facility Inventory

see National Medical Care Expenditure Survey

see National Medical Expenditure Survey

see National Mortality Survey

see National Natality Survey

see National Nursing Home Survey

see National Survey of Family Growth

National Heart, Lung, and Blood Institute

Activities and funding of NHLBI, FY87, annual narrative rpt, 4474–22

Activities and grants of NHLBI, and Advisory Council recommendations, FY77-94, annual rpt, 4474–11

Activities of NHLBI, and grants by recipient and location, FY88 with disease trends from 1940, annual rpt, 4474–15

Activities of NIH, funding, and advisory council recommendations, by inst, FY87-88, biennial rpt, 4434–16

National Highway Traffic Safety Administration

Acceleration (sudden) incidents involving Audi 5000 and selected other models, investigation results, 1986-88, 7768–107

Accidents (fatal), circumstances, and characteristics of persons and vehicles involved, 1988, semiannual rpt, 7762–11

Accidents (fatal), deaths, and rates, by circumstances, characteristics of persons and vehicles involved, and location, 1987, annual rpt, 7764–10

Accidents and safety data, fact sheet series, 7766–15

Accidents, injuries, and deaths, by circumstances and characteristics of persons and vehicles involved, 1970s-87, series, 7766–14

Auto safety, crash test results by domestic and foreign model, model years 1984-88, 7768–111

Auto safety, crash test results by domestic and foreign model, press release series, 7766–7

Budget of US Appendix, obligations, appropriations, and personnel, by program and agency, FY90, annual rpt, 104–3

Child traffic accident deaths and survivors, by restraint type and use, age, and seat position, 1982-87, 7768–104

Child traffic accident deaths, effects of State laws mandating safety restraint use, 1978-88, 7768–108

Deaths in traffic accidents by region, and death rates for miles traveled, monthly rpt, 7762–7

Drinking age laws impacts on traffic deaths, by State, 1975-87, 7768–103

Driving while intoxicated enforcement and publicity strategies, NHSTA deterrence project results, 1984-85, 7768–109

Drunk drivers and others involved in fatal accidents, alcohol levels by circumstances and characteristics of persons and vehicles, 1988, annual rpt, 7764–16

Employment of DOT, by subagency, occupation, and selected personnel characteristics, FY88, annual rpt, 7304–18

Expenditures of Fed Govt in States, by type, program, agency, and State, FY88, annual rpt, 2464–2

Motorcycle accident deaths, by whether helmet used, 1982-87, 7768–106

National Institute of Neurological and Communicative Disorders and Stroke

Activities of NIH, funding, and advisory council recommendations, by inst, FY87-88, biennial rpt, 4434–16

National Institute of Standards and Technology

Budget appropriations and staff for Commerce Dept, by subagency, FY88-90, annual rpt, 2004–6

Budget of US Appendix, obligations, appropriations, and personnel, by program and agency, FY90, annual rpt, 104–3

Computer systems of Fed Govt, security training activities, by agency, 1988, GAO rpt, 26125–31

Computer systems purchase and use, and data recording, processing, and transfer, Fed Govt standards, series, 2216–2

Energy-related inventions recommended by NIST for DOE support, awards, and evaluation status, 1988, annual listing, 2214–5

GATT Standards Code info activities of NIST, and proposed standards by agency and country, 1988, annual rpt, 2214–6

Intl standards assns participation by US and other countries, 1989, 2218–80

Publications of NIST, 1988, annual listing, 2214–1

Weights, measures, and performance standards dev, proposals, and policies, 1988 annual conf, 2214–7

National Institute on Aging

Activities of NIH, funding, and advisory council recommendations, by inst, FY87-88, biennial rpt, 4434–16

Cell cultures for aging research, availability and cultures shipped, 1989 listing, 4478–187

National Institute on Alcohol Abuse and Alcoholism

Abuse of alcohol, related injury and illness, series, 4486–1

Minority group alcohol use and abuse, and related problems, by selected characteristics, 1985 conf papers, 4488–13

Racial and ethnic groups alcohol use, abuse, treatment, and views, for US and native countries, by selected characteristics, 1988 compilation of papers, 4488–12

Research on alcoholism, treatment programs, and patient characteristics, quarterly journal, 4482–1

Treatment facilities for alcohol abuse, and related services use, by program, facility type, and State, biennial rpt, discontinued, 4484–5

Treatment facilities for drug and alcohol abuse, services, use, funding, and client characteristics, 1987, annual rpt, 4494–10

National Institute on Drug Abuse

Abuse of drugs and alcohol, by type, age, sex, race, and region, 1988 survey, biennial rpt, 4494–5

Abuse of drugs, emergency room admissions and deaths by drug type and major metro area, July-Dec 1988, semiannual rpt, 4492–3

Abuse of drugs, emergency room admissions and deaths by drug type and source, sex, race, age, and major metro area, 1988, annual rpt, 4494–8

Abuse of drugs, indicators for selected metro areas, research results, data collection, and policy issues, 1989 semiannual conf, 4492–5

Genetic and other factors in drug abuse, 1986 conf papers, 4498–60

Methamphetamine abuse, emergency room admissions and deaths by selected city, and lab seizures, 1980s-87, 4498–61

Research on drug abuse and treatment, summaries of findings, resource materials, and grant listings, periodic rpt, 4492–4

Treatment facilities for drug and alcohol abuse, services, use, funding, and client characteristics, 1987, annual rpt, 4494–10

Treatment facilities for drug and alcohol abuse, staff, and program characteristics, series, discontinued, 4496–8

Treatment facilities for drug and alcohol abuse, use, funding, and client and staff characteristics, series, discontinued, 4496–7

Youth drug, alcohol, and cigarette use and attitudes, by substance type and selected characteristics, 1975-88 surveys, annual rpt, 4494–4

National Institutes of Health

Activities of NIH, funding, and advisory council recommendations, by inst, FY87-88, biennial rpt, 4434–16

Activities of NIH, funding by program and recipient type, staff, and clinic patients, by inst, FY87, annual rpt, 4434–3

AIDS cases among children, by age, sex, and risk group, with related HHS funding, 1980s-88, 4438–15

AIDS research grants and contracts of NIH, by funding and approval status, and researcher age, experience, and sex, FY86, GAO rpt, 26121–267

Budget of US Appendix, obligations, appropriations, and personnel, by program and agency, FY90, annual rpt, 104–3

Financial aid of HHS, by program, recipient, State, and city, FY88, annual regional listings, 4004–3

Grants and awards of NIH, quarterly listing, 4432–1

Grants and contracts of NIH, by inst and type of recipient, FY79-88, annual rpt, 4434–9

Grants of NIH for R&D, training, construction, and medical libraries, by location and recipient, FY88, annual listings, 4434–7

Intl programs of NIH, activities and funding by inst and country, FY88, annual rpt, 4474–6

Nutrition biomedical and behavioral research and training, NIH activities and funding by inst, FY87, annual rpt, 4434–15

Publications of NIH, 1989 annual listing, 4434–2

R&D price index for medicine, NIH index by component, and compared to other indexes, FY79-86, article, 4042–3.901

Research and evaluation programs of HHS, 1970-FY87, annual listing, 4004–30

Research contract awards of NIH to higher education instns, and research staff, related charges, and time allocated to projects, 1984-88, 4008–89

Toxicology Natl Program research and testing activities, FY87 and planned FY88, annual rpt, 4044–16

see also Division of Research Resources, NIH

see also Fogarty International Center for Advanced Study in the Health Sciences

see also National Cancer Institute

see also National Center for Nursing Research

see also National Eye Institute

see also National Heart, Lung, and Blood Institute

see also National Institute of Allergy and Infectious Diseases

see also National Institute of Arthritis and Musculoskeletal and Skin Diseases

see also National Institute of Child Health and Human Development

see also National Institute of Dental Research

see also National Institute of Diabetes and Digestive and Kidney Diseases

see also National Institute of Environmental Health Sciences

see also National Institute of General Medical Sciences

see also National Institute of Neurological and Communicative Disorders and Stroke

see also National Institute on Aging

see also National Library of Medicine

National Labor Relations Board

Activities, cases, elections conducted, and litigation, FY85, annual rpt, 9584–1

Budget of US Appendix, obligations, appropriations, and personnel, by program and agency, FY90, annual rpt, 104–3

Budget of US, authoritative financial statements with appropriations, outlays, and receipts, by category and agency, FY88, annual rpt, 8104–2.2

Labor unions recognized in Fed Govt, agreements and membership by agency and facility, as of Jan 1989, biennial listing, 9844–14

Representation elections conducted by NLRB, results, monthly rpt, 9582–2

National Library of Medicine

Activities, holdings, and grants of Library, FY86-88, annual rpt, 4464–1

Activities of NIH, funding, and advisory council recommendations, by inst, FY87-88, biennial rpt, 4434–16

MEDLINE on-line data base user info needs and other characteristics, 1987 survey, 4468–3

National Longitudinal Study of High School Seniors

Educational attainment of high school classes of 1972, 1980, and 1982, by selected characteristics, 1976-87, 4848–36

High school class of 1972: education, employment, and family characteristics, activities, and attitudes, natl longitudinal study, series, 4836–1

Higher education enrollment and degrees by sex, race, and income level, for high school classes of 1972, 1980, and 1982, natl longitudinal surveys, 4848–35

National Low Income Housing Preservation Commission

"Preventing the Disappearance of Low-Income Housing", 21248–116.1

National Marine Fisheries Service

Aquaculture in US and Japan, mgmt, methods, and biological data for selected species, 1985 conf papers, annual rpt, 2164–15

Atlantic Ocean fish and shellfish distribution, bottom trawl survey evaluation with results by species and location, 1963-87, 2168–108

Atlantic Ocean fish and shellfish distribution, bottom trawl survey results by species and location, periodic rpt series, 2164–18

Bass (striped) stocks status on Atlantic coast, and sport and commercial catch by State, 1972-89, annual rpt, 5504–29

Cold storage holdings of fish and shellfish, by product and species, preliminary data, monthly press release, 2162–2

Endangered species recovery plans, and funding by Federal agencies and others, by species, FY72-87, GAO rpt, 26113–391

Fish and shellfish catch, wholesale receipts, prices, trade, and other market activities, weekly regional rpts, 2162–6

Fish catch, trade, use, and fishery operations, with selected foreign data, by species, 1970s-88, annual rpt, 2164–1

Fish meal and oil production and trade, quarterly tables, 2162–3

Fishing (ocean sport) catch and effort, and NMFS tagging and research activity, by species and location, 1987, annual rpt, 2164–7

Hudson-Raritan estuary pollution levels, and effects of refrigeration on pollutant samples, 1983-84, 2168–109

Japan fish catch, prices, trade by country, cold storage holdings, import quotas, and market devs, semimonthly press release, 2162–7

Marine Fisheries Review, US and foreign fisheries resources, dev, mgmt, and research, quarterly journal, 2162–1

Marine Mammal Protection Act admin, and populations, strandings, and catch permits by species and location, 1987-88, annual rpt, 2164–11

Nutrient and fatty acid composition of fish, by northeastern US species, 1985-87, 2168–111

Pacific coast fish and shellfish catch, prices, and fisheries economic status, 1986-87, annual rpt series, 2164–16

Production of processed fish by location, and trade, by species and product, 1987-88, annual rpts, 2166–6

R&D and mgmt of fisheries, Fed Govt grants by project and State, and rpts, 1987, annual listing, 2164–3

Southeastern US coastal fish distribution, by species, season, and location, 1980-82, 2168–112

Turbot (Greenland) catch, by Alaska coast fishery, 1960s-86, 2168–110

Women's employment in merchant marine, Natl Marine Fisheries Service, and fishing, with rpts of sexual assault, 1980s-88, GAO rpt, 26113–397

National Master Facility Inventory

Data coverage and availability, 1989 rpt, 4147–1.24

National Mediation Board

Activities and caseloads of NMB, and railroad and airline labor disputes, with data by carrier and union, FY85-86, annual rpt, 9604–1

Budget of US Appendix, obligations, appropriations, and personnel, by program and agency, FY90, annual rpt, 104–3

Budget of US, authoritative financial statements with appropriations, outlays, and receipts, by category and agency, FY88, annual rpt, 8104–2.2

see also National Railroad Adjustment Board

National Medical Care Expenditure Survey

Data coverage and availability, 1989 rpt, 4147–1.24

see also National Medical Expenditure Survey

National Medical Care Utilization and Expenditure Survey

Methodology and findings of natl survey and Medicare and Medicaid records, 1980, series, 4146–12

National Medical Expenditure Survey

Data on health care use and costs, methodology and findings of natl survey, series, 4186–8

Design and research methods for health surveys, 1989 conf proceedings, 4188–60

see also National Medical Care Expenditure Survey

National monuments

see Monuments and memorials

National Mortality Followback Survey

AIDS deaths, by health and other characteristics, 1986, 4146–8.178

Heart disease deaths, by health and other characteristics, 1986, 4146–8.177

National Mortality Survey

Data coverage and availability, 1989 rpt, 4147–1.24

National Narcotics Intelligence Consumers Committee

Supply of drugs in US by country of origin, abuse, deaths, prices, and seizures, by substance, 1988, annual rpt, 6284–2

National Natality Survey

Data coverage and availability, 1989 rpt, 4147–1.24

Hazardous substances exposure of parents and relation to adverse birth outcomes, 1980, article, 4042–3.945

Natality, marriage, and divorce trends, series, 4147–21

National Nursing Home Survey

Data coverage and availability, 1989 rpt, 4147–1.24

Use rates, charges, and resident length of stay, care needs, and other characteristics of nursing homes, 1985, 4147–13.102

National Occupational Exposure Survey

Hazardous substances and conditions occupational exposure, and prevention and control measures, 1981-83 survey, 4248–86

National Ocean Service

Alaska OCS environmental conditions and oil dev impacts, compilation of papers, series, 2176–1

Charting and Geodetic Service of Natl Ocean Service activities and funding, by State, FY89-90, biennial rpt, 2174–10

Coastal and estuarine environmental conditions, research results and methodology, series, 2176–7

Coastal and estuarine pollutant discharges, by source, pollutant type, and location, series, 2176–4

Coastal areas environmental conditions and mgmt, map series, 2176–5

Coastal areas environmental impacts of economic dev and population growth, 1980s and projected to 2000, series, 2176–8

Hudson-Raritan River basin pollutant levels and sources, model description and results, 1880s-1982, 2178–22

Oregon coastal and estuarine pollutant levels, by pollutant and location, 1960s-87, 2178–23

Pollutant (PCB and pesticide) concentrations in coastal and estuarine fish and shellfish, by species and location, 1965-84, 2178–21

Pollutant concentrations in coastal and estuarine fish, shellfish, and environment, series, 2176–3

Pollution of oceans, estuaries, and coastal waters monitoring and assessment, NOAA activities and funding, FY88, annual rpt, 2174–9

Pollution research, monitoring, and resources dev activities of Fed Govt, triennial rpt, issuing agency change, 2178–14

Tidal currents, daily time and velocity by station for North America and Asia coasts, forecast 1990, annual rpts, 2174–1

Tide height and time daily at coastal points worldwide, forecast 1990, annual rpt series, 2174–2

National Oceanic and Atmospheric Administration

Atlantic Oceanographic and Meteorological Lab research activities and bibl, FY88, annual rpt, 2144–19

Budget appropriations and staff for Commerce Dept, by subagency, FY88-90, annual rpt, 2004–6

Budget of US Appendix, obligations, appropriations, and personnel, by program and agency, FY90, annual rpt, 104–3

Diving (underwater sport and occupational) deaths, by circumstances, diver characteristics, and location, 1970-87, annual rpt, 2144–5

Drought of 1988, analysis of severity and factors, with worldwide conditions and trends from 1600, 2148–54

Environmental Research Labs staff publications, FY88, annual listing, 2144–25

Estuary environmental conditions and mgmt, for individual areas, conf series, 2146–6

Estuary environmental conditions and mgmt, research projects and funding, FY87, annual listing, 2144–24

Expenditures of Fed Govt in States, by type, program, agency, and State, FY88, annual rpt, 2464–2

Florida straits coastal currents, temperatures, and salinity, series, 2146–7

Great Lakes Environmental Research Lab activities, annual conf, discontinued, 2144–22

Great Lakes Environmental Research Lab activities, 1987 annual rpt, 2144–26

Great Lakes water levels impacts of water supply mgmt and weather, model description, 1900s-85, 2148-59

Maine coastal marine resources and ocean floor ecology, 1983-87, conf papers, 2148-55

Oceanographic research and distribution activities of World Data Center A by country, and cruises by ship, 1987, annual rpt, 2144-15

Pacific Marine Environmental Lab research activities and bibl, FY88, annual rpt, 2144-21

Paints used on ship hulls, impacts on environment and marine species, with bibl, 1960s-87, 2148-58

Pollution (marine) events, researchers rankings of seriousness by event type, 1987 survey, 2148-57

Research on ocean pollution, monitoring, and resources dev activities of Fed Govt, funding and project descriptions, FY87, annual listing, 2144-23

Research on ocean pollution, monitoring, and resources dev activities of Fed Govt, 5-year plan and funding by agency, FY84-89, triennial rpt, 2148-56

San Francisco Bay fish distribution by species, and water outflow, 1973-82, 2168-113

Storms (severe) natl lab research activities and bibl, FY88, annual rpt, 2144-20

Weather research, monitoring, and impact assessment activities of Fed Govt, and funding by agency, FY87, annual rpt, 2144-17

Weather services activities and funding, by Federal agency, planned FY89-90, annual rpt, 2144-2

see also National Environmental Satellite, Data, and Information Service

see also National Marine Fisheries Service

see also National Ocean Service

see also National Weather Service

National Park Service

Acreage of land under NPS mgmt, by site, ownership, and region, 1989 semiannual rpt, 5542-1

Bears (grizzly) in Yellowstone Natl Park area, monitoring results, 1988, annual rpt, 5544-4

Deaths of natl park system visitors, by cause, victim age, region, and park, 1978-88, annual rpt, 5544-6

Expenditures of Fed Govt in States, by type, program, agency, and State, FY88, annual rpt, 2464-2

Historic and natural natl landmarks damaged and threatened, with owner, location, damage type, and recommended remedial action, 1988, annual listing, 5544-16

Historic buildings rehabilitation tax incentives, projects, costs, ownership, use, and tax reform impacts, FY77-88, annual rpt, 5544-17

Historic Preservation Fund grants, by State, FY90, annual table, 5544-9

Visits and fees for Federal outdoor recreation facilities, by managing agency, 1988, annual rpt, 5544-14

Visits and overnight stays in natl park system, by park and State, monthly rpt, 5542-4

Visits and overnight stays in natl park system, by park and State, 1988 and trends from 1979, annual rpt, 5544-12

Wilderness areas acreage by Federal agency and location, and sources of damage, with data for foreign countries, 1988 conf papers, 1208-301

National parks

Acreage of land under Natl Park Service mgmt, by site, ownership, and region, 1989 semiannual rpt, 5542-1

Alaska land area by ownership, and availability for mineral exploration and dev, 1986, 5608-152

Bears (grizzly) in Yellowstone Natl Park area, monitoring results, 1988, annual rpt, 5544-4

Crimes committed in natl parks, by offense, 1975-88, annual rpt, 6064-6.3

Deaths of natl park system visitors, by cause, victim age, region, and park, 1978-88, annual rpt, 5544-6

Environmental quality and protection programs, and intl issues, 1988 annual rpt, 484-1

Inventory and costs of real property owned by Fed Govt, worldwide summary by location, agency, and use, 1987, annual rpt, 9454-5

Minerals resources and availability on public lands, State rpt series, 5606-7

Statistical Abstract of US, social, political, and economic data, 1790-2025, comprehensive annual compilation, 2324-1.1

Visits and fees for Federal outdoor recreation facilities, by managing agency, 1988, annual rpt, 5544-14

Visits and overnight stays in natl park system, by park and State, monthly rpt, 5542-4

Visits and overnight stays in natl park system, by park and State, 1988 and trends from 1979, annual rpt, 5544-12

Visits to natl parks, *Survey of Current Business*, monthly rpt, 2702-1.8

see also National forests

see also Wilderness areas

see also Wildlife refuges

National Petroleum Refiners Association

"U.S. Refining Industry Capability To Manufacture Ultra Low Sulfur Diesel Fuels", 21368-104.1

National planning

see Economic policy

see Fiscal policy

see Monetary policy

National Railroad Adjustment Board

Activities and caseloads of NRAB, and railroad and airline labor disputes, with data by carrier and union, FY85-86, annual rpt, 9604-1

National Railroad Passenger Corp.

Energy use by mode of transport, fuel supply, and demographic and economic factors of vehicle use, 1970s-88, annual rpt, 3304-5

Finances and ridership of Amtrak, FY75-85, annual rpt, 7304-1

Finances, operations, vehicles, equipment, accidents, and energy use, by mode of transport, 1955-88, annual rpt, 7304-2

Operations and finances of Amtrak, FY88, annual rpt, 29524-1

Salaries of Amtrak officers compared to industry average, 1986, hearing, 21368-103

National Rural Electric Cooperative Association

"NRECA Plans and the Minimum Health Benefit: A Comparison of Provisions and Costs", 25368-160

"NRECA Survey of Health Coverage in Smaller Firms: Evidence and Policy Implications", 25368-160

National school lunch and breakfast programs

see School lunch and breakfast programs

National Science Foundation

Activities of NSF, finances, and funding by program, FY88, annual rpt, 9624-6

Atmospheric sciences research activity of Fed Govt, and funding by agency and program, FY84-87, biennial rpt, 434-1

Black colleges R&D funding by source, and characteristics of grad students and research staff, by field of science and instn, 1980s-87, 9628-78

Budget of US Appendix, obligations, appropriations, and personnel, by program and agency, FY90, annual rpt, 104-3

Budget of US, authoritative financial statements with appropriations, outlays, and receipts, by category and agency, FY88, annual rpt, 8104-2.2

Degrees (PhD) in science and engineering, by field, instn, employment prospects, sex, race, and other characteristics, 1960s-88, 9627-30

Degrees in science and engineering, by field, level, and sex, 1950-86, 9628-77

Education funding by Federal agency, program, and recipient type, and instn spending, FY80-88, 4828-21

Education in science and engineering, enrollment, degrees, and student aid and sources, with data by field, race, sex, and instn, 1980s-87, 26358-202

Employment and other characteristics of science and engineering PhDs, by field and State, 1987, biennial rpt, 9627-18

Employment characteristics of scientists and engineers, by field, 1988, biennial rpt, 9627-16

Employment of scientists and engineers, and related topics, fact sheet series, 9626-2

Employment of scientists, engineers, and technicians, by nonmanufacturing industry and field, 1987, triennial rpt, 9627-31

Employment of scientists, engineers, and technicians in manufacturing, by field, occupation, and industry, 1986, triennial rpt, 9627-23

Employment of scientists, engineers, and technicians in transportation, utilities, and retail and wholesale trade, by field, occupation, and industry, 1985, triennial rpt, 9627-32

Engineering research and education grants of NSF, FY88, annual listing, 9624-24

Enrollment in science and engineering grad programs, by field, source of funds, and characteristics of student and instn, 1975-87, annual rpt, 9627-7

Expenditures of Fed Govt in States, by type, program, agency, and State, FY88, annual rpt, 2464-2

Fed Govt aid to higher education and nonprofit instns for R&D and related activities, by field, instn, agency, and State, FY87, annual rpt, 9627–17

Fed Govt science and engineering employment, by field, degree level, race, sex, agency, and State, 1987, annual rpt, 9627–5

Grants and contracts of NSF, by by field, inst, State, and country, FY88, annual rpt, 9624–26

Higher education instn R&D equipment, acquisition and service costs, condition, and financing, by field, 1982-83 and 1985-86, 9628–76

Immigrant scientists and engineers, by field, age, sex, country and world area of origin, and State, 1987 and trends from 1967, 9627–29

Intl exchange and training programs of Federal agencies, participants by world area, and funding, by program, FY87, annual rpt, 9854–8

Labor force, Federal and university research funding, and educational data, for science and engineering, series, 9626–6

Labor unions recognized in Fed Govt, agreements and membership by agency and facility, as of Jan 1989, biennial listing, 9844–14

NATO postdoctoral fellowships in science, recipients educational outcomes and other characteristics, 1959-81, 9628–80

Publications and project descriptions of NSF Science Resources Studies Div, 1988 annual listing, 9624–21

Publications of NSF Science Resources Studies Div, 1978-88, listing, 9627–22

Publications of NSF, 1989 annual listing, 9624–16

R&D Fed Govt policies and programs, 1985-88, biennial rpt, 424–2

R&D funding, and scientists and engineers education and employment, for US and selected foreign countries, 1988, annual rpt, 9624–23

R&D funding by Fed Govt, by detailed function, program, and agency, FY88-90, annual rpt, 9627–9

R&D funding by Fed Govt, by field, performer type, agency, and State, FY87-89, annual rpt, 9627–20

R&D funding by source and field, selected years 1953-89, annual rpt, 9624–18

R&D funding, labor supply, and other science indicators, with foreign comparisons, 1960s-89, annual chartbook, 9624–22

National security
see Internal security
see National defense

National Security Council
Budget of US Appendix, obligations, appropriations, and personnel, by program and agency, FY90, annual rpt, 104–3

Budget of US, authoritative financial statements with appropriations, outlays, and receipts, by category and agency, FY88, annual rpt, 8104–2.2

Presidential directives released through Natl Security Council, by purpose and admin, 1961-88, GAO rpt, 26123–224

Spacecraft debris in orbit, hazards, and tracking, with data for individual fragmented craft, 1961-88, 9508–34

National stockpiles
see Stockpiling

National Survey of Family Growth
Data coverage and availability, 1989 rpt, 4147–1.24

National Survey of Health and Sexual Behavior
Design and research methods for health surveys, 1989 conf proceedings, 4188–60

National Survey of Small Business Finances
Methodology, design, and response rates of survey, 1988, technical paper, 9366–6.207

National Technical Information Service
Activities, finances, and modernization plans of NTIS, FY88, annual rpt, 2224–6

Computer data files of NTIS, 1989 annual listing, 2224–3; 2224–5

EPA rpts in NTIS collection, quarterly listing, 9182–5

National Telecommunications and Information Administration
Budget appropriations and staff for Commerce Dept, by subagency, FY88-90, annual rpt, 2004–6

Budget of US Appendix, obligations, appropriations, and personnel, by program and agency, FY90, annual rpt, 104–3

Expenditures of Fed Govt in States, by type, program, agency, and State, FY88, annual rpt, 2464–2

Info services for home and business, availability, use, and market indicators, for US and other OECD countries, 1980s and projected to 1992, 2808–28

Publications of NTIA, FY88, annual listing, 2804–3

Radio frequency assignments for Federal use, by agency, 2nd half 1988, semiannual rpt, 2802–1

Telecommunications industry devs, finances, and operations, with data by service type, firm, and country, 1950s-80s, 2808–27

National Toxicology Program
Carcinogens chemistry, sources, environment and health risks, and regulation, by substance and brand, 1989, annual rpt, 4044–15

Research and testing activities under program, FY87 and planned FY88, annual rpt, 4044–16

National Transportation Safety Board
Activities of NTSB, with accident investigations and recommendations, 1988, annual rpt, 9614–1

Aircraft accidents and circumstances, for US operations of domestic and foreign airlines and general aviation, periodic rpt, 9612–1

Aircraft accidents, casualties, and damage, for commercial operations by detailed circumstances, 1986, annual rpt, 9614–2

Aircraft accidents, deaths, and circumstances, by carrier and carrier type, preliminary 1988, annual press release, 9614–9

Aircraft accidents in general aviation, by circumstances, characteristics of persons and aircraft involved, and type of flying, 1986, annual rpt, 9614–3

Budget of US Appendix, obligations, appropriations, and personnel, by program and agency, FY90, annual rpt, 104–3

Budget of US, authoritative financial statements with appropriations, outlays, and receipts, by category and agency, FY88, annual rpt, 8104–2.2

Deaths in transportation accidents, by mode, 1987-88, annual press release, 9614–6

Railroad accidents, circumstances, severity, and railroad involved, periodic rpt, 9612–3

National Veterinary Services Laboratories
Activities of NVSL, biologic drug product evaluation and disease testing, FY88, annual rpt, 1394–17

National Weather Service
Forecasts of precipitation and temperature for US and Northern Hemisphere, by location, semimonthly rpt, 2182–1

Hurricanes and tropical storms in north Atlantic and Caribbean area, paths, surveillance, deaths, damage, and landfall probabilities by city, 1988, annual rpt, 2184–7

Hurricanes and tropical storms in northeastern Pacific Ocean, paths and surveillance, 1988, annual rpt, 2184–8

Marine weather forecast areas, and broadcast schedules and stations worldwide, as of Nov 1988, annual rpt, 2184–3

Northeastern US water supply, precipitation and stream runoff by station, monthly rpt, 2182–3

Ocean surface temperature by ocean and for US coastal areas, and Bering Sea ice conditions, monthly rpt, 2182–5

Precipitation and temperature for US and foreign locations, major events and anomalies, weekly rpt, 2182–6

Western US water supply, streamflow and reservoir storage forecasts by stream and station, Jan-May monthly rpt, 1262–1

National Wildlife Refuge System
see Wildlife refuges

Nationality
see Citizenship

Nationalization
see Expropriation of alien property
see Government ownership
see Socialism

Nationwide Food Consumption Survey
Food consumption and nutrient intake by individuals, by food group, selected characteristics, and region, supplementary survey series, 1356–5

Native Americans
see Alaska Natives
see Indians

Nativity
see Birthplace

NATO
see North Atlantic Treaty Organization

Natural disasters
see Disasters
see Drought
see Earthquakes
see Floods
see Forest fires
see Storms
see Volcanoes

Natural fibers
County Business Patterns, 1987: employment, establishments, and payroll, by SIC 2- to 4-digit industry and county, annual State rpt series, 2326–8

Eastern Europe and USSR agricultural production, acreage, and consumption, by commodity and country, 1965-85, 1528–284

Employment and value added in food and fiber sectors, selected years 1975-87, annual rpt, 1544-19

Employment, earnings, and hours, by SIC 1- to 4-digit industry, monthly 1983-Feb 1989, annual rpt, 6744-4

Exports and imports (agricultural) of US, by commodity and country, bimonthly rpt with articles, 1522-1

Exports and imports (agricultural) of US, by detailed commodity and country, 1988, semiannual rpt, 1522-4

Exports and imports (agricultural) of US with Asia, Middle East, and North Africa, by commodity and country, 1962-86, 1528-277

Exports of US, detailed commodities by country, monthly rpt, 2422-3

Foreign and US agricultural production, trade, and weather devs, weekly press release, 1922-4

Foreign countries agricultural production, prices, and trade, by country, 1970s-89 and forecast 1990, annual world region rpt series, 1524-4

Imports of textiles, by country of origin, monthly rpt, 2042-27

Imports of textiles, by product and country of origin, periodic rpt series, 2046-8; 2046-9

Imports of textiles under Multifiber Arrangement by product and country, and status of bilateral agreements, 1986-88, annual rpt, 9884-18

Imports of US, detailed Schedule A commodities by country, monthly rpt, 2422-2

Manufacturers finances and operations, by SIC 2- to 4-digit industry, forecast 1989 and trends from 1950s, annual rpt, 2044-28

Manufacturing annual survey, 1986: financial and operating data, by SIC 2- to 4-digit industry, series, 2506-15

Manufacturing census, 1987: financial and operating data, for SIC 4-digit industries by product, preliminary rpt, 2491-1.11; 2491-1.14

OECD trade, total and for 4 major countries, and US trade by country, by commodity, 1970-87, world area rpt series, 9116-1

Price indexes (producer), by stage of processing and detailed commodity, monthly rpt, 6762-6

Price indexes (producer), by stage of processing and detailed commodity, monthly 1988, annual rpt, 6764-2

Production itemized costs, receipts, and returns, by commodity and region, 1985-87, annual rpt, 1544-20

Production itemized costs, receipts, and returns, by selected commodity and region, 1975-87, 1548-345

Production, prices, trade, and use of cotton, wool, and synthetic fibers, periodic situation rpt with articles, 1561-1

Production, trade, sales, stocks, and material used, by product, region, and State, periodic Current Industrial Rpt series, 2506-5

Statistical Abstract of US, social, political, and economic data, 1790-2025, comprehensive annual compilation, 2324-1.3

Stockpiling of strategic material by Fed Govt, activity, and inventory by commodity, as of Sept 1989, semiannual rpt, 3542-22; 3902-2

Stockpiling of strategic material, inventories and needs, by commodity, as of Sept 1988, annual rpt, 3544-37

see also Cotton

see also Silk

see also Wool and wool trade

see also under By Commodity in the "Index by Categories"

Natural gas and gas industry

Agriculture census, 1987: farms, farmland, production, finances, and operator characteristics, by county, final State rpt series, 2331-1

Buildings (commercial) energy use, costs, and conservation, by building characteristics, survey rpt series, 3166-8

Business statistics, detailed data for major industries and economic indicators, *Survey of Current Business*, monthly rpt, 2702-1.10

Communist, OECD, and selected other countries energy reserves, production, and use, and oil trade and revenue, 1960s-88, annual rpt, 9114-4.5

Construction industries census, 1987: establishments, employment, receipts, and expenditures, by SIC 4-digit industry and State, final industry rpt series, 2373-1

Construction industries census, 1987: financial and operating data, preliminary industry rpt series, 2371-1

Construction put in place (public and private), by type, bimonthly rpt, 2042-1.1

Construction put in place, value of new public and private structures, by type, monthly rpt, 2382-4

Consumer Expenditure Survey, household income by source, and itemized spending, by selected characteristics and location, 1984-86, annual rpt, 6764-5.2

Consumption, by detailed fuel type, end-use sector, and State, 1960-87, State Energy Data System annual rpt, 3164-39

Consumption of energy, by air pollutant source, fuel type, and State, 1986, annual rpt, 9194-14

County Business Patterns, 1987: employment, establishments, and payroll, by SIC 2- to 4-digit industry and county, annual State rpt series, 2326-8

Cuba economic conditions, agricultural and industrial production and distribution, trade, and intl economic relations, 1980-87 with trends from 1961, 9118-8

Defense Fuel Supply Center procurement, prices, stocks, transport, and other activities and finances, FY88, annual rpt, 3904-8

Earnings by major industry group, and personal income per capita and by source, by region and State, 1929-87, 2708-40

Electric power and industrial plants prohibited from oil and gas primary use, and gas use by State, 1988, annual rpt, 3104-8

Electric power plants (steam) fuel receipts, costs, and quality, by fuel, plant, utility, and State, 1988, annual rpt, 3164-42

Electric power plants and capacity, by fuel used, owner, location, and operating status, 1988 and for units planned 1989-98, annual listing, 3164-36

Electric power plants natural gas use, and fuel and electricity prices, with data by region, 1987-88 and alternative projections to 2000, 3166-6.31

Electric power plants production and capital costs, operations, and fuel use, by fuel type, plant, utility, and location, 1987, annual rpt, 3164-9

Electric power plants production, capacity, sales, and fuel stocks, use, and costs, by State, 1984-88, annual rpt, 3164-11

Electric power plants production, fuel use, stocks, and costs by fuel type, and sales, by State, monthly rpt, 3162-35

Electric utilities fuel cost, quality, use, receipts, and stocks, and power plant production, by energy source, State and utility, quarterly rpt, 3162-39

Employment, earnings, and hours, by SIC 1- to 4-digit industry, monthly 1983-Feb 1989, annual rpt, 6744-4

Employment of minorities and women, by occupation, SIC 1- to 3- digit industry, State, and MSA, 1986, annual rpt, 9244-1

Environmental impacts of energy technologies, 1960s-80s, handbook series, 3326-1

Farm production itemized costs, by farm sales size and region, 1988, annual rpt, 1614-3

Fed Govt energy use and efficiency, by agency and fuel type, FY88, annual rpt, 3304-22

Finances and operations, by SIC 2- to 4-digit industry, forecast 1989 with trends from 1950s, annual rpt, 2044-28

Finances and operations of energy producers, by energy type for US firms domestic and foreign operations, 1987, annual rpt, 3164-44

Foreign and US energy production, trade, use, and reserves, and oil and refined products supply and prices, by country, 1980-88, annual rpt, 3164-50

Foreign and US energy use by sector, and production, by fuel type, country, and country group, projected 1988-2000 and trends from 1970, annual rpt, 3164-84

Foreign and US natural gas plant liquids production, by country group and selected country, monthly rpt, 3162-42

Foreign and US natural gas production, by non-Communist country, monthly rpt, 9112-2

Foreign countries energy-intensive industry output and operations, and US investment barriers, for energy-rich countries, 1984-88, 9886-4.142

Foreign countries mineral production, reserves, and industry role in domestic economy and world supply, world area and country rpt series, 5606-1

Foreign direct investment in US energy sources by type and firm, and US affiliates operations, as of 1988, annual rpt, 3164-80

Govt employment and payroll, by function, level of govt, and jurisdiction, 1987-88, annual rpt series, 2466-1

Helium and other components of natural gas, analyses of individual wells and pipelines, 1917-88, annual rpt, 5604-2

Household utilities spending, by household size, income, householder age and race, and region, 1983, article, 1702-1.904

Housing (rental) market absorption rates, by whether utilities included in rent, 1987, annual Current Housing Rpt, 2484-2

Housing and households detailed characteristics, and unit and neighborhood quality, by location, 1985, biennial rpt, 2485-12

Housing and households detailed characteristics, and unit and neighborhood quality, MSA surveys, series, 2485-6

Housing energy use, costs, and conservation, and household and housing characteristics, survey rpt series, 3166-7

Housing heating and air conditioning equipment shipments by type of fuel used, monthly rpt, 2042-1.6

Housing natural gas use indicators, and conservation R&D spending of DOE and private sector, hearings, 21368-107

Housing units completed, single and multifamily units by structural and financial characteristics, inside-outside MSAs, and region, 1984-88, annual rpt, 2384-1

Labor productivity, indexes of output, hours, and employment by SIC 2- to 4-digit industry, 1963-87, annual rpt, 6824-1.4

Manufacturing energy use and prices, 1985 survey, series, 3166-13

Mergers of oil and gas companies impacts on domestic reserve purchases, exploration, and financial performance, 1982-86, 3168-112

Mineral industries census, 1987: financial and operating data, preliminary industry rpt, 2511-1.5

Minerals Yearbook, 1987, Vol 3: foreign country reviews of production, trade, and policy, by commodity, annual rpt, 5604-35

Minerals Yearbook, 1987, Vol 3 preprints: foreign country reviews of production, trade, and policy, by commodity, annual rpt series, 5604-23

Naval Petroleum and Oil Shale Reserves production and revenue by fuel type, sales by purchaser, and wells, by reserve, FY88, annual rpt, 3004-22

Occupational injury and illness rates, by SIC 2- to 4-digit industry, 1987, annual rpt, 6844-1

Oil fuel switching to other fuels, capability by end-use sector, 1989, annual rpt, 3164-88

Pollution (air) carbon dioxide emissions by fuel type and consuming sector, projected under alternative conservation methods, 1990s-2010, 3006-11.11

Pollution (air) levels for 5 pollutants, by detailed source and State, 1986, annual rpt, 9194-7

Pollution (air) levels for 6 pollutants, by source, 1970-87 and trends from 1940, annual rpt, 9194-13

Production and reserves of oil, gas, and gas liquids, by State and substate area, 1988, annual rpt, 3164-46

Production, dev, and distribution firms revenues and income, quarterly rpt, 3162-38

Production, prices, trade, use, reserves, pipeline finances, and wells classified, for natural and supplemental gas, by firm and State, monthly rpt with articles, 3162-4

Production, wells drilled, and contract prices, by Natural Gas Policy Act section, producer, State, and field, late 1970s-86, 3168-90

Regulatory and ratemaking standards of utilities, status and coverage of consumers and sales by standard, 1988, annual rpt, 3104-7

Science, engineering, and technical employment in transportation, utilities, and retail and wholesale trade, by field, occupation, and industry, 1985, triennial rpt, 9627-32

Statistical Abstract of US, social, political, and economic data, 1790-2025, comprehensive annual compilation, 2324-1.3

Supply, demand, and distribution of energy, and impacts of legislation, series, 3166-6

Supply, demand, and prices, by fuel type and end-use sector, projected under 3 oil price assumptions, 1988-2000, annual rpt, 3164-75

Supply, demand, and prices, by fuel type and end-use sector, with foreign comparisons, 1988 and trends from 1949, annual rpt, 3164-74

Supply, demand, and prices, by fuel type and end use, with foreign comparisons, 1976-88, annual summary rpt, 3164-76

Supply, demand, and prices, by fuel type, end-use sector, and country, detailed data, monthly rpt, 3162-24

Supply, demand, and prices of energy, forecasts by resource type, quarterly rpt, 3162-34

Supply, demand, and prices of oil and gas, alternative projections 1987-2000, annual rpt, 3164-89

Supply, demand, distribution, and prices of natural gas, by State, 1984-88, annual rpt, 3164-4

Tax (income) returns of corporations, income and tax items by asset size and detailed industry, 1986, annual rpt, 8304-4; 8304-21

Transportation energy use by mode, fuel supply, and demographic and economic factors of vehicle use, 1970s-88, annual rpt, 3304-5

Transportation finances, operations, vehicles, equipment, accidents, and energy use, by mode of transport, 1955-88, annual rpt, 7304-2

Utilities privately owned, detailed finances and operations by firm, 1987, annual rpt, 3164-23.1

Wages and employment by occupation, and benefits, by location for oil and gas extraction production workers, 1988 survey, 6787-6.240

see also Energy exploration and drilling
see also Liquefied petroleum gas
see also Natural gas exports and imports
see also Natural gas liquids
see also Natural gas prices
see also Natural gas reserves
see also Offshore oil and gas
see also Oil and gas leases
see also Pipelines
see also By Industry in the "Index by Categories"
see also under By Commodity in the "Index by Categories"

Natural gas exports and imports

China trade by SITC 1- to 5-digit commodity, 1970s-87, annual rpt, 9114-3

Eastern Europe and USSR natural gas trade, by country, monthly rpt, 9112-2

Exports and imports of gas, by country of origin and destination, 1987, annual rpt, 3164-50.3

Exports, imports, production, prices, use, reserves, and pipeline finances, for natural gas, by firm and State, monthly rpt with articles, 3162-4

Exports of US, detailed commodities by country, monthly rpt, 2422-3

Foreign countries mineral production, reserves, and industry role in domestic economy and world supply, world area and country rpt series, 5606-1

Imports and contracted supply of gas from Canada and Mexico, by US pipeline firm, 1987-88, annual rpt, 3164-33.6

Imports of US, detailed Schedule A commodities by country, monthly rpt, 2422-2

Liquids (gas) supply, demand, and movement, by PAD district and State, 1988 and trends from 1973, annual rpt, 3164-2

Liquids (gas) supply, demand, trade, stocks, and refining, by detailed product and PAD district, monthly rpt with articles, 3162-6

Minerals Yearbook, 1987, Vol 3 preprints: foreign country reviews of production, trade, and policy, by commodity, annual rpt series, 5604-23

Pipeline interstate company gas reserves and production, by firm, 1963-88 and deliverability projected to 2007, annual rpt, 3164-33

Statistical Abstract of US, social, political, and economic data, 1790-2025, comprehensive annual compilation, 2324-1.3

Supply, demand, and prices, by fuel type and end-use sector, projected under 3 oil price assumptions, 1988-2000, annual rpt, 3164-75

Supply, demand, and prices, by fuel type and end-use sector, with foreign comparisons, 1988 and trends from 1949, annual rpt, 3164-74

Supply, demand, and prices, by fuel type, end-use sector, and country, detailed data, monthly rpt, 3162-24

Supply, demand, and prices of energy, forecasts by resource type, quarterly rpt, 3162-34

Supply, demand, and prices of oil and gas, alternative projections 1987-2000, annual rpt, 3164-89

Natural gas liquids

Mineral industries census, 1987: financial and operating data, preliminary industry rpt, 2511-1.6

Minerals Yearbook, 1987, Vol 3: foreign country reviews of production, trade, and policy, by commodity, annual rpt, 5604-35

Minerals Yearbook, 1987, Vol 3 preprints: foreign country reviews of production, trade, and policy, by commodity, annual rpt series, 5604-23

see also Conservation of natural resources
see also Energy resources and consumption
see also Fish and fishing industry
see also Forests and forestry
see also Geothermal resources
see also Marine resources
see also Mines and mineral resources
see also Plants and vegetation
see also Reclamation of land
see also Severance taxes
see also Strategic materials
see also Water area
see also Water power
see also Water resources development
see also Water supply and use

Naturalization
see Citizenship

Naturopathy
see Chiropractic and naturopathy

Nauru
Economic, social, political, and geographic
summary data, by country, 1989, annual
factbook, 9114–2
Human rights conditions in 170 countries,
1988, annual rpt, 21384–3
Minerals Yearbook, 1987, Vol 3: foreign
country reviews of production, trade, and
policy, by commodity, annual rpt,
5604–35
Minerals Yearbook, 1987, Vol 3 preprints:
foreign country review of production,
trade, and policy, by commodity, annual
rpt, 5604–23.88
Population size, growth rates, and
components of change, by country,
projected 1989-2020 and trends from
1950, biennial rpt, 2324–9
see also under By Foreign Country in the
"Index by Categories"

Navajo and Hopi Indian Relocation Commission
Activities and caseloads of relocation
program, monthly rpt, 16002–1
Caseloads, activities and finances, FY88,
annual rpt, 16004–1
Caseloads, activities, and finances of
program, by location, annual rpt,
discontinued, 16004–4

Naval Acadmey
see Service academies

Naval Observatory
see U.S. Naval Observatory

Naval Oceanography Command
Hurricanes and tropical storms in Pacific
and Indian Oceans, paths and
surveillance, 1988, annual rpt, 3804–8
Research cruise schedules and ship
characteristics, by higher education instn
and Federal agency, 1989, annual listing,
3804–6

Naval Petroleum Reserves
Production and revenue by fuel type, sales
by purchaser, and wells, by reserve, FY88,
annual rpt, 3004–22
Property (real) of DOE owned and leased,
by type, subagency, contractor, and site,
FY87, annual rpt, 3004–28

Naval science
see also Navigation

Naval stores
see Gum and wood chemicals

Naval vessels
Budget of DOD, justification, programs, and
policies, FY90-91, annual rpt, 3544–2

Budget of DOD, organization, personnel,
weapons, and property, by service branch,
State, and country, 1989 annual summary
rpt, 3504–13
Budget of DOD, procurement appropriations
by item, service branch, and defense
agency, FY88-91, annual rpt, 3544–32
Budget of DOD, weapons acquisition costs
by system and service branch, FY89-91,
annual rpt, 3504–2
Customs Service activities, collections,
entries processed by mode of transport,
and seizures, FY84-88, annual rpt,
8144–1
DOD budget, manpower needs, costs, and
force readiness by service branch, FY90,
annual rpt, 3504–1
Drug and illegal alien enforcement activities
of Coast Guard, 2nd half FY89,
semiannual rpt, 7402–4
Expenditures and obligations of DOD, by
function and service branch, quarterly rpt,
3542–3
Foreign countries military aid and arms
sales of US, by weapon type, as of Sept
1988, annual rpt, 3904–3
Foreign countries military spending, arms
trade, and force strengths, with govt
spending and population, by country,
1977-87, annual rpt, 9824–1
Foreign-flag ships subject to US control, by
type and country of registry and
construction, as of July 1989, semiannual
rpt, 7702–3
Manufacturing annual survey, 1986:
financial and operating data, by SIC 2- to
4-digit industry, series, 2506–15
Manufacturing census, 1987: financial and
operating data, for SIC 4-digit industries
by product, preliminary rpt, 2491–1.77
Marine Corps amphibious ships,
procurement, and costs, projected under
alternative proposals, FY90-2000,
26308–90
Military Sealift Command shipping
operations, finances, and personnel, FY88,
annual rpt, 3804–14
Natl Defense Reserve Fleet inventory from
FY45, and ships and tonnage by vessel
type, with location, FY88, annual rpt,
7704–14.2; 7704–14.4
NATO and Japan military spending and
indicators of ability to support common
defense, by country, 1960s-87, annual rpt,
3544–28
Navy budget, manpower, procurement, and
equipment, planned FY89-91, annual fact
sheet, 3804–16
Pollution (water) incidents and discharges,
by type, source, cause, and location,
1984-86, annual rpt, 7404–3
Price indexes (producer), by stage of
processing and detailed commodity,
monthly 1988, annual rpt, 6764–2
Procurement cost estimates for weapons and
communications systems, by service
branch, quarterly summary rpt, 3502–1
Procurement, DOD prime contract awards
by category, contract and contractor type,
and service branch, FY79-88, semiannual
rpt, 3542–1
Procurement, DOD prime contract awards
by category, contractor type, and State,
FY86-88, annual rpt, 3544–11

Procurement, DOD prime contract awards
by detailed procurement category,
FY85-88, annual rpt, 3544–18
Procurement, DOD prime contract awards
by size and type of contract, service
branch, competitive status, category, and
labor standard, FY88, annual rpt,
3544–19
Reserve fleet inventory, by location, as of
Jan 1989, semiannual listing, 7702–2
Soviet Union and Warsaw Pact military
weapons systems, aid, presence, and force
strengths, and compared to US and
NATO, 1989 annual rpt, 3504–20
Wartime capability of commercial ships,
shipyards, and personnel, for merchant
and reserve fleet, revised estimates,
1985-2000, 11208–3
Wartime capability of commercial ships,
shipyards, and personnel, for merchant
and reserve fleet, 1988-2000, 11208–1
see also Nuclear-powered ships
see also Submarines

Navigation
Army Corps of Engineers water resources
dev projects, characteristics, and costs,
1950s-87, biennial State rpt series,
3756–2
Army Corps of Engineers water resources
dev projects, characteristics, and costs,
1950s-89, biennial State rpt series,
3756–1
Great Lakes ship pilotage activities, costs,
and traffic for US and Canada, and US
testing and certificates, 1960s-87,
7308–192
Manufacturing census, 1987: financial and
operating data, for SIC 4-digit industries
by product, preliminary rpt, 2491–1.78
Mariners Weather Log, quarterly journal,
2152–8
see also Aeronautical navigation
see also Lighthouses and lightships
see also Marine accidents and safety
see also Radar

Navy
Aircraft bird collisions, and related costs, by
service branch, 1975-88, GAO rpt,
26123–241
Criminal case processing in military courts,
and prisoners by facility, by service
branch, 1960s-87, annual rpt, 6064–6.6
Deaths by cause, age, race, and rank, and
personnel captured and missing, by
service branch, 2nd half FY88, semiannual
rpt, 3542–21
Drug and alcohol abuse by military
personnel, prevalence and consequences,
by selected characteristics, 1988, biennial
rpt, 3504–19
Drug and alcohol abuse education and
treatment programs activity of Navy, 2nd
half FY88, semiannual tables, 3802–6
Health care facilities of DOD in US and
abroad, beds, admissions, outpatient visits,
and births, by service branch, quarterly
rpt, 3542–15
Manpower active duty strength, civilian
personnel, and dependents, by service
branch and US and foreign location,
quarterly rpt, 3542–20
Manpower active duty strength, recruits,
and reenlistment, by race, sex, and service
branch, quarterly press release, 3542–7

Manpower, contracts, and payroll of DOD, by service branch and location, with top 5 contractors and maps, by State and country, FY88, annual rpt, 3544–29

Manpower needs, costs, and force readiness, by service branch, FY90, annual rpt, 3504–1

Manpower of DOD, and organization, budget, weapons, and property, by service branch, State, and country, 1989 annual summary rpt, 3504–13

Manpower of DOD, by service branch, major installation, and State, as of Sept 1988, annual rpt, 3544–7

Manpower, procurement, equipment, and budget of Navy, planned FY89-91, annual fact sheet, 3804–16

Manpower statistics for active duty, civilian, and reserve personnel, by service branch, FY88 and trends, annual rpt, 3544–1

Manpower statistics for active duty, civilian, and reserve personnel, by service branch, quarterly rpt, 3542–14

Manpower strengths, accessions, and attrition, detailed statistics for Navy and Naval Reserve, quarterly rpt, 3802–4

Manpower strengths in US and abroad, by service branch, world area, and country, quarterly press release, 3542–9

Manpower strengths, summary by service branch, monthly press release, 3542–2

Military Sealift Command shipping operations, finances, and personnel, FY88, annual rpt, 3804–14

NATO Europe members presence of US military and civilian personnel and dependents, by service branch, 1980-88, GAO rpt, 26123–252

NATO Europe members presence of US military and civilian personnel, and vacancies, by service branch, 1988, GAO rpt, 26123–251

Pilot proficiency program of Navy, aircraft hours flown and costs, FY83-87, GAO rpt, 26123–238

Reserve forces manpower strengths and characteristics, by component, quarterly rpt, 3542–4

Statistical Abstract of US, social, political, and economic data, 1790-2025, comprehensive annual compilation, 2324–1.2

Training and education programs of DOD, funding, staff, students, and facilities, by service branch, FY90, annual rpt, 3504–5

Women military personnel on active and reserve duty, by demographic and service characteristics and service branch, FY88, annual chartbook, 3544–26

see also Department of Navy
see also Marine Corps
see also Naval Petroleum Reserves
see also Naval vessels

Nduku, Willie
"Rhino Conservation Strategy in Zimbabwe Codenamed Operation Stronghold", 21708–125

Near East
see Middle East

Nebraska
Agriculture census, 1987: farms, farmland, production and costs, and operator characteristics, advance State and county rpts, 2330–1.31

Agriculture census, 1987: farms, farmland, production, finances, and operator characteristics, by county, final State rpt, 2331–1.27

Bank deposits in FDIC-insured commercial and savings banks, by instn, State, and county, as of June 1988, annual regional rpt, 9295–3.5

Bus (intercity) route in Nebraska, indicators of need, finances, and service and funding alternatives, 1980s, 7888–76

Corn and soybean futures contract yield and price risk hedging strategies, by selected county and State, model results, 1961-83, 1548–352

County Business Patterns, 1987: employment, establishments, and payroll, by SIC 2- to 4-digit industry and county, annual State rpt, 2326–8.29

Deaths and rates, by detailed location, cause, and demographic characteristics, 1987, US Vital Statistics annual rpt, 4144–3.1

DOD prime contract awards, by contractor, service branch, State, and city, FY88, annual rpt, 3544–22

Employment, earnings, and hours, by selected SIC 1- to 4-digit industry, State, and for 262 MSAs, 1972-87, 6748–81.3

Farm operators displaced worker programs under Job Training Partnership Act, funding, participation, and results by selected State, 1982-87, 15496–1.2

Fed Govt spending in States and local areas, by type, State, county, and city, FY88, annual rpt, 2464–3

Fed Govt spending in States, by type, program, agency, and State, FY88, annual rpt, 2464–2

HHS financial aid, by program, recipient, State, and city, FY88, annual regional listing, 4004–3.7

Homeless children educational enrollment and needs, 1988, annual State rpt, 4804–35.27

Income (personal) per capita and by source, and earnings by industry div, by State, MSA, and county, 1982-87, annual regional rpt, 2704–2.3

Mineral Industry Surveys, State reviews of production, 1988, preliminary annual rpt, 5614–6

Minerals Yearbook, 1987, Vol 2 preprints: State review of production and sales by commodity, and business activity, annual rpt, 5604–16.28

Minerals Yearbook, 1987, Vol 2: State reviews of production, sales, and firms, by commodity, and business activity, annual rpt, 5604–34

Nursing home compliance with Medicare and Medicaid regulations, and patient characteristics, by facility, 1987/88, annual State rpt, 4654–15.28

Retail trade census, 1987: employment, establishments, sales, and payroll, by SIC 2- to 4-digit kind of business, MSA, county, and city, State rpt, 2397–1.28

Savings instns, FHLB 10th District members finances and lending by State and MSA, monthly table, 9302–22

Savings instns, FHLB 10th District members financial condition, by State, quarterly rpt, 9302–34

Service industries census, 1987: employment, establishments, receipts, and payroll, by SIC 2- to 4-digit kind of business, MSA, county, and city, State rpt, 2391–1.28

Statistical Abstract of US, social, political, and economic data, with foreign comparisons, 1790-2025, comprehensive annual compilation, 2324–1

Water supply and quality in streams and lakes, and groundwater levels in wells, by drainage basin, 1987, annual State rpt, 5666–10.26

Wholesale trade census, 1987: employment, establishments, finances, and operations, by SIC 2- to 4-digit kind of business, MSA, county, and city, State rpt, 2405–1.28

Wildlife-related recreation, hunting, and fishing participation and spending, detailed data, 1985 survey, quinquennial State rpt, 5506–6.27

see also Grand Island, Nebr.
see also Hastings, Nebr.
see also Omaha, Nebr.
see also under By State in the "Index by Categories"

Neenah, Wis.
see also under By SMSA or MSA in the "Index by Categories"

Negotiable orders of withdrawal accounts
Banks (insured commercial) domestic and foreign office consolidated financial statements, monthly rpt, quarterly data, 9362–1.4

Banks (insured commercial and savings) finances, for foreign and domestic offices, by asset size, 1987, annual rpt, 9294–4.2

Debits, deposits, and deposit turnover, for commercial banks by type of account, monthly rpt, 9365–2.5

New England States, banks, thrifts, and financial statements by type of instn and Fed deposit insurance, and State, 1987, annual rpt, 9304–3

North Central States, FHLB 8th District savings instns financial operations by State and SMSA, monthly rpt, 9302–9

Savings instns (FSLIC-insured) assets, liabilities, and deposit and loan activity, and compared to all S&Ls, monthly rpt, 9312–4

Savings instns cost of funds index of FHLB of San Francisco, components and forecasting accuracy, 1987-89, working paper, 9306–1.10

Savings instns financial statements, FSLIC-insured instns by FHLB district and State, and FDIC-insured savings banks, 1988, annual rpt, 8434–1

Savings instns insured by Savings Assn Insurance Fund, assets, liabilities, and deposit and loan activity, by conservatorship status, monthly rpt, 8432–1

South Central States, FHLB 9th District savings instns finances and operations by State, quarterly rpt, 9302–31

Southeastern States, Fed Reserve 5th District insured commercial banks financial statements, by State, quarterly rpt, 9389–18

Statistical Abstract of US, social, political, and economic data, 1790-2025, comprehensive annual compilation, 2324–1.3

Negotiations
see Labor-management relations, general
see Labor-management relations in
government
see Labor-management relations, local and
regional
see Legal arbitration and mediation
see Strategic Arms Reduction Talks
see Treaties and conventions

Negroes
see Black Americans

Neidert, Lisa J.
"Analyzing the Characteristics of Blacks: A
Comparison of Data from SIPP and CPS",
2626–10.84

Neighborhood Reinvestment Corp.
Budget of US Appendix, obligations,
appropriations, and personnel, by program
and agency, FY90, annual rpt, 104–3
Budget of US, authoritative financial
statements with appropriations, outlays,
and receipts, by category and agency,
FY88, annual rpt, 8104–2.2

Neighborhoods
Crime and crime-related issues, public
opinion by respondent characteristics,
1970s-89, annual rpt, 6064–6.2
Mortgages by lender type and related to
neighborhood characteristics, for Boston,
Mass, 1982-87, article, 9373–1.915
Quality of housing and neighborhoods,
indicators and attitudes, by householder
type and location, 1985, biennial rpt,
2485–12
Quality of housing and neighborhoods,
indicators and attitudes, MSA surveys,
series, 2485–6
Services provided by Residential
Community Assns, and RCAs relations
with local govts, 1988 conf, 10048–75
see also Community development
see also ZIP codes

Nelson, Cheryl
"Office Visits to Cardiovascular Disease
Specialists, 1985", 4146–8.174

Nelson, Julie A.
"Food Quantity Data in the U.S. Consumer
Expenditure Survey: An Evaluation of
Usefulness for Economic and Statistical
Studies", 6886–6.43
"Household Economies of Scale in
Consumption: Theory and Evidence",
6886–6.40
"Individual Consumption Within the
Household: A Study of Expenditures on
Clothing", 6886–6.44
"Latent Family Influences on Individual
Expenditures for Clothing", 6886–6.61
"Quantity Aggregation and Price Variation
in U.S. Consumer Demand for Food",
6886–6.37

Nelson, Richard R.
"State Labor Legislation Enacted in 1988",
6722–1.904

Nelson, Susan
"Master Limited Partnerships: A View from
Their 1986 Tax Returns", 8006–3.59

Nelson, William J., Jr.
"Workers' Compensation: Coverage,
Benefits, and Costs, 1986", 4742–1.912

Neme, Laurel A.
"Survey of Government Assistance for the
World's Hard Coal Industries", 2048–144

Neoplasms
Agent Orange exposure health effects,
literature review, 1987, annual rpt series,
8706–1
Agent Orange exposure of Air Force
personnel, deaths and rates by cause and
selected characteristics, 1989 annual rpt,
3604–3
Alaska Natives cancer cases and risk, by
body site and ethnic group, 1969-83,
article, 4042–3.963
Alcohol use and abuse among minority
groups, and related problems, by selected
characteristics, 1985 conf papers,
4488–13
Asbestos in drinking water relation to
cancer incidence, by sex and cancer site,
1973-83, local area study, article,
4042–3.921
Breast and cervical cancer incidence, deaths,
and survival rates, by race, average
1973-81, article, 4042–3.952
Breast cancer screening, use and client
characteristics for low-income women's
mammography referral services, 1987-88
local area study, article, 4042–3.951
Breast cancer survival rates, for patients
receiving chemotherapy after surgery, for
diagnoses made 1975-85, GAO rpt,
26131–58
Cases of cancer, death, and survival rates,
by age, sex, race, and body site, 1973-86,
annual rpt, 4474–35
Cervical cancer screening and education
program for black women, effectiveness
and participant characteristics, 1988 local
area study, article, 4042–3.953
Child death rates, by age, sex, race, and
cause, for US and compared to 8 OECD
countries, 1985 and trends from 1900,
4147–3.27
Deaths and rates, by cause, age, sex, marital
status, race, and State, 1987, US Vital
Statistics advance annual rpt, 4146–5.113
Deaths and rates, by cause and age,
preliminary 1987-88, US Vital Statistics
annual rpt, 4144–7
Deaths and rates, by detailed cause and
demographic characteristics, 1986 and
trends from 1900, US Vital Statistics
annual rpt, 4144–2
Deaths and rates, by detailed location,
cause, and demographic characteristics,
1987, US Vital Statistics annual rpt,
4144–3
Deaths and rates from cancer, by body site,
provisional data, monthly rpt, 4142–1
Dioxin levels in paper products and pulp
mill effluents, and environmental and
health effects, 1988 hearing, 21368–112
Health condition and health care resources,
use, and spending, 1950s-87, annual data
compilation, 4144–11
HHS financial aid, by program, recipient,
State, and city, FY88, annual regional
listings, 4004–3
Hospital discharges and length of stay, by
diagnosis, patient age and sex, surgical
procedure performed, and region,
1965-86, 4147–13.101
Hospital discharges and length of stay, by
diagnosis, patient and instn characteristics,
procedure performed, and payment
source, 1987, annual rpt, 4147–13.99

Hospital discharges by detailed diagnostic
and procedure category, primary
diagnosis, and length of stay, by age, sex,
and region, 1987, annual rpt,
4147–13.100
Indian (Seneca Tribe) deaths and years of
potential life lost, by selected cause and
sex, various periods 1955-84, article,
4042–3.925
Indian Health Service and contract facilities
hospitalization, by diagnosis, age, sex, and
service area, FY87, annual rpt, 4104–16
Indian Health Service and contract facilities
hospitalization, by diagnosis, age, sex, and
service area, FY88, annual rpt, 4084–5
Indian Health Service facilities, funding,
operations, and Indian health and other
characteristics, 1950s-88, annual
chartbook, 4084–1
Kaposi's sarcoma deaths of AIDS patients,
weekly rpt, 4202–9
Military deaths by cause, age, race, and
rank, and personnel captured and missing,
by service branch, 2nd half FY88,
semiannual rpt, 3542–21
Natl Cancer Inst contracts and grants, by
recipient and location, FY88, annual
listing, 4474–28
Navy personnel radiation exposure on
nuclear-powered vessels and at support
facilities, and injury claims, 1950s-88,
annual rpt, 3804–10
Nursing home facility, staff, and resident
detailed characteristics, 1985,
4147–13.97
Older persons cancer screening by
physicians and compliance with American
Cancer Society schedules, by speciality,
1986 local area study, article,
4042–3.917
Pollutants health effects, concentrations in
food and environment, sources, and
human intake methodology and data
needs, series, 9186–9
Pollutants health effects, concentrations in
food and environment, sources, human
intake, and regulation, series, 9186–8
Research on cancer epidemiology and
biochemistry, semimonthly journal,
4472–1
Smoking and health effects, with trends in
smoking, related disease and death, and
public attitudes, literature review, 1989
annual rpt, 4204–18
Smoking and health research rpts, 1988, last
issue of annual listing, 4204–19
Smoking and health research summaries,
bimonthly rpt, 4202–8
Smoking prevalence, related disease and
deaths, and public attitudes, impact of
Surgeon General rpts and antismoking
campaigns, 1964-89, annual rpt, 4204–18
Statistical Abstract of US, social, political,
and economic data, 1790-2025,
comprehensive annual compilation,
2324–1.1
Treatments and health products not proven
safe or effective, use, costs, and user
characteristics, 1986 survey, 4008–86
West Virginia poverty conditions, food aid
participants, and birth outcomes, 1980-87,
hearing, 21968–49
see also Carcinogens
see also under By Disease in the "Index by
Categories"

Networks

see Computer networks

see Information storage and retrieval systems

see Public broadcasting

see Radio

see Television

Neuberger, Jonathan A.

"Capital Market Imperfections and the q-Theory of Investment: Theory and Evidence", 9393–10.9

Neumark, David

"After-Hours Stock Prices and Post-Crash Hangovers", 9366–6.164

"Market Structure and the Nature of Price Rigidity: Evidence from the Market for Consumer Deposits", 9366–6.166

Neurological disorders

Cases of acute and chronic conditions, disability, absenteeism, and health services use, by selected characteristics, 1988, annual rpt, 4147–10.170

Deaths and rates, by detailed cause and demographic characteristics, 1986 and trends from 1900, US Vital Statistics annual rpt, 4144–2

Disability Insurance and SSI eligibility determinations for mental impairment, caseload and review activities by impairment type and State, 1984-86, hearing, 21788–176

Epilepsy patients cancer risk relation to anticonvulsant drug treatment and radioactive thorium dioxide exposure, 1989 article, 4472–1.914

Epileptic persons employment discrimination, model description, 1988 working paper, 6886–6.59

HHS financial aid, by program, recipient, State, and city, FY88, annual regional listings, 4004–3

Hospital discharges and length of stay, by diagnosis, patient and instn characteristics, procedure performed, and payment source, 1987, annual rpt, 4147–13.99

Hospital discharges by detailed diagnostic and procedure category, primary diagnosis, and length of stay, by age, sex, and region, 1987, annual rpt, 4147–13.100

Hospital mental health care units, length of stay related to patient, instn, and State Medicaid program characteristics, 1981, article, 4652–1.924

Indian Health Service and contract facilities hospitalization, by diagnosis, age, sex, and service area, FY87, annual rpt, 4104–16

Indian Health Service and contract facilities hospitalization, by diagnosis, age, sex, and service area, FY88, annual rpt, 4084–5

Infectious notifiable disease cases, by age, State, and outlying area, and deaths, 1930s-88, annual rpt, 4204–1

Insurance (health) companies case mgmt for high-cost patients, savings, costs, and returns, 1984-86, article, 4652–1.914

Morbidity and Mortality Weekly Report, infectious notifiable disease cases by State, and public health issues, 4202–1

Nursing home facility, staff, and resident detailed characteristics, 1985, 4147–13.97

Patients and admissions of State and county mental hospitals, by age, diagnosis, and State, FY87, annual rpt, 4504–2

Pollutants health effects, concentrations in food and environment, sources, human intake, and regulation, series, 9186–8

Veterans disability and death compensation cases of VA, by entitlement type, period of service, sex, age, and State, FY88, annual rpt, 8604–7

see also Mental health and illness

see also Rabies

see also Spinal cord injuries

see also under By Disease in the "Index by Categories"

Nevada

Agriculture census, 1987: farms, farmland, production and costs, and operator characteristics, advance State and county rpts, 2330–1.32

Agriculture census, 1987: farms, farmland, production, finances, and operator characteristics, by county, final State rpt, 2331–1.28

Bank deposits in FDIC-insured commercial and savings banks, by instn, State, and county, as of June 1988, annual regional rpt, 9295–3.6

County Business Patterns, 1987: employment, establishments, and payroll, by SIC 2- to 4-digit industry and county, annual State rpt, 2326–8.30

Deaths and rates, by detailed location, cause, and demographic characteristics, 1987, US Vital Statistics annual rpt, 4144–3.1

DOD prime contract awards, by contractor, service branch, State, and city, FY88, annual rpt, 3544–22

Employment, earnings, and hours, by selected SIC 1- to 4-digit industry, State, and for 262 MSAs, 1972-87, 6748–81.3

Fed Govt spending in States and local areas, by type, State, county, and city, FY88, annual rpt, 2464–3

Fed Govt spending in States, by type, program, agency, and State, FY88, annual rpt, 2464–2

HHS financial aid, by program, recipient, State, and city, FY88, annual regional listing, 4004–3.9

Homeless children educational enrollment and needs, 1988, annual State rpt, 4804–35.28

Income (personal) per capita and by source, and earnings by industry div, by State, MSA, and county, 1982-87, annual regional rpt, 2704–2.5

Mineral Industry Surveys, State reviews of production, 1988, preliminary annual rpt, 5614–6

Minerals Yearbook, 1987, Vol 2 preprints: State review of production and sales by commodity, and business activity, annual rpt, 5604–16.29

Minerals Yearbook, 1987, Vol 2: State reviews of production, sales, and firms, by commodity, and business activity, annual rpt, 5604–34

Mining shares of gross product, employment, earnings, and other economic impacts, 1977-86, article, 5602–4.902

Nursing home compliance with Medicare and Medicaid regulations, and patient characteristics, by facility, 1987/88, annual State rpt, 4654–15.29

Radionuclide concentrations in air, water, humans, animals, and milk near Nevada and other nuclear test sites, 1988, annual rpt, 9194–17

Retail trade census, 1987: employment, establishments, sales, and payroll, by SIC 2- to 4-digit kind of business, MSA, county, and city, State rpt, 2397–1.29

River and stream environmental conditions, fish, wildlife, use, and mgmt, 1989 rpt, 5506–9.39

Savings instns, FHLB 11th District member offices, locations, savings balances, and accounts, quarterly listing, 9302–20

Service industries census, 1987: employment, establishments, receipts, and payroll, by SIC 2- to 4-digit kind of business, MSA, county, and city, State rpt, 2391–1.29

Statistical Abstract of US, social, political, and economic data, with foreign comparisons, 1790-2025, comprehensive annual compilation, 2324–1

Water supply and quality in streams and lakes, and groundwater levels in wells, by drainage basin, 1987, annual State rpt, 5666–10.27

Water supply, and snow survey results, monthly State rpt, 1266–2.6

Water supply, and snow survey results, 1988, annual State rpt, 1264–14.10

Wholesale trade census, 1987: employment, establishments, finances, and operations, by SIC 2- to 4-digit kind of business, MSA, county, and city, State rpt, 2405–1.29

Wildlife-related recreation, hunting, and fishing participation and spending, detailed data, 1985 survey, quinquennial State rpt, 5506–6.28

see also Las Vegas, Nev.

see also Reno, Nev.

see also Tonopah, Nev.

see also under By State in the "Index by Categories"

New Bedford, Mass.

Fish and shellfish catch, wholesale receipts, prices, trade, and other market activities, weekly regional rpt, 2162–6.1; 2162–6.2

see also under By SMSA or MSA in the "Index by Categories"

New Bern, N.C.

Wages by occupation, and benefits for office and plant workers, 1989 survey, periodic MSA rpt, 6785–3.2

New Britain, Conn.

see also under By SMSA or MSA in the "Index by Categories"

New Caledonia

Economic, social, political, and geographic summary data, by country, 1989, annual factbook, 9114–2

Minerals Yearbook, 1987, Vol 3: foreign country reviews of production, trade, and policy, by commodity, annual rpt, 5604–35

Minerals Yearbook, 1987, Vol 3 preprints: foreign country review of production, trade, and policy, by commodity, annual rpt, 5604–23.88

Population size, growth rates, and components of change, by country, projected 1989-2020 and trends from 1950, biennial rpt, 2324–9

New England
see Northeast States
see under By Census Division in the "Index by Categories"
New Guinea
see Papua New Guinea
New Hampshire
Agriculture census, 1987: farms, farmland, production, finances, and operator characteristics, by county, final State rpt, 2331–1.29
Bank deposits in FDIC-insured commercial and savings banks, by instn, State, and county, as of June 1988, annual regional rpt, 9295–3.1
Banks and thrifts in New England, financial statements by type of instn and Fed deposit insurance, and State, 1987, annual rpt, 9304–3
County Business Patterns, 1987: employment, establishments, and payroll, by SIC 2- to 4-digit industry and county, annual State rpt, 2326–8.31
Deaths and rates, by detailed location, cause, and demographic characteristics, 1987, US Vital Statistics annual rpt, 4144–3.1
DOD prime contract awards, by contractor, service branch, State, and city, FY88, annual rpt, 3544–22
Economic indicators for New England States, Fed Reserve 1st District, monthly rpt, 9373–24
Economic indicators for New England States, Fed Reserve 1st District, quarterly rpt with articles, 9373–2
Employment, earnings, and hours, by selected SIC 1- to 4-digit industry, State, and for 262 MSAs, 1972-87, 6748–81.3
Fed Govt spending in States and local areas, by type, State, county, and city, FY88, annual rpt, 2464–3
Fed Govt spending in States, by type, program, agency, and State, FY88, annual rpt, 2464–2
HHS financial aid, by program, recipient, State, and city, FY88, annual regional listing, 4004–3.1
Homeless children educational enrollment and needs, 1988, annual State rpt, 4804–35.29
Income (personal) per capita and by source, and earnings by industry div, by State, MSA, and county, 1982-87, annual regional rpt, 2704–2.2
Mineral Industry Surveys, State reviews of production, 1988, preliminary annual rpt, 5614–6
Minerals Yearbook, 1987, Vol 2 preprints: State review of production and sales by commodity, and business activity, annual rpt, 5604–16.30
Minerals Yearbook, 1987, Vol 2: State reviews of production, sales, and firms, by commodity, and business activity, annual rpt, 5604–34
Nursing home compliance with Medicare and Medicaid regulations, and patient characteristics, by facility, 1987/88, annual State rpt, 4654–15.30
Retail trade census, 1987: employment, establishments, sales, and payroll, by SIC 2- to 4-digit kind of business, MSA, county, and city, State rpt, 2397–1.30

Savings instns, FHLB 1st District members financial operations and related economic and housing indicators, monthly rpt, 9302–4
Service industries census, 1987: employment, establishments, receipts, and payroll, by SIC 2- to 4-digit kind of business, MSA, county, and city, State rpt, 2391–1.30
Statistical Abstract of US, social, political, and economic data, with foreign comparisons, 1790-2025, comprehensive annual compilation, 2324–1
Wages by occupation, for office and plant workers, 1989 survey, periodic labor market rpt, 6785–3.10
Water supply in northeastern US, precipitation and stream runoff by station, monthly rpt, 2182–3
Wholesale trade census, 1987: employment, establishments, finances, and operations, by SIC 2- to 4-digit kind of business, MSA, county, and city, State rpt, 2405–1.30
Wildlife-related recreation, hunting, and fishing participation and spending, detailed data, 1985 survey, quinquennial State rpt, 5506–6.29
see also under By State in the "Index by Categories"
New Haven, Conn.
AIDS cases, and health and social services availability, for 5 cities, 1988, GAO rpt, 26121–307
see also under By City and By SMSA or MSA in the "Index by Categories"
New Hebrides
see Vanuatu
New Jersey
Agriculture census, 1987: farms, farmland, production and costs, and operator characteristics, advance State and county rpts, 2330–1.34
Agriculture census, 1987: farms, farmland, production, finances, and operator characteristics, by county, final State rpt, 2331–1.30
Asian American earnings, and employment and other characteristics, by detailed origin and whether foreign-born, 1980, 11046–7.2
Bank deposits in FDIC-insured commercial and savings banks, by instn, State, and county, as of June 1988, annual regional rpt, 9295–3.1
County Business Patterns, 1987: employment, establishments, and payroll, by SIC 2- to 4-digit industry and county, annual State rpt, 2326–8.32
Cranberry production, prices, use, and acreage, for selected States, 1987-88 and forecast 1989, annual rpt, 1621–18.4
Deaths and rates, by detailed location, cause, and demographic characteristics, 1987, US Vital Statistics annual rpt, 4144–3.1
DOD prime contract awards, by contractor, service branch, State, and city, FY88, annual rpt, 3544–22
Economic and housing indicators for FHLB 2nd District, by State, quarterly rpt with articles, 9302–33
Employment by industry div in New York and northeastern New Jersey, unemployment, and consumer price changes by selected commodity, 1978-June 1989, press release, 6926–2.40

Employment, earnings, and hours, by selected SIC 1- to 4-digit industry, State, and for 262 MSAs, 1972-87, 6748–81.3
Employment growth and unemployment rates, Fed Reserve 3rd District, quarterly rpt, 9387–10
Fed Govt spending in States and local areas, by type, State, county, and city, FY88, annual rpt, 2464–3
Fed Govt spending in States, by type, program, agency, and State, FY88, annual rpt, 2464–2
HHS financial aid, by program, recipient, State, and city, FY88, annual regional listing, 4004–3.2
Homeless children educational enrollment and needs, 1988, annual State rpt, 4804–35.30
Hospital elective admissions relation to costs and length of stay, for New Jersey, 1982, article, 4652–1.930
Hudson-Raritan River basin pollutant levels and sources, model description and results, 1880s-1982, 2178–22
Income (personal) per capita and by source, and earnings by industry div, by State, MSA, and county, 1982-87, annual regional rpt, 2704–2.2
Mineral Industry Surveys, State reviews of production, 1988, preliminary annual rpt, 5614–6
Minerals Yearbook, 1987, Vol 2 preprints: State review of production and sales by commodity, and business activity, annual rpt, 5604–16.31
Minerals Yearbook, 1987, Vol 2: State reviews of production, sales, and firms, by commodity, and business activity, annual rpt, 5604–34
Nursing home compliance with Medicare and Medicaid regulations, and patient characteristics, by facility, 1987/88, annual State rpt, 4654–15.31
Retail trade census, 1987: employment, establishments, sales, and payroll, by SIC 2- to 4-digit kind of business, MSA, county, and city, State rpt, 2397–1.31
Savings instns, FHLB 2nd District members capital and assets under capital requirements increase proposal, by State, 3rd qtr 1988, article, 9302–33.901
Savings instns, FHLB 2nd District members finances and operations, by State, quarterly rpt, 9302–14
Service industries census, 1987: employment, establishments, receipts, and payroll, by SIC 2- to 4-digit kind of business, MSA, county, and city, State rpt, 2391–1.31
Smoking prevention program for black high school students in urban areas, teacher and student views, 1989 local areas surveys, article, 4042–3.956
Statistical Abstract of US, social, political, and economic data, with foreign comparisons, 1790-2025, comprehensive annual compilation, 2324–1
Unemployed displaced workers, labor-mgmt committee aid recipients by selected characteristics, for 4 State programs, 1988, GAO rpt, 26121–316
Unemployment insurance reemployment and training services, and bonus for early reemployment, New Jersey demonstration project results, 1987-88, 6406–6.27

Water supply and quality in streams and lakes, and groundwater levels in wells, by drainage basin, 1987, annual State rpt, 5666–10.29

Wholesale trade census, 1987: employment, establishments, finances, and operations, by SIC 2- to 4-digit kind of business, MSA, county, and city, State rpt, 2405–1.31

Wildlife-related recreation, hunting, and fishing participation and spending, detailed data, 1985 survey, quinquennial State rpt, 5506–6.30

see also Atlantic City, N.J.

see also Bergen County, N.J.

see also Monmouth County, N.J.

see also Newark, N.J.

see also Ocean County, N.J.

see also Passaic, N.J.

see also Trenton, N.J.

see also under By State in the "Index by Categories"

New London, Conn.

see also under By SMSA or MSA in the "Index by Categories"

New Mexico

Agriculture census, 1987: farms, farmland, production and costs, and operator characteristics, advance State and county rpts, 2330–1.35

Agriculture census, 1987: farms, farmland, production, finances, and operator characteristics, by county, final State rpt, 2331–1.31

Bank deposits in FDIC-insured commercial and savings banks, by instn, State, and county, as of June 1988, annual regional rpt, 9295–3.6

Coal production and mines by county, prices, productivity, miners, reserves, and stocks, by mining method and State, 1987-88, annual rpt, 3164–25

County Business Patterns, 1987: employment, establishments, and payroll, by SIC 2- to 4-digit industry and county, annual State rpt, 2326–8.33

Deaths and rates, by detailed location, cause, and demographic characteristics, 1987, US Vital Statistics annual rpt, 4144–3.1

DOD prime contract awards, by contractor, service branch, State, and city, FY88, annual rpt, 3544–22

Employment by industry div, earnings, and hours, by southwestern State, monthly rpt, 6962–2

Employment, earnings, and hours, by selected SIC 1- to 4-digit industry, State, and for 262 MSAs, 1972-87, 6748–81.3

Erosion (wind) damage costs to households, 1985, 1588–140

Fed Govt spending in States and local areas, by type, State, county, and city, FY88, annual rpt, 2464–3

Fed Govt spending in States, by type, program, agency, and State, FY88, annual rpt, 2464–2

HHS financial aid, by program, recipient, State, and city, FY88, annual regional listing, 4004–3.6

Homeless children educational enrollment and needs, 1988, annual State rpt, 4804–35.31

Income (personal) per capita and by source, and earnings by industry div, by State, MSA, and county, 1982-87, annual regional rpt, 2704–2.5

Indian (Navajo and Hopi) relocation program activities, caseloads, and finances, FY88, annual rpt, 16004–1

Indian diabetes cases, by tribe, for New Mexico, 1985, article, 4042–3.964

Mineral Industry Surveys, State reviews of production, 1988, preliminary annual rpt, 5614–6

Minerals resources and availability on public lands, 1987, State rpt, 5606–7.5

Minerals Yearbook, 1987, Vol 2 preprints: State review of production and sales by commodity, and business activity, annual rpt, 5604–16.32

Minerals Yearbook, 1987, Vol 2: State reviews of production, sales, and firms, by commodity, and business activity, annual rpt, 5604–34

Minerals Yearbook, 1988, Vol 2 rpts: State review of production and sales by commodity, and business activity, annual rpt, 5604–22.32

Nursing home compliance with Medicare and Medicaid regulations, and patient characteristics, by facility, 1987/88, annual State rpt, 4654–15.32

Oil and gas leasing activity on Federal land, production, revenue, and royalty rates, by whether competitively leased and western State, 1984-88, GAO rpt, 26113–413

Peppers (dried chili and paprika) acreage and production in California and New Mexico, 1971-88, FAS annual circular, 1925–15.1

Potash production, prices, trade by country, use, and sales, 1988 crop year, Mineral Industry Surveys, annual rpt, 5614–19

Radioactive waste (military) disposal at New Mexico Waste Isolation Pilot Plant, environmental impacts, 1989 supplemental statement, 3008–33

Retail trade census, 1987: employment, establishments, sales, and payroll, by SIC 2- to 4-digit kind of business, MSA, county, and city, State rpt, 2397–1.32

Savings instns, FHLB 9th District members finances and operations by State, monthly rpt, 9302–13

Savings instns, FHLB 9th District members finances and operations by State, quarterly rpt, 9302–31

Service industries census, 1987: employment, establishments, receipts, and payroll, by SIC 2- to 4-digit kind of business, MSA, county, and city, State rpt, 2391–1.32

Statistical Abstract of US, social, political, and economic data, with foreign comparisons, 1790-2025, comprehensive annual compilation, 2324–1

Timber in New Mexico, acreage and resources by species, ownership class, and county, 1986-87, series, 1206–23

Timber in New Mexico, production and mill residue, by species, ownership, and county, 1986, 1206–17.11

Timber in New Mexico, resources and harvest, 1987, 1208–310

Water resources data collection and analysis activities of USGS New Mexico District, with project descriptions, FY88, 5668–86

Water supply and quality in streams and lakes, and groundwater levels in wells, by drainage basin, 1987, annual State rpt, 5666–10.30

Water supply, and snow survey results, monthly State rpt, 1266–2.11

Water supply, and snow survey results, 1988, annual State rpt, 1264–14.1

Wholesale trade census, 1987: employment, establishments, and operations, by SIC 2- to 4-digit kind of business, MSA, county, and city, State rpt, 2405–1.32

Wildlife-related recreation, hunting, and fishing participation and spending, detailed data, 1985 survey, quinquennial State rpt, 5506–6.31

Wood fuel harvest in New Mexico, by species, ownership, and county, 1986, 1208–303

see also Alamogordo, N.Mex.

see also Albuquerque, N.Mex.

see also Las Cruces, N.Mex.

see also under By State in the "Index by Categories"

New Orleans, La.

AIDS cases, and health and social services availability, for 5 cities, 1988, GAO rpt, 26121–307

Drug abuse indicators for selected metro areas, research results, data collection, and policy issues, 1989 semiannual conf, 4492–5

Drug test results at arrest, by drug type, offense, and sex, for selected urban areas, quarterly rpt, 6062–3

Fish and shellfish catch, wholesale receipts, prices, trade, and other market activities, weekly regional rpt, 2162–6.3

Freight (waterborne domestic and foreign) by commodity, traffic, and passengers, by port and waterway, 1987, annual rpt, 3754–3.2

Fruit and vegetable shipments, and arrivals in US and Canada cities, by mode of transport and State and country of origin, 1988, annual rpt, 1311–4.2

Housing starts and completions authorized by building permits in 40 MSAs, quarterly rpt, 2382–9

Wages by occupation, for office and plant workers, 1988 survey, periodic MSA rpt, 6785–11.1

see also under By City and By SMSA or MSA in the "Index by Categories"

New York Bight

Fishing (sport) catch and hours fished in New York Bight, by type of boat rental, 1971, article, 2162–1.901

Freight (waterborne domestic and foreign) by commodity, traffic, and passengers, by port and waterway, 1987, annual rpt, 3754–3.1

Pollutant concentrations in coastal and estuarine sediments, by contaminant and selected site, 1984-87, 2176–3.7

Pollutant concentrations in coastal and estuarine shellfish, by pollutant and location, 1986-88, 2176–3.8

Pollutant levels and sources for Hudson-Raritan River basin, model description and results, 1880s-1982, 2178–22

New York City

Aliens exclusion and deportation cases, appeals, bond postings, and investigations, for NYC and Los Angeles, 1987, GAO rpt, 26119–271

Banks (commercial) debits to demand deposits, and demand deposits and turnover, monthly rpt, 9365–2.5

Banks balance sheets, by Fed Reserve District, for major banks in NYC, and for US branches and agencies of foreign banks, weekly rpt, 9365–1.3

CPI by component for US city average, and by region, population size, and for 15 metro areas, monthly rpt, 6762–1

CPI by component for US city average, and by region, population size, and for 27 metro areas, monthly rpt, 6762–2

Diplomats and staff with immunity for foreign missions in US and US missions abroad, and foreign diplomats criminal cases, 1978-87, hearing, 25388–51

Drug abuse emergency room admissions and deaths, by drug type and source, sex, race, age, and major metro area, 1988, annual rpt, 4494–8

Drug abuse indicators for selected metro areas, research results, data collection, and policy issues, 1989 semiannual conf, 4492–5

Drug test results at arrest, by drug type, offense, and sex, for selected urban areas, quarterly rpt, 6062–3

Employment by industry div in New York and northeastern New Jersey, unemployment, and consumer price changes by selected commodity, 1978-June 1989, press release, 6926–2.40

Fish and shellfish catch, wholesale receipts, prices, trade, and other market activities, weekly regional rpt, 2162–6.1

Freight (waterborne domestic and foreign) by commodity, traffic, and passengers, by port and waterway, 1987, annual rpt, 3754–3.1

Fruit and vegetable shipments, and arrivals in US and Canada cities, by mode of transport and State and country of origin, 1988, annual rpt, 1311–4.1

Fruit and vegetable wholesale prices in NYC, Chicago, and selected shipping points, by crop, 1988, annual rpt, 1311–8

Homeless persons aid programs, and shelter capacity and voucher programs, for 5 major cities, 1988, 5188–122

Homeless persons nutritional status, 1987 local area study, article, 4042–3.942

Household and family characteristics, by location, 1988, annual Current Population Rpt, 2546–1.437

Housing starts and completions authorized by building permits in 40 MSAs, quarterly rpt, 2382–9

Infectious notifiable disease cases, by age, State, and outlying area, and deaths, 1930s-88, annual rpt, 4204–1

Infectious notifiable diseases, cases and current outbreaks, by region and State, weekly rpt, 4202–1

Older frail persons HMO case mgmt and home care services, demonstration projects enrollment, 1986, article, 4652–1.913

Puerto Rico employee referrals and placements in NYC, FY84-88, annual GAO rpt, 26104–19

Wages by occupation, and benefits for office and plant workers, 1989 survey, periodic MSA rpt, 6785–12.7

see also under By City and By SMSA or MSA in the "Index by Categories"

New York State

Agriculture census, 1987: farms, farmland, production and costs, and operator characteristics, advance State and county rpts, 2330–1.36

Agriculture census, 1987: farms, farmland, production, finances, and operator characteristics, by county, final State rpt, 2331–1.32

Alien workers (unauthorized) employer sanctions, enforcement costs, compliance, and job discrimination, 1988 annual GAO rpt, 26104–19

Appalachian Regional Commission funding, by project and State, planned FY89, annual rpt, 9084–3

Asian American earnings, and employment and other characteristics, by detailed origin and whether foreign-born, 1980, 11046–7.2

Bank deposits in FDIC-insured commercial and savings banks, by instn, State, and county, as of June 1988, annual regional rpt, 9295–3.1

Banks (foreign) US branches assets and liabilities, total and for 3 States, monthly rpt, quarterly data, 9362–1.4

Banks (intl) facilities of foreign and US banks in New York and total US, assets and liabilities, monthly rpt, 9365–2.22

Celery acreage planted and growing, by growing area, monthly rpt, 1621–14

County Business Patterns, 1987: employment, establishments, and payroll, by SIC 2- to 4-digit industry and county, annual State rpt, 2326–8.34

Dairy production, and prices for cows, milk, and feed, by selected State, 1988, annual rpt, 1317–1.1; 1317–1.6

Deaths and rates, by detailed location, cause, and demographic characteristics, 1987, US Vital Statistics annual rpt, 4144–3.1

DOD prime contract awards, by contractor, service branch, State, and city, FY88, annual rpt, 3544–22

Drug abuse and trafficking reduction aid to States, and grant processing time, FY87-88, GAO rpt, 26119–258

Economic and housing indicators for FHLB 2nd District, by State, quarterly rpt with articles, 9302–33

Employment by industry div in New York and northeastern New Jersey, unemployment, and consumer price changes by selected commodity, 1978-June 1989, press release, 6926–2.40

Employment, earnings, and hours, by selected SIC 1- to 4-digit industry, State, and for 262 MSAs, 1972-87, 6748–81.3

Fed Govt spending in States and local areas, by type, State, county, and city, FY88, annual rpt, 2464–3

Fed Govt spending in States, by type, program, agency, and State, FY88, annual rpt, 2464–2

HHS financial aid, by program, recipient, State, and city, FY88, annual regional listing, 4004–3.2

Homeless children educational enrollment and needs, 1988, annual State rpt, 4804–35.32

Hospital reimbursement by Medicare under prospective payment system, impacts on subacute care, 1988 rpt, 17206–2.8

Hospital service area population care need indicators, and travel distances, for rural and urban instns in New York State, 1983, 4188–53

Hospital use and costs of Medicaid enrollees related to selected characteristics, 1980, article, 4652–1.949

Income (personal) per capita and by source, and earnings by industry div, by State, MSA, and county, 1982-87, annual regional rpt, 2704–2.2

Indian (Seneca Tribe) deaths and years of potential life lost, by selected cause and sex, various periods 1955-84, article, 4042–3.925

Medicaid enrollment, and service use and costs by service type, by eligibility type, for 5 States, 1980-84, article, 4652–1.919

Mineral Industry Surveys, State reviews of production, 1988, preliminary annual rpt, 5614–6

Minerals Yearbook, 1987, Vol 2 preprints: State review of production and sales by commodity, and business activity, annual rpt, 5604–16.33

Minerals Yearbook, 1987, Vol 2: State reviews of production, sales, and firms, by commodity, and business activity, annual rpt, 5604–34

Nursing home admissions and discharges for Medicaid patients with prior hospitalization, for 3 States, 1981, article, 4652–1.942

Nursing home compliance with Medicare and Medicaid regulations, and patient characteristics, by facility, 1987/88, annual State rpt, 4654–15.33

Nursing home reimbursement by Medicaid, case mix classification methodology, for New York State, 1987, article, 4652–1.910

Retail trade census, 1987: employment, establishments, sales, and payroll, by SIC 2- to 4-digit kind of business, MSA, county, and city, State rpt, 2397–1.33

Savings instns, FHLB 2nd District members capital and assets under capital requirements increase proposal, by State, 3rd qtr 1988, article, 9302–33.901

Savings instns, FHLB 2nd District members finances and operations, by State, quarterly rpt, 9302–14

Service industries census, 1987: employment, establishments, receipts, and payroll, by SIC 2- to 4-digit kind of business, MSA, county, and city, State rpt, 2391–1.33

Statistical Abstract of US, social, political, and economic data, with foreign comparisons, 1790-2025, comprehensive annual compilation, 2324–1

Truck driver multi-State license prohibition, FHwA enforcement activities by region, 1987-88, GAO rpt, 26113–396

Water supply and quality in streams and lakes, and groundwater levels in wells, by drainage basin, 1987, annual State rpt, 5666–10.31

Water supply in northeastern US, precipitation and stream runoff by station, monthly rpt, 2182–3

Wholesale trade census, 1987: employment, establishments, finances, and operations, by SIC 2- to 4-digit kind of business, MSA, county, and city, State rpt, 2405–1.33

Wildlife-related recreation, hunting, and fishing participation and spending, detailed data, 1985 survey, quinquennial State rpt, 5506–6.32

see also Buffalo, N.Y.

see also Long Island, N.Y.

see also Monroe County, N.Y.

see also Nassau County, N.Y.

see also New York Bight

see also New York City

see also Niagara Falls, N.Y.

see also Suffolk County, N.Y.

see also Woodstock, N.Y.

see also under By State in the "Index by Categories"

New York Stock Exchange

Capital gains tax rate changes effect on transactions by asset type, and stock exchange trading volume, late 1970s-88, article, 9373–1.901

Price indexes of NYSE for common stock, by type, 1966-88 with trends from 1949, annual rpt, 204–1.7

Statistical Abstract of US, social, political, and economic data, 1790-2025, comprehensive annual compilation, 2324–1.3

Stock market crash of 1987, US stock prices relation to prices on Tokyo and London exchanges, 1987-88, technical paper, 9366–6.164

Stockbrokers with NYSE membership, securities credit issues, as of June 1988, annual rpt, 9365–5.1

Trading volume and new issue registrations, monthly rpt, 9732–1

Trading volume on New York and American Stock Exchanges, monthly rpt, 9362–1.1

Trading volume, securities listed by type, and finances, by exchange, selected years 1935-88, annual rpt, 9734–2.1; 9734–2.3

New Zealand

Agricultural and food production and indexes, total and for selected commodities, by country, 1970s-88, annual rpt, 1524–12

Agricultural subsidies, consumer and producer equivalents by program, commodity, and major US trading partner, 1982-86, 1528–275

Agricultural trade and market impacts of eliminating foreign and US protectionist policies, model description and results, 1986, 1528–282

Agricultural trade of US, by detailed commodity and country, 1988, semiannual rpt, 1522–4

Background Notes, summary social, political, and economic data, 1989 rpt, 7006–2.39

Economic and military aid and loans from US and intl agencies, by program and country, FY46-87, annual rpt, 9914–5

Economic conditions in Communist and OECD countries, 1987, annual rpt, 7144–11

Economic conditions, income, production, prices, employment, and trade, 1989 periodic country rpt, 2046–4.10

Economic conditions, investment and export opportunities, and trade practices, 1989 country market research rpt, 2046–6.14

Economic conditions, policy, and trade practices, by country, 1986-88, annual rpt, 21384–5

Economic, social, political, and geographic summary data, by country, 1989, annual factbook, 9114–2

Exports and imports of US, by selected country, country group, and commodity group, 1988, annual rpt, 2044–37

Fish (groundfish) imports from Canada, New Zealand, and Australia to western US, by species, 1983-87, annual rpt, 2164–16.1

Fruit production, trade, use, and processing, by commodity for 5 countries, 1986-89, annual article, 1925–34.909

Human rights conditions in 170 countries, 1988, annual rpt, 21384–3

Imports of goods, services, and investment from US, trade barriers, impacts, and US actions, by country, 1988, annual rpt, 444–2

Military aid of US, arms sales, and training programs costs and budget requests, by program, world region, and country, FY88-90, annual rpt, 7144–13

Military spending, arms trade, and force strengths, with govt spending and population, by country, 1977-87, annual rpt, 9824–1

Minerals Yearbook, 1987, Vol 3: foreign country reviews of production, trade, and policy, by commodity, annual rpt, 5604–35

Minerals Yearbook, 1987, Vol 3 preprints: foreign country review of production, trade, and policy, by commodity, annual rpt, 5604–23.53

Multinatl US firms and foreign affiliates finances and operations, by industry of parent firm and affiliate, world area, and country, preliminary 1987, annual rpt, 2704–5

Oil production, trade, use, and stocks, by selected country and country group, monthly rpt, 3162–42

Population size, growth rates, and components of change, by country, projected 1989-2020 and trends from 1950, biennial rpt, 2324–9

R&D funding by Fed Govt, by field, performer type, agency, and State, FY87-89, annual rpt, 9627–20

Science and engineering immigrants, by field, age, sex, country and world area of birth and last residence, and State, 1987 and trends from 1967, 9627–29

Travel to US, market research, major magazine ad costs and circulation, and trade show data, for selected countries, 1989-90, annual rpt, 2904–11

UN voting record and share of votes in agreement with US, by issue, country, and world area, 1988, annual rpt, 7004–18

see also under By Foreign Country in the "Index by Categories"

Newark, N.J.

Drug abuse indicators for selected metro areas, research results, data collection, and policy issues, 1989 semiannual conf, 4492–5

Fruit and vegetable shipments, and arrivals in US and Canada cities, by mode of transport and State and country of origin, 1988, annual rpt, 1311–4.1

Wages by occupation, for office and plant workers, 1989 survey, periodic MSA rpt, 6785–12.4

see also under By City and By SMSA or MSA in the "Index by Categories"

Newell, Roger I.

"Blue Mussel. Species Profiles: Life Histories and Environmental Requirements of Coastal Fishes and Invertebrates (North and Mid-Atlantic)", 5506–8.108

Newhouse, Joseph P.

"Adjusting Capitation Rates Using Objective Health Measures and Prior Utilization", 4652–1.931

"Predicting Hospital Accounting Costs", 4652–1.948

Newman, James B.

"Overview of the Present Land-Use Situation and the Anticipated Ecological Impacts of Program Implementation", 1208–290

Newport News, Va.

Housing starts and completions authorized by building permits in 40 MSAs, quarterly rpt, 2382–9

Wages by occupation, for office and plant workers, 1989 survey, periodic MSA rpt, 6785–3.10

see also under By City and By SMSA or MSA in the "Index by Categories"

News reporting

see Freedom of the press

see Government and the press

see Journalism

Newspapers

Advertising in newspapers, spending by ad type, *Survey of Current Business*, monthly rpt, 2702–1.4

Bombing incidents, casualties, and damage, by target, circumstances, and State, 1988, annual rpt, 6224–5

Cigarette ad and promotion costs by media, and market shares, by cigarette type, with sales and use, 1963-87, annual rpt, 9404–4

County Business Patterns, 1987: employment, establishments, and payroll, by SIC 2- to 4-digit industry and county, annual State rpt series, 2326–8

CPI by component for US city average, and by region, population size, and for 27 metro areas, monthly rpt, 6762–2

Employment, earnings, and hours, by selected SIC 1- to 4-digit industry, State, and for 262 MSAs, 1972-87, 6748–81

Employment, earnings, and hours, by SIC 1- to 4-digit industry, monthly 1983-Feb 1989, annual rpt, 6744–14

Employment of minorities and women, by occupation, SIC 1- to 3- digit industry, State, and MSA, 1986, annual rpt, 9244–1

Exports of US, detailed commodities by country, monthly rpt, 2422–3

Fed Govt ad spending, and subcontracts to small and disadvantaged firms, by agency and medium, FY86, GAO rpt, 26113–428

Foreign travel to US and Canada, market analyses with detailed trip and traveler characteristics, country rpt series, 2906–2

Foreign travel to US, market research, major magazine ad costs and circulation, and trade show data, for selected countries, 1989-90, annual rpt, 2904–11

Imports of US, detailed Schedule A commodities by country, monthly rpt, 2422–2

Manufacturers finances and operations, by
SIC 2- to 4-digit industry, forecast 1989
and trends from 1950s, annual rpt,
2044–28

Manufacturing annual survey, 1986:
financial and operating data, by SIC 2- to
4-digit industry, series, 2506–15

Manufacturing census, 1987: financial and
operating data, for SIC 4-digit industries
by product, preliminary rpt, 2491–1.30;
2491–1.31

Occupational injury and illness rates, by SIC
2- to 4-digit industry, 1987, annual rpt,
6844–1

Price indexes (producer), by stage of
processing and detailed commodity,
monthly rpt, 6762–6

Price indexes (producer), by stage of
processing and detailed commodity,
monthly 1988, annual rpt, 6764–2

Retail trade census, 1987: employment,
establishments, sales, and payroll, by SIC
2- to 4-digit kind of business, MSA,
county, and city, State rpt series, 2397–1

Science, engineering, and technical
employment in manufacturing, by field,
occupation, and industry, 1986, triennial
rpt, 9627–23

Statistical Abstract of US, social, political,
and economic data, 1790-2025,
comprehensive annual compilation,
2324–1.3

Tax (income) returns of corporations,
income and tax items by asset size and
detailed industry, 1986, annual rpt,
8304–4; 8304–21

see also Journalism

Newton, John

"Effectiveness and Economic Development
Impact of Policy-Based Cash Transfer
Programs: The Case of Costa Rica",
9916–3.51

Niagara Falls, N.Y.

CPI by component for US city average, and
by region, population size, and for 27
metro areas, monthly rpt, 6762–2

see also under By SMSA or MSA in the
"Index by Categories"

Niagara River

Pollutant discharges, sources, and control
program activities for Great Lakes basin,
1987, biennial rpt, 14644–1

Nicaragua

Agricultural and food production and
indexes, total and for selected
commodities, by country, 1970s-88,
annual rpt, 1524–12

Agricultural trade of US, by detailed
commodity and country, 1988, semiannual
rpt, 1522–4

AID economic aid to developing countries,
obligations and disbursements by country,
quarterly rpt, 9912–4

AID loans repayment status and terms by
program and country, and status of
predecessor agency loans, quarterly rpt,
9912–3

Contra forces humanitarian aid of AID, by
type, 1988, GAO rpt, 26123–237

Economic and military aid and loans from
US and intl agencies, by program and
country, FY46-87, annual rpt, 9914–5

Economic conditions, policy, and trade
practices, by country, 1986-88, annual rpt,
21384–5

Economic, social, political, and geographic
summary data, by country, 1989, annual
factbook, 9114–2

Exports and imports of US, by commodity
and country, 1970-87, world area rpt,
9116–1.6

Exports and imports of US, by selected
country, country group, and commodity
group, 1988, annual rpt, 2044–37

Human rights conditions in 170 countries,
1988, annual rpt, 21384–3

Labor conditions, union coverage, and work
accidents, 1989 annual country rpt,
6366–4.7; 6366–4.41

Military spending, arms trade, and force
strengths, with govt spending and
population, by country, 1977-87, annual
rpt, 9824–1

Minerals Yearbook, 1987, Vol 3: foreign
country reviews of production, trade, and
policy, by commodity, annual rpt,
5604–35

Minerals Yearbook, 1987, Vol 3 preprints:
foreign country review of production,
trade, and policy, by commodity, annual
rpt, 5604–23.84

Population size, growth rates, and
components of change, by country,
projected 1989-2020 and trends from
1950, biennial rpt, 2324–9

Refugee resettlement programs and funding,
arrivals by country of origin, and
indicators of adjustment, by State, FY88,
annual rpt, 4694–5

Refugees from Nicaragua, El Salvador, and
Guatemala receiving UN aid, resettlement
in other Central American countries, and
repatriations, 1984-88, GAO rpt,
26123–232

Soviet Union arms sales to developing
countries and Nicaragua, 1981-86,
hearing, 23848–195

UN voting record and share of votes in
agreement with US, by issue, country, and
world area, 1988, annual rpt, 7004–18

see also under By Foreign Country in the
"Index by Categories"

Niccolucci, Michael J.

"Predicting Timber Sale Costs from Sale
Characteristics in the Intermountain
West", 1208–298

Nicholson, Walter

"Examination of Declining UI Claims
During the 1980s", 6406–6.24

Nickel

see Metals and metal industries

Nicotine

see Smoking

Nielsen, Elizabeth G.

"Farm Operating and Financial
Characteristics, 1986", 1544–27

"Investments in Soil Conservation and Land
Improvements: Factors Explaining
Farmers' Decisions", 1588–137

Niger

Agricultural and food production and
indexes, total and for selected
commodities, by country, 1970s-88,
annual rpt, 1524–12

Agricultural imports and food aid needs
under alternative weather assumptions, for
17 African countries, projected to 1995,
1528–279

Agricultural production, prices, and trade,
by country, 1960s-89, annual world region
rpt, 1524–4.2

Agricultural trade of US, by detailed
commodity and country, 1988, semiannual
rpt, 1522–4

AID activities and funding by project and
function, FY90, and developing countries
summary socioeconomic data from 1960s,
annual rpt, 9904–4.5

AID economic aid to developing countries,
obligations and disbursements by country,
quarterly rpt, 9912–4

AID loans repayment status and terms by
program and country, and status of
predecessor agency loans, quarterly rpt,
9912–3

Economic and military aid and loans from
US and intl agencies, by program and
country, FY46-87, annual rpt, 9914–5

Economic, social, political, and geographic
summary data, by country, 1989, annual
factbook, 9114–2

Food supply indicators for Sahel, by
country, 1960s-2000, 1528–290

Human rights conditions in 170 countries,
1988, annual rpt, 21384–3

Military aid of US, arms sales, and training
programs costs and budget requests, by
program, world region, and country,
FY88-90, annual rpt, 7144–13

Military spending, arms trade, and force
strengths, with govt spending and
population, by country, 1977-87, annual
rpt, 9824–1

Minerals Yearbook, 1987, Vol 3 preprints:
foreign country review of production,
trade, and policy, by commodity, annual
rpt, 5604–23.82

Population size, growth rates, and
components of change, by country,
projected 1989-2020 and trends from
1950, biennial rpt, 2324–9

UN voting record and share of votes in
agreement with US, by issue, country, and
world area, 1988, annual rpt, 7004–18

see also under By Foreign Country in the
"Index by Categories"

Nigeria

Agricultural and food production and
indexes, total and for selected
commodities, by country, 1970s-88,
annual rpt, 1524–12

Agricultural exports of Africa by
commodity, and relation to economic
conditions and other factors, by country,
1960s-87, 1528–280

Agricultural production, prices, and trade,
by country, 1960s-89, annual world region
rpt, 1524–4.2

Agricultural subsidies, consumer and
producer equivalents by program,
commodity, and major US trading partner,
1982-86, 1528–275

Agricultural trade of US, by detailed
commodity and country, 1988, semiannual
rpt, 1522–4

AID activities and funding by project and
function, FY90, and developing countries
summary socioeconomic data from 1960s,
annual rpt, 9904–4.5

AID economic aid to developing countries,
obligations and disbursements by country,
quarterly rpt, 9912–4

AID loans repayment status and terms by
program and country, and status of
predecessor agency loans, quarterly rpt,
9912–3

Economic and military aid and loans from US and intl agencies, by program and country, FY46-87, annual rpt, 9914-5

Economic conditions in Communist, OECD, and selected other countries, 1960s-88, annual rpt, 9114-4

Economic conditions, income, production, prices, employment, and trade, 1989 periodic country rpt, 2046-4.68

Economic conditions, policy, and trade practices, by country, 1986-88, annual rpt, 21384-5

Economic indicators of developing countries, problem debtors compared to other borrowers, by country, 1973-84, 1528-285

Economic, social, political, and geographic summary data, by country, 1989, annual factbook, 9114-2

Exports and imports of US, by commodity and country, 1970-87, world area rpt, 9116-1.4

Exports and imports of US, by selected country, country group, and commodity group, 1988, annual rpt, 2044-37

Human rights conditions in 170 countries, 1988, annual rpt, 21384-3

Imports of goods, services, and investment from US, trade barriers, impacts, and US actions, by country, 1988, annual rpt, 444-2

Labor conditions, union coverage, and work accidents, 1989 annual country rpt, 6366-4.5; 6366-4.38

Military aid of US, arms sales, and training programs costs and budget requests, by program, world region, and country, FY88-90, annual rpt, 7144-13

Military spending, arms trade, and force strengths, with govt spending and population, by country, 1977-87, annual rpt, 9824-1

Minerals Yearbook, 1987, Vol 3: foreign country reviews of production, trade, and policy, by commodity, annual rpt, 5604-35

Minerals Yearbook, 1987, Vol 3 preprints: foreign country review of production, trade, and policy, by commodity, annual rpt, 5604-23.54

Multinatl US firms and foreign affiliates finances and operations, by industry of parent firm and affiliate, world area, and country, preliminary 1987, annual rpt, 2704-5

Oil production, and exports and prices for US, by major exporting country, detailed data, monthly rpt, 3162-24

Oil production, trade, use, and stocks, by selected country and country group, monthly rpt, 3162-42

Population size, growth rates, and components of change, by country, projected 1989-2020 and trends from 1950, biennial rpt, 2324-9

UN voting record and share of votes in agreement with US, by issue, country, and world area, 1988, annual rpt, 7004-18

see also under By Foreign Country in the "Index by Categories"

NIH

see National Institutes of Health

Nikishka, Alaska

Tide height and time daily at coastal points, forecast 1990, annual rpt, 2174-2.1

NIMH

see National Institute of Mental Health

Nitrocellulose

see Chemicals and chemical industry

Nitrogen

see Gases

Nitrogen oxides

see Air pollution

NOAA

see National Oceanic and Atmospheric Administration

Noble, John A.

"Alcoholism Treatment in General Hospitals", 4186-9.3

Noise

Coastal areas environmental and socioeconomic conditions, and potential impact of oil and gas OCS leases, final statement series, 5736-1

Electric utilities privately owned, pollution abatement outlays by type of pollutant and equipment, and firm, 1987, annual rpt, 3164-23.1

Fed Govt financial and nonfinancial domestic aid, 1989 base edition with supplements, annual listing, 104-5

Health condition and health care resources, use, and spending, 1950s-87, annual data compilation, 4144-11

Mine safety and health enforcement, training, and funding, with casualties, by type of mine and State, FY87, annual rpt, 6664-6

Neighborhood and housing quality, indicators and attitudes, by householder type and location, 1985, biennial rpt, 2485-12

Neighborhood and housing quality, indicators and attitudes, MSA surveys, series, 2485-6

Uranium tailings at inactive mills, remedial action proposals, costs, site characteristics, and environmental, socioeconomic, and health impacts, series, 3356-4

Nolley, Jean W.

"Bulletin of Hardwood Market Statistics", 1202-4

Nolting, Louvan

"Forecasting and Long-Range Planning of Science and Technology in the USSR", 2326-18.45

Non-ferrous metals industry

see Aluminum and aluminum industry

see Copper and copper industry

see Lead and lead industry

see Metals and metal industries

see Tin and tin industry

see Zinc and zinc industry

Nonappropriated funds

Budget of US Appendix, obligations, appropriations, and personnel, by program and agency, FY90, annual rpt, 104-3

Budget of US, CBO analysis of revenue and spending alternatives and projections of economic indicators, FY90-94, annual rpt, 26304-3

Budget of US, compact budgets by activity, function, and agency, FY90 and projected to FY94, annual rpt, 104-2

Nonmarket economies

see Centrally planned economies

Nonmetallic minerals and mines

Alaska minerals resources, production, oil and gas leases, and exploratory wells, with maps and bibl, 1987, annual rpt, 5664-11

China trade by SITC 1- to 5-digit commodity, 1970s-87, annual rpt, 9114-3

County Business Patterns, 1987: employment, establishments, and payroll, by SIC 2- to 4-digit industry and county, annual State rpt series, 2326-8

Earnings by major industry group, and personal income per capita and by source, by region and State, 1929-87, 2708-40

Employment, earnings, and hours, by SIC 1- to 4-digit industry, monthly 1983-Feb 1989, annual rpt, 6744-4

Employment in nonmanufacturing industries, by detailed occupation and SIC 2-digit industry, 1987, triennial rpt, 6748-60

Employment of minorities and women, by occupation, SIC 1- to 3- digit industry, State, and MSA, 1986, annual rpt, 9244-1

Exports and imports of US, by commodity group, world area, selected country, US coastal area and port, and mode of transport, monthly rpt, 2422-9

Exports of US, detailed commodities by country, monthly rpt, 2422-3

Foreign and US minerals industries operations, trends, and projections for selected countries, series, 5606-5

Foreign and US minerals supply under alternative market conditions, reserves, and background industry data, series, 5606-4

Freight (waterborne domestic and foreign) by commodity, traffic, and passengers, by port and waterway, 1987, annual rpt, 3754-3

Imports, exports, and employment impacts, by SIC 2- to 4-digit industry and commodity, quarterly rpt, 2322-2

Imports of US, detailed Schedule A commodities by country, monthly rpt, 2422-2

Labor productivity, indexes of output, hours, and employment by SIC 2- to 4-digit industry, 1963-87, annual rpt, 6824-1.2

Manufacturing annual survey, 1986: financial and operating data, by SIC 2- to 4-digit industry, series, 2506-15

Manufacturing census, 1987: financial and operating data, for SIC 4-digit industries by product, preliminary industry rpt series, 2491-1

Mine employment by selected occupational and other characteristics, injuries, and workdays lost, for mines, 1986, 5606-8.2; 5606-8.6

Mineral industries census, 1987: financial and operating data, preliminary industry rpt series, 2511-1

Mineral Industry Surveys, commodity reviews of production, trade, stocks, and use, monthly rpt series, 5612-1

Mineral Industry Surveys, commodity reviews of production, trade, stocks, and use, quarterly rpt series, 5612-2

Mineral Industry Surveys, commodity reviews of production, trade, use, and industry operations, advance annual rpt series, 5614-5

Mineral Industry Surveys, State reviews of production, 1988, preliminary annual rpt, 5614–6

Minerals Yearbook, 1987, Vol 1: commodity reviews of production, use, trade, prices, and mining operations, annual rpt, 5604–33

Minerals Yearbook, 1987, Vol 1 preprints: commodity reviews of production, reserves, supply, use, and trade, annual rpt series, 5604–15

Minerals Yearbook, 1987, Vol 2 preprints: State reviews of production and sales by commodity, and business activity, annual rpt series, 5604–16

Minerals Yearbook, 1987, Vol 2: State reviews of production, sales, and firms, by commodity, and business activity, annual rpt, 5604–34

Minerals Yearbook, 1987, Vol 3: foreign country reviews of production, trade, and policy, by commodity, annual rpt, 5604–35

Minerals Yearbook, 1987, Vol 3 preprints: foreign country reviews of production, trade, and policy, by commodity, annual rpt series, 5604–23

Minerals Yearbook, 1988, Vol 1: commodity reviews of production, reserves, supply, use, and trade, annual rpt series, 5604–20

Minerals Yearbook, 1988, Vol 2 rpts: State reviews of production and sales by commodity, and business activity, annual rpt series, 5604–22

Multinatl US firms and foreign affiliates finances and operations, by industry of parent firm and affiliate, world area, and country, preliminary 1987, annual rpt, 2704–5

Occupational injuries and incidence, employment, and hours in nonmetallic minerals mines and related operations, 1987, annual rpt, 6664–1

Occupational injury and illness rates, by SIC 2- to 4-digit industry, 1987, annual rpt, 6844–1

Occupational safety and health enforcement, training, and funding, with casualties, by type of mine and State, FY87, annual rpt, 6664–6

Price indexes (producer), by stage of processing and detailed commodity, monthly rpt, 6762–6

Price indexes (producer), by stage of processing and detailed commodity, monthly 1988, annual rpt, 6764–2

Production, prices, trade, use, employment, tariffs, and stockpiles, by mineral, with foreign comparisons, 1984-88, annual rpt, 5604–18

Public lands minerals resources and availability, State rpt series, 5606–7

Publications and patents of Mines Bur, monthly listing, 5602–2

Rail shipments of grain and other commodities by car type, 1986, and rail car fleet size, 1978-88, 1278–15

Salt production capacity, and use in chlorine production, by firm and facility, 1988, annual listing, 5614–30

Science and engineering employment, by nonmanufacturing industry and field, 1987, triennial rpt, 9627–31

Science, engineering, and technical employment in manufacturing, by field, occupation, and industry, 1986, triennial rpt, 9627–23

Small business establishments, employment, and financial ratios, by SIC 1- to 2-digit industry and State, late 1960s-87, 9768–19

Soviet Union minerals production, trade, and use, by commodity, 1983-87, annual rpt, 5604–39

Statistical Abstract of US, social, political, and economic data, 1790-2025, comprehensive annual compilation, 2324–1.3

Talc production, use, and trade, with foreign comparisons, selected years 1977-87, 5608–158

Tax (income) returns of corporations, income and tax items by asset size and detailed industry, 1986, annual rpt, 8304–4; 8304–3

Tax (income) returns of partnerships, income statement items by industry group, 1986, annual article, 8302–2.903

Tax (income) returns of sole proprietorships, income statement items, by industry group, 1987, annual article, 8302–2.904; 8302–2.921

see also Asbestos contamination
see also Cement and concrete
see also Clay industry and products
see also Coal and coal mining
see also Fertilizers
see also Gases
see also Gemstones
see also Natural gas and gas industry
see also Offshore mineral resources
see also Offshore oil and gas
see also Oil shale
see also Petroleum and petroleum industry
see also Phosphate
see also Potash
see also Pottery and porcelain products
see also Stockpiling
see also Stone products and quarries
see also Strategic materials
see also Tar sands
see also By Industry in the "Index by Categories"
see also under By Commodity in the "Index by Categories"

Nonmetropolitan areas
see Rural areas
see under By Urban-Rural and Metro-Nonmetro in the "Index by Categories"

Nonprofit organizations and foundations

Advertising spending of Fed Govt, and subcontracts to small and disadvantaged firms, by agency and medium, FY86, GAO rpt, 26113–428

Agricultural exports shipped by voluntary relief agencies under federally financed programs, by commodity and country, bimonthly rpt, periodic data, 1522–1.4

AID loans repayment status and terms by program and country, and status of predecessor agency loans, quarterly rpt, 9912–3

Alcohol, Drug Abuse and Mental Health Admin research grants and awards, by recipient, FY88, annual listing, 4044–13

Allergy and Infectious Diseases Natl Inst activities, grants by recipient and location, and disease incidence, FY81-88, annual rpt, 4474–30

Arts Natl Endowment activities and grants, FY88, annual rpt, 9564–3

Assets and debts of private sector, balance sheets by segment, 1949-88, semiannual rpt, 9365–4.1

Blind and handicapped reading materials from nonprofit agencies, FY88, annual listing, 26404–3

County Business Patterns, 1987: employment, establishments, and payroll, by SIC 2- to 4-digit industry and county, annual State rpt series, 2326–8

Dental Research Natl Inst research and training grants, by recipient, FY88, annual listing, 4474–19

Developing countries disaster preparedness and economic, population, and political data, country rpt series, 9916–2

DOD prime contract awards, by category, contract and contractor type, and service branch, FY79-88, semiannual rpt, 3542–1

DOD prime contract awards, by category, contractor type, and State, FY86-88, annual rpt, 3544–11

DOD prime contract awards for R&D, for top 500 contractors, FY88, annual listing, 3544–4

DOD prime contract awards for R&D to US and foreign nonprofit instns and govt agencies, by instn and location, FY88, annual listing, 3544–17

Energy conservation grants of Fed Govt to public and nonprofit private instns, by building type and State, 1988, annual rpt, 3304–15

Fed Govt financial and nonfinancial domestic aid, 1989 base edition with supplements, annual listing, 104–5

Finances of nonprofit charitable organizations, and assets and grants of top 10, 1985, article, 8302–2.923

France and US hospital and long-term care beds, by facility type and ownership, 1981, 4147–5.4

Health care facilities for kidney end-stage disease treatment, by ownership and region, 1985, annual rpt, 4654–16.5

Health care R&D funding, by type of source and performer, 1978-87, annual rpt, 4434–3

HHS financial aid, by program, recipient, State, and city, FY88, annual regional listings, 4004–3

Homeless and runaway youth programs, funding, activities, and participant characteristics, FY86, annual rpt, 4604–3

Hospital reimbursement by Medicare under prospective payment system, impacts on instns, beneficiaries, and other care providers and payment sources, 1986, annual rpt, 4654–13

Humanities Natl Endowment activities and grants, FY88, annual rpt, 9564–2

Investment funds (collective) assets, instns involved, and accounts, by type of fund and holding, 1988, annual rpt, 13004–1.3

Kidney end-stage disease treatment facilities approved by Medicare, dialysis and transplant services and ownership, 1989 annual listing, 4654–17

Mail operating costs of USPS, itemized by class of mail, FY88, annual rpt, 9864–4

Mail revenue and appropriation for revenue forgone, by class of mail, FY88, annual rpt, 9864–5

Mail revenue and subsidy for revenue forgone, by class of mail, FY88, and volume from FY84, annual rpt, 9864–1

Mail revenue, costs, and volume, by class of mail, FY88, annual rpt, 9864–2

Mental health care facilities, staff, and patient characteristics, *Statistical Notes* series, 4506–3

Mentally retarded persons facilities, beds, and residents, by ownership, resident age and race, and State, 1986, 4147–14.34

NASA funding by program and type of performer, and contract awards by State, FY88, annual rpt, 9504–6.2

NASA procurement contract awards, by type, contractor, State, and country, FY89, semiannual rpt, 9502–6

Natl income and product accounts and components, *Survey of Current Business*, monthly rpt, 2702–1.21

Navy procurement, by contractor and location, FY88, annual rpt, 3804–13

NIH grants and contracts, by inst and type of recipient, FY79-88, annual rpt, 4434–9

NSF grants and contracts, by field, inst, State, and country, FY88, annual rpt, 9624–26

Nursing home compliance with Medicare and Medicaid regulations, and patient characteristics, by facility, 1987/88, annual State rpt series, 4654–15

Nursing home facility, staff, and resident detailed characteristics, 1985, 4147–13.97

Nursing homes, beds, and residents, by ownership, certification status, and State, 1986, 4147–14.33

PL 480 exports by commodity, and recipients, by program, sponsor, and country, FY87 and cumulative from FY55, annual rpt, 1924–7

R&D and related funding of Fed Govt to higher education and nonprofit instns, by field, instn, agency, and State, FY87, annual rpt, 9627–17.1

R&D funding by Fed Govt, by field, performer type, agency, and State, FY87-89, annual rpt, 9627–20

R&D funding by source and performer, and related employment, by State, 1975-87, 9626–6.32

R&D funding, by source, performer, and for top 10 States, 1977-89, 9626–2.185

R&D funding, performance by geographic division and State, and science and technology employment, selected years 1953-89, annual rpt, 9624–18.1

Refugee arrivals and resettlement in US, by age, sex, sponsoring agency, State, and country, monthly rpt, 4692–2

Refugee resettlement programs and funding, arrivals by country of origin, and indicators of adjustment, by State, FY88, annual rpt, 4694–5

Schools (public) partnerships with community organizations, participation, activities, and contributions, by school characteristics and location, 1987/88, 4826–1.27

Science and engineering employment characteristics, by field, 1988, biennial rpt, 9627–16

Science and engineering employment in R&D, earnings at DOE labs and non-DOE facilities, 1989, annual rpt, 3004–9

Science and engineering employment in R&D, earnings by field and educational, employment, and other characteristics, 1989, annual rpt, 3004–1

Science and engineering labor force, Federal and university research funding, and educational data, series, 9626–6

Science and engineering labor supply by region and employment characteristics, and salaries by years of experience, 1987, 9626–2.184

Science and engineering PhDs, by field, instn, employment prospects, sex, race, and other characteristics, 1960s-88, 9627–30

Science and engineering PhDs employment and other characteristics, by field and State, 1987, biennial rpt, 9627–18

Service industries census, 1987: establishments, receipts, employment, and payroll, by SIC 2- to 4-digit kind of business, MSA, county, and city, State rpt series, 2391–1

Service industries receipts, by SIC 2- to 4-digit kind of business, 1988, annual rpt, 2413–8

Statistical Abstract of US, social, political, and economic data, 1790-2025, comprehensive annual compilation, 2324–1.1; 2324–1.2

Tax (excise) collections of IRS, by type of tax, region, and State, FY88, annual rpt, 8304–3.3

Tax (property) revenue by level of govt, assessed values by locality, and exemptions, by property type and State, 1987 Census of Govts, 2453–1

see also Membership organizations

Noren, James

"New Look at Soviet Statistics: Implications for CIA Measures of the USSR's Economic Growth", 9118–4

Norfolk, Va.

Freight (waterborne domestic and foreign) by commodity, traffic, and passengers, by port and waterway, 1987, annual rpt, 3754–3.1

Housing starts and completions authorized by building permits in 40 MSAs, quarterly rpt, 2382–9

Wages by occupation, for office and plant workers, 1989 survey, periodic MSA rpt, 6785–3.10

see also under By City and By SMSA or MSA in the "Index by Categories"

Normal, Ill.

see also under By SMSA or MSA in the "Index by Categories"

Normile, Mary Anne

"European Community in the Uruguay Round: Agricultural Trade Negotiations and EC Policy", 1524–4.1

North America

Agricultural exports of US, for grains, oilseed products, hides, skins, and cotton, by country, weekly rpt, 1922–3

Agricultural trade of US, by commodity and country, bimonthly rpt with articles, 1522–1

Agricultural trade of US, by detailed commodity and country, 1988, semiannual rpt, 1522–4

Construction contracts awarded US firms, and share of construction market by country of contractor, by world area, 1982-87, annual article, 2042–1.902

Exports and imports (waterborne) of US, by type of service, customs district, port, and world area, monthly rpt, 2422–7

Exports and imports of US, by commodity group, world area, selected country, US coastal area and port, and mode of transport, monthly rpt, 2422–9

Fertilizer components use, by world area, 1978-88 and projected to 2010, 5608–154

Immigrant and nonimmigrant visas of US issued and refused, by class, issuing office, and nationality, FY88, annual rpt, 7184–1

Immigrants admitted to US, by class of admission, country of birth, and State and MSA of destination, FY88, annual rpt, 6264–4

Immigrants admitted to US, by occupational group and country of birth, preliminary FY88, annual table, 6264–1

Military spending, arms trade, and force strengths, with govt spending and population, by country, 1977-87, annual rpt, 9824–1

Oil and gas reserves and discoveries, by country and country group, quarterly rpt, 3162–43

Terrorist (intl) incidents, casualties, and attacks on US targets, by attack type and world area, 1968-88, annual rpt, 7004–13

Tidal currents, daily time and velocity by station for North America and Asia coasts, forecast 1990, annual rpts, 2174–1

Tide height and time daily at coastal points, forecast 1990, annual rpt, 2174–2.2; 2174–2.3

Travel to and from US on US and foreign flag air carriers, by country, world area, and US port, monthly rpt, 7302–2

Visas of US issued at Foreign Service posts, by category and world area, selected years FY84-88, annual rpt, 7184–4

Weather events and anomalies, precipitation and temperature for US and foreign locations, weekly rpt, 2182–6

Weather forecasts for US and Northern Hemisphere, precipitation and temperature by location, semimonthly rpt, 2182–1

see also Canada

see also Caribbean area

see also Greenland

see also Gulf of Mexico

see also Mexico

see also under By Foreign Country in the "Index by Categories"

North Atlantic Treaty Organization

DOD budget, procurement appropriations by item, service branch, and defense agency, FY88-91, annual rpt, 3544–32

DOD civilian and military personnel and dependents, by service branch and US and foreign location, quarterly rpt, 3542–20

DOD military and civilian personnel and dependents in NATO Europe countries, by service branch, 1980-88, GAO rpt, 26123–252

DOD military and civilian personnel, and vacancies, for NATO Europe countries, by service branch, 1988, GAO rpt, 26123–251

DOD military personnel abroad, by service branch, outlying area, and country, quarterly rpt, 3542–14.5

DOD military personnel abroad, by service branch, world area, and country, quarterly news release, 3542-9

Economic conditions in Communist and OECD countries, 1987, annual rpt, 7144-11

GNP and GNP growth of OECD members, by country, 1978-88, annual rpt, 7144-8

Helsinki Final Act implementation by NATO and Warsaw Pact, Oct 1988-Mar 1989, semiannual rpt, 7002-1

Military aid programs and related activities of US, costs by country and intl agency, FY85-87 and cumulative from FY50, GAO rpt, 26123-30

Military forces of NATO compared to Warsaw Pact, and selected economic indicators, by country, 1900s-87, conf papers, 3908-6

Military personnel of US abroad, by country, FY88, annual rpt, 3544-1.2

Military spending and indicators of ability to support common defense, for NATO members and Japan, 1971-87, annual rpt, 3544-28

Military spending, arms trade, and force strengths, with govt spending and population, by country, 1977-87, annual rpt, 9824-1

Military strength and spending of NATO, FY88, annual rpt, 3544-2

Military strength of USSR and Warsaw Pact, and proposed force reductions, with comparisons to NATO, 1980s-91, hearing, 21208-29

Military weapons systems, aid, presence, and force strengths of USSR and Warsaw Pact, and compared to US and NATO, 1989 annual rpt, 3504-20

Officials of NATO, admissions to US by country, FY78-88, annual rpt, 6264-2

Officials of NATO admissions to US, quarterly rpt, 6262-2

Science education, NATO postdoctoral fellowships recipients educational outcomes and other characteristics, 1959-81, 9628-80

Space satellites and other objects launched since 1957, quarterly listing, 9502-2

UN voting record and share of votes in agreement with US, by issue, country, and world area, 1988, annual rpt, 7004-18

North Carolina

Agriculture census, 1987: farms, farmland, production and costs, and operator characteristics, advance State and county rpts, 2330-1.37

Agriculture census, 1987: farms, farmland, production, finances, and operator characteristics, by county, final State rpt, 2331-1.33

Appalachian Regional Commission funding, by project and State, planned FY89, annual rpt, 9084-3

Bank deposits in FDIC-insured commercial and savings banks, by instn, State, and county, as of June 1988, annual regional rpt, 9295-3.2

Banks (insured commercial), Fed Reserve 5th District members financial statements, by State, quarterly rpt, 9389-18

Clothing (hosiery) production and related workers and wages by occupation and sex, and benefits, by location, 1987 survey, 6787-6.237

Collective bargaining calendar for southeastern States, 1989, annual rpt, 6946-1.73

Corn and soybean futures contract yield and price risk hedging strategies, by selected county and State, model results, 1961-83, 1548-352

County Business Patterns, 1987: employment, establishments, and payroll, by SIC 2- to 4-digit industry and county, annual State rpt, 2326-8.35

Deaths and rates, by detailed location, cause, and demographic characteristics, 1987, US Vital Statistics annual rpt, 4144-3.1

DOD prime contract awards, by contractor, service branch, State, and city, FY88, annual rpt, 3544-22

Economic indicators by State, Fed Reserve 5th District, quarterly rpt, 9389-16

Employment and housing market indicators by State, FHLB 4th District, quarterly rpt, 9302-36

Employment and unemployment, for 8 southeastern States, 1987-88, annual rpt, 6944-2

Employment by industry div, earnings, and hours, for 8 southeastern States, quarterly press release, 6942-7

Employment, earnings, and hours, by selected SIC 1- to 4-digit industry, State, and for 262 MSAs, 1972-87, 6748-81.4

Employment in North Carolina counties, by manufacturing industry group and whether urban, with exchange rate impacts, 1980-85, article, 9389-1.915

Fed Govt spending in States and local areas, by type, State, county, and city, FY88, annual rpt, 2464-3

Fed Govt spending in States, by type, program, agency, and State, FY88, annual rpt, 2464-2

Fish and shellfish catch, wholesale receipts, prices, trade, and other market activities, weekly regional rpt, 2162-6.3

HHS financial aid, by program, recipient, State, and city, FY88, annual regional listing, 4004-3.4

Homeless children educational enrollment and needs, 1988, annual State rpt, 4804-35.33

Hospital reimbursement by Medicare under prospective payment system, impacts on subacute care, 1988 rpt, 17206-2.8

Income (personal) per capita and by source, and earnings by industry div, by State, MSA, and county, 1982-87, annual regional rpt, 2704-2.4

Indian (Cherokee) Agency activities in North Carolina, FY89, annual rpt, 5704-4

Mineral Industry Surveys, State reviews of production, 1988, preliminary annual rpt, 5614-6

Minerals Yearbook, 1987, Vol 2 preprints: State review of production and sales by commodity, and business activity, annual rpt, 5604-16.34

Minerals Yearbook, 1987, Vol 2: State reviews of production, sales, and firms, by commodity, and business activity, annual rpt, 5604-34

Mobile home industry occupational injury and illness rates and workdays lost, by selected State, 1978-87, article, 6722-1.932

Nursing home compliance with Medicare and Medicaid regulations, and patient characteristics, by facility, 1987/88, annual State rpt, 4654-15.34

Retail trade census, 1987: employment, establishments, sales, and payroll, by SIC 2- to 4-digit kind of business, MSA, county, and city, State rpt, 2397-1.34

Savings instns, FHLB 4th District members finances and financial ratios, by State, quarterly rpt, 9302-3

Savings instns, FHLB 4th District members finances, by State, 1984-88, annual rpt, 9304-29.6

Service industries census, 1987: employment, establishments, receipts, and payroll, by SIC 2- to 4-digit kind of business, MSA, county, and city, State rpt, 2391-1.34

Small business contracts and obligations of Fed Govt, by program and recipient type, for North Carolina and total US, FY77-87, hearings, 21728-67

Statistical Abstract of US, social, political, and economic data, with foreign comparisons, 1790-2025, comprehensive annual compilation, 2324-1

Textile mill employment, earnings, and hours, for 8 Southeastern States, quarterly press release, 6942-1

Water supply and quality in streams and lakes, and groundwater levels in wells, by drainage basin, 1987, annual State rpt, 5666-10.32

Wholesale trade census, 1987: employment, establishments, finances, and operations, by SIC 2- to 4-digit kind of business, MSA, county, and city, State rpt, 2405-1.34

Wildlife-related recreation, hunting, and fishing participation and spending, detailed data, 1985 survey, quinquennial State rpt, 5506-6.33

see also Asheville, N.C.

see also Burlington, N.C.

see also Charlotte, N.C.

see also Durham, N.C.

see also Fayetteville, N.C.

see also Forsyth County, N.C.

see also Gastonia, N.C.

see also Goldsboro, N.C.

see also Greensboro, N.C.

see also Hickory, N.C.

see also High Point, N.C.

see also Jacksonville, N.C.

see also New Bern, N.C.

see also Raleigh, N.C.

see also Wilmington, N.C.

see also Winston-Salem, N.C.

see also under By State in the "Index by Categories"

North Central States

Banking industry structure, performance, and financial devs, for Fed Reserve 10th District, 1988, annual rpt, 9381-14

Banks financial performance, risk assessment, and regulation, 1988 annual conf papers, 9375-7

Birds (duck) breeding population, by species, State, and Canada Province, 1988-89 with trends from 1955, annual rpt, 5504-30

Business and economic conditions, Fed Reserve 9th District, quarterly journal, 9383-19

Corn yield impacts of weather, estimated 1989 with trends from 1965, article, 1561-4.902

CPI by component for US city average, and by region, population size, and for 27 metro areas, monthly rpt, 6762-2

Dairy prices, by product and selected area, with related marketing data, 1988, annual rpt, 1317-1

Economic conditions, Fed Reserve 9th District, quarterly rpt, 9383-18

Economic issues affecting North Central States, Fed Reserve 7th District, working paper series, 9375-13

Employment, income, and economic conditions, by Fed Reserve 7th District State, periodic rpt, discontinued, 9375-4

Farm credit conditions and economic devs, Fed Reserve 7th District, biweekly rpt, 9375-10

Farm credit conditions, earnings, and expenses, Fed Reserve 9th District, quarterly rpt, 9383-11

Farm production costs and prices, impacts of alternative crop, marketing, and futures contract purchase strategies, model results, 1971-86, 1548-353

Financial and economic devs, Fed Reserve Bank of Chicago bimonthly journal, 9375-1

Financial and economic devs, Fed Reserve Bank of Cleveland quarterly journal, 9377-1

Financial and economic devs, Fed Reserve Bank of Kansas City monthly journal, 9381-1

Financial and economic devs, Fed Reserve Bank of Minneapolis quarterly journal, 9383-6

Financial and economic devs, Fed Reserve Bank of St Louis bimonthly journal, 9391-1

Freight (waterborne domestic and foreign) by commodity, traffic, and passengers, by port and waterway, 1987, annual rpt, 3754-3.2; 3754-3.3

Head Start program operations, enrollment by handicap, and family characteristics, for North Central States, 1987/88, annual rpt, 4604-12

HHS financial aid, by program, recipient, State, and city, FY88, annual regional listing, 4004-3.5; 4004-3.7

Hogs inventory, value, farrowings, and farms, by State, quarterly release, 1623-3

Housing vacancy rates for single and multifamily units and mobile homes in FHLB 10th District, by ZIP code, annual MSA rpt series, 9304-22

Income (personal) per capita and by source, and earnings by industry div, by State, MSA, and county, 1982-87, annual regional rpt, 2704-2.2; 2704-2.3

Income (personal) per capita and by source, earnings by major industry group, and social insurance contributions, by region and State, 1929-87, 2708-40

Lumber (pulpwood) production and mill receipts in North Central States, by species, mill, State, and county, 1987, annual rpt, 1204-19

Manufacturing employment in Illinois compared to other Great Lakes States, by industry group, various periods 1960-88, working paper, 9375-13.14

Rangeland acreage, soil erosion, and other impacts of Conservation Reserve program, for Great Plains, 1987 conf papers, 1208-290

Reclamation Bur water storage and carriage facilities, capacity, and operating status, as of Sept 1988, biennial listing, 5824-7

Savings and loan assns, FHLB 6th District insured members financial condition and operations by State, quarterly rpt, 9302-23

Savings and loan assns, FHLB 8th District members, locations, assets, and savings, 1989, annual listing, 9304-9

Savings instns, FHLB 6th District members financial condition and operations by State, monthly rpt, 9302-11

Savings instns, FHLB 7th District and natl cost of funds indexes, and mortgage rates, monthly rpt, 9302-30

Savings instns, FHLB 8th District members financial operations by State and SMSA, monthly rpt, 9302-9

Savings instns, FHLB 10th District members finances and lending by State and MSA, monthly table, 9302-22

Savings instns, FHLB 10th District members financial condition, by State, quarterly rpt, 9302-34

Statistical Abstract of US, social, political, and economic data, with foreign comparisons, 1790-2025, comprehensive annual compilation, 2324-1

Wildlife damage to crops, livestock, and property in Great Plains, and effectiveness of mgmt methods, 1988 conf, 1208-304

see also under By Region in the "Index by Categories"

see also under names of individual States

North Dakota

Agriculture census, 1987: farms, farmland, production and costs, and operator characteristics, advance State and county rpts, 2330-1.38

Agriculture census, 1987: farms, farmland, production, finances, and operator characteristics, by county, final State rpt, 2331-1.34

Alcohol fuels (methanol) prices, distribution, and gasoline displacement, with background data, 1985-86 and projected to 2000, 3008-122

Bank deposits in FDIC-insured commercial and savings banks, by instn, State, and county, as of June 1988, annual regional rpt, 9295-3.5

Business and economic conditions, Fed Reserve 9th District, quarterly journal, 9383-19

Coal production and mines by county, prices, productivity, miners, reserves, and stocks, by mining method and State, 1987-88, annual rpt, 3164-25

Conservation of soil and wetlands, USDA programs costs and impacts on farm finances and operations, with background data, 1980s, hearing, 25168-69

County Business Patterns, 1987: employment, establishments, and payroll, by SIC 2- to 4-digit industry and county, annual State rpt, 2326-8.36

Deaths and rates, by detailed location, cause, and demographic characteristics, 1987, US Vital Statistics annual rpt, 4144-3.1

DOD prime contract awards, by contractor, service branch, State, and city, FY88, annual rpt, 3544-22

Economic conditions, Fed Reserve 9th District, quarterly rpt, 9383-18

Employment, earnings, and hours, by selected SIC 1- to 4-digit industry, State, and for 262 MSAs, 1972-87, 6748-81.4

Fed Govt spending in States and local areas, by type, State, county, and city, FY88, annual rpt, 2464-3

Fed Govt spending in States, by type, program, agency, and State, FY88, annual rpt, 2464-2

HHS financial aid, by program, recipient, State, and city, FY88, annual regional listing, 4004-3.8

Homeless children educational enrollment and needs, 1988, annual State rpt, 4804-35.34

Income (personal) per capita and by source, and earnings by industry div, by State, MSA, and county, 1982-87, annual regional rpt, 2704-2.3

Mineral Industry Surveys, State reviews of production, 1988, preliminary annual rpt, 5614-6

Minerals Yearbook, 1987, Vol 2 preprints: State review of production and sales by commodity, and business activity, annual rpt, 5604-16.35

Minerals Yearbook, 1987, Vol 2: State reviews of production, sales, and firms, by commodity, and business activity, annual rpt, 5604-34

Nursing home compliance with Medicare and Medicaid regulations, and patient characteristics, by facility, 1987/88, annual State rpt, 4654-15.35

Real estate investment by foreigners in North Dakota farm and commercial real estate, by owner country, 1977-89, GAO rpt, 26123-244

Retail trade census, 1987: employment, establishments, sales, and payroll, by SIC 2- to 4-digit kind of business, MSA, county, and city, State rpt, 2397-1.35

Savings instns, FHLB 8th District members financial operations by State and SMSA, monthly rpt, 9302-9

Service industries census, 1987: employment, establishments, receipts, and payroll, by SIC 2- to 4-digit kind of business, MSA, county, and city, State rpt, 2391-1.35

Statistical Abstract of US, social, political, and economic data, with foreign comparisons, 1790-2025, comprehensive annual compilation, 2324-1

Wages by occupation, for office and plant workers, 1989 survey, periodic labor market rpt, 6785-3.8

Water supply and quality in streams and lakes, and groundwater levels in wells, by drainage basin, 1987, annual State rpt, 5666-10.33

Wholesale trade census, 1987: employment, establishments, finances, and operations, by SIC 2- to 4-digit kind of business, MSA, county, and city, State rpt, 2405-1.35

Wildlife-related recreation, hunting, and fishing participation and spending, detailed data, 1985 survey, quinquennial State rpt, 5506-6.34

North Dakota

see also under By State in the "Index by Categories"

North Little Rock, Ark.

Housing vacancy rates for single and multifamily units and mobile homes, by city and ZIP code, 1989, annual MSA rpt, 9304–19.3

Wages by occupation, and benefits for office and plant workers, 1989 survey, periodic MSA rpt, 6785–12.7

North Sea

Plastic, tar, and other nondegradable ocean and beach debris, incidence and environmental impacts, 1970s-88, 14738–4

Northeast States

Banks and thrifts in New England, financial statements by type of instn and Fed deposit insurance, and State, 1987, annual rpt, 9304–3

Bond (municipal) yields relation to natl and regional financial indicators and issue and underwriter characteristics, by maturity and bond type, 1977-78, working paper, 9389–19.8

Coastal areas environmental conditions, fish, wildlife, use, and mgmt, 1989 rpt, 5506–9.35

CPI by component for US city average, and by region, population size, and for 27 metro areas, monthly rpt, 6762–2

Dairy prices, by product and selected area, with related marketing data, 1988, annual rpt, 1317–1

Distillate fuel production, imports, stocks, and prices, by selected PAD district and northern State, seasonal monthly rpt, 3162–40

Economic indicators for New England States, Fed Reserve 1st District, monthly rpt, 9373–24

Economic indicators for New England States, Fed Reserve 1st District, quarterly rpt with articles, 9373–2

Electric power trade of US with Canada, purchase agreements, and grid interconnection capacity, 1960s-88 and projected to 1992, GAO rpt, 26113–228

Exports and imports of New England States, impacts of Canada-US trade agreement, with data by industry, commodity, and State, 1987, article, 9373–2.902

Financial and economic devs, Fed Reserve Bank of Boston bimonthly journal, 9373–1

Fish and shellfish catch, life cycles, and environmental needs, for selected coastal species and regions, series, 5506–8

Fish and shellfish catch, wholesale receipts, prices, trade, and other market activities, weekly regional rpt, 2162–6.1; 2162–6.2

Fish and shellfish landings in New England, by port, State, and species, 1986-87, article, 2162–1.902

Freight (waterborne domestic and foreign) by commodity, traffic, and passengers, by port and waterway, 1987, annual rpt, 3754–3.1

Heart and cerebrovascular disease deaths in New England, and prevention programs, by State, 1989 article, 4042–3.909

HHS financial aid, by program, recipient, State, and city, FY88, annual regional listing, 4004–3.1

Income (personal) per capita and by source, and earnings by industry div, by State, MSA, and county, 1982-87, annual regional rpt, 2704–2.2

Income (personal) per capita and by source, earnings by major industry group, and social insurance contributions, by region and State, 1929-87, 2708–40

Lumber (pulpwood) production by species and county, and shipments, by northeastern State, 1987, annual rpt, 1204–18

Natural gas interstate pipeline company capacity, use, sales, deliveries, and prices, by firm and Northeast State, 1980-88, 3166–6.35

Savings instns, FHLB 1st District members, financial condition, and locations, 1989, annual listing, 9304–26

Savings instns, FHLB 1st District members financial operations and related economic and housing indicators, monthly rpt, 9302–4

Shipbuilding costs, deliveries, contracts, employment, and wage rates, by coastal district and shipyard, 1988, annual rpt, 7704–12

Statistical Abstract of US, social, political, and economic data, with foreign comparisons, 1790-2025, comprehensive annual compilation, 2324–1

Tide height and time daily at coastal points, forecast 1990, annual rpt, 2174–2.3

Timber in northeastern US, resources and removals by species, ownership class, and county, State rpt series, 1206–12

Water supply in northeastern US, precipitation and stream runoff by station, monthly rpt, 2182–3

Waterborne commerce (domestic) of US, freight by major commodity group, vessel type, and port, 1986, annual rpt, 7704–7

see also Appalachia

see also under By Region in the "Index by Categories"

see also under names of individual States

Northern Mariana Islands

Bank deposits in FDIC-insured commercial and savings banks, by instn, State, and county, as of June 1988, annual regional rpt, 9295–3.6

Census of Population and Housing, 1990: outlying areas preparations for count, hearings, 21628–74

Economic Censuses of Outlying Areas, 1987: Northern Mariana Islands employment, firms, payroll, and receipts, by SIC 1- to 4-digit industry, 2597–1

Economic, social, political, and geographic summary data, by country, 1989, annual factbook, 9114–2

Exports and imports between US and outlying areas, by detailed commodity and mode of transport, monthly rpt, 2422–4

Fed Govt spending in States and local areas, by type, State, county, and city, FY88, annual rpt, 2464–3

Fed Govt spending in States, by type, program, agency, and State, FY88, annual rpt, 2464–2

Harbor traffic, facilities, dev, funding, and needs, for Pacific territories and Hawaii by port, as of 1987, 7308–195

HHS financial aid, by program, recipient, State, and city, FY88, annual regional listing, 4004–3.9

Population size and components of change, by outlying area, 1980-88, annual Current Population Rpt, 2546–3.162

Population size, growth rates, and components of change, by country, projected 1989-2020 and trends from 1950, biennial rpt, 2324–9

Population social, economic, health, and govtl data, by TTPI govt, FY88 and selected trends, detailed annual rpt, 7004–6

Supplemental Security Income payments and beneficiaries by State and for Northern Mariana Islands, monthly rpt, 4742–1.4; 4742–1.12

Water supply and quality in streams and lakes, and groundwater levels in wells, by drainage basin, 1987, annual State rpt, 5666–10.10

see also under By Outlying Area in the "Index by Categories"

Norton, Jerry D.

"Railcar Shortages for Grain Shippers, A Current Overview", 1278–15

"Railcars for Grain: Future Need and Availability", 1278–14

"Rural Highway Finance: Federal Funding for Interstate and Non-Interstate Highways in Rural America", 1278–12

Norwalk, Conn.

see also under By SMSA or MSA in the "Index by Categories"

Norway

Agricultural and food production and indexes, total and for selected commodities, by country, 1970s-88, annual rpt, 1524–12

Agricultural production, prices, and trade, by country, 1970s-88 and forecast 1990, annual world region rpt, 1524–4.1

Agricultural trade of US, by detailed commodity and country, 1988, semiannual rpt, 1522–4

AID loans repayment status and terms by program and country, and status of predecessor agency loans, quarterly rpt, 9912–3

Apple exports of US to EC and 4 north European countries, 1984-89, article, 1925–34.939

Background Notes, summary social, political, and economic data, 1989 rpt, 7006–2.40

Economic and military aid and loans from US and intl agencies, by program and country, FY46-87, annual rpt, 9914–5

Economic conditions, policy, and trade practices, by country, 1986-88, annual rpt, 21384–5

Economic, social, political, and geographic summary data, by country, 1989, annual factbook, 9114–2

Exports and imports of US, by selected country, country group, and commodity group, 1988, annual rpt, 2044–37

Human rights conditions in 170 countries, 1988, annual rpt, 21384–3

Imports of goods, services, and investment from US, trade barriers, impacts, and US actions, by country, 1988, annual rpt, 444–2

Labor conditions, union coverage, and work accidents, 1989 annual country rpt, 6366–4.19

Manufacturing labor productivity and unit costs for 14 countries, 1950-88, annual press release, 6864–1

Military aid of US, arms sales, and training programs costs and budget requests, by program, world region, and country, FY88-90, annual rpt, 7144–13

Military spending, arms trade, and force strengths, with govt spending and population, by country, 1977-87, annual rpt, 9824–1

Minerals Yearbook, 1987, Vol 3: foreign country reviews of production, trade, and policy, by commodity, annual rpt, 5604–35

Minerals Yearbook, 1987, Vol 3 preprints: foreign country review of production, trade, and policy, by commodity, annual rpt, 5604–23.55

Multinatl US firms and foreign affiliates finances and operations, by industry of parent firm and affiliate, world area, and country, preliminary 1987, annual rpt, 2704–5

Oil production, trade, use, and stocks, by selected country and country group, monthly rpt, 3162–42

Population size, growth rates, and components of change, by country, projected 1989-2020 and trends from 1950, biennial rpt, 2324–9

UN voting record and share of votes in agreement with US, by issue, country, and world area, 1988, annual rpt, 7004–18

see also under By Foreign Country in the "Index by Categories"

Norwich, Conn.
see also under By SMSA or MSA in the "Index by Categories"

Norwood, Janet L.
"Developing Statistics To Meet Society's Needs", 6722–1.949

Nose and throat disorders
Cases of acute and chronic conditions, disability, absenteeism, and health services use, by selected characteristics, 1988, annual rpt, 4147–10.170

Deaths and rates, by detailed cause and demographic characteristics, 1986 and trends from 1900, US Vital Statistics annual rpt, 4144–2

Notifiable diseases
see Infective and parasitic diseases

Notions
see Clothing and clothing industry
see Household supplies and utensils

Nourse, Hugh O.
"Default Experience of the FHA Graduated-Payment Mortgage", 9316–1.147

Novara, Albert N.
"Preliminary Estimates of Age and Sex Compositions of Ducks and Geese Harvested in the 1988 Hunting Season in Comparison with Prior Years", 5504–32
"Sandhill Crane Harvest and Hunter Activity in the Central Flyway During the 1988-89 Hunting Season", 5504–31

NOW accounts
see Negotiable orders of withdrawal accounts

NSF
see National Science Foundation

Nuclear accidents and safety
Environmental impacts of energy technologies, 1960s-80s, handbook series, 3326–1

Inspection, regulatory, and licensing activities of NRC, budget and staff, by program, FY88-91, annual rpt, 9634–9

Inspection, regulatory, and licensing activities of NRC, with data for individual power plants, FY88, annual rpt, 9634–2

Inspections and operations of commercial reactors, by facility, monthly rpt, 9632–1

Power plants (nuclear) performance ratings, violations, penalties, and unplanned outages, by plant, 1970s-87, GAO rpt, 26113–416

Radiation exposure of population near commercial reactors, by body site, age group, and selected plant, 1986, annual rpt, 9634–7

Radiation exposure of workers at nuclear power plants and related facilities, by site, 1968-86, annual rpt, 9634–3

Radiation protection and health physics enrollment and degrees granted by instn and State, and women grads plans and employment, 1972-88, 3006–8.9

Reactor fuel assembly performance and failures, by fuel vendor and reactor, 1987, annual rpt, 9634–8

Safety standards and research, design, licensing, construction, operation, and finances, for nuclear power plants with data by reactor, quarterly journal, 3352–4

Nuclear explosives and explosions
Radionuclide concentrations in air, water, humans, animals, and milk near Nevada and other nuclear test sites, 1988, annual rpt, 9194–17
see also Nuclear weapons

Nuclear fallout
see Nuclear explosives and explosions
see Radiation

Nuclear industries
see Nuclear power

Nuclear medicine and radiology
Cancer (osteosarcoma) progress and deaths, by disease and treatment characteristics, 1977-85 study, article, 4472–1.901

Cancer cases linked to diagnostic radionuclide iodine-131, for Sweden, 1951-84 study, article, 4472–1.907

Community and migrant health services finances, operations, and staff, 1988 rpt, 4108–45.2

Drug prescriptions, by category, brand, and for new drugs, 1987, annual rpt, 4064–12.2

Epilepsy patients cancer risk relation to anticonvulsant drug treatment and radioactive thorium dioxide exposure, 1989 article, 4472–1.914

Equipment shipments, trade, use, and firms, for electronic medical equipment by product, 1988, annual Current Industrial Rpt, 2506–12.34

FDA investigations and regulatory activities, quarterly rpt, 4062–3

Hospital discharges and length of stay, by diagnosis, patient and instn characteristics, procedure performed, and payment source, 1987, annual rpt, 4147–13.99

Hospital discharges by detailed diagnostic and procedure category, primary diagnosis, and length of stay, by age, sex, and region, 1987, annual rpt, 4147–13.100

Medicare discharges, charges, and length of stay, by State and diagnosis, 1983 and 1985, article, 4652–1.925

Medicare enrollees physician and other services use, benefits, charges, and coinsurance and deductible obligations, 1982-86, article, 4652–1.901

Medicare physicians services use, charges, and reimbursement, by service type, setting, and specialty, 1986, article, 4652–1.936

Military health care personnel, and accessions by training source, by occupation, specialty, and service branch, FY87, annual rpt, 3544–24

Pregnancy-related services use and costs, for Medicaid beneficiaries in 3 States, 1983-84, article, 4652–1.938

Radiation exposure of workers at nuclear power plants and related facilities, by site, 1968-86, annual rpt, 9634–3

Radiation from electronic devices, incidents by type of device, and FDA control activities, 1988, annual rpt, 4064–13

Radiation protection and health physics enrollment and degrees granted by instn and State, and women grads plans and employment, 1972-88, 3006–8.9

VA health care facilities physicians, dentists, and nurses, by selected employment characteristics and VA district, quarterly rpt, 8602–6

VA health care facilities physicians staffing, vacancies, and positions filled, by speciality, 1982-87, hearing, 25768–48

VA Medicine and Surgery Dept trainees, by detailed program and city, FY88, annual rpt, 8704–4

see also X-rays

Nuclear power
Communist, OECD, and selected other countries energy reserves, production, and use, and oil trade and revenue, 1960s-88, annual rpt, 9114–4.5

Construction costs and status for nuclear power plants, and capacity, by plant, as of Dec 1988, annual rpt, 3164–69

Construction industries census, 1987: establishments, employment, receipts, and expenditures, by SIC 4-digit industry and State, final industry rpt series, 2373–1

Construction industries census, 1987: financial and operating data, preliminary industry rpt series, 2371–1

Consumption, by detailed fuel type, end-use sector, and State, 1960-87, State Energy Data System annual rpt, 3164–39

Criminal cases by type and disposition, and collections, for US attorneys, by Federal district, FY88, annual rpt, 6004–2.1

DOE real property owned and leased, by type, subagency, contractor, and site, FY87, annual rpt, 3004–28

Engineering (nuclear) enrollment and degrees by instn and State, and women grads plans and employment, 1972-88, 3006–8.8

Finances and operations of energy producers, by energy type for US firms domestic and foreign operations, 1987, annual rpt, 3164–44

Foreign and US energy production and use, by energy type and country, 1980-88, annual rpt, 3164–50.1; 3164–50.5; 3164–50.8

Foreign and US energy use by sector, and production, by fuel type, country, and country group, projected 1988-2000 and trends from 1970, annual rpt, 3164–84

Foreign and US nuclear power generation, by non-Communist country, monthly rpt, 9112–2

Foreign and US nuclear power plant capacity, generation, and construction and operating status, by plant and location, as of 1988 and projected to 2020, annual rpt, 3164–57

Fuel assembly performance and failures for nuclear power plants, by fuel vendor and reactor, 1987, annual rpt, 9634–8

Fuel cost, quality, use, receipts, and stocks, and power plant production, by energy source, State and utility, quarterly rpt, 3162–39

Great Lakes toxic spills and human error, with data by pollutant source and site, 1984-86, conf, 14648–21

Power plants and capacity, by fuel used, owner, location, and operating status, 1988, and for units planned 1989-98, annual listing, 3164–36

Power plants capacity and uranium needs, projected 1987-2000, annual rpt, 3164–82

Power plants capital and operating costs per kilowatt, by nuclear plant, semiannual rpt, discontinued, 9802–5

Power plants capital and production costs, operations, and fuel use, by fuel type, plant, utility, and location, 1987, annual rpt, 3164–9

Power plants production, capacity, and fuel use, by fuel type, census div, and State, 1984-88, annual rpt, 3164–11.1

Power plants production, fuel use, stocks, and costs by fuel type, and sales, by State, monthly rpt, 3162–35

Prices and spending for fuel, by type, end-use sector, and State, 1987, annual rpt, 3164–64

Reactors for domestic use and export by function and operating status, with owner, operating characteristics, and location, 1988, annual listing, 3004–26

Reactors inspections and operations, by commercial facility, monthly rpt, 9632–1

Regulatory, inspection, and licensing activities of NRC, budget and staff, by program, FY88-91, annual rpt, 9634–9

Regulatory, inspection, and licensing activities of NRC, with data for individual power plants, FY88, annual rpt, 9634–2

Rural Electrification Admin financed electric power plants, with location, capacity, and owner, as of Jan 1989, annual listing, 1244–6

Statistical Abstract of US, social, political, and economic data, 1790-2025, comprehensive annual compilation, 2324–1.3

Supply, demand, and prices, by fuel type and end-use sector, projected under 3 oil price assumptions, 1988-2000, annual rpt, 3164–75

Supply, demand, and prices, by fuel type and end-use sector, with foreign comparisons, 1988 and trends from 1949, annual rpt, 3164–74

Supply, demand, and prices, by fuel type and end use, with foreign comparisons, 1976-88, annual summary rpt, 3164–76

Supply, demand, and prices, by fuel type, end-use sector, and country, detailed data, monthly rpt, 3162–24

Supply, demand, and prices of energy, forecasts by resource type, quarterly rpt, 3162–34

TVA financial and operating data by program and facility, FY88, annual rpt, 9804–32

TVA nuclear power plant mgmt salaries by position, and plant capacity, compared to private utilities, 1985-87, hearing, 21648–57

Utilities finances and operations, detailed data for privately owned firms, and summary data for other utilities by type, 1987, annual rpt, 3164–23

see also Nuclear accidents and safety
see also Nuclear explosives and explosions
see also Nuclear-powered ships
see also Nuclear weapons
see also Radiation
see also Radioactive waste and disposal
see also Uranium

Nuclear-powered ships

Budget of DOD, justification, programs, and policies, FY90-91, annual rpt, 3544–2

Procurement cost estimates for weapons and communications systems, by service branch, quarterly summary rpt, 3502–1

Radiation exposure of Navy personnel on nuclear-powered vessels and at support facilities, and injury claims, 1950s-88, annual rpt, 3804–10

Radioactive waste from Navy nuclear-powered vessels and support facilities, releases in harbors, and public exposure, 1970s-88, annual rpt, 3804–11

Reactors for domestic use and export by function and operating status, with owner, operating characteristics, and location, 1988, annual listing, 3004–26

Soviet Union and Warsaw Pact military weapons systems, aid, presence, and force strengths, and compared to US and NATO, 1989 annual rpt, 3504–20

Nuclear radiation
see Radiation

Nuclear Regulatory Commission

Activities, finances, and staff of NRC, with data for individual power plants, FY88, annual rpt, 9634–2

Activities of NRC, budget, staff, and activities by program, FY88-91, annual rpt, 9634–9

Budget of US Appendix, obligations, appropriations, and personnel, by program and agency, FY90, annual rpt, 104–3

Budget of US, authoritative financial statements with appropriations, outlays, and receipts, by category and agency, FY88, annual rpt, 8104–2.2

Fuel assembly performance and failures for nuclear power plants, by fuel vendor and reactor, 1987, annual rpt, 9634–8

Fuel inventory discrepancies, by facility, 1st half 1988, semiannual rpt, 9632–3

Inspections and operations of commercial reactors, by facility, monthly rpt, 9632–1

Labor unions recognized in Fed Govt, agreements and membership by agency and facility, as of Jan 1989, biennial listing, 9844–14

Occupational radiation exposure at nuclear power plants and related facilities, by site, 1968-86, annual rpt, 9634–3

Power plants (nuclear) performance ratings, violations, penalties, and unplanned outages, by plant, 1970s-87, GAO rpt, 26113–416

R&D and related funding of Fed Govt to higher education and nonprofit instns, by field, instn, agency, and State, FY87, annual rpt, 9627–17

R&D funding by Fed Govt, by field, performer type, agency, and State, FY87-89, annual rpt, 9627–20

Radiation exposure of population near commercial reactors, by body site, age group, and selected plant, 1986, annual rpt, 9634–7

Radioactive waste from nuclear power plants, releases and waste composition by plant, 1986, annual rpt, 9634–1

Nuclear weapons

Budget deficit reduction under Gramm-Rudman Act, cancellation of budget authority by program, FY90, annual rpt, 104–27; 26304–6

Budget of US, historical data, selected years FY34-88 and projected to FY94, annual rpt, 104–22

DOD budget justification, programs, and policies, FY90-91, annual rpt, 3544–2

DOD prime contract awards, by detailed procurement category, FY85-88, annual rpt, 3544–18

DOD procurement cost estimates for weapons and communications systems, by service branch, quarterly summary rpt, 3502–1

NATO and Japan military spending and indicators of ability to support common defense, by country, 1960s-87, annual rpt, 3544–28

Reactors for domestic use and export by function and operating status, with owner, operating characteristics, and location, 1988, annual listing, 3004–26

Soviet Union and Warsaw Pact military weapons systems, aid, presence, and force strengths, and compared to US and NATO, 1989 annual rpt, 3504–20

Statistical Abstract of US, social, political, and economic data, 1790-2025, comprehensive annual compilation, 2324–1.2

Treaties on arms control, status and Arms Control and Disarmament Agency activities, 1988, annual rpt, 9824–2

Waste (radioactive) from DOE military activities, disposal plans and funding, FY87-93, last issue of annual rpt, 3344–1

Waste (radioactive) generation, inventory, and disposal, 1960s-88 and projected to 2020, annual rpt, 3364–2

Waste Isolation Pilot Plant, New Mexico, disposal of military radioactive waste, environmental impacts, 1989 supplemental statement, 3008–33

see also Nuclear explosives and explosions
see also Strategic Arms Reduction Talks

Numismatics
see Coins and coinage

Nurseries
see Child day care

Nurseries and nursery products
see Flowers and nursery products

Nursery schools

see Preschool education

Nurses and nursing

Alcohol and drug abuse coverage in nursing curricula, 1983 survey, article, 4482–1.902

Alien nurses with resident status and temporary work visas, by State and source country, 1985-90, GAO rpt, 26121–314

Collective bargaining coverage and membership of American Nurses Assn, 1956-88, article, 6722–1.946

Developing countries disaster preparedness and economic, population, and political data, country rpt series, 9916–2

Earnings, annual average percent changes for selected occupational groups, selected MSAs, monthly rpt, 6782–1.1

Educational and research grants and contracts of Health Professions Bur, by instn and program, FY88, annual listing, 4114–1

Enrollment in science and engineering grad programs, by field, source of funds, and characteristics of student and instn, 1975-87, annual rpt, 9627–7

Health condition and health care resources, use, and spending, 1950s-87, annual data compilation, 4144–11

HHS financial aid, by program, recipient, State, and city, FY88, annual regional listings, 4004–3

Home health care services use and costs for Medicare disabled and aged enrollees, by age, sex, service type, and diagnosis, mid 1970s-86, article, 4652–1.908

Hospital chief nursing officers activities, responsibilities, and role in nurse hiring and retention, 1988 survey, 4008–91

Hospital reimbursement by Medicare under prospective payment system, area wage index adjusted for health occupation mix, by location, 1984-85, article, 4652–1.950

Hospital reimbursement by Medicare under prospective payment system, urban area instn finances and operations, 1988 rpt, 17206–1.3

Indian Health Service facilities, funding, operations, and Indian health and other characteristics, 1950s-88, annual chartbook, 4084–1

Indian Health Service outpatient visits, by type of provider, selected hospital, and IHS service area, FY87-88, annual rpt, 4084–3

Insurance (health) coverage and provisions of employee benefit plans, by plan type and occupational group, 1988, annual rpt, 6784–19

Labor supply and shortage indicators, and earnings, for nursing, by State, 1970s-80s, 25148–41

Labor supply of nurses, recruitment and retention issues and indicators, 1988 conf papers, 4118–64

Labor supply of RNs, shortages, recruitment, and retention, findings and recommendations, 1988 rpt, 4008–88

Mental health care facilities, staff, and patient characteristics, *Statistical Notes* series, 4506–3

Military health care personnel, and accessions by training source, by occupation, specialty, and service branch, FY87, annual rpt, 3544–24

Military reserve medical personnel, by specialty and reserve component, FY88, annual rpt, 3544–31.2

Mississippi hospitals and community health centers, use, staff, and Medicare and other payments, 1988 hearing, 25548–97

Navy manpower strengths, accessions, and attrition, detailed statistics, quarterly rpt, 3802–4

Nursing home and home care case mix, quality of care, and outcomes, impacts of Medicare prospective payment system, 1980s-86, 4658–28

Nursing home compliance with Medicare and Medicaid regulations, and patient characteristics, by facility, 1987/88, annual State rpt series, 4654–15

Nursing home facility, staff, and resident detailed characteristics, 1985, 4147–13.97

Nursing home reimbursement by Medicaid, case mix classification methodology, for New York State, 1987, article, 4652–1.910

Occupational and environmental health care personnel supply and needs, by field, 1987 conf, 4118–65

Peer review organizations review of Medicare hospital claims, activities, and membership, 1984-88, GAO rpt, 26131–51

Statistical Abstract of US, social, political, and economic data, 1790-2025, comprehensive annual compilation, 2324–1.1

Tax (income) returns of partnerships, income statement items by industry group, 1986, annual article, 8302–2.903

Tax (income) returns of sole proprietorships, income statement items, by industry group, 1987, annual article, 8302–2.904; 8302–2.921

Texas-Mexico border area health facilities and services, with background data, by Texas county, 1980s-88, GAO rpt, 26121–261

Training support grants of Bur of Health Professions, by program, region, and State, FY80-87, 4118–62

VA health care facilities beds closed because of nurse shortages, and malpractice claim rates, FY85-88, hearing, 21768–48

VA health care facilities employment, FY64-88, annual rpt, 8604–5.1

VA health care facilities physicians, dentists, and nurses, by selected employment characteristics and VA district, quarterly rpt, 8602–6

VA health care professionals employment, by district and facility, quarterly rpt, 8602–4

VA Medicine and Surgery Dept trainees, by detailed program and city, FY88, annual rpt, 8704–4

see also Midwives

Nursing homes

Admissions and discharges from nursing homes for Medicaid patients with prior hospitalization, for 3 States, 1981, article, 4652–1.942

Admissions of nursing homes by prior hospitalization status and duration, and patient characteristics, with impacts of Medicare reimbursement under prospective payment system, mid 1970s-85, 4147–13.98

AIDS patients and persons with AIDS virus infection, Medicaid policies and State health insurance regulation, with background data, 1987-88, article, 4652–1.953

Construction put in place, private and public, by type and region, monthly rpt, annual tables, 2382–4

County Business Patterns, 1987: employment, establishments, and payroll, by SIC 2- to 4-digit industry and county, annual State rpt series, 2326–8

Data on health care spending, natl survey methodology, 1989 rpt, 4186–8.4

Employment, earnings, and hours, by SIC 1- to 4-digit industry, monthly 1983-Feb 1989, annual rpt, 6744–4

Energy use in commercial buildings, costs, and conservation, by building characteristics, survey rpt series, 3166–8

Expenditures for health care, by service type, payment source, and age, 1977 and 1987, article, 4652–1.946

Expenditures for health care, by service type, payment source, and sector, 1960s-87, annual article, 4652–1.926

Expenditures of aged for instnl and community care, under alternative community settings, 1979-84 study, article, 4652–1.932

Facilities, beds, and residents, by ownership, certification status, and State, 1986, 4147–14.33

Facility, staff, and resident detailed characteristics, 1985, 4147–13.97

France and US hospital and long-term care beds, by facility type and ownership, 1981, 4147–5.4

Govt finances, by level of govt, State, and for large cities and counties, annual rpt series, 2466–2

Health care and condition research, survey design and research methods, 1989 conf proceedings, 4188–60

Health Care Financing Review, provider prices, price inputs and indexes, and labor, quarterly journal, 4652–1.1

Health condition and health care resources, use, and spending, 1950s-87, annual data compilation, 4144–11

Insurance (health) for long term care, State regulation and enforcement actions, 1986-88, GAO rpt, 26121–282

Long-term health care case mix, quality of care, and outcomes, impacts of Medicare prospective payment system, 1980s-86, 4658–28

Long-term health care for aged, funding by Fed Govt, public views, 1987 survey, hearings, 21368–106

Long-term health care needs, ability to pay, and views on Federal aid for home care, 1988 survey, hearing, 21148–51

Long-term health care needs of aged with functional limitations, and costs by payment source, 1982-85, GAO rpt, 26121–266

Medicaid coverage, participation, payments, admin, and legislative history, with data by State, 1980s-88, 21368–105

Medicaid enrollment, and service use and costs by service type, by eligibility type, for 5 States, 1980-84, article, 4652–1.919

Medicaid reimbursement of nursing homes, case mix classification methodology, for New York State, 1987, article, 4652–1.910

Medicare and Medicaid beneficiaries and program operations, 1988, annual fact book, 4654-18

Medicare and Medicaid eligibility, participation, coverage, and program finances, various periods 1966-89, biennial rpt, 4654-1

Medicare and Medicaid enrollees, benefits, reimbursements, and services use, mid-1960s-87, annual rpt, 4744-3.5; 4744-3.6

Medicare and Medicaid regulations, nursing home compliance and patient characteristics, by facility, 1987/88, annual State rpt series, 4654-15

Medicare claims approved, charges, and reimbursements by type of service, from 1974, monthly rpt, quarterly data, 4742-1.11

Medicare discharges, charges, and length of stay, for facilities excluded from prospective payment system, FY84-88, article, 4652-1.935

Medicare enrollees skilled nursing facility use and costs, by selected characteristics and State, 1970s-87, article, 4652-1.954

Medicare payments for post-hospitalization care by diagnosis, for nursing home, home care, and rehabilitation, 1980s-87, article, 4652-1.909

Medicare reimbursement of hospitals under prospective payment system, and of physicians, effect on services, finances, and beneficiary payments, 1970s-88, annual rpt, 17204-2

Medicare reimbursement of hospitals under prospective payment system, impacts on industry structure, 1975-86, 17206-2.2

Medicare reimbursement of hospitals under prospective payment system, impacts on instns, beneficiaries, and other care providers and payment sources, 1986, annual rpt, 4654-13

Medicare reimbursement of hospitals under prospective payment system, impacts on subacute care, 1988 rpt, 17206-2.8

Medicare reimbursement of nursing homes under alternative payment systems, model results, 1988, article, 4652-1.929

Mentally retarded persons facilities, beds, and residents, by ownership, resident age and race, and State, 1986, 4147-14.34

Mortgage insurance programs of HUD, finances and lending activity by program, FY88, annual rpt, 5004-8

NIH grants for R&D, training, construction, and medical libraries, by location and recipient, FY88, annual listings, 4434-7

Nurses (RN) employment, shortages, recruitment, and retention, findings and recommendations, 1988 rpt, 4008-88

Occupational injury and illness rates, by SIC 2- to 4-digit industry, 1987, annual rpt, 6844-1

Older frail persons community and home-based care under prepaid care plan, enrollees health condition and services use, for San Francisco, 1987, article, 4652-1.912

Older persons care by family members, caregivers stress and respite services, for King County, Wash, 1983-87, article, 4652-1.916

Older persons eligible for nursing home care, cost of home and community services, Medicaid waiver program in 2 States, 1981-84, article, 4652-1.943

Older persons poverty risk from long-term care costs, by duration of care, income, and marital status, model results, 1987 rpt, 25928-7

Older persons socioeconomic characteristics, 1900s-86 and projected to 2050, biennial chartbook, 12904-1

Physicians Medicare services use, charges, and reimbursement, by service type, setting, and specialty, 1986, article, 4652-1.936

Productivity of labor and capital, indicators for health facilities excluded from Medicare prospective payment system by instn type, 1976-86, 17206-2.1

Receipts for services, by SIC 2- to 4-digit kind of business, 1988, annual rpt, 2413-8

Rehabilitation services of nursing homes, use by service type and patient characteristics, 1st qtr 1983, 4188-58

Retirement communities (continuing care) residents nursing home admissions compared to general population, late 1970s, article, 4652-1.917

Science and engineering employment, by nonmanufacturing industry and field, 1987, triennial rpt, 9627-31

Service industries census, 1987: establishments, receipts, employment, and payroll, by SIC 2- to 4-digit kind of business, MSA, county, and city, State rpt series, 2391-1

Statistical Abstract of US, social, political, and economic data, 1790-2025, comprehensive annual compilation, 2324-1.1

Supplemental Security Income and Medicaid eligibility and payment provisions, and beneficiaries living arrangements, by State, 1989, annual rpt, 4704-13

Supplemental Security Income beneficiaries Medicaid services use and costs, by diagnosis and whether covered by Medicare, 1984, article, 4652-1.947

Tax (income) returns of corporations, income and tax items by asset size and detailed industry, 1986, annual rpt, 8304-4; 8304-21

Tax (income) returns of partnerships, income statement items by industry group, 1986, annual article, 8302-2.903

Tax (income) returns of sole proprietorships, income statement items, by industry group, 1987, annual article, 8302-2.904; 8302-2.921

Veterans characteristics, and VA activities and programs, FY88, annual rpt, 8604-3

Veterans characteristics, and VA programs and activities, monthly rpt, 8602-3; 9922-2

Veterans health care, patients, visits, costs, and operating beds, by VA and contract facility, and region, quarterly rpt, 8602-4

Vital and Health Statistics series: health care facilities use and labor force, 4147-13

Nutrition and malnutrition

Agricultural Statistics, 1988, annual rpt, 1004-1.2

Cancer cases, and prevention and risk activities and attitudes, 1987 survey, annual rpt, 4474-35

Child health education programs for nutrition and smoking deterrence, effectiveness, 1979-85 local area study, article, 4472-1.916

Consumer food spending and consumption, housing, and other finances, 1960s-88, annual chartbook, 1504-3

Deaths and rates, by cause, age, sex, marital status, race, and State, 1987, US Vital Statistics advance annual rpt, 4146-5.113

Deaths and rates, by detailed cause and demographic characteristics, 1986 and trends from 1900, US Vital Statistics annual rpt, 4144-2

Deaths and rates, by detailed location, cause, and demographic characteristics, 1987, US Vital Statistics annual rpt, 4144-3

Developing countries disaster preparedness and economic, population, and political data, country rpt series, 9916-2

Developing countries economic and social conditions from 1960s, and Intl Dev Cooperation Agency and AID activities and funding, FY88-90, annual rpt, 9904-4

Developing countries food production and needs, and related economic outlook, by country, 1989/90, annual rpt, 1524-6

Farm financial and marketing conditions, forecast 1988, conf papers, annual rpt, 1004-16

Fed Govt financial and nonfinancial domestic aid, 1989 base edition with supplements, annual listing, 104-5

Foreign countries agricultural research grants of USDA, by program, subagency, and country, FY88, annual listing, 1954-3

Foreign countries human rights conditions in 170 countries, 1988, annual rpt, 21384-3

Health condition and practices related to nutritional status, by selected characteristics, 1970s-86, 4048-33

Health condition improvement and disease prevention goals and recommended activities for 2000, with trends 1970s-80s, 4048-10

HHS financial aid, by program, recipient, State, and city, FY88, annual regional listings, 4004-3

Homeless persons nutritional status, 1987 local area study, article, 4042-3.942

Indian Health Service facilities, funding, operations, and Indian health and other characteristics, 1950s-88, annual chartbook, 4084-1

Military personnel alcohol and drug abuse, prevalence and consequences, by selected characteristics, 1988, biennial rpt, 3504-19

NIH activities, funding by program and recipient type, staff, and clinic patients, by inst, FY87, annual rpt, 4434-3

NIH nutrition biomedical and behavioral research and training activities and funding, by inst, FY87, annual rpt, 4434-15

Nursing home compliance with Medicare and Medicaid regulations, and patient characteristics, by facility, 1987/88, annual State rpt series, 4654-15

Nutrient intake and food consumption by individuals, by food group, selected characteristics, and region, supplementary survey series, 1356-5

Research and education grants, USDA competitive awards by program and recipient, FY88, annual listing, 1764-1

Statistical Abstract of US, social, political, and economic data, 1790-2025, comprehensive annual compilation, 2324-1.1

see also Breast-feeding

see also Dietitians and nutritionists

see also Food assistance

see also Food consumption

see also Food ingredients and additives

see also Food supply

see also Obesity

see also School lunch and breakfast programs

see also Vitamins and nutrients

see also under By Disease in the "Index by Categories"

Nuts

Acreage planted, by selected crop and State, 1980-88 and planned 1989, annual rpt, 1621-22

Agricultural exports of US, impacts of foreign agricultural and trade policy, with data by commodity and country, 1988, annual rpt, 1924-8

Agricultural Statistics, 1988, annual rpt, 1004-1

Agriculture census, 1987: farms, farmland, production and costs, and operator characteristics, advance State and county rpt series, 2330-1

Agriculture census, 1987: farms, farmland, production, finances, and operator characteristics, by county, final State rpt series, 2331-1

Almond and hazelnut production, supply, trade, and use, by country, 1986-89, article, 1925-34.938

Cold storage food stocks by commodity and census div, and warehouse space use, by State, monthly rpt, 1631-5

Cold storage food stocks, by commodity and census div, 1988, annual rpt, 1631-11

Consumption of food and nutrient intake by individuals, by food group, selected characteristics, and region, supplementary survey series, 1356-5

Consumption, supply, trade, prices, spending, and indexes, by food commodity, 1987, annual rpt, 1544-4

Exports and imports (agricultural) of US, by commodity and country, bimonthly rpt with articles, 1522-1

Exports and imports (agricultural) of US, by commodity, monthly rpt, 1922-8

Exports and imports (agricultural) of US, by detailed commodity and country, 1988, semiannual rpt, 1522-4

Exports of US, detailed commodities by country, monthly rpt, 2422-3

Farm income, expenses, receipts by commodity, assets, liabilities, and ratios, 1988 and trends from 1945, annual rpt, 1544-16

Farm sector balance sheet, and receipts by detailed commodity, by State, 1984-88, annual rpt, 1544-18

Farm sector finances, income sources, expenses by type, assets, debts, and ratios, 1987, annual rpt, 1544-19

Foreign and US agricultural production, trade, and weather devs, weekly press release, 1922-4

Foreign and US fresh and processed fruit, vegetable, and nut production and trade, FAS monthly circular with articles, 1925-34

Imports of US, detailed Schedule A commodities by country, monthly rpt, 2422-2

Irrigation projects of Reclamation Bur in western US, crop production and acreage by commodity, State, and project, 1987, annual rpt, 5824-12.1

Manufacturing annual survey, 1986: financial and operating data, by SIC 2- to 4-digit industry, series, 2506-15

Manufacturing census, 1987: financial and operating data, for SIC 4-digit industries by product, preliminary rpt, 2491-1.6

Nutrient and caloric composition of food, for raw, processed, and prepared food, 1988 rpt, 1358-3

Pecan wholesale prices at selected shipping points, 1988, annual rpt, 1311-8

Pistachio production, trade, stocks, and use, for 5 countries, 1987/88-1989/90, annual article, 1925-34.942

Price indexes (producer), by stage of processing and detailed commodity, monthly rpt, 6762-6

Price indexes (producer), by stage of processing and detailed commodity, monthly 1988, annual rpt, 6764-2

Prices received and paid by farmers, by commodity and State, 1988, annual rpt, 1629-5

Prices received by farmers for major products, and paid for farm inputs and living items, by State, monthly rpt, 1629-1

Production, farms, acreage, and related data, by selected crop and State, monthly rpt, 1621-1

Production itemized costs, receipts, and returns, by commodity and region, 1985-87, annual rpt, 1544-20

Production of fruit and vegetables for processing, industries finances and operations, consumption, and trade, by commodity, 1970s-88, 1568-275

Production, prices, and use of fruit and nuts, 1986-89, annual rpt series, 1621-18

Production, prices, trade, stocks, and use, by selected crop, periodic situation rpt with articles, 1561-6

Statistical Abstract of US, social, political, and economic data, 1790-2025, comprehensive annual compilation, 2324-1.3

Turkey nut production, trade, use, and stocks, by type, 1979/80-1988/89, article, 1925-34.915

Walnut production, trade, stocks, and use, for 5 countries, 1987/88-1989/90, annual article, 1925-34.941

see also Oils, oilseeds, and fats

see also Peanuts

see also under By Commodity in the "Index by Categories"

Nuts, metal

see Hardware

Nyman, John A.

"Does the Average Cost of Home Health Care Vary with Case Mix?", 4042-3.932

Oak Ridge National Laboratory

"Effect of Lifestyle on Energy Use Estimations and Predicted Savings", 3226-2.11

"Energy Savings in New, Low-Rise Multifamily Buildings: Model Conservation Standards in Tacoma, Washington", 3308-92

"Integrated Data Base for 1989: Spent Fuel and Radioactive Waste Inventories, Projections, and Characteristics", 3364-2

"Light-Duty Vehicle Summary: Model Year 1976 to the First Half of Model Year 1989", 3302-4

"Transportation Energy Data Book: Edition 10", 3304-5

see also Department of Energy National Laboratories

Oakerson, Ronald J.

"Metropolitan Organization: The St. Louis Case", 10046-9.1

Oakland, Calif.

CPI by component for US city average, and by region, population size, and for 15 metro areas, monthly rpt, 6762-1

CPI by component for US city average, and by region, population size, and for 27 metro areas, monthly rpt, 6762-2

Fruit and vegetable shipments, and arrivals in US and Canada cities, by mode of transport and State and country of origin, 1988, annual rpt, 1311-4.2

Housing and households characteristics, 1985 survey, MSA fact sheet, 2485-11.9

Housing and households detailed characteristics, and unit and neighborhood quality, by location, 1985 survey, MSA rpt, 2485-6.10

Wages by occupation, for office and plant workers, 1989 survey, periodic MSA rpt, 6785-12.4

see also under By City and By SMSA or MSA in the "Index by Categories"

Oakland County, Mich.

Housing and households detailed characteristics, and unit and neighborhood quality, by location, 1985 survey, MSA rpt, 2485-6.9

OAPEC

see Organization of Petroleum Exporting Countries

OASDHI

see Old-Age, Survivors, Disability, and Health Insurance

Oats

see Animal feed

see Grains and grain products

Ober, Joyce A.

"Strontium: Uses, Supply, and Technology", 5606-9.2

Obesity

Deaths and rates, by detailed cause and demographic characteristics, 1986 and trends from 1900, US Vital Statistics annual rpt, 4144-2

Health condition and health care resources, use, and spending, 1950s-87, annual data compilation, 4144-11

Health-related behavior of runners, for 7 habits, by sex, age, education, income, and average miles run per week, 1985 survey, article, 4042-3.933

Hispanic Americans body measurements, obesity, and handedness, by detailed origin, age, and sex, 1982-84, 4147-11.207

Military personnel health-related behavior, for 7 habits, by age, education, race, and health status, 1985 survey, article, 4042-3.949

Nutritional status and related health condition and practices, by selected characteristics, 1970s-87, 4048–33

Older persons health care services use, persons with high and low levels of care by selected health and other characteristics, 1971 and 1980 studies, 4186–2.22

Vitamin and mineral supplements use by adults and children, by type and user characteristics, 1986, 4146–8.175

O'Brien, James M.

"Bank Equity Values, Bank Risk, and the Implied Market Value of Banks' Assets, Liabilities, and Deposit Insurance", 9366–6.212

"Bank Equity Values, Bank Risk, and the Implied Market Values of Banks' Assets and Liabilities", 9366–6.181

Obscenity and pornography

Child pornography investigations of USPS, arrests, and convictions, FY88, annual rpt, 9864–8; 9864–9

Criminal case processing in Federal district courts, and dispositions, by offense, district, and offender characteristics, 1984, annual rpt, 6064–29

Public opinion on crime and crime-related issues, by respondent characteristics, 1970s-89, annual rpt, 6064–6.2

Sentences for Federal offenses, guidelines by offense and circumstances, 1989 rpt, 17668–1

US attorneys civil and criminal cases by type and disposition, and collections, by Federal district, FY88, annual rpt, 6004–2.1

Obstetrics and gynecology

Cancer screening of aged by physicians and compliance with American Cancer Society schedules, by speciality, 1986 local area study, article, 4042–3.917

Cesarean section deliveries, by State, 1985 conf papers, 4148–28

Drugs (controlled) provided during physician office visits, by drug, patient, and provider characteristics, 1985, 4146–8.179

France and Germany physicians, and visits by reason and patient age and sex, by specialty, compared to US, 1981-83, 4147–5.5

France and US hospital and long-term care beds, by facility type and ownership, 1981, 4147–5.4

Health condition and health care resources, use, and spending, 1950s-87, annual data compilation, 4144–11

Hospital discharges and length of stay, by diagnosis, patient and instn characteristics, procedure performed, and payment source, 1987, annual rpt, 4147–13.99

Hospital discharges by detailed diagnostic and procedure category, primary diagnosis, and length of stay, by age, sex, and region, 1987, annual rpt, 4147–13.100

Indian Health Service and contract facilities hospitalization, by diagnosis, age, sex, and service area, FY87, annual rpt, 4104–16

Indian Health Service and contract facilities hospitalization, by diagnosis, age, sex, and service area, FY88, annual rpt, 4084–5

Indian Health Service outpatient visits, by reason for visit and age, FY87-88, annual rpt, 4084–2

Indian Health Service outpatient visits, by type of provider, selected hospital, and IHS service area, FY87-88, annual rpt, 4084–3

Malpractice claims and payments, by procedure and physician specialty, 1975-78, hearing, 21408–113

Medicaid beneficiaries maternity services use and costs, in 3 States, 1983-84, article, 4652–1.938

Military health care benefits and costs under Civilian Health and Medical Program of Uniformed Services, FY83-FY89, 3508–31

Military health care personnel, and accessions by training source, by occupation, specialty, and service branch, FY87, annual rpt, 3544–24

Military hospitals and CHAMPUS costs, and reduction in military hospital admissions, with background data, FY85-87, GAO rpt, 26121–288

Older persons preventive health care services use, and relation to selected characteristics, 1970s-80s, 26356–7.2

Physicians income, by specialty and other practice characteristics, 1975 and 1983-84, article, 4652–1.920

Surgical procedures performed in hospitals, by procedure type, age, sex, instn size, and payment source, 1983-87, 4146–8.171

VA health care facilities physicians, dentists, and nurses, by selected employment characteristics and VA district, quarterly rpt, 8602–6

see also Maternity

see also Prenatal care

Ocala, Fla.

see also under By SMSA or MSA in the "Index by Categories"

Occupational health and safety

AIDS virus transmission in health care settings, facilities compliance with OSHA guidelines for protecting workers, 1988 rpt, 26358–198

Aircraft accidents and circumstances, for US operations of domestic and foreign airlines and general aviation, periodic rpt, 9612–1

Aircraft accidents in general aviation, by circumstances, characteristics of persons and aircraft involved, and type of flying, 1986, annual rpt, 9614–3

Assistance (financial and nonfinancial) of Fed Govt, 1989 base edition with supplements, annual listing, 104–5

Aviation medicine research and test results, technical rpt series, 7506–10

Births of low birthweight and stillbirths risks relation to parental hazardous substance exposure, 1980, article, 4042–3.945

Cancer (bladder) risk for men in selected occupations, by employment characteristics, 1977-78, article, 4472–1.924; 4472–1.925

Carcinogens chemistry, sources, environment and health risks, and regulation, by substance and brand, 1989, annual rpt, 4044–15

Collective bargaining agreement provisions for labor-mgmt occupational health and safety committees, by major industry group, 1983 and 1986, 6306–3.4

Criminal cases by type and disposition, and collections, for US attorneys, by Federal district, FY88, annual rpt, 6004–2.1

Deaths and rates, by detailed cause and demographic characteristics, 1986 and trends from 1900, US Vital Statistics annual rpt, 4144–2

Deaths related to work, by equipment type, circumstances, and OSHA standards violated, series, 6606–2

Disability, acute and chronic health conditions, absenteeism, and health services use, by selected characteristics, 1988, annual rpt, 4147–10.170

Diving (underwater sport and occupational) deaths, by circumstances, diver characteristics, and location, 1970-87, annual rpt, 2144–5

Fed Govt block and categorical grant programs for State and local govts, FY89, biennial listing, 10044–8

Fed Govt spending in States, by type, program, agency, and State, FY88, annual rpt, 2464–2

Foreign countries labor conditions, union coverage, and work accidents, annual country rpt series, 6366–4

Hazardous substances and conditions occupational exposure, and prevention and control measures, 1981-83 survey, 4248–86

Health care personnel supply and needs, for environmental and occupational health fields, 1987 conf, 4118–65

Health condition and health care resources, use, and spending, 1950s-87, annual data compilation, 4144–11

Herbicide use in natl forests, exposure and cancer risk by type and application mode, 1988 rpt, 1208–295

HHS financial aid, by program, recipient, State, and city, FY88, annual regional listings, 4004–3

Injuries at workplace, by circumstances, body site, equipment type, and industry, with safety measures, series, 6846–1

Injuries from use of consumer products, by severity, victim age, and detailed product, 1988, annual rpt, 9164–6

Injuries, illnesses, and workdays lost, by industry div and major manufacturing group, Monthly Labor Review, 6722–1.7

Injuries, illnesses, and workdays lost, by SIC 2-digit industry, 1987-88, annual press release, 6844–3

Injuries on job, relation to increases in workers compensation benefits and employer premiums, model description and results, 1985 working paper, 6886–6.15

Injuries on job relation to increases in workers compensation benefits, model description and results, 1979-84, working paper, 6886–6.64

Injury and illness rates, by industry group, 1975-87, 6728–38.10

Injury and illness rates by SIC 2- to 4-digit industry, and deaths by cause and industry div, 1987, annual rpt, 6844–1

Inspections at firms with high injury rates, impacts on injury rates, 1979-85, working paper, 6886–6.63

Inspections at firms with high injury rates, impacts on injury reporting, 1979-85, working paper, 6886–6.41

Labor force health condition and services use, by occupation and industry of longest job held, income, age, sex, and race, 1980, 4147-10.168

Labor laws enacted, by State, 1988, annual article, 6722-1.904

Lumber mill occupational injury and illness rates and workdays lost, by selected State and SIC 4-digit industry, 1978-87, article, 6722-1.945

Meatpacking occupational injury and illness rates and workdays lost, 1977-86, article, 6722-1.901

Military deaths by cause, age, race, and rank, and personnel captured and missing, by service branch, 2nd half FY88, semiannual rpt, 3542-21

Minerals industry production cost impacts of occupational safety and environmental regulation, factors affecting US competitiveness, 1989 compilation of papers, 5606-5.7

Mobile home industry occupational injury and illness rates and workdays lost, by selected State, 1978-87, article, 6722-1.932

Navy personnel radiation exposure on nuclear-powered vessels and at support facilities, and injury claims, 1950s-88, annual rpt, 3804-10

Occupational Safety and Health Admin activities and grants, press release series, 6606-3

Oil and gas OCS operations accidents, spills, casualties, and circumstances, 1956-86, listing, 5738-7

Paper mill products and effluents levels of dioxins and other hazardous substances, and environmental and health effects, 1988 hearing, 21368-112

Pollutants health effects, concentrations in food and environment, sources, human intake, and regulation, series, 9186-8

Postal Service employees injury and motor vehicle accident frequency, FY85-88, annual rpt, 9864-5.2

Preventive disease and health improvement goals and recommended activities for 2000, with trends 1970s-80s, 4048-10

Radiation exposure of Federal employees, by age, occupation, and selected agency, 1986-87, biennial rpt, 4064-15

Radiation exposure of workers at nuclear power plants and related facilities, by site, 1968-86, annual rpt, 9634-3

Radiation protection and health physics enrollment and degrees granted by instn and State, and women grads plans and employment, 1972-88, 3006-8.9

Radioactive waste (military) disposal at New Mexico Waste Isolation Pilot Plant, environmental impacts, 1989 supplemental statement, 3008-33

Railroad accidents, casualties, and damage, by cause, railroad, and State, 1988, annual rpt, 7604-1

Railroad accidents, casualties, and damage, Fed Railroad Admin activities, and safety inspectors by State, 1987, annual rpt, 7604-12

Railroad accidents, casualties, and Federal safety activities, late 1970s-87, hearing, 21368-103

Railroad-hwy grade-crossing accidents, detailed data by State and railroad, 1988, annual rpt, 7604-2

Railroad safety violation claims settled, by carrier, FY88, annual rpt, 7604-10

Research and demonstration grants of NIOSH for occupational safety and health by State, and project listing, FY87, annual rpt, 4244-2

Smoking restrictions in the workplace, and attitudes of employees and managers, 1986-87 local area surveys, article, 4042-3.950

Smoking restrictions in workplace, and personnel directors views on morale, productivity, and smoking impacts, 1987 local area survey, article, 4472-1.904

Statistical Abstract of US, social, political, and economic data, 1790-2025, comprehensive annual compilation, 2324-1.3

Subway accidents, casualties, and damage, by circumstances and system, 1987, annual rpt, 7884-5

see also Agricultural accidents and safety

see also Assaults on police

see also Black lung disease

see also Mine accidents and safety

see also Workers compensation

Occupational Safety and Health Administration

Activities and grants of OSHA, press release series, 6606-3

Budget of US Appendix, obligations, appropriations, and personnel, by program and agency, FY90, annual rpt, 104-3

Deaths related to work, by equipment type, circumstances, and OSHA standards violated, series, 6606-2

Expenditures of Fed Govt in States, by type, program, agency, and State, FY88, annual rpt, 2464-2

Occupational Safety and Health Review Commission

Budget of US Appendix, obligations, appropriations, and personnel, by program and agency, FY90, annual rpt, 104-3

Labor unions recognized in Fed Govt, agreements and membership by agency and facility, as of Jan 1989, biennial listing, 9844-14

Occupational testing and certification

Air traffic control system safety, working conditions, and traffic volume, various periods 1981-88, GAO rpt series, 26113-220

Air traffic control training impacts on screening test performance, 1981-85, technical rpt, 7506-10.59

Aircraft pilots and nonpilots certified by FAA, by certificate type, age, sex, region, and State, 1988, annual rpt, 7504-2

Army Reserve and Natl Guard combat and critical job task training, resources, effectiveness, and officers views, FY87, GAO rpt, 26123-239

Foreign Service exam applications, participants, and pass rate, by sex and for minorities, 1986-87, GAO rpt, 26123-247

Health care professionals licensing and disciplinary actions of State medical boards, 1950s-87, series, 4006-8

Mental health services, staffing, research, and training programs in VA facilities, 1989 biennial listing, 8704-2

Physicians and dentists with board certification, VA employment by specialty, quarterly rpt, 8602-6

Physicians certification for alcohol and drug abuse specialty, applicants professional characteristics, 1986, article, 4482-1.901

Physicians with State medical board certification serving in peer review organizations, and PRO contact with State boards, 1984-88, GAO rpt, 26131-51

Red Cross activities, finances, volunteers, and certificates issued, by program, FY88, annual rpt, 29254-1

Ship pilotage activities, costs, and traffic for US and Canada, and US testing and certificates, for Great Lakes, 1960s-87, 7308-192

Teacher certification requirements, by State, 1982-88, annual table with supplements, 4804-32

Teacher testing for State certification, listing of laws, as of 1987, annual rpt, 4824-2.14

Teachers and other special education staff, training, degrees, and certification, by field and State, FY87, annual rpt, 4944-4

Occupational therapy

Medicare discharges, charges, and length of stay, by State and diagnosis, 1983 and 1985, article, 4652-1.925

Military health care personnel, and accessions by training source, by occupation, specialty, and service branch, FY87, annual rpt, 3544-24

Nursing home facility, staff, and resident detailed characteristics, 1985, 4147-13.97

Nursing home rehabilitation services use, by service type and patient characteristics, 1st qtr 1983, 4188-58

Special education programs, enrollment by age, staff, funding, and needs, by type of handicap and State, 1987/88, annual rpt, 4944-4

see also Vocational rehabilitation

Occupational training

see Employee development

see Vocational education and training

Occupational wage surveys

see Area wage surveys

see Industry wage surveys

Occupations

Census of Population and Housing, 1990: data item selection, questionnaire dev, and testing, 2626-11.3

Classifications of occupations and industries used in 1970 and 1980 censuses, impact on labor force counts by industry, occupation, and sex, 1970, technical paper, 2626-2.59

Consumer spending related to occupational group, 1986-87, article, 6722-1.961

Credit unions finances, by occupational membership category, as of June 1989, semiannual rpt, 9532-6

Criminal sentences for Federal offenses, guidelines by offense and circumstances, 1989 rpt, 17668-1

Degrees (bachelor and masters) awarded 1985/86, holders employment characteristics, 1987 survey, series, 4826-3

Employment conditions, alternative BLS projections to 2000 and trends 1970s-88, biennial article, 6722-1.955

Employment in nonmanufacturing industries, by detailed occupation and SIC 2-digit industry, 1987, triennial rpt, 6748-60

Labor force entrants, by age, sex, race, part-time status, and detailed occupation, Jan 1987, article, 6742–1.902

Labor mobility rates, job tenure, and other worker characteristics, factors in occupational changes, 1965-86, article, 6722–1.943

Occupational Outlook Quarterly, journal, 6742–1

Statistical Abstract of US, social, political, and economic data, 1790-2025, comprehensive annual compilation, 2324–1.3

Technological devs effect on labor force, composition, and productivity, by industry, 1960s-86 and projected to 2000, series, 6826–2

Wage differentials among employers, relation to occupation, sex, establishment size, and industry, 1975-82, working paper, 9377–9.78

see also Agricultural labor
see also Blue collar workers
see also Business management
see also Clergy
see also Clerical workers
see also Consultants
see also Domestic workers and services
see also Employee development
see also Engineers and engineering
see also Executives and managers
see also Health occupations
see also Job tenure
see also Judges
see also Lawyers and legal services
see also Librarians
see also Military personnel
see also Occupational testing and certification
see also Pilots
see also Postal employees
see also Production workers
see also Professional and technical workers
see also Sales workers
see also Scientists and technicians
see also Service workers
see also Teachers
see also Vocational education and training
see also Vocational guidance
see also Writers and writing
see also under By Occupation in the "Index by Categories"

Ocean County, N.J.

Wages by occupation, for office and plant workers, 1989 survey, periodic MSA rpt, 6785–12.4

see also under By SMSA or MSA in the "Index by Categories"

Ocean liners
see Passenger ships

Ocean pollution
see Marine pollution

Ocean resources
see Marine resources

Oceania

Agricultural exports of US, for grains, oilseed products, hides, skins, and cotton, by country, weekly rpt, 1922–3

Agricultural trade of US, by commodity and country, bimonthly rpt with articles, 1522–1

Agricultural trade of US, by detailed commodity and country, 1988, semiannual rpt, 1522–4

Businesses (foreign) activity in US, income tax returns, assets, and income statement items, by industry div, country, and world area, 1984-85, article, 8302–2.920

Economic and military aid and loans from US and intl agencies, by program and country, FY46-87, annual rpt, 9914–5

Exports and imports (waterborne) of US, by type of service, commodity, country, route, and US port, 1986-87, annual rpt, 7704–2

Exports and imports (waterborne) of US, by type of service, customs district, port, and world area, monthly rpt, 2422–7

Exports and imports of US, by commodity group, world area, selected country, US coastal area and port, and mode of transport, monthly rpt, 2422–9

Fertilizer components use, by world area, 1978-88 and projected to 2010, 5608–154

Immigrant and nonimmigrant visas of US issued and refused, by class, issuing office, and nationality, FY88, annual rpt, 7184–1

Immigrants admitted to US, by class of admission, country of birth, and State and MSA of destination, FY88, annual rpt, 6264–4

Immigrants admitted to US, by occupational group and country of birth, preliminary FY88, annual table, 6264–1

Immigration to US, alien workers, visitors, deportations, and naturalizations, by country, FY88 and trends from 1820, annual rpt, 6264–2

Military aid of US, arms sales, and training programs costs and budget requests, by program, world region, and country, FY88-90, annual rpt, 7144–13

Military aid programs and related activities of US, costs by country and intl agency, FY85-87 and cumulative from FY50, GAO rpt, 26123–30

Military spending, arms trade, and force strengths, with govt spending and population, by country, 1977-87, annual rpt, 9824–1

Minerals Yearbook, 1987, Vol 3: foreign country reviews of production, trade, and policy, by commodity, annual rpt, 5604–35

Oil and gas reserves and discoveries, by country and country group, quarterly rpt, 3162–43

Peace Corps activities, funding by program, and volunteers, by country, FY90, annual rpt, 9654–1

Population size, growth rates, and components of change, by country, projected 1989-2020 and trends from 1950, biennial rpt, 2324–9

Tide height and time daily at coastal points, forecast 1990, annual rpt, 2174–2.5

Travel to and from US on US and foreign flag air carriers, by country, world area, and US port, monthly rpt, 7302–2

Travel to and from US on US and foreign flag airlines, by world area, 1980-88, annual rpt, 2904–13

Travel to US, by characteristics of visit and traveler, country, port city, and State of destination, quarterly rpt, 2902–1

Travel to US, spending by category, world area of residence, census div, and State, model results, 1985-86, 2908–28

Visas of US issued at Foreign Service posts, by category and world area, selected years FY84-88, annual rpt, 7184–4

see also American Samoa
see also Australia
see also Cook Islands
see also Fiji
see also Guam
see also Kiribati
see also Marshall Islands
see also Micronesia Federated States
see also Nauru
see also New Caledonia
see also New Zealand
see also Northern Mariana Islands
see also Palau
see also Papua New Guinea
see also Solomon Islands
see also Tonga
see also Tuvalu
see also Vanuatu
see also Western Samoa
see also under By Foreign Country in the "Index by Categories"

Oceanography

Alaska OCS environmental conditions and oil dev impacts, compilation of papers, series, 2176–1

Atlantic Oceanographic and Meteorological Lab research activities and bibl, FY88, annual rpt, 2144–19

Carbon dioxide in atmosphere, measurement, methodology, and research results, series, 3006–11

Employment and earnings in science and engineering, by field and activity, and private and Federal R&D spending, by industry, 1975-88, 9626–6.29

Employment and other characteristics of science and engineering PhDs, by field and State, 1987, biennial rpt, 9627–18

Employment characteristics of scientists and engineers, by field, 1988, biennial rpt, 9627–16

Enrollment in science and engineering grad programs, by field, source of funds, and characteristics of student and instn, 1975-87, annual rpt, 9627–7

Estuary environmental conditions and mgmt, for individual areas, conf series, 2146–6

Fed Govt aid to higher education and nonprofit instns for R&D and related activities, by field, instn, agency, and State, FY87, annual rpt, 9627–17

Florida straits coastal currents, temperatures, and salinity, series, 2146–7

Maine coastal marine resources and ocean floor ecology, 1983-87, conf papers, 2148–55

Pacific Marine Environmental Lab research activities and bibl, FY88, annual rpt, 2144–21

Pacific Ocean subsurface temperature data collection activities, 1985-87, annual rpt, 2154–12

R&D funding by Fed Govt at large science facilities, by field, performer, and facility, FY86-88, hearings, 21708–128

R&D funding by Fed Govt, by field, performer type, agency, and State, FY87-89, annual rpt, 9627–20

R&D funding by higher education instns, by source and field, FY80-87, annual rpt, 9624–18.5

Research and distribution of oceanographic data, World Data Center A activities by country, and cruises by ship, 1987, annual rpt, 2144-15

Ships for oceanographic research, cruise schedules and vessel characteristics by higher education instn and Federal agency, 1989, annual listing, 3804-6

Temperature of sea surface by ocean and for US coastal areas, and Bering Sea ice conditions, monthly rpt, 2182-5

Wages of scientists and engineers in R&D, by field and educational, employment, and other characteristics, 1989, annual rpt, 3004-1

see also Ice conditions
see also Marine pollution
see also Marine resources
see also Marine resources conservation
see also Navigation
see also Tides and currents

Oceans
see Arctic Ocean
see Atlantic Ocean
see Bering Sea
see Chukchi Sea
see Coastal areas
see Continental shelf
see Coral reefs and islands
see Gulf of Alaska
see Gulf of Mexico
see Indian Ocean
see Marine pollution
see Marine resources
see Marine resources conservation
see Mediterranean Sea
see North Sea
see Oceanography
see Offshore mineral resources
see Offshore oil and gas
see Pacific Ocean
see Tides and currents
see Tsunamis

Oceanside, Calif.
see also under By City in the "Index by Categories"

O'Connell, Martin
"Maternity Leave Arrangements, 1961-85", 2328-62

O'Connor, Patrick J.
"Comparison of Metabolic Control Among Diabetic Subjects at Two Clinics", 4042-3.946

Odessa, Tex.
see also under By SMSA or MSA in the "Index by Categories"

OECD
see Organization for Economic Cooperation and Development

Office buildings
see Commercial buildings
see Public buildings

Office equipment
see Business machines and equipment
see Computer industry and products
see Office supplies

Office of Child Support Enforcement
see Family Support Administration

Office of Community Services
see Family Support Administration

Office of Education
see Department of Education

Office of Educational Research and Improvement
Activities of OERI, FY88, annual narrative rpt, 4814-1

Budget of US Appendix, obligations, appropriations, and personnel, by program and agency, FY90, annual rpt, 104-3

Condition of Education, detailed data on elementary, secondary, and higher education, 1920s-88 and projected to 1997, annual rpt, 4824-1

Degrees (bachelor and masters) awarded 1985/86, holders employment characteristics, 1987 survey, series, 4826-3

Digest of Education Statistics, detailed data on students, staff, finances, and facilities, 1989 edition, annual rpt, 4824-2

Education data, enrollment, degrees, teachers, and spending, 1974/75-1988/89 and alternative projections to 1999/2000, annual rpt, 4824-4

Educational data, projections, annual rpt series, 4826-8

Elementary and secondary education enrollment, teachers, high school grads, and spending, by State, 1988/89, annual rpt, 4834-19

Elementary and secondary public education agency revenues by source, and outlays, by State, FY86-87, annual rpt, 4834-6

Elementary and secondary public school agencies, by enrollment size and location, fall 1987, annual listing, 4834-1

Elementary and secondary public schools, enrollment and other characteristics, for top 55 districts, 1987-88, annual rpt, 4834-22

Elementary and secondary public schools, enrollment, and teachers, by level and State, 1987/88, annual rpt, 4834-17

Fast Response Survey System, estimates for education data, series, 4826-1

Fed Govt funding for education by agency, program, and recipient type, and instn spending, FY80-88, 4828-21

High school class of 1972: education, employment, and family characteristics, activities, and attitudes, natl longitudinal study, series, 4836-1

High school classes of 1972 and 1980: enrollment in 2-year colleges, credits earned and dropout rate, by student characteristics, as of 1984, 4848-38

High school classes of 1972, 1980, and 1982: educational attainment by selected characteristics, 1976-87, 4848-36

High school classes of 1972, 1980, and 1982: postsecondary enrollment and degrees, by sex, race, and income level, natl longitudinal surveys, 4848-35

High school classes of 1980 and 1982: education, employment, and family characteristics, activities, and attitudes, natl longitudinal study, series, 4826-2

High school dropout rates, and subsequent completion, by student and school characteristics, alternative estimates, 1988, annual rpt, 4834-23

Higher education enrollment and degrees awarded by sex, and instn finances, by instn level and control, 1987-88, annual rpt, 4844-14

Higher education instn student aid and other sources of support, with student

expenses and characteristics, by instn type and control, 1987 triennial study, series, 4846-3

Libraries (public) literacy project descriptions and funding, FY88, annual listing, 4874-3

Libraries (public), outlets, and staff, by hours open, service population size, and selected State, 1987, annual rpt, 4824-6

Libraries (public) services effectiveness, public opinion survey methodology and results, 1989 rpt, 4878-3

Libraries (public) services for Indians and Hawaii Natives, project listing and funding by tribe and State, FY88 rpt, 4874-5

Libraries (public) special programs, project descriptions and funding by level of govt, State, and city, 1984-87, annual rpt, 4874-4

Libraries (research) funding of Education Dept, by project, instn, and State, FY88, annual listing, 4874-2

Libraries literacy program activities, and relation to community and instn characteristics, 1986, 4878-2

Libraries technological aid, project descriptions and funding, FY88, annual listing, 4874-6

Library science training grants for disadvantaged students, by instn and State, FY89, annual listing, 4874-1

Minority group education, schools participating in natl surveys, 1969-88, listing, 4828-38

Private elementary and secondary schools, enrollment, teachers, and high school grads, by instn religious orientation, 1988/89, annual rpt, 4834-21

Publications of NCES, periodic listing, 4822-1

Publications of OERI, 1988-89, listing, 4868-9

Reading ability and literacy of young adults, relation to educational attainment and race, natl assessment, 1985, 4828-36

Reading ability test scores for natl assessment, comparison to scores on other tests, findings, 1989 rpt, 4828-37

Rural areas education conditions, and population characteristics, 1987 conf papers, 4818-6

School agencies (public elementary and secondary), by type and State, 1987/88, annual rpt, 4834-18

Teachers bachelor degrees, by field and other characteristics, 1985-86, 4838-39

Teachers in public and private schools, salaries by selected characteristics, 1984/85-1985/86, 4838-37

Teachers incentive programs of public schools, and participation, by instn and teacher characteristics, with effectiveness ratings, 1985, 4838-38

Teachers moonlighting, by selected employment and other characteristics, 1985, 4838-36

Vocational and academic AA degree and certificate recipients and credits, by field, and student and instn characteristics, 1984, 4848-37

Office of Energy Research
see Department of Energy

Employment and payroll (civilian) of Fed Govt, by occupation, pay grade, sex, agency, and location, 1987, biennial rpt, 9844-4

Employment and payroll (civilian) of Fed Govt, by pay system, agency, and location, 1988, annual rpt, 9844-6

Equal Opportunity Recruitment Program activity, and Fed Govt employment by sex, race, pay grade, and selected occupation, FY88, annual rpt, 9844-33

Exchange of employees between Fed Govt and other organizations, program activities and costs, with data by agency, FY84-88, GAO rpt, 26119-260

Incentive awards to Federal employees, costs, and benefits, by award type and agency, FY88, annual rpt, 9844-20

Labor unions recognized in Fed Govt, agreements and membership by agency and facility, as of Jan 1989, biennial listing, 9844-14

Merit system oversight and enforcement activities of OPM, series, 9496-2

Minority group, handicapped, and veteran employment in Fed Govt, and years of service, by occupation, age, sex, and agency, as of Sept 1988, biennial rpt, 9844-27

Senior Executive Service membership characteristics, entries, exits, and awards, FY80-1987, annual rpt, 9844-36

Temporary employment in Fed Govt, appointments and extensions, by occupational group, 1983-87, GAO rpt, 26119-129

Office of Policy Development

Budget of US Appendix, obligations, appropriations, and personnel, by program and agency, FY90, annual rpt, 104-3

Office of Policy, SSA

Employment and earnings covered under OASDHI, and social security contributions, by age, sex, race, State, and county, 1985, 4748-43

Social security programs, research rpt series, 4746-4

see also Office of International Policy, SSA

see also Office of Research and Statistics, SSA

Office of Refugee Resettlement

see Family Support Administration

Office of Research and Statistics, SSA

OASDHI, Medicaid, SSI, and related programs benefits, beneficiary characteristics, and trust funds, selected years 1937-87, annual rpt, 4744-3

OASDI benefits and beneficiaries, by type of benefit, State, and county, as of Dec 1987, annual rpt, 4744-28

Public welfare programs benefits, beneficiaries, and summary program data, selected years 1937-89, chartbook, 4748-42

Social Security Bulletin, indexes, 1980-88, 4748-32

Social Security Bulletin, OASDHI and other program operations and beneficiary characteristics, from 1940, monthly rpt with articles, 4742-1

Social security programs and related issues, technical paper series, 4746-26

Social security programs, research rpt series, 4746-4

Supplemental Security Income payments and beneficiaries, by type of eligibility, State, and county, Dec 1987, annual rpt, 4744-27

Office of Science and Technology Policy

Budget of US Appendix, obligations, appropriations, and personnel, by program and agency, FY90, annual rpt, 104-3

Budget of US, authoritative financial statements with appropriations, outlays, and receipts, by category and agency, FY88, annual rpt, 8104-2.2

R&D Fed Govt policies and programs, 1985-88, biennial rpt, 424-2

Office of Special Education and Rehabilitative Services

Blind-operated vending facilities on Federal and non-Federal property, finances and operations by agency and State, FY88, annual rpt, 4944-6

Budget of US Appendix, obligations, appropriations, and personnel, by program and agency, FY90, annual rpt, 104-3

Enrollment by age, staff, funding, and needs of special education programs, by type of handicap and State, 1987/88, annual rpt, 4944-4

Fed Govt and State rehabilitation activities and funding, FY88, annual rpt, 4944-1

Vocational rehabilitation cases of State agencies, by disposition and State, FY88 and trends from FY21, annual rpt, 4944-5

Office of Surface Mining Reclamation and Enforcement

Abandoned coal mines emergency complaint processing by OSMRE, efficiency, 1983-87, GAO rpt, 26113-398

Activities and funding of OSMRE, by State and Indian tribe, FY87, annual rpt, 5644-1

Expenditures of Fed Govt in States, by type, program, agency, and State, FY88, annual rpt, 2464-2

Office of Technology Assessment

Activities of OTA, and rpts, FY88, annual rpt, 26354-3

Alaska Arctic Natl Wildlife Refuge oil and gas production, reserves, exploration, and dev, 1981-89 and projected to 2003, 26358-200

Biotechnology legal, ethical, and economic issues, series, 26356-5

Dioxin levels in paper products and pulp mill effluents, and control technology, 1970s-87, 26358-204

Economic data series and collections of Fed Govt, adequacy to address devs and policy issues, 1989 rpt, 26358-207

Grain exports competitiveness and quality issues, with background data and comparisons to other countries, 1960s-88, 26358-201

Health care facilities medical waste disposal, hospital incinerator emissions, and regulation, 1988 rpt, 26358-198

HHS research and evaluation programs, 1970-FY87, annual listing, 4004-30

Insurance (health) coverage of adolescents by selected characteristics, and impacts of mandated employer and expanded Medicaid coverage, 1979-87, 26358-205

Older persons preventive health care services, effectiveness and costs of proposed Medicare coverage, series, 26356-7

Pollutant ozone levels, urban areas failure to meet natl standards, emissions sources, exposure, and costs and benefits of reduction strategies, 1983-87 and projected to 2004, 26358-203

Science and engineering education enrollment, degrees, and student aid and sources, with data by field, race, sex, and instn, 1980s-87, 26358-202

Science and engineering education in elementary and secondary schools, and student persistence in postsecondary education, 1977-88, 26358-199

Ship foreign and US flag competition in US Exclusive Economic Zone, impacts of extending cabotage laws, with background data, 1970s-80s, 26358-206

Office of Territorial and International Affairs

Expenditures of Fed Govt in States, by type, program, agency, and State, FY88, annual rpt, 2464-2

Office of the Comptroller of Currency

Activities of Comptroller, and natl banks operations, charters, and mergers, by instn and State, quarterly rpt, 8402-3

Banks (natl) financial performance, and OCC enforcement activities, 1978-88, 8408-18

Banks and other financial instns fraud and insider misconduct cases, Federal regulatory and enforcement activities, and losses, 1981-87, hearing, 21408-111

Budget of US Appendix, obligations, appropriations, and personnel, by program and agency, FY90, annual rpt, 104-3

Office of the Secretary of Defense

Base construction, renovation, and land acquisition, DOD budget requests by project, service branch, State, and country, FY90/91, annual rpt, 3544-15

Budget of DOD, justification, programs, and policies, FY90-91, annual rpt, 3544-2

Budget of DOD, procurement appropriations by item, service branch, and defense agency, FY88-91, annual rpt, 3544-32

Budget of DOD, R&D appropriations by item, service branch, and defense agency, FY88-91, annual rpt, 3544-33

Budget of DOD, summary justification, plans, and funding requests, FY90-91, annual rpt, 3544-30

Commercial activities of DOD performed in-house, and work-years, by service branch, installation, and State, FY88, annual rpt, 3544-25

Deaths by cause, age, race, and rank, and personnel captured and missing, by service branch, 2nd half FY88, semiannual rpt, 3542-21

Employment (civilian) of DOD, by service branch and defense agency, with summary military employment data, quarterly rpt, 3542-16

Employment (civilian and military) of DOD, by service branch, major installation, and State, as of Sept 1988, annual rpt, 3544-7

Expenditures and obligations of DOD, by function and service branch, quarterly rpt, 3542-3

Expenditures of DOD for contracts and payroll, and personnel, by service branch and location, with top 5 contractors and maps, by State and country, FY88, annual rpt, 3544-29

Fraud and abuse in DOD programs, audits and investigations, 1st half FY89, semiannual rpt, 3542-18

Hazardous waste site remedial action at military installations, activities and funding by site and State, FY88, annual rpt, 3544-36

Health care facilities of DOD in US and abroad, beds, admissions, outpatient visits, and births, by service branch, quarterly rpt, 3542-15

Health care personnel, and accessions by training source, by occupation, specialty, and service branch, FY87, annual rpt, 3544-24

Manpower active duty strength, civilian personnel, and dependents, by service branch and US and foreign location, quarterly rpt, 3542-20

Manpower active duty strength, recruits, and reenlistment, by race, sex, and service branch, quarterly press release, 3542-7

Manpower statistics for active duty, civilian, and reserve personnel, by service branch, FY88 and trends, annual rpt, 3544-1

Manpower statistics for active duty, civilian, and reserve personnel, by service branch, quarterly rpt, 3542-14

Manpower strengths in US and abroad, by service branch, world area, and country, quarterly press release, 3542-9

Manpower strengths, summary by service branch, monthly press release, 3542-2

Military women personnel on active and reserve duty, by demographic and service characteristics and service branch, FY88, annual chartbook, 3544-26

NATO and Japan military spending and indicators of ability to support common defense, by country, 1960s-87, annual rpt, 3544-28

Procurement, DOD prime contract awards by category, contract and contractor type, and service branch, FY79-88, semiannual rpt, 3542-1

Procurement, DOD prime contract awards by category, contractor type, and State, FY86-88, annual rpt, 3544-11

Procurement, DOD prime contract awards by contractor, service branch, State, and city, FY88, annual rpt, 3544-22

Procurement, DOD prime contract awards by detailed procurement category, FY85-88, annual rpt, 3544-18

Procurement, DOD prime contract awards by service branch and State, FY88, semiannual rpt, 3542-5

Procurement, DOD prime contract awards by size and type of contract, service branch, competitive status, category, and labor standard, FY88, annual rpt, 3544-19

Procurement, DOD prime contract awards for top 100 contractors, FY88, annual listing, 3544-5

Procurement, DOD prime contract awards in labor surplus areas, by service branch, State, and area, FY88, semiannual rpt, 3542-19

Procurement, subcontract awards by DOD contractors to small and disadvantaged business, by firm and service branch, quarterly rpt, 3542-17

Property, supply, and equipment inventory of DOD, by service branch, 1988, annual rpt, 3544-6

R&D prime contract awards of DOD, for top 500 contractors, FY88, annual listing, 3544-4

R&D prime contract awards of DOD to US and foreign nonprofit instns and govt agencies, by instn and location, FY88, annual listing, 3544-17

Reserve forces manpower and equipment strengths, and readiness, by reserve component, FY88, annual rpt, 3544-31

Reserve forces manpower strengths and characteristics, by component, quarterly rpt, 3542-4

Strategic material stockpile inventories and needs, by commodity, as of Sept 1988, annual rpt, 3544-37

Strategic material stockpiling by Fed Govt, activity, and inventory by commodity, as of Sept 1988, semiannual rpt, 3542-22

Office of the Secretary of Energy

Activities and finances of DOE, summary energy supply and demand data, and bibl, 1987, annual rpt, 3024-1

Electric power demand related to economic dev and weather, by census div, model results, quarterly 1977-85, 3028-2

Office of the Special Representative for Trade Negotiations

see Office of the U.S. Trade Representative

Office of the U.S. Trade Representative

Budget of US Appendix, obligations, appropriations, and personnel, by program and agency, FY90, annual rpt, 104-3

Budget of US, authoritative financial statements with appropriations, outlays, and receipts, by category and agency, FY88, annual rpt, 8104-2.2

Export and import agreements, negotiations, anticompetitive investigations, and related legislation, FY86-88, annual rpt, 444-1

Exports of goods, services, and investment, trade barriers, impacts, and US actions, by country, 1988, annual rpt, 444-2

Office of the Vice President

Budget of US Appendix, obligations, appropriations, and personnel, by program and agency, FY90, annual rpt, 104-3

Budget of US, authoritative financial statements with appropriations, outlays, and receipts, by category and agency, FY88, annual rpt, 8104-2.2

Congressional Directory, members of 101st Congress, other officials, elections, and districts, 1989-90, biennial rpt, 23874-1

Pay rates of Fed Govt civilian employees, by pay schedule and grade, 1989 and trends from 1789, annual rpt, 21624-4

Office of Thrift Supervision

Finances and operations of FHLB system and members, and savings instns regulatory issues and mgmt, monthly journal, 8432-2

Financial instns assets composition, growth, and distribution, by instn type, 1970s-88, 8438-1

Financial statements of FHLBB, FSLIC, Financing Corp, and FHLBs, 1988, annual rpt, 8434-2

Housing finance studies, technical paper series, 8436-1

Mortgage terms on conventional loans closed, and commitment rates, by type of loan and lender and for 32 SMSAs, monthly rpt, 8432-3

Savings instns financial statements, FSLIC-insured instns by FHLB district and State, and FDIC-insured savings banks, 1988, annual rpt, 8434-1

Savings instns insured by Savings Assn Insurance Fund, assets, liabilities, and deposit and loan activity, by conservatorship status, monthly rpt, 8432-1

Savings instns insured by Savings Assn Insurance Fund, finances by district, quarterly rpt, 8432-4

see also Federal Home Loan Bank Board

Office of Transportation, USDA

Airline service in rural areas, impacts of deregulation, and Federal subsidies, with data by location, 1978-87, 1278-17

Asia port facilities, operations, and impacts on US agricultural exports, for major Far East ports, 1970s-87, 1278-13

Bridges in rural areas, conditions, needs, and funding, with data by State and compared to urban areas, 1988, 1278-16

Budget of US Appendix, obligations, appropriations, and personnel, by program and agency, FY90, annual rpt, 104-3

Grain shipments, rail loadings, export sales and inspections, prices, and ocean freight rates, weekly rpt, 1272-2

Hwy Trust Fund obligations, by project and urban-rural location, 1982-86, 1278-12

Rail shipments of grain and other commodities by car type, 1986, and rail car fleet size, 1978-88, 1278-15

Rail shipments of grain, by commodity and port region, and car fleet requirements, 1949-88 with projections to 2001, 1278-14

Rural areas public transit services, operations and govt funding by region and State, 1986-87, 1278-11

Truck transport of fruit and vegetables, itemized costs per mile by item for fleets and owner-operator trucks, monthly table, 1272-1

Office of Youth Development

see Office of Human Development Services

Office on Smoking and Health

Intl research on smoking and health, biennial listing, suspended, 4044-7

Research on smoking and health, publications, 1988, last issue of annual listing, 4204-19

Research on smoking and health, summaries, bimonthly rpt, 4202-8

Research on smoking and health, with trends in smoking, related disease and death, and public attitudes, literature review, 1989 annual rpt, 4204-18

Office supplies

Banks in Fed Reserve System, expenses and operations itemized by service, office, and district, 1988, annual rpt, 9364-11

County Business Patterns, 1987: employment, establishments, and payroll, by SIC 2- to 4-digit industry and county, annual State rpt series, 2326-3

DOD prime contract awards, by detailed procurement category, FY85-88, annual rpt, 3544-18

Employment, earnings, and hours, by SIC 1- to 4-digit industry, monthly 1983-Feb 1989, annual rpt, 6744-4

Exports of US, detailed commodities by country, monthly rpt, 2422-3

House of Representatives salaries, expenses, and contingent fund disbursement, detailed listings, quarterly rpt, 21942-1

Injuries from use of consumer products and related activities, by victim age and sex, 1988, annual rpt, 9164-7

Injuries from use of consumer products, by severity, victim age, and detailed product, 1988, annual rpt, 9164-6

Manufacturing census, 1987: financial and operating data, for SIC 4-digit industries by product, preliminary rpt, 2491-1.31; 2491-1.82

Occupational injury and illness rates, by SIC 2- to 4-digit industry, 1987, annual rpt, 6844-1

Paper and pulp production, shipments, trade, stocks, and use, by product and State, 1988, annual Current Industrial Rpt, 2506-7.10

Pens, pencils, and marking devices shipments, trade, and use, by product, annual Current Industrial Rpt, discontinued, 2506-7.12

Price indexes (producer), by stage of processing and detailed commodity, monthly rpt, 6762-6

Price indexes (producer), by stage of processing and detailed commodity, monthly 1988, annual rpt, 6764-2

Science, engineering, and technical employment in manufacturing, by field, occupation, and industry, 1986, triennial rpt, 9627-23

Senate receipts, itemized expenses by payee, and balances, 1st half FY89, semiannual listing, 25922-1

Shipments, trade, and use of office supplies, by product, annual Current Industrial Rpt, discontinued, 2506-7.11; 2506-7.13

Wholesale trade census, 1987: employment, establishments, finances, and operations, by SIC 2- to 4-digit kind of business, MSA, county, and city, State rpt series, 2405-1

Office workers
see Clerical workers

Official publications
see Government documents

Officials
Census of Govts, 1987: elected officials, by level of govt, race, sex, and State, preliminary rpt, 2450-2

Corrupt govt officials prosecuted and convicted, by judicial district and level of govt, 1978-88, annual rpt, 6004-13

Criminal case processing in Federal courts, by offense, disposition, and jurisdiction, 1950s-88, annual rpt, 6064-6.5

Developing countries disaster preparedness and economic, population, and political data, country rpt series, 9916-2

Fed Govt civilian pay rates, by pay schedule and grade, 1989 and trends from 1789, annual rpt, 21624-4

Foreign and NATO officials admitted to US, by country, FY78-88, annual rpt, 6264-2

Foreign countries economic, social, political, and geographic summary data, by country, 1989, annual factbook, 9114-2

Foreign govt Chiefs of State and Cabinet members, by country, bimonthly listing, 9112-4

Foreign travelers and other aliens admitted to US, by class of admission, port, country, and State of destination, quarterly rpt, 6262-2

Soviet Union officials public appearances in and outside USSR, 1988, annual rpt, 9114-1

Workers compensation programs of States, top officials, salaries, and hours, by State, as of 1988, annual rpt, 6504-9

see also Congressional employees
see also Executives and managers
see also Federal employees
see also Government employees
see also International employees
see also Presidential appointments
see also State and local employees

Offshore mineral resources
Chukchi Sea mineral resources in sediment off north Alaska coast, 1985 study, 5668-95

Cobalt and other metals resources in manganese crusts of US Exclusive Economic Zone in Pacific Ocean, and cobalt production for onshore sites, 1988 article, 5602-4.901

Leasing activity, production, and revenue, for oil, gas, and minerals on Federal OCS lands by ocean region and State, 1950s-87, annual rpt, 5734-3

Mineral industries census, 1987: financial and operating data, preliminary summary rpt, 2511-1.13

see also Offshore oil and gas

Offshore oil and gas
Accidents, spills, casualties, and circumstances, for oil and gas OCS operations, 1956-86, listing, 5738-7

Alaska Arctic Natl Wildlife Refuge oil and gas resource assessment, with environmental impacts on North Slope and other locations, 1987 hearing, 21448-41

Alaska OCS environmental conditions and oil dev impacts, compilation of papers, series, 2176-1

Coastal and riparian areas environmental conditions, fish, wildlife, use, and mgmt, for individual ecosystems, series, 5506-9

Drilling rig construction financing guarantees of MarAd, FY88, annual rpt, 7704-14.1

Drilling rig removal using explosives, impacts on sea turtles and dolphins off Galveston, Tex, 1988 article, 2162-1.902

Environmental and socioeconomic conditions, and potential impact of oil and gas OCS leases, final statement series, 5736-1

Field codes and locations, for oil and gas, 1988, annual listing, 3164-70

Gulf of Mexico oil and gas leases, by company and tract, 1988, annual rpt, 5734-8

Gulf of Mexico oil and gas reserves, production, and leasing status, by location, 1987, annual rpt, 5734-6

Leasing activity, production, and revenue, for oil, gas, and minerals on Federal OCS lands by ocean region and State, 1950s-87, annual rpt, 5734-3

Leasing and other activities of Mineral Mgmt Service, press release series, 5736-4

Natural and supplemental gas production, prices, trade, use, reserves, and pipeline company finances, by firm and State, monthly rpt with articles, 3162-4

Natural gas production, wells drilled, and contract prices, by Natural Gas Policy Act section, producer, State, and field, late 1970s-86, 3168-90

Natural gas supply, demand, distribution, and prices, by State, 1984-88 annual rpt, 3164-4

Natural gas undiscovered reserves, analysis of alternative estimation methods, 1986, 3166-6.32

Pacific Ocean OCS oil and gas production, and wells, by drilling platform under Federal lease, 1960s-88, annual rpt, 5734-9

Pacific Ocean oil and gas production, reserves, and wells drilled, by location, 1988, annual rpt, 5734-7

Price indexes (producer), by stage of processing and detailed commodity, monthly 1988, annual rpt, 6764-2

Producers finances and operations, by energy type for US firms domestic and foreign operations, 1987, annual rpt, 3164-44.2

Production and reserves of oil, gas, and gas liquids, by State and substate area, 1988, annual rpt, 3164-46

Production and revenue from oil, gas, and minerals on Federal and Indian lands, by State, 1988 and trends from 1920, annual rpt, 5734-2

Production, leasing and exploration activity, revenue, and costs, for Fed Govt OCS oil and gas reserves, by ocean area, FY88, annual rpt, 5734-4

Reserves of OCS oil and gas, and leasing and dev activity, periodic regional rpt series, 5736-3

Seismic exploration crews and activity, monthly rpt, 3162-24.5

Statistical Abstract of US, social, political, and economic data, 1790-2025, comprehensive annual compilation, 2324-1.3

Supply, demand, and prices, by fuel type and end-use sector, with foreign comparisons, 1988 and trends from 1949, annual rpt, 3164-74.1; 3164-74.2

Supply, demand, and prices of oil and gas, alternative projections 1987-2000, annual rpt, 3164-89

Water discharges from oil and gas OCS production, and impacts on Gulf of Mexico coastal habitats, 1983-88, 5738-10

Water discharges from oil and gas OCS production, for Pacific lands under Federal lease by drilling platform, 1960s-88, annual rpt, 5734-9

Ogden, Utah
Housing starts and completions authorized by building permits in 40 MSAs, quarterly rpt, 2382-9

Wages by occupation, and benefits for office and plant workers, 1988 survey, periodic MSA rpt, 6785-11.3

see also under By SMSA or MSA in the "Index by Categories"

Environmental and socioeconomic conditions, and potential impact of oil and gas OCS leases, final statement series, 5736-1

Gulf of Mexico oil and gas leases, by company and tract, 1988, annual rpt, 5734-8

Gulf of Mexico oil and gas reserves, production, and leasing status, by location, 1987, annual rpt, 5734-6

Naval Petroleum and Oil Shale Reserves production and revenue by fuel type, sales by purchaser, and wells, by reserve, FY88, annual rpt, 3004-22

Offshore oil and gas leasing, and other activities of Mineral Mgmt Service, press release series, 5736-4

Offshore oil and gas reserves, and leasing and dev activity, periodic regional rpt series, 5736-3

Offshore oil and gas reserves of Fed Govt, production, leasing and exploration activity, revenue, and costs, by ocean area, FY88, annual rpt, 5734-4

Offshore oil, gas, and minerals production, revenue, and leasing activity, for Federal OCS lands by ocean area and State, 1950s-87, annual rpt, 5734-3

Pacific Ocean OCS oil and gas production, and wells, by drilling platform under Federal lease, 1960s-88, annual rpt, 5734-9

Production and revenue from oil, gas, and minerals on Federal and Indian lands, by State, 1988 and trends from 1920, annual rpt, 5734-2

Production, revenue, and royalty rates, for Federal lands by whether competitively bid, by western State, 1984-88, GAO rpt, 26113-413

Public lands acreage, grants, use, revenues, and allocations, by State, FY88, annual rpt, 5724-1.2

Statistical Abstract of US, social, political, and economic data, 1790-2025, comprehensive annual compilation, 2324-1.2; 2324-1.3

Oil depletion allowances

Producers finances and operations, by energy type for US firms domestic and foreign operations, 1987, annual rpt, 3164-44.1

Oil shale

Environmental impacts of energy technologies, 1960s-80s, handbook series, 3326-1

Naval Petroleum and Oil Shale Reserves production and revenue by fuel type, sales by purchaser, and wells, by reserve, FY88, annual rpt, 3004-22

Occupational injuries and incidence, employment, and hours in nonmetallic minerals mines and related operations, 1987, annual rpt, 6664-1

Oil spills

Accidents, spills, casualties, and circumstances, for oil and gas OCS operations, 1956-86, listing, 5738-7

Alaska Arctic Natl Wildlife Refuge oil and gas resource assessment, with environmental impacts on North Slope and other locations, 1987 hearing, 21448-41

Alaska OCS environmental conditions and oil dev impacts, compilation of papers, series, 2176-1

Alaska oil spill from tanker Exxon Valdez, impacts on gasoline and crude oil supply and prices, 1988-89, article, 3162-11.901; 3162-24.902

Coastal and estuarine pollutant discharges, by source, pollutant type, and location, series, 2176-4

Coastal and riparian areas environmental conditions, fish, wildlife, use, and mgmt, for individual ecosystems, series, 5506-9

Coastal areas environmental and socioeconomic conditions, and potential impact of oil and gas OCS leases, final statement series, 5736-1

Environmental quality and protection programs, and intl issues, 1988 annual rpt, 484-1

Estuary environmental conditions and mgmt, for individual areas, conf series, 2146-6

Great Lakes toxic spills and human error, with data by pollutant source and site, 1984-86, conf, 14648-21

Incidents and discharges, by type, source, cause, and location, 1984-86, annual rpt, 7404-3

Incidents of spills and well blowouts in waters under Federal lease, and tanker spills worldwide, selected years 1964-87, annual rpt, 5734-3.6

NOAA activities and funding for ocean pollution, estuary, and coastal waters monitoring and assessment, FY88, annual rpt, 2174-9

Statistical Abstract of US, social, political, and economic data, 1790-2025, comprehensive annual compilation, 2324-1.1

Tar, plastic, and other nondegradable ocean and beach debris, incidence and environmental impacts, 1970s-88, 14738-4

Oil wells

see Energy exploration and drilling

Oils, essential

see Spices and herbs

Oils, oilseeds, and fats

Acreage planted, by selected crop and State, 1980-88 and planned 1989, annual rpt, 1621-22

Africa agricultural exports by commodity, and relation to economic conditions and other factors, by country, 1960s-87, 1528-280

Agricultural exports of US, impacts of foreign agricultural and trade policy, with data by commodity and country, 1988, annual rpt, 1924-8

Agricultural Statistics, 1988, annual rpt, 1004-1

Agriculture census, 1987: farms, farmland, production and costs, and operator characteristics, advance State and county rpt series, 2330-1

Agriculture census, 1987: farms, farmland, production, finances, and operator characteristics, by county, final State rpt series, 2331-1

China trade by SITC 1- to 5-digit commodity, 1970s-87, annual rpt, 9114-3

Communist countries trade with US, by detailed commodity and country, quarterly rpt with articles, 9882-2

Consumer Expenditure Survey, household income by source, and itemized spending, by selected characteristics and location, 1984-86, annual rpt, 6764-5.2

Consumption of food and nutrient intake by individuals, by food group, selected characteristics, and region, supplementary survey series, 1356-5

Consumption, supply, trade, prices, spending, and indexes, by food commodity, 1987, annual rpt, 1544-4

Cotton linters production, stocks, use, and prices, monthly rpt, 1309-10

Cottonseed prices and quality, by State, seasonal weekly rpt, 1309-14

Cottonseed quality factors, by State, 1988 crop, annual rpt, 1309-5

County Business Patterns, 1987: employment, establishments, and payroll, by SIC 2- to 4-digit industry and county, annual State rpt series, 2326-8

CPI by component for US city average, and by region, population size, and for 27 metro areas, monthly rpt, 6762-2

Cuba economic conditions, agricultural and industrial production and distribution, trade, and intl economic relations, 1980-87 with trends from 1961, 9118-8

Developing countries agricultural and food aid, and impacts on US exports, with background data, 1960s-89, 26308-85

Developing countries food production and needs, and related economic outlook, by country, 1989/90, annual rpt, 1524-6

Eastern Europe agricultural production, consumption, and trade, by country, 1970s-88, annual rpt, 1524-11

Eastern Europe and USSR agricultural production, acreage, and consumption, by commodity and country, 1965-85, 1528-284

EC food supply and demand, market and support prices, and other economic indicators, by country and commodity, 1960-85, 1528-276

Employment, earnings, and hours, by SIC 1- to 4-digit industry, monthly 1983-Feb 1989, annual rpt, 6744-4

Exports and imports (agricultural) commodity and country, prices, and world market devs, monthly rpt, 1922-12

Exports and imports (agricultural) of US, by commodity and country, bimonthly rpt with articles, 1522-1

Exports and imports (agricultural) of US, by commodity, monthly rpt, 1922-8

Exports and imports (agricultural) of US, by detailed commodity and country, 1988, semiannual rpt, 1522-4

Exports and imports (agricultural) of US with Asia, Middle East, and North Africa, by commodity and country, 1962-86, 1528-277

Exports and imports of dairy, livestock, and poultry products, by commodity and country, FAS monthly circular, 1925-32

Exports and imports of US, by selected country, country group, and commodity group, 1988, annual rpt, 2044-37

Exports of grains, oilseed products, hides, skins, and cotton, by country, weekly rpt, 1922-3

Exports of US, detailed commodities by country, monthly rpt, 2422-3

Farm financial and marketing conditions, forecast 1988, conf papers, annual rpt, 1004–16

Farm income, expenses, receipts by commodity, assets, liabilities, and ratios, 1988 and trends from 1945, annual rpt, 1544–16

Farm sector balance sheet, and receipts by detailed commodity, by State, 1984-88, annual rpt, 1544–18

Farm sector finances, income sources, expenses by type, assets, debts, and ratios, 1987, annual rpt, 1544–19

Fish (processed) production by location, and trade, by species and product, 1987-88, annual rpts, 2166–6

Fish catch, prices, trade by country, cold storage holdings, and market devs, for Japan, semimonthly press release, 2162–7

Fish catch, trade, use, and fishery operations, with selected foreign data, by species, 1970s-88, annual rpt, 2164–1

Fish meal and oil production and trade, quarterly tables, 2162–3

Fish nutrient and fatty acid composition, by northeastern US species, 1985-87, 2168–111

Foreign and US agricultural production, prices, trade, and use, periodic rpt with articles, 1522–3

Foreign and US agricultural production, trade, and weather devs, weekly press release, 1922–4

Foreign and US agricultural trade and market impacts of eliminating protectionist policies, model description and results, 1986, 1528–282

Foreign and US oils, oilseeds, and fats production and trade, FAS periodic circular series, 1925–1

Foreign and US production, acreage, and yield for selected crops, forecasts by selected world region and country, FAS monthly circular, 1925–28

Foreign countries agricultural production, prices, and trade, by country, 1970s-89 and forecast 1990, annual world region rpt series, 1524–4

Freight (waterborne domestic and foreign) by commodity, traffic, and passengers, by port and waterway, 1987, annual rpt, 3754–3

Futures and options trading volume, by commodity and exchange, FY88, annual rpt, 11924–2

Imports of US, detailed Schedule A commodities by country, monthly rpt, 2422–2

Inspection of meat and poultry for domestic use and export, and rejections by cause, by type of animal and product, FY88, annual rpt, 1374–3

Lard production, monthly 1970-87, 1568–285.2

Lard production, 1988, annual rpt, 1623–10

Latin America trade, and balance of trade with US, by country, 1988, annual rpt, 2044–34

Manufacturing annual survey, 1986: financial and operating data, by SIC 2- to 4-digit industry, series, 2506–15

Manufacturing census, 1987: financial and operating data, for SIC 4-digit industries by product, preliminary rpt, 2491–1.4; 2491–1.7

Nutrient and caloric composition of food, for raw, processed, and prepared food, 1988 rpt, 1358–3

Occupational injury and illness rates, by SIC 2- to 4-digit industry, 1987, annual rpt, 6844–1

OECD trade, total and for 4 major countries, and US trade by country, by commodity, 1970-87, world area rpt series, 9116–1

PL 480 long-term credit sales allocations, by commodity and country, periodic press release, 1922–7

Price indexes (producer), by stage of processing and detailed commodity, monthly rpt, 6762–6

Price indexes (producer), by stage of processing and detailed commodity, monthly 1988, annual rpt, 6764–2

Prices (farm-retail) for food, marketing cost components, and industry finances and productivity, 1950s-88, annual rpt, 1544–9

Prices received and paid by farmers, by commodity and State, 1988, annual rpt, 1629–5

Prices received by farmers and production value, by detailed crop and State, 1986-88, annual rpt, 1621–2

Prices received by farmers for major products, and paid for farm inputs and living items, by State, monthly rpt, 1629–1

Production, farms, acreage, and related data, by selected crop and State, monthly rpt, 1621–1

Production inputs, output, and productivity for farms, by commodity and region, 1947-87, annual rpt, 1544–17

Production itemized costs, receipts, and returns, by crop and State, preliminary 1987, annual rpt, 1544–24

Production itemized costs, receipts, and returns, by selected commodity and region, 1975-87, 1548–345

Production of oil and fat, consumption by end use, and stocks, by type, monthly Current Industrial Rpt, 2506–4.4

Production of oil, crushings, and stocks, by oilseed type and State, monthly Current Industrial Rpt, 2506–4.3

Production, prices, trade, and export inspections by US port and country of destination, by grain type, weekly rpt, 1313–2

Production, prices, trade, and marketing, by commodity, current situation and forecast, monthly rpt with articles, 1502–4

Production, prices, trade, and use of oils and fats, periodic situation rpt with articles, 1561–3

Science, engineering, and technical employment in manufacturing, by field, occupation, and industry, 1986, triennial rpt, 9627–23

Sunflower seed stocks by region and market city, and seed inspected for export, weekly rpt, 1313–4

Tallow and grease foreign and US production, trade, and use, by selected country, forecast 1990, FAS annual circular, 1925–33

see also Animal feed

see also Corn

see also Peanuts

see also Soybeans

see also under By Commodity in the "Index by Categories"

Okada, M.

"'Bone Softening,' a Practical Way To Utilize Small Fish", 2162–1.902

Oklahoma

Agriculture census, 1987: farms, farmland, production and costs, and operator characteristics, advance State and county rpts, 2330–1.40

Agriculture census, 1987: farms, farmland, production, finances, and operator characteristics, by county, final State rpt, 2331–1.36

Bank deposits in FDIC-insured commercial and savings banks, by instn, State, and county, as of June 1988, annual regional rpt, 9295–3.4

Coal production and mines by county, prices, productivity, miners, reserves, and stocks, by mining method and State, 1987-88, annual rpt, 3164–25

Deaths and rates, by detailed location, cause, and demographic characteristics, 1987, US Vital Statistics annual rpt, 4144–3.1

DOD prime contract awards, by contractor, service branch, State, and city, FY88, annual rpt, 3544–22

Employment by industry div, earnings, and hours, by southwestern State, monthly rpt, 6962–2

Employment, earnings, and hours, by selected SIC 1- to 4-digit industry, State, and for 262 MSAs, 1972-87, 6748–81.4

Fed Govt spending in States and local areas, by type, State, county, and city, FY88, annual rpt, 2464–3

Fed Govt spending in States, by type, program, agency, and State, FY88, annual rpt, 2464–2

Fish farming finances and operations, for Oklahoma, 1989, article, 1561–15.901

HHS financial aid, by program, recipient, State, and city, FY88, annual regional listing, 4004–3.6

Homeless children educational enrollment and needs, 1988, annual State rpt, 4804–35.36

Income (personal) per capita and by source, and earnings by industry div, by State, MSA, and county, 1982-87, annual regional rpt, 2704–2.5

Mineral Industry Surveys, State reviews of production, 1988, preliminary annual rpt, 5614–6

Minerals Yearbook, 1987, Vol 2 preprints: State review of production and sales by commodity, and business activity, annual rpt, 5604–16.37

Minerals Yearbook, 1987, Vol 2: State reviews of production, sales, and firms, by commodity, and business activity, annual rpt, 5604–34

Nursing home compliance with Medicare and Medicaid regulations, and patient characteristics, by facility, 1987/88, annual State rpt, 4654–15.37

Oil and gas extraction production workers and wages by occupation, and benefits, by location, 1988 survey, 6787–6.240

Population, employment, and income characteristics of 3 northwestern Oklahoma counties, 1969 and 1984, article, 1502–7.914

Retail trade census, 1987: employment, establishments, sales, and payroll, by SIC 2- to 4-digit kind of business, MSA, county, and city, State rpt, 2397-1.37

Savings instns, FHLB 10th District members finances and lending by State and MSA, monthly table, 9302-22

Savings instns, FHLB 10th District members financial condition, by State, quarterly rpt, 9302-34

Service industries census, 1987: employment, establishments, receipts, and payroll, by SIC 2- to 4-digit kind of business, MSA, county, and city, State rpt, 2391-1.37

Statistical Abstract of US, social, political, and economic data, with foreign comparisons, 1790-2025, comprehensive annual compilation, 2324-1

Wholesale trade census, 1987: employment, establishments, finances, and operations, by SIC 2- to 4-digit kind of business, MSA, county, and city, State rpt, 2405-1.37

Wildlife-related recreation, hunting, and fishing participation and spending, detailed data, 1985 survey, quinquennial State rpt, 5506-6.36

see also Altus, Okla.

see also Cleveland County, Okla.

see also Lawton, Okla.

see also Oklahoma City, Okla.

see also Oklahoma County, Okla.

see also Tulsa, Okla.

see also under By State in the "Index by Categories"

Oklahoma City, Okla.

Housing and households characteristics, 1984 survey, MSA fact sheet, 2485-11.5

Housing and households detailed characteristics, and unit and neighborhood quality, by location, 1984 survey, MSA rpt, 2485-6.3

Wages by occupation, for office and plant workers, 1989 survey, periodic MSA rpt, 6785-3.9

see also under By City and By SMSA or MSA in the "Index by Categories"

Oklahoma County, Okla.

Housing and households detailed characteristics, and unit and neighborhood quality, by location, 1984 survey, MSA rpt, 2485-6.3

Okunade, Albert A.

"Price Forecasting Equations for Tree Nuts", 1561-6.904

Old age

see Aged and aging

Old age assistance

Assistance (financial and nonfinancial) of Fed Govt, 1989 base edition with supplements, annual listing, 104-5

Assistance of Fed Govt to aged, policies, and issues of aging, 1989 annual rpt, 25144-3

Food aid programs of USDA, costs and participation by program, region, and State, monthly rpt, 1362-14

Food stamp eligibility and payment errors, by type, recipient characteristics, and State, FY87, annual rpt, 1364-15

Health care (long-term) for aged, proposed insurance plan benefits and premiums, 1989 article, 4652-1.923

HHS financial aid, by program, recipient, State, and city, FY88, annual regional listings, 4004-3

Housing (rental) for low income aged, HUD construction and rehabilitation loans by recipient, 1989, press release, 5006-3.71

Income and poverty characteristics of aged, social security issues with data on Fed Govt spending and indicators of need, with bibl, 1988 compilation of papers, 25928-7

Medicaid and SSI recipients, by eligibility type, with data by State, 1970s-87, annual rpt, 4744-3.8

Medicaid coverage, participation, payments, admin, and legislative history, with data by State, 1980s-88, 21368-105

Older persons socioeconomic characteristics, 1900s-86 and projected to 2050, biennial chartbook, 12904-1

Outlying areas income maintenance beneficiaries and payments, by program and area, quarterly FY87, annual rpt, 4694-7.1; 4694-7.2

Outlying areas programs and provisions, FY88, annual rpt, 4694-4

Recreation (outdoor) at Federal facilities, Golden Age passports issued, 1988, annual rpt, 5544-14

see also Medicare

see also Old-Age, Survivors, Disability, and Health Insurance

see also Pensions and pension funds

see also Supplemental Security Income

Old-Age, Survivors, Disability, and Health Insurance

Actuarial studies, Medicare and OASDI future cost estimates and past experience analyses, series, 4706-1

Actuarial studies of OASDHI programs, series, 4706-2

Admin of OASDHI, and SSA activities, 1930s-89 and projected to 2063, data compilation, annual rpt, 4704-12

Assistance (financial and nonfinancial) of Fed Govt, 1989 base edition with supplements, annual listing, 104-5

Assistance of Fed Govt, by type, program, agency, and State, FY88, annual rpt, 2464-2

Benefits and beneficiaries of OASDI, by type of benefit, State, and county, as of Dec 1987, annual rpt, 4744-28

Benefits, beneficiaries, and summary program data for selected public welfare programs, selected years 1937-89, chartbook, 4748-42

Benefits, beneficiary characteristics, and trust funds of OASDHI, Medicaid, SSI, and related programs, selected years 1937-87, annual rpt, 4744-3

Benefits by county, FY88, annual regional listings, 4004-3

Budget deficit impact of OASDI trust fund surpluses, FY89-94, with surpluses projected to 2050, article, 9381-1.909

Budget of US Appendix, obligations, appropriations, and personnel, by program and agency, FY90, annual rpt, 104-3

Budget of US, balances of budget authority obligated and unobligated, by function and agency, FY88-90, annual rpt, 104-8

Budget of US, CBO analysis and review of FY90 budget by function, annual rpt, 26304-2

Budget of US, compact budgets by activity, function, and agency, FY90 and projected to FY94, annual rpt, 104-2

Budget of US, historical data, selected years FY34-88 and projected to FY94, annual rpt, 104-22

Budget of US, midsession review of FY90 budget, by function and agency, annual rpt, 104-7

Budget of US, Reagan Admin policy changes by program, FY90, annual rpt, 104-21

Budget of US, receipts by source, outlays by agency and program, and balances, monthly rpt, 8102-3

Court civil and criminal caseloads for Federal district, appeals, and special courts, June 1989, annual rpt, 18204-2; 18204-8

Disability Insurance and SSI admin of Fed Govt and States, benefits, caseloads, and operations, 1980s, 4708-11

Disability Insurance and SSI benefit denials, appeals processing, caseloads, dispositions, and allowances by disability, 1986-88, GAO rpt, 26121-278

Disability Insurance and SSI eligibility reviews, and State administrators views of review standards, 1986-88, GAO rpt, 26121-258

Disability Insurance beneficiaries health insurance coverage, by type and selected beneficiary characteristics, fall 1982, article, 4742-1.927

Disability Insurance eligibility claims reviewed by SSA administrative law judges and Appeals Council, and dispositions, FY81-88, GAO rpt, 26121-290

Disabled OASDI and SSI beneficiaries, by selected characteristics, 1986, article, 4742-1.916

Disabled persons employment, labor force status, and other characteristics, 1988, Current Population Rpt, 2546-2.147

Disabled worker OASDI beneficiaries, duration, and exits by reason, by selected characteristics, model description and results, 1972-80, article, 4742-1.923

Disabled worker OASDI beneficiaries recoveries and reentitlements, by selected characteristics, model description and results, 1989 article, 4742-1.924

Earnings limits for OASI beneficiaries, persons affected by selected characteristics, and Federal outlays, under alternative limits, 1986, 26306-3.110

Expenditures of Fed Govt by type, and other finances, selected years 1929-89, annual rpt, 10044-1

Fed Govt civilian employees demographic and employment characteristics, as of Sept 1988, article, 9842-1.901

Finances and operations of programs under Ways and Means Committee jurisdiction, FY70s-88, annual rpt, 21784-11

Finances of SSA programs, and litigation, FY88, annual rpt, 4704-6

Financial consolidated statements of Fed Govt based on business accounting methods, FY87-88, annual rpt, 8104-5

Household composition, income, benefits, and labor force status, Survey of Income and Program Participation methodology, working paper series, 2626-10

Income (household) and poverty status under alternative income definitions, by recipient characteristics, 1986, Current Population Rpt, 2546–6.58

Income (household) by source, and itemized spending, by selected characteristics and location, 1984-86 Consumer Expenditure Surveys, annual rpt, 6764–5.2

Income (personal) by source, and BEA and IRS adjusted gross income measures, 1984-86 with trends from 1947, article, 8302–2.914

Income (personal) by source, and BEA and IRS adjusted gross income measures, 1986-87, annual article, 2702–1.927

Income (personal) by source including transfer payments, and social insurance contributions, by region, 1948 and 1987 by type, by region, 1982, 2708–40

Income from transfer payments, natl income and product account, *Survey of Current Business*, monthly rpt, 2702–1.23

Income tax returns of individuals, selected income and tax items by income level, preliminary 1987, annual article, 8302–2.917

Mental illness and related disorders eligibility determinations for Disability Insurance and SSI, caseload and review activities by impairment type and State, 1984-86, hearing, 21788–176

Older persons labor force participation, unemployment, displacement, and reemployment, by selected characteristics, 1969-88, 6306–2.2

Older persons social security issues, Fed Govt spending, and indicators of need, with bibl, 1988 compilation of papers, 25928–7

Poverty status of families and persons, by detailed characteristics, 1987, annual Current Population Rpt, 2546–6.60

Railroad retirement and unemployment insurance accounts status, and interchange with OASDHI fund, FY85, annual rpt, 9704–2.1

Research on social security programs and related issues, technical paper series, 4746–26

Social Security Bulletin, OASDHI and other program operations and beneficiary characteristics, from 1940, monthly rpt with articles, 4742–1

Statistical Abstract of US, social, political, and economic data, 1790-2025, comprehensive annual compilation, 2324–1.2

Student aid Pell grants and applicants, by tuition, income level, instn type and control, and State, 1987/88, annual rpt, 4804–1

Tax (income) returns of individuals, by filing status, tax item, and income level, 1987, annual article, 8302–2.901

Tax (income) returns of individuals, detailed data, 1986, annual rpt, 8304–2

Tax expenditures, Federal revenues forgone through income tax deductions and exclusions by type, FY90-94, annual rpt, 21784–10

Trust funds finances of OASDI, and impact on Federal budget, 1987-88 and projected to 2050, GAO rpt, 26121–269

Trust funds financial condition, for Disability Insurance, monthly rpt, 8102–9.14

Trust funds financial condition, for OASI, monthly rpt, 8102–9.2

Trust funds surpluses impacts on budget deficit, projected FY89-2045, article, 9371–1.905

US attorneys civil cases, by type and disposition, FY88, annual rpt, 6004–2.5

see also Medicare

see also Social security tax

Older Americans Act

Social services for aged, funding under Act by program and State, and grants and contracts by grantee, 1989 annual rpt, 25144–3

Oleomargarine

see Oils, oilseeds, and fats

Oliner, Stephen D.

"Formation of Private Business Capital: Trends, Recent Developments, and Measurement Issues", 9362–1.910

Olive oil

see Oils, oilseeds, and fats

Oliveira, Victor J.

"Agricultural Work Force of 1987: A Statistical Profile", 1594–2

"Trends in the Hired Farm Work Force, 1945-87", 1598–246

Oliver, J. Douglas

"Bluefish. Species Profiles: Life Histories and Environmental Requirements of Coastal Fishes and Invertebrates (South Atlantic)", 5506–8.106

Olives

see Fruit and fruit products

Olmstead, Alan L.

"Dislocated Farmers: Number, Distribution, and Impacts", 15496–1.1

Olsen, Jorgen H.

"Cancer Among Epileptic Patients Exposed to Anticonvulsant Drugs", 4472–1.914

Olsenius, Christine

"Groundwater Quality: A Catalyst for a New Land Management Ethic", 1004–16.1

Olsson, Hakan

"Early Oral Contraceptive Use and Breast Cancer Among Premenopausal Woman: Final Report from a Study in Southern Sweden", 4472–1.917

Olympia, Wash.

see also under By SMSA or MSA in the "Index by Categories"

Omaha, Nebr.

Housing vacancy rates for single and multifamily units and mobile homes, by city and ZIP code, 1989, annual MSA rpt, 9304–22.3

Wages by occupation, for office and plant workers, 1988 survey, periodic MSA rpt, 6785–11.1

see also under By City and By SMSA or MSA in the "Index by Categories"

Oman

Agricultural and food production and indexes, total and for selected commodities, by country, 1970s-88, annual rpt, 1524–12

Agricultural trade of US, by detailed commodity and country, 1988, semiannual rpt, 1522–4

Agricultural trade of US with Asia, Middle East, and North Africa, by commodity and country, 1962-86, 1528–277

AID activities and funding by project and function, FY90, and developing countries summary socioeconomic data from 1960s, annual rpt, 9904–4.6

AID economic aid to developing countries, obligations and disbursements by country, quarterly rpt, 9912–4

AID loans repayment status and terms by program and country, and status of predecessor agency loans, quarterly rpt, 9912–3

Background Notes, summary social, political, and economic data, 1989 rpt, 7006–2.37

Economic and military aid and loans from US and intl agencies, by program and country, FY46-87, annual rpt, 9914–5

Economic conditions, income, production, prices, employment, and trade, 1989 periodic country rpt, 2046–4.50

Economic conditions, investment and export opportunities, and trade practices, 1988 country market research rpt, 2046–6.2

Economic conditions, policy, and trade practices, by country, 1986-88, annual rpt, 21384–5

Economic, social, political, and geographic summary data, by country, 1989, annual factbook, 9114–2

Exports and imports of US, by commodity and country, 1970-87, world area rpt, 9116–1.3

Human rights conditions in 170 countries, 1988, annual rpt, 21384–3

Military aid of US, arms sales, and training programs costs and budget requests, by program, world region, and country, FY88-90, annual rpt, 7144–13

Military spending, arms trade, and force strengths, with govt spending and population, by country, 1977-87, annual rpt, 9824–1

Minerals Yearbook, 1987, Vol 3: foreign country reviews of production, trade, and policy, by commodity, annual rpt, 5604–35

Minerals Yearbook, 1987, Vol 3 preprints: foreign country review of production, trade, and policy, by commodity, annual rpt, 5604–23.86

Population size, growth rates, and components of change, by country, projected 1989-2020 and trends from 1950, biennial rpt, 2324–9

UN voting record and share of votes in agreement with US, by issue, country, and world area, 1988, annual rpt, 7004–18

see also under By Foreign Country in the "Index by Categories"

Omnibus Budget Reconciliation Act

Medicaid eligibility extension to pregnant women and children with incomes over AFDC levels, with data by State, 1986-89, GAO rpt, 26121–303

Onions

see Vegetables and vegetable products

Ontario, Calif.

see also under By City in the "Index by Categories"

Ontario Province, Canada

Dioxin levels in paper products and pulp mill effluents, and environmental and health effects, 1988 hearing, 21368–112

Great Lakes basin pollutant discharges, sources, and control program activities, 1987, biennial rpt, 14644–1

OPEC

see Organization of Petroleum Exporting Countries

Food prices (farm-retail), marketing cost components, and industry finances and productivity, 1950s-88, annual rpt, 1544-9.2

Fruit and nut production, prices, trade, stocks, and use, by selected crop, periodic situation rpt with articles, 1561-6

Hospital operations, ownership, staffing, and other characteristics, by urban-rural location, 1960s-88, 25148-41

Hospital reimbursement by Medicare under prospective payment system, and physician reimbursement, effect on services, finances, and beneficiary payments, 1970s-88, annual rpt, 17204-2

Hospital reimbursement by Medicare under prospective payment system, capital cost reimbursement adjustments financial impacts by instn characteristics, 1978-87, 17206-1.1

Hospital reimbursement by Medicare under prospective payment system, impacts on costs, industry structure and operations, and quality of care, series, 17206-2

Hospital reimbursement by Medicare under prospective payment system, impacts on instns, beneficiaries, and other care providers and payment sources, 1986, annual rpt, 4654-13

Hospital reimbursement by Medicare under prospective payment system, methodology, inputs, and data by diagnostic group, 1989 annual rpt, 17204-1

Imports and tariff provisions effect on US industries and products, investigations with background financial and operating data, series, 9886-4

Imports injury to US industries from foreign subsidized products and sales at less than fair value, investigations with background financial and operating data, series, 9886-19

Imports injury to US industries from foreign subsidized products, investigations with background financial and operating data, series, 9886-15

Imports injury to US industries from sales at less than fair value, investigations with background financial and operating data, series, 9886-14

Industry (US) intl competitiveness, with selected foreign and US operating data by major firm and product, series, 2046-12

Industry finances and operations, by SIC 2- to 4-digit industry, forecast 1989 and trends from 1950s, annual rpt, 2044-28

Insurance (auto) industry profitability, income, and expenses, with premiums by company, 1977-87, 26119-267

Insurance (health) companies case mgmt for high-cost patients, savings, costs, and returns, 1984-86, article, 4652-1.914

Labor collective bargaining agreement concessions relation to economic and industry financial conditions, with data by major industry and union, 1970s-88, technical paper, 9385-8.41

Manufacturing and trade inventories, sales, and inventory/sales ratios, quarterly article, 2702-1.33

Manufacturing capital investment, capacity, and output relation to domestic demand and trade, 1970s-88, article, 9385-1.908

Manufacturing census, 1987: financial and operating data, for SIC 4-digit industries by product, preliminary industry rpt series, 2491-1

Mergers and acquisitions using leveraged buyout, financing characteristics and policy issues, 1970s-88, 21368-115

Minerals foreign and US supply under alternative market conditions, reserves, and background industry data, series, 5606-4

Natural gas interstate pipeline company detailed financial and operating data, by firm, 1988, annual rpt, 3164-38

North Central States banks finances and performance ratios, by State, quarterly journal, 9383-19

OASDI benefit payments, trust fund finances, and economic and demographic assumptions, 1970-87 and alternative projections to 1997, actuarial rpt, 4706-1.103

Oil and gas companies mergers, impacts on domestic reserve purchases, exploration, and financial performance, 1982-86, 3168-112

Oil company production and imports by type, and financial data, 1975-86, annual rpt, 3164-74.1

Partnerships (master limited) finances, firms, partners, and tax reform impacts, by industry, 1986, technical paper, 8006-3.59

Puerto Rico and other US possessions corporations tax incentives, finances, and operations by industry, and impacts on local economy, 1970s-83, biennial rpt, 8004-12

Railroad freight volume and revenue, by commodity and region of origin and destination, 1987, annual rpt, 7604-6

Railroad revenue, income, freight, and rate of return, by Class I freight railroad and district, quarterly rpt, 9482-2

Retail trade census, 1987: employment, establishments, sales, and payroll, by SIC 2- to 4-digit kind of business, MSA, county, and city, State rpt series, 2397-1

Retail trade inventory/sales ratios, by selected kind of business, monthly rpt, 2413-3.2

Retail trade sales, inventories, purchases, gross margin, and accounts receivable, by SIC 2- to 4-digit kind of business and form of ownership, 1987, annual rpt, 2413-5

Savings and loan assns assets composition, and alternative estimates of net worth for insolvent instns allowed to remain open, 1982-88, article, 9375-1.908

Savings and loan assns, FHLB 6th District insured members financial condition and operations by State, quarterly rpt, 9302-23

Savings instns (FSLIC-insured) assets, liabilities, and deposit and loan activity, and compared to all S&Ls, monthly rpt, 9312-4

Savings instns converting from mutual to stock ownership, stock sale proceeds related to stock index, interest rates, and instn finances, 1983-88, article, 9302-33.902

Savings instns failure resolution costs to FSLIC by State, and instn financial characteristics, 1979-88, technical paper, 9316-1.151

Savings instns, FHLB 1st District members financial operations and related economic and housing indicators, monthly rpt, 9302-4

Savings instns, FHLB 2nd District members capital and assets under capital requirements increase proposal, by State, 3rd qtr 1988, article, 9302-33.901

Savings instns, FHLB 2nd District members finances and operations, by State, quarterly rpt, 9302-14

Savings instns, FHLB 4th District members assets and financial ratios, by profitability and solvency status, various periods 1984-88, article, 9302-2.901

Savings instns, FHLB 4th District members finances and financial ratios, by State, quarterly rpt, 9302-3

Savings instns, FHLB 4th District members finances, by State, 1984-88, annual rpt series, 9304-29

Savings instns, FHLB 4th District members financial performance, by State and asset size, 1984-88, annual article, 9302-2.902

Savings instns, FHLB 6th District members financial condition and operations by State, monthly rpt, 9302-11

Savings instns, FHLB 9th District members finances and operations by State, monthly rpt, 9302-13

Savings instns, FHLB 9th District members finances and operations by State, quarterly rpt, 9302-31

Savings instns, FHLB 10th District members financial condition, by State, quarterly rpt, 9302-34

Savings instns finances and operations by district and State, mortgage lending activity and terms by MSA, and FHLB finances, 1987 with trends from 1900, annual rpt, 9314-3

Savings instns financial performance, for newly chartered instns by charter type, 1982-86, technical paper, 9316-1.146

Savings instns financial statements, FSLIC-insured instns by FHLB district and State, and FDIC-insured savings banks, 1988, annual rpt, 8434-1

Savings instns insured by Savings Assn Insurance Fund, assets, liabilities, and deposit and loan activity, by conservatorship status, monthly rpt, 8432-1

Savings instns insured by Savings Assn Insurance Fund, finances by district, quarterly rpt, 8432-4

Savings instns mortgage-backed securities share of assets, by asset size, capital ratio, and State, for FHLB 4th District, 1988, article, 9302-2.904

Savings instns off-balance-sheet hedging activity, by type, asset size, and State, for FHLB 4th District, 1984-88, article, 9302-2.903

Savings instns regulatory issues, mgmt, and FHLB system and member finances and operations, monthly journal, 8432-2; 9312-1

Securities industry finances, firms by type, and SEC applications and registrations, 1983-88, annual rpt, 9734-2.1

Service industries census, 1987: establishments, receipts, employment, and payroll, by SIC 2- to 4-digit kind of business, MSA, county, and city, State rpt series, 2391-1

Small business establishments, employment, and financial ratios, by SIC 1- to 2-digit industry and State, late 1960s-87, 9768–19

Small business financing sources, and business financial data by size, type, and industry, various periods 1980-88, annual rpt, 9764–6.2

South Central States farm yields by selected commodity, rainfall, and banks financial performance, with comparisons to US farm income trends, 1980s-88, annual article, 9391–1.911

Statistical Abstract of US, social, political, and economic data, 1790-2025, comprehensive annual compilation, 2324–1.3

Steel (stainless and alloy tool) production, employment, finances, and US producers inventories and unfilled orders, 1987-88, annual rpt, 9884–22

Steel imports of US under voluntary restraint agreement, by product, customs district, and country, with US industry operating data, monthly rpt, 9882–13

Steel industry finances and operations by product, and modernization efforts, as of June 1989, last issue of annual rpt, 9884–16

Stock performance of individual firms relative to market index, relation to firm characteristics by firm, alternative models results, 1963-81, technical paper, 9366–6.183

Telecommunications industry devs, finances, and operations, with data by service type, firm, and country, 1950s-80s, 2808–27

Telephone and telegraph firms detailed finances and operations, 1987, annual rpt, 9284–6

Telephone firms borrowing under Rural Telephone Program, and financial and operating data, 1988, annual rpt, 1244–2

Transit systems finances and operations, by mode of transport, size of fleet, and for 432 systems, 1986, annual rpt, 7884–4

Transit systems finances, costs, and needs, by State and selected system, 1980-88, biennial rpt, 7884–8

Transportation finances, operations, vehicles, equipment, accidents, and energy use, by mode of transport, 1955-88, annual rpt, 7304–2

Truck itemized costs per mile, finances, and operations, for agricultural carriers, 1988, annual rpt, 1311–15

Truck transport of fruit and vegetables, itemized costs per mile by item for fleets and owner-operator trucks, monthly table, 1272–1

Truck transport of household goods, financial and operating data by firm, quarterly rpt, 9482–14

Truck transport of property, financial and operating data by region and firm, quarterly rpt, 9482–5

Unemployment insurance programs of States, benefits, coverage, exhaustions, and finances by State, 1987, annual tables, 6404–10

Uranium mining and milling industries finances and operations, with selected foreign comparisons, 1970s-87 and projected to 2000, annual rpt, 3164–82

Vegetables production, prices, trade, stocks, and use, for selected fresh and processing crops, periodic situation rpt with articles, 1561–11

Wheat and rye foreign and US production, prices, trade, stocks, and use, quarterly situation rpt with articles, 1561–12

Wholesale trade census, 1987: employment, establishments, finances, and operations, by SIC 2- to 4-digit kind of business, MSA, county, and city, State rpt series, 2405–1

Wholesale trade sales, inventories, purchases, and gross margins, by SIC 2- to 3-digit kind of business and form of ownership, 1988, annual rpt, 2413–13

see also Agricultural productivity
see also Industrial capacity and utilization
see also Labor productivity
see also Productivity

OPIC
see Overseas Private Investment Corp.

Opinion and attitude surveys

AIDS info brochure of Surgeon General, public views by age, sex, race, education, and income, 1988 survey, 4042–3.908

AIDS public knowledge, attitudes, info sources, and testing, for blacks, 1988 survey, 4146–8.167

AIDS public knowledge, attitudes, info sources, and testing, for Hispanics, 1988 survey, 4146–8.168

AIDS public knowledge, attitudes, info sources, and testing, 1988 survey, 4146–8.165; 4146–8.169; 4146–8.173

AIDS public knowledge, attitudes, info sources, and testing, 1989 survey, 4146–8.176; 4146–8.180

AIDS public knowledge, by age and education, for Vermont, 1986-87 survey, article, 4042–3.938

AIDS risk knowledge and high-risk activities of homosexual men in cities with low and high AIDS rates, 1989 article, 4042–3.939

AIDS virus infection of patients and surgeons, orthopedists views on treatment and professional restriction, 1986 survey, article, 4042–3.907

Air traffic control system safety, working conditions, and traffic volume, various periods 1981-88, GAO rpt series, 26113–220

Air travel safety and congestion, public opinion, 1988 survey, hearing, 21788–180

Alcohol use, abuse, treatment, and views of racial and ethnic groups in US and native countries, by selected characteristics, 1988 compilation of papers, 4488–12

Alcohol use and abuse among minority groups, and related problems, by selected characteristics, 1985 conf papers, 4488–13

Alcoholic beverages warning labels and other consumer protection methods, public views by selected characteristics, 1988 survey, 8488–5

Apprenticeship issues and public opinion, 1988 rpt, 6408–72

Budget of US, balanced budget proposed constitutional amendment, economic impacts, projected to FY94 and background data from 1940s, hearings, 21528–72

Cancer (cervical) screening and education program for black women, effectiveness and participant characteristics, 1988 local area study, article, 4042–3.953

Cancer cases, and prevention and risk activities and attitudes, 1987 survey, annual rpt, 4474–35

Child care leave of absence for employees, policies, coverage, and attitudes, by employee characteristics, 1980-87, hearings, 25548–95

Crime and crime-related issues, public opinion by respondent characteristics, 1970s-89, annual rpt, 6064–6.2

Crime victimization rates, by offense and reasons for reporting and not reporting crime to police, 1987 survey, annual rpt, 6066–3.41

Drug, alcohol, and cigarette use and attitudes of youth, by substance type and selected characteristics, 1975-88 surveys, annual rpt, 4494–4

Drug and alcohol abuse by military personnel, prevalence and consequences, by selected characteristics, 1988, biennial rpt, 3504–19

Drunk driving enforcement and publicity strategies, NHSTA deterrence project results, 1984-85, 7768–109

Education data compilation, students, staff, finances, and facilities, 1989 edition, annual rpt, 4824–2

Education in science, methods, materials, and factors affecting elementary and secondary student proficiency, views of students, teachers, and administrators, 1983-85 surveys, 4828–37.1

Education statistics, detailed data on elementary and secondary education, 1920s-88 and projected to 1997, annual rpt, 4824–1.1

Food stamp program participation, and reasons for nonparticipation by eligible households, 1979 and 1986, GAO rpt, 26131–52

Health care (long-term) for aged, funding by Fed Govt, public views, 1987 survey, hearings, 21368–106

Health care (long-term) needs, ability to pay, and views on Federal aid for home care, 1988 survey, hearing, 21148–51

Hereditary disease mass screening, and access to results by employer, insurer, and others, foreign and US geneticists views, 1987 survey, article, 4042–3.902

High school class of 1972: education, employment, and family characteristics, activities, and attitudes, natl longitudinal study, series, 4836–1

High school classes of 1980 and 1982: education, employment, and family characteristics, activities, and attitudes, natl longitudinal study, series, 4826–2

Homeless and hungry assistance of Fed Govt, public opinion by respondent characteristics, 1988 survey, hearings, 25248–107

Housing and neighborhood quality, indicators and attitudes, by householder type and location, 1985, biennial rpt, 2485–12

Housing and neighborhood quality, indicators and attitudes, MSA surveys, series, 2485–6

Military reserve personnel social, economic, family, and service characteristics, and attitudes, by reserve component, 1986 survey, 3508–29

Military reserve spouses attitudes, and family social, economic, and other characteristics, 1986 survey, 3508–30

Ocean pollution events, researchers rankings of seriousness by event type, 1987 survey, 2148–57

Older persons employment, earnings, reasons for working, and job training preferences, by selected characteristics, 1960-87, 6306–2.3

Science proficiency, attitudes, factors affecting proficiency, and teacher background and views, natl assessment of elementary and high school students, 1977-86, 4898–25

Smoking and other tobacco use, by knowledge of health effects, and health and other characteristics, 1987, 4147–10.169

Smoking prevalence, related disease and deaths, and public attitudes, impact of Surgeon General rpts and antismoking campaigns, 1964-89, annual rpt, 4204–18

Tax (income) return processing, IRS workload forecasts, compliance, and enforcement, data compilation, 1989 annual rpt, 8304–8

Taxes, spending, and govt efficiency, public opinion by respondent characteristics, 1989 survey, annual rpt, 10044–2

Unemployment insurance long-term claimants employment services use, work experience, and reemployment, by selected characteristics and county, 1987-88, 6406–6.25; 6406–6.26

Veterans population, and benefits programs awareness and use, by age, sex, income, race, and period of service, 1987 survey, 8608–1

Youth sexual behavior, impact of popular music promoting responsibility, for Latin America, 1986, 9916–3.50

see also Business outlook and attitude surveys

see also Consumer surveys

see also Foreign opinion of U.S.

see also Market research

Opium

see Drug abuse and treatment

see Drugs

Optical instruments

see Instruments and measuring devices

see Scientific equipment and apparatus

Options

see Futures trading

see Options trading

Options trading

Banks (insured commercial and savings) finances, for foreign and domestic offices, by asset size, 1987, annual rpt, 9294–4.2

Exchange activity by commodity and exchange, and Commodity Futures Trading Commission oversight, FY88, annual rpt, 11924–2

Market crash of 1987, consumer complaints by reason, security type, and State, Nov-Dec 1987, hearings, 21368–111

Savings instns off-balance-sheet hedging activity, by type, asset size, and State, for FHLB 4th District, 1984-88, article, 9302–2.903

Stock price volatility forecasting performance of options on stock index futures, alternative model results, various periods 1983-88, article, 9371–1.908

Trading of options on commodity, financial instrument, and index futures contracts, NYC, Chicago, and other markets, monthly rpt, 11922–6

Trading volume and new issue registrations, monthly rpt, 9732–1

see also Futures trading

Optoelectronics

see Fiber optics

Optometric instruments

see Medical supplies and equipment

Optometry

County Business Patterns, 1987: employment, establishments, and payroll, by SIC 2- to 4-digit industry and county, annual State rpt series, 2326–8

CPI by component for US city average, and by region, population size, and for 27 metro areas, monthly rpt, 6762–2

France and Germany physicians, and visits by reason and patient age and sex, by specialty, compared to US, 1981-83, 4147–5.5

Glaucoma incidence, screening and treatment effectiveness, and costs under proposed Medicare coverage, 1988, 26356–7.1

Health condition and health care resources, use, and spending, 1950s-87, annual data compilation, 4144–11

Indian Health Service outpatient visits, by type of provider, selected hospital, and IHS service area, FY87-88, annual rpt, 4084–3

Insurance (health) coverage and provisions of employee benefit plans, by plan type and occupational group, 1988, annual rpt, 6784–19

Licensing and discipline of optometrists, by State medical boards, with medical school enrollment and applications, 1950s-87, 4006–8.2

Medicare physicians services use, charges, and reimbursement, by service type, setting, and specialty, 1986, article, 4652–1.936

Military health care personnel, and accessions by training source, by occupation, specialty, and service branch, FY87, annual rpt, 3544–24

Older persons preventive health care services use, and relation to selected characteristics, 1970s-80s, 26356–7.2

Ophthalmologist office visits, by characteristics of physician, practice, patient, and visit, with drug mentions by type and brand, 1985, 4146–8.166

Physicians income, by specialty and other practice characteristics, 1975 and 1983-84, article, 4652–1.920

Receipts for services, by SIC 2- to 4-digit kind of business, 1988, annual rpt, 2413–8

Service industries census, 1987: establishments, receipts, employment, and payroll, by SIC 2- to 4-digit kind of business, MSA, county, and city, State rpt series, 2391–1

Tax (income) returns of partnerships, income statement items by industry group, 1986, annual article, 8302–2.903

Tax (income) returns of sole proprietorships, income statement items, by industry group, 1987, annual article, 8302–2.904; 8302–2.921

Training support grants of Bur of Health Professions, by program, region, and State, FY80-87, 4118–62

VA Medicine and Surgery Dept trainees, by detailed program and city, FY88, annual rpt, 8704–4

Orange, Calif.

see also under By City in the "Index by Categories"

Orange County, N.Y.

see also under By SMSA or MSA in the "Index by Categories"

Oranges

see Citrus fruits

Orchards

see Fruit and fruit products

Orders

see Business orders

Ordnance

see Ammunition

see Military supplies and property

see Military weapons

Oregon

Agriculture census, 1987: farms, farmland, production and costs, and operator characteristics, advance State and county rpts, 2330–1.41

Agriculture census, 1987: farms, farmland, production, finances, and operator characteristics, by county, final State rpt, 2331–1.37

Alien workers (unauthorized) employer sanctions impacts on farm labor supply in Western US, with background data, 1986-89, GAO rpt, 26121–310

Bank deposits in FDIC-insured commercial and savings banks, by instn, State, and county, as of June 1988, annual regional rpt, 9295–3.6

Coastal and estuarine pollutant levels for Oregon, by pollutant and location, 1960s-87, 2178–23

County Business Patterns, 1987: employment, establishments, and payroll, by SIC 2- to 4-digit industry and county, annual State rpt, 2326–8.39

Cranberry production, prices, use, and acreage, for selected States, 1987-88 and forecast 1989, annual rpt, 1621–18.4

Deaths and rates, by detailed location, cause, and demographic characteristics, 1987, US Vital Statistics annual rpt, 4144–3.1

DOD prime contract awards, by contractor, service branch, State, and city, FY88, annual rpt, 3544–22

Employment, earnings, and hours, by selected SIC 1- to 4-digit industry, State, and for 262 MSAs, 1972-87, 6748–81.4

Estuary environmental conditions, research results and methodology, 1988 local area rpt, 2176–7.10

Fed Govt spending in States and local areas, by type, State, county, and city, FY88, annual rpt, 2464–3

Fed Govt spending in States, by type, program, agency, and State, FY88, annual rpt, 2464–2

Fish and shellfish catch, prices, and fisheries economic status, for Pacific coast, 1986-87, annual rpt series, 2164–16

Fish and shellfish catch, wholesale receipts, prices, trade, and other market activities, weekly regional rpt, 2162–6.5

HHS financial aid, by program, recipient, State, and city, FY88, annual regional listing, 4004–3.10

Homeless children educational enrollment and needs, 1988, annual State rpt, 4804–35.37

Hood River housing energy conservation program of Bonneville Power Admin, activities, cost effectiveness, and participation, 1983-86, series, 3226–2

Income (personal) per capita and by source, and earnings by industry div, by State, MSA, and county, 1982-87, annual regional rpt, 2704–2.5

Indian health clinic services use and staff, and effectiveness of prenatal care program, 1970s-86 local area study, article, 4042–3.960

Land (non-Federal) in western Oregon, by use and county, 1971-74 and 1982, 1206–19.9

Land Mgmt Bur activities and finances, and public land acreage and use, FY88, annual State rpt, 5724–11.3

Lumber mill occupational injury and illness rates and workdays lost, by selected State and SIC 4-digit industry, 1978-87, article, 6722–1.945

Mineral Industry Surveys, State reviews of production, 1988, preliminary annual rpt, 5614–6

Minerals Yearbook, 1987, Vol 2 preprints: State review of production and sales by commodity, and business activity, annual rpt, 5604–16.38

Minerals Yearbook, 1987, Vol 2: State reviews of production, sales, and firms, by commodity, and business activity, annual rpt, 5604–34

Nursing home compliance with Medicare and Medicaid regulations, and patient characteristics, by facility, 1987/88, annual State rpt, 4654–15.38

Population, households, employment, income, and fuel prices, for Pacific Northwest, alternative projections 1990-2010 with trends from 1960, annual rpt, 3224–5

Retail trade census, 1987: employment, establishments, sales, and payroll, by SIC 2- to 4-digit kind of business, MSA, county, and city, State rpt, 2397–1.38

River and stream environmental conditions, fish, wildlife, use, and mgmt, 1989 rpt, 5506–9.39

Savings instns, FHLB 12th District members deposits and lending, monthly press release, 9302–32.5

Service industries census, 1987: employment, establishments, receipts, and payroll, by SIC 2- to 4-digit kind of business, MSA, county, and city, State rpt, 2391–1.38

Statistical Abstract of US, social, political, and economic data, with foreign comparisons, 1790-2025, comprehensive annual compilation, 2324–1

Timber in northwestern US and British Columbia, production, prices, trade, and employment, quarterly rpt, 1202–3

Timber in Oregon, acreage on railroad grant lands returned to Federal ownership, by county, FY88, annual rpt, 5724–1.1

Timber in Oregon, resources by species, ownership, and county, 1983-86, series, 1206–19

Water supply and quality in streams and lakes, and groundwater levels in wells, by drainage basin, 1986, annual State rpt, 5666–23.36

Water supply, and snow survey results, monthly State rpt, 1266–2.7

Water supply, and snow survey results, 1988, annual State rpt, 1264–14.3

Water supply in Oregon, streamflow by station and reservoir storage, 1989, annual rpt, 1264–9

Wholesale trade census, 1987: employment, establishments, finances, and operations, by SIC 2- to 4-digit kind of business, MSA, county, and city, State rpt, 2405–1.38

Wildlife-related recreation, hunting, and fishing participation and spending, detailed data, 1985 survey, quinquennial State rpt, 5506–6.37

see also Eugene, Oreg.

see also Grants Pass, Oreg.

see also Klamath Falls, Oreg.

see also Medford, Oreg.

see also Portland, Oreg.

see also Roseburg, Oreg.

see also Springfield, Oreg.

see also under By State in the "Index by Categories"

Orem, Utah

see also under By SMSA or MSA in the "Index by Categories"

Organ transplants

see Medical transplants

Organization for Economic Cooperation and Development

Agricultural exports of high-value commodities from developing countries to OECD members, 1970s-87, article, 1522–3.921

Capital flows (intl) impacts on monetary policy instruments, and financial and economic indicators, 1987 compilation of papers, 9385–9

Caribbean Basin exports to OECD members, and US imports under preferential treatment programs, by commodity, 1980s-87, 2048–138

Dev aid of OECD and Arab countries, total, per capita, and share of GNP, by country, 1987, annual rpt, 9904–1.4

Economic conditions, and oil production, use, and imports, by country, biweekly rpt, 9112–1

Economic conditions in Communist and OECD countries, 1987, annual rpt, 7144–11

Economic conditions in Communist, OECD, and selected other countries, 1960s-88, annual rpt, 9114–4

Economic indicators, and dollar exchange rates, for selected OECD countries, 1980s-89, semiannual rpt, 8002–14

Economic indicators composite indexes, analysis of inputs, 1989 article, 2702–1.926

Energy prices, by fuel type and end use, for 10 countries, 1980-88 annual rpt, 3164–50.6

Energy production by type, and oil prices, trade, and use, by country group and selected country, monthly rpt, 9112–2

Energy use by sector, and production, by fuel type, country, and country group, projected 1988-2000 and trends from 1970, annual rpt, 3164–84

Exports and imports of OECD, total and for 4 major countries, and US trade by country, by commodity, 1970-87, world area rpt series, 9116–1

Exports and imports of US, by commodity group, world area, selected country, US coastal area and port, and mode of transport, monthly rpt, 2422–9

GNP and GNP growth of OECD members, by country, 1978-88, annual rpt, 7144–8

Imports of OECD countries covered by non-tariff trade barriers, by barrier type and commodity group, 1981-86, article, 9391–1.906

Industrial production, consumer price, and stock price indexes for 6 OECD countries and US, *Business Conditions Digest*, monthly rpt, 2702–3.10

Industrial production indexes and CPI, for US and 6 OECD countries, current data and annual trends, monthly rpt, 23842–1.7

Labor productivity related to govt spending, for 7 OECD countries, 1966-85, article, 9375–1.907

Manufacturing labor cost indexes, by selected country, 1980-89, article, 6722–1.926

Manufacturing labor costs and indexes, by selected country, 1975-88, annual rpt, 6824–3

Manufacturing labor costs and indexes, by selected country, 1975-88, semiannual rpt, 6822–3

Military spending, arms trade, and force strengths, with govt spending and population, by country, 1977-87, annual rpt, 9824–1

Nuclear power plant capacity, generation, and operating status, by plant and foreign and US location, 1988 and projected to 2020, annual rpt, 3164–57

Oil and refined products stocks of 7 OECD countries and OECD total, quarterly 1985-88, annual rpt, 3164–50.2

Oil production, trade, use, and stocks, by selected country and country group, monthly rpt, 3162–42

Oil stocks and use by OECD countries, selected years 1960-88, annual rpt, 3164–74.8

Oil use and stocks for selected OECD countries, monthly rpt, 3162–24.10

Productivity growth indicators, and impacts of pollution abatement spending and other factors, for US and selected OECD countries, various periods 1948-86, article, 9389–1.911

Social security programs and spending by type, with background data, for selected OECD countries, 1940s-80s and projected to 2040, 4742–1.908

see also International Energy Agency

Organization of Petroleum Exporting Countries

Economic conditions in Communist, OECD, and selected other countries, 1960s-88, annual rpt, 9114–4

Energy use by sector, and production, by fuel type, country, and country group, projected 1988-2000 and trends from 1970, annual rpt, 3164–84

Exports and imports of US, by commodity group, world area, selected country, US coastal area and port, and mode of transport, monthly rpt, 2422–9

Exports, imports, and balances of US by commodity group, world area, and country, and related employment, 1970s–88, annual rpt, 2044–26

Exports, imports, and balances of US with major trading partners, by product category, 1984-88, annual chartbook, 9884–21

Investment (direct) in US oil and other industries, by OPEC members, as of 1988, annual rpt, 3164–80

Loans of US banks to foreigners at all US and foreign offices, by country group and country, quarterly rpt, 13002–1

Military spending, arms trade, and force strengths, with govt spending and population, by country, 1977-87, annual rpt, 9824–1

Multinatl firms US affiliates, finances, and operations, by industry, world area of parent firm, and State, 1987, annual rpt, 2704–4

Multinatl US firms and foreign affiliates finances and operations, by industry of parent firm and affiliate, world area, and country, preliminary 1987, annual rpt, 2704–5

Oil and gas reserves and discoveries, by country and country group, quarterly rpt, 3162–43

Oil crude, gas liquids, and refined products supply, demand, and movement, by PAD district and State, 1988 and trends from 1973, annual rpt, 3164–2

Oil import costs, by crude type and country or group of origin, monthly rpt, 3162–11

Oil import costs, by crude type and country or group of origin, 1988, annual rpt, 3164–85

Oil prices and US and OPEC industry impacts of alternative US protective policies, projected 2037, technical paper, 9379–12.44

Oil prices of OPEC and non-OPEC countries, weekly rpt, 3162–32

Oil prices production by country, and OPEC prices by member, biweekly rpt, 9112–1

Oil production, and exports and prices for US, by major exporting country, detailed data, monthly rpt, 3162–24

Oil production and exports to US, by OPEC member, 1960-88, annual rpt, 3164–74.2; 3164–74.8

Oil production, capacity, use, exports by country, and prices, by OPEC member, monthly rpt, 9112–2

Oil production, trade, use, and stocks, by selected country and country group, monthly rpt, 3162–42

Oil, refined products, and gas liquids supply, demand, trade, stocks, and refining, by detailed product, State, and PAD district, monthly rpt with articles, 3162–6

Organized crime

Court civil and criminal caseloads for Federal district, appeals, and special courts, June 1989, annual rpt, 18204–2; 18204–8

Criminal case processing in Federal district courts, and dispositions, by offense, district, and offender characteristics, 1984, annual rpt, 6064–29

Drug enforcement regional task forces investigation of organized crime, activities by agency and region, and background data, FY83-88, annual rpt, 6004–17

Drug-related money laundering operations, US and foreign govts enforcement activities, 1988, annual rpt, 7004–17

Labor Dept programs fraud and abuse, audits and investigations, 2nd half FY89, semiannual rpt, 6302–2

Prison conditions, population, and problems, issues and bibl, 1989 compilation of papers, 25928–8

Sentences for Federal crimes, guidelines use and results by offense and district, and Sentencing Commission activities, 1988, annual rpt, 17664–1

Sentences for Federal offenses, guidelines by offense and circumstances, 1989 rpt, 17668–1

US attorneys civil and criminal cases by type and disposition, and collections, by Federal district, FY88, annual rpt, 6004–2.1; 6004–2.7

Wiretaps authorized, costs, arrests, trials, and convictions, by offense and jurisdiction, 1988, annual rpt, 18204–7

Organized Crime Drug Enforcement Task Forces

Activities of task forces by agency and region, and background data, FY83-88, annual rpt, 6004–17

Organized labor
see Labor unions

Organochlorides
see Chemicals and chemical industry
see Pesticides

Oriental Americans
see Asian Americans

Orlando, Fla.

Housing starts and completions authorized by building permits in 40 MSAs, quarterly rpt, 2382–9

Wages by occupation, and benefits for office and plant workers, 1988 survey, periodic MSA rpt, 6785–11.3

see also under By City and By SMSA or MSA in the "Index by Categories"

Orlando, S. Paul, Jr.

"Characterization of Salinity and Temperature for Mobile Bay", 2176–7.12

"Shoreline Modification, Dredged Channels and Dredged Material Disposal Areas in the Nation's Estuaries", 2176–7.6

Orr, James

"Performance of the U.S. Capital Goods Industry: Implications for Trade Adjustment", 9385–1.909

Orthopedic impairments
see Musculoskeletal diseases

Orthopedics

Malpractice claims and payments, by procedure and physician specialty, 1975-78, hearing, 21408–113

Medicare physicians services use, charges, and reimbursement, by service type, setting, and specialty, 1986, article, 4652–1.936

Military health care personnel, and accessions by training source, by occupation, specialty, and service branch, FY87, annual rpt, 3544–24

Physicians income, by specialty and other practice characteristics, 1975 and 1983-84, article, 4652–1.920

VA health care facilities physicians, dentists, and nurses, by selected employment characteristics and VA district, quarterly rpt, 8602–6

see also Podiatry
see also Prosthetics and orthotics

Orthotics
see Prosthetics and orthotics

Osborn, C. Tim

"Conservation Reserve Program: Enrollment Statistics for 1987-88 and Signup Periods 1-7", 1588–112

Oshkosh, Wis.

see also under By SMSA or MSA in the "Index by Categories"

Osteen, Craig

"Economic Importance of Cotton Insects and Mites", 1568–278

Osteopathy

County Business Patterns, 1987: employment, establishments, and payroll, by SIC 2- to 4-digit industry and county, annual State rpt series, 2326–8

Drugs (controlled) provided during physician office visits, by drug, patient, and provider characteristics, 1985, 4146–8.179

Health condition and health care resources, use, and spending, 1950s-87, annual data compilation, 4144–11

Labor supply of osteopaths and family practice MDs, 1978, and estimated 1990 supply and demand, 1989 article, 4042–3.926

Receipts for services, by SIC 2- to 4-digit kind of business, 1988, annual rpt, 2413–8

Service industries census, 1987: establishments, receipts, employment, and payroll, by SIC 2- to 4-digit kind of business, MSA, county, and city, State rpt series, 2391–1

Tax (income) returns of partnerships, income statement items by industry group, 1986, annual article, 8302–2.903

Tax (income) returns of sole proprietorships, income statement items, by industry group, 1987, annual article, 8302–2.904; 8302–2.921

Training support grants of Bur of Health Professions, by program, region, and State, FY80-87, 4118–62

Osterberg, William P.

"Intervention and the Risk Premium in Foreign Exchange Rates", 9377–9.80

O'Sullivan, Jennifer

"Medicaid Source Book: Background Data and Analysis", 21368–105

Otitis
see Ear diseases and infections

Ott, Mack

"Is America Being Sold Out?", 9391–1.910

Ott, Robert A., Jr.

"Accounting for Prepayment Risk on Gap Reports", 9316–1.142

Ottawa, Canada

Fruit and vegetable shipments, and arrivals in US and Canada cities, by mode of transport and State and country of origin, 1988, annual rpt, 1311–4.1

Outdoor recreation
see Recreation

Savings instns stock and mutual members of FHLB system by district, and conversions from mutual to stock ownership, monthly journal, 8432-2

Securities purchases, sales, and holdings, by issuer and type and ownership of security, monthly listing, 9732-2

Ships under foreign flag owned by US firms and foreign affiliates, by type, owner, and country of registry and construction, as of July 1989, semiannual rpt, 7702-3

Small business finances, operations, owner and employee characteristics, and Federal contracts, 1980s-88, annual rpt, 9764-6

Small Business Investment Companies capital holdings, SBA obligation, and ownership, as of June 1989, semiannual listing, 9762-4

Small Business Investment Companies finances, funding, licensing, and loan activity, 1st half FY89, semiannual rpt, 9762-3

Southeastern States banks and thrifts industry structure impacts of market entry and branching regulation, by State, 1982-88, article, 9302-2.907

Statistical Abstract of US, social, political, and economic data, 1790-2025, comprehensive annual compilation, 2324-1.3

Stockbrokers finances, firms by type of organization and State, and SEC applications and registrations, 1983-88, annual rpt, 9734-2.1

Tax (income) returns filed, by type of return and IRS region and service center, projected 1988-95 and trends from 1977, annual rpt, 8304-9

Virgin Islands economic censuses, 1987: employment, firms, payroll, and receipts, by SIC 1- to 4-digit industry, island, and city, 2593-1

Water supply in rural areas, public system financial and operating characteristics, by region, 1980, 1598-247

see also Bank holding companies
see also Business acquisitions and mergers
see also Consumer cooperatives
see also Cooperatives
see also Corporations
see also Divestiture
see also Foreign corporations
see also Franchises
see also Government corporations and enterprises
see also Government ownership
see also Holding companies
see also Joint ventures
see also Minority businesses
see also Multinational corporations
see also Partnerships
see also Proprietorships
see also Rural cooperatives
see also Securities
see also Self-employment
see also Women-owned businesses

Oxnard, Calif.
Housing vacancy rates for single and multifamily units and mobile homes, by city and ZIP code, 1988, annual MSA rpt, 9304-20.6

Wages by occupation, for office and plant workers, 1989 survey, periodic MSA rpt, 6785-3.9

see also under By City and By SMSA or MSA in the "Index by Categories"

Oxygen
see Gases

Ozanne, Larry
"Simulating the Revenue Effects of Changes in the Taxation of Capital Gains", 26306-3.106

Ozone
see Air pollution

Pacific Basin Development Council
"Ocean Transportation Needs of the American Pacific Islands: Report to Congress", 7308-195

Pacific Islands Americans
Agriculture census, 1987: farms, farmland, production, finances, and operator characteristics, by county, final State rpt series, 2331-1

Alcohol use, abuse, treatment, and views of racial and ethnic groups in US and native countries, by selected characteristics, 1988 compilation of papers, 4488-12

Alcohol use and abuse among minority groups, and related problems, by selected characteristics, 1985 conf papers, 4488-13

Census of Population, 1980: selected socioeconomic data for Asian and Pacific Island Americans, by detailed origin, young readers pamphlet, 2326-1.5

Deaths and rates, by detailed cause and demographic characteristics, 1986 and trends from 1900, US Vital Statistics annual rpt, 4144-2

Education data compilation, students, staff, finances, and facilities, 1989 edition, annual rpt, 4824-2

Statistical Abstract of US, social, political, and economic data, 1790-2025, comprehensive annual compilation, 2324-1.1

Pacific Marine Environmental Laboratory
see National Oceanic and Atmospheric Administration

Pacific Northwest
see Western States

Pacific Northwest Laboratory
"Fuel Performance Annual Report for 1987", 9634-8

"Population Dose Commitments Due to Radioactive Releases from Nuclear Power Plant Sites in 1986", 9634-7

see also Department of Energy National Laboratories

Pacific Ocean
Coastal areas environmental conditions and mgmt, map series, 2176-5

Coastal areas environmental conditions, fish, wildlife, use, and mgmt, 1989 rpt, 5506-9.36

Cobalt and other metals resources in manganese crusts of US Exclusive Economic Zone in Pacific Ocean, and cobalt production for onshore sites, 1988 article, 5602-4.901

Environmental summary data, and intl claims and disputes, 1989 annual factbook, 9114-2

Estuary environmental conditions and mgmt, for individual areas, conf series, 2146-6

Exports and imports (waterborne) of US, by type of service, commodity, country, route, and US port, 1986-87, annual rpt, 7704-2

Fish and shellfish catch, life cycles, and environmental needs, for selected coastal species and regions, series, 5506-8

Fish and shellfish catch, wholesale receipts, prices, trade, and other market activities, semiweekly regional rpt, 2162-6.4

Fish catch, trade, use, and fishery operations, with selected foreign data, by species, 1970s-88, annual rpt, 2164-1

Freight (waterborne domestic and foreign) by commodity, traffic, and passengers, by port and waterway, 1987, annual rpt, 3754-3.4

Hurricanes and tropical storms in north Pacific Ocean, characteristics, 1988, annual article, 2152-8.903

Hurricanes and tropical storms in north Pacific Ocean, selected characteristics, 1988 and trends from 1945, annual article, 2152-8.904

Hurricanes and tropical storms in northeastern Pacific Ocean, paths and surveillance, 1988, annual rpt, 2184-8

Hurricanes and tropical storms in Pacific and Indian Oceans, paths and surveillance, 1988, annual rpt, 3804-8

Japan fish catch, prices, trade by country, cold storage holdings, import quotas, and market devs, semimonthly press release, 2162-7

Marine Fisheries Review, US and foreign fisheries resources, dev, mgmt, and research, quarterly journal, 2162-1

Marine Mammal Protection Act admin, and populations, strandings, and catch permits by species and location, 1987-88, annual rpt, 2164-11

Mariners Weather Log, quarterly journal, 2152-8

Oil and gas OCS operations accidents, spills, casualties, and circumstances, 1956-86, listing, 5738-7

Oil and gas OCS production, and wells, for Pacific lands under Federal lease, by drilling platform, 1960s-88, annual rpt, 5734-9

Oil and gas OCS production, reserves, and wells drilled, for Pacific Ocean by location, 1988, annual rpt, 5734-7

Oil and gas OCS reserves of Fed Govt, leasing and exploration activity, production, revenue, and costs, by ocean area, FY88, annual rpt, 5734-4

Oil, gas, and minerals production, revenue, and leasing activity, for Federal OCS lands by ocean region and State, 1950s-87, annual rpt, 5734-3

Plastic, tar, and other nondegradable ocean and beach debris, incidence and environmental impacts, 1970s-88, 14738-4

Pollutant concentrations in coastal and estuarine sediments, by contaminant and selected site, 1984-87, 2176-3.7

Pollutant concentrations in coastal and estuarine shellfish, by pollutant and location, 1986-88, 2176-3.8

Pollution (water) incidents and discharges, by type, source, cause, and location, 1984-86, annual rpt, 7404-3

Health effects of hazardous substances, concentrations in environment, and household products composition, with data by selected location, 1988 hearings, 21408–112

Housewares (ceramic) lead and cadmium levels, FDA import inspection activity by country, and food safety funding and staff, 1983-88, hearing, 21368–108

Housing alteration and repair spending, by characteristics of property and region, 1984-88, annual rpt, 2384–4

Imports of US, detailed Schedule A commodities by country, monthly rpt, 2422–2

Injuries from use of consumer products and related activities, by victim age and sex, 1988, annual rpt, 9164–7

Injuries from use of consumer products, by severity, victim age, and detailed product, 1988, annual rpt, 9164–6

Input-output structure of US economy, detailed interindustry transactions for 84 industries, and components of final demand, 1983, annual article, 2702–1.909

Labor productivity, indexes of output, hours, and employment by SIC 2- to 4-digit industry, 1963-87, annual rpt, 6824–1.3

Lead paint abatement and other public and Indian housing renovation needs, series, 5186–15

Lead poisoning among children, and children at risk in Massachusetts, by city, 1985-87, hearing, 21248–119

Lead poisoning among children, and impacts of lead removal from housing, gasoline, and water, 1987 conf, 4108–46

Manufacturers finances and operations, by SIC 2- to 4-digit industry, forecast 1989 and trends from 1950s, annual rpt, 2044–28

Manufacturing annual survey, 1986: financial and operating data, by SIC 2- to 4-digit industry, series, 2506–15

Manufacturing census, 1987: financial and operating data, for SIC 4-digit industries by product, preliminary rpt, 2491–1.33; 2491–1.37

Minerals Yearbook, 1988, Vol 1: commodity review of production, reserves, supply, use, and trade, annual rpt, 5604–20.33

Occupational injury and illness rates, by SIC 2- to 4-digit industry, 1987, annual rpt, 6844–1

OECD trade, total and for 4 major countries, and US trade by country, by commodity, 1970-87, world area rpt series, 9116–1

Oil and fat production, consumption by end use, and stocks, by type, monthly Current Industrial Rpt, 2506–4.4

Oils, oilseeds, and fats production, prices, trade, and use, periodic situation rpt with articles, 1561–3

Price indexes (producer), by stage of processing and detailed commodity, monthly rpt, 6762–6

Price indexes (producer), by stage of processing and detailed commodity, monthly 1988, annual rpt, 6764–2

Production and sales of synthetic organic chemicals, and manufacturer listing, by product, 1988, annual rpt, 9884–3

Production of synthetic organic chemicals, by detailed product, quarterly rpt, 9882–1

Science, engineering, and technical employment in manufacturing, by field, occupation, and industry, 1986, triennial rpt, 9627–23

Ship hull paints impacts on environment and marine species, with bibl, 1960s-87, 2148–58

Shipments and PPI for building materials, by type, bimonthly rpt, 2042–1.5; 2042–1.6

Shipments, trade, and use of paint and related products, monthly Current Industrial Rpt, 2506–8.4

Talc production, use, and trade, with foreign comparisons, selected years 1977-87, 5608–158

Tax (income) returns of corporations, income and tax items by asset size and detailed industry, 1986, annual rpt, 8304–4; 8304–21

Wholesale trade census, 1987: employment, establishments, finances, and operations, by SIC 2- to 4-digit kind of business, MSA, county, and city, State rpt series, 2405–1

see also under By Commodity in the "Index by Categories"

Pait, Anthony S.

"Agricultural Pesticide Use in Estuarine Drainage Areas: A Preliminary Study for Selected Pesticides", 2176–4.9

Pakistan

Agricultural and food production and indexes, total and for selected commodities, by country, 1970s-88, annual rpt, 1524–12

Agricultural production, prices, and trade, by country, 1960s-89, annual world region rpt, 1524–4.2

Agricultural trade of US, by detailed commodity and country, 1988, semiannual rpt, 1522–4

Agricultural trade of US with Asia, Middle East, and North Africa, by commodity and country, 1962-86, 1528–277

AID activities and funding by project and function, FY90, and developing countries summary socioeconomic data from 1960s, annual rpt, 9904–4.6

AID economic aid to developing countries, obligations and disbursements by country, quarterly rpt, 9912–4

AID loans repayment status and terms by program and country, and status of predecessor agency loans, quarterly rpt, 9912–3

Cotton production, trade, and use, for selected countries, FAS monthly circular, 1925–4.2

Economic and military aid and loans from US and intl agencies, by program and country, FY46-87, annual rpt, 9914–5

Economic conditions in Communist, OECD, and selected other countries, 1960s-88, annual rpt, 9114–4

Economic conditions, income, production, prices, employment, and trade, 1988 periodic country rpt, 2046–4.4

Economic conditions, policy, and trade practices, by country, 1986-88, annual rpt, 21384–5

Economic, social, political, and geographic summary data, by country, 1989, annual factbook, 9114–2

Exports and imports of US, by commodity and country, 1970-87, world area rpt, 9116–1.2

Exports and imports of US, by selected country, country group, and commodity group, 1988, annual rpt, 2044–37

Human rights conditions in 170 countries, 1988, annual rpt, 21384–3

Imports of goods, services, and investment from US, trade barriers, impacts, and US actions, by country, 1988, annual rpt, 444–2

Labor conditions, union coverage, and work accidents, 1989 annual country rpt, 6366–4.9

Military aid of US, arms sales, and training programs costs and budget requests, by program, world region, and country, FY88-90, annual rpt, 7144–13

Military spending, arms trade, and force strengths, with govt spending and population, by country, 1977-87, annual rpt, 9824–1

Military strengths, spending, weapons systems, and arms imports, for Pakistan and India, 1980s-87, hearing, 21388–54

Minerals production, reserves, and industry role in domestic economy and world supply, 1988 country rpt, 5606–1.17

Minerals Yearbook, 1987, Vol 3: foreign country reviews of production, trade, and policy, by commodity, annual rpt, 5604–35

Minerals Yearbook, 1987, Vol 3 preprints: foreign country review of production, trade, and policy, by commodity, annual rpt, 5604–23.56

Nuclear power generation in US and 19 non-Communist countries, monthly rpt, 3162–24.10

Nuclear power plant capacity, generation, and operating status, by plant and foreign and US location, 1988 and projected to 2020, annual rpt, 3164–57

Population size, growth rates, and components of change, by country, projected 1989-2020 and trends from 1950, biennial rpt, 2324–9

UN voting record and share of votes in agreement with US, by issue, country, and world area, 1988, annual rpt, 7004–18

see also under By Foreign Country in the "Index by Categories"

Palau

Bank deposits in FDIC-insured commercial and savings banks, by instn, State, and county, as of June 1988, annual regional rpt, 9295–3.6

Economic, social, political, and geographic summary data, by country, 1989, annual factbook, 9114–2

Population social, economic, health, and govtl data, by TTPI govt, FY88 and selected trends, detailed annual rpt, 7004–6

Water supply and quality in streams and lakes, and groundwater levels in wells, by drainage basin, 1987, annual State rpt, 5666–10.10

Palm Bay, Fla.

Wages by occupation, for office and plant workers, 1989 survey, periodic MSA rpt, 6785–3.4

see also under By SMSA or MSA in the "Index by Categories"

Manufacturing annual survey, 1986:
financial and operating data, by SIC 2- to
4-digit industry, series, 2506–15

Manufacturing annual survey, 1986:
production indexes and exports by SIC
2-digit industry and State, with
comparisons to 1985, model results, series,
2506–16

Manufacturing census, 1987: financial and
operating data, for SIC 4-digit industries
by product, preliminary industry rpt
series, 2491–1

Manufacturing industries production,
shipments, inventories, orders, and
pollution control costs, periodic Current
Industrial Rpt series, 2506–3

Multinatl US firms and foreign affiliates
finances and operations, by industry of
parent firm and affiliate, world area, and
country, preliminary 1987, annual rpt,
2704–5

North Central States pulpwood production
and mill receipts, by species, mill, State,
and county, 1987, annual rpt, 1204–19

Northeastern US pulpwood production by
species and county, and shipments, by
State, 1987, annual rpt, 1204–18

Occupational injury and illness rates, by SIC
2- to 4-digit industry, 1987, annual rpt,
6844–1

OECD trade, total and for 4 major
countries, and US trade by country, by
commodity, 1970-87, world area rpt
series, 9116–1

Office supplies shipments, trade, and use, by
product, annual Current Industrial Rpt,
discontinued, 2506–7.11

Pacific Northwest population, households,
employment, income, and fuel prices,
alternative projections 1990-2010 with
trends from 1960, annual rpt, 3224–5

Pollution (air) abatement equipment
shipments by industry, exports, and new
and backlog orders, by product, 1988,
annual Current Industrial Rpt, 2506–12.5

Pollution abatement capital and operating
costs, by SIC 2-to 4-digit industry and
State, 1986, annual Current Industrial
Rpt, 2506–3.6

Price indexes (producer), by stage of
processing and detailed commodity,
monthly rpt, 6762–6

Price indexes (producer), by stage of
processing and detailed commodity,
monthly 1988, annual rpt, 6764–2

Production, shipments, trade, stocks, and
use, by paper and pulp product and State,
1988, annual Current Industrial Rpt,
2506–7.10

Retail trade census, 1987: employment,
establishments, sales, and payroll, by SIC
2- to 4-digit kind of business, MSA,
county, and city, State rpt series, 2397–1

Science, engineering, and technical
employment in manufacturing, by field,
occupation, and industry, 1986, triennial
rpt, 9627–23

Science, engineering, and technical
employment in transportation, utilities,
and retail and wholesale trade, by field,
occupation, and industry, 1985, triennial
rpt, 9627–32

Small business establishments, employment,
and financial ratios, by SIC 1- to 2-digit
industry and State, late 1960s-87,
9768–19

Southeastern US pulpwood and residue
prices, spending, and transport shares by
mode, 1986-87, annual rpt, 1204–22

Southern US lumber and paper industries
productivity, impact on economy, and
employment compared to other industries,
1970s-80, State rpt series, 1206–36

Statistical Abstract of US, social, political,
and economic data, 1790-2025,
comprehensive annual compilation,
2324–1.3

Talc production, use, and trade, with foreign
comparisons, selected years 1977-87,
5608–158

Tariff Schedule of US, classifications and
rates of duty by detailed imported
commodity, 1990 base edition and
supplements, 9886–13

Tax (income) returns of corporations,
income and tax items by asset size and
detailed industry, 1986, annual rpt,
8304–4; 8304–21

Transportation census, 1987: trucks, by
detailed characteristics, miles traveled,
and type of product carried, State rpt
series, 2573–1

Wages and employment by occupation, and
benefits, by location for pulp, paper, and
paperboard production workers, 1987
survey, 6787–6.238

Wholesale trade census, 1987: employment,
establishments, finances, and operations,
by SIC 2- to 4-digit kind of business,
MSA, county, and city, State rpt series,
2405–1

Wholesale trade sales and inventories, by
SIC 2- to 3-digit kind of business,
monthly rpt, 2413–7

Wholesale trade sales, inventories,
purchases, and gross margins, by SIC 2-
to 3-digit kind of business and form of
ownership, 1988, annual rpt, 2413–13

see also By Industry in the "Index by
Categories"

see also under By Commodity in the "Index
by Categories"

Paper gold

see Special Drawing Rights

Paperwork

see Government forms and paperwork

Paperwork Reduction Act

Info collection of Fed Govt under Act,
effects on requirements and respondent
burden by agency, FY87-89, annual rpt,
104–19

Info collection of Fed Govt under Act,
OMB review of agency requests of info
from public, 1982-87, GAO rpt,
26131–63

Info collection of Fed Govt under Act,
respondent burden by paperwork and
respondent type, 1985-87, GAO rpt,
26131–60

Info collection of Fed Govt under Act,
respondent burden, OMB reviews, and
violations, 1981-88, annual rpt, 104–26

Papua New Guinea

Agricultural and food production and
indexes, total and for selected
commodities, by country, 1970s-88,
annual rpt, 1524–12

Agricultural trade of US, by detailed
commodity and country, 1988, semiannual
rpt, 1522–4

Background Notes, summary social, political,
and economic data, 1989 rpt, 7006–2.41

Economic and military aid and loans from
US and intl agencies, by program and
country, FY46-87, annual rpt, 9914–5

Economic conditions, income, production,
prices, employment, and trade, 1989
periodic country rpt, 2046–4.39

Economic conditions, investment and export
opportunities, and trade practices, 1989
country market research rpt, 2046–6.12

Economic conditions, policy, and trade
practices, by country, 1986-88, annual rpt,
21384–5

Economic, social, political, and geographic
summary data, by country, 1989, annual
factbook, 9114–2

Human rights conditions in 170 countries,
1988, annual rpt, 21384–3

Military aid of US, arms sales, and training
programs costs and budget requests, by
program, world region, and country,
FY88-90, annual rpt, 7144–13

Military spending, arms trade, and force
strengths, with govt spending and
population, by country, 1977-87, annual
rpt, 9824–1

Minerals Yearbook, 1987, Vol 3: foreign
country reviews of production, trade, and
policy, by commodity, annual rpt,
5604–35

Minerals Yearbook, 1987, Vol 3 preprints:
foreign country review of production,
trade, and policy, by commodity, annual
rpt, 5604–23.88

Population size, growth rates, and
components of change, by country,
projected 1989-2020 and trends from
1950, biennial rpt, 2324–9

UN voting record and share of votes in
agreement with US, by issue, country, and
world area, 1988, annual rpt, 7004–18

see also under By Foreign Country in the
"Index by Categories"

Paraguay

Agricultural and food production and
indexes, total and for selected
commodities, by country, 1970s-88,
annual rpt, 1524–12

Agricultural trade of US, by detailed
commodity and country, 1988, semiannual
rpt, 1522–4

AID activities and funding by project and
function, FY90, and developing countries
summary socioeconomic data from 1960s,
annual rpt, 9904–4.7

AID economic aid to developing countries,
obligations and disbursements by country,
quarterly rpt, 9912–4

AID loans repayment status and terms by
program and country, and status of
predecessor agency loans, quarterly rpt,
9912–3

Economic and military aid and loans from
US and intl agencies, by program and
country, FY46-87, annual rpt, 9914–5

Economic conditions, income, production,
prices, employment, and trade, 1988
periodic country rpt, 2046–4.2

Economic conditions, policy, and trade
practices, by country, 1986-88, annual rpt,
21384–5

Economic, social, political, and geographic
summary data, by country, 1989, annual
factbook, 9114–2

Housing and households detailed characteristics, and unit and neighborhood quality, by location, 1985, biennial rpt, 2485-12

Housing and households detailed characteristics, and unit and neighborhood quality, MSA surveys, series, 2485-6

Housing units completed, single and multifamily units by structural and financial characteristics, inside-outside MSAs, and region, 1984-88, annual rpt, 2384-1

Occupational injury and illness rates, by SIC 2- to 4-digit industry, 1987, annual rpt, 6844-1

Service industries census, 1987: establishments, receipts, employment, and payroll, by SIC 2- to 4-digit kind of business, MSA, county, and city, State rpt series, 2391-1

Service industries receipts, by SIC 2- to 4-digit kind of business, 1988, annual rpt, 2413-8

Suburban areas land use, commuting, employment, and housing characteristics, detailed data for traffic planning, 1986, 7888-75

Tax (income) returns of partnerships, income statement items by industry group, 1986, annual article, 8302-2.903

Tax (income) returns of sole proprietorships, income statement items, by industry group, 1987, annual article, 8302-2.904; 8302-2.921

Urban areas traffic volume and detailed trip characteristics, by transport mode and city, 1950s-88, 7888-37

Parks

Acreage of land under Natl Park Service mgmt, by site, ownership, and region, 1989 semiannual rpt, 5542-1

Govt employment and payroll, by function, level of govt, and jurisdiction, 1987-88, annual rpt series, 2466-1

Service industries receipts, by SIC 2- to 4-digit kind of business, 1988, annual rpt, 2413-8

Statistical Abstract of US, social, political, and economic data, 1790-2025, comprehensive annual compilation, 2324-1.1

see also National parks

see also State parks

see also U.S. Park Police

Parks, Roger B.

"Metropolitan Organization: The St. Louis Case", 10046-9.1

Parks, William, II

"Labor Market Completes Sixth Year of Expansion in 1988", 6722-1.907

"Occupational Change: Pursuing a Different Kind of Work", 6722-1.943

Parlett, Ralph L.

"1989 Outlook for Food Prices", 1004-16.1

Parochial schools

see Private schools

Parole and probation

Crime, criminal justice admin and enforcement, and public opinion, data compilation, 1970s-88, annual rpt, 6064-6

Drug enforcement regional task forces investigation of organized crime, activities by agency and region, and background data, FY83-88, annual rpt, 6004-17

Employment of parole and probation officers, and entry salaries and requirements, by State and for Federal system, 1976-87, annual rpt, 6064-6.1

Employment, payroll, and spending for criminal justice, by level of govt, State, and selected city and county, FY71-85, annual rpt, 6064-9

Fed Probation System admissions, discharges, and caseloads, by type of supervision, June 1989, annual rpt, 18204-2; 18204-8.3; 18204-8.11; 18204-8.15

Fed Probation System caseload, by circuit and district, quarterly rpt, annual tables, 18202-1

Federal correctional instn parole and mandatory releases, and recidivism, by facility type and region, monthly rpt series, 6242-1

Federal district court criminal case processing and dispositions, by offense, district, and offender characteristics, 1984, annual rpt, 6064-29

Felony arrests by offender characteristics, prosecutions, convictions, and sentences by type, by offense, 1983-86, 6066-19.52

Juvenile court delinquency cases, by offense, referral source, disposition, age, sex, race, State, and county, 1985, annual rpt, 6064-12

Juvenile court referrals by offender characteristics, and dispositions, by offense, 1984, 6066-27.2

Parole and probation population, entries, and exits, by State, 1987, annual rpt, 6066-25.17

Prison conditions, population, and problems, issues and bibl, 1989 compilation of papers, 25928-8

Prisoners, movements, and characteristics, by State, 1986, annual rpt, 6064-26

Sentences for Federal crimes, guidelines use and results by offense and district, and Sentencing Commission activities, 1988, annual rpt, 17664-1

Sentences for Federal offenses, guidelines by offense and circumstances, 1989 rpt, 17668-1

State court sentences for felony offenses, and sentence lengths and time served, by offense, 1986, 6066-25.19

State probation and parole agencies problems and needs, 1986, 6066-26.4

Statistical Abstract of US, social, political, and economic data, 1790-2025, comprehensive annual compilation, 2324-1.1

US attorneys civil and criminal cases by type and disposition, and collections, by Federal district, FY88, annual rpt, 6004-2.1

Part-time employment

AFDC recipients demographic and financial characteristics, by State, FY87, annual rpt, 4694-1

Air traffic control system safety, working conditions, and traffic volume, various periods 1981-88, GAO rpt series, 26113-220

Child care arrangements and costs, by income and other characteristics of family, 1984-86, press release, 2328-61

Child care leave of absence for employees, policies, coverage, and attitudes, by employee characteristics, 1980-87, hearings, 25548-95

Child support and alimony awards, and payment status, by selected characteristics of woman, 1985, biennial Current Population Rpt, 2546-2.145

Consumer Income, socioeconomic characteristics of persons, families, and households, detailed cross-tabulations, Current Population Rpt series, 2546-6

Credit unions federally insured, finances by instn characteristics and State, as of June 1989, semiannual rpt, 9532-6

DOD civilian employment, by service branch and defense agency, with summary military employment data, quarterly rpt, 3542-16

DOT employment, by subagency, occupation, and selected personnel characteristics, FY88, annual rpt, 7304-18

Economic indicators and components, current data and annual trends, monthly rpt, 23842-1.2

Employment and Earnings, detailed data, monthly rpt, 6742-2

Employment, earnings, and hours, monthly press release, 6742-5

Employment situation, earnings, hours, and other BLS economic indicators, transcripts of BLS Commissioner's monthly testimony, periodic rpt, 23846-4

Employment, unemployment, and labor force characteristics, by region and State, 1988, annual rpt, 6744-7.1; 6744-7.2

Farm finances and operations, by size, commodity, and region, 1986, annual rpt, 1544-27

Fed Govt civilian employee work-years, pay rates, and benefits use and costs, by agency, FY87, annual rpt, 9844-31

Fed Govt civilian employees demographic and employment characteristics, as of Sept 1988, article, 9842-1.901

Fed Govt civilian employment and payroll, by agency in DC metro area, total US, and abroad, bimonthly rpt, 9842-1

Fed Govt civilian employment, by work schedule, selected agency, State, and MSA, as of Dec 1988, article, 9842-1.904

Federal district court magistrate full- and part-time positions, 1989, annual rpt, 18204-2.7; 18204-8.7

Govt employment and payroll, by function, level of govt, and jurisdiction, 1987-88, annual rpt series, 2466-1

Handbook of Labor Statistics, employment, unemployment, and labor force characteristics, 1940s-88 with trends from 1913, 6728-38.1; 6728-38.2

Health care (family) teaching faculty dev programs, Federal funding and trainees, by faculty status and region, 1978-87, 4118-63

High school class of 1988: college enrollment, and labor force participation of grads and dropouts, by race and sex, press release, 6726-1.22

Hospital reimbursement by Medicare under prospective payment system, and physician reimbursement, effect on services, finances, and beneficiary payments, 1970s-88, annual rpt, 17204-2

Hospitals, use, staff, and funding sources, by instn characteristics, for rural areas, 1980s-86, hearing, 25148-42

Household and family characteristics, by living arrangement, 1988 and trends from 1960, Current Population Rpt, 2546–2.148

Household composition, income, benefits, and labor force status, Survey of Income and Program Participation methodology, working paper series, 2626–10

Income (household) and poverty status under alternative income definitions, by recipient characteristics, 1986, Current Population Rpt, 2546–6.58

Insurance (health) coverage of total and working population, by selected characteristics, 1987, 4186–8.1

Insurance (health) coverage, uninsured persons employment and income characteristics, hospital charges, and care expenses, 1977-85, GAO rpt, 26121–274

Labor force entrants, by age, sex, race, part-time status, and detailed occupation, Jan 1987, article, 6742–1.902

Labor force, participation rates and unemployed persons by age and sex, and part-time employment, *Business Conditions Digest*, monthly rpt, 2702–3.7

Married couple earnings, by employment status, occupation, age, and education of spouses, and age of children, 1987, Current Population Rpt, 2546–6.61

Married couple families with both spouses working, effects on consumer spending by category, and income, by household characteristics, 1984-86, article, 6722–1.908

Maternity leave arrangements and work history of 1st-time mothers, by selected characteristics, 1960s-85, 2328–62

Mental health care hospitals, beds and caseload by State, patient characteristics, finances, and staff, for profit and nonprofit private instns, 1986, 4506–3.37

Military care health personnel, by full- and part-time status, occupation, and service branch, FY87, annual rpt, 3544–24.7

Military reserve personnel social, economic, family, and service characteristics, and attitudes, by reserve component, 1986 survey, 3508–29

Military reserve spouses attitudes, and family social, economic, and other characteristics, 1986 survey, 3508–30

Monthly Labor Review, current statistics and articles, 6722–1

NASA staff characteristics and personnel actions, FY88, annual rpt, 9504–1

Natl income and product accounts and components, *Survey of Current Business*, monthly rpt, 2702–1.27

Nursing home facility, staff, and resident detailed characteristics, 1985, 4147–13.97

Older persons community services employment funding, by recipient, 1989-90, press release, 6406–2.26

Older persons employment, earnings, reasons for working, and job training preferences, by selected characteristics, 1960-87, 6306–2.3

Older persons socioeconomic characteristics, 1900s-86 and projected to 2050, biennial chartbook, 12904–1

Pension and health insurance coverage for full- and part-time workers, 1985, article, 6722–1.913

Pension coverage, by plan type and worker characteristics, 1970s-88, article, 4742–1.925; 4746–26.7

Police agencies employment, spending, and operations, FY87, 6066–25.20

Poverty status of families and persons, by detailed characteristics, 1987, annual Current Population Rpt, 2546–6.60

State and local govt employment of minorities and women, by occupation, function, pay level, and State, 1986, annual rpt, 9244–6

Statistical Abstract of US, social, political, and economic data, 1790-2025, comprehensive annual compilation, 2324–1.3

Unemployed displaced workers, labor-mgmt committee aid recipients by selected characteristics, for 4 State programs, 1988, GAO rpt, 26121–316

VA employment characteristics and activities, FY88, annual rpt, 8604–3.8

VA health care facilities physicians, dentists, and nurses, by selected employment characteristics and VA district, quarterly rpt, 8602–6

Wage differentials between service and manufacturing sectors related to worker characteristics, 1987, article, 9377–1.901

Wages of full- and part-time workers, by selected characteristics, quarterly press release, 6742–20

see also Moonlighting

see also Temporary and seasonal employment

see also Underemployment

Particleboard

see Lumber industry and products

Particulates

see Air pollution

Partnerships

Agriculture census, 1987: farms, farmland, production, finances, and operator characteristics, by county, final State rpt series, 2331–1

Farm finances and operations, by size, commodity, and region, 1986, annual rpt, 1544–27

Guam economic censuses, 1987: employment, firms, payroll, and receipts, by SIC 1- to 4-digit industry and election district, 2595–1

Historic buildings rehabilitation tax incentives, projects, costs, ownership, use, and tax reform impacts, FY77-88, annual rpt, 5544–17

Limited partnerships (publicly traded), gross proceeds from offerings by industry, and securities registrations, monthly rpt, 9732–1.1

Master limited partnership finances, firms, partners, and tax reform impacts, by industry, 1986, technical paper, 8006–3.59

Natl income and product accounts and components, *Survey of Current Business*, monthly rpt, 2702–1.22

Northern Mariana Islands economic census, 1987: employment, firms, payroll, and receipts, by SIC 1- to 4-digit industry, 2597–1

Retail trade census, 1987: employment, establishments, sales, and payroll, by SIC 2- to 4-digit kind of business, MSA, county, and city, State rpt series, 2397–1

Retail trade sales, inventories, purchases, gross margin, and accounts receivable, by SIC 2- to 4-digit kind of business and form of ownership, 1987, annual rpt, 2413–5

Service industries census, 1987: establishments, receipts, employment, and payroll, by SIC 2- to 4-digit kind of business, MSA, county, and city, State rpt series, 2391–1

Small business finances, operations, owner and employee characteristics, and Federal contracts, 1980s-88, annual rpt, 9764–6

Small Business Investment Companies capital holdings, SBA obligation, and ownership, as of June 1989, semiannual listing, 9762–4

Small Business Investment Companies finances, funding, licensing, and loan activity, 1st half FY89, semiannual rpt, 9762–3

Statistical Abstract of US, social, political, and economic data, 1790-2025, comprehensive annual compilation, 2324–1.3

Stockbrokers finances, firms by type of organization and State, and SEC applications and registrations, 1983-88, annual rpt, 9734–2.1

Tax (income) collection, enforcement, and litigation activity of IRS, with data by type of tax, region, and State, FY88, annual rpt, 8304–3

Tax (income) returns and supplemental documents filed, by type, FY88 and projected to FY97, semiannual rpt, 8302–4

Tax (income) returns filed by type of filer, selected income items, quarterly rpt, 8302–2.1

Tax (income) returns filed, by type of return and IRS region and service center, projected 1988-95 and trends from 1977, annual rpt, 8304–9

Tax (income) returns of individuals, detailed data, 1986, annual rpt, 8304–2

Tax (income) returns of partnerships, income statement items by industry group, annual rpt, suspended, 8304–18

Tax (income) returns of partnerships, income statement items by industry group, 1986, annual article, 8302–2.903

Tax (income) withholding and related documents filed, by type and IRS service center, 1988 and projected 1989-96, annual rpt, 8304–22

Tax returns and supplemental documents filed, by type, FY88 and projected to FY97, semiannual rpt, 8302–2.916

Virgin Islands economic censuses, 1987: employment, firms, payroll, and receipts, by SIC 1- to 4-digit industry, island, and city, 2593–1

see also Joint ventures

Partyka, Susan C.

"Effect of Child Occupant Protection Laws on Fatalities", 7768–108

"Lives Saved by Child Restraints from 1982 Through 1987", 7768–104

"Lives Saved by Seat Belts from 1983 Through 1987", 7768–102

"Papers on Adult Seat Belts: Effectiveness and Use", 7766–14.1

"Papers on Car Size—Safety and Trends", 7766–14.4

"Papers on Vehicle Size: Cars and Trucks",
7766–14.3

"Papers on Victim Age: Pedestrians and
Occupants", 7766–14.2

Pasadena, Calif.
see also under By City in the "Index by
Categories"

Pasadena, Tex.
see also under By City in the "Index by
Categories"

Pascagoula, Miss.
Wages by occupation, and benefits for office
and plant workers, 1989 survey, periodic
MSA rpt, 6785–3.10
see also under By SMSA or MSA in the
"Index by Categories"

Pascal, Anthony
"State Policies and the Financing of
Acquired Immunodeficiency Syndrome
Care", 4652–1.953

Pasco, Wash.
see also under By SMSA or MSA in the
"Index by Categories"

Passaic, N.J.
Wages by occupation, for office and plant
workers, 1988 survey, periodic MSA rpt,
6785–11.1
see also under By SMSA or MSA in the
"Index by Categories"

Passenger ships
Canada travel to US by Province of
residence, and characteristics of visit, by
State, 1988, annual rpt, 2904–7

Caribbean area sugar production and
exports, and cruise ship tourist visits and
spending, by country, 1981-88, hearing,
21788–179

Competition in Exclusive Economic Zone
between foreign and US flag ships,
impacts of extending cabotage laws, with
background data, 1970s-80s, 26358–206

Construction and operating subsidies of
MarAd by firm, and ship deliveries and
fleet by country, by vessel type, FY88,
annual rpt, 7704–14.1; 7704–14.2

Cuba economic conditions, agricultural and
industrial production and distribution,
trade, and intl economic relations,
1980-87 with trends from 1961, 9118–8

Finances, operations, vehicles, equipment,
accidents, and energy use, by mode of
transport, 1955-88, annual rpt, 7304–2

Foreign-flag ships owned by US firms and
foreign affiliates, by type, owner, and
country of registry and construction, as of
July 1989, semiannual rpt, 7702–3

Foreign travel to US, by characteristics of
visit and traveler, country, port city, and
State of destination, monthly rpt, 2902–1

St Lawrence Seaway ship, cargo, and
passenger traffic, and toll revenue, 1988
and trends from 1959, annual rpt,
7744–2

Traffic, freight by commodity, and
passengers, domestic and foreign
waterborne commerce by port and
waterway, 1987, annual rpt, 3754–3

Wartime capability of commercial ships,
shipyards, and personnel, for merchant
and reserve fleet, 1988-2000, 11208–1

Passmore, S. Wayne
"Eleventh District Cost of Funds Index:
Description, Forecasting, and Pricing of
Index-Based Mortgages", 9306–1.10

Passport Office
see Bureau of Consular Affairs, State
Department

Passports and visas
Applicant screening for passports and visas,
State Dept info system records by reason
for exclusion, 1989, GAO rpt, 26125–36

Applications for passports handled by
Federal district courts, by circuit and
district, June 1988 and trends from 1970s,
annual rpt, 18204–8.11; 18204–8.24

Criminal cases by type and disposition, and
collections, for US attorneys, by Federal
district, FY88, annual rpt, 6004–2.1

Criminal sentences for Federal offenses,
guidelines by offense and circumstances,
1989 rpt, 17668–1

Developing countries disaster preparedness
and economic, population, and political
data, country rpt series, 9916–2

Family preference visas issued, and
admissions to US for relatives of US natls
and other immigrants, FY49-88 and
alternative projections to FY99, GAO rpt,
26131–59

Foreign travel to US, by characteristics of
visit and traveler, country, port city, and
State of destination, monthly rpt, 2902–1

Immigration reform affecting persons with
needed labor skills and persons otherwise
excluded, effect on admissions, visas, and
waiting periods, 1990-99, GAO rpt,
26131–64

Passports issued, *Survey of Current Business*,
monthly rpt, 2702–1.8

Statistical Abstract of US, social, political,
and economic data, 1790-2025,
comprehensive annual compilation,
2324–1.1

Visas of US issued and refused to
immigrants and nonimmigrants, by class,
issuing office, and nationality, FY88,
annual rpt, 7184–1

Visas of US issued at Foreign Service posts,
by category and world area, selected years
FY84-88, annual rpt, 7184–4

Pasture and rangeland
Acreage, erosion, and value of grazing land,
and livestock fed, by region and State,
1950-82, 1588–130

Acreage of farmland, finances, and
operations of farms, by size, commodity,
and region, 1985, annual rpt, 1544–27

Africa (Sahel) food supply indicators, by
country, 1960s-2000, 1528–290

Agricultural Statistics, 1988, annual rpt,
1004–1

Agriculture census, 1987: farms, farmland,
production, finances, and operator
characteristics, by county, final State rpt
series, 2331–1

Conservation and conditions of soil, water,
and environment, with data by State and
region, 1989 quinquennial rpt, 1268–24

Conservation program of USDA,
participation and payments by practice
and State, FY87, annual rpt, 1804–7

Eastern Europe and USSR agricultural
production, acreage, and consumption, by
commodity and country, 1965-85,
1528–284

Economic Indicators of the Farm Sector,
itemized production costs, receipts, and
returns, by commodity and region,
1985-87, annual rpt, 1544–20

Environmental quality and protection
programs, and intl issues, 1988 annual rpt,
484–1

Farm prices received for major products and
paid for farm inputs and living items, by
commodity and State, monthly rpt,
1629–1

Farm production itemized costs, by farm
sales size and region, 1988, annual rpt,
1614–3

Fires effects on forage nutrient
concentration, for Idaho aspen forests, by
species, 1982-83, 1208–309

FmHA activities, and loans and grants by
program and State, FY88 and trends from
FY69, annual rpt, 1184–17

FmHA borrowers, by type of borrower and
loan, and State, quarterly rpt, 1182–4

Foreign ownership of US farmland, holdings,
acquisitions, and disposals by land use,
owner type and country, and State, 1988,
annual rpt, 1584–2

Foreign ownership of US farmland, holdings,
acreage, and value by land use, owner
country, State, and county, 1988, annual
rpt, 1584–3

Forests (pinion-juniper) forage improvement
practices effectiveness, for Utah, 1955-85,
1208–307

Great Plains rangeland acreage, soil erosion,
and other impacts of Conservation
Reserve program, 1987 conf papers,
1208–290

Natl forests livestock grazing, acreage, use,
fees, and rancher costs and returns, by
region under alternative fee levels,
1980s-86, 1588–145

Natl forests livestock grazing, by region and
State, FY88, annual rpt, 1204–5

Natl forests revenue, by source, forest, and
State, FY88, annual rpt, 1204–34

Private land grazing fees, by western State,
1987, annual rpt, 1629–5

Public lands acreage, grants, use, revenues,
and allocations, by State, FY88, annual
rpt, 5724–1.2

Public lands grazing and receipts, by animal
type and State, FY88, annual rpt,
1204–1.1

Public lands mgmt and resources dev,
environmental, economic, and social
impacts of alternative Forest Service
programs, projected to 2030, 1208–24

Rental of pasture, and cattle grazing rates,
by region and State, 1985-89, article,
1561–16.902

Research and education grants, USDA
competitive awards by program and
recipient, FY88, annual listing, 1764–1

Soil and water conservation funding by
USDA, by program and State, FY86,
annual rpt, 1264–12

Southwestern States farm credit conditions
and real estate values, Fed Reserve 11th
District, quarterly rpt, 9379–11

Statistical Abstract of US, social, political,
and economic data, 1790-2025,
comprehensive annual compilation,
2324–1.1

Western US activities of Reclamation Bur,
land and population served, and recreation
areas, by location, 1987, annual rpt,
5824–12.1

Wilderness Natl Preservation System mgmt
by Forest Service, regulation of

commercial and recreational activities, and ranger views, 1985-88, GAO rpt, 26113–436

Wildlife damage to crops, livestock, and property in Great Plains, and effectiveness of mgmt methods, 1988 conf, 1208–304

see also National grasslands

Patent and Trademark Office

Activities of PTO, applications, grants, fees, and litigation, FY69-88, annual rpt, 2244–1

Activities of PTO, patent applications and grants, and trademark registrations and renewals, 1790-1988, 2248–2

Budget appropriations and staff for Commerce Dept, by subagency, FY88-90, annual rpt, 2004–6

Budget of US Appendix, obligations, appropriations, and personnel, by program and agency, FY90, annual rpt, 104–3

Patents (US) granted to US and foreign applicants, by applicant and country, 1960s-88, annual rpt, 2244–3

Patents (US) granted to US and foreign applicants, by State and country, 1987-88, annual press release, 2244–2

Patents

Applications and grants of patents, and Patent and Trademark Office activities, 1790-1988, 2248–2

Applications, grants, fees, and litigation, for patents and trademarks, FY69-88, annual rpt, 2244–1

Biotechnology patent issues, and time lapse between application and issue, 1988, GAO rpt, 26113–406

Biotechnology patent issues, for plants and animals, 1989 rpt, 26356–5.5

County Business Patterns, 1987: employment, establishments, and payroll, by SIC 2- to 4-digit industry and county, annual State rpt series, 2326–8

Court civil and criminal caseloads for Federal district, appeals, and special courts, June 1989, annual rpt, 18204–2; 18204–8

Energy-related inventions supported by DOE, sales, jobs created, and inventor characteristics, 1980-86, 3308–91

Exports of goods, services, and investment, trade barriers, impacts, and US actions, by country, 1988, annual rpt, 444–2

Fed Govt employee incentive awards, costs, and benefits, by award type and agency, FY88, annual rpt, 9844–20

Grants of patents to US and foreign applicants, by applicant and country, 1960s-88, annual rpt, 2244–3

Grants of patents to US and foreign applicants, by country, 1970-87, annual rpt, 9624–23.3

Grants of patents to US and foreign applicants, by State and country, 1988, annual press release, 2244–2

Grants of patents to US and foreign applicants, 1970-87, annual chartbook, 9624–22

Lands (public) acreage, grants, use, revenues, and allocations, by State, FY88, annual rpt, 5724–1.2

Mines Bur rpts and patents, monthly listing, 5602–2

Mining claims on public lands, patents by type and State, and applications by disposition, 1978-87, GAO rpt, 26113–403

Overseas Business Reports: economic conditions, investment and export opportunities, and trade practices, country market research rpt series, 2046–6

Productivity growth indicators, and impacts of pollution abatement spending and other factors, for US and selected OECD countries, various periods 1948-86, article, 9389–1.911

Statistical Abstract of US, social, political, and economic data, 1790-2025, comprehensive annual compilation, 2324–1.3

see also Trademarks

Paterson, N.J.

see also under By City in the "Index by Categories"

Pathology

Aviation medicine research and test results, technical rpt series, 7506–10

Enrollment in science and engineering grad programs, by field, source of funds, and characteristics of student and instn, 1975-87, annual rpt, 9627–7

Medicare physicians services use, charges, and reimbursement, by service type, setting, and specialty, 1986, article, 4652–1.936

Military health care personnel, and accessions by training source, by occupation, specialty, and service branch, FY87, annual rpt, 3544–24

VA health care facilities physicians, dentists, and nurses, by selected employment characteristics and VA district, quarterly rpt, 8602–6

VA health care facilities physicians staffing, vacancies, and positions filled, by speciality, 1982-87, hearing, 25768–48

see also Diseases and disorders

see also Medical examinations and tests

Patton, Larry T.

"Rural Health Care Challenge", 25148–41

"Rural Homeless", 4186–9.1

Pauley, Gilbert B.

"Amphipods. Species Profiles: Life Histories and Environmental Requirements of Coastal Fishes and Invertebrates", 5506–8.99

"Sea-Run Cutthroat Trout. Species Profiles: Life Histories and Environmental Requirements of Coastal Fishes and Invertebrates (Pacific Northwest)", 5506–8.93

Pawtucket, R.I.

Housing and households characteristics, 1984 survey, MSA fact sheet, 2485–11.3

see also under By SMSA or MSA in the "Index by Categories"

Payment-in-kind program, USDA

see Agricultural production quotas and price supports

Payne, James R.

"Development of a Predictive Model for the Weathering of Oil in the Presence of Sea Ice", 2176–1.25

Payroll

Banks (Fed Reserve) and branch officers, staff, and salary, 1988, annual rpt, 9364–1.1

Banks in Fed Reserve System, expenses and operations itemized by service, office, and district, 1988, annual rpt, 9364–11

Coal production and freight costs, and competitive position in selected markets, for Australia and US, 1987-89, 2048–143

Construction industries census, 1987: establishments, employment, receipts, and expenditures, by SIC 4-digit industry and State, final industry rpt series, 2373–1

Construction industries census, 1987: financial and operating data, preliminary industry rpt series, 2371–1

Costs (hourly) of labor, by component, occupational group, union coverage, industry div, and region, 1989, annual rpt, 6744–21

County Business Patterns, 1987: employment, establishments, and payroll, by SIC 2- to 4-digit industry and county, annual State rpt series, 2326–8

Credit unions federally insured, finances by instn characteristics and State, as of June 1989, semiannual rpt, 9532–6

Electric utilities privately owned, detailed finances and operations by firm, 1987, annual rpt, 3164–23.1

Fed Reserve System, Board of Governors, and district banks financial statements, performance, and fiscal services, 1987-89, annual rpt, 9364–10

Financial instns financial and operating statements by deposit size, Fed Reserve functional cost analysis, 1988, annual rpt, 9364–6

Foreign and US manufacturing hourly compensation costs, by industry and country, series, 6826–3

Foreign and US manufacturing labor costs and indexes, by selected country, 1975-88, annual rpt, 6824–3

Foreign and US manufacturing labor costs and indexes, by selected country, 1975-88, semiannual rpt, 6822–3

Foreign travelers spending in US by world area of residence, and economic impact, by spending category, census div, and State, model results, 1985-86, 2908–28

Guam economic censuses, 1987: employment, firms, payroll, and receipts, by SIC 1- to 4-digit industry and election district, 2595–1

Health Care Financing Review, provider prices, price inputs and indexes, and labor, quarterly journal, 4652–1.1

Hospital reimbursement by States under prospective payment programs, effects on operations, finances, and patient deaths, by State, 1970s-83, 4658–29

Manufacturing census, 1987: financial and operating data, for SIC 4-digit industries by product, preliminary industry rpt series, 2491–1

Mental health care hospitals, beds and caseload by State, patient characteristics, finances, and staff, for profit and nonprofit private instns, 1986, 4506–3.37

Mineral industries census, 1987: financial and operating data, preliminary industry rpt series, 2511–1

Multinatl firms US affiliates finances and operations, by industry div, country of parent firm, and State, 1986-87, annual article, 2702–1.925

Multinatl firms US affiliates, finances, and operations, by industry, world area of parent firm, and State, 1987, annual rpt, 2704–4

Multinatl US firms and foreign affiliates finances and operations, by industry of parent firm and affiliate, world area, and selected country, 1987, annual article, 2702–1.920; 2704–5

Natl income and product accounts and components, *Survey of Current Business*, monthly rpt, 2702-1.27

Natural gas interstate pipeline company detailed financial and operating data, by firm, 1988, annual rpt, 3164-38

Nonprofit charitable organizations finances, and assets and grants of top 10, 1985, article, 8302-2.923

Northern Mariana Islands economic census, 1987: employment, firms, payroll, and receipts, by SIC 1- to 4-digit industry, 2597-1

Pollution abatement labor costs, by SIC 2- to 4-digit industry and State, 1986, annual Current Industrial Rpt, 2506-3.6

Railroad (Class I) finances and operations, detailed data by firm, class of service, and district, 1987, annual rpt, 9486-6.1

Railroad (Class I) finances and operations, detailed data by firm, class of service, and district, 1988, annual rpt, 9486-5.1

Retail trade census, 1987: employment, establishments, sales, and payroll, by SIC 2- to 4-digit kind of business, MSA, county, and city, State rpt series, 2397-1

Savings instns financial statements, FSLIC-insured instns by FHLB district and State, and FDIC-insured savings banks, 1988, annual rpt, 8434-1

Service industries census, 1987: establishments, receipts, employment, and payroll, by SIC 2- to 4-digit kind of business, MSA, county, and city, State rpt series, 2391-1

Southeastern States, Fed Reserve 5th District insured commercial banks financial statements, by State, quarterly rpt, 9389-18

Statistical Abstract of US, social, political, and economic data, 1790-2025, comprehensive annual compilation, 2324-1.3

Steel imports of US under voluntary restraint agreement, by product, customs district, and country, with US industry operating data, monthly rpt, 9882-13

Steel industry finances and operations by product, and modernization efforts, as of June 1989, last issue of annual rpt, 9884-16

Tax (income) returns filed by type of filer, selected income items, quarterly rpt, 8302-2.1

Tax (income) returns of partnerships, income statement items by industry group, 1986, annual article, 8302-2.903

Tax (income) returns of sole proprietorships, income statement items, by industry group, 1987, annual article, 8302-2.904; 8302-2.921

Telephone and telegraph firms detailed finances and operations, 1987, annual rpt, 9284-6

Transportation employment, wages, and average annual earnings, by mode of transport, 1977-87, annual rpt, 7304-2.2

Truck and bus interstate carriers finances and operations, by district, 1987, annual rpt, 9486-6.3

Truck and warehouse services finances and inventory, by SIC 2- to 4-digit industry, 1988 survey, annual rpt, 2413-14

Truck interstate carriers finances and operations, by district, 1987, annual rpt, 9486-6.2

Virgin Islands economic censuses, 1987: employment, firms, payroll, and receipts, by SIC 1- to 4-digit industry, island, and city, 2593-1

Wholesale trade census, 1987: employment, establishments, finances, and operations, by SIC 2- to 4-digit kind of business, MSA, county, and city, State rpt series, 2405-1

see also Agricultural wages

see also Earnings, general

see also Earnings, specific industry

see also Educational employees pay

see also Federal pay

see also Military pay

see also Social security tax

see also State and local employees pay

see also Unemployment insurance tax

see also Wage deductions

Payroll tax

see Social security tax

see Unemployment insurance tax

PCBs

see Carcinogens

see Hazardous substances

see Hazardous waste and disposal

Peace Corps

Activities of PC, funding, and volunteers characteristics, FY62-88, GAO rpt, 26123-243

Activities of PC, funding by program, and volunteers, by country, FY90, annual rpt, 9654-1

Budget of US, authoritative financial statements with appropriations, outlays, and receipts, by category and agency, FY88, annual rpt, 8104-2.2

Economic and military aid of US, by country and program, FY86-88, annual rpt, 9904-1.4

Expenditures for economic and military aid, by program and country, FY46-87, annual rpt, 9914-5

Labor unions recognized in Fed Govt, agreements and membership by agency and facility, as of Jan 1989, biennial listing, 9844-14

Pacific territories social, economic, health, and govtl data, FY88 and trends, annual rpt, 7004-6

Participation by world area, and funding, for Fed Govt exchange and training programs, FY87, annual rpt, 9854-8

Peace Institute

see U.S. Institute of Peace

Peacekeeping forces

see International military forces

Peaches

see Fruit and fruit products

Peanuts

Acreage under Agricultural Stabilization and Conservation Service programs, rankings by commodity and congressional district, 1987, biennial rpt, 1804-17

Agriculture census, 1987: farms, farmland, production, finances, and operator characteristics, by county, final State rpt series, 2331-1

Exports and imports (agricultural) of US, by detailed commodity and country, 1988, semiannual rpt, 1522-4

Farm income, expenses, receipts by commodity, assets, liabilities, and ratios, 1988 and trends from 1945, annual rpt, 1544-16

Farm receipts for 25 leading crops, by State, 1960-87, 1548-347

Foreign and US oils, oilseeds, and fats production and trade, FAS periodic circular series, 1925-1

Manufacturing census, 1987: financial and operating data, for SIC 4-digit industries by product, preliminary rpt, 2491-1.6; 2491-1.9

Price indexes (producer), by stage of processing and detailed commodity, monthly 1988, annual rpt, 6764-2

Price support activity and policy options, with data on production, trade, use, and finances, and foreign comparisons, 1950s-89, commodity rpt, 1566-7.8

Prices received by farmers and production value, by detailed crop and State, 1986-88, annual rpt, 1621-2

Production and trade by country, prices, and stocks, of peanuts, weekly rpt, 1311-1

Production itemized costs, receipts, and returns, by selected commodity and region, 1975-87, 1548-345

Stocks, millings, and use, by peanut grade and type, monthly rpt, 1621-6

see also under By Commodity in the "Index by Categories"

Pearce, James E.

"Florida Thrifts Face a Changing Business Environment", 9302-2.905

"Incidence of Sanctions Against U.S. Employers of Illegal Aliens", 9379-12.33

Pearrow, Joan

"California Iceberg Lettuce: Prices and Spreads, 1980-88", 1561-11.904

"Washington Red Delicious Apples: Fresh Market Prices and Spreads, 1980/81-88/89", 1561-6.903

Pearson, Donald E.

"Survey of Fishes and Water Properties of South San Francisco Bay, California, 1973-82", 2168-113

Peas

see Vegetables and vegetable products

Peat

see Fertilizers

see Nonmetallic minerals and mines

Peat, Marwick, Mitchell & Co.

"Report to the American Retail Federation on Costs to Retailers of Sales and Use Tax Compliance", 21528-73

Pedersen, John R.

"Poultry Industry Outlook", 1004-16.1

Pedestrians

Accident deaths and rates, by cause, age, race, sex, and State, 1986, US Vital Statistics annual rpt, 4144-2

Accident deaths involving alcohol, by driver and victim blood alcohol levels, and other characteristics, 1977-87, annual rpt, 4486-1.2; 4486-1.5; 4486-1.8

Accidents (fatal), circumstances, and characteristics of persons and vehicles involved, 1988, semiannual rpt, 7762-11

Accidents (fatal), deaths, and rates, by circumstances, characteristics of persons and vehicles involved, and location, 1987, annual rpt, 7764-10

Accidents and deaths, by mode of transport, 1977-88, annual rpt, 7304-2

Accidents at hwy-railroad grade crossings, detailed data by State and railroad, 1988, annual rpt, 7604-2

Accidents, injuries, and deaths, by circumstances and characteristics of persons and vehicles involved, 1970s-87, series, 7766-14

Deaths from traffic accidents, for pedestrians by circumstances and characteristics of victim, injury, and vehicle, 1985-86 local area study, article, 4042-3.927

Suburban areas land use, commuting, employment, and housing characteristics, detailed data for traffic planning, 1986, 7888-75

Traffic volume in urban areas and detailed trip characteristics, by transport mode and city, 1950s-88, 7888-37

Pediatrics

Drug prescriptions dispensed in hospitals, by type and patient category, 1987, annual rpt, 4064-12.3

Drugs (controlled) provided during physician office visits, by drug, patient, and provider characteristics, 1985, 4146-8.179

France and Germany physicians, and visits by reason and patient age and sex, by specialty, compared to US, 1981-83, 4147-5.5

Health condition and health care resources, use, and spending, 1950s-87, annual data compilation, 4144-11

Indian Health Service and contract facilities hospitalization, by diagnosis, age, sex, and service area, FY87, annual rpt, 4104-16

Indian Health Service and contract facilities hospitalization, by diagnosis, age, sex, and service area, FY88, annual rpt, 4084-5

Indian Health Service outpatient visits, by reason for visit and age, FY87-88, annual rpt, 4084-2

Indian Health Service outpatient visits, by type of provider, selected hospital, and IHS service area, FY87-88, annual rpt, 4084-3

Insurance (health) companies case mgmt for high-cost patients, savings, costs, and returns, 1984-86, article, 4652-1.914

Medicare discharges, charges, and length of stay, for facilities excluded from prospective payment system, FY84-88, article, 4652-1.935

Military health care personnel, and accessions by training source, by occupation, specialty, and service branch, FY87, annual rpt, 3544-24

Physicians income, by specialty and other practice characteristics, 1975 and 1983-84, article, 4652-1.920

VA health care facilities physicians, dentists, and nurses, by selected employment characteristics and VA district, quarterly rpt, 8602-6

Pell grants

see Student aid

Penalties

see Judgments, civil procedure

see Sentences, criminal procedure

Pendlum, David W.

"Desk Reference Guide to U.S. Agricultural Trade", 1924-9

Pendlum, Stanley E.

"Oilseeds Outlook, Industry Reaction", 1004-16.1

Penn, J. B.

"Future Significance of the 1988 Drought: Impact on U.S. Policies and Programs", 1004-16.1

Pennipede, Sandra

"Bank Holding Company Performance", 9381-14.1

Pennsylvania

Agriculture census, 1987: farms, farmland, production and costs, and operator characteristics, advance State and county rpts, 2330-1.42

Agriculture census, 1987: farms, farmland, production, finances, and operator characteristics, by county, final State rpt, 2331-1.38

Appalachian Regional Commission funding, by project and State, planned FY89, annual rpt, 9084-3

Apple production, marketing, and prices, for Appalachia and compared to other States, various periods 1986-89, annual rpt, 1311-13

Bank deposits in FDIC-insured commercial and savings banks, by instn, State, and county, as of June 1988, annual regional rpt, 9295-3.1

Banks and thrifts market entry probability relation to market characteristics and competition, for rural areas, model description and results, 1980-84, working paper, 9377-9.76

Coal (Pennsylvania anthracite) production, use, and stocks, weekly rpt, 3162-1

Coal production and mines by county, prices, productivity, miners, reserves, and stocks, by mining method and State, 1987-88, annual rpt, 3164-25

County Business Patterns, 1987: employment, establishments, and payroll, by SIC 2- to 4-digit industry and county, annual State rpt, 2326-8.40

Dairy production, and prices for cows, milk, and feed, by selected State, 1988, annual rpt, 1317-1.1; 1317-1.6

Deaths and rates, by detailed location, cause, and demographic characteristics, 1987, US Vital Statistics annual rpt, 4144-3.1

DOD prime contract awards, by contractor, service branch, State, and city, FY88, annual rpt, 3544-22

Employment, earnings, and hours, by selected SIC 1- to 4-digit industry, State, and for 262 MSAs, 1972-87, 6748-81.4

Employment growth and unemployment rates, Fed Reserve 3rd District, quarterly rpt, 9387-10

Fed Govt spending in States and local areas, by type, State, county, and city, FY88, annual rpt, 2464-3

Fed Govt spending in States, by type, program, agency, and State, FY88, annual rpt, 2464-2

HHS financial aid, by program, recipient, State, and city, FY88, annual regional listing, 4004-3.3

Homeless children educational enrollment and needs, 1988, annual State rpt, 4804-35.38

Income (personal) per capita and by source, and earnings by industry div, by State, MSA, and county, 1982-87, annual regional rpt, 2704-2.2

Mineral Industry Surveys, State reviews of production, 1988, preliminary annual rpt, 5614-6

Minerals Yearbook, 1987, Vol 2 preprints: State review of production and sales by commodity, and business activity, annual rpt, 5604-16.39

Minerals Yearbook, 1987, Vol 2: State reviews of production, sales, and firms, by commodity, and business activity, annual rpt, 5604-34

Nursing home compliance with Medicare and Medicaid regulations, and patient characteristics, by facility, 1987/88, annual State rpt, 4654-15.39

Oil and gas extraction production workers and wages by occupation, and benefits, by location, 1988 survey, 6787-6.240

Railroad accidents, casualties, and damage, with data by carrier, for Pennsylvania and US, 1984-87, GAO rpt, 26113-390

Retail trade census, 1987: employment, establishments, sales, and payroll, by SIC 2- to 4-digit kind of business, MSA, county, and city, State rpt, 2397-1.39

Service industries census, 1987: employment, establishments, receipts, and payroll, by SIC 2- to 4-digit kind of business, MSA, county, and city, State rpt, 2391-1.39

Statistical Abstract of US, social, political, and economic data, with foreign comparisons, 1790-2025, comprehensive annual compilation, 2324-1

Uranium tailings at inactive mills, remedial action activities by site, and funding, FY88, annual rpt, 3354-9

Water quality effects of coal mining operations, sediment discharges effects of alternative mining and mgmt methods and reclamation, for Pennsylvania, 1980-83, 5668-93

Water supply and quality in streams and lakes, and groundwater levels in wells, by drainage basin, 1987, annual State rpt, 5666-10.37

Water supply and quality in streams and lakes, and groundwater levels in wells, by drainage basin, 1988, annual State rpt, 5666-16.37

Wholesale trade census, 1987: employment, establishments, finances, and operations, by SIC 2- to 4-digit kind of business, MSA, county, and city, State rpt, 2405-1.39

Wildlife-related recreation, hunting, and fishing participation and spending, detailed data, 1985 survey, quinquennial State rpt, 5506-6.38

see also Delaware County, Pa.

see also Montgomery County, Pa.

see also Philadelphia, Pa.

see also Pittsburgh, Pa.

see also Scranton, Pa.

see also Wilkes-Barre, Pa.

see also under By State in the "Index by Categories"

Pennsylvania Avenue Development Corp.

Budget of US Appendix, obligations, appropriations, and personnel, by program and agency, FY90, annual rpt, 104-3

Budget of US, authoritative financial statements with appropriations, outlays, and receipts, by category and agency, FY88, annual rpt, 8104-2.2

Pensacola, Fla.
see also under By SMSA or MSA in the "Index by Categories"

Pension Benefit Guaranty Corp.
Activities and finances of PBGC, FY88 and projected to FY98, annual rpt, 9674–1

Budget of US Appendix, obligations, appropriations, and personnel, by program and agency, FY90, annual rpt, 104–3

Finances and operations of programs under Ways and Means Committee jurisdiction, FY70s-88, annual rpt, 21784–11

Funding status of PBGC, impact of pension plan terminations, alternative projections 1986-96, article, 9385–1.903

Labor unions recognized in Fed Govt, agreements and membership by agency and facility, as of Jan 1989, biennial listing, 9844–14

Pensions and pension funds
Assets and debts of private sector, balance sheets by segment, 1949-88, semiannual rpt, 9365–4.1

Assets composition, growth, and distribution for financial instns, by instn type, 1970s-88, 8438–1

Assets of private and public pension funds, 1976-87, annual rpt, 9364–5.12

Bond (low-grade) issues by industry div, holdings by owner type, yields, and defaults, 1977-88, 21248–118

Consumer Expenditure Survey, spending by category, and income, by selected household characteristics and location, 1987, press release, 6726–1.23

Coverage and provisions of employee benefit plans, by plan type and occupational group, 1988, annual rpt, 6784–19

Coverage under pension and health insurance plans for full- and part-time workers, 1985, article, 6722–1.913

Coverage under pensions, by plan type and worker characteristics, 1970s-88, article, 4742–1.925; 4746–26.7

Disabled persons employment, labor force status, and other characteristics, 1988, Current Population Rpt, 2546–2.147

Employee Retirement Income Security Act (ERISA) admin and enforcement, 1987, annual rpt, 6304–4

Expenditures (private) for social welfare, by category, 1970s-87, annual article, 4742–1.928

Expenditures, coverage, and benefits for social welfare programs, late 1930s-87, annual rpt, 4744–3.1; 4744–3.3

Financial status of pension plans, impact of alternative accounting standards, 1978-87, technical paper, 9366–6.172

Flow-of-funds accounts, assets and liabilities by type and economic sector, outstanding at year-end 1965-88, annual rpt, 9364–3

Flow-of-funds accounts, savings, investments, and credit statements, quarterly rpt, 9365–3.3

Household composition, income, benefits, and labor force status, Survey of Income and Program Participation methodology, working paper series, 2626–10

Income (household) by source, and itemized spending, by selected characteristics and location, 1984-86 Consumer Expenditure Surveys, annual rpt, 6764–5.2

Income (household, family, and personal), by source, detailed characteristics, and region, 1987, annual Current Population Rpt, 2546–6.59

Income (personal) by source, and BEA and IRS adjusted gross income measures, 1984-86 with trends from 1947, article, 8302–2.914

Income (personal) by source, and BEA and IRS adjusted gross income measures, 1986-87, annual article, 2702–1.927

Income (personal) by source including transfer payments, and social insurance contributions, by region, 1948 and 1987, 2708–40

Labor hourly costs, by component, occupational group, union coverage, industry div, and region, 1989, annual rpt, 6744–21

Mortgage-backed securities investment by corporate and union pension funds and life insurance firms, by issuer, quarterly rpt, 5002–10

Mortgage loan activity, by type of lender, loan, and mortgaged property, monthly press release, 5142–18

Mortgage loan activity, by type of lender, loan, and mortgaged property, quarterly press release, 5142–30

Mortgage loan activity, by type of lender, loan, and mortgaged property, 1986-88, annual press release, 5144–22

OASI beneficiaries retiring before age 62, employment, income, and benefits, by selected characteristics, 1982, article, 4742–1.911

Older persons labor force participation, unemployment, displacement, and reemployment, by selected characteristics, 1969-88, 6306–2.2

Older persons socioeconomic characteristics, 1900s-86 and projected to 2050, biennial chartbook, 12904–1

Pension Benefit Guaranty Corp activities and finances, FY88 and projected to FY98, annual rpt, 9674–1

Poverty status of families and persons, by detailed characteristics, 1987, annual Current Population Rpt, 2546–6.60

Railroad (Amtrak) finances and operations, FY88, annual rpt, 29524–1

Railroad employee benefits and beneficiaries by type, and railroad employment and payroll, FY85, annual rpt, 9704–2

Railroad employee retirement, survivors, unemployment, and health insurance programs, monthly rpt, 9702–2

Railroad employment, and benefits program finances and beneficiaries, FY88, annual rpt, 9704–1

Railroad employment by occupation from 1957, and Railroad Retirement Account finances, alternative projections 1987-2010, GAO rpt, 26121–280

Regulation of pension plans, Labor Dept and IRS enforcement activity, violations, and penalties, FY85-88, GAO rpt, 26121–259

Soviet Union personal income by source, disposable income, wage deductions by type, and savings, 1950s-87, 9118–7

Statistical Abstract of US, social, political, and economic data, 1790-2025, comprehensive annual compilation, 2324–1.2; 2324–1.3

Tax (excise) collections of IRS, and returns examined, for employee plans, 1976-88, article, 8304–8.1

Tax (excise) collections of IRS, by source, quarterly rpt, 8302–1

Tax (income) returns filed by type of filer, selected income items, quarterly rpt, 8302–2.1

Tax (income) returns of individuals, detailed data, 1986, annual rpt, 8304–2

Tax (income) returns of individuals, selected income and tax items by income level, preliminary 1987, annual article, 8302–2.917

Tax (income) withholding and related documents filed, by type and IRS service center, 1988 and projected 1989-96, annual rpt, 8304–22

Tax Court of US caseloads and appeals by disposition, procedure duration, and recoveries, FY88, annual rpt, 18224–5

Tax expenditures from employee benefits, for income and payroll tax by benefit type, 1950-87 and projected to 2065, article, 9373–1.913

Telephone and telegraph firms detailed finances and operations, 1987, annual rpt, 9284–6.4; 9284–6.5

Telephone service of households, by composition, income sources, and other characteristics, 1984-87, 9288–11

Vestment and other provisions of pension plans by plan size, and compliance with Federal rules, 1984-85, GAO rpt, 26121–306

Women (older) pension coverage, sources, payments, and effect on income and poverty status, 1982, article, 4742–1.901

see also Area wage surveys
see also Civil service pensions
see also Disability benefits and insurance
see also Individual retirement arrangements
see also Military benefits and pensions
see also Old-Age, Survivors, Disability, and Health Insurance
see also Social security
see also Veterans benefits and pensions

People's Democratic Republic of Yemen
see Yemen, South

People's Republic of China
see China, Peoples Republic

Peoria, Ill.
Wages by occupation, for office and plant workers, 1989 survey, periodic MSA rpt, 6785–3.10

see also under By City and By SMSA or MSA in the "Index by Categories"

Per capita income
see Personal and household income

Percy, Stephen L.
"Disability Rights Mandates: Federal and State Compliance with Employment Protections and Architectural Barrier Removal", 10048–74

Pereira, Luiz C.
"Debtor's Approach to the Debt Crisis", 21248–122

Performing arts
Copyrights Register activities, registrations by material type, and fees, FY87 and trends from 1790, annual rpt, 26404–2

County Business Patterns, 1987: employment, establishments, and payroll, by SIC 2- to 4-digit industry and county, annual State rpt series, 2326–8

Natl Endowment for Arts activities and grants, FY88, annual rpt, 9564–3

Occupational injury and illness rates, by SIC 2- to 4-digit industry, 1987, annual rpt, 6844–1

Service industries census, 1987: establishments, receipts, employment, and payroll, by SIC 2- to 4-digit kind of business, MSA, county, and city, State rpt series, 2391–1

Service industries receipts, by SIC 2- to 4-digit kind of business, 1988, annual rpt, 2413–8

Statistical Abstract of US, social, political, and economic data, 1790-2025, comprehensive annual compilation, 2324–1.1

Tax (income) returns of sole proprietorships, income statement items, by industry group, 1987, annual article, 8302–2.904; 8302–2.921

see also Arts and the humanities

see also Dance

see also Motion pictures

see also Theater

Pergamit, Michael R.

"Earnings and Different Types of Training", 6886–6.34

"Regulation and Labor Earnings: Comment and Extension", 6886–6.33

"Wages in Regulated Industries", 6886–6.21

Periodicals

Cigarette ad and promotion costs by media, and market shares, by cigarette type, with sales and use, 1963-87, annual rpt, 9404–4

Cigarette ad revenues and articles on smoking and health of 14 magazines, 1960s-81, annual rpt, 4204–18

Construction trade periodicals and availability, 1989 listing, article, 2042–1.903

Copyrights Register activities, registrations by material type, and fees, FY87 and trends from 1790, annual rpt, 26404–2

County Business Patterns, 1987: employment, establishments, and payroll, by SIC 2- to 4-digit industry and county, annual State rpt series, 2326–8

Employment, earnings, and hours, by selected SIC 1- to 4-digit industry, State, and for 262 MSAs, 1972-87, 6748–81

Employment, earnings, and hours, by SIC 1- to 4-digit industry, monthly 1983-Feb 1989, annual rpt, 6744–4

Exports of US, detailed commodities by country, monthly rpt, 2422–3

Fed Govt ad spending, and subcontracts to small and disadvantaged firms, by agency and medium, FY86, GAO rpt, 26113–428

Foreign travel to US and Canada, market analyses with detailed trip and traveler characteristics, country rpt series, 2906–2

Foreign travel to US, market research, major magazine ad costs and circulation, and trade show data, for selected countries, 1989-90, annual rpt, 2904–11

Health care treatments and products not proven safe or effective, use, costs, and user characteristics, 1986 survey, 4008–86

Imports of US, detailed Schedule A commodities by country, monthly rpt, 2422–2

Libraries for blind and handicapped, readership, circulation, staff, funding, and holdings, FY88, annual listing, 26404–3

Library of Congress activities, acquisitions, services, and financial statements, FY88, annual rpt, 26404–1

Mail revenue and subsidy for revenue forgone, by class of mail, FY88, and volume from FY84, annual rpt, 9864–1

Manufacturers finances and operations, by SIC 2- to 4-digit industry, forecast 1989 and trends from 1950s, annual rpt, 2044–28

Manufacturing annual survey, 1986: financial and operating data, by SIC 2- to 4-digit industry, series, 2506–15

Manufacturing census, 1987: financial and operating data, for SIC 4-digit industries by product, preliminary rpt, 2491–1.30; 2491–1.31

Medicine Natl Library activities, holdings, and grants, FY86-88, annual rpt, 4464–1

Occupational injury and illness rates, by SIC 2- to 4-digit industry, 1987, annual rpt, 6844–1

Price indexes (producer), by stage of processing and detailed commodity, monthly rpt, 6762–6

Price indexes (producer), by stage of processing and detailed commodity, monthly 1988, annual rpt, 6764–2

Science, engineering, and technical employment in manufacturing, by field, occupation, and industry, 1986, triennial rpt, 9627–23

Senate receipts, itemized expenses by payee, and balances, 1st half FY89, semiannual listing, 25922–1

Statistical Abstract of US, social, political, and economic data, 1790-2025, comprehensive annual compilation, 2324–1.1; 2324–1.3

Tax (income) returns of corporations, income and tax items by asset size and detailed industry, 1986, annual rpt, 8304–4; 8304–21

USIA library holdings, use, and staff, by country and city, FY88, annual rpt, 9854–4

Wildlife-related recreation, hunting, and fishing participation and spending, detailed data by location, 1985 survey, quinquennial rpt, 5508–5

Wildlife-related recreation, hunting, and fishing participation and spending, detailed data, 1985 survey, quinquennial State rpt series, 5506–6

see also Newspapers

see also Research journals

Perlite

see Nonmetallic minerals and mines

Permits

see Building permits

see Drivers licenses

see Licenses and permits

see Occupational testing and certification

see Water permits

Perng, Shien

"Taxpayer Perceptions About the Quality of Taxpayer Service", 8304–8.1

Perquisites

see Employee benefits

see Employee bonuses and work incentives

Personal and household income

AFDC application denials and hearings decisions, by reason and State, FY87, annual rpt, 4694–7.3; 4694–7.4

AFDC recipients demographic and financial characteristics, by State, FY87, annual rpt, 4694–1

Alaska rural villages population characteristics and and subsistence activities, 1976-86, 5738–9

Alcohol use and abuse among minority groups, and related problems, by selected characteristics, 1985 conf papers, 4488–13

Alcoholic beverages warning labels and other consumer protection methods, public views by selected characteristics, 1988 survey, 8488–5

Alien nonresidents income from US sources and tax withheld by country and US tax treaty status, 1986, annual article, 8302–2.915

Asian American earnings, and employment and other characteristics, by detailed origin and whether foreign-born, 1980, 11046–7.2

Births, fertility rates, and childless women, by selected characteristics, 1988, annual Current Population Rpt, 2546–1.436

Black Americans household income, and expenses by type, by age and family composition, 1985, article, 1702–1.908

Business and financial statistics, historic trends, 1988 annual chartbook, 9364–2.4

Business Conditions Digest, economic, business, and financial devs and cyclical fluctuations, monthly rpt, 2702–3

Business statistics, detailed data for major industries and economic indicators, *Survey of Current Business*, monthly rpt, 2702–1

Child care arrangements and costs, by income and other characteristics of family, 1984-86, press release, 2328–61

Coastal areas environmental and socioeconomic conditions, and potential impact of oil and gas OCS leases, final statement series, 5736–1

Coastal States per capita personal income, by region and State, 1988, annual rpt, 7704–12.2

Consumer Expenditure Survey, household income by source, and itemized spending, by selected characteristics and region, 1984-87, annual rpt, 6764–5

Consumer food spending and consumption, housing, and other finances, 1960s-88, annual chartbook, 1504–3

Consumer Income, socioeconomic characteristics of persons, families, and households, detailed cross-tabulations, Current Population Rpt series, 2546–6

Consumer spending relation to income and earnings, alternative models description and results, various periods 1929-87, technical paper, 9366–6.171

Consumer spending relation to income, unemployment rate, and interest rate, various periods 1949-88, article, 9393–8.911

Developing countries aged population and selected characteristics, 1980s and projected to 2020, country rpt series, 2326–19

Developing countries aided by Peace Corps, quality of life indicators, FY90, annual rpt, 9654–1

Regional income and earnings per capita relative to US average, analysis of differential by census div, various periods 1969-87, article, 9373–1.909

Rent supplement programs evaluation, housing voucher demonstration compared to Section 8, series, 5186–14

Single-parent household income and spending, and selected characteristics, with comparison to households with married parents, 1984-86, article, 6722–1.916

Single-parent household income sources and spending by category, by sex, age, race, and household size, 1984-85, article, 1702–1.901

South Central States employment by industry div, and income, for 4 States, 1988 and forecast 1989, annual article, 9391–1.913

Southeastern States, Fed Reserve 5th District, economic indicators by State, quarterly rpt, 9389–16

Southeastern States, Fed Reserve 8th District banking and economic conditions, quarterly rpt with articles, 9391–16

Southeastern US economic and employment conditions, for 4 largest MSAs, 1977-87, article, 9391–16.902

Soviet Union personal income by source, disposable income, wage deductions by type, and savings, 1950s-87, 9118–7

St Louis metro area local govt finances, structure, and service delivery, mid-1980s, 10046–9.1

Statistical Abstract of US, social, political, and economic data, 1790-2025, comprehensive annual compilation, 2324–1.1; 2324–1.3

Student aid Pell grants and applicants, by tuition, income level, instn type and control, and State, 1987/88, annual rpt, 4804–1

Supplemental Security Income aged and disabled beneficiary characteristics, payments, and eligibility, for awards made 1981, 1985, article, 4742–1.907

Survey of Income and Program Participation, data collection, methodology, and availability, 1987 users guide, 2628–24

Survey of Income and Program Participation, data collection, methodology, and use, 1988 annual conf papers, 2624–1

Survey of Income and Program Participation, household composition, income, benefits, and labor force status, methodology, working paper series, 2626–10

Survey of Income and Program Participation, household income and socioeconomic characteristics, special study series, 2546–20

Tax (income) returns filed by type of filer, selected income items, quarterly rpt, 8302–2.1

Tax (income) returns of individuals, detailed data, 1986, annual rpt, 8304–2

Tax (income) returns of individuals, selected income and tax items by income level, preliminary 1987, annual article, 8302–2.917

Tax (income) returns of individuals, taxable income, and tax generated, by tax rate and income level, 1986, annual article, 8302–2.918

Telephone service of households, by composition, income sources, and other characteristics, 1984-87, 9288–11

Travel from US, characteristics of visit and traveler, and world area of destination, 1988 in-flight survey, annual rpt, 2904–14

Urban areas fiscal, economic, and social conditions, 1960s-87, biennial rpt, 5184–7.1; 5184–7.4

Wisconsin household income, and expenses by component, by urban-rural location, 1981, article, 1502–7.905

Women (older) pension coverage, sources, payments, and effect on income and poverty status, 1982, article, 4742–1.901

see also Child support and alimony

see also Earnings, general

see also Earnings, local and regional

see also Earnings, specific industry

see also Family budgets

see also Tips and tipping

see also under By Income in the "Index by Categories"

Personal assets

see Wealth

Personal care products

Carcinogens chemistry, sources, environment and health risks, and regulation, by substance and brand, 1989, annual rpt, 4044–15

Consumer Expenditure Survey, household income by source, and itemized spending, by selected characteristics and location, 1984-86, annual rpt, 6764–5.2

Consumer spending in metro and nonmetro areas, by item, 1987, article, 6722–1.962

Consumer spending, natl income and product account, *Survey of Current Business*, monthly rpt, 2702–1.23

Consumer spending related to occupational group, 1986-87, article, 6722–1.961

CPI by component for US city average, and by region, population size, and for 27 metro areas, monthly rpt, 6762–2

Health care treatments and products not proven safe or effective, use, costs, and user characteristics, 1986 survey, 4008–86

Injuries from use of consumer products and related activities, by victim age and sex, 1988, annual rpt, 9164–7

Injuries from use of consumer products, by severity, victim age, and detailed product, 1988, annual rpt, 9164–6

Manufacturing census, 1987: financial and operating data, for SIC 4-digit industries by product, preliminary rpt, 2491–1.29

Price indexes (producer), by stage of processing and detailed commodity, monthly rpt, 6762–6

Price indexes (producer), by stage of processing and detailed commodity, monthly 1988, annual rpt, 6764–2

Price indexes for department store inventories, by class of item, monthly table, 6762–7

Toxicology Natl Program research and testing activities, FY87 and planned FY88, annual rpt, 4044–16

see also Contraceptives

see also Cosmetics and toiletries

see also Drugs

see also Vitamins and nutrients

see also under By Commodity in the "Index by Categories"

Personal computers

see Computer industry and products

Personal consumption

Black Americans household income, and expenses by type, by age and family composition, 1985, article, 1702–1.908

Business and financial statistics, historic trends, 1988 annual chartbook, 9364–2.2

Business Conditions Digest, cyclical indicators, by economic process, monthly rpt, 2702–3.3

Cash holdings, interest rates, and other economic indicators related to consumer spending, 1950s-86, technical paper, 9379–12.38

Clothing price changes, spending, imports by fiber and country, and cotton share of textiles markets, mid 1970s-88, article, 1702–1.902

Consumer spending relation to income, unemployment rate, and interest rate, various periods 1949-88, article, 9393–8.911

Economic and employment conditions, alternative BLS projections to 2000 and trends 1970s-88, biennial article, 6722–1.953

Economic indicators and components, and Fed Reserve 4th District business and financial conditions, monthly chartbook, 9377–10

Economic indicators and components, current data and annual trends, monthly rpt, 23842–1.1

Economic indicators compounded annual rates of change, monthly rpt, 9391–3.2

Economic indicators compounded annual rates of change, 1969-88, annual rpt, 9391–9.2

Expenditures by category and age of household head, Consumer Expenditure Survey, 1987, semiannual pamphlet, 2322–3

Expenditures by category, and income, by selected household characteristics and location, Consumer Expenditure Survey, 1987, press release, 6726–1.23

Expenditures by category and selected household characteristics, 1986 survey, 6728–38.8

Expenditures by category, selected household characteristics, and region, Consumer Expenditure Survey, quarterly rpt, 6762–14

Expenditures for personal consumption, by expenditure type, 1929-88, annual rpt, 204–1.1

Expenditures for personal consumption, relation to income and earnings, alternative models description and results, various periods 1929-87, technical paper, 9366–6.171

Expenditures in metro and nonmetro areas, by item, 1987 survey, article, 6722–1.962

Expenditures related to occupational group, 1986-87, article, 6722–1.961

Family Economics Review, consumer goods prices and supply, and home economics, quarterly rpt with articles, 1702–1

Household debt and interest-earning assets, interest paid and received, and consumption expenditures, by selected characteristics, 1960s-88, article, 9385–1.913

Inflation measured by CPI and Personal Consumption Expenditure Index, under alternative weighting systems, monthly rpt, quarterly article, 6762-2

Input-output structure of US economy, detailed interindustry transactions for 84 industries, and components of final demand, 1983, annual article, 2702-1.909

Married couple families with both spouses working, effects on consumer spending by category, and income, by household characteristics, 1984-86, article, 6722-1.908

Metals (primary) demand relation to consumption patterns and economic, trade, and technological factors, 1960s-82, 5608-159

Natl income and product accounts and components, *Survey of Current Business*, monthly rpt, 2702-1.21; 2702-1.23

Older persons socioeconomic characteristics, 1900s-86 and projected to 2050, biennial chartbook, 12904-1

Older persons under financial stress, essential expenses cut and household economic characteristics, 1983, article, 1702-1.907

Pollution abatement spending by govts, business, and consumers, 1983-87, annual article, 2702-1.919

Retail trade sales per capita, 1987, annual rpt, 2413-5

Single-parent household income and spending, and selected characteristics, with comparison to households with married parents, 1984-86, article, 6722-1.916

Single-parent household income sources and spending by category, by sex, age, race, and household size, 1984-85, article, 1702-1.901

Soviet Union and US production and consumption of selected commodities, by commodity, 1960s-88, annual rpt, 9114-4.3

Soviet Union economic conditions and military activity, 1960s-86, hearing, 23848-195

Soviet Union economic conditions under General Secretary Gorbachev, 1988 and trends from 1956, annual rpt, 9114-6

Statistical Abstract of US, social, political, and economic data, 1790-2025, comprehensive annual compilation, 2324-1.3

Survey of Current Business, detailed financial and business data, and economic indicators, monthly rpt, 2702-1.1

Tax (excise) indexed to inflation, impacts on Federal revenue and family tax burden by commodity, projected under alternative proposals, 1989-93, GAO rpt, 26119-254

Transportation spending by mode of transport, and compared to other personal consumption, 1977-88, annual rpt, 7304-2.2

Wisconsin household income, and expenses by component, by urban-rural location, 1981, article, 1502-7.905

see also Cost of living
see also Family budgets
see also Food consumption
see also Housing energy use

see also Wealth

Personal debt

Debt and assets of private sector, balance sheets by segment, 1949-88, semiannual rpt, 9365-4.1

Debt outstanding, by sector and type of debt and holder, monthly rpt, 9362-1.1

Economic indicators and components, and Fed Reserve 4th District business and financial conditions, monthly chartbook, 9377-10

Financial and business statistics, historic trends, 1988 annual chartbook, 9364-2.7; 9364-2.11

Flow-of-funds accounts, assets and liabilities by type and economic sector, outstanding at year-end 1965-88, annual rpt, 9364-3

Flow-of-funds accounts, savings, investments, and credit statements, quarterly rpt, 9365-3.3

Household composition, income, benefits, and labor force status, Survey of Income and Program Participation methodology, working paper series, 2626-10

Household debt and interest-earning assets, interest paid and received, and consumption expenditures, by selected characteristics, 1960s-88, article, 9385-1.913

Older persons under financial stress, essential expenses cut and household economic characteristics, 1983, article, 1702-1.907

see also Consumer credit
see also Credit bureaus and agencies
see also Loans
see also Mortgages

Personal income

see Personal and household income

Personal property

see Housing tenure
see Land ownership and rights
see Ownership of enterprise
see Personal debt
see Property
see Savings
see Wealth

Personick, Martin E.

"Job Hazards Underscored in Woodworking Study", 6722-1.945

"Profiles in Safety and Health: Occupational Hazards of Meatpacking", 6722-1.901

"Profiles in Safety and Health: Work Hazards of Mobile Homes", 6722-1.932

Personick, Valerie A.

"Industry Output and Employment: A Slower Trend for the Nineties", 6722-1.954

Peru

Agricultural and food production and indexes, total and for selected commodities, by country, 1970s-88, annual rpt, 1524-12

Agricultural production, prices, and trade, by country, 1960s-89, annual world region rpt, 1524-4.2

Agricultural trade of US, by detailed commodity and country, 1988, semiannual rpt, 1522-4

AID activities and funding by project and function, FY90, and developing countries summary socioeconomic data from 1960s, annual rpt, 9904-4.7

AID economic aid to developing countries, obligations and disbursements by country, quarterly rpt, 9912-4

AID loans repayment status and terms by program and country, and status of predecessor agency loans, quarterly rpt, 9912-3

Auto imports from US, trade barriers by country, 1988, annual rpt, 444-2

Economic and military aid and loans from US and intl agencies, by program and country, FY46-87, annual rpt, 9914-5

Economic conditions, income, production, prices, employment, and trade, 1989 periodic country rpt, 2046-4.48

Economic conditions, policy, and trade practices, by country, 1986-88, annual rpt, 21384-5

Economic, social, political, and geographic summary data, by country, 1989, annual factbook, 9114-2

Exports and imports of Latin America, and balance of trade with US, by country, 1988, annual rpt, 2044-34

Exports and imports of US, by commodity and country, 1970-87, world area rpt, 9116-1.5

Exports and imports of US, by selected country, country group, and commodity group, 1988, annual rpt, 2044-37

Grain yield and production costs for alternative soil treatment and cropping practices in Peru, 1982-86, hearing, 21708-126

Human rights conditions in 170 countries, 1988, annual rpt, 21384-3

Labor conditions, union coverage, and work accidents, 1989 annual country rpt, 6366-4.42

Military aid of US, arms sales, and training programs costs and budget requests, by program, world region, and country, FY88-90, annual rpt, 7144-13

Military spending, arms trade, and force strengths, with govt spending and population, by country, 1977-87, annual rpt, 9824-1

Minerals Yearbook, 1987, Vol 3: foreign country reviews of production, trade, and policy, by commodity, annual rpt, 5604-35

Minerals Yearbook, 1987, Vol 3 preprints: foreign country review of production, trade, and policy, by commodity, annual rpt, 5604-23.57

Multinatl US firms and foreign affiliates finances and operations, by industry of parent firm and affiliate, world area, and country, preliminary 1987, annual rpt, 2704-5

Population size, growth rates, and components of change, by country, projected 1989-2020 and trends from 1950, biennial rpt, 2324-9

UN voting record and share of votes in agreement with US, by issue, country, and world area, 1988, annual rpt, 7004-18

see also under By Foreign Country in the "Index by Categories"

Peskin, Janice

"Work and Welfare: The Family Support Act of 1988", 26306-3.102

Pesticides

Agricultural Outlook, production, prices, marketing, and trade, by commodity, forecast and current situation, monthly rpt with articles, 1502-4

Developing countries disaster preparedness and economic, population, and political data, country rpt series, 9916–2

Forest Service mgmt of public lands and resources dev, environmental, economic, and social impacts of alternative programs, projected to 2030, 1208–24

Great Plains wildlife damage to crops, livestock, and property, and effectiveness of mgmt methods, 1988 conf, 1208–304

Housing and neighborhood quality, indicators and attitudes, by householder type and location, 1985, biennial rpt, 2485–12

Housing and neighborhood quality, indicators and attitudes, MSA surveys, series, 2485–6

Imports detained by FDA, by reason, product, shipper, brand, and country, monthly listing, 4062–2

Mountain pine beetle infestation in Western US and Canada, characteristics and control measures, 1988 conf papers, 1208–306

Plant pests and diseases entering US, by type of pest and host, country, and State, FY87, annual rpt, 1394–16

Receipts for services, by SIC 2- to 4-digit kind of business, 1988, annual rpt, 2413–8

Service industries census, 1987: establishments, receipts, employment, and payroll, by SIC 2- to 4-digit kind of business, MSA, county, and city, State rpt series, 2391–1

Sugarcane clones yields, stability, and fungi resistance, 1988/89, annual rpt, 1704–2

Timber (lodgepole pine) losses from beetle infestation, and effects of thinning stands, 1985 study, 1208–297

Timber in southeastern US, resources mgmt and research, 1988 biennial conf papers, 1204–35

Timber insect and disease incidence and damage, annual regional rpt series, 1206–11

Timber insect and disease incidence and damage, by State, 1988, annual rpt, 1204–8

see also Pesticides

Petaluma, Calif.

Housing vacancy rates for single and multifamily units and mobile homes, by city and ZIP code, 1988, annual MSA rpt, 9304–20.3

see also under By SMSA or MSA in the "Index by Categories"

Peters, Donald L.

"Receipts and Expenditures of State Governments and of Local Governments: Revised and Updated Estimates, 1985-88", 2702–1.935

Petersburg, Va.

Wages by occupation, and benefits for office and plant workers, 1989 survey, periodic MSA rpt, 6785–12.7

see also under By SMSA or MSA in the "Index by Categories"

Petersen, Bruce C.

"Investment Cyclicality in Manufacturing Industries", 9375–1.909

Petersen, James C.

"Statistical Summary of Selected Water-Quality Data (Water Years 1975-85) for Arkansas Rivers and Streams", 5668–83

Peterson, Linda S.

"Labor Force and Informal Employment in Mexico: Recent Characteristics and Trends", 2326–18.49

Peterson, Pamela P.

"Valuation Effects of New Capital Issues by Large Bank Holding Companies", 9371–10.34

Petrochemicals

China trade by SITC 1- to 5-digit commodity, 1970s-87, annual rpt, 9114–3

Consumption, by detailed fuel type, end-use sector, and State, 1960-87, State Energy Data System annual rpt, 3164–39

Consumption of fossil fuel by end use, and trade, by type, 1988 and trends from 1949, annual rpt, 3164–74.1; 3164–74.2

County Business Patterns, 1987: employment, establishments, and payroll, by SIC 2- to 4-digit industry and county, annual State rpt series, 2326–8

Employment, earnings, and hours, by selected SIC 1- to 4-digit industry, State, and for 262 MSAs, 1972-87, 6748–81

Employment, earnings, and hours, by SIC 1- to 4-digit industry, monthly 1983-Feb 1989, annual rpt, 6744–4

Exports of US, detailed commodities by country, monthly rpt, 2422–3

Freight (waterborne domestic and foreign) by commodity, traffic, and passengers, by port and waterway, 1987, annual rpt, 3754–3

Hudson-Raritan River basin pollutant levels and sources, model description and results, 1880s-1982, 2178–22

Imports of US, detailed Schedule A commodities by country, monthly rpt, 2422–2

Injuries from use of consumer products, by severity, victim age, and detailed product, 1988, annual rpt, 9164–6

Manufacturers finances and operations, by SIC 2- to 4-digit industry, forecast 1989 and trends from 1950s, annual rpt, 2044–28

Manufacturing annual survey, 1986: financial and operating data, by SIC 2- to 4-digit industry, series, 2506–15

Manufacturing census, 1987: financial and operating data, for SIC 4-digit industries by product, preliminary rpt, 2491–1.38; 2491–1.41

Occupational injury and illness rates, by SIC 2- to 4-digit industry, 1987, annual rpt, 6844–1

Price indexes (producer), by stage of processing and detailed commodity, monthly rpt, 6762–6

Price indexes (producer), by stage of processing and detailed commodity, monthly 1988, annual rpt, 6764–2

Prices and spending for fuel, by type, end-use sector, and State, 1987, annual rpt, 3164–64

Production and sales of synthetic organic chemicals, and manufacturer listing, by product, 1988, annual rpt, 9884–3

Production, dev, and distribution firms revenues and income, quarterly rpt, 3162–38

Production of synthetic organic chemicals, by detailed product, quarterly rpt, 9882–1

Supply, demand, and movement of crude oil, gas liquids, and refined products, by PAD district and State, 1988 and trends from 1973, annual rpt, 3164–2

Supply, demand, and prices, by fuel type and end-use sector, projected under 3 oil price assumptions, 1988-2000, annual rpt, 3164–75

Supply, demand, trade, stocks, and refining of oil and gas liquids, by detailed product, State, and PAD district, monthly rpt with articles, 3162–6

see also under By Commodity in the "Index by Categories"

Petroleum and petroleum industry

Agricultural cooperatives commercial member characteristics, and use of services, by region, 1980 and 1986, 1128–53

Agricultural production itemized costs, by farm sales size and region, 1988, annual rpt, 1614–3

Agriculture census, 1987: farms, farmland, production and costs, and operator characteristics, advance State and county rpt series, 2330–1

Agriculture census, 1987: farms, farmland, production, finances, and operator characteristics, by county, final State rpt series, 2331–1

Alaska Arctic Natl Wildlife Refuge oil and gas production, reserves, exploration, and dev, 1981-89 and projected to 2003, 26358–200

Business statistics, detailed data for major industries and economic indicators, *Survey of Current Business*, monthly rpt, 2702–1.15

Collective bargaining agreements expiring during year, and workers covered, by firm, union, industry group, and State, 1989, annual rpt, 6784–9

Communist, OECD, and selected other countries energy reserves, production, and use, and oil trade and revenue, 1960s-88, annual rpt, 9114–4.5

Consumption, by detailed fuel type, end-use sector, and State, 1960-87, State Energy Data System annual rpt, 3164–39

Consumption of energy, by air pollutant source, fuel type, and State, 1986, annual rpt, 9194–14

Consumption of oil related to GNP and oil prices, 1972-88 and alternative projections to 2000, article, 9379–1.901

Consumption of oil relation to crude oil prices, GNP, and industrial production, 1972-88, technical paper, 9379–12.39

Consumption of oil, switching to other fuels, capability by end-use sector, 1989, annual rpt, 3164–88

County Business Patterns, 1987: employment, establishments, and payroll, by SIC 2- to 4-digit industry and county, annual State rpt series, 2326–8

Cuba economic conditions, agricultural and industrial production and distribution, trade, and intl economic relations, 1980-87 with trends from 1961, 9118–8

Defense Fuel Supply Center procurement, prices, stocks, transport, and other activities and finances, FY88, annual rpt, 3904–8

Distillate fuel production, imports, stocks, and prices, by selected PAD district and northern State, seasonal monthly rpt, 3162–40

Petroleum stocks

Business statistics, detailed data for major industries and economic indicators, *Survey of Current Business*, monthly rpt, 2702–1.15

Distillate fuel production, imports, stocks, and prices, by selected PAD district and northern State, seasonal monthly rpt, 3162–40

Electric power plants production, capacity, sales, and fuel stocks, use, and costs, by State, 1984-88, annual rpt, 3164–11

Electric power plants production, fuel use, stocks, and costs by fuel type, and sales, by State, monthly rpt, 3162–35

Electric utilities fuel cost, quality, use, receipts, and stocks, and power plant production, by energy source, State and utility, quarterly rpt, 3162–39

Intl Energy Program countries oil stocks and conservation measures, 1987-88 and projected to 1990, GAO rpt, 26123–225

Manufacturing storage capacity for fuel oil and liquefied petroleum gas, by industry, 1985 survey, 3166–13.1

OECD oil crude and refined products stocks, for 7 countries and OECD total, quarterly 1985-88, annual rpt, 3164–50.2

OECD oil stocks, for US and 16 countries, monthly rpt, 9112–2

OECD oil stocks, monthly rpt, 3162–42

Statistical Abstract of US, social, political, and economic data, 1790-2025, comprehensive annual compilation, 2324–1.3

Supply and demand of oil and refined products, refinery capacity and use, and prices, weekly rpt, 3162–32

Supply, demand, and movement of crude oil, gas liquids, and refined products, by PAD district and State, 1988 and trends from 1973, annual rpt, 3164–2

Supply, demand, and prices, by fuel type and end-use sector, projected under 3 oil price assumptions, 1988-2000, annual rpt, 3164–75

Supply, demand, and prices, by fuel type and end-use sector, with foreign comparisons, 1988 and trends from 1949, annual rpt, 3164–74.2

Supply, demand, and prices, by fuel type, end-use sector, and country, detailed data, monthly rpt, 3162–24

Supply, demand, and prices of energy, forecasts by resource type, quarterly rpt, 3162–34

Supply, demand, trade, stocks, and refining of oil and gas liquids, by detailed product, State, and PAD district, monthly rpt with articles, 3162–6

see also Naval Petroleum Reserves

see also Strategic Petroleum Reserve

Petroni, Rita J.

"Nonresponse Adjustment Methods for Demographic Surveys at the U.S. Bureau of the Census", 2626–10.73

"Research and Evaluation Conducted on the Survey of Income and Program Participation", 2626–10.91

Pets

CPI by component for US city average, and by region, population size, and for 27 metro areas, monthly rpt, 6762–2

Feed for pets PPI, monthly rpt, 6762–6

Feed for pets PPI, monthly 1988, annual rpt, 6764–2

Injuries from use of consumer products, by severity, victim age, and detailed product, 1988, annual rpt, 9164–6

Rabies cases in animals and humans, by location for US, Mexico, and Canada, 1988, annual rpt, 4202–7.904

Retail trade census, 1987: employment, establishments, sales, and payroll, by SIC 2- to 4-digit kind of business, MSA, county, and city, State rpt series, 2397–1

Pharmaceutical industry

Cephalexin capsules (generic) from Canada at less than fair value, injury to US industry, investigation with background financial and operating data, 1989 rpt, 9886–14.267

County Business Patterns, 1987: employment, establishments, and payroll, by SIC 2- to 4-digit industry and county, annual State rpt series, 2326–8

Employment, earnings, and hours, by selected SIC 1- to 4-digit industry, State, and for 262 MSAs, 1972-87, 6748–81

Employment, earnings, and hours, by SIC 1- to 4-digit industry, monthly 1983-Feb 1989, annual rpt, 6744–4

Employment of minorities and women, by occupation, SIC 1- to 3- digit industry, State, and MSA, 1986, annual rpt, 9244–1

Finances and operations, by SIC 2- to 4-digit industry, forecast 1989 with trends from 1950s, annual rpt, 2044–28

Financial statements for manufacturing, mining, and trade corporations, by selected SIC 2- to 3-digit industry, quarterly rpt, 2502–1

Foreign and US technology dev and competition issues, fundings and recommendations, 1980s-87, 21708–123

Input-output structure of US economy, detailed interindustry transactions for 84 industries, and components of final demand, 1983, annual article, 2702–1.909

Labor productivity, indexes of output, hours, and employment by SIC 2- to 4-digit industry, 1963-87, annual rpt, 6824–1.3

Manufacturing annual survey, 1986: financial and operating data, by SIC 2- to 4-digit industry, series, 2506–15

Manufacturing census, 1987: financial and operating data, for SIC 4-digit industries by product, preliminary rpt, 2491–1.35

Multinatl US firms and foreign affiliates finances and operations, by industry of parent firm and affiliate, world area, and country, preliminary 1987, annual rpt, 2704–5

Occupational injury and illness rates, by SIC 2- to 4-digit industry, 1987, annual rpt, 6844–1

Price indexes (producer), by stage of processing and detailed commodity, monthly rpt, 6762–6

Price indexes (producer), by stage of processing and detailed commodity, monthly 1988, annual rpt, 6764–2

Production and sales of synthetic organic chemicals, and manufacturer listing, by product, 1988, annual rpt, 9884–3

Science, engineering, and technical employment in manufacturing, by field, occupation, and industry, 1986, triennial rpt, 9627–23

Science, engineering, and technical employment in transportation, utilities, and retail and wholesale trade, by field, occupation, and industry, 1985, triennial rpt, 9627–32

Tax (income) returns of corporations, income and tax items by asset size and detailed industry, 1986, annual rpt, 8304–4; 8304–21

Wholesale trade census, 1987: employment, establishments, finances, and operations, by SIC 2- to 4-digit kind of business, MSA, county, and city, State rpt series, 2405–1

Wholesale trade sales and inventories, by SIC 2- to 3-digit kind of business, monthly rpt, 2413–7

Wholesale trade sales, inventories, purchases, and gross margins, by SIC 2- to 3-digit kind of business and form of ownership, 1988, annual rpt, 2413–13

see also Biologic drug products

see also Drugs

see also Drugstores

see also Pharmacists and pharmacy

Pharmacists and pharmacy

Community and migrant health services finances, operations, and staff, 1988 rpt, 4108–45.3

Enrollment in science and engineering grad programs, by field, source of funds, and characteristics of student and instn, 1975-87, annual rpt, 9627–7

Health condition and health care resources, use, and spending, 1950s-87, annual data compilation, 4144–11

Indian Health Service outpatient visits, by type of provider, selected hospital, and IHS service area, FY87-88, annual rpt, 4084–3

Medicaid reimbursement for prescription drugs under alternative methods of determining pharmacy costs, for Wisconsin, 1986, article, 4652–1.933

Military health care personnel, and accessions by training source, by occupation, specialty, and service branch, FY87, annual rpt, 3544–24

Mississippi hospitals and community health centers, use, staff, and Medicare and other payments, 1988 hearing, 25548–97

Training support grants of Bur of Health Professions, by program, region, and State, FY80-87, 4118–62

VA Medicine and Surgery Dept trainees, by detailed program and city, FY88, annual rpt, 8704–4

VA pharmacies prescriptions issued and filled, FY87-88, annual rpt, 8604–3.4

see also Drugs

see also Drugstores

Phelps, Robert B.

"Outlook for Timber Products", 1004–16.1

Philadelphia, Pa.

AIDS cases, and health and social services availability, for 5 cities, 1988, GAO rpt, 26121–307

CPI by component for US city average, and by region, population size, and for 15 metro areas, monthly rpt, 6762–1

CPI by component for US city average, and by region, population size, and for 27 metro areas, monthly rpt, 6762–2

Drug abuse indicators for selected metro areas, research results, data collection, and policy issues, 1989 semiannual conf, 4492–5

Drug test results at arrest, by drug type, offense, and sex, for selected urban areas, quarterly rpt, 6062-3

Employment growth and unemployment rates, Fed Reserve 3rd District, quarterly rpt, 9387-10

Freight (waterborne domestic and foreign) by commodity, traffic, and passengers, by port and waterway, 1987, annual rpt, 3754-3.1

Fruit and vegetable shipments, and arrivals in US and Canada cities, by mode of transport and State and country of origin, 1988, annual rpt, 1311-4.1

Hazardous substances health effects, environmental levels, and household products composition, with data by selected location, 1988 hearings, 21408-112

Homeless persons aid programs, and shelter capacity and voucher programs, for 5 major cities, 1988, 5188-122

Housing and households characteristics, 1985 survey, MSA fact sheet, 2485-11.10

Housing and households detailed characteristics, and unit and neighborhood quality, by location, 1985 survey, MSA rpt, 2485-6.8

Wages by occupation, and benefits for office and plant workers, 1988 survey, periodic MSA rpt, 6785-11.3

see also under By City and By SMSA or MSA in the "Index by Categories"

Philanthropy
see Gifts and private contributions
see Nonprofit organizations and foundations

Philippine Americans
see Pacific Islands Americans

Philippines
Agricultural and food production and indexes, total and for selected commodities, by country, 1970s-88, annual rpt, 1524-12

Agricultural production, prices, and trade, by country, 1960s-89, annual world region rpt, 1524-4.2

Agricultural trade of US, by detailed commodity and country, 1988, semiannual rpt, 1522-4

Agricultural trade of US with Asia, Middle East, and North Africa, by commodity and country, 1962-86, 1528-277

AID activities and funding by project and function, FY90, and developing countries summary socioeconomic data from 1960s, annual rpt, 9904-4.6

AID economic aid to developing countries, obligations and disbursements by country, quarterly rpt, 9912-4

AID loans repayment status and terms by program and country, and status of predecessor agency loans, quarterly rpt, 9912-3

Background Notes, summary social, political, and economic data, 1989 rpt, 7006-2.49

Coal production, trade, and govt subsidies, by country and country group, 1973-87 and projected to 2000, 2048-144

Disaster preparedness and economic, population, and political data, 1988 country rpt, 9916-2.71

Economic and military aid and loans from US and intl agencies, by program and country, FY46-87, annual rpt, 9914-5

Economic conditions in Communist, OECD, and selected other countries, 1960s-88, annual rpt, 9114-4

Economic conditions, income, production, prices, employment, and trade, 1989 periodic country rpt, 2046-4.23; 2046-4.97

Economic conditions, policy, and trade practices, by country, 1986-88, annual rpt, 21384-5

Economic indicators of developing countries, problem debtors compared to other borrowers, by country, 1973-84, 1528-285

Economic, social, political, and geographic summary data, by country, 1989, annual factbook, 9114-2

Exports and imports of US, by commodity and country, 1970-87, world area rpt, 9116-1.2

Exports and imports of US, by selected country, country group, and commodity group, 1988, annual rpt, 2044-37

Human rights conditions in 170 countries, 1988, annual rpt, 21384-3

Imports of goods, services, and investment from US, trade barriers, impacts, and US actions, by country, 1988, annual rpt, 444-2

Military aid of US, arms sales, and training programs costs and budget requests, by program, world region, and country, FY88-90, annual rpt, 7144-13

Military spending, arms trade, and force strengths, with govt spending and population, by country, 1977-87, annual rpt, 9824-1

Minerals production, reserves, and industry role in domestic economy and world supply, 1988 country rpt, 5606-1.17

Minerals Yearbook, 1987, Vol 3: foreign country reviews of production, trade, and policy, by commodity, annual rpt, 5604-35

Minerals Yearbook, 1987, Vol 3 preprints: foreign country review of production, trade, and policy, by commodity, annual rpt, 5604-23.58

Multinatl US firms and foreign affiliates finances and operations, by industry of parent firm and affiliate, world area, and country, preliminary 1987, annual rpt, 2704-5

Nuclear power plant capacity, generation, and operating status, by plant and foreign and US location, 1988 and projected to 2020, annual rpt, 3164-57

Population size, growth rates, and components of change, by country, projected 1989-2020 and trends from 1950, biennial rpt, 2324-9

Port facilities, operations, and impacts on US agricultural exports, for major Far East Asia ports, 1970s-87, 1278-13

Ships in world merchant fleet, and tonnage, by country of registry, as of Jan 1988, annual rpt, 7704-3

Sugar exports, quotas of US, and displaced mill and farm workers, 1982-87, hearing, 21788-179

Tidal currents, daily time and velocity by station for North America and Asia coasts, forecast 1990, annual rpt, 2174-1.1

UN voting record and share of votes in agreement with US, by issue, country, and world area, 1988, annual rpt, 7004-18

US Air Force Pacific basin airlift of aircraft parts, traffic, shipments, and impacts on force readiness, 1986-88, GAO rpt, 26123-230

US veterans living abroad, disability and death compensation cases by entitlement type, period of service, sex, and age, FY88, annual rpt, 8604-7

US veterans living abroad, VA expenses by type and location, FY88, annual rpt, 8604-3.9

see also under By Foreign Country in the "Index by Categories"

Phillips, J. M.
"Spot. Species Profiles: Life Histories and Environmental Requirements of Coastal Fishes and Invertebrates", 5506-8.104

Phillips, Jane K.
"Honey: Background for 1990 Farm Legislation", 1566-7.3
"U.S. Honey Price Support Policy", 1561-14.902

Phillips, Keith R.
"Development and Uses of Regional Indexes of Leading Economic Indicators", 9379-12.30
"Diversifying Texas: Recent History and Prospects", 9379-1.907
"Econometric Analysis of U.S. Oil Demand", 9379-12.39
"Oil Demand and Prices in the 1990s", 9379-1.901
"Unionization and Unemployment Rates: Re-Examination of Olson's Labor Cartelization Hypothesis", 9379-12.29

Philosophy
see Arts and the humanities

Phoenix, Ariz.
Drug abuse indicators for selected metro areas, research results, data collection, and policy issues, 1989 semiannual conf, 4492-5

Drug test results at arrest, by drug type, offense, and sex, for selected urban areas, quarterly rpt, 6062-3

Housing and households detailed characteristics, and unit and neighborhood quality, by location, 1985 survey, MSA rpt, 2485-6.14

Housing starts and completions authorized by building permits in 40 MSAs, quarterly rpt, 2382-9

Wages by occupation, for office and plant workers, 1989 survey, periodic MSA rpt, 6785-12.6

see also under By City and By SMSA or MSA in the "Index by Categories"

Phonograph
see Home video and audio equipment

Phonograph records
see Recording industry

Phosphate
Africa agricultural exports by commodity, and relation to economic conditions and other factors, by country, 1960s-87, 1528-280

County Business Patterns, 1987: employment, establishments, and payroll, by SIC 2- to 4-digit industry and county, annual State rpt series, 2326-8

Exports and imports (agricultural) of US, by detailed commodity and country, 1988, semiannual rpt, 1522-4

Statistical Abstract of US, social, political, and economic data, 1790-2025, comprehensive annual compilation, 2324-1.1

see also Physical education and training

see also Sports and athletics

Physical sciences

Black colleges R&D funding by source, and characteristics of grad students and research staff, by field of science and instn, 1980s-87, 9628-78

Degrees (PhD) in science and engineering, by field, instn, employment prospects, sex, race, and other characteristics, 1960s-88, 9627-30

Degrees awarded in higher education, by level, field, race, and sex, 1989 edition, annual rpt, 4824-2.20

Degrees in science and engineering, by field, level, and sex, 1950-86, 9628-77

DOE R&D projects and funding at natl labs, universities, and other instns, periodic summary rpt series, 3004-18

Education in science, elementary and secondary students proficiency, attitudes, factors affecting proficiency, and teacher background and views, natl assessment, 1977-86, 4898-25

Employment and earnings in science and engineering, by field and activity, and private and Federal R&D spending, by industry, 1975-88, 9626-6.29

Employment and other characteristics of science and engineering PhDs, by field and State, 1987, biennial rpt, 9627-18

Employment characteristics of scientists and engineers, by field, 1988, biennial rpt, 9627-16

Employment of scientists and engineers, and related topics, fact sheet series, 9626-2

Employment of scientists, engineers, and technicians by nonmanufacturing industry and field, 1987, triennial rpt, 9627-31

Employment of scientists, engineers, and technicians in manufacturing, by field, occupation, and industry, 1986, triennial rpt, 9627-23

Employment of scientists, engineers, and technicians in transportation, utilities, and retail and wholesale trade, by field, occupation, and industry, 1985, triennial rpt, 9627-32

Enrollment in science and engineering, degrees, and student aid and sources, with data by field, race, sex, and instn, 1980s-87, 26358-202

Enrollment in science and engineering grad programs, by field, source of funds, and characteristics of student and instn, 1975-87, annual rpt, 9627-7

Fed Govt aid to higher education and nonprofit instns for R&D and related activities, by field, instn, agency, and State, FY87, annual rpt, 9627-17

Fed Govt science and engineering employment, by field, degree level, race, sex, agency, and State, 1987, annual rpt, 9627-5

Foreign and US funding for R&D, and scientists and engineering employment and education, 1988, annual rpt, 9624-23.1

NASA R&D funding to higher education instns, by field, instn, and State, FY88, annual listing, 9504-7

NSF activities, finances, and funding by program, FY88, annual rpt, 9624-6

R&D equipment of higher education instns, acquisition and service costs, condition, and financing, by field, 1982-83 and 1985-86, 9628-76

R&D funding by Fed Govt, by field, performer type, agency, and State, FY87-89, annual rpt, 9627-20

R&D funding by higher education instns, by source and field, FY80-87, annual rpt, 9624-18.5

R&D funding by source and performer, and related employment, by State, 1975-87, 9626-6.32

Teachers bachelor degrees, by field and other characteristics, 1985-86, 4838-39

Wages of scientists and engineers in R&D, by field and educational, employment, and other characteristics, 1989, annual rpt, 3004-1

see also Astronomy

see also Chemistry

see also Earth sciences

see also Environmental sciences

see also Geography

see also Mathematics

see also Oceanography

see also Physics

Physical therapy

Drugs (controlled) provided during physician office visits, by drug, patient, and provider characteristics, 1985, 4146-8.179

Home health care services use and costs for Medicare disabled and aged enrollees, by age, sex, service type, and diagnosis, mid 1970s-86, article, 4652-1.908

Indian Health Service outpatient visits, by type of provider, selected hospital, and IHS service area, FY87-88, annual rpt, 4084-3

Medicare and Medicaid beneficiaries and program operations, 1988, annual fact book, 4654-18

Medicare discharges, charges, and length of stay, by State and diagnosis, 1983 and 1985, article, 4652-1.925

Military health care personnel, and accessions by training source, by occupation, specialty, and service branch, FY87, annual rpt, 3544-24

Nursing home compliance with Medicare and Medicaid regulations, and patient characteristics, by facility, 1987/88, annual State rpt series, 4654-15

Nursing home facility, staff, and resident detailed characteristics, 1985, 4147-13.97

Nursing home rehabilitation services use, by service type and patient characteristics, 1st qtr 1983, 4188-58

Special education enrollment by disability, transfers to public schools from State instns, services provided, and Federal funding, with data by State, 1987-88, GAO rpt, 26121-294

Special education programs, enrollment by age, staff, funding, and needs, by type of handicap and State, 1987/88, annual rpt, 4944-4

Physically handicapped

see Blind

see Deaf

see Disabled and handicapped persons

Physicians

Acute and chronic health conditions, disability, absenteeism, and health services use, by selected characteristics, 1988, annual rpt, 4147-10.170

AIDS cases, and health and social services availability, for 5 cities, 1988, GAO rpt, 26121-307

AIDS deaths, by health and other characteristics, 1986, 4146-8.178

AIDS patients Medicaid claims and payments, by type of care and whether AIDS-related, race, sex, and diagnosis, 1984-87, article, 4042-3.940

Alcohol and drug abuse specialty certification for physicians, applicants professional characteristics, 1986, article, 4482-1.901

Allergy and Infectious Diseases Natl Inst activities, grants by recipient and location, and disease incidence, FY81-88, annual rpt, 4474-30

Births and rates, by characteristics of birth, infant, and parents, 1987 and trends from 1940, US Vital Statistics advance annual rpt, 4146-5.110

Cancer screening of aged by physicians and compliance with American Cancer Society schedules, by speciality, 1986 local area study, article, 4042-3.917

Cardiologist office visits, by characteristics of patient, physician, and visit, 1985, 4146-8.174

Cardiovascular diseases cases, health care services use and costs, and productivity losses, by selected characteristics, 1980, 4146-12.26

Children (handicapped) home health care and support services availability and need, 1988, GAO report, 26121-300

County Business Patterns, 1987: employment, establishments, and payroll, by SIC 2- to 4-digit industry and county, annual State rpt series, 2326-8

CPI by component for US city average, and by region, population size, and for 27 metro areas, monthly rpt, 6762-2

Developing countries disaster preparedness and economic, population, and political data, country rpt series, 9916-2

Drugs (controlled) provided during physician office visits, by drug, patient, and provider characteristics, 1985, 4146-8.179

Educational and research grants and contracts of Health Professions Bur, by instn and program, FY88, annual listing, 4114-1

Employment, earnings, and hours, by SIC 1- to 4-digit industry, monthly 1983-Feb 1989, annual rpt, 6744-4

Expenditures for health care, by service type, payment source, and age, 1977 and 1987, article, 4652-1.946

Expenditures for health care, by service type, payment source, and sector, 1960s-87, annual article, 4652-1.926

Expenditures for health care, share of GNP by component, 1960s-87, article, 4652-1.927

Family practice MDs by age, ratios to population, and residents, and percent women and foreign medical grads, 1960s-88 and projected to 2010, article, 4042–3.926

France and Germany physicians, and visits by reason and patient age and sex, by specialty, compared to US, 1981-83, 4147–5.5

Health Care Financing Review, provider prices, price inputs and indexes, and labor, quarterly journal, 4652–1.1

Health condition and health care resources, use, and spending, 1950s-87, annual data compilation, 4144–11

Heart disease deaths, by health and other characteristics, 1986, 4146–8.177

HHS financial aid, by program, recipient, State, and city, FY88, annual regional listings, 4004–3

Income of physicians, by specialty and other practice characteristics, 1975 and 1983-84, article, 4652–1.920

Indian Health Service outpatient visits, by type of provider, selected hospital, and IHS service area, FY87-88, annual rpt, 4084–3

Insurance (health) coverage and provisions of employee benefit plans, by plan type and occupational group, 1988, annual rpt, 6784–19

Insurance (health) coverage of employees, out-of-pocket expenses, benefits, and premiums, 1970s-86 and projected to 2000, 4188–56

Labor force health condition and services use, by occupation and industry of longest job held, income, age, sex, and race, 1980, 4147–10.168

Labor force health condition, disability days, health services use, and disease prevalence, by occupation and sex, 1983-85, 4146–8.170

Labs and medical equipment services owned by physicians, referrals to own businesses, and excess Medicare costs from referrals, 1987, 4008–90

Medicaid coverage, participation, payments, admin, and legislative history, with data by State, 1980s-88, 21368–105

Medicaid enrollment, and service use and costs by service type, by eligibility type, for 5 States, 1980-84, article, 4652–1.919

Medicare and Medicaid beneficiaries and program operations, 1988, annual fact book, 4654–18

Medicare and Medicaid eligibility, participation, coverage, and program finances, various periods 1966-89, biennial rpt, 4654–1

Medicare and Medicaid enrollees, benefits, reimbursements, and services use, mid-1960s-87, annual rpt, 4744–3.5; 4744–3.6

Medicare claims approved, charges, and reimbursements by type of service, from 1974, monthly rpt, quarterly data, 4742–1.11

Medicare enrollees health care alternatives, medical costs, training to select assigned-fee physicians, and physician attitudes, 1988 rpt, 4658–30

Medicare enrollees physician and other services use, benefits, charges, and coinsurance and deductible obligations, 1982-86, article, 4652–1.901

Medicare physicians assigned-fee laws of 4 States, impacts on care cost and availability, 1985-89, GAO rpt, 26121–312

Medicare physicians assigned fee participation related to selected physician, practice, and community characteristics, 1984, article, 4652–1.902

Medicare physicians services use, charges, and reimbursement, by service type, setting, and specialty, 1986, article, 4652–1.936

Medicare reimbursement of hospitals under prospective payment system, impacts on instns, beneficiaries, and other care providers and payment sources, 1986, annual rpt, 4654–13

Medicare supplementary care providers, program payments, copayment obligations, and balances billed, 1975-87, article, 4652–1.955

Mental health care in general hospitals, length of stay related to patient, instn, and State Medicaid program characteristics, 1981, article, 4652–1.924

Military health care benefits and costs under Civilian Health and Medical Program of Uniformed Services, FY83-FY89, 3508–31

Military health care personnel, and accessions by training source, by occupation, specialty, and service branch, FY87, annual rpt, 3544–24

Mississippi hospitals and community health centers, use, staff, and Medicare and other payments, 1988 hearing, 25548–97

Navy manpower strengths, accessions, and attrition, detailed statistics, quarterly rpt, 3802–4

Nursing home and home care case mix, quality of care, and outcomes, impacts of Medicare prospective payment system, 1980s-86, 4658–28

Nursing home compliance with Medicare and Medicaid regulations, and patient characteristics, by facility, 1987/88, annual State rpt series, 4654–15

Nursing home facility, staff, and resident detailed characteristics, 1985, 4147–13.97

Occupational and environmental health care personnel supply and needs, by field, 1987 conf, 4118–65

Older persons health care services use, persons with high and low levels of care by selected health and other characteristics, 1971 and 1980 studies, 4186–2.22

Older persons health care services use related to marital status, living arrangements, and other characteristics, 1977, 4188–54

Older persons visits to physicians, by age group, and compared to nonaged, 1986, 12904–1

Peer review organizations review of Medicare hospital claims, activities, and membership, 1984-88, GAO rpt, 26131–51

Receipts for services, by SIC 2- to 4-digit kind of business, 1988, annual rpt, 2413–8

Rural areas health care facilities, staffing, services accessibility, and indicators of need, 1960s-88, 25148–41

Service industries census, 1987: establishments, receipts, employment, and payroll, by SIC 2- to 4-digit kind of business, MSA, county, and city, State rpt series, 2391–1

Statistical Abstract of US, social, political, and economic data, 1790-2025, comprehensive annual compilation, 2324–1.1

Tax (income) returns of corporations, income and tax items by asset size and detailed industry, 1986, annual rpt, 8304–4; 8304–21

Tax (income) returns of partnerships, income statement items by industry group, 1986, annual article, 8302–2.903

Tax (income) returns of sole proprietorships, income statement items, by industry group, 1987, annual article, 8302–2.904; 8302–2.921

Texas-Mexico border area health facilities and services, with background data, by Texas county, 1980s-88, GAO rpt, 26121–261

VA health care facilities employment, FY64-88, annual rpt, 8604–5.1

VA health care facilities physicians, dentists, and nurses, by selected employment characteristics and VA district, quarterly rpt, 8602–6

VA health care facilities physicians staffing, vacancies, and positions filled, by speciality, 1982-87, hearing, 25768–48

VA health care professionals employment, by district and facility, quarterly rpt, 8602–4

VA Medicine and Surgery Dept trainees, by detailed program and city, FY88, annual rpt, 8704–4

Workers compensation laws of States and Fed Govt, 1989 semiannual rpt, 6502–1

see also Anesthesiology
see also Foreign medical graduates
see also Geriatrics
see also Medical education
see also Medical ethics
see also Medical malpractice
see also Nuclear medicine and radiology
see also Obstetrics and gynecology
see also Orthopedics
see also Osteopathy
see also Pathology
see also Pediatrics
see also Podiatry
see also Psychiatry
see also Surgeons and surgery

Physicians assistants
see Allied health personnel

Physics
Degrees (PhD) in science and engineering, by field, instn, employment prospects, sex, race, and other characteristics, 1960s-88, 9627–30

Degrees awarded in higher education, by level, field, race, and sex, 1989 edition, annual rpt, 4824–2.20

Degrees in science and engineering, by field, level, and sex, 1950-86, 9628–77

Employment and other characteristics of science and engineering PhDs, by field and State, 1987, biennial rpt, 9627–18

Energy use and prices for manufacturing industries, 1985 survey, series, 3166-13

Exports and imports of US, by commodity group, world area, selected country, US coastal area and port, and mode of transport, monthly rpt, 2422-9

Exports of US, detailed commodities by country, monthly rpt, 2422-3

Finances and operations, by SIC 2- to 4-digit industry, forecast 1989 with trends from 1950s, annual rpt, 2044-28

Financial statements for manufacturing, mining, and trade corporations, by selected SIC 2- to 3-digit industry, quarterly rpt, 2502-1

Freight (waterborne domestic and foreign) by commodity, traffic, and passengers, by port and waterway, 1987, annual rpt, 3754-3

Hose and belting shipments, trade, use, and firms, by product, 1988, annual Current Industrial Rpt, 2506-8.12

Imports, exports, and employment impacts, by SIC 2- to 4-digit industry and commodity, quarterly rpt, 2322-2

Imports of US, detailed Schedule A commodities by country, monthly rpt, 2422-2

Injuries from use of consumer products, by severity, victim age, and detailed product, 1988, annual rpt, 9164-6

Input-output structure of US economy, detailed interindustry transactions for 84 industries, and components of final demand, 1983, annual article, 2702-1.909

Labor productivity, indexes of output, hours, and employment by SIC 2- to 4-digit industry, 1963-87, annual rpt, 6824-1.3

Manufacturing annual survey, 1986: financial and operating data, by SIC 2- to 4-digit industry, series, 2506-15

Manufacturing census, 1987: financial and operating data, for SIC 4-digit industries by product, preliminary rpt, 2491-1.34; 2491-1.43

Multinatl US firms and foreign affiliates finances and operations, by industry of parent firm and affiliate, world area, and country, preliminary 1987, annual rpt, 2704-5

Occupational injury and illness rates, by SIC 2- to 4-digit industry, 1987, annual rpt, 6844-1

Ocean and beach plastic, tar, and other nondegradable debris, incidence and environmental impacts, 1970s-88, 14738-4

OECD trade, total and for 4 major countries, and US trade by country, by commodity, 1970-87, world area rpt series, 9116-1

Oil and fat production, consumption by end use, and stocks, by type, monthly Current Industrial Rpt, 2506-4.4

Plumbing fixtures shipments, stocks, trade, use, and firms, by product, quarterly Current Industrial Rpt, 2506-11.2

Pollution abatement capital and operating costs, by SIC 2-to 4-digit industry and State, 1986, annual Current Industrial Rpt, 2506-3.6

Polychloroprene from 2 countries at less than fair value, injury to US industry, investigation with background financial and operating data, 1989 rpt, 9886-14.271

Price indexes (producer), by stage of processing and detailed commodity, monthly rpt, 6762-6

Price indexes (producer), by stage of processing and detailed commodity, monthly 1988, annual rpt, 6764-2

Production and sales of synthetic organic chemicals, and manufacturer listing, by product, 1988, annual rpt, 9884-3

Production of synthetic organic chemicals, by detailed product, quarterly rpt, 9882-1

Science, engineering, and technical employment in manufacturing, by field, occupation, and industry, 1986, triennial rpt, 9627-23

Shoe production, shipments, trade, and use, by product, 1988, annual Current Industrial Rpt, 2506-6.8

Talc production, use, and trade, with foreign comparisons, selected years 1977-87, 5608-158

Tariff Schedule of US, classifications and rates of duty by detailed imported commodity, 1990 base edition and supplements, 9886-13

Tax (income) returns of corporations, income and tax items by asset size and detailed industry, 1986, annual rpt, 8304-4; 8304-21

Transportation census, 1987: trucks, by detailed characteristics, miles traveled, and type of product carried, State rpt series, 2573-1

Wholesale trade census, 1987: employment, establishments, finances, and operations, by SIC 2- to 4-digit kind of business, MSA, county, and city, State rpt series, 2405-1

see also Petrochemicals

see also under By Commodity in the "Index by Categories"

Platinum

see Metals and metal industries

Plotnick, Robert D.

"How Much Poverty Is Reduced by State Income Transfers?", 6722-1.933

Plumbing and heating

Business statistics, detailed data for major industries and economic indicators, *Survey of Current Business*, monthly rpt, 2702-1.14

Cancer (lung) risk relation to home heating and cooking facilities, air pollution exposure, and smoking, by sex, for Shenyang, PRC, 1985-87 study, article, 4472-1.931

China trade by SITC 1- to 5-digit commodity, 1970s-87, annual rpt, 9114-3

Construction industries census, 1987: financial and operating data, by SIC 4-digit industry, preliminary rpt, 2371-1.10

County Business Patterns, 1987: employment, establishments, and payroll, by SIC 2- to 4-digit industry and county, annual State rpt series, 2326-8

DOD prime contract awards, by detailed procurement category, FY85-88, annual rpt, 3544-18

Electric power rate schedules, by user type, utility, and city, as of Jan 1988, annual rpt, 3164-40

Employment, earnings, and hours, by selected SIC 1- to 4-digit industry, State, and for 262 MSAs, 1972-87, 6748-81

Employment, earnings, and hours, by SIC 1- to 4-digit industry, monthly 1983-Feb 1989, annual rpt, 6744-4

Energy conservation (housing) program of Bonneville Power Admin in Hood River, Oreg, cost effectiveness and participation, 1983-86, series, 3226-2

Energy supply, demand, and prices, by fuel type and end-use sector, with foreign comparisons, 1988 and trends from 1949, annual rpt, 3164-74

Energy use, costs, and conservation, and household and housing characteristics, survey rpt series, 3166-7

Energy use in commercial buildings, costs, and conservation, by building characteristics, survey rpt series, 3166-8

Exports of US, detailed commodities by country, monthly rpt, 2422-3

Furnace shipments, trade, use, and firms, 1988, annual Current Industrial Rpt, 2506-12.7

Housing alteration and repair spending, by characteristics of property and region, 1984-88, annual rpt, 2384-4

Housing and households characteristics, for rural and urban areas, 1930s-80, 1598-245

Housing and households detailed characteristics, and unit and neighborhood quality, by location, 1985, biennial rpt, 2485-12

Housing and households detailed characteristics, and unit and neighborhood quality, MSA surveys, series, 2485-6

Housing and households summary characteristics, 1985 and trends, biennial chartbook, 2486-1.7

Housing units completed, single and multifamily units by structural and financial characteristics, inside-outside MSAs, and region, 1984-88, annual rpt, 2384-1

Housing vacancy and occupancy rates, and vacant unit characteristics and costs, by region and metro-nonmetro location, quarterly rpt, 2482-1

Housing vacancy and occupancy rates, and vacant unit characteristics, by tenure, region, and metro-nonmetro location, selected years 1960-88, annual rpt, 2484-1

Imports of US, detailed Schedule A commodities by country, monthly rpt, 2422-2

Indian Health Service funding for housing sanitary facilities, and needs, FY60-88, annual rpt, 4084-1

Injuries from use of consumer products and related activities, by victim age and sex, 1988, annual rpt, 9164-7

Injuries from use of consumer products, by severity, victim age, and detailed product, 1988, annual rpt, 9164-6

Labor productivity, indexes of output, hours, and employment by SIC 2- to 4-digit industry, 1963-87, annual rpt, 6824-1.3

Manufacturing annual survey, 1986: financial and operating data, by SIC 2- to 4-digit industry, series, 2506-15

Manufacturing census, 1987: financial and operating data, for SIC 4-digit industries

by product, preliminary rpt, 2491–1.43; 2491–1.48; 2491–1.56; 2491–1.60; 2491–1.67

Occupational injury and illness rates, by SIC 2- to 4-digit industry, 1987, annual rpt, 6844–1

Pipes and tubes (light-walled steel) from Argentina at less than fair value, injury to US industry, investigation with background financial and operating data, 1989 rpt, 9886–14.262

Price indexes (producer), by stage of processing and detailed commodity, monthly rpt, 6762–6

Producer price indexes, by stage of processing and detailed commodity, monthly 1988, annual rpt, 6764–2

Production, shipments, and PPI for building materials, by type, bimonthly rpt, 2042–1.5; 2042–1.6

Solar collector and photovoltaic module shipments by end-use sector and State, R&D, and trade, 1988, annual rpt, 3164–62

Statistical Abstract of US, social, political, and economic data, 1790-2025, comprehensive annual compilation, 2324–1.3

Tax (income) returns of corporations, income and tax items by asset size and detailed industry, 1986, annual rpt, 8304–4; 8304–21

TVA electric power purchases of municipal and cooperative distributors, and prices and use by distributor and consumer sector, monthly rpt, 9802–1

Wholesale trade census, 1987: employment, establishments, finances, and operations, by SIC 2- to 4-digit kind of business, MSA, county, and city, State rpt series, 2405–1

see also Air conditioning

see also Electric power and heat cogeneration

see also Household appliances and equipment

Plumley, Alan H.

"Impacts of the Tax Reform Act of 1986 on the Income Tax Withholding System", 8304–8.1

Plums and prunes

see Fruit and fruit products

Plutonium

see Radioactive materials

Pneumonia and influenza

AIDS deaths, by opportunistic disease, weekly rpt, 4202–9

AIDS patients *pneumocystis carinii* pneumonia prevention and control, CDC guidelines, 1989 rpt, 4206–2.14

Cases of acute and chronic conditions, disability, absenteeism, and health services use, by selected characteristics, 1988, annual rpt, 4147–10.170

Deaths and rates, by cause, age, sex, marital status, race, and State, 1987, US Vital Statistics advance annual rpt, 4146–5.113

Deaths and rates, by cause and age, preliminary 1987-88, US Vital Statistics annual rpt, 4144–7

Deaths and rates, by detailed cause and demographic characteristics, 1986 and trends from 1900, US Vital Statistics annual rpt, 4144–2

Deaths and rates, by detailed location, cause, and demographic characteristics, 1987, US Vital Statistics annual rpt, 4144–3

Deaths recorded in 121 cities, weekly rpt, 4202–1

Health condition and health care resources, use, and spending, 1950s-87, annual data compilation, 4144–11

Hospital discharges and length of stay, by diagnosis, patient age and sex, surgical procedure performed, and region, 1965-86, 4147–13.101

Military deaths by cause, age, race, and rank, and personnel captured and missing, by service branch, 2nd half FY88, semiannual rpt, 3542–21

Morbidity and Mortality Weekly Report, infectious notifiable disease cases by State, and public health issues, 4202–1

Older persons pneumonia hospitalization and death rates, and risk relation to health status indicators, aggregate 1982-84, article, 4042–3.934

Statistical Abstract of US, social, political, and economic data, 1790-2025, comprehensive annual compilation, 2324–1.1

Vaccination activity, reactions, costs, and preventable disease cases and deaths, 1988 annual conf, 4204–15

see also under By Disease in the "Index by Categories"

Podgursky, Michael

"Do More-Educated Workers Fare Better Following Job Displacement?", 6722–1.942

Podiatry

Educational and research grants and contracts of Health Professions Bur, by instn and program, FY88, annual listing, 4114–1

Health condition and health care resources, use, and spending, 1950s-87, annual data compilation, 4144–11

HHS financial aid, by program, recipient, State, and city, FY88, annual regional listings, 4004–3

Indian Health Service outpatient visits, by type of provider, selected hospital, and IHS service area, FY87-88, annual rpt, 4084–3

Medicare physicians services use, charges, and reimbursement, by service type, setting, and specialty, 1986, article, 4652–1.936

Military health care personnel, and accessions by training source, by occupation, specialty, and service branch, FY87, annual rpt, 3544–24

Service industries census, 1987: establishments, receipts, employment, and payroll, by SIC 2- to 4-digit kind of business, MSA, county, and city, State rpt series, 2391–1

Training support grants of Bur of Health Professions, by program, region, and State, FY80-87, 4118–62

VA Medicine and Surgery Dept trainees, by detailed program and city, FY88, annual rpt, 8704–4

Pohnpei

see Micronesia Federated States

Poisoning and drug reaction

Deaths and rates, by detailed cause and demographic characteristics, 1986 and trends from 1900, US Vital Statistics annual rpt, 4144–2

Drug abuse, deaths, arrests, convictions, and seizures by drug type, for DC metro area, 1980-87, hearing, 21308–24

Drug abuse, deaths, prices, seizures, and supply by country of origin, by substance, 1988, annual rpt, 6284–2

Drug abuse emergency room admissions and deaths, by drug type and major metro area, July 1985-Dec 1988, semiannual rpt, 4492–3

Drug abuse emergency room admissions and deaths, by drug type and source, sex, race, age, and major metro area, 1988, annual rpt, 4494–8

Drug abuse indicators for selected metro areas, research results, data collection, and policy issues, 1989 semiannual conf, 4492–5

HHS financial aid, by program, recipient, State, and city, FY88, annual regional listings, 4004–3

Homicides, by circumstance, victim and offender relationship, and type of weapon, 1988, annual rpt, 6224–2.1

Injuries from use of consumer products, by severity, victim age, and detailed product, 1988, annual rpt, 9164–6

Isoniazid treatment for tuberculosis, relation to hepatitis risk for pregnant and postpartum women, by age group, 1981-82 study, article, 4042–3.911

Methamphetamine abuse, emergency room admissions and deaths by selected city, and lab seizures, 1980s-87, 4498–61

Military deaths by cause, age, race, and rank, and personnel captured and missing, by service branch, 2nd half FY88, semiannual rpt, 3542–21

Occupational illness rates, by cause and SIC 2- to 3-digit industry, 1987, annual rpt, 6844–1

PCP (phencyclidine) treatment admissions and deaths in selected areas, and emergency visits by patient sex, race, and age, 1987, article, 4042–3.931

Pollutants health effects, concentrations in food and environment, sources, and human intake methodology and data needs, series, 9186–9

Pollutants health effects, concentrations in food and environment, sources, human intake, and regulation, series, 9186–8

Research and testing activities under Natl Toxicology Program, FY87 and planned FY88, annual rpt, 4044–16

Vaccination activity, reactions, costs, and preventable disease cases and deaths, 1988 annual conf, 4204–15

Vaccine adverse reactions, *Morbidity and Mortality Weekly Report*, 4202–1

see also Food and waterborne diseases

see also Lead poisoning and pollution

Pokras, Robert

"Trends in Hospital Utilization: U.S., 1965-86", 4147–13.101

Poland

Agricultural and food production and indexes, total and for selected commodities, by country, 1970s-88, annual rpt, 1524–12

Political broadcasting
Broadcast and financial data for Radio Free Europe and Radio Liberty, and compared to other intl broadcasters, FY88, annual rpt, 10314-1
see also Radio Free Europe
see also Radio Liberty
see also Voice of America
Political campaign funds
see Campaign funds
see Political action committees
Political conventions
Financial activity reported to Fed Election Commission, by type of filer, 1988 natl elections, biennial rpt series, 9276-2
Political ethics
Govt employees political activities prohibited under Hatch Act, cases initiated, FY88, annual rpt, 9494-3
Public opinion on crime and crime-related issues, by respondent characteristics, 1970s-89, annual rpt, 6064-6.2
Public opinion on taxes, spending, and govt efficiency, by respondent characteristics, 1989 survey, annual rpt, 10044-2
Senior Executive Service former members reasons for leaving, and views on SES statutory compliance, 1988 survey, 9498-3
see also Conflict of interests
see also Corruption and bribery
see also Lobbying and lobbying groups
Political parties
Alcoholic beverages warning labels and other consumer protection methods, public views by selected characteristics, 1988 survey, 8488-5
Campaign finances and Fed Election Commission activities, various periods 1975-88, annual rpt, 9274-1
Campaign finances, elections, procedures, and Fed Election Commission activities, press release series, 9276-1
Campaign financial activity reported to Fed Election Commission, by type of filer, 1988 natl elections, biennial rpt series, 9276-2
County Business Patterns, 1987: employment, establishments, and payroll, by SIC 2- to 4-digit industry and county, annual State rpt series, 2326-8
Developing countries disaster preparedness and economic, population, and political data, country rpt series, 9916-2
Foreign countries *Background Notes*, summary social, political, and economic data, series, 7006-2
Foreign countries economic, social, political, and geographic summary data, by country, 1989, annual factbook, 9114-2
Foreign countries human rights conditions in 170 countries, 1988, annual rpt, 21384-3
Health care (long-term) needs, ability to pay, and views on Federal aid for home care, 1988 survey, hearing, 21148-51
Statistical Abstract of US, social, political, and economic data, 1790-2025, comprehensive annual compilation, 2324-1.2
Votes cast by party, candidate, and State, 1988 natl elections, biennial rpt, 9274-5; 21944-3
see also Communist parties
see also Democratic Party
see also Political conventions
see also Republican Party
Political rights
see Civil rights
Political science
Degrees (bachelor and masters) awarded 1985/86, holders employment characteristics, 1987 survey, series, 4826-3
Degrees awarded in higher education, by level, field, race, and sex, 1989 edition, annual rpt, 4824-2.20
Degrees in science and engineering, by field, level, and sex, 1950-86, 9628-77
Education Dept programs funding, operations, and effectiveness, FY88, annual rpt, 4804-5
Enrollment in science and engineering grad programs, by field, source of funds, and characteristics of student and instn, 1975-87, annual rpt, 9627-7
Fed Govt aid to higher education and nonprofit instns for R&D and related activities, by field, instn, agency, and State, FY87, annual rpt, 9627-17
R&D funding by Fed Govt, by field, performer type, agency, and State, FY87-89, annual rpt, 9627-20
R&D funding by higher education instns, by source and field, FY80-87, annual rpt, 9624-18.5
Polivka, Anne E.
"On the Definition of 'Contingent Work' ", 6722-1.958
Pollard, John
"Examination of Sudden Acceleration", 7768-107.1
Polls
see Elections
see Opinion and attitude surveys
Pollution
see Acid rain
see Air pollution
see Dioxins
see Environmental pollution and control
see Marine pollution
see Mercury pollution
see Motor vehicle exhaust
see Noise
see Radiation
see Radon
see Soil pollution
see Water pollution
Polychlorinated biphenyls
see Carcinogens
see Hazardous substances
see Hazardous waste and disposal
Polychloroprene
see Plastics and plastics industry
Polyester
see Synthetic fibers and fabrics
Pomar, M. Elena
"Coffee Prices Not Perking Up", 1522-3.923
Pomona, Calif.
see also under By City in the "Index by Categories"
Pompano Beach, Fla.
Housing starts and completions authorized by building permits in 40 MSAs, quarterly rpt, 2382-9

Wages by occupation, for office and plant workers, 1989 survey, periodic MSA rpt, 6785-3.10
see also under By SMSA or MSA in the "Index by Categories"
Ponce, P.R.
see also under By SMSA or MSA in the "Index by Categories"
Poor
see Homeless population
see Poverty
Pope, Gregory C.
"Occupational Adjustment of the Prospective Payment System Wage Index", 4652-1.950
"Trends in Hospital Labor and Total Factor Productivity, 1981-86", 4652-1.941
Popkin, Barry M.
"Food Choices: What and Why", 1004-16.1
Popoli, Gary
"Suicide in the State of Maryland, 1970-80", 4042-3.928
Popovich, Mark G.
"Entrepreneurs Find Niche Even in Rural Economies", 1502-7.913
Population census
see Census of Population
see Census of Population and Housing
Population characteristics
Agricultural research funding and staffing for USDA, State agencies, and other instns, by topic, FY88, annual rpt, 1744-2
Census Bur rpts and data files, coverage and availability, 1989 annual listing, 2304-2
Census of Population, 1980: selected socioeconomic data, young readers pamphlet series, 2326-1
Coastal areas environmental and socioeconomic conditions, and potential impact of oil and gas OCS leases, final statement series, 5736-1
Current Population Reports, demographic, social, and economic characteristics, series, 2546-1
Current Population Reports, demographic subjects, special study series, 2546-2
Current Population Reports, income and socioeconomic characteristics of persons, families, and households, detailed cross-tabulations, series, 2546-6
Developing countries disaster preparedness and economic, population, and political data, country rpt series, 9916-2
Developing countries economic and social conditions from 1960s, and Intl Dev Cooperation Agency and AID activities and funding, FY88-90, annual rpt, 9904-4
Developing countries sociodemographic data, and AID dev projects, special study series, 9916-3
Foreign countries *Background Notes*, summary social, political, and economic data, series, 7006-2
Foreign countries economic and social conditions, working paper series, 2326-18
Foreign countries economic, social, political, and geographic summary data, by country, 1989, annual factbook, 9114-2
Foreign countries population size, growth rates, and components of change, by country, projected 1989-2020 and trends from 1950, biennial rpt, 2324-9

Hazardous substances exposure factors, and methodological guidelines, 1989 rpt, 9188–109

Mental health care facilities needs assessment and program evaluation for communities, methodology, use of census data, analysis, and sample data, series, 4506–8

Overseas Business Reports: economic conditions, investment and export opportunities, and trade practices, country market research rpt series, 2046–6

Pacific territories social, economic, health, and govtl data, FY88 and trends, annual rpt, 7004–6

Population and housing data, and policy issues, fact sheet series, 2326–17

Research contracts and grants of Natl Inst of Child Health and Human Dev, by recipient and location, FY88, annual listing, 4474–36

Research on population and reproduction, Federal funding by project, FY87, annual listing, 4474–9

Research on population and reproduction, Natl Inst of Child Health and Human Dev funding and activities, 1988, annual rpt, 4474–33

Rural areas education conditions, and population characteristics, 1987 conf papers, 4818–6

Rural areas employment, economic conditions, and population characteristics, 1970s-85, compilation of papers, 1598–243

Statistical Abstract of US, social, political, and economic data, 1790-2025, comprehensive annual compilation, 2324–1.1

Survey of Income and Program Participation, household composition, income, benefits, and labor force status, methodology, working paper series, 2626–10

Texas-Mexico border area health facilities and services, with background data, by Texas county, 1980s-88, GAO rpt, 26121–261

Uranium tailings at inactive mills, remedial action proposals, costs, site characteristics, and environmental, socioeconomic, and health impacts, series, 3356–4

see also Aged and aging
see also Birthplace
see also Body measurements
see also Children
see also Disabled and handicapped persons
see also Earnings, general
see also Educational attainment
see also Educational enrollment
see also Employment and unemployment, general
see also Families and households
see also Farm population
see also Fertility
see also Health condition
see also Homeless population
see also Housing condition and occupancy
see also Intelligence levels
see also Labor supply and demand
see also Life expectancy
see also Living arrangements
see also Marriage and divorce
see also Men

see also Migration
see also Nutrition and malnutrition
see also Occupations
see also Personal and household income
see also Personal consumption
see also Physical characteristics
see also Population projections
see also Population size
see also Poverty
see also Quality of life
see also Vital statistics
see also Wealth
see also Women
see also Youth

Population projections

Aliens (illegal) and immigration impact on congressional apportionment, alternative estimates by State, 1950s-80 with projections to 2010, hearing, 21628–70

Coastal areas environmental impacts of economic dev and population growth, 1980s and projected to 2000, series, 2176–8

Current Population Reports, population estimates and projections, by region and State, series, 2546–3

Developing countries aged population and selected characteristics, 1980s and projected to 2020, country rpt series, 2326–19

Foreign countries economic and social conditions, working paper series, 2326–18

Foreign countries food and agricultural conditions, and relationship to population growth, with background data, 1950s-88 and projections to 2050, hearing, 21708–126

Foreign countries population size, growth rates, and components of change, by country, projected 1989-2020 and trends from 1950, biennial rpt, 2324–9

Immigration to US by category and for relatives of US natls, FY49-88 and alternative projections to FY99, GAO rpt, 26131–59

Mexico population, labor force, and emigration, alternative projections 1990-2000, working paper, 2326–18.46

Older persons socioeconomic characteristics, 1900s-86 and projected to 2050, biennial chartbook, 12904–1

Pacific Northwest population, households, employment, income, and fuel prices, alternative projections 1990-2010 with trends from 1960, annual rpt, 3224–5

Population size and components of change, alternative projections 1988-2080 and trends from 1900, annual actuarial rpt, 4706–1.104

Southern US in- and out-migration, by migrant characteristics and location, 1970s-87 and alternative projections to 2000, article, 9371–1.902

Statistical Abstract of US, social, political, and economic data, with foreign comparisons, 1790-2025, comprehensive annual compilation, 2324–1

Vermont older persons population by selected characteristics, 1900-85 and projected to 2050, hearing, 21148–54

Population size

Africa (Sahel) food supply indicators, by country, 1960s-2000, 1528–290

Appalachia population, by State and county, 1980 and 1987, annual rpt, 9084–1

Business and financial statistics, historic trends, 1988 annual chartbook, 9364–2.4

Census of Population, 1980: selected socioeconomic data, young readers pamphlet series, 2326–1

Child population from age 10 and from birth, by county, 1985, annual rpt, 6064–12

City population size for cities with population over 100,000, as of July 1988, biennial press release, 2324–7

Coastal areas environmental impacts of economic dev and population growth, 1980s and projected to 2000, series, 2176–8

Communist and OECD countries economic conditions, 1987, annual rpt, 7144–11

Communist, OECD, and selected other countries economic conditions, 1960s-88, annual rpt, 9114–4.2

Crimes, arrests by offender characteristics, and rates, by offense, and law enforcement employees, by population size and jurisdiction, 1988, annual rpt, 6224–2

Cuba economic conditions, agricultural and industrial production and distribution, trade, and intl economic relations, 1980-87 with trends from 1961, 9118–8

Current Population Reports, county population size, 1988, and components of change from 1980, annual rpt, 2544–3

Current Population Reports, demographic, social, and economic characteristics, series, 2546–1

Current Population Reports, demographic subjects, special study series, 2546–2

Current Population Reports, population estimates and projections, by region and State, series, 2546–3

Current Population Reports, population estimates for civilian, resident, and total population, monthly rpt, 2542–1

Developing countries aged population and selected characteristics, 1980s and projected to 2020, country rpt series, 2326–19

Developing countries aided by Peace Corps, quality of life indicators, FY90, annual rpt, 9654–1

Developing countries disaster preparedness and economic, population, and political data, country rpt series, 9916–2

Developing countries economic and social conditions from 1960s, and Intl Dev Cooperation Agency and AID activities and funding, FY88-90, annual rpt, 9904–4

Developing countries food production and needs, and related economic outlook, by country, 1989/90, annual rpt, 1524–6

Developing countries sociodemographic data, and AID dev projects, special study series, 9916–3

Eastern Europe and USSR agricultural production, acreage, and consumption, by commodity and country, 1965-85, 1528–284

EC food supply and demand, market and support prices, and other economic indicators, by country and commodity, 1960-85, 1528–276

Economic indicators and relation to govt finances by level of govt, selected years 1929-87, annual rpt, 10044-1

Economic Report of the President for 1989, Joint Economic Committee critique and policy recommendations, annual rpt, 23844-2

Energy use by mode of transport, fuel supply, and demographic and economic factors of vehicle use, 1970s-88, annual rpt, 3304-5

Environmental quality and protection programs, and intl issues, 1988 annual rpt, 484-1

Farms, sales, size, and operator tenure in metro and nonmetro areas, impacts of population growth, with data by State, 1969-82, 1598-253

Florida banks and thrifts deposits and mortgages, building permits, population, and migration, with comparisons to other areas, 1980s-88, article, 9302-2.905

Foreign and US agricultural and food production and indexes, total and for selected commodities, by country, 1970s-88, annual rpt, 1524-12

Foreign countries *Background Notes*, summary social, political, and economic data, series, 7006-2

Foreign countries economic and social conditions, working paper series, 2326-18

Foreign countries economic, social, political, and geographic summary data, by country, 1989, annual factbook, 9114-2

Foreign countries food and agricultural conditions, and relationship to population growth, with background data, 1950s-88 and projections to 2050, hearing, 21708-126

Foreign countries *Geographic Notes*, boundaries, claims, nomenclature, and other devs, periodic rpt, 7142-3

Foreign countries military spending, arms trade, and force strengths, with govt spending and population, by country, 1977-87, annual rpt, 9824-1

Foreign countries population size, growth rates, and components of change, by country, projected 1989-2020 and trends from 1950, biennial rpt, 2324-9

Health condition and health care resources, use, and spending, 1950s-87, annual data compilation, 4144-11

Household and family composition, and factors affecting change, 1960s-88, chartbook, 2546-2.149

Minority group population, and components of change, by race, State, metro-nonmetro location, MSA, and county, 1980-85, Current Population Rpt, 2546-3.159

MSA population size, by area, 1988, annual press release, 2324-8

NATO and Japan military spending and indicators of ability to support common defense, by country, 1960s-87, annual rpt, 3544-28

NATO military forces compared to Warsaw Pact, and selected economic indicators, by country, 1900s-87, conf papers, 3908-6

OASDI benefit payments, trust fund finances, and economic and demographic assumptions, 1970-87 and alternative projections to 1997, actuarial rpt, 4706-1.103

Older persons socioeconomic characteristics, 1900s-86 and projected to 2050, biennial chartbook, 12904-1

Outlying areas population size and components of change, by area, 1980-88, annual Current Population Rpt, 2546-3.162

Pacific basin countries military, economic, technological, and trade conditions, 1970s-85, compilation of papers, 3908-4

Pacific Northwest population, households, employment, income, and fuel prices, alternative projections 1990-2010 with trends from 1960, annual rpt, 3224-5

Pacific territories social, economic, health, and govtl data, FY88 and trends, annual rpt, 7004-6

Pollution (air) exposure of population and selected risk groups, by pollutant, MSA, and county, 1988, hearing, 21368-117

Population and housing data, and policy issues, fact sheet series, 2326-17

Population, income, earnings, and employment growth rates, by area population size and region, 1969-79 and 1979-87, article, 2702-1.915

Population size and households, by State, 1980 and 1988, annual press release, 2324-11

Population size, by age, selected years 1929-88, annual rpt, 204-1.2

Population size, July 1988 and compared to 1980 and 1987, and components of change, 1980-88, annual press release, 2324-10

Research on population and reproduction, Federal funding by project, FY87, annual listing, 4474-9

Research on population and reproduction, Natl Inst of Child Health and Human Dev funding and activities, 1988, annual rpt, 4474-33

Rural and urban areas population and economic data, 1960s-88, annual chartbook, 1504-3

Rural areas served by electric cooperatives, population by community, 1980, annual rpt, 3164-40.1

St Louis metro area local govt finances, structure, and service delivery, mid-1980s, 10046-9.1

Statistical Abstract of US, social, political, and economic data, 1790-2025, comprehensive annual compilation, 2324-1.1

Urban areas fiscal, economic, and social conditions, 1960s-87, biennial rpt, 5184-7.1; 5184-7.4

Vital statistics provisional data, monthly rpt, 4142-1

Western States, FHLB 11th District thrift offices, locations, savings balances, and accounts, quarterly listing, 9302-20

Western US activities of Reclamation Bur, land and population served, and recreation areas, by location, 1986, annual rpt, 5824-12.1

see also Births
see also Deaths
see also Family planning
see also Farm population
see also Fertility
see also Immigration and emigration
see also Migration

see also Population projections
see also Vital statistics

Porcelain products
see Pottery and porcelain products

Pork
see Meat and meat products

Pornography
see Obscenity and pornography

Port Arthur, Tex.
Wages by occupation, for office and plant workers, 1989 survey, periodic MSA rpt, 6785-3.6
see also under By SMSA or MSA in the "Index by Categories"

Port authorities
see Special districts

Porter, Jane M.
"Drought in the U.S.: A Short History", 1588-129

Porter, Joanell
"Occupational and Educational Outcomes of 1985-86 Bachelor's Degree Recipients", 4826-3.1

Porter, K. E.
"International Competitiveness of U.S. Copper Production, 1981-87", 5606-5.7

Porter, Richard D.
"Understanding the Behavior of M2 and V2", 9362-1.903

Porterville, Calif.
Wages by occupation, for office and plant workers, 1989 survey, periodic MSA rpt, 6785-12.7
see also under By SMSA or MSA in the "Index by Categories"

Portland, Maine
Fish and shellfish catch, wholesale receipts, prices, trade, and other market activities, weekly regional rpt, 2162-6.1; 2162-6.2
Wages by occupation, and benefits for office and plant workers, 1988 survey, periodic MSA rpt, 6785-11.3
see also under By SMSA or MSA in the "Index by Categories"

Portland, Oreg.
CPI by component for US city average, and by region, population size, and for 27 metro areas, monthly rpt, 6762-2
Drug test results at arrest, by drug type, offense, and sex, for selected urban areas, quarterly rpt, 6062-3
Freight (waterborne domestic and foreign) by commodity, traffic, and passengers, by port and waterway, 1987, annual rpt, 3754-3.4
Housing vacancy rates for single and multifamily units and mobile homes, by city and ZIP code, 1989, annual MSA rpt, 9304-21.3
Older frail persons HMO case mgmt and home care services, demonstration projects enrollment, 1986, article, 4652-1.913
see also under By City and By SMSA or MSA in the "Index by Categories"

Ports
see Harbors and ports

Portsmouth, N.H.
see also under By SMSA or MSA in the "Index by Categories"

Portsmouth, Ohio
Wages by occupation, for office and plant workers, 1989 survey, periodic MSA rpt, 6785-3.4

Electronic mail service volume, by firm, 1988 rpt, 2808–28

Finances of Fed Govt, cash and debt transactions, daily tables, 8102–4

Finances of govts, revenues by source and spending by function, natl income and product account, *Survey of Current Business*, monthly rpt, 2702–1.24

Finances, operations, and industry devs for telecommunications, with data by service type, firm, and country, 1950s-80s, 2808–27

Foreign and US domestic postal rates, for 14 countries, 1988, annual rpt, 9864–5.1

Foreign govt and private obligors debt to US, by country and program, periodic rpt, 8002–6

House of Representatives salaries, expenses, and contingent fund disbursement, detailed listings, quarterly rpt, 21942–1

Inspection activities of USPS, expenses, and staff, FY88, annual rpt, 9864–8

Inspection activities of USPS, FY88, annual rpt, 9864–9

Price indexes (producer), by stage of processing and detailed commodity, monthly rpt, 6762–6

Revenue and subsidy for revenue forgone, by class of mail, FY88, annual rpt, 9864–5

Revenue and volume by class of mail, and special service transactions, quarterly rpt, 9862–1

Revenue and volume, by class of mail and type of service, FY84-88, annual rpt, 9864–1

Revenue, costs, and volume, by class of mail, FY88, annual rpt, 9864–2

Senate receipts, itemized expenses by payee, and balances, 1st half FY89, semiannual listing, 25922–1

Statistical Abstract of US, social, political, and economic data, 1790-2025, comprehensive annual compilation, 2324–1.3

Tax (income) returns of individuals, use of preaddressed label and bar-coded envelope, 1986, annual article, 8302–2.901

see also Postal employees

see also ZIP codes

see also By Industry in the "Index by Categories"

Potash

Fertilizer consumption, by type and region, 1947-87, annual rpt, 1544–17.2

Fertilizer use by crop and State, and prices, by fertilizer type, 1960s-88, 1588–113

Minerals Yearbook, 1987, Vol 2: State reviews of production, sales, and firms, by commodity, and business activity, annual rpt, 5604–34

Minerals Yearbook, 1987, Vol 3: foreign country reviews of production, trade, and policy, by commodity, annual rpt, 5604–35

Minerals Yearbook, 1988, Vol 1: commodity review of production, reserves, supply, use, and trade, annual rpt, 5604–20.53

Price indexes (producer), by stage of processing and detailed commodity, monthly 1988, annual rpt, 6764–2

Production of potash, prices, trade by country, use, and sales, 1988 crop year, Mineral Industry Surveys, annual rpt, 5614–19

Potatoes

see Vegetables and vegetable products

Potomac River

Army Corps of Engineers water resources dev projects, characteristics, and costs, 1950s-89, biennial State rpt series, 3756–1

Fish (striped bass) stocks status on Atlantic coast, and sport and commercial catch by State, 1979-87, annual rpt, 5504–29

Freight (waterborne domestic and foreign) by commodity, traffic, and passengers, by port and waterway, 1987, annual rpt, 3754–3.1

Water supply and quality in streams and lakes, and groundwater levels in wells, by drainage basin, 1986, annual State rpt series, 5666–23

Water supply and quality in streams and lakes, and groundwater levels in wells, by drainage basin, 1987, annual State rpt series, 5666–10

Water supply and quality in streams and lakes, and groundwater levels in wells, by drainage basin, 1988, annual State rpt series, 5666–16

Water supply in US and southern Canada, streamflow, surface and groundwater conditions, and reservoir levels, by location, monthly rpt, 5662–3

Pottern, Gerald B.

"Bluefish. Species Profiles: Life Histories and Environmental Requirements of Coastal Fishes and Invertebrates", 5506–8.101

Pottery and porcelain products

Ceramics (advanced) technical info of Japan, US industry use and views on value, 1988 survey, 2008–28

County Business Patterns, 1987: employment, establishments, and payroll, by SIC 2- to 4-digit industry and county, annual State rpt series, 2326–8

Employment, earnings, and hours, by SIC 1- to 4-digit industry, monthly 1983-Feb 1989, annual rpt, 6744–4

Housewares (ceramic) lead and cadmium levels, FDA import inspection activity by country, and food safety funding and staff, 1983-88, hearing, 21368–108

Import restraint elimination, impact on domestic industry production and employment, by selected commodity, 1986-88, 9886–4.144

Plumbing fixtures shipments, stocks, trade, use, and firms, by product, quarterly Current Industrial Rpt, 2506–11.2

Price indexes (producer), by stage of processing and detailed commodity, monthly rpt, 6762–6

Price indexes (producer), by stage of processing and detailed commodity, monthly 1988, annual rpt, 6764–2

Science, engineering, and technical employment in manufacturing, by field, occupation, and industry, 1986, triennial rpt, 9627–23

Talc production, use, and trade, with foreign comparisons, selected years 1977-87, 5608–158

Poughkeepsie, N.Y.

see also under By SMSA or MSA in the "Index by Categories"

Poultry industry and products

Agricultural exports of US, impacts of foreign agricultural and trade policy, with data by commodity and country, 1988, annual rpt, 1924–8

Agricultural Statistics, 1988, annual rpt, 1004–1

Agriculture census, 1987: farms, farmland, production and costs, and operator characteristics, advance State and county rpt series, 2330–1

Agriculture census, 1987: farms, farmland, production, finances, and operator characteristics, by county, final State rpt series, 2331–1

Business statistics, detailed data for major industries and economic indicators, *Survey of Current Business*, monthly rpt, 2702–1.11

Cold storage food stocks by commodity and census div, and warehouse space use, by State, monthly rpt, 1631–5

Cold storage food stocks, by commodity and census div, 1988, annual rpt, 1631–11

Consumer Expenditure Survey, household income by source, and itemized spending, by selected characteristics and location, 1984-86, annual rpt, 6764–5.2

Consumption of food and nutrient intake by individuals, by food group, selected characteristics, and region, supplementary survey series, 1356–5

Consumption, supply, trade, prices, spending, and indexes, by food commodity, 1987, annual rpt, 1544–4

County Business Patterns, 1987: employment, establishments, and payroll, by SIC 2- to 4-digit industry and county, annual State rpt series, 2326–8

CPI by component for US city average, and by region, population size, and for 27 metro areas, monthly rpt, 6762–2

Cuba economic conditions, agricultural and industrial production and distribution, trade, and intl economic relations, 1980-87 with trends from 1961, 9118–8

Eastern Europe agricultural production, consumption, and trade, by country, 1970s-88, annual rpt, 1524–11

Eastern Europe and USSR agricultural production, acreage, and consumption, by commodity and country, 1965-85, 1528–284

EC food supply and demand, market and support prices, and other economic indicators, by country and commodity, 1960-85, 1528–276

Egg production and layer inventory, by State, revised estimates 1984-87, 1641–2

Egg production and layer inventory, by State, 1987-88, annual rpt, 1625–7

Egg production by type of product, and eggs broken under Federal inspection by region, monthly rpt, 1625–2

Employment, earnings, and hours, by selected SIC 1- to 4-digit industry, State, and for 262 MSAs, 1972-87, 6748–81

Employment, earnings, and hours, by SIC 1- to 4-digit industry, monthly 1983-Feb 1989, annual rpt, 6744–4

Exports and imports (agricultural) commodity and country, prices, and world market devs, monthly rpt, 1922–12

Exports and imports (agricultural) of US, by commodity and country, bimonthly rpt with articles, 1522–1

Exports and imports (agricultural) of US, by commodity, monthly rpt, 1922-8

Exports and imports (agricultural) of US, by detailed commodity and country, 1988, semiannual rpt, 1522-4

Exports and imports of dairy, livestock, and poultry products, by commodity and country, FAS monthly circular, 1925-32

Exports of US, detailed commodities by country, monthly rpt, 2422-3

Farm finances and operations, by size, commodity, and region, 1986, annual rpt, 1544-27

Farm financial and marketing conditions, forecast 1989, annual chartbook, 1504-8

Farm income, expenses, receipts by commodity, assets, liabilities, and ratios, 1988 and trends from 1945, annual rpt, 1544-16

Farm labor costs impacts of illegal aliens employer sanctions, by farm type, size, and region, 1986, 1598-250

Farm receipts for 25 leading crops, by State, 1960-87, 1548-347

Farm sector balance sheet, and receipts by detailed commodity, by State, 1984-88, annual rpt, 1544-18

Farm sector finances, income sources, expenses by type, assets, debts, and ratios, 1987, annual rpt, 1544-19

Financial ratios of farms, benchmarks by type of operation and region, 1984-86, 1548-342

Foreign and US agricultural production, trade, and weather devs, with EC price supports, weekly press release, 1922-4

Foreign and US production, trade, and use, by selected country, forecast 1990, FAS annual circular, 1925-33

Foreign countries agricultural production, prices, and trade, by country, 1970s-89 and forecast 1990, annual world region rpt series, 1524-4

Imports of US, detailed Schedule A commodities by country, monthly rpt, 2422-2

Inspection of meat and poultry, Federal, State, and foreign govts activities and staff, FY88, annual rpt, 1374-1

Inspection of meat and poultry for domestic use and export, and rejections by cause, by type of animal and product, FY88, annual rpt, 1374-3

Inspection of poultry slaughter by Fed Govt, pounds certified, and condemnations by cause, by State, monthly rpt, 1625-3

Labor productivity, indexes of output, hours, and employment by SIC 2- to 4-digit industry, 1963-87, annual rpt, 6824-1.3

Manufacturers finances and operations, by SIC 2- to 4-digit industry, forecast 1989 and trends from 1950s, annual rpt, 2044-28

Manufacturing annual survey, 1986: financial and operating data, by SIC 2- to 4-digit industry, series, 2506-15

Manufacturing census, 1987: financial and operating data, for SIC 4-digit industries by product, preliminary rpt, 2491-1.1

Natl Poultry Improvement Plan coverage of hatcheries and birds, by species, disease program, and State, 1988, annual rpt, 1394-15

Nutrient and caloric composition of food, for raw, processed, and prepared food, 1988 rpt, 1358-3

Occupational injury and illness rates, by SIC 2- to 4-digit industry, 1987, annual rpt, 6844-1

Price indexes (producer), by stage of processing and detailed commodity, monthly rpt, 6762-6

Price indexes (producer), by stage of processing and detailed commodity, monthly 1988, annual rpt, 6764-2

Prices (farm-retail) for food, marketing cost components, and industry finances and productivity, 1950s-88, annual rpt, 1544-9

Prices (producer and retail) of meat and fish, 1980-89, semiannual situation rpt, 1561-15.3

Prices and marketing of poultry and eggs, by selected region, State, and city, monthly and weekly 1988, annual rpt, 1317-2

Prices received and paid by farmers, by commodity and State, 1988, annual rpt, 1629-5

Prices received by farmers for major products, and paid for farm inputs and living items, by State, monthly rpt, 1629-1

Production and inventories for chickens, eggs, and turkeys, monthly rpt, 1625-1

Production and prices for chickens, eggs, and turkeys, by State, 1987-88, annual rpt, 1625-5

Production, consumption, and industry finances and operations, for livestock, meat, and poultry, 1950s-86, 1568-280

Production inputs, output, and productivity for farms, by commodity and region, 1947-87, annual rpt, 1544-17

Production itemized costs, by farm sales size and region, 1988, annual rpt, 1614-3

Production of chicken and turkey hatcheries, by State, 1987-88, annual rpt, 1625-8

Production, prices, receipts, trade, and disposition, for chickens, eggs, and turkeys, 1960-87, 1568-39

Production, prices, trade, and marketing, by commodity, current situation and forecast, monthly rpt with articles, 1502-4

Production, prices, trade, and stocks, monthly rpt, 1561-17

Production, prices, trade, stocks, and use, periodic situation rpt with articles, 1561-7

Production, receipts, and demand ratios, by commodity group and region, 1949-83, 1548-348

Production, slaughter, prices, and processing industry operations, for broilers, 1950s-87, 1568-279

Production, trade, and per capita consumption for chickens and turkeys, quarterly 1960-87, 1568-285.2

Statistical Abstract of US, social, political, and economic data, 1790-2025, comprehensive annual compilation, 2324-1.3

Supply and demand indicators for livestock and dairy products, and for selected foreign and US crops, monthly rpt, 1522-5

Tax (income) returns of partnerships, income statement items by industry group, 1986, annual article, 8302-2.903

Turkey consumption impacts of meat prices, and production related to net returns, 1950s-89, article, 1561-7.906

Turkey hatcheries egg inventory and poult placements, by region, monthly rpt, 1625-10

Turkeys raised by State, and losses by region, 1987-88, and hatchery plans, 1989, annual rpt, 1625-6

Wholesale trade census, 1987: employment, establishments, finances, and operations, by SIC 2- to 4-digit kind of business, MSA, county, and city, State rpt series, 2405-1

see also under By Commodity in the "Index by Categories"

Poverty

Agricultural Conservation Program participation by low-income farmers, by State, FY87, annual rpt, 1804-7

Asian American earnings, and employment and other characteristics, by detailed origin and whether foreign-born, 1980, 11046-7.2

Cardiovascular diseases cases, health care services use and costs, and productivity losses, by selected characteristics, 1980, 4146-12.26

CCC dairy price support program foreign donations and domestic donations to poor, schools, Prisons Bur, and VA, monthly rpt, 1802-2

Child care arrangements and costs, by income and other characteristics of family, 1984-86, press release, 2328-61

Child support and alimony awards, and payment status, by selected characteristics of woman, 1985, biennial Current Population Rpt, 2546-2.145

Consumer Income, socioeconomic characteristics of persons, families, and households, detailed cross-tabulations, Current Population Rpt series, 2546-6

Counties (nonmetro) employment by industry sector and degree of urbanization, and compared to metro counties, various periods 1969-86, 1598-244

Disabled OASDI and SSI beneficiaries, by selected characteristics, 1986, article, 4742-1.916

Disabled persons employment, labor force status, and other characteristics, 1988, Current Population Rpt, 2546-2.147

Education data, selected performance and financial indicators by State, 1982-88, annual table with supplements, 4804-32

Employment and unemployment in metro and nonmetro poverty and nonpoverty areas, monthly rpt, quarterly data, 6742-2.9

Employment, earnings, and other characteristics of poverty level labor force, 1987, article, 6722-1.948

Employment status of poor householders and reasons for not working, by sex, 1959-86, article, 6722-1.939

Employment, unemployment, and labor force characteristics, Labor Statistics Handbook, 1940s-88 with trends from 1913, 6728-38.1

Families and persons in poverty, by detailed socioeconomic characteristics, 1987 annual Current Population Rpt, 2546-6.60

Families and persons in poverty, by race, selected years 1960-87, annual rpt, 204-1.1

Food aid program of USDA for women, infants, and children, prenatal enrollees by trimester of enrollment and other characteristics, 1984, article, 4042-3.929

Food consumption and nutrient intake by individuals, by food group, selected characteristics, and region, supplementary survey series, 1356-5

Foreign countries labor conditions, union coverage, and work accidents, annual country rpt series, 6366-4

Health care (long-term) for aged, funding by Fed Govt, public views, 1987 survey, hearings, 21368-106

Hispanic Americans socioeconomic characteristics, by detailed origin, 1988, Current Population Rpt, 2546-1.430; 2546-1.438

Hospital reimbursement by Medicare under prospective payment system, dev of alternative indexes for diagnosis related group classification, with data by instn characteristics, 1984-86, 17206-2.6

Household and family characteristics, by living arrangement, 1988 and trends from 1960, Current Population Rpt, 2546-2.148

Household and family composition, and factors affecting change, 1960s-88, chartbook, 2546-2.149

Household composition, income, benefits, and labor force status, Survey of Income and Program Participation methodology, working paper series, 2626-10

Housing and households characteristics, MSA surveys, fact sheet series, 2485-11

Housing and households detailed characteristics, and unit and neighborhood quality, by location, 1985, biennial rpt, 2485-12

Housing and households detailed characteristics, and unit and neighborhood quality, MSA surveys, series, 2485-6

Income (household) and poverty status under alternative income definitions, by recipient characteristics, 1986, Current Population Rpt, 2546-6.58

Income (household) relation to poverty level by sex, and value of noncash benefits by type, by household type, 1959-86, article, 6722-1.927

Income (personal) and poverty status, change by selected socioeconomic characteristics, 1984-85, Current Population Rpt, 2546-20.10

Indian housing condition and other characteristics, for aged, 1987 survey, 21148-53

Insurance (health) coverage of adolescents by selected characteristics, and impacts of mandated employer and expanded Medicaid coverage, 1979-87, 26358-205

Job Training Partnership Act participants and eligible population, by selected characteristics, 1986, 15496-1.3

Mammography referral services for low-income women, use and client characteristics, 1987-88 local area study, article, 4042-3.951

Medicaid coverage, participation, payments, admin, and legislative history, with data by State, 1980s-88, 21368-105

Medicare and other insurance programs catastrophic illness coverage, benefits, premiums, costs, and program finances, projected 1988-93, 26306-3.105

Migration since 1986, mover characteristics by same or different area, and compared to nonmovers, 1987, annual Current Population Rpt, 2546-1.435

Nutritional status and related health condition and practices, by selected characteristics, 1970s-87, 4048-33

OASDI beneficiary households income, assets, and economic status changes, by beneficiary type, 1983-84, article, 4742-1.904

OASI beneficiaries affected by earnings limits by selected characteristics, and Federal outlays, under alternative limits, 1986, 26306-3.110

Older persons health condition and care access, data collection improvement needs, 1985 conf papers, 4147-4.26

Older persons social security issues, Fed Govt spending, and indicators of need, with bibl, 1988 compilation of papers, 25928-7

Older persons socioeconomic characteristics, 1900s-86 and projected to 2050, biennial chartbook, 12904-1

Population in poverty by selected characteristics, under measurement methods using income and wealth, 1983, article, 1502-7.908

Population poverty status by age group and living arrangements, and family poverty threshold, late 1930s-87, annual rpt, 4744-3.1

Population size and characteristics, 1969-88, Current Population Rpt, annual rpt, 2546-2.146

Public income transfers impact on poverty rate, by State, 1984-88, article, 6722-1.933

Rural and urban areas population and economic data, 1960s-88, annual chartbook, 1504-3

Rural and urban areas population, by months spent in poverty over previous year, 1983-84, article, 1502-7.915

Rural areas aid from Fed Govt compared to urban areas, by program and degree of urbanization, FY85, periodic rpt, 1598-248

Rural areas employment, economic conditions, and population characteristics, 1970s-85, compilation of papers, 1598-243

Single-parent household income and spending, and selected characteristics, with comparison to households with married parents, 1984-86, article, 6722-1.916

Southern US poverty rates, by household composition, race, and urban-rural location, 1986, article, 9371-1.903

St Louis metro area local govt finances, structure, and service delivery, mid-1980s, 10046-9.1

Statistical Abstract of US, social, political, and economic data, 1790-2025, comprehensive annual compilation, 2324-1.1; 2324-1.3

Telephone local service charges and low-income subsidies, by region, company, and city, 1940-June 1989, semiannual rpt, 9282-8

Telephone service of households, by composition, income sources, and other characteristics, 1984-87, 9288-11

Texas-Mexico border area health facilities and services, with background data, by Texas county, 1980s-88, GAO rpt, 26121-261

Vermont older persons employment, income, and other characteristics, by sex and age, 1900-86, hearing, 21148-54

Vitamin and mineral supplements use by adults and children, by type and user characteristics, 1986, 4146-8.175

Vocational education for disadvantaged and handicapped funding of Fed Govt, by selected State and district, 1985-89 and projected to 2000, GAO rpt, 26121-286

West Virginia poverty conditions, food aid participants, and birth outcomes, 1980-87, hearing, 21968-49

Women (older) pension coverage, sources, payments, and effect on income and poverty status, 1982, article, 4742-1.901

see also Homeless population

see also under By Income in the "Index by Categories"

Powell-Griner, Eve

"Characteristics of Persons Dying from AIDS. Preliminary Data from the 1986 National Mortality Followback Survey", 4146-8.178

"Characteristics of Persons Dying of Diseases of Heart. Preliminary Data from the 1986 National Mortality Followback Survey", 4146-8.177

"Induced Terminations of Pregnancy: Reporting States, 1984", 4147-24.2

"Perinatal Mortality in the U.S.: 1981-85", 4146-5.107

Power, Elaine J.

"Screening for Open-Angle Glaucoma in the Elderly", 26356-7.1

Power plants

see Electric power plants and equipment

Power resources

see terms listed under Energy resources and consumption

Power tools

see Tools

Powers, Susan G.

"Cyclical Movements in Bureau of Labor Statistics Multifactor Productivity Measures and Capacity Utilization", 6886-6.67

PRC

see China, Peoples Republic

Precious metals

see Gold

see Silver

Precious stones

see Gemstones

Precipitation

see Weather

Predictions

see Projections and forecasts

Prefabricated buildings

County Business Patterns, 1987: employment, establishments, and payroll, by SIC 2- to 4-digit industry and county, annual State rpt series, 2326-8

Employment, earnings, and hours, by SIC 1- to 4-digit industry, monthly 1983-Feb 1989, annual rpt, 6744-4

Exports of US, detailed commodities by country, monthly rpt, 2422-3

Imports of US, detailed Schedule A commodities by country, monthly rpt, 2422-2

Multinatl US firms and foreign affiliates finances and operations, by industry of parent firm and affiliate, world area, and country, preliminary 1987, annual rpt, 2704–5

Northern Mariana Islands economic census, 1987: employment, firms, payroll, and receipts, by SIC 1- to 4-digit industry, 2597–1

Occupational injury and illness rates, by SIC 2- to 4-digit industry, 1987, annual rpt, 6844–1

Pollutant ozone levels, urban areas failure to meet natl standards, emissions sources, exposure, and costs and benefits of reduction strategies, 1983-87 and projected to 2004, 26358–203

Pollution abatement capital and operating costs, by SIC 2-to 4-digit industry and State, 1986, annual Current Industrial Rpt, 2506–3.6

Price indexes (producer), by stage of processing and detailed commodity, monthly rpt, 6762–6

Price indexes (producer), by stage of processing and detailed commodity, monthly 1988, annual rpt, 6764–2

Science, engineering, and technical employment in manufacturing, by field, occupation, and industry, 1986, triennial rpt, 9627–23

Small business establishments, employment, and financial ratios, by SIC 1- to 2-digit industry and State, late 1960s-87, 9768–19

Statistical Abstract of US, social, political, and economic data, 1790-2025, comprehensive annual compilation, 2324–1.3

Tax (income) returns of corporations, income and tax items by asset size and detailed industry, 1986, annual rpt, 8304–4; 8304–21

Tax (income) returns of partnerships, income statement items by industry group, 1986, annual article, 8302–2.903

Tax (income) returns of sole proprietorships, income statement items, by industry group, 1987, annual article, 8302–2.904; 8302–2.921

Virgin Islands economic censuses, 1987: employment, firms, payroll, and receipts, by SIC 1- to 4-digit industry, island, and city, 2593–1

Wholesale trade census, 1987: employment, establishments, finances, and operations, by SIC 2- to 4-digit kind of business, MSA, county, and city, State rpt series, 2405–1

see also Books and bookselling

see also Copyright

see also Microforms

see also Newspapers

see also Periodicals

see also Writers and writing

see also By Industry in the "Index by Categories"

see also under By Commodity in the "Index by Categories"

Prison sentences

see Sentences, criminal procedure

Prison work programs

Fed Prison Industries finances and operations, FY88, annual rpt, 6244–3

Federal correctional instn inmates, by sex, prison, security level, contract facility type, and region, monthly rpt series, 6242–1

Participants of work release and other prison programs, and work release eligibility provisions, by State, various periods 1984-87, annual rpt, 6064–6.1; 6064–6.6

Private sector involvement in prison industries, operations by prison and firm, and State provisions, as of 1987, 6068–228

Prisoners

AIDS cases and AIDS virus infection prevalence, by risk group and other patient characteristics, 1981-88 and projected to 1992, 4206–2.13

AIDS cases in prisons, test results, and prevention and control policies, by location, 1988 survey, annual rpt, 6064–22

AIDS virus antibody testing of Federal prisoners, public opinion by respondent characteristics, 1987 survey, annual rpt, 6064–6.2

Criminal activity in prison, Federal sentencing guidelines by offense and circumstances, 1989 rpt, 17668–1

Drug abuse indicators for selected metro areas, research results, data collection, and policy issues, 1989 semiannual conf, 4492–5

Executions since 1930, and prisoners under death sentence by prison control and prisoner characteristics, by State, 1973-88, annual rpt, 6066–25.23

Fed Bur of Prisons activities, and inmate and staff characteristics, FY88, annual rpt, 6244–2

Federal correctional instn inmates, by sex, prison, security level, contract facility type, and region, monthly rpt series, 6242–1

Federal criminal sentencing, guidelines use and results by offense and district, and Sentencing Commission activities, 1988, annual rpt, 17664–1

Federal prisoners, admissions, and releases, by offense, selected prisoner characteristics, instn, and location, annual rpt, suspended, 6244–1

Foreign countries human rights conditions in 170 countries, 1988, annual rpt, 21384–3

Jail population by sex, race, and for 25 jurisdictions, and instn conditions, 1983-87, annual rpt, 6066–25.18

Marshals Service activities, FY88, annual rpt, 6294–1

Petitions of prisoners, and dispositions in Federal district and appeals courts, by type, June 1989, annual rpt, 18204–2; 18204–8

Population and movements of prisoners, by offense, location, and selected other characteristics, data compilation, 1930s-87, annual rpt, 6064–6.6

Population, conditions, and problems of prisons, issues and bibl, 1989 compilation of papers, 25928–8

Population of Federal and State instns by sex, admissions, and instn capacity and overcrowding, by State, 1980s-88, annual rpt, 6066–25.21

Population of prisoners, characteristics, and movements, by State, 1986, annual rpt, 6064–26

Recidivism rates of prisoners released in 1983, by offense and prisoner characteristics, 1983-86, 6066–19.48

State correctional instn prisoners, by offense, criminal history, family status and background, and victim and other inmate characteristics, 1986, annual rpt, 6064–26.3

Statistical Abstract of US, social, political, and economic data, 1790-2025, comprehensive annual compilation, 2324–1.1

Suicides in Maryland prisons, by selected characteristics, 1979-87, 4186–9.2

Time served ratio to offenses committed, by offense, 1958-86, 6068–229

US attorneys civil and criminal cases by type and disposition, and collections, by Federal district, FY88, annual rpt, 6004–2.1

see also Community-based correctional programs

see also Parole and probation

see also Prison work programs

see also Prisoners of war

Prisoners of war

Claims against foreign govts by US natls, by claim type and country, 1988, annual rpt, 6004–16

Military deaths by cause, age, race, and rank, and personnel captured and missing, by service branch, 2nd half FY88, semiannual rpt, 3542–1

VA activities and programs, monthly rpt, 8602–3; 9922–2

Veterans health care, patients, visits, costs, and operating beds, by VA and contract facility, and region, quarterly rpt, 8602–4

Vietnam Orderly Departure Program, former re-education camp prisoners arrivals in US and refugee camps, monthly rpt, 7002–4

Prisons

see Correctional institutions

see Juvenile detention and correctional institutions

see Military prisons

see Prison work programs

see Prisoners

see Sentences, criminal procedure

Privacy

see Right of privacy

Private schools

Black colleges R&D funding by source, and characteristics of grad students and research staff, by field of science and instn, 1980s-87, 9628–78

Compensatory education programs federally funded, private school students served, and costs, for selected districts, 1984-89, GAO rpt, 26121–308

Condition of Education, detailed data on elementary, secondary, and higher education, 1920s-88 and projected to 1997, annual rpt, 4824–1

Data on education, enrollment, degrees, teachers, and spending, 1974/75-1988/89 and alternative projections to 1999/2000, annual rpt, 4824–4

Desegregation of schools, indicators of integration plans effectiveness by school district and location, 1960s-85, 11048–189

Digest of Education Statistics, detailed data on students, staff, finances, and facilities, 1989 edition, annual rpt, 4824–2

see also Defective products
see also Food ingredients and additives
see also Food inspection
see also Hazardous substances
see also Inflammable materials
see also Motor vehicle safety devices
see also Poisoning and drug reaction
see also Quality control and testing
Production
see Agricultural production
see Industrial production
see Industrial production indexes
see Producer Price Index
see Production costs
see Productivity
see Value added tax
Production capacity and utilization
see Industrial capacity and utilization
Production costs
Auto quality changes since last model year, factory and retail value, 1990 model year, annual press release, 6764-3
Business Conditions Digest, economic, business, and financial devs and cyclical fluctuations, monthly rpt, 2702-3
Competitiveness (intl) of US industries, with selected foreign and US operating data by major firm and product, series, 2046-12
Food prices (farm-retail), marketing cost components, and industry finances and productivity, 1950s-88, annual rpt, 1544-9
Manufacturing census, 1987: financial and operating data, for SIC 4-digit industries by product, preliminary industry rpt series, 2491-1
Mineral industries census, 1987: financial and operating data, preliminary industry rpt series, 2511-1
Minerals foreign and US supply under alternative market conditions, reserves, and background industry data, series, 5606-4
Shipbuilding costs, deliveries, and contracts, by coastal district and shipyard, various periods 1971-88, annual rpt, 7704-12.1
Steel industry production costs relation to labor and other input changes, model description and results, 1954-85, working paper, 9377-9.83
Tax (income) returns of corporations, income and tax items by asset size and detailed industry, 1986, annual rpt, 8304-1; 8304-21
see also Agricultural production costs
see also Business income and expenses, general
see also Business income and expenses, specific industry
see also Capital investments, general
see also Capital investments, specific industry
see also Energy production costs
see also Labor costs and cost indexes
see also Payroll
see also Producer Price Index
Production Credit Associations
see Farm Credit System
Production workers
Construction industries census, 1987: establishments, employment, receipts, and expenditures, by SIC 4-digit industry and State, final industry rpt series, 2373-1
Dallas-Fort Worth metro area employment, earnings, hours, and CPI changes, 1970s-88, annual rpt, 6964-2

Earnings and hours, by industry div and major manufacturing group, Monthly Labor Review, 6722-1.2
Earnings, annual average percent changes for selected occupational groups, selected MSAs, monthly rpt, 6782-1.1
Employee benefit plan coverage and provisions, by plan type and occupational group, 1988, annual rpt, 6784-19
Employment and Earnings, detailed data, monthly rpt, 6742-2.6
Employment Cost Index and alternative measure of compensation costs, by component, occupation, industry group, union status, and location, 1975-89, annual rpt, 6744-20
Employment, earnings, and hours, by SIC 1- to 4-digit industry, monthly 1983-Feb 1989, annual rpt, 6744-4
Employment, earnings, and hours, monthly press release, 6742-5
Employment situation, earnings, hours, and other BLS economic indicators, transcripts of BLS Commissioner's monthly testimony, periodic rpt, 23846-4
Foreign countries labor cost indexes, by selected country, 1980-89, article, 6722-1.926
Handbook of Labor Statistics, employment, unemployment, and labor force characteristics, 1940s-88 with trends from 1913, 6728-38
Houston metro area employment, earnings, hours, and CPI changes, 1970s-88, annual rpt, 6964-1
Imports injury to US industries from foreign subsidized products, investigations with background financial and operating data, series, 9886-15
Imports injury to US industries from sales at less than fair value, investigations with background financial and operating data, series, 9886-14
Insurance (short term disability) coverage and provisions, by occupational group, 1986-87, article, 6722-1.925
Manufacturing employment change during periods of exchange rate volatility, by industry trade orientation and and census div, 1973-87, article, 9373-1.917
Natl income and product accounts and components, *Survey of Current Business*, monthly rpt, 2702-1.27
Puerto Rico economic conditions, 1986 hearings, 21448-39
Southeastern US manufacturing hours and earnings, for 8 States, quarterly press release, 6942-7
Southwestern States employment by industry div, earnings, and hours, by State, monthly rpt, 6962-2
see also under By Occupation in the "Index by Categories"
Productivity
Economic indicators, prices, labor costs, and productivity, BLS econometric analyses and methodology, working paper series, 6886-6
Foreign and US output, compensation, unit labor costs, and indexes, Monthly Labor Review, 6722-1.6
Foreign countries labor conditions, output, earnings, and price indexes, by selected country, 1950-88, 6728-38.11

Japan manufacturing capital stock relation to productivity, alternative measures, model results, 1955-81, working paper, 6886-6.58
Lumber and paper industries productivity, impact on southern US economy, and employment compared to other industries, 1970s-80, State rpt series, 1206-36
Manufacturing capacity, output, and productivity growth, and trade balance by major industry group, 1973-87, article, 9391-1.903
Monthly Labor Review, output, compensation, labor and nonlabor unit costs, and indexes, 6722-1.5
Shoe (nonrubber) industry productivity measures, 1958-86, article, 6722-1.920
Small business establishments, operations, owner characteristics, and job training, late 1950s-87, 9768-20
Soviet Union aggregate and industrial factor productivity annual growth rate, 1961-88, annual rpt, 9114-4.3
Soviet Union economic conditions and military activity, 1960s-86, hearing, 23848-195
Tire and inner tube industry productivity measures, 1958-86, article, 6722-1.928
see also Agricultural productivity
see also Government efficiency
see also Industrial capacity and utilization
see also Industrial production indexes
see also Labor productivity
Professional and technical workers
Aerospace industry employment and salaries, by sex and race, 1979-87, GAO rpt, 26121-315
Air traffic control and airway facilities staff, by selected employment and demographic characteristics, FY88, annual rpt, 7504-41
Aircraft mechanics certified by FAA, by age, sex, region, and State, 1988, annual rpt, 7504-2
Cancer (stomach) incidence and risk relation to diet and refrigerator use, 1985-87 local area study, article, 4472-1.919
Educational attainment, by sociodemographic characteristics and location, 1987 and trends from 1940, biennial Current Population Rpt, 2546-1.427; 2546-1.431
Employee benefit plan coverage and provisions, by plan type and occupational group, 1988, annual rpt, 6784-19
Employee flexible benefit plan coverage and provisions, by occupational group for private sector and govt workers, 1986-88, article, 6722-1.959
Employment and occupation of householder, by occupation of spouse, race, and family composition, 1988, annual Current Population Rpt, 2546-1.437
Employment Cost Index and alternative measure of compensation costs, by component, occupation, industry group, union status, and location, 1975-89, annual rpt, 6744-20
Employment, earnings, and hours, monthly press release, 6742-5
Employment in nonmanufacturing industries, by detailed occupation and SIC 2-digit industry, 1987, triennial rpt, 6748-60

Employment situation, earnings, hours, and other BLS economic indicators, transcripts of BLS Commissioner's monthly testimony, periodic rpt, 23846–4

Employment, unemployment, and labor force characteristics, by region, State, and selected metro area, 1988, annual rpt, 6744–7

Fed Govt civilian employment and payroll, by occupation, pay grade, sex, agency, and location, 1987, biennial rpt, 9844–4

Fed Govt civilian employment by occupation, agency, and location, and language and math skill needs, 1966-87 and projected to 2000, 9848–37

Fed Govt civilian employment, by occupation, pay schedule, grade, sex, and race, as of Sept 1988, article, 9842–1.902

Fed Govt pay comparability with private industry, and recommended and actual pay adjustments, 1970s-89, annual rpt, 10104–1

Fed Govt pay comparability with private industry, and recommended pay rate adjustments, 1989, annual rpt, 104–16

Fed Govt temporary employment, appointments and extensions, by occupational group, Jan-June 1983-85, GAO rpt, 26119–129

Handbook of Labor Statistics, employment, unemployment, and labor force characteristics, 1940s-88 with trends from 1913, 6728–38

Health condition of labor force, and services use, by occupation and industry of longest job held, income, age, sex, and race. 1980, 4147–10.168

Immigrants admitted to US, by occupational group and country of birth, preliminary FY88, annual table, 6264–1

Immigration to US, alien workers, visitors, deportations, and naturalizations, by country, FY88 and trends from 1820, annual rpt, 6264–2

Income (household, family, and personal), by source, detailed characteristics, and region, 1987, annual Current Population Rpt, 2546–6.59

Insurance (short term disability) coverage and provisions, by occupational group, 1986-87, article, 6722–1.925

Labor hourly costs, by component, occupational group, union coverage, industry div, and region, 1989, annual rpt, 6744–21

Labor unions recognized in Fed Govt, agreements and membership by agency and facility, as of Jan 1989, biennial listing, 9844–14

Minority group and women employment, by occupation, SIC 1- to 3- digit industry, State, and MSA, 1986, annual rpt, 9244–1

Occupational changes, by tenure and other worker characteristics, and labor mobility rates, 1965-86, article, 6722–1.943

State and local govt employment of minorities and women, by occupation, function, pay level, and State, 1986, annual rpt, 9244–6

Statistical Abstract of US, social, political, and economic data, 1790-2025, comprehensive annual compilation, 2324–1.3

Suburban areas land use, commuting, employment, and housing characteristics, detailed data for traffic planning, 1986, 7888–75

Transit systems finances and operations, by mode of transport, size of fleet, and for 432 systems, 1986, annual rpt, 7884–4

see also Area wage surveys

see also Consultants

see also Engineers and engineering

see also Executives and managers

see also Health occupations

see also Industry wage surveys

see also Paraprofessionals

see also Scientists and technicians

see also under By Occupation in the "Index by Categories"

see also under names of specific professions

Professional associations

see Associations

Professionals' fees

Health Care Financing Review, provider prices, price inputs and indexes, and labor, quarterly journal, 4652–1.1

Medicare claims approved, charges, and reimbursements by type of service, from 1974, monthly rpt, quarterly data, 4742–1.11

Medicare reimbursement of hospitals under prospective payment system, and of physicians, effect on services, finances, and beneficiary payments, 1970s-88, annual rpt, 17204–2

Physicians charges and reimbursement from Medicare, by enrollee characteristics and region, late 1960s-84, biennial rpt, 4654–1

Physicians income, by specialty and other practice characteristics, 1975 and 1983-84, article, 4652–1.920

Physicians Medicare assigned-fee laws of 4 States, impacts on care cost and availability, 1985-89, GAO rpt, 26121–312

Physicians Medicare assigned-fee participation related to selected physician, practice, and community characteristics, 1984, article, 4652–1.902

Physicians Medicare assigned-fee use, attitudes, and project to encourage patient use of assignment physician, 1988 rpt, 4658–30

Physicians Medicare services use, charges, and reimbursement, by service type, setting, and specialty, 1986, article, 4652–1.936

Physicians payment issues, HCFA research activities and grants, as of Mar 1989, annual listing, 4654–10

Service industries receipts, by SIC 2- to 4-digit kind of business, 1988, annual rpt, 2413–8

Profits

see Business income and expenses, general

see Business income and expenses, specific industry

see Farm income

see Operating ratios

Project HOPE

"Impact of Medicare Prospective Payment on the Use of Expensive Devices, 1984-86", 17206–2.3

"Trends in the Concentration of Six Surgical Procedures Under PPS and Their Implications for Patient Mortality and Medicare Cost", 17206–2.5

Project listings

see Demonstration and pilot projects

see Directories

Projections and forecasts

Africa (Sahel) food supply indicators, by country, 1960s-2000, 1528–290

Africa food imports and aid needs under alternative weather assumptions, for 17 African countries, projected to 1995, 1528–279

Agricultural Economics Research, quarterly journal, 1502–3

Agricultural production, acreage, and yield for selected crops, forecasts by selected world region and country, FAS monthly circular, 1925–28

Agricultural production, prices, and trade, by commodity and country, 1970s-89 and forecast 1990, annual world region rpt series, 1524–4

Agricultural supply and demand indicators for US and foreign countries, by selected crop, monthly rpt, 1522–5

Agricultural trade by commodity and country, prices, and world market devs, monthly rpt, 1922–12

Agricultural trade, outlook and current situation, quarterly rpt, 1542–4

AIDS cases and AIDS virus infection prevalence, by risk group and other patient characteristics, 1981-88 and projected to 1992, 4206–2.13

AIDS cases forecasts, analysis of CDC and other methodology, 1989 GAO rpt, 26131–55

AIDS health care services research status, needs, methods, and impacts on public health policy and funding, with data for selected cities, 1989 conf papers, 4188–59

Air traffic (passenger), and aircraft operations by type, by airport and State, projected FY89-2005 and trends from FY83, annual rpt, 7504–7

Air traffic and other aviation activity forecasts of FAA, 1989 annual conf, 7504–28

Air traffic control and airway facilities improvement activities under Natl Airspace System Plan, 1981-85 and projected to 2000, annual rpt, 7504–12

Air traffic, pilots, airports, and fuel use, forecast FY89-2000 and trends from FY80, annual rpt, 7504–6

Aircraft flight service station workload of FAA, pilot briefs, contacts, and flight plans by facility, projected FY88-99 and trends from FY80, annual rpt, 7504–39

Aircraft handled by instrument flight rule, by user type, FAA traffic control center, and region, FY80-88 and projected to FY2000, annual rpt, 7504–15

Airport traffic, delays, capacity improvement projects and funding, runway length, and navigational operations, for hub and reliever airports, 1986-87 and forecast to 1996, 7508–67

Alaska airport dev plans and air systems operations, FY89-98, annual rpt, 7504–36

Banks failure forecasting accuracy, and failure relation to financial, regulatory, and other indicators, with data by instn, 1960s-89, working paper, 9377–9.77

Money supply forecast accuracy impact of monetary target announcements, for US and Japan, 1978-88, working paper, 9393-10.8

North Central States business and economic conditions, Fed Reserve 9th District, quarterly journal, 9383-19

Northwestern US timber resources and removals, projected under 5 mgmt alternatives, 1988 rpt, 1208-300

OASDHI admin, and SSA activities, 1930s-89 and projected to 2063, data compilation, annual rpt, 4704-12

OASDHI future cost estimates, actuarial study series, 4706-1

OASDI trust funds finances, and impact on Federal budget, 1987-88 and projected to 2050, GAO rpt, 26121-269

OASDI trust funds finances, FY88 and projected to 2060s, annual article, 4742-1.918

OECD composite indexes of leading economic indicators, analysis of inputs, 1989 article, 2702-1.926

Older persons aid and policies of Fed Govt, and issues of aging, 1989 annual rpt, 25144-3

Pacific Northwest population, households, employment, income, and fuel prices, alternative projections 1990-2010 with trends from 1960, annual rpt, 3224-5

Pension Benefit Guaranty Corp activities and finances, FY88 and projected to FY98, annual rpt, 9674-1

Physicians (family practice) by age, ratios to population, and residents, and percent women and foreign medical grads, 1960s-88 and projected to 2010, article, 4042-3.926

Prisoner population impact of Federal sentencing guidelines, alternative projections 1989-2002, annual rpt, 17664-1

Radioactive waste and spent fuel generation, inventory, and disposal, 1960s-88 and projected to 2020, annual rpt, 3364-2

Radioactive waste containers for ocean disposal, performance criteria, with waste production and inventory, 1984-85 and projected to 2020, 9198-119

Rail shipments of grain, by commodity and port region, and car fleet requirements, 1949-88 with projections to 2001, 1278-14

Railroad employment by occupation from 1957, and Railroad Retirement Account finances, alternative projections 1987-2010, GAO rpt, 26121-280

Railroad retirement system actuarial evaluation, 1989 and projected to 2013, annual rpt, 9704-1

Savings and loan assns failure resolution costs, and FSLIC finances and promissory notes issued, with data by instn, FY80s and projected to FY99, hearing, 25258-22

Savings and loan assns insolvency crisis, Bush Admin resolution proposals funding by source and use, projected FY89-99, press release, 8008-134

Savings instns cost of funds index of FHLB of San Francisco, components and forecasting accuracy, 1987-89, working paper, 9306-1.10

Savings instns failure resolution costs, financing problems, and FSLIC and acquiring instns tax benefits, 1988 and projected to FY99, hearings, 21788-181

South Central States employment by industry div, and income, for 4 States, 1988 and forecast 1989, annual article, 9391-1.913

Statistical Abstract of US, social, political, and economic data, with foreign comparisons, 1790-2025, comprehensive annual compilation, 2324-1

Stock price volatility forecasting performance of options on stock index futures, alternative model results, various periods 1983-88, article, 9371-1.908

Stockpiling of strategic material, inventories and needs, by commodity, as of Sept 1988, annual rpt, 3544-37

Tax (income) return processing, IRS workload forecasts, compliance, and enforcement, data compilation, 1989 annual rpt, 8304-8

Tax (income) unpaid by reason, and compliance after audits and appeals, for individuals and corporations, 1970s-87 and projected to 1992, 8302-2.902; 8308-26

Tax (income) withholding and related documents filed, by type and IRS service center, 1988 and projected 1989-96, annual rpt, 8304-22

Tax expenditures, Federal revenues forgone through income tax deductions and exclusions by type, FY90-94, annual rpt, 21784-10

Tax expenditures from employee benefits, for income and payroll tax by benefit type, 1950-87 and projected to 2065, article, 9373-1.913

Tax reform revenue impacts, performance of alternative forecasts, 1981-83, technical paper, 8006-3.58

Tax returns and supplemental documents filed, by type, FY88 and projected to FY97, semiannual rpt, 8302-2.916; 8302-4

Tax returns filed, by type of tax and IRS region and service center, projected 1988-95 and trends from 1977, annual rpt, 8304-9

Tidal currents, daily time and velocity by station for North America and Asia coasts, forecast 1990, annual rpts, 2174-1

Treasury bill interest rate forecasts, performance of futures rates and survey forecasts, 1977-87, article, 9391-1.914

Wastewater treatment and collection facility construction funding needs and Fed Govt grants, by State, 1988 and projected to 2008, biennial rpt, 9204-7

Water supply in western US, streamflow and reservoir storage forecasts by stream and station, Jan-May monthly rpt, 1262-1

Weather forecasts for US and Northern Hemisphere, precipitation and temperature by location, semimonthly rpt, 2182-1

see also Energy projections

see also Population projections

Propaganda

see also Political broadcasting

Property

Divorce property settlement, by type, whether child support and alimony received, and selected characteristics of woman, 1985, biennial Current Population Rpt, 2546-2.145

see also Business assets and liabilities, general

see also Business assets and liabilities, specific industry

see also Capital investments, general

see also Capital investments, specific industry

see also Educational facilities

see also Farms and farmland

see also Government supplies and property

see also Housing condition and occupancy

see also Housing tenure

see also Land ownership and rights

see also Land use

see also Military bases, posts, and reservations

see also Military supplies and property

see also Mortgages

see also Property and casualty insurance

see also Property condemnation

see also Property damage and loss

see also Property tax

see also Property value

see also Public buildings

see also Public lands

see also Real estate business

see also Rent

see also Surplus government property

see also Vacant and abandoned property

see also Wealth

Property and casualty insurance

Aircraft operating costs by component for private planes, and Fed Govt mileage reimbursement rates, 1987, annual rpt, 9454-13

Arson incidents, casualties, property loss, and insurance savings in arson cases investigated by Bur of Alcohol, Tobacco and Firearms, FY79-88, annual rpt, 8484-4.3

County Business Patterns, 1987: employment, establishments, and payroll, by SIC 2- to 4-digit industry and county, annual State rpt series, 2326-8

Crime insurance policies under Federal program by State, and claims paid, 1988, annual rpt, 6064-6.3

Financial performance of property and casualty insurance industry, State monitoring activities, staff, and interstate info sharing, 1989 GAO rpt, 26119-273

Hazardous waste treatment site liability insurance costs and availability, and reasons for site closure, 1982-87, GAO rpt, 26131-54

Health Care Financing Review, provider prices, price inputs and indexes, and labor, quarterly journal, 4652-1.1

Housing and households detailed characteristics, and unit and neighborhood quality, by location, 1985, biennial rpt, 2485-12

Housing and households detailed characteristics, and unit and neighborhood quality, MSA surveys, series, 2485-6

Marine and war-risk insurance approved for US and foreign vessels, FY88, annual rpt, 7704-14.4

Medical malpractice insurance premium costs and growth rate for physicians, alternative estimates by risk class and State, 1975-85, 4658-27

Occupational injury and illness rates, by SIC 2- to 4-digit industry, 1987, annual rpt, 6844-1

Overseas Private Investment Corp activities, and lists of grants and insured projects and firms, FY88, annual rpt, 9904-3

Overseas Private Investment Corp finances and activities, with list of insured projects and firms, FY88, annual rpt, 9904-2

Transit systems finances and operations, by mode of transport, size of fleet, and for 432 systems, 1986, annual rpt, 7884-4

Truck itemized costs per mile, finances, and operations, for agricultural carriers, 1988, annual rpt, 1311-15

Truck transport of fruit and vegetables, itemized costs per mile by item for fleets and owner-operator trucks, monthly table, 1272-1

Property condemnation

Court caseloads for Federal district, appeals, and bankruptcy courts, by type of suit and offense, circuit, and district, quarterly rpt, 18202-1

Court caseloads for Federal district courts, June 1989, annual rpt, 18204-8.14

Court civil and criminal caseloads for Federal district, appeals, and special courts, June 1989, annual rpt, 18204-2; 18204-8

Housing characteristics of recent movers for new and previous unit, and household characteristics, by location, 1985, biennial rpt, 2485-12

US attorneys land condemnation cases, by disposition and district, FY88, annual rpt, 6004-2.6

Property damage and loss

Agricultural Statistics, 1988, annual rpt, 1004-1.2

Aircraft accidents and circumstances, for US operations of domestic and foreign airlines and general aviation, periodic rpt, 9612-1

Aircraft accidents, casualties, and damage, for commercial operations by detailed circumstances, 1986, annual rpt, 9614-2

Aircraft accidents in general aviation, by circumstances, characteristics of persons and aircraft involved, and type of flying, 1986, annual rpt, 9614-3

Arson incidents by whether structure occupied, property value, and arrest rate, by property type, 1988, annual rpt, 6224-2.1

Boat accidents, casualties, and damage, by cause, vessel characteristics, and State, 1988, annual rpt, 7404-1.1

Bombing incidents and casualties by target and circumstances, and explosives theft and recovery, by State, 1979-88, annual rpt, 8484-4

Bombing incidents, casualties, and damage, by target, circumstances, and State, 1988, annual rpt, 6224-5

Court civil and criminal caseloads for Federal district, appeals, and special courts, June 1989, annual rpt, 18204-2; 18204-8

Crime, by characteristics of victim and offender, circumstances, and location, 1970s-87, annual rpt, 6064-6.3

Crime victimization rates, by victim and offender characteristics, circumstances, and offense, 1987 survey, annual rpt, 6066-3.41

Farm income, expenses, receipts by commodity, assets, liabilities, and ratios, 1988 and trends from 1945, annual rpt, 1544-16

Farm sector finances, income sources, expenses by type, assets, debts, and ratios, 1987, annual rpt, 1544-19

Farmland damaged by natural disaster, Emergency Conservation Program funding by region and State, monthly table, 1802-13

Fish (trout) raised on farms, production, sales, prices, and losses, 1988-89, annual rpt, 1631-16

Hazardous material transport accidents, casualties, and damage, by mode of transport, with DOT control activities, 1988, annual rpt, 7304-4

Housing characteristics of recent movers for new and previous unit, and household characteristics, by location, 1985, biennial rpt, 2485-12

Hurricanes and tropical storms in north Atlantic and Caribbean area, paths, surveillance, deaths, damage, and landfall probabilities by city, 1988, annual rpt, 2184-7

Military personnel personal property shipped worldwide, and loss and damage claims, quarterly rpt, 3702-1

Panama Canal fires, and related property loss, FY87-88, annual rpt, 9664-3.2

Railroad accidents, casualties, and damage, by cause, railroad, and State, 1988, annual rpt, 7604-1

Railroad accidents, casualties, and damage, Fed Railroad Admin activities, and safety inspectors by State, 1987, annual rpt, 7604-12

Railroad accidents, casualties, and damage, with data by carrier, for Pennsylvania and US, 1984-87, GAO rpt, 26113-390

Railroad accidents, casualties, and Federal safety activities, late 1970s-87, hearing, 21368-103

Railroad accidents, casualties, damage, and circumstances, by incident, 1986, annual rpt, 7604-3

Railroad accidents, circumstances, severity, and railroad involved, periodic rpt, 9612-3

Railroad accidents reported and not reported to Fed Railroad Admin, injuries, damage, and workdays lost, for 5 carriers, 1983-87, GAO rpt, 26113-410

Ships in world merchant fleet, and tonnage, by country of registry, as of Jan 1988, annual rpt, 7704-3

Storms and unusual weather phenomena characteristics, casualties, and property damage, by State, monthly listing, 2152-3

Subway accidents, casualties, and damage, by circumstances and system, 1987, annual rpt, 7884-5

Tax (income) returns of individuals, by filing status, tax item, and income level, 1987, annual article, 8302-2.901

Tax (income) returns of individuals, detailed data, 1986, annual rpt, 8304-2

Tax (income) returns of individuals, selected income and tax items by income level, preliminary 1987, annual article, 8302-2.917

Thefts, and value of property stolen and recovered, by property type, 1988, annual rpt, 6224-2.1

Timber insect and disease incidence and damage, annual regional rpt series, 1206-11

Timber insect and disease incidence and damage, by State, 1988, annual rpt, 1204-8

Torts for product liability, dispositions, awards, case processing time, and plaintiff injury severity and other characteristics, 1983-85, GAO rpt, 26121-317

Truck transport of household goods, performance and disposition of damage claims, for selected carriers, 1988, annual rpt, 9484-11

Wilderness areas acreage by Federal agency and location, and sources of damage, with data for foreign countries, 1988 conf papers, 1208-301

Wildlife damage to crops, livestock, and property in Great Plains, and effectiveness of mgmt methods, 1988 conf, 1208-304

Property loss

see Property damage and loss

Property tax

Agricultural Statistics, 1988, annual rpt, 1004-1.2

Agriculture census, 1987: farms, farmland, production, finances, and operator characteristics, by county, final State rpt series, 2331-1

Banks in Fed Reserve System, expenses and operations itemized by service, office, and district, 1988, annual rpt, 9364-11

Census of Govts, 1987: property tax revenue by level of govt, assessed values by locality, and exemptions, by property type and State, 2453-1

Collections of taxes, by level of govt, type of tax, State, and selected counties, quarterly rpt, 2462-3

Consumer Expenditure Survey, household income by source, and itemized spending, by selected characteristics and location, 1984-86, annual rpt, 6764-5.2

Farm prices received for major products and paid for farm inputs and living items, by commodity and State, monthly rpt, 1629-1

Farm production itemized costs, by farm sales size and region, 1988, annual rpt, 1614-3

Farm sector finances, income sources, expenses by type, assets, debts, and ratios, 1983-87, annual rpt, 1544-19

Farmland value, rent, taxes, foreign ownership, and transfers by probable use and lender type, with data by region and State, 1975-89, article, 1561-16.902

Finances of govts, revenues by source and spending by function, natl income and product account, *Survey of Current Business,* monthly rpt, 2702-1.24

Govt finances, by level of govt, State, and for large cities and counties, annual rpt series, 2466-2

Govt finances, tax systems and revenue, and fiscal structure, by level of govt and State, selected years 1929-91, annual rpt, 10044-1

Southeastern States, Fed Reserve 5th District, economic indicators by State, quarterly rpt, 9389–16

Southeastern States, Fed Reserve 6th District, economic indicators by State and MSA, quarterly rpt, 9371–14

Southwestern States farm credit conditions and real estate values, Fed Reserve 11th District, quarterly rpt, 9379–11

St Louis metro area local govt finances, structure, and service delivery, mid-1980s, 10046–9.1

Tax (income) returns of corporations, income and tax items by asset size and detailed industry, 1986, annual rpt, 8304–4; 8304–21

Tax (property) revenue by level of govt, assessed values by locality, and exemptions, by property type and State, 1987 Census of Govts, 2453–1

Trust assets of banks, trust companies, and S&Ls, by type of asset and fund, selected firm, and State, 1988, annual rpt, 13004–1

Vacant housing characteristics and costs, and occupancy and vacancy rates, by region and metro-nonmetro location, quarterly rpt, 2482–1

Western States farm real estate values, and nonreal estate farm loan trends, monthly rpt, quarterly data, 9381–2

Wetlands acreage acquired by Fed Govt, and costs, by site and State, FY89, annual rpt, 14784–1

Wildlife refuges and other land under Fish and Wildlife Service mgmt, acreage by site and State, as of Sept 1988, annual rpt, 5504–8

Proprietorships

Agriculture census, 1987: farms, farmland, production, finances, and operator characteristics, by county, final State rpt series, 2331–1

Farm finances and operations, by size, commodity, and region, 1986, annual rpt, 1544–27

Guam economic censuses, 1987: employment, firms, payroll, and receipts, by SIC 1- to 4-digit industry and election district, 2595–1

Income (personal) by source, and BEA and IRS adjusted gross income measures, 1984-86 with trends from 1947, article, 8302–2.914

Natl income and product accounts and components, *Survey of Current Business*, monthly rpt, 2702–1.22

Northern Mariana Islands economic census, 1987: employment, firms, payroll, and receipts, by SIC 1- to 4-digit industry, 2597–1

Retail trade census, 1987: employment, establishments, sales, and payroll, by SIC 2- to 4-digit kind of business, MSA, county, and city, State rpt series, 2397–1

Retail trade sales, inventories, purchases, gross margin, and accounts receivable, by SIC 2- to 4-digit kind of business and form of ownership, 1987, annual rpt, 2413–5

Service industries census, 1987: establishments, receipts, employment, and payroll, by SIC 2- to 4-digit kind of business, MSA, county, and city, State rpt series, 2391–1

Small business establishments, employment, and financial ratios, by SIC 1- to 2-digit industry and State, late 1960s-87, 9768–19

Small business finances, operations, owner and employee characteristics, and Federal contracts, 1980s-88, annual rpt, 9764–6

Statistical Abstract of US, social, political, and economic data, 1790-2025, comprehensive annual compilation, 2324–1.3

Tax (income) returns filed by type of filer, selected income items, quarterly rpt, 8302–2.1

Tax (income) returns of sole proprietorships, income statement items, by industry group, 1987, annual article, 8302–2.904; 8302–2.921

Tax collection activity of IRS, by type of tax, FY88, annual rpt, 8304–3.3

Virgin Islands economic censuses, 1987: employment, firms, payroll, and receipts, by SIC 1- to 4-digit industry, island, and city, 2593–1

Prospective Payment Assessment Commission

Hospital reimbursement by Medicare under prospective payment system, analyses of alternative payment plans, series, 17206–1

Hospital reimbursement by Medicare under prospective payment system, and physician reimbursement, effect on services, finances, and beneficiary payments, 1970s-88, annual rpt, 17204–2

Hospital reimbursement by Medicare under prospective payment system, impacts on costs, industry structure and operations, and quality of care, series, 17206–2

Hospital reimbursement by Medicare under prospective payment system, methodology, inputs, and data by diagnostic group, 1989 annual rpt, 17204–1

Hospital reimbursement by Medicare under prospective payment system, regulatory adjustments review and diagnostic group weight calibration, FY90, annual rpt, 17204–3

Prosthetics and orthotics

Exports of US, detailed commodities by country, monthly rpt, 2422–3

FDA medical devices malfunction, injury, and death reports, and inspection findings and disposition, 1985-87, GAO rpt, 26131–57

Hospital discharges and length of stay, by diagnosis, patient and instn characteristics, procedure performed, and payment source, 1987, annual rpt, 4147–13.99

Imports of US, detailed Schedule A commodities by country, monthly rpt, 2422–2

Injuries from use of consumer products, by severity, victim age, and detailed product, 1988, annual rpt, 9164–6

Medicare reimbursement of hospitals under prospective payment system, impacts on use of surgical implants and prosthetics, with background data, 1984-86, 17206–2.3

Price indexes (producer), by stage of processing and detailed commodity, monthly rpt, 6762–6

Price indexes (producer), by stage of processing and detailed commodity, monthly 1988, annual rpt, 6764–2

VA Medicine and Surgery Dept trainees, by detailed program and city, FY88, annual rpt, 8704–4

Prostitution

Arrests and prisoners, by offense, offender characteristics, and location, 1970s-87, annual rpt, 6064–6.4; 6064–6.6

Arrests, by offense, offender characteristics, and location, 1988, annual rpt, 6224–2.2

Juvenile delinquent and status offenses, by sex, race, age, income, and urban-rural location, 1976-86 surveys, annual rpt, 6064–6.3

Sentences for Federal offenses, guidelines by offense and circumstances, 1989 rpt, 17668–1

US attorneys civil and criminal cases by type and disposition, and collections, by Federal district, FY88, annual rpt, 6004–2.1

Protective services

see Detective and protective services

Providence, R.I.

Housing and households characteristics, 1984 survey, MSA fact sheet, 2485–11.3

Housing and households detailed characteristics, and unit and neighborhood quality, by location, 1984 survey, MSA rpt, 2485–6.2

Wages by occupation, for office and plant workers, 1989 survey, periodic MSA rpt, 6785–3.7

see also under By City and By SMSA or MSA in the "Index by Categories"

Provo, Utah

see also under By SMSA or MSA in the "Index by Categories"

Prudhoe Bay, Alaska

Oil and gas resource assessment for Arctic Natl Wildlife Refuge with environmental impacts on North Slope and other locations, 1987 hearing, 21448–41

Pruiett, Bill

"Quality Revolution and Organizational Change", 8304–8.1

Psittacosis

see Animal diseases and zoonoses

Psychiatry

Alcohol and drug abuse specialty certification for physicians, applicants professional characteristics, 1986, article, 4482–1.901

Child mental health treatment in short-stay hospitals, by age, race, and facility and physician characteristics, 1977, 4188–55

Drugs (controlled) provided during physician office visits, by drug, patient, and provider characteristics, 1985, 4146–8.179

Education (special) enrollment by age, staff, funding, and needs, by type of handicap and State, 1987/88, annual rpt, 4944–4

France and Germany physicians, and visits by reason and patient age and sex, by specialty, compared to US, 1981-83, 4147–5.5

Indian Health Service outpatient visits, by type of provider, selected hospital, and IHS service area, FY87-88, annual rpt, 4084–3

Mental health care facilities, staff, and patient characteristics, *Statistical Notes* series, 4506–3

Military health care personnel, and accessions by training source, by occupation, specialty, and service branch, FY87, annual rpt, 3544–24

Physicians income, by specialty and other practice characteristics, 1975 and 1983-84, article, 4652-1.920

Rural areas health care facilities, staffing, services accessibility, and indicators of need, 1960s-88, 25148-41

Supply of psychiatrists, psychologists, and social workers, by selected State, 1983-87, hearing, 25148-42

VA health care facilities mental health services, staff, research, and training programs, 1989 biennial listing, 8704-2

VA health care facilities physicians, dentists, and nurses, by selected employment characteristics and VA district, quarterly rpt, 8602-6

VA health care facilities physicians staffing, vacancies, and positions filled, by speciality, 1982-87, hearing, 25768-48

VA Medicine and Surgery Dept trainees, by detailed program and city, FY88, annual rpt, 8704-4

Psychological disorders
see Mental health and illness

Psychology
Aviation medicine research and test results, technical rpt series, 7506-10

Black colleges R&D funding by source, and characteristics of grad students and research staff, by field of science and instn, 1980s-87, 9628-78

Degrees (bachelor and masters) awarded 1985/86, holders employment characteristics, 1987 survey, series, 4826-3

Degrees (PhD) in science and engineering, by field, instn, employment prospects, sex, race, and other characteristics, 1960s-88, 9627-30

Degrees awarded in higher education, by level, field, race, and sex, 1989 edition, annual rpt, 4824-2.20

Degrees in science and engineering, by field, level, and sex, 1950-86, 9628-77

Employment and earnings in science and engineering, by field and activity, and private and Federal R&D spending, by industry, 1975-88, 9626-6.29

Employment and other characteristics of science and engineering PhDs, by field and State, 1987, biennial rpt, 9627-18

Employment characteristics of scientists and engineers, by field, 1988, biennial rpt, 9627-16

Enrollment in science and engineering grad programs, by field, source of funds, and characteristics of student and instn, 1975-87, annual rpt, 9627-7

Fed Govt aid to higher education and nonprofit instns for R&D and related activities, by field, instn, agency, and State, FY87, annual rpt, 9627-17

Fed Govt science and engineering employment, by field, degree level, race, sex, agency, and State, 1987, annual rpt, 9627-5

Foreign and US funding for R&D, and scientists and engineering employment and education, 1988, annual rpt, 9624-23.1

Labor force, Federal and university research funding, and educational data, 1988 rpt, 9626-6.27

NASA R&D funding to higher education instns, by field, instn, and State, FY88, annual listing, 9504-7

R&D funding by Fed Govt, by field, performer type, agency, and State, FY87-89, annual rpt, 9627-20

R&D funding by higher education instns, by source and field, FY77-87, annual rpt, 9626-2.188

R&D funding by higher education instns, by source and field, FY80-87, annual rpt, 9624-18.5

Teachers bachelor degrees, by field and other characteristics, 1985-86, 4838-39

Public administration
Budget deficit reduction under Gramm-Rudman Act, cancellation of budget authority by program, FY90, annual rpt, 104-27

Budget of US Appendix, obligations, appropriations, and personnel, by program and agency, FY90, annual rpt, 104-3

Budget of US, CBO analysis and review of FY90 budget by function, annual rpt, 26304-2

Budget of US, compact budgets by activity, function, and agency, FY90 and projected to FY94, annual rpt, 104-2

Budget of US, historical data, selected years FY34-88 and projected to FY94, annual rpt, 104-22

Budget of US, House concurrent resolution, with spending and revenue targets, FY90, annual rpt, 21264-2

Budget of US, midsession review of FY90 budget, by function and agency, annual rpt, 104-7

Budget of US, receipts by source, outlays by agency and program, and balances, monthly rpt, 8102-3

Budget of US, Senate concurrent resolution, with spending and revenue targets, FY90, annual rpt, 25254-1

Census Bur rpts and data files, coverage and availability, 1989 annual listing, 2304-2

Employment and occupation of householder, by occupation of spouse, race, and family composition, 1988, annual Current Population Rpt, 2546-1.437

Employment and payroll, by function and level of govt, 1987-88, annual rpt series, 2466-1

Employment, unemployment, and labor force characteristics, Labor Statistics Handbook, 1940s-88 with trends from 1913, 6728-38

Finances of govts, by level of govt, State, and for large cities and counties, annual rpt series, 2466-2

Finances of govts, revenues by source and spending by function, natl income and product account, *Survey of Current Business*, monthly rpt, 2702-1.24

Labor force health condition and services use, by occupation and industry of longest job held, income, age, sex, and race, 1980, 4147-10.168

Minority group and women employment in State and local govt, by occupation, function, pay level, and State, 1986, annual rpt, 9244-6

Truman, Harry S, Scholarship Foundation finances, FY88, and awards by student characteristics from 1977, annual rpt, 14314-1

see also Administrative law and procedure
see also Civil service system
see also Federal boards, committees, and commissions
see also Federal employees
see also Federal executive departments
see also Federal independent agencies
see also Government and business
see also Government assets and liabilities
see also Government efficiency
see also Government employees
see also Government revenues
see also Government spending
see also Government supplies and property
see also Labor-management relations in government
see also Local government
see also Officials
see also Political science
see also Public services
see also School administration and staff
see also School boards
see also State and local employees
see also State government
see also under By Industry in the "Index by Categories"

Public assistance
see Public welfare programs

Public broadcasting
Expenditures of Fed Govt in States, by type, program, agency, and State, FY88, annual rpt, 2464-2

Licensing activities of FCC, by class of operation, FY88, annual rpt, 9284-4

Natl Endowment for Arts activities and grants, FY88, annual rpt, 9564-3

Statistical Abstract of US, social, political, and economic data, 1790-2025, comprehensive annual compilation, 2324-1.3

TV channel allocation and license status, for commercial and noncommercial UHF and VHF TV by market, as of June 1989, semiannual rpt, 9282-6

see also Educational broadcasting

Public buildings
Accident deaths and rates, by cause, age, race, sex, and State, 1986, annual rpt, 4144-2.5

Alteration and repair spending for commercial and public buildings, by type, size, age, and region, 1986, 2388-4

Alteration and repair spending for commercial and public buildings, by type, 1986, article, 2042-1.906

Arson incidents by whether structure occupied, property value, and arrest rate, by property type, 1988, annual rpt, 6224-2.1

Budget of US Appendix, obligations, appropriations, and personnel, by program and agency, FY90, annual rpt, 104-3

Budget of US, authoritative financial statements with appropriations, outlays, and receipts, by category and agency, FY88, annual rpt, 8104-2.2

Budget of US, historical data, selected years FY34-88 and projected to FY94, annual rpt, 104-22

Budget of US, special analysis of Federal capital spending by category, projected FY89-2005 and trends from FY81, annual rpt, 104-24

Capital (fixed), govt and private nonresidential structures and equipment,

residential capital, and consumer-owned durable goods, 1985-88, annual article, 2702-1.931

Capitol Architect activities, funding, costs, and contracts, FY86, annual rpt, 25944-1

Capitol Architect outlays for salaries, supplies, and services, itemized by payee and function, 1st half FY89, semiannual rpt, 25922-2

Capitol buildings and grounds, historical summary and floor plans, 1989-90, *Congressional Directory*, biennial rpt, 23874-1

Construction put in place, permits, housing sales, costs, material prices, and employment, bimonthly rpt with articles, 2042-1

Construction put in place, value of new public and private structures, by type, monthly rpt, 2382-4

Criminal cases by type and disposition, and collections, for US attorneys, by Federal district, FY88, annual rpt, 6004-2.1

DC metro area land acquisition and dev projects of Fed Govt, characteristics and funding by agency and project, FY90-94, annual rpt, 15454-1

Disabled persons access to election polling places, precincts by barrier type and State, 1988 natl elections, biennial rpt, 9274-6

Disabled persons access to Federal and federally funded facilities, complaints by disposition and agency, FY88, annual rpt, 17614-1

DOE energy use, costs, and conservation, by end use, fuel type, and field office, FY88, annual rpt, 3004-27

DOE real property owned and leased, by type, subagency, contractor, and site, FY87, annual rpt, 3004-28

Energy conservation grants of Fed Govt to public and nonprofit private instns, by building type and State, 1988, annual rpt, 3304-15

Energy use and efficiency of Fed Govt, by agency and fuel type, FY88, annual rpt, 3304-22

Energy use in commercial buildings, costs, and conservation, by building characteristics, survey rpt series, 3166-8

Fed Govt building energy use and efficiency, by agency, FY85-88, annual rpt, 3304-25

Fed Govt labor productivity, indexes of output and labor costs by function, FY67-87, annual rpt, 6824-1.6

Fed Reserve banks finances and staff, 1988, annual rpt, 9364-1.1

FmHA borrowers, by type of borrower and loan, and State, quarterly rpt, 1182-4

Govt finances, by level of govt, State, and for large cities and counties, annual rpt series, 2466-2

GSA activities and finances, FY88, annual rpt, 9454-1

Historic and natural natl landmarks damaged and threatened, with owner, location, damage type, and recommended remedial action, 1988, annual listing, 5544-16

Inventory and costs of real property owned by Fed Govt, worldwide summary by location, agency, and use, 1987, annual rpt, 9454-5

Inventory and rental costs of real property leased by Fed Govt, worldwide summary by location and agency, 1987, annual rpt, 9454-10

Pollution (air) indoor levels, effects of ventilation rates in commercial and public buildings, 1989 rpt, 3228-10

Postal Service finances, appropriations, and debt financing, selected years FY72-88, annual rpt, 9864-5.4

Postal Service operating costs, itemized by class of mail, FY88, annual rpt, 9864-4

Postal Service revenue, costs, and volume, by service type and class of mail, FY88, annual rpt, 9864-2

SSA activities, and OASDHI admin, 1930s-89 and projected to 2063, data compilation, annual rpt, 4704-12

Statistical Abstract of US, social, political, and economic data, 1790-2025, comprehensive annual compilation, 2324-1.2

TVA energy use by fuel type, and conservation costs and savings, FY88, annual rpt, 9804-26

see also Educational facilities

Public contracts
see Defense contracts and procurement
see Government contracts and procurement

Public debt
Budget deficit impact of OASDI trust fund surpluses, FY89-94, with surpluses projected to 2050, article, 9381-1.909

Budget deficit impact of OASDI trust fund surpluses, projected FY89-2045, article, 9371-1.905

Budget deficit projections of CBO, FY86-1994, article, 9383-6.902

Budget deficit reduction recommendations, background data and testimony, 1989 rpt, 15888-2

Budget deficit reduction recommendations, 1989 rpt, 15888-1

Budget deficit reduction through increased excise and income taxes, and proposed value-added tax, projected FY89-94, article, 9381-1.906

Budget deficit reduction under Gramm-Rudman Act, cancellation of budget authority by program, FY90, annual rpt, 104-27; 21924-1; 26304-6

Budget of US Appendix, obligations, appropriations, and personnel, by program and agency, FY90, annual rpt, 104-3

Budget of US, authoritative financial statements with appropriations, outlays, and receipts, by agency, FY88, annual rpt, 8104-2

Budget of US, CBO analysis of revenue and spending alternatives and projections of economic indicators, FY90-94, annual rpt, 26304-3

Budget of US, compact budgets by activity, function, and agency, FY90 and projected to FY94, annual rpt, 104-2

Budget of US, historical data, selected years FY34-88 and projected to FY94, annual rpt, 104-22

Budget of US, House concurrent resolution, with spending and revenue targets, FY90, annual rpt, 21264-2

Budget of US, midsession review of FY90 budget, by function and agency, annual rpt, 104-7

Budget of US, receipts by source, outlays by agency and program, and balances, monthly rpt, 8102-3

Budget of US, Senate concurrent resolution, with spending and revenue targets, FY90, annual rpt, 25254-1

Budget of US, special analysis of outstanding debt and interest costs, FY90, annual rpt, 104-1.5

Business statistics, detailed data for major industries and economic indicators, *Survey of Current Business*, monthly rpt, 2702-1.6

Economic indicators and components, and Fed Reserve 4th District business and financial conditions, monthly chartbook, 9377-10

Economic indicators targets and performance, 1960s-88 and projected to 1994, annual article, 9381-1.901

Economic Report of the President for 1989, Joint Economic Committee critique and policy recommendations, annual rpt, 23844-2

Fed Govt consolidated financial statements based on business accounting methods, FY87-88, annual rpt, 8104-5

Fed Govt debt, by type and holder, monthly rpt, 9362-1.1

Fed Govt debt, by type and holder, 1987, annual rpt, 9364-5.5

Fed Govt debt issued, redeemed, and outstanding, by series and source, and gifts to reduce debt, monthly rpt, 8242-2

Fed Govt finances, cash and debt transactions, daily tables, 8102-4

Fed Govt financial operations, detailed data, *Treasury Bulletin*, quarterly rpt, 8002-4

Fed Govt financial transactions, *Survey of Current Business*, monthly rpt, 2702-1.6

Fed Govt programs under Ways and Means Committee jurisdiction, finances and operations, FY70s-88, annual rpt, 21784-11

Fed Govt receipts, expenditures, and debt, Fed Reserve Bank of St Louis monthly rpt, 9391-2

Financial and business statistics, historic trends, 1988 annual chartbook, 9364-2.7; 9364-2.8; 9364-2.9

Flow-of-funds accounts, assets and liabilities by type and economic sector, outstanding at year-end 1965-88, annual rpt, 9364-3

Foreign countries economic conditions and implications for US, periodic country rpt series, 2046-4

Foreign countries economic conditions, policy, and trade practices, by country, 1986-88, annual rpt, 21384-5

Govt borrowing and debt issues, by level of govt, selected years 1929-88, annual rpt, 204-1.5; 204-1.6

Govt finances, by level of govt, State, and for large cities and counties, annual rpt series, 2466-2

Govt finances, tax systems and revenue, and fiscal structure, by level of govt and State, selected years 1929-91, annual rpt, 10044-1

Interest paid on Fed Govt debt, monthly rpt, quarterly and annual data, 23842-1.6

Interest rate impacts of Fed Govt deficit reduction, alternative model results, 1989 rpt, 26306-3.100; 26306-3.101

Public Health Service

see also National Institutes of Health
see also National Library of Medicine
see also Office on Smoking and Health

Public housing

American Housing Survey: unit and households detailed characteristics, and unit and neighborhood quality, MSA rpt series, 2485-6

American Housing Survey: unit and households detailed characteristics, and unit and neighborhood quality, 1985, biennial rpt, 2485-12

Assistance of Fed Govt to low-income housing, unit conditions, and household characteristics, 1985-FY88 and alternative projections to 2008, 26306-6.134

Chicago public housing projects structural and financial problems, and crime, 1979-88, GAO rpt, 26113-418

Construction put in place, permits, housing sales, costs, material prices, and employment, bimonthly rpt with articles, 2042-1

Construction put in place, value of new public and private structures, by type, monthly rpt, 2382-4

Disabled persons employment, labor force status, and other characteristics, 1988, Current Population Rpt, 2546-2.147

Employment and payroll, by function and level of govt, 1987-88, annual rpt series, 2466-1

Expenditures for public welfare by program, and private health care spending, FY50s-86, annual article, 4742-1.909

Expenditures of Fed Govt in States, by type, program, agency, and State, FY88, annual rpt, 2464-2

Govt finances, by level of govt, State, and for large cities and counties, annual rpt series, 2466-2

Household and family characteristics, by location, 1988, annual Current Population Rpt, 2546-1.437

Inventory and costs of real property owned by Fed Govt, worldwide summary by location, agency, and use, 1987, annual rpt, 9454-5

Poverty status of families and persons, by detailed characteristics, 1987, annual Current Population Rpt, 2546-6.60

Recreation and sports programs for youth in public housing projects, HUD grants by recipient, 1989, press release, 5006-3.73

Renovation needs and stock of public and Indian housing, series, 5186-15

Statistical Abstract of US, social, political, and economic data, 1790-2025, comprehensive annual compilation, 2324-1.3

see also Low-income housing

Public lands

Acreage and use of public lands, and Land Mgmt Bur activities and finances, annual State rpt series, 5724-11

Acreage, grants, use, revenues, and allocations, for public lands by State, FY88 and trends, annual rpt, 5724-1

Acreage of land under Natl Park Service mgmt, by site, ownership, and region, 1989 semiannual rpt, 5542-1

Agriculture census, 1987: farms, farmland, production, finances, and operator characteristics, by county, final State rpt series, 2331-1

Alaska land area by ownership, and availability for mineral exploration and dev, 1986, 5608-152

Arizona wood fuel harvest, by tree species, ownership, and county, 1984, 1208-293

Bur of Land Mgmt activities and funding by State, and receipts by program, FY87, annual rpt, 5724-13

Coal Surface Mining Reclamation and Enforcement Office activities and funding, by State and Indian tribe, FY87, annual rpt, 5644-1

Counties (nonmetro) employment by industry sector and degree of urbanization, and compared to metro counties, various periods 1969-86, 1598-244

Criminal cases by type and disposition, and collections, for US attorneys, by Federal district, FY88, annual rpt, 6004-2.1

DC metro area land acquisition and dev projects of Fed Govt, characteristics and funding by agency and project, FY90-94, annual rpt, 15454-1

Environmental quality and protection programs, and intl issues, 1988 annual rpt, 484-1

Fish and Wildlife Service restoration programs funding, land purchases, and project listing, by State, FY87, annual rpt, 5504-1

Forest Service mgmt of public lands and resources dev, environmental, economic, and social impacts of alternative programs, projected to 2030, 1208-24

Horse and burro wild herd areas in western States, population, adoption, and protection, and mgmt costs, as of FY87, biennial rpt, 5724-8

Illinois timber resources, removals, and products, by species, forest characteristics, ownership, and county, 1960s-85 and projected to 2015, 1208-292

Inventory and costs of real property owned by Fed Govt, worldwide summary by location, agency, and use, 1987, annual rpt, 9454-5

Landmarks (natl historic and natural) damaged and threatened, with owner, location, damage type, and recommended remedial action, 1988, annual listing, 5544-16

Local govt receipts from Fed Govt in lieu of property taxes on public lands, by State and county, FY89, annual rpt, 5724-9

Local govt receipts from Fed Govt in lieu of property taxes on public lands, by State, FY89, annual press release, 5306-4.2

Minerals (strategic) production, use, reserves, Federal lands availability for mining, and environmental impacts, 1950s-80s, 028-33

Minerals resources and availability on public lands, State rpt series, 5606-7

Mining claims on public lands, patents by type and State, and applications by disposition, 1978-87, GAO rpt, 26113-403

New Mexico timber acreage and resources, by species, ownership class, and county, 1986-87, series, 1206-23

Northeastern US timber resources and removals, by species, ownership, and county, State rpt series, 1206-12

Northwestern US and British Columbia forest industry production, prices, trade, and employment, quarterly rpt, 1202-3

Oregon timber resources, by species, ownership, and county, 1983-86, series, 1206-19

Reclamation Bur activities in western US, land and population served, and recreation areas, by location, 1987, annual rpt, 5824-12.1

Rocky Mountain States timber and mill residue production, by species, ownership, and county, series, 1206-17

Rural areas aid from Fed Govt compared to urban areas, by program and degree of urbanization, FY85, periodic rpt, 1598-248

Rural areas employment, economic conditions, and population characteristics, 1970s-85, compilation of papers, 1598-243

Statistical Abstract of US, social, political, and economic data, 1790-2025, comprehensive annual compilation, 2324-1.1; 2324-1.2

Tennessee timber acreage and resources, by species, ownership class, and county, 1989, series, 1206-27

Uranium reserves and industry operations, by region and State, various periods 1966-88, annual rpt, 3164-65.1

Wildlife-related recreation, hunting, and fishing participation and spending, detailed data by location, 1985 survey, quinquennial rpt, 5508-5

Wildlife-related recreation, hunting, and fishing participation and spending, detailed data, 1985 survey, quinquennial State rpt series, 5506-6

Wisconsin timber resources and removals, by species, forest type, ownership, and county, series, 1206-34

see also Homesteads
see also Military bases, posts, and reservations
see also Mineral leases
see also National forests
see also National grasslands
see also National parks
see also Oil and gas leases
see also Parks
see also Public buildings
see also State forests
see also State parks
see also Wilderness areas
see also Wildlife refuges

Public Law 480

Agricultural Statistics, 1988, annual rpt, 1004-1

CCC activities and finances, by program, FY87, last issue of annual rpt, 1824-1

CCC dairy price support program foreign donations and domestic donations to poor, schools, Prisons Bur, and VA, monthly rpt, 1802-2

CCC financial statements and operations, by program and commodity, FY88, annual rpt, 1824-4

Concessional sales program exports, by commodity and country, annual rpt, discontinued, 1924-10

Concessional sales program exports, by commodity and country, semiannual rpt, suspended, 1922-6

Natl income and product accounts govt
  transactions component estimates,
  methodology and bibl, 1988 technical rpt,
  2706–6.5
Poverty status of families and persons, by
  detailed characteristics, 1987, annual
  Current Population Rpt, 2546–6.60
R&D funding by Fed Govt, by detailed
  function, program, and agency, FY88-90,
  annual rpt, 9627–9
Refugee arrivals in US by world area of
  origin and State of settlement, and
  Federal aid, FY88-90, annual rpt,
  7004–16
Refugee resettlement programs and funding,
  arrivals by country of origin, and
  indicators of adjustment, by State, FY88,
  annual rpt, 4694–5
Research and evaluation programs of HHS,
  1970-FY87, annual listing, 4004–30
Rural areas aid from Fed Govt, by agency
  and program, with county classifications
  by population density, FY85 and FY87,
  GAO rpt, 26113–401
Rural areas aid from Fed Govt compared to
  urban areas, by program and degree of
  urbanization, FY85, periodic rpt,
  1598–248
Soviet Union personal income by source,
  disposable income, wage deductions by
  type, and savings, 1950s-87, 9118–7
State and local govt employment of
  minorities and women, by occupation,
  function, and pay level, 1986, annual rpt,
  9244–6.4
Statistical Abstract of US, social, political,
  and economic data, 1790-2025,
  comprehensive annual compilation,
  2324–1.2
*Survey of Income and Program
  Participation*, data collection,
  methodology, and availability, 1987 users
  guide, 2628–24
*Survey of Income and Program
  Participation*, data collection,
  methodology, and use, 1988 annual conf
  papers, 2624–1
*Survey of Income and Program
  Participation*, household composition,
  income, benefits, and labor force status,
  methodology, working paper series,
  2626–10
Telephone service of households, by
  composition, income sources, and other
  characteristics, 1984-87, 9288–11
West Virginia poverty conditions, food aid
  participants, and birth outcomes, 1980-87,
  hearing, 21968–49
Women awarded child support and alimony,
  award amount, and payment status, by
  selected characteristics of woman, 1985,
  biennial Current Population Rpt,
  2546–2.145
see also Aid to blind
see also Aid to disabled and handicapped
  persons
see also Aid to Families with Dependent
  Children
see also Child day care
see also Child welfare
see also Disability benefits and insurance
see also Disaster relief
see also Food assistance
see also Food stamp programs

see also Foster home care
see also Homemaker services
see also Income maintenance
see also Legal aid
see also Medicaid
see also Medical assistance
see also Medicare
see also Old age assistance
see also Public service employment
see also Rent supplements
see also School lunch and breakfast
  programs
see also Social security
see also Social services
see also Social work
see also State funding for social welfare
see also Supplemental Security Income
see also Vocational rehabilitation
see also Work incentive programs
Public works
Alaska rural villages population
  characteristics and and subsistence
  activities, 1976-86, 5738–9
Appalachian Regional Commission funding,
  by project and State, planned FY89,
  annual rpt, 9084–3
Army Corps of Engineers activities, FY87,
  annual rpt, 3754–1
Assistance (financial and nonfinancial) of
  Fed Govt, 1989 base edition with
  supplements, annual listing, 104–5
Budget of US Appendix, obligations,
  appropriations, and personnel, by program
  and agency, FY90, annual rpt, 104–3
Budget of US, authoritative financial
  statements with appropriations, outlays,
  and receipts, by category and agency,
  FY88, annual rpt, 8104–2.2
Budget of US, historical data, selected years
  FY34-88 and projected to FY94, annual
  rpt, 104–22
Budget of US, overview, FY90, annual rpt,
  104–6
Budget of US, special analysis of Federal
  capital spending by category, projected
  FY89-2005 and trends from FY81, annual
  rpt, 104–24
Canada construction products market trends
  and indicators, with imports by country,
  1960s-86, article, 2042–1.905
Community dev programs of HUD, funding
  and activities by program and State,
  FY88, annual rpt, 5124–5
Construction industries census, 1987:
  establishments, employment, receipts, and
  expenditures, by SIC 4-digit industry and
  State, final industry rpt series, 2373–1
Construction industries census, 1987:
  financial and operating data, preliminary
  industry rpt series, 2371–1
Construction put in place, housing starts,
  and Fed Govt public works spending,
  projected 1989-93 and trends from 1980,
  annual article, 2042–1.902
Construction put in place, permits, housing
  sales, costs, material prices, and
  employment, bimonthly rpt with articles,
  2042–1
Construction spending by Fed Govt, by
  program and type of structure, FY82-90,
  annual article, 2042–1.901
Economic Dev Admin activities, and
  funding by program, recipient, State, and
  county, FY87 and cumulative from FY66,
  annual rpt, 2064–2

Expenditures of Fed Govt in States, by type,
  program, agency, and State, FY88, annual
  rpt, 2464–2
Income (personal) regional impacts of public
  capital stock and investment, 1980-84,
  working paper, 9377–9.81
Lands (public) acreage, grants, use,
  revenues, and allocations, by State, FY88,
  annual rpt, 5724–1.2
Neighborhood and housing quality,
  indicators and attitudes, by householder
  type and location, 1985, biennial rpt,
  2485–12
Reclamation Bur activities, finances, and
  project impacts in western US, annual
  rpts, 5824–12
Rural areas aid from Fed Govt, by agency
  and program, with county classifications
  by population density, FY85 and FY87,
  GAO rpt, 26113–401
Statistical Abstract of US, social, political,
  and economic data, 1790-2025,
  comprehensive annual compilation,
  2324–1.2
Urban areas fiscal, economic, and social
  conditions, 1960s-87, biennial rpt,
  5184–7.3
Wastewater treatment and collection facility
  construction funding needs and Fed Govt
  grants, by State, 1988 and projected to
  2008, biennial rpt, 9204–7
see also Public buildings
see also Public service employment
see also Water resources development
Publications catalogs
see Bibliographies
see Government publications lists
Publishing industry
see Printing and publishing industry
Pueblo, Colo.
Wages by occupation, for office and plant
  workers, 1989 survey, periodic MSA rpt,
  6785–3.10
see also under By City and By SMSA or
  MSA in the "Index by Categories"
Puerto Ricans
see Hispanic Americans
see Puerto Rico
Puerto Rico
Agricultural and food production and
  indexes, total and for selected
  commodities, by country, 1970s-88,
  annual rpt, 1524–12
Agriculture census, 1987: farms, farmland,
  production, finances, and operator
  characteristics, by municipio, final State
  rpt, 2331–1.52
Aircraft (general aviation), flight hours, and
  equipment, by type, use, and model of
  aircraft, region, and State, 1988, annual
  rpt, 7504–29
Bank deposits in FDIC-insured commercial
  and savings banks, by instn, State, and
  county, as of June 1988, annual regional
  rpt, 9295–3.1
Cement (portland) shipments to Puerto
  Rico, bimonthly rpt, 2042–1.6
Corporations operating in Puerto Rico and
  other US possessions, tax incentives,
  finances, and operations by industry, and
  impacts on local economy, 1970s-83,
  annual rpt, 8004–12
Deaths and rates, by detailed location,
  cause, and demographic characteristics,
  1987, US Vital Statistics annual rpt,
  4144–3.2

Economic and housing indicators for FHLB 2nd District, by State, quarterly rpt with articles, 9302–33

Economic conditions and govt finances of Puerto Rico, 1975-89, GAO rpt, 26121–298

Economic conditions in Puerto Rico, 1986 hearings, 21448–39

Economic, social, political, and geographic summary data, by country, 1989, annual factbook, 9114–2

Employment, earnings, and hours, by selected SIC 1- to 4-digit industry, State, and for 262 MSAs, 1972-87, 6748–81.5

Exports and imports between US and outlying areas, by detailed commodity and mode of transport, monthly rpt, 2422–4

Fed Govt spending in States and local areas, by type, State, county, and city, FY88, annual rpt, 2464–3

Fed Govt spending in States, by type, program, agency, and State, FY88, annual rpt, 2464–2

Fish and shellfish catch, wholesale receipts, prices, trade, and other market activities, semiweekly regional rpt, 2162–6.4

Freight (waterborne domestic and foreign) by commodity, traffic, and passengers, by port and waterway, 1987, annual rpt, 3754–3.2

HHS financial aid, by program, recipient, State, and city, FY88, annual regional listing, 4004–3.2

Homeless children educational enrollment and needs, 1988, annual State rpt, 4804–35.51

Housing units authorized, by region, State, selected MSA, and permit-issuing place, monthly rpt, 2382–5

Marriages, divorces, and rates, by characteristics of spouses and county, 1984 and trends from 1940, US Vital Statistics annual rpt, 4144–4.3

Meat production, prices, consumption, and imports of Puerto Rico, and impact of import restrictions, 1950s-85, 1568–282

Mineral Industry Surveys, State reviews of production, 1988, preliminary annual rpt, 5614–6

Minerals Yearbook, 1987, Vol 2 preprints: State review of production and sales by commodity, and business activity, annual rpt, 5604–16.40

Minerals Yearbook, 1987, Vol 2: State reviews of production, sales, and firms, by commodity, and business activity, annual rpt, 5604–34

Nursing home compliance with Medicare and Medicaid regulations, and patient characteristics, by facility, 1987/88, annual State rpt, 4654–15.40

NYC employee referrals and placements from Puerto Rico, FY84-88, annual GAO rpt, 26104–19

Oil exports to US by OPEC and non-OPEC countries, monthly rpt, 3162–24.3

Population and housing census, 1980: outlying area data collection issues and procedural history, 2555–2.5

Population size and components of change, by outlying area, 1980-88, annual Current Population Rpt, 2546–3.162

Population size, growth rates, and components of change, by country, projected 1989-2020 and trends from 1950, biennial rpt, 2324–9

Poultry (chicken, egg, and turkey) production, prices, receipts, trade, and disposition, 1960-87, 1568–39

Rum production, trade by country, and use, 1987-88, annual rpt, 9884–15

Savings instns, FHLB 2nd District members capital and assets under capital requirements increase proposal, by State, 3rd qtr 1988, article, 9302–33.901

Savings instns, FHLB 2nd District members finances and operations, by State, quarterly rpt, 9302–14

Statistical Abstract of US, social, political, and economic data, with foreign comparisons, 1790-2025, comprehensive annual compilation, 2324–1

Sugar cane growers, acreage, yield, and cane sugar production, quarterly situation rpt with articles, 1561–14

Sugarcane area and yield, and raw sugar production, 1950-88, FAS periodic circular, 1925–14.4

Tax (excise) collections of IRS, by source, region, and State, quarterly rpt, annual table, 8302–1

Terrorist incidents in US, related activity, and casualties, by attack type, target, group, and location, 1988, annual rpt, 6224–6

Tobacco production, prices, stocks, taxes by State, and trade and production by country, 1988, annual rpt, 1319–1

Water supply and quality in streams and lakes, and groundwater levels in wells, by drainage basin, 1987, annual State rpt, 5666–10.48

Weather conditions and effect on agriculture, by US region, State, and city, and world area, weekly rpt, 2152–2

see also under By Outlying Area in the "Index by Categories"

Puget Sound

Estuary environmental and fishery conditions, research results and methodology, 1988 rpt, 2176–7.7

Pollutant concentrations in coastal and estuarine shellfish, by pollutant and location, 1986-88, 2176–3.8

Pulp

see Paper and paper products

Pulses

see Vegetables and vegetable products

Pumice

see Abrasive materials

Pumps and compressors

see Machines and machinery industry

Punishment

see Capital punishment

see Judgments, civil procedure

see Sentences, criminal procedure

see Student discipline

Purchasing

see Industrial purchasing

Purchasing power

see Personal and household income

Putnam, Judith J.

"Food Consumption, Prices, and Expenditures, 1966-87", 1544–4

Pyrite

see Nonmetallic minerals and mines

Pyrophyllite

see Nonmetallic minerals and mines

Qatar

Agricultural and food production and indexes, total and for selected commodities, by country, 1970s-88, annual rpt, 1524–12

Agricultural trade of US, by detailed commodity and country, 1988, semiannual rpt, 1522–4

Economic conditions, income, production, prices, employment, and trade, 1989 periodic country rpt, 2046–4.25

Economic conditions, policy, and trade practices, by country, 1986-88, annual rpt, 21384–5

Economic, social, political, and geographic summary data, by country, 1989, annual factbook, 9114–2

Exports and imports of US, by commodity and country, 1970-87, world area rpt, 9116–1.3

Human rights conditions in 170 countries, 1988, annual rpt, 21384–3

Military aid of US, arms sales, and training programs costs and budget requests, by program, world region, and country, FY88-90, annual rpt, 7144–13

Military spending, arms trade, and force strengths, with govt spending and population, by country, 1977-87, annual rpt, 9824–1

Minerals Yearbook, 1987, Vol 3: foreign country reviews of production, trade, and policy, by commodity, annual rpt, 5604–35

Minerals Yearbook, 1987, Vol 3 preprints: foreign country review of production, trade, and policy, by commodity, annual rpt, 5604–23.86

Oil production by major exporting countries, monthly rpt, 3162–24.10

Oil production, trade, use, and stocks, by selected country and country group, monthly rpt, 3162–42

Population size, growth rates, and components of change, by country, projected 1989-2020 and trends from 1950, biennial rpt, 2324–9

UN voting record and share of votes in agreement with US, by issue, country, and world area, 1988, annual rpt, 7004–18

see also under By Foreign Country in the "Index by Categories"

Quality control and testing

Cholesterol levels measurement using Reflotron analyzer, accuracy compared to lab assay, 1988 article, 4042–3.923

Coal purchases by Fed Govt, chemical analyses by mine and location, FY84, annual rpt, 3004–15

Cotton acreage planted by State and county, and fiber quality, by variety, 1989, annual rpt, 1309–6

Cotton fiber and processing test results, by staple, region, State, and production area, seasonal biweekly rpt, 1309–3

Cotton fiber and processing test results, by State, 1988, annual rpt, 1309–4

Cotton fiber grade, staple, and mike, for upland and American Pima cotton by State, monthly rpt, 1309–11

Cotton quality, by State, 1988, annual rpt, 1309–7

Cotton quality, supply, and carryover, 1988-89, annual rpt, 1309–8

Cottonseed prices and quality, by State, seasonal weekly rpt, 1309–14

Cottonseed quality factors, by State, 1988 crop, annual rpt, 1309–5

Equipment for industrial control, shipments, trade, use, and firms, 1988, annual Current Industrial Rpt, 2506–12.11

Fed Govt procurement contract awards, by procurement and contractor type, agency, State, and for top 100 contractors, quarterly rpt, 102–6

Fires in hotels and motels, casualties, and effectiveness of smoke detectors, sprinkler systems, and building and equipment design, 1989 hearing, 21708–127

Hearing aid performance test results, by make and model, 1989 annual rpt, 8704–3

Labs accreditation programs and requirements of Fed Govt, by agency, 1988–89, GAO rpt, 26113–405

Manufacturing high technology use and plans, with data by technology, selected industry, and firm and market characteristics, 1988 survey, 2508–1

Nuclear reactors for domestic use and export by function and operating status, with owner, operating characteristics, and location, 1988 annual listing, 3004–26

Radioactive waste containers for ocean disposal, performance criteria, with waste production and inventory, 1984-85 and projected to 2020, 9198–119

Science and engineering employment characteristics, by field, 1988, biennial rpt, 9627–16

Small business high technology sales, exports, siting, technology transfer, views on competitiveness, 1988 survey, hearing, 21728–69

Water quality data collection activities and quality, for 2 States, 1984, 5668–94

see also Food inspection

see also Government inspections

Quality of life

Communist, OECD, and selected other countries living standards and commodity production, 1960s-88, annual rpt, 9114–4.1

Data on health condition and quality of life measures, rpts and other info sources, quarterly listing, 4122–1

Homeless persons in rural areas, health condition, services use, and other characteristics, local area studies, 1989 rpt, 4186–9.1

Household composition, income, benefits, and labor force status, Survey of Income and Program Participation methodology, working paper series, 2626–10

Housing and neighborhood quality, indicators and attitudes, MSA surveys, series, 2485–6

Neighborhood and housing quality, indicators and attitudes, by householder type and location, 1985, biennial rpt, 2485–12

Nursing home facility, staff, and resident detailed characteristics, 1985, 4147–13.97

Older persons under financial stress, essential expenses cut and household economic characteristics, 1983, article, 1702–1.907

see also Health condition

see also Housing condition and occupancy

see also Living arrangements

see also Poverty

see also Work conditions

Quan, Choon K.

"Water Use in the Domestic Nonfuel Minerals Industry", 5608–153

Quarries

see Stone products and quarries

Quartz

see Nonmetallic minerals and mines

Quasi-official agencies

see American National Red Cross

see Government corporations and enterprises

see Legal Services Corp.

see National Railroad Passenger Corp.

see Smithsonian Institution

see U.S. Institute of Peace

see U.S. Railway Association

see U.S. Synthetic Fuels Corp.

Questionnaires

see Consumer surveys

see Opinion and attitude surveys

see Statistical programs and activities

see under names of individual surveys (listed under Surveys)

Quijano, Alicia M.

"Capital Expenditures by Majority-Owned Foreign Affiliates of U.S. Companies, 1989", 2702–1.910

Quinn, Heather

"Susceptibility and Status of Gulf of Mexico Estuaries to Nutrient Discharges", 2176–7.14

"Susceptibility of East Coast Estuaries to Nutrient Discharges: Albemarle/Pamlico Sound to Biscayne Bay", 2176–7.15

Quits

see Labor turnover

Rabchevsky, George A.

"Tungsten Industry of the USSR", 5606–5.8

Rabies

Cases of rabies in animals and humans, by location for US, Mexico, and Canada, 1988, annual rpt, 4202–7.904

Cases of rabies in animals and humans by State, and deaths, 1930s-88, annual rpt, 4204–1

Deaths and rates, by detailed cause and demographic characteristics, 1986 and trends from 1900, US Vital Statistics annual rpt, 4144–2

Foreign countries rabies-free, and disease prevention recommendations, 1989 annual rpt, 4204–11

Morbidity and Mortality Weekly Report, infectious notifiable disease cases by State, and public health issues, 4202–1

Race/ethnic groups

see Alaska Natives

see Asian Americans

see Black Americans

see Hispanic Americans

see Indians

see Minority groups

see Pacific Islands Americans

see Racial discrimination

see under By Race and Ethnic Group in the "Index by Categories"

Racial discrimination

Army personnel, promotion, and training by race and for women, discrimination issues, and career attitudes, FY88, annual rpt, 3704–10

Community Relations Service investigation and mediation of minority discrimination disputes, FY87, annual rpt, 6004–9

Education Dept Civil Rights Office, complaints, investigations, funding, and staff, various periods FY81-88, 21348–114

Employment of minorities and women, by occupation, SIC 1- to 3- digit industry, State, and MSA, 1986, annual rpt, 9244–1

Fed Equal Opportunity Recruitment Program activity, and employment by sex, race, pay grade, and selected occupation, FY88, annual rpt, 9844–33

Fed Govt personnel action appeals, decisions of Merit Systems Protection Board by agency and region, FY88, annual rpt, 9494–2

Foreign countries human rights conditions in 170 countries, 1988, annual rpt, 21384–3

Income and economic status of minority groups and women, and discrimination and govt policy impacts, series, 11046–7

Labor laws enacted, by State, 1988, annual article, 6722–1.904

School desegregation, indicators of integration plans effectiveness by school district and location, 1960s-85, 11048–189

State and local govt employment of minorities and women, by occupation, function, pay level, and State, 1986, annual rpt, 9244–6

Telecommunications industries minority employment and discrimination charges, with data by industry and selected firm, 1970s-88, hearings, 21368–113

Racine, Wis.

see also under By SMSA or MSA in the "Index by Categories"

Racketeering

see Organized crime

Rackowski, Joseph P.

"Pacific and Speckled Sanddabs. Species Profiles: Life Histories and Environmental Requirements of Coastal Fishes and Invertebrates (Pacific Southwest)", 5506–8.114

Radar

Air traffic levels at FAA-operated control facilities, including instrument operations, by airport and State, FY88, annual rpt, 7504–27

Aircraft (general aviation), flight hours, and equipment, by type, use, and model of aircraft, region, and State, 1988, annual rpt, 7504–29

DOD budget, weapons acquisition costs by system and service branch, FY89-91, annual rpt, 3504–2

DOD procurement cost estimates for weapons and communications systems, by service branch, quarterly summary rpt, 3502–1

Drug smuggling aircraft interdiction activities of Fed Govt, funding, and radar system capabilities, by agency, FY82-89, GAO rpt, 26119–259

Exports of US, detailed commodities by country, monthly rpt, 2422-3

Hurricanes and tropical storms in north Atlantic and Caribbean area, paths, surveillance, deaths, damage, and landfall probabilities by city, 1988, annual rpt, 2184-7

Hurricanes and tropical storms in northeastern Pacific Ocean, paths and surveillance, 1988, annual rpt, 2184-8

Hurricanes and tropical storms in Pacific and Indian Oceans, paths and surveillance, 1988, annual rpt, 3804-8

Imports of US, detailed Schedule A commodities by country, monthly rpt, 2422-2

Price indexes (producer), by stage of processing and detailed commodity, monthly 1988, annual rpt, 6764-2

Soviet Union and Warsaw Pact military weapons systems, aid, presence, and force strengths, and compared to US and NATO, 1989 annual rpt, 3504-20

Radecki, Lawrence J.

"Capital Mobility and Short-Term Interest Rates", 9385-9

"Globalization of Financial Markets and the Effectiveness of Monetary Policy Instruments", 9385-1.901

Radiation

Assistance (financial and nonfinancial) of Fed Govt, 1989 base edition with supplements, annual listing, 104-5

Births of low birthweight and stillbirths risks relation to parental hazardous substance exposure, 1980, article, 4042-3.945

Electronic devices radiation incidents by type of device, and FDA control activities, 1988, annual rpt, 4064-13

Environmental impacts of energy technologies, 1960s-80s, handbook series, 3326-1

Environmental radiation and radionuclide concentrations in air, water, and milk, monitoring results by State and site, quarterly rpt, 9192-5

Exposure to radiation of population near commercial reactors, by body site, age group, and selected plant, 1986, annual rpt, 9634-7

FDA investigations and regulatory activities, quarterly rpt, 4062-3

Fed Govt employees radiation exposure, by age, occupation, and selected agency, 1986-87, biennial rpt, 4064-15

Great Lakes toxic spills and human error, with data by pollutant source and site, 1984-86, conf, 14648-21

Health physics and radiation protection enrollment and degrees granted by instn and State, and women grads plans and employment, 1972-88, 3006-8.9

Idaho Natl Engineering Lab radiation monitoring results, for facilities and nearby areas, 1988, annual rpt, 3354-10

Mine safety and health enforcement, training, and funding, with casualties, by type of mine and State, FY87, annual rpt, 6664-6

Navy nuclear-powered vessels and support facilities radioactive waste, releases in harbors, and public exposure, 1970s-88, annual rpt, 3804-11

Navy personnel radiation exposure on nuclear-powered vessels and at support facilities, and injury claims, 1950s-88, annual rpt, 3804-10

Nuclear weapons test areas in Nevada and other sites, radionuclide concentrations in air, water, humans, animals, and milk, 1988, annual rpt, 9194-17

Research and testing activities under Natl Toxicology Program, FY87 and planned FY88, annual rpt, 4044-16

Uranium tailings at inactive mills, remedial action proposals, costs, site characteristics, and environmental, socioeconomic, and health impacts, series, 3356-4

Water supply and quality in streams and lakes, and groundwater levels in wells, by drainage basin, 1986, annual State rpt series, 5666-23

Water supply and quality in streams and lakes, and groundwater levels in wells, by drainage basin, 1987, annual State rpt series, 5666-10

Water supply and quality in streams and lakes, and groundwater levels in wells, by drainage basin, 1988, annual State rpt series, 5666-16

see also Nuclear accidents and safety

see also Nuclear explosives and explosions

see also Nuclear medicine and radiology

see also Nuclear power

see also Nuclear weapons

see also Radioactive materials

see also Radioactive waste and disposal

see also Radon

see also Uranium

see also X-rays

Radiation Control for Health and Safety Act

FDA admin of Act, and radiation incidents involving electronic devices, 1988, annual rpt, 4064-13

Radio

Business statistics, detailed data for major industries and economic indicators, *Survey of Current Business*, monthly rpt, 2702-1.14

Developing countries disaster preparedness and economic, population, and political data, country rpt series, 9916-2

Employment, earnings, and hours, by SIC 1- to 4-digit industry, monthly 1983-Feb 1989, annual rpt, 6744-4

Employment of minorities and discrimination charges in telecommunications industries, with data by industry and selected firm, 1970s-88, hearings, 21368-113

Exports of US, detailed commodities by country, monthly rpt, 2422-3

Fed Govt ad spending, and subcontracts to small and disadvantaged firms, by agency and medium, FY86, GAO rpt, 26113-428

Fed Govt radio frequency assignments, by agency, 2nd half 1988, semiannual rpt, 2802-1

Finances, operations, and industry devs for telecommunications, with data by service type, firm, and country, 1950s-80s, 2808-27

Foreign countries economic, social, political, and geographic summary data, by country, 1989, annual factbook, 9114-2

Imports of US, detailed Schedule A commodities by country, monthly rpt, 2422-2

Imports of US given duty-free treatment for value of US material sent abroad, and impacts on US industry and employment, by commodity and country, 1987, annual rpt, 9884-14

Injuries from use of consumer products, by severity, victim age, and detailed product, 1988, annual rpt, 9164-6

Licensing activities of FCC, by class of operation, FY88, annual rpt, 9284-4

Manufacturers finances and operations, by SIC 2- to 4-digit industry, forecast 1989 and trends from 1950s, annual rpt, 2044-28

Manufacturing annual survey, 1986: value of shipments, by SIC 4- to 5-digit product class, 2506-15.3

Manufacturing census, 1987: financial and operating data, for SIC 4-digit industries by product, preliminary rpt, 2491-1.72

OECD trade, total and for 4 major countries, and US trade by country, by commodity, 1970-87, world area rpt series, 9116-1

Price indexes (producer), by stage of processing and detailed commodity, monthly rpt, 6762-6

Price indexes (producer), by stage of processing and detailed commodity, monthly 1988, annual rpt, 6764-2

Stations on the air, by class of operation, monthly press release, 9282-4

Statistical Abstract of US, social, political, and economic data, 1790-2025, comprehensive annual compilation, 2324-1.3

see also Mobile radio

Radio Free Europe

Broadcast and financial data for Radio Free Europe and Radio Liberty, and compared to other intl broadcasters, FY88, annual rpt, 10314-1

Radio Liberty

Broadcast and financial data for Radio Free Europe and Radio Liberty, and compared to other intl broadcasters, FY88, annual rpt, 10314-1

Radioactive materials

Criminal sentences for Federal offenses, guidelines by offense and circumstances, 1989 rpt, 17668-1

Environmental quality and protection programs, and intl issues, 1988 annual rpt, 484-1

Exports of US, detailed commodities by country, monthly rpt, 2422-3

FDA investigations and regulatory activities, quarterly rpt, 4062-3

Freight (waterborne domestic and foreign) by commodity, traffic, and passengers, by port and waterway, 1987, annual rpt, 3754-3

Imports of US, detailed Schedule A commodities by country, monthly rpt, 2422-2

Inventory discrepancies for nuclear fuel, by facility, 1st half 1988, semiannual rpt, 9632-3

Inventory discrepancies for nuclear materials at DOE and contractor facilities, 2nd half FY87, semiannual rpt, 3002-4

Minerals Yearbook, 1987, Vol 1: commodity reviews of production, use, trade, prices, and mining operations, annual rpt, 5604-33

Minerals Yearbook, 1987, Vol 3: foreign country reviews of production, trade, and policy, by commodity, annual rpt, 5604-35

Nuclear Regulatory Commission activities, finances, and staff, with data for individual power plants, FY88, annual rpt, 9634-2

OECD trade, total and for 4 major countries, and US trade by country, by commodity, 1970-87, world area rpt series, 9116-1

Price indexes (producer), by stage of processing and detailed commodity, monthly rpt, 6762-6

Safety standards and research, design, licensing, construction, operation, and finances, for nuclear power plants with data by reactor, quarterly journal, 3352-4

Transportation census, 1987: trucks, by detailed characteristics, miles traveled, and type of product carried, State rpt series, 2573-1

Water chemistry, environmental impacts, analytic methods, and quality and mgmt issues, 1989 rpt, 5668-96

see also Radiation
see also Radioactive waste and disposal
see also Radon
see also Uranium

Radioactive waste and disposal
Budget of US, Bush Admin policy changes by program, FY90, 028-32

Budget of US, Reagan Admin policy changes by program, FY90, annual rpt, 104-21

DOE activities and finances, summary energy supply and demand data, and bibl, 1987, annual rpt, 3024-2

Environmental impacts of energy technologies, 1960s-80s, handbook series, 3326-1

Idaho Natl Engineering Lab radiation monitoring results, for facilities and nearby areas, 1988, annual rpt, 3354-10

Military activities of DOE, radioactive waste disposal plans and funding, FY87-93, last issue of annual rpt, 3344-1

Navy nuclear-powered vessels and support facilities radioactive waste, releases in harbors, and public exposure, 1970s-88, annual rpt, 3804-11

Nuclear Regulatory Commission activities, finances, and staff, with data for individual power plants, FY88, annual rpt, 9634-2

Nuclear Waste Fund finances, and DOE Civilian Radioactive Waste Mgmt Office activities, quarterly GAO rpt, 26102-4

Nuclear Waste Fund finances, and DOE Civilian Radioactive Waste Mgmt Office project budgets alternative projections, quarterly rpt, 3362-1

Ocean disposal of radioactive waste, containers performance criteria, with waste production and inventory, 1984-85 and projected to 2020, 9198-119

Radiation exposure of workers at nuclear power plants and related facilities, by site, 1968-86, annual rpt, 9634-3

Safety standards and research, design, licensing, construction, operation, and finances, for nuclear power plants with data by reactor, quarterly journal, 3352-4

Spent fuel and demand for uranium and enrichment services of nuclear power plants, for US and other country groups, projected 1989-2036, annual rpt, 3164-72

Spent fuel and radioactive waste generation, inventory, and disposal, 1960s-88 and projected to 2020, annual rpt, 3364-2

Spent fuel and radioactive waste, releases and waste composition by plant, 1986, annual rpt, 9634-1

Spent fuel from nuclear power plants and additional storage capacity needed, by reactor, 1987 and projected 1988-2007, annual rpt, 3354-2

Spent fuel storage capability, by nuclear power unit, monthly rpt, 9632-1.4

Uranium tailings at inactive mills, remedial action activities by site, and funding, FY88, annual rpt, 3354-9

Uranium tailings at inactive mills, remedial action proposals, costs, site characteristics, and environmental, socioeconomic, and health impacts, series, 3356-4

Waste Isolation Pilot Plant, New Mexico, disposal of military radioactive waste, environmental impacts, 1989 supplemental statement, 3008-33

Water movement through soil near radioactive waste repository sites in humid areas, 1989 rpt, 5668-98

Radiology
see Nuclear medicine and radiology
see X-rays

Radium
see Radioactive materials

Radner, Daniel B.
"Net Worth and Financial Assets of Age Groups in 1984", 4742-1.910
"Wealth of the Aged and Nonaged, 1984", 4746-26.5

Radon
Abatement activity of EPA, compliance, and monitoring stations operating status, 1987, annual rpt, 9194-4

Cancer (lung) risk relation to radon exposure, and death risk by smoking status, age, and sex, 1989 article, 4472-1.913

Indoor air pollution levels, effects of ventilation rates in commercial and public buildings, 1989 rpt, 3228-10

Indoor air radon levels, by county and State, 1989, annual rpt, 9194-19

Mine safety and health enforcement, training, and funding, with casualties, by type of mine and State, FY87, annual rpt, 6664-6

Raikes, Ronald
"Marketing Strategies for Commodity Producers", 1004-16.1

Raile, Gerhard K.
"Illinois' Forest Resource", 1208-292

Railpax
see National Railroad Passenger Corp.

Railroad accidents and safety
Accident deaths and rates, by cause, age, race, sex, and State, 1986, US Vital Statistics annual rpt, 4144-2

Accidents and deaths, by mode of transport, 1955-88, annual rpt, 7304-2

Accidents, casualties, and damage, by cause, railroad, and State, 1988, annual rpt, 7604-1

Accidents, casualties, and damage involving railroads, Fed Railroad Admin activities, and safety inspectors by State, 1987, annual rpt, 7604-12

Accidents, casualties, and damage, with data by rail carrier, for Pennsylvania and US, 1984-87, GAO rpt, 26113-390

Accidents, casualties, and Federal safety activities, for railroads late 1970s-87, hearing, 21368-103

Accidents, casualties, damage, and circumstances, by incident, 1986, annual rpt, 7604-3

Accidents, circumstances, severity, and railroad involved, periodic rpt, 9612-3

Accidents reported and not reported to Fed Railroad Admin, injuries, damage, and workdays lost, for 5 carriers, 1983-87, GAO rpt, 26113-410

DOT activities by subagency, budget, and summary accident data, FY85, annual rpt, 7304-1

Hazardous material transport accidents, casualties, and damage, by mode of transport, with DOT control activities, 1988, annual rpt, 7304-4

Hwy-railroad grade crossing accidents, detailed data by State and railroad, 1988, annual rpt, 7604-2

Hwy-railroad grade-crossing warning devices, costs and effectiveness of alternative devices, local area study, 1985-86, 7558-108

Hwy safety program funding, and accident and death reductions, by State, FY88, annual rpt, 7554-26

Injury and illness rates, by SIC 2- to 4-digit industry, 1987, annual rpt, 6844-1

Radioactive waste (military) disposal at New Mexico Waste Isolation Pilot Plant, environmental impacts, 1989 supplemental statement, 3008-33

Safety violation claims settled, by rail carrier, FY88, annual rpt, 7604-10

Short-line railroads operations and regulation, for lines established 1980-87 and trends from 1834, hearing, 21368-109

Railroad equipment and vehicles
Amtrak finances and operations, FY88, annual rpt, 29524-1

Business statistics, detailed data for major industries and economic indicators, *Survey of Current Business*, monthly rpt, 2702-1.20

Communist countries agricultural, mineral, and consumer and producer goods production, by commodity, 1960s-88, annual rpt, 9114-4.4

Construction put in place (public and private), by type, bimonthly rpt, 2042-1.1

Construction put in place, value of new public and private structures, by type, monthly rpt, 2382-4

County Business Patterns, 1987: employment, establishments, and payroll, by SIC 2- to 4-digit industry and county, annual State rpt series, 2326-8

Cuba economic conditions, agricultural and industrial production and distribution, trade, and intl economic relations, 1980-87 with trends from 1961, 9118-8

DOD prime contract awards, by detailed procurement category, FY85-88, annual rpt, 3544-18

Employment, earnings, and hours, by SIC 1- to 4-digit industry, monthly 1983-Feb 1989, annual rpt, 6744-4

Exports of US, detailed commodities by country, monthly rpt, 2422-3

Finances and operations of Class I railroads, detailed data by firm, class of service, and district, 1987, annual rpt, 9486–6.1

Finances and operations of Class I railroads, detailed data by firm, class of service, and district, 1988, annual rpt, 9486–5.1

Grain and other commodities shipments by rail by car type, 1986, and rail car fleet size, 1978-88, 1278–15

Grain shipments by rail, and car fleets and shortages, with data by firm, 1970s-88 and forecast to 1995, hearing, 21368–114

Grain shipments by rail, by commodity and port region, and car fleet requirements, 1949-88 with projections to 2001, 1278–14

Imports of US, detailed Schedule A commodities by country, monthly rpt, 2422–2

Imports of US given duty-free treatment for value of US material sent abroad, and impacts on US industry and employment, by commodity and country, 1987, annual rpt, 9884–14

Manufacturing annual survey, 1986: financial and operating data, by SIC 2- to 4-digit industry, series, 2506–15

Manufacturing census, 1987: financial and operating data, for SIC 4-digit industries by product, preliminary rpt, 2491–1.77

Occupational injury and illness rates, by SIC 2- to 4-digit industry, 1987, annual rpt, 6844–1

OECD trade, total and for 4 major countries, and US trade by country, by commodity, 1970-87, world area rpt series, 9116–1

Oil products sales, and purchases of refiners, processors, and distributors, by product, end-use sector, PAD district, and State, 1988, annual rpt, 3164–85

Pollution (air) levels for 6 pollutants, by source, 1970-87 and trends from 1940, annual rpt, 9194–13

Pollution (water) incidents and discharges, by type, source, cause, and location, 1984-86, annual rpt, 7404–3

Price indexes (producer), by stage of processing and detailed commodity, monthly rpt, 6762–6

Price indexes (producer), by stage of processing and detailed commodity, monthly 1988, annual rpt, 6764–2

Rails (steel) from Canada, injury to US industry from foreign subsidized and less than fair value imports, investigation with background financial and operating data, 1989 rpt, 9886–19.68

Science, engineering, and technical employment in manufacturing, by field, occupation, and industry, 1986, triennial rpt, 9627–23

Short-line railroads operations and regulation, for lines established 1980-87 and trends from 1834, hearing, 21368–109

Transportation finances, operations, vehicles, equipment, accidents, and energy use, by mode of transport, 1955-88, annual rpt, 7304–2

Urban areas traffic volume and detailed trip characteristics, by transport mode and city, 1950s-88, 7888–37

Urban Mass Transportation Admin grants for transit systems, by city and State, FY88, annual rpt, 7884–10

Urban transit systems services and vehicles, 1988 annual listing, 7884–9

see also Railroad accidents and safety

Railroad Retirement Board

Budget of US Appendix, obligations, appropriations, and personnel, by program and agency, FY90, annual rpt, 104–3

Budget of US, authoritative financial statements with appropriations, outlays, and receipts, by category and agency, FY88, annual rpt, 8104–2.2

Labor unions recognized in Fed Govt, agreements and membership by agency and facility, as of Jan 1989, biennial listing, 9844–14

Railroad employee benefits and beneficiaries by type, and railroad employment and payroll, FY85, annual rpt, 9704–2

Railroad employee retirement, survivors, unemployment, and health insurance programs, monthly rpt, 9702–2

Railroad employment, and benefits program finances and beneficiaries, FY88, annual rpt, 9704–1

Railroad employment by occupation from 1957, and Railroad Retirement Account finances, alternative projections 1987-2010, GAO rpt, 26121–280

Railroads

Business statistics, detailed data for major industries and economic indicators, *Survey of Current Business*, monthly rpt, 2702–1.8

Canada travel to US by Province of residence, and characteristics of visit, by State, 1988, annual rpt, 2904–7

Construction industries census, 1987: establishments, employment, receipts, and expenditures, by SIC 4-digit industry and State, final industry rpt series, 2373–1

Construction industries census, 1987: financial and operating data, preliminary industry rpt series, 2371–1

Cuba economic conditions, agricultural and industrial production and distribution, trade, and intl economic relations, 1980-87 with trends from 1961, 9118–8

Customs Service activities, collections, entries processed by mode of transport, and seizures, FY84-88, annual rpt, 8144–1

Developing countries disaster preparedness and economic, population, and political data, country rpt series, 9916–2

DOD shipments of military and personal property, passenger traffic, and costs, by service branch and mode of transport, quarterly rpt, 3702–1

Earnings by major industry group, and personal income per capita and by source, by region and State, 1929-87, 2708–40

Electric utilities finances and operations, detailed data for privately owned firms, and summary data for other utilities by type, 1987, annual rpt, 3164–23

Employee benefits and beneficiaries by type, and railroad employment and payroll, FY85, annual rpt, 9704–2

Employee retirement, disability, and unemployment insurance programs, beneficiaries and collections, monthly rpt, 4742–1.1

Employee retirement, survivors, unemployment, and health insurance programs, monthly rpt, 9702–2

Employee retirement, unemployment, and disability benefits, and program finances, late 1930s-87, annual rpt, 4744–3

Employment and retirees of railroads, 1945-88, annual rpt, 25144–3.1

Employment by functional group, for Class I line-haul railroads, monthly rpt, 9482–3

Employment by occupation from 1957, and Railroad Retirement Account finances, alternative projections 1987-2010, GAO rpt, 26121–280

Employment, earnings, and hours, by occupation for Class I railroads, 1988, annual table, 9484–5

Employment, earnings, and hours, by selected SIC 1- to 4-digit industry, State, and for 262 MSAs, 1972-87, 6748–81

Employment, earnings, and hours, by SIC 1- to 4-digit industry, monthly 1983-Feb 1989, annual rpt, 6744–4

Employment of railroads, and employee benefit program finances and beneficiaries, FY88, annual rpt, 9704–1

Energy use by mode of transport, fuel supply, and demographic and economic factors of vehicle use, 1970s-88, annual rpt, 3304–5

Finances and operations, by SIC 2- to 4-digit industry, forecast 1989 with trends from 1950s, annual rpt, 2044–28

Finances and operations of Class I railroads, detailed data by firm, class of service, and district, 1987, annual rpt, 9486–6.1

Finances and operations of Class I railroads, detailed data by firm, class of service, and district, 1988, annual rpt, 9486–5.1

Finances and operations of transit systems, by mode of transport, size of fleet, and for 432 systems, 1986, annual rpt, 7884–4

Finances, costs, and needs of transit systems, by State and selected system, 1980-88, biennial rpt, 7884–8

Finances, operations, vehicles, equipment, accidents, and energy use, by mode of transport, 1955-88, annual rpt, 7304–2

Foreign countries economic, social, political, and geographic summary data, by country, 1989, annual factbook, 9114–2

Grain shipments and rates, drought impacts, 1988, 1588–133

Grain shipments and rates for barge and rail loadings, periodic situation rpt with articles, 1561–4

Grain shipments for exports, effects of rail car availability and major river water levels, 1979-87, article, 1561–4.903

Grain shipping rates and revenues, impacts of rail deregulation, 1981-85, 1548–349

Labor disputes of railroads, and Federal mediation activities and caseloads, with data by carrier and union, FY85-86, annual rpt, 9604–1

Labor productivity, indexes of output, hours, and employment by SIC 2- to 4-digit industry, 1963-87, annual rpt, 6824–1.4

Pollution (air) levels for 5 pollutants, by detailed source and State, 1986, annual rpt, 9194–7

Price indexes (producer), by stage of processing and detailed commodity, monthly 1988, annual rpt, 6764–2

Revenue and volume for freight, by commodity and region of origin and destination, 1987, annual rpt, 7604–6

Revenue, charges, and employment of freight carriers, by transport mode, 1986, annual rpt, 7704–7.1

Revenue, income, freight, and rate of return, by Class I freight railroad and district, quarterly rpt, 9482–2

Science, engineering, and technical employment in transportation, utilities, and retail and wholesale trade, by field, occupation, and industry, 1985, triennial rpt, 9627–32

Short-line railroads operations and regulation, for lines established 1980-87 and trends from 1834, hearing, 21368–109

Soviet Union railroad productivity and operations, 1983-86, working paper, 2326–18.47

Statistical Abstract of US, social, political, and economic data, 1790-2025, comprehensive annual compilation, 2324–1.3

Tax (income) returns of corporations, income and tax items by asset size and detailed industry, 1986, annual rpt, 8304–4; 8304–21

Tax (property) revenue by level of govt, assessed values by locality, and exemptions, by property type and State, 1987 Census of Govts, 2453–1

Technological devs effect on labor force, composition, and productivity, by industry, 1960s-86 and projected to 2000, 6826–2.4

Unemployment insurance claims, by program, weekly press release, 6402–14

Urban areas traffic volume and detailed trip characteristics, by transport mode and city, 1950s-88, 7888–37

Urban transit systems services and vehicles, 1988 annual listing, 7884–9

see also Consolidated Rail Corp.

see also Federal aid to railroads

see also Freight

see also National Railroad Passenger Corp.

see also Railroad accidents and safety

see also Railroad equipment and vehicles

see also Subways

see also U.S. Railway Association

see also By Industry in the "Index by Categories"

Rainfall

see Weather

Rainy River

see Souris-Red-Rainy Rivers

Raisins

see Fruit and fruit products

Raleigh, N.C.

Wages by occupation, and benefits for office and plant workers, 1989 survey, periodic MSA rpt, 6785–3.7

see also under By City and By SMSA or MSA in the "Index by Categories"

Rand, Michael R.

"Households Touched by Crime, 1988", 6066–25.22

Randall, Richard E.

"Can the Market Evaluate Asset Quality Exposure in Banks?", 9373–1.911

Randolph, William C.

"Aggregation Consistent Restriction Based Improvement of Local Area Estimators", 6886–6.51

"Alternative Tests of the Error Components Model", 6886–6.38

"Consistent Least Squares Estimation of Error Covariance Parameters for Regression Models with Linear Covariance Structure", 6886–6.30

"Estimation of Housing Depreciation: Short Term Quality Change and Long Term Vintage Effects", 6886–6.29

"Housing Depreciation and Aging Bias in the Consumer Price Index", 6886–6.35

"Price Measurement When Designs Are Changed: Estimation Theory with Application to Computer Equipment", 6886–6.24

Rantoul, Ill.

Wages by occupation, and benefits for office and plant workers, 1988 survey, periodic MSA rpt, 6785–11.3

see also under By SMSA or MSA in the "Index by Categories"

Rape

Arrest rates, by offense, sex, age, and race, 1987, annual rpt, 6224–7

Crime, criminal justice admin and enforcement, and public opinion, data compilation, 1970s-88, annual rpt, 6064–6

Crime Index by population size and region, and offenses by large city, Jan-June 1989, semiannual rpt, 6222–1

Crimes, arrests by offender characteristics, and rates, by offense, and law enforcement employees, by population size and jurisdiction, 1988, annual rpt, 6224–2

Criminal case processing from arrest to sentencing, cases and duration by disposition, offense, and defendant characteristics, for selected cities, 1986, annual rpt, 6064–27

Criminal case processing in Federal district courts, and dispositions, by offense, district, and offender characteristics, 1984, annual rpt, 6064–29

Criminal case processing in Federal district courts, disposition by offense, 1980-87, 6066–19.50

Diplomats and staff with immunity for foreign missions in US and US missions abroad, and foreign diplomats criminal cases, 1978-87, hearing, 25388–51

Executions of prisoners, by offense and race, 1930-86, annual rpt, 6064–26.6

Juvenile court delinquency cases, by offense, referral source, disposition, age, sex, race, State, and county, 1985, annual rpt, 6064–12

Juvenile offenders recidivism rates, arrests, and court referrals, by offense, age, and sex, 1983 local area studies, 6068–227

Prison time served ratio to offenses committed, by offense, 1958-86, 6068–229

Prisoners in State instns, by offense, criminal history, and inmate, family, and victim characteristics, 1986, annual rpt, 6064–26.3

Recidivism rates of prisoners released in 1983, by offense and prisoner characteristics, 1983-86, 6066–19.48

Sentences by State courts for felony offenses, and sentence lengths and time served, by offense, 1986, 6066–25.19

Sentences for Federal offenses, guidelines by offense and circumstances, 1989 rpt, 17668–1

Sentences for felonies, by sentence type and offense, 1983-86, 6066–19.52

Statistical Abstract of US, social, political, and economic data, 1790-2025, comprehensive annual compilation, 2324–1.1

Victimization rates, by victim and offender characteristics, circumstances, and offense, survey rpt series, 6066–3

Victimizations and rates for attempted and completed rape, 1965-87, annual rpt, 6224–8

Victimizations, by offense, offender characteristics, and victim reactions and views, 1986-87, 6066–19.47

Victimizations of households, by offense, household characteristics, and location, 1975-88, annual rpt, 6066–25.22

Victimizations resulting in injury, by offense, type of injury and medical care received, and victim characteristics, 1979-86, 6066–19.49

Wiretaps authorized, costs, arrests, trials, and convictions, by offense and jurisdiction, 1988, annual rpt, 18204–7

Rapid City, S.Dak.

see also under By SMSA or MSA in the "Index by Categories"

Rapid transit

see Subways

see Urban transportation

Rare earths

see Nonmetallic minerals and mines

Ras al-Khaimah

see United Arab Emirates

Raskin, A. H.

"Cyrus S. Ching: Pioneer in Industrial Peacemaking", 6722–1.940

Rausser, Gordon

"Interest Rates and Commodity Prices", 1502–3.902

Raw materials

see Stockpiling

see Strategic materials

see terms listed under Agricultural commodities

see terms listed under Commodities

see terms listed under Natural resources

Rawlings, Steve W.

"Household and Family Characteristics: March 1988", 2546–1.437

"Single Parents and Their Children", 2546–2.148

Ray, Wayne A.

"Experience of a Medicaid Nursing Home Entry Cohort", 4652–1.942

Rayon

see Synthetic fibers and fabrics

RCA Global Communications

Finances and operations, detail for telegraph firms, 1987, annual rpt, 9284–6.5

REA

see Rural Electrification Administration

Reactors

see Electric power plants and equipment

see Nuclear power

Reading ability and habits

Condition of Education, detailed data on elementary and secondary education, 1920s-88 and projected to 1997, annual rpt, 4824–1.1

DOD Dependents Schools basic skills and college entrance test scores, 1988/89, annual rpt, 3504–16

Military reserve spouses attitudes, and family social, economic, and other characteristics, 1986 survey, 3508–30

New York and northeastern New Jersey employment by industry div, unemployment, and consumer price changes by selected commodity, 1978-June 1989, press release, 6926–2.40

Northern Mariana Islands economic census, 1987: employment, firms, payroll, and receipts, by SIC 1- to 4-digit industry, 2597–1

Occupational injury and illness rates, by SIC 2- to 4-digit industry, 1987, annual rpt, 6844–1

Ohio River basin waterway facilities, freight by commodity and port, and recreation, by waterway, 1986-87, annual rpt, 3754–6

Public lands acreage and use, and Land Mgmt Bur activities and finances, annual State rpt series, 5724–11

Public lands acreage, grants, use, revenues, and allocations, by State, FY88, annual rpt, 5724–1.2

Science and engineering employment, by nonmanufacturing industry and field, 1987, triennial rpt, 9627–31:

Service industries census, 1987: establishments, receipts, employment, and payroll, by SIC 2- to 4-digit kind of business, MSA, county, and city, State rpt series, 2391–1

Service industries receipts, by SIC 2- to 4-digit kind of business, 1988, annual rpt, 2413–8

Small business establishments, employment, and financial ratios, by SIC 1- to 2-digit industry and State, late 1960s-87, 9768–19

Statistical Abstract of US, social, political, and economic data, 1790-2025, comprehensive annual compilation, 2324–1.1

Tax (income) returns of corporations, income and tax items by asset size and detailed industry, 1986, annual rpt, 8304–4; 8304–21

Tax (income) returns of partnerships, income statement items by industry group, 1986, annual article, 8302–2.903

Tax (income) returns of sole proprietorships, income statement items, by industry group, 1987, annual article, 8302–2.904; 8302–2.921

Tax revenue potential of State and local systems relative to natl average tax burden, by type of tax and State, 1986, annual rpt, 10044–7

TVA financial and operating data by program and facility, FY88, annual rpt, 9804–32

VA Medicine and Surgery Dept trainees, by detailed program and city, FY88, annual rpt, 8704–4

Virgin Islands economic censuses, 1987: employment, firms, payroll, and receipts, by SIC 1- to 4-digit industry, island, and city, 2593–1

Western US activities of Reclamation Bur, land and population served, and recreation areas, by location, 1987, annual rpt, 5824–12.1

Wildlife refuge impacts of recreational, commercial, and military use, by type of activity, 1988-89, GAO rpt, 26113–434

Wildlife-related recreation, hunting, and fishing participation and spending, detailed data by location, 1985 survey, quinquennial rpt, 5508–5

Wildlife-related recreation, hunting, and fishing participation and spending, detailed data, 1985 survey, quinquennial State rpt series, 5506–6

see also Boats and boating
see also Camping
see also Fishing, sport
see also Horse racing
see also Hunting and trapping
see also Motion pictures
see also National forests
see also National parks
see also Parks
see also Recreational vehicles
see also Sporting goods
see also Sports and athletics
see also State forests
see also Swimming
see also Swimming pools
see also Travel and tourism
see also Wilderness areas
see also Winter sports
see also By Industry in the "Index by Categories"

Recreational vehicles

Accidents (fatal), deaths, and rates, by circumstances, characteristics of persons and vehicles involved, and location, 1987, annual rpt, 7764–10

Accidents involving consumer products and related activities, injuries by victim age and sex, 1988, annual rpt, 9164–7

Accidents involving consumer products, injuries by severity, victim age, and detailed product, 1988, annual rpt, 9164–6

All-terrain vehicles from Japan at less than fair value, injury to US industry, investigation with background financial and operating data, 1989 rpt, 9886–14.254

County Business Patterns, 1987: employment, establishments, and payroll, by SIC 2- to 4-digit industry and county, annual State rpt series, 2326–8

Employment, earnings, and hours, by SIC 1- to 4-digit industry, monthly 1983-Feb 1989, annual rpt, 6744–4

Energy use by mode of transport, fuel supply, and demographic and economic factors of vehicle use, 1970s-88, annual rpt, 3304–5

Exports of US, detailed commodities by country, monthly rpt, 2422–3

Imports of US, detailed Schedule A commodities by country, monthly rpt, 2422–2

Manufacturing annual survey, 1986: financial and operating data, by SIC 2- to 4-digit industry, series, 2506–15

Manufacturing census, 1987: financial and operating data, for SIC 4-digit industries by product, preliminary rpt, 2491–1.77

Natl park system visits and overnight stays, by park and State, 1988 and trends from 1979, annual rpt, 5544–12

Occupational injury and illness rates, by SIC 2- to 4-digit industry, 1987, annual rpt, 6844–1

OECD trade, total and for 4 major countries, and US trade by country, by commodity, 1970-87, world area rpt series, 9116–1

Park natl system visits and overnight stays, by park and State, monthly rpt, 5542–4

Price indexes (producer), by stage of processing and detailed commodity, monthly rpt, 6762–6

Price indexes (producer), by stage of processing and detailed commodity, monthly 1988, annual rpt, 6764–2

Retail trade census, 1987: employment, establishments, sales, and payroll, by SIC 2- to 4-digit kind of business, MSA, county, and city, State rpt series, 2397–1

Statistical Abstract of US, social, political, and economic data, 1790-2025, comprehensive annual compilation, 2324–1.3

Wildlife-related recreation, hunting, and fishing participation and spending, detailed data by location, 1985 survey, quinquennial rpt, 5508–5

Wildlife-related recreation, hunting, and fishing participation and spending, detailed data, 1985 survey, quinquennial State rpt series, 5506–6

Recruiting

see Voluntary military service

Recycling of waste materials

Chlorofluorocarbon use, and costs and benefits of proposed reductions, projected to 2010, 3166–6.34

Electric power plants and capacity, by fuel used, owner, location, and operating status, 1988 and for units planned 1989-98, annual listing, 3164–36

Employment, earnings, and hours, by SIC 1- to 4-digit industry, monthly 1983-Feb 1989, annual rpt, 6744–4

Energy prices and spending, by fuel type, end-use sector, and State, 1987, annual rpt, 3164–64

Energy use, by fuel pollutant source, fuel type, and State, 1986, annual rpt, 9194–14

Environmental quality and protection programs, and intl issues, 1988 annual rpt, 484–1

Exports of US, detailed commodities by country, monthly rpt, 2422–3

Industrial hazardous substances releases and reduction methods under EPA regulation, by chemical, source, industry, and location, 1987, annual rpt, 9234–6

Input-output structure of US economy, detailed interindustry transactions for 84 industries, and components of final demand, 1983, annual article, 2702–1.909

Lumber (pulpwood) production and mill receipts in North Central States, by species, mill, State, and county, 1987, annual rpt, 1204–19

Lumber production and mill residue for Rocky Mountain States, by species, ownership, and county, series, 1206–17

Lumber production from damaged and dead timber, feasibility of proposed Montana plant, 1989 rpt, 1208–308

Manufacturing pollution abatement costs recovered, by SIC 2- to 4-digit industry and State, 1986, annual Current Industrial Rpt, 2506–3.6

Minerals and metal recycling, by commodity, 1984-88, annual rpt, 5604–18

Employment, earnings, and hours, by SIC 1- to 4-digit industry, monthly 1983-Feb 1989, annual rpt, 6744-4

Environmental quality and protection programs, and intl issues, 1988 annual rpt, 484-1

Expenditures for pollution abatement by govts, business, and consumers, 1983-87, annual article, 2702-1.919

Expenditures for pollution abatement equipment by business, 1982-88, annual article, 2702-1.904

FmHA borrowers, by type of borrower and loan, and State, quarterly rpt, 1182-4

Govt employment and payroll, by function, level of govt, and jurisdiction, 1987-88, annual rpt series, 2466-1

Govt finances, by level of govt, State, and for large cities and counties, annual rpt series, 2466-2

Housing and households detailed characteristics, and unit and neighborhood quality, MSA surveys, series, 2485-6

Manufacturing pollution abatement capital and operating costs, by SIC 2- to 4-digit industry and State, 1986, annual Current Industrial Rpt, 2506-3.6

Neighborhood and housing quality, indicators and attitudes, by householder type and location, 1985, biennial rpt, 2485-12

Neighborhood and housing quality, indicators and attitudes, MSA surveys, series, 2485-6

Occupational injury and illness rates, by SIC 2- to 4-digit industry, 1987, annual rpt, 6844-1

Public opinion on taxes, spending, and govt efficiency, by respondent characteristics, 1989 survey, annual rpt, 10044-2

Science, engineering, and technical employment in transportation, utilities, and retail and wholesale trade, by field, occupation, and industry, 1985, triennial rpt, 9627-32

Spacecraft debris in orbit, hazards, and tracking, with data for individual fragmented craft, 1961-88, 9508-34

State and local govt employment of minorities and women, by occupation, function, and pay level, 1986, annual rpt, 9244-6.4

Statistical Abstract of US, social, political, and economic data, 1790-2025, comprehensive annual compilation, 2324-1.1

Tax (income) returns of partnerships, income statement items by industry group, 1986, annual article, 8302-2.903

Tax (income) returns of sole proprietorships, income statement items, by industry group, 1987, annual article, 8302-2.904; 8302-2.921

Tax expenditures, Federal revenues forgone through income tax deductions and exclusions by type, FY90-94, annual rpt, 21784-10

Transportation census, 1987: trucks, by detailed characteristics, miles traveled, and type of product carried, State rpt series, 2573-1

see also Hazardous waste and disposal
see also Landfills
see also Radioactive waste and disposal

see also Recycling of waste materials
see also Sewage and wastewater systems

Regional medical programs

Health Professions Bur training and research grants and contracts, by instn and program, FY88, annual listing, 4114-1

HHS financial aid, by program, recipient, State, and city, FY88, annual regional listings, 4004-3

Kidney end-stage disease treatment facilities, Medicare enrollment and reimbursement, survival, and patient characteristics, 1980-86, annual rpt, 4654-16

Rural areas health care facilities, staffing, services accessibility, and indicators of need, 1960s-88, 25148-41

Training support grants of Bur of Health Professions, by program, region, and State, FY80-87, 4118-62

VA and non-VA facilities health services sharing contracts, by service type and region, FY88, annual rpt, 8704-5

Regional planning

Appalachia local dev projects, and funding by source, by program and State, FY88, annual rpt, 9084-1

Appalachian Regional Commission funding, by project and State, planned FY89, annual rpt, 9084-3

Assistance (financial and nonfinancial) of Fed Govt, 1989 base edition with supplements, annual listing, 104-5

DC metro area land acquisition and dev projects of Fed Govt, characteristics and funding by agency and project, FY90-94, annual rpt, 15454-1

Estuary environmental conditions and mgmt, for individual areas, conf series, 2146-6

Fed Govt spending in States, by type, program, agency, and State, FY88, annual rpt, 2464-2

TVA financial and operating data by program and facility, FY88, annual rpt, 9804-32

see also Regional medical programs

Regions of the U.S.

see Middle Atlantic States
see North Central States
see Northeast States
see Southeastern States
see Southwestern States
see Western States
see under By Region, By Census Division, and By State in the "Index by Categories"
see under names of individual States

Regions of the world

see Africa
see Antarctica
see Asia
see Atlantic Ocean
see Caribbean area
see Central America
see Eastern Europe
see Europe
see Gulf of Mexico
see Indian Ocean
see Latin America
see Mediterranean Sea
see Middle East
see North America
see North Sea
see Oceania
see Pacific Ocean

see South America
see Southeast Asia

Regulatory commissions

see Administrative law and procedure
see under names of individual agencies (listed under Federal independent agencies)

Rehabilitation

see Drug abuse and treatment
see Housing maintenance and repair
see Rehabilitation of criminals
see Rehabilitation of the disabled
see Respiratory therapy
see Veterans rehabilitation
see Vocational rehabilitation

Rehabilitation of criminals

Drug and alcohol abuse treatment facilities, services, use, funding, and client characteristics, 1987, annual rpt, 4494-10

Education funding of Fed Govt, State allocation by program, recipient type, and State, 1987/88, annual rpt, 4804-8

Prison conditions, population, and problems, issues and bibl, 1989 compilation of papers, 25928-8

Sex offenders treatment programs for adults and juveniles, by program type and State, 1986-88, annual rpt, 6064-6.1

Vocational education aid recipients and sources, and characteristics of programs and students, 1970s-89, series, 4806-3

see also Community-based correctional programs
see also Pardons
see also Parole and probation
see also Prison work programs
see also Recidivism

Rehabilitation of the disabled

Facilities excluded from Medicare prospective payment system, labor and capital productivity indicators by instn type, 1976-86, 17206-2.1

Fed Govt and State rehabilitation activities and funding, FY88, annual rpt, 4944-1

Fed Govt spending in States, by type, program, agency, and State, FY88, annual rpt, 2464-2

Medicare and Medicaid beneficiaries and program operations, 1988, annual fact book, 4654-18

Medicare discharges, charges, and length of stay, for facilities excluded from prospective payment system, FY84-88, article, 4652-1.935

Medicare payments for post-hospitalization care by diagnosis, for nursing home, home care, and rehabilitation, 1980s-87, article, 4652-1.909

Medicare reimbursement of hospitals under prospective payment system, and of physicians, effect on services, finances, and beneficiary payments, 1970s-88, annual rpt, 17204-2

Nursing home rehabilitation services use, by service type and patient characteristics, 1st qtr 1983, 4188-58

Workers compensation laws of States and Fed Govt, 1989 semiannual rpt, 6502-1

see also Group homes for the handicapped
see also Occupational therapy
see also Physical therapy
see also Respiratory therapy
see also Sheltered workshops

see also Special education
see also Speech pathology and audiology
see also Veterans rehabilitation
see also Vocational rehabilitation

Reichelderfer, Katherine H.
"Water Quality Legislation Affecting Agriculture", 1004–16.1

Reid, J. Norman
"Do Federal Funds Help Spur Rural Development?", 1502–7.901

Reilly, John M.
"Economics of Ethanol Production in the U.S.", 1588–132

Reilly, Thomas
"Medicare and Medicaid Data Book, 1988", 4654–1

Reimund, Donn
"Farm Financial Situation in the Late 1980's: Farm Household Dependence on Farm Versus Off-Farm Income", 1504–4

Reinhart, Vincent
"Capital Mobility and Short-Term Interest Rates", 9385–9
"Globalization of Financial Markets and the Effectiveness of Monetary Policy Instruments", 9385–1.901
"Increasing Capital Mobility: Evidence from Short- and Long-Term Markets", 9385–9
"Strong Dollar and U.S. Inflation", 9375–14
"What Does Covered Interest Parity Reveal About Capital Mobility?", 9385–9

Reining, Robert
"Two Methods for Estimating Real Structural Change in Agriculture", 1502–3.901

Reinsdorf, Marshall B.
"Consumer Information and Industrial Profitability in an Equilibrium Price Dispersion Model", 6886–6.47
"Implications of Structural Retirement Models", 6886–6.31

Relief
see Disaster relief
see Food assistance
see Income maintenance
see International assistance
see Public welfare programs
see Refugees
see State funding for social welfare
see War relief

Religion
Abortions by patient characteristics, rates for all and 1st abortions, and related deaths in US and other countries, 1989 hearing, 21408–113
Alcohol use, abuse, treatment, and views of racial and ethnic groups in US and native countries, by selected characteristics, 1988 compilation of papers, 4488–12
Cancer (cervical) cases and risk relation to smoking and other characteristics, for 4 Latin American countries, 1986-87 study, article, 4472–1.905
Consumer spending, natl income and product account, *Survey of Current Business*, monthly rpt, 2702–1.23
Developing countries disaster preparedness and economic, population, and political data, country rpt series, 9916–2
Foreign countries *Background Notes*, summary social, political, and economic data, series, 7006–2
Foreign countries economic, social, political, and geographic summary data, by country, 1989, annual factbook, 9114–2

Health care (long-term) needs, ability to pay, and views on Federal aid for home care, 1988 survey, hearing, 21148–51
Health care treatments and products not proven safe or effective, use, costs, and user characteristics, 1986 survey, 4008–86
Mormons death risks from cancer and heart disease, by sex and health habits practiced, 1974 and 1979 studies, article, 4472–1.932
Older persons health care services use, persons with high and low levels of care ·by selected health and other characteristics, 1971 and 1980 studies, 4186–2.22
Statistical Abstract of US, social, political, and economic data, 1790-2025, comprehensive annual compilation, 2324–1.1
see also Clergy
see also Religious liberty
see also Religious organizations

Religious liberty
Foreign countries human rights conditions in 170 countries, 1988, annual rpt, 21384–3

Religious organizations
Buildings (commercial and public) alteration and repair spending, by type, size, age, and region, 1986, 2388–4
Construction industries census, 1987: establishments, employment, receipts, and expenditures, by SIC 4-digit industry and State, final industry rpt series, 2373–1
Construction industries census, 1987: financial and operating data, preliminary industry rpt series, 2371–1
Construction put in place, and authorized by selected MSA, by type and region, bimonthly rpt, 2042–1.1; 2042–1.3
Construction put in place, value of new public and private structures, by type, monthly rpt, 2382–4
County Business Patterns, 1987: employment, establishments, and payroll, by SIC 2- to 4-digit industry and county, annual State rpt series, 2326–8
Education data compilation, students, staff, finances, and facilities, 1989 edition, annual rpt, 4824–2
Education statistics, detailed data on elementary and secondary education, 1920s-88 and projected to 1997, annual rpt, 4824–1.1
Health care treatments and products not proven safe or effective, use, costs, and user characteristics, 1986 survey, 4008–86
Homeless children, by type of accommodation, urban-rural location, and State, alternative estimates, 1988, GAO rpt, 26131–61
Marriages, by prior marital status, interval between marriages, other characteristics of spouses, type of ceremony, and State, with divorces, 1970s-83, 4147–21.45
Marriages performed in civil and religious ceremonies, by characteristics of spouses and State, 1984, US Vital Statistics annual rpt, 4144–4.1
Nursing home compliance with Medicare and Medicaid regulations, and patient characteristics, by facility, 1987/88, annual State rpt series, 4654–15

Refugee resettlement programs and funding, arrivals by country of origin, and indicators of adjustment, by State, FY88, annual rpt, 4694–5
Schools (private) students federally funded compensatory education programs, and costs, for selected school districts, 1984-89, GAO rpt, 26121–308
Schools (private elementary and secondary), enrollment, teachers, and high school grads, by instn religious orientation, 1988/89, annual rpt, 4834–21
Schools (public) partnerships with community organizations, participation, activities, and contributions, by school characteristics and location, 1987/88, 4826–1.27
Science and engineering employment, by nonmanufacturing industry and field, 1987, triennial rpt, 9627–31
Statistical Abstract of US, social, political, and economic data, 1790-2025, comprehensive annual compilation, 2324–1.1
Tax (property) revenue by level of govt, assessed values by locality, and exemptions, by property type and State, 1987 Census of Govts, 2453–1
Terrorist (intl) incidents, casualties, and attacks on US targets, by attack type and country, 1980-88, 7008–56
Terrorist incidents in US, related activity, and casualties, by attack type, target, group, and location, 1988, annual rpt, 6224–6
see also Clergy

Relocation
Housing characteristics of recent movers for new and previous unit, and household characteristics, by location, 1985, biennial rpt, 2485–12
Housing characteristics of recent movers for new and previous unit, and household characteristics, MSA surveys, series, 2485–6
Indian (Navajo and Hopi) relocation program activities and caseloads, monthly rpt, 16002–1
Indian (Navajo and Hopi) relocation program activities, caseloads, and finances, by location, annual rpt, discontinued, 16004–4
Indian (Navajo and Hopi) relocation program activities, caseloads, and finances, FY88, annual rpt, 16004–1
Railroad accidents and cars releasing hazardous materials, and persons evacuated, for Pennsylvania and US, 1984-87, GAO rpt, 26113–390
Railroad accidents involving hazardous materials, damage, and persons evacuated, by cause, railroad, and State, 1988, annual rpt, 7604–1
Tax (income) returns of individuals, by filing status, tax item, and income level, 1987, annual article, 8302–2.901
see also Migration

Remedial education
Higher education instn remedial instruction and tutoring offerings, by instn type and control, 1980-88, annual rpt, 4824–2.21
Libraries literacy program activities, and relation to community and instn characteristics, 1986, 4878–2

Vocational and academic AA degree and certificate recipients and credits, by field, and student and instn characteristics, 1984, 4848–37

see also Compensatory education

see also Special education

Reno, Nev.

Wages by occupation, and benefits for office and plant workers, 1988 survey, periodic MSA rpt, 6785–3.1

see also under By City and By SMSA or MSA in the "Index by Categories"

Reno, Virginia P.

"Look at Very Early Retirees", 4742–1.911

Rent

Agriculture census, 1987: farms, farmland, production, finances, and operator characteristics, by county, final State rpt series, 2331–1

American Housing Survey: unit and households detailed characteristics, and unit and neighborhood quality, MSA rpt series, 2485–6

American Housing Survey: unit and households detailed characteristics, and unit and neighborhood quality, 1985, biennial rpt, 2485–12

Apartment and condominium completions by rent class and sales price, and market absorption rates, quarterly rpt, 2482–2

Apartment completions by region and metro-nonmetro location, and absorption rates, by size and rent class, preliminary 1988, annual Current Housing Rpt, 2484–3

Apartment market absorption rates and characteristics for nonsubsidized furnished and unfurnished units, 1987 and trends from 1970, annual Current Housing Rpt, 2484–2

Banks in Fed Reserve System, expenses and operations itemized by service, office, and district, 1988, annual rpt, 9364–11

Budget of US, authoritative financial statements with appropriations, outlays, and receipts, by category and agency, FY88, annual rpt, 8104–2.2

Business and financial statistics, historic trends, 1988 annual chartbook, 9364–2.6

Construction industries census, 1987: establishments, employment, receipts, and expenditures, by SIC 4-digit industry and State, final industry rpt series, 2373–1

Construction industries census, 1987: financial and operating data, preliminary industry rpt series, 2371–1

Consumer Expenditure Survey, household income by source, and itemized spending, by selected characteristics and region, 1984-87, annual rpt, 6764–5

Consumer spending, natl income and product account, *Survey of Current Business*, monthly rpt, 2702–1.23

CPI by component for US city average, and by region, population size, and for 27 metro areas, monthly rpt, 6762–2

CPI for rent, bimonthly rpt, 2042–1.5

CPI for rent, for US, Boston, San Francisco, and San Diego, 1980-88, article, 9373–1.907

Depreciation of rental housing, age as an indicator of unit quality, and other factors, model description and results, 1988 working paper, 6886–6.29; 6886–6.35

DOE real property owned and leased, by type, subagency, contractor, and site, FY87, annual rpt, 3004–28

Electric utilities privately owned, detailed finances and operations by firm, 1987, annual rpt, 3164–23.1

Farm finances and operations, by size, commodity, and region, 1986, annual rpt, 1544–27

Farm financial ratios, benchmarks by type of operation and region, 1984-86, 1548–342

Farm income, expenses, receipts by commodity, assets, liabilities, and ratios, 1988 and trends from 1945, annual rpt, 1544–16

Farm production itemized costs, by farm sales size and region, 1988, annual rpt, 1614–3

Farm production itemized costs, receipts, and returns, by commodity and region, 1985-87, annual rpt, 1544–20

Farm production itemized costs, receipts, and returns, by crop and State, preliminary 1987, annual rpt, 1544–24

Farm sector balance sheet, and marketing receipts by detailed commodity, by State, 1984-88, annual rpt, 1544–18

Farm sector finances, income sources, expenses by type, assets, debts, and ratios, 1983-87, annual rpt, 1544–19

Farmland value, rent, taxes, foreign ownership, and transfers by probable use and lender type, with data by region and State, 1975-89, article, 1561–16.902

Fed Govt-leased real property inventory and rental costs, worldwide summary by location and agency, 1987, annual rpt, 9454–10

Fed Govt obligations object class analysis, by agency, Budget of US, FY90, annual rpt, 104–9

Financial instns financial and operating statements by deposit size, Fed Reserve functional cost analysis, 1988, annual rpt, 9364–6

FmHA property acquired through foreclosure, 1-family homes, value, sales, and leases, by State, monthly rpt, 1182–7

Grazing land acreage, erosion, value, and livestock fed, by region and State, 1950-82, 1588–130

House of Representatives salaries, expenses, and contingent fund disbursement, detailed listings, quarterly rpt, 21942–1

Housing and households summary characteristics, 1985 and trends, biennial chartbook, 2486–1.7

Housing energy use, costs, and conservation, and household and housing characteristics, survey rpt series, 3166–7

Income (household, family, and personal), by source, detailed characteristics, and region, 1987, annual Current Population Rpt, 2546–6.59

Income (personal) by source, and BEA and IRS adjusted gross income measures, 1984-86 with trends from 1947, article, 8302–2.914

Income (personal) by source, and BEA and IRS adjusted gross income measures, 1986-87, annual article, 2702–1.927

Income (personal) per capita and by source, and earnings by industry div, by State, MSA, and county, 1982-87, annual regional rpts, 2704–2

Income from rent, *Business Conditions Digest*, monthly rpt, 2702–3.5

Natl income and product accounts and components, *Survey of Current Business*, monthly rpt, 2702–1.21; 2702–1.22

Natural gas interstate pipeline company detailed financial and operating data, by firm, 1988, annual rpt, 3164–38

Nonprofit charitable organizations finances, and assets and grants of top 10, 1985, article, 8302–2.923

Railroad (Class I) finances and operations, detailed data by firm, class of service, and district, 1987, annual rpt, 9486–6.1

Railroad (Class I) finances and operations, detailed data by firm, class of service, and district, 1988, annual rpt, 9486–5.1

Rural and urban areas housing and households characteristics, 1930s-80, 1598–245

Senate receipts, itemized expenses by payee, and balances, 1st half FY89, semiannual listing, 25922–1

Statistical Abstract of US, social, political, and economic data, 1790-2025, comprehensive annual compilation, 2324–1.3

Suburban areas land use, commuting, employment, and housing characteristics, detailed data for traffic planning, 1986, 7888–75

Survey of Current Business, detailed financial and business data, and economic indicators, monthly rpt, 2702–1.1

Tax (income) returns filed by type of filer, selected income items, quarterly rpt, 8302–2.1

Tax (income) returns of corporations, income and tax items by asset size and detailed industry, 1986, annual rpt, 8304–4; 8304–21

Tax (income) returns of individuals, detailed data, 1986, annual rpt, 8304–2

Tax (income) returns of partnerships, income statement items by industry group, 1986, annual article, 8302–2.903

Tax (income) returns of sole proprietorships, income statement items, by industry group, 1987, annual article, 8302–2.904; 8302–2.921

Telephone and telegraph firms detailed finances and operations, 1987, annual rpt, 9284–6.4

Telephone service of households, by composition, income sources, and other characteristics, 1984-87, 9288–11

Truck and warehouse services finances and inventory, by SIC 2- to 4-digit industry, 1988 survey, annual rpt, 2413–14

Vacant housing characteristics and costs, and occupancy and vacancy rates, by region and metro-nonmetro location, quarterly rpt, 2482–1

Vacant housing characteristics, and occupancy and vacancy rates, by tenure, region, and metro-nonmetro location, selected years 1960-88, annual rpt, 2484–1

see also Housing tenure

see also Motor vehicle rental

see also Rent control

see also Rent supplements

see also Rental industries

Receipts for services, by SIC 2- to 4-digit kind of business, 1988, annual rpt, 2413-8

Science and engineering employment, by nonmanufacturing industry and field, 1987, triennial rpt, 9627-31

Service industries census, 1987: establishments, receipts, employment, and payroll, by SIC 2- to 4-digit kind of business, MSA, county, and city, State rpt series, 2391-1

Tax (income) returns filed by type of filer, selected income items, quarterly rpt, 8302-2.1

Tax (income) returns of corporations, income and tax items by asset size and detailed industry, 1986, annual rpt, 8304-4; 8304-21

Tax (income) returns of partnerships, income statement items by industry group, 1986, annual article, 8302-2.903

Tax (income) returns of sole proprietorships, income statement items, by industry group, 1987, annual article, 8302-2.904; 8302-2.921

Transit systems finances and operations, by mode of transport, size of fleet, and for 432 systems, 1986, annual rpt, 7884-4

Transportation census, 1987: trucks, by detailed characteristics, miles traveled, and type of product carried, State rpt series, 2573-1

Virgin Islands economic censuses, 1987: employment, firms, payroll, and receipts, by SIC 1- to 4-digit industry, island, and city, 2593-1

see also Automobile repair and maintenance
see also Housing maintenance and repair
see also Shipbuilding and repairing
see also By Industry in the "Index by Categories"

Republic of China
see Taiwan

Republic of Korea
see Korea, South

Republican Party
Campaign finances, elections, procedures, and Fed Election Commission activities, press release series, 9276-1

Campaign financial activity reported to Fed Election Commission, by type of filer, 1988 natl elections, biennial rpt series, 9276-2

Congressional Directory, members of 101st Congress, other officials, elections, and districts, 1989-90, biennial rpt, 23874-1

Statistical Abstract of US, social, political, and economic data, 1790-2025, comprehensive annual compilation, 2324-1.2

Votes cast by party, candidate, and State, 1988 natl elections, biennial rpt, 9274-5; 21944-3

Research
County Business Patterns, 1987: employment, establishments, and payroll, by SIC 2- to 4-digit industry and county, annual State rpt series, 2326-8

Crime and criminal justice research results, series, 6066-20; 6066-26

Employment, earnings, and hours, by SIC 1- to 4-digit industry, monthly 1983-Feb 1989, annual rpt, 6744-4

Endangered animals and plants US trade and permits, by species, purpose, disposition, and country, 1987, annual rpt, 5504-19

Fulbright-Hays academic exchanges, grants by purpose, and foreign govt share of costs, by country, FY88, annual rpt, 10324-1

Juvenile justice issues, data on young offenders and victims, series, 6066-27

Occupational injury and illness rates, by SIC 2- to 4-digit industry, 1987, annual rpt, 6844-1

Science and engineering employment, by nonmanufacturing industry and field, 1987, triennial rpt, 9627-31

Science and engineering PhDs employment and other characteristics, by field and State, 1987, biennial rpt, 9627-18

Service industries census, 1987: establishments, receipts, employment, and payroll, by SIC 2- to 4-digit kind of business, MSA, county, and city, State rpt series, 2391-1

Tax (income) returns filed by type of filer, selected income items, quarterly rpt, 8302-2.1

Tax (income) returns of corporations, income and tax items by asset size and detailed industry, 1986, annual rpt, 8304-21

see also Agricultural sciences and research
see also Animal experimentation
see also Business outlook and attitude surveys
see also Consumer surveys
see also Defense research
see also Demonstration and pilot projects
see also Educational research
see also Energy research and development
see also Federal funding for research and development
see also Market research
see also Medical research
see also Opinion and attitude surveys
see also Research and development
see also Research journals
see also Statistical programs and activities
see also under specific academic and scientific disciplines

Research and development
Aerial survey R&D rpts, and sources of natural resource and environmental data, quarterly listing, 9502-3

Army Dept activities, manpower, logistics, R&D, and budget, FY86, annual rpt, 3704-11

Black colleges R&D funding by source, and characteristics of grad students and research staff, by field of science and instn, 1980s-87, 9628-78

Ceramics (advanced) technical info of Japan, US industry use and views on value, 1988 survey, 2008-28

County Business Patterns, 1987: employment, establishments, and payroll, by SIC 2- to 4-digit industry and county, annual State rpt series, 2326-8

Education statistics, detailed data on higher education, 1960s-88, annual rpt, 4824-1.2

Employment characteristics of scientists and engineers, by field, 1988, biennial rpt, 9627-16

Expenditures for R&D by source and field, selected years 1953-89, annual rpt, 9624-18

Expenditures for R&D by source and performer, and related employment, by State, 1975-87, 9626-6.32

Expenditures for R&D, by source, performer, and for top 10 States, 1977-89, 9626-2.185

Expenditures, labor supply, and other science indicators, with foreign comparisons, 1960s-89, annual chartbook, 9624-22

Food marketing sector R&D spending, 1984-88, annual rpt, 1544-22.3

Foreign and US technology dev and competition issues, fundings and recommendations, 1980s-87, 21708-123

Higher education instn R&D equipment, acquisition and service costs, condition, and financing, by field, 1982-83 and 1985-86, 9628-76

Higher education instn R&D equipment spending by funding source, and retirement and acquisition rates, by field, 1982/83-1985/86, 9626-2.180

Higher education instn R&D funding, by source and field, FY77-87, annual rpt, 9626-2.188

Hwy construction and design R&D, quarterly journal, 7552-3

India R&D funding, 1958-83, compilation of papers, 3908-1

Industry (US) intl competitiveness, with selected foreign and US operating data by major firm and product, series, 2046-12

Japan biotechnology R&D spending, industry finances, and govt involvement, FY85-86, 2048-139

Manufacturing R&D funding for 5 leading industry groups, 1986-89, 9626-2.186

Multinatl firms US affiliates, finances, and operations, by industry, world area of parent firm, and State, 1987, annual rpt, 2704-4

Pollution abatement spending by govts, business, and consumers, 1983-87, annual article, 2702-1.919

Productivity growth indicators, and impacts of pollution abatement spending and other factors, for US and selected OECD countries, various periods 1948-86, article, 9389-1.911

Science and engineering labor force, Federal and university research funding, and educational data, series, 9626-6

Science and engineering PhDs employment and other characteristics, by field and State, 1987, biennial rpt, 9627-18

Service industries census, 1987: establishments, receipts, employment, and payroll, by SIC 2- to 4-digit kind of business, MSA, county, and city, State rpt series, 2391-1

Service industries receipts, by SIC 2- to 4-digit kind of business, 1988, annual rpt, 2413-8

Small business high technology sales, exports, siting, technology transfer, views on competitiveness, 1988 survey, hearing, 21728-69

Soviet Union planning for science and technology, and relation to economic plans, 1989 working paper, 2326-18.45

Statistical Abstract of US, social, political, and economic data, 1790-2025, comprehensive annual compilation, 2324-1.3

Steel (stainless and alloy tool) production, employment, finances, and US producers inventories and unfilled orders, 1987-88, annual rpt, 9884-22

Steel industry finances and operations by product, and modernization efforts, as of June 1989, last issue of annual rpt, 9884–16

Superconductivity (high temperature) R&D spending by Federal agency, and US and Japan industry funding and employment, by application, 1981-89, hearing, 25408–100

Tax (income) returns of corporations, income and tax items by asset size and detailed industry, 1986, annual rpt, 8304–4

Telecommunications industry devs, finances, and operations, with data by service type, firm, and country, 1950s-80s, 2808–27

Transit systems research rpts, 1988, annual listing, 7884–11

Truck and bus engine R&D and alternative fuels to reduce exhaust emissions costs and economic impacts, 1988 hearing, 21708–124

Wages of scientists and engineers in R&D, by field and educational, employment, and other characteristics, 1989, annual rpt, 3004–1

see also Defense research
see also Demonstration and pilot projects
see also Energy research and development
see also Federal funding for research and development
see also Federally Funded R&D Centers
see also Inventions
see also Technological innovations

Research journals

Alcohol abuse research, treatment programs, and patient characteristics and health effects, quarterly journal, 4482–1

Drug abuse and treatment research summaries, and resource materials and grant listings, periodic rpt, 4492–4

Energy rpts from DOE and other sources, monthly listing, 3002–2

Geological Survey rpts and research journal articles, monthly listing, 5662–1

Health Care Financing Review, quarterly journal, 4652–1

Health care services delivery and costs, research rpts of NCHSR, 1985-July 1987, listing, 4188–57

Health condition and quality of life measurement, rpts and other info sources, quarterly listing, 4122–1

Morbidity and Mortality Weekly Report, infectious notifiable disease cases and deaths, and other public health issues, periodic journal, 4202–7

Morbidity and Mortality Weekly Report, infectious notifiable disease cases by State, and public health issues, 4202–1

NSF rpts, 1989 annual listing, 9624–16

Public Health Reports, bimonthly journal, 4042–3

Scientific and technical publications of US, share of world total, 1986, annual chartbook, 9624–22

Scientific journal articles and citations, by field for US sources, selected years 1973-84, annual rpt, 9624–23.3

Social Security Bulletin, OASDHI and other program operations and beneficiary characteristics, from 1940, monthly rpt with articles, 4742–1

Transit systems research rpts, 1988, annual listing, 7884–11

Vaccination research rpts, 1988 annual listing, 4204–16

Reserve components
see Armed services reserves
see Coast Guard Reserve
see Marine Reserve
see National Guard

Reserve Officers Training Corps

Enrollment in ROTC, and scholarship awards, by race and sex, FY87-88, annual rpt, 3704–10.1

Expenditures, staff, students, and facilities for DOD training and education programs, by service branch, FY90, annual rpt, 3504–5

Health care personnel, and accessions by training source, by occupation, specialty, and service branch, FY87, annual rpt, 3544–24

Manpower of DOD, and organization, budget, weapons, and property, by service branch, State, and country, 1989 annual summary rpt, 3504–13

Statistical Abstract of US, social, political, and economic data, 1790-2025, comprehensive annual compilation, 2324–1.2

Reservoirs

Agricultural Conservation Program participation and payments, by practice and State, FY87, annual rpt, 1804–7

Army Corps of Engineers activities and projects, FY87 and trends from 1800s, annual rpt, 3754–1.2

Army Corps of Engineers water resources dev projects, characteristics, and costs, 1950s-87, biennial State rpt series, 3756–2

Army Corps of Engineers water resources dev projects, characteristics, and costs, 1950s-89, biennial State rpt series, 3756–1

California, San Joaquin Valley reservoir water storage, 1982, article, 1502–4.903

Colorado River Basin Project reservoir and power operations and revenues, 1987-88, annual rpt, 5824–6

Colorado River Storage Project finances and activities in western States, FY88, annual rpt, 5824–3

Conservation and conditions of soil, water, and environment, with data by State and region, 1989 quinquennial rpt, 1268–24

Environmental quality and protection programs, and intl issues, 1988 annual rpt, 484–1

Fish Hatchery Natl System activities and deliveries, by species, hatchery, and jurisdiction of waters stocked, FY88, annual rpt, 5504–10

Fishery research of State fish and wildlife agencies, federally funded projects and costs by species and State, 1989, annual listing, 5504–23

Fishing, hunting, and other wildlife-related recreation participation and spending, detailed data by location, 1985 survey, quinquennial rpt, 5508–5

Fishing, hunting, and other wildlife-related recreation participation and spending, detailed data, 1985 survey, quinquennial State rpt series, 5506–6

Oregon water supply, streamflow by station and reservoir storage, 1989, annual rpt, 1264–9

Public lands acreage, grants, use, revenues, and allocations, by State, FY88, annual rpt, 5724–1.2

Reclamation Bur activities, finances, and project impacts in western US, annual rpts, 5824–12

Reclamation Bur water storage and carriage facilities, capacity, and operating status, as of Sept 1988, biennial listing, 5824–7

Rural areas public water supply system financial and operating characteristics, by region, 1980, 1598–247

Tennessee Valley river control activities, and hydroelectric power generation and capacity, 1984, annual rpt, 9804–7

TVA financial and operating data by program and facility, FY88, annual rpt, 9804–32

Water supply and quality in streams and lakes, and groundwater levels in wells, by drainage basin, 1986, annual State rpt series, 5666–23

Water supply and quality in streams and lakes, and groundwater levels in wells, by drainage basin, 1987, annual State rpt series, 5666–10

Water supply and quality in streams and lakes, and groundwater levels in wells, by drainage basin, 1988, annual State rpt series, 5666–16

Water supply in US and southern Canada, streamflow, surface and groundwater conditions, and reservoir levels, by location, monthly rpt, 5662–3

Western US water supply, and snow survey results, monthly State rpt series, 1266–2

Western US water supply, storage by reservoir and State, and streamflow conditions, as of Oct 1989, annual rpt, 1264–4

Western US water supply, streamflow and reservoir storage forecasts by stream and station, Jan-May monthly rpt, 1262–1

Residential energy use
see Housing energy use

Resins
see Chemicals and chemical industry
see Gum and wood chemicals
see Plastics and plastics industry

Resolution Trust Corp.

Savings instns failure resolution activity of RTC, with failed instn finances by instn, periodic press release, 9722–1

Resorts
see Hotels and motels

Resources Conservation Act

Soil, water, and environmental conservation and conditions, with data by State and region, 1989 quinquennial rpt, 1268–24

Respiratory diseases

Cancer (lung) incidence among smokers, by age and consumption level, 1989 article, 4472–1.911

Cancer (lung) incidence and death rates, by age, sex, and race, various periods 1950-86, article, 4472–1.926

Cancer (lung) risk, by intake of selected nutrients, fruits, and vegetables, by smoking history and sex, 1983-85 local area study, article, 4472–1.918

Cancer (lung) risk relation to radon exposure, and death risk by smoking status, age, and sex, 1989 article, 4472–1.913

North Central States economic conditions, Fed Reserve 9th District, quarterly rpt, 9383–18

Northern Mariana Islands economic census, 1987: employment, firms, payroll, and receipts, by SIC 1- to 4-digit industry, 2597–1

Occupational injuries, illnesses, and workdays lost, by SIC 2-digit industry, 1987-88, annual press release, 6844–3

Occupational injury and illness rates, by SIC 2- to 4-digit industry, 1987, annual rpt, 6844–1

Sales and inventories, by kind of retail business, region, and selected State, MSA, and city, monthly rpt, 2413–3

Sales and inventories, monthly rpt, 23842–1.3

Sales, inventories, and inventory/sales ratios for manufacturing and trade, quarterly article, 2702–1.33

Sales, inventories, purchases, gross margin, and accounts receivable, by SIC 2- to 4-digit kind of business and form of ownership, 1987, annual rpt, 2413–5

Sales of retailers, by kind of business, advance monthly rpt, 2413–2

Science, engineering, and technical employment in transportation, utilities, and retail and wholesale trade, by field, occupation, and industry, 1985, triennial rpt, 9627–32

SEC registration, firms required to file annual rpts, as of Sept 1988, annual listing, 9734–5

Small business establishments, employment, and financial ratios, by SIC 1- to 2-digit industry and State, late 1960s-87, 9768–19

Small business finances, operations, owner and employee characteristics, and Federal contracts, 1980s-88, annual rpt, 9764–6

Statistical Abstract of US, social, political, and economic data, 1790-2025, comprehensive annual compilation, 2324–1.3

Suburban areas land use, commuting, employment, and housing characteristics, detailed data for traffic planning, 1986, 7888–75

Tax (income) returns of corporations, income and tax items by asset size and detailed industry, 1986, annual rpt, 8304–4; 8304–21

Tax (income) returns of partnerships, income statement items by industry group, 1986, annual article, 8302–2.903

Tax (income) returns of sole proprietorships, income statement items, by industry group, 1987, annual article, 8302–2.904; 8302–2.921

Transportation census, 1987: trucks, by detailed characteristics, miles traveled, and type of product carried, State rpt series, 2573–1

Virgin Islands economic censuses, 1987: employment, firms, payroll, and receipts, by SIC 1- to 4-digit industry, island, and city, 2593–1

Wage and benefit changes from collective bargaining and mgmt decisions, by industry div, monthly rpt, 6782–1

Wages by occupation, and benefits for office and plant workers, periodic MSA survey rpt series, 6785–11; 6785–12

see also Advertising
see also Census of Retail Trade
see also Consumer credit
see also Consumer protection
see also Credit cards
see also Department stores
see also Direct marketing
see also Drugstores
see also Food stores
see also Franchises
see also Gasoline service stations
see also Labeling
see also Military post exchanges and commissaries
see also Packaging and containers
see also Restaurants and drinking places
see also Sales promotion
see also Sales workers
see also Shopping centers
see also Vending machines and stands
see also Warehouses
see also Wholesale trade
see also under By Industry in the "Index by Categories"
see also under names of specific commodities or commodity groups

Retired military personnel

Annuitants, DOD retired military personnel, FY50-88, annual rpt, 3544–1.4

Army personnel health condition, and use of Army medical services in US and abroad by personnel, retirees, and dependents, monthly rpt, 3702–4.1

Fed Govt civilian employees demographic and employment characteristics, as of Sept 1988, article, 9842–1.901

Health care costs for military hospitals and CHAMPUS, and reduction in military hospital admissions, with background data, FY85-87, GAO rpt, 26121–288

Health care facilities of DOD in US and abroad, beds, admissions, outpatient visits, and births, by service branch, quarterly rpt, 3542–15

Health care retired personnel, by specialty, FY87, annual rpt, 3544–24.8

Manpower of DOD, and organization, budget, weapons, and property, by service branch, State, and country, 1989 annual summary rpt, 3504–13

Navy manpower strengths, accessions, and attrition, detailed statistics, quarterly rpt, 3802–4

Reserve forces manpower and equipment strengths, and readiness, by reserve component, FY88, annual rpt, 3544–31

Reserve forces manpower strengths and characteristics, by component, quarterly rpt, 3542–4

Statistical Abstract of US, social, political, and economic data, 1790-2025, comprehensive annual compilation, 2324–1.2

see also Civilian Health and Medical Program of the Uniformed Services
see also Military benefits and pensions
see also Veterans

Retired Senior Volunteer Program

Activities of ACTION, by program, FY88, annual rpt, 9024–2

Retirement

Air traffic control and airway facilities staff, by selected employment and demographic characteristics, FY88, annual rpt, 7504–41

Air traffic control system safety, working conditions, and traffic volume, various periods 1981-88, GAO rpt series, 26113–220

Counties (nonmetro) employment by industry sector and degree of urbanization, and compared to metro counties, various periods 1969-86, 1598–244

DOT employment, by subagency, occupation, and selected personnel characteristics, FY88, annual rpt, 7304–18

Fed Govt personnel action appeals, decisions of Merit Systems Protection Board by agency and region, FY88, annual rpt, 9494–2

Fed Govt Senior Executive Service former members reasons for leaving, and views on SES statutory compliance, 1988 survey, 9498–3

Housing and community preferences of persons nearing retirement, by respondent characteristics, 1987 survey, article, 1702–1.905

Insurance (health) coverage of retirees, by source, and former industry and occupation, 1987, 4186–8.2

Insurance (health) for retirees, employer liabilities and costs by age group, 1988 and projected to 2043, GAO rpt, 26121–299

Insurance (health) plans of corporations for retirees, costs and liabilities under alternative accounting standards, 1983-88, technical paper, 9366–6.190

Labor force transition to retirement, timing and part-time employment, model description and results, 1987 working paper, 6886–6.31

Married couples retirement timing, differences in age and retirement age of spouses, 1982, article, 4742–1.906

NASA staff characteristics and personnel actions, FY88, annual rpt, 9504–1

OASDI benefit payments, trust fund finances, and economic and demographic assumptions, 1970-87 and alternative projections to 1997, actuarial rpt, 4706–1.103

Older persons aid and policies of Fed Govt, and issues of aging, 1989 annual rpt, 25144–3

Older persons socioeconomic characteristics, 1900s-86 and projected to 2050, biennial chartbook, 12904–1

Population size and components of change, alternative projections 1988-2080 and trends from 1900, annual actuarial rpt, 4706–1.104

Poverty status of families and persons, by detailed characteristics, 1987, annual Current Population Rpt, 2546–6.60

Rural areas aid from Fed Govt compared to urban areas, by program and degree of urbanization, FY85, periodic rpt, 1598–248

Rural areas employment, economic conditions, and population characteristics, 1970s-85, compilation of papers, 1598–243

Savings of retired persons, maintenance and liquidation, by selected financial and other characteristics, 1971-79, article, 1702–1.906

Science and engineering PhDs employment and other characteristics, by field and State, 1987, biennial rpt, 9627–18

Unemployed persons, by desire for job, reason for not seeking work, sex, and race, 1970-88, 6728–38.1

see also Civil service pensions
see also Employee benefits
see also Individual retirement arrangements
see also Old age assistance
see also Old-Age, Survivors, Disability, and Health Insurance
see also Pensions and pension funds
see also Retired military personnel
see also Retired Senior Volunteer Program
see also Retirement communities

Retirement communities
Continuing care retirement community residents nursing home admissions compared to general population, late 1970s, article, 4652–1.917

Reubens, Beatrice G.
"Unemployment Insurance in the U.S. and Europe, 1973-83", 6722–1.919

Reunion
Economic, social, political, and geographic summary data, by country, 1989, annual factbook, 9114–2
Minerals Yearbook, 1987, Vol 3: foreign country reviews of production, trade, and policy, by commodity, annual rpt, 5604–35
Minerals Yearbook, 1987, Vol 3 preprints: foreign country review of production, trade, and policy, by commodity, annual rpt, 5604–23.81
Population size, growth rates, and components of change, by country, projected 1989-2020 and trends from 1950, biennial rpt, 2324–9

Revenue sharing
Budget of US Appendix, obligations, appropriations, and personnel, by program and agency, FY90, annual rpt, 104–3
Budget of US, compact budgets by activity, function, and agency, FY90 and projected to FY94, annual rpt, 104–2
Budget of US, historical data, selected years FY34-88 and projected to FY94, annual rpt, 104–22
Expenditures of Fed Govt in States and local areas, by type, State, county, and city, FY88, annual rpt, 2464–3.2
Expenditures of Fed Govt in States, by type, program, agency, and State, FY88, annual rpt, 2464–2
Govt finances, by level of govt, State, and for large cities and counties, annual rpt series, 2466–2
Govt finances, tax systems and revenue, and fiscal structure, by level of govt and State, selected years 1929-91, annual rpt, 10044–1
Hwy funding by function, and revenue, by level of govt and type of hwy, 1960-87, biennial rpt, 7554–27.2
Hwy Trust Fund receipts by source, and apportionments, by State, 1988, annual rpt, 7554–1.3
Offshore oil and gas leases, revenue sharing payments by State, FY86-91, press release, 5736–4.1
Rural areas aid from Fed Govt compared to urban areas, by program and degree of urbanization, FY85, periodic rpt, 1598–248

Rural areas local govt budget impacts of revenue sharing reductions, and other funding sources, with data for Ohio, 1980s-86, 1598–254
Statistical Abstract of US, social, political, and economic data, 1790-2025, comprehensive annual compilation, 2324–1.2

Revolutions
see Insurgency

Revolvers
see Firearms

Reynolds, Bruce J.
"Co-ops Have a Distinct Commitment to Exporting Processed Foods", 1122–1.906

Rhenium
see Metals and metal industries

Rheumatism
see Musculoskeletal diseases

Rhode Island
Agriculture census, 1987: farms, farmland, production, finances, and operator characteristics, by county, final State rpt, 2331–1.39
Bank deposits in FDIC-insured commercial and savings banks, by instn, State, and county, as of June 1988, annual regional rpt, 9295–3.1
Banks and thrifts in New England, financial statements by type of instn and Fed deposit insurance, and State, 1987, annual rpt, 9304–3
County Business Patterns, 1987: employment, establishments, and payroll, by SIC 2- to 4-digit industry and county, annual State rpt, 2326–8.41
Deaths and rates, by detailed location, cause, and demographic characteristics, 1987, US Vital Statistics annual rpt, 4144–3.1
DOD prime contract awards, by contractor, service branch, State, and city, FY88, annual rpt, 3544–22
Economic indicators for New England States, Fed Reserve 1st District, monthly rpt, 9373–24
Economic indicators for New England States, Fed Reserve 1st District, quarterly rpt with articles, 9373–2
Employment, earnings, and hours, by selected SIC 1- to 4-digit industry, State, and for 262 MSAs, 1972-87, 6748–81.5
Fed Govt spending in States and local areas, by type, State, county, and city, FY88, annual rpt, 2464–3
Fed Govt spending in States, by type, . program, agency, and State, FY88, annual rpt, 2464–2
Fish and shellfish catch, wholesale receipts, prices, trade, and other market activities, weekly regional rpt, 2162–6.2
HHS financial aid, by program, recipient, State, and city, FY88, annual regional listing, 4004–3.1
Homeless children educational enrollment and needs, 1988, annual State rpt, 4804–35.39
Income (personal) per capita and by source, and earnings by industry div, by State, MSA, and county, 1982-87, annual regional rpt, 2704–2.2
Medicare physicians assigned-fee laws of 4 States, impacts on care cost and availability, 1985-89, GAO rpt, 26121–312

Mineral Industry Surveys, State reviews of production, 1988, preliminary annual rpt, 5614–6
Minerals Yearbook, 1987, Vol 2 preprints: State review of production and sales by commodity, and business activity, annual rpt, 5604–16.41
Minerals Yearbook, 1987, Vol 2: State reviews of production, sales, and firms, by commodity, and business activity, annual rpt, 5604–34
Nursing home compliance with Medicare and Medicaid regulations, and patient characteristics, by facility, 1987/88, annual State rpt, 4654–15.41
Retail trade census, 1987: employment, establishments, sales, and payroll, by SIC 2- to 4-digit kind of business, MSA, county, and city, State rpt, 2397–1.40
Savings instns, FHLB 1st District members financial operations and related economic and housing indicators, monthly rpt, 9302–4
Service industries census, 1987: employment, establishments, receipts, and payroll, by SIC 2- to 4-digit kind of business, MSA, county, and city, State rpt, 2391–1.40
Statistical Abstract of US, social, political, and economic data, with foreign comparisons, 1790-2025, comprehensive annual compilation, 2324–1
Transportation census, 1987: trucks, by detailed characteristics, miles traveled, and type of product carried, State rpt, 2573–1.40
Water resources dev projects of Army Corps of Engineers, characteristics, and costs, 1950s-87, biennial State rpt, 3756–2.40
Water supply and quality in streams and lakes, and groundwater levels in wells, by drainage basin, 1986, annual State rpt, 5666–23.20
Water supply and quality in streams and lakes, and groundwater levels in wells, by drainage basin, 1987, annual State rpt, 5666–10.20
Water supply in northeastern US, precipitation and stream runoff by station, monthly rpt, 2182–3
Wholesale trade census, 1987: employment, establishments, finances, and operations, by SIC 2- to 4-digit kind of business, MSA, county, and city, State rpt, 2405–1.40
Wildlife-related recreation, hunting, and fishing participation and spending, detailed data, 1985 survey, quinquennial State rpt, 5506–6.39
see also Cranston, R.I.
see also Pawtucket, R.I.
see also Providence, R.I.
see also Warwick, R.I.
see also under By State in the "Index by Categories"

Rhodesia
see Zimbabwe

Ribaudo, Marc O.
"Water Quality Benefits from the Conservation Reserve Program", 1588–134

Rice
Acreage planted, by selected crop and State, 1980-88 and planned 1989, annual rpt, 1621–22

Acreage under Agricultural Stabilization and Conservation Service programs, rankings by commodity and congressional district, 1987, biennial rpt, 1804–17

Agricultural Stabilization and Conservation Service producer payments, by program and State, 1988, annual rpt, 1804–12

Agricultural Stabilization and Conservation Service producer payments, by program, monthly rpt, 1802–10

Agricultural Statistics, 1988, annual rpt, 1004–1

Agriculture census, 1987: farms, farmland, production and costs, and operator characteristics, advance State and county rpt series, 2330–1

Agriculture census, 1987: farms, farmland, production, finances, and operator characteristics, by county, final State rpt series, 2331–1

Beer production, stocks, material used, tax-free removals, and taxable removals by State, monthly rpt, 8486–1.1

Business statistics, detailed data for major industries and economic indicators, *Survey of Current Business*, monthly rpt, 2702–1.11

CCC certificate exchange activity, by commodity, weekly press release, 1802–16

CCC loan and support programs payment activity, with data by commodity, 1986-88 and projected to 1994, 26308–86

Communist, OECD, and selected other countries agricultural production, by commodity, 1960s-88, annual rpt, 9114–4.6

Consumption, supply, trade, prices, spending, and indexes, by food commodity, 1987, annual rpt, 1544–4

County Business Patterns, 1987: employment, establishments, and payroll, by SIC 2- to 4-digit industry and county, annual State rpt series, 2326–1

Cuba economic conditions, agricultural and industrial production and distribution, trade, and intl economic relations, 1980-87 with trends from 1961, 9118–8

Eastern Europe agricultural production, consumption, and trade, by country, 1970s-88, annual rpt, 1524–11

Eastern Europe and USSR agricultural production, acreage, and consumption, by commodity and country, 1965-85, 1528–284

EC food supply and demand, market and support prices, and other economic indicators, by country and commodity, 1960-85, 1528–276

Export licensing, monitoring, and enforcement activities, FY88, annual rpt, 2024–1

Exports and imports (agricultural) commodity and country, prices, and world market devs, monthly rpt, 1922–12

Exports and imports (agricultural) of US, by commodity and country, bimonthly rpt with articles, 1522–1

Exports and imports (agricultural) of US, by detailed commodity and country, 1988, semiannual rpt, 1522–4

Exports of grains, oilseed products, hides, skins, and cotton, by country, weekly rpt, 1922–3

Exports of US, detailed commodities by country, monthly rpt, 2422–3

Farm financial ratios, benchmarks by type of operation and region, 1984-86, 1548–342

Farm income, expenses, receipts by commodity, assets, liabilities, and ratios, 1988 and trends from 1945, annual rpt, 1544–16

Farm receipts for 25 leading crops, by State, 1960-87, 1548–347

Farm sector balance sheet, and receipts by detailed commodity, by State, 1984-88, annual rpt, 1544–18

Farm sector finances, income sources, expenses by type, assets, debts, and ratios, 1987, annual rpt, 1544–19

Foreign and US agricultural supply and demand indicators, by selected crop, monthly rpt, 1522–5

Foreign and US agricultural trade and market impacts of eliminating protectionist policies, model description and results, 1986, 1528–282

Foreign and US grain production, prices, trade, stocks, and use, FAS periodic circular series, 1925–2

Foreign and US production, acreage, and yield for selected crops, forecasts by selected world region and country, FAS monthly circular, 1925–28

Foreign and US rice production, prices, trade, stocks, and use, periodic situation rpt, 1561–8

Foreign countries agricultural production, prices, and trade, by country, 1970s-89 and forecast 1990, annual world region rpt series, 1524–4

Freight (waterborne domestic and foreign) by commodity, traffic, and passengers, by port and waterway, 1987, annual rpt, 3754–3

Futures and options trading volume, by commodity and exchange, FY88, annual rpt, 11924–2

Futures trading in selected commodities and financial instruments and indexes, NYC, Chicago, and other markets activity, monthly rpt, 11922–5

Imports of US, detailed Schedule A commodities by country, monthly rpt, 2422–2

Irrigation projects of Reclamation Bur in western US, crop production and acreage by commodity, State, and project, 1987, annual rpt, 5824–12.1

Labor productivity, indexes of output, hours, and employment by SIC 2- to 4-digit industry, 1963-87, annual rpt, 6824–1.3

Loan support programs of USDA for grains, activity and status by grain and State, monthly rpt, 1802–3

Manufacturing annual survey, 1986: financial and operating data, by SIC 2- to 4-digit industry, series, 2506–15

Manufacturing census, 1987: financial and operating data, for SIC 4-digit industries by product, preliminary rpt, 2491–1.4

Mill production workers and wages, by occupation and sex, and benefits, by region, 1987 survey, 6787–6.239

Nutrient and caloric composition of food, for raw, processed, and prepared food, 1988 rpt, 1358–3

OECD trade, total and for 4 major countries, and US trade by country, by commodity, 1970-87, world area rpt series, 9116–1

PL 480 long-term credit sales allocations, by commodity and country, periodic press release, 1922–7

Price indexes (producer), by stage of processing and detailed commodity, monthly rpt, 6762–6

Price indexes (producer), by stage of processing and detailed commodity, monthly 1988, annual rpt, 6764–2

Prices, market activities, inspections, sales, trade, supply, and use of rice, for US and selected foreign markets, weekly rpt, 1313–8

Prices received and paid by farmers, by commodity and State, 1988, annual rpt, 1629–5

Prices received by farmers and production value, by detailed crop and State, 1986-88, annual rpt, 1621–2

Prices received by farmers for major products, and paid for farm inputs and living items, by State, monthly rpt, 1629–1

Production, farms, acreage, and related data, by selected crop and State, monthly rpt, 1621–1

Production itemized costs, receipts, and returns, by commodity and region, 1985-87, annual rpt, 1544–20

Production itemized costs, receipts, and returns, by crop and State, preliminary 1987, annual rpt, 1544–24

Production itemized costs, receipts, and returns, by selected commodity and region, 1975-87, 1548–345

Production, prices, trade, and marketing, by commodity, current situation and forecast, monthly rpt with articles, 1502–4

Shipments of rice, by end use, package size, and State of origin and destination, mid 1950s-87, biennial rpt, 1564–11

Stocks of grain on and off farms, by crop, quarterly rpt, 1621–4

Stocks of rice on and off farms and total, periodic rpt, 1621–7

Thailand rice production, consumption, exports, and subsidies, 1982-86, 1528–286

Thailand rice production, consumption, exports, and subsidies, 1982-87, article, 1522–3.915

see also under By Commodity in the "Index by Categories"

Rice, Stanley D.

"Lethal and Sublethal Effects of the Water-Soluble Fraction of Cook Inlet Crude Oil on Pacific Herring (Clupea harengus pallasi) Reproduction", 2176–1.29

Richards, Steven

"U.S. Import and Export Prices Continued To Register Sizeable Gains in 1988", 6722–1.922

Richardson, Philip

"Referral of Long-Term Unemployment Insurance (UI) Claimants to Reemployment Services", 6406–6.25; 6406–6.26

Richardson, Ralph M.

"Business Volume Up Slightly in 1987 for Nation's Agricultural Cooperatives", 1122–1.902

"Cooperative Business Volume, Net Income Up in 1988", 1122–1.912

"Farmer Cooperative Statistics, 1987",
1124–1

Richland, Wash.
see also under By SMSA or MSA in the
"Index by Categories"

Richmond, Va.
Wages by occupation, and benefits for office
and plant workers, 1989 survey, periodic
MSA rpt, 6785–12.7
see also under By City and By SMSA or
MSA in the "Index by Categories"

Ries, Peter W.
"Episodes of Persons Injured: U.S., 1975",
4147–16.2

Rifles
see Firearms

Right of assembly
Foreign countries human rights conditions in
170 countries, 1988, annual rpt, 21384–3

Right of privacy
AIDS health care and epidemiological
research, methodological issues, 1988
conf, 4188–61
AIDS patients and persons with AIDS virus
infection, Medicaid policies and State
health insurance regulation, with
background data, 1987-88, article,
4652–1.953
Criminal sentences for Federal offenses,
guidelines by offense and circumstances,
1989 rpt, 17668–1
Foreign countries human rights conditions in
170 countries, 1988, annual rpt, 21384–3
Hereditary disease mass screening, and
access to results by employer, insurer, and
others, foreign and US geneticists views,
1987 survey, article, 4042–3.902
Labor laws enacted, by State, 1988, annual
article, 6722–1.904
Nursing home compliance with Medicare
and Medicaid regulations, and patient
characteristics, by facility, 1987/88,
annual State rpt series, 4654–15
see also Electronic surveillance

Right to counsel
see also Legal aid

Riley, Fred J.
"Employee Plans Filings Since ERISA",
8304–8.1

Riley, Gerald F.
"Eliminating the Medicare Waiting Period
for Social Security Disabled-Worker
Beneficiaries", 4742–1.915
"Statistical Methods for the Estimation of
Costs in the Medicare Waiting Period for
Social Security Disabled-Worker
Beneficiaries", 4746–26.6

Riley, Margaret
"Private Foundation Returns, 1985",
8302–2.923

Riley, Peter A.
"World Trade in Barley Malt and the U.S.
Role", 1561–4.907

Rio Grande River
Water supply and quality in streams and
lakes, and groundwater levels in wells, by
drainage basin, 1986, annual State rpt
series, 5666–23
Water supply and quality in streams and
lakes, and groundwater levels in wells, by
drainage basin, 1987, annual State rpt
series, 5666–10
Water supply and quality in streams and
lakes, and groundwater levels in wells, by
drainage basin, 1988, annual State rpt
series, 5666–16

Water supply in US and southern Canada,
streamflow, surface and groundwater
conditions, and reservoir levels, by
location, monthly rpt, 5662–3

Riots and disorders
Police response to disturbances, officers
assaulted and killed, by circumstances,
1988, annual rpt, 6224–3
Prison conditions, population, and problems,
issues and bibl, 1989 compilation of
papers, 25928–8
Terrorist (intl) incidents, casualties, and
attacks on US targets, by attack type and
country, 1980-88, 7008–56
US attorneys civil and criminal cases by
type and disposition, and collections, by
Federal district, FY88, annual rpt,
6004–2.1

Ritchey, Joseph L.
"Cobalt-Rich Manganese Crust in the U.S.
Exclusive Economic Zone: A Potential
Source of Strategic Metals", 5602–4.901

Rivara, Fred P.
"Analysis of Fatal Pedestrian Injuries in
King County, Wash., and Prospects for
Prevention", 4042–3.927

Rivers and waterways
Alaska Arctic Natl Wildlife Refuge
resources, native hunting activity, and
energy exploration impact, 1985, last issue
of annual rpt, 5504–26
Army Corps of Engineers activities and
projects, FY87 and trends from 1800s,
annual rpt, 3754–1.2
Army Corps of Engineers water resources
dev projects, characteristics, and costs,
1950s-87, biennial State rpt series,
3756–2
Army Corps of Engineers water resources
dev projects, characteristics, and costs,
1950s-89, biennial State rpt series,
3756–1
Developing countries disaster preparedness
and economic, population, and political
data, country rpt series, 9916–2
Environmental conditions, fish, wildlife, use,
and mgmt, for individual coastal and
riparian ecosystems, series, 5506–9
Environmental quality and protection
programs, and intl issues, 1988 annual rpt,
484–1
Fish catch, trade, use, and fishery
operations, with selected foreign data, by
species, 1970s-88, annual rpt, 2164–1
Fish Hatchery Natl System activities and
deliveries, by species, hatchery, and
jurisdiction of waters stocked, FY88,
annual rpt, 5504–10
Fishery research of State fish and wildlife
agencies, federally funded projects and
costs by species and State, 1989, annual
listing, 5504–23
Fishing, hunting, and other wildlife-related
recreation participation and spending,
detailed data by location, 1985 survey,
quinquennial rpt, 5508–5
Fishing, hunting, and other wildlife-related
recreation participation and spending,
detailed data, 1985 survey, quinquennial
State rpt series, 5506–6
Foreign and US land, water, and energy
resources, by world area, 1960s-80s and
projected to 2050, article, 1522–3.908
Freight (waterborne domestic), by major
commodity group, vessel type, and port,
1986, annual rpt, 7704–7

Freight (waterborne domestic and foreign)
by commodity, traffic, and passengers, by
port and waterway, 1987, annual rpt,
3754–3
Hydroelectric power plants capacity, dev
status, and ownership, by State and river
basin, as of Jan 1988, quadrennial rpt,
3088–14
Hydroelectric power plants retired,
characteristics and location, as of 1989,
annual listing, 3084–12
Middle East water annual discharge for 4
rivers, 1989 hearing, 21708–126
Mississippi eastern coastal plain water
runoff, 1939-85, 5668–85
Natl forests and other lands under Forest
Service mgmt, acreage by forest and
location, 1988, annual rpt, 1204–2
Natl park system and other land under Natl
Park Service mgmt, acreage by site,
ownership, and region, 1989 semiannual
rpt, 5542–1
Natl park system visits and overnight stays,
by park and State, monthly rpt, 5542–4
Natl park system visits and overnight stays,
by park and State, 1988 and trends from
1979, annual rpt, 5544–12
Northeastern US water supply, precipitation
and stream runoff by station, monthly rpt,
2182–3
Oregon water supply, streamflow by station
and reservoir storage, 1989, annual rpt,
1264–9
Pollutant discharges in coastal areas and
estuaries, by source, pollutant type, and
location, series, 2176–4
Pollution (water) incidents and discharges,
by type, source, cause, and location,
1984-86, annual rpt, 7404–3
Public lands acreage, grants, use, revenues,
and allocations, by State, FY88, annual
rpt, 5724–1.2
Statistical Abstract of US, social, political,
and economic data, 1790-2025,
comprehensive annual compilation,
2324–1.1
Wastewater treatment and collection facility
construction funding needs and Fed Govt
grants, by State, 1988 and projected to
2008, biennial rpt, 9204–7
Water supply and quality in streams and
lakes, and groundwater levels in wells, by
drainage basin, 1986, annual State rpt
series, 5666–23
Water supply and quality in streams and
lakes, and groundwater levels in wells, by
drainage basin, 1987, annual State rpt
series, 5666–10
Water supply and quality in streams and
lakes, and groundwater levels in wells, by
drainage basin, 1988, annual State rpt
series, 5666–16
Water supply in US and southern Canada,
streamflow, surface and groundwater
conditions, and reservoir levels, by
location, monthly rpt, 5662–3
West Virginia streamflow, low flow
frequency by site, model description and
results, 1980-83, 5668–92
Western US water supply, and snow survey
results, monthly State rpt series, 1266–2
Western US water supply, storage by
reservoir and State, and streamflow
conditions, as of Oct 1989, annual rpt,
1264–4

Rivers and waterways

Western US water supply, streamflow and reservoir storage forecasts by stream and station, Jan-May monthly rpt, 1262-1

Wyoming streamflow, annual peak by site, model description and results, 1985, 5668-84

see also Arkansas River
see also Bridges and tunnels
see also Canals
see also Chesapeake Bay
see also Colorado River
see also Columbia River
see also Dams
see also Delaware River
see also Dredging
see also Estuaries
see also Floods
see also Great Lakes
see also Harbors and ports
see also Hudson River
see also Illinois River
see also James River
see also Lakes and lakeshores
see also Mississippi River
see also Missouri River
see also New York Bight
see also Niagara River
see also Ohio River
see also Potomac River
see also Puget Sound
see also Red River
see also Rio Grande River
see also San Francisco Bay
see also Snake River
see also Souris-Red-Rainy Rivers
see also St. Lawrence River
see also Susquehanna River
see also Tennessee River
see also Water resources development
see also Willamette River

Riverside, Calif.

CPI by component for US city average, and by region, population size, and for 15 metro areas, monthly rpt, 6762-1

CPI by component for US city average, and by region, population size, and for 27 metro areas, monthly rpt, 6762-2

Housing starts and completions authorized by building permits in 40 MSAs, quarterly rpt, 2382-9

see also under By City and By SMSA or MSA in the "Index by Categories"

Roads

see Highways, streets, and roads

Roanoke, Va.

see also under By City and By SMSA or MSA in the "Index by Categories"

see also under By SMSA or MSA in the "Index by Categories"

Robbery and theft

Arrest rates, by offense, sex, age, and race, 1987, annual rpt, 6224-7

Arrests by offender characteristics, prosecutions, convictions, and sentences by type, by felony offense, 1983-86, 6066-19.52

Court civil and criminal caseloads for Federal district, appeals, and special courts, June 1989, annual rpt, 18204-2; 18204-8

Crime, criminal justice admin and enforcement, and public opinion, data compilation, 1970s-88, annual rpt, 6064-6

Crime Index by population size and region, and offenses by large city, Jan-June 1989, semiannual rpt, 6222-1

Crimes, arrests by offender characteristics, and rates, by offense, and law enforcement employees, by population size and jurisdiction, 1988, annual rpt, 6224-2

Criminal case processing from arrest to sentencing, cases and duration by disposition, offense, and defendant characteristics, for selected cities, 1986, annual rpt, 6064-27

Criminal case processing in Federal district courts, and dispositions, by offense, district, and offender characteristics, 1984, annual rpt, 6064-29

Criminal case processing in Federal district courts, disposition by offense, 1980-87, 6066-19.50

Diplomats and staff with immunity for foreign missions in US and US missions abroad, and foreign diplomats criminal cases, 1978-87, hearing, 25388-51

Drug test results at arrest, by drug type, offense, and sex, for selected urban areas, quarterly rpt, 6062-3

Explosives theft and recovery, by type and State, 1979-88, annual rpt, 8484-4

Homicides, by circumstance, victim and offender relationship, and type of weapon, 1988, annual rpt, 6224-2.1

Juvenile court delinquency cases, by offense, referral source, disposition, age, sex, race, State, and county, 1985, annual rpt, 6064-12

Juvenile court referrals by offender characteristics, and dispositions, by offense, 1984, 6066-27.2

Juvenile delinquent and status offenses, by sex, race, age, income, and urban-rural location, 1976-86 surveys, annual rpt, 6064-6.3

Juvenile offenders recidivism rates, arrests, and court referrals, by offense, age, and sex, 1983 local area studies, 6068-227

Postal Service inspection activities, expenses, and staff, FY88, annual rpt, 9864-8

Postal Service inspection activities, FY88, annual rpt, 9864-9

Postal Service inspection and law enforcement activities, by type, FY88, annual rpt, 9864-5.3

Prison time served ratio to offenses committed, by offense, 1958-86, 6068-229

Prisoners in State instns, by offense, criminal history, and inmate, family, and victim characteristics, 1986, annual rpt, 6064-26.3

Recidivism rates of prisoners released in 1983, by offense and prisoner characteristics, 1983-86, 6066-19.48

Sentences by State courts for felony offenses, and sentence lengths and time served, by offense, 1986, 6066-25.19

Sentences for Federal crimes, guidelines use and results by offense and district, and Sentencing Commission activities, 1988, annual rpt, 17664-1

Sentences for Federal offenses, guidelines by offense and circumstances, 1989 rpt, 17668-1

Statistical Abstract of US, social, political, and economic data, 1790-2025, comprehensive annual compilation, 2324-1.1

US attorneys civil and criminal cases by type and disposition, and collections, by Federal district, FY88, annual rpt, 6004-2.1

Victimization rates, by victim and offender characteristics, circumstances, and offense, survey rpt series, 6066-3

Victimizations and rates, by type of premises and weapon, 1973-87, annual rpt, 6224-8

Victimizations, by offense, offender characteristics, and victim reactions and views, 1986-87, 6066-19.47

Victimizations of households, by offense, household characteristics, and location, 1975-88, annual rpt, 6066-25.22

Victimizations resulting in injury, by offense, type of injury and medical care received, and victim characteristics, 1979-86, 6066-19.49

Wiretaps authorized, costs, arrests, trials, and convictions, by offense and jurisdiction, 1988, annual rpt, 18204-7

see also Federal Inspectors General reports
see also Motor vehicle theft

Robbin, Alice

"Database Design for Large-Scale, Complex Data", 2626-10.103

Roberds, William

"How Little We Know About Budget Policy Effects", 9371-10.41

Roberts, Jean

"Blood Pressure of Persons 6-74 Years of Age in the U.S.", 4147-16.1

"Prevalence of Dermatological Disease Among Persons 1-74 Years of Age: U.S.", 4147-16.1

Roberts, Ralph T.

"Hydrologic Data for Experimental Agricultural Watersheds in the U.S., 1978-79", 1704-1

Roberts, Richard

"U.S. Economy in 1989: An Uncertain Outlook", 9381-1.901

Robilliard, Gordon A.

"Chukchi Sea Coastal Studies: Coastal Geomorphology, Environmental Sensitivity, and Persistence of Spilled Oil", 2176-1.28

Robins, Philip K.

"Why Are Child Support Awards Declining?", 4008-94

Robinson, Cynthia F.

"Mortality Among Production Workers in Pulp and Paper Mills", 21368-112

Robinson, Kenneth J.

"Further Evidence on the Liquidity Effect Using an Efficient-Markets Approach", 9379-12.34

"Money, Wages, and Factor Scarcity as Predictors of Inflation", 9379-1.906

"Stock Market and Inflation: A Synthesis of the Theory and Evidence", 9379-1.904

"Stock Returns and Inflation: Further Tests of the Proxy and Debt-Monetization Hypotheses", 9379-12.37

Robotics

see Automation
see Industrial robots

Rochester, Minn.

see also under By SMSA or MSA in the "Index by Categories"

Rochester, N.H.
see also under By SMSA or MSA in the "Index by Categories"

Rochester, N.Y.
see also under By City and By SMSA or MSA in the "Index by Categories"

Rock Hill, S.C.
Housing starts and completions authorized by building permits in 40 MSAs, quarterly rpt, 2382–9
Wages by occupation, for office and plant workers, 1988 survey, periodic MSA rpt, 6785–11.2
see also under By SMSA or MSA in the "Index by Categories"

Rock Island, Ill.
Freight (waterborne domestic and foreign) by commodity, traffic, and passengers, by port and waterway, 1987, annual rpt, 3754–3.2; 3754–3.3
Wages by occupation, and benefits for office and plant workers, 1989 survey, periodic MSA rpt, 6785–12.3
see also under By SMSA or MSA in the "Index by Categories"

Rockets
see Missiles and rockets

Rockford, Ill.
Housing vacancy rates for single and multifamily units and mobile homes, by city and ZIP code, 1989, annual MSA rpt, 9304–18.5
see also under By City and By SMSA or MSA in the "Index by Categories"

Rockwell, David C.
"Water Quality in the Middle Great Lakes: Results of the 1985 U.S. EPA Survey of Lakes Erie, Huron and Michigan", 9204–14

Rodano, Edith M.
"Technical Assistance and Safety Programs: FY88 Project Directory", 7884–1

Rodenhuis, David R.
"Meteorological Causes of Drought and Long-Term Climate Patterns", 1004–16.1

Rogers, Andrei
"Multistate Analysis of Active Life Expectancy", 4042–3.919

Rogers, R. Mark
"Tracking the Economy: Fundamentals for Understanding Data", 9371–1.906

Rogers, Robert P.
"Impact of State Price and Entry Regulation on Intrastate Long Distance Telephone Rates", 9406–1.55

Rogers, S. Gordon
"Atlantic Menhaden. Species Profiles: Life Histories and Environmental Requirements of Coastal Fishes and Invertebrates (Mid-Atlantic)", 5506–8.115

Rogers, Terrence J.
"Annual Southwestern Region Pest Conditions Report, 1988", 1206–11.1

Rohmann, Steven O.
"Pollutant Discharges to Coastal Areas: Improving Upstream Source Estimates. National Coastal Pollutant Discharge Inventory", 2176–4.11

Rollinson, Barbara L.
"Recent Issues in Transfer Pricing", 8006–3.57

Roman, Gail D.
"Rural and Urban Housing, 1930-80", 1598–245

Romania
Abortion-related deaths, complications, and low-birthweight births, impacts of law restricting abortion, for Romania, 1950s-83, hearing, 21408–113
Agricultural and food production and indexes, total and for selected commodities, by country, 1970s-88, annual rpt, 1524–12
Agricultural production, acreage, and consumption, by Eastern Europe country and commodity, 1965-85, 1528–284
Agricultural production, consumption, and trade, for Eastern Europe by country, 1970s-88, annual rpt, 1524–11
Agricultural trade of US, by detailed commodity and country, 1988, semiannual rpt, 1522–4
Auto imports from US, trade barriers by country, 1988, annual rpt, 444–2
Bearings (antifriction) from 9 countries, injury to US industry from foreign subsidized and less than fair value imports, investigation with background financial and operating data, 1989 rpt, 9886–19.65
Cuba economic conditions, agricultural and industrial production and distribution, trade, and intl economic relations, 1980-87 with trends from 1961, 9118–8
Debt, trade, and balances of Eastern Europe and USSR with US and other western countries, with background data, 1980s-87, hearing, 21248–120
Economic and military aid and loans from US and intl agencies, by program and country, FY46-87, annual rpt, 9914–5
Economic conditions in Communist, OECD, and selected other countries, 1960s-88, annual rpt, 9114–4
Economic conditions, income, production, prices, employment, and trade, 1989 periodic country rpt, 2046–4.47
Economic conditions, policy, and trade practices, by country, 1986-88, annual rpt, 21384–5
Economic, social, political, and geographic summary data, by country, 1989, annual factbook, 9114–2
Export licensing, monitoring, and enforcement activities, FY88, annual rpt, 2024–1
Exports and imports of US, by selected country, country group, and commodity group, 1988, annual rpt, 2044–37
Exports and imports of US with Communist countries, by detailed commodity and country, quarterly rpt with articles, 9882–2
Human rights conditions in 170 countries, 1988, annual rpt, 21384–3
Military spending, arms trade, and force strengths, with govt spending and population, by country, 1977-87, annual rpt, 9824–1
Military strength of USSR and Warsaw Pact, and proposed force reductions, with comparisons to NATO, 1980s-91, hearing, 21208–29
Minerals Yearbook, 1987, Vol 3: foreign country reviews of production, trade, and policy, by commodity, annual rpt, 5604–35

Minerals Yearbook, 1987, Vol 3 preprints: foreign country review of production, trade, and policy, by commodity, annual rpt, 5604–23.61
Nuclear power plant capacity and operating status, by plant and Communist country, as of Dec 1988, annual rpt, 3164–57.2
Population size, growth rates, and components of change, by country, projected 1989-2020 and trends from 1950, biennial rpt, 2324–9
Refugee resettlement programs and funding, arrivals by country of origin, and indicators of adjustment, by State, FY88, annual rpt, 4694–5
Steel export ceilings under voluntary restraint agreements, by country and product, with Western US steel industry impact, 1989 rpt, 9886–4.136
Steel imports of US under voluntary restraint agreement, by product, customs district, and country, with US industry operating data, monthly rpt, 9882–13
UN voting record and share of votes in agreement with US, by issue, country, and world area, 1988, annual rpt, 7004–18
see also under By Foreign Country in the "Index by Categories"

Rome, N.Y.
see also under By SMSA or MSA in the "Index by Categories"

Romieu, Isabelle
"Prospective Study of Oral Contraceptive Use and Risk of Breast Cancer in Women", 4472–1.923

Rones, Philip L.
"Institutional Barriers to Employment of Older Workers", 6722–1.918
"Labor Market Problems of Older Workers", 6306–2.2
"Profile of the Working Poor", 6722–1.948

Roney, John C.
"World and U.S. Outlook for Sugar and Sweeteners", 1004–16.1

Roningen, Vernon O.
"Economic Implications of Agricultural Policy Reforms in Industrial Market Economies", 1528–282

Rooming and boarding houses
Board and care homes conditions, State licensing and enforcement activity, and client characteristics, 1970s-88, 21148–55
Board and care homes licensing and inspection by States, and client characteristics, 1989 GAO rpt, 26121–275
County Business Patterns, 1987: employment, establishments, and payroll, by SIC 2- to 4-digit industry and county, annual State rpt series, 2326–8
Housing and households detailed characteristics, and unit and neighborhood quality, by location, 1985, biennial rpt, 2485–12
Service industries census, 1987: establishments, receipts, employment, and payroll, by SIC 2- to 4-digit kind of business, MSA, county, and city, State rpt series, 2391–1
Supplemental Security Income and Medicaid eligibility and payment provisions, and beneficiaries living arrangements, by State, 1989, annual rpt, 4704–13

Tax (income) returns of partnerships, income statement items by industry group, 1986, annual article, 8302–2.903

Tax (income) returns of sole proprietorships, income statement items, by industry group, 1987, annual article, 8302–2.904; 8302–2.921

Roos, Noralou P.
"Potential for Inpatient-Outpatient Substitution with Diagnosis-Related Groups", 4652–1.940

Rosa, Dan
"Statistics of Income Studies of Business Income and Taxes", 8302–2.910

Roseburg, Oreg.
Wages by occupation, and benefits for office and plant workers, 1989 survey, periodic MSA rpt, 6785–3.9

Rosen, Harvey S.
"Intertemporal Analysis of State and Local Government Spending: Theory and Tests", 9387–8.183

Rosen, Stacey
"Consumption Stability and the Potential Role of Food Aid in Africa", 1528–279
"Export Performance in Africa", 1528–280

Rosenberg, Michael J
"Reproductive Mortality in the U.S.: Recent Trends and Methodologic Considerations", 21408–113

Rosenblum, Harvey
"Money and Inflation in a Deregulated Financial Environment: An Overview", 9379–1.905

Rosenfeld, Arthur H.
"Conservation, Competition and National Security", 21368–107

Rosengren, Eric S.
"State Anti-Takeover Statutes", 9373–2.901

Rosenthal, Neal H.
"More Than Wages at Issue in Job Quality Debate", 6722–1.957

Rosenthal, Steven M.
"Reproductive Mortality in the U.S.: Recent Trends and Methodologic Considerations", 21408–113

Rosine, John
"Drought, Agriculture, and the Economy", 9362–1.901

Rosnow, Mark
"Milwaukee's Outreach to the Homeless Mentally Ill", 10048–73

ROTC
see Reserve Officers Training Corps

Roth, Dee
"Ohio's Coordinated Response to the Problems of Homelessness", 10048–73

Rothberg, James P.
"On the Determinants of Yield Spreads Between Mortgage Pass-Through and Treasury Securities", 9316–1.148

Rourke, John P.
"Producer Milk Marketed Under Federal Milk Orders by State of Origin", 1317–4.904

Royalties
Budget of US, authoritative financial statements with appropriations, outlays, and receipts, by category and agency, FY88, annual rpt, 8104–2.2

Cable TV royalties paid, 1978-87, 2808–27

Coal leasing activity on Federal land, acreage, production, and reserves, by coal region and State, FY88, annual rpt, 5724–10

Coal production and freight costs, and competitive position in selected markets, for Australia and US, 1987-89, 2048–143

Copyright royalty fees for cable TV and jukeboxes, and funds available for distribution, 1986-87, annual rpt, 26404–2

Fed Govt R&D labs technology transfer cooperative agreements, royalties, and incentive payments to employees, by agency, FY87-88, GAO rpt, 26113–422

Foreign countries military aid programs and related activities of US, costs by country and intl agency, FY85-87 and cumulative from FY50, GAO rpt, 26123–30

Foreign countries royalty and license fee payments to and from US, for OECD and other countries, 1972-85, annual chartbook, 9624–22

Foreign countries royalty payments and receipts for US, 1960-87, annual rpt, 9624–23.4

Forest Service activities and finances, by region and State, FY88, annual rpt, 1204–1.1

Multinatl US firms and foreign affiliates finances and operations, by industry of parent firm and affiliate, world area, and country, preliminary 1987, annual rpt, 2704–5

Natural gas interstate pipeline company detailed financial and operating data, by firm, 1988, annual rpt, 3164–38

Naval Petroleum and Oil Shale Reserves production and revenue by fuel type, sales by purchaser, and wells, by reserve, FY88, annual rpt, 3004–22

Oil, gas, and minerals production and revenue on Federal and Indian land, by State, 1988 and trends from 1920, annual rpt, 5734–2

Public lands acreage and use, and Land Mgmt Bur activities and finances, annual State rpt series, 5724–11

Tax (income) returns filed by type of filer, selected income items, quarterly rpt, 8302–2.1

Tax (income) returns of corporations, income and tax items by asset size and detailed industry, 1986, annual rpt, 8304–4; 8304–21

Tax (income) returns of individuals, detailed data, 1986, annual rpt, 8304–2

Tax (income) returns of partnerships, income statement items by industry group, 1986, annual article, 8302–2.903

Royer, Jeffrey S.
"Cooperatives' Net Income of $1.5 Billion Highest Since 1980; Assets Also Up", 1122–1.905

Rubber and rubber industry
Business statistics, detailed data for major industries and economic indicators, *Survey of Current Business*, monthly rpt, 2702–1.17

China trade by SITC 1- to 5-digit commodity, 1970s-87, annual rpt, 9114–3

Collective bargaining agreements expiring during year, and workers covered, by firm, union, industry group, and State, 1989, annual rpt, 6784–9

Communist, OECD, and selected other countries agricultural production, by commodity, 1960s-88, annual rpt, 9114–4.6

Communist, OECD, and selected other countries consumer and producer goods production, 1960s-88, annual rpt, 9114–4.8

County Business Patterns, 1987: employment, establishments, and payroll, by SIC 2- to 4-digit industry and county, annual State rpt series, 2326–8

Earnings by major industry group, and personal income per capita and by source, by region and State, 1929-87, 2708–40

Employment, earnings, and hours, by selected SIC 1- to 4-digit industry, State, and for 262 MSAs, 1972-87, 6748–81

Employment, earnings, and hours, by SIC 1- to 4-digit industry, monthly 1983-Feb 1989, annual rpt, 6744–4

Employment, unemployment, and labor force characteristics, by region and census div, 1988, annual rpt, 6744–7.1

Exports and imports (agricultural) of US, by commodity and country, bimonthly rpt with articles, 1522–1

Exports and imports (agricultural) of US, by commodity, monthly rpt, 1922–8

Exports and imports (agricultural) of US, by detailed commodity and country, 1988, semiannual rpt, 1522–4

Exports and imports of US, by commodity group, world area, selected country, US coastal area and port, and mode of transport, monthly rpt, 2422–9

Exports of US, detailed commodities by country, monthly rpt, 2422–3

Finances and operations, by SIC 2- to 4-digit industry, forecast 1989 with trends from 1950s, annual rpt, 2044–28

Financial statements for manufacturing, mining, and trade corporations, by selected SIC 2- to 3-digit industry, quarterly rpt, 2502–1

Footwear production, employment, use, prices, and US trade by country, quarterly rpt, 9882–6

Foreign countries agricultural production, prices, and trade, by country, 1970s-89 and forecast 1990, annual world region rpt series, 1524–4

Freight (waterborne domestic and foreign) by commodity, traffic, and passengers, by port and waterway, 1987, annual rpt, 3754–3

Hose and belting shipments, trade, use, and firms, by product, 1988, annual Current Industrial Rpt, 2506–8.12

Imports, exports, and employment impacts, by SIC 2- to 4-digit industry and commodity, quarterly rpt, 2322–2

Imports of US, detailed Schedule A commodities by country, monthly rpt, 2422–2

Input-output structure of US economy, detailed interindustry transactions for 84 industries, and components of final demand, 1983, annual article, 2702–1.909

Manufacturing annual survey, 1986: financial and operating data, by SIC 2- to 4-digit industry, series, 2506–15

Manufacturing census, 1987: financial and operating data, for SIC 4-digit industries by product, preliminary rpt, 2491–1.34; 2491–1.42

Manufacturing industries production, shipments, inventories, orders, and pollution control costs, periodic Current Industrial Rpt series, 2506–3

Multinatl US firms and foreign affiliates finances and operations, by industry of parent firm and affiliate, world area, and country, preliminary 1987, annual rpt, 2704–5

Occupational injury and illness rates, by SIC 2- to 4-digit industry, 1987, annual rpt, 6844–1

OECD trade, total and for 4 major countries, and US trade by country, by commodity, 1970-87, world area rpt series, 9116–1

Pollution abatement capital and operating costs, by SIC 2-to 4-digit industry and State, 1986, annual Current Industrial Rpt, 2506–3.6

Price indexes (producer), by stage of processing and detailed commodity, monthly rpt, 6762–6

Price indexes (producer), by stage of processing and detailed commodity, monthly 1988, annual rpt, 6764–2

Production and sales of synthetic organic chemicals, and manufacturer listing, by product, 1988, annual rpt, 9884–3

Science, engineering, and technical employment in manufacturing, by field, occupation, and industry, 1986, triennial rpt, 9627–23

Shipments of rubber mechanical goods, by product, 1988, annual Current Industrial Rpt, 2506–8.17

Shoe production, shipments, trade, and use, by product, 1988, annual Current Industrial Rpt, 2506–6.8

Statistical Abstract of US, social, political, and economic data, 1790-2025, comprehensive annual compilation, 2324–1.3

Stockpiling of strategic material by Fed Govt, activity, and inventory by commodity, as of Sept 1989, semiannual rpt, 3542–22; 3902–2

Stockpiling of strategic material, inventories and needs, by commodity, as of Sept 1988, annual rpt, 3544–37

Stockpiling of strategic material, inventories, costs, and goals by commodity, as of June 1989, semiannual rpt, 3902–3

Talc production, use, and trade, with foreign comparisons, selected years 1977-87, 5608–158

Tariff Schedule of US, classifications and rates of duty by detailed imported commodity, 1990 base edition and supplements, 9886–13

Tax (income) returns of corporations, income and tax items by asset size and detailed industry, 1986, annual rpt, 8304–4

Transportation census, 1987: trucks, by detailed characteristics, miles traveled, and type of product carried, State rpt series, 2573–1

see also Tires and tire industry

see also By Industry in the "Index by Categories"

see also under By Commodity in the "Index by Categories"

Rubella

see Infective and parasitic diseases

Ruben, George

"Collective Bargaining and Labor-Management Relations, 1988", 6722–1.903

Rubidium

see Metals and metal industries

Rubin, Mary

"Serving AFDC Recipients: Initial Findings on the Role of Performance Standards", 15496–1.4

Ruchlin, Hirsch S.

"Expenditures for Long-Term Care Services by Community Elders", 4652–1.932

Rudebusch, Glenn D.

"Forecasting Output with the Composite Leading Index: An Ex Ante Analysis", 9366–6.204

"Is Consumption Too Smooth? Long Memory and the Deaton Paradox", 9366–6.171

Ruebsamen, Rickey

"National Marine Fisheries Service Habitat Conservation Efforts in the Coastal Southeastern U.S. for 1987", 2162–1.902

Ruff, Craig

"Off-Balance-Sheet Hedging Activity in Southeast Thrifts", 9302–2.903

Ruffin, Marilyn D.

"Cutting Back on Consumption: The Experience of Older Households", 1702–1.907

Ruggles, Patricia

"Measuring the Duration of Poverty Spells", 2626–10.88

"Welfare Dependency and Its Causes: Determinants of the Duration of Welfare Spells", 2626–10.87

Rugs

see Carpets and rugs

Runaways

see Missing persons and runaways

Runkle, David E.

"Are Economic Forecasts Rational?", 9383–6.903

"U.S. Economy in 1989 and 1990: Walking a Fine Line", 9383–6.901

Runner, Diana

"Changes in Unemployment Insurance Legislation During 1988", 6722–1.905

Rupp, Kalman

"Who Is Served in JTPA Programs: Patterns of Participation and Intergroup Equity", 15496–1.3

Rural areas

AID dev projects, special study series, 9916–3

Airline service in rural areas, impacts of deregulation, and Federal subsidies, with data by location, 1978-87, 1278–17

Alaska rural villages population characteristics and and subsistence activities, 1976-86, 5738–9

Banks finances and operations, by metro-nonmetro location, 1986, annual rpt, 1544–29

Births, fertility rates, and childless women, by selected characteristics, 1988, annual Current Population Rpt, 2546–1.436

Bridges in rural areas, conditions, needs, and funding, with data by State and compared to urban areas, 1988, 1278–16

China rural areas surplus labor, urban jobs assigned, and employment by sector, urban-rural location, and Province, 1950s-87 and projected to 2000, working paper, 2326–18.48

Consumer spending in metro and nonmetro areas, by item, 1987, article, 6722–1.962

Crime Index by population size and region, and offenses by large city, Jan-June 1989, semiannual rpt, 6222–1

Crime victimization of households, by offense, household characteristics, and location, 1975-88, annual rpt, 6066–25.22

Crimes, arrests by offender characteristics, and rates, by offense, and law enforcement employees, by population size and jurisdiction, 1988, annual rpt, 6224–2

Drought of 1988, impacts on farm, rural areas, and food industry financial conditions, with trends from 1970, 1588–133

Economic and social conditions, dev, and problems in rural areas, periodic journal, 1502–7

Education conditions and population characteristics in rural areas, 1987 conf papers, 4818–6

Educational enrollment, by grade, instn type and control, and student characteristics, 1986 and trends from 1947, annual Current Population Rpt, 2546–1.429; 2546–1.432

Employment, economic conditions, and population characteristics of rural areas, 1970s-85, compilation of papers, 1598–243

Employment in nonmetro counties by industry sector and degree of urbanization, and compared to metro counties, various periods 1969-86, 1598–244

Employment stability in rural areas, impacts of industrial growth and other factors, 1979, 1598–255

Employment, unemployment, and labor force characteristics, Labor Statistics Handbook, 1940s-88 with trends from 1913, 6728–38.1

Farm financial and marketing conditions, forecast 1988, conf papers, annual rpt, 1004–16

Food consumption and nutrient intake by individuals, by food group, selected characteristics, and region, supplementary survey series, 1356–5

Health care facilities, staffing, services accessibility, and indicators of need, for rural areas, 1960s-88, 25148–41

Hospital service area population care need indicators, and travel distances, for rural and urban instns in New York State, 1983, 4188–53

Hospitals in rural areas, risk of closure by characteristics of service area and hospital, aggregate 1980-87, article, 4042–3.930

Hospitals, use, staff, and funding sources, by instn characteristics, for rural areas, 1980s-86, hearing, 25148–42

Household and family characteristics, by location, 1988, annual Current Population Rpt, 2546–1.437

Housing (rental) in rural areas, units, vacancy, and rent exceeding 30% of renter income, by type of rental aid and State, FY88, hearing, 21248–117

Housing and households characteristics, for rural and urban areas, 1930s-80, 1598–245

Budget of US Appendix, obligations, appropriations, and personnel, by program and agency, FY90, annual rpt, 104–3

Fed Financing Bank loans outstanding, and loan prepayment activity and costs, 1985-88, GAO rpt, 26111–63

Loans of REA, and borrower operating and financial data, by distribution firm and State, 1988, annual rpt, 1244–1

Loans of REA, by State, as of FY88, annual rpt, 1244–7

Plants financed by REA, with location, capacity, and owner, as of Jan 1989, annual listing, 1244–6

Purchases (wholesale) and costs for REA borrowers, by borrower, supplier, and State, 1940-87, annual rpt, 1244–5

see also Rural Telephone Bank

Rural Telephone Bank

Agricultural Statistics, 1988, annual rpt, 1004–1.2

Financial statements of Bank, FY87, annual rpt, 1244–4

Loans by State, and REA activities and finances, FY88 with trends from FY36, annual rpt, 1244–3

Loans to telephone firms under Rural Telephone Program, activity by State, FY88, annual tables, 1244–8

Loans to telephone firms under Rural Telephone Program, and borrower operations and finances, 1988, annual rpt, 1244–2

Ruser, John W.

"Effect of OSHA Records Check Inspections on Reported Occupational Injuries in Manufacturing Establishments", 6886–6.41

"Has Injury Reporting Changed? Looking Again at Firm Size and OSHA Effects", 6886–6.63

"Workers' Compensation and Occupational Injuries and Illnesses", 6886–6.64

"Workers' Compensation Benefits and Compensating Wage Differentials", 6886–6.22

"Workers' Compensation Insurance, Experience Rating, and Occupational Injuries", 6886–6.15

Russek, Frank

"Policies for Reducing the Current-Account Deficit", 26306–6.135

Russell, Julie C.

"Injuries to Seat Occupants of Light Airplanes", 7506–10.57

Russia

see Soviet Union

Russo, Philip A., Jr.

"Local Response to Federal Budget Policies: A Study of Nonmetropolitan Communities in Ohio", 1598–254

Ruther, Martin

"Medicare and Medicaid Data Book, 1988", 4654–1

"Use and Cost of Home Health Agency Services Under Medicare", 4652–1.908

Rutledge, Gary L.

"Plant and Equipment Expenditures by Business for Pollution Abatement, 1987 and Planned 1988", 2702–1.904

"Pollution Abatement and Control Expenditures, 1984-87", 2702–1.919

Ruttenberg, Ruth

"Role of Labor-Management Committees in Safeguarding Worker Safety and Health", 6306–3.4

Rwanda

Agricultural and food production and indexes, total and for selected commodities, by country, 1970s-88, annual rpt, 1524–12

Agricultural trade of US, by detailed commodity and country, 1988, semiannual rpt, 1522–4

AID activities and funding by project and function, FY90, and developing countries summary socioeconomic data from 1960s, annual rpt, 9904–4.5

AID economic aid to developing countries, obligations and disbursements by country, quarterly rpt, 9912–4

Background Notes, summary social, political, and economic data, 1989 rpt, 7006–2.15

Economic and military aid and loans from US and intl agencies, by program and country, FY46-87, annual rpt, 9914–5

Economic, social, political, and geographic summary data, by country, 1989, annual factbook, 9114–2

Human rights conditions in 170 countries, 1988, annual rpt, 21384–3

Military aid of US, arms sales, and training programs costs and budget requests, by program, world region, and country, FY88-90, annual rpt, 7144–13

Military spending, arms trade, and force strengths, with govt spending and population, by country, 1977-87, annual rpt, 9824–1

Minerals Yearbook, 1987, Vol 3: foreign country reviews of production, trade, and policy, by commodity, annual rpt, 5604–35

Minerals Yearbook, 1987, Vol 3 preprints: foreign country review of production, trade, and policy, by commodity, annual rpt, 5604–23.81

Population size, growth rates, and components of change, by country, projected 1989-2020 and trends from 1950, biennial rpt, 2324–9

UN voting record and share of votes in agreement with US, by issue, country, and world area, 1988, annual rpt, 7004–18

see also under By Foreign Country in the "Index by Categories"

Rye

see Animal feed

see Grains and grain products

see Pasture and rangeland

Ryscavage, Paul

"Longitudinal vs. Retrospective Measures of Work Experience", 2626–10.83

"Measuring Spells of Unemployment and Their Outcomes", 2626–10.86

"Spells of Job Search and Layoff...and Their Outcomes", 2546–20.9

Sabotage

Sentences for Federal offenses, guidelines by offense and circumstances, 1989 rpt, 17668–1

Terrorist (intl) incidents, casualties, and attacks on US targets, by attack type and country, 1980-88, 7008–56

Terrorist (intl) incidents, casualties, and attacks on US targets, by attack type and world area, 1968-88, annual rpt, 7004–13

US attorneys civil and criminal cases by type and disposition, and collections, by Federal district, FY88, annual rpt, 6004–2.1

Sachs, Jeffrey D.

"International Payments Imbalances of the East Asian Developing Economies", 9373–3.32

Sacramento, Calif.

Freight (waterborne domestic and foreign) by commodity, traffic, and passengers, by port and waterway, 1987, annual rpt, 3754–3.4

Housing starts and completions authorized by building permits in 40 MSAs, quarterly rpt, 2382–9

Housing vacancy rates for single and multifamily units and mobile homes, by city and ZIP code, 1988, annual MSA rpt, 9304–20.11

see also under By City and By SMSA or MSA in the "Index by Categories"

Safety

see Accidents and accident prevention

see Aviation accidents and safety

see Marine accidents and safety

see Mine accidents and safety

see Motor vehicle safety devices

see Occupational health and safety

see Product safety

see Railroad accidents and safety

see Traffic accident fatalities

see Traffic accidents and safety

see Transportation accidents and safety

Saginaw, Mich.

Wages by occupation, and benefits for office and plant workers, 1989 survey, periodic MSA rpt, 6785–3.10

see also under By SMSA or MSA in the "Index by Categories"

Sailors

see Merchant seamen

see Military personnel

Saint

see under terms beginning St.

Salant, Priscilla

"Programs and Policies To Assist Displaced Farmers", 15496–1.2

Salaries

see Agricultural wages

see Earnings, general

see Earnings, local and regional

see Earnings, specific industry

see Educational employees pay

see Federal pay

see Minimum wage

see Payroll

see Professionals' fees

see State and local employees pay

Salem, Mass.

CPI by component for US city average, and by region, population size, and for 15 metro areas, monthly rpt, 6762–1

CPI by component for US city average, and by region, population size, and for 27 metro areas, monthly rpt, 6762–2

see also under By SMSA or MSA in the "Index by Categories"

Salem, Oreg.

see also under By SMSA or MSA in the "Index by Categories"

Sales, business
see Business income and expenses, general
see Business income and expenses, specific industry
see Farm income

Sales promotion
Cigarette ad and promotion costs by media, and market shares, by cigarette type, with sales and use, 1963-87, annual rpt, 9404-4

Electric utilities finances and operations, detailed data for privately owned firms, and summary data for other utilities by type, 1987, annual rpt, 3164-23

Electric utilities finances and operations, detailed data for privately owned firms, 1986-88, annual rpt, 3164-11.4

Milk order advertising and promotion finances, and producer participation, by region, 1988, annual article, 1317-4.902

Natural gas interstate pipeline company detailed financial and operating data, by firm, 1988, annual rpt, 3164-38

see also Advertising
see also Foreign trade promotion
see also Market research
see also Sales workers

Sales tax
Auto operating costs by component, and Fed Govt mileage reimbursement rates, 1988, annual rpt, 9454-13

Collections of taxes, by level of govt, type of tax, State, and selected counties, quarterly rpt, 2462-3

Finances of govts, revenues by source and spending by function, natl income and product account, *Survey of Current Business*, monthly rpt, 2702-1.24

Govt finances, by level of govt, State, and for large cities and counties, annual rpt series, 2466-2

Govt finances, tax systems and revenue, and fiscal structure, by level of govt and State, selected years 1929-91, annual rpt, 10044-1

Income tax returns of individuals, detailed data, 1986, annual rpt, 8304-2

Local govt sales tax revenues and rates, and share of total revenue, by State and selected jurisdiction, 1960s-88, 10046-8.9

Mail order sales from out of State, tax revenues and rates under proposed collection system, by State, 1988 hearings, 21528-73

Natl income and product accounts and components, *Survey of Current Business*, monthly rpt, 2702-1.21

North Central States business and economic conditions, Fed Reserve 9th District, quarterly journal, 9383-19

North Central States economic conditions, Fed Reserve 9th District, quarterly rpt, 9383-18

Public opinion on taxes, spending, and govt efficiency, by respondent characteristics, 1989 survey, annual rpt, 10044-2

Puerto Rico economic conditions and govt finances, 1975-89, GAO rpt, 26121-298

Retail trade sales tax as share of sales, by SIC 2- to 4-digit kind of business, 1987, annual rpt, 2413-5

Retailer sales tax collection compliance costs, by industry group and for 7 States, 1981, hearings, 21528-73

State and local revenue potential relative to natl average tax burden, by type of tax and State, 1986, annual rpt, 10044-7

Transit systems finances and operations, by mode of transport, size of fleet, and for 432 systems, 1986, annual rpt, 7884-4

Transportation finances, operations, vehicles, equipment, accidents, and energy use, by mode of transport, 1955-88, annual rpt, 7304-2

see also Excise tax
see also Fuel tax
see also Value added tax

Sales workers
Educational attainment, by sociodemographic characteristics and location, 1987 and trends from 1940, biennial Current Population Rpt, 2546-1.427; 2546-1.431

Employment and earnings in marketing and sales industries, by occupation, 1986-87 and projected 2000, article, 6742-1.901

Employment and occupation of householder, by occupation of spouse, race, and family composition, 1988, annual Current Population Rpt, 2546-1.437

Employment Cost Index and alternative measure of compensation costs, by component, occupation, industry group, union status, and location, 1975-89, annual rpt, 6744-20

Employment, earnings, and hours, monthly press release, 6742-5

Employment in nonmanufacturing industries, by detailed occupation and SIC 2-digit industry, 1987, triennial rpt, 6748-60

Employment, unemployment, and labor force characteristics, by region, State, and selected metro area, 1988, annual rpt, 6744-7

Handbook of Labor Statistics, employment, unemployment, and labor force characteristics, 1940s-88 with trends from 1913, 6728-38

Health care treatments and products not proven safe or effective, use, costs, and user characteristics, 1986 survey, 4008-86

Health condition of labor force, and services use, by occupation and industry of longest job held, income, age, sex, and race. 1980, 4147-10.168

Immigrants admitted to US, by occupational group and country of birth, preliminary FY88, annual table, 6264-1

Immigration to US, alien workers, visitors, deportations, and naturalizations, by country, FY88 and trends from 1820, annual rpt, 6264-2

Income (household, family, and personal), by source, detailed characteristics, and region, 1987, annual Current Population Rpt, 2546-6.59

Minority group and women employment, by occupation, SIC 1- to 3- digit industry, State, and MSA, 1986, annual rpt, 9244-1

Occupational changes, by tenure and other worker characteristics, and labor mobility rates, 1965-86, article, 6722-1.943

Statistical Abstract of US, social, political, and economic data, 1790-2025, comprehensive annual compilation, 2324-1.3

Suburban areas land use, commuting, employment, and housing characteristics, detailed data for traffic planning, 1986, 7888-75

see also under By Occupation in the "Index by Categories"

Salinas, Calif.
Housing vacancy rates for single and multifamily units and mobile homes, by city and ZIP code, 1988, annual MSA rpt, 9304-20.4

see also under By City and By SMSA or MSA in the "Index by Categories"

Saline water conversion
Rural areas public water supply system financial and operating characteristics, by region, 1980, 1598-247

Salive, Marcel E.
"Suicide Mortality in the Maryland State Prison System: 1979-87", 4186-9.2

Salmonella
see Food and waterborne diseases

Salt Lake City, Utah
Housing starts and completions authorized by building permits in 40 MSAs, quarterly rpt, 2382-9

Wages by occupation, and benefits for office and plant workers, 1988 survey, periodic MSA rpt, 6785-11.3

see also under By City and By SMSA or MSA in the "Index by Categories"

Salt water conversion
see Saline water conversion

Saluter, Arlene F.
"Marital Status and Living Arrangements: March 1987", 2546-1.428

"Marital Status and Living Arrangements: March 1988", 2546-1.433

"Singleness in America", 2546-2.148

Salvage
see also Recycling of waste materials
see also Scrap metals

Samet, Jonathan M.
"Radon and Lung Cancer", 4472-1.913

Samoa
see American Samoa
see Western Samoa

San Angelo, Tex.
see also under By SMSA or MSA in the "Index by Categories"

San Antonio, Tex.
Drug test results at arrest, by drug type, offense, and sex, for selected urban areas, quarterly rpt, 6062-3

Housing starts and completions authorized by building permits in 40 MSAs, quarterly rpt, 2382-9

see also under By City and By SMSA or MSA in the "Index by Categories"

San Bernadino, Calif.
see also under By City and By SMSA or MSA in the "Index by Categories"

San Bernardino, Calif.
Housing starts and completions authorized by building permits in 40 MSAs, quarterly rpt, 2382-9

San Diego, Calif.
CPI by component for US city average, and by region, population size, and for 27 metro areas, monthly rpt, 6762-1

Drug abuse indicators for selected metro areas, research results, data collection, and policy issues, 1989 semiannual conf, 4492-5

Drug test results at arrest, by drug type, offense, and sex, for selected urban areas, quarterly rpt, 6062-3

Housing starts and completions authorized by building permits in 40 MSAs, quarterly rpt, 2382-9

Housing vacancy rates for single and multifamily units and mobile homes, by city and ZIP code, 1988, annual MSA rpt, 9304-20.9

Wages by occupation, for office and plant workers, 1988 survey, periodic MSA rpt, 6785-11.4

see also under By City and By SMSA or MSA in the "Index by Categories"

San Francisco Bay

Fish distribution by species, and water outflow, for south San Francisco Bay, 1973-82, 2168-113

Pollutant concentrations in coastal and estuarine sediments, by contaminant and selected site, 1984-87, 2176-3.7

Pollutant concentrations in coastal and estuarine shellfish, by pollutant and location, 1986-88, 2176-3.8

Ships in Natl Defense Reserve Fleet at Suisun Bay, as of Jan 1989, semiannual listing, 7702-2

San Francisco, Calif.

Child health and welfare programs of local agencies for high-risk infants and children, for Los Angeles and San Francisco, 1988 hearing, 21968-48

CPI by component for US city average, and by region, population size, and for 15 metro areas, monthly rpt, 6762-1

CPI by component for US city average, and by region, population size, and for 27 metro areas, monthly rpt, 6762-2

Drug abuse indicators for selected metro areas, research results, data collection, and policy issues, 1989 semiannual conf, 4492-5

Freight (waterborne domestic and foreign) by commodity, traffic, and passengers, by port and waterway, 1987, annual rpt, 3754-3.4

Fruit and vegetable shipments, and arrivals in US and Canada cities, by mode of transport and State and country of origin, 1988, annual rpt, 1311-4.2

Housing and households characteristics, 1985 survey, MSA fact sheet, 2485-11.9

Housing and households detailed characteristics, and unit and neighborhood quality, by location, 1985 survey, MSA rpt, 2485-6.10

Housing vacancy rates for single and multifamily units and mobile homes, by city and ZIP code, 1988, annual MSA rpt, 9304-20.8

Older frail persons community and home-based care under prepaid care plan, enrollees health condition and services use, for San Francisco, 1987, article, 4652-1.912

Wages by occupation, for office and plant workers, 1989 survey, periodic MSA rpt, 6785-12.2

see also under By City and By SMSA or MSA in the "Index by Categories"

San Jose, Calif.

CPI by component for US city average, and by region, population size, and for 15 metro areas, monthly rpt, 6762-1

CPI by component for US city average, and by region, population size, and for 27 metro areas, monthly rpt, 6762-2

Housing vacancy rates for single and multifamily units and mobile homes, by city and ZIP code, 1988, annual MSA rpt, 9304-20.5

Wages by occupation, for office and plant workers, 1989 survey, periodic MSA rpt, 6785-12.2

see also under By City and By SMSA or MSA in the "Index by Categories"

San Juan, P.R.

see also under By SMSA or MSA in the "Index by Categories"

San Marino

Economic, social, political, and geographic summary data, by country, 1989, annual factbook, 9114-2

Population size, growth rates, and components of change, by country, projected 1989-2020 and trends from 1950, biennial rpt, 2324-9

see also under By Foreign Country in the "Index by Categories"

San Mateo County, Calif.

Housing vacancy rates for single and multifamily units and mobile homes, by city and ZIP code, 1988, annual MSA rpt, 9304-20.8

Sana

see Yemen, North

Sanchez-Carrillo, Constanza I.

"Morbidity Following Mexico City's 1985 Earthquakes: Clinical and Epidemiologic Findings from Hospitals and Emergency Units", 4042-3.947

Sanchez, Pedro A.

"Low-Input Cropping for Acid Soils of the Humid Tropics", 21708-126

Sanctions

see International sanctions

Sand and gravel

see Stone products and quarries

Sandefur, Gary D.

"Small Gains for Rural Indians Who Move to Cities", 1502-7.904

Sandell, Steven H.

"Who Is Served in JTPA Programs: Patterns of Participation and Intergroup Equity", 15496-1.3

Sandia National Laboratories

see also Department of Energy National Laboratories

Sandusky, Ohio

Wages by occupation, for office and plant workers, 1989 survey, periodic MSA rpt, 6785-3.3

Sanford, Scott

"Factors Influencing U.S. Trade in Cotton and Manmade Fiber Textile Manufactures: Future Implications", 1561-1.906

"Portrait of Cotton Farm Operators and Their Farms: 1987 Census of Agriculture", 1561-1.907

Sanitary districts

see Special districts

Sanitary engineering

see Plumbing and heating

see Refuse and refuse disposal

see Sewage and wastewater systems

Santa Ana, Calif.

Housing starts and completions authorized by building permits in 40 MSAs, quarterly rpt, 2382-9

Wages by occupation, and benefits for office and plant workers, 1988 survey, periodic MSA rpt, 6785-11.3

see also under By City and By SMSA or MSA in the "Index by Categories"

Santa Barbara, Calif.

Wages by occupation, and benefits for office and plant workers, 1989 survey, periodic MSA rpt, 6785-3.9

see also under By SMSA or MSA in the "Index by Categories"

Santa Cruz, Calif.

Housing vacancy rates for single and multifamily units and mobile homes, by city and ZIP code, 1988, annual MSA rpt, 9304-20.10

see also under By SMSA or MSA in the "Index by Categories"

Santa Fe, N.Mex.

see also under By SMSA or MSA in the "Index by Categories"

Santa Maria, Calif.

Wages by occupation, and benefits for office and plant workers, 1989 survey, periodic MSA rpt, 6785-3.9

see also under By SMSA or MSA in the "Index by Categories"

Santa Rosa, Calif.

Housing vacancy rates for single and multifamily units and mobile homes, by city and ZIP code, 1988, annual MSA rpt, 9304-20.3

see also under By City and By SMSA or MSA in the "Index by Categories"

Sao Tome and Principe

AID activities and funding by project and function, FY90, and developing countries summary socioeconomic data from 1960s, annual rpt, 9904-4.5

AID economic aid to developing countries, obligations and disbursements by country, quarterly rpt, 9912-4

Economic and military aid and loans from US and intl agencies, by program and country, FY46-87, annual rpt, 9914-5

Economic, social, political, and geographic summary data, by country, 1989, annual factbook, 9114-2

Human rights conditions in 170 countries, 1988, annual rpt, 21384-3

Military aid of US, arms sales, and training programs costs and budget requests, by program, world region, and country, FY88-90, annual rpt, 7144-13

Military spending, arms trade, and force strengths, with govt spending and population, by country, 1977-87, annual rpt, 9824-1

Minerals Yearbook, 1987, Vol 3: foreign country reviews of production, trade, and policy, by commodity, annual rpt, 5604-35

Minerals Yearbook, 1987, Vol 3 preprints: foreign country review of production, trade, and policy, by commodity, annual rpt, 5604-23.80

Population size, growth rates, and components of change, by country, projected 1989-2020 and trends from 1950, biennial rpt, 2324-9

UN voting record and share of votes in agreement with US, by issue, country, and world area, 1988, annual rpt, 7004-18
see also under By Foreign Country in the "Index by Categories"

Sarasota, Fla.
see also under By SMSA or MSA in the "Index by Categories"

Satellites
Aerial survey R&D rpts, and sources of natural resource and environmental data, quarterly listing, 9502-7
DOD budget, weapons acquisition costs by system and service branch, FY89-91, annual rpt, 3504-2
Launches and other activities of NASA and Soviet Union, with flight data, 1957-88, annual rpt, 9504-6.1
Launchings of satellites and other space objects since 1957, quarterly listing, 9502-2
NASA project launch schedules and technical descriptions, press release series, 9506-2
Soviet Union space program activities, plans, and characteristics of flights and vehicles, 1981-87, 25268-76
see also Communications satellites
see also Meteorological satellites

Saudi Arabia
Agricultural and food production and indexes, total and for selected commodities, by country, 1970s-88, annual rpt, 1524-12
Agricultural production, prices, and trade, by country, 1960s-89, annual world region rpt, 1524-4.2
Agricultural trade of US, by detailed commodity and country, 1988, semiannual rpt, 1522-4
Auto imports from US, trade barriers by country, 1988, annual rpt, 444-2
Background Notes, summary social, political, and economic data, 1989 rpt, 7006-2.42
Economic and military aid and loans from US and intl agencies, by program and country, FY46-87, annual rpt, 9914-5
Economic conditions in Communist, OECD, and selected other countries, 1960s-88, annual rpt, 9114-4
Economic conditions, income, production, prices, employment, and trade, 1989 periodic country rpt, 2046-4.112
Economic conditions, policy, and trade practices, by country, 1986-88, annual rpt, 21384-5
Economic, social, political, and geographic summary data, by country, 1989, annual factbook, 9114-2
Energy-intensive industry output and operations, and US investment barriers, for energy-rich countries, 1984-88, 9886-4.142
Exports and imports of US, by commodity and country, 1970-87, world area rpt, 9116-1.3
Exports and imports of US, by selected country, country group, and commodity group, 1988, annual rpt, 2044-37
Human rights conditions in 170 countries, 1988, annual rpt, 21384-3
Military aid of US, arms sales, and training programs costs and budget requests, by program, world region, and country, FY88-90, annual rpt, 7144-13

Military spending, arms trade, and force strengths, with govt spending and population, by country, 1977-87, annual rpt, 9824-1
Minerals Yearbook, 1987, Vol 3: foreign country reviews of production, trade, and policy, by commodity, annual rpt, 5604-35
Minerals Yearbook, 1987, Vol 3 preprints: foreign country review of production, trade, and policy, by commodity, annual rpt, 5604-23.62
Multinatl US firms and foreign affiliates finances and operations, by industry of parent firm and affiliate, world area, and country, preliminary 1987, annual rpt, 2704-5
Oil production, and exports and prices for US, by major exporting country, detailed data, monthly rpt, 3162-24
Oil production, trade, use, and stocks, by selected country and country group, monthly rpt, 3162-42
Population size, growth rates, and components of change, by country, projected 1989-2020 and trends from 1950, biennial rpt, 2324-9
Space satellites and other objects launched since 1957, quarterly listing, 9502-2
UN voting record and share of votes in agreement with US, by issue, country, and world area, 1988, annual rpt, 7004-18
Wheat production, use, prices, and subsidies of Saudi Arabia, mid 1960s-89, article, 1522-3.903
see also under By Foreign Country in the "Index by Categories"

Saunders, Anthony
"Additions to Bank Loan-Loss Reserves Good News or Bad News?", 9387-8.186
"Incentives To Engage in Bank Window-Dressing: Manager vs. Stockholder Conflicts", 9387-8.188

Saunders, Norman C.
"Aggregate Structure of the Economy", 6722-1.953

Saupe, William E.
"Programs and Policies To Assist Displaced Farmers", 15496-1.2

Savannah, Ga.
Freight (waterborne domestic and foreign) by commodity, traffic, and passengers, by port and waterway, 1987, annual rpt, 3754-3.1
Wages by occupation, for office and plant workers, 1989 survey, periodic MSA rpt, 6785-3.4
see also under By City and By SMSA or MSA in the "Index by Categories"

Savannah River Plant, S.C.
Repository sites for nuclear waste, water movement through soil at sites in humid areas, 1989 rpt, 5668-98

Savings
Consumer food spending and consumption, housing, and other finances, 1960s-88, annual chartbook, 1504-3
Current account balance of US, components and relation to foreign and US investment and economic conditions, 1970s-88 and projected to 1990s, article, 9385-1.905; 9385-1.906
Deposits, debits, and deposit turnover at financial instns, 1987, annual rpt, 9364-5.1

Economic indicators and components, and Fed Reserve 4th District business and financial conditions, monthly chartbook, 9377-10
Economic indicators compounded annual rates of change, 1969-88, annual rpt, 9391-9.1
Economic indicators, monthly rpt, 9362-1.2
Economic indicators, monthly table, 9302-26
Farm sector finances, income sources, expenses by type, assets, debts, and ratios, 1987, annual rpt, 1544-19
Financial and business statistics, historic trends, 1988 annual chartbook, 9364-2.4; 9364-2.11
Financial and monetary conditions, selected US summary data, weekly rpt, 9391-4
Financial instns financial and operating statements by deposit size, Fed Reserve functional cost analysis, 1988, annual rpt, 9364-6
Flow-of-funds accounts, assets and liabilities by type and economic sector, outstanding at year-end 1965-88, annual rpt, 9364-3
Flow-of-funds accounts, savings, investments, and credit statements, quarterly rpt, 9365-3.3
Foreign countries economic conditions and implications for US, periodic country rpt series, 2046-4
Foreign countries economic conditions, policy, and trade practices, by country, 1986-88, annual rpt, 21384-5
Foreign debt of US, economic impact, 1970s-80s and projected to 2000, article, 9387-1.905
Monetary and Fed Govt budget trends, Fed Reserve Bank of St Louis monthly rpt, 9391-2
Natl income and product accounts and components, Survey of Current Business, monthly rpt, 2702-1.21; 2702-1.26
New England States, FHLB 1st District thrift instns financial operations and housing industry indicators, monthly rpt, 9302-4
North Central States, FHLB 6th District savings instns financial condition and operations by State, monthly rpt, 9302-11
North Central States, FHLB 8th District savings instns financial operations by State and SMSA, monthly rpt, 9302-9
OECD personal savings rates for selected countries, 1960s-88, annual rpt, 9114-4.2
Personal, business, and govt gross saving and investment from 1929, and personal savings by type, 1946-88, annual rpt, 204-1.1
Personal, business, and govt savings, Business Conditions Digest, monthly rpt, 2702-3.5
Retirees savings maintenance and liquidation, by selected financial and other characteristics, 1971-79, article, 1702-1.906
Southeastern States, Fed Reserve 5th District insured commercial banks financial statements, by State, quarterly rpt, 9389-18
Southeastern States, FHLB 4th District savings instns finances and financial ratios, by State, quarterly rpt, 9302-3

Mortgages by lender type and related to neighborhood characteristics, for Boston, Mass, 1982-87, article, 9373-1.915

New England States, banks, thrifts, and financial statements by type of instn and Fed deposit insurance, and State, 1987, annual rpt, 9304-3

New England States, FHLB 1st District thrift instns, financial condition, and locations, 1989, annual listing, 9304-26

New England States, FHLB 1st District thrift instns financial operations and housing industry indicators, monthly rpt, 9302-4

North Central States economic conditions, Fed Reserve 9th District, quarterly rpt, 9383-18

North Central States, FHLB 6th District insured S&Ls financial condition and operations by State, quarterly rpt, 9302-23

North Central States, FHLB 6th District savings instns financial condition and operations by State, monthly rpt, 9302-11

North Central States, FHLB 7th District and natl cost of funds indexes for savings instns, and mortgage rates, monthly rpt, 9302-30

North Central States, FHLB 7th District insured thrifts, offices, and savings, by county, 1986-87, annual rpt, 9304-5

North Central States, FHLB 8th District S&Ls, locations, assets, and savings, 1989, annual listing, 9304-9

North Central States, FHLB 8th District savings instns financial operations by State and SMSA, monthly rpt, 9302-9

Occupational injury and illness rates, by SIC 2- to 4-digit industry, 1987, annual rpt, 6844-1

Ohio savings instns crisis impact on certificates of deposit interest rates, 1983-85, technical paper, 9316-1.153

Regulatory issues for savings instns, 1988 annual conf, 9304-24

Science and engineering employment, by nonmanufacturing industry and field, 1987, triennial rpt, 9627-31

Securities (tax-exempt) holdings by investor type, and IRS enforcement of disallowance of interest deduction for financing holdings, mid 1970s-87, GAO rpt, 26119-239

Securities for subordinated debt issued by savings instns and banks, 1986-89, article, 9312-1.906

South Central States, FHLB 9th District savings instns finances and operations by State, monthly rpt, 9302-13

South Central States, FHLB 9th District savings instns finances and operations by State, quarterly rpt, 9302-31

Southeastern States, Fed Reserve 5th District, economic indicators by State, quarterly rpt, 9389-16

Southeastern States, FHLB 4th District savings instns finances and financial ratios, by State, quarterly rpt, 9302-3

Southeastern States, FHLB 4th District thrifts finances, by State, 1984-88 annual rpt series, 9304-29

Southeastern States savings instns, industry review, periodic journal, 9302-2

Southeastern States savings instns performance, and financial and economic devs, FHLB of Cincinnati quarterly journal, discontinued, 9302-29

Statistical Abstract of US, social, political, and economic data, 1790-2025, comprehensive annual compilation, 2324-1.3

Tax (income) returns of corporations, income and tax items by asset size and detailed industry, 1986, annual rpt, 8304-4; 8304-21

Trust assets of banks, trust companies, and S&Ls, by type of asset and fund, selected firm, and State, 1988, annual rpt, 13004-1

West Central States, FHLB 10th District savings instns finances and lending by State and MSA, monthly table, 9302-22

West Central States, FHLB 10th District savings instns financial condition, by State, quarterly rpt, 9302-34

West Central States, FHLB 10th District savings instns, locations, assets, and savings, 1989, annual listing, 9304-17

Western States, FHLB 11th District S&Ls, offices, and financial condition, 1989 annual listing, 9304-23

Western States, FHLB 11th District thrift offices, locations, savings balances, and accounts, quarterly listing, 9302-20

Western States, FHLB 12th District savings instns deposits and lending by State, monthly press release series, 9302-32

see also Mortgages

see also By Industry in the "Index by Categories"

Savitz, David A.
"Self-Reported Exposure to Pesticides and Radiation Related to Pregnancy Outcome: Results from National Natality and Fetal Mortality Surveys", 4042-3.945

SBA
see Small Business Administration

Scabies
see Infective and parasitic diseases

Scales and balances
see Instruments and measuring devices
see Scientific equipment and apparatus

Scaling, Wilson
"Implementing the 'Conservation Compliance,' 'Sodbuster,' and 'Swampbuster' Provisions of the 1985 Farm Bill", 1004-16.1

Schaible, Glenn D.
"Irrigated Acreage in the Conservation Reserve Program", 1588-143

Schallau, Con H
"Mississippi's Forest Products Industry: Performance and Contribution to the State's Economy, 1970-80", 1206-36.13

Schantz, Peter M.
"Trichinosis Surveillance, U.S., 1986", 4202-7.901

Schatzkin, Arthur
"Is Alcohol Consumption Related to Breast Cancer? Results from the Framingham Heart Study", 4472-1.902

Schaub, James D.
"Peanuts: Background for 1990 Farm Legislation", 1566-7.8

Schenectady, N.Y.
see also under By SMSA or MSA in the "Index by Categories"

Schenk, Christopher J.
"Bitumen-Bearing Deposits of the U.S.", 5668-88

Scheuren, Fritz
"Individual Income Tax Shares and Average Tax Rates, Tax Years 1916-50", 8302-2.913
"Individual Income Tax Shares and Average Tax Rates, Tax Years 1951-86", 8302-2.919

Schlegel, T. T.
"Comparison of Protective Breathing Equipment Performance at Ground Level and 8,000 Feet Altitude Using Parameters Prescribed by Portions of FAA Action Notice A-8150.2", 7506-10.62

Schmidt, D. R.
"Nearshore Fish Survey in the Western Beaufort Sea: Harrison Bay to Elson Lagoon", 2176-1.29

Schmidt, Ronald H.
"Natural Resources and Regional Growth", 9393-8.909

Schmitt, Charles
"Changes in Educational Attainment: Comparison Among 1972, 1980, and 1982 High School Seniors", 4848-36

Schneider, Don P.
"Case Mix for Nursing Home Payment: Resource Utilization Groups, Version II", 4652-1.910

Schnorbus, Robert H.
"New Approach to Regional Capital Stock Estimation: Measurement and Performance", 9375-13.13

Schoenborn, Charlotte A.
"Smoking and Other Tobacco Use: U.S., 1987", 4147-10.169

Scholarships
see Student aid

Scholastic Aptitude Test
see Educational tests

Scholl, Russell B.
"International Investment Position of the U.S. in 1988", 2702-1.922

School administration and staff
Black colleges R&D funding by source, and characteristics of grad students and research staff, by field of science and instn, 1980s-87, 9628-78

Community organizations partnerships with public schools, participation, activities, and contributions, by school characteristics and location, 1987/88, 4826-1.27

Condition of Education, detailed data on elementary and secondary education, 1920s-88 and projected to 1997, annual rpt, 4824-1.1

County Business Patterns, 1987: employment, establishments, and payroll, by SIC 2- to 4-digit industry and county, annual State rpt series, 2326-8

Digest of Education Statistics, detailed data on students, staff, finances, and facilities, 1989 edition, annual rpt, 4824-2

DOD Dependents Schools and Uniformed Services University of Health Sciences civilian and military personnel, quarterly rpt, 3542-14.1

Effective schools programs for improving academic achievement, characteristics of schools, districts, and students, 1987/88, GAO rpt, 26121-304

High school class of 1972: education, employment, and family characteristics, activities, and attitudes, natl longitudinal study, series, 4836-1

High school class of 1972: postsecondary enrollment, transfers, and completions, by selected characteristics, 1972-84, natl longitudinal study, 4836-1.12

High school class of 1980: postsecondary enrollment, transfers, part-time attendance, degrees, and dropouts, by selected characteristics, 1980-86, natl longitudinal study, 4826-2.50

High school class of 1988: college enrollment, and labor force participation of grads and dropouts, by race and sex, press release, 6726-1.22

High school classes of 1972 and 1980: enrollment in 2-year colleges, credits earned and dropout rate, by student characteristics, as of 1984, 4848-38

High school dropout rates, and subsequent completion, by student and school characteristics, alternative estimates, 1988, annual rpt, 4834-23

Homeless and runaway youth programs, funding, activities, and participant characteristics, FY86, annual rpt, 4604-3

Income (household) and poverty status under alternative income definitions, by recipient characteristics, 1986, Current Population Rpt, 2546-6.58

Job Training Partnership Act occupational training and other services provision, and outcomes, by participant characteristics, 1982-86, GAO rpt, 26106-8.8

Job Training Partnership Act participants and eligible population, by selected characteristics, 1986, 15496-1.3

Mexican American high school dropouts health condition, substance abuse, and involvement with violence, 1988-89 survey, article, 4042-3.957

Reading ability and literacy of young adults, relation to educational attainment and race, natl assessment, 1985, 4828-36

Science and engineering education enrollment, degrees, and student aid and sources, with data by field, race, sex, and instn, 1980s-87, 26358-202

Special education programs, enrollment by age, staff, funding, and needs, by type of handicap and State, 1987/88, annual rpt, 4944-4

Statistical Abstract of US, social, political, and economic data, 1790-2025, comprehensive annual compilation, 2324-1.1

see also Educational retention rates

School enrollment
see Educational enrollment

School finance
see Educational finance
see Tuition and fees

School lunch and breakfast programs

CCC dairy price support program foreign donations and domestic donations to poor, schools, Prisons Bur, and VA, monthly rpt, 1802-2

Community organizations partnerships with public schools, participation, activities, and contributions, by school characteristics and location, 1987/88, 4826-1.27

Consumer research, food marketing, legislation, and regulation devs, and consumption and price trends, quarterly journal, 1541-7

Effective schools programs for improving academic achievement, characteristics of schools, districts, and students, 1987/88, GAO rpt, 26121-304

Elementary and secondary public schools, enrollment and other characteristics, for top 55 districts, 1987-88, annual rpt, 4834-22

Eligibility for free lunch, share of enrollment by State, 1987/88, annual rpt, 4834-17

Expenditures for education by Federal agency, program, and recipient type, and instn spending, FY80-88, 4828-21

Fed Govt financial and nonfinancial domestic aid, 1989 base edition with supplements, annual listing, 104-5

Income (household) and poverty status under alternative income definitions, by recipient characteristics, 1986, Current Population Rpt, 2546-6.58

Milk order market sales, by container size and type, outlet type, and market area, 1987, biennial rpt, 1317-6

Participation and costs of USDA food aid programs, by program, region, and State, monthly rpt, 1362-14

PL 480 exports by commodity, and recipients, by program, sponsor, and country, FY87 and cumulative from FY55, annual rpt, 1924-7

Statistical Abstract of US, social, political, and economic data, 1790-2025, comprehensive annual compilation, 2324-1.2

USDA child nutrition programs evaluation, 1988, biennial narrative rpt, 14854-1

USDA child nutrition programs funding, by program and State, FY86-88, annual rpt, 4824-2.27

West Virginia poverty conditions, food aid participants, and birth outcomes, 1980-87, hearing, 21968-49

Schools
see Educational facilities
see Private schools
see terms listed under Education and beginning with School

Schreiber, Richard K.
"Artificial Intelligence Applications in the IRS", 8304-8.1

Schultz, Hyman
"Analyses of Tipple and Delivered Samples of Coal Collected During FY85", 3004-15

Schulz, Carl O.
"Review of Literature on Herbicides, Including Phenoxy Herbicides and Associated Dioxins. Volume XI: Analysis of Recent Literature on Health Effects Published in 1987; Volume XII: Annotated Bibliography of Recent Literature on Health Effects", 8706-1.1

Schur, Claudia L.
"Health Insurance Coverage of Retired Persons. National Medical Expenditure Survey", 4186-8.2

Schuster, Ervin G.
"Predicting Timber Sale Costs from Sale Characteristics in the Intermountain West", 1208-298

Science and technology

NSF grants and contracts, by field, inst, State, and country, FY88, annual rpt, 9624-26

NSF rpts, 1989 annual listing, 9624-16

NSF Science Resources Studies Div project descriptions and rpts, 1988 annual listing, 9624-21

Standards and Technology Natl Inst rpts, 1988, annual listing, 2214-1

Statistical Abstract of US, social, political, and economic data, 1790-2025, comprehensive annual compilation, 2324-1.3

see also Agricultural sciences and research
see also Astronomy
see also Atmospheric sciences
see also Aviation sciences
see also Biological sciences
see also Biotechnology
see also Botany
see also Chemistry
see also Computer sciences
see also Defense research
see also Department of Energy National Laboratories
see also Earth sciences
see also Educational research
see also Educational technology
see also Energy research and development
see also Engineers and engineering
see also Environmental sciences
see also Federal aid to medicine
see also Federal funding for energy programs
see also Federal funding for research and development
see also Federally Funded R&D Centers
see also Forensic sciences
see also Genetics
see also Information sciences
see also International cooperation in science and technology
see also Inventions
see also Mathematics
see also Medical research
see also Medicine
see also Meteorology
see also Military science
see also Oceanography
see also Physical sciences
see also Physics
see also Physiology
see also Psychology
see also Research
see also Research and development
see also Scientific education
see also Scientific equipment and apparatus
see also Scientific ethics
see also Scientists and technicians
see also Social sciences
see also Space programs
see also Space sciences
see also Technological innovations
see also Technology transfer
see also Zoology

Scientific education

Assistance (financial and nonfinancial) of Fed Govt, 1989 base edition with supplements, annual listing, 104-5

Black colleges R&D funding by source, and characteristics of grad students and research staff, by field of science and instn, 1980s-87, 9628-78

Condition of Education, detailed data on elementary, secondary, and higher education, 1920s-88 and projected to 1997, annual rpt, 4824-1

Natl park system visits and overnight stays, by park and State, monthly rpt, 5542–4

Natl park system visits and overnight stays, by park and State, 1988 and trends from 1979, annual rpt, 5544–12

Plastic, tar, and other nondegradable ocean and beach debris, incidence and environmental impacts, 1970s-88, 14738–4

Pollution (water) incidents and discharges, by type, source, cause, and location, 1984-86, annual rpt, 7404–3

Wildlife-related recreation, hunting, and fishing participation and spending, detailed data by location, 1985 survey, quinquennial rpt, 5508–5

Seaside, Calif.

Housing vacancy rates for single and multifamily units and mobile homes, by city and ZIP code, 1988, annual MSA rpt, 9304–20.4

see also under By SMSA or MSA in the "Index by Categories"

Seasonal adjustment factors

Balance of payments, seasonal adjustment statistical discrepancy, monthly rpt, 23842–1.7

Construction put in place, value of new public and private structures, by type, monthly rpt, 2382–4

Electric power demand related to economic dev and weather, by census div, model results, quarterly 1977-85, 3028–2

Employment, earnings, and hours benchmarks by SIC 2- to 4-digit industry, 1981-88, and revised seasonal adjustment factors by major industry group, 1989, semiannual article, 6742–2.903

Employment, earnings, and hours, by SIC 1- to 4-digit industry, monthly 1983-Feb 1989, annual rpt, 6744–4

Employment, earnings, and hours seasonal adjustment factors by major industry group, Oct 1989-Mar 1990, semiannual article, 6742–2.905

Employment situation, earnings, hours, and other BLS economic indicators, transcripts of BLS Commissioner's monthly testimony, periodic rpt, 23846–4

Housing starts, by units per structure and metro-nonmetro location, and mobile home placements and prices, by region, monthly rpt, 2382–1

Housing units (1-family) sold and for sale by price, stage of construction, months on market, and region, monthly rpt, 2382–3

Housing units authorized, by region, State, selected MSA, and permit-issuing place, monthly rpt, 2382–5

Labor force data series of BLS, seasonal adjustment factors, 1989, semiannual article, 6742–2.901; 6742–2.904

Labor force, revised estimates based on 1988 seasonal adjustment factors, monthly 1984-88, annual tables, 6742–2.902

Monetary aggregates and components weekly and monthly Fed Reserve seasonal adjustment factors, monthly rpt with articles, 9362–1

Retail trade sales and inventories, by kind of business, region, and selected State, MSA, and city, monthly rpt, 2413–3

Wholesale trade sales and inventories, by SIC 2- to 3-digit kind of business, monthly rpt, 2413–7

Seasonal and summer employment

see Temporary and seasonal employment

Seasonal variations

Crimes committed, monthly 1984-88, annual rpt, 6224–2.1

Electric and gas utility ratemaking and regulatory standards, status and coverage of consumers and sales, 1988, annual rpt, 3104–7

Energy supply, demand, and prices, forecasts by resource type, quarterly rpt, 3162–34

Fish distribution for coastal southeastern US and Caribbean, by season, species, and location, 1980-82, 2168–112

Great Lakes pollution loadings from nonpoint sources, for Lake Erie and Lake Ontario tributaries, 1982-85, 9208–129

Great Lakes water levels fluctuations, causes, and impacts of alternative mgmt strategies, 1900s-88, series, 14646–1

Statistical Abstract of US, social, political, and economic data, 1790-2025, comprehensive annual compilation, 2324–1.1

Traffic accidents, injuries, and deaths, by circumstances and characteristics of persons and vehicles involved, 1970s-87, series, 7766–14

Weather data by census div and State, historical trends, indexes, major events, and maps, series, 2156–17

see also Business cycles

see also Seasonal adjustment factors

Seat belts

see Motor vehicle safety devices

Seattle, Wash.

Aerospace industry employment and salaries, by sex and race, 1979-87, GAO rpt, 26121–315

AIDS cases, and health and social services availability, for 5 cities, 1988, GAO rpt, 26121–307

CPI by component for US city average, and by region, population size, and for 27 metro areas, monthly rpt, 6762–2

Drug abuse indicators for selected metro areas, research results, data collection, and policy issues, 1989 semiannual conf, 4492–5

Fish and shellfish catch, wholesale receipts, prices, trade, and other market activities, weekly regional rpt, 2162–6.5

Freight (waterborne domestic and foreign) by commodity, traffic, and passengers, by port and waterway, 1987, annual rpt, 3754–3.4

Fruit and vegetable shipments, and arrivals in US and Canada cities, by mode of transport and State and country of origin, 1988, annual rpt, 1311–4.2

Homeless population characteristics by city, and Federal funding by program, 1980s-89, hearings, 21248–123

Housing starts and completions authorized by building permits in 40 MSAs, quarterly rpt, 2382–9

Wages by occupation, and benefits for office and plant workers, 1988 survey, periodic MSA rpt, 6785–11.3

see also under By City and By SMSA or MSA in the "Index by Categories"

SEC

see Securities and Exchange Commission

Secondary education

see Elementary and secondary education

Secret Service

see U.S. Secret Service

Securities

Acquisitions (hostile takeover) defense through repurchase of stock, stock price changes for selected firms, 1985-86, article, 9373–2.901

Acquisitions (leveraged buyout), and stock price and economic impacts, 1960s-88, article, 9391–1.922

Assets and debts of private sector, balance sheets by segment, 1949-88, semiannual rpt, 9365–4.1

Bank holding companies stock market returns relation to nonbanking activities and selected financial ratios, 1979-85, technical paper, 9375–11.20

Bank holding company equity impact of credit and interest rate risk indicators and deposit insurance, 1986-87, technical paper, 9366–6.181; 9366–6.212

Bank holding company securities valuation, impact of new issue announcements by issue type, 1982-86, working paper, 9371–10.34

Bank holding company stock price effects of new issues and capital regulation, 1975-86, article, 9393–8.901

Bank holding company stock prices relative to indexes by instn, and bond and supervisory ratings impact of financial problems, 1970s-80s, article, 9373–1.911

Banking (interstate) laws of States, impacts of changes on bank stock returns, 1988 working paper, 9387–8.174

Banking and financial conditions, 1987, annual rpt, 9364–5

Banks (insured commercial and savings) finances, for foreign and domestic offices, by asset size, 1987, annual rpt, 9294–4.2

Banks (natl) domestic and intl operations, charters, mergers, and liquidations, by instn and State, quarterly rpt, 8402–3

Banks and thrifts in New England, financial statements by type of instn and Fed deposit insurance, and State, 1987, annual rpt, 9304–3

Banks in Fed Reserve System, expenses and operations itemized by service, office, and district, 1988, annual rpt, 9364–11

Banks market value accounting proposal, with assets and liabilities composition, loan ratios, and securities book and market value, 1984-88, working paper, 9389–19.12

Banks stock price and trading impact of loan-loss reserve additions, with data by instn, 1987, working paper, 9387–8.186

Banks stock returns for instns involved in acquisitions, 1982-87, technical paper, 9366–6.178

Budget of US, CBO analysis of revenue and spending alternatives and projections of economic indicators, FY90-94, annual rpt, 26304–3

Business Conditions Digest, economic, business, and financial devs and cyclical fluctuations, monthly rpt, 2702–3

Business statistics, detailed data for major industries and economic indicators, *Survey of Current Business*, monthly rpt, 2702–1.6

Savings instns, FHLB 9th District members finances and operations by State, quarterly rpt, 9302–31

Savings instns finances and operations by district and State, mortgage lending activity and terms by MSA, and FHLB finances, 1987 with trends from 1900, annual rpt, 9314–3

Savings instns financial statements, FSLIC-insured instns by FHLB district and State, and FDIC-insured savings banks, 1988, annual rpt, 8434–1

Savings instns insured by Savings Assn Insurance Fund, assets, liabilities, and deposit and loan activity, by conservatorship status, monthly rpt, 8432–1

Savings instns regulatory issues, mgmt, and FHLB system and member finances and operations, monthly journal, 8432–2; 9312–1

SEC activities, securities industry finances, and exchange activity, selected years 1935-88, annual rpt, 9734–2

Small business capital formation sources, 1988 annual conf, 9734–4

Small business financing sources, and business financial data by size, type, and industry, various periods 1980-88, annual rpt, 9764–6.2

Southeastern States, Fed Reserve 5th District insured commercial banks financial statements, by State, quarterly rpt, 9389–18

Southeastern States, Fed Reserve 8th District banking and economic conditions, quarterly rpt with articles, 9391–16

State and local govt retirement systems, cash and security holdings and finances, quarterly rpt, 2462–2

Statistical Abstract of US, social, political, and economic data, 1790-2025, comprehensive annual compilation, 2324–1.3

Steel industry bond ratings, by selected producer, various dates 1982-88, last issue of annual rpt, 9884–16

Tax (income) returns of corporations, income and tax items by asset size and detailed industry, 1986, annual rpt, 8304–4; 8304–21

Telephone and telegraph firms detailed finances and operations, 1987, annual rpt, 9284–6

Trust assets of banks, trust companies, and S&Ls, by type of asset and fund, selected firm, and State, 1988, annual rpt, 13004–1

UK and France govt-owned corporations stock issues, value, new shareholders, and revenue effects, 1960s-88, article, 9385–1.911

Venture capital-backed securities offerings by industry div, and venture capital firms financing by source, 1975-88, article, 9373–1.914

West Central States, Fed Reserve 10th District depository instns deposits, loans, investments, and borrowings, monthly rpt, 9381–2

West Central States, Fed Reserve 10th District depository instns financial activity by State, and large commercial banks by city, monthly rpt, 9381–11

Yields, interest rates, prices, and offerings, by type of bond and issuing sector, selected years 1929-88, annual rpt, 204–1.5; 204–1.7

Yields on corporate, Treasury, and municipal long-term bonds, *Treasury Bulletin*, quarterly rpt, 8002–4.8

Yields on govt and private issues, weekly rpt, 9391–4

Yields on stock, relation to inflation and monetary policy, 1969-87, technical paper, 9379–12.37

see also American Stock Exchange
see also Foreign investments
see also Government securities
see also Municipal bonds
see also Mutual funds
see also New York Stock Exchange
see also Options trading
see also Stockbrokers
see also Tax exempt securities
see also U.S. savings bonds

Securities and Exchange Commission

Activities of SEC, securities industry finances, and exchange activity, selected years 1935-FY88, annual rpt, 9734–2

Budget of US Appendix, obligations, appropriations, and personnel, by program and agency, FY90, annual rpt, 104–3

Budget of US, authoritative financial statements with appropriations, outlays, and receipts, by category and agency, FY88, annual rpt, 8104–2.2

Corporations required to file annual rpts with SEC, as of Sept 1988, annual listing, 9734–5

Employment discrimination complaints, and awards by funding source, for 3 Federal agencies, FY87-88, GAO rpt, 26121–313

Employment, pay, and turnover of SEC by occupation and city, with proposed fee revenues to improve work conditions, 1989 hearing, 21368–116

Labor unions recognized in Fed Govt, agreements and membership by agency and facility, as of Jan 1989, biennial listing, 9844–14

Securities purchases, sales, and holdings, by issuer and type and ownership of security, monthly listing, 9732–2

Small business capital formation sources, 1988 annual conf, 9734–4

Stock market transactions, and new issue registrations, monthly rpt, 9732–1

Securities exchange
see American Stock Exchange
see New York Stock Exchange
see Stock exchanges

Security clearance
see Internal security

Security services
see Detective and protective services
see Internal security

Sedatives
see Drug abuse and treatment
see Drugs

Sedberry, George R.
"Species Composition, Distribution, and Relative Abundance of Fishes in the Coastal Habitat off the Southeastern U.S.", 2168–112

Sedition
see Subversive activities
see Underground movements

Seeds

Agricultural Statistics, 1988, annual rpt, 1004–1

Agriculture census, 1987: farms, farmland, production, finances, and operator characteristics, by county, final State rpt series, 2331–1

Cooperatives commercial member characteristics, and use of services, by region, 1980 and 1986, 1128–53

Costs of production, receipts, and returns, itemized by selected commodity and region, 1975-87, 1548–345

Eastern Europe agricultural production, consumption, and trade, by country, 1970s-88, annual rpt, 1524–11

Exports and imports (agricultural) commodity and country, prices, and world market devs, monthly rpt, 1922–12

Exports and imports (agricultural) of US, by commodity and country, bimonthly rpt with articles, 1522–1

Exports and imports (agricultural) of US, by detailed commodity and country, 1988, semiannual rpt, 1522–4

Exports of seeds, by type, world region, and country, FAS quarterly rpt, 1925–13

Exports of US, detailed commodities by country, monthly rpt, 2422–3

Farm finances and operations, by size, commodity, and region, 1986, annual rpt, 1544–27

Farm finances, receipts by commodity, other income, expenses, assets, liabilities, and ratios, 1988, annual rpt, 1544–16

Farm production inputs supply, demand, and prices, 1970s-88 and projected to 1993, articles, 1561–16.901

Farm production itemized costs, by farm sales size and region, 1988, annual rpt, 1614–3

Farm production itemized costs, receipts, and returns, by commodity and region, 1985-87, annual rpt, 1544–20

Farm production itemized costs, receipts, and returns, by crop and State, preliminary 1987, annual rpt, 1544–24

Farm sector balance sheet, and marketing receipts by detailed commodity, by State, 1984-88, annual rpt, 1544–18

Farm sector finances, income sources, expenses by type, assets, debts, and ratios, 1983-87, annual rpt, 1544–19

Feed production, acreage, stocks, use, trade, prices, and price supports, periodic situation rpt with articles, 1561–4

Imports of US, detailed Schedule A commodities by country, monthly rpt, 2422–2

Irrigation projects of Reclamation Bur in western US, crop production and acreage by commodity, State, and project, 1987, annual rpt, 5824–12.1

Manufacturing census, 1987: financial and operating data, for SIC 4-digit industries by product, preliminary rpt, 2491–1.6

Potato production, prices, stocks, and use, by State, 1986-88, annual rpt, 1621–11

Prices received and paid by farmers, by commodity and State, 1988, annual rpt, 1629–5

Prices received by farmers for major products, and paid for farm inputs and living items, by State, monthly rpt, 1629–1

Production, farms, acreage, and related data, by selected crop and State, monthly rpt, 1621-1

Wheat (durum) acreage, production, prices, stocks, use, and US and Canada exports by country, quarterly rpt, 1313-6

see also Oils, oilseeds, and fats

Segregation

see Discrimination in education

see Discrimination in housing

see School busing

Seizures

see Searches and seizures

Seldovia, Alaska

Tide height and time daily at coastal points, forecast 1990, annual rpt, 2174-2.1

Selective service

Registrants by State, 2nd half FY88, semiannual rpt, 9742-1

see also Draft evasion and protest

see also Voluntary military service

Selective Service System

Activities of SSS, and registrants by State, 2nd half FY88, semiannual rpt, 9742-1

Budget of US Appendix, obligations, appropriations, and personnel, by program and agency, FY90, annual rpt, 104-3

Budget of US, authoritative financial statements with appropriations, outlays, and receipts, by category and agency, FY88, annual rpt, 8104-2.2

Labor unions recognized in Fed Govt, agreements and membership by agency and facility, as of Jan 1989, biennial listing, 9844-14

Selenium

see Nonmetallic minerals and mines

Self-employment

AFDC recipients demographic and financial characteristics, by State, FY87, annual rpt, 4694-1

Census of Population and Housing, 1990: data item selection, questionnaire dev, and testing, 2626-11.3

Consumer spending and income effects of wives' employment, by expenditure category and household characteristics, 1984-86, article, 6722-1.908

Disability Insurance beneficiaries health insurance coverage, by type and selected beneficiary characteristics, fall 1982, article, 4742-1.927

Disabled persons employment, labor force status, and other characteristics, 1988, Current Population Rpt, 2546-2.147

Employment and Earnings, detailed data, monthly rpt, 6742-2

Employment and occupation of householder, by occupation of spouse, race, and family composition, 1988, annual Current Population Rpt, 2546-1.437

Employment conditions, alternative BLS projections to 2000 and trends 1970s-88, biennial article, 6722-1.955

Employment, earnings, and hours, monthly press release, 6742-5

Employment situation, earnings, hours, and other BLS economic indicators, transcripts of BLS Commissioner's monthly testimony, periodic rpt, 23846-4

Farm labor, wages, hours, and perquisites, by State, quarterly rpt, 1631-1

Farm population, by employment and socioeconomic characteristics, and region, 1988, annual Current Population Rpt, 2546-1.439

Handbook of Labor Statistics, employment, unemployment, and labor force characteristics, 1940s-88 with trends from 1913, 6728-38

Hispanic Americans socioeconomic characteristics, by detailed origin, 1988, Current Population Rpt, 2546-1.430; 2546-1.438

Income (household) by source, and itemized spending, by selected characteristics and location, 1984-86 Consumer Expenditure Surveys, annual rpt, 6764-5.2

Income (household, family, and personal), by source, detailed characteristics, and region, 1987, annual Current Population Rpt, 2546-6.59

Insurance (health) coverage of total and working population, by selected characteristics, 1987, 4186-8.1

Mexico labor supply and conditions, with data by major city, selected years 1969-88, working paper, 2326-18.49

Moonlighting employment, by worker and primary and secondary job characteristics and reason, 1989, press release, 6726-1.24

Natl income and product accounts and components, *Survey of Current Business*, monthly rpt, 2702-1.27

OASDHI admin, and SSA activities, 1930s-89 and projected to 2063, data compilation, annual rpt, 4704-12

OASDHI coverage of employment and earnings, late 1930s-87, annual rpt, 4744-3.1; 4744-3.2

OASDI and Hospital Insurance tax rates for self-employed, 1988-89 and projected to 1990, article, 4742-1.921

OASDI benefit payments, trust fund finances, and economic and demographic assumptions, 1970-87 and alternative projections to 1997, actuarial rpt, 4706-1.103

Pension and health insurance coverage for full- and part-time workers, 1985, article, 6722-1.913

Poverty status of families and persons, by detailed characteristics, 1987, annual Current Population Rpt, 2546-6.60

Science and engineering employment characteristics, by field, 1988, biennial rpt, 9627-16

Science and engineering PhDs, by field, instn, employment prospects, sex, race, and other characteristics, 1960s-88, 9627-30

Small business finances, operations, owner and employee characteristics, and Federal contracts, 1980s-88, annual rpt, 9764-6

Statistical Abstract of US, social, political, and economic data, 1790-2025, comprehensive annual compilation, 2324-1.3

Tax (income) and other Fed Govt finances, selected years 1929-90, annual rpt, 10044-1.1

Tax (income) returns of individuals, by filing status, tax item, and income level, 1987, annual article, 8302-2.901

Tax (income) returns of individuals, detailed data, 1986, annual rpt, 8304-2

Telephone service of households, by composition, income sources, and other characteristics, 1984-87, 9288-11

Voting and registration, by socioeconomic and demographic characteristics, 1988 presidential election, biennial Current Population Rpt, 2546-1.440

Selma, Ala.

Wages by occupation, for office and plant workers, 1989 survey, periodic MSA rpt, 6785-3.9

Semiconductors

see Computer industry and products

see Electronics industry and products

Senate

Budget of US Appendix, obligations, appropriations, and personnel, by program and agency, FY90, annual rpt, 104-3

Budget of US, authoritative financial statements with appropriations, outlays, and receipts, by category and agency, FY88, annual rpt, 8104-2.2

Buildings and grounds under Capitol Architect supervision, itemized outlays by payee and function, 1st half FY89, semiannual rpt, 25922-2

Congressional Directory, members of 101st Congress, other officials, elections, and districts, 1989-90, biennial rpt, 23874-1

Election campaign finances and FEC activities, various periods 1975-88, annual rpt, 9274-1

Election campaign financial activity reported to FEC, by type of filer, 1988 natl elections, biennial rpt series, 9276-2

Election campaign funds raised and spent by party committees, by candidate, 1988, press release, 9276-1.64

Election campaign receipts and spending of congressional candidates, by candidate, 1987-88, press release, 9276-1.62; 9276-1.63

Election campaign receipts and spending of senatorial candidates, by party and State, 1989/90, press release, 9276-1.68

Finances of Senate, receipts, itemized expenses by payee, and balances, 1st half FY89, semiannual listing, 25922-1

Statistical Abstract of US, social, political, and economic data, 1790-2025, comprehensive annual compilation, 2324-1.2

Votes cast by party, candidate, and State, 1988 natl elections, biennial rpt, 9274-5; 21944-3

see also Senate Documents

see also Senate Special Publications

see also under names of individual committees (starting with Senate or Joint)

see also under names of individual subcommittees (starting with Subcommittee)

Senate Aging Committee, Special

Assistance of Fed Govt to aged, policies, and issues of aging, 1989 annual rpt, 25144-3

Older persons socioeconomic characteristics, 1900s-86 and projected to 2050, biennial chartbook, 12904-1

Rural areas health care facilities, staffing, services accessibility, and indicators of need, 1960s-88, 25148-41

Rural areas hospitals, use, staff, and funding sources, by instn characteristics, 1980s-86, hearing, 25148-42

Senate Agriculture and Forestry Committee
see Senate Agriculture, Nutrition, and Forestry Committee

Senate Agriculture, Nutrition, and Forestry Committee
Conservation of soil and wetlands, USDA programs costs and impacts on farm finances and operations, with background data, 1980s, hearing, 25168–69
Drought of 1988, impacts on food prices by selected item and city, hearing, 25168–71
Stock market crash of 1987, market performance, foreign futures market activity, and computer-aided trading impacts on price variability, 1980s-88, hearings, 25168–70

Senate Banking, Housing, and Urban Affairs Committee
Developing countries debt burden and economic conditions, and trade with industrialized countries, by country, 1970s-87, hearings, 25248–108
Fed Reserve monetary policy objectives and US and foreign economic indicators, 1988 hearing, 25248–109
Housing unit costs and homeownership rates, by income, age, family composition, and region, 1967-87, hearings, 25248–107

Senate Budget Committee
Budget of US, Senate concurrent resolution, with spending and revenue targets, FY90, annual rpt, 25254–1
Savings and loan assns failure resolution costs, and FSLIC finances and promissory notes issued, with data by instn, FY80s and projected to FY99, hearing, 25258–22

Senate Commerce, Science and Transportation Committee
Soviet Union space program activities, plans, and characteristics of flights and vehicles, 1981-87, 25268–76

Senate Documents
Capitol Architect outlays for salaries, supplies, and services, itemized by payee and function, 1st half FY89, semiannual rpt, 25922–2
Finances of Senate, receipts, itemized expenses by payee, and balances, 1st half FY89, semiannual listing, 25922–1
Older persons social security issues, Fed Govt spending, and indicators of need, with bibl, 1988 compilation of papers, 25928–7
Prison conditions, population, and problems, issues and bibl, 1989 compilation of papers, 25928–8

Senate Energy and Natural Resources Committee
Carbon dioxide and other pollutants in atmosphere, effects on climate, sea levels, and solar radiation, 1989 hearing, 25318–75

Senate Finance Committee
Foreign countries economic conditions, policy, and trade practices, by country, 1986-88, annual rpt, 21384–5
Insurance (health) provided by employer, coverage and characteristics of plan and employer, 1986-87, hearing, 25368–160
Medicare catastrophic illness coverage and premium collection, effects of revisions on Federal budget and enrollees, projected 1989-93, 25368–161

Tax expenditures, Federal revenues forgone through income tax deductions and exclusions by type, FY90-94, annual rpt, 21784–10

Senate Foreign Relations Committee
Diplomats and staff with immunity for foreign missions in US and US missions abroad, and foreign diplomats criminal cases, 1978-87, hearing, 25388–51
Economic conditions, policy, and trade practices, by country, 1986-88, annual rpt, 21384–5
Human rights conditions in 170 countries, 1988, annual rpt, 21384–3

Senate Governmental Affairs Committee
Census of Population and Housing, 1990: data collection procedure, and impacts on congressional apportionment by State, hearing, 25408–101
Labs (clinical) under HCFA regulation, and labs with violations by Medicare termination and license status, 1983-87, hearings, 25408–98
Regulatory costs by agency, reform proposals, and environmental regulation costs to govts and businesses, 1988 hearings, 25408–99
Superconductivity (high temperature) R&D spending by Federal agency, and US and Japan industry funding and employment, by application, 1981-89, hearing, 25408–100

Senate Human Resources Committee
see Senate Labor and Human Resources Committee

Senate Judiciary Committee
Airline computer reservation systems operating costs, fees, and market shares, by firm and location, 1984-87, hearing, 25528–108

Senate Labor and Human Resources Committee
Child care leave of absence for employees, policies, coverage, and attitudes, by employee characteristics, 1980-87, hearings, 25548–95
Mississippi hospitals and community health centers, use, staff, and Medicare and other payments, 1988 hearing, 25548–97
Student guaranteed loan defaults, rates, and borrowers in repayment status, by instn and State, FY86, with background data, 1980s, hearings, 25548–96

Senate Labor and Public Welfare Committee
see Senate Labor and Human Resources Committee

Senate Small Business Committee
Rural areas high-technology employment, by industry div and size of firm, and compared to urban areas, selected years 1972-86, hearing, 25728–41

Senate Special Publications
Capitol Architect activities, funding, costs, and contracts, FY86, annual rpt, 25944–1

Senate Veterans Affairs Committee
Board of Veterans Appeals caseloads and dispositions, 1988 hearing, 25768–47
Health care facilities physicians staffing, and rehabilitation programs admin and effectiveness, for VA, 1988 hearing, 25768–48
Mental illness (post-traumatic stress) cases of Vietnam veterans, claims, and VA disposition, 1985-88, hearing, 25768–46

Senegal
Agricultural and food production and indexes, total and for selected commodities, by country, 1970s-88, annual rpt, 1524–12
Agricultural exports of Africa by commodity, and relation to economic conditions and other factors, by country, 1960s-87, 1528–280
Agricultural imports and food aid needs under alternative weather assumptions, for 17 African countries, projected to 1995, 1528–279
Agricultural production, prices, and trade, by country, 1960s-89, annual world region rpt, 1524–4.2
Agricultural trade of US, by detailed commodity and country, 1988, semiannual rpt, 1522–4
AID activities and funding by project and function, FY90, and developing countries summary socioeconomic data from 1960s, annual rpt, 9904–4.5
AID economic aid to developing countries, obligations and disbursements by country, quarterly rpt, 9912–4
AID loans repayment status and terms by program and country, and status of predecessor agency loans, quarterly rpt, 9912–3
Economic and military aid and loans from US and intl agencies, by program and country, FY46-87, annual rpt, 9914–5
Economic conditions, policy, and trade practices, by country, 1986-88, annual rpt, 21384–5
Economic, social, political, and geographic summary data, by country, 1989, annual factbook, 9114–2
Food supply indicators for Sahel, by country, 1960s-2000, 1528–290
Human rights conditions in 170 countries, 1988, annual rpt, 21384–3
Military aid of US, arms sales, and training programs costs and budget requests, by program, world region, and country, FY88-90, annual rpt, 7144–13
Military spending, arms trade, and force strengths, with govt spending and population, by country, 1977-87, annual rpt, 9824–1
Minerals Yearbook, 1987, Vol 3 preprints: foreign country review of production, trade, and policy, by commodity, annual rpt, 5604–23.82
Population size, growth rates, and components of change, by country, projected 1989-2020 and trends from 1950, biennial rpt, 2324–9
UN voting record and share of votes in agreement with US, by issue, country, and world area, 1988, annual rpt, 7004–18
see also under By Foreign Country in the "Index by Categories"

Senior citizens
see Aged and aging

Senser, Robert A.
"How Poland's Solidarity Won Freedom of Association", 6722–1.947

Sentences, criminal procedure
AFDC fraud cases, referrals, and disposition, by State, FY87, annual rpt, 4694–7.5
Assaults and deaths of law enforcement officers, by circumstances, agency, victim and offender characteristics, and location, 1988, annual rpt, 6224–3

Employment, earnings, and hours, monthly press release, 6742–5

Employment in nonmanufacturing industries, by detailed occupation and SIC 2-digit industry, 1987, triennial rpt, 6748–60

Employment of minorities and women, by occupation, SIC 1- to 3- digit industry, State, and MSA, 1986, annual rpt, 9244–1

Employment shifts among industries, factors and impacts on wage growth, with data by industry group, 1948-87, 23848–207

Employment situation, earnings, hours, and other BLS economic indicators, transcripts of BLS Commissioner's monthly testimony, periodic rpt, 23846–4

Employment, unemployment, and labor force characteristics, by region, State, and selected metro area, 1988, annual rpt, 6744–7

Employment, unemployment, and labor force characteristics, Labor Statistics Handbook, 1940s-88 with trends from 1913, 6728–38

Export and import price indexes for goods and services, and dollar exchange rate indexes, quarterly press release, 6762–13

Export-related employment, by industry div, 1980s-87, 2048–103

Exports, imports, and balances of US by commodity group, world area, and country, and related employment, 1970s-88, annual rpt, 2044–26

Exports of goods, services, and investment, trade barriers, impacts, and US actions, by country, 1988, annual rpt, 444–2

Finances and operations, by SIC 2- to 4-digit industry, forecast 1989 with trends from 1950s, annual rpt, 2044–28

Foreign direct investment in US, major transactions by type, industry, country, and US location, 1987, annual rpt, 2044–20

Foreign direct investment of US, by selected industry group and world area, 1986-88, annual article, 2702–1.930

Guam economic censuses, 1987: employment, firms, payroll, and receipts, by SIC 1- to 4-digit industry and election district, 2595–1

Input-output structure of US economy, detailed interindustry transactions for 84 industries, and components of final demand, 1983, annual article, 2702–1.909

Intl transactions summary, 1980s-88, annual article, 9362–1.904

Japan and US labor force participation by selected characteristics, productivity, and unit labor costs, 1960s-87, article, 6722–1.910

Labor force health condition and services use, by occupation and industry of longest job held, income, age, sex, and race, 1980, 4147–10.168

Labor force supply and mobility, by age, and educational level needs, 1960-86 and projected to 2000, 6306–2.4

Labor hourly costs, by component, occupational group, union coverage, industry div, and region, 1989, annual rpt, 6744–21

Manufacturing annual survey, 1986: exports and export-related employment, by SIC

2-digit industry and State, and compared to 1985, model results, annual rpt, 2506–16.1

Manufacturing census, 1987: financial and operating data, for SIC 4-digit industries by product, preliminary rpt, 2491–1.67

Military post exchange operations, and sales by commodity, by facility and location worldwide, FY87, annual rpt, 3504–10

Multinatl firms US affiliates, finances, and operations, by industry, world area of parent firm, and State, 1987, annual rpt, 2704–4

Multinatl US firms and foreign affiliates finances and operations, by industry of parent firm and affiliate, world area, and country, preliminary 1987, annual rpt, 2704–5

New England States employment, BLS benchmark revisions by industry div and State, 1987-88, article, 9373–2.903

Northern Mariana Islands economic census, 1987: employment, firms, payroll, and receipts, by SIC 1- to 4-digit industry, 2597–1

Occupational injuries, illnesses, and workdays lost, by SIC 2-digit industry, 1987-88, annual press release, 6844–3

Occupational injury and illness rates, by SIC 2- to 4-digit industry, 1987, annual rpt, 6844–1

Price indexes, ITBusiness Conditions Digest, monthly rpt, 2702–3.11

Receipts for services, by SIC 2- to 4-digit kind of business, 1988, annual rpt, 2413–8

Rural areas employment, economic conditions, and population characteristics, 1970s-85, compilation of papers, 1598–243

Science and engineering employment and education, and R&D spending, for US and selected foreign countries, 1988, annual rpt, 9624–23.2

Science and engineering employment, by field and industry div, 1977, 1986, and alternative projections to 2000, 9626–2.181

Science and engineering employment, by nonmanufacturing industry and field, 1987, triennial rpt, 9627–31

SEC registration, firms required to file annual rpts, as of Sept 1988, annual listing, 9734–5

Senate receipts, itemized expenses by payee, and balances, 1st half FY89, semiannual listing, 25922–1

Small business establishments, employment, and financial ratios, by SIC 1- to 2-digit industry and State, late 1960s-87, 9768–19

Small business finances, operations, owner and employee characteristics, and Federal contracts, 1980s-88, annual rpt, 9764–6

Southeastern US industrial output, by major industry group, 1986 with growth since 1963, article, 9391–16.905

Statistical Abstract of US, social, political, and economic data, 1790-2025, comprehensive annual compilation, 2324–1.3

Suburban areas land use, commuting, employment, and housing characteristics, detailed data for traffic planning, 1986, 7888–75

Tax (income) returns filed by type of filer, selected income items, quarterly rpt, 8302–2.1

Tax (income) returns for foreign corporate activity in US, assets, and income statement items, by industry div, country, and world area, 1984-85, article, 8302–2.920

Tax (income) returns of corporations, income and tax items by asset size and detailed industry, 1986, annual rpt, 8304–4; 8304–21

Tax (income) returns of partnerships, income statement items by industry group, 1986, annual article, 8302–2.903

Tax (income) returns of sole proprietorships, income statement items, by industry group, 1987, annual article, 8302–2.904; 8302–2.921

Transportation census, 1987: trucks, by detailed characteristics, miles traveled, and type of product carried, State rpt series, 2573–1

Virgin Islands economic censuses, 1987: employment, firms, payroll, and receipts, by SIC 1- to 4-digit industry, island, and city, 2593–1

Wage and benefit changes from collective bargaining and mgmt decisions, by industry div, monthly rpt, 6782–1

Wage differentials between service and manufacturing sectors related to worker characteristics, 1987, article, 9377–1.901

Wages by occupation, and benefits for office and plant workers, periodic MSA survey rpt series, 6785–11; 6785–12

see also Accounting and auditing

see also Adult day care

see also Advertising

see also Agricultural services

see also Associations

see also Automobile repair and maintenance

see also Barber and beauty shops

see also Census of Service Industries

see also Child day care

see also Consultants

see also Credit bureaus and agencies

see also Detective and protective services

see also Direct marketing

see also Domestic workers and services

see also Franchises

see also Gasoline service stations

see also Health facilities and services

see also Hotels and motels

see also Information services

see also Janitorial and maintenance services

see also Labor unions

see also Laundry and cleaning services

see also Lawyers and legal services

see also Legal aid

see also Membership organizations

see also Motion pictures

see also Museums

see also Nonprofit organizations and foundations

see also Public relations

see also Public services

see also Rental industries

see also Repair industries

see also Service workers

see also Travel agencies

see also under By Industry in the "Index by Categories"

Service stations
see Gasoline service stations

Service workers

Educational attainment, by
sociodemographic characteristics and
location, 1987 and trends from 1940,
biennial Current Population Rpt,
2546–1.427; 2546–1.431

Employment and occupation of householder,
by occupation of spouse, race, and family
composition, 1988, annual Current
Population Rpt, 2546–1.437

Employment Cost Index and alternative
measure of compensation costs, by
component, occupation, industry group,
union status, and location, 1975–89,
annual rpt, 6744–20

Employment, earnings, and hours, monthly
press release, 6742–5

Employment in nonmanufacturing
industries, by detailed occupation and SIC
2-digit industry, 1987, triennial rpt,
6748–60

Employment situation, earnings, hours, and
other BLS economic indicators, transcripts
of BLS Commissioner's monthly
testimony, periodic rpt, 23846–4

Employment, unemployment, and labor
force characteristics, by region, State, and
selected metro area, 1988, annual rpt,
6744–7

Govt services transfer to private contractors,
impacts on govt workers, with data by
worker characteristics, level of govt, and
location, 1980s–87, 15496–1.5

Health condition of labor force, and services
use, by occupation and industry of longest
job held, income, age, sex, and race. 1980,
4147–10.168

Immigrants admitted to US, by occupational
group and country of birth, preliminary
FY88, annual table, 6264–1

Immigration to US, alien workers, visitors,
deportations, and naturalizations, by
country, FY88 and trends from 1820,
annual rpt, 6264–2

Income (household, family, and personal),
by source, detailed characteristics, and
region, 1987, annual Current Population
Rpt, 2546–6.59

Labor hourly costs, by component,
occupational group, union coverage,
industry div, and region, 1989, annual rpt,
6744–21

Minority group and women employment, by
occupation, SIC 1- to 3- digit industry,
State, and MSA, 1986, annual rpt,
9244–1

Occupational changes, by tenure and other
worker characteristics, and labor mobility
rates, 1965–86, article, 6722–1.943

State and local govt employment of
minorities and women, by occupation,
function, pay level, and State, 1986,
annual rpt, 9244–6

Statistical Abstract of US, social, political,
and economic data, 1790-2025,
comprehensive annual compilation,
2324–1.3

see also Area wage surveys
see also Domestic workers and services
see also Health occupations
see also Industry wage surveys
see also Police

see also Service industries
see also under By Occupation in the "Index
by Categories"

Servicepersons life insurance programs

Actuarial analysis of VA life insurance
programs for veterans and servicepersons,
1988, annual rpt, 8604–1

Finances and activities of VA life insurance
programs, FY64-88, annual rpt, 8604–5.3

Finances and coverage of VA life insurance
for veterans and servicepersons, by
program and State, 1988, annual rpt,
8604–4

Finances and operations of VA insurance
programs, FY88 and cumulative from
1965, annual rpt, 8604–3.7

Finances and operations of VA life
insurance programs, monthly rpt,
8602–3; 9922–2

Financial statements and death rates, for
servicepersons and veterans group life
insurance programs, as of June 1989,
annual rpt, 8654–1

Income (personal) by source including
transfer payments, and social insurance
contributions, by region, 1948 and 1987,
2708–40

see also Veterans benefits and pensions

Sesame seed
see Oils, oilseeds, and fats

Set-aside programs
see Agricultural production quotas and price
supports
see Defense contracts and procurement
see Small business

Seth, Rama
"Distributional Issues in Privatization",
9385–1.911

Severance taxes

Coal production and freight costs, and
competitive position in selected markets,
for Australia and US, 1987-89, 2048–143

Energy producers finances and operations,
by energy type for US firms domestic and
foreign operations, 1987, annual rpt,
3164–44

Finances of govts, revenues by source and
spending by function, natl income and
product account, Survey of Current
Business, monthly rpt, 2702–1.24

State and local revenue potential relative to
natl average tax burden, by type of tax
and State, 1986, annual rpt, 10044–7

State govt tax collections by detailed type of
tax, and tax rates, by State, FY88, annual
rpt, 2466–2.3

Statistical Abstract of US, social, political,
and economic data, 1790-2025,
comprehensive annual compilation,
2324–1.2

Sewage and wastewater systems

Army Corps of Engineers activities and
projects, FY87 and trends from 1800s,
annual rpt, 3754–1.2

Assistance (financial and nonfinancial) of
Fed Govt, 1989 base edition with
supplements, annual listing, 104–5

Bond tax-exempt issues for private activity,
by purpose, face value, major industry,
and State, 1986, annual article,
8302–2.905

Budget of US, special analysis of Federal
capital spending by category, projected
FY89-2005 and trends from FY81, annual
rpt, 104–24

Coastal and estuarine pollutant discharges,
by source, pollutant type, and location,
series, 2176–4

Coastal areas environmental impacts of
economic dev and population growth,
1980s and projected to 2000, 2176–8.1

Coastal areas sewage pipelines and
dumpsites authorized, status and EPA
enforcement activities by State, 1982-87,
hearings, 21568–45

Construction industries census, 1987:
establishments, employment, receipts, and
expenditures, by SIC 4-digit industry and
State, final industry rpt series, 2373–1

Construction industries census, 1987:
financial and operating data, preliminary
industry rpt series, 2371–1

Construction material PPI, by construction
industry, monthly rpt, 6762–6

Construction of wastewater treatment and
collection facilities, funding needs and
Federal grants, by State, 1988 and
projected to 2008, biennial rpt, 9204–7

Construction put in place (public and
private), by type, bimonthly rpt,
2042–1.1

Construction put in place, value of new
public and private structures, by type,
monthly rpt, 2382–4

Construction spending by Fed Govt, by
program and type of structure, FY82-90,
annual article, 2042–1.901; 2042–1.907

DOD prime contract awards, by detailed
procurement category, FY85-88, annual
rpt, 3544–18

EPA grants to State and local govts for
wastewater treatment facility construction,
by project, monthly listing, 9202–3

EPA pollution control grant program
activities, monthly rpt, 9182–8

Estuary environmental conditions and
mgmt, for individual areas, conf series,
2146–6

Expenditures for pollution abatement by
govts, business, and consumers, 1983-87,
annual article, 2702–1.919

Expenditures of Fed Govt in States, by type,
program, agency, and State, FY88, annual
rpt, 2464–2

Fed Govt wastewater facilities compliance
with pollution control regulations,
FY86-87, GAO rpt, 26113–388

FmHA activities, and loans and grants by
program and State, FY88 and trends from
FY69, annual rpt, 1184–17

Govt employment and payroll, by function,
level of govt, and jurisdiction, 1987-88,
annual rpt series, 2466–1

Govt finances, by level of govt, State, and
for large cities and counties, annual rpt
series, 2466–2

Great Lakes basin pollutant discharges,
sources, and control program activities,
1987, biennial rpt, 14644–1

Great Lakes toxic spills and human error,
with data by pollutant source and site,
1984-86, conf, 14648–21

Honduras health care projects of AID,
design and mgmt effects on sustainability,
1942-86, 9916–3.53

Housing and households detailed
characteristics, and unit and neighborhood
quality, by location, 1985, biennial rpt,
2485–12

Research on population and reproduction, Federal funding by project, FY87, annual listing, 4474–9

Statistical Abstract of US, social, political, and economic data, 1790-2025, comprehensive annual compilation, 2324–1.1

Sexually transmitted diseases

Army active duty personnel health condition, and use of Army medical services in US and abroad, monthly rpt, 3702–4.2

Cancer (anal) risk, by sex and history of urogenital disorders, homosexual activity, and smoking, 1989 article, 4472–1.930

Deaths and rates, by cause, age, sex, marital status, race, and State, 1987, US Vital Statistics advance annual rpt, 4146–5.113

Deaths and rates, by detailed cause and demographic characteristics, 1986 and trends from 1900, US Vital Statistics annual rpt, 4144–2

Deaths and rates, by detailed location, cause, and demographic characteristics, 1987, US Vital Statistics annual rpt, 4144–3

Health condition and health care resources, use, and spending, 1950s-87, annual data compilation, 4144–11

HHS financial aid, by program, recipient, State, and city, FY88, annual regional listings, 4004–3

Indian STD cases, by State, 1988, article, 4042–3.955

Minority group STD cases, by race, 1988, article, 4042–3.954

Morbidity and Mortality Weekly Report, infectious notifiable disease cases by age and State, and deaths, 1930s-88, annual rpt, 4204–1

Morbidity and Mortality Weekly Report, infectious notifiable disease cases by State, and public health issues, 4202–1

Natl Inst of Allergy and Infectious Diseases activities, grants by recipient and location, and disease incidence, FY81-88, annual rpt, 4474–30

Palau gonorrhea cases and rates, 1985-88, annual rpt, 7004–6

Preventive disease and health improvement goals and recommended activities for 2000, with trends 1970s-80s, 4048–10

Texas-Mexico border area health facilities and services, with background data, by Texas county, 1980s-88, GAO rpt, 26121–261

Treatment and diagnosis of STD, guidelines, 1989 rpt, 4206–2.17

see also Acquired immune deficiency syndrome

see also under By Disease in the "Index by Categories"

Seychelles

Agricultural trade of US, by detailed commodity and country, 1988, semiannual rpt, 1522–4

AID activities and funding by project and function, FY90, and developing countries summary socioeconomic data from 1960s, annual rpt, 9904–4.5

AID economic aid to developing countries, obligations and disbursements by country, quarterly rpt, 9912–4

Economic and military aid and loans from US and intl agencies, by program and country, FY46-87, annual rpt, 9914–5

Economic, social, political, and geographic summary data, by country, 1989, annual factbook, 9114–2

Human rights conditions in 170 countries, 1988, annual rpt, 21384–3

Military aid of US, arms sales, and training programs costs and budget requests, by program, world region, and country, FY88-90, annual rpt, 7144–13

Minerals Yearbook, 1987, Vol 3: foreign country reviews of production, trade, and policy, by commodity, annual rpt, 5604–35

Minerals Yearbook, 1987, Vol 3 preprints: foreign country review of production, trade, and policy, by commodity, annual rpt, 5604–23.81

Population size, growth rates, and components of change, by country, projected 1989-2020 and trends from 1950, biennial rpt, 2324–9

UN voting record and share of votes in agreement with US, by issue, country, and world area, 1988, annual rpt, 7004–18

see also under By Foreign Country in the "Index by Categories"

Shack-Marquez, Janice

"Earnings and Different Types of Training", 6886–6.34

"Interview Group Bias: Effects of Repeated Interviewing on Estimation of Labor Force Status", 6886–6.23

Shaffer, Sherrill

"Can the End User Improve an Econometric Forecast?", 9387–8.185

"Contestable Two-Part Tariffs with Income Effects", 9387–8.176

"Cournot Oligopoly with External Costs", 9387–8.196

"Pooling Intensifies Joint Failure Risk", 9387–8.180

"Structural Shifts and the Volatility of Chaotic Markets", 9387–8.175

"Transaction Costs and Option Configuration", 9387–8.197

Shagam, Shayle D.

"Trends in World Pork Production and Trade", 1561–7.904

Shale oil

see Oil shale

Shane, Mathew

"Agricultural Trade Between Asia/Near East Countries and the U.S., 1962-86", 1528–277

"Global Trade Environment and Agriculture", 1522–3.912

Shapouri, Hosein

"Livestock Costs and Returns, 1988-89", 1561–7.903

Shapouri, Shahla

"Export Performance in Africa", 1528–280

Sharjah

see United Arab Emirates

Sharon, Pa.

see also under By SMSA or MSA in the "Index by Categories"

Sharp, Kevin

"Summary of Public Attitude Survey Findings", 8304–8.1

Sharpe, Steven A.

"Animal Spirits, Margin Requirements, and Stock Price Volatility", 9366–6.205

"Asymmetric Information, Bank Lending, and Implicit Contracts: A Stylized Model of Customer Relationships", 9366–6.184

"Market Structure and the Nature of Price Rigidity: Evidence from the Market for Consumer Deposits", 9366–6.166

"Theory of Credit Rationing and the Maturity Structure of Debt", 9366–6.185

Shaughnessy, Peter

"Findings on Case Mix and Quality of Care in Nursing Homes and Home Health Agencies", 4658–28

Shaw, William F.

"Typical FHA First Time Home Buyer in 1988", 5148–8

Shaw, William N.

"Pismo Clam. Species Profiles: Life Histories and Environmental Requirements of Coastal Fishes and Invertebrates", 5506–8.102

Shea, Dennis

"Economic Resources of the Elderly: A Comprehensive Income Approach", 2626–10.93

Shear, Garrick R.

"Trends in Taxpayer Paperwork Burden", 8304–8.1

Sheboygan County, Wis.

see also under By SMSA or MSA in the "Index by Categories"

Sheep

see Livestock and livestock industry

Sheikh, Patricia

"China's Cotton Industry", 1561–1.901

Shelburne, Robert C.

"Trade and Employment Effects of the Caribbean Basin Economic Recovery Act", 6364–2

Shellfish

Agricultural Statistics, 1988, annual rpt, 1004–1.2

Alaska OCS environmental conditions and oil dev impacts, compilation of papers, series, 2176–1

Aquaculture in US and Japan, mgmt, methods, and biological data for selected species, 1985 conf papers, annual rpt, 2164–15

Atlantic Ocean estuary waters approved and prohibited for shellfish harvest, and pollution sources, 1985, 2176–7.11

Atlantic Ocean fish and shellfish distribution, bottom trawl survey evaluation with results by species and location, 1963-87, 2168–108

Atlantic Ocean fish and shellfish distribution, bottom trawl survey results by species and location, periodic rpt series, 2164–18

Coastal and estuarine environmental conditions, research results and methodology, series, 2176–7

Coastal and riparian areas environmental conditions, fish, wildlife, use, and mgmt, for individual ecosystems, series, 5506–9

Coastal areas environmental conditions and mgmt, 1988 map, 2176–5.6

Coastal areas fish and shellfish catch, life cycles, and environmental needs, for selected species and regions, series, 5506–8

Cold storage holdings of fish and shellfish, by product and species, preliminary data, monthly press release, 2162–2

Consumption, supply, trade, prices, spending, and indexes, by food commodity, 1987, annual rpt, 1544–4

Estuary environmental conditions and mgmt, for individual areas, conf series, 2146–6

Estuary waters approved and prohibited for shellfish harvest, by estuary, 1985, 2176–7.3

Exports and imports (agricultural) of US, by detailed commodity and country, 1988, semiannual rpt, 1522–4

Exports of US, detailed commodities by country, monthly rpt, 2422–3

Freight (waterborne domestic and foreign) by commodity, traffic, and passengers, by port and waterway, 1987, annual rpt, 3754–3

Gulf of Mexico estuary waters approved and prohibited for shellfish harvest, and pollution sources, 1985, 2176–7.5

Imports of US, detailed Schedule A commodities by country, monthly rpt, 2422–2

Japan fish catch, prices, trade by country, cold storage holdings, import quotas, and market devs, semimonthly press release, 2162–7

Landings and trade of commercial fisheries, by species, 1980-88, semiannual rpt, 1561–15.1

Landings, trade, use, and fishery operations, with selected foreign data, by species, 1970s-88, annual rpt, 2164–1

Landings, wholesale receipts, prices, trade, and other market activities, by region, weekly rpts, 2162–6

Manufacturing annual survey, 1986: financial and operating data, by SIC 2- to 4-digit industry, series, 2506–15

Manufacturing census, 1987: financial and operating data, for SIC 4-digit industries by product, preliminary rpt, 2491–1.9

Marine Fisheries Review, US and foreign fisheries resources, dev, mgmt, and research, quarterly journal, 2162–1

Nutrient and caloric composition of food, for raw, processed, and prepared food, 1988 rpt, 1358–3

Pacific coast fish and shellfish catch, prices, and fisheries economic status, 1986-87, annual rpt series, 2164–16

Pollutant (PCB and pesticide) concentrations in coastal and estuarine fish and shellfish, by species and location, 1965-84, 2178–21

Pollutant concentrations in coastal and estuarine fish, shellfish, and environment, series, 2176–3

Pollutants from ship hull paints, impacts on environment and marine species, with bibl, 1960s-87, 2148–58

Price indexes (producer), by stage of processing and detailed commodity, monthly rpt, 6762–6

Price indexes (producer), by stage of processing and detailed commodity, monthly 1988, annual rpt, 6764–2

Production of processed fish by location, and trade, by species and product, 1987-88, annual rpts, 2166–6

R&D and mgmt of fisheries, Fed Govt grants by project and State, and rpts, 1987, annual listing, 2164–3

Recreation related to wildlife, hunting, and fishing participation and spending, detailed data by location, 1985 survey, quinquennial rpt, 5508–5

Shrimp (bait) catch in Galveston Bay, 1959-87, article, 2162–1.901

Shrimp raised on farms, yield and production by country, and US imports, 1980-89, article, 1522–3.924

Statistical Abstract of US, social, political, and economic data, 1790-2025, comprehensive annual compilation, 2324–1.3

Sheltered workshops
Finances, operations, and Federal procurement from sheltered workshops, FY80-88, annual rpt, 11714–1

Shepard, Lloyd
"Analysis of Acid Precipitation Samples Collected by State Agencies: January-December 1987", 9194–20

Shepherd, William T.
"Human Factors Issues in Aircraft Maintenance and Inspection", 7506–10.63

Sherman, Sally R.
"Fast Facts and Figures About Social Security", 4748–42

Sherman, Tex.
Wages by occupation, for office and plant workers, 1989 survey, periodic MSA rpt, 6785–3.9
see also under By SMSA or MSA in the "Index by Categories"

Sherwood-Call, Carolyn
"Undocumented Workers and Regional Differences in Apparel Labor Markets", 9393–8.904

Shiells, Clinton R.
"Labor Market Changes and Adjustments: How Do the U.S. and Japan Compare?", 6722–1.910
"Trade and Employment Effects of the Caribbean Basin Economic Recovery Act", 6364–2

Shigella
see Food and waterborne diseases

Shiller, Robert J.
"Causes of Changing Financial Market Volatility", 9381–13.1

Shipbuilding and operating subsidies
Assistance (financial and nonfinancial) of Fed Govt, 1989 base edition with supplements, annual listing, 104–5

Contracts, deliveries, and costs, by coastal district and shipyard, various periods 1971-88, annual rpt, 7704–12.1

DOT activities by subagency, budget, and summary accident data, FY85, annual rpt, 7304–1

DOT planning and safety grants, by program, State, and for 38 SMSAs, FY88, annual rpt, 7304–7

Freight (waterborne) sponsored by Fed Govt, total and US-flag share by agency and program, 1987, annual rpt, 7704–14.3

MarAd activities, finances, subsidies, and world merchant fleet operations, FY88, annual rpt, 7704–14

Merchant ships in US fleet, operating subsidies, and ship-related employment, monthly rpt, 7702–1

Shipbuilding and repairing
Competition in Exclusive Economic Zone between foreign and US flag ships, impacts of extending cabotage laws, with background data, 1970s-80s, 26358–206

Construction and delivery of new ships, by vessel type and country of construction and registry, 1988, annual rpt, 7704–4

Costs, deliveries, contracts, employment, and wage rates, by coastal district and shipyard, 1988, annual rpt, 7704–12

County Business Patterns, 1987: employment, establishments, and payroll, by SIC 2- to 4-digit industry and county, annual State rpt series, 2326–8

DOD budget, procurement appropriations by item, service branch, and defense agency, FY88-91, annual rpt, 3544–32

Employment, earnings, and hours, by selected SIC 1- to 4-digit industry, State, and for 262 MSAs, 1972-87, 6748–81

Employment, earnings, and hours, by SIC 1- to 4-digit industry, monthly 1983-Feb 1989, annual rpt, 6744–4

Employment of minorities and women, by occupation, SIC 1- to 3- digit industry, State, and MSA, 1986, annual rpt, 9244–1

Employment shipboard, shipyard, and longshore, FY87-88, annual rpt, 7704–14.3

Exports of US, detailed commodities by country, monthly rpt, 2422–3

Facilities for shipbuilding and repair, capacity, and employment, by shipyard, 1988, annual rpt, 7704–9

Finances and operations, by SIC 2- to 4-digit industry, forecast 1989 with trends from 1950s, annual rpt, 2044–28

Foreign and US merchant ships, and tonnage, by country of registry, as of Jan 1988, annual rpt, 7704–3

Foreign-flag ships owned by US firms and foreign affiliates, by type, owner, and country of registry and construction, as of July 1989, semiannual rpt, 7702–3

Freight (waterborne domestic and foreign) by commodity, traffic, and passengers, by port and waterway, 1987, annual rpt, 3754–3

Manufacturing annual survey, 1986: financial and operating data, by SIC 2- to 4-digit industry, series, 2506–15

Manufacturing census, 1987: financial and operating data, for SIC 4-digit industries by product, preliminary rpt, 2491–1.77

Merchant ships in US fleet and Natl Defense Reserve Fleet, vessels, tonnage, and owner, as of Jan 1989, semiannual listing, 7702–2

Navy nuclear-powered vessels and support facilities radioactive waste, releases in harbors, and public exposure, 1970s-88, annual rpt, 3804–11

Navy personnel radiation exposure on nuclear-powered vessels and at support facilities, and injury claims, 1950s-88, annual rpt, 3804–10

Occupational injury and illness rates, by SIC 2- to 4-digit industry, 1987, annual rpt, 6844–1

OECD trade, total and for 4 major countries, and US trade by country, by commodity, 1970-87, world area rpt series, 9116–1

Pacific territories and Hawaii harbor traffic, facilities, dev, funding, and needs, by port, as of 1987, 7308–195

Paints used on ship hulls, impacts on environment and marine species, with bibl, 1960s-87, 2148–58

Price indexes (producer), by stage of processing and detailed commodity, monthly rpt, 6762-6

Price indexes (producer), by stage of processing and detailed commodity, monthly 1988, annual rpt, 6764-2

Science, engineering, and technical employment in manufacturing, by field, occupation, and industry, 1986, triennial rpt, 9627-23

Ships in US merchant fleet, operating subsidies, and ship-related employment, monthly rpt, dropped data, 7702-1

Statistical Abstract of US, social, political, and economic data, 1790-2025, comprehensive annual compilation, 2324-1.3

Tax (income) returns of corporations, income and tax items by asset size and detailed industry, 1986, annual rpt, 8304-4; 8304-21

Wartime capability of commercial ships, shipyards, and personnel, for merchant and reserve fleet, 1988-2000, 11208-1

see also Shipbuilding and operating subsidies

Shipley, Bernard E.

"Recidivism of Prisoners Released in 1983", 6066-19.48

Shipments, industrial

see Industrial production

Ships and shipping

Bulk carrier ships in world fleet, characteristics by country of registry, and for Great Lakes fleet by owner, as of Jan 1989, annual listing, 7704-13

Bunker fuel laden in US on vessels engaged in foreign trade, by fuel type and port, monthly rpt, 2422-5

Communist, OECD, and selected other countries freight and carrier inventories, by mode of transport, 1960s-88, annual rpt, 9114-4.10

Competition in Exclusive Economic Zone between foreign and US flag ships, impacts of extending cabotage laws, with background data, 1970s-80s, 26358-206

Containerized cargo carried over principal trade routes, by flag of vessel, port, and US coastal district, 1984, annual rpt, 7704-8

Containers (intermodal) and equipment owned by shipping and leasing companies, inventory by type and size, 1989, annual rpt, 7704-10

County Business Patterns, 1987: employment, establishments, and payroll, by SIC 2- to 4-digit industry and county, annual State rpt series, 2326-8

Customs Service activities, collections, entries processed by mode of transport, and seizures, FY84-88, annual rpt, 8144-1

Developing countries disaster preparedness and economic, population, and political data, country rpt series, 9916-2

Earnings by major industry group, and personal income per capita and by source, by region and State, 1929-87, 2708-40

Employment, earnings, and hours, by selected SIC 1- to 4-digit industry, State, and for 262 MSAs, 1972-87, 6748-81

Employment, earnings, and hours, by SIC 1- to 4-digit industry, monthly 1983-Feb 1989, annual rpt, 6744-4

Energy use, by fuel pollutant source, fuel type, and State, 1986, annual rpt, 9194-14

Energy use by mode of transport, fuel supply, and demographic and economic factors of vehicle use, 1970s-88, annual rpt, 3304-5

Estuary environmental conditions and mgmt, for individual areas, conf series, 2146-6

Exports and imports (waterborne) of US, by type of service, commodity, country, route, and US port, 1986-87, annual rpt, 7704-2

Exports and imports (waterborne) of US, by type of service, customs district, port, and world area, monthly rpt, 2422-7

Exports and imports between US and outlying areas, by detailed commodity and mode of transport, monthly rpt, 2422-4

Exports and imports of US, by commodity group, world area, selected country, US coastal area and port, and mode of transport, monthly rpt, 2422-9

Finances and operations, by SIC 2- to 4-digit industry, forecast 1989 with trends from 1950s, annual rpt, 2044-28

Finances, operations, vehicles, equipment, accidents, and energy use, by mode of transport, 1955-88, annual rpt, 7304-2

Fishery employment, vessels, plants, and cooperatives, by State, 1988 and trends from 1970, annual rpt, 2164-1.10

Foreign and US merchant ships, and tonnage, by country of registry, as of Jan 1988, annual rpt, 7704-3

Foreign and US merchant ships and tonnage, by vessel type, 1983-87, *Minerals Yearbook*, annual rpt, 5604-35.1

Foreign and US merchant ships, tonnage, shipments, crews, and other operations, as of 1988, annual rpt, 7704-14

Foreign-flag ships owned by US firms and foreign affiliates, by type, owner, and country of registry and construction, as of July 1989, semiannual rpt, 7702-3

Grain shipments and rates, drought impacts, 1988, 1588-133

Grain vessels in port, loaded, and due in Gulf coast, and freight rates for selected routes, weekly rpt, 1272-2

Great Lakes ship pilotage activities, costs, and traffic for US and Canada, and US testing and certificates, 1960s-87, 7308-192

Maritime Commission activities, case filings by type and disposition, and civil penalties by shipper, FY88, annual rpt, 9334-1

Merchant ships in US fleet and Natl Defense Reserve Fleet, vessels, tonnage, and owner, as of Jan 1989, semiannual listing, 7702-2

Ocean subsurface temperature data collection activities, for Pacific Ocean, 1985-87, annual rpt, 2154-14

Oceanographic research and distribution activities of World Data Center A by country, and cruises by ship, 1987, annual rpt, 2144-15

Oceanographic research cruise schedules and ship characteristics, by higher education instn and Federal agency, 1989, annual listing, 3804-6

Oil products sales, and purchases of refiners, processors, and distributors, by product, end-use sector, PAD district, and State, 1988, annual rpt, 3164-85

Overseas Business Reports: economic conditions, investment and export opportunities, and trade practices, country market research rpt series, 2046-6

Pacific territories and Hawaii harbor traffic, facilities, dev, funding, and needs, by port, as of 1987, 7308-195

Panama Canal traffic and tolls, by commodity, flag of vessel, and trade route, FY88, annual rpt, 9664-3.1

Pollution (air) levels for 5 pollutants, by detailed source and State, 1986, annual rpt, 9194-7

Pollution (air) levels for 6 pollutants, by source, 1970-87 and trends from 1940, annual rpt, 9194-13

Research vessels of higher education instns, purchases, 1982-83 and 1985-86, 9628-76

Science, engineering, and technical employment in transportation, utilities, and retail and wholesale trade, by field, occupation, and industry, 1985, triennial rpt, 9627-32

St Lawrence Seaway ship, cargo, and passenger traffic, and toll revenue, 1988 and trends from 1959, annual rpt, 7744-2

Statistical Abstract of US, social, political, and economic data, 1790-2025, comprehensive annual compilation, 2324-1.3

Tax (income) returns of corporations, income and tax items by asset size and detailed industry, 1986, annual rpt, 8304-4; 8304-21

Tax (income) returns of partnerships, income statement items by industry group, 1986, annual article, 8302-2.903

Tax (income) returns of sole proprietorships, income statement items, by industry group, 1987, annual article, 8302-2.904; 8302-2.921

Telephone and telegraph firms marine operations and revenue, 1987, annual rpt, 9284-6

Traffic, freight by commodity, and passengers, domestic and foreign waterborne commerce by port and waterway, 1987, annual rpt, 3754-3

Wartime capability of commercial ships, shipyards, and personnel, for merchant and reserve fleet, 1985-2000, revised estimates, 11208-3

Wartime capability of commercial ships, shipyards, and personnel, for merchant and reserve fleet, 1988-2000, 11208-1

Weather rpts and gale and wave observations received from ships, quarterly journal, 2152-8

Wholesale trade census, 1987: employment, establishments, finances, and operations, by SIC 2- to 4-digit kind of business, MSA, county, and city, State rpt series, 2405-1

see also Barges

see also Boats and boating

see also Freight

see also Harbors and ports

see also Inland water transportation

see also Longshoremen

see also Marine accidents and safety

see also Maritime law

see also Merchant seamen

see also Naval vessels
see also Navigation
see also Nuclear-powered ships
see also Oil spills
see also Passenger ships
see also Shipbuilding and operating subsidies
see also Shipbuilding and repairing
see also Tanker ships
see also By Industry in the "Index by Categories"

Shirkey, Charles P.
"Review of Valdez Oil Spill Market Impacts", 3162–11.901; 3162–24.902

Shirzad, Farzad F.
"Physical and Hydrologic Characteristics, the Oregon Estuaries", 2176–7.10
"Revised Physical and Hydrologic Characteristics for the Mississippi Delta Region Estuaries", 2176–7.13

Shoemaker, Robbin
"From the 1985 Farm Bill to 1990 and Beyond: The Resource Effects of Commodity Programs", 1561–16.904
"Long Run Determinants of Land Values", 1561–16.902

Shoenhair, John
"Interstate Banking: The Nation and Tenth District States", 9381–14.1

Shoes and shoe industry
Business statistics, detailed data for major industries and economic indicators, *Survey of Current Business*, monthly rpt, 2702–1.12
China trade by SITC 1- to 5-digit commodity, 1970s-87, annual rpt, 9114–3
Consumer Expenditure Survey, household income by source, and itemized spending, by selected characteristics and location, 1984-86, annual rpt, 6764–5.2
County Business Patterns, 1987: employment, establishments, and payroll, by SIC 2- to 4-digit industry and county, annual State rpt series, 2326–8
CPI by component for US city average, and by region, population size, and for 27 metro areas, monthly rpt, 6762–2
Cuba economic conditions, agricultural and industrial production and distribution, trade, and intl economic relations, 1980-87 with trends from 1961, 9118–8
Employment, earnings, and hours, by selected SIC 1- to 4-digit industry, State, and for 262 MSAs, 1972-87, 6748–81
Employment, earnings, and hours, by SIC 1- to 4-digit industry, monthly 1983-Feb 1989, annual rpt, 6744–4
Employment of minorities and women, by occupation, SIC 1- to 3- digit industry, State, and MSA, 1986, annual rpt, 9244–1
Exports and imports of US by country, and trade shifts by commodity, quarterly rpt, 9882–9
Exports of US, detailed commodities by country, monthly rpt, 2422–3
Finances and operations, by SIC 2- to 4-digit industry, forecast 1989 with trends from 1950s, annual rpt, 2044–28
Import restraint elimination, impact on domestic industry production and employment, by selected commodity, 1986-88, 9886–4.144
Imports of footwear, toys, and games from PRC and other countries, 1983-88, article, 9882–2.901

Imports of US, detailed Schedule A commodities by country, monthly rpt, 2422–2
Imports of US given duty-free treatment for value of US material sent abroad, and impacts on US industry and employment, by commodity and country, 1987, annual rpt, 9884–14
Injuries from use of consumer products, by severity, victim age, and detailed product, 1988, annual rpt, 9164–6
Input-output structure of US economy, detailed interindustry transactions for 84 industries, and components of final demand, 1983, annual article, 2702–1.909
Manufacturing annual survey, 1986: financial and operating data, by SIC 2- to 4-digit industry, series, 2506–15
Manufacturing census, 1987: financial and operating data, for SIC 4-digit industries by product, preliminary rpt, 2491–1.42; 2491–1.44
Occupational injury and illness rates, by SIC 2- to 4-digit industry, 1987, annual rpt, 6844–1
OECD trade, total and for 4 major countries, and US trade by country, by commodity, 1970-87, world area rpt series, 9116–1
Price indexes (producer), by stage of processing and detailed commodity, monthly rpt, 6762–6
Price indexes (producer), by stage of processing and detailed commodity, monthly 1988, annual rpt, 6764–2
Price indexes for department store inventories, by class of item, monthly table, 6762–7
Production, employment, use, prices, and US trade by country, quarterly rpt, 9882–6
Production, shipments, trade, and use of shoes, by product, 1988, annual Current Industrial Rpt, 2506–6.8
Production, shipments, trade, and use of shoes, monthly Current Industrial Rpt, 2506–6.7
Productivity measures for nonrubber footwear industry, 1958-86, article, 6722–1.920
Productivity of labor and capital, and indexes of output, hours, and employment, 1963-87, annual rpt, 6824–1.3; 6824–1.5
Retail trade census, 1987: employment, establishments, sales, and payroll, by SIC 2- to 4-digit kind of business, MSA, county, and city, State rpt series, 2397–1
Retail trade sales and inventories, by kind of business, region, and selected State, MSA, and city, monthly rpt, 2413–9
Retail trade sales, by kind of business, advance monthly rpt, 2413–2
Retail trade sales, inventories, purchases, gross margin, and accounts receivable, by SIC 2- to 4-digit kind of business and form of ownership, 1987, annual rpt, 2413–5
Science, engineering, and technical employment in manufacturing, by field, occupation, and industry, 1986, triennial rpt, 9627–23
Science, engineering, and technical employment in transportation, utilities,

and retail and wholesale trade, by field, occupation, and industry, 1985, triennial rpt, 9627–32
Service industries census, 1987: establishments, receipts, employment, and payroll, by SIC 2- to 4-digit kind of business, MSA, county, and city, State rpt series, 2391–1
Statistical Abstract of US, social, political, and economic data, 1790-2025, comprehensive annual compilation, 2324–1.3
Tax (income) returns of corporations, income and tax items by asset size and detailed industry, 1986, annual rpt, 8304–4; 8304–21
Wholesale trade census, 1987: employment, establishments, finances, and operations, by SIC 2- to 4-digit kind of business, MSA, county, and city, State rpt series, 2405–1
see also under By Commodity in the "Index by Categories"

Shook, Jonathan E.
"Corporation Income Tax Returns, Income Year 1986", 8302–2.922

Shopping centers
Suburban areas land use, commuting, employment, and housing characteristics, detailed data for traffic planning, 1986, 7888–75
Traffic volume in urban areas and detailed trip characteristics, by transport mode and city, 1950s-88, 7888–37
Urban Dev Action Grants, funding sources, project descriptions, and economic impacts, by city, periodic press releases, 5002–7

Short, Eugenie D.
"Further Evidence on the Liquidity Effect Using an Efficient-Markets Approach", 9379–12.34

Short, Kathleen S.
"Transitions in Income and Poverty Status: 1984-85", 2546–20.10

Short, Pamela F.
"Profile of Uninsured Americans. National Medical Expenditure Survey", 4186–8.1
"Trends in Employee Health Benefits", 4188–56

Short, Sara D.
"Financial Characteristics of Dairy Farms", 1561–2.902

Shorter, Rhoda
"National Urban Mass Transportation Statistics: 1986 Section 15 Annual Report", 7884–4

Shreveport, La.
Wages by occupation, and benefits for office and plant workers, 1988 survey, periodic MSA rpt, 6785–11.3
see also under By City and By SMSA or MSA in the "Index by Categories"

Shrimp
see Shellfish

Sibert, Anne
"Taxing Capital in an Open Economy", 9381–10.92

Sickle-cell anemia
Deaths and rates, by detailed cause and demographic characteristics, 1986 and trends from 1900, US Vital Statistics annual rpt, 4144–2

Sickness

see Absenteeism

see Diseases and disorders

see Health condition

see Hospitalization

Siegal, Harvey

"Alcohol and Other Drug Use Among Orthopedically Impaired College Students", 4482–1.904

Sierra Leone

Agricultural and food production and indexes, total and for selected commodities, by country, 1970s-88, annual rpt, 1524–12

Agricultural imports and food aid needs under alternative weather assumptions, for 17 African countries, projected to 1995, 1528–279

Agricultural trade of US, by detailed commodity and country, 1988, semiannual rpt, 1522–4

AID activities and funding by project and function, FY90, and developing countries summary socioeconomic data from 1960s, annual rpt, 9904–4.5

AID economic aid to developing countries, obligations and disbursements by country, quarterly rpt, 9912–4

Economic and military aid and loans from US and intl agencies, by program and country, FY46-87, annual rpt, 9914–5

Economic conditions, income, production, prices, employment, and trade, 1989 periodic country rpt, 2046–4.84

Economic, social, political, and geographic summary data, by country, 1989, annual factbook, 9114–2

Human rights conditions in 170 countries, 1988, annual rpt, 21384–3

Military aid of US, arms sales, and training programs costs and budget requests, by program, world region, and country, FY88-90, annual rpt, 7144–13

Military spending, arms trade, and force strengths, with govt spending and population, by country, 1977-87, annual rpt, 9824–1

Minerals Yearbook, 1987, Vol 3: foreign country reviews of production, trade, and policy, by commodity, annual rpt, 5604–35

Minerals Yearbook, 1987, Vol 3 preprints: foreign country review of production, trade, and policy, by commodity, annual rpt, 5604–23.63

Population size, growth rates, and components of change, by country, projected 1989-2020 and trends from 1950, biennial rpt, 2324–9

UN voting record and share of votes in agreement with US, by issue, country, and world area, 1988, annual rpt, 7004–18

see also under By Foreign Country in the "Index by Categories"

Sigler, Stella

"Analyses of Natural Gases, 1988", 5604–2

Silicon

see Nonmetallic minerals and mines

Silk

Broadwoven gray goods production, by fabric type, quarterly Current Industrial Rpt, 2506–5.11

Exports of US, detailed commodities by country, monthly rpt, 2422–3

Imports of silk-blend textiles, by product and country of origin, monthly rpt, 2046–8.6

Imports of textiles, by country of origin, monthly rpt, 2042–27

Imports of textiles, by product and country of origin, periodic rpt series, 2046–8; 2046–9

Imports of US, detailed Schedule A commodities by country, monthly rpt, 2422–2

Manufacturing annual survey, 1986: financial and operating data, by SIC 2- to 4-digit industry, series, 2506–15

Silver

Business statistics, detailed data for major industries and economic indicators, *Survey of Current Business,* monthly rpt, 2702–1.6

Coin production and monetary metals use and holdings of US Mint, by metal type, FY88, annual rpt, 8204–1

County Business Patterns, 1987: employment, establishments, and payroll, by SIC 2- to 4-digit industry and county, annual State rpt series, 2326–8

Exports of US, detailed commodities by country, monthly rpt, 2422–3

Foreign countries mineral production, reserves, and industry role in domestic economy and world supply, world area and country rpt series, 5606–1

Futures and options trading volume, by commodity and exchange, FY88, annual rpt, 11924–2

Futures contracts on commodities, financial instruments, and indexes, options trading in NYC, Chicago, and other markets, monthly rpt, 11922–6

Futures trading in selected commodities and financial instruments and indexes, NYC, Chicago, and other markets activity, monthly rpt, 11922–5

Idaho gold, silver, and other metals production, by location, late 1800s-1982, 5668–90

Imports of US, detailed Schedule A commodities by country, monthly rpt, 2422–2

Manufacturing census, 1987: financial and operating data, for SIC 4-digit industries by product, preliminary rpt, 2491–1.53; 2491–1.54; 2491–1.80

Mineral industries census, 1987: financial and operating data, preliminary industry rpt, 2511–1.2

Mineral Industry Surveys, commodity review of production, trade, stocks, and use, monthly rpt, 5612–1.10

Mineral Industry Surveys, State reviews of production, 1988, preliminary annual rpt, 5614–6

Minerals Yearbook, 1987, Vol 1: commodity reviews of production, use, trade, prices, and mining operations, annual rpt, 5604–33

Minerals Yearbook, 1987, Vol 1 preprints: commodity review of production, reserves, supply, use, and trade, annual rpt, 5604–15.60

Minerals Yearbook, 1987, Vol 2 preprints: State reviews of production and sales by commodity, and business activity, annual rpt series, 5604–16

Minerals Yearbook, 1987, Vol 2: State reviews of production, sales, and firms, by commodity, and business activity, annual rpt, 5604–34

Minerals Yearbook, 1987, Vol 3: foreign country reviews of production, trade, and policy, by commodity, annual rpt, 5604–35

Minerals Yearbook, 1987, Vol 3 preprints: foreign country reviews of production, trade, and policy, by commodity, annual rpt series, 5604–23

Minerals Yearbook, 1988, Vol 2 rpts: State reviews of production and sales by commodity, and business activity, annual rpt series, 5604–22

Mines (metal) and related operations occupational injuries and incidence, employment, and hours, 1987, annual rpt, 6664–3

Price indexes (producer), by stage of processing and detailed commodity, monthly rpt, 6762–6

Price indexes (producer), by stage of processing and detailed commodity, monthly 1988, annual rpt, 6764–2

Production, prices, trade, use, employment, tariffs, and stockpiles, by mineral, with foreign comparisons, 1984-88, annual rpt, 5604–18

Statistical Abstract of US, social, political, and economic data, 1790-2025, comprehensive annual compilation, 2324–1.3

Stockpiling of strategic material by Fed Govt, activity, and inventory by commodity, as of Sept 1989, semiannual rpt, 3542–22; 3902–2

Stockpiling of strategic material, inventories and needs, by commodity, as of Sept 1988, annual rpt, 3544–37

Stockpiling of strategic material, inventories, costs, and goals by commodity, as of June 1989, semiannual rpt, 3902–3

Silverman, Debra T.

"Occupational Risks of Bladder Cancer in the U.S.: I. White Men", 4472–1.924

"Occupational Risks of Bladder Cancer in the U.S.: II. Nonwhite Men", 4472–1.925

Silverman, Jane

"Characteristics and Prior Contraceptive Use of U.S. Abortion Patients", 21408–113

Silverware

see Household supplies and utensils

Silvestri, George

"Projections of Occupational Employment, 1988-2000", 6722–1.955

Simons, Douglas

"Pacific Razor Clam. Species Profiles: Life Histories and Environmental Requirements of Coastal Fishes and Invertebrates (Pacific Northwest)", 5506–8.96

Singapore

Agricultural and food production and indexes, total and for selected commodities, by country, 1970s-88, annual rpt, 1524–12

Agricultural trade of US, by detailed commodity and country, 1988, semiannual rpt, 1522–4

AID economic aid to developing countries, obligations and disbursements by country, quarterly rpt, 9912–4

DOE contracts and grants, by category, State, and for top contractors, FY88, annual rpt, 3004–21

DOE R&D projects and funding at natl labs, universities, and other instns, periodic summary rpt series, 3004–18

Establishments, employment, and financial ratios, for small business by SIC 1- to 2-digit industry and State, late 1960s-87, 9768–19

Establishments, operations, owner characteristics, and job training, for small businesses, late 1950s-87, 9768–20

Eximbank financial condition, credit and insurance authorizations, and loan activity and delinquencies, by country, FY88, annual rpt, 9254–1

Eximbank small businesses loans, by firm, 1984-88, hearing, 21728–70

Fed Govt financial and nonfinancial domestic aid, 1989 base edition with supplements, annual listing, 104–5

Fed Govt procurement contract awards, by procurement and contractor type, agency, State, and for top 100 contractors, quarterly rpt, 102–6

Fed Govt small business construction contracts, surety bonds use and fraud cases, by agency, 1985-89, GAO rpt, 26113–438

Fed Govt spending in States, by type, program, agency, and State, FY88, annual rpt, 2464–2

Finances, operations, owner and employee characteristics, and Federal contracts, for small business, 1980s-88, annual rpt, 9764–6

Forests (natl) set-aside sales in Pacific Northwest region, quarterly rpt, 1202–3

HHS financial aid, by program, recipient, State, and city, FY88, annual regional listings, 4004–3

Hwy construction contracts for Federal-aid system, awards to minority- and women-owned businesses, FHwA and State reviews, FY83-87, GAO rpt, 26113–389

Insurance (health) provided by employer, coverage and characteristics of plan and employer, 1986-87, hearing, 25368–160

Loans and finances of SBA, and small business contracts, by firm and location, FY88, annual rpt, 9764–1

Minority business funding, by program and Federal agency, FY86-88, annual rpt, 2104–5

NASA procurement contract awards, by type, contractor, State, and country, FY89, semiannual rpt, 9502–6

Navy procurement, by contractor and location, FY88, annual rpt, 3804–13

Navy small and disadvantaged business procurement offices and location, 1988 annual listing, 3804–5

NIH activities, funding by program and recipient type, staff, and clinic patients, by inst, FY87, annual rpt, 4434–3

NIH grants for R&D, by location and recipient, FY88, annual listing, 4434–7.1

R&D funding by Fed Govt to small business, by program area, agency, and State, FY88, annual rpt, 9764–7

R&D grants of Fed Govt to small business, administrators views on effectiveness, FY86-87, GAO rpt, 26113–393

Research and education grants, USDA competitive awards by program and recipient, FY88, annual listing, 1764–1

Schools (public) partnerships with community organizations, participation, activities, and contributions, by school characteristics and location, 1987/88, 4826–1.27

State govt financial and technical aid to small business, 1988 listing, 9768–15

Statistical Abstract of US, social, political, and economic data, 1790-2025, comprehensive annual compilation, 2324–1.3

Tax (income) returns filed by type of filer, selected income items, quarterly rpt, 8302–2.1

Tax (income) returns of corporations, income and tax items by asset size and detailed industry, 1986, annual rpt, 8304–4

Tax (income) returns of individuals, detailed data, 1986, annual rpt, 8304–2

Tax collection activity of IRS, by type of tax, FY88, annual rpt, 8304–3.3

Technology-intensive small businesses sales, exports, siting, technology transfer, views on competitiveness, 1988 survey, hearing, 21728–69

Workers compensation laws of States and Fed Govt, 1989 semiannual rpt, 6502–1

see also Franchises

see National Survey of Small Business Finances

see also Small Business Investment Companies

see also Venture capital

Small Business Administration

Activities of SBA, financial condition, and loans and contracts by firm, FY88, annual rpt, 9764–1

Budget deficit reduction under Gramm-Rudman Act, cancellation of budget authority by program, FY90, annual rpt, 104–27; 21924–1; 26304–6

Budget of US Appendix, obligations, appropriations, and personnel, by program and agency, FY90, annual rpt, 104–3

Budget of US, authoritative financial statements with appropriations, outlays, and receipts, by category and agency, FY88, annual rpt, 8104–2.2

Establishments, employment, and financial ratios, for small business by SIC 1- to 2-digit industry and State, late 1960s-87, 9768–19

Establishments, operations, owner characteristics, and job training, for small businesses, late 1950s-87, 9768–20

Fed Govt contracts and obligations for small business, by program and recipient type, for North Carolina and total US, FY77-87, hearings, 21728–67

Fraud and abuse in SBA programs, audits and investigations, 1st half FY89, semiannual rpt, 9762–5

Labor unions recognized in Fed Govt, agreements and membership by agency and facility, as of Jan 1989, biennial listing, 9844–14

Mgmt training confs of SBA, cosponsors by type, and compliance with SBA regulations, by region, 1988, GAO rpt, 26113–425

R&D funding by Fed Govt to small business, by program area, agency, and State, FY88, annual rpt, 9764–7

R&D grants of Fed Govt to small business, administrators views on effectiveness, FY86-87, GAO rpt, 26113–393

Small business finances, operations, owner and employee characteristics, and Federal contracts, 1980s-88, annual rpt, 9764–6

Small Business Investment Companies capital holdings, SBA obligation, and ownership, as of June 1989, semiannual listing, 9762–4

Small Business Investment Companies finances, funding, licensing, and loan activity, 1st half FY89, semiannual rpt, 9762–3

State govt financial and technical aid to small business, 1988 listing, 9768–15

Women-owned business mgmt issues, SBA loans, Federal contracts by agency, and owners views on Michigan business climate, FY79-88, hearings, 21728–68

Small Business Investment Companies

Capital holdings, SBA obligation, and ownership of SBICs, as of June 1989, semiannual listing, 9762–4

Finances, firms, and SEC registrations and terminations, by type of investment firm, 1983-88, annual rpt, 9734–2.2

Finances, funding, licensing, and loan activity of SBICs, 1st half FY89, semiannual rpt, 9762–3

Financing disbursements by SBICs, 1980-88, annual rpt, 9764–6.2

Financing disbursements by type of SBIC, and SBA loans and contracts by firm, various dates FY84-88, annual rpt, 9764–1

Financing disbursements of SBICs, by State, 1983-87, GAO rpt, 26113–417

Fraud and abuse in SBA programs, audits and investigations, 1st half FY89, semiannual rpt, 9762–5

Tax (income) returns of corporations, income and tax items by asset size and detailed industry, 1986, annual rpt, 8304–4; 8304–21

Small, David H.

"Understanding the Behavior of M2 and V2", 9362–1.903

Smith, Creston M.

"Social Security Administration's Continuous Work History Sample", 4742–1.926

Smith, Jeffrey W.

"Autocovariance of Expenditure Shares from Consumer Expenditure Survey Data", 6886–6.60

"Measures of Percentage Change and the View of Price Indexes as Averages of Percentage Change", 6886–6.57

Smith, Karen E.

"Methods of Processing Unit Data Longitudinally on the SIPP", 2626–10.89

Smith, Mark E.

"Review and Analysis of the EEP for Wheat", 1561–12.906

"Role of Government Programs in U.S. Rice Exports", 1561–8.903

Smith, Robert S.

"Effect of OSHA Records Check Inspections on Reported Occupational Injuries in Manufacturing Establishments", 6886–6.41

"Has Injury Reporting Changed? Looking Again at Firm Size and OSHA Effects", 6886–6.63.

Smith, Scott D.
"Deflators for Purchases of Computers in GNP: Revised and Extended Estimates, 1983-88", 2702–1.902

Smith, Shelley
"State Budget Implications: Child Support Enforcement", 4698–3

Smith, Stephen M.
"Contributions of High-Tech Manufacturing to Rural Economies", 1502–7.912

Smith, Tim R.
"Regional Exports of Manufactured Products", 9381–1.903

Smith, W. Brad
"Pulpwood Production in the North-Central Region by County, 1987", 1204–19
"Wisconsin's Forest Statistics, 1987: An Inventory Update", 1206–34.8

Smith, Wendy M.
"National Priorities in Marine Pollution", 2148–57

Smithsonian Institution
Activities and finances of Instn, FY88, annual rpt, 29574–1
American Historical Assn financial statements, and membership by State, 1988, annual rpt, 29574–2
Budget of US Appendix, obligations, appropriations, and personnel, by program and agency, FY90, annual rpt, 104–3
Budget of US, authoritative financial statements with appropriations, outlays, and receipts, by category and agency, FY88, annual rpt, 8104–2.2
Education funding by Federal agency, program, and recipient type, and instn spending, FY80-88, 4828–21
Labor unions recognized in Fed Govt, agreements and membership by agency and facility, as of Jan 1989, biennial listing, 9844–14
R&D funding by Fed Govt, by field, performer type, agency, and State, FY87-89, annual rpt, 9627–20

Smog
see Air pollution

Smoking
Air pollution indoor levels, effects of ventilation rates in commercial and public buildings, 1989 rpt, 3228–10
Airline consumer complaints to DOT about service, by reason and US and foreign carrier, monthly rpt, 7302–11
Alcoholic beverages warning labels and other consumer protection methods, public views by selected characteristics, 1988 survey, 8488–5
Algeria tobacco acreage, production, trade, and use, 1983-88, article, 1925–16.914
Cancer (anal) risk, by sex and history of urogenital disorders, homosexual activity, and smoking, 1989 article, 4472–1.930
Cancer (breast) risk for women by smoking history, and menopausal and estrogen receptor status, 1976-86 study, article, 4472–1.928
Cancer (cervical) cases and risk relation to smoking and other characteristics, for 4 Latin American countries, 1986-87 study, article, 4472–1.905
Cancer (lung) incidence among smokers, by age and consumption level, 1989 article, 4472–1.911

Cancer (lung) risk, by intake of selected nutrients, fruits, and vegetables, by smoking history and sex, 1983-85 local area study, article, 4472–1.918
Cancer (lung) risk relation to home heating and cooking facilities, air pollution exposure, and smoking, by sex, for Shenyang, PRC, 1985-87 study, article, 4472–1.931
Cancer (lung) risk relation to radon exposure, and death risk by smoking status, age, and sex, 1989 article, 4472–1.913
Cancer cases, and prevention and risk activities and attitudes, 1987 survey, annual rpt, 4474–35
Cessation of smoking, treatments and health products not proven safe or effective, use, costs, and user characteristics, 1986 survey, 4008–86
Child health education programs for nutrition and smoking deterrence, effectiveness, 1979-85 local area study, article, 4472–1.916
Consumers of cigarettes, by sex, age, race, occupation, region, and State, 1985 Current Population Survey, article, 4472–1.910
Consumption of cigarettes and cigars, *Survey of Current Business*, monthly rpt, 2702–1.11
Consumption of cigarettes and other tobacco products per capita, and total spending, 1983-88, annual rpt, 1319–1.4
Consumption of cigarettes and other tobacco products, users by knowledge of health effects, and health and other characteristics, 1987, 4147–10.169
Consumption of cigarettes and smokeless tobacco, by age, sex, race, and region, 1988 survey, biennial rpt, 4494–5
Deaths and rates, by detailed cause and demographic characteristics, 1986 and trends from 1900, US Vital Statistics annual rpt, 4144–2
Health condition and health care resources, use, and spending, 1950s-87, annual data compilation, 4144–11
Health-related behavior of runners, for 7 habits, by sex, age, education, income, and average miles run per week, 1985 survey, article, 4042–3.933
Human papillomavirus infection rates, by sexual and personal hygiene practices, and other patient characteristics, Brazil local area studies, 1989 article, 4472–1.908
Injuries from use of consumer products and related activities, by victim age and sex, 1988, annual rpt, 9164–7
Injuries from use of consumer products, by severity, victim age, and detailed product, 1988, annual rpt, 9164–6
Korea (South) tobacco and cigarette production, trade, and use, 1980-88, article, 1925–16.902
Labor laws enacted, by State, 1988, annual article, 6722–1.904
Military personnel alcohol and drug abuse, prevalence and consequences, by selected characteristics, 1988, biennial rpt, 3504–19
Military personnel health-related behavior, for 7 habits, by age, education, race, and health status, 1985 survey, article, 4042–3.949

Mormons death risks from cancer and heart disease, by sex and health habits practiced, 1974 and 1979 studies, article, 4472–1.932
Nicotine, tar, and carbon monoxide content of cigarettes, by brand, 1988, 9408–53
Older persons health care services use, persons with high and low levels of care by selected health and other characteristics, 1971 and 1980 studies, 4186–2.22
Pneumonia hospitalization and death rates for aged, and risk relation to health status indicators, aggregate 1982-84, article, 4042–3.934
Prevalence of smoking, related disease and deaths, and public attitudes, impact of Surgeon General rpts and antismoking campaigns, 1964-89, annual rpt, 4204–18
Preventive disease and health improvement goals and recommended activities for 2000, with trends 1970s-80s, 4048–10
Research on smoking and health, intl projects, biennial listing, suspended, 4044–7
Research on smoking and health, publications, 1988, last issue of annual listing, 4204–19
Research on smoking and health, summaries, bimonthly rpt, 4202–8
Research on smoking and health, with trends in smoking, related disease and death, and public attitudes, literature review, 1989 annual rpt, 4204–18
Smokeless tobacco use by youth and adults, user characteristics, and sales, 1970s-86, papers, 4478–188
Statistical Abstract of US, social, political, and economic data, 1790-2025, comprehensive annual compilation, 2324–1.1
Thailand tobacco and cigarette production, trade, and use, 1984-88, article, 1925–16.901
Turkey tobacco and cigarette production, trade, and use, 1985-88, article, 1925–16.910
Workplace smoking restrictions and attitudes of employees and managers, 1986-87 local area surveys, article, 4042–3.950
Workplace smoking restrictions, and personnel directors views on morale, productivity, and smoking impacts, 1987 local area survey, article, 4472–1.904
Youth drug, alcohol, and cigarette use and attitudes, by substance type and selected characteristics, 1975-88 surveys, annual rpt, 4494–4
Youth smoking prevention program for black high school students in urban areas, teacher and student views, 1989 local areas surveys, article, 4042–3.956
see also Tobacco industry and products

SMSA
see Metropolitan Statistical Areas
see under By SMSA or MSA in the "Index by Categories"

Smuggling
Aliens (illegal) smuggled into US, and smugglers located, FY82-88, annual rpt, 6264–2
Customs Service activities, collections, entries processed by mode of transport, and seizures, FY84-88, annual rpt, 8144–1

Drug enforcement regional task forces investigation of organized crime, activities by agency and region, and background data, FY83-88, annual rpt, 6004–17

Sentences for Federal offenses, guidelines by offense and circumstances, 1989 rpt, 17668–1

Snake River

Freight (waterborne domestic and foreign) by commodity, traffic, and passengers, by port and waterway, 1987, annual rpt, 3754–3.4

Water supply and quality in streams and lakes, and groundwater levels in wells, by drainage basin, 1986, annual State rpt series, 5666–23

Water supply and quality in streams and lakes, and groundwater levels in wells, by drainage basin, 1987, annual State rpt series, 5666–10

Water supply and quality in streams and lakes, and groundwater levels in wells, by drainage basin, 1988, annual State rpt series, 5666–16

Water supply in US and southern Canada, streamflow, surface and groundwater conditions, and reservoir levels, by location, monthly rpt, 5662–3

Snell, Sherri A.

"Energy-Related Inventions Program: An Assessment of Recent Commercial Progress", 3308–91

Snider, Dixie E., Jr.

"Tuberculosis: An Increasing Problem Among Minorities in the U.S.", 4042–3.962

Snipp, Matthew

"Small Gains for Rural Indians Who Move to Cities", 1502–7.904

Snitzler, James R.

"Far East Port Survey with Special Emphasis on the Transportation and Handling of U.S. Agricultural Exports", 1278–13

Snyder, Howard N.

"Court Careers of Juvenile Offenders", 6068–227

"Juvenile Court Statistics, 1985", 6064–12

Snyder, Thomas D.

"Digest of Education Statistics, 1989", 4824–2

Soap and detergent industry

County Business Patterns, 1987: employment, establishments, and payroll, by SIC 2- to 4-digit industry and county, annual State rpt series, 2326–8

CPI by component for US city average, and by region, population size, and for 27 metro areas, monthly rpt, 6762–2

Cuba economic conditions, agricultural and industrial production and distribution, trade, and intl economic relations, 1980-87 with trends from 1961, 9118–8

Employment, earnings, and hours, by selected SIC 1- to 4-digit industry, State, and for 262 MSAs, 1972-87, 6748–81

Employment, earnings, and hours, by SIC 1- to 4-digit industry, monthly 1983-Feb 1989, annual rpt, 6744–4

Employment of minorities and women, by occupation, SIC 1- to 3- digit industry, State, and MSA, 1986, annual rpt, 9244–1

Exports of US, detailed commodities by country, monthly rpt, 2422–3

Finances and operations, by SIC 2- to 4-digit industry, forecast 1989 with trends from 1950s, annual rpt, 2044–28

Freight (waterborne domestic and foreign) by commodity, traffic, and passengers, by port and waterway, 1987, annual rpt, 3754–3

Imports of US, detailed Schedule A commodities by country, monthly rpt, 2422–2

Injuries from use of consumer products and related activities, by victim age and sex, 1988, annual rpt, 9164–7

Injuries from use of consumer products, by severity, victim age, and detailed product, 1988, annual rpt, 9164–6

Labor productivity, indexes of output, hours, and employment by SIC 2- to 4-digit industry, 1963-87, annual rpt, 6824–1.3

Manufacturing annual survey, 1986: financial and operating data, by SIC 2- to 4-digit industry, series, 2506–15

Manufacturing census, 1987: financial and operating data, for SIC 4-digit industries by product, preliminary rpt, 2491–1.36

Multinatl US firms and foreign affiliates finances and operations, by industry of parent firm and affiliate, world area, and country, preliminary 1987, annual rpt, 2704–5

Occupational injury and illness rates, by SIC 2- to 4-digit industry, 1987, annual rpt, 6844–1

Oil and fat production, consumption by end use, and stocks, by type, monthly Current Industrial Rpt, 2506–4.4

Oils, oilseeds, and fats production, prices, trade, and use, periodic situation rpt with articles, 1561–3

Price indexes (producer), by stage of processing and detailed commodity, monthly rpt, 6762–6

Price indexes (producer), by stage of processing and detailed commodity, monthly 1988, annual rpt, 6764–2

Production and sales of synthetic organic chemicals, and manufacturer listing, by product, 1988, annual rpt, 9884–3

Science, engineering, and technical employment in manufacturing, by field, occupation, and industry, 1986, triennial rpt, 9627–23

Tax (income) returns of corporations, income and tax items by asset size and detailed industry, 1986, annual rpt, 8304–4; 8304–21

• Toxicology Natl Program research and testing activities, FY87 and planned FY88, annual rpt, 4044–16

see also under By Commodity in the "Index by Categories"

Soapstone

see Nonmetallic minerals and mines

Social indicators

see Quality of life

see under names of specific indicators (listed under Population characteristics)

Social sciences

Black colleges R&D funding by source, and characteristics of grad students and research staff, by field of science and instn, 1980s-87, 9628–78

Degrees (bachelor and masters) awarded 1985/86, holders employment characteristics, 1987 survey, series, 4826–3

Degrees (PhD) in science and engineering, by field, instn, employment prospects, sex, race, and other characteristics, 1960s-88, 9627–30

Degrees awarded in higher education, by level, field, race, and sex, 1989 edition, annual rpt, 4824–2.20

Degrees in science and engineering, by field, level, and sex, 1950-86, 9628–77

DOD Dependents Schools basic skills and college entrance test scores, 1988/89, annual rpt, 3504–16

Education statistics, detailed data on elementary, secondary, and higher education, 1920s-88 and projected to 1997, annual rpt, 4824–1

Employment and earnings in science and engineering, by field and activity, and private and Federal R&D spending, by industry, 1975-88, 9626–6.29

Employment and other characteristics of science and engineering PhDs, by field and State, 1987, biennial rpt, 9627–18

Employment characteristics of scientists and engineers, by field, 1988, biennial rpt, 9627–16

Employment of scientists and engineers, and related topics, fact sheet series, 9626–2

Employment of scientists and engineers, by field and industry div, 1977, 1986, and alternative projections to 2000, 9626–2.181

Employment of scientists, engineers, and technicians, by nonmanufacturing industry and field, 1987, triennial rpt, 9627–31

Employment of scientists, engineers, and technicians in transportation, utilities, and retail and wholesale trade, by field, occupation, and industry, 1985, triennial rpt, 9627–32

Enrollment in science and engineering, degrees, and student aid and sources, with data by field, race, sex, and instn, 1980s-87, 26358–202

Enrollment in science and engineering grad programs, by field, source of funds, and characteristics of student and instn, 1975-87, annual rpt, 9627–7

Fed Govt aid to higher education and nonprofit instns for R&D and related activities, by field, instn, agency, and State, FY87, annual rpt, 9627–17

Fed Govt science and engineering employment, by field, degree level, race, sex, agency, and State, 1987, annual rpt, 9627–5

Foreign and US funding for R&D, and scientists and engineering employment and education, 1988, annual rpt, 9624–23.1

Immigrant scientists and engineers, by field, age, sex, country and world area of origin, and State, 1987 and trends from 1967, 9627–29

NASA R&D funding to higher education instns, by field, instn, and State, FY88, annual listing, 9504–7

R&D funding by Fed Govt, by field, performer type, agency, and State, FY87-89, annual rpt, 9627–20

R&D funding by higher education instns, by source and field, FY77-87, annual rpt, 9626–2.188

see also Social services
Socialism
Cuba economic conditions, agricultural and
industrial production and distribution,
trade, and intl economic relations,
1980-87 with trends from 1961,
9118-8
Eastern Europe and USSR agricultural
production, acreage, and consumption, by
commodity and country, 1965-85,
1528-284
Sociology
Degrees awarded in higher education, by
level, field, race, and sex, 1989 edition,
annual rpt, 4824-2.20
Degrees in science and engineering, by field,
level, and sex, 1950-86, 9628-77
Employment and earnings in science and
engineering, by field and activity, and
private and Federal R&D spending, by
industry, 1975-88, 9626-6.29
Employment and other characteristics of
science and engineering PhDs, by field
and State, 1987, biennial rpt, 9627-18
Employment characteristics of scientists and
engineers, by field, 1988, biennial rpt,
9627-16
Enrollment in science and engineering grad
programs, by field, source of funds, and
characteristics of student and instn,
1975-87, annual rpt, 9627-7
Fed Govt aid to higher education and
nonprofit instns for R&D and related
activities, by field, instn, agency, and
State, FY87, annual rpt,
9627-17
R&D funding by Fed Govt, by field,
performer type, agency, and State,
FY87-89, annual rpt, 9627-20
R&D funding by higher education instns, by
source and field, FY80-87, annual rpt,
9624-18.5
Soffer, Evan
"Review of IRS Research Conferences",
8304-8.1
Soft drink industry and products
Consumption of food and nutrient intake by
individuals, by food group, selected
characteristics, and region, supplementary
survey series, 1356-5
Consumption, supply, trade, prices,
spending, and indexes, by food
commodity, 1987, annual rpt, 1544-4
County Business Patterns, 1987:
employment, establishments, and payroll,
by SIC 2- to 4-digit industry and county,
annual State rpt series, 2326-8
CPI by component for US city average, and
by region, population size, and for 27
metro areas, monthly rpt, 6762-2
Employment, earnings, and hours, by SIC 1-
to 4-digit industry, monthly 1983-Feb
1989, annual rpt, 6744-4
Exports of US, detailed commodities by
country, monthly rpt, 2422-3
Finances and operations, by SIC 2- to
4-digit industry, forecast 1989 with trends
from 1950s, annual rpt, 2044-28
Labor productivity, indexes of output, hours,
and employment by SIC 2- to 4-digit
industry, 1963-87, annual rpt, 6824-1.3
Manufacturing annual survey, 1986:
financial and operating data, by SIC 2- to
4-digit industry, series,
2506-15

Manufacturing census, 1987: financial and
operating data, for SIC 4-digit industries
by product, preliminary rpt, 2491-1.8
Nutrient and caloric composition of food,
for raw, processed, and prepared food,
1988 rpt, 1358-3
Occupational injury and illness rates, by SIC
2- to 4-digit industry, 1987, annual rpt,
6844-1
Price indexes (producer), by stage of
processing and detailed commodity,
monthly rpt, 6762-6
Price indexes (producer), by stage of
processing and detailed commodity,
monthly 1988, annual rpt, 6764-2
Tax (income) returns of corporations,
income and tax items by asset size and
detailed industry, 1986, annual rpt,
8304-4; 8304-21
Wholesale trade census, 1987: employment,
establishments, finances, and operations,
by SIC 2- to 4-digit kind of business,
MSA, county, and city, State rpt series,
2405-1
Software
see Computer industry and products
Soil Conservation Service
Activities of SCS, FY88, annual rpt,
1264-2
Budget of US Appendix, obligations,
appropriations, and personnel, by program
and agency, FY90, annual rpt, 104-3
Conservation and conditions of soil, water,
and environment, with data by State and
region, 1989 quinquennial rpt, 1268-24
Conservation of soil and water, USDA
funding by program and State, FY86,
annual rpt, 1264-12
County soil surveys and maps, 1899-1987,
annual listing, 1264-11
Expenditures of Fed Govt in States, by type,
program, agency, and State, FY88, annual
rpt, 2464-2
Montana water supply, precipitation, snow
cover, and reservoir storage, by river
basin, annual rpt, discontinued, 1264-7
Oregon water supply, streamflow by station
and reservoir storage, 1989, annual rpt,
1264-9
Sedimentation control and research activity
of Fed Govt, regional and project
summaries, 1987, annual narrative rpt,
5664-9
Western US water supply, and snow survey
results, monthly State rpt series, 1266-2
Western US water supply, and snow survey
results, 1988, annual State rpt series,
1264-14
Western US water supply, storage by
reservoir and State, and streamflow
conditions, as of Oct 1989, annual rpt,
1264-4
Western US water supply, streamflow and
reservoir storage forecasts by stream and
station, Jan-May monthly rpt, 1262-1
Soil pollution
Coastal and riparian areas environmental
conditions, fish, wildlife, use, and mgmt,
for individual ecosystems, series, 5506-9
Conservation and conditions of soil, water,
and environment, with data by State and
region, 1989 quinquennial rpt, 1268-24
Hazardous waste mgmt, effectiveness of
alternative technologies, 1989 conf papers,
biennial rpt, 9184-19

Hazardous waste site remedial action under
Superfund, current and proposed sites
descriptions and status, periodic listings,
series, 9216-3
Health effects of selected pollutants,
concentrations in food and environment,
sources, and human intake, methodology
and data needs, series, 9186-9
Health effects of selected pollutants,
concentrations in food and environment,
sources, human intake, and regulation,
series, 9186-8
Idaho Natl Engineering Lab radiation
monitoring results, for facilities and
nearby areas, 1988, annual rpt, 3354-10
Industrial hazardous substances releases and
reduction methods under EPA regulation,
by chemical, source, industry, and
location, 1987, annual rpt, 9234-6
Natl historic and natural landmarks
damaged and threatened, with owner,
location, damage type, and recommended
remedial action, 1988, annual listing,
5544-16
Polychlorinated biphenyls levels in Great
Lakes environment, humans, and animals,
and emissions sources, by site, 1970s-85,
conf, 14648-19
Radioactive waste (military) disposal at New
Mexico Waste Isolation Pilot Plant,
environmental impacts, 1989 supplemental
statement, 3008-33
Radioactive waste and spent fuel generation,
inventory, and disposal, 1960s-88 and
projected to 2020, annual rpt, 3364-2
Uranium tailings at inactive mills, remedial
action proposals, costs, site characteristics,
and environmental, socioeconomic, and
health impacts, series, 3356-4
Soils and soil conservation
Acreage covered under Soil Conservation
Service activities, FY88, annual rpt,
1264-2
Agricultural Stabilization and Conservation
Service producer payments, by program,
monthly rpt, 1802-10
Agricultural Statistics, 1988, annual rpt,
1004-1.2
Army Corps of Engineers activities and
projects, FY87 and trends from 1800s,
annual rpt, 3754-1.2
Capital investment for soil conservation and
other land improvement, impacts of govt
programs and economic factors, 1983-86,
1588-137
Census of Agriculture, 1987: farms,
farmland, production, finances, and
operator characteristics, by county, final
State rpt series, 2331-1
Coal mining effect on water quality,
sediment discharges effects of alternative
mining and mgmt methods and
reclamation, for Pennsylvania, 1980-83,
5668-93
Coastal and riparian areas environmental
conditions, fish, wildlife, use, and mgmt,
for individual ecosystems, series, 5506-9
Conservation and conditions of soil, water,
and environment, with data by State and
region, 1989 quinquennial rpt, 1268-24
Conservation of soil and water, USDA
activities, 1988-97, 1008-41
Conservation of soil and water, USDA
funding by program and State, FY86,
annual rpt, 1264-12

Conservation of soil and wetlands, USDA programs costs and impacts on farm finances and operations, with background data, 1980s, hearing, 25168–69

Conservation program of USDA, participation and payments by practice and State, FY87, annual rpt, 1804–7

County Business Patterns, 1987: employment, establishments, and payroll, by SIC 2- to 4-digit industry and county, annual State rpt series, 2326–8

County soil surveys and maps, 1899-1987, annual listing, 1264–11

Developing countries disaster preparedness and economic, population, and political data, country rpt series, 9916–2

Emergency Conservation Program for farmland damaged by natural disaster, aid and participation by State, FY87, annual rpt, 1804–22

Emergency Conservation Program for farmland damaged by natural disaster, funding by region and State, monthly table, 1802–13

Environmental quality and protection programs, and intl issues, 1988 annual rpt, 484–1

Erodibility of cropland related to crop yield and revenue, 1989 article, 1502–3.903

Erodible cropland acreage enrolled in conservation program by crop and State, and program costs, FY87-88, 1588–112

Erodible cropland set aside, potential productivity related to erodibility, model results, 1989 rpt, 1588–135

Erosion (wind) damage costs to households, 1985, 1588–140

Erosion control program acreage, costs of off-farm erosion damage, and sediment and other pollutants runoff, by region, 1988, 1588–134

Expenditures of Fed Govt in States, by type, program, agency, and State, FY88, annual rpt, 2464–2

Farm financial and marketing conditions, forecast 1988, conf papers, annual rpt, 1004–16

Farm production inputs, finances, mgmt, and land value and transfers, periodic situation rpt with articles, 1561–16

Fed Govt financial and nonfinancial domestic aid, 1989 base edition with supplements, annual listing, 104–5

FmHA borrowers, by type of borrower and loan, and State, quarterly rpt, 1182–4

FmHA loans, by type, borrower characteristics, and State, quarterly rpt, 1182–8

FmHA soil and water loans, by race, Hispanic origin, and State, quarterly rpt, 1182–5

Foreign and US land degradation, tropical deforestation, and salinization of irrigated cropland, by world area, late 1970s-84, article, 1522–3.910

Forest Service mgmt of public lands and resources dev, environmental, economic, and social impacts of alternative programs, projected to 2030, 1208–24

Grazing land acreage, erosion, value, and livestock fed, by region and State, 1950-82, 1588–130

Great Plains rangeland acreage, soil erosion, and other impacts of Conservation Reserve program, 1987 conf papers, 1208–290

Historic and natural natl landmarks damaged and threatened, with owner, location, damage type, and recommended remedial action, 1988, annual listing, 5544–16

Irrigated acreage covered and idled under Conservation Reserve Program, by western State, as of 1987 and projected 1990, 1588–143

Irrigation system sediment control costs and benefits, by technique, for Idaho project, 1981-86 and projected to 2030, 1588–138

Mali farm income and production impacts of alternative soil and water mgmt strategies, model results, 1989 rpt, 1528–289

Pesticide (soil fumigant) use, impacts of bans of selected fumigants on production, farm income, and retail prices, by crop and region, 1988 rpt, 1588–136

Production mandatory control programs impacts on farm income, acreage, govt payments, and consumers, projected under alternative program provisions, 1986-90, 1548–354

Public lands acreage, grants, use, revenues, and allocations, by State, FY88, annual rpt, 5724–1.2

Puerto Rico economic conditions, 1986 hearings, 21448–39

Saline soil impacts on yields and off-farm water quality, and costs and benefits of extending erosion control program to saline cropland, 1989 rpt, 1588–144

Sedimentation control and research activity of Fed Govt, regional and project summaries, 1987, annual narrative rpt, 5664–9

Timber in southeastern US, resources mgmt and research, 1988 biennial conf papers, 1204–35

Windbarrier planting and dev, by State, FY88, annual rpt, 1204–7

see also Flood control

see also Reclamation of land

see also Soil pollution

Solar energy

Collector (solar) and photovoltaic module shipments, by type and end use, 1974-87, annual rpt, 3164–74.7

Electric power plants and capacity, by fuel used, owner, location, and operating status, 1988 and for units planned 1989-98, annual listing, 3164–36

Environmental impacts of energy technologies, 1960s-80s, handbook series, 3326–1

Equipment shipments by end-use sector and State, R&D, and trade, for collectors and photovoltaic modules, 1988, annual rpt, 3164–62

Housing and households detailed characteristics, and unit and neighborhood quality, by location, 1985, biennial rpt, 2485–12

Housing and households detailed characteristics, and unit and neighborhood quality, MSA surveys, series, 2485–6

Housing energy use, costs, and conservation, and household and housing characteristics, survey rpt series, 3166–7

Photovoltaic R&D sponsored by DOE, projects, funding, and rpts, FY88, annual listing, 3304–20

Statistical Abstract of US, social, political, and economic data, 1790-2025, comprehensive annual compilation, 2324–1.3

Solar Energy Research Institute

"Photovoltaic Energy Program Summary, FY88", 3304–20

see also Department of Energy National Laboratories

Soldiers

see Military personnel

Soldiers' and Airmen's Home

Budget of US Appendix, obligations, appropriations, and personnel, by program and agency, FY90, annual rpt, 104–3

Labor unions recognized in Fed Govt, agreements and membership by agency and facility, as of Jan 1989, biennial listing, 9844–14

Soldiers pay and allowances

see Military benefits and pensions

see Military pay

Sole proprietorships

see Proprietorships

Solid waste

see Landfills

see Recycling of waste materials

see Refuse and refuse disposal

see Sewage and wastewater systems

Solomon, David J.

"Analysis of Michigan Medicaid Costs To Treat HIV Infection", 4042–3.940

Solomon Islands

Agricultural and food production and indexes, total and for selected commodities, by country, 1970s-88, annual rpt, 1524–12

Economic, social, political, and geographic summary data, by country, 1989, annual factbook, 9114–2

Human rights conditions in 170 countries, 1988, annual rpt, 21384–3

Military aid of US, arms sales, and training programs costs and budget requests, by program, world region, and country, FY88-90, annual rpt, 7144–13

Minerals Yearbook, 1987, Vol 3: foreign country reviews of production, trade, and policy, by commodity, annual rpt, 5604–35

Minerals Yearbook, 1987, Vol 3 preprints: foreign country review of production, trade, and policy, by commodity, annual rpt, 5604–23.88

Population size, growth rates, and components of change, by country, projected 1989-2020 and trends from 1950, biennial rpt, 2324–9

UN voting record and share of votes in agreement with US, by issue, country, and world area, 1988, annual rpt, 7004–18

see also under By Foreign Country in the "Index by Categories"

Somalia

Agricultural and food production and indexes, total and for selected commodities, by country, 1970s-88, annual rpt, 1524–12

Agricultural imports and food aid needs under alternative weather assumptions, for 17 African countries, projected to 1995, 1528–279

Agricultural production, prices, and trade, by country, 1960s-89, annual world region rpt, 1524–4.2

Economic and military aid and loans from US and intl agencies, by program and country, FY46-87, annual rpt, 9914–5

Exports and imports (waterborne) of US, by type of service, commodity, country, route, and US port, 1986-87, annual rpt, 7704–2

Exports and imports of Latin America, and balance of trade with US, by country, 1988, annual rpt, 2044–34

Exports and imports of OECD, total and for 4 major countries, and US trade by country, by commodity, 1970-87, world area rpt, 9116–1.5

Food production and needs, and related economic outlook, by country, 1989/90, annual rpt, 1524–6

Immigrants admitted to US, by class of admission, country of birth, and State and MSA of destination, FY88, annual rpt, 6264–4

Immigrants admitted to US, by occupational group and country of birth, preliminary FY88, annual table, 6264–1

Immigration to US, alien workers, visitors, deportations, and naturalizations, by country, FY88 and trends from 1820, annual rpt, 6264–2

Inter-American Foundation activities, grants by recipient, and fellowships, by country, FY88, annual rpt, 14424–1

Inter-American Foundation dev grants by program area, and fellowships by field and instn, by country, FY71-88, annual rpt, 14424–2

Investment (foreign direct) of US, by selected industry group and world area, 1986-88, annual article, 2702–1.930

Loans of US banks to foreigners at all US and foreign offices, by country group and country, quarterly rpt, 13002–1

Military aid of US, arms sales, and training, by country, FY50-88, annual rpt, 3904–3

Military aid of US, arms sales, and training programs costs and budget requests, by program, world region, and country, FY88-90, annual rpt, 7144–13

Oil and gas reserves and discoveries, by country and country group, quarterly rpt, 3162–43

Peace Corps activities, funding by program, and volunteers, by country, FY90, annual rpt, 9654–1

Population size, growth rates, and components of change, by country, projected 1989-2020 and trends from 1950, biennial rpt, 2324–9

R&D funding by Fed Govt, by field, performer type, agency, and State, FY87-89, annual rpt, 9627–20

Terrorist (intl) incidents, casualties, and attacks on US targets, by attack type and country, 1980-88, 7008–56

Travel to and from US on US and foreign flag airlines, by world area, 1980-88, annual rpt, 2904–13

Travel to US, by characteristics of visit and traveler, country, port city, and State of destination, quarterly rpt, 2902–1

Travel to US, market research, major magazine ad costs and circulation, and trade show data, for selected countries, 1989-90, annual rpt, 2904–11

Travel to US, spending by category, world area of residence, census div, and State, model results, 1985-86, 2908–28

see also Argentina
see also Bolivia
see also Brazil
see also Chile
see also Colombia
see also Ecuador
see also French Guiana
see also Guyana
see also Inter-American Development Bank
see also Latin American Integration Association
see also Paraguay
see also Peru
see also Suriname
see also Uruguay
see also Venezuela
see also under By Foreign Country in the "Index by Categories"

South Bend, Ind.
see also under By City and By SMSA or MSA in the "Index by Categories"

South Carolina
Agriculture census, 1987: farms, farmland, production and costs, and operator characteristics, advance State and county rpts, 2330–1.45

Agriculture census, 1987: farms, farmland, production, finances, and operator characteristics, by county, final State rpt, 2331–1.40

Appalachian Regional Commission funding, by project and State, planned FY89, annual rpt, 9084–3

Bank deposits in FDIC-insured commercial and savings banks, by instn, State, and county, as of June 1988, annual regional rpt, 9295–3.2

Banks (insured commercial), Fed Reserve 5th District members financial statements, by State, quarterly rpt, 9389–18

Collective bargaining calendar for southeastern States, 1989, annual rpt, 6946–1.73

County Business Patterns, 1987: employment, establishments, and payroll, by SIC 2- to 4-digit industry and county, annual State rpt, 2326–8.42

Deaths and rates, by detailed location, cause, and demographic characteristics, 1987, US Vital Statistics annual rpt, 4144–3.1

DOD prime contract awards, by contractor, service branch, State, and city, FY88, annual rpt, 3544–22

Economic indicators by State, Fed Reserve 5th District, quarterly rpt, 9389–16

Employment and housing market indicators by State, FHLB 4th District, quarterly rpt, 9302–36

Employment and unemployment, for 8 southeastern States, 1987-88, annual rpt, 6944–2

Employment by industry div, earnings, and hours, for 8 southeastern States, quarterly press release, 6942–7

Employment, earnings, and hours, by selected SIC 1- to 4-digit industry, State, and for 262 MSAs, 1972-87, 6748–81.5

Estuary environmental conditions and mgmt, 1989 conf, 2146–6.12; 2146–6.13

Fed Govt spending in States and local areas, by type, State, county, and city, FY88, annual rpt, 2464–3

Fed Govt spending in States, by type, program, agency, and State, FY88, annual rpt, 2464–2

HHS financial aid, by program, recipient, State, and city, FY88, annual regional listing, 4004–3.4

Homeless children educational enrollment and needs, 1988, annual State rpt, 4804–35.40

Income (personal) per capita and by source, and earnings by industry div, by State, MSA, and county, 1982-87, annual regional rpt, 2704–2.4

Mineral Industry Surveys, State reviews of production, 1988, preliminary annual rpt, 5614–6

Minerals Yearbook, 1987, Vol 2 preprints: State review of production and sales by commodity, and business activity, annual rpt, 5604–16.42

Minerals Yearbook, 1987, Vol 2: State reviews of production, sales, and firms, by commodity, and business activity, annual rpt, 5604–34

Nursing home compliance with Medicare and Medicaid regulations, and patient characteristics, by facility, 1987/88, annual State rpt, 4654–15.42

Peach production, marketing, and prices in 3 southeastern States and Appalachia, 1988, annual rpt, 1311–12

Retail trade census, 1987: employment, establishments, sales, and payroll, by SIC 2- to 4-digit kind of business, MSA, county, and city, State rpt, 2397–1.41

Savings instns, FHLB 4th District members finances and financial ratios, by State, quarterly rpt, 9302–3

Savings instns, FHLB 4th District members finances, by State, 1984-88, annual rpt, 9304–29.7

Service industries census, 1987: employment, establishments, receipts, and payroll, by SIC 2- to 4-digit kind of business, MSA, county, and city, State rpt, 2391–1.41

Statistical Abstract of US, social, political, and economic data, with foreign comparisons, 1790-2025, comprehensive annual compilation, 2324–1

Textile mill employment, earnings, and hours, for 8 Southeastern States, quarterly press release, 6942–1

Transportation census, 1987: trucks, by detailed characteristics, miles traveled, and type of product carried, State rpt, 2573–1.41

Water supply and quality in streams and lakes, and groundwater levels in wells, by drainage basin, 1987, annual State rpt, 5666–10.38

Wholesale trade census, 1987: employment, establishments, finances, and operations, by SIC 2- to 4-digit kind of business, MSA, county, and city, State rpt, 2405–1.41

Wildlife-related recreation, hunting, and fishing participation and spending, detailed data, 1985 survey, quinquennial State rpt, 5506–6.40

see also Charleston, S.C.
see also Columbia, S.C.
see also Greenville, S.C.
see also Rock Hill, S.C.
see also Spartanburg, S.C.
see also under By State in the "Index by Categories"

South Dakota

Agriculture census, 1987: farms, farmland, production and costs, and operator characteristics, advance State and county rpts, 2330-1.46

Agriculture census, 1987: farms, farmland, production, finances, and operator characteristics, by county, final State rpt, 2331-1.41

Bank deposits in FDIC-insured commercial and savings banks, by instn, State, and county, as of June 1988, annual regional rpt, 9295-3.5

Business and economic conditions, Fed Reserve 9th District, quarterly journal, 9383-19

County Business Patterns, 1987: employment, establishments, and payroll, by SIC 2- to 4-digit industry and county, annual State rpt, 2326-8.43

Deaths and rates, by detailed location, cause, and demographic characteristics, 1987, US Vital Statistics annual rpt, 4144-3.1

DOD prime contract awards, by contractor, service branch, State, and city, FY88, annual rpt, 3544-22

Economic conditions, Fed Reserve 9th District, quarterly rpt, 9383-18

Employment, earnings, and hours, by selected SIC 1- to 4-digit industry, State, and for 262 MSAs, 1972-87, 6748-81.5

Fed Govt spending in States and local areas, by type, State, county, and city, FY88, annual rpt, 2464-3

Fed Govt spending in States, by type, program, agency, and State, FY88, annual rpt, 2464-2

HHS financial aid, by program, recipient, State, and city, FY88, annual regional listing, 4004-3.8

Homeless children educational enrollment and needs, 1988, annual State rpt, 4804-35.41

Income (personal) per capita and by source, and earnings by industry div, by State, MSA, and county, 1982-87, annual regional rpt, 2704-2.3

Indian reservation water supply projects in South Dakota, costs and indicators of need, with health and housing data for other reservations, 1980s-87, hearing, 21448-37

Mineral Industry Surveys, State reviews of production, 1988, preliminary annual rpt, 5614-6

Minerals Yearbook, 1987, Vol 2 preprints: State review of production and sales by commodity, and business activity, annual rpt, 5604-16.43

Minerals Yearbook, 1987, Vol 2: State reviews of production, sales, and firms, by commodity, and business activity, annual rpt, 5604-34

Nursing home compliance with Medicare and Medicaid regulations, and patient characteristics, by facility, 1987/88, annual State rpt, 4654-15.43

Retail trade census, 1987: employment, establishments, sales, and payroll, by SIC 2- to 4-digit kind of business, MSA, county, and city, State rpt, 2397-1.42

Savings instns, FHLB 8th District members financial operations by State and SMSA, monthly rpt, 9302-9

Service industries census, 1987: employment, establishments, receipts, and payroll, by SIC 2- to 4-digit kind of business, MSA, county, and city, State rpt, 2391-1.42

Statistical Abstract of US, social, political, and economic data, with foreign comparisons, 1790-2025, comprehensive annual compilation, 2324-1

Wages by occupation, and benefits for office and plant workers, 1989 survey, periodic labor market rpt, 6785-3.10

Water supply and quality in streams and lakes, and groundwater levels in wells, by drainage basin, 1987, annual State rpt, 5666-10.39

Wholesale trade census, 1987: employment, establishments, finances, and operations, by SIC 2- to 4-digit kind of business, MSA, county, and city, State rpt, 2405-1.42

Wildlife-related recreation, hunting, and fishing participation and spending, detailed data, 1985 survey, quinquennial State rpt, 5506-6.41

see also under By State in the "Index by Categories"

South West Africa

see Namibia

Southeast Asia

Agricultural and food production and indexes, total and for selected commodities, by country, 1970s-88, annual rpt, 1524-12

Agricultural subsidies, consumer and producer equivalents by program, commodity, and major US trading partner, 1982-86, 1528-275

Agricultural trade of US, by detailed commodity and country, 1988, semiannual rpt, 1522-4

AID activities and funding by project and function, FY90, and developing countries summary socioeconomic data from 1960s, annual rpt, 9904-4.6

AID economic aid to developing countries, obligations and disbursements by country, quarterly rpt, 9912-4

AID loans authorized, signed, and canceled, by country and world area, quarterly rpt, 9912-2

Economic and military aid and loans from US and intl agencies, by program and country, FY46-87, annual rpt, 9914-5

Exports and imports (waterborne) of US, by type of service, commodity, country, route, and US port, 1986-87, annual rpt, 7704-2

Exports and imports of US, by commodity group, world area, selected country, US coastal area and port, and mode of transport, monthly rpt, 2422-9

Exports and imports of US, by selected country, country group, and commodity group, 1988, annual rpt, 2044-37

Exports and imports of US with Asian countries by commodity, and free trade area proposal, 1985-88, 9886-4.135

Exports, imports, and balances of US by commodity group, world area, and country, and related employment, 1970s-88, annual rpt, 2044-26

Food production and needs, and related economic outlook, by country, 1989/90, annual rpt, 1524-6

Southeastern Power Administration

Immigration to US, alien workers, visitors, deportations, and naturalizations, by country, FY88 and trends from 1820, annual rpt, 6264-2

Military aid of US, arms sales, and training, by country, FY50-88, annual rpt, 3904-3

Military aid programs and related activities of US, costs by country and intl agency, FY85-87 and cumulative from FY50, GAO rpt, 26123-30

Military, economic, technological, and trade conditions of Pacific Basin countries, 1970s-85, compilation of papers, 3908-4

Military spending, arms trade, and force strengths, with govt spending and population, by country, 1977-87, annual rpt, 9824-1

Minerals production, reserves, and industry role in domestic economy and world supply, 1988 world area rpt, 5606-1.17

Minerals Yearbook, 1987, Vol 3: foreign country reviews of production, trade, and policy, by commodity, annual rpt, 5604-35

Oil and gas reserves and discoveries, by country and country group, quarterly rpt, 3162-43

Refugee arrivals and resettlement in US, by age, sex, sponsoring agency, State, and country, monthly rpt, 4692-2

Refugee arrivals in US by world area of origin and State of settlement, and Federal aid, FY88-90, annual rpt, 7004-16

Refugee resettlement programs and funding, arrivals by country of origin, and indicators of adjustment, by State, FY88, annual rpt, 4694-5

Refugees from Indochina, arrivals, and departures, by country of origin and resettlement, camp, and ethnicity, monthly rpt, 7002-4

Refugees from Indochina, fertility indicators by ethnic group, 1970s-84, article, 4042-3.910

Tide height and time daily at coastal points, forecast 1990, annual rpt, 2174-2.5

Weather conditions and effect on agriculture, by US region, State, and city, and world area, weekly rpt, 2152-2

see also Association of Southeast Asian Nations

see also Brunei

see also Burma

see also Cambodia

see also Christmas Island

see also Indonesia

see also Laos

see also Malaysia

see also Philippines

see also Singapore

see also Thailand

see also Vietnam

see also under By Foreign Country in the "Index by Categories"

Southeastern Power Administration

Electric power wholesale purchases and costs for REA borrowers, by borrower, supplier, and State, 1940-87, annual rpt, 1244-5

Finances and operations of Federal power admins, as of Sept 1987, annual rpt, 3164-23.4

Sales by customer, plants, and capacity of SEPA, and Southeastern Fed Power Program financial statements, FY88, annual rpt, 3234-1

Wildlife damage to crops, livestock, and property in Great Plains, and effectiveness of mgmt methods, 1988 conf, 1208-304
see also under By Region in the "Index by Categories"
see also under names of individual States

Soviet Union

Agricultural and food production and indexes, total and for selected commodities, by country, 1970s-88, annual rpt, 1524-12

Agricultural exports of US, for grains, oilseed products, hides, skins, and cotton, by country, weekly rpt, 1922-3

Agricultural production, acreage, and consumption, by Eastern Europe country and commodity, 1965-85, 1528-284

Agricultural production cost efficiency of USSR, by Republic, model description and results, 1960s-85, 1528-292

Agricultural subsidies, consumer and producer equivalents by program, commodity, and major US trading partner, 1982-86, 1528-275

Agricultural trade by commodity and country, prices, and world market devs, monthly rpt, 1922-12

Agricultural trade of US, by detailed commodity and country, 1988, semiannual rpt, 1522-4

Arms control treaties status, and Arms Control and Disarmament Agency activities, 1988, annual rpt, 9824-2

Borders (maritime) between Turkey and USSR, geographic coordinates established under agreements of 1978 and 1983, 7006-8.4

Budget deficits and financing, revenues, and spending, with retail prices, for USSR, 1970-88, 9118-6

Coal production, trade, and govt subsidies, by country and country group, 1973-87 and projected to 2000, 2048-144

Cotton production, trade, and use, for selected countries, FAS monthly circular, 1925-4.2

Cuba economic conditions, agricultural and industrial production and distribution, trade, and intl economic relations, 1980-87 with trends from 1961, 9118-8

Debt, trade, and balances of Eastern Europe and USSR with US and other western countries, with background data, 1980s-87, hearing, 21248-120

Economic and military aid and loans from US and intl agencies, by program and country, FY46-87, annual rpt, 9914-5

Economic conditions and military activity, for USSR, 1960s-86, hearing, 23848-195

Economic conditions in Communist and OECD countries, 1987, annual rpt, 7144-11

Economic conditions in Communist, OECD, and selected other countries, 1960s-88, annual rpt, 9114-4

Economic conditions in USSR under General Secretary Gorbachev, Soviet and CIA measurement methods with background data, 1987 conf papers, 9118-4

Economic conditions in USSR under General Secretary Gorbachev, Soviet and CIA measures, 1950s-87, 9118-5

Economic conditions in USSR under General Secretary Gorbachev, 1988 and trends from 1956, annual rpt, 9114-6

Economic conditions, policy, and trade practices, by country, 1986-88, annual rpt, 21384-5

Economic, social, political, and geographic summary data, by country, 1989, annual factbook, 9114-2

Educational issues in USSR, 1988 conf, 4814-1

Energy-intensive industry output and operations, and US investment barriers, for energy-rich countries, 1984-88, 9886-4.142

Export licensing, monitoring, and enforcement activities, FY88, annual rpt, 2024-1

Exports and imports of US, by selected country, country group, and commodity group, 1988, annual rpt, 2044-37

Exports and imports of US with Communist countries, by detailed commodity and country, quarterly rpt with articles, 9882-2

Exports, imports, and balances of US by commodity group, world area, and country, and related employment, 1970s-88, annual rpt, 2044-26

Fertilizer components use, by world area, 1978-88 and projected to 2010, 5608-154

Food consumption by commodity, and food processing capacity, for USSR, 1960s-88, article, 1541-7.903

Grain area, yield, production, trade, supply, and use forecasts, FAS monthly circular, 1925-2.3

Grain exports to USSR and PRC under long-term bilateral agreements, 1976-88, 26123-227

Grain imports of USSR from US, 1970s-88 and commitments through 1990, FAS press release, 1928-10

Grain trade agreement of USSR with US, wheat, corn, and soybean imports, 1983-88, article, 9882-2.903

Helsinki Final Act implementation by NATO and Warsaw Pact, Oct 1988-Mar 1989, semiannual rpt, 7002-1

Human rights conditions in 170 countries, 1988, annual rpt, 21384-3

Income (personal) by source, disposable income, wage deductions by type, and savings, 1950s-87, 9118-7

Labor conditions and work accidents, 1989 annual country rpt, 6366-4.3

Livestock and poultry stocks and products production, for USSR, FAS monthly circular, 1925-2.3

Military aid of US, arms sales, and training, by country, FY50-88, annual rpt, 3904-3

Military spending, arms trade, and force strengths, with govt spending and population, by country, 1977-87, annual rpt, 9824-1

Military strength and spending of USSR and Warsaw Pact, FY88, annual rpt, 3544-2

Military strength of USSR and Warsaw Pact, and proposed force reductions, with comparisons to NATO, 1980s-91, hearing, 21208-29

Military weapons systems, aid, presence, and force strengths of USSR and Warsaw Pact, and compared to US and NATO, 1989 annual rpt, 3504-20

Minerals production, trade, and use, by commodity, for USSR, 1983-87, annual rpt, 5604-39

Minerals Yearbook, 1987, Vol 3: foreign country reviews of production, trade, and policy, by commodity, annual rpt, 5604-35

Minerals Yearbook, 1987, Vol 3 preprints: foreign country review of production, trade, and policy, by commodity, annual rpt, 5604-23.72

Nuclear power plant capacity and operating status, by plant and Communist country, as of Dec 1988, annual rpt, 3164-57.2

Officials appearances in and outside USSR, 1988, annual rpt, 9114-1

Oil and gas production, use, and trade by country, for Communist countries, monthly rpt, 9112-2

Oil production by major exporting countries, monthly rpt, 3162-24.10

Oil production, trade, use, and stocks, by selected country and country group, monthly rpt, 3162-42

Pakistan airspace violations by USSR and Afghanistan, and casualties, 1980-86, hearing, 21388-54

Population size, growth rates, and components of change, by country, projected 1989-2020 and trends from 1950, biennial rpt, 2324-9

Radio Free Europe and Radio Liberty broadcast and financial data, and compared to other intl broadcasters, FY88, annual rpt, 10314-1

Railroad productivity and operations, for USSR, 1983-86, working paper, 2326-18.47

Refugee arrivals in US by world area and country of origin, and quotas, monthly rpt, 7002-4

Refugee arrivals in US by world area of origin and State of settlement, and Federal aid, FY88-90, annual rpt, 7004-16

Refugee resettlement programs and funding, arrivals by country of origin, and indicators of adjustment, by State, FY88, annual rpt, 4694-5

Science and technology planning, and relation to economic plans, for USSR, 1989 working paper, 2326-18.45

Ships in world merchant fleet, and tonnage, by country of registry, as of Jan 1988, annual rpt, 7704-3

Space launches and other activities of NASA and USSR, with flight data, 1957-88, annual rpt, 9504-6.1

Space program of USSR, activities, plans, and characteristics of flights and vehicles, 1981-87, 25268-76

Space satellites and other objects launched since 1957, quarterly listing, 9502-2

Tungsten production, reserves, trade, and use, and operations of selected plants, for USSR, selected years 1915-86, 5606-5.8

UN voting record and share of votes in agreement with US, by issue, country, and world area, 1988, annual rpt, 7004-18

Weather conditions and effect on agriculture, by US region, State, and city, and world area, weekly rpt, 2152-2

Wheat procurement and prices paid to domestic producers under USSR govt programs, 1981-90, article, 1561-12.908
see also under By Foreign Country in the "Index by Categories"

Rail loadings of grain and soybeans, periodic situation rpt with articles, 1561–4

Rail shipments of grain and other commodities by car type, 1986, and rail car fleet size, 1978-88, 1278–15

Rail shipments of grain, by commodity and port region, and car fleet requirements, 1949-88 with projections to 2001, 1278–14

Railroad deregulation impacts on grain shipping rates and revenues, 1981-85, 1548–349

Soviet Union wheat, corn, and soybean imports from US under 5-year grain agreement, 1983-88, article, 9882–2.903

Statistical Abstract of US, social, political, and economic data, 1790-2025, comprehensive annual compilation, 2324–1.3

Stocks of grain by region and market city, and grain inspected for export, by type, weekly rpt, 1313–4

Stocks of grain on and off farms, by crop, quarterly rpt, 1621–4

see also under By Commodity in the "Index by Categories"

Space program accidents and safety

Debris from spacecraft in orbit, hazards, and tracking, with data for individual fragmented craft, 1961-88, 9508–34

Space programs

Aerial survey R&D rpts, and sources of natural resource and environmental data, quarterly listing, 9502–7

Budget of US Appendix, obligations, appropriations, and personnel, by program and agency, FY90, annual rpt, 104–3

Budget of US, compact budgets by activity, function, and agency, FY90 and projected to FY94, annual rpt, 104–2

Budget of US, historical data, selected years FY34-88 and projected to FY94, annual rpt, 104–22

Budget of US, Reagan Admin policy changes by program, FY90, annual rpt, 104–21

Budget of US, special analysis of Federal capital spending by category, projected FY89-2005 and trends from FY81, annual rpt, 104–24

DOD budget justification, programs, and policies, FY88, annual rpt, 3544–2

DOD budget, weapons acquisition costs by system and service branch, FY89-91, annual rpt, 3504–2

Employment and payroll, by function, level of govt, and State, 1988, annual rpt, 2466–1.1; 2466–1.5

Expenditures of Fed Govt in States, by type, program, agency, and State, FY88, annual rpt, 2464–2

Expenditures of govts, by function, natl income and product account, *Survey of Current Business*, monthly rpt, 2702–1.24

Expenditures of NASA and DOD for space programs, by category, FY81-89, GAO rpt, 26123–152

Finances and operations, by SIC 2- to 4-digit industry, forecast 1989 with trends from 1950s, annual rpt, 2044–28

Foreign and US funding for R&D, and scientists and engineering employment and education, 1988, annual rpt, 9624–23.1

Fraud and abuse in NASA programs, audits and investigations, 1st half FY89, semiannual rpt, 9502–9

NASA activities and finances, and data on US and USSR space launches, 1957-88, annual rpt, 9504–6

NASA project launch schedules and technical descriptions, press release series, 9506–2

Nuclear reactors for domestic use and export by function and operating status, with owner, operating characteristics, and location, 1988 annual listing, 3004–26

Procurement by NASA, economic benefits by industry group, jobs created, and sales, by State, FY90, 9508–35

Procurement contract awards of NASA, by type, contractor, State, and country, FY89, semiannual rpt, 9502–6

Rural areas aid from Fed Govt compared to urban areas, by program and degree of urbanization, FY85, periodic rpt, 1598–248

Soviet Union and Warsaw Pact military weapons systems, aid, presence, and force strengths, and compared to US and NATO, 1989 annual rpt, 3504–20

Soviet Union space program activities, plans, and characteristics of flights and vehicles, 1981-87, 25268–76

Statistical Abstract of US, social, political, and economic data, 1790-2025, comprehensive annual compilation, 2324–1.3

see also Communications satellites

see also Meteorological satellites

see also Satellites

see also Space program accidents and safety

see also Space sciences

see also Spacecraft

see also Strategic Defense Initiative

Space sciences

Aerial survey R&D rpts, and sources of natural resource and environmental data, quarterly listing, 9502–7

Employment characteristics of scientists and engineers, by field, 1988, biennial rpt, 9627–16

Expenditures for R&D by Fed Govt, by detailed function, program, and agency, FY88-90, annual rpt, 9627–9

NASA activities and finances, and data on US and USSR space launches, 1957-88, annual rpt, 9504–6

NASA project launch schedules and technical descriptions, press release series, 9506–2

NASA R&D funding to higher education instns, by field, instn, and State, FY88, annual listing, 9504–7

Procurement contract awards of NASA, by type, contractor, State, and country, FY89, semiannual rpt, 9502–6

R&D funding by Fed Govt at large science facilities, by field, performer, and facility, FY86-88, hearings, 21708–128

R&D funding by Fed Govt, by field, performer type, agency, and State, FY87-89, annual rpt, 9627–20

R&D funding by source and field, selected years 1953-89, annual rpt, 9624–18

Statistical Abstract of US, social, political, and economic data, 1790-2025, comprehensive annual compilation, 2324–1.3

Spacecraft

County Business Patterns, 1987: employment, establishments, and payroll, by SIC 2- to 4-digit industry and county, annual State rpt series, 2326–8

Debris from spacecraft in orbit, hazards, and tracking, with data for individual fragmented craft, 1961-88, 9508–34

DOD budget, weapons acquisition costs by system and service branch, FY89-91, annual rpt, 3504–2

DOD prime contract awards, by detailed procurement category, FY85-88, annual rpt, 3544–18

Launch schedules and technical descriptions of NASA projects, press release series, 9506–2

Launchings by US and USSR, 1957-88, annual rpt, 9504–6

Launchings of satellites and other space objects since 1957, quarterly listing, 9502–2

Manufacturers finances and operations, by SIC 2- to 4-digit industry, forecast 1989 and trends from 1950s, annual rpt, 2044–28

Manufacturing annual survey, 1986: value of shipments, by SIC 4- to 5-digit product class, 2506–15.3

Manufacturing census, 1987: financial and operating data, for SIC 4-digit industries by product, preliminary rpt, 2491–1.76

see also Communications satellites

see also Meteorological satellites

see also Satellites

see also Space program accidents and safety

Spain

Agricultural and food production and indexes, total and for selected commodities, by country, 1970s-88, annual rpt, 1524–12

Agricultural production, prices, and trade, by country, 1970s-88 and forecast 1990, annual world region rpt, 1524–4.1

Agricultural trade of US, by detailed commodity and country, 1988, semiannual rpt, 1522–4

AID activities and funding by project and function, FY90, and developing countries summary socioeconomic data from 1960s, annual rpt, 9904–4.6

AID loans repayment status and terms by program and country, and status of predecessor agency loans, quarterly rpt, 9912–3

Alcohol use, abuse, treatment, and views of racial and ethnic groups in US and native countries, by selected characteristics, 1988 compilation of papers, 4488–12

Coal production, trade, and govt subsidies, by country and country group, 1973-87 and projected to 2000, 2048–144

Drug abuse indicators, by world region and selected country, 1988 semiannual conf, 4492–5.1

Drug abuse indicators, for selected countries, 1989 semiannual conf, 4492–5.2

Economic and military aid and loans from US and intl agencies, by program and country, FY46-87, annual rpt, 9914–5

Economic and monetary trends, compounded annual rates of change for US and 13 trading partners, quarterly rpt annual supplement, 9391–7

Economic conditions in Communist, OECD, and selected other countries, 1960s-88, annual rpt, 9114–4

Economic conditions, income, production, prices, employment, and trade, 1988 periodic country rpt, 2046–4.11

Economic conditions, policy, and trade practices, by country, 1986-88, annual rpt, 21384–5

Economic, social, political, and geographic summary data, by country, 1989, annual factbook, 9114–2

Exports and imports of US, by selected country, country group, and commodity group, 1988, annual rpt, 2044–37

Human rights conditions in 170 countries, 1988, annual rpt, 21384–3

Imports of goods, services, and investment from US, trade barriers, impacts, and US actions, by country, 1988, annual rpt, 444–2

Military aid of US, arms sales, and training programs costs and budget requests, by program, world region, and country, FY88-90, annual rpt, 7144–13

Military spending, arms trade, and force strengths, with govt spending and population, by country, 1977-87, annual rpt, 9824–1

Minerals Yearbook, 1987, Vol 3: foreign country reviews of production, trade, and policy, by commodity, annual rpt, 5604–35

Minerals Yearbook, 1987, Vol 3 preprints: foreign country review of production, trade, and policy, by commodity, annual rpt, 5604–23.65

Multinatl US firms and foreign affiliates finances and operations, by industry of parent firm and affiliate, world area, and country, preliminary 1987, annual rpt, 2704–5

Nuclear power generation in US and 19 non-Communist countries, monthly rpt, 3162–24.10

Nuclear power plant capacity, generation, and operating status, by plant and foreign and US location, 1988 and projected to 2020, annual rpt, 3164–57

Oil production, trade, use, and stocks, by selected country and country group, monthly rpt, 3162–42

Population size, growth rates, and components of change, by country, projected 1989-2020 and trends from 1950, biennial rpt, 2324–9

Space satellites and other objects launched since 1957, quarterly listing, 9502–2

Steel export ceilings under voluntary restraint agreements, by country and product, with Western US steel industry impact, 1989 rpt, 9886–4.136

Steel imports of US under voluntary restraint agreement, by product, customs district, and country, with US industry operating data, monthly rpt, 9882–13

Stone (dimension) trade and price indexes by selected country, 1987, Mineral Industry Surveys, annual rpt, 5614–29

UN voting record and share of votes in agreement with US, by issue, country, and world area, 1988, annual rpt, 7004–18

see also under By Foreign Country in the "Index by Categories"

Spanish heritage Americans
see Hispanic Americans

Spanish Sahara
see Western Sahara

Sparks, Amy L.
"Situation and Prospects for Fresh Apple Markets", 1561–6.901

Sparta, Wis.
Wages by occupation, for office and plant workers, 1989 survey, periodic MSA rpt, 6785–3.9

Spartanburg, S.C.
Wages by occupation, for office and plant workers, 1989 survey, periodic MSA rpt, 6785–3.8

see also under By SMSA or MSA in the "Index by Categories"

Spatz, Karen J.
"Co-ops Have a Distinct Commitment to Exporting Processed Foods", 1122–1.906

Spear, Alden, Jr.
"Measuring Household Change at the Individual Level Using Data from SIPP", 2626–10.96

Special districts
Bus drivers pay impacts of taxes dedicated to local systems funding and other factors, 1950s-85, working paper, 9377–9.73

Census of Govts, 1987: elected officials, by level of govt, race, sex, and State, preliminary rpt, 2450–2

Census of Govts, 1987: property tax revenue by level of govt, assessed values by locality, and exemptions, by property type and State, 2453–1

Electric power wholesale purchases and costs for REA borrowers, by borrower, supplier, and State, 1940-87, annual rpt, 1244–5

Employment and payroll, by function, level of govt, and State, 1988, annual rpt, 2466–1.1; 2466–1.5

Enterprise zone program of Maryland, participants characteristics and views on incentives, and proposed Federal program tax expenditures, 1983-88, GAO rpt, 26131–53

Expenditures of local govts, impacts of competition among govtl units, migration, and other factors, 1976-77, working paper, 9377–9.82

Finances of govts, by level of govt, State, and for large cities and counties, annual rpt series, 2466–2

Finances, structure, and service delivery of local govts in metro areas, local area rpt series, 10046–9

Finances, tax systems and revenue, and fiscal structure, by level of govt and State, selected years 1929-91, annual rpt, 10044–1.2

Minority group and women employment in State and local govt, by occupation, function, and pay level, 1986, annual rpt, 9244–6.3

Statistical Abstract of US, social, political, and economic data, 1790-2025, comprehensive annual compilation, 2324–1.2

Water supply in rural areas, public system financial and operating characteristics, by region, 1980, 1598–247

see also School districts

Special Drawing Rights
Assets and debts of private sector, balance sheets by segment, 1949-88, semiannual rpt, 9365–4.1

Budget of US, authoritative financial statements with appropriations, outlays, and receipts, by category and agency, FY88, annual rpt, 8104–2.2

Economic indicators and components, current data and annual trends, monthly rpt, 23842–1.7

Fed Govt receipts by source and outlays by agency, *Treasury Bulletin,* quarterly rpt, 8002–4.1

Fed Reserve banks finances and staff, 1988, annual rpt, 9364–1.1

Financial and business statistics, historic trends, 1988 annual chartbook, 9364–2.17

Flow-of-funds accounts, assets and liabilities by type and economic sector, outstanding at year-end 1965-88, annual rpt, 9364–3

Flow-of-funds accounts, savings, investments, and credit statements, quarterly rpt, 9365–3.3

Intl finance and trade studies, 1987 biennial compilation, 9375–14

Investment (intl) position of US, by component, industry, world region, and country, 1987-88, annual article, 2702–1.922

Reserve assets of US by type, *Treasury Bulletin,* quarterly rpt, 8002–4.10

Reserve assets of US, monthly rpt, 9362–1.3

Special education
Assistance (financial and nonfinancial) of Fed Govt, 1989 base edition with supplements, annual listing, 104–5

Condition of Education, detailed data on elementary and secondary education, 1920s-88 and projected to 1997, annual rpt, 4824–1.1

Digest of Education Statistics, detailed data on students, staff, finances, and facilities, 1989 edition, annual rpt, 4824–2

Early childhood education for handicapped children, project descriptions, 1988/89, annual listing, 4944–10

Education Dept programs funding, operations, and effectiveness, FY88, annual rpt, 4804–5

Enrollment by age, staff, funding, and needs of special education programs, by type of handicap and State, 1987/88, annual rpt, 4944–4

Enrollment in public elementary and secondary schools, and facilities, by type and State, 1987/88, annual rpt, 4834–17

Enrollment in special education by disability, transfers to public schools from State instns, services provided, and Federal funding, with data by State, 1987-88, GAO rpt, 26121–294

Expenditures of Fed Govt in States, by type, program, agency, and State, FY88, annual rpt, 2464–2

Head Start enrollment, funding, and staff, FY88, annual rpt, 4604–8

Head Start handicapped enrollment, by handicap, State, and for Indian and migrant programs, 1985/86, annual rpt, 4604–1

Head Start program operations, enrollment by handicap, and family characteristics, for North Central States, 1987/88, annual rpt, 4604–12

Nursing home facility, staff, and resident
detailed characteristics, 1985,
4147–13.97

State allocation of Federal educational
funds, by program, recipient type, and
State, 1987/88, annual rpt, 4804–8

Statistical Abstract of US, social, political,
and economic data, 1790-2025,
comprehensive annual compilation,
2324–1.1

see also Compensatory education
see also Remedial education

Special foreign currency programs

AID local currency trust funds mgmt and
use, by country, FY83-87, GAO rpt,
26123–221

Currency (foreign) accounts owned by US
under AID admin and by foreign govts
with joint AID control, status by program
and country, quarterly rpt, 9912–1

Currency (foreign) holdings of US,
transactions and balances by program and
country, 1st half FY89, semiannual rpt,
8102–7

Developing countries economic and social
conditions from 1960s, and Intl Dev
Cooperation Agency and AID activities
and funding, FY88-90, annual rpt,
9904–4

DOD outlays and obligations, by function
and service branch, quarterly rpt, 3542–3

NIH intl program activities and funding, by
inst and country, FY88, annual rpt,
4474–6

PL 480 foreign currency status, by use,
agency, and country, as of FY87, annual
rpt, 1924–7

R&D funding by Fed Govt, by field,
performer type, agency, and State,
FY87-89, annual rpt, 9627–20

Special observances

see Vacations and holidays

Speech pathology and audiology

Educational enrollment of disabled in
postsecondary instns, by disability,
educational, and other characteristics, fall
1986, 4846–3.6

Enrollment in science and engineering grad
programs, by field, source of funds, and
characteristics of student and instn,
1975-87, annual rpt, 9627–7

Fed Govt employment of minorities,
handicapped, and veterans, and years of
service, by occupation, age, sex, and
agency, as of Sept 1988, biennial rpt,
9844–27

Head Start handicapped enrollment, by
handicap, State, and for Indian and
migrant programs, 1985/86, annual rpt,
4604–1

Head Start program operations, enrollment
by handicap, and family characteristics,
for North Central States, 1987/88, annual
rpt, 4604–12

Indian Health Service outpatient visits, by
type of provider, selected hospital, and
IHS service area, FY87-88, annual rpt,
4084–3

Medicare discharges, charges, and length of
stay, by State and diagnosis, 1983 and
1985, article, 4652–1.925

Military health care personnel, and
accessions by training source, by
occupation, specialty, and service branch,
FY87, annual rpt, 3544–24

Nursing home facility, staff, and resident
detailed characteristics, 1985,
4147–13.97

Nursing home rehabilitation services use, by
service type and patient characteristics,
1st qtr 1983, 4188–58

Special education enrollment by disability,
transfers to public schools from State
instns, services provided, and Federal
funding, with data by State, 1987-88,
GAO rpt, 26121–294

Special education programs, enrollment by
age, staff, funding, and needs, by type of
handicap and State, 1987/88, annual rpt,
4944–4

VA Medicine and Surgery Dept trainees, by
detailed program and city, FY88, annual
rpt, 8704–4

see also Ear diseases and infections

Speed limit

see Traffic laws and courts

Speich, Steven M.

"Catalog of Washington Seabird Colonies",
5508–101

Spencer, Gregory

"Projections of the Population of the U.S.,
by Age, Sex, and Race: 1988 to 2080",
2546–3.158

Spencer, John S., Jr.

"Wisconsin's Fourth Forest Inventory,
1983", 1206–34.7

Spendable earnings

see Earnings, general

see Personal and household income

Spices and herbs

Agricultural Statistics, 1988, annual rpt,
1004–1

Agriculture census, 1987: farms, farmland,
production, finances, and operator
characteristics, by county, final State rpt
series, 2331–1

Consumption, supply, trade, prices,
spending, and indexes, by food
commodity, 1987, annual rpt, 1544–4

CPI by component for US city average, and
by region, population size, and for 27
metro areas, monthly rpt, 6762–2

Exports and imports (agricultural) of US, by
commodity and country, bimonthly rpt
with articles, 1522–1

Exports and imports (agricultural) of US, by
commodity, monthly rpt, 1922–8

Exports and imports (agricultural) of US, by
detailed commodity and country, 1988,
semiannual rpt, 1522–4

Exports of essential oils, by type and
country, FAS monthly circular with
articles, 1925–34

Exports of US, detailed commodities by
country, monthly rpt, 2422–3

Farm income, expenses, receipts by
commodity, assets, liabilities, and ratios,
1988 and trends from 1945, annual rpt,
1544–16

Foreign and US production, prices, and
trade, FAS annual circular series,
1925–15

Foreign countries agricultural production,
prices, and trade, by country, 1970s-89
and forecast 1990, annual world region rpt
series, 1524–4

Health care treatments and products not
proven safe or effective, use, costs, and
user characteristics, 1986 survey,
4008–86

Imports of US, detailed Schedule A
commodities by country, monthly rpt,
2422–2

Irrigation projects of Reclamation Bur in
western US, crop production and acreage
by commodity, State, and project, 1987,
annual rpt, 5824–12.1

Manufacturing census, 1987: financial and
operating data, for SIC 4-digit industries
by product, preliminary rpt, 2491–1.9;
2491–1.40

Mint oil prices received by farmers and
production value, by State, 1986-88,
annual rpt, 1621–2

Nutrient and caloric composition of food,
for raw, processed, and prepared food,
1988 rpt, 1358–3

Price indexes (producer), by stage of
processing and detailed commodity,
monthly rpt, 6762–6

Price indexes (producer), by stage of
processing and detailed commodity,
monthly 1988, annual rpt, 6764–2

Production of fruit and vegetables for
processing, industries finances and
operations, consumption, and trade, by
commodity, 1970s-88, 1568–275

Spies

see Espionage

Spinal cord injuries

Deaths and rates, by detailed cause and
demographic characteristics, 1986 and
trends from 1900, US Vital Statistics
annual rpt, 4144–2

Insurance (health) companies case mgmt for
high-cost patients, savings, costs, and
returns, 1984-86, article, 4652–1.914

Spindt, Paul A.

"Underpricing of Seasoned Issues: The Case
of U.S. Treasury Bills", 9366–6.168

Spokane, Wash.

Wages by occupation, and benefits for office
and plant workers, 1989 survey, periodic
MSA rpt, 6785–3.10

see also under By City and By SMSA or
MSA in the "Index by Categories"

Sporting goods

County Business Patterns, 1987:
employment, establishments, and payroll,
by SIC 2- to 4-digit industry and county,
annual State rpt series, 2326–8

CPI by component for US city average, and
by region, population size, and for 27
metro areas, monthly rpt, 6762–2

DOD prime contract awards, by detailed
procurement category, FY85-88, annual
rpt, 3544–18

Employment, earnings, and hours, by
selected SIC 1- to 4-digit industry, State,
and for 262 MSAs, 1972-87, 6748–81

Employment, earnings, and hours, by SIC 1-
to 4-digit industry, monthly 1983-Feb
1989, annual rpt, 6744–4

Exports of US, detailed commodities by
country, monthly rpt, 2422–3

Imports of US, detailed Schedule A
commodities by country, monthly rpt,
2422–2

Imports of US given duty-free treatment for
value of US material sent abroad, and
impacts on US industry and employment,
by commodity and country, 1987, annual
rpt, 9884–14

Injuries from use of consumer products and
related activities, by victim age and sex,
1988, annual rpt, 9164–7

Minerals Yearbook, 1987, Vol 3: foreign country reviews of production, trade, and policy, by commodity, annual rpt, 5604–35

Minerals Yearbook, 1987, Vol 3 preprints: foreign country review of production, trade, and policy, by commodity, annual rpt, 5604–23.85

Population size, growth rates, and components of change, by country, projected 1989-2020 and trends from 1950, biennial rpt, 2324–9

UN voting record and share of votes in agreement with US, by issue, country, and world area, 1988, annual rpt, 7004–18

see also under By Foreign Country in the "Index by Categories"

Srinivasan, Aruna

"Costs of Financial Intermediation Under Regulation: Development Banks and Commercial Banks", 9371–10.39

"Measuring State and Local Fiscal Capacities in the Southeast", 9371–1.912

"Public Finance and Economic Growth in the Southeast", 9371–1.904

St. Christopher and Nevis

Economic, social, political, and geographic summary data, by country, 1989, annual factbook, 9114–2

Human rights conditions in 170 countries, 1988, annual rpt, 21384–3

Population size, growth rates, and components of change, by country, projected 1989-2020 and trends from 1950, biennial rpt, 2324–9

UN voting record and share of votes in agreement with US, by issue, country, and world area, 1988, annual rpt, 7004–18

see also under By Foreign Country in the "Index by Categories"

St. Cloud, Minn.

Wages by occupation, for office and plant workers, 1989 survey, periodic MSA rpt, 6785–12.7

see also under By SMSA or MSA in the "Index by Categories"

St. Joseph, Mo.

see also under By SMSA or MSA in the "Index by Categories"

St. Kitts-Nevis

see St. Christopher and Nevis

St. Lawrence, Janet S.

"Differences in Gay Men's AIDS Risk Knowledge and Behavior Patterns in High and Low AIDS Prevalence Cities", 4042–3.939

St. Lawrence River

Great Lakes water levels fluctuations, causes, and impacts of alternative mgmt strategies, 1900s-88, series, 14646–1

Pollutant discharges, sources, and control program activities for Great Lakes basin, 1987, biennial rpt, 14644–1

Traffic, costs, and other activities of US and Canada Great Lakes ship pilots, and US testing and certificates, 1960s-87, 7308–192

Traffic on Seaway for ships, cargo, and passengers, and toll revenue, 1988 and trends from 1959, annual rpt, 7744–2

Water levels of Great Lakes and connecting channels, and forecasts, semimonthly rpt, 3752–2

Water supply and quality in streams and lakes, and groundwater levels in wells, by drainage basin, 1986, annual State rpt series, 5666–23

Water supply and quality in streams and lakes, and groundwater levels in wells, by drainage basin, 1987, annual State rpt series, 5666–10

Water supply and quality in streams and lakes, and groundwater levels in wells, by drainage basin, 1988, annual State rpt series, 5666–16

Water supply in northeastern US, precipitation and stream runoff by station, monthly rpt, 2182–3

Water supply in US and southern Canada, streamflow, surface and groundwater conditions, and reservoir levels, by location, monthly rpt, 5662–3

St. Lawrence Seaway Development Corp.

Budget of US Appendix, obligations, appropriations, and personnel, by program and agency, FY90, annual rpt, 104–3

Employment of DOT, by subagency, occupation, and selected personnel characteristics, FY88, annual rpt, 7304–18

Traffic on Seaway for ships, cargo, and passengers, and toll revenue, 1988 and trends from 1959, annual rpt, 7744–2

St. Louis, Mo.

Airline merger of TWA and Ozark, impacts on fares and departures at St Louis, Mo, 1985-88, 7308–194

CPI by component for US city average, and by region, population size, and for 15 metro areas, monthly rpt, 6762–1

CPI by component for US city average, and by region, population size, and for 27 metro areas, monthly rpt, 6762–2

Drug abuse indicators for selected metro areas, research results, data collection, and policy issues, 1989 semiannual conf, 4492–5

Drug test results at arrest, by drug type, offense, and sex, for selected urban areas, quarterly rpt, 6062–3

Economic and banking conditions, for Fed Reserve 8th District, quarterly rpt with articles, 9391–16

Freight (waterborne domestic and foreign) by commodity, traffic, and passengers, by port and waterway, 1987, annual rpt, 3754–3.2

Fruit and vegetable shipments, and arrivals in US and Canada cities, by mode of transport and State and country of origin, 1988, annual rpt, 1311–4.2

Govt (local) finances, structure, and service delivery, for St Louis metro area, mid-1980s, 10046–9.1

Homeless population characteristics by city, and Federal funding by program, 1980s-89, hearings, 21248–123

Housing starts and completions authorized by building permits in 40 MSAs, quarterly rpt, 2382–9

Wages by occupation, and benefits for office and plant workers, 1989 survey, periodic MSA rpt, 6785–12.2

see also under By City and By SMSA or MSA in the "Index by Categories"

St. Lucia

Economic, social, political, and geographic summary data, by country, 1989, annual factbook, 9114–2

Human rights conditions in 170 countries, 1988, annual rpt, 21384–3

Population size, growth rates, and components of change, by country, projected 1989-2020 and trends from 1950, biennial rpt, 2324–9

UN voting record and share of votes in agreement with US, by issue, country, and world area, 1988, annual rpt, 7004–18

see also under By Foreign Country in the "Index by Categories"

St. Paul, Minn.

CPI by component for US city average, and by region, population size, and for 27 metro areas, monthly rpt, 6762–2

Drug abuse indicators for selected metro areas, research results, data collection, and policy issues, 1989 semiannual conf, 4492–5

Freight (waterborne domestic and foreign) by commodity, traffic, and passengers, by port and waterway, 1987, annual rpt, 3754–3.2; 3754–3.3

Housing and households characteristics, 1985 survey, MSA fact sheet, 2485–11.8

Housing and households detailed characteristics, and unit and neighborhood quality, by location, 1985 survey, MSA rpt, 2485–6.5

Housing starts and completions authorized by building permits in 40 MSAs, quarterly rpt, 2382–9

Wages by occupation, for office and plant workers, 1989 survey, periodic MSA rpt, 6785–12.4

see also under By City and By SMSA or MSA in the "Index by Categories"

St. Petersburg, Fla.

Housing and households characteristics, 1985 survey, MSA fact sheet, 2485–11.7

Housing and households detailed characteristics, and unit and neighborhood quality, by location, 1985 survey, MSA rpt, 2485–6.6

Housing starts and completions authorized by building permits in 40 MSAs, quarterly rpt, 2382–9

Wages by occupation, for office and plant workers, 1988 survey, periodic MSA rpt, 6785–11.2

Wages by occupation, for office and plant workers, 1989 survey, periodic MSA rpt, 6785–12.6

see also under By City and By SMSA or MSA in the "Index by Categories"

St. Vincent and The Grenadines

Economic conditions, income, production, prices, employment, and trade, 1989 periodic country rpt, 2046–4.43

Economic, social, political, and geographic summary data, by country, 1989, annual factbook, 9114–2

Human rights conditions in 170 countries, 1988, annual rpt, 21384–3

Investment (direct) incentives of Caribbean Basin Initiative, economic impacts, with finances and employment by country, 1984-88, 2048–141

Population size, growth rates, and components of change, by country, projected 1989-2020 and trends from 1950, biennial rpt, 2324–9

UN voting record and share of votes in agreement with US, by issue, country, and world area, 1988, annual rpt, 7004–18

see also under By Foreign Country in the "Index by Categories"

Stage, Albert R.
"Selected Yield Tables for Plantations and Natural Stands in Inland Northwest Forests", 1208–300

Staggers Rail Act
Short-line railroads operations and regulation, for lines established 1980-87 and trends from 1834, hearing, 21368–109

Stallings, David
"Global Trade Environment and Agriculture", 1522–3.912

Stam, Jerome M.
"Farm Sector Financial Stress and Farm Lender Acquired Property in the 1980s", 1541–1.903

Stamford, Conn.
see also under By City and By SMSA or MSA in the "Index by Categories"

Standard Consolidated Areas
see Metropolitan Statistical Areas

Standard Industrial Classification
Manufacturing and mineral industries censuses, 1987: SIC industry and SIC-based product codes, listing, 2628–10

Standard Metropolitan Statistical Areas
see Metropolitan Statistical Areas
see under By SMSA or MSA in the "Index by Categories"
see under By Urban-Rural and Metro-Nonmetro in the "Index by Categories"

Standard of living
see Cost of living
see Family budgets
see Personal and household income
see Quality of life

Standards
see Industrial standards
see Quality control and testing
see Weights and measures

Standish, Mich.
Wages by occupation, for office and plant workers, 1989 survey, periodic MSA rpt, 6785–3.8

Starsinic, Donald E.
"Patterns of Metropolitan Area and County Population Growth: 1980-87", 2546–3.160

START
see Strategic Arms Reduction Talks

State aid programs
see Aid to Families with Dependent Children
see Medicaid
see Medical assistance
see State funding for economic development
see State funding for education
see State funding for health and hospitals
see State funding for higher education
see State funding for local areas
see State funding for public safety
see State funding for social welfare
see State government spending
see Supplemental Security Income
see Unemployment insurance
see Workers compensation

State and local employees
Child support collection programs of States, operations, costs, and Federal incentive payments, by State, FY86-1987, 4698–3
Corrupt govt officials prosecuted and convicted, by judicial district and level of govt, 1978-88, annual rpt, 6004–13

Criminal justice spending, employment, and payroll, by level of govt, State, and selected city and county, FY71-85, annual rpt, 6064–9
DC govt workers compensation under Fed Govt admin, program finances and operations, FY87, annual rpt, 6504–10
Disabled persons employment and architectural barrier removal laws, Federal and State govt compliance, findings and recommendations, 1989 rpt, 10048–74
Employment and payroll, by function and level of govt, 1987-88, annual rpt series, 2466–1
Employment and payroll of State and local govts, monthly rpt, 6742–4
Employment Cost Index and percent change by occupational group, industry div, region, and metro-nonmetro area, quarterly press release, 6782–5
Employment, earnings, and hours, by selected SIC 1- to 4-digit industry, State, and for 262 MSAs, 1972-87, 6748–81
Employment, earnings, and hours, by SIC 1- to 4-digit industry, monthly 1983-Feb 1989, annual rpt, 6744–4
Employment situation, earnings, hours, and other BLS economic indicators, transcripts of BLS Commissioner's monthly testimony, periodic rpt, 23846–4
Epidemiologists in State health depts, ratios to population and professional characteristics, 1983, article, 4042–3.914
Exchange of employees between Fed Govt and other organizations, program activities and costs, with data by agency, FY84-88, GAO rpt, 26119–260
Health Care Financing Review, provider prices, price inputs and indexes, and labor, quarterly journal, 4652–1.1
Insurance (short term disability) coverage and provisions, by occupational group, 1986-87, article, 6722–1.925
Labor productivity of State and local employees, indexes of output by function, FY63-87, annual rpt, 6824–1.6
Law enforcement spending and employment, by activity and level of govt, 1970s-88, annual rpt, 6064–6.1
Meat and poultry inspection activities and staff of Federal, State, and foreign govts, FY88, annual rpt, 1374–1
Minority group and women employment in State and local govt, by occupation, function, pay level, and State, 1986, annual rpt, 9244–6
Prison employees drug testing, and training and treatment referrals provided, 1988 rpt, 6066–26.1
Railroad accidents, casualties, and damage, Fed Railroad Admin activities, and safety inspectors by State, 1987, annual rpt, 7604–12
Science and engineering employment characteristics, by field, 1988, biennial rpt, 9627–16
Science and engineering labor force, Federal and university research funding, and educational data, series, 9626–6
Science and engineering labor supply by region and employment characteristics, and salaries by years of experience, 1987, 9626–2.184
Science and engineering PhDs employment and other characteristics, by field and State, 1987, biennial rpt, 9627–18

Services transfer from govts to private contractors, impacts on govt workers, with data by worker characteristics, level of govt, and location, 1980s-87, 15496–1.5
Southwestern States employment by industry div, earnings, and hours, by State, monthly rpt, 6962–2
St Louis metro area local govt finances, structure, and service delivery, mid-1980s, 10046–9.1
Statistical Abstract of US, social, political, and economic data, 1790-2025, comprehensive annual compilation, 2324–1.2
Transit systems finances and operations, by mode of transport, size of fleet, and for 432 systems, 1986, annual rpt, 7884–4
Unemployment insurance administrative funding by Fed Govt, impacts of reductions on State program operations, FY80-88, GAO rpt, 26121–284
Unemployment insurance coverage of establishments, employment, and wages, by SIC 4-digit industry and State, 1988, annual rpt, 6744–16
see also Civil service system
see also Fire departments
see also Labor-management relations in government
see also Officials
see also Police
see also State and local employees pay
see also State police
see also Teachers

State and local employees pay
Bus drivers pay impacts of taxes dedicated to local systems funding and other factors, 1950s-85, working paper, 9377–9.73
Collective bargaining wage and benefit changes and coverage, monthly rpt, 6782–1
Collective bargaining wage and benefit changes and coverage, 1st half 1989, semiannual press release, 6782–6
Collective bargaining wage and benefit changes, by sector, 1954-88, 6728–38.7
Criminal justice spending, employment, and payroll, by level of govt, State, and selected city and county, FY71-85, annual rpt, 6064–9
Earnings by industry div, and personal income per capita and by source, by State, MSA, and county, 1982-87, annual regional rpts, 2704–2
Earnings by major industry group, and personal income per capita and by source, by region and State, 1929-87, 2708–40
Employee flexible benefit plan coverage and provisions, by occupational group for private sector and govt workers, 1986-88, article, 6722–1.959
Employment and payroll, by function and level of govt, 1987-88, annual rpt series, 2466–1
Employment Cost Index and alternative measure of compensation costs, by component, occupation, industry group, union status, and location, 1975-89, annual rpt, 6744–20
Finances of govts, by level of govt, State, and for large cities and counties, annual rpt series, 2466–2
Income (household, family, and personal), by source, detailed characteristics, and region, 1987, annual Current Population Rpt, 2546–6.59

Law enforcement spending and employment, by activity and level of govt, 1970s-88, annual rpt, 6064-6.1

Minority group and women employment in State and local govt, by occupation, function, pay level, and State, 1986, annual rpt, 9244-6

Natl income and product accounts and components, *Survey of Current Business*, monthly rpt, 2702-1.21

Natl income and product accounts govt transactions component estimates, methodology and bibl, 1988 technical rpt, 2706-6.5

Payroll and employment of State and local govts, monthly rpt, 6742-4

Police agencies employment, spending, and operations, FY87, 6066-25.20

Police dept operations, staff, and expenses, for large cities by population size, 1987, 6066-19.51

Police pay, benefits, and staffing, for US Park Police and compared to other Federal and local police units, FY85-88, GAO rpt, 26119-264

Science and engineering employment and earnings, by field and activity, and private and Federal R&D spending, by industry, 1975-88, 9626-6.29

Science and engineering PhDs employment and other characteristics, by field and State, 1987, biennial rpt, 9627-18

Services transfer from govts to private contractors, impacts on govt workers, with data by worker characteristics, level of govt, and location, 1980s-87, 15496-1.5

Statistical Abstract of US, social, political, and economic data, 1790-2025, comprehensive annual compilation, 2324-1.2

Transit systems finances and operations, by mode of transport, size of fleet, and for 432 systems, 1986, annual rpt, 7884-4

Unemployment insurance coverage of employment, establishments, and wages, by industry div and level of govt, 1978-87, 6728-38.5

Unemployment insurance coverage of establishments, employment, and wages, by SIC 4-digit industry and State, 1988, annual rpt, 6744-16

Workers compensation programs of States, top officials, salaries, and hours, by State, as of 1988, annual rpt, 6504-9

see also Civil service pensions

see also Educational employees pay

State and local taxes

Bus drivers pay impacts of taxes dedicated to local systems funding and other factors, 1950s-85, working paper, 9377-9.73

Collections of taxes, by level of govt, type of tax, State, and selected counties, quarterly rpt, 2462-3

Consumer Expenditure Survey, household income by source, and itemized spending, by selected characteristics and location, 1984-86, annual rpt, 6764-5.2

CPI tax liability components, by tax type, 1967-85, working paper, 6886-6.18

Energy producers finances and operations, by energy type for US firms domestic and foreign operations, 1987, annual rpt, 3164-44

Finances of govts, by level of govt, State, and for large cities and counties, annual rpt series, 2466-2

Finances of govts, revenue and spending by level of govt, natl income and product accounts, selected years 1929-88, annual rpt, 204-1.6

Finances of govts, tax systems and revenue, and fiscal structure, by level of govt and State, selected years 1929-91, annual rpt, 10044-1

Financial and business statistics, historic trends, 1988 annual chartbook, 9364-2.9

Foreign travelers spending in US by world area of residence, and economic impact, by spending category, census div, and State, model results, 1985-86, 2908-28

Hwy receipts by source, and spending by function, by level of govt and State, 1988, annual rpt, 7554-1.3

Income (household) and poverty status under alternative income definitions, by recipient characteristics, 1986, Current Population Rpt, 2546-6.58

Income tax deduction of State and local taxes, subsidy rates by State, 1985, article, 9373-1.910

Income tax deductions and exclusions, Federal tax expenditures by item, FY90-94, annual rpt, 21784-10

Income tax returns of individuals, detailed data, 1986, annual rpt, 8304-2

Income tax returns of individuals, selected income and tax items by income level, preliminary 1987, annual article, 8302-2.917

Insurance (health) for Federal employees, State taxes on plan underwriters, 1987, GAO rpt, 26119-262

Mail order sales from out of State, tax revenues and rates under proposed collection system, by State, 1988 hearings, 21528-73

Metro area employment and manufacturing output growth, relation to labor costs and area economic conditions, 1976-85, working paper, 9375-13.8

Natl income and product accounts and components, *Survey of Current Business*, monthly rpt, 2702-1.21

Natl income and product accounts govt transactions component estimates, methodology and bibl, 1988 technical rpt, 2706-6.5

New England States economic indicators, Fed Reserve 1st District, quarterly rpt, 9373-2.3

Older persons care by family members, tax subsidies in 2 States, 1981-84, article, 4652-1.915

Public opinion on taxes, spending, and govt efficiency, by respondent characteristics, 1989 survey, annual rpt, 10044-2

Retailer sales tax collection compliance costs, by industry group and for 7 States, 1981, hearings, 21528-73

Revenue potential of State and local tax systems relative to natl average tax burden, by type of tax and State, 1986, annual rpt, 10044-7

Southeastern States govt revenues by source, spending by purpose, and tax effort indexes, by State, 1970s-87, article, 9371-1.904

Southeastern States tax capacity and effort indexes, by State, 1982-86, article, 9371-1.912

Southeastern US economic and employment conditions, for 4 largest MSAs, 1977-87, article, 9391-16.902

St Louis metro area local govt finances, structure, and service delivery, mid-1980s, 10046-9.1

Statistical Abstract of US, social, political, and economic data, 1790-2025, comprehensive annual compilation, 2324-1.2

Telephone firms detailed finances and operations, 1987, annual rpt, 9284-6.4

Texas tax revenue by source, and govt spending by purpose, FY85, technical paper, 9379-12.28

Transit systems finances and operations, by mode of transport, size of fleet, and for 432 systems, 1986, annual rpt, 7884-4

Transportation finances, operations, vehicles, equipment, accidents, and energy use, by mode of transport, 1955-88, annual rpt, 7304-2

Unemployment insurance programs of States and Fed Govt, benefits, coverage, exhaustions, and finances, by State, and beneficiary characteristics, 1940s-FY89, 21788-175

Urban areas fiscal, economic, and social conditions, 1960s-87, biennial rpt, 5184-7.2

Urban Dev Action Grant eligibility rating system of HUD, and project costs and economic impacts, as of Nov 1988, GAO rpt, 26113-424

Urban Dev Action Grants, funding, and jobs and taxes generated, by city, FY88, annual rpt, 5124-5

Urban Dev Action Grants, funding sources, project descriptions, and economic impacts, by city, periodic press releases, 5002-7

see also Excise tax

see also Fuel tax

see also Property tax

see also Revenue sharing

see also Sales tax

see also Severance taxes

State College, Pa.

see also under By SMSA or MSA in the "Index by Categories"

State courts

Expenditures and employment for law enforcement, by activity and level of govt, 1984-87, annual rpt, 6064-6.1

Sentences by State courts for felony offenses, and sentence lengths and time served, by offense, 1986, 6066-25.19

Torts for product liability, dispositions, awards, case processing time, and plaintiff injury severity and other characteristics, 1983-85, GAO rpt, 26121-317

US attorneys work hours, by type of court and Federal district, FY88, annual rpt, 6004-2.6

Wiretaps authorized, costs, arrests, trials, and convictions, by offense and jurisdiction, 1988, annual rpt, 18204-7

State Department

see Department of State

State forests

Georgia timber resources and removals, by species, ownership class, and county, 1988-89, series, 1206-26

Mgmt of public lands and resources dev, environmental, economic, and social impacts of alternative Forest Service programs, projected to 2030, 1208-24

New Mexico timber acreage and resources, by species, ownership class, and county, 1986-87, series, 1206-23

Planting and dev of forests and windbarriers, by State, FY88, annual rpt, 1204-7

Tennessee timber acreage and resources, by species, ownership class, and county, 1989, series, 1206-27

Timber resources surveys of Forest Service, coverage and methodology, 1932-89, 9188-110

Wisconsin timber resources and removals, by species, forest type, ownership, and county, series, 1206-34

State funding for economic development

Appalachia local dev projects, and funding by source, by program and State, FY88, annual rpt, 9084-1

Construction put in place, value of new public and private structures, by type, monthly rpt, 2382-4

Enterprise zone program of Maryland, participants characteristics and views on incentives, and proposed Federal program tax expenditures, 1983-88, GAO rpt, 26131-53

Finances of govts, revenues by source and spending by function, natl income and product account, *Survey of Current Business*, monthly rpt, 2702-1.24

Small business financial and technical aid of States, 1988 listing, 9768-15

State funding for education

Condition of Education, detailed data on elementary and secondary education, 1920s-88 and projected to 1997, annual rpt, 4824-1.1

Data on education, selected performance and financial indicators by State, 1982-88, annual table with supplements, 4804-32

Digest of Education Statistics, detailed data on students, staff, finances, and facilities, 1989 edition, annual rpt, 4824-2

Elementary and secondary public education agency revenues by source and outlays, by State, FY86-87, annual rpt, 4834-6

Fed Govt education funds allocation by States, by program, recipient type, and State, 1987/88, annual rpt, 4804-8

Finances of govts, by level of govt, State, and for large cities and counties, annual rpt series, 2466-2

Libraries (public) special programs, project descriptions and funding by level of govt, State, and city, 1984-87, annual rpt, 4874-4

Special education programs, enrollment by age, staff, funding, and needs, by type of handicap and State, 1987/88, annual rpt, 4944-4

Statistical Abstract of US, social, political, and economic data, 1790-2025, comprehensive annual compilation, 2324-1.1

Vocational education aid recipients and sources, and characteristics of programs and students, 1970s-89, series, 4806-3

see also State funding for higher education

State funding for health and hospitals

AIDS patients and persons with AIDS virus infection, Medicaid policies and State health insurance regulation, with background data, 1987-88, article, 4652-1.953

Board and care homes conditions, State licensing and enforcement activity, and client characteristics, 1970s-88, 21148-55

Board and care homes licensing and inspection by States, and client characteristics, 1989 GAO rpt, 26121-275

Children (handicapped) health care services block grants of Fed Govt, State and other funding, and children served, by State, FY87, GAO rpt, 26121-301

Drug and alcohol abuse treatment facilities, services, use, funding, and client characteristics, 1987, annual rpt, 4494-10

Employment and payroll, by function, level of govt, and State, 1988, annual rpt, 2466-1.5

Finances of govts, by level of govt, State, and for large cities and counties, annual rpt series, 2466-2

Health condition and health care resources, use, and spending, 1950s-87, annual data compilation, 4144-11

Hospital reimbursement by States under prospective payment programs, effects on operations, finances, and patient deaths, by State, 1970s-83, 4658-29

Infant deaths, causes, and prevention, recommendations and findings, 1988 rpt, 15838-1

Insurance (health) for long term care, State regulation and enforcement actions, 1986-88, GAO rpt, 26121-282

Mental health care hospitals and costs per patient, by State, selected years 1969-87, 21148-55

Mental health care hospitals, beds and caseload by State, patient characteristics, finances, and staff, for profit and nonprofit private instns, 1986, 4506-3.37

Veterans health care, patients, visits, costs, and operating beds, by VA and contract facility, and region, quarterly rpt, 8602-4

see also Medicaid

State funding for higher education

Agricultural research funding and staffing for USDA, State agencies, and other instns, by topic, FY88, annual rpt, 1744-2

Allocation of Federal education funds by States, by program, recipient type, and State, 1987/88, annual rpt, 4804-8

Finances of govts, by level of govt, State, and for large cities and counties, annual rpt series, 2466-2

R&D equipment of higher education instns, acquisition and service costs, condition, and financing, by field, 1982-83 and 1985-86, 9628-76

Science and engineering education enrollment, degrees, and student aid and sources, with data by field, race, sex, and instn, 1980s-87, 26358-202

Student aid and other sources of support, with student expenses and characteristics, by instn type and control, 1987 triennial study, series, 4846-3

Student aid funding and participation, by Federal program, instn type and control, and State, various periods 1959-88, annual rpt, 4804-28

State funding for local areas

Alaska rural villages population characteristics and and subsistence activities, 1976-86, 5738-9

Appalachia local dev projects, and funding by source, by program and State, FY88, annual rpt, 9084-1

Education funding of Fed Govt, State allocation by program, recipient type, and State, 1987/88, annual rpt, 4804-8

Enterprise zone program of Maryland, participants characteristics and views on incentives, and proposed Federal program tax expenditures, 1983-88, GAO rpt, 26131-53

Finances of govts, by level of govt, State, and for large cities and counties, annual rpt series, 2466-2

Homeless persons aid programs, and shelter capacity and voucher programs, for 5 major cities, 1988, 5188-122

Hwy receipts by source, and spending by function, by level of govt and State, 1988, annual rpt, 7554-1.3

Hwy Statistics, summary data by State, 1987-88, annual rpt, 7554-24

Statistical Abstract of US, social, political, and economic data, 1790-2025, comprehensive annual compilation, 2324-1.2

Transit systems finances and operations, by mode of transport, size of fleet, and for 432 systems, 1986, annual rpt, 7884-4

Transit systems in rural areas, operations and govt funding by region and State, 1986-87, 1278-11

State funding for public safety

Crime and criminal justice data collection activities of Bur of Justice Statistics and States, FY88, annual rpt, 6064-21

Criminal justice spending, employment, and payroll, by level of govt, State, and selected city and county, FY71-85, annual rpt, 6064-9

Drug enforcement activities of State and local agencies, Federal aid by recipient, and background data, FY88, annual rpt, 6064-28

Employment and payroll, by function, level of govt, and State, 1988, annual rpt, 2466-1.5

Environmental protection budgets and aid of EPA and State, and regulation impacts on local govts credit availability and farm income, 1988 hearings, 25408-99

Finances of govts, by level of govt, State, and for large cities and counties, annual rpt series, 2466-2

Juvenile correctional and detention instns, inmates, and expenses, by instn and resident characteristics and State, 1975-85, biennial rpt, 6064-13

Landfills requiring cleanup under Federal and State programs, by operating status, disposition of site expansion applications, and State, 1986-88, GAO rpt, 26113-430

Law enforcement spending and employment, by activity and level of govt, 1970s-88, annual rpt, 6064-6.1

Prison conditions, population, and problems, issues and bibl, 1989 compilation of papers, 25928-8

see also State police

State funding for social welfare

Beneficiaries families and children, and total and average payments, by public assistance program and State, since 1940, monthly rpt, 4742–1.5

Disability Insurance and SSI admin of Fed Govt and States, benefits, caseloads, and operations, 1980s, 4708–11

Employment and payroll, by function, level of govt, and State, 1988, annual rpt, 2466–1.5

Farm operators displaced worker programs under Job Training Partnership Act, funding, participation, and results by selected State, 1982-87, 15496–1.2

Finances of govts, by level of govt, State, and for large cities and counties, annual rpt series, 2466–2

Indian social services funding by Federal, State, and tribal agencies, with reservation land property tax, for Montana, FY87, GAO rpt, 26121–257

Job Training Partnership Act performance standards use in serving AFDC recipients, State policies and effectiveness, 1983-86, 15496–1.4

Job Training Partnership Act State and local admin, funding, effectiveness, and participants, GAO rpt series, 26106–8

Poverty rate, impact of public income transfers by State, 1984-88, article, 6722–1.933

Vocational rehabilitation programs of Fed Govt and States, activities and funding, FY88, annual rpt, 4944–1

see also Medicaid

see also Supplemental Security Income

see also Unemployment insurance

State government

Finances of govts, by level of govt, State, and for large cities and counties, annual rpt series, 2466–2

Finances of govts, revenues by source and spending by function, natl income and product account, *Survey of Current Business*, monthly rpt, 2702–1.24

Finances of govts, tax systems and revenue, and fiscal structure, by level of govt and State, selected years 1929-91, annual rpt, 10044–1

Finances of State and local govts, revenues by source and outlays by type, 1985-88, annual article, 2702–1.908; 2702–1.935

Finances, policy, and intergovtl relations of Federal, State, and local govts, series, 10046–8

Financial and business statistics, historic trends, 1988 annual chartbook, 9364–2.9

Governors of States and territories, terms and salaries, 1989-90, *Congressional Directory*, biennial rpt, 23874–1

Public opinion on taxes, spending, and govt efficiency, by respondent characteristics, 1989 survey, annual rpt, 10044–2

Securities issued by State and local govts and corporations, 1987, annual rpt, 9364–5.5

Statistical Abstract of US, social, political, and economic data, 1790-2025, comprehensive annual compilation, 2324–1.2

see also Census of Governments

see also Federal aid to States

see also Federal-State relations

see also Interstate relations

see also State and local employees

see also State and local employees pay

see also State and local taxes

see also State courts

see also State forests

see also State funding for economic development

see also State funding for education

see also State funding for health and hospitals

see also State funding for higher education

see also State funding for local areas

see also State funding for public safety

see also State funding for social welfare

see also State government spending

see also State laws

see also State legislatures

see also State-local relations

see also State parks

see also State police

see also under By State in the "Index by Categories"

see also under names of individual States

State government spending

Contractor and private vendor prompt payment from govts, State law provisions and terms by State, 1988, GAO rpt, 26111–59

Contractor and private vendor prompt payment from govts, State procedures, 1988-89, GAO rpt, 26111–64

Expenditures of State and local govts relation to tax revenue and Federal aid, model description and results, 1960-87, working paper, 9387–8.183

Finances of govts, by level of govt, State, and for large cities and counties, annual rpt series, 2466–2

Finances of govts, revenues by source and spending by function, natl income and product account, *Survey of Current Business*, monthly rpt, 2702–1.24

Finances of State and local govts, revenues by source and outlays by type, 1985-88, annual article, 2702–1.908; 2702–1.935

Flow-of-funds accounts, savings, investments, and credit statements, quarterly rpt, 9365–3.3

Hwy admin and gasoline tax revenue proposed transfer from Fed Govt to States, issues, with motor fuel taxes by selected State, 1988 rpt, 10048–72

Hwy construction contracts awards of States to minority- and women-owned firms, FY85-88, GAO rpt, 26113–399

Hwy construction contracts for Federal-aid system, awards to minority- and women-owned businesses, FHwA and State reviews, FY83-87, GAO rpt, 26113–389

Hwy construction costs, funding, mileage, and traffic, for Middle Atlantic States by project, 1989 article, 9387–1.904

Hwy funding by function, and revenue, by level of govt and type of hwy, 1960-87, biennial rpt, 7554–27.2

Hwy Statistics, detailed data by State, 1988, annual rpt, 7554–1

Pacific territories social, economic, health, and govtl data, FY88 and trends, annual rpt, 7004–6

Procurement of goods and services by level of govt, *Business Conditions Digest*, monthly rpt, 2702–3.5

Public opinion on taxes, spending, and govt efficiency, by respondent characteristics, 1989 survey, annual rpt, 10044–2

Puerto Rico economic conditions and govt finances, 1975-89, GAO rpt, 26121–298

Transit systems finances, costs, and needs, by State and selected system, 1980-88, biennial rpt, 7884–8

Wildlife (endangered species) recovery plans, and funding by Federal agencies and others, by species, FY72-87, GAO rpt, 26113–391

see also Aid to Families with Dependent Children

see also Medicaid

see also Medical assistance

see also State funding for economic development

see also State funding for education

see also State funding for health and hospitals

see also State funding for higher education

see also State funding for local areas

see also State funding for public safety

see also State funding for social welfare

see also Supplemental Security Income

see also Unemployment insurance

see also Workers compensation

State laws

AFDC provisions, by State, FY88, annual rpt, 4694–4

Bank deposit insurance systems of States, banks, and bank failure rates, for selected States, various periods 1829-1930, article, 9375–1.904

Banking (interstate) laws of States, impacts of changes on bank stock returns, 1988 working paper, 9387–8.174

Banking (interstate) laws of States, status as of Feb 1989, article, 9371–1.909

Banks financial performance, impacts of State entry regulation and deposit insurance, model description and results, 1970-86, working paper, 9393–10.6

Banks market concentration relation to excess profits and State branching regulation, various periods 1966-86, technical paper, 9366–6.188

Banks profitability relation to market concentration, impact of local market entry barriers, 1983, working paper, 9381–10.93

Black lung benefits and claims by State, trust fund receipts by source, and disbursements, 1987, annual rpt, 6504–3

Coal ash contaminant levels, removal, EPA toxicity standards, and State disposal laws, 1988 rpt, 2048–140

Contractor and private vendor prompt payment from govts, State law provisions and terms by State, 1988, GAO rpt, 26111–59

Corporations anti-takeover laws of States, with merger announcements by type and stock price changes for firms paying greenmail by firm, 1970s-86, article, 9373–2.901

Criminal law statutes of States, and public opinion, various periods 1985-89, annual rpt, 6064–6.1; 6064–6.2

Disabled persons employment and architectural barrier removal laws, Federal and State govt compliance, findings and recommendations, 1989 rpt, 10048–74

Drinking age laws impacts on traffic deaths, by State, 1975-87, 7768-103

Execution methods, capital offenses, and minimum age for execution, provisions of States, 1988, annual rpt, 6066-25.23

Labor laws enacted, by State, 1988, annual article, 6722-1.904

Medicare physicians assigned-fee laws of 4 States, impacts on care cost and availability, 1985-89, GAO rpt, 26121-312

Prison industries involvement of private sector, operations by prison and firm, and State provisions, as of 1987, 6068-228

Sentencing provisions of States for death penalty, 1986, annual rpt, 6064-26.6

Small business financial and technical aid of States, 1988 listing, 9768-15

Smoking and cigarette sale regulation by States, and public attitudes toward laws, 1960s-88, annual rpt, 4204-18

Supplemental Security Income and Medicaid eligibility and payment provisions, and beneficiaries living arrangements, by State, 1989, annual rpt, 4704-13

Tax and spending provisions of State govts, and debt controls, by State, as of 1988, annual rpt, 10044-1.1

Telephone intrastate long distance call rates, impact of State entry and price regulation, 1983-87, 9406-1.55

Unemployment insurance coverage, impact of changes in labor market and UI policy, and trust fund finances of 11 States, 1971-86, 6406-6.24

Unemployment insurance laws of States, changes in coverage, benefits, tax rates, and penalties, by State, 1988, annual article, 6722-1.905

Unemployment insurance laws of States, comparison of provisions, as of Jan 1989, semiannual revisions to base edition, 6402-2

Unemployment insurance programs of States, benefits, coverage, and tax provisions, as of July 1989, semiannual listing, 6402-7

Water (groundwater) protection standards, States use of EPA and alternative standards by type of water use, and contaminant test results, 1976-88, GAO rpt, 26131-56

Workers compensation laws of States and Fed Govt, 1989 semiannual rpt, 6502-1

Workers compensation laws of States, changes in coverage, benefits, and premium rates, by State, 1988, annual article, 6722-1.906

Workers compensation programs of States, admin, coverage, benefits, finances, processing, and staff, 1984-88, annual rpt, 6504-9

see also Alcoholic beverages control laws

see also Traffic laws and courts

State legislatures

Statistical Abstract of US, social, political, and economic data, 1790-2025, comprehensive annual compilation, 2324-1.2

State-local relations

Hwy admin and gasoline tax revenue proposed transfer from Fed Govt to States, issues, with motor fuel taxes by selected State, 1988 rpt, 10048-72

see also State funding for local areas

State parks

Alaska land area by ownership, and availability for mineral exploration and dev, 1986, 5608-152

Statistical Abstract of US, social, political, and economic data, 1790-2025, comprehensive annual compilation, 2324-1.1

Wildlife-related recreation, hunting, and fishing participation and spending, detailed data by location, 1985 survey, quinquennial rpt, 5508-5

Wildlife-related recreation, hunting, and fishing participation and spending, detailed data, 1985 survey, quinquennial State rpt series, 5506-6

see also State forests

State police

Assaults and deaths of law enforcement officers, by circumstances, agency, victim and offender characteristics, and location, 1988, annual rpt, 6224-3

Drug enforcement activities of State and local agencies, Federal aid by recipient, and background data, FY88, annual rpt, 6064-28

Employment and spending for law enforcement, by activity and level of govt, 1984-87, annual rpt, 6064-6.1

Employment of State and local law enforcement personnel and officers, by sex, population size, census div, and jurisdiction, as of Oct 1988, annual rpt, 6224-2.3

Employment, payroll, and spending for criminal justice, by level of govt, State, and selected city and county, FY71-85, annual rpt, 6064-9

Employment, spending, and operations of law enforcement agencies, FY87, 6066-25.20

State prisons

see Correctional institutions

State taxation

see State and local taxes

States

see terms beginning with State

see under By State in the "Index by Categories"

see under names of individual States

States' rights

see Federal-State relations

Statistical programs and activities

Agricultural data collection, Economic Research Service activities, funding, and staff, by branch, planned FY89, annual rpt, 1504-6

Agricultural data collection, methodology, and use, for major time series of USDA, series, 1506-1

AIDS cases forecasts, analysis of CDC and other methodology, 1989 GAO rpt, 26131-55

AIDS health care and epidemiological research, methodological issues, 1988 conf, 4188-61

AIDS health care, social, and support services research, data collection methods with background data, 1984-88, 4186-9.5

AIDS virus antibody testing services demand, accuracy, and costs, data collection methods with background data, 1986-88, 4186-9.7

Alcohol use and abuse among minority groups, and related problems, by selected characteristics, 1985 conf papers, 4488-13

BLS major economic indicators, methodology, and time series revisions, transcripts of BLS Commissioner's monthly testimony, periodic rpt, 23846-4

Census Bur activities, rpts, and user services, monthly rpt, 2302-3

Census Bur data collection methodology, programs, and measurement techniques, technical paper series, 2626-2

Census Bur data coverage and availability for 1987 economic censuses and related statistics, 1989 preliminary guide, 2308-5

Census Bur rpts and data files, coverage and availability, 1989 annual listing, 2304-2

Census Bur rpts and data files, coverage, availability, and use, series, 2326-7

Census of Agriculture, 1987: data coverage and availability, for census and related statistics, 1989 guide, 2308-55

Computer systems purchase and use, and data recording, processing, and transfer, Fed Govt standards, series, 2216-2

CPI components relative importance, by selected SMSA, region, population size, and for US city average, 1988, annual rpt, 6884-1

Crime and criminal justice data collection activities of Bur of Justice Statistics and States, FY88, annual rpt, 6064-21

Crime and criminal justice data collection, methodology, and use, technical rpt series, 6066-23

Crime and criminal justice data collection programs and rpts, 1988, annual listing, 6064-25

Crime and criminal justice research results, series, 6066-20; 6066-26

Crime, criminal justice admin and enforcement, and public opinion, data compilation, 1970s-88, annual rpt, 6064-6

DOE data collection forms and related rpts, 1988, annual listing, 3164-86

Drug abuse indicators for selected metro areas, research results, data collection, and policy issues, 1989 semiannual conf, 4492-5

Economic data collection by Fed Govt, methods of improving existing surveys, 1988 conf papers, 2702-1.905; 2702-1.911

Economic data series and collections of Fed Govt, adequacy to address devs and policy issues, 1989 rpt, 26358-207

Education data, estimates from Fast Response Survey System, series, 4826-1

Education of minorities, schools participating in natl surveys, 1969-88, listing, 4828-38

Employment Cost Index methodology, occupational definitions, and coverage, quarterly press release, 6782-5

Energy Info Admin activities, 1988, annual rpt, 3164-29

Energy Info Admin and alternative estimates of energy supply, demand, prices, and trade, with methodology, series, 3166-12

Fed Govt financial and nonfinancial domestic aid, 1989 base edition with supplements, annual listing, 104-5

Fed Govt info collection effects of Paperwork Reduction Act, with respondent burden, OMB reviews, and violations, 1981-88, annual rpt, 104–26

Fed Govt policies relating to statistical programs technical operation, methodology, and use of data, working paper series, 106–4

Fed Govt statistical programs, funding by agency, FY87-89, annual rpt, 104–10

Fed Reserve data concordance for *Federal Reserve Bulletin* and *Annual Statistical Digest*, 1988 annual rpt, 9364–8

Fed Reserve System statistical series additions and revisions, monthly rpt with articles, 9362–1

Fishery mgmt and R&D, Fed Govt grants by project and State, and rpts, 1987, annual listing, 2164–3

Hazardous substances exposure factors, and methodological guidelines, 1989 rpt, 9188–109

Health care and condition research, survey design and research methods, 1989 conf proceedings, 4188–60

Health Care Financing Admin research activities and grants, by program, as of Mar 1989, annual listing, 4654–10

Health care resources geographic info system, data coverage and availability, 1989 rpt, 4118–61

HHS data projects and systems, by subagency, FY88, 4008–92

HHS financial aid, by program, recipient, State, and city, FY88, annual regional listings, 4004–3

HHS research and evaluation programs, 1970-FY87, annual listing, 4004–30

Infant deaths, causes, and prevention, recommendations and findings, 1988 rpt, 15838–1

Juvenile delinquency prevention funding, by program and Federal agency, FY88, annual rpt, 6064–11

Mental health care facilities data collection needs, implementation, uses, and costs, series, 4506–2

Mental health care facilities needs assessment and program evaluation for communities, methodology, use of census data, analysis, and sample data, series, 4506–8

Monetary aggregates components, with estimation data sources and availability of time series, as of 1988, article, 9389–1.906

OASDHI programs actuarial studies, series, 4706–2

Oil products supply, EIA and alternative estimates, 1979-88, annual article, 3162–6.903

Older persons health condition and care access, data collection improvement needs, 1985 conf papers, 4147–4.26

Population and reproduction research, Fed Govt funding by project, FY87, annual listing, 4474–9

Science Resources Studies Div of NSF, project descriptions and rpts, 1988 annual listing, 9624–21

Small business establishments, employment, and financial ratios, by SIC 1- to 2-digit industry and State, late 1960s-87, 9768–19

Soviet Union economic conditions under General Secretary Gorbachev, Soviet and CIA measurement methods with background data, 1987 conf papers, 9118–4

Timber resources surveys of Forest Service, coverage and methodology, 1932-89, 9188–110

Vital and Health Statistics series and other NCHS rpts, 1980-88, annual listing, 4124–1

Vital and Health Statistics series: methodology, survey design, and data evaluation, 4147–2

Vital and Health Statistics series: program and data collection procedures, 4147–1

Vital and Health Statistics series: survey questionnaire dev and testing, 4147–6

see also Business outlook and attitude surveys

see also Classifications

see also Computer data file guides

see also Consumer surveys

see also Economic and econometric models

see also Mathematic models and modeling

see also Methodology

see also Opinion and attitude surveys

see also Seasonal adjustment factors

see also Statisticians

see also under names of individual surveys (listed under Surveys)

Statisticians

Employment and earnings in science and engineering, by field and activity, and private and Federal R&D spending, by industry, 1975-88, 9626–6.29

Employment and other characteristics of science and engineering PhDs, by field and State, 1987, biennial rpt, 9627–18

Employment characteristics of scientists and engineers, by field, 1988, biennial rpt, 9627–16

Employment of scientists, engineers, and technicians in manufacturing, by field, occupation, and industry, 1986, triennial rpt, 9627–23

R&D funding by higher education instns, by source and field, FY80-87, annual rpt, 9624–18.5

Steel industry

see Iron and steel industry

Steele, Christine E.

"Federal Civilian Employment by State, Metropolitan Area, Overseas, Citizenship, Major Agency, Pay System Category, and Work Schedule as of Dec. 31, 1988", 9842–1.904

"Profile of the 'Typical' Federal Civilian Non-Postal Employee, as of Sept. 30, 1988", 9842–1.901

Steffens, Rebecca A.

"Apparent Per Capita Alcohol Consumption: National, State and Regional Trends, 1977-86", 4486–1.6

Stein, David

"Brown Rockfish, Copper Rockfish, and Black Rockfish. Species Profiles: Life Histories and Environmental Requirements of Coastal Fishes and Invertebrates (Pacific Southwest)", 5506–8.120

Stein, Ruth E.

"Measuring Health Variables Among Hispanic and Non-Hispanic Children with Chronic Conditions", 4042–3.936

Stergioulas, Nikolaos A.

"Plant and Equipment Expenditures by Business for Pollution Abatement, 1987 and Planned 1988", 2702–1.904

Sterilization

see Sexual sterilization

Sterling Heights, Mich.

see also under By City in the "Index by Categories"

Stern, Gary H.

"Case for Reforming Federal Deposit Insurance", 9383–2

Steubenville, Ohio

see also under By SMSA or MSA in the "Index by Categories"

Stevedores

see Longshoremen

Stevens, E. J.

"Pricing Daylight Overdrafts", 9377–9.71

Stevens, Robert J.

"Review of Lake Ontario Water Quality with Emphasis on the 1981-82 Intensive Years. Report to the Surveillance Subcommittee of the Great Lakes Water Quality Board", 14648–22

Stevens, Wallace

"Outlook for Aquaculture Products in the U.S. Marketplace", 1004–16.1

Stiles, Myrna

"Environmental Health Profile and Priority Projection for the Pine Ridge Reservation", 21448–37

Stillman, Richard

"Sheep Industry Trends", 1561–7.905

Stimulants

see Drug abuse and treatment

see Drugs

Stinson, Frederick S.

"Alcohol-Related Morbidity in the Aging Population", 4482–1.903

"Trends in Alcohol-Related Morbidity Among Short-Stay Community Hospital Discharges, U.S., 1979-84", 4486–1.1

Stinson, Thomas F.

"Public Water Supply in Rural Communities: Results from the National Rural Community Facilities Assessment Study", 1598–247

Stock exchanges

County Business Patterns, 1987: employment, establishments, and payroll, by SIC 2- to 4-digit industry and county, annual State rpt series, 2326–8

Financial and business statistics, historic trends, 1988 annual chartbook, 9364–2.15

Futures market trading abuses, Commodity Futures Trading Commission and exchanges enforcement activity, various periods 1984-FY90, GAO rpt, 26119–263

Futures market trading abuses, Commodity Futures Trading Commission, Chicago Board of Trade, and Chicago Mercantile Exchange enforcement activity, 1984-89, GAO rpt, 26119–247

Market crash of 1987, market performance, foreign futures market activity, and computer-aided trading impacts on price variability, 1980s-88, hearings, 25168–70

Price volatility of stock, with data by industry and country, 1970s-88, conf papers, 9381–13.1

Prices, trading, and customer financing, 1987, annual rpt, 9364–5.4

Science and engineering employment, by
nonmanufacturing industry and field,
1987, triennial rpt, 9627–31

Statistical Abstract of US, social, political,
and economic data, 1790-2025,
comprehensive annual compilation,
2324–1.3

Tax (income) returns of corporations,
income and tax items by asset size and
detailed industry, 1986, annual rpt,
8304–21

Trading volume and new issue registrations,
monthly rpt, 9732–1

Trading volume, securities listed by type,
and finances, by exchange, selected years
1935-88, annual rpt, 9734–2.1; 9734–2.3

see also American Stock Exchange
see also New York Stock Exchange
see also Securities

Stock market
see American Stock Exchange
see New York Stock Exchange
see Securities
see Stock exchanges
see Stockbrokers

Stockbrokers
Assets and liabilities of stockbrokers, 1987,
annual rpt, 9364–5.13

Assets composition, growth, and distribution
for financial instns, by instn type,
1970s-88, 8438–1

County Business Patterns, 1987:
employment, establishments, and payroll,
by SIC 2- to 4-digit industry and county,
annual State rpt series, 2326–8

Credit (securities) issues of stockbrokers and
other nonbank lenders, and brokers
balance sheet, as of June 1988, annual rpt,
9365–5.1

Employment, earnings, and hours, by SIC 1-
to 4-digit industry, monthly 1983-Feb
1989, annual rpt, 6744–4

Employment in nonmanufacturing
industries, by detailed occupation and SIC
2-digit industry, 1987, triennial rpt,
6748–60

Finances of stockbrokers, firms by type of
organization and State, and SEC
applications and registrations, 1983-88,
annual rpt, 9734–2.1

Flow-of-funds accounts, assets and liabilities
by type and economic sector, outstanding
at year-end 1965-88, annual rpt, 9364–3

Flow-of-funds accounts, savings,
investments, and credit statements,
quarterly rpt, 9365–3.3

Futures market trading abuses, Commodity
Futures Trading Commission and
exchanges enforcement activity, various
periods 1984-FY90, GAO rpt,
26119–263

Futures market trading abuses, Commodity
Futures Trading Commission, Chicago
Board of Trade, and Chicago Mercantile
Exchange enforcement activity, 1984-89,
GAO rpt, 26119–247

Market crash of 1987, consumer complaints
by reason, security type, and State,
Nov-Dec 1987, hearings, 21368–111

Occupational injury and illness rates, by SIC
2- to 4-digit industry, 1987, annual rpt,
6844–1

Science and engineering employment, by
nonmanufacturing industry and field,
1987, triennial rpt, 9627–31

Securities (tax-exempt) holdings by investor
type, and IRS enforcement of
disallowance of interest deduction for
financing holdings, mid 1970s-87, GAO
rpt, 26119–239

Securities purchases, sales, and holdings, by
issuer and type and ownership of security,
monthly listing, 9732–2

Tax (income) returns of corporations,
income and tax items by asset size and
detailed industry, 1986, annual rpt,
8304–4; 8304–21

Tax (income) returns of partnerships,
income statement items by industry group,
1986, annual article, 8302–2.903

Tax (income) returns of sole proprietorships,
income statement items, by industry
group, 1987, annual article, 8302–2.904;
8302–2.921

Tax (income) withholding and related
documents filed, by type and IRS service
center, 1988 and projected 1989-96,
annual rpt, 8304–22

Stockman, Alan C.
"Real Business Cycle Theory: A Guide, an
Evaluation, and New Directions",
9377–1.902

Stockpiling
GSA activities and finances, FY88, annual
rpt, 9454–1

Mineral Industry Surveys, commodity
reviews of production, trade, stocks, and
use, monthly rpt series, 5612–1

Mineral Industry Surveys, commodity
reviews of production, trade, use, and
industry operations, advance annual rpt
series, 5614–5

Minerals (strategic) supply, demand, trade,
and foreign and US industry devs by firm
and country, by commodity, bimonthly
rpt with articles, 5602–4

Minerals of strategic and technological
importance, supply, imports, and use, with
foreign comparisons, commodity rpt
series, 5606–9

Minerals production, prices, trade, use,
employment, tariffs, and stockpiles, by
mineral, with foreign comparisons,
1984-88, annual rpt, 5604–18

Statistical Abstract of US, social, political,
and economic data, 1790-2025,
comprehensive annual compilation,
2324–1.3

Strategic material stockpile inventories and
needs, by commodity, as of Sept 1988,
annual rpt, 3544–37

Strategic material stockpile inventories,
costs, and goals, by commodity, as of
June 1989, semiannual rpt, 3902–3

Strategic material stockpiling by Fed Govt,
activity, and inventory by commodity, as
of Sept 1989, semiannual rpt, 3542–22;
3902–2

Strategic minerals production, use, reserves,
Federal lands availability for mining, and
environmental impacts, 1950s-80s,
028–33

see also Naval Petroleum Reserves
see also Strategic Petroleum Reserve

Stocks
see Agricultural stocks
see Business inventories
see Coal stocks
see Energy stocks and inventories

see Options trading
see Petroleum stocks
see Securities
see Stock exchanges
see Stockbrokers
see Stockpiling

Stockton, Calif.
Wages by occupation, and benefits for office
and plant workers, 1989 survey, periodic
MSA rpt, 6785–3.9

see also under By City and By SMSA or
MSA in the "Index by Categories"

Stolte, Darwin E.
"Export Marketing Issues", 1004–16.1

Stolz, Richard W.
"Underpricing of Seasoned Issues: The Case
of U.S. Treasury Bills", 9366–6.168

Stommes, Eileen S.
"Reconnecting Rural America: Report on
Rural Intercity Passenger Transportation",
1278–11
"Rural Air Service", 1278–17

Stone, Jon P.
"Regulations of Minerals Industry Wastes",
5606–5.7

Stone products and quarries
Business statistics, detailed data for major
industries and economic indicators, *Survey
of Current Business*, monthly rpt,
2702–1.18

Collective bargaining agreements expiring
during year, and workers covered, by
firm, union, industry group, and State,
1989, annual rpt, 6784–9

Construction industries census, 1987:
financial and operating data, preliminary
industry rpt, 2371–1.13

County Business Patterns, 1987:
employment, establishments, and payroll,
by SIC 2- to 4-digit industry and county,
annual State rpt series, 2326–8

Cuba economic conditions, agricultural and
industrial production and distribution,
trade, and intl economic relations,
1980-87 with trends from 1961, 9118–8

Dimension stone trade and price indexes by
selected country, 1987, Mineral Industry
Surveys, annual rpt, 5614–29

Earnings by major industry group, and
personal income per capita and by source,
by region and State, 1929-87, 2708–40

Employment, earnings, and hours, by
selected SIC 1- to 4-digit industry, State,
and for 262 MSAs, 1972-87, 6748–81

Employment, earnings, and hours, by SIC 1-
to 4-digit industry, monthly 1983-Feb
1989, annual rpt, 6744–4

Employment, unemployment, and labor
force characteristics, by region and census
div, 1988, annual rpt, 6744–7.1

Energy use and prices for manufacturing
industries, 1985 survey, series, 3166–13

Exports and imports of US shipped through
Canada, by detailed commodity, customs
district, and country, 1987, annual rpt,
7704–11

Exports of US, detailed commodities by
country, monthly rpt, 2422–3

Foreign countries mineral production,
reserves, and industry role in domestic
economy and world supply, world area
and country rpt series, 5606–1

Freight (waterborne domestic and foreign)
by commodity, traffic, and passengers, by
port and waterway, 1987, annual rpt,
3754–3

Hazardous substances industrial releases and reduction methods under EPA regulation, by chemical, source, industry, and location, 1987, annual rpt, 9234–6

Hwy construction material use by type, and spending, by State, various periods 1944-88, annual rpt, 7554–29

Imports, exports, and employment impacts, by SIC 2- to 4-digit industry and commodity, quarterly rpt, 2322–2

Imports of US, detailed Schedule A commodities by country, monthly rpt, 2422–2

Indian (Cherokee) Agency activities in North Carolina, FY89, annual rpt, 5704–4

Input-output structure of US economy, detailed interindustry transactions for 84 industries, and components of final demand, 1983, annual article, 2702–1.909

Labor productivity, indexes of output, hours, and employment by SIC 2- to 4-digit industry, 1963-87, annual rpt, 6824–1.2

Lime industry competitiveness of US and Mexico, investigation with background financial and operating data, 1989 rpt, 9886–4.141

Manufacturing annual survey, 1986: financial and operating data, by SIC 2- to 4-digit industry, series, 2506–15

Manufacturing annual survey, 1986: production indexes and exports by SIC 2-digit industry and State, with comparisons to 1985, model results, series, 2506–16

Manufacturing census, 1987: financial and operating data, for SIC 4-digit industries by product, preliminary rpt, 2491–1.49

Manufacturing industries production, shipments, inventories, orders, and pollution control costs, periodic Current Industrial Rpt series, 2506–3

Mine employment by selected occupational and other characteristics, injuries, and workdays lost, for mines, 1986, 5606–8.2; 5606–8.4; 5606–8.5

Mineral industries census, 1987: financial and operating data, preliminary industry rpt, 2511–1.8; 2511–1.9

Mineral Industry Surveys, commodity review of production, trade, stocks, and use, quarterly rpt, 5612–2.20

Mineral Industry Surveys, commodity reviews of production, trade, use, and industry operations, advance annual rpt series, 5614–5

Mineral Industry Surveys, State reviews of production, 1988, preliminary annual rpt, 5614–6

Minerals Yearbook, 1987, Vol 1: commodity reviews of production, use, trade, prices, and mining operations, annual rpt, 5604–33

Minerals Yearbook, 1987, Vol 1 preprints: commodity review of production, reserves, supply, use, and trade, annual rpt, 5604–15.1; 5604–15.62

Minerals Yearbook, 1987, Vol 2 preprints: State reviews of production and sales by commodity, and business activity, annual rpt series, 5604–16

Minerals Yearbook, 1987, Vol 2: State reviews of production, sales, and firms, by commodity, and business activity, annual rpt, 5604–34

Minerals Yearbook, 1987, Vol 3: foreign country reviews of production, trade, and policy, by commodity, annual rpt, 5604–35

Minerals Yearbook, 1987, Vol 3 preprints: foreign country reviews of production, trade, and policy, by commodity, annual rpt series, 5604–23

Minerals Yearbook, 1988, Vol 2 rpts: State reviews of production and sales by commodity, and business activity, annual rpt series, 5604–22

Multinatl US firms and foreign affiliates finances and operations, by industry of parent firm and affiliate, world area, and country, preliminary 1987, annual rpt, 2704–5

Northern Mariana Islands economic census, 1987: employment, firms, payroll, and receipts, by SIC 1- to 4-digit industry, 2597–1

Occupational injuries and incidence, employment, and hours in sand and gravel mines and related operations, 1987, annual rpt, 6664–2

Occupational injuries and incidence, employment, and hours in stone mines and related operations, 1987, annual rpt, 6664–5

Occupational injuries by circumstances, employment, and hours, for mineral industries by type of operation and State, quarterly rpt, 6662–1

Occupational injury and illness rates, by SIC 2- to 4-digit industry, 1987, annual rpt, 6844–1

Ohio River basin waterway facilities, freight by commodity and port, and recreation, by waterway, 1986-87, annual rpt, 3754–6

Pollution abatement capital and operating costs, by SIC 2-to 4-digit industry and State, 1986, annual Current Industrial Rpt, 2506–3.6

Price indexes (producer), by stage of processing and detailed commodity, monthly rpt, 6762–6

Price indexes (producer), by stage of processing and detailed commodity, monthly 1988, annual rpt, 6764–2

Producer Price Index and sales of building materials, by type, bimonthly rpt, 2042–1.5; 2042–1.6

Production of stone, sand, and gravel, by end use, State, and district, 1985-86, 5608–157

Production, prices, trade, use, employment, tariffs, and stockpiles, by mineral, with foreign comparisons, 1984-88, annual rpt, 5604–18

Science and engineering employment, by nonmanufacturing industry and field, 1987, triennial rpt, 9627–31

Science, engineering, and technical employment in manufacturing, by field, occupation, and industry, 1986, triennial rpt, 9627–23

Small business establishments, employment, and financial ratios, by SIC 1- to 2-digit industry and State, late 1960s-87, 9768–19

Statistical Abstract of US, social, political, and economic data, 1790-2025, comprehensive annual compilation, 2324–1.3

Tariff Schedule of US, classifications and rates of duty by detailed imported commodity, 1990 base edition and supplements, 9886–13

Tax (income) returns of corporations, income and tax items by asset size and detailed industry, 1986, annual rpt, 8304–4; 8304–21

Tax (income) returns of partnerships, income statement items by industry group, 1986, annual article, 8302–2.903

Tax (income) returns of sole proprietorships, income statement items, by industry group, 1987, annual article, 8302–2.904; 8302–2.921

see also Abrasive materials
see also Cement and concrete
see also Oil shale
see also Phosphate
see also Potash
see also By Industry in the "Index by Categories"
see also under By Commodity in the "Index by Categories"

Stone, Robyn I.
"Spouses and Children of Disabled Elders: Potential and Active Caregivers", 4186–7.5

Storage
see Agricultural stocks
see Cold storage and refrigeration
see Packaging and containers
see Stockpiling
see Warehouses

Storms
Agricultural water supply, crop moisture, and drought indexes, weekly rpt, seasonal data, 2152–2

Deaths and rates, by detailed cause and demographic characteristics, 1986 and trends from 1900, US Vital Statistics annual rpt, 4144–2

Developing countries disaster preparedness and economic, population, and political data, country rpt series, 9916–2

Environmental quality and protection programs, and intl issues, 1988 annual rpt, 484–1

Estuary environmental conditions and mgmt, for individual areas, conf series, 2146–6

Farmland damaged by natural disaster, Emergency Conservation Program aid and participation by State, FY87, annual rpt, 1804–22

Hurricanes and tropical storms in north Atlantic and Caribbean area, paths, surveillance, deaths, damage, and landfall probabilities by city, 1988, annual rpt, 2184–7

Hurricanes and tropical storms in northeastern Pacific Ocean, paths and surveillance, 1988, annual rpt, 2184–8

Hurricanes and tropical storms in Pacific and Indian Oceans, paths and surveillance, 1988, annual rpt, 3804–8

Mariners Weather Log, quarterly journal, 2152–8

Precipitation and temperature for US and foreign locations, major events and anomalies, weekly rpt, 2182–6

Research activities of Natl Severe Storms Lab, and bibl, FY88, annual rpt, 2144–20

Statistical Abstract of US, social, political, and economic data, 1790-2025, comprehensive annual compilation, 2324–1.1

Watershed (agricultural) runoff, precipitation, weather conditions, and mgmt, for 72 projects, 1978-79, annual rpt, 1704-1

Weather phenomena and storm characteristics, casualties, and property damage, by State, monthly listing, 2152-3

see also Floods

Stovall, Therese K.
"Effect of Lifestyle on Energy Use Estimations and Predicted Savings", 3226-2.11

Strategic Arms Reduction Talks
Treaties on arms control, status and Arms Control and Disarmament Agency activities, 1988, annual rpt, 9824-2

Strategic Defense Initiative
R&D costs of SDI, and benefits, under alternative system capabilities, projected FY90-94, 26308-87

Strategic materials
Mineral Industry Surveys, commodity reviews of production, trade, stocks, and use, monthly rpt series, 5612-1

Mineral Industry Surveys, commodity reviews of production, trade, use, and industry operations, advance annual rpt series, 5614-5

Minerals (strategic) production, by country and for South Africa companies controlled by multinatl firms, 1987, GAO rpt, 26123-233

Minerals (strategic) production, use, reserves, Federal lands availability for mining, and environmental impacts, 1950s-80s, 028-33

Minerals (strategic) supply and characteristics of individual deposits, by country, commodity rpt series, 5666-21

Minerals (strategic) supply, demand, trade, and foreign and US industry devs by firm and country, by commodity, bimonthly rpt with articles, 5602-4

Nuclear material inventory discrepancies at DOE and contractor facilities, 2nd half FY87, semiannual rpt, 3002-4

Prices for sensitive materials, and indexes, *Business Conditions Digest*, cyclical indicators, monthly rpt, 2702-3.3

Supply, imports, and use of strategic and technologically important minerals, with foreign comparisons, commodity rpt series, 5606-9

see also Naval Petroleum Reserves
see also Stockpiling
see also Strategic Petroleum Reserve
see also Uranium

Strategic Petroleum Reserve
Activities and funding of SPR, by site, as of Sept 1988, semiannual GAO rpt, 26102-3

Capacity, inventory, fill rate, and finances of SPR, quarterly rpt, 3002-13

Crude oil imports, domestic deliveries, and stocks, 1977-88, annual rpt, 3164-74.2

Defense Fuel Supply Center procurement, prices, stocks, transport, and other activities and finances, FY88, annual rpt, 3904-8

Energy supply, demand, and prices, forecasts by resource type, quarterly rpt, 3162-34

Military Sealift Command shipping operations, finances, and personnel, FY88, annual rpt, 3804-14

Oil imports and withdrawals from stocks, monthly rpt, 3162-24.3

Property (real) of DOE owned and leased, by type, subagency, contractor, and site, FY87, annual rpt, 3004-28

Supply and demand of oil and refined products, refinery capacity and use, and prices, weekly rpt, 3162-32

Supply, demand, and movement of crude oil, gas liquids, and refined products, by PAD district and State, 1988 and trends from 1973, annual rpt, 3164-2

Supply, demand, and prices, by fuel type and end-use sector, projected under 3 oil price assumptions, 1988-2000, annual rpt, 3164-75

Supply, demand, and prices of oil and gas, alternative projections 1987-2000, annual rpt, 3164-89

Strauss, William A.
"Investment Cyclicality in Manufacturing Industries", 9375-1.909
"New Dollar Indexes Are No Different from the Old Ones", 9375-14

Strawberries
see Fruit and fruit products

Streams
see Rivers and waterways

Streetcars
see Urban transportation

Streets
see Highways, streets, and roads

Stress
see Mental health and illness

Strikes and lockouts
see Work stoppages

Stroke
see Cerebrovascular diseases

Strontium
see Radioactive materials

Strudler, Michael
"Sole Proprietorship Returns, 1987", 8302-2.921

Stuart, Bruce L.
"Changing U.S. Role in the International Dairy Market", 1004-16.1

Stuart, Hanson R.
"Opportunity and Challenge: The Story of BLM", 5728-30

Student aid
Alcohol, Drug Abuse and Mental Health Admin research grants and awards, by recipient, FY88, annual listing, 4044-13

Allergy and Infectious Diseases Natl Inst activities, grants by recipient and location, and disease incidence, FY81-88, annual rpt, 4474-30

Arts Natl Endowment activities and grants, FY88, annual rpt, 9564-3

Assistance (financial and nonfinancial) of Fed Govt, 1989 base edition with supplements, annual listing, 104-5

Assistance and other sources of support, with student expenses and characteristics, by instn type and control, 1987 triennial study, series, 4846-3

Assistance of Fed Govt, by type, program, agency, and State, FY88, annual rpt, 2464-2

Benefits overpayment recovery and judgment enforcement cases filed in Federal district courts, June 1988, annual rpt, 18204-8.11

Benefits overpayment recovery and judgment enforcement cases filed in Federal district courts, June 1989, annual rpt, 18204-2.12

Black colleges R&D funding by source, and characteristics of grad students and research staff, by field of science and instn, 1980s-87, 9628-78

Bond tax-exempt issues for private activity, by purpose, face value, major industry, and State, 1986, annual article, 8302-2.905

Budget deficit reduction under Gramm-Rudman Act, cancellation of budget authority by program, FY90, annual rpt, 104-27

Budget of US, midsession review of FY90 budget, by function and agency, annual rpt, 104-7

Child Health and Human Dev Natl Inst contracts and grants, by recipient and location, FY88, annual listing, 4474-36

Community organizations partnerships with public schools, participation, activities, and contributions, by school characteristics and location, 1987/88, 4826-1.27

Condition of Education, detailed data on higher education, 1960s-88, annual rpt, 4824-1.2

Dental Research Natl Inst research and training grants, by recipient, FY88, annual listing, 4474-19

DOD training and education programs funding, staff, students, and facilities, by service branch, FY90, annual rpt, 3504-5

Education Dept financial aid programs, 1989 annual listing, 4804-3

Education Dept programs funding, operations, and effectiveness, FY88, annual rpt, 4804-5

Expenditures and participation, by Federal student aid program, instn type and control, and State, various periods 1959-88, annual rpt, 4804-28

Expenditures for education by Federal agency, program, and recipient type, and instn spending, FY80-88, 4828-21

Expenditures for student aid supplemental grants, loans, and work-study awards, Federal shares by instn and State, 1989/90, annual listing, 4804-17

Flow-of-funds accounts, assets and liabilities by type and economic sector, outstanding at year-end 1965-88, annual rpt, 9364-3

Flow-of-funds accounts, savings, investments, and credit statements, quarterly rpt, 9365-3.3

Fulbright-Hays academic exchanges, grants by purpose, and foreign govt share of costs, by country, FY88, annual rpt, 10324-1

Guaranteed student loan default rates, and borrowers in repayment status, by instn, FY87, annual rpt, 4804-34

Guaranteed student loan default rates, and claims paid by guaranty agencies, by State, and borrower characteristics, FY87, GAO rpt, 26121-292

Guaranteed student loan defaults, losses, and rates, by instn, 1983-Sept 1987, GAO rpt, 26121-289

Guaranteed Student Loan Program defaults, rates, and borrowers in repayment status, by instn and State, FY86, with background data, 1980s, hearings, 25548-96

Health Professions Bur training and research grants and contracts, by instn and program, FY88, annual listing, 4114-1

Health Professions Bur training support grants, by program, region, and State, FY80-87, 4118-62

Heart, Lung, and Blood Natl Inst activities, and grants by recipient and location, FY88 with disease trends from 1940, annual rpt, 4474-15

HHS financial aid, by program, recipient, State, and city, FY88, annual regional listings, 4004-3

Higher education instn tuition, fees, and student aid awards, by State, 1960s-88, annual rpt, 4824-2.22

Humanities Natl Endowment activities and grants, FY88, annual rpt, 9564-2

Income (personal) by source including transfer payments, and social insurance contributions, by region, 1948 and 1987, 2708-40

Indian education funding of Fed Govt, enrollment, and degrees, late 1960s-FY88, annual rpt, 14874-1

Inter-American Foundation activities, grants by recipient, and fellowships, by country, FY88, annual rpt, 14424-1

Inter-American Foundation dev grants by program area, and fellowships by field and instn, by country, FY71-88, annual rpt, 14424-2

Japan-US Friendship Commission educational and cultural exchange activities, grants, and trust fund status, FY87-88, biennial report, 14694-1

Library science training grants for disadvantaged students, by instn and State, FY89, annual listing, 4874-1

Loan activity of FSLIC-insured savings instns by FHLB district and State, and for FDIC-insured savings banks, 1988, annual rpt, 8434-1

Loans and loan guarantees of of Fed Govt, outstanding amounts by agency and program, *Treasury Bulletin*, quarterly rpt, 8002-4.9

Loans of Fed Govt to students, defaults, losses, and rates, by instn and State, as of June 1988, annual rpt, 4804-18

Maritime academy students receiving Fed Govt aid, monthly rpt, 7702-1

Military health care personnel, and accessions by training source, by occupation, specialty, and service branch, FY87, annual rpt, 3544-24

Military reserve education benefits, eligible personnel and applications by component, 1988, annual rpt, 3544-31.1

NATO postdoctoral fellowships in science, recipients educational outcomes and other characteristics, 1959-81, 9628-80

NIH activities, funding by program and recipient type, staff, and clinic patients, by inst, FY87, annual rpt, 4434-3

NIH grants and awards, quarterly listing, 4432-1

NIH grants for R&D, training, construction, and medical libraries, by location and recipient, FY88, annual listings, 4434-7

Pell grants and applicants, by tuition, family and student income, instn type and control, and State, 1987/88, annual rpt, 4804-1

ROTC scholarship awards, by length of award, race, and sex, FY87-88, annual rpt, 3704-10.1

Science and engineering education enrollment, degrees, and student aid and sources, with data by field, race, sex, and instn, 1980s-87, 26358-202

Science and engineering grad enrollment, by field, source of funds, and characteristics of student and instn, 1975-87, annual rpt, 9627-7

Science fellowship and traineeship funding of Fed Govt, by field, instn, agency, and State, FY87, annual rpt, 9627-17

Science PhD recipients by whether foreign, race, and sex, and instnl support, 1978 and 1987-88, 9626-2.187

Soviet Union personal income by source, disposable income, wage deductions by type, and savings, 1950s-87, 9118-7

Statistical Abstract of US, social, political, and economic data, 1790-2025, comprehensive annual compilation, 2324-1.1

Truman, Harry S, Scholarship Foundation finances, FY88, and awards by student characteristics from 1977, annual rpt, 14314-1

Truman, Harry S, Scholarship Fund receipts by source, transfers, and investment holdings and transactions, monthly rpt, 14312-1

US attorneys civil and criminal cases by type and disposition, and collections, by Federal district, FY88, annual rpt, 6004-2.5

Vocational education aid recipients and sources, and characteristics of programs and students, 1970s-89, series, 4806-3

see also School lunch and breakfast programs

see also Veterans education

see also Work-study programs

Student Athlete Right-to-Know Act
Athlete grad rates for NCAA Div I college programs, and reporting of academic performance to Education Dept, 1987-89, GAO rpt, 26121-305

Student discipline
Condition of Education, detailed data on elementary and secondary education, 1920s-88 and projected to 1997, annual rpt, 4824-1.1

Digest of Education Statistics, detailed data on students, staff, finances, and facilities, 1989 edition, annual rpt, 4824-2

High school dropout rates, and subsequent completion, by student and school characteristics, alternative estimates, 1988, annual rpt, 4834-23

Student employment
see Work-study programs
see Youth employment

Student Loan Marketing Association
Budget of US Appendix, financial statements of federally sponsored enterprises, FY90, annual rpt, 104-3.4

Student loans
see Student aid

Students
Aircraft pilots and nonpilots certified by FAA, by certificate type, age, sex, region, and State, 1988, annual rpt, 7504-2

Aliens admitted to US, by class of admission, port, country, and State of destination, quarterly rpt, 6262-2

Bus (intercity) route in Nebraska, indicators of need, finances, and service and funding alternatives, 1980s, 7888-76

Condition of Education, detailed data on elementary, secondary, and higher education, 1920s-88 and projected to 1997, annual rpt, 4824-1

Crime and crime-related issues, public opinion by respondent characteristics, 1970s-89, annual rpt, 6064-6.2

Data on education, selected performance and financial indicators by State, 1982-88, annual table with supplements, 4804-32

Digest of Education Statistics, detailed data on students, staff, finances, and facilities, 1989 edition, annual rpt, 4824-2

Disabled college student alcohol and drug abuse, and prescription drug use, local area study, 1989 article, 4482-1.904

DOD Dependents Schools basic skills and college entrance test scores, 1988/89, annual rpt, 3504-16

Drug, alcohol, and cigarette use and attitudes of youth, by substance type and selected characteristics, 1975-88 surveys, annual rpt, 4494-4

Effective schools programs for improving academic achievement, characteristics of schools, districts, and students, 1987/88, GAO rpt, 26121-304

Elementary and secondary students performance in selected subjects, and factors affecting proficiency, natl assessments, 1969-86, 4898-26

Employment of high school students, academic and other characteristics, 1984-86, 4898-27

Employment, unemployment, and labor force characteristics, Labor Statistics Handbook, 1940s-88 with trends from 1913, 6728-38.2

Farm workers, earnings, and days worked, by selected characteristics and region, 1987, biennial rpt, 1594-2

High school class of 1972: education, employment, and family characteristics, activities, and attitudes, natl longitudinal study, series, 4836-1

High school classes of 1972 and 1980: enrollment in 2-year colleges, credits earned and dropout rate, by student characteristics, as of 1984, 4848-38

High school classes of 1972, 1980, and 1982: postsecondary enrollment and degrees, by sex, race, and income level, natl longitudinal surveys, 4848-35

High school classes of 1980 and 1982: education, employment, and family characteristics, activities, and attitudes, natl longitudinal study, series, 4826-2

Higher education instn student aid and other sources of support, with student expenses and characteristics, by instn type and control, 1987 triennial study, series, 4846-3

OASDI beneficiaries and benefits, selected characteristics with data by State, late 1930s-87, annual rpt, 4744-3.3; 4744-3.4

Science and engineering education in elementary and secondary schools, and student persistence in postsecondary education, 1977-88, 26358-199

Science education methods, materials, and factors affecting student proficiency, views of students, teachers, and administrators, 1983-85 surveys, 4828-37.1

Science proficiency, attitudes, factors affecting proficiency, and teacher background and views, natl assessment of elementary and high school students, 1977-86, 4898–25

Statistical Abstract of US, social, political, and economic data, 1790-2025, comprehensive annual compilation, 2324–1.1

see also Black students
see also Educational attainment
see also Educational enrollment
see also Educational tests
see also Foreign students
see also School dropouts
see also Student aid
see also Student discipline
see also Tuition and fees

Stullken, Lloyd E.
"Experiment in Representative Ground-Water Sampling for Water-Quality Analysis", 5668–97

Stults, Harold
"Cotton: Background for 1990 Farm Legislation", 1566–7.2

Sturrock, John
"Deficits and Interest Rates: Theoretical Issues and Empirical Evidence", 26306–3.101
"Deficits and Interest Rates: Theoretical Issues and Simulation Results", 26306–3.100

Subcommittee on Aging. Senate
Mississippi hospitals and community health centers, use, staff, and Medicare and other payments, 1988 hearing, 25548–97

Subcommittee on Antitrust, Monopolies and Business Rights. Senate
Airline computer reservation systems operating costs, fees, and market shares, by firm and location, 1984-87, hearing, 25528–108

Subcommittee on Arms Control, International Security, and Science. House
Pakistan military strengths, spending, weapons systems, and arms imports, with comparisons to India, 1980s-87, hearing, 21388–54

Subcommittee on Asian and Pacific Affairs. House
Pakistan military strengths, spending, weapons systems, and arms imports, with comparisons to India, 1980s-87, hearing, 21388–54

Subcommittee on Census and Population. House
Census of Population and Housing, 1990: data collection procedure improvement and preparation for count, hearing, 21628–71
Census of Population and Housing, 1990: outlying areas preparations for count, hearings, 21628–72; 21628–74

Subcommittee on Children, Family, Drugs, and Alcoholism. Senate
Employee parental leave of absence, policies, coverage, and attitudes, by employee characteristics, 1980-87, hearings, 25548–95

Subcommittee on Commerce, Consumer, and Monetary Affairs. House
Banks and other financial instns fraud and insider misconduct cases, Federal regulatory and enforcement activities, and losses, 1981-87, hearing, 21408–111

Subcommittee on Commerce, Consumer Protection, and Competitiveness. House
Auto insurance coverage, premiums, and theft losses, with data by model and State, 1988 hearings, 21368–110
Health care (long-term) for aged, funding by Fed Govt, public views, 1987 survey, hearings, 21368–106

Subcommittee on Compensation, Pension, and Insurance. House
VA benefit claims processing and efficiency at regional offices, and hearing officers salaries and travel costs, 1986-88, hearing, 21768–47

Subcommittee on Conservation and Forestry. Senate
Farm soil and wetland conservation programs of USDA, costs and impacts on farm finances and operations, with background data, 1980s, hearing, 25168–69

Subcommittee on Courts, Civil Liberties, and Administration of Justice. House
TV satellite dish and decoder sales, ownership, subscribers, and program ratings compared to local stations, 1980s-88, hearings, 21528–74

Subcommittee on Economic Development. House
Economic Dev Admin funding, and loans forgiven, with data by project and location, FY84-88, hearing, 21648–56

Subcommittee on Education, Arts and Humanities. Senate
Student guaranteed loan defaults, rates, and borrowers in repayment status, by instn and State, FY86, with background data, 1980s, hearings, 25548–96

Subcommittee on Employment Opportunities. House
Aerospace industry minority employment in Los Angeles area, by occupational group, 1980s-86, 21348–113

Subcommittee on Energy and Power. House
Conservation R&D spending of DOE and private sector, and housing natural gas use indicators, hearings, 21368–107

Subcommittee on Environment, Energy, and Natural Resources. House
Hazardous substances health effects, environmental levels, and household products composition, with data by selected location, 1988 hearings, 21408–112

Subcommittee on Europe and Middle East. House
Portugal and Turkey economic indicators and govt finances, 1982-86, hearing, 21388–53

Subcommittee on Exports, Tourism, and Special Problems. House
Small business loans of Eximbank, by firm, 1984-88, hearing, 21728–70

Subcommittee on Fiscal Affairs and Health. House
Drug abuse, deaths, arrests, convictions, and seizures by drug type, for DC metro area, 1980-87, hearing, 21308–24
Emergency fire and medical services operations, staff, and finances, for DC and compared to other US and Canadian cities, 1986, hearing, 21308–25

Subcommittee on Fisheries and Wildlife Conservation and Environment. House
Pollutant discharges in coastal areas and estuaries from agricultural, airborne, and other nonpoint sources, and regulatory issues, 1988 hearing, 21568–46
Sewage pipelines and dump sites authorized in coastal areas, status and EPA enforcement activities by State, 1982-87, hearings, 21568–45
Tuna fishery porpoise kill, purse seine vessels in Pacific Ocean, and porpoise population, 1960s-90, hearing, 21568–47

Subcommittee on Forests, Family Farms, and Energy. House
Production itemized costs, by selected commodity, projected 1986-97, hearing, 21168–40

Subcommittee on General Oversight and Investigations, Finance and Urban Affairs. House
Banks brokered deposit holdings and financial indicators, by size, region, and for failed instns, 1986-89, hearing, 21248–124
Bond (low-grade) issues by industry div, holdings by owner type, yields, and defaults, 1977-88, 21248–118

Subcommittee on General Oversight and Investigations, Interior and Insular Affairs. House
Connecticut energy use by consuming sector, and prices, by energy type, 1960s-86, hearing, 21448–38
Irrigation subsidies of Reclamation Bur, costs to Fed Govt and surplus crop production, 1985-86, 21448–40

Subcommittee on Government Information and Regulation. Senate
Census of Population and Housing, 1990: data collection procedure, and impacts on congressional apportionment by State, hearing, 25408–101

Subcommittee on Government Information, Justice, and Agriculture. House
Executions by whether writ of habeas corpus used to appeal, race, and State, with military death row inmates, 1977-87, hearing, 21408–110

Subcommittee on Health and Environment. House
Acid rain control economic impacts, and sulfur dioxide emissions and reductions of industrial and power plants, 1987 hearing, 21368–104
Dioxin levels in paper products and pulp mill effluents, and environmental and health effects, 1988 hearing, 21368–112
Medicaid coverage, participation, payments, admin, and legislative history, with data by State, 1980s-88, 21368–105
Pollution (air) exposure of population and selected risk groups, by pollutant, MSA, and county, 1988, hearing, 21368–117

Subcommittee on Health and Long-Term Care. House
Board and care homes conditions, State licensing and enforcement activity, and client characteristics, 1970s-88, 21148–55
Health care (long-term) needs, ability to pay, and views on Federal aid for home care, 1988 survey, hearing, 21148–51

Railroad (short-line) operations and regulation, for lines established 1834-1987, hearing, 21368–109

Railroad accidents, casualties, and Federal safety activities, late 1970s-87, hearing, 21368–103

Subcommittee on Water and Power Resources. House

Alaska Arctic Natl Wildlife Refuge oil and gas resource assessment, with environmental impacts on North Slope and other locations, 1987 hearing, 21448–41

Indian reservation water supply projects in South Dakota, costs and indicators of need, with health and housing data for other reservations, 1980s-87, hearing, 21448–37

Submarines

DOD budget, weapons acquisition costs by system and service branch, FY89-91, annual rpt, 3504–2

DOD procurement cost estimates for weapons and communications systems, by service branch, quarterly summary rpt, 3502–1

Foreign countries military spending, arms trade, and force strengths, with govt spending and population, by country, 1977-87, annual rpt, 9824–1

Radiation exposure of Navy personnel on nuclear-powered vessels and at support facilities, and injury claims, 1950s-88, annual rpt, 3804–10

Radioactive waste from Navy nuclear-powered vessels and support facilities, releases in harbors, and public exposure, 1970s-88, annual rpt, 3804–11

Soviet Union and Warsaw Pact military weapons systems, aid, presence, and force strengths, and compared to US and NATO, 1989 annual rpt, 3504–20

Submerged lands

see also Continental shelf

see also Offshore oil and gas

Subsidies

Budget of US Appendix, obligations, appropriations, and personnel, by program and agency, FY90, annual rpt, 104–3

Budget of US, compact budgets by activity, function, and agency, FY90 and projected to FY94, annual rpt, 104–2

Coal production, trade, and govt subsidies, by country and country group, 1973-87 and projected to 2000, 2048–144

Finances of govts, revenues by source and spending by function, natl income and product account, Survey of Current Business, monthly rpt, 2702–1.24

Minerals depletion allowance of foreign countries and US, by nonfuel mineral, 1984-88, annual rpt, 5604–18

Minority business funding, by program and Federal agency, FY86-88, annual rpt, 2104–5

Natl income and product accounts and components, Survey of Current Business, monthly rpt, 2702–1.21

Natl income and product accounts govt transactions component estimates, methodology and bibl, 1988 technical rpt, 2706–6.5

Oil prices and US and OPEC industry impacts of alternative US protective policies, projected 2037, technical paper, 9379–12.44

Postal Service operating costs, itemized by class of mail, FY88, annual rpt, 9864–4

Postal Service subsidy for revenue forgone, by class of mail, FY88, annual rpt, 9864–1; 9864–5

Telephone local service charges and low-income subsidies, by region, company, and city, 1940-June 1989, semiannual rpt, 9282–8

see also Agricultural production quotas and price supports

see also Agricultural subsidies

see also Federal aid programs

see also Federal aid to arts and humanities

see also Federal aid to education

see also Federal aid to higher education

see also Federal aid to highways

see also Federal aid to housing

see also Federal aid to law enforcement

see also Federal aid to libraries

see also Federal aid to local areas

see also Federal aid to medical education

see also Federal aid to medicine

see also Federal aid to railroads

see also Federal aid to rural areas

see also Federal aid to States

see also Federal aid to transportation

see also Federal aid to vocational education

see also Federal funding for energy programs

see also Federal funding for research and development

see also Rent supplements

see also Shipbuilding and operating subsidies

see also State funding for economic development

see also State funding for education

see also State funding for health and hospitals

see also State funding for higher education

see also State funding for local areas

see also State funding for public safety

see also State funding for social welfare

see also State government spending

see also Tax expenditures

see also Tax incentives and shelters

see also Trade adjustment assistance

Substance abuse

see Alcohol abuse and treatment

see Cocaine

see Drug abuse and treatment

see Marijuana

see Smoking

Suburbs

Births, fertility rates, and childless women, by selected characteristics, 1988, annual Current Population Rpt, 2546–1.436

Crime Index by population size and region, and offenses by large city, Jan-June 1989, semiannual rpt, 6222–1

Crime victimization of households, by offense, household characteristics, and location, 1975-88, annual rpt, 6066–25.22

Crimes, arrests by offender characteristics, and rates, by offense, and law enforcement employees, by population size and jurisdiction, 1988, annual rpt, 6224–2

Educational enrollment, by grade, instn type and control, and student characteristics, 1986 and trends from 1947, annual Current Population Rpt, 2546–1.429; 2546–1.432

Employment and unemployment in metro and nonmetro areas, monthly rpt, quarterly data, 6742–2.9

Employment, unemployment, and labor force characteristics, Labor Statistics Handbook, 1940s-88 with trends from 1913, 6728–38.1

Food consumption and nutrient intake by individuals, by food group, selected characteristics, and region, supplementary survey series, 1356–5

Household and family characteristics, by location, 1988, annual Current Population Rpt, 2546–1.437

Housing and households detailed characteristics, and unit and neighborhood quality, by location, 1985, biennial rpt, 2485–12

Housing and households detailed characteristics, and unit and neighborhood quality, MSA surveys, series, 2485–6

Housing vacancy and occupancy rates, and vacant unit characteristics and costs, by region and metro-nonmetro location, quarterly rpt, 2482–1

Income (household) and poverty status under alternative income definitions, by recipient characteristics, 1986, Current Population Rpt, 2546–6.58

Land use, commuting, employment, and housing characteristics for suburban areas, detailed data for traffic planning, 1986, 7888–75

Migration since 1986, mover characteristics by same or different area, and compared to nonmovers, 1987, annual Current Population Rpt, 2546–1.435

see also Neighborhoods

see also Urban renewal

see also under By Urban-Rural and Metro-Nonmetro in the "Index by Categories"

Subversive activities

Aliens excluded and deported from US by cause and country, 1892-1988, annual rpt, 6264–2

Bombing incidents and casualties, by target, circumstances, and State, 1979-88, annual rpt, 8484–4.1

Foreign countries human rights conditions in 170 countries, 1988, annual rpt, 21384–3

Prisoners and movements, by offense, location, and selected other characteristics, data compilation, 1930s-89, annual rpt, 6064–6.6

Sentences for Federal offenses, guidelines by offense and circumstances, 1989 rpt, 17668–1

US attorneys civil and criminal cases by type and disposition, and collections, by Federal district, FY88, annual rpt, 6004–2.1; 6004–2.7

see also Espionage

see also Insurgency

see also Internal security

see also Sabotage

see also Terrorism

see also Underground movements

Subways

Accidents, casualties, and damage, by circumstances and system, 1987, annual rpt, 7884–5

Construction industries census, 1987: establishments, employment, receipts, and expenditures, by SIC 4-digit industry and State, final industry rpt series, 2373–1

Construction industries census, 1987: financial and operating data, preliminary industry rpt series, 2371–1

Energy use by mode of transport, fuel supply, and demographic and economic factors of vehicle use, 1970s-88, annual rpt, 3304–5

Finances and operations of transit systems, by mode of transport, size of fleet, and for 432 systems, 1986, annual rpt, 7884–4

Finances, costs, and needs of transit systems, by State and selected system, 1980-88, biennial rpt, 7884–8

Finances, operations, vehicles, equipment, accidents, and energy use, by mode of transport, 1955-88, annual rpt, 7304–2

Manufacturing annual survey, 1986: financial and operating data, by SIC 2- to 4-digit industry, series, 2506–15

Urban areas traffic volume and detailed trip characteristics, by transport mode and city, 1950s-88, 7888–37

Urban Mass Transportation Admin grants for transit systems, by city and State, FY88, annual rpt, 7884–10

Urban transit systems services and vehicles, 1988 annual listing, 7884–9

Sudan

Agricultural and food production and indexes, total and for selected commodities, by country, 1970s-88, annual rpt, 1524–12

Agricultural exports of Africa by commodity, and relation to economic conditions and other factors, by country, 1960s-87, 1528–280

Agricultural imports and food aid needs under alternative weather assumptions, for 17 African countries, projected to 1995, 1528–279

Agricultural production, prices, and trade, by country, 1960s-89, annual world region rpt, 1524–4.2

Agricultural trade of US, by detailed commodity and country, 1988, semiannual rpt, 1522–4

AID activities and funding by project and function, FY90, and developing countries summary socioeconomic data from 1960s, annual rpt, 9904–4.5

AID economic aid to developing countries, obligations and disbursements by country, quarterly rpt, 9912–4

AID loans repayment status and terms by program and country, and status of predecessor agency loans, quarterly rpt, 9912–3

Economic and military aid and loans from US and intl agencies, by program and country, FY46-87, annual rpt, 9914–5

Economic conditions, income, production, prices, employment, and trade, 1989 periodic country rpt, 2046–4.90

Economic conditions, policy, and trade practices, by country, 1986-88, annual rpt, 21384–5

Economic, social, political, and geographic summary data, by country, 1989, annual factbook, 9114–2

Human rights conditions in 170 countries, 1988, annual rpt, 21384–3

Military aid of US, arms sales, and training programs costs and budget requests, by program, world region, and country, FY88-90, annual rpt, 7144–13

Military spending, arms trade, and force strengths, with govt spending and population, by country, 1977-87, annual rpt, 9824–1

Minerals Yearbook, 1987, Vol 3: foreign country reviews of production, trade, and policy, by commodity, annual rpt, 5604–35

Minerals Yearbook, 1987, Vol 3 preprints: foreign country review of production, trade, and policy, by commodity, annual rpt, 5604–23.81

Population size, growth rates, and components of change, by country, projected 1989-2020 and trends from 1950, biennial rpt, 2324–9

UN voting record and share of votes in agreement with US, by issue, country, and world area, 1988, annual rpt, 7004–18

see also under By Foreign Country in the "Index by Categories"

Suddendorf, Ronald F.

"Research on Alcohol Metabolism Among Asians and Its Implications for Understanding Causes of Alcoholism", 4042–3.959

Suez Canal

Traffic of Canal for minerals and other commodities, 1985-87, *Minerals Yearbook*, annual rpt, 5604–35.1

Suffolk County, N.Y.

Wages by occupation, for office and plant workers, 1988 survey, periodic MSA rpt, 6785–11.2

Wages by occupation, for office and plant workers, 1989 survey, periodic MSA rpt, 6785–12.7

see also under By SMSA or MSA in the "Index by Categories"

Sugar industry and products

Acreage planted, by selected crop and State, 1980-88 and planned 1989, annual rpt, 1621–22

Acreage under Agricultural Stabilization and Conservation Service programs, rankings by commodity and congressional district, 1987, biennial rpt, 1804–17

Agricultural Statistics, 1988, annual rpt, 1004–1

Agriculture census, 1987: farms, farmland, production and costs, and operator characteristics, advance State and county rpt series, 2330–8

Agriculture census, 1987: farms, farmland, production, finances, and operator characteristics, by county, final State rpt series, 2331–1

Alcohol fuels (ethanol) from Caribbean basin, impacts of duty-free treatment on US industry, investigation with background financial and operating data, 1989 rpt, 9886–4.134

Alcoholic beverages production, stocks, materials used, and taxable and tax-free removals, for beer and distilled spirits by State, monthly rpt, 8486–1.1; 8486–1.3

Business statistics, detailed data for major industries and economic indicators, *Survey of Current Business*, monthly rpt, 2702–1.11

Caribbean area sugar production and exports, and cruise ship tourist visits and spending, by country, 1981-88, hearing, 21788–179

China trade by SITC 1- to 5-digit commodity, 1970s-87, annual rpt, 9114–3

Cloned sugarcane yields, stability, and fungi resistance, 1988/89, annual rpt, 1704–2

Communist, OECD, and selected other countries agricultural production, by commodity, 1960s-88, annual rpt, 9114–4.6

Consumer Expenditure Survey, household income by source, and itemized spending, by selected characteristics and location, 1984-86, annual rpt, 6764–5.2

Consumption of food and nutrient intake by individuals, by food group, selected characteristics, and region, supplementary survey series, 1356–5

Consumption, supply, trade, prices, spending, and indexes, by food commodity, 1987, annual rpt, 1544–4

County Business Patterns, 1987: employment, establishments, and payroll, by SIC 2- to 4-digit industry and county, annual State rpt series, 2326–8

CPI by component for US city average, and by region, population size, and for 27 metro areas, monthly rpt, 6762–2

Cuba economic conditions, agricultural and industrial production and distribution, trade, and intl economic relations, 1980-87 with trends from 1961, 9118–8

Eastern Europe agricultural production, consumption, and trade, by country, 1970s-88, annual rpt, 1524–11

Eastern Europe and USSR agricultural production, acreage, and consumption, by commodity and country, 1965-85, 1528–284

Employment, earnings, and hours, by selected SIC 1- to 4-digit industry, State, and for 262 MSAs, 1972-87, 6748–81

Employment, earnings, and hours, by SIC 1- to 4-digit industry, monthly 1983-Feb 1989, annual rpt, 6744–4

Exports and imports (agricultural) commodity and country, prices, and world market devs, monthly rpt, 1922–12

Exports and imports (agricultural) of US, by commodity and country, bimonthly rpt with articles, 1522–1

Exports and imports (agricultural) of US, by commodity, monthly rpt, 1922–8

Exports and imports (agricultural) of US, by detailed commodity and country, 1988, semiannual rpt, 1522–4

Exports and imports (agricultural) of US with Asia, Middle East, and North Africa, by commodity and country, 1962-86, 1528–277

Exports of US, detailed commodities by country, monthly rpt, 2422–3

Farm financial and marketing conditions, forecast 1988, conf papers, annual rpt, 1004–16

Farm income, expenses, receipts by commodity, assets, liabilities, and ratios, 1988 and trends from 1945, annual rpt, 1544–16

Farm receipts for 25 leading crops, by State, 1960-87, 1548–347

Farm sector balance sheet, and receipts by detailed commodity, by State, 1984-88, annual rpt, 1544–18

Foreign and US agricultural trade and market impacts of eliminating protectionist policies, model description and results, 1986, 1528–282

Foreign and US production, prices, trade, and use, FAS periodic circular series, 1925–14

Suguiyama, Luis

Suicide

Sulfur

see Nonmetallic minerals and mines

Sulfur oxides

see Acid rain
see Air pollution

Sulfuric acid

see Chemicals and chemical industry

Sullivan, David F.

Sullivan, Gene D.

Sullivan, Patrick J.

Sulvetta, Margaret B.

Summer employment

see Temporary and seasonal employment

Sundberg, Mark W.

Sunflowers and sunflower seeds

see Oils, oilseeds, and fats

Sunnyvale, Calif.

see also under By City in the "Index by Categories"

Suntio, Leena R.

Superfund

see Hazardous waste and disposal

Supermarkets

see Food stores

Supervisors

see Business management
see Executives and managers

Supervisors and managers

see Executives and managers

Supplemental Security Income

Beneficiaries characteristics, payments, and eligibility, for aged and disabled SSI awards made 1981, 1985, article, 4742–1.907

Benefits and beneficiaries of SSI, by type of eligibility, State, and county, Dec 1987, annual rpt, 4744–27

Benefits, beneficiaries, and summary program data for selected public welfare programs, selected years 1937-89, chartbook, 4748–42

Benefits by county, FY88, annual regional listings, 4004–3

Board and care homes conditions, State licensing and enforcement activity, and client characteristics, 1970s-88, 21148–55

Court caseloads for SSI claims in Federal district courts, June 1989, annual rpt, 18204–2.12; 18204–8.11

Denials of Disability Insurance and SSI benefits, appeals processing, caseloads, dispositions, and allowances by disability, 1986-88, GAO rpt, 26121–278

Disabled OASDI and SSI beneficiaries, by selected characteristics, 1986, article, 4742–1.916

Disabled persons employment, labor force status, and other characteristics, 1988, Current Population Rpt, 2546–2.147

Eligibility and payment provisions for SSI and Medicaid, and beneficiaries living arrangements, by State, 1989, annual rpt, 4704–13

Eligibility reviews for Disability Insurance and SSI, and State administrators views of review standards, 1986-88, GAO rpt, 26121–258

Expenditures, coverage, and benefits for social welfare programs, late 1930s-87, annual rpt, 4744–3.1

Expenditures of Fed Govt in States, by type, program, agency, and State, FY88, annual rpt, 2464–2

Finances and operations of programs under Ways and Means Committee jurisdiction, FY70s-88, annual rpt, 21784–11

Finances of Fed Govt, cash and debt transactions, daily tables, 8102–4

Finances of SSA programs, and litigation, FY88, annual rpt, 4704–6

Household composition, income, benefits, and labor force status, Survey of Income and Program Participation methodology, working paper series, 2626–10

Household, family, and personal income, by source, detailed characteristics, and region, 1987, annual Current Population Rpt, 2546–6.59

Household income and poverty status under alternative income definitions, by recipient characteristics, 1986, Current Population Rpt, 2546–6.58

Income (personal) by source including transfer payments, and social insurance contributions, by region, 1984, 2708–40

Medicaid coverage, participation, payments, admin, and legislative history, with data by State, 1980s-88, 21368–105

Medicaid enrollment, and service use and costs by service type, by eligibility type, for 5 States, 1980-84, article, 4652–1.919

Medicaid enrollment, services use, and costs, by eligibility type and length of enrollment, for 2 States, 1980-83, article, 4652–1.906

Medicaid services use and costs for SSI beneficiaries, by diagnosis and whether covered by Medicare, 1984, article, 4652–1.947

Mental illness and related disorders eligibility determinations for Disability Insurance and SSI, caseload and review activities by impairment type and State, 1984-86, hearing, 21788–176

Older persons aid and policies of Fed Govt, with program funding, 1980s-89, annual rpt, 25144–3.1

Poverty status of families and persons, by detailed characteristics, 1987, annual Current Population Rpt, 2546–6.60

Social Security Bulletin, OASDHI and other program operations and beneficiary characteristics, from 1940, monthly rpt with articles, 4742–1

Statistical Abstract of US, social, political, and economic data, 1790-2025, comprehensive annual compilation, 2324–1.2

Telephone service of households, by composition, income sources, and other characteristics, 1984-87, 9288–11

Vocational rehabilitation programs of States, social, employment, and disability characteristics of clients, FY88, annual rpt, 4944–1

Supplementary Educational Opportunity Grant
see Student aid

Supplementary wage benefits
see Employee benefits

Supreme Court

Budget of US Appendix, obligations, appropriations, and personnel, by program and agency, FY90, annual rpt, 104–3

Budget of US, authoritative financial statements with appropriations, outlays, and receipts, by category and agency, FY88, annual rpt, 8104–2.2

Buildings and grounds under Capitol Architect supervision, itemized outlays by payee and function, 1st half FY89, semiannual rpt, 25922–2

Caseload, dispositions by type, and cases remaining, for Supreme Court, Oct 1983-87, annual rpt, 18204–8.12

Crime, criminal justice admin and enforcement, and public opinion, data compilation, 1970s-88, annual rpt, 6064–6

Pay rates of Fed Govt civilian employees, by pay schedule and grade, 1989 and trends from 1789, annual rpt, 21624–4

Statistical Abstract of US, social, political, and economic data, 1790-2025, comprehensive annual compilation, 2324–1.1

Tax Court of US caseloads and appeals by disposition, procedure duration, and recoveries, FY88, annual rpt, 18224–5

Tax litigation, prosecutions, and interpretive law decisions, FY88, annual rpt, 8304–3.2

Writs of certiorari for review by Supreme Court on writs filed in Federal courts of appeals, petitions and disposition, June 1988, annual rpt, 18204–8.13

Surety bonds

Aliens exclusion and deportation cases, appeals, bond postings, and investigations, for NYC and Los Angeles, 1987, GAO rpt, 26119–271

Companies (surety) authorized to post bonds with Fed Govt, location and bonding limits, as of July 1989, annual listing, 8104–4

Minority business funding, by program and Federal agency, FY86-88, annual rpt, 2104–5

Small Business Admin loans, contract awards, and surety bonds, by firm, State, and city, FY88, annual rpt, 9764–1

Small business construction contracts of Fed Govt, surety bonds use and fraud cases, by agency, 1985-89, GAO rpt, 26113–438

Surgeons and surgery

Admissions and costs for surgical inpatients and outpatients, by diagnostic group, for Manitoba, Canada, 1982-84, article, 4652–1.940

AIDS virus infection of patients and surgeons, orthopedists views on treatment and professional restriction, 1986 survey, article, 4042–3.907

Cancer (breast) survival rates, for patients receiving chemotherapy after surgery, for diagnoses made 1975-85, GAO rpt, 26131–58

Cancer (osteosarcoma) progress and deaths, by disease and treatment characteristics, 1977-85 study, article, 4472–1.901

Cardiovascular diseases cases, health care services use and costs, and productivity losses, by selected characteristics, 1980, 4146–12.26

Deaths related to surgery, and rates, by cause, age, race, sex, and State, 1986, US Vital Statistics annual rpt, 4144–2

Drugs (controlled) provided during physician office visits, by drug, patient, and provider characteristics, 1985, 4146–8.179

Health Care Financing Review, provider prices, price inputs and indexes, and labor, quarterly journal, 4652–1.1

Health condition and health care resources, use, and spending, 1950s-87, annual data compilation, 4144–11

Hepatitis cases by infection source, age, sex, race, and State, and deaths, by strain, 1987 and trends from 1966, 4205–2

Hospital discharges and length of stay, by diagnosis, patient age and sex, surgical procedure performed, and region, 1965-86, 4147–13.101

Hospital discharges and length of stay, by diagnosis, patient and instn characteristics, procedure performed, and payment source, 1987, annual rpt, 4147–13.99

Hospital discharges by detailed diagnostic and procedure category, primary diagnosis, and length of stay, by age, sex, and region, 1987, annual rpt, 4147–13.100

Hospital discharges, length of stay, and costs, for Medicare by type of beneficiary, procedure, diagnosis, and State, 1970s-86, article, 4652–1.945

Hospital elective admissions relation to costs and length of stay, for New Jersey, 1982, article, 4652–1.930

Hospital surgical procedures performed, by procedure type, age, sex, instn size, and payment source, 1983-87, 4146–8.171

Hospital use and costs of Medicaid enrollees related to selected characteristics, 1980, article, 4652–1.949

Insurance (health) coverage and provisions of employee benefit plans, by plan type and occupational group, 1988, annual rpt, 6784–19

Malpractice claims and payments, by procedure and physician specialty, 1975-78, hearing, 21408–113

Medicaid cost control measures, surgery 2nd opinion and preadmission review program characteristics, 1987 survey, article, 4652–1.944

Medicare and Medicaid beneficiaries and program operations, 1988, annual fact book, 4654–18

Medicare charges and reimbursements, by service type, 1966-86, annual rpt, 4744–3.5

Medicare claims approved, charges, and reimbursements by type of service, from 1974, monthly rpt, quarterly data, 4742–1.11

Medicare enrollees physician and other services use, benefits, charges, and coinsurance and deductible obligations, 1982-86, article, 4652–1.901

Medicare physicians services use, charges, and reimbursement, by service type, setting, and specialty, 1986, article, 4652–1.936

Medicare reimbursement of hospitals under prospective payment system, alternative case mix indexes, FY85-86, article, 4652–1.952

Medicare reimbursement of hospitals under prospective payment system, and of physicians, effect on services, finances, and beneficiary payments, 1970s-88, annual rpt, 17204–2

Medicare reimbursement of hospitals under prospective payment system, impacts on use of surgical implants and prosthetics, with background data, 1984-86, 17206–2.3

Medicare reimbursement of hospitals under prospective payment system, impacts on use of surgical procedures, costs, length of stay, and deaths, by procedure type, 1984-86, 17206–2.5

Military health care benefits and costs under Civilian Health and Medical Program of Uniformed Services, FY83-FY89, 3508–31

Military health care personnel, and accessions by training source, by occupation, specialty, and service branch, FY87, annual rpt, 3544–24

Military reserve medical personnel, by specialty and reserve component, FY88, annual rpt, 3544–31.2

Older persons health care services use, persons with high and low levels of care by selected health and other characteristics, 1971 and 1980 studies, 4186–2.22

Physicians income, by specialty and other practice characteristics, 1975 and 1983-84, article, 4652–1.920

Rural areas health care facilities, staffing, services accessibility, and indicators of need, 1960s-88, 25148–41

Rural areas hospitals surgeries performed by itinerant surgeons, quality of care issues and Medicare overpayments, 1985-86, 4008–93

Statistical Abstract of US, social, political, and economic data, 1790-2025, comprehensive annual compilation, 2324–1.1

Texas-Mexico border area health facilities and services, with background data, by Texas county, 1980s-88, GAO rpt, 26121–261

VA health care facilities mental health services, staff, research, and training programs, 1989 biennial listing, 8704–2

VA health care facilities physicians, dentists, and nurses, by selected employment characteristics and VA district, quarterly rpt, 8602–6

VA health care facilities physicians staffing, vacancies, and positions filled, by speciality, 1982-87, hearing, 25768–48

VA health care facilities surgery-related deaths and complications, by procedure and instn, and compared to non-VA instns, 1981-88, biennial rpt, 8704–1

VA hospitals admissions and discharges by diagnosis, facilities operating costs, and other VA activities, FY88, annual rpt, 8604–3.3

VA Medicine and Surgery Dept trainees, by detailed program and city, FY88, annual rpt, 8704–4

see also Medical transplants

Suriname

Agricultural and food production and indexes, total and for selected commodities, by country, 1970s-88, annual rpt, 1524–12

Agricultural trade of US, by detailed commodity and country, 1988, semiannual rpt, 1522–4

AID activities and funding by project and function, FY90, and developing countries summary socioeconomic data from 1960s, annual rpt, 9904–4.7

AID economic aid to developing countries, obligations and disbursements by country, quarterly rpt, 9912–4

AID loans repayment status and terms by program and country, and status of predecessor agency loans, quarterly rpt, 9912–3

Economic and military aid and loans from US and intl agencies, by program and country, FY46-87, annual rpt, 9914–5

Economic, social, political, and geographic summary data, by country, 1989, annual factbook, 9114–2

Human rights conditions in 170 countries, 1988, annual rpt, 21384–3

Labor conditions, union coverage, and work accidents, 1989 annual country rpt, 6366–4.17

Military aid of US, arms sales, and training programs costs and budget requests, by program, world region, and country, FY88-90, annual rpt, 7144–13

Military spending, arms trade, and force strengths, with govt spending and population, by country, 1977-87, annual rpt, 9824–1

Minerals Yearbook, 1987, Vol 3: foreign country reviews of production, trade, and policy, by commodity, annual rpt, 5604–35

Minerals Yearbook, 1987, Vol 3 preprints: foreign country review of production, trade, and policy, by commodity, annual rpt, 5604–23.87

Population size, growth rates, and components of change, by country, projected 1989-2020 and trends from 1950, biennial rpt, 2324–9

UN voting record and share of votes in agreement with US, by issue, country, and world area, 1988, annual rpt, 7004–18

see also under By Foreign Country in the "Index by Categories"

Surplus government property

Assistance (financial and nonfinancial) of Fed Govt, 1989 base edition with supplements, annual listing, 104–5

Budget of US, authoritative financial statements with appropriations, outlays, and receipts, by category and agency, FY88, annual rpt, 8104–2.2

Developing countries economic and social conditions from 1960s, and Intl Dev Cooperation Agency and AID activities and funding, FY88-90, annual rpt, 9904–4

DOD property, supply, and equipment inventory, by service branch, 1988, annual rpt, 3544–6

Foreign countries military aid of US, arms sales, and training, by country, FY50-88, annual rpt, 3904–3

Foreign countries military aid programs and related activities of US, costs by country and intl agency, FY85-87 and cumulative from FY50, GAO rpt, 26123–30

Surveillance

see Electronic surveillance

Survey of Income and Program Participation

Child care arrangements and costs, by income and other characteristics of family, 1984-86, press release, 2328–61

Data collection, methodology, and availability, 1987 users guide, 2628–24

Data collection, methodology, and comparisons to other data bases, working paper series, 2626–10

Data collection, methodology, and use, 1988 annual conf papers, 2624–1

Household Economic Studies, series, 2546–20

OASDI beneficiary classification under SIPP, methodology, 1989 article, 4742–1.905

Population and housing data, and policy issues, fact sheet series, 2326–17

Survey of Minority-Owned Business Enterprises

Data coverage and availability for 1987 economic censuses and related statistics, 1989 preliminary guide, 2308–5

Survey of Women-Owned Businesses

Data coverage and availability for 1987 economic censuses and related statistics, 1989 preliminary guide, 2308–5

Surveys

see American Housing Survey

see Annual Survey of Manufactures

see Area wage surveys

see Business outlook and attitude surveys

see Census of Agriculture

see Census of Construction Industries

see Census of Governments

see Census of Housing

see Census of Manufactures

see Census of Mineral Industries

see Census of Outlying Areas

see Census of Population

see Census of Population and Housing
see Census of Retail Trade
see Census of Service Industries
see Census of Transportation
see Census of Wholesale Trade
see Consumer Expenditure Survey
see Consumer surveys
see Continuing Survey of Food Intakes by Individuals
see Current Employment Survey
see Current Population Survey
see Economic censuses
see Enterprise Statistics Program
see Farm Costs and Returns Survey
see High School and Beyond Survey
see Hispanic Health and Nutrition Examination Survey
see Hospital Cost and Utilization Project
see Industry wage surveys
see Inventory of Long-Term Care Places
see Methodology
see Mineral Industry Surveys
see Motor Freight Transportation and Warehousing Survey
see National Ambulatory Medical Care Survey
see National Assessment of Educational Progress
see National Crime Survey
see National Drug and Alcoholism Treatment Utilization Survey
see National Fetal Mortality Survey
see National Health and Nutrition Examination Survey
see National Health Interview Survey
see National Health Interview Survey of Health Promotion and Disease Prevention
see National Hospital Discharge Survey
see National Household Seroprevalence Survey
see National Household Survey on Drug Abuse
see National Longitudinal Study of High School Seniors
see National Master Facility Inventory
see National Medical Care Expenditure Survey
see National Medical Care Utilization and Expenditure Survey
see National Medical Expenditure Survey
see National Mortality Followback Survey
see National Mortality Survey
see National Natality Survey
see National Nursing Home Survey
see National Occupational Exposure Survey
see National Survey of Family Growth
see National Survey of Health and Sexual Behavior
see National Survey of Small Business Finances
see Nationwide Food Consumption Survey
see Opinion and attitude surveys
see Recent College Graduates Survey
see Statistical programs and activities
see Survey of Income and Program Participation
see Survey of Minority-Owned Business Enterprises
see Survey of Women-Owned Businesses

Survivors
see Old-Age, Survivors, Disability, and Health Insurance
see Widows and widowers

Susquehanna River
Freight (waterborne domestic and foreign) by commodity, traffic, and passengers, by port and waterway, 1987, annual rpt, 3754–3.1
Water supply and quality in streams and lakes, and groundwater levels in wells, by drainage basin, 1986, annual State rpt series, 5666–23
Water supply and quality in streams and lakes, and groundwater levels in wells, by drainage basin, 1987, annual State rpt series, 5666–10
Water supply and quality in streams and lakes, and groundwater levels in wells, by drainage basin, 1988, annual State rpt series, 5666–16
Water supply in US and southern Canada, streamflow, surface and groundwater conditions, and reservoir levels, by location, monthly rpt, 5662–3

Susquehanna River Basin Commission
Budget of US, authoritative financial statements with appropriations, outlays, and receipts, by category and agency, FY88, annual rpt, 8104–2.2

Sussman, E. Donald
"Examination of Sudden Acceleration", 7768–107.1

Sutton, John
"Environmental Degradation and Agriculture", 1522–3.910

Svetlik, Mary A.
"Does the Average Cost of Home Health Care Vary with Case Mix?", 4042–3.932

Swaim, Paul
"Do More-Educated Workers Fare Better Following Job Displacement?", 6722–1.942

Swamps
see Wetlands

Swamy, P. A.
"Co-Integration: Is It a Property of the Real World?", 9366–6.210
"Coherent Methods of Estimating Technical Progress", 9366–6.191
"Forecasting Australian Monetary Aggregates", 9366–6.169
"Stochastic Coefficients Approach to Econometric Modeling, Part III: Estimation, Stability Testing, and Prediction", 1502–3.901

Swaziland
Agricultural and food production and indexes, total and for selected commodities, by country, 1970s-88, annual rpt, 1524–12
Agricultural trade of US, by detailed commodity and country, 1988, semiannual rpt, 1522–4
AID activities and funding by project and function, FY90, and developing countries summary socioeconomic data from 1960s, annual rpt, 9904–4.5
AID economic aid to developing countries, obligations and disbursements by country, quarterly rpt, 9912–4
AID loans repayment status and terms by program and country, and status of predecessor agency loans, quarterly rpt, 9912–3
Economic and military aid and loans from US and intl agencies, by program and country, FY46-87, annual rpt, 9914–5

Economic conditions, income, production, prices, employment, and trade, 1989 periodic country rpt, 2046–4.20
Economic conditions, policy, and trade practices, by country, 1986-88, annual rpt, 21384–5
Economic, social, political, and geographic summary data, by country, 1989, annual factbook, 9114–2
Human rights conditions in 170 countries, 1988, annual rpt, 21384–3
Military aid of US, arms sales, and training programs costs and budget requests, by program, world region, and country, FY88-90, annual rpt, 7144–13
Military spending, arms trade, and force strengths, with govt spending and population, by country, 1977-87, annual rpt, 9824–1
Minerals Yearbook, 1987, Vol 3: foreign country reviews of production, trade, and policy, by commodity, annual rpt, 5604–35
Minerals Yearbook, 1987, Vol 3 preprints: foreign country review of production, trade, and policy, by commodity, annual rpt, 5604–23.81
Population size, growth rates, and components of change, by country, projected 1989-2020 and trends from 1950, biennial rpt, 2324–9
UN voting record and share of votes in agreement with US, by issue, country, and world area, 1988, annual rpt, 7004–18
see also under By Foreign Country in the "Index by Categories"

Sweaters
see Clothing and clothing industry

Sweden
Agricultural and food production and indexes, total and for selected commodities, by country, 1970s-88, annual rpt, 1524–12
Agricultural production, prices, and trade, by country, 1970s-88 and forecast 1990, annual world region rpt, 1524–4.1
Agricultural trade of US, by detailed commodity and country, 1988, semiannual rpt, 1522–4
AID loans repayment status and terms by program and country, and status of predecessor agency loans, quarterly rpt, 9912–3
Aluminum sulfate (dry) from Sweden at less than fair value, injury to US industry, investigation with background financial and operating data, 1989 rpt, 9886–14.258
Apple exports of US to EC and 4 north European countries, 1984-89, article, 1925–34.939
Background Notes, summary social, political, and economic data, 1989 rpt, 7006–2.43
Bearings (antifriction) from 9 countries, injury to US industry from foreign subsidized and less than fair value imports, investigation with background financial and operating data, 1989 rpt, 9886–19.65
Businesses (foreign) activity in US, income tax returns, assets, and income statement items, by industry div, country, and world area, 1984-85, article, 8302–2.920
Cancer (breast) risk relation to oral contraceptives use, by age at first use and duration, Sweden study, 1979-85, article, 4472–1.917

Cancer (breast) tumor characteristics related to diet, number of children, and age, 1983-86, article, 4472-1.920

Cancer (melanoma) survival rates, by sex, for Sweden, for diagnoses made 1960-82, article, 4472-1.912

Cancer cases linked to diagnostic radionuclide iodine-131, for Sweden, 1951-84 study, article, 4472-1.907

Cancer survival rates 2- to 10-years following diagnosis, by sex, for Sweden and US, 1960s-84, article, 4472-1.929

Economic and military aid and loans from US and intl agencies, by program and country, FY46-87, annual rpt, 9914-5

Economic and monetary trends, compounded annual rates of change for US and 10 major trading partners, quarterly rpt, 9391-7

Economic conditions in Communist, OECD, and selected other countries, 1960s-88, annual rpt, 9114-4

Economic conditions, income, production, prices, employment, and trade, 1989 periodic country rpt, 2046-4.76

Economic conditions, investment and export opportunities, and trade practices, 1988 country market research rpt, 2046-6.13

Economic conditions, policy, and trade practices, by country, 1986-88, annual rpt, 21384-5

Economic, social, political, and geographic summary data, by country, 1989, annual factbook, 9114-2

Energy prices, by fuel type and end use, for 10 countries, 1980-88 annual rpt, 3164-50.6

Exports and imports of US, by selected country, country group, and commodity group, 1988, annual rpt, 2044-37

Human rights conditions in 170 countries, 1988, annual rpt, 21384-3

Imports of goods, services, and investment from US, trade barriers, impacts, and US actions, by country, 1988, annual rpt, 444-2

Imports of US given duty-free treatment for value of US material sent abroad, and impacts on US industry and employment, by commodity and country, 1987, annual rpt, 9884-14

Manufacturing labor productivity and unit costs for 14 countries, 1950-88, annual press release, 6864-1

Military aid of US, arms sales, and training programs costs and budget requests, by program, world region, and country, FY88-90, annual rpt, 7144-13

Military spending, arms trade, and force strengths, with govt spending and population, by country, 1977-87, annual rpt, 9824-1

Minerals Yearbook, 1987, Vol 3: foreign country reviews of production, trade, and policy, by commodity, annual rpt, 5604-35

Minerals Yearbook, 1987, Vol 3 preprints: foreign country review of production, trade, and policy, by commodity, annual rpt, 5604-23.66

Multinatl firms based in Sweden, domestic and foreign production, exports, employment, and sales, with data by commodity and firm, 1960s-86, conf, 23848-208

Multinatl US firms and foreign affiliates finances and operations, by industry of parent firm and affiliate, world area, and country, preliminary 1987, annual rpt, 2704-5

Nuclear power generation in US and 19 non-Communist countries, monthly rpt, 3162-24.10

Nuclear power plant capacity, generation, and operating status, by plant and foreign and US location, 1988 and projected to 2020, annual rpt, 3164-57

Oil production, trade, use, and stocks, by selected country and country group, monthly rpt, 3162-42

Paper mill products and effluents levels of dioxins and other hazardous substances, and environmental and health effects, 1988 hearing, 21368-112

Population size, growth rates, and components of change, by country, projected 1989-2020 and trends from 1950, biennial rpt, 2324-9

Social security trust funds surpluses impact on govt budgets, for 3 countries and US, 1960-86, article, 9373-1.905

Space satellites and other objects launched since 1957, quarterly listing, 9502-2

Stone (dimension) trade and price indexes by selected country, 1987, Mineral Industry Surveys, annual rpt, 5614-29

Transportation energy use, fuel prices, and vehicle registrations, by selected country, 1970s-88, annual rpt, 3304-5.1

UN voting record and share of votes in agreement with US, by issue, country, and world area, 1988, annual rpt, 7004-18

Unemployment insurance costs and beneficiaries, for US and 5 European countries, 1973-84, article, 6722-1.919

see also under By Foreign Country in the "Index by Categories"

Sweeteners
see Honey and beekeeping
see Sugar industry and products
see Syrups and sweeteners

Sweetpotatoes
see Vegetables and vegetable products

Swimming
Diving (underwater sport and occupational) deaths, by circumstances, diver characteristics, and location, 1970-87, annual rpt, 2144-5

Forest Service activities and finances, by region and State, FY88, annual rpt, 1204-1.1

Forests (natl) recreational use, by type of activity and State, 1988, annual rpt, 1204-17

Injuries from use of consumer products and related activities, by victim age and sex, 1988, annual rpt, 9164-7

Injuries from use of consumer products, by severity, victim age, and detailed product, 1988, annual rpt, 9164-6

Red Cross domestic and intl services, volunteers, and certificates issued, by program, FY88, annual rpt, 29254-1.1

see also Drowning
see also Swimming pools

Swimming pools
Apartment completions by region and metro-nonmetro location, and absorption rates, by size and rent class, preliminary 1988, annual Current Housing Rpt, 2484-3

Apartment market absorption rates and characteristics for nonsubsidized furnished and unfurnished units, 1987 and trends from 1970, annual Current Housing Rpt, 2484-2

Construction industries census, 1987: financial and operating data, preliminary industry rpt series, 2371-1

Injuries from use of consumer products, by severity, victim age, and detailed product, 1988, annual rpt, 9164-6

Solar collector and photovoltaic module shipments by end-use sector and State, R&D, and trade, 1988, annual rpt, 3164-62

Swine
see Livestock and livestock industry

Swisko, George M.
"Impact of Changes in the Nonfuel Mineral Industries to the State and Local Economies of Arizona and Nevada", 5602-4.902

Switzerland
Agricultural and food production and indexes, total and for selected commodities, by country, 1970s-88, annual rpt, 1524-12

Agricultural imports of Switzerland from US, and fresh produce import controls, by commodity, 1984-88, article, 1925-34.946

Agricultural production, prices, and trade, by country, 1970s-88 and forecast 1990, annual world region rpt, 1524-4.1

Agricultural trade of US, by detailed commodity and country, 1988, semiannual rpt, 1522-4

Background Notes, summary social, political, and economic data, 1989 rpt, 7006-2.21

Bank funds transfer system of Switzerland, payments, reserves, and daylight overdrafts, various periods 1987-88, article, 9389-1.910

Bank funds transfer system of Switzerland, system activity by payment size and time of day, monthly 1987-88, article, 9389-1.903

Businesses (foreign) activity in US, income tax returns, assets, and income statement items, by industry div, country, and world area, 1984-85, article, 8302-2.920

Economic and military aid and loans from US and intl agencies, by program and country, FY46-87, annual rpt, 9914-5

Economic and monetary trends, compounded annual rates of change for US and 10 major trading partners, quarterly rpt, 9391-7

Economic conditions in Communist, OECD, and selected other countries, 1960s-88, annual rpt, 9114-4

Economic conditions, income, production, prices, employment, and trade, 1989 periodic country rpt, 2046-4.36; 2046-4.91

Economic conditions, policy, and trade practices, by country, 1986-88, annual rpt, 21384-5

Economic, social, political, and geographic summary data, by country, 1989, annual factbook, 9114-2

Exports and imports of US, by selected country, country group, and commodity group, 1988, annual rpt, 2044-37

Human rights conditions in 170 countries, 1988, annual rpt, 21384–3

Imports of goods, services, and investment from US, trade barriers, impacts, and US actions, by country, 1988, annual rpt, 444–2

Imports of US given duty-free treatment for value of US material sent abroad, and impacts on US industry and employment, by commodity and country, 1987, annual rpt, 9884–14

Investment (foreign direct) in US, major transactions by type, industry, country, and US location, 1987, annual rpt, 2044–20

Military aid of US, arms sales, and training programs costs and budget requests, by program, world region, and country, FY88-90, annual rpt, 7144–13

Military spending, arms trade, and force strengths, with govt spending and population, by country, 1977-87, annual rpt, 9824–1

Minerals Yearbook, 1987, Vol 3: foreign country reviews of production, trade, and policy, by commodity, annual rpt, 5604–35

Minerals Yearbook, 1987, Vol 3 preprints: foreign country review of production, trade, and policy, by commodity, annual rpt, 5604–23.67

Monetary policy in Switzerland, impact on franc exchange rate against dollar and German mark, 1973-86, article, 9391–1.907

Multinatl firms US affiliates, finances, and operations, by industry, world area of parent firm, and State, 1987, annual rpt, 2704–4

Multinatl US firms and foreign affiliates finances and operations, by industry of parent firm and affiliate, world area, and country, preliminary 1987, annual rpt, 2704–5

Nuclear power generation in US and 19 non-Communist countries, monthly rpt, 3162–24.10

Nuclear power plant capacity, generation, and operating status, by plant and foreign and US location, 1988 and projected to 2020, annual rpt, 3164–57

Oil production, trade, use, and stocks, by selected country and country group, monthly rpt, 3162–42

Population size, growth rates, and components of change, by country, projected 1989-2020 and trends from 1950, biennial rpt, 2324–9

see also under By Foreign Country in the "Index by Categories"

Symposiums

see Conferences

Synthetic fibers and fabrics

Business statistics, detailed data for major industries and economic indicators, *Survey of Current Business*, monthly rpt, 2702–1.19

Clothing production, by fiber and product, quarterly Current Industrial Rpt, 2506–6.12

Communist, OECD, and selected other countries consumer and producer goods production, 1960s-88, annual rpt, 9114–4.8

County Business Patterns, 1987: employment, establishments, and payroll, by SIC 2- to 4-digit industry and county, annual State rpt series, 2326–8

Cuba economic conditions, agricultural and industrial production and distribution, trade, and intl economic relations, 1980-87 with trends from 1961, 9118–8

Employment, earnings, and hours, by SIC 1- to 4-digit industry, monthly 1983-Feb 1989, annual rpt, 6744–4

Exports of US, detailed commodities by country, monthly rpt, 2422–3

Freight (waterborne domestic and foreign) by commodity, traffic, and passengers, by port and waterway, 1987, annual rpt, 3754–3

Glass (fibrous) production, shipments, and firms, by product, 1976-88, annual Current Industrial Rpt, 2506–9.5

Import restraint elimination, impact on domestic industry production and employment, by selected commodity, 1986-88, 9886–4.144

Imports of textiles, by country of origin, monthly rpt, 2042–27

Imports of textiles, by product and country of origin, periodic rpt series, 2046–8; 2046–9

Imports of textiles, production, and imports share of use, by Multifiber Arrangement product, quarterly rpt, 2042–32

Imports of textiles under Multifiber Arrangement by product and country, and status of bilateral agreements, 1986-88, annual rpt, 9884–18

Imports of US, detailed Schedule A commodities by country, monthly rpt, 2422–2

Labor productivity, indexes of output, hours, and employment by SIC 2- to 4-digit industry, 1963-87, annual rpt, 6824–1.3

Manufacturers finances and operations, by SIC 2- to 4-digit industry, forecast 1989 and trends from 1950s, annual rpt, 2044–28

Manufacturing annual survey, 1986: financial and operating data, by SIC 2- to 4-digit industry, series, 2506–15

Manufacturing census, 1987: financial and operating data, for SIC 4-digit industries by product, preliminary rpt, 2491–1.11; 2491–1.13; 2491–1.14; 2491–1.34

Occupational injury and illness rates, by SIC 2- to 4-digit industry, 1987, annual rpt, 6844–1

Price indexes (producer), by stage of processing and detailed commodity, monthly rpt, 6762–6

Price indexes (producer), by stage of processing and detailed commodity, monthly 1988, annual rpt, 6764–2

Production, prices, trade, and use of cotton, wool, and synthetic fibers, periodic situation rpt with articles, 1561–1

Production, trade, sales, stocks, and material used, by product, region, and State, periodic Current Industrial Rpt series, 2506–5

Science, engineering, and technical employment in manufacturing, by field, occupation, and industry, 1986, triennial rpt, 9627–23

Stockpiling of strategic material, inventories, costs, and goals by commodity, as of June 1989, semiannual rpt, 3902–3

Synthetic food products

Manufacturing census, 1987: financial and operating data, for SIC 4-digit industries by product, preliminary rpt, 2491–1.2; 2491–1.38; 2491–1.40

Nutrient, caloric, and waste composition of food, detailed data for raw, processed, and prepared foods, series, 1356–3

Synthetic fuels

Environmental impacts of energy technologies, 1960s-80s, handbook series, 3326–1

Pollution (air) carbon dioxide emissions by fuel type and consuming sector, projected under alternative conservation methods, 1990s-2010, 3006–11.11

Synthetic Fuels Corp.

see U.S. Synthetic Fuels Corp.

Synthetic products

see Chemicals and chemical industry

see Plastics and plastics industry

see Synthetic fibers and fabrics

see Synthetic food products

see Synthetic fuels

Syphilis

see Sexually transmitted diseases

Syracuse, N.Y.

see also under By City and By SMSA or MSA in the "Index by Categories"

Syria

Agricultural and food production and indexes, total and for selected commodities, by country, 1970s-88, annual rpt, 1524–12

Agricultural production, prices, and trade, by country, 1960s-89, annual world region rpt, 1524–4.2

Agricultural trade of US, by detailed commodity and country, 1988, semiannual rpt, 1522–4

AID economic aid to developing countries, obligations and disbursements by country, quarterly rpt, 9912–4

AID loans repayment status and terms by program and country, and status of predecessor agency loans, quarterly rpt, 9912–3

Economic and military aid and loans from US and intl agencies, by program and country, FY46-87, annual rpt, 9914–5

Economic conditions, income, production, prices, employment, and trade, 1989 periodic country rpt, 2046–4.111

Economic conditions, policy, and trade practices, by country, 1986-88, annual rpt, 21384–5

Economic, social, political, and geographic summary data, by country, 1989, annual factbook, 9114–2

Exports and imports of US, by commodity and country, 1970-87, world area rpt, 9116–1.3

Human rights conditions in 170 countries, 1988, annual rpt, 21384–3

Military spending, arms trade, and force strengths, with govt spending and population, by country, 1977-87, annual rpt, 9824–1

Minerals Yearbook, 1987, Vol 3: foreign country reviews of production, trade, and policy, by commodity, annual rpt, 5604–35

Minerals Yearbook, 1987, Vol 3 preprints: foreign country review of production, trade, and policy, by commodity, annual rpt, 5604–23.86

Population size, growth rates, and components of change, by country, projected 1989-2020 and trends from 1950, biennial rpt, 2324–9

UN voting record and share of votes in agreement with US, by issue, country, and world area, 1988, annual rpt, 7004–18

see also under By Foreign Country in the "Index by Categories"

Syrups and sweeteners

Agricultural Statistics, 1988, annual rpt, 1004–1

Carcinogens chemistry, sources, environment and health risks, and regulation, by substance and brand, 1989, annual rpt, 4044–15

Consumption and trade by commodity, quarterly situation rpt with articles, 1561–14

Consumption, supply, trade, prices, spending, and indexes, by food commodity, 1987, annual rpt, 1544–4

County Business Patterns, 1987: employment, establishments, and payroll, by SIC 2- to 4-digit industry and county, annual State rpt series, 2326–8

Exports and imports (agricultural) of US, by commodity and country, bimonthly rpt with articles, 1522–1

Exports and imports (agricultural) of US, by detailed commodity and country, 1988, semiannual rpt, 1522–4

Exports of US, detailed commodities by country, monthly rpt, 2422–3

Farm financial and marketing conditions, forecast 1988, conf papers, annual rpt, 1004–16

Farm income, expenses, receipts by commodity, assets, liabilities, and ratios, 1988 and trends from 1945, annual rpt, 1544–16

Futures and options trading volume, by commodity and exchange, FY88, annual rpt, 11924–2

Imports of US, detailed Schedule A commodities by country, monthly rpt, 2422–2

Manufacturing annual survey, 1986: financial and operating data, by SIC 2- to 4-digit industry, series, 2506–15

Manufacturing census, 1987: financial and operating data, for SIC 4-digit industries by product, preliminary rpt, 2491–1.4; 2491–1.6; 2491–1.8; 2491–1.9

Molasses (feed) production, wholesale prices by market area, and US imports and country, weekly rpt, 1311–16

Molasses supply, use, wholesale prices by market, and trade and production by country, 1983-88, annual rpt, 1311–19

Nutrient and caloric composition of food, for raw, processed, and prepared food, 1988 rpt, 1358–3

Occupational injury and illness rates, by SIC 2- to 4-digit industry, 1987, annual rpt, 6844–1

Price indexes (producer), by stage of processing and detailed commodity, monthly rpt, 6762–6

Price indexes (producer), by stage of processing and detailed commodity, monthly 1988, annual rpt, 6764–2

see also Honey and beekeeping

see also Sugar industry and products

SysteMetrics/McGraw-Hill, Inc.

"Analysis of Hospital Sensitivity to DRG Price Variation in the Medicare Prospective Payment System", 17206–2.7

"Assessing the Adequacy of the Medicare Cost Report Data", 17206–2.4

"Developing a Measure of Complexity of Illness Within DRGs", 17206–2.6

Tableware

see Household supplies and utensils

Tacoma, Wash.

CPI by component for US city average, and by region, population size, and for 27 metro areas, monthly rpt, 6762–2

Energy-efficiency building codes effect on apartment building electricity use, for Tacoma, Wash, 1986-87, 3308–92

Fruit and vegetable shipments, and arrivals in US and Canada cities, by mode of transport and State and country of origin, 1988, annual rpt, 1311–4.2

Housing starts and completions authorized by building permits in 40 MSAs, quarterly rpt, 2382–9

Wages by occupation, and benefits for office and plant workers, 1989 survey, periodic MSA rpt, 6785–3.5

see also under By City and By SMSA or MSA in the "Index by Categories"

Taffel, Selma M.

"Characteristics of American Indian and Alaska Native Births: U.S., 1984", 4147–24.2

"Trends in Low Birth Weight: U.S., 1975-85", 4147–21.48

Taha, Fawzi A.

"Patterns of Change in Japanese Cereal Production, Consumption, and Trade", 1522–3.913

Taiwan

Agricultural and food production and indexes, total and for selected commodities, by country, 1970s-88, annual rpt, 1524–12

Agricultural subsidies, consumer and producer equivalents by program, commodity, and major US trading partner, 1982-86, 1528–275

Agricultural trade by commodity and country, prices, and world market devs, monthly rpt, 1922–12

Agricultural trade of US, by detailed commodity and country, 1988, semiannual rpt, 1522–4

AID loans repayment status and terms by program and country, and status of predecessor agency loans, quarterly rpt, 9912–3

Alcohol use, abuse, treatment, and views of racial and ethnic groups in US and native countries, by selected characteristics, 1988 compilation of papers, 4488–12

Batteries for motorcycles from Taiwan at less than fair value, injury to US industry, investigation with background financial and operating data, 1989 rpt, 9886–14.268

Coal production, trade, and govt subsidies, by country and country group, 1973-87 and projected to 2000, 2048–144

Cooking appliance thermostatic plugs from 4 countries, injury to US industry from foreign subsidized and less than fair value

imports, investigation with background financial and operating data, 1988 rpt, 9886–19.63

Dollar exchange rates, and impacts of currency appreciation on current account and trade balances and economic indicators, for 3 Asian countries, 1980s-90, GAO rpt, 26123–234

Economic and military aid and loans from US and intl agencies, by program and country, FY46-87, annual rpt, 9914–5

Economic conditions in Communist, OECD, and selected other countries, 1960s-88, annual rpt, 9114–4

Economic conditions, income, production, prices, employment, and trade, 1989 periodic country rpt, 2046–4.40; 2046–4.93

Economic conditions, policy, and trade practices, by country, 1986-88, annual rpt, 21384–5

Economic indicators of developing countries, problem debtors compared to other borrowers, by country, 1973-84, 1528–285

Economic, social, political, and geographic summary data, by country, 1989, annual factbook, 9114–2

Export and import balance impacts of exchange rates and foreign and domestic economic indicators, for Taiwan and South Korea, 1974-87, article, 9393–8.905

Export and import balances of US, and dollar exchange rates, with 4 Asian countries 1980s-89, semiannual rpt, 8002–14

Exports and imports of US, by commodity and country, 1970-87, world area rpt, 9116–1.2

Exports and imports of US, by selected country, country group, and commodity group, 1988, annual rpt, 2044–37

Exports and imports of US with Asian countries by commodity, and free trade area proposal, 1985-88, 9886–4.135

Exports and imports, trade agreements and relations, and USITC investigations, 1988, annual rpt, 9884–5

Exports, imports, and trade balance of Taiwan and South Korea with US, 1985-88, article, 9385–1.904

Human rights conditions in 170 countries, 1988, annual rpt, 21384–3

Import restraint elimination by US, impact on domestic industry production and employment, by selected commodity, 1987, 9886–4.144

Imports of goods, services, and investment from US, trade barriers, impacts, and US actions, by country, 1988, annual rpt, 444–2

Locks (residential door) from Taiwan at less than fair value, injury to US industry, investigation with background financial and operating data, 1989 rpt, 9886–14.264

Machinery belts from 8 countries, injury to US industry from foreign subsidized and less than fair value imports, investigation with background financial and operating data, 1989 rpt, 9886–19.66

Manufacturing labor productivity and unit costs for 14 countries, 1950-88, annual press release, 6864–1

Military aid of US, arms sales, and training programs costs and budget requests, by program, world region, and country, FY88-90, annual rpt, 7144–13

Military spending, arms trade, and force strengths, with govt spending and population, by country, 1977-87, annual rpt, 9824–1

Minerals production, reserves, and industry role in domestic economy and world supply, 1988 country rpt, 5606–1.17

Minerals Yearbook, 1987, Vol 3: foreign country reviews of production, trade, and policy, by commodity, annual rpt, 5604–35

Minerals Yearbook, 1987, Vol 3 preprints: foreign country review of production, trade, and policy, by commodity, annual rpt, 5604–23.68

Multinatl US firms and foreign affiliates finances and operations, by industry of parent firm and affiliate, world area, and country, preliminary 1987, annual rpt, 2704–5

Mushroom (canned) trade by selected country, supply and use for 2 Asia countries, and US production and imports, various periods 1979-89, annual article, 1925–34.935

Nuclear power generation in US and 19 non-Communist countries, monthly rpt, 3162–24.10

Nuclear power plant capacity, generation, and operating status, by plant and foreign and US location, 1988 and projected to 2020, annual rpt, 3164–57

Pineapple and asparagus (canned) exports of Taiwan, by country, selected years 1970-88, article, 1925–34.936

Population size, growth rates, and components of change, by country, projected 1989-2020 and trends from 1950, biennial rpt, 2324–9

Port facilities, operations, and impacts on US agricultural exports, for major Far East Asia ports, 1970s-87, 1278–13

Space satellites and other objects launched since 1957, quarterly listing, 9502–2

Steel pipes and tubes from Taiwan at less than fair value, injury to US industry, investigation with background financial and operating data, 1989 rpt, 9886–14.256

Sweaters from 3 countries at less than fair value, injury to US industry, investigation with background financial and operating data, 1989 rpt, 9886–14.272

Telephones and equipment from 3 countries at less than fair value, injury to US industry, investigation with background financial and operating data, 1989 rpt, 9886–14.251; 9886–14.274

Tobacco trade of US with 3 Asian countries, 1984-88, article, 1925–16.908

Uniforms (martial arts) from Taiwan at less than fair value, injury to US industry, investigation with background financial and operating data, 1989 rpt, 9886–14.247; 9886–14.269

Talc
see Nonmetallic minerals and mines
Tallahassee, Fla.
see also under By City and By SMSA or MSA in the "Index by Categories"

Tallow and greases
see Oils, oilseeds, and fats
Tampa, Fla.
Housing and households characteristics, 1985 survey, MSA fact sheet, 2485–11.7

Housing and households detailed characteristics, and unit and neighborhood quality, by location, 1985 survey, MSA rpt, 2485–6.6

Housing starts and completions authorized by building permits in 40 MSAs, quarterly rpt, 2382–9

Wages by occupation, for office and plant workers, 1988 survey, periodic MSA rpt, 6785–11.2

Wages by occupation, for office and plant workers, 1989 survey, periodic MSA rpt, 6785–12.6

see also under By City and By SMSA or MSA in the "Index by Categories"

Tanker ships
Communist, OECD, and selected other countries freight and carrier inventories, by mode of transport, 1960s-88, annual rpt, 9114–4.10

Competition in Exclusive Economic Zone between foreign and US flag ships, impacts of extending cabotage laws, with background data, 1970s-80s, 26358–206

Construction and delivery of new ships, by vessel type and country of construction and registry, 1988, annual rpt, 7704–4

Construction and operating subsidies of MarAd by firm, and ship deliveries and fleet by country, by vessel type, FY88, annual rpt, 7704–14.1; 7704–14.2

Construction and repair facilities, capacity, and employment, by shipyard, 1988, annual rpt, 7704–9

Defense Fuel Supply Center procurement, prices, stocks, transport, and other activities and finances, FY88, annual rpt, 3904–8

Exports and imports (waterborne) of US, by type of service, commodity, country, route, and US port, 1986-87, annual rpt, 7704–2

Exports and imports (waterborne) of US, by type of service, customs district, port, and world area, monthly rpt, 2422–7

Finances, operations, vehicles, equipment, accidents, and energy use, by mode of transport, 1955-88, annual rpt, 7304–2

Foreign and US merchant ships, and tonnage, by country of registry, as of Jan 1988, annual rpt, 7704–3

Foreign and US merchant ships and tonnage, by vessel type, 1983-87, *Minerals Yearbook*, annual rpt, 5604–35.1

Foreign-flag ships owned by US firms and foreign affiliates, by type, owner, and country of registry and construction, as of July 1989, semiannual rpt, 7702–3

Freight (waterborne domestic), by major commodity group, vessel type, and port, 1986, annual rpt, 7704–7

Freight (waterborne domestic and foreign) by commodity, traffic, and passengers, by port and waterway, 1987, annual rpt, 3754–3

Manufacturing census, 1987: financial and operating data, for SIC 4-digit industries by product, preliminary rpt, 2491–1.77

Merchant ships in US fleet and Natl Defense Reserve Fleet, vessels, tonnage, and owner, as of Jan 1989, semiannual listing, 7702–2

Merchant ships in US fleet, operating subsidies, and ship-related employment, monthly rpt, 7702–1

Military Sealift Command shipping operations, finances, and personnel, FY88, annual rpt, 3804–14

Oil and refined products stocks, and interdistrict shipments by mode of transport, monthly rpt, 3162–6.3

Oil refinery crude received, by mode of transport and PAD district, 1988, annual rpt, 3164–2.1

Oil spills from tankers worldwide, selected years 1964-87, annual rpt, 5734–3.6

Oil tanker inbound freight price indexes, quarterly press release, 6762–13

Pollution (water) incidents and discharges, by type, source, cause, and location, 1984-86, annual rpt, 7404–3

Ships in world tanker fleet, characteristics by country of registry, as of Jan 1989, annual listing, 7704–17

St Lawrence Seaway ship, cargo, and passenger traffic, and toll revenue, 1988 and trends from 1959, annual rpt, 7744–2

Wartime capability of commercial ships, shipyards, and personnel, for merchant and reserve fleet, 1988-2000, 11208–1

Tanks
see Military vehicles
Tann, Helen M.
"Directory of Urban Public Transportation Service", 7884–9
Tannenwald, Robert
"Changing Level and Mix of Federal Aid to State and Local Governments", 9373–1.910
Tanning industry
see Hides and skins
see Leather industry and products
Tanzania
Agricultural and food production and indexes, total and for selected commodities, by country, 1970s-88, annual rpt, 1524–12

Agricultural exports of Africa by commodity, and relation to economic conditions and other factors, by country, 1960s-87, 1528–280

Agricultural imports and food aid needs under alternative weather assumptions, for 17 African countries, projected to 1995, 1528–279

Agricultural production, prices, and trade, by country, 1960s-89, annual world region rpt, 1524–4.2

Agricultural trade of US, by detailed commodity and country, 1988, semiannual rpt, 1522–4

AID activities and funding by project and function, FY90, and developing countries summary socioeconomic data from 1960s, annual rpt, 9904–4.5

AID economic aid to developing countries, obligations and disbursements by country, quarterly rpt, 9912–4

AID loans repayment status and terms by program and country, and status of predecessor agency loans, quarterly rpt, 9912–3

Auto imports from US, trade barriers by country, 1988, annual rpt, 444–2

Economic and military aid and loans from US and intl agencies, by program and country, FY46-87, annual rpt, 9914–5

Economic conditions, income, production, prices, employment, and trade, 1989 periodic country rpt, 2046–4.38

Economic conditions, policy, and trade practices, by country, 1986-88, annual rpt, 21384–5

Economic, social, political, and geographic summary data, by country, 1989, annual factbook, 9114–2

Exports and imports of US, by commodity and country, 1970-87, world area rpt, 9116–1.4

Human rights conditions in 170 countries, 1988, annual rpt, 21384–3

Military aid of US, arms sales, and training programs costs and budget requests, by program, world region, and country, FY88-90, annual rpt, 7144–13

Military spending, arms trade, and force strengths, with govt spending and population, by country, 1977-87, annual rpt, 9824–1

Minerals Yearbook, 1987, Vol 3: foreign country reviews of production, trade, and policy, by commodity, annual rpt, 5604–35

Minerals Yearbook, 1987, Vol 3 preprints: foreign country review of production, trade, and policy, by commodity, annual rpt, 5604–23.81

Population size, growth rates, and components of change, by country, projected 1989-2020 and trends from 1950, biennial rpt, 2324–9

UN voting record and share of votes in agreement with US, by issue, country, and world area, 1988, annual rpt, 7004–18

see also under By Foreign Country in the "Index by Categories"

Tape recordings
see Recording industry

Tar
see Asphalt and tar
see Gum and wood chemicals
see Tar sands

Tar sands
Bitumen-bearing tar sand deposits locations and characteristics, as of 1984, 5668–88

Tariff Commission
see U.S. International Trade Commission

Tariffs and foreign trade controls
Agricultural exports of US, impacts of foreign agricultural and trade policy, with data by commodity and country, 1988, annual rpt, 1924–8

Agricultural production, trade, and weather devs, foreign and US, weekly press release, 1922–4

Agricultural subsidies, consumer and producer equivalents by program, commodity, and major US trading partner, 1982-86, 1528–275

Agricultural trade among western hemisphere countries, and US duty-free imports, with listing of trade disputes and outcomes, 1960s-85, 1528–278

Agricultural trade and market impacts of eliminating foreign and US protectionist policies, model description and results, 1986, 1528–282

Auto trade of Canada and US, and production, sales, prices, and employment, selected years 1965-85, annual rpt, 2044–35

Bean (dried) prices by State, market activity, and foreign and US production, use, stocks, and trade, weekly rpt, 1311–17

Budget of US, authoritative financial statements with appropriations, outlays, and receipts, by category and agency, FY88, annual rpt, 8104–2.2

Budget of US, historical data, selected years FY34-88 and projected to FY94, annual rpt, 104–22

Budget of US, midsession review of FY90 budget, by function and agency, annual rpt, 104–7

Budget of US, receipts by source, outlays by agency and program, and balances, monthly rpt, 8102–3

Business America, foreign and domestic commerce, and US investment and trade opportunities, biweekly journal, 2042–24

Canada-US trade agreement impacts on New England States trade, with data by industry, commodity, and State, 1987, article, 9373–2.902

Caribbean area agricultural exports to US, by whether duty levied, commodity, and country, 1983-88, annual article, 1925–34.923

Caribbean area duty-free exports to US, and imports from US, by country, and impact on US employment, by commodity, 1988, annual rpt, 6364–2

Caribbean area duty-free exports to US, and US exports and import duties on other goods, by commodity and country, 1984-88, annual rpt, 9884–20

Caribbean area sugar production and exports, and cruise ship tourist visits and spending, by country, 1981-88, hearing, 21788–179

China high technology trade, US export license applications by disposition, 1973-84, compilation of papers, 3908–4

Coal production, trade, and govt subsidies, by country and country group, 1973-87 and projected to 2000, 2048–144

Coffee production, trade and quotas, and use, by country, with US and intl prices, FAS periodic circular, 1925–5

Cotton textile import quotas filled, by product and country of origin, 1987-88, article, 1561–1.905

Cotton, wool, and synthetic fiber production, prices, trade, and use, periodic situation rpt with articles, 1561–1

Criminal sentences for Federal offenses, guidelines by offense and circumstances, 1989 rpt, 17668–1

Customs collections, for top 15 ports, quarterly rpt, 8142–1

Customs Service activities, collections, entries processed by mode of transport, and seizures, FY84-88, annual rpt, 8144–1

Dairy imports under quota by commodity, and meat imports under Meat Import Act, by country of origin, FAS monthly rpt, 1925–31

Developing countries export revenue effects of trade policy changes in developing and developed countries, model results, 1989 article, 1522–3.922

EC economic integration impact on EC employment, GDP, and other economic indicators, projected 1992, article, 9373–1.908

EC economic integration, proposed duty rates and ad valorem taxes on alcohol, tobacco, and fuel, 1989 rpt, 9886–4.140

EC food supply and demand, market and support prices, and other economic indicators, by country and commodity, 1960-85, 1528–276

Economic Report of the President for 1989, with economic trends from 1929, annual rpt, 204–1

Endangered animals and plants US trade and permits, by species, purpose, disposition, and country, 1987, annual rpt, 5504–19

Energy producers finances and operations, by energy type for US firms domestic and foreign operations, 1987, annual rpt, 3164–44.1

Export and import agreements, negotiations, anticompetitive investigations, and related legislation, FY86-88, annual rpt, 444–1

Export licensing, monitoring, and enforcement activities, FY88, annual rpt, 2024–1

Exports and imports, trade agreements and relations, and USITC investigations, 1988, annual rpt, 9884–5

Exports of goods, services, and investment, trade barriers, impacts, and US actions, by country, 1988, annual rpt, 444–2

Fed Govt consolidated financial statements based on business accounting methods, FY87-88, annual rpt, 8104–5

Fed Govt receipts by source and outlays by agency, *Treasury Bulletin*, quarterly rpt, 8002–4.1

Fed Govt tax revenues, by type of tax, quarterly rpt, 2462–3

Finances of govts, revenues by source and spending by function, natl income and product account, *Survey of Current Business*, monthly rpt, 2702–1.24

Fish import duties collected, 1979-88, annual rpt, 2164–1.6

Foreign countries economic conditions, policy, and trade practices, by country, 1986-88, annual rpt, 21384–5

GATT Standards Code info activities of Natl Inst of Standards and Technology, and proposed standards by agency and country, 1988, annual rpt, 2214–6

Generalized System of Preferences status, and US tariffs, trade by country, production, and use, for selected commodities, 1984-88, annual rpt, 9884–23

Import duties of US under antidumping and countervailing orders, and duty assessment and reporting errors, 1987-88, GAO rpt, 26119–270

Import quotas on steel, autos, and textiles, employment and income impacts by industry, model description and results, 1984, 9406–1.57

Imports and tariff provisions effect on US industries and products, investigations with background financial and operating data, series, 9886–4

Imports injury to US industries from foreign subsidized products and sales at less than fair value, investigations with background financial and operating data, series, 9886–19

Imports injury to US industries from foreign subsidized products, investigations with background financial and operating data, series, 9886–15

Imports injury to US industries from sales at less than fair value, investigations with background financial and operating data, series, 9886-14

Imports of US, by whether duty levied, commodity group, world area, selected country, and US coastal area and port, monthly rpt, 2422-9

Imports of US given duty-free treatment for value of US material sent abroad, and impacts on US industry and employment, by commodity and country, 1987, annual rpt, 9884-14

Japan grape wine production, imports by country, and duty, selected years 1978-89, article, 1925-34.928

Korea (South) fruit production, consumption, trade, and tariffs, by commodity, 1977-88, article, 1925-34.907

Maritime Commission activities, case filings by type and disposition, and civil penalties by shipper, FY88, annual rpt, 9334-1

Meat plants inspected and certified for exporting to US, by country, 1988, annual listing, 1374-2

Military use potential of US exports, DOD and Commerce Dept licensing activities, staff, and costs, 1986-88, GAO rpt, 26123-250

Mineral Industry Surveys, commodity reviews of production, trade, use, and industry operations, advance annual rpt series, 5614-5

Minerals of strategic and technological importance, supply, imports, and use, with foreign comparisons, commodity rpt series, 5606-9

Minerals production, prices, trade, use, employment, tariffs, and stockpiles, by mineral, with foreign comparisons, 1984-88, annual rpt, 5604-18

Natl income and product accounts and components, *Survey of Current Business*, monthly rpt, 2702-1.21

OECD countries imports covered by non-tariff trade barriers, by barrier type and commodity group, 1981-86, article, 9391-1.906

Oil prices and US and OPEC industry impacts of alternative US protective policies, projected 2037, technical paper, 9379-12.44

Overseas Business Reports: economic conditions, investment and export opportunities, and trade practices, country market research rpt series, 2046-6

Puerto Rico meat production, prices, consumption, imports, and impact of import restrictions, 1950s-85, 1568-282

Rum imports (duty-free) of US under Caribbean Basin Initiative, by country, 1987-88, annual rpt, 9884-15

Sugar and honey foreign and US production, prices, trade, and use, FAS periodic circular series, 1925-14

Sugar and sugar product imports of US under quota, by country, periodic rpt, 1922-9

Sugar import tariff impacts on imports of sugar-containing products, by product, 1977-88, article, 1561-14.905

Switzerland fresh fruit and vegetable import controls, and imports from US, by commodity, 1984-88, article, 1925-34.946

Tariff Schedule of US, classifications and rates of duty for detailed imported commodities, and codes for ports and foreign countries, 1990 base edition and supplements, 9886-13

US attorneys civil and criminal cases by type and disposition, and collections, by Federal district, FY88, annual rpt, 6004-2.1

USITC activities, investigations, and rpts, FY88, annual rpt, 9884-1

USITC rpts, 1982-88, annual listing, 9884-12

Vegetables (winter fresh) from Florida, Mexico, and Caribbean area, shipments and costs by commodity, 1970s-87, article, 1561-11.902

Watches duty-free imports, injury to US industry, investigation with background financial and operating data, 1989 rpt, 9886-4.143

see also Common markets and free trade areas

see also Dumping

see also International sanctions

Tarr, David G.
"General Equilibrium Analysis of the Welfare and Employment Effects of U.S. Quotas in Textiles, Autos and Steel", 9406-1.57

Tarrant County, Tex.
Housing and households detailed characteristics, and unit and neighborhood quality, by location, 1985 survey, MSA rpt, 2485-6.7

Tatom, John A.
"Link Between the Value of the Dollar, U.S. Trade and Manufacturing Output: Some Recent Evidence", 9391-1.903

Tavlas, George S.
"Forecasting Australian Monetary Aggregates", 9366-6.169

Tawas City, Mich.
Wages by occupation, for office and plant workers, 1989 survey, periodic MSA rpt, 6785-3.8

Tax appeals
see Tax protests and appeals

Tax Court of the U.S.
Budget of US Appendix, obligations, appropriations, and personnel, by program and agency, FY90, annual rpt, 104-3

Budget of US, authoritative financial statements with appropriations, outlays, and receipts, by category and agency, FY88, annual rpt, 8104-2.2

Caseloads of Court and appeals by disposition, procedure duration, and recoveries, FY88, annual rpt, 18224-5

Caseloads of US Tax Court, and tax due, by disposition, FY89, annual tables, 18224-3

IRS collections, enforcement, and litigation activity, with data by type of tax, region, and State, FY88, annual rpt, 8304-3

Tax courts
see Tax Court of the U.S.
see Tax laws and courts

Tax credits
see Tax expenditures
see Tax incentives and shelters

Tax delinquency and evasion
Criminal case processing in Federal district courts, and dispositions, by offense, district, and offender characteristics, 1984, annual rpt, 6064-29

Criminal case processing in Federal district courts, disposition by offense, 1980-87, 6066-19.50

Criminal investigations of IRS resulting in tax assessment and collection, by violation type, 1984, GAO rpt, 26119-244

Drug enforcement regional task forces investigation of organized crime, activities by agency and region, and background data, FY83-88, annual rpt, 6004-17

Fed Govt mgmt cost control proposals, Reagan Admin initiatives, savings, and status, FY85-94, annual rpt, 104-23

Income (personal) by source, BEA and IRS adjusted gross income and income tax noncompliance measures, 1984-86 with trends from 1947, article, 8302-2.914

Income tax return processing, IRS workload forecasts, compliance, and enforcement, data compilation, 1989 annual rpt, 8304-8

Income tax unpaid by reason, and compliance after audits and appeals, for individuals and corporations, 1970s-87 and projected to 1992, 8302-2.902; 8308-26

Litigation, enforcement, and collection activity of IRS, with data by type of tax, region, and State, FY88, annual rpt, 8304-3

Penalties (civil) assessed and abated for income tax law violations, FY87-88, GAO rpt, 26119-265

Securities (tax-exempt) holdings by investor type, and IRS enforcement of disallowance of interest deduction for financing holdings, mid 1970s-87, GAO rpt, 26119-239

Sentences for Federal crimes, guidelines use and results by offense and district, and Sentencing Commission activities, 1988, annual rpt, 17664-1

Sentences for Federal offenses, guidelines by offense and circumstances, 1989 rpt, 17668-1

Tax exempt organizations
Court caseloads and appeals by disposition, procedure duration, and recoveries, for US Tax Court, FY88, annual rpt, 18224-5

IRS collections, by excise tax source, quarterly rpt, 8302-1

IRS collections, enforcement, and litigation activity, with data by type of tax, region, and State, FY88, annual rpt, 8304-3

IRS tax returns and supplemental documents filed, by type, FY88 and projected to FY97, semiannual rpt, 8302-2.916; 8302-4

IRS tax returns filed by type of filer, quarterly rpt, 8302-2.1

IRS tax returns filed, by type of tax and IRS region and service center, projected 1988-95 and trends from 1977, annual rpt, 8304-9

Service industries census, 1987: establishments, receipts, employment, and payroll, by SIC 2- to 4-digit kind of business, MSA, county, and city, State rpt series, 2391-1

Service industries receipts, by SIC 2- to 4-digit kind of business, 1988, annual rpt, 2413-8

Tax exempt securities

Assets and debts of private sector, balance
sheets by segment, 1949-88, semiannual
rpt, 9365-4.1

Budget of US, special analysis of credit
programs, FY90, annual rpt, 104-1.6

Flow-of-funds accounts, assets and liabilities
by type and economic sector, outstanding
at year-end 1965-88, annual rpt, 9364-3

Flow-of-funds accounts, savings,
investments, and credit statements,
quarterly rpt, 9365-3.3

Interest deduction for financing tax exempt
securities holdings, IRS enforcement of
disallowance, with holdings by investor
type, mid 1970s-87, GAO rpt,
26119-239

Issues of tax-exempt bonds for private
activity, by purpose, face value, major
industry, and State, 1986, annual article,
8302-2.905

Ownership of govt securities, dealer
transactions and financing sources, and
new State and local issues, monthly rpt,
9362-1.1

Urban Dev Action Grants, funding sources,
project descriptions, and economic
impacts, by city, periodic press releases,
5002-7

see also Municipal bonds

Tax expenditures

Budget of US, compact budgets by activity,
function, and agency, FY90 and projected
to FY94, annual rpt, 104-2

Budget of US, House concurrent resolution,
with spending and revenue targets, FY90,
annual rpt, 21264-2

Budget of US, overview, FY90, annual rpt,
104-6

Budget of US, Senate concurrent resolution,
with spending and revenue targets, FY90,
annual rpt, 25254-1

Budget of US, special analysis of tax
expenditures, FY90, annual rpt, 104-1.7

Employee benefits impact on income and
payroll tax revenue, by benefit type,
1950-87 and projected to 2065, article,
9373-1.913

Enterprise zone program of Maryland,
participants characteristics and views on
incentives, and proposed Federal program
tax expenditures, 1983-88, GAO rpt,
26131-53

Fed Govt consolidated financial statements
based on business accounting methods,
FY87-88, annual rpt, 8104-5

Fed Govt programs under Ways and Means
Committee jurisdiction, finances and
operations, FY70s-88, annual rpt,
21784-11

Income tax deduction of State and local
taxes, subsidy rates by State, 1985, article,
9373-1.910

Income tax deductions and exclusions,
Federal tax expenditures by item,
FY90-94, annual rpt, 21784-10

Property tax revenue by level of govt,
assessed values by locality, and
exemptions, by property type and State,
1987 Census of Govts, 2453-1

Puerto Rico and other US possessions
corporations tax incentives, finances, and
operations by industry, and impacts on
local economy, 1970s-83, biennial rpt,
8004-12

Savings instns failure resolution costs,
financing problems, and FSLIC and
acquiring instns tax benefits, 1988 and
projected to FY99, hearings, 21788-181

Statistical Abstract of US, social, political,
and economic data, 1790-2025,
comprehensive annual compilation,
2324-1.2

Tax incentives and shelters

Abusive tax shelter promoters civil penalties
assessed and abated, FY87-88, GAO rpt,
26119-265

AFDC recipients demographic and financial
characteristics, by State, FY87, annual rpt,
4694-1

Capital gains tax rate changes effect on
transactions by asset type, and stock
exchange trading volume, late 1970s-88,
article, 9373-1.901

Charitable contributions impacts of tax
deductibility, model description and
results, 1985 working paper, 6886-6.16

Corporations income tax returns, income
and tax items by asset size and detailed
industry, 1986, annual rpt, 8304-4;
8304-21

Corporations income tax returns, summary
data by asset size and industry div, 1986,
annual article, 8302-2.922

Electric utilities privately owned, detailed
finances and operations by firm, 1987,
annual rpt, 3164-23.1

Employee tax deferred savings plans
coverage, by worker characteristics,
1970s-88, article, 4742-1.925;
4746-26.7

Energy producers finances and operations,
by energy type for US firms domestic and
foreign operations, 1987, annual rpt,
3164-44.1

Enterprise zone program of Maryland,
participants characteristics and views on
incentives, and proposed Federal program
tax expenditures, 1983-88, GAO rpt,
26131-53

Fed Govt programs under Ways and Means
Committee jurisdiction, finances and
operations, FY70s-88, annual rpt,
21784-11

Foreign corporate activity in US, income tax
returns, assets, and income statement
items, by industry div, country, and world
area, 1984-85, article, 8302-2.920

Foreign earned income on US individual
returns, exclusions, credits, and US
revenue losses, with data by country,
1983, quadrennial rpt, 8308-34

Historic buildings rehabilitation tax
incentives, projects, costs, ownership, use,
and tax reform impacts, FY77-88, annual
rpt, 5544-17

Income tax unpaid by reason, and
compliance after audits and appeals, for
individuals and corporations, 1970s-87
and projected to 1992, 8302-2.902;
8308-26

Individual income tax returns, detailed data,
1986, annual rpt, 8304-2

Individual income tax returns, selected
income and tax items by income level,
preliminary 1987, annual article,
8302-2.917

Insurance (life) industry income, income
taxes, and alternative methods of taxing
dividends, for stock and mutual
companies, 1980s-87, GAO rpt,
26119-274

Interest deduction for financing tax exempt
securities holdings, IRS enforcement of
disallowance, with holdings by investor
type, mid 1970s-87, GAO rpt,
26119-239

Litigation, enforcement, and collection
activity of IRS, with data by type of tax,
region, and State, FY88, annual rpt,
8304-3

Mergers and acquisitions using leveraged
buyout, financing characteristics and
policy issues, 1970s-88, 21368-115

Mortgage interest and property tax income
tax deductions, by income, 1987, hearings,
25248-107

Natural gas interstate pipeline company
detailed financial and operating data, by
firm, 1988, annual rpt, 3164-38

Older persons care by family members, tax
subsidies in 2 States, 1981-84, article,
4652-1.915

Partnerships (master limited) finances, firms,
partners, and tax reform impacts, by
industry, 1986, technical paper,
8006-3.59

Puerto Rico and other US possessions
corporations tax incentives, finances, and
operations by industry, and impacts on
local economy, 1970s-83, biennial rpt,
8004-12

Returns filed, by type of filer, detailed
preliminary and supplementary data,
quarterly rpt with articles, 8302-2

Savings and loan assns failure resolution
costs, and FSLIC finances and promissory
notes issued, with data by instn, FY80s
and projected to FY99, hearing,
25258-22

Savings instns failure resolution costs to
FSLIC for liquidation and sale, and
financial characteristics of instn, 1988,
technical paper, 8436-1.2

Savings instns failures, financial condition
indicators, and liquidation and acquisition
costs and tax benefits by instn and
acquiring company, 1985-98, hearing,
21268-41

see also Individual retirement arrangements
see also Oil depletion allowances
see also Tax exempt organizations
see also Tax exempt securities
see also Tax expenditures

Tax laws and courts

Assets (depreciable) class lives
measurement, investment, and industry
operations, asset class rpt series, 8006-5

Court caseloads and appeals by disposition,
procedure duration, and recoveries, for US
Tax Court, FY88, annual rpt, 18224-5

Court caseloads of US Tax Court, and tax
due, by disposition, FY89, annual tables,
18224-3

Court civil and criminal caseloads for
Federal district, appeals, and special
courts, June 1989, annual rpt, 18204-2;
18204-8

Criminal case processing in Federal courts
by disposition, and prisoners, by offense
and jurisdiction, 1976-88, annual rpt,
6064-6.5; 6064-6.6

Income tax law changes, 1916-50, article,
8302-2.913

Income tax return processing, IRS workload
forecasts, compliance, and enforcement,
data compilation, 1989 annual rpt,
8304-8

Litigation, enforcement, and collection activity of IRS, with data by type of tax, region, and State, FY88, annual rpt, 8304–3

Penalties (civil) assessed and abated for income tax law violations, FY87-88, GAO rpt, 26119–265

Sentences for Federal offenses, guidelines by offense and circumstances, 1989 rpt, 17668–1

Unemployment insurance programs of States, benefits, coverage, and tax provisions, as of July 1989, semiannual listing, 6402–7

US attorneys civil and criminal cases by type and disposition, and collections, by Federal district, FY88, annual rpt, 6004–2.1; 6004–2.5

see also Tax delinquency and evasion
see also Tax protests and appeals
see also Tax reform

Tax loopholes
see Tax incentives and shelters

Tax protests and appeals
Court caseloads and appeals by disposition, procedure duration, and recoveries, for US Tax Court, FY88, annual rpt, 18224–5

Court civil and criminal caseloads for Federal district, appeals, and special courts, June 1989, annual rpt, 18204–2; 18204–8

Income tax unpaid by reason, and compliance after audits and appeals, for individuals and corporations, 1970s-87 and projected to 1992, 8302–2.902; 8308–26

IRS collections, enforcement, and litigation activity, with data by type of tax, region, and State, FY88, annual rpt, 8304–3

Tax reform
Budget of US, CBO analysis of revenue and spending alternatives and projections of economic indicators, FY90-94, annual rpt, 26304–3

Capital gains tax rate changes effect on transactions by asset type, and stock exchange trading volume, late 1970s-88, article, 9373–1.901

Capital gains tax rate changes effects on revenue, alternative model results, 1988, 26306–3.106

Historic buildings rehabilitation tax incentives, projects, costs, ownership, use, and tax reform impacts, FY77-88, annual rpt, 5544–17

Income tax returns of individuals, by filing status, tax item, and income level, 1987, annual article, 8302–2.901

Insurance (life) companies financial and tax impacts of Deficit Reduction Act and proposed reforms, for stock and mutual firms, 1984-88 and projected to FY94, 8008–138

Labor force participation rate impact of Reagan Admin tax policy and business cycle indicators, by sex and age, 1976-88, article, 9389–1.914

Partnerships (master limited) finances, firms, partners, and tax reform impacts, by industry, 1986, technical paper, 8006–3.59

Returns and supplemental documents filed, by type, FY88 and projected to FY97, semiannual rpt, 8302–2.916

Revenue impacts of tax reform, performance of alternative forecasts, 1981-83, technical paper, 8006–3.58

Tax (income) returns filed, impacts of tax reform provisions, projected FY88-97, semiannual rpt, 8302–4

Tax sharing
see Revenue sharing

Taxation
Banks in Fed Reserve System, expenses and operations itemized by service, office, and district, 1988, annual rpt, 9364–11

Budget deficit reduction through increased excise and income taxes, and proposed value-added tax, projected FY89-94, article, 9381–1.906

Budget of US, authoritative financial statements with appropriations, outlays, and receipts, by agency, FY88, annual rpt, 8104–2

Budget of US, authoritative financial statements with appropriations, outlays, and receipts, by category and agency, FY88, annual rpt, 8104–2.2

Budget of US, CBO analysis and review of FY90 budget by function, annual rpt, 26304–2

Budget of US, CBO analysis of revenue and spending alternatives and projections of economic indicators, FY90-94, annual rpt, 26304–3

Budget of US, compact budgets by activity, function, and agency, FY90 and projected to FY94, annual rpt, 104–2

Budget of US, House concurrent resolution, with spending and revenue targets, FY90, annual rpt, 21264–2

Budget of US, midsession review of FY90 budget, by function and agency, annual rpt, 104–7

Budget of US, receipts by source, outlays by agency and program, and balances, monthly rpt, 8102–3

Budget of US, Senate concurrent resolution, with spending and revenue targets, FY90, annual rpt, 25254–1

Coal production and freight costs, and competitive position in selected markets, for Australia and US, 1987-89, 2048–143

Corporations income tax returns, income and tax items by asset size and detailed industry, 1986, annual rpt, 8304–4; 8304–21

Economic Report of the President for 1989, with economic trends from 1929, annual rpt, 204–1

Electric power plants production and capital costs, operations, and fuel use, by fuel type, plant, utility, and location, 1987, annual rpt, 3164–9

Farm finances and operations, by size, commodity, and region, 1986, annual rpt, 1544–27

Farm income, expenses, receipts by commodity, assets, liabilities, and ratios, 1988 and trends from 1945, annual rpt, 1544–16

Farm production inputs, output, and productivity, by commodity and region, 1947-87, annual rpt, 1544–17

Fed Govt consolidated financial statements based on business accounting methods, FY87-88, annual rpt, 8104–5

Fed Govt finances, cash and debt transactions, daily tables, 8102–4

Fed Govt internal revenue and refunds, by type of tax, quarterly rpt, 8302–2.1

Fed Govt receipts by source and outlays by agency, *Treasury Bulletin*, quarterly rpt, 8002–4.1

Fed Govt tax receipts, monthly rpt, quarterly and annual data, 23842–1.6

Finances of govts, tax systems and revenue, and fiscal structure, by level of govt and State, selected years 1929-91, annual rpt, 10044–1

Flow-of-funds accounts, assets and liabilities by type and economic sector, outstanding at year-end 1965-88, annual rpt, 9364–3

Flow-of-funds accounts, savings, investments, and credit statements, quarterly rpt, 9365–3.3

Foreign travelers spending in US by world area of residence, and economic impact, by spending category, census div, and State, model results, 1985-86, 2908–28

Household composition, income, benefits, and labor force status, Survey of Income and Program Participation methodology, working paper series, 2626–10

Income (personal) per capita impacts of Federal and defense spending and taxation, by State, 1950s-87, article, 9391–1.918

IRS collections, enforcement, and litigation activity, with data by type of tax, region, and State, FY88, annual rpt, 8304–3

Multinatl firms US affiliates, finances, and operations, by industry, world area of parent firm, and State, 1987, annual rpt, 2704–4

Multinatl US firms and foreign affiliates finances and operations, by industry of parent firm and affiliate, world area, and country, preliminary 1987, annual rpt, 2704–5

Natl income and product accounts and components, *Survey of Current Business*, monthly rpt, 2702–1.21

Natl income and product accounts govt transactions component estimates, methodology and bibl, 1988 technical rpt, 2706–6.5

Natural gas interstate pipeline company detailed financial and operating data, by firm, 1988, annual rpt, 3164–38

Nonprofit charitable organizations finances, and assets and grants of top 10, 1985, article, 8302–2.923

Public opinion on taxes, spending, and govt efficiency, by respondent characteristics, 1989 survey, annual rpt, 10044–2

Rural areas dev spending of Fed Govt, and aid/tax ratio by State, FY85, article, 1502–7.901

Soviet Union budget deficits and financing, revenues, and spending, with retail prices, 1970-88, 9118–6

Soviet Union personal income by source, disposable income, wage deductions by type, and savings, 1950s-87, 9118–7

Statistical Abstract of US, social, political, and economic data, 1790-2025, comprehensive annual compilation, 2324–1.2

Tax-related economic and fiscal topics, technical paper series, 8006–3

Telephone and telegraph firms detailed finances and operations, 1987, annual rpt, 9284–6

Telephone firms borrowing under Rural
Telephone Program, and financial and
operating data, 1988, annual rpt, 1244–2

Truck and warehouse services finances and
inventory, by SIC 2- to 4-digit industry,
1988 survey, annual rpt, 2413–14

Truck interstate carriers finances and
operations, by district, 1987, annual rpt,
9486–6.2

see also Estate tax

see also Excise tax

see also Fuel tax

see also Gift tax

see also Income taxes

see also Licenses and permits

see also Oil depletion allowances

see also Property tax

see also Revenue sharing

see also Sales tax

see also Severance taxes

see also Social security tax

see also State and local taxes

see also Tariffs and foreign trade controls

see also Tax delinquency and evasion

see also Tax exempt organizations

see also Tax exempt securities

see also Tax expenditures

see also Tax incentives and shelters

see also Tax laws and courts

see also Tax protests and appeals

see also Tax reform

see also Unemployment insurance tax

see also Value added tax

see also Windfall profit tax

see also Withholding tax

Taxicabs

Auto fleet size, trip characteristics, and
energy use, by fleet type, 1970s-88,
annual rpt, 3304–5.3

County Business Patterns, 1987:
employment, establishments, and payroll,
by SIC 2- to 4-digit industry and county,
annual State rpt series, 2326–8

Drivers licenses issued and in force by age
and sex, fees, and renewal, by license
class and State, 1987, annual rpt,
7554–16

Employment, earnings, and hours, by SIC 1-
to 4-digit industry, monthly 1983-Feb
1989, annual rpt, 6744–4

Finances, operations, vehicles, equipment,
accidents, and energy use, by mode of
transport, 1955-88, annual rpt, 7304–2

Occupational injury and illness rates, by SIC
2- to 4-digit industry, 1987, annual rpt,
6844–1

Science, engineering, and technical
employment in transportation, utilities,
and retail and wholesale trade, by field,
occupation, and industry, 1985, triennial
rpt, 9627–32

Tax (income) returns of partnerships,
income statement items by industry group,
1986, annual article, 8302–2.903

Tax (income) returns of sole proprietorships,
income statement items, by industry
group, 1987, annual article, 8302–2.904;
8302–2.921

Urban areas traffic volume and detailed trip
characteristics, by transport mode and
city, 1950s-88, 7888–37

Taylor, Bruce M.

"New Directions for the National Crime
Survey", 6066–23.5

"Redesign of the National Crime Survey",
6066–3.40

Taylor, Harold

"Timing of Fertilizer Applications",
1561–16.903

Taylor, Herbert E.

"Optimal Response of Monetary Policy to
Oil Price Shocks", 9387–8.193

Taylor, Jeffrey R.

"China: The Problem of Employing Surplus
Rural Labor", 2326–18.48

Taylor-Shirley, Katherine

"Profiles in Safety and Health: Occupational
Hazards of Meatpacking", 6722–1.901

Taylor, William F.

"Prognostic Variables in Osteosarcoma: A
Multi-Institutional Study", 4472–1.901

Tea

Africa agricultural exports by commodity,
and relation to economic conditions and
other factors, by country, 1960s-87,
1528–280

Agricultural Statistics, 1988, annual rpt,
1004–1

Business statistics, detailed data for major
industries and economic indicators, *Survey
of Current Business*, monthly rpt,
2702–1.11

Consumption of food and nutrient intake by
individuals, by food group, selected
characteristics, and region, supplementary
survey series, 1356–5

Consumption, supply, trade, prices,
spending, and indexes, by food
commodity, 1987, annual rpt, 1544–4

Developing countries export revenue effects
of trade policy changes in developing and
developed countries, model results, 1989
article, 1522–3.922

Exports and imports (agricultural) of US, by
commodity and country, bimonthly rpt
with articles, 1522–1

Exports and imports (agricultural) of US, by
commodity, monthly rpt, 1922–8

Exports and imports (agricultural) of US, by
detailed commodity and country, 1988,
semiannual rpt, 1522–4

Exports and imports (agricultural) of US
with Asia, Middle East, and North Africa,
by commodity and country, 1962-86,
1528–277

Exports of US, detailed commodities by
country, monthly rpt, 2422–3

Foreign and US agricultural production,
trade, and weather devs, weekly press
release, 1922–4

Foreign and US production, prices, and
trade, FAS annual circular series,
1925–15

Foreign countries agricultural production,
prices, and trade, by country, 1970s-89
and forecast 1990, annual world region rpt
series, 1524–4

Imports of US, detailed Schedule A
commodities by country, monthly rpt,
2422–2

Manufacturing annual survey, 1986:
financial and operating data, by SIC 2- to
4-digit industry, series, 2506–15

Manufacturing census, 1987: financial and
operating data, for SIC 4-digit industries
by product, preliminary rpt, 2491–1.9

Mormons death risks from cancer and heart
disease, by sex and health habits
practiced, 1974 and 1979 studies, article,
4472–1.932

Price indexes (producer), by stage of
processing and detailed commodity,
monthly rpt, 6762–6

Price indexes (producer), by stage of
processing and detailed commodity,
monthly 1988, annual rpt, 6764–2

Teacher education

Assistance (financial and nonfinancial) of
Fed Govt, 1989 base edition with
supplements, annual listing, 104–5

Bilingual education program activities,
Federal and State aid, and enrollment,
FY86-87, biennial rpt, 4804–14

Condition of Education, detailed data on
elementary, secondary, and higher
education, 1920s-88 and projected to
1997, annual rpt, 4824–1

Degrees (bachelor) held by teachers, by field
and other characteristics, 1985-86,
4838–39

Degrees (bachelor and masters) awarded
1985/86, holders employment
characteristics, 1987 survey, series,
4826–3

Degrees awarded in higher education, by
level, field, race, and sex, 1989 edition,
annual rpt, 4824–2.20

Digest of Education Statistics, detailed data
on students, staff, finances, and facilities,
1989 edition, annual rpt, 4824–2

Education Dept programs funding,
operations, and effectiveness, FY88,
annual rpt, 4804–5

Fulbright-Hays academic exchanges, grants
by purpose, and foreign govt share of
costs, by country, FY88, annual rpt,
10324–1

Health care (family) teaching faculty dev
programs, Federal funding and trainees,
by faculty status and region, 1978-87,
4118–63

Incentive programs for public school
teachers, and participation, by instn and
teacher characteristics, with effectiveness
ratings, 1985, 4838–38

Salaries of public and private schools
teachers, by selected characteristics,
1984/85-1985/86, 4838–37

Science and math teacher training and high
school course requirements, by State,
1988 rpt, 26358–199

Science proficiency, attitudes, factors
affecting proficiency, and teacher
background and views, natl assessment of
elementary and high school students,
1977-86, 4898–25

Special education staff, training, degrees,
and certification, by field and State,
FY87, annual rpt, 4944–4

State allocation of Federal educational
funds, by program, recipient type, and
State, 1987/88, annual rpt, 4804–8

Teachers moonlighting, by selected
employment and other characteristics,
1985, 4838–36

USIA English language program enrollment
and staff, by instn, world area, and
country, FY88, annual rpt, 9854–2

Teachers

American Federation of Teachers
membership, 1955-87, article,
6722–1.931

Community organizations partnerships with
public schools, participation, activities,
and contributions, by school
characteristics and location, 1987/88,
4826–1.27

Condition of Education, detailed data on elementary and secondary education, 1920s-88 and projected to 1997, annual rpt, 4824-1.1

Data on education, enrollment, degrees, teachers, and spending, 1974/75-1988/89 and alternative projections to 1999/2000, annual rpt, 4824-4

Data on education, selected performance and financial indicators by State, 1982-88, annual table with supplements, 4804-32

Digest of Education Statistics, detailed data on students, staff, finances, and facilities, 1989 edition, annual rpt, 4824-2

DOD Dependents Schools teachers hired, by whether living abroad, dependent, and permanent position, and world area, 1983/84-1987/88, GAO rpt, 26119-257

DOD training and education programs funding, staff, students, and facilities, by service branch, FY90, annual rpt, 3504-5

Elementary and secondary education enrollment, teachers, high school grads, and spending, by State, 1988/89, annual rpt, 4834-19

Elementary and secondary public education agency revenues by source, and outlays, by State, FY86-87, annual rpt, 4834-6

Elementary and secondary public schools, enrollment and other characteristics, for top 55 districts, 1987-88, annual rpt, 4834-22

Elementary and secondary public schools, enrollment, and teachers, by level and State, 1987/88, annual rpt, 4834-17

Elementary and secondary school teachers, fall 1987 and projected to 1993, annual rpt, 4826-8.6

Employment and payroll, by function and level of govt, 1987-88, annual rpt series, 2466-1

Employment, enrollment, and spending, by instn level and control, and teachers salaries, 1980s-90, annual press release, 4804-19

Employment, unemployment, and labor force characteristics, by region and census div, 1988, annual rpt, 6744-7.1

Flight and ground instructors certified by FAA, by age, sex, region, and State, 1988, annual rpt, 7504-2

Fulbright-Hays academic exchanges, grants by purpose, and foreign govt share of costs, by country, FY88, annual rpt, 10324-1

Incentive programs for public school teachers, and participation, by instn and teacher characteristics, with effectiveness ratings, 1985, 4838-38

Moonlighting by teachers, by selected employment and other characteristics, 1985, 4838-36

Natl Education Assn membership, 1955-87, article, 6722-1.931

Private elementary and secondary schools, enrollment, teachers, and high school grads, by instn religious orientation, 1988/89, annual rpt, 4834-21

Red Cross domestic and intl services, volunteers, and certificates issued, by program, FY88, annual rpt, 29254-1.1

Science and engineering education in elementary and secondary schools, and student persistence in postsecondary education, 1977-88, 26358-199

Science and engineering employment characteristics, by field, 1988, biennial rpt, 9627-16

Science and engineering labor force, Federal and university research funding, and educational data, series, 9626-6

Science and engineering PhDs employment and other characteristics, by field and State, 1987, biennial rpt, 9627-18

Science education methods, materials, and factors affecting student proficiency, views of students, teachers, and administrators, 1983-85 surveys, 4828-37.1

Science proficiency, attitudes, factors affecting proficiency, and teacher background and views, natl assessment of elementary and high school students, 1977-86, 4898-25

Smoking prevention program for black high school students in urban areas, teacher and student views, 1989 local areas surveys, article, 4042-3.956

Special education programs, enrollment by age, staff, funding, and needs, by type of handicap and State, 1987/88, annual rpt, 4944-4

Statistical Abstract of US, social, political, and economic data, 1790-2025, comprehensive annual compilation, 2324-1.1

USIA English language program enrollment and staff, by instn, world area, and country, FY88, annual rpt, 9854-2

see also Educational employees pay

see also Teacher education

Teaching aids and devices

see Educational materials

see Educational technology

Technical assistance

see International assistance

see Military assistance

Technical education

see Vocational education and training

Technicians

see Clinical laboratory technicians

see Scientists and technicians

Technological innovations

Auto and home supply stores productivity trends and technological devs, 1972-87, article, 6722-1.941

Autos powered by electricity, R&D activity and DOE funding shares, FY88, annual rpt, 3304-2

Banks employment relation to labor costs, output, and technological change, US and 5 OECD countries, 1980-86, working paper, 9371-10.42

Banks technological devs adoption relation to asset size, regression results, 1980s-86, working paper, 9371-10.33

Dioxin levels in paper products and pulp mill effluents, and control technology, 1970s-87, 26358-204

Economic indicators, prices, labor costs, and productivity, BLS econometric analyses and methodology, working paper series, 6886-6

Engine carburetors, pistons, and valves, industry productivity and technological devs, for 1972-86, article, 6722-1.911

Engineering research and education grants of NSF, FY88, annual listing, 9624-24

Export-related employment, by industry div, 1980s-87, 2048-103

Exports, imports, and balances of US by commodity group, world area, and country, and related employment, 1970s-88, annual rpt, 2044-26

Fertilizer and pesticide industry productivity of labor, indexes and annual rates of change, 1972-86, article, 6722-1.915

Foreign and US technology dev and competition issues, fundings and recommendations, 1980s-87, 21708-123

Hazardous waste mgmt, effectiveness of alternative technologies, 1989 conf papers, biennial rpt, 9184-19

Labor force, composition, and productivity effects of technological devs, by industry, 1960s-86 and projected to 2000, series, 6826-2

Manufacturing high technology use and plans, with data by technology, selected industry, and firm and market characteristics, 1988 survey, 2508-1

Metals (primary) demand relation to consumption patterns and economic, trade, and technological factors, 1960s-82, 5608-159

Minerals of strategic and technological importance, supply, imports, and use, with foreign comparisons, commodity rpt series, 5606-9

NSF Science Resources Studies Div project descriptions and rpts, 1988 annual listing, 9624-21

Rural areas high-technology employment, by industry div and size of firm, and compared to urban areas, selected years 1972-86, hearing, 25728-41

Small business R&D grants of Fed Govt, administrators views on effectiveness, FY86-87, GAO rpt, 26113-393

Small business R&D grants of Fed Govt, by program area, agency, and State, FY88, annual rpt, 9764-7

Soviet Union planning for science and technology, and relation to economic plans, 1989 working paper, 2326-18.45

Transit systems research rpts, 1988, annual listing, 7884-11

see also Automation

see also Energy research and development

see also Fiber optics

see also Industrial robots

see also Inventions

see also Lasers

see also Patents

see also Research

see also Research and development

see also Technology transfer

Technology

see Inventions

see Research

see Research and development

see Science and technology

see Technological innovations

see Technology transfer

Technology Policy Task Force. House

Foreign and US technology dev and competition issues, fundings and recommendations, 1980s-87, 21708-123

Technology transfer

AID contracts and grants for technical and support services, by instn, country, and State, FY88, annual listing, 9914-7

AID economic aid to developing countries, obligations and disbursements by country, quarterly rpt, 9912-4

Arms sales of US, foreign conditions on sales and impacts on US industry, with data by industry group and country, 1988 annual rpt, 104-25

Biotechnology in Japan, R&D spending, industry finances, and govt involvement, FY85-86, 2048-139

Ceramics (advanced) technical info of Japan, US industry use and views on value, 1988 survey, 2008-28

Developing countries economic and social conditions from 1960s, and Intl Dev Cooperation Agency and AID activities and funding, FY88-90, annual rpt, 9904-4

Export licensing, monitoring, and enforcement activities, FY88, annual rpt, 2024-1

Fed Govt R&D labs technology transfer cooperative agreements, royalties, and incentive payments to employees, by agency, FY87-88, GAO rpt, 26113-422

Pacific basin countries military, economic, technological, and trade conditions, 1970s-85, compilation of papers, 3908-4

Small business high technology sales, exports, siting, technology transfer, views on competitiveness, 1988 survey, hearing, 21728-69

Superconductivity (high temperature) R&D spending by Federal agency, and US and Japan industry funding and employment, by application, 1981-89, hearing, 25408-100

Teenage pregnancy

Abortions, and patient characteristics, 1972-85, article, 4202-7.906

Abortions, by method, pregnancy history, and other characteristics of woman, 1985-86, US Vital Statistics annual rpt, 4146-5.108

Births and rates, by characteristics of birth, infant, and parents, 1987 and trends from 1940, US Vital Statistics advance annual rpt, 4146-5.110

Deaths related to pregnancy, and rates, by detailed cause and demographic characteristics, 1986, US Vital Statistics annual rpt, 4144-2

Fetal deaths and rates, by characteristics of mother and birth, 1986, US Vital Statistics annual rpt, 4144-2.3

Head Start program operations, enrollment by handicap, and family characteristics, for North Central States, 1987/88, annual rpt, 4604-12

HHS financial aid, by program, recipient, State, and city, FY88, annual regional listings, 4004-3

Infant deaths, causes, and prevention, recommendations and findings, 1988 rpt, 15838-1

Mexican American high school dropouts health condition, substance abuse, and involvement with violence, 1988-89 survey, article, 4042-3.957

Research on population and reproduction, Federal funding by project, FY87, annual listing, 4474-9

Teenagers

see Elementary and secondary education
see Juvenile delinquency
see School dropouts
see Teenage pregnancy

see Youth
see Youth employment

Teigen, Lloyd D.

"Weather in U.S. Agriculture: Monthly Temperature and Precipitation by State and Farm Production Region, 1950-88", 1544-28

Telecommunication

Air traffic control and airway facilities improvement activities under Natl Airspace System Plan, 1981-85 and projected to 2000, annual rpt, 7504-12

Budget of US, special analysis of Federal capital spending by category, projected FY89-2005 and trends from FY81, annual rpt, 104-24

Construction industries census, 1987: establishments, employment, receipts, and expenditures, by SIC 4-digit industry and State, final industry rpt series, 2373-1

Construction industries census, 1987: financial and operating data, preliminary industry rpt series, 2371-1

Construction put in place, value of new public and private structures, by type, monthly rpt, 2382-4

County Business Patterns, 1987: employment, establishments, and payroll, by SIC 2- to 4-digit industry and county, annual State rpt series, 2326-8

Developing countries disaster preparedness and economic, population, and political data, country rpt series, 9916-2

DOD budget justification, programs, and policies, FY88-91, annual rpt, 3544-2

Exports of US, detailed commodities by country, monthly rpt, 2422-3

Fed Govt labor productivity, indexes of output and labor costs by function, FY67-87, annual rpt, 6824-1.6

Finances, operations, and industry devs for telecommunications, with data by service type, firm, and country, 1950s-80s, 2808-27

Foreign countries economic, social, political, and geographic summary data, by country, 1989, annual factbook, 9114-2

GSA activities and finances, FY88, annual rpt, 9454-1

Imports of US, detailed Schedule A commodities by country, monthly rpt, 2422-2

Info services for home and business, availability, use, and market indicators, for US and other OECD countries, 1980s and projected to 1992, 2808-28

Manufacturers finances and operations, by SIC 2- to 4-digit industry, forecast 1989 and trends from 1950s, annual rpt, 2044-28

Modem availability to households, 1980s and projected to 1992, 2808-28

Natl Telecommunications and Info Admin rpts, FY88, annual listing, 2804-3

Price indexes (producer), by stage of processing and detailed commodity, monthly rpt, 6762-6

Price indexes (producer), by stage of processing and detailed commodity, monthly 1988, annual rpt, 6764-2

Rates for domestic and overseas service, by type of service and area served, various dates 1988, annual rpt, 9284-6.6

Science, engineering, and technical employment in transportation, utilities,

and retail and wholesale trade, by field, occupation, and industry, 1985, triennial rpt, 9627-32

Tax (excise) collections of IRS, by type of tax, region, and State, FY88, annual rpt, 8304-3.3

Tax rates and provisions, by type of service and State, 1988, annual rpt, 10044-1.1

Wire and cable (insulated) shipments, trade, use, and firms, by product, 1987-88, annual Current Industrial Rpt, 2506-10.8

see also Communications satellites
see also Educational broadcasting
see also Mobile radio
see also Public broadcasting
see also Radio
see also Telegraph
see also Telephones and telephone industry
see also Television

Telegraph

County Business Patterns, 1987: employment, establishments, and payroll, by SIC 2- to 4-digit industry and county, annual State rpt series, 2326-8

Exports of US, detailed commodities by country, monthly rpt, 2422-3

Finances and operations, detail for telegraph firms, 1987, annual rpt, 9284-6

Manufacturers finances and operations, by SIC 2- to 4-digit industry, forecast 1989 and trends from 1950s, annual rpt, 2044-28

Manufacturing annual survey, 1986: financial and operating data, by SIC 2- to 4-digit industry, series, 2506-15

Rates for domestic and overseas service, by type of service and area served, various dates 1988, annual rpt, 9284-6.6

Science, engineering, and technical employment in transportation, utilities, and retail and wholesale trade, by field, occupation, and industry, 1985, triennial rpt, 9627-32

Statistical Abstract of US, social, political, and economic data, 1790-2025, comprehensive annual compilation, 2324-1.3

Telephones and telephone industry

Agricultural Statistics, 1988, annual rpt, 1004-1.2

Banks in Fed Reserve System, expenses and operations itemized by service, office, and district, 1988, annual rpt, 9364-11

Business statistics, detailed data for major industries and economic indicators, *Survey of Current Business*, monthly rpt, 2702-1.8

Construction put in place and cost indexes, by type of construction, bimonthly rpt, 2042-1.1

Consumer Expenditure Survey, household income by source, and itemized spending, by selected characteristics and location, 1984-86, annual rpt, 6764-5.2

Consumer spending, natl income and product account, *Survey of Current Business*, monthly rpt, 2702-1.23

County Business Patterns, 1987: employment, establishments, and payroll, by SIC 2- to 4-digit industry and county, annual State rpt series, 2326-8

CPI by component for US city average, and by region, population size, and for 27 metro areas, monthly rpt, 6762-2

Criminal cases by type and disposition, and collections, for US attorneys, by Federal district, FY88, annual rpt, 6004–2.1

Developing countries disaster preparedness and economic, population, and political data, country rpt series, 9916–2

Employment, earnings, and hours, by SIC 1- to 4-digit industry, monthly 1983-Feb 1989, annual rpt, 6744–4

Employment of minorities and discrimination charges in telecommunications industries, with data by industry and selected firm, 1970s-88, hearings, 21368–113

Employment of minorities and women, by occupation, SIC 1- to 3- digit industry, State, and MSA, 1986, annual rpt, 9244–1

Exports of US, detailed commodities by country, monthly rpt, 2422–3

Farm average monthly local and total telephone bill, monthly rpt, annual table, 1629–1

Finances and operations, by SIC 2- to 4-digit industry, forecast 1989 with trends from 1950s, annual rpt, 2044–28

Finances and operations, detail for telephone firms, 1987, annual rpt, 9284–6

Finances and operations of local and long distance firms, subscribership, and charges, 1970s-FY89, semiannual rpt, 9282–7

Finances, operations, and industry devs for telecommunications, with data by service type, firm, and country, 1950s-80s, 2808–27

Foreign countries economic, social, political, and geographic summary data, by country, 1989, annual factbook, 9114–2

Health care treatments and products not proven safe or effective, use, costs, and user characteristics, 1986 survey, 4008–86

House of Representatives salaries, expenses, and contingent fund disbursement, detailed listings, quarterly rpt, 21942–1

Household utilities spending, by household size, income, householder age and race, and region, 1983, article, 1702–1.904

Households receipt of telephone service, by composition, income sources, and other characteristics, 1984-87, 9288–11

Households with telephones, MSA surveys, series, 2485–6

Imports of telephones and equipment from 3 countries at less than fair value, injury to US industry, investigation with background financial and operating data, 1989 rpt, 9886–14.251; 9886–14.274

Imports of US, detailed Schedule A commodities by country, monthly rpt, 2422–2

Injuries from use of consumer products, by severity, victim age, and detailed product, 1988, annual rpt, 9164–6

Labor productivity, indexes of output, hours, and employment by SIC 2- to 4-digit industry, 1963-87, annual rpt, 6824–1.4

Local telephone rates and low-income subsidies, by region, company, and city, 1940-June 1989, semiannual rpt, 9282–8

Manufacturing annual survey, 1986: financial and operating data, by SIC 2- to 4-digit industry, series, 2506–15

Manufacturing census, 1987: financial and operating data, for SIC 4-digit industries by product, preliminary rpt, 2491–1.72

Occupational injury and illness rates, by SIC 2- to 4-digit industry, 1987, annual rpt, 6844–1

Older persons functional limitations, by activity type and selected characteristics, 1984, 4147–10.167

Pacific territories social, economic, health, and govtl data, FY88 and trends, annual rpt, 7004–6

Price indexes (producer), by stage of processing and detailed commodity, monthly rpt, 6762–6

Price indexes (producer), by stage of processing and detailed commodity, monthly 1988, annual rpt, 6764–2

Rates for domestic and overseas service, by type of service and area served, various dates 1988, annual rpt, 9284–6.6

Rates for long distance intrastate calls, impact of State entry and price regulation, 1983-87, 9406–1.55

Rural areas electric and telephone loans by State, and REA activities and finances, FY88 with trends from FY36, annual rpt, 1244–3

Rural areas telecommunication technologies availability and use, 1986-87, article, 1502–7.910

Rural Telephone Bank financial statements, FY87, annual rpt, 1244–4

Rural Telephone Cooperatives, membership, and revenue, by State, 1987, annual rpt, 1124–1

Rural Telephone Program loan activity, by State, FY88, annual tables, 1244–8

Rural Telephone Program loans, and borrower operations and finances, 1988, annual rpt, 1244–2

Science, engineering, and technical employment in transportation, utilities, and retail and wholesale trade, by field, occupation, and industry, 1985, triennial rpt, 9627–32

Service industries census, 1987: establishments, receipts, employment, and payroll, by SIC 2- to 4-digit kind of business, MSA, county, and city, State rpt series, 2391–1

Statistical Abstract of US, social, political, and economic data, 1790-2025, comprehensive annual compilation, 2324–1.3

Tax (excise) collections of IRS, by source, quarterly rpt, 8302–1; 8302–2.1

Tax (income) aid telephone system of IRS, accessibility and accuracy, and other IRS workload indicators, 1988 hearing, 21788–178

Tax (income) aid telephone system of IRS, accessibility and accuracy, 1988 survey, GAO rpt, 26119–190

see also Mobile radio

Television

Business statistics, detailed data for major industries and economic indicators, *Survey of Current Business*, monthly rpt, 2702–1.14

CPI by component for US city average, and by region, population size, and for 27 metro areas, monthly rpt, 6762–2

Developing countries disaster preparedness and economic, population, and political data, country rpt series, 9916–2

Educational progress by subject and selected student characteristics, standard test results and credits, 1989 edition, annual rpt, 4824–2.12

Employment, earnings, and hours, by SIC 1- to 4-digit industry, monthly 1983-Feb 1989, annual rpt, 6744–4

Employment of minorities and discrimination charges in telecommunications industries, with data by industry and selected firm, 1970s-88, hearings, 21368–113

Exports of US, detailed commodities by country, monthly rpt, 2422–3

Fed Govt ad spending, and subcontracts to small and disadvantaged firms, by agency and medium, FY86, GAO rpt, 26113–428

Finances, operations, and industry devs for telecommunications, with data by service type, firm, and country, 1950s-80s, 2808–27

Foreign countries economic, social, political, and geographic summary data, by country, 1989, annual factbook, 9114–2

Health care treatments and products not proven safe or effective, use, costs, and user characteristics, 1986 survey, 4008–86

High-definition TV sales, alternative projections 1990-2010, 26306–3.109

High school students employment, hours spent on homework and watching TV, 1984-86, 4898–27

Hwy speed limit increase coverage by newspapers and TV, 1987, 7768–110

Imports of US, detailed Schedule A commodities by country, monthly rpt, 2422–2

Imports of US given duty-free treatment for value of US material sent abroad, and impacts on US industry and employment, by commodity and country, 1987, annual rpt, 9884–14

Injuries from use of consumer products and related activities, by victim age and sex, 1988, annual rpt, 9164–7

Injuries from use of consumer products, by severity, victim age, and detailed product, 1988, annual rpt, 9164–6

License status and allocation of commercial and noncommercial UHF and VHF TV channels, by market, as of Dec 1988, semiannual rpt, 9282–6

Licensing activities of FCC, by class of operation, FY88, annual rpt, 9284–4

Manufacturing annual survey, 1986: value of shipments, by SIC 4- to 5-digit product class, 2506–15.3

Manufacturing census, 1987: financial and operating data, for SIC 4-digit industries by product, preliminary rpt, 2491–1.72

OECD trade, total and for 4 major countries, and US trade by country, by commodity, 1970-87, world area rpt series, 9116–1

Pacific territories social, economic, health, and govtl data, FY88 and trends, annual rpt, 7004–6

Price indexes (producer), by stage of processing and detailed commodity, monthly rpt, 6762–6

Price indexes (producer), by stage of processing and detailed commodity, monthly 1988, annual rpt, 6764–2

Satellite TV dish and decoder sales, ownership, subscribers, and program ratings compared to local stations, 1980s-88, hearings, 21528-74

Science proficiency, attitudes, factors affecting proficiency, and teacher background and views, natl assessment of elementary and high school students, 1977-86, 4898-25

Service industries census, 1987: establishments, receipts, employment, and payroll, by SIC 2- to 4-digit kind of business, MSA, county, and city, State rpt series, 2391-1

Stations on the air, by class of operation, monthly press release, 9282-4

Statistical Abstract of US, social, political, and economic data, 1790-2025, comprehensive annual compilation, 2324-1.3

see also Cable television

see also Video recordings and equipment

Tellurium

see Metals and metal industries

Tempe, Ariz.

see also under By City and By SMSA or MSA in the "Index by Categories"

Temperature

see Weather

Temporary and seasonal employment

Agriculture census, 1987: farms, farmland, production, finances, and operator characteristics, by county, final State rpt series, 2331-1

Air traffic control and airway facilities staff, by selected employment and demographic characteristics, FY88, annual rpt, 7504-41

Aliens admitted to US, by class of admission, port, country, and State of destination, quarterly rpt, 6262-2

Capitol Architect outlays for salaries, supplies, and services, itemized by payee and function, 1st half FY89, semiannual rpt, 25922-2

DOD Dependents Schools teachers hired, by whether living abroad, dependent, and permanent position, 1983/84-1987/88, GAO rpt, 26119-257

DOT employment, by subagency, occupation, and selected personnel characteristics, FY88, annual rpt, 7304-18

Earnings and employment for permanent and temporary workers in temporary help supply services industry, by occupation, Sept 1987, article, 6722-1.912

Farm finances and operations, by size, commodity, and region, 1986, annual rpt, 1544-27

Farm workers, earnings, and days worked, by selected characteristics and region, 1987, biennial rpt, 1594-2

Fed Govt civilian employee work-years, pay rates, and benefits use and costs, by agency, FY87, annual rpt, 9844-31

Fed Govt civilian employment and payroll, by agency in DC metro area, total US, and abroad, bimonthly rpt, 9842-1

Fed Govt temporary employment, appointments and extensions, by occupational group, Jan-June 1983-85, GAO rpt, 26119-129

Immigration to US, alien workers, visitors, deportations, and naturalizations, by country, FY88 and trends from 1820, annual rpt, 6264-2

Income (household, family, and personal), by source, detailed characteristics, and region, 1987, annual Current Population Rpt, 2546-6.59

Nursing home facility, staff, and resident detailed characteristics, 1985, 4147-13.97

Pension and health insurance coverage for full- and part-time workers, 1985, article, 6722-1.913

Poverty status of families and persons, by detailed characteristics, 1987, annual Current Population Rpt, 2546-6.60

Radiation exposure of workers at nuclear power plants and related facilities, by site, 1968-86, annual rpt, 9634-3

Service industries census, 1987: establishments, receipts, employment, and payroll, by SIC 2- to 4-digit kind of business, MSA, county, and city, State rpt series, 2391-1

Teachers moonlighting, by selected employment and other characteristics, 1985, 4838-36

Unemployed displaced workers, by reason, industry, selected characteristics, and State, 1988, annual rpt, 6744-18

Wages, hours, and employment by occupation, and benefits, for selected locations, industry survey rpt series, 6787-6

Youth labor force participation by age, Apr and July 1989 and change from 1988, annual press release, 6744-13

Youth labor force status, by sex and race, summer 1985-89, annual press release, 6744-14

see also Migrant workers

see also Part-time employment

Tennessee

Agriculture census, 1987: farms, farmland, production and costs, and operator characteristics, advance State and county rpts, 2330-1.47

Agriculture census, 1987: farms, farmland, production, finances, and operator characteristics, by county, final State rpt, 2331-1.42

Appalachian Regional Commission funding, by project and State, planned FY89, annual rpt, 9084-3

Bank deposits in FDIC-insured commercial and savings banks, by instn, State, and county, as of June 1988, annual regional rpt, 9295-3.4

Clothing (hosiery) production and related workers and wages by occupation and sex, and benefits, by location, 1987 survey, 6787-6.237

Coal production and mines by county, prices, productivity, miners, reserves, and stocks, by mining method and State, 1987-88, annual rpt, 3164-25

Collective bargaining calendar for southeastern States, 1989, annual rpt, 6946-1.73

County Business Patterns, 1987: employment, establishments, and payroll, by SIC 2- to 4-digit industry and county, annual State rpt, 2326-8.44

Deaths and rates, by detailed location, cause, and demographic characteristics, 1987, US Vital Statistics annual rpt, 4144-3.1

Disabled SSI beneficiaries Medicaid services use and costs, by diagnosis and whether covered by Medicare, 1984, article, 4652-1.947

DOD prime contract awards, by contractor, service branch, State, and city, FY88, annual rpt, 3544-22

Economic and banking conditions, for Fed Reserve 8th District, quarterly rpt with articles, 9391-16

Economic indicators by State and MSA, Fed Reserve 6th District, quarterly rpt, 9371-14

Employment and unemployment, for 8 southeastern States, 1987-88, annual rpt, 6944-2

Employment by industry div, earnings, and hours, for 8 southeastern States, quarterly press release, 6942-7

Employment, earnings, and hours, by selected SIC 1- to 4-digit industry, State, and for 262 MSAs, 1972-87, 6748-81.5

Fed Govt spending in States and local areas, by type, State, county, and city, FY88, annual rpt, 2464-3

Fed Govt spending in States, by type, program, agency, and State, FY88, annual rpt, 2464-2

HHS financial aid, by program, recipient, State, and city, FY88, annual regional listing, 4004-3.4

Homeless children educational enrollment and needs, 1988, annual State rpt, 4804-35.42

Income (personal) per capita and by source, and earnings by industry div, by State, MSA, and county, 1982-87, annual regional rpt, 2704-2.4

Medicaid enrollment, and service use and costs by service type, by eligibility type, for 5 States, 1980-84, article, 4652-1.919

Mineral Industry Surveys, State reviews of production, 1988, preliminary annual rpt, 5614-6

Minerals Yearbook, 1987, Vol 2 preprints: State review of production and sales by commodity, and business activity, annual rpt, 5604-16.44

Minerals Yearbook, 1987, Vol 2: State reviews of production, sales, and firms, by commodity, and business activity, annual rpt, 5604-34

Nursing home compliance with Medicare and Medicaid regulations, and patient characteristics, by facility, 1987/88, annual State rpt, 4654-15.44

Retail trade census, 1987: employment, establishments, sales, and payroll, by SIC 2- to 4-digit kind of business, MSA, county, and city, State rpt, 2397-1.43

Savings instns, FHLB 5th District members finances and lending by State, monthly rpt, 9302-8

Service industries census, 1987: employment, establishments, receipts, and payroll, by SIC 2- to 4-digit kind of business, MSA, county, and city, State rpt, 2391-1.43

Statistical Abstract of US, social, political, and economic data, with foreign comparisons, 1790-2025, comprehensive annual compilation, 2324-1

Textile mill employment, earnings, and hours, for 8 Southeastern States, quarterly press release, 6942-1

Timber in Tennessee, acreage and resources by species, ownership class, and county, 1989, series, 1206–27

Tobacco (burley) finances, operations, and labor, for Kentucky and Tennessee, 1984, 1568–277

Water resources dev projects of Army Corps of Engineers, characteristics, and costs, 1950s-87, biennial State rpt, 3756–2.43

Water supply and quality in streams and lakes, and groundwater levels in wells, by drainage basin, 1987, annual State rpt, 5666–10.40

Wholesale trade census, 1987: employment, establishments, finances, and operations, by SIC 2- to 4-digit kind of business, MSA, county, and city, State rpt, 2405–1.43

Wildlife-related recreation, hunting, and fishing participation and spending, detailed data, 1985 survey, quinquennial State rpt, 5506–6.42

see also Chattanooga, Tenn.
see also Clarksville, Tenn.
see also Knoxville, Tenn.
see also Memphis, Tenn.
see also Nashville, Tenn.
see also Tennessee River
see also Tennessee Valley
see also under By State in the "Index by Categories"

Tennessee River
Army Corps of Engineers water resources dev projects, characteristics, and costs, 1950s-87, biennial State rpt, 3756–2.43

Army Corps of Engineers water resources dev projects, characteristics, and costs, 1950s-87, biennial State rpt series, 3756–2

Army Corps of Engineers water resources dev projects, characteristics, and costs, 1950s-89, biennial State rpt series, 3756–1

Freight (waterborne) by commodity and port, waterway facilities, and recreation, for Ohio River basin by waterway, 1986-87, annual rpt, 3754–6

Freight (waterborne domestic and foreign) by commodity, traffic, and passengers, by port and waterway, 1987, annual rpt, 3754–3.2

TVA river control activities, and hydroelectric power generation and capacity, 1984, annual rpt, 9804–7

Water supply and quality in streams and lakes, and groundwater levels in wells, by drainage basin, 1986, annual State rpt series, 5666–23

Water supply and quality in streams and lakes, and groundwater levels in wells, by drainage basin, 1987, annual State rpt series, 5666–10

Water supply and quality in streams and lakes, and groundwater levels in wells, by drainage basin, 1988, annual State rpt series, 5666–16

see also Tennessee Valley

Tennessee Valley
Economic conditions in Tennessee Valley, and compared to US, alternative projections and trends, annual rpt, discontinued, 9804–27

Electric power distributors of TVA, finances and operations by firm, annual rpt, discontinued, 9804–19

Industrial dev, employment, and electricity demand, for Tennessee Valley by SIC 2-digit industry, firm, and location, 1988, annual rpt, 9804–3

River control activities of TVA, and hydroelectric power generation and capacity, 1984, annual rpt, 9804–7

Timber in Tennessee Valley, resources, use, and mgmt, technical paper series, discontinued, 9806–2

TVA financial and operating data by program and facility, FY88, annual rpt, 9804–32

Tennessee Valley Authority
Budget of US Appendix, obligations, appropriations, and personnel, by program and agency, FY90, annual rpt, 104–3

Budget of US, authoritative financial statements with appropriations, outlays, and receipts, by category and agency, FY88, annual rpt, 8104–2.2

Economic conditions in Tennessee Valley, and compared to US, alternative projections and trends, annual rpt, discontinued, 9804–27

Electric power demand and peak load of TVA, annual rpt, discontinued, 9804–25

Electric power distributors of TVA, finances and operations by firm, annual rpt, discontinued, 9804–19

Electric power purchases from TVA and resales, with use, average bills, and rates by customer class, by distributor, 1988, annual rpt, 9804–14

Electric power purchases of municipal and cooperative distributors, and prices and use by distributor and consumer sector, for TVA, monthly rpt, 9802–1

Electric power wholesale purchases and costs for REA borrowers, by borrower, supplier, and State, 1940-87, annual rpt, 1244–5

Employment (civilian) of Fed Govt, work-years, pay rates, and benefits use and costs, by agency, FY87, annual rpt, 9844–31

Energy use of TVA by fuel type, and conservation costs and savings, FY88, annual rpt, 9804–26

Expenditures of Fed Govt in States, by type, program, agency, and State, FY88, annual rpt, 2464–2

Fertilizer use and costs by type, and farm income and expenses, by State, 1988 and trends from 1965, biennial rpt, 9804–5

Fertilizer use, by fertilizer type and State, 1987-88, annual rpt, 9804–30

Finances and operations of Federal power admins, as of Sept 1987, annual rpt, 3164–23.4

Finances and power sales, FY88, annual rpt, 9804–1

Financial and operating data by program and facility, FY88, annual rpt, 9804–32

Industrial dev, employment, and electricity demand, for Tennessee Valley by SIC 2-digit industry, firm, and location, 1988, annual rpt, 9804–3

Labor unions recognized in Fed Govt, agreements and membership by agency and facility, as of Jan 1989, biennial listing, 9844–14

Managers salaries, incentive payments by program, and supplemental pensions, for TVA, 1979-88, GAO rpt, 26113–420

Nuclear power plant capital and operating costs per kilowatt, by plant, semiannual rpt, discontinued, 9802–5

Nuclear power plant mgmt salaries by position, and plant capacity, for TVA compared to private utilities, 1985-87, hearing, 21648–57

Publications of TVA on fertilizer and agriculture, 1989 annual listing, 9804–28

R&D funding by Fed Govt, by field, performer type, agency, and State, FY87-89, annual rpt, 9627–20

Recreation (outdoor) facilities of Fed Govt, fees and visitors by managing agency, 1988, annual rpt, 5544–14

River control activities of TVA, and hydroelectric power generation and capacity, 1984, annual rpt, 9804–7

Science and engineering employment in Fed Govt, by field, degree level, race, sex, agency, and State, 1987, annual rpt, 9627–5

Timber in Tennessee Valley, resources, use, and mgmt, technical paper series, discontinued, 9806–2

Tennessen, Alan J.
"Serving Oilseed Customers in International Markets", 1004–16.1

Tenure
see Housing tenure
see Job tenure

Tepordei, Valentin V.
"Crushed Stone and Sand and Gravel Production by State Districts, 1985-86", 5608–157

Terre Haut, Ind.
see also under By SMSA or MSA in the "Index by Categories"

Terrell, Henry S.
"Bank Lending to Developing Countries: Recent Developments and Some Considerations for the Future", 9375–14

Territorial waters
Developing countries disaster preparedness and economic, population, and political data, country rpt series, 9916–2

Foreign countries economic, social, political, and geographic summary data, by country, 1989, annual factbook, 9114–2

Foreign countries Geographic Notes, boundaries, claims, nomenclature, and other devs, periodic rpt, 7142–3

Foreign countries maritime claims and boundary agreements, series, 7006–8

Pollution (water) incidents and discharges, by type, source, cause, and location, 1984-86, annual rpt, 7404–3

Ship foreign and US flag competition in US Exclusive Economic Zone, impacts of extending cabotage laws, with background data, 1970s-80s, 26358–206

see also Continental shelf

Territories of the U.S.
Aircraft (general aviation), flight hours, and equipment, by type, use, and model of aircraft, region, and State, 1988, annual rpt, 7504–29

Assistance (financial and nonfinancial) of Fed Govt, 1989 base edition with supplements, annual listing, 104–5

Businesses (foreign) activity in US, income tax returns, assets, and income statement items, by industry div, country, and world area, 1984-85, article, 8302–2.920

Census of Population and Housing, 1990: outlying areas preparations for count, hearings, 21628–72; 21628–74

Corporations operating in Puerto Rico and other US possessions, tax incentives, finances, and operations by industry, and impacts on local economy, 1970s-83, annual rpt, 8004–12

DOD budget, organization, personnel, weapons, and property, by service branch, State, and country, 1989 annual summary rpt, 3504–13

DOD civilian and military personnel and dependents, by service branch and US and foreign location, quarterly rpt, 3542–20

Fed Govt civil service pension beneficiaries and benefits overseas, FY87, annual rpt, 9844–34

Fed Govt civilian employee accessions and separations, by agency for DC metro area and elsewhere, bimonthly rpt, 9842–1.3

Fed Govt civilian employment and payroll, by pay system and location, 1988, annual rpt, 9844–6.1

Fed Govt-leased real property inventory and rental costs, worldwide summary by location and agency, 1987, annual rpt, 9454–10

Fed Govt-owned real property inventory and costs, worldwide summary by purpose, agency, and location, 1987, annual rpt, 9454–5

Fed Govt spending in States and local areas, by type, State, county, and city, FY88, annual rpt, 2464–3

Governors of States and territories, terms and salaries, 1989-90, *Congressional Directory*, biennial rpt, 23874–1

HHS financial aid, by program, recipient, State, and city, FY88, annual regional listing, 4004–3.2; 4004–3.9

Income maintenance beneficiaries and payments, by program and outlying area, quarterly FY87, annual rpt, 4694–7.1; 4694–7.2

Interior Dept programs fraud and abuse, audits and investigations, 2nd half FY89, semiannual rpt, 5302–2

Medicare enrollment, and use by type of service, by age, sex, race, region, State, and MSA, 1986-87, annual rpt, 4657–5

Medicare enrollment, by region and abroad, 1966-87, article, 4652–1.937

Minerals Yearbook, 1987, Vol 2: State reviews of production, sales, and firms, by commodity, and business activity, annual rpt, 5604–34

Pacific territories social, economic, health, and govtl data, FY88 and trends, annual rpt, 7004–6

Population and housing census, 1980: outlying area data collection issues and procedural history, 2555–2.5

Population size and components of change, by outlying area, 1980-88, annual Current Population Rpt, 2546–3.162

Population size, growth rates, and components of change, by country, projected 1989-2020 and trends from 1950, biennial rpt, 2324–9

R&D funding by Fed Govt, by field, performer type, agency, and State, FY87-89, annual rpt, 9627–20

Refugee resettlement programs and funding, arrivals by country of origin, and indicators of adjustment, by State, FY88, annual rpt, 4694–5

Science and engineering grad enrollment, by field, source of funds, and characteristics of student and instn, 1975-87, annual rpt, 9627–7

Science and engineering immigrants, by field, age, sex, country and world area of birth and last residence, and State, 1987 and trends from 1967, 9627–29

Statistical Abstract of US, social, political, and economic data, by outlying area and country, 1950s-87, comprehensive annual compilation, 2324–1.4

Taxes levied on underwriters of Fed Govt employees health insurance plans, 1987, GAO rpt, 26119–262

Tsunamis intensity, time, location, and other characteristics, for US and territories, 1690-1988, 2158–52

TV channel allocation and license status, for commercial and noncommercial UHF and VHF TV by market, as of June 1989, semiannual rpt, 9282–6

VA expenses, by type and location, FY88, annual rpt, 8604–3.9

Waterborne commerce (domestic) of US, freight by major commodity group, vessel type, and port, 1986, annual rpt, 7704–7

Weather data for stations in continental US and outlying areas, 1988 and historic trends, annual rpt, 2154–8

see also American Samoa
see also Guam
see also Midway Islands
see also Northern Mariana Islands
see also Puerto Rico
see also U.S. Virgin Islands
see also Wake Island
see also under By Outlying Area in the "Index by Categories"

Terrorism

Incidents of terrorism in US, related activity, and casualties, by attack type, target, group, and location, 1988, annual rpt, 6224–6

Intl terrorism incidents involving US targets, by type of attack, and casualties, by target type, 1981-88, annual rpt, 6064–6.3

Intl terrorist incidents, casualties, and attacks on US targets, by attack type and country, 1980-88, 7008–56

Intl terrorist incidents, casualties, and attacks on US targets, by attack type and world area, 1968-88, annual rpt, 7004–13

Wiretaps authorized, costs, arrests, trials, and convictions, by offense and jurisdiction, 1988, annual rpt, 18204–7

see also Air piracy
see also Assassination
see also Hostages
see also Sabotage

Testa, William A.

"Determining Manufacturing Output for States and Regions", 9375–13.11

"Geography of Value Added", 9375–1.906

"Metro Area Growth from 1976-85: Theory and Evidence", 9375–13.8

"Regional Specialization and Technology in Manufacturing", 9375–13.15

"Unemployment Insurance: A State Economic Development Perspective", 9375–13.9

"Unemployment Insurance and Regional Economic Development", 9375–1.902

"Why Has Illinois Manufacturing Fallen Behind the Region?", 9375–13.14

Tests

see Drug and alcohol testing
see Educational tests
see Medical examinations and tests
see Occupational testing and certification
see Quality control and testing

Tetanus

see Infective and parasitic diseases

Teutsch, Steven M.

"Chronic Disease Reports in the Morbidity and Mortality Weekly Report (MMWR)", 4206–2.10

Texarkana, Ark.

see also under By SMSA or MSA in the "Index by Categories"

Texarkana, Tex.

see also under By SMSA or MSA in the "Index by Categories"

Texas

Agriculture census, 1987: farms, farmland, production and costs, and operator characteristics, advance State and county rpts, 2330–1.48

Agriculture census, 1987: farms, farmland, production, finances, and operator characteristics, by county, final State rpt, 2331–1.43

Alien workers (unauthorized) employer sanctions, enforcement costs, compliance, and job discrimination, 1988 annual GAO rpt, 26104–19

Asian American earnings, and employment and other characteristics, by detailed origin and whether foreign-born, 1980, 11046–7.2

Bank deposits in FDIC-insured commercial and savings banks, by instn, State, and county, as of June 1988, annual regional rpt, 9295–3.4

Citrus production and use, by crop and State, 1981/82-1986/87, 1641–4

Coal production and mines by county, prices, productivity, miners, reserves, and stocks, by mining method and State, 1987-88, annual rpt, 3164–25

Dairy prices for cows, milk, and feed, by selected State, and cows slaughtered by region, 1988, annual rpt, 1317–1.6

Deaths and rates, by detailed location, cause, and demographic characteristics, 1987, US Vital Statistics annual rpt, 4144–3.1

Disaster relief program of Fed Emergency Mgmt Agency under State admin, impact of mgmt changes on benefits processing, 1986-88, GAO rpt, 26113–412

DOD prime contract awards, by contractor, service branch, State, and city, FY88, annual rpt, 3544–22

Drug abuse indicators for selected metro areas, research results, data collection, and policy issues, 1989 semiannual conf, 4492–5

Employment by industry div, earnings, and hours, by southwestern State, with CPI by major component for 2 Texas MSAs, monthly rpt, 6962–2

Employment, earnings, and hours, by selected SIC 1- to 4-digit industry, State, and for 262 MSAs, 1972-87, 6748–81.5

Employment in Texas by major industry group, and relation to oil prices and employment in other States, mid 1970s-88, article, 9379–1.902

Employment variability, employment shares, and potential impact of diversification, for Texas by major industry group, 1970s-88, article, 9379-1.907

Estuary environmental and fishery conditions, research results and methodology, 1989 rpt, 2176-7.16

Estuary environmental conditions and mgmt, 1988 conf, 2146-6.10

Fed Govt spending in States and local areas, by type, State, county, and city, FY88, annual rpt, 2464-3

Fed Govt spending in States, by type, program, agency, and State, FY88, annual rpt, 2464-2

Finance companies loan terms relation to borrower socioeconomic characteristics, for Texas, 1973, technical paper, 9366-6.174

Fish and shellfish catch, wholesale receipts, prices, trade, and other market activities, weekly regional rpt, 2162-6.3

Goat inventory in Texas, 1987-89, annual press release, 1623-4

Health care facilities and services in the Texas-Mexico border area, and background data, by county, 1980-88, GAO rpt, 26121-261

HHS financial aid, by program, recipient, State, and city, FY88, annual regional listing, 4004-3.6

Homeless children educational enrollment and needs, 1988, annual State rpt, 4804-35.43

Hospital use and costs of Medicaid enrollees related to selected characteristics, 1980, article, 4652-1.949

Income (personal) per capita and by source, and earnings by industry div, by State, MSA, and county, 1982-87, annual regional rpt, 2704-2.5

Industrial production shares, and labor and capital index weights, for Texas by industry group, 1986, article, 9379-1.908

Mineral Industry Surveys, State reviews of production, 1988, preliminary annual rpt, 5614-6

Minerals Yearbook, 1987, Vol 2 preprints: State review of production and sales by commodity, and business activity, annual rpt, 5604-16.45

Minerals Yearbook, 1987, Vol 2: State reviews of production, sales, and firms, by commodity, and business activity, annual rpt, 5604-34

Nursing home compliance with Medicare and Medicaid regulations, and patient characteristics, by facility, 1987/88, annual State rpt, 4654-15.45

Oil and gas extraction production workers and wages by occupation, and benefits, by location, 1988 survey, 6787-6.240

Oil and gas OCS production water discharges, and impacts on Gulf of Mexico coastal habitats, 1983-88, 5738-10

Retail trade census, 1987: employment, establishments, sales, and payroll, by SIC 2- to 4-digit kind of business, MSA, county, and city, State rpt, 2397-1.44

Rice market activities, prices, inspections, sales, trade, supply, and use, for US and selected foreign markets, weekly rpt, 1313-8

Savings and loan assns failure resolution costs, and FSLIC finances and promissory notes issued, with data by instn, FY80s and projected to FY99, hearing, 25258-22

Savings and loan assns failures, assets, and FSLIC resolution costs and promissory notes, with data for acquired and acquiring instn in US and Texas, 1988 hearings, 21248-121

Savings instns, FHLB 9th District members finances and operations by State, monthly rpt, 9302-13

Savings instns, FHLB 9th District members finances and operations by State, quarterly rpt, 9302-31

Service industries census, 1987: employment, establishments, receipts, and payroll, by SIC 2- to 4-digit kind of business, MSA, county, and city, State rpt, 2391-1.44

Statistical Abstract of US, social, political, and economic data, with foreign comparisons, 1790-2025, comprehensive annual compilation, 2324-1

Tax revenue by source, and govt spending by purpose, for Texas, FY85, technical paper, 9379-12.28

Wages by occupation, for office and plant workers, 1989 survey, periodic labor market rpt, 6785-3.10

Water supply and quality in streams and lakes, and groundwater levels in wells, by drainage basin, 1987, annual State rpt, 5666-10.41

Wholesale trade census, 1987: employment, establishments, finances, and operations, by SIC 2- to 4-digit kind of business, MSA, county, and city, State rpt, 2405-1.44

Wildlife-related recreation, hunting, and fishing participation and spending, detailed data, 1985 survey, quinquennial State rpt, 5506-6.43

see also Arlington, Tex.
see also Austin, Tex.
see also Beaumont, Tex.
see also Brazoria, Tex.
see also Collin County, Tex.
see also Dallas County, Tex.
see also Dallas, Tex.
see also Denison, Tex.
see also El Paso, Tex.
see also Fort Worth, Tex.
see also Galveston, Tex.
see also Houston, Tex.
see also Longview, Tex.
see also Marshall, Tex.
see also Port Arthur, Tex.
see also San Antonio, Tex.
see also Sherman, Tex.
see also Tarrant County, Tex.
see also Wichita Falls, Tex.
see also under By State in the "Index by Categories"

Texas City, Tex.
see also under By SMSA or MSA in the "Index by Categories"

Textbooks
see Educational materials

Textile industry and fabrics
Business statistics, detailed data for major industries and economic indicators, *Survey of Current Business*, monthly rpt, 2702-1.19

Caribbean Basin Initiative investment incentives, economic impacts, with finances and employment by country, 1984-88, 2048-141

China trade by SITC 1- to 5-digit commodity, 1970s-87, annual rpt, 9114-3

Collective bargaining agreements expiring during year, and workers covered, by firm, union, industry group, and State, 1989, annual rpt, 6784-9

County Business Patterns, 1987: employment, establishments, and payroll, by SIC 2- to 4-digit industry and county, annual State rpt series, 2326-8

Earnings by major industry group, and personal income per capita and by source, by region and State, 1929-87, 2708-40

Electric power use and prices, shipments, and trade, for 25 SIC 4-digit manufacturing industries, 1972-86, 2048-137

Employment, earnings, and hours, by selected SIC 1- to 4-digit industry, State, and for 262 MSAs, 1972-87, 6748-81

Employment, earnings, and hours, by SIC 1- to 4-digit industry, monthly 1983-Feb 1989, annual rpt, 6744-4

Employment of minorities and women, by occupation, SIC 1- to 3-digit industry, State, and MSA, 1986, annual rpt, 9244-1

Employment, unemployment, and labor force characteristics, by region and census div, 1988, annual rpt, 6744-7.1

Energy use and prices for manufacturing industries, 1985 survey, series, 3166-13

Exports and imports between US and outlying areas, by detailed commodity and mode of transport, monthly rpt, 2422-4

Exports and imports of US, by commodity group, world area, selected country, US coastal area and port, and mode of transport, monthly rpt, 2422-9

Exports and imports of US by country, and trade shifts by commodity, quarterly rpt, 9882-9

Exports and imports of US, by selected country, country group, and commodity group, 1988, annual rpt, 2044-37

Exports of US, detailed commodities by country, monthly rpt, 2422-3

Finances and operations, by SIC 2- to 4-digit industry, forecast 1989 with trends from 1950s, annual rpt, 2044-28

Financial statements for manufacturing, mining, and trade corporations, by selected SIC 2- to 3-digit industry, quarterly rpt, 2502-1

Freight (waterborne domestic and foreign) by commodity, traffic, and passengers, by port and waterway, 1987, annual rpt, 3754-3

Hazardous substances industrial releases and reduction methods under EPA regulation, by chemical, source, industry, and location, 1987, annual rpt, 9234-6

Import classification codes under Textile Agreement Category System, correlation with TSUSA, 1988 annual rpt, 2044-31

Import quotas on steel, autos, and textiles, employment and income impacts by industry, model description and results, 1984, 9406-1.57

Import restraint elimination, impact on domestic industry production and employment, by selected commodity, 1986-88, 9886-4.144

Imports, exports, and employment impacts, by SIC 2- to 4-digit industry and commodity, quarterly rpt, 2322-2

Imports of textiles, by country of origin, monthly rpt, 2042-27

Imports of textiles, by product and country of origin, periodic rpt series, 2046-8; 2046-9

Imports of textiles, production, and imports share of use, by Multifiber Arrangement product, quarterly rpt, 2042-32

Imports of textiles under Multifiber Arrangement by product and country, and status of bilateral agreements, 1986-88, annual rpt, 9884-18

Imports of US, detailed Schedule A commodities by country, monthly rpt, 2422-2

Imports of US given duty-free treatment for value of US material sent abroad, and impacts on US industry and employment, by commodity and country, 1987, annual rpt, 9884-14

Input-output structure of US economy, detailed interindustry transactions for 84 industries, and components of final demand, 1983, annual article, 2702-1.909

Labor productivity, indexes of output, hours, and employment by SIC 2- to 4-digit industry, 1963-87, annual rpt, 6824-1.3

Manufacturing annual survey, 1986: financial and operating data, by SIC 2- to 4-digit industry, series, 2506-15

Manufacturing annual survey, 1986: production indexes and exports by SIC 2-digit industry and State, with comparisons to 1985, model results, series, 2506-16

Manufacturing census, 1987: financial and operating data, for SIC 4-digit industries by product, preliminary industry rpt series, 2491-1

Manufacturing industries production, shipments, inventories, orders, and pollution control costs, periodic Current Industrial Rpt series, 2506-3

Multinatl US firms and foreign affiliates finances and operations, by industry of parent firm and affiliate, world area, and country, preliminary 1987, annual rpt, 2704-5

Northern Mariana Islands economic census, 1987: employment, firms, payroll, and receipts, by SIC 1- to 4-digit industry, 2597-1

Occupational injury and illness rates, by SIC 2- to 4-digit industry, 1987, annual rpt, 6844-1

OECD trade, total and for 4 major countries, and US trade by country, by commodity, 1970-87, world area rpt series, 9116-1

Pollution (air) levels for 5 pollutants, by detailed source and State, 1986, annual rpt, 9194-7

Pollution abatement capital and operating costs, by SIC 2-to 4-digit industry and State, 1986, annual Current Industrial Rpt, 2506-3.6

Price indexes (producer), by stage of processing and detailed commodity, monthly rpt, 6762-6

Price indexes (producer), by stage of processing and detailed commodity, monthly 1988, annual rpt, 6764-2

Price indexes for department store inventories, by class of item, monthly table, 6762-7

Production, prices, trade, and use of cotton, wool, and synthetic fibers, periodic situation rpt with articles, 1561-1

Production, trade, sales, stocks, and material used, by product, region, and State, periodic Current Industrial Rpt series, 2506-5

Research (agricultural) funding and staffing for USDA, State agencies, and other instns, by topic, FY88, annual rpt, 1744-2

Retail trade census, 1987: employment, establishments, sales, and payroll, by SIC 2- to 4-digit kind of business, MSA, county, and city, State rpt series, 2397-1

Science, engineering, and technical employment in manufacturing, by field, occupation, and industry, 1986, triennial rpt, 9627-23

Small business establishments, employment, and financial ratios, by SIC 1- to 2-digit industry and State, late 1960s-87, 9768-19

Southeastern US textile mill employment, earnings, and hours, for 8 States, quarterly press release, 6942-1

Southern US textile mill employment, 1951-88, annual rpt, 6944-1

Statistical Abstract of US, social, political, and economic data, 1790-2025, comprehensive annual compilation, 2324-1.3

Tariff Schedule of US, classifications and rates of duty by detailed imported commodity, 1990 base edition and supplements, 9886-13

Tax (income) returns of corporations, income and tax items by asset size and detailed industry, 1986, annual rpt, 8304-4; 8304-21

Tax (income) returns of partnerships, income statement items by industry group, 1986, annual article, 8302-2.903

Tax (income) returns of sole proprietorships, income statement items, by industry group, 1987, annual article, 8302-2.904; 8302-2.921

Transportation census, 1987: trucks, by detailed characteristics, miles traveled, and type of product carried, State rpt series, 2573-1

Wholesale trade census, 1987: employment, establishments, finances, and operations, by SIC 2- to 4-digit kind of business, MSA, county, and city, State rpt series, 2405-1

Wholesale trade sales, inventories, purchases, and gross margins, by SIC 2- to 3-digit kind of business and form of ownership, 1988, annual rpt, 2413-13

see also Carpets and rugs
see also Clothing and clothing industry
see also Cotton
see also Natural fibers
see also Silk

see also Synthetic fibers and fabrics
see also Wool and wool trade
see also By Industry in the "Index by Categories"
see also under By Commodity in the "Index by Categories"

Thackray, Richard I.
"Comparison of Detection Efficiency on an Air Traffic Control Monitoring Task with and Without Computer Aiding", 7506-10.56

Thailand
Agricultural and food production and indexes, total and for selected commodities, by country, 1970s-88, annual rpt, 1524-12

Agricultural policy impacts on economic dev, with background data for 6 developing countries, 1960s-86, 1528-283

Agricultural production, prices, and trade, by country, 1960s-89, annual world region rpt, 1524-4.2

Agricultural trade of US, by detailed commodity and country, 1988, semiannual rpt, 1522-4

Agricultural trade of US with Asia, Middle East, and North Africa, by commodity and country, 1962-86, 1528-277

AID activities and funding by project and function, FY90, and developing countries summary socioeconomic data from 1960s, annual rpt, 9904-4.6

AID economic aid to developing countries, obligations and disbursements by country, quarterly rpt, 9912-4

AID loans repayment status and terms by program and country, and status of predecessor agency loans, quarterly rpt, 9912-3

Bearings (antifriction) from 9 countries, injury to US industry from foreign subsidized and less than fair value imports, investigation with background financial and operating data, 1989 rpt, 9886-19.65

Economic and military aid and loans from US and intl agencies, by program and country, FY46-87, annual rpt, 9914-5

Economic conditions in Communist, OECD, and selected other countries, 1960s-88, annual rpt, 9114-4

Economic conditions, income, production, prices, employment, and trade, 1988 periodic country rpt, 2046-4.7

Economic conditions, income, production, prices, employment, and trade, 1989 periodic country rpt, 2046-4.55

Economic conditions, policy, and trade practices, by country, 1986-88, annual rpt, 21384-5

Economic indicators of developing countries, problem debtors compared to other borrowers, by country, 1973-84, 1528-285

Economic, social, political, and geographic summary data, by country, 1989, annual factbook, 9114-2

Exports and imports of US, by commodity and country, 1970-87, world area rpt, 9116-1.2

Exports and imports of US, by selected country, country group, and commodity group, 1988, annual rpt, 2044-37

Human rights conditions in 170 countries, 1988, annual rpt, 21384–3

Imports of goods, services, and investment from US, trade barriers, impacts, and US actions, by country, 1988, annual rpt, 444–2

Labor conditions, union coverage, and work accidents, 1989 annual country rpt, 6366–4.30

Military aid of US, arms sales, and training programs costs and budget requests, by program, world region, and country, FY88-90, annual rpt, 7144–13

Military spending, arms trade, and force strengths, with govt spending and population, by country, 1977-87, annual rpt, 9824–1

Minerals production, reserves, and industry role in domestic economy and world supply, 1988 country rpt, 5606–1.17

Minerals Yearbook, 1987, Vol 3: foreign country reviews of production, trade, and policy, by commodity, annual rpt, 5604–35

Minerals Yearbook, 1987, Vol 3 preprints: foreign country review of production, trade, and policy, by commodity, annual rpt, 5604–23.69

Multinatl US firms and foreign affiliates finances and operations, by industry of parent firm and affiliate, world area, and country, preliminary 1987, annual rpt, 2704–5

Older persons population and selected characteristics, 1980s and projected to 2020, country rpt, 2326–19.3

Population size, growth rates, and components of change, by country, projected 1989-2020 and trends from 1950, biennial rpt, 2324–9

Rice acreage, supply, use, and exports by country, for Thailand, 1960s-90, article, 1561–8.904

Rice market activities, prices, inspections, sales, trade, supply, and use, for US and selected foreign markets, weekly rpt, 1313–8

Rice production, consumption, exports, and subsidies of Thailand, 1982-86, 1528–286

Rice production, consumption, exports, and subsidies of Thailand, 1982-87, article, 1522–3.915

Tobacco and cigarette production, trade, and use, for Thailand, 1984-88, article, 1925–16.901

UN voting record and share of votes in agreement with US, by issue, country, and world area, 1988, annual rpt, 7004–18

see also under By Foreign Country in the "Index by Categories"

Thallium
see Metals and metal industries

Theater
County Business Patterns, 1987: employment, establishments, and payroll, by SIC 2- to 4-digit industry and county, annual State rpt series, 2326–8

Natl Endowment for Arts activities and grants, FY88, annual rpt, 9564–3

Service industries census, 1987: establishments, receipts, employment, and payroll, by SIC 2- to 4-digit kind of business, MSA, county, and city, State rpt series, 2391–1

Theft
see Robbery and theft

Theisen, Gary
"Indonesia: The Bogor Institute of Agriculture", 9916–1.68

Theology
see Religion

Therapy
see Chemotherapy
see Occupational therapy
see Physical therapy
see Rehabilitation of the disabled
see Respiratory therapy
see Speech pathology and audiology

Thermal power
see Electric power and heat cogeneration
see Geothermal resources

Thibodaux, La.
see also under By SMSA or MSA in the "Index by Categories"

Third World countries
see Developing countries

Thomas, Paul R.
"International Competitiveness of U.S. Copper Production, 1981-87", 5606–5.7

Thombs, Dennis L.
"Review of PCP Abuse Trends and Perceptions", 4042–3.931

Thompson, Andrew F.
"Who Does Rate Swaps?", 9312–1.902

Thompson, Cynthia
"Compensation for Death and Dismemberment", 6722–1.944

Thompson, Frances E.
"Where's the Fat? Where's the Fiber?", 1004–16.1

Thompson, Michael T.
"Forest Statistics for Central Georgia, 1989", 1206–26.10
"Forest Statistics for Georgia, 1989", 1206–26.13
"Forest Statistics for North Georgia, 1989", 1206–26.11

Thompson, Nancy B.
"Status of Loggerhead, *Caretta caretta;* Kemp's Ridley, *Lepidochelys kempi;* and Green, *Chelonia mydas,* Sea Turtles in U.S. Waters", 2162–1.902

Thompson, Thomas A.
"Estimates of Restaurant Tipping: 1983-86", 8304–8.1

Thompson, W. Douglas
"Hypertension, Pregnancy, and Risk of Breast Cancer", 4472–1.927

Thor, Eric P.
"One Year Later: The Farm Credit System Assistance Board", 1004–16.1

Thorium
see Radioactive materials

Thorn, Magnus
"Trends in Survival from Malignant Melanoma: Remarkable Improvement in 23 Years", 4472–1.912

Thornberry, Owen T.
"Health Characteristics of Workers by Occupation and Sex: U.S., 1983-85", 4146–8.170

Thornton, Daniel L.
"Link Between M1 and the Monetary Base in the 1980s", 9391–1.923
"Tests of Covered Interest Rate Parity", 9391–1.920

Thorpe, Kenneth E.
"Are the Diagnosis-Related Group Case Weights Compressed?", 4652–1.922

Thousand Oaks, Calif.
see also under By City in the "Index by Categories"

Thrift institutions
see Credit unions
see Savings institutions

Throat disorders
see Nose and throat disorders

Throop, Adrian W.
"Fiscal Policy, the Dollar, and International Trade: A Synthesis of Two Views", 9393–8.908
"Macroeconometric Model of the U.S. Economy", 9393–10.4
"Reagan Fiscal Policy and the Dollar", 9393–8.907

Thurman, Jane L.
"Hydrologic Data for Experimental Agricultural Watersheds in the U.S., 1978-79", 1704–1

Thurston, Linda
"Federal Offshore Statistics: 1987, Leasing, Exploration, Production, and Revenues", 5734–3

Tibbs, Belva D.
"Profile of Small or Rural Hospitals 1980-86", 25148–42

Tice, Helen S.
"Government Transactions", 2706–6.5

Tichler, J.
"Radioactive Materials Released from Nuclear Power Plants, Annual Report, 1986", 9634–1

Ticks
see Animal diseases and zoonoses
see Infective and parasitic diseases

Tidal waves
see Tsunamis

Tides and currents
Alaska OCS environmental conditions and oil dev impacts, compilation of papers, series, 2176–1

Coastal and estuarine environmental conditions, research results and methodology, series, 2176–7

Coastal currents, for US by ocean region, monthly rpt, 2182–5

Coastal tidal currents, daily time and velocity by station for North America and Asia, forecast 1990, annual rpts, 2174–1

Coastal tide height and time daily at points worldwide, forecast 1990, annual rpt series, 2174–2

Estuary environmental conditions and mgmt, for individual areas, conf series, 2146–6

Florida straits coastal currents, temperatures, and salinity, series, 2146–7

Mariners Weather Log, quarterly journal, 2152–8

San Francisco Bay fish distribution by species, and water outflow, 1973-82, 2168–113

Tilley, Daniel S.
"Oklahoma Net-Pen Catfish Production: Estimated Attainable Production Levels and Their Associated Costs", 1561–15.901

Timber
see Forests and forestry
see Lumber industry and products

Tax revenues, by level of govt, type of tax, State, and selected large county, quarterly rpt, 2462–3

Toxicology Natl Program research and testing activities, FY87 and planned FY88, annual rpt, 4044–16

VA health care centers canteen services discontinuing tobacco sales, impacts on finances, FY83-FY88, hearing, 21768–49

Wholesale trade census, 1987: employment, establishments, finances, and operations, by SIC 2- to 4-digit kind of business, MSA, county, and city, State rpt series, 2405–1

see also Smoking

see also By Industry in the "Index by Categories"

see also under By Commodity in the "Index by Categories"

Tobin, James

"Natural Gas Production in the Post-NGPA Decade", 3162–4.904

Toder, Eric

"Simulating the Revenue Effects of Changes in the Taxation of Capital Gains", 26306–3.106

Togo

Agricultural and food production and indexes, total and for selected commodities, by country, 1970s-88, annual rpt, 1524–12

Agricultural exports of Africa by commodity, and relation to economic conditions and other factors, by country, 1960s-87, 1528–280

Agricultural trade of US, by detailed commodity and country, 1988, semiannual rpt, 1522–4

AID activities and funding by project and function, FY90, and developing countries summary socioeconomic data from 1960s, annual rpt, 9904–4.5

AID economic aid to developing countries, obligations and disbursements by country, quarterly rpt, 9912–4

Economic and military aid and loans from US and intl agencies, by program and country, FY46-87, annual rpt, 9914–5

Economic, social, political, and geographic summary data, by country, 1989, annual factbook, 9114–2

Human rights conditions in 170 countries, 1988, annual rpt, 21384–3

Military aid of US, arms sales, and training programs costs and budget requests, by program, world region, and country, FY88-90, annual rpt, 7144–13

Military spending, arms trade, and force strengths, with govt spending and population, by country, 1977-87, annual rpt, 9824–1

Minerals Yearbook, 1987, Vol 3 preprints: foreign country review of production, trade, and policy, by commodity, annual rpt, 5604–23.82

Population size, growth rates, and components of change, by country, projected 1989-2020 and trends from 1950, biennial rpt, 2324–9

UN voting record and share of votes in agreement with US, by issue, country, and world area, 1988, annual rpt, 7004–18

see also under By Foreign Country in the "Index by Categories"

Toiletries

see Cosmetics and toiletries

Toledo, Ohio

Wages by occupation, and benefits for office and plant workers, 1988 survey, periodic MSA rpt, 6785–11.3

see also under By City and By SMSA or MSA in the "Index by Categories"

Tolls

Hwy funding, costs, and completion status of Federal-aid system, by State, as of June 1989, semiannual rpt, 7552–5

Hwy receipts by source, and spending by function, by level of govt and State, 1988, annual rpt, 7554–1.3

Panama Canal Commission finances and activities, with Canal traffic and local govt operations, FY88, annual rpt, 9664–3

St Lawrence Seaway ship, cargo, and passenger traffic, and toll revenue, 1988 and trends from 1959, annual rpt, 7744–2

Tolson, John P.

"Land Use and the Nation's Estuaries", 2176–7.4

Tomatoes

see Vegetables and vegetable products

Tomita, Dianne K.

"Drug Utilization in the U.S., 1987: Ninth Annual Review", 4064–12

Tonga

Economic, social, political, and geographic summary data, by country, 1989, annual factbook, 9114–2

Human rights conditions in 170 countries, 1988, annual rpt, 21384–3

Military aid of US, arms sales, and training programs costs and budget requests, by program, world region, and country, FY88-90, annual rpt, 7144–13

Minerals Yearbook, 1987, Vol 3: foreign country reviews of production, trade, and policy, by commodity, annual rpt, 5604–35

Population size, growth rates, and components of change, by country, projected 1989-2020 and trends from 1950, biennial rpt, 2324–9

see also under By Foreign Country in the "Index by Categories"

Toniolo, Paolo

"Calorie-Providing Nutrients and Risk of Breast Cancer", 4472–1.906

Tonn, Bruce E.

"Energy Savings in New, Low-Rise Multifamily Buildings: Model Conservation Standards in Tacoma, Washington", 3308–92

Tonopah, Nev.

Wages by occupation, for office and plant workers, 1988 survey, periodic MSA rpt, 6785–3.1

Tool and die industry

see Machines and machinery industry

Tools

County Business Patterns, 1987: employment, establishments, and payroll, by SIC 2- to 4-digit industry and county, annual State rpt series, 2326–8

DOD prime contract awards, by detailed procurement category, FY85-88, annual rpt, 3544–18

Employment, earnings, and hours, by SIC 1- to 4-digit industry, monthly 1983-Feb 1989, annual rpt, 6744–4

Exports of US, detailed commodities by country, monthly rpt, 2422–3

Imports of US, detailed Schedule A commodities by country, monthly rpt, 2422–2

Imports of US given duty-free treatment for value of US material sent abroad, and impacts on US industry and employment, by commodity and country, 1987, annual rpt, 9884–14

Injuries from use of consumer products and related activities, by victim age and sex, 1988, annual rpt, 9164–7

Injuries from use of consumer products, by severity, victim age, and detailed product, 1988, annual rpt, 9164–6

Injuries from use of consumer products, related deaths and costs, and recalls by brand, by product type, FY87, annual rpt, 9164–2

Labor productivity, indexes of output, hours, and employment by SIC 2- to 4-digit industry, 1963-87, annual rpt, 6824–1.3

Manufacturers finances and operations, by SIC 2- to 4-digit industry, forecast 1989 and trends from 1950s, annual rpt, 2044–28

Manufacturing annual survey, 1986: financial and operating data, by SIC 2- to 4-digit industry, series, 2506–15

Manufacturing census, 1987: financial and operating data, for SIC 4-digit industries by product, preliminary rpt, 2491–1.55; 2491–1.63

Occupational injury and illness rates, by SIC 2- to 4-digit industry, 1987, annual rpt, 6844–1

OECD trade, total and for 4 major countries, and US trade by country, by commodity, 1970-87, world area rpt series, 9116–1

Price indexes (producer), by stage of processing and detailed commodity, monthly rpt, 6762–6

Price indexes (producer), by stage of processing and detailed commodity, monthly 1988, annual rpt, 6764–2

see also Agricultural machinery and equipment

see also Hardware

see also Household supplies and utensils

see also Lawn and garden equipment

see also Machines and machinery industry

see also under By Commodity in the "Index by Categories"

Toomey, Kathleen E.

"Sexually Transmitted Diseases and Native Americans: Trends in Reported Gonorrhea and Syphilis Morbidity, 1984-88", 4042–3.955

Topeka, Kans.

Housing vacancy rates for single and multifamily units and mobile homes, by city and ZIP code, 1989, annual MSA rpt, 9304–22.6

see also under By City and By SMSA or MSA in the "Index by Categories"

Topography

Charting and Geodetic Service of Natl Ocean Service activities and funding, by State, FY89-90, biennial rpt, 2174–10

Foreign countries *Background Notes*, summary social, political, and economic data, series, 7006–2

Foreign countries economic, social, political, and geographic summary data, by country, 1989, annual factbook, 9114–2

Puerto Rico land area and topography, 1986 hearings, 21448–39

see also Arid zones
see also Cartography
see also Coastal areas
see also Lakes and lakeshores
see also Land area
see also Rivers and waterways
see also Seashores
see also Water area

Tornadoes
see Storms

Tornberg, Sven A.
"Cancer Incidence and Cancer Mortality in Relation to Serum Cholesterol", 4472–1.936

Toronto, Canada
Fruit and vegetable shipments, and arrivals in US and Canada cities, by mode of transport and State and country of origin, 1988, annual rpt, 1311–4.1

Torpedoes
DOD budget, weapons acquisition costs by system and service branch, FY89-91, annual rpt, 3504–2

Torrance, Calif.
see also under By City in the "Index by Categories"

Torts
Court caseloads for Federal district, appeals, and bankruptcy courts, by type of suit and offense, circuit, and district, quarterly rpt, 18202–1

Court civil and criminal caseloads for Federal district, appeals, and special courts, June 1989, annual rpt, 18204–2; 18204–8

Product liability torts dispositions, awards, case processing time, and plaintiff injury severity and other characteristics, 1983-85, GAO rpt, 26121–317

US attorneys civil cases, by type and disposition, FY88, annual rpt, 6004–2.5

Touchstone, R. Mark
"Comparison of Detection Efficiency on an Air Traffic Control Monitoring Task with and Without Computer Aiding", 7506–10.56

Tourist travel
see Travel and tourism

Towels
see Household supplies and utensils

Town planning
see City and town planning

Towner, Roy R.
"International Strategic Minerals Inventory Summary Report: Titanium", 5666–21.7

Towns
see Central cities
see Cities
see Rural areas
see Suburbs
see Urban areas

Toxic substances
see Dioxins
see Hazardous substances
see Hazardous waste and disposal
see Pesticides
see Poisoning and drug reaction

Toys and games
County Business Patterns, 1987: employment, establishments, and payroll, by SIC 2- to 4-digit industry and county, annual State rpt series, 2326–8

CPI by component for US city average, and by region, population size, and for 27 metro areas, monthly rpt, 6762–2

Employment, earnings, and hours, by selected SIC 1- to 4-digit industry, State, and for 262 MSAs, 1972-87, 6748–81

Employment, earnings, and hours, by SIC 1- to 4-digit industry, monthly 1983-Feb 1989, annual rpt, 6744–4

Employment of minorities and women, by occupation, SIC 1- to 3- digit industry, State, and MSA, 1986, annual rpt, 9244–1

Exports of US, detailed commodities by country, monthly rpt, 2422–3

Finances and operations, by SIC 2- to 4-digit industry, forecast 1989 with trends from 1950s, annual rpt, 2044–28

Import restraint elimination, impact on domestic industry production and employment, by selected commodity, 1986-88, 9886–4.144

Imports of footwear, toys, and games from PRC and other countries, 1983-88, article, 9882–2.901

Imports of US, detailed Schedule A commodities by country, monthly rpt, 2422–2

Imports of US given duty-free treatment for value of US material sent abroad, and impacts on US industry and employment, by commodity and country, 1987, annual rpt, 9884–14

Injuries from use of consumer products and related activities, by victim age and sex, 1988, annual rpt, 9164–7

Injuries from use of consumer products, by severity, victim age, and detailed product, 1988, annual rpt, 9164–6

Injuries from use of consumer products, related deaths and costs, and recalls by brand, by product type, FY87, annual rpt, 9164–2

Manufacturing annual survey, 1986: financial and operating data, by SIC 2- to 4-digit industry, series, 2506–15

Manufacturing census, 1987: financial and operating data, for SIC 4-digit industries by product, preliminary rpt, 2491–1.81

Occupational injury and illness rates, by SIC 2- to 4-digit industry, 1987, annual rpt, 6844–1

OECD trade, total and for 4 major countries, and US trade by country, by commodity, 1970-87, world area rpt series, 9116–1

Pollution abatement capital and operating costs, by SIC 2-to 4-digit industry and State, 1986, annual Current Industrial Rpt, 2506–3.6

Price indexes (producer), by stage of processing and detailed commodity, monthly rpt, 6762–6

Price indexes (producer), by stage of processing and detailed commodity, monthly 1988, annual rpt, 6764–2

Retail trade census, 1987: employment, establishments, sales, and payroll, by SIC 2- to 4-digit kind of business, MSA, county, and city, State rpt series, 2397–1

Science, engineering, and technical employment in manufacturing, by field, occupation, and industry, 1986, triennial rpt, 9627–23

Wholesale trade census, 1987: employment, establishments, finances, and operations, by SIC 2- to 4-digit kind of business, MSA, county, and city, State rpt series, 2405–1

see also Sporting goods
see also under By Commodity in the "Index by Categories"

Trace metals
Acid rain distribution, pH levels, and composition, monitoring results by site, 1987, annual rpt, 9194–20

Alaska OCS environmental conditions and oil dev impacts, compilation of papers, series, 2176–1

Arkansas water quality in streams and rivers, by monitoring site, 1975-85, 5668–83

California water quality, trace metal concentrations in San Joaquin river bed sediment, 1985, 5668–91

Coastal and estuarine pollutant concentrations in fish, shellfish, and environment, series, 2176–3

Coastal and estuarine pollutant discharges, by source, pollutant type, and location, series, 2176–4

Environmental quality and protection programs, and intl issues, 1988 annual rpt, 484–1

Estuary environmental conditions and mgmt, for individual areas, conf series, 2146–6

Fish hazardous substances toxicity levels, by detailed compound, 1989 rpt, 9238–68; 9238–69

Great Lakes basin pollutant discharges, sources, and control program activities, 1987, biennial rpt, 14644–1

Health effects of selected pollutants, concentrations in food and environment, sources, and human intake, methodology and data needs, series, 9186–9

Health effects of selected pollutants, concentrations in food and environment, sources, human intake, and regulation, series, 9186–8

Housewares (ceramic) lead and cadmium levels, FDA import inspection activity by country, and food safety funding and staff, 1983-88, hearing, 21368–108

Hudson-Raritan estuary pollution levels, and effects of refrigeration on pollutant samples, 1983-84, 2168–109

Hudson-Raritan River basin pollutant levels and sources, model description and results, 1880s-1982, 2178–22

Industrial hazardous substances releases and reduction methods under EPA regulation, by chemical, source, industry, and location, 1987, annual rpt, 9234–6

Lake Ontario eutrophication and pollutant levels, by contaminant type and site, 1967-85, 14648–22

Oil and gas OCS production water discharges, and impacts on Gulf of Mexico coastal habitats, 1983-88, 5738–10

Oregon coastal and estuarine pollutant levels, by pollutant and location, 1960s-87, 2178–23

Waste (hazardous) mgmt, effectiveness of alternative technologies, 1989 conf papers, biennial rpt, 9184-19

Water chemistry, environmental impacts, analytic methods, and quality and mgmt issues, 1989 rpt, 5668-96

Water supply and quality in streams and lakes, and groundwater levels in wells, by drainage basin, 1986, annual State rpt series, 5666-23

Water supply and quality in streams and lakes, and groundwater levels in wells, by drainage basin, 1987, annual State rpt series, 5666-10

Water supply and quality in streams and lakes, and groundwater levels in wells, by drainage basin, 1988, annual State rpt series, 5666-16

see also Lead poisoning and pollution

see also Mercury pollution

Tractors

see Agricultural machinery and equipment

Trade

see Agricultural exports and imports

see Arms trade

see Balance of payments

see Coal exports and imports

see Common markets and free trade areas

see Contraband

see Customs administration

see East-West trade

see Energy exports and imports

see Foreign competition

see Foreign trade

see Foreign trade promotion

see International assistance

see Interstate commerce

see Marketing

see Military assistance

see Motor vehicle exports and imports

see Natural gas exports and imports

see Petroleum exports and imports

see Retail trade

see Smuggling

see Tariffs and foreign trade controls

see Trade adjustment assistance

see Trade agreements

see Wholesale trade

Trade adjustment assistance

Assistance programs under Ways and Means Committee jurisdiction, finances and operations, FY70s-88, annual rpt, 21784-11

Eligibility of workers, petitions by disposition, selected industry, union, and State, monthly rpt, 6402-13

Employment and Training Admin activities, funding, and participant characteristics, by program, FY80-86, 6408-71

Fed Govt financial and nonfinancial domestic aid, 1989 base edition with supplements, annual listing, 104-5

Trade agreements

Agricultural trade among western hemisphere countries, and US duty-free imports, with listing of trade disputes and outcomes, 1960s-85, 1528-278

Arms sales of US, foreign conditions on sales and impacts on US industry, with data by industry group and country, 1988 annual rpt, 104-25

Bilateral and multilateral treaties and other agreements in force, by country, as of Jan 1989, annual listing, 7004-1

Canada-US trade agreement impacts on New England States trade, with data by industry, commodity, and State, 1987, article, 9373-2.902

Caribbean Basin exports to OECD members, and US imports under preferential treatment programs, by commodity, 1980s-87, 2048-138

Caribbean Basin Initiative investment incentives, economic impacts, with finances and employment by country, 1984-88, 2048-141

Coal production, trade, and govt subsidies, by country and country group, 1973-87 and projected to 2000, 2048-144

Economic conditions, and trade devs and balances, with data by selected country and country group, monthly rpt, 9882-14

Export and import agreements, negotiations, anticompetitive investigations, and related legislation, FY86-88, annual rpt, 444-1

Exports and imports, trade agreements and relations, and USITC investigations, 1988, annual rpt, 9884-5

GATT agricultural trade reform proposals in Uruguay round, impact on farm production and income, 1983-87, article, 9381-1.908

GATT agricultural trade reform proposals in Uruguay round, price and income effects projected to 1995 with background data from 1970s, article, 9381-1.904

GATT Standards Code info activities of Natl Inst of Standards and Technology, and proposed standards by agency and country, 1988, annual rpt, 2214-6

Grain exports to USSR and PRC under long-term bilateral agreements, 1976-88, 26123-227

Grain exports under long-term bilateral and countertrade agreements, by major exporting and importing country, 1975-87, GAO rpt, 26123-229

Import restraint elimination, impact on domestic industry production and employment, by selected commodity, 1986-88, 9886-4.144

OECD countries imports covered by non-tariff trade barriers, by barrier type and commodity group, 1981-86, article, 9391-1.906

Overseas Business Reports: economic conditions, investment and export opportunities, and trade practices, country market research rpt series, 2046-6

Soviet Union grain imports from US, 1970s-88 and commitments through 1990, FAS press release, 1928-10

Steel export ceilings under voluntary restraint agreements, by country and product, with Western US steel industry impact, 1989 rpt, 9886-4.136

Steel import voluntary restraint agreements, ITA review of requests for restraint waivers because of supply shortages, 1985-88, GAO rpt, 26123-240

Steel imports from EC and other countries, impact of voluntary restraint agreements on US user industries exports, sales, and prices, 1989 rpt, 9886-4.138

Steel imports of US under voluntary restraint agreement, by product, customs district, and country, with US industry operating data, monthly rpt, 9882-13

Steel imports of US under voluntary restraint agreements, with industry finances, operations, and foreign comparisons, various periods 1979-89, 21788-182

Textile Agreement Category System import classification codes, correlation with TSUSA, 1989 annual rpt, 2044-31

Textile imports under Multifiber Arrangement by product and country, and status of bilateral agreements, 1986-88, annual rpt, 9884-18

USITC activities, investigations, and rpts, FY88, annual rpt, 9884-1

see also Common markets and free trade areas

see also Tariffs and foreign trade controls

Trade balances

see Balance of payments

see Foreign trade

Trade fairs

see Exhibitions and trade fairs

Trade investigations

see Government investigations

Trade promotion

see Foreign trade promotion

Trade regulation

see Antitrust law

see Consumer protection

see Copyright

see Fuel allocation

see Government and business

see Licenses and permits

see Patents

see Price regulation

see Tariffs and foreign trade controls

see Trade adjustment assistance

see Trademarks

Trade unions

see Labor unions

Trademarks

Applications, grants, fees, and litigation, for patents and trademarks, FY69-88, annual rpt, 2244-1

Court civil and criminal caseloads for Federal district, appeals, and special courts, June 1989, annual rpt, 18204-2; 18204-8

Criminal sentences for Federal offenses, guidelines by offense and circumstances, 1989 rpt, 17668-1

Registrations and renewals of trademarks, and Patent and Trademark Office activities, 1790-1988, 2248-2

Statistical Abstract of US, social, political, and economic data, 1790-2025, comprehensive annual compilation, 2324-1.3

Traffic accident fatalities

Accidents (fatal), circumstances, and characteristics of persons and vehicles involved, 1988, semiannual rpt, 7762-11

Accidents (fatal), deaths, and rates, by circumstances, characteristics of persons and vehicles involved, and location, 1987, annual rpt, 7764-10

Child death rates, by age, sex, race, and cause, for US and compared to 8 OECD countries, 1985 and trends from 1900, 4147-3.27

Child traffic accident deaths and survivors, by restraint type and use, age, and seat position, 1982-87, 7768-104

Child traffic accident deaths, effects of State laws mandating safety restraint use, 1978-88, 7768-108

Exports of US, detailed commodities by country, monthly rpt, 2422-3

Fed Govt procurement contract awards, by procurement and contractor type, agency, State, and for top 100 contractors, quarterly rpt, 102-6

Finances and operations of Class I rail and motor carriers, detailed data, 1987, annual rpt series, 9486-6

Finances and operations of Class I rail and motor carriers, detailed data, 1988, annual rpt series, 9486-5

Finances and operations of transit systems, by mode of transport, size of fleet, and for 432 systems, 1986, annual rpt, 7884-4

Finances, operations, vehicles, equipment, accidents, and energy use, by mode of transport, 1955-88, annual rpt, 7304-2

Financial statements for manufacturing, mining, and trade corporations, by selected SIC 2- to 3-digit industry, quarterly rpt, 2502-1

Foreign countries economic, social, political, and geographic summary data, by country, 1989, annual factbook, 9114-2

Foreign direct investment in US, major transactions by type, industry, country, and US location, 1987, annual rpt, 2044-20

Foreign direct investment of US, by selected industry group and world area, 1986-88, annual article, 2702-1.930

Freight (waterborne domestic and foreign) by commodity, traffic, and passengers, by port and waterway, 1987, annual rpt, 3754-3

Imports, exports, and employment impacts, by SIC 2- to 4-digit industry and commodity, quarterly rpt, 2322-2

Imports of US, detailed Schedule A commodities by country, monthly rpt, 2422-2

Imports of US given duty-free treatment for value of US material sent abroad, and impacts on US industry and employment, by commodity and country, 1987, annual rpt, 9884-14

Industry finances and operations, by SIC 2- to 4-digit industry, forecast 1989 and trends from 1950s, annual rpt, 2044-28

Input-output structure of US economy, detailed interindustry transactions for 84 industries, and components of final demand, 1983, annual article, 2702-1.909

Manufacturing annual survey, 1986: financial and operating data, by SIC 2- to 4-digit industry, series, 2506-15

Manufacturing annual survey, 1986: production indexes and exports by SIC 2-digit industry and State, with comparisons to 1985, model results, series, 2506-16

Manufacturing census, 1987: financial and operating data, for SIC 4-digit industries by product, preliminary industry rpt series, 2491-1

Manufacturing industries production, shipments, inventories, orders, and pollution control costs, periodic Current Industrial Rpt series, 2506-3

Multinatl US firms and foreign affiliates finances and operations, by industry of parent firm and affiliate, world area, and country, preliminary 1987, annual rpt, 2704-5

Natl income and product accounts and components, *Survey of Current Business*, monthly rpt, 2702-1.21; 2702-1.27

New York and northeastern New Jersey employment by industry div, unemployment, and consumer price changes by selected commodity, 1978-June 1989, press release, 6926-2.40

Occupational injury and illness rates, by SIC 2- to 4-digit industry, 1987, annual rpt, 6844-1

OECD trade, total and for 4 major countries, and US trade by country, by commodity, 1970-87, world area rpt series, 9116-1

Pollution abatement capital and operating costs, by SIC 2-to 4-digit industry and State, 1986, annual Current Industrial Rpt, 2506-3.6

Price indexes (producer), by stage of processing and detailed commodity, monthly rpt, 6762-6

Price indexes (producer), by stage of processing and detailed commodity, monthly 1988, annual rpt, 6764-2

Science, engineering, and technical employment in manufacturing, by field, occupation, and industry, 1986, triennial rpt, 9627-23

Science, engineering, and technical employment in transportation, utilities, and retail and wholesale trade, by field, occupation, and industry, 1985, triennial rpt, 9627-32

SEC registration, firms required to file annual rpts, as of Sept 1988, annual listing, 9734-5

Small business establishments, employment, and financial ratios, by SIC 1- to 2-digit industry and State, late 1960s-87, 9768-19

Small business finances, operations, owner and employee characteristics, and Federal contracts, 1980s-88, annual rpt, 9764-6

Statistical Abstract of US, social, political, and economic data, 1790-2025, comprehensive annual compilation, 2324-1.3

Stock (common) prices and yields, current data and annual trends, monthly rpt, 23842-1.5

Tariff Schedule of US, classifications and rates of duty by detailed imported commodity, 1990 base edition and supplements, 9886-13

Tax (income) returns of corporations, income and tax items by asset size and detailed industry, 1986, annual rpt, 8304-4; 8304-21

Tax (income) returns of partnerships, income statement items by industry group, 1986, annual article, 8302-2.903

Tax (income) returns of sole proprietorships, income statement items, by industry group, 1987, annual article, 8302-2.904; 8302-2.921

Technology-intensive manufacturing methods use and plans, with data by technology, selected industry, and firm and market characteristics, 1988 survey, 2508-1

Wage and benefit changes from collective bargaining and mgmt decisions, by industry div, monthly rpt, 6782-1

Wholesale trade census, 1987: employment, establishments, finances, and operations, by SIC 2- to 4-digit kind of business, MSA, county, and city, State rpt series, 2405-1

see also Air travel
see also Aircraft
see also Airlines
see also Automobile repair and maintenance
see also Automobiles
see also Aviation accidents and safety
see also Bicycles
see also Boats and boating
see also Bridges and tunnels
see also Buses
see also Canals
see also Census of Transportation
see also Civil aviation
see also Commuting
see also Drivers licenses
see also Federal aid to transportation
see also Ferries
see also Freight
see also Gasoline
see also General aviation
see also Harbors and ports
see also Hazardous substances transport
see also Helicopters
see also Highways, streets, and roads
see also Inland water transportation
see also Marine accidents and safety
see also Military vehicles
see also Motor fuels
see also Motor vehicle exhaust
see also Motor vehicle exports and imports
see also Motor vehicle fleets
see also Motor vehicle industry
see also Motor vehicle registrations
see also Motor vehicle rental
see also Motor vehicle safety devices
see also Motor vehicle theft
see also Motorcycles
see also Parking facilities
see also Passenger ships
see also Pipelines
see also Railroad accidents and safety
see also Railroad equipment and vehicles
see also Railroads
see also Recreational vehicles
see also Rivers and waterways
see also School busing
see also Shipbuilding and repairing
see also Ships and shipping
see also Subways
see also Tanker ships
see also Taxicabs
see also Traffic accident fatalities
see also Traffic accidents and safety
see also Transportation accidents and safety
see also Transportation energy use
see also Travel agencies
see also Travel and tourism
see also Trucks and trucking industry
see also Urban transportation
see also under By Commodity in the "Index by Categories"
see also under By Industry in the "Index by Categories"

Transportation census
see Census of Transportation

Transportation Department
see Department of Transportation

Farm production itemized costs, by farm sales size and region, 1988, annual rpt, 1614–3

Farm sector finances, income sources, expenses by type, assets, debts, and ratios, 1983-87, annual rpt, 1544–19

Fed Govt motor vehicle fleet costs and operating data, by agency, FY87, annual rpt, 9454–9

Finances and inventory of truck and warehouse services, by SIC 2- to 4-digit industry, 1988 survey, annual rpt, 2413–14

Finances and operations, by SIC 2- to 4-digit industry, forecast 1989 with trends from 1950s, annual rpt, 2044–28

Finances and operations for carriers of property, by region and firm, quarterly rpt, 9482–5

Finances and operations of interstate carriers, by district, 1987, annual rpt, 9486–6.2; 9486–6.3

Finances, operations, vehicles, equipment, accidents, and energy use, by mode of transport, 1955-88, annual rpt, 7304–2

Household goods carriers financial and operating data by firm, quarterly rpt, 9482–14

Household goods carriers performance and disposition of damage claims, for selected carriers, 1988, annual rpt, 9484–11

Households with autos and trucks available, by location, 1985, biennial rpt, 2485–12

Households with autos and trucks available, MSA surveys, series, 2485–6

Hwy Statistics, detailed data by State, 1988, annual rpt, 7554–1

Hwy Statistics, summary data by State, 1987-88, annual rpt, 7554–24

Imports of US, detailed Schedule A commodities by country, monthly rpt, 2422–2

Labor productivity, indexes of output, hours, and employment by SIC 2- to 4-digit industry, 1963-87, annual rpt, 6824–1.4

Manufacturing annual survey, 1986: financial and operating data, by SIC 2- to 4-digit industry, series, 2506–15

Manufacturing census, 1987: financial and operating data, for SIC 4-digit industries by product, preliminary rpt, 2491–1.75

Natl income and product accounts and components, *Survey of Current Business*, monthly rpt, 2702–1.21; 2702–1.22

Occupational injury and illness rates, by SIC 2- to 4-digit industry, 1987, annual rpt, 6844–1

OECD trade, total and for 4 major countries, and US trade by country, by commodity, 1970-87, world area rpt series, 9116–1

Pollution (air) levels for 5 pollutants, by detailed source and State, 1986, annual rpt, 9194–7

Price indexes (producer), by stage of processing and detailed commodity, monthly rpt, 6762–6

Price indexes (producer), by stage of processing and detailed commodity, monthly 1988, annual rpt, 6764–2

Rental of autos and trucks, industry receipts, 1988, annual rpt, 2413–8

Revenue, charges, and employment of freight carriers, by transport mode, 1986, annual rpt, 7704–7.1

Safety of domestic and foreign autos, crash test results by model, model years 1984-88, 7768–111

Safety of domestic and foreign autos, crash test results by model, press release series, 7766–7

Sales and prices for domestic and import autos and trucks, and auto production and inventories, 1988 model year, annual article, 2702–1.901

Science, engineering, and technical employment in transportation, utilities, and retail and wholesale trade, by field, occupation, and industry, 1985, triennial rpt, 9627–32

Statistical Abstract of US, social, political, and economic data, 1790-2025, comprehensive annual compilation, 2324–1.3

Tax (excise) collections of IRS, by source, quarterly rpt, 8302–1

Tax (income) returns of corporations, income and tax items by asset size and detailed industry, 1986, annual rpt, 8304–4; 8304–21

Tax (income) returns of partnerships, income statement items by industry group, 1986, annual article, 8302–2.903

Tax (income) returns of sole proprietorships, income statement items, by industry group, 1987, annual article, 8302–2.904; 8302–2.921

Trailer shipments, exports, and firms, by trailer type, monthly Current Industrial Rpt, 2506–12.25

Urban areas traffic volume and detailed trip characteristics, by transport mode and city, 1950s-88, 7888–37

Wholesale trade census, 1987: employment, establishments, finances, and operations, by SIC 2- to 4-digit kind of business, MSA, county, and city, State rpt series, 2405–1

see also Freight

see also Motor vehicle industry

see also By Industry in the "Index by Categories"

Truett, Joe C.

"Environmental Characterization and Biological Utilization of the North Aleutian Shelf Nearshore Zone", 2176–1.26

"Evaluation of Environmental Information for the Unimak Pass Area, Alaska", 2176–1.24

Truk

see Micronesia Federated States

Truman, Harry S., Scholarship Foundation

Awards by student characteristics from 1977, and Foundation finances, FY88, annual rpt, 14314–1

Budget of US Appendix, obligations, appropriations, and personnel, by program and agency, FY90, annual rpt, 104–3

Budget of US, authoritative financial statements with appropriations, outlays, and receipts, by category and agency, FY88, annual rpt, 8104–2.2

Trust fund receipts by source, transfers, and investment holdings and transactions, monthly rpt, 14312–1

Trust funds

American Historical Assn financial statements, and membership by State, 1988, annual rpt, 29574–2

Assets of collective investment funds, instns involved, and accounts, by type of fund and holding, 1988, annual rpt, 13004–1.3

Assets of trusts under mgmt of banks, trust companies, and S&Ls, by type of asset and fund, selected firm, and State, 1988, annual rpt, 13004–1

County Business Patterns, 1987: employment, establishments, and payroll, by SIC 2- to 4-digit industry and county, annual State rpt series, 2326–8

Higher education instn endowment funds, for top 100 instns, FY86, annual rpt, 4824–2.25

Mortgage loan activity, by type of lender, loan, and mortgaged property, monthly press release, 5142–18

Mortgage loan activity, by type of lender, loan, and mortgaged property, quarterly press release, 5142–30

Science and engineering employment, by nonmanufacturing industry and field, 1987, triennial rpt, 9627–31

Tax (income) returns of individuals, detailed data, 1986, annual rpt, 8304–2

Tax (income) returns of partnerships, income statement items by industry group, 1986, annual article, 8302–2.903

see also Government trust funds

see also Pensions and pension funds

see also Unemployment trust funds

Trust Territory of the Pacific Islands

see Marshall Islands

see Micronesia Federated States

see Northern Mariana Islands

see Palau

see Territories of the U.S.

Tryon, A. E.

"Occupational Radiation Exposure from U.S. Naval Nuclear Propulsion Plants and Their Support Facilities, 1988", 3804–10

Tsui, Ted L.

"Avoid the Typhoon", 2152–8.901

Tsunamis

Intensity, time, location, and other characteristics of tsunamis, for US and territories, 1690-1988, 2158–52

Tuberculosis

Cases of TB and deaths, by patient characteristics, State, and city, 1987 and trends from 1953, annual rpt, 4204–10

Cattle TB cases and cooperative Federal-State eradication activities, by State, FY88, annual rpt, 1394–13

Deaths and rates, by cause, age, sex, marital status, race, and State, 1987, US Vital Statistics advance annual rpt, 4146–5.113

Deaths and rates, by detailed cause and demographic characteristics, 1986 and trends from 1900, US Vital Statistics annual rpt, 4144–2

Deaths and rates, by detailed location, cause, and demographic characteristics, 1987, US Vital Statistics annual rpt, 4144–3

Drug (isoniazid) treatment for tuberculosis, relation to hepatitis risk for pregnant and postpartum women, by age group, 1981-82 study, article, 4042–3.911

France and US hospital and long-term care beds, by facility type and ownership, 1981, 4147–5.4

Health condition and health care resources, use, and spending, 1950s-87, annual data compilation, 4144–11

HHS financial aid, by program, recipient, State, and city, FY88, annual regional listings, 4004–3

Indian Health Service facilities, funding, operations, and Indian health and other characteristics, 1950s-88, annual chartbook, 4084–1

Meat and poultry inspection for domestic use and export, and rejections by cause, by type of animal and product, FY88, annual rpt, 1374–3

Minority group TB cases, by age and race, 1987, article, 4042–3.962

Morbidity and Mortality Weekly Report, infectious notifiable disease cases by age and State, and deaths, 1930s-88, annual rpt, 4204–1

Morbidity and Mortality Weekly Report, infectious notifiable disease cases by State, and public health issues, 4202–1

Prevention and control technologies for TB, status and needs, 1989 rpt, 4206–2.12

Texas-Mexico border area health facilities and services, with background data, by Texas county, 1980s-88, GAO rpt, 26121–261

see also under By Disease in the "Index by Categories"

Tucson, Ariz.

Housing starts and completions authorized by building permits in 40 MSAs, quarterly rpt, 2382–9

Wages by occupation, and benefits for office and plant workers, 1989 survey, periodic MSA rpt, 6785–3.10

see also under By City and By SMSA or MSA in the "Index by Categories"

Tuition and fees

Condition of Education, detailed data on higher education, 1960s-88, annual rpt, 4824–1.2

Consumer spending, natl income and product account, *Survey of Current Business*, monthly rpt, 2702–1.23

CPI by component for US city average, and by region, population size, and for 27 metro areas, monthly rpt, 6762–2

Digest of Education Statistics, detailed data on students, staff, finances, and facilities, 1989 edition, annual rpt, 4824–2

Higher education instn student aid and other sources of support, with student expenses and characteristics, by instn type and control, 1987 triennial study, series, 4846–3

Statistical Abstract of US, social, political, and economic data, 1790-2025, comprehensive annual compilation, 2324–1.1

see also Student aid

Tulare, Calif.

see also under By SMSA or MSA in the "Index by Categories"

Tulare County, Calif.

Wages by occupation, for office and plant workers, 1989 survey, periodic MSA rpt, 6785–12.7

Tulsa, Okla.

Wages by occupation, for office and plant workers, 1989 survey, periodic MSA rpt, 6785–3.7

see also under By City and By SMSA or MSA in the "Index by Categories"

Tung nuts and oil

see Oils, oilseeds, and fats

Tungsten

see Metals and metal industries

Tunisia

Agricultural and food production and indexes, total and for selected commodities, by country, 1970s-88, annual rpt, 1524–12

Agricultural imports and food aid needs under alternative weather assumptions, for 17 African countries, projected to 1995, 1528–279

Agricultural production, prices, and trade, by country, 1960s-89, annual world region rpt, 1524–4.2

Agricultural trade of US, by detailed commodity and country, 1988, semiannual rpt, 1522–4

Agricultural trade of US with Asia, Middle East, and North Africa, by commodity and country, 1962-86, 1528–277

AID activities and funding by project and function, FY90, and developing countries summary socioeconomic data from 1960s, annual rpt, 9904–4.6

AID economic aid to developing countries, obligations and disbursements by country, quarterly rpt, 9912–4

AID loans repayment status and terms by program and country, and status of predecessor agency loans, quarterly rpt, 9912–3

Economic and military aid and loans from US and intl agencies, by program and country, FY46-87, annual rpt, 9914–5

Economic conditions, income, production, prices, employment, and trade, 1989 periodic country rpt, 2046–4.66

Economic conditions, policy, and trade practices, by country, 1986-88, annual rpt, 21384–5

Economic, social, political, and geographic summary data, by country, 1989, annual factbook, 9114–2

Exports and imports of US, by commodity and country, 1970-87, world area rpt, 9116–1.3

Exports and imports of US, by selected country, country group, and commodity group, 1988, annual rpt, 2044–37

Human rights conditions in 170 countries, 1988, annual rpt, 21384–3

Labor conditions, union coverage, and work accidents, 1989 annual country rpt, 6366–4.26; 6366–4.63

Military aid of US, arms sales, and training programs costs and budget requests, by program, world region, and country, FY88-90, annual rpt, 7144–13

Military spending, arms trade, and force strengths, with govt spending and population, by country, 1977-87, annual rpt, 9824–1

Minerals Yearbook, 1987, Vol 3: foreign country reviews of production, trade, and policy, by commodity, annual rpt, 5604–35

Minerals Yearbook, 1987, Vol 3 preprints: foreign country review of production, trade, and policy, by commodity, annual rpt, 5604–23.70

Population size, growth rates, and components of change, by country, projected 1989-2020 and trends from 1950, biennial rpt, 2324–9

UN voting record and share of votes in agreement with US, by issue, country, and world area, 1988, annual rpt, 7004–18

see also under By Foreign Country in the "Index by Categories"

Tunnels

see Bridges and tunnels

Turk, B. H.

"Indoor Air Quality in Commercial Buildings", 3228–10

Turkey

Agricultural and food production and indexes, total and for selected commodities, by country, 1970s-88, annual rpt, 1524–12

Agricultural production and exports, by commodity, 1984-87, article, 1925–34.902

Agricultural production, prices, and trade, by country, 1960s-89, annual world region rpt, 1524–4.2

Agricultural trade of US, by detailed commodity and country, 1988, semiannual rpt, 1522–4

AID activities and funding by project and function, FY90, and developing countries summary socioeconomic data from 1960s, annual rpt, 9904–4.6

AID economic aid to developing countries, obligations and disbursements by country, quarterly rpt, 9912–4

AID loans repayment status and terms by program and country, and status of predecessor agency loans, quarterly rpt, 9912–3

Borders (maritime) between Turkey and USSR, geographic coordinates established under agreements of 1978 and 1983, 7006–8.4

Economic and military aid and loans from US and intl agencies, by program and country, FY46-87, annual rpt, 9914–5

Economic conditions, income, production, prices, employment, and trade, 1989 periodic country rpt, 2046–4.103

Economic conditions, investment and export opportunities, and trade practices, 1989 country market research rpt, 2046–6.5

Economic conditions, policy, and trade practices, by country, 1986-88, annual rpt, 21384–5

Economic indicators and govt finances, for Portugal and Turkey, 1982-86, hearing, 21388–53

Economic indicators of developing countries, problem debtors compared to other borrowers, by country, 1973-84, 1528–285

Economic, social, political, and geographic summary data, by country, 1989, annual factbook, 9114–2

Exports and imports of US, by selected country, country group, and commodity group, 1988, annual rpt, 2044–37

Human rights conditions in 170 countries, 1988, annual rpt, 21384–3

Imports of goods, services, and investment from US, trade barriers, impacts, and US actions, by country, 1988, annual rpt, 444–2

Labor conditions, union coverage, and work accidents, 1989 annual country rpt, 6366–4.48

Military aid of US, arms sales, and training programs costs and budget requests, by program, world region, and country, FY88-90, annual rpt, 7144–13

Military spending, arms trade, and force strengths, with govt spending and population, by country, 1977-87, annual rpt, 9824–1

Minerals Yearbook, 1987, Vol 3: foreign country reviews of production, trade, and policy, by commodity, annual rpt, 5604–35

Minerals Yearbook, 1987, Vol 3 preprints: foreign country review of production, trade, and policy, by commodity, annual rpt, 5604–23.71

Multinatl US firms and foreign affiliates finances and operations, by industry of parent firm and affiliate, world area, and country, preliminary 1987, annual rpt, 2704–5

Nuclear power plant capacity, generation, and operating status, by plant and foreign and US location, 1988 and projected to 2020, annual rpt, 3164–57

Nut production, exports, use, and stocks, by type, for Turkey, 1979/80-1988/89, article, 1925–34.915

Oil production, trade, use, and stocks, by selected country and country group, monthly rpt, 3162–42

Population size, growth rates, and components of change, by country, projected 1989-2020 and trends from 1950, biennial rpt, 2324–9

Raisin production, trade, use, and stocks for selected countries, and EC subsidies, various periods 1981-90, annual article, 1925–34.944

Tobacco and cigarette production, trade, and use, for Turkey, 1985-88, article, 1925–16.910

UN voting record and share of votes in agreement with US, by issue, country, and world area, 1988, annual rpt, 7004–18

see also under By Foreign Country in the "Index by Categories"

Turkeys
see Poultry industry and products

Turner, Marshall L.
"1990 Census: Redistricting by the Numbers", 9278–7

Turnover of labor
see Job tenure
see Labor turnover

Turpentine
see Gum and wood chemicals

Tuscaloosa, Ala.
see also under By SMSA or MSA in the "Index by Categories"

Tuvalu
Economic, social, political, and geographic summary data, by country, 1989, annual factbook, 9114–2
Population size, growth rates, and components of change, by country, projected 1989-2020 and trends from 1950, biennial rpt, 2324–9
see also under By Foreign Country in the "Index by Categories"

TVA
see Tennessee Valley Authority

Tyler, Tex.
see also under By SMSA or MSA in the "Index by Categories"

Typewriters
see Business machines and equipment

Udell, Gregory F.
"Collateral, Loan Quality, and Bank Risk", 9366–6.165

Ueber, Edward
"Traditional Central California Setnet Fishery", 2162–1.901

Uganda
Agricultural and food production and indexes, total and for selected commodities, by country, 1970s-88, annual rpt, 1524–12
Agricultural production, prices, and trade, by country, 1960s-89, annual world region rpt, 1524–4.2
Agricultural trade of US, by detailed commodity and country, 1988, semiannual rpt, 1522–4
AID activities and funding by project and function, FY90, and developing countries summary socioeconomic data from 1960s, annual rpt, 9904–4.5
AID economic aid to developing countries, obligations and disbursements by country, quarterly rpt, 9912–4
AID loans repayment status and terms by program and country, and status of predecessor agency loans, quarterly rpt, 9912–3
Economic and military aid and loans from US and intl agencies, by program and country, FY46-87, annual rpt, 9914–5
Economic conditions, income, production, prices, employment, and trade, 1989 periodic country rpt, 2046–4.56
Economic conditions, policy, and trade practices, by country, 1986-88, annual rpt, 21384–5
Economic, social, political, and geographic summary data, by country, 1989, annual factbook, 9114–2
Human rights conditions in 170 countries, 1988, annual rpt, 21384–3
Military aid of US, arms sales, and training programs costs and budget requests, by program, world region, and country, FY88-90, annual rpt, 7144–13
Military spending, arms trade, and force strengths, with govt spending and population, by country, 1977-87, annual rpt, 9824–1
Minerals Yearbook, 1987, Vol 3: foreign country reviews of production, trade, and policy, by commodity, annual rpt, 5604–35
Minerals Yearbook, 1987, Vol 3 preprints: foreign country review of production, trade, and policy, by commodity, annual rpt, 5604–23.81
Population size, growth rates, and components of change, by country, projected 1989-2020 and trends from 1950, biennial rpt, 2324–9
UN voting record and share of votes in agreement with US, by issue, country, and world area, 1988, annual rpt, 7004–18
see also under By Foreign Country in the "Index by Categories"

Ulbrich, Holley
"Local Revenue Diversification: Local Sales Taxes", 10046–8.9

Ulcers
see Digestive diseases

Umm al-Qaiwain
see United Arab Emirates

Unconventional warfare
see Chemical and biological warfare agents
see Underground movements

Underdeveloped countries
see Developing countries

Underemployment
Earnings losses related to unemployment and underemployment, by worker characteristics and location, 1986, 1598–251
Employment, earnings, and hours, monthly press release, 6742–5
Handbook of Labor Statistics, employment, unemployment, and labor force characteristics, 1940s-88 with trends from 1913, 6728–38.1
Mexico labor supply and conditions, with data by major city, selected years 1969-88, working paper, 2326–18.49
Poverty level labor force employment, earnings, and other characteristics, 1987, article, 6722–1.948
Science and engineering PhDs employment and other characteristics, by field and State, 1987, biennial rpt, 9627–18
Youth labor force status, by sex and race, summer 1985-89, annual press release, 6744–14

Underground economy
Drug enforcement regional task forces investigation of organized crime, activities by agency and region, and background data, FY83-88, annual rpt, 6004–17
Drug-related money laundering operations, US and foreign govts enforcement activities, 1988, annual rpt, 7004–17
Money laundering and related activity, Federal sentencing guidelines by offense and circumstances, 1989 rpt, 17668–1

Underground movements
Terrorist (intl) incidents, casualties, and attacks on US targets, by attack type and country, 1980-88, 7008–56
Terrorist (intl) incidents, casualties, and attacks on US targets, by attack type and world area, 1968-88, annual rpt, 7004–13
UN voting record and share of votes in agreement with US, by issue, country, and world area, 1988, annual rpt, 7004–18
see also Terrorism

Unemployment
see Employment and unemployment, general
see Employment and unemployment, local and regional
see Employment and unemployment, specific industry
see Labor turnover
see Public welfare programs
see Underemployment
see Unemployment insurance
see Unemployment insurance tax
see Work incentive programs

Unemployment insurance
AFDC recipients demographic and financial characteristics, by State, FY87, annual rpt, 4694–1
Beneficiaries, taxes collected, and State program operations by State, since 1940, monthly rpt, 4742–1.1; 4742–1.7
Benefits adequacy, State and Federal programs, and work disincentives, series, 6406–6

State UI benefits, coverage, and tax provisions, as of July 1989, semiannual listing, 6402–7

State UI laws, changes in coverage, benefits, tax rates, and penalties, by State, 1988, annual article, 6722–1.905

State UI laws, comparison of provisions, as of Jan 1989, semiannual revisions to base edition, 6402–2

State UI programs benefits, coverage, exhaustions, and finances by State, 1987, annual tables, 6404–10

State UI tax rates based on benefits paid former employees, and taxes and benefits share of payroll costs, by major industry group and State, 1969-88, 6406–6.29

Transit systems finances and operations, by mode of transport, size of fleet, and for 432 systems, 1986, annual rpt, 7884–4

Unemployment trust funds

Financial condition of Federal UI trust funds, quarterly rpt, 8102–9.1

Financial condition of UI trust funds, by State, monthly rpt, 8102–9.16

Financial condition of UI trust funds, for 11 States, 1971-86, 6406–6.24

State and Federal UI programs coverage, benefits, exhaustions, and finances, by State, and beneficiary characteristics, 1940s-FY89, 21788–175

State UI programs benefits, coverage, exhaustions, and finances by State, 1987, annual tables, 6404–10

Unicon Research Corp.

"New Evidence on School Desegregation", 11048–189

UNICOR

see Federal Prison Industries

Uniforms

see Clothing and clothing industry

Unions

see Labor unions

United Arab Emirates

Agricultural and food production and indexes, total and for selected commodities, by country, 1970s-88, annual rpt, 1524–12

Agricultural trade of US, by detailed commodity and country, 1988, semiannual rpt, 1522–4

AID loans repayment status and terms by program and country, and status of predecessor agency loans, quarterly rpt, 9912–3

Economic conditions, income, production, prices, employment, and trade, 1988 periodic country rpt, 2046–4.3

Economic conditions, policy, and trade practices, by country, 1986-88, annual rpt, 21384–5

Economic, social, political, and geographic summary data, by country, 1989, annual factbook, 9114–2

Exports and imports of US, by commodity and country, 1970-87, world area rpt, 9116–1.3

Exports and imports of US, by selected country, country group, and commodity group, 1988, annual rpt, 2044–37

Human rights conditions in 170 countries, 1988, annual rpt, 21384–3

Military aid of US, arms sales, and training programs costs and budget requests, by program, world region, and country, FY88-90, annual rpt, 7144–13

Military spending, arms trade, and force strengths, with govt spending and population, by country, 1977-87, annual rpt, 9824–1

Minerals Yearbook, 1987, Vol 3: foreign country reviews of production, trade, and policy, by commodity, annual rpt, 5604–35

Minerals Yearbook, 1987, Vol 3 preprints: foreign country review of production, trade, and policy, by commodity, annual rpt, 5604–23.73

Multinatl US firms and foreign affiliates finances and operations, by industry of parent firm and affiliate, world area, and country, preliminary 1987, annual rpt, 2704–5

Oil production and exports, by major exporting country, detailed data, monthly rpt, 3162–24

Oil production, trade, use, and stocks, by selected country and country group, monthly rpt, 3162–42

Population size, growth rates, and components of change, by country, projected 1989-2020 and trends from 1950, biennial rpt, 2324–9

UN voting record and share of votes in agreement with US, by issue, country, and world area, 1988, annual rpt, 7004–18

see also under By Foreign Country in the "Index by Categories"

United Arab Republic

see Egypt

United Kingdom

Agricultural and food production and indexes, total and for selected commodities, by country, 1970s-88, annual rpt, 1524–12

Agricultural production, prices, and trade, by country, 1970s-88 and forecast 1990, annual world region rpt, 1524–4.1

Agricultural trade of US, by detailed commodity and country, 1988, semiannual rpt, 1522–4

AID loans repayment status and terms by program and country, and status of predecessor agency loans, quarterly rpt, 9912–3

Apprentices in US and 4 European countries, 1987, article, 6722–1.936

Background Notes, summary social, political, and economic data, 1989 rpt, 7006–2.33

Bearings (antifriction) from 9 countries, injury to US industry from foreign subsidized and less than fair value imports, investigation with background financial and operating data, 1989 rpt, 9886–19.65

Businesses (foreign) activity in US, income tax returns, assets, and income statement items, by industry div, country, and world area, 1984-85, article, 8302–2.920

Cancer (stomach) incidence and risk relation to diet and refrigerator use, 1985-87 local area study, article, 4472–1.919

Capital cost indicators for US, Japan, West Germany, and UK, various periods 1977-88, article, 9385–1.910

Coal production, trade, and govt subsidies, by country and country group, 1973-87 and projected to 2000, 2048–144

Current account balance and related economic indicators, for US and 4 countries, 1980s-87, article, 9389–1.908

Current account balance of US, components and relation to foreign and US investment and economic conditions, 1970s-88 and projected to 1990s, article, 9385–1.907

Developing countries loans from banks and govts, debt exposure of 7 developed countries, various periods 1980-88, GAO rpt, 26123–255

Economic and military aid and loans from US and intl agencies, by program and country, FY46-87, annual rpt, 9914–5

Economic and monetary trends, compounded annual rates of change for US and 10 major trading partners, quarterly rpt, 9391–7

Economic conditions, and oil production, use, and imports, by country, biweekly rpt, 9112–1

Economic conditions, consumer and stock prices and production indexes, 6 OECD countries and US, *Business Conditions Digest*, monthly rpt, 2702–3.10

Economic conditions in Communist, OECD, and selected other countries, 1960s-88, annual rpt, 9114–4

Economic conditions, policy, and trade practices, by country, 1986-88, annual rpt, 21384–5

Economic indicators, and dollar exchange rates, for selected OECD countries, 1980s-89, semiannual rpt, 8002–14

Economic indicators variability and correlation with GNP, for US, Japan, and UK, alternative estimates, for business cycles 1954-86, article, 9377–1.902

Economic, social, political, and geographic summary data, by country, 1989, annual factbook, 9114–2

Energy prices, by fuel type and end use, for 10 countries, 1980-88 annual rpt, 3164–50.6

Energy production by type, and oil prices, trade, and use, by country group and selected country, monthly rpt, 9112–2

Export credit activity of Eximbank and 6 OECD countries, 1988, annual rpt, 9254–3

Exports and imports of OECD, total and for 4 major countries, and US trade by country, by commodity, 1970-87, world area rpt series, 9116–1

Exports and imports of US, by commodity group, world area, selected country, US coastal area and port, and mode of transport, monthly rpt, 2422–9

Exports and imports of US, by selected country, country group, and commodity group, 1988, annual rpt, 2044–37

Farmland (US) owned by foreigners, holdings, acreage, and value by land use, owner country, State, and county, 1988, annual rpt, 1584–3

Food supply and demand, market and support prices, and other economic indicators, by EC country and commodity, 1960-85, 1528–276

Govt-owned corporations stock issues, value, new shareholders, and revenue effects, for UK and France, 1960s-88, article, 9385–1.911

Human rights conditions in 170 countries, 1988, annual rpt, 21384–3

Imports of goods, services, and investment from US, trade barriers, impacts, and US actions, by country, 1988, annual rpt, 444–2

Imports of US given duty-free treatment for value of US material sent abroad, and impacts on US industry and employment, by commodity and country, 1987, annual rpt, 9884–14

Interest rate differentials among countries, US and 4 industrialized countries, 1960s-88, article, 9385–1.902

Investment (foreign direct) in US, major transactions by type, industry, country, and US location, 1987, annual rpt, 2044–20

Labor conditions, union coverage, and work accidents, 1989 annual country rpt, 6366–4.11

Machinery belts from 8 countries, injury to US industry from foreign subsidized and less than fair value imports, investigation with background financial and operating data, 1989 rpt, 9886–19.66

Manufacturing labor productivity and unit costs for 14 countries, 1950-88, annual press release, 6864–1

Military aid of US, arms sales, and training programs costs and budget requests, by program, world region, and country, FY88-90, annual rpt, 7144–13

Military spending, arms trade, and force strengths, with govt spending and population, by country, 1977-87, annual rpt, 9824–1

Minerals Yearbook, 1987, Vol 3: foreign country reviews of production, trade, and policy, by commodity, annual rpt, 5604–35

Minerals Yearbook, 1987, Vol 3 preprints: foreign country review of production, trade, and policy, by commodity, annual rpt, 5604–23.74

Mortgages outstanding, by type of holder, as of Dec 1987, article, 9312–1.901

Multinatl firms US affiliates, finances, and operations, by industry, world area of parent firm, and State, 1987, annual rpt, 2704–4

Multinatl US firms and foreign affiliates finances and operations, by industry of parent firm and affiliate, world area, and country, preliminary 1987, annual rpt, 2704–5

Nuclear power generation in US and 19 non-Communist countries, monthly rpt, 3162–24.10

Nuclear power plant capacity, generation, and operating status, by plant and foreign and US location, 1988 and projected to 2020, annual rpt, 3164–57

Oil production, trade, use, and stocks, by selected country and country group, monthly rpt, 3162–42

Oil production, use, stocks, and exports and prices for US, by country, detailed data, monthly rpt, 3162–24

Population size, growth rates, and components of change, by country, projected 1989-2020 and trends from 1950, biennial rpt, 2324–9

R&D funding and science and technology employment for selected countries, selected years 1961-87, annual rpt, 9624–18.2

Science and engineering employment and education, and R&D spending, for US and selected foreign countries, 1988, annual rpt, 9624–23

Ships in world merchant fleet, and tonnage, by country of registry, as of Jan 1988, annual rpt, 7704–3

Space satellites and other objects launched since 1957, quarterly listing, 9502–2

Stock market crash of 1987, US stock prices relation to prices on Tokyo and London exchanges, 1987-88, technical paper, 9366–6.164

Stock price index correlations among US and 3 countries, various periods 1957-88, article, 9391–1.901

Tea imports of UK by country, and London auction prices, various periods 1975-89, FAS annual circular, 1925–15.3

Transportation energy use, fuel prices, and vehicle registrations, by selected country, 1970s-88, annual rpt, 3304–5.1

Travel to US, market research, major magazine ad costs and circulation, and trade show data, for selected countries, 1989-90, annual rpt, 2904–11

UN voting record and share of votes in agreement with US, by issue, country, and world area, 1988, annual rpt, 7004–18

Unemployment insurance costs and beneficiaries, for US and 5 European countries, 1973-84, article, 6722–1.919

see also Gibraltar

see also under By Foreign Country in the "Index by Categories"

United Nations

Background Notes, UN history, structure, and programs, 1988 rpt, 7006–2.11

Diplomats and staff with immunity for foreign missions in US and US missions abroad, and foreign diplomats criminal cases, 1978-87, hearing, 25388–51

Environment Program activities, and funding by source, program, and country, 1986-89, GAO rpt, 26123–246

Loans and grants for economic and military aid from US and intl agencies, by program and country, FY46-87, annual rpt, 9914–5

PL 480 exports by commodity, and recipients, by program, sponsor, and country, FY87 and cumulative from FY55, annual rpt, 1924–7

US participation in UN, and member and nonmember shares of UN budget by country, FY86-88, annual rpt, 7004–5

Voting record in UN and share of votes in agreement with US, by issue, country, and world area, 1988, annual rpt, 7004–18

see also International Bank for Reconstruction and Development

see also International Development Association

see also International Finance Corp.

see also International Monetary Fund

Universities

see Higher education

University of Colorado Center for Health Services Research

"Findings on Case Mix and Quality of Care in Nursing Homes and Home Health Agencies", 4658–28

University of Minnesota

"Employer-Based Health Insurance", 4186–2.23

Unmanned space programs

see Communications satellites

see Meteorological satellites

see Satellites

see Space programs

Unpaid family workers

Census of Population and Housing, 1990: data item selection, questionnaire dev, and testing, 2626–11.3

Disabled persons employment, labor force status, and other characteristics, 1988, Current Population Rpt, 2546–2.147

Employment and Earnings, detailed data, monthly rpt, 6742–2

Employment conditions, alternative BLS projections to 2000 and trends 1970s-88, biennial article, 6722–1.955

Employment, earnings, and hours, monthly press release, 6742–5

Employment situation, earnings, hours, and other BLS economic indicators, transcripts of BLS Commissioner's monthly testimony, periodic rpt, 23846–4

Farm population, by employment and socioeconomic characteristics, and region, 1988, annual Current Population Rpt, 2546–1.439

Farm workers, earnings, and days worked, by selected characteristics and region, 1987, biennial rpt, 1594–2

Handbook of Labor Statistics, employment, unemployment, and labor force characteristics, 1940s-88 with trends from 1913, 6728–38

Hispanic Americans socioeconomic characteristics, by detailed origin, 1988, Current Population Rpt, 2546–1.438

Mexico labor supply and conditions, with data by major city, selected years 1969-88, working paper, 2326–18.49

Moonlighting employment, by worker and primary and secondary job characteristics and reason, 1989, press release, 6726–1.24

Virgin Islands economic censuses, 1987: employment, firms, payroll, and receipts, by SIC 1- to 4-digit industry, island, and city, 2593–1

Youth labor force status, by sex and race, summer 1985-89, annual press release, 6744–14

Unreported income

see Tax delinquency and evasion

see Underground economy

Upper Volta

see Burkina Faso

Uranium

County Business Patterns, 1987: employment, establishments, and payroll, by SIC 2- to 4-digit industry and county, annual State rpt series, 2326–8

Demand for uranium and enrichment services, and nuclear power plant spent fuel, for US and other country groups, projected 1989-2036, annual rpt, 3164–72

Enrichment facilities of DOE, financial statements, operations, and stocks, FY88, annual rpt, 3354–7

Environmental impacts of energy technologies, 1960s-80s, handbook series, 3326–1

Exports of US, detailed commodities by country, monthly rpt, 2422–3

Foreign countries mineral production, reserves, and industry role in domestic economy and world supply, world area and country rpt series, 5606–1

Urban Institute
"Experience Rating in Unemployment Insurance: Some Current Issues", 6406–6.29

Urban Mass Transportation Administration
Budget of US Appendix, obligations, appropriations, and personnel, by program and agency, FY90, annual rpt, 104–3

Bus (intercity) route in Nebraska, indicators of need, finances, and service and funding alternatives, 1980s, 7888–76

Employment of DOT, by subagency, occupation, and selected personnel characteristics, FY88, annual rpt, 7304–18

Expenditures of Fed Govt in States, by type, program, agency, and State, FY88, annual rpt, 2464–2

Grants of UMTA for transit systems, by city and State, FY88, annual rpt, 7884–10

Grants of UMTA to higher education instns for research and training, by project, FY88, annual listing, 7884–7

R&D projects and funding of UMTA, FY88, annual listing, 7884–1

Research on transit systems, rpts, semiannual listing, periodicity change, 7882–1

Research on transit systems, rpts, 1988, annual listing, 7884–11

Suburban areas land use, commuting, employment, and housing characteristics, detailed data for traffic planning, 1986, 7888–75

Subway accidents, casualties, and damage, by circumstances and system, 1987, annual rpt, 7884–5

Traffic volume in urban areas and detailed trip characteristics, by transport mode and city, 1950s-88, 7888–37

Transit systems finances and operations, by mode of transport, size of fleet, and for 432 systems, 1986, annual rpt, 7884–4

Transit systems finances, costs, and needs, by State and selected system, 1980-88, biennial rpt, 7884–8

Transit systems in urban areas, services and vehicles, 1988 annual listing, 7884–9

Urban planning
see City and town planning

Urban renewal
Govt finances, by level of govt, State, and for large cities and counties, annual rpt series, 2466–2

Mortgage insurance programs of HUD, finances and lending activity by program, FY88, annual rpt, 5004–8

see also Community Development Block Grants

see also Relocation

see also Urban beautification

see also Urban Development Action Grants

Urban transportation
Bond tax-exempt issues for private activity, by purpose, face value, major industry, and State, 1986, annual article, 8302–2.905

Budget of US, special analysis of Federal capital spending by category, projected FY89-2005 and trends from FY81, annual rpt, 104–24

Business statistics, detailed data for major industries and economic indicators, *Survey of Current Business*, monthly rpt, 2702–1.8

Collective bargaining agreements expiring during year, and workers covered, by firm, union, industry group, and State, 1989, annual rpt, 6784–9

Construction industries census, 1987: financial and operating data, preliminary industry rpt series, 2371–1

Consumer Expenditure Survey, household income by source, and itemized spending, by selected characteristics and location, 1984-86, annual rpt, 6764–5.2

Consumer Expenditure Survey, spending by category, and income, by selected household characteristics and location, 1987, press release, 6726–1.23

Consumer spending and income effects of wives' employment, by expenditure category and household characteristics, 1984-86, article, 6722–1.908

Consumer spending in metro and nonmetro areas, by item, 1987, article, 6722–1.962

County Business Patterns, 1987: employment, establishments, and payroll, by SIC 2- to 4-digit industry and county, annual State rpt series, 2326–8

CPI by component for US city average, and by region, population size, and for 27 metro areas, monthly rpt, 6762–1

Crime victimization rates, by victim and offender characteristics, circumstances, and offense, 1987 survey, annual rpt, 6066–3.41

DOT planning and safety grants, by program, State, and for 38 SMSAs, FY88, annual rpt, 7304–7

Employment, earnings, and hours, by selected SIC 1- to 4-digit industry, State, and for 262 MSAs, 1972-87, 6748–81

Employment, earnings, and hours, by SIC 1- to 4-digit industry, monthly 1983-Feb 1989, annual rpt, 6744–4

Energy use by mode of transport, fuel supply, and demographic and economic factors of vehicle use, 1970s-88, annual rpt, 3304–5

Fed Govt financial and nonfinancial domestic aid, 1989 base edition with supplements, annual listing, 104–5

Fed Govt spending in States, by type, program, agency, and State, FY88, annual rpt, 2464–2

Finances and operations of interstate carriers, 1987, annual rpt, 9486–6.3

Finances and operations of transit systems, by mode of transport, size of fleet, and for 432 systems, 1986, annual rpt, 7884–4

Finances, costs, and needs of transit systems, by State and selected system, 1980-88, biennial rpt, 7884–8

Finances, operations, vehicles, equipment, accidents, and energy use, by mode of transport, 1955-88, annual rpt, 7304–2

Govt employment and payroll, by function, level of govt, and jurisdiction, 1987-88, annual rpt series, 2466–1

Manufacturing census, 1987: financial and operating data, for SIC 4-digit industries by product, preliminary rpt, 2491–1.77

New York and northeastern New Jersey employment by industry div, unemployment, and consumer price changes by selected commodity, 1978-June 1989, press release, 6926–2.40

Occupational injury and illness rates, by SIC 2- to 4-digit industry, 1987, annual rpt, 6844–1

Operations of urban transit systems, services and vehicles, 1988 annual listing, 7884–9

R&D projects and funding of Urban Mass Transportation Admin, FY88, annual listing, 7884–1

Research and training grants of UMTA to higher education instns, by project, FY88, annual listing, 7884–7

Research on transit systems, rpts, 1988, annual listing, 7884–11

Statistical Abstract of US, social, political, and economic data, 1790-2025, comprehensive annual compilation, 2324–1.3

Tax (income) returns of corporations, income and tax items by asset size and detailed industry, 1986, annual rpt, 8304–4; 8304–21

Tax (income) returns of partnerships, income statement items by industry group, 1986, annual article, 8302–2.903

Tax (income) returns of sole proprietorships, income statement items, by industry group, 1987, annual article, 8302–2.904; 8302–2.921

Traffic volume in urban areas and detailed trip characteristics, by transport mode and city, 1950s-88, 7888–37

Traffic volume on rural roads and city streets, monthly rpt, 7552–8

Urban Mass Transportation Admin grants for transit systems, by city and State, FY88, annual rpt, 7884–10

see also Buses

see also Commuting

see also Subways

see also Taxicabs

see also Traffic engineering

see also By Industry in the "Index by Categories"

Urbana, Ill.
Wages by occupation, and benefits for office and plant workers, 1988 survey, periodic MSA rpt, 6785–11.3

see also under By SMSA or MSA in the "Index by Categories"

Urogenital diseases
Breast enhancement, use of treatments and products not proven safe or effective, costs, and user characteristics, 1986 survey, 4008–86

Cancer (anal) risk, by sex and history of urogenital disorders, homosexual activity, and smoking, 1989 article, 4472–1.930

Cancer (bladder) risk for men in selected occupations, by employment characteristics, 1977-78, article, 4472–1.924; 4472–1.925

Cancer (breast) long-term risk among women with selected risk factors, model description and results, 1989 article, 4472–1.934

Cancer (breast) risk, by alcohol use and other risk factors, aggregate 1950-80, article, 4472–1.902

Cancer (breast) risk, by oral contraceptives use and menopausal status, 1976-86 study, article, 4472–1.923

Cancer (breast) risk for women by smoking history, and menopausal and estrogen receptor status, 1976-86 study, article, 4472–1.928

Cancer (breast) risk of scoliosis patients x-rayed during childhood, by diagnosis and other characteristics, 1922-86, local area study, article, 4472–1.922

Cancer (breast) risk relation to diet and nutrient intake, for northwestern Italy, 1983-85 study, article, 4472-1.906

Cancer (breast) risk, relation to hypertension diagnosis before and after pregnancy, 1989 article, 4472-1.927

Cancer (breast) risk relation to oral contraceptives use, by age at first use and duration, Sweden study, 1979-85, article, 4472-1.917

Cancer (breast) screening, use and client characteristics for low-income women's mammography referral services, 1987-88 local area study, article, 4042-3.951

Cancer (breast) survival rates, for patients receiving chemotherapy after surgery, for diagnoses made 1975-85, GAO rpt, 26131-58

Cancer (breast) tumor characteristics related to diet, number of children, and age, 1983-86, article, 4472-1.920

Cancer (breast and cervical) incidence, deaths, and survival rates, by race, average 1973-81, article, 4042-3.952

Cancer (cervical) cases and risk relation to smoking and other characteristics, for 4 Latin American countries, 1986-87 study, article, 4472-1.905

Cancer (cervical) screening and education program for black women, effectiveness and participant characteristics, 1988 local area study, article, 4042-3.953

Cancer incidence, death, and survival rates, by sex, race, age, and body site, 1973-86, annual rpt, 4474-35

Cases of acute and chronic conditions, disability, absenteeism, and health services use, by selected characteristics, 1988, annual rpt, 4147-10.170

Deaths and rates, by cause, age, sex, marital status, race, and State, 1987, US Vital Statistics advance annual rpt, 4146-5.113

Deaths and rates, by cause and age, preliminary 1987-88, US Vital Statistics annual rpt, 4144-7

Deaths and rates, by detailed cause and demographic characteristics, 1986 and trends from 1900, US Vital Statistics annual rpt, 4144-2

Deaths and rates, by detailed location, cause, and demographic characteristics, 1987, US Vital Statistics annual rpt, 4144-3

Health condition and health care resources, use, and spending, 1950s-87, annual data compilation, 4144-11

HHS financial aid, by program, recipient, State, and city, FY88, annual regional listings, 4004-3

Hospital discharges and length of stay, by diagnosis, patient and instn characteristics, procedure performed, and payment source, 1987, annual rpt, 4147-13.99

Hospital discharges by detailed diagnostic and procedure category, primary diagnosis, and length of stay, by age, sex, and region, 1987, annual rpt, 4147-13.100

Human papillomavirus infection rates, by sexual and personal hygiene practices, and other patient characteristics, Brazil local area studies, 1989 article, 4472-1.908

Incontinence of aged, by activity type and selected characteristics, 1984, 4147-10.167

Incontinence of nursing home residents, incidence, and instn compliance with care regulations, by facility, annual State rpt series, 4654-15

Indian Health Service and contract facilities hospitalization, by diagnosis, age, sex, and service area, FY87, annual rpt, 4104-16

Indian Health Service and contract facilities hospitalization, by diagnosis, age, sex, and service area, FY88, annual rpt, 4084-5

Kidney end-stage disease Medicare enrollees, by age, sex, race, and region, 1975-87, annual rpt, 4744-3.5

Kidney end-stage disease Medicare enrollees, hospitalization, and survival rates, 1980-85, annual rpt, 4654-13

Kidney end-stage disease Medicare enrollment, by State, 1987, annual rpt, 4657-5.1

Kidney end-stage disease patients Medicare reimbursements, various periods 1966-84, biennial rpt, 4654-1

Kidney end-stage disease program of Medicare, enrollment and program operations, 1989, annual fact book, 4654-18

Kidney end-stage disease treatment facilities approved by Medicare, dialysis and transplant services and ownership, 1989 annual listing, 4654-17

Kidney end-stage disease treatment facilities, Medicare enrollment and reimbursement, survival, and patient characteristics, 1980-86, annual rpt, 4654-16

Kidney end-stage disease treatment facilities, physicians Medicare services use, charges, and reimbursement, 1986, article, 4652-1.936

Nursing home facility, staff, and resident detailed characteristics, 1985, 4147-13.97

Pollutants health effects, concentrations in food and environment, sources, human intake, and regulation, series, 9186-8

Research on population and reproduction, Federal funding by project, FY87, annual listing, 4474-9

Surgical procedures performed, costs, length of stay, and deaths, impacts of Medicare prospective payment system by procedure type, 1984-86, 17206-2.5

see also Sexually transmitted diseases

see also under By Disease in the "Index by Categories"

Uruguay

Agricultural and food production and indexes, total and for selected commodities, by country, 1970s-88, annual rpt, 1524-12

Agricultural trade of US, by detailed commodity and country, 1988, semiannual rpt, 1522-4

AID activities and funding by project and function, FY90, and developing countries summary socioeconomic data from 1960s, annual rpt, 9904-4.7

AID economic aid to developing countries, obligations and disbursements by country, quarterly rpt, 9912-4

AID loans repayment status and terms by program and country, and status of predecessor agency loans, quarterly rpt, 9912-3

Auto imports from US, trade barriers by country, 1988, annual rpt, 444-2

Economic and military aid and loans from US and intl agencies, by program and country, FY46-87, annual rpt, 9914-5

Economic conditions, policy, and trade practices, by country, 1986-88, annual rpt, 21384-5

Economic, social, political, and geographic summary data, by country, 1989, annual factbook, 9114-2

Exports and imports of Latin America, and balance of trade with US, by country, 1988, annual rpt, 2044-34

Exports and imports of US, by commodity and country, 1970-87, world area rpt, 9116-1.5

Exports and imports of US, by selected country, country group, and commodity group, 1988, annual rpt, 2044-37

Human rights conditions in 170 countries, 1988, annual rpt, 21384-3

Labor conditions, union coverage, and work accidents, 1989 annual country rpt, 6366-4.32

Military aid of US, arms sales, and training programs costs and budget requests, by program, world region, and country, FY88-90, annual rpt, 7144-13

Military spending, arms trade, and force strengths, with govt spending and population, by country, 1977-87, annual rpt, 9824-1

Minerals Yearbook, 1987, Vol 3: foreign country reviews of production, trade, and policy, by commodity, annual rpt, 5604-35

Minerals Yearbook, 1987, Vol 3 preprints: foreign country review of production, trade, and policy, by commodity, annual rpt, 5604-23.87

Population size, growth rates, and components of change, by country, projected 1989-2020 and trends from 1950, biennial rpt, 2324-9

UN voting record and share of votes in agreement with US, by issue, country, and world area, 1988, annual rpt, 7004-18

see also under By Foreign Country in the "Index by Categories"

U.S. Advisory Commission on Public Diplomacy

USIA activities, finances, and info services, FY89, annual rpt, 17594-1

U.S. Architectural and Transportation Barriers Compliance Board

Budget of US Appendix, obligations, appropriations, and personnel, by program and agency, FY90, annual rpt, 104-3

Budget of US, authoritative financial statements with appropriations, outlays, and receipts, by category and agency, FY88, annual rpt, 8104-2.2

Building access for disabled to Federal and federally funded facilities, complaints by disposition and agency, FY88, annual rpt, 17614-1

Complaints received by ATBCB, by disposition, 1977-87, 10048-74

U.S. Arms Control and Disarmament Agency

Activities of ACDA, and status of arms control treaties, 1988, annual rpt, 9824-2

Budget of US Appendix, obligations, appropriations, and personnel, by program and agency, FY90, annual rpt, 104-3

Budget of US, authoritative financial statements with appropriations, outlays, and receipts, by category and agency, FY88, annual rpt, 8104-2.2

Foreign countries military spending, arms trade, and force strengths, with govt spending and population, by country, 1977-87, annual rpt, 9824–1

R&D funding by Fed Govt, by field, performer type, agency, and State, FY87-89, annual rpt, 9627–20

U.S. Army Corps of Engineers
see Army Corps of Engineers

U.S. attorneys
Case processing and collections of US attorneys, by case type and Federal district, FY88, annual rpt, 6004–2

Criminal case processing in Federal courts, by offense, disposition, and jurisdiction, 1950s-88, annual rpt, 6064–6.5

Criminal case processing in Federal district courts, and dispositions, by offense, district, and offender characteristics, 1984, annual rpt, 6064–29

Indian reservation crimes and enforcement activity in Montana, and Bur of Indian Affairs law enforcement officers training, 1985-87, GAO rpt, 26113–402

U.S. Budget
see Budget of the U.S.

U.S. Claims Court
Caseloads of Court by type of suit, and judgments, FY89, annual rpt, 18224–1

Cases, judgments, and appeals, 1988, annual rpt, 18204–8.19

Pay rates of Fed Govt civilian employees, by pay schedule and grade, 1989 and trends from 1789, annual rpt, 21624–4

Tax litigation, prosecutions, and interpretive law decisions, FY88, annual rpt, 8304–3.2

U.S. Coast Guard
see Coast Guard

U.S. Commission on Civil Rights
see Commission on Civil Rights

U.S. Court of Appeals for the Federal Circuit
Budget of US Appendix, obligations, appropriations, and personnel, by program and agency, FY90, annual rpt, 104–3

Cases filed and terminated, by source of appeal, 1989, annual rpt, 18204–2.10; 18204–8.18

Intl Trade Court decisions appealed to Appeals Court, and dispositions, FY88-89, annual rpt, 18224–2

U.S. Court of International Trade
see Court of International Trade

U.S. Customs Service
Activities, collections, entries processed by mode of transport, and seizures, FY84-88, annual rpt, 8144–1

Automated system of Customs Service for selecting imports for inspection, operations, FY88-1st qtr FY89, GAO rpt, 26125–35

Budget of US Appendix, obligations, appropriations, and personnel, by program and agency, FY90, annual rpt, 104–3

Customs collections, for top 15 ports, quarterly rpt, 8142–1

Drug enforcement training of US for foreign govts, enrollment in US and host countries by program, FY88, annual rpt, 7004–17

Drug smuggling aircraft interdiction activities of Fed Govt, funding, and radar system capabilities, by agency, FY82-89, GAO rpt, 26119–259

U.S. Employment and Training Service
see Employment and Training Administration

U.S. Fish and Wildlife Service
see Fish and Wildlife Service

U.S. Geological Survey
see Geological Survey

U.S. Holocaust Memorial Council
Budget of US Appendix, obligations, appropriations, and personnel, by program and agency, FY90, annual rpt, 104–3

Budget of US, authoritative financial statements with appropriations, outlays, and receipts, by category and agency, FY88, annual rpt, 8104–2.2

U.S. Information Agency
Activities, finances, and info services of USIA, FY89, annual rpt, 17594–1

Budget of US Appendix, obligations, appropriations, and personnel, by program and agency, FY90, annual rpt, 104–3

Budget of US, authoritative financial statements with appropriations, outlays, and receipts, by category and agency, FY88, annual rpt, 8104–2.2

English language program of USIA, enrollment and staff, by instn, world area, and country, FY88, annual rpt, 9854–2

Exchange and training programs of Federal agencies, participants by world area, and funding, by program, FY87, annual rpt, 9854–8

Fulbright-Hays academic exchanges, grants by purpose, and foreign govt share of costs, by country, FY88, annual rpt, 10324–1

Labor unions recognized in Fed Govt, agreements and membership by agency and facility, as of Jan 1989, biennial listing, 9844–14

Libraries of USIA, holdings, use, and staff by country and city, FY88, annual rpt, 9854–4

R&D funding by Fed Govt, by field, performer type, agency, and State, FY87-89, annual rpt, 9627–20
see also Voice of America

U.S. Institute of Peace
Budget of US Appendix, obligations, appropriations, and personnel, by program and agency, FY90, annual rpt, 104–3

Education funding by Federal agency, program, and recipient type, and instn spending, FY80-88, 4828–21

U.S. International Development Cooperation Agency
Activities and funding of IDCA and AID, FY86-88, and developing countries economic and social conditions from 1960s, annual rpt, 9904–4

Developing countries economic aid from US, bilateral and through intl dev banks, by world region and country, 1970s-FY88, annual rpt, 9904–1
see also Agency for International Development
see also Overseas Private Investment Corp.

U.S. International Trade Commission
Activities, investigations, and rpts of USITC, FY88, annual rpt, 9884–1

Auto industry finances and operations, trade by country, and prices of selected US and foreign models, monthly rpt, 9882–8

Budget of US Appendix, obligations, appropriations, and personnel, by program and agency, FY90, annual rpt, 104–3

Budget of US, authoritative financial statements with appropriations, outlays, and receipts, by category and agency, FY88, annual rpt, 8104–2.2

Caribbean area duty-free exports to US, and US exports and import duties on other goods, by commodity and country, 1984-88, annual rpt, 9884–20

Chemicals (synthetic organic) production, by detailed product, quarterly rpt, 9882–1

Chemicals (synthetic organic) production, sales, and manufacturer listing, by product, 1988, annual rpt, 9884–3

Communist countries trade with US, by detailed commodity and country, quarterly rpt with articles, 9882–2

Exports and imports of US by country, and trade shifts by commodity, quarterly rpt, 9882–9

Exports and imports, trade agreements and relations, and USITC investigations, 1988, annual rpt, 9884–5

Exports, imports, and balances of US with major trading partners, by product category, 1984-88, annual chartbook, 9884–21

Footwear production, employment, use, prices, and US trade by country, quarterly rpt, 9882–6

Foreign and US economic conditions, and trade devs and balances, with data by selected country and country group, monthly rpt, 9882–14

Generalized System of Preferences status, and US tariffs, trade by country, production, and use, for selected commodities, 1984-88, annual rpt, 9884–23

Imports and tariff provisions effect on US industries and products, investigations with background financial and operating data, series, 9886–4

Imports injury to US industries from foreign subsidized products and sales at less than fair value, investigations with background financial and operating data, series, 9886–19

Imports injury to US industries from foreign subsidized products, investigations with background financial and operating data, series, 9886–15

Imports injury to US industries from sales at less than fair value, investigations with background financial and operating data, series, 9886–14

Imports of US given duty-free treatment for value of US material sent abroad, and impacts on US industry and employment, by commodity and country, 1987, annual rpt, 9884–14

Labor unions recognized in Fed Govt, agreements and membership by agency and facility, as of Jan 1989, biennial listing, 9844–14

Publications of USITC, 1982-88, annual listing, 9884–12

R&D funding by Fed Govt, by field, performer type, agency, and State, FY87-89, annual rpt, 9627–20

Rum production, trade by country, and use, 1987-88, annual rpt, 9884–15

Steel (stainless and alloy tool) production, employment, finances, and US producers inventories and unfilled orders, 1987-88, annual rpt, 9884–22

Harbor traffic, facilities, dev, funding, and needs, for Pacific territories and Hawaii by port, as of 1987, 7308–195

HHS Freedom of Info Act requests, disposition, costs, and fees, 1988, annual rpt, 4004–21

Hwy use taxes paid by trucking industry for Federal and State hwys, 1986-87, annual rpt, 7304–2

Land Mgmt Bur activities and finances, and public land acreage and use, annual State rpt series, 5724–11

Land Mgmt Bur activities and funding by State, and receipts by program, FY87, annual rpt, 5724–13

Lands (public) acreage, grants, use, revenues, and allocations, by State, FY88, annual rpt, 5724–1.2; 5724–1.3

Mail revenue and appropriation for revenue forgone, by class of mail, FY88, annual rpt, 9864–5.4

Minority Business Dev Centers mgmt and financial aid, and characteristics of businesses, by region and State, FY88, annual rpt, 2104–6

Nuclear Waste Fund finances, and DOE Civilian Radioactive Waste Mgmt Office activities, quarterly GAO rpt, 26102–4

Nuclear Waste Fund finances, and DOE Civilian Radioactive Waste Mgmt Office project budgets alternative projections, quarterly rpt, 3362–1

Recreation (outdoor) facilities of Fed Govt, fees and visitors by managing agency, 1988, annual rpt, 5544–14

SEC staffing, pay, and turnover by occupation and city, with proposed fee revenues to improve work conditions, 1989 hearing, 21368–116

Ship pilotage activities, costs, and traffic for US and Canada, and US testing and certificates, for Great Lakes, 1960s-87, 7308–192

Southeastern States govt revenues by source, spending by purpose, and tax effort indexes, by State, 1970s-87, article, 9371–1.904

State and local revenue potential relative to natl average tax burden, by type of tax and State, 1986, annual rpt, 10044–7

Transit systems finances and operations, by mode of transport, size of fleet, and for 432 systems, 1986, annual rpt, 7884–4

Wildlife-related recreation, hunting, and fishing participation and spending, detailed data by location, 1985 survey, quinquennial rpt, 5508–5

Wildlife-related recreation, hunting, and fishing participation and spending, detailed data, 1985 survey, quinquennial State rpt series, 5506–6

see also Royalties
see also Tolls

Usher, Lisa

"Multifactor Productivity Slips in the Nonrubber Footwear Industry", 6722–1.920

USIA
see U.S. Information Agency

USMC
see Marine Corps

USSR
see Soviet Union

Utah

Agriculture census, 1987: farms, farmland, production and costs, and operator characteristics, advance State and county rpts, 2330–1.49

Agriculture census, 1987: farms, farmland, production, finances, and operator characteristics, by county, final State rpt, 2331–1.44

Bank deposits in FDIC-insured commercial and savings banks, by instn, State, and county, as of June 1988, annual regional rpt, 9295–3.6

Coal production and mines by county, prices, productivity, miners, reserves, and stocks, by mining method and State, 1987-88, annual rpt, 3164–25

County Business Patterns, 1987: employment, establishments, and payroll, by SIC 2- to 4-digit industry and county, annual State rpt, 2326–8.46

Deaths and rates, by detailed location, cause, and demographic characteristics, 1987, US Vital Statistics annual rpt, 4144–3.1

DOD prime contract awards, by contractor, service branch, State, and city, FY88, annual rpt, 3544–22

Employment, earnings, and hours, by selected SIC 1- to 4-digit industry, State, and for 262 MSAs, 1972-87, 6748–81.5

Fed Govt spending in States and local areas, by type, State, county, and city, FY88, annual rpt, 2464–3

Fed Govt spending in States, by type, program, agency, and State, FY88, annual rpt, 2464–2

Forests (pinion-juniper) forage improvement practices effectiveness, for Utah, 1955-85, 1208–307

HHS financial aid, by program, recipient, State, and city, FY88, annual regional listing, 4004–3.8

Homeless children educational enrollment and needs, 1988, annual State rpt, 4804–35.44

Income (personal) per capita and by source, and earnings by industry div, by State, MSA, and county, 1982-87, annual regional rpt, 2704–2.5

Indian (Navajo and Hopi) relocation program activities, caseloads, and finances, FY88, annual rpt, 16004–1

Juvenile offenders recidivism rates, arrests, and court referrals, by offense, age, and sex, 1983 local area studies, 6068–227

Mineral Industry Surveys, State reviews of production, 1988, preliminary annual rpt, 5614–6

Minerals Yearbook, 1987, Vol 2 preprints: State review of production and sales by commodity, and business activity, annual rpt, 5604–16.46

Minerals Yearbook, 1987, Vol 2: State reviews of production, sales, and firms, by commodity, and business activity, annual rpt, 5604–34

Nursing home compliance with Medicare and Medicaid regulations, and patient characteristics, by facility, 1987/88, annual State rpt, 4654–15.46

Oil and gas leasing activity on Federal land, production, revenue, and royalty rates, by whether competitively leased and western State, 1984-88, GAO rpt, 26113–413

Retail trade census, 1987: employment, establishments, sales, and payroll, by SIC 2- to 4-digit kind of business, MSA, county, and city, State rpt, 2397–1.45

River and stream environmental conditions, fish, wildlife, use, and mgmt, 1989 rpt, 5506–9.39

Savings instns, FHLB 12th District members deposits and lending, monthly press release, 9302–32.8

Service industries census, 1987: employment, establishments, receipts, and payroll, by SIC 2- to 4-digit kind of business, MSA, county, and city, State rpt, 2391–1.45

Statistical Abstract of US, social, political, and economic data, with foreign comparisons, 1790-2025, comprehensive annual compilation, 2324–1

Transportation census, 1987: trucks, by detailed characteristics, miles traveled, and type of product carried, State rpt, 2573–1.45

Uranium tailings at inactive Green River mill, remedial action proposals, costs, site characteristics, and environmental, socioeconomic, and health impacts, 1988 rpt, 3356–4.7

Water supply and quality in streams and lakes, and groundwater levels in wells, by drainage basin, 1987, annual State rpt, 5666–10.42

Water supply, and snow survey results, monthly State rpt, 1266–2.8

Water supply, and snow survey results, 1987, annual State rpt, 1264–14.11

Wholesale trade census, 1987: employment, establishments, and operations, by SIC 2- to 4-digit kind of business, MSA, county, and city, State rpt, 2405–1.45

Wildlife-related recreation, hunting, and fishing participation and spending, detailed data, 1985 survey, quinquennial State rpt, 5506–6.44

see also Ogden, Utah
see also Salt Lake City, Utah
see also under By State in the "Index by Categories"

Utica, N.Y.
see also under By SMSA or MSA in the "Index by Categories"

Utilities
see Public utilities

VA
see Department of Veterans Affairs
see Veterans Administration

Vacant and abandoned property

Alteration and repair spending for commercial and public buildings, by type, size, age, and region, 1986, 2388–4

Arson incidents by whether structure occupied, property value, and arrest rate, by property type, 1988, annual rpt, 6224–2.1

Coal mines (abandoned) emergency complaint processing by Office of Surface Mining Reclamation and Enforcement, efficiency, 1983-87, GAO rpt, 26113–398

Coal Surface Mining Reclamation and Enforcement Office activities and funding, by State and Indian tribe, FY87, annual rpt, 5644–1

Commercial buildings energy use, costs, and conservation, by building characteristics, survey rpt series, 3166-8

Fed Govt-owned real property inventory and costs, worldwide summary by purpose, agency, and location, 1987, annual rpt, 9454-5

Hospital closures in 1987, operating characteristics, current use, and location, 1989 rpt, 4008-87

Neighborhood and housing quality, indicators and attitudes, by householder type and location, 1985, biennial rpt, 2485-12

Neighborhood and housing quality, indicators and attitudes, MSA surveys, series, 2485-6

Office building vacancy rates in 16 cities, 1960s-87, article, 9387-1.903

Railroad (short-line) operations and regulation, for lines established 1834-1987, hearing, 21368-109

Statistical Abstract of US, social, political, and economic data, 1790-2025, comprehensive annual compilation, 2324-1.3

Tax (property) revenue by level of govt, assessed values by locality, and exemptions, by property type and State, 1987 Census of Govts, 2453-1

Uranium tailings at inactive mills, remedial action proposals, costs, site characteristics, and environmental, socioeconomic, and health impacts, series, 3356-4

see also Housing condition and occupancy

Vacations and holidays

Developing countries disaster preparedness and economic, population, and political data, country rpt series, 9916-2

Employee benefit plan coverage and provisions, by plan type and occupational group, 1988, annual rpt, 6784-19

Employee vacations, holidays, and relative pay levels, regional and metro area differences, 1983-86, article, 6722-1.909

Fed Govt civilian employee leave use and costs, by type of leave, 1987-88, annual article, 9842-1.906

Fed Govt civilian employee work-years, pay rates, and benefits use and costs, by agency, FY87, annual rpt, 9844-31

Fed Govt civilian regular work-years by schedule, overtime, holidays, and personnel cost components, FY87-88, annual article, 9842-1.905

Foreign countries economic, social, political, and geographic summary by country, 1989, annual factbook, 9114-2

Foreign countries holidays observed by businesses, by country, biweekly rpt, annual listing, 2042-24

Foreign countries labor hours, holidays, and paid leave days, for 19 countries, 1987, 2908-30

Labor force not at work, by reason, whether absence paid, and sex, 1957-83, 6728-38.1

Labor force not at work, unemployed, and working less than 35 hours, by reason, sex, race, region, and State, 1988, annual rpt, 6744-7.1; 6744-7.2

Labor hourly costs, by component, occupational group, union coverage, industry div, and region, 1989, annual rpt, 6744-21

Overseas Business Reports: economic conditions, investment and export opportunities, and trade practices, country market research rpt series, 2046-6

Transit systems finances and operations, by mode of transport, size of fleet, and for 432 systems, 1986, annual rpt, 7884-4

see also Area wage surveys

see also Industry wage surveys

see also Wage surveys

Vaccination and vaccines

Child and adult immunization activity, reactions, costs, and preventable disease cases and deaths, 1988 conf, 4204-15

Exports of US, detailed commodities by country, monthly rpt, 2422-3

Foreign travel vaccination needs by country, and disease prevention recommendations, 1989 annual rpt, 4204-11

Head Start program operations, enrollment by handicap, and family characteristics, for North Central States, 1987/88, annual rpt, 4604-12

Health condition and health care resources, use, and spending, 1950s-87, annual data compilation, 4144-11

Health condition improvement and disease prevention goals and recommended activities for 2000, with trends 1970s-80s, 4048-10

HHS financial aid, by program, recipient, State, and city, FY88, annual regional listings, 4004-3

Manufacturing annual survey, 1986: value of shipments, by SIC 4- to 5-digit product class, 2506-15.3

Manufacturing census, 1987: financial and operating data, for SIC 4-digit industries by product, preliminary rpt, 2491-1.35

Morbidity and Mortality Weekly Report, infectious notifiable disease cases by State, and public health issues, 4202-1

Natl Inst of Allergy and Infectious Diseases activities, grants by recipient and location, and disease incidence, FY81-88, annual rpt, 4474-30

Prescriptions for new drugs, by category and brand, 1987, annual rpt, 4064-12.2

Price indexes (producer), by stage of processing and detailed commodity, monthly rpt, 6762-6

Price indexes (producer), by stage of processing and detailed commodity, monthly 1988, annual rpt, 6764-2

Research on immunization, 1988 annual listing, 4204-16

Shipments of vaccines and toxoids, by product type, July-Dec 1986, 4205-22

Tax (excise) collections of IRS, by source, quarterly rpt, 8302-1

Valdez, Alaska

Oil spill from tanker Exxon Valdez, impacts on gasoline and crude oil supply and prices, 1988-89, article, 3162-11.901; 3162-24.902

Tide height and time daily at coastal points, forecast 1990, annual rpt, 2174-2.1

Vallejo, Calif.

Housing vacancy rates for single and multifamily units and mobile homes, by city and ZIP code, 1988, annual MSA rpt, 9304-20.1

Wages by occupation, for office and plant workers, 1989 survey, periodic MSA rpt, 6785-3.9

see also under By City and By SMSA or MSA in the "Index by Categories"

Value added tax

EC economic integration, proposed duty rates and ad valorem taxes on alcohol, tobacco, and fuel, 1989 rpt, 9886-4.140

Van Den Avyle, Michael J.

"Alewife and Blueback Herring. Species Profiles: Life Histories and Environmental Requirements of Coastal Fishes and Invertebrates (South Atlantic)", 5506-8.118

"Atlantic Menhaden. Species Profiles: Life Histories and Environmental Requirements of Coastal Fishes and Invertebrates (Mid-Atlantic)", 5506-8.115

"Spot. Species Profiles: Life Histories and Environmental Requirements of Coastal Fishes and Invertebrates (South Atlantic)", 5506-8.98

Van Dyke, John

"Impact of Minimum Drinking Age Laws on Fatal Crash Involvements: An Update of the NHTSA Analyses", 7768-103

Van Hooser, Dwane D.

"Timberland and Woodland Resources Outside National Forests in Northeastern New Mexico, 1987", 1206-23.9

"Timberland and Woodland Resources Outside National Forests in Southern New Mexico, 1987", 1206-23.10

Van House, Nancy A.

"Public Library Effectiveness Study: Final Report", 4878-3

Van Meir, Larry

"Trends in Concentrate Use", 1561-4.906

Vanadium

see Metals and metal industries

Vancouver, Canada

Fruit and vegetable shipments, and arrivals in US and Canada cities, by mode of transport and State and country of origin, 1988, annual rpt, 1311-4.2

Vancouver, Wash.

CPI by component for US city average, and by region, population size, and for 27 metro areas, monthly rpt, 6762-2

Housing vacancy rates for single and multifamily units and mobile homes, by city and ZIP code, 1989, annual MSA rpt, 9304-21.1

see also under By SMSA or MSA in the "Index by Categories"

Vandalism

Arrests, by offense, offender characteristics, and location, 1970s-87, annual rpt, 6064-6.4

Arrests, by offense, offender characteristics, and location, 1988, annual rpt, 6224-2.2

Bombing incidents and casualties, by target, circumstances, and State, 1979-88, annual rpt, 8484-4.1

Diplomats and staff with immunity for foreign missions in US and US missions abroad, and foreign diplomats criminal cases, 1978-87, hearing, 25388-51

Historic and natural natl landmarks damaged and threatened, with owner, location, damage type, and recommended remedial action, 1988, annual listing, 5544-16

Juvenile court delinquency cases, by offense, referral source, disposition, age, sex, race, State, and county, 1985, annual rpt, 6064-12

Tax (income) returns of sole proprietorships, income statement items, by industry group, 1987, annual article, 8302–2.904; 8302–2.921

Thefts, and value of property stolen and recovered, by property type, 1988, annual rpt, 6224–2.1

Thefts, by property type, 1973-87, annual rpt, 6224–8

Venereal diseases

see Sexually transmitted diseases

Venezuela

Agricultural and food production and indexes, total and for selected commodities, by country, 1970s-88, annual rpt, 1524–12

Agricultural production, prices, and trade, by country, 1960s-89, annual world region rpt, 1524–4.2

Agricultural trade by commodity and country, prices, and world market devs, monthly rpt, 1922–12

Agricultural trade of US, by detailed commodity and country, 1988, semiannual rpt, 1522–4

AID economic aid to developing countries, obligations and disbursements by country, quarterly rpt, 9912–4

AID loans repayment status and terms by program and country, and status of predecessor agency loans, quarterly rpt, 9912–3

Aluminum sulfate from Venezuela, injury to US industry from foreign subsidized and less than fair value imports, investigation with background financial and operating data, 1989 rpt, 9886–19.64; 9886–19.69

Coal production, trade, and govt subsidies, by country and country group, 1973-87 and projected to 2000, 2048–144

Economic and military aid and loans from US and intl agencies, by program and country, FY46-87, annual rpt, 9914–5

Economic conditions in Communist, OECD, and selected other countries, 1960s-88, annual rpt, 9114–4

Economic conditions, income, production, prices, employment, and trade, 1989 periodic country rpt, 2046–4.63

Economic conditions, investment and export opportunities, and trade practices, 1989 country market research rpt, 2046–6.8

Economic conditions, policy, and trade practices, by country, 1986-88, annual rpt, 21384–5

Economic indicators of developing countries, problem debtors compared to other borrowers, by country, 1973-84, 1528–285

Economic, social, political, and geographic summary data, by country, 1989, annual factbook, 9114–2

Energy-intensive industry output and operations, and US investment barriers, for energy-rich countries, 1984-88, 9886–4.142

Exports and imports of Latin America, and balance of trade with US, by country, 1988, annual rpt, 2044–34

Exports and imports of US, by commodity and country, 1970-87, world area rpt, 9116–1.5

Exports and imports of US, by selected country, country group, and commodity group, 1988, annual rpt, 2044–37

Human rights conditions in 170 countries, 1988, annual rpt, 21384–3

Imports of goods, services, and investment from US, trade barriers, impacts, and US actions, by country, 1988, annual rpt, 444–2

Intl transactions of US with 9 countries, 1986-88, *Survey of Current Business*, monthly rpt, annual table, 2702–1.31

Labor conditions, union coverage, and work accidents, 1989 annual country rpt, 6366–4.52

Military aid of US, arms sales, and training programs costs and budget requests, by program, world region, and country, FY88-90, annual rpt, 7144–13

Military spending, arms trade, and force strengths, with govt spending and population, by country, 1977-87, annual rpt, 9824–1

Minerals Yearbook, 1987, Vol 3: foreign country reviews of production, trade, and policy, by commodity, annual rpt, 5604–35

Minerals Yearbook, 1987, Vol 3 preprints: foreign country review of production, trade, and policy, by commodity, annual rpt, 5604–23.75

Multinatl US firms and foreign affiliates finances and operations, by industry of parent firm and affiliate, world area, and country, preliminary 1987, annual rpt, 2704–5

Oil production, and exports and prices for US, by major exporting country, detailed data, monthly rpt, 3162–24

Oil production, trade, use, and stocks, by selected country and country group, monthly rpt, 3162–42

Population size, growth rates, and components of change, by country, projected 1989-2020 and trends from 1950, biennial rpt, 2324–9

Steel export ceilings under voluntary restraint agreements, by country and product, with Western US steel industry impact, 1989 rpt, 9886–4.136

Steel imports of US under voluntary restraint agreement, by product, customs district, and country, with US industry operating data, monthly rpt, 9882–13

UN voting record and share of votes in agreement with US, by issue, country, and world area, 1988, annual rpt, 7004–18

see also under By Foreign Country in the "Index by Categories"

Ventura, Calif.

Housing vacancy rates for single and multifamily units and mobile homes, by city and ZIP code, 1988, annual MSA rpt, 9304–20.6

Wages by occupation, for office and plant workers, 1989 survey, periodic MSA rpt, 6785–3.9

see also under By SMSA or MSA in the "Index by Categories"

Ventura, Stephanie J.

"Births of Hispanic Parentage, 1983 and 1984", 4147–24.2

"Births of Hispanic Parentage, 1985", 4147–24.2

"Trends and Variations in First Births to Older Women, 1970-86", 4147–21.47

"Trends in Marital Status of Mothers at Conception and Birth of First Child: U.S., 1964-66, 1972, and 1980", 4147–24.2

Venture capital

Japan venture capital investment in US, and industry and govt biotechnology R&D spending, FY85-86, 2048–139

Securities offerings of venture capital-backed firms by industry div, and venture capital firms financing by source, 1975-88, article, 9373–1.914

Small business capital formation sources, 1988 annual conf, 9734–4

Small business financial and technical aid of States, 1988 listing, 9768–15

Small business financing sources, and business financial data by size, type, and industry, various periods 1980-88, annual rpt, 9764–6.2

see also Small Business Investment Companies

Vermiculite

see Nonmetallic minerals and mines

Vermont

Agriculture census, 1987: farms, farmland, production, finances, and operator characteristics, by county, final State rpt, 2331–1.45

AIDS public knowledge, by age and education, for Vermont, 1986-87 survey, article, 4042–3.938

Bank deposits in FDIC-insured commercial and savings banks, by instn, State, and county, as of June 1988, annual regional rpt, 9295–3.1

Banks and thrifts in New England, financial statements by type of instn and Fed deposit insurance, and State, 1987, annual rpt, 9304–3

County Business Patterns, 1987: employment, establishments, and payroll, by SIC 2- to 4-digit industry and county, annual State rpt, 2326–8.47

Deaths and rates, by detailed location, cause, and demographic characteristics, 1987, US Vital Statistics annual rpt, 4144–3.1

DOD prime contract awards, by contractor, service branch, State, and city, FY88, annual rpt, 3544–22

Economic indicators for New England States, Fed Reserve 1st District, monthly rpt, 9373–24

Economic indicators for New England States, Fed Reserve 1st District, quarterly rpt with articles, 9373–2

Employment, earnings, and hours, by selected SIC 1- to 4-digit industry, State, and for 262 MSAs, 1972-87, 6748–81.5

Fed Govt spending in States and local areas, by type, State, county, and city, FY88, annual rpt, 2464–3

Fed Govt spending in States, by type, program, agency, and State, FY88, annual rpt, 2464–2

HHS financial aid, by program, recipient, State, and city, FY88, annual regional listing, 4004–3.1

Homeless children educational enrollment and needs, 1988, annual State rpt, 4804–35.45

Income (personal) per capita and by source, and earnings by industry div, by State, MSA, and county, 1982-87, annual regional rpt, 2704–2.2

Medicare physicians assigned-fee laws of 4 States, impacts on care cost and availability, 1985-89, GAO rpt, 26121–312

Mineral Industry Surveys, State reviews of production, 1988, preliminary annual rpt, 5614-6

Minerals Yearbook, 1987, Vol 2 preprints: State review of production and sales by commodity, and business activity, annual rpt, 5604-16.47

Minerals Yearbook, 1987, Vol 2: State reviews of production, sales, and firms, by commodity, and business activity, annual rpt, 5604-34

Nursing home compliance with Medicare and Medicaid regulations, and patient characteristics, by facility, 1987/88, annual State rpt, 4654-15.47

Older persons employment, income, and other characteristics, by sex and age, 1900-86, hearing, 21148-54

Retail trade census, 1987: employment, establishments, sales, and payroll, by SIC 2- to 4-digit kind of business, MSA, county, and city, State rpt, 2397-1.46

Savings instns, FHLB 1st District members financial operations and related economic and housing indicators, monthly rpt, 9302-4

Service industries census, 1987: employment, establishments, receipts, and payroll, by SIC 2- to 4-digit kind of business, MSA, county, and city, State rpt, 2391-1.46

Statistical Abstract of US, social, political, and economic data, with foreign comparisons, 1790-2025, comprehensive annual compilation, 2324-1

Unemployed displaced workers, labor-mgmt committee aid recipients by selected characteristics, for 4 State programs, 1988, GAO rpt, 26121-316

Water supply in northeastern US, precipitation and stream runoff by station, monthly rpt, 2182-3

Wholesale trade census, 1987: employment, establishments, finances, and operations, by SIC 2- to 4-digit kind of business, MSA, county, and city, State rpt, 2405-1.46

Wildlife-related recreation, hunting, and fishing participation and spending, detailed data, 1985 survey, quinquennial State rpt, 5506-6.45

see also under By State in the "Index by Categories"

Vertrees, James C.

"Cost Effectiveness of Home and Community-Based Care", 4652-1.943

Veterans

Agent Orange exposure health effects, literature review, 1987, annual rpt series, 8706-1

Agent Orange exposure of Air Force personnel, deaths and rates by cause and selected characteristics, 1989 annual rpt, 3604-3

Census of Population and Housing, 1990: data item selection, questionnaire dev, and testing, 2626-11.2

Deaths of military personnel by service branch and age group, and veterans death rates, 1966-88, annual rpt, 8654-1

Homeless population characteristics by city, and Federal funding by program, 1980s-89, hearings, 21248-123

Insurance (health) coverage of total and working population, by selected characteristics, 1987, 4186-8.1

Older persons socioeconomic characteristics, 1900s-86 and projected to 2050, biennial chartbook, 12904-1

Population and characteristics of veterans, and VA activities and programs, FY88, annual rpt, 8604-3

Population of veterans, and benefits programs awareness and use, by age, sex, income, race, and period of service, 1987 survey, 8608-1

Population of veterans, by period of service, age, and State, as of Mar 1989, semiannual rpt, 8602-7

Population of veterans, by period of service, FY64-88, annual rpt, 8604-5.1

Prisoners in State instns, by offense, criminal history, and inmate, family, and victim characteristics, 1986, annual rpt, 6064-26.3

Puerto Rico veterans and war casualties, by period of service, 1986 hearings, 21448-39

Statistical Abstract of US, social, political, and economic data, 1790-2025, comprehensive annual compilation, 2324-1.2

War participants, deaths, veterans living, and compensation and pension recipients, for each US war, 1775-1988, annual rpt, 8604-2

see also Retired military personnel

see also Servicepersons life insurance programs

see also Veterans benefits and pensions

see also Veterans education

see also Veterans employment

see also Veterans health facilities and services

see also Veterans housing

see also Veterans rehabilitation

Veterans Administration

Activities and programs of VA, monthly rpt, 9922-2

Agent Orange exposure health effects, literature review, annual rpt series, issuing agency change, 9926-7

AIDS cases at VA health care centers, by facility and region, periodic tables, 9922-15

Benefits claims processing and efficiency at regional VA offices, and hearing officers salaries and travel costs, 1986-88, hearing, 21768-47

Budget of US, authoritative financial statements with appropriations, outlays, and receipts, by category and agency, FY88, annual rpt, 8104-2.2

Compensation and pension cases of VA, by type of entitlement and period of service, monthly rpt, 9922-10

Disability and death compensation cases of VA, by entitlement type, period of service, and sex, semiannual rpt, issuing agency change, 9922-9

Disability and death compensation cases of VA, by entitlement type, period of service, sex, age, and State, annual rpt, issuing agency change, 9924-20

Disability ratings system of VA, evaluation of methods, 1987 survey, GAO rpt, 26121-264

Education funding by Federal agency, program, and recipient type, and instn spending, FY80-88, 4828-21

Employment (civilian) of Fed Govt, by work schedule, selected agency, State, and MSA, as of Dec 1988, article, 9842-1.904

Expenditures and beneficiaries of VA compensation, health, and rehabilitation programs, annual rpt, issuing agency change, 9924-13

Expenditures for VA programs, by State, county, and congressional district, annual rpt, issuing agency change, 9924-14

Expenditures of Fed Govt in States, by type, program, agency, and State, FY88, annual rpt, 2464-2

Fraud and abuse in VA programs, audits and investigations, semiannual rpt, issuing agency change, 9922-13

Health care centers canteen services discontinuing tobacco sales, impacts on finances, FY83-FY88, hearing, 21768-49

Health care employment and average salary of VA, by pay system and occupational group, 1988, annual rpt, 9844-6

Health care employment of VA, work-years, pay rates, and benefits use and costs, by agency, FY87, annual rpt, 9844-31

Health care facilities of VA, beds closed because of nurse shortages, and malpractice claim rates, FY85-88, hearing, 21768-48

Health care facilities of VA, surgery-related deaths by procedure and instn, biennial rpt, issuing agency change, 9924-26

Health care for veterans, patients, visits, costs, and operating beds, quarterly rpt, issuing agency change, 9922-5

Health care professionals of VA, by selected employment characteristics and VA district, quarterly rpt, issuing agency change, 9922-11

Health care services sharing contracts among VA and non-VA facilities, annual rpt, issuing agency change, 9924-18

Hearing aid performance test results, by make and model, annual rpt, issuing agency change, 9924-5

Insurance (life) for veterans and servicepersons, actuarial analysis of 5 VA programs, annual rpt, issuing agency change, 9924-16

Insurance (life) for veterans and servicepersons, finances and coverage by program and State, annual rpt, issuing agency change, 9924-2

Insurance (life) for veterans and servicepersons, financial statements of programs and death rates, annual rpt, issuing agency change, 9924-3

Loan guarantee operations of VA, quarterly rpt, issuing agency change, 9922-1

Medicine and Surgery Dept of VA, trainees by detailed program and city, annual rpt, issuing agency change, 9924-21

Mental health services in VA facilities, annual listing, issuing agency change, 9924-10

Pay rates of Fed Govt civilian employees, by pay schedule and grade, 1989 and trends from 1789, annual rpt, 21624-4

Population of veterans, by period of service, age, and State, semiannual rpt, issuing agency change, 9922-3

Science and engineering employment in Fed Govt, by field, degree level, race, sex, agency, and State, 1987, annual rpt, 9627-5

Small business construction contracts of Fed Govt, surety bonds use and fraud cases, by agency, 1985-89, GAO rpt, 26113–438

Veterans characteristics, and VA programs and activities, FY87, annual rpt, issuing agency change, 9924–1

War participants, deaths, veterans living, and compensation and pension recipients, for each US war, annual rpt, issuing agency change, 9924–11

see also Department of Veterans Affairs

Veterans Benefits Administration

Insurance (life) for veterans and servicepersons, financial statements of programs and death rates, as of June 1989, annual rpt, 8654–1

Veterans benefits and pensions

Assistance (financial and nonfinancial) of Fed Govt, 1989 base edition with supplements, annual listing, 104–5

Beneficiaries and taxes collected for social insurance programs since 1940, monthly rpt, 4742–1.1

Benefits claims processing and efficiency at regional VA offices, and hearing officers salaries and travel costs, 1986-88, hearing, 21768–47

Benefits overpayment recovery and judgment enforcement cases filed in Federal district courts, June 1988, annual rpt, 18204–8.11

Benefits overpayment recovery and judgment enforcement cases filed in Federal district courts, June 1989, annual rpt, 18204–2.12

Board of Veterans Appeals caseloads and dispositions, 1988 hearing, 25768–47

Budget deficit reduction under Gramm-Rudman Act, cancellation of budget authority by program, FY90, annual rpt, 104–27; 26304–6

Budget of US Appendix, obligations, appropriations, and personnel, by program and agency, FY90, annual rpt, 104–3

Budget of US, compact budgets by activity, function, and agency, FY90 and projected to FY94, annual rpt, 104–2

Budget of US, historical data, selected years FY34-88 and projected to FY94, annual rpt, 104–22

Budget of US, House concurrent resolution, with spending and revenue targets, FY90, annual rpt, 21264–2

Budget of US, midsession review of FY90 budget, by function and agency, annual rpt, 104–7

Budget of US, Reagan Admin policy changes by program, FY90, annual rpt, 104–21

Budget of US, receipts by source, outlays by agency and program, and balances, monthly rpt, 8102–3

Budget of US, Senate concurrent resolution, with spending and revenue targets, FY90, annual rpt, 25254–1

Compensation and pension cases of VA, by type of entitlement and period of service, monthly rpt, 8602–5; 9922–10

Disability and death compensation cases of VA, by entitlement type, period of service, and sex, as of Mar 1989, semiannual rpt, 8602–8

Disability and death compensation cases of VA, by entitlement type, period of service, sex, age, and State, FY88, annual rpt, 8604–7

Disability compensation and pensions, VA claims processing and disposition, FY87, GAO rpt, 26121–293

Disability compensation cases of VA, effects of eliminating non-service connected disabilities, with background data, 1986, GAO rpt, 26121–295

Disability ratings system of VA, evaluation of methods, 1987 survey, GAO rpt, 26121–264

Expenditures and beneficiaries of VA compensation, health, and rehabilitation programs, FY64-88, annual rpt, 8604–5

Expenditures, coverage, and benefits for social welfare programs, late 1930s-87, annual rpt, 4744–3.1; 4744–3.3; 4744–3.7

Expenditures for public welfare by program, and private health care spending, FY50s-86, annual article, 4742–1.909

Expenditures for public welfare programs, by program type and level of govt, FY50s-87, annual article, 4742–1.929

Expenditures for VA programs, by State, county, and congressional district, FY88, annual rpt, 8604–6

Expenditures of Fed Govt in States, by type, program, agency, and State, FY88, annual rpt, 2464–2

Finances of govts, revenues by source and spending by function, natl income and product account, *Survey of Current Business*, monthly rpt, 2702–1.24

Fraud and abuse in VA programs, audits and investigations, 2nd half FY89, semiannual rpt, 8602–1

Homeless persons aid by program and Federal agency, and indicators of need, 1988, annual rpt, 14364–1

Household composition, income, benefits, and labor force status, Survey of Income and Program Participation methodology, working paper series, 2626–10

Income (household, family, and personal), by source, detailed characteristics, and region, 1987, annual Current Population Rpt, 2546–6.59

Income (personal) by source including transfer payments, and social insurance contributions, by region, 1948 and 1987, 2708–40

Income from transfer payments, natl income and product account, *Survey of Current Business*, monthly rpt, 2702–1.23

Insurance (life) for veterans and servicepersons, actuarial analysis of VA programs, 1988, annual rpt, 8604–1

Insurance (life) for veterans and servicepersons, finances and coverage by program and State, 1988, annual rpt, 8604–4

Insurance (life) for veterans and servicepersons, financial statements of programs and death rates, as of June 1989, annual rpt, 8654–1

Lands (public) acreage and grants, by State, FY88 and trends, annual rpt, 5724–1.1

Loans and loan guarantees of of Fed Govt, outstanding amounts by agency and program, *Treasury Bulletin*, quarterly rpt, 8002–4.9

Mental illness (post-traumatic stress) cases of Vietnam veterans, claims, and VA disposition, 1985-88, hearing, 25768–46

R&D funding by Fed Govt, by detailed function, program, and agency, FY88-90, annual rpt, 9627–9

Red Cross activities, finances, volunteers, and certificates issued, by program, FY88, annual rpt, 29254–1

Rural areas aid from Fed Govt compared to urban areas, by program and degree of urbanization, FY85, periodic rpt, 1598–248

Statistical Abstract of US, social, political, and economic data, 1790-2025, comprehensive annual compilation, 2324–1.2

Tax expenditures, Federal revenues forgone through income tax deductions and exclusions by type, FY90-94, annual rpt, 21784–10

Telephone service of households, by composition, income sources, and other characteristics, 1984-87, 9288–11

US attorneys civil and criminal cases by type and disposition, and collections, by Federal district, FY88, annual rpt, 6004–2.1; 6004–2.5

VA activities and programs, and veterans characteristics, FY88, annual rpt, 8604–3

VA activities and programs, monthly rpt, 8602–3; 9922–2

VA programs awareness and use, by age, sex, income, race, and period of service, 1987 survey, 8608–1

War participants, deaths, veterans living, and compensation and pension recipients, for each US war, 1775-1988, annual rpt, 8604–2

see also Military benefits and pensions

see also Servicepersons life insurance programs

see also Veterans education

see also Veterans health facilities and services

see also Veterans housing

Veterans education

Assistance and other sources of support, with student expenses and characteristics, by instn type and control, 1987 triennial study, series, 4846–3

Education Dept programs funding, operations, and effectiveness, FY88, annual rpt, 4804–5

Expenditures and beneficiaries of VA compensation, health, and rehabilitation programs, FY64-88, annual rpt, 8604–5

Higher education instn support from Fed Govt, by program and instn type and control, FY85-88, annual rpt, 4804–28.4

Pell grants and applicants, by tuition, family and student income, instn type and control, and State, 1987/88, annual rpt, 4804–1

Training benefits and participation, and other VA activities, FY88, annual rpt, 8604–3.7

VA activities and programs, monthly rpt, 8602–3; 9922–2

VA programs awareness and use, by age, sex, income, race, and period of service, 1987 survey, 8608–1

Veterans employment

Disability and death compensation cases of VA, by entitlement type, period of service, and sex, as of Mar 1989, semiannual rpt, 8602–8

Disabled persons employment, labor force status, and other characteristics, 1988, Current Population Rpt, 2546–2.147

DOT employment, by subagency, occupation, and selected personnel characteristics, FY88, annual rpt, 7304–18

Employment and Training Admin activities, funding, and participant characteristics, by program, FY80-86, 6408–71

Fed Govt civilian employees demographic and employment characteristics, as of Sept 1988, article, 9842–1.901

Fed Govt civilian employment, by occupation, pay schedule, grade, sex, and race, as of Sept 1988, article, 9842–1.902

Fed Govt employment and promotion of disabled veterans by agency, and recruitment coordinator activities, FY81-87, GAO rpt, 26119–245

Fed Govt employment of minorities, handicapped, and veterans, and years of service, by occupation, age, sex, and agency, as of Sept 1988, biennial rpt, 9844–27

Postal Service employment of veterans, FY88, annual rpt, 9864–5.1

Rehabilitation of veterans, participants earnings and tax liability before and after training, and program admin, 1988 hearing, 25768–48

Unemployment insurance claims, by program, weekly press release, 6402–14

VA employment characteristics and activities, FY88, annual rpt, 8604–3.8

Vietnam veterans employment status, by age and race, monthly rpt, 6742–2

Vietnam veterans employment status, by age, monthly press release, 6742–5

Vietnam veterans employment status, by age, race, and Hispanic origin, 1970-88, 6728–38.1

Vietnam veterans employment status, transcripts of BLS Commissioner's monthly testimony, periodic rpt, 23846–4

Veterans health facilities and services

AIDS cases at VA health care centers, by facility and region, periodic tables, 8702–1; 9922–15

Assistance (block and categorical grants) programs for State and local govts, FY89, biennial listing, 10044–8

Assistance (financial and nonfinancial) of Fed Govt, 1989 base edition with supplements, annual listing, 104–5

Budget of US, CBO analysis of revenue and spending alternatives and projections of economic indicators, FY90-94, annual rpt, 26304–3

Budget of US, historical data, selected years FY34-88 and projected to FY94, annual rpt, 104–22

Budget of US, special analysis of Federal capital spending by category, projected FY89-2005 and trends from FY81, annual rpt, 104–24

Canteen services of VA health care centers, discontinuation of tobacco sales impacts on finances, FY83-FY88, hearing, 21768–49

Clinics outpatient care applications, denials, appointments, and waiting periods, for 4 Florida VA clinics, FY88, GAO rpt, 26121–283

Contracts for sharing health services among VA and non-VA facilities, by service type and region, FY88, annual rpt, 8704–5

Expenditures and beneficiaries of VA compensation, health, and rehabilitation programs, FY64-88, annual rpt, 8604–5

Expenditures for public welfare by program, and private health care spending, FY50s-86, annual article, 4742–1.909

Expenditures for VA programs, by State, county, and congressional district, FY88, annual rpt, 8604–6

Fraud and abuse in VA programs, audits and investigations, 2nd half FY89, semiannual rpt, 8602–1

Health care personnel of VA born abroad, and English proficiency, as of Mar 1988, GAO rpt, 26121–273

Health condition and health care resources, use, and spending, 1950s-87, annual data compilation, 4144–11

Medicine and Surgery Dept of VA, trainees by detailed program and city, FY88, annual rpt, 8704–4

Mental health care facilities, staff, and patient characteristics, *Statistical Notes* series, 4506–3

Mental health services, staffing, research, and training programs in VA facilities, 1989 biennial listing, 8704–2

Mental illness (post-traumatic stress) cases of Vietnam veterans, claims, and VA disposition, 1985-88, hearing, 25768–46

Nurses (RN) employment, shortages, recruitment, and retention, findings and recommendations, 1988 rpt, 4008–88

Nurses shortages impacts on VA health facilities bed size, and malpractice claim rates against physicians, FY85-88, hearing, 21768–48

Older persons with functional limitations, long-term health care needs, and costs by payment source, 1982-85, GAO rpt, 26121–266

Patients, visits, costs, and operating beds, by VA and contract facility, and region, quarterly rpt, 8602–4

Physicians staffing, vacancies, and positions filled, for VA health care facilities, 1982-87, hearing, 25768–48

Statistical Abstract of US, social, political, and economic data, 1790-2025, comprehensive annual compilation, 2324–1.2

Surgery-related deaths and complications, by procedure and VA facility, and compared to non-VA instns, 1981-88, biennial rpt, 8704–1

VA activities and programs, and veterans characteristics, FY88, annual rpt, 8604–3

VA activities and programs, monthly rpt, 8602–3; 9922–2

VA programs awareness and use, by age, sex, income, race, and period of service, 1987 survey, 8608–1

see also Military health facilities and services

see also Veterans benefits and pensions

see also Veterans rehabilitation

Veterans Health Services and Research Administration

Agent Orange exposure health effects, literature review, 1987, annual rpt series, 8706–1

AIDS cases at VA health care centers, by facility and region, periodic tables, 8702–1

Contracts for sharing health services among VA and non-VA facilities, by service type and region, FY88, annual rpt, 8704–5

Hearing aid performance test results, by make and model, 1989 annual rpt, 8704–3

Medicine and Surgery Dept of VA, trainees by detailed program and city, FY88, annual rpt, 8704–4

Mental health services, staffing, research, and training programs in VA facilities, 1989 biennial listing, 8704–2

Surgery-related deaths and complications, by procedure and VA facility, and compared to non-VA instns, 1981-88, biennial rpt, 8704–1

Veterans hospitals

see Veterans health facilities and services

Veterans housing

American Housing Survey: unit and households detailed characteristics, and unit and neighborhood quality, MSA rpt series, 2485–6

American Housing Survey: unit and households detailed characteristics, and unit and neighborhood quality, 1985, biennial rpt, 2485–12

Expenditures for VA programs, by State, county, and congressional district, FY88, annual rpt, 8604–6

Expenditures of Fed Govt in States, by type, program, agency, and State, FY88, annual rpt, 2464–2

Loan guarantee operations of VA, quarterly rpt, 8602–2

Mortgage loan activity, by type of lender, loan, and mortgaged property, quarterly press release, 5142–30

Mortgage loan activity, by type of lender, loan, and mortgaged property, 1986-88, annual press release, 5144–22

Mortgage loan activity of VA, defaults, and property acquired, FY64-88, annual rpt, 8604–5.3

Mortgage loans guaranteed by VA, and other activities, FY88, annual rpt, 8604–3.7

Mortgages FHA-insured for 1-family units, by loan type and mortgage characteristics, quarterly rpt, 5142–45

New single and multifamily units, by structural and financial characteristics, inside-outside MSAs, and region, 1984-88, annual rpt, 2384–1

New single-family houses sold and sales price by type of financing, monthly rpt, quarterly tables, 2382–3.2

Statistical Abstract of US, social, political, and economic data, 1790-2025, comprehensive annual compilation, 2324–1.2

Tax (property) revenue by level of govt, assessed values by locality, and exemptions, by property type and State, 1987 Census of Govts, 2453–1

VA activities and programs, monthly rpt, 8602–3; 9922–2

VA programs awareness and use, by age, sex, income, race, and period of service, 1987 survey, 8608–1

Veterans loans
see Veterans benefits and pensions
see Veterans housing

Veterans pensions
see Veterans benefits and pensions

Veterans rehabilitation
Expenditures and beneficiaries of VA
compensation, health, and rehabilitation
programs, FY64-88, annual rpt, 8604-5

Expenditures for VA programs, by State,
county, and congressional district, FY88,
annual rpt, 8604-6

Medicine and Surgery Dept of VA, trainees
by detailed program and city, FY88,
annual rpt, 8704-4

Mental health services, staffing, research,
and training programs in VA facilities,
1989 biennial listing, 8704-2

Participants in veterans rehabilitation,
earnings and tax liability before and after
training, and program admin, 1988
hearing, 25768-48

VA activities and programs, and veterans
characteristics, FY88, annual rpt, 8604-3

VA activities and programs, monthly rpt,
8602-3; 9922-2

VA health care facilities physicians, dentists,
and nurses, by selected employment
characteristics and VA district, quarterly
rpt, 8602-6

VA programs awareness and use, by age,
sex, income, race, and period of service,
1987 survey, 8608-1

Veterinary medicine
Agricultural Statistics, 1988, annual rpt,
1004-1.1

Cattle tuberculosis cases and cooperative
Federal-State eradication activities, by
State, FY88, annual rpt, 1394-13

County Business Patterns, 1987:
employment, establishments, and payroll,
by SIC 2- to 4-digit industry and county,
annual State rpt series, 2326-8

Dairy Herd Improvement Program
cooperatives and cows tested, by State,
1987, annual rpt, 1124-1

Drugs (veterinary) PPI, monthly rpt,
6762-6

Drugs (veterinary) PPI, monthly 1988,
annual rpt, 6764-2

Enrollment in science and engineering grad
programs, by field, source of funds, and
characteristics of student and instn,
1975-87, annual rpt, 9627-7

Farm production itemized costs, by farm
sales size and region, 1988, annual rpt,
1614-3

Farm production itemized costs, receipts,
and returns, by commodity and region,
1985-87, annual rpt, 1544-20

FDA investigations and regulatory activities,
quarterly rpt, 4062-3

Foreign countries agricultural research
grants of USDA, by program, subagency,
and country, FY88, annual listing,
1954-3

Health condition and health care resources,
use, and spending, 1950s-87, annual data
compilation, 4144-11

Lab animals protection, licensing, and
inspection activities of USDA, by State,
FY88, annual rpt, 1394-10

Military health care personnel, and
accessions by training source, by
occupation, specialty, and service branch,
FY87, annual rpt, 3544-24

Natl Veterinary Services Labs activities,
biologic drug products evaluation and
disease testing, FY88, annual rpt,
1394-17

Research (agricultural) funding and staffing
for USDA, State agencies, and other
instns, by topic, FY88, annual rpt,
1744-2

Research and education grants, USDA
competitive awards by program and
recipient, FY88, annual listing, 1764-1

Tax (income) returns of partnerships,
income statement items by industry group,
1986, annual article, 8302-2.903

Tax (income) returns of sole proprietorships,
income statement items, by industry
group, 1987, annual article, 8302-2.904;
8302-2.921

Training support grants of Bur of Health
Professions, by program, region, and
State, FY80-87, 4118-62
see also Animal diseases and zoonoses

Vice Presidency of the U.S.
see Office of the Vice President

Vicksburg, Miss.
Freight (waterborne domestic and foreign)
by commodity, traffic, and passengers, by
port and waterway, 1987, annual rpt,
3754-3.2

Victoria, Tex.
see also under By SMSA or MSA in the
"Index by Categories"

Video recordings and equipment
Cassette rentals and sales, projected
1987-89, 2808-27

Courtroom videotaping, permissibility and
effective date, by State, 1987, annual rpt,
6064-6.1

Criminal justice issues and research, rpts
and videotapes, 1984-88, listing,
6066-26.2

Fed Govt audiovisual activities and
spending, by whether performed in-house
and agency, FY87, annual rpt, 9514-1

Guam economic censuses, 1987:
employment, firms, payroll, and receipts,
by SIC 1- to 4-digit industry and election
district, 2595-1

Library of Congress rpts and recordings,
1989, biennial listing, 26404-5

Natl Archives and Records Admin
activities, finances, holdings, and staff,
FY88, annual rpt, 9514-2

Northern Mariana Islands economic census,
1987: employment, firms, payroll, and
receipts, by SIC 1- to 4-digit industry,
2597-1

Price indexes (producer), by stage of
processing and detailed commodity,
monthly rpt, 6762-6

Price indexes (producer), by stage of
processing and detailed commodity,
monthly 1988, annual rpt, 6764-2

Service industries census, 1987:
establishments, receipts, employment, and
payroll, by SIC 2- to 4-digit kind of
business, MSA, county, and city, State rpt
series, 2391-1

Vietnam
Agricultural and food production and
indexes, total and for selected
commodities, by country, 1970s-88,
annual rpt, 1524-12

Agricultural production, prices, and trade,
by country, 1960s-89, annual world region
rpt, 1524-4.2

Agricultural trade of US, by detailed
commodity and country, 1988, semiannual
rpt, 1522-4

AID loans repayment status and terms by
program and country, and status of
predecessor agency loans, quarterly rpt,
9912-3

Cuba economic conditions, agricultural and
industrial production and distribution,
trade, and intl economic relations,
1980-87 with trends from 1961, 9118-8

Economic and military aid and loans from
US and intl agencies, by program and
country, FY46-87, annual rpt, 9914-5

Economic conditions in Communist, OECD,
and selected other countries, 1960s-88,
annual rpt, 9114-4

Economic, social, political, and geographic
summary data, by country, 1989, annual
factbook, 9114-2

Exports and imports of US with Communist
countries, by detailed commodity and
country, quarterly rpt with articles,
9882-2

Human rights conditions in 170 countries,
1988, annual rpt, 21384-3

Military spending, arms trade, and force
strengths, with govt spending and
population, by country, 1977-87, annual
rpt, 9824-1

Minerals production, reserves, and industry
role in domestic economy and world
supply, 1988 country rpt, 5606-1.17

Minerals Yearbook, 1987, Vol 3: foreign
country reviews of production, trade, and
policy, by commodity, annual rpt,
5604-35

Minerals Yearbook, 1987, Vol 3 preprints:
foreign country review of production,
trade, and policy, by commodity, annual
rpt, 5604-23.85

Population size, growth rates, and
components of change, by country,
projected 1989-2020 and trends from
1950, biennial rpt, 2324-9

Refugee arrivals in US by world area of
origin and State of settlement, and
Federal aid, FY88-90, annual rpt,
7004-16

Refugee resettlement programs and funding,
arrivals by country of origin, and
indicators of adjustment, by State, FY88,
annual rpt, 4694-5

Refugees from Indochina, arrivals, and
departures, by country of origin and
resettlement, camp, and ethnicity,
monthly rpt, 7002-4

UN voting record and share of votes in
agreement with US, by issue, country, and
world area, 1988, annual rpt, 7004-18
see also under By Foreign Country in the
"Index by Categories"

Vietnam War
see Veterans benefits and pensions
see War

Villa, Luisa L.
"Epidemiologic Correlates of Cervical
Neoplasia and Risk of Human
Papillomavirus Infection in Asymptomatic
Women in Brazil", 4472-1.908

Vince, Susan W.
"Ecology of Hydric Hammocks: A
Community Profile", 5506-9.37

Vineland, N.J.
see also under By SMSA or MSA in the "Index by Categories"

Vines, Paula L.
"Relationship Between the 1970 and 1980 Industry and Occupation Classification Systems", 2626–2.59

Vinyl chloride
see Chemicals and chemical industry

Vinyl materials
see Plastics and plastics industry
see Synthetic fibers and fabrics

Violence
Crime, by characteristics of victim and offender, circumstances, and location, 1970s-87, annual rpt, 6064–6.3

Juvenile delinquency prevention funding, by program and Federal agency, FY88, annual rpt, 6064–11

Mexican American high school dropouts health condition, substance abuse, and involvement with violence, 1988-89 survey, article, 4042–3.957

Preventive disease and health improvement goals and recommended activities for 2000, with trends 1970s-80s, 4048–10

Prison conditions, population, and problems, issues and bibl, 1989 compilation of papers, 25928–8

see also Assassination
see also Assault
see also Assaults on police
see also Child abuse and neglect
see also Crime and criminals
see also Domestic violence
see also Homicide
see also Rape
see also Riots and disorders
see also Terrorism
see also Vandalism
see also War
see also War casualties

Virgin Islands
see British Virgin Islands
see U.S. Virgin Islands

Virginia
Agriculture census, 1987: farms, farmland, production and costs, and operator characteristics, advance State and county rpts, 2330–1.51

Agriculture census, 1987: farms, farmland, production, finances, and operator characteristics, by county, final State rpt, 2331–1.46

Appalachian Regional Commission funding, by project and State, planned FY89, annual rpt, 9084–3

Apple production, marketing, and prices, for Appalachia and compared to other States, various periods 1986-89, annual rpt, 1311–13

Bank deposits in FDIC-insured commercial and savings banks, by instn, State, and county, as of June 1988, annual regional rpt, 9295–3.2

Banks (insured commercial), Fed Reserve 5th District members financial statements, by State, quarterly rpt, 9389–18

Coal production and mines by county, prices, productivity, miners, reserves, and stocks, by mining method and State, 1987-88, annual rpt, 3164–25

County Business Patterns, 1987: employment, establishments, and payroll, by SIC 2- to 4-digit industry and county, annual State rpt, 2326–8.48

Deaths and rates, by detailed location, cause, and demographic characteristics, 1987, US Vital Statistics annual rpt, 4144–3.1

DOD prime contract awards, by contractor, service branch, State, and city, FY88, annual rpt, 3544–22

Economic indicators by State, Fed Reserve 5th District, quarterly rpt, 9389–16

Employment and housing market indicators by State, FHLB 4th District, quarterly rpt, 9302–36

Employment, earnings, and hours, by selected SIC 1- to 4-digit industry, State, and for 262 MSAs, 1972-87, 6748–81.5

Fed Govt spending in States and local areas, by type, State, county, and city, FY88, annual rpt, 2464–3

Fed Govt spending in States, by type, program, agency, and State, FY88, annual rpt, 2464–2

HHS financial aid, by program, recipient, State, and city, FY88, annual regional listing, 4004–3.3

Homeless children educational enrollment and needs, 1988, annual State rpt, 4804–35.46

Housing and households characteristics, 1985 survey, MSA fact sheet, 2485–11.6

Income (personal) per capita and by source, and earnings by industry div, by State, MSA, and county, 1982-87, annual regional rpt, 2704–2.4

Mineral Industry Surveys, State reviews of production, 1988, preliminary annual rpt, 5614–6

Minerals Yearbook, 1987, Vol 2 preprints: State review of production and sales by commodity, and business activity, annual rpt, 5604–16.48

Minerals Yearbook, 1987, Vol 2: State reviews of production, sales, and firms, by commodity, and business activity, annual rpt, 5604–34

Retail trade census, 1987: employment, establishments, sales, and payroll, by SIC 2- to 4-digit kind of business, MSA, county, and city, State rpt, 2397–1.47

Savings instns, FHLB 4th District members finances and financial ratios, by State, quarterly rpt, 9302–3

Savings instns, FHLB 4th District members finances, by State, 1984-88, annual rpt, 9304–29.8

Service industries census, 1987: employment, establishments, receipts, and payroll, by SIC 2- to 4-digit kind of business, MSA, county, and city, State rpt, 2391–1.47

Statistical Abstract of US, social, political, and economic data, with foreign comparisons, 1790-2025, comprehensive annual compilation, 2324–1

Wages by occupation, and benefits for office and plant workers in southwestern Virginia, 1988 survey, periodic labor market rpt, 6785–3.2

Wages by occupation, and benefits for office and plant workers, 1989 survey, periodic labor market rpt, 6785–3.9

Water supply and quality in streams and lakes, and groundwater levels in wells, by drainage basin, 1987, annual State rpt, 5666–10.43

Water supply and quality in streams and lakes, and groundwater levels in wells, by drainage basin, 1988, annual State rpt, 5666–16.43

Wholesale trade census, 1987: employment, establishments, finances, and operations, by SIC 2- to 4-digit kind of business, MSA, county, and city, State rpt, 2405–1.47

Wildlife-related recreation, hunting, and fishing participation and spending, detailed data, 1985 survey, quinquennial State rpt, 5506–6.46

see also Alexandria, Va.
see also Arlington, Va.
see also Fairfax County, Va.
see also Loudoun County, Va.
see also Newport News, Va.
see also Norfolk, Va.
see also Petersburg, Va.
see also Prince William County, Va.
see also Richmond, Va.
see also Virginia Beach, Va.
see also under By State in the "Index by Categories"

Virginia Beach, Va.
Housing starts and completions authorized by building permits in 40 MSAs, quarterly rpt, 2382–9

Wages by occupation, for office and plant workers, 1989 survey, periodic MSA rpt, 6785–3.10

see also under By City and By SMSA or MSA in the "Index by Categories"

Virta, Robert L.
"Talc Industry—An Overview", 5608–158

Visalia, Calif.
Wages by occupation, for office and plant workers, 1989 survey, periodic MSA rpt, 6785–12.7

see also under By SMSA or MSA in the "Index by Categories"

Viscusi, W. Kip
"Presidential Oversight: Controlling the Regulators", 25408–99

Vision
see also Blind
see also Eye diseases and defects
see also Optometry

VisionQuest National, Ltd.
Cuba refugees entering US during 1980 boatlift, Federal funding for youth mental health services, and participation, 1981-88, GAO rpt, 26121–270

Vissage, John S.
"Forest Statistics for East Tennessee Counties", 1206–27.6

VISTA
Activities of ACTION, by program, FY88, annual rpt, 9024–2

Vital, Christian
"SIC: Switzerland's New Electronic Interbank Payment System", 9389–1.903

Vital statistics
Developing countries disaster preparedness and economic, population, and political data, country rpt series, 9916–2

Developing countries sociodemographic data, and AID dev projects, special study series, 9916–3

Foreign countries economic and social conditions, working paper series, 2326–18

Foreign countries population size, growth rates, and components of change, by country, projected 1989-2020 and trends from 1950, biennial rpt, 2324–9

Health condition and health care resources, use, and spending, 1950s-87, annual data compilation, 4144–11

Natl Vital and Health Statistics Committee activities, FY88, annual narrative rpt, 4164–1

Pacific territories social, economic, health, and govtl data, FY88 and trends, annual rpt, 7004–6

Statistical Abstract of US, social, political, and economic data, 1790-2025, comprehensive annual compilation, 2324–1.1

Survey programs and data collection procedures, Vital and Health Statistics series, 4147–1

Vital and Health Statistics series: advance data rpts, 4146–8

Vital and Health Statistics series: analytical and epidemiological studies, 4147–3

Vital and Health Statistics series and other NCHS rpts, 1980-88, annual listing, 4124–1

Vital and Health Statistics series: foreign and US comparative data, 4147–5

Vital and Health Statistics series: methodology, survey design, and data evaluation, 4147–2

Vital and Health Statistics series: natality, marriage, and divorce trends, 4147–21

Vital and Health Statistics series: reprints of advance data rpts, 4147–16

Vital and Health Statistics series: reprints of monthly rpt supplements, 4147–24

Vital and Health Statistics series: survey questionnaire dev and testing, 4147–6

Vital statistics, preliminary 1987-88 and trends from 1950, annual rpt, 4144–7

Vital statistics provisional data, monthly rpt, 4142–1

Vital statistics provisional data, supplements to monthly rpts, series, 4146–5

see also Births
see also Child mortality
see also Deaths
see also Infant mortality
see also Life expectancy
see also Marriage and divorce

Vitamins and nutrients

Agricultural Statistics, 1988, annual rpt, 1004–1.2

Animal feed mill operations, detailed data by State, 1984, 1568–281

Cancer (breast) risk relation to diet and nutrient intake, for northwestern Italy, 1983-85 study, article, 4472–1.906

Cancer (breast) tumor characteristics related to diet, number of children, and age, 1983-86, article, 4472–1.920

Cancer (lung) risk, by intake of selected nutrients, fruits, and vegetables, by smoking history and sex, 1983-85 local area study, article, 4472–1.918

Cholesterol levels in blood, relation to cancer dev and death risk, and death risk from other causes, by sex, 1963-84 study, article, 4472–1.936

Cholesterol levels measurement using Reflotron analyzer, accuracy compared to lab assay, 1988 article, 4042–3.923

Cholesterol screening, results, and referrals, under alternative guidelines, local area study, 1989 article, 4042–3.941

Consumer research, food marketing, legislation, and regulation devs, and consumption and price trends, quarterly journal, 1541–7

Consumption of food and nutrient intake by individuals, by food group, selected characteristics, and region, supplementary survey series, 1356–5

Consumption of food, daily supply of nutrients and other food components per capita, 1900s-85, annual rpt, 1544–4.3

Consumption of nutrients, nutritional status, and related health condition and practices, by selected characteristics, 1970s-86, 4048–33

Consumption of vitamin and mineral supplements by adults and children, by type and user characteristics, 1986, 4146–8.175

Exports of US, detailed commodities by country, monthly rpt, 2422–3

Fiber content in breakfast cereal and bread, health claim ads, and other factors affecting consumption, 1978-88, 9406–1.60

Fiber supplements effects on rectal polyp dev, local area study, 1989 article, 4472–1.921

Fish nutrient and fatty acid composition, by northeastern US species, 1985-87, 2168–111

Fish nutrient composition and taste effects of alternative processing methods, for selected species, 1988 article, 2162–1.902

Food composition, detailed data on nutrients, calories, and waste, for raw, processed, and prepared foods, series, 1356–3

Food composition, nutrients and calories for raw, processed, and prepared food, 1988 rpt, 1358–3

Imports of US, detailed Schedule A commodities by country, monthly rpt, 2422–2

Manufacturing annual survey, 1986: value of shipments, by SIC 4- to 5-digit product class, 2506–15.3

NIH nutrition biomedical and behavioral research and training activities and funding, by inst, FY87, annual rpt, 4434–15

Prescriptions for drugs, by drug type and brand, and for new drugs, 1987, annual rpt, 4064–12

Price indexes (producer), by stage of processing and detailed commodity, monthly rpt, 6762–6

Price indexes (producer), by stage of processing and detailed commodity, monthly 1988 annual rpt, 6764–2

Production and sales of synthetic organic chemicals, and manufacturer listing, by product, 1988, annual rpt, 9884–3

Rice treated with vitamins and other additives, 1987, biennial rpt, 1564–11.1

Safety and effectiveness of health care, use of unproven treatments and products, costs, and user characteristics, 1986 survey, 4008–86

Smoking and other tobacco use, by knowledge of health effects, and health and other characteristics, 1987, 4147–10.169

Statistical Abstract of US, social, political, and economic data, 1790-2025, comprehensive annual compilation, 2324–1.1

Vocational education and training

Assistance for vocational education by type of recipient and source, and characteristics of programs and students, 1970s-89, series, 4806–3

Degrees (2-yr vocational and academic) recipients and credits, by field, and student and instn characteristics, 1984, 4848–37

Earnings relation to job training, by source of training and employee characteristics, model results, 1983, working paper, 6886–6.34

Employment programs, training, and unemployment compensation, current devs and grants to States, press release series, 6406–2

Enrollment and other data for adult and vocational education programs, by student characteristics, 1980s-88, annual rpt, 4824–2.26

Enrollment in public elementary and secondary schools, and facilities, by type and State, 1987/88, annual rpt, 4834–17

Foreign countries labor conditions, union coverage, and work accidents, annual country rpt series, 6366–4

High school classes of 1972 and 1980: enrollment in 2-year colleges, credits earned and dropout rate, by student characteristics, as of 1984, 4848–38

High school dropout rates, and subsequent completion, by student and school characteristics, alternative estimates, 1988, annual rpt, 4834–23

Homeless shelters services, operations, and client characteristics, 1988 survey, 5188–123

Job Training Partnership Act participant occupational training and placements by occupation and skill level, and placement wages, by sex, 1982-86, GAO rpt, 26106–8.9

Juvenile correctional and detention instns, inmates, and expenses, by instn and resident characteristics and State, 1975-85, biennial rpt, 6064–13

Labor laws enacted, by State, 1988, annual article, 6722–1.904

Occupational injury and illness rates, by SIC 2- to 4-digit industry, 1987, annual rpt, 6844–1

Older persons employment, earnings, reasons for working, and job training preferences, by selected characteristics, 1960-87, 6306–2.3

Participant characteristics, and sources of training, with data by employer size and major industry group, 1982-88, 6408–73

Science and engineering education in elementary and secondary schools, and student persistence in postsecondary education, 1977-88, 26358–199

Service industries census, 1987: establishments, receipts, employment, and payroll, by SIC 2- to 4-digit kind of business, MSA, county, and city, State rpt series, 2391–1

Small business establishments, operations, owner characteristics, and job training, late 1950s-87, 9768–20

Special education programs, enrollment by age, staff, funding, and needs, by type of handicap and State, 1987/88, annual rpt, 4944–4

Student guaranteed loan defaults, losses, and rates, by instn, 1983-Sept 1987, GAO rpt, 26121–289

Teachers bachelor degrees, by field and other characteristics, 1985-86, 4838–39

Truck drivers training in private and public programs, requirements, cost, and staffing, 1989, GAO rpt, 26113–432

Unemployment insurance long-term claimants employment services use, work experience, and reemployment, by selected characteristics and county, 1987-88, 6406–6.25; 6406–6.26

Veterans education benefits and job training, and other VA activities, FY88, annual rpt, 8604–3.7

see also Apprenticeship
see also Employee development
see also Federal aid to vocational education
see also Manpower training programs
see also Sheltered workshops
see also Vocational guidance
see also Vocational rehabilitation

Vocational guidance

Employment and Training Admin activities, funding, and participant characteristics, by program, FY80-86, 6408–71

Occupational Outlook Quarterly, journal, 6742–1

Vocational rehabilitation

Assistance for vocational education by type of recipient and source, and characteristics of programs and students, 1970s-89, series, 4806–3

Blind-operated vending facilities on Federal and non-Federal property, finances and operations by agency and State, FY88, annual rpt, 4944–2

Disability Insurance and SSI admin of Fed Govt and States, benefits, caseloads, and operations, 1980s, 4708–11

Education (special) enrollment by age, staff, funding, and needs, by type of handicap and State, 1987/88, annual rpt, 4944–4

Education Dept programs funding, operations, and effectiveness, FY88, annual rpt, 4804–5

Expenditures for public welfare by program, and private health care spending, FY50s-86, annual article, 4742–1.909

Fed Govt and State rehabilitation activities and funding, FY88, annual rpt, 4944–1

Govt spending, coverage, and benefits for social welfare programs, late 1930s-87, annual rpt, 4744–3.1

Nursing home facility, staff, and resident detailed characteristics, 1985, 4147–13.97

OASDI benefit payments, trust fund finances, and economic and demographic assumptions, 1970-87 and alternative projections to 1997, actuarial rpt, 4706–1.103

Service industries census, 1987: establishments, receipts, employment, and payroll, by SIC 2- to 4-digit kind of business, MSA, county, and city, State rpt series, 2391–1

State vocational rehabilitation agency cases and disposition, by State, FY88 and trends from FY21, annual rpt, 4944–5

Statistical Abstract of US, social, political, and economic data, 1790-2025, comprehensive annual compilation, 2324–1.2

Workers compensation laws of States and Fed Govt, 1989 semiannual rpt, 6502–1

see also Sheltered workshops
see also Veterans rehabilitation

Vocke, Gary

"New Technology Is Increasing Saltwater Shrimp Exports to the U.S.", 1522–3.924

"Third World Increasingly Competitive in Nitrogen Fertilizer Industry", 1522–3.905

Voice of America

Broadcast data for Radio Free Europe, Radio Liberty, and other intl broadcasters, FY88, annual rpt, 10314–1

Voith, Richard

"Unequal Subsidies in Highway Investment: What Are the Consequences?", 9387–1.904

Volcanoes

Alaska OCS environmental conditions and oil dev impacts, compilation of papers, series, 2176–1

Developing countries disaster preparedness and economic, population, and political data, country rpt series, 9916–2

Vollrath, Thomas L.

"Indicators of Competitiveness", 1522–3.901

Voluntary military service

Army enlistment by race and for women, and attitudes toward reenlistment, FY87, annual rpt, 3704–10.1

Budget of DOD, manpower needs, costs, and force readiness by service branch, FY90, annual rpt, 3504–1

Enlistments and reenlistment rates, by service branch, FY79-88, annual rpt, 3544–1.2

Enlistments and reenlistment rates, by service branch, quarterly rpt, 3542–14.4

Enlistments and reenlistments, by race, sex, and service branch, quarterly press release, 3542–7

Manpower of DOD, and organization, budget, weapons, and property, by service branch, State, and country, 1989 annual summary rpt, 3504–13

Manpower statistics for active duty and reserve recruits, aptitude test scores and retention rates, with data by sex, race, and service branch, various periods 1980-87, 26306–6.136

Natl Guard (Army and Air) activities, manpower, and facilities, FY88, annual rpt, 3504–22

Navy budget, manpower, procurement, and equipment, planned FY89-91, annual fact sheet, 3804–16

Reserve forces manpower strengths and characteristics, by component, quarterly rpt, 3542–4

Reserve personnel reenlistment, attitudes by reserve component, 1986 survey, 3508–29

Reserve personnel reenlistment, spouses attitudes, 1986 survey, 3508–30

Women military personnel on active and reserve duty, by demographic and service characteristics and service branch, FY88, annual chartbook, 3544–26

see also Selective service

Volunteers

ACTION activities, by program, FY88, annual rpt, 9024–2

Budget of US, Bush Admin policy changes by program, FY90, 028–32

Crime victim aid programs of law enforcement agencies, funding levels, staff, and needs, 1986, 6066–26.3

Forest Service activities and finances, by region and State, FY88, annual rpt, 1204–1.4

Head Start enrollment, funding, and staff, FY88, annual rpt, 4604–8

Head Start program operations, enrollment by handicap, and family characteristics, for North Central States, 1987/88, annual rpt, 4604–12

Health care (family) teaching faculty dev programs, Federal funding and trainees, by faculty status and region, 1978-87, 4118–63

High school and college grads employment status and income, 1989 edition, annual rpt, 4824–2.28

Military reserve spouses attitudes, and family social, economic, and other characteristics, 1986 survey, 3508–30

Older persons aid and policies of Fed Govt, and issues of aging, 1989 annual rpt, 25144–3

Peace Corps activities, funding, and volunteers characteristics, FY62-88, GAO rpt, 26123–243

Peace Corps activities, funding by program, and volunteers, by country, FY90, annual rpt, 9654–1

Red Cross activities, finances, volunteers, and certificates issued, by program, FY88, annual rpt, 29254–1

Statistical Abstract of US, social, political, and economic data, 1790-2025, comprehensive annual compilation, 2324–1.2

see also Foster Grandparent Program
see also Retired Senior Volunteer Program
see also VISTA
see also Voluntary military service

Volunteers in Service to America

see VISTA

von Hagen, Jurgen

"Monetary Targeting with Exchange Rate Constraints: The Bundesbank in the 1980s", 9391–1.924

Voting

see Elections

Vroman, Wayne

"Experience Rating in Unemployment Insurance: Some Current Issues", 6406–6.29

Vroomen, Harry

"Fertilizer Trade Statistics, 1970-88", 1588–142

"Fertilizer Use and Price Statistics, 1960-88", 1588–113

"Timing of Fertilizer Applications", 1561–16.903

Vuilleumier, Stephen W.

"World and Domestic Outlook for Corn Sweeteners", 1004–16.1

Waco, Tex.

see also under By City and By SMSA or MSA in the "Index by Categories"

Wade, Alice H.

"Social Security Area Population Projections: 1989", 4706–1.104

Wage controls
see also Minimum wage

Wage deductions
Soviet Union personal income by source, disposable income, wage deductions by type, and savings, 1950s-87, 9118-7
see also Employee benefits
see also Social security tax
see also Unemployment insurance tax
see also Withholding tax

Wage garnishment
see Wage deductions

Wage surveys
Farm labor wage surveys to set minimum wage for US and alien workers, evaluation with data by location, 1980s-87, GAO rpt, 26131-50
see also Area wage surveys
see also Industry wage surveys

Wages and salaries
see Agricultural wages
see Earnings, general
see Earnings, local and regional
see Earnings, specific industry
see Educational employees pay
see Federal pay
see Labor costs and cost indexes
see Minimum wage
see Payroll
see Professionals' fees
see State and local employees pay
see Wage surveys

Wagley, Henry
"China's Cotton Industry", 1561-1.901

Wagner, Janet
"Gift-Giving Behavior: An Economic Perspective", 6886-6.49

Wahl, Jenny
"Operation and Effect of the Possessions Corporation System of Taxation: 6th Report", 8004-12

Wahl, Terence R.
"Catalog of Washington Seabird Colonies", 5508-101

Wake Island
Economic, social, political, and geographic summary data, by country, 1989, annual factbook, 9114-2
HHS financial aid, by program, recipient, State, and city, FY88, annual regional listing, 4004-3.9

Wakefield, Joseph C.
"Federal Fiscal Programs", 2702-1.907

Walcoff, Carol
"Examination of Media Coverage of Increasing the Speed Limit to 65 mph", 7768-110

Waldo, Daniel R.
"Health Expenditures by Age Group, 1977 and 1987", 4652-1.946

Wales
see United Kingdom

Walker County, Ala.
Housing and households detailed characteristics, and unit and neighborhood quality, by location, 1984 survey, MSA rpt, 2485-6.1

Wall, Larry D.
"Bank Merger Motivations: A Review of the Evidence and an Examination of Key Target Bank Characteristics", 9371-1.911
"Valuation Effects of New Capital Issues by Large Bank Holding Companies", 9371-10.34

Walla Walla, Wash.
Freight (waterborne domestic and foreign) by commodity, traffic, and passengers, by port and waterway, 1987, annual rpt, 3754-3.4

Wallen, Jacqueline
"Alcoholism Treatment in General Hospitals", 4186-9.3
"Care of Children with Psychiatric Disorders at Community Hospitals", 4188-55

Waller, Christopher J.
"Discretion, Wage Indexation, and Inflation", 9381-10.97

Walraven, Nicholas
"Drought, Agriculture, and the Economy", 9362-1.901

Walter, Heather J.
"Primary Prevention of Cancer Among Children: Changes in Cigarette Smoking and Diet After Six Years of Intervention", 4472-1.916

Walter, John R.
"Fifth District Banks' Return on Assets: Highest in Decade", 9389-1.909
"Monetary Aggregates: A User's Guide", 9389-1.906

War
Claims against foreign govts by US natls, by claim type and country, 1988, annual rpt, 6004-16
Participants and casualties in principal US wars, by service branch, 1775-1973, annual rpt, 3544-1.2
Participants and casualties in principal US wars, 1775-1973, annual summary rpt, 3504-13
Participants, deaths, veterans living, and compensation and pension recipients, for each US war, 1775-1988, annual rpt, 8604-2
Statistical Abstract of US, social, political, and economic data, 1790-2025, comprehensive annual compilation, 2324-1.2
Vietnam veterans exposure to Agent Orange, Air Force personnel deaths and rates by cause and selected characteristics, 1988 annual rpt, 3604-3
see also Arms control and disarmament
see also Civil defense
see also Military science
see also Military strategy
see also National defense
see also Prisoners of war
see also Veterans
see also Veterans benefits and pensions
see also War casualties
see also War relief

War casualties
Casualties and participants in principal US wars, by service branch, 1775-1973, annual rpt, 3544-1.2
Casualties and participants in principal US wars, 1775-1973, annual summary rpt, 3504-13
Deaths and rates, by detailed cause and demographic characteristics, 1986 and trends from 1900, US Vital Statistics annual rpt, 4144-2
Deaths by cause, age, race, and rank, and personnel captured and missing, by service branch, 2nd half FY88, semiannual rpt, 3542-21

Deaths, participants, veterans living, and compensation and pension recipients, for each US war, 1775-1988, annual rpt, 8604-2
Mental illness (post-traumatic stress) cases of Vietnam veterans, claims, and VA disposition, 1985-88, hearing, 25768-46
Pakistan airspace violations by USSR and Afghanistan, and casualties, 1980-86, hearing, 21388-54
Puerto Rico veterans and war casualties, by period of service, 1986 hearings, 21448-39
Statistical Abstract of US, social, political, and economic data, 1790-2025, comprehensive annual compilation, 2324-1.2

War prisoners
see Prisoners of war

War relief
Reparations debt burden, indicators for France, 1872-75, and Germany, 1925-32, conf papers, 9373-3.32
World War I debt to US of foreign govts, by country and program, periodic rpt, 8002-6

Warehouses
Agricultural Stabilization and Conservation Service producer payments, by program and State, 1988, annual rpt, 1804-12
Alteration and repair spending for commercial and public buildings, by type, size, age, and region, 1986, 2388-4
Arson incidents by whether structure occupied, property value, and arrest rate, by property type, 1988, annual rpt, 6224-2.1
Asia port facilities, operations, and impacts on US agricultural exports, for major Far East ports, 1970s-87, 1278-13
Construction industries census, 1987: establishments, employment, receipts, and expenditures, by SIC 4-digit industry and State, final industry rpt series, 2373-1
Construction industries census, 1987: financial and operating data, preliminary industry rpt series, 2371-1
Construction put in place, private and public, by type and region, monthly rpt, annual tables, 2382-4
Cotton ginning activity and charges, by State, 1988/89, annual rpt, 1564-3
County Business Patterns, 1987: employment, establishments, and payroll, by SIC 2- to 4-digit industry and county, annual State rpt series, 2326-8
Customs Service activities, collections, entries processed by mode of transport, and seizures, FY84-88, annual rpt, 8144-1
Earnings by major industry group, and personal income per capita and by source, by region and State, 1929-87, 2708-40
Employment, earnings, and hours, by SIC 1- to 4-digit industry, monthly 1983-Feb 1989, annual rpt, 6744-4
Employment of minorities and women, by occupation, SIC 1- to 3- digit industry, State, and MSA, 1986, annual rpt, 9244-1
Energy use in commercial buildings, costs, and conservation, by building characteristics, survey rpt series, 3166-8
Finances of warehouse services, by SIC 2- to 4-digit industry, 1988 survey, annual rpt, 2413-14

Foreign trade zones (US) operations and movement of goods, by zone and commodity, FY86, annual rpt, 2044–30

Grain storage facility and equipment loans to farmers under CCC program, by State, FY68-89, annual table, 1804–14

Grain storage facility and equipment loans to farmers under CCC program, by State, monthly table, 1802–9

Grain support loan programs of USDA, activity and status by grain and State, monthly rpt, 1802–3

Occupational injury and illness rates, by SIC 2- to 4-digit industry, 1987, annual rpt, 6844–1

Oil and fat production, consumption by end use, and stocks, by type, monthly Current Industrial Rpt, 2506–4.4

Pacific territories and Hawaii harbor traffic, facilities, dev, funding, and needs, by port, as of 1987, 7308–195

Rice stocks on and off farms and total in all positions, periodic rpt, 1621–7

Science, engineering, and technical employment in transportation, utilities, and retail and wholesale trade, by field, occupation, and industry, 1985, triennial rpt, 9627–32

Statistical Abstract of US, social, political, and economic data, 1790-2025, comprehensive annual compilation, 2324–1.3

Tax (income) returns of partnerships, income statement items by industry group, 1986, annual article, 8302–2.903

Tax (income) returns of sole proprietorships, income statement items, by industry group, 1987, annual article, 8302–2.904; 8302–2.921

Tobacco marketing activity, prices, and sales, by grade, type, market, and State, 1988, annual rpt series, 1319–5

see also Cold storage and refrigeration

see also By Industry in the "Index by Categories"

Warner, Michael
"Farmer's Perspective on Sugar Policy and Where It Is Headed", 1004–16.1

Warner Robins, Ga.
Wages by occupation, and benefits for office and plant workers, 1988 survey, periodic MSA rpt, 6785–3.1

see also under By SMSA or MSA in the "Index by Categories"

Warren, Charles W.
"Trends and Variations in Post Partum Sterilization in the U.S., 1972 and 1980", 4147–24.2

Warren, Mich.
see also under By City in the "Index by Categories"

Warren, Ohio
see also under By SMSA or MSA in the "Index by Categories"

Warsaw Pact
Helsinki Final Act implementation by NATO and Warsaw Pact, Oct 1988-Mar 1989, semiannual rpt, 7002–1

Military forces of NATO compared to Warsaw Pact, and selected economic indicators, by country, 1900s-87, conf papers, 3908–6

Military spending, arms trade, and force strengths, with govt spending and population, by country, 1977-87, annual rpt, 9824–1

Military strength and spending of USSR and Warsaw Pact, FY88, annual rpt, 3544–2

Military strength of USSR and Warsaw Pact, and proposed force reductions, with comparisons to NATO, 1980s-91, hearing, 21208–29

Military weapons systems, aid, presence, and force strengths of USSR and Warsaw Pact, and compared to US and NATO, 1989 annual rpt, 3504–20

UN voting record and share of votes in agreement with US, by issue, country, and world area, 1988, annual rpt, 7004–18

Warshawsky, Mark J.
"Adequacy of Funding of Private Defined Benefit Pension Plans", 9366–6.172

"Postretirement Health Benefit Plans Costs and Liabilities for Private Employers", 9366–6.190

Warships
see Naval vessels

Warwick, R.I.
Housing and households characteristics, 1984 survey, MSA fact sheet, 2485–11.3

Housing and households detailed characteristics, and unit and neighborhood quality, by location, 1984 survey, MSA rpt, 2485–6.2

Washington
see D.C.
see Washington State

Washington Metropolitan Area Transit Authority
Budget of US, authoritative financial statements with appropriations, outlays, and receipts, by category and agency, FY88, annual rpt, 8104–2.2

Washington State
Agriculture census, 1987: farms, farmland, production and costs, and operator characteristics, advance State and county rpts, 2330–1.53

Agriculture census, 1987: farms, farmland, production, finances, and operator characteristics, by county, final State rpt, 2331–1.47

Alien workers (unauthorized) employer sanctions impacts on farm labor supply in Western US, with background data, 1986-89, GAO rpt, 26121–310

Apple (red delicious) prices by marketing stage, and trucking rates, 1980-89, article, 1561–6.903

Apple price impacts of consumer awareness of use of chemical growth regulator Alar, monthly 1986-June 1989, article, 1561–6.902

Asian American earnings, and employment and other characteristics, by detailed origin and whether foreign-born, 1980, 11046–7.2

Bank deposits in FDIC-insured commercial and savings banks, by instn, State, and county, as of June 1988, annual regional rpt, 9295–3.6

Birds (waterfowl) coastal breeding population and colonies, by species and location for Washington, 1978-82, atlas, 5508–101

Coal production and mines by county, prices, productivity, miners, reserves, and stocks, by mining method and State, 1987-88, annual rpt, 3164–25

County Business Patterns, 1987: employment, establishments, and payroll, by SIC 2- to 4-digit industry and county, annual State rpt, 2326–8.49

Cranberry production, prices, use, and acreage, for selected States, 1987-88 and forecast 1989, annual rpt, 1621–18.4

Dairy prices for cows, milk, and feed, by selected State, and cows slaughtered by region, 1988, annual rpt, 1317–1.6

Deaths and rates, by detailed location, cause, and demographic characteristics, 1987, US Vital Statistics annual rpt, 4144–3.1

DOD prime contract awards, by contractor, service branch, State, and city, FY88, annual rpt, 3544–22

Employment, earnings, and hours, by selected SIC 1- to 4-digit industry, State, and for 262 MSAs, 1972-87, 6748–81.5

Estuary environmental and fishery conditions, research results and methodology, 1988 rpt, 2176–7.7

Fed Govt spending in States and local areas, by type, State, county, and city, FY88, annual rpt, 2464–3

Fed Govt spending in States, by type, program, agency, and State, FY88, annual rpt, 2464–2

Fish and shellfish catch, prices, and fisheries economic status, for Pacific coast, 1986-87, annual rpt series, 2164–16

Fish and shellfish catch, wholesale receipts, prices, trade, and other market activities, weekly regional rpt, 2162–6.5

HHS financial aid, by program, recipient, State, and city, FY88, annual regional listing, 4004–3.10

Homeless children educational enrollment and needs, 1988, annual State rpt, 4804–35.47

Hospital reimbursement by Medicare under prospective payment system, impacts on subacute care, 1988 rpt, 17206–2.8

Income (personal) per capita and by source, and earnings by industry div, by State, MSA, and county, 1982-87, annual regional rpt, 2704–2.5

Irrigation subsidies of Reclamation Bur, costs to Fed Govt and surplus crop production, 1985-86, 21448–40

Irrigation water supply restriction and compensatory use of other production inputs, 1984-85, 1588–139

Land Mgmt Bur activities and finances, and public land acreage and use, FY88, annual State rpt, 5724–11.3

Lumber mill occupational injury and illness rates and workdays lost, by selected State and SIC 4-digit industry, 1978-87, article, 6722–1.945

Mineral Industry Surveys, State reviews of production, 1988, preliminary annual rpt, 5614–6

Minerals Yearbook, 1987, Vol 2 preprints: State review of production and sales by commodity, and business activity, annual rpt, 5604–16.49

Minerals Yearbook, 1987, Vol 2: State reviews of production, sales, and firms, by commodity, and business activity, annual rpt, 5604–34

Nursing home compliance with Medicare and Medicaid regulations, and patient characteristics, by facility, 1987/88, annual State rpt, 4654–15.49

Population, households, employment, income, and fuel prices, for Pacific Northwest, alternative projections 1990-2010 with trends from 1960, annual rpt, 3224–5

Retail trade census, 1987: employment, establishments, sales, and payroll, by SIC 2- to 4-digit kind of business, MSA, county, and city, State rpt, 2397–1.48

Rural areas telecommunication technologies availability and use, 1986-87, article, 1502–7.910

Savings instns, FHLB 12th District members deposits and lending, monthly press release, 9302–32.6

Service industries census, 1987: employment, establishments, receipts, and payroll, by SIC 2- to 4-digit kind of business, MSA, county, and city, State rpt, 2391–1.48

Statistical Abstract of US, social, political, and economic data, with foreign comparisons, 1790-2025, comprehensive annual compilation, 2324–1

Timber in northwestern US and British Columbia, production, prices, trade, and employment, quarterly rpt, 1202–3

Water supply and quality in streams and lakes, and groundwater levels in wells, by drainage basin, 1987, annual State rpt, 5666–10.44

Water supply, and snow survey results, monthly State rpt, 1266–2.9

Water supply, and snow survey results, 1988, annual State rpt, 1264–14.5

Wholesale trade census, 1987: employment, establishments, finances, and operations, by SIC 2- to 4-digit kind of business, MSA, county, and city, State rpt, 2405–1.48

Wildlife-related recreation, hunting, and fishing participation and spending, detailed data, 1985 survey, quinquennial State rpt, 5506–6.48

see also Kelso, Wash.

see also King County, Wash.

see also Longview, Wash.

see also Seattle, Wash.

see also Spokane, Wash.

see also Tacoma, Wash.

see also Vancouver, Wash.

see also Walla Walla, Wash.

see also under By State in the "Index by Categories"

Waste Isolation Pilot Plant

see Radioactive waste and disposal

Waste management

see Hazardous waste and disposal

see Landfills

see Radioactive waste and disposal

see Recycling of waste materials

see Refuse and refuse disposal

see Sewage and wastewater systems

Wastewater treatment

see Sewage and wastewater systems

Watches and clocks

County Business Patterns, 1987: employment, establishments, and payroll, by SIC 2- to 4-digit industry and county, annual State rpt series, 2326–8

CPI by component for US city average, and by region, population size, and for 27 metro areas, monthly rpt, 6762–2

Employment, earnings, and hours, by SIC 1- to 4-digit industry, monthly 1983-Feb 1989, annual rpt, 6744–4

Imports of watches duty-free, injury to US industry, investigation with background financial and operating data, 1989 rpt, 9886–4.143

Price indexes (producer), by stage of processing and detailed commodity, monthly rpt, 6762–6

Price indexes (producer), by stage of processing and detailed commodity, monthly 1988, annual rpt, 6764–2

Science, engineering, and technical employment in manufacturing, by field, occupation, and industry, 1986, triennial rpt, 9627–23

Virgin Islands economic censuses, 1987: employment, firms, payroll, and receipts, by SIC 1- to 4-digit industry, island, and city, 2593–1

Water area

Coastal and estuarine environmental conditions, research results and methodology, series, 2176–7

Coastal and riparian areas environmental conditions, fish, wildlife, use, and mgmt, for individual ecosystems, series, 5506–9

Conservation and conditions of soil, water, and environment, with data by State and region, 1989 quinquennial rpt, 1268–24

Foreign countries economic, social, political, and geographic summary data, by country, 1989, annual factbook, 9114–2

Great Lakes water area, depth, and shoreline acreage by land use, 1989 rpt, 14646–1.1

Indiana water supply, annual high and low levels by lake, 1940s-85, 5668–89

Park natl system and other land under Natl Park Service mgmt, acreage by site, ownership, and region, 1989, semiannual rpt, 5542–1

Public lands acreage and use, and Land Mgmt Bur activities and finances, annual State rpt series, 5724–11

Public lands acreage, grants, use, revenues, and allocations, by State, FY88 and trends, annual rpt, 5724–1

Tennessee Valley river control activities, and hydroelectric power generation and capacity, 1984, annual rpt, 9804–7

Water supply and quality in streams and lakes, and groundwater levels in wells, by drainage basin, 1986, annual State rpt series, 5666–23

Water supply and quality in streams and lakes, and groundwater levels in wells, by drainage basin, 1987, annual State rpt series, 5666–10

Water supply and quality in streams and lakes, and groundwater levels in wells, by drainage basin, 1988, annual State rpt series, 5666–16

see also Water supply and use

Water fluoridation

Rural areas public water supply system financial and operating characteristics, by region, 1980, 1598–247

Water permits

Coastal and riparian areas environmental conditions, fish, wildlife, use, and mgmt, for individual ecosystems, series, 5506–9

Coastal areas environmental and socioeconomic conditions, and potential impact of oil and gas OCS leases, final statement series, 5736–1

Water pollution

Abatement equipment spending of business, 1982-88, annual article, 2702–1.904

Abatement spending by govts, business, and consumers, 1983-87, annual article, 2702–1.919

Abatement spending, capital and operating costs by SIC 2- to 4-digit industry and State, 1986, annual Current Industrial Rpt, 2506–3.6

Agricultural Conservation Program participation and payments, by practice and State, FY87, annual rpt, 1804–7

Agricultural sources of water pollution, USDA abatement program benefits and costs, projected 1990, 1588–141

Agricultural Stabilization and Conservation Service producer payments, by program and State, 1988, annual rpt, 1804–12

Agricultural Stabilization and Conservation Service producer payments, by program, monthly rpt, 1802–10

Arkansas water quality in streams and rivers, by monitoring site, 1975-85, 5668–83

Army Corps of Engineers water resources dev projects, characteristics, and costs, 1950s-87, biennial State rpt series, 3756–2

Army Corps of Engineers water resources dev projects, characteristics, and costs, 1950s-89, biennial State rpt series, 3756–1

Asbestos in drinking water relation to cancer incidence, by sex and cancer site, 1973-83, local area study, article, 4042–3.921

Assistance (financial and nonfinancial) of Fed Govt, 1989 base edition with supplements, annual listing, 104–5

California water quality, trace metal concentrations in San Joaquin river bed sediment, 1985, 5668–91

Chemistry of surface and groundwater, environmental impacts, analytic methods, and quality and mgmt issues, 1989 rpt, 5668–96

Coal mining effect on water quality, sediment discharges effects of alternative mining and mgmt methods and reclamation, for Pennsylvania, 1980-83, 5668–93

Coastal and estuarine environmental conditions, research results and methodology, series, 2176–7

Coastal and estuarine pollutant discharges from agricultural, airborne, and other nonpoint sources, and regulatory issues, 1988 hearing, 21568–46

Coastal and riparian areas environmental conditions, fish, wildlife, use, and mgmt, for individual ecosystems, series, 5506–9

Conservation and conditions of soil, water, and environment, with data by State and region, 1989 quinquennial rpt, 1268–24

Data on water quality, aquifer hydrologic and chemical properties impacts on representative groundwater sampling, local area study, 1988 rpt, 5668–97

Data on water quality, collection methods and data quality, for 2 States, 1984, 5668–94

Dioxin levels in paper products and pulp mill effluents, and control technology, 1970s-87, 26358–204

Dioxin levels in paper products and pulp mill effluents, and environmental and health effects, 1988 hearing, 21368–112

Electric utilities privately owned, pollution abatement outlays by type of pollutant and equipment, and firm, 1987, annual rpt, 3164–23.1

Environmental quality and protection programs, and intl issues, 1988 annual rpt, 484–1

EPA pollution control grant program activities, monthly rpt, 9182–8

Farm financial and marketing conditions, forecast 1988, conf papers, annual rpt, 1004–16

Farm irrigation system sediment control costs and benefits, by technique, for Idaho project, 1981-86 and projected to 2030, 1588–138

Fed Govt wastewater facilities compliance with pollution control regulations, FY86-87, GAO rpt, 26113–388

Fish hazardous substances toxicity levels, by detailed compound, 1989 rpt, 9238–68; 9238–69

Fishery research of State fish and wildlife agencies, federally funded projects and costs by species and State, 1989, annual listing, 5504–23

Great Lakes basin pollutant discharges, sources, and control program activities, 1987, biennial rpt, 14644–1

Great Lakes pollution loadings from nonpoint sources, for Lake Erie and Lake Ontario tributaries, 1982-85, 9208–129

Great Lakes toxic spills and human error, with data by pollutant source and site, 1984-86, conf, 14648–21

Great Lakes water quality indicators, by water basin and lake, 1970s-85, annual rpt, 9204–14

Groundwater pollution from soil injection of oil and gas refining wastes, by State, 1987, GAO rpt, 26113–429

Groundwater protection standards, States use of EPA and alternative standards by type of water use, and contaminant test results, 1976-88, GAO rpt, 26131–56

Hazardous waste mgmt, effectiveness of alternative technologies, 1989 conf papers, biennial rpt, 9184–19

Hazardous waste site remedial action under Superfund, current and proposed sites descriptions and status, periodic listings, series, 9216–3

Health effects of hazardous substances, concentrations in environment, and household products composition, with data by selected location, 1988 hearings, 21408–112

Health effects of selected pollutants, concentrations in food and environment, sources, and human intake, methodology and data needs, series, 9186–9

Health effects of selected pollutants, concentrations in food and environment, sources, human intake, and regulation, series, 9186–8

Hudson-Raritan estuary pollution levels, and effects of refrigeration on pollutant samples, 1983-84, 2168–109

Hudson-Raritan River basin pollutant levels and sources, model description and results, 1880s-1982, 2178–22

Idaho Natl Engineering Lab radiation monitoring results, for facilities and nearby areas, 1988, annual rpt, 3354–10

Incidents and discharges, by type, source, cause, and location, 1984-86, annual rpt, 7404–3

Industrial hazardous substances releases and reduction methods under EPA regulation, by chemical, source, industry, and location, 1987, annual rpt, 9234–6

Lake Ontario eutrophication and pollutant levels, by contaminant type and site, 1967-85, 14648–22

Lead poisoning among children, and impacts of lead removal from housing, gasoline, and water, 1987 conf, 4108–46

Natl historic and natural landmarks damaged and threatened, with owner, location, damage type, and recommended remedial action, 1988, annual listing, 5544–16

Polychlorinated biphenyls levels in Great Lakes environment, humans, and animals, and emissions sources, by site, 1970s-85, conf, 14648–19

Quality and supply of water in streams and lakes, and groundwater levels in wells, by drainage basin, 1986, annual State rpt series, 5666–23

Quality and supply of water in streams and lakes, and groundwater levels in wells, by drainage basin, 1987, annual State rpt series, 5666–10

Quality and supply of water in streams and lakes, and groundwater levels in wells, by drainage basin, 1988, annual State rpt series, 5666–16

Radiation and radionuclide concentrations in air, water, and milk, monitoring results by State and site, quarterly rpt, 9192–5

Radiation exposure of population near commercial reactors, by body site, age group, and selected plant, 1986, annual rpt, 9634–7

Radioactive waste from nuclear power plants, releases and waste composition by plant, 1986, annual rpt, 9634–1

Radioactive waste repository sites, water movement through soil near sites in humid areas, 1989 rpt, 5668–98

Radionuclide concentrations in air, water, humans, animals, and milk near Nevada and other nuclear test sites, 1988, annual rpt, 9194–17

Rivers dissolved solids and water temperatures, for 6 rivers by monitoring site, monthly rpt, 5662–3

Rural areas public water supply system financial and operating characteristics, by region, 1980, 1598–247

Rural Clean Water Program funding for control of water pollution from farming, by project and State, monthly table, 1802–14

Sedimentation control and research activity of Fed Govt, regional and project summaries, 1987, annual narrative rpt, 5664–9

Soil erosion control program acreage, costs of off-farm erosion damage, and sediment and other pollutants runoff, by region, 1988, 1588–134

Soil salinity impacts on yields and off-farm water quality, and costs and benefits of extending erosion control program to saline cropland, 1989 rpt, 1588–144

Statistical Abstract of US, social, political, and economic data, 1790-2025, comprehensive annual compilation, 2324–1.1

TVA financial and operating data by program and facility, FY88, annual rpt, 9804–32

Uranium tailings at inactive mills, remedial action proposals, costs, site characteristics, and environmental, socioeconomic, and health impacts, series, 3356–4

see also Eutrophication
see also Food and waterborne diseases
see also Marine pollution
see also Oil spills

Water power

Shipments and firms for fluid power products, by type, 1988, annual Current Industrial Rpt, 2506–12.31

see also Dams
see also Hydroelectric power

Water Resources Council

Budget of US, authoritative financial statements with appropriations, outlays, and receipts, by category and agency, FY88, annual rpt, 8104–2.2

Water resources development

Agricultural Conservation Program participation and payments, by practice and State, FY87, annual rpt, 1804–7

Agricultural Stabilization and Conservation Service producer payments, by program and State, 1988, annual rpt, 1804–12

Agricultural Stabilization and Conservation Service producer payments, by program, monthly rpt, 1802–10

Agricultural Statistics, 1988, annual rpt, 1004–1.2

Army Corps of Engineers activities, FY87, annual rpt, 3754–1

Army Corps of Engineers water resources dev projects, characteristics, and costs, 1950s-87, biennial State rpt series, 3756–2

Army Corps of Engineers water resources dev projects, characteristics, and costs, 1950s-89, biennial State rpt series, 3756–1

Assistance (block and categorical grants) programs for State and local govts, FY89, biennial listing, 10044–8

Bond tax-exempt issues for private activity, by purpose, face value, major industry, and State, 1986, annual article, 8302–2.905

Budget of US, historical data, selected years FY34-88 and projected to FY94, annual rpt, 104–22

Budget of US, special analysis of Federal capital spending by category, projected FY89-2005 and trends from FY81, annual rpt, 104–24

Colorado River Storage Project finances and activities in western States, FY88, annual rpt, 5824–3

Conservation and conditions of soil, water, and environment, with data by State and region, 1989 quinquennial rpt, 1268–24

Conservation of soil and water, USDA activities, 1988-97, 1008–41

Conservation of soil and water, USDA funding by program and State, FY86, annual rpt, 1264–12

Construction industries census, 1987: financial and operating data, preliminary industry rpt, 2371–1.20

Construction industries census, 1987: financial and operating data, preliminary industry rpt series, 2371–1

Construction put in place (public and private), by type, bimonthly rpt, 2042–1.1

Construction put in place, value of new public and private structures, by type, monthly rpt, 2382–4

Electric utilities privately owned, detailed finances and operations by firm, 1987, annual rpt, 3164-23.1

FmHA activities, and loans and grants by program and State, FY88 and trends from FY69, annual rpt, 1184-17

FmHA borrowers, by type of borrower and loan, and State, quarterly rpt, 1182-4

Forest Service activities and finances, by region and State, FY88, annual rpt, 1204-1

Forest Service mgmt of public lands and resources dev, environmental, economic, and social impacts of alternative programs, projected to 2030, 1208-24

Indian reservation water supply projects in South Dakota, costs and indicators of need, with health and housing data for other reservations, 1980s-87, hearing, 21448-37

Public lands acreage and use, and Land Mgmt Bur activities and finances, annual State rpt series, 5724-11

Reclamation Bur activities and finances, FY88, annual rpt, 5824-1

Reclamation Bur activities, finances, and project impacts in western US, annual rpts, 5824-12

Reclamation Bur water storage and carriage facilities, capacity, and operating status, as of Sept 1988, biennial listing, 5824-7

Soil Conservation Service activities, FY88, annual rpt, 1264-2

Water Bank Program agreements, payments to farmers, and wetlands acreage, by State, FY72-89, annual rpt, 1804-21

Water Bank program agreements, payments to farmers, and wetlands acreage, by State, monthly rpt, 1802-5

see also Aquaculture
see also Canals
see also Dredging
see also Flood control
see also Hydroelectric power
see also Inland water transportation
see also Irrigation
see also Marine resources
see also Saline water conversion
see also Water power
see also Water supply and use
see also Watershed projects

Water supply and use

Aerial survey R&D rpts, and sources of natural resource and environmental data, quarterly listing, 9502-7

Agricultural Stabilization and Conservation Service producer payments, by program, monthly rpt, 1802-10

Agriculture census, 1987: equipment and facilities on farms, by election district, final outlying area rpt, 2331-1.53

Agriculture census, 1987: equipment and facilities on farms, by island and island group, final outlying area rpt, 2331-1.54

Arkansas water quality in streams and rivers, by monitoring site, 1975-85, 5668-83

Army Corps of Engineers activities and projects, FY87 and trends from 1800s, annual rpt, 3754-1.2

Army Corps of Engineers water resources dev projects, characteristics, and costs, 1950s-87, biennial State rpt series, 3756-2

Army Corps of Engineers water resources dev projects, characteristics, and costs, 1950s-89, biennial State rpt series, 3756-1

Assistance (financial and nonfinancial) of Fed Govt, 1989 base edition with supplements, annual listing, 104-5

Catfish raised on farms, operations, water use, and acreage, by State, 1988-89, semiannual situation rpt, 1561-15.2

Chemistry of surface and groundwater, environmental impacts, analytic methods, and quality and mgmt issues, 1989 rpt, 5668-96

Coastal areas environmental impacts of economic dev and population growth, 1980s and projected to 2000, 2176-8.1

Colorado River Basin Project reservoir and power operations and revenues, 1987-88, annual rpt, 5824-6

Colorado River Storage Project finances and activities in western States, FY88, annual rpt, 5824-3

Conservation and conditions of soil, water, and environment, with data by State and region, 1989 quinquennial rpt, 1268-24

County Business Patterns, 1987: employment, establishments, and payroll, by SIC 2- to 4-digit industry and county, annual State rpt series, 2326-8

Criminal sentences for Federal offenses, guidelines by offense and circumstances, 1989 rpt, 17668-1

DC metro area land acquisition and dev projects of Fed Govt, characteristics, funding, and impacts, by agency and project, FY90-94, annual rpt, 15454-1

Developing countries economic and social conditions from 1960s, and Intl Dev Cooperation Agency and AID activities and funding, FY88-90, annual rpt, 9904-4

Environmental quality and protection programs, and intl issues, 1988 annual rpt, 484-1

EPA pollution control grant program activities, monthly rpt, 9182-8

Farm production itemized costs, by farm sales size and region, 1988, annual rpt, 1614-3

FmHA soil and water loans, by race, Hispanic origin, and State, quarterly rpt, 1182-5

Foreign and US land, water, and energy resources, by world area, 1960s-80s and projected to 2050, article, 1522-3.908

Forest Service mgmt of public lands and resources dev, environmental, economic, and social impacts of alternative programs, projected to 2030, 1208-24

Freight (waterborne domestic and foreign) by commodity, traffic, and passengers, by port and waterway, 1987, annual rpt, 3754-3

Govt employment and payroll, by function, level of govt, and jurisdiction, 1987-88, annual rpt series, 2466-1

Govt finances, by level of govt, State, and for large cities and counties, annual rpt series, 2466-2

Hazardous substances exposure factors, and methodological guidelines, 1989 rpt, 9188-109

Honduras health care projects of AID, design and mgmt effects on sustainability, 1942-86, 9916-3.53

Household utilities spending, by household size, income, householder age and race, and region, 1983, article, 1702-1.904

Housing and household characteristics of units with septic tanks, cesspools, and other nonpublic sewer systems, 1970 and 1980, 9208-128

Housing and households detailed characteristics, and unit and neighborhood quality, by location, 1985, biennial rpt, 2485-12

Housing and households detailed characteristics, and unit and neighborhood quality, MSA surveys, series, 2485-6

Housing and households summary characteristics, 1985 and trends, biennial chartbook, 2486-1.7

Indian reservation water supply projects in South Dakota, costs and indicators of need, with health and housing data for other reservations, 1980s-87, hearing, 21448-37

Mali farm income and production impacts of alternative soil and water mgmt strategies, model results, 1989 rpt, 1528-289

Minerals industries water supply and use, and production, by commodity and State, 1950s-84 and projected to 2000, 5608-153

Mississippi eastern coastal plain water runoff, 1939-85, 5668-85

Montana water supply, precipitation, snow cover, and reservoir storage, by river basin, annual rpt, discontinued, 1264-7

New Mexico water resources data collection and analysis activities of USGS, with project descriptions, FY88, 5668-86

Northeastern US water supply, precipitation and stream runoff by station, monthly rpt, 2182-3

Occupational injury and illness rates, by SIC 2- to 4-digit industry, 1987, annual rpt, 6844-1

Oregon water supply, streamflow by station and reservoir storage, 1989, annual rpt, 1264-9

Panama Canal water supply and use, FY87-88, annual rpt, 9664-3.2

Reclamation Bur activities in western US, land and population served, and recreation areas, by location, 1987, annual rpt, 5824-12.1

Research (agricultural) funding and staffing for USDA, State agencies, and other instns, by topic, FY88, annual rpt, 1744-2

Rural areas public water supply system financial and operating characteristics, by region, 1980, 1598-247

Science, engineering, and technical employment in transportation, utilities, and retail and wholesale trade, by field, occupation, and industry, 1985, triennial rpt, 9627-32

Statistical Abstract of US, social, political, and economic data, 1790-2025, comprehensive annual compilation, 2324-1.1

Streamflow conditions in US and Puerto Rico, weekly rpt, monthly data, 2152-2

Supply and quality of water in streams and lakes, and groundwater levels in wells, by drainage basin, 1986, annual State rpt series, 5666-23

Supply and quality of water in streams and lakes, and groundwater levels in wells, by drainage basin, 1987, annual State rpt series, 5666–10

Supply and quality of water in streams and lakes, and groundwater levels in wells, by drainage basin, 1988, annual State rpt series, 5666–16

Supply in US and southern Canada, streamflow, surface and groundwater conditions, and reservoir levels, by location, monthly rpt, 5662–3

Tax (income) returns of corporations, income and tax items by asset size and detailed industry, 1986, annual rpt, 8304–21

Transportation census, 1987: trucks, by detailed characteristics, miles traveled, and type of product carried, State rpt series, 2573–1

Western US water supply, and snow survey results, monthly State rpt series, 1266–2

Western US water supply, and snow survey results, 1988, annual State rpt series, 1264–14

Western US water supply, storage by reservoir and State, and streamflow conditions, as of Oct 1989, annual rpt, 1264–4

Western US water supply, streamflow and reservoir storage forecasts by stream and station, Jan-May monthly rpt, 1262–1

see also Dams
see also Food and waterborne diseases
see also Hydroelectric power
see also Irrigation
see also Reservoirs
see also Saline water conversion
see also Water area
see also Water fluoridation
see also Water permits
see also Water pollution
see also Water power
see also Water resources development
see also Watershed projects
see also Weather
see also Wetlands

Waterbury, Conn.
see also under By City and By SMSA or MSA in the "Index by Categories"

Waterloo, Iowa
see also under By SMSA or MSA in the "Index by Categories"

Watershed projects
Acreage, grants, use, revenues, and allocations, for public lands by State, FY88, annual rpt, 5724–1.2

Agricultural Conservation Program participation and payments, by practice and State, FY87, annual rpt, 1804–7

Agricultural Statistics, 1988, annual rpt, 1004–1.2

Agricultural watershed runoff, precipitation, weather conditions, and mgmt, for 72 projects, 1978-79, annual rpt, 1704–1

Army Corps of Engineers activities and projects, FY87 and trends from 1800s, annual rpt, 3754–1.2

Army Corps of Engineers water resources dev projects, characteristics, and costs, 1950s-87, biennial State rpt series, 3756–2

Army Corps of Engineers water resources dev projects, characteristics, and costs, 1950s-89, biennial State rpt series, 3756–1

Colorado River Storage Project finances and activities in western States, FY88, annual rpt, 5824–3

Forest Service activities and finances, by region and State, FY88, annual rpt, 1204–1

Reclamation Bur activities, finances, and project impacts in western US, annual rpts, 5824–12

Soil Conservation Service activities, FY88, annual rpt, 1264–2

Waterways
see Canals
see Harbors and ports
see Inland water transportation
see Lakes and lakeshores
see Rivers and waterways

Wausau, Wis.
Housing vacancy rates for single and multifamily units and mobile homes, by city and ZIP code, 1989, annual MSA rpt, 9304–18.6

see also under By SMSA or MSA in the "Index by Categories"

Wayne County, Mich.
Housing and households detailed characteristics, and unit and neighborhood quality, by location, 1985 survey, MSA rpt, 2485–6.9

Wealth
Assets and debts of private sector, balance sheets by segment, 1949-88, semiannual rpt, 9365–4.1

Financial and business statistics, historic trends, 1988 annual chartbook, 9364–2.11

Household composition, income, benefits, and labor force status, Survey of Income and Program Participation methodology, working paper series, 2626–10

OASDI beneficiary households income, assets, and economic status changes, by beneficiary type, 1983-84, article, 4742–1.904

OASI beneficiaries retiring before age 62, employment, income, and benefits, by selected characteristics, 1982, article, 4742–1.911

Older persons assets and relation to income, by selected characteristics, 1984, article, 4742–1.910

Older persons assets and relation to income, 1984, technical paper, 4746–26.5

Retirees savings maintenance and liquidation, by selected financial and other characteristics, 1971-79, article, 1702–1.906

Statistical Abstract of US, social, political, and economic data, 1790-2025, comprehensive annual compilation, 2324–1.3

Student aid Pell grants and applicants, by tuition, income level, instn type and control, and State, 1987/88, annual rpt, 4804–1

Supplemental Security Income beneficiaries, assets by type and eligibility class, FY87, article, 4742–1.922

see also Business assets and liabilities, general
see also Business assets and liabilities, specific industry
see also Gross National Product
see also Investments

see also Money supply
see also National income and product accounts
see also Personal and household income
see also Personal debt
see also Poverty
see also Property
see also Savings

Weapons
Arrest rates, by offense, sex, age, and race, 1987, annual rpt, 6224–7

Assaults and rates, by type of weapon, 1965-87, annual rpt, 6224–8

Court civil and criminal caseloads for Federal district, appeals, and special courts, June 1989, annual rpt, 18204–2; 18204–8

Criminal case processing from arrest to sentencing, cases and duration by disposition, offense, and defendant characteristics, for selected cities, 1986, annual rpt, 6064–27

Criminal case processing in Federal district courts, and dispositions, by offense, district, and offender characteristics, 1984, annual rpt, 6064–29

Criminal case processing in Federal district courts, disposition by offense, 1980-87, 6066–19.50

Criminal sentences, by sentence type and felony offense, 1983-86, 6066–19.52

Criminal sentences for Federal offenses, guidelines by offense and circumstances, 1989 rpt, 17668–1

Deaths and rates, by detailed cause and demographic characteristics, 1986 and trends from 1900, US Vital Statistics annual rpt, 4144–2

Diplomats and staff with immunity for foreign missions in US and US missions abroad, and foreign diplomats criminal cases, 1978-87, hearing, 25388–51

Drug enforcement activities of State and local agencies, Federal aid by recipient, and background data, FY88, annual rpt, 6064–28

Drug test results at arrest, by drug type, offense, and sex, for selected urban areas, quarterly rpt, 6062–3

Input-output structure of US economy, detailed interindustry transactions for 84 industries, and components of final demand, 1983, annual article, 2702–1.909

Juvenile court delinquency cases, by offense, referral source, disposition, age, sex, race, State, and county, 1985, annual rpt, 6064–12

Juvenile offenders recidivism rates, arrests, and court referrals, by offense, age, and sex, 1983 local area studies, 6068–227

Marijuana crop eradication activities of DEA and local agencies, and weapons and assets seized, by State, 1982-88, annual rpt, 6284–4

Prisoners in State instns, by offense, criminal history, and inmate, family, and victim characteristics, 1986, annual rpt, 6064–26.3

Recidivism rates of prisoners released in 1983, by offense and prisoner characteristics, 1983-86, 6066–19.48

Robberies and rates, by type of premises and weapon, 1973-87, annual rpt, 6224–8

Statistical Abstract of US, social, political, and economic data, 1790-2025, comprehensive annual compilation, 2324–1.1

Wiretaps authorized, costs, arrests, trials, and convictions, by offense and jurisdiction, 1988, annual rpt, 18204–7

see also Ammunition

see also Arms trade

see also Bombs

see also Chemical and biological warfare agents

see also Firearms

see also Military assistance

see also Military weapons

see also Missiles and rockets

see also Nuclear weapons

see also Torpedoes

Weather

Africa food imports and aid needs under alternative weather assumptions, for 17 African countries, projected to 1995, 1528–279

Aircraft (general aviation) flight hours, by weather and light conditions, aircraft type and model, and region, 1988, annual rpt, 7504–29.2

Aircraft accidents and circumstances, for US operations of domestic and foreign airlines and general aviation, periodic rpt, 9612–1

Aircraft accidents, casualties, and damage, for commercial operations by detailed circumstances, 1986, annual rpt, 9614–2

Aircraft accidents in general aviation, by circumstances, characteristics of persons and aircraft involved, and type of flying, 1986, annual rpt, 9614–3

Alaska OCS environmental conditions and oil dev impacts, compilation of papers, series, 2176–1

Boat accidents, casualties, and damage, by cause, vessel and operator characteristics, and State, 1988, annual rpt, 7404–1.2

Carbon dioxide and other pollutants in atmosphere, effects on climate, sea levels, and solar radiation, 1989 hearing, 25318–75

Carbon dioxide in atmosphere, measurement, methodology, and research results, series, 3006–11

Coastal areas environmental and socioeconomic conditions, and potential impact of oil and gas OCS leases, final statement series, 5736–1

Coastal currents driven by wind, velocity and direction by station for North America, forecast 1990, annual rpts, 2174–1

Corn yield impacts of weather, estimated 1989 with trends from 1965, article, 1561–4.902

Deaths and rates, by detailed cause and demographic characteristics, 1986 and trends from 1900, US Vital Statistics annual rpt, 4144–2

Deaths, injuries, and damage from weather phenomena, and storm characteristics, by State, monthly listing, 2152–3

Deaths of natl park system visitors, by cause, victim age, region, and park, 1978-88, annual rpt, 5544–6

Developing countries disaster preparedness and economic, population, and political data, country rpt series, 9916–2

Diving (underwater sport and occupational) deaths, by circumstances, diver characteristics, and location, 1970-87, annual rpt, 2144–5

Electric power demand related to economic dev and weather, by census div, model results, quarterly 1977-85, 3028–2

Energy supply, demand, and price forecasts, economic and weather assumptions, quarterly rpt, 3162–34

Environmental quality and protection programs, and intl issues, 1988 annual rpt, 484–1

Estuary environmental conditions and mgmt, for individual areas, conf series, 2146–6

Farmland precipitation and temperature, average by State, monthly 1950-88, biennial rpt, 1544–28

Foreign and US agricultural production, trade, and weather devs, weekly press release, 1922–4

Foreign countries economic, social, political, and geographic summary data, by country, 1989, annual factbook, 9114–2

Great Lakes water levels fluctuations, causes, and impacts of alternative mgmt strategies, 1900s-88, series, 14646–1

Heating and cooling degree days, by census div, monthly and cumulative for season, monthly rpt, 3162–24.1

Heating and cooling degree days, distribution for commercial buildings by building type, survey rpt series, 3166–8

Heating and cooling degree days, for 45 cities and total US, cumulative for season, weekly rpt, 3162–32.2

Heating and cooling degree days weighted by population, by census div and State, with area-weighted temperature and precipitation, monthly rpt, 2152–13

Labor force not at work, unemployed, and working less than 35 hours, by reason, sex, race, region, and State, 1988, annual rpt, 6744–7.1; 6744–7.2

Mali farm income and production impacts of alternative soil and water mgmt strategies, model results, 1989 rpt, 1528–289

Mali food supply indicators, 1960s-2000, 1528–290

Marine weather forecast areas, and broadcast schedules and stations worldwide, as of Nov 1988, annual rpt, 2184–3

Mariners Weather Log, quarterly journal, 2152–8

Northeastern US water supply, precipitation and stream runoff by station, monthly rpt, 2182–3

Precipitation, and groundwater and surface water supply and conditions, monthly rpt, 5662–3

Precipitation and temperature, and effect on agriculture, by US region, State, and city, and world area, weekly rpt, 2152–2

Precipitation and temperature for US and foreign locations, major events and anomalies, weekly rpt, 2182–6

Precipitation and temperature forecasts for US and Northern Hemisphere, by location, semimonthly rpt, 2182–1

Railroad accidents, casualties, and damage, by cause, railroad, and State, 1988, annual rpt, 7604–1

Railroad accidents, circumstances, severity, and railroad involved, periodic rpt, 9612–3

Railroad-hwy grade-crossing accidents, detailed data by State and railroad, 1988, annual rpt, 7604–2

Statistical Abstract of US, social, political, and economic data, 1790-2025, comprehensive annual compilation, 2324–1.1

Timber in southeastern US, resources mgmt and research, 1988 biennial conf papers, 1204–35

Traffic accident impacts of speed limits, with accident circumstances and speed averages, for States with 55 and 65 mph limit, 1986-87, annual rpt, 7764–15

Traffic accidents, injuries, and deaths, by circumstances and characteristics of persons and vehicles involved, 1970s-87, series, 7766–14

Traffic fatal accidents, deaths, and rates, by circumstances, characteristics of persons and vehicles involved, and location, 1987, annual rpt, 7764–10

Unemployed displaced workers, by reason, industry, selected characteristics, and State, 1988, annual rpt, 6744–18

Uranium tailings at inactive mills, remedial action proposals, costs, site characteristics, and environmental, socioeconomic, and health impacts, series, 3356–4

Watershed (agricultural) runoff, precipitation, weather conditions, and mgmt, for 72 projects, 1978-79, annual rpt, 1704–1

Weather data by census div and State, historical trends, indexes, major events, and maps, series, 2156–17

Weather data for stations in continental US and outlying areas, 1988 and historic trends, annual rpt, 2154–8

Weather data for surface and upper air, averages by foreign and US station, monthly rpt, 2152–4

Western US water supply, and snow survey results, monthly State rpt series, 1266–2

Western US water supply, and snow survey results, 1988, annual State rpt series, 1264–14

Western US water supply, streamflow and reservoir storage forecasts by stream and station, Jan-May monthly rpt, 1262–1

see also Drought

see also Floods

see also Ice conditions

see also Meteorological satellites

see also Meteorology

see also Storms

see also Wind energy

Weather Bureau

see National Environmental Satellite, Data, and Information Service

see National Weather Service

Weather satellites

see Meteorological satellites

Webb, Roy H.

"Commodity Prices as Predictors of Aggregate Price Change", 9389–1.902

Webb, Shwu-Eng H.

"Agricultural Commodity Policies in China: Estimates of PSE's and CSE's, 1982-87", 1524–4.3

"China's Grain Policy at a Crossroads", 1522–3.914

Weber, Bruce R.
"Food Grain Outlook", 1004–16.1

Weber, Michael E.
"Individual Income Tax Returns for 1987: Selected Characteristics from the Taxpayer Usage Study", 8302–2.901

Webre, Philip C.
"Scope of the High-Definition Television Market and Its Implications for Competitiveness", 26306–3.109

Webster, Barbara
"Victim Assistance Programs Report Increased Workload", 6066–26.3

Weeks, John R.
"High Fertility Among Indochinese Refugees", 4042–3.910

Weems, Kerry
"Disabled-Worker Beneficiaries and Disabled SSI Recipients: A Profile of Demographic and Program Characteristics", 4742–1.916

Wei-Cheng You
"Allium Vegetables and Reduced Risk of Stomach Cancer", 4472–1.903

Weight
see Body measurements
see Obesity

Weights and measures
Auto and light truck fuel economy, sales, and market shares, by size and model for US and foreign makes, 1989 model year, semiannual rpt, 3302–4
Natl Inst of Standards and Technology rpts, 1988, annual listing, 2214–1
Standards dev, proposals, and policies, for weights, measures, and performance, 1988 annual conf, 2214–7
Statistical Abstract of US, social, political, and economic data, with foreign comparisons, 1790-2025, comprehensive annual compilation, 2324–1
see also Industrial standards

Weikel, Joseph R.
"Review of IRS Research Conferences", 8304–8.1

Weiler, Philip G.
"Statewide Preventive Health Care Program for the Aged", 4042–3.918

Weiller, Kenneth J.
"Developments in International Capital Mobility: A Perspective on the Underlying Forces and the Empirical Literature", 9385–9
"Increasing Capital Mobility: Evidence from Short- and Long-Term Markets", 9385–9
"Substitutability of U.S. and Foreign Assets", 9385–9
"What Does Covered Interest Parity Reveal About Capital Mobility?", 9385–9

Weimar, Mark R.
"Factors Affecting Growth in Turkey Consumption", 1561–7.906
"Outlook for Poultry and Eggs", 1004–16.1
"U.S. Egg and Poultry Statistical Series, 1960-87", 1568–39

Weinstock, Martin A.
"Moles and Site-Specific Risk of Nonfamilial Cutaneous Malignant Melanoma in Women", 4472–1.915

Weir, Paula E.
"Comparison of Selected EIA-782 Data with Other Data Sources", 3162–11.903

Weirton, W.Va.
see also under By SMSA or MSA in the "Index by Categories"

Weisman, Carol W.
"Cancer Screening Services for the Elderly", 4042–3.917

Welch, Finis
"New Evidence on School Desegregation", 11048–189

Welfare
see Aid to Families with Dependent Children
see Public welfare programs
see Social security
see State funding for social welfare

Welker, Donald L.
"Fifth District Banks' Return on Assets: Highest in Decade", 9389–1.909

Welniak, Edward J.
"Money Income of Households, Families, and Persons in the U.S.: 1987", 2546–6.59

Welty, Thomas K.
"Health Problems Among Aberdeen Area Indians Related to Inadequate Water and Sanitation", 21448–37

Wendland, Bruce
"Peanuts: Background for 1990 Farm Legislation", 1566–7.8
"Proposed Changes in the Cu-Sum Plan: What Will Be the Impact on the U.S. Soybean Industry?", 1561–3.903

Wenner, Charles A.
"Species Composition, Distribution, and Relative Abundance of Fishes in the Coastal Habitat off the Southeastern U.S.", 2168–112

Wenninger, John
"Exploring the Effects of Capital Movements on M1 and the Economy", 9385–9

Wertz, Dorothy C.
"International Survey of Attitudes of Medical Geneticists Toward Mass Screening and Access to Results", 4042–3.902

West Indies
see Caribbean area

West Palm Beach, Fla.
Housing starts and completions authorized by building permits in 40 MSAs, quarterly rpt, 2382–9
Wages by occupation, for office and plant workers, 1989 survey, periodic MSA rpt, 6785–3.10
see also under By SMSA or MSA in the "Index by Categories"

West Point
see Service academies

West Virginia
Agriculture census, 1987: farms, farmland, production and costs, and operator characteristics, advance State and county rpts, 2330–1.54
Agriculture census, 1987: farms, farmland, production, finances, and operator characteristics, by county, final State rpt, 2331–1.48
Appalachian Regional Commission funding, by project and State, planned FY89, annual rpt, 9084–3
Apple production, marketing, and prices, for Appalachia and compared to other States, various periods 1986-89, annual rpt, 1311–13

Bank deposits in FDIC-insured commercial and savings banks, by instn, State, and county, as of June 1988, annual regional rpt, 9295–3.2
Banks (insured commercial), Fed Reserve 5th District members financial statements, by State, quarterly rpt, 9389–18
Coal production and mines by county, prices, productivity, miners, reserves, and stocks, by mining method and State, 1987-88, annual rpt, 3164–25
County Business Patterns, 1987: employment, establishments, and payroll, by SIC 2- to 4-digit industry and county, annual State rpt, 2326–8.50
Deaths and rates, by detailed location, cause, and demographic characteristics, 1987, US Vital Statistics annual rpt, 4144–3.1
DOD prime contract awards, by contractor, service branch, State, and city, FY88, annual rpt, 3544–22
Economic indicators by State, Fed Reserve 5th District, quarterly rpt, 9389–16
Employment, earnings, and hours, by selected SIC 1- to 4-digit industry, State, and for 262 MSAs, 1972-87, 6748–81.5
Fed Govt spending in States and local areas, by type, State, county, and city, FY88, annual rpt, 2464–3
Fed Govt spending in States, by type, program, agency, and State, FY88, annual rpt, 2464–2
HHS financial aid, by program, recipient, State, and city, FY88, annual regional listing, 4004–3.3
Homeless children educational enrollment and needs, 1988, annual State rpt, 4804–35.48
Income (personal) per capita and by source, and earnings by industry div, by State, MSA, and county, 1982-87, annual regional rpt, 2704–2.4
Mineral Industry Surveys, State reviews of production, 1988, preliminary annual rpt, 5614–6
Minerals Yearbook, 1987, Vol 2 preprints: State review of production and sales by commodity, and business activity, annual rpt, 5604–16.50
Minerals Yearbook, 1987, Vol 2: State reviews of production, sales, and firms, by commodity, and business activity, annual rpt, 5604–34
Nursing home compliance with Medicare and Medicaid regulations, and patient characteristics, by facility, 1987/88, annual State rpt, 4654–15.50
Poverty conditions in West Virginia, food assistance participants and birth outcomes, 1980-87, hearing, 21968–49
Retail trade census, 1987: employment, establishments, sales, and payroll, by SIC 2- to 4-digit kind of business, MSA, county, and city, State rpt, 2397–1.49
Service industries census, 1987: employment, establishments, receipts, and payroll, by SIC 2- to 4-digit kind of business, MSA, county, and city, State rpt, 2391–1.49
Statistical Abstract of US, social, political, and economic data, with foreign comparisons, 1790-2025, comprehensive annual compilation, 2324–1

Transportation census, 1987: trucks, by detailed characteristics, miles traveled, and type of product carried, State rpt, 2573–1.49

Wages by occupation, and benefits for office and plant workers, 1989 survey, periodic labor market rpt, 6785–3.8

Water supply and quality in streams and lakes, and groundwater levels in wells, by drainage basin, 1987, annual State rpt, 5666–10.45

Water supply in West Virginia, low streamflow frequency by site, model description and results, 1980-83, 5668–92

Wholesale trade census, 1987: employment, establishments, finances, and operations, by SIC 2- to 4-digit kind of business, MSA, county, and city, State rpt, 2405–1.49

Wildlife-related recreation, hunting, and fishing participation and spending, detailed data, 1985 survey, quinquennial State rpt, 5506–6.47

see also Huntington, W.Va.

see also under By State in the "Index by Categories"

Westat, Inc.

"End of Academic Year Student Financial Aid Update Report", 4846–3.4

Westcott, Paul C.

"Agricultural Policy Provisions Affecting Soybean Plantings", 1004–16.1

"Analysis of Factors Influencing Corn Yields", 1561–4.902

"Effects of the Triple Base Proposal on Planting Decisions for Potatoes and Dry Edible Beans", 1561–11.905

"Effects of the Triple Base Proposal on Soybeans and Sunflowers", 1561–3.905

"Net Returns Analysis of the Flexible Plantings Provision for Soybeans and Sunflowers", 1561–3.902

"Winter Wheat Plantings and Soybean Double Cropping", 1561–3.901

Westerfield, Janice M.

"How U.S. Multinationals Manage Currency Risk", 9375–14

Western Area Power Administration

Activities of WAPA by plant, financial statements, and sales by customer, FY88, annual rpt, 3254–1

Electric power wholesale purchases and costs for REA borrowers, by borrower, supplier, and State, 1940-87, annual rpt, 1244–5

Finances and operations of Federal power admins, as of Sept 1987, annual rpt, 3164–23.4

Property (real) of DOE owned and leased, by type, subagency, contractor, and site, FY87, annual rpt, 3004–28

Western Sahara

Agricultural trade of US, by detailed commodity and country, 1988, semiannual rpt, 1522–4

Economic, social, political, and geographic summary data, by country, 1989, annual factbook, 9114–2

Human rights conditions in 170 countries, 1988, annual rpt, 21384–3

Population size, growth rates, and components of change, by country, projected 1989-2020 and trends from 1950, biennial rpt, 2324–9

Western Samoa

Agricultural and food production and indexes, total and for selected commodities, by country, 1970s-88, annual rpt, 1524–12

Agricultural trade of US, by detailed commodity and country, 1988, semiannual rpt, 1522–4

Economic and military aid and loans from US and intl agencies, by program and country, FY46-87, annual rpt, 9914–5

Economic, social, political, and geographic summary data, by country, 1989, annual factbook, 9114–2

Human rights conditions in 170 countries, 1988, annual rpt, 21384–3

Population size, growth rates, and components of change, by country, projected 1989-2020 and trends from 1950, biennial rpt, 2324–9

UN voting record and share of votes in agreement with US, by issue, country, and world area, 1988, annual rpt, 7004–18

see also under By Foreign Country in the "Index by Categories"

Western States

Bank deposits, loans, investments, and borrowings, Fed Reserve 10th District depository instns, monthly rpt, 9381–2

Banking industry structure, performance, and financial devs, for Fed Reserve 10th District, 1988, annual rpt, 9381–14

Banks financial activity, Fed Reserve 10th District depository instns by State, and large commercial banks by city, monthly rpt, 9381–11

Birds (duck) breeding population, by species, State, and Canada Province, 1988-89 with trends from 1955, annual rpt, 5504–30

Bonneville Power Admin mgmt of Fed Columbia River Power System, finances and sales, summary data, quarterly rpt, 3222–2

Bonneville Power Admin mgmt of Fed Columbia River Power System, finances, operations, and sales by customer, FY88, annual rpt, 3224–1

Bonneville Power Admin sales, revenues, and rates, by customer and customer type, 1988, semiannual rpt, 3222–1

Coal production and mines by county, prices, productivity, miners, reserves, and stocks, by mining method and State, 1987-88, annual rpt, 3164–25

Colorado River Storage Project finances and activities in western States, FY88, annual rpt, 5824–3

CPI by component for US city average, and by region, population size, and for 27 metro areas, monthly rpt, 6762–2

Dairy prices, by product and selected area, with related marketing data, 1988, annual rpt, 1317–1

Electric power capacity and use in Pacific Northwest, by end-use sector, projected under alternative fuel price cases, 1987-2010, annual rpt, 3224–4

Electric power capacity and use in Pacific Northwest, by energy source, projected under alternative load and demand cases, 1989-2008, annual rpt, 3224–3

Electric power sales by customer, activities by plant, and financial statements of Western Area Power Admin, FY88, annual rpt, 3254–1

Estuary environmental and fishery conditions, research results and methodology, 1986 rpt, 2176–7.1

Financial and economic devs, Fed Reserve Bank of Kansas City monthly journal, 9381–1

Financial and economic devs, Fed Reserve Bank of San Francisco quarterly journal, 9393–8

Fish and shellfish catch, life cycles, and environmental needs, for selected coastal species and regions, series, 5506–8

Fish and shellfish catch, prices, and fisheries economic status, for Pacific coast, 1986-87, annual rpt series, 2164–16

Freight (waterborne domestic and foreign) by commodity, traffic, and passengers, by port and waterway, 1987, annual rpt, 3754–3.4

Herbicide use in natl forests, exposure and cancer risk by type and application mode, 1988 rpt, 1208–295

HHS financial aid, by program, recipient, State, and city, FY88, annual regional listing, 4004–3.8; 4004–3.9; 4004–3.10

Horse and burro wild herd areas in western States, population, adoption, and protection, and mgmt costs, as of FY87, biennial rpt, 5724–8

Housing energy conservation program of BPA, energy savings and indoor air quality under alternative methods, projected 1986-2006, 3228–9

Housing finance studies, technical paper series, 9306–1

Housing vacancy rates for single and multifamily units and mobile homes in FHLB 10th District, by ZIP code, annual MSA rpt series, 9304–22

Housing vacancy rates for single and multifamily units and mobile homes in FHLB 11th District, by ZIP code, annual MSA rpt series, 9304–20

Housing vacancy rates for single and multifamily units and mobile homes in FHLB 12th District, by ZIP code, annual MSA rpt series, 9304–21

Income (personal) per capita and by source, and earnings by industry div, by State, MSA, and county, 1982-87, annual regional rpt, 2704–2.5

Income (personal) per capita and by source, earnings by major industry group, and social insurance contributions, by region and State, 1929-87, 2708–40

Irrigated acreage covered and idled under Conservation Reserve Program, by western State, as of 1987 and projected 1990, 1588–143

Irrigation subsidies of Reclamation Bur, costs to Fed Govt and surplus crop production, 1985-86, 21448–40

Minerals resources and availability on public lands, State rpt series, 5606–7

Population, households, employment, income, and fuel prices, for Pacific Northwest, alternative projections 1990-2010 with trends from 1960, annual rpt, 3224–5

Radionuclide concentrations in air, water, humans, animals, and milk near Nevada and other nuclear test sites, 1988, annual rpt, 9194–17

Reclamation Bur activities and finances, FY88, annual rpt, 5824–1

Reclamation Bur water storage and carriage facilities, capacity, and operating status, as of Sept 1988, biennial listing, 5824–7

River and stream environmental conditions, fish, wildlife, use, and mgmt, 1989 rpt, 5506–9.39

Savings and loan assns, FHLB 11th District members, offices, and financial condition, 1989 annual listing, 9304–23

Savings instns, FHLB 10th District members, locations, assets, and savings, 1989, annual listing, 9304–17

Savings instns, FHLB 11th District member offices, locations, savings balances, and accounts, quarterly listing, 9302–20

Savings instns, FHLB 12th District members deposits and lending by State, monthly press release series, 9302–32

Shipbuilding costs, deliveries, contracts, employment, and wage rates, by coastal district and shipyard, 1988, annual rpt, 7704–12

Statistical Abstract of US, social, political, and economic data, with foreign comparisons, 1790-2025, comprehensive annual compilation, 2324–1

Steel export ceilings under voluntary restraint agreements, by country and product, with Western US steel industry impact, 1989 rpt, 9886–4.136

Technology-intensive manufacturing employment in rural areas of western States, by occupational group, 1986 survey results, article, 1502–7.912

Tidal currents, daily time and velocity by station for North America and Asia coasts, forecast 1990, annual rpt, 2174–1.1

Tide height and time daily at coastal points, forecast 1990, annual rpt, 2174–2.2

Timber in northwestern US and British Columbia, production, prices, trade, and employment, quarterly rpt, 1202–3

Timber in northwestern US, resources and removals projected under 5 mgmt alternatives, 1988 rpt, 1208–300

Timber in Rocky Mountain States, production and mill residue, by species, ownership, and county, series, 1206–17

Timber insect and disease incidence and damage, 1988, annual regional rpt, 1206–11.2

Timber mountain pine beetle infestation in Western US and Canada, characteristics and control measures, 1988 conf papers, 1208–306

Timber sales in natl forests, logging and road construction costs, model results, 1989 rpt, 1208–298

Uranium tailings at inactive mills, remedial action activities by site, and funding, FY88, annual rpt, 3354–9

Uranium tailings at inactive mills, remedial action proposals, costs, site characteristics, and environmental, socioeconomic, and health impacts, series, 3356–4

Water supply in western US, and snow survey results, monthly State rpt series, 1266–2

Water supply in western US, and snow survey results, 1988, annual State rpt series, 1264–14

Water supply in western US, storage by reservoir and State, and streamflow conditions, as of Oct 1989, annual rpt, 1264–4

Water supply in western US, streamflow and reservoir storage forecasts by stream and station, Jan-May monthly rpt, 1262–1

Waterborne commerce (domestic) of US, freight by major commodity group, vessel type, and port, 1986, annual rpt, 7704–7

see also under By Region in the "Index by Categories"

see also under names of individual States

Western Union Telegraph Co.

Finances and operations, detail for telegraph firms, 1987, annual rpt, 9284–6.5

Wetlands

Agricultural Stabilization and Conservation Service producer payments, by program, monthly rpt, 1802–10

Alaska OCS environmental conditions and oil dev impacts, compilation of papers, series, 2176–1

Birds (waterfowl) population, breeding areas, and habitat conditions, with detail for North Dakota, 1955-87, hearing, 25168–69

Birds (waterfowl) population, habitat conditions, and migratory flight forecasts, for Canada and US by region, 1989 and trends from 1955, annual rpt, 5504–27

Birds (waterfowl) refuge and breeding area acreage acquired by Fed Govt, and costs, by site and State, FY89, annual rpt, 14784–1

Conservation and conditions of soil, water, and environment, with data by State and region, 1989 quinquennial rpt, 1268–24

Conservation of soil and wetlands, USDA programs costs and impacts on farm finances and operations, with background data, 1980s, hearing, 25168–69

Environmental and socioeconomic conditions, and potential impact of oil and gas OCS leases, final statement series, 5736–1

Environmental conditions, fish, wildlife, use, and mgmt, for individual coastal and riparian ecosystems, series, 5506–9

Environmental conditions of coastal areas and estuaries, research results and methodology, series, 2176–7

Environmental quality and protection programs, and intl issues, 1988 annual rpt, 484–1

Oil and gas OCS production water discharges, and impacts on Gulf of Mexico coastal habitats, 1983-88, 5738–10

Public lands acreage, grants, use, revenues, and allocations, by State, FY88, annual rpt, 5724–1.2

Soil salinity impacts on yields and off-farm water quality, and costs and benefits of extending erosion control program to saline cropland, 1989 rpt, 1588–144

Southeastern US wetlands acreage conserved and disturbed, by disturbance type and State, 1987, article, 2162–1.902

Water Bank Program agreements, payments to farmers, and wetlands acreage, by State, FY72-89, annual rpt, 1804–21

Water Bank program agreements, payments to farmers, and wetlands acreage, by State, monthly rpt, 1802–5

Wildlife-related recreation, hunting, and fishing participation and spending, detailed data by location, 1985 survey, quinquennial rpt, 5508–5

Wildlife research of State fish and wildlife agencies, federally funded projects and costs by species and State, 1989, annual listing, 5504–24

Wetterau, John M.

"Fluid Milk Sales by Method of Distribution", 1317–4.901

Wever, Kirsten R.

"Western Airlines and Its Four Major Unions: The Air Line Pilots Association, the Air Transport Employees, the Association of Flight Attendants, and the International Brotherhood of Teamsters", 6306–3.2

Whalen, Gary

"Predicting De Novo Branch Entry into Rural Markets", 9377–9.76

Whales

see Marine mammals

Wheat

Acreage of wheat and rye seeded, by State, 1987-89, annual rpt, 1621–30

Acreage planted, by selected crop and State, 1980-88 and planned 1989, annual rpt, 1621–22

Acreage under Agricultural Stabilization and Conservation Service programs, rankings by commodity and congressional district, 1987, biennial rpt, 1804–17

Agricultural data compilation, 1987/88 and trends from 1920, annual rpt, 1004–14

Agricultural Stabilization and Conservation Service producer payments, by program and State, 1988, annual rpt, 1804–12

Agricultural Stabilization and Conservation Service producer payments, by program, monthly rpt, 1802–10

Agricultural Stabilization and Conservation Service wheat program, 1960-89, annual fact sheet, 1806–4.10

Agricultural Statistics, 1988, annual rpt, 1004–1

Agriculture census, 1987: farms, farmland, production and costs, and operator characteristics, advance State and county rpt series, 2330–1

Agriculture census, 1987: farms, farmland, production, finances, and operator characteristics, by county, final State rpt series, 2331–1

Alcoholic beverages production, stocks, materials used, and taxable and tax-free removals, for beer and distilled spirits by State, monthly rpt, 8486–1.1; 8486–1.3

Business statistics, detailed data for major industries and economic indicators, *Survey of Current Business*, monthly rpt, 2702–1.11

CCC certificate (generic commodity) issues and exchanges by commodity, and wheat auction sales, 1987-89, article, 1502–4.904

CCC certificate exchange activity, by commodity, weekly press release, 1802–16

CCC loan and support programs payment activity, with data by commodity, 1986-88 and projected to 1994, 26308–86

Communist, OECD, and selected other countries agricultural production, by commodity, 1960s-88, annual rpt, 9114–4.6

Consumption, supply, trade, prices, spending, and indexes, by food commodity, 1987, annual rpt, 1544–4

Tax (income) returns of corporations, income and tax items by asset size and detailed industry, 1986, annual rpt, 8304–4; 8304–21

Tax (income) returns of partnerships, income statement items by industry group, 1986, annual article, 8302–2.903

Tax (income) returns of sole proprietorships, income statement items, by industry group, 1987, annual article, 8302–2.904; 8302–2.921

Transportation census, 1987: trucks, by detailed characteristics, miles traveled, and type of product carried, State rpt series, 2573–1

Virgin Islands economic censuses, 1987: employment, firms, payroll, and receipts, by SIC 1- to 4-digit industry, island, and city, 2593–1

Wage and benefit changes from collective bargaining and mgmt decisions, by industry div, monthly rpt, 6782–1

Wages by occupation, and benefits for office and plant workers, periodic MSA survey rpt series, 6785–11; 6785–12

see also Agricultural marketing

see also Census of Wholesale Trade

see also Industrial purchasing

see also Retail trade

see also Warehouses

see also under By Industry in the "Index by Categories"

see also under names of specific commodities or commodity groups

Wiatrowski, William J.

"Analyzing Short-Term Disability Benefits", 6722–1.925

"Flexible Benefits Plans: Employees Who Have a Choice", 6722–1.959

Wichita Falls, Tex.

Wages by occupation, for office and plant workers, 1989 survey, periodic MSA rpt, 6785–3.4

see also under By SMSA or MSA in the "Index by Categories"

Wichita, Kans.

Wages by occupation, and benefits for office and plant workers, 1989 survey, periodic MSA rpt, 6785–3.5

see also under By City and By SMSA or MSA in the "Index by Categories"

Widmann, Richard H.

"Pulpwood Production in the Northeast, 1987", 1204–18

Widows and widowers

Black lung beneficiaries and benefits by recipient type, from 1970, and by State, 1987, annual rpt, 4744–3.7

Civil service retirement system actuarial valuation, and benefits and coverage by age, type of beneficiary, and State, FY87, annual rpt, 9844–34

Consumer Income, socioeconomic characteristics of persons, families, and households, detailed cross-tabulations, Current Population Rpt series, 2546–6

Deaths and rates, by cause, marital status, age, race, and sex, 1986, annual rpt, 4144–2.1

Educational attainment, by sociodemographic characteristics and location, 1987 and trends from 1940, biennial Current Population Rpt, 2546–1.427; 2546–1.431

Employment, unemployment, and labor force characteristics, Labor Statistics Handbook, 1940s-88 with trends from 1913, 6728–38.2

Farm population, by employment and socioeconomic characteristics, and region, 1988, annual Current Population Rpt, 2546–1.439

Hispanic Americans socioeconomic characteristics, by detailed origin, 1988, Current Population Rpt, 2546–1.430; 2546–1.438

Household and family characteristics, by living arrangement, 1988 and trends from 1960, Current Population Rpt, 2546–2.148

Household and family characteristics, by location, 1988, annual Current Population Rpt, 2546–1.437

Living arrangements, family relationships, and marital status, by selected characteristics, 1988, annual Current Population Rpt, 2546–1.428; 2546–1.433

Marriages and rates, by age, race, education, previous marital status of spouses, and State, 1986, US Vital Statistics advance annual rpt, 4146–5.111; 4146–5.112

Marriages, by prior marital status and other characteristics of spouses, and State, 1984, US Vital Statistics annual rpt, 4144–4.1

Marriages, by prior marital status, interval between marriages, other characteristics of spouses, type of ceremony, and State, with divorces, 1970s-83, 4147–21.45

OASDI benefit payments, trust fund finances, and economic and demographic assumptions, 1970-87 and alternative projections to 1997, actuarial rpt, 4706–1.103

Older persons socioeconomic characteristics, 1900s-86 and projected to 2050, biennial chartbook, 12904–1

Population size and components of change, alternative projections 1988-2080 and trends from 1900, annual actuarial rpt, 4706–1.104

Railroad employee retirement, survivors, unemployment, and health insurance programs, monthly rpt, 9702–2

Railroad employment, and benefits program finances and beneficiaries, FY88, annual rpt, 9704–1

Statistical Abstract of US, social, political, and economic data, 1790-2025, comprehensive annual compilation, 2324–1.1

Tax (income) returns of individuals, by filing status, tax item, and income level, 1987, annual article, 8302–2.901

Veterans compensation and pension recipients, for each US war, 1775-1988, annual rpt, 8604–2

Veterans disability and death compensation and pension cases, by type of entitlement and period of service, monthly rpt, 8602–5; 9922–10

Veterans disability and death compensation cases of VA, by entitlement type, period of service, and sex, as of Mar 1989, semiannual rpt, 8602–8

Veterans disability and death compensation cases of VA, by entitlement type, period of service, sex, age, and State, FY88, annual rpt, 8604–7

Workers compensation laws of States and Fed Govt, 1989 semiannual rpt, 6502–1

see also Old-Age, Survivors, Disability, and Health Insurance

see also under By Marital Status in the "Index by Categories"

Wiest, Philip R.

"Consolidation and Restructuring of the U.S. Thrift Industry Under the Financial Institutions Reform, Recovery, and Enforcement Act", 8436–1.1

Wilburn, Anne M.

"Current Velocity and Hydrographic Observations in the Straits of Florida, the Caribbean Sea and Offshore of the Antillean Archipelago: Subtropical Atlantic Climate Studies (STACS) 1986", 2146–7.4

Wilcox, James A.

"Liquidity Constraints on Consumption: The Real Effects of 'Real' Lending Policies", 9393–8.911

Wilder, Patricia S.

"Productivity in the Retail Auto and Home Supply Store Industry", 6722–1.941

Wilderness areas

Acreage and use of public lands, and Land Mgmt Bur activities and finances, annual State rpt series, 5724–11

Acreage, grants, use, revenues, and allocations, for public lands by State, FY88, annual rpt, 5724–1.2

Acreage of land under Forest Service mgmt, by forest and location, 1988, annual rpt, 1204–2

Acreage of land under Natl Park Service mgmt, by site, ownership, and region, 1989 semiannual rpt, 5542–1

Acreage of Natl Wilderness Preservation System, by site and State, 1987, annual rpt, 1004–15

Acreage of refuges and other land under Fish and Wildlife Service mgmt, by site and State, as of Sept 1988, annual rpt, 5504–8

Acreage of wilderness areas by Federal agency and location, and sources of damage, with data for foreign countries, 1988 conf papers, 1208–301

Environmental quality and protection programs, and intl issues, 1988 annual rpt, 484–1

Forest Service activities and finances, by region and State, FY88, annual rpt, 1204–1.1

Forest Service mgmt of Natl Wilderness Preservation System, regulation of commercial and recreational activities, and ranger views, 1985-88, GAO rpt, 26113–436

Forest Service mgmt of public lands and resources dev, environmental, economic, and social impacts of alternative programs, projected to 2030, 1208–24

Forests (natl) recreational use, by type of activity and State, 1988, annual rpt, 1204–17

Land Mgmt Bur activities and funding by State, and receipts by program, FY87, annual rpt, 5724–13

Minerals resources and availability on public lands, State rpt series, 5606–7

Visits and overnight stays in natl park system, by park and State, monthly rpt, 5542–4

"Trade Journals and Professional Periodicals of the U.S. Construction and Building Materials Industries", 2042–1.903

Williams, Gerald D.
"Trends in Alcohol-Related Morbidity Among Short-Stay Community Hospital Discharges, U.S., 1979-84", 4486–1.1

Williams, Harry B.
"What Temporary Workers Earn: Findings from New BLS Survey", 6722–1.912

Williams, Jeffrey
"Teacher Compensation: A Comparison of Public and Private School Teachers, 1984-86", 4838–37

Williams, Jennifer D.
"Proposed Exclusion of Illegal Aliens from the Population Used To Apportion the House of Representatives: A Methodological and Policy Analysis", 21628–70

Williams, Linda S.
"Light-Duty Vehicle Summary: Model Year 1976 to the First Half of Model Year 1989", 3302–4

Williams, Robert P.
"Leading Commodity Cash Receipts, 1960-87", 1548–347

Williams, Roberton
"Economic Status of the Elderly", 26306–3.111
"Measuring the Duration of Poverty Spells", 2626–10.88
"Social Security Earnings Test and Options for Change", 26306–3.110

Williamson, Stephen D.
"Bank Failures, Financial Restrictions, and Aggregate Fluctuations: Canada and the U.S., 1870-1913", 9383–6.904

Williamsport, Pa.
see also under By SMSA or MSA in the "Index by Categories"

Wilmington, Del.
CPI by component for US city average, and by region, population size, and for 15 metro areas, monthly rpt, 6762–1
CPI by component for US city average, and by region, population size, and for 27 metro areas, monthly rpt, 6762–1
see also under By SMSA or MSA in the "Index by Categories"

Wilmington, N.C.
Freight (waterborne domestic and foreign) by commodity, traffic, and passengers, by port and waterway, 1987, annual rpt, 3754–3.1
see also under By SMSA or MSA in the "Index by Categories"

Wilmot, Richard L.
"Genetic Stock Identification of Sockeye and Chum Salmon from Bristol Bay, Alaska", 2176–1.29
"Population Genetic Structure of Arctic Char (Salvelinus alpinus) from Rivers of the North Slope of Alaska", 2176–1.29

Wilson, Barbara F.
"Remarriages and Subsequent Divorces, U.S.", 4147–21.45

Wilson, Donna C.
"Effectiveness of Motorcycle Helmets in Preventing Fatalities", 7768–106

Wilson, Ewen M.
"Implications of the 1988 Drought for Agricultural Production and Stocks", 1004–16.1

Wilson, John F.
"Reconciliation of Flow of Funds and Commerce Department Statistics on U.S. International Transactions and Foreign Investment Position", 9366–6.198

Wilson, Robert A.
"Statistics of Income: A By-Product of the U.S. Tax System", 8302–2.911
"Statistics of Income: 75 Years of Service", 8302–2.906

Wilson, Robert H.
"Sources of Increasing Inequality in Wages and Salaries, 1960-80", 6722–1.917

Winch, Kevin F.
"Corporate Finance Trends: 1989", 21368–118
"Junk Bonds: 1988 Status Report", 21248–118

Wind
see Meteorology
see Storms
see Weather
see Wind energy

Wind energy
California wind energy production, turbines, and air pollutant reductions, 1988 and projected to 2000, hearing, 25318–75
Electric power plants and capacity, by fuel used, owner, location, and operating status, 1988 and for units planned 1989-98, annual listing, 3164–36
Environmental impacts of energy technologies, 1960s-80s, handbook series, 3326–1

Windfall profit tax
Collections of excise tax, by source, quarterly rpt, 8302–1; 8302–2.1
Collections, refunds, and taxes due IRS, by State and region, FY86, annual rpt, 8304–3.3
Finances of govts, revenues by source and spending by function, natl income and product account, *Survey of Current Business*, monthly rpt, 2702–1.24
Income tax returns of individuals, detailed data, 1986, annual rpt, 8304–2
Producers finances and operations, by energy type for US firms domestic and foreign operations, 1987, annual rpt, 3164–44

Wine and winemaking
Agricultural exports of US, impacts of foreign agricultural and trade policy, with data by commodity and country, 1988, annual rpt, 1924–8
Business statistics, detailed data for major industries and economic indicators, *Survey of Current Business*, monthly rpt, 2702–1.11
Consumption of alcohol, by beverage type, region, and State, 1977-87, annual rpt, 4486–1.3; 4486–1.6; 4486–1.9
Consumption, supply, trade, prices, spending, and indexes, by food commodity, 1987, annual rpt, 1544–4
County Business Patterns, 1987: employment, establishments, and payroll, by SIC 2- to 4-digit industry and county, annual State rpt series, 2326–8
CPI by component for US city average, and by region, population size, and for 27 metro areas, monthly rpt, 6762–2
Exports and imports (agricultural) of US, by commodity and country, bimonthly rpt with articles, 1522–1

Exports and imports (agricultural) of US, by detailed commodity and country, 1988, semiannual rpt, 1522–4
Exports of US, detailed commodities by country, monthly rpt, 2422–3
Foreign and US fresh and processed fruit, vegetable, and nut production and trade, FAS monthly circular with articles, 1925–34
Imports of US, detailed Schedule A commodities by country, monthly rpt, 2422–2
Inventory and supply of wine, by type of wine, source, and selected State, periodic situation rpt with articles, 1561–6
Japan grape wine production, imports by country, and duty, selected years 1978-89, article, 1925–34.928
Manufacturing annual survey, 1986: financial and operating data, by SIC 2- to 4-digit industry, series, 2506–15
Manufacturing census, 1987: financial and operating data, for SIC 4-digit industries by product, preliminary rpt, 2491–1.8
Military personnel alcohol and drug abuse, prevalence and consequences, by selected characteristics, 1988, biennial rpt, 3504–19
Nutrient and caloric composition of food, for raw, processed, and prepared food, 1988 rpt, 1358–3
Occupational injury and illness rates, by SIC 2- to 4-digit industry, 1987, annual rpt, 6844–1
Price indexes (producer), by stage of processing and detailed commodity, monthly 1988, annual rpt, 6764–2
Production, prices, and use of noncitrus fruit and nuts, by crop and State, 1986-88, annual rpt, 1621–18.1; 1621–18.2
Production, stocks, and taxable and tax-free removals, for wine by State, monthly rpt, 8486–1.2
Tax (excise) collections of IRS, by source, quarterly rpt, 8302–1
Tax (excise) indexed to inflation, impacts on Federal revenue and family tax burden by commodity, projected under alternative proposals, 1989-93, GAO rpt, 26119–254
Tax revenue potential of State and local systems relative to natl average tax burden, by type of tax and State, 1986, annual rpt, 10044–7

Winnipeg, Canada
Fruit and vegetable shipments, and arrivals in US and Canada cities, by mode of transport and State and country of origin, 1988, annual rpt, 1311–4.2

Winston-Salem, N.C.
Clothing (hosiery) production and related workers and wages by occupation and sex, and benefits, by location, 1987 survey, 6787–6.237
see also under By City and By SMSA or MSA in the "Index by Categories"

Winter Haven, Fla.
see also under By SMSA or MSA in the "Index by Categories"

Winter sports
Forest Service activities and finances, by region and State, FY88, annual rpt, 1204–1.1
Forests (natl) recreational use, by type of activity and State, 1988, annual rpt, 1204–17

Injuries from use of consumer products and related activities, by victim age and sex, 1988, annual rpt, 9164–7

Injuries from use of consumer products, by severity, victim age, and detailed product, 1988, annual rpt, 9164–6

Public lands acreage, grants, use, revenues, and allocations, by State, FY88, annual rpt, 5724–1.2

Wiretapping
see Electronic surveillance

Wiring, electrical
see Electrical machinery and equipment
see Electronics industry and products

Wirt, John G.
"Handicapped and Disadvantaged Students: Access to Quality Vocational Education. National Assessment of Vocational Education", 4806–3.6

Wisconsin
Agriculture census, 1987: farms, farmland, production and costs, and operator characteristics, advance State and county rpts, 2330–1.55

Agriculture census, 1987: farms, farmland, production, finances, and operator characteristics, by county, final State rpt, 2331–1.49

Bank deposits in FDIC-insured commercial and savings banks, by instn, State, and county, as of June 1988, annual regional rpt, 9295–3.3

Business and economic conditions, Fed Reserve 9th District, quarterly journal, 9383–19

Cranberry production, prices, use, and acreage, for selected States, 1987-88 and forecast 1989, annual rpt, 1621–18.4

Dairy prices, by product and selected area, with related marketing data, 1988, annual rpt, 1317–1

Deaths and rates, by detailed location, cause, and demographic characteristics, 1987, US Vital Statistics annual rpt, 4144–3.1

Disaster relief program of Fed Emergency Mgmt Agency under State admin, impact of mgmt changes on benefits processing, 1986-88, GAO rpt, 26113–412

DOD prime contract awards, by contractor, service branch, State, and city, FY88, annual rpt, 3544–22

Drugs (prescription) reimbursement by Medicaid under alternative methods of determining pharmacy costs, for Wisconsin, 1986, article, 4652–1.933

Economic conditions, Fed Reserve 9th District, quarterly rpt, 9383–18

Employment, earnings, and hours, by selected SIC 1- to 4-digit industry, State, and for 262 MSAs, 1972-87, 6748–81.5

Farm operators displaced worker programs under Job Training Partnership Act, funding, participation, and results by selected State, 1982-87, 15496–1.2

Fed Govt spending in States and local areas, by type, State, county, and city, FY88, annual rpt, 2464–1

Fed Govt spending in States, by type, program, agency, and State, FY88, annual rpt, 2464–2

Food stamp program temporary termination of benefits, by reason and duration, for 2 States, FY87, GAO rpt, 26113–423

Head Start program operations, enrollment by handicap, and family characteristics, for North Central States, 1987/88, annual rpt, 4604–12

HHS financial aid, by program, recipient, State, and city, FY88, annual regional listing, 4004–3.5

Homeless children educational enrollment and needs, 1988, annual State rpt, 4804–35.49

Housing and households characteristics, 1985 survey, MSA fact sheet, 2485–11.8

Housing vacancy rates for single and multifamily units and mobile homes in FHLB 7th District, by ZIP code, annual MSA rpt series, 9304–18

Income (household), and expenses by component, by urban-rural location, for Wisconsin, 1981, article, 1502–7.905

Income (personal) per capita and by source, and earnings by industry div, by State, MSA, and county, 1982-87, annual regional rpt, 2704–2.2

Mineral Industry Surveys, State reviews of production, 1988, preliminary annual rpt, 5614–6

Minerals Yearbook, 1987, Vol 2 preprints: State review of production and sales by commodity, and business activity, annual rpt, 5604–16.51

Minerals Yearbook, 1987, Vol 2: State reviews of production, sales, and firms, by commodity, and business activity, annual rpt, 5604–34

Mortgage interest fixed and adjustable rates and fees offered by Wisconsin S&Ls, monthly rpt, 9302–7

Nursing home compliance with Medicare and Medicaid regulations, and patient characteristics, by facility, 1987/88, annual State rpt, 4654–15.51

Retail trade census, 1987: employment, establishments, sales, and payroll, by SIC 2- to 4-digit kind of business, MSA, county, and city, State rpt, 2397–1.50

Savings instns, FHLB 7th District and natl cost of funds indexes, and mortgage rates, monthly rpt, 9302–30

Savings instns, FHLB 7th District insured members, offices, and savings, by county, 1985-86, annual rpt, 9304–5

Service industries census, 1987: employment, establishments, receipts, and payroll, by SIC 2- to 4-digit kind of business, MSA, county, and city, State rpt, 2391–1.50

Statistical Abstract of US, social, political, and economic data, with foreign comparisons, 1790-2025, comprehensive annual compilation, 2324–1

Timber in Wisconsin, resources and removals by species, forest type, ownership, and county, series, 1206–34

Water supply and quality in streams and lakes, and groundwater levels in wells, by drainage basin, 1987, annual State rpt, 5666–10.46

Wholesale trade census, 1987: employment, establishments, finances, and operations, by SIC 2- to 4-digit kind of business, MSA, county, and city, State rpt, 2405–1.50

Wildlife-related recreation, hunting, and fishing participation and spending, detailed data, 1985 survey, quinquennial State rpt, 5506–6.49

see also Green Bay, Wis.
see also La Crosse, Wis.
see also Madison, Wis.
see also Milwaukee, Wis.
see also Sparta, Wis.
see also Wausau, Wis.
see also under By State in the "Index by Categories"

Wissman, Roger
"Co-op Share of Supply Sales Up: Marketings Slip During 1980s", 1122–1.901

Withholding tax
Alien nonresidents income from US sources and tax withheld by country and US tax treaty status, 1986, annual article, 8302–2.915

Budget of US, authoritative financial statements with appropriations, outlays, and receipts, by category and agency, FY88, annual rpt, 8104–2.2

Employee benefits impact on income and payroll tax revenue, by benefit type, 1950-87 and projected to 2065, article, 9373–1.913

Finances of govts, revenues by source and spending by function, natl income and product account, *Survey of Current Business*, monthly rpt, 2702–1.24

Returns and supplemental documents filed, by type, FY88 and projected to FY97, semiannual rpt, 8302–2.916; 8302–4

Returns filed, by type of tax, region, and IRS service center, projected 1988-95 and trends from 1977, annual rpt, 8304–9

Returns filed for individual income tax, detailed data, 1986, annual rpt, 8304–2

Returns processing, IRS workload forecasts, compliance, and enforcement, data compilation, 1989 annual rpt, 8304–8

Statements of income tax withholding and related documents filed, by type and IRS service center, 1988 and projected 1989-96, annual rpt, 8304–22

Violations of income tax law, civil penalties assessed and abated, FY87-88, GAO rpt, 26119–265

see also Social security tax

Witnesses
Criminal case processing from arrest to sentencing, cases and duration by disposition, offense, and defendant characteristics, for selected cities, 1986, annual rpt, 6064–27

Criminal sentences for Federal offenses, guidelines by offense and circumstances, 1989 rpt, 17668–1

Immunity requests by Federal prosecutors to US Attorney General, and witnesses involved, FY73-88, annual rpt, 6064–6.5

Marshals Service activities, FY88, annual rpt, 6294–1

Woburn, Mass.
Hazardous substances health effects, environmental levels, and household products composition, with data by selected location, 1988 hearings, 21408–112

Wolfe, Raymond M.
"Sole Proprietorship Returns, 1986", 8302–2.904

Wolfe, William H.
"Project Ranch Hand II: An Epidemiologic Investigation of Health Effects in Air Force Personnel Following Exposure to Herbicides, Mortality Update, 1989", 3604–3

Wolfson, Martin H.
"Causes of Financial Instability",
9366–6.192
"Recent Developments in the Profitability
and Lending Practices of Commercial
Banks", 9362–1.907
Wolfson, Steven A.
"Estimated Oil and Gas Reserves: Pacific
Outer Continental Shelf (as of Dec. 31,
1988)", 5734–7
Wolken, John D.
"Returns to Bidders and Targets in the
Acquisition Process: Evidence from the
Banking Industry", 9366–6.178
"Systematic Risk, Market Structure and
Entry Barriers", 9366–6.182
Womble, Kathleen
"Impact of Minimum Drinking Age Laws
on Fatal Crash Involvements: An Update
of the NHTSA Analyses", 7768–103
Women
AIDS cases by risk group, race, sex, age,
State, and MSA, and deaths, monthly rpt,
4202–9
Arrest rates, by offense, sex, age, and race,
1987, annual rpt, 6224–7
Breast enhancement, use of treatments and
products not proven safe or effective,
costs, and user characteristics, 1986
survey, 4008–86
Cancer (breast) long-term risk among
women with selected risk factors, model
description and results, 1989 article,
4472–1.934
Cancer (breast) risk, by alcohol use and
other risk factors, aggregate 1950-80,
article, 4472–1.902
Cancer (breast) risk, by oral contraceptives
use and menopausal status, 1976-86 study,
article, 4472–1.923
Cancer (breast) risk for women by smoking
history, and menopausal and estrogen
receptor status, 1976-86 study, article,
4472–1.928
Cancer (breast) risk of scoliosis patients
x-rayed during childhood, by diagnosis
and other characteristics, 1922-86, local
area study, article, 4472–1.922
Cancer (breast) risk relation to diet and
nutrient intake, for northwestern Italy,
1983-85 study, article, 4472–1.906
Cancer (breast) risk, relation to hypertension
diagnosis before and after pregnancy,
1989 article, 4472–1.927
Cancer (breast) risk relation to oral
contraceptives use, by age at first use and
duration, Sweden study, 1979-85, article,
4472–1.917
Cancer (breast) survival rates, for patients
receiving chemotherapy after surgery, for
diagnoses made 1975-85, GAO rpt,
26131–58
Cancer (breast) tumor characteristics related
to diet, number of children, and age,
1983-86, article, 4472–1.920
Cancer (breast and cervical) incidence,
deaths, and survival rates, by race,
average 1973-81, article, 4042–3.952
Cancer (cervical) cases and risk relation to
smoking and other characteristics, for 4
Latin American countries, 1986-87 study,
article, 4472–1.905
Cancer (cervical) screening and education
program for black women, effectiveness
and participant characteristics, 1988 local
area study, article, 4042–3.953

Cancer (melanoma) risk relation to mole
count, by body site, 1989 article,
4472–1.915
Child support and alimony awards, and
payment status, by selected characteristics
of woman, 1985, biennial Current
Population Rpt, 2546–2.145
Childless women, by selected characteristics,
1988, annual Current Population Rpt,
2546–1.436
Crime, criminal justice admin and
enforcement, and public opinion, data
compilation, 1970s-88, annual rpt,
6064–6
Crimes, arrests, and rates, by offense,
offender characteristics, population size,
and jurisdiction, 1988, annual rpt,
6224–2.1; 6224–2.2
Deaths and rates, by detailed cause and
demographic characteristics, 1986 and
trends from 1900, US Vital Statistics
annual rpt, 4144–2
Deaths and rates, by detailed location,
cause, and demographic characteristics,
1987, US Vital Statistics annual rpt,
4144–3
Divorces by age of spouses and duration of
marriage, and children involved, by State,
1986 with trends from 1940, US Vital
Statistics advance annual rpt, 4146–5.109
Drug, alcohol, and cigarette use, by
substance, age, sex, race, and region, 1988
survey, biennial rpt, 4494–5
Drug and alcohol abuse treatment facilities,
services, use, funding, and client
characteristics, 1987, annual rpt,
4494–10
Education Dept programs funding,
operations, and effectiveness, FY88,
annual rpt, 4804–5
Education statistics, detailed data on higher
education, 1960s-88, annual rpt,
4824–1.2
Fiber content in breakfast cereal and bread,
health claim ads, and other factors
affecting consumption, 1978-88,
9406–1.60
Food aid program of USDA for women,
infants, and children, participants and
costs by State and Indian agency, FY87,
annual rpt, 1364–12
Food consumption and nutrient intake by
individuals, by food group, selected
characteristics, and region, 1986
supplementary survey, 1356–5.1
Health condition and health care resources,
use, and spending, 1950s-87, annual data
compilation, 4144–11
Homicide rates, and lifetime probability of
victimization, by age, sex, and race, 1987,
annual rpt, 6224–8
Household composition, income, benefits,
and labor force status, Survey of Income
and Program Participation methodology,
working paper series, 2626–10
Human papillomavirus infection rates, by
sexual and personal hygiene practices, and
other patient characteristics, Brazil local
area studies, 1989 article, 4472–1.908
Income (household) and poverty status
under alternative income definitions, by
recipient characteristics, 1986, Current
Population Rpt, 2546–6.58
Mammography referral services for
low-income women, use and client
characteristics, 1987-88 local area study,
article, 4042–3.951

Marriages and rates, by age, race, education,
previous marital status of spouses, and
State, 1986, US Vital Statistics advance
annual rpt, 4146–5.111; 4146–5.112
Marriages, by prior marital status, interval
between marriages, other characteristics of
spouses, type of ceremony, and State,
with divorces, 1970s-83, 4147–21.45
Marriages, divorces, and rates, by
characteristics of spouses, State, and
county, 1984 and trends from 1920, US
Vital Statistics annual rpt, 4144–4
Nutritional status and related health
condition and practices, by selected
characteristics, 1970s-87, 4048–33
OASDHI, Medicaid, SSI, and related
programs benefits, beneficiary
characteristics, and trust funds, selected
years 1937-87, annual rpt, 4744–3
Pension coverage, sources, payments, and
effect on income and poverty status, for
older women, 1982, article, 4742–1.901
Population size, by age, sex, and race, and
components of change, alternative
projections 1988-2080, Current Population
Rpt, 2546–3.158
Prisoners, movements, and characteristics,
by State, 1986, annual rpt, 6064–26
Prisoners under death sentence by prison
control and prisoner characteristics, and
executions from 1930, by State, 1973-88,
annual rpt, 6066–25.23
Science and engineering grad enrollment, by
field, source of funds, and characteristics
of student and instn, 1975-87, annual rpt,
9627–7
Statistical Abstract of US, social, political,
and economic data, with foreign
comparisons, 1790-2025, comprehensive
annual compilation, 2324–1
Veteran women population, by period of
service, FY70-88, annual rpt, 8604–5.1
Veterans disability and death compensation
cases of VA, by entitlement type, period
of service, sex, age, and State, FY88,
annual rpt, 8604–7
Veterans population, by period of service
and age, as of Mar 1989, semiannual rpt,
8602–7
Voting and registration, by socioeconomic
and demographic characteristics, 1988
presidential election, biennial Current
Population Rpt, 2546–1.440
see also Families and households
see also Fertility
see also Maternity
see also Maternity benefits
see also Prenatal care
see also Sex discrimination
see also Teenage pregnancy
see also Women-owned businesses
see also Women's employment
see also under By Sex in the "Index by
Categories"
Women-Owned Business Enterprise Survey
see Survey of Women-Owned Businesses
Women-owned businesses
Agriculture census, 1987: farms, farmland,
production, finances, and operator
characteristics, by county, final State rpt
series, 2331–1
AID contracts to minority and
women-owned businesses, awards and
goals, FY88, annual rpt, 9904–1.2

Fed Govt contracts and obligations for small business, by program and recipient type, for North Carolina and total US, FY77-87, hearings, 21728-67

Fed Govt procurement contract awards to women-owned businesses, by agency, quarterly rpt, 102-6

FmHA loans, by type, borrower characteristics, and State, quarterly rpt, 1182-8

Hwy construction contracts awards of States to minority- and women-owned firms, FY85-88, GAO rpt, 26113-399

Hwy construction contracts for Federal-aid system, awards to minority- and women-owned businesses, FHwA and State reviews, FY83-87, GAO rpt, 26113-389

Mgmt and financial aid from Minority Business Dev Centers, and characteristics of businesses, by region and State, FY88, annual rpt, 2104-6

Mgmt issues for women-owned businesses, SBA loans, Federal contracts by agency, and owners views on Michigan business climate, FY79-88, hearings, 21728-68

NASA procurement contract awards, by type, contractor, State, and country, FY89, semiannual rpt, 9502-6

Navy procurement awards to disadvantaged and women-owned businesses, FY88, annual rpt, 3804-13.3

Small business establishments, operations, owner characteristics, and job training, late 1950s-87, 9768-20

Small business finances, operations, owner and employee characteristics, and Federal contracts, 1980s-88, annual rpt, 9764-6

Small business financial and technical aid of States, 1988 listing, 9768-15

Statistical Abstract of US, social, political, and economic data, 1790-2025, comprehensive annual compilation, 2324-1.3

Telecommunications industries purchases from minority- and women-owned businesses, 1986-87, hearings, 21368-113

see also Survey of Women-Owned Businesses

Women's employment

Aerospace industry employment and salaries, by sex and race, 1979-87, GAO rpt, 26121-315

Aerospace industry minority employment in Los Angeles area, by occupational group, 1980s-86, 21348-113

AFDC recipients demographic and financial characteristics, by State, FY87, annual rpt, 4694-1

Aircraft pilots and nonpilots certified by FAA, by certificate type, age, sex, region, and State, 1988, annual rpt, 7504-2

Army personnel, promotion, and training by race and for women, discrimination issues, and career attitudes, FY88, annual rpt, 3704-10

Asian American earnings, and employment and other characteristics, by detailed origin and whether foreign-born, 1980, 11046-7.2

Births, fertility rates, and childless women, by selected characteristics, 1988, annual Current Population Rpt, 2546-1.436

Child care arrangements and costs, by income and other characteristics of family, 1984-86, press release, 2328-61

Child care costs relation to mothers labor force participation, 1984, Survey of Income and Program Participation, working paper, 2626-10.97

Child care leave of absence for employees, policies, coverage, and attitudes, by employee characteristics, 1980-87, hearings, 25548-95

Child support and alimony awards, and payment status, by selected characteristics of woman, 1985, biennial Current Population Rpt, 2546-2.145

Child support awards related to selected variables, 1970s-85, 4008-94

Consumer spending and income effects of wives' employment, by expenditure category and household characteristics, 1984-86, article, 6722-1.908

Dallas-Fort Worth metro area employment, earnings, hours, and CPI changes, 1970s-88, annual rpt, 6964-2

Defense Fuel Supply Center procurement, prices, stocks, transport, and other activities and finances, FY88, annual rpt, 3904-8

Disabled persons employment, labor force status, and other characteristics, 1988, Current Population Rpt, 2546-2.147

DOT activities by subagency, budget, and summary accident data, FY85, annual rpt, 7304-1

DOT employment, by subagency, occupation, and selected personnel characteristics, FY88, annual rpt, 7304-18

Earnings of married couples, by employment status, occupation, age, and education of spouses, and age of children, 1987, Current Population Rpt, 2546-6.61

Employment and earnings covered under OASDHI, and social security contributions, by age, sex, race, State, and county, 1985, 4748-43

Employment and Earnings, detailed data, monthly rpt, 6742-2.5

Employment, earnings, and hours, by SIC 1- to 4-digit industry, monthly 1983-Feb 1989, annual rpt, 6744-1

Employment of minorities and women, by occupation, SIC 1- to 3- digit industry, State, and MSA, 1986, annual rpt, 9244-1

Employment situation, earnings, hours, and other BLS economic indicators, transcripts of BLS Commissioner's monthly testimony, periodic rpt, 23846-4

Employment status of family members and earnings, by family composition and race, quarterly press release, 6742-21

Employment, unemployment, and labor force characteristics, by region, State, and selected metro area, 1988, annual rpt, 6744-7

Energy-related employment of scientists and engineers with PhDs, by field and work activity, various periods 1975-87, 3006-8.10

Farm population, by employment and socioeconomic characteristics, and region, 1988, annual Current Population Rpt, 2546-1.439

Fed Equal Opportunity Recruitment Program activity, and employment by sex, race, pay grade, and selected occupation, FY88, annual rpt, 9844-33

Fed Govt civilian employment and payroll, by occupation, pay grade, sex, agency, and location, 1987, biennial rpt, 9844-4

Fed Govt civilian employment, by occupation, pay schedule, grade, sex, and race, as of Sept 1988, article, 9842-1.902

Fed Govt civilian employment of minorities and women, by pay grade, 1976-86, 9848-37

Fed Govt employment of minorities and women by occupation, and handicapped employment, by agency, FY87, annual rpt, 9244-10

Fed Govt employment of minorities, handicapped, and veterans, and years of service, by occupation, age, sex, and agency, as of Sept 1988, biennial rpt, 9844-27

Foreign Service minority and women employment, hires, and promotions, 1981-87, GAO rpt, 26123-247

Handbook of Labor Statistics, employment, unemployment, and labor force characteristics, 1940s-88 with trends from 1913, 6728-38

Hispanic Americans socioeconomic characteristics, by detailed origin, 1988, Current Population Rpt, 2546-1.430; 2546-1.438

Household and family characteristics, by living arrangement, 1988 and trends from 1960, Current Population Rpt, 2546-2.148

Household and family characteristics, by location, 1988, annual Current Population Rpt, 2546-1.437

Houston metro area employment, earnings, hours, and CPI changes, 1970s-88, annual rpt, 6964-1

Income (household) and poverty status under alternative income definitions, by recipient characteristics, 1986, Current Population Rpt, 2546-6.58

Income (household, family, and personal), by source, detailed characteristics, and region, 1987, annual Current Population Rpt, 2546-6.59

Job Training Partnership Act participants and eligible population, by selected characteristics, 1986, 15496-1.3

Labor force composition, and wages relation to inflation and unemployment, late 1930s-88, article, 9373-1.902

Labor force participation of women, by age, race, and family status, quarterly rpt, 6742-17

Labor force status by race and sex, employment by industry div, and unemployment duration and reason, selected years 1929-88, annual rpt, 204-1.2

Labor force status, by worker characteristics and industry group, 1982-1st half 1989, semiannual article, 6722-1.907; 6722-1.937

Labor force supply and mobility, by age, and educational level needs, 1960-86 and projected to 2000, 6306-2.4

Labor force, wages, hours, and payroll costs, by major industry group and demographic characteristics, *Survey of Current Business*, monthly rpt, 2702-1.5

Maternity leave arrangements and work history of 1st-time mothers, by selected characteristics, 1960s-85, 2328-62

Military health care personnel, by sex, occupation, and service branch, FY87, annual rpt, 3544–24.1

Military officers, enlisted, and reserve personnel, by sex and service branch, FY88 and trends from 1945, annual rpt, 3544–1.2; 3544–1.5

Military personnel on active duty, recruits, and reenlistment, by race, sex, and service branch, quarterly press release, 3542–7

Military reserve officer and enlisted personnel, by component, FY88, annual rpt, 3544–31.1

Military reserve personnel social, economic, family, and service characteristics, and attitudes, by reserve component, 1986 survey, 3508–29

Military reserve spouses attitudes, and family social, economic, and other characteristics, 1986 survey, 3508–30

Military women personnel on active and reserve duty, by demographic and service characteristics and service branch, FY88, annual chartbook, 3544–26

Military women personnel on active duty, by rank, grade, and service branch, quarterly rpt, 3542–14.3

Navy manpower strengths, accessions, and attrition, detailed statistics, quarterly rpt, 3802–4

Nuclear engineering enrollment and degrees by instn and State, and women grads plans and employment, 1972-88, 3006–8.8

Pension and health insurance coverage for full- and part-time workers, 1985, article, 6722–1.913

Police dept operations, staff, and expenses, for large cities by population size, 1987, 6066–19.51

Population size and characteristics, 1969-88, Current Population Rpt, annual rpt, 2546–2.146

Postal Service employment of minority groups and women, by pay level, FY87-88, annual rpt, 9864–5.1

Poverty status of families and persons, by detailed characteristics, 1987, annual Current Population Rpt, 2546–6.60

Public welfare programs beneficiaries, and benefits duration and share of income, by selected characteristics, 1983-86, 2546–20.8

Radiation protection and health physics enrollment and degrees granted by instn and State, and women grads plans and employment, 1972-88, 3006–8.9

Railroad employee benefits and beneficiaries by type, and railroad employment and payroll, FY85, annual rpt, 9704–2

Science and engineering employment and education, and R&D spending, for US and selected foreign countries, 1988, annual rpt, 9624–23.2

Science and engineering labor supply, R&D funding, and other science indicators, with foreign comparisons, 1960s-89, annual chartbook, 9624–22

Science and engineering PhDs employment and other characteristics, by field and State, 1987, biennial rpt, 9627–18

Shipboard employment of women in merchant marine, Natl Marine Fisheries Service, and fishing, with rpts of sexual assault, 1980s-88, GAO rpt, 26113–397

Small Business Admin employment, by sex, race, and pay grade, and SBA activities, FY84-88, annual rpt, 9764–1

SSA minority, handicapped, and women employees, by pay grade, FY88, annual rpt, 4704–6

State and local govt employment of minorities and women, by occupation, function, pay level, and State, 1986, annual rpt, 9244–6

State Dept and Foreign Service minority and women employment, FY88, annual rpt, 7004–21

Statistical Abstract of US, social, political, and economic data, 1790-2025, comprehensive annual compilation, 2324–1.3

Tax policy of Reagan Admin and business cycle indicators, impacts on labor force participation rate by sex and age, 1976-88, article, 9389–1.914

Taxes, spending, and govt efficiency, public opinion by respondent characteristics, 1989 survey, annual rpt, 10044–2

Telecommunications industries minority employment and discrimination charges, with data by industry and selected firm, 1970s-88, hearings, 21368–113

Unemployed displaced workers, by reason, industry, selected characteristics, and State, 1988, annual rpt, 6744–18

Unemployment rates, current data and annual trends, monthly rpt, 23842–1.2

VA employment characteristics and activities, FY88, annual rpt, 8604–3.8

VA health care facilities physicians, dentists, and nurses, by selected employment characteristics and VA district, quarterly rpt, 8602–6

Voting and registration, by socioeconomic and demographic characteristics, 1988 presidential election, biennial Current Population Rpt, 2546–1.440

see also Women-owned businesses

see also under By Sex in the "Index by Categories"

Wonder, Bernard
"Future Significance of the North American Drought", 1004–16.1

Wones, Robert G.
"Comparisons of Referral Criteria for Public Screening of Blood Cholesterol Levels", 4042–3.941

Wood
see Lumber industry and products
see Wood fuel

Wood, E. M.
"Toxicity of 3,400 Chemicals to Fish", 9238–68

Wood fuel
Arizona timber harvest, mill receipts, and residues, with methodology, 1984-85, 1208–294

Arizona wood fuel harvest, by tree species, ownership, and county, 1984, 1208–293

Buildings (commercial) energy use, costs, and conservation, by building characteristics, survey rpt series, 3166–8

Consumption of energy, by air pollutant source, fuel type, and State, 1986, annual rpt, 9194–14

Consumption of wood, waste, and alcohol fuels, by region, 1980-84, and characteristics of wood-burning households, 1984, annual rpt, 3164–74.7

Cuba economic conditions, agricultural and industrial production and distribution, trade, and intl economic relations, 1980-87 with trends from 1961, 9118–8

Electric power plants and capacity, by fuel used, owner, location, and operating status, 1988 and for units planned 1989-98, annual listing, 3164–36

Environmental impacts of energy technologies, 1960s-80s, handbook series, 3326–1

Exports of US, detailed commodities by country, monthly rpt, 2422–3

Freight (waterborne domestic and foreign) by commodity, traffic, and passengers, by port and waterway, 1987, annual rpt, 3754–3

Housing and households detailed characteristics, and unit and neighborhood quality, by location, 1985, biennial rpt, 2485–12

Housing and households detailed characteristics, and unit and neighborhood quality, MSA surveys, series, 2485–6

Housing energy use, costs, and conservation, and household and housing characteristics, survey rpt series, 3166–7

Illinois timber resources, removals, and products, by species, forest characteristics, ownership, and county, 1960s-85 and projected to 2015, 1208–292

Imports of US, detailed Schedule A commodities by country, monthly rpt, 2422–2

New Mexico fuelwood harvest, by species, ownership, and county, 1986, 1208–303

New Mexico timber resources and harvest, 1987, 1208–310

Pollution (air) levels for 5 pollutants, by detailed source and State, 1986, annual rpt, 9194–7

Pollution (air) levels for 6 pollutants, by source, 1970-87 and trends from 1940, annual rpt, 9194–13

Prices and spending for fuel, by type, end-use sector, and State, 1987, annual rpt, 3164–64

Rocky Mountain States timber and mill residue production, by species, ownership, and county, series, 1206–17

Statistical Abstract of US, social, political, and economic data, 1790-2025, comprehensive annual compilation, 2324–1.3

Wisconsin timber resources and removals, by species, forest type, ownership, and county, series, 1206–34

Wood, Geoffrey E.
"Introduction to Non-Tariff Barriers to Trade", 9391–1.906

Wood, John H.
"Are Reserve Requirement Changes Really Exogenous? An Example of Regulatory Accommodation of Industry Goals", 9379–12.43

Woods, John R.
"Pension Coverage Among Private Wage and Salary Workers: Preliminary Findings from the 1988 Survey of Employee Benefits", 4742–1.925; 4746–26.7

"Retirement-Age Women and Pensions: Findings from the New Beneficiary Survey", 4742–1.901

Woodstock, N.Y.

Cancer incidence relation to exposure to asbestos in drinking water, by sex and cancer site, 1973-83, local area study, article, 4042-3.921

Wool and wool trade

Acreage under Agricultural Stabilization and Conservation Service programs, rankings by commodity and congressional district, 1987, biennial rpt, 1804-17

Agricultural Stabilization and Conservation Service producer payments, by program and State, 1988, annual rpt, 1804-12

Agricultural Stabilization and Conservation Service producer payments, by program, monthly rpt, 1802-10

Agricultural Stabilization and Conservation Service wool and mohair programs, 1955-89, annual fact sheet, 1806-4.3; 1806-4.4

Agricultural Statistics, 1988, annual rpt, 1004-1

Agriculture census, 1987: farms, farmland, production, finances, and operator characteristics, by county, final State rpt series, 2331-1

Business statistics, detailed data for major industries and economic indicators, *Survey of Current Business*, monthly rpt, 2702-1.19

Clothing production, by fiber and product, quarterly Current Industrial Rpt, 2506-6.12

Communist countries agricultural, mineral, and consumer and producer goods production, by commodity, 1960s-88, annual rpt, 9114-4.4

County Business Patterns, 1987: employment, establishments, and payroll, by SIC 2- to 4-digit industry and county, annual State rpt series, 2326-8

Eastern Europe and USSR agricultural production, acreage, and consumption, by commodity and country, 1965-85, 1528-284

Employment, earnings, and hours, by SIC 1- to 4-digit industry, monthly 1983-Feb 1989, annual rpt, 6744-4

Exports and imports (agricultural) of US, by commodity and country, bimonthly rpt with articles, 1522-1

Exports and imports (agricultural) of US, by detailed commodity and country, 1988, semiannual rpt, 1522-4

Exports and imports of dairy, livestock, and poultry products, by commodity and country, FAS monthly circular, 1925-32

Exports of US, detailed commodities by country, monthly rpt, 2422-3

Farm sector balance sheet, and receipts by detailed commodity, by State, 1984-88, annual rpt, 1544-18

Farm sector finances, income sources, expenses by type, assets, debts, and ratios, 1987, annual rpt, 1544-19

Foreign countries agricultural production, prices, and trade, by country, 1970s-89 and forecast 1990, annual world region rpt series, 1524-4

Import restraint elimination, impact on domestic industry production and employment, by selected commodity, 1986-88, 9886-4.144

Imports of textiles, by country of origin, monthly rpt, 2042-27

Imports of textiles, by product and country of origin, periodic rpt series, 2046-8; 2046-9

Imports of textiles, production, and imports share of use, by Multifiber Arrangement product, quarterly rpt, 2042-32

Imports of textiles under Multifiber Arrangement by product and country, and status of bilateral agreements, 1986-88, annual rpt, 9884-18

Imports of US, detailed Schedule A commodities by country, monthly rpt, 2422-2

Manufacturing annual survey, 1986: financial and operating data, by SIC 2- to 4-digit industry, series, 2506-15

Manufacturing census, 1987: financial and operating data, for SIC 4-digit industries by product, preliminary rpt, 2491-1.11; 2491-1.14

Marketing data for livestock, meat, and wool, by species and market, weekly rpt, 1315-1

Occupational injury and illness rates, by SIC 2- to 4-digit industry, 1987, annual rpt, 6844-1

Price indexes (producer), by stage of processing and detailed commodity, monthly rpt, 6762-6

Price indexes (producer), by stage of processing and detailed commodity, monthly 1988, annual rpt, 6764-2

Prices received and paid by farmers, by commodity and State, 1988, annual rpt, 1629-5

Prices received by farmers for major products, and paid for farm inputs and living items, by State, monthly rpt, 1629-1

Prices, sales, trade, and stocks of wool, and sheep inventory, weekly and biweekly rpt, 1315-2

Production and prices of wool and mohair, by State, 1988, annual press release, 1623-6

Production itemized costs, receipts, and returns, by commodity and region, 1985-87, annual rpt, 1544-20

Production, prices, and value of wool and mohair, 1970-87, 1568-285.1; 1568-285.3

Production, prices, trade, and marketing, by commodity, current situation and forecast, monthly rpt with articles, 1502-4

Production, prices, trade, and use of wool, mohair, and other fibers, periodic situation rpt with articles, 1561-1

Production, trade, sales, stocks, and material used, by product, region, and State, periodic Current Industrial Rpt series, 2506-5

Science, engineering, and technical employment in manufacturing, by field, occupation, and industry, 1986, triennial rpt, 9627-23

Wholesale trade census, 1987: employment, establishments, finances, and operations, by SIC 2- to 4-digit kind of business, MSA, county, and city, State rpt series, 2405-1

Woonsocket, R.I.

see also under By SMSA or MSA in the "Index by Categories"

Worcester, Mass.

see also under By City and By SMSA or MSA in the "Index by Categories"

Word, David L.

"Population Estimates by Race and Hispanic Origin for States, Metropolitan Areas, and Selected Counties: 1980-85", 2546-3.159

Word processing

see Computer industry and products
see Computer use

Work conditions

Air pollution indoor levels, effects of ventilation rates in commercial and industrial buildings, 1989 rpt, 3228-10

Air traffic control system safety, working conditions, and traffic volume, various periods 1981-88, GAO rpt series, 26113-220

Military reserve personnel social, economic, family, and service characteristics, and attitudes, by reserve component, 1986 survey, 3508-29

Military reserve spouses attitudes, and family social, economic, and other characteristics, 1986 survey, 3508-30

Teachers in public schools, demographic and employment characteristics, 1989 edition, annual rpt, 4824-2.9

Technological devs effect on labor force, composition, and productivity, by industry, 1960s-86 and projected to 2000, series, 6826-2

see also Agricultural accidents and safety
see also Job tenure
see also Mine accidents and safety
see also Occupational health and safety

Work incentive programs

AFDC job training and related aid, participants, costs, and budget impact, projected FY89-93, 26306-3.102

AFDC recipients demographic and financial characteristics, by State, FY87, annual rpt, 4694-1

Assistance (financial and nonfinancial) of Fed Govt, 1989 base edition with supplements, annual listing, 104-5

Disability Insurance and SSI admin of Fed Govt and States, benefits, caseloads, and operations, 1980s, 4708-11

Expenditures of Fed Govt in States, by type, program, agency, and State, FY88, annual rpt, 2464-2

HHS financial aid, by program, recipient, State, and city, FY88, annual regional listings, 4004-3

Participant characteristics, activities, and funding, for Employment and Training Admin programs, FY80-86, 6408-71

Rural and urban areas jobs created under AFDC workfare program, 1986 and estimated 1988, article, 1502-7.902

Tax (income) returns filed by type of filer, selected income items, quarterly rpt, 8302-2.1

Work stoppages

Air traffic control system safety, working conditions, and traffic volume, various periods 1981-88, GAO rpt series, 26113-220

Foreign countries labor conditions, output, earnings, and price indexes, by selected country, 1950-88, 6728-38.11

Foreign countries labor conditions, union coverage, and work accidents, annual country rpt series, 6366-4

Labor force, wages, hours, and payroll costs, by major industry group and demographic characteristics, *Survey of Current Business*, monthly rpt, 2702–1.5

Mediation and arbitration activities of Fed Mediation and Conciliation Service, and cases by issue, region, and State, FY82-87, annual rpt, 9344–1

Monthly Labor Review, work stoppages involving 1,000 workers or more, workers involved, and days idle, 6722–1.3

Railroad and airline labor disputes, and Federal mediation activities and caseloads, with data by carrier and union, FY85-86, annual rpt, 9604–1

Statistical Abstract of US, social, political, and economic data, 1790-2025, comprehensive annual compilation, 2324–1.3

Wage and benefit changes from collective bargaining and mgmt decisions, by industry div, monthly rpt, 6782–1

Work stoppages, workers involved, and days idle, by industry group, 1984-88 with trends from 1947, 6728–38.9

Work stoppages, workers involved, and days idle, 1988 and trends from 1947, annual press release, 6784–12

Work-study programs

Assistance and other sources of support, with student expenses and characteristics, by instn type and control, 1987 triennial study, series, 4846–3

Community dev work-study program of HUD, students and awards by sponsor instn, 1988-89, press release, 5006–3.64

Education Dept programs funding, operations, and effectiveness, FY88, annual rpt, 4804–5

Fed Govt funding for education by agency, program, and recipient type, and instn spending, FY80-88, 4828–21

Fed Govt share of student aid supplemental grants, loans, and work-study awards, by instn and State, 1989/90, annual listing, 4804–17

Science and engineering grad enrollment, by field, source of funds, and characteristics of student and instn, 1975-87, annual rpt, 9627–7

Special education programs, enrollment by age, staff, funding, and needs, by type of handicap and State, 1987/88, annual rpt, 4944–4

Student aid funding and participation, by Federal program, instn type and control, and State, various periods 1959-88, annual rpt, 4804–28

Work training

see Employee development

see Manpower training programs

see Vocational education and training

Worker adjustment assistance

see Trade adjustment assistance

Worker incentives

see Employee bonuses and work incentives

Workers

see Agricultural labor

see Blue collar workers

see Clerical workers

see Employment and unemployment, general

see Employment and unemployment, local and regional

see Employment and unemployment, specific industry

see Government employees

see Job tenure

see Labor supply and demand

see Migrant workers

see Occupational testing and certification

see Production workers

see Professional and technical workers

see Sales workers

see Unpaid family workers

see Women's employment

see Work conditions

Workers compensation

Beneficiaries and taxes collected for social insurance programs since 1940, monthly rpt, 4742–1.1

Benefits and benefit duration under workers compensation, by State, 1988, article, 4742–1.921

Benefits and coverage under workers compensation, by type of program and insurer, and State, 1985-86, annual article, 4742–1.912

Black lung benefits and claims by State, trust fund receipts by source, and disbursements, 1987, annual rpt, 6504–3

Black lung benefits by county, FY88, annual regional listings, 4004–3

Black lung benefits to miners, widows, and dependents, with data by State reported quarterly, monthly rpt, 4742–1.6; 4742–1.13

Black lung trust funds financial condition, monthly rpt, 8102–9.10

Costs (hourly) of labor, by component, occupational group, union coverage, industry div, and region, 1989, annual rpt, 6744–21

Economic conditions relation to UI and workers compensation programs costs, for North Central States, 1970s-88, working paper, 9375–13.9

Expenditures (private) for social welfare, by category, 1970s-87, annual article, 4742–1.928

Expenditures, coverage, and benefits for social welfare programs, late 1930s-87, annual rpt, 4744–3.1; 4744–3.7

Expenditures for health care of business, households, and govts, 1965-87, article, 4652–1.928

Expenditures for public welfare by program, and private health care spending, FY50s-86, annual article, 4742–1.909

Expenditures of Fed Govt in States, by type, program, agency, and State, FY88, annual rpt, 2464–2

Fed Govt civilian employee work-years, pay rates, and benefits use and costs, by agency, FY87, annual rpt, 9844–31

Fed Govt workers compensation program finances and operations, FY87, annual rpt, 6504–10

Foreign countries social security programs coverage, funding, eligibility, and benefits, by country, 1987, biennial rpt, 4746–4.60

France and US hospital beds, and use by diagnosis and patient characteristics, by instn ownership, with deaths by cause, 1981, 4147–5.4

Hospital discharges and length of stay, by diagnosis, patient and instn characteristics, procedure performed, and payment source, 1987, annual rpt, 4147–13.99

Income (household, family, and personal), by source, detailed characteristics, and region, 1987, annual Current Population Rpt, 2546–6.59

Income (personal) by source including transfer payments, and social insurance contributions, by region, 1948 and 1987, 2708–40

Injuries on job, relation to increases in workers compensation benefits and employer premiums, model description and results, 1985 working paper, 6886–6.15

Injuries on job relation to increases in workers compensation benefits, model description and results, 1979-84, working paper, 6886–6.64

Police pay, benefits, and staffing, for US Park Police and compared to other Federal and local police units, FY85-88, GAO rpt, 26119–264

Postal Service activities, finances, and mail volume and subsidies, FY88, annual rpt, 9864–5

State workers compensation laws, and Fed Govt provisions, 1989 semiannual rpt, 6502–1

State workers compensation laws, changes in coverage, benefits, and premium rates, by State, 1988, annual article, 6722–1.906

State workers compensation programs, admin, coverage, benefits, finances, processing, and staff, various periods 1984-88, annual rpt, 6504–9

Statistical Abstract of US, social, political, and economic data, 1790-2025, comprehensive annual compilation, 2324–1.2

Telephone service of households, by composition, income sources, and other characteristics, 1984-87, 9288–11

Transit systems finances and operations, by mode of transport, size of fleet, and for 432 systems, 1986, annual rpt, 7884–4

Wages relation to workers compensation benefits, model description and results, 1985 working paper, 6886–6.22

Working women

see Women-owned businesses

see Women's employment

World Bank

see International Bank for Reconstruction and Development

see International Development Association

World Meteorological Organization

Weather data for surface and upper air, averages by foreign and US station, monthly rpt, 2152–4

World Wars

see Veterans benefits and pensions

see War

Wrecking and demolition

Construction industries census, 1987: financial and operating data, preliminary industry rpt, 2371–1.24

County Business Patterns, 1987: employment, establishments, and payroll, by SIC 2- to 4-digit industry and county, annual State rpt series, 2326–8

Historic and natural natl landmarks damaged and threatened, with owner, location, damage type, and recommended remedial action, 1988, annual listing, 5544–16

Transportation census, 1987: trucks, by detailed characteristics, miles traveled, and type of product carried, State rpt series, 2573–1

Agricultural trade of US with Asia, Middle East, and North Africa, by commodity and country, 1962-86, 1528–277

AID activities and funding by project and function, FY90, and developing countries summary socioeconomic data from 1960s, annual rpt, 9904-4.6

AID economic aid to developing countries, obligations and disbursements by country, quarterly rpt, 9912-4

AID loans repayment status and terms by program and country, and status of predecessor agency loans, quarterly rpt, 9912-3

Economic and military aid and loans from US and intl agencies, by program and country, FY46-87, annual rpt, 9914-5

Economic conditions, income, production, prices, employment, and trade, 1989 periodic country rpt, 2046-4.110

Economic conditions, policy, and trade practices, by country, 1986-88, annual rpt, 21384-5

Economic, social, political, and geographic summary data, by country, 1989, annual factbook, 9114-2

Human rights conditions in 170 countries, 1988, annual rpt, 21384-3

Military aid of US, arms sales, and training programs costs and budget requests, by program, world region, and country, FY88-90, annual rpt, 7144-13

Military spending, arms trade, and force strengths, with govt spending and population, by country, 1977-87, annual rpt, 9824-1

Minerals Yearbook, 1987, Vol 3: foreign country reviews of production, trade, and policy, by commodity, annual rpt, 5604-35

Minerals Yearbook, 1987, Vol 3 preprints: foreign country review of production, trade, and policy, by commodity, annual rpt, 5604-23.86

Population size, growth rates, and components of change, by country, projected 1989-2020 and trends from 1950, biennial rpt, 2324-9

UN voting record and share of votes in agreement with US, by issue, country, and world area, 1988, annual rpt, 7004-18

see also under By Foreign Country in the "Index by Categories"

Yemen, South

Agricultural and food production and indexes, total and for selected commodities, by country, 1970s-88, annual rpt, 1524-12

Agricultural trade of US, by detailed commodity and country, 1988, semiannual rpt, 1522-4

Economic and military aid and loans from US and intl agencies, by program and country, FY46-87, annual rpt, 9914-5

Economic, social, political, and geographic summary data, by country, 1989, annual factbook, 9114-2

Human rights conditions in 170 countries, 1988, annual rpt, 21384-3

Military spending, arms trade, and force strengths, with govt spending and population, by country, 1977-87, annual rpt, 9824-1

Minerals Yearbook, 1987, Vol 3: foreign country reviews of production, trade, and policy, by commodity, annual rpt, 5604-35

Minerals Yearbook, 1987, Vol 3 preprints: foreign country review of production, trade, and policy, by commodity, annual rpt, 5604-23.86

Population size, growth rates, and components of change, by country, projected 1989-2020 and trends from 1950, biennial rpt, 2324-9

UN voting record and share of votes in agreement with US, by issue, country, and world area, 1988, annual rpt, 7004-18

see also under By Foreign Country in the "Index by Categories"

Yetley, Mervin J.
"Economic Cost of Unemployment and Underemployment", 1598–251

Yeutter, Clayton
"Status of Trade Negotiations and Trade Issues", 1004–16.1

Yonkers, N.Y.
see also under By City in the "Index by Categories"

Yordi, Cathleen L.
"Case Management in the Social Health Maintenance Organization Demonstrations", 4652–1.913

York, Pa.
see also under By SMSA or MSA in the "Index by Categories"

Young, Allan H.
"Alternative Measures of Real GNP", 2702–1.913
"BEA's Measurement of Computer Output", 2702–1.924

Young, C. Edwin
"Costs of Combining Dockage and Foreign Material in the Grading Standards for Wheat Exports", 1561–12.901
"Economic Effects of Mandatory Production Controls", 1548–354
"Effects of the CRP: Focus on Wheat Production", 1561–12.904
"Wheat: Background for 1990 Farm Legislation", 1566–7.7

Young, Nathan
"Wave Seam Effects in the SIPP", 2626–10.101

Youngstown, Ohio
see also under By City and By SMSA or MSA in the "Index by Categories"

Youth

AIDS cases among children, by age, sex, and risk group, with related HHS funding, 1980s-88, 4438-15

Arrest rates, by offense, sex, age, and race, 1987, annual rpt, 6224-7

Assistance (financial and nonfinancial) of Fed Govt, 1989 base edition with supplements, annual listing, 104-5

Cholesterol levels of youth related to physical characteristics, age, sex, and race, 1966-70 natl study, article, 4042-3.922

Crime and crime-related issues, public opinion by respondent characteristics, 1970s-89, annual rpt, 6064-6.2

Cuba refugees entering US during 1980 boatlift, Federal funding for youth mental health services, and participation, 1981-88, GAO rpt, 26121-270

Death rates of children, by age, sex, race, and cause, for US and compared to 8 OECD countries, 1985 and trends from 1900, 4147-3.27

Deaths and rates, by detailed cause and demographic characteristics, 1986 and trends from 1900, US Vital Statistics annual rpt, 4144-2

Drinking age laws impacts on traffic deaths, by State, 1975-87, 7768–103

Drug, alcohol, and cigarette use and attitudes of youth, by substance type and selected characteristics, 1975-88 surveys, annual rpt, 4494-4

Drug, alcohol, and cigarette use, by substance, age, sex, race, and region, 1988 survey, biennial rpt, 4494-5

Drug and alcohol abuse treatment facilities, services, use, funding, and client characteristics, 1987, annual rpt, 4494-10

Firearms-related deaths of children, by motive, age, sex, and race, 1968-87, 4146-8.181

FmHA loans, by type, borrower race, and State, quarterly rpt, 1182-5

Health condition and health care resources, use, and spending, 1950s-87, annual data compilation, 4144-11

HHS financial aid, by program, recipient, State, and city, FY88, annual regional listings, 4004-3

Homeless and runaway youth programs, funding, activities, and participant characteristics, FY86, annual rpt, 4604-3

Homeless population characteristics by city, and Federal funding by program, 1980s-89, hearings, 21248-123

Household and family characteristics, by living arrangement, 1988 and trends from 1960, Current Population Rpt, 2546-2.148

Housing (public) projects youth recreation and sports programs, HUD grants by recipient, 1989, press release, 5006-3.73

Indian youth health center use, by type of visit, for demonstration projects in New Mexico, 1987-88, article, 4042-3.924

Indian youth suicide attempts, potential, and risk factors, longitudinal study, 1989 article, 4042-3.958

Insurance (health) coverage of adolescents by selected characteristics, and impacts of mandated employer and expanded Medicaid coverage, 1979-87, 26358-205

Living arrangements, family relationships, and marital status, by selected characteristics, 1988, annual Current Population Rpt, 2546-1.433

Population of 16 and 18 year olds, for US and selected foreign countries, 1966-94, annual rpt, 9624-23.2

Population size, by age, sex, and race, and components of change, alternative projections 1988-2080, Current Population Rpt, 2546-3.158

Radiation exposure of population near commercial reactors, by body site, age group, and selected plant, 1986, annual rpt, 9634-7

Red Cross domestic and intl services, volunteers, and certificates issued, by program, FY88, annual rpt, 29254-1.1

Sexual behavior of youth, impact of popular music promoting responsibility, for Latin America, 1986, 9916-3.50

Smoking prevalence, related disease and deaths, and public attitudes, impact of Surgeon General rpts and antismoking campaigns, 1964-89, annual rpt, 4204-18

Statistical Abstract of US, social, political, and economic data, with foreign comparisons, 1790-2025, comprehensive annual compilation, 2324-1

Tobacco (smokeless) use by youth and adults, user characteristics, and sales, 1970s-86, papers, 4478-188

Traffic accident deaths involving alcohol, by driver and victim blood alcohol levels and other characteristics, 1977-87, annual rpt, 4486-1.2; 4486-1.5; 4486-1.8

Voting and registration, by socioeconomic and demographic characteristics, 1988 presidential election, biennial Current Population Rpt, 2546-1.440

see also Child mortality

see also Children

see also Elementary and secondary education

see also Foster home care

see also Higher education

see also Juvenile courts and cases

see also Juvenile delinquency

see also Juvenile detention and correctional institutions

see also School dropouts

see also Students

see also Teenage pregnancy

see also Youth employment

see also under By Age in the "Index by Categories"

Youth Conservation Corps

Forest Service activities and finances, by region and State, FY88, annual rpt, 1204-1.4

Participation in YCC, by sponsoring agency and participant characteristics, annual rpt, discontinued, 5304-12

Youth employment

Business and financial statistics, historic trends, 1988 annual chartbook, 9364-2.4

Community organizations partnerships with public schools, participation, activities, and contributions, by school characteristics and location, 1987/88, 4826-1.27

Dallas-Fort Worth metro area employment, earnings, hours, and CPI changes, 1970s-88, annual rpt, 6964-2

Disabled persons employment, labor force status, and other characteristics, 1988, Current Population Rpt, 2546-2.147

Employment and earnings covered under OASDHI, and social security contributions, by age, sex, race, State, and county, 1985, 4748-43

Employment situation, earnings, hours, and other BLS economic indicators, transcripts of BLS Commissioner's monthly testimony, periodic rpt, 23846-4

Employment, unemployment, and labor force characteristics, by region, State, and selected metro area, 1988, annual rpt, 6744-7

Fed Govt funding for juvenile delinquency prevention, by program and agency, FY88, annual rpt, 6064-11

Georgia employment and unemployment, by sex and race, 1988, press release, 6946-3.13

Handbook of Labor Statistics, employment, unemployment, and labor force characteristics, 1940s-88 with trends from 1913, 6728-38.1; 6728-38.2

High school and college grads and dropouts employment status and income, 1989 edition, annual rpt, 4824-2.28

High school students employment, academic and other characteristics, 1984-86, 4898-27

Hispanic Americans socioeconomic characteristics, by detailed origin, 1988, Current Population Rpt, 2546-1.430; 2546-1.438

Houston metro area employment, earnings, hours, and CPI changes, 1970s-88, annual rpt, 6964-1

Japan and US labor force participation by selected characteristics, productivity, and unit labor costs, 1960s-87, article, 6722-1.910

Labor force composition, and wages relation to inflation and unemployment, late 1930s-88, article, 9373-1.902

Labor force participation of youth, by age, Apr and July 1989 and change from 1988, annual press release, 6744-13

Labor force status by race and sex, employment by industry div, and unemployment duration and reason, selected years 1929-88, annual rpt, 204-1.2

Labor force status by sex, and employment by class, for youth by race, summer 1985-89, annual press release, 6744-14

Labor force status, by worker characteristics and industry group, 1982-1st half 1989, semiannual article, 6722-1.907; 6722-1.937

Labor force status of youth, by school enrollment, educational attainment, sex, and race, monthly rpt, 6742-2.1

Special education programs, enrollment by age, staff, funding, and needs, by type of handicap and State, 1987/88, annual rpt, 4944-4

Statistical Abstract of US, social, political, and economic data, 1790-2025, comprehensive annual compilation, 2324-1.3

see also Apprenticeship

see also Child labor

Yuba City, Calif.

Housing vacancy rates for single and multifamily units and mobile homes, by city and ZIP code, 1988, annual MSA rpt, 9304-20.7

see also under By SMSA or MSA in the "Index by Categories"

Yucel, Mine

"Dynamic Comparison of an Oil Tariff, a Producer Subsidy, and a Gasoline Tax", 9379-12.44

Yugoslavia

Agricultural and food production and indexes, total and for selected commodities, by country, 1970s-88, annual rpt, 1524-12

Agricultural production, acreage, and consumption, by Eastern Europe country and commodity, 1965-85, 1528-284

Agricultural production, consumption, and trade, for Eastern Europe by country, 1970s-88, annual rpt, 1524-11

Agricultural trade of US, by detailed commodity and country, 1988, semiannual rpt, 1522-4

AID loans repayment status and terms by program and country, and status of predecessor agency loans, quarterly rpt, 9912-3

Background Notes, summary social, political, and economic data, 1989 rpt, 7006-2.28

Economic and military aid and loans from US and intl agencies, by program and country, FY46-87, annual rpt, 9914-5

Economic conditions in Communist and OECD countries, 1987, annual rpt, 7144-11

Economic conditions in Communist, OECD, and selected other countries, 1960s-88, annual rpt, 9114-4

Economic conditions, policy, and trade practices, by country, 1986-88, annual rpt, 21384-5

Economic, social, political, and geographic summary data, by country, 1989, annual factbook, 9114-2

Exports and imports of US, by selected country, country group, and commodity group, 1988, annual rpt, 2044-37

Human rights conditions in 170 countries, 1988, annual rpt, 21384-3

Imports of goods, services, and investment from US, trade barriers, impacts, and US actions, by country, 1988, annual rpt, 444-2

Labor conditions and work accidents, 1989 annual country rpt, 6366-4.40

Military aid of US, arms sales, and training programs costs and budget requests, by program, world region, and country, FY88-90, annual rpt, 7144-13

Military spending, arms trade, and force strengths, with govt spending and population, by country, 1977-87, annual rpt, 9824-1

Minerals Yearbook, 1987, Vol 3: foreign country reviews of production, trade, and policy, by commodity, annual rpt, 5604-35

Minerals Yearbook, 1987, Vol 3 preprints: foreign country review of production, trade, and policy, by commodity, annual rpt, 5604-23.76

Nitrocellulose (industrial) from 7 countries at less than fair value, injury to US industry, investigation with background financial and operating data, 1989 rpt, 9886-14.270

Nuclear power plant capacity, generation, and operating status, by plant and foreign and US location, 1988 and projected to 2020, annual rpt, 3164-57

Population size, growth rates, and components of change, by country, projected 1989-2020 and trends from 1950, biennial rpt, 2324-9

Steel export ceilings under voluntary restraint agreements, by country and product, with Western US steel industry impact, 1989 rpt, 9886-4.136

Steel imports of US under voluntary restraint agreement, by product, customs district, and country, with US industry operating data, monthly rpt, 9882-13

UN voting record and share of votes in agreement with US, by issue, country, and world area, 1988, annual rpt, 7004-18

see also under By Foreign Country in the "Index by Categories"

Zaire

Agricultural and food production and indexes, total and for selected commodities, by country, 1970s-88, annual rpt, 1524-12

Agricultural exports of Africa by commodity, and relation to economic conditions and other factors, by country, 1960s-87, 1528-280

Agricultural imports and food aid needs
under alternative weather assumptions, for
17 African countries, projected to 1995,
1528–279

Agricultural production, prices, and trade,
by country, 1960s-89, annual world region
rpt, 1524–4.2

Agricultural trade of US, by detailed
commodity and country, 1988, semiannual
rpt, 1522–4

AID activities and funding by project and
function, FY90, and developing countries
summary socioeconomic data from 1960s,
annual rpt, 9904–4.5

AID economic aid to developing countries,
obligations and disbursements by country,
quarterly rpt, 9912–4

AID loans repayment status and terms by
program and country, and status of
predecessor agency loans, quarterly rpt,
9912–3

Economic and military aid and loans from
US and intl agencies, by program and
country, FY46-87, annual rpt, 9914–5

Economic conditions, income, production,
prices, employment, and trade, 1989
periodic country rpt, 2046–4.98

Economic conditions, policy, and trade
practices, by country, 1986-88, annual rpt,
21384–5

Economic, social, political, and geographic
summary data, by country, 1989, annual
factbook, 9114–2

Exports and imports of US, by commodity
and country, 1970-87, world area rpt,
9116–1.4

Exports and imports of US, by selected
country, country group, and commodity
group, 1988, annual rpt, 2044–37

Human rights conditions in 170 countries,
1988, annual rpt, 21384–3

Military aid of US, arms sales, and training
programs costs and budget requests, by
program, world region, and country,
FY88-90, annual rpt, 7144–13

Military spending, arms trade, and force
strengths, with govt spending and
population, by country, 1977-87, annual
rpt, 9824–1

Minerals Yearbook, 1987, Vol 3: foreign
country reviews of production, trade, and
policy, by commodity, annual rpt,
5604–35

Minerals Yearbook, 1987, Vol 3 preprints:
foreign country review of production,
trade, and policy, by commodity, annual
rpt, 5604–23.77

Population size, growth rates, and
components of change, by country,
projected 1989-2020 and trends from
1950, biennial rpt, 2324–9

UN voting record and share of votes in
agreement with US, by issue, country, and
world area, 1988, annual rpt, 7004–18

see also under By Foreign Country in the
"Index by Categories"

Zale, Alexander V.

"Ladyfish and Tarpon. Species Profiles: Life
Histories and Environmental
Requirements of Coastal Fishes and
Invertebrates (South Florida)",
5506–8.111

Zambia

Agricultural and food production and
indexes, total and for selected
commodities, by country, 1970s-88,
annual rpt, 1524–12

Agricultural exports of Africa by
commodity, and relation to economic
conditions and other factors, by country,
1960s-87, 1528–280

Agricultural imports and food aid needs
under alternative weather assumptions, for
17 African countries, projected to 1995,
1528–279

Agricultural production, prices, and trade,
by country, 1960s-89, annual world region
rpt, 1524–4.2

Agricultural trade of US, by detailed
commodity and country, 1988, semiannual
rpt, 1522–4

AID activities and funding by project and
function, FY90, and developing countries
summary socioeconomic data from 1960s,
annual rpt, 9904–4.5

AID economic aid to developing countries,
obligations and disbursements by country,
quarterly rpt, 9912–4

AID loans repayment status and terms by
program and country, and status of
predecessor agency loans, quarterly rpt,
9912–3

Economic and military aid and loans from
US and intl agencies, by program and
country, FY46-87, annual rpt, 9914–5

Economic conditions, income, production,
prices, employment, and trade, 1989
periodic country rpt, 2046–4.92

Economic, social, political, and geographic
summary data, by country, 1989, annual
factbook, 9114–2

Exports and imports of US, by commodity
and country, 1970-87, world area rpt,
9116–1.4

Human rights conditions in 170 countries,
1988, annual rpt, 21384–3

Military aid of US, arms sales, and training
programs costs and budget requests, by
program, world region, and country,
FY88-90, annual rpt, 7144–13

Military spending, arms trade, and force
strengths, with govt spending and
population, by country, 1977-87, annual
rpt, 9824–1

Minerals Yearbook, 1987, Vol 3: foreign
country reviews of production, trade, and
policy, by commodity, annual rpt,
5604–35

Minerals Yearbook, 1987, Vol 3 preprints:
foreign country review of production,
trade, and policy, by commodity, annual
rpt, 5604–23.78

Population size, growth rates, and
components of change, by country,
projected 1989-2020 and trends from
1950, biennial rpt, 2324–9

UN voting record and share of votes in
agreement with US, by issue, country, and
world area, 1988, annual rpt, 7004–18

see also under By Foreign Country in the
"Index by Categories"

Zawadski, Rick T.

"Case Management in Capitated Long-Term
Care", 4652–1.912

Zempel, Alan

"Partnership Returns, 1986", 8302–2.903

Zepp, Glenn

"Effects of the Triple Base Proposal on
Planting Decisions for Potatoes and Dry
Edible Beans", 1561–11.905

Zervos, David

"Policies To Change the Priority of
Claimants: The Case of Depositor
Preference Laws", 9316–1.154

Zieman, Joseph C.

"Ecology of the Seagrass Meadows of the
West Coast of Florida: A Community
Profile", 5506–9.40

Zieman, Rita T.

"Ecology of the Seagrass Meadows of the
West Coast of Florida: A Community
Profile", 5506–9.40

Zieschang, Kimberly D.

"Aggregation Consistent Restriction Based
Improvement of Local Area Estimators",
6886–6.51

"Characteristics Approach to the Problem of
New and Disappearing Goods in Price
Indexes", 6886–6.52

"Consistent Estimation of the Impact of Tax
Deductibility on the Level of Charitable
Contributions", 6886–6.16

"Indexes of the Terms of Trade: Theory and
Application", 6886–6.14

"Measuring the Nominal Value of Financial
Services in the National Income
Accounts", 6886–6.62

"Output Price Measurement When Output
Characteristics Are Endogenous",
6886–6.19

Zimbabwe

Agricultural and food production and
indexes, total and for selected
commodities, by country, 1970s-88,
annual rpt, 1524–12

Agricultural exports of Africa by
commodity, and relation to economic
conditions and other factors, by country,
1960s-87, 1528–280

Agricultural production, prices, and trade,
by country, 1960s-89, annual world region
rpt, 1524–4.2

Agricultural trade of US, by detailed
commodity and country, 1988, semiannual
rpt, 1522–4

AID activities and funding by project and
function, FY90, and developing countries
summary socioeconomic data from 1960s,
annual rpt, 9904–4.5

AID economic aid to developing countries,
obligations and disbursements by country,
quarterly rpt, 9912–4

AID loans repayment status and terms by
program and country, and status of
predecessor agency loans, quarterly rpt,
9912–3

Economic and military aid and loans from
US and intl agencies, by program and
country, FY46-87, annual rpt, 9914–5

Economic conditions, income, production,
prices, employment, and trade, 1989
periodic country rpt, 2046–4.67

Economic conditions, policy, and trade
practices, by country, 1986-88, annual rpt,
21384–5

Economic, social, political, and geographic
summary data, by country, 1989, annual
factbook, 9114–2

Exports and imports of US, by commodity and country, 1970-87, world area rpt, 9116–1.4

Human rights conditions in 170 countries, 1988, annual rpt, 21384–3

Labor conditions, union coverage, and work accidents, 1989 annual country rpt, 6366–4.25

Military aid of US, arms sales, and training programs costs and budget requests, by program, world region, and country, FY88-90, annual rpt, 7144–13

Military spending, arms trade, and force strengths, with govt spending and population, by country, 1977-87, annual rpt, 9824–1

Minerals Yearbook, 1987, Vol 3: foreign country reviews of production, trade, and policy, by commodity, annual rpt, 5604–35

Minerals Yearbook, 1987, Vol 3 preprints: foreign country review of production, trade, and policy, by commodity, annual rpt, 5604–23.79

Population size, growth rates, and components of change, by country, projected 1989-2020 and trends from 1950, biennial rpt, 2324–9

Rhinoceros wild and captive population, poacher kills and enforcement action, and conservation issues, 1988 hearing, 21708–125

UN voting record and share of votes in agreement with US, by issue, country, and world area, 1988, annual rpt, 7004–18

see also under By Foreign Country in the "Index by Categories"

Zimbler, Linda
"Profile of Handicapped Students in Postsecondary Education, 1987", 4846–3.6

Zimmer, Steven A.
"Explaining International Differences in the Cost of Capital", 9385–1.910

Zimmerman, Gary C.
"Growing Presence of Japanese Banks in California", 9393–8.906

Zinc and zinc industry
Business statistics, detailed data for major industries and economic indicators, *Survey of Current Business*, monthly rpt, 2702–1.14

Castings (nonferrous) shipments, by metal type, monthly Current Industrial Rpt, 2506–10.5

Coin production and monetary metals use and holdings of US Mint, by metal type, FY88, annual rpt, 8204–1

Communist countries agricultural, mineral, and consumer and producer goods production, by commodity, 1960s-88, annual rpt, 9114–4.4

Exports of US, detailed commodities by country, monthly rpt, 2422–3

Finances and operations, by SIC 2- to 4-digit industry, forecast 1989 with trends from 1950s, annual rpt, 2044–28

Foreign countries mineral production, reserves, and industry role in domestic economy and world supply, world area and country rpt series, 5606–1

Imports of US, detailed Schedule A commodities by country, monthly rpt, 2422–2

Manufacturing annual survey, 1986: financial and operating data, by SIC 2- to 4-digit industry, series, 2506–15

Manufacturing census, 1987: financial and operating data, for SIC 4-digit industries by product, preliminary rpt, 2491–1.53; 2491–1.54

Mineral industries census, 1987: financial and operating data, preliminary industry rpt, 2511–1.2

Mineral Industry Surveys, commodity review of production, trade, stocks, and use, monthly rpt, 5612–1.27

Mineral Industry Surveys, State reviews of production, 1988, preliminary annual rpt, 5614–6

Minerals Yearbook, 1987, Vol 1: commodity reviews of production, use, trade, prices, and mining operations, annual rpt, 5604–33

Minerals Yearbook, 1987, Vol 1 preprints: commodity review of production, reserves, supply, use, and trade, annual rpt, 5604–15.71

Minerals Yearbook, 1987, Vol 2 preprints: State reviews of production and sales by commodity, and business activity, annual rpt series, 5604–16

Minerals Yearbook, 1987, Vol 2: State reviews of production, sales, and firms, by commodity, and business activity, annual rpt, 5604–34

Minerals Yearbook, 1987, Vol 3: foreign country reviews of production, trade, and policy, by commodity, annual rpt, 5604–35

Minerals Yearbook, 1987, Vol 3 preprints: foreign country reviews of production, trade, and policy, by commodity, annual rpt series, 5604–23

Minerals Yearbook, 1988, Vol 2 rpts: State reviews of production and sales by commodity, and business activity, annual rpt series, 5604–22

Occupational injuries and incidence, employment, and hours in metal mines and related operations, 1987, annual rpt, 6664–3

Occupational injury and illness rates, by SIC 2- to 4-digit industry, 1987, annual rpt, 6844–1

OECD trade, total and for 4 major countries, and US trade by country, by commodity, 1970-87, world area rpt series, 9116–1

Price indexes (producer), by stage of processing and detailed commodity, monthly rpt, 6762–6

Price indexes (producer), by stage of processing and detailed commodity, monthly 1988, annual rpt, 6764–2

Production, prices, trade, use, employment, tariffs, and stockpiles, by mineral, with foreign comparisons, 1984-88, annual rpt, 5604–18

Statistical Abstract of US, social, political, and economic data, 1790-2025, comprehensive annual compilation, 2324–1.3

Stockpiling of strategic material by Fed Govt, activity, and inventory by commodity, as of Sept 1989, semiannual rpt, 3542–22; 3902–2

Stockpiling of strategic material, inventories and needs, by commodity, as of Sept 1988, annual rpt, 3544–37

Stockpiling of strategic material, inventories, costs, and goals by commodity, as of June 1989, semiannual rpt, 3902–3

Supply, demand, trade, and foreign and US industry devs by firm and country, for strategic minerals by commodity, bimonthly rpt with articles, 5602–4

see also under By Commodity in the "Index by Categories"

ZIP codes
North Central States, FHLB 7th District housing vacancy rates for single and multifamily units and mobile homes, by ZIP code, annual MSA rpt series, 9304–18

South Central States, FHLB 9th District housing vacancy rates for single and multifamily units and mobile homes by ZIP code, annual MSA rpt series, 9304–19

West Central States, FHLB 10th District housing vacancy rates for single and multifamily units and mobile homes, by ZIP code, annual MSA rpt series, 9304–22

Western States, FHLB 11th District housing vacancy rates for single and multifamily units and mobile homes, by ZIP code, annual MSA rpt series, 9304–20

Western States, FHLB 12th District housing vacancy rates for single and multifamily units and mobile homes, by ZIP code, annual MSA rpt series, 9304–21

Zirconium
see Metals and metal industries

Zlatoper, Thomas J.
"Determinants of Direct Air Fares to Cleveland: How Competitive?", 9377–1.903

Zobeck, Terry S.
"Liver Cirrhosis Mortality in the U.S., 1972-86", 4486–1.7

"Trends in Alcohol-Related Fatal Traffic Accidents, U.S.: 1977-85", 4486–1.2

"Trends in Alcohol-Related Fatal Traffic Accidents, U.S.: 1977-86", 4486–1.5

"Trends in Alcohol-Related Fatal Traffic Crashes, U.S.: 1977-87", 4486–1.8

Zoning and zoning laws
see also Building permits

Zoological parks
County Business Patterns, 1987: employment, establishments, and payroll, by SIC 2- to 4-digit industry and county, annual State rpt series, 2326–8

Earnings by major industry group, and personal income per capita and by source, by region and State, 1929-87, 2708–40

Endangered animals and plants US trade and permits, by species, purpose, disposition, and country, 1987, annual rpt, 5504–19

Inst of Museum Services grants, by recipient, FY89, annual press release series, 9564–6

Licensing and inspection of facilities, and other animal protection activities of USDA, with animals used in research, by State, FY88, annual rpt, 1394–10

Rhinoceros wild and captive population, poacher kills and enforcement action, and conservation issues, 1988 hearing, 21708–125

Smithsonian Instn activities and finances, FY88, annual rpt, 29574–1

Zoology

Degrees awarded in higher education, by
level, field, race, and sex, 1989 edition,
annual rpt, 4824-2.20

Enrollment in science and engineering grad
programs, by field, source of funds, and
characteristics of student and instn,
1975-87, annual rpt, 9627-7

Research on population and reproduction,
Federal funding by project, FY87, annual
listing, 4474-9

see also Animals

see also Birds and bird conservation

see also Wildlife and wildlife conservation

see also Zoological parks

Zornitsky, Jeffrey

"Serving AFDC Recipients: Initial Findings
on the Role of Performance Standards",
15496-1.4

Zweizig, Douglas L.

"Libraries and Literacy Education:
Comprehensive Survey Report", 4878-2

Index by
Categories

Index by Categories

INTRODUCTION

The Index by Categories contains references to all publications, tables, and groups of tables that contain breakdowns of statistical data by any or several of the following 21 standard categories:

GEOGRAPHIC BREAKDOWNS

By Census Division	By Outlying Area
By City	By Region
By County	By SMSA or MSA
By Foreign Country	By State
	By Urban-Rural

ECONOMIC BREAKDOWNS

By Commodity	By Individual
By Federal Agency	Company
By Income	or Institution
By Industry	By Occupation

DEMOGRAPHIC BREAKDOWNS

By Age	By Marital Status
By Disease	By Race and Ethnic
By Educational	Group
Attainment	By Sex

SUBJECT SUBHEADINGS

Within each of the categories listed above, references have been grouped according to the subject matter of the publication or the statistical content being indexed. Nineteen subheadings have been used for this purpose; they are listed below. The kinds of material referenced under each subheading are noted, as well as cross-references to other, related subheadings.

Agriculture and Food — Covers all agricultural data, including commercial fishing and the fertilizer industry; agricultural credit of all kinds; agricultural land; farm population and labor; and all data on food except retail prices.

See also Natural Resources, Environment, and Pollution, for forestry data, additional conservation data

Prices and Cost of Living, for retail food prices

Banking, Finance, and Insurance — Covers all data on financial institutions and their activities; all banking and insurance data; consumer credit; bankruptcy; securities markets; and money supply, interest rates, and other financial indicators.

See also Other specific subheadings, for Federal insurance programs

Agriculture and Food, for agricultural credit

Government and Defense, for Government debt and securities

Health and Vital Statistics, for health insurance data

Housing and Construction, for mortgage data

Industry and Commerce, for general economic indicators

Communications and Transportation — Covers all data on industries in these sectors, including their finances, employment, occupational safety, and rates and regulation; highway data; Postal Service; all travel and tourism data, including accidents; and propaganda.

See also Energy Resources and Demand, for pipeline data

Industry and Commerce, for equipment and parts manufacturing and trade.

Education — Covers all data on education in general, including schools, faculty, students, graduates, and finances.

See also Government and Defense, for military academies

Health and Vital Statistics, for medical and dental schools and all data on health manpower training

Labor and Employment, for employment training programs, such as CETA and WIN, and for apprenticeships

Science and Technology, for education exclusively in science and engineering

Veterans Affairs, for GI Bill and other veterans' education

Energy Resources and Demand — Covers supply, consumption, and conservation of all types of energy. Includes exploration, extraction, R&D, transportation, distribution, and waste disposal of all energy forms; all data on energy industries; and energy use and costs.

See also Health and Vital Statistics, for accidents and occupational health in energy industries, including mines

Natural Resources, Environment, and Pollution, for additional data exclusively on energy reserves, and for pollution and radioactivity from energy resources

Prices and Cost of Living, for consumer utility bills

Geography and Climate — Covers all data on weather, climate, oceanography, and storms and other natural disasters.

See also Natural Resources, Environment, and Pollution, for data on water supply and land use

Government and Defense — Covers all data on government in general, including activities, finances, programs, and personnel; all data on defense activities and foreign affairs; taxes; coinage; passports; and elections and voting.

See also Other specific subheadings for data on government aid, employment, or regulation in specific areas

Health and Vital Statistics, for military medicine

Health and Vital Statistics—Covers all data on health condition, disease, and disability; occupational health and safety in general; medical care, costs, and insurance; medical facilities; health personnel and their education; and vital statistics.

See also Communications and Transportation, for all transportation accidents, including occupational accidents and health

Labor and Employment, for vocational rehabilitation and other training programs for disabled persons

Public Welfare and Social Security, for data on Medicare, Medicaid, and social security recipients

Veterans Affairs, for data on veterans' health and VA medical facilities

Housing and Construction — Covers all data on housing condition, finance, and occupancy; all data on the construction industry; all mortgages; urban renewal and community development; and government aid for housing or communities.

See also Communications and Transportation, for construction of highways and bridges

Natural Resources, Environment, and Pollution, for construction of dams, sewer plants, etc.

Industry and Commerce — Covers all data on industry in general, including production, finances, payrolls, and profits; productivity; trade and marketing; foreign trade, tariffs, and balance of payments; and economic indicators in general.

See also Other more specific subheadings for data on specific industry sectors

Government and Defense, for corporate income tax data

Labor and Employment — Covers all data on the labor force and employment in general, including characteristics, earnings, hours, working conditions, and employee benefits; unemployment; labor unions; and employment training programs, such as CETA and WIN.

See also Other more specific subheadings for employment and employees in specific disciplines, such as health or science, or in specific industry sectors, such as agriculture or transportation

Industry and Commerce, for general industry data including employment and payrolls

Law Enforcement — Covers all data on crime and the characteristics of criminals; and all data on the criminal justice system, including police, lawyers, courts, prisons, and sentences.

See also Other specific subheadings for civil proceedings and government regulation in specific areas

Natural Resources, Environment, and Pollution— Covers all data on natural resource supply and conservation, including energy reserves, forests, public lands, and wildlife; land use; water supply, dams, and flood control; environmental quality; all types of pollutants; wastes in general, including sewage disposal; oil spills; and radioactivity in the environment.

See also Agriculture and Food, for conservation specifically related to agriculture

Energy Resources and Demand, for additional data on energy reserves, disposal of wastes from energy production, and nuclear power

Health and Vital Statistics, for occupational hazards and for the health effects of pollutants

Population—Covers all data on population size; characteristics of the population in general; demographic groups such as youth, women, or blacks; and migration.

See also Other specific subheadings for data on special population groups such

as farmers, veterans, or mortgagors

Health and Vital Statistics, for data on births and deaths

Prices and Cost of Living—Covers prices in general, both wholesale and retail; price indexes; consumer costs; and inflation.

See also Education, for tuition costs

Health and Vital Statistics, for medical costs

Industry and Commerce or other more specific subheadings, for data on production costs, farm value, etc.

Public Welfare and Social Security—Covers everything related to the social security program, including Medicare and disability insurance; everything related to welfare, public assistance, and medical assistance (Medicaid); food stamps and school lunch programs; and social services.

See also Health and Vital Statistics, for data on workers compensation and disabled persons in general

Labor and Employment, for unemployment insurance

Recreation and Leisure—Covers all data on recreation activities and recreation industries. Includes sport fishing, hunting, parks, museums, and the arts; and tourists promotion.

See also Communications and Transportation, for data on travel

Education, for libraries

Science and Technology—Covers activities, private and government funding, employment, and education, exclusively in scientific fields; all data on space programs; and inventions and patents.

See also Agriculture and Food, for agricultural sciences

Energy Resources and Demand, for R&D in energy fields

Geography and Climate, for meteorology, oceanography, etc.

Veterans Affairs—Covers everything that relates exclusively to veterans, including education, health, VA hospitals, housing and VA home loans, employment and employment programs, pensions, and disability payments.

See also Government and Defense, for data on the armed services

---

USING THE INDEX

In using the Category Index, you must keep in mind that the amount of detail provided in the various tabular breakdowns may vary considerably.

Breakdowns "By sex" or "By urban-rural" are, by definition, complete. Breakdowns "By census division," "By region," or "By State" are generally complete unless specific limitations are noted.

Breakdowns "By race and ethnic group" generally show white and nonwhite or white, black, and other. When substantial data on race/ethnic breakdowns are included, they are indexed specifically in the Index of Subjects and Names (i.e. Black Americans, Asian Americans, Indians, Hispanic Americans) as well as under the category "By race."

The greatest variation in the detail of category breakdowns occurs in such categories as "By city," "By county," "By foreign country," "By industry," "By commodity," and "By occupation." For these categories, we try, whenever possible, to indicate the degree of detail in the notations of content listed under the category terms and in the abstract of the publication.

For further information about using the Category Index, see the User Guide.

For use in conjunction with the Category Index, we have printed several standard classification systems that are frequently used in Federal statistical publications (see p. 1003). These classifications include regions of the U.S., SMSAs, Standard Industrial Classification, and Standard International Trade Classification.

Index by Categories

GEOGRAPHIC BREAKDOWNS

BY CENSUS DIVISION

Agriculture and Food

Cold storage food stocks by commodity and census div, and warehouse space use, by State, monthly rpt, 1631-5

Cold storage food stocks, by commodity and census div, 1988, annual rpt, 1631-11

Fertilizer (inorganic) shipments, trade, use, and firms, by product and State, with stocks, 1988, annual Current Industrial Rpt, 2506-8.13

Fertilizer use, by fertilizer type and State, 1987-88, annual rpt, 9804-30

Rice shipments, by end use, package size, and State of origin and destination, mid 1950s-87, biennial rpt, 1564-11

Statistical Abstract of US, social, political, and economic data, 1790-2025, comprehensive annual compilation, 2324-1.3

Banking, Finance, and Insurance

Statistical Abstract of US, social, political, and economic data, 1790-2025, comprehensive annual compilation, 2324-1.3

Communications and Transportation

Canada travel to US by Province of residence, and characteristics of visit, by State, 1988, annual rpt, 2904-7

Travel to US, spending by category, world area of residence, census div, and State, model results, 1985-86, 2908-28

Education

Statistical Abstract of US, social, political, and economic data, 1790-2025, comprehensive annual compilation, 2324-1.1

Energy Resources and Demand

Buildings (commercial) energy use, costs, and conservation, by building characteristics, survey rpt series, 3166-8

Coal, coke, and breeze supply, demand, prices, trade, and stocks, by end-use sector and State, quarterly rpt with articles, 3162-37

Coal production and stocks by district, and shipments by district of origin, State of destination, end-use sector, and mode of transport, quarterly rpt, 3162-8

Coal production, reserves, use, and prices by State, exports by country, and employment, 1900s-87, biennial rpt, 3164-79

Coal stocks at electric utilities, by census div and State, weekly rpt, monthly data, 3162-1.2

Electric power demand related to economic dev and weather, by census div, model results, quarterly 1977-85, 3028-2

Electric power plants (steam) fuel receipts, costs, and quality, by fuel, plant, utility, and State, 1988, annual rpt, 3164-42

Electric power plants and capacity, by fuel used, owner, location, and operating status, 1988 and for units planned 1989-98, annual listing, 3164-36

Electric power plants natural gas use, by State, 1977 and 1988, annual rpt, 3104-8

Electric power plants production, capacity, sales, and fuel stocks, use, and costs, by State, 1984-88, annual rpt, 3164-11

Electric power plants production, fuel use, stocks, and costs by fuel type, and sales, by State, monthly rpt, 3162-35

Electric power sales, by end-use sector, census div, and State, and fuel use and costs, EIA and alternative estimates, with methodology, 1982-87, 3166-12.5

Electric utilities fuel cost, quality, use, receipts, and stocks, and power plant production, by energy source, State and utility, quarterly rpt, 3162-39

Housing energy use, costs, and conservation, and household and housing characteristics, survey rpt series, 3166-7

Hydroelectric power plants capacity, dev status, and ownership, by State and river basin, as of Jan 1988, quadrennial rpt, 3088-14

Natural gas interstate pipeline company capacity, use, sales, deliveries, and prices, by firm and Northeast State, 1980-88, 3166-6.35

Natural gas interstate pipeline company sales, contract deliveries, and prices, with data by firm and location, 1982-87, 3168-113

Natural gas supply, demand, distribution, and prices, by State, 1984-88 annual rpt, 3164-4

Statistical Abstract of US, social, political, and economic data, 1790-2025, comprehensive annual compilation, 2324-1.3

Geography and Climate

Heating and cooling degree days, by census div, monthly and cumulative for season, monthly rpt, 3162-24.1

Heating and cooling degree days weighted by population, by census div and State, with area-weighted temperature and precipitation, monthly rpt, 2152-13

Statistical Abstract of US, social, political, and economic data, 1790-2025, comprehensive annual compilation, 2324-1.1

Weather data by census div and State, historical trends, indexes, major events, and maps, series, 2156-17

Government and Defense

DOD prime contract awards, by category, contractor type, and State, FY86-88, annual rpt, 3544-11

Statistical Abstract of US, social, political, and economic data, 1790-2025, comprehensive annual compilation, 2324-1.2

Voting and registration, by socioeconomic and demographic characteristics, 1988 presidential election, biennial Current Population Rpt, 2546-1.440

Health and Vital Statistics

Births and rates, by characteristics of birth, infant, and parents, 1987 and trends from 1940, US Vital Statistics advance annual rpt, 4146-5.110

Deaths and rates, by cause, age, sex, marital status, race, and State, 1987, US Vital Statistics advance annual rpt, 4146-5.113

Deaths and rates, by detailed cause and demographic characteristics, 1986 and trends from 1900, US Vital Statistics annual rpt, 4144-2

Divorces by age of spouses and duration of marriage, and children involved, by State, 1986 with trends from 1940, US Vital Statistics advance annual rpt, 4146-5.109

Health condition and health care resources, use, and spending, 1950s-87, annual data compilation, 4144-11

Hospital discharges, length of stay, and costs, for Medicare by type of beneficiary, procedure, diagnosis, and State, 1970s-86, article, 4652-1.945

Hospital reimbursement by Medicare under prospective payment system, capital cost reimbursement adjustments financial impacts by instn characteristics, 1978-87, 17206-1.1

Hospital reimbursement by Medicare under prospective payment system, dev of alternative indexes for diagnosis related group classification, with data by instn characteristics, 1984-86, 17206-2.6

Hospital reimbursement by Medicare under prospective payment system, urban area instn finances and operations, 1988 rpt, 17206-1.3

Infant and fetal deaths and rates, by race, sex, State, census div, and metro-nonmetro location, 1950s-85, 4146-5.107

Infectious notifiable disease cases, by age, State, and outlying area, and deaths, 1930s-88, annual rpt, 4204-1

Marriages and rates, by age, race, education, previous marital status of spouses, and State, 1986, US Vital Statistics advance annual rpt, 4146-5.111; 4146-5.112

Marriages, divorces, and rates, by characteristics of spouses, State, and county, 1984 and trends from 1920, US Vital Statistics annual rpt, 4144-4

Nursing facility service use and costs for Medicare enrollees, by selected characteristics and State, 1970s-87, article, 4652-1.954

Physicians Medicare services use, charges, and reimbursement, by service type, setting, and specialty, 1986, article, 4652-1.936

Rural areas health care facilities, staffing, services accessibility, and indicators of need, 1960s-88, 25148-41

Smoking rates, by sex, age, race, occupation, region, and State, 1985 Current Population Survey, article, 4472-1.910

Statistical Abstract of US, social, political, and economic data, 1790-2025, comprehensive annual compilation, 2324-1.1

Tobacco (smokeless) use by youth and adults, user characteristics, and sales, 1970s-86, papers, 4478-188

Tuberculosis cases and deaths, by patient characteristics, State, and city, 1987 and trends from 1953, annual rpt, 4204-10

Vital statistics provisional data, monthly rpt, 4142-1

Housing and Construction

Construction put in place, value of new public and private structures, by type, monthly rpt, 2382-4

Mobile home placements by structural characteristics, and price, by census div and State, monthly rpt, annual tables, 2382-1

New housing units authorized, by region, State, selected MSA, and permit-issuing place, monthly rpt, 2382-5

New housing units authorized, by State, MSA, and permit-issuing place, 1988, annual rpt, 2384-2

Statistical Abstract of US, social, political, and economic data, 1790-2025, comprehensive annual compilation, 2324-1.3

Industry and Commerce

Cement (portland) shipments to census divs, bimonthly rpt, 2042-1.6

Clay construction products production and shipments by region and State, trade, and use, by product, monthly Current Industrial Rpt, 2506-9.2

Foreign direct investment in North Central States and other US regions by country and major industry group, and for auto industry, 1978-88, working paper, 9375-13.12

Retail trade sales and inventories, by kind of business, region, and selected State, MSA, and city, monthly rpt, 2413-3

Small business establishments, employment, and financial ratios, by SIC 1- to 2-digit industry and State, late 1960s-87, 9768-19

Small business finances, operations, owner and employee characteristics, and Federal contracts, 1980s-88, annual rpt, 9764-6

Labor and Employment

Employment, unemployment, and labor force characteristics, by region and census div, 1988, annual rpt, 6744-7.1

Handbook of Labor Statistics, employment, unemployment, and labor force characteristics, 1940s-88 with trends from 1913, 6728-38.1

Income and earnings per capita relative to US average, analysis of differential by census div, various periods 1969-87, article, 9373-1.909

Labor Relations Natl Board activities, cases, elections conducted, and litigation, FY85, annual rpt, 9584-1

Manufacturing employment change during periods of exchange rate volatility, by industry trade orientation and and census div, 1973-87, article, 9373-1.917

Restaurant tips and rates, with data by metro-nonmetro location and census div, 1983-86, article, 8304-8.1

Small business establishments, operations, owner characteristics, and job training, late 1950s-87, 9768-20

Statistical Abstract of US, social, political, and economic data, 1790-2025, comprehensive annual compilation, 2324-1.3

Urban areas fiscal, economic, and social conditions, 1960s-87, biennial rpt, 5184-7.1

Wage differentials among census divs related to worker and job characteristics, 1973-87, article, 9377-1.905

Law Enforcement

Assaults and deaths of law enforcement officers, by circumstances, agency, victim and offender characteristics, and location, 1988, annual rpt, 6224-3

Crimes and rates by offense, and law enforcement employment, by population size and jurisdiction, 1988, annual rpt, 6224-2.1; 6224-2.3

Police employment and expenditures, by population size, metro status, and location, 1984-87, annual rpt, 6064-6.1

Statistical Abstract of US, social, political, and economic data, 1790-2025, comprehensive annual compilation, 2324-1.1

Natural Resources, Environment, and Pollution

Electric utilities privately owned, air pollution emissions and abatement equipment by fuel type and State,, 1987-88, annual rpt, 3164-11.5

Population

Households and population size, by State, 1980 and 1988, annual press release, 2324-11

Income (household) before and after taxes, and discretionary, by sociodemographic characteristics, 1986, 2308-54

Income (household, family, and personal), by source, detailed characteristics, and region, 1987, annual Current Population Rpt, 2546-6.59

Income (personal) totals, by region, census div, and State, quarterly article, 2702-1.32

Migration to and from Southern US, by migrant characteristics and location, 1970s-87 and alternative projections to 2000, article, 9371-1.902

Population estimates and projections, by region and State, Current Population Rpt series, 2546-3

Population size, July 1988 and compared to 1980 and 1987, and components of change, 1980-88, annual press release, 2324-10

Statistical Abstract of US, social, political, and economic data, 1790-2025, comprehensive annual compilation, 2324-1.1

Prices and Cost of Living

Electric power rate schedules, by user type, utility, and city, as of Jan 1988, annual rpt, 3164-40

Public Welfare and Social Security

Medicare and Medicaid eligibility, participation, coverage, and program finances, various periods 1966-89, biennial rpt, 4654-1

Medicare disabled enrollee costs related to patient characteristics, model description and results, 1974-81, technical paper, 4746-26.6

Medicare enrollment, and use by type of service, by age, sex, race, region, State, and MSA, 1986-87, annual rpt, 4657-5

Medicare reimbursement of hospitals under prospective payment system, and of physicians, effect on services, finances, and beneficiary payments, 1970s-88, annual rpt, 17204-2

Medicare reimbursement of hospitals under prospective payment system, costs related to hospital characteristics, and alternative case mix indexes, 1984, article, 4652-1.922

Medicare reimbursement of hospitals under prospective payment system, costs under alternative cost updating procedures, model estimates, 1976-84, article, 4652-1.921

Medicare reimbursement of hospitals under prospective payment system, impacts on instns, beneficiaries, and other care providers and payment sources, 1986, annual rpt, 4654-13

Medicare reimbursement of hospitals under prospective payment system, methodology, inputs, and data by diagnostic group, 1989 annual rpt, 17204-1

OASDHI, Medicaid, SSI, and related programs benefits, beneficiary characteristics, and trust funds, selected years 1937-87, annual rpt, 4744-3

Statistical Abstract of US, social, political, and economic data, 1790-2025, comprehensive annual compilation, 2324-1.2

Recreation and Leisure

Wildlife-related recreation, hunting, and fishing participation and spending, detailed data by location, 1985 survey, quinquennial rpt, 5508-5

Science and Technology

Employment and other characteristics of science and engineering PhDs, by field and State, 1987, biennial rpt, 9627-18

Employment concentration of scientists and engineers, by industry group and census div, 1989 working paper, 9375-13.15

Enrollment in science and engineering grad programs, by field, source of funds, and characteristics of student and instn, 1975-87, annual rpt, 9627-7

Immigrant scientists and engineers, by field, age, sex, country and world area of origin, and State, 1987 and trends from 1967, 9627-29

R&D and related funding of Fed Govt to higher education and nonprofit instns, by field, instn, agency, and State, FY87, annual rpt, 9627-17

R&D funding by Fed Govt, by field, performer type, agency, and State, FY87-89, annual rpt, 9627-20

R&D funding by source and performer, and related employment, by State, 1975-87, 9626-6.32

BY CITY

Agriculture and Food

Cotton prices in 8 spot markets, futures prices at NYC exchange, farm prices, and CCC loan stocks, monthly rpt, 1309-1

Drought of 1988, impacts on food prices by selected item and city, hearing, 25168-71

Exports and imports (agricultural) of US, by commodity, country, and US port, 1950s-89, annual rpt, 1924-9

Fish and shellfish catch, wholesale receipts, prices, trade, and other market activities, weekly regional rpts, 2162-6

Fish catch, by species, use, region, State, and major port, 1970s-88, annual rpt, 2164-1.1

Fruit and vegetable shipments, and arrivals in US and Canada cities, by mode of transport and State and country of origin, 1988, annual rpt series, 1311-4

Grain stocks by region and market city, and grain inspected for export, by type, weekly rpt, 1313–4

Molasses (feed) production, wholesale prices by market area, and US imports and country, weekly rpt, 1311–16

Molasses supply, use, wholesale prices by market, and trade and production by country, 1983–88, annual rpt, 1311–19

Tobacco marketing activity, prices, and sales, by grade, type, market, and State, 1988, annual rpt series, 1319–5

Banking, Finance, and Insurance

Bond (municipal) yields relation to natl and regional financial indicators and issue and underwriter characteristics, by maturity and bond type, 1977–78, working paper, 9389–19.8

Fed Financing Bank holdings and transactions, by borrower, monthly press release, 12802–1

Fed Reserve banks expenses and operations, itemized by service, office, and district, 1988, annual rpt, 9364–11

New England States, FHLB 1st District thrift instns, financial condition, and locations, 1989, annual listing, 9304–26

Savings and loan assns, FHLB 8th District members, locations, assets, and savings, 1989, annual listing, 9304–9

West Central States, Fed Reserve 10th District depository instns financial activity by State, and large commercial banks by city, monthly rpt, 9381–11

West Central States, FHLB 10th District savings instns, locations, assets, and savings, 1989, annual listing, 9304–17

Western States, FHLB 11th District thrift offices, locations, savings balances, and accounts, quarterly listing, 9302–20

Communications and Transportation

Air traffic (passenger), and aircraft operations by type, by airport and State, projected FY89-2005 and trends from FY83, annual rpt, 7504–7

Air traffic levels at FAA-operated control facilities, by airport and State, FY88, annual rpt, 7504–27

Aircraft accidents and circumstances, for US operations of domestic and foreign airlines and general aviation, periodic rpt, 9612–1

Aircraft flight service station workload of FAA, pilot briefs, contacts, and flight plans by facility, projected FY88-99 and trends from FY80, annual rpt, 7504–39

Aircraft handled by instrument flight rule, by user type, FAA traffic control center, and region, FY80-88 and projected to FY2000, annual rpt, 7504–15

Airline computer reservation systems finances, operations, and impacts on airline competitiveness, 1980s-86, 7308–193

Airline computer reservation systems operating costs, fees, and market shares, by firm and location, 1984-87, hearing, 25528–108

Airline consumer complaints by reason, passengers denied boarding, and late flights, by reporting carrier and airport, monthly rpt, 7302–11

Airline flight delays caused by air traffic control procedures and problems, and costs, with data by airport, 1976-86, 7508–68

Airline service in rural areas, impacts of deregulation, and Federal subsidies, with data by location, 1978-87, 1278–17

Airport improvement program of FAA, grants and activities by State and airport, FY88, annual rpt, 7504–38

Airport planning and dev project grants of FAA, by airport and location, quarterly press release, 7502–14

Airport traffic, delays, capacity improvement projects and funding, runway length, and navigational operations, for hub and reliever airports, 1986-87 and forecast to 1996, 7508–67

Alaska airport dev plans and air systems operations, FY89-98, annual rpt, 7504–36

AT&T workers membership in Intl Brotherhood of Electrical Workers, by local, 1981 and 1987, hearings, 21368–113

Great Lakes ship pilotage activities, costs, and traffic for US and Canada, and US testing and certificates, 1960s-87, 7308–192

Harbor traffic, facilities, dev, funding, and needs, for Pacific territories and Hawaii by port, as of 1987, 7308–195

Hwy toll facilities of State and local govts, receipts and disbursements by facility, 1987-88, annual rpt, 7554–1.3

Ohio River basin waterway facilities, freight by commodity and port, and recreation, by waterway, 1986-87, annual rpt, 3754–6

Ports accessible to tankers of 200,000 tons and larger, by country, Jan 1989, annual rpt, 9114–4.10

Railroad accidents, casualties, damage, and circumstances, by incident, 1986, annual rpt, 7604–3

Railroad accidents, circumstances, severity, and railroad involved, periodic rpt, 9612–3

Seat belt use in 19 cities, 1988, press release, 7306–10.1

Shipborne commerce (domestic and foreign) of US, freight by commodity, traffic, and passengers, by port and waterway, 1987, annual rpt, 3754–3

Shipborne trade of US, by type of service, commodity, country, route, and US port, 1986-87, annual rpt, 7704–2

St Lawrence Seaway ship, cargo, and passenger traffic, and toll revenue, 1988 and trends from 1959, annual rpt, 7744–2

Statistical Abstract of US, social, political, and economic data, 1790-2025, comprehensive annual compilation, 2324–1.3

Telephone local service charges and low-income subsidies, by region, company, and city, 1940-June 1989, semiannual rpt, 9282–8

Traffic volume in urban areas and detailed trip characteristics, by transport mode and city, 1950s-88, 7888–37

Transit systems finances and operations, by mode of transport, size of fleet, and for 432 systems, 1986, annual rpt, 7884–4

Transit systems finances, costs, and needs, by State and selected system, 1980-88, biennial rpt, 7884–8

Transit systems grants of Urban Mass Transportation Admin, by city and State, FY88, annual rpt, 7884–10

Transit systems in urban areas, services and vehicles, 1988 annual listing, 7884–9

Travel to and from US on US and foreign flag air carriers, by country, world area, and US port, monthly rpt, 7302–2

Travel to US, by characteristics of visit and traveler, country, port city, and State of destination, quarterly rpt, 2902–1

Travel to US, characteristics of visit and traveler, world area of origin, and US destination, 1988 survey, annual rpt, 2904–12

Truck rates for fresh vegetables, by crop, growing area, and market, periodic situation rpt with articles, 1561–11

Truck rates for fruit and vegetables, by growing area and market, weekly 1988, annual rpt, 1311–15

TV channel allocation and license status, for commercial and noncommercial UHF and VHF TV by market, as of June 1989, semiannual rpt, 9282–6

TV satellite dish and decoder sales, ownership, subscribers, and program ratings compared to local stations, 1980s-88, hearings, 21528–74

Waterborne commerce (domestic) of US, freight by major commodity group, vessel type, and port, 1986, annual rpt, 7704–7

Waterborne containerized cargo carried over principal trade routes, by flag of vessel, port, and US coastal district, 1984, annual rpt, 7704–8

Waterborne trade of US, by type of service, customs district, port, and world area, monthly rpt, 2422–7

Education

Desegregation of schools, indicators of integration plans effectiveness by school district and location, 1960s-85, 11048–189

Elementary and secondary public schools, enrollment and other characteristics, for top 55 districts, 1987-88, annual rpt, 4834–22

Libraries (public) special programs, project descriptions and funding by level of govt, State, and city, 1984-87, annual rpt, 4874–4

USIA library holdings, use, and staff, by country and city, FY88, annual rpt, 9854–4

Vocational education for disadvantaged and handicapped funding of Fed Govt, by selected State and district, 1985-89 and projected to 2000, GAO rpt, 26121–286

Energy Resources and Demand

Bonneville Power Admin mgmt of Fed Columbia River Power System, finances, operations, and sales by customer, FY88, annual rpt, 3224–1

Bonneville Power Admin sales, revenues, and rates, by customer and customer type, 1988, semiannual rpt, 3222–1

Bunker fuel laden in US on vessels engaged in foreign trade, by fuel type and port, monthly rpt, 2422–5

Coal purchases by Fed Govt, chemical analyses by mine and location, FY84, annual rpt, 3004–15

Electric power and industrial plants exempt from oil and gas primary use prohibition, 1988, annual rpt, 3104–8

Electric utilities fuel cost, quality, use, receipts, and stocks, and power plant production, by energy source, State and utility, quarterly rpt, 3162–39

Nuclear reactors for domestic use and export by function and operating status, with owner, operating characteristics, and location, 1988 annual listing, 3004–26

Southeastern Power Admin sales by customer, plants, capacity, and Southeastern Fed Power Program financial statements, FY88, annual rpt, 3234–1

Southwestern Fed Power System financial statements, sales by customer, and operations and costs by project, FY88, annual rpt, 3244–1

TVA electric power purchases and resales, with electricity use, average bills, and rates by customer class, by distributor, 1988, annual tables, 9804–14

TVA electric power purchases of municipal and cooperative distributors, and prices and use by distributor and consumer sector, monthly rpt, 9802–1

Western Area Power Admin activities by plant, financial statements, and sales by customer, FY88, annual rpt, 3254–1

Geography and Climate

Earthquakes and other ground motion, intensity by station, and info sources, 1986, annual rpt, 5664–14

Heating and cooling degree days, for 45 cities and total US, cumulative for season, weekly rpt, 3162–32.2

Hurricanes and tropical storms in north Atlantic and Caribbean area, paths, surveillance, deaths, damage, and landfall probabilities by city, 1988, annual rpt, 2184–7

Statistical Abstract of US, social, political, and economic data, 1790-2025, comprehensive annual compilation, 2324–1.1

Tidal currents, daily time and velocity by station for North America and Asia coasts, forecast 1990, annual rpts, 2174–1

Tide height and time daily at coastal points worldwide, forecast 1990, annual rpt series, 2174–2

Weather conditions and effect on agriculture, by US region, State, and city, and world area, weekly rpt, 2152–2

Weather data for stations in continental US and outlying areas, 1988 and historic trends, annual rpt, 2154–8

Weather data for surface and upper air, averages by foreign and US station, monthly rpt, 2152–4

Weather events and anomalies, precipitation and temperature for US and foreign locations, weekly rpt, 2182–6

Weather forecasts for US and Northern Hemisphere, precipitation and temperature by location, semimonthly rpt, 2182–1

Government and Defense

Aliens admitted to US, by class of admission, port, country, and State of destination, quarterly rpt, 6262–2

Census of Govts, 1987: property tax revenue by level of govt, assessed values by locality, and exemptions, by property type and State, 2453–1

Customs collections, by district and port, FY88, annual rpt, 8104–2.2

Customs collections, for top 15 ports, quarterly rpt, 8142–1

DOD contracts, payroll, and personnel, by service branch and location, with top 5 contractors and maps, by State and country, FY88, annual rpt, 3544–29

DOD in-house commercial activities work-years, by service branch, State, and installation, FY88, annual rpt, 3544–25

DOD prime contract awards, by contractor, service branch, State, and city, FY88, annual rpt, 3544–22

DOD prime contract awards for R&D to US and foreign nonprofit instns and govt agencies, by instn and location, FY88, annual listing, 3544–17

DOD prime contract awards in labor surplus areas, by service branch, State, and area, FY88, semiannual rpt, 3542–19

Employment and payroll of city govts, by function, for 295 largest cities, 1988, annual rpt, 2466–1.3; 2466–1.6

Fed Govt spending in States and local areas, by type, State, county, and city, FY88, annual rpt, 2464–3.2

Finances of govts, by level of govt, State, and for large cities and counties, annual rpt series, 2466–2

Govt finances, tax systems and revenue, and fiscal structure, by level of govt and State, selected years 1929-91, annual rpt, 10044–1

Immigrant and nonimmigrant visas of US issued and refused, by class, issuing office, and nationality, FY88, annual rpt, 7184–1

Immigration to US, alien workers, visitors, deportations, and naturalizations, by country, FY88 and trends from 1820, annual rpt, 6264–2

Military communities population, 1980, annual rpt, 3164–40.1

Natl Guard emergency response and strengths, by incident and location, FY88, annual rpt, 3504–22.1

Navy nuclear-powered vessels and support facilities radioactive waste, releases in harbors, and public exposure, 1970s-88, annual rpt, 3804–11

Navy procurement, by contractor and location, FY88, annual rpt, 3804–13

Property (real) of Fed Govt, leased inventory and rental costs, worldwide summary by location and agency, 1987, annual rpt, 9454–10

SEC staffing, pay, and turnover by occupation and city, with proposed fee revenues to improve work conditions, 1989 hearing, 21368–116

Services transfer from govts to private contractors, impacts on govt workers, with data by worker characteristics, level of govt, and location, 1980s-87, 15496–1.5

Ships, shipyards, and personnel wartime capability, for merchant and reserve fleet, 1988-2000, 11208–1

Statistical Abstract of US, social, political, and economic data, 1790-2025, comprehensive annual compilation, 2324–1.2

Tax (sales) revenues and rates of local govts, and share of total revenue, by State and selected jurisdiction, 1960s-88, 10046–8.9

Urban areas fiscal, economic, and social conditions, 1960s-87, biennial rpt, 5184–7.2

Health and Vital Statistics

AIDS cases and AIDS virus infection prevalence, by risk group and other patient characteristics, 1981-88 and projected to 1992, 4206–2.13

AIDS health care services research status, needs, methods, and impacts on public health policy and funding, with data for selected cities, 1989 conf papers, 4188–59

Alcohol, Drug Abuse and Mental Health Admin research grants and awards, by recipient, FY88, annual listing, 4044–13

Alcohol use, abuse, treatment, and views of racial and ethnic groups in US and native countries, by selected characteristics, 1988 compilation of papers, 4488–12

Cancer Natl Inst contracts and grants, by recipient and location, FY88, annual listing, 4474–28

Deaths and rates, by detailed location, cause, and demographic characteristics, 1987, US Vital Statistics annual rpt, 4144–3

Deaths recorded in 121 cities, weekly rpt, 4202–1

Drug (methamphetamine) abuse, emergency room admissions and deaths by selected city, and lab seizures, 1980s-87, 4498–61

Drug abuse indicators for selected metro areas, research results, data collection, and policy issues, 1989 semiannual conf, 4492–5

Emergency fire and medical services operations, staff, and finances, for DC and compared to other US and Canadian cities, 1986, hearing, 21308–25

Health Professions Bur training and research grants and contracts, by instn and program, FY88, annual listing, 4114–1

HHS financial aid, by program, recipient, State, and city, FY88, annual regional listings, 4004–3

Lead poisoning among children, and impacts of lead removal from housing, gasoline, and water, 1987 conf, 4108–46

NIH grants for R&D, training, construction, and medical libraries, by location and recipient, FY88, annual listings, 4434–7

Nursing home compliance with Medicare and Medicaid regulations, and patient characteristics, by facility, 1987/88, annual State rpt series, 4654–15

Tuberculosis cases and deaths, by patient characteristics, State, and city, 1987 and trends from 1953, annual rpt, 4204–10

Housing and Construction

American Housing Survey: unit and households detailed characteristics, and unit and neighborhood quality, MSA rpt series, 2485–6

Community dev programs of HUD, funding and activities by program and State, FY88, annual rpt, 5124–5

Housing finance, construction, and improvement aid programs of HUD, press release series, 5006–3

Indian (Navajo and Hopi) relocation program activities, caseloads, and finances, FY88, annual rpt, 16004–1

New housing units authorized, by region, State, selected MSA, and permit-issuing place, monthly rpt, 2382–5

New housing units authorized, by State, MSA, and permit-issuing place, 1988, annual rpt, 2384–2

North Central States, FHLB 7th District housing vacancy rates for single and multifamily units and mobile homes, by ZIP code, annual MSA rpt series, 9304–18

Office building vacancy rates in 16 cities, 1960s-87, article, 9387–1.903

Public housing projects youth recreation and sports programs, HUD grants by recipient, 1989, press release, 5006–3.73

Rent supplement programs evaluation, housing voucher demonstration compared to Section 8, series, 5186–14

South Central States, FHLB 9th District housing vacancy rates for single and multifamily units and mobile homes by ZIP code, annual MSA rpt series, 9304–19

Southeastern States community dev grants from HUD, by purpose and location, quarterly rpt, 9389–16

Urban Dev Action Grant projects and funding, impacts of changes in selection criteria, by city and State, 1988, GAO rpt, 26113–395

Urban Dev Action Grants, funding, and jobs and taxes generated, by city, FY88, annual rpt, 5124–5

Urban Dev Action Grants, funding sources, project descriptions, and economic impacts, by city, periodic press releases, 5002–7

Wage rates for construction trades union, by coastal region and for 10 port cities, 1988, annual rpt, 7704–12.2

West Central States, FHLB 10th District housing vacancy rates for single and multifamily units and mobile homes, by ZIP code, annual MSA rpt series, 9304–22

Western States, FHLB 11th District housing vacancy rates for single and multifamily units and mobile homes, by ZIP code, annual MSA rpt series, 9304–20

Western States, FHLB 12th District housing vacancy rates for single and multifamily units and mobile homes, by ZIP code, annual MSA rpt series, 9304–21

Industry and Commerce

Exports and imports of US, by commodity group, world area, selected country, US coastal area and port, and mode of transport, monthly rpt, 2422–9

Foreign trade zones (US) operations and movement of goods, by zone and commodity, FY86, annual rpt, 2044–30

Guam economic censuses, 1987: employment, firms, payroll, and receipts, by SIC 1- to 4-digit industry and election district, 2595–1

Northern Mariana Islands economic census, 1987: employment, firms, payroll, and receipts, by SIC 1- to 4-digit industry, 2597–1

Retail trade census, 1987: employment, establishments, sales, and payroll, by SIC 2- to 4-digit kind of business, MSA, county, and city, State rpt series, 2397–1

Retail trade sales and inventories, by kind of business, region, and selected State, MSA, and city, monthly rpt, 2413–3

Salt production capacity, and use in chlorine production, by firm and facility, 1988, annual listing, 5614–30

Service industries census, 1987: establishments, receipts, employment, and payroll, by SIC 2- to 4-digit kind of business, MSA, county, and city, State rpt series, 2391–1

Small Business Admin loans, contract awards, and surety bonds, by firm, State, and city, FY88, annual rpt, 9764–1

Tennessee Valley industrial dev, employment, and electricity demand, by SIC 2-digit industry, firm, and location, 1988, annual rpt, 9804–3

Virgin Islands economic censuses, 1987: employment, firms, payroll, and receipts, by SIC 1- to 4-digit industry, island, and city, 2593–1

Wholesale trade census, 1987: employment, establishments, finances, and operations, by SIC 2- to 4-digit kind of business, MSA, county, and city, State rpt series, 2405–1

Labor and Employment

Employment and Earnings, detailed data, monthly rpt, 6742–2.8

Employment, unemployment, and labor force characteristics, by selected metro area and large city, 1988, annual rpt, 6744–7.3

Unemployment, employment, and labor force, by State, MSA, and city, monthly rpt, 6742–22

Unemployment insurance extended benefits provision in substate areas, model results and cost estimates, 1980-86, 6406–6.28

Law Enforcement

Aircraft hijackings, on-board explosions, and other crime, US and foreign incidents, 1983-87, annual rpt, 7504–31

Assaults and deaths of law enforcement officers, by circumstances, agency, victim and offender characteristics, and location, 1988, annual rpt, 6224–3

Crime, by characteristics of victim and offender, circumstances, and location, 1970s-87, annual rpt, 6064–6.3

Crime Index by population size and region, and offenses by large city, Jan-June 1989, semiannual rpt, 6222–1

Crimes and rates by offense, and law enforcement employment, by population size and jurisdiction, 1988, annual rpt, 6224–2.1; 6224–2.3

Criminal case processing from arrest to sentencing, cases and duration by disposition, offense, and defendant characteristics, for selected cities, 1986, annual rpt, 6064–27

Criminal justice spending, employment, and payroll, by level of govt, State, and selected city and county, FY71-85, annual rpt, 6064–9

Drug enforcement activities of State and local agencies, Federal aid by recipient, and background data, FY88, annual rpt, 6064–28

Drug smuggling interdiction aircraft deployed by Customs Service and Coast Guard, by aircraft type and location, as of Feb 1989, GAO rpt, 26119–259

Drug test results at arrest, by drug type, offense, and sex, for selected urban areas, quarterly rpt, 6062–3

Jail population by sex, race, and for 25 jurisdictions, and instn conditions, 1983-87, annual rpt, 6066–25.18

Police dept operations, staff, and expenses, for large cities by population size, 1987, 6066–19.51

Statistical Abstract of US, social, political, and economic data, 1790-2025, comprehensive annual compilation, 2324–1.1

Terrorist incidents in US, related activity, and casualties, by attack type, target, group, and location, 1988, annual rpt, 6224–6

Natural Resources, Environment, and Pollution

Acid rain distribution, pH levels, and composition, monitoring results by site, 1987, annual rpt, 9194–20

Air pollution levels for 6 pollutants, and measurements exceeding natl standards, by site, 1987-88, annual rpt, 9194–5

Arkansas water quality in streams and rivers, by monitoring site, 1975-85, 5668–83

Army Corps of Engineers activities and projects, FY87 and trends from 1800s, annual rpt, 3754–1.2

Auto emissions control device tampering and fuel-switching incidence in 15 urban areas, 1988, annual rpt, 9194–15

Coastal and estuarine pollutant concentrations in sediments, by contaminant and selected site, 1984-87, 2176–3.7

Coastal and estuarine pollutant concentrations in shellfish, by contaminant and selected site, 1986-88, 2176–3.8

Coastal and estuarine pollutant discharges, by source, pollutant type, and location, series, 2176–4

Great Lakes basin pollutant discharges, sources, and control program activities, 1987, biennial rpt, 14644–1

Great Lakes polychlorinated biphenyls levels in environment, humans, and animals, and emissions sources, by site, 1970s-85, conf, 14648–19

Great Lakes toxic spills and human error, with data by pollutant source and site, 1984-86, conf, 14648–21

Hazardous waste site remedial action under Superfund, current and proposed sites descriptions and status, periodic listings, series, 9216–3

Hazardous waste site remedial action under Superfund, current and proposed sites priority ranking and status by location, as of July 1989, listing, 9218–64

Military installations hazardous waste site remedial action, activities and funding by site and State, FY88, annual rpt, 3544–36

Minerals resources and availability on public lands, State rpt series, 5606–7

New Mexico water resources data collection and analysis activities of USGS, with project descriptions, FY88, 5668–86

Ozone levels, urban areas failure to meet natl standards, emissions sources, exposure, and costs and benefits of reduction strategies, 1983-87 and projected to 2004, 26358–203

Ozone peak concentrations by selected city, 1983 and 1988, and health effects clinical test results, 1989 hearing, 21368–117

Radiation and radionuclide concentrations in air, water, and milk, monitoring results by State and site, quarterly rpt, 9192–5

Radioactive waste from Navy nuclear-powered vessels and support facilities, releases in harbors, and public exposure, 1970s-88, annual rpt, 3804–11

Radionuclide concentrations in air, water, humans, animals, and milk near Nevada and other nuclear test sites, 1988, annual rpt, 9194–17

Tennessee Valley river control activities, and hydroelectric power generation and capacity, 1984, annual rpt, 9804–7

Timber sales of Forest Service, expenses, and operations, by region, State, and natl forest, FY88, annual rpts, 1204–36

Uranium tailings at inactive mills, remedial action activities by site, and funding, FY88, annual rpt, 3354–9

Uranium tailings at inactive mills, remedial action proposals, costs, site characteristics, and environmental, socioeconomic, and health impacts, series, 3356-4

Wastewater treatment facility construction grants of EPA to State and local govts, by project, monthly listing, 9202-3

Water resources dev projects of Army Corps of Engineers, characteristics, and costs, 1950s-87, biennial State rpt series, 3756-2

Water resources dev projects of Army Corps of Engineers, characteristics, and costs, 1950s-89, biennial State rpt series, 3756-1

Water supply and quality in streams and lakes, and groundwater levels in wells, by drainage basin, 1986, annual State rpt series, 5666-23

Water supply and quality in streams and lakes, and groundwater levels in wells, by drainage basin, 1987, annual State rpt series, 5666-10

Water supply and quality in streams and lakes, and groundwater levels in wells, by drainage basin, 1988, annual State rpt series, 5666-16

Water supply in northeastern US, precipitation and stream runoff by station, monthly rpt, 2182-3

Water supply in western US, streamflow and reservoir storage forecasts by stream and station, Jan-May monthly rpt, 1262-1

Watershed (agricultural) runoff, precipitation, weather conditions, and mgmt, for 72 projects, 1978-79, annual rpt, 1704-1

Population

Developing countries disaster preparedness and economic, population, and political data, country rpt series, 9916-2

Foreign countries population size, growth rate, and area, for 94 largest cities, 1989 biennial rpt, 2324-9

Homeless children educational enrollment and needs, 1988, annual State rpt series, 4804-35

Homeless population characteristics by city, and Federal funding by program, 1980s-89, hearings, 21248-123

Population size, by MSA, county, metro-nonmetro location, and State, 1987, and for cities, 1986, with change from 1980 and trends from 1960, Current Population Rpt, 2546-3.160

Population size of cities with population over 100,000, as of July 1988, biennial press release, 2324-7

Refugees from Indochina, arrivals, and departures, by country of origin and resettlement, camp, and ethnicity, monthly rpt, 7002-4

Rural areas served by electric cooperatives, population by community, 1980, annual rpt, 3164-40.1

Statistical Abstract of US, social, political, and economic data, 1790-2025, comprehensive annual compilation, 2324-1.1

Prices and Cost of Living

Cost of living indexes for metro areas, relation of expenditure items and quality of life indicators, model results, 1973, working paper, 6886-6.9

Cotton prices at selected spot markets, NYC futures prices, and CCC loan rates, 1988/89 and trends from 1940, annual rpt, 1309-2

Dairy prices, by product and selected area, with related marketing data, 1988, annual rpt, 1317-1

Electric power rate schedules, by user type, utility, and city, as of Jan 1988, annual rpt, 3164-40

Food prices for 15 items in DC and 15 foreign capital cities, weekly press release, periodic table, 1922-4

Foreign countries living costs, State Dept indexes, housing allowances, and hardship differentials by country and major city, quarterly rpt, 6862-1

Milk order and cooperative prices, by selected area, 1988, annual rpt, 1317-1.5

Poultry and egg prices and marketing, by selected region, State, and city, monthly and weekly 1988, annual rpt, 1317-2

Statistical Abstract of US, social, political, and economic data, 1790-2025, comprehensive annual compilation, 2324-1.3

Public Welfare and Social Security

Food aid programs purchases, by commodity, firm, and shipping point or destination, weekly rpt, 1302-3

Head Start demonstration program grants, by recipient, 1985, 4608-25

HHS financial aid, by program, recipient, State, and city, FY88, annual regional listings, 4004-3

Homeless persons aid programs, and shelter capacity and voucher programs, for 5 major cities, 1988, 5188-122

SSA activities, and OASDHI admin, 1930s-89 and projected to 2063, data compilation, annual rpt, 4704-12

Recreation and Leisure

Fishing (ocean sport) catch and effort, and Natl Marine Fisheries Service tagging and research activity, by species and location, 1987, annual rpt, 2164-7

Park natl system and other land under Natl Park Service mgmt, acreage by site, ownership, and region, 1989, semiannual rpt, 5542-1

Veterans Affairs

Health care for veterans, patients, visits, costs, and operating beds, by VA and contract facility, and region, quarterly rpt, 8602-4

Health care professionals of VA, by selected employment characteristics and VA district and duty station, quarterly rpt, 8602-6

Medicine and Surgery Dept of VA, trainees by detailed program and city, FY88, annual rpt, 8704-4

BY COUNTY

Agriculture and Food

California vegetable production by leading county and crop, 1982, article, 1502-4.903

Census of Agriculture, 1987: farms, farmland, production and costs, and operator characteristics, advance State and county rpt series, 2330-1

Census of Agriculture, 1987: farms, farmland, production, finances, and operator characteristics, by county, final State rpt series, 2331-1

Corn and soybean futures contract yield and price risk hedging strategies, by selected county and State, model results, 1961-83, 1548-352

Cotton acreage planted by State and county, and fiber quality, by variety, 1989, annual rpt, 1309-6

Cotton ginnings and production, by State and county, 1988, annual rpt, 2344-1

Cotton ginnings, by State and county, seasonal monthly rpt, 2342-2

Farmland (US) owned by foreigners, holdings, acreage, and value by land use, owner country, State, and county, 1988, annual rpt, 1584-3

Milk order market producer deliveries, by State and county, 1986-87, periodic rpt, 1317-5

Soil and water conservation funding by USDA, by program and State, FY86, annual rpt, 1264-12

Banking, Finance, and Insurance

Banks (commercial and savings) FDIC-insured, deposits by instn, State, MSA, and county, as of June 1988, annual regional rpt series, 9295-3

North Central States, FHLB 7th District insured thrifts, offices, and savings, by county, 1986-87, annual rpt, 9304-5

Savings instns FSLIC-insured, offices, and deposits, by FHLB district, State, SMSA, and county, 1988, annual rpt, 9314-4

Western States, FHLB 11th District thrift offices, locations, savings balances, and accounts, quarterly listing, 9302-20

Communications and Transportation

Aircraft registered with FAA, by type and characteristics of aircraft, make, carrier, State, and county, 1988, annual rpt, 7504-3

Education

Desegregation of schools, indicators of integration plans effectiveness by school district and location, 1960s-85, 11048-189

Energy Resources and Demand

Arizona wood fuel harvest, by tree species, ownership, and county, 1984, 1208-293

Bonneville Power Admin mgmt of Fed Columbia River Power System, finances, operations, and sales by customer, FY88, annual rpt, 3224-1

Coal production and mines by county, prices, productivity, miners, reserves, and stocks, by mining method and State, 1987-88, annual rpt, 3164-25

Coal purchases by Fed Govt, chemical analyses by mine and location, FY84, annual rpt, 3004-15

New Mexico fuelwood harvest, by species, ownership, and county, 1986, 1208-303

Government and Defense

Census of Govts, 1987: property tax revenue by level of govt, assessed values by locality, and exemptions, by property type and State, 2453-1

DOD prime contract awards in labor surplus areas, by service branch, State, and area, FY88, semiannual rpt, 3542-19

Economic Dev Admin activities, and funding by program, recipient, State, and county, FY87 and cumulative from FY66, annual rpt, 2064-2

Economic Dev Admin funding, and loans forgiven, with data by project and location, FY84-88, hearing, 21648-56

Employment and payroll of county govts, by function and population size, for 398 largest counties, 1987, annual rpt, 2466-1.4

Grain production, prices, trade, and export inspections by US port and country of destination, by grain type, weekly rpt, 1313-2

Honey production, prices, trade, stocks, marketing, and CCC honey loan and distribution activities, monthly rpt, 1311-2

Hops production, stocks, use, and US trade by country, monthly rpt, 1313-7

Japan fish catch, prices, trade by country, cold storage holdings, import quotas, and market devs, semimonthly press release, 2162-7

Livestock and meat trade of US, by country, 1970-87, 1568-285.4

Livestock, meat, poultry, and egg production, prices, trade, and stocks, monthly rpt, 1561-17

Livestock, poultry, and dairy trade, by commodity and country, FAS monthly circular, 1925-32

Livestock, poultry, and products foreign and US production, trade, and use, by selected country, forecast 1990, FAS annual circular, 1925-33

Meat and poultry inspection activities and staff of Federal, State, and foreign govts, FY88, annual rpt, 1374-1

Meat and poultry inspection for export and import, by product and country, FY88, annual rpt, 1374-3.3

Meat imports under Meat Import Act, by country of origin, FAS monthly circular, 1925-31

Meat plants inspected and certified for exporting to US, by country, 1988, annual listing, 1374-2

Molasses (feed) production, wholesale prices by market area, and US imports and country, weekly rpt, 1311-16

Molasses supply, use, wholesale prices by market, and trade and production by country, 1983-88, annual rpt, 1311-19

Oils, oilseeds, and fats foreign and US production and trade, FAS periodic circular series, 1925-1

Peanut production and trade by country, prices, and stocks, weekly rpt, 1311-1

Pests and diseases of plants entering US, by type of pest and host, country, and State, FY87, annual rpt, 1394-16

PL 480 exports by commodity, and recipients, by program, sponsor, and country, FY87 and cumulative from FY55, annual rpt, 1924-7

PL 480 long-term credit sales allocations, by commodity and country, periodic press release, 1922-7

Production, acreage, and yield for selected crops, forecasts by selected world region and country, FAS monthly circular, 1925-28

Production and indexes, total and for selected commodities, by country, 1970s-88, annual rpt, 1524-12

Production, consumption, and policies for selected countries, and US export dev and promotion, monthly journal, 1922-2

Production, prices, and trade of agricultural commodities, by country, 1970s-89 and forecast 1990, annual world region rpt series, 1524-4

Production, prices, trade, and use, for foreign and US agriculture, periodic rpt with articles, 1522-3

Production, trade, and price support activity and policy options, with foreign comparisons, 1950s-89, commodity rpt series, 1566-7

Research (agricultural) of US, staffing by topic, performing organization, and for 6 countries, FY88, annual rpt, 1744-2.2

Research grants of USDA, by program, subagency, and country, FY88, annual listing, 1954-3

Rice foreign and US production, prices, trade, stocks, and use, periodic situation rpt, 1561-8

Rice market activities, prices, inspections, sales, trade, supply, and use, for US and selected foreign markets, weekly rpt, 1313-8

Rum imports (duty-free) of US under Caribbean Basin Initiative, by country, 1987-88, annual rpt, 9884-15

Seed exports, by type, world region, and country, FAS quarterly rpt, 1925-13

Soybean exports related to foreign market prices, and price and income elasticities of demand, by selected country, alternative forecast model results, 1989 article, 1502-3.903

Spice, essential oil, and tea foreign and US production, prices, and trade, FAS annual circular series, 1925-15

Statistical Abstract of US, social, political, and economic data, by outlying area and country, 1950s-87, comprehensive annual compilation, 2324-1.4

Subsidies for agriculture, consumer and producer equivalents by program, commodity, and major US trading partner, 1982-86, 1528-275

Sugar and honey foreign and US production, prices, trade, and use, FAS periodic circular series, 1925-14

Sugar and sugar product imports of US under quota, by country, periodic rpt, 1922-9

Sugar and sweeteners production, prices, trade, supply, and use, quarterly situation rpt with articles, 1561-14

Sugar production, supply, trade, and use, quarterly rpt, 1621-28

Supply and demand indicators for selected foreign and US crops, monthly rpt, 1522-5

Sweetpotato and yam production by State and leading foreign country, and US consumption, 1970s-88, article, 1561-11.901

Taiwan canned pineapple and asparagus exports, by country, selected years 1970-88, article, 1925-34.936

Technical aid of USDA, personnel and agreements by project, world area, and country, FY87, annual rpt, 1954-2

Tobacco and products foreign and US industry review, FAS monthly circular articles, 1925-16

Tobacco leaf stocks, production, sales, and import inspections by country, by product, quarterly rpt, 1319-3

Tobacco production and US trade, by country, 1985-88, annual rpt, 1319-1

Tobacco production, use, prices, and trade, by country, 1981-86 and trends from 1935, 1568-276

Wheat (durum) acreage, production, prices, stocks, use, and US and Canada exports by country, quarterly rpt, 1313-6

Wheat and rye foreign and US production, prices, trade, stocks, and use, quarterly situation rpt with articles, 1561-12

Wheat exports impacts of subsidies and exchange rates, by importing and exporting country, alternative model results, 1986/87, 1548-351

Banking, Finance, and Insurance

AID local currency trust funds mgmt and use, by country, FY83-87, GAO rpt, 26123-221

Banks (US) and nonbanking firms liabilities to and claims on foreigners, by country, 1986-87, annual rpt, 9364-5.10

Banks (US) foreign branches assets and liabilities, by world region and country, quarterly rpt, 9365-3.7

Banks employment relation to labor costs, output, and technological change, US and 5 OECD countries, 1980-86, working paper, 9371-10.42

Capital flows (intl) impacts on monetary policy instruments, and financial and economic indicators, 1987 compilation of papers, 9385-9

Capital movements between US and foreign countries, *Treasury Bulletin*, quarterly rpt, 8002-4.11

Debt to US of foreign govts and private obligors, by country and program, periodic rpt, 8002-6

Developing countries debt burden and economic conditions, and trade with industrialized countries, by country, 1970s-87, hearings, 25248-108

Developing countries debt reduction proposals, and Eximbank export financing programs, with background data, 1986-89, 2048-142

Developing countries foreign debt and debt burden indicators, for selected countries, 1989 hearings, 21248-122

Dollar exchange rate variability, with comparisons to other currencies, 1914-89, working paper, 9381-10.98

Dollar exchange rates of 22 developing countries, 1972-86, article, 1522-3.917

Dollar exchange rates of 35 countries, and interest rates and security yields for US and selected foreign countries, weekly chartbook, 9365-1.5

Dollar exchange rates offered by US disbursing offices, by country, quarterly rpt, 8102-6

Eastern Europe and USSR debt, trade, and balances with US and other western countries, with background data, 1980s-87, hearing, 21248-120

Eximbank financial condition, credit and insurance authorizations, and loan activity and delinquencies, by country, FY88, annual rpt, 9254-1

Export credit activity of Eximbank and 6 OECD countries, 1988, annual rpt, 9254-3

Fed Financing Bank holdings and transactions, by borrower, monthly press release, 12802-1

Fed Financing Bank loans outstanding, and loan prepayment activity and costs, 1985-88, GAO rpt, 26111-63

Finance (intl) statistics, monthly rpt, 9362-1.3

Interest rates relation to intl rates, exchange rates, and US money supply, for 7 OECD countries, 1979-88, article, 9391-1.920

Loans and grants for economic and military aid from US and intl agencies, by program and country, FY46-87, annual rpt, 9914-5

Loans of banks and govts to developing countries, debt exposure of 7 developed countries, various periods 1980-88, GAO rpt, 26123-255

Loans of US banks to foreigners at all US and foreign offices, by country group and country, quarterly rpt, 13002-1

Monetary aggregates velocity relation to inflation, for US and 39 countries, various periods 1908-87, working paper, 9377-9.74

Overseas Private Investment Corp finances and activities, with list of insured projects and firms, FY88, annual rpt, 9904-2

Real estate investment by foreigners in US farm and commercial land, by owner country, 1977-89, GAO rpt, 26123-244

Securities intl transaction activity, by country, 1982-88, GAO rpt, 26123-235

Stock market crash of 1987, market performance, foreign futures market activity, and computer-aided trading impacts on price variability, 1980s-88, hearings, 25168-70

Stock price volatility, with data by industry and country, 1970s-88, conf papers, 9381-13.1

Stock prices correlation with inflation rates in US and 6 other countries, 1950s-86, article, 9379-1.904

Communications and Transportation

Aircraft registered with FAA, by type and characteristics of aircraft, and country, 1988, annual rpt, 7504-3

Developing countries disaster preparedness and economic, population, and political data, country rpt series, 9916-2

Info services for home and business, availability, use, and market indicators, for US and other OECD countries, 1980s and projected to 1992, 2808-28

Mail (domestic) postal rates, for 14 countries, 1988, annual rpt, 9864-5.1

Panama Canal traffic and tolls, by commodity, flag of vessel, and trade route, FY88, annual rpt, 9664-3.1

Ship foreign and US flag competition in US Exclusive Economic Zone, impacts of extending cabotage laws, with background data, 1970s-80s, 26358-206

Shipborne trade of US, by type of service, commodity, country, route, and US port, 1986-87, annual rpt, 7704-2

Shipbuilding and deliveries, by vessel type and country of construction and registry, 1988, annual rpt, 7704-4

Ships in world bulk carrier fleet, characteristics by country of registry, as of Jan 1989, annual listing, 7704-13

Ships in world merchant fleet, and deliveries, by vessel type and country, FY88, annual rpt, 7704-14.1

Ships in world merchant fleet, and tonnage, by country of registry, as of Jan 1988, annual rpt, 7704-3

Ships in world merchant fleet, US transfers to foreign firms, and deliveries, by vessel type and country, FY88, annual rpt, 7704-14.2

Ships in world tanker fleet, by country, selected years 1970-88, annual rpt, 9114-4.10

Ships in world tanker fleet, characteristics by country of registry, as of Jan 1989, annual listing, 7704-17

Ships under foreign flag owned by US firms and foreign affiliates, by type, owner, and country of registry and construction, as of July 1989, semiannual rpt, 7702-3

St Lawrence Seaway ship, cargo, and passenger traffic, and toll revenue, 1988 and trends from 1959, annual rpt, 7744-2

Statistical Abstract of US, social, political, and economic data, by outlying area and country, 1950s-87, comprehensive annual compilation, 2324-1.1; 2324-1.4

Telephone and telegraph overseas operations, revenue, and rates, by world area and country, various dates 1987-88, annual rpt, 9284-6

Transportation finances, operations, vehicles, equipment, accidents, and energy use, by mode of transport, 1955-88, annual rpt, 7304-2

Travel to and from US, and travel receipts and payments, by world area, with data by country, 1984-88, annual rpt, 2904-10

Travel to and from US, by world area, forecast 1989-90, annual rpt, 2904-9

Travel to and from US on US and foreign flag air carriers, by country, world area, and US port, monthly rpt, 7302-2

Travel to US and Canada, market analysis with detailed trip and traveler characteristics, country rpt series, 2906-2

Travel to US, by characteristics of visit and traveler, country, port city, and State of destination, quarterly rpt, 2902-1

Travel to US, market research, major magazine ad costs and circulation, and trade show data, for selected countries, 1989-90, annual rpt, 2904-11

Travel to US, receipts, and Travel and Tourism Admin spending, by country and world area, 1960s-88 and projected to 2000, 2908-30

Travel to US, spending by category, world area of residence, census div, and State, model results, 1985-86, 2908-28

Waterborne containerized cargo carried over principal trade routes, by flag of vessel, port, and US coastal district, 1984, annual rpt, 7704-8

Waterborne freight rates for grain, by US loading port and country of destination, weekly rpt, 1272-2

Education

Condition of Education, detailed data on elementary and secondary education, 1920s-88 and projected to 1997, annual rpt, 4824-1.1

Education data for foreign countries, and students enrolled in US higher education instns, 1989 edition, annual rpt, 4824-2.29

English language program of USIA, enrollment and staff, by instn, world area, and country, FY88, annual rpt, 9854-2

Exchange and training programs of Federal agencies, participants by world area, and funding, by program, FY87, annual rpt, 9854-8

Fulbright-Hays academic exchanges, grants by purpose, and foreign govt share of costs, by country, FY88, annual rpt, 10324-1

Statistical Abstract of US, social, political, and economic data, by outlying area and country, 1950s-87, comprehensive annual compilation, 2324-1.1; 2324-1.4

US students receiving credit for study abroad, by country, 1986, 2048-142

USIA library holdings, use, and staff, by country and city, FY88, annual rpt, 9854-4

Energy Resources and Demand

Coal imports of US electric utilities, by utility and country of origin, 1984-88, annual rpt, 3164-42

Coal production, trade, and govt subsidies, by country and country group, 1973-87 and projected to 2000, 2048-144

Coal trade and average price, by country of destination and origin and customs district, weekly rpt, monthly data, 3162-1.2

Coal trade and average price, by world region, country, and customs district, quarterly rpt, 3162-37

Coal trade flows and reserves, by country, 1970s-87 and projected to 2000, annual rpt, 3164-77

Energy-intensive industry output and operations, and US investment barriers, for energy-rich countries, 1984-88, 9886-4.142

Energy production by type, and oil prices, trade, and use, by country group and selected country, monthly rpt, 9112-2

Energy production, trade, use, and reserves, and oil and refined products supply and prices, by country, 1980-88, annual rpt, 3164-50

Energy supply, demand, and prices, by fuel type and end-use sector, with foreign comparisons, 1988 and trends from 1949, annual rpt, 3164-74

Energy supply, demand, and prices, by fuel type, end-use sector, and country, detailed data, monthly rpt, 3162-24

Energy use by sector, and production, by fuel type, country, and country group, projected 1988-2000 and trends from 1970, annual rpt, 3164-84

Nuclear power generation in US and 19 non-Communist countries, monthly rpt, 3162-24.10

Nuclear power plant capacity, generation, and operating status, by plant and foreign and US location, 1988 and projected to 2020, annual rpt, 3164-57

Nuclear power plant spent fuel and demand for uranium and enrichment service, for US and other country groups, projected 1989-2036, annual rpt, 3164-72

Nuclear reactors for domestic use and export by function and operating status, with owner, operating characteristics, and location, 1988 annual listing, 3004-26

Oil and gas reserves and discoveries, by country and country group, quarterly rpt, 3162-43

Oil crude, gas liquids, and refined products supply, demand, and movement, by PAD district and State, 1988 and trends from 1973, annual rpt, 3164-2

Oil import costs, by crude type and country or group of origin, monthly rpt, 3162-11

Oil import costs, by crude type and country or group of origin, 1988, annual rpt, 3164-85

Oil industry mergers and acquisitions impacts on market concentration, with background data, 1970-84, 9406-1.58

Oil prices of OPEC and non-OPEC countries, weekly rpt, 3162-32

Oil production by country, use and imports for US and 6 OECD countries, and OPEC member prices, biweekly rpt, 9112-1

Oil production, trade, use, and stocks, by selected country and country group, monthly rpt, 3162-42

Oil production, use, stocks, and exports and prices for US, by country, detailed data, monthly rpt, 3162-24

Oil, refined products, and gas liquids supply, demand, trade, stocks, and refining, by detailed product, State, and PAD district, monthly rpt with articles, 3162-6

Oil reserves, production, and production costs of OPEC, by country, 1987, technical paper, 9379-12.44

Statistical Abstract of US, social, political, and economic data, by outlying area and country, 1950s-87, comprehensive annual compilation, 2324-1.4

Strategic Petroleum Reserve oil deliveries, by country and State of origin, quarterly rpt, annual data, 3002-13

Transportation energy use, fuel prices, and vehicle registrations, by selected country, 1970s-88, annual rpt, 3304-5.1

Uranium mining and milling industries finances and operations, with selected foreign comparisons, 1970s-87 and projected to 2000, annual rpt, 3164-82

Geography and Climate

Borders (maritime) agreements and claims of coastal countries, series, 7006-8

Disaster preparedness and economic, population, and political data, country rpt series, 9916-2

Geographic Notes, foreign countries boundaries, claims, nomenclature, and other devs, periodic rpt, 7142-3

Oceanographic research and distribution activities of World Data Center A by country, and cruises by ship, 1987, annual rpt, 2144-15

Tide height and time daily at coastal points worldwide, forecast 1990, annual rpt series, 2174-2

Weather conditions and effect on agriculture, by US region, State, and city, and world area, weekly rpt, 2152-2

Weather data for surface and upper air, averages by foreign and US station, monthly rpt, 2152-4

Weather events and anomalies, precipitation and temperature for US and foreign locations, weekly rpt, 2182-6

Government and Defense

AID contracts and grants for technical and support services, by instn, country, and State, FY88, annual listing, 9914-7

AID dev projects and socioeconomic impacts, evaluation rpt series, 9916-1

AID dev projects, special study series, 9916-3

AID economic aid to developing countries, obligations and disbursements by country, quarterly rpt, 9912-4

AID loans authorized, signed, and canceled, by country and world area, quarterly rpt, 9912-2

AID loans repayment status and terms by program and country, and status of predecessor agency loans, quarterly rpt, 9912-3

Aliens (illegal) enforcement activity of Coast Guard, by nationality, 2nd half FY89, semiannual rpt, 7402-4

Aliens admitted to US, by class of admission, port, country, and State of destination, quarterly rpt, 6262-2

Arms control treaties status, and Arms Control and Disarmament Agency activities, 1988, annual rpt, 9824-2

Arms sales of US, foreign conditions on sales and impacts on US industry, with data by industry group and country, 1988 annual rpt, 104-25

Background Notes, foreign countries summary social, political, and economic data, series, 7006-2

Chiefs of State and Cabinet members, by country, bimonthly listing, 9112-4

Claims against foreign govts by US natls, by claim type and country, 1988, annual rpt, 6004-16

Coin production of US Mint, for US by denomination and mint, and for foreign countries, monthly table, 8202-1

Currency (foreign) accounts owned by US under AID admin and by foreign govts with joint AID control, status by program and country, quarterly rpt, 9912-1

Currency (foreign) holdings of US, transactions and balances by program and country, 1st half FY89, semiannual rpt, 8102-7

Currency (foreign) purchases of US with dollars, by country, 1st half FY89, semiannual rpt, 8102-5

Developing countries disaster preparedness and economic, population, and political data, country rpt series, 9916-2

Developing countries economic aid from US, bilateral and through intl dev banks, by world region and country, 1970s-FY88, annual rpt, 9904-1

Developing countries economic and social conditions from 1960s, and Intl Dev Cooperation Agency and AID activities and funding, FY88-90, annual rpt, 9904-4

Diplomats and staff with immunity for foreign missions in US and US missions abroad, and foreign diplomats criminal cases, 1978-87, hearing, 25388-51

Economic and military aid and loans from US and intl agencies, by program and country, FY46-87, annual rpt, 9914-5

Economic conditions, policy, and trade practices, by country, 1986-88, annual rpt, 21384-5

Economic, social, political, and geographic summary data, by country, 1989, annual factbook, 9114-2

Helsinki Final Act implementation by NATO and Warsaw Pact, Oct 1988-Mar 1989, semiannual rpt, 7002-1

Human rights conditions in 170 countries, 1988, annual rpt, 21384-3

Immigrants admitted to US, by class of admission, country of birth, and State and MSA of destination, FY88, annual rpt, 6264-4

Immigration reform affecting persons with needed labor skills and persons otherwise excluded, effect on admissions, visas, and waiting periods, 1990-99, GAO rpt, 26131-64

Immigration to US, alien workers, visitors, deportations, and naturalizations, by country, FY88 and trends from 1820, annual rpt, 6264-2

Latin America dev grants of Inter-American Foundation by program area, and fellowships by field and instn, by country, FY71-88, annual rpt, 14424-2

Latin America dev grants of Inter-American Foundation by recipient, and fellowships, by country, FY88, annual rpt, 14424-1

Military aid of US, arms sales, and training, by country, FY50-88, annual rpt, 3904-3

Military aid of US, arms sales, and training programs costs and budget requests, by program, world region, and country, FY88-90, annual rpt, 7144-13

Military aid of US, DOD notifications to Congress of changes from Admin budget request, and funds affected by country, FY86-87, GAO rpt, 26123-219

Military aid programs and related activities of US, costs by country and intl agency, FY85-87 and cumulative from FY50, GAO rpt, 26123-30

Military sales program loans outstanding, prepayments, delinquency, and refinancing, by country, 1988-89, GAO rpt, 26123-253

Military spending and imports of developing countries, measures to determine eligibility for US economic aid, by country, 1985-86, annual rpt, 9914-1

Military spending, arms trade, and force strengths, with govt spending and population, by country, 1977-87, annual rpt, 9824-1

NATO and Japan military spending and indicators of ability to support common defense, by country, 1960s-87, annual rpt, 3544-28

NATO Europe members presence of US military and civilian personnel and dependents, by service branch, 1980-88, GAO rpt, 26123-252

NATO Europe members presence of US military and civilian personnel, and vacancies, by service branch, 1988, GAO rpt, 26123-251

NATO military forces compared to Warsaw Pact, and selected economic indicators, by country, 1900s-87, conf papers, 3908-6

Pacific basin countries military, economic, technological, and trade conditions, 1970s-85, compilation of papers, 3908-4

Peace Corps activities, funding by program, and volunteers, by country, FY90, annual rpt, 9654-1

Statistical Abstract of US, social, political, and economic data, by outlying area and country, 1950s-87, comprehensive annual compilation, 2324-1.2; 2324-1.4

Tax (income) returns for foreign corporate activity in US, assets, and income statement items, by industry div, country, and world area, 1984-85, article, 8302-2.920

Tax (income) returns of individuals with foreign earned income, returns, exclusions, credits, and US revenue losses, with data by country, 1983, quadrennial rpt, 8308-34

Tax withheld and income from US sources for foreign natls not residing in US, by country and tax treaty status, 1986, annual article, 8302-2.915

UN participation of US, and member and nonmember shares of UN budget by country, FY86-88, annual rpt, 7004-5

UN voting record and share of votes in agreement with US, by issue, country, and world area, 1988, annual rpt, 7004–18

US govt contingent liabilities and claims paid on federally insured and guaranteed contracts with foreign obligors, by country and program, periodic rpt, 8002–12

US govt-leased real property inventory and rental costs, worldwide summary by location and agency, 1987, annual rpt, 9454–10

US govt-owned real property inventory and costs, worldwide summary by location, agency, and use, 1987, annual rpt, 9454–5

US military and civilian personnel and dependents, by service branch and location, FY88, annual rpt, 3544–1

US military and civilian personnel and dependents, by service branch, world area, and country, quarterly rpt, 3542–20

US military base construction, renovation, and land acquisition, budget requests by project, service branch, State, and country, FY90/91, annual rpt, 3544–15

US military contracts, payroll, and personnel, by service branch and location, with top 5 contractors and maps, by State and country, FY88, annual rpt, 3544–29

US military deaths, by service branch and country, 2nd half FY88, semiannual rpt, 3542–21

US military employment of civilians, by country, quarterly rpt, 3542–16

US military personnel abroad, by service branch, outlying area, and country, quarterly rpt, 3542–14.5

US military personnel abroad, by service branch, world area, and country, quarterly news release, 3542–9

US military post exchange operations, and sales by commodity, by facility and location worldwide, FY87, annual rpt, 3504–10

US military presence abroad, by service branch and country, 1989 annual summary rpt, 3504–13

US military prime contract awards for R&D, for top 500 contractors, FY88, annual listing, 3544–4

US military prime contract awards for R&D to US and foreign nonprofit instns and govt agencies, by instn and location, FY88, annual listing, 3544–17

US Navy procurement, by contractor and location, FY88, annual rpt, 3804–13.5

Visas of US issued and refused to immigrants and nonimmigrants, by class, issuing office, and nationality, FY88, annual rpt, 7184–1

Visas of US issued at Foreign Service posts, by category and world area, selected years FY84-88, annual rpt, 7184–4

Warsaw Pact and USSR military strength, and proposed force reductions, with comparisons to NATO, 1980s-91, hearing, 21208–29

Warsaw Pact and USSR military weapons systems, aid, presence, and force strengths, and compared to US and NATO, 1989 annual rpt, 3504–20

Health and Vital Statistics

Abortion-related deaths and hospitalization, for selected countries restricting abortions, 1950s-83, hearing, 21408–113

Cancer Natl Inst contracts and grants, by recipient and location, FY88, annual listing, 4474–28

Child death rates, by age, sex, race, and cause, for US and compared to 8 OECD countries, 1985 and trends from 1900, 4147–3.27

Child Health and Human Dev Natl Inst contracts and grants, by recipient and location, FY88, annual listing, 4474–36

Diving (underwater sport and occupational) deaths, by circumstances, diver characteristics, and location, 1970-87, annual rpt, 2144–5

Health condition and health care resources, use, and spending, 1950s-87, annual data compilation, 4144–11

Health, welfare, and research aid from HHS, by program, recipient, and country, FY88, annual listing, 4004–3.10

Heart, Lung, and Blood Natl Inst activities, and grants by recipient and location, FY88 with disease trends from 1940, annual rpt, 4474–15

Hereditary disease mass screening, and access to results by employer, insurer, and others, foreign and US geneticists views, 1987 survey, article, 4042–3.902

Infant death rates, for 21 countries, 1985, 15838–1.1

Infant deaths and prevention issues, for OECD, 1985 conf papers, 4148–28

Kidney end-stage disease cases, new patients by country, 1980-85, annual rpt, 4654–16.1

Malaria cases in US, for military personnel and US and foreign civilians, and by country of infection, 1966-87, annual rpt, 4205–4

NIH grants for R&D, training, construction, and medical libraries, by location and recipient, FY88, annual listings, 4434–7

NIH intl program activities and funding, by inst and country, FY88, annual rpt, 4474–6

Nurses with alien resident status and temporary work visas, by State and source country, 1985-90, GAO rpt, 26121–314

Older persons institutionalization in medical and other care facilities, rates by selected country, 1980 and 1985, article, 4652–1.918

Statistical Abstract of US, social, political, and economic data, by outlying area and country, 1950s-87, comprehensive annual compilation, 2324–1.4

Tuberculosis cases in the US, by country of origin, 1987, annual rpt, 4204–10

Vaccination needs for intl travel by country, and disease prevention recommendations, 1989 annual rpt, 4204–11

Housing and Construction

AID housing and urban dev program financial statements, and loan guarantees by country, FY88, annual rpt, 9914–4

Canada construction products market trends and indicators, with imports by country, 1960s-86, article, 2042–1.905

Construction contracts awarded US firms, and share of construction market by country of contractor, by world area, 1982-87, annual article, 2042–1.902

Industry and Commerce

Aluminum plant ownership, capacity, energy and aluminum sources, and startup and closing dates, by US and foreign plant and location, 1988, annual listing, 5604–49

Auto industry finances and operations, trade by country, and prices of selected US and foreign models, monthly rpt, 9882–8

Auto trade of Canada and US, by country, 1983-85, annual rpt, 2044–35

Business America, foreign and domestic commerce, and US investment and trade opportunities, biweekly journal, 2042–24

Caribbean area duty-free exports to US, and imports from US, by country, and impact on US employment, by commodity, 1988, annual rpt, 6364–2

Caribbean area duty-free exports to US, and US exports and import duties on other goods, by commodity and country, 1984-88, annual rpt, 9884–20

Caribbean Basin exports to OECD members, and US imports under preferential treatment programs, by commodity, 1980s-87, 2048–138

Caribbean Basin Initiative investment incentives, economic impacts, with finances and employment by country, 1984-88, 2048–141

China trade, by commodity, world area, and country, 1985-87, 9118–10

China trade with US by commodity, and foreign investment by source country, 1988, 9118–9

Clothing price changes, spending, imports by fiber and country, and cotton share of textiles markets, mid 1970s-88, article, 1702–1.902

Communist countries trade with US, by detailed commodity and country, quarterly rpt with articles, 9882–2

Communist, OECD, and selected other countries economic conditions, 1960s-88, annual rpt, 9114–4

Competitiveness (intl) of US industries, with selected foreign and US operating data by major firm and product, series, 2046–12

Cuba economic conditions, agricultural and industrial production and distribution, trade, and intl economic relations, 1980-87 with trends from 1961, 9118–8

Cuba trade with multinatl US firms foreign affiliates, by country, FY82-87, press release, 8008–137

Current account balance of US, components and relation to foreign and US investment and economic conditions, 1970s-88 and projected to 1990s, 9385–1.906

Developing countries economic indicators, problem debtors compared to other borrowers, by country, 1973-84, 1528–285

EC economic integration impacts on domestic economic conditions and US trade, with trade by commodity and country, 1984-87, 9886–4.140

EC trade with US by country, and total agricultural trade, selected years 1958-88, annual rpt, 7144–7

Economic and monetary trends, compounded annual rates of change for US and 10 major trading partners, quarterly rpt, 9391–7

Economic and social conditions of foreign countries, working paper series, 2326–18

Economic conditions, and trade devs and balances, with data by selected country and country group, monthly rpt, 9882–14

Economic conditions and trade devs and policy, for US and foreign countries, 1988 conf papers, 9373–3.32

R&D funding and science and technology employment for selected countries, selected years 1961-87, annual rpt, 9624-18.2

R&D funding, and scientists and engineers education and employment, for US and selected foreign countries, 1988, annual rpt, 9624-23

R&D funding by Fed Govt, by field, performer type, agency, and State, FY87-89, annual rpt, 9627-20

Space satellites and other objects launched since 1957, quarterly listing, 9502-2

BY OUTLYING AREA

Agriculture and Food

Agricultural Stabilization and Conservation Service producer payments, by program and State, 1988, annual rpt, 1804-12

Agricultural Statistics, 1988, annual rpt, 1004-1

Animal protection, licensing, and inspection activities of USDA, and animals used in research, by State, FY88, annual rpt, 1394-10

Cattle tuberculosis cases and cooperative Federal-State eradication activities, by State, FY88, annual rpt, 1394-13

Census of Agriculture, 1987: farms, farmland, production and costs, and operator characteristics, advance State and county rpt series, 2330-1

Census of Agriculture, 1987: farms, farmland, production, finances, and operator characteristics, by county, final State rpt series, 2331-1

Conservation program of USDA, participation and payments by practice and State, FY85, monthly table, 1802-15

Fish (processed) production by location, and trade, by species and product, 1987-88, annual rpts, 2166-6

Fishery employment, vessels, plants, and cooperatives, by State, 1988 and trends from 1970, annual rpt, 2164-1.10

Fishery mgmt and R&D, Fed Govt grants by project and State, and rpts, 1987, annual listing, 2164-3

FmHA borrowers, by type of borrower and loan, and State, quarterly rpt, 1182-4

FmHA guaranteed loans from private lenders outstanding, delinquencies, and losses, by State, FY83-88, GAO rpt, 26113-433

FmHA loans and borrower supervision activities in farm and housing programs, by type and State, monthly rpt, 1182-1

FmHA loans, by type, borrower characteristics, and State, quarterly rpt, 1182-8

FmHA loans, by type, borrower race, and State, quarterly rpt, 1182-5

FmHA property acquired through foreclosure, acreage, value, and sales, for farm and nonfarm property by State, monthly rpt, 1182-6

Meat and poultry inspection activities and staff of Federal, State, and foreign govts, FY88, annual rpt, 1374-1

Research (agricultural) funding and staffing for USDA, State agencies, and other instns, by topic, FY88, annual rpt, 1744-2

Rice shipments, by end use, package size, and State of origin and destination, mid 1950s-87, biennial rpt, 1564-11

Statistical Abstract of US, social, political, and economic data, by outlying area and country, 1950s-87, comprehensive annual compilation, 2324-1.4

Tobacco production, prices, stocks, taxes by State, and trade and production by country, 1988, annual rpt, 1319-1

Banking, Finance, and Insurance

Banks (commercial and savings) FDIC-insured, deposits by instn, State, MSA, and county, as of June 1988, annual regional rpt series, 9295-3

Banks (insured commercial) assets, income, and financial ratios, by asset size and State, quarterly rpt, 13002-3

Banks (insured commercial and savings) finances, and changes in status, by State, 1987, annual rpt, 9294-4.1

Credit unions federally insured, finances by instn characteristics and State, as of June 1989, semiannual rpt, 9532-6

Credit unions federally insured, finances, 1987-88, annual rpt, 9534-1

Savings and loan assns assets and liabilities, by FHLB district and State, 1987 and trends from 1930, annual rpt, 9314-1

Savings instns finances and operations by district and State, mortgage lending activity and terms by MSA, and FHLB finances, 1987 with trends from 1900, annual rpt, 9314-3.2

Savings instns financial statements, FSLIC-insured instns by FHLB district and State, and FDIC-insured savings banks, 1988, annual rpt, 8434-1

Savings instns FSLIC-insured, offices, and deposits, by FHLB district, State, SMSA, and county, 1988, annual rpt, 9314-4

Savings instns insured by Savings Assn Insurance Fund, finances by district, quarterly rpt, 8432-4

Communications and Transportation

Air traffic (passenger), and aircraft operations by type, by airport and State, projected FY89-2005 and trends from FY83, annual rpt, 7504-7

Air traffic levels at FAA-operated control facilities, by airport and State, FY88, annual rpt, 7504-27

Aircraft registered with FAA, by type and characteristics of aircraft, make, carrier, State, and county, 1988, annual rpt, 7504-3

Airport improvement program of FAA, grants and activities by State and airport, FY88, annual rpt, 7504-38

Airport planning and dev project grants of FAA, by airport and location, quarterly press release, 7502-14

DOT planning and safety grants, by program, State, and for 38 SMSAs, FY88, annual rpt, 7304-7

Hwy Statistics, detailed data by outlying area, 1988, annual rpt, 7554-1.5

Hwy Statistics, detailed data by State, 1988, annual rpt, 7554-1

Hwy Trust Fund status and net revenues, FY57-88, annual rpt, 7554-24

Rural areas electric and telephone loans by State, and REA activities and finances, FY88 with trends from FY36, annual rpt, 1244-3

Shipborne trade of US, by type of service, commodity, country, route, and US port, 1986-87, annual rpt, 7704-2

Telephone firms borrowing under Rural Telephone Program, and financial and operating data, by State, 1988, annual rpt, 1244-2.3

Telephone firms borrowing under Rural Telephone Program, loan activity by State, FY88, annual tables, 1244-8

Telephones in residences and businesses, carriage equipment miles, and calls placed, by State, 1987, annual rpt, 9284-6.2

Urban Mass Transportation Admin grants for transit systems, by city and State, FY88, annual rpt, 7884-10

Waterborne commerce (domestic) of US, freight by major commodity group, vessel type, and port, 1986, annual rpt, 7704-7

Education

American Historical Assn financial statements, and membership by State, 1988, annual rpt, 29574-2

Digest of Education Statistics, detailed data on students, staff, finances, and facilities, 1989 edition, annual rpt, 4824-2

Elementary and secondary public education agency revenues by source, and outlays, by State, FY86-87, annual rpt, 4834-6

Elementary and secondary public school agencies, by enrollment size and location, fall 1987, annual listing, 4834-1

Elementary and secondary public schools, enrollment, and teachers, by level and State, 1987/88, annual rpt, 4834-17

Head Start enrollment, funding, and staff, FY88, annual rpt, 4604-2

Head Start handicapped enrollment, by handicap, State, and for Indian and migrant programs, 1985/86, annual rpt, 4604-1

Libraries for blind and handicapped, readership, circulation, staff, funding, and holdings, FY88, annual listing, 26404-3

School agencies (public elementary and secondary), by type and State, 1987/88, annual rpt, 4834-18

Special education programs, enrollment by age, staff, funding, and needs, by type of handicap and State, 1987/88, annual rpt, 4944-4

Statistical Abstract of US, social, political, and economic data, by outlying area and country, 1950s-87, comprehensive annual compilation, 2324-1.4

Student aid funding and participation, by Federal program, instn type and control, and State, various periods 1959-88, annual rpt, 4804-28

Student aid supplemental grants, loans, and work-study awards, Federal share by instn and State, 1989/90, annual listing, 4804-17

Student guaranteed loan default rates, and claims paid by guaranty agencies, by State, and borrower characteristics, FY87, GAO rpt, 26121-292

Student guaranteed loan defaults, rates, and borrowers in repayment status, by instn and State, FY86, with background data, 1980s, hearings, 25548-96

Student loans of Fed Govt in default, losses, and rates, by instn and State, as of June 1988, annual rpt, 4804-18

Energy Resources and Demand

Conservation aid of DOE, activities, funding, and grants by State, by program, FY88 annual rpt, 3304-21

Conservation grants of Fed Govt to public and nonprofit private instns, by building type and State, 1988, annual rpt, 3304–15

Consumption of energy, by air pollutant source, fuel type, and State, 1986, annual rpt, 9194–14

Oil crude, gas liquids, and refined products supply, demand, and movement, by PAD district and State, 1988 and trends from 1973, annual rpt, 3164–2

Rural areas electric and telephone loans by State, and REA activities and finances, FY88 with trends from FY36, annual rpt, 1244–3

Rural Electrification Program lending, by State, as of FY88, annual rpt, 1244–7

Geography and Climate

Charting and Geodetic Service of Natl Ocean Service activities and funding, by State, FY89-90, biennial rpt, 2174–10

Statistical Abstract of US, social, political, and economic data, by outlying area and country, 1950s-87, comprehensive annual compilation, 2324–1.1

Storms and unusual weather phenomena characteristics, casualties, and property damage, by State, monthly listing, 2152–3

Tsunamis intensity, time, location, and other characteristics, for US and territories, 1690-1988, 2158–52

Government and Defense

Congressional Directory, members of 101st Congress, other officials, elections, and districts, 1989-90, biennial rpt, 23874–1

DOD budget requests for base construction, renovation, and land acquisition, by project, service branch, State, and country, FY90/91, annual rpt, 3544–15

DOD civilian and military personnel and dependents, by service branch and location, FY88, annual rpt, 3544–1

DOD civilian and military personnel and dependents, by service branch and US and foreign location, quarterly rpt, 3542–20

DOD contracts, payroll, and personnel, by service branch and location, with top 5 contractors and maps, by State and country, FY88, annual rpt, 3544–29

DOD in-house commercial activities work-years, by service branch, State, and installation, FY88, annual rpt, 3544–25

DOD military personnel abroad, by service branch, outlying area, and country, quarterly rpt, 3542–14.5

DOD military personnel abroad, by service branch, world area, and country, quarterly news release, 3542–9

DOT employment, by subagency, occupation, and selected personnel characteristics, FY88, annual rpt, 7304–18

Economic Dev Admin activities, and funding by program, recipient, State, and county, FY87 and cumulative from FY66, annual rpt, 2064–2

Economic Dev Admin funding, and loans forgiven, with data by project and location, FY84-88, hearing, 21648–56

Fed Govt spending in States and local areas, by type, State, county, and city, FY88, annual rpt, 2464–3

Fed Govt spending in States, by type, program, agency, and State, FY88, annual rpt, 2464–2

Local govt receipts from Fed Govt in lieu of property taxes on public lands, by State and county, FY89, annual rpt, 5724–9

Local govt receipts from Fed Govt in lieu of property taxes on public lands, by State, FY89, annual press release, 5306–4.2

Military deaths, by service branch and home State, 2nd half FY88, semiannual rpt, 3542–21

Military draft registrants by State, 2nd half FY88, semiannual rpt, 9742–1

Military reserve forces manpower strengths and characteristics, by component, quarterly rpt, 3542–4

Navy procurement, by contractor and location, FY88, annual rpt, 3804–13.5

Property (real) of Fed Govt, inventory and costs, worldwide summary by location, agency, and use, 1987, annual rpt, 9454–5

Savings bonds sold and sales quotas for Series EE, by State, monthly table, 8442–2

Statistical Abstract of US, social, political, and economic data, by outlying area and country, 1950s-87, comprehensive annual compilation, 2324–1.2; 2324–1.4

Votes cast by party, candidate, and State, 1988 natl elections, biennial rpt, 9274–5; 21944–3

Health and Vital Statistics

Abortions, by place of woman's residence and selected State of occurrence, 1986, US Vital Statistics annual rpt, 4146–5.108

AIDS cases by risk group, race, sex, age, State, and MSA, and deaths, monthly rpt, 4202–9

Deaths and rates, by detailed location, cause, and demographic characteristics, 1987, US Vital Statistics annual rpt, 4144–3.2

Deaths in US, by State of occurrence and birthplace abroad, 1986, US Vital Statistics annual rpt, 4144–2.1

Disabled persons rehabilitation, Federal and State activities and funding, FY88, annual rpt, 4944–1

Diving (underwater sport and occupational) deaths, by circumstances, diver characteristics, and location, 1970-87, annual rpt, 2144–5

Drug abuse and trafficking reduction aid to States, and grant processing time, FY87-88, GAO rpt, 26119–258

Health Professions Bur training and research grants and contracts, by instn and program, FY88, annual listing, 4114–1

Health Professions Bur training support grants, by program, region, and State, FY80-87, 4118–62

Hepatitis cases by infection source, age, sex, race, and State, and deaths, by strain, 1987 and trends from 1966, 4205–2

HHS financial aid, by program, recipient, State, and city, FY88, annual regional listing, 4004–3.2; 4004–3.9

Infectious notifiable disease cases, by age, State, and outlying area, and deaths, 1930s-88, annual rpt, 4204–1

Infectious notifiable diseases, cases and current outbreaks, by region and State, weekly rpt, 4202–1

Kidney end-stage disease program of Medicare, enrollment, eligibility, inpatient and home treatment, and facilities, by State, 1985, annual rpt, 4654–16.1; 4654–16.2

Minerals industries injuries by circumstances, employment, and hours, by type of operation and State, quarterly rpt, 6662–1

NIH activities, funding by program and recipient type, staff, and clinic patients, by inst, FY87, annual rpt, 4434–3

NIH grants for R&D, training, construction, and medical libraries, by location and recipient, FY88, annual listings, 4434–7

Statistical Abstract of US, social, political, and economic data, by outlying area and country, 1950s-87, comprehensive annual compilation, 2324–1.4

Tuberculosis cases and deaths, by patient characteristics, State, and city, 1987 and trends from 1953, annual rpt, 4204–10

Workers compensation benefits and benefit duration, by State, 1988, article, 4742–1.921

Workers compensation laws of States and Fed Govt, 1989 semiannual rpt, 6502–1

Housing and Construction

FmHA property acquired through foreclosure, 1-family homes, value, sales, and leases, by State, monthly rpt, 1182–7

Mortgage originations, by State, 1978-88, annual press release, 5144–21

New housing units authorized, by State, MSA, and permit-issuing place, 1988, annual rpt, 2384–2

Industry and Commerce

Exports and imports between US and outlying areas, by detailed commodity and mode of transport, monthly rpt, 2422–4

Mineral Industry Surveys, commodity reviews of production, trade, stocks, and use, monthly rpt series, 5612–1

Mineral Industry Surveys, commodity reviews of production, trade, stocks, and use, quarterly rpt series, 5612–2

Minerals Yearbook, 1987, Vol 1: commodity reviews of production, use, trade, prices, and mining operations, annual rpt, 5604–33

Minerals Yearbook, 1987, Vol 2 preprints: State reviews of production and sales by commodity, and business activity, annual rpt series, 5604–16

Minerals Yearbook, 1987, Vol 2: State reviews of production, sales, and firms, by commodity, and business activity, annual rpt, 5604–34

Minerals Yearbook, 1988, Vol 2 rpts: State reviews of production and sales by commodity, and business activity, annual rpt series, 5604–22

Small Business Admin loans, contract awards, and surety bonds, by firm, State, and city, FY88, annual rpt, 9764–1

Statistical Abstract of US, social, political, and economic data, by outlying area and country, 1950s-87, comprehensive annual compilation, 2324–1.4

Vending facilities run by blind on Federal and non-Federal property, finances and operations by agency and State, FY88, annual rpt, 4944–2

Labor and Employment

Employment and Earnings, detailed data, monthly rpt, 6742–2.5; 6742–2.6

Employment and Training Admin activities, funding, and participant characteristics, by program, FY80-86, 6408–71

Employment and unemployment, by age, sex, race, marital and family status, industry div, and State, Monthly Labor Review, 6722–1.2

Recreation and Leisure

Boat registrations, and accidents, casualties, and damage by cause, by vessel characteristics and State, 1988, annual rpt, 7404-1

Fishing (ocean sport) catch and effort, and Natl Marine Fisheries Service tagging and research activity, by species and location, 1987, annual rpt, 2164-7

Historic and natural natl landmarks damaged and threatened, with owner, location, damage type, and recommended remedial action, 1988, annual listing, 5544-16

Historic Preservation Fund grants, by State, FY90, annual table, 5544-9

Lighthouses historic preservation grants, by State, FY89, press release, 5306-4.1

Park natl system visits and overnight stays, by park and State, 1988 and trends from 1979, annual rpt, 5544-12

Science and Technology

Patents (US) granted to US and foreign applicants, by State and country, 1987-88, annual press release, 2244-2

Patents granted to US residents, by State, FY81-88, annual rpt, 2244-1.2

R&D and related funding of Fed Govt to higher education and nonprofit instns, by field, instn, agency, and State, FY87, annual rpt, 9627-17

BY REGION

Agriculture and Food

Agricultural Statistics, 1988, annual rpt, 1004-1.2

Alien workers (unauthorized) employer sanctions impacts on farm labor costs, by farm type, size, and region, 1986, 1598-250

Animal feed mill operations, detailed data by State, 1984, 1568-281

Banks (agricultural) financial performance, impacts of drought by region, 1988, article, 1502-7.916

Conservation program of USDA, funding by region and State, monthly table, 1802-15

Cooperatives commercial member characteristics, and use of services, by region, 1980 and 1986, 1128-53

Cooperatives loans, assets, net worth, and assns, for FCS by district, 1987, annual rpt, 1124-1

Cooperatives member characteristics, and use of services, by region, 1980 and 1986, 1128-54

Cotton acreage related to prices and acreage reduction programs, by region, 1989 article, 1561-1.903

Cotton fiber and processing test results, by staple, region, State, and production area, seasonal biweekly rpt, 1309-3

Cotton fiber and processing test results, by State, 1988, annual rpt, 1309-4

Cotton, wool, and synthetic fiber production, prices, trade, and use, periodic situation rpt with articles, 1561-1

Cottonseed prices and quality, by State, seasonal weekly rpt, 1309-14

Dairy farm financial statement and balance sheet, by size and region, 1985-88, article, 1561-2.902

Drought of 1988, impacts on farm, rural areas, and food industry financial conditions, with trends from 1970, 1588-133

Economic Indicators of the Farm Sector, itemized production costs, receipts, and returns, by commodity and region, 1985-87, annual rpt, 1544-20

Economic Indicators of the Farm Sector, production inputs, output, and productivity, by commodity and region, 1947-87, annual rpt, 1544-17

Egg production and layer inventory, by State, revised estimates 1984-87, 1641-2

Egg production and layer inventory, by State, 1987-88, annual rpt, 1625-7

Egg production by type of product, and eggs broken under Federal inspection by region, monthly rpt, 1625-2

Emergency Conservation Program for farmland damaged by natural disaster, funding by region and State, monthly table, 1802-13

Employment, earnings, and days worked, for farm workers by selected characteristics and region, 1987, biennial rpt, 1594-2

Employment on farms, wages, hours, and perquisites, by State, quarterly rpt, 1631-1

Erodible cropland acreage enrolled in conservation program by crop and State, and program costs, FY87-88, 1588-112

Erosion control program acreage, costs of off-farm erosion damage, and sediment and other pollutants runoff, by region, 1988, 1588-134

Farm Credit System financial statements and loan activity by lender type and district, and borrower characteristics, 1988, annual rpt, 9264-2

Farm Credit System income, nonperforming loans, and property acquired, by district, 1988, annual GAO rpt, 26104-16

Farms, sales, size, and operator tenure in metro and nonmetro areas, impacts of population growth, with data by State, 1969-82, 1598-253

Fertilizer use and costs by type, and farm income and expenses, by State, 1988 and trends from 1965, biennial rpt, 9804-5

Finances and operations of farms, by size, commodity, and region, 1986, annual rpt, 1544-27

Finances of farms, debts, assets, and receipts, and lenders financial condition, quarterly rpt with articles, 1541-1

Financial condition of farms, and farm household income by source, 1970-88, annual rpt, 1504-4

Financial ratios of farms, benchmarks by type of operation and region, 1984-86, 1548-342

Financial ratios of farms, model description and results, 1986, 1548-341

Fish (processed) production by location, and trade, by species and product, 1987-88, annual rpts, 2166-6

Fish and shellfish catch, wholesale receipts, prices, trade, and other market activities, weekly regional rpts, 2162-6

Fish catch, trade, use, and fishery operations, with selected foreign data, by species, 1970s-88, annual rpt, 2164-1

Fish Hatchery Natl System activities and deliveries, by species, hatchery, and jurisdiction of waters stocked, FY88, annual rpt, 5504-10

Food consumption and nutrient intake by individuals, by food group, selected characteristics, and region, supplementary survey series, 1356-5

Fruit and vegetable shipments, and arrivals in US and Canada cities, by mode of transport and State and country of origin, 1988, annual rpt series, 1311-4

Grain exports by port area of origin, weekly rpt, 1272-2

Grain inspected for export, test results by commodity and port region, 1988, annual rpt, 1294-2

Grain production, prices, trade, and export inspections by US port and country of destination, by grain type, weekly rpt, 1313-2

Grain stocks by region and market city, and grain inspected for export, by type, weekly rpt, 1313-4

Grazing land acreage, erosion, value, and livestock fed, by region and State, 1950-82, 1588-130

Honey production, prices, trade, stocks, marketing, and CCC honey loan and distribution activities, monthly rpt, 1311-2

Irrigation projects of Reclamation Bur in western US, crop production and acreage by commodity, State, and project, 1987, annual rpt, 5824-12.1

Livestock grazing on natl forest land, acreage, use, fees, and rancher costs and returns, by region under alternative fee levels, 1980s-86, 1588-145

Livestock grazing on natl forest lands, by region and State, FY88, annual rpt, 1204-5

Livestock, meat, and poultry production, consumption, and industry finances and operations, 1950s-86, 1568-280

Livestock packers purchases and feeding, and livestock markets, dealers, and sales, by State, 1987, annual rpt, 1384-1

Livestock slaughter and meat products prepared under Federal inspection, by type, monthly 1970-87, 1568-285.2

Livestock slaughter, meat production, and slaughter plants, by species and State, 1988, annual rpt, 1623-10

Livestock slaughter under Fed Govt inspection, by livestock type and region, monthly rpt, 1623-9

Milk home delivery, and sales by wholesale outlet type, by region, 1987 survey, article, 1317-4.901

Milk itemized production costs, by region 1985-87, article, 1561-2.901

Milk itemized production costs, by region, 1985-89, article, 1561-2.903

Milk order market policy alternatives impact on producer costs and income, prices, and supply, by region, 1985, 1568-274

Milk order market prices and detailed operations, by State and market area, 1987-88, annual rpt, 1317-3

Milk order market prices and detailed operations, monthly rpt with articles, 1317-4

Milk order market producer deliveries, by State and county, 1986-87, periodic rpt, 1317-5

Milk order market sales, by container size and type, outlet type, and market area, 1987, biennial rpt, 1317-6

Molasses (feed) production, wholesale prices by market area, and US imports and country, weekly rpt, 1311-16

Molasses supply, use, wholesale prices by market, and trade and production by country, 1983-88, annual rpt, 1311-19

Mushroom production, sales, and prices, by State, 1966/67-1988/89 and planned 1989/90, annual rpt, 1631–9

Oils, oilseeds, and fats production, prices, trade, and use, periodic situation rpt with articles, 1561–3

Peanut production and trade by country, prices, and stocks, weekly rpt, 1311–1

Pesticide (soil fumigant) use, impacts of bans of selected fumigants on production, farm income, and retail prices, by crop and region, 1988 rpt, 1588–136

Population of farm operators and farming-dependent households, by selected characteristics, under alternative definitions, 1987, 1598–252

Population on farms, by employment and socioeconomic characteristics, and region, 1988, annual Current Population Rpt, 2546–1.439

Population on farms under alternative definitions, by selected characteristics, 1983, 1598–249

Potato chip plants and potatoes processed, by region, 1986-88, annual rpt, 1621–11

Poultry (broiler) production, slaughter, prices, and processing industry operations, 1950s-87, 1568–279

Poultry (chicken and turkey) hatchery production, 1987-88, annual rpt, 1625–8

Poultry (chicken, egg, and turkey) production and inventories, monthly rpt, 1625–1

Poultry Natl Improvement Plan coverage of hatcheries and birds, by species, disease program, and State, 1988, annual rpt, 1394–15

Price support activity and policy options, with data on production, trade, use, and finances, and foreign comparisons, 1950s-89, commodity rpt series, 1566–7

Prices received and paid by farmers, by commodity and State, 1988, annual rpt, 1629–5

Prices received by farmers for major products, and paid for farm inputs and living items, by State, monthly rpt, 1629–1

Production inputs, finances, mgmt, and land value and transfers, periodic situation rpt with articles, 1561–16

Production itemized costs, by farm sales size and region, 1988, annual rpt, 1614–3

Production itemized costs, receipts, and returns, by selected commodity and region, 1975-87, 1548–345

Production, receipts, and demand ratios, by commodity group and region, 1949-83, 1548–348

Rail shipments of grain, by commodity and port region, and car fleet requirements, 1949-88 with projections to 2001, 1278–14

Research (agricultural) funding and staffing for USDA, State agencies, and other instns, by topic, FY88, annual rpt, 1744–2

Soil and water conservation funding by USDA, by program and State, FY86, annual rpt, 1264–12

Soil conservation and other land improvement capital investment, impacts of govt programs and economic factors, 1983-86, 1588–137

Soil salinity impacts on yields and off-farm water quality, and costs and benefits of extending erosion control program to saline cropland, 1989 rpt, 1588–144

Soybean production itemized costs, by region, for US, Argentina, and Brazil, 1986-88, article, 1522–3.902

Statistical Abstract of US, social, political, and economic data, 1790-2025, comprehensive annual compilation, 2324–1.3

Sugar and sweeteners production, prices, trade, supply, and use, quarterly situation rpt with articles, 1561–14

Turkey hatcheries egg inventory and poult placements, by region, monthly rpt, 1625–10

Turkeys raised by State, and losses by region, 1987-88, and hatchery plans, 1989, annual rpt, 1625–6

Urban areas farms, acreage, finances, and operators, under alternative MSA definitions, 1960s-82, 1598–256

Vegetables (fresh and processed) consumption by type, and spending by consumer characteristics, 1960s-87, article, 1561–11.903

Vegetables for processing, production and value, by selected commodity and State, 1970s-85, 1568–275

Vegetables production, prices, trade, stocks, and use, for selected fresh and processing crops, periodic situation rpt with articles, 1561–11

Wage surveys to set minimum wage for US and alien farm workers, evaluation with data by location, 1980s-87, GAO rpt, 26131–50

Banking, Finance, and Insurance

Banks (commercial) specializing in real estate loans, financial condition, 1989 technical paper, 9366–6.202

Banks (commercial and savings) FDIC-insured, deposits by instn, State, MSA, and county, as of June 1988, annual regional rpt series, 9295–3

Banks (insured commercial) financial condition and performance, by asset size and region, quarterly rpt, 9292–1

Banks balance sheets, by Fed Reserve District, for major banks in NYC, and for US branches and agencies of foreign banks, weekly rpt, 9365–1.3

Banks brokered deposit holdings and financial indicators, by size, region, and for failed instns, 1986-89, hearing, 21248–124

Banks failures by bank type, asset size, region, and State, 1984-88, article, 9391–16.901

Banks failures, by type of charter and mgmt weakness, audit activity, asset size, age, and State, 1984-88, GAO rpt, 26111–61

Banks finances and operations, by metro-nonmetro location, 1986, annual rpt, 1544–29

Banks status changes, instns, assets, and concentration ratios by size, ownership, and location, and compared to other financial instns, 1976-87, article, 9362–1.902

Check collection systems of Fed Reserve and private services, competition issues, finances, and operations, 1984-87, GAO rpt, 26119–255

Credit unions federally insured, finances by instn characteristics and State, as of June 1989, semiannual rpt, 9532–6

Fed Home Loan Banks, FHLBB, FSLIC, and Financing Corp financial statements, 1988, annual rpt, 8434–2

Fed Home Loan Banks financial statements, monthly tables, 9442–1

Fed Home Loan Mortgage Corp activities and financial statements, 1988, annual rpt, 9414–1

Fed Reserve banks expenses and operations, itemized by service, office, and district, 1988, annual rpt, 9364–11

Fed Reserve banks finances and staff, 1988, annual rpt, 9364–1.1

Fed Reserve banks financial statements and performance, by district, 1988-89, annual rpt, 9364–10.6

Fed Reserve services provided depository instns, costs and revenue by service and district bank, 1987-88, article, 9362–1.908

Fraud and insider misconduct at financial instns, cases, Federal regulatory and enforcement activities, and losses, 1981-87, hearing, 21408–111

Savings and loan assns assets and liabilities, by FHLB district and State, 1987 and trends from 1930, annual rpt, 9314–1

Savings instns failures by State, with exam of mgmt weaknesses and regulatory activity, 1980s-87, GAO rpt, 26111–62

Savings instns finances and operations by district and State, mortgage lending activity and terms by MSA, and FHLB finances, 1987 with trends from 1900, annual rpt, 9314–3.2

Savings instns financial statements, FSLIC-insured instns by FHLB district and State, and FDIC-insured savings banks, 1988, annual rpt, 8434–1

Savings instns FSLIC-insured, offices, and deposits, by FHLB district, State, SMSA, and county, 1988, annual rpt, 9314–4

Savings instns insured by Savings Assn Insurance Fund, finances by district, quarterly rpt, 8432–4

Savings instns regulatory issues, mgmt, and FHLB system and member finances and operations, monthly journal, 8432–2; 9312–1

Small Business Investment Companies finances, funding, licensing, and loan activity, 1st half FY89, semiannual rpt, 9762–3

Statistical Abstract of US, social, political, and economic data, 1790-2025, comprehensive annual compilation, 2324–1.3

Treasury bill offerings, auction results by Fed Reserve District, and terms, periodic press release series, 8002–7

Communications and Transportation

Air traffic (passenger), and aircraft operations by type, by airport and State, projected FY89-2005 and trends from FY83, annual rpt, 7504–7

Air traffic control and airway facilities staff, by selected employment and demographic characteristics, FY88, annual rpt, 7504–41

Air traffic levels at FAA-operated control facilities, by airport and State, FY88, annual rpt, 7504–27

Air traffic, pilots, airports, and fuel use, forecast FY89-2000 and trends from FY80, annual rpt, 7504–6

Aircraft (general aviation), flight hours, and equipment, by type, use, and model of aircraft, region, and State, 1988, annual rpt, 7504–29

Aircraft handled by instrument flight rule, by user type, FAA traffic control center, and region, FY80-88 and projected to FY2000, annual rpt, 7504–15

Aircraft pilots and nonpilots certified by FAA, by certificate type, age, sex, region, and State, 1988, annual rpt, 7504–2

Aircraft registered with FAA, by type and characteristics of aircraft, make, carrier, State, and county, 1988, annual rpt, 7504–3

DOT planning and safety grants, by program, State, and for 38 SMSAs, FY88, annual rpt, 7304–7

FAA activities and finances, and staff by region, FY87-88, annual rpt, 7504–10

Hwy construction material prices and indexes for Federal-aid system, by type of material and urban-rural location, quarterly rpt, 7552–7

Hwy traffic and pavement condition, by type of hwy and State, 1983-87, biennial rpt, 7554–27.3

Hwy traffic volume on rural roads and city streets, monthly rpt, 7552–8

Motorcycle operating costs by component, for 4 makes, and Fed Govt mileage reimbursement rates, 1987, annual rpt, 9454–13

Postal Service employee disciplinary actions, by type of infraction and penalty, and region, 1985-88, GAO rpt, 26119–256

Railroad (Class I) finances and operations, detailed data by firm, class of service, and district, 1987, annual rpt, 9486–6.1

Railroad (Class I) finances and operations, detailed data by firm, class of service, and district, 1988, annual rpt, 9486–5.1

Railroad freight volume and revenue, by commodity and region of origin and destination, 1987, annual rpt, 7604–6

Railroad revenue, income, freight, and rate of return, by Class I freight railroad and district, quarterly rpt, 9482–2

Rural areas public transit services, operations and govt funding by region and State, 1986-87, 1278–11

Shipborne commerce (domestic and foreign) of US, freight by commodity, traffic, and passengers, by port and waterway, 1987, annual rpt, 3754–3

Shipborne trade of US, by type of service, commodity, country, route, and US port, 1986-87, annual rpt, 7704–2

Shipbuilding and repair facilities, capacity, and employment, by shipyard, 1988, annual rpt, 7704–9

Shipbuilding costs, deliveries, contracts, employment, and wage rates, by coastal district and shipyard, 1988, annual rpt, 7704–12

Telephone local service charges and low-income subsidies, by region, company, and city, 1940-June 1989, semiannual rpt, 9282–8

Traffic deaths by region, and death rates for miles traveled, monthly rpt, 7762–7

Travel from US, characteristics of visit and traveler, and world area of destination, 1988 in-flight survey, annual rpt, 2904–14

Travel to US and Canada, market analysis with detailed trip and traveler characteristics, country rpt series, 2906–2

Travel to US, characteristics of visit and traveler, world area of origin, and US destination, 1988 survey, annual rpt, 2904–12

Truck and bus interstate carriers finances and operations, by district, 1987, annual rpt, 9486–6.3

Truck driver multi-State license prohibition, FHwA enforcement activities by region, 1987-88, GAO rpt, 26113–396

Truck interstate carriers finances and operations, by district, 1987, annual rpt, 9486–6.2

Truck rates for fruit and vegetables, by growing area and market, weekly 1988, annual rpt, 1311–15

Truck transport of property, financial and operating data by region and firm, quarterly rpt, 9482–5

Waterborne commerce (domestic) of US, freight by major commodity group, vessel type, and port, 1986, annual rpt, 7704–7

Waterborne containerized cargo carried over principal trade routes, by flag of vessel, port, and US coastal district, 1984, annual rpt, 7704–8

Waterborne freight rates for grain, by US loading port and country of destination, weekly rpt, 1272–2

Waterborne trade of US, by type of service, customs district, port, and world area, monthly rpt, 2422–7

Education

American Historical Assn financial statements, and membership by State, 1988, annual rpt, 29574–2

Athlete grad rates for NCAA Div I college programs, by region, aggregate 1982-87, GAO rpt, 26121–285

Community organizations partnerships with public schools, participation, activities, and contributions, by school characteristics and location, 1987/88, 4826–1.27

Condition of Education, detailed data on elementary and secondary education, 1920s-88 and projected to 1997, annual rpt, 4824–1.1

Desegregation of schools, indicators of integration plans effectiveness by school district and location, 1960s-85, 11048–189

Early childhood education centers, services, costs, and teacher salaries, FY88, GAO rpt, 26121–297

Education Dept Civil Rights Office, complaints, investigations, funding, and staff, various periods FY81-88, 21348–114

Enrollment, by grade, instn type and control, and student characteristics, 1986 and trends from 1947, annual Current Population Rpt, 2546–1.429; 2546–1.432

High school class of 1972: education, employment, and family characteristics, activities, and attitudes, natl longitudinal study, series, 4836–1

High school dropout rates, and subsequent completion, by student and school characteristics, alternative estimates, 1988, annual rpt, 4834–23

High school students employment, academic and other characteristics, 1984-86, 4898–27

Libraries (depository), and users by selected characteristics, for academic and public instns, 1988 survey, 26208–1

Libraries technological aid, project descriptions and funding, FY88, annual listing, 4874–6

Natl Archives and Records Admin activities, finances, holdings, and staff, FY88, annual rpt, 9514–2

Statistical Abstract of US, social, political, and economic data, 1790-2025, comprehensive annual compilation, 2324–1.1

Teachers in public and private schools, salaries by selected characteristics, 1984/85-1985/86, 4838–37

Teachers incentive programs of public schools, and participation, by instn and teacher characteristics, with effectiveness ratings, 1985, 4838–38

Teachers moonlighting, by selected employment and other characteristics, 1985, 4838–36

Vocational education aid recipients and sources, and characteristics of programs and students, 1970s-89, series, 4806–3

Energy Resources and Demand

Business energy demand indicators, and use by fuel type and region, 1983, 3166–6.33

Coal production and mines by county, prices, productivity, miners, reserves, and stocks, by mining method and State, 1987-88, annual rpt, 3164–25

Coal production and stocks by district, and shipments by district of origin, State of destination, end-use sector, and mode of transport, quarterly rpt, 3162–8

Coal production by region, exports, and use by sector, projected 1988-2000 and trends from 1975, annual rpt, 3164–68

Coal production by State and region, trade, use, and stocks, weekly rpt, 3162–1

Coal reserves, by heat and sulfur content, mining method, and State, 1987, 3168–114

Coal trade and average price, by world region, country, and customs district, quarterly rpt, 3162–37

Distillate fuel production, imports, stocks, and prices, by selected PAD district and northern State, seasonal monthly rpt, 3162–40

Electric power plants and capacity, by fuel used, owner, location, and operating status, 1988 and for units planned 1989-98, annual listing, 3164–36

Electric power plants capacity use, by fuel type and region, projected 1990-2000, 3166–6.33

Electric power plants fuel switching from oil to natural gas, capability by region, 1989 annual rpt, 3164–88

Electric power plants natural gas use, and fuel and electricity prices, with data by region, 1987-88 and alternative projections to 2000, 3166–6.31

Electric power plants production, by North American Electric Reliability Council region, monthly rpt, 3162–35

Electric power plants production, capacity, sales, and fuel stocks, use, and costs, by State, 1984-88, annual rpt, 3164–11

Electric power seasonal peak demand and generating capacity, by region, 1987 and projected 1988-97, annual rpt, 3404–6

Electric power trade of US with Canada, purchase agreements, and grid interconnection capacity, 1960s-88 and projected to 1992, GAO rpt, 26113–228

Energy supply, demand, and prices, by fuel type and end-use sector, with foreign comparisons, 1988 and trends from 1949, annual rpt, 3164–74

Housing energy use, costs, and conservation, and household and housing characteristics, survey rpt series, 3166–7

Manufacturing energy use and prices, 1985 survey, series, 3166–13

Natural gas production, wells drilled, and contract prices, by Natural Gas Policy Act section, producer, State, and field, late 1970s-86, 3168–90

Natural gas undiscovered reserves, alternative estimates by region, 1986, article, 3162–4.902

Natural gas use indicators for housing, and conservation R&D spending of DOE and private sector, hearings, 21368–107

Nuclear power plant capacity, generation, and operating status, by plant and foreign and US location, 1988 and projected to 2020, annual rpt, 3164–57

Offshore oil and gas reserves, and leasing and dev activity, periodic regional rpt series, 5736–3

Offshore oil, gas, and minerals production, revenue, and leasing activity, for Federal OCS lands by ocean area and State, 1950s-87, annual rpt, 5734–3

Oil and gas leasing activity on Federal land, production, revenue, and royalty rates, by whether competitively leased and western State, 1984-88, GAO rpt, 26113–413

Oil and gas supply, demand, and prices, alternative projections 1987-2000, annual rpt, 3164–89

Oil crude, gas liquids, and refined products supply, demand, and movement, by PAD district and State, 1988 and trends from 1973, annual rpt, 3164–2

Oil industry mergers and acquisitions impacts on market concentration, with background data, 1970-84, 9406–1.58

Oil products sales and purchases of refiners, processors, and distributors, by product, end-use sector, PAD district, and State, monthly rpt with articles, 3162–11

Oil products sales, and purchases of refiners, processors, and distributors, by product, end-use sector, PAD district, and State, 1988, annual rpt, 3164–85

Oil, refined products, and gas liquids supply, demand, trade, stocks, and refining, by detailed product, State, and PAD district, monthly rpt with articles, 3162–6

Oil refinery production workers and wages by occupation and sex, and benefits, by region, 1988 survey, 6787–6.243

Rural Electrification Admin loans, and borrower operating and financial data, by distribution firm and State, 1988, annual rpt, 1244–1

Statistical Abstract of US, social, political, and economic data, 1790-2025, comprehensive annual compilation, 2324–1.3

Uranium mining and milling industries finances and operations, with selected foreign comparisons, 1970s-87 and projected to 2000, annual rpt, 3164–82

Uranium reserves and industry operations, by region and State, various periods 1966-88, annual rpt, 3164–65.1

Geography and Climate

Statistical Abstract of US, social, political, and economic data, 1790-2025, comprehensive annual compilation, 2324–1.1

Weather data for farmland, average precipitation and temperature by State, monthly 1950-88, biennial rpt, 1544–28

Weather events and anomalies, precipitation and temperature for US and foreign locations, weekly rpt, 2182–6

Government and Defense

Aliens (illegal) and immigration impact on congressional apportionment, alternative estimates by State, 1950s-80 with projections to 2010, hearing, 21628–70

Budget of US, special analysis of grants-in-aid, by agency, function, and region, FY90, annual rpt, 104–1.8

Counterfeiting and other Secret Service investigations and arrests by type, and dispositions, by field office, FY88 and trends from FY79, annual rpt, 8464–1

Customs collections and entries processed, by district, FY84-88, annual rpt, 8144–1

Customs collections, by custom region, quarterly rpt, annual data, 8142–1

Customs collections, by district and port, FY88, annual rpt, 8104–2.2

Defense Fuel Supply Center procurement, prices, stocks, transport, and other activities and finances, FY88, annual rpt, 3904–8

Employment (civilian) of Fed Govt by occupation, agency, and location, and language and math skill needs, 1966-87 and projected to 2000, 9848–37

Fed Govt personnel action appeals, decisions of Merit Systems Protection Board by agency and region, FY88, annual rpt, 9494–2

Govt finances, tax systems and revenue, and fiscal structure, by level of govt and State, selected years 1929-91, annual rpt, 10044–1

Immigration to US, alien workers, visitors, deportations, and naturalizations, by country, FY88 and trends from 1820, annual rpt, 6264–2

Military post exchange operations, and sales by commodity, by facility and location worldwide, FY87, annual rpt, 3504–10

Statistical Abstract of US, social, political, and economic data, 1790-2025, comprehensive annual compilation, 2324–1.2

Tax (excise) collections of IRS, by source, region, and State, quarterly rpt, annual table, 8302–1

Tax (income) return processing, IRS workload forecasts, compliance, and enforcement, data compilation, 1989 annual rpt, 8304–8

Tax (income) withholding and related documents filed, by type and IRS service center, 1988 and projected 1989-96, annual rpt, 8304–22

Tax collection, enforcement, and litigation activity of IRS, with data by type of tax, region, and State, FY88, annual rpt, 8304–3

Tax returns filed, by type of tax and IRS region and service center, projected 1988-95 and trends from 1977, annual rpt, 8304–9

Taxes, spending, and govt efficiency, public opinion by respondent characteristics, 1989 survey, annual rpt, 10044–2

Voting and registration, by socioeconomic and demographic characteristics, 1988 presidential election, biennial Current Population Rpt, 2546–1.440

Health and Vital Statistics

Acute and chronic health conditions, disability, absenteeism, and health services use, by selected characteristics, 1988, annual rpt, 4147–10.170

AIDS cases in prisons, test results, and prevention and control policies, by location, 1988 survey, annual rpt, 6064–22

AIDS health care, social, and support services research, data collection methods with background data, 1984-88, 4186–9.5

Alcohol use and abuse among minority groups, and related problems, by selected characteristics, 1985 conf papers, 4488–13

Alcohol use, by type of beverage, region, and State, 1977-87, annual rpt, 4486–1.3; 4486–1.6; 4486–1.9

Births, fertility rates, and childless women, by selected characteristics, 1988, annual Current Population Rpt, 2546–1.436

Births of low birthweight, by race of child, and characteristics of mother, prenatal care, and birth, selected years 1975-87, 4147–21.48

Deaths and rates, by region and State, preliminary 1987-88 and trends from 1960, US Vital Statistics annual rpt, 4144–7

Disability Insurance and SSI eligibility determinations for mental impairment, caseload and review activities by impairment type and State, 1984-86, hearing, 21788–176

Disabled persons employment, labor force status, and other characteristics, 1988, Current Population Rpt, 2546–2.147

Disabled persons rehabilitation, Federal and State activities and funding, FY88, annual rpt, 4944–1

Divorces by age of spouses and duration of marriage, and children involved, by State, 1986 with trends from 1940, US Vital Statistics advance annual rpt, 4146–5.109

Drug, alcohol, and cigarette use and attitudes of youth, by substance type and selected characteristics, 1975-88 surveys, annual rpt, 4494–4

Drug, alcohol, and cigarette use, by substance, age, sex, race, and region, 1988 survey, biennial rpt, 4494–5

Health care use and costs, methodology and findings of natl survey, series, 4186–8

Health condition and health care resources, use, and spending, 1950s-87, annual data compilation, 4144–11

Health Professions Bur training and research grants and contracts, by instn and program, FY88, annual listing, 4114–1

Health Professions Bur training support grants, by program, region, and State, FY80-87, 4118–62

Heart transplants performed by hospital, charges, payment sources, nonpaying patients, and waiting periods, 1986-88, GAO rpt, 26121–281

HHS financial aid, by program, recipient, State, and city, FY88, annual regional listings, 4004–3

Hospice services awareness of aged, by age, sex, education, region, SMSA/non-SMSA residence, and cancer history, 1984 survey, article, 4042–3.915

Hospital discharges and length of stay, by diagnosis, patient age and sex, surgical procedure performed, and region, 1965-86, 4147–13.101

Hospital discharges and length of stay, by diagnosis, patient and instn characteristics, procedure performed, and payment source, 1987, annual rpt, 4147-13.99

Hospital discharges by detailed diagnostic and procedure category, primary diagnosis, and length of stay, by age, sex, and region, 1987, annual rpt, 4147-13.100

Indian Health Service and contract facilities hospitalization, by diagnosis, age, sex, and service area, FY87, annual rpt, 4104-16

Indian Health Service and contract facilities hospitalization, by diagnosis, age, sex, and service area, FY88, annual rpt, 4084-5

Indian Health Service hospital admissions, length of stay, beds, births, and outpatient visits, by facility and IHS service area, FY70-88, annual rpt, 4084-4

Indian Health Service hospital capacity, use, births, and outpatient visits, by area and facility, quarterly rpt, 4082-1

Indian Health Service outpatient visits, by type of provider, selected hospital, and IHS service area, FY87-88, annual rpt, 4084-3

Infectious notifiable disease cases, by age, State, and outlying area, and deaths, 1930s-88, annual rpt, 4204-1

Infectious notifiable diseases, cases and current outbreaks, by region and State, weekly rpt, 4202-1

Insurance (health) coverage of adolescents by selected characteristics, and impacts of mandated employer and expanded Medicaid coverage, 1979-87, 26358-205

Insurance (health) provided by employer, coverage, employer and employee contributions, and plan operations, by carrier type, 1987, article, 4652-1.934

Kidney end-stage disease treatment facilities approved by Medicare, dialysis and transplant services and ownership, 1989 annual listing, 4654-17

Kidney end-stage disease treatment facilities, by ownership and region, 1985, annual rpt, 4654-16.5

Labs (clinical) under HCFA regulation, and labs with violations by Medicare termination and license status, 1983-87, hearings, 25408-98

Long-term health care needs, ability to pay, and views on Federal aid for home care, 1988 survey, hearing, 21148-51

Malpractice insurance premium costs and growth rate for physicians, alternative estimates by risk class and State, 1975-85, 4658-27

Marriages and rates, by age, race, education, previous marital status of spouses, and State, 1986, US Vital Statistics advance annual rpt, 4146-5.111; 4146-5.112

Marriages, divorces, and rates, by characteristics of spouses, State, and county, 1984 and trends from 1920, US Vital Statistics annual rpt, 4144-4

Mental health care hospitals, beds and caseload by State, patient characteristics, finances, and staff, for profit and nonprofit private instns, 1986, 4506-3.37

NIH grants for R&D, training, construction, and medical libraries, by location and recipient, FY88, annual listings, 4434-7

Nursing home facility, staff, and resident detailed characteristics, 1985, 4147-13.97

Nursing homes, beds, and residents, by ownership, certification status, and State, 1986, 4147-14.33

Nutritional status and related health condition and practices, by selected characteristics, 1970s-87, 4048-33

Occupational safety and health research and demonstration grants by State, and project listing, FY87, annual rpt, 4244-2

Older persons functional limitations, by activity type and selected characteristics, 1984, 4147-10.167

Physicians Medicare services use, charges, and reimbursement, by service type, setting, and specialty, 1986, article, 4652-1.936

Pregnancies (ectopic) and related deaths, by race, age, and region, 1970-86, article, 4202-7.902; 4202-7.905

Rural areas hospitals, use, staff, and funding sources, by instn characteristics, 1980s-86, hearing, 25148-42

Smoking and other tobacco use, by knowledge of health effects, and health and other characteristics, 1987, 4147-10.169

Smoking prevalence, related disease and deaths, and public attitudes, impact of Surgeon General rpts and antismoking campaigns, 1964-89, annual rpt, 4204-18

Smoking rates, by sex, age, race, occupation, region, and State, 1985 Current Population Survey, article, 4472-1.910

Statistical Abstract of US, social, political, and economic data, 1790-2025, comprehensive annual compilation, 2324-1.1

Teaching faculty dev programs for family medicine, Federal funding and trainees, by faculty status and region, 1978-87, 4118-63

Tobacco (smokeless) use by youth and adults, user characteristics, and sales, 1970s-86, papers, 4478-188

Tuberculosis cases and deaths, by patient characteristics, State, and city, 1987 and trends from 1953, annual rpt, 4204-10

Vitamin and mineral supplements use by adults and children, by type and user characteristics, 1986, 4146-8.175

Housing and Construction

American Housing Survey: unit and households detailed characteristics, and unit and neighborhood quality, 1985, biennial rpt, 2485-12

Apartment and condominium completions by rent class and sales price, and market absorption rates, quarterly rpt, 2482-2

Apartment completions by region and metro-nonmetro location, and absorption rates, by size and rent class, preliminary 1988, annual Current Housing Rpt, 2484-3

Apartment market absorption rates and characteristics for nonsubsidized furnished and unfurnished units, 1987 and trends from 1970, annual Current Housing Rpt, 2484-2

Buildings (commercial and public) alteration and repair spending, by type, size, age, and region, 1986, 2388-4

Construction put in place, permits, housing sales, costs, material prices, and employment, bimonthly rpt with articles, 2042-1

Construction put in place, value of new public and private structures, by type, monthly rpt, 2382-4

Historic buildings rehabilitation tax incentives, projects, costs, ownership, use, and tax reform impacts, FY77-88, annual rpt, 5544-17

Homeless shelters services, operations, and client characteristics, 1988 survey, 5188-123

Housing alteration and repair spending, by characteristics of property and region, 1984-88, annual rpt, 2384-4

Housing and households summary characteristics, 1985 and trends, biennial chartbook, 2486-1.7

Housing unit costs and homeownership rates, by income, age, family composition, and region, 1967-87, hearings, 25248-107

Indian and Alaska Native housing and economic development program operations, by region, FY86-87, annual rpt, 5004-5

Mortgages FHA-insured, secondary market prices and yields, and interest rates on construction and conventional mortgage loans, by region, monthly press release, 5142-20

New housing unit starts, by units per structure and metro-nonmetro location, and mobile home placements and prices, by region, monthly rpt, 2382-1

New housing units authorized, by region, State, selected MSA, and permit-issuing place, monthly rpt, 2382-5

New housing units authorized, by State, MSA, and permit-issuing place, 1988, annual rpt, 2384-2

New housing units completed and under construction, by units per structure, region, and inside-outside MSAs, monthly rpt, 2382-2

New single and multifamily units, by structural and financial characteristics, inside-outside MSAs, and region, 1984-88, annual rpt, 2384-1

New single-family houses sold and for sale, by price, stage of construction, months on market, and region, monthly rpt, 2382-3

Public and Indian housing stock and renovation needs, series, 5186-15

Rental housing voucher program of HUD, allocations by region, 1989, press release, 5006-3.65

Statistical Abstract of US, social, political, and economic data, 1790-2025, comprehensive annual compilation, 2324-1.3

Urban Dev Action Grant projects and funding, impacts of changes in selection criteria, by city and State, 1988, GAO rpt, 26113-395

Vacant housing characteristics and costs, and occupancy and vacancy rates, by region and metro-nonmetro location, quarterly rpt, 2482-1

Vacant housing characteristics, and occupancy and vacancy rates, by tenure, region, and metro-nonmetro location, selected years 1960-88, annual rpt, 2484-1

Industry and Commerce

Clay construction products production and shipments by region and State, trade, and use, by product, monthly Current Industrial Rpt, 2506-9.2

Exports and imports of US, by commodity group, world area, selected country, US coastal area and port, and mode of transport, monthly rpt, 2422-9

Exports and imports of US shipped through Canada, by detailed commodity, customs district, and country, 1987, annual rpt, 7704–11

Exports of manufactured goods, shares by industry group, region, and country of destination, 1987, article, 9381–1.903

Imports detained by FDA, by reason, product, shipper, brand, and country, monthly listing, 4062–2

Lumber production, prices, trade, and employment, for northwestern US and British Columbia, quarterly rpt, 1202–3

Minority Business Dev Centers mgmt and financial aid, and characteristics of businesses, by region and State, FY88, annual rpt, 2104–6

Multinatl firms US affiliates finances and operations, by industry div, country of parent firm, and State, 1986-87, annual article, 2702–1.925

Phosphate rock production, sales, trade, and use, 1989, Mineral Industry Surveys, annual rpt, 5614–20

Retail trade sales and inventories, by kind of business, region, and selected State, MSA, and city, monthly rpt, 2413–3

Small business finances, operations, owner and employee characteristics, and Federal contracts, 1980s-88, annual rpt, 9764–6

Small business training confs of SBA, cosponsors by type, and compliance with SBA regulations, by region, 1988, GAO rpt, 26113–425

Statistical Abstract of US, social, political, and economic data, 1790-2025, comprehensive annual compilation, 2324–1.3

Steel imports of US under voluntary restraint agreement, by product, customs district, and country, with US industry operating data, monthly rpt, 9882–13

Textile mill production, trade, sales, stocks, and material used, by product, region, and State, periodic Current Industrial Rpt series, 2506–5

Vending facilities run by blind on Federal and non-Federal property, finances and operations by agency and State, FY88, annual rpt, 4944–2

Labor and Employment

Counties (nonmetro) employment by industry sector and degree of urbanization, and compared to metro counties, various periods 1969-86, 1598–244

Drug testing of employees, coverage, policies, sponsors, treatment aid provided, and results, by industry div, 1988, 6728–37

Earnings by major industry group, and personal income per capita and by source, by region and State, 1929-87, 2708–40

Earnings by occupation, industry div, sex, region, and selected MSA, 1961-88, 6728–38.7

Earnings distribution measures by race, sex, industry sector, and region, 1960-80, article, 6722–1.917

Employment Cost Index and alternative measure of compensation costs, by component, occupation, industry group, union status, and location, 1975-89, annual rpt, 6744–20

Employment Cost Index and percent change by occupational group, industry div, region, and metro-nonmetro area, quarterly press release, 6782–5

Employment Cost Index, by region, selected quarters 1988-89, press release, 6946–3.15

Employment Cost Index changes for nonfarm workers, by occupation, industry div, region, and bargaining status, monthly rpt, 6782–1

Employment cost indexes, by occupation, industry div, and region, Monthly Labor Review, 6722–1.3

Employment, unemployment, and labor force characteristics, by region and census div, 1988, annual rpt, 6744–7.1

Farm operators leaving farming, employment prospects, indicators by region, various periods 1969-86, article, 1502–7.911

Grain mill production workers and wages, by occupation and sex, and benefits, by region, 1987 survey, 6787–6.239

Handbook of Labor Statistics, employment, unemployment, and labor force characteristics, 1940s-88 with trends from 1913, 6728–38.1

Labor Dept activities and funding, by program and State, FY88, annual rpt, 6304–1

Labor hourly costs, by component, occupational group, union coverage, industry div, and region, 1989, annual rpt, 6744–21

Labor Relations Natl Board activities, cases, elections conducted, and litigation, FY85, annual rpt, 9584–1

Longshore employment in 4 coastal regions, monthly rpt, 7702–1

Mediation and arbitration activities of Fed Mediation and Conciliation Service, and cases by issue, region, and State, FY82-87, annual rpt, 9344–1

Rural areas employment, economic conditions, and population characteristics, 1970s-85, compilation of papers, 1598–243

Statistical Abstract of US, social, political, and economic data, 1790-2025, comprehensive annual compilation, 2324–1.3

Vacations, holidays, and relative pay levels, regional and metro area differences, 1983-86, article, 6722–1.909

Vocational rehabilitation cases of State agencies, by disposition and State, FY88 and trends from FY21, annual rpt, 4944–5

Wages by occupation, for office and plant workers in metro areas, by industry div and region, Aug 1988, annual rpt, 6785–9

Wages by occupation, for office and plant workers in selected MSAs, 1989 survey, annual rpt, 6785–5

Wages, hours, and employment by occupation, and benefits, for selected locations, industry survey rpt series, 6787–6

Law Enforcement

Assaults and deaths of law enforcement officers, by circumstances, agency, victim and offender characteristics, and location, 1988, annual rpt, 6224–3

Bombing incidents, casualties, and damage, by target, circumstances, and State, 1988, annual rpt, 6224–5

Burglaries by time of day, and household victimization probability by region and State, 1965-87, annual rpt, 6224–8

Corrupt govt officials prosecuted and convicted, by judicial district and level of govt, 1978-88, annual rpt, 6004–13

Court caseloads, actions, procedure duration, judges, and jurors, by Federal district and appeals court, 1984-89, annual rpt, 18204–3

Court caseloads for Federal district, appeals, and bankruptcy courts, by type of suit and offense, circuit, and district, quarterly rpt, 18202–1

Court civil and criminal caseloads for Federal district, appeals, and special courts, June 1989, annual rpt, 18204–2; 18204–8

Crime, criminal justice admin and enforcement, and public opinion, data compilation, 1970s-88, annual rpt, 6064–6

Crime Index by population size and region, and offenses by large city, Jan-June 1989, semiannual rpt, 6222–1

Crime victimization of households, by offense, household characteristics, and location, 1975-88, annual rpt, 6066–25.22

Crimes, arrests by offender characteristics, and rates, by offense, and law enforcement employees, by population size and jurisdiction, 1988, annual rpt, 6224–2

Drug enforcement regional task forces investigation of organized crime, activities by agency and region, and background data, FY83-88, annual rpt, 6004–17

Executions by whether writ of habeas corpus used to appeal, race, and State, with military death row inmates, 1977-87, hearing, 21408–110

Firearms violations enhanced and mandatory sentences, for cases under Bur of Alcohol, Tobacco, and Firearms investigation program, FY87-88, 8488–6

Juror (grand and petit) use and costs, trials, and trial days, by Federal district court, 1981-88, annual rpt, 18204–4

Parole and probation population, entries, and exits, by State, 1987, annual rpt, 6066–25.17

Prison cases of AIDS, test results, and prevention and control policies, by location, 1988 survey, annual rpt, 6064–22

Prison conditions, population, and problems, issues and bibl, 1989 compilation of papers, 25928–8

Prisoners in Federal instns, by sex, prison, security level, contract facility type, and region, monthly rpt series, 6242–1

Prisoners, movements, and characteristics, by State, 1986, annual rpt, 6064–26

Sentences for Federal crimes, guidelines use and results by offense and district, and Sentencing Commission activities, 1988, annual rpt, 17664–1

Statistical Abstract of US, social, political, and economic data, 1790-2025, comprehensive annual compilation, 2324–1.1

Terrorist incidents in US, related activity, and casualties, by attack type, target, group, and location, 1988, annual rpt, 6224–6

Natural Resources, Environment, and Pollution

Acid rain control economic impacts, and sulfur dioxide emissions and reductions of industrial and power plants, 1987 hearing, 21368–104

Air pollution levels for 6 pollutants, by source, region, and selected MSA, 1978-87, annual rpt, 9194–1

Army Corps of Engineers activities and projects, FY87 and trends from 1800s, annual rpt, 3754–1.2

Army Corps of Engineers activities, FY87, annual rpt, 3754-1

Birds (mourning dove) population, by hunting and nonhunting State, 1966-89, annual rpt, 5504-15

Birds (waterfowl) hunter harvest, age and sex ratios by species, State, and flyway, 1984-88, annual rpt, 5504-32

Birds (waterfowl) hunter harvest and unretrieved kills, and duck stamps sold, by species, State, and flyway, 1987-88, annual rpt, 5504-28

Birds (waterfowl) population, habitat conditions, and migratory flight forecasts, for Canada and US by region, 1989 and trends from 1955, annual rpt, 5504-27

Birds (woodcock) population in US and Canada from 1968, and hunter harvest, by State, 1989, annual rpt, 5504-11

Coastal and estuarine pollutant discharges, by source, pollutant type, and location, series, 2176-4

Coastal and riparian areas environmental conditions, fish, wildlife, use, and mgmt, for individual ecosystems, series, 5506-9

Energy technologies environmental impacts, 1960s-80s, handbook series, 3326-1

Environmental quality and protection programs, and intl issues, 1988 annual rpt, 484-1

EPA pollution control grant program activities, monthly rpt, 9182-8

Fish and Wildlife Service restoration programs finances by State, and excise tax collections, FY88, annual rpt, 5504-13

Forest Service activities and finances, by region and State, FY88, annual rpt, 1204-1

Forest Service revenue, share paid to States and natl forest acreage by forest, region, county, and congressional district, FY88, annual rpt, 1204-33

Forests (natl) and other lands under Forest Service mgmt, acreage by forest and location, 1988, annual rpt, 1204-2

Forests (natl) revenue, by source, forest, and State, FY88, annual rpt, 1204-34

Forests improvement program for private timberland, Fed Govt cost-sharing funds by region and State, monthly table, 1802-11

Hazardous waste site remedial action under Superfund, current and proposed sites priority ranking and status by location, as of July 1989, listing, 9218-64

Hazardous waste site remedial action under Superfund, enforcement, spending, and cost recovery, 1986-88, GAO rpt, 26113-386

Helium resources in storage and natural gas reserves, by State, 1950-87 and projected to 2020, biennial rpt, 5604-44

Reclamation Bur activities, finances, and project impacts in western US, annual rpts, 5824-12

Soil, water, and environmental conservation and conditions, with data by State and region, 1989 quinquennial rpt, 1268-24

Timber insect and disease incidence and damage, annual regional rpt series, 1206-11

Timber insect and disease incidence and damage, by State, 1988, annual rpt, 1204-8

Timber sales of Forest Service, expenses, and operations, by region and natl forest, FY88, annual rpt, 1204-36.2

Timber stumpage prices, for sawtimber sold from natl forests by species and region, quarterly rpt, 1202-1

Wastewater treatment and collection facility construction funding needs and Fed Govt grants, by State, 1988 and projected to 2008, biennial rpt, 9204-7

Water supply in rural areas, public system financial and operating characteristics, by region, 1980, 1598-247

Wilderness areas acreage by Federal agency and location, and sources of damage, with data for foreign countries, 1988 conf papers, 1208-301

Population

Asian American earnings, and employment and other characteristics, by detailed origin and whether foreign-born, 1980, 11046-7.2

Consumer Income, socioeconomic characteristics of persons, families, and households, detailed cross-tabulations, Current Population Rpt series, 2546-6

Educational attainment, by sociodemographic characteristics and location, 1987 and trends from 1940, biennial Current Population Rpt, 2546-1.427; 2546-1.431

Household and family characteristics, by location, 1988, annual Current Population Rpt, 2546-1.437

Households and population size, by State, 1980 and 1988, annual press release, 2324-11

Income (household) and poverty status under alternative income definitions, by recipient characteristics, 1986, Current Population Rpt, 2546-6.58

Income (personal) per capita and by source, and earnings by industry div, by State, MSA, and county, 1982-87, annual regional rpts, 2704-2

Income (personal) per capita and by source, earnings by major industry group, and social insurance contributions, by region and State, 1929-87, 2708-40

Income (personal) per capita and total, and earnings by industry group, by region and State, 1986-88, annual article, 2702-1.928

Income (personal) per capita, by region and for lowest- and highest-income States, 1982 and 1988, article, 2702-1.914

Income (personal), population, earnings, and employment growth rates, by area population size and region, 1969-79 and 1979-87, article, 2702-1.915

Income (personal) totals, by region, census div, and State, quarterly article, 2702-1.32

Living arrangements, family relationships, and marital status, by selected characteristics, 1988, annual Current Population Rpt, 2546-1.428; 2546-1.433

Migration since 1986, mover characteristics by same or different area, and compared to nonmovers, 1987, annual Current Population Rpt, 2546-1.435

Migration to and from Southern US, by migrant characteristics and location, 1970s-87 and alternative projections to 2000, article, 9371-1.902

Older persons socioeconomic characteristics, 1900s-86 and projected to 2050, biennial chartbook, 12904-1

Population estimates and projections, by region and State, Current Population Rpt series, 2546-3

Population size, July 1988 and compared to 1980 and 1987, and components of change, 1980-88, annual press release, 2324-10

Poverty status of families and persons, by detailed characteristics, 1987, annual Current Population Rpt, 2546-6.60

Statistical Abstract of US, social, political, and economic data, 1790-2025, comprehensive annual compilation, 2324-1.1

Urban areas fiscal, economic, and social conditions, 1960s-87, biennial rpt, 5184-7.1; 5184-7.4

Prices and Cost of Living

Child rearing costs, by age, region, and urban-rural location, quarterly rpt, 1702-1

Consumer Expenditure Survey, household income by source, and itemized spending, by selected characteristics and region, 1984-87, annual rpt, 6764-5

Consumer Expenditure Survey, spending by category, and income, by selected household characteristics and location, 1987, press release, 6726-1.23

Consumer Expenditure Survey, spending by category, selected household characteristics, and region, quarterly rpt, 6762-14

CPI by component for US city average, and by region, population size, and for 15 metro areas, monthly rpt, 6762-1

CPI by component for US city average, and by region, population size, and for 27 metro areas, monthly rpt, 6762-2

CPI components relative importance, by selected SMSA, region, population size, and for US city average, 1988, annual rpt, 6884-1

CPI current statistics, Monthly Labor Review, 6722-1.4

Dairy prices, by product and selected area, with related marketing data, 1988, annual rpt, 1317-1

Farm prices received and paid, by commodity and State, 1988, annual rpt, 1629-5

Housing prices and price index for new single-family units sold, by region, quarterly rpt, 2382-8

Poultry and egg prices and marketing, by selected region, State, and city, monthly and weekly 1988, annual rpt, 1317-2

Producer price indexes, by stage of processing and detailed commodity, monthly 1988, annual rpt, 6764-2

Statistical Abstract of US, social, political, and economic data, 1790-2025, comprehensive annual compilation, 2324-1.3

Utilities spending of households, by household size, income, householder age and race, and region, 1983, article, 1702-1.904

Public Welfare and Social Security

Child care arrangements and costs, by income and other characteristics of family, 1984-86, press release, 2328-61

Child support and alimony awards, and payment status, by selected characteristics of woman, 1985, biennial Current Population Rpt, 2546-2.145

Food aid program of USDA for women, infants, and children, participants and costs by State and Indian agency, FY87, annual rpt, 1364-12

Food aid program of USDA for women,
infants, and children, participants, clinics,
and costs by State and Indian agency,
monthly tables, 1362-16

Food aid programs of USDA, costs and
participation by program, region, and State,
monthly rpt, 1362-14

Food stamp issues and participation, by State
and county, as of July 1988, semiannual
rpt, 1362-6

HHS financial aid, by program, recipient,
State, and city, FY88, annual regional
listings, 4004-3

Homeless and runaway youth programs,
funding, activities, and participant
characteristics, FY86, annual rpt, 4604-3

Medicare and Medicaid beneficiaries and
program operations, 1988, annual fact
book, 4654-18

Medicare and Medicaid eligibility,
participation, coverage, and program
finances, various periods 1966-89, biennial
rpt, 4654-1

Medicare enrollment, and use by type of
service, by age, sex, race, region, State, and
MSA, 1986-87, annual rpt, 4657-5

Medicare physicians assigned fee
participation related to selected physician,
practice, and community characteristics,
1984, article, 4652-1.902

Medicare reimbursement of hospitals under
prospective payment system, alternative
case mix indexes, FY85-86, article,
4652-1.952

Medicare reimbursement of hospitals under
prospective payment system, area wage
index adjusted for health occupation mix,
by location, 1984-85, article, 4652-1.950

Medicare reimbursement of hospitals under
prospective payment system, cost
accounting alternatives, model description
and results, FY84, article, 4652-1.948

Medicare reimbursement of hospitals under
prospective payment system, costs under
alternative cost updating procedures, model
estimates, 1976-84, article, 4652-1.921

Medicare reimbursement of hospitals under
prospective payment system, proposed
inclusion of capital costs, with background
data, FY84-88 and projected to 2008,
26308-83

Mental health care in general hospitals,
length of stay related to patient, instn, and
State Medicaid program characteristics,
1981, article, 4652-1.924

Public welfare programs beneficiaries, and
benefits duration and share of income, by
selected characteristics, 1983-86,
2546-20.8

Statistical Abstract of US, social, political,
and economic data, 1790-2025,
comprehensive annual compilation,
2324-1.2

Recreation and Leisure

Fishing (ocean sport) catch, by species, mode
of fishing, and coastal region, 1988, annual
rpt, 2164-1.2

Foreign travel to US, tour promotion by
region of destination and country of
traveler, 1987, 2908-31

Forests (natl) trail construction and
maintenance needs by region, and Forest
Service budget, FY80-89 and projected to
1993, GAO rpt, 26113-435

Park natl system and other land under Natl
Park Service mgmt, acreage by site,
ownership, and region, 1988, semiannual
rpt, 5542-1.2

Park natl system and other land under Natl
Park Service mgmt, acreage by site,
ownership, and region, 1989, semiannual
rpt, 5542-1.4

Park natl system visitor deaths, by cause,
victim age, region, and park, 1978-88,
annual rpt, 5544-6

Park natl system visits and overnight stays,
by park and State, monthly rpt, 5542-4

Park natl system visits and overnight stays,
by park and State, 1988 and trends from
1979, annual rpt, 5544-12

Science and Technology

Earnings of scientists and engineers in R&D
at DOE labs and non-DOE facilities, 1989,
annual rpt, 3004-9

Education in science and engineering in
elementary and secondary schools, and
student persistence in postsecondary
education, 1977-88, 26358-199

R&D funding by source and performer, and
related employment, by State, 1975-87,
9626-6.32

R&D funding, performance by geographic
division and State, and science and
technology employment, selected years
1953-89, annual rpt, 9624-18.1

Science and engineering labor supply by
region and employment characteristics, and
salaries by years of experience, 1987,
9626-2.184

Wages of scientists and engineers in R&D, by
field and educational, employment, and
other characteristics, 1989, annual rpt,
3004-1

Veterans Affairs

AIDS cases at VA health care centers, by
facility and region, periodic tables,
8702-1; 9922-15

Health care centers canteen services
discontinuing tobacco sales, impacts on
finances, FY83-FY88, hearing, 21768-49

Health care professionals of VA, by selected
employment characteristics and VA district
and duty station, quarterly rpt, 8602-6

Health care services sharing contracts among
VA and non-VA facilities, by service type
and region, FY88, annual rpt, 8704-5

Housing loans of VA outstanding, by loan
type and annual totals by regional office,
quarterly rpt, annual table, 8602-2

VA benefit claims processing and efficiency
at regional offices, and hearing officers
salaries and travel costs, 1986-88, hearing,
21768-47

BY SMSA OR MSA

Banking, Finance, and Insurance

Bank deposits in FDIC-insured commercial
and savings banks, by State, MSA, and
county, as of June 1988, annual rpt,
9295-3.7

New England States economic indicators,
Fed Reserve 1st District, quarterly rpt,
9373-2.5

New England States, FHLB 1st District thrift
instns financial operations and housing
industry indicators, monthly rpt, 9302-4

North Central States, FHLB 8th District
savings instns financial operations by State
and SMSA, monthly rpt, 9302-9

Ohio savings instns crisis impact on
certificates of deposit interest rates,
1983-85, technical paper, 9316-1.153

Savings instns finances and operations by
district and State, mortgage lending activity
and terms by MSA, and FHLB finances,
1987 with trends from 1900, annual rpt,
9314-3.4

Savings instns FSLIC-insured, offices, and
deposits, by FHLB district, State, SMSA,
and county, 1988, annual rpt, 9314-4

Southeastern States banks and thrifts deposit
concentration index, by selected MSA,
1984 and 1988, article, 9302-2.905

West Central States, FHLB 10th District
savings instns finances and lending by State
and MSA, monthly table, 9302-22

Western States, FHLB 11th District thrift
offices, locations, savings balances, and
accounts, quarterly listing, 9302-20

Communications and Transportation

DOT planning and safety grants, by program,
State, and for 38 SMSAs, FY88, annual
rpt, 7304-7

Education

Desegregation of schools, indicators of
integration plans effectiveness by school
district and location, 1960s-85, 11048-189

Government and Defense

Employment (civilian) of Fed Govt, by work
schedule, selected agency, State, and MSA,
as of Dec 1988, article, 9842-1.904

Employment and payroll (civilian) of Fed
Govt, by pay system and location, 1988,
annual rpt, 9844-6.6

Expenditures of local govts, impacts of
competition among govtl units, migration,
and other factors, 1976-77, working paper,
9377-9.82

Immigrants admitted to US, by class of
admission, country of birth, and State and
MSA of destination, FY88, annual rpt,
6264-4

Health and Vital Statistics

AIDS cases by risk group, race, sex, age,
State, and MSA, and deaths, monthly rpt,
4202-9

Deaths and infant deaths, by cause, age, sex,
race, and location, 1986, annual rpt,
4144-2.1; 4144-2.2

Deaths and rates, by detailed location, cause,
and demographic characteristics, 1987, US
Vital Statistics annual rpt, 4144-3

Drug abuse emergency room admissions and
deaths, by drug type and major metro area,
July 1985-Dec 1988, semiannual rpt,
4492-3

Drug abuse emergency room admissions and
deaths, by drug type and source, sex, race,
age, and major metro area, 1988, annual
rpt, 4494-8

Drug abuse indicators for selected metro
areas, research results, data collection, and
policy issues, 1989 semiannual conf,
4492-5

Marriages, divorces, and rates, by
characteristics of spouses, State, and
county, 1984 and trends from 1920, US
Vital Statistics annual rpt, 4144-4

Pollution (air) exposure of population and
selected risk groups, by pollutant, MSA,
and county, 1988, hearing, 21368-117

Housing and Construction

American Housing Survey: unit and households characteristics, MSA fact sheet series, 2485–11

American Housing Survey: unit and households detailed characteristics, and unit and neighborhood quality, MSA rpt series, 2485–6

Construction authorized by building permits, by type of construction, region, State, and MSA, bimonthly rpt, 2042–1.3

Florida housing starts and population growth rates, by MSA, 1988, article, 9302–2.906

Mortgage terms on conventional loans closed, and commitment rates, by type of loan and lender and for 32 SMSAs, monthly rpt, 8432–3; 9312–2

New housing starts and completions authorized by building permits in 40 MSAs, quarterly rpt, 2382–9

New housing units authorized, by region, State, selected MSA, and permit-issuing place, monthly rpt, 2382–5

New housing units authorized, by State, MSA, and permit-issuing place, 1988, annual rpt, 2384–2

North Central States, FHLB 7th District housing vacancy rates for single and multifamily units and mobile homes, by ZIP code, annual MSA rpt series, 9304–18

South Central States, FHLB 9th District housing vacancy rates for single and multifamily units and mobile homes by ZIP code, annual MSA rpt series, 9304–19

Statistical Abstract of US, social, political, and economic data, 1790-2025, comprehensive annual compilation, 2324–1.3

West Central States, FHLB 10th District housing vacancy rates for single and multifamily units and mobile homes, by ZIP code, annual MSA rpt series, 9304–22

Western States, FHLB 11th District housing vacancy rates for single and multifamily units and mobile homes, by ZIP code, annual MSA rpt series, 9304–20

Western States, FHLB 12th District housing vacancy rates for single and multifamily units and mobile homes, by ZIP code, annual MSA rpt series, 9304–21

Industry and Commerce

Exports, imports, and balances of US by commodity group, world area, and country, and related employment, 1970s-88, annual rpt, 2044–26

New England States economic indicators, Fed Reserve 1st District, quarterly rpt with articles, 9373–2

Retail trade census, 1987: employment, establishments, sales, and payroll, by SIC 2- to 4-digit kind of business, MSA, county, and city, State rpt series, 2397–1

Retail trade sales and inventories, by kind of business, region, and selected State, MSA, and city, monthly rpt, 2413–3

Service industries census, 1987: establishments, receipts, employment, and payroll, by SIC 2- to 4-digit kind of business, MSA, county, and city, State rpt series, 2391–1

Small business establishments, employment, and financial ratios, by SIC 1- to 2-digit industry and State, late 1960s-87, 9768–19

Southeastern States, Fed Reserve 6th District, economic indicators by State and MSA, quarterly rpt, 9371–14

Southeastern US economic and employment conditions, for 4 largest MSAs, 1977-87, article, 9391–16.902

Wholesale trade census, 1987: employment, establishments, finances, and operations, by SIC 2- to 4-digit kind of business, MSA, county, and city, State rpt series, 2405–1

Labor and Employment

Auto dealer repair workers and wages by occupation, and benefits, by selected MSA, 1988 survey, 6787–6.241

Earnings, annual average percent changes for selected occupational groups, selected MSAs, monthly rpt, 6782–1.1

Earnings by occupation, industry div, sex, region, and selected MSA, 1961-88, 6728–38.7

Earnings of production workers, average weekly gross by coastal region and MSA, 1988, annual rpt, 7704–12.2

Employment and Earnings, detailed data, monthly rpt, 6742–2.5; 6742–2.6; 6742–2.8

Employment, earnings, and hours, by selected SIC 1- to 4-digit industry, State, and for 262 MSAs, 1972-87, 6748–81

Employment in manufacturing and nonagricultural industries, by MSA, 1987-88, annual press release, 6946–3.12

Employment, unemployment, and labor force characteristics, by selected metro area and large city, 1988, annual rpt, 6744–7.3

Hotel and motel service workers and wages by occupation and sex, and benefits, for 18 MSAs, 1988 survey, 6787–6.242

Minority group and women employment, by occupation, SIC 1- to 3- digit industry, State, and MSA, 1986, annual rpt, 9244–1

New England States economic indicators, Fed Reserve 1st District, quarterly rpt, 9373–2.1

North Central States business and economic conditions, Fed Reserve 9th District, quarterly journal, 9383–19

North Central States economic conditions, Fed Reserve 9th District, quarterly rpt, 9383–18

Southeastern US employment, by selected MSA, 1987-88, annual rpt, 6944–2

Southeastern US wages of office and plant workers, for 36 MSAs, 1988, press release, 6946–3.14

Unemployment, by State and metro area, monthly press release, 6742–12

Unemployment, employment, and labor force, by State, MSA, and city, monthly rpt, 6742–22

Vacations, holidays, and relative pay levels, regional and metro area differences, 1983-86, article, 6722–1.909

Wages by occupation, and benefits for office and plant workers in selected MSAs, 1988, annual rpt, 6785–1

Wages by occupation, and benefits for office and plant workers, periodic MSA survey rpt series, 6785–3; 6785–11; 6785–12

Wages by occupation, for office and plant workers in selected MSAs, 1989 survey, annual rpt, 6785–5

Wages by occupation, for office and plant workers in selected MSAs, 1989 survey, annual summary rpts, 6785–6

Wages for 3 occupational groups, relative pay levels in 92 labor market areas, 1988, annual rpt, 6785–13

Wages for 4 occupational groups, relative pay levels in 61 MSAs, 1988, annual rpt, 6785–8

Wages, hours, and employment by occupation, and benefits, for selected locations, industry survey rpt series, 6787–6

Wages of workers covered by unemployment insurance, by MSA, 1987-88, annual press release, 6784–17.2

Natural Resources, Environment, and Pollution

Air pollutants ozone and carbon monoxide levels exceeding EPA standards, by MSA, 1988, annual press release, 9194–18

Air pollution levels for 6 pollutants, by source, region, and selected MSA, 1978-87, annual rpt, 9194–1

Statistical Abstract of US, social, political, and economic data, 1790-2025, comprehensive annual compilation, 2324–1.1

Population

Educational attainment, by sociodemographic characteristics and location, 1987 and trends from 1940, biennial Current Population Rpt, 2546–1.427; 2546–1.431

Immigration to US, alien workers, visitors, deportations, and naturalizations, by country, FY88 and trends from 1820, annual rpt, 6264–2

Income (personal) per capita and by source, and earnings by industry div, by State, MSA, and county, 1982-87, annual regional rpts, 2704–2

Income (personal) per capita and total, by State, MSA, county, and metro-nonmetro location, 1985-87, article, 2702–1.916

Minority group population, and components of change, by race, State, metro-nonmetro location, MSA, and county, 1980-85, Current Population Rpt, 2546–3.159

Population size, by MSA, county, metro-nonmetro location, and State, 1987, and for cities, 1986, with change from 1980 and trends from 1960, Current Population Rpt, 2546–3.160

Population size, by MSA, 1988, annual press release, 2324–8

Statistical Abstract of US, social, political, and economic data, 1790-2025, comprehensive annual compilation, 2324–1.1

Urban areas fiscal, economic, and social conditions, 1960s-87, biennial rpt, 5184–7.1

Prices and Cost of Living

Consumer Expenditure Survey, household income by source, and itemized spending, by selected MSA, 1984-85, annual rpt, 6764–5.2

CPI by component for US city average, and by region, population size, and for 15 metro areas, monthly rpt, 6762–1

CPI by component for US city average, and by region, population size, and for 27 metro areas, monthly rpt, 6762–2

CPI by major component and selected metro area, 1940s-88 with trends from 1913, 6728–38.8

CPI components relative importance, by selected SMSA, region, population size, and for US city average, 1988, annual rpt, 6884–1

Fish and shellfish catch, prices, and fisheries economic status, for Pacific coast, 1986-87, annual rpt series, 2164–16

Fish catch, by species, use, region, State, and major port, 1970s-88, annual rpt, 2164–1.1

Fish Hatchery Natl System activities and deliveries, by species, hatchery, and jurisdiction of waters stocked, FY88, annual rpt, 5504–10

Fishery employment, vessels, plants, and cooperatives, by State, 1988 and trends from 1970, annual rpt, 2164–1.10

Fishery mgmt and R&D, Fed Govt grants by project and State, and rpts, 1987, annual listing, 2164–3

Flour milling production by State, stocks, daily capacity, and exports by country, monthly Current Industrial Rpt, 2506–4.1

Flower and foliage plant production, sales, prices, and growers, by crop and State, 1987-88 and planting planned 1989, annual rpt, 1631–8

FmHA activities, and loans and grants by program and State, FY88 and trends from FY69, annual rpt, 1184–17

FmHA borrowers, by type of borrower and loan, and State, quarterly rpt, 1182–4

FmHA guaranteed loans from private lenders outstanding, delinquencies, and losses, by State, FY83-88, GAO rpt, 26113–433

FmHA loans and borrower supervision activities in farm and housing programs, by type and State, monthly rpt, 1182–1

FmHA loans, borrowers, and interest rate reduction program repayments to lenders, by State, FY86-88, GAO rpt, 26113–419

FmHA loans, by type, borrower characteristics, and State, quarterly rpt, 1182–8

FmHA loans, by type, borrower race, and State, quarterly rpt, 1182–5

FmHA property acquired through foreclosure, acreage, value, and sales, for farm and nonfarm property by State, monthly rpt, 1182–6

Food (processed) production and stocks by State, shipments, exports, ingredients, and use, periodic Current Industrial Rpt series, 2506–4

Fruit (noncitrus) and nut production, prices, and use, by crop and State, 1986-88, annual rpt, 1621–18.1; 1621–18.2

Fruit and nut production, prices, trade, stocks, and use, by selected crop, periodic situation rpt with articles, 1561–6

Fruit and vegetable shipments, and arrivals in US and Canada cities, by mode of transport and State and country of origin, 1988, annual rpt series, 1311–4

Fruit and vegetable shipments by mode of transport, arrivals, and imports, by commodity and State and country of origin, weekly rpt, 1311–3

Fruit and vegetable shipments by truck, monthly by State and country of origin, and rates weekly by growing area and market, 1988, annual rpt, 1311–15

Grain inspected, test results by commodity and State, 1988, annual rpt series, 1294–3

Grain stocks on and off farms, by crop, quarterly rpt, 1621–4

Grain storage facility and equipment loans to farmers under CCC program, by State, FY68-89, annual table, 1804–14

Grain support loan programs of USDA, activity and status by grain and State, monthly rpt, 1802–3

Grazing land acreage, erosion, value, and livestock fed, by region and State, 1950-82, 1588–130

Hay (alfalfa and prairie) prices, for selected areas, weekly rpt, 1313–5

Hogs and pigs production, inventory, and farms, by State, 1983-87, 1641–10

Hogs inventory, value, farrowings, and farms, by State, quarterly release, 1623–3

Honey production, prices, stocks, and bee colonies, by State, 1987-88, annual rpt, 1631–6

Honey production, prices, trade, stocks, marketing, and CCC honey loan and distribution activities, monthly rpt, 1311–2

Income of farms, for 25 leading crops, by State, 1960-87, 1548–347

Irrigated acreage covered and idled under Conservation Reserve Program, by western State, as of 1987 and projected 1990, 1588–143

Irrigated farms, by selected characteristics of farm and operator, and State, 1982, 1588–131

Irrigation projects of Reclamation Bur in western US, crop production and acreage by commodity, State, and project, 1987, annual rpt, 5824–12.1

Livestock and meat production, prices, and trade, 1970-88, 1568–285

Livestock grazing on natl forest lands, by region and State, FY88, annual rpt, 1204–5

Livestock inspected by Fed Govt, by type, weekly rpt, 1315–1

Livestock packers purchases and feeding, and livestock markets, dealers, and sales, by State, 1987, annual rpt, 1384–1

Livestock production, prices, receipts, and disposition, by species and State, 1987-88, annual rpt, 1623–8

Livestock slaughter and meat production, by livestock type and State, monthly rpt, 1623–9

Livestock slaughter, meat production, and slaughter plants, by species and State, 1988, annual rpt, 1623–10

Meat and poultry inspection activities and staff of Federal, State, and foreign govts, FY88, annual rpt, 1374–1

Milk order market deliveries, by State of origin, 1968-88, annual article, 1317–4.904

Milk order market prices and detailed operations, by State and market area, 1987-88, annual rpt, 1317–3

Milk order market producer deliveries, by State and county, 1986-87, periodic rpt, 1317–5

Milk order market sales, by container size and type, outlet type, and market area, 1987, biennial rpt, 1317–6

Milk production, use, and receipts, and milk cow inventory, by State, 1986-88, annual rpt, 1627–4

Mink and pelt production, prices, and farms, selected years 1969-89, annual rpt, 1631–7

Mint oil production, yield, and farm prices by State, and NYC spot prices, various periods 1986-1989, FAS annual circular, 1925–15.2

Mushroom production, sales, and prices, by State, 1966/67-1988/89 and planned 1989/90, annual rpt, 1631–9

Peach production, marketing, and prices in 3 southeastern States and Appalachia, 1988, annual rpt, 1311–12

Peanut production and trade by country, prices, and stocks, weekly rpt, 1311–1

Pesticide use, costs, toxicity, and application rates, and losses from pests, for cotton by pest type and State, 1981-84, 1568–278

Pests and diseases of plants entering US, by type of pest and host, country, and State, FY87, annual rpt, 1394–16

Potato and sweet potato production, stocks, prices, acreage, and yield, 1982-87, 1641–14

Potato production, prices, stocks, and use, by State, 1986-88, annual rpt, 1621–11

Potato production, stocks, processing, yields, and harvest losses, by State, periodic rpt, 1621–10

Poultry (broiler) production, slaughter, prices, and processing industry operations, 1950s-87, 1568–279

Poultry (chicken and turkey) hatchery production, 1987-88, annual rpt, 1625–8

Poultry (chicken, egg, and turkey) production and inventories, monthly rpt, 1625–1

Poultry (chicken, egg, and turkey) production and prices, by State, 1987-88, annual rpt, 1625–5

Poultry Natl Improvement Plan coverage of hatcheries and birds, by species, disease program, and State, 1988, annual rpt, 1394–15

Poultry slaughtered, by class of bird and State, FY88, annual rpt, 1374–3.2

Poultry slaughtered under Fed Govt inspection, pounds certified, and condemnations by cause, by State, monthly rpt, 1625–3

Price support activity and policy options, with data on production, trade, use, and finances, and foreign comparisons, 1950s-89, commodity rpt series, 1566–7

Prices received and paid by farmers, by commodity and State, 1988, annual rpt, 1629–5

Prices received by farmers and production value, by detailed crop and State, 1986-88, annual rpt, 1621–2

Prices received by farmers for major products, and paid for farm inputs and living items, by State, monthly rpt, 1629–1

Production inputs, finances, mgmt, and land value and transfers, periodic situation rpt with articles, 1561–16

Production itemized costs, receipts, and returns, by crop and State, preliminary 1987, annual rpt, 1544–24

Production mandatory control programs impacts on farm income, acreage, govt payments, and consumers, projected under alternative program provisions, 1986-90, 1548–354

Research (agricultural) funding and staffing for USDA, State agencies, and other instns, by topic, FY88, annual rpt, 1744–1

Rice foreign and US production, prices, trade, stocks, and use, periodic situation rpt, 1561–8

Rice market activities, prices, inspections, sales, trade, supply, and use, for US and selected foreign markets, weekly rpt, 1313–8

Rice shipments, by end use, package size, and State of origin and destination, mid 1950s-87, biennial rpt, 1564–11

Sheep, lamb, and goat inventory, by State, 1987-89, annual press release, 1623-4

Soil and water conservation funding by USDA, by program and State, FY86, annual rpt, 1264-12

South Central States farm yields by selected commodity, rainfall, and banks financial performance, with comparisons to US farm income trends, 1980s-88, annual article, 9391-1.911

Statistical Abstract of US, social, political, and economic data, 1790-2025, comprehensive annual compilation, 2324-1.3

Storage facility and equipment loans to farmers under CCC grain program, by State, monthly table, 1802-9

Sugar and sweeteners production, prices, trade, supply, and use, quarterly situation rpt with articles, 1561-14

Sugar production, supply, trade, and use, quarterly rpt, 1621-28

Sweetpotato and yam production by State and leading foreign country, and US consumption, 1970s-88, article, 1561-11.901

Tobacco marketing activity, prices, and sales, by grade, type, market, and State, 1988, annual rpt series, 1319-5

Tobacco production, prices, stocks, taxes by State, and trade and production by country, 1988, annual rpt, 1319-1

Turkeys raised by State, and losses by region, 1987-88, and hatchery plans, 1989, annual rpt, 1625-6

Vegetables farms, acreage, and sales, by whether Federal farm program participant and State, 1987, article, 1561-11.907

Vegetables for processing, production and value, by selected commodity and State, 1970s-85, 1568-275

Vegetables production, acreage, and yield, current and forecast for selected fresh and processing crops by State, periodic rpt, 1621-12

Vegetables production, prices, and acreage, for selected fresh and processing crops by State, 1986-88, annual rpts, 1621-25

Vegetables production, prices, trade, stocks, and use, for selected fresh and processing crops, periodic situation rpt with articles, 1561-11

Wage surveys to set minimum wage for US and alien farm workers, evaluation with data by location, 1980s-87, GAO rpt, 26131-50

Wheat and rye acreage seeded, by State, 1987-89, annual rpt, 1621-30

Wheat and rye foreign and US production, prices, trade, stocks, and use, quarterly situation rpt with articles, 1561-12

Wheat production, acreage, and sales, for winter, durum, and other wheat, by State, 1949-88, 1568-284

Wool and mohair production and prices, by State, 1988, annual press release, 1623-6

Banking, Finance, and Insurance

Appalachian States, FHLB 5th District savings instns finances and lending by State, monthly rpt, 9302-8

Bank holding company acquisitions in southeastern States, as of Oct 1988, article, 9389-1.907

Banks (commercial) specializing in real estate loans, financial condition, 1989 technical paper, 9366-6.202

Banks (commercial and savings) FDIC-insured, deposits by instn, State, MSA, and county, as of June 1988, annual regional rpt series, 9295-3

Banks (insured commercial) assets, income, and financial ratios, by asset size and State, quarterly rpt, 13002-3

Banks (insured commercial) financial ratios, by State, 1984-87, annual rpt, 9294-4.4

Banks (insured commercial and savings) finances, and changes in status, by State, 1987, annual rpt, 9294-4.1

Banks (insured commercial and savings) finances, by State, 1987, annual rpt, 9294-4.3

Banks (natl) domestic and intl operations, charters, mergers, and liquidations, by instn and State, quarterly rpt, 8402-3

Banks, branches, earnings, assets, and deposits, 1987, annual rpt, 9364-5.11

Banks failures by bank type, asset size, region, and State, 1984-88, article, 9391-16.901

Banks failures, by type of charter and mgmt weakness, audit activity, asset size, age, and State, 1984-88, GAO rpt, 26111-61

Banks status changes, instns, assets, and concentration ratios by size, ownership, and location, and compared to other financial instns, 1976-87, article, 9362-1.902

Bond tax-exempt issues for private activity, by purpose, face value, major industry, and State, 1986, annual article, 8302-2.905

Credit unions federally insured, finances by instn characteristics and State, as of June 1989, semiannual rpt, 9532-6

Credit unions federally insured, finances, 1987-88, annual rpt, 9534-1

Deposit insurance systems, banks, and bank failure rates, for selected States, various periods 1829-1930, article, 9375-1.904

Fraud and insider misconduct at financial instns, cases, Federal regulatory and enforcement activities, and losses, 1981-87, hearing, 21408-111

Futures industry registered traders, by type and State, FY88, annual rpt, 11924-2

Insurance (auto) coverage, premiums, and theft losses, with data by model and State, 1988 hearings, 21368-110

Interstate banking offices by type of controlling organization and State, 1982-Feb 1989, article, 9371-1.909

Middle Atlantic States, FHLB 2nd District economic and housing indicators, by State, quarterly rpt with articles, 9302-33

New England States, banks, thrifts, and financial statements by type of instn and Fed deposit insurance, and State, 1987, annual rpt, 9304-3

New England States economic indicators, Fed Reserve 1st District, monthly rpt, 9373-24

New England States economic indicators, Fed Reserve 1st District, quarterly rpt with articles, 9373-2

New England States, FHLB 1st District thrift instns, financial condition, and locations, 1989, annual listing, 9304-26

New England States, FHLB 1st District thrift instns financial operations and housing industry indicators, monthly rpt, 9302-4

North Central States business and economic conditions, Fed Reserve 9th District, quarterly journal, 9383-19

North Central States, Fed Reserve 7th District, economic issues, working paper series, 9375-13

North Central States, FHLB 8th District savings instns financial operations by State and SMSA, monthly rpt, 9302-9

Rural areas banks, control by urban-based firms, and financial and market characteristics, 1960s-88, article, 1502-7.906

Savings and loan assns assets and liabilities, by FHLB district and State, 1987 and trends from 1930, annual rpt, 9314-1

Savings and loan assns assets composition, and alternative estimates of net worth for insolvent instns allowed to remain open, 1982-88, article, 9375-1.908

Savings instns failure resolution costs, financing problems, and FSLIC and acquiring instns tax benefits, 1988 and projected to FY99, hearings, 21788-181

Savings instns failure resolution costs to FSLIC by State, and instn financial characteristics, 1979-88, technical paper, 9316-1.151

Savings instns failures by State, with exam of mgmt weaknesses and regulatory activity, 1980s-87, GAO rpt, 26111-62

Savings instns failures resolution costs to FSLIC relation to discount rate, instn financial characteristics, and State, alternative model results, 1980s-88, technical paper, 8436-1.3

Savings instns finances and operations by district and State, mortgage lending activity and terms by MSA, and FHLB finances, 1987 with trends from 1900, annual rpt, 9314-3.2

Savings instns financial statements, FSLIC-insured instns by FHLB district and State, and FDIC-insured savings banks, 1988, annual rpt, 8434-1

Savings instns FSLIC-insured, offices, and deposits, by FHLB district, State, SMSA, and county, 1988, annual rpt, 9314-4

Savings instns insured by Savings Assn Insurance Fund, finances by district, quarterly rpt, 8432-4

Savings instns mortgage-backed securities share of assets, by asset size, capital ratio, and State, for FHLB 4th District, 1988, article, 9302-2.904

Savings instns off-balance-sheet hedging activity, by type, asset size, and State, for FHLB 4th District, 1984-88, article, 9302-2.903

Small Business Investment Companies finances, funding, licensing, and loan activity, 1st half FY89, semiannual rpt, 9762-3

South Central States, FHLB 9th District savings instns finances and operations by State, monthly rpt, 9302-13

South Central States, FHLB 9th District savings instns finances and operations by State, quarterly rpt, 9302-31

Southeastern States banks and thrifts industry structure impacts of market entry and branching regulation, by State, 1982-88, article, 9302-2.907

Southeastern States, Fed Reserve 5th District banks financial performance, 1984-88, annual article, 9389-1.909

Southeastern States, Fed Reserve 5th District insured commercial banks financial statements, by State, quarterly rpt, 9389-18

Southeastern States, Fed Reserve 8th District banks financial ratios, by State, 1985-88, article, 9391–16.903

Southeastern States, FHLB 4th District members financial performance, by State and asset size, 1984-88, annual article, 9302–2.902

Southeastern States, FHLB 4th District savings instns finances and financial ratios, by State, quarterly rpt, 9302–3

Southeastern States, FHLB 4th District thrifts finances, by State, 1984-88 annual rpt series, 9304–29

Statistical Abstract of US, social, political, and economic data, 1790-2025, comprehensive annual compilation, 2324–1.3

Stock market crash of 1987, consumer complaints by reason, security type, and State, Nov-Dec 1987, hearings, 21368–111

Stockbrokers finances, firms by type of organization and State, and SEC applications and registrations, 1983-88, annual rpt, 9734–2.1

Trust assets of banks, trust companies, and S&Ls, by type of asset and fund, selected firm, and State, 1988, annual rpt, 13004–1

West Central States, Fed Reserve 10th District banking industry structure, performance, and financial devs, 1988, annual rpt, 9381–14

West Central States, Fed Reserve 10th District depository instns financial activity by State, and large commercial banks by city, monthly rpt, 9381–11

West Central States, FHLB 10th District savings instns finances and lending by State and MSA, monthly table, 9302–22

West Central States, FHLB 10th District savings instns financial condition, by State, quarterly rpt, 9302–34

West Central States, FHLB 10th District savings instns, locations, assets, and savings, 1989, annual listing, 9304–17

Western States, FHLB 11th District thrift offices, locations, savings balances, and accounts, quarterly listing, 9302–20

Western States, FHLB 12th District savings instns deposits and lending by State, monthly press release series, 9302–32

Communications and Transportation

Air traffic (passenger), and aircraft operations by type, by airport and State, projected FY89-2005 and trends from FY83, annual rpt, 7504–7

Air traffic levels at FAA-operated control facilities, by airport and State, FY88, annual rpt, 7504–27

Aircraft (general aviation), flight hours, and equipment, by type, use, and model of aircraft, region, and State, 1988, annual rpt, 7504–29

Aircraft accidents and circumstances, for US operations of domestic and foreign airlines and general aviation, periodic rpt, 9612–1

Aircraft accidents, by State, 1986, annual rpt, 9614–3

Aircraft flight service station workload of FAA, pilot briefs, contacts, and flight plans by facility, projected FY88-99 and trends from FY80, annual rpt, 7504–39

Aircraft pilots and nonpilots certified by FAA, by certificate type, age, sex, region, and State, 1988, annual rpt, 7504–2

Aircraft registered with FAA, by type and characteristics of aircraft, make, carrier, State, and county, 1988, annual rpt, 7504–3

Airline computer reservation systems operating costs, fees, and market shares, by firm and location, 1984-87, hearing, 25528–108

Airport improvement program of FAA, grants and activities by State and airport, FY88, annual rpt, 7504–38

Airport planning and dev project grants of FAA, by airport and location, quarterly press release, 7502–14

Appalachia hwy system and access roads funding and completion status, by State, quarterly tables, 9082–1

Bridges in rural areas, conditions, needs, and funding, with data by State and compared to urban areas, 1988, 1278–16

Canada travel to US by Province of residence, and characteristics of visit, by State, 1988, annual rpt, 2904–7

DOT planning and safety grants, by program, State, and for 38 SMSAs, FY88, annual rpt, 7304–7

Drivers licenses issued and in force by age and sex, fees, and renewal, by license class and State, 1987, annual rpt, 7554–16

Gasoline octane labeling, State testing programs, violations, and penalties, as of Feb 1988, GAO rpt, 26113–409

Hazardous material transport accidents, casualties, and damage, by mode of transport, with DOT control activities, 1988, annual rpt, 7304–4

Hwy (interstate) system expenditures, costs, and mileage, by State, as of 1988 and forecast FY91-92, 21648–58

Hwy admin and gasoline tax revenue proposed transfer from Fed Govt to States, issues, with motor fuel taxes by selected State, 1988 rpt, 10048–72

Hwy construction bids and contracts for Federal-aid hwys, by State, 1st half 1989, semiannual rpt, 7552–12

Hwy construction contracts awards of States to minority- and women-owned firms, FY85-88, GAO rpt, 26113–399

Hwy construction material prices and indexes for Federal-aid system, by type of material and urban-rural location, quarterly rpt, 7552–7

Hwy construction material use by type, and spending, by State, various periods 1944-88, annual rpt, 7554–29

Hwy funding, costs, and completion status of Federal-aid system, by State, as of June 1989, semiannual rpt, 7552–5

Hwy safety program funding, and accident and death reductions, by State, FY88, annual rpt, 7554–26

Hwy speed averages and vehicles exceeding 55 mph, by State, quarterly rpt, 7552–14

Hwy speed limit increase coverage by newspapers and TV, 1987, 7768–110

Hwy Statistics, detailed data by State, 1988, annual rpt, 7554–1

Hwy Statistics, summary data by State, 1987-88, annual rpt, 7554–24

Hwy traffic and pavement condition, by type of hwy and State, 1983-87, biennial rpt, 7554–27.3

Hwy traffic daily mileage, by State, 1987 and forecast 2005, biennial rpt, 7554–27.6

Hwy traffic volume on rural roads and city streets, monthly rpt, 7552–8

Ohio River basin waterway facilities, freight by commodity and port, and recreation, by waterway, 1986-87, annual rpt, 3754–6

Pipeline accidents, casualties, safety enforcement activity, and Federal funding, by State, 1987, annual rpt, 7304–5

Railroad accidents, casualties, and damage, by cause, railroad, and State, 1988, annual rpt, 7604–1

Railroad accidents, casualties, and damage, Fed Railroad Admin activities, and safety inspectors by State, 1987, annual rpt, 7604–12

Railroad employee benefits and beneficiaries by type, and railroad employment and payroll, FY85, annual rpt, 9704–2

Railroad employment, and benefits program finances and beneficiaries, FY88, annual rpt, 9704–1

Railroad-hwy grade-crossing accidents, detailed data by State and railroad, 1988, annual rpt, 7604–2

Rural areas electric and telephone loans by State, and REA activities and finances, FY88 with trends from FY36, annual rpt, 1244–3

Rural areas public transit services, operations and govt funding by region and State, 1986-87, 1278–11

Telephone firms borrowing under Rural Telephone Program, and financial and operating data, by State, 1988, annual rpt, 1244–2.3

Telephone firms borrowing under Rural Telephone Program, loan activity by State, FY88, annual tables, 1244–8

Telephone intrastate long distance call rates, impact of State entry and price regulation, 1983-87, 9406–1.55

Telephone service subscribership, charges, and local and long distance firm finances and operations, 1970s-FY89, semiannual rpt, 9282–7

Telephones in residences and businesses, carriage equipment miles, and calls placed, by State, 1987, annual rpt, 9284–6.2

Traffic accident impacts of speed limits, with accident circumstances and speed averages, for States with 55 and 65 mph limit, 1986-87, annual rpt, 7764–15

Traffic accidents impacts of drinking age laws, by State, 1975-87, 7768–103

Traffic accidents, injuries, and deaths, by circumstances and characteristics of persons and vehicles involved, 1970s-87, series, 7766–14

Traffic deaths by circumstances and State, drunk drivers involved in fatal accidents, and impacts of minimum age drinking laws, 1982-88, fact sheet, 7766–15.2

Traffic fatal accidents, deaths, and rates, by circumstances, characteristics of persons and vehicles involved, and location, 1987, annual rpt, 7764–10

Transit systems finances, costs, and needs, by State and selected system, 1980-88, biennial rpt, 7884–8

Transit systems in urban areas, services and vehicles, 1988 annual listing, 7884–9

Transportation census, 1987: trucks, by detailed characteristics, miles traveled, and type of product carried, State rpt series, 2573–1

Travel to US and Canada, market analysis
with detailed trip and traveler
characteristics, country rpt series, 2906–2

Travel to US, by characteristics of visit and
traveler, country, port city, and State of
destination, quarterly rpt, 2902–1

Travel to US, characteristics of visit and
traveler, world area of origin, and US
destination, 1988 survey, annual rpt,
2904–12

Travel to US, spending by category, world
area of residence, census div, and State,
model results, 1985-86, 2908–28

Urban Mass Transportation Admin grants for
transit systems, by city and State, FY88,
annual rpt, 7884–10

Education

American Historical Assn financial
statements, and membership by State,
1988, annual rpt, 29574–2

Bilingual education program activities,
Federal and State aid, and enrollment,
FY86-87, biennial rpt, 4804–14

Digest of Education Statistics, detailed data
on students, staff, finances, and facilities,
1989 edition, annual rpt, 4824–2

Education data, selected performance and
financial indicators by State, 1982-88,
annual table with supplements, 4804–32

Elementary and secondary education
enrollment, teachers, high school grads,
and spending, by State, 1988/89, annual
rpt, 4834–19

Elementary and secondary public education
agency revenues by source, and outlays, by
State, FY86-87, annual rpt, 4834–6

Elementary and secondary public school
agencies, by enrollment size and location,
fall 1987, annual listing, 4834–1

Elementary and secondary public schools,
enrollment, and teachers, by level and
State, 1987/88, annual rpt, 4834–17

Enrollment in public elementary and
secondary schools, by State, 1980s-90,
annual press release, 4804–19

Expenditures for education by Fed Govt,
State allocation by program, recipient type,
and State, 1987/88, annual rpt, 4804–8

Head Start enrollment, funding, and staff,
FY88, annual rpt, 4604–8

Head Start handicapped enrollment, by
handicap, State, and for Indian and migrant
programs, 1985/86, annual rpt, 4604–1

Head Start program operations, enrollment by
handicap, and family characteristics, for
North Central States, 1987/88, annual rpt,
4604–12

Historical Publications and Records Natl
Commission grants, by recipient and State,
FY88, annual rpt, 9514–2

Homeless children educational enrollment
and needs, 1988, annual State rpt series,
4804–35

Humanities Natl Endowment activities and
grants, FY88, annual rpt, 9564–2

Libraries (public), outlets, and staff, by hours
open, service population size, and selected
State, 1987, annual rpt, 4824–6

Libraries (public) services for Indians and
Hawaii Natives, project listing and funding
by tribe and State, FY88 rpt, 4874–5

Libraries (public) special programs, project
descriptions and funding by level of govt,
State, and city, 1984-87, annual rpt,
4874–4

Libraries (research) funding of Education
Dept, by project, instn, and State, FY88,
annual listing, 4874–2

Libraries for blind and handicapped,
readership, circulation, staff, funding, and
holdings, FY88, annual listing, 26404–3

Libraries technological aid, project
descriptions and funding, FY88, annual
listing, 4874–6

Library science training grants for
disadvantaged students, by instn and State,
FY89, annual listing, 4874–1

Nuclear engineering enrollment and degrees
by instn and State, and women grads plans
and employment, 1972-88, 3006–8.8

Private elementary and secondary schools,
enrollment, teachers, and high school
grads, by instn religious orientation,
1988/89, annual rpt, 4834–21

Radiation protection and health physics
enrollment and degrees granted by instn
and State, and women grads plans and
employment, 1972-88, 3006–8.9

School agencies (public elementary and
secondary), by type and State, 1987/88,
annual rpt, 4834–18

Special education enrollment by disability,
transfers to public schools from State
instns, services provided, and Federal
funding, with data by State, 1987-88, GAO
rpt, 26121–294

Special education programs, enrollment by
age, staff, funding, and needs, by type of
handicap and State, 1987/88, annual rpt,
4944–4

Statistical Abstract of US, social, political,
and economic data, 1790-2025,
comprehensive annual compilation,
2324–1.1

Student aid funding and participation, by
Federal program, instn type and control,
and State, various periods 1959-88, annual
rpt, 4804–28

Student aid Pell grants and applicants, by
tuition, income level, instn type and
control, and State, 1987/88, annual rpt,
4804–1

Student aid supplemental grants, loans, and
work-study awards, Federal share by instn
and State, 1989/90, annual listing,
4804–17

Student guaranteed loan default rates, and
claims paid by guaranty agencies, by State,
and borrower characteristics, FY87, GAO
rpt, 26121–292

Student guaranteed loan defaults, rates, and
borrowers in repayment status, by instn
and State, FY86, with background data,
1980s, hearings, 25548–96

Student loans of Fed Govt in default, losses,
and rates, by instn and State, as of June
1988, annual rpt, 4804–18

Vocational education for disadvantaged and
handicapped funding of Fed Govt, by
selected State and district, 1985-89 and
projected to 2000, GAO rpt, 26121–286

Energy Resources and Demand

Coal, coke, and breeze supply, demand,
prices, trade, and stocks, by end-use sector
and State, quarterly rpt with articles,
3162–37

Coal leasing activity on Federal land, acreage,
production, and reserves, by coal region
and State, FY88, annual rpt, 5724–10

Coal production and freight costs, and
competitive position in selected markets,
for Australia and US, 1987-89, 2048–143

Coal production and mines by county, prices,
productivity, miners, reserves, and stocks,
by mining method and State, 1987-88,
annual rpt, 3164–25

Coal production and stocks by district, and
shipments by district of origin, State of
destination, end-use sector, and mode of
transport, quarterly rpt, 3162–8

Coal production by State and region, trade,
use, and stocks, weekly rpt, 3162–1

Coal production, reserves, use, and prices by
State, exports by country, and employment,
1900s-87, biennial rpt, 3164–79

Coal reserves, by heat and sulfur content,
mining method, and State, 1987,
3168–114

Coal reserves, by type, region, and State, as
of Jan 1988, annual rpt, 3164–74.1

Conservation aid of DOE, activities, funding,
and grants by State, by program, FY88
annual rpt, 3304–21

Conservation grants of Fed Govt to public
and nonprofit private instns, by building
type and State, 1988, annual rpt, 3304–15

Consumption, by detailed fuel type, end-use
sector, and State, 1960-87, State Energy
Data System annual rpt, 3164–39

Consumption of energy, by air pollutant
source, fuel type, and State, 1986, annual
rpt, 9194–14

Distillate fuel production, imports, stocks,
and prices, by selected PAD district and
northern State, seasonal monthly rpt,
3162–40 •

DOE contracts and grants, by category,
State, and for top contractors, FY88,
annual rpt, 3004–21

Electric power plants (steam) fuel receipts,
costs, and quality, by fuel, plant, utility,
and State, 1988, annual rpt, 3164–42

Electric power plants and capacity, by fuel
used, owner, location, and operating status,
1988 and for units planned 1989-98, annual
listing, 3164–36

Electric power plants natural gas use, by
State, 1977 and 1988, annual rpt, 3104–8

Electric power plants production, capacity,
sales, and fuel stocks, use, and costs, by
State, 1984-88, annual rpt, 3164–11

Electric power plants production, fuel use,
stocks, and costs by fuel type, and sales, by
State, monthly rpt, 3162–35

Electric power sales, by end-use sector,
census div, and State, and fuel use and
costs, EIA and alternative estimates, with
methodology, 1982-87, 3166–12.5

Electric power trade of US with Canada,
purchase agreements, and grid
interconnection capacity, 1960s-88 and
projected to 1992, GAO rpt, 26113–228

Electric power wholesale purchases and costs
for REA borrowers, by borrower, supplier,
and State, 1940-87, annual rpt, 1244–5

Electric utilities fuel cost, quality, use,
receipts, and stocks, and power plant
production, by energy source, State and
utility, quarterly rpt, 3162–39

Electric utilities privately owned, detailed
finances and operations by firm, 1987,
annual rpt, 3164–23.1

Fed Govt and Indian land oil, gas, and
minerals production and revenue, by State,
1988 and trends from 1920, annual rpt,
5734–2

Gasohol consumption, by State, 1980-87, annual rpt, 3304-5.2

Gasohol use, and tax rates on all motor fuels, by State, 1987-88, annual rpt, 3304-9

Gasoline and other motor fuel use and tax rates, by State, monthly rpt, 7552-1

Hydroelectric power plants capacity, dev status, and ownership, by State and river basin, as of Jan 1988, quadrennial rpt, 3088-14

Hydroelectric power plants retired, characteristics and location, as of 1989, annual listing, 3084-12

Natural and supplemental gas production, prices, trade, use, reserves, and pipeline company finances, by firm and State, monthly rpt with articles, 3162-4

Natural gas interstate pipeline company capacity, use, sales, deliveries, and prices, by firm and Northeast State, 1980-88, 3166-6.35

Natural gas interstate pipeline company reserves and production, by firm, 1963-88 and deliverability projected to 2008, annual rpt, 3164-33

Natural gas interstate pipeline company sales, by customer, SIC 2-digit industry group, and State, monthly rpt, annual tables, 3162-4.6

Natural gas production, wells drilled, and contract prices, by Natural Gas Policy Act section, producer, State, and field, late 1970s-86, 3168-90

Natural gas supply, demand, distribution, and prices, by State, 1984-88 annual rpt, 3164-4

Nuclear power plant capacity, generation, and operating status, by plant and foreign and US location, 1988 and projected to 2020, annual rpt, 3164-57

Nuclear reactors for domestic use and export by function and operating status, with owner, operating characteristics, and location, 1988 annual listing, 3004-26

Offshore oil and gas leases, revenue sharing payments by State, FY86-91, press release, 5736-4.1

Offshore oil, gas, and minerals production, revenue, and leasing activity, for Federal OCS lands by ocean area and State, 1950s-87, annual rpt, 5734-3

Oil and gas leasing activity on Federal land, production, revenue, and royalty rates, by whether competitively leased and western State, 1984-88, GAO rpt, 26113-413

Oil crude, gas liquids, and refined products supply, demand, and movement, by PAD district and State, 1998 and trends from 1973, annual rpt, 3164-2

Oil, gas, and gas liquids reserves and production, by State and substate area, 1988, annual rpt, 3164-46

Oil products sales and purchases of refiners, processors, and distributors, by product, end-use sector, PAD district, and State, monthly rpt with articles, 3162-11

Oil products sales, and purchases of refiners, processors, and distributors, by product, end-use sector, PAD district, and State, 1988, annual rpt, 3164-85

Oil, refined products, and gas liquids supply, demand, trade, stocks, and refining, by detailed product, State, and PAD district, monthly rpt with articles, 3162-6

Rural areas electric and telephone loans by State, and REA activities and finances, FY88 with trends from FY36, annual rpt, 1244-3

Rural Electrification Admin loans, and borrower operating and financial data, by distribution firm and State, 1988, annual rpt, 1244-1

Rural Electrification Program lending, by State, as of FY88, annual rpt, 1244-7

Solar collector and photovoltaic module shipments by end-use sector and State, R&D, and trade, 1988, annual rpt, 3164-62

Southeastern Power Admin sales by customer, plants, capacity, and Southeastern Fed Power Program financial statements, FY88, annual rpt, 3234-1

Statistical Abstract of US, social, political, and economic data, 1790-2025, comprehensive annual compilation, 2324-1.3

Uranium mining and milling industries finances and operations, with selected foreign comparisons, 1970s-87 and projected to 2000, annual rpt, 3164-82

Uranium reserves and industry operations, by region and State, various periods 1966-88, annual rpt, 3164-65.1

Western Area Power Admin activities by plant, financial statements, and sales by customer, FY88, annual rpt, 3254-1

Geography and Climate

Charting and Geodetic Service of Natl Ocean Service activities and funding, by State, FY89-90, biennial rpt, 2174-10

Heating and cooling degree days weighted by population, by census div and State, with area-weighted temperature and precipitation, monthly rpt, 2152-13

Statistical Abstract of US, social, political, and economic data, 1790-2025, comprehensive annual compilation, 2324-1.1

Storms and unusual weather phenomena characteristics, casualties, and property damage, by State, monthly listing, 2152-3

Weather conditions and effect on agriculture, by US region, State, and city, and world area, weekly rpt, 2152-2

Weather data by census div and State, historical trends, indexes, major events, and maps, series, 2156-17

Weather data for farmland, average precipitation and temperature by State, monthly 1950-88, biennial rpt, 1544-28

Government and Defense

AID contracts and grants for technical and support services, by instn, country, and State, FY88, annual listing, 9914-7

Aliens admitted to US, by class of admission, port, country, and State of destination, quarterly rpt, 6262-2

Appalachia local dev projects, and funding by source, by program and State, FY88, annual rpt, 9084-1

Census of Govts, 1987: elected officials, by level of govt, race, sex, and State, preliminary rpt, 2450-2

Census of Govts, 1987: property tax revenue by level of govt, assessed values by locality, and exemptions, by property type and State, 2453-1

Census of Population and Housing, 1990: data collection procedure, and impacts on congressional apportionment by State, hearing, 25408-101

Congressional Directory, members of 101st Congress, other officials, elections, and districts, 1989-90, biennial rpt, 23874-1

DOD budget, organization, personnel, weapons, and property, by service branch, State, and country, 1989 annual summary rpt, 3504-13

DOD budget requests for base construction, renovation, and land acquisition, by project, service branch, State, and country, FY90/91, annual rpt, 3544-15

DOD civilian and military employment, by service branch and State, FY88, annual rpt, 3544-1.1

DOD civilian and military employment, by service branch, major installation, and State, as of Sept 1988, annual rpt, 3544-7

DOD contracts, payroll, and personnel, by service branch and location, with top 5 contractors and maps, by State and country, FY88, annual rpt, 3544-29

DOD in-house commercial activities work-years, by service branch, State, and installation, FY88, annual rpt, 3544-25

DOD prime contract awards, by category, contractor type, and State, FY86-88, annual rpt, 3544-11

DOD prime contract awards, by contractor, service branch, State, and city, FY88, annual rpt, 3544-22

DOD prime contract awards, by service branch and State, FY88, semiannual rpt, 3542-5

DOD prime contract awards in labor surplus areas, by service branch, State, and area, FY88, semiannual rpt, 3542-19

DOE real property owned and leased, by type, subagency, contractor, and site, FY87, annual rpt, 3004-28

DOT employment, by subagency, occupation, and selected personnel characteristics, FY88, annual rpt, 7304-18

Economic Dev Admin activities, and funding by program, recipient, State, and county, FY87 and cumulative from FY66, annual rpt, 2064-2

Economic Dev Admin funding, and loans forgiven, with data by project and location, FY84-88, hearing, 21648-56

Election campaign financial activity reported to FEC, by type of filer, 1988 natl elections, biennial rpt series, 9276-2

Election campaign receipts and spending of senatorial candidates, by party and State, 1989/90, press release, 9276-1.68

Election polling places accessibility to aged and disabled, precincts by barrier type and State, 1988 natl elections, biennial rpt, 9274-6

Election returns, by candidate and State, 1988 presidential election, press release, 9276-1.66

Employment (civilian) of Fed Govt, by work schedule, selected agency, State, and MSA, as of Dec 1988, article, 9842-1.904

Employment and payroll (civilian) of Fed Govt, by pay system and location, 1988, annual rpt, 9844-6.6

Employment and payroll, by function, level of govt, and State, 1988, annual rpt, 2466-1.1; 2466-1.5

Fed Govt revenue by source and State, *Treasury Bulletin*, quarterly rpt, annual data, 8002-4.1

Health Professions Bur training support grants, by program, region, and State, FY80-87, 4118–62

Heart, Lung, and Blood Natl Inst activities, and grants by recipient and location, FY88 with disease trends from 1940, annual rpt, 4474–15

Hepatitis cases by infection source, age, sex, race, and State, and deaths, by strain, 1987 and trends from 1966, 4205–2

HHS financial aid, by program, recipient, State, and city, FY88, annual regional listings, 4004–3

Hospital closures in 1987, operating characteristics, current use, and location, 1989 rpt, 4008–87

Hospital discharges, length of stay, and costs, for Medicare by type of beneficiary, procedure, diagnosis, and State, 1970s-86, article, 4652–1.945

Hospital Medicare discharges, charges, and length of stay, by State and diagnosis, 1983 and 1985, article, 4652–1.925

Hospital reimbursement by States under prospective payment programs, effects on operations, finances, and patient deaths, by State, 1970s-83, 4658–29

Infant and fetal deaths and rates, by race, sex, State, census div, and metro-nonmetro location, 1950s-85, 4146–5.107

Infectious notifiable disease cases, by age, State, and outlying area, and deaths, 1930s-88, annual rpt, 4204–1

Infectious notifiable diseases, cases and current outbreaks, by region and State, weekly rpt, 4202–1

Insurance (health) provided by employer, coverage and characteristics of plan and employer, 1986-87, hearing, 25368–160

Kidney end-stage disease program of Medicare, enrollment, eligibility, inpatient and home treatment, and facilities, by State, 1985, annual rpt, 4654–16.1; 4654–16.2

Kidney end-stage disease treatment facilities approved by Medicare, dialysis and transplant services and ownership, 1989 annual listing, 4654–17

Labs (clinical) under HCFA regulation, and labs with violations by Medicare termination and license status, 1983-87, hearings, 25408–98

Malpractice insurance premium costs and growth rate for physicians, alternative estimates by risk class and State, 1975-85, 4658–27

Marriages and rates, by age, race, education, previous marital status of spouses, and State, 1986, US Vital Statistics advance annual rpt, 4146–5.111; 4146–5.112

Marriages, divorces, and rates, by characteristics of spouses, State, and county, 1984 and trends from 1920, US Vital Statistics annual rpt, 4144–4

Mental health care hospitals of States and counties, patients and admissions by age, diagnosis, and State, FY87, annual rpt, 4504–2

Mentally retarded persons facilities, beds, and residents, by ownership, resident age and race, and State, 1986, 4147–14.34

Mine safety and health enforcement, training, and funding, with casualties, by type of mine and State, FY87, annual rpt, 6664–6

Minerals industries injuries by circumstances, employment, and hours, by type of operation and State, quarterly rpt, 6662–1

Mines (coal) and related operations occupational injuries and incidence, employment, and hours, 1987, annual rpt, 6664–4

Mines (metal) and related operations occupational injuries and incidence, employment, and hours, 1987, annual rpt, 6664–3

Mines (nonmetallic minerals) and related operations occupational injuries and incidence, employment, and hours, 1987, annual rpt, 6664–1

Mines (sand and gravel) and related operations occupational injuries and incidence, employment, and hours, 1987, annual rpt, 6664–2

Mines (stone) and related operations occupational injuries and incidence, employment, and hours, 1987, annual rpt, 6664–5

NIH activities, funding by program and recipient type, staff, and clinic patients, by inst, FY87, annual rpt, 4434–3

NIH grant and contract awards, for top 15 States, FY79-88, annual rpt, 4434–9

NIH grants for R&D, training, construction, and medical libraries, by location and recipient, FY88, annual listings, 4434–7

Nurses with alien resident status and temporary work visas, by State and source country, 1985-90, GAO rpt, 26121–314

Nursing facility service use and costs for Medicare enrollees, by selected characteristics and State, 1970s-87, article, 4652–1.954

Nursing home compliance with Medicare and Medicaid regulations, and patient characteristics, by facility, 1987/88, annual State rpt series, 4654–15

Nursing homes, beds, and residents, by ownership, certification status, and State, 1986, 4147–14.33

Occupational safety and health research and demonstration grants by State, and project listing, FY87, annual rpt, 4244–2

Psychiatrists, psychologists, and social workers supply, by selected State, 1983-87, hearing, 25148–42

Rabies cases in animals and humans, by location for US, Mexico, and Canada, 1988, annual rpt, 4202–7.904

Rural areas health care facilities, staffing, services accessibility, and indicators of need, 1960s-88, 25148–41

Sexually transmitted disease cases among Indians, by State, 1988, article, 4042–3.955

Smoking prevalence, related disease and deaths, and public attitudes, impact of Surgeon General rpts and antismoking campaigns, 1964-89, annual rpt, 4204–18

Smoking rates, by sex, age, race, occupation, region, and State, 1985 Current Population Survey, article, 4472–1.910

Statistical Abstract of US, social, political, and economic data, 1790-2025, comprehensive annual compilation, 2324–1.1

Tobacco (smokeless) use by youth and adults, user characteristics, and sales, 1970s-86, papers, 4478–188

Traffic accident deaths involving alcohol, by driver and victim blood alcohol levels and other characteristics, 1977-87, annual rpt, 4486–1.2; 4486–1.5; 4486–1.8

Trichinosis cases in US, by type of meat and State, 1986, article, 4202–7.901

Tuberculosis cases and deaths, by patient characteristics, State, and city, 1987 and trends from 1953, annual rpt, 4204–10

Vital statistics, preliminary 1987-88 and trends from 1950, annual rpt, 4144–7

Vital statistics provisional data, monthly rpt, 4142–1

Workers compensation benefits and benefit duration, by State, 1988, article, 4742–1.921

Workers compensation coverage and benefits, by type of program and insurer, and State, 1985-86, annual article, 4742–1.912

Workers compensation laws of States and Fed Govt, 1989 semiannual rpt, 6502–1

Workers compensation laws of States, changes in coverage, benefits, and premium rates, by State, 1988, annual article, 6722–1.906

Workers compensation programs of States, admin, coverage, benefits, finances, processing, and staff, 1984-88, annual rpt, 6504–9

Housing and Construction

Census of Construction Industries, 1987: financial and operating data, by SIC 4-digit industry and State, final rpt series, 2373–1

Community dev programs of HUD, funding and activities by program and State, FY88, annual rpt, 5124–5

Construction authorized by building permits, by type of construction, region, State, and MSA, bimonthly rpt, 2042–1.3

FmHA property acquired through foreclosure, 1-family homes, value, sales, and leases, by State, monthly rpt, 1182–7

Homeless children, by type of accommodation, urban-rural location, and State, alternative estimates, 1988, GAO rpt, 26131–61

Low-income housing stock, units eligible for subsidized mortgage prepayment, and index of affordable housing needs, by State, 1982-2006, article, 1702–1.903

Mobile home placements by structural characteristics, and price, by census div and State, monthly rpt, annual tables, 2382–1

Mobile home shipments from manufacturers, by State, monthly rpt, quarterly table, 2382–5

Mortgage originations, by State, 1978-88, annual press release, 5144–21

New England States economic indicators, Fed Reserve 1st District, monthly rpt, 9373–24

New England States economic indicators, Fed Reserve 1st District, quarterly rpt, 9373–2.4

New housing units authorized, by region, State, selected MSA, and permit-issuing place, monthly rpt, 2382–5

New housing units authorized, by State, MSA, and permit-issuing place, 1988, annual rpt, 2384–2

Rural areas rental housing units, vacancy, and rent exceeding 30% of renter income, by type of rental aid and State, FY88, hearing, 21248–117

Vending facilities run by blind on Federal and non-Federal property, finances and operations by agency and State, FY88, annual rpt, 4944–2

Wholesale trade census, 1987: employment, establishments, finances, and operations, by SIC 2- to 4-digit kind of business, MSA, county, and city, State rpt series, 2405–1

Labor and Employment

Clothing industry employment and wages impact of prohibition against hiring undocumented aliens, with data by State, 1975-85, article, 9393–8.904

Collective bargaining agreements expiring during year, and workers covered, by firm, union, industry group, and State, 1989, annual rpt, 6784–9

Earnings by major industry group, and personal income per capita and by source, by region and State, 1929-87, 2708–40

Employment and Earnings, detailed data, monthly rpt, 6742–2.5; 6742–2.6; 6742–2.8

Employment and Training Admin activities, funding, and participant characteristics, by program, FY80-86, 6408–71

Employment and unemployment, by age, sex, race, marital and family status, industry div, and State, Monthly Labor Review, 6722–1.2

Employment and unemployment, for 11 large States, monthly press release, 6742–5

Employment, earnings, and hours, by selected SIC 1- to 4-digit industry, State, and for 262 MSAs, 1972-87, 6748–81 ˎ

Employment programs, training, and unemployment compensation, current devs and grants to States, press release series, 6406–2

Employment services participation, placement rates, wages relative to community rates, and Federal funding, 1980-87, GAO rpt, 26121–296

Employment, unemployment, and labor force characteristics, by State, 1988, annual rpt, 6744–7.2

Exports and export-related employment, by SIC 2-digit industry and State, 1985-86 surveys, model results, annual rpt, 2506–16.1

Handbook of Labor Statistics, employment, unemployment, and labor force characteristics, 1940s-88 with trends from 1913, 6728–38.1; 6728–38.3

Labor Dept activities and funding, by program and State, FY88, annual rpt, 6304–1

Labor Relations Natl Board activities, cases, elections conducted, and litigation, FY85, annual rpt, 9584–1

Mediation and arbitration activities of Fed Mediation and Conciliation Service, and cases by issue, region, and State, FY82-87, annual rpt, 9344–1

Middle Atlantic States economic conditions, Fed Reserve 3rd District, quarterly rpt, 9387–10

Minority group and women employment, by occupation, SIC 1- to 3- digit industry, State, and MSA, 1986, annual rpt, 9244–1

New England States economic indicators, Fed Reserve 1st District, monthly rpt, 9373–24

New England States economic indicators, Fed Reserve 1st District, quarterly rpt, 9373–2.1

New England States employment, BLS benchmark revisions by industry div and State, 1987-88, article, 9373–2.903

Southeastern States collective bargaining calendar, 1989, annual rpt, 6946–1.73

Southeastern States, FHLB 4th District, employment and housing market indicators by State, quarterly rpt, 9302–36

Southeastern States manufacturing employment and earnings, by industry group, State, and urban-rural location, 1970s-85, article, 9371–1.901

Southeastern US employment and unemployment, for 8 States, 1987-88, annual rpt, 6944–2

Southeastern US employment by industry div, earnings, and hours, for 8 States, quarterly press release, 6942–7

Southeastern US employment conditions, series, 6946–1

Southeastern US employment conditions, with comparisons to other regions, press release series, 6946–3

Southeastern US textile mill employment, earnings, and hours, for 8 States, quarterly press release, 6942–1

Southwestern States employment by industry div, earnings, and hours, by State, monthly rpt, 6962–2

Statistical Abstract of US, social, political, and economic data, 1790-2025, comprehensive annual compilation, 2324–1.3

Trade adjustment aid for workers, petitions by disposition, selected industry, union, and State, monthly rpt, 6402–13

Unemployed displaced workers, by reason, industry, selected characteristics, and State, 1988, annual rpt, 6744–18

Unemployment, by State and metro area, monthly press release, 6742–12

Unemployment, employment, and labor force, by State, MSA, and city, monthly rpt, 6742–22

Unemployment insurance benefits and benefit duration, by State, 1988, article, 4742–1.921

Unemployment insurance coverage of establishments, employment, and wages, by SIC 4-digit industry and State, 1988, annual rpt, 6744–16

Unemployment insurance laws of States, comparison of provisions, as of Jan 1989, semiannual revisions to base edition, 6402–2

Unemployment insurance programs costs relation to local economic conditions, for North Central States, 1970s-88, working paper, 9375–13.9

Unemployment insurance programs of States and Fed Govt, benefits adequacy, and work disincentives, series, 6406–6

Unemployment insurance programs of States and Fed Govt, benefits, coverage, exhaustions, and finances, by State, and beneficiary characteristics, 1940s-FY89, 21788–175

Unemployment insurance programs of States, benefits, coverage, and tax provisions, as of July 1989, semiannual listing, 6402–7

Unemployment insurance programs of States, benefits, coverage, exhaustions, and finances by State, 1987, annual tables, 6404–10

Unemployment insurance programs of States, quality appraisal results, FY88, annual rpt, 6404–16

Unemployment insurance tax rates of States based on benefits paid former employees, and taxes and benefits share of payroll costs, by major industry group and State, 1969-88, 6406–6.29

Unemployment trust funds financial condition, by State, monthly rpt, 8102–9.16

Unemployment, underemployment, and related earnings losses, by worker characteristics and location, 1986, 1598–251

Vocational rehabilitation cases of State agencies, by disposition and State, FY88 and trends from FY21, annual rpt, 4944–5

Vocational rehabilitation programs of Fed Govt and States, activities and funding, FY88, annual rpt, 4944–1

Wages of workers covered by unemployment insurance, by State and industry div, 1987-88, annual press release, 6784–17.1

Law Enforcement

Assaults and deaths of law enforcement officers, by circumstances, agency, victim and offender characteristics, and location, 1988, annual rpt, 6224–3

Bombing incidents and casualties by target and circumstances, and explosives theft and recovery, by State, 1979-88, annual rpt, 8484–4

Bombing incidents, casualties, and damage, by target, circumstances, and State, 1988, annual rpt, 6224–5

Burglaries by time of day, and household victimization probability by region and State, 1965-87, annual rpt, 6224–8

Corrupt govt officials prosecuted and convicted, by judicial district and level of govt, 1978-88, annual rpt, 6004–13

Court caseloads, actions, procedure duration, judges, and jurors, by Federal district and appeals court, 1984-89, annual rpt, 18204–3

Court caseloads for Federal district, appeals, and bankruptcy courts, by type of suit and offense, circuit, and district, quarterly rpt, 18202–1

Court civil and criminal caseloads for Federal district, appeals, and special courts, June 1989, annual rpt, 18204–2; 18204–8

Crime, criminal justice admin and enforcement, and public opinion, data compilation, 1970s-88, annual rpt, 6064–6

Crimes, arrests by offender characteristics, and rates, by offense, and law enforcement employees, by population size and jurisdiction, 1988, annual rpt, 6224–2

Criminal case processing in Federal district courts, and dispositions, by offense, district, and offender characteristics, 1984, annual rpt, 6064–29

Criminal justice spending, employment, and payroll, by level of govt, State, and selected city and county, FY71-85, annual rpt, 6064–9

Drug enforcement activities of State and local agencies, Federal aid by recipient, and background data, FY88, annual rpt, 6064–28

Executions by whether writ of habeas corpus used to appeal, race, and State, with military death row inmates, 1977-87, hearing, 21408–110

Executions since 1930, and prisoners under death sentence by prison control and prisoner characteristics, by State, 1973-88, annual rpt, 6066-25.23

Juror (grand and petit) use and costs, trials, and trial days, by Federal district court, 1981-88, annual rpt, 18204-4

Juvenile correctional and detention instns, inmates, and expenses, by State, 1975-85, biennial rpt, 6064-13.1

Juvenile court delinquency cases, by offense, referral source, disposition, age, sex, race, State, and county, 1985, annual rpt, 6064-12

Marijuana crop eradication activities of DEA and local agencies by State, and drug potency, 1982-88, annual rpt, 6284-4

Parole and probation population, entries, and exits, by State, 1987, annual rpt, 6066-25.17

Prison cases of AIDS, test results, and prevention and control policies, by location, 1988 survey, annual rpt, 6064-22

Prison conditions, population, and problems, issues and bibl, 1989 compilation of papers, 25928-8

Prisoners in Federal and State instns by sex, admissions, and instn capacity and overcrowding, by State, 1980s-88, annual rpt, 6066-25.21

Prisoners, movements, and characteristics, by State, 1986, annual rpt, 6064-26

Public defender grants, by State, FY90-91, Judicial Conf proceedings, semiannual rpt, 18202-2

Sentences for Federal crimes, guidelines use and results by offense and district, and Sentencing Commission activities, 1988, annual rpt, 17664-1

Statistical Abstract of US, social, political, and economic data, 1790-2025, comprehensive annual compilation, 2324-1.1

US attorneys case processing and collections, by case type and Federal district, FY88, annual rpt, 6004-2

Wiretaps authorized, costs, arrests, trials, and convictions, by offense and jurisdiction, 1988, annual rpt, 18204-7

Natural Resources, Environment, and Pollution

Air pollution levels for 5 pollutants, by detailed source and State, 1986, annual rpt, 9194-7

Army Corps of Engineers activities and projects, FY87 and trends from 1800s, annual rpt, 3754-1.2

Asbestos abatement and technical aid, funding by State, 1985-88, hearing, 21248-119

Birds (duck) breeding population, by species, State, and Canada Province, 1988-89 with trends from 1955, annual rpt, 5504-30

Birds (mourning dove) population, by hunting and nonhunting State, 1966-89, annual rpt, 5504-15

Birds (sandhill crane) hunting activity and permits, by State and county, 1987/88-1988/89, annual rpt, 5504-31

Birds (waterfowl) coastal breeding population and colonies, by species and location, 1976-82 surveys, 5508-100

Birds (waterfowl) hunter harvest, age and sex ratios by species, State, and flyway, 1984-88, annual rpt, 5504-32

Birds (waterfowl) hunter harvest and unretrieved kills, and duck stamps sold, by species, State, and flyway, 1987-88, annual rpt, 5504-28

Birds (waterfowl) population, habitat conditions, and migratory flight forecasts, for Canada and US by region, 1989 and trends from 1955, annual rpt, 5504-27

Birds (woodcock) population in US and Canada from 1968, and hunter harvest, by State, 1989, annual rpt, 5504-11

Bitumen-bearing tar sand deposits locations and characteristics, as of 1984, 5668-88

Coal Surface Mining Reclamation and Enforcement Office activities and funding, by State and Indian tribe, FY87, annual rpt, 5644-1

Coastal and estuarine pollutant discharges, by source, pollutant type, and location, series, 2176-4

Coastal and riparian areas environmental conditions, fish, wildlife, use, and mgmt, for individual ecosystems, series, 5506-9

Coastal areas environmental impacts of economic dev and population growth, 1980s and projected to 2000, series, 2176-8

Conservation of soil and wetlands, USDA programs costs and impacts on farm finances and operations, with background data, 1980s, hearing, 25168-69

Electric utilities privately owned, air pollution emissions and abatement equipment by fuel type and State, 1987-88, annual rpt, 3164-11.5

Energy technologies environmental impacts, 1960s-80s, handbook series, 3326-1

Environmental quality and protection programs, and intl issues, 1988 annual rpt, 484-1

EPA pollution control grant program activities, monthly rpt, 9182-8

Estuary environmental conditions and mgmt, for individual areas, conf series, 2146-6

Fish (striped bass) stocks status on Atlantic coast, and sport and commercial catch by State, 1979-87, annual rpt, 5504-29

Fish and Wildlife Service restoration programs finances by State, and excise tax collections, FY88, annual rpt, 5504-13

Fish and Wildlife Service restoration programs funding, land purchases, and project listing, by State, FY87, annual rpt, 5504-1

Fishery research of State fish and wildlife agencies, federally funded projects and costs by species and State, 1989, annual listing, 5504-23

Forest Service activities and finances, by region and State, FY88, annual rpt, 1204-1

Forest Service revenue, share paid to States and natl forest acreage by forest, region, county, and congressional district, FY88, annual rpt, 1204-33

Forests (natl) and other lands under Forest Service mgmt, acreage by forest and location, 1988, annual rpt, 1204-2

Forests (natl) revenue, by source, forest, and State, FY88, annual rpt, 1204-34

Forests improvement program for private timberland, Fed Govt cost-sharing funds by region and State, monthly table, 1802-11

Great Lakes basin pollutant discharges, sources, and control program activities, 1987, biennial rpt, 14644-1

Groundwater pollution from soil injection of oil and gas refining wastes, by State, 1987, GAO rpt, 26113-429

Hazardous substances industrial releases and reduction methods under EPA regulation, by chemical, source, industry, and location, 1987, annual rpt, 9234-6

Hazardous waste site remedial action under Superfund, current and proposed sites descriptions and status, periodic listings, series, 9216-3

Hazardous waste site remedial action under Superfund, current and proposed sites priority ranking and status by location, as of July 1989, listing, 9218-64

Helium and other components of natural gas, analyses of individual wells and pipelines, 1917-88, annual rpt, 5604-2

Helium resources in storage and natural gas reserves, by State, 1950-87 and projected to 2020, biennial rpt, 5604-44

Horse and burro wild herd areas in western States, population, adoption, and protection, and mgmt costs, as of FY87, biennial rpt, 5724-8

Land Mgmt Bur activities and funding by State, and receipts by program, FY87, annual rpt, 5724-13

Landfills requiring cleanup under Federal and State programs, by operating status, disposition of site expansion applications, and State, 1986-88, GAO rpt, 26113-430

Landmarks (natl historic and natural) damaged and threatened, with owner, location, damage type, and recommended remedial action, 1988, annual listing, 5544-16

Military installations hazardous waste site remedial action, activities and funding by site and State, FY88, annual rpt, 3544-36

Minerals industries water supply and use, and production, by commodity and State, 1950s-84 and projected to 2000, 5608-153

Minerals production and revenue on Federal and Indian land, by State, 1988 and trends from 1920, annual rpt, 5734-2

Minerals resources and availability on public lands, State rpt series, 5606-7

Mining claims on public lands, patents by type and State, and applications by disposition, 1978-87, GAO rpt, 26113-403

Pollution abatement capital and operating costs, by SIC 2-to 4-digit industry and State, 1986, annual Current Industrial Rpt, 2506-3.6

Public lands acreage and use, and Land Mgmt Bur activities and finances, annual State rpt series, 5724-11

Public lands acreage, grants, use, revenues, and allocations, by State, FY88 and trends, annual rpt, 5724-1

Radiation and radionuclide concentrations in air, water, and milk, monitoring results by State and site, quarterly rpt, 9192-5

Radioactive waste and spent fuel generation, inventory, and disposal, 1960s-88 and projected to 2020, annual rpt, 3364-2

Radon indoor air pollution levels, by county and State, 1989, annual rpt, 9194-19

Reclamation Bur activities, finances, and project impacts in western US, annual rpts, 5824-12

Sewage pipelines and dump sites authorized in coastal areas, status and EPA enforcement activities by State, 1982-87, hearings, 21568-45

Soil, water, and environmental conservation and conditions, with data by State and region, 1989 quinquennial rpt, 1268–24

Timber and windbarrier planting and dev, by State, FY88, annual rpt, 1204–7

Timber improvement program for private land, participation and payments by State, as of FY87, annual rpt, 1804–20

Timber in northeastern US, resources and removals by species, ownership class, and county, State rpt series, 1206–12

Timber insect and disease incidence and damage, annual regional rpt series, 1206–11

Timber insect and disease incidence and damage, by State, 1988, annual rpt, 1204–8

Timber sales of Forest Service, expenses, and operations, by State and natl forest, FY88, annual rpt, 1204–36.3

Wastewater treatment and collection facility construction funding needs and Fed Govt grants, by State, 1988 and projected to 2008, biennial rpt, 9204–7

Wastewater treatment facility construction grants of EPA to State and local govts, by project, monthly listing, 9202–3

Water pollution from farming, funding for control under Rural Clean Water Program by project and State, monthly table, 1802–14

Water pollution incidents and discharges, by type, source, cause, and location, 1984-86, annual rpt, 7404–3

Water resources dev projects of Army Corps of Engineers, characteristics, and costs, 1950s-87, biennial State rpt series, 3756–2

Water resources dev projects of Army Corps of Engineers, characteristics, and costs, 1950s-89, biennial State rpt series, 3756–1

Water supply and quality in streams and lakes, and groundwater levels in wells, by drainage basin, 1986, annual State rpt series, 5666–23

Water supply and quality in streams and lakes, and groundwater levels in wells, by drainage basin, 1987, annual State rpt series, 5666–10

Water supply and quality in streams and lakes, and groundwater levels in wells, by drainage basin, 1988, annual State rpt series, 5666–16

Water supply in western US, and snow survey results, monthly State rpt series, 1266–2

Water supply in western US, and snow survey results, 1988, annual State rpt series, 1264–14

Water supply in western US, storage by reservoir and State, and streamflow conditions, as of Oct 1989, annual rpt, 1264–4

Water use from Colorado River Basin Project, by State and for Mexico, 1981-85, annual rpt, 5824–6

Wetlands acreage acquired by Fed Govt, and costs, by site and State, FY89, annual rpt, 14784–1

Wetlands acreage, and agreements and payments to farmers under Water Bank Program, by State, FY72-89, annual rpt, 1804–21

Wetlands acreage conserved and disturbed in southeastern US, by disturbance type and State, 1987, article, 2162–1.902

Wetlands preservation under Water Bank Program, acreage, agreements, and payments, by State, monthly rpt, 1802–5

Wilderness areas acreage by Federal agency and location, and sources of damage, with data for foreign countries, 1988 conf papers, 1208–301

Wilderness Preservation Natl System acreage, by site and State, 1987, annual rpt, 1004–15

Wildlife refuges and other land under Fish and Wildlife Service mgmt, acreage by site and State, as of Sept 1988, annual rpt, 5504–8

Wildlife research of State fish and wildlife agencies, federally funded projects and costs by species and State, 1989, annual listing, 5504–24

Population

Asian American earnings, and employment and other characteristics, by detailed origin and whether foreign-born, 1980, 11046–7.2

Educational attainment, by sociodemographic characteristics and location, 1987 and trends from 1940, biennial Current Population Rpt, 2546–1.427; 2546–1.431

Households and population size, by State, 1980 and 1988, annual press release, 2324–11

Immigration to US, alien workers, visitors, deportations, and naturalizations, by country, FY88 and trends from 1820, annual rpt, 6264–2

Income (household), median for 4-person families by State, 1969 and 1974-86, 2548–10

Income (personal) per capita and by source, and earnings by industry div, by State, MSA, and county, 1982-87, annual regional rpts, 2704–2

Income (personal) per capita and by source, earnings by major industry group, and social insurance contributions, by region and State, 1929-87, 2708–40

Income (personal) per capita and total, and earnings by industry group, by region and State, 1986-88, annual article, 2702–1.928

Income (personal) per capita and total, by State, MSA, county, and metro-nonmetro location, 1985-87, article, 2702–1.916

Income (personal) per capita, by coastal region and State, 1988, annual rpt, 7704–12.2

Income (personal) per capita, by region and for lowest- and highest-income States, 1982 and 1988, article, 2702–1.914

Income (personal) per capita impacts of Federal and defense spending and taxation, by State, 1950s-87, article, 9391–1.918

Income (personal) totals, by region, census div, and State, quarterly article, 2702–1.32

Migration to and from Southern US, by migrant characteristics and location, 1970s-87 and alternative projections to 2000, article, 9371–1.902

Minority group population, and components of change, by race, State, metro-nonmetro location, MSA, and county, 1980-85, Current Population Rpt, 2580–3.159

Older persons socioeconomic characteristics, 1900s-86 and projected to 2050, biennial chartbook, 12904–1

Population estimates and projections, by region and State, Current Population Rpt series, 2546–3

Population size, July 1988 and compared to 1980 and 1987, and components of change, 1980-88, annual press release, 2324–10

Population size of counties, 1988, and components of change from 1980, annual Current Population Rpt, 2544–3

Refugee arrivals and resettlement in US, by age, sex, sponsoring agency, State, and country, monthly rpt, 4692–2

Refugee arrivals in US by world area of origin and State of settlement, and Federal aid, FY88-90, annual rpt, 7004–16

Statistical Abstract of US, social, political, and economic data, 1790-2025, comprehensive annual compilation, 2324–1.1

Prices and Cost of Living

Dairy prices, by product and selected area, with related marketing data, 1988, annual rpt, 1317–1

Electric power billings for housing, and rankings, by State, as of Jan 1988, annual rpt, 1244–1.6

Electric power rate schedules, by user type, utility, and city, as of Jan 1988, annual rpt, 3164–40

Energy prices and spending, by fuel type, end-use sector, and State, 1987, annual rpt, 3164–64

Farm prices received and paid, by commodity and State, 1988, annual rpt, 1629–5

Farm prices received and production value, by detailed crop and State, 1986-88, annual rpt, 1621–2

Fruit and vegetable wholesale prices in NYC, Chicago, and selected shipping points, by crop, 1988, annual rpt, 1311–8

Heating oil retail prices, by State, and wholesale prices and dealer margins, monthly rpt, 3162–24.9

Poultry and egg prices and marketing, by selected region, State, and city, monthly and weekly 1988, annual rpt, 1317–2

Statistical Abstract of US, social, political, and economic data, 1790-2025, comprehensive annual compilation, 2324–1.3

Public Welfare and Social Security

AFDC beneficiaries by county, payments, application processing and disposition, hearings, and fraud cases, by State, FY87, annual rpt, 4694–7

AFDC provisions, by State, FY88, annual rpt, 4694–4

AFDC recipients demographic and financial characteristics, by State, FY87, annual rpt, 4694–1

Aliens (illegal) welfare benefits, operations of Federal-State system to prevent payment, State official views, 1988, GAO rpt, 26121–276

Child support collection programs of States, operations, costs, and Federal incentive payments, by State, FY86-1987, 4698–3

Child support enforcement automated systems of States, operational status by State and whether federally funded, 1985-88, GAO rpt, 26121–272

Disability Insurance and SSI admin of Fed Govt and States, benefits, caseloads, and operations, 1980s, 4708–11

Disability Insurance and SSI eligibility determinations for mental impairment, caseload and review activities by impairment type and State, 1984-86, hearing, 21788–176

Employment and earnings covered under OASDHI, and social security contributions, by age, sex, race, State, and county, 1985, 4748–43

Fed Govt programs under Ways and Means Committee jurisdiction, finances and operations, FY70s-88, annual rpt, 21784–11

Fed Govt spending in States, by type, program, agency, and State, FY88, annual rpt, 2464–2

Food aid program of USDA for women, infants, and children, participants and costs by State and Indian agency, FY87, annual rpt, 1364–12

Food aid program of USDA for women, infants, and children, participants, clinics, and costs by State and Indian agency, monthly tables, 1362–16

Food aid programs of USDA, costs and participation by program, region, and State, monthly rpt, 1362–14

Food stamp eligibility and payment errors, by type, recipient characteristics, and State, FY87, annual rpt, 1364–15

Food stamp issues and participation, by State and county, as of July 1988, semiannual rpt, 1362–6

HHS financial aid, by program, recipient, State, and city, FY88, annual regional listings, 4004–3

Medicaid coverage, participation, payments, admin, and legislative history, with data by State, 1980s-88, 21368–105

Medicaid eligibility extension to pregnant women and children with incomes over AFDC levels, with data by State, 1986-89, GAO rpt, 26121–303

Medicaid policies and State health insurance regulation for AIDS patients and persons with AIDS virus infection, with background data, 1987-88, article, 4652–1.953

Medicare and Medicaid eligibility, participation, coverage, and program finances, various periods 1966-89, biennial rpt, 4654–1

Medicare and Medicaid outlays per enrollee, for aged and disabled beneficiaries by State, 1986, Current Population Rpt, 2546–6.58

Medicare enrollment, and use by type of service, by age, sex, race, region, State, and MSA, 1986-87, annual rpt, 4657–5

Nursing home certifications by Medicare, beds, and coverage of Medicare enrollees, by State, 1981 and 1985, annual rpt, 4654–13

OASDHI, Medicaid, SSI, and related programs benefits, beneficiary characteristics, and trust funds, selected years 1937-87, annual rpt, 4744–3

OASDI and SSI disabled beneficiaries, by selected characteristics, 1986, article, 4742–1.916

OASDI benefits and beneficiaries, by type of benefit, State, and county, as of Dec 1987, annual rpt, 4744–28

Older persons aid and policies of Fed Govt, program funding, and grants awarded, FY80-89, annual rpt, 25144–3.2

Poverty rate, impact of public income transfers by State, 1984-88, article, 6722–1.933

Refugee resettlement programs and funding, arrivals by country of origin, and indicators of adjustment, by State, FY88, annual rpt, 4694–5

Social Security Bulletin, OASDHI and other program operations and beneficiary characteristics, from 1940, monthly rpt with articles, 4742–1

Statistical Abstract of US, social, political, and economic data, 1790-2025, comprehensive annual compilation, 2324–1.2

Supplemental Security Income and Medicaid eligibility and payment provisions, and beneficiaries living arrangements, by State, 1989, annual rpt, 4704–13

Supplemental Security Income payments and beneficiaries, by type of eligibility, State, and county, Dec 1987, annual rpt, 4744–27

Unemployment insurance programs costs relation to local economic conditions, for North Central States, 1970s-88, working paper, 9375–1.902

Recreation and Leisure

Boat registrations and accidents, casualties, and damage by cause, by vessel characteristics and State, 1988, annual rpt, 7404–1

Fishing (ocean sport) catch and effort, and Natl Marine Fisheries Service tagging and research activity, by species and location, 1987, annual rpt, 2164–7

Fishing and hunting licenses issued, and costs, by State, FY88, annual press release, 5504–16

Foreign travel to US, tour promotion by region of destination and country of traveler, 1987, 2908–31

Forests (natl) recreational use, by type of activity and State, 1988, annual rpt, 1204–17

Historic and natural natl landmarks damaged and threatened, with owner, location, damage type, and recommended remedial action, 1988, annual listing, 5544–16

Historic Preservation Fund grants, by State, FY90, annual table, 5544–9

Lighthouses historic preservation grants, by State, FY89, press release, 5306–4.1

Park natl system visits and overnight stays, by park and State, 1988 and trends from 1979, annual rpt, 5544–12

Statistical Abstract of US, social, political, and economic data, 1790-2025, comprehensive annual compilation, 2324–1.1

Wildlife-related recreation, hunting, and fishing participation and spending, detailed data by location, 1985 survey, quinquennial rpt, 5508–5

Wildlife-related recreation, hunting, and fishing participation and spending, detailed data, 1985 survey, quinquennial State rpt series, 5506–6

Science and Technology

Animal protection, licensing, and inspection activities of USDA, and animals used in research, by State, FY88, annual rpt, 1394–10

Degrees (PhD) in science and engineering, by field, instn, employment prospects, sex, race, and other characteristics, 1960s-88, 9627–30

Employment and other characteristics of science and engineering PhDs, by field and State, 1987, biennial rpt, 9627–18

Energy-related inventions recommended by Natl Inst of Standards and Technology for DOE support, awards, and evaluation status, 1988, annual listing, 2214–5

Enrollment in science and engineering grad programs, by field, source of funds, and characteristics of student and instn, 1975-87, annual rpt, 9627–7

Fed Govt science and engineering employment, by field, degree level, race, sex, agency, and State, 1987, annual rpt, 9627–5

Immigrant scientists and engineers, by field, age, sex, country and world area of origin, and State, 1987 and trends from 1967, 9627–29

NASA funding by program and type of performer, and contract awards by State, FY88, annual rpt, 9504–6.2

NASA procurement contract awards, by type, contractor, State, and country, FY89, semiannual rpt, 9502–6

NASA procurement economic benefits by industry group, jobs created, and sales, by State, FY90, 9508–35

NSF grants and contracts, by field, inst, State, and country, FY88, annual rpt, 9624–26

Patents (US) granted to US and foreign applicants, by State and country, 1987-88, annual press release, 2244–2

Patents granted to US residents, by State, FY81-88, annual rpt, 2244–1.2

R&D and related funding of Fed Govt to higher education and nonprofit instns, by field, instn, agency, and State, FY87, annual rpt, 9627–17

R&D funding by Fed Govt, by field, performer type, agency, and State, FY87-89, annual rpt, 9627–20

R&D funding by source and performer, and related employment, by State, 1975-87, 9626–6.32

R&D funding, by source, performer, and for top 10 States, 1977-89, 9626–2.185

R&D funding, performance by geographic division and State, and science and technology employment, selected years 1953-89, annual rpt, 9624–18.1

Science and math teacher training and high school course requirements, by State, 1988 rpt, 26358–199

Small business R&D grants of Fed Govt, by program area, agency, and State, FY88, annual rpt, 9764–7

Veterans Affairs

Disability and death compensation cases of VA, by entitlement type, period of service, sex, age, and State, FY88, annual rpt, 8604–7

Insurance (life) for veterans and servicepersons, finances and coverage by program and State, 1988, annual rpt, 8604–4

Population and characteristics of veterans, and VA hospital and other activities, by State, FY88, annual rpt, 8604–3

Population of veterans, by period of service, age, and State, as of Mar 1989, semiannual rpt, 8602–7

Statistical Abstract of US, social, political, and economic data, 1790-2025, comprehensive annual compilation, 2324–1.2

VA programs spending, by State, county, and congressional district, FY88, annual rpt, 8604-6

BY URBAN-RURAL AND METRO-NONMETRO

Agriculture and Food
Africa (Sahel) food supply indicators, by country, 1960s-2000, 1528-290

Farms, sales, size, and operator tenure in metro and nonmetro areas, impacts of population growth, with data by State, 1969-82, 1598-253

Financial condition of farms, and farm household income by source, 1970-88, annual rpt, 1504-4

Food consumption and nutrient intake by individuals, by food group, selected characteristics, and region, supplementary survey series, 1356-5

Banking, Finance, and Insurance
Banks (commercial) specializing in real estate loans, financial condition, 1989 technical paper, 9366-6.202

Banks finances and operations, by metro-nonmetro location, 1986, annual rpt, 1544-29

Banks status changes, instns, assets, and concentration ratios by size, ownership, and location, and compared to other financial instns, 1976-87, article, 9362-1.902

Economic and population data for rural and urban areas, 1960s-88, annual chartbook, 1504-3

Communications and Transportation
Bridges in rural areas, conditions, needs, and funding, with data by State and compared to urban areas, 1988, 1278-16

Hwy and bridge conditions, travel, and funding, by type of hwy, 1960s-87 and projected to 2005, biennial rpt, 7554-27

Hwy construction material prices and indexes for Federal-aid system, by type of material and urban-rural location, quarterly rpt, 7552-7

Hwy Statistics, summary data by State, 1987-88, annual rpt, 7554-24

Hwy Trust Fund obligations, by project and urban-rural location, 1982-86, 1278-12

Railroad-hwy grade-crossing accidents, detailed data by State and railroad, 1988, annual rpt, 7604-2

Traffic accident impacts of speed limits, with accident circumstances and speed averages, for States with 55 and 65 mph limit, 1986-87, annual rpt, 7764-15

Traffic fatal accidents, alcohol levels of drivers and others, by circumstances and characteristics of persons and vehicles, 1988, annual rpt, 7764-16

Traffic fatal accidents, circumstances, and characteristics of persons and vehicles involved, 1988, semiannual rpt, 7762-11

Traffic fatal accidents, deaths, and rates, by circumstances, characteristics of persons and vehicles involved, and location, 1987, annual rpt, 7764-10

Education
Community organizations partnerships with public schools, participation, activities, and contributions, by school characteristics and location, 1987/88, 4826-1.27

Desegregation of schools, indicators of integration plans effectiveness by school district and location, 1960s-85, 11048-189

Effective schools programs for improving academic achievement, characteristics of schools, districts, and students, 1987/88, GAO rpt, 26121-304

Elementary and secondary public school agencies, by enrollment size and location, fall 1987, annual listing, 4834-1

Enrollment, by grade, instn type and control, and student characteristics, 1986 and trends from 1947, annual Current Population Rpt, 2546-1.429; 2546-1.432

High school dropout rates, and subsequent completion, by student and school characteristics, alternative estimates, 1988, annual rpt, 4834-23

Energy Resources and Demand
Buildings (commercial) energy use, costs, and conservation, by building characteristics, survey rpt series, 3166-8

Housing energy use, costs, and conservation, and household and housing characteristics, survey rpt series, 3166-7

Government and Defense
Fed Govt aid to rural areas compared to urban areas, by program and degree of urbanization, FY85, periodic rpt, 1598-248

Military reserve spouses attitudes, and family social, economic, and other characteristics, 1986 survey, 3508-30

Property (real) of Fed Govt, inventory and costs, worldwide summary by location, agency, and use, 1987, annual rpt, 9454-5

Property (real) of Fed Govt, leased inventory and rental costs, worldwide summary by location and agency, 1987, annual rpt, 9454-10

Taxes, spending, and govt efficiency, public opinion by respondent characteristics, 1989 survey, annual rpt, 10044-2

Voting and registration, by socioeconomic and demographic characteristics, 1988 presidential election, biennial Current Population Rpt, 2546-1.440

Health and Vital Statistics
Abortions, by method, pregnancy history, and other characteristics of woman, 1985-86, US Vital Statistics annual rpt, 4146-5.108

Abortions by patient characteristics, rates for all and 1st abortions, and related deaths in US and other countries, 1989 hearing, 21408-113

Acute and chronic health conditions, disability, absenteeism, and health services use, by selected characteristics, 1988, annual rpt, 4147-10.170

Alcohol use, abuse, treatment, and views of racial and ethnic groups in US and native countries, by selected characteristics, 1988 compilation of papers, 4488-12

Alcohol use and abuse among minority groups, and related problems, by selected characteristics, 1985 conf papers, 4488-13

Births, fertility rates, and childless women, by selected characteristics, 1988, annual Current Population Rpt, 2546-1.436

Deaths and rates, by detailed location, cause, and demographic characteristics, 1987, US Vital Statistics annual rpt, 4144-3.1

Diabetes control levels, and other health indicators, for non-insulin-dependent Indians treated at rural and urban clinics, 1984-86 study, article, 4042-3.946

Disabled persons employment, labor force status, and other characteristics, 1988, Current Population Rpt, 2546-2.147

Drug, alcohol, and cigarette use and attitudes of youth, by substance type and selected characteristics, 1975-88 surveys, annual rpt, 4494-4

Health care facilities, staffing, services accessibility, and indicators of need, for rural areas, 1960s-88, 25148-41

Health care treatments and products not proven safe or effective, use, costs, and user characteristics, 1986 survey, 4008-86

Health condition and health care resources, use, and spending, 1950s-87, annual data compilation, 4144-11

Hospice services awareness of aged, by age, sex, education, region, SMSA/non-SMSA residence, and cancer history, 1984 survey, article, 4042-3.915

Hospital closures in 1987, operating characteristics, current use, and location, 1989 rpt, 4008-87

Hospital reimbursement by Medicare under prospective payment system, capital cost reimbursement adjustments financial impacts by instn characteristics, 1978-87, 17206-1.1

Hospital reimbursement by Medicare under prospective payment system, impacts on costs, industry structure and operations, and quality of care, series, 17206-2

Hospital reimbursement by Medicare under prospective payment system, impacts on profit margins, and instn characteristics, 1986/87, hearing, 21148-52

Hospital service area population care need indicators, and travel distances, for rural and urban instns in New York State, 1983, 4188-53

Infant and fetal deaths and rates, by race, sex, State, census div, and metro-nonmetro location, 1950s-85, 4146-5.107

Insurance (health) coverage of adolescents by selected characteristics, and impacts of mandated employer and expanded Medicaid coverage, 1979-87, 26358-205

Insurance (health) coverage of total and working population, by selected characteristics, 1987, 4186-8.1

Lead poisoning among children, and impacts of lead removal from housing, gasoline, and water, 1987 conf, 4108-46

Long-term health care needs, ability to pay, and views on Federal aid for home care, 1988 survey, hearing, 21148-51

Nursing chief officers in hospitals, activities, responsibilities, and role in nurse hiring and retention, 1988 survey, 4008-91

Nursing home facility, staff, and resident detailed characteristics, 1985, 4147-13.97

Nutritional status and related health condition and practices, by selected characteristics, 1970s-87, 4048-33

Older persons functional limitations, by activity type and selected characteristics, 1984, 4147-10.167

Older persons preventive health care services use, and relation to selected characteristics, 1970s-80s, 26356-7.2

Ophthalmologist office visits, by characteristics of physician, practice, patient, and visit, with drug mentions by type and brand, 1985, 4146-8.166

Physicians income, by specialty and other practice characteristics, 1975 and 1983-84, article, 4652-1.920

Poverty population under alternative definitions and metro-nonmetro location, 1983-84, Survey of Income and Program Participation, working paper, 2626–10.72

Poverty status of families and persons, by detailed characteristics, 1987, annual Current Population Rpt, 2546–6.60

Retirees savings maintenance and liquidation, by selected financial and other characteristics, 1971-79, article, 1702–1.906

Southern US poverty rates, by household composition, race, and urban-rural location, 1986, article, 9371–1.903

Statistical Abstract of US, social, political, and economic data, 1790-2025, comprehensive annual compilation, 2324–1.1

Prices and Cost of Living

Child rearing costs, by age, region, and urban-rural location, quarterly rpt, 1702–1

Consumer Expenditure Survey, household income by source, and itemized spending, by selected characteristics and location, 1984-86, annual rpt, 6764–5.2

Consumer Expenditure Survey, spending by category, and income, by selected household characteristics and location, 1987, press release, 6726–1.23

Consumer spending in metro and nonmetro areas, by item, 1987, article, 6722–1.962

Public Welfare and Social Security

Child support and alimony awards, and payment status, by selected characteristics of woman, 1985, biennial Current Population Rpt, 2546–2.145

Medicare enrollment, and use by type of service, by age, sex, race, region, State, and MSA, 1986-87, annual rpt, 4657–5

Medicare physicians assigned fee participation related to selected physician, practice, and community characteristics, 1984, article, 4652–1.902

Medicare reimbursement of hospitals under prospective payment system, alternative case mix indexes, FY85-86, article, 4652–1.952

Medicare reimbursement of hospitals under prospective payment system, and of physicians, effect on services, finances, and beneficiary payments, 1970s-88, annual rpt, 17204–2

Medicare reimbursement of hospitals under prospective payment system, area wage index adjusted for health occupation mix, by location, 1984-85, article, 4652–1.950

Medicare reimbursement of hospitals under prospective payment system, cost accounting alternatives, model description and results, FY84, article, 4652–1.948

Medicare reimbursement of hospitals under prospective payment system, costs under alternative cost updating procedures, model estimates, 1976-84, article, 4652–1.921

Medicare reimbursement of hospitals under prospective payment system, impacts on instns, beneficiaries, and other care providers and payment sources, 1986, annual rpt, 4654–13

Medicare reimbursement of hospitals under prospective payment system, methodology, inputs, and data by diagnostic group, 1989 annual rpt, 17204–1

Medicare reimbursement of hospitals under prospective payment system, proposed inclusion of capital costs, with background data, FY84-88 and projected to 2008, 26308–83

Medicare reimbursement of hospitals under prospective payment system, regulatory adjustments review and diagnostic group weight calibration, FY90, annual rpt, 17204–3

OASDI and SSI disabled beneficiaries, by selected characteristics, 1986, article, 4742–1.916

Public welfare programs beneficiaries, and benefits duration and share of income, by selected characteristics, 1983-86, 2546–20.8

Recreation and Leisure

Park natl system visits and overnight stays, by park and State, monthly rpt, 5542–4

Park natl system visits and overnight stays, by park and State, 1988 and trends from 1979, annual rpt, 5544–12

Wildlife-related recreation, hunting, and fishing participation and spending, detailed data by location, 1985 survey, quinquennial rpt, 5508–5

Wildlife-related recreation, hunting, and fishing participation and spending, detailed data, 1985 survey, quinquennial State rpt series, 5506–6

Science and Technology

Education in science and engineering in elementary and secondary schools, and student persistence in postsecondary education, 1977-88, 26358–199

ECONOMIC BREAKDOWNS

BY COMMODITY

Agriculture and Food

Acreage planted, by selected crop and State, 1980-88 and planned 1989, annual rpt, 1621–22

Acreage under Agricultural Stabilization and Conservation Service programs, rankings by commodity and congressional district, 1987, biennial rpt, 1804–17

Africa agricultural exports by commodity, and relation to economic conditions and other factors, by country, 1960s-87, 1528–280

Agricultural data compilation, 1987/88 and trends from 1920, annual rpt, 1004–14

Agricultural Outlook, production, prices, marketing, and trade, by commodity, forecast and current situation, monthly rpt with articles, 1502–4

Agricultural Stabilization and Conservation Service programs, annual commodity fact sheet series, 1806–4

Agricultural Statistics, 1988, annual rpt, 1004–1

Alien workers (unauthorized) employer sanctions impacts on farm labor costs, by farm type, size, and region, 1986, 1598–250

Business statistics, detailed data for major industries and economic indicators, *Survey of Current Business*, monthly rpt, 2702–1.11

CCC activities and finances, by program, FY87, last issue of annual rpt, 1824–1

CCC certificate (generic commodity) issues and exchanges by commodity, and wheat auction sales, 1987-89, article, 1502–4.904

CCC certificate exchange activity, by commodity, weekly press release, 1802–16

CCC commodities for sale, and prices, monthly press release, 1802–4

CCC financial statements and operations, by program and commodity, FY88, annual rpt, 1824–4

CCC loan activities by commodity, and agency operating results, monthly press release, 1802–7

CCC loan and support programs payment activity, with data by commodity, 1986-88 and projected to 1994, 26308–86

Census of Agriculture, 1987: farms, farmland, production and costs, and operator characteristics, advance State and county rpt series, 2330–1

Census of Agriculture, 1987: farms, farmland, production, finances, and operator characteristics, by county, final State rpt series, 2331–1

Cold storage food stocks by commodity and census div, and warehouse space use, by State, monthly rpt, 1631–5

Cold storage food stocks, by commodity and census div, 1988, annual rpt, 1631–11

Communist countries agricultural, mineral, and consumer and producer goods production, by commodity, 1960s-88, annual rpt, 9114–4.4

Communist, OECD, and selected other countries agricultural production, by commodity, 1960s-88, annual rpt, 9114–4.6

Conservation of soil and wetlands, USDA programs costs and impacts on farm finances and operations, with background data, 1980s, hearing, 25168–69

Cooperatives finances, aggregate for top 100 assns by commodity group, FY87, annual rpt, 1124–3

Cooperatives, finances, and membership, by type of service, commodity, and State, 1987, annual rpt, 1124–1

Cooperatives finances, operations, activities, and current issues, monthly journal, 1122–1

Developing countries agricultural policy impacts on economic dev, with background data for 6 countries, 1960s-86, 1528–283

Developing countries food production and needs, and related economic outlook, by country, 1989/90, annual rpt, 1524–6

Eastern Europe agricultural production, consumption, and trade, by country, 1970s-88, annual rpt, 1524–11

Eastern Europe and USSR agricultural production, acreage, and consumption, by commodity and country, 1965-85, 1528–284

EC and US trade of high-value agricultural commodities, 1985-87, article, 1502–4.905

EC food supply and demand, market and support prices, and other economic indicators, by country and commodity, 1960-85, 1528–276

Economic Indicators of the Farm Sector, balance sheets, and receipts by detailed commodity, by State, 1984-88, annual rpt, 1544–18

Economic Indicators of the Farm Sector, finances, income sources, expenses by type, assets, debts, and ratios, 1987, annual rpt, 1544–19

performance, with comparisons to US farm income trends, 1980s-88, annual article, 9391–1.911

Statistical Abstract of US, social, political, and economic data, 1790-2025, comprehensive annual compilation, 2324–1.1; 2324–1.3

Urban areas farms, acreage, finances, and operators, under alternative MSA definitions, 1960s-82, 1598–256

Vegetables farms, acreage, and sales, by whether Federal farm program participant and State, 1987, article, 1561–11.907

Vegetables production, acreage, and yield, current and forecast for selected fresh and processing crops by State, periodic rpt, 1621–12

Vegetables production, prices, and acreage, for selected fresh and processing crops by State, 1986-88, annual rpts, 1621–25

Vegetables production, prices, trade, stocks, and use, for selected fresh and processing crops, periodic situation rpt with articles, 1561–11

Weather conditions and effect on agriculture, by US region, State, and city, and world area, weekly rpt, 2152–2

Banking, Finance, and Insurance

Futures and options trading volume, by commodity and exchange, FY88, annual rpt, 11924–2

Futures contracts on commodities, financial instruments, and indexes, options trading in NYC, Chicago, and other markets, monthly rpt, 11922–6

Futures trading in selected commodities and financial instruments and indexes, NYC, Chicago, and other markets activity, monthly rpt, 11922–5

Communications and Transportation

Freight (waterborne domestic), by major commodity group, 1981-86, annual rpt, 3754–1.1

Freight and distance hauled, by commodity and mode of transport, selected years 1970-88, annual rpt, 3304–5.4

Great Lakes ship pilotage activities, costs, and traffic for US and Canada, and US testing and certificates, 1960s-87, 7308–192

Ohio River basin waterway facilities, freight by commodity and port, and recreation, by waterway, 1986-87, annual rpt, 3754–6

Panama Canal traffic and tolls, by commodity, flag of vessel, and trade route, FY88, annual rpt, 9664–3.1

Rail shipments of grain and other commodities by car type, 1986, and rail car fleet size, 1978-88, 1278–15

Railroad freight volume and revenue, by commodity and region of origin and destination, 1987, annual rpt, 7604–6

Shipborne commerce (domestic and foreign) of US, freight by commodity, traffic, and passengers, by port and waterway, 1987, annual rpt, 3754–3

Shipborne trade of US, by type of service, commodity, country, route, and US port, 1986-87, annual rpt, 7704–2

St Lawrence Seaway ship, cargo, and passenger traffic, and toll revenue, 1988 and trends from 1959, annual rpt, 7744–2

Transportation census, 1987: trucks, by detailed characteristics, miles traveled, and type of product carried, State rpt series, 2573–1

Truck freight revenue, by commodity, 1988 survey, annual rpt, 2413–14

Truck rates for fruit and vegetables, by growing area and market, weekly 1988, annual rpt, 1311–15

Waterborne commerce (domestic) of US, freight by major commodity group, vessel type, and port, 1986, annual rpt, 7704–7

Government and Defense

DOD prime contract awards, by detailed procurement category, FY85-88, annual rpt, 3544–18

DOD shipments of military and personal property, passenger traffic, and costs, by service branch and mode of transport, quarterly rpt, 3702–1

Military post exchange operations, and sales by commodity, by facility and location worldwide, FY87, annual rpt, 3504–10

Strategic material stockpile inventories and needs, by commodity, as of Sept 1988, annual rpt, 3544–37

Strategic material stockpile inventories, costs, and goals, by commodity, as of June 1989, semiannual rpt, 3902–3

Strategic material stockpiling by Fed Govt, activity, and inventory by commodity, as of Sept 1989, semiannual rpt, 3542–22; 3902–2

Tax (excise) collections of IRS, by source, quarterly rpt, 8302–1

Tax (excise) indexed to inflation, impacts on Federal revenue and family tax burden by commodity, projected under alternative proposals, 1989-93, GAO rpt, 26119–254

Health and Vital Statistics

Carcinogens chemistry, sources, environment and health risks, and regulation, by substance and brand, 1989, annual rpt, 4044–15

Injuries from use of consumer products and related activities, by victim age and sex, 1988, annual rpt, 9164–7

Injuries from use of consumer products, by severity, victim age, and detailed product, 1988, annual rpt, 9164–6

Injuries from use of consumer products, related deaths and costs, and recalls by brand, by product type, FY87, annual rpt, 9164–2

Industry and Commerce

Asia countries trade with US by commodity, and free trade area proposal, 1985-88, 9886–4.135

Building materials production, shipments, and PPI, by type, bimonthly rpt, 2042–1.5; 2042–1.6

Business statistics, detailed data for major industries and economic indicators, *Survey of Current Business*, monthly rpt, 2702–1

Caribbean area duty-free exports to US, and imports from US, by country, and impact on US employment, by commodity, 1988, annual rpt, 6364–2

Caribbean area duty-free exports to US, and US exports and import duties on other goods, by commodity and country, 1984-88, annual rpt, 9884–20

Caribbean Basin exports to OECD members, and US imports under preferential treatment programs, by commodity, 1980s-87, 2048–138

Caribbean Basin Initiative investment incentives, economic impacts, with finances and employment by country, 1984-88, 2048–141

China trade, by commodity, world area, and country, 1985-87, 9118–10

China trade by SITC 1- to 5-digit commodity, 1970s-87, annual rpt, 9114–3

China trade with US by commodity, and foreign investment by source country, 1988, 9118–9

Communist countries agricultural, mineral, and consumer and producer goods production, by commodity, 1960s-88, annual rpt, 9114–4.4

Communist countries trade with US, by detailed commodity and country, quarterly rpt with articles, 9882–2

Communist, OECD, and selected other countries industrial production and trade, by commodity, 1960s-88, annual rpt, 9114–4

Competitiveness (intl) of US industries, with selected foreign and US operating data by major firm and product, series, 2046–12

Consumer holdings of durable goods, by type, in current and constant dollars, 1985-88, annual article, 2702–1.931

Cuba economic conditions, agricultural and industrial production and distribution, trade, and intl economic relations, 1980-87 with trends from 1961, 9118–8

EC economic integration impacts on domestic economic conditions and US trade, with trade by commodity and country, 1984-87, 9886–4.140

Export and import balances of US, by major commodity group, monthly rpt, 9882–14

Export licensing, monitoring, and enforcement activities, FY88, annual rpt, 2024–1

Exports and imports between US and outlying areas, by detailed commodity and mode of transport, monthly rpt, 2422–4

Exports and imports of US, by commodity group, world area, selected country, US coastal area and port, and mode of transport, monthly rpt, 2422–9

Exports and imports of US by country, and trade shifts by commodity, quarterly rpt, 9882–9

Exports and imports of US, by selected country, country group, and commodity group, 1988, annual rpt, 2044–37

Exports and imports of US shipped through Canada, by detailed commodity, customs district, and country, 1987, annual rpt, 7704–11

Exports and imports, trade agreements and relations, and USITC investigations, 1988, annual rpt, 9884–5

Exports, imports, and balances of US by commodity group, world area, and country, and related employment, 1970s-88, annual rpt, 2044–26

Exports of US, detailed commodities by country, monthly rpt, 2422–3

Foreign countries economic conditions and implications for US, periodic country rpt series, 2046–4

Foreign trade zones (US) operations and movement of goods, by zone and commodity, FY86, annual rpt, 2044–30

Import duties of US under antidumping and countervailing orders, and duty assessment and reporting errors, 1987-88, GAO rpt, 26119–270

Import restraint elimination, impact on domestic industry production and employment, by selected commodity, 1986-88, 9886–4.144

OECD economic conditions for 6 countries
and US, biweekly rpt, 9112–1
Price indexes (consumer and producer), by
commodity group, selected years 1929-88,
annual rpt, 204–1.4
Price indexes (consumer and producer)
changes for selected items, 1982-88, annual
article, 6722–1.921
Producer Price Index, by major commodity
group and subgroup, and processing stage,
monthly press release, 6762–5
Producer price indexes, by stage of
processing and detailed commodity,
monthly rpt, 6762–6
Producer price indexes, by stage of
processing and detailed commodity,
monthly 1988, annual rpt, 6764–2
Statistical Abstract of US, social, political,
and economic data, 1790-2025,
comprehensive annual compilation,
2324–1.3
Texas, Dallas-Ft Worth and Houston MSAs,
CPI by major component, monthly rpt,
6962–2

Public Welfare and Social Security
Food aid programs purchases, by commodity,
firm, and shipping point or destination,
weekly rpt, 1302–3

BY FEDERAL AGENCY

Agriculture and Food
PL 480 exports by commodity, and
recipients, by program, sponsor, and
country, FY87 and cumulative from FY55,
annual rpt, 1924–7

Banking, Finance, and Insurance
Fed Financing Bank holdings and
transactions, by borrower, monthly press
release, 12802–1
Fed Financing Bank loans outstanding, and
loan prepayment activity and costs,
1985-88, GAO rpt, 26111–63
Minority-owned banks, deposits from Fed
Govt by agency, FY86-88, annual rpt,
2104–5

Communications and Transportation
Audiovisual activities and spending of Fed
Govt, by whether performed in-house and
agency, FY87, annual rpt, 9514–1
Auto fleet of Fed Govt, costs and operating
data by agency, FY87, annual rpt, 9454–9
Waterborne cargo sponsored by Fed Govt,
total and US-flag share by agency and
program, 1987, annual rpt, 7704–14.3

Education
Employment training and vocational
education programs funding and
participation, for 6 Federal agencies,
FY89-90, GAO rpt, 26121–277
Exchange and training programs of Federal
agencies, participants by world area, and
funding, by program, FY87, annual rpt,
9854–8
Expenditures for education by Federal
agency, program, and recipient type, and
instn spending, FY80-88, 4828–21
Expenditures for education, by Federal
agency, program, and State, FY80-89,
annual rpt, 4824–2.27

Energy Resources and Demand
Bonneville Power Admin mgmt of Fed
Columbia River Power System, finances,
operations, and sales by customer, FY88,
annual rpt, 3224–1

Consumption of energy, by Federal agency
and fuel type, FY77-88, annual rpt,
7304–2.3
Energy use and efficiency in Federal
buildings, by agency, FY85-88, annual rpt,
3304–25
Energy use and efficiency of Fed Govt, by
agency and fuel type, FY88, annual rpt,
3304–22
Energy use, by Federal agency and fuel type,
FY76-88, annual rpt, 3164–74.1

Geography and Climate
Weather research, monitoring, and impact
assessment activities of Fed Govt, and
funding by agency, FY87, annual rpt,
2144–17
Weather services activities and funding, by
Federal agency, planned FY89-90, annual
rpt, 2144–2

Government and Defense
Advertising spending of Fed Govt, and
subcontracts to small and disadvantaged
firms, by agency and medium, FY86, GAO
rpt, 26113–428
Advisory committees of Fed Govt, and
members, staff, meetings, and costs by
agency, FY88, annual rpt, 9454–18
Assistance (financial and nonfinancial) of Fed
Govt, 1989 base edition with supplements,
annual listing, 104–5
Audits and investigations of fraud and abuse
by Inspectors General, by agency, FY88,
annual rpt, 104–29
Audits and investigations of fraud and abuse
by Inspectors General, by agency, 2nd half
FY87, semiannual rpt, 102–5
Budget deficit reduction under
Gramm-Rudman Act, cancellation of
budget authority by program, FY90, annual
rpt, 104–27; 21924–1; 26304–6
Budget of US Appendix, obligations,
appropriations, and personnel, by program
and agency, FY90, annual rpt, 104–3
Budget of US, authoritative financial
statements with appropriations, outlays,
and receipts, by agency, FY88, annual rpt,
8104–2
Budget of US, authority rescissions and
deferrals, monthly rpt, 102–2
Budget of US, balances of budget authority
obligated and unobligated, by function and
agency, FY88-90, annual rpt, 104–8
Budget of US, Bush Admin policy changes by
program, FY90, 028–32
Budget of US, compact budgets by activity,
function, and agency, FY90 and projected
to FY94, annual rpt, 104–2
Budget of US, historical data, selected years
FY34-88 and projected to FY94, annual
rpt, 104–22
Budget of US, midsession review of FY90
budget, by function and agency, annual rpt,
104–7
Budget of US, object class analysis of
obligations, by agency, FY90, annual rpt,
104–9
Budget of US, overview, FY90, annual rpt,
104–6
Budget of US, Reagan Admin policy changes
by program, FY90, annual rpt, 104–21
Budget of US, receipts by source, outlays by
agency and program, and balances,
monthly rpt, 8102–3
Budget of US, special analyses by activity,
function, and agency, FY90, annual rpt,
104–1

Budget of US, special analysis of Federal
capital spending by category, projected
FY89-2005 and trends from FY81, annual
rpt, 104–24
Collective bargaining multi-unit agreements
of Fed Govt, by agency and labor union, as
of Aug 1988, annual listing, 9847–4
Computer systems of Fed Govt, mgmt
deficiencies, and corrective actions and
delays, by agency, 1983-87, GAO rpt,
26125–33
Cost control proposals for Fed Govt mgmt,
Reagan Admin initiatives, savings, and
status, FY85-94, annual rpt, 104–23
Currency (foreign) holdings of US,
transactions and balances by program and
country, 1st half FY89, semiannual rpt,
8102–7
Employee appeals of personnel actions,
decisions of Merit Systems Protection
Board by agency and region, FY88, annual
rpt, 9494–2
Employee exchange between Fed Govt and
other organizations, program activities and
costs, with data by agency, FY84-88, GAO
rpt, 26119–260
Employee incentive awards, costs, and
benefits, by award type and agency, FY88,
annual rpt, 9844–20
Employee productivity improvement program
of Fed Govt, coverage and impacts by
function for selected agencies, FY86-87
and projected to 1992, 26306–3.103
Employment (civilian) of Fed Govt by
occupation, agency, and location, and
language and math skill needs, 1966-87 and
projected to 2000, 9848–37
Employment (civilian) of Fed Govt,
work-years, pay rates, and benefits use and
costs, by agency, FY87, annual rpt,
9844–31
Employment (noncareer) of Fed Govt,
conversions to career appointments, by
agency, quarterly rpt, 26102–5
Employment (noncareer) of Fed Govt,
conversions to career appointments
unreported, by agency, 1987-88, GAO rpt,
26119–250
Employment and payroll (civilian) of Fed
Govt, by agency in DC metro area, total
US, and abroad, bimonthly rpt, 9842–1
Employment and payroll (civilian) of Fed
Govt, by occupation, pay grade, sex,
agency, and location, 1987, biennial rpt,
9844–4
Employment and payroll (civilian) of Fed
Govt, by pay system, agency, and location,
1988, annual rpt, 9844–6.1; 9844–6.2
Employment discrimination complaints,
processing, and disposition, by complaint
type and Federal agency, FY87, annual rpt,
9244–11
Employment of minorities, handicapped, and
veterans in Fed Govt, and years of service,
by occupation, age, sex, and agency, as of
Sept 1988, biennial rpt, 9844–27
Executive and excepted service employees,
and political appointments, by category,
branch, and selected agency, Sept 1988,
article, 9842–1.903
Expenditures of Fed Govt in States, by type,
program, agency, and State, FY88, annual
rpt, 2464–2
Financial consolidated statements of Fed
Govt based on business accounting
methods, FY87-88, annual rpt, 8104–5

Financial operations of Fed Govt, detailed data, *Treasury Bulletin*, quarterly rpt, 8002-4

Info collection of Fed Govt under Paperwork Reduction Act, effects on requirements and respondent burden by agency, FY87-89, annual rpt, 104-19

Info collection of Fed Govt under Paperwork Reduction Act, respondent burden by paperwork and respondent type, 1985-87, GAO rpt, 26131-60

Info collection of Fed Govt under Paperwork Reduction Act, respondent burden, OMB reviews, and violations, 1981-88, annual rpt, 104-26

Info Security Oversight Office monitoring of Federal security measures and classification actions, FY88, annual rpt, 9454-21

Labor Relations Fed Authority and Fed Service Impasses Panel activities, and cases by union, agency, and State, FY79-87, annual rpt, 13364-1

Labor unions recognized in Fed Govt, agreements and membership by agency and facility, as of Jan 1989, biennial listing, 9844-14

Land acquisition and dev projects of Fed Govt in DC metro area, characteristics and funding by agency and project, FY90-94, annual rpt, 15454-1

Loans, loan guarantees, and insurance programs of Fed Govt, outstanding amounts by agency and program, FY65-88, GAO rpt, 26111-65

Minority group and women employment of Fed Govt by occupation, and handicapped employment, by agency, FY87, annual rpt, 9244-10

Procurement contract awards of Fed Govt, by State, agency, procurement and contractor type, and for top 100 contractors, quarterly rpt, 102-6

Property (real) of Fed Govt, inventory and costs, worldwide summary by location, agency, and use, 1987, annual rpt, 9454-5

Property (real) of Fed Govt, leased inventory and rental costs, worldwide summary by location and agency, 1987, annual rpt, 9454-10

Regulatory costs by agency, reform proposals, and environmental regulation costs to govts and businesses, 1988 hearings, 25408-99

Regulatory review procedures of OMB, proposed and final rules by disposition and agency, 1981-89, GAO rpt, 26119-261

Rural areas aid from Fed Govt, by agency and program, with county classifications by population density, FY85 and FY87, GAO rpt, 26113-401

Senior Executive Service career position longterm vacancies, by reason and agency, 1989, GAO rpt, 26119-252

Senior Executive Service membership characteristics, entries, exits, and awards, FY80-1987, annual rpt, 9844-36

Service contracts of Fed Govt compared with work performed in-house, savings and employment effects by agency, 1978-87, GAO rpt, 26119-238

Small business finances, operations, owner and employee characteristics, and Federal contracts, 1980s-88, annual rpt, 9764-6

Statistical Abstract of US, social, political, and economic data, 1790-2025, comprehensive annual compilation, 2324-1.2

Statistical programs of Fed Govt, funding by agency, FY87-89, annual rpt, 104-10

Surety bonds use to guarantee Federal small business construction contracts, and fraud cases, by agency, 1985-89, GAO rpt, 26113-438

Trust funds of Fed Govt, financial condition, periodic rpt series, 8102-9

Trust funds of Fed Govt, financial status by agency, and impacts on budget balance, FY47-93 and projected to FY93, GAO rpt, 26111-58

Women-owned business mgmt issues, SBA loans, Federal contracts by agency, and owners views on Michigan business climate, FY79-88, hearings, 21728-68

Health and Vital Statistics

Carcinogens chemistry, sources, environment and health risks, and regulation, by substance and brand, 1989, annual rpt, 4044-15

Diabetes research and care services programs and funding, by Federal agency and NIH inst, FY88, annual rpt, 4474-34

Disabled persons employment in Fed Govt, by agency, 1986, 10048-74

Disabled persons rehabilitation, Federal and State activities and funding, FY88, annual rpt, 4944-1

Health condition and health care resources, use, and spending, 1950s-87, annual data compilation, 4144-11

R&D in medicine, funding by type of source and performer, 1978-87, annual rpt, 4434-3

Radiation exposure of Federal employees, by age, occupation, and selected agency, 1986-87, biennial rpt, 4064-15

Reproduction and population research, Fed Govt funding by project, FY87, annual listing, 4474-9

Housing and Construction

Construction spending by Fed Govt, by program and type of structure, FY82-90, annual article, 2042-1.901

Disabled persons access to Federal and federally funded facilities, complaints by disposition and agency, FY88, annual rpt, 17614-1

Industry and Commerce

Export and import product standards under GATT, Natl Inst of Standards and Technology info activities, and proposed standards by agency and country, 1988, annual rpt, 2214-6

Minority business funding, by program and Federal agency, FY86-88, annual rpt, 2104-5

Vending facilities run by blind on Federal and non-Federal property, finances and operations by agency and State, FY88, annual rpt, 4944-2

Law Enforcement

Appeals filed involving Federal agency decisions, by circuit and agency, 1988, annual rpt, 18204-8.10

Assaults and deaths of law enforcement officers, by circumstances, agency, victim and offender characteristics, and location, 1988, annual rpt, 6224-3

Drug abuse and trafficking reduction programs funding by Federal agency, and Bush Admin budget request, by program area, FY87-90, 238-1

Drug enforcement regional task forces investigation of organized crime, activities by agency and region, and background data, FY83-88, annual rpt, 6004-17

Employment and hiring of Federal law enforcement personnel, by agency, 1982-FY87, GAO rpt, 26119-242

Juvenile delinquency prevention funding, by program and Federal agency, FY88, annual rpt, 6064-11

US attorneys civil cases and amounts involved, and criminal cases declined, by agency, FY88, annual rpt, 6004-2.5; 6004-2.7

Natural Resources, Environment, and Pollution

Alaska land area by ownership, and availability for mineral exploration and dev, 1986, 5608-152

Geological Survey reimbursable program funds from other Federal agencies, by program and agency, FY85-88, annual rpt, 5664-8

Hazardous waste site remedial action under Superfund, deadlines and compliance of govts and businesses, as of Mar 1989, GAO rpt, 26113-394

Lands (public) disposition and withdrawals from inventory, by agency and State, FY88, annual rpt, 5724-1.2

Minerals resources and availability on public lands, State rpt series, 5606-7

Ocean pollution research, monitoring, and resources dev activities of Fed Govt, funding and project descriptions, FY87, annual rpt, 2144-23

Ocean pollution research, monitoring, and resources dev activities of Fed Govt, 5-year plan and funding by agency, FY84-89, triennial rpt, 2148-56

Wastewater facilities of Fed Govt, compliance with pollution control regulations, FY86-87, GAO rpt, 26113-388

Wilderness areas acreage by Federal agency and location, and sources of damage, with data for foreign countries, 1988 conf papers, 1208-301

Public Welfare and Social Security

Expenditures of Fed Govt in States, by type, program, agency, and State, FY88, annual rpt, 2464-2

Homeless persons aid by program and Federal agency, and indicators of need, 1988, annual rpt, 14364-1

Older persons aid and policies of Fed Govt, program funding, and grants awarded, FY80-89, annual rpt, 25144-3.2

Recreation and Leisure

Visits and fees for Federal outdoor recreation facilities, by managing agency, 1988, annual rpt, 5544-14

Science and Technology

Atmospheric sciences research activity of Fed Govt, and funding by agency and program, FY84-87, biennial rpt, 434-1

Black colleges R&D funding by source, and characteristics of grad students and research staff, by field of science and instn, 1980s-87, 9628-78

Computer systems and equipment of Fed Govt, by type, make, and agency, 1st half FY89, semiannual listing, 9452-9

Computer systems of Fed Govt, security training activities, by agency, 1988, GAO rpt, 26125-31

Computer systems of Fed Govt with sensitive info, and plans submitted to oversight agencies, by agency, 1989, GAO rpt, 26125-34

DOD prime contract awards for R&D to US and foreign nonprofit instns and govt agencies, by instn and location, FY88, annual listing, 3544-17

Employment of scientists and engineers in Fed Govt, by field, degree level, race, sex, agency, and State, 1987, annual rpt, 9627-5

Enrollment in science and engineering grad programs, by field, source of funds, and characteristics of student and instn, 1975-87, annual rpt, 9627-7

Labor force, Federal and university research funding, and educational data, for science and engineering, series, 9626-6

Labs accreditation programs and requirements of Fed Govt, by agency, 1988-89, GAO rpt, 26113-405

Labs of Fed Govt, technology transfer cooperative agreements, royalties, and incentive payments to employees, by agency, FY87-88, GAO rpt, 26113-422

NASA procurement contract awards, by type, contractor, State, and country, FY89, semiannual rpt, 9502-6

Oceanographic research cruise schedules and ship characteristics, by higher education instn and Federal agency, 1989, annual listing, 3804-6

Patents granted to Federal agencies, FY78-88, annual rpt, 2244-1.2

R&D and related funding of Fed Govt to higher education and nonprofit instns, by field, instn, agency, and State, FY87, annual rpt, 9627-17

R&D facilities of higher education instns, equipment spending by funding source, and retirement and acquisition rates, by field, 1982/83-1985/86, 9626-2.180

R&D funding by Fed Govt, by agency and performer, FY80-89, annual rpt, 9624-18.3

R&D funding by Fed Govt, by detailed function, program, and agency, FY88-90, annual rpt, 9627-9

R&D funding by Fed Govt, by field, performer type, agency, and State, FY87-89, annual rpt, 9627-20

R&D funding by source and performer, and related employment, by State, 1975-87, 9626-6.32

R&D prime contract awards of DOD, for top 500 contractors, FY88, annual listing, 3544-4

Small business R&D grants of Fed Govt, administrators views on effectiveness, FY86-87, GAO rpt, 26113-393

Small business R&D grants of Fed Govt, by program area, agency, and State, FY88, annual rpt, 9764-7

Smithsonian Instn grants and contracts from other agencies, FY87-88, annual rpt, 29574-1

Space launches and other activities of NASA and USSR, with flight data, 1957-88, annual rpt, 9504-6.1

Statistical Abstract of US, social, political, and economic data, 1790-2025, comprehensive annual compilation, 2324-1.3

Superconductivity (high temperature) R&D spending by Federal agency, and US and Japan industry funding and employment, by application, 1981-89, hearing, 25408-100

Veterans Affairs

Employment and promotion of disabled veterans in Fed Govt by agency, and recruitment coordinator activities, FY81-87, GAO rpt, 26119-245

BY INCOME

Agriculture and Food

Census of Agriculture, 1987: farms, farmland, production and costs, and operator characteristics, advance State and county rpt series, 2330-1

Cooperatives commercial member characteristics, and use of services, by region, 1980 and 1986, 1128-53

Cooperatives member characteristics, and use of services, by region, 1980 and 1986, 1128-54

Employment, earnings, and days worked, for farm workers by selected characteristics and region, 1987, biennial rpt, 1594-2

Food consumption and nutrient intake by individuals, by food group, selected characteristics, and region, supplementary survey series, 1356-5

Households (farm), by income level, 1987, annual Current Population Rpt, 2546-1.439

Population of farm operators and farming-dependent households, by selected characteristics, under alternative definitions, 1987, 1598-252

Population on farms under alternative definitions, by selected characteristics, 1983, 1598-249

Production itemized costs, by farm sales size and region, 1988, annual rpt, 1614-3

Vegetables (fresh and processed) consumption by type, and spending by consumer characteristics, 1960s-87, article, 1561-11.903

Banking, Finance, and Insurance

Checking accounts service fees burden by income level, 1980s, hearing, 21788-181

Communications and Transportation

Telephone service of households, by composition, income sources, and other characteristics, 1984-87, 9288-11

Traffic volume in urban areas and detailed trip characteristics, by transport mode and city, 1950s-88, 7888-37

Travel to US and Canada, market analysis with detailed trip and traveler characteristics, country rpt series, 2906-2

Education

American Historical Assn financial statements, and membership by State, 1988, annual rpt, 29574-2

Enrollment, by grade, instn type and control, and student characteristics, 1986 and trends from 1947, annual Current Population Rpt, 2546-1.429; 2546-1.432

High school classes of 1972, 1980, and 1982: educational attainment by selected characteristics, 1976-87, 4848-36

High school classes of 1972, 1980, and 1982: postsecondary enrollment and degrees, by sex, race, and income level, natl longitudinal surveys, 4848-35

Higher education instn student aid and other sources of support, with student expenses and characteristics, by instn type and control, 1987 triennial study, series, 4846-3

Statistical Abstract of US, social, political, and economic data, 1790-2025, comprehensive annual compilation, 2324-1.1

Student aid awards, by Federal program and student income level, FY86-88, annual rpt, 4804-28.2

Student aid Pell grants and applicants, by tuition, income level, instn type and control, and State, 1987/88, annual rpt, 4804-1

Student guaranteed loan default rates, and claims paid by guaranty agencies, by State, and borrower characteristics, FY87, GAO rpt, 26121-292

Vocational and academic AA degree and certificate recipients and credits, by field, and student and instn characteristics, 1984, 4848-37

Vocational education aid recipients and sources, and characteristics of programs and students, 1970s-89, series, 4806-3

Energy Resources and Demand

Household, housing, and fuel use characteristics, survey rpt series, 3166-7

Government and Defense

Tax (excise) indexed to inflation, impacts on Federal revenue and family tax burden by commodity, projected under alternative proposals, 1989-93, GAO rpt, 26119-254

Tax (income) returns filed by type of filer, selected income items, quarterly rpt, 8302-2.1

Tax (income) returns of individuals, by filing status, tax item, and income level, 1987, annual article, 8302-2.901

Tax (income) returns of individuals, detailed data, 1986, annual rpt, 8304-2

Tax (income) returns of individuals, income and tax shares, and tax rates, by income level, 1916-50, article, 8302-2.913

Tax (income) returns of individuals, income and tax shares, and tax rates, by income level, 1951-86, article, 8302-2.919

Tax (income) returns of individuals, selected income and tax items by income level, preliminary 1987, annual article, 8302-2.917

Tax (income) returns of individuals, taxable income, and tax generated, by tax rate and income level, 1986, annual article, 8302-2.918

Tax returns filed, by type of tax and IRS region and service center, projected 1988-95 and trends from 1977, annual rpt, 8304-9

Taxes, spending, and govt efficiency, public opinion by respondent characteristics, 1989 survey, annual rpt, 10044-2

Voting and registration, by socioeconomic and demographic characteristics, 1988 presidential election, biennial Current Population Rpt, 2546-1.440

Health and Vital Statistics

Abortions by patient characteristics, rates for all and 1st abortions, and related deaths in US and other countries, 1989 hearing, 21408-113

Acute and chronic health conditions, disability, absenteeism, and health services use, by selected characteristics, 1988, annual rpt, 4147-10.170

BY INCOME

Public Welfare and Social Security

Child care arrangements and costs, by income and other characteristics of family, 1984-86, press release, 2328-61

Child support and alimony awards, and payment status, by selected characteristics of woman, 1985, biennial Current Population Rpt, 2546-2.145

Disability Insurance beneficiaries health insurance coverage, by type and selected beneficiary characteristics, fall 1982, article, 4742-1.927

Food stamp eligibility and payment errors, by type, recipient characteristics, and State, FY87, annual rpt, 1364-15

Medicare and other insurance programs catastrophic illness coverage, benefits, premiums, costs, and program finances, projected 1988-93, 26306-3.105

Medicare catastrophic illness coverage and premium collection, effects of revisions on Federal budget and enrollees, projected 1989-93, 25368-161

OASDHI, Medicaid, SSI, and related programs benefits, beneficiary characteristics, and trust funds, selected years 1937-87, annual rpt, 4744-3

OASI beneficiaries affected by earnings limits by selected characteristics, and Federal outlays, under alternative limits, 1986, 26306-3.110

Recreation and Leisure

Wildlife-related recreation, hunting, and fishing participation and spending, detailed data by location, 1985 survey, quinquennial rpt, 5508-5

Wildlife-related recreation, hunting, and fishing participation and spending, detailed data, 1985 survey, quinquennial State rpt series, 5506-6

Veterans Affairs

Population of veterans, and benefits programs awareness and use, by age, sex, income, race, and period of service, 1987 survey, 8608-1

BY INDIVIDUAL COMPANY OR INSTITUTION

Agriculture and Food

Cooperative sales, for 13 coops on *Fortune* 500 list, 1988, article, 1122-1.907

Fiber content in breakfast cereal and bread, health claim ads, and other factors affecting consumption, 1978-88, 9406-1.60

Fish Hatchery Natl System activities and deliveries, by species, hatchery, and jurisdiction of waters stocked, FY88, annual rpt, 5504-10

Fishery mgmt and R&D, Fed Govt grants by project and State, and rpts, 1987, annual listing, 2164-3

Food marketing sector finances, operations, and merger activity, for processors and distributors, as of 1988, annual rpt, 1544-22

Food retailers after-tax profits, aggregate and for 14 supermarket chains, 1988, annual rpt, 1544-9.2

Foreign countries agricultural research grants of USDA, by program, subagency, and country, FY88, annual listing, 1954-3

Grain handling facility explosions and casualties, by firm, FY88, annual rpt, 1294-1

Livestock, meat, and wool, market news summary statistics by animal type and market, weekly rpt, 1315-1

Meat plants inspected and certified for exporting to US, by country, 1988, annual listing, 1374-2

Meat, poultry, and livestock production, consumption, and industry finances and operations, 1950s-86, 1568-280

PL 480 exports by commodity, and recipients, by program, sponsor, and country, FY87 and cumulative from FY55, annual rpt, 1924-7

Research (agricultural) funding and staffing for USDA, State agencies, and other instns, by topic, FY88, annual rpt, 1744-2

Research and education grants, USDA competitive awards by program and recipient, FY88, annual listing, 1764-1

Banking, Finance, and Insurance

Acquisitions (hostile takeover) defense through repurchase of stock, stock price changes for selected firms, 1985-86, article, 9373-2.901

Bank holding company stock prices relative to indexes by instn, and bond and supervisory ratings impact of financial problems, 1970s-80s, article, 9373-1.911

Bankruptcy filings with SEC participation, by firm, FY88, annual rpt, 9734-2.6

Banks (commercial and savings) FDIC-insured, deposits by instn, State, MSA, and county, as of June 1988, annual regional rpt series, 9295-3

Banks (natl) domestic and intl operations, charters, mergers, and liquidations, by instn and State, quarterly rpt, 8402-3

Banks (US) loans to developing countries, and loan loss reserves, by money center bank, Sept 1988, hearings, 21248-122

Banks (US) loans to developing countries, ratios and reserves as share of loans, for leading instns, 1988, working paper, 9389-19.12

Banks and bank branch formations, mergers, liquidations, and other changes in status, listing by instn, monthly rpt, 9365-2.23

Banks assets, income, and rates of return, by major instn for Fed Reserve 3rd District, quarterly rpt, annual table, 9387-10

Banks brokered deposit holdings and financial indicators, by size, region, and for failed instns, 1986-89, hearing, 21248-124

Banks failure forecasting accuracy, and failure relation to financial, regulatory, and other indicators, with data by instn, 1960s-89, working paper, 9377-9.77

Banks financial performance, risk assessment, and regulation, 1988 annual conf papers, 9375-7

Banks mergers and consolidations approved by Fed Reserve Board of Governors, 1988, annual rpt, 9364-1.2

Banks needing FDIC aid, finances and operations, 1988, annual rpt, 9294-1

Banks stock price and trading impact of loan-loss reserve additions, with data by instn, 1987, working paper, 9387-8.186

Bond (low-grade) issues by industry div, holdings by owner type, yields, and defaults, 1977-88, 21248-118

Credit unions assets and location, 1989 annual listing, 9534-6

Credit unions federally insured, finances by instn characteristics and State, as of June 1989, semiannual rpt, 9532-6

Credit unions federally insured, finances, mergers, closings, and insurance fund losses and financial statements, FY88, annual rpt, 9534-7

Credit unions federally insured, finances, 1987-88, annual rpt, 9534-1

Eximbank financial condition, credit and insurance authorizations, and loan activity and delinquencies, by country, FY88, annual rpt, 9254-1

Eximbank loans for energy-related products and services, by country and firm, 1988, annual rpt, 9254-3

Fed Financing Bank holdings and transactions, by borrower, monthly press release, 12802-1

Fed Home Loan Bank System members and assets, 1988, annual listing, 9314-5

Fed Home Loan Banks, FHLBB, FSLIC, and Financing Corp financial statements, 1988, annual rpt, 8434-2

Foreign firms hostile takeover of US firms, attempts by outcome, and transaction value, with data by firm, 1984-88, GAO rpt, 26123-222

Futures and options trading volume, by commodity and exchange, FY88, annual rpt, 11924-2

Futures market trading abuses, Commodity Futures Trading Commission and exchanges enforcement activity, various periods 1984-FY90, GAO rpt, 26119-263

Insurance (auto) coverage, premiums, and theft losses, with data by model and State, 1988 hearings, 21368-110

Insurance (auto) industry profitability, income, and expenses, with premiums by company, 1977-87, 26119-267

Interstate banking offices by type of controlling organization and State, 1982-Feb 1989, article, 9371-1.909

Investment advisors for trust, employee benefit, and other accounts, assets involved for all and top 15 firms, 1988, annual rpt, 13004-1

Mergers and acquisitions using leveraged buyout, financing characteristics and policy issues, 1970s-88, 21368-115

New England States, FHLB 1st District thrift instns, financial condition, and locations, 1989, annual listing, 9304-26

North Central States, FHLB 8th District S&Ls, locations, assets, and savings, 1989, annual listing, 9304-9

Ohio savings instns crisis impact on certificates of deposit interest rates, 1983-85, technical paper, 9316-1.153

Overseas Private Investment Corp finances and activities, with list of insured projects and firms, FY88, annual rpt, 9904-2

Savings and loan assns failure resolution costs, and FSLIC finances and promissory notes issued, with data by instn, FY80s and projected to FY99, hearing, 25258-22

Savings and loan assns failures, assets, and FSLIC resolution costs and promissory notes, with data for acquired and acquiring instn in US and Texas, 1988 hearings, 21248-121

Savings instns failure resolution activity of Resolution Trust Corp, with failed instn finances by instn, periodic press release, 9722-1

Savings instns failure resolution costs, financing problems, and FSLIC and acquiring instns tax benefits, 1988 and projected to FY99, hearings, 21788-181

Hydroelectric power plants retired, characteristics and location, as of 1989, annual listing, 3084–12

Hydrogen energy R&D activity and funding of DOE, and project listing, FY88, annual rpt, 3304–18

Natural and supplemental gas production, prices, trade, use, reserves, and pipeline company finances, by firm and State, monthly rpt with articles, 3162–4

Natural gas interstate pipeline company capacity, use, sales, deliveries, and prices, by firm and Northeast State, 1980-88, 3166–6.35

Natural gas interstate pipeline company detailed financial and operating data, by firm, 1988, annual rpt, 3164–38

Natural gas interstate pipeline company reserves and production, by firm, 1963-88 and deliverability projected to 2008, annual rpt, 3164–33

Natural gas interstate pipeline company sales, by customer, SIC 2-digit industry group, and State, monthly rpt, annual tables, 3162–4.6

Natural gas interstate pipeline company sales, contract deliveries, and prices, with data by firm and location, 1982-87, 3168–113

Naval Petroleum and Oil Shale Reserves sales and contract prices, by purchaser and reserve, FY88, annual rpt, 3004–22

Nuclear fuel inventory discrepancy, by facility, 1st half 1988, semiannual rpt, 9632–3

Nuclear material inventory discrepancies at DOE and contractor facilities, 2nd half FY87, semiannual rpt, 3002–4

Nuclear power plant capacity, generation, and operating status, by plant and foreign and US location, 1988 and projected to 2020, annual rpt, 3164–57

Nuclear power plant construction costs and status, and capacity, by plant, as of Dec 1988, annual rpt, 3164–69

Nuclear power plant fuel assembly performance and failures, by fuel vendor and reactor, 1987, annual rpt, 9634–8

Nuclear power plant fuel processing and waste facilities capacity, owner, and foreign and US location, projected 1989-2036, annual rpt, 3164–72

Nuclear power plant mgmt salaries by position, and plant capacity, for TVA compared to private utilities, 1985-87, hearing, 21648–57

Nuclear power plant safety standards and research, design, licensing, construction, operation, and finances, with data by reactor, quarterly journal, 3352–4

Nuclear power plant spent fuel discharges and additional storage capacity needed, by reactor, 1987 and projected 1988-2007, annual rpt, 3354–2

Nuclear reactors for domestic use and export by function and operating status, with owner, operating characteristics, and location, 1988 annual listing, 3004–26

Nuclear reactors inspections and operations, by commercial facility, monthly rpt, 9632–1

Nuclear Regulatory Commission activities, finances, and staff, with data for individual power plants, FY88, annual rpt, 9634–2

Nuclear Waste Fund program costs, by contractor, quarterly GAO rpt, supplemental data, 26102–4

Offshore oil and gas production by operator, for Federal leases in 2 ocean areas, 1987, annual rpt, 5734–3.4

Offshore oil and gas reserves, and leasing and dev activity, periodic regional rpt series, 5736–3

Oil (crude) and products imports, by company, 1988, article, 3162–6.902

Oil and gas OCS lease sales in Gulf of Mexico, by company and tract, 1988, annual rpt, 5734–8

Oil enhanced recovery research contracts of DOE, project summaries, funding, and bibl, quarterly rpt, 3002–14

Oil industry mergers and acquisitions impacts on market concentration, with background data, 1970-84, 9406–1.58

Oil refinery capacity, closings, and acquisitions by plant, and fuel used, by PAD district, 1973-88, annual rpt, 3164–2.1

Pacific Northwest electric power capacity and use, by energy source, projected under alternative load and demand cases, 1989-2008, annual rpt, 3224–3

R&D projects and funding of DOE at natl labs, universities, and other instns, periodic summary rpt series, 3004–18

Rural Electrification Admin financed electric power plants, with location, capacity, and owner, as of Jan 1989, annual listing, 1244–6

Rural Electrification Admin loans, and borrower operating and financial data, by distribution firm and State, 1988, annual rpt, 1244–1

Solar photovoltaic R&D sponsored by DOE, projects, funding, and rpts, FY88, annual listing, 3304–20

Southeastern Power Admin sales by customer, plants, capacity, and Southeastern Fed Power Program financial statements, FY88, annual rpt, 3234–1

Southwestern Fed Power System financial statements, sales by customer, and operations and costs by project, FY88, annual rpt, 3244–1

Tennessee Valley river control activities, and hydroelectric power generation and capacity, 1984, annual rpt, 9804–7

TVA electric power purchases and resales, with electricity use, average bills, and rates by customer class, by distributor, 1988, annual tables, 9804–14

TVA electric power purchases of municipal and cooperative distributors, and prices and use by distributor and consumer sector, monthly rpt, 9802–1

Uranium mill capacity by plant, and production, by operating status, 1985-88, annual rpt, 3164–65.1

Uranium mining and milling industries finances and operations, with selected foreign comparisons, 1970s-87 and projected to 2000, annual rpt, 3164–82

Western Area Power Admin activities by plant, financial statements, and sales by customer, FY88, annual rpt, 3254–1

Geography and Climate

Oceanographic research and distribution activities of World Data Center A by country, and cruises by ship, 1987, annual rpt, 2144–15

Government and Defense

AID contracts and grants for technical and support services, by instn, country, and State, FY88, annual listing, 9914–7

AID loans repayment status and terms by program and country, and status of predecessor agency loans, quarterly rpt, 9912–3

Capitol Architect outlays for salaries, supplies, and services, itemized by payee and function, 1st half FY89, semiannual rpt, 25922–2

Coin production of US Mint, for US by denomination and mint, and for foreign countries, monthly table, 8202–1

Collective bargaining multi-unit agreements of Fed Govt, by agency and labor union, as of Aug 1988, annual listing, 9847–4

DC metro area land acquisition and dev projects of Fed Govt, characteristics and funding by agency and project, FY90-94, annual rpt, 15454–1

Developing countries economic and social conditions from 1960s, and Intl Dev Cooperation Agency and AID activities and funding, FY88-90, annual rpt, 9904–4

DOD budget requests for base construction, renovation, and land acquisition, by project, service branch, State, and country, FY90/91, annual rpt, 3544–15

DOD budget, weapons acquisition costs by prime contractor and system, FY89-91, annual rpt, 3504–2

DOD civilian and military employment, by service branch, major installation, and State, as of Sept 1988, annual rpt, 3544–7

DOD contractor subcontract awards to small and disadvantaged business, by firm and service branch, quarterly rpt, 3542–17

DOD contracts, payroll, and personnel, by service branch and location, with top 5 contractors and maps, by State and country, FY88, annual rpt, 3544–29

DOD prime contract awards, by contractor, service branch, State, and city, FY88, annual rpt, 3544–22

DOD prime contract awards for R&D, for top 500 contractors, FY88, annual listing, 3544–4

DOD prime contract awards for R&D to US and foreign nonprofit instns and govt agencies, by instn and location, FY88, annual listing, 3544–17

DOD prime contract awards, for top 100 contractors, FY88, annual rpt, 3504–13; 3544–5

DOD training and education programs funding, staff, students, and facilities, by service branch, FY90, annual rpt, 3504–5

DOE real property owned and leased, by type, subagency, contractor, and site, FY87, annual rpt, 3004–28

Economic Dev Admin activities, and funding by program, recipient, State, and county, FY87 and cumulative from FY66, annual rpt, 2064–2

Economic Dev Admin funding, and loans forgiven, with data by project and location, FY84-88, hearing, 21648–56

Election campaign financial activity reported to FEC, by type of filer, 1988 natl elections, biennial rpt series, 9276–2

House of Representatives salaries, expenses, and contingent fund disbursement, detailed listings, quarterly rpt, 21942–1

Insurance (health) for Federal employees, State taxes on plan underwriters, 1987, GAO rpt, 26119-262

Inter-American Foundation activities, grants by recipient, and fellowships, by country, FY88, annual rpt, 14424-1

Inter-American Foundation dev grants by program area, and fellowships by field and instn, by country, FY71-88, annual rpt, 14424-2

Labor unions recognized in Fed Govt, agreements and membership by agency and facility, as of Jan 1989, biennial listing, 9844-14

Military equipment foreign sales, by top contractor, FY85-88, GAO rpt, 26123-30

Military post exchange operations, and sales by commodity, by facility and location worldwide, FY87, annual rpt, 3504-10

Military prisons population and capacity, by service branch and facility, 1970s-87, annual rpt, 6064-6.6

NASA funding by program and type of performer, and contract awards by State, FY88, annual rpt, 9504-6.2

Navy procurement, by contractor and location, FY88, annual rpt, 3804-13

Political action committees contributions by office and party, and finances by PAC, 1988 natl elections, press release, 9276-1.65

Presidential libraries holdings, use, and costs, by instn, FY88, annual rpt, 9514-2

Procurement contract awards of Fed Govt, by State, agency, procurement and contractor type, and for top 100 contractors, quarterly rpt, 102-6

Senate receipts, itemized expenses by payee, and balances, 1st half FY89, semiannual listing, 25922-1

Ships, shipyards, and personnel wartime capability, for merchant and reserve fleet, 1988-2000, 11208-1

Health and Vital Statistics

Alcohol, Drug Abuse and Mental Health Admin research grants and awards, by recipient, FY88, annual listing, 4044-13

Allergy and Infectious Diseases Natl Inst activities, grants by recipient and location, and disease incidence, FY81-88, annual rpt, 4474-30

Cancer Natl Inst contracts and grants, by recipient and location, FY88, annual listing, 4474-28

Carcinogens chemistry, sources, environment and health risks, and regulation, by substance and brand, 1989, annual rpt, 4044-15

Child Health and Human Dev Natl Inst contracts and grants, by recipient and location, FY88, annual listing, 4474-36

Cigarette ad revenues and articles on smoking and health of 14 magazines, 1960s-81, annual rpt, 4204-18

Cigarette smoke tar, nicotine, and carbon monoxide content, by brand, 1988, 9408-53

Dental Research Natl Inst research and training grants, by recipient, FY88, annual listing, 4474-19

Drug abuse emergency room admissions and deaths, by drug type and major metro area, July 1985-Dec 1988, semiannual rpt, 4492-3

Drug mentions during cardiologist office visits, by drug type and brand, 1985, 4146-8.174

Drug mentions during ophthalmologist office visits, for generic and brand name products, 1985, 4146-8.166

Drug prescriptions, by drug type and brand, and for new drugs, 1987, annual rpt, 4064-12

Health Care Financing Admin research activities and grants, by program, as of Mar 1989, annual listing, 4654-10

Health Professions Bur training and research grants and contracts, by instn and program, FY88, annual listing, 4114-1

Hearing aid performance test results, by make and model, 1989 annual rpt, 8704-3

Heart, Lung, and Blood Natl Inst activities, and grants by recipient and location, FY88 with disease trends from 1940, annual rpt, 4474-15

Heart transplants performed by hospital, charges, payment sources, nonpaying patients, and waiting periods, 1986-88, GAO rpt, 26121-281

HHS financial aid, by program, recipient, State, and city, FY88, annual regional listings, 4004-3

HHS research and evaluation programs, 1970-FY87, annual listing, 4004-30

Indian Health Service hospital admissions, length of stay, beds, births, and outpatient visits, by facility and IHS service area, FY70-88, annual rpt, 4084-4

Indian Health Service hospital capacity, use, births, and outpatient visits, by area and facility, quarterly rpt, 4082-1

Indian Health Service outpatient visits, by type of provider, selected hospital, and IHS service area, FY87-88, annual rpt, 4084-3

Insurance (health) companies case mgmt for high-cost patients, savings, costs, and returns, 1984-86, article, 4652-1.914

Insurance (health) for Federal employees and annuitants, enrollment, costs, and Medicare coverage, with data for selected plans, 1980-89, 21628-73

Kidney end-stage disease research of CDC and HCFA, project listing, 1988 annual rpt, 4654-16

Mental health services use, spending, facility ownership, and Medicaid reimbursement, with data for 9 multifacility firms, 1987 conf papers, 4508-9

Mississippi hospitals and community health centers, use, staff, and Medicare and other payments, 1988 hearing, 25548-97

NIH grants and awards, quarterly listing, 4432-1

NIH grants and contracts to top recipients, FY88, annual rpt, 4434-9

NIH grants for R&D, training, construction, and medical libraries, by location and recipient, FY88, annual listings, 4434-7

Nursing home compliance with Medicare and Medicaid regulations, and patient characteristics, by facility, 1987/88, annual State rpt series, 4654-15

Occupational safety and health education grants, by recipient, 1989, press release, 6606-3.9

Occupational safety and health research and demonstration grants by State, and project listing, FY87, annual rpt, 4244-2

Radiation exposure of workers at nuclear power plants and related facilities, by site, 1968-86, annual rpt, 9634-3

Reproduction and population research, Fed Govt funding by project, FY87, annual listing, 4474-9

Housing and Construction

Disabled persons housing, HUD loans by recipient, 1989, press release, 5006-3.72

Homeless persons housing aid of HUD, project listing, 1988 rpt, 5188-121

Homeless persons housing in rehabilitated single occupancy units, HUD grants by recipient, 1989, press release, 5006-3.68

Homeless persons transitional housing, HUD grants by recipient, 1989, press release, 5006-3.66

Homeless persons with handicaps, HUD group housing grants by recipient, 1989, press release, 5006-3.67

HUD grants for moderate-income homeownership loans, by recipient, 1989, press release, 5006-3.70

Older persons low-income rental housing construction and rehabilitation loans, by recipient, 1989, press release HUD loans for older persons low-income rental housing construction and rehabilitation, by recipient, 1989, press release, 5006-3.71

Industry and Commerce

Aluminum plant ownership, capacity, energy and aluminum sources, and startup and closing dates, by US and foreign plant and location, 1988, annual listing, 5604-49

Auto and auto equipment recalls for safety-related defects, by make, quarterly listing, 7762-2

Auto and light truck fuel economy, sales, and market shares, by size and model for US and foreign makes, 1989 model year, semiannual rpt, 3302-4

Auto industry sales, profits, and loss, by US make, monthly rpt, annual data, 9882-8

Chemicals (synthetic organic) production, sales, and manufacturer listing, by product, 1988, annual rpt, 9884-3

Competitiveness (intl) of US industries, with selected foreign and US operating data by major firm and product, series, 2046-12

Exporters (US) antiboycott law violations and fines by firm, and invitations to boycott by country, FY88, annual rpt, 2024-1

Foreign direct investment in US, major transactions by type, industry, country, and US location, 1987, annual rpt, 2044-20

Imports detained by FDA, by reason, product, shipper, brand, and country, monthly listing, 4062-2

Japan auto exports to US, and quotas under voluntary restraints, by make, 1987-88, 9886-4.144

Lumber (pulpwood) production and mill receipts in North Central States, by species, mill, State, and county, 1987, annual rpt, 1204-19

Lumber (pulpwood) production by county, and mill capacity by firm, by southern State, 1987, annual rpt, 1204-23

Minerals (strategic) production, by country and for South Africa companies controlled by multinatl firms, 1987, GAO rpt, 26123-233

Minerals (strategic) supply, demand, trade, and foreign and US industry devs by firm and country, by commodity, bimonthly rpt with articles, 5602-4

Minerals foreign and US supply under alternative market conditions, reserves, and background industry data, series, 5606–4

Minerals production, reserves, and industry role in domestic economy and world supply, world area and country rpt, series, 5606–1

Minerals Yearbook, 1987, Vol 1 preprints: commodity reviews of production, reserves, supply, use, and trade, annual rpt series, 5604–15

Minerals Yearbook, 1987, Vol 2: State reviews of production, sales, and firms, by commodity, and business activity, annual rpt, 5604–34

Minerals Yearbook, 1988, Vol 1: commodity reviews of production, reserves, supply, use, and trade, annual rpt series, 5604–20

Overseas Private Investment Corp activities, and lists of grants and insured projects and firms, FY88, annual rpt, 9904–3

Paper and wood products production and trade, and industry operations by firm, by country, world region rpt series, 2046–14

Salt production capacity, and use in chlorine production, by firm and facility, 1988, annual listing, 5614–30

Small Business Admin loans, contract awards, and surety bonds, by firm, State, and city, FY88, annual rpt, 9764–1

Small Business Investment Companies capital holdings, SBA obligation, and ownership, as of June 1989, semiannual listing, 9762–4

Stock performance of individual firms relative to market index, relation to firm characteristics by firm, alternative models results, 1963–81, technical paper, 9366–6.183

Sweden multinatl firms domestic and foreign production, exports, employment, and sales, with data by commodity and firm, 1960s–86, conf, 23848–208

Tennessee Valley industrial dev, employment, and electricity demand, by SIC 2-digit industry, firm, and location, 1988, annual rpt, 9804–3

UK and France govt-owned corporations stock issues, value, new shareholders, and revenue effects, 1960s–88, article, 9385–1.911

Labor and Employment

Collective bargaining agreement concessions relation to economic and industry financial conditions, with data by major industry and union, 1970s–88, technical paper, 9385–8.41

Collective bargaining agreements expiring during year, and workers covered, by firm, union, industry group, and State, 1989, annual rpt, 6784–9

Fed Labor Relations Authority and Fed Service Impasses Panel activities, and cases by union, agency, and State, FY79–87, annual rpt, 13364–1

Labor union membership and percent of workers accepting concessionary contracts, 1975–88, article, 9385–1.912

Labor union representation elections conducted by NLRB, results, monthly rpt, 9582–2

Older persons community services employment funding, by recipient, 1989-90, press release, 6406–2.26

Research contracts of Bur of Intl Labor Affairs, FY83-89, annual listing, 6364–1

Southeastern States collective bargaining calendar, 1989, annual rpt, 6946–1.73

Trade adjustment aid for workers, petitions by disposition, selected industry, union, and State, monthly rpt, 6402–13

Wage and benefit changes from collective bargaining and mgmt decisions, by industry div, monthly rpt, 6782–1

Work stoppages, workers involved, and days idle, 1988 and trends from 1947, annual press release, 6784–12

Law Enforcement

Aircraft hijackings, on-board explosions, and other crime, US and foreign incidents, 1983-87, annual rpt, 7504–31

Capital punishment public defender resource centers, grants by organization, FY90, Judicial Conf proceedings, semiannual rpt, 18202–2

Coal surface mining-related civil actions, attorneys fees and expenses awarded by case, 1989, GAO rpt, 26113–421

Drug enforcement activities of State and local agencies, Federal aid by recipient, and background data, FY88, annual rpt, 6064–28

Higher education instn law enforcement personnel, and crimes by offense, by instn, 1988, annual rpt, 6224–2.1; 6224–2.3

Prison industries involvement of private sector, operations by prison and firm, and State provisions, as of 1987, 6068–228

Prisoners in Federal instns, by sex, prison, security level, contract facility type, and region, monthly rpt series, 6242–1

Terrorist incidents in US, related activity, and casualties, by attack type, target, group, and location, 1988, annual rpt, 6224–6

Trials (civil and criminal) of 20 days or more terminated in Federal district courts, case and trial characteristics, June 1988, annual rpt, 18204–8.14

Natural Resources, Environment, and Pollution

Coastal and estuarine pollutant discharges, by source, pollutant type, and location, series, 2176–4

Electric utilities serving aluminum smelters, effects of proposed sulfur dioxide abatement legislation on operating costs, 1985, 5608–155

Estuary environmental conditions and mgmt, research projects and funding, FY87, annual listing, 2144–24

Great Lakes basin pollutant discharges, sources, and control program activities, 1987, biennial rpt, 14644–1

Hazardous substances industrial releases and reduction methods under EPA regulation, by chemical, source, industry, and location, 1987, annual rpt, 9234–6

Hazardous waste site remedial action under Superfund, current and proposed sites descriptions and status, periodic listings, series, 9216–3

Hazardous waste site remedial action under Superfund, current and proposed sites priority ranking and status by location, as of July 1989, listing, 9218–64

Ocean pollution research, monitoring, and resources dev activities of Fed Govt, funding and project descriptions, FY87, annual rpt, 2144–23

Radiation exposure of population near commercial reactors, by body site, age group, and selected plant, 1986, annual rpt, 9634–7

Radioactive waste and spent fuel generation, inventory, and disposal, 1960s–88 and projected to 2020, annual rpt, 3364–2

Radioactive waste from nuclear power plants, releases and waste composition by plant, 1986, annual rpt, 9634–1

Uranium tailings at inactive mills, remedial action proposals, costs, site characteristics, and environmental, socioeconomic, and health impacts, series, 3356–4

Water storage and carriage facilities of Reclamation Bur, capacity, and operating status, as of Sept 1988, biennial listing, 5824–7

Prices and Cost of Living

Auto industry finances and operations, trade by country, and prices of selected US and foreign models, monthly rpt, 9882–8

Electric power rate schedules, by user type, utility, and city, as of Jan 1988, annual rpt, 3164–40

Public Welfare and Social Security

Food aid programs purchases, by commodity, firm, and shipping point or destination, weekly rpt, 1302–3

Health maintenance organization Medicare enrollees, reimbursement and other characteristics by plan, and compared to fee-for-service, mid-1980s, 4658–31

Medicare program provisions affecting hospice participation, and claims processing time by carrier, 1987-89, GAO rpt, 26121–311

Nonprofit charitable organizations finances, and assets and grants of top 10, 1985, article, 8302–2.923

Older persons aid and policies of Fed Govt, program funding, and grants awarded, FY80-89, annual rpt, 25144–3.2

Refugee arrivals and resettlement in US, by age, sex, sponsoring agency, State, and country, monthly rpt, 4692–2

Refugee resettlement programs and funding, arrivals by country of origin, and indicators of adjustment, by State, FY88, annual rpt, 4694–5

Recreation and Leisure

Arts Natl Endowment activities and grants, FY88, annual rpt, 9564–3

Historic and natural natl landmarks damaged and threatened, with owner, location, damage type, and recommended remedial action, 1988, annual listing, 5544–16

Museum Services Inst activities and finances, and grants by recipient, FY88, annual rpt, 9564–7

Museum Services Inst grants, by recipient, FY89, annual press release series, 9564–6

Smithsonian Instn activities, rpts, and funding by donor, FY88, annual rpt, 29574–1.2

Science and Technology

Astronomical tables, time conversion factors, and listing of observatories worldwide, 1990, annual rpt, 3804–7

Black colleges R&D funding by source, and characteristics of grad students and research staff, by field of science and instn, 1980s–87, 9628–78

Computer mainframe and related equipment procurement, compatibility, and operating system contracts, for Navy, FY86-89, GAO rpt, 26125–37

Computer systems and equipment of Fed Govt, by type, make, and agency, 1st half FY89, semiannual listing, 9452–9

Degrees (PhD) in science and engineering, by field, instn, employment prospects, sex, race, and other characteristics, 1960s-88, 9627–30

Energy-related inventions recommended by Natl Inst of Standards and Technology for DOE support, awards, and evaluation status, 1988, annual listing, 2214–5

Enrollment in science and engineering, degrees, and student aid and sources, with data by field, race, sex, and instn, 1980s-87, 26358–202

Enrollment in science and engineering grad programs, by field, source of funds, and characteristics of student and instn, 1975-87, annual rpt, 9627–7

Labor force, Federal and university research funding, and educational data, for science and engineering, series, 9626–6

NASA procurement contract awards, by type, contractor, State, and country, FY89, semiannual rpt, 9502–6

NASA R&D funding to higher education instns, by field, instn, and State, FY88, annual listing, 9504–7

NATO postdoctoral fellowships in science, recipients educational outcomes and other characteristics, 1959-81, 9628–80

NSF grants and contracts, by field, inst, State, and country, FY88, annual rpt, 9624–26

Oceanographic research cruise schedules and ship characteristics, by higher education instn and Federal agency, 1989, annual listing, 3804–6

Patents (US) granted to US and foreign applicants, by applicant and country, 1960s-88, annual rpt, 2244–3

R&D and related funding of Fed Govt to higher education and nonprofit instns, by field, instn, agency, and State, FY87, annual rpt, 9627–17

R&D funding by Fed Govt at large science facilities, by field, performer, and facility, FY86-88, hearings, 21708–128

R&D funding by Fed Govt, by field, performer type, agency, and State, FY87-89, annual rpt, 9627–20

Space launches and other activities of NASA and USSR, with flight data, 1957-88, annual rpt, 9504–6.1

Spacecraft debris in orbit, hazards, and tracking, with data for individual fragmented craft, 1961-88, 9508–34

Veterans Affairs

AIDS cases at VA health care centers, by facility and region, periodic tables, 8702–1; 9922–15

Health care for veterans, patients, visits, costs, and operating beds, by VA and contract facility, and region, quarterly rpt, 8602–4

Hospital and nursing home use, beds, daily census, and construction projects, by VA facility, FY88, annual rpt, 8604–3

Medicine and Surgery Dept of VA, trainees by detailed program and city, FY88, annual rpt, 8704–4

Mental health services, staffing, research, and training programs in VA facilities, 1989 biennial listing, 8704–2

Surgery-related deaths and complications, by procedure and VA facility, and compared to non-VA instns, 1981-88, biennial rpt, 8704–1

BY INDUSTRY

Banking, Finance, and Insurance

Bond (low-grade) issues by industry div, holdings by owner type, yields, and defaults, 1977-88, 21248–118

Bond tax-exempt issues for private activity, by purpose, face value, major industry, and State, 1986, annual article, 8302–2.905

Small business common stock offerings, by distribution method and industry div, 1978-87, annual conf, 9734–4

Small Business Investment Companies finances, funding, licensing, and loan activity, 1st half FY89, semiannual rpt, 9762–3

Stock market transactions, and new issue registrations, monthly rpt, 9732–1

Stock price volatility, with data by industry and country, 1970s-88, conf papers, 9381–13.1

Venture capital-backed securities offerings by industry div, and venture capital firms financing by source, 1975-88, article, 9373–1.914

Communications and Transportation

Freight carriage for trucks, rail, and water, by industry group, 1985, 3166–6.33

Transportation census, 1987: trucks, by detailed characteristics, miles traveled, and type of product carried, State rpt series, 2573–1

Energy Resources and Demand

Coal receipts and prices at manufacturing plants, by SIC 2-digit industry, quarterly rpt, 3162–37.2

Electric power use and prices, shipments, and trade, for 25 SIC 4-digit manufacturing industries, 1972-86, 2048–137

Electric power use indexes, by SIC 2- to 4-digit industry, monthly rpt, 9365–2.10

Energy supply, demand, and prices, by fuel type and end use, with foreign comparisons, 1976-88, annual summary rpt, 3164–76

Foreign countries energy-intensive industry output and operations, and US investment barriers, for energy-rich countries, 1984-88, 9886–4.142

Manufacturing energy use and prices, 1985 survey, series, 3166–13

Natural gas interstate pipeline company sales, by customer, SIC 2-digit industry group, and State, monthly rpt, annual tables, 3162–4.6

Oil fuel switching to other fuels, capability by end-use sector, 1989, annual rpt, 3164–88

Government and Defense

Arms sales of US, foreign conditions on sales and impacts on US industry, with data by industry group and country, 1988 annual rpt, 104–25

DOD in-house commercial activities work-years, by service branch, State, and installation, FY88, annual rpt, 3544–25

Partnerships (master limited) finances, firms, partners, and tax reform impacts, by industry, 1986, technical paper, 8006–3.59

Puerto Rico and other US possessions corporations tax incentives, finances, and

operations by industry, and impacts on local economy, 1970s-83, biennial rpt, 8004–12

Tax (income) returns filed by type of filer, selected income items, quarterly rpt, 8302–2.1

Tax (income) returns for foreign corporate activity in US, assets, and income statement items, by industry div, country, and world area, 1984-85, article, 8302–2.920

Tax (income) returns of corporations, income and tax items by asset size and detailed industry, 1986, annual rpt, 8304–4; 8304–21

Tax (income) returns of corporations, summary data by asset size and industry div, 1986, annual article, 8302–2.922

Tax (income) returns of partnerships, income statement items by industry group, 1986, annual article, 8302–2.903

Tax (income) returns of sole proprietorships, income statement items, by industry group, 1987, annual article, 8302–2.904; 8302–2.921

Tax (sales) retailer collections as share of sales, by SIC 2- to 4-digit kind of business, 1987, annual rpt, 2413–5

Tax (sales) retailer collections, compliance costs by industry group and for 7 States, 1981, hearings, 21528–73

Health and Vital Statistics

Disabled persons employment, labor force status, and other characteristics, 1988, Current Population Rpt, 2546–2.147

Injuries at workplace, by circumstances, body site, equipment type, and industry, with safety measures, series, 6846–1

Injuries, illnesses, and workdays lost, by industry div and major manufacturing group, Monthly Labor Review, 6722–1.7

Injury and illness rates by SIC 2- to 4-digit industry, and deaths by cause and industry div, 1987, annual rpt, 6844–1

Insurance (health) coverage of retirees, by source, and former industry and occupation, 1987, 4186–8.2

Insurance (health) coverage of total and working population, by selected characteristics, 1987, 4186–8.1

Insurance (health) coverage, uninsured persons employment and income characteristics, hospital charges, and care expenses, 1977-85, GAO rpt, 26121–274

Insurance (health) provided by employer, coverage and characteristics of plan and employer, 1986-87, hearing, 25368–160

Labor force health condition and services use, by occupation and industry of longest job held, income, age, sex, and race, 1980, 4147–10.168

Occupational deaths, by equipment type, circumstances, and OSHA standards violated, series, 6606–2

Occupational injuries, illnesses, and workdays lost, by SIC 2-digit industry, 1987-88, annual press release, 6844–3

Occupational injury and illness rates, by industry group, 1975-87, 6728–38.10

Industry and Commerce

Assets (depreciable) class lives measurement, investment, and industry operations, asset class rpt series, 8006–5

Business activity indicators, 1987, annual rpt, 9364–5.9

Disabled persons rehabilitation, Federal and State activities and funding, FY88, annual rpt, 4944-1

Health condition of labor force, disability days, health services use, and disease prevalence, by occupation and sex, 1983-85, 4146-8.170

Heart disease deaths, by health and other characteristics, 1986, 4146-8.177

Hospital labor and total factor productivity, with background data, 1980-86, article, 4652-1.941

Injuries at workplace, by circumstances, body site, equipment type, and industry, with safety measures, series, 6846-1

Insurance (health) coverage of retirees, by source, and former industry and occupation, 1987, 4186-8.2

Insurance (short term disability) coverage and provisions, by occupational group, 1986-87, article, 6722-1.925

Labor force health condition and services use, by occupation and industry of longest job held, income, age, sex, and race, 1980, 4147-10.168

Long-term health care needs, ability to pay, and views on Federal aid for home care, 1988 survey, hearing, 21148-51

Mine safety and health enforcement, training, and funding, with casualties, by type of mine and State, FY87, annual rpt, 6664-6

Mines (coal) and related operations occupational injuries and incidence, employment, and hours, 1987, annual rpt, 6664-4

Mines (metal) and related operations occupational injuries and incidence, employment, and hours, 1987, annual rpt, 6664-3

Mines (nonmetallic minerals) and related operations occupational injuries and incidence, employment, and hours, 1987, annual rpt, 6664-1

Mines (sand and gravel) and related operations occupational injuries and incidence, employment, and hours, 1987, annual rpt, 6664-2

Mines (stone) and related operations occupational injuries and incidence, employment, and hours, 1987, annual rpt, 6664-5

Occupational deaths, by equipment type, circumstances, and OSHA standards violated, series, 6606-2

Radiation exposure of Federal employees, by age, occupation, and selected agency, 1986-87, biennial rpt, 4064-15

Smoking prevalence, related disease and deaths, and public attitudes, impact of Surgeon General rpts and antismoking campaigns, 1964-89, annual rpt, 4204-18

Smoking rates, by sex, age, race, occupation, region, and State, 1985 Current Population Survey, article, 4472-1.910

Industry and Commerce

Mine employees by selected occupational and other characteristics, injuries, and workdays lost, 1986, series, 5606-8

Labor and Employment

Aerospace industry employment and salaries, by sex and race, 1979-87, GAO rpt, 26121-315

Aerospace industry minority employment in Los Angeles area, by occupational group, 1980s-86, 21348-113

Dallas-Fort Worth metro area employment, earnings, hours, and CPI changes, 1970s-88, annual rpt, 6964-2

Earnings, annual average percent changes for selected occupational groups, selected MSAs, monthly rpt, 6782-1.1

Earnings of married couples, by employment status, occupation, age, and education of spouses, and age of children, 1987, Current Population Rpt, 2546-6.61

Employee benefit plan coverage and provisions, by plan type and occupational group, 1988, annual rpt, 6784-19

Employment and Earnings, detailed data, monthly rpt, 6742-2

Employment conditions, alternative BLS projections to 2000 and trends 1970s-88, biennial article, 6722-1.955

Employment Cost Index and alternative measure of compensation costs, by component, occupation, industry group, union status, and location, 1975-89, annual rpt, 6744-20

Employment Cost Index and percent change by occupational group, industry div, region, and metro-nonmetro area, quarterly press release, 6782-5

Employment Cost Index changes for nonfarm workers, by occupation, industry div, region, and bargaining status, monthly rpt, 6782-1

Employment cost indexes, by occupation, industry div, and region, Monthly Labor Review, 6722-1.3

Employment in nonmanufacturing industries, by detailed occupation and SIC 2-digit industry, 1987, triennial rpt, 6748-60

Employment, unemployment, and labor force characteristics, by region, State, and selected metro area, 1988, annual rpt, 6744-7

Farm population, by employment and socioeconomic characteristics, and region, 1988, annual Current Population Rpt, 2546-1.439

Foreign countries labor conditions, union coverage, and work accidents, annual country rpt series, 6366-4

Handbook of Labor Statistics, employment, unemployment, and labor force characteristics, 1940s-88 with trends from 1913, 6728-38

High school and college grads employment status and income, 1989 edition, annual rpt, 4824-2.28

Hispanic Americans socioeconomic characteristics, by detailed origin, 1988, Current Population Rpt, 2546-1.430; 2546-1.438

Household and family characteristics, by location, 1988, annual Current Population Rpt, 2546-1.437

Houston metro area employment, earnings, hours, and CPI changes, 1970s-88, annual rpt, 6964-1

Immigrants admitted to US, by occupational group and country of birth, preliminary FY88, annual table, 6264-1

Japan and US labor force participation by selected characteristics, productivity, and unit labor costs, 1960s-87, article, 6722-1.910

Job Training Partnership Act occupational training and other services provision, and outcomes, by participant characteristics, 1982-86, GAO rpt, 26106-8.8

Job Training Partnership Act participant occupational training and placements by occupation and skill level, and placement wages, by sex, 1982-86, GAO rpt, 26106-8.9

Labor force counts under occupation and industry classifications used in 1970 and 1980 censuses, by industry, occupation, and sex, 1970, technical paper, 2626-2.59

Labor force entrants, by age, sex, race, part-time status, and detailed occupation, Jan 1987, article, 6742-1.902

Labor force status, by worker characteristics and industry group, 1982-1st half 1989, semiannual article, 6722-1.907

Labor force, wages, hours, and payroll costs, by major industry group and demographic characteristics, *Survey of Current Business*, monthly rpt, 2702-1.5

Labor hourly costs, by component, occupational group, union coverage, industry div, and region, 1989, annual rpt, 6744-21

Mexico labor supply and conditions, with data by major city, selected years 1969-88, working paper, 2326-18.49

Minority group and women employment, by occupation, SIC 1- to 3- digit industry, State, and MSA, 1986, annual rpt, 9244-1

Moonlighting employment, by worker and primary and secondary job characteristics and reason, 1989, press release, 6726-1.24

Occupational changes, by tenure and other worker characteristics, and labor mobility rates, 1965-86, article, 6722-1.943

Older persons socioeconomic characteristics, 1900s-86 and projected to 2050, biennial chartbook, 12904-1

Rural areas employment, economic conditions, and population characteristics, 1970s-85, compilation of papers, 1598-243

Rural areas high-technology employment, by industry div and size of firm, and compared to urban areas, selected years 1972-86, hearing, 25728-41

Rural areas high-technology manufacturing employment in western States, by occupational group, 1986 survey results, article, 1502-7.912

Small business establishments, operations, owner characteristics, and job training, late 1950s-87, 9768-20

Southeastern US wages of office and plant workers, for 36 MSAs, 1988, press release, 6946-3.14

Statistical Abstract of US, social, political, and economic data, 1790-2025, comprehensive annual compilation, 2324-1.3

Technological devs effect on labor force, composition, and productivity, by industry, 1960s-86 and projected to 2000, series, 6826-2

Temporary help supply services industry employment and earnings for permanent and temporary workers, by occupation, Sept 1987, article, 6722-1.912

Training for job, relation to earnings by source of training and employee characteristics, model results, 1983, working paper, 6886-6.34

Training for job, sources and participant characteristics, with data by employer size and major industry group, 1982-88, 6408-73

DEMOGRAPHIC BREAKDOWNS

BY AGE

Aircraft accidents and circumstances, for US operations of domestic and foreign airlines and general aviation, periodic rpt, 9612-1

Aircraft accidents, pilots involved by age, 1986, annual rpt, 9614-3

Aircraft pilots and nonpilots certified by FAA, by certificate type, age, sex, region, and State, 1988, annual rpt, 7504-2

Drivers licenses in force, by age, sex, and State, 1987-88, annual rpt, 7554-24

Drivers licenses in force by license type, sex, and age, and revenues, by State, 1988, annual rpt, 7554-1.2

Drivers licenses issued and in force by age and sex, fees, and renewal, by license class and State, 1987, annual rpt, 7554-16

Pedestrian deaths, by circumstances and characteristics of victim, injury, and vehicle, 1985-86 local area study, article, 4042-3.927

Railroad employee benefits and beneficiaries by type, and railroad employment and payroll, FY85, annual rpt, 9704-2

Railroad employment, and benefits program finances and beneficiaries, FY88, annual rpt, 9704-1

Statistical Abstract of US, social, political, and economic data, 1790-2025, comprehensive annual compilation, 2324-1.1

Telephone service of households, by composition, income sources, and other characteristics, 1984-87, 9288-11

Traffic accident impacts of speed limits, with accident circumstances and speed averages, for States with 55 and 65 mph limit, 1986-87, annual rpt, 7764-15

Traffic accidents, injuries, and deaths, by circumstances and characteristics of persons and vehicles involved, 1970s-87, series, 7766-14

Traffic accidents, injuries, and deaths of older drivers, compared to other age groups, 1986, 7768-105

Traffic fatal accidents, alcohol levels of drivers and others, by circumstances and characteristics of persons and vehicles, 1988, annual rpt, 7764-16

Traffic fatal accidents, circumstances, and characteristics of persons and vehicles involved, 1988, semiannual rpt, 7762-11

Traffic fatal accidents, deaths, and rates, by circumstances, characteristics of persons and vehicles involved, and location, 1987, annual rpt, 7764-10

Travel to US and Canada, market analysis with detailed trip and traveler characteristics, country rpt series, 2906-2

Travel to US, by characteristics of visit and traveler, country, port city, and State of destination, quarterly rpt, 2902-1

Education

Condition of Education, detailed data on elementary and secondary education, 1920s-88 and projected to 1997, annual rpt, 4824-1.1

Digest of Education Statistics, detailed data on students, staff, finances, and facilities, 1989 edition, annual rpt, 4824-2

Elementary and secondary public schools, enrollment and other characteristics, for top 55 districts, 1987-88, annual rpt, 4834-22

Elementary and secondary students performance in selected subjects, and factors affecting proficiency, natl assessments, 1969-86, 4898-26

Enrollment, by grade, instn type and control, and student characteristics, 1986 and trends from 1947, annual Current Population Rpt, 2546-1.429; 2546-1.432

High school dropout rates, and subsequent completion, by student and school characteristics, alternative estimates, 1988, annual rpt, 4834-23

Higher education enrollment by age and instn type, and degrees by level, by sex, 1974/75-1988/89 and alternative projections to 1999/2000, annual rpt, 4824-4

Higher education instn student aid and other sources of support, with student expenses and characteristics, by instn type and control, 1987 triennial study, series, 4846-3

Special education programs, enrollment by age, staff, funding, and needs, by type of handicap and State, 1987/88, annual rpt, 4944-4

Statistical Abstract of US, social, political, and economic data, 1790-2025, comprehensive annual compilation, 2324-1.1

Student aid Pell grants and applicants, by tuition, income level, instn type and control, and State, 1987/88, annual rpt, 4804-1

Teachers bachelor degrees, by field and other characteristics, 1985-86, 4838-39

Teachers moonlighting, by selected employment and other characteristics, 1985, 4838-36

Vocational education aid recipients and sources, and characteristics of programs and students, 1970s-89, series, 4806-3

Energy Resources and Demand

Coal production, reserves, use, and prices by State, exports by country, and employment, 1900s-87, biennial rpt, 3164-79

Household, housing, and fuel use characteristics, survey rpt series, 3166-7

Government and Defense

Employment of minorities, handicapped, and veterans in Fed Govt, and years of service, by occupation, age, sex, and agency, as of Sept 1988, biennial rpt, 9844-27

Immigration to US, alien workers, visitors, deportations, and naturalizations, by country, FY88 and trends from 1820, annual rpt, 6264-2

Military deaths by cause, age, race, and rank, and personnel captured and missing, by service branch, 2nd half FY88, semiannual rpt, 3542-21

Military personnel alcohol and drug abuse, prevalence and consequences, by selected characteristics, 1988, biennial rpt, 3504-19

Military personnel, by selected characteristics, 1989 annual summary rpt, 3504-13

Military personnel deaths by service branch and age group, and veterans death rates, 1966-88, annual rpt, 8654-1

Military personnel on active duty, by age, 1963-88, annual rpt, 3544-1.2

Military reserve forces manpower strengths and characteristics, by component, quarterly rpt, 3542-4

Military reserve personnel social, economic, family, and service characteristics, and attitudes, by reserve component, 1986 survey, 3508-29

Military reserve spouses attitudes, and family social, economic, and other characteristics, 1986 survey, 3508-30

Navy manpower strengths, accessions, and attrition, detailed statistics, quarterly rpt, 3802-4

Pension program of Fed Govt, benefits and coverage by age, type of beneficiary, and State, FY87, annual rpt, 9844-34

Senior Executive Service membership characteristics, entries, exits, and awards, FY80-1987, annual rpt, 9844-36

Statistical Abstract of US, social, political, and economic data, 1790-2025, comprehensive annual compilation, 2324-1.2

Taxes, spending, and govt efficiency, public opinion by respondent characteristics, 1989 survey, annual rpt, 10044-2

Voting and registration, by race, Hispanic origin, sex, age, and State, 1988 presidential election, advance Current Population Rpt, 2546-1.434

Voting and registration, by socioeconomic and demographic characteristics, 1988 presidential election, biennial Current Population Rpt, 2546-1.440

Health and Vital Statistics

Abortions, and patient characteristics, 1972-85, article, 4202-7.906

Abortions, by method, pregnancy history, and other characteristics of woman, 1985-86, US Vital Statistics annual rpt, 4146-5.108

Abortions by patient characteristics, rates for all and 1st abortions, and related deaths in US and other countries, 1989 hearing, 21408-113

Acute and chronic health conditions, disability, absenteeism, and health services use, by selected characteristics, 1988, annual rpt, 4147-10.170

Agent Orange exposure of Air Force personnel, deaths and rates by cause and selected characteristics, 1989 annual rpt, 3604-3

AIDS cases by risk group, race, sex, age, State, and MSA, and deaths, monthly rpt, 4202-9

AIDS deaths, by health and other characteristics, 1986, 4146-8.178

AIDS health care services research status, needs, methods, and impacts on public health policy and funding, with data for selected cities, 1989 conf papers, 4188-59

AIDS info brochure of Surgeon General, public views by age, sex, race, education, and income, 1988 survey, 4042-3.908

AIDS public knowledge, attitudes, info sources, and testing, for blacks, 1988 survey, 4146-8.167

AIDS public knowledge, attitudes, info sources, and testing, for Hispanics, 1988 survey, 4146-8.168

AIDS public knowledge, attitudes, info sources, and testing, 1988 survey, 4146-8.165; 4146-8.169; 4146-8.173

AIDS public knowledge, attitudes, info sources, and testing, 1989 survey, 4146-8.176; 4146-8.180

AIDS public knowledge, by age and education, for Vermont, 1986-87 survey, article, 4042-3.938

Aircraft pilots disease rates, by disease and age, 1988 technical rpt, 7506-10.55

Alcohol-related hospitalization, discharges by diagnosis and age, 1979-85, article, 4482-1.903

Alcohol use, abuse, treatment, and views of racial and ethnic groups in US and native countries, by selected characteristics, 1988 compilation of papers, 4488-12

Alcohol use and abuse among minority groups, and related problems, by selected characteristics, 1985 conf papers, 4488-13

Alcoholic beverages warning labels and other consumer protection methods, public views by selected characteristics, 1988 survey, 8488-5

Births and first births to women over age 30, by age and race, 1970-86, 4147-21.47

Births and rates, by characteristics of birth, infant, and parents, 1987 and trends from 1940, US Vital Statistics advance annual rpt, 4146-5.110

Births at home, and hospital, by whether planned, outcome, and characteristics of mother and prenatal care, for Calgary, Canada, 1984-87, article, 4042-3.935

Births, fertility rates, and childless women, by selected characteristics, 1988, annual Current Population Rpt, 2546-1.436

Births of low birthweight, by race of child, and characteristics of mother, prenatal care, and birth, selected years 1975-87, 4147-21.48

Birthweight relation to child health condition, indicators for low and normal weight by age, sex, mothers education, and race, 1981, article, 4042-3.904

Cancer (breast) risk, by oral contraceptives use and menopausal status, 1976-86 study, article, 4472-1.923

Cancer (breast and cervical) incidence, deaths, and survival rates, by race, average 1973-81, article, 4042-3.952

Cancer (cervical) screening and education program for black women, effectiveness and participant characteristics, 1988 local area study, article, 4042-3.953

Cancer incidence by body site and population characteristics, research results, semimonthly journal, 4472-1

Cancer incidence, death, and survival rates, by sex, race, age, and body site, 1973-86, annual rpt, 4474-35

Cardiologist office visits, by characteristics of patient, physician, and visit, 1985, 4146-8.174

Cardiovascular diseases cases, health care services use and costs, and productivity losses, by selected characteristics, 1980, 4146-12.26

Child death rates, by age, sex, race, and cause, for US and compared to 8 OECD countries, 1985 and trends from 1900, 4147-3.27

Cholesterol levels among aged, screening and treatment effectiveness, and costs under proposed Medicare coverage, 1978-89, 26356-7.3

Cholesterol levels of youth related to physical characteristics, age, sex, and race, 1966-70 natl study, article, 4042-3.922

Cirrhosis of liver deaths, by age, sex, race, and whether alcohol involved, 1986 and trends from 1910, 4486-1.4; 4486-1.7

Contraceptives use by women, by age and country, 1989 biennial rpt, 2324-9

Deaths and rates, by cause, age, sex, marital status, race, and State, 1987, US Vital Statistics advance annual rpt, 4146-5.113

Deaths and rates, by cause, age, sex, race, and State, preliminary 1987-88 and trends from 1960, US Vital Statistics annual rpt, 4144-7

Deaths and rates, by detailed cause and demographic characteristics, 1986 and trends from 1900, US Vital Statistics annual rpt, 4144-2

Deaths and rates, by detailed location, cause, and demographic characteristics, 1987, US Vital Statistics annual rpt, 4144-3

Deaths and rates, provisional data, monthly rpt, 4142-1

Deaths recorded in 121 cities, by age group and for infants, weekly rpt, 4202-1

Disabled persons employment, labor force status, and other characteristics, 1988, Current Population Rpt, 2546-2.147

Disabled persons rehabilitation, Federal and State activities and funding, FY88, annual rpt, 4944-1

Diving (underwater sport and occupational) deaths, by circumstances, diver characteristics, and location, 1970-87, annual rpt, 2144-5

Divorces and children involved, by characteristics of spouses and whether 1st marriage, 1950s-84, 4147-21.46

Divorces by age of spouses and duration of marriage, and children involved, by State, 1986 with trends from 1940, US Vital Statistics advance annual rpt, 4146-5.109

Drug (PCP) treatment admissions and deaths in selected areas, and emergency room visits by patient sex, race, and age, 1987, article, 4042-3.931

Drug abuse emergency room admissions and deaths, by drug type and source, sex, race, age, and major metro area, 1988, annual rpt, 4494-8

Drug abuse indicators for selected metro areas, research results, data collection, and policy issues, 1989 semiannual conf, 4492-5

Drug, alcohol, and cigarette use, by substance, age, sex, race, and region, 1988 survey, biennial rpt, 4494-5

Drug and alcohol abuse treatment facilities, services, use, funding, and client characteristics, 1987, annual rpt, 4494-10

Drugs (controlled) provided during physician office visits, by drug, patient, and provider characteristics, 1985, 4146-8.179

Expenditures for health care, by service type, payment source, and age, 1977 and 1987, article, 4652-1.946

Firearms-related deaths of children, by motive, age, sex, and race, 1968-87, 4146-8.181

France and Germany physicians, and visits by reason and patient age and sex, by specialty, compared to US, 1981-83, 4147-5.5

France and US hospital beds, and use by diagnosis and patient characteristics, by instn ownership, with deaths by cause, 1981, 4147-5.4

Glaucoma incidence, screening and treatment effectiveness, and costs under proposed Medicare coverage, 1988, 26356-7.1

Health care treatments and products not proven safe or effective, use, costs, and user characteristics, 1986 survey, 4008-86

Health care use and costs, methodology and findings of natl survey, series, 4186-8

Health condition and health care resources, use, and spending, 1950s-87, annual data compilation, 4144-11

Health maintenance organization enrollment of Medicare enrollees, services use, charges, and survival, compared to fee-for-service, 1980-82 study, article, 4652-1.904

Health-related behavior of runners, for 7 habits, by sex, age, education, income, and average miles run per week, 1985 survey, article, 4042-3.933

Heart disease deaths, by health and other characteristics, 1986, 4146-8.177

Hepatitis cases by infection source, age, sex, race, and State, and deaths, by strain, 1987 and trends from 1966, 4205-2

Hepatitis risk for pregnant and postpartum women related to isoniazid treatment for tuberculosis, by age group, 1981-82 study, article, 4042-3.911

Hispanic Americans body measurements, obesity, and handedness, by detailed origin, age, and sex, 1982-84, 4147-11.207

Home health care services use and costs for Medicare disabled and aged enrollees, by age, sex, service type, and diagnosis, mid 1970s-86, article, 4652-1.908

Hospice services awareness of aged, by age, sex, education, region, SMSA/non-SMSA residence, and cancer history, 1984 survey, article, 4042-3.915

Hospital discharges and length of stay, by diagnosis, patient age and sex, surgical procedure performed, and region, 1965-86, 4147-13.101

Hospital discharges and length of stay, by diagnosis, patient and instn characteristics, procedure performed, and payment source, 1987, annual rpt, 4147-13.99

Hospital discharges by detailed diagnostic and procedure category, primary diagnosis, and length of stay, by age, sex, and region, 1987, annual rpt, 4147-13.100

Human papillomavirus infection rates, by sexual and personal hygiene practices, and other patient characteristics, Brazil local area studies, 1989 article, 4472-1.908

Indian Health Service and contract facilities hospitalization, by diagnosis, age, sex, and service area, FY87, annual rpt, 4104-16

Indian Health Service and contract facilities hospitalization, by diagnosis, age, sex, and service area, FY88, annual rpt, 4084-5

Indian Health Service facilities, funding, operations, and Indian health and other characteristics, 1950s-88, annual chartbook, 4084-1

Indian Health Service outpatient visits, by reason for visit and age, FY87-88, annual rpt, 4084-2

Infectious notifiable disease cases, by age, State, and outlying area, and deaths, 1930s-88, annual rpt, 4204-1

Injuries from use of consumer products and related activities, by victim age and sex, 1988, annual rpt, 9164-7

Injuries from use of consumer products, by severity, victim age, and detailed product, 1988, annual rpt, 9164-6

Injuries from use of consumer products, related deaths and costs, and recalls by brand, by product type, FY87, annual rpt, 9164-2

Insurance (health) coverage of adolescents by selected characteristics, and impacts of mandated employer and expanded Medicaid coverage, 1979-87, 26358-205

Kidney end-stage disease treatment facilities, Medicare enrollment and reimbursement, survival, and patient characteristics, 1980-86, annual rpt, 4654-16

Labor force health condition and services use, by occupation and industry of longest job held, income, age, sex, and race, 1980, 4147-10.168

Life tables, 1986 and trends from 1900, US Vital Statistics annual rpt, 4144-2.6

Long-term health care for aged, funding by Fed Govt, public views, 1987 survey, hearings, 21368-106

Long-term health care needs, ability to pay, and views on Federal aid for home care, 1988 survey, hearing, 21148-51

Mammography referral services for low-income women, use and client characteristics, 1987-88 local area study, article, 4042-3.951

Marriages and rates, by age, race, education, previous marital status of spouses, and State, 1986, US Vital Statistics advance annual rpt, 4146-5.111; 4146-5.112

Marriages, by prior marital status, interval between marriages, other characteristics of spouses, type of ceremony, and State, with divorces, 1970s-83, 4147-21.45

Marriages, divorces, and rates, by characteristics of spouses, State, and county, 1984 and trends from 1920, US Vital Statistics annual rpt, 4144-4

Maternal postpartum exercise intention relationship to age, education, and exercise attitudes and habits, local area study, 1989 article, 4042-3.916

Mental health care hospitals, beds and caseload by State, patient characteristics, finances, and staff, for profit and nonprofit private instns, 1986, 4506-3.37

Mental health care hospitals of States and counties, patients and admissions by age, diagnosis, and State, FY87, annual rpt, 4504-2

Mental health treatment of children in short-stay hospitals, by age, race, and facility and physician characteristics, 1977, 4188-55

Mentally retarded persons facilities, beds, and residents, by ownership, resident age and race, and State, 1986, 4147-14.34

Military personnel health-related behavior, for 7 habits, by age, education, race, and health status, 1985 survey, article, 4042-3.949

Nurses recruitment and retention issues and indicators, 1988 conf papers, 4118-64

Nursing facility service use and costs for Medicare enrollees, by selected characteristics and State, 1970s-87, article, 4652-1.954

Nursing home facility, staff, and resident detailed characteristics, 1985, 4147-13.97

Nursing home rehabilitation services use, by service type and patient characteristics, 1st qtr 1983, 4188-58

Nursing home reimbursement by Medicare under prospective payment system, and admissions by prior hospitalization status and duration, and patient characteristics, mid 1970s-85, 4147-13.98

Nursing home use rates, charges, and resident length of stay, care needs, and other characteristics, 1985, 4147-13.102

Nursing homes, beds, and residents, by ownership, certification status, and State, 1986, 4147-14.33

Nutritional status and related health condition and practices, by selected characteristics, 1970s-87, 4048-33

Occupational injuries, by circumstances, body site, equipment type, and industry, with safety measures, series, 6846-1

Older persons care by family members, caregivers and potential caregivers by relation and other characteristics, 1984, 4186-7.5

Older persons functional limitations, by activity type and selected characteristics, 1984, 4147-10.167

Older persons health care services use, persons with high and low levels of care by selected health and other characteristics, 1971 and 1980 studies, 4186-2.22

Older persons health condition, chronic and multiple illness prevalence by sex and age group, 1984, 4146-8.172

Ophthalmologist office visits, by characteristics of physician, practice, patient, and visit, with drug mentions by type and brand, 1985, 4146-8.166

Physicians (family practice) by age, ratios to population, and residents, and percent women and foreign medical grads, 1960s-88 and projected to 2010, article, 4042-3.926

Pollutants health effects, concentrations in food and environment, sources, and human intake methodology and data needs, series, 9186-9

Pollutants health effects, concentrations in food and environment, sources, human intake, and regulation, series, 9186-8

Pregnancies (ectopic) and related deaths, by race, age, and region, 1970-86, article, 4202-7.902; 4202-7.905

Pregnancy-related deaths, rates, and risk, by pregnancy outcome, cause, and maternal characteristics, 1980-85, article, 4202-7.903

Radiation exposure of Federal employees, by age, occupation, and selected agency, 1986-87, biennial rpt, 4064-15

Smoking and other tobacco use, by knowledge of health effects, and health and other characteristics, 1987, 4147-10.169

Smoking prevalence, related disease and deaths, and public attitudes, impact of Surgeon General rpts and antismoking campaigns, 1964-89, annual rpt, 4204-18

Smoking rates, by sex, age, race, occupation, region, and State, 1985 Current Population Survey, article, 4472-1.910

Statistical Abstract of US, social, political, and economic data, 1790-2025, comprehensive annual compilation, 2324-1.1

Suicide incidence rates related to age, sex, race, marital status, and month, for Maryland, 1970-80, article, 4042-3.928

Surgical procedures performed in hospitals, by procedure type, age, sex, instn size, and payment source, 1983-87, 4146-8.171

Tobacco (smokeless) use by youth and adults, user characteristics, and sales, 1970s-86, papers, 4478-188

Traffic accident deaths involving alcohol, by driver and victim blood alcohol levels and other characteristics, 1977-87, annual rpt, 4486-1.2; 4486-1.5; 4486-1.8

TTPI deaths by age, and births by age of mother, by sex, 1981-87, annual rpt, 7004-6

Tuberculosis cases among minorities, by age and race, 1987, article, 4042-3.962

Tuberculosis cases and deaths, by patient characteristics, State, and city, 1987 and trends from 1953, annual rpt, 4204-10

Vaccination activity, reactions, costs, and preventable disease cases and deaths, 1988 annual conf, 4204-15

Vitamin and mineral supplements use by adults and children, by type and user characteristics, 1986, 4146-8.175

Housing and Construction

American Housing Survey: unit and households detailed characteristics, and unit and neighborhood quality, MSA rpt series, 2485-6

American Housing Survey: unit and households detailed characteristics, and unit and neighborhood quality, 1985, biennial rpt, 2485-12

Home ownership rate, by age of household head, 1974-87, article, 1702-1.903

Homeless shelters services, operations, and client characteristics, 1988 survey, 5188-123

Housing and households summary characteristics, 1985 and trends, biennial chartbook, 2486-1.7

Housing unit costs and homeownership rates, by income, age, family composition, and region, 1967-87, hearings, 25248-107

Retirees housing and community preferences, by respondent characteristics, 1987 survey, article, 1702-1.905

Rural and urban areas housing and households characteristics, 1930s-80, 1598-245

Industry and Commerce

Mine employees by selected occupational and other characteristics, injuries, and workdays lost, 1986, series, 5606-8

Labor and Employment

Earnings of married couples, by employment status, occupation, age, and education of spouses, and age of children, 1987, Current Population Rpt, 2546-6.61

Employment and Earnings, detailed data, monthly rpt, 6742-2

Employment and Training Admin activities, funding, and participant characteristics, by program, FY80-86, 6408-71

Employment and unemployment, by age, sex, race, marital and family status, industry div, and State, Monthly Labor Review, 6722-1.2

Employment conditions, alternative BLS projections to 2000 and trends 1970s-88, biennial article, 6722-1.952

Employment, earnings, and hours, monthly press release, 6742-5

Employment situation, earnings, hours, and other BLS economic indicators, transcripts of BLS Commissioner's monthly testimony, periodic rpt, 23846-4

Handbook of Labor Statistics, employment, unemployment, and labor force characteristics, 1940s-88 with trends from 1913, 6728-38.1; 6728-38.2

Insurance (health) for retirees, employer
liabilities and costs by age group, 1988 and
projected to 2043, GAO rpt, 26121-299

Insurance (life) coverage and benefits of
employee plans, by length of service and
other employee characteristics, 1988,
article, 6722-1.951

Job Training Partnership Act participants and
eligible population, by selected
characteristics, 1986, 15496-1.3

Job Training Partnership Act participants, by
selected characteristics, FY88, annual rpt,
6304-1

Labor force composition, and wages relation
to inflation and unemployment, late
1930s-88, article, 9373-1.902

Labor force entrants, by age, sex, race,
part-time status, and detailed occupation,
Jan 1987, article, 6742-1.902

Labor force participation rate impact of
Reagan Admin tax policy and business
cycle indicators, by sex and age, 1976-88,
article, 9389-1.914

Labor force, participation rates and
unemployed persons by age and sex, and
part-time employment, *Business Conditions
Digest*, monthly rpt, 2702-3.7

Labor force status, by worker characteristics
and industry group, 1982-1st half 1989,
semiannual article, 6722-1.907;
6722-1.937

Labor force supply and mobility, by age, and
educational level needs, 1960-86 and
projected to 2000, 6306-2.4

Maternity leave arrangements and work
history of 1st-time mothers, by selected
characteristics, 1960s-85, 2328-62

Mexico labor supply and conditions, with
data by major city, selected years 1969-88,
working paper, 2326-18.49

Mexico population, labor force, and
emigration, alternative projections
1990-2000, working paper, 2326-18.46

Moonlighting employment, by worker and
primary and secondary job characteristics
and reason, 1989, press release, 6726-1.24

Occupational changes, by tenure and other
worker characteristics, and labor mobility
rates, 1965-86, article, 6722-1.943

Older persons employment, earnings, reasons
for working, and job training preferences,
by selected characteristics, 1960-87,
6306-2.3

Older persons labor force participation,
unemployment, displacement, and
reemployment, by selected characteristics,
1969-88, 6306-2.2

Pension coverage, by plan type and worker
characteristics, 1970s-88, article,
4742-1.925; 4746-26.7

Pension coverage in private sector, age and
length of service requirements by
occupational group, 1988, annual rpt,
6784-19

Poverty level labor force employment,
earnings, and other characteristics, 1987,
article, 6722-1.948

Retirement timing of married couples,
differences in age and retirement age of
spouses, 1982, article, 4742-1.906

Statistical Abstract of US, social, political,
and economic data, 1790-2025,
comprehensive annual compilation,
2324-1.3

Training for job, sources and participant
characteristics, with data by employer size
and major industry group, 1982-88,
6408-73

Unemployed displaced workers, labor-mgmt
committee aid recipients by selected
characteristics, for 4 State programs, 1988,
GAO rpt, 26121-316

Unemployment insurance long-term claimants
employment services use, work experience,
and reemployment, by selected
characteristics and county, 1987-88,
6406-6.25; 6406-6.26

Unemployment rates, current data and annual
trends, monthly rpt, 23842-1.2

Unemployment spells duration, frequency,
insurance coverage, and outcome, by age,
sex, and race, 1984, Current Population
Rpt, 2546-20.9

Union coverage of workers and earnings, by
age, sex, race, occupational group, and
industry div, annual article, 6782-1.2

Vermont older persons employment, income,
and other characteristics, by sex and age,
1900-86, hearing, 21148-54

Wage differentials between service and
manufacturing sectors related to worker
characteristics, 1987, article, 9377-1.901

Wages of full- and part-time workers, by
selected characteristics, quarterly press
release, 6742-20

Women's labor force participation, by age,
race, and family status, quarterly rpt,
6742-17

Youth labor force participation by age, Apr
and July 1989 and change from 1988,
annual press release, 6744-13

Law Enforcement

Arrest rates, by offense, sex, age, and race,
1987, annual rpt, 6224-7

Arrests by offender characteristics,
prosecutions, convictions, and sentences by
type, by felony offense, 1983-86,
6066-19.52

Assaults and deaths of law enforcement
officers, by circumstances, agency, victim
and offender characteristics, and location,
1988, annual rpt, 6224-3

Children abducted and murdered by
strangers, and rates, by victim sex, age, and
race, 1976-84, 6066-27.1

Crime, criminal justice admin and
enforcement, and public opinion, data
compilation, 1970s-88, annual rpt, 6064-6

Crime victimization rates, by victim and
offender characteristics, circumstances, and
offense, 1987 survey, annual rpt,
6066-3.41

Crime victimizations resulting in injury, by
offense, type of injury and medical care
received, and victim characteristics,
1979-86, 6066-19.49

Crimes, arrests, and rates, by offense,
offender characteristics, population size,
and jurisdiction, 1988, annual rpt,
6224-2.1; 6224-2.2

Criminal case processing from arrest to
sentencing, cases and duration by
disposition, offense, and defendant
characteristics, for selected cities, 1986,
annual rpt, 6064-27

Criminal case processing in Federal district
courts, and dispositions, by offense, district,
and offender characteristics, 1984, annual
rpt, 6064-29

Homicide rates, and lifetime probability of
victimization, by age, sex, and race, 1987,
annual rpt, 6224-8

Juvenile correctional and detention instns,
inmates, and expenses, by instn and
resident characteristics and State, 1975-85,
biennial rpt, 6064-13

Juvenile court delinquency cases, by offense,
referral source, disposition, age, sex, race,
State, and county, 1985, annual rpt,
6064-12

Juvenile court referrals by offender
characteristics, and dispositions, by offense,
1984, 6066-27.2

Juvenile offenders recidivism rates, arrests,
and court referrals, by offense, age, and
sex, 1983 local area studies, 6068-227

Prison conditions, population, and problems,
issues and bibl, 1989 compilation of papers,
25928-8

Prisoners in State instns, by offense, criminal
history, and inmate, family, and victim
characteristics, 1986, annual rpt,
6064-26.3

Prisoners under death sentence, and
executions from 1930, by offense, prisoner
characteristics, and State, 1986, annual rpt,
6064-26.6

Prisoners under death sentence by prison
control and prisoner characteristics, and
executions from 1930, by State, 1973-88,
annual rpt, 6066-25.23

Recidivism rates of prisoners released in
1983, by offense and prisoner
characteristics, 1983-86, 6066-19.48

Statistical Abstract of US, social, political,
and economic data, 1790-2025,
comprehensive annual compilation,
2324-1.1

Suicides in Maryland prisons, by selected
characteristics, 1979-87, 4186-9.2

Natural Resources, Environment, and Pollution

Radiation exposure of population near
commercial reactors, by body site, age
group, and selected plant, 1986, annual rpt,
9634-7

Population

Alaska rural villages population
characteristics and and subsistence
activities, 1976-86, 5738-9

Children, and family income, by family
characteristics, 1974-88, article,
6722-1.963

Consumer Income, socioeconomic
characteristics of persons, families, and
households, detailed cross-tabulations,
Current Population Rpt series, 2546-6

Educational attainment, by sociodemographic
characteristics and location, 1987 and
trends from 1940, biennial Current
Population Rpt, 2546-1.427; 2546-1.431

Hispanic Americans socioeconomic
characteristics, by detailed origin, 1988,
Current Population Rpt, 2546-1.430;
2546-1.438

Household and family characteristics, by
living arrangement, 1988 and trends from
1960, Current Population Rpt, 2546-2.148

Household and family characteristics, by
location, 1988, annual Current Population
Rpt, 2546-1.437

Household and family composition, and
factors affecting change, 1960s-88,
chartbook, 2546-2.149

Wildlife-related recreation, hunting, and fishing participation and spending, detailed data, 1985 survey, quinquennial State rpt series, 5506-6

Science and Technology

Earnings of scientists and engineers in R&D at DOE labs and non-DOE facilities, 1989, annual rpt, 3004-9

Education in science and engineering in elementary and secondary schools, and student persistence in postsecondary education, 1977-88, 26358-199

Education in science, elementary and secondary students proficiency, attitudes, factors affecting proficiency, and teacher background and views, natl assessment, 1977-86, 4898-25

Education in science, methods, materials, and factors affecting elementary and secondary student proficiency, views of students, teachers, and administrators, 1983-85 surveys, 4828-37.1

Employment and education of scientists and engineers, and R&D spending, for US and selected foreign countries, 1988, annual rpt, 9624-23.2

Employment and other characteristics of science and engineering PhDs, by field and State, 1987, biennial rpt, 9627-18

Immigrant scientists and engineers, by field, age, sex, country and world area of origin, and State, 1987 and trends from 1967, 9627-29

Labor force, Federal and university research funding, and educational data, for science and engineering, series, 9626-6

NASA staff characteristics and personnel actions, FY88, annual rpt, 9504-1

Veterans Affairs

Disability and death compensation cases of VA, by entitlement type, period of service, sex, age, and State, FY88, annual rpt, 8604-7

Insurance (life) for veterans and servicepersons, actuarial analysis of VA programs, 1988, annual rpt, 8604-1

Population and characteristics of veterans, and VA hospital and other activities, by State, FY88, annual rpt, 8604-3

Population of veterans, and benefits programs awareness and use, by age, sex, income, race, and period of service, 1987 survey, 8608-1

Population of veterans, by period of service, age, and State, as of Mar 1989, semiannual rpt, 8602-7

Statistical Abstract of US, social, political, and economic data, 1790-2025, comprehensive annual compilation, 2324-1.2

BY DISEASE

Communications and Transportation

Aircraft pilots disease rates, by disease and age, 1988 technical rpt, 7506-10.55

Railroad accidents, casualties, and damage, by cause, railroad, and State, 1988, annual rpt, 7604-1

Railroad employee sickness benefits and beneficiaries, by age, occupation, and disease, 1984/85, annual rpt, 9704-2.3

Education

Head Start handicapped enrollment, by handicap, State, and for Indian and migrant programs, 1985/86, annual rpt, 4604-1

Head Start program operations, enrollment by handicap, and family characteristics, for North Central States, 1987/88, annual rpt, 4604-12

Higher education enrollment of disabled, by disability, educational, and other characteristics, fall 1986, 4846-3.6

Special education programs, enrollment by age, staff, funding, and needs, by type of handicap and State, 1987/88, annual rpt, 4944-4

Statistical Abstract of US, social, political, and economic data, 1790-2025, comprehensive annual compilation, 2324-1.1

Government and Defense

Army active duty personnel health condition, and use of Army medical services in US and abroad, monthly rpt, 3702-4.2

Employment of disabled in Fed Govt, by disability and agency, FY87, annual rpt, 9244-10.2

Employment of minorities, handicapped, and veterans in Fed Govt, and years of service, by occupation, age, sex, and agency, as of Sept 1988, biennial rpt, 9844-27

Military deaths by cause, age, race, and rank, and personnel captured and missing, by service branch, 2nd half FY88, semiannual rpt, 3542-21

Health and Vital Statistics

Acute and chronic health conditions, disability, absenteeism, and health services use, by selected characteristics, 1988, annual rpt, 4147-10.170

Agent Orange exposure of Air Force personnel, deaths and rates by cause and selected characteristics, 1989 annual rpt, 3604-3

AIDS patients Medicaid claims and payments, by type of care and whether AIDS-related, race, sex, and diagnosis, 1984-87, article, 4042-3.940

Alcohol-related disorder hospital discharges, by sex, 1979-84, annual rpt, 4486-1.1

Alcohol-related hospitalization, discharges by diagnosis and age, 1979-85, article, 4482-1.903

Alcohol-related illness hospital discharges for disabled Medicare beneficiaries, by diagnosis, 1985, article, 4482-1.905

Alcohol use and abuse among minority groups, and related problems, by selected characteristics, 1985 conf papers, 4488-13

Birthweight relation to child health condition, indicators for low and normal weight by age, sex, mothers education, and race, 1981, article, 4042-3.904

Cardiologist office visits, by characteristics of patient, physician, and visit, 1985, 4146-8.174

Children (handicapped) home health care and support services availability and need, 1988, GAO report, 26121-300

Costs (direct and indirect) of disease, by diagnosis, 1986, annual rpt, 4474-15

Costs of health care related to cost of prior hospitalization, model description and results, 1974-80, article, 4652-1.939

Death rates by cause, age, and sex, average change 1968-86, annual actuarial rpt, 4706-1.104

Deaths and rates, by cause, age, sex, marital status, race, and State, 1987, US Vital Statistics advance annual rpt, 4146-5.113

Deaths and rates, by cause and age, preliminary 1987-88, US Vital Statistics annual rpt, 4144-7

Deaths and rates, by detailed cause and demographic characteristics, 1986 and trends from 1900, US Vital Statistics annual rpt, 4144-2

Deaths and rates, by detailed location, cause, and demographic characteristics, 1987, US Vital Statistics annual rpt, 4144-3

Deaths and rates, provisional data, monthly rpt, 4142-1

Deaths from 10 leading causes, 1987, annual rpt, 4474-15

Disability Insurance and SSI eligibility determinations for mental impairment, caseload and review activities by impairment type and State, 1984-86, hearing, 21788-176

Disabled persons rehabilitation, Federal and State activities and funding, FY88, annual rpt, 4944-1

Drug prescriptions, by drug type and brand, and for new drugs, 1987, annual rpt, 4064-12

Drugs (controlled) provided during physician office visits, by drug, patient, and provider characteristics, 1985, 4146-8.179

Foreign travel vaccination needs by country, and disease prevention recommendations, 1989 annual rpt, 4204-11

France and Germany physicians, and visits by reason and patient age and sex, by specialty, compared to US, 1981-83, 4147-5.5

France and US hospital beds, and use by diagnosis and patient characteristics, by instn ownership, with deaths by cause, 1981, 4147-5.4

Health condition and health care resources, use, and spending, 1950s-87, annual data compilation, 4144-11

Home health care services use and costs for Medicare disabled and aged enrollees, by age, sex, service type, and diagnosis, mid 1970s-86, article, 4652-1.908

Homeless persons in rural areas, health condition, services use, and other characteristics, local area studies, 1989 rpt, 4186-9.1

Hospital discharges and length of stay, by diagnosis, patient age and sex, surgical procedure performed, and region, 1965-86, 4147-13.101

Hospital discharges and length of stay, by diagnosis, patient and instn characteristics, procedure performed, and payment source, 1987, annual rpt, 4147-13.99

Hospital discharges by detailed diagnostic and procedure category, primary diagnosis, and length of stay, by age, sex, and region, 1987, annual rpt, 4147-13.100

Hospital discharges, length of stay, and costs, for Medicare by type of beneficiary, procedure, diagnosis, and State, 1970s-86, article, 4652-1.945

Hospital Medicare discharges, charges, and length of stay, by State and diagnosis, 1983 and 1985, article, 4652-1.925

Indian Health Service and contract facilities hospitalization, by diagnosis, age, sex, and service area, FY87, annual rpt, 4104-16

Wildlife-related recreation, hunting, and fishing participation and spending, detailed data, 1985 survey, quinquennial State rpt series, 5506-6

Science and Technology
Earnings of scientists and engineers in R&D at DOE labs and non-DOE facilities, 1989, annual rpt, 3004-9

Employment and education of scientists and engineers, and R&D spending, for US and selected foreign countries, 1988, annual rpt, 9624-23.2

Fed Govt science and engineering employment, by field, degree level, race, sex, agency, and State, 1987, annual rpt, 9627-5

Labor force, Federal and university research funding, and educational data, for science and engineering, series, 9626-6

NASA staff characteristics and personnel actions, FY88, annual rpt, 9504-1

Wages of scientists and engineers in R&D, by field and educational, employment, and other characteristics, 1989, annual rpt, 3004-1

Veterans Affairs
Population of veterans, and benefits programs awareness and use, by age, sex, income, race, and period of service, 1987 survey, 8608-1

BY MARITAL STATUS

Agriculture and Food
FmHA loans, by type, borrower characteristics, and State, quarterly rpt, 1182-8

Population on farms, by employment and socioeconomic characteristics, and region, 1988, annual Current Population Rpt, 2546-1.439

Communications and Transportation
Telephone service of households, by composition, income sources, and other characteristics, 1984-87, 9288-11

Travel to US and Canada, market analysis with detailed trip and traveler characteristics, country rpt series, 2906-2

Nursing home reimbursement by Medicare under prospective payment system, and admissions by prior hospitalization status and duration, and patient characteristics, mid 1970s-85, 4147-13.98

Education
Enrollment, by grade, instn type and control, and student characteristics, 1986 and trends from 1947, annual Current Population Rpt, 2546-1.429; 2546-1.432

High school class of 1972: education, employment, and family characteristics, activities, and attitudes, natl longitudinal study, series, 4836-1

High school dropout rates, and subsequent completion, by student and school characteristics, alternative estimates, 1988, annual rpt, 4834-23

Higher education instn student aid and other sources of support, with student expenses and characteristics, by instn type and control, 1987 triennial study, series, 4846-3

Teachers in public schools, demographic and employment characteristics, 1989 edition, annual rpt, 4824-2.9

Government and Defense
Immigration to US, alien workers, visitors, deportations, and naturalizations, by country, FY88 and trends from 1820, annual rpt, 6264-2

Military personnel alcohol and drug abuse, prevalence and consequences, by selected characteristics, 1988, biennial rpt, 3504-19

Military reserve personnel social, economic, family, and service characteristics, and attitudes, by reserve component, 1986 survey, 3508-29

Military reserve spouses attitudes, and family social, economic, and other characteristics, 1986 survey, 3508-30

Military women personnel on active and reserve duty, by demographic and service characteristics and service branch, FY88, annual chartbook, 3544-26

Tax (income) returns of individuals, by filing status, tax item, and income level, 1987, annual article, 8302-2.901

Tax (income) returns of individuals, detailed data, 1986, annual rpt, 8304-2

Tax (income) returns of individuals, taxable income, and tax generated, by tax rate and income level, 1986, annual article, 8302-2.918

Taxes, spending, and govt efficiency, public opinion by respondent characteristics, 1989 survey, annual rpt, 10044-2

Health and Vital Statistics
Abortions, and patient characteristics, 1972-85, article, 4202-7.906

Abortions, by method, pregnancy history, and other characteristics of woman, 1985-86, US Vital Statistics annual rpt, 4146-5.108

Abortions by patient characteristics, rates for all and 1st abortions, and related deaths in US and other countries, 1989 hearing, 21408-113

Alcohol use, abuse, treatment, and views of racial and ethnic groups in US and native countries, by selected characteristics, 1988 compilation of papers, 4488-12

Alcohol use and abuse among minority groups, and related problems, by selected characteristics, 1985 conf papers, 4488-13

Alcoholic beverages warning labels and other consumer protection methods, public views by selected characteristics, 1988 survey, 8488-5

Births at home, and hospital, by whether planned, outcome, and characteristics of mother and prenatal care, for Calgary, Canada, 1984-87, article, 4042-3.935

Births, fertility rates, and childless women, by selected characteristics, 1988, annual Current Population Rpt, 2546-1.436

Births of low birthweight, by race of child, and characteristics of mother, prenatal care, and birth, selected years 1975-87, 4147-21.48

Cancer (cervical) screening and education program for black women, effectiveness and participant characteristics, 1988 local area study, article, 4042-3.953

Deaths and rates, by cause, age, sex, marital status, race, and State, 1987, US Vital Statistics advance annual rpt, 4146-5.113

Deaths and rates, by cause, marital status, age, race, and sex, 1986, annual rpt, 4144-2.1

Disabled persons employment, labor force status, and other characteristics, 1988, Current Population Rpt, 2546-2.147

Drug abuse indicators for selected metro areas, research results, data collection, and policy issues, 1989 semiannual conf, 4492-5

Fetal deaths and rates, by characteristics of mother and birth, 1986, US Vital Statistics annual rpt, 4144-2.3

France and US hospital beds, and use by diagnosis and patient characteristics, by instn ownership, with deaths by cause, 1981, 4147-5.4

Health care use and costs, methodology and findings of natl survey, series, 4186-8

Heart disease deaths, by health and other characteristics, 1986, 4146-8.177

Human papillomavirus infection rates, by sexual and personal hygiene practices, and other patient characteristics, Brazil local area studies, 1989 article, 4472-1.908

Mammography referral services for low-income women, use and client characteristics, 1987-88 local area study, article, 4042-3.951

Marriages and rates, by age, race, education, previous marital status of spouses, and State, 1986, US Vital Statistics advance annual rpt, 4146-5.111; 4146-5.112

Marriages, by prior marital status, interval between marriages, other characteristics of spouses, type of ceremony, and State, with divorces, 1970s-83, 4147-21.45

Marriages, divorces, and rates, by characteristics of spouses, State, and county, 1984 and trends from 1920, US Vital Statistics annual rpt, 4144-4

Nurses recruitment and retention issues and indicators, 1988 conf papers, 4118-64

Nursing home facility, staff, and resident detailed characteristics, 1985, 4147-13.97

Nursing home use rates, charges, and resident length of stay, care needs, and other characteristics, 1985, 4147-13.102

OASDI disabled workers Medicare enrollment waiting period, proposed elimination impact on costs, with background data, 1974-81, article, 4742-1.915

Older persons care by family members, caregivers and potential caregivers by relation and other characteristics, 1984, 4186-7.5

Older persons functional limitations, by activity type and selected characteristics, 1984, 4147-10.167

Older persons health care services use, persons with high and low levels of care by selected health and other characteristics, 1971 and 1980 studies, 4186-2.22

Older persons poverty risk from long-term care costs, by duration of care, income, and marital status, model results, 1987 rpt, 25928-7

Pregnancy-related deaths, rates, and risk, by pregnancy outcome, cause, and maternal characteristics, 1980-85, article, 4202-7.903

Smoking and other tobacco use, by knowledge of health effects, and health and other characteristics, 1987, 4147-10.169

Smoking prevalence, related disease and deaths, and public attitudes, impact of Surgeon General rpts and antismoking campaigns, 1964-89, annual rpt, 4204-18

Suicide incidence rates related to age, sex, race, marital status, and month, for Maryland, 1970-80, article, 4042-3.928

Index by Categories

Vitamin and mineral supplements use by adults and children, by type and user characteristics, 1986, 4146-8.175

Housing and Construction

American Housing Survey: unit and households detailed characteristics, and unit and neighborhood quality, MSA rpt series, 2485-6

American Housing Survey: unit and households detailed characteristics, and unit and neighborhood quality, 1985, biennial rpt, 2485-12

Homeless shelters residents characteristics, local area study, 1983-87, 21248-123

Homeless shelters services, operations, and client characteristics, 1988 survey, 5188-123

Housing and households summary characteristics, 1985 and trends, biennial chartbook, 2486-1.7

Housing unit costs and homeownership rates, by income, age, family composition, and region, 1967-87, hearings, 25248-107

Retirees housing and community preferences, by respondent characteristics, 1987 survey, article, 1702-1.905

Labor and Employment

Employment and Earnings, detailed data, monthly rpt, 6742-2.2; 6742-2.3; 6742-2.4

Employment and unemployment, by age, sex, race, marital and family status, industry div, and State, Monthly Labor Review, 6722-1.2

Employment status of family members and earnings, by family composition and race, quarterly press release, 6742-21

Employment, unemployment, and labor force characteristics, by region, State, and selected metro area, 1988, annual rpt, 6744-7

Handbook of Labor Statistics, employment, unemployment, and labor force characteristics, 1940s-88 with trends from 1913, 6728-38.1; 6728-38.2

Labor force, wages, hours, and payroll costs, by major industry group and demographic characteristics, *Survey of Current Business*, monthly rpt, 2702-1.5

Maternity leave arrangements and work history of 1st-time mothers, by selected characteristics, 1960s-85, 2328-62

Moonlighting employment, by worker and primary and secondary job characteristics and reason, 1989, press release, 6726-1.24

Statistical Abstract of US, social, political, and economic data, 1790-2025, comprehensive annual compilation, 2324-1.3

Unemployment insurance long-term claimants employment services use, work experience, and reemployment, by selected characteristics and county, 1987-88, 6406-6.25; 6406-6.26

Wages of full- and part-time workers, by selected characteristics, quarterly press release, 6742-20

Women's labor force participation, by age, race, and family status, quarterly rpt, 6742-17

Law Enforcement

Crime victimization rates, by victim and offender characteristics, circumstances, and offense, 1987 survey, annual rpt, 6066-3.41

Crime victimizations resulting in injury, by offense, type of injury and medical care received, and victim characteristics, 1979-86, 6066-19.49

Criminal case processing in Federal district courts, and dispositions, by offense, district, and offender characteristics, 1984, annual rpt, 6064-29

Prisoners and movements, by offense, location, and selected other characteristics, data compilation, 1930s-89, annual rpt, 6064-6.6

Prisoners in State instns, by offense, criminal history, and inmate, family, and victim characteristics, 1986, annual rpt, 6064-26.3

Prisoners under death sentence, and executions from 1930, by offense, prisoner characteristics, and State, 1986, annual rpt, 6064-26.6

Prisoners under death sentence by prison control and prisoner characteristics, and executions from 1930, by State, 1973-88, annual rpt, 6066-25.23

Torts for product liability, dispositions, awards, case processing time, and plaintiff injury severity and other characteristics, 1983-85, GAO rpt, 26121-317

Population

Alaska rural villages population characteristics and and subsistence activities, 1976-86, 5738-9

Child support awards related to selected variables, 1970s-85, 4008-94

Consumer Income, socioeconomic characteristics of persons, families, and households, detailed cross-tabulations, Current Population Rpt series, 2546-6

Educational attainment, by sociodemographic characteristics and location, 1987 and trends from 1940, biennial Current Population Rpt, 2546-1.427; 2546-1.431

Hispanic Americans socioeconomic characteristics, by detailed origin, 1988, Current Population Rpt, 2546-1.430; 2546-1.438

Household and family characteristics, by living arrangement, 1988 and trends from 1960, Current Population Rpt, 2546-2.148

Income (household) and spending, and selected characteristics, for single-parent and married-couple households, 1984-86, article, 6722-1.916

Income (personal) and poverty status, change by selected socioeconomic characteristics, 1984-85, Current Population Rpt, 2546-20.10

Migration since 1986, mover characteristics by same or different area, and compared to nonmovers, 1987, annual Current Population Rpt, 2546-1.435

Older persons assets and relation to income, by selected characteristics, 1984, article, 4742-1.910

Older persons socioeconomic characteristics, 1900s-86 and projected to 2050, biennial chartbook, 12904-1

Population size and characteristics, 1969-88, Current Population Rpt, annual rpt, 2546-2.146

Population size and components of change, alternative projections 1988-2080 and trends from 1900, annual actuarial rpt, 4706-1.104

BY RACE AND ETHNIC GROUP

Poverty status of families and persons, by detailed characteristics, 1987, annual Current Population Rpt, 2546-6.60

Retirees savings maintenance and liquidation, by selected financial and other characteristics, 1971-79, article, 1702-1.906

Statistical Abstract of US, social, political, and economic data, 1790-2025, comprehensive annual compilation, 2324-1.1

Women (older) pension coverage, sources, payments, and effect on income and poverty status, 1982, article, 4742-1.901

Public Welfare and Social Security

Child support and alimony awards, and payment status, by selected characteristics of woman, 1985, biennial Current Population Rpt, 2546-2.145

Disability Insurance beneficiaries health insurance coverage, by type and selected beneficiary characteristics, fall 1982, article, 4742-1.927

Food stamp eligibility and payment errors, by type, recipient characteristics, and State, FY87, annual rpt, 1364-15

OASDHI, Medicaid, SSI, and related programs benefits, beneficiary characteristics, and trust funds, selected years 1937-87, annual rpt, 4744-3

OASDI benefit payments, trust fund finances, and economic and demographic assumptions, 1970-87 and alternative projections to 1997, actuarial rpt, 4706-1.103

OASI beneficiaries affected by earnings limits by selected characteristics, and Federal outlays, under alternative limits, 1986, 26306-3.110

OASI beneficiaries retiring before age 62, employment, income, and benefits, by selected characteristics, 1982, article, 4742-1.911

Public welfare programs beneficiaries, and benefits duration and share of income, by selected characteristics, 1983-86, 2546-20.8

Supplemental Security Income beneficiaries, assets by type and eligibility class, FY87, article, 4742-1.922

Science and Technology

NATO postdoctoral fellowships in science, recipients educational outcomes and other characteristics, 1959-81, 9628-80

Veterans Affairs

Hospitals of VA, patients discharged by diagnosis, compensation and pension status, and other characteristics, FY88, annual rpt, 8604-3.3

Population of veterans, and benefits programs awareness and use, by age, sex, income, race, and period of service, 1987 survey, 8608-1

BY RACE AND ETHNIC GROUP

Agriculture and Food

Census of Agriculture, 1987: farms, farmland, production, finances, and operator characteristics, by county, final State rpt series, 2331-1

Cotton farm operators by selected characteristics, and farms by size, by State, 1982 and 1987, article, 1561-1.907

Employment, earnings, and days worked, for farm workers by selected characteristics and region, 1987, biennial rpt, 1594-2

FmHA borrowers, by type of borrower and loan, and State, quarterly rpt, 1182-4

FmHA loans, by type, borrower characteristics, and State, quarterly rpt, 1182-8

FmHA loans, by type, borrower race, and State, quarterly rpt, 1182-5

Food consumption and nutrient intake by individuals, by food group, selected characteristics, and region, supplementary survey series, 1356-5

Population of farm operators and farming-dependent households, by selected characteristics, under alternative definitions, 1987, 1598-252

Population on farms, by employment and socioeconomic characteristics, and region, 1988, annual Current Population Rpt, 2546-1.439

Population on farms under alternative definitions, by selected characteristics, 1983, 1598-249

Vegetables (fresh and processed) consumption by type, and spending by consumer characteristics, 1960s-87, article, 1561-11.903

Communications and Transportation

Air traffic control and airway facilities staff, by selected employment and demographic characteristics, FY88, annual rpt, 7504-41

Hwy construction contracts awards of States to minority- and women-owned firms, FY85-88, GAO rpt, 26113-399

Telecommunications industries minority employment and discrimination charges, with data by industry and selected firm, 1970s-88, hearings, 21368-113

Education

Condition of Education, detailed data on elementary, secondary, and higher education, 1920s-88 and projected to 1997, annual rpt, 4824-1

Desegregation of schools, indicators of integration plans effectiveness by school district and location, 1960s-85, 11048-189

Digest of Education Statistics, detailed data on students, staff, finances, and facilities, 1989 edition, annual rpt, 4824-1

Elementary and secondary public schools, enrollment and other characteristics, for top 55 districts, 1987-88, annual rpt, 4834-22

Elementary and secondary students performance in selected subjects, and factors affecting proficiency, natl assessments, 1969-86, 4898-26

Enrollment, by grade, instn type and control, and student characteristics, 1986 and trends from 1947, annual Current Population Rpt, 2546-1.429; 2546-1.432

Enrollment in public schools, minorities share by group and State, 1987/88, annual rpt, 4834-17

Enrollment in science and engineering, degrees, and student aid and sources, with data by field, race, sex, and instn, 1980s-87, 26358-202

Head Start enrollment, funding, and staff, FY88, annual rpt, 4604-8

High school class of 1972: education, employment, and family characteristics, activities, and attitudes, natl longitudinal study, series, 4836-1

High school class of 1988: college enrollment, and labor force participation of grads and dropouts, by race and sex, press release, 6726-1.22

High school classes of 1972 and 1980: enrollment in 2-year colleges, credits earned and dropout rate, by student characteristics, as of 1984, 4848-38

High school classes of 1972, 1980, and 1982: educational attainment by selected characteristics, 1976-87, 4848-36

High school classes of 1972, 1980, and 1982: postsecondary enrollment and degrees, by sex, race, and income level, natl longitudinal surveys, 4848-35

High school classes of 1980 and 1982: education, employment, and family characteristics, activities, and attitudes, natl longitudinal study, series, 4826-2

High school dropout rates, and subsequent completion, by student and school characteristics, alternative estimates, 1988, annual rpt, 4834-23

High school students employment, academic and other characteristics, 1984-86, 4898-27

Higher education instn student aid and other sources of support, with student expenses and characteristics, by instn type and control, 1987 triennial study, series, 4846-3

Reading ability and literacy of young adults, relation to educational attainment and race, natl assessment, 1985, 4828-36

Statistical Abstract of US, social, political, and economic data, 1790-2025, comprehensive annual compilation, 2324-1.1

Teachers bachelor degrees, by field and other characteristics, 1985-86, 4838-39

Teachers in public and private schools, salaries by selected characteristics, 1984/85-1985/86, 4838-37

Teachers incentive programs of public schools, and participation, by instn and teacher characteristics, with effectiveness ratings, 1985, 4838-38

Teachers moonlighting, by selected employment and other characteristics, 1985, 4838-36

Truman, Harry S, Scholarship Foundation finances, FY88, and awards by student characteristics from 1977, annual rpt, 14314-1

Vocational and academic AA degree and certificate recipients and credits, by field, and student and instn characteristics, 1984, 4848-37

Vocational education aid recipients and sources, and characteristics of programs and students, 1970s-89, series, 4806-3

Energy Resources and Demand

Coal production, reserves, use, and prices by State, exports by country, and employment, 1900s-87, biennial rpt, 3164-79

Household, housing, and fuel use characteristics, survey rpt series, 3166-7

Government and Defense

Army personnel, promotion, and training by race and for women, discrimination issues, and career attitudes, FY88, annual rpt, 3704-10

Census of Govts, 1987: elected officials, by level of govt, race, sex, and State, preliminary rpt, 2450-2

DOT employment, by subagency, occupation, and selected personnel characteristics, FY88, annual rpt, 7304-18

Employment (civilian) of Fed Govt, by demographic and employment characteristics, as of Sept 1988, article, 9842-1.901

Employment (civilian) of Fed Govt, by occupation, pay schedule, grade, sex, and race, as of Sept 1988, article, 9842-1.902

Employment (civilian) of minorities and women in Fed Govt, by pay grade, 1977-86, 9848-37

Employment of minorities and women in Fed Govt by occupation, and handicapped employment, by agency, FY87, annual rpt, 9244-10

Employment of minorities, handicapped, and veterans in Fed Govt, and years of service, by occupation, age, sex, and agency, as of Sept 1988, biennial rpt, 9844-27

Employment of Small Business Admin, by sex, race, and pay grade, and SBA activities, FY84-88, annual rpt, 9764-1

Equal Opportunity Recruitment Program activity, and Fed Govt employment by sex, race, pay grade, and selected occupation, FY88, annual rpt, 9844-33

Foreign Service minority and women employment, hires, and promotions, 1981-87, GAO rpt, 26123-247

Military deaths by cause, age, race, and rank, and personnel captured and missing, by service branch, 2nd half FY88, semiannual rpt, 3542-21

Military personnel alcohol and drug abuse, prevalence and consequences, by selected characteristics, 1988, biennial rpt, 3504-19

Military personnel, by selected characteristics, 1989 annual summary rpt, 3504-13

Military personnel on active duty, recruits, and reenlistment, by race, sex, and service branch, quarterly press release, 3542-7

Military recruits for active duty and reserve, aptitude test scores and retention rates, with data by sex, race, and service branch, various periods 1980-87, 26306-6.136

Military reserve forces manpower strengths and characteristics, by component, quarterly rpt, 3542-4

Military reserve personnel social, economic, family, and service characteristics, and attitudes, by reserve component, 1986 survey, 3508-29

Military reserve spouses attitudes, and family social, economic, and other characteristics, 1986 survey, 3508-30

Military reserves strengths, by selected characteristics and reserve component, FY88, annual rpt, 3544-1.5

Military women personnel on active and reserve duty, by demographic and service characteristics and service branch, FY88, annual chartbook, 3544-26

Natl Guard officers and enlisted personnel, by race and sex, FY88, annual rpt, 3504-22.1

Postal Service employment of minority groups and women, by pay level, FY87-88, annual rpt, 9864-5.1

Senior Executive Service membership characteristics, entries, exits, and awards, FY80-1987, annual rpt, 9844-36

Services transfer from govts to private
contractors, impacts on govt workers, with
data by worker characteristics, level of
govt, and location, 1980s-87, 15496–1.5

State and local govt employment of
minorities and women, by occupation,
function, pay level, and State, 1986, annual
rpt, 9244–6

State Dept and Foreign Service minority and
women employment, FY88, annual rpt,
7004–21

Statistical Abstract of US, social, political,
and economic data, 1790-2025,
comprehensive annual compilation,
2324–1.2

Taxes, spending, and govt efficiency, public
opinion by respondent characteristics, 1989
survey, annual rpt, 10044–2

Voting and registration, by race, Hispanic
origin, sex, age, and State, 1988
presidential election, advance Current
Population Rpt, 2546–1.434

Voting and registration, by socioeconomic
and demographic characteristics, 1988
presidential election, biennial Current
Population Rpt, 2546–1.440

Health and Vital Statistics

Abortions, and patient characteristics,
1972-85, article, 4202–7.906

Abortions, by method, pregnancy history, and
other characteristics of woman, 1985-86,
US Vital Statistics annual rpt, 4146–5.108

Abortions by patient characteristics, rates for
all and 1st abortions, and related deaths in
US and other countries, 1989 hearing,
21408–113

Acute and chronic health conditions,
disability, absenteeism, and health services
use, by selected characteristics, 1988,
annual rpt, 4147–10.170

Agent Orange exposure of Air Force
personnel, deaths and rates by cause and
selected characteristics, 1989 annual rpt,
3604–3

AIDS cases and AIDS virus infection
prevalence, by risk group and other patient
characteristics, 1981-88 and projected to
1992, 4206–2.13

AIDS cases, and health and social services
availability, for 5 cities, 1988, GAO rpt,
26121–307

AIDS cases by risk group, race, sex, age,
State, and MSA, and deaths, monthly rpt,
4202–9

AIDS deaths, by health and other
characteristics, 1986, 4146–8.178

AIDS health care services research status,
needs, methods, and impacts on public
health policy and funding, with data for
selected cities, 1989 conf papers, 4188–59

AIDS info brochure of Surgeon General,
public views by age, sex, race, education,
and income, 1988 survey, 4042–3.908

AIDS patients Medicaid claims and
payments, by type of care and whether
AIDS-related, race, sex, and diagnosis,
1984-87, article, 4042–3.940

AIDS public knowledge, attitudes, info
sources, and testing, for blacks, 1988
survey, 4146–8.167

AIDS public knowledge, attitudes, info
sources, and testing, 1988 survey,
4146–8.165; 4146–8.169; 4146–8.173

AIDS public knowledge, attitudes, info
sources, and testing, 1989 survey,
4146–8.176; 4146–8.180

Alcohol use, abuse, treatment, and views of
racial and ethnic groups in US and native
countries, by selected characteristics, 1988
compilation of papers, 4488–12

Alcohol use and abuse among minority
groups, and related problems, by selected
characteristics, 1985 conf papers, 4488–13

Alcoholic beverages warning labels and other
consumer protection methods, public views
by selected characteristics, 1988 survey,
8488–5

Births and first births to women over age 30,
by age and race, 1970-86, 4147–21.47

Births and rates, by characteristics of birth,
infant, and parents, 1987 and trends from
1940, US Vital Statistics advance annual
rpt, 4146–5.110

Births, fertility rates, and childless women, by
selected characteristics, 1988, annual
Current Population Rpt, 2546–1.436

Births of low birthweight, by race of child,
and characteristics of mother, prenatal
care, and birth, selected years 1975-87,
4147–21.48

Birthweight relation to child health condition,
indicators for low and normal weight by
age, sex, mothers education, and race,
1981, article, 4042–3.904

Cancer (breast and cervical) incidence,
deaths, and survival rates, by race, average
1973-81, article, 4042–3.952

Cancer incidence by body site and population
characteristics, research results,
semimonthly journal, 4472–1

Cancer incidence, death, and survival rates,
by sex, race, age, and body site, 1973-86,
annual rpt, 4474–35

Cardiologist office visits, by characteristics of
patient, physician, and visit, 1985,
4146–8.174

Cardiovascular diseases cases, health care
services use and costs, and productivity
losses, by selected characteristics, 1980,
4146–12.26

Child death rates, by age, sex, race, and
cause, for US and compared to 8 OECD
countries, 1985 and trends from 1900,
4147–3.27

Child mental health treatment in short-stay
hospitals, by age, race, and facility and
physician characteristics, 1977, 4188–55

Cholesterol levels among aged, screening and
treatment effectiveness, and costs under
proposed Medicare coverage, 1978-89,
26356–7.3

Cholesterol levels of youth related to physical
characteristics, age, sex, and race, 1966-70
natl study, article, 4042–3.922

Cirrhosis of liver deaths, by age, sex, race,
and whether alcohol involved, 1986 and
trends from 1910, 4486–1.4; 4486–1.7

Deaths and rates by age, and life expectancy,
by sex and race, preliminary 1987-88 and
trends from 1950, US Vital Statistics
annual rpt, 4144–7

Deaths and rates, by cause, age, sex, marital
status, race, and State, 1987, US Vital
Statistics advance annual rpt, 4146–5.113

Deaths and rates, by detailed cause and
demographic characteristics, 1986 and
trends from 1900, US Vital Statistics
annual rpt, 4144–2

Deaths and rates, by detailed location, cause,
and demographic characteristics, 1987, US
Vital Statistics annual rpt, 4144–3

Deaths and rates, provisional data, monthly
rpt, 4142–1

Disabled persons employment, labor force
status, and other characteristics, 1988,
Current Population Rpt, 2546–2.147

Disabled persons rehabilitation, Federal and
State activities and funding, FY88, annual
rpt, 4944–1

Drug (PCP) treatment admissions and deaths
in selected areas, and emergency room
visits by patient sex, race, and age, 1987,
article, 4042–3.931

Drug abuse emergency room admissions and
deaths, by drug type and source, sex, race,
age, and major metro area, 1988, annual
rpt, 4494–8

Drug abuse indicators for selected metro
areas, research results, data collection, and
policy issues, 1989 semiannual conf,
4492–5

Drug, alcohol, and cigarette use, by
substance, age, sex, race, and region, 1988
survey, biennial rpt, 4494–5

Drug and alcohol abuse treatment facilities,
services, use, funding, and client
characteristics, 1987, annual rpt, 4494–10

Drugs (controlled) provided during physician
office visits, by drug, patient, and provider
characteristics, 1985, 4146–8.179

Firearms-related deaths of children, by
motive, age, sex, and race, 1968-87,
4146–8.181

Food aid program of USDA for women,
infants, and children, prenatal enrollees by
trimester of enrollment and other
characteristics, 1984, article, 4042–3.929

Health care treatments and products not
proven safe or effective, use, costs, and
user characteristics, 1986 survey, 4008–86

Health care use and costs, methodology and
findings of natl survey, series, 4186–8

Health condition and health care resources,
use, and spending, 1950s-87, annual data
compilation, 4144–11

Health-related behavior of runners, for 7
habits, by sex, age, education, income, and
average miles run per week, 1985 survey,
article, 4042–3.933

Heart disease deaths, by health and other
characteristics, 1986, 4146–8.177

Hepatitis cases by infection source, age, sex,
race, and State, and deaths, by strain, 1987
and trends from 1966, 4205–2

Hospital discharges and length of stay, by
diagnosis, patient and instn characteristics,
procedure performed, and payment source,
1987, annual rpt, 4147–13.99

Human papillomavirus infection rates, by
sexual and personal hygiene practices, and
other patient characteristics, Brazil local
area studies, 1989 article, 4472–1.908

Infant and fetal deaths and rates, by race,
sex, State, census div, and metro-nonmetro
location, 1950s-85, 4146–5.107

Infectious notifiable diseases reporting to
CDC, cases and rates by race, 1987,
article, 4042–3.943

Insurance (health) companies case mgmt for
high-cost patients, savings, costs, and
returns, 1984-86, article, 4652–1.914

Insurance (health) coverage of adolescents by
selected characteristics, and impacts of
mandated employer and expanded
Medicaid coverage, 1979-87, 26358–205

Migration to and from Southern US, by migrant characteristics and location, 1970s-87 and alternative projections to 2000, article, 9371–1.902

Minority group population, and components of change, by race, State, metro-nonmetro location, MSA, and county, 1980-85, Current Population Rpt, 2546–3.159

Older persons socioeconomic characteristics, 1900s-86 and projected to 2050, biennial chartbook, 12904–1

Population size, by age, sex, and race, and components of change, alternative projections 1988-2080, Current Population Rpt, 2546–3.158

Poverty status of families and persons, by detailed characteristics, 1987, annual Current Population Rpt, 2546–6.60

Retirees savings maintenance and liquidation, by selected financial and other characteristics, 1971-79, article, 1702–1.906

Single-parent household income and spending, and selected characteristics, with comparison to households with married parents, 1984-86, article, 6722–1.916

Single-parent household income sources and spending by category, by sex, age, race, and household size, 1984-85, article, 1702–1.901

Southern US poverty rates, by household composition, race, and urban-rural location, 1986, article, 9371–1.903

Statistical Abstract of US, social, political, and economic data, 1790-2025, comprehensive annual compilation, 2324–1.1

Prices and Cost of Living
Consumer Expenditure Survey, household income by source, and itemized spending, by selected characteristics and location, 1984-86, annual rpt, 6764–5.2

Consumer Expenditure Survey, spending by category, and income, by selected household characteristics and location, 1987, press release, 6726–1.23

Consumer spending and income effects of wives' employment, by expenditure category and household characteristics, 1984-86, article, 6722–1.908

Utilities spending of households, by household size, income, householder age and race, and region, 1983, article, 1702–1.904

Public Welfare and Social Security
AFDC recipients demographic and financial characteristics, by State, FY87, annual rpt, 4694–1

Child care arrangements and costs, by income and other characteristics of family, 1984-86, press release, 2328–61

Child support and alimony awards, and payment status, by selected characteristics of woman, 1985, biennial Current Population Rpt, 2546–2.145

Disability Insurance and SSI admin of Fed Govt and States, benefits, caseloads, and operations, 1980s, 4708–11

Employment and earnings covered under OASDHI, and social security contributions, by age, sex, race, State, and county, 1985, 4748–43

Medicare and Medicaid beneficiaries and program operations, 1988, annual fact book, 4654–18

Medicare and Medicaid eligibility, participation, coverage, and program finances, various periods 1966-89, biennial rpt, 4654–1

Medicare disabled enrollee costs related to patient characteristics, model description and results, 1974-81, technical paper, 4746–26.6

Medicare enrollment, and use by type of service, by age, sex, race, region, State, and MSA, 1986-87, annual rpt, 4657–5

Medicare reimbursement of hospitals under prospective payment system, impacts on instns, beneficiaries, and other care providers and payment sources, 1986, annual rpt, 4654–13

OASDHI admin, and SSA activities, 1930s-89 and projected to 2063, data compilation, annual rpt, 4704–12

OASDHI, Medicaid, SSI, and related programs benefits, beneficiary characteristics, and trust funds, selected years 1937-87, annual rpt, 4744–3

OASDI and SSI disabled beneficiaries, by selected characteristics, 1986, article, 4742–1.916

OASDI disabled worker beneficiaries, duration, and exits by reason, by selected characteristics, model description and results, 1972-80, article, 4742–1.923

OASDI disabled worker beneficiaries recoveries and reentitlements, by selected characteristics, model description and results, 1989 article, 4742–1.924

OASDI disabled workers Medicare enrollment waiting period, proposed elimination impact on costs, with background data, 1974-81, article, 4742–1.915

Public welfare programs beneficiaries, and benefits duration and share of income, by selected characteristics, 1983-86, 2546–20.8

Statistical Abstract of US, social, political, and economic data, 1790-2025, comprehensive annual compilation, 2324–1.2

Supplemental Security Income beneficiaries, by race and sex, monthly rpt, 4742–1.12

Recreation and Leisure
Wildlife-related recreation, hunting, and fishing participation and spending, detailed data by location, 1985 survey, quinquennial rpt, 5508–5

Wildlife-related recreation, hunting, and fishing participation and spending, detailed data, 1985 survey, quinquennial State rpt series, 5506–6

Science and Technology
Black colleges R&D funding by source, and characteristics of grad students and research staff, by field of science and instn, 1980s-87, 9628–78

Degrees (PhD) in science and engineering, by field, instn, employment prospects, sex, race, and other characteristics, 1960s-88, 9627–30

Degrees (PhD) in science, recipients by whether foreign, race, and sex, and instnl support, 1978 and 1987-88, 9626–2.187

Education in science and engineering in elementary and secondary schools, and student persistence in postsecondary education, 1977-88, 26358–199

Education in science, elementary and secondary students proficiency, attitudes, factors affecting proficiency, and teacher background and views, natl assessment, 1977-86, 4898–25

Employment and other characteristics of science and engineering PhDs, by field and State, 1987, biennial rpt, 9627–18

Engineering PhD awards to US and foreign students, and minority bachelors and masters degree recipients, 1977-87, 9626–2.182

Enrollment in science and engineering grad programs, by field, source of funds, and characteristics of student and instn, 1975-87, annual rpt, 9627–7

Fed Govt science and engineering employment, by field, degree level, race, sex, agency, and State, 1987, annual rpt, 9627–5

Labor force, Federal and university research funding, and educational data, for science and engineering, series, 9626–6

NASA staff characteristics and personnel actions, FY88, annual rpt, 9504–1

NATO postdoctoral fellowships in science, recipients educational outcomes and other characteristics, 1959-81, 9628–80

Veterans Affairs
Population of veterans, and benefits programs awareness and use, by age, sex, income, race, and period of service, 1987 survey, 8608–1

VA employment characteristics and activities, FY88, annual rpt, 8604–3.8

BY SEX

Agriculture and Food
Census of Agriculture, 1987: farms, farmland, production, finances, and operator characteristics, by county, final State rpt series, 2331–1

Cotton farm operators by selected characteristics, and farms by size, by State, 1982 and 1987, article, 1561–1.907

Employment, earnings, and days worked, for farm workers by selected characteristics and region, 1987, biennial rpt, 1594–2

FmHA loans, by type, borrower characteristics, and State, quarterly rpt, 1182–8

Food consumption and nutrient intake by individuals, by food group, selected characteristics, and region, supplementary survey series, 1356–5

Population of farm operators and farming-dependent households, by selected characteristics, under alternative definitions, 1987, 1598–252

Population on farms, by employment and socioeconomic characteristics, and region, 1988, annual Current Population Rpt, 2546–1.439

Population on farms under alternative definitions, by selected characteristics, 1983, 1598–249

Communications and Transportation
Air traffic control and airway facilities staff, by selected employment and demographic characteristics, FY88, annual rpt, 7504–41

Aircraft pilots and nonpilots certified by FAA, by certificate type, age, sex, region, and State, 1988, annual rpt, 7504–2

Military reserve spouses attitudes, and family social, economic, and other characteristics, 1986 survey, 3508–30

Military reserves strengths, by selected characteristics and reserve component, FY88, annual rpt, 3544–1.5

Natl Guard officers and enlisted personnel, by race and sex, FY88, annual rpt, 3504–22.1

Navy manpower strengths, accessions, and attrition, detailed statistics, quarterly rpt, 3802–4

Senior Executive Service membership characteristics, entries, exits, and awards, FY80-1987, annual rpt, 9844–36

Services transfer from govts to private contractors, impacts on govt workers, with data by worker characteristics, level of govt, and location, 1980s-87, 15496–1.5

SSA employment of Hispanics by regional office, and Spanish-speaking employees in California, 1987, GAO rpt, 26121–268

State and local govt employment of minorities and women, by occupation, function, pay level, and State, 1986, annual rpt, 9244–6

State Dept and Foreign Service minority and women employment, FY88, annual rpt, 7004–21

Statistical Abstract of US, social, political, and economic data, 1790-2025, comprehensive annual compilation, 2324–1.2

Taxes, spending, and govt efficiency, public opinion by respondent characteristics, 1989 survey, annual rpt, 10044–2

Voting and registration, by race, Hispanic origin, sex, age, and State, 1988 presidential election, advance Current Population Rpt, 2546–1.434

Voting and registration, by socioeconomic and demographic characteristics, 1988 presidential election, biennial Current Population Rpt, 2546–1.440

Health and Vital Statistics

Acute and chronic health conditions, disability, absenteeism, and health services use, by selected characteristics, 1988, annual rpt, 4147–10.170

AIDS cases and AIDS virus infection prevalence, by risk group and other patient characteristics, 1981-88 and projected to 1992, 4206–2.13

AIDS cases, and health and social services availability, for 5 cities, 1988, GAO rpt, 26121–307

AIDS cases by risk group, race, sex, age, State, and MSA, and deaths, monthly rpt, 4202–9

AIDS deaths, by health and other characteristics, 1986, 4146–8.178

AIDS health care services research status, needs, methods, and impacts on public health policy and funding, with data for selected cities, 1989 conf papers, 4188–59

AIDS info brochure of Surgeon General, public views by age, sex, race, education, and income, 1988 survey, 4042–3.908

AIDS patients Medicaid claims and payments, by type of care and whether AIDS-related, race, sex, and diagnosis, 1984-87, article, 4042–3.940

AIDS public knowledge, attitudes, info sources, and testing, for blacks, 1988 survey, 4146–8.167

AIDS public knowledge, attitudes, info sources, and testing, for Hispanics, 1988 survey, 4146–8.168

AIDS public knowledge, attitudes, info sources, and testing, 1988 survey, 4146–8.165; 4146–8.169; 4146–8.173

AIDS public knowledge, attitudes, info sources, and testing, 1989 survey, 4146–8.176; 4146–8.180

AIDS research grants and contracts of NIH, by funding and approval status, and researcher age, experience, and sex, FY86, GAO rpt, 26121–267

Alaska Natives cancer cases and risk, by body site and ethnic group, 1969-83, article, 4042–3.963

Alcohol-related disorder hospital discharges, by sex, 1979-84, annual rpt, 4486–1.1

Alcohol use, abuse, treatment, and views of racial and ethnic groups in US and native countries, by selected characteristics, 1988 compilation of papers, 4488–12

Alcohol use and abuse among minority groups, and related problems, by selected characteristics, 1985 conf papers, 4488–13

Alcoholic beverages warning labels and other consumer protection methods, public views by selected characteristics, 1988 survey, 8488–5

Births and rates, by characteristics of birth, infant, and parents, 1987 and trends from 1940, US Vital Statistics advance annual rpt, 4146–5.110

Birthweight relation to child health condition, indicators for low and normal weight by age, sex, mothers education, and race, 1981, article, 4042–3.904

Cancer incidence by body site and population characteristics, research results, semimonthly journal, 4472–1

Cancer incidence, death, and survival rates, by sex, race, age, and body site, 1973-86, annual rpt, 4474–35

Cancer incidence relation to exposure to asbestos in drinking water, by sex and cancer site, 1973-83, local area study, article, 4042–3.921

Cardiologist office visits, by characteristics of patient, physician, and visit, 1985, 4146–8.174

Cardiovascular diseases cases, health care services use and costs, and productivity losses, by selected characteristics, 1980, 4146–12.26

Child death rates, by age, sex, race, and cause, for US and compared to 8 OECD countries, 1985 and trends from 1900, 4147–3.27

Cholesterol levels among aged, screening and treatment effectiveness, and costs under proposed Medicare coverage, 1978-89, 26356–7.3

Cholesterol levels of youth related to physical characteristics, age, sex, and race, 1966-70 natl study, article, 4042–3.922

Cirrhosis of liver deaths, by age, sex, race, and whether alcohol involved, 1986 and trends from 1910, 4486–1.4; 4486–1.7

Costs of health care related to cost of prior hospitalization, model description and results, 1974-80, article, 4652–1.939

Deaths and rates by age, and life expectancy, by sex and race, preliminary 1987-88 and trends from 1950, US Vital Statistics annual rpt, 4144–7

Deaths and rates, by cause, age, sex, marital status, race, and State, 1987, US Vital Statistics advance annual rpt, 4146–5.113

Deaths and rates, by detailed cause and demographic characteristics, 1986 and trends from 1900, US Vital Statistics annual rpt, 4144–2

Deaths and rates, by detailed location, cause, and demographic characteristics, 1987, US Vital Statistics annual rpt, 4144–3

Deaths and rates, provisional data, monthly rpt, 4142–1

Disabled persons employment, labor force status, and other characteristics, 1988, Current Population Rpt, 2546–2.147

Disabled persons rehabilitation, Federal and State activities and funding, FY88, annual rpt, 4944–1

Diving (underwater sport and occupational) deaths, by circumstances, diver characteristics, and location, 1970-87, annual rpt, 2144–5

Divorces and children involved, by characteristics of spouses and whether 1st marriage, 1950s-84, 4147–21.46

Drug (PCP) treatment admissions and deaths in selected areas, and emergency room visits by patient sex, race, and age, 1987, article, 4042–3.931

Drug abuse emergency room admissions and deaths, by drug type and source, sex, race, age, and major metro area, 1988, annual rpt, 4494–8

Drug abuse indicators for selected metro areas, research results, data collection, and policy issues, 1989 semiannual conf, 4492–5

Drug, alcohol, and cigarette use and attitudes of youth, by substance type and selected characteristics, 1975-88 surveys, annual rpt, 4494–4

Drug, alcohol, and cigarette use, by substance, age, sex, race, and region, 1988 survey, biennial rpt, 4494–5

Drug and alcohol abuse treatment facilities, services, use, funding, and client characteristics, 1987, annual rpt, 4494–10

Drugs (controlled) provided during physician office visits, by drug, patient, and provider characteristics, 1985, 4146–8.179

Firearms-related deaths of children, by motive, age, sex, and race, 1968-87, 4146–8.181

Foreign countries infant mortality rate and life expectancy, by sex and country, 1989 biennial rpt, 2324–9

France and Germany physicians, and visits by reason and patient age and sex, by specialty, compared to US, 1981-83, 4147–5.5

France and US hospital beds, and use by diagnosis and patient characteristics, by instn ownership, with deaths by cause, 1981, 4147–5.4

Health care treatments and products not proven safe or effective, use, costs, and user characteristics, 1986 survey, 4008–86

Health care use and costs, methodology and findings of natl survey, series, 4186–8

Health condition and health care resources, use, and spending, 1950s-87, annual data compilation, 4144–11

Health maintenance organization enrollment of Medicare enrollees, services use, charges, and survival, compared to fee-for-service, 1980-82 study, article, 4652–1.904

Wage differentials between service and manufacturing sectors related to worker characteristics, 1987, article, 9377–1.901

Wages by occupation, and benefits for office and plant workers, periodic MSA survey rpt series, 6785–11; 6785–12

Wages, hours, and employment by occupation, and benefits, for selected locations, industry survey rpt series, 6787–6

Wages of full- and part-time workers, by selected characteristics, quarterly press release, 6742–20

Youth labor force status, by sex and race, summer 1985-89, annual press release, 6744–14

Law Enforcement

Aircraft hijackings, on-board explosions, and other crime, US and foreign incidents, 1983-87, annual rpt, 7504–31

Arrest rates, by offense, sex, age, and race, 1987, annual rpt, 6224–7

Arrests by offender characteristics, prosecutions, convictions, and sentences by type, by felony offense, 1983-86, 6066–19.52

Assaults and deaths of law enforcement officers, by circumstances, agency, victim and offender characteristics, and location, 1988, annual rpt, 6224–3

Children abducted and murdered by strangers, and rates, by victim sex, age, and race, 1976-84, 6066–27.1

Crime, criminal justice admin and enforcement, and public opinion, data compilation, 1970s-88, annual rpt, 6064–6

Crime victimization rates, by victim and offender characteristics, circumstances, and offense, 1987 survey, annual rpt, 6066–3.41

Crime victimizations resulting in injury, by offense, type of injury and medical care received, and victim characteristics, 1979-86, 6066–19.49

Crimes, arrests, and rates, by offense, offender characteristics, population size, and jurisdiction, 1988, annual rpt, 6224–2.1; 6224–2.2

Criminal case processing from arrest to sentencing, cases and duration by disposition, offense, and defendant characteristics, for selected cities, 1986, annual rpt, 6064–27

Criminal case processing in Federal district courts, and dispositions, by offense, district, and offender characteristics, 1984, annual rpt, 6064–29

Criminal sentences for Federal offenses, guidelines use and results by offense and offender characteristics, and Sentencing Commission activities, 1988, annual rpt, 17664–1

Drug test results at arrest, by drug type, offense, and sex, for selected urban areas, quarterly rpt, 6062–3

Employment of State and local law enforcement personnel and officers, by sex, population size, census div, and jurisdiction, as of Oct 1988, annual rpt, 6224–2.3

Homicide rates, and lifetime probability of victimization, by age, sex, and race, 1987, annual rpt, 6224–8

Jail population by sex, race, and for 25 jurisdictions, and instn conditions, 1983-87, annual rpt, 6066–25.18

Juvenile correctional and detention instns, inmates, and expenses, by instn and resident characteristics and State, 1975-85, biennial rpt, 6064–13

Juvenile court delinquency cases, by offense, referral source, disposition, age, sex, race, State, and county, 1985, annual rpt, 6064–12

Juvenile court referrals by offender characteristics, and dispositions, by offense, 1984, 6066–27.2

Juvenile offenders recidivism rates, arrests, and court referrals, by offense, age, and sex, 1983 local area studies, 6068–227

Police agencies employment, spending, and operations, FY87, 6066–25.20

Postal Service inspection activities, expenses, and staff, FY88, annual rpt, 9864–8

Prison conditions, population, and problems, issues and bibl, 1989 compilation of papers, 25928–8

Prisoners in Federal and State instns by sex, admissions, and instn capacity and overcrowding, by State, 1980s-88, annual rpt, 6066–25.21

Prisoners in Federal instns, by sex, prison, security level, contract facility type, and region, monthly rpt series, 6242–1

Prisoners in State instns, by offense, criminal history, and inmate, family, and victim characteristics, 1986, annual rpt, 6064–26.3

Prisoners, movements, and characteristics, by State, 1986, annual rpt, 6064–26

Prisoners under death sentence by prison control and prisoner characteristics, and executions from 1930, by State, 1973-88, annual rpt, 6066–25.23

Recidivism rates of prisoners released in 1983, by offense and prisoner characteristics, 1983-86, 6066–19.48

Statistical Abstract of US, social, political, and economic data, 1790-2025, comprehensive annual compilation, 2324–1.1

Suicides in Maryland prisons, by selected characteristics, 1979-87, 4186–9.2

Torts for product liability, dispositions, awards, case processing time, and plaintiff injury severity and other characteristics, 1983-85, GAO rpt, 26121–317

Population

Alaska rural villages population characteristics and and subsistence activities, 1976-86, 5738–9

Consumer Income, socioeconomic characteristics of persons, families, and households, detailed cross-tabulations, Current Population Rpt series, 2546–6

Developing countries aged population and selected characteristics, 1980s and projected to 2020, country rpt series, 2326–19

Educational attainment, by sociodemographic characteristics and location, 1987 and trends from 1940, biennial Current Population Rpt, 2546–1.427; 2546–1.431

Hispanic Americans socioeconomic characteristics, by detailed origin, 1988, Current Population Rpt, 2546–1.430; 2546–1.438

Homeless population characteristics by city, and Federal funding by program, 1980s-89, hearings, 21248–123

Household and family characteristics, by living arrangement, 1988 and trends from 1960, Current Population Rpt, 2546–2.148

Household and family characteristics, by location, 1988, annual Current Population Rpt, 2546–1.437

Household and family composition, and factors affecting change, 1960s-88, chartbook, 2546–2.149

Income (household) and poverty status under alternative income definitions, by recipient characteristics, 1986, Current Population Rpt, 2546–6.58

Income (personal) and poverty status, change by selected socioeconomic characteristics, 1984-85, Current Population Rpt, 2546–20.10

Income (personal), by sex and race, selected years 1965-87, annual rpt, 204–1.1

Living arrangements and household composition, 1988, advance annual Current Population Rpt, 2546–1.441

Living arrangements, family relationships, and marital status, by selected characteristics, 1988, annual Current Population Rpt, 2546–1.428; 2546–1.433

Migration since 1986, mover characteristics by same or different area, and compared to nonmovers, 1987, annual Current Population Rpt, 2546–1.435

Migration to and from Southern US, by migrant characteristics and location, 1970s-87 and alternative projections to 2000, article, 9371–1.902

Older persons income, ratios for couples to single persons, by age and sex, 1987, 26306–3.111

Older persons socioeconomic characteristics, 1900s-86 and projected to 2050, biennial chartbook, 12904–1

Population size and characteristics, 1969-88, Current Population Rpt, annual rpt, 2546–2.146

Population size and components of change, alternative projections 1988-2080 and trends from 1900, annual actuarial rpt, 4706–1.104

Population size by age and sex, components of change, and households, by State, 1980-88, Current Population Rpt, 2546–3.161

Population size, by age, sex, and race, and components of change, alternative projections 1988-2080, Current Population Rpt, 2546–3.158

Poverty status of families and persons, by detailed characteristics, 1987, annual Current Population Rpt, 2546–6.60

Refugee arrivals and resettlement in US, by age, sex, sponsoring agency, State, and country, monthly rpt, 4692–2

Retirees savings maintenance and liquidation, by selected financial and other characteristics, 1971-79, article, 1702–1.906

Single-parent household income sources and spending by category, by sex, age, race, and household size, 1984-85, article, 1702–1.901

Southern US poverty rates, by household composition, race, and urban-rural location, 1986, article, 9371–1.903

Statistical Abstract of US, social, political, and economic data, 1790-2025, comprehensive annual compilation, 2324–1.1

Women (older) pension coverage, sources, payments, and effect on income and poverty status, 1982, article, 4742–1.901

Public Welfare and Social Security

AFDC recipients demographic and financial characteristics, by State, FY87, annual rpt, 4694–1

Disability Insurance and SSI admin of Fed Govt and States, benefits, caseloads, and operations, 1980s, 4708–11

Disability Insurance beneficiaries health insurance coverage, by type and selected beneficiary characteristics, fall 1982, article, 4742–1.927

Employment and earnings covered under OASDHI, and social security contributions, by age, sex, race, State, and county, 1985, 4748–43

Homeless and runaway youth programs, funding, activities, and participant characteristics, FY86, annual rpt, 4604–3

Medicaid enrollment, and service use and costs by service type, by eligibility type, for 5 States, 1980-84, article, 4652–1.919

Medicare and Medicaid beneficiaries and program operations, 1988, annual fact book, 4654–18

Medicare and Medicaid eligibility, participation, coverage, and program finances, various periods 1966-89, biennial rpt, 4654–1

Medicare disabled enrollee costs related to patient characteristics, model description and results, 1974-81, technical paper, 4746–26.6

Medicare enrollment, and use by type of service, by age, sex, race, region, State, and MSA, 1986-87, annual rpt, 4657–5

Medicare reimbursement of hospitals under prospective payment system, impacts on instns, beneficiaries, and other care providers and payment sources, 1986, annual rpt, 4654–13

OASDHI admin, and SSA activities, 1930s-89 and projected to 2063, data compilation, annual rpt, 4704–12

OASDHI, Medicaid, SSI, and related programs benefits, beneficiary characteristics, and trust funds, selected years 1937-87, annual rpt, 4744–3

OASDI and SSI disabled beneficiaries, by selected characteristics, 1986, article, 4742–1.916

OASDI benefit payments, trust fund finances, and economic and demographic assumptions, 1970-87 and alternative projections to 1997, actuarial rpt, 4706–1.103

OASDI benefits and beneficiaries, by type of benefit, State, and county, as of Dec 1987, annual rpt, 4744–28

OASDI benefits and beneficiaries, for aged by sex and State, monthly rpt, 4742–1.10

OASDI disabled worker beneficiaries, duration, and exits by reason, by selected characteristics, model description and results, 1972-80, article, 4742–1.923

OASDI disabled worker beneficiaries recoveries and reentitlements, by selected characteristics, model description and results, 1989 article, 4742–1.924

OASDI disabled workers Medicare enrollment waiting period, proposed elimination impact on costs, with background data, 1974-81, article, 4742–1.915

OASI beneficiaries affected by earnings limits by selected characteristics, and Federal outlays, under alternative limits, 1986, 26306–3.110

OASI beneficiaries retiring before age 62, employment, income, and benefits, by selected characteristics, 1982, article, 4742–1.911

Public welfare programs beneficiaries, and benefits duration and share of income, by selected characteristics, 1983-86, 2546–20.8

Statistical Abstract of US, social, political, and economic data, 1790-2025, comprehensive annual compilation, 2324–1.2

Supplemental Security Income aged and disabled beneficiary characteristics, payments, and eligibility, for awards made 1981, 1985, article, 4742–1.907

Supplemental Security Income beneficiaries, by race and sex, monthly rpt, 4742–1.12

Recreation and Leisure

Wildlife-related recreation, hunting, and fishing participation and spending, detailed data by location, 1985 survey, quinquennial rpt, 5508–5

Wildlife-related recreation, hunting, and fishing participation and spending, detailed data, 1985 survey, quinquennial State rpt series, 5506–6

Science and Technology

Black colleges R&D funding by source, and characteristics of grad students and research staff, by field of science and instn, 1980s-87, 9628–78

Computer and data processing services workers and wages by occupation and sex, and benefits, by selected MSA, 1987 survey, 6787–6.236

Degrees (PhD) in science and engineering, by field, instn, employment prospects, sex, race, and other characteristics, 1960s-88, 9627–30

Degrees (PhD) in science, recipients by whether foreign, race, and sex, and instnl support, 1978 and 1987-88, 9626–2.187

Degrees in science and engineering, by field, level, and sex, 1950-86, 9628–77

Education in science and engineering in elementary and secondary schools, and student persistence in postsecondary education, 1977-88, 26358–199

Education in science, elementary and secondary students proficiency, attitudes, factors affecting proficiency, and teacher background and views, natl assessment, 1977-86, 4898–25

Employment and education of scientists and engineers, and R&D spending, for US and selected foreign countries, 1988, annual rpt, 9624–23.2

Employment and other characteristics of science and engineering PhDs, by field and State, 1987, biennial rpt, 9627–18

Enrollment in science and engineering grad programs, and total and foreign natl employment in higher education, by field, 1986-87, 9626–2.183

Enrollment in science and engineering grad programs, by field, source of funds, and characteristics of student and instn, 1975-87, annual rpt, 9627–7

Fed Govt science and engineering employment, by field, degree level, race, sex, agency, and State, 1987, annual rpt, 9627–5

Immigrant scientists and engineers, by field, age, sex, country and world area of origin, and State, 1987 and trends from 1967, 9627–29

Labor force, Federal and university research funding, and educational data, for science and engineering, series, 9626–6

NASA staff characteristics and personnel actions, FY88, annual rpt, 9504–1

NATO postdoctoral fellowships in science, recipients educational outcomes and other characteristics, 1959-81, 9628–80

Veterans Affairs

Disability and death compensation cases of VA, by entitlement type, period of service, and sex, as of Mar 1989, semiannual rpt, 8602–8

Disability and death compensation cases of VA, by entitlement type, period of service, sex, age, and State, FY88, annual rpt, 8604–7

Hospitals of VA, patients discharged by diagnosis, compensation and pension status, and other characteristics, FY88, annual rpt, 8604–3.3

Population of veterans, and benefits programs awareness and use, by age, sex, income, race, and period of service, 1987 survey, 8608–1

VA employment characteristics and activities, FY88, annual rpt, 8604–3.8

Index by
Titles

Index by Titles

It's Time To Tax Employee Benefits,
9373–1.913

Jail Inmates, 1987, 6066–25.18
Japan Has Increased Its Contributions but
Could Do More. U.S.-Japan Burden Sharing,
26123–249
Japanese Market Opens Wider to Imported
Citrus, 1925–34.901
Japanese Solid Wood Products Market: Profile
and Outlook, 2046–14.2
Japanese Wine Market, 1925–34.928
Japan-U.S. Friendship Commission Annual
Report, 1987-88, 14694–1
Jewelry, Silverware, and Plated Ware
(Industries 3911, 3914, and 3915): 1987
Census of Manufactures. Preliminary
Report. Industry Series, 2491–1.80
Job Hazards Underscored in Woodworking
Study, 6722–1.945
Job Patterns for Minorities and Women in
Private Industry, 1986, 9244–1
Job Patterns for Minorities and Women in
State and Local Government, 1986, 9244–6
Job Training Partnership Act, 26106–8
Job Training Partnership Act: Information on
Training, Placements, and Wages of Male
and Female Participants, 26106–8.9
Job Training Partnership Act: Services and
Outcomes for Participants with Differing
Needs, 26106–8.8
John R. Commons: Pioneer of Labor
Economics, 6722–1.924
Joint Economic Report, 1989, 23844–2
Joint Retirement Decision of Husbands and
Wives, 4742–1.906
Jones Announces $19 Million To Automate
State Unemployment Insurance Systems,
6406–2.24
Journal of Agricultural Economics Research,
1502–3
Journal of the National Cancer Institute,
4472–1
JTPA Grants Will Aid Dislocated Workers in
Nine States, 6406–2.25
Junk Bonds: 1988 Status Report, 21248–118
Justice Expenditure and Employment in the
U.S., 1985, 6064–9
Juvenile Court Statistics, 1985, 6064–12
Juvenile Court's Response to Violent Crime,
6066–27.2
Juvenile Justice Bulletin, 6066–27

Kemp Announces Additional Housing
Vouchers, 5006–3.65
Kemp Announces $18.9 Million in Grants for
Nehemiah Housing Opportunity Program,
5006–3.70
Kemp Announces $45 Million in Rental
Assistance for Single Room Occupancy
Dwellings for the Homeless, 5006–3.68
Kemp Announces $85.8 Million in Awards for
Operation Bootstrap, 5006–3.69
Kemp Announces $112.8 Million in Loans To
House People with Handicaps, 5006–3.72
Kemp Announces $327.1 in Housing Loans To
Assist Elderly Families, 5006–3.71
Kemp Announces $89.2 Million in Grants for
Transitional Housing for the Homeless,
5006–3.66
Kemp Announces $9.9 Million for Permanent
Housing for Handicapped Homeless,
5006–3.67

Kemp's Ridley, Lepidochelys kempi, Sea
Turtle Head Start Tag Recoveries:
Distribution, Habitat, and Method of
Recovery, 2162–1.902
Key Statistics for Private Elementary and
Secondary Education: Early Estimates,
School Year 1988-89, 4834–21
Key Statistics for Public Elementary and
Secondary Education: Early Estimates,
School Year 1988-89, 4834–19
Knitting Mills (Industries 2251, 2252, 2253,
2254, 2257, 2258, and 2259): 1987 Census
of Manufactures. Preliminary Report.
Industry Series, 2491–1.12

Labor and IRS Enforcement of the Employee
Retirement Income Security Act. Pension
Plans, 26121–259
Labor Expenditures Help Determine Farms
Affected by Immigration Reform,
1598–250
Labor Force and Informal Employment in
Mexico: Recent Characteristics and Trends,
2326–18.49
Labor Force Status and Other Characteristics
of Persons with a Work Disability: 1981-88,
2546–2.147
Labor Force, Unemployment Rates, and Wage
Pressures, 9373–1.902
Labor Force. 1990 Census of Population and
Housing: Content Determination Reports,
2626–11.1
Labor Issues in the Telecommunications
Industry, 21368–113
Labor Market Changes and Adjustments: How
Do the U.S. and Japan Compare?,
6722–1.910
Labor Market Completes Sixth Year of
Expansion in 1988, 6722–1.907
Labor Market Problems of Older Workers,
6306–2.2
Labor Market Shortages, 6306–2.4
Laboratory Accreditation: Requirements Vary
Throughout the Federal Government,
26113–405
Laboratory and X-Ray Services in Community
and Migrant Health Centers, 4108–45.2
Labor-Management Committees Enhance
Reemployment Assistance. Dislocated
Workers, 26121–316
Labor-Management Conflict and Cooperation:
The Role of Shop Floor Leaders, 6306–3.3
Lack of Health Insurance Coverage in the U.S.
(Part 1), 25368–160
Lake Erie Estuarine Systems: Issues,
Resources, Status, and Management,
2146–6.11
Land Areas of the National Forest System, As
of Sept. 30, 1988, 1204–2
Land Subdividers and Developers, Except
Cemeteries (Industry 6552): 1987 Census of
Construction Industries. Preliminary Report.
Industry Series, 2371–1.27
Land Use and the Nation's Estuaries,
2176–7.4
Lands Under Control of the U.S. Fish and
Wildlife Service, as of Sept. 30, 1988,
Annual Report, 5504–8
Language Barriers Between Providers and
Patients Have Been Reduced: VA Health
Care, 26121–273
Large Class I Household Goods Carriers
Selected Earnings Data, 9482–14

Large Class I Motor Carriers of Passengers
Selected Earnings Data, 9482–13
Large Class I Motor Carriers of Property
Selected Earnings Data, 9482–5
Latent Family Influences on Individual
Expenditures for Clothing, 6886–6.61
Latest Sales Figures Show Hunting and
Fishing License Sales Up, Revenues
Increasing, 5504–16
Latin America Trade Review, 1988: A U.S.
Perspective, 2044–34
Law Allows Compensation for Disabilities
Unrelated to Military Service. VA Benefits,
26121–295
Law Enforcement Officers Killed and
Assaulted, 1988, 6224–3
Layers and Egg Production, 1988 Summary,
1625–7
Lead in Housewares, 21368–108
Lead Industry: Mineral Industry Surveys,
5612–1.13
Lead: Minerals Yearbook Preprint, Volume 1,
1987, 5604–15.38
Lead Poisoning Needs Assessment,
21248–119
Lead-Based Paint Poisoning Prevention Act,
21248–119
Leading Commodity Cash Receipts, 1960-87,
1548–347
Leading Indicators and the "Prime Mover"
View, 2702–1.926
Leaking Underground Storage Tanks Trust
Fund, 8102–9.11
Learning Enterprise, 6408–73
Learning in the Marketplace: Free Entry Is
Free Riding, 9387–8.192
Leather Gloves; Luggage; and Miscellaneous
Leather Goods (Industries 3151, 3161, 3171,
3172, and 3199): 1987 Census of
Manufactures. Preliminary Report. Industry
Series, 2491–1.45
Less Profit, Less Care? Reassessing the Impact
of Medicare and Medicaid Cuts on Patients,
21148–52
Lessons from the Maryland Experience.
Enterprise Zones, 26131–53
Lessons from West German Monetary Policy,
9381–1.907
Lethal and Sublethal Effects of the
Water-Soluble Fraction of Cook Inlet Crude
Oil on Pacific Herring (Clupea harengus
pallasi) Reproduction, 2176–1.29
Leveraged Buyouts and the Pot of Gold: 1989
Update, 21368–115
Libraries and Literacy Education:
Comprehensive Survey Report, 4878–2
Library Literacy Program, Analysis of Funded
Projects, 1988, 4874–3
Library of Congress Publications in Print,
1989, 26404–5
Library Programs: College Library Technology
and Cooperation Grants Program, HEA
Title II-D. Abstracts of Funded Projects,
1988, 4874–6
Library Programs: Library Career Training
Program, Abstracts of Funded Projects,
1988, 4874–1
Library Programs: Library Career Training
Program, Abstracts of Funded Projects,
1989, 4874–1
Library Programs: Library Literacy Program,
Analysis of Funded Projects, 1988, 4874–3
Library Programs: Library Services for Indian
Tribes and Hawaiian Natives Program,
Library Services and Construction Act, Title
IV, Abstracts of Funded Projects, 1988,
4874–5

Nurse Educators Look at Alcohol Education for the Profession, 4482–1.902

Nurse Participation in Hospital Decision Making: Potential Impact on the Nursing Shortage, 4008–91

Nursing Home Characteristics: 1986 Inventory of Long-Term Care Places. Vital and Health Statistics Series 14, 4147–14.33

Nursing Home Reimbursement and the Allocation of Rehabilitation Therapy Resources, 4188–58

Nursing Home Utilization by Current Residents: U.S., 1985. Vital and Health Statistics Series 13, 4147–13.102

Nursing Shortage: Strategies for Nursing Practice and Education. Report of the National Invitational Workshop, Feb. 22-24, 1988, 4118–64

Nutrition Monitoring in the U.S. An Update Report on Nutrition Monitoring, 4048–33

Nutrition Monitoring in the U.S. The Directory of Federal Nutrition Monitoring Activities, 4048–33

Nutritional Adequacy of Primary Food Programs on Four Indian Reservations. Food Assistance Programs, 26113–439

Nutritive Value of American Foods in Common Units, 1358–3

Nutritive Value of Foods, 1358–3

OASDI Beneficiaries by State and County, December 1987, 4744–28

Oats: Background for 1990 Farm Legislation, 1566–7.5

Object Class Analysis: Budget of the U.S. Government, FY90, 104–9

Occupant Protection Facts, 7766–15.1

Occupational Adjustment of the Prospective Payment System Wage Index, 4652–1.950

Occupational and Educational Outcomes of 1985-86 Bachelor's Degree Recipients, 4826–3.1

Occupational Change: Pursuing a Different Kind of Work, 6722–1.943

Occupational Earnings and Wage Trends in Metropolitan Areas, 6785–5

Occupational Earnings in All Metropolitan Areas, August 1988, 6785–9

Occupational Earnings in Selected Areas, 6785–6

Occupational Employment in Mining, Construction, Finance, and Services, 6748–60

Occupational Fatalities as Found in Reports of OSHA Fatality/Catastrophe Investigations, 6606–2

Occupational Injuries and Illnesses in the U.S., By Industry, 1987, 6844–1

Occupational Outlook Quarterly, 6742–1

Occupational Radiation Exposure at Commercial Nuclear Power Reactors and Other Facilities, 1986, 9634–3

Occupational Radiation Exposure from U.S. Naval Nuclear Propulsion Plants and Their Support Facilities, 1988, 3804–10

Occupational Risks of Bladder Cancer in the U.S.: I. White Men, 4472–1.924

Occupational Risks of Bladder Cancer in the U.S.: II. Nonwhite Men, 4472–1.925

Occupational Safety and Health Administration Press Releases, 6606–3

Occupations of Federal White-Collar and Blue-Collar Workers, Federal Civilian Workforce Statistics, 9844–4

Occurrence and Fate of PCDDs and PCDFs in Five Bleached Kraft Pulp and Paper Mills, 21368–112

Occurrence of PCDD and PCDF in Different Kinds of Paper, 21368–112

Ocean Transportation Needs of the American Pacific Islands: Report to Congress, 7308–195

Ocean-Ice Oil-Weathering Computer Program User's Manual, 2176–1.25

Oceanographic Data Exchange, 1987, 2144–15

Oceanographic Monthly Summary, 2182–5

OECD Trade Series, 9116–1

OECD Trade with Asia, 9116–1.2

OECD Trade with Mexico and Central America, 9116–1.6

OECD Trade with Middle East, 9116–1.3

OECD Trade with South America, 9116–1.5

OECD Trade with Sub-Saharan Africa, 9116–1.4

OECD Trade with the Caribbean, 9116–1.1

OERI Publications Catalog, 1988-89, 4868–9

Off-Balance-Sheet Hedging Activity in Southeast Thrifts, 9302–2.903

Office and Computing Machines (Industries 3571, 3572, 3575, 3577, 3578, and 3579): 1987 Census of Manufactures. Preliminary Report. Industry Series, 2491–1.66

Office of Aviation Medicine Reports, 7506–10

Office of Energy Research Program Summaries, 3004–18

Office of Housing and Urban Programs Annual Report, FY88, 9914–4

Office of Inspector General Report to the Congress, Department of Housing and Urban Development, for the Six Month Period Oct. 1, 1988-Mar. 31, 1989, Pursuant to Section 5(b) of Public Law 95-452, 5002–8

Office of Inspector General Report to the Congress, Department of Housing and Urban Development, for the Six Month Period Apr. 1-Sept. 30, 1989, Pursuant to Section 5(b) of Public Law 95-452, 5002–8

Office of Inspector General Semiannual Report, Department of Interior, Oct. 1, 1988-Mar. 31, 1989, 5302–2

Office of Inspector General Semiannual Report, Department of Interior, Apr. 1-Sept. 30, 1989, 5302–2

Office of Inspector General Semiannual Report, NASA, Oct. 1, 1988-Mar. 30, 1989, 9502–9

Office of Inspector General, Semiannual Report to Congress, General Services Administration, Apr.1-Sept. 30, 1988, 9452–8

Office of Inspector General, Semiannual Report to Congress, General Services Administration, Oct. 1, 1988-Mar. 31, 1989, 9452–8

Office of Inspector General, Semiannual Report to Congress, General Services Administration, Apr. 1-Sept. 30, 1989, 9452–8

Office of Inspector General Semiannual Report to Congress: U.S. Department of Education, Apr. 1-Sept. 30, 1988, 4802–1

Office of Inspector General Semiannual Report to Congress: U.S. Department of Education, Oct. 1, 1988-Mar. 31, 1989, 4802–1

Office of Inspector General Semiannual Report to Congress: U.S. Department of Education, Apr. 1-Sept. 30, 1989, 4802–1

Office of Inspector General Semiannual Report to the Congress, Department of Energy, Oct. 1, 1988-Mar. 31, 1989, 3002–12

Office of Inspector General Semiannual Report to the Congress, Department of Energy, Apr. 1-Sept. 30, 1989, 3002–12

Office of Inspector General Semiannual Report to the Congress, Department of Health and Human Services, Oct. 1, 1988-Mar. 31, 1989, 4002–6

Office of Inspector General Semiannual Report to the Congress, Department of Health and Human Services, Apr. 1-Sept. 30, 1989, 4002–6

Office of Inspector General Semiannual Report to the Congress, Department of State, Apr. 1-Sept. 30, 1989, 7002–6

Office of Inspector General Special Report: An Analysis of the Comprehensive Annual Financial Report of the Government of the Virgin Islands, 5304–10

Office of Management and Budget, Initial Sequester Report to the President and Congress for FY90, 104–27

Office of Management and Budget, Final Sequester Report to the President and Congress for FY90, 104–27

Office of Refugee Resettlement Monthly Data Report, 4692–2

Office of Surface Mining Annual Report, 5644–1

Office of Tax Analysis Papers, 8006–3

Office of the Inspector General Semiannual Report to the Congress, Environmental Protection Agency, Oct. 1, 1988-Mar. 31, 1989, 9182–10

Office of the Inspector General Semiannual Report to the Congress, Environmental Protection Agency, Apr. 1-Sept. 30, 1989, 9182–10

Office of Thrift Supervision Journal, 8432–2

Office of Thrift Supervision Research Papers, 8436–1

Office, Public Building, and Miscellaneous Furniture; Office and Store Fixtures (Industries 2521, 2522, 2531, 2541, 2542, 2591, and 2599): 1987 Census of Manufactures. Preliminary Report. Industry Series, 2491–1.26

Office Supplies, Costume Jewelry and Notions (Industries 3951, 3952, 3953, 3955, 3961, and 3965): 1987 Census of Manufactures. Preliminary Report. Industry Series, 2491–1.82

Office Vacancy Rates: How Should We Interpret Them?, 9387–1.903

Office Visits to Cardiovascular Disease Specialists, 1985, 4146–8.174

Office Visits to Internists: National Ambulatory Medical Care Survey, U.S., 1975, 4147–16.2

Office Visits to Obstetrician-Gynecologists: National Ambulatory Medical Care Survey, U.S., 1975, 4147–16.2

Official Guard and Reserve Manpower: Strengths and Statistics, 3542–4

Official Summary of Security Transactions and Holdings, 9732–2

Official Tabulation of 1988 Presidential Election Votes Released by Federal Election Commission, 9276–1.66

Index by Agency Report Numbers

Index by Agency Report Numbers

Agency report number practices vary from agency to agency, and from publication to publication within an agency. Sometimes a number is noted on the publication, sometimes it is not. In the following list an attempt is made to include every agency report number available in the form in which it appears on the publication.

Those publications covered that did not have identifiable assigned numbers are not included in the list.

EXECUTIVE OFFICE OF THE PRESIDENT

Office of Management and Budget

OMB 89-11 .... 108–35.1
Stat. Policy Working Paper
  No. 15 .... 106–4.9

Federal Coordinating Council for Science, Engineering and Technology

NSF 89-66 434–1
SAR-3 FY 84-87 434–1

DEPARTMENT OF AGRICULTURE

ACS Res. Rpt. 77 1128–54
ACS Res. Rpt. 81 1128–53
ACS Service Rpt. 24 1124–1
AER 589 1568–276
AER 591 1568–279
AER 595 1548–354
AER 598 1568–274
AER 599 1568–278
AER 600 1568–277
AER 601 1588–137
AER 602 1588–136
AER 603 1548–343
AER 604 1588–135
AER 605 1568–282
AER 606 1588–134
AER 607 1588–132
AER 608 1548–346
AER 609 1594–2
AER 610 1588–143
AER 612 1528–290
AER 614 1544–22
AER 615 1544–9
AER 618 1588–144
AER 619 1598–256
AFO-(nos.) 1541–1
Agric. Hndbk. 8-17 .... 1356–3.11
Agric. Hndbk. 8-20 .... 1356–3.12
Agric. Hndbk. 456 1358–3
Agric. Hndbk. 671 1506–1
Agric. Hndbk. 683 1924–9
Agric. Hndbk. 684 1504–3
Agric. Info. Bull. 545 1568–280
Agric. Info. Bull. 557 1598–250
Agric. Info. Bull. 561 1598–246
AO-(nos.) 1502–4
APHIS 82-14 1394–16
APHIS 91-43 1394–15

AQUA 2 1561–15
AQUA 3 1561–15
AR-(nos.) 1561–16
CEP-16R 1802–15
CEP-18R 1802–13
CEP-25R 1802–14
CoSt 1(date) 1631–5
CoSt 1(89) 1631–11
CrPr 2-1(date) 1621–1
CrPr 2-1(89) 1621–2
CrPr 2-2(date) 1621–1
CrPr 2-3(1-89) 1621–30
CrPr 2-4(3-89) 1621–22
CWS-(nos.) 1561–1
Da 1-1(date) 1627–1
Da 1-2(89) 1627–4
Da 2-1(89) 1627–5
Da 2-6(date) 1627–3
DS-(nos.) 1561–2
ECIFS 7-3 1544–20
ECIFS 7-4 1544–19
ECIFS 7-5 1544–17
ECIFS 8-1 1544–16
ECIFS 8-2 1544–18
EMG (nos.) 1925–2.4
ERS Staff Rpt. 89-26 1588–140
ERS Staff Rpt. AGES 89-4 1598–247
ERS Staff Rpt. AGES 89-6 1548–351
ERS Staff Rpt. AGES 89-7 1598–248
ERS Staff Rpt. AGES 89-8 1588–133
ERS Staff Rpt. AGES 89-9 1598–249
ERS Staff Rpt. AGES
  89-13 1544–24
ERS Staff Rpt. AGES
  89-14 1584–2
ERS Staff Rpt. AGES
  89-15 1584–3
ERS Staff Rpt. AGES
  89-16 1528–280
ERS Staff Rpt. AGES
  89-17 1598–251
ERS Staff Rpt. AGES
  89-18 1588–141
ERS Staff Rpt. AGES
  89-19 1528–283
ERS Staff Rpt. AGES
  89-22 1548–345
ERS Staff Rpt. AGES
  89-24 1598–254
ERS Staff Rpt. AGES
  89-25 1548–348
ERS Staff Rpt. AGES
  89-27 1548–350
ERS Staff Rpt. AGES
  89-28 1528–278
ERS Staff Rpt. AGES
  89-29 1528–279
ERS Staff Rpt. AGES
  89-30 1528–286
ERS Staff Rpt. AGES
  89-31 1598–255
ERS Staff Rpt. AGES
  89-33 1588–138
ERS Staff Rpt. AGES
  89-35 1528–289
ERS Staff Rpt. AGES
  89-36 1528–282
ERS Staff Rpt. AGES
  89-37 1598–253

ERS Staff Rpt. AGES
  89-38 1524–11
ERS Staff Rpt. AGES
  89-40 1528–288
ERS Staff Rpt. AGES
  89-41 .... 1566–7.1
ERS Staff Rpt. AGES
  89-42 .... 1566–7.2
ERS Staff Rpt. AGES
  89-43 .... 1566–7.3
ERS Staff Rpt. AGES
  89-44 1528–287
ERS Staff Rpt. AGES
  89-46 .... 1566–7.5
ERS Staff Rpt. AGES
  89-47 .... 1566–7.4
ERS Staff Rpt. AGES
  89-48 .... 1566–7.6
ERS Staff Rpt. AGES
  89-50 1564–3
ERS Staff Rpt. AGES
  89-51 1588–145
ERS Staff Rpt. AGES
  89-54 1528–292
ERS Staff Rpt. AGES
  89-55 1528–293
ERS Staff Rpt. AGES
  89-56 .... 1566–7.7
ERS Staff Rpt. AGES
  89-61 .... 1566–7.8
ERS Staff Rpt. AGES
  89-67 .... 1566–7.9
ERS Staff Rpt. AGES
  871210 1598–245
ERS Staff Rpt. AGES
  880216 1568–275
ERS Staff Rpt. AGES
  880720 1598–244
ERS Staff Rpt. AGES
  880802 1528–275
ERS Staff Rpt. AGES
  881020 1588–129
ERS Staff Rpt.
  AGES881025 1524–11
FAER 238 1528–291
FC (nos.) 1925–4.2
FCB 1-89 .... 1925–9.1
FCB 2-89 .... 1925–9.2
FCOF (nos.) 1925–5
FD 1-89 1925–10
FD 2-89 1925–10
FDL-MT (nos.) 1925–31
FDLP (nos.) 1925–32
FdS-(nos.) 1561–4
FFVS (nos.) 1925–13
FG (nos.) 1925–2.1
FHORT (nos.) 1925–34
FL&P (nos.) 1925–33
FL&P 1-89 .... 1925–33.1
FL&P 2-89 .... 1925–33.2
FMOS (nos.) 1317–4
FOP (nos.) 1925–1
—   1925–1.1
FrNt 1-3(7-89) 1621–18.2
FrNt 1-3(89) 1621–18.1
FrNt 2-4(6-89) 1621–18.3
FrNt 3-1(89) 1621–18.5
—   1641–4
FS 1-89 .... 1925–14.2

DEPARTMENT OF COMMERCE

DEPARTMENT OF HEALTH AND HUMAN SERVICES

DEPARTMENT OF HOUSING AND URBAN DEVELOPMENT

Interstate Commerce Commission

National Aeronautics and Space Administration

National Credit Union Administration

National Labor Relations Board

National Science Foundation

National Transportation Safety Board

Nuclear Regulatory Commission

Office of Personnel Management

Tennessee Valley Authority

U.S. Arms Control and Disarmament Agency

U.S. International Development Cooperation Agency

U.S. International Trade Commission

SPECIAL BOARDS, COMMITTEES, AND COMMISSIONS

Advisory Commission on Intergovernmental Relations

Commission on Civil Rights

Federal Financial Institutions Examination Council

National Commission for Employment Policy

Presidential Commission on World Hunger

UNITED STATES COURTS

Federal Judicial Center

CONGRESS

Congressional Committees

General Accounting Office

Office of Technology Assessment

QUASI-OFFICIAL AGENCIES

American National Red Cross

Index by
Superintendent of
Documents Numbers

Index of Superintendent of Documents Numbers

This index presents, in shelf list order, the Superintendent of Documents (SuDocs) Classification Numbers of publications abstracted by ASI in this Annual, and provides references from SuDoc Numbers to ASI accession numbers.

A1.1:988	1004–3
A1.1/3:989	1002–4
A1.1/3:989-2	1002–4
A1.2:So3/7/989	1268–24
A1.2:So3/988-97/update	1008–41
A1.10:989	1004–18
A1.34:767	1588–131
A1.34:768	1568–281
A1.34:770	1528–276
A1.34:771	1588–130
A1.34:772	1544–27
A1.34:774	1528–277
A1.34:775	1568–39
A1.34:777	1548–347
A1.34:778	1528–284
A1.34:779	1568–284
A1.34:780	1588–113
A1.34:781	1524–12
A1.34:782	1588–142
A1.34:784	1568–285
A1.34:785	1588–112
A1.34:787	1544–29
A1.34:789	1544–28
A1.34/3:(yrs.)	1524–5
A1.34/4:987	1544–4
A1.36:1747	1548–342
A1.36:1749	1548–344
A1.36:1751	1548–352
A1.36:1753	1548–341
A1.36:1756	1548–353
A1.36:1759	1548–349
A1.36:1763	1528–281
A1.36:1765	1588–139
A1.36:1767	1528–285
A1.38:1469	1704–1
A1.38/2:989	1004–14
A1.47:988	1004–1
A1.75:545	1568–280
A1.75:557	1598–250
A1.75:561	1598–246
A1.76:(nos.)	1356–3
A1.76:8-17	1356–3.11
A1.76:8-20	1356–3.12
A1.76:456/988	1358–3
A1.76:671/(v.nos.)	1506–1
A1.76:671/v.2	1506–1.10
A1.76:671/v.5	1506–1.11
A1.76:671/v.7	1506–1.7
A1.76:671/v.9	1506–1.9
A1.76:671/v.11	1506–1.8
A1.76:683	1924–9
A1.76/2:989	1504–3
A1.101:(date)	1802–4
A1.107:589	1568–276
A1.107:591	1568–279
A1.107:595	1548–354
A1.107:598	1568–274
A1.107:599	1568–278

A1.107:600	1568–277
A1.107:601	1588–137
A1.107:602	1588–136
A1.107:603	1548–343
A1.107:604	1588–135
A1.107:605	1568–282
A1.107:606	1588–134
A1.107:607	1588–132
A1.107:608	1548–346
A1.107:609	1594–2
A1.107:610	1588–143
A1.107:612	1528–290
A1.107:618	1588–144
A1.107:619	1598–256
A1.107/2:988	1544–9
A1.107/3:988	1544–22
A1.116:R88/2/987	1244–4
A13.1/3:988	1204–1
A13.10:988	1204–2
A13.52/2:988	1204–8
A13.52/11:987	1206–11.1
A13.52/11:988	1206–11.1
A13.58/2:(date)	1202–1
A13.66/13:(date)	1202–3
A13.78:INT-394	1208–300
A13.78:INT-396	1208–297
A13.78:INT-403	1208–307
A13.78:INT-404	1208–309
A13.78:INT-405	1208–305
A13.78:INT-406	1208–298
A13.78:PNW-RP(nos.)	1206–36
A13.78:PNW-RP-397	1206–36.12
A13.78:PNW-RP-398	1206–36.13
A13.78:RM-208	1208–299
A13.78:SE-272	1208–296
A13.79/2:987	1204–22
A13.80:INT-(nos.)	1206–17
—	1206–23
A13.80:INT-57	1208–293
A13.80:INT-58	1208–294
A13.80:INT-59	1206–17.11
A13.80:INT-60	1208–303
A13.80:INT-62	1208–310
A13.80:INT-63	1206–23.9
A13.80:INT-64	1206–23.10
A13.80:NC-105	1208–292
A13.80:NC-107	1206–34.7
A13.80:NE-(nos.)	1206–12
A13.80:NE-106	1206–12.12
A13.80:PNW-RB-148	1208–291
A13.80:PNW-RB-165	1206–19.9
A13.80:SE-(nos.)	1206–26
A13.80:SE-105	1206–26.10
A13.80:SE-107	1206–26.11
A13.80:SE-108	1206–26.12
A13.80:SE-109	1206–26.13
A13.80:SO-(nos.)	1206–27
A13.80:SO-143	1206–27.6
A13.80/3:987	1204–18
A13.80/4:987	1204–23
A13.80/5:987	1204–19
A13.83:988	1204–5
A13.88:INT-258	1208–308
A13.88:INT-262	1208–306
A13.88:NC-130	1206–34.8
A13.88:NE-(nos.)	1202–4
A13.88:RM-158	1208–290

A13.88:RM-166	1208–302
A13.88:RM-171	1208–304
A13.88:SE-51	1208–301
A13.88:SO-74	1204–35
A13.109:988	1204–7
A57.9/a:C765/988	1264–2
A57.38:list/988	1264–11
A57.46:(date)	1266–2.2
A57.46/3:(date)	1266–2.5
A57.46/4:(date)	1266–2.6
A57.46/5:(date)	1266–2.7
A57.46/5-3:988	1264–14.3
A57.46/6:(date)	1266–2.8
A57.46/6-3:987	1264–14.11
A57.46/7:(date)	1266–2.9
A57.46/8:989	1264–4
A57.46/10:(date)	1266–2.10
A57.46/11:(date)	1266–2.4
A57.46/12-2:(date/nos.)	1262–1
A57.46/13:(date)	1266–2.1
A57.46/18:(date)	1266–2.11
A57.46/18-2:988	1264–14.1
A57.46/19:(date)	1266–2.3
A57.46/19-2:988	1264–14.4
A67.2:Ex7/8/(yr.)	1922–6
A67.7/3:(v.nos.&nos.)	1922–2
A67.18:(ltrs.-nos.)	1925–2
A67.18:(nos.)	1925–4
A67.18:EMG(nos.)	1925–2.4
A67.18:FC(nos)	1925–4.2
A67.18:FCOF(nos.)	1925–5
A67.18:FD2-89	1925–10
A67.18:FDL-MT(nos.)	1925–31
A67.18:FDLP(nos.)	1925–32
A67.18:FFVS(nos.)	1925–13
A67.18:FG(nos.)	1925–2.1
A67.18:FHORT(nos.)	1925–34
A67.18:FL&P(nos.)	1925–33
A67.18:FL&P1-89	1925–33.1
A67.18:FL&P2-89	1925–33.2
A67.18:FOP(nos.)	1925–1
—	1925–1.1
A67.18:FS(nos.)	1925–14
A67.18:FS1-89/supp	1925–14.1
A67.18:FS1-89	1925–14.2
A67.18:FS2-89	1925–14.3
A67.18:FS3-89	1925–14.4
A67.18:FT(nos.)	1925–16
A67.18:FTEA(nos.)	1925–15
A67.18:FTEA1-89	1925–15.1
A67.18:FTEA2-89	1925–15.2
A67.18:FTEA3-89	1925–15.3
A67.18:SG(nos.)	1925–2.3
A67.18:WAP(nos.)	1925–28
A67.18:WP(nos.)	1925–36
A67.18/2:FCB(nos.)	1925–9
A67.18/2:FCB1-89	1925–9.1
A67.18/2:FCB2-89	1925–9.2
A67.40:(date)	1922–3
A67.42:(yr.)/supp.(nos.)	1922–8
A67.42:WR(nos.)	1922–4
A67.42/2:(nos.)	1922–9
A67.44:987	1924–7
A67.45:(date)	1922–12
A68.1:988	1244–3
A68.1/2:988	1244–1
A68.1/3:988	1244–2

C61.11:Ug1	2046–4.56	D5.19:(yr.)	3564–1	E3.11/7-3:988	3164–25
C61.11:Un3/988	2046–4.3	D5.402:M71/6	3908–6	E3.11/7-7:987	3164–79
C61.11:V55/989	2046–4.63	D5.402:P11/985	3908–4	E3.11/7-8:989	3164–68
C61.11:Y3/989	2046–4.110	D7.1/6-2:988	3904–8	E3.11/7-9:989	3164–77
C61.11:Z1/2/989	2046–4.92	D12.1:988	3504–22	E3.11/7-10:989	3164–89
C61.11:Z1/989	2046–4.98	D103.1:(yr.)/v.(nos.)	3754–1	E3.11/9:(yr./nos.)	3162–37
C61.11:Z6/989	2046–4.67	D103.1:987/v.1	3754–1.1	E3.11/15-2:988	3164–42
C61.12:(yr.-nos.)	2046–6	D103.1:987/v.2	3754–1.2	E3.11/17-8:(date)	3162–35
C61.12:88-13	2046–6.1	D103.1/2:987/(pt.nos.)	3754–3	E3.11/17-10:988	3164–11
C61.12:88-14	2046–6.2	D103.1/2:987/pt.1	3754–3.1	E3.11/17-11:(date)	3162–39
C61.12:88-15	2046–6.3	D103.1/2:987/pt.2	3754–3.2	E3.11/20:988	3164–50
C61.12:89-01	2046–6.4	D103.1/2:987/pt.3	3754–3.3	E3.11/20-3:989	3164–84
C61.12:89-02	2046–6.5	D103.1/2:987/pt.4	3754–3.4	E3.11/20-4.(date)	3162–43
C61.12:89-03	2046–6.8	D103.1/2:987/pt.5	3754–3.5	E3.13/4:(yr./nos.)	3162–11
C61.12:89-04	2046–6.6	D103.35/(nos.):987	3756–2	E3.13/4-2:988	3164–85
C61.12:89-05	2046–6.7	D103.35/(nos.):989	3756–1	E3.17/4-2:987	3164–9
C61.12:89-06	2046–6.10	D103.35/14.987	3756–2.15	E3.17/6:988	3164–69
C61.12:89-07	2046–6.9	D103.35/15:989	3756–1.16	E3.18/4:987	3164–23
C61.12:89-08	2046–6.11	D103.35/17:987	3756–2.18	E3.19/2:988	3164–62
C61.12:89-09	2046–6.12	D103.35/39:987	3756–2.40	E3.22:988	3164–40
C61.12:89-10	2046–6.13	D103.35/42:987	3756–2.43	E3.25:987	3164–38
C61.12:89-11	2046–6.14	D103.116:(date)	3752–1	E3.25:988	3164–38
C61.12:89-12	2046–6.15	D201.6/14:987	3804–13	E3.25/2:988	3164–33
C61.12:89-13	2046–6.16	D201.6/14:988	3804–13	E3.29:988	3164–36
C61.18:(v.nos.&nos.)	2042–24	D203.33:989	3804–6	E3.31:(nos.)	3162–34
C61.24:987	2024–1	D208.25:(date)	3802–4	E3.32:(date)	3162–32
C61.24:988	2024–1	D213.8:990	3804–7	E3.34:988	3164–46
C61.25/2:987	2044–20	D216.1:988	3804–14	E3.34/2:988	3164–70
C61.28:988	2044–26	D220.11:988	3804–8	E3.37:987	3164–44
C61.28/2:988	2044–37	D301.73:(v.nos.&nos.)	3602–1	E3.42:960-87	3164–39
C61.31:(yr.)	2044–27	E1.1:987	3024–2	E3.42/3:987	3164–64
C61.31/2:(yrs.)	2044–2	E1.11:(v.nos.&nos.)	3002–2	E3.43/2-2:986	3166–8.8
C61.34:989	2044–28	E1.15/2:988-2	3002–4	E3.43/3:987	3166–7.29
C61.37:(v.nos.&nos.)	2042–1	E1.19:(nos.)	3004–18	E3.43/4:987	3166–7.30
C61.38:988	2044–34	E1.19:0397	3004–18.1	E3.45:988	3164–86
CC1.1:988	9284–4	E1.19:0401	3004–18.2	E3.46/3:987	3164–82
CC1.35:985	9284–6	E1.19:0424	3004–18.3	E3.46/4:989	3164–72
CC1.35:986	9284–6	E1.24:988	3004–1	E3.46/5:988	3164–65
CC1.35:987	9284–6	E1.24:989	3004–1	E3.49:988	3164–76
CR1.10:95	11046–7.2	E1.28:DOE/OSTI-8200-R52	3004–26	E3.51:989	3164–57
D1.1:990/91	3544–2	E1.35/2-2:(yr.)	3004–14	E3.52:988	3164–80
D1.1/3-2:988	3544–31	E1.45/2:988	3304–2	E5.1:988	3224–1
D1.1/4:990-91	3544–30	E1.50/2:988	3004–27	E5.14:988	3222–1
D1.19:987-88	3504–3	E1.68:0025/4/988	3354–9	E5.14:988-2	3222–1
D1.57:988	3544–5	E1.81:0083	3028–2	E6.1:988	3254–1.1
D1.57/2:988	3544–4	E1.84/2:988	3004–22	E6.1:988/app	3254–1.2
D1.57/3:(date)	3542–7	E1.89:0019/8	3304–11	ED1.2:As7/2/v.1	4806–3.3
D1.57/3:988-2	3542–1	E1.89:0019/8/990	3304–11	ED1.2:As7/2/v.2	4806–3.4
D1.57/3-5:988	3544–19	E1.89:0242	3304–18	ED1.2:G76/2/986-87	4804–1
D1.57/4:985-88	3544–18	E1.90/2:(date)	3002–13	ED1.2:G76/2/987-88	4804–1
D1.57/5:986-88	3544–11	E1.93:(v.nos.&nos.)	3352–4	ED1.10/2:989	4804–3
D1.57/6:988	3542–5	E1.95:988	3234–1	ED1.14:90-1	4804–17
D1.57/6:988-2	3542–5	E1.95/2:988	3244–1	ED1.18:988	4874–2
D1.57/7:988-2	3542–19	E1.104:21400-H6	3008–122	ED1.18/2:988	4874–3
D1.57/8:988	3544–17	E2.1:988	3084–9	ED1.18/3:988	4874–5
D1.57/9:(date)	3542–17	E2.2:H99/2	3088–14	ED1.18/4:989	4874–1
D1.58/2:988	3544–6	E2.12/3:988	3084–13	ED1.26:988	4802–1
D1.58/4:987	3544–29	E3.1:988	3164–29	ED1.26:988-2	4802–1
D1.58/4:988	3544–29	E3.1/2:988	3164–74	ED1.26:989	4802–1
D1.61:(date)	3542–14	E3.1/4:989	3164–75	ED1.29/2:987-88	4804–28
D1.61/2:(date)	3542–16	E3.2:C63/18	3168–114	ED1.32:989	4944–4
D1.61/3:(date)	3542–20	E3.2:N21/3	3168–113	ED1.32/4:988-89	4944–10
D1.61/4:988	3544–1	E3.2:Oi5/16	3168–112	ED1.37:St2/4	4804–32.2
D1.61/5:988	3544–7	E3.9:(date)	3162–24	ED1.37:St2/5	4804–32.1
D1.61/6:988	3542–21	E3.11:(yr./nos.)	3162–4	ED1.39:988	4804–5
D1.62:(date)	3542–15	E3.11/2-2:988/v.(nos.)	3164–4	ED1.40/4:988	4804–18
D1.62/2:987	3544–24	E3.11/2-2:988/v.1	3164–4.1	ED1.109:989/v.1	4824–1.1
D1.64:988	3544–25	E3.11/2-2:988/v.2	3164–4.2	ED1.109:989/v.2	4824–1.2
D1.66:988	3904–3	E3.11/4:(yr./nos.)	3162–1	ED1.109/2:989	4824–1.3
D1.74:989	3504–20	E3.11/5:(date)	3162–6	ED1.111/2:988	4834–1
D1.82:988	3508–31	E3.11/5-5:988/v.(nos.)	3164–2	ED1.120:998-2000	4824–4
D1.85:990	7144–13	E3.11/5-5:988/v.1	3164–2.1	ED1.125:32	4826–1.27
D1.90:989	3544–26	E3.11/5-5:988/v.2	3164–2.2	ED1.210:988	4944–1
D2.15/3:989	3504–13	E3.11/7:(date)	3162–8	ED1.302:M66/2	4828–38

Guide
to Selected
Standard
Classifications

Guide to Selected Standard Classifications
(This guide outlines the major standard classification systems used by various Federal agencies to arrange and present social and economic statistical data.)

Census Regions and Divisions

**CENSUS REGIONS SHOWING
DIVISIONS INCLUDED IN EACH:**

Northeast
New England, Middle Atlantic

Midwest
East North Central, West North Central

South
South Atlantic, East South Central,
West South Central

West
Mountain, Pacific

**CENSUS DIVISIONS SHOWING
STATES INCLUDED IN EACH:**

New England
Maine, New Hampshire, Vermont,
Massachusetts, Rhode Island, Connecticut

Middle Atlantic
New York, New Jersey, Pennsylvania

East North Central
Ohio, Indiana, Illinois, Michigan, Wisconsin

West North Central
Minnesota, Iowa, Missouri, North Dakota,
South Dakota, Nebraska, Kansas

South Atlantic
Delaware, Maryland, District of Columbia,
Virginia, West Virginia, North Carolina,
South Carolina, Georgia, Florida

East South Central
Kentucky, Tennessee, Alabama, Mississippi

West South Central
Arkansas, Louisiana, Oklahoma, Texas

Mountain
Montana, Idaho, Wyoming, Colorado, New
Mexico, Arizona, Utah, Nevada

Pacific
Washington, Oregon, California, Alaska,
Hawaii

Outlying Areas of the United States

American Samoa
Guam

Northern Mariana Islands
Puerto Rico

Trust Territory of the Pacific Islands
Virgin Islands

Standard Federal Administrative Regions

Region I
Connecticut, Maine, Massachusetts,
New Hampshire, Rhode Island, and
Vermont

Region II
New Jersey, New York, Puerto Rico,
and the Virgin Islands

Region III
Delaware, District of Columbia,
Maryland, Pennsylvania, Virginia,
and West Virginia

Region IV
Alabama, Florida, Georgia, Kentucky,
Mississippi, North Carolina, South
Carolina, and Tennessee

Region V
Illinois, Indiana, Michigan, Minnesota,
Ohio, and Wisconsin

Region VI
Arkansas, Louisiana, New Mexico,
Oklahoma, and Texas

Region VII
Iowa, Kansas, Missouri, and Nebraska

Region VIII
Colorado, Montana, North Dakota,
South Dakota, Utah, and Wyoming

Region IX
American Samoa, Arizona, California,
Guam, Hawaii, and Nevada

Region X
Alaska, Idaho, Oregon, and Washington

Farm Production Regions

National agricultural data are frequently
grouped into 10 farm production regions,
covering the 48 contiguous States. Alaska, Hawaii,
and Puerto Rico are each shown separately, if included.

Appalachian
Kentucky, North Carolina, Tennessee,
Virginia, West Virginia

Corn Belt
Illinois, Indiana, Iowa, Missouri, Ohio

Delta States
Arkansas, Louisiana, Mississippi

Lake States
Michigan, Minnesota, Wisconsin

Mountain
Arizona, Colorado, Idaho, Montana,
Nevada, New Mexico, Utah, Wyoming

Northeast
Connecticut, Delaware, Maine,
Maryland, Massachusetts, New
Hampshire, New Jersey, New York,
Pennsylvania, Rhode Island, Vermont

Northern Plains
Kansas, Nebraska, North Dakota,
South Dakota

Pacific
California, Oregon, Washington

Southeast
Alabama, Florida, Georgia,
South Carolina

Southern Plains
Oklahoma, Texas

Federal Reserve Districts

District 1 (Boston)
Maine, Massachusetts, New Hampshire, Rhode Island, Vermont; most of Connecticut

District 2 (New York)
New York, Puerto Rico, Virgin Islands; portions of New Jersey; Fairfield Co., Connecticut

District 3 (Philadelphia)
Delaware; portions of New Jersey and Pennsylvania

District 4 (Cleveland)
Ohio; portions of Kentucky, Pennsylvania, West Virginia

District 5 (Richmond)
District of Columbia, Maryland, North & South Carolina, Virginia; portions of West Virginia

District 6 (Atlanta)
Alabama, Florida, Georgia; portions of Louisiana, Mississippi, Tennessee

District 7 (Chicago)
Iowa; portions of Michigan, Illinois, Indiana, Wisconsin

District 8 (St. Louis)
Arkansas; portions of Kentucky, Illinois, Indiana, Mississippi, Missouri, Tennessee

District 9 (Minneapolis)
Minnesota, Montana, North & South Dakota; portions of Michigan and Wisconsin

District 10 (Kansas City)
Colorado, Kansas, Nebraska, Oklahoma Wyoming; portions of Missouri, New Mexico

District 11 (Dallas)
Texas; portions of Louisiana, New Mexico

District 12 (San Francisco)
Alaska, Arizona, California, Guam, Hawaii, Idaho, Nevada, Oregon, Utah, Washington

Federal Home Loan Bank Districts

District 1 (Boston)
Connecticut, Maine, Massachusetts, New Hampshire, Rhode Island, and Vermont

District 2 (New York)
New Jersey, New York, Puerto Rico, and Virgin Islands

District 3 (Pittsburgh)
Delaware, Pennsylvania, and West Virginia

District 4 (Atlanta)
Alabama, District of Columbia, Florida, Georgia, Maryland, North Carolina, South Carolina, and Virginia

District 5 (Cincinnati)
Kentucky, Ohio, and Tennessee

District 6 (Indianapolis)
Indiana and Michigan

District 7 (Chicago)
Illinois and Wisconsin

District 8 (Des Moines)
Iowa, Minnesota, Missouri, North Dakota, and South Dakota

District 9 (Dallas)
Arkansas, Louisiana, Mississippi, New Mexico, and Texas

District 10 (Topeka)
Colorado, Kansas, Nebraska, and Oklahoma

District 11 (San Francisco)
Arizona, Nevada, and California

District 12 (Seattle)
Alaska, Hawaii, Guam, Idaho, Montana, Oregon, Utah, Washington, and Wyoming

Bureau of Labor Statistics Regions
(And Regional Offices)

Region 1: New England (Boston)
Connecticut, Maine, Massachusetts, New Hampshire, Rhode Island, Vermont

Region 2: Middle Atlantic Region (New York)
New Jersey, New York, Puerto Rico, Virgin Islands

Region 3: Mideast Region (Philadelphia)
Delaware, District of Columbia, Maryland, Pennsylvania, Virginia, West Virginia

Region 4: Southeast Region (Atlanta)
Alabama, Florida, Georgia, Kentucky, Mississippi, North Carolina, South Carolina, Tennessee

Region 5: North Central Region (Chicago)
Illinois, Indiana, Michigan, Minnesota, Ohio, Wisconsin

Region 6: Southwest Region (Dallas)
Arkansas, Louisiana, New Mexico, Oklahoma, Texas

Region 7 and 8: Mountain-Plains Region (Kansas City)
Colorado, Iowa, Kansas, Missouri, Montana, Nebraska, North Dakota, South Dakota, Utah, Wyoming

Region 9 and 10: Pacific Region (San Francisco)
Alaska, American Samoa, Arizona, California, Guam, Hawaii, Idaho, Nevada, Oregon, Trust Territory of the Pacific Islands, Washington

Metropolitan Statistical Areas

Metropolitan Statistical Areas (MSAs) were developed to enable all Federal statistical agencies to use the same boundaries in publishing urban data.

As part of the Federal Government's July 1983 revision of its metropolitan area classification, Standard Metropolitan Statistical Areas (SMSAs) were replaced by MSAs and Primary Metropolitan Statistical Areas (PSMAs). In addition, some new areas were designated, and the titles or definitions of several areas were changed. OMB issues supplemental announcements annually to account for new data.

MSAs and PSMAs are listed below. SMSA titles in use through June 1983 are listed in ASI 1983 Annual.

Area Code	Area Title
0040	Abilene, Tex.
0060	Aguadilla, P.R.
0080	Akron, Ohio
0120	Albany, Ga.
0160	Albany-Schenectady-Troy, N.Y.
0200	Albuquerque, N. Mex.
0220	Alexandria, La.
0240	Allentown-Bethlehem, Pa.-N.J.
0275	Alton-Granite City, Ill.
0280	Altoona, Pa.
0320	Amarillo, Tex.
0360	Anaheim-Santa Ana, Calif.
0380	Anchorage, Alaska
0400	Anderson, Ind.
0405	Anderson, S.C.
0440	Ann Arbor, Mich.
0450	Anniston, Ala.
0460	Appleton-Oshkosh-Neenah, Wis.
0470	Arecibo, P.R.
0480	Asheville, N.C.
0500	Athens, Ga.
0520	Atlanta, Ga.
0560	Atlantic City, N.J.
0600	Augusta, Ga.-S.C.
0620	Aurora-Elgin, Ill.
0640	Austin, Tex.
0680	Bakersfield, Calif.
0720	Baltimore, Md.
0730	Bangor, Maine
0760	Baton Rouge, La.
0780	Battle Creek, Mich.
0840	Beaumont-Port Arthur, Tex.
0845	Beaver County, Pa.
0860	Bellingham, Wash.
0870	Benton Harbor, Mich.
0875	Bergen-Passaic, N.J.
0880	Billings, Mont.
0920	Biloxi-Gulfport, Miss.
0960	Binghamton, N.Y.
1000	Birmingham, Ala.
1010	Bismarck, N.Dak.
1020	Bloomington, Ind.
1040	Bloomington-Normal, Ill.
1080	Boise City, Idaho
1120	Boston, Mass.
1125	Boulder-Longmont, Colo.

Area Code	Area Title
1140	Bradenton, Fla.
1145	Brazoria, Tex.
1150	Bremerton, Wash.
1160	Bridgeport-Milford, Conn.
1170	Bristol, Conn.
1200	Brockton, Mass.
1240	Brownsville-Harlingen, Tex.
1260	Bryan-College Station, Tex.
1280	Buffalo, N.Y.
1300	Burlington, N.C.
1305	Burlington, Vt.
1310	Caguas, P.R.
1320	Canton, Ohio
1350	Casper, Wyo.
1360	Cedar Rapids, Iowa
1400	Champaign-Urbana-Rantoul, Ill.
1440	Charleston, S.C.
1480	Charleston, W.Va.
1520	Charlotte-Gastonia-Rock Hill, N.C.-S.C.
1540	Charlottesville, Va.
1560	Chattanooga, Tenn.-Ga.
1580	Cheyenne, Wyo.
1600	Chicago, Ill.
1620	Chico, Calif.
1640	Cincinnati, Ohio-Ky.-Ind.
1660	Clarksville-Hopkinsville, Tenn.-Ky.
1680	Cleveland, Ohio
1720	Colorado Springs, Colo.
1740	Columbia, Mo.
1760	Columbia, S.C.
1800	Columbus, Ga.-Ala.
1840	Columbus, Ohio
1880	Corpus Christi, Tex.
1900	Cumberland, Md.-W.Va.
1920	Dallas, Tex.
1930	Danbury, Conn.
1950	Danville, Va.
1960	Davenport-Rock Island-Moline, Iowa-Ill.
2000	Dayton-Springfield, Ohio
2020	Daytona Beach, Fla.
2040	Decatur, Ill.
2080	Denver, Colo.
2120	Des Moines, Iowa
2160	Detroit, Mich.

Area Code	Area Title
2180	Dothan, Ala.
2200	Dubuque, Iowa
2240	Duluth, Minn.-Wis.
2285	East St. Louis-Belleville, Ill.
2290	Eau Claire, Wis.
2320	El Paso, Tex.
2330	Elkhart-Goshen, Ind.
2335	Elmira, N.Y.
2340	Enid, Okla.
2360	Erie, Pa.
2400	Eugene-Springfield, Oreg.
2440	Evansville, Ind.-Ky.
2480	Fall River, Mass.-R.I.
2520	Fargo-Moorhead, N. Dak.-Minn.
2560	Fayetteville, N.C.
2580	Fayetteville-Springdale, Ark.
2600	Fitchburg-Leominster, Mass.
2640	Flint, Mich.
2650	Florence, Ala.
2655	Florence, S.C.
2670	Fort Collins-Loveland, Colo.
2680	Fort Lauderdale-Hollywood-Pompano Beach, Fla.
2700	Fort Myers-Cape Coral, Fla.
2710	Fort Pierce, Fla.
2720	Fort Smith, Ark.-Okla.
2750	Fort Walton Beach, Fla.
2760	Fort Wayne, Ind.
2800	Fort Worth-Arlington, Tex.
2840	Fresno, Calif.
2880	Gadsden, Ala.
2900	Gainesville, Fla.
2920	Galveston-Texas City, Tex.
2960	Gary-Hammond, Ind.
2975	Glens Falls, N.Y.
2985	Grand Forks, N.Dak.
3000	Grand Rapids, Mich.
3040	Great Falls, Mont.
3060	Greeley, Colo.
3080	Green Bay, Wis.
3120	Greensboro-Winston-Salem-High Point, N.C.
3160	Greenville-Spartanburg, S.C.
3180	Hagerstown, Md.
3200	Hamilton-Middletown, Ohio
3240	Harrisburg-Lebanon-Carlisle, Pa.
3280	Hartford, Conn.
3290	Hickory, N.C.
3320	Honolulu, Hawaii
3350	Houma-Thibodaux, La.
3360	Houston, Tex.

Area Code	Area Title
3400	Huntington-Ashland, W.Va.-Ky.-Ohio
3440	Huntsville, Ala.
3480	Indianapolis, Ind.
3500	Iowa City, Iowa
3520	Jackson, Mich.
3560	Jackson, Miss.
3580	Jackson, Tenn.
3600	Jacksonville, Fla.
3605	Jacksonville, N.C.
3620	Janesville-Beloit, Wis.
3640	Jersey City, N.J.
3660	Johnson City-Kingsport-Bristol, Tenn.-Va.
3680	Johnstown, Pa.
3690	Joliet, Ill.
3710	Joplin, Mo.
3720	Kalamazoo, Mich.
3740	Kankakee, Ill.
3760	Kansas City, Mo.-Kans.
3800	Kenosha, Wis.
3810	Killeen-Temple, Tex.
3840	Knoxville, Tenn.
3850	Kokomo, Ind.
3870	LaCrosse, Wis.
3880	Lafayette, La.
3920	Lafayette-West Lafayette, Ind.
3960	Lake Charles, La.
3965	Lake County, Ill.
3980	Lakeland-Winter Haven, Fla.
4000	Lancaster, Pa.
4040	Lansing-East Lansing, Mich.
4080	Laredo, Tex.
4100	Las Cruces, N. Mex.
4120	Las Vegas, Nev.
4150	Lawrence, Kans.
4160	Lawrence-Haverhill, Mass.-N.H.
4200	Lawton, Okla.
4240	Lewiston-Auburn, Maine
4280	Lexington-Fayette, Ky.
4320	Lima, Ohio
4360	Lincoln, Nebr.
4400	Little Rock-North Little Rock, Ark.
4420	Longview-Marshall, Tex.
4440	Lorain-Elyria, Ohio
4480	Los Angeles-Long Beach, Calif.
4520	Louisville, Ky.-Ind.
4560	Lowell, Mass.-N.H.
4600	Lubbock, Tex.
4640	Lynchburg, Va.
4680	Macon-Warner Robins, Ga.
4720	Madison, Wis.

4760	Manchester, N.H.	5880	Oklahoma City, Okla.	6920	Sacramento, Calif.	8280	Tampa-St. Petersburg-Clearwater, Fla.
4800	Mansfield, Ohio	5910	Olympia, Wash.	6960	Saginaw-Bay City-Midland, Mich.	8320	Terre Haute, Ind.
4840	Mayaguez, P.R.	5920	Omaha, Nebr.-Iowa			8360	Texarkana, Tex.-Ark.
4880	McAllen-Edinburg-Mission, Tex.	5950	Orange County, N.Y.	6980	St. Cloud, Minn.	8400	Toledo, Ohio
4890	Medford, Oreg.	5960	Orlando, Fla.	7000	St. Joseph, Mo.	8440	Topeka, Kans.
4900	Melbourne-Titusville-Palm Bay, Fla.	5990	Owensboro, Ky.	7040	St. Louis, Mo.-Ill.	8480	Trenton, N.J.
		6000	Oxnard-Ventura, Calif.	7080	Salem, Oreg.	8520	Tucson, Ariz.
4920	Memphis, Tenn.-Ark.-Miss.			7090	Salem-Gloucester, Mass.	8560	Tulsa, Okla.
5000	Miami-Hialeah, Fla.	6015	Panama City, Fla.	7120	Salinas-Seaside-Monterey, Calif.	8600	Tuscaloosa, Ala.
5015	Middlesex-Somerset-Hunterdon, N.J.	6020	Parkersburg-Marietta, W.Va.-Ohio	7160	Salt Lake City-Ogden, Utah	8640	Tyler, Tex.
5020	Middletown, Conn.	6025	Pascagoula, Miss.	7200	San Angelo, Tex.		
5040	Midland, Tex.	6060	Pawtucket-Woonsocket-Attleboro, R.I.-Mass.	7240	San Antonio, Tex.	8680	Utica-Rome, N.Y.
5080	Milwaukee, Wis.			7320	San Diego, Calif.		
5120	Minneapolis-St. Paul, Minn.-Wis.	6080	Pensacola, Fla.	7360	San Francisco, Calif.		
		6120	Peoria, Ill.	7400	San Jose, Calif.	8720	Vallejo-Fairfield-Napa, Calif.
5160	Mobile, Ala.	6160	Philadelphia, Pa.-N.J.	7440	San Juan, P.R.	8725	Vancouver, Wash.
5170	Modesto, Calif.	6200	Phoenix, Ariz.	7480	Santa Barbara-Santa Maria-Lompoc, Calif.	8750	Victoria, Tex.
5190	Monmouth-Ocean, N.J.	6240	Pine Bluff, Ark.			8760	Vineland-Millville-Bridgeton, N.J.
5200	Monroe, La.	6280	Pittsburgh, Pa.	7485	Santa Cruz, Calif.		
5240	Montgomery, Ala.	6320	Pittsfield, Mass.	7490	Santa Fe, N. Mex.	8780	Visalia-Tulare-Porterville, Calif.
5280	Muncie, Ind.	6360	Ponce, P.R.	7500	Santa Rosa-Petaluma, Calif.		
5320	Muskegon, Mich.	6400	Portland, Maine	7510	Sarasota, Fla.		
		6440	Portland, Oreg.	7520	Savannah, Ga.		
5345	Naples, Fla.	6450	Portsmouth-Dover-Rochester, N.H.-Maine	7560	Scranton-Wilkes-Barre, Pa.	8800	Waco, Tex.
5350	Nashua, N.H.			7600	Seattle, Wash.	8840	Washington, D.C.-Md.-Va.
5360	Nashville, Tenn.	6460	Poughkeepsie, N.Y.	7610	Sharon, Pa.	8880	Waterbury, Conn.
5380	Nassau-Suffolk, N.Y.	6480	Providence, R.I.	7620	Sheboygan, Wis.	8920	Waterloo-Cedar Falls, Iowa
5400	New Bedford, Mass.	6520	Provo-Orem, Utah	7640	Sherman-Denison, Tex.		
5440	New Britain, Conn.	6560	Pueblo, Colo.	7680	Shreveport, La.	8940	Wausau, Wis.
5480	New Haven-Meriden, Conn.			7720	Sioux City, Iowa-Nebr.	8960	West Palm Beach-Boca Raton-Delray Beach, Fla.
5520	New London-Norwich, Conn.-R.I.	6600	Racine, Wis.	7760	Sioux Falls, S.Dak.		
		6640	Raleigh-Durham, N.C.	7800	South Bend-Mishawaka, Ind.	9000	Wheeling, W.Va.-Ohio
5560	New Orleans, La.	6660	Rapid City, S. Dak.			9040	Wichita, Kans.
5600	New York, N.Y.	6680	Reading, Pa.	7840	Spokane, Wash.	9080	Wichita Falls, Tex.
5640	Newark, N.J.	6690	Redding, Calif.	7880	Springfield, Ill.	9140	Williamsport, Pa.
5700	Niagara Falls, N.Y.	6720	Reno, Nev.	7920	Springfield, Mo.	9160	Wilmington, Del.-N.J.-Md.
5720	Norfolk-Virginia Beach-Newport News, Va.	6740	Richland-Kennewick-Pasco, Wash.	8000	Springfield, Mass.	9200	Wilmington, N.C.
				8040	Stamford, Conn.	9240	Worcester, Mass.
5760	Norwalk, Conn.	6760	Richmond-Petersburg, Va.	8050	State College, Pa.		
		6780	Riverside-San Bernardino, Calif.	8080	Steubenville-Weirton, Ohio-W. Va.		
				8120	Stockton, Calif.	9260	Yakima, Wash.
		6800	Roanoke, Va.	8160	Syracuse, N.Y.	9280	York, Pa.
5775	Oakland, Calif.	6820	Rochester, Minn.	8200	Tacoma, Wash.	9320	Youngstown-Warren, Ohio
5790	Ocala, Fla.	6840	Rochester, N.Y.	8240	Tallahassee, Fla.	9340	Yuba City, Calif.
5800	Odessa, Tex.	6880	Rockford, Ill.				

Consolidated Metropolitan Statistical Areas

Consolidated Metropolitan Statistical Areas (CSMAs) consist of component Primary Metropolitan Statistical Areas.

As part of the Federal Government's July 1983 revision of its metropolitan area classification, the term CSMA replaced "Standard Consolidated Statistical Areas." In addition, some new areas were designated, and the titles or definitions of several areas were changed.

CSMAs are listed below. Standard Consolidated Statistical Area titles in use through June 1983 are listed in ASI 1983 Annual.

Area Code	Area Title				
07	Boston-Lawrence-Salem, Mass.-N.H.	34	Denver-Boulder, Colo.	77	Philadelphia-Wilmington-Trenton, Pa.-Del.-N.J.-Md.
10	Buffalo-Niagara Falls, N.Y.	35	Detroit-Ann Arbor, Mich.	78	Pittsburgh-Beaver Valley, Pa.
14	Chicago-Gary-Lake County, Ill.-Ind.-Wis.	41	Hartford-New Britain-Middletown, Conn.	79	Portland-Vancouver, Oreg.-Wash.
21	Cincinnati-Hamilton, Ohio-Ky.-Ind.	42	Houston-Galveston-Brazoria, Tex.	80	Providence-Fall River, R.I.-Mass.
28	Cleveland-Akron-Lorain, Ohio	49	Los Angeles-Anaheim-Riverside, Calif.	84	San Francisco-Oakland-San Jose, Calif.
31	Dallas-Fort Worth, Tex.	56	Miami-Fort Lauderdale, Fla.	87	San Juan-Caguas, P.R.
		63	Milwaukee-Racine, Wis.	91	Seattle-Tacoma, Wash.
		70	New York-Northern New Jersey-Long Island, N.Y.-N.J.-Conn.		

Cities With Population Over 100,000

1988 Rank and Population

1 New York, N.Y.	7,352,700
2 Los Angeles, Calif.	3,352,710
3 Chicago, Ill	2,977,520
4 Houston, Tex.	1,698,090
5 Philadelphia, Pa.	1,647,000
6 San Diego, Calif.	1,070,310
7 Detroit, Mich.	1,035,920
8 Dallas, Tex.	987,360
9 San Antonio, Tex.	941,150
10 Phoenix, Ariz.	923,750
11 Baltimore, Md.	751,400
12 San Jose, Calif.	738,420
13 San Francisco, Calif.	731,600
14 Indianapolis, Ind.	727,130
15 Memphis, Tenn.	645,190
16 Jacksonville, Fla.	635,430
17 Washington, D.C.	617,000
18 Milwaukee, Wis.	599,380
19 Boston, Mass.	577,830
20 Columbus, Ohio	569,570
21 New Orleans, La.	531,700
22 Cleveland, Ohio	521,370
23 El Paso, Tex.	510,970
24 Seattle, Wash	502,200
25 Denver, Colo.	492,200
26 Nashville-Davidson, Tenn.	481,400
27 Austin, Tex.	464,690
28 Kansas City, Mo.	438,950
29 Oklahoma City, Okla.	434,380
30 Fort Worth, Tex.	426,610
31 Atlanta, Ga.	420,220
32 Portland, Ore.	418,470
33 Long Beach, Calif	415,040
34 St. Louis, Mo.	403,700
35 Tucson, Ariz.	385,720
36 Albuquerque, N.M.	378,480
37 Honolulu, Hawaii	376,110
38 Pittsburgh, Pa.	375,230
39 Miami, Fla.	371,100
40 Cincinnati, Ohio	370,480
41 Tulsa, Okla.	368,330
42 Charlotte, N.C.	367,860
43 Virginia Beach, Va.	365,300
44 Oakland, Calif.	356,860
45 Omaha, Nebr.	353,170
46 Minneapolis, Minn.	344,670
47 Toledo, Ohio	340,760
48 Sacramento, Calif.	338,220
49 Newark, N.J.	313,800
50 Buffalo, N.Y.	313,570
51 Fresno, Calif.	307,090
52 Wichita, Kan.	295,320
53 Norfolk, Va.	286,500
54 Colorado Springs, Colo.	283,110
55 Louisville, Ky.	281,880
56 Tampa, Fla.	281,790
57 Mesa, Ariz.	280,360
58 Birmingham, Ala.	277,280
59 Corpus Christi, Tex.	260,930
60 St. Paul, Minn.	259,110
61 Arlington, Tex.	257,460
62 Anaheim, Calif.	244,670
63 Santa Ana, Calif.	239,540
64 St. Petersburg, Fla.	235,450
65 Baton Rouge, La.	235,270
66 Rochester, N.Y.	229,780
67 Lexington-Fayette, Ky.	225,700
68 Akron, Ohio	221,510
69 Aurora, Colo.	218,720
70 Anchorage, Alaska	218,500
71 Shreveport, La.	218,010
72 Jersey City, N.J.	217,630
73 Richmond, Va.	213,300
74 Riverside, Calif.	210,630
75 Las Vegas, Nev.	210,620
76 Mobile, Ala.	208,820

77 Jackson, Miss	201,250
78 Montgomery, Ala.	193,510
79 Des Moines, Iowa	192,910
80 Stockton, Calif.	190,680
81 Lubbock, Tex.	188,090
82 Lincoln, Nebr.	187,890
83 Huntington Beach, Calif.	186,880
84 Raleigh, N.C.	186,720
85 Grand Rapids, Mich.	185,370
86 Yonkers, N.Y.	183,000
87 Greensboro, N.C.	181,970
88 Garland, Tex.	180,450
89 Little Rock, Ark.	180,090
90 Fort Wayne, Ind.	179,810
91 Madison, Wis.	178,180
92 Dayton, Ohio	178,000
93 Columbus, Ga.	177,680
94 Knoxville, Tenn	172,080
95 Spokane, Wash.	170,900
96 Fremont, Calif	166,590
97 Amarillo, Tex.	166,010
98 Tacoma, Wash.	163,960
99 Chattanooga, Tenn.	162,670
100 Hialeah, Fla.	162,080
101 Glendale, Calif.	161,210
102 Kansas City, Kan.	160,630
103 Newport News, Va.	160,100
104 Huntsville, Ala.	159,450
105 Bakersfield, Calif.	157,650
106 Worcester, Mass	156,190
107 Providence, R.I.	156,160
108 Orlando, Fla.	155,950
109 Syracuse, N.Y.	153,610
110 Salt Lake City, Utah	152,740
111 Springfield, Mass.	150,320
112 Winston-Salem, N.C.	148,690
113 Modesto, Calif.	148,670
114 San Bernardino, Calif.	148,420
115 Chesapeake, Va.	147,800
116 Savannah, Ga.	145,980
117 Fort Lauderdale, Fla.	145,610
118 Warren, Mich.	145,410
119 Springfield, Mo.	142,690
120 Flint, Mich.	141,620
121 Tempe, Ariz.	140,440
122 Glendale, Ariz.	140,170
123 Bridgeport, Conn.	139,770
124 Paterson, N.J.	138,620
125 Torrance, Calif.	137,940
126 Garden Grove, Calif.	135,310
127 Rockford, Ill.	134,500
128 Irving, Tex.	133,000
129 Gary, Ind.	132,460
130 Pasadena, Calif.	132,010
131 Hartford, Conn.	131,300
132 Hampton, Va.	130,800
133 Oxnard, Calif.	130,080
134 Evansville, Ind.	128,210
135 Chula Vista, Calif.	126,240
136 Tallahassee, Fla.	125,640
137 Lansing, Mich.	124,960
138 Laredo, Tex.	124,730
139 New Haven, Conn.	123,840
140 Ontario, Calif.	123,380
141 Topeka, Kan.	122,360
142 Scottsdale, Ariz.	121,740
143 Pomona, Calif.	120,470
144 Hollywood, Fla.	120,140
145 Lakewood, Colo.	119,340
146 Plano, Tex.	118,790
147 Macon, Ga.	117,940
148 Pasadena, Tex.	116,880
149 Sunnyvale, Calif.	116,180
150 Durham, N.C.	115,430
151 Reno, Nev.	115,130
152 Independence, Mo.	115,090
153 Sterling Heights, Mich.	114,720

154 Beaumont, Tex.	114,210
155 Erie, Pa.	112,800
156 Oceanside, Calif.	112,630
157 Boise City, Idaho	111,030
158 Cedar Rapids, Iowa	110,300
159 Fullerton, Calif.	109,740
160 Peoria, Ill.	109,560
161 Abilene, Tex.	109,110
162 Ann Arbor, Mich.	108,440
163 Alexandria, Va.	108,400
164 Santa Rosa, Calif.	108,220
165 Concord, Calif.	108,040
166 Eugene, Ore.	108,030
167 Portsmouth, Va.	107,500
168 Overland Park, Kan.	106,860
169 South Bend, Ind.	106,190
170 Orange, Calif.	105,710
171 Allentown, Pa.	105,200
172 Elizabeth, N.J.	105,150
173 Waterbury, Conn.	104,520
174 Brownsville, Tex.	104,510
175 Inglewood, Calif	103,920
176 Berkeley, Calif.	103,660
177 Hayward, Calif.	103,600
178 Waco, Tex.	103,420
179 Thousand Oaks, Calif.	101,530
180 Youngstown, Ohio	101,150
181 Livonia, Mich.	101,100
182 Salinas, Calif.	101,090
183 Pueblo, Colo.	101,070
184 Vallejo, Calif.	100,730
185 Stamford, Conn.	100,260
186 Irvine, Calif.	100,130

Consumer Price Index Cities

Consumer Price Index data are collected for the following Metropolitan Statistical Areas:

Anchorage, Alaska
Atlanta, Ga.
Baltimore, Md.
Boston, Mass.
Buffalo-Niagara Falls, N.Y.
Chicago, Ill.-Northwestern Ind.
Cincinnati-Hamilton, Ohio-Ky.-Ind.
Cleveland, Ohio
Dallas-Ft. Worth, Tex.
Denver-Boulder, Colo.
Detroit, Mich.
Honolulu, Hawaii
Houston, Tex.
Kansas City, Mo.-Kans.
Los Angeles-Long Beach, Anaheim, Calif.
Miami, Fla.
Milwaukee, Wis.
Minneapolis-St. Paul, Minn.-Wis.
New York, N.Y.-Northeastern N.J.
Philadelphia, Pa.-N.J.
Pittsburgh, Pa.
Portland-Vancouver, Oreg.-Wash.
St. Louis, Mo.-Ill.
San Diego, Calif.
San Francisco-Oakland, Calif.
Seattle-Tacoma, Wash.
Washington, D.C.-Md.-Va.

Standard Industrial Classification

The Standard Industrial Classification (SIC) was developed to classify industrial establishments by the type of activity in which they are engaged, for the purpose of promoting uniformity and comparability of statistical data collected by Federal and State agencies, trade associations, and others. The classification system is at 4 levels: industry divisions, major groups, groups, and individual industries—represented by 1- to 4-digit codes. The following list is taken from the 1987 *Standard Industrial Classification Manual,* which revises the 1972 edition and 1977 supplement. For description of the 1987 Manual, see 108-4 in ASI 1987 Annual.

Group and
Industry
Code

AGRICULTURE, FORESTRY, AND FISHING

01 AGRICULTURAL PRODUCTION— CROPS

011 Cash Grains
0111 Wheat
0112 Rice
0115 Corn
0116 Soybeans
0119 Cash grains, nec

013 Field Crops, Except Cash Grains
0131 Cotton
0132 Tobacco
0133 Sugarcane and sugar beets
0134 Irish potatoes
0139 Field crops, except cash grains, nec

016 Vegetables and Melons
0161 Vegetables and melons

017 Fruits and Tree Nuts
0171 Berry crops
0172 Grapes
0173 Tree nuts
0174 Citrus fruits
0175 Deciduous tree fruits
0179 Fruits and tree nuts, nec

018 Horticultural Specialties
0181 Ornamental nursery products
0182 Food crops grown under cover

019 General Farms, Primarily Crop
0191 General farms, primarily crop

02 AGRICULTURAL PRODUCTION— LIVESTOCK

021 Livestock, Except Dairy and Poultry
0211 Beef cattle feedlots
0212 Beef cattle, except feedlots
0213 Hogs
0214 Sheep and goats
0219 General livestock, nec

024 Dairy Farms
0241 Dairy farms

025 Poultry and Eggs
0251 Broiler, fryer, and roaster chickens
0252 Chicken eggs
0253 Turkeys and turkey eggs
0254 Poultry hatcheries
0259 Poultry and eggs, nec

027 Animal Specialties
0271 Fur-bearing animals and rabbits
0272 Horses and other equines
0273 Animal aquaculture
0279 Animal specialties, nec

029 General Farms, Primarily Animal
0291 General farms, primarily animal

07 AGRICULTURAL SERVICES

071 Soil Preparation Services
0711 Soil preparation services

072 Crop Services
0721 Crop planting and protecting
0722 Crop harvesting
0723 Crop preparation services for market
0724 Cotton ginning

074 Veterinary Services
0741 Veterinary services for livestock
0742 Veterinary services, specialties

075 Animal Services, Except Veterinary
0751 Livestock services, exc. veterinary
0752 Animal specialty services

076 Farm Labor and Management Services
0761 Farm labor contractors
0762 Farm management services

078 Landscape and Horticultural Services
0781 Landscape counseling and planning
0782 Lawn and garden services
0783 Ornamental shrub and tree services

08 FORESTRY

081 Timber Tracts
0811 Timber tracts

083 Forest Products
0831 Forest products

085 Forestry Services
0851 Forestry services

09 FISHING, HUNTING, AND TRAPPING

091 Commercial Fishing
0912 Finfish
0913 Shellfish
0919 Miscellaneous marine products

092 Fish Hatcheries and Preserves
0921 Fish hatcheries and preserves

097 Hunting, Trapping, Game Propagation
0971 Hunting, trapping, game propagation

MINING

10 METAL MINING

101 Iron Ores
1011 Iron ores

102 Copper Ores
1021 Copper ores

103 Lead and Zinc Ores
1031 Lead and zinc ores

104 Gold and Silver Ores
1041 Gold ores
1044 Silver ores

106 Ferroalloy Ores, Except Vanadium
1061 Ferroalloy ores, except vanadium

108 Metal Mining Services
1081 Metal mining services

109 Miscellaneous Metal Ores
1094 Uranium-radium-vanadium ores
1099 Metal ores, nec

12 COAL MINING

122 Bituminous Coal and Lignite Mining
1221 Bituminous coal and lignite—surface
1222 Bituminous coal—underground

123 Anthracite Mining
1231 Anthracite mining

124 Coal Mining Services
1241 Coal mining services

13 OIL AND GAS EXTRACTION

131 Crude Petroleum and Natural Gas
1311 Crude petroleum and natural gas

132 Natural Gas Liquids
1321 Natural gas liquids

138 Oil and Gas Field Services
1381 Drilling oil and gas wells
1382 Oil and gas exploration services
1389 Oil and gas field services, nec

14 NONMETALLIC MINERALS, EXCEPT FUELS

141 Dimension Stone
1411 Dimension stone

142 Crushed and Broken Stone
1422 Crushed and broken limestone
1423 Crushed and broken granite
1429 Crushed and broken stone, nec

144 Sand and Gravel
1442 Construction sand and gravel
1446 Industrial sand

145 Clay, Ceramic, & Refractory Minerals
1455 Kaolin and ball clay
1459 Clay and related minerals, nec

147 Chemical and Fertilizer Minerals
1474 Potash, soda, and borate minerals
1475 Phosphate rock
1479 Chemical and fertilizer mining, nec

148 Nonmetallic Minerals Services
1481 Nonmetallic minerals services

149 Miscellaneous Nonmetallic Minerals
1499 Miscellaneous nonmetallic minerals

CONSTRUCTION

15 GENERAL BUILDING CONTRACTORS

152 Residential Building Construction
1521 Single-family housing construction
1522 Residential construction, nec

153 Operative Builders
1531 Operative builders

154 Nonresidential Building Construction
1541 Industrial buildings and warehouses
1542 Nonresidential construction, nec

16 HEAVY CONSTRUCTION, EX. BUILDING

161 Highway and Street Construction
1611 Highway and street construction

162 Heavy Construction, Except Highway
1622 Bridge, tunnel, & elevated highway
1623 Water, sewer, and utility lines
1629 Heavy construction, nec

17 SPECIAL TRADE CONTRACTORS

171 Plumbing, Heating, Air-Conditioning
1711 Plumbing, heating, air-conditioning

172 Painting and Paper Hanging
1721 Painting and paper hanging

173 Electrical Work
1731 Electrical work

174 Masonry, Stonework, and Plastering
1741 Masonry and other stonework
1742 Plastering, drywall, and insulation
1743 Terrazzo, tile, marble, mosaic work

175 Carpentry and Floor Work
1751 Carpentry work
1752 Floor laying and floor work, nec

176 Roofing, Siding, and Sheet Metal Work
1761 Roofing, siding, and sheet metal work

177 Concrete Work
1771 Concrete work

178 Water Well Drilling
1781 Water well drilling

179 Misc. Special Trade Contractors
1791 Structural steel erection
1793 Glass and glazing work
1794 Excavation work
1795 Wrecking and demolition work
1796 Installing building equipment, nec
1799 Special trade contractors, nec

MANUFACTURING

20 FOOD AND KINDRED PRODUCTS

201 Meat Products
2011 Meat packing plants
2013 Sausages and other prepared meats
2015 Poultry slaughtering and processing

202 Dairy Products
2021 Creamery butter
2022 Cheese, natural and processed
2023 Dry, condensed, evaporated products
2024 Ice cream and frozen desserts
2026 Fluid milk

203 Preserved Fruits and Vegetables
2032 Canned specialties
2033 Canned fruits and vegetables
2034 Dehydrated fruits, vegetables, soups
2035 Pickles, sauces, and salad dressings
2037 Frozen fruits and vegetables
2038 Frozen specialties, nec

204 Grain Mill Products
2041 Flour and other grain mill products
2043 Cereal breakfast foods
2044 Rice milling
2045 Prepared flour mixes and doughs
2046 Wet corn milling
2047 Dog and cat food
2048 Prepared feeds, nec

205 Bakery Products
2051 Bread, cake, and related products
2052 Cookies and crackers
2053 Frozen bakery products, except bread

206 Sugar and Confectionery Products
2061 Raw cane sugar
2062 Cane sugar refining
2063 Beet sugar
2064 Candy & other confectionery products

2066 Chocolate and cocoa products
2067 Chewing gum
2068 Salted and roasted nuts and seeds

207 Fats and Oils
2074 Cottonseed oil mills
2075 Soybean oil mills
2076 Vegetable oil mills, nec
2077 Animal and marine fats and oils
2079 Edible fats and oils, nec

208 Beverages
2082 Malt beverages
2083 Malt
2084 Wines, brandy, and brandy spirits
2085 Distilled and blended liquors
2086 Bottled and canned soft drinks
2087 Flavoring extracts and syrups, nec

209 Misc. Food and Kindred Products
2091 Canned and cured fish and seafoods
2092 Fresh or frozen prepared fish
2095 Roasted coffee
2096 Potato chips and similar snacks
2097 Manufactured ice
2098 Macaroni and spaghetti
2099 Food preparations, nec

21 TOBACCO PRODUCTS

211 Cigarettes
2111 Cigarettes

212 Cigars
2121 Cigars

213 Chewing and Smoking Tobacco
2131 Chewing and smoking tobacco

214 Tobacco Stemming and Redrying
2141 Tobacco stemming and redrying

22 TEXTILE MILL PRODUCTS

221 Broadwoven Fabric Mills, Cotton
2211 Broadwoven fabric mills, cotton

222 Broadwoven Fabric Mills, Manmade
2221 Broadwoven fabric mills, manmade

223 Broadwoven Fabric Mills, Wool
2231 Broadwoven fabric mills, wool

224 Narrow Fabric Mills
2241 Narrow fabric mills

225 Knitting Mills
2251 Women's hosiery, except socks
2252 Hosiery, nec
2253 Knit outerwear mills
2254 Knit underwear mills
2257 Weft knit fabric mills
2258 Lace & warp knit fabric mills
2259 Knitting mills, nec

226 Textile Finishing, Except Wool
2261 Finishing plants, cotton
2262 Finishing plants, manmade
2269 Finishing plants, nec

227 Carpets and Rugs
2273 Carpets and rugs

228 Yarn and Thread Mills
2281 Yarn spinning mills
2282 Throwing and winding mills
2284 Thread mills

229 Miscellaneous Textile Goods
2295 Coated fabrics, not rubberized
2296 Tire cord and fabrics
2297 Nonwoven fabrics
2298 Cordage and twine
2299 Textile goods, nec

23 APPAREL AND OTHER TEXTILE PRODUCTS

231 Men's and Boys' Suits and Coats
2311 Men's and boys' suits and coats

232 Men's and Boys' Furnishings
2321 Men's and boys' shirts
2322 Men's & boys' underwear & nightwear
2323 Men's and boys' neckwear
2325 Men's and boys' trousers and slacks
2326 Men's and boys' work clothing
2329 Men's and boys' clothing, nec

233 Women's and Misses' Outerwear
2331 Women's & misses' blouses & shirts
2335 Women's, juniors', & misses' dresses
2337 Women's and misses' suits and coats
2339 Women's and misses' outerwear, nec

234 Women's and Children's Undergarments
2341 Women's and children's underwear
2342 Bras, girdles, and allied garments

235 Hats, Caps, and Millinery
2353 Hats, caps, and millinery

236 Girls' and Children's Outerwear
2361 Girls' & children's dresses, blouses
2369 Girls' and children's outerwear, nec

237 Fur Goods
2371 Fur goods

238 Miscellaneous Apparel and Accessories
2381 Fabric dress and work gloves
2384 Robes and dressing gowns
2385 Waterproof outerwear
2386 Leather and sheep-lined clothing
2387 Apparel belts
2389 Apparel and accessories, nec

239 Misc. Fabricated Textile Products
2391 Curtains and draperies
2392 Housefurnishings, nec
2393 Textile bags
2394 Canvas and related products
2395 Pleating and stitching
2396 Automotive and apparel trimmings
2397 Schiffli machine embroideries
2399 Fabricated textile products, nec

24 LUMBER AND WOOD PRODUCTS

241 Logging
2411 Logging

242 Sawmills and Planing Mills
2421 Sawmills and planing mills, general
2426 Hardwood dimension & flooring mills
2429 Special product sawmills, nec

243 Millwork, Plywood & Structural Members
2431 Millwork
2434 Wood kitchen cabinets
2435 Hardwood veneer and plywood
2436 Softwood veneer and plywood
2439 Structural wood members, nec

244 Wood Containers
2441 Nailed wood boxes and shook
2448 Wood pallets and skids
2449 Wood containers, nec

245 Wood Buildings and Mobile Homes
2451 Mobile homes
2452 Prefabricated wood buildings

249 Miscellaneous Wood Products
2491 Wood preserving
2493 Reconstituted wood products
2499 Wood products, nec

25 FURNITURE AND FIXTURES

251 Household Furniture
2511 Wood household furniture
2512 Upholstered household furniture
2514 Metal household furniture
2515 Mattresses and bedsprings
2517 Wood TV and radio cabinets
2519 Household furniture, nec

252 Office Furniture
2521 Wood office furniture
2522 Office furniture, except wood

253 Public Building & Related Furniture
2531 Public building & related furniture

254 Partitions and Fixtures
2541 Wood partitions and fixtures
2542 Partitions and fixtures, except wood

259 Miscellaneous Furniture and Fixtures
2591 Drapery hardware & blinds & shades
2599 Furniture and fixtures, nec

26 PAPER AND ALLIED PRODUCTS

261 Pulp Mills
2611 Pulp mills

262 Paper Mills
2621 Paper mills

263 Paperboard Mills
2631 Paperboard mills

265 Paperboard Containers and Boxes
2652 Setup paperboard boxes
2653 Corrugated and solid fiber boxes
2655 Fiber cans, drums & similar products
2656 Sanitary food containers
2657 Folding paperboard boxes

267 Misc. Converted Paper Products
2671 Paper coated & laminated, packaging
2672 Paper coated and laminated, nec
2673 Bags: plastics, laminated, & coated
2674 Bags: uncoated paper & multiwall
2675 Die-cut paper and board
2676 Sanitary paper products
2677 Envelopes
2678 Stationery products
2679 Converted paper products, nec

27 PRINTING AND PUBLISHING

271 Newspapers
2711 Newspapers

272 Periodicals
2721 Periodicals

273 Books
2731 Book publishing
2732 Book printing

274 Miscellaneous Publishing
2741 Miscellaneous publishing

275 Commercial Printing
2752 Commercial printing, lithographic
2754 Commercial printing, gravure
2759 Commercial printing, nec

276 Manifold Business Forms
2761 Manifold business forms

277 Greeting Cards
2771 Greeting cards

278 Blankbooks and Bookbinding
2782 Blankbooks and looseleaf binders
2789 Bookbinding and related work

279 Printing Trade Services
2791 Typesetting
2796 Platemaking services

28 CHEMICALS AND ALLIED PRODUCTS

281 Industrial Inorganic Chemicals
2812 Alkalies and chlorine
2813 Industrial gases
2816 Inorganic pigments
2819 Industrial inorganic chemicals, nec

282 Plastics Materials and Synthetics
2821 Plastics materials and resins
2822 Synthetic rubber
2823 Cellulosic manmade fibers
2824 Organic fibers, noncellulosic

283 Drugs
2833 Medicinals and botanicals
2834 Pharmaceutical preparations
2835 Diagnostic substances
2836 Biological products exc. diagnostic

284 Soap, Cleaners, and Toilet Goods
2841 Soap and other detergents
2842 Polishes and sanitation goods
2843 Surface active agents
2844 Toilet preparations

285 Paints and Allied Products
2851 Paints and allied products

286 Industrial Organic Chemicals
2861 Gum and wood chemicals
2865 Cyclic crudes and intermediates
2869 Industrial organic chemicals, nec

287 Agricultural Chemicals
2873 Nitrogenous fertilizers
2874 Phosphatic fertilizers
2875 Fertilizers, mixing only
2879 Agricultural chemicals, nec

289 Miscellaneous Chemical Products
2891 Adhesives and sealants
2892 Explosives
2893 Printing ink
2895 Carbon black
2899 Chemical preparations, nec

29 PETROLEUM AND COAL PRODUCTS

291 Petroleum Refining
2911 Petroleum refining

295 Asphalt Paving and Roofing Materials
2951 Asphalt paving mixtures and blocks
2952 Asphalt felts and coatings

299 Misc. Petroleum and Coal Products
2992 Lubricating oils and greases
2999 Petroleum and coal products, nec

30 RUBBER AND MISC. PLASTICS PRODUCTS

301 Tires and Inner Tubes
3011 Tires and inner tubes

302 Rubber and Plastics Footwear
3021 Rubber and plastics footwear

305 Hose & Belting & Gaskets & Packing
3052 Rubber & plastics hose & belting
3053 Gaskets, packing and sealing devices

306 Fabricated Rubber Products, NEC
3061 Mechanical rubber goods
3069 Fabricated rubber products, nec

308 Miscellaneous Plastics Products, NEC
3081 Unsupported plastics film & sheet
3082 Unsupported plastics profile shapes
3083 Laminated plastics plate & sheet
3084 Plastics pipe
3085 Plastics bottles
3086 Plastics foam products
3087 Custom compound purchased resins
3088 Plastics plumbing fixtures
3089 Plastics products, nec

31 LEATHER AND LEATHER PRODUCTS

311 Leather Tanning and Finishing
3111 Leather tanning and finishing

313 Footwear Cut Stock
3131 Footwear cut stock

314 Footwear, Except Rubber
3142 House slippers
3143 Men's footwear, except athletic
3144 Women's footwear, except athletic
3149 Footwear, except rubber, nec

315 Leather Gloves and Mittens
3151 Leather gloves and mittens

316 Luggage
3161 Luggage

317 Handbags and Personal Leather Goods
3171 Women's handbags and purses
3172 Personal leather goods, nec

319 Leather Goods, NEC
3199 Leather goods, nec

32 STONE, CLAY, AND GLASS PRODUCTS

321 Flat Glass
3211 Flat glass

322 Glass and Glassware, Pressed or Blown
3221 Glass containers
3229 Pressed and blown glass, nec

323 Products of Purchased Glass
3231 Products of purchased glass

324 Cement, Hydraulic
3241 Cement, hydraulic

325 Structural Clay Products
3251 Brick and structural clay tile
3253 Ceramic wall and floor tile
3255 Clay refractories
3259 Structural clay products, nec

326 Pottery and Related Products
3261 Vitreous plumbing fixtures
3262 Vitreous china table & kitchenware
3263 Semivitreous table & kitchenware
3264 Porcelain electrical supplies
3269 Pottery products, nec

327 Concrete, Gypsum, and Plaster Products
3271 Concrete block and brick
3272 Concrete products, nec
3273 Ready-mixed concrete
3274 Lime
3275 Gypsum products

328 Cut Stone and Stone Products
3281 Cut stone and stone products

329 Misc. Nonmetallic Mineral Products
3291 Abrasive products
3292 Asbestos products
3295 Minerals, ground or treated
3296 Mineral wool
3297 Nonclay refractories
3299 Nonmetallic mineral products, nec

33 PRIMARY METAL INDUSTRIES

331 Blast Furnace and Basic Steel Products
3312 Blast furnaces and steel mills
3313 Electrometallurgical products
3315 Steel wire and related products
3316 Cold finishing of steel shapes
3317 Steel pipe and tubes

332 Iron and Steel Foundries
3321 Gray and ductile iron foundries
3322 Malleable iron foundries
3324 Steel investment foundries
3325 Steel foundries, nec

333 **Primary Nonferrous Metals**
  3331 Primary copper
  3334 Primary aluminum
  3339 Primary nonferrous metals, nec

334 **Secondary Nonferrous Metals**
  3341 Secondary nonferrous metals

335 **Nonferrous Rolling and Drawing**
  3351 Copper rolling and drawing
  3353 Aluminum sheet, plate, and foil
  3354 Aluminum extruded products
  3355 Aluminum rolling and drawing, nec
  3356 Nonferrous rolling and drawing, nec
  3357 Nonferrous wiredrawing & insulating

336 **Nonferrous Foundries (Castings)**
  3363 Aluminum die-castings
  3364 Nonferrous die-casting exc. aluminum
  3365 Aluminum foundries
  3366 Copper foundries
  3369 Nonferrous foundries, nec

339 **Miscellaneous Primary Metal Products**
  3398 Metal heat treating
  3399 Primary metal products, nec

34 **FABRICATED METAL PRODUCTS**

341 **Metal Cans and Shipping Containers**
  3411 Metal cans
  3412 Metal barrels, drums, and pails

342 **Cutlery, Handtools, and Hardware**
  3421 Cutlery
  3423 Hand and edge tools, nec
  3425 Saw blades and handsaws
  3429 Hardware, nec

343 **Plumbing and Heating, Except Electric**
  3431 Metal sanitary ware
  3432 Plumbing fixture fittings and trim
  3433 Heating equipment, except electric

344 **Fabricated Structural Metal Products**
  3441 Fabricated structural metal
  3442 Metal doors, sash, and trim
  3443 Fabricated plate work (boiler shops)
  3444 Sheet metal work
  3446 Architectural metal work
  3448 Prefabricated metal buildings
  3449 Miscellaneous metal work

345 **Screw Machine Products, Bolts, Etc.**
  3451 Screw machine products
  3452 Bolts, nuts, rivets, and washers

346 **Metal Forgings and Stampings**
  3462 Iron and steel forgings
  3463 Nonferrous forgings
  3465 Automotive stampings
  3466 Crowns and closures
  3469 Metal stampings, nec

347 **Metal Services, NEC**
  3471 Plating and polishing
  3479 Metal coating and allied services

348 **Ordnance and Accessories, NEC**
  3482 Small arms ammunition
  3483 Ammunition, exc. for small arms, nec
  3484 Small arms
  3489 Ordnance and accessories, nec

349 **Misc. Fabricated Metal Products**
  3491 Industrial valves
  3492 Fluid power valves & hose fittings
  3493 Steel springs, except wire
  3494 Valves and pipe fittings, nec
  3495 Wire springs
  3496 Misc. fabricated wire products
  3497 Metal foil and leaf
  3498 Fabricated pipe and fittings
  3499 Fabricated metal products, nec

35 **INDUSTRIAL MACHINERY AND EQUIPMENT**

351 **Engines and Turbines**
  3511 Turbines and turbine generator sets
  3519 Internal combustion engines, nec

352 **Farm and Garden Machinery**
  3523 Farm machinery and equipment
  3524 Lawn and garden equipment

353 **Construction and Related Machinery**
  3531 Construction machinery
  3532 Mining machinery
  3533 Oil and gas field machinery
  3534 Elevators and moving stairways
  3535 Conveyors and conveying equipment
  3536 Hoists, cranes, and monorails
  3537 Industrial trucks and tractors

354 **Metalworking Machinery**
  3541 Machine tools, metal cutting types
  3542 Machine tools, metal forming types
  3543 Industrial patterns
  3544 Special dies, tools, jigs & fixtures
  3545 Machine tool accessories
  3546 Power-driven handtools
  3547 Rolling mill machinery
  3548 Welding apparatus
  3549 Metalworking machinery, nec

355 **Special Industry Machinery**
  3552 Textile machinery
  3553 Woodworking machinery
  3554 Paper industries machinery
  3555 Printing trades machinery
  3556 Food products machinery
  3559 Special industry machinery, nec

356 **General Industrial Machinery**
  3561 Pumps and pumping equipment
  3562 Ball and roller bearings
  3563 Air and gas compressors
  3564 Blowers and fans
  3565 Packaging machinery
  3566 Speed changers, drives, and gears
  3567 Industrial furnaces and ovens
  3568 Power transmission equipment, nec
  3569 General industrial machinery, nec

357 **Computer and Office Equipment**
  3571 Electronic computers
  3572 Computer storage devices
  3575 Computer terminals
  3577 Computer peripheral equipment, nec
  3578 Calculating and accounting equipment
  3579 Office machines, nec

358 **Refrigeration and Service Machinery**
  3581 Automatic vending machines
  3582 Commercial laundry equipment
  3585 Refrigeration and heating equipment
  3586 Measuring and dispensing pumps
  3589 Service industry machinery, nec

359 **Industrial Machinery, NEC**
  3592 Carburetors, pistons, rings, valves
  3593 Fluid power cylinders & actuators
  3594 Fluid power pumps and motors
  3596 Scales and balances, exc. laboratory
  3599 Industrial machinery, nec

36 **ELECTRONIC & OTHER ELECTRIC EQUIPMENT**

361 **Electric Distribution Equipment**
  3612 Transformers, except electronic
  3613 Switchgear and switchboard apparatus

362 **Electrical Industrial Apparatus**
  3621 Motors and generators

  3624 Carbon and graphite products
  3625 Relays and industrial controls
  3629 Electrical industrial apparatus, nec

363 **Household Appliances**
  3631 Household cooking equipment
  3632 Household refrigerators and freezers
  3633 Household laundry equipment
  3634 Electric housewares and fans
  3635 Household vacuum cleaners
  3639 Household appliances, nec

364 **Electric Lighting and Wiring Equipment**
  3641 Electric lamps
  3643 Current-carrying wiring devices
  3644 Noncurrent-carrying wiring devices
  3645 Residential lighting fixtures
  3646 Commercial lighting fixtures
  3647 Vehicular lighting equipment
  3648 Lighting equipment, nec

365 **Household Audio and Video Equipment**
  3651 Household audio and video equipment
  3652 Prerecorded records and tapes

366 **Communications Equipment**
  3661 Telephone and telegraph apparatus
  3663 Radio & TV communications equipment
  3669 Communications equipment, nec

367 **Electronic Components and Accessories**
  3671 Electron tubes
  3672 Printed circuit boards
  3674 Semiconductors and related devices
  3675 Electronic capacitors
  3676 Electronic resistors
  3677 Electronic coils and transformers
  3678 Electronic connectors
  3679 Electronic components, nec

369 **Misc. Electrical Equipment & Supplies**
  3691 Storage batteries
  3692 Primary batteries, dry and wet
  3694 Engine electrical equipment
  3695 Magnetic and optical recording media
  3699 Electrical equipment & supplies, nec

37 **TRANSPORTATION EQUIPMENT**

371 **Motor Vehicles and Equipment**
  3711 Motor vehicles and car bodies
  3713 Truck and bus bodies
  3714 Motor vehicle parts and accessories
  3715 Truck trailers
  3716 Motor homes

372 **Aircraft and Parts**
  3721 Aircraft
  3724 Aircraft engines and engine parts
  3728 Aircraft parts and equipment, nec

373 **Ship and Boat Building and Repairing**
  3731 Ship building and repairing
  3732 Boat building and repairing

374 **Railroad Equipment**
  3743 Railroad equipment

375 **Motorcycles, Bicycles, and Parts**
  3751 Motorcycles, bicycles, and parts

376 **Guided Missiles, Space Vehicles, Parts**
  3761 Guided missiles and space vehicles
  3764 Space propulsion units and parts
  3769 Space vehicle equipment, nec

379 **Miscellaneous Transportation Equipment**
  3792 Travel trailers and campers
  3795 Tanks and tank components
  3799 Transportation equipment, nec

38 INSTRUMENTS AND RELATED PRODUCTS

381 Search and Navigation Equipment
3812 Search and navigation equipment

382 Measuring and Controlling Devices
3821 Laboratory apparatus and furniture
3822 Environmental controls
3823 Process control instruments
3824 Fluid meters and counting devices
3825 Instruments to measure electricity
3826 Analytical instruments
3827 Optical instruments and lenses
3829 Measuring & controlling devices, nec

384 Medical Instruments and Supplies
3841 Surgical and medical instruments
3842 Surgical appliances and supplies
3843 Dental equipment and supplies
3844 X-ray apparatus and tubes
3845 Electromedical equipment

385 Ophthalmic Goods
3851 Ophthalmic goods

386 Photographic Equipment and Supplies
3861 Photographic equipment and supplies

387 Watches, Clocks, Watchcases & Parts
3873 Watches, clocks, watchcases & parts

39 MISCELLANEOUS MANUFACTURING INDUSTRIES

391 Jewelry, Silverware, and Plated Ware
3911 Jewelry, precious metal
3914 Silverware and plated ware
3915 Jewelers' materials & lapidary work

393 Musical Instruments
3931 Musical instruments

394 Toys and Sporting Goods
3942 Dolls and stuffed toys
3944 Games, toys, and children's vehicles
3949 Sporting and athletic goods, nec

395 Pens, Pencils, Office, & Art Supplies
3951 Pens and mechanical pencils
3952 Lead pencils and art goods
3953 Marking devices
3955 Carbon paper and inked ribbons

396 Costume Jewelry and Notions
3961 Costume jewelry
3965 Fasteners, buttons, needles, & pins

399 Miscellaneous Manufactures
3991 Brooms and brushes
3993 Signs and advertising specialities
3995 Burial caskets
3996 Hard surface floor coverings, nec
3999 Manufacturing industries, nec

TRANSPORTATION AND PUBLIC UTILITIES

40 RAILROAD TRANSPORTATION

401 Railroads
4011 Railroads, line-haul operating
4013 Switching and terminal services

41 LOCAL AND INTERURBAN PASSENGER TRANSIT

411 Local and Suburban Transportation
4111 Local and suburban transit
4119 Local passenger transportation, nec

412 Taxicabs
4121 Taxicabs

413 Intercity and Rural Bus Transportation
4131 Intercity & rural bus transportation

414 Bus Charter Service
4141 Local bus charter service
4142 Bus charter service, except local

415 School Buses
4151 School buses

417 Bus Terminal and Service Facilities
4173 Bus terminal and service facilities

42 TRUCKING AND WAREHOUSING

421 Trucking & Courier Services, Ex. Air
4212 Local trucking, without storage
4213 Trucking, except local
4214 Local trucking with storage
4215 Courier services, except by air

422 Public Warehousing and Storage
4221 Farm product warehousing and storage
4222 Refrigerated warehousing and storage
4225 General warehousing and storage
4226 Special warehousing and storage, nec

423 Trucking Terminal Facilities
4231 Trucking terminal facilities

43 U.S. POSTAL SERVICE

431 U.S. Postal Service
4311 U.S. Postal Service

44 WATER TRANSPORTATION

441 Deep Sea Foreign Trans. of Freight
4412 Deep sea foreign trans. of freight

442 Deep Sea Domestic Trans. of Freight
4424 Deep sea domestic trans. of freight

443 Freight Trans. on the Great Lakes
4432 Freight trans. on the Great Lakes

444 Water Transportation of Freight, NEC
4449 Water transportation of freight, nec

448 Water Transportation of Passengers
4481 Deep sea passenger trans., ex. ferry
4482 Ferries
4489 Water passenger transportation, nec

449 Water Transportation Services
4491 Marine cargo handling
4492 Towing and tugboat service
4493 Marinas
4499 Water transportation services, nec

45 TRANSPORTATION BY AIR

451 Air Transportation, Scheduled
4512 Air transportation, scheduled
4513 Air courier services

452 Air Transportation, Nonscheduled
4522 Air transportation, nonscheduled

458 Airports, Flying Fields, & Services
4581 Airports, flying fields, & services

46 PIPELINES, EXCEPT NATURAL GAS

461 Pipelines, Except Natural Gas
4612 Crude petroleum pipelines
4613 Refined petroleum pipelines
4619 Pipelines, nec

47 TRANSPORTATION SERVICES

472 Passenger Transportation Arrangement
4724 Travel agencies
4725 Tour operators
4729 Passenger transport arrangement, nec

473 Freight Transportation Arrangement
4731 Freight transportation arrangement

474 Rental of Railroad Cars
4741 Rental of railroad cars

478 Miscellaneous Transportation Services
4783 Packing and crating
4785 Inspection & fixed facilities
4789 Transportation services, nec

48 COMMUNICATIONS

481 Telephone Communications
4812 Radiotelephone communications
4813 Telephone communications, exc. radio

482 Telegraph & Other Communications
4822 Telegraph & other communications

483 Radio and Television Broadcasting
4832 Radio broadcasting stations
4833 Television broadcasting stations

484 Cable and Other Pay TV Services
4841 Cable and other pay TV services

489 Communications Services, NEC
4899 Communications services, nec

49 ELECTRIC, GAS, AND SANITARY SERVICES

491 Electric Services
4911 Electric services

492 Gas Production and Distribution
4922 Natural gas transmission
4923 Gas transmission and distribution
4924 Natural gas distribution
4925 Gas production and/or distribution

493 Combination Utility Services
4931 Electric and other services combined
4932 Gas and other services combined
4939 Combination utilities, nec

494 Water Supply
4941 Water supply

495 Sanitary Services
4952 Sewerage systems
4953 Refuse systems
4959 Sanitary services, nec

496 Steam and Air-Conditioning Supply
4961 Steam and air-conditioning supply

497 Irrigation Systems
4971 Irrigation systems

WHOLESALE TRADE

50 WHOLESALE TRADE—DURABLE GOODS

501 Motor Vehicles, Parts, and Supplies
5012 Automobiles and other motor vehicles
5013 Motor vehicle supplies and new parts
5014 Tires and tubes
5015 Motor vehicle parts, used

502 Furniture and Homefurnishings
5021 Furniture
5023 Homefurnishings

503 Lumber and Construction Materials
5031 Lumber, plywood, and millwork
5032 Brick, stone, & related materials
5033 Roofing, siding, & insulation
5039 Construction materials, nec

504 Professional & Commercial Equipment
5043 Photographic equipment and supplies
5044 Office equipment
5045 Computers, peripherals & software

5046 Commercial equipment, nec
5047 Medical and hospital equipment
5048 Ophthalmic goods
5049 Professional equipment, nec

505 Metals and Minerals, Except Petroleum
5051 Metals service centers and offices
5052 Coal and other minerals and ores

506 Electrical Goods
5063 Electrical apparatus and equipment
5064 Electrical appliances, TV & radios
5065 Electronic parts and equipment

507 Hardware, Plumbing & Heating Equipment
5072 Hardware
5074 Plumbing & hydronic heating supplies
5075 Warm air heating & air-conditioning
5078 Refrigeration equipment and supplies

508 Machinery, Equipment, and Supplies
5082 Construction and mining machinery
5083 Farm and garden machinery
5084 Industrial machinery and equipment
5085 Industrial supplies
5087 Service establishment equipment
5088 Transportation equipment & supplies

509 Miscellaneous Durable Goods
5091 Sporting & recreational goods
5092 Toys and hobby goods and supplies
5093 Scrap and waste materials
5094 Jewelry & precious stones
5099 Durable goods, nec

51 WHOLESALE TRADE— NONDURABLE GOODS

511 Paper and Paper Products
5111 Printing and writing paper
5112 Stationery and office supplies
5113 Industrial & personal service paper

512 Drugs, Proprietaries, and Sundries
5122 Drugs, proprietaries, and sundries

513 Apparel, Piece Goods, and Notions
5131 Piece goods & notions
5136 Men's and boys' clothing
5137 Women's and children's clothing
5139 Footwear

514 Groceries and Related Products
5141 Groceries, general line
5142 Packaged frozen foods
5143 Dairy products, exc. dried or canned
5144 Poultry and poultry products
5145 Confectionery
5146 Fish and seafoods
5147 Meats and meat products
5148 Fresh fruits and vegetables
5149 Groceries and related products, nec

515 Farm-Product Raw Materials
5153 Grain and field beans
5154 Livestock
5159 Farm-product raw materials, nec

516 Chemicals and Allied Products
5162 Plastics materials & basic shapes
5169 Chemicals & allied products, nec

517 Petroleum and Petroleum Products
5171 Petroleum bulk stations & terminals
5172 Petroleum products, nec

518 Beer, Wine, and Distilled Beverages
5181 Beer and ale
5182 Wine and distilled beverages

519 Misc. Nondurable Goods
5191 Farm supplies

5192 Books, periodicals, & newspapers
5193 Flowers & florists' supplies
5194 Tobacco and tobacco products
5198 Paints, varnishes, and supplies
5199 Nondurable goods, nec

RETAIL TRADE

52 BUILDING MATERIALS & GARDEN SUPPLIES

521 Lumber and Other Building Materials
5211 Lumber and other building materials

523 Paint, Glass, and Wallpaper Stores
5231 Paint, glass, and wallpaper stores

525 Hardware Stores
5251 Hardware stores

526 Retail Nurseries and Garden Stores
5261 Retail nurseries and garden stores

527 Mobile Home Dealers
5271 Mobile home dealers

53 GENERAL MERCHANDISE STORES

531 Department Stores
5311 Department stores

533 Variety Stores
5331 Variety stores

539 Misc. General Merchandise Stores
5399 Misc. general merchandise stores

54 FOOD STORES

541 Grocery Stores
5411 Grocery stores

542 Meat and Fish Markets
5421 Meat and fish markets

543 Fruit and Vegetable Markets
5431 Fruit and vegetable markets

544 Candy, Nut, and Confectionery Stores
5441 Candy, nut, and confectionery stores

545 Dairy Products Stores
5451 Dairy products stores

546 Retail Bakeries
5461 Retail bakeries

549 Miscellaneous Food Stores
5499 Miscellaneous food stores

55 AUTOMOTIVE DEALERS & SERVICE STATIONS

551 New and Used Car Dealers
5511 New and used car dealers

552 Used Car Dealers
5521 Used car dealers

553 Auto and Home Supply Stores
5531 Auto and home supply stores

554 Gasoline Service Stations
5541 Gasoline service stations

555 Boat Dealers
5551 Boat dealers

556 Recreational Vehicle Dealers
5561 Recreational vehicle dealers

557 Motorcycle Dealers
5571 Motorcycle dealers

559 Automotive Dealers, NEC
5599 Automotive dealers, nec

56 APPAREL AND ACCESSORY STORES

561 Men's & Boys' Clothing Stores
5611 Men's & boys' clothing stores

562 Women's Clothing Stores
5621 Women's clothing stores

563 Women's Accessory & Specialty Stores
5632 Women's accessory & specialty stores

564 Children's and Infants' Wear Stores
5641 Children's and infants' wear stores

565 Family Clothing Stores
5651 Family clothing stores

566 Shoe Stores
5661 Shoe stores

569 Misc. Apparel & Accessory Stores
5699 Misc. apparel & accessory stores

57 FURNITURE AND HOMEFURNISHINGS STORES

571 Furniture and Homefurnishings Stores
5712 Furniture stores
5713 Floor covering stores
5714 Drapery and upholstery stores
5719 Misc. homefurnishings stores

572 Household Appliance Stores
5722 Household appliance stores

573 Radio, Television, & Computer Stores
5731 Radio, TV, & electronic stores
5734 Computer and software stores
5735 Record & prerecorded tape stores
5736 Musical instrument stores

58 EATING AND DRINKING PLACES

581 Eating and Drinking Places
5812 Eating places
5813 Drinking places

59 MISCELLANEOUS RETAIL

591 Drug Stores and Proprietary Stores
5912 Drug stores and proprietary stores

592 Liquor Stores
5921 Liquor stores

593 Used Merchandise Stores
5932 Used merchandise stores

594 Miscellaneous Shopping Goods Stores
5941 Sporting goods and bicycle shops
5942 Book stores
5943 Stationery stores
5944 Jewelry stores
5945 Hobby, toy, and game shops
5946 Camera & photographic supply stores
5947 Gift, novelty, and souvenir shops
5948 Luggage and leather goods stores
5949 Sewing, needlework, and piece goods

596 Nonstore Retailers
5961 Catalog and mail-order houses
5962 Merchandising machine operators
5963 Direct selling establishments

598 Fuel Dealers
5983 Fuel oil dealers
5984 Liquefied petroleum gas dealers
5989 Fuel dealers, nec

599 Retail Stores, NEC
5992 Florists
5993 Tobacco stores and stands
5994 News dealers and newsstands
5995 Optical goods stores
5999 Miscellaneous retail stores, nec

FINANCE, INSURANCE, AND REAL ESTATE

60 DEPOSITORY INSTITUTIONS

601 Central Reserve Depositories
6011 Federal reserve banks
6019 Central reserve depository, nec

602 Commercial Banks
6021 National commercial banks
6022 State commercial banks
6029 Commercial banks, nec

603 Savings Institutions
6035 Federal savings institutions
6036 Savings institutions, except federal

606 Credit Unions
6061 Federal credit unions
6062 State credit unions

608 Foreign Bank & Branches & Agencies
6081 Foreign bank & branches & agencies
6082 Foreign trade & international banks

609 Functions Closely Related to Banking
6091 Nondeposit trust facilities
6099 Functions related to deposit banking

61 NONDEPOSITORY INSTITUTIONS

611 Federal & Fed.-Sponsored Credit
6111 Federal & fed.-sponsored credit

614 Personal Credit Institutions
6141 Personal credit institutions

615 Business Credit Institutions
6153 Short-term business credit
6159 Misc. business credit institutions

616 Mortgage Bankers and Brokers
6162 Mortgage bankers and correspondents
6163 Loan brokers

62 SECURITY AND COMMODITY BROKERS

621 Security Brokers and Dealers
6211 Security brokers and dealers

622 Commodity Contracts Brokers, Dealers
6221 Commodity contracts brokers, dealers

623 Security and Commodity Exchanges
6231 Security and commodity exchanges

628 Security and Commodity Services
6282 Investment advice
6289 Security & commodity services, nec

63 INSURANCE CARRIERS

631 Life Insurance
6311 Life insurance

632 Medical Service and Health Insurance
6321 Accident and health insurance
6324 Hospital and medical service plans

633 Fire, Marine, and Casualty Insurance
6331 Fire, marine, and casualty insurance

635 Surety Insurance
6351 Surety insurance

636 Title Insurance
6361 Title insurance

637 Pension, Health, and Welfare Funds
6371 Pension, health, and welfare funds

639 Insurance Carriers, NEC
6399 Insurance carriers, nec

64 INSURANCE AGENTS, BROKERS, & SERVICE

641 Insurance Agents, Brokers, & Service
6411 Insurance agents, brokers, & service

65 REAL ESTATE

651 Real Estate Operators and Lessors
6512 Nonresidential building operators
6513 Apartment building operators
6514 Dwelling operators, exc. apartments
6515 Mobile home site operators

6517 Railroad property lessors
6519 Real property lessors, nec

653 Real Estate Agents and Managers
6531 Real estate agents and managers

654 Title Abstract Offices
6541 Title abstract offices

655 Subdividers and Developers
6552 Subdividers and developers, nec
6553 Cemetery subdividers and developers

67 HOLDING AND OTHER INVESTMENT OFFICES

671 Holding Offices
6712 Bank holding companies
6719 Holding companies, nec

672 Investment Offices
6722 Management investment, open-end
6726 Investment offices, nec

673 Trusts
6732 Educational, religious, etc. trusts
6733 Trusts, nec

679 Miscellaneous Investing
6792 Oil royalty traders
6794 Patent owners and lessors
6798 Real estate investment trusts
6799 Investors, nec

SERVICES

70 HOTELS AND OTHER LODGING PLACES

701 Hotels and Motels
7011 Hotels and motels

702 Rooming and Boarding Houses
7021 Rooming and boarding houses

703 Camps and Recreational Vehicle Parks
7032 Sporting and recreational camps
7033 Trailer parks and campsites

704 Membership-Basis Organization Hotels
7041 Membership-basis organization hotels

72 PERSONAL SERVICES

721 Laundry, Cleaning, & Garment Services
7211 Power Laundries, family & commercial
7212 Garment pressing & cleaners' agents
7213 Linen supply
7215 Coin-operated laundries and cleaning
7216 Drycleaning plants, except rug
7217 Carpet and upholstery cleaning
7218 Industrial launderers
7219 Laundry and garment services, nec

722 Photographic Studios, Portrait
7221 Photographic studios, portrait

723 Beauty Shops
7231 Beauty shops

724 Barber Shops
7241 Barber shops

725 Shoe Repair and Shoeshine Parlors
7251 Shoe repair and shoeshine parlors

726 Funeral Service and Crematories
7261 Funeral service and crematories

729 Miscellaneous Personal Services
7291 Tax return preparation services
7299 Miscellaneous personal services, nec

73 BUSINESS SERVICES

731 Advertising
7311 Advertising agencies

7312 Outdoor advertising services
7313 Radio, TV, publisher representatives
7319 Advertising, nec

732 Credit Reporting and Collection
7322 Adjustment & collection services
7323 Credit reporting services

733 Mailing, Reproduction, Stenographic
7331 Direct mail advertising services
7334 Photocopying & duplicating services
7335 Commercial photography
7336 Commercial art and graphic design
7338 Secretarial & court reporting

734 Services to Buildings
7342 Disinfecting & pest control services
7349 Building maintenance services, nec

735 Misc. Equipment Rental & Leasing
7352 Medical equipment rental
7353 Heavy construction equipment rental
7359 Equipment rental & leasing, nec

736 Personnel Supply Services
7361 Employment agencies
7363 Help supply services

737 Computer and Data Processing Services
7371 Computer programming services
7372 Prepackaged software
7373 Computer integrated systems design
7374 Data processing and preparation
7375 Information retrieval services
7376 Computer facilities management
7377 Computer rental & leasing
7378 Computer maintenance & repair
7379 Computer related services, nec

738 Miscellaneous Business Services
7381 Detective & armored car services
7382 Security systems services
7383 News syndicates
7384 Photofinishing laboratories
7389 Business services, nec

75 AUTO REPAIR, SERVICES, AND PARKING

751 Automotive Rentals, No Drivers
7513 Truck rental and leasing, no drivers
7514 Passenger car rental
7515 Passenger car leasing
7519 Utility trailer rental

752 Automobile Parking
7521 Automobile parking

753 Automotive Repair Shops
7532 Top & body repair & paint shops
7533 Auto exhaust system repair shops
7534 Tire retreading and repair shops
7536 Automotive glass replacement shops
7537 Automotive transmission repair shops
7538 General automotive repair shops
7539 Automotive repair shops, nec

754 Automotive Services, Except Repair
7542 Carwashes
7549 Automotive services, nec

76 MISCELLANEOUS REPAIR SERVICES

762 Electrical Repair Shops
7622 Radio and television repair
7623 Refrigeration service and repair
7629 Electrical repair shops, nec

763 Watch, Clock, and Jewelry Repair
7631 Watch, clock, and jewelry repair

764 Reupholstery and Furniture Repair
7641 Reupholstery and furniture repair

769 Miscellaneous Repair Shops
7692 Welding repair
7694 Armature rewinding shops
7699 Repair services, nec

78 MOTION PICTURES

781 Motion Picture Production & Services
7812 Motion picture & video production
7819 Services allied to motion pictures

782 Motion Picture Distribution & Services
7822 Motion picture and tape distribution
7829 Motion picture distribution services

783 Motion Picture Theaters
7832 Motion picture theaters, ex drive-in
7833 Drive-in motion picture theaters

784 Video Tape Rental
7841 Video tape rental

79 AMUSEMENT & RECREATION SERVICES

791 Dance Studios, Schools, and Halls
7911 Dance studios, schools, and halls

792 Producers, Orchestras, Entertainers
7922 Theatrical producers and services
7929 Entertainers & entertainment groups

793 Bowling Centers
7933 Bowling centers

794 Commercial Sports
7941 Sports clubs, managers, & promoters
7948 Racing, including track operation

799 Misc. Amusement, Recreation Services
7991 Physical fitness facilities
7992 Public golf courses
7993 Coin-operated amusement devices
7996 Amusement parks
7997 Membership sports & recreation clubs
7999 Amusement and recreation, nec

80 HEALTH SERVICES

801 Offices & Clinics of Medical Doctors
8011 Offices & clinics of medical doctors

802 Offices and Clinics of Dentists
8021 Offices and clinics of dentists

803 Offices of Osteopathic Physicians
8031 Offices of osteopathic physicians

804 Offices of Other Health Practitioners
8041 Offices and clinics of chiropractors
8042 Offices and clinics of optometrists
8043 Offices and clinics of podiatrists
8049 Offices of health practitioners, nec

805 Nursing and Personal Care Facilities
8051 Skilled nursing care facilities
8052 Intermediate care facilities
8059 Nursing and personal care, nec

806 Hospitals
8062 General medical & surgical hospitals
8063 Psychiatric hospitals
8069 Specialty hospitals exc. psychiatric

807 Medical and Dental Laboratories
8071 Medical laboratories
8072 Dental laboratories

808 Home Health Care Services
8082 Home health care services

809 Health and Allied Services, NEC
8092 Kidney dialysis centers
8093 Specialty outpatient clinics, nec
8099 Health and allied services, nec

81 LEGAL SERVICES

811 Legal Services
8111 Legal services

82 EDUCATIONAL SERVICES

821 Elementary and Secondary Schools
8211 Elementary and secondary schools

822 Colleges and Universities
8221 Colleges and universities
8222 Junior colleges

823 Libraries
8231 Libraries

824 Vocational Schools
8243 Data processing schools
8244 Business and secretarial schools
8249 Vocational schools, nec

829 Schools & Educational Services, NEC
8299 Schools & educational services, nec

83 SOCIAL SERVICES

832 Individual and Family Services
8322 Individual and family services

833 Job Training and Related Services
8331 Job training and related services

835 Child Day Care Services
8351 Child day care services

836 Residential Care
8361 Residential care

839 Social Services, NEC
8399 Social services, nec

84 MUSEUMS, BOTANICAL, ZOOLOGICAL GARDENS

841 Museums and Art Galleries
8412 Museums and art galleries

842 Botanical and Zoological Gardens
8422 Botanical and zoological gardens

86 MEMBERSHIP ORGANIZATIONS

861 Business Associations
8611 Business associations

862 Professional Organizations
8621 Professional organizations

863 Labor Organizations
8631 Labor organizations

864 Civic and Social Associations
8641 Civic and social associations

865 Political Organizations
8651 Political organizations

866 Religious Organizations
8661 Religious organizations

869 Membership Organizations, NEC
8699 Membership organizations, nec

87 ENGINEERING & MANAGEMENT SERVICES

871 Engineering & Architectural Services
8711 Engineering services
8712 Architectural services
8713 Surveying services

872 Accounting, Auditing, & Bookkeeping
8721 Accounting, auditing, & bookkeeping

873 Research and Testing Services
8731 Commercial physical research
8732 Commercial nonphysical research
8733 Noncommercial research organizations
8734 Testing laboratories

874 Management and Public Relations
8741 Management services
8742 Management consulting services
8743 Public relations services
8744 Facilities support services
8748 Business consulting, nec

88 PRIVATE HOUSEHOLDS

881 Private Households
8811 Private households

89 SERVICES, NEC

899 Services, NEC
8999 Services, nec

PUBLIC ADMINISTRATION

91 EXECUTIVE, LEGISLATIVE, AND GENERAL

911 Executive Offices
9111 Executive offices

912 Legislative Bodies
9121 Legislative bodies

913 Executive and Legislative Combined
9131 Executive and legislative combined

919 General Government, NEC
9199 General government, nec

92 JUSTICE, PUBLIC ORDER, AND SAFETY

921 Courts
9211 Courts

922 Public Order and Safety
9221 Police protection
9222 Legal counsel and prosecution
9223 Correctional institutions
9224 Fire protection
9229 Public order and safety, nec

93 FINANCE, TAXATION, & MONETARY POLICY

931 Finance, Taxation, & Monetary Policy
9311 Finance, taxation, & monetary policy

94 ADMINISTRATION OF HUMAN RESOURCES

941 Admin. of Educational Programs
9411 Admin. of educational programs

943 Admin. of Public Health Programs
9431 Admin. of public health programs

944 Admin. of Social & Manpower Programs
9441 Admin. of social & manpower programs

945 Administration of Veterans' Affairs
9451 Administration of veterans' affairs

95 ENVIRONMENTAL QUALITY AND HOUSING

951 Environmental Quality
9511 Air, water, & solid waste management
9512 Land, mineral, wildlife conservation

953 Housing and Urban Development
9531 Housing programs
9532 Urban and community development

96 ADMINISTRATION OF ECONOMIC PROGRAMS

961 Admin. of General Economic Programs
9611 Admin. of general economic programs

962 Regulation, Admin. of Transportation
9621 Regulation, admin. of transportation

963 Regulation, Admin. of Utilities
9631 Regulation, admin. of utilities

964 Regulation of Agricultural Marketing
9641 Regulation of agricultural marketing

965 Regulation Misc. Commercial Sectors
9651 Regulation misc. commercial sectors

966 Space Research and Technology
9661 Space research and technology

97 NATIONAL SECURITY AND INTL. AFFAIRS

971 National Security
9711 National security

972 International Affairs
9721 International affairs

NONCLASSIFIABLE ESTABLISHMENTS

99 NONCLASSIFIABLE ESTABLISHMENTS

999 Nonclassifiable Establishments
9999 Nonclassifiable establishments

Standard Occupational Classification

The Standard Occupational Classification was developed to provide a standardized system of job descriptions and classification codes for all occupations performed for pay or profit, for use in the presentation and analysis of statistical data about occupations. The classification system is at 4 levels, with division titles, 2- and 3-digit occupation group codes, and 4-digit unit group codes. The classification was used in the 1980 Census of Population and in Labor Department programs.

The classification is presented in the revised 1980 *Standard Occupational Classification Manual,* from which the following list is taken (for description, see ASI 1981 Annual, 2088-2).

Occupation
Group Code

EXECUTIVE, ADMINISTRATIVE AND MANAGERIAL OCCUPATIONS

11 **Officials and Administrators, Public Administration**
- 111 Legislators
- 112 Chief Executives and General Administrators
- 113 Officials and Administrators, Government Agencies

12-13 **Officials and Administrators, Other**
- 121 General Managers and Other Top Executives
- 122 Financial Managers
- 123 Personnel and Labor Relations Managers
- 124 Purchasing Managers
- 125 Managers; Marketing, Advertising, and Public Relations
- 126 Managers; Engineering, Mathematics, and Natural Sciences
- 127 Managers; Social Sciences and Related Fields
- 128 Administrators; Education and Related Fields
- 131 Managers; Medicine and Health
- 132 Production Managers, Industrial
- 133 Construction Managers
- 134 Public Utilities Managers
- 135 Managers; Service Organizations
- 136 Managers; Mining, Quarrying, Well Drilling, and Similar Operations
- 137 Managers; Administrative Services
- 139 Officials and Administrators; Other, Not Elsewhere Classified

14 **Management Related Occupations**
- 141 Accountants, Auditors, and Other Financial Specialists
- 142 Management Analysts
- 143 Personnel, Training, and Labor Relations Specialists
- 144 Purchasing Agents and Buyers
- 145 Business and Promotion Agents
- 147 Inspectors and Compliance Officers
- 149 Management Related Occupations, Not Elsewhere Classified

ENGINEERS, SURVEYORS AND ARCHITECTS

16 **Engineers, Surveyors and Architects**
- 161 Architects
- 162-3 Engineers
- 164 Surveyors and Mapping Scientists

NATURAL SCIENTISTS AND MATHEMATICIANS

17 **Computer, Mathematical, and Operations Research Occupations**
- 171 Computer Scientists
- 172 Operations and Systems Researchers and Analysts
- 173 Mathematical Scientists

18 **Natural Scientists**
- 184 Physical Scientists
- 185 Life Scientists

SOCIAL SCIENTISTS, SOCIAL WORKERS, RELIGIOUS WORKERS, AND LAWYERS

19 **Social Scientists and Urban Planners**
- 191 Social Scientists
- 192 Urban and Regional Planners

20 **Social, Recreation, and Religious Workers**
- 203 Social and Recreation Workers
- 204 Religious Workers

21 **Lawyers and Judges**
- 211 Lawyers
- 212 Judges

TEACHERS, LIBRARIANS, AND COUNSELORS

22 **Teachers; College, University and Other Postsecondary Institution**

23 **Teachers, Except Postsecondary Institution**
- 231 Prekindergarten and Kindergarten Teachers
- 232 Elementary School Teachers
- 233 Secondary School Teachers
- 235 Teachers; Special Education
- 236 Instructional Coordinators
- 239 Adult Education and Other Teachers, Not Elsewhere Classified

24 **Vocational and Educational Counselors**

25 **Librarians, Archivists, and Curators**
- 251 Librarians
- 252 Archivists and Curators

HEALTH DIAGNOSING AND TREATING PRACTITIONERS

26 **Physicians and Dentists**
- 261 Physicians
- 262 Dentists

27 **Veterinarians**

28 **Other Health Diagnosing and Treating Practitioners**
- 281 Optometrists
- 283 Podiatrists
- 289 Health Diagnosing and Treating Practitioners, Not Elsewhere Classified

REGISTERED NURSES, PHARMACISTS, DIETITIANS, THERAPISTS, AND PHYSICIAN'S ASSISTANTS

29 **Registered Nurses**

30 **Pharmacists, Dietitians, Therapists, and Physician's Assistants**
- 301 Pharmacists
- 302 Dietitians
- 303 Therapists
- 304 Physician's Assistants

WRITERS, ARTISTS, ENTERTAINERS, AND ATHLETES

32 **Writers, Artists, Performers, and Related Workers**
- 321 Authors
- 322 Designers
- 323 Musicians and Composers
- 324 Actors and Directors
- 325 Painters, Sculptors, Craft-Artists and Artist-Printmakers
- 326 Photographers
- 327 Dancers
- 328 Performers, Not Elsewhere Classified
- 329 Writers, Artists, and Related Workers; Not Elsewhere Classified

33 **Editors, Reporters, Public Relations Specialists, and Announcers**
- 331 Editors and Reporters
- 332 Public Relations Specialists and Publicity Writers
- 333 Radio, Television and Other Announcers

34 **Athletes and Related Workers**

HEALTH TECHNOLOGISTS AND TECHNICIANS

36 Health Technologists and Technicians
362 Clinical Laboratory Technologists and Technicians
363 Dental Hygienists
364 Health Record Technologists and Technicians
365 Radiologic Technologists and Technicians
366 Licensed Practical Nurses
369 Health Technologists and Technicians, Not Elsewhere Classified

TECHNOLOGISTS AND TECHNICIANS, EXCEPT HEALTH

37 Engineering and Related Technologists and Technicians
371 Engineering Technologists and Technicians
372 Drafting Occupations
373 Surveying and Mapping Technicians

38 Science Technologists and Technicians
382 Biological Technologists and Technicians, Except Health
383 Chemical and Nuclear Technologists and Technicians
384 Mathematical Technicians
389 Science Technologists and Technicians, Not Elsewhere Classified

39 Technicians; Except Health, Engineering, and Science
392 Air Traffic Controllers
393 Radio and Related Operators
396 Legal Technicians
397 Programmers
398 Technical Writers
399 Technicians, Not Elsewhere Classified

MARKETING AND SALES OCCUPATIONS

40 Supervisors; Marketing and Sales Occupations
401 Supervisors; Sales Occupations, Insurance, Real Estate, and Business Services
402 Supervisors; Sales Occupations, Commodities Except Retail
403 Supervisors; Sales Occupations, Retail

41 Insurance, Securities, Real Estate, and Business Service Sales Occupations
412 Insurance, Real Estate, and Securities Sales Occupations
415 Business Service Sales Occupations

42 Sales Occupations, Commodities Except Retail
421 Sales Engineers
423 Technical Sales Workers and Service Advisors
424 Sales Representatives

43 Sales Occupations, Retail
434-5 Salespersons, Commodities
436 Sales Occupations; Other

44 Sales Related Occupations
444 Appraisers and Related Occupations
445 Demonstrators, Promoters, and Models
446 Shoppers
447 Auctioneers
449 Sales Occupations; Other, Not Elsewhere Classified

ADMINISTRATIVE SUPPORT OCCUPATIONS, INCLUDING CLERICAL

45 Supervisors; Administrative Support Occupations, Including Clerical
46-47 Administrative Support Occupations, Including Clerical
461 Computer and Peripheral Equipment Operators
462 Secretaries, Stenographers and Typists
463 General Office Occupations
464 Information Clerks
466 Correspondence Clerks and Order Clerks
469 Record Clerks
471 Financial Record Processing Occupations
472 Duplicating, Mail and Other Office Machine Operators
473 Communications Equipment Operators
474 Mail and Message Distributing Occupations
475 Material Recording, Scheduling, and Distributing Clerks
478 Adjusters, Investigators, and Collectors
479 Miscellaneous Administrative Support Occupations, Including Clerical

SERVICE OCCUPATIONS

50 Private Household Occupations
502 Day Workers
503 Launderers and Ironers
504 Cooks, Private Household
505 Housekeepers and Butlers
506 Child Care Workers, Private Household
507 Private Household Cleaners and Servants
509 Private Household Occupations, Not Elsewhere Classified

51 Protective Service Occupations
511 Supervisors; Service Occupations, Protective
512 Firefighting and Fire Prevention Occupations
513 Police and Detectives
514 Guards

52 Service Occupations, Except Private Household and Protective
521 Food and Beverage Preparation and Service Occupations
523 Health Service Occupations
524 Cleaning and Building Service Occupations, Except Private Household
525-6 Personal Service Occupations

AGRICULTURAL, FORESTRY AND FISHING OCCUPATIONS

55 Farm Operators and Managers
551 Farmers (Working Proprietors)
552 Farm Managers

56 Other Agricultural and Related Occupations
561 Farm Occupations, Except Managerial
562 Related Agricultural Occupations

57 Forestry and Logging Occupations
571 Supervisors; Forestry and Logging Workers
572 Forestry Workers, Except Logging
573 Timber Cutting and Related Occupations
579 Logging Occupations, Not Elsewhere Classified

58 Fishers, Hunters, and Trappers
583 Fishers
584 Hunters and Trappers

MECHANICS AND REPAIRERS

60 Supervisors; Mechanics and Repairers
61 Mechanics and Repairers
611 Vehicle and Mobile Equipment Mechanics and Repairers
613 Industrial Machinery Repairers
614 Machinery Maintenance Occupations
615 Electrical and Electronic Equipment Repairers
616 Heating, Air-Conditioning, and Refrigeration Mechanics
617 Miscellaneous Mechanics and Repairers

CONSTRUCTION AND EXTRACTIVE OCCUPATIONS

63 Supervisors; Construction and Extractive Occupations
631 Supervisors; Construction
632 Supervisors; Extractive Occupations

64 Construction Trades
641 Brickmasons, Stonemasons, and Hard Tile Setters
642 Carpenters and Related Workers
643 Electricians and Power Transmission Installers
644 Painters, Paperhangers, and Plasterers
645 Plumbers, Pipefitters and Steamfitters
646-7 Other Construction Trades

65 Extractive Occupations
652 Drillers, Oil Well
653 Explosive Workers
654 Mining Machine Operators
656 Extractive Occupations, Not Elsewhere Classified

PRECISION PRODUCTION OCCUPATIONS

67　**Supervisors; Precision Production Occupations**

68　**Precision Production Occupations**
681-2　Precision Metal Workers
683　Precision Woodworkers
684　Precision Printing Occupations
685　Precision Textile, Apparel and Furnishings Workers
686　Precision Workers; Assorted Materials
687　Precision Food Production Occupations
688　Precision Inspectors, Testers, and Related Workers

69　**Plant and System Operators**
691　Water and Sewage Treatment Plant Operators
692　Gas Plant Operators
693　Power Plant Operators
694　Chemical Plant Operators
695　Petroleum Plant Operators
696　Miscellaneous Plant or System Operators

PRODUCTION WORKING OCCUPATIONS

71　**Supervisors; Production Occupations**
73-74　**Machine Setup Operators**
731-2　Metalworking and Plastic Working Machine Setup Operators
733　Metal Fabricating Machine Setup Operators
734　Metal and Plastic Processing Machine Setup Operators
743　Woodworking Machine Setup Operators
744　Printing Machine Setup Operators
745　Textile Machine Setup Operators
746-7　Assorted Materials: Machine Setup Operators

75-76　**Machine Operators and Tenders**
751-2　Metalworking and Plastic Working Machine Operators and Tenders
753　Metal Fabricating Machine Operators and Tenders
754　Metal and Plastic Processing Machine Operators and Tenders
763　Woodworking Machine Operators and Tenders
764　Printing Machine Operators and Tenders
765　Textile, Apparel and Furnishings Machine Operators and Tenders
766-7　Machine Operators and Tenders; Assorted Materials

77　**Fabricators, Assemblers, and Hand Working Occupations**
771　Welders and Solderers
772　Assemblers
774　Fabricators, Not Elsewhere Classified
775　Hand Working Occupations

78　**Production Inspectors, Testers, Samplers, and Weighers**
782　Production Inspectors, Checkers and Examiners
783　Production Testers
784　Production Samplers and Weighers
785　Graders and Sorters, Except Agricultural
787　Production Expediters

TRANSPORTATION AND MATERIAL MOVING OCCUPATIONS

81　**Supervisors; Transportation and Material Moving Occupations**
811　Supervisors; Motorized Equipment Operators
812　Supervisors; Material Moving Equipment Operators

82　**Transportation Occupations**
821　Motor Vehicle Operators
823　Rail Transportation Occupations
824　Water Transportation Occupations
825　Airplane Pilots and Navigators
828　Transportation Inspectors

83　**Material Moving Occupations, Except Transportation**
831　Material Moving Equipment Operators

HANDLERS, EQUIPMENT CLEANERS, HELPERS AND LABORERS

85　**Supervisors; Handlers, Equipment Cleaners, Helpers, and Laborers**

86　**Helpers**
861　Helpers; Machine Operators and Tenders
862　Helpers; Fabricators and Inspectors
863　Helpers; Mechanics and Repairers
864　Helpers; Construction Trades
865　Helpers; Extractive Occupations

87　**Handlers, Equipment Cleaners and Laborers**
871　Construction Laborers
872　Freight, Stock, and Material Movers; Hand
873　Garage and Service Station Related Occupations
874　Parking Lot Attendants
875　Vehicle Washers and Equipment Cleaners
876　Miscellaneous Manual Occupations

MILITARY OCCUPATIONS

91　**Military Occupations**

MISCELLANEOUS OCCUPATIONS

99　**Miscellaneous Occupations**

Standard International Trade Classification, Revision 2

The Standard International Trade Classification (SITC) is a statistical classification of commodities in world trade, developed by the United Nations to facilitate international comparison of commodity trade data. Revision 2 was published in 1975.

In U.S. foreign trade statistics, commodities are primarily classified according to two systems developed and maintained by the Census Bureau: *Schedule A, Statistical Classification of Commodities Imported into the U.S.*, and *Schedule E, SITC Based Classification of Domestic and Foreign Commodities Exported from the U.S.*

Import data are initially collected in terms of the 10,000 codes of the *Tariff Schedules of the U.S.* (TSUS). These data are then rearranged and reported in terms of 1978 Schedule A, which is based on SITC Revision 2.

Export data are initially collected in terms of Schedule B, which is consistent with the TSUS classification used for imports. These data are then rearranged and reported in terms of 1978 Schedule E, which is also based on SITC Revision 2.

Both Schedules A and E, which provide commodity codes to the detailed 7-digit level, are essentially identical at the 1-, 2-, and 3-digit level to the SITC, Revision 2. A modified classification scheme, Revision 3, was published in 1986. However, most Federal reports continue to publish data classified according to Revision 2. Therefore, the 1- to 3-digit codes of Revision 2 are listed below.

Section, Division,
and Group Codes

0 FOOD AND LIVE ANIMALS CHIEFLY FOR FOOD

00 Live Animals Chiefly for Food
001 Live animals chiefly for food

01 Meat and Meat Preparations
011 Meat and edible meat offals, fresh, chilled or frozen
012 Meat and edible meat offals (except poultry liver), salted, in brine, dried or smoked
014 Meat and edible meat offals, prepared or preserved, n.e.s.; fish extracts

02 Dairy Products and Birds' Eggs
022 Milk and cream
023 Butter
024 Cheese and curd
025 Eggs, birds', and egg yolks, fresh, dried, or otherwise preserved, sweetened or not

03 Fish, Crustaceans and Molluscs, and Preparations Thereof
034 Fish, fresh (live or dead), chilled or frozen
035 Fish, dried, salted or in brine; smoked fish
036 Crustaceans and molluscs, whether in shell or not, fresh (live or dead), chilled, frozen, salted, in brine or dried; crustaceans, in shell, simply boiled in water
037 Fish, crustaceans and molluscs, prepared or preserved, n.e.s.

04 Cereals and Cereal Preparations
041 Wheat (including spelt) and meslin, unmilled
042 Rice
043 Barley, unmilled
044 Maize (corn), unmilled
045 Cereals, unmilled (other than wheat, rice, barley and maize)
046 Meal and flour of wheat and flour of meslin

047 Other cereal meals and flours
048 Cereal preparations and preparations of flour or starch of fruits or vegetables

05 Vegetables and Fruit
054 Vegetables, fresh, chilled, frozen or simply preserved
056 Vegetables, roots and tubers, prepared or preserved, n.e.s.
057 Fruit and nuts (not including oil nuts), fresh or dried
058 Fruit, preserved, and fruit preparations

06 Sugar, Sugar Preparations and Honey
061 Sugar and honey
062 Sugar confectionery (except chocolate confectionery) and other sugar preparations

07 Coffee, Tea, Cocoa, Spices, and Manufacturers Thereof
071 Coffee and coffee substitutes
072 Cocoa
073 Chocolate and other food preparations containing cocoa, n.e.s.
074 Tea and mate
075 Spices

08 Feeding Stuff for Animals (Not Including Unmilled Cereals)
081 Feeding stuff for animals (not including unmilled cereals)

09 Miscellaneous Edible Products and Preparations
091 Margarine and shortening
098 Edible products and preparations, n.e.s.

1 BEVERAGES AND TOBACCO

11 Beverages
111 Non-alcoholic beverages, n.e.s.
112 Alcoholic beverages

12 Tobacco and Tobacco Manufactures
121 Tobacco, unmanufactured; tobacco refuse
122 Tobacco, manufactured

2 CRUDE MATERIALS, INEDIBLE, EXCEPT FUELS

21 Hides, Skins and Furskins, Raw
211 Hides and skins (except furskins), raw
212 Furskins, raw (including astrakhan, caracul, Persian lamb, broadtail and similar skins)

22 Oil Seeds and Oleaginous Fruit
222 Oil seeds and oleaginous fruit, whole or broken, of a kind used for the extraction of 'soft' fixed vegetable oils (excluding flours and meals)
223 Oilseeds and oleaginous fruit, whole or broken, of a kind used for the extraction of other fixed vegetable oils

23 Crude Rubber (Including Synthetic and Reclaimed)
232 Natural rubber latex; natural rubber and similar natural gums
233 Synthetic rubber latex; synthetic rubber and reclaimed rubber; waste and scrap of unhardened rubber

24 Cork and Wood
244 Cork, natural, raw and waste (including natural cork in blocks or sheets)
245 Fuel wood (excluding wood waste) and wood charcoal
246 Pulpwood (including chips and wood waste)
247 Other wood in the rough or roughly squared
248 Wood, simply worked, and railway sleepers of wood

25 Pulp and Waste Paper
251 Pulp and waste paper

26 Textile Fibres (Other Than Wool Tops) and Their Wastes (Not Manufactured Into Yarn or Fabric)
261 Silk
263 Cotton
264 Jute and other textile bast fibres, n.e.s., raw or processed but not spun; tow and waste thereof
265 Vegetable textile fibres (other)
266 Synthetic fibres suitable for spinning
267 Other man-made fibres suitable for spinning and waste of man-made fibres
268 Wool and other animal hair (excluding wool tops)
269 Old clothing and other old textile articles; rags

27 Crude Fertilizers and Crude Minerals (excluding Coal, and Precious Stones)
271 Fertilizers, crude
273 Stone, sand and gravel
274 Sulphur and unroasted iron pyrites

277 Natural abrasives, n.e.s. (including industrial diamonds)
278 Other crude minerals

28 Metalliferous Ores and Metal Scrap
281 Iron ore and concentrates
282 Waste and scrap metal of iron or steel
286 Ores and concentrates of uranium and thorium
287 Ores and concentrates of base metals, n.e.s.
288 Non-ferrous base metal waste and scrap, n.e.s.
289 Ores and concentrates of precious metals; waste, scrap and sweepings of precious metals (other than of gold)

29 Crude Animal and Vegetable Materials, n.e.s.
291 Crude animal materials, n.e.s.
292 Crude vegetable materials, n.e.s.

3 MINERAL FUELS, LUBRICANTS AND RELATED MATERIALS

32 Coal, Coke and Briquettes
322 Coal, lignite and peat
323 Briquettes; coke and semi-coke of coal, lignite or peat; retort carbon

33 Petroleum, Petroleum Products and Related Materials
333 Petroleum oils, crude, and crude oils obtained from bituminous minerals
334 Petroleum products, refined
335 Residual petroleum products, n.e.s. and related materials

34 Gas, Natural and Manufactured
341 Gas, natural and manufactured

35 Electric Current
351 Electric current

4 ANIMAL AND VEGETABLE OILS, FATS AND WAXES

41 Animal Oils and Fats
411 Animal oils and fats

42 Fixed Vegetable Oils and Fats
423 Fixed vegetable oils, 'soft', crude, refined or purified
424 Other fixed vegetable oils, fluid or solid, crude, refined or purified

43 Animal and Vegetable Oils and Fats, Processed, and Waxes of Animal or Vegetable Origin
431 Animal and vegetable oils and fats, processed, and waxes of animal or vegetable origin

5 CHEMICALS AND RELATED PRODUCTS, N.E.S.

51 Organic Chemicals
511 Hydrocarbons, n.e.s., and their halogenated, sulphonated, nitrated or nitrosated derivatives

512 Alcohols, phenols, phenol-alcohols, and their halogenated, sulphonated, nitrated or nitrosated derivatives
513 Carboxylic acids, and their anhydrides, halides, peroxides and peracids, and their halogenated, sulphonated, nitrated or nitrosated derivatives
514 Nitrogen-function compounds
515 Organo-inorganic and heterocyclic compounds
516 Other organic chemicals

52 Inorganic Chemicals
522 Inorganic chemical elements, oxides, and halogen salts
523 Other inorganic chemicals; organic and inorganic compounds of precious metals
524 Radio-active and associated materials

53 Dyeing, Tanning and Colouring Materials
531 Synthetic organic dyestuffs, etc., natural indigo and colour lakes
532 Dyeing and tanning extracts, and synthetic tanning materials
533 Pigments, paints, varnishes and related materials

54 Medicinal and Pharmaceutical Products
541 Medicinal and pharmaceutical products

55 Essential Oils and Perfume Materials; Toilet, Polishing and Cleansing Preparations
551 Essential oils, perfume and flavour materials
553 Perfumery, cosmetics and toilet preparations (excluding soaps)
554 Soap, cleansing and polishing preparations

56 Fertilizers, Manufactured
562 Fertilizers, manufactured

57 Explosives and Pyrotechnic Products
572 Explosives and pyrotechnic products

58 Artificial Resins and Plastic Materials, and Cellulose Esters and Ethers
582 Condensation, polycondensation and polyaddition products
583 Polymerization and copolymerization products
584 Regenerated cellulose; cellulose nitrate, cellulose acetate and other cellulose esters, cellulose ethers and other chemical derivatives of cellulose, plasticized or not (e.g., collodions, celluloid); vulcanized fibre
585 Other artificial resins and plastic materials

59 Chemical Materials and Products, n.e.s.
591 Disinfectants, insecticides, fungicides, weed killers, anti-sprouting products, rat poisons and similar products, put up in forms or packings for sale by retail
592 Starches, inulin and wheat gluten; albuminoidal substances; glues
598 Miscellaneous chemical products, n.e.s.

6 MANUFACTURED GOODS CLASSIFIED CHIEFLY BY MATERIAL

61 Leather, Leather Manufactures, n.e.s., and Dressed Furskins
611 Leather
612 Manufactures of leather or of composition leather, n.e.s; saddlery and harness; parts of footwear, n.e.s.
613 Furskins, tanned or dressed

62 Rubber Manufactures, n.e.s.
621 Materials of rubber (e.g., pastes, plates, sheets, rods, thread, tubes, of rubber)
625 Rubber tyres, tyre cases, interchangeable tyre treads, inner tubes and tyre flaps, for wheels of all kinds
628 Articles of rubber, n.e.s.

63 Cork and Wood Manufactures (Excluding Furniture)
633 Cork manufactures
634 Veneers, plywood, "improved" or reconstituted wood, and other wood, worked, n.e.s.
635 Wood manufactures, n.e.s.

64 Paper, Paperboard, and Articles of Paper Pulp, of Paper or of Paperboard
641 Paper and paperboard
642 Paper and paperboard, cut to size or shape, and articles of paper or paperboard

65 Textile Yarn, Fabrics, Made-Up Articles, n.e.s., and Related Products
651 Textile yarn
652 Cotton fabrics, woven (not including narrow or special fabrics)
653 Fabrics, woven, of man-made fibres (not including narrow or special fabrics)
654 Textile fabrics, woven, other than of cotton or man-made fibres
655 Knitted or crocheted fabrics (including tubular knit fabrics, pile fabrics and open-work fabrics)
656 Tulle, lace, embroidery, ribbons, trimmings and other small wares
657 Special textile fabrics and related products
658 Made-up articles, wholly or chiefly of textile materials, n.e.s.
659 Floor coverings, etc.

66 Non-Metallic Mineral Manufactures, n.e.s.
661 Lime, cement, and fabricated construction materials (except glass and clay materials)
662 Clay construction materials and refractory construction materials
663 Mineral manufactures, n.e.s.
664 Glass
665 Glassware
666 Pottery
667 Pearls, precious and semi-precious stones, unworked or worked

67 Iron and Steel
671 Pig iron, spiegeleisen, sponge iron, iron or steel powders and shot, and ferro-alloys

672 Ingots and other primary forms, of iron or steel
673 Iron and steel bars, rods, angles, shapes and sections (including sheet piling)
674 Universals, plates and sheets, of iron or steel
675 Hoop and strip, of iron or steel, hot-rolled or cold-rolled
676 Rails and railway track construction material, of iron or steel
677 Iron or steel wire (excluding wire rod), whether or not coated, but not insulated
678 Tubes, pipes and fittings, of iron or steel
679 Iron and steel castings, forgings and stampings, in the rough state, n.e.s.

68 Non-Ferrous Metals
681 Silver, platinum and other metals of the platinum group
682 Copper
683 Nickel
684 Aluminum
685 Lead
686 Zinc
687 Tin
688 Uranium depleted in U235 and thorium, and their alloys, unwrought or wrought, and articles thereof, n.e.s.
689 Miscellaneous non-ferrous base metals employed in metallurgy, and cermets

69 Manufactures of Metal, n.e.s.
691 Structures and parts of structures, n.e.s., of iron, steel or aluminum
692 Metal containers for storage and transport
693 Wire products (excluding insulated electrical wiring) and fencing grills
694 Nails, screws, nuts, bolts, rivets and the like, of iron, steel or copper
695 Tools for use in the hand or in machines
696 Cutlery
697 Household equipment of base metal, n.e.s.
699 Manufactures of base metal, n.e.s.

---

7 MACHINERY AND TRANSPORT EQUIPMENT

71 Power Generating Machinery and Equipment
711 Steam and other vapour generating boilers, superheated water boilers, and auxiliary plant for use therewith; and parts thereof, n.e.s.
712 Steam and other vapour power units, not incorporating boilers; steam engines (including mobile engines) with self-contained boilers; and parts thereof, n.e.s.
713 Internal combustion piston engines, and parts thereof, n.e.s.
714 Engines and motors, non-electric (other); parts, n.e.s.
716 Rotating electric plant and parts thereof, n.e.s.

718 Other power generating machinery and parts thereof, n.e.s.

72 Machinery Specialized For Particular Industries
721 Agricultural machinery (excluding tractors) and parts thereof, n.e.s.
722 Tractors (other), whether or not fitted with power take-offs, winches or pulleys
723 Civil engineering and contractors' plant and equipment and parts thereof, n.e.s.
724 Textile and leather machinery, and parts thereof, n.e.s.
725 Paper mill and pulp mill machinery, paper cutting machines and other machinery for the manufacture of paper articles; and parts thereof, n.e.s.
726 Printing and bookbinding machinery, and parts thereof, n.e.s.
727 Food-processing machines (excluding domestic) and parts thereof, n.e.s.
728 Other machinery and equipment specialized for particular industries, and parts thereof, n.e.s.

73 Metalworking Machinery
736 Machine-tools for working metal or metal carbides, and parts and accessories thereof, n.e.s.
737 Metalworking machinery (other than machine-tools), and parts thereof, n.e.s.

74 General Industrial Machinery and Equipment, n.e.s., and Machine Parts, n.e.s.
741 Heating and cooling equipment and parts thereof, n.e.s.
742 Pumps (including motor and turbo pumps) for liquids, whether or not fitted with measuring devices; liquid elevators of bucket, chain, screw, band and similar kinds; parts, n.e.s.
743 Pumps (other than pumps for liquids) and compressors; fans and blowers; centrifuges; filtering and purifying apparatus; and parts thereof, n.e.s.
744 Mechanical handling equipment, and parts thereof, n.e.s.
745 Other non-electrical machinery, tools and mechanical apparatus, and parts thereof, n.e.s.
749 Non-electric parts and accessories of machinery, n.e.s.

75 Office Machines and Automatic Data Processing Equipment
751 Office machines
752 Automatic data processing machines and units thereof; magnetic or optical readers, machines for transcribing data onto data media in coded form and machines for processing such data, n.e.s.
759 Parts, n.e.s. of and accessories (other than covers, carrying cases and the like) suitable for use with machines of a kind falling within heading 751 or 752

76 Telecommunications and Sound Recording and Reproducing Apparatus and Equipment
761 Television receivers (including receivers incorporating radio-broadcast receivers or sound recorders or reproducers)
762 Radio-broadcast receivers (including receivers incorporating sound recorders or reproducers)
763 Gramophones (phonographs), dictating machines and other sound recorders and reproducers (including record players and tape decks, with or without sound-heads); television image and sound recorders and reproducers, magnetic
764 Telecommunications equipment, n.e.s.; and parts, n.e.s. of and accessories for the apparatus and equipment falling within division 76

77 Electrical Machinery, Apparatus and Appliances, n.e.s., and Electrical Parts Thereof (Including Non-Electrical Counterparts, n.e.s. of Electrical Household Type Equipment)
771 Electric power machinery (other), and parts thereof, n.e.s.
772 Electrical apparatus for making and breaking electrical circuits
773 Equipment for distributing electricity
774 Electric apparatus for medical purposes and radiological apparatus
775 Household type, electrical and non-electrical equipment, n.e.s.
776 Thermionic, cold cathode and photo-cathode valves and tubes; photocells; mounted piezoelectric crystals; diodes, transistors and similar semi-conductor devices; electronic microcircuits; and parts thereof, n.e.s.
778 Electrical machinery and apparatus, n.e.s.

78 Road Vehicles (Including Air-Cushion Vehicles)
781 Passenger motor cars (other than public-service type vehicles), including vehicles designed for the transport of both passengers and goods
782 Motor vehicles for the transport of goods or materials and special purpose motor vehicles
783 Road motor vehicles, n.e.s.
784 Parts and accessories, n.e.s.
785 Motorcycles, motor scooters and other cycles, motorized and non-motorized; invalid carriages
786 Trailers and other vehicles, not motorized, n.e.s. and specially designed and equipped transport containers

79 Other Transport Equipment
791 Railway vehicles (including hovertrains) and associated equipment

792 Aircraft and associated equipment, and parts thereof, n.e.s.
793 Ships, boats (including hovercraft) and floating structures

8 MISCELLANEOUS MANUFACTURED ARTICLES

81 Sanitary, Plumbing, Heating and Lighting Fixtures and Fittings, n.e.s.
812 Sanitary, plumbing, heating and lighting fixtures and fittings, n.e.s.

82 Furniture and Parts Thereof
821 Furniture and parts thereof

83 Travel Goods, Handbags and Similar Containers
831 Travel goods, shopping bags, handbags, satchels, brief-cases, wallets, purses, etc.

84 Articles of Apparel and Clothing Accessories
842 Outer garments, men's and boys', of textile fabrics (other than knitted or crocheted goods)
843 Outer garments, women's, girls' and infants', of textile fabrics (other than knitted or crocheted)
844 Under garments of textile fabrics (other than knitted or crocheted goods)
845 Outer garments and other articles, knitted or crocheted, not elastic nor rubberized
846 Under garments, knitted or crocheted

847 Clothing accessories, of textile fabrics, n.e.s.
848 Articles of apparel and clothing accessories of other than textile fabrics; headgear of all materials

85 Footwear
851 Footwear

87 Professional, scientific and Controlling Instruments and Apparatus, n.e.s.
871 Optical instruments and apparatus
872 Medical instruments and appliances, n.e.s.
873 Meters and counters, n.e.s.
874 Measuring, checking, analysing and controlling instruments and apparatus, n.e.s.; parts and accessories, n.e.s.

88 Photographic Apparatus, Equipment and Supplies and Optical Goods, n.e.s.; Watches and Clocks
881 Photographic apparatus and equipment, n.e.s.
882 Photographic and cinematographic supplies
883 Cinematograph film, exposed and developed, whether or not incorporating sound track or consisting only of sound track, negative or positive
884 Optical goods, n.e.s.
885 Watches and clocks

89 Miscellaneous Manufactured Articles, n.e.s.
892 Printed matter
893 Articles, n.e.s. of materials of the kinds described in division 58

894 Baby carriages, toys, games and sporting goods
895 Office and stationery supplies, n.e.s.
896 Works of art, collectors' pieces and antiques
897 Jewellery, goldsmiths' and silver-smiths' wares, and other articles of precious or semi-precious materials, n.e.s.
898 Musical instruments and parts and accessories thereof (including phonograph records and the like)
899 Other miscellaneous manufactured articles, n.e.s.

9 COMMODITIES AND TRANSACTIONS NOT CLASSIFIED ELSEWHERE IN THE SITC

911.0 Postal packages not classified according to kind
931.0 Special transactions and commodities not classified according to kind
941.0 Animals, live, n.e.s. (including zoo animals, dogs, cats, insects, etc.)
951.0 Armoured fighting vehicles, arms of war and ammunition therefor, and parts of arms, n.e.s.
961.0 Coin (other than gold coin), not being legal tender
971.0 Gold, non-monetary (excluding gold ores and concentrates)